The New

WEBSTER

Encyclopedic

DICTIONARY

of The English Language

The New
WEBSTER
Encyclopedic
DICTIONARY
of The English Language

VOLUME I

VIRGINIA S. THATCHER
Editor in chief

ALEXANDER McQUEEN
Advisory Editor and Lexicographer

Editorial Staff

Margaret L. Smith • Clarice Geels
Anne Tomkin • Peter Morrison
Walter Eckart • David Phelps
George Malayil
Willard Grayson Smythe • Ava Friedmann

1971

 Grolier
INCORPORATED
NEW YORK

LIBRARY OF CONGRESS CATALOG CARD NUMBER: 75-128779

STANDARD BOOK NUMBER: 8326-0000-8

Preface

This dictionary is based on a wider experience with the usage of words than any one person can ever have in his own lifetime. A great body of information about words has been built up over many years, and lexicographers have made it their business to collect it and to organize it in dictionary form. We have endeavored to bring you authoritative data on every word you are likely to use in school, office, or home and in your daily contacts with people.

A great quantity of matter has been compiled in this work in very moderate compass, and the wide scope of this volume should meet the needs of the most exacting dictionary user. It is recognized that a dictionary suited to the popular demand for such a work should possess the three important qualities of accuracy, completeness, and convenience. This work carries an outstanding background of authority and scholarship and is a source to which you may turn with complete confidence for an understanding of the meaning, pronunciation, spelling, and proper use of the words with which you are unfamiliar.

In selecting the words for inclusion in this dictionary, the net has been cast fairly widely. The greatest importance is naturally attached to words in literary and colloquial use at the present day. At the same time, a large number of purely technical and scientific words and terms have been included since many of these necessarily play a considerable part in the lives of important sections of the community. Meanings and shades of meaning are carefully distinguished and explained, not with synonyms or confusing technical terms, but in clearly worded, simplified form, illustrated by quotations or brief phrases whenever necessary for lucidity.

The compilers of this dictionary have made it possible for the reader to find instantly the word or information he seeks, including at the same time such details as the spelling and pronunciation, as well as the origin of words so that he can appreciate how far reaching are the sources of our language. For easy reference, main entries are displayed in large, extra bold type the full width of the column, with definitions and other text matter slightly indented.

In order to carry out the principle of conciseness, the method of grouping related words in a single paragraph has been adopted. Particularly, primary words followed by a number of derivatives are thus grouped, and compounds are listed under the word that forms their first element.

We have included the name of WEBSTER, the great American lexicographer, in the title of this dictionary in recognition of his important contribution to the principles of lexicography.

The Publishers

ON THE ORIGIN OF WORDS

Alexander McQueen

On almost every page of this dictionary are clues to the origin and development of our language. Such clues may be traced from mankind's earliest days—through the ancient civilizations of Greece and Rome—and into the modern period, where, with the piling up of new discoveries in the arts and sciences, the invention of new words has become almost commonplace.

Every word we use has a history, and in almost every case it is a story of action—a story of something happening. This word-forming activity has been going on for thousands of years, ever since the first human beings uttered the first human sounds. We have inherited a rich legacy from the past.

SOUND AND SENSE

Many of our most stirring impressions come to us through elementary speech sounds. Conclusive proof of this statement can be found in the radio script that depends for dramatic effect not only on words but also on other sounds—of closing doors, tramping feet, rippling water, howling wind, ticking clocks, crashing collisions, and no end of other noises.

The use of sound effects is as old as man. Early men got along with a small stock of words, and they probably began with sound effects. For telling about violence, such as shattering or breaking, they made noises with smashing sounds, which in time became such dictionary words as *smash, dash, bash, mash, clash, crash.* It is easy to add to such a list of words ending in *-sh,* meaning something to do with violence.

To show how a sound might suggest a whole group of words, let us take an imaginary situation. Suppose that an ancient Teuton has gone to sleep. He sleeps with his mouth open, and as he breathes he makes a queer noise, a mixture of whistling and nasal humming. Someone observing the sleeping man imitates him like this: "Sss-norr!" In the evolution of language these sounds have been retained; today when we refer to this noise made by a sleeper, we call it a *snore.* Other nasal words have been built on the same pattern. A more abrupt sound, in waking hours, became a *snort.* A growl through the nose was called a *snarl.* A sudden breathing into the nose was called a *sniff.* A laugh like "eh-eh-eh" was called a *snicker.* The nose of an animal was called a *snout.* A scornful glance, with upturned nose, became a *sneer.* And a sort of nasal explosion became a *sneeze.* One could make a long list of words starting with *sn,* all related to the nose. It isn't by accident that sense and sound go together. The Choctaws have a very expressive word for *sneeze;* it has three syllables, *ha-bish-ko.* When the Choctaw says it quickly, with stress on the *bish,* it's a perfect sound effect for a sneeze.

In a dictionary are hundreds of these imitative words: the *tick-tick* of the clock, the *ding-dong* of the bell, the *boom* of the cannon. To describe an overabundance of talking, we use such words as *chatter* or *jabber.* Then there is *babble,* not very different from jabbering. It is possible that *babble* came from the simple sound *ba-ba* and from the prattle of a baby, whose first words are usually made with the lips. The sound *ba-ba* reminds us of a more complicated word—*barbarian.* In ancient times, when there was little travel from one land to another, men seldom had a chance to learn foreign languages. When they met a foreigner, they had to talk through an interpreter. And although most of the men of the Old World knew only one language, they despised people of other countries who also knew only their own native tongue. In fact, the Greeks used to say that the language of foreigners sounded like "bar-bar-bar." In time foreigners began to be nicknamed the "bar-bar" people. That particular nickname found its way into the regular language of the Greeks, then of the Romans, and we have it in a form that came through the Latin—*barbarian.* So even the ancient Greeks, with their keen sense of the niceties of language, sometimes made a dictionary word out of a simple sound. In doing so they were giving a sort of classic approval to the methods of our remotest ancestors, who enriched our speech with sounds that made sense.

WORDS FROM GREEK

The classic tongue of Greece — the language of Homer and Plato and Aristotle — is one of the most important sources of our everyday speech. You have already learned something of the Greek language. You started when you learned your ABC's; when you referred to the alphabet, you were just saying the names of the two Greek letters alpha and beta, that is, A and B. A little later, when you talked about arithmetic, you were very nearly saying *arithmos,* the Greek word for "numbers."

You can't go into the kitchen and wash dishes without handling something with a Greek name. The very word *dish* is Greek. At first it was *diskos,* meaning "quoit." Later the meaning was extended to include dishes.

One word from the ancient Greek shows how meanings change. The rich men in Greece had an easy life —no tiresome work to do—plenty of leisure time. To this spare time they gave the name of *scho-le.* In their *scho-lē* they were devoted to discussion, study, and instruction. Because they studied in their *scho-lē,* they were called scholars; and the place where they studied came to be called school. So schooltime was spare time, and the pleasure found in that spare time was the pleasure of study.

Among familiar personal names are many that come from the Greek, as George, Philip, and Eugene. The name George means "landman, or farmer." The *geo* in the name George is simply the Greek word for "earth." It is in *geography* and *geology* and *geometry;* they all have something to do with the earth.

The name Philip means one who loves horses; *philos,* "loving"; *hippos,* "horse." A hippodrome is a racecourse where horses run. A hippopotamus is a river horse; *potamos* is Greek for "river."

The name Eugene means "well-born": *eu-,* "good, well"; *genesis,* "birth." Most words starting with *eu* have a sense that is good, pleasant, or beautiful. *Euphony* has to do with pleasant sounds; *eulogy,* pleasant sayings or words. A speech praising someone is a eulogy.

Now for some girls' names: Margaret, she's a pearl; Dora, she's a gift; Catherine, she's pure; Irene, she's peaceful—that is, if you go by their Greek names. And the Greeks did have a name for almost everything. When you say that this great nation of ours is a democracy, you're talking Greek—*demos-kratein,* "people-governing." Democracy is government by the people. The same Greeks who gave us the name of our kind of government gave us the word *politics.* It comes from the Greek *polis,* "city." The Greeks gave us also the precious word *economy.* They called it *oikonomos,* from *oikos,* "house," and *nomos,* "management." That's the spirit of economy—the management of a house. And because economy has so much to do with the home, some of the world's best economists are women.

Speaking of women and housekeeping, marriage customs in ancient Greece emphasized business rather than romance. Sometimes the man never saw his wife until the wedding day. However, even if he didn't see her face, he always wanted to be sure about her dowry, that is, the money and other things of value that she would bring to him, as a sort of premium. Almost everything she owned became his. But under the old Greek law every bride was allowed to keep certain articles as her own, such as personal belongings and articles of adornment. These things would be carefully listed, and it was understood that the husband would have no control over them. What he got was the *phernē,* or dowry. The things the bride kept were the *parapherna: para,* "independent of"; *phernē,* "dowry." On the day of an ancient Greek wedding the bride came home, taking great care to keep her own special treasures separate from the ones that would belong to her husband. It might be a strange collection of unrelated things, but it was her very own —her *parapherna.* And that's how we came by our word *paraphernalia,* meaning "a miscellaneous collection of accessories or equipment."

People who guess at the derivation of words and then refer to the dictionary often find that their guess was wrong. Guessing is not safe. A comet and a comma look somewhat alike (each has a round part and a tail); so someone says, "They must be related." But they're not. *Comet* is from Greek *kometes,* "long-haired," because of the trail of light the comet leaves behind. *Comma,* Greek *komma,* means "a section or segment, something cut off"; a comma slightly cuts off part of a sentence. Now someone may say, "Is a comic long-haired?" No. He gets his name from Greek *kōsmos,* "a revel." Today many children give the word *comic* an entirely new meaning; they use it to mean any pictured story in strip form. They even talk about "Bible comics," an example of how the meaning of a word gets "pushed around."

Pharmacist is from Greek *pharmakon,* "poison." Many ancient medicinal drugs were more or less poisonous; hence the name of their dispenser.

Glamour is merely another form of *grammar.* Because *grammar* at one time meant "magic" or "fascination," *glamour* took on the meaning "witchery, allurement." This word also is Greek.

A dilemma is not an animal, in spite of its two horns. The word comes from Greek *di,* "double," and *lemma,* "proposition or assumption." When we have to choose between two propositions, each unfavorable to us, we are said to be "on the horns of a dilemma."

WORDS FROM LATIN

Latin is not a dead language, for it plays a lively part in our everyday speech. Sometimes we recognize it and applaud it. That word *applaud* is Latin; in Latin it's *applaudere* and usually means the clapping of hands. It is one of the thousands of Latin words that help give life to our language. So were I to say that Latin is totally dead, I would not be entirely candid. *Candid* is another Latin word; it means "fair, frank, or just." *Candid,* the Latin *candidus,* really meant "white, pure." In ancient Rome when a politician was running for office and went on a speechmaking tour, he wore white garments as a sign of good, clean politics. So our own officeseekers are called candidates. Next time you burn a candle, remember that its name is also from the Latin *candidus,* "white." Our republic gets its name from Latin *respublica: res,* "thing, interest"; *publica,* "public." Many of our political terms are derived from the Latin. Take the word *senate;* it's just another form of the Latin *senatus,* "council of old men." Senators are supposed to be old enough to be wise. Men who are *junior* (pure Latin for "younger") are seldom found in a senate. The senate calls for men who are *senior* ("older"). In fact, *senior* and *senate* are of the same origin.

Many of the Latin words in our language are quite

lively. Take the word *rivals*. We know what rivals are. If several men are competitors in business or are running a race, they are rivals. If several young men are courting the same girl, they are rivals in love. But why are they called rivals? The Latin word for stream is *rivus;* when two men lived near a stream and had to share that stream between them, they were called *rivales,* or rivals. The word originally meant "partners"; but when two persons have to share something, it is easy for partnership to lead to contention. So the Latin word for stream became our word for rivalry in sports, in business, in love, or in war.

Speaking of war, Roman soldiers usually got part of their wages in salt, because salt was considered essential to human life. The Latin word for salt was *sal;* the salt pay was called *salarium.* From that word came our word *salary.* Sometimes, if we consider that a man is lazy and isn't earning his salary, we say, "He isn't earning his salt." Note that word *consider,* which means "to study, to meditate, to reflect upon something." It's a simple word with a romantic origin. In Latin it was two words: *con,* "with"; *sider,* "a star." It comes from the days when men, for guidance in their decisions, turned for help to the stars. This use of *consider* is found in the English of Psalm 8: "When I consider Thy heavens . . . the moon and the stars, which thou hast ordained."

We take our words from old Roman politicians, stream dwellers, senators, soldiers—and farmers. When a Roman farmer was plowing and became careless, his plowshare would turn out of the furrow; and when his neighbors saw that his plowing had gone awry, they would say, "He has turned from the furrow." In Latin a furrow is *lira;* and "to turn out of the furrow" is *de-lira,* the source of our word *delirious.* When a man is temporarily out of his mind, he has turned aside from his proper mental furrow. When he comes to himself, and we might say that he's back on the right track, the old Romans said, "He's back in the right furrow."

The Rome of 20 centuries ago was built on seven hills. One was called the Palatium; on this Palatium, or Palatine Hill, the Emperor Augustus built a magnificent house. It was thought to be the last word in royal residences. But it wasn't, for a little later the Emperor Nero built another on the self-same hill. His house, called the Golden House, was still grander than the one built by Augustus. These royal houses gave their name to all royal houses to come. Because they were built on the Palatine Hill, they were called palatial; and it is from them that we get our word *palace.*

When you listen carefully, you are paying attention, or attending to what is being said. *Attention* is from *attentio,* the Latin word for a "stretching of the mind toward something." The same idea is in our word *tension,* which also means "stretching." And speaking of stretching, let us imagine a Roman strong man showing the remarkable development of his muscles. As he stretches out his arm and makes one of his muscles move between his elbow and his shoulder, somebody says, "It looks like a little mouse!" Now

the Latin word for mouse is *mus,* and a little mouse is *musculus. Musculus* in time was changed to *muscule,* and now we call it *muscle.*

Consider the words *host* and *guest.* Both are derived from the Latin *hostis.* One offers hospitality, the other receives it—a friendly arrangement. But, oddly enough, *hostis* also meant "an enemy," which does not sound so friendly. The history of the words provides an explanation. In the days before hotels the person needing hospitality was a stranger, and all strangers were feared as possible enemies.

Another tricky word is *miniature.* Because a miniature is something small, one might suppose that it is related to *minus* and *minimum.* But it comes from the Latin *minium,* meaning "red lead," with which certain ancient pictures were painted. The word came to be connected with small pictures and then with small objects.

We have considered *candid* and *candidate,* both coming from Latin *candidus,* "white." What about candy? Did it, too, come from this source? No. Candy gets its name from the Arabic word *qand,* meaning "sugar."

Confute is a dignified word; it means "to disprove" or "to show that an argument is false." Its original significance, however, from the Latin was "to throw water on something." And *absurd,* another word from the Latin, joins *ab,* "from," to *surdus,* "deaf," suggesting an amusing misunderstanding by a deaf person.

WORDS THAT STAND OR STAY

One of the simplest words in our language is *stand.* It is very old and is related to many other words. It has been traced to an ancient Indo-European root, *sta,* which appears in many Greek and Latin words. *Sta* suggests stability, "strength to stand without being moved or overthrown." A stable is a place where horses stand. A stage is a platform whereon someone stands to act. An establishment is something that is fixed, reliable, standing. A standard is a flag or other sign around which loyal soldiers can stand; it is also a norm by which the standing of other things may be measured.

The *sta* root is seen unchanged in hundreds of words. A staple is an item of merchandise that is kept in stock, that is, a standing, always available, item. A staple is also a fastening device, to keep things, as it were, standing. A stall is a place where people stand to buy and sell goods. If the customer stands too long without buying, he may be charged with stalling. Things become stale from standing too long. A man's status indicates his standing in the community. When the man becomes old, he may need a staff to aid him in standing. Ecstasy might be described as a kind of "out-standing emotion."

To recite all of the *sta* words would be tiring. And even if we exhausted the list of *sta* words, we would encounter scores of related *ste* words. The homestead is where the home stands. One who is steady is one who is able to stand well. The printer's notation *stet* is pure Latin for "let it stand." In such words as *destiny,* the *sta* element appears as *sti;* destiny is a sort of predetermined stand in a person's future.

NONCLASSICAL WORD SOURCES

English, with its richness, power, and beauty, is indebted to many languages other than Greek and Latin. A few examples will illustrate this debt.

Long ago in a town in France a young man was in his workshop. As he worked, a group of his friends came by and called, "Come along, Pierre, don't work so hard. Come with us and have a good time; you can leave your shop." Now, the old French word for shop was *bauche* or *bawtch;* and the French word for luring a man away from his shop, or, as we might say, un-shopping him, was *dé-baucher.* Today if we entice a man away from his duty and attempt to corrupt him, we are said to be debauching him.

Among the ancient French a man and his wife sometimes had arguments. If the husband shouted at his wife, she might begin to look pathetic, with tear-filled eyes and pouting lips. Now her husband couldn't bear to see her lips sticking out like that, so he built a special little room into which she might retire to pout. Since the French word for pouting was *bouder,* the lady's pouting room came to be called the *boudoir,* a household word today.

In the days of Richard II of England men lost their heads for uttering a single word; it was the word *havoc.* *Havoc* was a dangerous word. In war the shout "Havoc" was a signal for soldiers to lay waste the countryside and to plunder and kill without mercy. That's what Shakespeare meant in his famous line in *Julius Caesar,* "Cry 'Havoc!' and let slip the dogs of war." When the cry "Havoc" was raised in a rebellion, it was a call to revolt against the government; for shouting "Havoc" in such a case, the shouter was condemned to lose his head.

The ancient Scottish Highlanders believed in battle cries. They called them army yells. In the Gaelic tongue, army is *sluagh;* yell is *ghairm.* Put them together, and it's *sluagh-ghairm,* or, as it is pronounced today, *slogan.* A good slogan is always short, something one can yell out easily while rushing full tilt at his opponent. Slogans are handy in advertising.

In Hungary, not far from the twin cities of Buda and Pest, is a town named Kocs. In Hungarian it's pronounced "kotch." In the little town of Kocs more than 500 years ago a man designed a special carriage for the king. It was a large four-wheeled carriage, with a roof. To make it ride easier on the rough roads, it was suspended on springs. In time such carriages became very popular. Because they were first made at the town of Kocs, they were called *coaches;* and that's what we call them today. Even when we use the word *coach* for a tutor or an athletic trainer, such as a football coach, we're carrying out the same idea. A human coach, like the oldtime carriage, helps the student get along faster.

Let's change the scene to East India, about a hundred years ago, and pay a visit to an Indian prince. He offers us a cool drink, of pleasant taste. We ask him what it is. He explains that it is made of arrack, tea, sugar, lemon, and water—five different elements. Now the Hindustani word for five is *panch,* pronounced almost like *punch.* So we call the drink punch.

In London, in the days of Queen Victoria, the people often wondered whether the national income was going to be enough to pay the national expenses. They called it "balancing the budget." The expression sounds perfectly natural to us, for we too have budgets to balance. But why is an annual statement of finances called a budget? It's from the old British custom of enclosing the annual estimates of revenue and expenditures in a leather purse or bag for presentation to the House of Commons. The name of the bag came from an old French word, *bougette,* or, as we pronounce it, "budget."

In delving into the history of the English language we find a group of unfortunates—people who have come down in the world: a villain, a hussy, a boor, a pagan, a savage, an imp, a knave, a silly, an idiot, and a hypocrite. All have seen better days. They are victims of change and, to some extent, of carelessness. Take, for example, the villain. He was a farm laborer working on a country estate. The estate was called a villa, and the man was called a villain. It was only after centuries, during which his master sometimes called to him impatiently, "Villain, come here!" that the name began to suggest a scoundrel.

So it is with the others. The hussy, at one time, was a respectable housewife. But *housewife* was pronounced *huzzif;* that word, shortened to *hussy,* was sometimes applied jokingly to a girl. Today we forget the good meaning and remember only the disrespectful one. A boor was merely a farmer; that's what *boor* meant, not very long ago. The pagan was simply a countryman, a peasant; *paganus* in Latin meant "a dweller in the country." The savage, as shown by his Franco-Latin name, was simply a *sauvage,* "a dweller in the woods."

We usually employ the word *imp* for the boy next door when we want to suggest that he's up to mischief. Yet the name comes from the days when *imp* was merely another word for "child." In one oldtime book a young English prince is called "that most angelic imp." *Knave* today means "a rascal, a rogue." At one time it was the word for "boy" or "youth."

The final trio—the silly, the idiot, and the hypocrite—were all perfectly normal. A silly today is one who is weak in intellect; in ancient times, *silly* meant "happy, fortunate, blessed." Our idiot received his name many centuries ago, when *idiot* meant "a private person." As to the hypocrite—he dates his name from the old days in classic Greece, when a hypocrite was not a deceitful person at all but merely a mimic, an actor.

AMERICA'S CONTRIBUTIONS

If a language belongs to the people who speak it, the English language surely belongs to America. Today about 60 percent of the world's English-speaking people are citizens of the United States; about 20 percent are found in the British Isles; the other 20 percent live elsewhere.

Since the establishment of the first English settlement in America in the 17th century, American influence on the language of the mother country has grown so great that today an Englishman cannot speak his own language without using words and expressions originating in the New World. Some years ago Dr. Mitford M. Mathews, of the University of Chicago, began to make a list of English words of American origin, and at last count he had reached a total of well over 50,000. These words were not merely terms of American Indian origin (such as *tomahawk, wampum, squaw)* or of Spanish origin (such as *bronco, lariat, stampede)* but a host of others that can fairly be classed as household words. Here are a few of them:

advertising	chop suey	lengthy
agent	cute	lipstick
anesthesia	elevator (lift)	moron
appendicitis	faculty	movie
automobile	(of school)	O. K.
balance	filibuster	overcoat
(remainder)	fraternity	phonograph
beeline	(college)	refrigerator
belittle	gerrymander	Santa Claus
boss	girl friend	single tax
boy friend	governmental	sorority
cablegram	hamburger	telephone
cafeteria	interview	typewriter
casket (coffin)	iron lung	undershirt

Multiplying this list by 1,100 will give some idea of the vast number of words in the English language that are of American origin. The British can accept the situation without embarrassment, for they know that English, the language of Shakespeare and Lincoln, was not created by the people of any single nation. English is a polyglot river, fed by the streams of every land and age, forever changing, ever flowing on. And we have done our share to keep it flowing.

OUR HOSPITABLE LANGUAGE

Our language is rich because it is hospitable. It receives, naturalizes, and uses words from many tongues. Thousands of words of Greek, Latin, French, and German origin will be found in the dictionary pages. In addition, there are many words from other languages.

From Arabic we get *coffee, cotton, magazine, mattress, sofa, syrup, tariff, zero.* Also from Arabic are such words as *alcohol, alcove, algebra,* and *alkali,* in all of which the *al-* means "the."

Among Chinese contributions are *tea, china, typhoon.*

From Dutch we borrow *boss, skate, snoop, skipper, yacht,* and many other seafaring terms.

From Hebrew: *amen, hallelujah, cherub,* and *satan.*

From Hindustani: *khaki* and probably *calico.*

From Hungarian: *coach, hussar, shako.*

From Italian: *alarm, bandit, bankrupt, carnival,* *ditto, gazette, influenza, piano, sonnet, stucco, studio, umbrella, volcano.*

From Japanese: *geisha, mikado.*

From Malay: *bamboo, bantam, caddy* (for tea), *gong, sago, gutta-percha, ketchup, batik.*

From Persian: *bazaar, check, shawl, turban, paradise.*

From Portuguese: *caste, marmalade, cobra.*

From Russian: *babushka, czar, knout, soviet.*

From the Scandinavian languages: *fiord, ski, skoal, viking.*

From Turkish: *ottoman, tulip, caviar.*

BEAUTIFUL WORDS

Every few years, presumably when there is a shortage of news, some enterprising reporter asks a number of prominent men and women to make lists of the ten "most beautiful" words in the language. As might be expected, the nominations include a great diversity of words; no two persons have the same eye or ear for words. Beauty in words is somewhat elusive, but ugliness is easy to recognize. No one would give a beauty prize to *scratch,* or *shredded,* or *eschew.*

Popular in many lists of beautiful words are *mother, love, truth,* and *justice,* yet all of these have been disallowed on the ground that they are not euphonious. They are beautiful in concept but not in sound. *Love* may be supremely beautiful in our thoughts, but as a word it is a mere monosyllable that closes on the uninspiring sound of *v.* The Romance languages are much more fortunate in their words for love: Latin and Spanish *amor,* French *amour,* and, notably, the flowing Italian *amore,* ah-mo'reh, which sounds and sings very well.

The word *lullaby* is a great vote getter, partly from its sound but probably also from its association with the slumber of innocent infants. *Slumber,* by the way, is a popular word.

High on many lists are *golden, murmuring,* and *melody;* also *glow, noble,* and *soul.* The *o* sound is always liked. *Twilight, home,* and *romance* are favored by many voters, and it will be noticed that two of these words contain the *o* sound, unstressed in *romance* but definite in *home.* (The word *home* also profits from its sentimental associations.)

Smoothness seems to be the deciding factor in judging verbal beauty. The "good round *O*" is smooth sounding; perhaps even more so is the *oo* sound as in *moon, coo,* and the Irish pet name *mavourneen.* The 18th-century Emanuel Swedenborg, whose studies in words are unique, pictured the language of heaven as containing many long-vowel sounds, with *oo* as the most important. The *oo* sound can be tested in a sort of one-sided conversation with a young baby by gently saying "oo" and then waiting for the infantile response. You may have to wait as long as 15 or 20 seconds, but the reaction is almost sure to come in the form of a pleased smile.

Famous among allegedly beautiful English words is *cellar-door.* This word was chosen many years ago by the Italian patriot Mazzini, when he began to learn

English. To him the sound of *cellar-door* was fascinating. As he formed his opinion in England, we may assume that he heard the word with its 19th-century British pronunciation of *selladaw*.

George Whitefield, 18th-century English preacher, who spent some years in America, gave a vogue to the long word *Mesopotamia*. It is said that by merely uttering that word he could reduce a great audience to tears. To this day some public speakers talk about "the true Mesopotamia ring," referring to an utterance with more ring to it than reason.

NEW WORDS

New words are always entering the language. The ways in which new words come into existence are many, and the rate at which they enter varies with the times. Four of the main sources of new words are borrowing, construction, compounding, and affixing. In the past, as we have seen, English borrowed a large number of words, called loan-words, from other languages.

In our own time, constructed words probably account for most of the additions to the vocabulary. Constructed words are formed from word elements of other languages, usually Greek or Latin. For instance, *bathyscaph* is from the Greek *bathys,* deep, and *skaphe,* boat. Most constructed words appear in technical vocabularies. Some, however, do gain wide currency: *antibiotic* and *transistor,* for example.

Another important source of new words is compounding, the joining of two existing words: *paperback* and *spacewalk,* for example.

Many new words are formed by affixing, the addition of living prefixes or suffixes (such as *pre-, non-,* and *-ize*) to a word. Affixed words often originate in conversation to satisfy the needs of a particular situation. Thus, even an unabridged dictionary does not contain all of the many affixed words in use.

A short description of some other sources of new words follows: Conversion is the transfer of a word from one part of speech to another. Conversion of a noun to a verb, for example, *to invoice* and *to contact,* is common. Blending is the combination of parts of different words: *brunch* from *br*eakfast and *lunch*. Acronyms are words formed from the initial letters of a phrase: *laser* and *radar*. Proper or trade names are sometimes adapted as common nouns: *diesel* and *nylon*. Shortening usually involves a single word, rather than a phrase: *phone* from *telephone*.

Many words are transitory and are not in currency long enough to be included in a dictionary. Other words (such as the Latin additions of the 16th century or new words of the Space Age) are relatively permanent members of the language and are altered or eliminated only in the long, slow, complex process of language change.

The following list is composed of three types of current words: (1) new words, such as *spacewalk,* (2) words with new meanings or applications, such as *abort* and *Augmented Roman,* and (3) existing words that are new to popular usage, such as *LSD-25*.

abort, a·bạrt′, *v.t.* To cancel or cut short a space flight, usually because of the craft's failure to perform its purposes.

aerospace, âr′ō·spās′, *a.* Referring to the earth's atmosphere and space.

aquanaut, ak′wa·nat, *n.* One who explores underwater phenomena.

Augmented Roman, *n.* A phonetic alphabet system that utilizes 43 characters to represent the speech sounds of English, used in teaching reading.

bathyscaph, bath′i·skaf, *n.* A submarine-like craft used in exploring extreme depths of the oceans and in other oceanographic research.

biodegrade, bi′ō·di·grād″, *v.t.* To break down a substance by means of bacterial action.

bistatic radar, *n.* A radar system that utilizes three bodies: the earth, the object of study, and an artificial satellite, which carries receiving equipment (conventional, monostatic radar having the transmitter and receiver in one place).

booster rocket, *n.* A rocket engine that provides the necessary thrust, or pushing force, to launch a spacecraft and place it in orbit. (Also referred to as a *launch vehicle.*)

centrifuge, sen′tri·fūj, *n.* An apparatus in which equipment, human beings, or animals are rotated and subjected to conditions simulating the accelerations encountered in a spacecraft.

collision course, *n.* A course taken by a craft, especially a missile, that will cause it to intercept and collide with another craft.

comsat, käm′sat, *n.* A blending of *com*munications and *sat*ellite.

countdown, kount′doun, *n.* The period during which the sequence of actions necessary to launch a spacecraft is carried out.

deep space probe, *n.* A space vehicle designed to explore regions near the moon and beyond.

destruct, dē·strukt′, *v.t.* To deliberately destroy a spacecraft before it has completed its course, usually because of a malfunction that makes the craft a hazard.

docking, dok′ing, *n.* The operation of bringing together and joining two craft in space.

escape velocity, *n.* The speed that a body must attain in order to leave the gravitational pull of a celestial body.

exobiology, eks′ō·bi·o″lo·ji, *n.* The study of living organisms that exist on celestial bodies other than the earth.

garbage, gar′bij, *n.* Miscellaneous objects in orbit that have been ejected or have broken away from spacecraft.

hold, hōld, *n.* The temporary halt of a countdown to remove an impediment so that the countdown can be continued (compare with **abort** and **scrub**).

laser, lā′zer, *n.* [An acronyn for *l*ight *a*mplification by *s*timulated *e*mission of *r*adiation.] A device that generates a concentrated light beam that can be used to carry communications signals, to weld hard materials (such as the exotic metals used in the aerospace industry), to perform some kinds of surgery, etc.

LEM, lem, *n.* [An acronym for *l*unar *e*xcursion *mod-*

ule.] A small spacecraft that is designed to carry two men and equipment and to be launched from another manned craft in order to make a landing on the moon.

LSD-25 (lysergic acid diethylamide), *n.* A drug that can cause hallucinations and other simulated symptoms of mental disorders, used primarily in psychological experimentation.

magnetosphere, mag·net″ō·sfēr′, *n.* The region of space around a celestial body that is dominated by that body's magnetic field.

microelectronics, mi′krō·ē·lek·tron″iks, *n.* A branch of electronics concerned with extreme miniaturization of components, especially circuits. [Amplifier circuits smaller than an aspirin tablet have been produced.]

module, mod′ūl, *n.* A self-contained unit of a spacecraft that serves as a functional part of the craft.

op art, *n.* A form of painting that evinces strong visual responses by utilizing various optical effects; optical art.

OSO, ō′sō, *n.* [An acronym for *orbiting solar observatory.*] A series of U.S. artificial satellites used in solar research.

plus count, *n.* The count, in seconds, that immediately follows the launching of a spacecraft, used to check the sequence of events after the countdown has ended.

pop art, *n.* A form of painting and sculpture that uses as subject matter such things as comic strip characters, advertisements, product packages, etc.

rendezvous, ran′dā·vö, *n.* The meeting of two or more spacecraft in space at a prescheduled time and place.

retrorocket, re″trō·rok′et, *n.* A rocket used to retard the forward motion of a spacecraft.

roll, rōl, *n.* The rotational movement of a craft about its longitudinal axis.

scrub, skrub, *v.t.* To cancel a rocket firing, either before or during the countdown.

shutdown, shut′doun, *n.* The automatic switching off of the booster rocket in order to prevent a liftoff, possibly because of a malfunction in one of the spacecraft's systems.

soft landing, *n.* A landing, on a celestial body other than the earth, that avoids a crash of the landing vehicle.

spacewalk, spās′wak, *n.* The activity of an astronaut that takes place outside the spacecraft; extra vehicular activity (EVA).

staging, stāg′ing, *n.* The method of using a booster and one or more rockets in a spacecraft, in which each state, as it burns out, is jettisoned.

sustainer engine, *n.* A rocket that maintains the velocity a spacecraft attains from its booster rocket.

tracking, trak′ing, *n.* The various means of observing the movements of spacecraft.

T-time, *n.* Any specific time either before or after the launching of a spacecraft, for instance, "T minus 40," meaning 40 minutes prior to launch.

voiceprint, vois′print, *n.* A spectograph, or visible representation, of the sound patterns of the human voice.

weightlessness, wāt′les·nes, *n.* The absence of apparent gravitational pull on an object.

yaw, ya, *n.* The lateral rotational movement of a craft about its vertical axis.

HOW TO USE THIS DICTIONARY

For most users of this dictionary the entries will explain themselves. None the less, a few words of introduction may be useful.

To find a word, we must know how it is spelled. When several spellings are in use, they appear under cross-entries. Thus the main entry for *czar* is indexed also under *tsar* and *tzar.* The order of information is as follows: (1) The word itself. (2) Its pronunciation, according to the sound-spelling system at the foot of each page and explained in the key to pronunciation. Stress is shown by this sign (′) *after* the stressed syllable. In some words an additional heavier stress is indicated by the same sign doubled (″). (3) The part of speech, shown by *n.* for noun, *v.* for verb, *a.* for adjective, and so forth, and explained in the list of abbreviations and signs used in this dictionary. (4) The derivation of the word, in brackets, with related words in other languages. (5) The meaning or meanings of the word, often followed by idioms or familiar phrases.

PRONUNCIATION

In speaking, choice of the right word is important, but that word must be given an acceptable pronunciation. Absolute uniformity of pronunciation is neither possible nor necessary. A dictionary noting local speech variations heard in all fifty States of the Union would

be confusing. The pronunciations in the present work represent an American standard, acceptable wherever English is spoken.

Sometimes a sound-spelling may seem strange, as when *exhibit* is spelled ig·zib′it. Possibly at one time the word was pronounced eks·hib′it, but not now. Long ago the *eks,* because it was unstressed, was worn down to *igs,* and the *h,* because its utterance called for more breath, was dropped entirely. Today only a foreign student would carefully say eks-hib-it. *Exhibition,* on the other hand, is pronounced eg′zi·bish″on, because here the *eks,* somewhat stressed, was protected from vowel change.

Stress, in speech as in music, is a valuable aid to expression, but when it is placed on the wrong syllable, the effect is absurd, especially when it is put on an unaccented syllable. A person may be heard talking about CREE-ation, YEW-nited States, DEE-mocracy, REE-publicanism, and so forth. Such a practice, presumably used to emphasize the words, only distorts them. The case is similar with final unstressed syllables; for example, there is no *age* in damage, no *page* in rampage, no *sage* in message. The accepted pronunciations are, respectively, dam′ij, ramp′ij, mes′ij.

Stress is important even with monosyllables. In the sentence "He asked her boy to call James" (hē askt hẽr boi tu kal jāmz), the word *to* is pronounced tu,

xiii

because it is obscure and unstressed. Only when stressed is it given its full sound tö, rhyming with "moo."

Early in the 20th century an American publisher issued a book entitled *25,000 Words Frequently Mispronounced*. This is a most discouraging title, until we realize that the list included many geographic, theological, scientific, and foreign terms seldom used by the average citizen.

Pronunciation of English varies to some extent, which is not to be wondered at, for the language is spoken by about 300 million people. Some variation is noted even in the pronunciation of the well educated.

Here is a short list of words that are often mispronounced. Preferred pronunciations for them are found in the dictionary entries.

accessory	column	liqueur
accompanist	coupé	perfume *(n.)*
address	decade	presentation
adult	envoy	program
ally	exemplary	promulgate
anti-	exquisite	respite
arctic	genuine	semi-
athletic	gesture	statistics
bade	gist	suite
bulwark	lingerie	vagary

KEY TO PRONUNCIATION

In showing the pronunciation the simplest and most easily understood method has been adopted, that of rewriting the word with a set of letters that have invariably the same sound, no matter by what letter or letters the sounds may be expressed in the word whose pronunciation is shown. The key by this means is greatly simplified, the reader having only to bear in mind one mark for each sound. Sounds and letters, it must be remembered, are often very different things. In English there are a great many more sounds than letters to represent them, so that some of the letters stand for more than one sound. The letter *a,* for instance, has at least six or seven, namely, those given in the accompanying table and two more, as in the words *any* and *quality,* which may be better represented by *e* and *o* respectively. Our alphabet is therefore very far from being a perfect alphabet, which would have a distinct letter for each sound and would always represent the same sound by the same letter. The following is a list of characters and key-words used to show the pronunciation in the dictionary.

VOWELS

ā ....as in....... *fate*	i ....as in .... *pin*
ä ....as in........ *far*	ō ....as in........ *note*
â ....as in........ *fare*	o ....as in........ *not*
a ....as in........ *fat*	ö ....as in....... *move*
a̞ ....as in....... *fall*	ū ....as in........ *tube*
ē ....as in........ *me*	u ....as in........ *tub*
e ....as in....... *met*	u̞ ....as in........ *bull*
ė ....as in .... *her*	oi ....as in........ *oil*
ī ....as in........ *pine*	ou ...as in...... *pound*

CONSONANTS

ch ...as in....... *ch*ain	ng ...as in......... si*ng*
ch ...as in..... Sc. lo*ch*	TH ...as in....... *then*
Ger. na*ch*t	th....as in....... *th*in
g ....as in........ *g*o	w ....as in .... *w*ig
j ....as in .... *j*ob	hw ...as in ...... *wh*ig
zh...as in...... a*z*ure	

This system, it is believed, will be sufficient for all practical purposes, and the intelligent reader will not care for greater nicety. Consonants not in the list are used simply with their ordinary sounds.

Accent.—Words consisting of more than one syllable receive an accent, as the first syllable of the word *labor,* the second of *delay,* and the third of *comprehension.* The accented syllable is the most prominent part of the word and is denoted by the mark ('), as in the words *la'bor, delay',* and *comprehen'sion.*

Many polysyllabic words are pronounced with two accents, the primary and the secondary accent, as the word *excommunication,* in which the third as well as the fifth syllable is commonly accented. The accent on the fifth syllable is the primary accent, and when it requires to be indicated in the pronunciation it receives a double mark, thus ("), the secondary or inferior accent receiving only the single mark ('), as in *excommu'nica"tion.*

ABBREVIATIONS AND SIGNS
USED IN THIS DICTIONARY

a. or *adj.* adjective	*antiq.* antiquities	at. wt. atomic weight	*chem.* chemistry
abbrev. abbreviation,	aor. aorist, aoristic	aug. augmentative	*chron.* chronology
abbreviated	Ar. Arabic	*avi.* aviation	Class. Classical
acc. accusative	*arch.* architecture	*bact.* bacteriology	(=Greek and Latin)
adv. adverb	*archaeol.* archaeology	*biol.* biology	cog. cognate,
agri. agriculture	*arith.* arithmetic	*bot.* botany	cognate with
alg. algebra	Armor. Armoric	Bret. Breton	colloq. colloquial
Amer. American	art. article	(=Armoric)	*com.* commerce
anat. anatomy	A.Sax. Anglo-Saxon	*Carl.* Carlyle	comp. compare
anc. ancient	*astrol.* astrology	*carp.* carpentry	compar. comparative
anthropol.	*astron.* astronomy	caus. causative	*conch.* conchology
anthropology	at. no. atomic number	Celt. Celtic	*conj.* conjunction

xiv

contr. contraction, contracted
crystal. crystallography
D. Dutch
Dan. Danish
dat. dative
def. definite
dial. dialect, dialectal
dict. dictionary
dim. diminutive
distrib. distributive
dram. drama, dramatic
dyn. dynamics
E., Eng. English
eccles. ecclesiastical, in ecclesiastical affairs
econ. economics
educ. education
elect. electricity
engin. engineering
engr. engraving
entom. entomology
ethn. ethnology
etym. etymology
exclam. exclamation
fem. feminine
fig. figuratively
Fl. Flemish
fort. fortification
Fr. French
freq. frequentative
Fris. Frisian
fut. future
G. German
Gael. Gaelic
galv. galvanism
genit. genitive
geog. geography
geol. geology
geom. geometry
Goth. Gothic
Gr. Greek
gram. grammar
gun. gunnery
Heb. Hebrew
her. heraldry
Hind. Hindustani, or Hindi
hist. history
hort. horticulture
Hung. Hungarian
hydros. hydrostatics
Icel. Icelandic
ich. ichthyology

imper. imperative
imperf. imperfect
impers. impersonal
incept. inceptive
ind. indicative
Ind. Indian
indef. indefinite
Indo-Eur. Indo-European
inf. infinitive
intens. intensive
interj. interjection
Ir. Irish
It. Italian
L. Latin
L.G. Low German
lit. literal, literally
Lith. Lithuanian
L.L. Late Latin
mach. machinery
manuf. manufactures
masc. masculine
math. mathematics
mech. mechanics
med. medicine
Med. L. Medieval Latin
mensur. mensuration
metal. metallurgy
metaph. metaphysics
meteor. meteorology
M.H.G. Middle High German
Mil. Milton
milit. military, in military affairs
mineral. mineralogy
Mod. Fr. Modern French
Ms manuscript
Mss manuscripts
mus. music
myth. mythology
N. Norse, Norwegian
n. noun
nat. hist. natural history
nat. order natural order
nat. phil. natural philosophy
naut. nautical
navig. navigation
neg. negative
neut. neuter
N.H.G. New High German

N.L. New Latin
nom. nominative
Norm. Norman
North. E. Northern English
N.T. New Testament
numis. numismatics
obj. objective
obs. obsolete
obsoles. obsolescent
O.E. Old English (*i.e.,* English between A. Saxon and Modern English)
O.Fr. Old French
O.H.G. Old High German
O. Sax. Old Saxon
O.T. Old Testament
ornith. ornithology
p. or *part.* participle
paint. painting
paleon. paleontology
pass. passive
pathol. pathology
pejor. pejorative
Per. Persian
perf. perfect
pers. person
persp. perspective
Pg. Portuguese
phar. pharmacy
philol. philology
philos. philosophy
Phoen. Phoenician
photog. photography
phren. phrenology
phys. physics
phys. geog. physical geography
physiol. physiology
pl. plural
pneum. pneumatics
poet. poetical
Pol. Polish
poss. possessive
pp. past participle
ppr. present participle
Pr. Provençal
prep. preposition
pres. present
pret. preterite
print. printing
priv. privative
pron. pronunciation, pronounced

pron. pronoun
pros. prosody
prov. provincial
psych. psychology
rail. railways
refl. reflexively, with a reflexive pronoun
R. Cath. Ch. Roman Catholic Church
rhet. rhetoric
Rom. antiq. Roman antiquities
Rus. Russian
Sax. Saxon
Sc. Scottish
Scand. Scandinavian
Scrip. Scripture
sculp. sculpture
Shak. Shakespeare
sing. singular
Skr. Sanskrit
Slav. Slavonic, or Slavic
sociol. sociology
Sp. Spanish
sp. gr. specific gravity
subj. subjunctive
superl. superlative
surg. surgery
surv. surveying
Sw. Swedish
sym. symbol
syn. synonym
technol. technology
tel. telegraphy and telephony
teleg. telegraphy
Tenn. Tennyson
term. termination
Teut. Teutonic
Thack. Thackeray
theol. theology
trigon. trigonometry
Turk. Turkish
typog. typography
v.i. verb intransitive
v.t. verb transitive
W. Welsh
zool. zoology
† rare
‡ obsolete
= equivalent to
. comparison of
.. synonyms

Cross-references in this dictionary are printed in two kinds of type. When a word is printed in small capital letters, as NAIL, *the reader should look under that entry for more information. When a word is capitalized and italicized, it is a variant and directs the reader to the desired information.*

PREFIXES AND SUFFIXES

PREFIXES

A-. From A. Sax. *a-* intensive, as in *arise, awake.*

A-. From A. Sax. *of,* as in *adown, athirst, anew, akin.*

A-. From A. Sax. *of, o',* as in *o'clock (a-clock).*

A-. From A. Sax. *on,* as in *afoot, abed, aboard.*

A-. From L. *ab,* from, as in *avert.*

A-. From L. *ad,* to, as in *achieve, ascend.*

A-. From A. Sax. *and-, against,* as in *along.*

A-. From L. *ex,* out, modified by Angl. Fr. *a* from O. Fr. *e,* as in *amend, affray.*

A-. From Gr. *a-* privative or negative, sometimes through L. or Fr. as in *abysm, agnostic, amorphous*

Ab-, from, away, as in *abduct, abjure.* From L. *ab,* from, preposition and prefix; allied to E. *of, off,* Gr. *apo,* from or away. Before *c* and *t,* generally assumes the lengthened form *abs,* also appears as *a-* (*see* **A-**).

Abs-. *See* **Ab-.**

Ac-. A form of **Ad-.**

Ad-, to, toward, at or near, as in *adapt, admit.* From L. *ad,* to, preposition and prefix; allied to E. *at.* Takes by assimilation the forms *ac-, af-, ag-, al-, an-, ap-, ar-, as-, at-,* as in *accede, affirm, aggregate, allude, annex, applaud, arrogant, assume, attribute,* also appears as *a-* in *ascend.*

Af-, Ag-, Al-. Forms of **Ad-.**

Al- (Arabic *al,* the), as in *alchemy, alcohol, algebra, alkali.*

Ambi-, Amb-, about, around, as in *ambition, amputate.* From L. *ambi-, amb-,* on both sides, around; allied to Gr. *amphi,* about, L. *ambo,* both; A. Sax. *emb, ymb,* G. *um,* about.

Amphi-, about, around, on both or all sides, as in *amphibious, amphitheater.* From Gr. *amphi,* about, around, preposition and prefix. *See* **Ambi-.**

An-. (1)=**Ad-.** (2) Not, negation or privation, from Gr. *an-* or *a-,* the negative prefix, as in *anarchy.* Allied to E. *un-,* L. *in-,* not. (3)=A. Sax. *and-,* against, opposite, as in *answer.* Appears as *a-,* in *along.* Same as Goth. *and-,* Gr. *ant-, ent-,* Gr. *anti.*

Ana-, up, through, throughout, as in *analysis, anatomy, anabasis.* From Gr. *ana,* up, preposition and prefix; allied to E. *on.*

Ant-, against, as in *antagonist, antacid.* Same as **Anti-.**

Ante-, before, as in *antecedent, antedate.* From L. *ante,* before, preposition and prefix. *See* **Anti-.**

Anti-, against, in opposition, as in *antichrist, anticlimax.* From Gr. *anti,* against, preposition and prefix; allied to L. *ante,* before, and to the A. Sax. prefix *and-, an-,* seen in *answer.* *See* **An-.**

Ap-. A form of **Ad-.**

Apo-, Aph-, away, apart, off, as in *apostle, apostate, aphelion.* From Gr. *apo,* from, away, preposition and prefix; allied to L. *ab,* from, E. *off.* *See* **Ab-.**

Ar-. A form of **Ad-.**

Arch-, Archi-, chief, head, ruling, as in *archbishop, architect, archangel.* From Gr. *archi-,* chief, from *archē,* rule, beginning.

As-, At-. Forms of **Ad-.**

Auto-, self, of one's self, as in *autograph, automatic.* From Gr. *auto-,* from pronoun *autos,* self.

Be-. From A. Sax. *be-, bi-,* from *bi, big*=E. *by.* Has various meanings: by or near, or denoting locality, as in *beside, beneath, below;* with a causative or intensive force, as in *benumb, besprinkle, bemire;* with a privative force, in *behead;* upon or against, as in *befall.*

Bi-, twice, two ways, double, as in *bicycle, biennial, bisect.* From L. *bi-,* double, for older *dui-,* akin to *duo,* two (compare *bellum,* war, for *duellum*), and to E. *two.*

Bis-, twice, double, as in *biscuit.* Longer form of **Bi-.**

Cata-, Cath-, Cat-, down, downward, through, according to, as in *cataract, cataclysm, catarrh, catholic, catechism.* From Gr. *kata,* down, through; preposition and prefix.

Circum-, around, all round, as in *circumnavigate, circumspect, circumstance.* From L. *circum,* round, preposition and prefix; from *circus,* a circle. Seen also in *circuit.*

Cis-, on this side of, as in *cisalpine.* From L. *cis,* preposition and prefix.

Co-, Col-. Same as **Com-.**

Com-, with, together, altogether (intensively), as in *combine, compound, command.* From L. *com-,* prefix, used for preposition *cum,* with, allied to Gr. *syn,* Skr. *sam,* with. Appears also as *co-, col-, con-, cor-,* as in *co-exist, collect, connect, correspond.*

Con-. Same as **Com-.**

Contra-, against, as in *contradict, contravene.* From L. *contra,* against, preposition and prefix, from *con-,* or *cum-* and *-tra* (as in *intra,* within, *extra,* beyond), akin to *trans,* across, Skr. *tar,* to pass.

Cor-. Same as **Com-.**

Counter-, against; same as **Contra,** but directly from Fr. *contre,* against.

De-, down, from, away, as in *descend, denude, depart, describe.* From L. *de,* from, out of, preposition and prefix. In some cases, represents O. Fr. *des-,* from L. *dis-,* apart, as in *decry, defeat.*

Demi-, half, semi-. From Fr. *demi.* *See* dictionary.

Di-, double, as in *dimorphous.* From Gr. *di-,* double, akin to *dis-, bis-.*

Dia-, through, between, double, as in *diameter, diagnosis, dialogue.* From Gr. *dia,* through, between, preposition and prefix; akin to *di-, dis-.*

Dif-. A form of **Dis-.**

Dis-, apart, asunder, in two, as in *disarm, discharge, distract;* also used negatively, as in *disbelief, disapprove.* From L. *dis,* asunder, preposition and prefix; allied to Gr. *dis, di-,* double, and to L. *bis,* twice.

Dys-, bad, ill, difficult, as in *dysentery, dyspepsia.* From Gr. *dys-,* prefix.

E. Same as **Ex-.** In *enough,* e- represents A. Sax. prefix *ge-;* in *esquire, estate,* it is a mere euphonic element prefixed for ease in pronunciation.

Ec-, Ex-, out, as in *ecstasy, eclectic, exodus.* From Gr. *ek, ex,* out, preposition and prefix, akin to L. *ex.*

Ef-. A form of **Ex-.**

Em-, En-, in, as in *embrace, enclose, enlist;* or used with a causal force, as in *enable, enlarge.* From Fr. *em-, en-,* L. *im-, in-,* preposition and prefix. *See* **In-.**

En-, in, as in *encaustic, energy.* From Gr. *en,* in, preposition and prefix, akin to L. *in,* A. Sax. *in,* in.

Enter-, between, among, as in *enterprise.* From Fr. *entre,* L. *inter.* *See* **Inter-.**

Epi-, Eph-, Ep-, upon, over, as in *epitaph, epithet, epidermis, ephemeral.* From Gr. *epi,* upon; akin to Skr. *api.*

Es-, out, away, as in *escape, escheat.* From L. *ex, q.v.*

Eu-, well, as in *eulogy, euphony.* From. Gr. *eu-,* well, prefix, neuter of *eus,* good, for *esus,* from root *as,* to be (seen in E. *is*).

Ex-, out of, out, from, as in *exceed, exclude;* also used intensively, as in *exacerbate, exasperate.* From L. *ex,* out, akin to Gr. *ek, ex,* out. *See* **Ec-.** Appears also as *e-, ef-, es-.*

Extra-, beyond, without, as in *extraordinary, extrajudicial.* From L. *extra,* without, preposition and prefix, from *ex* and *-tra. See* **Contra-.**

For-. Used intensively or almost negatively, as in *forgive, forbid, forgo.* From A. Sax. *for-,* same as Icel. and Dan. *for-,* D. and G. *ver-,* Goth. *fra-;* allied to *far,* L. *per.*

Fore-, beforehand, in advance, as in *foretell, foreshow, foreground. See* FORE, in dictionary.

Hemi-, half, as in *hemisphere.* From Gr. prefix *hēmi-,* half, akin to L. *semi.*

Hetero-, other, different, as in *heterodox, heterogeneous.* From Gr. *heteros,* other.

Holo-, whole, entire, as in *holograph, holocaust.* From Gr. *holos,* whole.

Homo-, same, as in *homonym.* From Gr. *homos,* same; allied to E. *same.*

Hyper-, over, beyond, too; *hyperborean, hypercritical.* From Gr. *hyper,* above, over, preposition and prefix; allied to L. *super,* E. *over, up.*

Hypo-, under, beneath, as in *hypocaust, hypotenuse, hypothesis.* From Gr. *hypo,* under, preposition and prefix; allied to L. *sub,* under.

Il-. A form of **In-** (2 and 3).

Im-. A form of **In-.**

In-. (1) In, as in *inborn, insight.* From A. Sax. and E. preposition *in,* cog. with L. *in,* in (whence next **In-**). It may become *im-,* as in *imbed, imbody.* (2) In, into, as in *include, inclose.* From L. *in,* in, preposition and prefix; cog. with Gr. *en,* E. and Goth. *in,* Icel. *inn,* G. *ein.* Before *m, b, p,* it becomes *im-,* as in *immune, imbibe, implant;* before *l, il-;* before *r, ir-.* (3) Not—the negative prefix, as in *inactive, incapable.* From L. *in-,* not, prefix; Gr. *an-,* E. *un-,* not (see **Un-**). Like the preceding it appears also as *il-, im-, ir-,* as in *illegitimate, immaculate, irrational.*

Infra-, below, as in *infracostal, infraorbital, infrared.* From L. *infra,* below.

Inter-, between, among, as in *intercede, intermingle, interchange.* From L. *inter,* between, among, preposition and prefix; a comparative form akin to *intra-, intro-,* within, *interior,* inner, *internus,* internal. *See* UNDER in dictionary. It also takes the form **Intel-,** as in *intellect.*

Intra-, within, as in *intramural.* From L. *intra,* within. *See* **Inter-.**

Intro-, within, into, as in *introduce, introspection. See* **Inter-.**

Ir-. A form of **In-.**

Juxta-, near, nigh, as in *juxtaposition.* From L. preposition *juxta,* near.

Kata-. *See* **Cata-.**

Mal-, Male-, ill, badly, as in *maladministration, maladroit, malcontent, malefactor.* From Fr. *mal-,* L. *male,* badly, *malus,* evil.

Meta-, Met-, after, beyond, among, or denoting change, as in *metaphysics, metaphor, metamorphosis, metathesis, metonymy.* From Gr. *meta,* with, among, preposition and prefix; cog. with A. Sax. *mid,* G. *mit,* Goth. *mith,* with.

Mis-. (1) Wrong, wrongly, bad, badly, as in *misdeed, mistake, misshapen, mishap, misinformed.* From A. Sax., Icel., Dan., and D. *mis-,* Sw. *miss-,* Goth. *missa-,* wrongly; akin to verb *miss.* (2) Ill, unfortunate, as in *misadventure, misalliance, mischance.* From O. Fr. *mes-,* from L. *minus,* less. *See* dictionary.

Mono-, Mon-, single, sole, having only one, as in *monarch, monody, monogram, monomaniac.* From Gr. *monos,* sole, single.

Multi-, Mult-, many, as in *multangular, multiform, multivalve.* From L. *multus,* many, much.

N-, negative element, as in *never, none.* From A. Sax. *ne,* not; cog. with L. *ne,* not, Skr. *na,* E. *no. See* NO in dictionary.

Non-, not; often used as *in-,* negative, or as *un-.* From L. *non,* not, from *ne unum,* not one. *See* above.

Ob-, against, before, in the way of, as in *object, obstacle, obstruct.* From L. *ob,* against, preposition and prefix; allied to Gr. *epi,* upon, Skr. *api,* moreover. It appears also as *o-, oc-, of-, op-,* as in *omit, occur, offend, oppress.*

Oc-, Of-. Forms of **Ob-.**

Off-, from, as in *offshoot, offspring. See* OFF in dictionary.

On-, on, against, as in *onset, onslaught. See* ON in dictionary.

Op-. A form of **Ob-.**

Out-, out, beyond, as in *outbid, outburst. See* OUT in dictionary.

Over-, above, beyond, too much, as in *overhead, overhang, overburden, overcharge. See* OVER in dictionary.

Palin-, back again, as in *palindrome.* From Gr. *palin,* again.

Pan-, Panto-, all, as in *panacea, pantheism, pantograph.* From Gr. *pan, pantos,* all.

Para-, Par-, beside, beyond or aside from, as in *parallel, paradox, parable, parody.* From Gr. *para,* beside, preposition and prefix; allied to *peri,* around, L. *per,* through, E. *for-. See* **For-.**

Pel-. A form of **Per-.**

Pen-, almost, as in *peninsula, penultimate.* From L. *pene, paene,* almost.

Per-, through, throughout, thoroughly, as in *perforate, pervade, perfect, perdition;* sometimes has the effect of E. *for-* (in *forswear, forget*), as in *perfidy, perjury.* From L. *per,* through, preposition and prefix; allied to Gr. *para,* E. *for-;* in *pellucid* it appears as *pel.*

Peri-, around, about, as in *periphery, peripatetic, periphrasis.* From Gr. *peri,* about, preposition and prefix; allied to Gr. *para,* L. *per.*

Pol-. A form of **Por-.**

Poly-, many, as in *polygamy, polygon, polysyllable.* From Gr. *polys,* many; same root as E. *full.*

Por-, Pol-, forward, forth, as in *portend, pollute.* From L. prefix *por-, pol-,* akin to *pro,* before, Gr. *pro,* Skr. *pra,* E. *forth.*

Post-, after, behind, as in *postdate, postpone.* From L. *post,* after, preposition and prefix.

Pre-, Prae-, before, beforehand, in advance, as in *predict, prefer, prefigure, preeminent.* From L. *prae,* before, preposition and prefix; akin to *pro, per, primus.* It is the *pr* of *prison,* the *pro* of *provost.*

Preter-, beyond, above, as in *preternatural, preterit.* From L. *praeter,* beyond, a comparative form of *prae. See* **Prae.**

Pro-, before, forth, forward, as in *produce, project, pro-*

fess, promise; also instead of, as in *pronoun, proconsul.* From L. *pro,* before, for, preposition and prefix; akin to *prae* and to Gr. *pro,* before, Skr. *pra,* away, E. *for-, q.v.* In some words *pro-* is the Gr. *pro,* as in *prologue.*

Pros-, toward, in addition, as in *proselyte, prosody.* From Gr. *pros,* toward, preposition and prefix; akin to Skr. *prati,* toward, E. *forth.*

Proto-, Prot-, first, original, as in *protocol, protoplasm, protagonist.* From Gr. *prōtos,* first, akin to *pro,* before.

Re-, Red-, back, again, as in *recall, regain, return, retract;* also change of place, as in *remove.* From L. *re-, red-,* prefix, the latter form being used before vowels, as in *redeem, redolent, redundant.*

Retro-, backward, as in *retroact, retrograde.* From L. prefix *retro-,* backward, a comparative of **Re-** (compare *intro-* and *in-*).

Se-, aside, apart, as in *secede, seduce, seclude;* also without, as in *secure.* From L. *se-,* originally *sed-,* only used as a prefix.

Semi-, half, as in *semicircle.* From L. prefix *semi-,* half; akin to Skr. *sāmi,* half, Gr. *hēmi-.* See **Hemi-.**

Sine-, without, as in *sinecure.* From L. *sine,* without, preposition and prefix, from *si,* if, and *ne,* not.

Sub-, under, beneath, inferior, as in *subject, subordinate, submarine, submerge, submit;* also slightly, as in *subacid, subobtuse.* From L. *sub,* under, preposition and prefix; allied to Gr. *hypo,* under, Skr. *upa,* near, and to E. *up, over;* appears also as *su-, suc-, suf-, sug-, sum-, sup-, sur-,* as in *suspect, succeed, suffer, suggest, summon, suppress, surreptitious.*

Subter-, beneath, as in *subterfuge.* From L. *subter,* beneath, preposition and prefix; comparative of *sub, q.v.*

Suc-, Suf-, Sug-, Sum-, Sup-. Forms of **Sub-.**

Super-, above, over, more than, as in *superabound, superadd, supersede, superhuman.* From L. *super,* over, above, preposition and prefix; a comparative form

akin to *sub* and to Gr. *hyper,* over, E. *over.* See SUPER in dictionary.

Supra-, above, as in *supracostal.* From L. *supra,* above, akin to *super.*

Sur-, over, above, as in *surface, surmount;* from Fr. *sur,* above, from L. *super, q.v.*

Sur-. A form of **Sub-.**

Syn-, Sym-, Syl-, with, together with, in company, as in *synagogue, synclinal, symmetry, sympathy, syllable, syllogism.* From Gr. *syn,* with, preposition and prefix; allied to L. *cum.* See **Com-.**

To-, this, on this, as in *today, tonight, together, toward.* From preposition *to.*

Trans-, Tra-, across, over, through, beyond, as in *transmit, transport, transfix, transgress, traverse, traduce.* From L. *trans,* across, preposition and prefix; same root as E. *through.* See THROUGH in dictionary.

Tri-, three, thrice, threefold, as in *triangle, tricolor, trident, trilobite, trilogy.* From L. and Gr. *tri-,* prefix, three, thrice; allied to E. *three.*

Ultra-, beyond, as in *ultramarine, ultramontane.* From L. *ultra,* beyond, preposition and prefix. See ULTRA in dictionary.

Un- (1) The negative prefix = not, as in *unavailing, unanswerable.* From A. Sax. *un-,* not; allied to L. *in-,* not. (2) Denoting reversal of an action; as in *undo, untie.* From A. Sax. *un-,* akin to G. *ent-,* Goth. *and-,* E. *an-* in *answer.* See UN- in dictionary.

Under-, below, beneath, as in *undercurrent, underlie, underhand, undersell.* See UNDER in dictionary.

Up-, up, as in *upheave.* See UP in dictionary.

Utter-, outer, further, as in *uttermost.* From A. Sax. *uter,* comparative of *ut,* out.

With-, against, back, as in *withstand, withdraw, withhold.* From A. Sax. *with,* against, same as preposition *with.* See dictionary.

SUFFIXES

-able, that may be, capable of being, as in *lovable, affable.* L. *-abilis.*

-ac, pertaining to, as in *cardiac, demoniac.* Gr. *-akos.*

-aceous, partaking of the properties of, as in *arenaceous, herbaceous.* L. *-aceus.*

-acious, characterized by, as in *tenacious, pugnacious.* Fr. *-acieux,* L. *-ax, -acis.*

-acity, character, quality, as in *veracity.* From L. *acitas.*

-ad, toward, as in *ventrad, dorsad.* From Lat. *-ad,* toward.

-ade, a more or less continuous action, usually by a group of persons, as in *cavalcade, cannonade, fusillade.* From L. suffix *-ata,* through F., Sp., etc.

-age, abstract or collective, also locality, as in *advantage, foliage, parsonage.* Fr. *-age,* L.L. *-aticum,* L. *-aticus,* adjective termination.

-ain, giving adjectives and nouns, as in *certain, captain.* Fr. *-ain,* L. *-anus.*

-air, -aire, as in *corsair, millionaire.* From L. *arius,* through F. *aire.*

-al, pertaining to, as in *annual, filial.* L. *-alis.*

-an, noun and adjective suffix, as in *pagan, Roman, human.* L. *-anus.*

-ana (iana), items of information about places, persons, or things, as in *Americana, Swedenborgiana, Californiana.* From L. *ana,* pertaining to.

-ance, -ancy, denoting state or action, as in *abundance,*

acceptance. L. *-antia.* See **-nce.**

-ane, adjective suffix, as in *mundane, humane.* L. *-anus.*

-aneous, belonging to, as in *contemporaneous.* L.*-aneus.*

-ant, equivalent to E. suffix *-ing,* as in *abundant, accordant.* L. *-ans, -antis,* termination of present participle.

-ar, pertaining to, as in *angular, familiar, polar.* L. *-aris.*

-ard, denoting disposition or character, as in *coward, niggard, sluggard.* Partly from A. Sax. *-heard,* literally hard, partly from Fr. *-ard,* from G. *hart,* hard.

-ary, adjective and noun suffix, as in *auxiliary, contrary, library, secretary, antiquary, seminary.* L. *-arius,-arium.*

-asm. See **-ism.**

-aster, denoting contempt, as in *poetaster, criticaster.* O. Fr. *-astre,* L. *-aster,* having somewhat of, adjective termination.

-ate, seen in verbs, adjectives, and nouns, as *animate, agitate.* From L. *-atus,* termination of past participle.

-ble. See **-able, -ible.**

-ble, as in *treble.* See **-ple.**

-cle, -cule, diminutive suffix, as in *article, particle, animalcule.* L. *-culus, -cula, -culum.*

-cy, state of, as in *idiocy.* Fr. *-cie,* L. *-tia.*

-d. See **-ed.**

-dom, power or jurisdiction, state, as in *kingdom, earldom, wisdom, martyrdom.* A. Sax. *dóm,* judgment, authority; akin G. *-thum.* See DOOM in dictionary.

xviii

-ed, -d, suffix of past tense. A. Sax. *-de,* shortened for *-dide,* past tense of *dón,* E. to do.

-ed, -d, suffix of past participle and some adjectives and nouns, as in *loved, booted, horned.* Originally *-th,* and corresponding to L. *-tus,* of past participle; same as the *-d, -t, -th,* of *cold, dead, fight, height, death, health.*

-ee, denoting one who is acted on, a recipient, as in *legatee, referee, trustee.* Fr. *-é, -ée,* from L. *-atus* of past participle. *See* **-ate.**

-eer, -ier, denoting profession or employment, as in *brigadier, charioteer.* Fr. *-ier,* L. *-arius.*

-el, diminutive. *See* **-le.**

-en, -n, made of, as in *golden, waxen, leathern;* also pertaining to, as in *heathen.* A. Sax. *-en,* G. *-en,* Goth. *-ein;* akin to L. *-nus,* Gr. *-nos,* Skr. *-nas.*

-en, diminutive, as in *chicken, kitten.* A. Sax. *-en.*

-en, plural, as in *oxen, kine, shoon.* A. Sax *-an.*

-en, to make, verbal termination, as in *soften, whiten.* A. Sax and Goth. infinitive *-nan,* originally an intransitive form.

-ence, -ency. Similar to **-ance, ancy.**

-eous, pertaining to, containing, as in *aqueous.* L. *-eus.* [In *courteous, -eous* is from L. *-ensis;* in *righteous,* also of different origin.]

-er, one who does, as in *baker, singer, writer.* A. Sax. *ere,* G. *-er,* Goth. *-areis,* allied to L. *-arius.* Sometimes takes *y* before it, as in *bowyer, lawyer, sawyer;* in *liar* takes form of *-ar.*

-er, frequentative, as in *flicker, sputter.* A. Sax. *-erian,* G. *-ern.*

-er, comparative suffix. A. Sax. *-er, -or,* G. *-er,* L. *-or.*

-erel, diminutive, as in *cockerel, mongrel.* O. Fr. *-erel.*

-erly, to or from in direction, as in *northerly, easterly.* For *-ern-ly.*

-ern, expressing direction, as in *southern.* A. Sax. *-ern.*

-ery, business or place where it is carried on, also with collective force, as in *archery, brewery, cutlery, finery, soldiery.* From nouns in *-er* with Fr. *-ie,* L. *-ia.*

-es, -s, denoting plurals. A. Sax. *-as;* common to the Aryan languages.

-escent, becoming gradually, as in *convalescent, effervescent.* L. *-escens, -escentis,* present participle of inceptive verbs in *-esco.*

-ese, belonging to a country or city, as in *Siamese, Maltese.* Fr. *-ais, -ois,* It. *-ese,* from L. *-ensis.*

-esque, partaking of, as in *picturesque.* Fr. *-esque,* from L. *-iscus,* a form of *-icus.*

-ess, feminine suffix, as in *authoress, countess, giantess.* Fr. *-esse,* L. *-issa,* from Gr. *-issa.*

-est, suffix of superlatives. A. Sax. *-est, -ost,* G. *-est;* allied to Gr. *-istos,* Skr. *-ishthas.*

-et, -ette, diminutive suffix, as in *billet, coronet, palette.* Fr. *-et, -ette.*

-ey, adjective suffix. *See* **-y.**

-ferous, bearing, producing, as in *auriferous, quartziferous.* L. *-fer,* from *fero,* to bear.

-fold, denoting multiplication, as in *threefold, manifold.* From *fold,* noun or verb.

-ful, full of, as in *fanciful, mournful.* A. Sax. *-ful*=E. *full.*

-fy, to make, as in *beautify.* Fr. *-fier,* L. *ficare,* from *facio,* to make.

-geneous, -genous, as in *homogeneous.* From Gr. and L. root *-gen,* to produce.

-graph, -graphy. From Gr. *-graphos, -graphia,* from *grapho,* to write.

-head, -hood, state, condition, as in *Godhead, widowhood.* A. Sax. *had,* state, rank=G. *-heit.*

-iana. *See* **-ana.**

-ible, same meaning as **-able,** as in *accessible.*

-ic, pertaining to, as in *botanic, periodic, public.* L. *-icus,* Gr. *-ikos,* Skr. *-ikas.*

-ical, pertaining to, as in *logical.* From L. *-icus* and *-alis* combined.

-ics, properly plural, but used as a singular in names of branches of knowledge, as in *mathematics, ethics.* Gr. *ika,* literally things belonging to.

-id, adjective suffix, as in *arid, fluid, torpid.* L. *-idus.*

-id, -idae, suffix of family names of animals. Gr. *-ides,* denoting descent.

-ide, suffix of certain chemical compounds, as *chloride.* Gr. *-eidos,* form.

-ie, -y, diminutive suffix, as in *wifie, Johnnie.* From *-ick,* weaker form of *-ock.*

-ier. Same as **-eer.**

-ile, capable of being, as in *docile, fragile.* L. *-ilis.*

-ile, belonging to, as in *puerile, senile, Gentile.* L. *-ilis.*

-im, a Hebrew plural sign, as in *cherubim.*

-ine, feminine suffix, as in *heroine.* Fr. *-ine,* L. *-ina.*

-ine, suffix of adjectives and nouns, as in *divine, iodine.* L. *-inus, -ina.*

-ing, noun suffix, as in *whiting, shilling.* A. Sax. *-ing.*

-ing, termination of present participles. Corrupted from A. Sax. *-ende.*

-ing, termination of verbal nouns. A. Sax. *-ung.*

-ion. *See* **-sion, -tion.**

-ique, adjective suffix, as in *antique, unique.* Fr. *-ique,* L. *-iquus,* a form of *-icus.*

-ise. *See* **-ize.**

-ish, pertaining to, having somewhat of, as in *childish, foolish, dwarfish, whitish, English.* A. Sax. *-isc,* G. *-isch,* Goth. *-isk.*

-ish, verbal suffix, as in *nourish, perish.* From forms in *-iss-* of French verbs, from L. *-esc-* of inceptive verbs (as *abolesco—abolish*).

-ism, -asm, suffix of nouns, often implying state, system, doctrines, as in *barbarism, atheism, organism, skepticism, pleonasm.* L. *-ismus, -asmus,* from Gr. *-ismos, -asmos.*

-ist, -ast, one who; suffix often corresponding to *-ism, -asm,* as in *atheist, gymnast.*

-ite, one of, a follower of, as in *Israelite, Spinozite.* L. *-ita,* Gr. *-itēs.*

-ite, a geological suffix=*-lite.* Also a chemical suffix, from L. adjective suffix *-itus.*

-itis, suffix denoting inflammation; used in medical terms, as in *laryngitis.* Gr. *-itis.*

-ity, state, as in *ability.* L. *-itas. See* **-ty.**

-ix. *See* **-trix.**

-ize, -ise, to make, to act, as in *civilize, economize.* Fr. *-iser,* O. Fr. *-izer,* L.L. *izare,* from Gr. *-izein.*

-kin, diminutive suffix, as in *lambkin.* Not in A. Sax.; same as D. *-ek-en,* Gr. *-ch-en;* equivalent to *-ock-en,* and thus a double diminutive.

-le, -el, a suffix in nouns denoting instrument, as in *needle, saddle, steeple, navel, weasel.* A. Sax. *-el, -ol, -ul, -ela,* G. *-el,* Aryan *-al, -ar.* Also in some adjectives, as *idle.*

-le, diminutive and frequent suffix of verbs, as in *frizzle, nibble, sparkle.*

-lence, suffix in abstract nouns, corresponds to **-lent.**

-lent, full of, as in *violent, purulent.* L. *-lentus.*

-less, free from, without, as in *artless, fatherless.* A. Sax. *-leás,* G. *-los;* akin *lose, loss.*

-let, diminutive suffix, as in *leaflet, streamlet.* From *-le* or *-el,* and *-et.*

-ling, diminutive suffix, as in *darling, lordling, starveling.* From *-ing,* A. Sax. *-ing,* with prefixed *-le* or *-el.*

-ling, -long, adverbial suffix, as in *darkling, endlong*. A. Sax. *-linga, -lunga,* adverbial datives.

-lite, in mineralogical terms, stone, as in *aerolite*. Gr. *lithos,* a stone.

-logy, doctrine, science, as in *biology*. Gr. *-logia,* from *logos,* a word, speech.

-ly, like, an adjective and adverbial suffix, as in *lovely, truly*. A form of adjective *like;* A. Sax. *-lic,* adjective suffix, *-lice,* adverbial suffix.

-ment, act of, state of, as in *agreement, argument, experiment*. Fr. *-ment,* L. *mentum*.

-meter, a measure, as in *hydrometer*. Gr. *metron,* a measure.

-mony, state, as in *matrimony, parsimony*. L. *-monium, -monia*.

-most, suffix in superlatives, as *foremost*. Not the same as *most,* superlative of *much,* but a double superlative composed of superlative suffixes *-ma* and *-est*. See FORE-MOST in dictionary.

-nce, -ncy, suffix of abstract nouns usually denoting state, as in *vigilance, brilliancy, abhorrence, excellency*. Fr. *-nce,* L. *-ntia,* from present participles in *-ans, -antis, ens, -entis,* with suffix *-ia*.

-ness, denoting state of being, as in *barrenness, fullness, redness*. A. Sax. *-nes,* same as G. *-nis,* Goth. *-nassus*.

-ock, diminutive suffix, as in *hillock, bullock*. A. Sax. *-uca*.

-oid, -oidal, resembling, as in *elephantoid, spheroidal*. Gr. *-oeidēs,* from *eidos,* form.

-on, noun suffix, as in *dragon, falcon*. Fr. *-on,* L. *-onem,* accusative suffix of nouns in *-o, -onis*.

-or, one who, as in *emperor, sailor*. Fr. *-eur,* from L. *-torem,* accusative of nouns in *-tor*.

-ory. See **-tory**.

-our, -or, suffix of abstract nouns, as in *colour* or *color, favor, honor*. Fr. *eur,* L. *-oreum,* accusative of nouns in *-or, -oris*.

-ous, -ose, full of, abounding with, as in *copious, famous, operose, verbose*. Fr. *-eux,* L. *-osus*.

-pathy, state of feeling, as in *antipathy*. Gr. *-pathia,* from *pathos,* suffering.

-phorous, bearing, carrying, as in *phyllophorous*. Gr. *-phoros,* from *pherō,* to bear.

-ple, same sense as *-fold,* as in *triple, quadruple*. L. *-plus,* akin to *-pleo,* to fill.

-red. See HATRED in dictionary.

-ric. See BISHOPRIC in dictionary.

-ry, collective noun suffix, an art, as in *nunnery, cookery, poetry*. Fr. *-rie,* L. *-ria*.

-'s, suffix of the possessive. A. Sax. *-es*=G. *-s, -es,* L. *-is*. [The old notion that it stands for *his* is quite erroneous, though this may be the origin of the apostrophe sign.]

-scope, -scopy, what assists sight, a seeing. Gr. *-skopes, -skopia,* from *skopeō,* to see.

-ship, state of, office of, as in *apprenticeship, censorship,*

rectorship. A. Sax. *-scipe,* akin to *ship, shape*.

-sion, state or action abstractly, as in *explosion, tension*. L. *-sio, sionis,* akin *-tion*.

-some, full of, abounding in, as in *gladsome, frolicsome, troublesome*. A. Sax. *-sum,* Icel. and G. *-sam;* akin to *same*.

-some, noun suffix for two or more persons working or playing together, as in *twosome, foursome*.

-ster, one who, as in *gamester, maltster, songster*. A. Sax. *-estre,* originally a feminine suffix, as still in *spinster*.

-sy, state, as in *heresy, fantasy*. Gr. *-sis, -sia*.

-t, suffix of nouns, as in *height, flight*. Same as *-th*.

-teen, ten, as in *fifteen*. A. Sax. *-tyne*.

-ter, -ther, a comparative suffix, as in *after, other*. A. Sax. *-ter, -der, -ther*. See AFTER in dictionary.

-th, suffix of abstract nouns, as in *breadth, death, health*. A. Sax. *-th,* allied to L. *-tus,* as in *juventus,* youth.

-th, suffix of ordinals, as *sixth*. A. Sax. *-tha;* allied to *-tus,* in L. *sextus,* sixth.

-ther, an agent, as in *father, mother, brother*. A. Sax. *-der, -dor, thor;* allied to L. *-tor,* Skr. *-tar,* denoting an agent.

-tion, state or action abstractly, as in *conception, perception*. L. *-tio, -tionis;* akin *-sion*.

-tor, an agent, as in *actor*. See **-ther**.

-tory, adjective suffix, as in *amatory, confirmatory, explanatory*. L. *-torius,* corresponding to nouns in *-tor*. From the neuter *-torium* comes the termination when signifying place, as in *dormitory, lavatory*.

-trix, feminine suffix corresponding to *-tor,* as in *testatrix*. L. *-trix*.

-tude, suffix of abstract nouns, as in *fortitude, gratitude*. L. *-tudo, -tudinis*.

-ture, See **-ure**.

-ty, suffix of abstract nouns, as in *gravity, levity*. Fr. *-té,* L. *-tas, -tatis*.

-ty, ten times, as in *fifty*. A. Sax. *-tig;* akin to *ten, -teen*.

-ule, diminutive suffix, as in *globule*. L. *-ulus, -ula, -ulum*.

-ure, act, thing produced, as in *capture, gesture, creature, picture*. L. *-ura*.

-ward, -wards, suffix of direction, as in *homeward, homewards;* when with *-s* an adverbial genitive. A. Sax. *-weard, -weardes;* akin to *worth* (verb), L. *verto,* to turn.

-way, -ways, suffix of manner, as in *always, straightway*. From *way,* manner; *-ways* is an adverbial genitive.

-wise, suffix of manner, as in *lengthwise, likewise*. See WISE in dictionary.

-y, -ey, adjective suffix, as in *bloody, clayey, dirty, filthy, skyey, woody*. A. Sax. *-ig,* G. *-ig;* allied to L. *-icus,* Gr. *-ikos*. In *hasty, jolly,* represents Fr. *-if,* L. *-ivus*.

-y, noun suffix. Sometimes, as in *company, fallacy,* it represents Fr. *-ie,* L. *-ia,* or Gr. *-ia* (as in *apology*); sometimes L. *-ium,* as in *remedy, subsidy;* sometimes L. *-ius,* as in *notary;* sometimes L. *-atus,* as in *deputy*.

A

A, a, ā, the first letter in the English and other alphabets derived from the Latin and Greek alphabets. In *music*, it designates the sixth note of the model or diatonic scale of C, the note sounded by the open second string of the violin.

a, ā, the indefinite article, a contraction of *an*, used before nouns singular beginning with a consonant sound. AN.

aardvark, ärd'värk, *n.* [D.=earth pig.] The groundhog of South Africa, a burrowing, insectivorous, edentate animal.

aardwolf, ärd'wụlf, *n.* [D.=earth wolf.] The earth wolf of South Africa, an animal allied to the hyenas and civets.

Aaronic, Aaronical, â·ron'ik, â·ron'-ik·al, *a.* Pertaining to Aaron, or to his priesthood.

abaca, ab'a·ka, *n.* Native name of the plant which yields Manila hemp.

aback, a·bak', *adv.* [Prefix *a*, on, and *back*.] Backward: *naut.* catching the wind so as to urge a sailing vessel backward; *fig.* by surprise; unexpectedly: as, to take a person *aback*.

ab·a·cus ab'a·kus, *n.* [L.] A frame holding beaded rods for making calculations; *arch.* a slab or table forming the crowning of a column and its capital.

Abaddon, a·bad'on, *n.* [Heb. destruction.] Hell. Rev. ix. 11.

abaft, a·bäft', *adv.* or *prep.* [Prefix *a*, and A. Sax. *be-aeftan, baeftan.* AFT.] On or toward the aft or hinder part of a ship.

abalone, ab·a·lō'ni, *n.* [Spanish, of unknown origin.] A name in California for a marine mollusk, a species of ear shell which furnishes mother-of-pearl.

abandon, a·ban'dun, *v.t.* [Fr. *abandonner*, from *a*, to, and O.Fr. *bandon*, control, liberty; to leave at liberty. BAN.] To detach or withdraw one's self from; desert; forsake; give up; resign; yield up; *refl.* to yield one's self up without attempt at restraint; as, to *abandon one's self* to grief.—*n.*

Abandonment†; heartiness; frank, unrestrained demeanor (a French usage).—**abandoned,** a·ban'dund, *a.* Given up to vice; shamelessly and recklessly wicked; profligate; depraved; vicious.—**abandoner,** a·ban'dun·ér, *n.* One who abandons.—**abandonment,** a·ban'dun·ment, *n.* The act of abandoning or state of being abandoned; relinquishment; desertion; giving up.

abase, a·bās', *v.t.*—*abased, abasing.* [Fr. *abaisser—a*, to, and *baisser*, to lower, from L.L. *bassus*, low. BASE.] To lower or depress (of material objects)‡; to reduce lower, as in rank; humble; degrade.—**abasement,** a·bās'ment, *n.* The act of abasing; a state of depression, degradation, or humiliation.

abash, a·bash', *v.t.* [O.Fr. *esbahir*, ppr. *esbahissant*, from *es=ex*, intens., *bair, baer*, to gape; Mod.Fr. *s'ebahir*, to be astonished; probably from *bah!* exclamation of astonishment.] To confuse or confound, as by consciousness of guilt, inferiority, etc; make ashamed; put to confusion. *Abash* is a stronger word than *confuse*, but not so strong as *confound.* —**abashment,** a·bash'ment, *n.* Act of, state of being, abashed.

abate, a·bāt', *v.t.*—*abated, abating.* [Fr. *abattre*, to beat down, from L. *batere*, a form of *batuere*, to beat. BATTER.] To beat down‡; to lessen; diminish; remit; moderate (zeal, a demand, a tax); *law*, to annul; put an end to.—*v.i.* To decrease or become less in strength or violence.—**abatable,** a·bāt'a·bl, *a.* Capable of being abated.—**abatement,** a·bāt'ment, *n.* The act of, or state of being, abated; decrease; decline; mitigation; amount or sum deducted; deduction; decrease.—**abater,** a·bāt'-ér, *n.* One who or that abates.

abatis, ab'a·tis, *n.* [Fr. *abattis, abattis*, from *abattre*, to beat down. ABATE.] *Fort.* a collection of felled trees, from which the smaller branches have been cut off, and which are laid side by side, with the branched ends toward assailants, forming an obstruction to their progress.

abattoir, a·bat·wär', *n.* [Fr., from *abattre*, to beat or knock down.

ABATE.] A public slaughterhouse.

abaxial, ab·ak'si·al, *a.* [Prefix *ab*, from, *axis*.] Not in the axis.

abbacy, ab'ba·si, *n.* The dignity, rights, and privileges of an abbot.—**abbatial,** ab·bā'shi·al), *a.* Belonging to an abbey.

abbé, ab'bā, *n.* [Fr., an abbot.] In France, especially before the Revolution, one who devoted himself to divinity, or who had pursued a course of study in a theological seminary; many of them became tutors, professors, and men of letters.

abbess, ab'bes, *n.* [Fr. *abbesse*, L.L. *abbatissa.*] A female superior of an abbey, possessing, in general, the same dignity and authority as an abbot, except that she cannot exercise the spiritual functions appertaining to the priesthood.—**abbey,** ab'bi, *n.* [Fr. *abbaye*, from L.L. *abbatia*, an abbey. ABBOT.] A monastery or monastic establishment of the highest rank; a society of persons of either sex, secluded from the world, and devoted to religion and celibacy, governed by an *abbot* or *abbess.*—**abbot,** ab'but, *n.* [Formerly *abbat*, L.L. *abbas, abbatis*, from Syr. and Chal. *abba*, father.] The male head or superior of an abbey or monastery. Some abbots were *mitred* abbots, almost equal in rank with bishops. Laymen were sometimes abbots, enjoying the abbey revenues.—*Abbot of Misrule*, of unreason; burlesque figure in medieval mystery plays and revels.—**abbotship,** ab'but·ship, *n.* The state or office of an abbot.

abbreviate, ab·brē'vi·āt, *v.t.*—*abbreviated, abbreviating.* [L. *abbrevio, abbreviatum*, to shorten—*ab* for *ad*, and *brevis*, short. BRIEF, ABRIDGE (which is really the same word).] To make briefer; shorten; abridge; reduce to smaller compass.—**abbreviation,** ab·brē'vi·ā"shon, *n.* Act of abbreviating, shortening, or contracting; that which is abbreviated; a syllable, letter, or series of letters, standing for a word or words; as *Ph.D.* for *doctor of philosophy; D.A.R.* for *Daughters of the American Revolution.*—**abbreviator,** ab·brē'vi·ā·tér, *n.* One who abbreviates.

abdicate, ab'di·kāt, *v.t.*—*abdicated,*

abdicating. [L. *abdico, abdicatum—ab,* from, and *dico, dicatum,* to declare publicly.] To give up, renounce, lay down, or withdraw from in a voluntary, public, or formal manner, as a throne, duties, etc.; vacate; resign.—*v.i.* To renounce or give up power voluntarily.—**abdication,** ab·di·kā′shon, *n.* The act of abdicating an office, especially the kingly office.—**abdicator,** ab′di·kāt·ėr, *n.* One who abdicates.

abdomen, ab·dō′men or ab′do·men, *n.* [L.] That part of the human body which lies between the thorax and the pelvis, containing the stomach, liver, spleen, pancreas, kidneys, bladder, and intestines; the posterior of the three parts of a perfect insect.—**abdominal,** ab·dom′in·al, *a.* Pertaining to the abdomen or belly.—*abdominal regions,* certain regions into which the abdomen in man is arbitrarily divided for convenience in anatomical or medical descriptions.—**abdominous,**† ab·dom′in·us, *a.* Abdominal; potbellied.

abduce, ab·dūs′, *v.t.*—*abduced, abducing.* [L. *abduco,* to lead away—*ab,* and *duco,* to lead, to draw. DUKE.] To draw or conduct away.—**abducent,** ab·dūs′ent, *a.* Drawing away; pulling back.—*Abducent muscles,* muscles which pull back certain parts of the body from the mesial line.—**abduct,** ab·dukt′, *v.t.* To draw or lead away; to take away surreptitiously, and by force.—**abduction,** ab·duk′shon, *n.* The act of abducting; *anat.* the action by which muscles withdraw a limb or other part from the axis of the body; *law,* the unlawful leading away of a person, as a young woman, by fraud, persuasion, or open violence.—**abductor,** ab·duk′tėr, *n.* One who or that which abducts; *anat.* a muscle which moves certain parts from the axis of the body.

abeam, a·bēm′, *adv. Naut.* in the direction of the beams, that is, at right angles to the keel of a ship.

abecedarian, ā′bē·sē·dâ′′ri·an, *n,* [From the letters *a, b, c, d.*] One who teaches the letters of the alphabet, or a learner of the letters.—**abecedary,**† ā·bē·sē′dâ·ri, *a.* Pertaining to or formed by the letters of the alphabet.—*n.* A first principle or element; rudiment.

abed, a·bed′, *adv.* In bed; gone to bed.

abele, a·bēl′, *n.* [D. *abeel,* G. *albele,* L. *albus,* white.] The white poplar.

aberr, ab·er′, *v.i.* [L. *aberro, aberratum—ab,* from, and *erro,* to wander, to err.] *Obs.* To wander; to err.—**aberrance,**† **aberrancy,**† ab·er′rans, ab·er′ran·si, *n.* A wandering; aberration.—**aberrant,** ab·er′rant, *a.* Characterized by aberration; wandering; straying from the right way; differing from a common type.—**aberration,** ab·er·rā′shon, *n.* [L. *aberratio.*] The act of wandering from the right way; deviation from truth or rectitude or from a type or standard; partial alienation of mind; mental wandering; the difference between the true and the observed

position of a heavenly body.

abet, a·bet′, *v.t.*—*abetted, abetting.* [O.Fr. *abetter, abeter,* to incite, to lure; *abet,* a bait—prefix *a,* and word=*bait,* to incite, set on. BAIT, BITE.] To encourage by aid, countenance, or approval: used chiefly in a bad sense; incite; support, encourage; back up.—**abetment,** a·bet′ment, *n.* The act of abetting; aid.—**abetter, abettor,** a·bet′ėr, *n.* One who abets or incites; a supporter or encourager, generally of something bad.

abeyance, a·bā′ans, *n.* [O.Fr. *abaiaunce,* expectation, from *abbayer,* to listen with the mouth open, from *bayer, baer,* to gape, as in crying *bah!* ABASH.] A state of expectation, or waiting for an occupant or holder: said of lands, honors, or dignities; a state of temporary suspension.—**abeyant,** a·bā′ant, *a.* Being in abeyance.

abhor, ab·hạr′, *v.t.*—*abhorred, abhorring.* [L. *abhorreo,* to shrink back—*ab,* from, and *horreo,* to feel horror. HORRIBLE.] To hate extremely or with loathing; loathe, detest, or abominate; shrink from with horror; fill with horror and loathing (*Shak.*)‡.—**abhorrence,** ab·hor′rens, *n.* Extreme hatred; detestation; great aversion.—**abhorrent,** ab·hor′rent, *a.* Struck with abhorrence; hating; detesting; utterly repugnant: in the last sense used formerly with *from,* now with *to.*—**abhorrently,** ab·hor′rent·li, *adv.* With abhorrence.—**abhorrer,** ab·hor′ėr, *n.* One who abhors; petitioner to Charles II in 1680 against the change of succession.

abide, a·bīd′, *v.i.*—*abode* (pret. and pp.), *abiding.* [A. Sax. *abîdan, gebîdan,* to abide, from *bîdan,* to bide. See BIDE.] To take up one's abode; dwell; stay; not to depart.—*To abide by,* to remain beside; to adhere to: to maintain; to remain satisfied with.—*v.t.* To be prepared for; to await; be able to endure or sustain; remain firm under; to put up with; to tolerate.—**abider,** a·bīd′ėr, *n.* One who abides.—**abiding,** a·bīd′ing, *a.* Continuing; permanent; steadfast; as an *abiding* faith.—**abidingly,** a·bīd′·ing·li, *adv.* In such a manner as to continue; permanently.

Abigail, ab′i·gāl, *n.* [From the title of *handmaid* assumed to herself by *Abigail,* wife of Nabal. See 1 Sam. xxv. 3.] A general name for a waiting woman or lady's-maid. [Colloq.]

ability, a·bil′i·ti, *n.* [Fr. *habilité,* L. *habilitas,* ableness. ABLE.] The state or condition of being able; power, whether bodily or mental; *pl.* talents; powers of the mind; mental gifts or endowments.

abiogenesis, abiogeny, a·bī′ō·jen′′e·sis, a·bī·oj′en·i, *n.* [Gr. *a,* not, *bios,* life, and *genesis,* generation.] The doctrine that living matter may be produced by nonliving matter. BIOGENESIS, HETEROGENESIS.—**abiogenist,** a·bī·oj′en·ist, *n.* A believer in the doctrine of abiogenesis.—**abiogenetic,** a·bī′ō·jen·et′′ik, *a.* Of, pertaining to, or produced by abiogenesis.—**abiogenetically,** a·bī′ō·

jenet′′ik·al·li, *adv.* In an abiogenetic manner.

abject, ab′jekt, *a.* [L. *abjectus,* from *abjicio,* to throw away—*ab,* and *jacio,* to throw.] Sunk to a low condition; worthless, mean, despicable; low, groveling.—*n.* A person in a low or abject condition.—**abjection,** ab·jek′shon, *n.* A low state; meanness of spirit; abjectness.—**abjectly,** ab·jekt′·li, *adv.* In an abject or contemptible manner; meanly; servilely.—**abjectness,** ab·jekt′nes, *n.* The state of being abject; meanness; servility.

abjure, ab·jūr′, *v.t.*—*abjured, abjuring.* [L. *abjuro,* to deny upon oath—*ab,* and *juro,* to swear. JURY.] To renounce upon oath; to reject or withdraw from with solemnity; abandon (as allegiance, errors); to recant or retract.—**abjurer,** ab·jūr′ėr, *n.* One who abjures.—**abjuration,** ab·jū·rā′shon, *n.* The act of abjuring; a renunciation upon oath; a rejection or denial with solemnity; a total abandonment.—**abjuratory,** ab·jū′ra·to·ri, *a.* Pertaining to abjuration.

ablactate, ab·lak′tāt, *v.t.* [L. *ablacto,* to wean—*ab,* from, and *lac,* milk.] To wean from the breast.—**ablactation,** ab·lak·tā′shon, *n.* The weaning of a child from the breast; *hort.* same as *inarching.*

ablative, ab′la·tiv, *a.* [L. *ablativus,* from *ablatus,* carried away—*ab,* away, and *latus,* carried.] Taking or tending to take away†: applied to a case of nouns in Sanskrit, Latin, and some other languages, originally given to the case in Latin because separation from was considered to be one of the chief ideas expressed by it.—**ablation,**† ab·lā′shon, *n.* A carrying or taking away.

ablaut, ab′lout, *n.* [G., from *ab,* off, and *laut,* sound.] *Philol.* a substitution of one vowel for another in the body of a word, to indicate a corresponding modification of use or meaning; as, *bind, band, bound, bond;* especially the change of a vowel to indicate tense change in verbs, instead of the addition of a syllable (·*ed*); as, *sink, sank, sunk.*

ablaze, a·blāz′, *adv.* or *a.* In a blaze; in a state of eager excitement or desire.

able, ā′bl, *a.* [O. Fr. *able, hable, habile,* skillful, fit, from L. *habilis,* suitable, fit, from *habeo,* to have; akin are *ability, habiliment, habit,* suffix·*able.*] Having the power, means, or qualification sufficient; competent; qualified; having strong or unusual powers of mind, or intellectual qualifications; gifted; vigorous; active.—**able,**‡ ā′bl, *v.t.* To make able; to enable; to warrant or answer for. [*Shak.*]—**able-bodied,** *a.* Having a sound, strong body; having strength sufficient for work; often applied to a seaman who is well skilled in seamanship, and classed in the ship's books as A.B.—**ably,** ā′bli, *adv.* In an able manner; with ability.

abloom, a·blöm′, *a.* or *adv.* In a blooming state.

abluent, ab′lū·ent, *a.* [L. *abluens, abluentis,* ppr. of *abluo,* to wash off—*ab,* from, and *luo,* to wash.]

Washing clean; cleansing by water or liquids.—*n.* That which washes or carries off impurities; a detergent.—**ablution,** ab·lū′shon, *n.* The act of washing; cleansing or purification by water or other liquid; specifically, a washing of the body preparatory to religious rites.—**ablutionary,** ab·lū′shon·a·ri, *a.* Pertaining to ablution.

abnegate, ab′nē·gāt, *v.t.*—abnegated, abnegating. [L. abnego, abnegatum—ab, from, and nego, to deny. NEGATIVE, DENY.] To deny; to renounce.—**abnegation,** ab·nē·gā′shon, *n.* [L. abnegatio.] The act of abnegating; denial; renunciation.—**abnegator,** ab′nē·gā·tẽr, *n.* One who abnegates, denies, or renounces.

abnormal, ab·nọr′mal, *a.* [L. abnormis—ab, from, and norma, a rule. NORMAL.] Not conformed or conforming to rule; deviating from a type or standard; irregular; contrary to system or law.—**abnormality,** ab·nor·mal′i·ti, *n.* The state or quality of being abnormal; deviation from a standard, rule, or type; irregularity; that which is abnormal.—**abnormity,**† ab·nor′mi·ti, *n.* Abnormality.

aboard, a·bōrd′, *adv.* On board; within a ship or boat.—*prep.* On board; into (to go *aboard* a ship).

abode, a·bōd′, pret. of abide.—**abode,** a·bōd′, *n.* [From abide.] Residence or place of residence; a place where a person abides, a dwelling; habitation.—*To make abode,* to dwell or reside.

abolish, a·bol′ish, *v.t.* [Fr. abolir; L. abolere, to annul, abolish—ab, from, and oleo, to grow. ADULT.] To do away with; to put an end to; to destroy; to efface or obliterate; to make void; to annul; to put out of existence.—**abolishable,** a·bol′ish·a·bl, *a.* Capable of being abolished.—**abolisher,** a·bol′ish·ẽr, *n.* One who or that which abolishes.—**abolishment,**† a·bol′ish·ment, *n.* Abolition. —**abolition,** ab·ō·li′shon, *n.* The act of abolishing, or the state of being abolished.—**abolitionism,** ab·ō·li′shon-izm, *n.* The principles of an abolitionist.—**abolitionist,** ab·ō·li′shon·ist, *n.* A person who favors the abolition of anything; applied especially to those who favored the abolition of slavery in the United States.

abomasus, abomasum, ab·ō·mā′sus, ab·ō·mā′sum, *n.* [L. prefix ab, from, and omasum.] The fourth stomach of ruminating animals, lying next to the omasum or third stomach.

abominate, a·bom′in·āt, *v.t.*—abominated, abominating. [L. abominor, abominatus, to deprecate, as of ill omen—ab, from, and omen, an omen.] To hate extremely; to abhor; to detest.—**abominable,** abom′in·a·bl, *a.* Deserving or liable to be abominated; detestable; loathsome; odious in the utmost degree; execrable.—**abominableness,** a·bom′in·a·bl·nes, *n.* The quality or state of being abominable, detestable, or odious.—**abominably,** a·bom′in·a·bli, *adv.* In an abominable manner or degree.—**abomination,** a·bom′-

in·ā″shon, *n.* The act of abominating or state of being abominated; detestation; that which is abominated or abominable; hence, hateful or shameful vice.

aboriginal, ab·o·rij′in·al, *a.* [L. ab, from, and origo, origin.] Inhabiting a country from the earliest known times; as, *aboriginal* tribes.—*n.* An original inhabitant; one of an aboriginal race.—**aboriginally,** ab·o·rij′-in·al·li, *adv.* In or of first origin; originally; from the very first.—**aborigines,** ab·o·rij′in·ēz, *n. pl.* [L.] The people found in a country at the time of the earliest known settlement.

abort, a·bạrt′, *v.i.* [L. aborior, abortus, to miscarry—ab, and orior, ortus, to arise. ORIENT.] To miscarry in giving birth; to appear in a rudimentary or undeveloped state.—**abortion,** a·bor′shon, *n.* The act of miscarrying, or producing young before the natural time, or before the fetus is perfectly formed; the product of untimely birth; a misshapen being; a monster; anything which fails before it is matured or perfect, as a design.—**abortive,** a·bort′iv, *a.* Brought forth in an immature state; rudimentary; imperfectly formed or developed; producing or intended to produce abortion; not brought to completion or to a successful issue; coming to nought.—**abortive,** a·bort′iv, *n.* A drug causing or thought to cause abortion.—**abortively,** a·bort′iv·li, *adv.* In an abortive manner; immaturely.—**abortiveness,** a·bort′iv·nes, *n.* The state of being abortive.

abound, a·bound′, *v.i.* [Fr. abonder, from L. abundare, to overflow—ab, and unda, a wave. UNDULATE, WATER.] To be in great plenty; be very prevalent; have or possess in great quantity; be copiously supplied: in the latter sense followed by *with* or *in.*

about, a·bout′, *prep.* [A.Sax. âbûtan, onbûtan, about, around—prefixes â, on, on, and bûtan, without. BUT.] Around; on the outside or surface of; in a circle surrounding; round (two yards *about* the stem); near to in place, time, size, number, quantity, etc.; near to in action; on the point of (to be *about* to speak): in this sense followed by the infinitive; concerned in; engaged in (what is he *about?*) concerning; relating to; respecting.—*adv.* Around the outside; in circuit; in a circle; near to in number, time, place, quality, or degree (*about* as high); here and there; around; in one place and another; in different directions.—*To bring about,* to cause to happen; to effect or accomplish.—*To come about,* to come to pass; to happen.—*To go about,* to prepare to do.—*Turn about, week about,* etc.; alternately, on each alternate week, and the like.

above, a·buv′, *prep.* [A.Sax. âbúfan, above: a triple compound of â, on, at, be, by, and úfan, upward, akin to E. over, L. super, Gr. hyper, above.] In or to a higher place than; superior to in any respect; too high for

(*above* mean actions); more in number, quantity, or degree than; in excess of (*above* a ton).—*Above all,* above or before everything else; before every other consideration.—*adv.* In or to a higher place; overhead; before, in rank or order, especially in a book or writing (what has been said *above*); besides, in the expression *over and above. Above* is often used elliptically as a noun, meaning (1) heaven; (2) the aforesaid; as, from the *above* you will learn. It is equal to an adjective in such phrases as, the *above* particulars, in which *cited* or *mentioned* is understood.—**aboveboard,** *adv.* [Said to mean lit. above the table, not with hands below the table, as one trying to cheat at cards.] In open sight; without tricks or disguise.—**aboveground,** *adv.* Alive; not buried.

abracadabra, ab′ra·ka·dab″ra, *n.* A word of eastern origin used in incantations. When written on paper so as to form a triangle, the first line contained the word in full, the one below it omitted the last letter, and so on each time until only one letter remained. Worn as an amulet, it was supposed to be an antidote against certain diseases.

abrade, a·brād′, *v.t.*—abraded, abrading. [L. abrado, to scrape off—ab, away, and rado, to scrape, whence raze, razor, etc.] To rub or wear down; to rub or grate off.—**abradant,** a·brād′ant, *n.* A material for grinding, usually in powder, such as emery, sand, glass, etc.—**abrasion,** ab·rā′zhon, *n.* The act of abrading, wearing, or rubbing off; an injury of the skin by removal of cuticle.—**abrasive,** ab·rā′ziv, *a.* and *n.* Serving to abrade; an abradant.

Abrahamic, ā·bra·ham′ik, *a.* pertaining to Abraham, the patriarch.

abranchiate, a·brang′ki·āt, *a.* [Gr. a, without, and branchia, gills.] Devoid of branchiae or gills.—*n.* A vertebrate animal (mammal, bird, reptile) that at no period of its existence possesses gills.

abrasion. See ABRADE.

abreaction, ab′rē·ak″shon, *n.* [L. ab, away, and reaction.] In psychoanalysis, getting rid of a past disagreeable experience by living it through again in speech or action in the course of treatment.

abreast, a·brest′, *adv.* Side by side, with the breasts in a line; hence, up to a level or standard (to keep *abreast* of science).

abridge, a·brij′, *v.t.*—abridged, abridging. [Fr. abréger, from L. abbreviare, to shorten. ABBREVIATE.] To make shorter; to curtail; to epitomize; to shorten by using fewer words; to condense; to lessen; to diminish; to deprive or cut off from: in the last sense followed by *of* (to abridge one *of* his *rights*).—**abridger,** a·brij′-ẽr, *n.* One who or that which abridges.—**abridgment,** a·brij′ment, *n.* The act of abridging or state of being; that which is abridged; an epitome; a summary, as of a book; an abstract. ∴ An *abridgment* is a larger work shortened; a *compendium* is a condensed view of a particular subject regarded as complete in itself; an *epitome* has more reference to the selection of essential facts than an *abridgment*; an *abstract* is a bare statement of facts contained in, or of the leading features of, a work.

abroach, a·brōch', *a.* or *adv.* Tapped; in a position for letting out liquor: said of a cask; broached.

abroad, a·brạd', *adv.* At large; without being confined to narrow limits; with expansion (to spread its branches *abroad*); beyond or out of the walls of a house or other inclosure; beyond the bounds of a country; in foreign countries.

abrogate, ab'rō·gāt, *v.t.*—*abrogated*, *abrogating*. [L. *abrogo*, to repeal—*ab*, from, and *rogo*, to ask, propose as a law.] To repeal; to make void; to do away with; to annul by an authoritative act.—**abrogable,** ab'rō·ga·bl, *a.* Capable of being abrogated.—**abrogation,** ab·rō·gā'shon, *n.* The act of abrogating; repeal by authority.—**abrogative,** ab'rō·gā·tiv, *a.* Capable of abrogating; tending to abrogate.

abrupt, ab·rupt', *a.* [L. *abruptus*, from *abrumpo*, to break off—*ab*, off, from, and *rumpo, ruptum*, to break, whence *rupture*, etc.] Steep; craggy (of rocks, precipices, etc.); sudden; without notice to prepare the mind for the event (an *abrupt* entrance); disconnected; having sudden transitions (an *abrupt* style).—*Abrupt leaf, root, bot.,* one terminating suddenly as if the end were cut off.—**abruption,** ab·rup'shon, *n.* A sudden and violent breaking off.—**abruptly,** ab·rupt'li, *adv.* In an abrupt manner; suddenly; without any notice or warning; precipitously.—**abruptness,** ab·rupt'nes, *n.* The state or quality of being abrupt; precipitousness; suddenness; unceremonious haste or vehemence.

abscess, ab'ses, *n.* [L. *abscessus*, from *abscedere*, to separate, to gather into an abscess—*abs*, away, and *cedo, cessum*, to go, whence *cession, cede*, etc.] A collection of purulent matter in the tissue of a body organ or part, with pain and heat.

abscind, ab·sind', *v.t.* L. *abscindo, abscissum*, to cut off—*ab*, from, and *scindo*, to cut.] To cut off.—**abscissa,** ab·sis'sa, *n.* Any part of the diameter or transverse axis of a conic section (as an ellipse), intercepted between the vertex and a line at right angles to the axis; the *x*-coordinate of a point.—**abscission,** ab·si'zhon, *n.* The act of cutting off; severance; removal.

abscond, ab·skond', *v.i.* [L. *abscondo*, to hide—*abs*, from, and *condo*, to hide.] To withdraw or absent one's self in a private manner; run away in order to avoid a legal process; decamp.—**absconder,** ab·skond'·ėr, *n.* One who absconds.

absence, ab'sens, *n.* L. *absentia*, from *absens, absentis*, absent, pres. part. of *absum*, to be absent—*ab* or *abs*, away, and *sum, esse*, to be.] The state of being absent; opposite of *presence*;

the state of being at a distance in place; the state of being wanting; nonexistence within a certain sphere (*absence* of evidence); inattention.—**absent,** ab'sent, *a.* Not present; away; somewhere else; wanting; having the mind withdrawn from what is passing; characterized by absence of mind (an *absent* man).—**absent,** ab·sent', *v.t.* To keep away intentionally: used *refl.*; as, to *absent* one's self from a meeting.—**absentee,** ab·sen·tē', *n.* One who is absent; one who absents himself: often applied to landlords who, deriving their income from one country, reside and spend it in another.—**absenteeism,** ab·sen·tē'izm, *n.* The practice or habit of an absentee.—**absenter,** ab·sent'ėr, *n.* One who absents himself.—**absently,** ab'sent·li, *adv.* In an absent or inattentive manner.—**absent-minded,** ab'sent·mīn'ded, *a.* Preoccupied; forgetful of one's immediate surroundings.

absinthe, ab·sanṫ' or ab'sinth, *n.* [Fr., from L. *absinthium*, wormwood.] A popular French liqueur or cordial consisting of brandy flavored with wormwood. The sale and consumption of absinthe are prohibited because of its harmful effects on the nervous system.

absolute, ab'sō·lūt, *a.* [L. *absolutus*. ABSOLVE.] Freed from limitation or condition; unconditional (an *absolute* promise); unlimited by extraneous power or control (an *absolute* government or prince); complete in itself; finished; perfect (*absolute* beauty); free from mixture (*absolute* alcohol); positive; decided; peremptory (now rare); *metaph.* (*a*) not relative; considered without reference to other things; (*absolute* knowledge); (*b*) existing independent of any other cause; self-existing; unconditioned; *gram.* applied to the case which is not determined by any other word in the sentence.—**absolute temperature.** Temperature measured in degrees centigrade from absolute zero, which is -273.16° centigrade.—**absolutely,** ab'sō·lūt·li, *adv.* In an absolute manner; completely; without restriction, limitation, or qualification; unconditionally; positively.—**absoluteness,** ab'sō·lūt·nes, *n.* The state of being.—**absolutism,** ab'sō·lūt·izm, *n.* State of being absolute, or principles of absolute government.—**absolutist,** ab'sō·lūt·ist, *n.* An advocate for absolute government.—**absolutistic,** ab'sō·lūt·ist″ik, ab'sō·lūt·ist, *a.* Pertaining to absolutism.

absolution, ab·sō·lū'shon, *n.* The act of absolving or state of being absolved; specifically, in the Roman Catholic and some other churches, a remission of sins pronounced by a priest in favor of a penitent.

absolve, ab·solv', *v.t.*—*absolved, absolving*. [L. *absolvo, absolutum*, to set free—*ab*, from, and *solvo*, to loose. SOLVE.] To set free or release from some duty, obligation, or responsibility (to *absolve* a person *from* a promise); acquit; to forgive

or grant remission of sins to (with *from*).—**absolvable,** ab·solv'·a·bl, *a.* Capable of being absolved.—**absolver,** ab·solv'ėr, *n.* One who absolves.

absorb, ab·sorb', *v.t.* [L. *absorbeo*—*ab*, from, and *sorbeo*, to suck in.] To drink in; suck up; imbibe, as a sponge; take in by capillarity; swallow up; engross or engage wholly.—**absorbability,** ab·sorb'a·bil'i·ti, *n.* The state or quality of being absorbable.—**absorbable,** ab·sorb'a·bl, *a.* Capable of being absorbed or imbibed.—**absorbent,** ab·sorb'ent, *a.* Capable of absorbing fluids; performing the function of absorption.—**absorbent,** ab·sorb'ent, *n.* Anything which absorbs; a vessel in an animal body which takes in nutritive matters into the system; a substance applied to a wound to stanch or arrest the flow of blood.—**absorption,** ab·sorp'shon, *n.* The act or process of absorbing; state of being absorbed or engrossed.—**absorptive,** ab·sorp'tiv, *a.* Having power to absorb or imbibe.—**absorptivity,** ab·sorp·tiv'i·ti, *n.* The power or capacity of absorption.

abstain, ab·stān', *v.i.* [O.Fr. *abstener*, Mod.Fr. *abstenir*, from L. *abstineo*, to keep from—*abs*, from, and *teneo*, to hold, whence *contain, tenant, tenacious*, etc.] To forbear or refrain voluntarily; to withhold.—**abstainer,** ab·stān'ėr, *n.* One who abstains; specifically, one who abstains from the use of intoxicating liquors.—**abstention,** ab·sten'shon, *n.* The act of holding off or abstaining; abstinence.—**abstinence,** ab'sti·nens, *n.* The act or practice of voluntarily refraining from the use of anything within our reach, especially from some bodily indulgence; partaking sparingly of food or drink.—**abstinent,** ab'sti·nent, *a.* Practicing abstinence.—**abstinently,** ab'sti·nent·li, *adv.* In an abstinent manner.

abstemious, ab·stē'mi·us, *a.* [L. *abstemius*—*abs*, and root seen in *temetum*, strong drink, *temulentus*, drunken; Skr. *tim*, to be wet.] Sparing in diet; refraining from a free use of food and strong drinks; temperate; devoted to or spent in abstemiousness or abstinence (an *abstemious* life); very moderate and plain; very sparing (*abstemious* diet).—**abstemiously,** ab·stē'mi·us·li, *adv.* In an abstemious manner.—**abstemiousness,** ab·stē'mi·us·nes, *n.*

abstention. See ABSTAIN.

absterge, ab·stėrj', *v.t.*—*absterged, absterging*. [L. *abstergeo*, to wipe off—*abs*, and *tergeo, tersum*, to wipe, whence *terse*.] To wipe, or make clean by wiping; to wash away; to deterge.—**abstergent,** ab·stėrj'ent, *a.* Having cleansing or purgative properties.—**abstergent,** ab·stėrj'ent, *n.* Whatever aids in scouring or cleansing; a detergent.—**abstersion,** ab·stėr'shon, *n.* The act of absterging or cleansing.

abstinence, abstinent, abstinently. See ABSTAIN.

abstract, ab·strakt', *v.t.* [From L. *abstraho, abstractum*, to draw away—

abs, and *traho, tractum,* to draw, seen also in *trace, contract, detract, retract,* etc.] To draw or take away; to withdraw; to purloin; to take away mentally; consider separately; epitomize or reduce to a summary.—**abstract,** ab′strakt, *a.* Considered or thought of in itself; not concrete; considered and treated apart from any particular object (*abstract* mathematics; *abstract* logic). In *gram.* and *logic, abstract nouns* or *terms* are names of qualities, in opposition to *concrete,* which are names of things. —*n.* A summary or epitome containing the substance; a bare or brief statement of facts detailed elsewhere. *Syn.* under ABRIDGMENT. —**abstracted,** ab·strakt′ed, *a.* Absent in mind; inattentive.—**abstractedly,** ab·strakt′ed·li, *adv.* In an abstracted or absent manner.—**abstractedness,** ab·strakt′ed·nes, *n.*—**abstracter,** ab·-strakt′ér. *n.* One who abstracts or purloins.—**abstraction,** ab·strak′-shon, *n.* The act of abstracting or separating; the act of withdrawing; the act of considering separately what is united in a complex object; something abstract; an idea or notion of an abstract character; absence of mind; the state of being entirely engrossed in thought.—In *art,* an artistic composition intended to suggest an idea or emotion without imitating recognizable objects.—**abstractive,** ab·strakt′iv, *a.* Having the power or quality of abstracting.—**abstractively,** ab·strakt′iv·li, *adv.* In an abstractive manner.

abstriction,† ab·strik′shon, *n.* [L. *ab,* from, and *stringo, strictum,* to bind.] The act of unbinding.

abstruse, ab·strūs′, *a.* [L. *abstrusus,* pp. of *abstrudo,* to thrust away.] Remote from ordinary minds or notions; difficult to be comprehended or understood; profound; recondite. —**abstrusely,** ab·strūs′li, *adv.* In an abstruse manner; profoundly; with terms or notions remote from such as are obvious.—**abstruseness,** ab·-strūs′nes, *n.* The quality of being abstruse.

absurd, ab·sérd′, *a.* [L. *absurdus—ab,* and *surdus,* deaf, insensible. SURD.] Inconsistent with reason or common sense; ridiculous; nonsensical; logically contradictory.—**absurdity,** ab·sérd′i·ti, *n.* The state or quality of being absurd; that which is absurd; an absurd action, statement, etc.—**absurdly,** ab·sérd′li, *adv.* In an absurd manner.—**absurdness,** ab·-sérd′nes, *n.* The quality of being absurd.

abundance, a·bun′dans, *n.* [L. *abundantia,* abundance, from *abundo,* to abound (which see).] A fullness or plenteousness great to overflowing; ample sufficiency; plenteousness; copiousness.—**abundant,** a·bun′-dant, *a.* Plentiful; ample; fully sufficient; abounding; overflowing. —**abundantly,** a·bun′dant·li, *adv.* In a plentiful or sufficient degree; amply; plentifully.

abuse, a·būz′, *v.t.*—*abused, abusing.* [Fr. *abuser;* L. *abutor, abusus—ab,* and *utor,* to use. USE.] To misuse;

to put to a wrong or bad use; to do wrong to; injure; dishonor; violate; deceive; impose on; take undue advantage of.—**abuse,** a·būs′, *n.* Improper treatment or employment; improper use or application; misuse; a corrupt practice or custom (the *abuses* of government); injury; scurrilous or contumelious language.—**abuser,** a·būz′ér. One who abuses, in speech or behavior.—**abusive,** a·būs′iv, *a.* Practicing abuse; offering harsh words or ill-treatment; scurrilous; opprobrious; insulting.—**abusively,** a·būs′iv·li, *adv.* In an abusive manner.—**abusiveness,** a·bū′-siv·nes, *n.* The quality of being abusive; rudeness of language.

abut, a·but′, *v.i.*—*abutted, abutting.* [Fr. *aboutir,* to meet at the end, to border on—*a,* at, and *bout,* extremity. BUTT.] To be contiguous; to join at a border or boundary; to form a point or line of contact: with *on, upon, against.*—**abutment,** a·but′ment, *n.* The condition of abutting; the part abutting; the solid part of a pier or wall against which an arch abuts or from which it springs.—**abuttal,** a·but′al, *n.* The abutting part of a piece of land.—**abutter,** a·but′ér, *n.*—That which abuts.

abyss, a·bis′, *n.* [L. *abyssus,* Gr. *abyssos,* bottomless—*a,* not, and *byssos,* bottom.] A bottomless gulf; anything profound and unfathomable, literally or figuratively.—**abysmal,** a·biz′mal, *a.* Pertaining to an abyss; profound; immeasurable.—**abyssal,** a·bis′al, *a.* Relating to or like an abyss; pertaining to the deeper parts of the sea.

Abyssinian, ab·is·sin′i·an, *a.* Belonging to Abyssinia or its inhabitants.—*n.* A native or inhabitant of Abyssinia; a member of the Abyssinian Church.

Acacia, a·kā′shi·a, *n.* [L. *acacia,* Gr. *akakia,* from *ake,* a point.] A genus of ornamental plants, some species of which produce catechu, and some exude gum arabic. *Acacia-tree,* a name sometimes given to the locust-tree, *Robinia pseudoacacia.*

academy, a·kad′e·mi, *n.* [L. *academia,* Gr. *akadēmeia,* the Academy, from the hero *Acadēmus,* to whom the ground originally belonged which formed the garden in which Plato taught.] A school holding a rank between a college and an elementary school; a seminary of learning of the higher class; an association for the promotion of literature, science, or art, established sometimes by government, and sometimes by the voluntary union of private individuals, the members of which are called *academicians.* The Academy of Plato was the philosophical school founded by that Greek philosopher.—**academe,** *n.* An academy. [Poet.]—**academic, academical,** ak·a·dem′ik, ak·a·dem′ik·al, *a.* Belonging to an academy, or to a college or university; as, *academic* studies.—**academic,** ak·a·dem′ik, *n.* A student in a college or university.—**academical,** ak·a·dem′i·kal, *n.* A member of an

academy; *pl.* the costume proper to the officers and students of a school or college.—**academically,** ak′a·dem″ik·al·li, *adv.* In an academical manner.—**academician,** a·kad′e·mish″an, *n.* A member of an academy or society for promoting arts and sciences.—**academicism,** ak·a·dem′-i·sizm, *n.* The system or mode of teaching at an academy; an academical mannerism.

Acadian, a·kā′di·an, *a.* Belonging to Acadia, a former name of Nova Scotia.—*n.* A native or inhabitant of Acadia.

Acalephae, a·ka·lē′fē, *n. pl.* [Gr. *akalēphē,* a nettle.] A name sometimes applied to the marine animals commonly known as sea nettles, jellyfish, etc.—**acaleph, acalephan,** ak′a·lef, ak·a·lē′fan, *n.* A member of the Acalephae.—**acalephoid,** a·ka-lē′foid, *a.* Like an acaleph or medusa; medusoid.

acantha, a·kan′tha, *n.* [Gr. *akantha,* a spine or thorn.] A prickle of a plant; a spine of an animal; one of the acute processes of the vertebrae of animals.—**acanthaceous,** ak·an·thā′-shus, *a.* Armed with prickles, as a plant.—**acanthine,** a·kan′thīn, *a.* Pertaining to or resembling the plant acanthus; prickly.—**acantho-cephalous,** a·kan·thō·sef′a·lus, *a.* [Gr. *akantha,* thorn, *kephalē,* head.] *Zool.* having spines or hooks on the head, as certain intestinal worms (the Acanthocephala), which are thus attached within the bodies of animals.—**acanthoid, acanthous,** a·kan′thoid, a·kan′thus, *a.* Spiny.— **acanthorous,** ak·an·tho′for·us, *a.* Having or producing spines.

acanthus, a·kan′thus, *n.* [Gr. *akanthos,* from its prickly leaves.] Any of a genus of plants of the Mediterranean region having large spiny leaves; an architectural ornament used in capitals of the Corinthian and Composite orders, and resembling somewhat the foliage of this plant.

Acanthopterygii, a·kan′thop·te·rij″-i·ī, *n. pl.* [Gr. *akantha,* a thorn, and *pterygion,* the fin of a fish, from *pteryx,* a wing.] One of the two primary divisions of the osseous fishes, characterized by having one or more of the first rays of the fins in the form of spines.—**acanthopterygian,** a·kan′thop·te·rij″i·an, *a.* Of or pertaining to the Acanthopterygii. —**acanthopterygian,** a·kan′thop-te·rij″i·an, *n.* An acanthopterygian fish.

acanthus, a·kan′thus, *n.* See ACANTHA.

Acarida, a·kar′i·da, *n. pl.* (Gr. *akarēs,* too short to be cut, small, tiny—*a,* not, and *keirō,* to cut.] A division of Arachnida, including the mites, ticks, and water mites. The mouth in all is formed for suction.—**acarid,** ak′a·rid, *n.* One of the Acarida.—**acaricide,** a·kär′i-sīd, *n.* A substance that destroys mites.

acaroid resin, ak′a·roid rez′in, *n.* A resin that exudes from the grass trees of Australia, used in varnishes.

acarpous, a·kär′pus, *a.* [Gr. *akarpos,*

unfruitful—*a*, not, and *karpos*, fruit.] *Bot.* not producing fruit; sterile; barren.

acatalectic, a′kat·a·lek″tik, *a.* [Gr. *akatalēktos.*] Having the complete number of syllables (an *acatalectic* verse).

acaulous, acaulescent, a·kạl′us, a··kạl·es′ent, *a.* [Gr. *a*, not, and *kaulos*, a stalk.] *Bot.* without a conspicuous stem; stemless; *acauline, acaulose*, are also used in same sense.

accede, ak·sēd′, *v.i.*—*acceded, acceding.* [Fr. *accéder*, to assent, from L. *accedo*—*ad*, to, and *cedo*, to move, to give place. CEDE.] To agree or assent, as to a proposition, or to terms proposed by another; to become a party by agreeing to terms; to join or be added; to succeed, as an heir; come to by inheritance: said especially of a sovereign.—**accession,** ak·se′shon, *n.* The act of acceding; the act of agreeing or assenting; increase by something added; that which is added; the act of succeeding to a throne, office, or dignity; the attack or commencement of a disease.

accelerate, ak·sel′ėr·āt, *v.t.*—*accelerated, accelerating.* [L. *accelero, acceleratum*, to hasten—*ad*, to, and *celer*, swift. CELERITY.] To make quicker; to cause to move or advance faster; hasten; add to the velocity of; bring about or help to bring about more speedily.—**acceleration,** ak′sel·ėr·ā″shon, *n.* The act of accelerating or state of being accelerated; increase of velocity.—**acceleration of gravity.** *Phys.* the acceleration of a falling body due to the gravity, which is a little more than 32 feet per second per second at sea level and which varies with latitude and altitude.—**accelerative,** ak·sel′ėr·ā·tiv, *a.* Tending to accelerate; adding to velocity.—**accelerator,** ak·sel′ėr·āt·ėr, *n.* One who or that which accelerates; a hastener. In *chem.* a catalyst; *phys.* any device that increases the speed of charged particles.—**acceleratory,** ak·sel′ėr··a·to·ri, *a.* Accelerating or tending to accelerate.

accent, ak′sent, *n.* [L. *accentus*, an accent—*ad*, to, and *cano, cantum*, to sing. CHANT.] A superior stress or force of voice upon certain syllables of words, which distinguishes them from the other syllables, and forms an element in correct pronunciation; a mark or character used in writing to direct the stress of the voice in pronunciation, or to mark a particular tone, length of vowel sound, or the like; a peculiar or characteristic modulation or modification of the voice, such as that found in a given district; *pl.* words or expressions; *music*, stress or emphasis on particular notes.—*v.t.* ak·sent′. To give an accent or accents to in speaking; mark with an accent or accents.—**accentual,** ak·sent′ū·al, *a.* Pertaining to accent. —**accentuate,** ak·sent′ū·āt, *v.t.*—*accentuated, accentuating.* To mark or pronounce with an accent or with

accents; to emphasize or give prominence to.—**accentuation,** ak·sent′·ū·ā″shon, *n.* The act of accentuating or state of being accentuated.

accept, ak·sept′, *v.t.* [L. *acceptare*, freq. of *accipio, acceptum*, to accept—*ad*, to, and *capio*, to take. CAPABLE, HAVE.] To take or receive, as something offered; receive with approbation or favor; take as it comes; accede or assent to (a treaty, a proposal); to acknowledge, especially by signature, and thus to promise to pay (a bill of exchange).—**acceptable,** ak·sep′ta·bl, *a.* Capable, worthy, or sure of being accepted or received; pleasing to a receiver; gratifying; agreeable; welcome.—**acceptableness, acceptability,** ak·sep′ta·bl·nes, ak·sep′ta·bil″i·ti, *n.* The quality of being acceptable.—**acceptably,** ak·sep′ta·bli, *adv.* In an acceptable manner; in a manner to please.—**acceptance,** ak·sep′tans, *n.* The act of accepting; a taking or receiving; favorable reception; an agreeing to terms; a written engagement to pay money, made by a person signing his name across or at the end of a bill of exchange; an accepted bill, or the amount contained in it.—**acceptation,** ak·sep·tā′shon, *n.* The act of accepting or receiving; kind or favorable reception; the meaning or sense in which a word or expression is understood, or generally received.—**accepter, acceptor,** ak·sept′ėr, ak·sept′or, *n.* A person who accepts; specifically, the person who accepts a bill of exchange.

access, ak′ses, *n.* [L. *accessus*, from *accedo*, to come near, to approach. ACCEDE.] A coming to; near approach; admittance; admission; the means or way of approach; passage allowing communication; increase or accession; attack or return of a disease.—**accessibility,** ak′ses·si·bil″i·ti, *n.* The condition or quality of being accessible or of admitting approach.—**accessible,** ak·ses′si·bl, *a.* Capable of being approached or reached; easy of access; approachable; attainable.—**accession,** ak·se′shon, *n.* See ACCEDE.—**accessional,** ak·se′shon··al, *a.* Additional.

accessory, accessary, ak·ses′o·ri, ak·ses′a·ri, *a.* [L. *accessorius*, from *accessus, accedo.* ACCEDE.] Contributing; aiding in producing some effect, or acting in subordination to the principal agent: contributing to a general effect; belonging to something else as principal; accompanying.—*n.* One who aids or gives countenance to a crime; that which belongs to something else, as its principal; that which contributes to the effect of something more important; an accompaniment.—**accessorial,** ak·ses·sō′ri·al, *a.* Pertaining to an accessory.—**accessorily,** ak′ses·so″ri·li, *adv.* In the manner of an accessory; not as principal but as a subordinate agent.—**accessoriness,** ak′ses·so·ri·nes, *n.* The state of being accessory, or of being or acting in a secondary character.

accident, ak′si·dent, *n.* [L. *accidens,*

falling—*ad*, and *cado*, to fall, whence *case, cadence, casual, decadence*, etc.] Chance or what happens by chance; an event that happens when quite unlooked for; an unforeseen and undesigned injury to a person; casualty; mishap; a property or quality of a thing which is not essential to it nor is one of its invariable signs (as whiteness in paper).—**accidence,** ak′si·dens, *n.* [A corruption of *accidents* in the old sense of inflections of words.] That part of grammar which treats of the inflection of words, or the declension of nouns, adjectives, etc., and the conjugation of verbs; a small book containing the rudiments of grammar.—**accidental,** ak·si·dent′·al, *a.* Happening by chance or accident, or unexpectedly; casual; fortuitous; nonessential; not necessarily belonging; adventitious.—*n.* A casualty; a property not essential; *music*, a sharp, flat, or natural which does not occur in the clef, and which implies some change of key or modulation different from that in which the piece began.—**accidentally,** ak·si·dent′al·li, *adv.* In an accidental manner; by chance; fortuitously; not essentially.

accipiter, ak·sip′i·tėr, *n.* [L. *accipiter*, a bird of prey, from root *ak*, signifying sharpness and swiftness, and *pet*, to fly, like Gr. *ōkypteros*, swift-winged.] A genus of the order of birds Falconiformes.—**accipitres,** ak·sip′i·trēz, *n. pl.* An order of rapacious birds, now usually called Falconiformes.—**accipitral, accipitrine,** ak·sip′i·tral, ak·sip″i·trin, *a.* Of or pertaining to a hawk; having the character of a bird of prey; rapacious.

acclaim,† ak·klām′, *v.t.* [L. *acclamo*—*ac* for *ad*, and *clamo*, to cry out, whence *claim*, clamor, etc.] To applaud; to declare or salute by acclamation.—**acclaim,** ak·klām′, *n.* A shout of joy; acclamation.—**acclamation,** ak·kla·mā′shon, *n.* A shout or other demonstration of applause made by a multitude, indicating joy, hearty assent, approbation, or good wishes.—**acclamatory,** ak·klam′a·to·ri, *a.* Expressing joy or applause by acclamation.

acclimate, acclimatize, ak·klī′māt, ak·klī′mat·iz, *v.t.*—*acclimated, acclimating; acclimatized, acclimatizing.* [Fr. *acclimater*, to acclimate. CLIMATE.] To habituate to a foreign climate; to render proof against the prejudicial influences of a foreign climate; to adopt for permanent existence and propagation in a foreign climate.—**acclimation, acclimatization,** ak·kli·mā′shon, ak′kli··mat·iz·ā″shon, *n.* The act or process of acclimating or acclimatizing, or state of being acclimatized.

acclivity, ak·kliv′i·ti, *n.* [L. *acclivitas*, an acclivity—*ac* for *ad*, and *clivus*, a slope, from root *cli* seen in *clino, inclino*, to incline, Gr. *klinō*, to bend, incline; akin E. to *lean*.] A slope or inclination of the earth, as the side of a hill, considered as *ascending*, in opposition to *declivity*.

—**acclivitous, acclivous,** ak·kliv′i·tus, ak·klīv′us, *a.* Rising, as a hill with a slope; sloping upwards.

accolade, ak·kō·lād′, *n.* Fr. *accolade,* the accolade, lit. an embracing of the neck—L. *ad,* to, and *collum,* the neck; Fr. *accoler,* to embrace, *donner l'accolade,* to dub a knight. COLLAR.] A ceremony used in conferring knighthood, anciently consisting in putting the hand on the knight's neck, now usually a blow over the neck or shoulder with the flat of a sword; a salutation or rite performed in recognition of special merit; an award.

accommodate, ak·kom′mō·dāt, *v.t.* —*accommodated, accommodating.* [L. *accommodo,* to apply or suit—*ac* for *ad,* to, and *commodo,* to profit or help, from *con,* with, and *modus,* measure, proportion, limit, or manner. MODE.] To make suitable, correspondent, or consistent; to fit; adapt; conform; adjust; reconcile (with *to* after the object); to supply or furnish with required conveniences (with *with* after the object, as a friend *with* money).—**accommodating,** ak·kom′mō·dāt·ing, *a.* Obliging; yielding to the desires of others; disposed to comply and to oblige another.—**accommodation,** ak·kom′mō·dā″shon, *n.* The act of accommodating; adjustment; adaptation; adjustment of differences; anything which supplies a want, as in respect of ease, refreshment, and the like; a convenience; lodgings; a loan of money.—*Accommodation bill,* a bill of exchange not given like a genuine bill of exchange in payment of a debt, but merely intended to accommodate the drawer.—*Accommodation ladder,* a light ladder hung over the side of a ship to facilitate ascending from, or descending to, boats.—**accommodative,** ak·kom′mō·dāt·iv, *a.* Furnishing accommodation.

accompany, ak·kum′pa·ni, *v.t.*—*accompanied, accompanying.* [Fr. *accompagner,* to accompany—*ac* for *ad,* to, and *compagnon,* a companion. COMPANION.] To go with or attend as a companion or associate; to go together; to be associated or connected with; to play a subordinate musical part to, as to a singer or other performer of a musical composition.—**accompaniment,** ak·kum′pa·ni·ment, *n.* Something that attends as a circumstance, or which is added by way of ornament to the principal thing, or for the sake of symmetry; the subordinate part or parts performed by instruments accompanying a voice, or several voices, or a principal instrument.—**accompanist,** ak·kum′pan·ist, *n.* The performer in music who plays the accompaniment.

accomplice, ak·kom′plis, *n.* [Prefix *ac* for *ad,* to, and the older E. *complice,* Fr. *complice,* L. *complex, complicis,* confederate, participant—*con,* with, and *plico,* to fold, *plica,* a fold, a stem which appears also in E. *comply, ply, triple,* etc. PLY, etc.] An associate or confederate, espe-

cially in a crime; a partner or partaker in guilt.

accomplish, ak·kom′plish, *v.t.* [Fr. *accomplir,* to finish—prefix *ac* for *ad,* to, and L. *compleo,* to complete. COMPLETE.] To complete; to finish entirely; to execute; to carry out; to fulfill or bring to pass.—**accomplishable,** ak·kom′plish·a·bl, *a.* Capable of accomplishment.—**accomplished,** ak·kom′plisht, *a.* Perfected; finished; consummate; having the attainments and graces regarded as necessary for cultivated or fashionable society.—**accomplisher,** ak·kom′plish·ėr, *n.* One who accomplishes.—**accomplishment,** ak·kom′plish·ment, *n.* The act of accomplishing or carrying into effect; fulfillment; acquirement; attainment, especially such as belongs to cultivated or fashionable society.

accord, ak·kord′, *n.* [Fr. *accord,* agreement—prefix *ac* for *ad,* to, and L. *cor, cordis,* the heart, formed like L. *concors, discors,* E. *concord, discord.*] Agreement; harmony of minds; as, to do a thing with one *accord;* just correspondence of things; concord; harmony of sound; voluntary or spontaneous impulse or act; in this sense in such phrases as *of my, of his, of its, of their own accord.*—*v.t.* To make to agree or correspond†; to grant; to give; to concede; as, to *accord* to one due praise.—*v.i.* To be in correspondence or harmony.—**accordance,** ak·kord′ans, *n.* The state of being in accord; agreement with a person; conformity with a thing.—**accordant,** ak·kord′ant, *a.* Corresponding; consonant; agreeable; of the same mind.—**accordantly,** ak·kord′ant·li, *adv.* In accordance or agreement.—**according,** ak·kord′ing, *a.* Agreeing; agreeable; in accordance.—*According as,* agreeably, conformably, or proportionately as.—*According to,* agreeably to or in accordance with (zeal *according to* knowledge): followed by a personal object it refers to a statement of the person (*according to him* you are wrong).—**accordingly,** ak·kord′ing·li, *adv.* Agreeably; suitably; in a manner conformable; consequently.

accordion, ak·kord′i·on, *n.* [From *accord.*] A small keyed wind instrument, whose tones are generated by the play of wind upon metallic reeds.—**accordionist,** ak·kord′i·on·ist, *n.* A player on the accordion.

accost, ak·kost′, *v.t.* [Fr. *accoster,* L.L. *accostare*—*ac* for *ad,* to, and L. *costa* (Fr. *côte*), a rib, a side. COAST.] To speak first to; to address before oneself is addressed.

accoucheur, ak·kö·shėr′, *n.* [Fr., a man-midwife—*ac* for *ad,* and *coucher,* to lie or lay down. COUCH.] A surgeon who attends women in childbirth.—**accoucheuse,** ak·kö·shėz′, *n.* A midwife.—**accouchement,** ak·kösh′ment, *n.* Childbirth.

account, ak·kount′, *n.* [O.E. *accompt*—*ac* for *ad,* and O.Fr. *compte,* a calculation, from L. *computo,* to compute, reckon. The Mod.Fr. *conte, conter,* present the same change

of *m* into *n* as our own word.] A reckoning, enumeration, or computation; a list of debits and credits, or charges; a statement of things bought or sold, of payments, services, etc.; an explanatory statement of particulars, facts, or events; narrative; relation; description; reason or consideration; ground (on all *accounts*); profit; advantage (to turn to *account*); regard; behalf; sake (trouble incurred on one's *account*); *stockbroking,* the operations on the stock exchange performed during the period before the ordinary settlement day.—*To make account of,* to hold in estimation or esteem; to value: with an adjective of quantity, as *much, little, no,* etc.—*Account current,* the statement of the successive mercantile transactions of one person with another, drawn out in the form of debtor and creditor, and in the order of their dates.—**account,** ak·kount′, *v.t.* To deem, judge, think, or hold in opinion,—*v.i.* To render an account or relation of particulars; to answer in a responsible character; to give reasons; to explain: followed by *to* before a person, *for* before a thing.—**accountability,** ak·kount′a·bil″i·ti, *n.* The state of being accountable or answerable.—**accountable,** ak·kount′a·bl, *a.* Liable to pay or make good in case of loss; responsible for a trust; liable to be called to account; answerable to a superior.—**accountableness,** ak·kount′a·bl·nes, *n.* The state of being accountable; accountability.—**accountably,** ak·kount′a·bli, *adv.* In an accountable manner.—**accountant,** ak·kount′ant, *n.* One who makes the keeping or examination of accounts his profession; an officer in a public office who has charge of the accounts.—**accountantship,** ak·kount′ant·ship, *n.* The office or employment of an accountant.—**accounting,** a·koun′ting, *n.* The theory and system of setting up, maintaining, and auditing the books of a firm; the art of analyzing the financial position and operating results of a business house from a study of its sales, purchases, etc.

accouter, accoutre, ak·kö′tėr, *v.t.* —*accoutred, accoutring.* [Fr. *accoutrer*—prefix *ac* for *ad,* to, and *couture,* a seam, from L. *consutura,* a stitching together, from *con,* together, and *suo, sutum,* to sew.] To equip or furnish with personal trappings; especially, to array in a military dress and arms; to equip for military service.—**accouterments,** ak·kö′tėr·ments, *n. pl.* Military dress and arms; fighting array.

accredit ak·kred′it, *v. t.* [Fr. *accréditer,* to accredit—L. *ad,* to, and *credo, creditum,* to trust.] To repose confidence in; to trust (a person); to give credit to; to believe (a story); to confer credit or authority on; to send with credentials, as an envoy.

accresce, ak·kres′, *v.i.* [L. *accresco, accretum,* to increase, to grow to—*ad,* to, and *cresco,* to grow, increase.] To accrue (which see).—**accrescence,** ak·kres′ens, *n.* Act of increasing;

gradual growth or increase; accretion.—**accrescent,** ak·kres'ent, *a.* Increasing; growing.—**accrete,†** ak·krēt', *v.i.* To grow by accretion; to be added by growth.—**accretion,** ak·krē'shon, *n.* The act of accreting or accrescing; a growing to; an increase by natural growth; an increase by an accession of parts externally; *med.* the growing together of parts naturally separate, as the fingers or toes; the thing added by growth; an accession.—**accretive,** ak·krēt'iv, *a.* Of or pertaining to accretion.

accrue, ak·krö', *v.i.*—**accrued,** *accruing.* [Fr. *accrue,* increase, from *accrū,* pp. of *accroitre,* to increase, from L. *accrescere—ac* for *ad,* to, and *cresco* to grow, seen also in *crescent, decrease, increase.*] To be gained or obtained; to proceed, arise, or spring; as, a profit or a loss *accrues* from a commercial transaction.—**accrual,** a·krö'al, *n.* Act or process of accruing; accretion.—**accrument,†** ak·krö'ment, *n.* That which accrues; addition; increase.

accumbent, ak·kum'bent, *a.* [L. *accumbens,* ppr. of *accumbo,* from *ad,* to, and *cumbo,* to lie down.] Leaning or reclining; lying against anything.—**accumbency,** ak·kum'ben·si, *n.* State of being accumbent.

accumulate, ak·kū'mū·lāt, *v.t.*—*accumulated, accumulating.* [L. *accumulo, accumulatum,* to heap up—*ad,* to, and *cumulus,* a heap.] To heap or pile up; to amass; to collect or bring together.—*v.i.* To grow to be extensive in number or quantity; to increase greatly.—**accumulation,** ak·kū'mū·lā'shon, *n.* The act of accumulating; a collecting or being heaped up; that which has accumulated; a mass that has been collected.—**accumulative,** ak·kū'mū·lāt·iv, *a.* Causing accumulation; heaping up.—**accumulatively,** ak·kū'mū·lāt·iv·li, *adv.* In an accumulative manner; in heaps.—**accumulator,** ak·kū'mū·lāt·ėr, *n.* One who or that which accumulates; a contrivance, such as a spring, that by being coiled up serves as a store of force.

accurate, ak'kū·rāt, *a.* [L. *accuratus,* prepared with care—*ac* for *ad,* to, and *cura,* care. CURE.] In exact conformity to truth, or to a standard or rule, or to a model; free from error or defect; exact; precise; strictly correct; adhering to exactness or correctness.—**accuracy, accurateness,** ak'kū·ra·si, ak'kū·rāt·nes, *n.* The condition or quality of being accurate; extreme precision or exactness; exact conformity to truth, or to a rule or model; correctness.—**accurately,** ak'kū·rāt·li, *adv.* In an accurate manner.

accurse, ak·kėrs', *v.t.* [Prefix *ac* for *ad,* or A. Sax. *â,* intens., and *curse.*] To call down curses on; to curse.—**accursed, accurst,** ak·kėrst' or ak·kėrs'ėd, ak·kėrst', *a.* Lying under a curse; blasted; ruined; execrable; cursed.

accuse, ak·kūz', *v.t.*—*accused, accusing.* [L. *accuso,* to call to account, blame, indict—*ad,* to, and *causa,* cause, process. CAUSE.] To charge

with a crime, offense, or fault; to blame (with *of* before the crime or offense). ∴ *Accuse* is both a legal and a general term, and commonly expresses something more formal than *charge.* The construction of the two verbs is also different: *accuse of, charge with.*—**accusation,** ak·kū·zā'shon, *n.* The act of accusing; that of which one is accused; a charge brought against one.—**accusative,** ak·kūz'at·iv, *a.* Accusatory. —**accusative,** ak·kūz'at·iv, *n.* The fourth case of nouns and other declinable words in Latin, Greek, etc., corresponding to the *objective* in English.—**accusatively,** ak·kūz'at·iv·li, *adv.* By way of accusation; in the position or relation of an accusative case.—**accusatory, accusatorial,** ak·kūz'a·to·ri, ak·kūz'a·tō'ri·al, *a.* Accusing; containing an accusation; as, an *accusatory* libel.—**accused,** ak·kūzd', *pp.* used as a *noun.* A person or persons charged with a crime.—**accuser,** ak·kūz'ėr, *n.* One who accuses; one who formally brings a charge.

accustom, ak·kus'tum, *v.t.* [O.Fr. *accoustumer,* to accustom—*ac* for L. *ad,* to, and O.Fr. *coustume,* custom. CUSTOM.] To familiarize by use or habit; to habituate or inure.—**accustomed,** ak·kus'tumd, *a.* Often practiced; customary; habitual; wonted; familiar; as, in their *accustomed* manner.

ace, ās, *n.* [Fr. *as,* ace at dice or cards; L. *as,* a unit, a pound, a foot, etc., from Doric Gr. *as, ais,* Attic Gr. *heis,* one.] A unit; a single pip on a card or die, or the card or face of a die so marked; a trifle or insignificant quantity or distance (within an *ace* of it); the ace in certain card games counting as ten; an expert; a champion; one proficient in a particular field of endeavor. In *aviation,* the name given to a combat pilot officially credited with shooting down five or more enemy planes.—*a.* Excellent; first in quality.

Aceldama, a·kel'da·ma, *n.* [Heb.] Field of blood. Acts, i. 19.

acentric, a·sen'trik, *a.* [Prefix *a,* neg., and *centre.*] Not centric; away from a center.—*n.* An airplane so designed that the line of the propeller thrust does not pass through the center of gravity.

Acephala, a·sef'a·la, *n. pl.* [Gr. *akephalos,* headless—*a,* not, and *kephalē,* head.] Molluscous animals, like the oyster and scallop, that do not have a distinct head.—**acephalist,** a·sef'al·ist, *n.* One who acknowledges no head or superior.—**acephalous,** a·sef'al·us, *a.* Without a head; headless.

acerb, a·sėrb', *a.* [L. *acerbus,* unripe, harsh, sour, from *acer,* sharp; same root as in *acid.*] Sour, bitter, and harsh to the taste; sour with astringency and roughness.—**acerbity,** a·sėrb'it·i, *n.* Sourness, with roughness or astringency of taste; poignancy or severity; painfulness; sharpness; harshness or severity of temper; sourness.

acerous, acerose, as'ėr·us, as'ėr·ōz,

a. [L. *acerosus,* chaffy, from *acus, aceris,* chaff.] *Bot.* resembling chaff; narrow and slender, with a sharp point.

acervate,† a·sėrv'āt, *v.t.* [L. *acervo,* to heap up, from *acervus,* a heap.] To heap up.

acetabulum, as·ē·tab'ū·lum, *n. pl.* **acetabula,** as·ē·tab'ū·la. [L., vinegar cruet, a cup-shaped vessel, from *acetum,* vinegar. ACID.] The cavity which receives the head of the thigh bone; the socket in which the leg of an insect is inserted; the cuplike sucker with which the arms of the cuttlefish are provided; the cuplike or saucer-like fructification of many lichens; the receptacle of certain fungi.

acetic, a·set'ik, *a.* [L. *acetum,* vinegar.] Having the properties of vinegar; sour.—*Acetic acid,* an acid often prepared by the oxidation of alcohol (acetous fermentation), and along with water forming the chief ingredient of vinegar.—**acetate,** as'ē·tāt, *n.* A salt formed by the union of acetic acid with a base; a product made from cellulose acetate, for example, acetate rayon.—**acetification,** a·set'i·fi·kā'shon, *n.* The act of acetifying or making acetous or sour; the process of becoming acetous; the operation of making vinegar.—**acetifier,** a·set'i·fī·ėr, *n.* An apparatus used in making vinegar.—**acetify,** a·set'i·fī, *v.t.*—*acetified, acetifying.* To convert into acid or vinegar.—*v.i.* To become acid; to be converted into vinegar.—**acetimeter, acetometer,** as·et·im'et·ėr, as·et·om'et·ėr, *n.* An instrument for ascertaining the strength or purity of acids; an acidimeter.—**acetone,** as'ē·tōn, *n.* [*acetic* and *ketone.*] A chemical compound used as a solvent for fats, rubber, and plastic.

acetylcholine, as'ē·til·ko'lēn, *n.* A chemical compound liberated from nerve endings, involved in transmission of nerve impulses.

acetylene, a·set'i·lēn, *n.* [From *acetic,* and Gr. *hylē,* matter.] A flammable gas made with calcium carbide and water; used as a fuel in welding.

acetylsalicylic acid, as'ē·til·sal'e·sil'ik as'id, *n.* Aspirin.

ache, āk, *n.* [A.Sax, *ace, æce, ece,* ache, pain; *acan,* to ache; akin to Icel. *aka,* to drive, press hard; cog. L. *ago,* to drive.] Pain, or continued pain, in opposition to sudden twinges, or spasmodic pain; a continued gnawing pain as in toothache or earache; feeling of distress (heartache).—*v.i.*—*ached, aching.* To suffer from an ache or pain.

achene, a·kēn', *n.* [Gr. *a,* priv., and *chainō,* to yawn, to gape.] *Bot.* a small dry carpel, containing a single seed, which does not open when ripe.

achieve, a·chēv', *v.t.*—*achieved, achieving,* [Fr. *achever,* to finish—*a,* to, and O.Fr. *cheve,* Fr. *chef,* the head or end, from L. *caput,* the head. CHIEF.] To perform or execute; to finish or carry on to a final and prosperous close; to obtain or bring about, as by effort.—**achievable,** a·chēv'a·bl, *a.* Capable of being achieved or performed.—**achievement,** a·chĕv′ment, *n.* The act of achieving or performing; accomplishment; an exploit; a great or heroic deed; an escutcheon or ensign armorial; a hatchment.—**achiever,** a·chĕv′ẽr, *n.* One who achieves or accomplishes.

achlamydate, a·klam′id·āt, *a.* [Gr. *a,* not, and *chlamys, chlamydos,* a cloak.] *Zool.* not possessing a mantle, as certain mollusks.—**achlamydeous,** a·kla·mid′ē·us, *a. Bot.* having neither calyx nor corolla, the flowers being without floral envelope.

achromatic, ak·rō·mat′ik, *a.* [Gr. *a,* not, and *chrōma, chrōmatos,* color.] Destitute of color; transmitting light without decomposing it into its primary colors; as, an *achromatic* lens or telescope.—**achromaticity, achromatism,** ak′rō·ma·tis″i·ti, ak·rō′ma·tizm, *n.* The state of being achromatic; want of color.—**achromatize,** a·krō′ma·tīz, *v.t.* To deprive of color; to render achromatic.

acicula, a·sik′ū·la, *n.* pl.—**aciculae,** a·sik′ū·lē. [L., dim. of *acus,* a needle. ACID.] A name given by naturalists to a spine or prickle of an animal or plant.—**acicular, aciculate, aciform,** a·sik′ū·lẽr, a·sik′ū·lāt, as′i·form, *a.* Having the shape of a needle; having sharp points like needles; needle shaped.—**acicularly,** a·sik′ū·lẽr·li, *adv.* In an acicular manner.

acid, as′id, *a.* [L. *acidus,* sour, from root *ac, ak,* a point, seen in *acus,* a needle; *acuo,* to sharpen; *acer,* sharp; *aceo,* to be sour; *acetum,* vinegar; giving such English words as *acrid, acumen, acute, ague, eager,* etc.] Sour, sharp, or biting to the taste; not sweet; not alkaline.—**acid,** as′id, *n.* A sour substance; specifically, in *chem.* a compound of which hydrogen is an essential constituent. Acids possess a sour taste, change blue vegetable colors to red, and combine with bases to form salts.—**acidic,** a·sid′ik, *a. Chem.* pertaining to acid; containing a large amount of an acid constituent.—**acidify,** a·sid′i·fī, *v.t.*—*acidified, acidifying.* To make acid; to convert into an acid.—**acidifiable,** a·sid′i·fī·a·bl, *a.* Capable of being acidified or converted into an acid.—**acidification,** a·sid′i·fi·kā″shon, *n.* The act or process of acidifying.—**acidimeter,** as·id·im′et·ẽr, *n.* Same as *acetimeter.*—**acidity,** a·sid′i·ti, *n.* The quality of being acid or sour; sourness; tartness.—**acidulate,** a·sid′ū·lāt, *v.t.*—*acidulated, acidulating.* [Pr. *aciduler,* to make slightly sour; L. *acidulus,* slightly sour.] To make acid in a moderate degree.—**acidulent,** a·sid′ū·lent, *a.* Somewhat acid or sour; tart; peevish.—**acidulous,** a·sid′ū·lus, *a.* Slightly sour; subacid; as cream of tartar, oranges, etc.

aciform, as′i·form, *a.* See ACICULA.

acinaceous, as·in·ā′shus, *a.* [L. *acinus,* a grapestone or kernel.] Full of kernels.—**acinarious,** as·in·ā′ri·us, *a. Bot.* covered with little spherical stalked vesicles resembling grapeseeds, as in some algae.—**aciniform,**

a·sin′i·form, *a.* Having the form of grapes, or being in clusters like grapes.—**acinose, acinous,** as′in·ōs, as′in·us, *a.* Consisting of minute, granular concretions.

acinaciform, as·in·as′i·form, *a.* [L. *acinaces,* Gr. *akinakēs,* a scimitar.] Formed like or resembling a scimitar; as, an *acinaciform* leaf.

ack-ack, ak·ak, *a.* [From pronunciation of AA, antiaircraft, by British radio operators.] Pertaining to antiaircraft.—*n.* An antiaircraft gun; antiaircraft artillery; antiaircraft fire.

acknowledge, ak·nol′ej, *v.t.*—*acknowledged, acknowledging.* [Prefix *a,* on, and *knowledge.*] To own or recognize by avowal or by some act; to assent to the truth or claims of; to admit to be; to own or confess; to avow receiving. ...We *acknowledge* what is in some way brought or set before our notice; when we *confess* we make known, and often of our own free will.—**acknowledger,** ak·nol′ej·ẽr, *n.* One who acknowledges.

acknowledgment, ak·nol′ej·ment, *n.* The act of acknowledging; owning; recognition; avowal; confession; expression of thanks; something given or done in return for a favor; a receipt for money received.

acme, ak′mē, *n.* [Gr. *akmē,* a point. Root *ak.* ACID.] The top or highest point; the furthest point attained; maturity or perfection; the height or crisis of a disease.

acne, ak′nē, *n.* [Origin unknown.] An eruption of hard, inflamed tubercles or pimples on the face.

acolyte, ak′o·līt, *n.* [Fr. from L.L. *acolythus,* an acolyte; Gr. *akolouthos,* a follower.] An attendant; in the *R. Cath. Ch.* one of an inferior order of clergy, who attends during service on the superior orders; a lay attendant so employed.

aconite, ak′on·īt, *n.* L. *aconitum,* Gr. *akoniton,* a poisonous plant, like monkshood.] The plant wolfsbane or monkshood, *Aconitum napellus.*

acorn, ā′korn, *n.* [A. Sax. *æceren, æcern,* an acorn; Goth. *akram,* fruit; Icel. *akarn,* Dan. *agern,* O.H.G. *ackeran,* an acorn; the word originally meant simply fruit, fruit of the field, being allied to *acre.*] The fruit of the oak, a one-celled, one-seeded, oval nut, which grows in a permanent cup.

acotyledon, a·kot′il·ē″don, *n.* [Gr. *a,* not, and *kotylēdon,* any cupshaped cavity, from *kotylē,* a hollow.] *Bot.* a plant whose seeds, called spores, are not furnished with cotyledons or seed lobes.—**acotyledonous,** a·kot′il·ē″don·us, *a.* Having no seed lobes.

acoustic, acoustical, a·kös′tik, a·kös′tik·al, *a.* [Gr. *akoustikos,* from *akouō,* to hear.] Pertaining to the sense or organs of hearing, or to the science of acoustics.—**acoustic,** *n.* A remedy for deafness or imperfect hearing.—**acoustically,** a·kös′tik·al·li, *adv.* In relation to or in a manner adapted to acoustics.—**acoustics,** a·kös′·tiks, *n.* The science of sound, teaching the cause, nature, and phenomena of the vibrations

of elastic bodies which affect the organ of hearing.

acquaint, ak·kwānt′, *v.t.* [O.Fr. *accointer;* L.L. *accognitare,* to make known, from L. *ad,* to, and *cognitus,* known, from *cognosco, cognitum,* to know; same root as in *know.*] To make to know; to make aware of; to apprise; to make familiar; inform: *with* is used before the subject of information, if a noun (*acquaint* a person *with* facts).—**acquaintance,** ak·kwānt′ans, *n.* A state of being acquainted, or of having more or less intimate knowledge; knowledge; familiarity (followed by *with*); a person known to one; the whole body of those with whom one is acquainted.—**acquaintanceship,** ak·kwānt′ans·ship, *n.* State of being acquainted.—**acquainted,** ak·kwānt′ed, *a.* Having acquaintance; knowing, but not a close or intimate friend.

acquiesce, ak·kwi·es′, *v.i.*—*acquiesced, acquiescing.* [Fr. *acquiescer,* L. *acquiesco,* to rest, to acquiesce—*ad,* to, and *quiesco,* to be quiet. QUIET.] To rest satisfied, or apparently satisfied, or to rest without opposition and discontent; to assent quietly; to agree.—**acquiescence,** ak·kwi·es′ens, *n.* The act of acquiescing or giving a quiet assent.—**acquiescent,** ak·kwi·es′ent, *a.* Disposed to acquiesce; disposed to submit; quietly assenting.—**acquiescently,** ak·kwi·es′ent·li, *adv.*

acquire, ak·kwīr′, *v.t.*—*acquired, acquiring.* [L. *acquiro,* to get—*ad,* to and *quaero,* to look or search for. QUEST.] To get or gain, the object being something which is more or less permanent (as fortune, title, habits, etc.) A mere temporary possession is not expressed by *acquire,* but by *obtain, procure,* etc.; as, to *obtain* (not *acquire*) a book on loan.—**acquirable,** ak·kwīr′a·bl, *a.* Capable of being acquired.—**acquirement,** ak·kwīr′ment, *n.* The act of acquiring, or of making acquisition; that which is acquired; attainment, especially personal attainment (as contrasted with a natural *gift* or *endowment*).—**acquirer,** ak·kwīr′ẽr, *n.* A person who acquires.—**acquisition,** ak·kwi·zi′shon, *n.* The act of acquiring; the thing acquired or gained; generally applied to material gains.—**acquisitive,** ak·kwiz′it·iv, *a.* Disposed to make acquisitions; having a propensity to acquire property.—**acquisitively,** ak·kwiz′it·iv·li, *adv.* In an acquisitive manner; by way of acquisition.—**acquisitiveness,** ak·kwiz′i·tiv·nes, *n.* Quality of being acquisitive.

acquired character, *n.* A biological change that results from use or environment rather than from heredity.

acquit, ak·kwit′, *v.t.*—*acquitted, acquitting.* [Fr. *acquitter,* to discharge, to set at rest with respect to a claim—L. *ad,* to, and *quietus,* at rest, quiet. QUIET.] To release or discharge from an obligation, accusation, or the like; to pronounce not guilty (with *of* before the thing; *refl.* to behave; to bear or conduct one's self.—**acquittal**, ak·kwit′al, *n.* The act of acquitting; a judicial setting free from the charge of an offense.—**acquittance**, ak·kwit′ans, *n.* An acquitting or discharging from a debt or any other liability; the writing which is evidence of such a discharge.

acre, ā′kėr, *n.* [A.Sax. *acer*, *æcer*, a field=D. *akker*, Icel. *akr*, Dan. *ager*, G. *acker*, Goth. *akrs*, arable land, a field; L. *ager*, Gr. *agros*, Skr. *ajra*, a field. From root, *ag*, *ak*, as in L. *ago*. Icel. *aka*, to drive; the word probably meaning originally the place to or over which cattle were driven; a pasture. *Acorn* is from this root.] A definite quantity of land. The United States and British statute acre contains 160 square rods or perches, or 4,840 square yards.—**acreage**, ā′kėr·āj, *n.* The number of acres in a piece of land; acres taken collectively.

acrid, ak′rid, *a.* [From L. *acer*, *acris*, *acre*, sharp: with *id*, from the common L. adjective termination -*idus*. ACID.] Sharp or biting to the taste; pungent; bitter; virulent; bitter (as in temper or disposition).—**acrid**, ak′rid, *n.* An acrid or irritant poison.—**acridity**, **acridness**, a··krid′i·ti, ak′rid·nes, *n.* The quality of being acrid or pungent.

acrimony, ak′ri·mo·ni, *n.* [L. *acrimonia*, from *acris*, sharp.] Acridity; pungency; sharpness or severity of temper; bitterness of expression; acerbity; asperity.—**acrimonious**, ak·ri·mō′ni·us, *a.* Abounding in acrimony; severe; bitter; virulent; caustic; stinging.—**acrimoniously**, ak·ri·mō′ni·us·li, *adv.* In an acrimonious manner; sharply; bitterly; pungently.—**acrimoniousness**, ak··ri·mō′ni·us·nes, *n.* The quality of being acrimonious.

acrobat, ak′rō·bat, *n.* [Gr. *akrobatos*—*akros*, high, and *bainō*, to go.] A rope-dancer; also, one who practices vaulting, tumbling, throwing somersaults, etc.—**acrobatic**, ak′rō·bat·ik, *a.* Of or pertaining to an acrobat or his performance.

acrocarpous, ak·rō·kärp′us, *a.* [Gr. *akros*, highest, and *karpos*, fruit.] *Bot.* applied to mosses whose flower terminates the growth of a primary axis.

acrogen, ak′rō·jen, *n.* [Gr. *akros*, high, on the top, and root *gen*, to produce.] A plant (as a moss, fern, horsetail) increasing by extension of the stem or axis of growth at the top.—**acrogenous**, a·kroj′en·us, *a.* Increasing by growth at the summit, as the tree ferns; pertaining to the acrogens.

acromegaly, ak′ro·meg″a·le, *n.* [Gr. *akros*, an extremity; *megale*, large.] A rare disease, associated with overgrowth of bone, especially in the jaws, hands, and feet.

acronical, a·kron′ik·al, *a.* [Gr. *akros*, extreme, and *nyx*, night.] *Astron,* culminating at midnight: said of a star which rises as the sun sets, and sets as the sun rises.—**acronically**, a·kron′ik·al·li, *adv.* In an acronical manner.

acronym, ak′ru·nim, *n.* [From *acro*- and Gr. *onoma*, name.] A word formed from the initial syllables or letters of other words, as *radar* from "*radio detecting and ranging.*"

acrophobia, ak′ro·fo″bi·a, *n.* [Gr. *akron*, a height; *phobos*, fear.] A pathological dread of high places.

acropolis, a·krop′o·lis, *n.* [Gr. *akros*, high, and *polis*, a city.] The citadel or highest part of a Grecian city, usually situated on an eminence commanding the town.

acrospire, ak′rō·spīr, *n.* [Gr. *akros*, highest, and *speira*, a spire or spiral line.] The first leaf which rises above the ground when corn germinates; also the rudimentary stem or first leaf which appears in malted grain.

across, a·kros′, *prep.* and *adv.* [Prefix *a*, and *cross*.] From side to side: opposed to *along*; athwart; quite over; intersecting; passing over at any angle; from one side to another; crosswise.

acrostic, a·kros′tik, *n.* [Gr. *akrostichion*, an acrostic—*akros*, extreme, and *stichos*, order or verse.] A composition in verse, in which the first, or the first and last, or certain other letters of the lines, taken in order, form a name, title, motto, etc., which is the subject of the poem.—*a.* Relating to or containing an acrostic.—**acrostically**, a·kros′tik·al·li, *adv.* In the manner of an acrostic.

acrotic, a·krot′ik, *a.* [L.L. *acroticus*, from Gr. *akros*, extreme.] *Med.* belonging to or affecting external surfaces.

acrotism, ak′rō·tizm, *n.* [Gr. *a*, not, and *krotos*, a beating.] An absence or weakness of the pulse.

acrylic, a′kril″ik, *adj.* Pertaining to the acid CH₂: CH.COOH obtained from acrolein.—**acrylic resin**, *n.* Thermoplastic resin from polymerization of acrylic or methacrylic acid esters, used for transparent airplane parts, lenses, dentures.

act, akt, *v.i.* [L. *ago*, *actum*, to exert power, to put in motion, to do; Gr. *agō*, to lead; allied to Icel. *aka*, to drive, and to E. *acre* (which see).] To exert power; to produce effects; to be in action or motion; to carry into effect a purpose or determination of the mind; to behave, demean, or conduct oneself; to perform, as an actor.—*v.t.* To transact; to do or perform; to represent as real; to perform on or as on the stage; to play; hence, to feign or counterfeit.—**act**, akt, *n.* That which is being done or which has been done; a deed; an exploit; the exertion of power; the effect of which power exerted is the cause; a state of reality or real existence, as opposed to a possibility; actuality; a part or division of a play, generally subdivided into smaller portions called *scenes*; a decree, edict, or law, especially one proceeding from a legislative body. ACTION.—*In the act*, in the actual performance or commission of some misdeed.—*In act to*, prepared or ready to, by being in a suitable posture.—**actable**, akt′-

a·bl, *a.* Capable of being acted or performed; practically possible.—**acting**, akt′ing, *a.* Performing duty, service, or functions; doing the real work of an office for a nominal or honorary holder of the post.—*n.* A playing on the stage.—**actor**, ak′-tėr, *n.* One who acts or performs; one who represents a character or acts a part in a play.—**actress**, ak′-tres, *n.* A female actor.

ACTH, ā′sē′tē′āch′, *n.* Initials for adrenocorticotropic hormone, a pituitary hormone that stimulates the cortex of the adrenal glands.

actinia, ak·tin′i·a, *n.* pl. **actiniae**, [Gr. *aktis*, *aktinos*, a ray; from their tentacles being ray-like.] A sea anemone; a polyp having the mouth surrounded by tentacles in concentric circles, which when spread resemble the petals of a flower: often of brilliant colors.

actinic, ak·tin′ik, *a.* [Gr. *aktis*, *aktinos*, a ray.] Pertaining to rays; pertaining to the chemical rays of the sun.—**actinism**, ak′tin·izm, *n.* The radiation of heat or light; the property of the chemical part of the sun's rays, which, as seen in photography, produces chemical combinations and decompositions.—**actinium**, ak·tin′i·um, *n.* Radioactive element discovered in pitchblende. Symbol, Ac; at. no., 89; at. wt., 227.—**actinoid**, ak′tin·oid, *a.* Resembling a ray or rays; radiated.—**actinograph**, ak·tin′ō·graf, *n.* An instrument for measuring and registering the variations of actinic or chemical influence in the solar rays.—**actinology**, ak·ti·nol′ō·ji, *n.* The science which investigates the power of sunlight to cause chemical action.—**actinolitic**, ak·tin′ō·lit″ik, *a.* Like or pertaining to actinolite.—**actinometer**, ak·tin·om′et·ėr, *n.* An instrument for measuring the intensity of the sun's actinic rays.—**actinometric**, ak·tin′ō·met″rik, *a.* Of or belonging to the actinometer or its use.

action, ak′shon, *n.* [L. *actio*. ACT.] The state or manner of acting or being active, as opposed to *rest*; activity; an act or thing done; the performance of a function; a deed; an exploit; a battle or engagement; the mechanism or movement of a compound instrument, or the like; agency; operation; impulse; the connected series of events on which the interest of a drama or work of fiction depends; gesture or gesticulation; a suit or process at law... *Action* and *Act* have some meanings in common, but others are peculiar to each. Thus, the meanings battle, lawsuit, mechanism, belong only to the former; those of law, part of a play, to the latter. So we speak of a *course of action*. But we may speak of performing a noble *action* or a noble *act*.—**actionable**, ak′shon·a·bl, *a.* Furnishing ground for an action at law.—**actionably**, ak′shon·a·bli, *adv.* In an actionable manner.

active, ak′tiv, *a.* [Fr. *actif*, *active*; L. *activus*. ACT.] Having the power or property of acting; exerting or having the power to exert an influence (as opposed to *passive*); performing actions quickly; quick; nimble; brisk; agile; constantly engaged in action; busy; assiduous; accompanied or characterized by action, work, or by the performance of business (an *active* demand for goods); actually proceeding (*active* hostilities); *gram.* expressing action, especially action affecting an object; transitive.—**actively,** ak′tiv·li, *adv.* In an active manner.—**activity,** ak·tiv′i·ti, *n.* The state or quality of being active; the active faculty; active force; nimbleness; agility; briskness.—**activeness,** ak′tiv·nes, *n.* State of being active.

actor, actress. See ACT.

actual, ak′tū·al, *a.* Acting or existing really and objectively; real; effectively operative; effectual: opposed to *potential* or *nominal*; now existing; present.—*n.* Something actual or real.—**actualness,** ak′tū·al·nes, *n.* The quality of being actual.—**actuality,** ak·tū·al′i·ti, *n.* The state of being actual; that which is real or actual.—**actualization,** ak′tū·al·iz·ā″shon, *n.* A making real or actual.—**actualize,** ak′tū·al·īz, *v.t.*—*actualized, actualizing.* To make actual.—**actually,** ak′tū·al·li, *adv.* In fact; really; with active manifestation.

actuary, ak′tū·a·ri, *n.* [L. *actuarius,* a clerk, a registrar, from *acta,* records, acts.] A registrar or clerk; an official in a joint-stock company, particularly an insurance company, whose duty it is to make the necessary computations, especially computations of some complexity.—**actuarial,** ak·tū·ā′ri·al, *a.* Of or pertaining to an actuary or to his business.

actuate, ak′tū·āt, *v.t.*—*actuated, actuating,* [From *act.*] To put into action; to move or incite to action.—**actuation,** ak·tū·ā′shon, *n.* The state of being put in action.—**actuator,** ak′tū·āt·ėr, *n.* One who actuates or puts in action.

aculeate, aculeated, a·kū′lē·āt, a·kū′lē·āt·ed, *a.* [L. *aculeus,* a spine, a prickle, dim. of *acus,* a needle. ACID.] *Bot.* having prickles or sharp points; *zool.* having a sting.

acumen, a·kū′men, *n.* [L. *acumen,* from *acuo,* to sharpen. ACID.] Quickness of perception; mental acuteness or penetration; keenness of insight; sagacity.—**acuminate,** a·kū′min·āt, *a.* [L. *acuminatus,* sharpened.] Pointed; acute.—**acuminate,** a·kū′min·āt, *v.t.* —*acuminated, acuminating.* To render sharp or keen.—*v.i.* † To taper to a point.—**acumination,** a·kū′min·ā″shon, *n.* Act of acuminating or sharpening; a pointed extremity; a sharp point or jag.

acupuncture, ak·ū·pungk′tūr, *n.* [L. *acus,* a needle, and *punctura,* a pricking. PUNCTURE.] A surgical operation resorted to in certain complaints, as in headaches, neuralgia, rheumatism, etc., and consisting in the insertion of a delicate needle or set of needles beneath the tissues.

acute, a·kūt′, *a.* [L. *acutus,* sharp-pointed, from *acuo,* to sharpen.

From root, *ac, ak,* a point. ACID.] Sharp at the end; ending in a sharp point: opposed to *blunt* or *obtuse*; intellectually sharp; perceiving minute distinctions, or characterized by the use of such; characterized by keenness of insight: opposed to *dull* or *stupid*; having nice or quick sensibility; susceptible of slight impressions (*acute* hearing); keen; sharp; said of pain; high in pitch; shrill: said of sound; *med,* a term applied to a disease which is attended with more or less violent symptoms, and comes speedily to a crisis; *geom.* less than a right angle.—**acutely,** a·kūt′li, *adv.* In an acute manner; sharply; keenly; with nice discrimination.—**acuteness,** a·kūt′nes, *n.* The quality of being acute; sharpness; keenness; sagacity; acumen.

adage, ad′āj, *n.* [Fr. *adage,* L. *adagium,* a proverb.] A proverb; an old saying, which has obtained credit by long use.

adagio, a·dä′jō, *a.* and *adv.* [It.] *Music,* slow; slowly, leisurely, and with grace.—*n.* A slow movement.

Adam, ad′am, *n.* The name of the first man; hence, the frailty inherent in human nature.—*Adam's apple,* the prominence on the fore part of the throat.—*Adam's needle,* the popular name of the plants otherwise called *Yucca.*—**Adamic,** a·dam′ik, *a.* Pertaining to Adam.

adamant, ad′a·mant, *n.* [L. *adamas, adamantis,* Gr. *adamas,* the hardest iron or steel, anything inflexibly hard, the diamond, lit. the unconquerable—Gr. *a,* not, and *damaō,* to tame. TAME, DIAMOND.] Any substance of impenetrable hardness: chiefly a rhetorical or poetical word. (Formerly it sometimes meant the diamond, sometimes loadstone, from confusion with L. *adamantem* through the loving-attractive quality). — **adamantean, adamantine,** ad′a·mant·ē″an, ad·a·mant′īn, *a.* Made of adamant; having the qualities of adamant; impenetrable.

adapt, a·dapt′, *v.t.* [L. *adapto—ad,* to, and *apto,* to fit. APT.] To make suitable; to make to correspond; to fit or suit; to proportion; to remodel, work up, and render fit for representation on the stage, as a play from a foreign language or a novel. — **adaptability, adaptableness,** a·dapt′a·bil″i·ti, a·dapt′a·bl·nes, *n.* The quality of being capable of adaptation.—**adaptable,** a·dapt′a·bl, *a.* Capable of being adapted.—**adaptation,** ad·ap·tā′shon, *n.* The act of adapting or making suitable; the state of being suitable or fit; that which is adapted.—**adapter,** a·dapt′ėr, *n.* One who or that which adapts.—**adaptive,**† a·dapt′iv, *a.* Tending to adapt; suitable.

Adar, ā′där, *n.* A Hebrew month, answering to the latter part of February and the beginning of March, the twelfth of the sacred and sixth of the civil year.

add, ad, *v.t.* [L. *addo,* to add—*ad,* to, and *do,* to put, to place, to give.] To set or put together; to join or

unite; to put into one sum; to annex; subjoin; say further.—*v.i.* To be or serve as an addition (with *to*); also, to perform the arithmetical operation of addition.—**addible,** ad′i·bl, *a.* Capable of being added.—**addition,** ad·di′shon, *n.* The act or process of adding; the uniting of two or more numbers in one sum; the rule or branch of arithmetic which treats of adding numbers; an increase; something added; a title coming after a personal name (*Shak.*).—**additional,** ad·di′shon·al, *a.* Added; supplementary.—**additionally,** ad·di′shon·al·li, *adv.* By way of addition.—**additive,** ad′it·iv, *a.* Additional; helping to increase.

addax, ad′aks, *n.* A species of large antelope inhabiting Africa, with long and beautifully twisted horns.

addendum, ad·den′dum, *n.* pl. **addenda,** ad·den′da. [L.] A thing to be added; an addition; an appendix to a work.

adder, ad′ėr, *n.* [O.E. *addre, addere,* by loss of initial *n* from A. Sax. *nædre, næddre,* O. and Prov. E. *nedder,* Icel. *nadr.* Goth. *nadrs,* G. *natter.*] A variety of venomous serpents, as the common viper, found in America and over Europe. —**adder's-tongue,** *n.* A species of fern.—**Adderwort,** *n.* Snakeweed, a kind of plant.

addible. See ADD.

addict, ad·dikt′, *v.t.* [L. *addico, addictum,* to devote—*ad,* to, and *dico,* to dedicate.] To apply habitually; to habituate: generally with a reflexive pronoun, and usually in a bad sense (followed by *to*); as, to *addict* one's self to intemperance. —*n.* (ad′dikt). One who is addicted. —**addicted,** ad·dikt′ed, *a.* Habitually practicing; given up; devoted; habituated (followed by *to*).—**addiction,** ad·dik′shon, *n.* The act of devoting or giving up one's self to a practice; the state of being devoted; devotion.

addition, additional, etc. See ADD.

addle, ad′l, *a.* [From A.Sax. *adela,* filth; Sw. *adel* (seen in *ko adel,* cow urine), urine; Sc. *addle,* putrid water, urine.] Having lost the power of development and become rotten, putrid: applied to eggs; hence, barren; producing nothing.—*v.t.*— *addled, addling.* To make rotten, as eggs.—**addleheaded, addlepated,** *a.* Stupid; muddled.

address, ad·dres′, *v.t.* [Fr. *adresser.* DRESS.] To direct or aim words; to pronounce; to apply to by words or writings; to accost; to speak to; to direct in writing; to write an address on; to court or make suit to.—*To address one's self to,* to speak to; to address.—*n.* The act of addressing one's self to a person; a speaking to; any speech or writing in which one person or set of persons makes a communication to another person or set of persons; manner of speaking to another; a person's bearing in conversation; courtship (in this sense generally in the plural); skill; dexterity; adroitness; direction of a letter.—**addressee,** ad·

dres·ē′, n. One who is addressed.—
addresser, ad·dres′ér, n. One who
addresses or petitions.

adduce, ad·dūs′, v.t.—adduced, adducing. [L. adduco, to lead or bring
to—ad, to, and duco, to lead. DUKE.]
To cite; to name or instance as
authority or evidence; to bring to
notice as bearing on a subject.—
adducent, ad·dūs′ent, a. Bringing
forward or together (an adducent
muscle).—**adducer**, ad·dūs′ér, n. One
that adduces.—**adducible**, ad·dūs′i-
bl, a. Capable of being adduced.—
adduction, ad·duk′shon, n. The act
of adducing; anat. the action by
which a part of the body is drawn
towards the bodily axis.—**adduc-
tive**, ad·dukt′iv, a.

adenalgy, ad·en·al′ji, n. [Gr. aden, a
gland, and algos, pain.] Pain in a
gland.—**adenoid**, ad′en·oid, a. Of a
glandlike shape or character; glandular.—**adenitis**, ad·e·nī′tis, n. Inflammation of one or more of the
lymphatic glands.—**adenoids**, ad′e-
noidz, n. pl. Glandlike morbid
growths in the throat behind the
soft palate.—**adenoma**, ad·e·nō′ma,
n. A tumor originating in a gland.

adenosine diphosphate, ad·en″o-
sin dī·fos′fāt, n. A coenzyme important to the transfer of energy through
the cell.

adenosine triphosphate, ad·en″o-
sin trī·fos′fāt, n. A nucleotide that
occurs in all cells. It represents the
reserve energy of muscle and is important to many biochemical processes that produce or require energy.

adept, a·dept′, n. [L. adeptus, pp. of
adipiscor, to obtain. Alchemists who
were reputed to have obtained the
philosopher's stone were termed
adepts; hence adept, a proficient.]
One fully skilled or well versed
in any art; a proficient.—a. Well
skilled.

adequate, ad′ē·kwāt, a. [L. adaequa-
tus, made equal, pp. of adaequo—ad,
to, and aequus, equal.] Equal; proportionate; exactly correspondent;
fully sufficient.—**adequacy**, ad′ē-
kwa·si, n. The state of being adequate; a sufficiency for a particular
purpose.—**adequately**, ad′ē·kwāt·li,
adv. In an adequate manner; sufficiently.—**adequateness**, ad′ē·kwāt-
nes, n. The state of being adequate;
sufficiency.

adhere, ad·hēr′, v.i.—adhered, adhering. [L. adhaereo—ad, to, and
haereo, to stick, whence hesitate.]
To stick together; to cleave; to
become closely joined or united;
to be fixed in attachment or devotion.
—**adherence**, ad·hēr′ens, n. The
quality or state of adhering; fidelity;
steady attachment.—**adherent**, ad-
hēr′ent, a. Sticking fast to something;
clinging; attached.—**adherent**, ad-
hēr′ent, n. One who adheres; one
who follows a leader, party, or
profession; a follower or partisan.—
adherently, ad·hēr′ent·li, adv. In an
adherent manner.—**adhesion**, ad-
hē′zhon, n. L. adhaesio, from adhaereo, to adhere.] The act or state
of adhering, or being united and
attached; a sticking together of the

surface of bodies; close connection
or association; steady attachment
of the mind or feelings; assent;
concurrence (adhesion to a treaty).—
adhesive, ad·hē′siv, a. Sticky; tenacious.—**adhesively**, ad·hē′siv·li, adv.
In an adhesive manner.—**adhesive-
ness**, ad·hē′siv·nes, n. The state or
quality of being adhesive; phren.
an organ which is said to promote
attachment to objects.

adhibit, ad·hib′it, v.t. [L. adhibeo,
adhibitum—ad, to, and habeo, to
hold.] To apply†; to attach (one's
signature).—**adhibition**, ad·hi·bi′-
shon, n. The act of adhibiting.

adiabatic, a·di·a·bat′ik, a. [Gr. a,
not, diabainō, pass through.] Of
physical changes without gain or
loss of heat; adiabatic curve, curve
showing relation between the volume
and the pressure of a fluid which
changes its volume without gain or
loss of heat.

adieu, a·dū′. [Fr. à, to, and Dieu,
God, It. addio, Span. a dios, all
forms of L. ad, to, and Deus, God.]
Lit. to God: an ellipsis for I commend you to God; farewell; an
expression of kind wishes at the
parting of friends.—n. pl. **adieus**, or
adieux, a·dūz′. A farewell or commendation to the care of God.

adipocere, ad′i·pō·sēr, n. [L. adeps,
fat, and cera, wax.] A soft, unctuous,
or waxy substance, into which the
flesh of dead animals is converted
when protected from atmospheric
air, and under certain circumstances
of temperature and humidity.

adipose, ad′i·pōs, a. [From L. adeps,
adipis, fat.] Fatty; consisting of or
resembling fat.—n. Fat; the fat
on the kidneys.

adit, ad′it, n. [L. aditus—ad, to,
and eo, itum, to go.] Approach;
access; passage; a more or less
horizontal passage into a mine.

adjacent, ad·jā′sent, a. [L. adjacens,
adjacentis, pp. of adjaceo, to lie
contiguous—ad, to, and jaceo, to
lie.] Lying near or close; bordering
upon; neighboring; adjoining.—**ad-
jacency**, ad·jā′sen·si, n. The state
of being adjacent.—**adjacently**, ad-
jā′sent·li, adv. So as to be adjacent.

adjective, ad′jek·tiv, n. [L. adjec-
tivum, adjectivus, added—ad, to, and
jacio, to throw.] Gram. a word used
with a noun to express a quality of
the thing named, or something
attributed to it, or to specify or
describe a thing as distinct from
something else, and so to limit and
define it.—**adjectival**, ad·jek·tīv′al,
a. Belonging to or like an adjective;
having the import of an adjective.—
adjectivally, **adjectively**, ad·jek·tī-
v′al·li, ad′jek·tiv·li, adv. By way of,
or as, an adjective.

adjoin, ad·join′, v.t. [Fr. adjoindre;
L. adjungo—ad, to, and jungo, to
join. JOIN.] To join or add; to
unite; to annex or append.—v.i. To
lie or be next or in contact; to be
contiguous.—**adjoining**, ad·join′ing,
a. Adjacent; contiguous; neighboring.

adjourn, ad·jérn′, v.t. [Fr. ajourner,
O.Fr. ajorner, adjorner—prefix a,

ad, to, and O.Fr. jorn (now jour),
a day, L. diurnus, diurnal, from dies,
a day. DIURNAL.] To put off or
defer to another day or until a later
period; to suspend the meeting of,
as of a public or private body, to a
future day; to postpone to a future
meeting of the same body.—v.i. To
cease sitting and carrying on business
for a time.—**adjournment**, ad·jérn′-
ment, n. The act of adjourning; the
period during which a public body
adjourns its sittings.

adjudge, ad·juj′, v.t.—adjudged, adjudging. [Prefix ad, and judge.
JUDGE.] To award judicially; to
adjudicate upon; to settle.—

adjudicate, ad·jū′di·kāt, v.t.—adjudi-
cated, adjudicating. [L. adjudico, to
give sentence—ad, to, and judico, to
judge. JUDGE.] To adjudge; to award
judicially.—v.i. To sit in judgment;
to give a judicial decision.—**adju-
dication**, ad·jū·di·kā′shon, n. The
act of adjudicating; the act or process
of trying and determining judicially;
judgment or decision of a court.—
adjudicator, ad·jū′di·kāt·ér, n. One
who adjudicates.

adjunct, ad′jungkt, n. [L. adjunctus,
joined, from adjungo—ad, to, and
jungo, junctum, to join. JOIN.] Something added to another, but not
essentially a part of it.—a. United
with in office or in action of any
kind; conjoined with.—**adjunctive**,
ad·jungk′tiv, a. Joining; having the
quality of joining.—n. One who or
that which is joined.

adjure, ad·jūr′, v.t.—adjured, adjuring. [L. adjuro—ad, to, and juro, to
swear.] To charge, bind, or command, earnestly and solemnly.—
adjuration, ad·jū·rā′shon, n. The
act of adjuring; a solemn charging
on oath; a solemn oath.—**adjurato-
ry**, ad·jūr′a·to·ri, a. Containing an
adjuration, or characterized by adjurations.—**adjurer**, ad·jūr′ér, n. One
who adjures.

adjust, ad·just′, v.t. [Fr. ajuster,
Mod.Fr. adjouter, L.L. adjuxtare,]
to bring together—ad and juxta.
To fit; to make correspondent; to
adapt; to accommodate; to put in
order; to regulate or reduce to system;
to settle or bring to a satisfactory
state, so that parties are agreed in the
result.—**adjustable**, ad·just′a·bl, a.
Capable of being adjusted.—**ad-
juster**, ad·just′ér, n. One who or
that which adjusts.—**adjustment**,
ad·just′ment, n. The act of adjusting.

adjutant, ad′jū·tant, n. [L. adjutans,
ppr. of adjuto, to assist—ad, and
juvo, jutum, to help.] Milit. an
officer whose business is to assist
a commanding officer by receiving
and communicating orders.—**adju-
tancy**, ad′jū·tan·si, n. The office of
an adjutant.—**adjutant bird**, **adjutant crane**, **adjutant stork**, n. A
very large grallatorial bird allied
to the storks, a native of the warmer
parts of India. It feeds on carrion,
and is most voracious.

adjutor, ad·jūt′ér, n. obs. A helper;
a coadjutor.—**adjutrix**,† ad·jū′triks,
n. A female assistant.—**adjuvant**,
ad′jū·vant or ad·jū′vant, n. An

assistant; *med.* a substance added to a prescription to aid the operation of the principal ingredient or basis.

admeasure, ad·me′zhŭr, *v.t.*—*admeasured, admeasuring.* [L. *ad*, to, and E. *measure.* MEASURE.] To ascertain the dimensions, size, or capacity of; to measure.—**admeasurement,** ad·me′zhŭr·ment, *n.* The act of admeasuring; the measure of a thing, or dimensions ascertained.

adminicular, ad·min·ik′ū·lêr, *a.* [L. *adminiculum*, a prop, stay, or support.] Supplying help; helpful; lending aid or support.

administer, ad·min′is·têr, *v.t.* [L. *administro*—*ad*, to, and *ministro*, to serve. MINISTER.] To manage or conduct as chief agent or directing and controlling official; to direct or superintend the execution of, as of laws; to afford, give, furnish, or supply; to give, as a dose of medicine; to dispense or distribute; to tender, as an oath; *law*, to manage, as the estate of a deceased person, collecting debts, paying legacies, etc. —*v.i.* To contribute assistance; to bring aid or supplies: with *to*; as, to *administer to* one's necessities; *law*, to perform the office of administrator.—**administrable,** ad·min′is·tra·bl, *a.* Capable of being administered.—**administration,** ad·min′is·trā″shon, *n.* The act of administering; direction; management; government of public affairs; the executive functions of government; the persons, collectively, who are intrusted with such functions; the executive; *law*, the management of the estate of a deceased person, consisting in collecting debts, paying debts and legacies, and distributing the property among the heirs.—**administrative,** ad·min′is·trāt·iv, *a.* Pertaining to administration.—**administrator,** ad·min′is·trāt·êr, *n.* One who administers, or who directs, manages, distributes, or dispenses; one who has the charge of the goods and estate of a person dying without a will.—**administratorship,** ad·min′is·trāt·êr·ship, *n.* The office of an administrator.—**administratrix,** ad·min′is·trāt·riks, *n.* A female administrator.

admirable, etc. See ADMIRE.

admiral, ad′mi·ral, *n.* [O.E. *amiral*, Fr. *amiral*, from Ar. *amir, emir*, a prince, chief, with the Ar. article suffixed.] Commander in chief of a fleet; highest rank of naval officer; high rank of naval officer. In U.S. Navy grades are fleet admiral, admiral, vice admiral, and rear admiral. Two species of butterflies, *Vanessa atalanta*, or red admiral, and *Limenitis camilla*, or white admiral.—**admiralship,** ad′mi·ral·ship, *n.* The office or power of an admiral.—**admiralty,** ad′mi·ral·ti, *n.* Jurisdiction of an admiral; department of state having charge of naval affairs.—**the admiralty,** official building of British commission for naval affairs in London.

admire, ad·mīr′, *v.t.*—*admired, admiring.* [Fr. *admirer*, L. *admiror*—*ad*, and *miror*, to wonder.] To wonder at‡; to regard with wonder mingled with approbation, esteem, reverence, or affection; to take pleasure in the beauty of; to look on or contemplate with pleasure.—*v.i.* To feel or express admiration.—**admirer,** ad·mīr′êr, *n.* One who admires; one who esteems greatly; one who openly shows his admiration of a woman; a lover.—**admiringly,** ad·mīr′ing·li, *adv.* In an admiring manner; with admiration.—**admiration,** ad·mi·rā′shon, *n.* Wonder‡; wonder mingled with pleasing emotions, as approbation, esteem, love, or veneration; an emotion excited by something beautiful or excellent.—**admirable,** ad′mi·ra·bl, *a.* Worthy of admiration; most excellent.—**admirableness,** ad′mi·ra·bl·nes, *n.* —**admirably,** ad′mi·ra·bli, *adv.* In an admirable manner; excellently; exceedingly well.

admissible, etc. See ADMIT.

admit, ad·mit′, *v.t.*—*admitted, admitting.* [L. *admitto*—*ad*, to, and *mitto, missum*, to send, seen also in *commit, submit, mission*, etc.] To suffer to enter; to grant entrance to; to give right of entrance to; to grant in argument; to receive as true; to permit, grant, or allow, or to be capable of; to acknowledge; to own; to confess.—*v.i.* To give warrant or allowance; to grant opportunity; to permit: with *of* (the words do not *admit of* this interpretation).—**admittance,** ad·mit′ans, *n.* The act of admitting; permission to enter; entrance.—**admittedly,** ad·mit′ed·li, *adv.* By admission, acknowledgment, or concession.—**admissible,** ad·mis′i·bl, *a.* [Fr. *admissible*, L.L. *admissibilis*, from *admitto, admissum*, to admit.] Capable of being admitted, allowed, or conceded.—**admissibility,** ad·mis′i·bil″i·ti, *n.* The quality of being admissible.—**admissibly,** ad·mis′i·bli, *adv.* In an admissible manner; so as to be admitted.—**admission,** ad·mi′shon, *n.* [L. *admissio.*] The act of admitting; power or permission to enter; entrance; access; power to approach; the granting of an argument or position not fully proved; a point or statement admitted; acknowledgment; confession of a charge, error, or crime.—**admissive,** ad·mis′iv, *a.* Having the nature of an admission.

admix, ad·miks′, *v.t.* [Prefix *ad*, to, and *mix*.] To mingle with something else.—**admixture,** ad·miks′tūr, *n.* The act of mingling or mixing; that which is formed by mingling.

admonish, ad·mon′ish, *v.t.* [O.E. *amoneste*, O.Fr. *amonester*, to admonish—prefix *a, ad*, and L.L. *monestum*, for L. *monitum*, pp. of *moneo*, to warn. MONITION.] To warn or notify of a fault; to reprove with mildness; to counsel against wrong practices; to caution or advise; to instruct or direct; to remind; to recall or incite to duty.—**admonisher,** ad·mon′ish·êr, *n.* One who admonishes.—**admonishment,†** ad·mon′ish·ment, *n.* Admonition.—**ad-**

monition, ad·mō·ni′shon, *n.* The act of admonishing; counsel or advice; gentle reproof; instruction in duties; caution; direction.—**admonitor,** ad·mon′it·êr, *n.* An admonisher; a monitor.—**admonitory,** ad·mon′i·to·ri, *a.* Containing admonition; tending or serving to admonish.

adnascent,† ad·nas′ent, *a.* [L. *ad*, to, *nascens*, growing.] Growing on something else.—**adnate,** ad′nāt, *a.* [L. *adnatus*—*ad*, to, and *natus*, grown.] Growing attached: chiefly a term in *bot.*

ado, a·dö′, *n.* [Prefix *a* for *at*, and *do*, that is, to do; *at* being here the sign of the infinitive, as in Icelandic.] Bustle; trouble; labor; difficulty.

adobe, a·dö′be, *n.* [Sp.] A sun-dried brick.

adolescence, ad·ō·les′ens, *n.* [L. *adolescentia*—*ad*, and *olesco*, to grow.] The state of growing: applied almost exclusively to the young of the human race; youth, or the period of life between childhood and the full development of the frame.—**adolescent,** ad·ō·les′ent, *a.* Growing up; advancing from childhood to manhood.

Adonic, Adonean, a·don′ik, ad·ō·nē′an, *a.* [From *Adonis*, a mythical personage among the Greeks, originally the Phoenician sun god.] Of or pertaining to Adonis.—*Adonic verse*, in Greek and Latin poetry, a verse consisting of a dactyl and a spondee or trochee.—**Adonis,** a·dōn′is, *n.* Beautiful person; a beau.

adopt, a·dopt′, *v.t.* [L. *adopto*—*ad*, and *opto*, to desire or choose. OPTION.] To take into one's family and treat as one's own child; to take to one's self by choice or approval, as principles, opinions, a course of conduct, etc.—**adoptable,** a·dopt′a·bl, *a.* Capable of, fit for, or worthy of being adopted.—**adopter,** a·dopt′êr, *n.* One who adopts.—**adoption,** a·dop′shon, *n.* [L. *adoptio.*] The act of adopting, or the state of being adopted.—**adoptive,** a·dopt′iv, *a.* [L. *adoptivus.*] Constituted by adoption; adopting or adopted; assumed.

adore, a·dōr′, *v.t.*—*adored, adoring.* [L. *adoro*, to pray, to adore,—*ad*, to, and *oro*, to ask. ORACLE.] To worship with profound reverence; to pay divine honors to; to regard with the utmost esteem, love, and respect; to love in the highest degree, as a man a woman.—**adorability,** a·dōr′a·bil″i·ti, *n.* Quality of being adorable.—**adorable,** a·dōr′a·bl, *a.* Demanding adoration; worthy of being adored; exquisitely charming; lovable. —**adorableness,** a·dōr′a·bl·nes, *n.*—**adorably,** a·dōr′a·bli, *adv.* In a manner worthy of adoration.—**adoration,** ad·ōr·ā′shon, *n.* The act of adoring; the act of paying honors, as to a divine being; worship addressed to a deity; the highest degree of love, as of a man for a woman.—**adorer,** a·dōr′êr, *n.* One who adores; one who worships or honors as divine; a lover; an admirer.—**adoringly,** a·dōr′ing·li, *adv.* With adoration.

adorn, a·dorn′, *v.t.* [L. *adorno*—*ad*, to, and *orno*, to deck or beautify.]

To deck or decorate; to add to the attractiveness of by dress or ornaments; to set off to advantage; beautify; embellish.—**adornment**, a·dorn′ment, *n*. An ornament or decoration.

ADP. See ADENOSINE DIPHOSPHATE.

adrenal, ad·rē′nal, *a*. [L. *ad*, near, and *renes*, kidney.] On or near the kidney.—*n*. An adrenal gland.—**adrenal gland**, ad·rē′nal gland, *n*. A small endocrine gland attached to the kidney.

adrenalin, ad·ren′al·in, *n*. A name for epinephrine, a hormone secreted by the medulla of the adrenal gland; a drug used as a heart stimulant, muscle relaxant, etc.

adrift, a·drift′, *a*. or *adv*. [Prefix *a*, on, and *drift*, a driving or floating. DRIVE.] Floating at random; impelled or moving without direction; at the mercy of winds and currents; swayed by any chance impulse; at sea; at a loss.

adroit, a·droit′, *a*. [Fr. *adroit*, dexterous—*a*, to, and *droit*, right, as opposed to left (comp. *dexterous*, from L. *dexter*, right); from L. *directus*, straight, direct.] Dexterous; skillful; expert; active in the use of the hand, and, figuratively, in the exercise of the mental faculties; ready in invention or execution.—**adroitly**, a·droit′li, *adv*.—**adroitness**, a·droit′nes, *n*.

adsorb, ad·sorb′, *v.t*. To collect, as molecules of gases, dissolved substances, or liquids, in a thin layer on a surface.—**adsorption**, ad·sorp′shun, *n*. The adhesion of molecules to a surface, to be distinguished from *absorption*.

adularia, ad·ū·lā′ri·a, *n*. [From *Adula*, the summit of the St. Gothard, where fine specimens are got.] A very pure, limpid, translucent variety of the common feldspar, called also *Moonstone*.

adulation, ad·ū·lā′shon, *n*. [L. *adulatio, adulationis*, a fawning, *adulor, adulatus*, to flatter.] Servile flattery; praise in excess, or beyond what is merited; high compliment.—**adulate**, ad′ū·lāt, *v.t*. To show feigned devotion to; to flatter servilely.—**adulator**, ad′ū·lāt·ẽr, *n*. A flatterer.—**adulatory**, ad′ū·lāt·o·ri, *a*. Flattering.

adult, a·dult′, *a*. [L. *adultus*, grown to maturity, from *ad*, to, *oleo*, to grow. ADOLESCENCE.] Having arrived at mature years, or to full size and strength; pertaining or relating to full strength; suitable for an adult.—**adult**, a·dult′, *n*. A person grown to full size and strength.

adulterate, a·dul′tẽr·āt, *v.t*.—*adulterated, adulterating*. [L. *adultero*, from *adulter*, mixed, an adulterer—*ad*, to, and *alter*, other.] To debase or deteriorate by an admixture of foreign or baser materials.—**adulterant**, a·dul′tẽr·ant, *n*. The person or thing that adulterates.—**adulteration**, a·dul′tẽr·ā′shon, *n*. The act of adulterating, or the state of being adulterated or debased by foreign mixture.—**adulterator**, a·dul′tẽr·ā·tẽr, *n*. One who adulterates.

adultery, a·dul′tẽr·i, *n*. [L. *adulte-*

rium, from *adulter*, an adulterer. ADULTERATE.] Violation of the marriage bed; sexual commerce by a married person with one who is not his or her wife or husband.—**adulterer**, a·dul′tẽr·ẽr, *n*. A man guilty of adultery.—**adulteress**, a·dul′tẽr·es, *n*. A woman guilty of adultery.—**adulterine**, a·dul′tẽr·īn, Proceeding from adulterous commerce.—**adulterous**, a·dul′tẽr·us, *a*. Guilty of adultery; pertaining to adultery; illicit.—**adulterously**, a·dul′tẽr·us·li, *adv*. In an adulterous manner.

adumbrate, ad·um′brāt, *v.t*.—*adumbrated, adumbrating*. [L. *adumbro*, to shade—*ad*, and *umbra*, a shade.] To give a faint shadow of; to exhibit a faint resemblance of, like a shadow; to shadow forth.—**adumbration**, ad·um·brā′shon, *n*. The act of adumbrating or shadowing forth; a faint or imperfect representation of a thing.—**adumbrative**, ad·um′bra·tiv, *a*. Shadowing forth; faintly resembling.—**adumbratively**, ad·um′bra·tiv·li, *adv*. In an adumbrative manner.

aduncous, ad·ungk′us, *a*. [L. *aduncus*, hooked—*ad*, to, and *uncus*, a hook.] Hooked; bent or made in the form of a hook.—**aduncity**, ad·un′si·ti, *n*. Hookedness.

adust, a·dust′, *a*. [L. *adustus*, burned—*ad*, to, and *uro, ustum*, to burn.] Burned; scorched; parched up; looking as if burned or scorched.

advance, ad·vans′, *v.t*.—*advanced, advancing*. [Fr. *avancer*, from *avant*, forward (whence also E. *van*), L. *abante*, from before, in front—*ab*, from, *ante*, before.] To bring forward; to move further in front; to promote; to raise to a higher rank; to forward or further; to encourage the progress of; to enhance (price); to accelerate the growth of; to offer or propose; to bring to view or notice, as something one is prepared to abide by; to allege; to supply beforehand; to furnish on credit, or before goods are delivered, or work done.—*v.i*. To move or go forward; to proceed; to make progress; to grow better, greater, wiser, or older; to rise in rank, office, or consequence.—*n*. A moving forward or toward the front; a march forward; gradual progression; improvement; advancement; promotion; a proposal; a first step toward; addition to price; rise in price; a giving beforehand; that which is given beforehand, especially money.—*In advance*, in front, before; beforehand; before an equivalent is received.—**advancement**, ad·vans′ment, *n*. The act of advancing; the state of being advanced; the act of promoting; preferment; promotion; improvement; furtherance.

advantage, ad·van′tāj, *n*. [O.Fr. *advantage*, Fr. *avantage*, from *avant*, before. ADVANCE.] Any state, condition, circumstance, opportunity, or means specially favorable to success, prosperity, or any desired end (the *advantage* of a good constitution, of an excellent education); superiority; benefit; gain; profit.—*v.t*.—*advan-*

taged, advantaging. To bring advantage to; to be of service to; to benefit; to yield profit or gain to.—**advantageous**, ad·van·tā′jus, *a*. Being of advantage; profitable; useful; beneficial.—**advantageously**, ad·van·tā′jus·li, *adv*. In an advantageous manner.—**advantageousness**, ad·van·tā′jus·nes, *n*.

advene, ad·vēn′, *v.i*. [L. *advenio*, to come to—*ad*, to, and *venio*, to come. VENTURE.] To accede or be superadded; to become a part, though not essential.—**advent**, ad′vent, *n*. [L. *adventus*, an arrival.] A coming; approach; visitation; [*cap*] the coming of the Saviour; an ecclesiastical division of the year embracing the four weeks before Christmas.—**adventitious**, ad·ven·tish′us, *a*. [L. *adventitius*.] Added extrinsically; not essentially inherent; accidentally or casually acquired.—**adventitiously**, ad·ven·tish′us·li, *adv*.—**adventitiousness**, ad·ven·tish′us·nes, *n*.

adventure, ad·ven′tūr, *n*. [O.Fr. *adventure*, Fr. *aventure*, L.L. *adventura, aventura*, from L. *adventurus*, about to arrive, fut. part. of *advenio*, to arrive. ADVENE.] Hazard; risk; chance; a hazardous enterprise; a bold and dangerous undertaking of uncertain issue; a commercial speculation; a speculation in goods sent abroad; a remarkable occurrence in one's personal history; a noteworthy event or experience in one's life.—*v.t*.—*adventured, adventuring*. To risk or hazard; to venture on; to attempt.—**adventurer**, ad·ven′tūr·ẽr, *n*. One who engages in an adventure or speculation; one who attempts or takes part in bold, novel, or extraordinary enterprises; one who lives by underhand means, or by a system of imposition.—**adventuress**, ad·ven′tūr·es, *n*. A female adventurer.—**adventurous**, ad·ven′tūr·us, *a*. Bold to encounter danger; daring; courageous; enterprising; full of hazard; attended with risk.—**adventurously**, ad·ven′tūr·us·li, *adv*. In an adventurous manner.—**adventurousness**, ad·ven′tūr·us·nes, *n*.

adverb, ad′vẽrb, *n*. [L. *adverbium*—*ad*, to, and *verbum*, a word, a verb.] *Gram*. one of the indeclinable parts of speech, so called from being frequently joined to verbs for the purpose of limiting or extending their signification.—**adverbial**, ad·vẽrb′i·al, *a*. Pertaining to or having the character or structure of an adverb.—**adverbially**, ad·vẽrb′i·al·li, *adv*. In the manner or with the force or character of an adverb.

adversary, ad′vẽr·se·ri, *n*. [L. *adversarius*. ADVERSE.] An enemy; a foe; an antagonist; an opponent... An *adversary* is one who is opposed to another, without necessarily having hostile feelings; an *antagonist* is one who strives personally against another for victory; an *enemy* is one who entertains feelings of personal hostility.

adversative, ad·vẽrs′at·iv, *a*. Expressing difference, contrariety, or opposition (an *adversative* conjunction).—*n*. A word denoting contrariety or opposition.

adverse, ad′vėrs, *a.* [L. *adversus,* opposite—*ad,* to, and *versus,* turned, from *verto,* to turn.] Acting in a contrary direction; counteracting; opposing (*adverse* winds; hostile; inimical (a party, criticism); unfortunate; calamitous; unprosperous (fate or circumstances).—**adversely,** ad′vėrs·li, *adv.* In an adverse manner. —**adverseness,** ad′vėrs·nes, *n.* The state or quality of being adverse.— **adversity,** ad·vėrs′i·ti, *n.* An event, or series of events, which oppose success or desire; misfortune; calamity; affliction; distress; state of unhappiness.

advert, a·dvėrt′, *v.i.* [L. *advert*—*ad,* to, and *verto,* to turn.] To turn the mind or attention; to regard, observe, or notice; to refer or allude: followed by *to.* ∴ *Advert* is to turn directly, and it may be abruptly; *allude* is to touch slightly, and it may be in a very vague and uncertain manner; *refer, lit.* to carry back, is to bring a thing already well known into notice; to mention or speak of directly.—**advertence, advertency,** ad·vėrt′ens, ad·vėrt′en·si, *n.* Attention; notice; regard; heedfulness.— **advertent,** ad·vėrt′ent, *a.* Attentive; heedful.—**advertently,** ad·vėrt′ent·li, *adv.* In an advertent manner.

advertise, ad·vėr·tīz′, *v.t.*—*advertised, advertising.* [Fr. *avertir, avertissant,* to warn, inform, from L. *adverto,* to turn towards—*ad, verto,* to turn.] To inform or give notice; to make public intimation of, especially by printed notice.—*v.i.* To announce one's wishes or intentions by a public and usually a printed notice.—**advertisement,** ad·vėr′tiz·ment, *n.* Warning, advice, or admonition (*Shak.*); a written or printed notice intended to make something known to the public; especially a printed and paid notice in a newspaper or other public print.— **advertiser,** ad·vėr·tīz′ėr, *n.* One who advertises.

advice, ad·vīs′, *n.* [O.Fr. *advis,* opinion, counsel—L. *ad,* to, and *visum,* what is seen or judged proper. VISION.] An opinion recommended, or offered, as worthy to be followed; counsel; suggestion; information; notice; intelligence; a notification in respect of a business transaction.— *To take advice,* to consult with others; specifically, to take the opinion of a professional or skillful man, as a physician or lawyer.—**advisability,** ad·vīz′a·bil″i·ti, *n.* Advisableness; expediency.—**advisable,** ad·vīz′a·bl, *a.* Proper to be advised; expedient; proper to be done or practiced; open to advice.—**advisableness,** ad·vīz′a·bl·nes, *n.* The quality of being advisable or expedient.—**advisably,** ad·vīz′a·bli, *adv.* With advice.—**advise,** ad·vīz′, *v.t.*—*advised, advising.* [Fr. *aviser.* ADVICE.] To give counsel to; to counsel; to give information to; to inform; to acquaint.—*v.i.* To consider; to reflect; to take counsel. —**advised,** ad·vīzd′, *a.* Cautious; prudent; done, formed, or taken with advice or deliberation (an *advised*

act).—**advisedly,** ad·vīz′ed·li, *adv.* With deliberation or advice; heedfully; purposely; by design.—**advisedness,** ad·vīz′ed·nes, *n.* The state of being advised; prudent procedure. —**adviser,** ad·vīz′ėr, *n.* One who gives advice or admonition; a counsellor.—**advisory,** ad·vīz′o·ri, *a.* Having power to advise; containing advice.

advocate, ad′vō·kāt, *n.* [L. *advocatus,* one summoned to aid—*ad,* to, and *voco, vocatum,* to call. VOICE, VOCAL.] One who pleads the cause of another in a court of law; one who defends, vindicates, or espouses a cause by argument; a pleader in favor of something; an upholder; a defender. —*v.t. advocated, advocating.* To plead in favor of (a thing, not a person); to defend by argument before a tribunal; to support or vindicate.— **advocacy,** ad′vō·ka·si, *n.* The act of pleading for; intercession; defense.

advocation, ad·vō·kā′shon, *n.* The act of advocating; a pleading for.

advowson, ad·vou′sn, *n.* [O.Fr. *advoeson, advouson,* protection, patronage; L. *advocatio, advocationis,* a calling to one for help. ADVOCATE.] The right of presentation to a vacant benefice in the Established Church of England.

adynamia, ad″·i·nā′mi·a, *n.* [Gr. *a,* not, and *dynamis,* power.] Weakness; want of strength occasioned by disease; a deficiency of vital power.— **adynamic,** a·di·nam′ik, *a.* Weak; destitute of strength.

adytum, ad′i·tum, *n.* pl. **adyta,** ad′i·ta. [L. *adytum,* Gr. *adyton,* lit. a place not to be entered—*a,* not, and *dyō,* to enter.] An innermost sanctuary or shrine; the chancel or altar-end of a church.

adz, adze, adz, *n.* [O.E. *addice,* A.Sax. *adese,* an adze.] An instrument of the ax kind used for chipping the surface of timber, the cutting edge being at right angles to the handle.— *v.t.* To chip or shape with an adz.

aedile. Same as *Edile.*

aegis, ē′jis, *n.* [Gr. *aigis.*] Among the ancient Greeks the shield of Zeus; in later times part of the armor of Pallas Athena, a kind of breastplate; hence, anything that protects or shields; protecting power or influence.

aeolian. Same as *Eolian.*

aeolotropic, ē′ol·ō·trop″ik, *a.* [Gr. *aiolos,* varied, *tropē,* a turn.] Applied to bodies unequally elastic in different directions: opposed to *isotropic.*

aeon, *n.* Same as *Eon.*

aerate, ā′ėr·āt, *v.t.*—*aerated, aerating.* [L. *aer,* air. AIR.] To combine with carbonic acid or other gas, or with air.—**aerial,** ā·ē′ri·al, *a.* [L. *aerius.*] Belonging or pertaining to the air or atmosphere; inhabiting or frequenting the air; produced by or in the air; reaching far into the air; high; lofty; possessed of a light and graceful beauty.—*n.* Radio or television antenna.—**aerially,** ā·ē′ri·al·li, *adv.* **aerify,** ā′ėr·i·fī, *v.t.*—*aerified, aerifying.* To infuse air into; to fill with air, or to combine air with; to change into an aeriform state.

aerie, ē′rē or ā′ėr·i, *n.* [Fr. and Pr. *aire,* L.L. *aeria, aerea, area,* an aerie; origin doubtful.] The nest of a bird of prey, as of an eagle or hawk; a brood of eagles or hawks.

aerify. See AERATE.

aerobic, ā·ėr·ob′ik, *a.* [Gr. *aēr,* air, *bios,* life.] Requiring air or free oxygen in order to live and thrive, as certain bacteria.

aerodynamics, ā′ėr·ō·dī·nam″iks, *n.* [Gr. *aēr, dynamis,* power.] The science treating of the motion of the air and gases, and of their effects when in motion.

aerolite, ā′ėr·ō·līt, *n.* [Gr. *aēr,* air, and *lithos,* a stone.] A meteoric stone; a meteorite.—**aerolitic,** ā′ėr·ō·lit″ik, *a.* Relating to aerolites.

aerology, ā·ėr·ol′o·ji, *n.* [Gr. *aēr, aeros,* air, *logos,* description, *gnōsis,* knowledge.] That branch of physics which treats of the air, its constituent parts, properties, and phenomena.— **aerologic, aerological,** ā′ėr·ō·loj″ik, ā′ėr·ō·loj″ik·al, *a.* Pertaining to aerology.—**aerologist,** ā·ėr·ol′o·jist, *n.* One who is versed in aerology.

aeromechanics, ā′ėr·ō·me·kan″iks, *n.* [Gr. *aēr,* and *mechanikos, mechane,* a machine.] Study of air and other gases in motion or equilibrium, or of solid bodies immersed in gases.

aerometer, ā·ėr·om′et·ėr, *n.* [Gr. *aēr,* air, and *metron,* measure.] An instrument for weighing air, or for ascertaining the density of air and gases.— **aerometric,** ā′ėr·ō·met″rik, *a.* Pertaining to aerometry.—**aerometry,** ā·ėr·om′et·ri, *n.* The science of measuring the weight or density of air and gases.

aeronaut, ā′ėr·ō·nạt, *n.* [Gr. *aēr,* air, and *nautes,* a sailor, from *naus,* a ship.] An aerial navigator; a balloonist.—**aeronautic, aeronautical,** ā′ėr·ō·nạt″ik, ā′ėr·ō·nạt″ik·al, *a.* Pertaining to aeronautics or aerial sailing.—**aeronautics,** ā′ėr·ō·nạt″iks, *n.* The doctrine, science, or art of floating in the air, as by means of a balloon.

aeropause, ā′ėr·ō·pạz, *n.* [Gr. *aēr,* air, and *pausis,* stop.] The dividing line between outer space and areas in which man and aircraft can function.

aerophore, ā′ėr·o·for, *n.* [Gr. *aēr, pherō,* to bring.] A kind of ventilating apparatus; a portable receptacle by which air is supplied artificially under water or elsewhere.

aerophysics, ā′ėr·ō·fiz′iks, *n.* [*aer,* and *physics.*] A branch of physics that deals with the design, construction, and operation of high-speed, rocket-type aircraft.

aerophyte, ā′ėr·o·fīt, *n.* [Gr. *aēr,* air, and *phyton,* a plant.] A plant which lives exclusively in air; an air plant.

aerosol, ā″er·o·sōl′, *n. Phys. Chem.* A suspension of fine particles, solid or liquid, in a gas; a smoke or fog.— **aerosol bomb.** A device that sprays insecticide in a mist.

aerostat, ā′ėr·ō·stat, *n.* [Fr. *aérostat,* a balloon—Gr. *aēr,* air, and *statos,* standing, from *histemi,* to stand.] A machine or vessel sustaining weights in the air; a name given to air balloons.—**aerostatic, aerostatical,**

ā′ėr·ō stat″ik, ā′ėr·ō·stat″ik·al, *a*. Pertaining to aerostatics; pertaining to aerostation, or aerial navigation.—**aerostatics**, ā′ėr·ō·stat″iks, *n*. The science which treats of the weight, pressure, and equilibrium of air and other elastic fluids, and of the equilibrium of bodies sustained in them.—**aerostation**, ā′ėr·ō·stā″shon, *n*. Aerial navigation.

aery, ā′ėr·i, *a*. Airy; breezy; aerial. [Poetic.]

Aesculapian, ēs·kul·āp′i·an, *a*. Med. of or pertaining to Aesculapius, the ancient healing god.

aesthete, ēs′thēt, *n*. [From *aesthetic*.] One devoted to the principles or doctrines of aesthetics; a lover of the beautiful.—**aesthetic**, **aesthetical**, ēs·thet′ik, ēs·thet′ik·al, *a*. [Gr. *aisthētikos*, from *aisthanomai*, to perceive by the senses.] Pertaining to the science of taste or beauty; pertaining to the sense of the beautiful.—**aesthetically**, ēs·thet′ik·al·li, *adv*. According to the principles of aesthetics; with reference to the sense of the beautiful.—**aestheticism**, ēs·thet′i·sizm, *n*. The principles or doctrines of aesthetics; attachment to aesthetics.—**aesthetics**, ēs·thet′iks, *n*. The theory of the fine arts; the science or that branch of philosophy which deals with the beautiful; the doctrines of taste.

afar, a·fär′, *adv*. At a distance in place; to or from a distance: often with *from* preceding or *off* following, or both.

affable, af′fa·bl, *a*. [L. *affabilis*, affable—*af* for *ad*, to, *fari*, to speak.] Easy of conversation; admitting others to free conversation without reserve; courteous; complaisant; of easy manners; condescending.—**affability**, **affableness**, af·fa·bil′i·ti, af′fa·bl·nes, *n*. The quality of being affable.—**affably**, af′fa·bli, *adv*. In an affable manner; courteously.

affair, af·fär′, *n*. [Fr. *affaire—a*, to, and *faire*, to do, L. *facere*, to make, to do.] Business of any kind; that which is done, or is to be done; matter; concern; sometimes used by itself in the plural with the specific sense of public affairs or pecuniary affairs; special business; personal concern; a rencontre; a skirmish.—*Affair of honor*, a duel.

affect, af·fekt′, *v.t.* [L. *affecto*, to desire, to strive after, freq. of *afficio*, *affectum*, to affect the mind or body—*af* for *ad*, to, and *facio*, to do.] To act upon; to produce an effect or change upon; to influence; to move or touch by exciting the feelings; to aspire to; to endeavor after; to choose commonly; to habitually follow after; make a show of; to assume the appearance of; to pretend.—**affectation**, **affectedness**, af·fek·tā′shon, af·fekt′ed·nes, *n*. [L. *affectatio*.] An attempt to assume or exhibit what is not natural or real; false pretense, especially of what is praiseworthy or uncommon; artificial appearance or show.—**affected**, af·fekt′ed, *a*. Inclined or disposed (especially with *well*, *ill*, etc.); given to affectation; assuming or pretending

to possess what is not natural or real; assumed artificially; not natural.—**affectedly**, af·fekt′ed·li, *adv*. In an affected or assumed manner; with affectation.—**affecter**, af·fekt′ėr, *n*. One who affects, pretends, or assumes.—**affecting**, af·fekt′ing, *a*. Having power to excite emotion; suited to affect; pathetic.—**affectingly**, af·fekt′ing·li, *adv*. In an affecting or impressive manner.

affection, af·fek′shon, *n*. [L. *affectio*, *affectionis*, the being affected or touched. AFFECT.] The state of having one's feelings affected in some way; bent or disposition of mind; sentiment or moral feeling (as esteem, envy, jealousy); appetite; inclination; a settled good-will, love, or zealous attachment; a property or attribute inseparable from its object (as figure from bodies); any particular morbid state of the body (a gouty *affection*).—**affectionate**, af·fek′shon·āt, *a*. Having great love or affection; warmly attached; fond; kind; loving; proceeding from affection; tender.—**affectionately**, af·fek′shon·āt·li, *adv*. In an affectionate manner; fondly; tenderly; kindly.—**affectionateness**, af·fek′shon·āt·nes, *n*. The quality of being affectionate; fondness; affection.

affenpinscher, af″en·pin′·shėr, *n*. Breed of small dog having stiff red, black, or gray coat, pointed ears, and shaggy hairs about nose, eyes, and chin; also called *monkey dog* from monkeyish expression.

afferent, af′fėr·ent, *a*. [L. *afferens*, *afferentis*, ppr. of *affero—af* for *ad*, to, and *fero*, to carry. Carrying to or inward (of vessels or nerves in animals).

affiance, af·fī′ans, *n*. [O.Fr., from *af* for *ad*, to, and *fiancer*, to betroth. L. *fidans*, *fidantis*, ppr. of *fido*, to pledge one's faith, *fides*, faith.] Marriage contract or promise; faith pledged; confidence; reliance.—*v.t.*—*affianced*, *affiancing*. To betroth; to bind by promise of marriage.

affidavit, af·fi·dā′vit, *n*. [3rd pers. sing. perf. ind. of L.L. *affido*, to pledge one's faith—L. *af* for *ad*, to, and *fides*, faith.] A written declaration upon oath; a statement of facts in writing signed by the party, and sworn to or confirmed by declaration before an authorized magistrate.

affiliate, af·fil′i·āt, *v.t.*—*affiliated*, *affiliating*. [L.L. *adfiliare*, to adopt as a son—L. *ad*, to, and *filius*, a son.] To adopt; to receive into a family as a son; to establish the paternity of, as of a bastard child; to connect in the way of descent; to receive into a society as a member.—**affiliation**, af·fil′i·ā″shon, *n*. The act of one who affiliates; the settlement of the paternity of a child on its true father.

affined,‡ af·fīnd′, *a*. [O.Fr. *affiner* to unite. AFFINITY.] Joined in affinity; akin; bound or impelled by any kind of affinity. [*Shak*.]

affinity, af·fin′i·ti, *n*. [L. *affinitas*, from *affinis*, adjacent, related—*af* for *ad*, to, and *finis*, boundary.] The relation contracted by marriage,

in contradistinction from *consanguinity*, or relation by blood; relation, connection, or alliance in general (as of languages, sounds, etc.); similarity in kind or nature; *chem*. that force by which bodies of dissimilar nature unite in certain definite proportions to form a compound, different in its nature from any of its constituents.

affirm, af·fėrm′, *v.t.* [L. *affirmo—af* for *ad*, to, and *firmo*, to make firm.] To assert positively; to tell with confidence; to aver; declare; allege: opposed to *deny*; to confirm or ratify.—*v.i.* To make a solemn assertion or declaration; to make a legal affirmation.—**affirmable**, af·fėrm′abl, *a*. Capable of being affirmed, asserted, or declared.—**affirmably**, af·fėrm′a·bli, *adv*. In a way capable of affirmation.—**affirmance**,† af·fėrm′ans, *n*. Confirmation; ratification; affirmation.—**affirmant**, **affirmer**, af·fėrm′ant, af·fėrm′ėr, *a*. One who affirms or asserts; one who makes affirmation instead of an oath.—**affirmation**, af·fėr·mā′shon, *n*. The act of affirming or asserting as true; that which is asserted; averment; confirmation; ratification; a solemn declaration made in lieu of an oath by one who has scruples about taking the oath.—**affirmative**, af·fėrm′at·iv, *a*. Affirming or asserting, opposed to *negative*.—*n*. A word or phrase expressing assent or affirmation or answering a question affirmatively; the opposite of a negative.—*The affirmative*, that side of a debated question which maintains the truth of the affirmative proposition.—**affirmatively**, af·fėrm′at·iv·li, *adv*. In an affirmative manner; positively.

affix, af·fiks′, *v.t.* [L. *affigo*, *affixum—af* for *ad*, to, and *figo*, *fixum*, to fix.] To subjoin, annex, unite, or add at the close or end; to append; to attach.—**affix**, af′fiks, *n*. A syllable or letter added to the end of a word; a suffix; a post-fix.

afflation, af·flā′shon, *n*. [L. *afflo*, *afflatum—af* for *ad*, to, and *flo*, to blow.] A blowing or breathing on.—**afflatus**, af·flā′tus, *n*. [L.] A breath or blast of wind; inspiration; the inspiration of the poet.

afflict, af·flikt′, *v.t.* [L. *afflicto*, intens. of *affligo*, to dash down—*af* for *ad*, to, and *fligo*, to strike.] To give (to the body or mind) pain which is continued or of some permanence; to trouble, grieve, harass, or distress.—**afflicter**, af·flikt′ėr, *n*. One who afflicts.—**affliction**, af·flik′shon, *n*. The state of being afflicted; a state of acute pain or distress of body or mind; the cause of continued pain of body or mind… *Affliction* is stronger than *grief*, and *grief* than *sorrow*. *Affliction* is acute mental suffering caused by the loss of something cherished, as friends, health, or fortune.—**afflictive**, af·flikt′iv, *a*. Painful; distressing.—**afflictively**, af·flikt′iv·li, *adv*.

affluence, af′flu·ens, *n*. [L. *affluentia*, from *affluo*, to flow to—*ad*, to, and *fluo*, to flow. FLUENT.] A flowing to or concourse; an abundant supply; great plenty of worldly goods; wealth.—**affluent**, af'flu·ent, *a*. Flowing to; wealthy; abundant.—*n*. A tributary stream.—**affluently**, af'-flu·ent·li, *adv*.

afflux, af'fluks, *n*. [From L. *affluo, affluxum*. AFFLUENCE.] The act of flowing to; a flowing to, or that which flows to.

afford, af·fōrd', *v.t*. [O.E. *aforth*, to afford, from prefix *a*, and *forth*; A.Sax. *forthian*, to further.] To give forth; to yield, supply, or produce (fruit, profit); to grant or confer (as consolation, gratification); to buy, sell, expend, etc., from having a sufficiency of means; to bear the expense of (with *can, could, may, might*. etc.).

afforest, af·for'est, *v.t*. [Prefix *af* for *ad*, to, and *forest*.] To convert into a forest; to turn into forest land.—**afforestation**, af·for'es·tā''shon, *n*. The act of converting into a forest.

affranchise, af·fran'chiz, *v.t*. [Prefix *af*, and *franchise*.] To make free; to liberate from servitude.

affray, af·frā', *v.t*. [O. or Prov. Fr. *affraier, effroyer*, Fr. *effrayer*, to frighten; from L.L. *exfrediare*—L. *ex*, intens., and O.H.G. *fridu*, G. *friede*, peace. AFRAID.] To frighten; to terrify.—*n*. Fear‡; a noisy quarrel; a brawl; a tumult; disturbance.

affright, af·frīt', *v.t*. [A. Sax. *afyrhtian, afyrhtan*—prefix *a*, intens., and *fyrhtan*, to frighten. FRIGHT.] To impress with sudden fear; to frighten.—*n*. Sudden or great fear; terror.

affront, af·frunt', *v.t*. [Fr. *affronter*, to encounter face to face—*af* for *ad*, to, and L. *frons, frontis*, front, face.] To confront (*Shak*.)‡; to offend by an open manifestation of disrespect; to insult; to put out of countenance.—*n*. An open manifestation of disrespect or contumely; an outrage to the feelings; an insult; anything producing a feeling of shame or disgrace.—**affronter**, af·frunt'ėr, *n*. One who affronts.

affuse, af·fūz', *v.t*.—*affused, affusing*. [L. *affundo, affusum*—*af* for *ad*, to, and *fundo, fusum*, to pour out.] To pour upon; to sprinkle, as with a liquid.—**affusion**, af·fū'zhon, *n*. The act of pouring or sprinkling liquid upon; *med*. the act of pouring water on the body as a curative means.

afield, a·fēld', *adv*. To the field; in the field; astray.

afire, a·fīr', *a*. or *adv*. On fire.

aflame, a·flām', *a*. or *adv*. Flaming; glowing.

afloat, a·flōt', *a*. or *adv*. Borne on the water; floating; passing from one person to another; in circulation (as a rumor).

afoot, a·fut', *a*. or *adv*. On foot; borne by the feet; walking; in a state of being planned for execution (as a plan or plot).

afore, a·fōr', *adv*. [Prefix *a*, at, and *fore*; A.Sax. *onforan*.] Before in time or place: now mainly a nautical term; in the fore part of a vessel.—

prep. Before in time, position, rank, etc.; in presence of: now a *naut*. term.; more toward the head of a ship than; nearer the stem than.— *Afore the mast*, applied to a common sailor.—**aforesaid**, a·fōr'sed, *a*. Mentioned before in the same writing or discourse.—**aforethought**, a·fōr'-that, *a*. Thought of beforehand; premeditated; prepense.— **afore-time**,‡ a·fōr'tīm, *adv*. In time past; formerly. [N.T.]

afraid, a·frād', *a*. or *pp*. [O.E. *affrayd, afrayde*, etc., pp. of *affray*. AFFRAY.] Impressed with fear or apprehension; fearful: not used attributively. [Colloquially, *I am afraid* is often nearly equivalent to I suspect, I am inclined to think, or the like.]

afreet, af·rēt'. *n. Mohammedan myth*. a powerful evil jinni or demon. Written also *Efreet, Afrite*.

afresh, a·fresh', *adv*. Anew; again; after intermission.

African, af'rik·an, *a*. Pertaining to Africa.—*n*. A native of Africa.

Afrikaans, af'ra·käns'', *n*. [Variation of D. *Afrikansch*.] An official language of the Republic of South Africa, developed from Dutch.

Afrikaner, af'ra·kän''ėr, *n*. [D.] A native of the Republic of South Africa of European (especially Dutch) descent.

aft, aft, *a*. or *adv*. [A.Sax. *æft, eft*, after, behind; Goth. *afta*; from A.Sax. *af, æf*, Goth. *af*, E. *of, off*.] *Naut*. a word used to denote position at or near, or direction toward the stern of a ship.

after, aft'ėr, *a*. [A.Sax. *æfter*, a compar. from *af*, E. *of, off, -ter* being the compar. syllable, seen as *-ther* in *whether, hither*, as *-der* in *under*. OF.] Later in time; subsequent; succeeding; as, an *after* period of life: in this sense often combined with the following noun.— *prep*. Behind in place; later in time; in pursuit of; in search of; with or in desire for; in imitation of, or in imitation of the style of (*after* a model); according to; in proportion to (*after* our deserts); below in rank or excellence; next to; concerning (inquire *after*).—*After all*, at last; upon the whole; at the most; notwithstanding.—*adv*. Later in time; behind; in pursuit.—**afterbirth**, *n*. That which is expelled from the uterus after the birth of a child. —**afterburner**, *n*. A turbojet device that provides extra thrust by forcing fuel into hot exhaust gases; tail-pipe burner.—**aftereffect**, *n*. A delayed effect; *med*. a result appearing after the immediate effect; secondary effect.—**afterglow**, *n*. The glow in the west after sunset.—**afterimage**, *n*. The image of a bright object left for a time on the retina.—**afternoon**, *n*. The part of the day which follows noon, between noon and evening. —**afterthought**, *n*. Reflection after act to which it refers.—**aftertime**, *n*. Succeeding time: more commonly in the plural.

aftermost, aft'ėr·mōst, *a. superl*. [A.Sax. *æftemest*, a double superla-

tive, *mest* being from *ma+st*, two superlative suffixes.] Hindmost: opposed to *foremost*.

afterward, afterwards, aft'ėr·wėrd, aft'ėr·wėrdz, *adv*. [A.Sax. *æfterweard*. *Afterwards* is an adverbial genitive. WARD.] In later or subsequent time.

again, a·gen' or a·gān', *adv*. [A.Sax. *ongeân*, again; *geân*, against. AGAINST.] A second time; once more; on another occasion; on the other hand; moreover; besides; further; in return; back; in answer.

against, a·genst', *prep*. [O.E. *agayns, ongaenes*, A.Sax. *ongeân*, against. The *es* is an adverbial or genitive termination and the *t* has been added, like that in *amidst, betwixt*. A.Sax. *geân*, again or against, is the same as *gain* in *gainsay*; G. *gegen*, against.] Opposite in place (often preceded by *over*); in opposition to; adverse or hostile to (*against* law or public opinion); towards or upon; so as to meet (to strike *against* a rock); bearing or resting upon (to lean *against*); in preparation for (an event).

agamic, a·gam'ik, *a*. [Gr. *a*, not, and *gamos*, marriage.] Reproduced without the congress of individuals of the opposite sex.

agamogenesis, a·gam'ō·jen''e·sis, *n*. [Gr. *a*, not, *gamos*, marriage, and *genesis*, production.] The production of young without the congress of the sexes.—**agamogenetic**, a·gam'ō·jen·et''ik, *a*. Of or pertaining to agamogenesis.

agape, a·gāp', *adv*. or *a*. Gaping as with wonder; having the mouth wide open.

agape, ag'a·pē, *n*. [Gr. *agapē*, love.] Among the primitive Christians a love feast or feast of charity, held before or after the communion, when contributions were made for the poor.

agar-agar, āgar·ā'gar, *n*. The native name of a dried seaweed much used in the East for soups and jellies.

agaric, a·gar'ik, *n*. [Gr. *agarikon*.] A genus of various fungi. Many of the species are edible like the common mushroom, while others are deleterious and even poisonous.

agate, ag'āt, *n*. [Fr. *agate*, from L. *achates*, so called because found near a river of that name in Sicily.] A semipellucid mineral, consisting of bands or layers of various colors blended together, the base generally being chalcedony, and this mixed with jasper, amethyst, quartz, opal, etc.: used for rings, seals, cups, beads, etc.; an instrument used by gold-wire drawers, so called from the agate in the middle of it; a gilder's tool; a kind of type, called also *Ruby*.

agave, a·gā'vē, *n*. [Gr. *agauos*, noble. A genus of plants, comprehending the American aloe. They live for many years—ten to seventy—before flowering.

age, āj, *n*. [Fr. *âge*, O.Fr. *eage*, L.L. *aeταticum*, from L. *aetas, aetatis*, abbrev. of *aevitas*, from *aevum*, an age. EVER.] A period of time representing the whole or a part of the duration of any individual thing or being; the time during which an individual has lived; the latter part of life; the state of being old; oldness; old people collectively; the state of having arrived at legal maturity (the completion of the first twenty-one years of one's life); great length of time; a long or protracted period, sometimes definitely a century; a historical epoch; an epoch having a particular character; the people who live at a particular period.—*The age*, the times we live in.—*v.i.*—*aged* (ājd), *aging.* To grow old; to assume the appearance of old age.—*v.t.* To give the character of age or ripeness to (to *age* wine).—**aged,** āj´ed, *a.* Old; having lived long; having a certain age (*aged* forty years); in this sense often (ājd).—**agedly,** āj´ed·li, *adv.* Like an aged person.—**agedness,** āj´ed·nes, *n.* The state or condition of being aged; oldness.

agenda, a·jen´da, *n. pl.* [L., things to be done.] Memoranda; a memorandum-book; a church service; a ritual or liturgy.

agent, ā´jent, *n.* [L. *agens, agentis,* acting. ACT.] One who or that which acts; an actor; one that exerts power or has the power to act; an active power or cause; a body or substance that causes a certain action to begin; a person entrusted with the business of another.—**agency,** ā´jen·si, *n.* The state of being in action or of exerting power; operation; instrumentality; the office or business of an agent or factor.—**agential,** ā·jen´shal, *a.* Pertaining to an agent or agency.

agglomerate, ag·glom´ėr·āt, *v.t.*— *agglomerated, agglomerating.* [L. *agglomero*—*ad,* and *glomus, glomeris,* a ball of yarn.] To collect or gather into a mass.—*v.i.* To become collected into a ball or mass.—*n. Geol.* a collective name for masses consisting of angular fragments ejected from volcanoes. — **agglomeration,** ag·glom´ėr·ā˝shon, *n.* The act of agglomerating; a collection; a heap. —**agglomerative,** ag·glom´ėr·āt·iv, *a.* Disposed to agglomerate.

agglutinate, ag·glū´tin·āt, *v.t.*— *glutinated, agglutinating.* [L. *agglutino*—*ad,* and *glutino,* from *gluten,* glue. GLUE.] To unite or cause to adhere, as with glue or other viscous substance; to glue together.—*a.* United as by glue; joined.—*Agglutinate* or *Agglutinating languages,* in *philol.* those languages in which the suffixes for inflection retain a kind of independence, and are felt to be distinct from the root or main significant element of the word.— **agglutinant,** ag·glū´tin·ant, *a.* Uniting as glue; tending to cause adhesion.—*n.* Any viscous substance which agglutinates or unites other substances.—**agglutination,** ag·glū´tin·ā˝shon, *n.* The act of agglutinating or the state of; adhesion of parts; the marked feature of agglutinate languages.—**agglutinative,** ag·glū´tin·āt·iv, *a.* Tending or having power

to agglutinate.

aggrandize, ag´gran·dīz, *v.t.*— *aggrandized, aggrandizing.* [Fr. *agrandir*—L. prefix *a* for *ad,* to, and *grandis,* grand.] To make great or greater: especially to make greater in power, wealth, rank, or honor; to exalt; to elevate; extend; enlarge. —**aggrandizement,** ag´gran·dīz˝ment or ag·gran´diz·ment, *n.* The act of aggrandizing; the act of increasing one's own power, rank, or honor; advancement.—**aggrandizer,** ag´gran·dīz·ėr, *n.* One that aggrandizes.

aggravate, ag´gra·vāt, *v.t.*—*aggravated, aggravating.* [L. *aggravo*—*ad,* to, and *gravis,* heavy. whence *grave, grief,* etc.] To make worse, more severe, or less tolerable; to make more enormous, or less excusable; to intensify; to exaggerate; to provoke; irritate; tease.—**aggravating,** ag´gra·vāt·ing, *a.* Provoking; annoying.—**aggravatingly,** ag´gra·vāt·ing·li, *adv.* In an aggravating manner.—**aggravation,** ag´gra·vā˝shon, *n.* The act of aggravating or making worse; addition to that which is evil or improper; provocation; irritation.

aggregate, ag´grē·gāt, *v.t.*—*aggregated, aggregating.* [L. *aggrego, aggregatum*—*ad,* and *grex, gregis,* a herd or band.] To bring together; to collect into a sum, mass, or body.—*a.* Formed by the conjunction or collection of particulars into a whole mass or sum; total.—*n.* A sum, mass, or assemblage of particulars; a whole or total.—*In the aggregate,* taken altogether; considered as a whole; collectively.—**aggregately,** ag´grē·gāt·li, *adv.* Collectively; taken in a sum or mass.— **aggregation,** ag·grē·gā´shon, *n.* The act of aggregating; the state of; an aggregate.—**aggregative,** ag´grē·gāt·iv, *a.* Tending to aggregate; collective.

aggress, ag·gres´, *v.i.* [L. *aggredior, aggressus*—*ad,* and *gradior,* to go.] To make a first attack; to commit the first act of hostility or offence.— *v.t.†* To attack.—**aggression,** ag·gre´shon, *n.* The first attack or act of hostility; the first act leading to a war or controversy.—**aggressive,** ag·gres´iv, *a.* Characterized by aggression; tending to aggress.—**aggressiveness,** ag·gres´iv·nes, *n.* The quality of being aggressive.—**aggressor,** ag·gres´ėr, *n.* The person who aggresses; an assaulter; an invader.

aggrieve, ag·grēv´, *v.t.*—*aggrieved, aggrieving.* [O.Fr. *agrever,* to weigh down, from *grever,* to oppress, from L. *gravis,* heavy, whence also *grief, grave,* etc.] To give pain or sorrow; to afflict; to grieve; to bear hard upon; to oppress or injure in one's rights.

aghast, a·gast´, *a.* or *p.* [A participial form from O.E. *agasten, agesten,* to terrify—prefix *a,* intens., and A.Sax. *gaestan,* to terrify; allied to Goth. *gaisjan; usgaisjan,* to terrify; comp. Prov. E. *gast,* to terrify, *gast,* fear, *gastful.*] Struck with amazement;

stupefied with sudden fright or horror. Written also *agast,* which is etymologically the better spelling.

agile, aj´il, *a.* [Fr. *agile;* L. *agilis,* from *ago.* ACT.] Nimble; quick in movement; brisk; active.—**agilely,** aj´il·li, *adv.* In an agile or nimble manner.—**agility, agileness,** a·jil´i·ti, aj´il·nes, *n.* The state or quality of being agile; nimbleness; briskness; activity.

agio, a·ji·ō, *n.* [It.] The difference in value between one sort of money and another, especially between paper money and metallic coin.— **agiotage,** a·ji·ot·āj, *n.* The maneuvers by which speculators in stocks contrive to lower or enhance their price; stock jobbing.

agitate, aj´it·āt, *v.t.* agitated, agitating. [L. *agito, agitatum,* freq. from *ago.* ACT.] To move or force into violent irregular action; to shake or move briskly; to disturb; to perturb; to discuss; debate; arouse public attention to, as by speeches, pamphlets, etc.—*v.i.* To engage in agitation.—**agitable,** aj´it·a·bl, *a.* Capable of being agitated.—**agitated,** aj´it·āt·ed, *a.* Disturbed; perturbed; excited; expressing agitation (countenance, manner).—**agitation,** aj·it·ā´shon, *n.* The act of agitating, or state of being agitated; perturbation of mind or feelings; commotion; disturbance.—**agitator,** aj´it·āt·ėr, *n.* One who or that which agitates, rouses, or stirs up.

aglet, ag´let, *n.* [Fr. *aiguillette,* a point, from *aiguille,* a needle; L. *acus,* a needle.] A metal tag at the end of a lace or point, formerly worn on dresses.

aglow, a·glō´, *a.* In a glow; glowing.

agnail, ag´nāl, *n.* [A.Sax. *angnægl* = *ange,* pain, and *nægl,* nail.] A sore hard as a nail; a corn; corrupted to *hangnail,* from false idea of sore on fingernail.

agnate, ag´nāt, *n.* [L. *agnatus*—*ad,* and *nascor, natus,* to be born.] Any male relation by the father's side.— *a.* Related or akin by the father's side.—**agnatic,** ag·nat´ik, *a.* Pertaining to descent by the male line, of ancestors.—**agnation,** ag·nā´shon, *n.* Relation by the father's side only or descent in the male line.

agnomen, ag·nō´men, *n.* [L.—*ag* for *ad,* to, and *nomen,* a name.] An additional name or epithet conferred on a person.

agnostic, ag·nos´tik, *n.* [Gr. *agnōstos,* unknowing, unknown, from *a,* not, and stem of *gignōskō,* to know. Same root as *know.*] One of those persons who disclaim any knowledge of God or of the origin of the universe or of anything but material phenomena, holding that with regard to such matters nothing can be known.—*a.* Pertaining to the agnostics or their doctrines.—**agnosticism,** ag·nos´ti·sizm, *n.* The doctrines or belief of agnostics.

agnus, ag´nus, *n.* [L., a lamb.] An image of a lamb as emblematical of the Saviour; an Agnus Dei.— *Agnus Dei.* [L., Lamb of God.] A medal, or more frequently a cake of wax, consecrated by the pope, stamped with the figure of a lamb supporting the banner of the cross; supposed to possess great virtues, such as preserving those who carry it in faith from accidents, etc.

ago, a·gō′, *a.* or *adv.* [Really a *pp.*, being shortened form of *agone*, formerly used in same sense; A. Sax. *âgân*, gone by—*â*, away, *gân*, to go.] Past; gone; as, a year ago.

agog, a·gog′, *adv.* [Prefix *a*, on, and W. *gog*, activity, *gogi*, to shake.] In eager excitement; highly excited by eagerness for an object.

agone,‡ a·gon′, *adv.* Ago, [O.T.]

agonic, a·gon′ik, *a.* [Gr. *a*, not, and *gōnia*, an angle.] Not forming an angle.—*Agonic lines*, two lines on the earth's surface, on which the magnetic needle points to the true north, or where the magnetic meridian coincides with the geographical.

agonist,† ag′ō·nist, *n.* [Gr. *agōnistēs*. AGONY.] One who contends for the prize in public games; a combatant; a champion.—**agonistics**, ag·ō·nist′iks, *n.* The art of contending in public games.

agony, ag′ō·ni, *n.* [Gr. *agōnia*, struggle, anguish, from *agōn*, a contest or struggle, from *agō*, to lead, to bring together.] A violent contest or striving‡; the struggle, frequently unconscious, that precedes natural death; the death throe or pang (often in plural); extreme bodily or mental pain; intense suffering; anguish; torment. ∴ *Agony* is extreme bodily pain; *anguish* is mental pain or the effect of extreme distress on the mind.—**agonize**, ag′ō·nīz, *v.i.*—*agonized*, *agonizing*. To writhe with agony or extreme pain.—*v.t.* To distress with extreme pain; to torture.

agoraphobia, ag″ō·ra·fō′bē·a, *n.* [L., from Gr. *agora*, a marketplace, Gr. *phŏbŏs*, fear.] Morbid fear of open spaces.

agouta, a·gö′ta, *n.* [W. Indian name.] An insectivorous animal peculiar to Haiti, of the tanrec family, and rather larger than a rat.

agouti, a·gö′ti, *n.* The native American name of several species of rodent mammals allied to the guinea pig.

agraffe, a·graf′, *n.* [Fr. *agrafe*.] A sort of hook or clasp, often jewelled.

agraphia, a·graf′i·a, *n.* [Gr. *a*, not, and *graphō*, to write.] A form of aphasia, in which the patient is unable to express ideas by written signs.

agrarian, a·grā′ri·an, *a.* [L. *agrarius*, from *ager*, a field. ACRE.] Relating to lands, especially public lands; growing wild in fields†.—*Agrarian laws*, in ancient Rome, laws for regulating the distribution of the public lands among the citizens.—*n.* One in favor of an equal division of landed property.—**agrarianism**, a·grā′ri·an·izm, *n.* The upholding of an equal division of lands and property; the principles of one who does so.

agree, a·grē′, *v.i.*—*agreed*, *agreeing*. [Fr. *agréer*—*a*, to, and *gré*, O.Fr.

gret, good-will, favor, from L. *gratus*, pleasant, whence *gratitude*, *grateful*, etc.] To be of one mind; to harmonize in opinion; to live in concord or without contention; to come to an arrangement or understanding; to arrive at a settlement (*agree to* a proposal; *agree with* a person); to be consistent; to harmonize; not to contradict or be repugnant (stories *agree with* each other); to tally; to match; to correspond; to suit; to be accommodated or adapted (food *agrees with* a person); *gram.* to correspond in number, case, gender, or person.—**agreeability**, a·grē′a·bil″i·ti, *n.* Agreeableness.—**agreeable**, a·grē′a·bl, *a.* Suitable; conformable; correspondent; pleasing, either to the mind or senses (*agreeable* manners; *agreeable* to the taste); willing or ready to agree or consent; giving consent; with *to*.—**agreeableness**, a·grē′a·bl·nes, *n.* The state or quality of being agreeable; the quality of pleasing.—**agreeably**, a·grē′a·bli, *adv.* In an agreeable manner; suitably; consistently; conformably; in a manner to give pleasure; pleasingly.—**agreement**, a·grē′ment, *n.* The state of agreeing or being agreed; harmony; conformity; union of opinions or sentiments; bargain; compact; contract.

agrestic,† a·gres′tik, *a.* [L. *agrestis*, from *ager*, a field.] Rural; rustic.

agriculture, ag′ri·kul·tūr, *n.* [L. *agricultura*—*ager*, a field, and *cultura*, cultivation. ACRE and CULTURE.] The cultivation of the ground, more especially with the plough and in large areas or fields; it may include also the raising and feeding of cattle or other live stock; husbandry; tillage; farming.—**agricultural**, ag·ri·kul′tūr·al, *a.* Pertaining to, connected with, or engaged in agriculture.—**agriculturist, agriculturalist**, ag·ri·kul′tūr·ist, ag·ri·kul′tūr·al·ist, *n.* One engaged or skilled in agriculture; a husbandman.

agrimony, ag′ri·mon·i, *n.*]L. *argemonia*, from Gr. *argema*, a whitish ulceration on the eye (which this plant was supposed to cure), from *argos*, white.] A British plant formerly of much repute as a medicine. Its leaves and rootstock are astringent, and the latter yields a yellow dye.

agriology, ag·ri·ol′o·ji, *n.* [Gr. *agrios*, pertaining to a wild state, and *logos*, a discourse.] The comparative study of human customs, especially of the customs of man in a rude or uncivilized state.—**agriologist**, ag·ri·ol′o·jist, *n.* A student of agriology.

agronomy, a·gron′ō·mi, *n.* [Gr. *agronomos*, rural, from *agros*, a field.] Agriculture and other rural pursuits. —**agronomic, agronomical**, ag·rō·nom′ik, a·grō·nom′ik·al, *a.* Relating to agronomy.—**agronomist**, a·gron′ō·mist, *n.* One who studies agronomy.

agrostography, a·gros·tog′ra·fi, *n.* [Gr. *agrŏstis*, a grass.] A description of grasses.—**agrostology**, a·gros·tol′o·ji, *n.* That part of botany which relates to grasses.

aground, a·ground′, *adv.* or *a.* On

the ground; run ashore; stranded.

ague, ā′gū, *n.* [Fr. *aigu*, acute; *fièvre aiguë* (L.L. *febris acuta*), acute fever; L. *acutus*, sharp.] The cold fit or rigor which precedes a fever or a paroxysm of fever in intermittents; a fever coming in periodical fits accompanied by shivering; a chill or state of shaking not resulting from disease.—**aguish**, ā′gū·ish, *a.* Having the qualities of an ague; productive of agues; chilly, shivering.—

ah, ä. [A natural cry expressive of sudden emotion; comp. G. *ach*, L. *ah*, Skr. *â*, *âh*, ah.] An exclamation expressive of pain, surprise, pity, compassion, complaint, contempt, dislike, joy, exultation, etc., according to the manner of utterance.

aha, ä·hä′, [A lengthened form of *ah*, or formed of *ah* and *ha*; comp. G. *aha*, Skr. *ahô*, *ahaha*.] An exclamation expressing triumph, contempt, surprise, etc.

ahead, a·hed′, *adv.* Headlong; head foremost‡; in or to the front; in advance; before; further on (to walk *ahead of* a person; *naut.* opposite to *astern*.

ahoy, a·hoi′, *exclam.* [Longer form of *hoy!*] A word used chiefly at sea in hailing.

ai, ä′ē, *n.* The three-toed sloth, so called from its cry.

aid, ād, *v.t.* [Fr. *aider*, O.Fr. *ajuder*, from L. *adjutare*, freq. of *adjuvo*, *adjutum*, to help—*ad*, to, and *juvo*, *jutum*, to help.] To help; to assist; to come to the support or relief of; to succor;—**aid**, ād, *n.* [Fr. *aide*.] Help; succor; support; assistance; the person or thing that aids or yields assistance; a helper; an auxiliary; an assistant; a subsidy or tax formerly granted by Parliament to the crown; a tax paid by a feudal tenant to his lord.—**aider**, ād′ér, *n.*

aide, ād, *n.* [Fr.] A person acting as an assistant.

aide-de-camp, ād′de·koṅ, *n.* pl. **aides-de-camp,** ādz′de·koṅ. [Fr., lit. field assistant.] *Milit.* an officer whose duty is to receive and communicate the orders of a general officer, to act as his secretary, etc.

aigrette, ā·gret′, *n.* [EGRET.] A plume or ornament for the head composed of feathers or precious stones.

aiguille, ā′gwil, *n.* [Fr., a needle.] A name given to the needle-like points or tops of rocks and mountain masses, or to sharp-pointed masses of ice on glaciers, etc.

ail, āl, *v.t.* [O.E. *eylen*, A.Sax. *eglian*, to feel pain; to ail; *eglan*, to give pain; *egle*, trouble, grief; comp. Goth. *aglo*, affliction, Sw. *agg*, á prick.] To affect with pain or uneasiness, either of body or mind; to trouble; to be the matter with. —*v.i.* To be in pain or trouble.—**ailment**, āl′ment, *n.* Disease; indisposition; morbid affection of the body.

ailanthus, ā·lan′thus, *n.* [From *ailanto*, the Malacca name.] A handsome Asiatic tree, the tree-of-heaven, widely grown in cities.

aileron, ā′ler·on, *n.* [Fr. *aile*, wing.]

ch, *ch*ain; *ch*, Sc. lo*ch*; g, go; j, job; ng, sing; TH, *th*en; th, *th*in; w, wig; hw, *wh*ig; zh, azure.

Any one of certain small movable planes fixed to the main planes of an airplane and used as balancing flaps, or to give stability, being actuated by suitable leverage.

aim, ām, *v.i.* [O. Fr. *esmer, aesmer*—L. *ad*, to, and *aestimare*, to estimate.] To direct a missile towards an object; to direct the mind or intention; to make an attempt; to endeavor (followed by *at* before the object).—*v.t.* To direct or point to a particular object with the intention of hitting it; to level at.—*n.* The pointing or directing of a missile; the point intended to be hit, or object intended to be affected; the mark; a purpose; intention; design; scheme.—**aimless,** ām′les, *a.* Without aim; purposeless.—**aimlessly,** ām′les·li, *adv.* Purposelessly.

air, âr, *n.* [Fr. *air*, L. *aër*, from Gr. *aēr, air*.] A heterogeneous mixture of tasteless, odorless, colorless, and invisible gases surrounding the earth, which consists of 78.03% nitrogen, 20.99% oxygen, 0.94% argon, 0.03% carbon dioxide, 0.01% hydrogen, and traces of krypton, neon, helium, and xenon; that which we breathe and which is essential to all plant and animal life; a breeze; air in motion; a tune; a melody; the principal melody part in a harmonized piece of music; outward appearance, mien, bearing, manner of a person or thing as, an *air of importance;* semblance; an affected manner as, *to put on airs.*—*v.t.* To expose to, put out in, the air; to let air into, to ventilate, as *to air a room;* to state publicly, as *to air one's views, one's grievances,* etc.—**air base,** *n.* The base of operations for aircraft.—**air bladder,** *n.* A sac or vesicle filled with air located under the backbone of most fishes, and responsible for their buoyancy.—**air brake,** *n.* A mechanical brake worked by air pressure.—**airbrush,** *n.* A device attached to a compressed-air hose, for the spraying of paint.—**air castle,** *n.* A daydream; an unrealizable scheme.—**air cell,** *n.* A minute cavity containing air; one of the cells of the lungs.—**air chamber,** *n.* Any cavity filled with air.—**air compressor,** *n.* A device used for compressing air.—**air conditioning,** *n.* The process of controlling the quality, temperature, humidity, and circulation of air in a space enclosure. —**aircooled,** *a.* Cooled by air, as in an engine that is cooled by a current of air.—**aircraft,** *n.* Any kind of flying machine.—**aircraft carrier,** *n.* A ship designed to carry naval airplanes, with special decks for taking off and landing.—**airfield,** *n.* A level area where airplanes take off and land; an airport.—**airfoil,** *n.* Wing, rudder, or any aircraft surface designed to obtain reaction from a moving air stream.—**air force,** *n.* That branch of the armed forces which fights in the air.—**air gun,** *n.* A gun that uses compressed air to propel bullets.—**air hole,** *n.* A hole made to admit or to pass in or out; an *air pocket.*—**airily,** *adv.* In an airy manner; in a light, gay manner.

—**airing,** *n.* An exposure to air as, *to give clothes an airing;* a short walk or drive out of doors.—**air lane,** *n.* A particular route through the air traversed by aircraft.—**airless,** *adj.* Lacking air; stuffy.—**airlift,** *n.* A supply line operated by aircraft.—*v.* To transport by air.—**airline,** *n.* A transportation system of airplanes making regularly scheduled flights and transporting passengers and freight between its points of flight. —**air lock,** *n.* Airtight area at the entrance of a pressure chamber.—**air mail,** *n.* Mail carried by airplanes. —**airman,** *n.* A flier; an aviator. —**airminded,** *a.* Interested in, and approving of, air travel or things aeronautic.—**airplane,** *n.* Any one of the different kinds of flying machines which are heavier than air and which are supported in the air by planes or wings, driven forward by a propeller or a jet.—**air pocket,** *n.* A disturbance of the atmosphere that causes aircraft to drop suddenly for a considerable distance; an air hole.—**airport,** *n.* An airfield; a field, with a hangar or hangars, for the landing, taking-off, and servicing of aircraft.—**air raid,** *n.* A hostile destructive incursion by enemy aircraft.—**air rifle,** *n.* A rifle that uses compressed air to propel bullets. —**air shaft,** *n.* A passage for admitting fresh air into a mine or tunnel; a passage in a building which affords ventilation and light.—**airship,** *n.* A machine for navigating the air, capable of being steered, supported by gas bags, and propelled by an engine or engines; a dirigible. —**airsickness,** *n.* Illness when flying at high altitudes.—**airtight,** *a.* Impermeable to air; hermetically sealed. —**airway,** *n.* A passage for air currents; a chartered route for aircraft.—**airy,** *a.* Consisting of or having the character of air; ethereal; exposed to air; gay and sprightly; lively.—**air-cushion vehicle,** *n.* A vehicle that hovers and travels near the ground or water on a cushion of air; GEM.

Airedale, ar′dāl, *n.* [From *Airedale,* Yorkshire, Eng.] A large terrier with coarse wiry hair.

aisle, īl, *n.* [O.Fr. *aisle.* Fr. *aile,* a wing, an aisle; L. *ala,* a wing; the *s* does not properly belong to the word.] A lateral division of a cathedral or other church, separated from the central part, called the nave, by pillars or piers.—**aisled,** īld, *a.* Furnished with aisles.

ait, āt, *n.* [A form of *eyot,* an islet.] A small island in a river or lake.

aitchbone, āch′bōn, *n.* [For *natch-bone* (by loss of initial *n* as in *apron*), from Fr. *nache,* L.L. *naticae,* L. *nates,* the rump.] The rump-bone of an ox. Called also *Edgebone* (by false etymology).

ajar, a·jar′, *adv.* [O.E. *achar, onchar,* lit. on the turn—prefix *a,* on, *jar, char,* A. Sax. *cerre,* a turn, seen also in *chare, char*-woman.] On the turn; neither quite open nor shut; partly opened; said of a door.

akimbo, a·kim′bō, *a.* or *adv.* [Prefix *a,* on, and *kimbo,* from Icel. *keng-boginn,* lit. crook-bowed, *kengr,* a crook.] With the elbow pointing outwards and the hand resting on the hip; said of the arm.

akin, a·kin′, *a.* or *adv.* [Prefix *a,* of, and *kin.*] Related by blood; allied by nature; partaking of the same properties.

alabaster, al′a·bas·tér, *n.* [L. *alabaster,* Gr. *alabastros,* from Alabastron, a village in Egypt where it was got.] A soft, semi-transparent, marble-like mineral of which there are two well-known varieties—the gypseous and the calcareous. Small works of art are often made of it.— **alabastrine,** al·a·bas′trīn, *a.* Of or pertaining to.

alack, a·lak′, *interj.* [Probably a corruption of *alas;* but comp. *lauk!* euphemism for Lord.] An explanation expressive of sorrow.—**alackaday,** a·lak′a·dā, *interj.* [Comp. *Well-a-day!*] An exclamation uttered to express regret or sorrow.

alacrity, a·lak′ri·ti, *n.* [L. *alacritas,* from *alacer, alacris,* cheerful.] A cheerful readiness or promptitude to do some act; cheerful willingness; briskness.

alamode, a·la·mōd′, *adv.* [Fr. *à la mode,* after the fashion.] According to the fashion or prevailing mode: sometimes used as an adjective.

alar, ā′lér, *a.* [L. *ala,* a wing.] Pertaining to wings; having the character of a wing.

alarm, a·lärm′, *n.* [Fr. *alarme,* alarm, from It. *all'arme*=L. *ad arma,* to arms.] A summons to arms; an outcry or other notice of approaching danger; a tumult; a disturbance; a sudden fear or painful suspense excited by an apprehension of danger; apprehension; terror; a mechanical contrivance for awakening persons from sleep or rousing their attention.—*v.t.* To call to arms for defense; to give notice of danger; to rouse to vigilance; to disturb with terror; to fill with anxiety by the prospect of evil.—**alarming,** a·lärm′ing, *a.* Calculated to rouse alarm; causing apprehension.—**alarmingly,** a·lärm′ing·li, *adv.* In an alarming manner.—**alarmist,** a·lärm′ist, *n.* One that excites alarm; one who is prone to take alarm, and to circulate and exaggerate any sort of bad news.

alary, ā′la·ri, *a.* Alar.

alas, a·las′, *exclam.* [O.Fr. *alas,* from interj. *a, ah,* L. *lassus,* weary.] An exclamation expressive of sorrow, grief, pity, concern, or apprehension of evil.

alate, ā′lāt, *a.* [L. *alatus,* winged, *ala,* a wing.] Winged; having membranous expansions like wings.

alb, alb, *n.* [L. *alba,* white (*vestis,* garment, understood).] A clerical vestment worn by priests, a long robe of white linen bound with a girdle.

albacore, al′ba·kōr, *n.* [Sp. *albacora,* Fr. *albicore,* from Ar. *al,* the, *bakr,* a young cow or heifer.] A name given to several fishes of the tunny kind, especially to the Pacific tunny.

albata, al·bā′ta, *n.* [L. *albus,* white.]

An alloy consisting of a combination of nickel, zinc, tin, and copper, often with antimony and silver; German silver.

albatross, al′ba·tros, *n.* [Fr. *albatros,* a corruption of Sp. and Pg. *alcatraz,* a pelican, from Ar. *al-qādūs,* the bucket of a water wheel, the pelican being supposed to carry water to its young ones in the pouch below its bill.] An aquatic bird, the largest sea bird known, some measuring 17½ feet from tip to tip of the wings, met with at immense distances from land.

albeit, al·bē′it, *conj.* [*Al* in old sense of though, *be,* and *it,* and equivalent to *be it so,*] Be it so; admit all that; although; notwithstanding; even though.

albescent, al·bes′ent, *a.* [L. *albesco,* to grow white, an incept. from *albus,* white.] Becoming white or rather whitish; moderately white; of a pale, hoary aspect.

Albigenses, al·bi·jens′ez, *n. pl.* A party of religious reformers in the twelfth century, who were ruthlessly persecuted: so called from *Albi,* a town of Languedoc in France, where they resided.

albino, al·bī′nō, *n. pl.* **albinos,** al·bī′nōz. [Pg., from L. *albus,* white.] A person of abnormally pale, milky complexion, with light hair and pink eyes; an animal characterized by the same peculiarity in physical constitution.—**albinism,** al′bin·izm, *n.* The state or condition of an albino; leucopathy.

albite, al′bīt, *n.* [L. *albus,* white.] A name given to feldspar whose alkali is composed of soda instead of potash.

album, al′bum, *n.* [L., from *albus,* white.] A book originally blank, in which may be inserted autographs of celebrated persons or favorite pieces of poetry or prose, generally contributed by friends; a book for preserving photographs, drawings, portraits, etc.

albumen, al·bū′men, *n.* [L., from *albus,* white.] The white of an egg.—**albumenize,** al·bū′men·īz, *v.t.*—**albumenized, albumenizing.** To convert into albumen; to cover or impregnate with albumen.—**albumin,** al·bū′min, *n.* Any of a group of simple proteins widely found in plant and animal tissues, especially in the white of eggs.—**albuminoid,** al·bū′min·oid, *a.* Like albumin.—*n.* A substance resembling albumin; proteide.—**albuminose, albuminous,** al·bū′min·ōs, al·bū′min·us, *a.* Pertaining to or having the properties of albumin; applied to plants whose seeds have a store of albumin, as all kinds of grain, palms, etc.—**albuminuria,** al·bū′mi·nū″ri·a. [*Albumen* and Gr. *ouron,* urine.] *Pathol.* a condition in which the urine contains albumin, indicating a diseased state of the kidneys.

alburnum, al·bėr′num, *n.* [L. *alburnum,* sapwood, from *albus,* white.] The white and softer part of the wood of exogenous plants between the inner bark and the heartwood; the sapwood.

Alcaic, al·kā′ik, *a.* [L. *alcaicus.*] Pertaining to *Alcaeus,* a lyric poet of Mitylene.—*Alcaic verse,* a variety of verse used in Greek and Latin poetry, consisting of five feet, a spondee or iambus, an iambus, a long syllable, and two dactyls.

alcalde, alcaide, äl·käl′dä, äl·kä′i·dä, *n.* [Sp. and Pg. from Ar.] In Spain, Portugal, etc., a commander of a fortress; the chief civil magistrate of a town; also, a jailer.

alchemy, alchymy, al′ke·mi, al′ki·mi, *n.* [O.F. *alquimie,* L.L. *alchimia,* from Ar. *al-Kimia—al,* the, and *Khemia,* the name of Egypt; confusion with Gr. *kheō,* I pour, *khumeia,* gives alchemy. CHEMISTRY.] The art which had for its main objects the transmuting of the baser metals into gold or silver, the discovery of an elixir of life, a universal solvent, etc.—**alchemic, alchemical, alchemistic, alchemistical,** al·kem′ik, al·kem′ik·al, al·kem·ist′ik, al·kem·ist′ik·al, *a.* Relating to, produced by, or practicing alchemy. Also spelled with *y* for *e.*—**alchemically,** al·kem′ik·al·li, *adv.* In the manner of alchemy.—**alchemist,** al′kem·ist, *n.* One who practices alchemy.—**alchemise,†** al′kem·iz, *v.t.* To change by alchemy; to transmute, as metals.—**alchymy,** A mixed metal (Mil.).

alcohol, al′kō·hol, *n.* [Sp. Pg. *alcohol*—Ar. *al,* the, and *kohl,* a fine powder of antimony, hence anything very fine or purified, as rectified spirits.] Any of a class of chemical compounds derived from hydrocarbons by replacing one or more of the hydrogen atoms with an equal number of hydroxyl radicals; term for ethyl alcohol (ethanol), the alcohol of commerce and medicine.—**alcoholic,** al·kō·hol′ik, *a.* Pertaining to alcohol, or partaking of its qualities.—*n.* An alcoholic liquid.—**alcoholism,** al′kō·hol·izm, *n.* A disease condition due to over-indulgence of alcohol; dipsomania.—**alcoholize,** al′kō·hol·īz, *v.t.* To convert into alcohol; to rectify (spirit) till it is wholly purified.—**alcoholometer,** al′kō·hol·om″et·er, *n.* An instrument for determining the quantity of pure alcohol in any liquid.—**alcoholometry,** al′kō·hol·om″et·ri, *n.* The determination of the percentage of absolute alcohol in a liquid.

Alcoran. See ALKORAN.

alcove, al′kōv, *n.* [Fr. *alcove,* Sp. *alcoba—*Ar. *al,* the, and *kubbeh,* an alcove, a little chamber.] A wide and deep recess in a room, intended for the reception of a bed or seats, etc.; any natural recess.

aldehyde, al′dē·hīd, *n.* [*Al,* first syllable of *alcohol,* and *dehyd,* the first two of *dehydrogenatus,* deprived of hydrogen.] A transparent colorless liquid produced by the oxidation of pure alcohol; one of a class of organic compounds, derived from alcohol by the abstraction of two atoms of hydrogen, and converted into acids by the addition of one atom of oxygen.

alder, ol′dėr, *n.* [O.E. *aller* (the *d* being a more modern insertion), A. Sax. *aler, alr;* Icel. *ölr,* G. *eller;* allied to L. *alnus,* an alder.] The popular name of plants of the genus *Alnus. A. glutinosa* is the common alder, usually growing in moist land.

alderman, ol′dėr·man, *n. pl.* **aldermen,** ol′dėr·men. [A.Sax. *aldorman, ealdorman—ealdor,* an elder, from *eald,* old, and *man.*] Anciently, an Anglo-Saxon nobleman, often a governor of a shire; now a magistrate or officer of a town corporate, next in rank below the mayor.—**aldermanic,** ol·dėr·man′ik, *a.* Relating to or becoming an alderman.

Aldine, ol′dīn, *a.* Proceeding from the printing press of *Aldus* Manutius, of Venice, and his family, from 1490 to 1597.—**Aldine type**=Italic type invented by the printer for his 1501 edition of Virgil.

ale, āl, *n.* [A.Sax. *ealu,* Dan. Sw. and Icel. *öl,* ale.] A liquor made from an infusion of malt by fermentation; beer, or a kind of beer; a merry meeting in English country places, so called from the liquor drunk.—**alehouse,** *n.* A house where ale is retailed; a beer shop.—**alewife,** *n.* A woman who keeps an alehouse.

aleatory, al′ē·a·to·ri, *a.* [L. *alea,* a die, chance.] Pertaining to chance or contingency; depending on a contingency.

alee, a·lē′, *adv. Naut.* on the lee side; on the side opposite to that on which the wind strikes: opposite of *a-weather.*

alembic, a·lem′bik, *n.* [L.L. *alembicum;* Sp. *alambique—*Ar. *al,* the, *ambik,* an alembic, from Gr. *ambix,* a cup.] A chemical vessel formerly used in distillation, usually made of glass or copper.

alert, a·lėrt′, *a.* [Fr. *alerte,* alert, and (as noun) alarm or notice of danger, formerly *allerte,* and *a l'erte,* from It. *all'erta,* to the watchtower, the lookout—*erta,* fem. p.p. of L. *erigere,* erect.] Active in vigilance; watchful; vigilant; brisk; nimble.—*On* or *upon the alert,* upon the watch; on the lookout; guarding against surprise or danger.—**alertness,** a·lėrt′nes, *n.* The state or quality of being alert.

aleurone, a·lū′rōn, *n.* [Gr. *aleuron,* fine flour.] Albuminoid granules found in seeds.

alewife, āl′wif, *n.* A fish of the shad genus, caught in the Severn; also a similar N. American fish much used as food.

Alexandrian, al·egz·an′dri·an, *a.* Pertaining to *Alexandria* in Egypt, more especially ancient Alexandria.—**alexandrine,** al·egz·an′drin, *n.* A kind of verse consisting of twelve syllables in English poetry, or in French of twelve and thirteen in alternate couplets: so called from a poem written in French on the life of *Alexander the Great.*

alexipharmic, a·lek′si·farm″ik, *a.* [Gr. *alexō,* to ward off, *pharmakon,* a drug, remedy, poison.] Acting as a means of warding off disease or the effects of poison; acting as a remedy.—*n.* A remedy; an antidote.

alfalfa, alf·al·fa, *n.* [Sp.] A common name in the United States for the fodder plant lucerne.

alga, al′ga, *n.* pl. algae, al′jē, [L.] A seaweed; one of an order of cryptogamic plants found for the most part in the sea and fresh water, comprising seaweeds.—**algal,** al′gal, *n.* One of the Algae.—**algal,** al′gal, *a.* Of or pertaining to the Algae; having the nature of the Algae.—**algology,** al·gol′o·ji, *n.* The study or science of Algae.

algebra, al′je·bra, *n.* [Sp. *algebra,* from Ar. *al-jabr,* the putting together of broken things, reduction of fractions to whole numbers, from Ar. *jabara,* to bind together, to consolidate.] That branch of mathematical analysis in which signs are employed to denote arithmetical operations, and letters are used to represent numbers and quantities; a kind of universal arithmetic.—**algebraic, algebraical,** al·je·brā′ik, al·je·brā′ik·al, *a.* Pertaining to algebra; containing an operation of algebra.—**algebraically,** al·je·brā′ik·al·li, *adv.* By algebraic process.—**algebraist,** al·je·brā′ist, *n.* One versed in the science of algebra.

algid, al′jid, *a.* [L. *algidus,* cold, *algeo,* to be cold.] Cold.—*Algid cholera,* Asiatic cholera.—**algidity, algidness,** al·jid′i·ti, al′jid·nes, *n.* The state of being algid; chilliness; coldness.—**algific,** al·jif′ik, *a.* [L. *algificus.*] Producing cold.—**algor,** al′gor, *n.* [L.] An unusual coldness in the human system.—**algose,** al′gōs, *a.* [L. *algosus.*] Cold in a high degree.

algology. See ALGA.

algorithm, algorism, al′gō·rithm, al′gō·rizm, *n.* [O.F. *augorisme,* L. *algorismus,* Ar. *al-khowarazmi,* the man of Khiva, name of a mathematician; confused with Gr. *arithmos,* number.] Arabic decimal notation; the art of computing or reckoning in reference to some particular subject, or in some particular way (the *algorithm* of the differential calculus).

Alhambresque, al·am′bresk, *a.* Of or pertaining to the *Alhambra* (lit. red house), a Moorish palace near Granada in Spain; built or decorated after the fanciful manner of the Alhambra, in which arabesques are a notable feature.

alias, ā′li·as, *adv.* [L.] Otherwise; used especially of persons who assume various names (John Smith *alias* Thomas Jones).—*n.* pl. aliases, ā′li·as·ez. An assumed name; another name.

alibi, al′i·bī, *n.* [L., elsewhere.] *Law,* a plea which avers that the accused was in another place at the time of the commission of the offense, and therefore cannot be guilty.

alien, āl′yen, *a.* [L. *alienus,* alien, from *alius,* another. The same root appears in E. *else.*] Not belonging to the same country, land, or government; foreign; different in nature; estranged; adverse: with *to* or *from.* —*n.* A foreigner; one born in or belonging to another country; one

who is not a denizen, or entitled to the privileges of a citizen.—**alienability,** āl′yen·a·bil″i·ti, *n.* The state or quality of being alienable.—**alienable,** āl′yen·a·bl, *a.* Capable of being alienated, sold, or transferred to another.—**alienage,** āl′yen·āj, *n.* The state of being an alien.—**alienate,** āl′yen·āt, *v.t.*—alienated, alienating. [L. *alieno, alienatum,* to alienate.] To transfer or convey, as title, property, or other right, to another; to withdraw, as the affections; to make indifferent or averse, where love or friendship before existed; to estrange; to wean; with *from.*—**alienation,** āl·yen·ā′shon, *n.* [L. *alienatio.*] The act of alienating or the state of being alienated.—**alienator,** āl·yen·ā′tėr, *n.* One who alienates.—**alienee,** āl·yen·ē′, *n.* One to whom the title of property is transferred.— **alienism,** āl′yen·izm, *n.* The state of being an alien; the scientific study and treatment of mental alienation or insanity.—**alienist,** āl′yen·ist, *n.* One who studies or practices alienism.—**alienor,** āl′yen·or, *n.* One who transfers property.

aliferous, aligerous, a·lif′ér·us, a·lij′ér·us, *a.* [L. *ala,* wing, and *fero, gero,* to bear.] Having wings.— **aliform,** ā′li·form, *a.* [L. *ala,* wing, and *forma,* shape.] Having the shape of a wing or wings.

alight, a·līt′, *v.i.* [A.Sax. *âlihtan, gelihtan,* to alight or light. See LIGHT in this sense.] To get down or descend, as from horseback or from a carriage; to settle or lodge, as a bird on a tree; to light down.

alight, a·līt′, *a.* or *adv.* Lighted; kindled; made to burn by having a light applied.

align, a·līn′, *v.t.* [Fr. *aligner,* to align—*a,* to, and *ligne,* L. *linea,* a line.] To lay out or regulate by a line; to form in line, as troops.— **alignment,** a·līn′ment, *n.* The act of aligning; an adjusting to a line; the line of adjustment; the groundplan of a railway or other road; a row of things.

alike, a·līk′, *a.* [Prefix *a,* and *like ;* A.Sax. *gelic,* alike. LIKE.] Having resemblance or similitude; similar; without difference (always used as a predicate).—**alike,** a·līk′, *adv.* In the same manner, form, or degree; in common (all have erred *alike*).

aliment, al′i·ment, *n.* [L. *alimentum,* nourishment—*alo,* to nourish.] That which nourishes; food; nutriment.— **alimental,** al·i·ment′al, *a.* Of or pertaining to aliment.—**alimentally,** al·i·ment′al·li, *adv.* In an alimental manner.—**alimentary,** al·i·ment′a·ri, *a.* Pertaining to aliment or food.— **alimentary canal,** *n. Anat.* the canal from the mouth to the anus through which food passes; digestive tract.—**alimentation,** al′i·ment·ā″-shon, *n.* The act or power of affording nutriment; the state of being nourished.

alimony, al′i·mo·ni, *n.* [L. *alimonia.*] An allowance out of her husband's estate made for the support of a woman legally separated from him.

aliped, al′i·ped, *a.* [L. *ala,* wing, and

pes, pedis, a foot.] Wing-footed; having the toes connected by a membrane, which serves as a wing, as the bats.—*n.* An animal whose toes are so connected.

aliquant, al′i·kwant, *a.* [L. *aliquantum,* somewhat.] *Arith.* applied to a number which does not measure another without a remainder.—**aliquot,** al′i·kwot, *a.* [L. *aliquot,* some, several.] *Arith.* applied to a part of a number or quantity which will measure it without a remainder.

alive, a·līv′, *a.* [Prefix *a* for *on,* and *life ;* in old English it was written *on live, on lyve,* where *live, lyve* is a dat. form of *life.*] Having life; living; not dead; in a state of action; in force or operation (keep an agitation *alive*); full of alacrity; sprightly (*alive* with excitement); easily impressed; sensitive to; susceptible (*alive* to the beauties of nature); used always after its noun.

alizarin, al′i·za·rin, *n.* [Fr. *alizarine,* from *alizari,* an Eastern name of madder, from the (Ar.) root of *azure,* with the article prefixed.] A red coloring matter obtained from madder, but made for commercial purposes from coal-tar products, and now largely used instead of madder.

alkahest, al′ka·hest, *n.* [Etym. unknown.] The pretended universal solvent or menstruum of the alchemists.

alkali, al′ka·lī, *n.* pl. alkalies, or alkalis, al′ka·līz. [Sp. *alcali,* Ar. *al-qali,* the plant from which soda was first obtained.] A term applied to an important class of bases which combine with acids to form salts, turn vegetable yellows to red and vegetable blues to green, and unite with oil or fat to form soap. The proper alkalies are hydroxide of potassium (potash), hydroxide of sodium (soda), hydroxide of lithium (lithia), and hydroxide of ammonium (an aqueous solution of ammonia).— **alkalescent,** al·ka·les′ent, *a.* Tending to the properties of an alkali; slightly alkaline. — **alkalescence, alkalescency,** al·ka·les′ens, al·ka·les′en·si, *n.* A tendency to become alkaline.—**alkalifiable,** al′ka·li·fī·a·bl or al·kal′i·fī·a·bl, *a.* Capable of being alkalified. —**alkalify,** al′ka·li·fī or al·kal′i·fī, *v.t.*—alkalified, alkalifying; **alkalize,** al′ka·līz, *v.t.*—alkalized, alkalizing. To form or to convert into an alkali; to make alkaline.—*v.i.* To become an alkali.—**alkalimeter,** al·ka·lim′-et·ér, *n.* An instrument for ascertaining the strength of alkalies.— **alkalimetry,** al·ka·lim′et·ri, *n.* The finding of the amount of real alkali in an alkaline mixture or liquid.— **alkaline,** al′ka·līn, *a.* Having the properties of an alkali.—**alkaline earths,** oxides of barium, strontium, calcium, and sometimes magnesium. —**alkalinity,** al·ka·lin′i·ti, *n.* The state of being alkaline; the quality which constitutes an alkali.—**alkalization,** al′ka·liz·ā″shon, *n.* The act or process of rendering alkaline.— **alkaloid,** al′ka·loid, *n.* A term applied to a class of nitrogenized compounds found in living plants, and con-

fāte, fär, fâre, fat, fạll; mē, met, hėr; pīne, pin; nōte, not, möve; tūbe, tub, bụll; oil, pound.

taining their active principles, such as *morphine, quinine, aconitine, caffeine*, etc.—*a.* Relating to or containing alkali.

alkanet, al′ka·net, *n.* [Sp. *alcaneta*, dim. of *alcana, alcanna*, from Ar. *al-hinna*, henna.] A plant, *Alkanna* (*Anchusa tinctoria*) whose root yields a red dye.

Alkoran, al·kō·ran′ or al′kō·ran, *n.* [Ar.—*al*, the, *qurân*, book.] The book which contains the religious and moral code of the Mohammedans, and by which indeed all their transactions, civil, legal, military, etc., are regulated; the Koran.

all, al, *a.* [A.Sax. *eal* (sing.), *ealle* (pl.); Icel. *allr*, Goth. *alls*, G. *all*, all. Common to all the Teutonic tongues; also in Celtic.] Every one of; the whole number or quantity of. It goes before an article or adj. belonging to the same noun: *all the* men, *all good* men, *all my* labor, etc. With nouns of time it is equivalent to during the whole (*all day, all* night).—*adv.* Wholly; completely; entirely; altogether; quite (*all* alone, *all* unarmed).—*All but*, nearly; almost; not quite.—*All one*, the same thing in effect; quite the same.—*n.* The whole number; the entire thing; the aggregate; the total.—*At all*, in the least degree; to the least extent; under any circumstances.—*In all*, everything reckoned or taken into account; all included.—*All*, in composition, has often the force of an adverb; as in *almighty, all-powerful, all-perfect, all-important;* sometimes of a noun in the objective case; as, *all-seeing.*—**All Fools' Day.** The first day of April.—**all fours.** A game of cards, so called from the four chances of which it consists, for each of which a point is scored.—**On all fours**, on four legs, or on two legs and two arms or hands; hence, fig. even or evenly; as a parallel case.—**all hail,** *exclam.* and *n.* All health: a phrase of salutation.—**Allhallows,** *n.* All Saints' Day.—**Allhallowmas, Allhallowtide,** *n.* The time near All Saints or November 1.—**allheal,** *n.* A plant, cat's or common wild valerian, so called from its medicinal virtues.—**All Saints' Day.** A church festival held on November 1; Hallowmas.—**All Souls' Day.** A church festival held on November 2, when prayers are offered up for the dead.—**allspice,** *n.* A spice of a mildly pungent taste, the fruit of a West Indian tree, so called from being regarded as combining many different flavors; pimento.

Allah, al′la, *n.* The Arabic name of the Supreme Being.

allantois, al·lan′tois, *n.* [Gr. *allas, allantos*, a sausage, and *eidos*, form.] A sac developed from the posterior end of the abdominal cavity in vertebrate embryos.—**allantoic,** al·lan·tō′ik, al·lan·toid′al, *a.* Pertaining to or contained in the allantois.

allay, al·lā′, *v.t.* [A.Sax. *âlecgan*, to lay down, suppress, tranquilize, from prefix *â*, and *lecgan*, to lay. LAY.] To make quiet; to pacify or appease (a tumult); to abate, mitigate, or

subdue; to relieve or alleviate (grief, thirst).—*v.i.* To subside; to grow calm.—**allayer,** al·lā′ẽr, *n.* One who or that which allays.

allege, al·lej′, *v.t.*—*alleged, alleging.* [O.Fr. *esligier*, L.L. *exlitigare*, to clear at law (confused with L.L. *allegare*).] To assert; to pronounce with positiveness; to declare; to affirm; to assert; to produce as an argument, plea, or excuse; cite; quote; bring forward.—**allegation,** al·lē·gā′shon, *n.*—**alleged,** al·lej′id, *a.*—**allegedly,** al·lej′id·li, *adv.*

allegiance, al·lē′jans, *n.* [Prefix *a*, to, and O.Fr. *ligence*, allegiance, loyalty, from *lige*, loyal. LIEGE.] The tie or obligation of a subject to his sovereign or government; the duty of fidelity to a king, government, or state.

allegory, al′lē·go·ri, *n.* [Gr. *allegoria*—*allos*, other, and *agoreuō*, to speak, from *agora*, a forum, an oration.] A figurative discourse, in which the principal subject is described by another subject resembling it in its properties and circumstances; a narrative in which abstract ideas are personified; a continued metaphor.—**allegoric, allegorical,** al·lē·gor′ik, al·lē·gor′ik·al, *a.* Pertaining to allegory; in the manner of allegory.—**allegorically,** al·lē·gor′ik·al·li, *adv.* In an allegorical manner; by way of allegory.—**allegorist, allegorizer,** al′lē·go·rist, al′lē·go·rīz·ẽr, *n.* One who allegorizes; a writer of allegory.—**allegorize,** al′lē·go·rīz, *v.t.*—*allegorized, allegorizing.* To turn into allegory; to narrate in allegory; to explain in an allegorical sense.—*v.i.* To use allegory.—**allegorization,** al′lē·gor·i·zā″shon, *n.* The act of turning into allegory.

allegro, äl·lā′grō, *a.* and *n.* [It., merry, cheerful.] *Music*, a word denoting a brisk movement; a sprightly part or strain.—**allegretto,** äl·lē·gret′to. Time quicker than *andante*, but not so quick as *allegro.*

alleluia, al·lā·lū′ya, *n.* and *interj.* [Heb. *halelûyâh*, praise to Jah—*halal*, to praise, and *Yâh*, Jehovah.] Praise Jehovah; a word used to denote pious joy and exultation, chiefly in hymns and anthems. Written also *hallelujah.*

allergen, al′ẽr·jin, *n.* [Gr. *allos*, other, *ergon*, work, and *gen*, to produce.] Any substance that induces allergy.

allergy, al′ẽr·ji, *n.* [Gr. *allos* other and *ergon* work.] Excess sensitiveness to certain substances, as food, pollen, drugs, or heat or cold, which are harmless to most persons. Common allergies are hay fever, hives, and asthma.—**allergic,** al·ẽr′jik, *a.*

alleviate, al·lē′vi·āt, *v.t.*—*alleviated, alleviating.* [L.L. *alleviare, alleviatus*, L. *allevare, allevatus*—*ad*, to, and *levo*, to ease, from *levis*, light. LEVITY.] To make light, in a figurative sense; to lessen, mitigate, or make easier to be endured (sorrow, pain, distress).—**alleviation,** al·lē′vi·ā″shon, *n.* The act of alleviating: that which lessens, mitigates, or makes more tolerable.—**alleviative,** al·lē′vi·āt·iv, *a.* Tending to alleviate;

mitigative.—*n.* That which alleviates or mitigates.—**alleviator,** al·lē′vi·āt·ẽr, *n.* One who or that which alleviates.

alley, al′li, *n.* [Fr. *allée*, from *aller*, to go, from O.Fr. *aner*, from L. *adnare*, lit. to swim to—*ad*, to, and *nare*, to swim.] A passage; especially, a narrow passage or way in a town.

alliaceous, al·li·ā′shus, *a.* [L. *allium*, garlic.] Pertaining to garlic and allied plants; having the properties of garlic.

alliance. See ALLY.

alligator, al′li·gā·tẽr, *n.* [A corruption of Sp. *el lagarto*, lit. the lizard—*el*, the, and *lagarto*, a lizard, from L. *lacertus*, whence E. *lizard*.] A large reptile of the crocodile family found in tropical America. The alligators differ from the true crocodiles in having a shorter and flatter head, in having cavities or pits in the upper jaw, into which the long canine teeth of the under jaw fit, and in having the feet much less webbed.

alliteration, al·lit·ẽr·ā′shon, *n.* [L. *al* for *ad*, to, and *litera*, a letter.] The repetition of the same letter at the beginning of two or more words immediately succeeding each other, or at short intervals (as in 'apt *alliteration*'s artful aid').—**alliterative,** al·lit′ẽr·āt·iv, *a.* Pertaining to or consisting in alliteration; characterized by alliteration.—**alliterativeness,** al·lit′ẽr·āt·iv·nes, *n.* Quality of being alliterative.

allocate, al′lō·kāt, *v.t.*—*allocated, allocating.* [L. *ad*, to, and *loco, locatum*, to place, from *locus*, a place.] To assign or allot to a person or persons; to set apart for a particular purpose; to apportion or distribute (shares in a public company or the like).—**allocation,** al·lō·kā′shon, *n.* The act of allocating, alloting, or assigning; allotment; assignment; apportionment.

allocution, al·lō·kū′shon, *n.* [L. *allocutio*—*ad*, to, and *loquor*, to speak.] A speaking to; an address, especially a formal address.

allodium, al·lō′di·um, *n.* [L.L. *allodium*, of Ger. or Scand. origin *allod*, all, *od*, estate. UDAL. Comp. Icel. *odal*, Dan. and Sw. *odel*, a patrimonial estate.] Freehold estate; real estate held in absolute independence, without being subject to any rent, service, or acknowledgment to a superior.—**allodial,** al·lō′di·al, *a.* Pertaining to allodium or freehold; held independent of a lord paramount: opposed to *feudal.*

allomorphism, al·lō·mar′fizm, *n.* [Gr. *allos*, other, and *morphē*, form.] That property of certain substances of assuming a different form, the substance remaining otherwise unchanged.—**allomorphic,** al·lō·mar′fik, *a.* Pertaining to, or possessing the qualities of allomorphism.

allopathy, al·lop′a·thi, *n.* [Gr. *allos*, other, and *pathos*, morbid condition.] That method of treating disease by which it is endeavored to produce a condition of the system either different from, opposite to, or incompatible with the condition essential to the disease: it is opposed to *homeopathy*, and is the common method of treatment.—**allopathic,** al·lo·path′ik, *a.* Pertaining to allopathy.—**allopathically,** al·lo·path′-ik·al·li, *adv.* In a manner conformable to allopathy.—**allopathist,** al·lop′a·thist, *n.* One who practices allopathy.

allophane, al′lō·fān, *n.* [Gr. *allos,* other, and *phainō,* to appear.] A mineral of a pale blue, or sometimes of a green or brown color.

allot, al·lot′, *v.t.*—*allotted, allotting.* O.Fr. *allotir, alloter,* to divide, part—*al* for *ad,* to, and *lotir,* to cast lots for, from *lot,* a share, which itself is a Teutonic word=A. Sax. *hlot.* LOT.] To distribute or parcel out in parts or portions; to assign; to set apart; to destine.—**allotment,** al·lot′ment, *n.* The act of allotting; that which is allotted; a share, part, or portion granted or distributed; a place or piece of ground appropriated.—*Allotment-system,* the system of allotting small portions of land to farm laborers or others, to be cultivated, after regular work, by themselves and families.—**allottee,** al·lot′tē, *n.* One to whom anything is allotted.

allotropy, allotropism, al·lot′ro·pi, al·lot′ro·pizm, *n.* [Gr. *allos,* another, and *tropos,* condition.] The capability exhibited by some substances of existing in more than one form, and with different characteristics (thus carbon forms both the diamond and charcoal).—**allotropic,** al·lō-trop′ik, *a.* Of or pertaining to allotropy.

allow, al·lou′, *v.t.* [Fr. *allouer,* to grant, settle, L.L. *allocare—ad,* to, and *locare,* to place. (ALLOCATE.) O.Fr. *allouer,* to approve or praise, from L. *ad,* and *laudare,* to praise, from *laus, laudis,* praise, has also influenced the meaning.] To grant, give, or make over; to assign (to *allow* him $300 a year); to admit; to own or acknowledge (*allow* a claim); to abate or deduct; to set apart (*allow* so much for loss); to grant permission to; to permit.—*v.i.* To concede; to make abatement or concession.—**allowable,** al·lou′-a·bl, *a.* Proper to be or capable of being allowed or permitted; not forbidden; permissible.—**allowably,** al·lou′a·bli, *adv.* In an allowable manner; with propriety.—**allowance,** al·lou′ans, *n.* Permission; license; sanction; a quantity allowed or granted; relaxation of severity in censure; a deduction or abatement.—**allowance,** al·lou′ans, *v.t.* To put upon allowance.—**allowedly,**† al·-lou′ed·li, *adv.* Admittedly.

alloy, al·loi′, *n.* [Originally *allay,* O.F. *aley,* L. *alligare,* bind, with confusion of Fr. *aloi,* legal standard of coin, *a,* according, and *loi,* law.] A baser metal mixed with a finer; a mixture of different metals; any metallic compound; *fig.* evil mixed with good.—**alloy,** al·loi′, *v.t.* To reduce the purity of (a metal) by

mixing with it a portion of less valuable metal; to reduce, abate, or impair by mixture.

allspice, al′spīs, *n.* See ALL.

allude, al·lūd′, *v.i.*—*alluded, alluding,* [L. *alludo,* to play upon, to allude—*ad,* and *ludo,* to play.] To refer to something not directly mentioned; to hint at by remote suggestions (followed by *to*). Syn. under ADVERT.—**allusion,** al·lū′zhon, *n.* The act of alluding; a reference to something not explicitly mentioned; an indirect or incidental suggestion; a hint.—**allusive,** al·lū′siv, *a.* Having allusion or reference to something not fully expressed; containing allusions.—**allusively,** al·lū′-siv·li, *adv.* In an allusive manner; by way of allusion.—**allusiveness,** al·lū′siv·nes, *n.*

allure, al·lūr′, *v.t.*—*allured, alluring.* [Prefix *al* for *ad,* to, and *lure,* Fr. *leurrer,* to decoy. LURE.] To tempt by the offer of some good, real or apparent; to draw or try to draw by some proposed pleasure or advantage; to entice, decoy, tempt, attract.—**allurement,** al·lūr′ment, *n.* The act of alluring, or that which allures.—**allurer,** al·lūr′ėr, *n.* One who, or that which, allures.—**alluring,** al·lūr′ing, *a.* Inviting; having the quality of attracting or tempting.—**alluringly,** al·lūr′ing·li, *adv.* In an alluring manner; enticingly.

alluvium, al·lū′vi·um, *n.* [L. *alluvius,* alluvial—*ad,* to, and *luo*=Gr. *louō,* L. *lavo,* to wash; akin *deluge, lotion, dilute,* etc.] Soil deposited by means of the action of water, often washed down from mountains or high grounds.—**alluvial,** al·lū′vi·al, *a.* Pertaining to or having the character of alluvium; deposited by the action of waves or currents of water.

ally, al·lī′, *v.t.*—*allied, allying.* [Fr. *allier,* to join, to unite, *s'allier,* to confederate or become allied—*al* for *ad,* to, and *lier,* to tie or unite; L. *ligare,* to bind, whence *league, ligament.*] To unite by marriage, treaty, league, or confederacy; to connect by formal agreement; to bind together or connect (as by friendship or pursuits).—*v.i.* To be closely united.—*n.* A prince or state united by treaty or league; a confederate.—**alliance,** al·lī′ans, *n.* [O.Fr. *alliance.*] The state of being allied or connected; the relation or union between families, contracted by marriage; a union between nations, contracted by compact, treaty, or league; any union or connection of interests; a compact or treaty; the persons or parties allied.

almagest, al′ma·jest, *n.* [Ar. *al,* the, Gr. *megistē,* greatest.] The great astronomical and geographical compilation of Ptolemy; great books on astrology and kindred arts.

Alma Mater, al′ma mā′tėr. [L., benign mother, fostering mother.] An epithet applied by students to the university where they have been trained.

almanac, al′ma·nak, *n.* [Fr. *almanach.*

Sp. *almanaque,* Ar. *al-manakh,* probably from a root meaning to reckon; Heb. *manah.*] A table, book, or publication of some kind, generally annual, comprising a calendar of days, weeks, and months, with the times of the rising of the sun and moon, changes of the moon, eclipses, stated festivals of churches, etc., for a certain year or years.

almandine, al′man·dīn, *n.* [Fr. *almandine,* L.L. *alamandina, alavandina, alabandina,* a gem brought from *Alabanda,* a city in Asia Minor.] A name given to the violet or violet-red varieties of the spinel ruby, and also to precious or noble garnet.

alme, almeh, al′mē, *n.* The name given in some parts of the East, and especially in Egypt, to singing and dancing girls.

almighty, al·mī′ti, *a.* [All and *mighty.*] Possessing all power; omnipotent; being of unlimited might.—*The Almighty,* the omnipotent God.—**almightily,**† al·mī′ti·li, *adv.* In an almighty manner; with almighty power.—**almightiness,** al·mī′ti·nes, *n.* The quality of being almighty; omnipotence.

almond, ä′mund, *n.* [O. Fr. *almandre,* Fr. *amande,* It. *amandola,* corrupted from L. *amygdala,* Gr. *amygdale,* an almond.] The seed or kernel of a tree allied to the peach; the tree itself. There are two varieties, *sweet* and *bitter.* The name is also given to the seeds of some other species of plants; also to a tonsil or gland of the throat.

almoner,† al′mon·ėr, *n.* [O.Fr. *almosnier,* L.L. *eleemosynarius,* from Gr. *eleēmosynē*=E. *alms.*] A dispenser of alms or charity; more especially an officer who directs or carries out the distribution of charitable doles in connection with religious communities, hospitals, or almshouses, or on behalf of some superior.—**almonry,** al′mon·ri, *n.* The place where an almoner resides, or where alms are distributed.

almost, al′mōst, *adv.* [All and *most.*] Nearly; well nigh; for the greatest part.

alms, ämz, *n.* [O.E. *almesse, almes,* A. Sax, *almes, aelmesse,* borrowed from L. *eleemosyna,* alms, from Gr. *eleēmosynē,* pity.] Anything given gratuitously to relieve the poor; a charitable dole; charity. [This word (like *riches*) is strictly a singular, but its form has caused it to be often regarded as grammatically plural.]—**almsgiver,** *n.* One who gives alms.—**almsgiving,** *n.* The act of giving alms.—**almsman,** *n.* A person supported by charity or by public provision.

aloe, al′ō, *n.* [Gr. *aloē.*] The common name of the plants of the genus *Aloe,* of the same order as the lily. They are natives of warm climates, and especially abundant in Africa. Several species yield *aloes,* the well-known bitter purgative medicine.—**aloetic,** al·ō·et′ik, *a.* Pertaining to or obtained from the aloe or aloes; partaking of the qualities or containing the properties of aloes.

---

fāte, fär, fâre, fat, fạll; mē, met, hėr; pīne, pin; nōte, not, mōve; tūbe, tub, bụll; oil, pound.

aloft, a·loft′, adv. [Icel. à lopt (pron. loft). LOFT.] On high; in the air; high above the ground; naut. on the higher yards or rigging.

alone, a·lōn′, a, or adv. [All and one—the all and one being formerly printed as separate words; G. allein, Dan. allene, D. alleen, alone, are formed in the same way.] Apart from another or others; single; solitary (to remain alone, to walk alone); only; to the exclusion of other persons or things; solely (he alone remained, two men alone returned). Rarely used before a noun, as one alone verse.—To let alone, to leave untouched or not meddled with.

along, a·long′, adv. [A.Sax, andlang, anlong—prefix and, an (in answer), and lang, long.] By the length; lengthwise; in a line with the length (stretched along); in a line or with a progressive motion; onward (to walk along); in company; together (followed by with).—prep. By the length of, as distinguished from across; in a longitudinal direction over or near.—**alongshore,** along′-shōr, adv. By the shore or coast; lengthwise and near the shore.—**alongside,** a·long′sīd, adv. Along or by the side; beside each other (to lie alongside or alongside of).—prep. Beside; by the side of.

aloof, a·lōf′, adv. (O.E. a·lofe—prefix a, on, and loof or luff, windward.] At a distance, but within view; apart; separated.

alopecia, al′o·pe″shi·a, n. [L. alopecia, Gr. alòpekia, from alòpex, a fox, because foxes are said to be subject to this disease.] Loss of hair; baldness.

aloud, a·loud′, adv. With a loud voice or great noise; loudly.

alow, a·lō′, adv. In a low place, or a lower part; opposed to aloft.

alp, alp, n. [From the Alps, well-known mountains in Central Europe.] A high mountain.—**alpenhorn,** al′pen·horn, n. [G. Alpen, the Alps, and horn, a horn.] A very long, powerful, nearly straight horn, but curving slightly and widening towards its extremity, used on the Alps to convey signals. Called also Alphorn.—**alpenstock,** al′pen·stok, n. [G. Alpen, the Alps, and stock, a stick.] A strong tall stick shod with iron, pointed at the end, used in climbing the Alps and other high mountains.—**Alpine,** al′pīn, a. Of, pertaining to, or connected with the Alps, or any lofty mountain; mountainous. [not cap.]

alpaca, al·pak′a, n. [Peruv. alpaco.] A ruminant mammal, of the camel tribe, a native of the Andes, valued for its long, soft, and silky wool, which is woven into fabrics of great beauty: a fabric manufactured from the wool of the alpaca.

alpha, al′fa, n. The first letter in the Greek alphabet, answering to A, sometimes used to denote what is first or a beginning.—Alpha and Omega. The first and last letters of the Greek alphabet; the beginning and the end.—**alphabet,** al′fa·bet, n.

[Gr. alpha and beta, A and B.] The letters of a language arranged in the customary order; any series of elementary signs or symbols used for a similar purpose; hence, first elements; simplest rudiments.—**alphabetic, alphabetical,** al·fa·bet′ik, al·fa·bet′ik-al, a. Pertaining to an alphabet; furnished with an alphabet; expressed by an alphabet; in the order of an alphabet.—**alphabetically,** al·fa·bet′ik·al·li, adv. In an alphabetical manner; in the customary order of the letters.—**alphabetize,** al′fa·bet·īz, v.t. To arrange alphabetically.—**alpha particle,** Phys. a positively charged particle composed of two protons and two neutrons and therefore the equivalent of the nucleus of a helium atom.

already, al·red′i, adv. [All and ready.] Before the present time; before some specified time.

Alsatian, al·sā′shon, a. Of or pertaining to Alsace in France.—n. A native of Alsatia.

also, al′so, adv. and conj. [All and so; A.Sax. eall-swâ, ealswâ, alswâ, from eall, eal, all, quite, and swâ, so. As is this word contracted.] In like manner; likewise; in addition; too; further.

Altaic, Altaian, al·tā′ik, al·tā′yan, a. Pertaining to the Altai, a vast range of mountains in Eastern Asia.—Altaic or Altaian family of languages, a family of languages which includes Hungarian, Finnish, Turkish, etc. Also called Scythian and Turanian.

altar, al′ter, n. [L. altare, from a root seen in L. altus, high.] An elevated place on which sacrifices were offered or incense burned to a deity; a table in a church for the celebration of the eucharist.—**altarpiece,** n. A painting or piece of sculpture placed behind or above an altar in a church.

altazimuth, alt·az′i·muth, n. [From altitude and azimuth.] An astronomical instrument for determining the altitude and azimuth of heavenly bodies, consisting of a vertical circle and attached telescope, the two having both a vertical and a horizontal motion.

alter, al′ter, v.t. [L.L. altero, to change, from L. alter, another of two—root al, another (seen in alius, Gr. allos, another, E. else), and compar. suffix -ter=E. -ther in other, etc.] To make other or different; to make some change in; to vary in some degree, without an entire change;—v.i. To become, in some respects, different; to vary; to change.—**alterability,** al′ter·a·bil′i·ti, n. The quality of being susceptible of alteration.—**alterable,** al′ter·a·bl, a. Capable of being altered, varied, or made different.—**alterableness,** al′ter·a·bl·nes, n. The quality of being alterable.—**alterably,** al′ter·a·bli, adv. In an alterable manner; so as to be altered or varied.—**alteration,** al′ter·ā′shon, n. The act of altering; the state of being altered; also, the change made.—**alterative,** al′ter·āt·iv, a. Causing alteration; having the power

to alter; med. having the power to restore healthy functions of the body without sensible evacuations.—n. A medicine having this character.

altercate, al′ter·kāt, v.i. [L. altercor, altercatus, to wrangle, from alter, another. ALTER.] To contend in words; to wrangle.—**altercation,** al·ter·kā′shon, n. The act of altercating; warm contention in words; heated argument; a wrangle.

altern,† al′tern, a. [L. alternus, from alter, another. ALTER.] Acting by turns; alternate. [Mil.]—**alternate,** al·ter′nāt, a. [L. alternatus, pp. of alterno, to do by turns.] Being by turns; following one another in time or place by turns; first one, then another successively; reciprocal; having one intervening between each pair; occupying every second place; consisting of parts or members proceeding in this way (an alternate series).—Alternate generation, that species of generation among animals by which the young do not resemble their parent, but their grandparent or some more ancestor; heterogenesis.—**alternate,** al′ter·nāt or al·ter′nāt, v. t.—**alternated, alternating.** To perform by turns or in succession; to cause to succeed or follow by turns.—v.i. To follow one another in time or place by turns.—**alternating current,** Elect. a current that reverses direction in cycles.—**alternately,** al·ter′nāt·li, adv. In an alternate manner.—**alternation,** al·ter·nā′shon, n. The act of alternating, or state of being alternate; the act of following and being followed in turn.—**alternative,** al·ter′na·tiv, a. Offering a choice or possibility of one of two things.—n. A choice between two things, so that if one is taken the other must be left; a possibility of one of two things, so that if one thing is false the other must be true.—**alternatively,** al·ter′na·tiv·li, adv. In an alternative manner.—**alternativeness,** al·ter′na·tiv·nes, n.

although, al·THō′, conj. [All, if, even, and though; comp. albeit.] Grant all this; be it so; suppose that; admit all that. Although differs very little from though, but is perhaps rather stronger.

altimeter, al·tim′et·er, n. [L. altus, high, and Gr. metron, measure.] An instrument for taking altitudes by geometrical principles, as a quadrant.—**altimetry,** al·tim′et·ri, n. The art of ascertaining altitudes.

altitude, al′ti·tūd, n. [L. altitudo, from altus, high (whence exalt, haughty).] Height; amount of space to a point above from one below; measure of elevation; pl. haughty airs (colloq.).

alto, al′tō or äl′tō, n. [It., from L. altus, high, being above the tenor.] Mus. contralto; the deepest voice among women and boys, and the highest among men, a special voice above the tenor; a singer in this voice.—a. Pertaining to this voice.—**altorilievo,** äl′tō·rē·lyä″vo, n. High relief; sculpture in which the figures stand out prominently from the background; sculpture in high relief.

altogether, al·tu·geTH′ĕr, *adv.* [*All*, quite, and *together*.] Wholly; entirely; completely; quite.

altruism, al′trö·izm, *n.* [It. *altrui*, others, from L. *alter*, another.] Devotion to others or to humanity: the opposite of *selfishness*.—**altruist,** al′trö·ist. *n.* One who practices altruism.—**altruistic,** al·trö·ist′ik, *a.* Pertaining to altruism.

alum, al′um, *n.* [L. *alumen*.] A general name for a class of double sulfates containing aluminum and such metals as potassium, ammonium, iron, etc. Common or potash alum is used medicinally as an astringent and a styptic; in dyeing, as a mordant; in tanning, for restoring the cohesion of skins.—*v.t.* To steep in or impregnate with a solution of alum.—**alumina,** al·ū′min·a, *n.* The oxide of aluminum, the most abundant of the earths, widely diffused in the shape of clay, loam, etc.—**aluminiferous,** al·ū′min·if″ĕr·us, *a.* Containing alum or alumina.—**aluminum,** al·ū′min·um, *n.* Chemical sym. Al; sp. gr., 2.7; at. no., 13; at. wt., 26.98. The metallic base of alumina; a white metal with a bluish tinge, and a luster somewhat resembling, but far inferior to, that of silver.—*Aluminum bronze*, an alloy of aluminum and copper, possessed of great tenacity, for industrial purposes.—*Aluminum gold*, an alloy of 10 parts of aluminum to 90 of copper.—**aluminous,** al·ū′min·us, *a.* Pertaining to or containing alum or alumina.—**alumroot,** *n.* A name given to the astringent root of several plants.

alumnus, a·lum′nus, *n.* pl. **alumni,** a·lum′nī. [L., a disciple, from *alo*, to nourish.] Formerly a pupil; now a graduate of an educational institution.—**alumna,** a·lum′na, *n.* Feminine for alumnus.

alveary, al′vē·a·ri, *n.* [L. *alvearium*, a bee-hive.] A beehive, or something resembling a beehive; the hollow of the external ear.—**alveolar,** al′vē·o·lĕr, *a.* Containing sockets, hollow cells, or pits; pertaining to sockets, specifically the sockets of the teeth.—**alveolate,** al′vē·o·lāt, *a.* Deeply pitted, so as to resemble a honeycomb.—**alveolus,** al′vē·o·lus, *n.* pl. **alveoli,** al·vē′o·lī. [L., a little hollow, dim. of *alveus*.] A cell, as in a honeycomb or in a fossil; the socket of a tooth.

alvine, al′vīn, *a.* [From L. *alvus*, the belly.] Belonging to the belly or intestines; relating to the intestinal excrements.

always, al′wāz, *adv.* [*All* and *way*, *-ways* being an adverbial genitive.] Perpetually; uninterruptedly; continually (*always* the same); as often as occasion recurs (he is *always* late).

am, am. [For hypothetical *arm*, *asm*; comp. Goth. *im* for *ism*, Icel. *em* for *erm*, *esm*, Lith. *esmi*, L. *sum*, Skr. *asmi*, made up of root *as*, to breathe, exist, be, and *mi*, cognate with E. *me*. In the conjugation of this verb three different roots are employed; seen in *am*, *was*, *be*. BE, WAS.] The first person of the verb *to be*, in the indicative mood, present tense.

amadavat, am·a·da·vat′, *n.* [East Indian name.] A small granivorous bird of India, having a red conical beak and red and black plumage, often imported as a cage bird.

amadou, am′a·dö, *n.* [Fr. *amadou*, a word of Scandinavian origin.] A soft leathery substance used for tinder, prepared from a fungus growing on trees; German tinder.

amain, a·mān′, *adv.* [Prefix *a*, in, on, and *main*, force.] With force, strength, or violence; suddenly; at once.

amalgam, a·mal′gam, *n.* [Fr. *amalgame*, Gr. *malagma*, a soft mass.] A compound of mercury or quicksilver with another metal; any metallic alloy of which mercury forms an essential constituent part; a mixture or compound of different things.—**amalgamate,** a·mal′gam·āt, *v.t.*—*amalgamated, amalgamating.* To compound or mix (a metal) with quicksilver; commonly, to blend, unite, or combine generally into one mass or whole.—*v.i.* To combine to form an amalgam; to unite or coalesce generally; to become mixed or blended together.—**amalgamation,** a·mal′ga·mā″shon, *n.* The act or operation of amalgamating; the state of being amalgamated; union or junction into one body or whole; the process of separating gold and silver from their ores by combining them with mercury, which dissolves and separates the other metal, and is afterward driven off by heat.

amanuensis, a·man′ū·en″sis, *n.* pl. **amanuenses,** a·man′ū·en″sēz. [L. *a*, by, and *manus*, the hand.] A person whose employment is to write what another dictates, or to copy what has been written by another.

amaranth, am′a·ranth, *n.* [Gr. *amarantos*, unfading—*a*, not, and *marainō*, to wither.] A poetical name loosely used to signify a flower supposed never to fade; a color inclining to purple.—**amaranthine,** am·a·ranth′in, *a.* Belonging to, consisting of, or resembling amaranth; never fading; of a purplish color.

Amaryllis, am·a·ril′lis, *n.* [Greek female name.] A genus of bulbous-rooted plants with fine flowers. Some of them, called lilies, form the type of a natural family of plants, the Amaryllidaceae.

amass, a·mas′, *v.t.* [Fr. *amasser—a*, to, and *masse*, L. *massa*, a mass.] To collect into a heap; to gather a great quantity or number of; to accumulate.—**amassment,** a·mas′ment, *n.* The act of amassing.

amateur, am′a·tūr, am·a·tĕr (ê long), *n.* [Fr., from L. *amator*, *amatoris*; a lover, from *amo*, to love.] One who cultivates any study or art from taste or attachment without pursuing it professionally or with a view to gain; one who has a taste for the arts.—**amateurish,** am·a·tūr′ish, *a.* Pertaining to or characteristic of an amateur; wanting the skill, finish, or other faculties of a professional.

amative, am′at·iv, *a.* [L. *amo*, *amatum*, to love.] Full of love; amorous; amatory.—**amativeness,** am′at·iv·nes, *n. Phren.* that propensity which impels to sexual passion.—**amatorial,**† am·a·tō′ri·al, *a.* Pertaining to love; amatory.—**amatory,** am′a·to·ri, *a.* Pertaining to or producing love; expressive of love (verses, sighs, etc.).

amaurosis, am·a·rō′sis, *n.* [Gr. *amaurōsis*, from *amauros*, obscure.] A partial or complete loss of sight from loss of power in the optic nerve or retina, without any visible defect in the eye except an immovable pupil.—**amaurotic,** a·ma·rot′ik, *a.* Pertaining to or affected with amaurosis.

amaze, a·māz′, *v.t.* [Prefix *a*, on or in, and *maze* (which see),] To confound with fear, sudden surprise, or wonder; to confuse utterly; to perplex; to astound; to astonish; to surprise.—*n.* Astonishment; confusion; amazement: used chiefly in poetry.—**amazedly,** a·māz′ed·li, *adv.* With amazement.—**amazedness,** a·māz′ed·nes, *n.* The state of being amazed; amazement.—**amazement,** a·māz′ment, *n.* The state of being amazed or astounded; astonishment; great surprise.—**amazing,** a·māz′ing, *a.* Very wonderful; exciting astonishment.—**amazingly,** a·māz′ing·li, *adv.* In an amazing manner or degree.

Amazon, am′a·zon, *n.* [Gr. *amazōn*: of unknown origin.] One of a fabled race of female warriors who are mentioned by the ancient Greek writers; hence, a warlike or masculine woman; a virago.—**Amazonian,** am·a·zō′ni·an, *a.* Pertaining to or resembling an Amazon; of masculine manners; also, belonging to the river Amazon in South America.

ambages,† am·bā′jēz, *n. pl.* [L.] Windings or turnings; hence, circumlocution; subterfuges; evasions.—**ambagious,**† am·bā′jus, *a.* Circumlocutory; roundabout.

ambassador, am·bas′sa·dor, *n.* [Fr. *ambassadeur*, from *ambassade*, an embassy, from L. *ambactus*, a vassal, a dependent, from a Teutonic word = Goth. *andbathts*, A.Sax. *ambiht*, *ambeht*, a servant, from prefix *and* (the *an* in *an*swer), and a root allied to Skr. *bhaj*, to serve or honor.] A minister of the highest rank employed by one prince or state at the court of another to transact state affairs. [The spelling *Embassador* is obsolete, though *Embassy*, not *Ambassy* is used.]—**ambassadorial,** am·bas′sa·dō″ri·al, *a.* Belonging to an ambassador.—**ambassadress,** am·bas′sa·dres, *n.* The wife of an ambassador; a female ambassador.

amber, am′bĕr, *n.* [Fr. *ambre*, It. *ambra*, Sp. *ambar*, from Ar. *ambar*, ambergris, from its resemblance to this.] A mineralized pale-yellow, and sometimes reddish or brownish, resin of extinct pine trees, found most abundantly on the shores of the Baltic. *a.* Of or like amber.

---

fāte, fär, fâre, fat, fall; mē, met, hėr; pīne, pin; nōte, not, mŏve; tūbe, tub, bull; oil, pound.

ambergris, am′bėr·grēs, n. [Fr. ambre gris (gris, gray), gray amber.] A solid, opaque, ash-colored substance used in perfumery. It is a morbid secretion obtained from the sperm whale.

ambidexter,† am·bi·deks′tėr, n. [L. ambo, both, and dexter, the right hand.] A person who uses both hands with equal facility; one equally ready to act on either side.—**ambidexterity,† ambidextrousness,†** am′bi·deks·ter″i·ti, am·bi··deks′trus·nes, n. The quality of being ambidextrous; double-dealing.—**ambidextrous,** am·bi·deks′trus, a. Having the faculty of using both hands with equal ease; double-dealing.

ambient, am′bi·ent, a. [L. ambiens, ambientis—amb, around, and iens, ppr. of ire, to go]. Surrounding; encompassing on all sides: applied to fluids or diffusible substances (the ambient air).

ambiguous, am·big′ū·us, a. [L. ambiguus, from ambigo, to go about—ambi, about, and ago, to drive.] Doubtful or uncertain, especially in respect to signification; liable to be interpreted two ways; equivocal; indefinite.—**ambiguously,** am·big′ū·us·li, adv. In an ambiguous manner; with doubtful meaning.—**ambiguity, ambiguousness,** am·bi·gū′i·ti, am·big′ū·us·nes, n. The state or quality of being ambiguous; doubtfulness or uncertainty, particularly of signification.

ambition, am·bi′shon. n. [L. ambitio, ambitionis, the going about of candidates for office in Rome, hence flattery, ambition—amb, around, round about, and eo, itum, to go, from L. Gr. and Skr. root i, to go.] An eager and sometimes inordinate desire after honor, power, fame, or whatever confers distinction; desire to distinguish one's self among others.—v.t.† To seek after ambitiously.—**ambitious,** am·bi′shus, a. [L. ambitiosus.] Possessing ambition; eagerly or inordinately desirous of power, honor, fame, office, superiority, or distinction; strongly desirous (with of or after); springing from, indicating, or characterized by ambition; showy; pretentious (ambitious ornament).—**ambitiously,** am·bi′shus·li, adv. In an ambitious manner.—**ambitiousness,** am·bi′shus·nes, n. The quality of being ambitious.

ambivalence, am·biv′a·lans, n. [L. ambo, both, and valere, to be strong.] Coexistence of contradictory feelings about a particular person, object, or action.

amble, am′bl, v.i.—ambled, ambling, [O.Fr. ambler, to amble, from L. ambulo, to walk, from amb, about.] To move by lifting both legs on each side alternately: said of horses, etc.; hence, to move easily and gently.—n. The pace of a horse or like animal when ambling; easy motion; gentle pace.—**ambler,** am′blėr, n. One who ambles.

amblygon, am′bli·gon, n. [Gr. amblys, obtuse, and gōnia, an angle.] An obtuse-angled triangle.—**ambly-**

gonite, am·blig′on·īt, n. A greenish-colored mineral, of different pale shades, marked with reddish and yellowish brown spots.

amblyopia, am·bli·ō′pi·a, n. [From Gr. amblys, dull, and ōps, ōpos, the eye.] Dullness or dimness of eyesight without any apparent defect in the organs—the first stage in amaurosis.

ambo, am′bo, n. [Gr. ambōn, a stage, a pulpit.] In early Christian churches a raised desk or pulpit.

Amboina wood, am·boi′na wụd, n. [Amboyna, one of the Molucca Islands.] A beautifully mottled and curled wood employed in cabinet work.

ambrosia, am·brō′zhi·a, n. [Gr. ambrosia, from ambrotos, immortal—a, not, and same root as L. mors, death, E. murder.] The fabled food of the ancient Greek gods, which conferred immortality on those who partook of it; hence, anything pleasing to the taste or smell, as a perfumed draught, unguent, or the like.—**ambrosial,** am·brō′zhi·al, a. Of or pertaining to ambrosia; anointed or fragrant with ambrosia; delicious; fragrant.—**ambrosially,** am·brō′zhi·al·li, adv. In an ambrosial manner; with an ambrosial odor.

ambry, am′bri, n. [From L. armarium, tool chest. Scottish aumry, through French.] An almonry‡; a niche or recess in the wall of ancient churches near the altar in which the sacred utensils were deposited; a cupboard†.

ambsace, āmz′ās, n. [O.F. ambes ace.] Ambsace; complete bad luck, the two aces being the lowest throw at dice.

ambulacrum, am·bū·lā′krum, n. pl. **ambulacra,** am·bū·lā′kra. [L. ambulacrum, an alley.] One of the perforated spaces or avenues through which are protruded the tube feet, by means of which locomotion is effected in the sea urchins, etc.—**ambulacral,** am·bū·lā′kral, a. Pertaining to ambulacra.

ambulance, am′bū·lans, n. [Fr. AMBULATE.] A vehicle fitted with suitable appliances for conveying the injured and sick. Also a mobile hospital unit which accompanies an army in its movements in the field.

ambulate,† am′bū·lāt, v.i.—ambulated, ambulating. [L. ambulo, ambulatum, to go about. AMBLE.] To move backward and forward; to walk.—**ambulant,** am′bū·lant, a. Walking; moving from place to place.—**ambulation,** am·bū·lā′shon, n. The act of ambulating or walking about.—**ambulatory,** am′bū·la·to·ri, a. Having the power or faculty of walking; adapted for walking; pertaining to a walk; accustomed to move from place to place; not stationary (an ambulatory court).—n. Any part of a building intended for walking in.

ambuscade, am·bus·kād′, n. [Fr. embuscade, from It. imboscare, to lie in bushes—in, in, and bosco, a wood, the same word as E. bush.] A lying in wait and concealed for the purpose of attacking an enemy by surprise; a place where one party lies con-

cealed with a view to attack another by surprise; those lying so concealed; ambush.—v.t. and i.—ambuscaded, ambuscading. To lie in wait in order to attack from a concealed position.—**ambush,** am′bụsh, n. [O. Fr. embusche, verb embuscher, to lie in wait.] Same as Ambuscade.—v.t. To post or place in ambush.—v.i. To lie or be posted in ambush.—**ambushment,** am′bụshment, n.

ameba. See AMOEBA.

ameer, amir, a·mēr′, n. [Ar.] A nobleman; a chief; a ruler; an emir.

ameliorate, a·mēl′yor·āt, v.t.—ameliorated, ameliorating. [Fr. améliorer, from L. ad, to, and melioro, melioratum, to make better, from melior, better.] To make better; to improve; to meliorate.—v.i. To grow better; to meliorate.—**ameliorable,** a·mēl′yor·a·bl, a. Capable of being ameliorated.—**amelioration,** a·mēl′yor·ā″shon, n. The act of ameliorating; improvement; melioration.—**ameliorative,** a·mēl′yor·āt·iv, a. Producing, or having a tendency to produce, amelioration.—**ameliorator,** a·mēl′yor·āt·ėr, n. One who ameliorates.

Amen, ä·men′, ā·men′. [Heb. āmen, verily, certainly.] A term occurring generally at the end of a prayer, and meaning So be it. In the N. T. it is used as a noun to denote Christ as being one who is true and faithful, and as an adjective to signify made true, verified, fulfilled.

amenable, a·mē′na·bl, a. [Fr. amener, to bring or lead to—a, to, and mener, to lead. DEMEAN.] Liable to answer or be called to account; responsible; ready to yield or submit, as to advice; submissive.—**amenableness, amenability,** a·mē′na·bl·nes, a·mē′na·bil″i·ti, n. The state of being amenable.—**amenably,** a·mē′na·bli, adv. In an amenable manner.

amend, a·mend′, v.t. [Fr. amender, for emender, to correct, from L. emendo, to free from faults—e, out, out of, and menda, a fault. MEND.] To make better, or change for the better, by removing what is faulty; to correct; to improve; to reform.—v.i. To grow or become better by reformation or rectifying something wrong in manners or morals.∴ Amend differs from improve in this, that to amend implies something previously wrong, while to improve does not necessarily do so.—**amendable,** a·mend′a·bl, a. Capable of being amended or corrected.—**amendatory,** a·mend′a·to·ri, a. Supplying amendment; corrective.—**amender,** a·mend′ėr, n. One who amends.—**amendment,** a·mend′ment, n. The act of amending, or changing for the better, in any way; the act of becoming better, or state of having become better; an alteration proposed to be made in the draft of a parliamentary bill, or in the terms of any motion under discussion before a meeting.—**amends,** a·mendz′, n. pl. Compensation for a loss or injury; recompense; satisfaction; equivalent.

amende, ä·mänd′, n. [Fr. amende, L.L. amenda, a penalty, reparation. AMEND.] A pecuniary punishment or

---

ch, chain; ch, Sc. loch; g, go; j, job; ng, sing; TH, then; th, thin; w, wig; hw, whig; zh, azure.

fine; a recantation or reparation.—
Amende honorable, a public or open
recantation and reparation to an
injured party.

amenity, a·men'i·ti, *n*. [Fr. *amenité*,
L. *amaenitas, amaenus*, pleasant.] The
quality of being pleasant or agreeable,
in respect of situation, prospect,
climate, etc., as also of temper,
disposition, or manners.

amenorrhea, a·men·o·rē'a, *n*. [Gr.
a, not, *mén*, month, *rheo*, to flow.]
Med. a morbid or unnatural suppression of menstruation.

amentia, a·men'shi·a, *n*. [L., want
of reason—*a*, from, and *mens, mentis*,
mind.] Imbecility of mind; idiocy
or dotage.

amentum, ament, a·men'tum, am'·
ent, *n*. pl. **amenta**, a·men'ta. *Bot.* a
kind of inflorescence consisting of
unisexual apetalous flowers in the
axils of scales or bracts ranged along
a stalk or axis; a catkin.—**amenta-
ceous**, a·men·tā'shus, *a*. Consisting
of, resembling, or furnished with
an amentum or amenta.

amerce, a·mèrs', *v.t.*—*amerced, amercing*. [Fr. *amercié*, fined at the mercy
of the court—*a*, at, and *merci*, mercy.]
To punish by a pecuniary penalty,
the amount of which is left to the
discretion of the court; hence, to
punish by deprivation of any kind†.
—**amerceable**, a·mèrs'a·bl, *a*. Liable
to amercement.—**amercement**, a··
mèrs'ment, *n*. The act of amercing;
a pecuniary penalty inflicted on an
offender at the discretion of the
court.—**amercer**, a·mèrs'ér, *n*. One
who amerces.

American, a·mer'i·kan, *a*. Pertaining
to America; often, in a restricted
sense, pertaining to the United
States.—*n*. A native of America; in
a restricted sense, one of the inhabitants of the United States.—**Amer-
icanism**, a·mer'i·kan·izm, *n*. The
feelings of nationality which distinguish American citizens; the exhibition of national prejudice by Americans; a word, phrase, or idiom
peculiar to Americans.—**American-
ize**, a·mer'i·kan·īz, *v.t.*—*American-
ized, Americanizing*. To render American or like what prevails in or is
characteristic of America (especially
the United States); to naturalize in
America.

americium, am'er·ish"i·um, *n*. Radi-
active element produced by the
bombardment of uranium with high-
energy helium ions. Symbol, Am;
at. no., 95.

amethyst, am'ē·thist, *n*. [Gr. *ame-
thystos—a*, not, and *methyō*, to
inebriate, from its supposed power
of preventing or curing intoxication.]
A violet-blue or purple variety of
quartz which is wrought into various
articles of jewelry.—*Oriental Amethyst*, a rare violet-colored gem, a
variety of corundum, of extraordinary brilliancy and beauty.—**ame-
thystine**, a·mē·thist'īn, *a*. Pertaining
to, composed of, or resembling amethyst.

amiable, ā'mi·a·bl, *a*. [Partly from
Fr. *aimable*, lovely, amiable, from
L. *amabilis*, from *amo*, to love, partly

from Fr. *amiable*, amicable, L. *amica-
bilis*.] Worthy of love; delightful or
pleasing (said of things)‡; possessing
agreeable moral qualities; having an
excellent and attractive disposition;
lovable.—**amiability, amiableness**,
ā'mi·a·bil"i·ti, ā'mi·a·bl·nes, *n*. The
quality of being amiable or lovable;
sweetness of temper.—**amiably**, ā'-
mi·a·bli, *adv*. In an amiable manner.

amianthus, am·i·an'thus, *n*. [Gr.
amiantos—a, not, and *miainō*, to
pollute or vitiate; so called from its
incombustibility.] Flexible asbestos,
earth flax, or mountain flax; an
incombustible mineral composed of
delicate filaments, very flexible, and
somewhat elastic, often long and
resembling threads of silk.

amicable, am'ik·a·bl, *a*. [L. *amica-
bilis*, from *amicus*, a friend, from *amo*,
to love.] Characterized by or exhibiting friendship, peaceableness, or
harmony; friendly; peaceable; harmonious in social or mutual transactions. *Amicable* is a weaker word
than *friendly*. *Friendly* is active and
positive; *amicable* simply implies a
degree of friendship such as makes
us unwilling to disagree with those
with whom we are on harmonious
terms.—**amicability, amicableness**,
am'ik·a·bil"i·ti, am'ik·a·bl·nes, *n*.
Quality of being amicable.—**amicably**, am'ik·a·bli, *adv*. In an amicable or friendly manner; with harmony.

amice, am'is, *n*. [Confusion of O.F.
amit, L. *amictus*, garment, with O.F.
amusse, cap, mutch.] A flowing cloak
formerly worn by priests and pilgrims; an oblong embroidered piece
or strip of fine linen, falling down
the shoulders like a cope, worn under
the alb by priests in the service of
the mass.

amid, amidst, a·mid', a·midst', *prep*.
[Prefix *a*, on, in, and *mid, midst*.
O.E. *amidde, amiddes* (the latter a
genitive form); A.Sax. *on-middan*;
the *t* has been tacked on as in
against.] In the midst or middle of;
surrounded or encompassed by;
mingled with; among.—**amidships**,
a·mid'ships, *adv*. In or towards the
middle or the middle line of a ship.

amide, am'id, *n*. [From *am* of
ammonia.] *Chem*. any chemical compound derived from ammonia by the
substitution of acid or acyl groups
for the atoms of hydrogen.

amine, am'in, *n*. [From *am* of
ammonia.] Chemical compound
formed from ammonia by replacing
one or more hydrogen atoms of the
ammonia molecule with a corresponding number of organic radicals.—
aminic, a·mi'nik, *a*.

amino acid, a·mē'no as'id. *Chem*.
an acid containing the amino group,
NH_2. These acids are the basic
constituents of proteins.

amiss, a·mis', *a*. [Prefix *a*, on, and
miss.] Wrong; faulty; out of time
or order; improper.—*adv*. In a faulty
manner.—*To be not amiss*, to be
passable or suitable.

amity, am'i·ti, *n*. [Fr. *amitié*, from
L.L. *amicitas*, friendship; L. *amicus*,
a friend, from *amo*, to love.] Friend-

ship; harmony; good understanding,
especially between nations.

ammeter, am'mē·ter, *n*. [*Ampere* and
meter.] An instrument for measuring
electric current.

ammonia, am·mō'ni·a, *n*. [Gr. *ammo-
niakon*, sal ammoniac, from being
first obtained near the Temple of
Ammon in Libya.] A gaseous compound whose molecules contain one
atom of nitrogen and three of
hydrogen. Very soluble in water and
easily liquefied, it is widely used in
industry, agriculture, and medicine,
frequently in solution in water, under
the names of *liquid ammonia* or *spirits
of hartshorn*.—**ammoniac, ammoniacal**, am·mō'ni·ak, am·mō·ni'ak·al,
a. Pertaining to ammonia, or possessing its properties.—**ammoniac**, am··
mō'ni·ak, *n*. An exudation of an
umbelliferous plant with a fetid
smell, used as an antispasmodic and
expectorant, and in plasters.—**ammonium**, am·mo'ni·um, *n*. The
radical NH_4 formed by the reaction
of ammonia with acids.

ammonite, am'mon·it, *n*. [Resem-
bling the horns with which Jupiter
Ammon was furnished when represented by statues.] One of the fossil
shells of an extensive genus of extinct
cuttle-fishes, coiled in a plane spiral,
and chambered within like that of
the nautilus, to which the ammonites
were allied.

ammunition, am·mū·ni'shon, *n*. [Fr.
amunition, L. *munitio*, defence, from
munio, to fortify.] Military stores,
especially such articles as are used
in the discharge of firearms and
ordnance of all kinds, as powder,
balls, shells, shot, etc.

amnesia, am·nē'zha, *n*. [Gr. *a*. not,
and *mnēsis*, memory.] Loss of memory.

amnesty, am'nes·ti, *n*. [L. *amnestia*,
from Gr. *amnestia*, oblivion—*a*, not,
and root *mna*, to remember.] An act
of oblivion; a general pardon of the
offenses of subjects against the government, or the proclamation of
such pardon.—*v.t.*—*amnestied, am-
nestying*. To grant an amnesty to;
to pardon.

amnion, am'ni·on, *n*. [Gr.] The
innermost membrane surrounding
the fetus of mammals, birds, and reptiles; also a thin, semitransparent,
gelatinous fluid, in which the embryo
of a seed is suspended when it first
appears.

amoeba, a·mē'ba, *n*. [Gr. *amoibē*,
change.] The generic name of various
microscopic Protozoa, one of which
is common in our fresh-water ponds
and ditches. It consists of a gelatinous mass, and from continually
altering its shape it received this as
well as its former name of *proteus-
animalcule*.—**amoeboid**, a·mē'boid,
a. Of or pertaining to or resembling
the amoeba.

amok, a·mok', *n*. Same as *Amuck*.

among, amongst, a·mung', a·-
mungst', *prep*. [O.E. *amonge, amon-
ges, amongest*, A.Sax. *amang, on-
mang*, from *mengan*, to mingle; the
es being an adverbial genitive termination, and the *t* tacked on, as in

---

fāte, fär, fâre, fat, fall; mē, met, hèr; pīne, pin; nōte, not, möve; tūbe, tub, bull; oil, pound.

amidst. MINGLE.] Mixed or mingled with (implying a number); in or into the midst of; in or into the number of (one _among_ a thousand); jointly or with a reference to some one or other (they killed him _among_ them).

amontillado, a·mon′til·ä″dō, _n._ [Sp.] A dry kind of sherry of a light color.

amoral, ã·mor′al, _a._ [_a_, not, and _moral._] Lacking, or indifferent to, moral responsibility; independent of moral distinctions.

amoretto, am·o·ret′tō (pl. **amoretti**); **amorino,** am·o·rē′nō (pl. **amorini**), _n._ [It. from _amor_, love.] Terms in art for loves or cupids.

amorous, am′or·us, _a._ [Fr. _amoureux_, L.L. _amorosus_, L. _amor_, love; akin _amity_, _amiable_, etc.] Inclined to love persons of the opposite sex; having a propensity to love, or to sexual enjoyment; loving; fond; pertaining or relating to love; produced by love; indicating love; enamored (in this sense with _of_).—**amorously,** am′or·us·li, _adv._ In an amorous manner; fondly, lovingly. — **amorousness,** am′or·us·nes, _n._

amorphous, a·mor′fus, _a._ [Gr. _amorphos_—_a_, neg., and _morphē_, form.] Having no determinate form; of irregular shape; not having the regular forms exhibited by the crystals of minerals; being without crystallization; formless; characterless.—**amorphism,** a·mor′fizm, _n._

amortize, a·mor′tīz, _v.t._—_amortized_, _amortizing._ [L.L. _amortisare_, to sell in _mort_-main—L. _ad_, to, and _mors_, _mortis_, death.] To extinguish a debt by means of a sinking fund.—**amortization,** a·mor′tiz·ā″shon, _n._

amount, a·mount′, _v.i._ [O.Fr. _amonter_ to advance, increase, _amont_, upwards—_a_, to, and _mont_, L. _mons_, _montis_, a hill.] To add up to a sum; to reach a certain total by an accumulation of particulars; to come in the aggregate or whole; to result in; to be equivalent: followed by _to_.—_n._ The sum total of two or more particular sums or quantities; the aggregate; the effect, substance, or result.

amour, a·mör′, _n._ [Fr., from L. _amor_, love.] A love intrigue; an affair of gallantry.

amperage, am·pâr′ij, _n._ [From _Ampere_, a French physicist.] The strength of an electric current measured in amperes.

ampere, am·pār′, _n. Elect._ the unit employed in measuring the strength of an electric current.

ampersand, am′pér·sand, _n._ [_and_, _per se_, and _and._] The character &, symbol for _and_.

amphetamine, am·fet′a·min, _n._ [_alphamethyl-phenethyl_, and _amine._] A drug used as an inhalant in colds or hay fever, or internally as a mental stimulant.

amphibian, am·fib′i·an, _n._ [Gr. _amphibios_, living a double life—_amphi_, both, and _bios_, life.] Any of a class of vertebrates intermediate between fishes and reptiles; an animal or plant that is adapted to live both on land and in the water; sea plane; hydroplane.—_a._ Amphibious. —**amphibious,** am·fib′i·us, _a._ Ca-

pable of living both on land and in water; _mil._ executed by the combined action of sea, land, and air forces; trained for such action; having two lives, natures, characteristics, etc.— **amphibiously,** am·fib′i·us·li, _adv._— **amphibiousness,** am·fib′i·us·nes, _n._

amphibole, am′fi·bōl, _n._ [Gr. _amphibolos_, doubtful, equivocal.] A name given to hornblende, from its resemblance to augite, for which it may readily be mistaken.—**amphibolic,** am·fi·bol′ik, _a._ Pertaining to or resembling amphibole.—**amphibolite,** am·fib′o·līt, _n._ A rock with a base of amphibole or hornblende.

amphibology, am·fi·bol′o·ji, _n._ Gr. _amphibologia_—_amphi_, in two ways, _ballō_, to throw, and _logos_, discourse.] A phrase or discourse susceptible of two interpretations; and hence, a phrase of uncertain meaning.—**amphibological,** am·fib′o·loj″ik·al, _a._ Of or pertaining to amphibology; of doubtful meaning; ambiguous.

amphibrach, am′fi·brak, _n._ [Gr.— _amphi_, on both sides, and _brachys_, short.] _Pros._ a foot of three syllables, the middle one long, the first and last short.

amphictyonic, am·fikt′i·on·ik, _a._ Of or belonging to the Amphictyonic Council, or council of amphictyones or neighbors, meeting in spring at Thermopylae, in autumn at Delphi.

amphigory, am′fi·gōr·i, _n._ [Fr. _amphigouri._] A meaningless rigmarole; a nonsensical parody.—**amphigoric,** am·fi·gor′ik, _a._ Of, relating to, or consisting of amphigory; absurd; nonsensical.

amphimacer, am·fim′a·sėr, _a._ [Gr. _amphimakros_, long on both sides.] _Pros._ a foot of three syllables, the middle one short and the others long.

amphioxus, am·fi·oks′us, _n._ [Gr. _amphi_, on both sides, and _oxus_ or _oxys_, sharp, because sharp at both ends.] A kind of fish of a very rudimentary type, the lancelet.

amphipod, am′fi·pod, _n._ [Gr. _amphi_, on both sides, and _pous_, _podos_, a foot.] Any of a large group of crustaceans having both swimming and leaping appendages, as beach fleas, sand hoppers, and fresh-water shrimps.—_a._ Of or pertaining to amphipods.

amphiprostyle, am·fip′ro·stīl, _a._ [Gr. _amphi_, on both sides, _pro_, before, and _stylē_, a column.] Having a prostyle or portico on both ends or fronts, but with no columns on the sides.

amphisbaena, am·fis·bē′na, _n._ [Gr. _amphisbaina_—_amphis_, on both sides, and _bainō_, to go, from the belief that it moved with either end foremost.] The generic name of small serpentlike reptiles, formerly but erroneously deemed poisonous.

amphiscii, amphiscians, am·fish′i·ī, am·fish′i·anz, _n. pl._ [Gr. _amphi_, on both sides, and _skia_, shadow.] The inhabitants of the intertropical regions, whose shadows at noon in one part of the year are cast to the north and in the other to the south.

amphitheater, am·fi·thē′a·tėr, _n._ [Gr. _amphitheatron_—_amphi_, on both sides, and _theatron_, theater.] An

ancient edifice of an oval form, having a central area encompassed with rows of seats, rising higher as they receded from the center, on which people used to sit to view some spectacle or performance; a similar modern edifice; anything, as a natural hollow among hills, resembling an amphitheater in form. —**amphitheatric, amphitheatrical,** am′fi·thē·at″rik, am′fi·thē·at″rik·al, _a._ Pertaining to or resembling an amphitheater; exhibited in an amphitheater.

Amphitryon, am·fit′ri·ōn, _n._ King of Thebes, used for host, the man who provides dinner, from Molière's play of that name.

amphora, am′fo·ra, _n. pl._ **amphorae,** am′fo·rē. [L. _amphora_, Gr. _amphoreus_—_amphi_, on both sides, and _phoreō_, to carry, from its two handles.] Among the Greeks and Romans, a vessel, usually tall and narrow, with two handles or ears and a narrow neck, used for holding wine, oil, honey, and the like.

ample, am′pl, _a._ [Fr. _ample_, L. _amplus_ —prefix _am_, _amb_, round, about, and root of _pleo_, to fill; akin _double_.] Large in dimensions; of great size, extent, capacity, or bulk; wide; spacious; extended (_ample_ room); fully sufficient for some purpose intended; abundant; copious; plentiful (an _ample_ supply; _ample_ justice). —**ampleness,** am′pl·nes, _n._ The state of being ample; largeness; sufficiency; abundance.—**amplification,** am′pli·fi·kā″shon, _n._ The act of amplifying; an enlargement; extension; diffusive description or discussion.—**amplificatory,** am′pli·fi·kā·tō·ri, _a._ Serving or tending to amplify.—**amplifier,** am′pli·fī·ėr, _n._ One who amplifies or enlarges.— _Elect._ a device for increasing the amplitude of electric waves or impulses, commonly including one or more vacuum tubes.—**amplify,** am′-pli·fī, _v.t._—_amplified_, _amplifying_. [Fr. _amplifier_, to enlarge—L. _amplus_, ample, and _facio_, to make.] To make more ample, larger, more extended, more copious, and the like. _v.i._—To grow or become ample or more ample; to be diffuse in argument or description.—**amplitude,** am′pli-tūd, _n._ [L. _amplitudo._] State of being ample; largeness of dimensions; extent of surface or space; greatness; _astron._ an arc of the horizon intercepted between the east or west point and the center of the sun or star at its rising or setting.—**amplitude modulation.** _Elect._ a system of radio transmission in which the amplitude of the carrier wave is modulated (contrasted with frequency modulation).—**amply,** am′-pli, _adv._ In an ample manner; largely; sufficiently; copiously.

amplectant, am·plek′tant, _a._ [L. _am-plectens_, _amplectentis_, ppr. of _am-plector_, to embrace.] _Bot._ embracing; clasping.—**amplexicaul,** am·plek′-si·kal, _a._ [L. _amplexus_, embracing, and _caulis_, a stem.] _Bot._ nearly surrounding, clasping, or embracing the stem, as some leaves do at their base.

ampulla, am·pul′la, n. pl. **ampullae,** am·pul′lē. [L.] A more or less globular bottle, used by the Romans for holding oil; a vessel for holding the consecrated oil used in various church rites and at the coronation of kings; a small sac or baglike appendage of a plant; a hollow flask-shaped leaf.—**ampullaceous,** am·pul·lā′shus, a. Of or pertaining to or like an ampulla.

amputate, am′pū·tāt, v.t.—amputated, amputating. [L. amputo, amputatum—amb, about, and puto, to prune.] To cut off, especially a human limb or that of an animal.—**amputation,** am·pū·tā′shon, n. The act of amputating, or the operation of cutting off a limb or other projecting part of the body.

amuck, a·muk′, n. [Malay or Javanese.] A furious, reckless onset; a term used in the Eastern Archipelago by Malays, who are occasionally seen to rush out in a frantic state with daggers in their hands, yelling 'Amuck, amuck,' and attacking all that come in their way.—To run amuck, to rush about frantically, attacking all that come in the way; to attack all and sundry.

amulet, am′ū·let, n. [L. amuletum, Fr. amulette, from Ar. hamâlat, anything worn, from hamala, to carry, to wear.] Something worn or carried about the person, intended to act as a charm or preservative against evils or mischief, such as diseases and witchcraft.

amuse, a·mūz′, v.t.—amused, amusing. [Fr. amuser, to amuse, to divert, to hold in play—a, to, and O.Fr. muser, to muse. MUSE, v.] To entertain the mind of agreeably; to occupy or detain the attention of in a pleasant manner or with agreeable objects; to divert; entertain; often refl.; to keep in expectation, as by flattery, plausible pretenses and the like; to keep in play. ∴ Amuse is to occupy lightly and pleasantly; divert generally implies something absolutely lively or sportive; entertain, to keep in a continuous state of interest, often by something instructive.—**amusable,** a·mūz′a·bl, a. Capable of being amused.—**amusement,** a·mūz′ment, n. The act of amusing, or state of being amused; a slight amount of mirth or tendency towards merriment; that which amuses; entertainment; sport; pastime.—**amuser,** a·mūz′ėr, n. One who amuses.—**amusing,** a·mūz′ing, a. Giving amusement; pleasing; diverting.—**amusingly,** a·mūz′ing·li, adv. In an amusing manner.

amygdalate, a·mig′da·lāt, n. [L. amygdalus, an almond.] An emulsion made of almonds; milk of almonds.—**amygdaline,** a·mig′da·lin, a. Pertaining to, resembling, or made of almonds.—**amygdaloid,** a·mig′da·loid, n. A term applied to igneous rock, especially trap, containing round or almond-shaped vesicles or cavities partly or wholly filled with crystalline nodules of various minerals.—**amygdaloidal,** a·mig′da·loid′al, a. Pertaining to amygdaloid;

shaped like an almond.

amyl, am′il, n. [Gr. amylon, starch.] Chem. a hypothetical radical said to exist in many compounds, as amylic alcohol, etc.—Nitrite of amyl, an amber-colored fluid with a pleasant odor, having the property when inhaled of quickening the heart's action.—**amylaceous,** am·il·ā′shus, a. Pertaining to starch, or the farinaceous part of grain; resembling starch.—**amylene,** am′il·ēn, n. A hydrocarbon obtained from amylic alcohol, and possessing anesthetic properties.—**amylic,** am·il′ik, a. Pertaining to amyl.—**amyloid,** am′il·oid, a. Resembling or being of the nature of amyl.—n. A semigelatinous substance, analogous to starch, met with in some seeds.

amylase, am′i·lās, n. [Gr. amylon, starch.] A digestive enzyme that converts starch into sugar, as in saliva and germinating seeds.

an, a, an, ā, indef. art. [A.Sax. án, one, an, the former being the original, the latter a developed meaning; the same word as one. ONE.] A word used before nouns in the singular number to denote an individual as one among more belonging to the same class, and not marking singleness like one, nor pointing to something known and definitive like the. The form a is used before consonants (including the name sound of u as in unit, European=yu); an is used before words beginning with a vowel sound, or the sound of h when the accent falls on any syllable except the first, as, an inn, an umpire, an heir, an historian (but also a historian).

ana, ā′na, n. pl. [The neuter plural termination of Latin adjectives in -anus, often forming an affix to the names of eminent men to denote a collection of their memorable sayings—thus Scaligeriana, Johnsoniana.] The sayings of notable men; personal gossip or anecdotes.

Anabaptist, an·a·bap′tist, n. [Gr. ana, again, and baptistēs, a baptist.] One who holds the invalidity of infant baptism, and the necessity of re-baptism, generally by immersion, at an adult age.—**Anabaptism,** an·a·bap′tizm, n. The doctrine or practices of the Anabaptists.

anabasis, an·ab′a·sis, n. [Gr.—ana, up, and basis, a going, from bainō, to go.] A going up; an expedition from the coast inland; [cap.] the expedition of Cyrus the Younger against Persia in 401 B.C. described by Xenophon.

anabolism, an·ab′o·lizm, n. [anabole, build up, and ism.] Constructive metabolism.

anachronism, an·ak′ron·izm, n. [Gr. ana, implying inversion, error, and chronos, time.] An error in computing historical time; any error which implies the misplacing of persons or events in time; anything foreign to or out of keeping with a specified epoch (as where Shakespeare makes Hector quote Aristotle). —**anachronous, anachronistic,** an·ak′ron·us, an·ak′ron·ist″ik, a.

anaclastic, an·a·klas′tik, a. [Gr. ana-klasis, a bending back—Gr. ana,

back, and klasis, a breaking, from klaō, to break.] Pertaining to or produced by the refraction of light; bending back; flexible.

anacoluthon, an′a·kol·ū″thon, n. [Gr. anakolouthos, wanting sequence—neg. prefix an, and akolouthos, following.] Gram. want of sequence in a sentence, owing to the latter member of it belonging to a different grammatical construction from the preceding; as, 'He that curseth father or mother, let him die the death.'—Mat. xv. 4.—**anacoluthic,** an′a·kol·ū″thik, a.

anaconda, an·a·kon′da, n. The popular name of two of the largest species of the serpent tribe, namely, a Ceylonese species and a South American species, both growing to the length of over 30 feet.

Anacreontic, a·nak′rē·on″tik, a. Pertaining to or after the manner of Anacreon; relating to the praise of love and wine; convivial; amatory.—**Anacreontic,** a·nak′rē·on″tik, n. A poem by Anacreon, or composed in the manner of Anacreon; a little poem in praise of love or wine.

anacrusis, an′a·krü′sis, n. [Gr. ana-krousis, striking up.] The unstressed syllable at the beginning of a verse.

anadem, an′a·dem, n. [Gr. anadēma, a head-band or fillet—ana, up, and deō, to bind.] A band, fillet, garland, or wreath.

anadromous, a·nad′rom·us, a. [Gr. ana, up, and dromos, course.] Passing from the sea into fresh waters at stated seasons, as the salmon.

anaerobe, an·âr′ōb, n. [Gr. an, without, aer, air, and bios, life.] A micro-organism that lives without air or free oxygen.—**anaerobic,** an·âr·ōb′ik, a.

anaglyph, an′a·glif, n. [Gr. anaglyphon, embossed work—ana, up, and glyphō, to engrave.] An ornament in relief chased or embossed.—**anaglyphic,** an·a·glif′ik, a.

anagoge, anagogy, an′a·gō·jē, an′a·go·ji, n. [Gr. anagōgē—ana, upward, and agōgē, a leading, from agō, to lead.] An elevation of mind to things celestial; the spiritual meaning or application of words; a mysterious or allegorical interpretation, especially of Scripture.—**anagogic, anagogical,** an·a·goj′ik, an·a·goj′ik·al, a. Of or pertaining to anagoge; mysterious; elevated; spiritual.—**anagogically,** an·a·goj′ik·al·li, adv.

anagram, an′a·gram, n. [Gr. ana, up, again, and gramma, a letter.] A transposition of the letters of a word or sentence, to form a new word or sentence.—**anagrammatic, anagrammatical,** an′a·gram·mat′ik, an′a·gram·mat″ik·al, a. Pertaining to or forming an anagram.—**anagrammatize,** an·a·gram′mat·īz, v.t. To transpose, as the letters of a word, so as to form an anagram,—v.i. To make anagrams.

anal, ā′nal, a. [L. anus, the fundament.] Pertaining to or situated near the anus.

analcime, a·nal′sim, n. [Gr. an, priv., and alkimos, strong, from alkē, strength.] A mineral of frequent occurrence in traprocks, especially in the cavities of amygdaloids. By friction it acquires a *weak* electricity; hence its name.

analecta, analects, an·a·lek′ta, an′·a·lekts, *n. pl.* [Gr. neut. pl. of *analektos,* select—*ana,* up, and *legō,* to gather.] Extracts or small pieces selected from different authors.

analepsis, an·a·lep′sis, *n.* [Gr., from *ana,* up or again, and *lepsis,* a taking, from *lambanō,* to take.] *Med.* recovery of strength after disease.—**analeptic,** an·a·lep′tik, *a.* Invigorating; giving strength after disease; awakening, especially from drug stupor.—*n.* an analeptic remedy.

analgesia, an·al·jēz′i·a, *n.* [Gr. *analgesia*—*an,* not, and *algos,* pain.] *Pathol.* incapacity for feeling pain in some part of the body.

analogy, an·al′o·ji, *n.* [Gr. *analogia*—*ana,* according to, and *logos,* ratio, proportion.] An agreement or likeness between things in some circumstances or effects, when the things are otherwise entirely different; relationship; conformity; parallelism; likeness. ∴ *Analogy* is sometimes confounded with *similarity,* but the latter properly denotes general likeness or resemblance; the former implies general difference, with identity or sameness in one or more relations. Thus there is *analogy,* but no *similarity* between the wing of a bird and that of a bat. [We say analogy *between* things, one thing has an analogy *to* or *with* another.]—**analogical,** an·a·loj′ik·al, *a.* Having analogy; analogous; used by way of analogy; expressing or implying analogy.—**analogically,** an·a·loj′ik·al·li, *adv.* In an analogical manner.—**analogist,** an·al′o·jist, *n.* One who adheres to analogy.—**analogize,** an·al′o·jīz, *v.t.*—analogized, analogizing. To explain by analogy; to consider with regard to its analogy to something else.—**analogous,** an·al′og·us, *a.* Having analogy; bearing some resemblance in the midst of differences (followed by *to* or *with*).—**analogously,** an·al′og·us·li, *adv.* In an analogous manner.—**analogue,** an′a·log, *n.* Something having analogy with something else.—**analogue computer.** A calculating machine that uses directly measurable quantities (voltages, resistances, etc.) to solve problems by physical analogy. Also spelled *analog computer.*

analysis, an·al′i·sis, *n. pl.* **analyses,** an·al′i·sēz. [Gr.—prefix *ana,* implying distribution, and *lysis,* a loosing, resolving, from *lyō,* to loosen.] The resolution of a compound object whether of the senses or the intellect into its constituent elements or component parts; a consideration of anything in its separate parts and their relation to each other; opposed to *synthesis;* the process of subjecting to chemical tests to determine ingredients; a syllabus or table of the principal heads of a discourse or treatise.—**analyzable,** an·a·līz′a·bl, *a.* Capable of being analyzed.—**analyzation,** an′a·līz·ā″shon, *n.* The act of analyzing.—**analyze,** an′a·līz,

v.t.—analyzed, analyzing. [Fr. *analyser.*] To resolve into its elements; to separate, as a compound subject, into its parts or propositions.—**analyzer,** an′a·līz·ėr, *n.* One who or that which analyzes.—**analyst,** an′a·list, *n.* One who analyzes or is versed in analysis; one who subjects articles to chemical tests to find out their ingredients.—**analytic, analytical,** an·a·lit′ik, an·a·lit′ik·al, *a.* Pertaining to analysis; resolving into first principles or elements.—**analytically,** an·a·lit′ik·al·li, *adv.* In an analytical manner; in the manner of analysis.—**analytics,** an·a·lit′iks, *n.* The science of analysis.

anandrous, an·an′drus, *a.* [Gr. *an,* not, and *anēr, andros,* a male or stamen.] *Bot.* applied to flowers that are destitute of a stamen (female flowers).

anapaest, anapest, an′a·pest, *n.* [L. *anapaestus,* from Gr. *anapaistos.*] A poetical foot consisting of three syllables, the first two short or unaccented, the last long or accented.—**anapaestic,** an·a·pes′tik, *a.* Pertaining to an anapest; consisting of anapests.

anaphrodisiac, an·af′ro·diz″i·ak, *n.* [Gr. neg. prefix *an,* and *aphrodisiakos,* venereal.] A substance capable of dulling sexual appetite.

anaplasty, an′a·plas·ti, *n.* [Gr. *ana,* again, and *plassō,* to fashion.] *Surg.* an operation to supply by the employment of adjacent healthy structure the loss of small portions of flesh.—**anaplastic,** an·a·plas′tik, *a.* Of or pertaining to anaplasty.

anarchy, an′ar·ki, *n.* [Gr. *anarchia,* lawlessness—*an,* not, and *archē,* rule.] Want of government; a state of society when there is no law or supreme power; political confusion.—**anarchic, anarchical,** an·ärk′ik, an·ärk′ik·al, *a.* Of or pertaining to anarchy or anarchism; in a state of anarchy or confusion; lawless.—**anarchism,** an′ärk·izm, *n.* The doctrine of the abolition of formal government, free action for the individual, land and other resources being common property.—**anarchist,** **anarch,** an′ärk·ist, an′ärk, *n.* One who excites disorder in a state; an advocate of anarchy or anarchism.

anastomose, a·nas′tō·mōz, *v.i.*—anastomosed, anastomosing. [Fr. *anastomoser,* Gr. *anastomoō*—*ana,* again, anew, and *stoma,* a mouth.] *Anat.* and *bot.* to inosculate or run into each other, to communicate with each other by minute branches or ramifications, as the arteries and veins.—**anastomosis,** a·nas·tō·mō′sis, *n.* The inosculation of vessels in vegetable or animal bodies.—**anastomotic,** a·nas·tō·mot″ik, *a.* Pertaining to anastomosis.

anastrophe, a·nas′tro·fe, *n.* [Gr.—*ana,* back, *strephō,* to turn.] An inversion of the natural order of words.

anathema, a·nath′ē·ma, *n.* [Gr. *anathema,* a thing devoted to evil, from *anatithēmi,* to dedicate—*ana,* up, and *tithēmi,* to place.] A curse or denunciation pronounced with

religious solemnity by ecclesiastical authority, and accompanied by excommunication; execration generally; curse.—**anathematization,** a·nath′-ē·mat·iz·a″shon, *n.* The act of anathematizing.—**anathematize,** a·nath′ē·mat·īz, *v.t.*—anathematized, anathematizing. To pronounce an anathema against.—*v.i.* To pronounce anathemas; to curse.

anatomy, a·nat′o·mi, *n.* [Gr. *anatomē*—*ana,* up, and *tomē,* a cutting.] The art of dissecting or artificially separating the different parts of an organized body, to discover their situation, structure, and economy; the science which treats of the internal structure of organized bodies, as elucidated by dissection; when used alone it refers to the human body, *vegetable anatomy* being the anatomy of plants, *zootomy* that of the lower animals; the act of taking to pieces something for the purpose of examining in detail (the *anatomy* of a discourse); a skeleton (colloq.); hence, a thin meager person.—**anatomic, anatomical,** an·a·tom′ik, an·a·tom′ik·al, *a.* Belonging to anatomy or dissection.—**anatomically,** an·a·tom′ik·al·li, *adv.* In an anatomical manner; by means of dissection.—**anatomist,** a·nat′o·mist, *n.* One who is skilled in dissection, or in the doctrine and principles of anatomy.—**anatomization,** a·nat′o·miz·ā″shon, *n.* The act of anatomizing.—**anatomize,** a·nat′o·mīz, *v.t.*—anatomized, anatomizing. To cut up or dissect for the purpose of displaying or examining the structure; *fig.* to lay open or expose minutely; to analyze (to *anatomize* an argument).

ancestor, an′ses·tėr, *n.* [O.Fr. *ancestre, ancessor,* Fr. *ancêtre,* an ancestor, from L. *antecessor,* a predecessor—*ante,* before, and *cedo, cessum,* to go. CEDE.] One from whom a person descends, either by the father or mother, at any distance of time; a progenitor; a forefather; one from whom an inheritance is derived.—**ancestress,†** an′ses·tres, *n.* A female ancestor.—**ancestry,** an′ses·tri, *n.* A series of ancestors; lineage; honorable descent; high birth.

anchor, ang′kėr, *n.* [A.Sax. *ancor,* borrowed from L. *ancora,* Gr. *angkyra,* an anchor. From a root meaning crooked, bent, seen in L. *angulus,* a corner, E. *ankle, angle,* a fish-hook.] An iron implement, consisting usually of a straight bar called the shank, at the upper end of which is a transverse piece called the stock, and of two curved arms at the lower end of the shank, each of which arms terminates in a triangular plate called a fluke, and used for holding a ship or other vessel at rest in comparatively shallow water; something serving a purpose analogous to that of a ship's anchor; *fig.* that which gives stability or security; that on which we place dependence for safety.—*At anchor,* floating attached to an anchor; anchored.—*v.t.* To hold at rest by lowering the anchor; to place at anchor; *fig.* to fix or fasten on; to fix in a stable condition.—*v.i.* To cast anchor; to come to anchor.—**anchorage,** ang'kėr·aj, *n.* Anchoring ground; a place where a ship can anchor; a duty imposed on ships for anchoring in a harbor.

anchoret, anchorite, ang'kō·ret, ang'kō·rīt, *n.* [L. *anachoreta;* Gr. *anachorētēs—ana,* back, and *chōreō,* to retire, from *chōros,* a place.] A hermit; a recluse; one who retires from society to avoid the temptations of the world and devote himself to religious duties.—**anchoress,** ang'kō·res, *n.* A female anchoret.—**anchoretic,** ang·kō·ret'ik, *a.* Pertaining to a hermit, or his mode of life.

anchovy, an·chō'vi, *n.* [Pg. and Sp. *anchova,* an anchovy, from Basque *anchua, anchuva,* dry.] A small fish belonging to the herring family, caught in vast numbers in the Mediterranean, and pickled for exportation. An esteemed sauce is also made from them.

anchylose, ang'ki·lōs. A common but erroneous spelling of *Ankylose.*

ancient, ān'shent, *a.* [Fr. *ancien,* L.L. *antianus,* from L. prep. *ante,* before. The final *t* has no right to its place in this word.] That happened or existed in former times, usually at a great distance of time; associated with, or bearing marks of the times of long ago (*ancient* authors); of long standing; having lasted from a remote period; of great age; old (an *ancient* city); having lived long (an *ancient* man—poetical). ∴ *Old* refers to the duration of the thing itself; *ancient,* to the period with which it is associated. *Ancient* is opposed to *modern; old* to *young, new, fresh.* An *old* dress, custom, etc., is one which has lasted a long time, and which still exists; an *ancient* dress, custom, etc., is one which prevailed in former ages.—*n.* A person living at an early period of history (generally in plural, and opposed to *moderns*); a very old man; an elder or person of influence.—**anciently,** ān'shent·li, *adv.* In old times; in times long past.—**ancientness,** ān'shent·nes, *n.* The state or character of being ancient; antiquity.

ancillary, an'sil·la·ri, *a.* [L. *ancillaris,* from *ancilla,* a maid-servant.] Subservient; aiding; auxiliary; subordinate.

ancipital, an·sip'it·al, *a.* [L. *anceps, ancipitis,* two-headed, ambiguous— *an* for *amb,* on both sides, and *caput,* the head.] Doubtful or double; ambiguous; *bot.* two-edged.

ancon, ang'kon, *n.* pl. **ancones,** ang·- kō'nēz. [L. *ancon,* Gr. *angknō,* the elbow.] *Anat.* the upper end of the ulna or elbow; *arch.* a console, cantilever, corbel, or other stone projection.

and, and, *conj.* [A.Sax. *and,* D. *en, ende,* G. *und,* O.H.G. *anti,* all signifying and; and Icel. *enda,* and yet, and if.] A particle joining words and sentences, and expressing the relations of connection or addition; sometimes used to introduce interrogative and other clauses.

andalusite, an·da·lū'sīt, *n.* A pellucid mineral of the garnet family, of a gray, green, bluish, flesh or rose-red color: so called from *Andalusia* in Spain, where it was first discovered.

andante, an·dan'tā, *a.* [It. *andante,* walking moderately, from *andare,* to go.] *Music,* moving with a moderate, even, graceful, onward progression. —*n.* A movement or piece composed in *andante* time.—**andantino,** an·- dan·tē'no, *a.* Applied to a movement quicker than *andante.*

Andean, an·dē'an, *a.* Pertaining to the Andes, the great mountain chain of South America.

andiron, and'ī·ėrn, *n.* [O.E. *andiren, aundirin, aundire,* O.F. *andier;* origin unknown.] A horizontal iron bar raised on short legs, with an upright standard at one end, used to support pieces of wood when burning on an open hearth, one being placed on each side; a firedog.

andraecium, an·drē'si·um, *n.* [Gr. *anēr, andros,* a man, a male, and *oikos,* a house.] *Bot.* the male system of a flower; the assemblage of the stamens.

androgynal, androgynous, an·- droj'in·al, an·droj'in·us, *a.* [Gr. *androgynos—anēr, andros,* a man, and *gynē,* woman.] Having two sexes; being male and female; hermaphroditical; having or partaking of the mental and physical characteristics of both sexes.

androsphinx, an'dro·sfingks, *n.* [Gr. *anēr, andros,* a man, and *sphingx,* a sphinx.] A sphinx with a human head.

androus, an'drus, *a.* [Gr. *anēr, andros,* a male.] *Bot.* producing stamens only; staminate; male.

anecdote, an'ek·dōt, *n.* [Gr. *anekdotos,* not published—*a,* neg., *ek,* out, and *dotos,* given, from *didōmi,* to give.] A short story, narrating a detached incident or fact of an interesting nature; a biographical incident; a single passage of private life.—**anecdotage.** The garrulity of dotage, or old age.—**anecdotic, anecdotal, anecdotical,** an·ek·dot'ik, an'ek·dōt·al, an·ek·dot'ik·al, *a.* Pertaining to anecdotes; consisting of or of the nature of anecdotes.—**anecdotist,** an'ek·dōt·ist, *n.* One who deals in anecdotes.

anele, an·ēl' *v.t.* [O.E. *ele,* L. *oleum,* oil.] Anoint, with extreme unction. [*Shak.*]

anelectric, an·ē·lek'trik, *a.* [Gr. *an,* not, and E. *electric.*] Having no electric properties; nonelectric.

anemia, a·nē'mi·a, *n.* [Gr. *an,* not, and *haima,* blood.] *Med.* a deficiency of blood; a state of the system marked by a deficiency in certain constituents of the blood.—**anemic,** a·ne'mik, *a.* Pertaining to or affected with anemia.

anemograph, a·nem'o·graf, *n.* [Gr. *anemos,* the wind.] An instrument for measuring and recording the force and direction of the wind.— **anemology,** an·e·mol'o·ji, *n.* The doctrine of or a treatise on winds.— **anemometer,** an·e·mom'et·ėr, *n.* An instrument for measuring force and velocity of the wind.—**anemometry,** an·e·mom'et·ri, *n.* The process of determining the pressure or force of the wind by an anemometer.

anemone, a·nem'o·nē, *n.* [Gr. *anem- ōnē,* the wind-flower, from *anemos,* the wind, being easily stripped of its petals by the wind.] Any plant of the genus *Anemone,* especially *Anemone quinquefolia,* a spring flower with slender stem and delicate whitish blossoms. *Sea anemone.* ACTINIA.

anemophilous, an·e·mof'i·lus, *a.* [Gr. *anemos,* wind, *philos,* loving.] *Bot.* having the pollen conveyed and fertilization effected by the wind.

anemoscope, a·nem'o·skōp, *n.* [Gr. *anemos,* wind, and *skopeō,* to view.] A contrivance which shows the direction of the wind; a weathercock; a wind vane.

anent, a·nent', *prep.* [A.Sax. *on efn, on emn,* on a level, near, lit. on even. The *t,* as in *ancient,* is superfluous.] About; respecting; regarding.

anergy, an'ėr·ji, *n.* [Gr. *an,* not, *ergon,* work.] *Pathol.* morbid loss of energy.

aneroid, an'ē·roid, *a.* [Gr. *a,* not, *nēros,* moisture, and *eidos,* form.] Dispensing with fluid, as with quicksilver.—*Aneroid barometer,* a barometer the action of which depends on the pressure of the atmosphere on a circular metallic box exhausted of air, hermetically sealed, and having a slightly elastic top, the vacuum serving the purpose of the column of mercury in the ordinary barometer.

anesthesia, an·es·thē'zha, *n.* [Gr. *anaisthēsia—an,* not, and *aisthanomai,* to feel.] Diminished or lost sense of feeling; an artificially produced state of insensibility, especially to the sense of pain.—**anesthetic,** an·es·thet'ik, *a.* Of or belonging to anesthesia; having the power of depriving of feeling or sensation.— *n.* A substance which has the power of depriving of feeling or sensation, as chloroform when its vapor is inhaled.—**anesthetize,** an·es'the·tīz, *v.t.*—*anesthetized, anesthetizing.* To bring under the influence of an anesthetic agent; to render insensible to the feeling of pain.

anew, a·nū', *adv.* [Prefix *a,* of or on, and *new.*] Over again; in a new form; afresh.

anfractuous, an·frak'tū·us, *a.* [Fr. *anfractueux,* L. *anfractus,* winding— *frango, fractum,* to break.] Winding; full of windings and turnings; sinuous.—**anfractuose,** an·frak'tū·ōs, *a.* *Bot.* twisted or sinuous.—**anfractuosity,** an·frak·tū·os"i·ti, *n.* A state of being anfractuous; *anat.* a sinuous depression.

angel, ān'jel, *n.* [L. *angelus,* Gr. *angelos,* a messenger.] A divine messenger; a spiritual being employed in the service of God; also applied to an evil being of similar powers; a gold coin, formerly current in England, varying in value from 6*s.* 8*d.* to 10*s.,* bearing the figure of the archangel Michael.—**angelic, angelical,** an·jel'lik, an·jel'ik·al, *a.* Resembling or belonging to, or partaking of the nature and dignity of angels.—*Angelic doctor,* Thomas Aquinas.—**angelica,** an·jel'ik·a, *n.*

[From possessing what were regarded as *angelic* powers or virtues.] Any plant of the genus *Angelica*, tall umbelliferous plants found in both hemispheres, especially *Angelica Archangelica*, cultivated in Europe for its aromatic odor and its medicinal roots, also for its roots, which are candied.—**angelically**, an·jel′ik·al·li, *adv.* In an angelic manner.—**angelology**, ān·jel·ol′o·ji, *n.* A discourse on angels, or the doctrine of angelic beings.—**Angelus**, an′jel·us, *n.* R. Cath. Ch. a solemn devotion in memory of the Incarnation; the bell tolled to indicate the time when the Angelus is to be recited.—**angelfish**, ān′jel·fish, *n.* A fish nearly allied to the sharks: so called from its pectoral fins, which are so large as to spread like wings.

anger, ang′gėr, *n.* [Originally grief, from Icel. *angr*, grief, sorrow, *angra*, to grieve, annoy; Dan. *anger*, sorrow; same root as in A.Sax. *ange*, vexed, narrow, G. *enge*, narrow; L. *ango*, to trouble, *angor*, vexation, Gr. *angchō*, to choke.] A violent, revengeful passion or emotion, excited by a real or supposed injury to one's self or others; passion; ire; choler; rage; wrath. ∴ *Anger* is more general and expresses a less strong feeling than *wrath* and *rage*, both of which imply a certain outward manifestation, and the latter violence and want of self-command.—*v.t.* To excite to anger; to rouse resentment in; to make angry; to exasperate.—**angrily**, [*Tenn.*]—**angrily**, ang′gri·li, *adv.* In an angry manner.—**angriness**, ang′gri·nes, *n.* The state of being angry.—**angry**, ang′gri, *a.* Feeling resentment; provoked; showing anger; caused by anger; raging; tumultuous.

Angevin, an′je·vin, *a.* Of or pertaining to *Anjou*, a former province of France.

angina, an·ji′na, *n.* [L. from *ango*, to choke. ANGER.] *Med.* an inflammatory affection of the throat or fauces.—*Angina pectoris*, a fatal disease characterized by paroxysms of intense pain and a feeling of constriction in the chest. (Also pron. an′-ji·na.)

angiocarpous, an′ji·ō·kär″pus, *a.* [Gr. *angeion*, a capsule, and *karpos*, fruit.] *Bot.* having a fruit whose seed vessels are enclosed within a covering that does not form a part of themselves, as the acorn.

angiography, **angiology**, an·ji·og′ra·fi, an·ji·ol′o·ji, *n.* [Gr. *angeion*, a vessel.] *Med.* a description of the vessels of the body.

angioma, an·ji·ō′ma, *n.* [Gr. *angeion*, a vessel.] *Med.* a tumor produced by the enlargement of a blood vessel.

angiosperm, an′ji·ō·spėrm, *n.* [Gr. *angeion*, a vessel, and *sperma*, seed.] *Bot.* a plant which has its seeds enclosed in a seed vessel.—**angiospermous**, an′ji·ō·spėrm″us, *a.* *Bot.* having seeds enclosed in a seed vessel.

angle, ang′gl, *n.* [L. *angulus*, a corner. ANCHOR.] The point where two lines or planes meet that do not run in the same straight line; a corner; the degree of opening or divergence of two straight lines which meet one another.—**angled**, ang′gld, *a.* Having angles: used chiefly in compounds.—**angular**, ang′gū·lėr, *a.* Having an angle or angles; having corners; pointed; consisting of or forming an angle.—*Angular motion*, *angular velocity*, the motion or velocity of a body or a point moving circularly.—**angularity**, ang·gū·lar′i·ti, *n.* The quality of being angular.—**angularly**, ang′gū·lėr·li, *adv.* In an angular manner.—**angularness**, ang′gū·lėr·nes, *n.* The quality of being angular.—**angulate**, **angulated**, ang′gū·lāt, ang′gū·lāt·ed, *a.* Angled; cornered.—**angulation**, ang·gū·lā′shon, *n.* The state of being angulated; that which is angulated.—**angle iron**, *n.* A piece of rolled iron in the shape of the letter L, used for forming the joints of iron plates in girders, boilers, etc., to which it is riveted.

angle, ang′gl, *v.i.*—*angled*, *angling*. [A. Sax. *angel*, a fishhook; G. *angel*, Icel. *öngull*, a hook; from a root meaning crooked, seen also in ANCHOR.] To fish with an angle, or with line and hook.—**angler**, ang′glėr, *n.* One who fishes with an angle; a fish having long filamentous appendages in its head, which attract the smaller fishes and thus provide it with prey. —**angleworm**, ang′gl·wėrm, *n.* An earth worm used as bait.—**angling**, ang′gling, *n.* The act or art of fishing with a rod and line.

Angles, ang′glz, *n. pl.* [A.Sax. *Angle*, *Engle*, the Angles.] A Low German tribe who in the fifth century and subsequently crossed over to Britain along with bands of Saxons, Jutes, and others, and colonized a great part of what from them has received the name of England.—**Anglian**, ang′gli·an, *a.* Of or pertaining to the tribe of the Angles.—*n.* A member of the tribe of the Angles.

Anglican, ang′glik·an, *a.* [L.L. *anglicus*, English.] English; pertaining to the English Church.—*Anglican Church*, the Church of England and the Protestant Episcopal churches in Ireland, Scotland, and the colonies; sometimes including also the Episcopal churches of the United States.—*n.* A member of the Anglican Church.—**Anglicanism**, ang′glik·an·izm, *n.* The principles of or adherence to the Established Church of England.—**Anglicism**, ang′gli·sizm, *n.* The quality of being English; an English idiom.—**Anglicize**, **Anglify**, ang′gli·sīz, ang′gli·fī, *v.t.*—*anglicized*, *anglicizing*. To make English; to render conformable to the English idiom or to English analogies.

Anglo-, ang′glō, prefix. [L.L. *Anglus*, an Englishman.] A prefix signifying *English*, or connected with England. —**Anglo-American**, *n.* A descendant from English ancestors born in America or the United States: used also as an adj.—**Anglo-Catholic**, *n.* A member of the Church of England who lays stress on the claim that his church is historically a part of the Catholic Church: used also as an adj.—**Anglo-Catholicism**, *n.* The principles or doctrines of the Anglo-Catholics.—**Anglo-Indian**, *n.* One of the English race born or resident in the East Indies. Also as an adj.—**Anglo-Irish**, *n. pl.* English people born or resident in Ireland; descendants of parents English on the one side and Irish on the other. Also as an adj.—**Anglomania**, ang·glō·mā′ni·a, *n.* [Gr. *mania*, madness.] An excessive or undue attachment to, respect for, or imitation of Englishmen or English institutions and customs by a foreigner.—**Anglophobia**, ang·glō·fō′bi·a, *n.* [Gr. *phobos*, fear.] An excessive hatred or dread of English people, customs, or institutions.—**Anglo-Saxon**, *n.* [ANGLES, SAXON.] One of the nation formed by the union of the Angles, Saxons, and other early Teutonic settlers in Britain, or one of their descendants; one belonging to the English race; the language of the Anglo-Saxons, or the English language in its first stage.—*a.* Pertaining to the Anglo-Saxons or to the oldest form of English.

Angora, an·gō′ra, *n.* A light cloth, made from the wool or long silky hair of the Angora goat, a native of Asia Minor.—*Angora cat.* A large variety of the domestic cat originally from Angora, with beautiful long silky hair.

angostura, ang·gos·tū′ra, *a.* Belonging to or brought from the town of Angostura in Venezuela—an epithet of a kind of bark having febrifugal properties and of a kind of bitters made from it.

angrily, **angriness**, **angry**. See ANGER.

angstrom unit, **angstrom**, ang′-strum. [After A. J. Angström (1814-1874), Sw. physicist.] One tenth of a millimicron or one hundred-millionth of a centimeter; a unit used to express the length of light waves.

anguish, ang′gwish, *n.* [O.E. *anguis*, *angoise*, Fr. *angoisse*, from L. *angustia*, a strait, perplexity, from *angustus*, narrow; root *ang* as in E. *anger*.] Extreme pain, either of body or mind; any keen affection of the emotions or feelings ('an *anguish* of delight.' *Thack.*)—**anguish**,† ang′-gwish, *v.t.* To distress extremely.

angular, **angularity**, etc. See ANGLE.

angustifoliate, ang·gus′ti·fō′li·āt, *a.* [L. *angustus*, narrow, and *folium*, a leaf.] *Bot.* having narrow leaves.

anhydrous, an·hī′drus, *a.* [Gr. *anydros*, dry—neg. prefix *an*, and *hydōr*, water.] Destitute of water; specifically, *chem.* destitute of the water of crystallization.—**anhydride**, an·hī′-drid, *n.* One of a class of oxygen compounds in which there is no water.—**anhydrite**, an·hī′drīt, *n.* Anhydrous sulfate of calcium, a mineral resembling a coarse-grained granite.

anil, an′il, *n.* [Sp. *anil*, Ar. *neel*, Skr. *nîlam*, indigo, *nîlî*, the indigo-plant.] A shrub from whose leaves and stalks the West Indian indigo is made.—**aniline**, an′i·lin, *n.* A substance obtained from indigo and other organic substances, though the aniline of commerce is obtained from benzol, a product of coal tar. It furnishes a number of brilliant dyes.

anile, an′īl, *a.* [L. *anilis*, from *anus*, an old woman.] Old-womanish; aged; imbecile.—**anility,** a·nil′i·ti, *n.* The state of being anile.

animadvert, an″i·mad·vėrt′, *v.i.* [L. *anidmadverto—animus*, mind, and *adverto*, to turn to.] To perceive or take cognizance; usually, to make remark by way of criticism; to pass strictures or criticisms (followed by *on*, *upon*). —**animadversion,** an″i·mad·vėr′-shon, *n.* The act of one who animadverts; a remark by way of criticism or censure; stricture; censure.

animal, an′i·mal, *n.* [L. *animal*, a living being, from *anima*, air, breath, life, the soul, from a root *an*, to breathe or blow.] A living being characterized by sensation and voluntary motion; an inferior or irrational being, in contradistinction to man; also often popularly used to signify a quadruped.—*a.* Belonging or relating to animals (*animal* functions); pertaining to the merely sentient part of a living being, as distinguished from the intellectual or spiritual part (*animal* passions); of or pertaining to, or consisting of, the flesh of animals.—**animalism,** an′i·mal·izm, *n.* The state of a mere animal; the state of being actuated by sensual appetites only; sensuality. —**animality,** an·i·mal′i·ti, *n.* The state of being an animal; *physiol.* those vital phenomena which, superadded to vegetative powers, constitute animal existence.—**animalization,** an′i·mal·iz·ā″shon, *n.* The act of animalizing; conversion into animal matter by the process of assimilation.—**animalize,** an′i·mal·īz, *v.t.* —*animalized*, *animalizing*. To give animal life to; to convert into animal matter; to bring under the sway of animal appetites.

animalcule, an·i·mal′kūl, *n.* [L.L. *animalculum*, dim. of L. *animal*, an animal.] A minute animal, especially one that is microscopic or invisible to the naked eye.—**animalcular,** an·i·mal′kū·lėr, *a.* Pertaining to or resembling animalcules.—**animalculum,** an·i·mal′kū·lum, *n.* pl. **animalcula,** an·i·mal′kū·la. An animalcule.

animate, an′i·māt, *v.t.* —*animated*, *animating*. [L. *animatus*, animated, pp. of *animo*, to fill with breath. ANIMAL.] To give natural life to; to quicken; to make alive; to give life, spirit, or liveliness to; to heighten the powers or effect of; to stimulate or incite; to inspirit; to rouse.—**animate,** an′i·māt, *a.* Alive; possessing animal life.—**animated,** an′i·māt·ed, *a.* Endowed with animal life; lively; vigorous; full of spirit (an *animated* discourse).—**animater,** **animator,** an′i·māt·ėr, *n.* One who animates.—**animating,** an′i·māt·ing, *a.* Giving life; infusing spirit; enlivening; rousing.—**animatingly,** an′i·māt·ing·li, *adv.* So as to animate. —**animation,** an·i·mā′shon, *n.* The act of animating or state of being animated; state of having life;

liveliness; briskness; vivacity.

animé, an′i·mā, *n.* [Sp.] A resin exuding from a large American tree, called in the West Indies *locust tree.* It produces a fine varnish. The name is also given to Indian copal.

animism, an′i·mizm, *n.* [L. *anima*, the soul.] The old hypothesis of a force (*Anima mundi*, soul of the world) immaterial but inseparable from matter, and giving to matter its form and movements; the attribution of spirit or soul to inanimate things.—**animist,** an′i·mist, *n.* One who holds to or believes in animism. —**animistic,** an·i·mist′ik, *a.* Pertaining to, or founded on, animism.

animosity, an·i·mos′i·ti, *n.* [L. *animositas*, from *animosus*, full of courage, ardent, from *animus*, the mind, courage, pride.] Courage‡; rancorous feeling; bitter and active enmity.

animus, an′i·mus, *n.* [L., spirit, temper.] Intention; purpose; spirit; temper; especially, hostile spirit or angry temper.

anion, an′i·on, *n.* [Gr. *ana*, upward, and *iōn*, going.] *Elect.* the element of an electrolyte which is evolved at the positive pole or *anode.*

anise, an′is, *n.* [Fr., from L. *anisum.*] An annual umbelliferous plant (*Pimpinella Anisum*), the seeds of which have an aromatic smell and a pleasant warm taste, and are employed in the manufacture of liqueurs.—**aniseed,** an′i·sēd, *n.* The seed of the anise. —**anisette,** an·i·set, *n.* [Fr.] A liqueur flavored with anise.

anisotrope, anisotropic, an′i·sō-trōp, an·i·sō·trōp′ik, *a.* Same as *Aelotropic.*

ankle, ang′kl, *n.* [A.Sax. *ancleow*, O. Fris. *ankel*, Dan. and Sw. *ankel*, G. *enkel*; from a root *ang*, meaning crooked. ANCHOR.] The joint which connects the foot with the leg.— **anklet,** ang′klet, *n.* An ornament, support, or protection for the ankle.

ankylosis, ang·ki·lō′sis, *n.* [Gr., from *angkylos*, crooked.] Stiffness and immovability of a joint; morbid adhesion of the articular ends of contiguous bones.—**ankylose,** ang′-ki·lōs, *v.t.* —*ankylosed*, *ankylosing.* To affect with ankylosis.—*v.i.* To become ankylosed.—**ankylotic,** ang·-ki·lot′ik, *a.* Pertaining to ankylosis.

anna, an′na, *n.* In the East Indies, the sixteenth part of a rupee, or about 1 English penny.

annals, an′nalz, *n. pl.* [L. *annales* (*libri*, books, understood), *annalis*, pertaining to a year, from *annus*, a year.] A history or relation of events in chronological order, each event being recorded under the year in which it happened.—**annalist,** an′nal·ist, *n.* A writer of annals.—**annalistic,** an·nal·ist′ik, *a.* Pertaining or peculiar to an annalist.

annats, annates, an′nats, an′nāts, *n. pl.* [L.L. *annata*, from L. *annus*, a year.] The first year's income of a see or benefice.

annatto, an·nät′tō, *n.* A small tropical American tree, the seeds of which yield an orange-red dye-stuff.

anneal, an·nēl′, *v.t.* [A.Sax. *anaelan*,

onaelan, to set on fire, to anneal—*an* or *on*, on, and *ælan*, to kindle.] To heat, as glass or iron vessels, in an oven or furnace, and then cool slowly, for the purpose of rendering less brittle; to temper by a gradually diminishing heat; to heat in order to fix colors; to bake.

annelid, annelidan, an′ne·lid, an·nel′i·dan, *n.* [L. *annellus*, a little ring, and Gr. *eidos*, form.] One of an extensive division or class of annulose animals, so called because their bodies are formed of a great number of small rings, as in the earthworm.

annex, an·neks′, *v.t.* [L. *annecto*, *annexum*, to bind to—*ad*, to, and *necto*, *nexum*, to bind.] To unite at the end; to subjoin; to unite, as a smaller thing to a greater; to connect, especially as a consequence (to *annex* a penalty).—*n.* Something annexed.—**annexation,** an·neks·ā′-shon, *n.* The act of annexing; what is annexed; addition; union.—**annexationist,** an·neks·ā′shon·ist, *n.* One favorable to annexation, as of a portion of another country to his own.

annihilate, an·nī′hil·āt, *v.t.* —*annihilated*, *annihilating.* [L. *annihilo—ad*, to, and *nihil*, nothing.] To reduce to nothing; to destroy the existence of; to cause to cease to be; to destroy the form or peculiar distinctive properties of.—**annihilable,** an·nī′hil·a·bl, *a.* Capable of being annihilated.—**annihilation,** an·nī′-hi·lā·shon, *n.* The act of annihilating or the state of being annihilated.— **annihilator,** an·nī′hil·āt·ėr, *n.* One who, or that which annihilates.

anniversary, an·ni·vėrs′a·ri, *a.* [L. *anniversarius—annus*, a year, and *verto*, *versum*, to turn.] Returning with the year at a stated time; annual; yearly.—*n.* A stated day on which some event is annually celebrated; the annual celebration in honor of an event.

annotate, an′nō·tāt, *v.t.* —*annotated*, *annotating.* [L. *annoto*, *annotatum—ad*, to, and *noto*, to note.] To comment upon; to make remarks on by notes.—*v.i.* To act as an annotator; to make annotations or notes (with *on*).—**annotation,** an·nō·tā′ shon, *n.* The act of annotating or making notes on; an illustrative note on some passage of a book.—**annotator,** an′nō·tāt·ėr, *n.* A writer of annotations or notes; a commentator.

announce, an·nouns′, *v.t.* —*announced*, *announcing.* [Fr. *annoncer*, from L. *annuncio—ad*, and *nuncio*, to tell, from *nuncius*, a messenger.] To publish; to proclaim; to give notice or first notice of.—**announcement,** an·nouns′ment, *n.* The act of announcing or giving notice; proclamation; publication.—**announcer,** an·-nouns′ėr, *n.* One that announces; a proclaimer.

annoy, an·noi′, *v.t.* [O.Fr. *anoier*, from *anoi*, annoyance, vexation, from L. *in odio*, in hatred, common in such phrases as *est mihi in odio*, it is hateful to me. ODIUM.] To torment or disturb, especially by continued or repeated acts; to tease, vex, pester, or molest.—*n.* Molestation; annoyance (chiefly a poetical word).—**annoyance**, an·noi′ans, *n.* The act of annoying; the state of being annoyed; that which annoys; trouble.—**annoyer**, an·noi′ẻr, *n.* One that annoys.—**annoying**, an·noi′ing, *a.* Vexatious; troublesome.

annual, an′nū·al, *a.* [L.L. *annualis*, from L. *annus*, a year.] Returning every year; coming yearly; lasting or continuing only one year or one yearly season; performed in a year; reckoned by the year.—*n.* A plant that grows from seed, flowers, and perishes in the course of the same season; a literary production published annually.—**annually**, an′nū·al·li, *adv.* Yearly; returning every year; year by year.

annuity, an·nū′i·ti, *n.* [Fr. *annuité*, from *annus*, a year.] A yearly payment of money which a person receives for life or for a term of years, the person being usually entitled to such payment in consideration of money advanced to those who pay.—**annuitant**, an·nū′it·ant, *n.* One receiving an annuity.

annul, an·nul′, *v.t.*—*annulled, annulling.*[Fr. *annuler*, from L. *ad nullum*, to nothing.] To reduce to nothing or annihilate (*Mil.*)‡; to make void; to nullify; to abrogate; cancel (laws, decrees, compacts, etc.).—**annulment**, an·nul′ment, *n.* The act of.

annular, † an′nū·lẻr, *a.* [L. *annularis*, from *annulus, anulus*, dim. of *anus*, a ring, akin to *annus*, a year, ANNUAL.] Having the form of a ring; pertaining to a ring.—*Annular eclipse*, an eclipse of the sun in which a ring of light formed by the sun's disk is visible around the dark shadow of the moon.—**annularly**, an′nū·lẻr·li, *adv.* In the manner of a ring.—**annulate, annulated**, an′nū·lāt, an′nū·lāt·ed, *a.* Furnished with rings, or circles like rings; having belts.—**annulation**, an·nū·lā′shon, *n.* A circular or ringlike formation.—**annulet**, an′nū·let, *n.* [A dim. from L. *annulus*, a ring.] A little ring or ringlike body.—**annulose**, an′nū·lōs, *a.* Furnished with rings; having a body composed of rings; a term applied to animals forming a subkingdom which embraces the worms, leeches, crabs, spiders, insects.

annunciate, an·nun′shi·āt, *v.t.*—*annunciated, annunciating.* [ANNOUNCE.] To bring tidings of; to announce.—**annunciation**, an·nun′shi·ā″shon, *n.* The act of announcing; announcement. [*cap.*] The tidings brought by the angel to Mary of the Incarnation of Christ; the church festival in memory of this announcement, falling on March 25.—**annunciator**, an·nun′shi·āt·ẻr, *n.* One who announces.

anode, an′ōd, *n.* [Gr. *ana*, upwards, and *hodos*, a way.] The part of the surface of an electrolyte which the electric current enters: opposed to *cathode.*—**anodize**, an′ōd·īz, *v.t.* To coat a metal with a protective film

by subjecting it to electrolytic action as the anode of a cell.

anodyne, an′ō·dĭn, *n.* [Gr. neg. prefix *an*, and *odynē*, pain.] Any medicine which allays pain.—*a.* Assuaging pain.

anoint, a·noint′, *v.t.* [O.E. *anointen, enointen*; O.Fr. *enoindre*, part. *enoint*, from L. *inungere, inunctum*, from *in*, in, on, and *ungo, unctum*, to anoint. UNGUENT.] To pour oil upon; to smear or rub with oil or unctuous substances; to consecrate by unction, or the use of oil.—**anointer**, a·noint′ẻr, *n.* One who anoints.—**anointment**, a·noint′ment, *n.* The act of anointing.

anomaly, a·nom′a·li, *n.* [Fr. *anomalie*; L. *anomalia*, Gr. *anōmalia*, inequality, neg. prefix *an*, and *homalos*, equal, similar, from *homos*, the same. SAME.] Deviation from the common rule; something abnormal; irregularity; *astron.* the angular distance of a planet from its perihelion, as seen from the sun; also the angle measuring apparent irregularities in the motion of a planet.—**anomalism**, a·nom′al·izm, *n.* An anomaly; a deviation from rule.—**anomalistic**, a·nom′a·list″ik, *a.* Pertaining to an anomaly.—*Anomalistic year*, the interval between two occasions when the earth is in perihelion, rather longer than the civil year.—**anomalous**, a·nom′a·lus, *a.* [L. *anomalus*, Gr. *anomalos*.] Forming an anomaly; deviating from a general rule, method, or analogy; irregular; abnormal.—**anomalously**, a·nom′a·lus·li, *adv.*—**anomalousness**, a·nom′a·lus·nes, *n.*

anon, a·non′, *adv.* [O.E. *anan, anoon*, A.Sax. *on ân, an ân*=on one, that is, without break.] Forthwith; immediately; quickly; at another time; thereafter; sometimes.—*Ever and anon*, every now and then.

anonymous, a·non′im·us, *a.* [Gr. *anōnymos*—neg. prefix *an*, and *onoma*, name. NAME.] Wanting a name; without any name acknowledged as that of author, contributor, and the like.—**anonymously**, a·non′im·us·li, *adv.* In an anonymous manner; without a name.—**anonyme**, an′on·īm, *n.* An assumed or false name.—**anonymity, anonymousness**, an·o·nim′i·ti, a·non′im·us·nes, *n.* The state of being anonymous.

anorthic, an·or′thik, *a.* [Gr. neg. prefix *an*, and *orthos*, straight, right.] Without right angles; *mineral.* having unequal oblique axes.—**anorthite**, an·or′thīt, *n.* A mineral of the feldspar family.

anosmia, an·os′mi·a, *n.* [Gr. neg. prefix *an*, and *osmē*, smell.] *Med.* a loss of the sense of smell.

another, an·uTH′ẻr, *a.* [*An*, indefinite art., and *other*.] Not the same; different; one more, in addition to a former number; any other; any one else. Often used without a noun, as a substitute for the name of a person or thing, and much used in opposition to *one*; as, *one* went *one* way, *another another.* Also frequently used with *one* in a reciprocal sense; as, 'Love *one*

another '; any other; some other.

anserine, an′sẻr·in, *a.* [L. *anserinus*, from *anser*, a goose.] Relating to or resembling a goose, or the skin of a goose: applied to the skin when roughened by cold or disease.—**anserous**,† an′sẻr·us, *a.* Of or pertaining to a goose; foolish; silly.

answer, an′sẻr, *v.t.* [A.Sax. *andswerian*, to answer—*and*, a prefix meaning against (=*a in* along, L. *ante*, before, Gr. *anti*, against), and *swerian*, to swear.] To speak or write in return to; to reply to; to refute; to say or do in reply; to act in compliance with, or in fulfilment or satisfaction of; to render account to or for; to be security for (*Shak.*); to be equivalent or adequate to; to serve; to suit.—*v.i.* To reply; to speak or write by way of return; to respond to some call; to be fit or suitable.—*To answer for*, to be accountable for; to guarantee.—*To answer to*, to be known by; to correspond to, in the way of resemblance, fitness, or correlation.—**answer**, an′sẻr, *n.* A reply; that which is said, written, or done, in return to a call, question, argument, challenge, allegation, petition, prayer, or address; the result of an arithmetical or mathematical operation; a solution; something done in return for, or in consequence of, something else; *law*, a counterstatement of facts in a course of pleadings.—**answerable**, an′sẻr·a·bl, *a.* Capable of being answered: obliged to give an account; amenable; responsible; correspondent.—**answerableness**, an′sẻr·a·bl·nes, *n.* The quality of being answerable.—**answerably**, an′sẻr·a·bli, *adv.* In due proportion, correspondence, or conformity; suitably.

ant, ant, *n.* [From A.Sax. *aemete*, an emmet (like *aunt*, from L. *amita*). EMMET.] An emmet; a pismire; a hymenopterous insect living in communities which consist of males, females, and neuters. The name is also given to the neuropterous insects more correctly called *Termites*.—**antbear**, *n.* A kind of large anteater.—**anteater**, *n.* A quadruped that eats ants, especially an edentate animal (genus *Myrmecophaga*) which feeds on ants and other insects, catching them by thrusting among them the long tongue covered with a viscid saliva.—**ant lion**, *n.* The larva of a neuropterous insect which prepares a kind of pitfall for the destruction of ants, etc.

antacid, ant·as′id, *n.* [*Anti*, against, and *acid*.] An alkali, or a remedy for acidity in the stomach.—*a.* Counteracting acidity.

antagonist, an·tag′ō·nist, *n.* [Gr. *antagōnistēs*—*anti*, against, and *agōnistēs*, a champion, a combatant, from *agōn*, a contest (whence *agony*).] One who contends with another; an opponent; a competitor; an adversary. ∴ *Syn.* under ADVERSARY.—*a.* Counteracting; opposing (said of muscles).—**antagonistic**, an·tag′ō·nist″ik, *a.* Contending against; acting in opposition; op-

---

ch, *ch*ain; *ch*, Sc. lo*ch*; g, *g*o; j, *j*ob; ng, si*ng*; TH. *then*; th, *th*in; w, *w*ig; hw, *wh*ig; zh, a*z*ure.

posing.—**antagonistic**, *n*. A muscle whose action counteracts that of another.—**antagonistically**, an·tag′-ō·nis″tik·al·li, *adv*. In an antagonistical manner.—**antagonize**, an·tag′-ō·niz, *v.i.*—*antagonized*, *antagonizing* To contend against; to act in opposition.—**antagonism**, an·tag′ō·nizm, *n*. Character of being an antagonist or antagonistic; counteraction or contrariety of things or principles.

antalkali, ant·al′ka·li, *n*. [*Anti* against, and *alkali*.] A substance which neutralizes an alkali.—**antalkaline**, ant·al′ka·lin, *a*. Having the property of neutralizing alkalies.

antarctic, ant·ärk′tik, *a*. [L. *antarcticus*, Gr. *antarktikos*—*anti*, against, and *arktos*, the north. ARCTIC.] Opposite to the northern or arctic pole; relating to the southern pole or to the region near it, and applied to a circle parallel to the equator and distant from the pole 23° 28′.

ante, an′tē, *prefix*. [L. *ante*, before, in front.] Before.—*n*. Poker stake.

antebellum, an′ti·bel′lum, *a*. [*ante*, before, and *bellum*, war.] Before the war; before the American Civil War.

antecede, an·tē·sēd′, *v.t.*—*anteceded*, *anteceding*. [L. *ante*, before, and *cedo*, to go. CEDE.] To go before in time; to precede.—**antecedence**, an·tē·sē′dens, *n*. The act or state of going before in time; precedence. —**antecedent**, an·tē·sē′dent, *a*. Going before; prior; anterior; preceding.—*n*. One who or that which goes before in time or place; *gram*. the noun to which a relative or other pronoun refers; *pl*. the earlier events of a man's life; previous course, conduct, or avowed principles.

antechamber, **anteroom**, an′tē--chām·bėr, an′tē·rōm, *n*. A chamber or room before or leading to another apartment.

antedate, an′tē·dāt, *n*. [Prefix *ante*, before, and *date*.] Prior date; a date antecedent to another.—*v.t.* *antedated*, *antedating*. To date before the true time or beforehand; to give an earlier date than the real one to; to anticipate or give effect to before the due time.

antediluvian, an′tē·di·lū″vi·an, *a*. [L. *ante*, before, and *diluvium*, a flood.] Existing, happening, or relating to what happened before the deluge.— *n*. One who lived before the deluge.

antelope, an′tē·lōp, *n*. [Doubtfully derived from a Gr. *antholōns*, an antelope, supposed to be compounded of *anthos*, a flower, and *ōps*, an eye.] A name applied to many species of ruminant mammals resembling the deer in general appearance, but essentially different in nature from them, having hollow, unbranched horns that are not deciduous.

antemeridian, an′tē·me·rid″i·an, *a*. [L. *ante*, before, and *meridies*, noon.] Being before noon; pertaining to the forenoon.

antenna, an·ten′na, *n. pl.* **antennae**, an·ten′nē. [L. *antenna*, a sail-yard.] One of the hornlike filaments that project from the head in insects, crustacea, and myriapods, and are considered as organs of touch and hearing; a feeler.

antepast, an′tē·past, *n*. [L. *ante*, before, *pastus*, food.] A foretaste.

antependium, ant·ē·pen′di·um, *n*. [L. *ante*, before, and *pendo*, to hang.] The hanging with which the front of an altar is covered.

antepenult, an′tē·pē·nult, *n*. [L. *ante*, before, *pene*, almost, and *ultimus*, last.] The last syllable of a word except two.—**antepenultimate**, an′-tē·pē·nul″ti·māt, *a*. Pertaining to the last syllable but two.—*n*. The antepenult.

anterior, an·tē′ri·ėr, *a*. [L., a comparative from *ante*, before.] Before in time; prior; antecedent; before in place; in front.—**anteriority**, an·tē′ri·or″i·ti, *n*. The state of being anterior in time or place.—**anteriorly**, an·tē′ri·ėr·li, *adv*. In an anterior manner; before.

anteroom, an′tē·rōm, *n*. See ANTECHAMBER.

anteroposterior, an·tē″rō·pos·tē′-ri·ėr, *a*. [L. *anterior*, from *ante*, before, and *posterior*, from *post*, behind.] Lying in a direction from behind forward.

anthelion, ant·hē′li·on, *n. pl.* **anthelia**, ant·hē′li·a. [Gr. *anti*, opposite to, and *hēlios*, the sun.] A luminous ring, or rings, caused by the diffraction of light, seen in alpine and polar regions opposite the sun when rising or setting.

anthelmintic, an·thel·min′tic, *a*. [Gr. *anti*, against, and *helmius*, *helminthos*, a worm.] *Med*. destroying or expelling worms in the intestines. —*n*. A vermifuge; a remedy for worms in the intestines.

anthem, an′them, *n*. [O.E. *antempne*, *antemne*, *antefne*, etc., A.Sax. *antefen*, an anthem; from L.L. *antiphona*, from Gr. *antiphōnon*, an antiphon—*anti*, against, and *phōne*, sound, the voice.] A hymn sung in alternate parts; in modern usage, a sacred tune or piece of music set to words taken from the Psalms or other parts of the Scriptures.

anther, an′thėr. *n*. [Gr. *anthēros*, flowery, from *anthos*, a flower.] The essential part of the stamen of a plant containing the pollen or fertilizing dust.

anthesis, an·thē′sis, *n*. [Gr., from *antheō*, to bloom, from *anthos*, a flower.] The period when flowers expand; expansion into a flower.

anthocyanin, an·tho·si′an·in, *n*. [Gr. *anthos* a flower, and *kyanos*, blue.] The blue coloring matter of plants.

anthodium, an·thō′di·um, *n*. [Gr. *anthōdēs*, from *anthos*, a flower.] *Bot*. the head of flowers of composite plants, as of a thistle or daisy.

anthology, an·thol′o·ji, *n*. [Gr. *anthologia*, from *anthologos*, flower-gathering—*anthos*, a flower, and *legō*, to gather.] A collection of passages from authors; a collection of selected poems.—**anthological**, an·tho·loj′ik·al, *a*. Pertaining to anthology.

anthophore, an′tho·fōr, *n*. [Gr. *anthos*, a flower, and *pherein*, to bear.] *Bot*. a columnar process arising from the bottom of the calyx, and having at its apex the petals, stamens, and pistil.

anthracene, an′thra·sēn, *n*. [ANTHRACITE.] A hydrocarbon obtained from coal tar and furnishing alizarine.

anthracite, an′thra·sīt, *n*. [Gr. *anthrax*, *anthrakos*, coal.] Glance or blind coal, a nonbituminous coal of a shining luster, approaching to metallic, and which burns without smoke, with a weak or no flame, and with intense heat.—**anthracitic**, an·thra·sit′ik, *a*. Pertaining to anthracite.

anthrax, an′thraks, *n*. [Gr.] *Med*. a carbuncle; a malignant ulcer.

anthropogeny, an·thro·poj′en·i, *n*. [Gr. *anthrōpos*, a man, and root *gen*. to beget.] the science of the origin and development of man.

anthropography, an·thro·pog′ra·fi, *n*. [Gr. *anthrōpos*, a man, and *graphē*, a description.] A description of man or of the human race; ethnography.

anthropoid, an′thro·poid, *a*. [Gr. *anthrōpos*, a man, and *eidos*, resemblance.] Resembling man: specifically applied to such apes as most closely approach the human race.

anthropology, an·thro·pol′o·ji, *n*. [Gr. *anthrōpos*, a man, and *logos*, discourse.] The science of man and mankind, including the study of the physical and mental constitution of man, or his whole nature, as exhibited both in the present and the past.—**anthropologic**, **anthropological**, an·thrō′pō·loj″ik, an·thrō·pō·loj″ik·al, *a*. Pertaining to anthropology.—**anthropologist**, an·thrō·pol′o·jist, *n*. One who writes on or studies anthropology.

anthropometry, an·thro·pom′et·ri, *n*. [Gr. *anthrōpos*, a man, and *metron*, measure.] The measurement of the human body.

anthropomorphism, an·thrō′pō--morf″izm, *n*. [Gr. *anthrōpos*, a man, and *morphē*, form.] The representation or conception of the Deity under a human form, or with human attributes and affections.—**anthropomorphic**, an·thrō′pō·mor″fik, *a*. Relating to or characterized by anthropomorphism; resembling man. —**anthropomorphist**, an·thrō′pō--morf″ist, *n*. One who believes that the Supreme Being has a human form and human attributes.— **anthropomorphitism**, an·thrō′pō--morf″it·izm, *n*. The doctrines of anthropomorphites.—**anthropomorphous**, an·thrō′pō·morf″us, *a*. Having the figure of or resemblance to a man.

anthropophagi, an·thrō·pof′a·ji, *n. pl*. [Gr. *anthrōpos*, a man, and *phagō*, to eat.] Maneaters; cannibals; men that eat human flesh.— **anthropophagite**, an·thrō·pof′a·jīt *n*. A cannibal.—**anthropophagous**, an·-thrō·pof′a·gus, *a*. Feeding on human flesh.—**anthropophagy**, an·thrō-pof′a·ji, *n*. Cannibalism.

antiaircraft, an′ti·âr″kraft, *adj*. Used for defense against enemy aircraft.

antiar, an′ti·är, *n*. [Javanese.] The milky juice which exudes from wounds made in the upas-tree, and which is one of the most acrid and virulent vegetable poisons.

antibiotic, an′ti·bi·ot″ik, *n.* A substance produced by living organisms (a bacterium or fungus) and having the power to kill or inhibit the growth of bacteria, as penicillin.

antibody, an′ti·bod″i, *n.* [*anti* and *body.*] A substance produced by body tissue as a reaction to the introduction of a foreign substance; an antigen.

antic, an′tik, *a.* [A form of *antique,* L. *antiquus,* ancient. The modern sense of this word is derived from the grotesque figures seen in the antique sculpture of the Middle Ages. ANTIQUE.] Odd; fanciful; grotesque; fantastic (tricks, postures).—*n.* An absurd or ridiculous gesture, an odd gesticulation; a piece of buffoonery; a caper.

antichlor, an′ti·klōr, *n.* [Gr. *anti,* against, and the *chlor-* of *chlorine.*] A substance employed to remove, or neutralize the effects of, the free chlorine left in goods bleached by means of chloride of lime, etc.

antichrist, an′ti·krīst, *n.* An opponent of Christ; a person or power antagonistic to Christ.—**antichristian,** an·ti·kris′tyan, *a.* Opposite to or opposing the Christian religion.

anticipate, an·tis′i·pāt, *v.t.*—*anticipated, anticipating.* [L. *anticipo* for *antecipo,* to *take* beforehand—*ante,* before, and *capio,* to take.] To be before in doing something; to prevent or preclude by prior action; to forestall; to realize beforehand; to foretaste or foresee; to look forward to; to expect.—*v.i.* To treat of something, as in a narrative, before the proper time.—**anticipant,** an·tis′i·pant, *a.* Anticipating; anticipative.—**anticipation,** an·tis′i·pā″shon, *n.* The act of anticipating; expectation; foretaste; realization beforehand; previous notion; preconceived opinion.—**anticipative,** an·tis′i·pāt·iv, *a.* Anticipating or tending to anticipate; containing anticipation.—**anticipatively,** an·tis′i·pāt·iv·li, *adv.* By anticipation.—**anticipator,** an·tis′i·pāt·ėr, *n.* One who anticipates.—**anticipatory,** an·tis′i·pā·to·ri, *a.* Anticipative.

anticlimax, an·ti·klī′maks, *n.* A passage in which the ideas first increase in force, and then terminate in something less important and striking: opposed to climax.

anticlinal, an·ti·klī′nal, *a.* [Gr. *anti,* opposite, and *klinō,* to incline.] Inclining in opposite directions.—*Anticlinal axis, geol.* a line from which strata dip on either side as from the ridge of a house: opposed to synclinal.—*n.* An anticlinal line or axis.

anticyclone, an″ti·sī′klōn, *n.* A meteorological phenomenon consisting of a region of high barometric pressure, the pressure being greatest in the center, with light winds flowing outward from the center and not inward as in the cyclone.

antidote, an′ti·dōt, *n.* [L. *antidotum,* from Gr. *antidoton,* an antidote—*anti,* against, and *dotos,* given, from

didōmi, to give.] A medicine to counteract the effects of poison, or of anything noxious taken into the stomach; *fig.* anything that prevents or counteracts evil.—**antidotal,** an·ti·dōt′al, *a.* Having the qualities of an antidote; serving as an antidote.

antifebrile, an·ti·feb′ril or an·ti·fē′bril, *a.* Having the quality of abating fever; opposing or tending to cure fever.

antifederal, an·ti·fed′ėr·al, *a.* Opposed to or opposing federalism or a federal constitution.—**antifederalism,** an·ti·fed′ėr·al·izm, *n.* Opposition to federalism.—**antifederalist,** an·ti·fed′ėr·al·ist, *n.* One who is averse to federalism.

antifreeze, an′ti·frēz″, *n.* A substance added to water to lower its freezing temperature and used to keep the cooling systems of internal-combustion engines from freezing during the cold weather.

antifriction, an·ti·frik′shon, *a.* Obviating or lessening friction.

antigen, an′ti·jen, *n.* [Gr. *anti,* against, and *gen,* to form.] A substance that gives rise to an antibody when introduced into blood or tissue.

antihistamine, an·ti·his″ta·mēn, *n. Med.* any of a number of compounds that inactivate histamine in the body, used mainly for the treatment of allergy.

antilogy, an·til′o·ji, *n.* [Gr. *antilogia*—*anti,* against, and *legō,* to speak.] A contradiction between any words or passages in an author, or between members of the same body.

antimacassar, an′ti·ma·kas″ar, *n.* [Gr. *anti,* against, and E. *macassar-oil.*] A covering for chairs, sofas, couches, etc., made of open cotton or worsted work, to preserve them from being soiled.

antimatter, an′ti·mat′ėr, *n.* [*anti* and *matter.*] Matter composed of particles with charges opposite to those of ordinary matter.

antimere, an′ti·mēr, *n.* [Gr. *anti,* opposite, *meros,* part.] *Biol.* one of two or more corresponding parts on opposite sides of animals.

antimissile, an′ti·mis″il, *adj.* Designed for use in the defense against enemy missiles, such as rockets.

antimonarchic, an′ti·mon·ärk″ik, *a.* Opposed to monarchy; opposing a kingly government.

antimony, an′ti·mo·ni, *n.* [L. of twelfth century *antimonium;* origin doubtful.] A metallic element, brittle, lustrous, and white in color, used chiefly in alloys and (in compounds) in medicine and such as rockets. Symbol, Sb (stibium); at. no., 51; at. wt., 121.75.—**antimonial,** an·ti·mō′ni·al, *a.* Pertaining to antimony, or partaking of its qualities.

antineutrino, an′ti·nu·trē″nō, *n. Phys.* a hypothetical subnuclear particle having the same relation to the neutrino as the positron has to the electron, having near zero mass, no electric charge, and a spin opposite in direction to that of the neutrino.

antineutron, an′ti·nū″tron, *n. Phys.* a hypothetical particle of mass equal

to that of the neutron, without electric charge, and with a magnetic moment opposite to that of the neutron.

antinomy, an·tin′om·i, *n.* [Gr. *anti,* against, and *nomos,* a law.] The opposition of one law or rule to another law or rule; anything, as a law, statement, etc., opposite or contrary.— **antinomian,** an·ti·nō′mi·an, *a.* Opposed to law; pertaining to the Antinomians.—*n.* One of a sect who maintains that, under the gospel dispensation, the moral law is of no use or obligation.—**antinomianism,** an·ti·nō′mi·an·izm, *n.* The tenets of the Antinomians.

antioxidant, an′ti·ok″si·dant, *n.* A substance added to rubber that inhibits its deterioration; any substance inhibiting oxidation.

antipathy, an·tip′a·thi, *n.* [Gr. *antipatheia*—*anti,* against, and *pathos,* feeling. PATHOS.] Natural aversion; instinctive contrariety or opposition in feeling; an aversion felt at the presence of an object; repugnance; contrariety in nature: commonly with *to* before the object.—**antipathetic, antipathetical,** an′ti·pa·thet″ik, an′ti·pa·thet″ik·al, *a.* Having antipathy.

antipersonnel, an′ti·pér″so·nel′, *adj. Milit.* used to destroy or obstruct individuals rather than matériel.

antiphlogistic, an′ti·flo·jis″tik, *a.* Opposed to the theory of phlogiston; counteracting inflammation, or an excited state of the system.—*n.* A medicine which checks inflammation.

antiphon, antiphony, an′ti·fon, an·tif′o·ni, *n.* [Gr. *anti,* in response to, and *phōnē,* voice. Anthem is the same word.] The answer of one choir or one portion of a congregation to another when an anthem or psalm is sung alternately; alternate singing; a short versicle sung before and after the psalms.—**antiphonal, antiphonary,** an·tif′o·nal, an·tif′o·na·ri, *n.* A book of antiphons or anthems.—**antiphonal, antiphonic,** an·tif′on·al, an·ti·fon′ik, *a.* Pertaining to antiphony or alternate singing.

antipodes, an·tip′o·dēz, *n. pl.* [Gr.—*anti,* opposite, and *pous, podos,* foot.] Those who live on the opposite side of the globe; the region directly on the opposite side of the globe; *fig.* anything diametrically opposite or opposed to another; a contrary.—**antipodal, antipodean,** an·tip′o·dal, an·tip′o·dē″an, *a.* Pertaining to antipodes.—**antipode,** an′ti·pōd, *n.* One who or that which is in opposition or opposite.

antipope, an′ti·pōp, *n.* One who usurps the papal power in opposition to the pope; a pretender to the papacy.

antiproton, an′ti·prō″ton, *n. Phys.* a hypothetical particle with mass equal to that of a proton but carrying a negative charge, postulated as existing in the nuclei of hypothetical inverted atoms.

antipyretic, an′ti·pi·ret″ik, *n.* [Gr. *anti,* against, and *pyretos,* fever.] *Med.* a remedy efficacious against fever.

antiquary, an′ti·kwa·ri, *n.* [L. *anti-*

quarius, from *antiquus*, old, ancient, from *ante*, before.] One devoted to the study of ancient times through their relics; one versed in antiquity: an archaeologist.—**antiquarian**, an·ti·kwā′ri·an, *a*. Pertaining to antiquaries or to antiquity.—*n*. An antiquary. —**antiquated**, an′ti·kwāt·ed, *a*. Grown old fashioned; obsolete; out of use; behind the times.—**antique**, an·tēk′, *a*. [Fr., from L. *antiquus*, ancient. *Antic* is a form of this word.] Having existed in ancient times; belonging to or having come down from antiquity; ancient (an *antique* statue); having the characteristics of an earlier day; smacking of bygone days; of old fashion (an *antique* robe).—*n*. Anything very old; specifically, a term applied to the remains of ancient art, more especially to the works of Grecian and Roman antiquity.—**antiquity**, an·tik′wi·ti, *n*. [L. *antiquitas* from *antiquus*, ancient.] The quality of being ancient; ancientness; great age; ancient times; former ages; the people of ancient times; *pl*. the remains of ancient times; institutions, customs, etc., belonging to ancient nations.

antirrhinum, an·ti·rī′num, *n*. [Gr. *anti*, like, and *rhin*, a nose. The flowers of most of the species bear a resemblance to the snout of some animal.] Snapdragon, the generic name of various plants with showy flowers, much cultivated in gardens.

antiscorbutic, an″ti·skạr·bū′tik, *a*. *Med*. counteracting scurvy or a scorbutic tendency.—*n*. A remedy for or preventive of scurvy.

anti-Semitism, an·ti·sem′i·tizm, *n*. Hostility or discrimination against Jews.

antisepsis, an·ti·sep′sis, *n*. [Gr. *anti*, against, and *septos*, putrid, from *sepō*, to putrefy.] The inhibition or destruction of microorganisms; prevention of sepsis.—**antiseptic**, an·ti··sep′tik, *a*.—*n*. An agent that inhibits the growth of microorganisms.

antislavery, an′ti·slā·vėr·i, *a*. Against slavery.

antisocial, an′ti·sō′shal, *a*. Contrary to the laws and standards of society.

antispasmodic, an′ti·spaz·mod″ik, *a*. *Med*. opposing spasm; resisting convulsions.—*n*. A remedy for spasm.

antistrophe, an·tis′tro·fe, *n*. [Gr.—*anti*, opposite, and *strophē*, a turning.] A part of an ancient Greek choral ode alternating with the strophe.—**antistrophic**, an·ti·strof′ik, *a*. Relating to the antistrophe.

antisyphilitic, an·ti·sif′il·it″ik, *a*. Efficacious against syphilis, or the venereal poison.—*n*. A medicine of this kind.

antithesis, an·tith′e·sis, *n*. pl. **antitheses**, an·tith′e·sēz. [Gr. *antithesis* —*anti*, against, and *thesis*, a setting, from *tithēmi*, to place.] Opposition; contrast; *rhet*. a figure by which contraries are opposed to contraries; a contrast or opposition of words or sentiments; as, the prodigal *robs his heir*, the miser *robs himself*.—**antithetic, antithetical**, an·ti·thet′ik, an·ti·thet′ik·al, *a*. Pertaining to or characterized by antithesis.—**anti-**

thetically, an·ti·thet′ik·al·li, *adv*. In an antithetical manner.

antitoxin, an·ti·tok′sin, *n*. [Gr. *anti*, against. TOXIC.] *Med*. a fluid introduced into the blood to counteract the poison of a disease.

antitrades, an′ti·trādz, *n*. A tropical wind blowing above a trade wind and in the opposite direction.

anti-Trinitarian, an·ti·trin′i·tā″ri·an, *n*. One who denies the doctrine of the Trinity, or the existence of three persons in the Godhead.—*a*. Opposing the doctrine of the Trinity.

antitrust, an′ti·trust, *a*. Against monopoly.

antitype, an′ti·tīp, *n*. That which is correlative to a type; that which is prefigured or represented by the type.—**antitypical**, an·ti·tip′ik·al, *a*.

antler, ant′lėr, *n*. [O.Fr. *antoillier*, *entoillier;* origin doubtful.] A branch of the horn of a deer, particularly of a stag; one of the horns of the cervine animals.—**antlered**, ant′lėrd, *a*.

antonym, ant′ō·nim, *n*. [Gr. *anti*, against, *onoma*, name.] A word of directly contrary signification to another: the opposite of a synonym.

antrorse, an·trors′, *a*. [From L. *ante*, before, and *versus*, turned.] *Bot*. forward or upward in direction.

antrum, an′trum, *n*. [Gr. *antron*, cave.] Chamber or cavern; *anat*. cavity in a hollow organ; a sinus, esp. the maxillary antrum.

anus, ā′nus, *n*. [L.] *Anat*. the inferior opening of the alimentary canal; the fundament.

anvil, an′vil, *n*. [A.Sax. *anfilt*, O.H.G. *anafalz*—*an*, on, and A.Sax. *fealdan*, G. *falten*, *falzen*, to *fold*.] An iron block with a smooth, usually steel, face, and often a projecting horn, on which metals are hammered and shaped.—*v.t.*† To form or shape on an anvil.

anxiety, ang·zī′e·ti, *n*. [L. *anxietas*, from *anxius*, solicitous, from *ango*, to vex. ANGER.] Pain or uneasiness of mind respecting some event, future or uncertain; concern; solicitude; care; disquietude.—**anxious**, angk′shus, *a*. Full of anxiety or solicitude respecting something future or unknown; being in painful suspense (of persons); attended with or proceeding from solicitude or uneasiness (of things): followed often by *for*, *about*, *on account of*.—**anxiously**, angk′shus·li, *adv*. In an anxious manner; solicitously.—**anxiousness**, angk′shus·nes, *n*. Anxiety.

any, en′ni, *a*. [A.Sax. *ænig*, from *ân*, one, and term. *ig* (parallel to *naenig*, none); like G. *einig*, D. *eenig*, *any*.] One out of many indefinitely (*any* man); some; an indefinite number or quantity (*any* men, *any* money): often used as a pronoun, the noun being understood.—*adv*. In any degree; to any extent; at all (*any* better).—**anybody**, en′ni·bo·di, *n*. Any one person.—**anyhow**, en′ni··hou, *adv*. In any manner, at any rate; in any event; on any account.—**anyone**, en′ni·wun, *pron*. Any person at all; anybody.—**anything**, en′ni··thing, *pron*. Any object or fact whatever.—**anyway**, en′ni·wā, *adv*.

Anyhow; at least.—**anywhere**, en′ni·whār, *adv*. In any place.—**anywise**, en′ni·wīz, *adv*. [*wise=guise*.] In any way.

Anzac, an′zak, *n*. The Australian—New Zealand Army Corps, at Gallipoli during the war of 1915: from the initial letters.

aorist, ā′or·ist, *n*. [Gr. *aoristos*, indefinite—*a*, not, and *horos*, limit.] *Gram*. a tense in the Greek verb which expresses past time indefinitely (like E. *did* or *saw*).—**aoristic**, ā·or·ist′ik, *a*. Pertaining to or having the character of an aorist.

aorta, ā·or′ta, *n*. [Gr. *aortē*, from *aeirō*, to lift, to heave.] *Anat*. the great artery or trunk of the arterial system, proceeding from the left ventricle of the heart, and giving origin to all the arteries except the pulmonary.—**aortal, aortic**, ā·or′tal, ā·or′tik, *a*. Pertaining to the aorta.

apace, a·pās′, *adv*. With a quick pace; fast; speedily; with haste.

apache, a·pash′, *n*. [American Indian tribe.] A French street ruffian or desperado.

apart, a·pärt′, *adv*. [Fr. *à part*, aside, separate—*à*, from L. *ad*, to, *part*=E. *part*, side.] Separately; in a state of separation; distinct or away from others; at some distance.—**apartment**, a·pärt′ment, *n*. [Fr. *appartement*.] A room in a building; a division in a house separated from others by partitions; *pl*. a suite, or set, of rooms; lodgings (a French usage).

apartheid, a·pärt′āt, *n*. [Afrik. lit, separateness.] The system of separation of the racial groups in the Republic of South Africa.

apathy, ap′a·thi, *n*. [L. *apathia*, Gr. *apatheia*—*a*, not, and *pathos*, suffering.] Want of feeling; privation of passion, emotion, or excitement; insensibility; indifference.—**apathetic, apathetical**, ap·a·thet′ik, ap·a·thet′ik·al, *a*. Affected with or proceeding from apathy; devoid of feeling; insensible.

apatite, ap′a·tīt, *n*. [From Gr. *apatē*, deceit, it having been mistaken for other minerals.] A mineral consisting chiefly of phosphate of lime, used as a fertilizer.

ape, āp, *n*. [A.Sax. *apa*, Icel. *api*, D. *aap*, Dan. *abe*, G. *affe*, O.H.G. *affo*, Ir. and Gael. *apa*: an initial guttural has been lost, seen in Gr. *kēpos*, Skr. *kapi*, an ape.] One of a family of quadrumanous animals found in both continents, having the teeth of the same number and form as in man, and possessing neither tails nor cheek pouches; *fig*. one who imitates servilely.—*v.t*. aped, aping. To imitate servilely; to mimic.—**apish**, āp′ish, *a*. Having the qualities of an ape; inclined to imitate superiors.—**apishly**, āp′ish·li, *adv*. In an apish manner.—**apishness**, āp′ish·nes, *n*.

apeak, a·pēk′, *adv*. [Fr. *à-pic*, to the summit.] On the point; in a posture to pierce; *naut*. perpendicular, or inclining to the perpendicular: said of the anchor or yards.

aperient, a·pē′ri·ent, *a*. [L. *aperiens*, *aperientis*, part. of *aperio*, to open.]

---

fāte, fär, fâre, fat, fạll; mē, met, hėr; pīne, pin; nōte, not, mōve; tūbe, tub, bụll; oil, pound.

Med. gently purgative; having the quality of opening; deobstruent; laxative.—*n.* A medicine which gently opens the bowels; a laxative.

apert, a·pėrt′, *a.* [L. *apertus*, open.] Open; evident.—**aperture,** ap′ėr·tūr, *n.* [L. *apertura*, from *aperio, apertum*, to open.] An opening; a mouth, entrance, gap, cleft, etc.; a passage; a perforation; the diameter of the exposed part of the object glass of a telescope or other optical instrument.

apetalous, a·pet′al·us, *a.* [Gr. *a*, neg., and *petalon*, a petal.] *Bot.* having no petals or corolla.—**apetalousness,** a·pet′al·us·nes, *n.*

apex, ā′peks, *n.* pl. **apices, apexes,** ā′pi·sēz, ā′peks·ez. [L. *apex*, pl. *apices.*] The tip, point, or summit of anything.

aphaeresis, apheresis, a·fē′re·sis, *n.* [Gr. *aphairesis*, a taking away—*apo*, from, and *haireō*, to take.] *Gram.* the taking of a letter or syllable from the beginning of a word; *med.* the removal of anything noxious; *surg.* amputation.

aphanite, af′an·īt, *n.* [Gr. *aphanēs*, indistinct—*a*, not, and *phainō*, to appear.] A name of fine-grained minerals whose structure cannot be detected by the naked eye.—**aphanitic,** af·an·it′ik, *a.* Pertaining to aphanite or of similar character.

aphasia, a·fā′zha, *n.* [Gr. *a*, not, *phasis*, speech.] Loss of the faculty of speech, or of connecting words and ideas, owing to morbid conditions of brain, while the speech organs and general intelligence remain unaffected.

aphelion, a·fē′li·on, *n.* pl. **aphelia,** a·fē′li·a. [Gr. *apo*, from, and *hēlios*, the sun.] That point of a planet's or comet's orbit which is most distant from the sun: opposed to *perihelion.*

aphesis, af′e·sis, *n.* [Gr. *aphesis*, a letting go.] Loss of a short unaccented syllable at the beginning of a word; as *squire* for *esquire.*—**aphetic,** a·fet′ik, *a.* Pertaining to.

aphid, ā′fid, *n.* pl. **aphides,** af′i·dēz. [A term of modern origin, perhaps from Gr. *aphyssō*, to draw or drink up liquids.] A plant louse. The aphides are small insects, some of them wingless; they are very numerous and destructive, almost every species of plant supporting a different variety.—**aphidian,** a·fid′i·an, *a.* Pertaining to the aphides.

aphonia, a·fō′ni·a, *n.* [Gr. *a*, not, and *phōne*, voice.] A loss of voice; dumbness; speechlessness.—**aphonous,** af′ō·nus, *a.* Destitute of voice.

aphorism, af′or·izm, *n.* [Gr. *aphorismos*, from *aphorizō*, to mark out, to define—*apo*, from, and *horos*, a boundary.] A precept or principle expressed in a few words; a brief sentence containing some important truth; a maxim. ∴ *Aphorism* is the brief statement of a doctrine. *Axiom*, a statement claiming to be considered as a self-evident truth. *Maxim*, a formula referring rather to practical than to abstract truth; a rule of conduct. *Apophthegm*, a terse sententious saying.—**aphorist,** af′or·ist, *n.* A writer of aphorisms.—**aphor-**

istic, af·or·ist′ik, *a.* Pertaining to, resembling, or containing aphorisms; in the form of an aphorism.—**aphoristically,** af·or·ist′ik·al·li, *adv.* In the form or manner of aphorisms. —**aphorize,** af′or·īz, *v.i.* To make aphorisms.

aphrodisiac, af·ro·diz′i·ak, *a.* [Gr. *aphrodisios, aphrodisiakos*, from *Aphrodite*, goddess of love.] Exciting venereal desire.—**aphrodisiac,** *n.* Food or a medicine exciting sexual desire.

aphyllous, af′il·lus or a·fil′us, *a.* [Gr. *a*, neg., and *phyllon*, a leaf.] *Bot.* destitute of leaves.

apiary, ā′pi·a·ri, *n.* [L. *apiarium*, from *apis*, a bee.] The place where bees are kept; a stand or shed for bees.—**apiarian,** ā·pi·ā′ri·an, *a.* Relating to bees.—*n.* A bee keeper; an apiarist.—**apiarist,** ā′pi·a·rist, *n.* One who keeps bees.—**apiculture,** āp·i·kul′tūr, *n.* The art of managing bees in hives; beekeeping.

apical, ap′ik·al, *a.* [L. *apex*, an apex, a sharp point or peak.] Relating to the apex or top; belonging to the pointed end of a cone-shaped body. —**apices, apexes,** pl. of *apex.*—**apiculate,** a·pik′ū·lāt, *a. Bot.* tipped with a short and abrupt point.

apiece, a·pēs′, *adv.* To each; as the share of each; each by itself; by the individual.

apish, apishly. See APE.

aplacental, ap·la·sen′tal, *a.* [Prefix *a*, not, and *placental.*] Applied to those mammals in which the young are destitute of a placenta (as the kangaroo, duck mole, etc.).

aplanatic, ap·la·nat′ik, *a.* [Gr. *a*, not, and *planaō*, to wander.] *Optics*, corrective of the defect by which rays of light diverge and do not come to a focus (an *aplanatic* lens).

aplomb, a·plom′, *n.* [Fr., lit. the state of being perpendicular, or true to the *plumb*-line.] Self-possession springing from perfect self-confidence; assurance.

apocalypse, a·pok′a·lips, *n.* [Gr. *apokalypsis*, from *apokalyptō*, to disclose—prefix *apo*, and *kalyptō*, to cover.] Revelation; discovery; disclosure. The name of the last book of the New Testament.—**apocalyptic, apocalyptical,** a·pok′a·lip″tik, a·pok′a·lip″tik·al, *a.* Containing or pertaining to revelation; pertaining to the Revelation of St. John.—**apocalyptic,** a·pok′a·lip″tik, *n.* A writer on the Apocalypse.—**apocalyptically,** a·pok′a·lip″tik·al·li, *adv.* In an apocalyptic manner; by revelation.

apocarpous, ap·o·kär′pus, *a.* [Gr. *apo*, denoting separation, and *karpos*, fruit.] In *bot.* having the carpels, or at least their styles, disunited.

apocope, a·pok′o·pe, *n.* [Gr. *apokopē*, a cutting off—*apo*, and *kopē*, a cutting.] The cutting off or omission of the last letter or syllable of a word, as *th'* for *the.*—**apocopate,** a·pok′ō·pāt, *v.t.*—**apocopated, apocopating.** To cut off or drop the last letter or syllable of.

Apocrypha, a·pok′ri·fa, *n.* [Gr. *apok-ryphos*, hidden, spurious—*apo*, away,

and *kryptō*, to conceal. CRYPT.] The collective name of certain books admitted by the R. Catholics into the Old Testament canon, but whose authenticity as inspired writings is not generally admitted.—**apocryphal,** a·pok′ri·fal, *a.* Pertaining to the Apocrypha; not canonical; of uncertain authority or credit; fictitious. —**apocryphally,** a·pok′ri·fal·li, *adv.* In an apocryphal manner; equivocally; doubtfully.—**apocryphalness,** a·pok′ri·fal·nes, *n.*

apodal, ap′o·dal, *a.* Having no feet: also said of fishes having no ventral fins, as the eel, swordfish, etc.

apodictic, apodictical, ap·o·dik′tik, ap·o·dik′tik·al, *a.* [Gr. *apodeiktikos—apo*, forth, and *deiknymi*, to show.] Demonstrative; evident beyond contradiction.—**apodictically,** ap·o·dik′tik·al·li, *adv.* Demonstratively.

apodosis, a·pod′o·sis, *n.* [Gr. *apodosis*, a giving back—*apo*, from, and *didōmi*, to give.] *Gram.* the latter part of a conditional sentence (or one beginning with *if, though*, etc.), dependent on the *protasis* or condition.

apogee, ap′o·jē, *n.* [Gr. *apo*, from, and *ge*, the earth.] That point in the orbit of a planet or other heavenly body which is at the greatest distance from the earth; properly this particular point of the moon's orbit. —**apogean,** ap·o·jē′an, *a.* Pertaining to or connected with the apogee.

Apollyon, a·pol′yon, *n.* [Gr. *apollūmi*, to destroy.] The Devil.

apologue, ap′o·log, *n.* [Gr. *apologos*, an apologue, a fable—*apo*, from, and *logos*, discourse.] A moral fable; a relation of fictitious events intended to convey useful truths, such as the fables of Aesop.

apology, a·pol′o·ji, *n.* [Gr. *apologia*, a speech in defence—*apo*, away from, and *logos*, a discourse.] Something said or written in defense; justification; vindication; an acknowledgment, usually accompanied by an expression of regret, for some improper remark or act; a temporary substitute or makeshift (colloq.)— **apologetic, apologetical,** a·pol′o·jet″ik, a·pol′o·jet″ik·al, *a.* Of or pertaining to or containing apology; defending by words or arguments.— **apologetically,** a·pol′o·jet″ik·al·li, *adv.* In an apologetic manner; by way of apology.—**apologetics,** a·pol′-o·jet″iks, *n.* That branch of theology by which Christians are enabled scientifically to justify and defend the peculiarities of their faith, and to answer its opponents.—**apologist, apologizer,** a·pol′o·jist, a·pol′o·jīz·er, *n.* One who makes an apology.— **apologize,** a·pol′o·jīz, *v.i.*—*apologized, apologizing.* To make an apology.

aponeurosis, ap′o·nū·rō″sis, *n.* pl. **aponeuroses,** ap′o·nū·rō″sēz. [Gr. *aponeurōsis—apo*, from, and *neuron*, a nerve, because formerly supposed to be an expansion of a nerve or nerves.] A white, shining, and very resisting membrane, composed of interlaced fibers, found surrounding the voluntary muscles, large arteries,

ch, *chain*; ch, Sc. lo*ch*; g, *go*; j, *job*; ng, si*ng*; TH, *then*; th, *thin*; w, *wig*; hw, *whig*; zh, a*z*ure.

and other parts of the body.—
aponeurotic, ap′o·nū·rot″ik, *a.* Relating to the aponeuroses.

apophthegm, ap′o·them, *n.* [Gr. *apo*, from, and *phthēgma*, word.] A short, pithy, and instructive saying; a sententious precept or maxim. Written also *Apothegm. Syn.* under APHORISM.—**apophthegmatic, apophthegmatical,** ap′o·theg·mat″ik, ap′o·theg·mat″ik·al, *a.* Pertaining to or having the character of an apophthegm; sententious.—**apophthegmatize,** ap·o·theg′mat·īz, *v.i.* To utter apophthegms.

apophyllite, a·pof′i·līt, *n.* [Gr. *apo*, from, and *phyllon*, a leaf, from its tendency to exfoliate.] A mineral of a foliated structure, and readily separating into thin laminae, with a peculiar luster.

apophysis, a·pof′i·sis, *n.* pl. **apophyses,** a·pof′i·sēz. [Gr.—*apo*, from, and *physis*, growth.] *Anat.* a prominence; a prominent part of a bone.

apoplexy, ap′o·plek·si, *n.* [Gr. *apoplēxia*, apoplexy—*apo*, from, and *plēssō, plēxō*, to strike.] Abolition or sudden diminution of sensation and voluntary motion, resulting from congestion or rupture of the blood vessels of the brain.—**apoplectic, apoplectical,** ap·o·plek′tik, ap·o·plek′tik·al, *a.* Pertaining to or consisting in apoplexy; predisposed to apoplexy.—**apoplectic,** ap·o·plek′tik, *n.* A person affected with apoplexy.

aposiopesis, ap′o·sī·ō·pē″sis, *n.* [Gr.—*apo*, from, and *siopaō*, to be silent.] *Rhet.* sudden stopping short and leaving a statement unfinished for the sake of effect.

apostasy, a·pos′ta·si, *n.* [Gr. *apostasia*, a standing away from, a defection—*apo*, from, and root *sta*, to stand.] An abandonment of what one has professed; a total desertion or departure from one's faith, principles, or party.—**apostate,** a·pos′tāt, *n.* One who has forsaken his faith, principles, or party.—*a.* False, traitorous.—**apostatize,** a·pos′ta·tīz, *v.i.* —*apostatized, apostatizing.* To turn apostate; to abandon principles, faith, or party.

a posteriori, a pos·tē′ri·ō″ri. [L. *posterior*, after.] A phrase applied to a mode of reasoning founded on observation of effects, consequences, or facts, whereby we reach the causes; inductive: opposed to *a priori.*

apostle, a·pos′l, *n.* [Gr. *apostolos, lit.* one sent forth, a messenger—*apo*, forth, and *stellō*, to send.] One of the twelve disciples of Christ, who were commissioned to preach the gospel; one regarded as having a similar mission.—**apostleship,** a·pos′l·ship, *n.* The office or dignity of an apostle. —**apostolate,** a·pos′tol·āt, *n.* The dignity or office of an apostle; a mission; the dignity or office of the pope, the holder of the apostolic see. —**apostolic, apostolical,** ap·os·tol′ik, ap·os·tol′ik·al, *a.* Pertaining or relating to or characteristic of an apostle, more especially of the twelve apostles; according to the doctrines of the apostles; proceeding from an apostle.

—*Apostolic see*, the see of the bishop of Rome, as directly founded by the apostle Peter.—*Apostolic succession,* the uninterrupted succession of bishops, and, through them, of priests and deacons, in the church by regular ordination from the first apostles down to the present day.—**apostolicism, apostolicity,**† ap·os·tol′i·sizm, ap·os′tol·is″i·ti, *n.* The character of being apostolical.

apostrophe, a·pos′tro·fe, *n.* [Gr. *apo*, from, and *strophē*, a turning.] A sudden change in discourse; a sudden and direct address to a person or thing in the course of a speech; *gram.* the omission of a letter or letters from a word marked by a sign ('); the sign used to mark the omission, or merely as the sign of the possessive case in nouns.—**apostrophic,** ap·os·trof′ik, *a.* Pertaining to an apostrophe.—**apostrophize,** a·pos′trof·īz, *v.t.*—*apostrophized, apostrophizing.* To address by apostrophe; to make a direct address to in course of a speech; to mark with an apostrophe.—*v.i.* To make an apostrophe in speaking.

apothecary, a·poth′e·ka·ri, *n.* [L.L. *apothecarius*, a shopkeeper, from Gr. *apothēkē*, a repository—*apo*, away, and *thēkē*, a chest, from *tithēmi*, to place.] One who practices pharmacy; a skilled person who prepares drugs for medicinal uses, and keeps them for sale.

apothecium, ap·o·thē′si·um, *n.* pl. **apothecia,** ap·o·thē′si·a. [APOTHECARY.] *Bot.* the receptacle of lichens, the sporecase.

apothegm, apothegmatic, ap′o·them, ap′o·theg·mat″ik. Same as *Apophthegm, Apophthegmatic.*

apotheosis, ap″o·thē·o′sis or -thē′o·sis, *n.* [Gr. *apo*, away, and *theos*, God.] Deification; the placing or ranking of a person among deities.— **apotheosize,** ap·o·thē′ō·sīz, *v.t.* To exalt to the dignity of a deity; to deify.

appall, appal, ap·pạl′, *v.t.*—*appalled, appalling.* [O.Fr. *appalir*, to make pale, from prefix *ap* for *ad*, and *palle*, pale, from L. *pallidus*, pallid.] To impress with overpowering fear; to confound with terror; to dismay.—*n.* Terror; affright; dismay. [*Cowper*.] —**appalling,** ap·pạl′ing, *a.* Calculated to cause dismay or horror.—**appallingly,** ap·pạl′ing·li, *adv.* In a manner to appall.

appanage, ap′pan·āj, *n.* [Fr. *appanage, apanage*, from O.Fr. *apaner*, L.L. *apanare*, to furnish with bread —L. *ad*, to, and *panis*, bread.] An allowance to the younger branches of a sovereign house out of the revenues of the country, generally together with a grant of public domains; whatever belongs or falls to one from rank or station in life.

apparatus, ap·pa·rā′tus, *n. sing.* and *pl.*; pl. rarely **apparatuses,** ap·pa·rā′tus·ez. [L. from *apparo*, to prepare—*ad*, and *paro*, to make ready.] Things provided as means to some end; a collection or combination of articles or materials for the accomplishment of some purpose, opera-

tion, or experiment; *physiol* a collection of organs all ministering to the same function.

apparel, ap·par′el, *n.* (no pl.). [Fr. *appareil*, dress, *appareiller*, to match, to fit. to suit—*a*, to, and *pareil*, like, L.L. *pariculus*, from L. *par*, equal.] Clothing; vesture; garments; dress; external array; the furniture of a ship.—*v.t.*—*appareled, appareling.* To dress or clothe; to cover as with garments.

apparent, ap·pā′rent, *a.* [L. *apparens, apparentis*, ppr. of *appareo.* APPEAR.] Visible to the eye; within sight or view; appearing to the eye or to the judgment; seeming (often in distinction to *real*); obvious; plain; evident: in the latter sense now used only as a predicate.—*Heir apparent*, the heir who is certain to inherit if he survive the present holder.—*n.*† Heir apparent; one who has a claim. [*Shak.*]—**apparently,** ap·pā′rent·li, *adv.* Openly; evidently; seemingly; in appearance.—**apparentness,** ap·pā′rent·nes, *n.*

apparition, ap·pa·ri′shon, *n.* [AP-PEAR.] The act of appearing; appearance; the thing appearing; especially, a ghost; a specter, a visible spirit.—**apparitional,** ap·pa·ri′shon·al, *a.* Pertaining to an apparition.

apparitor, ap·par′it·or, *n.* [L., from *appareo*, to attend. APPEAR.] A messenger or officer who serves the process of a spiritual court; the beadle in a university.

appeal, ap·pēl′, *v.i.* [Fr. *appeler*, from L. *appellare*, to call, address, appeal to.] To call, as for aid, mercy, sympathy, and the like; to refer to another person or authority for the decision of a question controverted; to refer to a superior judge or court for a final settlement.—*v.t.* To summon or to challenge†; to remove (a cause) from an inferior to a superior judge or court; to charge with a crime; to accuse.—*n.* A call for sympathy, mercy, aid, and the like; a supplication; an entreaty; the removal of a cause or suit from an inferior to a superior tribunal, that the latter may, if needful, amend the decision of the former; a challenge; a reference to another for proof or decision; resort; recourse (*appeal* to arms).—**appealable,** ap·pēl′a·bl, *a.* Liable to be appealed; removable to a higher tribunal for decision.— **appealer,** ap·pēl′ėr, *n.* One who appeals; an appellant.—**appellant,** ap·pel′ant, *n.* One who appeals; one who removes a cause from a lower to a higher tribunal.—**appellate,** ap·pel′āt, *a.* Relating to appeals; having cognizance of appeals.—**appellee,** ap·pel·lē′, *n.* One against whom an appeal is brought.—**appellor,** ap·pel′or, *n.* One who appeals.

appear, ap·pēr′, *v.i.* [O.Fr. *apparoir*, L. *appareo—ad*, to, and *pareo*, to show one's self.] To come or be in sight; to be or become visible to the eye; to stand in presence of some one; to be obvious; to be clear or made clear by evidence; to seem; to look like.—**appearance,** ap·pēr′ans, *n.* The act of appearing or coming into sight; a coming into the presence of a person or persons; the thing seen; a phenomenon; an apparition; external show; semblance, in opposition to reality or substance; mien; build and carriage; figure.

appease, ap·pēz´, v.t.—*appeased, appeasing.* [Fr. *appaiser*, to pacify—*a*, from L. *ad*, to, and O.Fr. *pais* (Fr. *paix*), L. *pax, pacis*, peace.] To make quiet; to still; to assuage (hunger); to tranquilize; to calm or pacify (a person, anger).—**appeasable,** ap·pēz´a·bl, a. Capable of being appeased.—**appeasement,** ap·pēz´ment, n. Act of appeasing; appeased state.—**appeaser,** ap·pēz´ẽr, n. One who appeases.

appellant, appellate, etc. See APPEAL.

appellation, ap·pel·ā´shon, n. [L. *appellatio*, from *appellare*, to address, accost, appeal to.] The word by which a thing or person is known; name; title.—**appellative,** ap·pel´a·tiv, a. Serving as an appellation; naming or marking out; denominative.—n. An appellation.

append, ap·pend´, v.t. [L. *appendo*—*ad*, to, and *pendo*, to hang. PENDANT.] To hang on or attach; to add, as accessory or adjunct to a thing; to subjoin; to annex.—**appendage,** ap·pend´āj, n. Something appended or attached; what is attached to a greater thing.—**appendectomy,** ap·pen·dek´to·mi, n. [Gr. *appendix* and *ectomy*, excision.] Removal of the appendix by surgical operation.—**appendix,** ap·pen´diks, n. pl. **appendixes** and **appendices,** ap·pen´di·sez. [L. *appendix, appendicis*, from *appendo*.] Something appended or added; an addition appended to a book relating, but not essential, to the main work; *anat.* an appendage, process, or projecting part.—**appendicitis,** ap·pen´di·sī˝tis, n. Inflammation of the vermiform appendix, a small hollow blind process attached to the cecum in man and some animals, an ailment sometimes fatal.

apperception, ap·pẽr·sep´shon, n. [Prefix *ap* for *ad*, and *perception*.] Perception that reflects upon itself; consciousness; spontaneous thought.

appertain, ap·pẽr·tān´, v.i. [Fr. *appartenir*—L. *ad*, and *pertineo*, to pertain.] To belong or pertain: with *to*.

appetence, appetency, ap´pē·tens, ap´pē·ten·si, n. [L. *appetentia*, from *appetens, appetentis*, ppr. of *appeto*, to desire—*ad*, and *peto*, to desire. PETITION.] Desire; inclination; propensity; strong natural craving or tendency; appetite.—**appetite,** ap´pe·tīt, n. [L. *appetitus*, desire.] The natural desire of pleasure or good; taste; inclination; a desire to supply a bodily want or craving; a desire for food or drink; eagerness or longing.—**appetizer,** ap´pē·tīz·ẽr, n. That which appetizes or whets the appetite.—**appetizing,** ap´pē·tīz·ing, a. Whetting the appetite; appealing to the appetite.

applaud, ap·plad´, v.t. [L. *applaudo, applausum*—*ad*, and *plaudo*, to make a noise by clapping the hands.]

To show approbation of by clapping the hands, acclamation, or other significant sign; to praise highly; to extol.—v.i. To give praise; to express approbation.—**applause,** ap·plaz´, n. Praise loudly expressed; approbation expressed by clapping the hands or shouting; commendation; approval.—**applausive,** ap·plaz´iv, a. Applauding; containing applause.

apple, ap´l, n. [A. Sax, *aeppel, aepl*, a word common to the Teutonic, Celtic, Slavonic, and Lithuanian tongues; root unknown.] A fruit of a well-known fruit tree, or the tree itself; also a name popularly given to various exotic fruits or trees having little or nothing in common with the apple, as the pineapple, etc.—*Apple of the eye*, the pupil.—*Apple of Sodom*, a fruit described by old writers as externally of fair appearance, but turning to ashes when plucked.—*Adam's apple*, a prominence on the throat.

appliqué, ap·pli·kā´, a. [Fr. *appliqué*, applied.] Cut out from one material and fastened on another as an ornament.—n. Any such ornament.

apply, ap·plī´, v.t.—*applied, applying.* [O. Fr. *applier*, from L. *applicare*, to fasten to —*ad*, to, and *plico*, to fold. PLY.] To lay on (the hand to a table); to put or place on another thing; to use or employ for a particular purpose or in a particular case (a remedy, a sum of money); to put, refer, or use as suitable or relative to some person or thing (a proverb, etc.); to engage and employ with attention; to occupy (the mind, or *refl.*).—v.i. To suit; to agree; to have some connection, agreement, analogy, or reference; to make request; to solicit; to have recourse with a view to gain something; followed by *to*.—**appliance,** ap·plī´ans, n. The act of applying; the thing applied; means to an end; a device; an application; a remedy (*Shak.*)—**applicability,** ap´pli·ka·bil˝i·ti, n. The quality of being applicable.—**applicable,** ap´pli·ka·bl, a. Capable of being applied; fit to be applied; having relevance.—**applicableness,** ap´pli·ka·bl·nes, n. The state or quality of being applicable.—**applicably,** ap´pli·ka·bli, adv. In an applicable manner.—**applicant,** ap´pli·kant, n. One who applies; a petitioner; a candidate.—**application,** ap·pli·kā´shon, n. The act of applying or putting to; the thing applied; the act of making request or soliciting; the employment of means; close study; attention; the testing of something theoretical by applying it in practice.—**applicative, applicatory,** ap´pli·kāt·iv, ap´pli·ka·to·ri, a. Having an application; that which may be applied.—**applier,** ap·plī´ẽr, n. One that applies.

appoggiatura, ap·poj´a·tö˝ra, n. [It.] *Mus.* a grace note: an added note of embellishment to an original passage.

appoint, ap·point´, v.t. [Fr. *appointer*, from L.L. *appunctare*, to bring to the

point—L. *ad*, to, and *punctum*, a point. POINT.] To make firm, establish, or secure (O.T.)‡; to constitute, ordain, or decree; to allot, set apart, or designate; to nominate, as to an office; to settle; to fix, name, or determine by authority or upon agreement; to equip.—v.i. To ordain; to determine.—**appointer,** ap·point´ẽr, n. One who appoints.—**appointment,** ap·point´ment, n. The act of appointing; designation to office; an office held; the act of fixing by mutual agreement; arrangement; decree; direction; command; equipment, furniture, etc. (*Shak.*); an allowance; a salary or pension.

apportion, ap·pōr´shon, v.t. [O.Fr. *apportioner*—L. *ad*, and *portio*, portion.] To divide and assign in just proportion; to distribute in proper shares; to allot.—**apportionment,** ap·pōr´shon·ment, n. The act of apportioning.

apposite, ap´pō·zit, a. [L. *appositus*, set or put to, from *appono, appositum*—*ad*, and *pono*, to put or place.] Suitable; fit; appropriate; very applicable; well adapted; followed by *to*, and said of answers, arguments, etc.—**appositely,** ap´pō·zit·li, adv. In an apposite manner; suitably; fitly.—**appositeness,** ap´pō·zit·nes, n. The state or quality of being apposite; fitness.—**apposition,** ap·pō·zi´shon, n. The act of adding to; addition; a setting to; *gram.* the relation in which a noun or a substantive phrase or clause stands to a noun or pronoun when it explains without being predicated of it, at the same time agreeing in case; as, Cicero, the orator, was there.—**appositional,** ap·pō·zi´shon·al, a. Pertaining to apposition.—**appositive,** ap·poz´it·iv, a. Placed in apposition.

appraise, ap·prāz´, v.t.—*appraised, appraising.* [O. Fr. *appreiser*; L. *appretiare*, to set a price on—*ad*, to, and *pretium*, a price. PRAISE, PRICE, PRECIOUS.] To set a price upon; to estimate the value of under the direction of a competent authority; to estimate generally.—**appraisement,** ap·prāz´ment, n. The act of appraising; the value fixed; the valuation.—**appraiser,** ap·prāz´ẽr, n. One who appraises; a person licensed and sworn to estimate and fix the value of goods and estate.

appreciate, ap·prē´shi·āt, v.t.—*appreciated, appreciating.* [Fr. *apprécier*, to set a value, L. *appretio, appretiatum*. APPRAISE.] To set a just price, value, or estimate on; to estimate or value properly.—v.i. To rise in value; to become of more value.—**appreciable,** ap·prē´shi·a·bl, a. Capable of being appreciated or estimated; sufficiently great to be capable of estimation.—**appreciably,** ap·prē´shi·a·bli, adv. To a degree that may be appreciated or estimated; perceptibly.—**appreciation,** ap·prē´shi·ā˝shon, n. The act of appreciating; the act of valuing or estimating; the act of setting a due price or value on.—**appreciative,** ap·prē´shi·ā·tiv, *a.* Capable of appreciating; manifesting, due appreciation.— **appreciatory**, ap·prē′shi·a·to·ri, *a.* Pertaining to appreciation.

apprehend, ap·prē·hend′, *v.t.* [L. *apprehendo—ad*, and *prehendo*, to take or seize, *prae*, before, and *hendo* (not used), to seize.] To take or seize (a person); to arrest; to take or lay hold of by the mind; to become cognizant of; to understand; to entertain suspicion or fear of; to dread or be apprehensive of.— *v.t.* To form a conception; to conceive; to believe or be of opinion without positive certainty; to be apprehensive; to be in fear of a future evil.— **apprehensible**, ap·prē·hen′si·bl, *a.* Capable of being apprehended or conceived.— **apprehension**, ap·prē·hen′shon, *n.* The act of apprehending; a seizing or arresting by legal process; the operation of the mind in contemplating ideas, or merely taking them into the mind; opinion; belief; the power of perceiving and understanding; distrust or fear at the prospect of future evil, accompanied with uneasiness of mind.— **apprehensive**, ap·prē·hen′siv, *a.* Quick of apprehension (*Shak.*); inclined to believe, fear, or dread; anticipating, or in expectation of, evil (*apprehensive of* evil; *apprehensive for* our lives).— **apprehensively**, ap·prē·hen′siv·li, *adv.* In an apprehensive manner.— **apprehensiveness**, ap·prē·hen′siv·nes, *n.* The character of being apprehensive.

apprentice, ap·pren′tis, *n.* [L.L. *apprenticius*, from L. *apprehendo*, *apprendo*, to seize, to apprehend. APPREHEND.] One bound, often by legal document, to learn some art, trade, or profession; a learner in any subject; one not well versed in a subject.— *v.t.* *apprenticed*, *apprenticing*. To make an apprentice of; to put under the care of a master, for the purpose of learning a trade or profession.— **apprenticeship**, ap·pren′tis·ship, *n.* The state or condition of an apprentice; the term during which one is an apprentice.

apprize, ap·prīz′, *v.t.*—*apprized*, *apprizing*. [O.E. *apprise*, notice, information, from Fr. *appris*, *apprise*, pp. of *apprendre*, to inform, to learn, L. *apprehendo*. APPREHEND.] To give notice, verbal or written; to inform; followed by *of* before that of which notice is given.

approach, ap·prōch′, *v.i.* [Fr. *approcher*, from L.L. *appropiare*, to approach—L. *ad*, to, and *prope*, near. PROPINQUITY.] To come or go near in place or time; to draw near; to advance nearer; to approximate.— *v.t.* To bring near; to advance or put near; to come or draw near to, either literally or figuratively; to come near to, so as to be compared with,—*n.* The act of approaching or drawing near; a coming or advancing near; access; a passage or avenue by which buildings are approached.— **approachable**, ap·prōch′a·bl, *a.* Capable of being approached; accessible.

approbate, † ap′prō·bāt, *v.t.* [L. *approbo*, *approbatum*, to approve. APPROVE.] To express satisfaction with; to express approval of; to approve.— **approbation**, ap·prō·bā′shon, *n.* [L. *approbatio*.] The act of approving; that state or disposition of the mind in which we assent to the propriety of a thing with some degree of pleasure or satisfaction; approval.— **approbative**, ap′prō·bāt·iv, *a.* Approving; implying approbation.

appropriate, ap·prō′pri·āt, *v.t.*—*appropriated*, *appropriating*. [L. *approprio*, *appropriatum*, to make one's own—*ad*, to, *proprius*, one's own. PROPER, PROPRIETY.] To claim or take to one's self in exclusion of others; to claim or use as by an exclusive right; to set apart for or assign to a particular purpose.—*a.* Set apart for a particular use or person; hence, belonging peculiarly; peculiar; suitable; fit; proper.— **appropriable**, ap·prō′pri·a·bl, *a.* Capable of being appropriated, set apart, or assigned to a particular use.— **appropriately**, ap·prō′pri·āt·li, *adv.* In an appropriate manner.— **appropriateness**, ap·prō′pri·āt·nes, *n.* The quality of being appropriate.— **appropriation**, ap·prō′pri·ā″shon, *n.* The act of appropriating; application to a special use or purpose; the act of making one's own; anything appropriated or set apart.— **appropriative**, ap·prō′pri·āt·iv, *a.* Appropriating; making appropriation.— **appropriator**, ap·prō′pri·āt·er, *n.* One who appropriates.

approve, ap·pröv′, *v.t.*—*approved*, *approving*. [Fr. *approuver*, *approver*, from L. *approbo*, to approve, to find good—*ad*, to and *probare*, to try, test, prove, from *probus*, good.] To admit the propriety or excellence of; to think or judge well or favorably of; to find to be satisfactory; to show to be real or true (to *approve* one's bravery); to prove by trial (*Shak.*,)‡.—*v.i.* To be pleased; to feel or express approbation; to think or judge well or favorably: followed by *of*.— **approvable**, ap·pröv′a·bl, *a.* Capable of being approved.— **approval**, ap·pröv′al, *n.* The act of approving; approbation; commendation; sanction; ratification.— **approver**, ap·pröv′er, *n.* One who approves; one who confesses a crime and accuses another.— **approvingly**, ap·pröv′ing·li, *adv.* In an approving manner.

approximate, ap·prok′si·māt, *v.t.*—*approximated*, *approximating*. [L.L. *approximo*, *approximatum*, to bring or come near—L. *ad*, to, and *proximus*, nearest. PROXIMATE, APPROACH.] To carry or advance near; to cause to approach (especially said of amount, state, or degree).—*v.i.* To come near; to approach (especially as regards amount, state, or character).—*a.* Being near in state, place, or quantity; approaching; nearly equal or like.— **approximately**, ap·prok′si·māt·li, *adv.* In an approximate manner; by approximation.— **approximation**, ap·prok′-

si·mā″shon, *n.* The act of approximating; an approximate estimate or amount; approach.

appurtenance, ap·per′ten·ans, *n.* [Fr. *appartenance*. APPERTAIN.] That which appertains or belongs to something else; something belonging to another thing as principal; an adjunct; an appendage.— **appurtenant**, ap·per′ten·ant, *a.* Appertaining or belonging; pertaining; being an appurtenance.

apricot, ā′pri·kot, *n.* [O.E. *apricock*, *abricot*, Fr. *abricot*, Sp. *albarcoque*, from Ar. *alburqūq*, from *al*, the article, and L. Gr. *praikokkion*, from L. *praecox*, *praecoquus*, early ripe. PRECOCIOUS.] A roundish fruit of a delicious flavor, the produce of a tree of the plum kind.

April, ā·pril, *n.* [L. *aprilis*, the month in which the earth opens for the growth of plants, from *aperio*, to open.] The fourth month of the year.—*April fool*, one who is sportively imposed upon by others on April 1, as by being sent on some absurd errand.

a priori, ā prī·ō′ri. [L., from something prior or going before.] A phrase applied to a mode of reasoning by which we proceed from the cause to the effect, as opposed to *a posteriori* reasoning, by which we proceed from the effect to the cause; also a term applied to knowledge independent of all experience.

apron, ā′prun, *n.* [O.E. *napron*, Fr. *napperon*, from *nape*, *nappe*, a tablecloth, etc. (whence E. *napkin*), *nappe* being another form of *mappe*, E. *map*. *Apron*, like *adder*, *auger*, has lost the initial *n.*] A piece of cloth or leather worn on the forepart of the body to keep the clothes clean or defend them from injury; a covering for the front part of a body.—*v.t.* To put an apron on; to furnish with an apron.

apropos, ap′ro·pō′, *a.* [Fr.—*à*, to, according to, and *propos*, purpose, L. *propositum*, a thing proposed.] Opportune; seasonable; to the purpose (an *apropos* remark).

apse, aps, *n.* [Gr. (*h*)*apsis*, (*h*)*apsidos*, an arch, vault. joining, from (*h*)*aptō*, to join.] A portion of any building forming a termination or projection semicircular or polygonal in plan, and having a dome or vaulted roof; especially such a structure at the east end of a church.— **apsidal**, ap′si′dal, *a.* Pertaining to or resembling an apse; pertaining to apsides.— **apsis**, ap′sis, *n.* pl. **apsides**, ap·sī′dēz. *Arch.* an apse; *astron.* one of the two points in the orbit of a heavenly body which mark its greatest and its least distance from the primary round which it revolves.

apt, apt, *a.* [L. *aptus*, fitted, fit.] Fit; suitable; apposite; pertinent; appropriate; having a tendency; liable; inclined; disposed; ready; prompt.— **aptitude**, ap′ti·tūd, *n.* The state or quality of being apt; disposition; tendency; fitness; suitableness; readiness in learning; docility.— **aptly**, apt′li, *adv.* In an apt or suitable manner; justly; pertinently; readily;

quickly; cleverly.—**aptness**, apt′nes, *n.* The state or quality of being apt; fitness; tendency; quickness of apprehension; readiness in learning; docility.

apteral, apterous, ap′ter·al, ap′ter·us, *a.* [Gr. *apteros*, without wings—*a*, not, and *pteron*, a wing.] Destitute of wings.

apteryx, ap′tėr·iks, *n.* [Gr. *a*, not, and *pteryx*, a wing.] A bird peculiar to but now nearly extinct in New Zealand, having no tail and very short rudimentary wings.

aqua, ak′wa, *n.* [L.] Water: a word forming an element in various terms; also used by itself as a commercial name of whisky.—*Aqua fortis* (= strong water), a name given to weak and impure nitric acid.—*Aqua regia* (= royal water), a mixture of nitric and hydrochloric acids, so called from its power of dissolving gold and other noble metals.—*Aqua vitae* (=water of life), ardent spirits, as whisky, brandy, etc.—**aquarium**, a·kwā′ri·um, *n.* A case, vessel, tank, or the like, in which aquatic plants and animals are kept; a place containing a collection of such vessels or tanks.—**Aquarius**, a·kwā′ri·us, *n.* [L.] The Waterbearer; a sign in the zodiac which the sun enters about 15 January.—**aquatic**, a·kwat′ik, *a.* Pertaining to water; living in or frequenting water.—*n.* A plant which grows in water; *pl.* sports or exercises practiced on or in water, as rowing or swimming.—**aqueous**, ak′wē·us, *a.* Partaking of the nature of water, or abounding with or formed by it; watery.

aquacade, ak′wa·kād, *n.* Water show with musical accompaniment including exhibitions of swimming, diving, and acrobatics.

aqualung, ak′wa·lung, *n.* A device to permit breathing under water, consisting of a watertight face mask and cylinders of compressed air.

aquamarine, ak′wa·ma·rēn, *n.* [L. *aqua*, water, and *marinus*, pertaining to the sea.] The finest beryl, so called from its bluish or sea-green tint.

aquanaut, ak′wa·nạt, *n.* [*Aqua*, water, and *nautēs*, sailor.] A deep-sea explorer who uses a capsule, resting on the ocean floor, as a base for his exploration.

aquaplane, ak′wa·plān″, *n.* A board on which a person stands as it is pulled over the water by a speedboat.—*v.i.* To ride an aquaplane.

aquarelle, ak·wa·rel′, [Fr., from L. *aqua*, water.] Watercolor painting.

aquatint, ak′wa·tint, *n.* [L. *aqua*, water, and It. *tinta*, dye, tint.] A method of etching on copper by which a beautiful effect is produced, resembling a fine drawing in watercolors or India ink.

aqueduct, ak′wē·dukt, *n.* [L. *aquaeductus*—*aqua*, water, and *ductus*, a pipe or canal, from *duco*, to lead.] A conduit or channel for conveying water from one place to another; a structure for conveying water for the supply of a town.

aqueous. See AQUA.

aquiline, ak′wil·īn, *a.* [L. *aquilinus*, from *aquila*, an eagle.] Of or belonging to the eagle; resembling an eagle's beak; curving; hooked.

Arab, ar′ab, *n.* A native of Arabia; a neglected outcast boy or girl of the streets.—*a.* Of or pertaining to the Arabs or Arabia.—**arabesque**, ar′ab·esk, *n.* [Fr., from the *Arabs*, who brought the style to high perfection.] A species of architectural ornamentation for enriching flat surfaces, either painted, inlaid, or wrought in low relief, often consisting of fanciful figures, human or animal, combined with floral forms.—**Arabian**, a·rā′bi·an, *a.* Pertaining to Arabia.—*n.* A native of Arabia; an Arab.—**Arabic**, ar′ab·ik, *a.* Belonging to Arabia or the language of its inhabitants.—*n.* The language of the Arabians.

arable, ar′a·bl, *a.* [Fr. *arable*, L. *arabilis*, from *aro*, to plow, from root seen also in A.Sax. *erian*, E. to *ear*, Icel. *erja*, Goth. *erjan*, Lith. *arti*, Rus. *orati*, to plow, to till; Ir. and W. *ar*, tillage; W. *aru*, to plow.] Fit for plowing or tillage.

Arachnida, a·rak′ni·da, *n. pl.* [Gr. *arachnē*, a spider.] A class of annulose, wingless animals, intermediate between the insects and the Crustacea, including spiders, mites, and scorpions.—**arachnidan**, a·rak′ni·dan, *n.* One of the Arachnida.—**arachnoid**, a·rak′noid, *a.* Resembling a spider's web; *anat.* applied to a semitransparent thin membrane which is spread over the brain and pia mater; *bot.* having hair that gives an appearance of being covered with cobweb.

Aramaic, ar·a·mā′ik, *n.* [From *Aram*, a son of Shem, the supposed ancestor of the Chaldeans and Syrians.] A language or group of languages anciently spoken in Syria, the earliest specimens being the Chaldee passages in the Old Testament and Apocrypha; Chaldaic; Chaldee.

Araucaria, ar·ạ·kā′ri·a, *n.* [From the *Araucanos*, a tribe of Indians in Chili.] The generic name of some fine coniferous trees found chiefly in South America, but now also commonly grown in Britain.—**Araucarian**, ar·ạ·kā′ri·an, *a.*

arbalist, arbalest, är′bal·ist, är′bal·est, *n.* [O.Fr. *arbaleste*, from L. *arcus*, a bow, and *ballista, balista*, an engine to throw stones.] A kind of powerful crossbow formerly used.—**arbalister**, är′bal·ist·ėr, *n.* A crossbowman.

arbiter, är′bit·ėr, *n.* [L., an arbiter, umpire, judge.] A person appointed or chosen by parties in controversy to decide their differences; one who judges and determines without control; one whose power of deciding and governing is not limited; an arbitrator.—**arbitrage**, är′bi·träj, *n.* The calculation of the best mode by which advantage may be taken of differences in the value of money, stocks, etc., at different places in the same time; the dealing in bills of exchange, stocks, etc., for the pur-

pose of making profit by such calculations.—**arbitrament**, är·bit′ra·ment, *n.* Determination; decision; settlement; award (the *arbitrament* of the sword).—**arbitrary**, är′bi·tra·ri, *a.* [L. *arbitrarius*.] Given, adjudged, or done according to one's will or discretion; exercised according to one's will or discretion; capricious; despotic; imperious; tyrannical; uncontrolled.—**arbitrarily**, är′bi·tra·ri·li, *adv.* In an arbitrary manner; capriciously.—**arbitrariness**, är′bi·tra·ri·nes, *n.* The quality of being arbitrary.—**arbitrate**, är′bi·trāt, *v.i.* arbitrated, arbitrating. [L. *arbitror, arbitratus*.] To act as an arbiter or umpire; to hear and decide in a dispute.—*v.t.* To hear and decide on.—**arbitration**, är·bi·trā′shon, *n.* The act of arbitrating; the hearing and determination of a cause between parties in controversy, by a person or persons chosen by the parties.—**arbitrator**, är′bi·trāt·ėr, *n.* One who arbitrates; an arbiter.

arbor, är′bor, *n.* [L., a tree, a wooden bar, etc.] The principal spindle or axis of a machine, communicating motion to the other moving parts.—**arboreous, arboreal**, är·bō′rē·us, är·bō′rē·al, *a.* Pertaining to trees; living on or among trees; having the character of a tree.—**arborescence**, är·bor·es′ens, *n.* The state of being arborescent; an arborescent form or growth.—**arborescent**, är·bor·es′ent, *a.* [L. *arborescens*, pp. of *arboresco*, to grow to a tree.] Resembling a tree; *bot.* partaking of the nature and habits of a tree; dendritic.—**arboretum**, är·bo·rē′tum, *n.* [L.] A place in which a collection of different trees and shrubs is cultivated for scientific or educational purposes.—**arborization**, är′bor·i·zā″shon, *n.* A mineral or other body with a treelike form.

arbor, arbour, är′bėr, *n.* [O.E. *herber*, O.Fr. *herbier*, L. *herba*, herb; the spelling influenced by L. *arbor*, tree.] A seat in the open air sheltered by intertwining branches or climbing plants; a bower.—**arborous**, är′bor·us, *a.* Having the appearance or nature of an arbor. (*Mil.*)

arboriculture, är″bo·ri·kul′tūr, *n.* [L. *arbor*, a tree, and *cultura*, cultivation. CULTURE.] The cultivation of trees; the art of planting, dressing, and managing trees and shrubs.—**arboricultural**, är·bor′i·kul″tūr·al, *a.* Relating to arboriculture.—**arboriculturist**, är″bo·ri·kul′tūr·ist, *n.* One who practices arboriculture.

arbor vitae, är′bor vī′tē, *n.* [L., the tree of life.] A common name of certain coniferous trees; a treelike arrangement which appears in the medullary substance of the brain when the cerebellum is cut vertically.

arbutus, är·bu′tus, *n.* [L., the strawberry-tree.] The generic name of an evergreen tree or shrub, with bright red or yellow berries, somewhat like the strawberry, having an unpleasant taste and narcotic properties.

---

ch, *ch*ain; *ch*, Sc. lo*ch*; g, go; j, *j*ob; ng, si*ng*; TH, *th*en; th, *th*in; w, *w*ig; hw, *wh*ig; zh, a*z*ure.

arc, ärk, *n.* [L. *arcus,* a bow. ARCH.] *Geom.* a curve line forming or that might form part of the circumference of a circle; formerly also an arch.—**arcade,** är·kād′, *n.* [Fr., L.L. *arcata,* L. *arcus,* an arch.] A series of arches supported on pillars, often used as a roof support or as an ornamental dressing to a wall; a covered-in passage containing shops or stalls.

Arcadian, är·kā′di·an, *a.* Pertaining to Arcadia, a mountainous district in southern Greece; hence, rustic; rural; pastoral.

arcanum, är·kā′num, *n.* pl. **arcana,** är·kā′na. [L.] A secret; a mystery: generally used in the plural (the *arcana* of nature).

arch, ärch, *n.* [Fr. *arche,* L.L. *archia,* from L. *arcus,* a bow, arch, arc.] A structure composed of separate wedge-shaped pieces, arranged on a curved line, so as to retain their position by mutual pressure; a covering, or structure, of a bow shape; a vault.—*Court of arches,* an ecclesiastical court of appeal pertaining to the archbishopric of Canterbury, anciently held in the church of St. Mary-le-bow, called also St. Mary-of-the-arches.—*v.t.* To cover or span with an arch.—**archway,** ärch′wā, *n.* A passage under an arch.

arch, ärch, *a.* [From next word, from being often used in such phrases as *arch* wag, *arch* rogue.] Cunning, sly, shrewd; waggish; mischievous for sport; roguish.—**archly,** ärch′li, *adv.* In an arch or roguish manner.—**archness,** ärch′nes, *n.*

arch, ärch, *a.* [From Gr. *archi,* in compound words, from stem of *archē,* power or rule.] Chief; of the first class or rank: principally used in composition as the first part of many words; as, *arch*bishop, *arch*priest, etc.—*n.‡* A leader; a chief. (*Shak.*)

Archaean, är·kē′an, *a.* [Gr. *archaios,* ancient.] *Geol.* applied to the oldest rocks of the earth's crust, crystalline in character, and embracing granite, syenite, gneiss.

archaeology, är·kē·ol′o·ji, *n.* [Gr. *archaios,* ancient, and *logos,* discourse.] The science of antiquities, especially prehistoric antiquities, which investigates the history of peoples by the remains belonging to the earlier periods of their existence.—**archaeological, archaeologic,** är′ke·o·loj″ik·al, är′kē·o·loj″ik, *a.* Pertaining to archaeology.—**archaeologist,** är·kē·ol′o·jist, *n.* One skilled in archaeology.

archaeopteryx, är·kē·op′tėr·iks, *n.* [Gr. *archaios,* ancient, and *pteryx,* wing.] A fossil bird of the size of a rook, having two claws representing the thumb and forefinger projecting from the wing, and about twenty tail vertebrae prolonged as in mammals.

archaic, är·kā′ik, *a.* [Gr. *archaïkos,* old-fashioned, from *archaios,* ancient.] Old fashioned; obsolete; antiquated.—**archaism,** är′kā·izm, *n.* An ancient or obsolete word or idiom; antiquity of style or use; obsoleteness.

archangel, ärk·ān′jel, *n.* An angel of the highest order in the celestial hierarchy.—**archangelic,** ärk·an·jel′-ik, *a.* Of or pertaining to archangels.

archbishop, ärch·bish′up, *n.* A bishop who has the supervision of other bishops (the sees of whom form his province), and also exercises episcopal authority in his own diocese.—**archbishopric,** ärch·bish′-up·rik, *n.*

archdeacon, ärch·dē′kn, *n.* In England, an ecclesiastical dignitary, next in rank below a bishop, who has jurisdiction either over a part of or over the whole diocese.—**archdeaconate,** ärch·dē′kn·āt, *n.*

archdiocese, ärch·dī′ō·sēs, *n.* [*arch* and *diocese.*] Diocese of an archbishop.

archduke, ärch·dūk′, *n.* A prince belonging to the reigning family of the Austrian empire.—**archducal,** ärch·dūk′al, *a.* Pertaining to an archduke.—**archduchess,** ärch·duch′es, *n.* The wife of an archduke.—**archduchy,** ärch·duch′i, *n.* The territory or rank of an archduke or archduchess.

archenemy, ärch·en′ē·mi, *n.* A principal enemy; Satan.

archer, ärch′ėr, *n.* [Fr. *archer,* from *arc,* L. *arcus,* a bow. ARCH.] One who uses, or is skilled in the use of the bow and arrow; a bowman.—**archery,** ärch′ėr·i, *n.* The practice, art, or skill of shooting with a bow and arrow.

archetype, är′kē·tīp, *n.* [Gr. *archetypon*—*archē,* beginning, and *typos,* form.] A model or first form; the original pattern after which a thing is made, or to which it corresponds.—**archetypal,** är′kē·tīp·al, *a.* Of or pertaining to an archetype.

archidiaconal, är′ki·dī·ak″on·al, *a.* [Gr. *archi,* chief, *diakonos,* deacon.] Pertaining to an archdeacon.

archiepiscopacy, archiepiscopate, är′ki·ē·pis″kō·pa·si, är′ki·ē·pis″kō·-pāt, *n.* The dignity, office, or province of an archbishop.—**archiepiscopal,** är′ki·ē·pis″kō·pal, *a.* Belonging to an archbishop.

archil, är′kil, *n.* A violet, mauve, or purple coloring matter obtained from lichens.

archimandrite, är·ki·man′drīt, *n.* [Gr. *archi,* chief, *mandra,* a monastery.] *Greek Ch.* an abbot, or abbot general, who has the superintendence of other abbots and convents.

Archimedean, är′ki·mē·dē″an, *a.* Pertaining to Archimedes, the Greek philosopher.—*Archimedean screw,* an instrument for raising water, formed by winding a flexible tube round a cylinder in the form of a screw, being placed in an inclined position, and the lower end immersed in water; by causing the screw to revolve, the water is raised to the upper end.

archipelago, är·ki·pel′a·gō, *n.* [Gr. *archi,* chief, and *pelagos,* the sea.] Originally the Aegean Sea, which is studded with a number of small islands; hence any water space interspersed with many islands; a group of many islands.—**archipelagic,** är′ki·pe·laj″ik, *a.* Relating to an archipelago.

architect, är′ki·tekt, *n.* [Fr. *architecte,* L. *architectus,* Gr. prefix *archi,* chief, and *tektōn,* a workman.] A person skilled in the art and science of building; one who makes it his occupation to form plans and designs of buildings, and superintend their erection; a former or maker. **architectonic,** är′ki·tek·ton″ik; *a.* Pertaining to or skilled in architecture.—**architectonics,** är′ki·tek·ton″iks, *n.* The science of architecture.—**architectural,** är′ki·tek′tūr·al, *a.* Pertaining to architecture or the art of building.—**architecture,** är′ki·tek·tūr, *n.* [L. *architectura.*] The art or science of building; that branch of the fine arts which has for its object the production of edifices pleasing to a cultivated and artistic taste; construction.

architrave, är′ki·trāv, *n.* [It. *architrave*—prefix *archi,* chief, and *trave,* from L. *trabs,* a beam.] *Arch.* the lower division of an entablature, or that part which rests immediately on the column.

archive, är′kīv, *n.* [L.L. *archivum,* a place for keeping public records, from Gr. *archeion,* a government building, from *archē,* rule, government.] A record or document preserved in evidence of something; almost always in plural and signifying documents or records relating to the affairs of a family, corporation, community, city, or kingdom.—**archival,** är′kīv·al, *a.* Pertaining to or contained in archives or records.—**archivist,** är′kīv·ist or är′ki·vist, *n.* The keeper of archives or records.

archon, är′kon, *n.* [Gr.] One of the chief magistrates of ancient Athens chosen to superintend civil and religious concerns.

arctic, ärk′tik, *a.* [L. *arcticus;* Gr. *arktikos,* from *arctos,* a bear, the northern constellation Ursa Major.] Northern; surrounding or lying near the north pole. The *arctic* circle is a circle parallel to the Equator, 23° 28′ from the north pole.

Arcturus, ärk·tū′rus, *n.* [Gr. *arktos,* a bear, and *oura,* tail.] A fixed star of the first magnitude near the tail of the Great Bear.

arcuate, ärk′ū·āt, *a.* [L. *arcuatus,* from *arcus,* a bow.] Bent or curved in the form of a bow.

ardent, är′dent, *a.* [L. *ardens, ardentis,* pp. of *ardeo,* to burn, to be eager.] Burning; causing a sensation of burning; warm: applied to the passions and affections; vehement; passionate; eager; fervent; fervid; zealous.—*Ardent spirits,* alcoholic drinks, as brandy, whisky, rum, etc.—**ardently,** är′dent·li, *adv.* In an ardent manner; with warmth.—**ardency,** är′den·si, *n.* The quality of being ardent; warmth; ardor; eagerness.—**ardor,** är′dėr, *n.* [L. *ardor.*] Heat in a literal sense; warmth or heat, as of the passions and affections; eagerness.

arduous, är′dū·us, *a.* [L. *arduus;* allied to Ir. and Gael, *ard,* high.]

Steep, and therefore difficult of ascent; hard to climb; attended with great labor; difficult; hard (task or employment).—**arduously,** är′·dū·us·li, *adv.* In an arduous manner.—**arduousness,** är′dū·us·nes, *n.*

are, är. [O. Northumbrian *aron, arn,* we (you, they) are; the A.Sax. form proper is *sind* or *sindon.* The *r* is changed from *s,* the root being *as.* AM.] The present tense plural of the verb *to be, art* being the second pers. sing.

are, är or är, *n.* [L. *area.*] The unit of French superficial or square measure, containing 100 square meters or 119.6 square yards.

area, ä′rē·a, *n.* [L. *area,* a threshing floor, then any level open piece of land.] Any plain surface within boundaries, as the floor of a hall, etc.; a space sunk below the general surface of the ground before windows in the basement story of a building; a yard; the superficial contents of any space; a surface, as given in square inches, feet, yards, etc.—**areal,** ä′rē·al, *a.* Pertaining to an area.

areca, a·rē′ka, *n.* [The Malabar name.] A genus of palms, including the betel nut and cabbage trees.

arena, a·rē′na, *n.* [L. *arena,* lit. sand, a sandy place.] The inclosed space (usually covered with sand) in the central part of the Roman amphitheater; hence, the scene or theater of exertion or contest of any kind.—**arenaceous,** ar·ē·ē·nā′shus, *a.* Abounding with sand; having the properties of sand; sandy; granular.

areola, a·rē′ō·la, *n.* pl. **areolae,** a·rē′-ō·lē. [L., dim. of *area* (which see).] A small area or space; a small interstice; the colored circle or halo surrounding the nipple or surrounding a pustule.—**areolar,** a·rē′ō·lêr, *a.* Pertaining to an areola.—**areolate,** a·rē′ō·lāt, *a.* Marked by areolae or small spots.—**areolation,** a·rē′ō·lā″-shon, *n.* Any small space or spot differing from the rest of a surface in color, texture, etc.

areometer, ar·ē·om′et·êr, *n.* [Gr. *araios,* rare, thin, and *metron,* a measure.] An instrument for measuring the specific gravity of liquids; a hydrometer.

Areopagus, ar·ē·op′a·gus, *n.* [Gr., lit. hill of Ares or Mars.] A tribunal at ancient Athens, so called because held on a hill of this name.—**Areopagite,** ar·ē·op′a·jīt, *n.* A member of the Areopagus.—**Areopagitic,** ar·ē·op′a·jit″ik, *a.* Pertaining to the Areopagus.

argal, argol, är′gal, är′gol, *n.* Unrefined or crude tartar; a hard crust formed on the sides of vessels in which wine has been kept.

argali, är′ga·li, *n.* [Mongolian name.] A species of wild Asiatic sheep with very large horns, nearly as bulky as a moderately sized ox.

argent, är′jent, *n.* [Fr., from L. *argentum,* silver: cog. Gr. *argyros,* silver, *argos,* white; Ir. *arg,* white, *airgiod,* silver, money.] Silver‡; whiteness, like that of silver; *her.* the white color in coats of arms, intended

to represent silver, etc.—*a.* Resembling silver; bright like silver; silvery.—**argentic,** är·jent′ik, *a.* Pertaining to, like, or containing silver.—**gentiferous,** är·jen·tif′ér·us, *a.* Producing or containing silver (*argentiferous* ore).—**argentine,** är′jen·tīn, *a.* Pertaining to, resembling, or sounding like silver; silvery.—*n.* White metal coated with silver; the Argentine Republic, S. America.—**argentite,** är′jen·tīt, *n.* Sulfide of silver, a valuable ore of this metal, a blackish, lead-gray mineral.

argil, är′jil, *n.* [L. *argilla,* white clay, allied to *argentum,* silver. ARGENT.] Clay or potter's earth; sometimes, pure clay or alumina.—**argillaceous,** är·jil·lā′shus, *a.* Partaking of the nature of argil or clay; clayey.—**argilliferous,** är·jil·lif′ér·us, *a.* Producing or containing clay or argil.—**argillite,** är′jil·līt, *n.* Clay-slate.

Argive, är′jīv, *n.* A native or inhabitant of Argos, in ancient Greece; an ancient Greek. [Poetical.]

argon, är′gon, *n.* [Gr. *argos,* inert.] A colorless, odorless, gaseous element, chemically inactive. Symbol, A; at. no., 18; at. wt., 39.948.

Argonaut, är′gō·nạt, *n.* [Gr. *Argō,* and *nautēs,* a sailor.] One of the persons who, in the Greek legend, sailed with Jason, in the ship Argo, in quest of the golden fleece; a kind of cuttlefish, the paper nautilus or paper sailor of the Mediterranean, the female having a boatlike shell, in which its eggs are received. It was fabled to float with its arms extended to catch the breeze, and with other arms as oars.—**Argonautic,** är·gō·nạ′tik, *a.*

argosy, är′gō·si, *n.* [From *Ragusa.*] A large merchantman or other ship, especially if richly laden. [Poetical.]

argot, är′gō, *n.* [Fr.] Slang.

argue, är′gū, *v.i.*—*argued, arguing.* [L. *arguo,* to show, argue, to make clear.] To offer reasons to support or overthrow a proposition, opinion, or measure; to reason; to discuss; to debate; to dispute.—*v.t.* To debate or discuss (*argue* a cause in court); to prove, show, or evince; to cause to be inferred (his conduct *argued* suspicion).—**arguable,** är′gū·a·bl, *a.* Capable of being argued.—**arguer,** är′gū·êr, *n.* One who argues.—**argument,** är′gū·ment, *n.* [L. *argumentum,* proof, theme, subject-matter.] The subject of a discourse or writing; an abstract or summary of a book or section of a book; a reason offered for or against something; a debate, controversy, or discussion; a process of reasoning.—*Argumentum ad hominem,* an argument which presses a man with consequences drawn from his own principles and concessions, or his own conduct.—**argumentation,** är·gū·men·tā′shon, *n.* The act of arguing, discussing, or debating; reasoning.—**argumentative,** är·gū·ment′a·tiv, *a.* Consisting of argument; addicted to argument, disputing, or debating.—**argumentatively,** är·gū·ment′a·tiv·li, *adv.*—**argumentativeness,** är·gū·ment′a·tiv·nes, *n.*

Argus, är′gus, *n.* A being in Greek mythology having a hundred watchful eyes; hence, any watchful person; a species of pheasant having its plumage marked with eyelike spots.

Argyrol, är′ji·rol, *n.* [Gr. *argyros,* silver.] Trade-mark for a silver-protein compound used as a mild local antiseptic.

aria, ä′ri·a, *n.* [It. *aria.*] A song; an operatic air for single voice.

Arian, ä′ri·an, *n.* One maintaining the doctrines of *Arius* (fourth century A.D.), who held Christ to be a created being inferior to God.—**Arian,** ä′ri·-an, *a.* Pertaining to Arius or to his doctrines.—**Arianism,** ä′ri·an·izm, *n.*

arid, ar′id, *a.* [L. *aridus.*] Dry; exhausted of moisture; parched with heat.—**aridity,** a·rid′i·ti, *n.* The state of being arid; dryness; want of interest.

Aries, ä′ri·ēz, *n.* [L. *aries,* a ram.] The Ram, a northern constellation, the first of the twelve signs in the zodiac, which the sun enters at the vernal equinox.

aright, a·rīt′, *adv.* In a right way or form; properly; correctly; rightly.

aril, ar′il, *n.* [L. *areo,* to be dry, because it falls off when dry.] An extra covering of the seed of some plants (as the nutmeg) outside the true seed coats, falling off spontaneously.

arise, a·rīz′, *v.i.*—*arose* (pret.), *arisen* (pp.), *arising.* [Prefix *a,* and *rise;* A.Sax. *arisan.* RISE.] To move to a higher place; to mount up; to ascend; to come into view; to get out of bed, or quit a sitting or lying posture; to spring; to originate; to start into action; to rise.

arista, a·ris′ta, *n.* [L.] *Bot.* an awn or beard.—**aristate,** a·ris′tāt, *a.* Awned.

aristocracy, ar·is·tok′ra·si, *n.* [Gr. *aristokratia*—*aristos,* best, and *kratos,* rule.] Government by the nobility or persons of rank in the state; the nobility or chief persons in a state.—**aristocrat,** a·ris′to·krat, *n.* A member of the aristocracy; one who favors an aristocracy; one who apes the aristocracy.—**aristocratic, aristocratical,** a·ris′to·krat″ik, a·ris′to·krat″-ik·al, *a.* Pertaining or belonging to the aristocracy or to the rule of aristocrats; resembling the aristocracy.—**aristocratically,** a·ris′to·krat′ik·al·li, *adv.*

Aristotelian, a·ris′to·tē″li·an, *a.* Pertaining to *Aristotle* (born 384 B.C.), the celebrated Greek philosopher, and founder of the Peripatetic school.—*n.* A follower of Aristotle; a peripatetic.—**Aristotelianism,** a·ris′to·tē″-li·an·izm, *n.* The philosophy or doctrines of Aristotle.

arithmetic, a·rith′met·ik, *n.* [Gr. *arithmētikē,* from *arithmos,* number.] The science of numbers or the art of computation by figures or numerals.—**arithmetical,** ar·ith·met′-ik·al, *a.* Pertaining to arithmetic; according to the rules or methods used in arithmetic.—*Arithmetical progression,* series of numbers showing increase or decrease by a constant quantity, as 1, 2, 3, 4, etc.—9, 7, 5, 3; opposed to *geometrical progression,* q.v.—**arithmetically**, ar·ith·met´ik·al·li, adv. By the rules or methods of arithmetic.—**arithmetician**, a·rith´me·ti˝shan, n. One skilled in arithmetic.

ark, ärk, n. [A.Sax. arc, from L. arca, a chest.] A small chest or coffer‡; Scrip. the repository of the covenant or tables of the law, over which was placed the golden covering or mercy seat; the large floating vessel in which Noah and his family were preserved during the deluge; hence, a place of safety or shelter.

arm, ärm, n. [A.Sax. arm, earm= Goth. arms, Icel. armr, G. Fris. D. Dan. and Sw. arm; cog. L. armus, the shoulder; Gr. armos, a fitting, from arō, to fit.] The limb of the human body which extends from the shoulder to the hand; an anterior limb; anything projecting from a main body, as a branch of a tree, a narrow inlet of waters from the sea; fig. power, might, strength.— **armful**, ärm´ful, n. As much as the arms can hold; that which is embraced by the arms.—**armchair**, n. A chair with arms to support the elbows.—**armhole**, n. The armpit†; a hole for the arm in a garment.— **armpit**, n. The cavity under the shoulder or upper arm.

arm, ärm, n. [Fr. arme, a weapon, from L. arma, arms.] A weapon; a branch of the military service; pl. war; the military profession; armor; armorial bearings.—Small arms, arms that can be carried by those who use them.—A stand of arms, a complete set of arms for one soldier.—v.t. To furnish or equip with arms or weapons; to cover or provide with whatever will add strength, force, or security; to fortify.—v.i. To provide one's self with arms; to take arms.—**armada**, är·mä´da, n. [Sp.] A fleet of armed ships; a squadron. [cap.] Usually applied to the Spanish fleet intended to act against England in the reign of Queen Elizabeth I, A.D. 1588.— **armadillo**, är·ma·dil´lō, n. [Sp. dim. of armado, one who is armed, so called from its bony shell.] A mammal peculiar to South America, covered with a hard bony shell, divided into belts, composed of small separate plates like a coat of mail.—**armament**, är´ma·ment, n. A body of forces equipped for war; a land force or a naval force.—**armature**, är´ma·tūr, n. Armor; hence, anything serving as a defense, as the prickles and spines of plants; a piece of iron connecting the two poles of a magnet.

Armageddon, är´ma·ged˝on, n. [Possibly from Plain of Megiddo.] The scene of the final conflict of nations. Rev. xvi. 16.

Armenian, är·mē´ni·an, a. Pertaining to Armenia.—n. A native of Armenia; the language of the Armenians.

armilla, är·mil´la, n. [L., from armus, the shoulder.] An armlet; a bracelet; an iron ring, hoop, or brace, in which the gudgeons of a wheel move; a circular ligament of the wrist binding the tendons of the whole hand.— **armillary**, är´mil·la·ri, a. Resembling

an armilla; consisting of rings or circles.—Armillary sphere, an arrangement of rings, all circles of one sphere, intended to show the relative positions of the principal circles of the heavens.

Arminian, är·min´i·an, n. A member of the Protestant sect who follows the teaching of Arminius, a Dutch theologian (died 1609), specially opposed to the Calvinistic doctrine of predestination.—a. Pertaining to Arminius or his principles.—**Arminianism**, är·min´i·an·izm, n. The peculiar doctrines or tenets of the Arminians.

armipotent, är·mip´ō·tent, a. [L. armipotens, armipotentis—arma, arms, and potens, powerful.] Powerful in arms; mighty in battle.

armistice, är´mis·tis, n. [L. arma, arms, sisto, to stand still.] A temporary suspension of hostilities by agreement of the parties; a truce.

armor, armour, är´mėr, n. [O.E. armure, O.Fr. armeure, from L. armatura, armor, from armare, to arm.] Defensive arms; any covering worn to protect the body in battle: also called Harness; the steel or iron covering intended as a protection for a ship of war.—**armorial**, är·mō´ri·al, a. Belonging to armor, or to the arms or escutcheon of a family.— **armorer**, är´mėr·ėr, n. A maker of armor or arms, or one who keeps them in repair; one who has the care of arms and armor.—**armory**, **armoury**, är´mėr·i, n. A place where arms and instruments of war are made or deposited for safekeeping; a collection of arms.

Armoric, Armorican, är·mor´ik, är·mor´ik·an, a. [Celt. ar, upon, and mor, the sea.] Pertaining to the northwestern part of France, formerly called Armorica, now Brittany. —n. The language of the Celtic inhabitants of Brittany, allied to the Welsh.

army, är´mi, n. [Fr. armée, an armed force or army, from armer, to arm. ARM, a weapon.] A collection or body of men armed for war, and organized in regiments, brigades, or similar divisions, under proper officers; a host; a vast multitude; a great number.—**army worm**, n. The larva of a moth, so called from its marching in compact and enormous bodies, devouring green things.

arnica, är´ni·ka, n. A composite plant, otherwise called mountain tobacco. The roots yield tannin, and a tincture of the plant is used as an application to wounds and bruises.

aroint, v.t. AROYNT.

aroma, a·rō´ma, n. [Gr. arōma, spice, sweet herb.] An agreeable odor; fragrance; perfume; fig. delicate intellectual quality; flavor.—**aromatic**, ar·ō·mat´ik, a. Giving out an aroma; fragrant; sweetscented; odoriferous. Also **aromatical**, ar·ō·mat´ik·al.— Aromatic vinegar, a perfume made by adding oil of lavender, cloves, etc., to acetic acid.—**aromatic**, ar·ō·mat´ik, n. A plant or drug which yields a fragrant smell, and often a warm, pungent taste.—**aromatize**, a·rō´-

mat·īz, v.t.—aromatized, aromatizing. To impregnate with aroma; to render fragrant; to perfume.

arose, a·rōz´, pret. of arise.

around, a·round´, prep. About; on all sides; encircling; encompassing.— adv. In a circle; on every side.

arouse, a·rouz´, v.t.—aroused, arousing. [Prefix a, with intens. force, and rouse.] To excite into action that which is at rest; to stir or put in motion or exertion; to rouse; to animate; to awaken.

arpeggio, är·ped´jē·ō, n. [It., from arpa, a harp.] The distinct sound of the notes of a chord, heard when the notes are struck in rapid succession.

arquebus, är´kwē·bus, n. [Fr. arquebuse, corrupted from D. haakbus, a gun fired from a rest, from haak, a hook, a forked rest, and bus, a gun= E. hagbut, hackbut.] An old-fashioned hand gun fired from a rest. Spelled also Harquebus, etc.—**arquebusier**, är´kwē·bus·ēr˝, n. A soldier armed with an arquebus.

arrack, ar´ak, n. [Ar. araq, juice, spirits, from araqa, to sweat.] A spirituous liquor distilled in the East Indies from rice, the juice of the coconut, and other palms, etc.

arraign, a·rān´, v.t. [O.Fr. arraigner, aresner, etc., to arraign—L. ad, to, and ratio, rationis, account, a pleading in a suit. REASON.] To call or set at the bar of a court of justice; to call before the bar of reason or taste; to accuse or charge; to censure publicly; to impeach.—**arraignment**, a·rān´ment, n. The act of arraigning.

arrange, a·rānj´, v.t.—arranged, arranging. [Fr. arranger—ar=L. ad, and ranger, to range, from rang, a rank. RANGE, RANK.] To put in proper order; to dispose or set out; to give a certain collocation to; to adjust; to settle; to come to an agreement or understanding regarding.—v.i. To make or come to terms; to come to a settlement or agreement. —**arrangement**, a·rānj´ment, n. The act of arranging; disposition in suitable form; that which is arranged; preparatory measure; preparation; settlement; adjustment.—**arranger**, a·rānj´ėr, n. One that arranges or puts in order.

arrant, ar´ant, a. [A form of errant, wandering, hence vagrant, vagabond, thorough, in a bad sense.] Wandering‡; vagrant‡; shameless; notorious; thorough; out-and-out; downright.—**arrantly**, ar´ant·li, adv. In an arrant manner.

arras, ar´as, n. [From Arras, in France, where this article was manufactured.] Tapestry; hangings, consisting of woven stuffs ornamented with figures.

array, a·rā´, n. [O.Fr. arrai, order, arrangement, dress—prefix ar- (L. ad, to), and rai, order, from the Teutonic root seen in E. ready.] A collection or assemblage of men or things disposed in regular order, as an army in order of battle; raiment; dress; apparel.—v.t. To place or dispose in order, as troops for battle; to marshal; to deck or dress; to attire.

arrear, a·rēr´, n. [Fr. arrière, behind

—L. *ad*, to, and *retro*, behind.] The state of being behindhand; that which remains unpaid or undone when the due time is past: usually in the plural.

arrest, a·rest′, *v.t.* [O.Fr. *arrester*, Fr. *arrêter*—L. *ad*, to, and *restare*, to remain. REST.] To check or hinder the motion or action of; to stop; to seize or apprehend by virtue of a warrant from authority; to seize and fix (attention); to engage; to secure; to catch.—*n.* The act of arresting; apprehension; stoppage; stay; restraint.—**arrester, arrestor**, a·rest′ér, a·rest′or, *n.* One who arrests.—**arrestment**, a·rest′ment, *n.* The act of arresting; detention; arrest.

arride, a·rīd′, *v.t.* [L. *arrideo*—*ad*, and *rideo*, to smile.] To please or gratify. (*C. Lamb.*)

arris, ar′is, *n.* [O.Fr. *areste*, an arris.] The line in which two meeting surfaces of a body form an angle.

arrive, a·rīv′, *v.i.*—*arrived, arriving*. [Fr. *arriver*, from L.L. *adripare*, to come to shore—L. *ad*, to, and *ripa*, Fr. *rive*, the shore or bank.] To come to a certain place or point; to get to a destination; to reach a point or stage; to attain to a certain result or state: followed by *at*.—*v.t.*† To reach or arrive at. (*Mil.*)—**arrival**, a·rī′val, *n.* The act of arriving; a coming to or reaching; attainment; the person or thing which arrives.

arrogance, a′rō·gans, *n.* [L. *arrogantia, arrogo, arrogatum*—*ad*, to, and *rogo*, to ask or desire.] The character of being arrogant; the disposition to make exorbitant claims of rank, dignity, or estimation; the pride which exalts one's own importance; pride with contempt of others; presumption; haughtiness; disdain.—**arrogant**, a′rō·gant, *a.* Making exorbitant claims on account of one's rank, power, worth; presumptuous; haughty; overbearing; proud and assuming.—**arrogantly**, a′rō·gant·li, *adv.* In an arrogant manner.—**arrogate**, a′rō·gāt, *v.t.*—*arrogated, arrogating*. To claim or demand unduly or presumptuously; to lay claim to in an overbearing manner.—**arrogation**, a·rō·gā′shon, *n.* The act of arrogating; the claiming of superior consideration or privileges.

arrow, a′rō, *n.* [A.Sax. *arewe, aruwe, arwe*; allied to A.Sax. *earu*, swift, Icel. *ör*, pl. *örvar*, an arrow, *örr*, swift.] A missile weapon, straight, slender, pointed, and barbed, to be shot with a bow; anything resembling this.—**arrowy**, a′rō·i, *a.* Resembling an arrow in shape, in rapidity of flight, or the like.—**arrowroot**, *n.* A flour or starch obtained from the rootstocks of several West Indian reedlike plants, and much used as an article of food.

arsenal, är′se·nal, *n.* [Fr. *arsenal*, Sp. *arsenal*, from an Ar. word.] A repository or magazine of arms and military stores for land or naval service; a public establishment where arms or warlike equipments are manufactured or stored.

arsenic, är′sen·ik, *n.* [From Ar. *az-zernikh*, the orpiment (q.v.).] An element, a grayish-white substance having a metallic luster and forming poisonous compounds. Symbol, As; at. no., 33; at. wt., 74.92.—**arsenic trioxide**, *n.* As_2O_3, a white or transparent, highly poisonous substance.—**arsenical**, är·sen′ik·al, *a.*

arsis, är′sis, *n.* [Gr. *arsis*, from *airō*, to elevate.] Elevation of the voice at a word or syllable, in distinction from *thesis*, or its depression; *pros.* a greater stress or force on a syllable.

arson, är′son, *n.* [O.Fr. *arson*, from L. *ardeo, arsum*, to burn.] The malicious burning of a house, shop, church, or other building, agricultural produce, ship, etc., which by the common law is felony.

art, ärt. Second pers. sing. ARE.

art, ärt, *n.* [L. *ars, artis*, art, from same root as Gr. *arō*, to join, to fit. ARM.] The use or employment of things to answer some special purpose; the employment of means to accomplish some end: opposed to *nature*; a system of rules to facilitate the performance of certain actions; skill in applying such rules (the *art* of building or of engraving; the fine *arts*): opposed to *science*; one of the fine arts or the fine arts collectively, that is those that appeal to the taste or sense of beauty, as painting, sculpture, music; the profession of a painter or sculptor; the special skill required by those who practice these arts; artistic faculty; skill; dexterity; knack; artfulness; cunning; duplicity.—*Art union*, an association for encouraging art.—**artful**, ärt′ful, *a.* Cunning; sly; deceitful; crafty.—**artfully**, ärt′ful·li, *adv.* In an artful manner; cunningly; craftily.—**artfulness**, ärt′ful·nes, *n.* The quality of being artful.—**artless**, ärt′les, *a.* Devoid of art, skill, or cunning; natural; simple.—**artlessly**, ärt′les·li, *adv.* In an artless manner; naturally; simply.—**artlessness**, ärt′les·nes, *n.* Naturalness; simplicity; ingenuousness.

artery, är′tér·i, *n.* [L. *artēria*, Gr. *arteria*.] One of a system of cylindrical vessels or tubes, which convey the blood from the heart to all parts of the body, to be brought back again by the veins.—**arterial**, är·tē′ri·al, *a.* Pertaining to or contained in an artery or the arteries.—**arterialization**, är·tē·ri·al·iz·ā′shon, *n.* The conversion of the venous into the arterial blood.—**arterialize**, är·tē′ri·al·īz, *v.t.*—*arterialized, arterializing*. To communicate, as to venous blood, the qualities of arterial blood, a result effected by the oxygen of the air taken into the lungs.—**sclerosis**, är·tér′ri·o·sklī·rō″sis, *n.* [Gr. *arteria*, artery, and *scleros*, hard.] A disease in which thickening of the walls of arteries impedes circulation of the blood.

artesian, är·tē′zi·an, *a.* [Fr. *artésien*, lit. pertaining to *Artois*.] Term descriptive of a kind of well formed by a perpendicular boring into the ground, often of great depth, through which water rises to the surface of the soil by natural gravitation, producing a constant flow or stream.

arthritis, är·thrī′tis, *n.* [Gr., from *arthron*, a joint.] Any inflammation of the joints; the gout.—**arthritic**, är·thrit′ik, *a.*

arthropod, är′thro·pod, *n.* [Gr. *arthron*, joint, and *podos, poús*, foot.] Any member of the Arthropoda, a phylum of invertebrates with segmented bodies and jointed limbs. Included are myriapods, arachnids, crustaceans, and insects.

artichoke, är′ti·chōk, *n.* [It. *articiocco*, probably of Ar. origin.] A composite plant somewhat resembling a thistle, cultivated in gardens for the thick and fleshy receptacle (or part supporting the flower), which is eaten. The *Jerusalem artichoke* is quite different, being a species of sunflower whose roots are used like potatoes. See GIRASOLE.

article, är′ti·kl, *n.* [L. *articulus*, a joint, division, part, or member, dim. of *artus*, a joint.] A single clause, item, point, or particular; a point of faith, doctrine, or duty; a prose contribution to a newspaper, magazine, or other periodical; a particular commodity or substance; a part of speech used before nouns to limit or define their application—in English *a* or *an* and *the*.—*v.t.*—*articled, articling*. To draw up under distinct heads or particulars; to bind, as an apprentice; to indenture.—**articular**, är·tik′ū·lér, *a.* [L. *articularis*.] Belonging to the joints or to a joint.—**articulate**, är·tik′ū·lāt, *a.* [L. *articulatus*, jointed, distinct.] Jointed; formed with joints (an *articulate* animal); formed by the distinct and intelligent movement of the organs of speech; pronounced distinctly; expressed clearly; distinct (*articulate* speech or utterance).—*v.t.* *articulated, articulating*. To joint; to unite by means of a joint; to utter by intelligent and appropriate movement of the vocal organs; to enunciate, pronounce, or speak; to draw up or write in separate particulars or in articles (*Shak.*)‡.—*v.i.* To utter articulate sounds; to utter distinct syllables or words; to treat or stipulate (*Shak.*)‡.—**articulately**, är·tik′ū·lāt·li, *adv.* In an articulate manner; with distinct utterance.—**articulateness**, är·tik′ū·lāt·nes, *n.* The quality of being articulate.—**articulation**, är·tik·ū·lā′shon, *n.* The act or manner of articulating or being articulated; a joining or juncture, as of the bones; a joint; a part between two joints.—**articulator**, är·tik′ū·lāt·ér, *n.* One who articulates.

artifact, är′ti·fakt, *n.* [L. *arte*, by art, and *factum*, made.] Any man-made object; *biol.* any unnatural change in structure or tissue.

artifice, är′ti·fis, *n.* [L. *artificium*—*ars, artis*, art, and *facio*, to make.] Artful, skillful, or ingenious contrivance; a crafty device; trick; shift; stratagem; deception; cunning; guile; fraud.—**artificial**, är·ti·fish′al, *a.* Made or contrived by art, or by human skill and labor; feigned; fictitious; assumed; affected; not genuine or natural.—**artificiality**, är·ti·fish′i·al″i·ti, *n.* The quality of being artificial.—**artificially,** är·ti·fish'al·li, *adv.* In an artificial manner; by human skill and contrivance.—**artificialness,** är·ti·fish'al·nes, *n.* Artificiality.

artillery, är·til'lėr·i, *n.* (No pl.) [Fr. *artillerie,* from *artiller,* to work with art, to fortify, from L. *ars, artis,* art.] Formerly offensive weapons of war in general whether large or small (see 1 *Sa.* xx. 40); now, cannon; great guns; ordnance; ordnance and its equipment both in men and material; the men and officers that manage the guns; the science which treats of the use and management of great guns.—**artillerist,** är·til'lėr·ist, *n.* A person skilled in gunnery.—**artilleryman,** *n.* A man engaged in the management of large guns.

artiodactyl, är'ti·ō·dak"til, *n.* [Gr. *artios,* even-numbered, and *daktylos,* a toe.] A hoofed mammal in which the number of toes is even (two or four), as the ox and other ruminants, the pig, etc.

artisan, är'ti·zan, *n.* [Fr. *artisan,* It. *artigiano,* L.L. *artitianus,* from L. *ars, artis,* art.] One skilled in any art or trade; a handicraftsman; a mechanic.

artist, ärt'ist, *n.* [Fr. *artiste,* It. *artista,* from L. *ars, artis,* art.] One skilled in an art or profession, especially, one who professes and practices one of the fine arts, as painting, sculpture, engraving, and architecture; specifically, and most frequently, a painter.—**artiste,** är·tēst', *n.* [Fr.] One who is peculiarly skillful in almost any art, as a public singer, an opera dancer, and even a cook.—**artistic, artistical,** är·tist'ik, är·tist'ik·al, *a.* Pertaining to art or artists; trained in art; conformable to or characterized by art.—**artistically,** är·tist'ik·al·li, *adv.* In an artistic manner.

artless, etc. See ART.

arum, ā'rum, *n.* [L. *arum,* Gr. *aron.*] The generic name of certain plants, one of which is the common arum, wake-robin, or lords-and-ladies.

arundinaceous, a·run'di·nā"shus, *a.* [L. *arundo,* a reed.] Pertaining to reeds; resembling a reed.

aruspex, a·rus'peks, *n.* [L. *aruspex* or *haruspex.*] One of a class of priests in ancient Rome whose business was to inspect the entrails of victims killed in sacrifice, and by them to foretell future events.—**aruspicy,** a·rus'pi·si, *n.* The art of an aruspex; augury; prognostication.

Aryan, är'i·an or ā'ri·an, *n.* [Skr. *ârya,* noble, eminent.] An Indo-European; a member of that division of the human race which includes the Hindus and Persians and most Europeans (except Turks, Hungarians, Finns, etc.).—*a.* Pertaining or belonging to the Aryans; Indo-European.

as, az, *adv.* and *conj.* [Contr. from A.Sax. *eallswa,* that is, *all so,* through the forms *alswa, also, alse, als, ase;* similarly G. *als, also,* as.] A word expressing equality, similarity of manner or character, likeness, proportion, accordance; in the same manner in which (ye shall be *as* gods; I live *as* I did); while; when (he whistled *as* he went); for example; for instance; thus; because; since (*as* the wind was fair we set sail); often equivalent to the relative *that* after *such* (give us *such* things as you please).

as, as, *n.* pl. **asses** as'ez, A Roman weight of 12 oz.; also, a Roman copper or bronze coin, latterly weighing ½ oz.

asafetida, asafoetida, as·a·fe'tid·a, *n.* [Per. *aza,* gum, and L. *fœtidus,* fetid.] A fetid inspissated sap from a large umbelliferous plant found in Central Asia, used in medicine as an antispasmodic, in flatulency, hysteric paroxysms, etc.

asbestos, asbestus, as·bes'tos, as·bes'tus, ♠ [Gr. *asbestos,* inextinguishable—*a,* neg., and *sbennynai,* to extinguish.] A fibrous variety of several members of the hornblende family, having fine, elastic, flexible filaments, which are incombustible, and are made into fireproof cloth, paper, etc.—**asbestine,** as·bes'tin, *a.* Pertaining to asbestos, or partaking of its nature and qualities.

ascend, as·send', *v.i.* [L. *ascendo—ad,* to, and *scando,* to climb. SCAN.] To move upward; to mount; to go up from a lower to a higher place; to rise; to proceed from an inferior to a superior degree, from mean to noble objects, from particulars to generals, etc.; to pass from a grave tone to one more acute.—*v.t.* To go or move upward upon; to climb; to move upward along; to go toward the source of (a river).—**ascendable, ascendible,** as·send'a·bl, as·send'i·bl, *a.* Capable of being ascended.—**ascendant,** as·send'ant, *n.* An ancestor, or one who precedes in genealogy or degrees of kindred; superiority or commanding influence; predominance.—**ascendant, ascendent,** as·send'ant, as·send'ent, *a.* Directed upward; rising; superior; predominant; surpassing.—**ascendancy,** as·send'en·si, *n.* Governing or controlling influence; power; sway; control.—**ascension,** as·sen'shon, *n.* [L. *ascensio.*] The act of ascending; a rising; *the Ascension,* the visible elevation of the Saviour to heaven.—*Ascension Day,* the day on which the ascension of the Saviour is commemorated, falling on the Thursday but one before Whitsuntide.—*Right ascension* of the sun or of a star, the arc of the equator intercepted between the first point of Aries and that point of the equator which comes to the meridian at the same instant with the star.—**ascensional,** as·sen'shon·al, *a.* Relating to ascension; ascending or rising up.—**ascent,** as·sent', *n.* The act of rising; motion upward; rise; the way by which one ascends; acclivity; an upward slope; the act of proceeding from an inferior to a superior degree, from particulars to generals, etc.

ascertain, as·sėr·tān', *v.t.* [O.Fr. *ascertainer—as* for *ad,* to, *certain,* from L. *certus,* sure. CERTAIN.] To make certain; to make sure or find out by trial or examination; to establish; to determine with certainty.—**ascertainable,** as·sėr·tān'a·bl, *a.* Capable of being ascertained. —**ascertainment,** as·sėr·tān'ment, *n.* The act of ascertaining.

ascetic, as·set'ik, *a.* [Gr. *askētos,* exercised, disciplined, from *askeō,* to exercise.] Excessively strict or rigid in devotions or mortifications; severe; austere.—**ascetic,** as·set'ik, *n.* One who retires from the world and devotes himself to a strictly devout life; one who practices excessive rigor and self-denial; a hermit; a recluse.—**asceticism** as·set'i·sizm, *n.* The condition or practice of ascetics.

ascidian, as·sid'i·an, *n.* [Gr. *askidion,* a little bottle.] One of certain marine molluscous animals of a low type; a tunicate animal.—**ascidium,** as·sid'i·um, *n. Bot.* a pitcher-like appendage found in some plants.

ascites, as·sī'tēz, *n.* [Gr. *askos,* a bladder.] *Med.* dropsy of the abdomen, or of the peritoneal cavity.

ascorbic acid, a·skor'bik. The antiscorbutic vitamin, vitamin C, abundant in citrus fruits, tomatoes, and green vegetables and also occurring in animal products.

ascot, as'kot, *n.* [*Ascot* Heath, a racetrack in England.] A wide neck scarf that is looped under the chin.

ascribe, as·krīb', *v.t.*—*ascribed, ascribing.* [L. *ascribo—ad,* to, and *scribo,* to write. SCRIBE.] To attribute, impute, or refer, as to a cause; to assign; to set down; to attribute, as a quality or appurtenance.—**ascribable,** as·krīb'a·bl, *a.* Capable of being ascribed or attributed.—**ascription,** as·krip'shon, *n.*

ascus, as'kus, *n.* pl. **asci,** as'kī. [Gh *askos,* a leather bottle.] *Bot.* one of the little membranous bags or cells in which the spores of lichens, some fungi, and some other cryptogams are produced.

asepsis, a·sep'sis, *n.* [Gr. *a,* without, and *sepsis,* putrefaction.] Absence of microorganisms; prevention of sepsis.—**aseptic,** a·sep'tik, *a.* Free or freed from septic material.

asexual, a·seks'ū·al, *a.* [Prefix *a,* neg., *sexual.*] Not sexual; having no distinctive organs of sex, or imperfect organs; performed without the union of males and females.—**asexually,** a·seks'ū·al·li, *adv.*

ash, ash, *n.* [A.Sax. *æsc* = Icel. *askr,* Sw. and Dan. *ask,* D. *esh,* G. *esche.*] A well-known tree cultivated extensively for its hard and tough timber; the timber of this tree.—**ash, ashen,** ash, ash'en, *a.*

ash, ash, *n.* [A.Sax. *æsce, asce*—a word common to the Teutonic tongues.] What remains of a body that is burnt; the dust or powdery substance to which a body is reduced by the action of fire: generally used in the plural; incombustible residue; the remains of a human body when burnt or otherwise decayed; *fig.* a corpse.—*Ash Wednesday,* the first day of Lent, so called from the ancient custom of sprinkling ashes on

the heads of penitents on that day.—
ashy, ash'i. *a.* Composed of or resembling ashes; lifeless and pale.
ashame, a·shām', *v.t.*—ashamed, a-shaming. [Prefix *a*, intens., for *of*, and *shame*.] To make ashamed; to shame. —**ashamed**, a·shāmd', *p.* and *a.* Affected or touched by shame; feeling shame; exhibiting shame (an *ashamed* look): with *of* before the object.—**ashamedly**, a·shām'ed·li, *adv.* In a shamefaced manner.
ashlar, ashler, ash'lẽr, *n.* [O.Fr. *aisselle, aissil*, a shingle, from L. *assula*, a small board, a chip or splinter.] Common freestones rough from the quarry; a facing made of squared stones on the front of buildings; hewn stone for such facing.
ashore, a·shōr', *adv* On the shore, bank, or beach; on the land adjacent to water, to the shore.
Asian, ā'zhen, *a.* Pertaining to Asia, one of the continents of the globe.— **Asiatic**, ā·zhi·at'ik, *a.* Belonging to Asia or its inhabitants.—*n.* A native of Asia.
aside, a·sīd', *adv.* On or to one side; to or at a short distance off; apart; away from some normal direction; out of one's thoughts, consideration, or regard; away; off (to lay cares *aside*); so as not to be heard, or supposed not to be heard, by someone present.—**aside**, a·sīd', *n.* Something spoken and not heard, or supposed not to be heard, by someone present, as something uttered by an actor on the stage.
asinine. See ASS.
ask, ask, *v.t.* [A.Sax. *ascian, acsian, axian*, = Dan. *æske*, D. *eischen*, O.Fris. *askia*, O.G. *eiscôn*.] To request; to seek to obtain by words; to petition (with *of* before the person); to require, expect or claim; to demand; to interrogate or inquire of; to question; to inquire concerning; to seek to be informed about (to *ask* the way); to invite. [This verb may take two objects; as, to *ask* a person the time.]—*v.i.* To make a request or petition (with *for* before an object); to inquire or seek by request (often followed by *after*).—**asker**, ask'ẽr, *n.* One who asks; a questioner, inquirer, petitioner.
askance, a·skans', *adv.* [Etymology doubtful; perhaps It. *scansare*, to slip aside.] Sideways; obliquely; out of one corner of the eye.—**askant**, a·skant', *adv.* A less common form of *Askance.*
askew, a·skū', *adv.* In an oblique or skew position; obliquely; awry.
aslant, a·slant', *a.* or *adv.* Slantwise; on one side; obliquely; not perpendicularly or at right angles.
asleep, a·slēp', *a.* or *adv.* In or into a state of sleep; at rest.
aslope, a·slōp', *a.* or *adv.* Sloping; deflected from the perpendicular.
asp, aspic, asp, as'pik, *n.* [L. and Gr. *aspis*, an asp.] A deadly species of viper found in Egypt; also, a species of viper found on the continent of Europe.
asparagus, as·par'a·gus, *n.* [Gr. *asparagos*.] A perennial herb of the

lily family cultivated in gardens, the young shoots being used at table.
aspect, as'pekt, *n.* [L. *aspectus*, from *aspicio*, to look on—*ad*, to, and *specio*, to see or look.] Look; view; appearance to the eye or the mind (to present a subject in its true *aspect*); countenance; look or particular appearance of the face; mien; air (a severe *aspect*); view commanded; prospect; outlook (a house with a southern *aspect*); *astrol.* the situation of one planet with respect to another.
aspen, asp'en, *n.* [A.Sax. *aspen, æspe*, the aspen; D. *esp*, Icel. *ösp*, Sw. and Dan. *asp*, G. *espe*, the aspen-tree.] A species of poplar that has become proverbial for the trembling of its leaves, which move with the slightest impulse of the air.
aspergillum, as'pẽr·jil'um, *n.* [Dim. from L. *aspergo*, to sprinkle—*ad*, to, and *spargo*, to sprinkle.] *R. Cath. Ch.* the brush used for sprinkling holy water on the people, said to have been originally made of hyssop.
asperity, as·per'i·ti, *n.* [L. *asperitas*, from *asper*, rough.] The quality or state of being rough; roughness or harshness to the touch, taste, hearing, or feelings; tartness; crabbedness; severity; acrimony.
asperse, as·pẽrs', *v.t.*—aspersed, aspersing. [L. *aspergo, aspersus—ad*, and *spargo*, to scatter or sprinkle.] To bespatter with foul reports or false and injurious charges; to slander or calumniate.—**aspersion**, as·pẽr'zhun, *n.* A sprinkling, as of water (*Shak.*)†; the spread of calumnious reports or charges; calumny; censure.
asphalt, as'falt', [Gr. *asphaltos*, from the Phoenician.] The most common variety of bitumen; mineral pitch; a black or brown substance which melts readily and has a strong pitchy odor; a mixture of asphalt or bitumen and sand or other substances, used for pavements, floors, the lining of tanks, etc.—*Asphalt rock* or *stone*, a dark-colored bituminous limestone.—**asphaltic**, as-falt'ik, *a.* Pertaining to or containing asphalt; bituminous.
asphodel, as'fō·del, *n.* [Gr. *asphodelos*.] The name given to various species of plants of the lily family: the asphodel of the older English poets is the daffodil.
asphyxia, as·fik'si·a, *n.* [Gr. *asphyxia—a*, not, and *sphyxis*, the pulse, from *sphyzō*, to throb.] Suspended animation or loss of consciousness, with temporary stoppage of the heart's action, caused by interrupted respiration, particularly from suffocation or drowning, or the inhalation of irrespirable gases.— **asphyxiate**, as·fik'si·āt, *v.t.* To bring to a state of asphyxia; to cause asphyxia in.—**asphyxiation**, as·fik'si·ā'shon, *n.* The act of causing asphyxia; a state of asphyxia.
aspic. See ASP.
aspic, as'pik, *n.* [Fr.; origin unknown.] A dish consisting of a clear, savory, meat jelly, and containing fowl, game, fish, etc.

aspire, as·pīr', *v.i.*—aspired, aspiring. [L. *aspiro*, to breathe—*ad*, to, and *spiro*, to breathe, to endeavor after (in *expire, respire*, etc.). SPIRIT.] To desire with eagerness; to pant after a great or noble object; to aim at something elevated or above one; to be ambitious: followed by *to* or *after*; to ascend; to tower; to point upward; to soar.—**aspirant**, as·pīr'ant, *n.* One who aspires or seeks with eagerness; a candidate.— **aspirate**, as'pi·rāt, *v.t.*—aspirated, aspirating. To pronounce with a breathing or audible emission of breath; to pronounce with such a sound as our letter *h* has; to add an *h*-sound to (the word *horse* is aspirated, but not the word *hour*). —*n.* An aspirated sound like that of *h*; the letter *h* itself, or any mark of aspiration.—**aspiration**, as·pi·rā'shon, *n.* The act of aspirating; an aspirated sound; the act of aspiring or of ardently desiring; an ardent wish or desire chiefly after what is great and good.—**aspirator**, as'pi·rā·tẽr, *n.* A device that uses suction to move air, liquids, or granular substances.
aspirin, as'pi·rēn, *n. Pharm.* a white crystalline derivative of salicylic acid, $C_9H_8O_4$, used to relieve pain and reduce fever.
asportation, as·pōr·tā'shon, *n.* [L. *asportatio—abs*, from, and *porto*, to carry.] A carrying away; specifically, the felonious removal of goods from the place where they were deposited.
asquint, a·skwint', *adv.* In a squinting manner; not in the straight line of vision; obliquely.
ass, as, *n.* [A.Sax. *assa*, a male ass, *assen*, the female, also *esol, asal*; Goth. *asilus*, D. *ezel*, G. *esel*, Icel. *asni, asna*, Dan. *asen*, Lith. *asilas*, Gael. *asal*, W. *asyn*, L. *asinus*; ultimate origin unknown.] A well-known quadruped of the horse family, supposed to be a native of Asia, in parts of which vast troops roam in a wild state; from the slowness and want of spirit of the domestic ass, the type of obstinacy and stupidity; hence, a dull, stupid fellow; a dolt; a blockhead.—**asinine**, as'i·nīn, *a.* [L. *asininus*, from *asinus*, an ass.] Belonging to or having the qualities of an ass.
assafetida, *n.* Same as *Asafetida.*
assagai, as'sa·gā, *n.* [Pg. *azagaia*, Ar. *alzagāya—al*, the, and *zagaya*, a Berber word for a kind of weapon.] An instrument of warfare among the Kaffirs; a throwing spear; a species of javelin.
assail, as·sāl', *v.t.* [Fr. *assaillir*, from L. *assilio*, to leap or rush upon—*ad*, to, and *salio*, to leap, to rise. ASSAULT.] To fall upon with violence; to set upon; assault; attack, with actual weapons or with arguments, censure, abuse, criticism, entreaties, or the like. *Assail* is not so strong as *assault*, which implies more violence, and is more frequently used in a figurative sense.—**assailable**, as·sāl'a·bl, *a.* Capable of being assailed.—**assailant**, as·sāl'-ant, *n.* One who assails, attacks,

or assaults.—*a.* Assaulting; attacking.—**assailer**, as·sāl′ėr, *n.* One who assails.

assassin, as·sas′in, *n.* [Ar. *hashāshin*, *hashishin*, one who murders when infuriated by *hashish*, a maddening drink made from hemp.] One of a strange sect in Palestine in the time of the Crusades, the followers of the Old Man of the Mountains, distinguished for their secret murders; one who kills or attempts to kill by surprise or secret assault; a secret murderer; a cut-throat.—**assassinate**, as·sas′sin·āt, *v.t.*—*assassinated*, *assassinating*. To kill or attempt to kill by surprise or secret assault; to murder by sudden violence.—*n.*‡ [Fr. *assassinat*.] An assassin; assassination.—**assassination**, as·sas′sin·ā″shon, *n.* The act of assassinating; a killing or murdering by surprise or secret assault.—**assassinator**, as·sas′sin·āt·ėr, *n.* An assassin.

assault, as·salt′, *n.* [O.Fr. *assault* (Fr. *assaut*), from L.L. *assaltus*, from L. *ad*, to, and *saltus*, a leap, from *salio*, to leap. *Assail*, *insult*, *result*, etc., are akin.] An attack or violent onset; an onslaught; a violent attack with the intention of injuring a person; specifically, a sudden and vigorous attack on a fortified post; a storm.—*Assault at arms*, a name sometimes given to an exhibition of fencing or similar military exercises.—*v.t.* To fall upon by violence or with a hostile intention; to fall on with force; to assail. ASSAIL.—**assaulter**, as·salt′ėr, *n.* One who assaults.

assay, as·sā′, *n.* [O.Fr. *assai*, *essay*, a trial, examination, *essayer*, to test, from L. *exagium*, Gr. *exagion*, a weighing—*ex*, out, *agō*, to bring. *Essay* is the same word.] Examination; trial; the trial of the goodness, purity, weight, value, etc., of metals or metallic substances, especially gold and silver, their ores and alloys.—**assay**, as·sā′, *v.t.* To make an assay of; to examine by trial; to test the purity or metallic constituents of; to attempt, endeavor, essay (*Shak.*)‡—**assayer**, as·sā′ėr, *n.* One who assays.

assegai, *n.* Same as *Assagai*.

assemble, as·sem′bl, *v.t.*—*assembled*, *assembling*. [Fr. *assembler*, from L.L. *assimulo*, to assemble—L. *ad*, to, and *simul*, together; akin, *similar*, *simulate*, *assimilate*, etc.; same root as E. *same*.] To collect into one place or body; to bring or call together; to convene; to congregate; to fit together (pieces of mechanism).—*v.i.* To meet or come together; to gather; to convene.—**assemblage**, as·sem′blāj, *n.* The act of assembling, or state of being assembled; a collection of individuals or of particular things; a gathering or company.—**assembler**, as·sem′blėr, *n.* —**assembly**, as·sem′bli, *n.* [Fr. *assemblée*.] A company or collection of human beings in the same place, usually for the same purpose; the name given to the legislative body or one of the divisions of it in various states.—*General Assembly*, the legis-

lative body of the United Nations.—**assembly line**, as·sem′bli līn, *n.* Production line along which successive operations are performed until the final product is made.—**assemblyman**, as·sem′bli·man, *n.* Member of a law-making body, usually the lower house.

assent, as·sent′, *n.* [O.Fr. *assent*—L. *ad*, and *sentio*, to think (also in *consent*, *dissent*, *sense*, etc.)] The act of the mind in admitting or agreeing to the truth of a proposition; consent; concurrence; acquiescence; agreement to a proposal; accord; agreement; approval.— *Royal assent*, the approbation given by the British sovereign in parliament to a bill which has passed both houses, after which it becomes law.—*v.i.* To express an agreement of the mind to what is alleged or proposed; to concur; to acquiesce.—**assentation**, as·sen·tā′shon, *n.* [L. *assentatio*, flattery; from *assentor*, to assent from interested motives, to flatter.] Flattery; adulation.—**assentor**, as·sent′ėr, *n.* One who assents.

assert, as·sėrt′, *v.t.* [L. *assero*, *assertum*—*ad*, to, and *sero*, *sertum*, to join, connect, bind, from root of *series*.] To support the cause or claims of (rights, liberties); to vindicate a claim or title to; to affirm positively; to asseverate; to aver; *refl.* to come forward and assume one's rights, claims, etc.—**assertion**, as·sėr′shon, *n.* The act of affirming; the maintaining of a claim; a positive declaration or averment; an affirmation.—**assertive**, **assertory**, as·sėrt′iv, as·sėrt′o·ri, *a.* Positive; affirming confidently; peremptory; declaratory.—**assertively**, as·sėrt′iv·li, *adv.* In an assertive manner; affirmatively.—**assertor**, **asserter**, as·sėrt′ėr, *n.* One who asserts; one who affirms positively; one who maintains or vindicates.

assess, as·ses′, *v.t.* [O.Fr. *assesser*, L.L. *assessare*, from L. *assideo*, *assessum*, to sit beside, and hence to act as assessor—*ad*, to, and *sedeo*, to sit; akin, *assiduous*, *reside*, *sedentary*, etc.] To set, fix, or charge a certain sum upon (a person), by way of tax; to value, as property or the amount of yearly income, for the purpose of being taxed; to settle or determine the amount of (damages).—**assessable**, as·ses′a·bl, *a.* Capable of being assessed; liable to be assessed.—**assessably**, as·ses′a·bli, *adv.* By assessment.—**assessment**, as·ses′ment, *n.* The act of assessing; a valuation of property, profits, or income, for the purpose of taxation; a tax or specific sum charged on a person or property.—**assessor**, as·ses′ėr, *n.* One appointed to make assessments; an officer of justice who sits to assist a judge.—**assessorial**, as·ses·sō′ri·al, *a.* Pertaining to an assessor or assessors.

asset, as′set, *n.* [O.Fr. *aset*, *assetz*, Fr. *assez*, enough, from L. *ad*. to, and *satis*, enough.] An article of goods or property available for the payment of a person's obligations

or debts: generally used in the plural; any portion of the entire effects belonging to a person.

asseverate, as·sev′ėr·āt, *v.t.*—*asseverated*, *asseverating*. [L. *assevero*, *asseveratum*—*ad*, to, and *severus*, serious, severe.] To affirm or aver positively, or with solemnity.—**asseveration**, as·sev′ėr·ā″shon, *n.* The act of asseverating; positive affirmation or assertion.

assiduous, as·sid′ū·us, *a.* [L. *assiduus*, from *assideo*, to sit close—*ad*, and *sedeo*, to sit. ASSESS.] Constant in application; attentive; devoted; unremitting; performed with constant diligence or attention.—**assiduously**, as·sid′ū·us·li, *adv.* In an assiduous manner.—**assiduousness**, **assiduity**, as·sid′ū·us·nes, as·si·dū′i·ti, *n.* The quality of being assiduous; constant or diligent application to any business or enterprise; diligence.

assign, as·sīn′, *v.t.* [Fr. *assigner*, L. *assigno*,—*ad*, and *signo*, to allot, mark out, from *signum*, a mark (whence *sign*, *consign*, etc.).] To mark out as a portion allotted; to apportion; to allot; to fix or specify; *law*, to transfer or make over to another.—*n.* A person to whom property or an interest is transferred; an assignee.—**assignable**, as·sīn′a·bl, *a.* Capable of being assigned. —**assignation**, as·sig·nā·shon, *n.* The act of assigning or allotting; the act of fixing or specifying; a making over by transfer of title; an appointment of time and place for meeting: used chiefly of love meetings.—**assignee**, as·sin·ē′, *n.* A person to whom an assignment is made; a person appointed or deputed to perform some act or business, or enjoy some right.—**assigner**, **assignor**, as·sīn′ėr, as·sīn′or, *n.* One who assigns or appoints.— **assignment**, as·sīn′ment, *n.* The act of assigning, fixing, or specifying; the writing by which an interest is transferred.—**assignat**, as′sig·nat or as·sin·yä′, *n.* [Fr., from L. *assignatus*, assigned.] A public note or bill in France during the first revolution.

assimilate, as·sim′il·āt, *v.t.*—*assimilated*, *assimilating*. [L. *assimilo*—*ad*, to, and *similis*, like. ASSEMBLE.] To make alike; to cause to resemble; to absorb and incorporate (food) into the system; to incorporate with organic tissues; to liken or compare†.—*v.i.* To become similar; to harmonize; to become incorporated with the body; to perform the act of converting food to the substance of the body.—**assimilability**, as·sim′il·a·bil″i·ti, *n.* The quality of being assimilable.—**assimilable**, as·sim′il·a·bl, *a.* Capable of being assimilated.—**assimilation**, as·sim′il·ā″shon, *n.* The act or process of assimilating or being assimilated; the process by which animals and plants convert and absorb nutriment so that it becomes part of the substances composing them.—**assimilative**, **assimilatory**, as·sim′il·āt·iv, as·sim′il·a·to·ri, *a.* Having the power of assimilating; tending to assimilate; producing assimilation.

assist, as·sist′, *v.t.* [Fr. *assister*, to stand by, help; L. *assisto*—*ad*, to, and *sisto*, to stand.] To help; to aid; to succor.—*v.i.* To lend aid; to be present; to take part in a ceremony or discussion.—**assistance,** as·sist′ans, *n.* Help; aid; succor; a contribution in aid.—**assistant,** as·sist′ant, *a.* Helping; lending aid or support; auxiliary.—*n.* One who aids or assists another; one engaged to work along with another; an auxiliary.

assize, as·sīz′, *n.* [Fr. *assises*, assizes, *assise*, a fixed rate, a tax, from L. *assideo*, to be an assessor.—ASSESS.] A jury or similar assembly‡; the periodical sessions held at stated intervals by at least two judges in each of the counties of England and Wales (except Middlesex), for the purpose of trying criminal and certain other cases before a jury; generally in the plural; an ordinance; a decree; an assessment; particularly, an ordinance formerly fixing the weight, measure, and price of articles (hence the word *size*).—*v.t.*—*assized, assizing; assised, assising.* To fix the weight, measure, or price of; to fix the rate of; to assess‡.

associate, as·sō′shi·āt, *v.t.*—*associated, associating.* [L. *associo*, *associatum*—*ad*, to, and *socius*, a companion. SOCIAL.] To join in company (another with ourselves); to adopt as a partner, companion, and the like; to join or connect intimately (things together); to unite; to combine.—*v.i.* To unite in company; to join in a confederacy or association.—*a.* Joined in interest, object, office, etc.; combined together; joined with another or others.—*n.* A companion; a mate; a fellow; a partner; a confederate; an accomplice; an ally.—**associable,** as·sō′shi·a·bl, *a.* Capable of being associated; companionable; social.—**associability, association,** as·sō′shi·a·bil′i·ti, as·sō·shi·ā″shon, *n.* The act of associating or state of being associated; connection; union; a society, the members of which are united by mutual interests or for a common purpose; *philos.* the tendency which one idea, feeling, etc., has for one reason or another to recall another.—**associational,** as·sō′shi·ā″shon·al, *a.* Pertaining to association.—**associative,** as·sō′shi·āt·iv, *a.* Capable of associating; tending to associate or unite; leading to association.

assonant, as′sō·nant, *a.* [L. *assonans*, ppr. of *assono*—*ad*, to, and *sono*, to sound.] Having a resemblance of sounds; *pros.* rhyming only so far as the vowels are concerned.—**assonance,** as′sō·nans, *n.* Resemblance of sounds; *pros.* a species of imperfect rhyme which consists in using the same vowel with different consonants.

assort, as·sort′, [Fr. *assortir*, to sort, to assort—*as* for L. *ad*, to, and *sors, sortis*, a lot. SORT.] To separate and distribute into sorts, classes,

or kinds; to furnish with a suitable variety of goods (to *assort* a cargo); to adapt or suit.—*v.i.* To agree; to suit together; to associate; to keep company.—**assortment,** as·sort′ment, *n.* The act of assorting; a collection of things assorted.

assuage, as·swāj′, *v.t.*—*assuaged, assuaging.* [O.Fr. *assouager, assouagier*, from L. *ad*, to, and *suavis*, sweet.] To allay, mitigate, ease, or lessen (pain or grief); to moderate; to appease or pacify (passion or tumult).—**assuagement,** as·swaj′ment, *n.* The act of assuaging; mitigation; abatement.

assume, as·sūm′, *v.t.*—*assumed, assuming,* [L. *assumo*—*ad*, to, and *sumo*, to take, also seen in *consume, presume, sumptuous,* etc.] To take upon one's self; to take on; to appear in (*assume* a figure or shape); to appropriate; to take for granted; suppose as a fact; to pretend to possess; to put on (*assume* a wise air).—*v.i.* To be arrogant; to claim more than is due; *law,* to undertake or promise.—**assuming,** as·sūm′ing, *a.* Putting on airs of superiority; haughty; arrogant; overbearing.—**assumption,** as·sum′shon, *n.* [L. *assumptio.*] The act of assuming; a taking upon one's self; the act of taking for granted; supposition; the thing supposed; a postulate or proposition assumed; a church festival in honor of the miraculous ascent to heaven of the Virgin Mary's body after death, celebrated August 15.—**assumptive,** as·sum′tiv, *a.* Capable of being assumed; assumed.

assure, a·shör′, *v.t.*—*assured, assuring,* [Fr. *assurer*, O.Fr. *asseürer*, L.L. *assecurare*—L. *ad*, to, and *securus*, secure.] To make (a person) sure or certain; to convince (to *assure* a person of a thing); to declare or affirm solemnly to; to confirm; to ensure; to secure (to *assure* success to a person); to insure; to embolden or make confident (N.T.); to affiance or betroth (*Shak.*).—**assurable,** a·shör′a·bl, *a.* Capable of being assured; suitable for insurance.—**assurance,** a·shör′ans, *n.* The act of assuring; a pledge furnishing ground of full confidence; firm persuasion; certain expectation; undoubting steadiness; intrepidity; excess of boldness; impudence; laudable confidence; self-reliance; insurance.—**assured,** a·shörd′, *a.* Certain; convinced; not doubting or doubtful; bold to excess; confident; having life or goods insured (in this sense often a noun, sing. or pl.). —**assuredly,** a·shör′ed·li, *adv.* Certainly; indubitably.—**assuredness,** a·shör′ed·nes, *n.* The state of being assured; certainty; full confidence.—**assurer,** a·shör′ėr, *n.* One who assures; an insurer or underwriter.

assurgent, as·sėr′jent, *a.* [L. *assurgens, assurgentis,* ppr. of *assurgo*—*ad*, to, and *surgo*, to rise. SURGE.] Rising or directed upward.—**assurgency,**† as·sėr′jen·si, *n.* The act of rising upward.

Assyrian, as·sir′i·an, *a.* Pertaining or

relating to Assyria or to its inhabitants.—*n.* A native or inhabitant of Assyria; the language of the Assyrians.—**Assyriologist,** as·sir′i·ol″o·jist, *n.* One skilled in the antiquities, language (as exhibited in the cuneiform inscriptions), etc., of ancient Assyria.

astatic, a·stat′ik, *a.* [Gr. *a*, not, and root *sta*, to stand.] Being without polarity.—*Astatic needle*, a magnetic needle having its directive property destroyed by the proximity of another needle of the same intensity fixed parallel to it, but with the poles reversed.—**astatically,** a·stat′ik·al·li, *adv.* In an astatic manner.

astatine, as′ta·tēn, *n.* [Gr. *astatos* unstable.] An unstable element belonging to the halogen family and produced by bombardment of bismuth with alpha particles. Symbol, At; at. no., 85.

aster, as′tėr, *n.* [Gr. *astēr*, a star.] A large genus of composite plants, the flowers of which somewhat resemble stars.—**asterisk,** as′tėr·isk, *n.* [Gr. *asteriskos*, a little star.] The figure of a star, thus *, used in printing and writing, as a reference to a note or to fill the space where something is omitted.—**asterism,** as′tėr·izm, *n.* [Gr. *asterismos.*] A small collection of stars; an asterisk, or several asterisks together†.

astern, a·stėrn′, *adv.* In or at or toward the stern of a ship; behind a ship; backward; with the stern foremost.

asteroid, as′tėr·oid, *n.* [Gr. *astēr*, a star, and *eidos*, form.] One of the small planets between the orbits of Mars and Jupiter, more accurately called *planetoids.*—**asteroid, asteroidal,** as′tėr·oid, as·tėr·oid′al, *a.* Resembling a star; pertaining to the asteroids, or to the starfishes.

asthenia, as·thē·nī′a, *n.* [Gr. *astheneia*—*a*, not, and *sthenos*, strength.] Debility; want of strength.—**asthenic,** as·then′ik, *a.* Characterized by asthenia or debility.

asthma, as′ma, *n.* [Gr. *asthma*, shortdrawn breath.] A chronic disorder of respiration, characterized by difficulty of breathing, a cough, and expectoration.—**asthmatic, asthmatical,** ast·mat′ik, ast·mat′ik·al, *a.* Pertaining to asthma; affected by asthma.—*n.* A person troubled with asthma.—**asthmatically,** ast·mat′ik·al·li, *adv.* In an asthmatical manner.

astigmatism, a·stig′mat·izm, *n.* [Gr. *a*, neg., and *stigma, stigmatos,* a mark.] A malformation of the lens of the eye, such that rays of light are not brought to converge in the same point.

astir, a·stėr′, *adv.* or *a.* On the stir; on the move; stirring; active; not used attributively.

astomatous, as·tom′a·tus, *a.* [Gr. *a*, without, and *stoma*, a mouth.] Without a mouth.

astonish, as·ton′ish, *v.t.* [Partly from O.Fr. *estonner*, L.L. *extonare*, lit. to make thunder-struck, from *ex*, intens., and *tono*, to thunder; partly from A.Sax. *âstunian*—*â*, intensive,

ch, *ch*ain; *ch*, Sc. lo*ch*; g, *g*o; j, *j*ob; ng, si*ng*; TH, *th*en; th, *th*in; w, *w*ig; hw, *wh*ig; zh, a*z*ure.

and *stunian*, to stun.] To strike or impress with wonder, surprise, or admiration; to surprise; to amaze; to stun†; to confound‡.—**astonishing**, as·ton´ish·ing, *a.* Calculated to astonish; amazing; wonderful.—**astonishingly**, as·ton´ish·ing·li, *adv.* In an astonishing manner.—**astonishment**, as·ton´ish·ment, *n.* The state or feeling of being astonished; amazement; great surprise; a cause or matter of astonishment (O.T.).—**astound**, as·tound´, *v.t.* [For old *astoune*, A.Sax. *astunian*, with *d* added, as in *sound*, *expound*.] To astonish; to strike dumb with amazement.—**astounding**, as·tound´ing, *a.* Fitted or calculated to astound; causing terror; astonishing.

astraddle, a·strad´l, *adv.* Straddling; with one leg on either side; astride.

astragal, as´tra·gal, *n.* [Gr. *astragalos*, a huckle-bone, a moulding.] A small semi-circular molding separating the shaft of a column from the capital; one of the bars which hold the panes of a window; the huckle or ankle bone; the upper bone of the foot.

astrakhan, as´tra·kan, *n.* [From *Astrakhan* in the U.S.S.R.] A rough kind of cloth with a curled pile.

astral, as´tral, *a.* [L. *astralis*, from *astrum*, a star.] Belonging to the stars; starry.

astray, a·strā´, *adv.* Having strayed; out of the right way or proper place.

astrict,† as·trikt´, *v.t.* [L. *astrictum*. ASTRINGE.] To constrict; to contract; to limit.—**astriction**, as·trik´shon. *n.* The act of binding close, contracting, or restricting; limitation.—**astrictive**, as·trikt´iv, *a.* Binding; compressing.

astride, a·strīd´, *adv.* With one leg on each side; with the legs wide apart.

astringent, as·trin´jent, *a.* [L. *astringo*—*ad*, to, and *stringo*, to strain. STRAIN.] Contracting; especially contracting the organic tissues and canals of the body, and thereby checking or diminishing excessive discharges.—*n.* An astringent substance.

astrodynamics, as´trō·dī·nam″iks, *n.* [Gr. *astron*, star, and *dynamis*, power.] The science of adapting celestial mechanics to space flight.

astrolabe, as´trō·lāb, *n.* [Gr. *astēr*, a star, and root *lab*, seen in *lambanō*, to take.] An instrument formerly used for taking the altitude of the sun or stars at sea, now superseded by the quadrant and sextant.

astrology, as·trol´o·ji, *n.* [Gr. *astron*, a star, and *logos*, discourse, theory.] The pseudoscience which pretends to enable men to discover effects and influences of the heavenly bodies on human and other mundane affairs and to foretell the future.—**astrologer**, as·trol´o·jèr, *n.* One who practices astrology.—**astrological**, as·trō·loj´ik·al, *a.*—**astrologically**, as·trō·loj´ik·al·li, *adv.*

astronaut, as´tro·nat, *n.* A person who travels through interplanetary space; a space-age enthusiast.—**astronautics**, as·tro·na̧´tiks, *n.* The

science of space flight.

astronomy, as·tron´o·mi, *n.* [Gr. *astron*, a star, and *nomos*, a law or rule.] The science which treats of the celestial bodies, their nature, magnitudes, motions, distances, periods of revolution, etc.—**astronomer**, as·tron´o·mèr, *n.* One who is versed in astronomy.—**astronomic, astronomical**, as·trō·nom´ik, as·trō·nom´ik·al, *a.*—**astronomically**, as·trō·nom´ik·al·li, *adv.*—**astronomical unit**, as·trō·nom´ik·al ū´nit, *n.* A basic measurement of astronomy. It is the mean distance between the earth and the sun.

astrophysics, as´tro·fiz″iks, *n.* Astronomical physics, the science that deals with the physical properties and phenomena of celestial bodies.

astucious, as·tū´shus, *a.* [Fr. *astucieux*, L. *astus*, craft.] Astute; crafty.

astute, as·tūt´, *a.* [L. *astutus*, from *astus*, craft, subtlety.] Of a shrewd and penetrating turn; cunning; sagacious; keen.—**astutely**, as·tūt´li, *adv.* In an astute manner; shrewdly; sharply; cunningly.—**astuteness**, as·tūt´nes, *n.* The quality of being astute; cunning; shrewdness.

astylar, a·stī´lèr, *a.* [Gr. *a*, not, and *stylos*, a column.] *Arch.* having no columns.

asunder, a·sun´dèr, *adv.* In sunder; apart; into parts; separately.

asylum, a·sī´lum, *n.* [L. *asylum*, Gr. *asylon*—*a*, not, and *sylaō*, to strip, plunder.] A sanctuary or place of refuge; any place of retreat and security; an institution for receiving and maintaining persons laboring under certain bodily defects or mental maladies; a refuge for the unfortunate.

asymmetry, a·sim´met·ri, *n.* [Gr. *a*, not, and *symmetria*, symmetry.] The want of symmetry or proportion between the parts of a thing.—**asymmetrical**, a·sim·met´rik·al, *a.* Not having symmetry; inharmonious; not reconcilable.

asymptote, as´im·tōt, *n.* [Gr. *asymptōtos*, not falling together—*a*, not, *syn*, with, and *piptō*, to fall.] *Math.* a line which approaches nearer and nearer to some curve, but though infinitely extended would never meet it.—**asymptotic, asymptotical**, as·im·tot´ik, as·im·tot´ik·al, *a.* Belonging to or having the character of an asymptote.—**asymptotically**, as·im·tot´ik·al·li, *adv.* In an asymptotic manner.

asyndeton, a·sin´de·ton, *n.* [Gr. *a*, not, *syn*, together, *deō*, to bind.] A figure of speech by which connectives are omitted; as, *veni, vidi, vici*; I came, I saw, I conquered.—**asyndetic**, as·in·det´ik, *a.* Pertaining to or characterized by the use of asyndeton.

at, at, *prep.* [A.Sax. *æt*, Goth. O.Sax. Icel. *at*, Dan. *ad*, O.H.G. *az*; allied to L. *ad*, to, Skr. *adhi*, upon.] Denoting coincidence or contiguity: in time (*at* first); in space (*at* home, *at* church); in occupation or condition (*at* work, *at* prayer); in degree or condition (*at* best, *at* the worst); in effect, as coincident with the cause

(*at* the sight); in relation, as existing between two objects (*at* your command); in value (*at* a dollar a head); also, direction toward (fire *at* the target).—**At large**, at liberty; unconfined; also, generally; as a whole (the country *at large*).

Atabrine, at´a·brin, *n.* Trade-mark for quinacrine hydrochloride. It is used in the treatment of malaria.

ataractic, at·a·rak´tik, *n.* [Gr. *ataraktos*, without confusion.] A drug that decreases anxiety or tension.—*a.* tranquillizing.

atavism, at´a·vizm, *n.* [L. *atavus*, an ancestor.] The resemblance of off-spring to a remote ancestor; the return or reversion among animals to the original type; *med.* the recurrence of any peculiarity or disease of an ancestor.

ataxia, a·tak´si·a, *n.* [Gr. *a*, not, and *taxis*, order.] Want of order; disturbance; *med.* irregularity in the functions of the body or in the crisis and paroxysms of disease.—**ataxic**, a·tak´sik, *a.*

atelier, at´el·yā, *n.* [Fr., a workshop.] A workshop; specifically, the workroom of sculptors and painters.

Athanasian, ath·a·nā´zhen, *a.* Pertaining to *Athanasius*, bishop of Alexandria, in the fourth century.—*Athanasian creed*, a creed of the Christian church, erroneously attributed to Athanasius, and also ascribed to Hilary, bishop of Arles (about A.D. 430). It defines the doctrines of the Trinity and the Incarnation in very precise and emphatic language, declaring damnation to be the lot of those who do not hold the right faith.

atheism, ā´thē·izm, *n.* [Gr. *atheos*, an atheist—*a*, not, and *theos*, God.] The disbelief in the existence of a God or Supreme Being.—**atheist**, ā´thē·ist, *n.* One who professes atheism or disbelief in God.—**atheistic, atheistical**, ā·thē·ist´ik, ā·thē·ist´ik·al, *a.*

atheling, ath´el·ing [A.Sax. *ætheling*, from *æthele*, noble = G. *edel*, noble.] In Anglo-Saxon times, a prince; one of the royal family; a nobleman.

athenaeum, atheneum, ath·e·nē´um, *n.* [L. from Gr. *Athēnē*, the goddess of wisdom.] An institution for the encouragement of literature and art, where a library, periodicals, etc., are kept for the use of the members.

athermanous, a·thèr´man·us, *a.* [Gr. *a*, not, and *thermainō*, to heat, from *thermē*, heat.] A term applied to those substances which have the power of absorbing radiant heat.—**athermancy**, a·thèr´man·si, *n.* The power or property of absorbing radiant heat.

athirst, a·thèrst´, *a.* or *adv.* Thirsty; wanting drink; having a keen appetite or desire (with *for*).

athlete, ath´lēt, *n.* [Gr. *athlētēs*, from *athlon*, a contest.] One trained to exercises of agility and strength.—**athletic**, ath·let´ik, *a.* Pertaining to athletes or such exercises as are practiced by athletes; strong; robust; vigorous.—**athletics**, ath·let´iks, *n. pl.* Athletic exercises.—**athletically**, ath·let´ik·al·li, *adv.* In an athletic manner.—**athleticism,** ath·let′i·sizm, *n.* The practice of athletics; the profession of an athlete.

athwart, a·thwạrt′, *prep.* Across; from side to side of; *naut,* across the line of a ship's course.—*adv.* In a manner to cross and perplex; crossly; wrong. (*Shak.*)

atilt, a·tilt′, *adv.* In the manner of a tilter; in the manner of a cask tilted up.

atlas, at′las, *n.* [Gr. *Atlas,* one of the Titans, who, according to the legend, bore the earth on his shoulders.] A collection of maps in a volume; a volume of plates or tables illustrative or explanatory of some subject; the first vertebra of the neck (so named because it supports the head).—**Atlantean,** at·lan·tē′an, *a.* Pertaining to Atlas; resembling Atlas.—**atlantes,** at·lan′tēz, *n. pl.* [Gr., pl. of *Atlas.*] Sculptured figures or half figures of men used in the place of columns or pilasters in buildings, supporting or seeming to support some mass above them.—**Atlantic,** at·lan′tik, *a.* Pertaining to or descended from Atlas (*Mil.*); pertaining to that division of the ocean which lies between Europe and Africa on the east and America on the west (named from *Mt. Atlas*).

atmosphere, at′mos·fẽr, *n.* [Gr. *atmos,* vapor, and *sphaira,* a sphere.] The whole mass of aeriform fluid surrounding the earth and generally supposed to extend to the height of 40 or 50 miles above its surface; any similar gaseous envelope or medium; the amount of pressure of a column of the atmosphere on a square inch (=14.69lbs.); *fig.* pervading influence (to live in an *atmosphere* of doubt).—**atmospheric, atmospherical,** at·mos·fẽr′ik, at·mos·fẽr′ik·al, *a.* Pertaining to, existing in, or consisting of the atmosphere; caused, produced, or operated on by the atmosphere. *Atmospheric railway,* a railway, the motive power of which is derived from the pressure of the atmosphere, brought to act when air is exhausted from a tube of uniform bore, laid from one place to another.

atoll, a·tol′, *n.* [Name in the Maldive group.] A coral island, consisting of a strip or ring of coral surrounding a central lagoon or lake: such islands are very common in the Pacific Ocean.

atom, at′om, *n.* [L. *atomus,* Gr. *atomos,* an atom, lit. what is indivisible—*a,* not, and *temnō,* to cut.]—*Chem. & Phys.* the smallest particle of an element; it is composed of subatomic particles (protons, neutrons, electrons) whose number and arrangement characterize the element. A minute quantity.—**atomic,** a·tom′ik, *a.* Pertaining to atoms; consisting of atoms; extremely minute.—**atomic bomb.** A bomb whose explosive power is derived from the splitting (fission) of nuclei of atoms (plutonium, uranium) by bombardment with neutrons to release atomic energy.—**atomic energy.** Energy obtained from changes within the nucleus of an atom, by

fission of a heavy nucleus or by fusion of light nuclei into heavier ones with loss of mass.—**atomic number.** *Chem & Phys.* a number giving the position of an element in the periodic table of elements; it is the number of positive charges on the nucleus of an atom of a given element.—**atomic philosophy,** a system of philosophy which taught that atoms, by virtue of their own properties, brought all things into being without the aid of a Creator.—**atomic theory,** the theory that all chemical combinations take place in a definite manner between the ultimate particles or atoms of bodies.—**atomic weight.** *Chem & Phys.* the weight of an atom of an element relative to the weight of a carbon atom, which is taken as 12.—**atomical,** a·tom′ik·al, *a.* Atomic.—**atomist,** at′om·ist, *n.* An adherent of the atomic philosophy or theory.—**atomism,** at′om·izm, *n.* The doctrine of atoms; atomic philosophy.—**atomistic,** at·om·ist′ik, *a.* Pertaining to atomism.—**atomize,** at′om·īz, *v.t.* —*atomized, atomizing.* To reduce to atoms.—**atomizer,** at′om·īz·ẽr, *n.* One who or that which atomizes or reduces to atoms; an apparatus for reducing a liquid into spray for disinfecting, cooling, perfuming, etc. —**atomy,** at′om·i, *n.* An atom; a minute creature. (*Shak.*)

atone, a·tōn′, *v.i.* —*atoned, atoning.* [Compounded of *at* and *one,* often found together in such phrases as 'to be *at one,*' 'to set *at one.*'] To be at one‡; to agree or accord (*Shak.*)‡; to make reparation, amends, or satisfaction, as for an offense or a crime.—*v.t.* To expiate; to answer or make satisfaction for; to reconcile, as parties at variance.‡—**atonement,** a·tōn′ment, *n.* The act of atoning, reconciling, or making reparation; reconciliation after enmity or controversy; specifically, the reconciliation of God with man through Christ; satisfaction; expiation.— **atoner,** a·tōn′ẽr, *n.* One who makes atonement.

atony, at′o·ni, *n.* [Gr. *atonia*—*a,* not, *tonos,* tone.] *Med.* a want of tone; defect of muscular power; weakness of every organ; debility.—**atonic,** a·ton′ik, *a. Med.* characterized by atony.

atop, a·top′, *adv.* On or at the top.

atrabilarian, atrabilarious, at′ra·bi·lā″ri·an, at′ra·bi·lā″ri·us, *a.* [L. *atra bilis,* black bile.] Affected with melancholy, which the ancients attributed to black bile; very bilious.— **atrabiliar, atrabilious,** at·ra·bil′i·ar, at·ra·bil′i·us, *a.* Melancholic or hypochondriacal; atrabilarian.

atrip, a·trip′, *a.* Of anchor loosed from bottom by means of a cable: of sails turned from horizontal to vertical position.

atrium, ā′tri·um, *n.* [L.] The entrance hall and usually the most splendid apartment of an ancient Roman house; *zool.* the chamber into which the intestine opens in ascidians.

atrocious, a·trō′shus, *a.* [L. *atrox,*

atrocis, fierce, cruel.] Extremely heinous, criminal, or cruel; enormously or outrageously wicked; enormous; horrible.—**atrociously,** a·trō′shus·li, *adv.* In an atrocious manner.— **atrociousness,** a·trō′shus·nes, *n.* The quality of being atrocious.— **atrocity,** a·tros′i·ti, *n.* The state or quality of being atrocious; enormous wickedness or cruelty; a specific act of extreme heinousness or cruelty.

atrophy, at′ro·fi, *n.* [Gr. *atrophia*—*a,* not, and *trephō,* to nourish.] A wasting of the flesh with loss of strength; emaciation.

atropin, atropine, at′rō·pin, *n.* A very poisonous substance obtained from the deadly nightshade (*Atropa belladonna*).

attach, at·tach′, *v.t.* [Fr. *attacher,* same word as *attaquer,* to attack, from Arm. *tach,* Ir. *taca,* a peg, a nail=E. *tack,* a small nail.] To make to adhere; to tie, bind, or fasten; to connect or associate; to gain over, win, charm, or attract; to arrest or seize (a person or goods) by lawful authority, as in case of debt, etc.— *v.i.* To be attached or connected; to be joined or bound up with; to belong: with *to* (interest *attaches* to a subject).—**attachable,** at·tach′a·bl, *a.* Capable of being attached.— **attache,** a·ta·shā′, *n.* [Fr.] One attached to an embassy or legation to a foreign court.—**attachment,** at·tach′ment, *n.* The act of attaching; the state of being attached; close adherence or affection; any passion or liking which binds one person to another or to a place, etc.; love; regard; that which attaches one object to another; the object attached; an adjunct; *law,* a taking of a person or goods by legal means to secure a debt.

attack, at·tak′, *v.t.* [Fr. *attaquer.* ATTACH.] To assault; to fall upon with force or violence; to make a hostile onset on; to assail; to endeavor or to injure by any act, speech, or writing; to come or fall upon; to seize, as a disease.—*v.i.* To make an attack or onset; to begin an assault.—*n.* A falling on, with force or violence, or with calumny, satire, etc.; an onset; an assault; a seizure by a disease.

attain, at·tān′, *v.t.* [O.Fr. *ataindre,* Fr. *atteindre,* L. *attingere*—*ad,* to, and *tango,* to touch. Akin *attaint, attainder, tact, tangent,* etc.] To reach by effort; to achieve or accomplish; to acquire; to gain: said of an end or object; to come to; to arrive at; to reach: said of a place.—*v.i.* To reach; to come or arrive; followed by *to.*—**attainable,** at·tān′a·bl, *a.* Capable of being attained, reached, achieved, or accomplished.—**attainability, attainableness,** at·tān′a·bil″i·ti, at·tān′a·bl·nes, *n.* The quality of being attainable.—**attainment,** at·tān′ment, *n.* The act of attaining; that which is attained, an acquisition; an acquirement.

attainder, at·tān′dẽr, *n.* [O.Fr. *atteindre, attaindre,* to touch or reach, as with law; to attaint, from L. *attingo.* ATTAIN, *v.t.*] The act or legal process of subjecting a person to the consequences of judgment of death or outlawry pronounced in respect of treason or felony; forfeiture of civil privileges; a bringing under some disgrace or dishonor (*Shak*).—**attaint,** at·tānt′, *v.t.* [O.Fr. *attaint*, pp. of *attaindre, ataindre*.] To affect with attainder; to find guilty of a crime, as of felony or treason, involving forfeiture of civil privileges.

attaint,‡ at·tānt′, *n.* [Prefix *at*, from L. *ad*, to, and *taint*, from L. *tinctus*, pp. of *tingo*, to dye. TAINT.] A spot, taint, stain, disgrace. (*Shak*.)—*a*.‡ Tainted; corrupted; infected. (*Shak*.)

attar, at′tär, *n.* [Ar. *atr*, perfume.] A perfume from flowers.—*Attar* or *otto of roses*, an essential oil made from various species of roses, which forms a valuable perfume.

attemper, at·tem′pėr, *v.t.* [L. *attempero—ad*, and *tempero*, to temper, mix, or moderate. TEMPER.] To reduce, mollify, or moderate by mixture; to soften, modify, or regulate; to accommodate or make fit.

attempt, at·temt′, *v.t.* [O.Fr. *attempter*, from L. *attemptare—ad*, to and *tempto*, to try.] To make an effort to effect; to endeavor to perform; to undertake; to try; to attack; to make an effort upon (a person's life); to try to win or seduce.—*n.* An essay, trial, or endeavor; an effort to gain a point; an attack, onset, or assault.—**attemptable,** at·temt′a·bl, *a.* Capable of being attempted.

attend, at·tend′, *v.t.* [Fr. *attendre*, L. *attendo*, to turn one's mind to, to turn to—*ad*, to, and *tendo*, to stretch. TEND.] To accompany or be present with, as a companion or servant; to be present at or in for some purpose (church, a concert, etc.); to accompany or follow in immediate sequence, especially from a causal connection (a cold *attended* with fever); to wait for‡.—*v.i.* To pay regard or heed; to be present, in pursuance of duty; to act as an attendant; to be concomitant: by itself or followed by *on* or *upon*.—**attendance,** at·tend′ans, *n.* The act of attending or attending on; the act of waiting on or serving; service; ministry; the persons attending for any purpose; a train; a retinue.—**attendant,** at·tend′ant, *a.* Accompanying; being present or in attendance upon; connected with, or immediately following.—*n.* One who attends or accompanies another; one who belongs to a person's retinue; a follower; one who is present or regularly present; that which accompanies or is consequent on.—**attention,** at·ten′shon, *n.* [L. *attentio, attentionis*, from *attendo*.] The act of attending or heeding; the application of the ear to sounds, or of the mind to objects presented to its contemplation; heedfulness; observation; an act of civility or courtesy.—**attentive,** at·tent′iv, *a.* Paying or giving attention; heedful; intent; observant; regarding with care; mindful; habitually heedful or mindful; sedulous.—**attentively,** at·tent′iv·li, *adv.* In an attentive man-

ner.—**attentiveness,** at·tent′iv·nes, *n.* The state of being attentive; attention.

attenuate, at·ten′ū·āt, *v.t.*—*attenuated, attenuating.* [L. *attenuo, attenuatum—ad*, and *tenuo*, to make thin; *tenuis*, thin; same root as in E. *thin, tender*.] To make thin, fine, or slender; to reduce the thickness of either liquids or solid bodies; to reduce the strength of; to render meager or jejune.—*v.i.* To become thin, slender, or fine; to diminish; to lessen.—**attenuation,** at·ten′ū·ā″shon, *n.* The act of attenuating or making thin, as fluids, or slender and fine, as solid bodies.—**attenuant,** at·ten′ū·ant, *a.* Attenuating; making thin, as fluids; diluting.—*n.* A medicine which increases the fluidity of the humors; a diluent.

attest, at·test′, *v.t.* [Fr. *attester*, L. *attestor—ad*, and *testor*, to witness. TESTAMENT, DETEST.] To bear witness to; to certify; to affirm to be true or genuine; to declare the truth of; to manifest (one's joy, etc.).—**attestation,** at·test·ā′shon, *n.* The act of attesting; a solemn declaration, verbal or written, in support of a fact; evidence; testimony.

Attic, at′tik, *a.* [L. *Atticus*, Gr. *Attikos*.] Pertaining to *Attica*, in Greece, or to its principal city, Athens; marked by the qualities characteristic of the Athenians; as, *Attic* wit, *Attic* salt, a delicate wit for which the Athenians were famous.—*n.* The dialect spoken in Attica or Athens; the chief literary and most elegant language of ancient Greece; [*not cap.*] *arch.* a low story erected over a principal; an apartment in the uppermost part of a house, with windows in the cornice or the roof; a garret.—**Atticism,** at′ti·sizm, *n.* A peculiarity or characteristic of the Attic dialect of Greek; elegance of diction.—**Atticize,** at′ti·sīz, *v.t.* and *i.* To conform to the Attic dialect.

attire, at·tīr′, *v.t.*—*attired, attiring.* [O.Fr. *attirer*, to array, from prefix *at*, L. *ad*, to, and same word as G. *zier*, ornament, A.Sax. *tir*, splendor, Dan. *ziir*, ornament.] To dress; to deck; to array; to adorn with elegant or splendid garments.—*n.* (no pl.). Dress; clothes; garb; apparel.

attitude, at′ti·tūd, *n.* [Fr., from It. *attitudine*, fitness, posture, L.L. *aptitudo*, fitness, L. *aptus*, fit. APT.] Posture or position of a person, or the manner in which the parts of his body are disposed; state, condition, or conjuncture, as likely to have a certain result; aspect (the *attitude* of affairs).—**attitudinize,** at·ti·tūd′in·īz, *v.i.*—*attitudinized, attitudinizing.* To assume affected attitudes, airs, or postures.

attorney, at·tėr′ni, *n.* [O.Fr. *attorné*, pp. of *attorner*, to transfer—*at*, L. *ad*, to, and *torner*, to turn. TURN.] One who is appointed or admitted in the place of another to transact any business for him.—*Letter* or *power of attorney*, a formal instrument by which one person authorizes

another to do some act or acts for him.—*v.t.*‡—**district attorney,** the prosecuting officer of a Federal judicial district, or of a state, or any district thereof.—**attorney general,** *n.* Head of the Federal Department of Justice; also the chief officer of a Federal judicial district; also legal adviser to the state legislature.

attract, at·trakt′, *v.t.* [L. *attraho, attractum—ad*, to, and *traho*, to draw, whence *tract, treat, trace*, etc.] To draw to or toward, either in a physical or mental sense; to cause to draw near or close to by some influence; to invite or allure; to entice; to win.—*v.i.* To possess or exert the power of attraction; to be attractive or winning.—**attractable,** at·trakt′a·bl, *a.* Capable of being attracted; subject to attraction.—**attractor,** *n.* One who or that which attracts.—**attraction,** at·trak′shon, *n.* The act, power, or property of attracting; *physics*, the tendency, force, or forces through which all particles of matter, as well as all individual masses of matter are attracted or drawn towards each other; the inherent tendency in bodies to approach each other, to unite and to remain united; the power or act of alluring, drawing to, inviting, or engaging; allurement; enticement; that which attracts; a charm; an allurement.—**attractive,** at·trakt′iv, *a.* [Fr. *attractif*.] Having the quality of attracting; having the power of charming or alluring; inviting; engaging; enticing.—*n.* That which attracts; a charm or allurement.—**attractively,** at·trakt′iv·li, *adv.* In an attractive manner.—**attractiveness,** at·trakt′iv·nes, *n.* The quality of being attractive or engaging.

attrahent,† at′tra·hent, *a.* [L. *attrahens, attrahentis*, ppr. of *attraho*. ATTRACT.] Drawing to; attracting; dragging or pulling.

attribute, at·trib′ūt, *v.t.*—*attributed, attributing.* [L. *attribuo, attributum—ad*, and *tribuo*, to assign.] To ascribe; to impute; to consider as belonging or as due; to assign.—**attribute,** at′tri·būt, *n.* Any property, quality, or characteristic that can be ascribed to a person or thing; *fine arts*, a symbol of office or character added to any figure (thus the eagle is the *attribute* of Jupiter).—**attributable,** at·trib′ūt·a·bl, *a.* Capable of being, or liable to be attributed; ascribable; imputable.—**attribution,** at·tri·bū′shon, *n.* The act of attributing; that which is ascribed; attribute.—**attributive,** at·trib′ū·tiv, *a.* Pertaining to or expressing an attribute; *gram.* coming before the noun it qualifies.—*n. Gram.* a word expressive of an attribute; an adjective.—**attributively,** at·trib′ū·tiv·li, *adv. Gram.* in an attributive manner; used before the noun.

attrition, at·tri′shon, *n.* [L. *attritio*, from *attero, attritum*, to rub down—*ad*, to, and *tero, tritum*, to rub.] The act of wearing or rubbing down; the state of being worn down or smoothed by friction; abrasion.

attune, at·tūn′, v.t.—attuned, attuning. [Prefix at for ad, to, and tune.] To tune or put in tune; to adjust one sound to another; to make accordant; fig. to arrange fitly; to bring into harmony, concord, or agreement.

atypic, a·tip′ik, a. [Gr. a, not, and typos, a type.] Devoid of typical character; irregular.

auburn, a̱′bėrn, a. [L.L. alburnus, whitish, from L. albus, white.] Originally, whitish or flaxen colored; now reddish brown or rich chestnut; generally applied to hair.

auction, ak′shon, n. [L. auctio, from augeo, auctum, to increase (from the rising in successive bids); allied to Icel. auka, Goth. aukan, E. ake, to increase. AUGMENT, AUXILIARY.] A public sale of property to the highest bidder.—v.t. To sell by auction.—**auctioneer,** ak′shon·ēr′, n. One whose business it is to sell things by auction.—v.t† To sell by auction.

audacious, a̱·dā′shus, a. [L. audax, audacis, from audeo, to dare.] Over bold or daring; bold in wickedness; insolent; imprudent; shameless; unabashed.—**audaciously,** a̱·dā′shus·li, adv. In an audacious manner.—**audaciousness, audacity,** a̱·dā′shus·nes, a̱·das′i·ti, n. The quality of being audacious; impudence; effrontery; insolence.

audible, a̱′di·bl, a. [L. audibilis, from audio, to hear; same root as in E. ear.] Capable of being heard; perceivable by the ear; loud enough to be heard.—**audibleness, audibility,** a̱′di·bl·nes, a̱·di·bil′i·ti, n. The quality of being audible.—**audibly,** a̱′di·bli, adv. In an audible manner.

audience, a̱′di·ens, n. [L. audientia.] The act of listening; a hearing; liberty or opportunity of being heard before a person or assembly; an assembly of hearers.

audiofrequency, a̱′di·ō·frē″kwen·si, adj. Elec. Pertaining to a frequency corresponding to audible frequencies of sound waves, that is, from 15 to 20,000 cycles per second.

audiometer, a̱·di·om′et·ėr, n. [L. audio, to hear, and Gr. metron, measure.] An instrument for testing the sense of hearing.

audio-visual aid, nontextual materials such as films, recordings, and charts used in teaching; so called because of their appeal to sight and hearing.

audiphone, a̱′di·fōn, n. [L. audio, to hear, and Gr. phōnē, voice.] An instrument for enabling the deaf to hear, essentially consisting of a fan-shaped vibratory plate of caoutchouc which is applied to the upper teeth, through which the sound vibrations are conveyed to the auditory nerve.

audit, a̱′dit, n. [L. audit, he hears, or auditus, a hearing, from audio, to hear. AUDIBLE.] An examination into accounts or dealings with money or property by proper officers, or persons appointed for that purpose, hence, a calling to account; an examination into one's actions; also, an audience or hearing†.—v.t. To

make audit of; to examine, as an account or accounts.—**audition,** a̱·di′shon, n. [L. auditio, a hearing.] The act of hearing; a hearing or listening.—**auditor,** a̱′dit·ėr, [L.] A hearer; a listener; a person appointed and authorized to audit or examine an account or accounts.—**auditorium,** a̱·di·tō′ri·um, n. [L.] In an opera house, public hall, etc., the space allotted to the hearers.—**auditory,** a̱′di·to·ri, a. [L. auditorius.] Relating to hearing or to the sense or organs of hearing.—n. [L. auditorium.] An audience; an assembly of hearers; a place for hearing or for the accommodation of hearers; an auditorium.

Augean, a̱·jē′an, a. Of or pertaining to the mythical Augeas, King of Elis, in Greece.—Augean stable, the stable of this king, in which he kept 3000 oxen, and the cleaning out of which, after it had remained uncleaned for thirty years, was assigned as a task to Hercules, who accomplished it in a single day. Hence cleaning the Augean stables became a synonym for the removal of accumulated nuisances, abuses, etc.

auger, a̱′gėr, n. [For nauger, initial n having been lost (as in adder, apron), this word being from A. Sax. nafe-gâr, nafugâr, from nafu, nafa, the nave of a wheel; and gâr, a sharp-pointed thing, a dart or javelin. NAVE, GORE, to pierce.] An instrument for boring holes larger than those bored by a gimlet, chiefly used by carpenters, joiners, etc., and made in a great many forms; instruments on the same plan are used for boring into the soil.

aught, a̱t, n. [A.Sax. âwiht, from â for ân, one, and wiht=E. whit, wight; lit. a whit, its negative being naught, not a whit.] Anything, indefinitely; any part or quantity.

augite, a̱′jit, n. [Gr. augē, brightness.] The name given to a class of minerals, greenish black, pitch or velvet black, or leek green in color, and consisting of silicates of lime, magnesia, and iron, with alumina in the darker varieties.—**augitic,** a̱·jit′ik, a. Pertaining to, consisting of, resembling, or containing augite.

augment, ag·ment′, v.t. [Fr. augmenter, L. augmento, from augmentum, increase, from augeo, to increase. AUCTION.] To increase; to enlarge in size or extent; to swell; to make bigger.—v.i. To increase; to grow larger.—**augment,** ag′ment, n. Increase; enlargement by addition†; gram. an increase at the beginning of certain inflectional forms of a verb, as the e prefixed in certain tenses of the Greek verb, and the ge in the past participle of the German verb.—**augmentable,** ag·ment′a·bl, a. Capable of being augmented or increased.—**augmentation,** ag·men·tā′shon, n. The act of augmenting; the act of adding to or enlarging; the state or condition of being made larger; increase; enlargement; accession; the thing added by way of enlargement;

addition.—**augmentative,** ag·ment′a·tiv, a. Having the quality or power of augmenting.—n. A word formed to express greatness: opposed to a diminutive.—**augmenter,** ag·ment′ėr, n. One who or that which augments.

augur, a̱′gėr, n. [L. augur, from avis, a bird, and L. garrio, to chatter.] Among the ancient Romans a functionary whose duty was to derive signs concerning future events from the flight or other actions of birds, from certain appearances in quadrupeds, from lightning and other unusual occurrences; hence, one who foretells future events by omens; a soothsayer; a prophet.—v.i. To guess; to conjecture, as from signs or omens; to be a sign; to bode (to augur well or ill for a project).—v.t. To guess or conjecture; to predict; to anticipate: said of persons; to betoken; to forebode: said of things.—**augury,** a̱′gū·ri or a̱′gėr·i, n. The art or practice of an augur; that which forebodes; that from which a prediction is drawn; a prognostication.

august, a̱·gust′, a. [L. augustus, from augeo, to increase, the same word as the name Augustus. AUGMENT, AUCTION.] Grand; magnificent, majestic; impressing awe; inspiring reverence.—**augustly,** a̱·gust′li, adv. In an august manner.—**augustness,** a̱·gust′nes, n. The quality of being august.

August, a̱′gust, n. [L. Augustus, from the Roman Emperor Augustus.] The eighth month of the year, containing thirty-one days.—**Augustan,** a̱·gust′an, a. Pertaining to the Emperor Augustus; as, the Augustan Age, which was the most brilliant period in Roman literature; hence, any brilliant period in the literary history of other countries.

Augustinian, a̱·gust·in′i·an, n. A member of one of the fraternities who follow rules framed by St. Augustine or deduced from his writings.

auk, a̱k, n. [Dan. alke, Icel. alka, álka, an auk.] The name of several swimming birds found in the colder parts of the Northern Hemisphere, having their legs placed so far back as to cause them to stand nearly upright, and with very short wings more useful for swimming and diving than for flight.

aulic, a̱′lik, a. [L. aulicus, from aula, Gr. aulē, a court.] Pertaining to a royal court.

aunt, änt, n. [O.Fr. ante, from L. amita, contracted in the same way as emmet is contracted into ant.] The sister of one's father or mother, a term correlative to nephew or niece.

aura, a̱′ra, n. [L. aura, a breath of air.] An air; an effluvium or odor; an exhalation.—**aural,** a̱′ral, a. Pertaining to an aura.

aural, a̱′ral, a. [L. auris, the ear.] Relating to the ear (aural surgery).—**auriform,** a̱′ri·form, a. Ear-shaped; having the form of the human ear.—**aurist,** a̱′rist, n. One skilled in disorders of the ear, or who professes to cure them; an otologist.

aureate, a̞′rē·āt, a. [L. aureatus.] Golden; gilded.

aureola, aureole, a̞·rē′ō·la, a̞′rē·ōl, n. [Fr. auréole, from L. aureolus, dim. of aureus, golden, from aurum, gold.] Painting, an illumination surrounding a holy person, as Christ, a saint, etc.; anything resembling an aureola; a halo.

aureomycin, a̞′re·o·mī″sin, n. Antibiotic isolated from Streptomyces aureofaciens and effective against certain diseases.

auricle, a̞′ri·kl, n. [L. auricula, dim. from auris, the ear.] The external ear, or that part which is prominent from the head; either of the two cavities in the mammalian heart, placed above the two ventricles, and resembling in shape the external ear.—**auricula,** a̞·rik′ū·la, n. A garden flower of the primrose family, found native in the Swiss Alps, and sometimes called bear's-ear from the shape of its leaves.—**auricular,** a̞·rik′ū·lėr, a. Pertaining to the ear or the sense of hearing, or to an auricle; confided to one's ear, especially privately confided to the ear of a priest (auricular confession).—**auriculate,** a̞·rik′ū·lāt, a. Shaped like the ear; having ears or some kind of expansions resembling ears; eared, as a leaf.

auriferous, a̞·rif′ėr·us, a. [L. aurifer—aurum, gold, and fero, to produce.] Yielding or producing gold; containing gold.

aurist. See AURAL.

aurochs, a̞′roks, n. [G.] A species of wild bull or buffalo, once abundant on the continent of Europe, but now reduced to a few herds inhabiting the forests of Lithuania.

aurora, a̞·rō′ra, n. [L., the goddess of morning, the dawn; same root as L. uro, to burn, aurum, gold.] The dawn, or morning twilight; the goddess of the morning, or dawn deified; the aurora borealis (in this sense with the plural aurorœ).—Aurora borealis, the northern lights or streamers, a luminous meteoric phenomenon of varying brilliancy seen in the northern heavens, and in greatest magnificence in the arctic regions, believed to be electric in origin.—Aurora australis, the aurora of the Southern Hemisphere, quite a similar phenomenon to that of the north.—**auroral,** a̞·rō′ral, a. Belonging to or resembling the dawn; belonging to or resembling the polar lights; roseate; rosy.

auscultation, as·kul·tā′shon, n. [L. auscultatio, a listening, from ausculto, to listen, from auris, the ear.] Med. a method of distinguishing the state of the internal parts of the body, particularly of the chest, by observing the sounds arising there either through the application of the ear or by the stethoscope.—**auscultator,** as′kul·tāt·ėr, n. One who practices auscultation.—**auscultatory,** as·kul′ta·to·ri, a. Pertaining to auscultation.

auspice, a̞′spis, n. [L. auspicium, from auspex, an augur—avis, a bird, and specio, to view.] An augury from birds; an omen or sign in general; protection; favorable influence.—**auspicate,**† a̞′spi·kāt, v.t. [L. auspicor, to take the auspices.] To initiate with pomp or ceremony; to inaugurate.—**auspicious,** a̞·spi′shus, a. Having omens of success, or favorable appearances; propitious; favorable; prosperous; happy.—**auspiciously,** a̞·spi′shus·li, adv. In an auspicious manner.—**auspiciousness,** a̞·spi′shus·nes, n.

austere, a̞·stēr′, a. [L. austerus, Gr. austēros, harsh.] Harsh; tart; sour; rough to the taste; fig. severe; harsh; rigid; rigorous; stern.—**austerely,** a̞·stėr′li, adv. In an austere manner; severely; rigidly; harshly.—**austereness, austerity,** a̞·stėr′nes, a̞·stė′ri·ti, n. The state or quality of being austere; severity; rigor; strictness; harshness.

austral, as′tral, a. [L. australis, from auster, the south wind, or south.] Southern; lying or being in the south.—**Australian,** as·trā′li·an, a. Pertaining to Australia.—n. A native or inhabitant of Australia.

autarchy, a̞′tär·ki, n. [Gr. autos, self, and archos, ruler.] Absolute rule; despotism.

autarky, a̞′tär·ki, n. [Gr. atarkeia, sufficiency.] Economic self-sufficiency; an economically independent area.

authentic, a̞·then′tik, a. [L. authenticus, from Gr. authentikos, original, genuine, from authentēs, one who does anything with his own hand.] Being what it purports to be; not false or fictitious; genuine; valid; authoritative; reliable.—**authentically,** a̞·then′tik·al·li, adv.—**authenticate,** a̞·then′ti·kāt, v.t.—authenticated, authenticating. To render authentic; to give authority to by proof, attestation, etc.; to prove authentic; to determine as genuine.—**authenticity,** a̞·then·tis′i·ti, n.

author, a̞′thor, n. [O.F. autheur, L. auctor, improperly written autor, author, from augeo, auctum, to increase, to produce. AUGMENT.] The beginner, former, or first mover of anything (author of our being): the originator or creator; efficient cause; the original composer of a literary work; the writer of a book or other literary production.—**authoress,** a̞′thor·es, n. A female author.—**authoritative,** a̞·thor′i·tā·tiv, a. Having authority; having the sanction or appearance of authority; positive; peremptory; dictatorial.—**authoritatively,** a̞·thor′i·tā·tiv·li, adv. In an authoritative manner; with a show of authority.—**authoritativeness,** a̞·thor′i·tā·tiv·nes, n. The quality of being authoritative.—**authority,** a̞·thor′i·ti, n. [O.Fr. authorité.] Power or right to command or act; dominion; control; the power derived from opinion, respect, or esteem; influence conferred by character, station, mental superiority, etc.; a person or persons exercising power or command: generally in the plural (the civil and military authorities); that to which or one to whom reference may be made in support of any fact, opinion, action, etc. (a person's authority for a statement); credit or credibility (a work of no authority).—**authorize,** a̞′thor·īz, vt.—authorized, authorizing. To give authority, warrant, or legal power to; to give a right to act; to empower; to make legal; to establish by authority or by usage or public opinion (an authorized idiom); to warrant; to sanction; to justify.—**authorization,** a̞′thor·iz·ā″shon, n. The act of authorizing.—**authorship,** a̞′thor·ship, n. The character or state of being an author; the source from which a work proceeds.

autobiography, a̞′tō·bī·og″ra·fi, n. [Gr. autos, self, and E. biography.] Biography or memoirs of a person written by himself.—**autobiographer,** a̞·tō·bī·og″ra·fėr, n. One who writes an autobiography.—**autobiographic, autobiographical,** a̞·tō·bī′o·graf″ik, a̞·tō·bī′o·graf″ik·al, a. Pertaining to, consisting of, or containing autobiography.—**autobiographically,** a̞·tō·bī′o·graf″ik·al·li, adv. In an autobiographical manner.

autochthon, a̞·tok′thon, n. pl. **autochthones,** a̞·tok′thon·ēz. [Gr. autochthōn—autos, self, and chthōn, the earth.] One of the primitive inhabitants of a country; an aboriginal inhabitant; that which is original to a particular country.—**autochthonous,** a̞·tok′thon·us, a. Aboriginal; primitive; indigenous.

autoclave, a̞′tō·klāv, n. [Gr. auto, self, and L. clavism, key.] Airtight vessel for sterilizing, cooking, etc., by high-pressure steam; pressure cooker.

autocracy, a̞·tok′ra·si, n. [Gr. autokrateia—autos, self, and kratos, power.] Supreme power invested in a single person; the government or power of an absolute monarch.—**autocrat,** a̞′tō·krat, n. [Gr. autokratēs.] An absolute sovereign; a monarch who governs without being subject to restriction: a title assumed by the emperors of Russia; hence, one who is invested with or assumes unlimited authority in any relation.—**autocratic, autocratical,** a̞″tō·krat′ik, a̞″tō·krat′ik·al, a. Pertaining to autocracy; absolute; holding unlimited powers of government.—**autocratically,** adv. In an autocratic manner.

auto-da-fé, a̞′tō·da·fā″, n. pl. **autos-da-fé,** a̞′tōz·da·fā″. [Sp., lit. act (in sense of decree, judgment, sentence) of faith—auto=L. actum, an act, de, of, and fe=L. fides, faith.] A public solemnity, formerly held by the courts of the Inquisition in Spain and Portugal and their dependencies at the execution of heretics condemned to the stake.

autogenous, a̞·toj′en·us, a. [Gr. autos, self, and root gen, to generate.] Self-produced; self-generated; produced independently.

autograph, a̞′tō·graf, n. [Gr. autos, self, and graphē, writing.] A person's own handwriting; an original manuscript or signature.—**autographic, autographical,** a̞·tō·graf′ik, a̞·tō·graf′ik·al, a. Pertaining or relating to an autograph, or one's own handwriting; relating to or used in the process of autography.—**autography,** a̱·tog′ra·fi. *n.* A person's own handwriting†; a process in lithography by which a writing or drawing is transferred from paper to stone.

automatic, a̱·tō·mat′ik, *a.* [Gr. *automatos,* self-acting—*autos,* self, and root *ma,* to strive.] Belonging to or proceeding by spontaneous movement; having the power of self-motion; self-acting: said especially of mechanism.—**automat,** a̱′tō·mat, *n.* A restaurant in which food is delivered through self-operating mechanical devices.—**automaton,** a̱·tom′a·ton, *n.* That which is self-moving; a self-acting machine; a mechanical contrivance which imitates the arbitrary or voluntary motions of living beings; a person who acts mechanically.—**automation,** a̱·to·mā′shun, *n.* The technique of making an industrial process or system operate automatically; the use of electronic devices for controlling processes or systems.

automobile, a̱·tō·mō·bil′, *n.* [Gr. *autos,* self. MOBILE.] A vehicle propelled by self-contained power and used for carrying passengers.—**automotive,** a̱·to·mō′tiv, *a.* Self-moving; related to automobiles.

autonomy, a̱·tono′·mi, *n.* [Gr. *autonomia*—*autos,* self, and *nomos,* law, rule.] The power or right of self-government.—**autonomic, autonomous,** a̱·tō·nom′ik, a̱·ton′o·mus, *a.* Relating to autonomy; independent in government.

autoplasty, a̱·tō·plas·ti, *n.* [Gr. *autos,* self, and *plassō,* to form.] *Surg.* same as *Anaplasty.*

autopsy, a̱′top·si, *n.* [Gr., from *autos,* self, and *opsis,* sight.] Personal observation; ocular view; *med.* post-mortem examination.

autotype, a̱′tō·tīp, *n.* [Gr. *autos,* self, *typos,* a stamp.] A photographic process resembling heliotype; a picture produced by the process.

autumn, a̱′tum, *n.* [L. *autumnus,* for *auctumnus,* the season of increase, from *augeo, auctum,* to increase. AUGMENT.] The third season of the year, or the season between summer and winter, popularly regarded as comprising Aug., Sept., and Oct., but astronomically beginning at the autumnal equinox, September 23, and ending at the winter solstice, December 21.—**autumnal,** a̱·tum′nal, *a.* Belonging to autumn; produced or gathered in autumn; *fig.* belonging to the period past the middle stage of life.

auxiliary, ag·zil′i·a·ri, *a.* [L. *auxiliaris,* from *auxilium,* aid, from *augeo,* to increase, whence also *auction, augment, autumn,* etc.] Conferring aid or support; helping; aiding; assisting; subsidiary.—**auxiliary,** ag·zil′i·a·ri, *n.* A helper; an assistant; an associate in some undertaking; *pl.* foreign troops in the service of a nation at war; *gram.* a verb which helps to form the moods and tenses of other verbs; as, *have, may, shall,* and *will.*

auxin, a̱k′sän, *n.* [Gr. *auxein,* to increase, and *in,* of, or belonging to.] *Biol.* any of several organic compounds, acting as plant hormones, which in minute quantities promote plant cell growth.

avail, a̱·vāl′, *v.t.* [O.Fr. *valeir,* to be worth, from L. *valeo,* to be strong, with prefix *a* for L. *ad.*] To be for the advantage of; to assist or profit; to benefit.—*To avail one's self of,* to take advantage of.—*v.i.* To be of use, benefit, or advantage; to answer a purpose; to have strength, force, or efficacy sufficient.—*n.* Advantage tending to promote success; benefit; service; utility; efficacy: used in such phrases as, of little *avail;* of much *avail.*—**available,** a̱·vāl′a·bl, *a.* Advantageous; having efficacy: capable of being used; attainable; accessible.—**availableness, availability,** a̱·vāl′a·bl·nes, a̱·vāl′a·bil″i·ti, *n.* State of being available; power or efficacy; legal force; validity.—**availably,** a̱·vāl′a·bli, *adv.* In an available manner.

avalanche, av′a·lansh, *n.* [Fr. *avalanche,* from *avaler,* to descend—*a,* to, *val,* a valley.] A vast body of snow or ice sliding down a mountain, or over a precipice.

avant-courier, a̱·vaṅ′kō′rēr, *n.* [Fr. *avant,* before, from L. *ab,* from *ante,* before.] A person despatched before another person or a company, to give notice of their approach.—**avant-guard,** a̱·väṅ′gärd′, *n.* [Fr. *avant-garde.*] The van or advanced body of an army; the vanguard.

avarice, av′a·ris, *n.* [L. *avaritia* from *avarus,* greedy, from *aveo,* to covet.] An inordinate desire of gaining and possessing wealth; covetousness; cupidity; greediness.—**avaricious,** av·a·ri′shus, *a.* Characterized by avarice; greedy of gain; miserly; covetous.—**avariciously,** av·a·ri′shus·li, *adv.* In an avaricious manner; covetously; greedily.—**avariciousness,** av·a·ri′shus·nes, *n.* The quality of being avaricious.

avast, a̱·vast′, *exclam.* [From D. *houd vast,* hold fast, stop.] *Naut.* the order to stop, hold, cease, or stay in any operation: sometimes used colloquially, without reference to ships.

avatar, av·a·tär′, *n.* [Skr. *avatāra*—*ava,* down, and root *tri,* to go,] A descent from heaven; the incarnation of the Hindu deities, or their appearance in some manifest shape upon earth.

avaunt, a̱·vant′, *interj.* [Fr. *avant, en avant,* forward, march!—from L. *ab.* from *ante,* before. *Van* is the same word.] Begone; depart; an exclamation of contempt or abhorrence.

ave, ä′vā, *interj.* [L.] Hail! farewell! God bless you! [*cap.*] Sometimes used as a noun for an Ave Maria.— **Ave Maria,** ä′vā ma·rē′a, *n.* [L. = hail Mary!—the first words of Gabriel's salutation to the Virgin Mary.] Devotional words often repeated in the Roman Catholic Church, chaplets and rosaries being divided into a certain number of Ave Marias and paternosters.

avenaceous, av·e·nā′shus, *a.* [L. *avena,* oats.] Belonging to or partaking of the nature of oats.

avenge, a̱·venj′, *v.t.*—*avenged, avenging.* [O.Fr. *avengier*—prefix *a,* and L. *vindicare,* to avenge, vindicate.] To vindicate by inflicting pain or evil on the wrong doer; to deal punishment for injury done to, with a person as object; to take satisfaction for, by pain or punishment inflicted on the injuring party; to deal punishment on account of: with a thing as object.—**avenger,** a̱·venj′ér, *n.* One who avenges; one who takes vengeance.

avens, av′enz, *n.* The popular name of several species of rosaceous plants growing wild: common avens is also called herb bennet.

aventurine, a̱·ven′tū·rin, *n.* [Fr. *aventure,* chance.] A variety of artificial gem consisting of glass, oxide of copper, and oxide of iron: a compound discovered accidentally (*par aventure*); also, a variety of quartz rock containing spangles of mica or quartz.

avenue, av′e·nū, *n.* [Fr., from *avenir,* to arrive, L. *advenio.* ADVENE ADVENT.] A passage; a way or opening for entrance; a wide straight roadway or street; an alley or walk planted on each side with trees; *fig.* means of access or attainment.

aver, a̱·vér′, *v.t.*—*averred, averring.* [Fr. *averer,* from L. *ad,* to, and *verus,* true.] To affirm with confidence; to declare in a positive or peremptory manner; to assert.—**averment,** a̱·vér′ment, *n.* The act of averring; affirmation; a positive assertion or declaration.

average, av′ér·āj, *n.* [Fr. *avarie,* Sp. *averia,* damage sustained by goods at sea; from Ar. *avär,* defect, flaw, modified by the influence of L.L. *averagium,* the carriage of goods by *averia* or draft cattle, a contribution towards loss of things carried; from O.Fr. *aver,* a work horse, from L. *habere,* to have.] A contribution falling on the owners of a ship's freight and cargo, in proportion to their several interests, to make good a loss that has been sustained; a sum or quantity intermediate to a number of different sums or quantities; a mean or medial amount; a general estimate based on comparison of a number of diverse cases; a medium.—*a.* Exhibiting a mean proportion or mean quality; forming an average; medium; not extreme; ordinary; *com.* estimated in accordance with the rules of average.—*v.t.*—*averaged, averaging.* To find the average of; to reduce to a mean sum or quantity; to show or have as an average or mean (trees average 50 feet in height).

avert, a̱·vért′, *v.t.* [L. *averto, aversum,* to turn away—*a,* from, and *verto, versum,* to turn, whence *verse, convert, converse, diverse,* etc.] To turn or direct away from; to turn or to cause to turn off or away (the eyes, calamity, etc.).—**averse,** a̱·vérs′, *a.* [L. *aversus,* turned from, pp. of *averto.*] Turned away from;

averted (*Mil.*); unwilling; having repugnance; now regularly followed by *to*, not by *from*.—**aversely,** a‧vèrs′li, *adv.* In an averse manner; with repugnance; unwillingly.—**averseness,** a‧vèrs′nes, *n.* The state of being averse.—**aversion,** a‧vèr′zhen, *n.* Opposition or repugnance of mind; dislike; disinclination; reluctance; hatred: used absolutely or with *to*; the cause of dislike; the object of repugnance.

Avesta, a‧ves′ta, *n.* The sacred writings attributed to Zoroaster; the Zend-Avesta.—**Avestan,** a‧ves′tan, *n.* The language of the Avesta; Zend.

avian, ā′vi‧an, *a.* [L. *avis*, a bird.] Pertaining to birds.—**aviary,** ā′vi‧a‧ri, *n.* [L. *aviarium.*] A building or enclosure for the breeding, rearing, and keeping of birds.—**aviation,** ā‧vi‧ā′shon, *n.* Aerial navigation by machines heavier than air.—**aviator,** ā′vi‧ā‧tèr, *n.* One who engages in aviation.—**aviculture,** ā′vi‧kul″tür, *n.* The breeding and rearing of birds.—**avifauna,** ā′vi‧fạ‧na, *n.* A collective name for the birds or avian fauna of a district.

avid, av′id, *a.* [L. *avidus*, from *aveo*, to desire; akin *avarice.*] Eager; greedy: with *of.*—**avidity,** a‧vid′i‧ti, *n.* [L. *aviditas.*] Greediness; strong appetite; eagerness; intenseness of desire.

avocado, av‧ō‧kä′dō, *n.* [Corrupted from Mexican name.] The fruit of a small tree of the laurel family, common in tropical America and the West Indies: also called *alligator pear.*

avocate,† av′ō‧kät, *v.t.* [L. *avoco, avocatum—a*, from, and *voco*, to call.] To call off or away; to remove from an inferior to a superior court.—**avocation,** av‧ō‧kā′shon, *n.* A chosen spare-time occupation, distinct from one's regular calling; the authoritative removal of a case from an inferior to a superior court; that which calls a man away from his proper business; a distraction; a hindrance.

avocet, av′ō‧set, *n.* Same as *Avoset.*

avoid, a‧void′, *v.t.* [Originally to empty; from prefix *a*, and *void.*] To make void (in legal phraseology); to shun; to keep away from; to eschew; to evade; to elude (expense, danger, bad company).—*v.i.* To become void or vacant; to retire‡; to withdraw‡.—**avoidable,** a‧void′a‧bl, *a.* That may be vacated or annulled; capable of being avoided, shunned, or escaped.—**avoidance,** a‧void′ans, *n.* The act of annulling or making void; the act of avoiding or shunning.

avoirdupois, av‧èr′dū‧poiz″, *n.* [O.Fr. *avoir du pois*, to have weight—L. *habeo*, to have, *pensum*, something weighed out. POISE.] A system of weight of which 1 lb. contains 16 oz., in distinction to troy weight, which has only 12—the system by which commodities in general are weighed.

avoset, av′ō‧set, *n.* [Fr. *avocette*, It. *avocetta.*] A wading bird of the size of a lapwing, with very long legs, feathers variegated with black and

white, and a long slender bill bent upward toward the tip.

avouch, a‧vouch′, *v.t.* [Prefix *a* (=L. *ad*, to), and *vouch;* O.Fr. *avochier, avocher.*] To affirm openly; to avow; to maintain, vindicate, or justify (a statement); to establish; guarantee; substantiate.—*n.*‡ Evidence; testimony. (*Shak.*).

avow, a‧vou′, *v.t.* [Fr. *avouer—a* (from L. *ad*, to), and *vouer*, to vow. VOW.] To declare openly, with a view to justify, maintain, or defend (sentiments, etc.); to acknowledge; to own.—**avowal,** a‧vou′al, *n.* An open declaration; frank acknowledgment. —**avowed,** a‧voud′, *a.* Declared; open (an *avowed* enemy).—**avowedly,** a‧vou′ed‧li, *adv.* In an avowed or open manner; with frank acknowledgment.—**avower,** a‧vou′èr, *n.* One who avows, owns, or asserts.

avulsion, a‧vul′shon, *n.* [L. *avulsio*, from *avello—a*, from, away, and *vello, vulsum*, to pull.] A pulling or tearing asunder or off.

avuncular, a‧vung′kü‧lèr, *a.* [L. *avunculus*, an uncle.] Of or pertaining to an uncle.

await, a‧wāt′, *v.t.* To wait for; to look for or expect; to be in store for; to be ready for (a reward *awaits* him).

awake, a‧wāk′, *v.t.*—*awoke* or *awaked* (pret. & pp.), *awaking.* [Prefix *a*, intens., and *wake;* A.Sax. *áwacan*, pret. *áwóc*, also *áwacian*, to awake. WAKE.] To rouse from sleep or from a state resembling sleep; to put into action or new life.—*v.i.* To cease to sleep; to bestir or rouse one's self from a state resembling sleep.—*a.* [A.Sax. *áwacen*, pp. of *áwacan.*] Not sleeping; in a state of vigilance or action.—**awaken,** a‧wāk′n, *v.i.* [A.Sax. *áwacnan, áwacnian*, to awake (intrans.).] To become awake; to awake. —*v.t.* To rouse from sleep; to awake. —**awakening,** a‧wāk′n‧ing, *n.* Act of awaking from sleep; a revival of religion.—*a.* Rousing; alarming.

award, a‧ward′, *v.t.* [O.Fr. *awarder*, to have under *ward*, to inspect, to pronounce as to the sufficiency of. WARD.] To adjudge; to assign judicially or by sentence (as an arbitrator pronouncing upon the rights of parties).—*v.i.* To make an award.— *n.* Judgment; decision; the decision of arbitrators on points submitted to them.—**awarder,** a‧ward′er, *n.* One that awards or makes an award.

aware, a‧wār′, *a.* [Prefix *a*, and *ware* (as in be*ware*); A.Sax. *gewær*, wary, cautious; G. *gewahr*, aware. WARE, WARY.] Apprised; cognizant; informed; conscious; followed by *of.* [Not used attributively.]

away, a‧wā′, *adv.* [A.Sax. *onweg—on.* on and *weg*, way.] Absent; at a distance; apart; to a distance (to go *away*). It is often used elliptically (whither *away* so fast?). With many verbs it conveys a notion of using up or consuming (to squander *away*, to idle or loiter *away*); it has also merely an intensive force (eat *away*, laugh *away*).—*int.* Begone! depart! go away.

awe, ạ, *n.* [O.E. *aghe, eghe*, A.Sax.

ege, fear, dread; Icel. *agi*, awe, terror; Goth. *agis*, fear; allied to Gael. *agh*, fear; Gr. *achos*, anguish—from root seen in *anguish, anger*, etc. ANGER.] Dread or great fear; fear mingled with admiration or reverence; reverential fear; feeling inspired by something sublime.—*v.t. awed, awing.* To strike with awe; to influence by fear, reverence, or respect.— **aweless, awless,** ạ′les, *a.* Devoid of awe; wanting the power of inspiring reverence or awe.—**awful,** ạ′ful, *a.* Striking or inspiring with awe; filling with dread, or dread mingled with profound reverence; proceeding from awe; extraordinary or highly remarkable (colloq.).—**awfully,** ạ′ful‧li, *adv.* In an awful manner; in a manner to fill with awe; terribly; excessively.—**awfulness,** ạ′ful‧nes, *n.* The quality of being awful, or of striking with awe, reverence, or terror.

aweary, a‧wē′ri, *a.* Weary. [Poetical.]

aweather, a‧weTH′èr, *a.* or *adv.* On or to the weather side of a ship: opposed to *alee.*

awhile, a‧hwīl′, *adv.* [O.E. *ane hwile*, a while.] For a space of time; for some time.

awkward, ạk′wèrd, *a.* [O.E. *awk, awke*, wrong, backward, reverse. and term. *-ward.* *Awk* corresponds to Icel. *öfigr, öfugr*, Sw. *afvig*, turned the wrong way, from *af*=E. *off.*] Wanting dexterity in the use of the hands or of instruments; bungling; clumsy; ungraceful in manners; uncouth.—**awkwardly,** ạk′wèrd‧li, *adv.* In an awkward manner; clumsily.— **awkwardness,** ạk′wèrd‧nes, *n.* The quality of being awkward.

awl, ạl, *n.* [A.Sax. *awul, ael, ál;* Icel. *alr*, G. *ahle.*] A pointed instrument for piercing small holes in leather, wood, etc.

awn, ạn, *n.* [Icel. *ögn*, Dan. *avne*, Sw. *agne*, chaff, husk; akin to Gr. *achnē*, chaff.] The bristle or beard of corn or grass, or any similar bristlelike appendage.—**awned,** *a.* Having awns.

awning, ạn′ing, *n.* [L.G. *havenung*, a shelter, from *haven*, a haven.] A covering of canvas or other cloth spread over any place as a protection from the sun's rays.

awry, a‧rī′, *a.* or *adv.* In a wry position; turned or twisted toward one side; asquint; crooked; perverse.

ax, axe, aks, *n.* [A.Sax. *ax, æx*, Icel. *ox*, Dan. *oxe*, D. *aakse*, G. *ax, axt;* allied to Gr. *axinē*, L. *ascia* for *acsia* —an axe. From root *ac, ak*, a point. ACID.] An instrument, consisting of a head, with an arching edge of steel in the plane of the sweep of the tool, attached to a handle, and used for hewing timber and chopping wood.

axial, axially, etc. See AXIS.

axil, axilla, aks′il, aks‧il′la, *n.* [L. *axilla*, the arm-pit.] The armpit; a cavity under the upper part of the arm or shoulder, *bot.* the angle on the upper side between an axis and any organ growing from it.— **axillar, axillary,** aks′il‧lèr, aks′il‧la‧ri, *a.* Pertaining to the armpit or to the axil of plants.

axiom, aks′i‧om, *n.* [Gr. *axiōma.*]

A self-evident truth or proposition; a proposition whose truth is so evident at first sight that no process of reasoning or demonstration can make it plainer; an established principle in some art or science; a principle universally received.—*Syn.* under APHORISM.—**axiomatic, axiomatical,** aks′i·ō·mat″ik, aks′·iō·mat″ik·al, *a.* Pertaining to, consisting of, or having the character of an axiom. —**axiomatically,** aks′i·ō·mat″ik·al·li, *adv.* In an axiomatic manner.

axis, aks′is, *n.* pl. **axes,** aks′ēz. [L.] The straight line, real or imaginary, passing through a body or magnitude, on which it revolves, or may be supposed to revolve; an agreement between two or more leading powers by which lesser powers may align themselves for or against the general principles set forth; specifically the Rome-Berlin axis; *bot.* the central line or column about which other parts are arranged; *anat.* the second vertebra of the neck.—**axial,** aks′i·al, *a.* Pertaining to an axis.—**axially,** aks′i·al·li, *adv.* According to or in line with the axis.

axle, axletree, aks′l, aks′l·trē, *n.* [A dim. from A.Sax. *eax, ex,* an axle; same root as L. *axis,* namely, *ag,* to drive. ACRE.] A piece of timber or bar of iron on which the wheels of a vehicle, etc., turn.

axolotl, aks′ō·lotl, *n.* [Mexican name.] A remarkable member of the tailed amphibians found in Mexican lakes, possessing four limbs resembling those of a frog, and usually having throughout life both lungs and gills, but sometimes losing the latter.

ay, aye, ī, *adv.* [Of doubtful origin.] Yes; yea; a word expressing assent or affirmation; truly; certainly; indeed.—*n.* The word by which assent is expressed in Parliament; hence, an affirmative vote.—*The ayes have it,* the affirmative votes are in a majority.

ayah, ä′yä, *n.* In the East Indies, a native lady's maid.

aye-aye, ī′ī, *n.* [From its cry.] A nocturnal quadruped, about the size of a hare, found in Madagascar, allied to the lemurs, and in its habits resembling the sloth.

azalea, a·zā′lē·a, *n.* [Gr. *azaleos,* dry, from inhabiting dry localities.] The generic name of certain plants belonging to the heath family, remarkable for the beauty and fragrance of their flowers, and distinguished from the rhododendrons chiefly by the flowers having five stamens instead of ten.

azimuth, az′i·muth, *n.* [Ar. *as-sumuth,* pl. of *as-samt,* a way, a path. *Zenith* has the same origin.] *Astron.* an arc of the horizon intercepted between the meridian of a place and the vertical circle passing through the center of a celestial object and the zenith.—*Azimuth circle,* a circle passing through the zenith and cutting the horizon perpendicularly.—*Azimuth compass,* a kind of compass used for finding the azimuth of a heavenly object.—**azimuthal,** az′i·muth·al, *a.* Pertaining or relating to the azimuth.

azoic, a·zō′ik, *a.* [Gr. *a,* not, and *zōē,* life.] Destitute of any vestige of organic life: applied to rocks, especially some very old rocks, in which no fossils have as yet been found.

azote, az′ōt, *n.* [Gr. *a,* not, and *zōē,* life.] A name formerly given to nitrogen because it is unfit for respiration.

Aztec, az′tek, *n.* and *a.* One of or pertaining to the Aztecs, the ruling tribe in Mexico at the time of the Spanish invasion.

azure, a′zhūr, *a.* [Fr. *azur,* L.L. *azurrum, lazurum,* etc., from Arab. *lazwerd,* blue.] Resembling the clear blue color of the sky; sky blue.—*n.* The fine blue color of the sky; a name common to several sky-colored or blue pigments, as ultramarine or smalt; the sky or vault of heaven.—*v.t.* To color blue.—**azurite,** a′zhūr·īt, *n.* A blue mineral, an ore of copper, composed chiefly of hydrous carbonate: called also *Azure stone.*

azygous, az′i·gus, *a.* [Gr. *azygos—a,* not, and *zygon,* a yoke.] Not one of a pair; single: applied to certain muscles, etc.

B

B, b, bē, the second letter and the first consonant in the English and most other alphabets; *mus.* the seventh note of the model diatonic scale or scale of C.

baa, bä, *v.i.* [Imitation of the sound.] Bleating of a sheep.

Baal, bā′al, *n.* [Heb. *ba′al,* lord.] A deity worshiped among the Canaanites, Phoenicians, etc., and supposed to represent the sun.—**Baalism,** bā′al·izm, *n.* The worship of Baal; gross idolatry.—**Baalite,** bā′al·īt, *n.* A worshiper of Baal; a groveling idolizer.

Babbitt metal, bab′it·met·al, *n.* [From the name of the inventor.] An alloy of copper, zinc, and tin, used for obviating friction in the bearing of cranks, axles, etc.

babble, bab′bl, *v.i.* [From *ba,* a sound uttered by an infant; D. and G. *babbeln,* Icel. *babbla,* Dan. *bable,* Fr. *babiller.*] To utter words imperfectly or indistinctly; to talk idly or irrationally; to make a continuous murmuring sound; to prate; to tell secrets.—*v.t.* To utter idly or irrationally.—*n.* Idle talk; senseless prattle; murmur as of a stream.—**babblement,**† bab′bl·ment, *n.* Idle talk; babble. (*Mil.*)—**babbler,** bab′bler, *n.* One who babbles; a teller of secrets.

babe, baby, bāb, bā′bi, *n.* [From the Celtic; W. Ir. and Gael. *baban,* Gael. and Ir. *bab,* child, infant.] An infant; a young child of either sex.—**babyish,** bā′bi·ish, *a.* Like a babe; childish.—**babyhood,** bā′bi·hud, *n.* The state of being a baby; infancy.—**baby farm,** *n.* The establishment of a baby farmer.—**baby farmer,** *n.* One who receives infants, generally illegitimate, along with a sum of money for their bringing up, and whose object is to get rid of the children, by neglect or ill usage, as soon as possible.—**baby farming,** *n.* The system or practices of a baby farmer.

Babel, bā′bel, *n.* The city mentioned in Scripture where the confusion of tongues took place; any great city where confusion may be supposed to prevail; a confused mixture of sounds; confusion; disorder.

babiroussa, bab·i·rös′sa, *n.* A species of the swine family with long curved tusks in the upper jaw, inhabiting the islands of the East Indies and the Malayan Peninsula, and allied to the wild boars of Europe.

bablah, bab′la, *n.* The pod of several species of acacia sometimes used in dyeing, to produce a drab color.

baboo, babu, ba·bö′, *n.* A Hindu title of respect paid to gentlemen, equivalent to master, sir.—**babu.** *Babu-English.* The broken English of Bengal.

baboon, ba·bön′, *n.* [Fr. *babouin.*] A term applied to certain quadrumanous animals of the Old World having elongated muzzles like a dog, strong canine teeth, short tails, cheek pouches, small deep eyes with huge eyebrows, and naked callosities on the hips.

baby, etc. See BABE.

Babylon, bab′i·lon, *n.* Type of any great or evil city; capital of Chaldean Empire.—**Babylonian, Babylonish,** bab·i·lō′ni·an, ba·bi·lo′nish, *a.* Pertaining to Babylon; like the confusion of tongues at Babel; mixed; confused.

bacca, bak′ka, *n.* [L.] *Bot.* a berry; a one-celled fruit, with several naked seeds immersed in a pulpy mass.—**baccate,** bak′kāt, *a. Bot.* having a pulpy texture like a berry; bearing berries; berried.—**bacciferous,** bak·sif′er·us, *a.* [L. *bacca,* and *fero,* to bear.] Bearing or producing berries.—**baccivorous,** bak·siv′ō·rus, *a* [L. *bacca,* and *voro,* to devour.] Eating or subsisting on berries.

baccalaureate, bak·ka·lạ′rē·āt, *n.* [L.L. *baccalaureatus,* from *baccalaureus,* a corrupted form, through *bacca lauri,* laurel berry, of L.L. *baccalarius,* Fr. *bachelier,* a bachelor, or one who has attained the lowest degree in a university. BACHELOR, LAUREATE.] The degree of Bachelor of Arts.—*a.* Pertaining to a Bachelor of Arts.

baccarat, bak′ka·rat or bak·ka·rä, *n.* [Fr.] A game of cards played by any number of players or rather betters.

bacchanal, bacchanalian, bak′a·nal, bak·a·nā′li·an, *a.* [L. *bacchanalis,* from *Bacchus,* the god of wine.] Revelling in or characterized by intemperate drinking; riotous; noisy. —*n.* A votary of Bacchus; one who indulges in drunken revels; a drunken feast.—**Bacchanalia,** bak·a·nā′li·a, *n. pl.* [L.] Feasts or festive rites in honor of Bacchus.—**bacchanalianism,** bak·a·nā′li·an·izm, *n.* The practice of bacchanalian rites; drunken

ch, *chain*; ch, Sc. *loch*; g, *go*; j, *job*; ng, si*ng*; TH, *then*; th, *thin*; w, *wig*; hw, *whig*; zh, a*zure*.

revelry.—**bacchant**, ba·kant′, n. [L. *bacchans*, ppr. of *bacchor*, to celebrate the feast of Bacchus.] A priest of Bacchus; a bacchanal.—**bacchante**, ba·kan′tē, n. [It. *baccante*.] A priestess of Bacchus, or one who joined in the feasts of Bacchus, one in a state of Bacchic frenzy; a female bacchanal. — **Bacchic**, **Bacchical**, bak′ik, bak′ik·al, a. Relating to Bacchus; jovial; drunken; mad with intoxication.

bachelor, bach′el·ėr, n. [O.Fr. *bacheler*, *bachiler*, Fr. *bachelier*, from L.L. *baccalarius*, the owner of a small farm or a herd of cows, a vassal, from *bacca*, for L. *vacca*, a cow.] Formerly, a young man in the first or probationary stage of knighthood; hence, a man who has not been married; one who has taken the degree below that of Master or Doctor in Arts, Science, or other subjects at a university.—*Knight bachelor*, a man who has been knighted without being made a member of any of the orders of knighthood, as the Bath.—**bachelorhood**, **bachelorship**, bach′el·ėr·hud, bach′el·ėr·ship, n. The state of being a bachelor.

bacillus, ba·sil′us, n. pl. **bacilli**, ba·sil′ī. [L., a little rod.] Any rod-shaped bacteria that produce spores in the presence of free oxygen; a bacterium.—**bacillary**, ba·sil′a·ri, a. Relating to bacilli.

back, bak, n. [A.Sax. *bæc*, Icel. Sw. and L.G. *bak*.] The posterior part of the trunk; the region of the spine; the hinder part of the body in man and the upper in other animals; that which is behind or furthest from the face or front; the rear (the *back* of a house); that which is behind or in the furthest distance; the part which comes behind in the ordinary movements of a thing, or when it is used (the *back* of the hand, a knife, saw, etc.); a reserve or secondary resource; a support or second; pl. among leather dealers the thickest and best-tanned hides.—*Behind one's back*, in secret, or when one is absent.—adv. [Short for *aback*, A.Sax. on *bæc*, back.] To or toward a former place, state, or condition; not advancing; in a state of restraint or hindrance (to keep *back*); toward times or things past (to look *back*); again; in return (to give *back*); away from contact; by reverse movement; in withdrawal or resilement from an undertaking or engagement (to draw *back*).—*To go or give back*, to retreat, to recede; to give way; to succumb.—a. Belonging to the back; lying in the rear; remote; in a backward direction: chiefly in compounds.—v.t. to furnish with a back or backing; to support; to second or strengthen by aid (often with *up*); to bet or wager in favor of; to get upon the back of; to mount; to write something on the back of; to endorse; to put backward; to cause to move backwards or recede.—v.i. To move or go back; to move with the back foremost.—**backed**, bakt, a. Having a back: used chiefly in composition. —**backer**, bak′ėr, n. One who backs

or gets on the back; one who supports another; one who bets in favor of a particular party in a contest.—**backing**, bak′ing, n. Something put at or attached to the back of something else by way of support or finish.

back, bak, n. [Fr. *bac*, a back or ferry-boat, a brewer's or distiller's back; Armor. *bac*, a boat; D. *bak*, a bowl; Dan. *bakke*, a tray. The word may be originally Celtic. *Basin* is akin to this word.] A ferryboat, especially one adapted for carrying vehicles, and worked by a chain or rope fastened on each side of the ferry; *brewing* and *distilling*, a large tub or vessel into which the wort, etc., is drawn for the purpose of cooling, straining, mixing, etc.

backbite, bak′bīt, v.t.—**backbit** (pret.), *backbit* or *backbitten* (pp.), *backbiting*. To censure, slander, or speak evil of, in the absence of the person traduced.—**backbiter**, bak′bīt·ėr, n. One who backbites; a calumniator of the absent.

backboard, bak′bōrd, n. A board for the back; a board used to support the back and give erectness to the figure.

backbone, bak′bōn, n. The bone of the back; the spine; the vertebral column; *fig.* firmness; decision of character; resolution.—*To the backbone*, to the utmost extent; out and out; all through or over (a soldier *to the backbone*).

backdoor, bak′dōr, n. A door in the back part of a building.

backgammon, bak·gam′mon, n. [Dan. *bakke*, a tray, *gammen*, mirth.] A game played by two persons upon a table or board made for the purpose, with pieces or men, dice-boxes, and dice.

background, bak′ground, n. The part of a picture represented as farthest from the spectator; *fig.* a situation little seen or noticed; a state of being out of view (to keep a fact in the *background*).

backhand, bak′hand, n. Writing sloping backwards or to the left.—**backhand**, **backhanded**, bak′hand, bak′hand·ed, a. With the hand turned backward (a *backhanded* blow); unfair; oblique; indirect; sloping back or to the left (of writing).—**backhandedness**, bak′hand·ed·nes, n.

backshish, **backsheesh**, bak′shēsh, n. Same as BAKSHISH.

backside, bak′sīd, n. The back part of anything; the side opposite to the front or behind that which is presented to the spectator.

backslide, bak′slīd, v.i. (conjugated as *slide*). To slide back; to fall off or turn away from religion or morality; to apostatize.—**backslider**, bak′slīd·ėr, n. One who backslides; one who falls away from religion or morality.

backstair, **backstairs**, bak′stār, bak′stārz, n. A stair or stairs in the back part of a house; private stairs.—a. Of or pertaining to backstairs; hence, indirect; underhand; secret and unfair (*backstairs* influence).

backstay, n. A long rope or stay, extending from the top of a mast

backwards to the side of a ship to assist the shrouds in supporting the mast.

backward, **backwards**, bak′wėrd, bak′wėrdz, adv. [*Back* and *ward*, denoting direction.] With the back in advance; toward the back; in a direction opposite to forward; toward past times or events; from a better to a worse state; in a contrary or reverse manner, way, or direction.—**backward**, a. Being in the back or at the back; turned or directed back (a *backward* look); unwilling; reluctant; slow; dull; not quick of apprehension; late; behind in time.—**backwardly**, bak′wėrd·li, adv. Unwillingly; reluctantly; aversely; perversely†.—**backwardness**, bak′wėrd·nes, n. The state or quality of being backward.—**backwater**, n. Ebbtide.—v.i. To fall back in the boat course.

backwoods, bak′wudz, n. pl. Woody or forest districts of a country situated back or away from the more thickly settled parts: more especially used in regard to the United States and Canada.—**backwoodsman**, bak′wudz·man, n. An inhabitant of the backwoods.

bacon, bā′kn, n. [O.Fr. *bacon*, from O.D. *baken*, bacon, from *bak*, *bake*, a pig; G. *bache*, a wild sow.] Swine's flesh salted or pickled and dried, usually in smoke.

Baconian, bā·kō′ni·an, a. Pertaining to Francis *Bacon*, or his system of philosophy.

bacteria, bak·tē′ri·a, n. pl. [Gr. *bakterion*, a stick.] Simple microscopic organisms that reproduce themselves by fission. Some, such as pathogenic bacteria, cause disease; others, such as denitrifying bacteria, are useful.—**bactericide**, bak·tē′ri·sīd, n. Anything capable of destroying bacteria.—**bacteriology**, bak·tē′ri·ol′o·ji, n. The study of bacteria.—**bacteriologist**, bak·tē′ri·ol′o·jist, n.—**bacteriophage**, bak·tē′ri·o·fāj, n. Any of various viruses that destroy bacteria.

bactericide, bak·tēr′i·sīd, n. Anything capable of destroying bacteria.

bacteriostasis, bak·tēr′i·o·stā′sis, n. *Bact.* prevention of the development of bacteria without killing them.

Bactrian, bak′tri·an, a. Of or pertaining to Bactria, an ancient province of the Persian empire (the *Bactrian* camel).

bad, bad, a. compar. (from quite a different root) *worse*, superl. *worst*. [Perhaps of Celtic origin; comp. Corn. *bad*, Gael. *baodh*, *baoth*, vain, foolish, etc.] The opposite of good; wanting good qualities, physical or moral; not coming up to a certain type or standard or the average of individuals of the particular class; wicked, unprincipled, depraved, immoral, vicious; pernicious, debasing, corrupting (influence, habits); ill, infirm (health); unwholesome, noxious (air, climate, food); defective, insufficient (work, crop); infertile, sterile (soil); unfortunate or unhappy (result, marriage); incompetent (workman), etc. etc.—n. That which is bad.—*To go to the bad*, to fall into bad company, bad ways, or bad circumstances; to fall into vicious courses and ruin one's life.—**badly,** bad′li, *adv.* In a bad manner; not well; unskillfully.—**badness,** bad′nes, *n.* The state of being bad; want of good qualities, physical or moral.

badderlocks, bad′ėr·loks, *n.* A common name for a seaweed found on the shores of the north of Europe, the midrib of which is edible.

badge, baj, *n.* [L.L. *bagia,* a sign, probably from O.Sax. *bag,* A.Sax. *beag,* Icel. *baugr,* a bracelet, ring, garland.] A mark, sign, token, or cognizance worn to show the relation of the weaver to any person, occupation, or order.—*v.t.*† To mark or distinguish with a badge or as with a badge. (*Shak.*)

badger, baj′ėr, *n.* [For *bladger,* from O.Fr. *blaage,* store of corn (the animal being supposed to steal corn), from L.L. *bladum,* wheat (Fr. *blé*); L. *ablatum*—*ab,* from, and *latum,* carried.] A plantigrade carnivorous mammal belonging to a family intermediate between the bears and the weasels, living in a burrow, nocturnal in habits, and feeding on vegetables, small quadrupeds, etc.—*v.t.* To attack (a person), as the badger is attacked when being drawn or baited; to assail (as with importunities, commands, etc.); to worry; to pester.

badinage, bad′i·nāj or bä·dē·näzh, *n.* [Fr., from *badin,* facetious.] Light or playful discourse.

badminton, bad′min·ton, *n.* [From a residence of the Dukes of Beaufort.] An outdoor game, the same as lawn tennis but played with shuttlecocks; a kind of claret cup or summer beverage.

baffle, baf′fl, *v.t.*—*baffled, baffling.* [Origin unknown.] To elude; to foil; to frustrate; to defeat; to thwart.—*n.* A plate or screen that deflects or regulates flow of a gas, liquid, or the distribution of soundwaves.—**baffler,** baf′flėr, *n.*

bag, bag, *n.* [Icel. *baggi, böggr,* a bag, a bundle; comp. O.Fr. *bague,* a bundle, Gael. *bag,* a bag.] A sack; a wallet; a pouch; what is contained in a bag (as the animals shot by a sportsman); a definite quantity of certain commodities.—*v.t.*—*bagged, bagging.* To put into a bag; to distend; to swell; to shoot or otherwise lay hold of (game).—*v.i.* To swell or hang like a bag.—**bagging,** bag′ing, *n.* The cloth or other materials for bags.—**baggy,** bag′i, *a.* Having the appearance of a bag; puffy.—**bagginess,** bag′i·nes, *n.* Character of being baggy.—**bagpipe,** bag′pīp, *n.* A musical wind instrument consisting of a leathern bag which receives the air from the mouth or from a bellows; and of pipes into which the air is pressed from the bag by the performer's elbow.—**bagpiper,** bag′pīp·ėr, *n.* One who plays on a bagpipe.—**bagwig,** *n.* A wig with a sort of purse attached to it.

bagasse, ba·gas′, *n.* [Fr.] The sugarcane in its dry crushed state as delivered from the sugar mill.

bagatelle, bag·a·tel′, *n.* [Fr., from It. *bagatella,* a dim. of *bagata,* a trifle, L.L. *baga,* a bundle, a bag.] A trifle; a thing of no importance; a game played on a board having at the end nine holes, into which balls are to be struck with a cue or mace.

baggage, bag′āj, *n.* [Fr. *bagage,* baggage, O.Fr. *bague,* a bundle. BAG.] The necessaries of an army, or other body of men on the move; luggage; things required for a journey.

baggage, bag′āj, *n.* [Fr. *bagasse,* It. *bagascia,* Sp. *bagazo,* a strumpet.] A low worthless woman; a strumpet; now usually a playful epithet applied familiarly to any young woman.

bagnio, bän′yo, *n.* [It. *bagno,* from L. *balneum,* a bath.] A bath; a brothel; a stew.

bah, bä, *interj.* An exclamation expressing contempt, disgust, or incredulity.

bail, bāl, *v.t.* [O.Fr. *bailler,* to bail, to guard, from L. *bajulus,* a bearer, later a tutor or governor. Hence *bailiff.*] To liberate from arrest and imprisonment, upon security that the person liberated shall appear and answer in court.—*n.* The person or persons who procure the release of a prisoner from custody by becoming surety for his appearance in court; the security given for the release; not used with a plural termination (we were his *bail*).—**bailable,** bāl′a·bl, *a.* Capable of being admitted to bail; admitting of bail (a *bailable* offense).—**bailer,** bāl′ėr, *n.* One who or that which bails.

bail, bāl, *n.* [O.Fr. *baille,* a palisade, from L. *baculum,* a rod or staff.] A little stick laid on the tops of the stumps in playing cricket.

bail, bāl, *v.t.* [Fr. *baille,* a bucket, Armor. *bal,* a tub.] To free (a boat) from water with a bucket or other utensil.

bailiff, bā′lif, *n.* [O.Fr. *baillij, bailli,* from *baillir, bailler,* to hold, to govern, L. *bajulare,* to bear, *bajulus,* a porter. BAIL, to liberate.] A civil officer or functionary, a sheriff's deputy, a court officer who executes writs, processes, distraints, and arrests; who also acts as a messenger or usher in court.—**bailiwick,** bā′li·wik, *n.* [*-wick* from A.Sax. *wic,* dwelling, station, L. *vicus,* a village.] The precincts in which a bailiff has jurisdiction.

bailment, bāl′ment, *n.* The act of bailing an arrested person.

Baily's beads, *n.* [From F. *Baily,* astronomer.] The belt of bright sunlight shining through mountains on the moon's surface that is seen just before and just after a total eclipse of the sun.

Bairam, bā′ram, *n.* The name of two Mohammedan festivals, one held at the close of the fast Ramadan, the other seventy days after.

bait, bāt, *v.t.* [From Icel. *beita,* to make to eat, to feed, to bait a hook—a causative of *bita,* E. *bite.*] To give a portion of food and drink to a beast when traveling; to furnish with a piece of flesh or other substance which acts as a lure to fish or other animals (to *bait* a hook); to provoke and harass by dogs (as a bull, badger, or bear); to annoy.—*v.i.* To take a portion of food and drink for refreshment on a journey.—*n.* A portion of food and drink, or a refreshment taken on a journey; any substance used as a lure to catch fish or other animals; an allurement; enticement.

bait, bāt, *v.i.* [Fr. *battre,* to beat. BATE.] To clap the wings; to hover above prey. (*Shak.*)

baize, bāz, *n.* [A modified plural; O.E. *bayes,* Fr. *baie,* coarse woolen cloth, originally of a bay color; from L. *badius,* bay-colored.] A coarse woolen stuff with a long nap, sometimes friezed on one side.

bake, bāk, *v.t.*—*baked, baking* (old pp. *baken*). [A.Sax. *bacan*=Icel. and Sw. *baka,* Dan. *bage,* D. *bakken,* G. *backen.*] To dry and harden by heat, in an oven, kiln, or furnace, or by the solar rays (as bread, bricks, pottery); to prepare in an oven.—*v.i.* To do the work of baking; to dry and harden in heat.—**baker,** bāk′ėr, *n.* One whose occupation is to bake bread, biscuit, etc.—**baker's dozen.** Thirteen, the extra as retailer's profit.—**bakery,** bāk′ėr·i, *n.* A place used for the business of baking bread, etc.

bakelite, bā′ke·līt, *n.* [From L. H. *Baekeland,* chemist.] Trade name of a substance of coal tar origin used in making plastic ware.

baking powder, *n.* A mixture of baking soda, starch or flour, and an acid substance, used as a leavening agent.—**baking soda,** *n.* Sodium bicarbonate.

bakshish, bak′shēsh, *n.* [Pers., from *bakkshidan,* to give.] A present or gratuity of money: used in Eastern countries.

balance, bal′ans, *n.* [Fr., from L. *bilanx*—*bis,* double, and *lanx,* a dish, the scale of a balance.] An instrument for ascertaining the weight of bodies, consisting in its common form of a beam or lever suspended exactly at the middle, and having a scale or basin hung to each extremity of exactly the same weight, so that the beam rests horizontally when nothing is in either scale or when they are loaded with equal weights; the excess by which one thing is greater than another; surplus; the difference of two sums; the sum due on an account; an equality of weight, power, advantage, and the like; the part of a clock or watch which regulates the beats; the balance wheel.—*v.t.*—*balanced, balancing.* To bring to an equipoise; to keep in equilibrium on a small support; to poise; to compare by estimating the relative importance or value of; to weigh; to serve as a counterpoise to; to settle (an account) by paying what remains due; to examine (a merchant's books) by summations and show how debits and credits stand.—*v.i.* To be in equipoise; to have equal weight or importance; to be employed in finding balances on accounts.—**balancer,** bal´ans·ėr, *n.* One who or that which balances; an organ of an insect useful in balancing the body.—**balance sheet,** A statement of the assets and liabilities of a trading concern.—**balance wheel,** *n.* That part of a watch or chronometer which, like a pendulum, regulates the beat or strike.

balas, bal´as, ba·las´, *n.* [From Ar. *balakhsh,* from *Badakhshan,* in Central Asia.] A variety of spinel ruby, of a pale rose-red color, sometimes inclining to orange.

balata, ba·lä´ta, *n.* A gum obtained from a S. American tree, used for similar purposes to india-rubber, and in the United States as a chewing-gum. BULLET TREE.

balcony, bal´kō·ni (nineteenth century), bal·kō´ni (previously), *n.* [It. *balcone,* from *balco,* a scaffold, from O.H.G. *balcho,* G. *balken*=E. *balk,* a beam.] A platform projecting from the front of a building, supported by columns, pillars, or consoles, and encompassed with a balustrade, railing, or parapet; a projecting gallery in the interior of a building, as of a theater.

bald, bald, *a.* [O.E. *balled,* lit. marked with a white spot; of Celtic origin, comp. Armor. *bal,* a white mark on an animal's face; Ir. and Gael. *bal,* a spot.] Having white on the face (said of animals); destitute of hair, especially on the top and back of the head; destitute of the natural or usual covering of the head or top; destitute of appropriate ornament; unadorned (said of style or language); *bot.* destitute of beard or awn.—**baldly,** bald´li, *adv.* Nakedly; meanly; inelegantly.—**baldness,** bald´nes, *n.* The state or quality of being bald.—**bald eagle,** the white-headed eagle of America.—**bald-faced,** *a.* Having a white face or white on the face; said of animals. —**bald head,** *n.* A person bald on the head. [O.T.] **bald-headed,** *a.* (*to go*). Having a bald head. In a wild, reckless manner.

baldachin, baldaquin, bal´da·kin, bal´da·kin, *n.* [It. *baldacchino,* Sp. *baldaquino,* from *Baldacco,* Italian form of *Bagdad,* where the cloth was manufactured.] A canopy or covering; a canopy on four poles held over the pope; a canopy on four columns over an altar; a canopy over a throne.

balderdash, bal´dėr·dash, *n.* [W. *baldordus,* prattling, *baldordd,* prattle.] Senseless prate; a jargon of words; noisy nonsense.

baldpate, *n.* Same as *Bald head.*

baldric, bald´rik, *n.* [O.E. *baudric, baldric,* etc., O.Fr. *baudric,* from O.G. *balderich,* from *balz,* a belt. BELT.] A broad belt, stretching from the right or left shoulder diagonally across the body, either as an ornament or to suspend a sword, dagger, or horn.

bale, bāl, *n.* [O.Fr. *bale,* the same word as *ball,* meaning originally a round package.] A bundle or package of goods.—*v.t.*—**baled, baling.** To

make up into a bale or bundle.

bale, bāl, *v.t.*—**baled, baling.** To free from water by laving; to bail.

bale, bāl, *n.* [A.Sax. *bealu,* O.Sax. *balu,* Icel. *böl,* calamity, sorrow.] Misery; calamity; that which causes ruin, destruction, or sorrow.—**baleful,** bāl´ful, *a.* Full of bale, destruction, or mischief; destructive; pernicious; calamitous; deadly.—**balefully,** bāl´ful·li, *adv.* In a baleful or calamitous manner.—**balefulness,** bāl´ful·nes, *n.* The state or quality of being baleful.

baleen, ba·lēn´, *n.* [Fr. *baleine,* from L. *balæna,* a whale.] The whalebone of commerce.

balefire, bāl´fīr, *n.* [A.Sax. *bael,* fire, flame, a funeral pile; Icel. *bal,* flame, a funeral pile.] A signal fire; an alarm fire.

balk, bak, *n.* [A.Sax. *balca,* a balk or ridge, a beam; Icel. *balkr,* Sw. *balk,* a balk, a partition; Dan. *bjelke,* G. *balken,* a beam.] A ridge of land left unplowed; an uncultivated strip of land serving as a boundary; a beam or piece of timber of considerable length and thickness; a barrier or check; a disappointment.—*v.t.* To bar the way of; to disappoint. to frustrate.—*v.i.* To turn aside or stop in one's course (as a horse).—**balker,** bak´ėr, *n.* One who balks.—**balkingly,** bak´ing·li, *adv.* In a manner to balk or frustrate.

ball, bal, *n.* [Fr. *balle,* from O.H.G. *balla,* G. *ball,* Icel. *böllr,* ball. *Bale,* a package, is another form, and *balloon, ballot* are derivatives.] A round body; a small spherical body often covered with leather and used in many games; any part of a thing that is rounded or protuberant; *farriery,* a form of medicine, corresponding to the term *bolus* in pharmacy; *metal.* a mass of half-melted iron; a loop; the projectile of a firearm; a bullet (in this sense also used collectively).—Ball-and-socket joint, a joint (as in the human hip) formed by a ball or rounded end playing within a socket so as to admit of motion in all directions.—**ball,** bal, *v.t.* To make into a ball.—*v.i.* To form or gather into a ball. —**ball cock,** *n.* A kind of self-acting stop cock opened and shut by means of a hollow sphere or ball of metal floating on the surface of a liquid, and attached to the end of a lever connected with the cock.—**ballpoint pen.** A pen with a tiny steel ball as a writing point, inked by rotating against an inking magazine.

ball, bal, *n.* [Fr. *bal,* L.L. *ballare,* to dance, to shake, from Gr. *ballizō,* to dance. Akin *ballad, ballet.*] A social assembly of persons of both sexes for the purpose of dancing.

ballad, bal´lad, *n.* [Fr. *ballade,* from L.L. (and It.) *ballare,* to dance. BALL, a dance, BALLET]. A short narrative poem, especially such as is adapted for singing; a poem partaking of the nature both of the epic and the lyric.—**ballad,†** bal´lad, *v.t.* To celebrate in a ballad. (*Shak.*) —**ballade,** ba·lad´, *n.* [Fr. *ballade.*]

Poem consisting in its normal form of three stanzas of eight lines each, with a closing stanza or envoy of four lines, the rhymes throughout being not more than three.

ballast, bal´ast, *n.* [D. *ballast,* ballast, literally worthless load (being worthless in itself), from *bal* (akin to E. *bale,* misery, bad, and *last,* a load. LAST.) In Danish it was modified to *baglast,* lit. a back-load—*bag,* back after, and *last,* load.] Heavy matter, as stone, sand, or iron, carried in the bottom of a ship or other vessel, to prevent it from being readily overset (the vessel being said to be in *ballast* when she sails without a cargo); sand carried in bags in the car of a balloon to steady it, and enable the aeronaut to lighten the balloon by throwing part of it out; material filling up the space between the rails on a railroad in order to make it firm and solid; *fig.* that which confers steadiness on a person. —*v.t.* To place ballast in or on (a ship, a railroad track); *fig.* to steady; to counterbalance.

ballerina, bal·e·rē´na, *n.* A female ballet dancer.

ballet, bal·lā´or bal´let, *n.* [Fr. *ballet,* It. *balletto.* BALL, a dance.] A dance, more or less elaborate, in which several persons take part; a theatrical representation, in which a story is told by gesture, accompanied with dancing, scenery, etc.

ballista, bal·lis´ta, *n.* pl. **ballistae,** bal·lis´tē, [L., from Gr. *ballō,* to throw.] A military engine used by the ancients for discharging heavy stones or other missiles especially against a besieged place.—**ballistic,** bal·lis´tik, *a.* —**ballistic missile,** a projectile that uses rocket power in its first stage but continues to its target unguided and without propulsion.—**ballistics,** bal·lis´tiks, *n.* The science that studies the motion of projectiles.

balloon, bal·lön´, *n.* [Fr. *ballon,* an aug. of *balle,* a ball. BALL.] A large hollow spherical body; a very large bag, usually made of light fabric or plastic material and filled with hydrogen gas or heated air, or any other gaseous fluid lighter than common air, the contained gas causing the balloon to rise and float in the atmosphere.—**balloonist,** bal·lön´ist, *n.*

ballot, bal´lot, *n.* [Fr. *ballotte,* a ball used in voting, dim. of *balle,* a ball. BALL.] A ball, ticket, paper, or the like, by which one votes, and which gives no indication of who the voter is; the system of voting by means of this kind.—*v.i.* To vote or decide by ballot: frequently with *for.*—**balloter,** bal´lot·ėr, *n.* One who ballots or votes by ballot.

balm, bäm, *n.* [O.Fr. *baulme,* Fr. *baume;* a contr. of *balsam.*] A name common to several species of odoriferous or aromatic trees or shrubs, and to the fragrant medicinal exudations from them; any fragrant or valuable ointment; anything which heals, soothes, or mitigates pain.—**balm,** bäm, *v.t.* To anoint as with balm or with anything fragrant or medicinal; to soothe; to mitigate; to assuage; to heal.—**balmily,** bäm′-i·li, *adv.* In a balmy manner.—**balminess,** bäm′i·nes, *n.* The state or quality of being balmy.—**balmy,** bäm′i, *a.* Having the qualities of balm; aromatic; fragrant; healing; soothing; assuaging; refreshing.

balsam, bạl′sam, *n.* [L. *balsamum,* Gr. *balsamon,* a fragrant gum.] An oily, aromatic, resinous substance, flowing spontaneously or by incision from certain plants and used in medicine and perfumery; balm. —**balsamic,** bạl·sam′ik, *a.* Having the qualities of balsam, stimulating; unctuous; soft; mitigating; mild.— *n.* A warm, stimulating, demulcent medicine, of a smooth and oily consistence.—**balsamiferous,** bạl·-sam·if′ėr·us, *a.* Producing or yielding balm or balsam.

baluster, bal′us·tėr, *n.* [Fr. *balustre.* It. *balaustro,* a baluster, from L. *balaustium,* Gr. *balaustion,* the flower of the wild pomegranate, being so called from some resemblance of form.] A small column or pilaster, of various forms and dimensions, used for balustrades.—**balustrade,** bal·us·trād′, *n.* [Fr. *balustrade.*] A row of small columns or pilasters, joined by a rail, serving as an enclosure for altars, balconies, stair-cases, terraces, etc., or used merely as an ornament.

bamboo, bam·bö, *n.* [Malay.] A tropical plant of the family of the grasses, with large jointed stems, the thickest being much used in India, China, etc., for building purposes, and the slenderest for walking canes.—**bamboo curtain.** The condition of censorship, prohibition of free travel, and secrecy in Communist China.

bamboozle, bam·bö′zl, *v.t.* [Origin doubtful.] To impose or practice upon; to hoax; to humbug; to deceive.—**bamboozler,** bam·bö′zlėr, *n.* One who bamboozles.

ban, ban, *n.* [A.Sax. *ban, gebann,* interdict, proclamation, edict; D. *ban,* excommunication; Icel. and Sw. *bann,* proclamation; Dan. *band.* a ban, *bande,* to curse. Akin *bandit, banish, abandon,* etc.] An edict or proclamation in general; an edict of interdiction or proscription; interdiction; prohibition; curse; excommunication; anathema; *pl.* proclamation of marriage (BANNS).— *v.t.*—**banned, banning.** To curse; to execrate; to prohibit; to interdict.— *v.i.* To curse.

ban, ban, *n.* [Serv. *ban,* a lord.] A Croatian or Hungarian military chief or ruler.

banal, ban′al, *a.* [Fr.] Hackneyed; commonplace; vulgar; properly, a *bannal mill* was by feudal custom the mill common by *ban* or order to *all* the vassals.—**banality,** ban·-al′i·ti, *n.* Banal character; what is banal.

banana, ba·nä′na, *n.* [Sp., from the native name.] A herbaceous plant closely allied to the plantain, and extensively cultivated in tropical countries for its soft luscious fruit, which is the staple food of millions of people.

band, band, *n.* [A.Sax. *bend,* a band, from *bindan,* to bind; D. Icel. Sw. and G. *band,* in sense of body of men, from Fr. *bande,* G. *bande,* from same root. BIND.] That which binds together; a bond or means of attachment in general; a fetter or similar fastening; a narrow strip or ribbon-shaped ligature, tie, or connection; a fillet; a border or strip on an article of dress; that which resembles a band, tie, or ligature; *pl.* the linen ornament about the neck of a clergyman, with the ends hanging down in front; a company of persons united together by some common bond, especially a body of armed men; a company of soldiers; an organized body of instrumental musicians; an orchestra.—*v.t.*—To bind with a band; to mark with a band; to unite in a troop, company, or confederacy.—*v.i.* To associate or unite for some common purpose.—**bandage,** ban′dij, *n.* A fillet, roller, or swathe used in dressing and binding up wounds, restraining hemorrhages, etc.; a band or ligature in general.—*v.t.* **bandaged, bandaging.** To put a bandage on.—**bandbox,** band′box, *n.* A box made of pasteboard, or thin flexible pieces of wood and paper, for holding bands, bonnets, or other light articles.—**bandmaster,** *n.* The conductor and trainer of a band of musicians.—**bandsaw,** *n.* A saw formed of a long flexible belt of steel revolving on pulleys.—**bandwagon,** *n.* A wagon in which a band of musicians rides.—*Get on the bandwagon,* side with the apparent victor in a contest or cause.

bandana, bandanna, ban·dan′a, *n.* [Hind. *bândhnû,* to tie.] An Indian silk handkerchief having a pattern formed by tying little bits so as to keep them from being dyed; hence, a silk or cotton handkerchief having a somewhat similar pattern, that is, a uniform ground, usually of bright red or blue, with white or yellow figures of simple form.

bandeau, ban′dō, *n.* pl. **bandeaux,** ban′dō. [Fr., dim. from *bande,* a band.] A fillet worn round the head; a head band.

banderole, ban′de·rōl, *n.* [Fr. *banderole,* Sp. *banderola,* a little banner, from *bandera,* a banner, from G. *band.* BAND.] A little flag or streamer affixed to a mast, a military weapon, or a trumpet; a pennon; a banderole. *Arch.* stone band with inscription.

bandicoot, ban′di·kut, *n.* [Corruption of the Telinga name *pandikoku,* lit. pig-rat.] A large species of rat, attaining the weight of 2 or 3 lbs., a native of India and Ceylon, where its flesh is a favorite article of food among the coolies.

bandit, ban′dit, *n.* pl. **bandits,** ban′dits, **banditti,** ban·dit′ti. [It. *bandito,* pp. of *bandire,* L.L. *bannire,* to banish. BAN, BANISH.] An out-

law; more commonly a robber; a highwayman.

bandog, ban′dog, *n.* [*Band* and *dog,* lit. bound-dog.] A large, fierce kind of dog, generally a mastiff, usually kept chained.

bandoleer, ban·dō·lēr′, *n.* [Sp. *bandolera,* Fr. *bandoulière,* from Sp. *banda,* a sash.] A large leather belt carrying a bag for balls and a number of charges of gunpowder, worn by musketeers; a shoulder belt carrying ball cartridges.

bandoline, ban′dō·lēn, *n.* A gummy perfumed substance used to impart a glossiness and stiffness to the hair.

bandore, ban′dōr, *n.* [Fr., from It. *pandora,* L. *pandura,* Gr. *pandoura,* a musical instrument ascribed to *Pan.*] A musical stringed instrument like a lute.

bandy, ban′di, *n.* [Fr. *bandé,* bent, from *bander,* to bend a bow, to bind, to swathe, from G. *band,* a band. BAND.] A club bent at the end for striking a ball at play; a game played with such clubs.—*v.t.*—**bandied, bandying.** To beat to and fro, as a ball in play; to toss from one to another; to exchange contentiously; to give and receive reciprocally (words, compliments).—*v.i.* To contend; to strive. (*Shak.*)—**bandy,** ban′di, *a.* Bent, especially having a bend or crook outwards: said of a person's legs.—**bandy-legged,** *a.* Having bandy or crooked legs.

bane, bān, *n.* [A.Sax. *bana,* destruction, death, bane; Icel. *bani,* Dan. and Sw. *bane,* O.H.G. *bana;* allied to Gr. *phonos,* murder.] Any fatal cause of mischief, injury, or destruction; ruin; destruction; deadly poison.—**baneful,** bān′fụl, *a.* Destructive; pernicious; poisonous.—**banefully,** bān′fụl·li, *adv.* In a baneful manner.—**banefulness,** bān′-fụl·nes, *n.* The quality of being baneful.

bang, bang, *v.t.* [Comp. Icel. *bang,* a knocking; G. *bängel,* a club, the clapper of a bell; D. *bangel,* a bell.] To beat, as with a club or cudgel; to thump; to cudgel; to beat or handle roughly or with violence (*Shak.*); to bring a loud noise from or by, as in slamming a door, and the like.—*v.i.* To resound with a loud noise; to produce a loud noise; to thump violently.—*n.* A loud, sudden, resonant sound; a blow as with a club; a heavy blow.

bang, bang, *n.* See BHANG.

bangle, bang′gl, *n.* [Hind. *bangri.*] An ornamental ring worn upon the arms or ankles in India, Africa, and elsewhere.

banian, ban′yan, *n.* [Hind. *banyá,* a merchant.] An Indian trader or merchant; a Hindu trader strict in regard to food.

banish, ban′ish, *v.t.* [Fr. *bannir,* ppr. *bannissant,* to banish, from L.L. *bannire,* to proclaim, denounce, from O.H.G. *bannan,* to proclaim. BAN.] To condemn to exile; to send (a person) from a country as a punishment; to drive away; to exile; to cast from the mind (thoughts, care, business).—**banisher**, ban´ish·ẻr, n. One who banishes.—**banishment**, ban´ish·ment, n. The act of banishing; the state of being banished; enforced absence; exile.

banister, ban´is·tẻr, n. [Form of *baluster*.] A baluster; an upright in a stair rail.

banjo, ban´jō, n. [Negro corruption of *bandore*.] A musical instrument having six strings, a body like a tambourine, and a neck like a guitar.

bank, bangk, n. [A.Sax. *banc*, a bank, a hillock, also *benc*, a bench; Sw. and Dan. *bank*, bänk, Icel. *bakki* (for *banki*), D. and G. *bank*, a bank, a bench. In sense of establishment dealing in money the word is directly from the Fr. *banque*, a banking establishment; It. *banco*, a bench, counter, a bank, this being from the German. *Bench* is the same word.] A mound or heap of earth; any steep acclivity, as one rising from a river, the sea, or forming the side of a ravine or the like; a rising ground in the sea, partly above water or covered everywhere with shoal water; a shoal; the face of coal at which miners are working; a bench or seat for the rowers in a galley; one of the rows of oars; an establishment which trades in money; an establishment for the deposit, custody, remittance, and issue of money; the office in which the transactions of a banking company are conducted; the funds of a gaming establishment; a fund in certain games at cards.—*v.t.* To enclose, defend, or fortify with a bank; to embank; to lay up or deposit in a bank.—*v.i.* To deposit money in a bank.—*To bank* (*upon*), to stake or rest hopes upon an event (recent use).—**bankable**, bangk´a·bl, a. **banker**, bangk´ẻr, n. One who keeps a bank; one who traffics in money, receives and remits money, negotiates bills of exchange, etc.—**banking**, bangk´ing, n. The business or profession of a banker; the system followed by banks in carrying on their business; the tilting up of an airplane at a sharp angle sideways when flying swiftly round a curve, on the same principle as that on which a cycle track is ' banked ' steeply at corners rounded at high speed.—**banknote**, n. A promissory note issued by a banking company payable on demand.

bankrupt, bangk´rupt, n. [*Bank*, a bench, and L. *ruptus*, broken, lit. one whose bench has been broken, the bench or table which a merchant or banker formerly used in the exchange having been broken on his bankruptcy.] A person declared by legal authority unable to pay his debts; popularly, one who has wholly or partially failed to pay his debts; one who has compounded with his creditors; an insolvent.—*a.* Insolvent; unable to meet one's obligations.— **bankruptcy**, bangk´rupt·si, n. The state of being a bankrupt; inability to pay all debts; failure in trade.

banner, ban´ẻr, n. [Fr. *bannière*, L.L.

banderia, from *bandum*, banner, standard, from G. *band*, a band or strip of cloth, from *binden*, to bind.] A piece of cloth usually bearing some warlike or heraldic device or national emblem, attached to the upper part of a pole or staff; an ensign; a standard; a square flag.— **bannerol**, ban´ẻr·ol, n. A little flag; a banderole.—**banneret**, ban´ẻr·et, n. A knight of a rank between a baron and an ordinary knight, raised to this rank for bravery on the field.

bannock, ban´ok, n. [A.Sax. *bannue*, Gael. *bannach*.] An unleavened cake of oatmeal or other meal baked at an open fire, and generally on an iron plate. [Scotch.]

banns, banz, n.pl. [See BAN.] The proclamation in church previous to a marriage, made by calling over the names of the parties intending matrimony.

banquet, bang´kwet, n. [Fr. *banquet*, dim. of *banque*, a bench, a seat, and hence a feast. BANK.] A feast; a rich entertainment of meat and drink; *fig.* something specially delicious or enjoyable.—*v.t.* To treat with a feast or rich entertainment.—*v.i.* To feast; to regale one's self; to fare daintily.—**banqueter**, bang´kwet·ẻr, n. A feaster; one who provides feasts or rich entertainments.

banquette, ban·ket´, n. [Fr. from *banc*, a bench, a bank.] *Fort.* A little raised way or bank running along the inside of a parapet, on which musketeers or riflemen stand to fire upon the enemy in the moat or covered way; the footway of a bridge when raised above the carriage way.

banshee, ban´shē, n. [Ir. *bean-sith*, Gael. *ban-sith*, from Ir. and Gael. *bean*, *ban*, woman, and *sith*, fairy.] A kind of female fairy believed in Ireland and some parts of Scotland to attach herself to a particular house, and to appear before the death of one of the family.

Bantam, ban´tam, n. A small but spirited breed of domestic fowl with feathered shanks, first brought from the East Indies, and supposed to derive its name from *Bantam* in Java.—*a.* [not cap.] Pertaining to or resembling the bantam; of the breed of the bantam; hence, diminutive; puny.

banter, ban´tẻr, v.t. [Origin unknown.] To address humorous raillery to; to attack with jokes or jests; to make fun of; to rally.—*n.* (no pl.) A joking or jesting; humorous raillery: pleasantry with which a person is attacked.—**banterer**, ban´tẻr·ẻr, n. One who banters.

bantling, bant´ling, n. [Probably from *band*, a wrapping, and the dim. suffix- *ling*, meaning properly a child in swaddling clothes.] A young child; an infant: a term carrying with it a shade of contempt.

banyan, ban´yan, n. [From the connection of one such tree with certain *banians* or Indian merchants.] An Indian tree of the fig genus, remarkable for its horizontal bran-

ches sending down shoots which take root when they reach the ground and enlarge into trunks, which in their turn send out branches; the tree in this manner covering a prodigious extent of ground.

baobab, bā´ō·bab, n. [The name in Senegal.] A large African tree usually from 40 to 70 feet high, and often 30 feet in diameter, having an oblong pulpy fruit called monkey bread; the sour-gourd or calabash tree.

baptism, bap´tizm, n. [Gr. *baptisma*, from *baptizō*, to baptize, from *baptō*, to dip in water.] The application of water by sprinkling or immersion to a person, as a sacrament or religious ceremony.—**baptismal**, bap·tiz´mal, a. Pertaining to baptism.—**baptismally**, bap·tiz´mal·li, adv. In a baptismal manner.— **Baptist**, bap´tist, n. [Gr. *baptistēs*.] One who administers baptism: specifically applied to John, the forerunner of Christ; as a contraction of *Anabaptist*, one who objects to infant baptism.—**baptistery**, bap´tis·tẻr·i, n. A building or a portion of a building in which is administered the rite of baptism.—**baptize**, bap·tīz´, v.t.—*baptized*, *baptizing*. [Gr. *baptizō*.] To administer the sacrament of baptism to; to christen. —**baptizer**, bap·tīz´ẻr, n. One who baptizes.

bar, bär, n. [Fr. *barre*; from the Celtic; W. and Armor. *bar*, the top branch of a tree, a rail, a bar. *Barrier*, *barrister*, *barricade*, *embarrass*, etc., are derivatives.] A piece of wood, metal, or other solid matter, long in proportion to its thickness; a pole; a connecting piece in various positions and structures, often for a hindrance or obstruction; anything which obstructs, hinders, or impedes; an obstruction; an obstacle; a barrier; a bank of sand, gravel, or earth forming an obstruction at the mouth of a river or harbor; the railing enclosing the place which counsel occupy in courts of justice; the place in court where prisoners are stationed for arraignment, trial, or sentence; all those who can plead in a court; lawyers in general; the profession of the law; the railing or partition which separates a space near the door from the body of either house of parliament; a tribunal in general; the enclosed place of a tavern, inn, or other establishment where liquors, etc., are served out; the counter over which such articles are served out; military mark of distinction, stripe added to medal; *music*, a line drawn perpendicularly across the staff dividing it into equal measures of time; the space and notes included between two such lines.—*v.t.*—*barred*, *barring*. To fasten with a bar or as with a bar; to hinder; to obstruct; to prevent; to prohibit; to restrain; to except; to exclude by exception; to provide with a bar or bars; to mark with bars; to cross with one or more stripes or lines.—**barmaid,** *n.* A maid or woman who serves at the bar of an inn or other place of refreshment.— **Bar-room,** *n.* The room in a public house, hotel, etc., containing the bar or counter where refreshments are served.

barb, bärb, *n.* [Fr. *barbe,* L. *barba,* beard.] The sharp point projecting backward from the penetrating extremity of an arrow, fishhook, or other instrument for piercing, intended to prevent its being extracted; a barbel; a beard.—*v.t.* To shave or dress the beard‡; to furnish with barbs, as an arrow.

barb, bärb, *n.* [Contr. from *Barbary.*] A horse of the Barbary breed, remarkable for speed, endurance, and docility.

barbarian, bär·bā′ri·an, *n.* [L. *barbarus,* from Gr. *barbaros,* one whose language is unintelligible, a foreigner.] A foreigner‡ (N.T.); a man in his rude savage state; an uncivilized person; a cruel, savage, brutal man; one destitute of pity or humanity.—*a.* Of or pertaining to savages; rude; uncivilized; cruel; inhuman.—**barbaric,** bär·bar′ik, *a.* Of or pertaining to, or characteristic of a barbarian; uncivilized; savage; wild; ornate without being in accordance with sound taste.—**barbarism,** bär′bar·izm, *n.* An uncivilized state; want of civilization; rudeness of manners; an act of barbarity, cruelty, or brutality; an outrage; an offense against purity of style or language; any form of speech contrary to correct idiom.—**barbarity,** bär·bar′i·ti, *n.* The state of being barbarous; barbarousness; savageness; ferociousness; inhumanity; a barbarous act.—**barbarization,** bär′bar·iz·ā″shon, *n.* The act or process of rendering barbarous or of becoming barbarous.—**barbarize,** bär′bar·īz, *v.i.* To become barbarous.—*v.t.* To make barbarous.—**barbarous,** bär′ba·rus, *a.* Unacquainted with arts and civilization; uncivilized; rude and ignorant; pertaining to or characteristic of barbarians; adapted to the taste of barbarians; barbaric; cruel; ferocious; inhuman.—**barbarously,** bär′ba·rus·li, *adv.* In a barbarous manner; without knowledge or arts; savagely; cruelly; ferociously; inhumanly.—**barbarousness,** bär′ba·rus·nes, *n.* The state or quality of being barbarous; barbarity.

barbecue,† bär′bē·kū, *n.* [Conjectured to be from Fr. *barbe-à-queue,* from beard to tail; more probably from Carib *barbacoa,* a kind of large gridiron.] a hog or other large animal dressed whole;—*v.t.*— *barbecued, barbecuing.* To dress and cook whole by splitting to the backbone and roasting on a gridiron; to cook meat on a revolving spit, often drenching it in a sauce.

barbel, bär′bel, *n.* [O.Fr. *barbel,* from L. *barbus,* a barbel (the fish), from *barba,* a beard. In sense of appendage it is rather for *barbule.*] A fresh-water fish having four beard-like appendages on its upper

jaw; a vermiform process appended to the mouth of certain fishes, serving as an organ of touch.

barber, bär′bėr, *n.* [Fr. *barbier,* from *barbe,* L. *barba,* a beard.] One whose occupation is to shave the beard or to cut and dress hair.—*v.t.* To shave and dress the hair of. (*Shak.*)

barberry, bär′be·ri, *n.* [Fr. *berberis,* from Ar. *barbāris,* the barberry, but the spelling has been modified so as to give the word an English appearance.] A shrubby plant bearing small acid and astringent, red berries, common in hedges.

barbet, bär′bet, *a.* [Fr. *barbet,* from L. *barba,* a beard.] A variety of dog having long, curly hair; a poodle; one of a group of climbing birds, approaching the cuckoos, having a large conical beak, and at its base tufts of stiff bristles.

barbette, bär·bet′, *n.* [Fr. *barbette.*] A fixed armored shelter on a warship, inside which a gun revolves on a turntable.

barbican, bär′bi·kan, *n.* [Fr. *barbacane,* It. *barbacane,* from Ar. *bâbkhânah,* a gateway or gatehouse.] A kind of watchtower; an advanced work defending the entrance to a castle or fortified town, as before the gate or drawbridge.

barbiturate, bär·bit′ū·rāt, *n. Chem.* a derivative of barbituric acid; any **of a group of drugs used as sedatives.—barbital,** bär′bi·tal, *n.* A drug containing barbituric acid, used as a hypnotic.—**barbituric acid,** bär·bi·tūr′ik as′id, *n.* A crystalline substance, $C_4H_4O_3N_2$, that is the basis **for many sedative and hypnotic drugs.**

barbule, bär′būl, *n.* [L. *barbula,* dim. of *barba,* a beard.] A small barb; a little beard.

barcarole, bär′ka·rōl, *n.* [Fr., from It. *barcarolo,* a boatman, from *barca,* a boat or barge.] A simple song or melody sung by Venetian gondoliers; a piece of instrumental music composed in imitation of such a song.

bard, bärd, *n.* [Celtic.] A poet and singer among the ancient Celts; a poet generally.—**bardic,** bärd′ik, *a.* Pertaining to bards or to their poetry.

bare, bâr, *a.* [A.Sax. *bær,* Icel. *ber,* Sw. Dan. *bar,* D. *bāar,* G. *bar, baar,* probably from root meaning shining seen in Skr. *bhas,* to shine.] Naked; without covering; laid open to view; detected; no longer concealed; poor; destitute; indigent; ill-supplied; empty; unfurnished; unprovided: often followed by *of* (bare *of* money); threadbare; much worn.—*v.t.*— *bared, baring.* To strip off the covering from; to make naked.—**barely,** bâr′li, *adv.* In a bare manner; nakedly; poorly; without decoration; scarcely; hardly.—**bareness,** bâr′nes, *n.* The state of being bare; want of clothing or covering; nakedness; deficiency of appropriate covering, ornament, and the like; poverty; indigence.— **barefaced,** bâr′fâst, *a.* Having the face uncovered; unreserved; shameless; impudent.—**barefoot, barefooted,** bâr′fut, bâr′fut·ed, *a.* and *adv.* Without shoes or stockings.

barege, ba·räzh′, *n.* [From *Baréges,* a village of the Pyrenees.] A thin, gauzelike fabric for ladies' dresses, usually made of silk and worsted, but, in the inferior sorts, with cotton instead of silk.

bargain, bär′gin, *n.* [O.Fr. *bargaine,* L.L. *barcania,* a bargain, traffic; believed to be from L. L. *barca,* a bark.] A contract or agreement between two or more parties; a compact settling that something shall be done, sold, transferred, etc.; the thing purchased or stipulated for; what is obtained by an agreement; something bought or sold at a low price.—*v.i.* To make a bargain or agreement; to make an agreement about the transfer of property.—*v.t.* To sell; to transfer for a consideration: generally followed by *away.*— **bargainer,** bär′gin·ėr, *n.* One who bargains or stipulates.

barge, bärj, *n.* [O.Fr. *barge,* L.L. *bargia, barga, barca,* bark. BARQUE.] A vessel or boat elegantly fitted up and decorated, used on occasions of state and pomp; a flat-bottomed vessel for loading and unloading ships or conveying goods from one place to another.—**bargee,** bär·jē′, *n.* One of the crew of a barge or canal-boat. —**bargeman,** bärj′man, *n.* The man who manages a barge.

barilla, ba·ril′la, *n.* [Sp.] An impure soda or carbonate and sulfate of soda obtained in Spain and elsewhere by burning several species of plants; a kind of kelp; Spanish soda.

baritone, bar′i·tōn, *n.* [Gr. *barys,* heavy, and *tonos,* tone.] Ranging between tenor and bass; having a voice ranging between tenor and bass.—*n.* A male voice, the compass of which partakes of the bass and the tenor, but which does not descend so low as the one nor rise as high as the other; a person with a voice of this quality; a deep brass instrument.

barium, bâr′i·um, *n.* [Gr. *barys,* heavy.] Chemical element belonging to the alkaline-earth series, a whitish malleable metal occurring in combination. Symbol, Ba; at. no., 56; at. wt., 137. 34.

bark, bärk, *n.* [Dan. and Sw. *bark,* Icel. *börkr,* G. *borke,* bark.] The outer rind of a tree, shrub, etc.; the exterior covering of exogenous plants, composed of cellular and vascular tissue.—*v.i.* To strip bark off; to peel; to apply bark to; to treat with bark in tanning.—**barker,** bärk′ėr, *n.* One who barks; one who removes the bark from trees.

bark, bärk, *n.* Same as *Barque.*

bark, bärk, *v.i.* [A.Sax. *beorcan.*] To emit the cry of a dog, or a similar sound.—*n.* The cry of the domestic dog; a cry resembling that of the dog.—**barker,** bärk′ėr, *n.* An animal that barks; a person who clamors unreasonably.

barley, bär′li, *n.* [O.E. *barlic, berlic,* from A.Sax. *bere* (= Sc. *bear*), barley, and *leac,* a plant (also a *leek*); comp. *garlic.*] A kind of grain commonly grown and used especially for making malt; the plant yielding the grain.—

barleycorn, bär′li·korn, *n.* A grain of barley; a measure equal to the third part of an inch.—John Barleycorn, a surname of malted drink.

barm, bärm, *n.* [A.Sax. *beorma*= Sw. *bärma,* Dan. *bärme,* L.G. *barme,* G. *bärme,* barm; from root of *brew.*] Yeast.—**barmy,** bärm′i, *a.* Containing or consisting of barm; frothy, as beer.

Barmecidal, bar′me·sīd·al, *a.* Disappointing, fallacious.—**Barmecide feast.** Rich apparent feast given in the *Arabian Nights,* by prince to guest, with nothing but names for the dishes.

barn, bärn, *n.* [A.Sax. *berern—bere,* barley, and *ern,* a house.] A covered building for securing grain, hay, or other farm produce.—*v.t.* To store up in a barn.

barnacle, bär′na·kl, *n.* [Fr. *bernacle, barnacle,* L.L. *bernacula,* for *pernacula,* dim. of L. *perna,* a ham, a kind of shellfish. In sense of goose origin doubtful.] A stalked cirriped, often found on the bottoms of ships, on timber fixed below the surface of the sea, etc.; a species of goose found in the northern seas, but visiting more southern climates in winter.

barnacle, bär′na·kl, *n. pl.* [Origin unknown.] An instrument to put upon a horse's nose, to confine him for shoeing, bleeding, or dressing.

barograph, bar′ō·graf, *n.* [Gr. *baros,* weight, and *graphō,* to write.] A self-registering barometric instrument for recording the variations in the pressure of the atmosphere.

barometer, ba·rom′et·ér, *n.* [Gr. *baros,* weight, and *metron,* measure.] An instrument for measuring the weight or pressure of the atmosphere, consisting ordinarily of a glass tube containing a column of mercury, its lower end dipping into a cup containing the same metal; the mercury in the tube, having a vacuum above it, rises and falls according to the varying pressure of the air on the mercury in the cup. In the aneroid barometer no fluid is used.—**barometric, barometrical,** bar·ō·met′rik, bar·ō·met′rik·al, *a.* Pertaining or relating to the barometer; made by a barometer.—**barometrically,** bar·ō·met′rik·al·li, *adv.* By means of a barometer.

baron, bar′on, *n.* [Fr. *baron,* from O.H.G. *bar,* a man, from *beran*= E. to *bear,* the original sense being probably that of one who could *bear,* as being strong and robust.] In Great Britain, a title or degree of nobility; one who holds the lowest rank in the peerage; a title of certain judges or officers; as, *barons of the exchequer,* the judges of the court of exchequer.—*Baron of beef,* two sirloins not cut asunder.—**baronage,** bar′on·āj, *n.* The whole body of barons or peers; the dignity or condition of a baron.—**baroness,** bar′on·es, *n.* A baron's wife or lady; a holder of the title in her own right.—**baronet,** bar′on·et, *n.* [Dim. of *baron.*] One who possesses a hereditary rank or degree of honor next below a baron, and therefore not a member of the peerage; one belonging to an order founded by James I in 1611.—**baronetage,** bar′on·et·āj, *n.* The baronets as a body; the dignity of a baronet.—**baronetcy,** bar′on·et·si, *n.* The title and dignity of a baronet.—**baronial,** bar·ō′ni·al, *a.* Pertaining to a baron or a barony. —**barony,** bar′on·i, *n.*

baroque, ba·rōk′, *a.* [Fr., from It. *barocco.*] Pertaining to a style of architecture, music, and literature that involves elaborate and sometimes grotesque forms; ornate.

baroscope, bar′ō·skōp, *n.* [Gr. *baros,* weight, *skopeō,* to view.] An instrument for exhibiting changes of atmospheric pressure; a kind of weatherglass.

barouche, ba·rösh′, *n.* [From G. *barutsche,* from It. *baroccio, biroccio,* from L. *birotus,* two-wheeled—*bis,* double, and *rota,* a wheel.] A four-wheeled carriage with a falling top.

barque, bärk, *n.* [Fr. *barque,* L.L. *barca,* a barque, through a dim. form *barica,* from Gr. *baris,* a skiff. *Barge* is a form of this word.] A sailing vessel of any kind; *naut.* a three-masted vessel with only fore-and-aft sails on the mizzenmast, the other two masts being square rigged.

barquentine, bärk′an·tīn, *n.* [From *barque,* in imitation of *brigantine.*] A three-masted vessel square rigged in the foremast and fore-and-aft rigged in the main and mizzenmasts.

barrack, bar′ak, *n.* [Fr. *baraque,* It. *baracca,* from L.L. *bárra,* a bar, from the Celtic; comp. Ir. *barrachad,* a hut or booth.] A hut or house for soldiers, especially in garrison; permanent buildings in which both officers and men are lodged; a large building, or a collection of huts for a body of workpeople: generally in pl.—**barracoon,** bar·a·kön′, *n.* A Negro barrack; a slave depot or bazaar.

barracuda, ba·ra·kö′da, *n.* A large voracious game fish of tropical seas related to gray mullets.

barrage, ba·räzh′, *n.* [Fr. *barre.*] Damming up; the discharge of artillery so as to keep a zone under continuous fire.

barranca, bar·rang′ka, *n.* [Sp.] A deep gully or ravine.

barrator, bar′a·tor, *n.* [O.Fr. *barateur,* a cheater, *barate,* deceit. BARTER.] One who frequently excites suits at law; an encourager of litigation; the master or one of the crew of a ship who commits any fraud in the management of the ship or cargo, by which the owner, freighters, or insurers are injured.—**barratrous,** bar′a·trus, *a.* Characterized by or tainted with barratry.—**barratrously,** bar′a·trus·li, *adv.*—**barratry,** bar′a·tri, *n.* The act or practice of a barrator; the exciting and encouraging of lawsuits and quarrels; fraud in a shipmaster to the injury of the owners, freighters, or insurers, as by running away with the ship, sinking, or deserting her.

barrel, bar′el, *n.* [O.Fr. *bareil,* Fr. *baril,* from Celt; comp. W. *baril,* Gael. *barail,* a barrel; so called because made of *bars* or staves. BAR.] A somewhat cylindrical wooden vessel made of staves and bound with hoops; a cask; anything resembling a barrel in shape; a hollow cylinder or tube (as the *barrel* of a gun).—*v.t.* —*barreled, barreling.* To put in a barrel.—**barrel organ,** *n.* An organ in which a barrel or cylinder furnished with pegs or staples, when turned round, opens a series of valves to admit a current of air to a set of pipes, or acts on wires, so as to produce a tune.

barren, bar′en, *a.* [From O.Fr. *baraigne, brehaine, brehaigne,* sterile, possibly from Armor. *brec′han,* sterile.] Incapable of producing its kind; not prolific: applied to animals and vegetables; unproductive; unfruitful; sterile: applied to land; *fig.* not producing or leading to anything (*barren* speculation, *barren* of ideas); unsuggestive; uninstructive.—*n.* A barren or unproductive tract of land. —**barrenly,** bar′en·li, *adv.* Unfruitfully.—**barrenness,** bar′en·nes, *n.* The state or quality of being barren; sterility; want of fertility, instructiveness, interest, or the like (*barrenness* of invention).

barret, bar′et, *a.* [Fr. *barrette.*] Flat cap, or biretta.

barricade, bar·i·kād′, *n.* [From Sp. *barricada,* blocking with *barricas* or casks.] A temporary fortification made of trees, earth, stones, or anything that will obstruct the progress of an enemy or serve for defense or security against his shot; a fence around or along the side of a space to be kept clear; any barrier or obstruction.—*v.t.* —*barricaded, barricading.* To stop up by a barricade; to erect a barricade across; to obstruct.

barrier, bar′i·ér, *n.* [Fr. *barrière,* a barrier, from *barre,* a bar. BAR.] A fence; a railing; any obstruction; what hinders approach, attack, or progress; what stands in the way; an obstacle; a limit or boundary of any kind; a line of separation.— *Barrier reef,* a coral reef rising from a great depth to the level of low tide, encircling an island like a barrier, or running parallel to a coast, with a navigable channel inside, as on the northeast coast of Australia.

barring, bär′ing, *part.* of verb to *bar,* used as *prep.* Excepting; leaving out of account. (Colloq.).

barrister, bar′is·tér, *n.* [From *bar.*] A counselor or advocate admitted to plead at the bar of a court of law in protection and defense of clients: a term more especially used in England and Ireland, the corresponding term in Scotland being *advocate,* in the United States *lawyer.*

barrow, bar′ō, *n.* [A.Sax. *beorg, beorh, berg,* a hill or funeral mound; Dan. Sw. G. *berg,* a hill; allied to *burgh.*] A prehistoric or at least ancient sepulchral mound formed of earth or stones, found in Britain and elsewhere, and met with in various forms: often containing remains of the dead, implements, etc.

barter, bär′tér, *v.i.* [O.Fr. *bareter,*

barater, to cheat, to barter, barat, barate, deceit, barter; origin doubtful.] To traffic or trade by exchanging one commodity for another (and not for money).—*v.t.* To give in exchange; to exchange, as one commodity for another.—*n.* The act of exchanging commodities; the thing given in exchange.—**barterer,** bär′-têr·êr, *n.* One who barters or traffics by exchanging commodities.

bartizan, bär′ti·zan, *n.* [Comp. O.Fr. bretesche, a fortification of timber; G. bret, a board.] A small turret projecting from the top part of a tower or wall, with apertures for archers to shoot through.

baryta, ba·rī′ta, *n.* [Gr. barys, heavy, barytēs, weight.] Oxide of barium, called sometimes *heavy earth,* generally found in combination with sulfuric and carbonic acids, forming sulfate and carbonate of baryta, the former of which is called *heavy spar.* Baryta is a gray powder with a sharp caustic alkaline taste.—**barytes,** ba·rī′tēz, *n.* A name of baryta or its sulfate (heavy spar).—**barytic,** ba·rī′tik, *a.* Of or containing baryta.

barytone, bar′i·tōn, *a.* [Gr. barys, heavy, and tonos, tone.] *Greek gram.* having no accent marked on the last syllable, the grave being understood.

basal metabolism, *n.* The heat produced by an organism in the resting and fasting state. It represents the minimum amount of energy needed to maintain respiration, circulation, and other vital functions.

basalt, ba·salt′, *n.* [Gr. basaltēs, of unknown origin.] A well-known igneous dark-gray or black rock, remarkable as often assuming the form of regularly prismatic columns.

bascule, bas′kūl, *n.* [Fr.] An arrangement in bridges by which one portion balances another.—*Bascule bridge,* a kind of drawbridge in which the roadway may be raised at will and kept in an upright position by means of weights or otherwise.

base, bās, *a.* [Fr. bas, low, from L.L. bassus, low, short, allied to Ir, bass, W. bas, Armor. baz, shallow.] Of little or no value; coarse in comparison (the *base* metals); worthless; fraudulently debased in value; spurious (*base* coin); of or pertaining to humble or illegitimate birth; of low station; lowly; of mean spirit; morally low; showing or proceeding from a mean spirit; deep; grave; applied to sounds.—*n. pl.* An old name for a skirt or something similar worn by knights, etc. (*Mil.*)—**basely,** bās′li, *adv.* In a base manner or condition; meanly; humbly; vilely.—**baseness,** bās′nes, *n.* The state or quality of being base; meanness; lowness; vileness; worthlessness.—**baseborn,** *a.* Born in a base condition; of illegitimate birth.

base, bās, *n.* [Fr. base, L. basis, a base, a pedestal, from Gr. basis, a going, a foot, a base, from bainō, to go.] The bottom of anything, considered as its support, or the part of a thing on which it stands or rests; the opposite extremity to the apex; *arch.* the part between the bottom of a column and the pedestal or the floor; *chem.* one of those compound substances which unite with acids to form salts; *dyeing,* a mordant; *geom.* the line or surface forming that part of a figure on which it is supposed to stand; *mus.* the bass; *milit.* a tract of country protected by fortifications, or strong by natural advantages, from which the operations of an army proceed; the place from which racers or tilters start; a starting post; the game of baseball or prisoner's base, or an old game somewhat similar.—*v.t.*—based, basing. To lay the base or foundation of; to place on a basis; to found.—**basal, basilar basilary,** bās′al, bas′il·êr, bas·il·a·ri, *a.* Of or pertaining to a base; situated at the base.—**baseless,** bās′les, *a.* Without a base; without grounds or foundation (a *baseless* rumor).—**basement,** bās′ment, *n.* Arch. the lowest story of a building, whether above or below the ground.—**basic,** bās′ik, *a.* Relating to a base; *chem.* performing the place of a base in a salt, or having the base in excess.—**basic slag,** *n.* The slag or refuse matter got in making basic steel, a valuable fertilizer from the phosphate of lime it contains.—**basicity,** bās·is′·iti, *n.* Chem. the state of being a base; the power of an acid to unite with one or more atoms of a base.

baseball, *n.* The national American game or sport played with bat and ball, four bases indicating the points of the diamond marking the course each player takes in making a run (scoring), played by two teams of nine players each, one team being at bat while the other is in the field alternately; a horsehide-covered ball used in the game of baseball.

bash, bash, *v.t.* [Scand., Dan. bask, a slap, baske, to slap; akin to box, to fight.] To beat violently; to knock out of shape. (Colloq.)

bashaw, ba·shä′, *n.* [Per. bâshâ, pâshâh.] A pasha.

bashful, bash′ful, *a.* [For abashful.] Easily put to confusion; modest to excess; diffident; shy.—**bashfully,** bash′ful·li, *adv.*—**bashfulness,** bash′-ful·nes, *n.*

bashi-bazouk, bash′ē·ba·zök″, *n.* [Turk.] A kind of irregular soldier in the Turkish army, a member of a corps collected hastily in a time of emergency.

Basic English, *n.* A simplified system of English consisting of 850 essential words.

basic, basicity. See BASE.

basidium, ba·sid′i·um, *n. pl.* **basidia,** ba·sid′i·a. [Gr. basis, a base, and eidos, likeness.] Bot. the cell to which the spores of some fungi are attached.

basil, baz′il, *n.* [Shortened from O.Fr. basilic, from Gr. basilikos, royal, basileus, a king.] A plant, a native of India, cultivated in Europe as an aromatic potherb, and used for flavoring dishes.

basilar. See BASE, *n.*

basilica, ba·sil′ik·a, *n.* [L., from Gr. basilikē, a colonnade; lit. a royal colonnade or porch, from basileus, a king.] Originally, the name applied by the Romans to their public halls: usually of rectangular form, with a middle and two side aisles and an apse at the end. The ground plan of these was followed in the early Christian churches, and the name is now applied to some of the churches in Rome by way of distinction, or to other churches built in imitation of the Roman basilicas.—**basilican,** ba·sil′ik·an, *a.* In the manner of or pertaining to a basilica.

basilisk, bas′il·isk, *n.* [Gr. basiliskos, lit. little king, from basileus, king.] A fabulous creature formerly believed in, and variously regarded as a kind of serpent, lizard, or dragon, and sometimes identified with the cockatrice; a name of several reptiles of the lizard tribe with a crest or hood; a large piece of ordnance formerly used.

basin, bā′sn, *n.* [Fr. bassin, O.Fr. bacin, a dim. of bac, a wide open vessel, same as E. back, a brewer's vat. BACK.] A vessel or dish of some size, usually circular, rather broad and not very deep, used to hold water for washing, and for various other purposes; any reservoir for water, natural or artificial; the whole tract of country drained by a river and its tributaries; *geol.* an aggregate of strata dipping toward a common axis or center; strata or deposits lying in a depression in older rocks.

basis, bās′is, *n. pl.* **bases,** bās′ēz. [L. and Gr. basis, the foundation. BASE.] A base; a foundation or part on which something rests; *fig.* grounds or foundation. BASE.

bask, bask, *v.i.* [Formerly to bathe, a word of Scandinavian origin—Icel. batha sik, to bathe one's self—sik being the reflexive pronoun. Busk is a similar form.] To lie in warmth; to be exposed to genial heat; *fig.* to be at ease and thriving under benign influences.—*v.t.* To warm by continued exposure to heat; to warm with genial heat.

basket, bas′ket, *n.* [Possibly of Celtic origin; comp. W. basged or basgawd, Ir. bascaid, a basket; W. basg, a netting or piece of wickerwork.] A vessel made of twigs, rushes, thin strips of wood, or other flexible materials interwoven; as much as a basket will hold.—*v.t.* To put in a basket.

basketball, bas′ketbạl, *n.* A game played by teams of five, using basket-like nets as goals.

Basque, bask, *n.* A language of unknown affinities spoken in parts of France and Spain on both sides of the Pyrenees at the angle of the Bay of Biscay, supposed to represent the tongue of the ancient Iberians, the primitive inhabitants of Spain; Biscayan or Euskarian.—*a.* Pertaining to the people or language of Biscay.

bas-relief, basso-rilievo, bas′ or bä′rē·lēf, bäs′sō·rē·lyä′vō, *n.* [Fr. bas, It. basso, low, and relief, It. rilievo, relief.] A sculpture in low relief; a mode of sculpturing figures on a flat surface, the figures being raised above the surface, but not so much as in high relief or *alto-rilievo*.

bass, bas, *n.* [A corruption of *barse*, A.Sax. *bærs*, G. *bars*, D. *baars*, a perch.] The name of various British and American sea fishes allied to the perch, some of them of considerable size and used as food.

bass, bas, *n.* [Same as *bast*, the *t* being dropped or changed to *s*. BAST.] The American linden or lime tree; a mat made of bast; a hassock.—**basswood** *n.* The American lime tree or its timber.

bass, bās, *n.* [It. *basso*, deep, low. BASE, *a.*] *Mus.* the lowest part in the harmony of a musical composition, whether vocal or instrumental; the lowest male voice.—*a. Mus.* low; deep; grave.—**bass clef,** *n.* The character shaped like an inverted C put at the beginning of the bass staff. —**bass drum,** *n.* A large drum having two heads and producing a deep sound when struck.—**bass horn,** *n.* A tuba.

basset, bas´set or bas·set´, *n.* [Fr. *bassette;* It. *bassetta*.] An old game at cards, resembling modern faro.

basset, bas´set, *n.* A miner's term for the outcrop or surface edge of any inclined stratum.—*v.i. Mining,* to incline upward, so as to appear at the surface; to crop out.

basset, bas´set, *n.* [Fr. *basset*, diminutive of *bas*, low.] A dog with short crooked legs and a long body, used for hunting; also *basset hound.*

basset horn, bas´set·horn, *n.* [It. *bassetto*, somewhat low, and E. *horn*.] A musical instrument, a sort of clarinet of enlarged dimensions and extended compass.

bassinet, bas´i·net, *n.* [Probably a dim. from Fr. *berceau*, a cradle.] A wicker basket with a covering or hood over one end, in which young children are placed by way of cradle.

bassoon, bas·sön´, *n.* [Fr. *basson;* It. *bassone*, aug. of *basso*, low.] A musical wind instrument of the reed order, blown with a bent metal mouthpiece.

bast, bast, *n.* [A.Sax. *bæst*=Icel. Sw. D. Dan. and G. *bast*, bark, perhaps from root of *bind*.] The inner bark of exogenous trees, especially of the lime, consisting of several layers of fibers; rope or matting made of this.

bastard, bas´tėrd, *n.* [O.Fr. *bastard*, from *bast* (Fr. *bât*), a packsaddle, with the common termination *-ard* added to it, referring to the old locution *fils de bast*, son of a packsaddle, the old saddles being often used by way of beds or to serve as pillows.] A natural child; a child begotten and born out of wedlock; an illegitimate or spurious child; what is spurious or inferior in quality; a kind of impure, soft, brown sugar; a kind of sweet, heady Spanish wine (*Shak.*).—*a.* Begotten and born out of lawful matrimony; illegitimate; spurious; not genuine; false; adulterate; impure; not of the first or usual order or character.— **bastardize,** bas´tėrd·īz, *v. t.*—*bastardized, bastardizing.* To make or prove to be a bastard.—**bastardly,** bas´-tėrd·li, *a.* Bastard; spurious.—**bas-**

tardy, bas´tėrd·i, *n.* The state of being a bastard, or begotten and born out of lawful wedlock.—**bastard wing,** *n.* A group of stiff feathers attached to the bone of a bird's wing that represents the thumb.

baste, bāst, *v.t.*—*basted, basting.* [Allied to Icel. *beysta*, to strike, to beat, Dan. *böste*, to beat. As term in cookery the origin may be different.] To beat with a stick; to cudgel; to give a beating to; to drip butter or fat upon meat in roasting it.

baste, bāst, *v.t.* [O.Fr. *bastir*, lit. to sew with *bast*, the fibers of bast having been used as thread. BAST.] To sew with long stitches, and usually to keep parts together temporarily; to sew slightly.—**basting,** bāst´ing, *n.* The long stitches by which pieces of garments are loosely attached to each other.

bastille, bastile, bas·tēl´ *n.* [Fr. *bastille*, a fortress, O.Fr. *bastir*, to build.] A tower or fortification.—*The Bastille,* an old castle in Paris used as a state prison, demolished by the enraged populace in 1789.

bastinado, bas·ti·nā´dō, *n.* [Sp. *bastonada*, from *baston*, a stick, a baton.] A sound beating with a stick or cudgel; a mode of punishment in oriental countries, especially Mohammedan, by beating the soles of the feet with a rod.—*v.t.* To beat with a stick or cudgel; to beat on the soles of the feet, as a judicial punishment.

bastion, bas´ti·on, *n.* [Fr. and Sp. *bastion,* from O.Fr. and Sp. *bastir,* Fr. *bâtir,* to build.] *Fort.* a huge mass of earth, faced with sods, brick, or stones, standing out with an angular form from the rampart at the angles of a fortification.— **bastioned,** bas´ti·ond, *a.* Provided with bastions.

bat, bat, *n.* [A Celtic word: Ir. and Armor. *bat,* a stick.] A heavy stick or club; a piece of wood used in driving the ball in baseball and similar games; a turn at batting; a piece of a brick; a brickbat.— *v.t.* and *i.*—*batted, batting.*—**batsman, batter,** bats´man, bat´ėr, *n.*

bat, bat, *n.* [Corruption of O.E. *back, bak;* Sc. *bak, bakie-bird,* a bat. Dan. *bakke* (in *aften-bakke,* a bat, lit. evening-bird), the word having lost an *l,* seen in Icel. *lethrblaka,* 'leather-flapper', a bat, from *blaka,* to flutter.] One of a group of mammals possessing a pair of leathery wings which extend between the fore and the posterior limbs, the former being specially modified for flying, the bones of the forefeet being extremely elongated.—**batty,** bat´i, *a.* Pertaining to or resembling a bat. (*Shak.*)— **batfowling,** *n.* A mode of catching birds at night by means of a light and nets; the birds being roused fly toward the light and are entangled in the nets.

batch, bach, *n.* [From the verb to *bake.*] The quantity of bread baked at one time; any quantity of a thing made at once; a number of individuals or articles similar to each other.

bate, bāt, *v.t.*—*bated, bating.* [Abbrev. of *abate.*] To abate, lessen, or reduce; to leave out; to take away; to weaken, dull, or blunt (*Shak.*).‡ To grow or become less; to lessen.— **bating,** bāt´ing, *ppr.* used as *prep.* Abating; taking away; deducting; excepting.

bateau, bä·tō´, *n.* [Fr.] A light broad and flat boat used in Canada; also the pontoon of a floating bridge.

bath, bäth, *n.* [A.Sax. *bœth,* a bath= Icel. *bath,* Dan. D. G. *bad.*] From root of *bake; bask* is akin.] The immersion of the body or a part of it in water or other fluid or medium; an apparatus or contrivance for exposing the surface of the body to water or other diffusible body (as oil, medicated fluids, steam, etc.); a building in which people may bathe; an apparatus for regulating the heat in chemical processes, by interposing a quantity of sand, water, etc., between the fire and the vessel to be heated.—*Knights of the Bath,* a British order established in 1725 by George I, patterned after a legendary order connected with the coronation of Henry IV in 1399. Candidates were put into a bath the preceding evening, to denote a purification or absolution from evil deeds.—**bathe,** bāTH, *v.t.*— *bathed, bathing.* [A.Sax. *bathian,* from *bœth.* a bath=Icel. *batha.* Dan. *bade.* D. and G. *baden.* BATH.] To subject to a bath; to immerse in water for pleasure, health, or cleanliness; to wash, moisten, or suffuse with any liquid; to immerse in or surround with anything analogous to water.— *v.i.* To take a bath; to be or lie in a bath; to be in water or in other liquid; to be immersed or surrounded as if with water.—**bather,** bāTH´ėr, *n.* One who bathes.—**bathroom,** *n.* A room for bathing in.

bath, bäth, *n.* [Heb.] A Hebrew liquid measure, the tenth part of a homer.

Bath brick, bäth´brik, *n.* [From the town of *Bath,* in Somersetshire.] A preparation of siliceous earth in the form of a brick, used for cleaning knives, etc.—**bath chair,** *n.* A small carriage capable of being pushed along by an attendant; used by invalids.

bathometer, ba·thom´e·tėr, *n.* [Gr. *bathos,* depth, and *metron,* a measure.] An apparatus for taking soundings, especially one in which a sounding line is dispensed with.

bathos, bā´thos, *n.* [Gr. *bathos,* from *bathys,* deep.] A ludicrous descent from the elevated to the mean in writing or speech.

bathyscaph, bath´i·skaf, *n.* [Gr.— *bathys,* deep, and *skaphe,* light boat.] A deep-sea craft that uses gasoline and lead pellets for ballast control.

bathysphere, bath´i·sfēr, *n.* A diving sphere for deep-sea observation and study developed by William Beebe.

bating. See BATE.

batiste, ba·tēst´, *n.* [Fr. *batiste,* from its inventor *Baptiste.*] A fine linen cloth made in Flanders and Picardy, a kind of cambric.

batman, ba´man, *n.* [Fr. *bât,* a packsaddle.] In the British army a person having charge of the cooking utensils of each company of a regiment of soldiers on foreign service, and of the horse (bat horse) that carries them.—**bat money,** bạ'mun·i, *n.* Money paid to a batman.

baton, ba·ton', *n.* [Fr. *bâton*, O.Fr. *baston;* akin *baste*, to beat.] A staff or club; a truncheon, the official badge of various officials of widely different rank; the stick with which a conductor of music beats time.

batrachian, ba·trā'ki·an, *a.* [Gr. *batracheios*, of a frog.] Relating to or pertaining to a frog.—*n.* A frog, toad, or other froglike animal.

battalion, bat·tal'yon, *n.* [Fr. *bataillon*, It. *battaglione*, aug. of *battaglia*, a battle or body of soldiers. BATTLE.] A body of infantry usually forming part of a regiment.

batten, bat'n, *v.t.* [Icel. *batna*, to grow better, from root *bat*, *bet* in *better*.] To fatten; to make fat; to make plump by plenteous feeding.—*v.i.* To grow or become fat; to feed greedily; to gorge.

batten, bat'n, *n.* [Fr. *bâton*, a stick.] A long piece of wood from 1 inch to 7 inches broad, and from ½ in. to 2½ in. thick; a plank; *naut.* one of the slips of wood used to keep a tarpaulin close over a hatchway; *weav.* a lathe.—*v.t.* To fasten with battens (to *batten* down the hatches).

batter, bat'ėr, *v.t.* [Fr. *battre*, It. *battere*, from L.L. *batere*, a form of L. *batuere*, to beat, whence also *battle*.] To beat with successive blows; to beat with violence, so as to bruise or dent; to assail by a battering-ram or ordnance; to wear or impair, as by beating, long service, or the like (usually in pp.).—*v.i.* To make attacks, as by a battering-ram or ordnance.—**batter,** bat'ėr, *n.* A mixture of several ingredients, as flour, eggs, etc., beaten together with some liquor into a paste, and used in cookery.—**battering-ram,** *n.* An engine formerly used to beat down the walls of besieged places, consisting of a large beam, with a head of iron somewhat resembling the head of a ram, whence its name.—**battery,** bat'ėr·i, *n.* [Fr. *batterie*.] The act of battering‡; a small body of cannon for field operations, with complement of wagons, artillerymen, etc.; a parapet thrown up to cover a gun or guns and the men employed in loading, etc.; a number of guns placed near each other and intended to act in concert; *elect.* an apparatus for originating an electric current; a series of connected Leyden jars that may be discharged together; *law*, the unlawful beating of a person.

battle, bat'l, *n.* [Fr. *bataille*, from L.L. *batalia*, *batualia*, a fight; from L. *batuere*, to beat, to fence. BATTER.] A fight or encounter between enemies or opposing armies; an engagement; more especially a general engagement between large bodies of troops; a combat, conflict, or struggle; a division of an army‡.—*To give battle*, to attack; *to join battle*, to meet in hostile encounter. ∴ *Battle* is the appropriate word for great engage-ments. *Fight* has reference to actual conflict; a man may take part in a *battle*, and have no share in the *fighting. Combat* is a word of greater dignity than *fight*, but agrees with it in denoting close encounter.—*v.i.* —*battled, battling.* To join in battle; to contend; to struggle; to strive or exert one's self.—**battle-ax,** *n.* An ax anciently used as a weapon of war.—**battlefield,** *n.* The field or scene of a battle.—**battlement,** bat'l·ment, *n.* [Perhaps from O.Fr. *bastille*, a fortress, *bastiller*, to fortify, to embattle modified by the influence of E. *battle*.] A notched or indented parapet, originally constructed for defenses, afterward for ornament, formed by a series of rising parts called cops or merlons, separated by openings called crenelles or embrasures, the latter intended to be fired through.

battledore, bat'l·dōr, *n.* [From Sp. *batidor*, a beater, from *batir*, to beat.] An instrument with a handle and a flat board or palm, used to strike a ball or shuttlecock; a racket.

battue, bat·tü', *n.* [Fr., from *battre*, to beat.] A kind of sport in which the game is driven by a body of beaters from under cover into a limited area where the animals may be easily shot.

bauble, ba'bl, *n.* [O.Fr. *babole*, a toy or baby-thing; from same Celtic root as *babe*.] A short stick with a fool's head, anciently carried by the fools attached to great houses; a trifling piece of finery; something showy without real value; a gewgaw; a trifle.

baulk, bạk. Same as *Balk.*

bauxite, bạx'īt, *n.* [From Fr. *Baux*, near Arles, France.] A clay mineral from which aluminum is derived.

bawd, bạd, *n.* [O.Fr. *baud*, bold, wanton, from G. *bald*=E. *bold*.] A person who keeps a house of prostitution or acts as a go-between in illicit amours.—**bawdy,** bạ'di, *a.* Obscene; lewd; indecent; smutty; unchaste. Hence **bawdily, bawdiness.**

bawl, bạl, *v.i.* A word imitative of sound; akin, *bell*, *bellow*; L. *balo*, to bleat.] To cry out with a loud full sound; to make vehement or clamorous outcries; to shout.—*v.t.* To proclaim by outcry; to shout out. —*n.* A vehement cry or clamor.— **bawler,** bạl'ėr, *n.* One who bawls.

bay, bā, *n.* [Fr. *baie*, L.L. *baia*, a bay; of doubtful origin.] A rather wide recess in the shore of a sea or lake; the expanse of water between two capes or headlands; a gulf; any recess resembling a bay.—**bay rum,** bā·rum', *n.* A spirituous liquor containing the oil of the bayberry of Jamaica, a species of pimento, and used for the hair.—**baywood,** *n.* A variety of mahogany exported from Honduras, or the Bay of Honduras.

bay, bā, *n.* [Fr. *baie*, L. *bacca*, a berry.] The laurel tree, noble laurel, or sweet bay; a garland or crown bestowed as a prize for victory or excellence, consisting of branches of the laurel; hence, fame or renown; laurels: in this sense chiefly in plural.

bay, bā, *n.* [O.Fr. *abai*, *abbai*, a barking, *abbayer*, to bark; Mod. Fr. *aboi*, a barking, *aux abois*, at bay; comp. Fr. *bayer*, to gape, or stand gaping. ABASH.] The bark of a dog; especially, a deep-toned bark.—*At bay*, so hard pressed by enemies as to be compelled to turn round and face them from impossibility of escape.—*v.i.* To bark; to bark with a deep sound. —*v.t.* To bark at; to follow with barking (*Shak.*); to express by barking.

bay, bā, *n.* [Fr. *bai*, L. *badius*, brown or chestnut colored; akin *baize*.] Red or reddish, inclining to a chestnut color.—**Bayard,** bā'yard, *n.* A brave man, from the Chevalier Bayard; [*not cap.*] a horse, from *Bayard*, the horse given by Charlemagne to Renaud.

bayadere, bā·ya·dēr', *n.* [Pg. *bailadeira*, from *bailar*, to dance.] In the East Indies, a professional dancing girl.

bayberry, bā'be·ri, *n.* The fruit of the bay tree; also the wax myrtle and its fruit.

bayonet, bā'on·et, *n.* [O.Fr. *bayonnette*, Fr. *baïonnette*, usually derived from *Bayonne* in France, because bayonets are said to have been first made there.] A short triangular sword or dagger, made so that it may be fixed upon the muzzle of a rifle or musket.—*v.t.* To stab with a bayonet; to compel or drive by the bayonet.

bayou, bī'ō, *n.* [Fr. *boyau*, a gut, a long narrow passage.] A channel proceeding from a lake or a river.

bazaar, bazar, ba·zär', *n.* [Per. *bâzâr.*] In the East, a place where goods are exposed for sale, usually consisting of small shops or stalls in a narrow street or series of streets; a series of connected shops or stalls in a European town; a sale of miscellaneous articles in furtherance of some charitable or other purpose; a fancy fair.

bazooka, ba·zö'ka, *n.* [From *bazooka*, a musical instrument.] An antitank rocket weapon; a rocket launcher.

bdellium, del'li·um, *n.* [L. *bdellium*, Gr. *bdellion*, from Heb.] An aromatic gum resin brought chiefly from Africa and India, in pieces of different sizes and figures, used as a perfume and a medicine, externally of a dark reddish brown, internally clear, and not unlike glue.

be, bē, *v.i. substantive verb*, pres. *am, art, is, are;* pret. *was, wast* or *wert, were;* subj. pres. *be;* pret. *were;* imper. *be;* pp. *been;* ppr. *being.* [One of the three verbal roots required in the conjugation of the substantive verb, the others being *am* and *was*. A.Sax. *beó*, I am, *beón* to be; G. *bin*, I am; allied to L. *fui*, I was, Skr. *bhû*, to be. It is now chiefly used in the subjunctive, imperative, infinitive, and participles, being seldom used in the present tense. AM and WAS.] To have a real state or existence; to exist in the world of fact, whether physical or mental; to exist in or have a certain state or quality; to become; to remain. ∴ The most common use of the verb *to be* is to assert connection between a subject and a predicate, forming what is called the copula; as, he *is* good; John *was* at home; or to form the compound tenses of other verbs.—**being,** bē′ing, *n.* Existence, whether real or only in the mind; that which has life; a living existence; a creature.

beach, bēch, *n.* [Origin doubtful; comp. Icel. *bakki,* Sw. *backe,* Dan. *bakke,* a bank, the shore; or from old *bealch,* to belch, alluding to the washing up of pebbles, etc.] That part of the shore of a sea or lake which is washed by the tide and waves; the strand.—*Raised beaches,* in *geol.* a term applied to those long terraced level pieces of land, consisting of sand and gravel, and containing marine shells, now, it may be, a considerable distance above and away from the sea.—*v.t.* To run (a vessel) on a beach.—**beachcomber,** bēch′kōm·ėr, *n.* A long rolling wave breaking on the beach; a seashore idler or vacationist.—**beachhead,** bēch′hed, *n.* A foothold on enemy shore from which further attacks can be made.

beacon, bē·kn, *n.* [A.Sax. *bécn, beácen,* a beacon; hence *beck, beckon.*] An object visible to some distance, and serving to denote the presence of danger, as a light or signal shown to signify the approach of an enemy, or to warn seamen of the presence of rocks, shoals, etc.; hence, anything used for a kindred purpose. A revolving light supported by a structure for the guidance of aviators.—*v.t.* To light up by a beacon; to illuminate; to signal.

bead, bēd, *n.* [A.Sax. *bed, bead,* a prayer, from *biddan,* to pray. From beads being used to count prayers (as in the rosary), the word which originally meant prayer came to mean what counted the prayers. BID.] A little perforated ball of gold, amber, glass, etc., strung with others on a thread, and often worn round the neck as an ornament, or used to form a rosary; any small globular body, as a drop of liquid and the like; *arch.* and *joinery,* a small round molding sometimes cut so as to resemble a series of beads or pearls; an astragal. —*v.t.* To mark or ornament with beads.—**beady,** bēd′i, *a.* Consisting of or containing beads; beadlike.— **bead roll,** *n.* A list of persons for the repose of whose souls a certain number of prayers is to be said; hence, any list or catalogue.—**beads man,** *n.* A man employed in praying, generally in praying for another; one privileged to claim certain alms or charities.—**beads woman,** *n.* The feminine equivalent of *beads man.*

beadle, bē′dl, *n.* [A.Sax. *bydel,* a herald, a beadle, from *beódan,* to bid. BID.] A messenger or crier of a court; a parish officer whose business is to punish petty offenders; a church officer with various subordinate duties.

beagle, bē′gl, *n.* [Comp. Ir. and Gael. *beag,* little.] A small smooth-haired, hanging-eared hound, for-

merly kept to hunt hares.

beak, bēk, *n.* [Fr. *bec,* from the Celtic—Armor. *bek, beg,* Ir. and Gael. *bec,* a beak.] The bill or neb of a bird; anything in some way resembling a bird's bill; the bill-like mouth of some fishes, reptiles, etc.; a pointed piece of wood fortified with brass, fastened to the prow of ancient galleys, and intended to pierce the vessels of an enemy; a similar, but infinitely more powerful appendage of iron or steel in modern warships; a magistrate. (Colloq.)— **beaked,** bēkt, *a.* Having a beak or something resembling a beak; beak shaped; rostrate.

beaker, bēk′ėr, *n.* [Icel. *bikarr,* D. *beker,* G. *becher,* from L.L. *bicarium,* a cup, from Gr. *bikos,* a wine-jar.] A large drinking cup or glass.

beam, bēm, *n.* [A.Sax. *beam,* a beam, a post, a tree, a ray of light; D. *boom,* G. *baum,* a tree.] A long straight and strong piece of wood or iron, especially when holding an important place in some structure, and serving for support or consolidation; a horizontal piece of timber in a structure; the part of a balance from the ends of which the scales are suspended; the pole of a carriage which runs between the horses; a cylindrical piece of wood, making part of a loom, on which the warp is wound before weaving; one of the strong timbers stretching across a ship from one side to the other to support the decks and retain the sides at their proper distance; the oscillating lever of a steam engine forming the communication between the piston rod and the crankshaft; a ray of light, or more strictly a collection of parallel rays emitted from the sun or other body; a constant unidirectional radio signal to guide airplane pilots.—*v.i.* To emit rays of light or beams; to give out radiance; to shine.—**beamy,** bēm′i, *a.* Like a beam; heavy or massive; emitting beams or rays of light: radiant.

bean, bēn, *n.* [A.Sax. *beán*=Icel. *baun,* Sw. *bōna,* Dan. *bonne,* D. *boon,* G. *bohne.*] A name given to several kinds of valuable leguminous seeds contained in a bivalve pod, and to the plants producing them, as the common bean, cultivated both in fields and gardens for man and beast, the French bean, the kidney bean, etc.—**bean caper,** *n.* A small tree growing in warm climates, the flowerbuds of which are used as capers.

bear, bâr, *v.t.* pret. *bore* (formerly *bare*); pp. *borne*; ppr. *bearing.* [A.Sax. *beran*=Icel. *bera,* Dan. *bære,* to bear, to carry, to bring forth; D. *baren,* G. *(ge)bären,* to bring forth; cog. L. *ferre,* Gr. *pherein,* Skr. *bhri,* to bear, to support. Akin are *birth, burden, bairn, barrow.*] To support, hold up, or sustain, as a weight; to suffer, endure, undergo, or tolerate, as pain, loss, blame, etc.; to carry or convey; to have, possess, have on, or contain; to bring forth or produce, as the fruit of plants or the young of animals. [*Born* is the passive parti-

ciple in the sense of brought forth by a female, as the child was *born*; but we say actively, she has *borne* a child. *Born* is also used attributively, *borne* not.]—*To bear down,* to overcome by force.—*To bear out,* to give support or countenance to (a person or thing); to uphold, corroborate, establish, justify.—*To bear up,* to support; to keep from sinking. —*To bear a hand,* to lend aid; to give assistance.—*To bear in mind,* to remember.—*v.i.* To suffer, as with pain, to be patient; to endure; to produce (fruit); to be fruitful; to lean, weigh, or rest burdensomely; to tend; to be directed or move in a certain way (to *bear* back, to *bear* out to sea, to *bear* down upon the enemy); to relate; to refer: with *upon;* to be situated as to some point of the compass, with respect to something else.—*To bear up,* to have fortitude; to be firm; not to sink.— *To bear with,* to tolerate; to be indulgent; to forbear to resent, oppose, or punish.—**bearable,** bâr′a·bl, *a.* Capable of being borne, endured, or tolerated.—**bearably,** bâr′a·bli, *adv.* In a bearable manner.— **bearer,** bâr′ėr, *n.* One who or that which bears, sustains, supports, carries, conveys, etc.—**bearing,** bâr′ing, *n.* The act of one who bears; manner in which a person comports himself; carriage, mien, or behavior; import, effect, or force (of words); that part of a shaft or axle which is in connection with its support; the direction or point of the compass in which an object is seen; relative position or direction; a figure on a heraldic shield.—**bearing rein,** *n.* The rein by which the head of a horse is held up in driving.

bear, bâr, *n.* [A.Sax. *bera,* a bear=D. *beer,* G. *bär,* Icel. *bera.*] A name common to various quadrupeds of the carnivorous order and of the plantigrade group, having shaggy hair and a very short tail, the most notable being the brown or black bear of Europe, the grizzly bear of the Rocky Mountains, the white or Polar bear, etc.; the name of two constellations in the northern hemisphere, called the Greater and Lesser Bear; *fig.* a rude or uncouth man; in stock-exchange slang, a person who does all he can to bring down the price of stock in order that he may buy cheap: opposed to a *bull,* who tries to raise the price that he may sell dear.—**bearish,** bâr′ish, *a.* Resembling a bear; rude; violent in conduct; surly.—**bearbaiting,** *n.* The sport of baiting bears with dogs.— **bear garden,** *n.* A place in which bears are kept for sport, as bearbaiting, etc.; *fig.* a place of disorder or tumult.—**bearberry,** bâr′ber·i, *n.* An evergreen shrub of the heath family, growing on barren moors in the colder parts of the northern hemisphere, the leaves being used as an astringent and tonic under the name *uva-ursi.*—**bear's-ear,** *n.* A species of primrose, so called from the shape of the leaf.—**bear's-foot,** *n.* A herbaceous plant of the hellebore

fāte, fär, fâre, fat, fall; mē, met, hėr; pīne, pin; nōte, not, mȯve; tūbe, tub, bu̞ll; oil, pound.

genus, having a rank smell and purgative and emetic properties.

bear, bēr, *n.* Same as *Bere.*

beard, bērd, *n.* [A.Sax. *beard,* a beard = D. *baard,* G. *bart;* L. *barba,* W. and Armor. *barf*—beard.] The hair that grows on the chin, lips, and adjacent parts of the face of male adults; anything resembling this; a hairy, bristly, or threadlike appendage of various kinds, such as the filaments by which some shellfish attach themselves to foreign bodies, etc.; the awn on the ears of grain; a barb, as of an arrow.—*v.t.* To take by the beard; to oppose to the face; to set at defiance.—**bearded,** bērd′ed, *a.* Having a beard in any of the senses of that word.—**beardless,** bērd′les, *a.* Without a beard; hence, of persons of the male sex, young; not having arrived at manhood.

beast, bēst, *n.* [O.Fr. *beste,* from L. *bestia,* a beast.] Any four-footed animal, as distinguished from birds, insects, fishes, and man; as opposed to *man,* any irrational animal; a brutal man; a disgusting person.—**beastliness,** bēst′li·nes, *n.* The state or quality of being beastly; brutality; filthiness.—**beastly,** bēst′li, *a.* Like a beast; brutish; brutal; filthy; contrary to the nature and dignity of man.

beat, bēt, *v.t.* pret. *beat;* pp. *beat, beaten;* ppr. *beating.* [A.Sax. *beatan* = Icel. *bauta, bjáta,* O.H.G. *pózan,* to beat; akin *butt, abut, beetle* (a mallet).] To strike repeatedly; to lay repeated blows upon; to knock, rap, or dash against often; to pound; to strike for the purpose of producing sound (a drum); to shape by hammer; to scour with bustle and outcry in order to raise game; to overcome, vanquish, or conquer in a battle, contest, competition, etc.; to surpass or excel; to be too difficult for; to be beyond the power or skill of; to baffle; to fatigue utterly; to prostrate; to flutter (the wings).—*To beat back,* to compel to retire or return.—*To beat down,* to dash down by beating or battering, as a wall; to lay flat; to cause to lower a price by importunity or argument; to lessen the price or value of; to depress or crush.—*To beat off,* to repel or drive back.—*To beat out,* to extend by hammering.—*To beat up,* to attack suddenly; to alarm or disturb, as an enemy's quarters.—*To beat time,* to regulate time in music by the motion of the hand or foot.—*To beat a retreat,* to give a signal to retreat by a drum; hence, generally, to retreat or retire.—*v.i.* To strike or knock repeatedly; to move with pulsation; to throb (as the pulse, heart, etc.); to dash or fall with force or violence (as a storm, flood, etc.); to summon or signal by beating a drum; *naut.* to make progress against the direction of the wind by sailing in a zigzag.—*To beat about,* to make search by various means or ways.—*To beat up for* (recruits); to search earnestly or carefully for.—*n.* A stroke; a blow; a pulsation; a throb; a footfall; a round or course which is frequently gone over, as by a policeman, etc.; *music,* the beating or pulsation resulting from the joint vibrations of two sounds of the same strength, and all but in unison.—**beaten,** bēt′n, *p.* and *a.* Made smooth by beating or treading; worn by use; conquered; vanquished; exhausted; baffled. [*Beat* is so far synonymous with *beaten,* but is less of an adjective, not being used attributively as the latter is; thus we do not say *beat* gold.]—**beater,** bēt′ėr, *n.* One who or that which beats; an instrument for pounding or comminuting substances; the striking part in various machines.

beatify, bē·at′i·fī, *v.t.*—*beatified, beatifying.* [Fr. *beatifier,* L. *beatificare*—*beatus,* blessed, and *facere,* to make.] To make happy; to bless with the completion of celestial enjoyment; *R. Cath. Ch.* to declare that a person is to be reverenced as blessed, though not canonized.—**beatific,** bē·a·tif′ik, *a.* Blessing of making happy; imparting bliss.—**beatification,** bē·at′i·fi·kā″shon, *n.* The act of beatifying; the state of being blessed; blessedness; *R. Cath. Ch.* an act of the pope by which he declares a person beatified; an inferior kind of canonization.—**beatitude,** bē·at′i·tūd, *n.* [L. *beatitudo.*] Blessedness; felicity; one of the declarations of blessedness to particular virtues, made by the Saviour in the Sermon on the Mount.

beatnik, bēt′nik, *n.* [Beat, and *nik,* Rus. suffix meaning person.] A person (often) characterized by unconventional behavior and dress and by an emotional disengagement from society.

beau, bō, *n.* pl. **beaux,** bōz. [Fr. *beau,* O.Fr. *bel,* from L. *bellus,* beautiful.] One whose great care is to deck his person according to the first fashion of the times; male sweetheart or lover.—**beau ideal,** bō ī·dē′al or ē·dā′al, *n.* [Fr. *beau idéal,* beautiful ideal.] A conception of any object in its perfect typical form; a model of excellence in the mind or fancy.—**beau monde,** bō″ mond′, *n.* [Fr. *beau,* fine, and *monde,* world.] The fashionable world.

beauty, bū′ti, *n.* [O.Fr. *biaute,* Fr. *beauté,* beauty, from L.L. *bellitas, bellitatis,* beauty, from L. *bellus,* beautiful.] An assemblage of perfections through which an object is rendered pleasing to the eye; those qualities in the aggregate that give pleasure to the aesthetic sense; qualities that delight the eye, the ear, or the mind; loveliness; elegance; grace; a particular grace or ornament; that which is beautiful; a part which surpasses in beauty that with which it is united; a beautiful person, especially, a beautiful woman.—**beauty shop,** an establishment where a woman may receive a hairdress, manicure, and other beauty treatments.—**beauteous,** bū′tē·us, *a.* Possessing beauty; beautiful.—**beauteously,** bū′tē·us·li, *adv.*—**beautician,** bū·tish′an, one whose business is to improve the appearance of women's hair, nails, complexion, etc.—**beau-**

tification, bū′ti·fi·kā″shon, *n.* The act of beautifying or rendering beautiful; decoration; adornment; embellishment.—**beautiful,** bū′ti·ful, *a.* Having the qualities that constitute beauty; highly pleasing to the eye, the ear, or the mind (a *beautiful* scene, melody, poem, character, but not a *beautiful* taste or smell); beauteous; lovely; handsome; fair; charming; comely.—*The beautiful,* all that possess beauty; beauty in the abstract.—**beautifully,** bū′ti·ful·li, *adv.* In a beautiful manner.—**beautifulness,** bū′ti·ful·nes, *n.* The quality of being beautiful; beauty.—**beautify,** bū′ti·fī, *v.t.*—*beautified, beautifying.* To make or render beautiful; to adorn; to deck; to decorate.

beaver, bē′vėr, *n.* [A.Sax. *befer* = D. *bever,* Dan. *bæver,* Sw. *bäfver,* Icel. *bjórr,* G. *biber,* L. *fiber.*] A rodent quadruped valued for its fur, about 2 feet in length, haunting streams and lakes, now found in considerable numbers only in North America, and generally living in colonies, with large webbed hind feet and a flat tail covered with scales on its upper surface; beaver fur; a hat or cap made of beaver fur.

beaver, bē′vėr, *n.* [O.Fr. *baviere,* a child's bib, a beaver, *bave,* slaver.] The faceguard of a helmet, so constructed with joints or otherwise that the wearer could raise or lower it to eat and drink; a visor.

bebeeru, bē·bē′rö, *n.* [Native name.] A tree of British Guiana of the laurel family, the timber of which, known as *greenheart,* is used for building ships and submarine structures.

bebop, bē″bop′, *n.* Jazz style characterized by dissonance, complex rhythms, and experimental instrumentation.

becalm, bē·käm′, *v.t.* To render calm, still, or quiet (the sea, passions, etc.)†; to keep from motion for want of wind (as a ship); to delay (a person) by a calm.

became, bi·kām′, pret. of *become.*

because, bē·kaz′, *conj.* [*Be* for *by,* and *cause;* O.E. *bicause, bycause* = by or for the cause that.] By cause, or by the cause that; on this account that; for the cause or reason next explained; as, he fled *because* (as the reason given) he was afraid.

beccafico, bek·a·fē′kō, *n.* [It., lit. figpecker.] A bird resembling the nightingale; the greater pettichaps or garden warbler.

bechamel, besh′a·mel, *n.* [Named after its inventor.] A fine white broth or sauce thickened with cream.

bechance,† bē·chans′, *v.t.* To befall; to happen to. (*Shak.*)

beck, bek, *n.* [Shortened form of *beckon.*] To nod or make a significant gesture.—*v.t.* To call by a nod; to intimate a command or desire to by gesture.—*n.* A nod of the head or other significant gesture intended as a sign or signal.

becket, bek′et, *n.* A contrivance in ships for confining loose ropes, etc.

beckon, bek′n, *v.i.* [A.Sax. *beácnian, bécnian,* to beckon, from *beácn, bécn,* a beacon.] To make a sign to another by a motion of the hand or finger, etc., intended as a hint or intimation.—v.t. To make a significant sign to; to direct by making signs (*beckon* him to us).

become, bē·kum', v.i.—*became* (pret.) *become* (pp.), *becoming*. [A.Sax. *becuman, bicuman*, to arrive, happen, turn out—prefix *be=by*, and *cuman*, to come, to happen.] To pass from one state to another; to change, grow, or develop into (the boy *becomes* a man).—*To become of* (usually with *what* preceding), to be the fate of; to be the end of; to be the final or subsequent condition.—v.t. To suit or to be suitable to (anger *becomes* him not); to befit; to accord with, in character or circumstances; to be worthy of, or proper to; to grace or suit as regards outward appearance (a garment *becomes* a person).— **becoming,** bē·kum'ing, a. Suitable; meet: proper; appropriate; befitting; seemly.—**becomingly,** bē·kum'ing·li, adv. After a becoming or proper manner.

bed, bed, n. [A.Sax. *bed=*D. *bed, bedde*, Dan. *bed*, Goth. *badi*, G. *bett.*] That on or in which one sleeps, or which is specially intended to give ease to the body at night; especially, a large flat bag filled with feathers or other soft materials: the word may include or even be used for the bedstead; a plat or piece of tilled ground in a garden; the bottom of a river or other stream, or of any body of water; a layer; a stratum; an extended mass of anything, whether upon the earth or within it; that on which anything lies, rests, or is supported.—v.t.—*bedded*, *bedding*. To place in, or as in, a bed; to plant, as flowers, in beds.—**bedding,** bed'ing, n. A bed and its furniture; materials of a bed.—**bedrid, bedridden,** bed'rid, bed'rid·n, a. [A.Sax. *bed-rida*, lit. a bedrider.] Long confined to bed by age or infirmity.— **bedstead,** bed'sted, n. The framework of a bed.—**bedstraw,** bed'strạ, n. Straw for packing into a bed; also, a herbaceous perennial plant bearing yellow or white flowers growing in waste places in Britain.—**bedchamber,** n. An apartment intended for sleeping in, or in which there is a bed; a bedroom.—**bedclothes,** n. pl. Blankets, coverlets, etc., for beds.— **bedfellow,** n. One who occupies the same bed with another.—**bed linen,** n. Sheets, pillow covers, etc., for beds.—**bedpan,** n. A pan for warming a bed; also a necessary utensil for bedridden persons.—**bedplate.** The soleplate or foundation plate of an engine, etc.—**bedpost,** n. One of the posts forming part of the framework and often supporting the canopy of a bed.—**bedroom,** n. A room intended for sleeping in; a sleeping room or bedchamber.—**bedsore,** n. A sore liable to occur on bedridden persons on the parts of the body subjected to most pressure.—**bedtick,** n. A tick or stout linen or cotton bag for containing the feathers or other packing material of a bed.—**bedtime,** n. The time to go to bed; the usual

hour of retiring to rest.

bedaub, bē·dạb', v.t. To daub over; to soil with anything thick, slimy, and dirty.

bedeck, bē·dek', v.t. To deck; to adorn; to grace.

bedell, bedel, bē'dl, n. [L.L. *bedellus* =E. *beadle.*] A beadle in a university or connected with a law court.

bedevil, bē·dev'il, v.t. To throw into utter disorder and confusion; spoil or corrupt, as by evil spirits.

bedizen, bē·diz'n, v.t. [DIZEN.] To deck or trick out; especially, to deck in a tawdry manner or with false taste.

bedlam, bed'lam, n. [Corrupted from *Bethlehem*, the name of a religious house in London, afterward converted into a hospital for lunatics.] A madhouse; a place appropriated for lunatics; hence, any scene of wild uproar and madness.—**bedlamite,** bed'lam·it, n. A madman.

Bedouin, bed'ö·in, n. [Ar. *bedâwî*, dwellers in the desert.] A nomadic Arab living in tents in Arabia, Syria, Egypt, and elsewhere.

bedraggle, bē·drag'l, v.t.—*bedraggled*, *bedraggling*. To soil by draggling; to soil by drawing along on mud.

bee, bē, n. [A.Sax. *beó, bi=*Icel. *by*, Sw. Dan. *bi*, D. *bij, bije*, O. and Prov. G. *beie*, Ir. and Gael. *beach*, a bee.] An insect, of which there are numerous species, the honey or hive bee being the most familiar and typical species, having been kept in hives from the earliest periods for its wax and honey.—**bee bread,** n. A brown substance, the pollen of flowers, collected by bees as food for their young.—**bee eater,** n. A bird of several species that feeds on bees.— **beehive,** n. A case or box intended as a habitation for bees, and in which they may store honey for the use of their owners.—**beeline,** n. The direct line or nearest distance between two places.—**beeswax,** n. The wax secreted by bees, and of which their cells are constructed.—**beeswing,** n. A gauzy film in port wines indicative of age, and much esteemed by connoisseurs.

beech, bēch, n. [A.Sax. *béce*, from *bóc*, a beech, a book=*Icel. *bók*, Dan. *bög*, D. *beuk*, G. *buche*, a beech; cog. L. *fugus*, a beech; Gr. *phēgos*, the esculent oak, from root seen in Gr. *phagein*, Skr. *bhag*, to eat, from its nuts being eaten. BOOK.] A large-sized tree with a smooth bark yielding a hard timber made into tools, etc., and nuts from which an oil is expressed.—**beechen,** bēch'en, a. Consisting of the wood of the beech; belonging to the beech.—**beechnut,** n. One of the nuts or fruits of the beech.

beef, bēf, n. [Fr. *bœuf*, from L. *bos, bovis*, an ox; cog. Ir. and Gael. *bo*, W. *buw*, Skr. *go*, a cow.] Originally an animal of the ox kind in the full-grown state (in this sense with the plural *beeves*, but the singular is no longer used); the flesh of an ox, bull, or cow when killed.—**beefeater,** bēf'-ēt·er, n. An eater of beef; a yeoman of

the royal guard (of England), a body of men who attend the sovereign at state banquets and on other occasions; an African bird that picks the larvae of insects from the hides of oxen.—**beefsteak,** n. A steak or slice of beef for broiling.—**beef-witted,** a. With no more wit than an ox; dull; stupid. (*Shak.*)

Beelzebub, bē·el'zē·bub, n. [Heb. *baal*, lord, and *zebub*, a fly.] A god of the Philistines; in the N.T. the prince of devils.

beer, bēr, n. [A.Sax. *beór=*D. and G. *bier;* origin doubtful.] A fermented alcoholic liquor made from any farinaceous grain, but generally from malted barley flavored with hops, and yielding a spirit on being distilled; a fermented drink prepared with various substances, as ginger, molasses, etc.—**beery,** bē'ri, a. Pertaining to beer; soiled or stained with beer; affected by beer; intoxicated.

beestings, bēst'ingz, n. pl. [A.Sax. *býsting, byst, beóst*, D. *biest, biestemelk* G. *biestmilch.*] The first milk given, by a cow after calving.

beet, bēt, n. [A.Sax. *béte*, D. *biet*, G. *beeta*, from L. *beta*, beet.] A plant of various species cultivated for its thick fleshy roots, the red varieties of which are much used as a kitchen vegetable, while the white varieties yield a large portion of sugar, and are now extensively cultivated.

beetle, bē'tl, n. [A.Sax. *bytl, bitel*, a mallet from *bedtan*, to beat; L.G. *betel, bötel.*] A heavy wooden mallet used to drive wedges, consolidate earth, etc.—v.t. To use a beetle on; to beat with a heavy wooden mallet as a substitute for mangling.

beetle, bē'tl, n. [A.Sax. *bitel*, from *bitan*, to bite.] A general name of many insects having four wings, the anterior pair of which are of a horny nature and form a sheath or protection to the posterior pair; a coleopterous insect.

beetle, bē'tl, v.i. [From A.Sax. *bitel*, sharp, hence prominent, from *bitan*, to bite.] To be prominent (as a cliff, a battlement); to hang or extend out; to overhang; to jut.—**beetle-browed,** a. Having prominent brows.

befall, bē·fạl', v.t.—*befell, befallen, befalling*. [A.Sax. *befeallan*—prefix *be*, and *feallan*, to fall.] To happen to; to occur to.—v.i. To happen; to come to pass.

befit, bē·fit', v.t.—*befitted, befitting*. [Prefix *be*, and *fit*.] To be fitting for; to suit; to be suitable or proper to.

befog, bē·fog', v.t.—*befogged, befogging*. To involve in fog; hence, to confuse.

befool, bē·föl', v.t. To fool; to make a fool of; to delude or lead into error.

before, bē·fōr', prep. [A.Sax. *beforan* —prefix *be*, and *foran*, fore.] In front of; preceding in space; in presence of; in sight of; under the cognizance or consideration of (a court, a meeting); preceding in time; earlier than; ere; in preference to; prior to; having precedence of in rank, dignity, etc.— *Before the mast*, in or into the condition of a common sailor, the portion of a ship behind the mainmast being reserved for the officers.—*adv.* Further onward in place; in front; in the forepart; in time preceding; previously; formerly; already.—**beforehand,** bē·fōr'hand, *a.* In good pecuniary circumstances; having enough to meet one's obligations and something over.—*adv.* In anticipation; in advance.—**beforetime,**‡ bē·fōr'tīm, *adv.* Formerly; of old time. (O.T.)

befoul, bē·foul', *v.t.* To make foul; to soil.

befriend, bē·frend', *v.t.* To act as a friend to; to aid, benefit, or assist.

beg, beg, *v.t.*—begged, begging. [Contr. it is believed from A.Sax. *bedegian* or *bedecian,* to beg; from stem of *bid,* A.Sax. *biddan,* to beg, to ask; comp. Goth. *bidagwa,* a beggar, from same root.] To ask or supplicate in charity; to ask for earnestly (alms); to ask earnestly (a person); to beseech; to implore; to entreat or supplicate with humility; to take for granted; to assume without proof. [The phrase *I beg to* is often used as a polite formula for introducing a question or communication; as, *I beg to* inquire, *I beg to* state. It may be regarded as elliptical for *I beg leave to.*]—*v.i.* To ask alms or charity; to live by asking alms.—**beggar,** beg'ẻr, *n.* One that begs; a person who lives by asking alms; one who supplicates with humility; a petitioner.—*v.t.* To reduce to beggary; to impoverish; to exhaust the resources of (to *beggar* description); to exhaust.—**beggarliness,** beg'ẻr·li·nes, *n.* The character of being beggarly; meanness; extreme poverty.—**beggarly,** beg'ẻr·li, *a.* Like or belonging to a beggar; poor; mean; contemptible.—**beggary,** beg'ẻr·i, *n.* The state of a beggar; a state of extreme indigence.

began, bē·gan', *pret.* of begin.

beget, bē·get', *v.t.*—begat (pret. the latter now almost obsolete), *begot, begotten* (pp.), *begetting.* (A. Sax. *begitan, bigitan*—prefix *be,* and *gitan,* to get.] To procreate, as a father or sire; to produce, as an effect; to cause to exist; to generate. —**begetter,** bē·get'ẻr, *n.* One who begets or procreates; a father.

begin, bē·gin', *v.i.*—began (pret.), *begun* (pp.), *beginning.* [A.Sax. *beginnan,* to begin—prefix *be,* and *ginnan,* to begin.] To take rise; to originate; to commence; to do the first act; to enter upon something new; to take the first step.—**begin,** bē·gin', *v.t.* To do the first act of; to enter on; to commence.—**beginner,** bē·gin'ẻr, *n.* A person who begins or originates; the agent who is the cause; one who first enters upon any art, science, or business; a young practitioner; a novice; a tyro.—**beginning,** bē·gin'ing, *n.* The first cause; origin; the first state; commencement; entrance into being; that from which a greater thing proceeds or grows.

begird, bē·gẻrd', *v.t.*—begirt (pret. etc. pp.), *begirding.* [A.Sax. *begyrdan.*] To gird or bind with a band or girdle; to surround; to encompass.

begone, bē·gon', *interj.* Go away; hence!—the imperative *be* and pp. *gone* combined.

begonia, bē·gō'ni·a, *n.* [From M. *Begon,* a French botanist.] The generic name of tropical plants much cultivated in hothouses for the beauty of their leaves and flowers.

begot, bē·got' (pret. and pp.) **begotten,** bē·got'n. pp. of beget.

begrudge, bē·gruj', *v.t.*—begrudged, *begrudging.* To grudge; to envy the possession of: with two objects (to *begrudge* a person something).

beguile, bē·gīl', *v.t.*—beguiled, *beguiling.* To practice guile upon; to delude; to deceive; to cheat; to trick; to dupe; to impose on by artifice or craft; to dispel or render unfelt by diverting the mind (cares); to while away (time).—**beguilement,** bē·gīl'ment, *n.* The act or state of beguiling.—**beguiler,** bē·gīl'ẻr, *n.* One who beguiles.

Beguine, bā·gēn', *n.* [Fr. *béguine;* from founder's name. Lambert Begue, 1180.] One of an order of females in Holland, Belgium, and Germany, who, without taking the monastic vows, form societies for the purposes of devotion and charity.

begum, bē'gum, *n.* In the East Indies, a princess or lady of high rank.

begun, bē·gun', pp. of begin.

behalf, bē·häf', *n.* [Prefix *be,* and *half,* in old sense of side.] Interest; profit; support; defense; always in such phrases as in or on *behalf* of, in my, his, some person's *behalf.*

behave, bē·hāv', *v.i.*—behaved, *behaving.* [Prefix *be,* and *have.*] To conduct one's self; to demean one's self: used *refl.*—*v.i.* To act; to conduct one's self.—**behavior,** bē·hāv'yẻr, *n.* Manner of behaving; conduct; deportment; mode of acting (of a person, a machine, etc.).

behead, bē·hed', *v.t.* To cut off the head of; to sever the head from the body of.

beheld, bē·held', *pret.* and pp. of *behold.*

behemoth, bē'hē·moth, *n.* [Heb.] An animal described in Job xl. 15-24, and which some suppose to be an elephant, others a hippopotamus, crocodile, etc.

behest, bē·hest', *n.* [Prefix *be,* and *hest;* A.Sax. *behaes.* HEST.] A command; precept; mandate. [Poetical.]

behind, bē·hīnd', *prep.* [A.Sax. *behindan,* behind—prefix *be,* and *hindan,* behind. HIND.] On the side opposite the front or nearest part of, or opposite to that which fronts a person; at the back of; toward the back or back part of; remaining after; later in point of time than; farther back than; in an inferior position to.—*adv.* At the back; in the rear; out of sight; not exhibited; remaining; toward the back part; backward; remaining after one's departure.—**behindhand,** bē·hīnd'hand, *adv.* or *a.* In a state in which means are not adequate to the supply of wants in arrear; in a

backward state; not sufficiently advanced; not equally advanced with another; tardy.

behold, bē·hōld', *v.t.*—beheld (pret. and pp.), *beholding.* [A.Sax. *behealdan* —prefix *be,* and *healdan,* to hold.] To fix the eyes upon; to look at with attention; to observe with care; to contemplate, view, survey, regard, or see.—*v.i.* To look; to direct the eyes to an object; to fix the attention upon an object; to attend or fix the mind; in this sense chiefly in the imperative, and used interjectionally.—**beholden,** bē·hōld'n, *a.* Under obligation; bound in gratitude; obliged; indebted.— **beholder,** bē·hōld'ẻr, *n.* One who beholds; a spectator.

behoof, bē·höf', *n.* [A.Sax. *behóf=* D. *behoef,* G. *behuf*—prefix *be,* and word equivalent to Icel. *hóf,* measure, moderation.] That which is advantageous to a person; behalf; interest; advantage; profit; benefit: always in such phrases as in or for *behoof* of, for a person's *behoof.*—**behoove,** bē·höv', *v.t.*—behooved, behooving. [A. Sax. *behófian,* from the noun.] To be fit or meet for, with respect to necessity, duty, or convenience; to be necessary for: used impersonally (*it* behooves us, or the like).

belabor, bē·lā'bẻr, *v.t.* [Prefix *be,* and *labor;* comp. G. *bearbeiten,* to labor, and to beat soundly—prefix *be,* and *arbeit,* work.] To beat soundly; to deal blows to; to thump.

belay, bē·lā', *v.t.* [Prefix *be,* and *lay.*] *Naut.* to make fast by winding round something.—**belaying pin,** *n. Naut.* a pin for belaying ropes to.

belch, belsh, *v.t.* [O.E. *belken, belke,* A. Sax. *bealcian,* to belch.] To throw out or eject with violence, as from the stomach or from a deep hollow place; to cast forth (a volcano *belches* flames or ashes).—*v.i.* To eject wind from the stomach; to issue out, as with eructation.—*n.* The act of one who or that which belches; eructation.

beldam, beldame, bel'dam, bel'dām, *n.* [Fr. *belle,* fine, handsome, and *dame,* lady; it was at one time, applied respectfully to elderly females.] A grandmother (*Shak.*)‡; an old woman in general, especially an ugly old woman; a hag.

beleaguer, bē·lēg'ẻr, *v.t.* [Prefix *be,* and *leaguer.*] To besiege; to surround with an army so as to preclude escape; to blockade.

belemnite, bel'em·nīt, *n.* [Gr. *belemnon,* a dart or arrow, from *belos,* a dart, from the root of *ballō,* to throw.] A straight, tapering, dartshaped fossil; the internal bone or shell of animals allied to the cuttlefishes, common in the chalk formation; the animal to which such a bone belonged.

belfry, bel'fri, *n.* [O.Fr. *belfroi, beffroit,* etc., a watch-tower, from O.G. *bervrit, bercvrit,* a tower or castle for defense, from *bergen,* to protect, and *frid,* a strong place (Mod. G. *friede,* peace). False etymology connected the word with *bell,* hence its modern English meaning.] A bell tower, generally attached to a church or other building; that part of a building in which a bell is hung.

Belgian, bel′ji·an, *a.* Pertaining to Belgium.—*n.* A native of Belgium.

Belgravian, bel·grā′vi·an, *a.* Belonging to *Belgravia,* an aristocratic portion of London; aristocratic; fashionable.—*n.* An inhabitant of Belgravia; a member of the upper classes. (*Thack.*)

Belial, bē′li·al, *n.* [Heb. *belial—beli,* not, without, and *yaal,* use, profit.] Wickedness; a wicked and unprincipled person; an evil spirit; Satan.

belie, bē·lī′, *v.t.—belied, belying.* [Prefix *be,* and *lie,* to speak falsely; like G. *belugan,* to belie. LIE.] To tell lies concerning; to calumniate by false reports; to show to be false; to be in contradiction to (his terror *belies* his words); to fail to equal or come up to; to disappoint (*belie* one's hopes).

believe, bē·lēv′, *v.t.—believed, believing.* [O.E. *bileve, beleve,* from A.Sax. *gelyfan, gelēfan,* to believe, the initial particle being changed; *-lieve* is akin to *lief* and *leave,* n.] To credit upon the ground of authority, testimony, argument, or any other circumstances than personal knowledge; to expect or hope with confidence.—*v.i.* To be more or less firmly persuaded of the truth of anything.—*To believe in,* to hold as an object of faith; to have belief of.—**belief,** bē·lēf′, *n.* An assent of the mind to the truth of a declaration, proposition, or alleged fact, on the ground of evidence, distinct from personal knowledge; *theol.* faith, or a firm persuasion of the truths of religion; the thing believed; the object of belief; the body of tenets held by the professors of any faith; a creed.—**believable,** bē·lēv′a·bl, *a.* Capable of being believed; credible.—**believer,** bē·lēv′ėr, *n.* One who believes; an adherent of a religious faith; a professor of Christianity.—**believingly,** bē·lēv′ing·li, *adv.* In a believing manner.

belittle, bē·lit′l, *v.t.* To make smaller; to lower; speak disparagingly of.

bell, bel, *n.* [A.Sax. *belle;* allied to *bellan,* to bellow, E. to *bell,* as a deer; akin *bellow,* and G. *bellen,* to bark.] A metallic vessel which gives forth a clear, musical, ringing sound on being struck, generally cup shaped; anything in form of a bell; *pl.* the phrase employed on shipboard to denote the divisions of daily time, from their being marked by strokes on a bell each half hour.—*To bear the bell,* to be the first or leader, in allusion to the bell wether of a flock.—*Passing bell,* a bell which used to be rung when a person was on the point of death.—*v.i.* To flower; to put out bell-shaped blossoms.—*v.t.* To put a bell on.—**bell bird,** *n.* A South American passerine bird, and also an Australian insessorial bird; so named from their bell-like notes.—**bell**

buoy, *n.* A buoy on which is fixed a bell, which is rung by the heaving of the sea.—**bellflower,** *n.* A common name of plants of the genus *Campanula,* from the shape of the flower.—**bellman,** *n.* A public crier who uses a bell.—**bell metal,** *n.* An alloy of copper and tin, used for making bells.—**bellmouthed,** *a.* Gradually expanded at the mouth in the form of a bell.—**bell-punch,** *n.* A small punch fitted to the jaws of a pincers-shaped instrument, combined with a little bell which sounds when the punch makes a perforation, used as a check on streetcar conductors, etc.—**bellwether,** *n.* A wether or sheep which leads the flock, with a bell on his neck.

bell, bel, *v.i.* [A.Sax. *bellan,* Icel. *belja,* to bellow. BELLOW.] To roar; to bellow, as a bull or a deer in rutting time.

belladonna, bel·la·don′na, *n.* [It., beautiful lady.] A plant of the nightshade family, containing atropine; *med.* a drug prepared from the plant.

belle, bel, *n.* [Fr., from L. *bellus,* beautiful.] A young lady; a lady of superior beauty and much admired.

belles-lettres, bel·let·tr, *n. pl.* [Fr. BELLE and LETTER.] Polite or elegant literature, a term including rhetoric, poetry, history, criticism, with the languages in which the literature is written.

bellicose, bel′li·kōs, *a.* [L. *bellicosus,* from *bellum,* war.] Inclined to war; warlike; pugnacious; indicating warlike feelings.

belligerent, bel·lij′ėr·ent, *a.* [L. *bellum,* war, and *gerens, gerentis,* carrying on.] Waging war; carrying on war; pertaining to war or warfare.—*n.* A nation, power, or state carrying on war; one engaged in fighting.—**belligerence,**† bel·lij′ėr·ens, *n.* The act of carrying on war; warfare.

bellow, bel′lō, *v.i.* [A.Sax. *bylgean,* to bellow, allied to *bellan,* to bell, Icel. *belja,* to bellow. BELL.] To utter a hollow, loud sound, as a bull; to make a loud noise or outcry; to roar.—*n.* A loud outcry; roar.—**bellower,** bel′lō·ėr, *n.* One who bellows.

bellows, bel′lōz, *n. sing.* and *pl.* [Really a plural form of the word *belly,* A.Sax. *bœlg, belg, bœlig,* a bag, a belly, bellows. BELLY.] An instrument for producing a strong current of air, and principally used for blowing fire, either in private dwellings or in forges, furnaces, mines, etc., or for supplying the pipes of an organ with wind.

belly, bel′li, *n.* [A.Sax. *bœlg, belg, bœlig,* bag, belly=Icel. *belgr,* D. *balg,* Dan. *bœlg,* G. *balg,* the belly; akin to *bulge;* comp. Gael. and Ir. *bolg, balg,* the belly, a bag, bellows. *Bellows* is a plural form of this word.] That part of the human body which extends from the breast to the thighs, containing the bowels; the abdomen; the corresponding part of a beast; the part of anything which resembles the human belly in

protuberance or cavity.—*v.t. bellied, bellying.* To fill; to swell out.—*v.i.* To swell and become protuberant like the belly.—**bellyband,** *n.* A band that goes round the belly of a horse as part of its harness.

belong, bē·long′, *v.i.* [Prefix *be,* and O.E. *long,* to belong (to extend in length to), from the adjective *long;* comp. D. and G. *belangen,* to concern, from *lang,* long.] To be the property of; to appertain; to be the concern or affair; to be appendant or connected; to be suitable; to be due; to have a settled residence; to be domiciliated; to be a native of a place; to have original residence: in all senses followed by *to.*—**belonging,** bē·long′ing, *n.* That which belongs to one: used generally in plural; qualities, endowments, property, possessions, appendages.

beloved, bē·luv′ed, *a.* Loved; greatly loved; dear to the heart.

below, bē·lō′, *prep.* [Prefix *be,* and *low.*] Under in place; beneath; not so high as; inferior to in rank, excellence, or dignity.—*adv.* In a lower place, with respect to any object; beneath; on the earth, as opposed to the heavens; in hell, or the regions of the dead; in a court of inferior jurisdiction.

belt, belt, *n.* [A.Sax. *belt*=Dan. *bœlte,* Icel. *belti,* a belt, a girdle, from L. *balteus,* a belt. Comp. Ir. and Gael. *balt,* a border, a welt.] A girdle; a band, usually of leather, in which a sword or other weapon is hung; anything resembling a belt; a strip; a stripe; a band; a band passing round two wheels, and communicating motion from one to the other.—*v.t.* To encircle; to surround.—**belted,** belt′ed, *a.* Wearing a belt; marked or distinguished with a belt.—**belting,** belt′ing, *n.* Belts taken generally; the material of which the belts used in machinery are made.

Beltane, bel′tān, *n.* [A Celtic word; Gael. *bealltainn,* Ir. *bealltaine;* the first of May; origin unknown.] The name of a sort of festival formerly observed among all the Celtic tribes of Europe. It was celebrated in Scotland on the first day of May (o.s.), and in Ireland on June 21 by kindling fires on the hills and eminences.

beluga, bē·lū′ga, *n.* [Rus. *bieluga,* from *bielyi,* white.] A kind of whale found in northern seas, the white whale or white fish, from 12 to 18 feet in length, killed for its oil and skin.

belvedere, bel′ve·dēr, *n.* [It., lit. a beautiful view—*bello, bel,* beautiful, and *vedere,* to see.] In Italy an open erection on the top of a house for the purpose of obtaining a view of the country; in France, a summerhouse on an eminence.

bema, bē′ma, *n.* [Gr.] A stage or platform for an orator; part of a church raised above the rest and reserved for the higher clergy.

bemire, bē·mīr′, *v.t.—bemired, bemiring.* To drag or stall in the mire; to soil, as by passing through mud.

---

fāte, fär, fâre, fat, fạll; mē, met, hėr; pīne, pin; nōte, not, mŏve; tūbe, tub, bụll; oil, pound.

bemoan, bē·mōn′, v.t. To moan or mourn for; to lament; to bewail; to express sorrow for.

bemock, bē·mok′, v.t. To treat with mockery; to mock.

bemused, bē·mūzd′, a. Originally, overcome with musing; sunk in reverie; hence, muddled; stupefied.

ben, ben, n. A tree of India, called also horse-radish tree, having seeds or nuts that yield an oil (oil of ben) which keeps without becoming rancid for many years.

bench, bensh, n. [A.Sax. benc, a bench = Dan. bænk, a parallel form with bank. BANK.] A long seat; a strong table on which carpenters or other mechanics prepare their work; the seat on which judges sit in court; the seat of justice; the persons who sit as judges; the court.—Bench of bishops, or episcopal bench, a collective designation of the bishops who have seats in the House of Lords.—King's (or Queen's) Bench, a superior English court of civil and criminal jurisdiction, now incorporated in the High Court of Justice.—v.t. To furnish with benches; to seat on a bench or seat of honor (Shak.)‡.—v.i.‡ To sit on a seat of justice. (Shak.)

bend, bend, v.t.—bended or bent (pret. & pp.), bending. [A.Sax. bendan, to bend, lit. to bend and keep bent by the string, from bend, a band; comp. Fr. bander un arc, to bend a bow, from bande, a string.] To curve or make crooked; to deflect from a normal condition of straightness; to direct to a certain point (one's mind, course, steps); to subdue; to cause to yield.—v.i. To be or become curved or crooked; to incline; to lean or turn; to be directed; to bow or be submissive.—n. A curve; a crook; a turn; flexure; incurvation.

beneath, bē·nēth′, prep. [A.Sax. beneoth, beneothan—prefix be, and neothan, below. NETHER.] Under; lower in place than something which rests above; burdened or overburdened with; lower than in rank, dignity, or excellence; below the level of.—adv. In a lower place; below.

benedicite, ben·e·dis′i·tē, n. [L., lit. bless ye, the first word of the hymn.] A canticle or hymn in the Book of Common Prayer, as old as the time of St. Chrysostom.

benedick, benedict, ben′e·dik, ben′e·dikt, n. A sportive name for a married man, especially one who has been long a bachelor: from one of the characters (Benedick) in Shakespeare's Much Ado about Nothing.

Benedictine, ben·e·dik′tin, a. Pertaining to the monks of St. Benedict. —n. A Blackmonk; a member of the order of monks founded at Monte Cassino about the year 530 by St. Benedict, and wearing a loose black gown with large wide sleeves, and a cowl on the head; a liqueur made by the Benedictine monks at Fécamp, in Normandy, consisting of spirits containing juices of certain aromatic herbs. CHARTREUSE.

benediction, ben·e·dik′shon, n. [L. benedictio—bene, well, and dictio, speaking.] The act of invoking a blessing; blessing, prayer, or kind wishes uttered in favor of any person or thing; a solemn or affectionate invocation of happiness.—benedictory, ben·e·dik′to·ri, a. Giving a blessing; expressing a benediction, or wishes for good.

Benedictus, ben·e·dik′tus, n. [L., blessed—' Blessed be the Lord God of Israel ', etc.] The song of Zacharias in Luke i, used in the service of the Roman Catholic Church and introduced with English words into the morning prayer of the English Church.

benefaction, ben·e·fak′shon, n. [L. benefactio, from benefacio, to do good to one. BENEFICE.] The act of conferring a benefit; a benefit conferred, especially a charitable donation.—benefactor, ben·e·fak′tĕr, n. One who confers a benefit.—benefactress, ben·e·fak′tres, n. A female who confers a benefit.

benefice, ben′e·fis, n. [Fr. bénéfice, a benefice, from L. beneficium, a kindness, in late L. an estate granted for life—bene, well, and facio, to do.] An ecclesiastical living; a church endowed with a revenue for the maintenance of divine service, or the revenue itself.—beneficed, ben′e·fist, a. Possessed of a benefice or church preferment.—beneficence, be·nef′i·sens, n. [L. beneficentia.] The practice of doing good; active goodness, kindness, or charity. ∴ Beneficence, lit. well-doing, is the outcome and visible expression of benevolence, or well-willing. Benevolence may exist without beneficence, but beneficence always presupposes benevolence.—beneficent, beneficient,‡ be·nef′i·sent, ben·e·fi′shent, a. Doing good; performing acts of kindness and charity.—beneficently, be·nef′i·sent·li, adv. In a beneficent manner.—beneficial, ben·e·fi′shal, a. Contributing to a valuable end; conferring benefit; advantageous; useful; profitable; helpful. —beneficially, ben·e·fi′shal·li, adv. In a beneficial manner; advantageously; profitably; helpfully.—beneficialness, ben·e·fi′shal·nes, n.—beneficiary, ben·e·fi′shi·a·ri, a. Connected with the receipt of benefits, profits, or advantages.—n. One who holds a benefice; one who is in the receipt of benefits, profits, or advantages; one who receives something as a free gift.

benefit, ben′e·fit, n. [O.E. benfite, bienfete, O.Fr. bienfet, from L. benefactum, a benefit. BENEFICE.] An act of kindness; a favor conferred; whatever is for the good or advantage of a person or thing; advantage; profit; a performance at a theater or other place of public entertainment, the proceeds of which go to one of the actors, or towards some charitable object.—v.t. To do good to; to be of service to; to advantage.—v.i. To gain advantage; to make improvement.

benevolence, bē·nev′ō·lens, n. [L. benevolentia—bene, well, and volens, volentis, ppr. of volo, to will or wish.] The disposition to do good; the love of mankind, accompanied with a desire to promote their happiness; good will; kindness; charitableness; an act of kindness; a contribution or tax illegally exacted by arbitrary kings of England. ∴ BENEFICENCE.—benevolent, bē·nev′ō·lent, a. Possessing love to mankind, and a desire to promote their prosperity and happiness; inclined to charitable actions.—benevolently, bē·nev′ō·lent·li, adv. In a benevolent manner.

bengali, ben·gal·ē′, n. The language or dialect spoken in Bengal.—bengal light, n. A species of fireworks used as signals by night or otherwise, producing a steady and vivid blue-colored fire.

benign, bē·nīn′, a. [L. benignus for benigenus, kind-hearted—benus for bonus, good, and genus, kind, race.] Of a kind disposition; gracious; kind (benign sovereign); proceeding from or expressive of gentleness, kindness, or benignity; salutary (benign influences); med. mild; not severe or violent.—benignant, bē·nig′nant, a. Kind; gracious; favorable: frequently, like benign, used of the kindness of superiors; but benign is more a poetical word.—benignantly, bē·nig′nant·li, adv. In a benignant manner.—benignity, bē·nig′ni·ti, n. The state or quality of being benign or benignant; kindness of nature; graciousness; beneficence.—benignly, bē·nīn′li, adv. In a benign manner; favorably; kindly; graciously.

benison, ben′i·zn, n. [O.Fr. beneison, from L. benedictio, a benediction. Benediction is thus the same word.] A blessing uttered by a person; a benediction.

Benjamin, ben′ja·min, n. [Proper name. O.T.] The youngest son of family.

benjamin, ben′ja·min, n. [Fr. benjoin, benzoin.] A common form of the name of the gum benzoin.

benne, ben′e, n. [Malay.] Sesame.

bent, bent, pret. & pp. of bend.—n. Originally, a condition of being bent (as a bow); flexure; hence, fig. turn; inclination; disposition; natural tendency; leaning or bias of the mind.

bent, bent grass, bent, bent′gras, n. [A.Sax. beonet = G. binse, a rush.] A wiry grass, such as grows on common or neglected ground.

Benthamism, ben′tham·izm, n. The doctrine according to Jeremy Bentham, by which man's actions are regulated purely by utilitarian considerations; profit-and-loss morality.

benumb, bē·num′, v.t. [NUMB.] To make numb or torpid; to deprive of sensation; to stupefy; to render inactive; to drug, deaden, or paralyze.

benzene, ben′zēn, n. A clear, colorless, flammable liquid obtained from coal or petroleum and used as a solvent, an ingredient of motor fuel, and a chemical raw material.

benzine, ben′zēn, n. A volatile,

highly flammable liquid composed chiefly of hydrocarbons of the methane series obtained from the distillation of petroleum and used as a cleaning agent and an ingredient of paints and varnishes.

benzoin, ben·zō′in, or ben′zoin, *n.* [Of Ar. origin = Fr. *benjoin*, Pg. *beijoim*.] Gum benjamin; a concrete resinous juice or balsam flowing from incisions made in the stem of a tree of Sumatra, etc., chiefly used in cosmetics and perfumes, and in incense, having a fragrant and agreeable smell.—**benzoic,** ben·zō′ik, *a.* Pertaining to or obtained from benzoin.

bequeath, bē·kwēth′, *v.t.* [A.Sax. *becwethan*—prefix *be,* and *cwethan,* to say. QUOTH.] To give or leave by will; to devise by testament; to hand down; to transmit.—**bequest,** bē·kwest′, *n.* The act of bequeathing or leaving by will; something left by will, a legacy.

berate, bē·rāt′, *v.t.*—*berated, berating.* To rate or chide vehemently; to scold.

Berber, bėr′bėr, *n.* A person belonging to, or the language spoken by, certain tribes of North Africa (Barbary).

berberine, bėr′bėr·in, *n.* A substance obtained from the root of the barberry tree, used in dyeing yellow.

bere, bēr, *n.* [A.Sax. *bere,* barley. BARLEY.] A species of barley having six rows in the ear.

bereave, bē·rēv′, *v.t.*—*bereaved* or *bereft* (pret. & pp.), *bereaving.* [Prefix *be,* and *reave*; A.Sax. *bereafian.* REAVE.] To deprive of something that is prized; to make destitute; to rob; to strip; with *of* before the thing taken away.—**bereavement,** bē·rēv′ment, *n.* The act of bereaving, or state of being bereaved, deprivation, particularly the loss of a friend by death.

berg, bėrg, *n.* [A.Sax. and G. *berg,* a hill.] A large mass or mountain, as of ice; an iceberg.

bergamot, bėr′ga·mot, *n.* [Fr. *bergamote,* It. *bergamotta,* from *Bergamo,* in Italy.] A variety of pear; the lime or its fruit, the rind of which yields a fragrant oil; an essence or perfume from the fruit of the lime; a coarse tapestry manufactured originally at *Bergamo,* in Italy.

beri-beri, ber′i·ber′i, *n.* [Singhalese, *beri,* weakness.] A dangerous disease endemic in parts of India and Ceylon, characterized by paralysis, difficult breathing, and other symptoms. It is due to a lack of vitamin B.

berkelium, bėr·kē′li·um, *n.* [From *Berkeley,* Calif., where it was discovered.] Radioactive element first produced by helium-ion bombardment of americium 241. Symbol, Bk; at. no., 97.

berlin, bėr′lin or bėr·lin′, *n.* A fourwheeled vehicle of the chariot kind, first made at Berlin; Berlin wool; a knitted glove.—*Berlin blue,* Prussian blue.—*Berlin wool,* a kind of fine dyed wool used for tapestry,

knitting, etc.—*Berlin work,* fancy work in Berlin wools or worsted.

berm, berme, bėrm, *n.* [O.Fr. *barme,* from G. *brame, bräme* = E. *brim,* border.] *Fort.* a space of ground of 3, 4, or 5 feet in width, between the rampart and the moat or fosse; the bank or side of a canal which is opposite to the towpath.

berry, be′ri, *n.* [A.Sax. *berie,* a berry; Icel. *ber,* Sw. and D. *bär,* G. *beere,* Goth. *basi*; root seen in Skr. *bhas,* to eat.] A succulent or pulpy fruit, containing many seeds, and usually of no great size, such as the gooseberry, the strawberry, etc.; what resembles a berry, as one of the eggs of the lobster.—*v.i.* To bear or produce berries.—**berried,** be′rid, *a.* Furnished with berries.

berserk, bėr′sėrk, or bėr·sėrk′, *n.* [Icel. *berserkr,* lit. 'bearsark', or bear-shirt.] A berserker.—*a.* Extremely agitated; crazed; frenzied. —**berserker,** bėr′sėr·kėr, *n.* A wild warrior in Scandinavian folklore.

berth, bėrth, *n.* [From the root of *bear.*] A station in which a ship lies or can lie; a small room in a ship set apart for one or more persons; a box or place for sleeping in a ship or railroad car; a post or appointment; a situation.—*v.t.* To assign a berth or anchoring ground to; to allot a berth or berths to.

beryl, ber′il, *n.* [L. *beryllus,* Gr. *bēryllos,* of Eastern origin.] A colorless, yellowish, bluish, or less brilliant green variety of emerald, the prevailing hue being green.— **beryllium,** be·ril′li·um, *n.* A hard, light metallic element (also called glucinum) always occurring in combination. Symbol, Be (also Gl); at. no., 4; at. wt., 9.0122.

beseech, bē·sēch′, *v.t.* besought (pret. & pp.), *beseeching.* [O.E. *beseke, biseke*—prefix *be,* and *seek.*] To entreat; to supplicate; to implore; to beg eagerly for; to solicit.— **beseecher,** bē·sēch′ėr, *n.* One who beseeches.—**beseechingly,** bē·sēch′ing·li, *adv.* In a beseeching manner.

beseem, bē·sēm′, *v.t.* [Prefix *be,* and *seem,* in old sense of become, be seemly.] To become; to be fit for or worthy of.

beset, bē·set′, *v.t.*—*beset, besetting.* [A.Sax. *besettan,* to set near, to surround—prefix *be,* and *settan,* to set.] To distribute over; to intersperse through or among; to surround; to enclose; to hem in (*beset* with enemies, a city *beset* with troops; to press on all sides, so as to perplex (temptations that *beset* us); to press hard upon.— **besetment,** bē·set′ment, *n.* The condition of being beset; the sin or failing to which one is most liable; a besetting sin.—**besetting,** bē·set′ing, *a.* Habitually attending or assailing us (a *besetting* sin).

beshrew, bē·shrö′, *v.t.* [Prefix *be,* and *shrew.* SHREWD.] To wish a curse to; to execrate: generally used impersonally in phrases intended as mild imprecations or maledictions (*beshrew* me! *beshrew* the fellow!).

beside, bē·sīd′, *prep.* [Prefix *be,* by,

and *side.*] At the side of a person or thing; near to; apart from; not connected with (*beside* the present subject).—*To be beside one's self,* to be out of one's wits or senses.—**beside, besides,** bē·sīdz′, *adv.* Moreover; over and above; not included in the number, or in what has been mentioned. [*Besides* is now the commoner form.]—**besides,** *prep.* Over and above; separate or distinct from; in addition to.

besiege, bē·sēj′, *v.t.*—*besieged, besieging.* To lay siege to; beset or surround with armed forces for the purpose of compelling to surrender; to beset; to harass (*besieged* with applications).—**besieger,** bē·sēj′ėr, *n.* One who besieges.

besmear, bē·smēr′, *v.t.* To smear all over; to bedaub; to overspread with some viscous, glutinous, or soft substance that adheres; to foul; to soil.

besom, bē′zum, *n.* [A.Sax. *besema, besma,* a besom = D. *bezem,* G. *besem, besen*: root unknown.] A broom; a brush of twigs or other materials for sweeping.—*v.t.†* To sweep, as with a besom. (*Cowper.*)

besot, bē·sot′, *v.t.*—*besotted, besotting.* To make sottish, as with drink; to infatuate; to stupefy; to make dull, stupid, or senseless.—**besotted,** bē·sot′ed, *a.* Made sottish by drink; indicating or proceeding from gross stupidity; stupid; infatuated.

bespatter, bē·spat′ėr, *v.t.* To soil by spattering; *fig.* to asperse with calumny or reproach.

bespeak, bē·spēk′, *v.t.*—*bespoke* (pret.), *bespoke, bespoken* (pp.), *bespeaking.* To speak for (something wanted) beforehand; to order or engage against a future time; to betoken; to indicate by outward appearance (an action that *bespoke* a kind heart).—*n.* Among actors, a benefit.

bespread, bē·spred′, *v.t.* To spread over; to cover or form a coating over.

besprent, bē·sprent′, *pp.* [A participle of the obsolete verb *besprenge,* to besprinkle.] Sprinkled or scattered. [Poetical.]

besprinkle, bē·spring′kl, *v.t.* To sprinkle over; to cover by scattering or being scattered over.

Bessemer steel, bes′e·mėr·stēl, *n.* [From Sir H. *Bessemer,* the inventor of the process.] Steel made directly from molten cast iron by driving through it currents of air so as to oxidize and carry off the carbon and impurities, the proper quantity of carbon for making steel being then introduced.

best, best, *a. superl.* [A.Sax. *betest, betst, best,* serving as the superl. of *gód, good* = D. and G. *best,* Dan. *beste,* Icel. *bestr,* Sw. *bästa.* The root is *bat, bet,* seen also in *better,* Goth. *batista,* best. BETTER.] Most good; having good qualities or attainments in the highest degree; possessing the highest advantages.— *Best man,* the right-hand man or supporter of the bridegroom at a wedding.—*adv.* In the highest degree.—*n.* Highest possible state of excellence (*Shak.*); all that one can do, or show in one's self: often used in this sense with the possessive pronouns *my*, *thy*, *his*, *their*, etc. —*At best*, considered or looked at in the most favorable light.—*To make the best of*, to use to the best advantage; to get all that one can out of; to put up with as well as one can.

bestead, bē-sted', *pp.* of an obs. verb. [Prefix *be*, and *stead*, place.] Placed, disposed, or circumstanced as to convenience, benefit, and the like; situated: now always with *ill*, *well*, *sore*, etc.

bestial, bes'ti·al, *a.* [L. *bestialis*, from *bestia*, a beast.] Belonging to a beast or to the class of beasts; animal; having the qualities of a beast; brutal; brutish.—**bestiality**, bes·ti·al'i·ti, *n.* The quality of a beast; beastliness.—**bestialize**, bes'ti·al·īz, *v.t.*—*bestialized*, *bestializing*. To make like a beast; to bring or reduce to the condition of a beast.— **bestially**, bes'ti·al·li, *adv.* In a bestial manner.

bestir, bē-stėr', *v.t.* To stir; to put into brisk or vigorous action; usually *refl.*

bestow, bē-stō', *v.t.* To stow away; to lay up in store: to deposit; to lodge; to place (often *refl.*); to give; to confer; to impart: followed by *on* or *upon* before the recipient.— **bestowal**, bē-stō'al, *n.* The act of bestowing.

bestrew, bē-strū' or bē-strō', *v.t.* To scatter over; to besprinkle; to strew.

bestride, bē-strīd', *v.t.*—*bestrid*, *bestrode* (pret.), *bestrid*, *bestridden* (pp.), *bestriding*. To stride over; to stand or sit on with the legs on either side; to step over; to cross by stepping (*Shak.*).

bet, bet, *v.t.* and *i.*—*bet* or *betted*, *betting.* [A contraction of *abet*, to encourage, back up.] To lay or stake in wagering; to stake or pledge something upon the event of a contest; to wager.—*n.* A wager; that which is laid, staked, or pledged on any uncertain question or event; the terms on which a bet is laid.— **better**, **bettor**, bet'ėr, bet'or, *n.* One who lays bets or wagers.

beta, bā'ta, *n.* The second letter of the Greek alphabet.—**beta particle**, *n.* *Phys.* one of the high-speed electrons ejected from the nucleus during radioactive disintegration.— **beta ray**, *n.* *Phys.* a stream of high-speed electrons from radioactive disintegration.

betake, bē-tāk', *v.t.*—*betook* (pret.), *betaken* (pp.), *betaking.* [Prefix *be*, and *take*.] To repair; to resort; to have recourse: with the reflexive pronouns.

betatron, bē'ta·tron, *n.* *Phys.* a device for the high-speed acceleration of electrons to form a beam of beta rays.

betel, bē'tl, *n.* [An Oriental word.] A species of pepper, a creeping or climbing plant, cultivated throughout the East Indies for its leaf, which is chewed with the betel nut and lime.—**betel nut**, *n.* The kernel of the nut of the betel palm.—**betel palm**, *n.* An Asiatic palm tree.

bethink, bē-thingk', *v.t.* [Prefix *be*, and *think*.] To call or recall to mind; to bring to consideration: always with a reflexive pronoun (to *bethink* one's self *of* a thing). —*v.i.*† To have in recollection; to consider.

betide, bē-tīd', *v.t.*—*betid*, *betided* (pret.), *betid* (pp.), *betiding.* [Prefix *be*, and *tide*, from A.Sax. *tidan*, to happen. TIDE.] To happen to; to befall; to come to.—*v.i.* To come to pass; to happen.

betimes, bē-tīmz', *adv.* [Prefix *be* for *by* and *time*, with adverbial genitive termination.] Seasonably; in good season or time; early; at an early hour; soon; in a short time.

betoken, bē-tō'kn, *v.t.* To be or serve as a token of; to foreshow; to indicate as future by that which is seen.

betony, bet'o·ni, *n.* [L. *betonica*.] A plant formerly much employed in medicine, and sometimes used to dye wool of a fine dark yellow.

betook, bē-tuk', *pret.* of *betake*.

betray, bē-trā', *v.t.* [Prefix *be*, and O.Fr. *traïr*, Fr. *trahir*, to betray, from L. *tradere*, to give up or over. TRADITION.] To deliver into the hands of an enemy by treachery in violation of trust; to violate by fraud or unfaithfulness (to *betray* a cause or trust); to play false to; to reveal or disclose (secrets, designs) to let appear or be seen inadvertently (to *betray* ignorance).—**betrayal**, bē-trā'al, *n.* Act of betraying.—**betrayer**, bē-trā'ér, *n.* One who betrays; a traitor.

betroth, bē-trōth', *v.t.* [Prefix *be*, and *troth*. TROTH.] To contract to any one in order to a future marriage; to affiance; to pledge one's troth to (O.T.).—**betrothal**, **betrothment**, bē-trōth'al, bē-trōth'ment, *n.* The act of betrothing.

better, bet'ér, *a.* serving as the compar. of *good*. [A.Sax. *betera*, *betra*, with corresponding forms in the other Teutonic languages. BEST.] Having good qualities in a greater degree than another; preferable, in regard to use, fitness, or the like; improved in health.—*To be better off*, to be in improved or in superior circumstances.—*adv.* In a more excellent or superior manner; more correctly or fully; in a higher or greater degree; with greater advantage; more, in extent or amount (*better* than a mile).—*v.t.* To make better; to improve; to ameliorate; to increase the good qualities of (soil, etc.); to advance the interest or worldly position of; to surpass; to exceed; to improve on (as a previous effort).—*v.i.* To grow better; to become better; to improve.—*n.* A superior; one who has a claim to precedence; generally in the plural, and with possessive pronouns.— *The better*, a state of improvement; generally in adverbial phrase *for the better* (to alter a thing *for the better*); advantage; superiority; victory (to have or get *the better*

of).—**betterment**, bet'ér·ment, *n.* A making better; improvement; value added to property from public improvements.

between, bē-twēn', *prep.* [A.Sax. *betweónum*, *betweónan*—prefix *be*, and dat. pl. of *tweon*, twain, from *twá*, two; akin *twain*, *twin*.] In the space, place, or interval of any kind separating; in intermediate relation to; from one to another of (letters passing *between* them); in partnership among (shared *between* them); so as to affect both of; pertaining to one or other of two (the blame lies *between* you).—**betwixt**, bē-twikst', *prep.* [A.Sax. *betweox*, *betweohs*—prefix *be*, and *tweoh*, from *twá*, two. The *t* is excrescent as in *amidst*, etc.] Between; passing between; from one to another.

bevel, bev'el, *n.* [O.Fr. *bevel*; origin unknown.] The obliquity or inclination of one surface of a solid body to another surface of the same body; an instrument for drawing or measuring angles.—*a.* Having the form of a bevel; slant; not upright, (*Shak.*).—*v.t.*—*beveled*, *beveling.* To cut to a bevel.—*v.i.* To slant or incline on to a bevel angle.—**bevel gear**, *n.*—A species of wheel-work in which the axis or shaft of the driving wheel forms an angle with the axis or shaft of the wheel driven.—**beveled**, bev'eld, *a.* Having a bevel; formed with a bevel angle.— **beveling**, bev'el·ing, *a.* Inclining from a right line; slanting towards a bevel angle.

beverage, bev'ér·āj, *n.* [O.Fr. *beuvrage*, from *boivre*, *bevre*, L. *bibere*, to drink.] Drink; liquor for drinking.

bevy, bev'i, *n.* [Perhaps of similar origin with *beverage*, and originally a drinking company, or animals collected at a watering-place.] A flock of birds; a company of females.

bewail, bē-wāl', *v.t.* and *i.* To wail or weep aloud for; to lament.

beware, bē-wār', *v.t.* and *i.* [*Be*, imperative of verb to *be*, and *ware*= wary. WARE, WARY.] To be wary or cautious; to be suspicious of danger; to take care; now used only in imperative and infinitive, with *of* before the noun denoting what is to be avoided.

bewilder, bē-wil'dėr, *v.t.* [Prefix *be*, and old *wilder*, to lead astray. WILD.] To lead into perplexity or confusion; to perplex; to puzzle; to confuse.—**bewilderingly**, bē-wil'dėr·ing·li, *adv.* So as to bewilder.— **bewilderment**, bē-wil'dėr·ment, *n.* State of being bewildered.

bewitch, bē-wich', *v.t.* To subject to the influence of witchcraft; to throw a charm or spell over; to please to such a degree as to take away the power of resistance.— **bewitcher**, bē-wich'ér, *n.* One that bewitches or fascinates.— **bewitchery**, bē-wich'ér·i, *n.* Witchery; fascination; charm.—**bewitching**, bē-wich'ing. *a.* Having power to bewitch or to control by the arts of pleasing. —**bewitchingly**, bē-wich'ing·li, *adv.* **bewitchment**, bē-wich'ment, *n.* Fascination; the power of charming.

---

ch, *ch*ain; ch, Sc. lo*ch*; g, *g*o; j, *j*ob; ng, si*ng*; TH, *th*en; th, *th*in; w, *w*ig; hw, *wh*ig; zh, a*z*ure.

bey, bā, *n*. [Turk. *beg*, pron. as *bey*.] A governor of a town or district in the Turkish dominions; also, a prince; a beg.

beyond, bē·yond', *prep*. [A.Sax. *begeond*, *begeondam*—prefix *be*, and *geond*, yond, yonder.—YON.] On the further side of; out of reach of; further than the scope or extent of; above; in a degree exceeding or surpassing.

bezant, bez'ant, *n*. [From *Byzantium*.] A gold coin of Byzantium; a coin current in England from the tenth century till the time of Edward III.

bezel, bez'el, *n*. [A form of *basil*, Fr. *beseau*, a slope. BASIL.] The part of a finger ring which surrounds and holds fast the stone; the groove in which the glass of a watch is set.

bezique, be·zēk', *n*. [Fr.] A simple game at cards, played by two, three, or four persons.

bezoar, bē'zōr, *n*. [O.Fr. *bezoar*, from Per. *pâdzahr*—*pâd*, dispelling, and *zâhr*, poison.] A name for certain concretions found in the intestines of some animals (especially ruminants), formerly (and still in some places) supposed to be an antidote to poison.

bhang, bang, *n*. An Indian variety of the common hemp.

biangular, bī·ang'gū·lėr, *a*. Having two angles or corners.

biannual, bī·an'nū·al, *a*. [Prefix *bi*, twice, and *annual*.] Occurring twice a year.

bias, bī'as, *n*. [Fr. *biais*, from L.L. *bifax*, *bifacis*, two-faced—L. *bi*, double, and *facies*, the face.] A weight on the side of a bowl which turns it from a straight line; that which causes the mind to incline towards a particular object or course; inclination; bent; prepossession.—*v.t. biassed* or *biased*, *biassing* or *biasing*. To give a bias or particular direction to; to prejudice; to prepossess.—*adv*. In a slanting manner; obliquely.

biaxial, bī·aks'i·al, *a*. Having two axes, as in biaxial polarization.

bib, bib, *n*. A fish of the cod family, about a foot in length.

bib,‡ bib, *v.t*. and *i.*—*bibbed*, *bibbing*. [L. *bibo*, *bibere*, to drink.] To sip; to tipple; to drink frequently.—*n*. A small piece of linen or other cloth worn by children over the breast, so called because protective of the child's dress when drinking.—**bibber**, bib'ėr, *n*. A tippler; a man given to drinking.—**bibulous**, bib'ū·lus, *a*. [L. *bibulus*.] Having the quality of imbibing fluids; spongy; addicted to drinking intoxicants; pertaining to the drinking of intoxicants (*bibulous* propensities).

Bible, bī'bl, *n*. [Fr. *bible*, Gr. *biblia*, the books, pl. of *biblion*, dim. from *biblos*, papyrus, paper, a book.] Originally a book, but specifically restricted now to THE BOOK, by way of eminence; the sacred Scriptures, consisting of two parts, the Old Testament, originally written in Hebrew, the New Testament in Greek.—**Biblical**, bib'lik·al, *a*. Pertaining to the Bible or to the sacred writings.—**Biblically**, bib'lik·al·li, *adv*. In a Biblical manner; according to the Bible.—**Biblicist**, bib'li·sist, *n*. One skilled in the knowledge and interpretation of the Bible.—**Biblist**, bī'blist, *n*. One conversant with the Bible; one who makes the Bible the sole rule of faith.

bibliography, bib·li·og'ra·fi, *n*. [Gr. *biblion*, a book, and *grapho*, to write.] A history or description of books or manuscripts, with notices of the different editions, the times when they were printed, etc.—**bibliographer**, bib·li·og'ra·fėr, *n*. One versed in bibliography; one who composes or compiles the history of books.—**bibliographic**, **bibliographical**, bib'li·o·graf″ik, bib'li·ō·graf″ik·al, *a*. Pertaining to bibliography.

bibliolatry, bib·li·ol'a·tri, *n*. [Gr. *biblion*, a book, and *latreia*, worship.] Worship or homage paid to books; excessive reverence for any book, especially the Scriptures.

bibliology, bib·li·ol'o·ji, *n*. [Gr. *biblion*, a book, and *logos*, discourse.] Biblical literature, doctrine, or theology; a treatise on books; bibliography.

bibliomancy, bib'li·ō·man·si, *n*. [Gr. *biblion*, a book, and *manteia*, divination.] Divination performed by means of a book; divination by means of the Bible, consisting of selecting passages of Scripture at hazard and drawing from them indications concerning future things.

bibliomania, bib'li·ō·mā″ni·a, *n*. [Gr. *biblion*, a book, and *mania*, madness.] Book-madness; a rage for possessing rare and curious books.—**bibliomaniac**, bib'li·ō·mā″ni·ak, *n*. One affected with bibliomania.—**bibliomaniacal**, bib'li·ō·ma·nī″ak·al, *a*. Pertaining to bibliomania.

bibliopegy, bib·li·op'e·ji, *n*. [Gr. *biblion*, a book, and *pegnumi*, to make firm.] The art of bookbinding.

bibliophile, bib'li·ō·fil, *n*. [Gr. *biblion*, book, and *phileō*, to love.] A lover of books.—**bibliophilism**, bib·li·of'il·izm, *n*. Love of bibliography or of books.—**bibliophilist**, bib·li·of'il·ist, *n*. A bibliophile.

bibliopole, bib'li·ō·pōl, *n*. [Gr. *biblion*, a book, and *pōleō*, to sell.] A bookseller.—**bibliopolist**, bib·li·op'ol·ist, *n*. A bibliopole.

bibliotheca, bib'li·ō·thē″ka, *n*. [L., from Gr. *biblion*, a book, and *thēkē*, a repository.] A library.

bibulous. See BIB.

bicameral, bī·kam'ėr·al, *a*. [L. prefix *bi*, twice, and *camera*, a chamber]. Pertaining to or consisting of two legislative or other chambers.

bicarbonate, bī·kär'bon·āt, *n*. A carbonate containing two equivalents of carbonic acid to one of a base.

bice, bīs, *n*. [Fr. *bis*; etymology unknown.] A name given to two colors used in painting, one blue, the other green, and both native carbonates of copper.

bicentenary, bī·sen'te·na·ri, *n*. [L. *bi*, twice, and E. *centenary*.] The period of two hundred years; the commemoration of an event that happened two hundred years before.—*a*. Relating to a bicentenary; occurring once in two hundred years.

biceps, bī'seps, *n*. [L., from *bi*, double, and *caput*, the head.] A muscle having two heads or origins; the name of two muscles, one of the arm the other of the thigh.—**bicipital**, bī·sip'it·al, *a*. Having two heads; two-headed; pertaining to a biceps.

bicker, bik'ėr, *v.i*. [W. *bicra*, to fight, *bicre*, conflict.] To skirmish; to quarrel; to contend in words; to scold; to run rapidly; to move quickly with some noise, as a stream; to quiver; to be tremulous, like flame or water; to make a confused noise; to clatter.—*n*. A fight, especially a confused fight.

biconcave, bī·kon'kāv, *a*. Hollow or concave on both sides.

bicorn, bī'korn, *a*. [L. *bi*, double, and *cornu*, a horn.] Having two horns or antlers; crescent-shaped.

bicuspid, bī·kus'pid, *a*. [L. prefix *bi* two, and *cuspis*, a prong.] With two, cusps or points; two-fanged: often applied to teeth, as to the two first pairs of grinders in each jaw.

bicycle, bī'si·kl, *n*. [L. prefix *bi*, two, and Gr. *kyklos*, a circle or wheel.] A two-wheeled velocipede; a vehicle consisting of two wheels, one behind the other, connected by a light metal frame carrying a seat, the vehicle being propelled by the feet of the rider pressing on treadles which act directly or through gearing.—**bicyclist**, bī'sik·list, *n*. One who rides on a bicycle.

bid, bid, *v.t.*—*bid* or *bade* (pret.), *bid*, *bidden* (pp.), *bidding*. [Partly from A.Sax. *biddan*, to pray, ask, declare, command=Icel. *bidja*, G. *bitten*, Goth. *bidjan*, to ask, to pray; partly from A. Sax. *beódan*, to offer, to bid=Goth. *biudan*, G. *bieten*, to offer, command.] To ask, request, or invite (a person); to pray; to wish; to say to by way of greeting or benediction (to *bid* good-day, farewell); to command; to order or direct; to enjoin: followed by an objective and infinitive without *to* (*bid* him come); to offer; to propose, as a price at an auction.—*n*. An offer of a price, especially at an auction.—**bidder**, bid'ėr, *n*. One who bids or offers a price.

bide, bīd, *v.i*. [A. Sax. *bidan*=Icel. *bida*, D. *beiden*, Goth. *beidan*. Hence *abide*.] To be or remain in a place or state; to dwell; to inhabit.—*v.t*. To endure; to suffer; to bear; to wait for (chiefly in phrase *to bide one's time*).

bidentate, bī·den'tāt, *a*. [L. *bidens*—prefix *bi*, and *dens*, a tooth.] Having two teeth, or processes like teeth; two-toothed.

biennial, bī·en'ni·al, *a*. [L. *biennium*, a space of two years—prefix *bi*, twice, *annus*, a year.] Happening or taking place once in two years; *bot.* continuing for two years and then perishing; taking two years to produce its flowers and fruit.—*n*. A biennial plant.—**biennially**, bī·-

en′ni·al·li, *adv.* Once in two years; at the return of two years.

bier, bēr, *n.* [O.E. *beere, bere,* A. Sax. *baer,* a bier; from the root of *bear,* to carry.] A carriage or frame of wood for conveying a corpse to the grave.

biestings, bēst′ingz. See BEESTINGS.

bifacial, bī·fā′shi·al, *a.* [L. prefix *bi,* twice, *facies,* a face.] Having the opposite surfaces alike.

bifid, bī′fid, *a.* [L. *bifidus*—prefix *bi,* twice, *findo, fidi,* to split.] Cleft or divided into two parts; forked; *bot.* divided half-way down into two parts; opening with a cleft.

bifilar, bī·fī′lėr, *a.* [L. prefix *bi,* twice, and *filum,* a thread.] Two-threaded; fitted or furnished with two threads (a *bifilar* micrometer).

bifocal, bī·fō′kal, *a.* Having two focuses.—**bifocal lens,** a lens with two parts: one for near vision and one for distant vision.—*n. pl.* Eyeglasses with bifocal lenses.

bifoliate, bī·fō′li·āt, *a.* [L. *bi,* twice, two, and *folium,* a leaf.] In *bot.* having two leaves.

biform, biformed, bī′form, bī′-formd, *a.* [L. *biformis,* double-formed—*bi,* twice, and *forma,* form.] Having two forms, bodies, or shapes; double-shaped.

bifurcate, bī·fėr′kāt, *a.* [L. *bi,* twice, and *furca,* a fork.] Forked; divided into two branches.—**bifurcation,** bī·fėr·kā′shon, *n.* A forking or division into two branches.

big, big, *a.* [Etymology doubtful; perhaps connected with Sc. or North. E. to *big,* Icel. *byggja,* Dan. *bygge,* to build.] Having size, whether large or small; more especially, great; large; bulky; great with young; pregnant; hence, *fig.* full of something important; teeming; distended; full, as with grief or passion; tumid; haughty in air or mien; pompous. —**bighorn,** *n.* The Rocky Mountain sheep.—**bigwig,** *n.* A person of great importance.

bigamy, big′a·mi, *n.* [Prefix *bi,* twice, and Gr. *gamos,* marriage.] The crime, fact, or state of having two wives or husbands at once.— **bigamist,** big′a·mist, *n.* One who has committed bigamy.—**bigamous,** big′a·mus, *a.* Of or pertaining to bigamy; guilty of bigamy.

biggin, big′in, *n.* [Fr. *beguin,* the cap of the *Beguines.*] A child's cap; a nightcap; a coif. (Shak.)

bight, bīt, *n.* [A.Sax. *byht,* from *bigan, bugan,* to *bow* or bend=L.G. Dan. Icel. *bugt,* a bending, a bay. BOW.] A bend in a coastline; a bay; the double of a rope when folded; a bend anywhere except at the ends; a loop.

bignonia, big·nō′ni·a, *n.* [After M. *Bignon,* librarian to Louis XIV.] The generic name of a number of plants, inhabitants of hot climates, usually climbing shrubs with beautiful trumpet-shaped flowers, hence their name of *trumpet flower.*

bigot, big′ot, *n.* [Fr. *bigot,* a bigot; It. *bigotto, bigozzo.* Etymology uncertain; Some suppose it a corruption of *Visigoth,* as intolerant Arians, persecuting in Spain, others refer it to

the oath *bi Gott* (by God) common among the Norse settlers in Normandy.] A person obstinately and unreasonably wedded to a particular religious creed, opinion, or practice; a person blindly attached to any opinion, system, or party.—**bigoted,** big′ot·ed, *a.* Having the character of a bigot; belonging to a bigot; showing blind attachment to opinions.—**bigotedly,** big′ot·ed·li, *adv.* In a bigoted manner.—**bigotry,** big′ot·ri, *n.* The practice or tenets of a bigot; obstinate or blind attachment to a particular creed or to certain tenets; unreasoning zeal; intolerance.

bijou, bē′zhö, *n.* [Fr.] A jewel; something small and pretty.—**bijouterie,** bē·zhö′trē, *n.* Jewelry; trinkets.

bijugous, bijugate, bī′jū·gus, bī′jū-gāt, *a.* [L. *bijugus*—*bi,* two, *jugum,* a yoke.] Having two pairs of leaflets.

bike, bīk, *n.* A bicycle. [Colloq.]

bilabiate, bī·lā′bi·āt, *a.* [L. *bi,* twice, and *labium,* a lip.] *Bot.* applied to a corolla having two lips, the one placed over the other.

bilander, bī′lan·dėr, *n.* [D. *bijlander*—*bij,* by, near, and *land,* land.] A small merchant vessel with two masts, used chiefly in the Dutch canals; a kind of hoy.

bilateral, bī·lat′ėr·al, *a.* [L. *bi,* twice, and *latus, lateris,* a side.] Having two sides; of or pertaining to two sides; two sided.

bilberry, bil′be·ri, *n.* [Dan. *böllebaer,* bilberry—*bölle,* of doubtful meaning, and *baer,* a berry.] Any of several species of blueberry of the genus *Vaccinium;* the European whortleberry (*Vaccinium myrtillus*).

bilbo,‡ bil′bō, *n.* [From *Bilbao* in Spain, famous for their manufacture.] A rapier; a sword.—**bilboes,** bil′bōz, *n. pl.* A contrivance for confining the feet of prisoners—a long bar or bolt of iron with shackles sliding on it and a lock at the end.

bile, bīl, *n.* [Fr. *bile,* L. *bilis,* bile, also anger, spleen.] A yellow bitter liquid, separated from the blood by the action of the liver, and discharged into the gallbladder, its most obvious use being to assist in the process of digestion; ill-nature; bitterness of feeling; spleen.—**biliary,** bil′i-a·ri, *n.* Pertaining to or containing bile.—**bilious,** bil′i·us, *a.* Consisting of, or affected by bile; having an excess of bile; having the health deranged from excess of bile in the system.—**biliousness,** bil′i·us·nes, *n.* The state or quality of being bilious, or of suffering from an excessive secretion of bile.

bilge, bilj, *n.* [A different orthography of *bulge.*] The protuberant part of a cask; the breadth of a ship's bottom, or that part of her floor which approaches to a horizontal direction.—*v.i. Naut.* to spring a leak in the bilge.—**bilge water,** *n.* A water which enters a ship and lies upon her bilge or bottom.

bilingual, bī·ling′gwal, *a.* [L. *bilinguis*—*bi,* double, and *lingua,* a tongue, a language.] Containing, or expressed in, two different lan-

guages (a *bilingual* dictionary).

bilk, bilk, *v.t.* [Probably a form of *balk.*] To deceive or defraud by nonfulfillment of engagement; to leave in the lurch; to decamp without paying (a person).

bill, bil, *n.* [A.Sax. *bile,* a beak.] The beak of a fowl.—*v.t.* To join bills or beaks, as doves; to caress fondly.

bill, bil, *n.* [A.Sax. *bil, bill,* a bill, a sword, etc.; D. and G. *bille,* a pick; Dan. *biil,* D. *bijl,* G. *beil,* a hatchet; root in Skr. *bhil,* to split.] A cutting instrument hook-shaped toward the point, or with a concave cutting edge, used in pruning, etc.; a billhook; an ancient military weapon, consisting of a broad hook-shaped blade, having a short pike at the back and another at the summit, attached to a long handle.— **billhook,** *n.* A small variety of hatchet with a hook at the end of the cutting edge.

bill, bil, *n.* [O.Fr. *bille,* a label or note, from L.L. *billa, bulla,* a seal, a letter, a roll, from L. *bulla,* a boss, a stud, whence *bull,* a papal edict.] A sheet or piece of paper containing a statement of certain particulars; a sheet containing a public notice or advertisement; a note of charges for goods supplied, work done, or the like, with the amount due on each item; a declaration of certain facts in legal proceedings; a written promise to pay or document binding one to pay a specified sum at a certain date; a bill of exchange (see below); a draft of a law presented to a legislature to be passed into an act: also applied to various measures that are really acts.—*Bill of divorce,* a writing given by a husband to his wife among the Jews by which their marriage was dissolved.—*Bill of entry,* a written account of goods entered at the custom house.— *Bill of exchange,* an order drawn by one person (the drawer) on another (the drawee) who is either in the same or in some distant country, requesting or directing him to pay money at a specified time to some person assigned (the payee), who may either be the drawer himself or some other person. The person on whom the bill is drawn becomes the ' acceptor ' by writing his name on it as such.—*Bill of fare,* in a hotel, restaurant, etc., a list of refreshments ready to be supplied.— *Bill of health,* a certificate signed by consuls or other authorities as to the health of a ship's company at the time of her clearing any port, a *clean bill* being given when no disorder is supposed to exist, and a *foul bill* when it is known to exist.— *Bill of lading,* a memorandum of goods shipped on board of a vessel, signed by way of receipt by the master of the vessel.—*Bill of mortality,* an official return of the number of deaths occurring in a place within a certain time.—*Bill of sale,* a formal instrument for the transfer of personal property (as furniture, the stock in a shop), often given in security for a debt, empowering the receiver to sell the goods if the money is not repaid at the appointed time.—**billboard**, *n.* A board, fence, etc., on which advertisements are posted.

billet, bil′et, *n.* [A dim of *bill* = Fr. *billet*. BILL.] A small paper or note in writing; a short letter; a ticket directing soldiers at what house to lodge.—**billet**, bil′et, *v.t.* To quarter or place in lodgings, as soldiers in private houses.—*v.i.* To be quartered; to lodge: specifically applied to soldiers.

billet, bil′et, *n.* [Fr. *billot*, a log, from *bille*, the stock of a tree, from the Celtic.] A small stick or round piece of wood used for various purposes; *arch.* an imitation of a wooden billet placed in a hollow molding at intervals apart, usually equal to its own length.

billet-doux, bil·le·dö′, *n. pl.* **billets-doux**, bil·le·döz′. [Fr., lit. sweet billet or note.] A love note or short love letter.

billiards, bil′yẽrdz, *n.* [Fr. *billard*, the game of billiards, a billiard cue, from *bille*, a piece of wood.] A game played on a long rectangular, cloth-covered table, without pockets, with three ivory balls. Scoring is made by the use of a cue to cause one ball to strike the other two. Pocket billiards are played on the same kind of table but having six pockets and fifteen numbered balls and one cue ball, the object being to drive the numbered balls into pockets with the cue ball.

billingsgate, bil′ingz·gāt, *n.* [From a fish-market of this name in London, celebrated for the use of foul language.] Profane or foul language; ribaldry.

billion, bil′yon, *n.* [Fr., contr. from L. *bis*, twice, and *million*.] A thousand millions, in the U.S. and France; a million millions in Great Britain and Germany.

billon, bil′on, *n.* [Fr.] An alloy of copper and silver, used in some countries for coins of low value.

billow, bil′ō, *n.* [Icel. *bylgja*, Dan. *bölge*, Sw. *bölja*, a swell, a billow, from root of *bulge, belly, bellows*.] A great wave or surge of the sea.—*v.i.* To swell; to rise and roll in large waves or surges.—**billowy**, bil′lō·i, *a.* Swelling into large waves; full of surges; belonging to billows; wavy.

billy goat, bil′i·gōt, *n.* A he-goat, after the man's name.

bilobate, bī·lō′bāt, *a.* [Prefix *bi*, and *lobate*.] Divided into two lobes (a *bilobate* leaf).

bilocular, bī·lok′ū·lẽr, *a.* [L. *bi*, twice, and *loculus*, a cell, from *locus*, a place.] Divided into two cells or small compartments.

biltong, bil′tong, *n.* An African name for lean meat cut in strips and dried.

bimensal, bī·men′sal, *a.* [L. *bi*, two, twice, and *mensis*, a month.] Occurring once in two months.

bimetallic, bī·me·tal′ik, *a.* [Prefix *bi*, twice, and *metallic*.] Of or pertaining to two metals; pertaining to the use of a double metallic standard in currency.—**bimetallism**, bī·met′al·izm, *n.* That system of currency which recognizes coins of two metals, as silver and gold, as legal tender to any amount.—**bimetallist**, met′al·ist, *n.* One who favors bimetallism.

bimonthly, bī·munth′li, *a.* [Prefix *bi*, twice, and *monthly*.] Occurring every two months.

bin, bin, *n.* [A.Sax. *bin, binn*, a bin, a hutch; D. *ben*, G. *benne, binne*, a basket.] A box or enclosed place used as a repository of any commodity; one of the subdivisions of a cellar for wine bottles.

binary, bī′na·ri, *a.* [L. *binus*, double. two and two.] Consisting or composed of two or of two parts; double; twofold; dual.—*Binary compound, chem.* a compound of two elements or radicals.—*Binary system, math.* a system of numerical notation with a base of 2, used in digital computers. —*Binary star*, a double star, one of two stars associated together so as to form a system, the one revolving round the other, or both round their common center of gravity.

binaural broadcasting. Radio broadcasting via both FM and AM microphones so arranged that pickup on FM and AM receivers provides a stereophonic effect.

bind, bīnd, *v.t.*—*bound* (pret. & pp.), *binding*. [A. Sax. *bindan*, pret. *band*, pp. *bunden* = Icel. Sw. *binda*, Dan. *binde*, D. and G. *binden*, same root as Skr. *bandh*, to bind.] To tie or confine with a cord, or anything that is flexible; to fasten or encircle, as with a band or ligature; to put a ligature or bandage on; to put in bonds or fetters; to hold in, confine, or restrain; to engage by a promise, agreement, vow, law, duty, or any other moral or legal tie; to form a border on, or strengthen by a border; to sew together and cover (a book). —*v.i.* To exercise an obligatory influence; to be obligatory; to tie up; to tie sheaves up; to grow hard or stiff (of soil).—**binder**, bīnd′ẽr, *n.* A person who binds; one whose occupation is to bind books; one who binds sheaves; anything that binds, as a fillet, cord, rope, or band; a bandage.—**bindery**, bīnd′ẽr·i *n.* A place where books are bound.— **binding**, bīnd′ing, *a.* Serving to bind; having power to bind or oblige; obligatory; making fast; astringent.— *n.* The act of one who binds; anything which binds; the cover of a book, with the sewing and accompanying work; something that secures the edges of cloth.—**bindingly**, bīnd′ing·li, *adv.* In a binding manner; so as to bind.—**bindingness**, bīnd′ing·nes. *n.* The character of being binding or obligatory.—**bindweed**, *n.* The common name for twining or trailing plants of the convolvulus family, common in cornfields and waste places and overrunning hedges.

bine, bīn, *n.* [From the verb to *bind*.] The slender stem of a climbing plant: sometimes written *Bind*.

bing, bing, *n.* [Dan. *binge*, Icel. *bingr*, a heap.] A large heap, as of corn, coal, ore, etc.

binnacle, bin′a·kl, *n.* [Formerly, *bittacle*, from Fr. *habitacle*, a little house for pilot and steersman, from L. *habitaculum*, an abode, from *habito*, to dwell. HABITATION.] A box on the deck of a vessel, near the helm, containing the compass and lights by which it can be read at night.

binocular, bī·nok′ū·lẽr, *a.* [L. *binus* double and *oculus*, an eye.] Involving two eyes.—*n. pl.* Field glasses.

binomial, bī·nō′mi·al, *n.* [L. *bi*, two, twice, and *nomen*, a name.] *Alg.* an expression or quantity consisting of two terms connected by the sign *plus* (+) or *minus* (—).—*a.* Pertaining to binomials.—*Binomial theorem*, a celebrated theorem by Sir Isaac Newton, for raising a binomial to any power, or for extracting any root of it.

bioastronautics, bī·ō·as·trō·nạ′tiks, *n.* [Gr. *bios*, life, and E. *astronautics*.] The study of the effects of air flight and space travel on plant and animal life; space medicine.

biochemistry, bī·ō·kem′ist·ri, *n.* [Gr. *bios*, life, and *chemistry*.] The science that studies the chemical processes of plant and animal life.

biodynamics, bī′ō·di·nam″iks, *n.* [Gr. *bios*, life, and E. *dynamics* (which see).] The doctrine of vital forces or energy.

biogenesis, bī·ō·jen′e·sis, *n.* [Gr. *bios*, life, and *genesis*, generation.] The origin of what has life (vegetable or animal) from living matter; the doctrine which holds that living organisms can spring only from living parents: as opposed to *abiogenesis;* the history of the life development of organized existences. —**biogenetic**, bī·ō·je·net′ik, *a.* Of or pertaining to biogenesis.

biography, bī·og′ra·fi, *n.* [Gr. *bios*, life, and *graphō*, to write.] The history of the life and character of a particular person; a life; a memoir. —**biographer**, bī·og′ra·fẽr, *n.* One who writes a biography.—**biographic, biographical**, bī·ō·graf′ik, bī·ō·graf′ik·al, *a.*—**biographically**, bī·ō·graf′ik·al·li, *adv.*

biology, bī·ol′o·ji, *n.* [Gr. *bios*, life, and *logos*, a discourse.] The science of life, or which treats generally of the life of animals and plants, including their morphology, physiology, origin, development, and distribution.—**biologic, biological**, bī·ō·loj′ik, bī·ō·loj′ik·al, *a.* Pertaining to biology.—**biological warfare.** Warfare using bacteria or viruses or their products against man, domestic animals, or food plants.—**biologist**, bī·ol′o·jist, *n.* One skilled in or who studies biology.

bioluminescence, bī·ō·lu·me·nes′ens, *n.* [Gr. *bios*, life, and *luminescence*.] The emission of light from living organisms such as fireflies.

biopsy, bī′op·si, *n.* [Gr. *bios*, life, and *opsis*, appearance.] The examination of specimens of fluid, cells, or tissue taken from a living body.

biparous, bip′a·rus, *a.* [L. *bi*, twice, and *pario*, to bear.] Bringing forth two at a birth. *Bot.* bearing two axes.

fāte, fär, fâre, fat, fạll; mē, met, hẽr; pīne, pin; nōte, not, möve; tūbe, tub, bụll; oil, pound.

bipartible, bipartile, bī·pär′ti·bl, bī·pär′til, *a.* [L. prefix *bi*, twice, and *partio*, to divide.] Capable of being divided into two parts.— **bipartite,** bī·pär′tīt, *a.* In two parts; having two correspondent parts; double; *bot.* divided into two parts nearly to the base, as leaves.— **bipartition,** bī·pär·ti′shon, *n.* The act of making bipartite.

bipartisan, bī·pär′ti·zan, *n.* [Prefix *bi* and *partisan*.] Composed or representative of two parties.

biped, bī′ped, *n.* [L. *bipes*—*bi*, twice, and *pes*, *pedis*, a foot.] An animal having two feet, as man.—**bipedal,** bī′ped·al, *a.* [L. *bipedalis*.] Having two feet.

bipinnate, bī·pin′nāt, *a.* [L. *bi*, double, and *pinnatus*, winged.] *Bot.* doubly pinnate; having pinnae which are pinnate.

biplane, bī′plān, *n.* [Prefix *bi*, and *plane*.] A flying machine with an upper and an under plane or carrying surface.

bipropellant, bī·prō·pel′ant, *n.* [Prefix *bi* and *propellant*.] Rocket fuel consisting of two unmixed chemicals that combine in a combustion chamber.

biquadratic, bī·kwod·rat′ik, *n.* [L. *bi*, double, twice, and *quadratus*, squared.] *Math.* the fourth power, arising from the multiplication of a square by itself; the square of the square.—*a.* Pertaining to this power.

birch, bėrch, *n.* [A. Sax. *byrc, beorc*= Icel. and Sw. *björk*, Dan. and Sc. *birk* (comp. Sc. *kirk*, E. *church*), D. *berk*, G. *birke*, Rus. *bereza*, Lith. *berzas*, Skr. *bhurja*—a birch.] A graceful tree having small leaves, slender, often drooping branches, and a smooth whitish bark; a kind of wine is made from its spring sap, its bark is much used in tanning, and its timber is employed in turnery; an instrument of punishment used by schoolmasters, generally made of the tough, slender twigs of the common birch.— **birchen,** bėrch′en, *a.* Made of birch; consisting of birch.

bird, bėrd, *n.* [A. Sax. *brid*, a young bird, from the root of *brood*, *breed*. *Fowl* was originally the word for bird in general.] A feathered, warm-blooded animal, with two legs and two wings, producing young from eggs; one of the feathered class (Aves) of the vertebrate animals.— *v.i.* To catch birds.—**birdcall,** *n.* An instrument for imitating the cry of birds in order to attract or decoy them.— **bird cherry,** *n.* A species of cherry having the flowers in racemes and fruit only fit for birds.— **birdlime,** *n.* A viscous substance prepared from holly bark, etc., used for entangling birds; twigs being for this purpose smeared with it at places where birds resort.—*v.t.* To besmear with birdlime.— **bird of paradise,** *n.* One of a family of conirostral birds found in the islands of the Indian Archipelago, the male birds being celebrated for their gorgeous plumage.—**bird's-eye,** *n.* The popular name of a species of

primrose or wild germander and several other plants; a kind of cut tobacco, the minute slices of the stems of which are marked somewhat like a bird's eye.—*Bird's-eye maple*, the wood of the sugar maple, which is marked by little knotty spots resembling birds' eyes, and is much used in cabinetmaking.—*Bird's-eye view*, a view or landscape shown as it might appear to a flying bird; hence, a rapid and comprehensive view of a subject.—**bird's-foot,** *n.* A common name for several plants, having legumes somewhat resembling the claws of a bird.—**bird's-nest,** *n.* A name of several plants, especially a British orchid having a root resembling a nest.

bireme, bī′rēm, *n.* [L. *biremis*—*bi*, two, and *remus*, an oar.] An ancient Greek or Roman vessel with two banks or tiers of oars.

biretta, beretta, bē·ret′ta, bā·ret′ta, *n.* [It. *berretta*, L.L. *birettum*, *birretum*, dim. of *birrus*, a hood.] A square cap worn by ecclesiastics; priests have it black, bishops purple, cardinals red: written also *Birretta*.

birr, bir, *n.* [Imitative of the sound.] A whirring noise.—*v.i.* To make a whirring noise.

birth, bėrth, *n.* [A. Sax. *beorth, byrth*, from *beran*, to bear; Goth. *gabaurths*, G. *geburt*.] The act or process of being born; the occasion of an individual's coming into life; the act of bearing or bringing forth; parturition; the condition in which a person is born; lineage; extraction; descent; that which is born or produced; origin; beginning.— **birthday,** *n.* The day on which any person is born, or the anniversary of the day; day or time of origin.— **birthmark,** *n.* Some congenital mark or blemish on a person's body.— **birthplace,** *n.* The place of one's birth; place of origin.—**birthright,** *n.* Any right or privilege to which a person is entitled by birth; right of primogeniture.—**birthroot,** *n.* A North American plant, the roots of which are esteemed as astringent, tonic, and antiseptic.

biscuit, bis′ket, *n.* [Fr. *bis*, twice, and *cuit* (L. *coctus*), cooked. COOK.] Bread baked in pieces from dough leavened with soda, yeast, or baking-powder; unraised bread, plain, sweet, or fancy, formed into flat cakes, and baked hard, commonly called *cracker* in the United States.

bisect, bī·sekt′, *v.t.* [L. *bi*, two, and *seco*, *sectum*, to cut.] To cut or divide into two parts, more especially into two equal parts, as a line, etc.— **bisection,** bī·sek′shon, *n.* The act of bisecting; the division of a line, angle, etc., into two equal parts.

bisexual, bī·seks′ū·al. *a.* Having the organs of both sexes in one individual; of two sexes; hermaphrodite; *bot.* having both stamen and pistil within the same envelope.

bishop, bish′up, *n.* [A. Sax. *biscop*, a bishop, from Gr. *episcopos*, an overseer—*epi*, over, and *skopeō*, to look. *Bishop* is the same word as Fr. *évêque* (a bishop), though they

have not a letter in common.] A member of the highest order of the Christian ministry; a prelate having the spiritual direction and government of a diocese, the oversight of the clergy within it, and with whom rests the power of ordination, confirmation, and consecration; a piece in the game of chess having its upper section cleft in the form of a bishop's miter.—**bishopric,** bish′up·rik, *n.* [*Bishop*, and *ric*, jurisdiction= A. Sax. *rice*, D. *rijk*, G. *reich*, realm, dominion.] The office or dignity of a bishop; the district over which the jurisdiction of a bishop extends; a diocese.

bismuth, bis′muth or biz′muth, *n.* [G. *bismuth*, *wismuth*.] Chemical element. Symbol, Bi; at. no., 83; at. wt., 208.980.

bison, bī′son, *n.* [L. *bison*, Gr. *bisōn*, a name borrowed from the ancient Germans.] The name of two bovine quadrupeds, the European bison or aurochs, and the American bison, usually called the buffalo, having short, black, rounded horns, and on the shoulders a large hunch, consisting of a fleshy substance.

bisque, bisk, *n.* [Fr.] Unglazed white porcelain; a reddish-yellow color; a rich soup, usually of meat or fish.

bissextile, bis·seks′til, *n.* [L. *bisextilis* (*annus*), leap year, from *bi*, twice, and *sextus*, sixth, because the sixth day before the calends of March (=our 24th Feb.) was reckoned twice every fourth year, a day (the *bisextus*) being intercalated.] Leap year.—*a.* Pertaining to leap year.

bistort, bis′tort *n.* [L. *bistorta*—*bis*, twice, and *tortus*, twisted.] A plant, so called because of its twisted roots.

bistre, bister, bis′tėr, *n.* [Fr. *bistre*.] A brown pigment prepared from the soot of wood, especially of the beech.

bisulcate, bī·sul′kāt, *a.* [L. *bi*, double, and *sulcus*, a furrow.] Cloven-footed, or having two-hoofed digits, as oxen or swine.

bisulfate, bī·sul′fāt, *n.* In *chem.* a salt of sulfuric acid, in which one-half of the hydrogen of the acid is replaced by a metal.—**bisulfite,** bī·sul′fīt, *n.* A salt of sulfurous acid, in which one-half of the hydrogen of the acid is replaced by a metal.

bit, bit, *n.* [From the verbal stem *bite*. In sense of piece it is the A. Sax. *bita*, *bite*, Icel. *biti*, a bite, a morsel; in sense of part of a bridle it corresponds to A. Sax. *bitol*, D. *bit*, Icel. *bitill*, G. *gebiss*.] A small piece of anything; a piece, morsel, fragment, or part; any small coin; the metal part of a bridle which is inserted in the mouth of a horse, and its appendages, to which the reins are fastened; a boring tool for wood or metal, fixed in a stock, brace, lathe, or the like; the part of a key which enters the lock and acts on the bolts and tumblers; the cutting blade of a plane. ∴ In certain phrases *a bit* often means somewhat, a little, a whit; as, he is *a bit* of a painter; not *a bit* better.—*A bit of* *one's mind*, one's candid opinions expressed in clear and unflattering terms.—*v.t.*—*bitted, bitting*. To put a horse's bit into the mouth of.

bit, bit, *n*. [A blend of *bi*nary and digi*t*.] *Communication theory*, the basic unit of the measurement of information.

bitch, bich, *n*. [A. Sax. *bicce* = Sc. *bick*, Icel. *bikkja*, Dan. *bikke*.] The female of canine animals, as of the dog, wolf, and fox; a term of reproach for a woman.

bite, bīt, *v.t.* bit (pret.), *bit, bitten* (pp.), *biting*. [A. Sax. *bītan* = Icel. *bíta*, D. *bijten*, Goth. *beitan*, G. *beiszen*; *allied* to L. *findo, fidi*, Skr. *bhid*, to split. *Bit, bitter, beetle* are from this stem.] To cut, break, or crush with the teeth; to penetrate or seize with the teeth; to cause a sharp or smarting pain to (pepper *bites* the mouth); to pinch or nip as with frost; to blast or blight; to grip or catch into or on, so as to act with effect (as an anchor, a file, etc.); to corrode or eat into, by aqua fortis or other acid.—*v.i.* To have a habit of biting persons; to seize a bait with the mouth; to grip or catch into another object, so as to act on it with effect (the anchor *bites*).—*n.* The seizure of anything by the teeth or with the mouth; a wound made by the mouth; a mouthful; a bit; a cheat, trick, fraud‡; catch or hold of one object on another.—**biter**, bīt′ėr, *n.* One who or that which bites; an animal given to biting; one who cheats or deceives‡ (in phrase now, 'the *biter* bit').—**biting**, bīt′ing, *a.* Sharp; severe; cutting; pungent; sarcastic. —**bitingly**, bīt′ing·li, *adv.* In a biting manner; sarcastically; sneeringly.

bitt, bit, *n.* [Comp. Icel. *biti*, a cross-beam or girder.] *Naut.* a piece of wood or frame secured to the deck, on which to make fast the cables.

bitter, bit′ėr, *a.* [A.Sax. *biter*, from *bītan*, to bite, from causing the tongue to smart = D. G. Dan. and Sw. *bitter*, Icel. *bitr*.] Acrid, biting, pungent to taste; keen, cruel, poignant, severe, sharp, harsh, painful, distressing, piercing to the feelings or to the mind; reproachful, sarcastic, or cutting, as words.—**bitterish**, bit′ėr·ish, *a.* Somewhat bitter, especially to the taste.—**bitterly**, bit′ėr·li, *adv.* In a bitter manner; keenly, sharply, severely, intensely. —**bittern**, bit′ėrn, *n.* The residual brine in saltworks, used for making Epsom salts.—**bitterness**, bit′ėr·nes, *n.* The state or quality of being bitter in all its senses, whether to the taste, feelings, or mind.—**bitters**, bit′ėrz, *n. pl.* A liquor prepared with bitter herbs or roots, and used as a stomachic, etc.—**bittersweet**, *n.* The woody nightshade, a trailing plant with small scarlet berries and strongly narcotic leaves, so called because the root and branches when chewed produce first a bitter, then a sweet taste.

bittern, bit·ėrn, *n.* [O.E. *bitore, bittor, bittour*; Fr. *butor*, Sp. *bitor*; origin uncertain.] A name given to several grallatorial or wading birds of the heron family, celebrated for the singular booming or drumming noise they make.

bitumen, bi·tū′men, *n.* [L.] A mineral substance of a resinous nature and highly inflammable, appearing in a variety of forms which are known by different names, *naphtha* being the most fluid, *petroleum* and *mineral tar* less so, and *asphalt* being solid.— **bituminization**, bi·tū′min·iz·ā″shon, *n.* Transformation into a bituminous substance.—**bituminize**, bi·tū′min-īz, *v.t.*—*bituminized, bituminizing*. To form into or impregnate with bitumen; to convert (as wood) into a bituminous body.—**bituminous**, bi·tū′min·us, *a.* Having the qualities of bitumen; containing or yielding bitumen.

bivalve, bī′valv, *n.* [L. prefix *bi*, double, and *valva*, a valve.] An animal of the molluscous class, having two valves, or a shell consisting of two parts which open by an elastic hinge and are closed by muscles, as the oyster, cockle, mussel, etc.; *bot.* a pericarp in which the seedcase opens or splits into two parts.— **bivalve, bivalvular**, bī′valv, bī·val′-vū·lėr, *a.* Having two valves: said especially of the shells of mollusks.

bivouac, biv′ö·ak, *n.* [Fr. *bivouac, bivac*, from G. *beiwache*; lit. by-or near-watch. WAKE, WATCH.] An encampment of soldiers in the open air without tents, each remaining dressed and with his weapons by him; a similar encampment of travelers, hunters, etc.—*v.i.* bivouacked, bivouacking. To encamp in bivouac; to pass the night in the open air without tents or covering.

biweekly, bī·wēk′li, *a.* Occurring or appearing every two weeks (a *biweekly* magazine).

bizarre, bi·zär′, *a.* [Fr., from Sp. *bizarro*, gallant, of Basque origin.] Old in appearance; fanciful; fantastical; formed of incongruous parts.

blab, blab, *v.t.*—*blabbed, blabbing.* [Allied to L.G. *blabben*, Dan. *blabbre*, G. *plappern*, to gabble; Gael. *bla-baran*, a stutterer; *blubber*-lipped, *blob*, etc.] To utter or tell in a thoughtless or unnecessary manner what ought to be kept secret; to let out (secrets).—*v.i.* To talk indiscreetly; to tattle; to tell tales.—*n.* One who blabs; a telltale. (*Mil.*)— **blabber**, blab′ėr, *n.* A blab; a tattler; a telltale.

black, blak, *a.* [A.Sax. *blæc, blac*, black = Icel. *blakkr*, O.H.G. *plak*, black; comp. D. and L.G. *blaken*, to burn or scorch, Gr. *phlegō*, to burn, the original meaning perhaps referring to blackness caused by fire.] Of the darkest color; the opposite of white; very dark in hue (though not absolutely incapable of reflecting light; destitute of light, or nearly so; dismal, gloomy, sullen, forbidding, or the like; destitute of moral light or goodness; mournful; calamitous; evil; wicked; atrocious. —*Black art*, the art of performing wonderful feats by supernatural means, or aided by evil spirits; necromancy; magic.—*Black beer*, a kind of beer of a black color and syrupy consistence.—*Black cattle*, oxen, cows, etc., reared for slaughter, as distinguished from dairy cattle; used without reference to color.— *Black death*, an oriental plague which first visited Europe in the fourteenth century, characterized by inflammatory boils and black spots all over the skin.—*Black flag*, the flag formerly assumed by pirates.— *Black list*, a printed list circulated among commercial men, containing the names of persons who have become bankrupt or unable to meet their bills, etc.—*Black snake*, a name given to some snakes of a black color, such as a large non-venomous North American snake which feeds on birds and small quadrupeds.— *Black spruce*, a spruce tree belonging to North America, which furnishes the spruce deals of commerce.—*n.* The opposite of white; a black dye or pigment or a hue produced by such; a black part of something, as of the eye; a black dress of mourning; frequently in plural; **a** small flake of soot; a member of one of the dark-colored races; a Negro or other dark-skinned person. —*v.t.* To make black; to apply blacking to (shoes); to blacken; to soil.—**blacken**, blak′n, *v.t.* To make black; to polish with blacking; to sully; to stain; to defame; to vilify; to slander.—*v.i.* To become black or dark.—**blacking**, blak′ing, *n.* A composition for polishing boots, shoes, harness, etc., consisting usually of a mixture of lampblack, oil, vinegar. etc.—**blackish**, blak′ish, *a.* Somewhat black.—**blackly**, blak′li, *adv.* In a black manner; darkly; gloomily; threateningly; angrily; atrociously.—**blackness**, blak′nes, *n.* The state or quality of being black; black color; darkness; gloominess; somberness; sullen or severe aspect; atrocity.—**blackamoor**, blak′a·mör, *a.* [*Black.* and *Moor.* in the old sense of black man or Negro, formerly written also *blackmoor*.] A Negro; a black man or woman.— **blackball**, *v.t.* To reject, as a proposed member of a club; to exclude by vote.—**blackberry**, *n.* The berry of the bramble.—**blackbird**, blak′-bėrd, *n.* An insessorial bird of the thrush family, the male bird being characterized by its black plumage and its rich mellow note; the merle. —**blackboard**, *n.* A board painted black, used in schools and lecture rooms for writing or drawing lines on for instruction.—**blackcap**, *n.* A dentirostral European bird of the warbler family, noted for the sweetness of its song, and so called from its black tufted crown; a species of raspberry having black fruit, native to North America.—**black-cock**, *n.* A bird of the grouse family, so called from the glossy black plumage of the male; the heath cock or black grouse.—**Black Friar**, *n.* A friar of the Dominican order, so called from the color of

the dress; a Dominican.—**black-guard**, black'gärd or bla'gärd, n. [Formerly a name given to the scullions and lowest menials connected with a great household, who attended to the pots, coals, etc.] A man of coarse and offensive manners; a fellow of low character; a scamp; a scoundrel.—v.t. To revile in low or scurrilous language.—**blackguardism**, blak'gärd·izm, or bla'gärd·izm, n. The conduct or language of a blackguard.—**blackguardly**, blak'gärd·li or bla'gärd·li, a. Characteristic of a blackguard; rascally; villainous.—**black hole**, n. Formerly a dungeon or dark cell in a prison; now more specifically applied to a place of confinement for soldiers.—**blackjack**, n. A capacious can, now made of tin, but formerly of waxed leather; the flag or ensign of a pirate; a small leather-covered club or billy weighted at the head and having an elastic shaft; a card game.—**blacklead**, n. Amorphous graphite; plumbago. GRAPHITE.—**blackleg**, n. [Origin undecided.] One who systematically tries to win money by cheating in connection with races, or with cards, billiards, or other game; a rook; a swindler; also same as Black-quarter, a disease of cattle.—**black letter**, n. The old English or Gothic type used in early printed books, being an imitation of the written character in use before the art of printing, still in general use in German books.—**blackmail**, n. [-mail is from Icel. mâl, stipulation, agreement, mœla, to stipulate.] Money or an equivalent, anciently paid, in the north of England and in Scotland, to certain men allied with robbers, to be protected by them from pillage; hence, the act of demanding payment by means of intimidation; also extortion of money from a person by threats of public accusation or censure.—**black market**, n. Trade in violation of official prices or quantities.—**blackout**, n. The dimming of a city's lights as a precaution against air raids; temporary loss of consciousness.—**Black Rod**, n. In England, the usher belonging to the order of the Garter and one of the official messengers of the House of Lords, so called from the black rod which he carries.—**black sheep**, n. A member of a family or society distinguished from his fellows by low habits or loose conduct.—**blacksmith**, blak'smith, n. A smith who works in iron and makes iron utensils; an ironsmith: opposed to a whitesmith or tinsmith.—**blackthorn**, n. The sloe.—**black vomit**, n. A blackish substance vomited in yellow fever; the fever itself.—**black widow spider**, n. The name given to the female of an American spider that devours its mate. Its bite is poisonous.
bladder, blad'ėr, n. [A.Sax. blœdr, blœddre, a bladder, pustule, blister = Icel. blathra, Sw. bläddra, L.G. bladere, bledder, O.H.G. plâtara, a bladder, G. blatter, a pustule; the root is probably in E. to blow.] A

thin membranous bag in animals, which serves as the receptacle of some secreted fluid, as the urine, the gall, etc.; any vesicle, blister, or pustule, especially if filled with air or a thin watery liquid; a hollow appendage in some plants.—v.t. To put up in a bladder, as lard; to puff up; to fill with wind†.—**bladdery**, blad'ėr·i, a. Resembling or containing bladders.
blade, blād, n. [A.Sax. blœd, a leaf = D. Dan. Sw. blad, Icel. blath, G. blatt, a leaf; from root of to blow, and allied to bloom, blossom.] The leaf of a plant, especially the leaf or the young stalk or spire of grass or corn plants; a thing resembling a blade in shape, etc., as the cutting part of an instrument; the broad part of an oar; a dashing or rollicking fellow; a swaggerer; a rakish fellow.—v.t. To furnish with a blade.—v.i. To come into blade; to produce blades.—**bladed**, blād'ed, a. Having a blade or blades.
blain, blān, n. [A.Sax. blegen = D. blein, Dan. blegn, a blain, a blister; probably from root of to blow, and allied to bladder.] A pustule; a botch; a blister.
blame, blām, v.t.—blamed, blaming. [Fr. blâmer, O. Fr. blasmer, from L.L. blasphemare, from Gr. blasphemein, to calumniate. Blaspheme is the same word.] To express disapprobation of (a person or thing); to find fault with; to censure; to reproach; to chide; to condemn; to upbraid. ∴ In such phrases as ' he is to blame,' to blame has the passive meaning = to be blamed, like ' a house to let,' etc.—n. An expression of disapprobation for something deemed to be wrong; imputation of a fault; censure; reproach; reprehension; that which is deserving of censure (the blame is yours); fault; crime; sin.—**blamable**, blām'a·bl, a. Deserving of blame or censure; faulty; culpable; reprehensible; censurable.—**blamableness**, blām'a·bl·nes, n. The state or quality of being blamable.—**blamably**, blām'a·bli, adv. In a blamable manner; culpably.—**blameful**, blām'ful, a. Meriting blame; reprehensible; faulty; guilty; criminal.—**blameless**, blām'les, a. Not meriting blame or censure; without fault; undeserving of reproof; innocent; guiltless.—**blamelessly**, blām'les·li, adv. In a blameless manner.—**blamelessness**, blām'les·nes, n.—**blameworthy**, blām'wėr·ᴛʜi, a. Deserving blame; censurable, culpable; reprehensible. —**blameworthiness**, blām'wėr·ᴛʜi·nes, n.
blanch, blansh, v.t. [Fr. blanchir, to whiten, from blanc, white. BLANK.] To whiten by depriving of color; to render white, pale, or colorless (fear blanches the cheek); hort. to whiten or prevent from turning green by excluding the light, a process applied to kitchen vegetables, such as celery, lettuce, sea kale, etc.; to whiten or make lustrous, as metals, by acids or other means.—

v.i. To become white; to bleach.—**blancher**, blansh'ėr, n. One who blanches or whitens.
blanc-mange, blanc-manger, bla·manzh', blaṅ·maṅ·zhä', n. [Fr. blanc, white, and manger, food.] Cookery, a preparation of the consistency of a jelly, variously composed of dissolved isinglass, arrow root, cornstarch, etc., with milk and flavoring substances.
bland, bland, a. [L. blandus, mild.] Mild; soft; gentle (bland zephyrs); affable; suave (his manner is very bland); soothing; kindly.—**blandness**, bland'nes, n. State of being bland; mildness; gentleness.
blandish, blan'dish, v.t. & i. [O.Fr. blandir, blandissant, L. blandior, to flatter, from blandus, bland.] To render pleasing, alluring, or enticing; to caress, soothe, fawn, or flatter.—**blandisher**, blan'dish·ėr, n. One that blandishes; one that flatters with soft words.—**blandishment**, blan'dish·ment, n. Words or actions expressive of affection or kindness, and tending to win the heart; artful caresses; flattering attention; cajolery; endearment.
blank, blangk, a. [Fr. blanc, white, blank, from G. blank, white, lustrous, blank, from blinken, to blink, to glimmer; cog. D. Dan. and Sw. blank, white. BLINK.] White or pale†; void of written or printed characters, as paper; wanting something necessary to completeness; vacant; unoccupied; void; empty; pale from fear or terror; hence, confused; confounded; dispirited; dejected; unrhymed; applied to verse.—n. A piece of paper without writing or printed matter on it; a void space on paper or in any written or printed document; a document remaining incomplete till something essential is filled in; any void space; a void; a vacancy; a ticket in a lottery on which no prize is indicated; a lot by which nothing is gained; archery, the white mark in the center of a butt or target to which an arrow is directed; hence, the object to which anything is directed; aim; a piece of metal prepared to be formed into something useful by a further operation; a plate, or piece of gold or silver, cut and shaped, but not stamped into a coin.—v.t.‡ To make white or pale; confuse, confound, dispirit. (Shak.)—**blankly**, blangk'li, adv. In a blank manner; with paleness or confusion.—**blankness**, blangk'nes, n. State of being blank.
blanket, blang'ket, n. [O.Fr. blanket, dim. from blanc, white. BLANK.] A soft thick cloth made of wool loosely woven, and used as a covering in beds; any similar fabric used as covering, etc.—v.t. To toss in a blanket by way of punishment; to cover or clothe with a blanket (Shak.).
blare, blār, v.i.—blared, blaring. [Probably an imitative word; comp. D. blaren, L.G. blarren, blaren, G. blarren, blärren, to bellow, bleat, blare.] To give forth a loud sound

like a trumpet; to give out a brazen sound; to bellow.— *v.t.* To sound loudly; to proclaim noisily.—*n.* Sound like that of a trumpet; noise; roar.

blarney, blär'ni, *n.* [From Castle *Blarney*, near Cork, in the wall of which is a stone said to endow any one who kisses it with skill in the use of flattery.] Excessively complimentary language; gross flattery; smooth, deceitful talk; gammon. (Colloq.)—*v.t.* To talk over by soft delusive speeches; to flatter; to humbug with talk (colloq.).

blasé, blä·zā'. [Fr.] Lost to the power of enjoyment; used up; having the healthy energies exhausted.

blaspheme, blas·fēm', *v.t.*—*blasphemed, blaspheming.* [L. *blasphemare,* Gr. *blasphēmein,* to calumniate—from *blapsis,* injury, and *phēmi,* to speak. *Blame* is a shortened form of this word.] To speak in terms of impious irreverence of; to revile or speak reproachfully of instead of reverentially: used of speaking against God or things sacred.—*v.i.* To utter blasphemy; to use blasphemous language.—**blasphemer,** blas·fēm'ėr, *n.* One who blasphemes; one who speaks of God in impious and irreverent terms.—**blasphemous,** blas'fē·mus, *a.* Containing or exhibiting blasphemy; impiously irreverent or reproachful toward God.—**blasphemously,** blas'fē·mus·li, *adv.* In a blasphemous manner.—**blasphemy,** blas'fē·mi, *n.* The language of one who blasphemes; words uttered impiously against God; grossly irreverent or outrageous language.

blast, blast, *n.* [A.Sax. *blaest,* a puff of wind; from *blaesan,* to blow = Icel. *blástr,* Dan. *blœst,* a blowing; Icel. *blása,* Dan. *blœse,* G. *blasen,* to blow; same root as E. *blow, blase.*] A gust or puff of wind; a sudden gust of wind; the sound made by blowing a wind-instrument, as a horn or trumpet; the sound produced by one's breath; a blight or sudden pernicious influence on animals or plants; a forcible stream of air from the mouth, bellows etc.; a violent explosion of gunpowder or other explosive in splitting rocks, etc.—*v.t.* To injure by a blast; to cause to fade, shrivel, or wither; to blight or cause to come to nothing; to ruin; to split by an explosion.—*v.i.* To wither or be blighted. (*Shak.*)—**blast furnace,***n.* The smelting furnace used for obtaining iron from its ores with the aid of a powerful blast of air, usually a lofty furnace of masonry, in which the iron is smelted from its ore by being mixed with coal and the whole mass kept burning, the melted metal being run off at the bottom. —**blast-pipe,** *n.* The pipe of a locomotive steam engine which carries the waste steam up the chimney, and thus induces a stronger draught. **blastema,** blas·tē'ma, *n.* [Gr. *blastēma,* a shoot, growth, from *blastano,* to bud.] *Bot.* the axis of growth of an embryo; that part of the embryo comprising the radicle and

plumule, with the intervening portion.

blastocarpous, blas·tō·kär'pus, *a.* [Gr. *blastos,* a germ, and *karpos,* fruit.] Having the germ beginning to grow inside the pericarp of the fruit.—**blastoderm,** blas'tō·dėrm, *n.* [Gr. *derma,* a skin.] *Anat.* the germinal skin or membrane; the superficial layer of the embryo in its earliest condition.—**blastodermic,** blas·tō·dėr'mik, *a.* Relating to the blastoderm.—**blastogenesis,** blas·tō·jen'e·sis, *n. Biol.* reproduction by germination or budding.

blastula, blas'tū·la, *n.* [From Gr. *blastos,* a germ.] An embryo so far developed from a germ or ovum as to consist of a sack formed of a single layer of cells.

blatant, blā'tant, *a.* [From Prov. E. *blate,* to *bleat,* with suffix -*ant,* as in *errant,* etc.] Bellowing; bawling; noisy.

blaze, blāz, *n.* [A.Sax. *blœse,* a blaze, a torch, from root of *blow*; comp. Icel. *blys,* Dan. *blus,* a torch; akin to *blast.*] The stream of light and heat from any body when burning; a flame; brilliant sunlight; effulgence; brilliance; a bursting out; an active or violent display (a *blaze* of wrath).—*v.i.*—*blazed, blazing.* To flame; to send forth or show a bright and expanded light.—**blazer,** blāz'ėr, *n.* That which blazes; a bright-colored jacket or short coat suited for sports, etc.

blaze, blāz, *v.t.*—*blazed, blazing,* [A.Sax. *blaesan,* to blow = Icel. *blása,* Dan. *blœse,* G. *blasen,* to blow, to sound as a trumpet. BLAST, BLOW.] To make known to all; to noise or bruit abroad; to proclaim.

blaze, blāz, *n.* [D. *bles,* Icel. *blesi,* Dan. *blis,* a white spot or streak on the forehead.] A white spot on the forehead or face of a horse or other quadruped; a white spot on a tree by removing the bark with a hatchet.—*v.t.* To set a blaze on, by paring off part of the bark; to indicate or mark out, as a path, by paring off the bark of a number of trees in succession.

blazon, blā'zn, *n.* [O.E. *blasoun, blason,* Fr. *blason,* heraldry, *blasonner,* to blazon, from a G. word equivalent to E. *blaze,* to spread abroad or make known.] The drawing or representation on coats of arms; a heraldic figure; show; pompous display, by words or other means (*Shak.*).—*v.t.* To explain, in proper terms, the figures on ensigns armorial; to deck; to embellish; to adorn; to display; to publish; to celebrate.— **blazoner,** blā'zn·ėr, *n.* One that blazons; a herald; one prone to spread reports; a propagator of scandal. — **blazonment,** blā'zn·ment, *n.* The act of blazoning; emblazonment.—**blazonry,** blā'zn·ri, *n.* The art of describing or explaining coats of arms in proper heraldic terms and method; emblazonry.

bleach, blēch, *v.t.* [A.Sax. *blaecan,* from *blaec,* pale, white. BLEAK.] To make white or whiter by taking out color; to whiten; to blanch; to

whiten by exposure to the action of the air and sunlight or of chemical preparations.—*v.i.* To grow white in any manner.—**bleacher,** blēch'ėr, *n.* One who bleaches; one whose occupation is to whiten cloth.— **bleachers,** blēch'ėrz, *n.* Seats, usually uncovered, for spectators at baseball and other outdoor sporting events.— **bleachery,** blēch'ėr·i, *n.* An establishment where bleaching textile fabrics or the like is carried on.— **bleaching powder,** *n.* Chloride of lime made by exposing slaked lime to the action of chlorine.

bleak, blēk, *a.* [A.Sax. *blaec* = Icel. *bleikr,* D. *bleek,* G. *bleich,* pale, pallid, white; allied to A.Sax. *blican,* Icel. *blíkja,* G. *blicken,* to shine, to gleam, E. to *blink. Bleach* is from this word.] Exposed to cold and winds (situation, tract of land); desolate; ungenial; cheerless; dreary; cold; chill (*bleak* winds).— **bleakish,** blēk'ish, *a.* Moderately bleak.—**bleakly,** blēk'li, *adv.* In a bleak manner; coldly.—**bleakness,** blēk'nes, *n.* State of being bleak; coldness; desolation.—**bleaky,** †blēk'-i, *a.* Bleak; unsheltered; cold; chill.

bleak, blēk, *n.* [So called from the *bleak* or pale color of its scales.] A small river fish, 5 or 6 inches long, belonging to the carp family, occurring in many European rivers.

blear, blēr, *a.* [L.G. *blarr, blerr,* blear; Sw. *blira,* Dan. *blire, plire,* to twinkle, to wink; Dan. *pliirōiet,* blear-eyed.] Sore, with a watery rheum; said of the eyes.—*v.t.* To make sore so that the sight is indistinct; to affect with soreness of eyes; to make rheumy and dim; *fig.* to hoodwink or deceive.—**bleareyed,** *a.* Having sore eyes; having the eyes dim with rheum; dimsighted; wanting in perception or understanding.

bleat, blēt, *v.i.* [A.Sax. *blaetan* = D. *blaten, bleeten,* L.G. *blaten, bleten,* to bleat, probably an imitative word.] To utter the cry of a sheep or a similar cry.—**bleat,** *n.* The cry of a sheep.—**bleater,** blēt'ėr, *n.* One who bleats; a sheep.

bleed, blēd, *v.i.*—*bled* (pret. & pp.), *bleeding.* [A.Sax. *blédan,* from *blód,* blood = D. *blœden,* Icel. *blœtha,* Dan. *blóde,* to bleed.] To lose blood; to be drained of blood; to run with blood; to let sap or other moisture flow from itself; to trickle or flow, as from an incision; to have money extorted, or to part with it freely to some wheedling or unworthy party (colloq.).—*v.t.* To take blood from by opening a vein; to emit (a tree *bleeds* juice, sap, or gum); to extort or extract money from (colloq.).

blemish, blem'ish, *v.t.* [O.Fr. *blemir, blemissant,* to spot, to beat one blue, from Icel. *bláman,* the livid color of a wound, from *blár,* blue, livid. BLUE.] To injure or impair; to mar or make defective; to deface; to sully; to tarnish, as reputation or character; to defame.—*n.* A defect, flaw, or imperfection; something that mars beauty, completeness, perfection, or reputation; a blot or stain.

blench, blensh, *v.i.* [Probably a softened form of *blink*, in old sense to wink; hence, to turn aside, to flinch; *blanch* seems to have been partly confounded with it.] To shrink; to start back; to give way; to flinch; to turn aside, as from pain, fear, repugnance, etc.—*n.* A start back; a deviation; aberration.

blend, blend, *v.t.*—*blended* (pret.), *blended* or *blent* (pp.), *blending.* [A.Sax. *blandan*, to mix=Icel. and Sw. *blanda*, Dan. *blande*, to mix; allied to *blind*, originally turbid. BLIND.] To mix or mingle together; to confound so that the separate things mixed cannot be distinguished.—*v.i.* To be mixed; to become united; to merge insensibly the one into the other (as colors).—*n.* A mixture, as of liquids, colors, etc.; a mixture of spirits from different distilleries.

blende, blend, *n.* [G. *blende*, blend. from *blenden*, to blind, to dazzle.] An ore of zinc, of which there are several varieties; a native sulfide of zinc. This word is also employed in such compound terms as manganese blende, zinc blende, ruby blende.

Blenheim, blen'em, *n.* One of a breed of dogs of the spaniel kind, preserved in perfection at Blenheim Palace in Oxfordshire, England.

blenny, blen'i, *n.* [L. *blennius*, from Gr. *blennos*, slime.] The name of several small fishes frequenting rocky coasts.

blepharitis, blef·a·rī'tis, *n.* [Gr. *bleh-paron*, eyelid.] Inflammation of the eyelids.

blesbok, bles'bok, *n.* [D. *bles*, a blaze or spot on the forehead, and *bok*, a buck.] An antelope of Cape Colony, with a white face.

bless, bles, *v.t.*—*blessed* or *blest*, *blessing.* [A.Sax. *bletsian, bledsian*, to bless, from *blód*, blood; originally perhaps to consecrate by sprinkling blood.] To invoke the divine favor on; to express a wish for the good fortune or happiness of; to bestow happiness, prosperity, or good things of any kind upon (*blest* with peace and plenty); to make and pronounce holy; to consecrate; to glorify for benefits received; to extol for excellencies (to *bless* the Lord; to esteem or account happy: with the reflexive pronoun.—*Bless me! bless my soul!* expressions of surprise.—**blessed,** bles'ed, *a.* [As pret. and pp. *blessed* is now commonly pronounced *blest*]. Enjoying happiness; favored with blessings; highly favored; happy; fortunate; enjoying spiritual blessings and the favor of God; fraught with or imparting blessings; sacred; hallowed; holy.—**blessedly,** bles'ed·li, *adv.* In a blessed or fortunate manner; joyfully.—**blessedness,** bles'ed·nes, *n.* The state of being blessed; happiness; felicity; heavenly joys; the favor of God.—*Single blessedness*, the unmarried state; celibacy.—**blessing,** bles'ing, *n.* The act of one who blesses; a prayer or solemn wish imploring happiness upon another; a benediction; the act of pronounc-ing a benediction or blessing; that which promotes temporal prosperity and welfare or secures immortal felicity; any good thing falling to one's lot; a mercy.

blew, blö, pret. of *blow.*

blight, blīt, *n.* [Possibly from prefix *be*, and *light*, the original meaning being perhaps to scorch or blast as by lightning.] Something that nips, blasts, or destroys plants; a diseased state of plants; smut, mildew, or other plant disease; *fig.* something that frustrates, blasts, destroys, brings to nought, etc.—*v.t.* To affect with blight; to cause to wither or decay; to blast; to frustrate.—*v.i.* To injure or blast as blight does.

blimp, blimp, *n.* A nonrigid airship of the smallest size.

blind, blīnd, *a.* [A.Sax. D. Icel. Sw. Dan. G. *blind*; originally meaning turbid or cloudy, and allied to *blend*, to mix.] Destitute of the sense of sight; not having sight; not having the faculty of discernment; destitute of intellectual, moral, or spiritual light; not easily discernible; dark; obscure (*blind* paths, *blind* mazes); indiscriminate; heedless (*blind* wrath); without openings for admitting light (*blind* window), or otherwise wanting something ordinarily essential; closed at one end; having no outlet (a *blind* alley).—*v.t.* To make physically, morally, or intellectually blind; to render incapable of clear vision (*blinded* by passion); to darken; to obscure to the eye or to the mind; to conceal ('to *blind* the truth'. *Tenn.*); to eclipse.—*n.* Something to hinder sight, to intercept a view, or keep out light; a screen of some sort to prevent too strong a light from shining in at a window, or to keep people from seeing in; something ostensible to conceal a covert design; a cover; a pretext.—**blinder,** blīnd'-ér, *n.* One who or that which blinds; a blinker on a horse's bridle.—**blindfold,** blīnd'fōld, *a.* Having the eyes covered, as with a bandage; having the mental eye darkened (*Shak.*).—*v.t.* To cover the eyes of; to hinder from seeing by binding something round the eyes.—**blinding,** blīnd'ing, *a.* Making blind; preventing from seeing clearly; depriving of sight or of understanding.—**blindingly,** blīnd'ing·li, *adv.* In a blinding manner; so as to blind.—**blindly,** blīnd'li, *adv.* In a blind manner; without sight or understanding; without examination; regardlessly; recklessly.—**blindman's buff,** *n.* A play in which one person is blindfolded and tries to catch some one of the company and tell who it is.—**blindness,** blīnd'nes, *n.* State of being blind; want of bodily sight; mental darkness; ignorance.—**blindworm,** *n.* [So called because its eyes being very minute, it has popularly been supposed to be blind.] A small harmless wormlike reptile, called also slowworm, connecting the serpents and lizards.

blink, blingk, *v.i.* [Same word as D. *blinken*, Dan. *blinke*, Sw. *blinka*, G. *blinken*, to shine, glance, twinkle; allied to A. Sax. *blican*, to gleam, D. *blikken*, Dan. *blikke*, G. *blicken*, to glance, to glimpse. Akin *blank*, *blench*, *bleach*.] To wink; to twinkle; to see with the eyes half shut or with frequent winking; to get a glimpse; to peep (*Shak.*); to intermit light; to glimmer.—*v.t.* To shut one's eyes to; to avoid or purposely evade (to *blink* a question or topic).—*n.* A glance of the eye; a glimpse; a gleam; a glimmer; the gleam or glimmer reflected from ice in the Arctic regions.—**blinker,** bling'ker, *n.* One who blinks; a leather flap placed on either side of a horse's head, to prevent him from seeing sideways or backward; a warning light.

bliss, blis, *n.* [A.Sax. *blis, bliss*, joy, alacrity, exultation, from *blithe*, blithe. BLITHE.] The highest degree of happiness; blessedness; felicity; often specifically heavenly felicity.—**blissful,** blis'ful, *a.* Full of, abounding in, enjoying, or conferring bliss. —**blissfully,** blis'ful·li, *adv.* In a blissful manner.—**blissfulness,** blis'-ful·nes, *n.* Exalted happiness; felicity; fullness of joy.

blister, blis'tėr, *n.* [Connected with *blast*, to blow or puff, from same root as to *blow.* com. G. *blase*, a blister, a bladder.] A thin vesicle on the skin, containing watery matter or serum; a pustule; an elevation made by the separation of an external film or skin, as on plants; something applied to the skin to raise a blister; a vesicatory.—*v.t.* To raise a blister or blisters on.—*v.i.* To rise in blisters or become blistered.—**blister beetle,** *n.* A beetle used to raise a blister on the skin; the Spanish fly.—**blister steel,** *n.* Iron bars which, when converted into steel, have their surface covered with blisters.—**blistery,** blis'tėr·i, *a.* Full of blisters.

blithe, blīTH, *a.* [A.Sax. *blithe*, blithe, joyful; O.Sax. *blithi*, clear, joyful; Goth. *bleiths*, merciful; Icel. *blithr*, Dan. *blid*, bland; D. *blijde*, blithe. Hence *bliss*.] Gay; merry; joyous; sprightly; mirthful; characterized by blitheness or joy.—**blithely,** blīTH'li, *adv.* In a blithe, gay, or joyful manner.—**blithesome,** blīTH'sum, *a.* Full of blitheness or gaiety; gay; merry; cheerful.

blitzkrieg, blits'krēg, *n.* [G. *Blitz*, lightning, and *Krieg*, war.] A technique of warfare developed by German strategists, consisting of swift strokes designed to pierce the enemy's lines, disrupt his communications and supply systems, and separate his forces so that they can be destroyed piecemeal.

blizzard, bliz'ard, *n.* [Akin to *blaze, blast.* Originally provincial English, but general in American literature since 1880.] A biting-cold snowstorm.

bloat, blōt, *v.t.* [Allied to Icel. *blautr*, soaked and soft; Sw. *blöt*, soaked, *blöta*, to soak, to cure fish by soaking.] To make turgid or swollen, as with air, water, etc.; to cause to swell, as in adenia; to inflate; to make vain; to cure by smoking, as herrings.—*v.i.* To become swollen; to dilate.

blob, blob, *n.* [Also in form *bleb,* and allied to *blab, blubber.*] A small globe of liquid; a dewdrop; a blister.

bloc, blok, *n.* [Fr. for block or lump.] A combination of groups or nations united to further their joint interests.

block, blok, *n.* [Same word as D. and Dan. *blok,* G. and Sw. *block,* a block, a log, a lump; Ir. *blog,* a fragment.] Any solid mass of matter, usually with one or more plane or approximately plane faces; a lump; a stock or stupid person; the mass of wood on which criminals lay their necks when they are beheaded; any obstruction or cause of obstruction; a stop; the state of being blocked or stopped up; a casing or shell containing one or more pulleys over which a rope or chain works; a connected mass of buildings; a portion of a city enclosed by streets; a mold or piece on which something is shaped, or placed to make it keep in shape; a piece of wood on which an engraving is cut.—*v.t.* To hinder egress or passage from or to; to stop up or barricade; to obstruct; to act in opposition or by interference, as in boxing, football, cricket; to mold, shape, or stretch on a block.—*To block out,* to begin to reduce to the required shape; to shape out.—**blockade,** blok·ād', *n.* [Comp. such words as *barricade, stockade, palisade,* etc.] The shutting up of a place by surrounding it with hostile troops or ships with a view to compel a surrender, by hunger and want, without regular attacks.—*To raise a blockade,* to remove or break up a blockade.—*v.t.* *blockaded, blockading.* To subject to a blockade; to prevent ingress to or egress from by warlike means; to shut up or in by obstacles of any kind; to obstruct.

block and tackle, *n.* A set of pulleys and ropes for lifting or hauling.—**blockhead,** blok'hed, *n.* A stupid fellow.—**blockhouse,** *n.* *Milit.* a building of one or more stories, so named because constructed chiefly of logs or beams of timber, having loopholes for musketry.—**blockish,** blok'ish, *a.* Like a block; stupid; dull; deficient in understanding. (*Shak.*)—**block system,** *n.* The system of working the traffic on a railroad, according to which the line is divided into short sections, and no train is allowed to enter upon any one section till it is signalled wholly clear, so that between two successive trains there is an interval of time as well as one of space.—**block tin,** *n.* Tin cast into ingots or blocks.

blond, blonde, blond, *a.* [Fr. *blond, blonde,* a word of Teutonic origin; comp. D. and G. *blond,* fair, flaxen; A.Sax. *blonden,* grayish or grizzled; allied to *blend.*] Of a fair color or complexion.—*n.* A person (especially a woman) of very fair complexion, with light hair and light-blue eyes.

blood, blud, *n.* [O.E. *blod, blode,* etc., A.Sax. *blōd*=Goth. *bloth,* Icel. *blōth,*

Dan. Sw. *blod,* L.G. *blood,* D. *bloed,* G. *blut;* root probably seen in to *blow* (as a flower), *bloom,* from the brightness of its color.] The fluid which circulates through the arteries and veins of the human body and that of other animals, and which is essential to life and nutrition—in man and the higher animals of a more or less red color; relationship by descent from a common ancestor (allied by *blood*); consanguinity; lineage; kindred; family; birth; extraction; often high birth; good extraction; natural disposition; temper; spirit (to do a thing in hot *blood* or cold *blood,* that is in anger or deliberately); mettle; passion; anger (his *blood* was up).—*The blood,* royal family or royal lineage; thus it is common to speak of princes of the blood.—*Flesh and blood,* human nature; mortal man.—*v.t.* To let blood; to bleed; to stain with blood; to inure to blood; to give a taste of blood.—**bloodguiltiness,** *n.* The state of being blood-guilty; the guilt or crime of shedding blood.—**bloodguilty,** *a.* Guilty of murder.—**bloodhound,** *n.* A large variety of dog with long smooth and pendulous ears, remarkable for the acuteness of its smell, and employed to recover game or prey by scent.—**bloodily,** blud'i·li, *adv.* In a bloody manner; cruelly.—**bloodiness,** blud'i·nes, *n.* The state of being bloody; disposition to shed blood; murderousness. —**bloodless,** blud'les, *a.* Without blood; drained of blood; dead; without shedding of blood or slaughter (a *bloodless* victory); without spirit or activity.—**bloodlessly,** blud'les·li, *adv.* In a bloodless manner; without bloodshed.—**bloodletting,** blud'let·ing, *u.* The act of letting blood by opening a vein.—**blood money,** *n.* Money earned by the shedding of blood or by laying, or supporting, a charge implying peril to the life of an accused person. —**bloodshed,** blud'shed, *n.* The shedding or spilling of blood; slaughter; waste of life.—**bloodshedder,** blud'shed·ėr, *n.* One who sheds blood; a murderer.—**bloodshedding,** blud'shed·ing, *n.* The crime of shedding blood or taking human life.—**bloodshot,** blud'shot, *a.* Red and inflamed by a turgid state of the blood vessels: said of the eye.—**bloodstained,** *a.* Stained with blood; guilty of slaughter.—**bloodstone,** *n.* A stone worn as an amulet, to prevent bleeding at the nose; red hematite; a species of heliotrope dotted with spots of jasper. —**bloodsucker,** *n.* Any animal that sucks blood, as a leech, a fly, etc.; a hard niggardly man; an extortioner. —**bloodthirstiness,** blud'thėrs·ti·nes, *n.* Thirst for shedding blood.—**bloodthirsty,** blud thėrs·ti, *a.* Desirous to shed blood; murderous.—**blood vessel,** *n.* Any vessel in which blood circulates in an animal body; an artery or a vein.—**bloody,** blud'i, *a.* Of or pertaining to blood; consisting of, containing, or exhibiting blood; bloodstained; cruel; murder-

ous; given to the shedding of blood; attended with much bloodshed.

bloom, blöm, *n.* [Same word as Icel. *blóm,* Sw. *blomma,* Dan. *blomme,* Goth. *bloma,* D. *bloem,* G. *blume,* a flower, from stem of *blow,* to blossom; akin *blossom.*] A blossom; the flower of a plant; the act or state of blossoming; fullness of life and vigor; a period of high success; a flourishing condition; the delicate rose hue on the cheek indicative of youth and health; a glow; a flush; a superficial coating or appearance upon certain things, as the delicate powdery coating upon certain fruits when newly gathered.—*v.i.* To produce or yield blossoms; to blossom; to flower; to show the beauty of youth; to glow.—*v.t.‡* To put forth, as blossoms. (O.T.)— **blooming,** blöm'ing, *a.* Showing blooms; glowing as with youthful vigor.—**bloomingly,** blöm'ing·li, *adv.* In a blooming manner.—**bloomy,** blö'mi, *a.* Full of bloom or blossoms; flowery; having freshness or vigor as of youth; having a delicate powdery appearance, as fresh fruit.

bloom, blöm, *n.* [A.Sax, *blóma,* a mass or lump of metal.] A lump of puddled iron, which leaves the furnace in a rough state, to be subsequently rolled into the bars or other material into which. it may be desired to convert the metal.—**bloomery,** blöm'ėr·i, *n.* The first forge through which iron passes after it is melted from the ore.

bloomers, blöm'ėrz, *n.* A woman's knee-length undergarment; originally loose trousers, gathered at the ankles; named for Amelia Bloomer, American, who advocated their use in 1849.

blossom, blos'om, *n.* [A.Sax. *blóstma,* a blossom, from same root as *bloom* (which see).] The flower of a plant, consisting of one or more colored leaflets, generally of more delicate texture than the leaves; the bloom; blooming state or period (the plant is in *bloom*).—*v.i.* To put forth blossoms or flowers; to bloom; to flourish.—**blossomy,†** blos'om·i, *a.* Full of or covered with blossoms.

blot, blot, *n.* [Same word as Icel. *blettr,* Dan. *plet,* a blot; Dan. dial. *blat,* a drop, a spot of something wet.] A spot or stain, as of ink on paper; a blur; an obliteration of something written or printed; a spot in reputation; a blemish.—*v.t.*— *blotted, blotting.* To spot, to stain, as with ink; to stain with infamy; to tarnish; to obliterate or efface: in this sense generally with *out;* to dry by means of blotting paper or the like.—**blotter,** blot'ėr, *n.* One who or that which blots.—**blotting paper,** *n.* A species of unsized paper, serving to imbibe the superfluous ink from newly written manuscript, etc.

blotch, bloch, *n.* [For *blatch, blach,* a softened form of *black* (comp. *bleak, bleach*), the meaning being influenced by *botch,* a pustule.] A pustule or eruption on the skin; an irregular spot.—*v.t.* To mark with blotches.—**blotchy,** bloch'i, *a.* Marked with blotches, spots, or blurs.

blouse, blouz or blous, _n._ [Fr.] A light loose upper garment, resembling a smock frock, made of linen or cotton, and worn by men as a protection from dust or in place of a coat; also, a garment of nearly the same form and of various materials worn by women and children.

blow, blō, _v.i._—blew, blown, blowing. [A.Sax. _bláwan;_ allied to G. _blähen,_ to blow, Icel. _blása,_ Goth. _blésan,_ G. _blasen,_ to blow, to blow a wind instrument; also to E. _blow,_ to bloom, _bladder, blast,_ etc., and L. _flo, flare,_ to breathe or blow.] To make a current of air, as with the mouth, a bellows, etc.; to constitute or form a current of air; to be a wind: often used with an indefinite _it_ for the subject (_it blew_ strongly yesterday); to pant; to puff; to breathe hard or quick; to give out sound by being blown, as a horn or trumpet; to boast; to brag: in this sense colloq.—_To blow over,_ to pass away after having spent its force (the storm _blew over_).—_To blow up,_ to be broken and scattered by an explosion.—_To blow upon,_ to bring into disfavor or discredit; to render stale, unsavory, or worthless; also to inform upon.—_v.t._ To throw or drive a current of air upon; to drive by a current of air; to sound by the breath (a wind instrument); to form by inflation (to _blow_ a glass bottle); to swell by injecting air into; to put out of breath by fatigue; to scatter or shatter by explosives (to _blow_ up, to _blow_ to pieces).—_To blow out,_ to extinguish by a current of air; to scatter (one's brains) by firearms.—_To blow up,_ to fill with air; to swell; to inflate; to puff up; to blow into a blaze; to burst in pieces and scatter by explosion; to scold: in this sense colloq.—_n._ A gale of wind; a blast; the breathing or spouting of a whale.—**blower,** blō′ér, _n._ One who or that which blows; a blowing engine.—**blowy,** blō′i, _a._ Windy; gusty.—**blowfly,** _n._ A name of various species of flies (dipterous insects) which deposit their eggs on flesh, and thus taint it.—**blowhole,** _n._ The nostril of a cetacean, situated on the highest part of the head; a hole in the ice to which whales and seals come to breathe.—**blowpipe,** _n._ An instrument by which a current of air or gas is driven through a flame so as to direct it upon a substance, an intense heat being created by the rapid supply of oxygen and the concentration of the flame; a pipe or tube through which poisoned arrows are blown by the breath, used by South American Indians and natives of Borneo.

blow, blō, _v.i._—blew, blown. [A.Sax. _blówan,_ to bloom or blossom; D. _bloeijen,_ G. _blühen;_ allied to the other verb _to blow,_ and to L. _florere,_ to bloom.] To flower; to blossom; to bloom, as plants.—_v.t._‡ To make to blow or blossom.—_n._ A mass of blossoms; the state or condition of blossoming or flowering; the highest state of anything; bloom; an ovum or egg deposited by a fly; a flyblow.—

blown, blōn, _p._ and _a._ Fully expanded or opened, as a flower.

blow, blō, _n._ [Akin to O.D. _blauwen,_ to strike; D. _blouwen,_ to beat flax; G. _bleuen,_ to cudgel; and perhaps also with _blue._ BLUE.] A stroke with the hand or fist, or a weapon; a knock; an act of hostility; a sudden calamity; a sudden or severe evil; mischief or damage received.—_At a blow,_ by one single action; at one effort; suddenly.

blowze, blouz, _n._ [From the same root as _blush._] _Obs._ A ruddy fat-faced woman; a blowzy woman.—**blowzed, blowzy,** blouzd, blou′zi, _a._ Ruddyfaced; fat and ruddy; highcolored.

blubber, blub′ér, _n._ [A lengthened form of _blub, blob, bleb;_ perhaps from same root as that of _blow, bladder._] The fat of whales and other large sea animals, from which train oil is obtained; a gelatinous mass of various kinds; the sea-nettle; a jellyfish.—_v.i._ To weep, especially in such a manner as to swell the cheeks or disfigure the face.—_v.t._ To disfigure with weeping.

blucher, blöch′ér, _n._ A strong leather half boot or high shoe, named after Field Marshal von _Blücher._

bludgeon, bluj′on, _n._ [Origin unknown; perhaps allied to G. _blotzen,_ to strike, D. _blutsen,_ to bruise.] A short stick, with one end loaded or thicker and heavier than the other, and used as an offensive weapon.

blue, blū, _n._ [Same as Sc. _blae,_ Icel. _blár,_ livid; Dan. _blaa,_ D. _blaauw,_ G. _blau,_ blue; connected with _blow,_ a blow producing a blue color. Akin _blemish._] One of the primary colors; the color of the clear sky or deep sea; azure; what is blue; a dye or pigment of this hue.—_a._ Of the color of blue; sky-colored; azure.—_v.t._—blued, bluing. To make blue; to dye of a blue color.—**bluely,** blū′li, _adv._ With a blue hue or shade.—**blueness,** blū′nes, _n._ The quality of being blue; a blue hue or color.—**blues,** blūz, _n._ A type of song of melancholy character and slow tempo written in characteristic key.—**bluish,** blū′ish, _a._ Blue in a slight degree; somewhat blue.—**bluishness,** blū′ish·nes, _n._—**blue baby,** An infant with a bluish color from congenital heart disease.—**Bluebeard,** _n._ Personage in medieval tale, synonymous with wife-murderer.—**bluebird,** _n._ A small bluish bird with a red breast very common in the United States.—**bluebook,** _n._ In the U. S. a directory of persons of social prominence. In colleges, a blue-covered booklet for writing examinations.—**bluebottle,** _n._ A composite plant found frequently in cornfields; a fly with a large blue belly.—**bluecap,** _n._ The blue titmouse.—**bluecoat,** _n._ A person wearing a blue coat as a special dress.—**bluefish,** _n._ A name of certain American fishes, one of them a food fish allied to the mackerel, common on the Atlantic coast of N. America. —**blue devils,** _n. pl._ A colloquial phrase for dejection, hypochondria, or lowness of spirits; also for de-

lirium tremens. Often called simply _the blues._—**bluegrass,** _n._ A name of several grasses, more especially a grass of Kentucky, highly valued for pasturage and hay.—**blue gum,** _n._ A species of Eucalyptus or gum-tree with valuable medicinal properties, and now planted in malarious localities with beneficial results. It yields the drug Eucalyptol.—**bluejacket,** _n._ A sailor, from the color of his jacket. —**blueprint,** _n._ A photographic printing method using sensitized paper for the reproduction of engineering drawings; the print itself.— **blue ribbon,** _n._ The broad, dark-blue ribbon, worn by members of the order of the Garter; a piece of blue ribbon, usually with suitable words or markings, awarded as evidence of the winning of a highest award; hence a prize, a distinction.— **bluestone, blue vitriol,** _n._ Sulfate of copper.

bluff, bluf, _a._ [Perhaps from or allied to O.D. _blaf,_ applied to a broad full face, also to a forehead rising straight up.] Broad and full: specially applied to a full countenance, indicative of frankness and good humor; rough and hearty; somewhat boisterous and unconventional; having a steep front (a _bluff_ bank).—_v.t._ To deceive or impose upon, by boisterous talk or action.—_n._ A high bank with a steep front; a bold headland; bold words or acts intended to daunt or test an opponent.

bluing, blū′ing, _n._ A blue liquid used in laundering to offset the yellow tinge of linen or cotton.

blunder, blun′dér, _v.i._ [Allied to Icel. _blunda,_ to doze, _blundr,_ slumber, Dan. and Sw. _blund,_ a nap, also to _blind, blend._] To make a gross mistake, especially through mental confusion; to err stupidly; to move without direction or steady guidance; to flounder; to stumble, literally or figuratively.—_n._ A mistake through precipitance or mental confusion; a gross and stupid mistake.— **blunderer,** blun′dér·ér, _n._ One who is apt to blunder or to make gross mistakes.—**blunderingly,** blun′dér·ing·li, _adv._ In a blundering manner.

blunderbuss, blun′dér·bus, _n._ [A humorous corruption of D. _donderbus,_ a blunderbuss—_donder,_ thunder, and _bus,_ a tube, gun, originally a box.] A short gun or firearm, with a large bore.

blunt, blunt, _a._ [Akin to Prov. G. _bludde,_ a dull or blunt knife; Dan. _blunde,_ Sw. and Icel. _blunda,_ to doze, E. _blunder._] Having a thick edge or point, as an instrument; dull; not sharp; dull in understanding; slow of discernment; abrupt in address; plain; unceremonious.—_v.t._ To dull the edge or point of, by making it thicker; to impair the force, keenness, or susceptibility of.—**bluntly,** blunt′li, _adv._ In a blunt manner; plainly; abruptly; without delicacy or the usual forms of civility.— **bluntness,** blunt′nes, _n._ The state or quality of being blunt.

blur, blér, _n._ [Probably a form of _blear._] Something that obscures or soils; a blot; a stain; confused appearance, as produced by indistinct vision.—*v.t.*—*blurred, blurring.* To obscure without quite effacing; to render indistinct; to confuse and bedim; to cause imperfection of vision in; to dim; to sully; to stain; to blemish (reputation).

blurt, blẽrt, *v.t.* [Perhaps imitative of abrupt sound made by the lips.] To utter suddenly or inadvertently; to divulge unadvisedly: commonly with *out.*

blush, blush, *v.i.* [A.Sax. *blísian, blysian,* allied to Dan. *blusse,* to blaze, to blush, D. *blos,* a blush, *blozen,* to blush; akin *blaze, blow.*] To redden in the cheeks or over the face, as from a sense of guilt, shame, confusion, or modesty; to exhibit a red or rosy color; to bloom.—*n.* The act of blushing; the suffusion of the cheeks or the face generally with a red color through confusion, shame, diffidence, or the like; a red or reddish color; a rosy tint.—*At the first blush,* at the first review or consideration of a matter.—**blushful,** blush′fụl, *a.* Full of blushes.—**blushingly,** blush′ing·li, *adv.* In a blushing manner; with blushes.

bluster, blus′tẽr, *v.i.* [A kind of intens. of *blow;* akin to *blast, blister.*] To roar and be tumultuous, as wind; to be boisterous; to be loud, noisy, or swaggering; to bully; to swagger. —*v.t.* To utter or effect in a blustering manner or with noise and violence; with *out,* or other prep.—*n.* A violent blast of wind; a gust; noisy talk; swaggering; boisterousness.— **blusterer,** blus′tẽr·ẽr, *n.* One who blusters; a swaggerer; a bully.— **blusteringly,** blus′tẽr·ing·li, *adv.* In a blustering manner.—**blusterous, blustery,** blus′tẽr·us, blus′tẽr·i, *a.* Noisy; tumultuous; tempestuous.

boa, bō′a, *n.* [L., a water-serpent.] The generic and common name of certain serpents destitute of fangs and venom, having a prehensile tail, and including some of the largest species of serpents, the constrictor being 30 or 40 feet long; a long round article of dress for the neck, made of fur.

boar, bōr, *n.* [A.Sax. *bár*=D. *beer,* O.H.G. *pér,* M.H.G. *ber,* a boar; perhaps akin to *bear* (the animal).] The male of swine: when applied to the wild species the term is used without reference to sex.—**boarish,** bōr′ish, *a.* Pertaining to or resembling a boar; swinish; brutal.

board, bōrd, *n.* [A.Sax. *bord,* table, plank, deck or side of a ship = Icel. Dan. G. *bord,* Goth. *baurd,* D. *boord;* allied probably to verb *bear. Border, broider,* are akin.] A piece of timber sawed thin, and of considerable length and breadth compared with the thickness; a table; hence, what is served on a board or table; food; diet; specifically, daily food obtained for a stipulated sum at the table of another; a council table; a number of persons having the management, direction, or superintendence of some public or private office or trust; the deck or side of a ship or boat, or its

interior part (on *board,* to fall over *board*); a table or frame for a game, as chess, checkers, etc.; a kind of thick stiff paper; a sheet of substance formed by layers of paper pasted together, usually in compounds (as, card*board,* mill-*board*); one of the two stiff covers on the sides of a book.—*The boards,* the stage of a theater.—*v.t.* To lay or spread with boards; to cover with boards; to place at board, or where food or food and lodging are to be had; to furnish with food, or food and lodging, for a compensation; to go on board a vessel; to enter a vessel by force in combat.—*v.t.* To live at board; to live as a boarder.—**boarder,** bōrd′ẽr, *n.* One furnished with food or food and lodging at another's house at a stated charge; one who boards a ship in action.—**boarding-house,** *n.* A house where board or board and lodging is furnished.—**boarding school,** *n.* A school in which pupils are boarded and lodged as well as taught.

boast, bōst, *v.i.* [Probably of Celtic origin; comp. W. *bost,* a boast, *bostio,* to boast. Corn. *bostye,* to boast.] To speak in high praise of one's self or belongings; to use exulting, pompous, or pretentious language; to brag; to exult; to glory; to vaunt; to bluster.—*v.t.* To display in ostentatious language; to speak of with pride, vanity, or exultation; to magnify or exalt (strength, genius); to vaunt; often *refl.*—*n.* A statement expressive of ostentation, pride, or vanity; a vaunting or bragging; a brag; the cause of boasting; occasion of pride, vanity, or laudable exultation.—**boaster,** bōst′ẽr, *n.* One who boasts, glories, or vaunts with exaggeration or ostentatiously; a bragger.—**boastful,** bōst′fụl, *a.* Given to boasting.—**boastfully,** bōst′fụl·li, *adv.* In a boastful manner.—**boastfulness,** bōst′fụl·nes, *n.*—**boastingly,** bōst′ing·li, *adv.* Boastfully; with boasting.

boat, bōt, *n.* [A.Sax. *bát*=Icel. *bátr,* D. L.G. and G. *boot,* a boat. Similar forms occur also in Celtic, as Ir. W. *bad.* Cael. *bata.*] A small open vessel or watercraft, usually moved by oars or rowing; any sailing vessel, but usually described by another word denoting its use or mode of propulsion; as, a packet-*boat,* steam-*boat,* etc.—*v.t.* To transport in a boat.—*v.i.* To go or sail in a boat.—**boatbill,** *n.* A bird of the heron family, inhabiting South America, and named from having a bill resembling a boat with the keel uppermost.—**boat hook,** *n.* An iron hook with a point on the back, fixed to a long pole, to pull or push a boat. —**boathouse,** *n.* A house or shed for protecting boats from the weather.—**boatman,** bōt′man, *n.* A man who manages a boat; a rower of a boat.—**boatswain,** bōt′swān or bō′sn, *n.* [A.Sax. *bátswan*-*bát,* boat, and *swan,* swain.] A ship's officer who has charge of the sails, rigging, anchors, cables, etc., and who pipes or summons the crew to their duty.

bob, bob, *n.* [Perhaps imitative or suggestive of abrupt, jerky motion; in some of its senses allied to Gael. *babag, baban,* a tassel.] A general name for any small round object playing loosely at the end of a cord, line, chain, etc., as a knot of worms on a string used in fishing for eels, the bail or weight at the end of a pendulum, plumbline, and the like; a short jerking action or motion; a shake or jog; a blow.—**bob,** bob, *n.* A shilling. [Colloq.] Bell-ringing, a peal of courses or sets of changes.— *v.t.* bobbed, bobbing. To move in a short, jerking manner; to perform with a jerky movement; to cut short, as hair or a horse's tail; to beat or strike; to deceive; to defraud of (*Shak.*)‡.—*v.i.* To play backward and forward; to play loosely against anything; to make a quick, jerky motion, as a rapid bow or obeisance; to angle or fish with a bob, or by giving the hook a jerking motion in the water.—**bobtail,** bob′tāl, *n.* A short tail or a tail cut short; the rabble; used in contempt, as in the phrase *ragtag and bobtail.*

bobbin, bob′in, *n.* [Fr. *bobine,* from L. *bombus,* a humming sound, or more probably connected with E. *bob.*] A small cylindrical piece of wood with a head or flange at one or both ends, on which thread or yarn is wound for use in sewing, weaving, etc.—**bobbinet,** bob′in·et, *n.* A machine-made cotton net, originally imitated from the lace made by means of a pillow and bobbins.

bobolink, bob′ō·lingk, *n.* American migratory bird known in southern U. S. as the reedbird or ricebird.

Boche, bosh, *n.* [Fr. of disputed origin. Perhaps short form of *Alboche,* slang for *Allemand,* a German.] A term of opprobrium for a German.

bode, bōd, *v.t.*—boded, boding. [A. Sax. *bodian,* to announce; to proclaim, from *bod,* an edict. a message; Icel, *botha,* to proclaim; to bode; A. Sax. *boda,* D. *bode,* G. *bote,* a messenger; allied to *bid.*] To portend; to foreshow; to presage; to indicate something future by signs; to be the omen of.—*v.i.* To be ominous.— **bodement,** bōd′ment, *n.* An omen; portent; prognostic.—**boding,** bōd′-ing, *a.* Portentous; ominous.—*n.* A portent; an omen.

bode, bōd, pret. of *bide.*

bodice, bod′is, *n.* [Formerly *bodies,* pl. of *body,* being originally in two pieces.] The body part of a woman's dress; a kind of waistcoat; stays; a corset.

bodkin, bod′kin, *n.* [From W. *bidogyn,* a dagger, dim. of *bidog,* Gael. *biodag,* a short sword.] Originally a dagger; now a pointed pin of steel, ivory, or the like, for piercing holes in cloth; a blunted needle for drawing a ribbon, cord, or string through a loop, or a pin for keeping up the hair; to sit *bodkin,* to sit squeezed between two persons.

body, bod′i, *n.* [A.Sax. *bodig,* a body —O.H.G. *potach,* later *botech, bodech;* body; comp. Gael. *bodhaig,* the body.] The frame or material organized substance of an animal, in distinction from the soul, spirit, or vital principle; the main central or principal part of anything, as distinguished from subordinate parts, such as the extremities, branches, wings, etc.; a person; a human being; now generally forming a compound with *some* or *no* preceding; a number of individuals spoken of collectively, united by some common tie or by some occupation; a corporation; any extended solid substance; matter; any substance or mass distinct from others; a united mass; a general collection; a code; a system; a certain consistency or density; substance; strength (as of liquors, paper, etc.).—*v.t.*—*bodied, bodying.* To produce in some form; to embody; to invest with a body.—**bodiless,** bod'i·les, *a.* Having no body or material form; incorporeal. —**bodily,** bod'i·li, *a.* Pertaining to or concerning the body; of or belonging to the body or to the physical constitution; not mental; corporeal. ∴ *Bodily,* relating to or connected with the body as a whole; opposed to *mental; corporal,* relating to the body as regards outward bearings; *corporeal,* relating to its nature; opposed to *spiritual.* Hence *bodily* form, *corporal* punishment, *corporeal* existence.—*adv.* Corporeally; united with a body or matter; entirely; completely (to remove a thing *bodily*). —**bodyguard,** *n.* The guard that protects or defends one's person; lifeguard.—**body snatcher,** *n.* One who robs burying-places of dead bodies.

Boeotian, bē·ō'shun, *a.* Of or relating to Boeotia, thick-witted, dull, in distinction from *Attic,* the inhabitants of Attica.

Boer, bör or bö'er, *n.* [D., a peasant, farmer.] The name applied to the Dutch colonists of South Africa engaged in agriculture or cattle-breeding.

bog, bog, *n.* [Gael. and Ir. *bog,* soft, moist, *bogan, bogach,* a quagmire.] A piece of wet, soft, and spongy ground, where the soil is composed mainly of decaying and decayed vegetable matter; a piece of mossy ground or where peat is found; a quagmire or morass.—*v.t.*—*bogged, bogging.* To whelm or plunge in mud or mire.—**boggy,** bog'i. *a.* Pertaining to or resembling a bog; full of bogs; marshy; swampy; miry.—**bogtrotter,** *n.* A derisive term for an inhabitant of a boggy country, applied especially to the Irish peasantry.

bogey, bogy, bō'gi, *n.* [W. *bwg, bwgan,* a hobgoblin, scarecrow, *bugbear.*] A hobgoblin; a wicked spirit. —*Old Bogey,* the devil.

boggle, bog'l, *v.i.*—*boggled, boggling.* [Probably connected with *bogey,* Prov. E. *bogle,* a goblin.] To doubt; to hesitate; to stop, as if afraid to proceed or as if impeded by unforeseen difficulties; to waver; to shrink; to play fast and loose; to shilly-shally.—**boggler,** bog'lér, *n.* A doubter; a timorous man; a waverer; an inconstant person.

bogus, bō'gus, *a.* [A word of uncertain origin. It first appeared in America, having been originally applied, it is said, in 1827, to an apparatus for coining spurious money.] Counterfeit; spurious; sham; pretended. [Originally Amer.]

bohea, bō·hē' *n.* [Said to be from a mountain in China called *Voo-y.*] An inferior kind of black tea: sometimes applied to black teas in general.

Bohemian, bō·hē'mi·an, *n.* [Fr. *Bohémien,* a gypsy, because the first of that wandering race that entered France were believed to be Hussites driven from Bohemia, their native country.] A person, especially an artist or literary man, who leads a free, often somewhat dissipated life, despising conventionalities generally. —**Bohemianism,** bō·hē'mi·an·izm, *n.* The life or habits of a Bohemian.

boil, boil, *v.i.* [O.Fr. *boiller,* Fr. *bouillir,* L. *bullare, bullire,* to boil, to bubble, from *bulla,* a bubble. *Bill* (a paper), *billet, bullet,* are of same origin.] To be in a state of ebullition; to bubble by the action of heat, as water or other fluids; to exibit a swirling or swelling motion; to seethe, as waves; to be violently agitated or excited, as the blood; to be subjected to the action of boiling water in cooking, etc., as meat.—*v.t.* To put into a state of ebullition; to cause to be agitated or bubble by the application of heat; to collect, form, or separate by the application of heat, as sugar, salt; to subject to the action of heat in a boiling liquid, as meat in cooking; to prepare in a boiling liquid; to seethe.—**boiler,** boil'ér, *n.* A person who boils; a vessel, generally a large vessel of iron, copper, etc., in which anything is boiled in great quantities; a strong metallic vessel, usually of wrought iron or steel plates riveted together, in which steam is generated for driving engines or other purposes.—*Boiling point,* the degree of heat at which a fluid is converted into vapor with ebullition, as water at 212° Fahr., mercury at 675°, etc.— *Boiling springs,* springs or fountains which give out water at the boiling point or at a high temperature, as the geysers of Iceland and in the Yellowstone region in the United States.

boil, boil, *n.* [O.E. *bile, byle,* A.Sax. *byl,* a blotch, a sore; D. *buil,* G. *beule,* a boil; Icel. *bóla,* a blain or blister; Dan. *byld,* a boil.] An inflamed and painful suppurating tumor.

boisterous, bois'tér·us, *a.* [Probably from W. *bwystus,* brutal, ferocious, *bwyst,* wildness, ferocity; perhaps connected with *boast.*] Violent; stormy; turbulent; furious; tumultuous; noisy.—**boisterously,** bois'tér·us·li, *adv.* In a boisterous manner.— **boisterousness,** bois'tér·us·nes, *n.* The state or quality of being boisterous.

bold, bōld, *a.* [A.Sax. *beald, bald,* bold, courageous=Icel. *ballr,* D. *bout,* O.H.G. *bald,* bold.] Daring; courageous; brave; intrepid; fear-

less, as a man; requiring or exhibiting courage in execution; executed with courage and spirit, as a deed; rude; forward; impudent; overstepping usual bounds; presuming upon sympathy or forbearance; showing liberty or license; striking to the eye; markedly conspicuous; steep; abrupt; prominent.—**boldly,** bōld'li, *adv.* In a bold manner; courageously; intrepidly; forwardly; insolently; abruptly, etc.—**boldness,** bōld'nes, *n.* The quality of being bold, in all the senses of the word; courage; bravery; confidence; assurance; forwardness; steepness; abruptness.—**bold-faced,** *a.* Impudent.

bole, bōl, *n.* [From Icel. *bolr, bulr,* Dan. *bul,* trunk, stem of a tree; probably of same root as *bowl, bulge,* etc.] The body or stem of a tree.

bole, bōl, *n.* [Fr. *bol,* bole, a bolus, L. *bolus,* from Gr. *bolos,* a clod of earth.] A friable clayey shale or earth of various kinds used as a pigment, generally yellow, or yellowish-red, or brownish-black, from the presence of iron oxide. These earths were formerly employed as astringent, absorbent, and tonic medicines, and they are still in repute in the East; they are also used occasionally as veterinary medicines in Europe. Armenian bole is used as a coarse red pigment.

bolero, bō·ler'ō, *n.* [Sp., from *bola,* a ball.] A favorite dance in Spain.

boll, bōl, *n.* [G. *bolle,* a seed vessel of flax, D. *bol,* a round body; same root as *bole,* a stem.] The pod or capsule of a plant, as of flax.—**boll weevil,** *n.* A weevil, the larva of which feeds on cotton bolls.

bollard, bol'lärd, *n.* [Allied to *bole,* the stem of a tree.] A strong post fixed vertically into the ground on a wharf or quay; a kind of stanchion in a ship or boat.

bologna, bo·lō'nya, *n.* A large sausage made of bacon, veal, and pork suet, chopped fine, and enclosed in a skin.

Bolshevik, bōl·she'vik, *n.* The Russian name for the majority party, as opposed to the minority (*mensheviki*), that took over the government in 1917.—**bolshevism,** bōl'she·vizm, *n.*

bolster, bōl'stér, *n.* [A.Sax. D. Dan. and Sw. *bolster,* Icel. *bólstr,* G. *polster,* a cushion, a bolster; root *bol, bul,* as in *bulge,* etc., and term. *-ster,* as in *holster.*] A long pillow or cushion used to support the head of persons lying on a bed; something resembling a bolster more or less in form or application, as a pad or quilt used to prevent pressure; a compress, a cushioned or padded part of a saddle; the part of a cutting tool which joins the end of the handle; a hollow tool for punching holes, etc.— *v.t.* To furnish or support with a bolster, pillow, or any soft pad; to pad; to stuff; *fig.* to support; to maintain: usually implying support of an unworthy cause or object and generally with *up* (to *bolster up* his pretentions with lies).—**bolsterer,** bōl'stér·ér, *n.* One who bolsters; a supporter; an upholder; a standby.

bolt, bōlt, *n.* [A.Sax. *bolt*, an arrow, a bolt; Dan. *bolt*, a bolt, an iron peg, a fetter, G. *bolz*, *bolzen*, an arrow, a bolt or large nail.] An arrow; a thunderbolt; a stream of lightning; a stout metallic pin used for holding objects together, frequently screw-threaded at one extremity to receive a nut; a movable bar for fastening a door, gate, window sash, or the like; especially that portion of a lock which is protruded from or retracted within the case by the action of the key; an iron to fasten the legs of a prisoner; a shackle.—*v.t.* To fasten or secure with a bolt or iron pin, as a door, a plank, fetters, etc.; to swallow hurriedly or without chewing, as food (colloq.); to start or spring game.—*v.i.* To shoot forth suddenly; to spring out with speed and suddenness; to start forth like a bolt; to run out of the regular path; to start and run off; to take flight; to make one's escape (colloq.).—*adv.* As straight as a bolt; suddenly; with sudden meeting or collision (to come *bolt* against a person).—**bolter**, bōlt'-ėr, *n.* One who fastens with a bolt; one who makes his escape or runs away; a horse given to starting off or running away.

bolt, bōlt, *v.t.* [O.Fr. *buleter*, *bulter* (Mod. Fr. *bluter*), with change of *r* into *l*, from an older form *bureter*, from *bure*, the thick woolen cloth of which bolting-sieves are made, from L. *burra*, coarse cloth.] To sift or pass through a sieve so as to separate the coarser from the finer particles, as bran from flour; *fig.* to sift or separate good from bad, or the like.—**bolter**, bōlt'ėr, *n.* One who bolts; a sieve or apparatus for bolting.—**bolthead**, *n.* A long straight-necked glass vessel for chemical distillations; a matrass or receiver.—**boltrope**, *n.* A rope to which the edges of sails are sewed to strengthen them.

bolus, bō'lus, *n.* [L. *bolus*, a bit, a morsel, a lump, Gr. *bōlos*, a clod, a lump.] A soft round mass of anything medicinal to be swallowed at once, larger and less solid than an ordinary pill.

bomb, bom, *n.* [Fr. *bombe*, a bomb, from L. *bombus*, Gr. *bombos*, a hollow deep sound. Probably imitative, like E. *bum*, *boom*, to make a deep hollow sound.] A projectile filled with explosive or flammable materials fired from a mortar or dropped from an airplane.—**bombproof**, *a.* Secure against the force of bombs; capable of resisting the shock or explosion of shells.—**bombshell**, *n.* A spherical shell; a bomb.—**bombsight**, bom'-sīt, *n.* A sighting device for controlling the dropping of aerial bombs on a specific target.—**bombard**, bom'bärd, *n.* [Fr. *bombarde*, a piece of ordnance.] A piece of short thick ordnance with a large mouth, formerly used; a barrel; a drinking vessel (*Shak.*).—*v.t.*, bom·bärd'. To attack with bombs; to fire shells at or into; to shell: sometimes used somewhat loosely for to assault with artillery of any kind.—**bombardier**,

bom·bär·dēr', *n.* In the British army, a noncommissioned artillery officer; a crew member on a bomber who aims and releases aerial bombs.—*Bombardier beetle*, the common name of many coleopterous insects, possessing a remarkable power of violently expelling from the anus a pungent, acrid fluid, accompanied by a smart report.—**bombardment**, bom·bärd'ment, *n.* The act of bombarding; the act of throwing shells and shot into a town, fortress, etc.—**bombardon**, bom·bär'don, *n.* [Fr., ultimately from L. *bombus*, a hollow sound.] A large-sized and grave-toned musical instrument of the trumpet kind, in sound not unlike the ophicleide.

bombasine, bombazine, bom·ba-zēn', *n.* [Fr. *bombasin*, *bombasine*, It. *bombicina*, *bombasin*, L. *bombycinus*, made of silk or cotton, from Gr. *bombyx*, *bombykos*, a silkworm, silk.] A slight twilled fabric, of which the warp is silk (or cotton) and the weft worsted.

bombast, bom'bast, *n.* [Originally padding made of cotton, of same origin as *bombasine*.] Cotton or other stuff of soft, loose texture used to stuff garments‡; hence, high-sounding words; inflated or turgid language; fustian; words too big and high-sounding for the occasion.—**bombastic**, bom·bas'tik, *a.* Characterized by bombast; high-sounding; turgid; inflated. —**bombastically**, bom·bas'tik·al·li, *adv.* In a bombastic or inflated manner or style.

bona fide, bō'na fī'dē. [L.] With good faith; without fraud or deception: frequently used as a sort of adjective.

bonanza, bo·nan'zä, *n.* [Sp. good weather, L. *bonus*.] Good luck, good output of farms, mines, stocks.

Bonapartist, bō'na·pärt·ist, *n.* One attached to the policy or the dynasty of the Bonapartes; one who favors the claims of the Bonaparte family to the throne of France.

bonbon, bon'bon, *n.* [Fr.] Some article of sugar confectionery; a sugarplum.

bond, bond, *n.* [A form of *band*. BAND, BIND.] Anything that binds, fastens, confines, or holds things together, as a cord, a chain, a rope; hence, *pl.* fetters, chains, and so imprisonment, captivity; a binding power or influence; a uniting tie (the *bond* of affection); an obligation imposing a moral duty, as by a vow or promise; an obligation or deed by which a person binds himself, his heirs, etc., to do or not to do a certain act, usually to pay a certain sum on or before a certain day; *masonry*, the connection of one stone or brick with another by lapping them over each other in building so that an inseparable mass may be formed, which could not be the case if every vertical joint were over that below it; the state of being bonded, as goods in bond, that is stored in a bonded warehouse until customs or excise duties have been paid on them.—*a.* [For *bound*.]

In a state of servitude or slavery; captive.—*v.t.* To put in bond or into a bonded warehouse, as goods liable for customs or excise duties, the duties remaining unpaid till the goods are taken out.—*Bonded warehouse*, a licensed warehouse or store in which goods liable to government duties may be lodged after bond has been given on behalf of the owners of the goods, for the payment of such duty on their removal for home consumption.—**bondage**, bon'dij, *n.* Slavery or involuntary servitude; thraldom; captivity; imprisonment; restraint of a person's liberty by compulsion.—**bonder**, bon'dėr, *n.* One who bonds; one who deposits goods in a bonded warehouse; one of the stones which reach a considerable distance into or entirely through a wall for the purpose of binding it together.—**bondholder**, *n.* A person who holds a bond for money lent.—**bondmaid**, bond'mād, *n.* A female slave, or one bound to service without wages, in opposition to a hired servant.—**bondman, bondsman**, bond'man, bondz'man, *n.* [Dan. *bonde*, pl. *bönder*, yeoman, peasant. Same as A.S. *bonda*, a house-holder, the -*band* of *husband*.] Serf, with mistaken meaning of one bound by bond. At the Norman Conquest the yeoman sank to a serf, and the meaning changed to suit. A man slave, or one bound to service without wages. —**bond servant**, *n.* A slave; a bondman or bondwoman.—**bondwoman**, *n.* A woman slave.

bone, bōn, *n.* [A.Sax. *bán*, a bone; cog. D. and Dan. *been*, Icel. and G. *bein*, a bone, the lower part of the leg.] One of the pieces of which the skeleton of an animal is composed; the substance of which the skeleton of vertebrate animals is composed; a firm hard substance of a dull white color, more or less hollow or cellular internally, and consisting of earthy matters (chiefly calcium phosphate and some calcium carbonate) about 67 per cent, and animal matter 33 per cent; *pl.* pieces of bone held between the fingers somewhat after the manner of castanets, and struck together in time to music of the Negro minstrel type.—*Bone of contention*, a subject of dispute and rivalry, probably from ·the manner in which dogs quarrel over a bone.—*To make no bones*, to make no scruple: a metaphor taken from a dog, which greedily swallows meat, bones included.—*v.t.*—*boned, boning.* To take out the bones from, as in cookery; to put whalebone into (stays).—**bony**, bō'-ni, *a.* Pertaining to, consisting of, or resembling bone; having prominent bones.—**bone black**, *n.* Animal charcoal; the black carbonaceous substance into which bones are converted by charring in close vessels.

bonfire, bon'fīr, *n.* [M. E. *banfyre*, bone-fire, a ceremonial burning of bones.] A fire made as an expression of public joy and exultation.

fāte, fär, fâre, fat, fạll; mē, met, hėr; pīne, pin; nōte, not, mõve; tūbe, tub, bụll; oil, pound.

Boniface, bon'i·fās, n. [The name of the landlord in Farquhar's *Beaux' Stratagem*.] A sleek, jolly, good-natured landlord or innkeeper.

bonito, bo·nē'to, n. [Sp.] A fish of several species, one of which is the striped-bellied tunny common in tropical seas, one of the fishes which pursue the flying fish.

bon-mot, bon·mō', n. [Fr. *bon*, good, and *mot*, a word.] A witticism; a witty repartee.

bonnet, bon'et, n. [Fr. *bonnet*, Sp. and Pg. *bonete*, L.L. *bonetus, boneta*, originally a sort of stuff so called; perhaps of Oriental origin.] A covering for the head worn by men; a cap; a covering for the head worn by women, and distinguished from a hat by details which vary according to the fashion; anything that covers the head or top of an object, as the cowl or wind-cap of a chimney, etc.—*v.t.* To force the hat over the eyes of, with the view of mobbing or hustling.—*v.i.* To pull off the bonnet; to make obeisance. (*Shak.*)

bonny, bon'i, a. [Doubtfully derived from Fr. *bonne*, good.] Handsome; beautiful; fair or pleasant to look upon; pretty; fine.

bonspiel, bon'spēl, n. [Dan. *bondespil*, a rustic game, from *bonde*, a rustic (A.Sax. *bonda*), and *spil*, G. *spiel*, a game.] In Scotland, a match in the game of curling between parties belonging to different districts.

bon ton, bon ton', n. [Fr. 'good tone'.] The style of persons in high life; high mode or fashion; fashionable society.

bonus, bō'nus, n. [L. *bonus*, good.] A sum given or paid over and above what is required to be paid, as a premium given for a loan, or for a charter or other privilege granted to a company; an extra dividend or allowance to the shareholders of a joint stock company, holders of insurance policies, etc., out of accumulated profits; a sum paid to an employe over and above his stated pay in recognition of successful exertions.

bony, a. See BONE.

bonze, bonz, n. [Pg., a corruption of Japanese *busso*, a pious man.] The European name for a priest or monk of the religion of Fo or Buddha in China, Burma, Japan, etc.; there are both male and female bonzes living in monasteries.

booby, bö'bi, n. [Sp. *bobo*, a fool, the bird called the booby.] A dunce; a stupid fellow; a lubber; a bird allied to the gannet, apparently so stupid as to allow itself to be knocked on the head by a stick or caught by the hand.

boodle, bö'dl, n. [D. *boedel*, goods, lumber.] Goods fraudulently obtained; gain made by cheating in public office; lot, crowd, or pack.

boogie-woogie, bö'gi wö'gi, n. A blues style using melodic variations over a persistent bass rhythm.

book, buk, n. [A.Sax. *boc*, a book, originally a beech tree; Icel. *bók*, a beech; D. *boek*, a book, a beech; G. *buch*, a book, *buche*, a beech; Slav. *bukva*, a book, *buk*, a beech. The words *book* and *beech* are closely akin, beechen tablets or pieces of beech bark having probably formed the early books.] A number of sheets of paper or other material folded, stitched, and bound together on edge, blank, written, or printed; a volume; a particular part (generally including several chapters or sections) of a literary composition; a division of a subject in the same volume; a register or record; a register containing commercial transactions or facts in proper form.—*v.t.* To enter, write, or register in a book; to secure the carriage or transmission of by purchasing a ticket for coach, rail, or steamer.—**bookish,** buk'ish, a. Given to reading or study; more acquainted with books than with the world; pertaining to, contained in, or learned from books; theoretical.—**bookishness,** buk'ish·nes, n. Addictedness to books; fondness for study.—**booklet,** buk'let, n. A little book.—**bookbinder,** buk'bīnd·er, n. One whose occupation is to bind books.—**bookbindery,** buk'bīnd·er·i, n. A place where books are bound.—**bookbinding,** buk'bīnd·ing, n. The act or practice of binding books; or of sewing the sheets and covering them with leather or other material.—**bookcase,** n. An upright case with shelves for holding books.—**bookkeeper,** n. One who keeps accounts; a person who has the charge of entering or recording business transactions or items of debit and credit in the regular set of books belonging to business houses.—**bookkeeping,** n. The art of recording mercantile transactions by keeping accounts in a book or set of books in such a manner as to give a permanent record of business transactions, so that at any time the true state of one's pecuniary affairs and mercantile dealings may be exhibited.—**bookmaker,** n. One who writes and publishes books; especially, a compiler; in betting phraseology, a person, generally a professional betting man, who wagers on the defeat of a specified horse or other competitor in a race; a layer as opposed to a backer.—**bookseller,** buk'sel·er, n. One whose occupation is to sell books.—**bookstall,** n. A stall on which books are placed which are offered for sale.—**bookstand,** n. A stand or support to hold books for reading or reference.—**bookworm,** n. A worm or mite that eats holes in books; a person too much addicted to books or study.

boom, böm, n. [Akin to *beam*, from D. *boom*, a tree, a pole, a beam, Dan. *bom*, a rail or bar.] A long pole or spar run out from various parts of a vessel for extending the bottom of particular sails, as the jib-*boom*, main-*boom*, etc.; a strong beam, or an iron chain or cable, extended across a river or harbor to prevent ships from passing.

boom, böm, v.i. [An imitative word; comp. D. *bomme*, a drum; *bommen*, to drum; L. *bombus*, a humming sound. BOMB.] To make a sonorous, hollow, humming, or droning sound. —*n.* A deep hollow noise, as the roar of waves or the sound of distant guns: applied also to the cry of the bittern and the buzz of the beetle; a sudden briskness or rise in prices.

boomerang, böm'e·rang, n. A missile formed generally of a piece of hard wood, parabolic in shape, used by the Australian aborigines, and remarkable from the fact that when thrown returns near the thrower; a scheme or plan that recoils upon the user.—*v.i.* To reverse or recoil like a boomerang.

boon, bön, n. [Icel. *bón*, a request, a boon, Dan. and Sw. *bón*=A.Sax. *ben*, Icel. *bæn*, a prayer.] Originally a prayer, petition, or request; hence, that which is asked; a petition, favor; a grant; a benefaction; a benefit; a blessing; a great privilege.

boon, bön, a. [Norm. Fr. *boon*, Fr. *bon*, from L. *bonus*, good.] Gay; jovial; merry (a *boon* companion).

boor, bör, n. [A.Sax. (ge)*búr*, a countryman or farmer=D. *boer*, G. *bauer*; from A.Sax. *buan*, Icel. *búa*, to dwell, to inhabit, to cultivate; D. *bouwen*, G. *bauen*, to cultivate.] A countryman; a peasant; a rustic; a clown; hence, one who is rude in manners and illiterate.—**boorish,** bör'ish, a. Clownish; rustic; awkward in manners, illiterate.—**boorishly,** bör'ish·li, adv. In a clownish manner.—**boorishness,** bör'ish·nes, n. The state of being boorish.

boost, böst, n. A push that helps one over an obstacle; any help given; an increase in price, etc.—*v.t.* To give a boost to.—**booster,** böst'-er, n. A person who enthusiastically promotes the welfare of another person or thing; a device that increases pressure or force.

boot, böt, n. [A.Sax. *bót*, reparation, amends; Icel. *bót*, remedy, amends; same root as in *better*.] Profit; gain; advantage; that which is given to supply the deficiency of value in one of the things exchanged.—*To boot* [A.Sax. *to-bóte*], in addition to; over and above; into the bargain.—*v.t.* To profit; to advantage; to avail; used impersonally (it *boots* us little; what *boots* it?).—**bootless,** böt'les, a. Without boot, profit, or advantage; unprofitable; unavailing; useless.—**bootlessly,** böt'les·li, adv. In a bootless or unprofitable manner.—**bootlessness,** böt'les·nes, n.

boot, böt, n. [Fr. *botte*, a butt, and also a boot, from resemblance in shape. BUTT.] An article of dress, generally of leather, covering the foot and extending to a greater or less distance up the leg; an instrument of torture fastened on to the leg, between which and the boot wedges were introduced and hammered in, often crushing both muscles and bones; the luggage box in a stagecoach, either on the front or the hind part; *pl.*, used as a singular noun, the servant in hotels who cleans the shoes of the guests, or part of whose work was originally to do so.—*v.t.* To put boots on.— **booted**, böt'ed, *a.* Equipped with boots having boots on.—**bootee**, böt·ē', *n.* A half or short boot; also a child's knitted boot.—**bootjack**, *n.* An instrument for drawing off boots.—**bootrack**, *n.* A frame or stand to hold boots, especially with their tops downward.—**boot tree**, *n.* A shoe tree; an instrument for blocking or stretching boots or shoes.

Boötes, bo·ō'tēz, *n.* [Gr. *boötēs*, a herdsman, from *bous*, an ox or cow.] A northern constellation, containing the star Arcturus.

booth, böth, *n.* [Icel. *búth*, Dan. and Sw. *bod*, G. *bude*, a booth; allied to Gael. *buth*, Slav. *bauda*, *buda*, Lith. *buda*, a booth, a hut.] A covered stall at a fair, market, exposition or polling place; a closed stall for privacy when telephoning.

booty, bö'ti, *n.* [Same as Icel. *byii*, Dan. *bytte*, exchange, barter, booty, from *byta*, to divide into portions, to deal out.] Spoil taken from an enemy in war; that which is seized by violence and robbery; plunder; pillage.

booze, böz, [M.E. *baus*, a drink.] *n.* Intoxicating liquor, generally of inferior quality.—*v.i.* To drink intoxicating liquor, especially excessively.—**boozer**, böz'er, *n.* One who boozes; a drunkard.

borage, bor'ij, *n.* [L.L. *borrago*, *borago*, from *borra*, hair, from its hairy leaves.] A plant allied to the forget-me-not, having very rough hairy leaves and pretty blue flowers, which were supposed to be cordial and were infused in drinks.

borax, bō'raks, *n.* [Sp. *borax*, Ar. *búrag*, saltpeter, from *barak*, to shine.] A natural salt, sodium tetraborate; also, obtained from boric acid in reaction to soda: used as a flux in soldering metals, and in making glass and artificial gems.— **boracic**, bō·ras'ik, *a.* Of, pertaining to, or produced from boron: same as *boric*.

border, bor'der, *n.* [Fr. *bordure*, *bord*, a border, *border*, to border, from the German. BOARD.] The outer part or edge of anything, as of a garment, piece of cloth, a country, etc.; margin; verge; brink; boundary; confine; frontier.—*v.i.* To have the edge or boundary adjoining; to be contiguous or adjacent; to approach; to come near: with *on* or *upon*.—*v.t.* To make a border to; to adorn with a border of ornaments; to form a border to; to touch at the edge or end; to be contiguous to; to limit.—**borderer**, bor'der·er, *n.* One who dwells on a border, or at the extreme part or confines of a country, region, or tract of land.— **borderland**, *n.* Land forming a border or frontier; an uncertain intermediate district.

bore, bōr, *v.t.*—*bored*, *boring.* [A.Sax. *borian*; Icel. *bora*, Sw. *borra*, Dan. *bore*, D. *boren*, G. *bohren*, to bore; of same root with L. *foro*, to bore.] To pierce or perforate and make a round hole in; to drill a hole in;

to form by piercing or drilling (to *bore* a hole); to force a narrow and difficult passage through; to weary by tedious iteration or repetition; to tire by insufferable dullness; to tease; to annoy; to pester.—*v.i.* To pierce or enter by drilling, etc.; to push forward toward a certain point.—*n.* The hole made by boring; hence, the cavity or hollow of a gun, cannon, pistol, or other firearm; the caliber whether formed by boring or not; a person that tires or wearies, especially by trying the patience; a dull person who forces his company and conversation upon us; anything troublesome or annoying.—**boredom**, bōr'dum, *n.* The domain of bores; bores collectively; the state of being bored or of being a bore.— **borer**, bōr'er, *n.* One who or that which bores; a term sometimes applied to certain worms, insects, fishes, which penetrate foreign bodies.

bore, bōr, *n.* [Icel. *bára*, a wave or swell.] A sudden influx of the tide into the estuary of a river from the sea, the inflowing water rising and advancing like a wall and rushing with a tremendous noise against the current for a considerable distance.

bore, bōr, pret. of *bear* (which see).

boreal, bō'rē·al, *a.* [L. *borealis*, from *boreas*, the north wind.] Northern; pertaining to the north or the north wind.

boric, bōr'ik, *a.* [From *boron*.] Of, or pertaining to, the element boron.— *Boric acid*, boron in combination with oxygen and hydrogen.—**borate**, bō'rāt, *n.* A salt of boric acid.

born, born, pp. of *bear*, to bring forth.

borne, bōrn, pp. of *bear*, to carry, etc.

boron, bō'ron, *n.* [From *borax*.] Nonmetallic element present in combination, as in borax. Symbol, B; at. no., 5; at. wt., 10.811.

borough, bur'ō, *n.* [A.Sax. *burg*, *burh*, a fort, town, city; Icel. Sw. Dan. *borg*, Goth. *baurgo*, G. D. *burg*; root in A. Sax. *beorgan*, Goth. *bairgan*, G. *bergen*, to protect. From same root as *bury*, *borrow*, *burrow*, *barrow* (grave mound), etc.] A corporate town or township; a town with a properly organized municipal government.—**borough-English**, *n.* *Law*, a customary descent of estates to the youngest son instead of the eldest, or, if the owner leaves no son, descent to the youngest brother.

borrow, bor'rō, *v.t.* [A.Sax. *borgian*, properly to take on security, from *borg*, *borh*, security, from *beorgan*, to protect; G. and D. *borgen*, to borrow. BOROUGH.] To ask and obtain on loan, trust, or on credit, with the intention of returning or giving an equivalent for; to take or adopt from another or from a foreign source and use as one's own; to adopt; to appropriate; to imitate; to copy—**borrower**, bor'rō·er, *n.* One who borrows; one who takes what belongs to another and

uses it as his own; a copier; an imitator; a plagiarist.

bort, bort, *n.* Diamonds too coarse for ornamental setting, or small fragments of pure diamonds, used, when reduced to a powder, for polishing and grinding.

boscage, bos'kij, *n.* [O.Fr. *boscage*, from the German. BUSH.] A mass of growing trees or shrubs; woods; groves or thickets; sylvan foliage.

bosh, bosh, *n.* [Turk., empty, vain, useless.] Nonsense; absurdity; trash.

bosk,† bosk, *n.* [An old form of *bush*.] A thicket; a small close natural wood, especially of bushes. (*Tenn.*)—**boskage**, *n.* BOSCAGE.— **bosky**, bos'ki, *a.* Bushy; covered with groves or thickets. (*Mil.*)

bosom, bu'zum, *n.* [A.Sax. *bósm*, D. *boezem*, G. *busen*, probably from root of *bow*, meaning literally a swelling or protruding part.] The breast of a human being; the folds of the dress about the breast; the seat of the tender affections, passions, inmost thoughts, wishes, secrets, etc.; embrace or compass (the *bosom* of the church); something likened to the human bosom (the *bosom* of the earth, of a lake, etc.).—*a.* Intimate; familiar; close; dear.—*v.t.* To enclose or harbor in the bosom; to embrace; to keep with care; to cherish intimately; to conceal; embosom.

boss, bos, *n.* [Fr. *bosse*, a swelling, from O.H.G. *bózo*, a bunch or bundle, same root as G. *boszen*, to beat; E. *beat*.] A protuberant part; a round, swelling body; a projecting mass; a stud or knob; a protuberant ornament of silver, ivory, or other material, used on bridles, harness, etc.; *arch.* an ornament placed at the intersection of the ribs or groins in vaulted or flat roofs.—*v.t.* To ornament with bosses; to bestud; to emboss. (*Shak.*) —**bossy**, bos'i, *a.* Containing a boss; ornamented with bosses.

boss, bos, *n.* [D. *baas*, a master.] An employer; a master; a superintendent; a chief man.—*v.t.* and *i.* To control; to superintend.

bot, botfly. See BOTT.

botany, bot'a·ni, *n.* [As if from a form *botaneia*, from Gr. *botane*, herbage, a plant, from *boskō*, to feed.] The science which treats of the vegetable kingdom, dealing with the forms, structure, and tissues of plants, the laws or conditions which regulate their growth or development, the functions of their various organs, the classification of the various specific forms of plants, their distribution over the face of the globe, and their condition at various geological epochs.—*Botany Bay*, Sydney, N.S.W., from its botanical richness when discovered by Captain Cook, 1770; as a penal settlement, in 1787.—**botanic**, **botanical**, bo·tan'ik, bo·tan'ik·al, *a.* Pertaining to botany; relating to plants in general.—**botanically**, bo·tan'ik·al·li, *adv.* In a botanical manner; after the manner of a botanist;

according to a system of botany.—
botanist, bot'an·ist, n. One skilled in botany; one versed in the knowledge of plants or vegetables, their structure, and generic and specific differences.—**botanize,** bot'an·īz, v.i. —botanized, botanizing. To study plants; to investigate the vegetable kingdom; to seek for plants with a view to study them.

botch, boch, n. [O.E. bocche, botche, a sore, a swelling, O.Fr. boce, a boss, a botch, a boil, a parallel form of boss; comp. O.D. butse, a boil, a swelling.] A swelling on the skin; a large ulcerous affection; a boil or blotch; a patch, or the part of a garment patched or mended in a clumsy manner; a part in any work bungled or ill-finished; bungled work generally.—v.t. To mark or cover with botches or boils†; to mend or patch in a clumsy manner; to perform or express in a bungling manner.—**botcher,** boch'ėr, n. One who botches; a clumsy workman at mending; a mender of old clothes; a bungler.—**botchery,**† boch'ėr·i, n. A botching, or that which is done by botching; clumsy workmanship. —**botchy,** boch'i, a. marked with botches; full of botches.

both, bōth, a. and pron. [A Scandinavian word = Icel. báthir, baethi, Sc. baith, Dan. baade, Goth. bajoths, G. beide, both. The first element is seen in A.Sax. bátwa, bothtwo, both, Goth. bai, both, L. ambo, G. amphö, Skr. ubha, both.] The one and the other; the two; the pair or the couple. In such a sentence as 'both men were there', it is an adjective; in 'he invited James and John, and both went', it is a pronoun; in 'the men both went', 'he took them both', it is a pronoun in apposition to men, them. It is often used as a conjunction in connection with and—both. ∴ and being equivalent to as well the one as the other; not only this but also that; equally the former and the latter.

bother, boTH'ėr, v.t. [Probably a word of Irish origin; comp. Ir. buaidhirt, trouble, affliction; buaidhrim, I vex, disturb; Ir. and Gael. buair, to vex, trouble.] To perplex; to perturb; to tease; to annoy.—v.i. To trouble or worry one's self; to make many words or much ado.—n. A trouble, vexation, or plague.— **botheration,** boTH·ėr·ā'shon, n. The act of bothering, or state of being bothered; annoyance; trouble; vexation; perplexity.

bothy, both'i, n. [Gael. bothag, a cot, from same root as booth.] In Scotland a house for the accommodation of workpeople engaged in the same employment; a farm building in which the unmarried male or female servants or laborers are lodged.

botryoid, botryoidal, bot'ri·oid, bot·ri·oi'dal, a. [Gr. botrys, a bunch of grapes, and eidos, form.] Having the form of a bunch of grapes; like grapes, as a mineral presenting an aggregation of small globes.

bott, bot, bot, n. [Gael, botus, a bott, boithag, a maggot.] A name given to the larvae or maggots of several species of gadfly when found in the intestines of horses, under the hides of oxen, in the nostrils of sheep, etc.; generally in plural.—**botfly,** n. A fly that produces botts.

bottle, bot'l, n. [Fr. bouteille, from L.L. buticula, a dim. from butica, a kind of vessel, from Gr. boutis, a flask.] A hollow vessel of glass, leather, or other material, with a narrow mouth, for holding and carrying liquors; the contents of a bottle; as much as a bottle contains; hence, fig. the bottle is used as equivalent to strong drink in general; the practice of drinking (to be fond of the bottle).—v.t.—bottled, bottling. To put into bottles.—**bottler,** bot'lėr, n. One whose occupation it is to bottle wines, spirits, beer, or the like.—**bottlenose,** n. A whale measuring from 22 to 28 feet long, and having a beaked snout, occurring in high north latitudes; also, the caaing whale.

bottom, bot'om, n. [A.Sax. botm, bottom = D. bodem, Icel. botn, O.H.G. podam, Mod. G. boden, from same root as L. fundus, Gr. pythmen, base, bottom.] The lowest or deepest part of anything, as distinguished from the top; that on which anything rests or is founded; utmost depth either literally or figuratively; base; foundation; the ground under any body of water; the lower or hinder extremity of the trunk of an animal; the buttocks; the portion of a chair for sitting on; the seat; low land formed by alluvial deposits along a river; a dale; a valley; the part of a ship below the wales; hence, the ship itself; power of endurance; stamina; native strength.—a. At the bottom; lowest; undermost; having a low situation; alluvial.—v.t. To found or build upon; to base; to furnish with a bottom.—**bottomless,** bot'om·les, a. Without a bottom; hence, fathomless; whose bottom cannot be found by sounding.—**bottomry,** bot'om·ri, n. The act of borrowing money, and pledging the bottom of the ship, that is, the ship itself, as security for the repayment of the money.

bottom, bot'om, n. [W. botwm, a boss, a bud, a button.] A ball or skein of thread; a cocoon.—v.t. To wind round something, as in making a ball of thread.

botulism, bot'ū·lizm, n. [L. botulus.] Poisoning caused by a toxin from the bacillus Clostridium botulinum, occurring in improperly preserved food, usually home canned, and affecting the nervous system.

boudoir, bö'dwär, n. [Fr., from bouder, to pout, to sulk.] A small room to which a lady may retire to be alone, or in which she may receive her intimate friends.

bough, bou, n. [A. Sax. bóg, bóh, an arm, a shoulder, a bough; Icel. bógr, Dan. boug, bov, the shoulder, a vessel's bow; allied to Gr. péchys, the fore-arm, Skr. bāhus, the arm.

Bow (of a ship) is the same word]. An arm or large branch of a tree.

bought, bat, pret. & pp. of buy (which see).

bougie, bö'zhē, n. [Fr., a wax-candle, from Sp. bugia, from Bugia, in North Africa, whence wax candles were first brought.] A wax taper; surg. a slender flexible cylinder made of waxed linen or silk cord, or of caoutchouc, steel, German silver, etc., intended for introduction into the urethra, esophagus, or rectum, when those passages are obstructed, as by stricture.

bouillon, bö'yon, n. [Fr.] Broth; soup.

boulder, bōl'dėr, n. From Dan. buldre, E. dial. bolder, Sw. bullra, to make a loud noise, to thunder; Sw. dial bullersten (sten = stone), a large pebble; lit. a stone that makes a thundering noise.] A water-worn roundish stone of considerable size, and larger than a pebble; geol. applied to iceworn and smoothed blocks lying on the surface of the soil, or imbedded in the clays and gravels of the drift formation.

boule, boule-work, böl, böl'wėrk, n. Same as Buhl.

boulevard, böl'e·värd, n. [Fr., older forms boulevert, bouleverse, borrowed and altered from G. bollwerk. BULWARK.] Originally, a bulwark or rampart of a fortification or fortified town; hence a public walk or street occupying the site of demolished fortifications; now sometimes extended to any wide street or walk.

bounce, bouns, v.i.—bounced, bouncing. [O.E. bounsen, bunsen, to strike suddenly; L.G. bunsen, to knock; D. bonzen, to strike, bounce; bons, a bounce; imitative of the noise of a blow.] To make a sudden leap or spring; to jump or rush suddenly; to knock or thump; to boast or bluster; to brag.—v.t. To drive against anything suddenly and violently.—n. A heavy blow, thrust, or thump; a loud heavy sound; a sudden crack or noise; a boast; a piece of brag or bluster; boastful language; exaggeration; a bold or impudent lie.—adv. With a bounce or abrupt movement; abruptly (to come bounce into a room).—**bouncer,** bouns'ėr, n. One that bounces; a boaster; a bully; a bragging liar; a barefaced lie; something big or large of its kind.—**bouncing,** bouns'ing, a. Vigorous; strong; stout; exaggerated; excessive; big.

bound, bound, n. [O.Fr. bodne, bonne, a bound, limit (Fr. borne), from L.L. bodina, bonna, a boundary, from Armor. boden, a cluster of trees serving as a boundary.] That which limits or circumscribes; the external or limiting line of any object or of space (to pass beyond the bounds); hence, that which keeps in or restrains; limit (to set bounds to ambition).—v.t. To set bounds or limits to; to act as a bound or limit to; to limit; to terminate; to restrain or confine; to circumscribe.—**boundary,** boun'de·ri, n. [From bound, with a Latin termination.] That which marks a bound or limit; a limit; a bound.—

bounder, boun'dėr, *n.* One who or that which bounds; assertive, unduly forceful person. [Colloq.] **boundless,** bound'les, *a.* Without bounds or limits; unlimited; limitless; immeasurable; illimitable; infinite.—**boundlessly,** bound'les·li, *adv.* In a boundless manner; infinitely. — **boundlessness,** bound'les·nes, *n.* The state or quality of being boundless or without limits.

bound, bound, *v.i.* [Fr. *bondir,* to leap, O.Fr. to ring, to echo; from L.L. *bombitare,* to resound, from L. *bombus,* a humming. BOMB.] To leap; to jump; to spring; to move forward by leaps; to rebound.—*n.* A leap; a spring; a jump; a rebound.

bound, bound, *pp.* of *bind* (also *pret.*). Made fast by a band or by chains, fetters, etc.; hemmed in; kept back; tied; having a binding; obliged by moral ties; confined; restrained. Colloquially the word is often used as equivalent to certain, sure; as, he is *bound* to succeed; the town is *bound* to increase.

bound, bound, *a.* [Formerly *boun,* from Icel. *buinn,* pp. of *bua,* to till, prepare, get ready. The *d* is parasitic, as in *sound,* from L. *sonus.* Same root as *boor, bower.*] Prepared; ready, hence, going or intending to go (outward *bound*); destined: often with *to* or *for* (a ship *bound for* London).

bounden, boun'den, *a.* [An old participle of *bind*] Obliged or beholden†; appointed; indispensable; obligatory (our *bounden* duty).

bounty, boun'ti, *n.* [O.Fr. *bonteit,* Fr. *bonte,* goodness, favor, from L. *bonitas,* goodness, from *bonus,* good.] Liberality in bestowing gifts and favors; generosity; munificence; a favor bestowed from a benevolent disposition; that which is given bounteously; a free gift; a premium offered to induce men to enlist into the public service, or to encourage some branch of industry.—**bounteous,** boun'tē·us, *a.* Disposed to give freely; free in bestowing gifts; bountiful; liberal; generous; munificent.—**bounteously,** boun'tē·us·li, *adv.* In a bounteous manner; liberally.—**bounteousness,** boun'tē·us·nes, *n.* The quality of being bounteous.—**bountiful,** boun'ti·fụl, *a.* Liberal in bestowing gifts, favors, or bounties; munificent; generous.—**bountifully,** boun'ti·fụl·li, *adv.* In a bountiful manner; liberally.—**bountifulness,** boun'ti·fụl·nes, *n.*

bouquet, bö·kā', *n.* [Fr., O.Fr. *bousquet, bosquet,* a little wood, dim. of *bosc,* a wood. BUSH.] A nosegay; a bunch of flowers; something resembling a bunch of flowers; an agreeable aromatic odor, such as that of the finer wines.

bourbon, bėr'bon, *n.* [Bourbon County, Kentucky.] A whiskey made from corn or rye.

bourdon, bör'don, *n.* [Fr.] The drone of the bagpipe; a bass stop in the organ or harmonium having a drone-like quality of tone.

bourgeois, börzh·wä', *n.* [Fr., sing. & pl.] A member of the middle class; a kind of printing type.—*a.* Ordinary.

bourgeon, bėr'jon, *n.* [Fr. *bourgeon,* a bud.] A bud.—*v.i.* To sprout; to put forth buds.

bourn, börn, bōrn, *n.* [Fr. *borne,* a limit, corruption of *bonne,* a boundary. BOUND.] A bound; a limit.

bourn,‡ börn, *n.* [Prov. E. and Sc. *burn,* A.Sax. *burna,* a stream=D. *born,* Icel. *brunnr,* Sw. *brunn,* Goth. *brunna,* G. *brunnen,* a spring, a well.] A brook; a torrent; a rivulet; a burn. (*Shak.*)

bourse, börs, *n.* [Fr., a purse, an exchange, from L. *bursa,* a hide, leather.] An exchange; a place where merchants assemble for general business.

bout, bout, *n.* [Older form *bought;* same word as Dan. *bugt,* a bend, a bight; closely akin to E. *bight,* and verb to *bow.*] A twist or turn; a bend or flexure; a going and returning, as in plowing, reaping, etc.; as much as is performed at one time; a trial; a set-to; a contest; a debauch.

boutonnière, bö·tan·yėr', *n.* [Fr. *boutonnière,* buttonhole.] A small flower worn in the buttonhole.

bovine, bō'vīn, *a.* [L.L. *bovinus,* from L. *bos, bovis,* an ox.] Pertaining to oxen and cows, or other quadrupeds of the same family.

bow, bou, *v.t.* [A.Sax. *búgan,* to bend (trans. and intrans.)=D. *buigen,* Dan. *boie,* Goth. *biugan,* G. *beugen;* cog. L. *fugio,* Gr. *pheugō,* to flee; Skr. *bhuj,* to bend. From same stem are *bow* (for arrows), *bight, bout.*] To make crooked or curved; to bend; to bend or incline, as the head or the body, in token of respect or civility; to bend or cause to yield; to subdue (to *bow* the will); to make a bow to (to *bow* a person out, etc.).—*v.i.* To bend in token of reverence, respect, or civility; to be bent or inflected; to curve.—*n.* An inclination of the head, or a bending of the body, in token of reverence, respect, or submission. —**bower,** bou'ėr, *n.* One who bows.

bow, bou, *n.* [Icel. *bógr,* Dan. *bov, boug,* a shoulder, the bow of a vessel; same words as *bough.*] *Naut.* the rounding part of a ship's side forward, on either side, terminating at the stem or prow.—**bower,** bou'ėr, *n.* One of two anchors at the bow of a vessel, which are both kept in constant working use: called also *Bower-anchor.*—**bowline,** bō'lin, *n.* A rope fastened near the middle of the perpendicular edge of the square sails, and used to keep the weather edge of the sails tight forward toward the bow.—**bowsprit,** bō'sprit, *n.* The large spar or boom projecting over the bow or stem of a vessel.

bow, bō, *n.* [A.Sax. *boga,* Icel. *bogi,* Dan. *bue,* D. *boog;* from root of verb to *bow.*] A missile weapon made of a strip of wood or other elastic material, which, being bent by means of a string fastened to its two ends, can discharge an arrow placed endwise on the string by the latter being drawn back and suddenly let go;

anything bent or in form of a curve, as the rain*bow;* an implement strung with horsehair, by means of which the tone is produced from instruments of the violin kind; an instrument in use among smiths for turning a drill, with turners for turning wood, with hatters for breaking fur and wool, and consisting of a piece of wood more or less curved, and having a string extending from one extremity to the other; a kind of ornamental knot of ribbon or other material.—*v.t.* or *i. Mus.* to perform or play with the *bow.*—**bowman,** bō'man, *n.* One who shoots with or is skilled in the use of the bow; an archer.—**bowyer,** bō'yėr, *n.* An archer or bowman; a maker of bows. —**bowknot,** *n.* A ⏤ipknot made by a ribbon or other material.—**bowleg,** *n.* A crooked or bandy leg.—**bowlegged,** *a.* Having crooked or bandy legs.—**bowshot,** *n.* The distance a bow can propel an arrow.—**bowstring,** *n.* The string with which a bow is bent; a similar string used by the Turks for strangling offenders.—*v.t.* To strangle with a bowstring.—**bow window,** *n.* A window built so as to project from a wall, properly one that forms a segment of a circle.

bowdlerize, boud'lėr·īz, *v.t.* To abbreviate, or expunge texts of objectionable matter, on moral grounds. From Thomas Bowdler, who in 1818 issued an edition of Shakespeare in which " those words and expressions are omitted which cannot with propriety be read aloud in a family. "

bowel, bou'el, *n.* [O.Fr. *boel,* from L. *botellus,* a small sausage, an intestine.] One of the intestines of an animal; a gut, especially of man; *pl.* the supposed seat of pity or tenderness; hence kindness, compassion, or affection; the interior part of anything (the *bowels* of the earth).—*v.t.*—**boweled, boweling.** To take out the bowels of; to eviscerate.

bower, bou'ėr, *n.* [A.Sax. *búr,* a chamber, from *búan,* to dwell; Icel. *búr,* a chamber, from *búa,* to live; akin *boor, bound* (ready).] A woman's private apartment; any room in a house except the hall (in these senses now only poetical); a shelter made with boughs or twining plants; an arbor; a shady recess.—**bowerbird,** *n.* A name of certain Australian birds of the oriole family, about the size of a large starling, and remarkable for erecting bowers and adorning them with gay feathers, shells, and other bright-colored objects, these bowers being used as places of resort, but not as nests.

bower, bou'ėr, *n.* [G. *bauer,* peasant, knave.] One of two cards at Euchre. The right bower is the knave of trumps, the left is the knave of same color.

bowie knife, bō'i, *n.* [After its inventor, Colonel James *Bowie.*] A knife from 10 to 15 inches long and about 2 inches broad.

bowl, bōl, *n.* [O.E. *bolle,* A.Sax. *bolla,* a bowl; Icel. *bolli,* M.H.G. *bolle,* a bowl; allied to *ball.*] A concave vessel

bowl, bōl, n. [O.E. bowle, Fr. boule, from L. bulla, a bubble (whence verb to boil).] A ball of wood or other material used for rolling on a level surface at play; a ball of wood loaded on one side used in a game played on a level plat of greensward; pl. the game played with such balls.—v.i. To play with bowls or at bowling; to roll a bowl, as in the game of bowls; to deliver the ball to be played by the batsman at cricket; to move rapidly and like a ball (bowl along).—v.t. To roll in the manner of a bowl; to pelt with or as with bowls.—bowler, bōl′ėr, n. One who plays at bowls; cricket, the player who delivers the ball in order to be played by the batsman.—bowling alley, n. A covered place for the game of bowls.—bowling green, n. A level piece of greensward kept smooth for bowling.—bowlder, bōl′-dėr, n. Same as boulder.

box, boks, n. [A.Sax. box, a box, from L. buxus, buxum, the box tree, and something made of its wood.] A case or receptacle of any size and made of any material; the driver's seat on a carriage; a present, especially a Christmas present; a compartment for the accommodation of a small number of people, as in a theater; a narrow confined enclosed place; a place of shelter for one or two men engaged in certain duties, as sentries, signalmen, etc.; a small house for sportsmen during the shooting season or the like.—v.t. To enclose, as in a box; to confine.—To box the compass, to repeat or go over the points of the compass in order, or to answer any questions regarding the divisions of the compass; to perform a swift change in politics.—Boxing day, n. The day after Christmas day when Christmas boxes and presents are given [in England].

box, boks, n. [Corresponding by metathesis to Dan. bask, a slap, baske, to beat; akin bash.] A blow with the fist.—v.t. To strike with the fist or hand.—v.i. To fight with the fists; to practice fighting with the fists.—boxer, bok′sėr, n. One who fights with his fists; a pugilist; a breed of short-haired, medium-sized dog.—boxing, n. Fist fighting with padded gloves, practiced as a sport.—boxing glove, n. A large padded glove used for sparring.

box, boks, n. [L. buxus, Gr. pyxos, the box-tree. Box, a case.] The name given to several species of trees or shrubs, the most important being a small evergreen tree with small shining leaves, and yielding a hard close-grained wood, and the dwarf variety used as edgings of garden walks.—boxwood, n. The fine hard-grained timber of the box tree, much used by wood engravers and in the manufacture of musical and mathematical instruments, etc.

boy, boi, n. [Fris. boi, boy, a boy; allied to D. boef, G. bube, Sw. bue, a boy.] A male child from birth to the age of puberty; a lad; a man wanting in vigor, experience, judgment; a familiar term applied in addressing or speaking of grown persons, especially one's associates; in compounds sometimes applied to grown men without any idea of youth or contempt; as, a postboy, a potboy.—boyhood, boi′hud, n. The state of being a boy or of immature age.—boyish, boi′ish, a. Belonging to a boy; pertaining to boyhood; in a disparaging sense; childish; trifling; puerile.—boyishly, boi′ish·li, adv. In a boyish manner.—boyishness, boi′-ish·nes, n. The quality of being boyish.

boyar, boi′är, n. A member of an order of the old Russian aristocracy next in rank to the ruling princes.

boycott, boi′kot, v.t. [From Capt. Boycott, an Irish land agent, the first prominent victim of the system in 1880.] To combine in refusing to work for, to buy from or sell to, or to have any dealings with, as a means to show disapproval or to coerce.—n. The process of boycotting.

brabble, brab′l, n. [D. brabbelen, to confound, to stammer.] A broil; a wrangle.—v.i.—brabbled, brabbling. To dispute or quarrel noisily.—brabblement, brab′l·ment, n. A clamorous contest; a brabble.

brace, brās, n. [O.Fr. brace, brasse, etc., from L. brachia, the arms, pl. of brachium, an arm; allied to Gael. brac, W. braic, the arm.] That which holds anything tight, tense, firm, or secure, or which supports, binds, or strengthens, as a piece of timber placed near and across the angles in the frame of a building; a thick strap which supports a carriage on wheels; the crank-shaped stock in which boring tools, etc., are held, serving as a lever for turning them, etc.; a mark { or } used in written or printed matter connecting two or more words or lines; a couple or pair (not of persons unless in contempt).—v.t.—braced, bracing. To bind or tie closely; to make tense; to strain up; to increase the tension, tone, or vigor of (the nerves, the system); to strengthen; to invigorate.—bracer, brās′ėr, n. One who or that which braces; an archery guard for the left forearm.—bracing, brās′-ing, a. Giving vigor or tone to the bodily system.

bracelet, brās′let, n. [Fr. bracelet, a dim. of O.Fr. bracel, brachel, an armlet, from L. brachile, from brachium, the arm. BRACE.] An ornament encircling the wrist, now worn mostly by ladies.

brachial, brā′ki·al, a. [L. brachium, the arm.] Belonging to the arm; of the nature of an arm; resembling an arm.—brachiate, brā′ki·āt, a. Bot. having branches in pairs, nearly horizontal, and each pair at right angles with the next.

Brachiopoda, brā·ki·op′o·da, n. pl. [Gr. brachiōn, an arm, and pous, a foot.] A class of marine, bivalve, molluscoid animals, including the lamp shells, etc., so named from the development of a long spirally-coiled fringed respiratory appendage or arm on either side of the mouth.—brachiopod, brā′ki·o·pod, n. One of the Brachiopoda.

brachycephalic, brachycephalous, brak′i·se·fal″ik, brak·i·sef′al·us, a. [Gr. brachys, short, and kephalé, the head.] In ethn. terms applied to heads (or races possessing such heads) whose diameter from side to side is not much less than that from front to back, their ratio being as 8 to 10, as those of the Mongolian type.

Brachyura, brak·i·ū′ra, n. pl. [Gr. brachys, short, and oura, tail.] A section of ten-footed crustaceans (Decapoda), with the abdomen forming a very short, jointed tail, folded forward closely under the thorax, as in the common edible crab.—brachyurous, brak·i·ū′rus, a. Short-tailed: applied to certain Crustacea, as the crab, to distinguish them from the macrurous or long-tailed crustaceans, as the lobster.—brachyuran, brak·i·ū′ran, n. One of the Brachyura.

bracken, brak′en, n. [A Scandinavian word; same as Sw. bräken, Dan. bregne, fern; closely allied to brake.] Fern. BRAKE.

bracket, brak′et, n. [Ultimately perhaps from L. brachium, an arm.] A kind of short supporting piece projecting from a perpendicular surface, either plain or ornamentally carved, as an ornamental projection from the face of a wall to support a statue; a triangular wooden support for a shelf or the like; an ornamental piece supporting a hammer beam; one of two projecting pieces attached to a wall, beam, etc., for carrying or supporting a line of shafting; printing, one of two marks [ ] used to enclose a reference, note, or explanation, to indicate an interpolation, rectify a mistake, etc.; a gas pipe projecting from a wall, usually more or less ornamental.—v.t. To furnish with a bracket or with brackets; printing, to place within brackets; to connect by brackets.

brackish, brak′ish, a. [D. and L.G. brak, G. brack, brackish.] Possessing a salt or somewhat salt taste; salt in a moderate degree; applied to water.—brackishness, brak′ish·nes, n. The quality of being brackish.

bract, brakt, n. [L. bractea, a thin plate of metal.] Bot. a modified leaf differing from other leaves in shape or color, and generally situated on the peduncle near the flower.—bracteate, brak′tē·it, a. Furnished with bracts.—bracteole, bractlet, brak′tē·ōl, brakt′let, n. A little bract on a partial flower stalk or pedicel in a many-flowered inflorescence.

brad, brad, n. [Same word as Icel. broddr, a spike, a nail; Dan. brodde, a frost nail; A.Sax. brord, a prick, a spire of grass; comp. Gael. and Ir. brod, goad, sting.] A finishing nail with little or no head used where it is deemed proper to drive nails entirely into the wood.—bradawl, n.

An awl to make holes for brads or other nails.

brae, brā, *n.* [Icel. *brá*, eyelid, akin to G. *braue*, eyebrow.] A sloping bank, acclivity. [Scottish.]

brag, brag, *v.i.*—*bragged, bragging.* [From the Celtic; W. *bragiaw*, Ir. *braghaim*, to boast; Gael. *bragaire-achd*, boasting; Armor. *braga*, to make a display; from root of *break*.] To use boastful language; to speak vaingloriously; to boast; to vaunt; to swagger; to bluster.—*n.* A boast or boasting; a vaunt; the thing boasted of; a game at cards: so called because one player *brags* he has a better hand than the others, staking a sum of money on the issue.— **braggadocio**, brag·a·dō′shi·ō, *n.* [From *Braggadochio*, a boastful character in Spenser's 'Faery Queen', from the verb to *brag*.] A boasting fellow; a braggart; empty boasting; brag.—**braggart**, brag′ärt, *n.* [*Brag*, and suffix *-art*, *-ard*.] A boaster; a vain fellow.—*a.* Boastful; vainly ostentatious.

Brahman, brä′man, *n.* Among the Hindus a member of the sacred or sacerdotal caste, who claim to have proceeded from the mouth of Brahmā (the Creator, one of the deities of the Hindu triad or trinity), and who are noted for their many minute religious observances, their abstemiousness, and their severe penances.— **Brahmanic, Brahmanical**, brä·man′ik, brä·man′ik·al, *a.* Of or pertaining to the Brahmans or their doctrines and worship.—**Brahmanism**, brä′man·izm, *n.* The religion or system of doctrines of the Brahmans.—**Brahmanist**, brä′man·ist, *n.* An adherent of Brahmanism. These words are also spelled *Brahmin, Braminic*, etc.

braid, brād, *v.t.* [A.Sax. *bredan, bregdan*, to weave, to braid; Icel. *bregtha*, to braid, *bragth*, a sudden movement; O.H.G. *brettan*, to braid.] To weave or intertwine, as hair, by forming three or more strands into one; to plait.—*n.* A sort of narrow textile band formed by plaiting or weaving several strands of silk, cotton, woolen, etc., together; a plait or plaited tress of hair.—**braiding**, brād′ing, *n.* Braid, or trimming made of braid collectively.

brail, brāl, *n.* [O.Fr. *braiel, braieul*, etc., a trouser band, from *braies*, breeches, from L. *bracae*, breeches.] BREECHES.] *Naut.* a rope attached to a fore-and-aft sail, or a jib to assist in taking in the sail.—*v.t.* To haul in by means of the brails: followed by *up.*

braille, brāl, *n.* [Fr. *Braille*, inventor's name.] A system of reading with raised letters for the blind.

brain, brān, *n.* [A.Sax. *braegen, bregen*, D. and O.Fris. *brein*.] The soft whitish mass enclosed in the skull in man and other vertebrate animals, forming the center of the nervous system, and the seat of consciousness and volition, and in which the nerves and spinal marrow terminate; the cerebrum: sometimes used to include also the cerebellum; the understand-

ing; the fancy; the imagination.— *v.t.* To dash out the brains of; to kill by beating out the brains.—**brainless**, brān′les, *a.* Without understanding or judgment; silly; stupid.—**brainy**, brān′i, *a.* Provided with brains; intellectual.—**brainpan**, *n.* The skull which encloses the brain. (*Shak.*)— **brainsick**, *a.* Disordered in the understanding; fantastic; crotchety; crazed.—**brainsickness**, *n.* Disorder of the understanding.—**brainstorming**, brān′storm·ing, *n.* A group technique for stimulating creative thinking.—**brain washing.** Systematic indoctrination by psychological manipulation to undermine or change political beliefs.

braise, brāz, *v.t.* [Fr. *braiser*, to braise, from Dan. *brase*, to fry; Sw. *brasa*, to flame. BRASS.] To bake, broil, or stew with herbs, spices, etc., in a closely covered pan.

brake, brāk, *n.* [A.Sax. *bracce*, fern, bracken; L.G. *brake*, brushwood; allied to D. *braak*, Dan. *brak*, G. *brach*, fallow.] A fern; bracken; a place overgrown with brakes or brushwood, shrubs, and brambles; a thicket, as of canes, etc.

brake, brāk, *n.* [From the verb to *break*; comp. L.G. *brake*, G. *breche*, an instrument for breaking flax; O.D. *brake*, a fetter for the neck, *braake*, an instrument for holding an animal by the nose.] An instrument or machine to break flax or hemp; a pump handle; a kneading trough; a sharp bit or snaffle; a frame for confining refractory horses while shoeing; a large heavy barrow for breaking clods; a kind of wagonette; a strong heavy vehicle with a seat only for the driver, used for breaking in young horses to harness; an appliance used to stop or retard the motion of a machine or vehicle by friction, and generally consisting of a simple or compound lever which can be pressed forcibly against the rim of a wheel on one of the axles of the machine or carriage.—**brakeman**, brāk′man, *n.* The man whose business is to stop a railroad train by applying the brake; *mining*, the man in charge of a winding engine.

bramble, bram′bl, *n.* [A.Sax. *bremel, brembel*, from stem *bram, brem* (seen also in *broom*), *el* being simply a termination and *b* inserted as in *number*, etc., comp. L.G. *brummel-beere*, Dan. *brambär*, G. *brombeere*, Sw. *brom-*bär, a blackberry.] A prickly trailing shrub of the rose family growing in hedges and waste places, and bearing a black berry somewhat like a raspberry; the berry itself; the blackberry.—**brambly**, bram′bli, *adv.* Full of brambles.

bran, bran, *n.* [A Celtic word = W. Ir. Gael. *bran*, bran, chaff; Armor. *brenn*, bran, whence O.Fr. *bren*.] The outer coat of wheat, rye, or other farinaceous grain, separated from the flour by grinding.

branch, bransh, *n.* [From Fr. *branche*, a branch, from Armor. *branc*, an arm; connected with L.L. *branca*, a claw, W. *braich*, L. *brachium*, an arm.] A portion of a tree, shrub, or

other plant springing from the stem, or from a part ultimately supported by the stem; a bough; a shoot; something resembling a branch; an offshoot or part extending from the main body of a thing; any member or part of a body or system; a department, section, or subdivision; a line of family descent, in distinction from some other line or lines from the same stock.—*v.i.* To spread in branches; to send out branches as a plant; to divide into separate parts or subdivisions; to diverge (a road *branches* off); to ramify.—*v.t.*† To divide, as into branches; to adorn, as with needlework, representing branches, flowers, or twigs.

branchiae, brang′ki·ē, *n. pl.* [L.] The respiratory organs of fishes, etc.; the gills.—**branchial**, brang′ki·al, *a.* Relating to the branchiae or gills; performed by means of branchiae.

Branchiopoda, brang·ki·op′o·da, *n. pl.* [Gr. *branchia*, gills, and *pous, podos*, a foot.] An order of crustaceous animals, so called because their branchiae, or gills, are situated on the feet, as in the water fleas, brine shrimps, etc.—**branchiopod**, brang′-ki·o·pod, *n.* An animal belonging to the order Branchiopoda.

brand, brand, *n.* [A.Sax. *brand*, a burning, a sword = Icel. *brandr*, fire-brand, sword; Dan. D. and G. *brand*, a burning. The sword is so called from its gleaming. Akin to verb *burn*.] A piece of wood burning or partly burned; a sword; a mark made by burning with a hot iron or by other means, as on commodities to indicate the quality or manufacturer, on sheep to indicate the owner, or on criminals to indicate their crime or for identification; a trademark; hence, kind or quality; a mark of infamy; a stigma; a disease in vegetables by which their leaves and tender bark are partially destroyed as if they had been burned.—*v.t.* To burn or impress a mark upon with a hot iron, or to distinguish by a similar mark; to fix a mark or character of infamy upon; to stigmatize as infamous.—**brander**, brand′-ėr, *n.* One who brands.—**brand-new**, *a.* A more correct form of *bran-new* (which see).

brandish, bran′dish, *v.t.* [From Fr. *brandir, brandissant*, from Teut. *brand*, a sword. BRAND.] To move or wave, as a weapon; to raise and move in various directions; to shake or flourish.—**brandisher**, bran′dish-ėr, *n.* One who brandishes.

brandling, brand′ling, *n.* The parr or young of the salmon, so named from having, as it were, branded markings; also, a small red worm used for bait in fresh-water fishing.

brandy, bran′di, *n.* [O.E. *brandywine*, D. *brandewijn*, lit. burnt wine—D. *branden*, to burn, to distil, and *wijn*, wine, like G. *branntwein—brennen*, to burn, and *wein*, wine. BRAND.] A spirituous liquor obtained by the distillation of wine, or the refuse of the wine press; a name now also given to spirit distilled from other liquors or from some fruit juices.

brangle, brang´gl, n. [Perhaps for *braggle*, from *brag*.] A wrangle; a squabble; a noisy contest or dispute. —*v.i.* To wrangle; to dispute contentiously; to squabble.

branks, brangks, n. [From the Celtic: Gael. *brangas*, a kind of pillory; Ir. *brancas*, a halter.] An instrument of the nature of a bridle formerly used for correcting scolding women; a scolding bridle.

bran-new, bran´nū, a. [For *brand-new*, the original form, from *brand*, a burning, and *new*.] *Lit.* glowing like metal newly out of the fire or forge; hence, quite new.

brash, brash, n. [From Fr. *brèche*, a breach, broken stuff, breccia.] A confused heap of fragments, as masses of loose, broken, or angular fragments of rocks; small fragments of crushed ice, collected by winds or currents, near the shore; refuse boughs of trees.

brasier, brā´zi·êr, n. [Fr. *brasier*, *braisier*, from *braise*, embers, live coals; same origin as *braze, brass*.] An open pan for burning wood or coal.

brasier, brā´zi·êr, n. [From *brass* or from *braze*.] An artificer who works in brass.

brass, bras, n. [A.Sax. *braes*, brass= Icel. *bras*, solder; from verbal stem seen in Icel. *brasa*, to harden by fire; Sw. *brasa*, to blaze; Dan. *brase*, to fry (whence Fr. *braise*, live embers, *braser*, to braze, *braiser*, to braise).] A malleable and fusible alloy of copper and zinc, of a yellow color, usually containing about one-third of its weight of zinc; a utensil, ornament, or other article made of brass, as a monumental plate bearing effigies, coats of arms, etc., inlaid in a slab of stone, common in the pavements of medieval churches; *pl.* musical instruments of the trumpet kind; brazenness or impudence (colloq.); money (colloq.).—*v.t.* To cover or coat over with brass.—**brassy,** bras´i, a. Resembling or composed of brass; brazen.—*n.* A golf club shod with brass.—**brassiness,** bras´i·nes, n.

brassard, bras´êrd, n. [Fr., from *bras*, arm.] A protecting piece, or a badge, for the arm. Also *Brassart*.

brassiere, bras·yâr´, bra·zēr´, n. (Fr., from *bras*, arm.) An undergarment worn by women to support the breasts. Also (colloq.) **bra,** brä.

brat, brat, n. [Ir. and Gael. *brat*, a rag, an apron.] A child: so called in contempt.

brattice, brat´is, n. [O.Fr. *breteche*, a bartizan; probably from G. *bret*, a board, a plank.] A partition which divides a mining shaft into two chambers, serving as the upcast and downcast shafts for ventilation, or placed across a gallery to keep back noxious gases, or prevent the escape of water; a fence put round dangerous machinery.

bravado, bra·vä´dō, n. [Sp. *bravada*, Fr. *bravade*. BRAVE.] An arrogant menace, intended to intimidate; a boast; a brag.

brave, brāv, a. [Fr. *brave*, brave, gay, proud, braggard; Sp. and It.

bravo, brave, courageous; perhaps from the Celtic; comp. Armor. *brao*, *brav*, gaily dressed, fine, handsome; also O.Sw. *braf*, good.] Courageous; bold; daring; intrepid; high-spirited; valiant; fearless; making a fine display in bearing, dress, or appearance generally; excellent‡; capital‡.—*n.* A brave, bold, or daring person; a man daring beyond discretion; a North American Indian warrior.—*v.t.*—*braved, braving.* To encounter with courage and fortitude, or without being moved; to defy; to dare.—**bravely,** brāv´li, adv. In a brave manner; courageously; gallantly; prosperously.—**braveness,** brāv´nes, n. The quality of being brave.—**bravery,** brāv´êr·i, n. The quality of being brave; courage; undaunted spirit; intrepidity; gallantry; splendor‡; show‡; bravado‡.

bravo, brä´vō, interj. [It. BRAVE.] Well done! The word being an Italian adjective, the correct usage is to say *bravo* to a male singer or actor, *brava* to a female, and *bravi* to a company.

bravo, brä´vō, n. pl. **bravoes,** brä´vōz. [It. and Sp., lit. a daring man.] A daring villain; an assassin or murderer for hire.

bravura, brä·vö´ra, a. [It., bravery, spirit.] *Mus.* applied to a florid air, serving to display a performer's flexibility of voice and distinctness of articulation.

brawl, brạl, v.i. [Perhaps from W. *brawl*, a boast, *broliaw*, to boast, *bragal*, to vociferate; or akin to D. *brallen*, to boast, Dan. *bralle*, to jabber, to prate, *brölle*, to roar.] To be clamorous or noisy; to quarrel noisily; to make the noise of rushing or running water; to flow with a noise (a brook *brawls* along).—*n.* A noisy quarrel; loud angry contention; an uproar, row, or squabble; a kind of dance‡.—**brawler,** brạl´êr, n. One who brawls; a noisy fellow; a wrangler.

brawn, brạn, n. [O.Fr. *braon*, the muscular parts of the body, from O.H.G. *brato, braton*, meat for roasting, from *braten*, to roast.] Boar's flesh; the flesh of the boar or swine, collared so as to squeeze out much of the fat, boiled, and pickled; the flesh of a pig's head and ox feet cut in pieces and boiled, pickled, and pressed into a shape; a fleshy, protuberant, muscular part of the body, as on the thigh or the arm; muscular strength; muscle; the arm‡.—**brawniness,** brạ´ni·nes, n. The quality of being brawny; strength, hardiness.—**brawny,** brạ´ni, a. Having large strong muscles; muscular; fleshy; bulky; strong.

braxy, brak´si, n. [Perhaps from the verb to *break*; comp. G. *brechen*, vomiting, *brechen*, to break; or from Gael. *bragsaidh*, a disease of sheep.] The name given to several diseases of sheep; a sheep having the braxy; the mutton of such a sheep.—*a.* Affected or tainted with braxy.

bray, brā, n. [O.Fr. *brayer* (Fr. *broyer*), to pound, from G. *brechen*, to break.] To pound, beat, or

grind small, especially in a mortar.

bray, brā, v.i. [Fr. *braire*, to bray; L.L. *bragire*, *bragare*, to bray, from Celtic root seen in *brag*.] To utter a harsh cry: said especially of the ass; to make a loud, harsh, disagreeable sound.—*v.t.* To utter with a loud harsh sound: sometimes with *out*.—*n.* The harsh sound or roar of an ass; a harsh or grating sound.—**brayer,** brā´êr, n. One that brays like an ass.

braze, brāz, v.t.—*brazed, brazing.* [Fr. *braser*, to braze, from the Scandinavian. BRASS.] To solder with hard solder, such as an alloy of brass and zinc; to cover or ornament with brass; to harden; to harden to impudence (*Shak.*).‡—**brazen,** brā´zn, a. Made of brass; also, from brass often serving as a type of strength or impenetrability, extremely strong; impenetrable; pertaining to brass; proceeding from brass (a *brazen* sound); impudent; having a front like brass.—*v.t.* To behave with insolence or effrontery: with an indefinite *it*.—*To brazen out*, to persevere in treating with effrontery: with an indefinite *it*, or a noun like *matter, affair, business.*—**brazenly,** brā´zn·li, adv. In a brazen manner; boldly; impudently.—**brazenness,** brā´zn·nes, n. Appearance like brass; brassiness; impudence. — **brazier,** brā´zi·êr, n. Same as *Brasier.*—**brazenface,** n. An impudent person; one remarkable for effrontery.—**brazen-faced,** a. Impudent; bold to excess.

brazil, brazil-wood, bra·zil´, n. [Pg. *brasil*, from *braza*, a live coal, the name being given to the wood from its color, and the country being called after the wood.] A very heavy wood of a red color, growing in Brazil and other tropical countries, used for dyeing red.—**brazilin,** braz´il·in, n. The red coloring matter of Brazil-wood.—**Brazil nut,** n. The seeds of a very lofty tree growing throughout tropical America. The fruit is nearly round and about 6 inches in diameter, having an extremely hard shell, and containing from eighteen to twenty-four triangular wrinkled seeds, which, besides being eaten, yield an oil, used by watchmakers and others.

breach, brēch, n. [From A.Sax. *brece*, *brice*, a breach or breaking, from *brecan*, to break; partly also from Fr. *brèche*, a breach, from the same stem, but directly from the German.] The act of breaking in a figurative sense; the act of violating or neglecting some law, contract, obligation, or custom; the space between the several parts of a mass parted by violence; a rupture; a break; a gap (a *breach* in a wall); separation between persons through ill feeling; difference; quarrel; injury; wound (O.T.); the breaking of waves; the surf (*Shak.*).—*v.t.* To make a breach or opening in.

bread, bred, n. [A.Sax. *bread*=D. *brood*, Sw. and Dan. *bröd*, G. *brod*, *brot*. Root doubtful; perhaps *brew*.] A kind of food made by moistening and kneading the flour or meal of some species of grain, or that prepared from other plants, and baking it, the dough being often caused to ferment; food or sustenance in general.—**breadfruit,** n. The fruit of a tree which grows in the islands of the Pacific Ocean, producing a large round fruit used as a substitute for bread, and forming the principal food of a considerable population.—**breadstuff,** bred′stuf, n. Breadcorn: used frequently in the plural to signify all the different varieties of grain and flour from which bread is made collectively.— **breadwinner,** n. One who works for the support of himself or of himself and a family.

breadth, bredth, n. [O.E. brede, with th added, from A.Sax. braedu, breadth, from brád, broad; comp. length, width. BROAD.] The measure or extent of any plane surface from side to side; width; fig. largeness of mind; liberality; wide intellectual grasp; fine arts, an impression of largeness, freedom, and space produced by bold or simple touches and strokes of the pencil.—**breadthways,** bredth′wāz, adv. In the direction of the breadth.

break, brāk, v.t.—broke (pret. brake is still used in archaic style); broken or broke (pp.); breaking. [A.Sax. brecan, to break, weaken, vanquish, etc.=D. breken, Dan. braekke, G. brechen, Goth. brikan, to break, to crush, etc.; Icel. braka, to creak; same root as L. frango, Gr. (f)rēgnymi, to break.] To part or divide by force and violence (as a stick, a rope); fig. to sever or interrupt (connection, friendship); to cause to give way (to break an enemy's lines); to destroy, weaken, or impair (health, constitution); to subdue; to quell (to break one's spirit); to train to obedience; to make tractable (to break a horse); to dismiss or cashier; pay off (troops); to reduce in rank or condition (an officer); to give a superficial wound to so as to lacerate (the skin); to violate, as a contract, law, or promise; to stop; to interrupt (sleep); to cause to discontinue (to break a person of a habit); to check; to lessen the force of (a fall or a blow); to make a first and partial disclosure of; to impart or tell cautiously so as not to startle or shock (to break unwelcome news); to destroy the completeness of; to remove a part from (a sum of money, a set of things).—To break off, to sever by breaking; to put a sudden stop to (a marriage); to discontinue; to leave off (intimacy, a conversation).—To break up, to open forcibly (a door); to lay open (to break up ground); to dissolve or put an end to (a meeting); to separate; to disband.—To break ground, to begin to plow or dig; to commence excavation; fig. to begin to execute any plan.—To break the heart, to afflict grievously; to cause to die of grief.—To break one's mind to, to reveal one's thoughts to.—To break the ice, to overcome

obstacles and make a beginning; to get over the feeling of restraint incident to a new acquaintanceship. —v.i. To become broken; to burst forth violently (a storm, a deluge); to open spontaneously or by force from within; to burst (a bubble, a tumor); to show the first light of morning; to dawn (the day, the morning breaks); to become bankrupt; to decline or fail in health and strength; to fail, change in tone, or falter, as the voice.—To break away, to disengage one's self abruptly; to rush off.—To break down, to come down by breaking; to fail and be unable to proceed in an undertaking.—To break forth, to burst out; to be suddenly manifested (rage, light, noise); to rush or issue out; to give vent to one's feelings. —To break from, to disengage one's self from; to leave abruptly or violently.—To break in or into, to enter by force; to start into suddenly (break into a gallop).— To break loose, to get free by force; to shake off restraint.—To break off, to part; to become separated; to desist suddenly.—To break out, to issue forth; to arise or spring up (fire, fever, sedition); to appear in eruptions.—To break up, to dissolve and separate (as a company).— To break with, to cease to be friends with; to quarrel; to broach a subject to (Shak.)†.—n. An opening made by force; a rupture; a breach; an interruption of continuity (five years without a break); a line in writing or printing, noting a suspension of the sense or a stop in the sentence; a contrivance to check the velocity of a wheeled carriage; a brake; a contrivance for interrupting or changing the direction of electric currents; a large high-set four-wheeled vehicle; a brake; in cricket, a sudden swerve of the ball after pitching, in direction of the batsman; in billiards, a continuous score of points.—Break of day, the dawn.— **breakable,** brāk′a·bl, a. Capable of being broken.—**breakage,** brāk′ij, n. The act of breaking; allowance for what is accidentally broken.— **breakdown,** n. An overthrow, as of a carriage; a downfall; a crash; a failure; a collapse; a lively, noisy dance.—**breaker,** brāk′ér, n. The person who or that which breaks anything; a violator or transgressor; a wave broken into foam against the shore, a sand bank, or a rock near the surface; a small flat water cask (in this sense perhaps a corruption of Sp. barrica, a keg.— **breakfast,** brek′fast, n. The first meal in the day; the meal which enables one to break the fast lasting from the previous day; the food eaten at the first meal.—v.t. To furnish with breakfast.—v.i. To eat breakfast.—**breakneck,**† brāk′nek, n. A fall that breaks the neck; a dangerous business (Shak.).—a Endangering life; extremely hazardous.— **breakthrough,** brāk′thrö, n. Milit. penetration beyond an enemy's defense line; a major advance in

solving a problem.—**breakup,** n. A disruption; a dissolution of connection; a disintegration; a disbandment.—**breakwater,** brāk′wạ·tér, n. Any structure or contrivance serving to break the force of waves.

bream, brēm, n. [Fr. brème, O.Fr. bresme, from O.H.G. brahsema, G. bressem, the bream.] The name of several fresh-water soft-finned fishes belonging to the carp family; the name is also given to some spiny-finned sea fishes resembling the perches.

bream, brēm, v.t. [D. brem, broom, furze, from the materials commonly used; the verb broom is also used in same sense.] Naut. to clear of shells, seaweed, ooze, etc., by fire— an operation applied to a ship's bottom.

breast, brest, n. [A.Sax. breóst=Icel. brjóst, Sw. bröst, Dan. bryst, D. borst, Goth. brusts, G. brust; allied to E. burst, and primarily signifying a protuberance, a swelling.] The soft protuberant body adhering to the thorax in females, in which the milk is secreted for the nourishment of infants; the fore part of the thorax, or the fore part of the body between the neck and the belly in man or animals; fig. the seat of the affections and emotions; the repository of consciousness, designs, and secrets; anything resembling or likened to the breast.—To make a clean breast, to make full confession. —v.t. To meet in front boldly or openly; to oppose with the breast; to bear the breast against (a current); to stem.—**breastbone,** n. The bone of the breast; the sternum.—**breastplate,** brest′plāt, n. A plate worn on the breast as a part of defensive armor; Jewish antiq. a part of the vestment of the high priest.—**breast stroke,** n. A swimming stroke in which both arms are simultaneously moved forward and then backward.— **breastwork,** n. Fort, a hastily constructed work thrown up breasthigh for defense; the parapet of a building.

breath, breth, n. [A.Sax. braeth, odor, scent, breath, allied to G. bradem, brodem, steam, vapor, breath, brod, vapor, a bubble; same root as E. broth and brew.] The air inhaled and expelled in the respiration of animals, the power of breathing, life; the state or power of breathing freely (to be out of breath from violent exercise), a pause; time to breathe, a single respiration; the time of a single respiration; a very slight breeze; air in gentle motion, an exhalation; an odor, a perfume.— Out of breath, breathless.—**breathable,** brēTH′a·bl, a. Capable of being breathed.—**breathe,** brēTH, v.i.—breathed, breathing. To respire; to inspire and expire air; to live; to make a single respiration; to take breath; to rest from action; to pass or blow gently, as air; to exhale, as odor; to emanate; fig. to be instinct with life; to be alive.—v.t. To inhale and exhale in respiration; to inspire or infuse (breathe life into), to exhale; to send out; to utter; to speak; to whisper (vows, etc.); to suffer to take or recover breath (a horse); to put out of breath; to exhaust.—**breathed**, *a.* Endowed with breath; *philol.* uttered with breath as distinguished from *voice;* surd or mute.—**breather**, brĒTH´ėr, *n.* One who breathes; one who lives (*Shak.*); a sharp spell of exercise.—**breathing**, brĒTH´ing, *n.* Respiration; the act of inhaling and exhaling air; a gentle breeze; *fig.* a gentle influence or operation; inspiration; soft or secret utterance (*Shak.*); time taken to recover breath; a stop; a delay; *gram.* an aspiration; an aspirate.—**breathless**, breth´les, *a.* Being out of breath; spent with labor or violent action; without breath; dead; incapable of breathing, as with wonder or admiration.—**breathlessness**, breth´les·nes *n.* The state of being breathless.

breccia, brech´i·a, *n.* [It., a breach, a breccia.] *Geol.* an aggregate composed of angular fragments of the same rock or of different rocks united by a matrix or cement.

bred, bred, *pp.* of *breed.*

breech, brēch, *n.* [A singular developed from a plural. BREECHES.] The lower part of the body behind; the hinder part of anything: the large thick end of a cannon or other firearm.—*v.t.* To put into breeches; to whip on the breech; to fit or furnish with a breech; to fasten by a breeching.—**breechblock**, *n.* A movable piece at the breech of a breech-loading gun which is withdrawn for the insertion of the charge, and closed before firing.—**breeches**, brēch´ez, *n. pl.* [A double plural, from A.Sax. *brēc*, breeches, pl. of *brōc*, as *feet* is the pl. of *foot*=Fris. *brôck*, pl. *brêk*, breeches; D. *broek*, breeches; Dan. *brog*, breeches, the breeching of a gun; Icel. *brók*, pl. *brœkr*, breeches; Ir. *brog*, Gael. *briogais*, Armor. *brœges*—breeches.] A garment worn by men, covering the hips and thighs; less properly used in the sense of trousers.—*To wear the breeches*, to usurp the authority of the husband: said of a wife.—**breeching**, brēch´ing, *n.* A whipping on the breech; a strong rope to prevent a cannon from recoiling too much when fired; that part of a horse's harness attached to the saddle and hooked on the shafts, which enables him to push back the vehicle to which he is harnessed; a bifurcated smoke pipe of a furnace.—**breechloader**, *n.* A cannon or smaller firearm loaded at the breech instead of the muzzle.—**breech-loading**, *a.* Receiving the charge at the breech instead of the muzzle: applied to firearms.

breed, brēd, *v.t.*—bred, breeding. [A.Sax. *brēdan*, to nourish, cherish, keep warm; allied to D. *broeden*, G. *brüten*, to brood, hatch, and to E. *brew*, W. *brwd*, warm.] To procreate; to beget; to engender; to hatch; to cause; to occasion; to produce; to originate (to *breed* dissension); to produce; to yield or

give birth to; to bring up; to nurse and foster; to train; to rear, as live stock.—*v.i.* To beget or bear a child or children; to be fruitful; to be produced; to take rise (dissensions *breed* among them); to engage in raising live stock.—*n.* A race or progeny from the same parents or stock; kind or sort in a general sense.—**breeder**, brēd´ėr, *n.* One who breeds, procreates, or produces young; one who or that which rears or brings up; one who or that which produces, causes, brings about; one who takes care to raise a particular breed or breeds, as of horses or cattle.—**breeding**, brēd´ing, *n.* The act of generating or producing; the raising of cattle or live stock of different kinds; upbringing; nurture; education; deportment or behavior in social life; manners, especially good manners.—*Cross breeding*, breeding from individuals of two different offsprings or varieties.—*In-and-in breeding*, breeding from animals of the same parentage.

breeze, brēz, *n.* [Fr. *brise*, Sp. *brisa*, a breeze.] A wind, generally a light or not very strong wind; a gentle gale.—**breezy**, brēz´i, *a.* Fanned with gentle winds or breezes; subject to frequent breezes; vivacious; hilarious.

breeze, brēz, *n.* [A.Sax. *briosa*, *breosa*, a gadfly; comp. A.Sax. *brimse*, a gadfly, a horsefly; D. *brems*, G. *bremse*; O.H.G. *bremen*, to hum.] A name given to flies of various species, the most noted of which is the great horsefly, which sucks the blood of horses.

breeze, brēz, *n.* [Fr. *bris*, *débris*, rubbish, fragments, from *briser*, to break.] House sweepings, as fluff, dust, ashes, etc.; small ashes and cinders used for burning bricks.

brent, brant, brent, brant, *n.* [D. and G. *brent-gans*, Icel. *brand-gás*, probably from its color being likened to that caused by burning. BRAND.] A species of goose much smaller than the common goose, which breeds in the far north, but migrates for the winter as low down as the middle of France.

brethren, breTH´ren, *n. pl.* of *brother.*

Breton, bret´on, *a.* Relating to Brittany, or Bretagne in France, or the language of its people.—*n.* The native language of Brittany; Armoric.

breve, brēv, *n.* [From L. *brevis*, short.] *Music*, a note or character of time, ◌, equivalent to two semibreves or four minims; *printing*, a mark (˘) used to indicate that the syllable over which it is placed is short.

brevet, bre·vet´, *n.* [Fr., commission, license. BRIEF.] A commission to an officer which entitles him to a rank in the army above that which he holds in his regiment, without, however, conferring a right to receive corresponding advance in pay; a patent; a warrant; license.—*a.* Taking rank by brevet.—*v.t.* To confer brevet rank upon.

breviary, brē´vi·e·ri, *n.* [Fr. *breviaire*, L. *breviarium*, from *brevis*, short.

BRIEF.] *R. Cath. Ch.* a book containing the daily offices which all who are in orders are bound to read. It consists of prayers or offices to be used at the canonical hours, and is an abridgment (whence the name) of the services of the early church.

brevier, bre·vēr´, *n.* [G. *brevier*, Fr. *breviaire*: so called from being originally used in printing breviaries.] A kind of printing type in size between bourgeois and minion.

brevipennate, brev´i·pen·āt, *a.* [L. *brevis*, short, and *penna*, a feather, a wing.] Having short wings: said of such birds as the ostrich, emu, cassowary, dodo, etc.—*n.* A bird having short wings.

brevirostrate, brev·i·ros´trāt, *a.* [L. *brevis*, short, and *rostrum*, a beak.] Having a short beak or bill.

brevity, brev´i·ti, *n.* [L. *brevitas*, from *brevis*, short. BRIEF.] The state or character of being brief; shortness; conciseness; fewness of words.

brew, brö, *v.t.* [A.Sax. *brēowan*, to brew; D. *brouwen*, Icel. *brugga*, Dan. *brygge*, G. *brauen*, to brew; akin *broth*.] To prepare, as beer, ale, or other similar liquor is prepared, from malt or other materials, by steeping, boiling, and fermentation; to mingle; to mix; to concoct (a bowl of punch, a philter); to contrive; to plot.—*v.i.* To perform the business of brewing or making beer; to be mixing, forming, or collecting (a storm *brews*).—*n.* The mixture formed by brewing; that which is brewed.—**brewage**, brö´ij, *n.* A mixed drink; drink brewed or prepared in any way.—**brewer**, brö´ėr, *n.* One who brews; one whose occupation is to brew malt liquors.—**brewery**, brö´ėr·i, *n.* The establishment and apparatus where brewing is carried on.—**brewing**, brö´ing, *n.* The act or process of making ale, or other fermented liquor; the quantity brewed at a time.

briar, briary, etc. See BRIER, BRIERY.

Briarean, bri·â´ri·an, *a.* Pertaining to or resembling *Briareus*, a giant with a hundred hands.

bribe, brīb, *n.* [Fr. *bribe*, Prov. Fr. *brife*, broken victuals, such as are given to beggars, something given away; from root seen in Armor. *breva*, to break; W. *briw*, a fragment.] A price, reward, gift, or favor bestowed or promised with a view to pervert the judgment or corrupt the conduct.—*v.t.*—bribed, bribing. To induce to a certain course of action, especially a wrong course, by the gift or offer of something valued; to gain over by a bribe.—*v.i.* To practice bribery; to give a bribe to a person.—**bribable**, brī´ba·bl, *a.* Capable of being bribed; liable to be bribed.—**briber**, brī´bėr, *n.* One who bribes or pays for corrupt practices.—**bribery**, brī´bėr·i, *n.* The act or practice of giving or taking a bribe or bribes; the giving or receiving of money by which one's conduct in some public capacity is influenced.

bric-a-brac, brik´a″brak, *n.* [Fr.

Origin doubtful.] Articles of vertu; a collection of objects having a certain interest or value from their rarity, antiquity, or the like.

brick, brik, n. [Fr. *brique,* a brick, also a piece, a fragment, from O.D. *brick,* a piece, a fragment, a brick or tile, from *breken,* to *break.*] A kind of artificial stone made principally of clay moistened and made fine by kneading, formed usually into a rectangular shape in a mold and hardened by being burned in a kiln; bricks collectively or as designating the material of which any structure is composed; a mass or object resembling a brick; a jolly good fellow (colloq. or slang.)—*a.* Made of brick; resembling brick.—*v.t.* To lay or pave with bricks, or to surround, close, or wall in with bricks.—**brickbat,** brik′bat, n. A piece or fragment of a brick.—**brickkiln,** n. A kiln or furnace in which bricks are baked or burned; or a pile of bricks, laid loose, with arches underneath to receive the fuel.—**bricklayer,** brik′lā·ėr, n. One whose occupation is to build with bricks.—**bricklaying,** brik′lā·ing, n. The art of building with bricks.—**brickwork,** brik′wėrk, n. The laying of bricks; masonry consisting of bricks; a place where bricks are made.

bride, brīd, n. [A.Sax. *brýd, bríd;* cog. D. *bruid,* Icel. *brúthr,* Dan. *brud,* Goth. *bruths,* G. *braut*—a bride.] A woman newly married, or on the eve of being married.—**bridal,** brī′dal, n. [Formerly *bride-ale,* from *bride,* and *ale,* in the sense of a feast; comp. *church-ale,* etc.] A nuptial festival; a marriage; a wedding.—*a.* Belonging to a bride or to a wedding.—**bridegroom,** brīd′-grŏm, n. [A.Sax. *brydguma,* from *bryd,* a bride, and *guma,* a man—D. *bruidegom,* Icel. *brúthgumi,* Dan. *brudgom,* G. *bräutigam.* A.Sax. is cognate with L. *homo,* a man.] A man newly married, or just about to be married.—**bridesmaid,** brīdz′-mād, n. A woman or girl who attends on or accompanies a bride at her wedding.

bridewell, brīd′wel, n. A house of correction for the confinement of disorderly persons: so called from the palace of King John, 1210, built near *St. Bride's* or *Bridget's Well,* in London, which was turned into a penal workhouse by Edward VI in 1553.

bridge, brij, n. [O.E. *brig, brigge,* Sc. *brig,* A.Sax. *bricg, brycg,* Icel. *bryggja,* Dan. *brygge,* a pier, D. *brug,* G. *brücke,* a bridge; akin to Icel. *bru,* Dan. *bro,* a bridge.] Any structure of wood, stone, brick, or iron, raised over a river, pond, lake, road, valley, or the like, for the purpose of a convenient passage; in *furnaces,* a low wall or vertical partition for compelling the flame and heated vapor to ascend; the part of a stringed instrument over which the strings are stretched, and by which they are raised above the sounding board; the upper bony part of the

nose; a platform above the deck of a ship for the commanding officer; a device for fastening false teeth to natural teeth; a card game.—**bridge-head,** brij′hed, n. A commanding position in hostile territory.—*v.t.*—*bridged, bridging.* To build a bridge on or over; to make a bridge or bridges for (a road); *fig.* to find a way of overcoming or getting over: generally with *over* (to *bridge over* a difficulty).

bridle, brī′dl, n. [A.Sax. *bridel,* a bridle=D. *bridel,* O.H.G. *bridel.* Probably from A.Sax. *bredan,* to braid.] The portion of gear or harness fitted to the head of a horse (or animal similarly used), and by which he is governed and restrained; a restraint; a curb; a check.—*v.t.*—*bridled, bridling.* To put a bridle on; to restrain, guide, or govern; to check, curb, or control.—*v.i.* To hold the head up and backward; to assume a lofty manner so as to assert one's dignity or express indignation at its being offended; to toss the head: generally with *up.*—**bridle path,** n. A path or road which can be traveled on horseback but not by wheeled carriages.

bridoon, bri·dön′, n. [Fr. *bridon,* from *bride,* a bridle.] A light snaffle or bit of a bridle in addition to the principal bit, and having a distinct rein.

brief, brēf, a. [O.Fr. *brief,* Fr. *bref,* from L. *brevis,* short, seen also in *brevity, breve, abbreviate, abridge.*] Short in duration; lasting a short time; short in expression; using few words; concise; succinct.—*In brief,* in few words; in short.—*n.* An epitome; a short or concise writing (*Shak.*); an abridged relation of the facts of a litigated case drawn up for the instruction of an advocate or barrister in conducting proceedings in a court of justice; a formal letter from the pope on some matter of discipline.—*v.t.* To furnish (a barrister) with a brief.—**briefless,** brēf′les, a. Receiving or having received no briefs (a *briefless* barrister).—**briefly,** brēf′li, adv. In a brief manner; concisely; in few words.—**briefness,** brēf′nes, n. The state or quality of being brief; shortness; conciseness; brevity.

brier, briar, brī′ėr, n. [A.Sax. *braer, brér,* a brier; probably borrowed from the Celtic; comp. Ir. *briar,* a thorn, a pin, a brier; Gael. *preas,* a bush, a brier.] A prickly plant or shrub in general; the sweetbrier and the wild brier, species of the rose; the wild rose.—**briery, briary,** brī′-ėr·i, a. Full of briers; rough; thorny.

brig, brig, n. [An abbrev. of *brigantine.*] A vessel with two masts, square rigged nearly like a ship's mainmast and foremast.

brigade, bri·gād′, n. [Fr. *brigade,* from It. *brigata,* a brigade, from *brigare,* to fight. BRIGAND.] A party or division of troops, consisting of several regiments, squadrons, or battalions; in the U.S. army for-

mation, three regiments ordinarily constitute a *brigade,* and three *brigades* a division; an organized body of individuals, usually wearing a uniform, and acting under an authorized head (a fire *brigade*).—**brigadier,** brig·a·dēr′, **brigadier general,** n. The general officer next in rank below a major general.

brigand, brig′and, n. [Fr. *brigand,* from It. *brigante,* a pirate, a brigand, from *brigare,* to intrigue, to quarrel (whence also *brigade*), from *briga,* an intrigue, a quarrel.] A robber; a freebooter; a highwayman; especially, one of those robbers who live in gangs in secret retreats in mountains or forests.—**brigandage,** brig′an·dij, n. The life and practices of a brigand; highway robbery.

brigandine, brig′an·dēn, n. [Fr. *brig-andine,* from *brigand,* in old sense of foot soldier. BRIGAND.] Body armor composed of iron rings or small thin iron plates sewed upon canvas, linen, or leather, and covered over with similar materials.

brigantine, brig′an·tēn, n. [Fr. *brig-antin,* from It. *brigantino,* a pirate vessel, from *brigante,* a pirate. BRIGAND. *Brig* is an abbrev. of this word.] A kind of light sailing vessel formerly much used by corsairs; a two-masted vessel partly square rigged and resembling a brig.

bright, brīt, a. [A.Sax. *beorht, bryht,* clear, shining=Goth. *bairhts,* O.H.G. *berht,* bright; same root as L. *flagro* (anciently *fragro*), to flame, *flamma* (*flagma*), flame, Skr. *bhraj,* to shine.] Radiating or reflecting light; blazing with light; brilliant; shining; luminous; resplendent; sparkling; illustrious; glorious (name, period); quick in wit; witty; clever; not dull; lively; vivacious; animated; cheerful.—**brighten,** brīt′n. v.t. To make bright or brighter; to shed light on; to make to shine; to cheer; to make gay or cheerful; to heighten the splendor of; to add luster to; to make acute or witty; to sharpen the faculties of.—*v.i.* To grow bright or more bright; to clear up; to become less dark or gloomy.—**brightly,** brīt′li, adv. In a bright manner; splendidly; with luster.—**brightness,** brīt′nes, n. The state or quality of being bright; splendor; luster; acuteness of mental faculties; sharpness of wit.—**Bright's disease** (Dr. Bright). Granular kidney degeneration.

brill, bril, n. [Probably from Corn. *brithel,* a mackerel, pl. *brithelli, brilli,* from *brith,* streaked, variegated.] A kind of flatfish resembling the turbot, but inferior to it both in size and quality.

brilliant, bril′yant, a. [Fr. *brillant,* sparkling, from *briller,* to shine or sparkle, L.L. *beryllare,* to shine like a beryl, from L. *beryllus,* a beryl.] Sparkling or gleaming with luster; glittering; bright; distinguished by such qualities as command admiration; splendid; shining (a *brilliant* achievement, a *brilliant* writer).—*n.* A diamond of the finest cut, formed into faces and facets so as to reflect and refract the light in the most vivid manner possible; *printing*, a very small type, a size less than diamond.—**brilliance, brilliancy,** bril′yans, bril′yan·si, *n*. Great brightness; splendor; luster.—**brilliantly,** bril′yant·li, *adv*. In a brilliant manner; splendidly.—**brilliantness,** bril′yant·nes, *n*.

brim, brim, *n*. [A.Sax. *brim*, the surf, the sea=Icel. *brim*, the surf; akin Dan. *braemme*, G. *bräme*, the edge, border; from root seen in L. *fremere*, to roar, Skr. *bhram*, to whirl, *bhrimi*, a whirlpool, *brim* being thus the part where the surf roars or rages.] The brink, edge, or margin of a river or sheet of water; the upper edge of anything hollow, as a cup; a projecting edge, border, or rim round anything hollow, as a hat.— *v.t.*—**brimmed, brimming.** To fill to the brim, upper edge, or top; to furnish with a brim, as a hat.—*v.i.* To be full to the brim; to be full to overflowing.—*To brim over*, to run over the brim; to be so full as to overflow.—**brimful,** brim′f_ul, *a*. Full to the top; completely full; used predicatively.—**brimmer,** brim′ėr, *n*. A bowl or glass full to the top.

brimstone, brim′stōn, *n*. [O.E. *bremstone, brenston*, etc., Sc. *bruntstane, brunstane*; lit. *burn-stone*, or *burning-stone*, like Icel. *brennisteinn*, brimstone.] Sulfur.

brinded, brin′ded, *a*. [Equivalent to Prov. E. and Sc. *branded*, of a reddish-brown color with darker markings; lit. of a burnt color, the root being in *burn, brand*, etc.] Obs., of a gray or tawny color with bars or streaks of a darker hue; having a hide variegated by streaks or blotches lighter and darker in hue.—**brindled,** brin′dld, *a*. Same as *Brinded*, and now the more commonly used word.

brine, brīn, *n*. [A.Sax. *bryne*, brine, so called from its burning taste= A.Sax. *bryne*, a burning. BURN.] Water saturated or strongly impregnated with salt, like the water of the ocean; salt water; hence used for tears, and for the sea or ocean.— *v.t.*—**brined, brining.** To steep in brine.—**brinish,** brī′nish, *a*. Like brine; somewhat salt; saltish.— **briny,** brī′ni, *a*. Consisting of or resembling brine; of the nature of brine; salt.

bring, bring, *v.t.*—**brought, bringing.** [A.Sax. *bringan, brang, brungen*, later *brengan, brohte, broht*=D. *brengen*, Goth. *briggan* (pron. *bringan*), G. *bringen*; same root as *bear*, to carry.] To bear or convey from a distant to a nearer place, or to a person; to fetch; to carry; to make to come (honor, wisdom, strength, sleep); to procure; to conduct or attend in going; to accompany; to change in state or condition (*bring* to nought, etc.); to persuade (*bring* to reason, to terms).—*To bring about*, to effect; to accomplish.— *To bring down*, to cause to come down; to lower; to humiliate; to abase.—*To bring forth*, to produce, as young or fruit; to beget; to cause.—*To bring forward*,

to produce to view or notice (*bring forward* arguments).—*To bring in*, to introduce; to supply; to furnish (income, rent).—*To bring off*, to bear or convey from a place; to procure to be acquitted; to clear from condemnation.—*To bring on*, to cause to begin (a battle, etc.); to originate (*bring on* a disease).— *To bring over*, to convey over; to convert by persuasion or other means; to cause to change sides or an opinion.—*To bring (a ship) to*, to check the course of (a ship) by making the sails counteract each other and keep her nearly stationary.—*To bring to light*, to reveal.— *To bring to mind*, to recall what has been forgotten or out of the thoughts. —*To bring to pass*, to effect.—*To bring under*, to subdue; to reduce to obedience.—*To bring up*, to nurse, feed, and tend; to rear; to educate; to introduce to notice (to *bring up* a subject); to cause to advance near (troops); to cause to stop (a horse); to pull up.—*To bring up the rear*, to move onward in the rear; to form the rear portion.— **bringer,** bring′ėr, *n*. One who brings or conveys.

brink, bringk, *n*. [A Scandinavian word; Dan. and Sw. *brink*, a hill, declivity; allied to W. *bryncyn*, a hillock, from *bryn*, a hill.] The edge, margin, or border of a steep place, as of a precipice or the bank of a river; verge; hence, close proximity to danger.

briquette, bri·ket′, *n*. [Dim. of Fr. *brique*, a brick.] A lump of fuel, in the form of a brick, made from coal dust, with some binding material such as coal tar.

brisk, brisk, *a*. [From the Celtic: W. *brysg*, Ir. *brisg*, quick, lively.] Lively; active; nimble; gay; sprightly; vivacious; effervescing vigorously; sparkling (liquor); burning freely; rapid; quick (movement, pace).—*v.t.* To make brisk.—*v.i.* To become brisk, lively, or alert: often with *up*.—**briskly,** brisk′li, *adv*. In a brisk manner; actively; vigorously; with life and spirit.— **briskness,** brisk′nes, *n*. The state or quality of being brisk.

brisket, bris′ket, *n*. [O.Fr. *brischet* or *bruschet* (Fr. *bréchet*), from Armor. *brusk*, the breast.] The breast of an animal, or that part of the breast that lies next to the ribs; in a horse, the fore part of the neck at the shoulder down to the forelegs.

bristle, bris′l, *n*. [A diminutive from A. Sax. *byrst*, a bristle=D. *borstel*, a bristle; akin Icel. *burst*, Dan. *börste*, G. *borste*, a bristle.] One of the stiff, coarse, glossy hairs of the hog and the wild boar, especially one of the hairs growing on the back; a stiff roundish hair or similar appendage.—*v.t.*—**bristled, bristling.** To erect in bristles; to make bristly; to erect in defiance or anger, like a swine; to furnish with bristles or stiff hairs.—*v.i.* To rise up or stand on end like bristles; to appear as if covered with bristles; to show anger, resentment, or

defiance: generally followed by *up*.— **bristly,** bris′li, *a*. Thick set with bristles, or with hairs like bristles; rough; resembling a bristle or bristles.

Bristol board, *n*. [From the city of *Bristol*, in England.] A fine kind of pasteboard, smooth, and sometimes glazed on the surface.

britannia metal, *n*. A metallic compound or alloy of tin, with a little copper and antimony, used chiefly for teapots, spoons, etc.

Britannic, bri·tan′ik, *a*. Pertaining to Britain.—**British,** brit′ish, *a*. Pertaining to Great Britain or its inhabitants: sometimes applied distinctively to the original Celtic inhabitants.—**Britisher,** brit′ish·ėr, *n*. A patriot or typical British subject.—**Briton,** brit′on, *n*. A native of Britain or the British islands.

British Thermal Unit. The amount of heat needed to raise one pound of water one degree Fahrenheit. Abbrev. B.T.U.

brittle, brit′l, *a*. [O.E. *britel*, from A.Sax. *brytan, breótan*, to break= Icel. *brjóta*, Dan. *bryde*, to break.] Easily broken, or easily breaking short, without splinters or loose parts rent from the substance; fragile; not tough or tenacious.— **brittleness,** brit′l·nes, *n*. Aptness to break; fragility.

britzska, brits′ka, *n*. [A Polish word.] An open carriage with a calash top, and space for reclining when used for a journey.

broach, brōch, *n*. [Fr. *broche*, from L.L. *brocca*, a spit, a point; allied to Gael. *brog*, to goad, *brog*, an awl.] A spit‡; a spire, especially a spire springing directly from a tower; a general name for all tapered boring bits or drills.—*v.t.* To pierce with or as with a spit‡; to open for the first time for the purpose of taking out something; more especially to tap: to pierce, as a cask in order to draw the liquor; to begin conversation or discussion about; to open up (a topic or subject).—*To broach to* (*naut.*), to incline suddenly to windward, so as to lay the sails aback and expose the vessel to the danger of oversetting; to overset, by death.—**broacher,** brōch′ėr, *n*. One who broaches, opens, or utters.

broad, brad, *n*. [A.Sax. *brád*=D. *breed*, Icel. *breithr*, Dan. and Sw. *bred*, Goth. *braids*, G. *breit*, broad; root unknown.] Having extent from side to side, as distinguished from *long*, or extended from end to end; having breadth; having a great extent from side to side, as opposed to *narrow*; wide; extensive; vast; *fig*. not limited or narrow; liberal; comprehensive; enlarged; widely diffused; open; full (*broad* daylight); plain or unmistakable; free; unrestrained (*broad* humor); somewhat gross, coarse, or unpolished; indelicate; indecent; bold; unreserved; characterized by vigor, boldness, or freedom of style, as in art, so that strong and striking effects or impressions are produced by simple unelaborate means.—*Broad Church*, a section of the Church of England contrasted with the High Church and the Low Church; a section of any church holding moderate or not very rigid views.—**broaden,** brăd′n, *v.t.* To make broad or broader; to increase the width of; to render more comprehensive, extensive, or open.—*v.i.* To become broad or broader.—**broadly,** brăd′li, *adv.* In a broad manner; widely; comprehensively; fully; openly; plainly. —**broad arrow** *n.* A stamp resembling the barbed head of an arrow put upon stores, etc., belonging to the British government.—**broadbrim,** *n.* A hat with a very broad brim, such as is worn by members of the Society of Friends; *cap.* hence, a member of said society; a Quaker. (Colloq.)— **broadcast,** brăd′kast, *n. Agri.* a casting or throwing seed from the hand for dispersion in sowing; act of disseminating; transmission by radio or television.—*v.t.* To scatter widely; to send out by radio or television.—*a.* Widely scattered; made public by radio or television. —**broadcaster,** *n.*—**broadcloth,** *n.* A kind of fine woolen cloth woven about twice the usual breadth, and dyed in the piece.—**broadside,** brăd′sīd, *n.* The side of a ship above the water from the bow to the quarter; a simultaneous discharge of all the guns on one side of a ship; a sheet of paper, one side of which is covered by printed matter, often of a popular character.—**broadsword,** brăd′sōrd, *n.* A sword with a broad blade and cutting edges.

Brobdingnagian, brob·ding·nag′i-an, *a.* Gigantic, like an inhabitant of the fabled region of Brobdingnag in Swift's *Gulliver's Travels.*

brocade, brō·kād′, *n.* [Sp. *brocado*, from an old *brocar*, equivalent to Fr. *brocher*, to pick, emboss. BROACH.] Silk stuff variegated with gold and silver, or having raised flowers, foliage, and other ornaments; also applied to other stuffs wrought and enriched in like manner.—**brocaded,** brō·kād′ed, *a.* Woven or worked into a brocade; dressed in brocade.

brocatel, brok·a·tel′, *n.* [Sp. *brocatel*, Fr. *brocatelle*, It. *brocatello*, from root of *brocade*.] Sienna marble, a species of brecciated marble composed of fragments of various colors; a kind of light thin woolen cloth of silky surface used for linings, etc.; linsey-woolsey. Spelled also *Brocatelle.*

broccoli, brok′o·li, *n.* [It. *broccoli*, pl. of *broccolo*, sprout, cabbage sprout, dim. of *brocco*, a skewer, a shoot. BROACH.] One of the many varieties of the common cabbage, closely resembling the cauliflower.

brochure, brō·shōr′, *n.* [Fr., from *brocher*, to stitch.] A pamphlet, especially a slight pamphlet, or one on a matter of transitory interest.

brock, brok, *n.* [A.Sax. *broc*=Dan. *brok*, Ir. and Gael. *broc*, W. *broch*, a badger, from the white-streaked face of the animal; comp. Gael. *brocach*, speckled; Dan. *broget*, Sw. *brokug*, parti-colored.] A badger.

brocket, brok′et, *n.* [Fr. *brocart*, because it has one *broche* or snag to its antler.] A red deer two years old; a pricket.

brogue, brōg, *n.* [Ir. and Gael. *brog*, a shoe of rough hide. From this shoe being used by the Irish the word came to designate their manner of speaking English.] A kind of shoe made of raw or half-tanned leather, of one entire piece; a stout, coarse shoe; a dialectical manner of pronunciation; especially the pronunciation peculiar to the Irish.

broil, broil, *n.* [Fr. *brouiller*, to jumble or mix up, to throw into bustle or confusion; origin doubtful.] A tumult; a noisy quarrel; contention; discord; a brawl.—**broiler,** broil′ér, *n.* One who excites broils or quarrels, or who readily takes part in tumults or contentions.

broil, broil, *v.t.*[O.Fr. *bruiller;* origin doubtful.] To dress or cook over a fire, generally upon a gridiron; to subject to a strong heat.—*v.i.* To be subjected to the action of heat, like meat over the fire; to be greatly heated or to sweat with heat.— **broiler,** broil′ér, *n.* One who or that which dresses by broiling; a gridiron.

broke, brōk. Pret. and obsolescent or poetical pp. of *break.*—**broken,** brō′-kn, pp. of *break*, often used as an *a.* Parted by violence; separated into fragments, as by a blow; not integral or entire; fractional, as numbers; humble; contrite; violated; transgressed (a *broken* vow); interrupted by sobs or imperfect utterance.— **brokenly,** brō′kn·li, *adv.* In a broken interrupted manner.—**brokenness,** brō′kn·nes, *n.* The state of being broken.—**brokenhearted,** *a.* Having the spirits quite crushed by grief or despair.—**broken wind,** *n.* A disease in horses, characterized by a difficult expiration of the air from the lungs, and often accompanied with an enlargement of the lungs and heart. —**broken-winded,** *a.* Affected with broken wind.

broker, brō′kér, *n.* [O.Fr. *brokeor*, *brokiere*, from a verb meaning to tap or *broach;* originally a retailer of liquor.] An agent who buys and sells goods or shares or transacts other business for others, being generally paid at a rate per cent on the value of the transaction, such as exchange brokers, ship brokers, stockbrokers, etc.; one who deals in second-hand household goods, clothes, and the like.—**brokerage,** brō′kér·ij, *n.* The fee, reward, or commission given or charged for transacting business as a broker; the business or employment of a broker.

brom, brŏm, *n.* [Gr. *bromos*, oats.] A name of several oatlike species of grass.

bromine, brō′mīn or brō′min, *n.* [Gr. *brōmos*, a fetid odor.] An element occurring as a dark-red fuming liquid, the vapor being irritating and evil smelling. Symbol, Br; at. no., 35; at. wt., 79.904.—**bromal,** brō′-mal, *n.* A colorless oily fluid of a penetrating odor, obtained by the action of bromine on alcohol.—

bromate, brō′māt, *n.* A salt formed of bromic acid.—**bromic,** brō′mik, *a.* Pertaining to or obtained from bromine, as *bromic* acid, a compound of oxygen and bromine.—**bromide,** brō′mīd, *n.* A compound formed by the union of bromine with another element.

bronchia, brong′ki·a, *n. pl.* [Gr. and L.] The two tubes, with their ramifications, arising from the bifurcation of the windpipe in the lungs, and conveying air to the latter; the bronchi.—**bronchial,** brong′ki·al, *a.* Belonging to the bronchia.—*Bronchial tubes*, the ramifications of the bronchia, terminating in the bronchial cells, or air cells of the lungs.— **bronchic,** brong′kik, *a.* Same as *Bronchial.*—**bronchitis,** brong·kī′tis, *n.* [The term. -*itis* signifies inflammation.] An inflammation of the lining membrane of the bronchi or bronchia, often a troublesome ailment.—**bronchotomy,** brong·kot′o-mi, *n.* [Gr. *tome*, a cutting.] *Surg.* an incision into the windpipe or larynx between the rings, to afford a passage for the air into and out of the lungs when respiration in the usual way is prevented.—**bronchus,** brong′kus, *n. pl.* **bronchi,** brong′kī. [Gr. *bronchos*, the windpipe.] One of the two bronchia or bifurcations of the trachea.

brontosaurus, bron·to·sạ′rus, *n.* [Gr. *bronte*, thunder, *sauros*, a lizard.] A fossil reptile with a remarkably small skull.

bronze, bronz, *n.* [Fr. *bronze*, from It. *bronzo*, bronze, L. *Aes Brundusianum*, the brass of Brundusium.] A compound or alloy of from 2 to 20 parts of copper to 1 of tin, to which other metallic substances are sometimes added, especially zinc, used for statues, bells, cannon, coins, etc.; any statue, bust, urn, medal, or other work of art, cast of bronze; a brown color resembling bronze; a pigment prepared for the purpose of imitating bronze.—*v.t.* *bronzed, bronzing.* To give the appearance or color of bronze to, by covering with bronze leaf, copper dust, etc.; to make brown or tan, as the skin by exposure to the sun.— **bronzy,** bron′zi, *a.* Belonging to or resembling bronze.

brooch, brōch, *n.* [A form of *broach* (which see).] An ornamental pin or clasp used for fastening the dress or merely for display.

brood, brŏd, *n.* [A.Sax. *brod*, a brood=D. *broed*, G. *brut*, a brood; from root of *breed.*] Offspring; progeny; the young birds hatched at once; that which is bred or produced.—*v.i.* To sit upon eggs or upon young, as a hen for the purpose of hatching, warming, or protecting them; hence, to remain steadfastly settled over something; to have the mind dwelling for a long time uninterruptedly on a subject; with *on* or *over.*—*v.t.* To sit over, cover, and cherish; to nourish; to foster.

brook, bruk, *n.* [A.Sax. *brōc*, a spring, a brook, from *brecan*, to burst forth; comp. D. *brock*, G. *bruch*, a marsh.

A brook is a breaking forth of water; comp. *spring*.] A small natural stream of water, or a current flowing from a spring or fountain less than a river.— **brooklet**, bruk′let, *n*. A small brook. **brook**, bruk, *v.t*. [A.Sax. *brúcan*, to use, enjoy = D. *gebruiken*, Icel. *bruka*, Goth. *brukjan*, to use; allied to L. *frui*, to enjoy (whence *fruition*).] To bear; to endure; to support; usually in negative or interrogative sentences (they cannot *brook* restraint). **broom**, bröm, *n*. [A.Sax. *bróm* = L.G. *brâm*, D. *brem*, broom; allied to *bramble*. BRAMBLE, BRIM.] A leguminous shrub growing abundantly on sandy pastures and heaths, distinguished by having large, yellow, papilionaceous flowers, leaves in threes, and single, and the branches angular; a besom or brush with a long handle for sweeping floors; so called from being originally made of the broom plant.—**broomcorn**, *n*. The common millet or Guinea corn, a cereal plant so called from its branched panicles being made into carpet brooms.—**broomrape**, *n*. A parasitic plant growing on the roots of broom, furze, etc.—**broomstick**, bröm′stik, *n*. The stick or handle of a broom. **broth**, broth, *n*. [A.Sax. *broth*, from root of *brew*.] Liquor in which flesh is boiled and macerated, usually with certain vegetables to give it a better relish. **brothel**, broth′el, *n*. [O.E. *brothel*, a wretch, from *brothen*, ruined, destroyed, from *breóthan*, to destroy.] A house appropriated to the purposes of prostitution; a bawdyhouse. **brother**, bruTH′er, *n*. pl. **brothers**, bruTH′erz, or **brethren**, breTH′ren. [A.Sax. *bróthor* = D. *broeder*, Icel. *bróthir*, Dan. and Sw. *broder*, Goth. *brothar*, G. *bruder*, Ir. and Gael. *brathair*, W. *brawd*, Rus. *brat'*, Bohem. *brátr*, L. *frater*, Gr. *phrater*, Skr. *bhratr*, brother; the root meaning of the word is unknown.] Strictly a human male born of the same father and mother (also used of animals); a male born of the same father or mother (more strictly called a *half*-brother); a relation or kinsman; an associate; one of the same rank, profession, or occupation; or more generally, a fellow creature; specifically, a member of a religious order; one that resembles another in manners or disposition. [The plural *brethren* is now used only in the wider meanings of the word.]—**brotherhood**, bruTH′er·hud, *n*. The state of being a brother or brotherly; an association of men for any purpose; a class of individuals of the same kind, profession, or occupation; a fraternity.—**brotherly**, bruTH′er·li, *a*. Pertaining to brothers; such as is natural for brothers; becoming brothers (*brotherly* love).—**brotherliness**, bruTH′er·li·nes, *n*. State of being brotherly.—**brother-in-law**, *n*. The brother of one's husband or wife; also, a sister's husband. **brougham**, brö′am or bröm, *n*. [After the first Lord *Brougham*.] A one-horse closed carriage, either two or

four wheeled, and adapted to carry either two or four persons. **brought**, brat, pret. & pp. of *bring*. **brow**, brou, *n*. [A.Sax. *brú*, the eyebrow = D. *braauw*, Icel. *brun*, G. *braue*, the eyebrow; cog. with Gr. *ophrys*, Per. *abru*, Skr. *bhrú*, the eyebrow.] The prominent ridge over the eye, forming an arch above the orbit; the arch of hair over the eye; the eyebrow; the forehead; the edge of a steep place; the upper portion of a slope.—**browbeat**, brou′bēt, *v.t*. To abash or bear down with haughty, stern looks, or with arrogant speech and dogmatic assertions. **brown**, broun, *a*. [A.Sax. *brun* = Icel. *brúnn*, Dan. *bruun*, Sw. *brun*, D. *bruin*, G. *braun*, brown; lit. of a *burnt* color, from root of *burn*, *bronze*, etc.] Of a dark or dusky color, inclining to redness.—*n*. A dark color inclining to red or yellow of various degrees of depth, and resulting from a mixture of red, black, and yellow.— *Brown bread*, wheaten bread made from unbolted flour, which thus includes the bran, and hence is of a brown color.—*Brown coal*, lignite. —*Brown study*, a fit of mental abstraction or meditation; a reverie.— *v.t*. To make brown or dusky; to give a brown color to.—*v.i*. To become brown.—**brownie**, *n*. Household servant of a fairy or goblin nature, in Scottish mythology. Milton's 'drudging-goblin', 'lubberfiend'.—**brownish**, broun′ish, *a*. Somewhat brown; inclined to brown. **browse**, brouz, *v.t*.—browsed, browsing. [O.Fr. *brouster* (Fr. *brouter*), to browse, from *brost*, *broust*, a sprout, a shoot, from O.H.G. *broz*, G. *bross*, sprout.] To feed on: said of cattle, deer, etc.; to pasture on; to graze.— *v.i*. To feed on pasture or on the leaves, shoots, etc., of shrubs and trees: said of cattle, deer, etc.—*n*. The tender shoots or twigs of trees and shrubs, such as cattle may eat; green food fit for cattle, deer, etc. **brucine**, brö′sin, *n*. [From name *Bruce*.] A vegetable alkaloid akin to strychnine, bitter and acid, but less powerful in its action. **bruin**, brö′in, *n*. [The bear's name in the celebrated fable Reynard the Fox; from the D. *bruin*, brown.] A name given to the bear. **bruise**, bröz, *v.t*.—bruised, bruising. [O.Fr. *bruiser*, *bruser*, *briser*, to break, to shiver, from O.G. *brestan*, to break, to burst.] To injure by a blow without laceration; to contuse; to crush by beating or pounding; to pound; to bray, as drugs or articles of food; to make a dent or dint in.— *v.i*. To fight with the fists; to box (colloq.).—*n*. A contusion; a hurt upon the flesh of animals, upon plants or other bodies, with a blunt or heavy object.—**bruiser**, bröz′er, *n*. The person or thing that bruises; an instrument or machine for bruising substances; a pugilist, boxer, or prize fighter (colloq.). **bruit**, bröt, *v.t*. [Fr. *bruit*, noise, uproar, rumor, from *bruire*, to make a noise.]—*v.t*. To announce with noise; to report; to noise abroad.

brumal, brumous, brö′mal, brö′mus, *a*. [L. *brumalis*, from *bruma*, winter.] Belonging to the winter. **brunet**, brö·net′, *n*. [Fr., a dim. from *brun*, brown. BROWN.] A woman with a brown or dark complexion. **brunt**, brunt, *n*. [From the root or stem of to *burn*; comp. Sc. *brunt*, burnt; Icel. *bruni*, a burning; Dan. *brynde* and *brunst*, ardor, ardency, burning heat. BURN.] The heat or utmost violence of an onset; the first or severest shock of a battle or struggle; the force of a blow; violence; shock of any kind. **brush**, brush, *n*. [O.Fr. *broche*, *brosse*, brushwood; Mod.Fr. *brosse*, a brush; from O.H.G. *broz*, a sprout. BROWSE.] An instrument made of bristles or other similar material bound together, used for various purposes, as for dressing the hair, removing dust from clothes, laying on colors, whitewash, and the like; the small trees and shrubs of a wood, or a thicket of small trees; electricity issuing in a diverging manner from a point; the bushy tail of some animals, as the fox, squirrel, etc.; the act of using a brush, or of applying a brush to; a slight encounter; a skirmish.—*v.t*. To sweep or rub with a brush; to strike lightly by passing over the surface; to pass lightly over; to remove by brushing or by lightly passing over.—*To brush up*, to furbish; to polish; to improve; especially, to improve the appearance of.—*v.i*. To move nimbly in haste; to move so lightly as scarcely to be perceived; to move over lightly.—**brushy**, brush′i, *a*. Resembling a brush; rough; shaggy; having long hair.— **brushwood**, *n*. Small trees or shrubs forming a thicket or coppice; branches of trees cut off. **brusque, brusk**, brusk, *a*. [Fr. *brusque*, from It. *brusco*, brusque, sharp, sour.] Abrupt in manner; blunt; rude.—**brusqueness**, brusk′nes, *n*. A rude, abrupt, or blunt manner. **Brussels carpet**, *n*. A carpet having a heavy linen web enclosing worsted yarns of different colors, which are raised in loops to form the patterns. —**Brussels sprouts**, *n*. pl. A variety of cabbage, characterized by little clusters of leaves which form miniature heads of cabbage. **brute**, bröt, *n*. [L. *brutus*, stupid, insensible, irrational.] A beast; any animal destitute of reason; a brutal person; a savage in disposition or manners; a low-bred, unfeeling human being.—*a*. Insensible, irrational, or unintelligent; not proceeding from or inspired by reason and intelligence (*brute* force, the *brute* earth).—**brutal**, brö′tal, *a*. Pertaining to a brute; like a brute; savage; cruel; inhuman; brutish.—**brutality**, brö·tal′i·ti, *n*. The quality of being brutal; inhumanity; savageness; gross cruelty; insensibility to pity or shame; a savage, shameless, and inhuman act.— **brutalize**, brö′tal·īz, *v.t*.—brutalized, brutalizing. To make brutal, coarse, gross, or inhuman; to degrade to the level of a brute.—**brutally**, brö′tal·li, *adv.* In a brutal manner; cruelly; inhumanly; in a coarse, gross, or unfeeling manner.—**brutify,** brö´ti-fī, *v.t.*—**brutified,** *brutifying.* To make a person a brute; to make senseless, stupid, or unfeeling.—**brutish,** brö´tish, *a.* Pertaining to or resembling a brute; uncultured; ignorant; stupid; unfeeling; savage; brutal; gross; carnal; bestial.—**brutishly,** brö´tish-li, *adv.* In a brutish manner.—**brutishness,** brö´tish-nes, *n.* The quality of being brutish.

bryology, brī-ol´o-ji, *n.* [Gr. *bryon,* moss, and *logos,* discourse.] The science of mosses, their structure, affinities, classification, etc.—**bryological,** brī-o-loj´ik-al, *a.* Pertaining to bryology, or to the mosses.

bryony, brī´o-ni, *n.* [L. *bryonia,* Gr. *bryōnia,* bryony, from *bryō,* to swell, to sprout, from the quick growth of the stems.] A climbing plant of various species; *white bryony,* found in the hedgerows of England, has small red berries and abounds in an acrid fetid juice, which acts as a cathartic and emetic; *black bryony* is a plant of the yam family, and has a tuberous rootstalk, also with cathartic and emetic properties.

Bryozoa, brī-o-zō´a, *n. pl.* [Gr. *bryon,* moss, and *zōon,* animal.] A group of minute molluscoid animals living together in mosslike masses; now commonly called *Polyzoa* (which see).—**bryozoan,** brī-o-zō´an, *n.* One of the Bryozoa.

bubble, bub´l, *n.* [Dan. *boble,* Sw. *bubbla,* D. *bobbel,* a bubble; akin to *blob.*] A small vesicle of water or other fluid inflated with air; a blob of air in a fluid; *fig.* something that wants firmness or solidity; a vain project; a false show; a delusive or fraudulent scheme of speculation; a fraud.—*v.i.* *bubbled, bubbling.* To rise in bubbles, as liquids when boiling or agitated; to run with a gurgling noise; to gurgle.—*v.t.* To cause to bubble; to cheat; to deceive; to trick.—**bubbly,** bub´li, *a.* Full of bubbles.

bubo, bū´bō, *n.* [Gr. *boubōn,* the groin, a swelling in the groin.] A tumor or abscess, with inflammation, which rises in certain glandular parts of the body, as in the groin or armpit.

buccal, buk´al, *a.* [L. *bucca,* the cheek.] Pertaining to the cheek.—*Buccal glands,* the small glands of the mouth which secrete a viscous fluid that mixes with the saliva.

buccaneer, buk-a-nēr´, *n.* [Fr. *boucanier,* a pirate, originally a hunter who smoked the flesh of the animals killed, from *boucaner,* to smoke meat, from *boucan,* a place for smoking meat, a Carib word.] A pirate; a sea robber; more especially, one of the piratical adventurers, English and French, who combined to make depredations on the Spaniards in America in the 17th and 18th centuries.—*v.i.* To act the part of a pirate or sea robber.

bucentaur, bū-sen´tar, *n.* [Gr. *bous,* an ox, and *kentauros,* a centaur.] A mythological monster, half man and half ox; the state barge of Venice, in which the doge and senate went to wed the Adriatic.

Bucephalus, bū-sef´a-lus, *n.* A war horse, the steed of Alexander the Great.

buck, buk, *n.* [Ir. and Gael. *buac,* cow dung used in bleaching, bleaching liquid, lye; from W. *bu, buw,* Gael. *bo,* a cow.] Lye or suds in which clothes are soaked in the operation of bleaching.—*v.t.* To soak or wash in lye, a process in bleaching; to break up and pulverize, as ores.

buck, buk, *n.* [A.Sax. *bucca,* a he-goat, a buck=D. *bok,* Icel. *bokkr,* a he-goat; Dan. *buk,* a buck, a he-goat, a ram; G. *bock,* a he-goat, a buck; W. *bwch,* a buck, Ir. *boc,* a he-goat.] The male of the fallow deer, of the goat, the rabbit and hare; often used specifically of the male of the fallow deer; a roebuck; a dashing fellow; a fop, swell, or dandy.—**buckish,** buk´ish, *a.* Pertaining to a buck or dashing fellow; foppish.—**buckeye,** *n.* A name for several species of American horse chestnut.—**buckhound,** *n.* A kind of hound, less than the staghound, for hunting bucks or fallow deer.—**buckskin,** buk´skin, *n.* A kind of soft, yellowish or grayish leather originally made of the skin of the deer, but now of that of the sheep; *pl.* breeches made of this leather.—**buckshot,** *n.* A large kind of shot used for killing deer or other large game.—**buckthorn,** *n.* A somewhat spiny shrub of various species; as the purging buckthorn, a native of Britain, having small shining black berries with powerful cathartic properties; another species yields the Persian or yellow berries of commerce.—**bucktooth,** *n.* A projecting tooth in a person's jaw; a prominent canine tooth.

bucket, buk´et, *n.* [A.Sax. *buc,* a bucket, a flagon, a pitcher, with dim. term. added. Probably allied to *back,* a vessel.] A vessel made of wood, leather, metal, or other material, for drawing or holding water or other liquids; one of the cavities on the circumference of a water wheel, into which the water is delivered to move the wheel; the scoop of a dredging machine or of a grain elevator.—**bucketful,** buk´et-ful, *n.* As much as a bucket will hold.

buckle, buk´l, *n.* [Fr. *boucle,* buckle, from L.L. *buccula,* the central part of the buckler, the boss, dim. of L. *bucca,* a cheek.] An instrument, usually made of some kind of metal, and consisting of a rim with a chape and tongue, used for fastening harness, belts, or parts of dress together; a curl of hair; a state of being curled or crisped (as a wig).—*v.t.* *buckled, buckling.* To fasten with a buckle or buckles; *refl.* to set vigorously to work at anything; to join together, as in marriage (colloq.).—*v.i.* To bend or bow (*Shak.*)‡; to apply with vigor; to engage with zeal: followed by *to.*

buckler, buk´lėr, *n.* [O.Fr. *bocler,* Fr. *bouclier,* a protuberance, a boss on the shield. BUCKLE.] A kind of shield, a piece of defensive armor anciently used in war, and worn on the left arm.—*v.t.*† To be a buckler or shield to; to shield; to defend.

buckra, buk´ra, *n.* [W. African word meaning supernatural being or demon.] A Negro term for a white man.

buckram, buk´ram, *n.* [O.E. *bokeram,* from O.Fr. *boucaran, boqueran,* M. H.G. *buckeram, buckeran,* L.L. *boquerannus,* etc.; perhaps stuff made originally of goat's hair (G. *bock,* a goat) BUCK.] A coarse linen cloth, stiffened with glue, used in garments to keep them in the form intended, and for wrappers to some kinds of merchandise; imaginary or phantom foemen, *men in buckram* (Shak. 1 Henry IV).—*a.* Made of buckram or resembling buckram; hence, stiff, precise, formal.

buckshot, buk´shot, *n.* A coarse leaden pellet used as a projectile for killing large game.

buckwheat, buk´hwēt, *n.* [From Prov. E. *buck,* beech and *wheat,* D. *boekweit,* G. *buchweizen* (D. *boek,* G. *buche* a beech); from the resemblance of its triangular seeds to beech-nuts.] A plant with a branched and jointed herbaceous stem, somewhat arrow-shaped leaves, purplish-white flowers, and bearing small triangular seeds, which are ground into flour.

bucolic, bū-kol´ik, *a.* [L. *bucolicus,* from Gr. *boukolikos,* pertaining to cattle, pastoral, from *bous,* an ox.] Pastoral, relating to country affairs and to a herdsman's life and occupation.—*n.* A pastoral poem.

bud, bud, *n.* [Allied to D. *bot,* a bud; O.Fr. *boter,* to bud; Fr. *bouton,* a bud; E. *button.*] A small, generally more or less ovoid, protuberance on the stem or branches of a plant, being the form in which leaves or flowers exist before expanding; a prominence on or in certain animals of low organization, as polyps, which becomes developed into an independent being, which may or may not remain permanently attached to the parent organism.—*v.i.* *budded, budding.* To put forth or produce buds; to sprout; to begin to grow from a stock like a bud, as a horn, *fig.* to be in an early stage of development.—*v.t.* To graft by inserting a bud under the bark of another tree.

Buddhism, böd´izm, *n.* [*Buddha,* from Skr. *buddh; pp.* from Skr. *budh,* to awake, the Enlightened, known otherwise as Sakyamuni, Gautama: the sacred name of the founder of the system, who appears to have lived in the 6th cent. B.C.] The religious system founded by Buddha, one of the most prominent doctrines of which is that *nirvâna,* or an absolute release from existence, is the chief good; it prevails in China, Japan, Kashmir, Tibet, Burma, Ceylon, etc., its adherents comprising about a third of the human race.—**Buddhist,** böd´ist, *n.* A worshiper of Buddha; one who adheres to the system of Buddhism. —**Buddhistic,** böd-ist´ik, *a.* Relating to Buddha or to Buddhism.

buddle, bud´l, *n.* [Comp. G. *butteln,* to shake.] *Mining,* a large square frame of boards used in washing metalliferous ore.—*v.t.* or *i.* To wash ore in a buddle.

budge, buj, *v.i.* [Fr. *bouger*, to stir, to move = Pr. *bolegar*, to be agitated, It. *bolicare*, to bubble, from L. *bullire*, to boil. BOIL.] To move off; to stir; to remove from a spot a little; to flinch; to take one's self off.

budge, buj, *n.* [O.Fr. *bouge*, L. *bulga*, a leather bag, from a Gallic word seen in Ir. and Gael. *balg*, *bolg*, a bag; akin *bellows*, *belly*.] Lambskin with the wool dressed outward, formerly used as an ornamental border for scholastic habits.—*a.‡* Trimmed or adorned with budge; scholastic; pedantic; austere; stiff; formal. (*Mil.*)

budget, buj′et, *n.* [O.E. *boget*, *bouget*, from Fr. *bougette*, dim. of *bouge*, a leather bag. BUDGE, *n.*] A little sack, with its contents; hence, a stock or store; a financial statement of estimated income and expenditures of a country for a fiscal year; a plan of financing a government, based on such a statement; in general, the *weekly budget* of a family, estimating costs of living.

buff, buf, *n.* [Abbrev. of *buffalo*, O.E. *buffle*, Fr. *buffle*, a buffalo.] A sort of leather prepared from the skin of the buffalo, ox, etc., dressed with oil, like shammy, the color of buff; a light yellow.—*a.* Made of buff; of the color of buff.—**buffing wheel,** *n.* A wheel covered with cloth or leather, used in polishing metal.

buffalo, buf′fa·lō, *n.* [From Sp. *bufalo*, Fr. *buffle*, L. *bubalus*, *bufalus*, from Gr. *boubalos* from *bous*, an ox.] A ruminant mammal of the ox family somewhat larger than the common ox and with stouter limbs; in North America, it is called the *bison*, while in India it is named *water buffalo*, in Africa, the *cape buffalo*.—*v.t.* To bewilder; to bamboozle; to get one *buffaloed*. [*American Slang.*]—**buffalo grass,** *n.* A species of short grass growing on the prairies of North America.

buffer, buf′ėr, *n.* [O.E. *buff*, to strike; *buffet*, a blow.] Any apparatus for deadening the concussion between a moving body and the one on which it strikes; an apparatus with powerful springs attached to railroad carriages to prevent injury from violent contact.—**buffer state,** *n.* [Name invented by Archibald Forbes to express the position of Afghanistan in relation to India.] A state between two rival nations.

buffer, buf′ėr, *n.* [From O.E. *buffe*, to stammer, Fr. *bufer*, to puff out the cheeks; comp. Sc. *buff*, nonsense.] A foolish fellow; a fellow: a term expressive of extreme familiarity, and generally having a flavor of contempt.

buffet, bu̇·fā′, *n.* [Fr. *buffet*, a sideboard, a cupboard.] A cupboard, sideboard, or closet, to hold china, crystal, plate, and other like articles; the space set apart for refreshments in public places.

buffet, buf′et, *n.* [O.Fr. *buffet*, *bufet*, a slap, a blow, dim. from *buffe*, *bufe*, a blow.] A blow with the fist; a box; a cuff; a slap; hence, hard usage of

any kind suggestive of blows (Fortune's *buffets*).—*v.t.* To strike with the hand or fist; to box; to beat; to beat in contention; to contend against (*buffet* the billows).—*v.i.* To deal blows or buffets; to make one's way by buffeting.

buffoon, buf·fön′, *n.* [Fr. *bouffon*, from It. *buffone*, from *buffare*, to jest or sport, from *buffa*, a trick, a piece of sport.] A man who makes a practice of amusing others by low tricks, odd gestures and postures, jokes, etc.; a merry-andrew; a clown; a jester.—*v.t.* To make ridiculous.—*v.i.* To play the buffoon.—*a.* Characteristic of a buffoon.—**buffoonery,** buf·fön′ėr·i, *n.* The arts and practices of a buffoon; low jests; ridiculous pranks.—**buffoonish,** buf·fön′ish, *a.* Like a buffoon; consisting in low jests or gestures.

bug, bug, *n.* [W. *bwg*, a hobgoblin, a scarecrow; akin to E. *bogey*, Sc. *bogle*.] A hobgoblin, specter, or bugbear (*Shak.*)‡; a name applied to insects of various kinds, as the may-bug, the lady-bug.—**bugaboo,** bug′a·bö, *n.* An imagined object of fright; a bogeyman; a bugbear.—**bugbear,** bug′bâr, *n.* [Lit. a *bug* or hobgoblin in the shape of a *bear*.] Something real or imaginary that causes terror.—**buggy,** bug′i, *a.* Abounding with bugs.

buggy, bug′i, *n.* A name given to several species of light one-horse carriages or gigs.

bugle, bū′gl, *n.* [Lit. a buffalo-horn, from O.E. *bugle*, a buffalo, from L. *buculus*, a young bullock.] A hunting horn; a military musical brass wind instrument, now frequently furnished with keys so as to be capable of producing all the notes of the scale.—**bugler,** būg′lėr, *n.* One who plays a bugle; a soldier whose duty is to convey the commands of the officers by sounding a bugle.

bugle, bū′gl, *n.* [L.L. *bugulus*, a female ornament, from root seen in A.Sax. *bugan*, to bend, to *bow*, G. *bügel*, a bent piece of metal.] A shining elongated glass bead, usually black, used in decorating female apparel, etc.—*a.‡* Black as a bugle or bead; jet black. (*Shak.*)

bugloss, bū′glos, *n.* [L. *buglossus*, Gr. *bouglōssos*—*bous*, an ox, and *glōssa*, tongue.] A bristly plant of several species, with narrow oblong leaves and deep purple flowers, a common weed, and so called from the shape and roughness of its leaves; oxtongue.

buhl, būl, *n.* [From *Boule*, an Italian woodcarver, who introduced this style of work into France in the reign of Louis XIV.] Unburnished gold, brass, or mother-of-pearl worked into complicated and ornamental patterns, used for inlaying; articles ornamented in this style.—**buhlwork,** būl′wėrk, *n.* Work in which wood, tortoise-shell, etc., is inlaid with buhl.

buhrstone, bör′stōn, *n.* Same as *Burrstone.*

build, bild, *v.i.*—*built, building.* The pret. & pp. *builded* are now confined to poetry. [Of obscure origin, but

connected with A.Sax. *bold*, a house, a building; Icel. *ból*, Dan. *bol*, a house, a dwelling, from same root as Icel. *búa*, to dwell, G. *bauen*, to build or cultivate.] To frame, construct, and raise, as an edifice or fabric of almost any kind; to construct; to frame; to raise on a support or foundation; to rear; to erect; to settle or establish (fame, hopes, etc.).—*v.i.* To exercise the art or practice the business of building; to rest or depend (to *build* on another's foundation); to base; to rely.—*n.* Construction; make; form.—**builder,** bil′dėr, *n.* One who builds; one whose occupation is to build, as an architect, shipwright, mason, etc.—**building,** bild′ing, *n.* The act of one who builds; the thing built, as a house, a church, etc.; fabric; edifice.—**built,** bilt, *p.* and *a.* Formed; shaped (of the human body, etc.): frequently in composition; constructed of different pieces instead of one, as a mast, beam, etc.

bulb, bulb, *n.* [L. *bulbus*, a bulbous root.] The rounded part or head of an onion or similar plant; strictly, a modified leaf bud, consisting of imbricated scales or concentric coats or layers, formed on a plant usually beneath the surface of the ground, emitting roots from its base, and producing a stem from its center, as in the onion, lily, hyacinth, etc.; any protuberance or expansion resembling a bulb, especially an expansion at the end of a stalk or long and slender body, as in the tube of a thermometer.—*v.i.* To project or be protuberant: with *out.*—**bulbil,** bul′bil, *n. Bot.* a separable bulb formed on certain flowering plants; a small axillary bulb.—**bulbiferous,** bul·bif′ėr·us, *a.* Producing bulbs.—**bulbous,** bul′bus, *a.* Having or pertaining to bulbs or a bulb; growing from bulbs; resembling a bulb in shape; swelling out.

bulbul, bul′bul, *n.* The Persian name of the nightingale, or a species of nightingale; an Eastern name of other singing birds.

Bulgarian, bul·gâ′ri·an, *a.* Pertaining to Bulgaria.—*n.* A Bulgarian; the language of the Bulgarians, a Slavonic tongue.

bulge, bulj, *v.i.*—*bulged, bulging.* [From the Scandinavian; O.Sw. *bulgja*, to swell; Icel. *bólginn*, swollen; the same word as A.Sax. *belgan*, to swell, in sense of be angry; akin, *belly*, *bellows*, *bowl*, *billow*, *bulk*, etc. *Bilge* is another spelling.] To swell out; to be protuberant; to bilge, as a ship.

bulimia, bulimy, bū·lim′i·a, bū′li·mi, *n.* [Gr. *boulimia*—*bous*, an ox, in composition, huge, great, and *limos*, hunger.] Morbidly voracious, insatiable appetite.

bulk, bulk, *n.* [Same root as *bulge*; Icel. *bulki*, a heap, the freight of a vessel; Dan. *bulk*, a lump, a clod; O.Sw. *bolk*, a crowd, a mass.] Magnitude of material substance; whole dimensions; size; the gross; the majority; the main mass or body (the *bulk* of a nation); the whole contents of a ship's hold.— *In bulk*, loose or open, that is not packed in bags, boxes, etc.—*v.i.* To grow large; to swell; to appear large or important.—**bulky**, bul'ki, *a.* Of great bulk or dimensions; of great size; large.—**bulkiness**, bul'ki·nes, *n.* The state or quality of being bulky.—**bulkhead**, *n.* A partition in a ship made with boards, to form separate apartments.

bull, bul, *n.* [A.Sax. *bull* (only found in dim. *bulluca*, a bullock); L.G. *bulle*, *bolle*, D. *bul*, Icel. *boli*, a bull. The root may be in A.Sax. *bellan*, to bellow.] The male of any bovine quadruped or animal of the ox or cow kind; an old male whale; *stock-exchange slang*, one who operates in order to effect a rise in the price of stock in order to sell out at a profit; the opposite of a *bear*; —*a.* Male, or of large size; characteristic of a bull, as coarse, loud, obstinate, or the like: used in composition; as, a *bull*trout, *bull*head, *bul*rush, etc.—**bullock**, bul'ok, *n.* [A.Sax. *bulluca*, dim. of *bull*.] An ox or castrated bull; a full-grown steer.—**bulldog**, *n.* A very strong muscular variety of dog, with large head, broad muzzle, short hair, and of remarkable courage and ferocity: formerly much used in bullbaiting.—**bullfight**, *n.* A combat between armed men and bulls in a closed arena; a popular amusement in Spain, Portugal, and Latin America.—**bullfighter**, *n.* A man who engages in bullfights.—**bullfinch**, *n.* A species of finch, distinguished by the large size of the head, the stoutness of the bill, and by having the beak and crown of the head black; a European song-bird.—**bullfrog**, *n.* A large species of frog living in marshy places, having a loud bass voice which resembles the bellowing of a bull.—**bullhead**, *n.* A name given to several species of fish with wide and flattened heads, as the *catfish*; **bullheaded**, *a.* Headstrong; obstinate; opinionated.—**bull's-eye**, *n.* *Arch.* any circular opening for the admission of light or air; a round piece of thick glass convex on one side let into the deck, port, or skylight of a vessel for the purpose of admitting light; a small lantern with a lens on one side to concentrate the light in a given direction; the center of a target of a different color from the rest of it, and usually round, also a shot that hits the bull's-eye.—**bull terrier**, *n.* Breed of dog with characteristics of terrier and bulldog.

bull, bul, *n.* [L. *bulla*, a boss, an ornament worn on a child's neck, later a leaden seal.] Originally the seal appended to the edicts and briefs of the pope, hence, a letter, edict, or rescript of the pope, published or transmitted to the churches over which he is head, containing some decree, order, or decision.

bull, bul, *n.* [Origin doubtful.] A gross inconsistency in language; a ludicrous blunder involving a contradiction in terms.

bullate, bul'lāt, *a.* [L. *bullatus*, from *bulla*, a bubble.] In *bot.* having elevations like bubbles or blisters, as a leaf whose membranous part rises between the veins in elevations like blisters.

bullet, bul'et, *n.* [Fr. *boulet*, a dim. from *boule*, a ball, from L. *bulla*, a bubble, a boss, a seal. Akin *bullion*, *bulletin*, to *boil*, a papal *bull*.] A small ball; a projectile generally of lead intended to be discharged from small arms, as rifles, muskets, pistols, etc.—**bulletproof**, *a.* Capable of resisting the force of a bullet.

bulletin, bul'e·tin, *n.* [Fr. from It. *bulletino*, dim. of *bulla*, an edict of the pope.] An official report concerning some public event, such as military operations, etc., issued for the information of the public; any public announcement, especially of news recently received.

bullion, bul'yon, *n.* [From L.L. *bullio*, *bulliona*, a mass of gold or silver, from L. *bulla*, a boss, a stud, a seal. BULLET.] Uncoined gold or silver in the mass; gold or silver not in the form of current coin; the precious metals in bars, ingots, or in any uncoined form; foreign or uncurrent coins; a kind of heavy twisted fringe frequently made of silk and covered with fine gold or silver wire.

bullock. See BULL.

bully, bul'i, *n.* [From root of *bull*, *bellow*; originally the first element in compounds such as *bully-rook*, *bully-Jack*, and other old terms; comp. Sw. *bullerbas*, a noisy person, from *bullra*, to make a noise.] A blustering, quarrelsome, overbearing fellow, more distinguished for insolence than for courage; a swaggerer; one who domineers or browbeats; a brisk, dashing fellow: a familiar term of address (*Shak.*)‡.—*v.t.*—**bullied**, **bullying.** To act the bully toward; to overbear with bluster or menaces.—*v.i.* To be loudly arrogant and overbearing; to be noisy and quarrelsome; to bluster, swagger, hector, or domineer.

bully, bul'i, [Fr. *bouilli*.] Tinned beef.

bulrush, bul'rush, *n.* [From *bull*, implying largeness, and *rush*.] A name given to large rushlike plants, of various genera, growing in marshes.—**bulrushy**, bul'rush·i, *a.* Abounding in bulrushes, resembling or pertaining to bulrushes.

bulwark, bul'werk, *n.* [Lit. a *work* built of the *boles* or trunks of trees, from Dan. *bulwerk*, D. *bolwerk*, G. *bollwerk*, rampart; hence by corruption Fr. *boulevard*.] A mound of earth round a place, capable of resisting cannon shot, and formed with bastions, curtains, etc.; a rampart; a fortification; that which protects or secures against attack; means of protection and safety; the boarding round the sides of a ship, above the level of the decks, to prevent them being swept by the waves, etc.—*v.t.* To fortify with a bul-

wark or rampart; to protect; defend.

bum,† bum, *v.i.* [A different spelling of *boom*, D. *bommen*, to boom or sound hollow.] To make a hollow noise; to boom.—*n.* A droning or humming sound, as that made by the bee; a hum.

bum, bum, *n.* An inebriate; a mendicant; a loafer; one who prefers charity to work; a panhandler.—*v.i.* To travel without expense to oneself, by begging or stealing food and lodging.

bumblebee, bum'bl·bē, *n.* [From *bum*, to hum or boom.] A large bee; a humblebee: so named from its sound.

bumboat, bum'bōt, *n.* [D. *bumboot*, a wide fishing-boat, from *bun*, a tank in a boat in which fish are kept alive, and *boot*, a boat.] A boat for carrying provisions to a ship at a distance from shore.

bump, bump, *v.t.* [Perhaps imitative of sound; comp. L.G. *bumsen*, to strike or fall on with a hollow noise; also W. *pwmp*, a round mass; *pwmpiaw*, to thump.] To make to come in violent contact; to give a shock to; to strike; to thump.—*v.i.* To come in collision; to strike against something.—*n.* A swelling or protuberance (especially on the body); *phren.* one of the natural protuberances on the surface of the skull regarded as indicative of distinct qualities, affections, propensities, etc. of the mind; a shock from a collision.

bumper, bum'pér, *n.* [Corrupted from older *bumbard*, *bombard*.] A cup or glass filled to the brim; something well or completely filled; device for absorbing shock in a collision, especially a bar across the end of an automobile.

bumpkin, bump'kin, *n.* [For *bumkin*, a short boom; a bumpkin being a blockish fellow, a blockhead.] An awkward, clumsy rustic; a clown or country lout.

bumptious, bump'shus, *a.* [For *bumpish*, from *bump*, apt to strike against or come in contact with others.] Offensively self-assertive; disposed to quarrel; domineering. (Colloq.)—**bumptiousness**, bump'shus·nes, *n.* (Colloq.)

bun, bun, *n.* [O.Fr. *bugne*, a swelling; Fr. *bugnet*, a little puffed loaf.] A kind of cake; a kind of sweet bread.

bunch, bunsh, *n.* [From O.Sw. and Dan. *bunke*, Icel. *bunki*, a heap. BUNK.] A protuberance; a bunch; a knob or lump; a collection, cluster, or tuft of things of the same kind connected together in growth or tied together; any cluster or aggregate.—*v.i.* To swell out in a protuberance; to cluster, as into bunches.—*v.t.* To form or tie in a bunch.—**bunchy**, bunsh'i, *a.* Having a bunch or hunch; having knobs or protuberances; growing in a bunch; like a bunch.

bundle, bun'dl, *n.* [A dim. from *bind*; equivalent to D. *bondel*, G. *bundel*, bundle.] A number of things bound or rolled into a convenient form for conveyance or handling; a package.—*v.t.*—**bundled**, **bundling.** To tie or bind in a bundle or roll: often followed by *up*; to place or dispose of in a hurried unceremonious manner.—*To bundle off*, to send a person off in a hurry; to send off unceremoniously.—*To bundle out*, to expel summarily.—*v.i.* To depart in a hurry or unceremoniously; often with *off*.

bung, bung, *n.* [Allied to D. *bom*, O.D. *bonne*, a bung; Ir. *buinne*, a tap, a spigot; W. *bwng*, a bung-hole.] A large cork or stopper for closing the hole in a cask through which it is filled.—*v.t.* To stop the orifice of with a bung; to close up.—**bunghole,** *n.* The hole or orifice in a cask through which it is filled, and which is closed by a bung.

bungalow, bung'ga·lō, *n.* [Per. *bangalah*, from *Bengal*; lit. a Bengalese house.] A house or residence, generally of a single floor, and surrounded by a veranda.

bungle, bung'gl, *v.i.*—*bungled, bungling*. [Akin to *bang*, G. dial. *bungen* O.Sw. *bunga*, to beat, to bang.] To perform in a clumsy awkward manner.—*v.t.* To make or mend clumsily; to botch; to manage awkwardly; to perform inefficiently.—*n.* A clumsy performance; a piece of awkward work; a botch.—**bungler,** bung'glêr, *n.* One who bungles; one who performs without skill.—**bungling,** bung'gling, *a.* Prone to bungle, clumsy; characterized by bungling. —**bunglingly,** bung'gling·li, *adv.* In a bungling manner; clumsily; awkwardly.

bunion, bun'yon, *n.* [From It. *bugnone*, a round knot or bunch, a boil. *Bun* is of the same origin.] An excrescence or knob on some of the joints of the feet, generally at the side of the ball of the great toe, which causes an inflammation of the small membranous sac called *bursa mucosa*.

bunk, bungk, *n.* [Sw. *bunke*, a wooden vessel, a coop, in O.Sw. also part of a vessel's deck.] A wooden box or case, serving as a seat during the day and a bed at night; one of a series of sleeping berths arranged above each other.—**bunker,** bung'kêr, *n.* A sort of fixed chest or box; a large bin or receptacle (a coal-*bunker*).

bunker, *n.* A sandy hollow in golf links.—**bunker,** *v.t.* To block, to check.

bunkum, buncombe, bung'kum, *n.* [From *Buncombe*, in N. Carolina, whose member of Congress had on one occasion admitted that he was talking simply ' for Buncombe ', that is, to please his constituents.] Talking for talking's sake; bombastic speechmaking; mere words.

bunny, bun'i, *n.* [Ir. and Gael. *bun*, root, stump; lit. the short-tailed animal.] A sort of pet name for the rabbit.

Bunsen burner, bun'sen, *n.* [From inventor, Baron *Bunsen*.] A kind of lamp or gas burner producing an intensely hot flame.

bunt, bunt, *v.t.* To tap a baseball lightly with a loosely held bat.—

buntline, bunt'līn, *n.* *Naut.* one of the ropes fastened on the bottoms of square sails, to draw them up to their yards.

bunt, bunt, *n.* [Supposed to be a corruption of *burnt*.] A disease of wheat; smut; also, the fungus producing the disease.

bunting, bun'ting, *n.* [O.E. *bunting, bounting, buntel,* Sc. *buntlin*; origin unknown.] The popular name of a number of insessorial birds closely allied to finches and sparrows.

bunting, buntine, bun'ting, bun'tin, *n.* [Probably from G. *bunt*, D. *bont*, particolored, of different colors.] A thin woolen stuff, of which the colors, or flags and signals, of ships are made; a vessel's flags collectively.

buoy, boi, *n.* [D. *boei*, a buoy, a fetter, O.Fr. *boye*, from L. *boiae*, a kind of fetter or shackle; a buoy being fettered at a fixed point.] A floating object fixed at a certain place to show the position of objects beneath the water, as shoals, rocks, etc., or to mark out the course a ship is to follow, etc.; a floating object used to throw overboard for a person who has fallen into the water to lay hold of, and to keep him afloat till he can be taken out; more particularly called a *life buoy*.—*v.i.* To keep afloat in a fluid, as in water or air; generally with *up*; *fig.* to keep from sinking into despondency; to fix buoys in as a direction to mariners.—**buoyancy,** boi'an·si, *n.* The quality of being buoyant, that is of floating on the surface of water or in the atmosphere; *fig.* lightheartedness; cheerfulness; hopefulness; elasticity of spirit.—**buoyant,** boi'ant, *a.* Floating; light; having the quality of rising or floating in a fluid; *fig.* cheerful; hopeful; not easily depressed.—**buoyantly,** boi'ant·li, *adv.* In a buoyant manner.

bur, burr, bêr, *n.* [A.Sax. *burr*, a bur, a burdock; Dan. *borre*, Sw. *kardborre*, a burdock; the root is probably seen in Ir. *borr*, a knob, *borraim*, to swell.] A rough prickly covering of the seeds of certain plants, as of the chestnut and burdock; the plant burdock; *engr.* a slight ridge of metal left by the graver on the edges of a line, and which is removed by a scraper; the guttural pronunciation of the rough *r* common in some of the northern counties of England.

Burberry, bêr'be·ri, *n.* [Maker's name.] Waterproof overcoat of material specially treated by Burberry process.

burbot, bêr'bot, *n.* [Fr. *barbote*, from *barbe* L. *barba*, a beard.] A fish of the cod family, shaped like an eel but shorter, with a flat head and two small beards on the nose and another on the chin.

burden, burthen, bêr'dn, bêr'THn, *n.* [A.Sax. *byrthen*, from *beran*, to bear, like Icel. *byrthr, byrthi*, Dan. *byrde*, Goth. *baurthei*, G. *bürde*, a burden. BEAR.] That which is borne or carried; a load; that which is grievous, wearisome, or oppressive;

the quantity or number of tons a vessel will carry.—*v.t.* To load; to lay a heavy load on; to encumber with weight; to oppress with anything grievous; to surcharge.—**burdensome,** bêr'dn·sum, *a.* Weighing like a heavy burden; grievous to be borne; causing uneasiness or fatigue; oppressive; heavy; wearisome.—**burdensomely,** bêr'dn·sum·li, *adv.* In a burdensome manner.—**burdensomeness,** bêr'dn·sum·nes, *n.* The quality of being burdensome; heaviness; oppressiveness.

burden, bêr'dn, *n.* [Fr. *bourdon*, a drone or bass, the humble-bee, from L.L. *burdo*, a drone.] The part in a song which is repeated at the end of each verse; the chorus or refrain; a subject on which one dwells.

burdock, bêr'dok, *n.* [*Bur* and *dock*.] The popular name of a large rough-leaved perennial plant belonging to the composite family, common on roadsides and waste places, and a troublesome weed in cultivated grounds.

bureau, bū'rō, pl. **bureaux, bureaus,** bū'rōz, *n.* [Fr. *bureau*, an office, a desk or writing table, originally a kind of russet stuff with which writing tables were covered; from L. *burrus*, red or reddish.] An office or place where business is transacted; a department for the transaction of public business; a chest of drawers for clothes, etc.—**bureaucracy,** bū·ro'kra·si, *n.* The system of centralizing the administration of a country, through regularly graded series of government officials; such officials collectively.—**bureaucrat,** bū'rō·krat, *n.* An advocate for or supporter of bureaucracy.—**bureaucratic,** bū·rō·krat'ik, *a.* Relating to bureaucracy.

burette, bū·ret', *n.* [Fr. from *buire*, a flagon, L. *bibere*, to drink.] A tube used in chemistry for accurately measuring out quantities of fluids.

burgee, bêr'jē, *n.* A flag or pennant which ends in two points; a kind of small coal suited for burning in furnaces.

burgeon, bêr'jon, *n.* and *v.i.* Same as *Bourgeon*.

burgh, bêrg, bu're, *n.* [BOROUGH.] A corporate town or borough; the Scotch term corresponding to the English *borough*, applied to several different kinds of corporations.—**burgess,** bêr'jes, *n.* [O.Fr. *burgeis*, Fr. *bourgeois*, from *bourg*, L.L. *burgus*, a borough.] An inhabitant of a borough or walled town, especially one who possesses a tenement therein; a citizen or freeman of a borough; a parliamentary representative of a borough.—**burgher,** bêr'gêr, *n.* An inhabitant of a burgh or borough, who enjoys the privileges of the borough of which he is a freeman.

burglar, bêrg'lêr, *n.* [From Fr. *bourg*, a town, and O.Fr. *laire*, Pr. *lairo*, L. *latro*, a thief.] One guilty of housebreaking. — **burglarious,** bêrg·lâ'ri·us, *a.* Pertaining to burglary; constituting the crime of burglary.—**burglariously,** bêrg·lâ'ri·us·li, *adv.* With an intent to commit burglary; in the manner of a burglar.—**burglary**, bẽrg′la·ri, *n.* The act or crime of housebreaking, with an intent to commit a felony.

burgomaster, bẽr′go·mas·tẽr, *n.* [D. *burgemeester*=E. *borough-master.*]The chief magistrate of a municipal town in Holland, Flanders, and Germany, nearly corresponding to *mayor* in England and the United States.

burgonet, bẽr′go·net, *n.* [Fr. *bourguignotte*, properly a Burgundian helmet.] A kind of helmet with a small visor formerly worn.

burgoo, bẽr′gö, *n.* A kind of oatmeal porridge, a dish used at sea; contemptuous Russian anarchist expression for middle-class or bourgeois politics.

burgrave, bẽr′grāv, *n.* [L.L. *burggravius*, from G. *burggraf*—*burg*, a town, and *graf*, a count, an earl.] In some European countries an hereditary governor of a town or castle.

Burgundy, bẽr′gun·di, *n.* A kind of wine, so called from Burgundy, in France.—*Burgundy pitch*, a pitch obtained from the Norway spruce, used in plasters.

burial, be′ri·al, *n.* See BURY.

burin, bü′rin, *n.* [Fr. *burin*, from root of *bore.*] A graver; an instrument for engraving made of tempered steel, of a prismatic form, and with the graving end ground off obliquely so as to produce a sharp point.

burke, bẽrk, *v.t.* [From the name of an Irishman who first committed the crime, in 1829, in Edinburgh, with the view of selling the dead bodies for dissection.] To murder by suffocation; *fig.* to smother.

burl, bẽrl, *n.* [Fr. *bourre*, a flock of wool as for stuffing, L.L. *burra*, a flock of wool.] A small knot or lump in thread, whether woven into cloth or not.—*v.t.* To pick knots, loose threads, etc., from, as in finishing cloth.—**burler**, bẽr′lẽr, *n.* One who burls cloth.

burlap, bẽr′lap, *n.* [Origin uncertain.] A fabric made from jute and used to make bags and upholstery.

burlesque, bẽr·lesk′, *a.* [Fr. *burlesque*, from It. *burlesco*, ridiculous, from *burlare*, to ridicule, *burla*, mockery.] Tending to excite laughter by ludicrous images, or by a contrast between the subject and the manner of treating it.—*n.* That kind of literary composition which exhibits a contrast between the subject and the manner of treating it so as to excite laughter or ridicule; travesty; caricature; a kind of dramatic extravaganza with more or less singing in it; a ludicrous or debasing caricature of any kind; a gross perversion.—*v.t.*—**burlesqued**, **burlesquing**. To make ridiculous by burlesque representation; to turn into a burlesque.—*v.i.*† To use burlesque.—**burlesquer**, bẽr·lesk′ẽr, *n.* One who burlesques or turns to ridicule.

burly, bẽr′li, *a.* [Of same origin as *bur*, *burr*, Ir. and Gael. *borr*, a knob, with term. *-ly.*] Great in bodily size; bulky; lusty: the word, now used only of persons, includes the idea of some degree of coarseness.—**burliness**, bẽr′li·nes, *n.* The state or quality of being burly.

Burmese, bur·mēz′, *a.* Of or pertaining to Burma.—*n.* An inhabitant or inhabitants of Burma; the language of the people of Burma.

burn, bẽrn, *v.t.—burned* or *burnt*, *burning.* [A.Sax. *bernan*, *byrnan*, *beornan*, *brinnan*, to burn=Icel. *brenna*, Dan. *braende*, O.D. *bernen*, Goth. *brinnan*, G. *brennen*, to burn, *Brand*, *brown*, *brine*, *brimstone*, etc., are akin.] To consume with fire; to reduce to ashes; to injure by fire; to scorch, to act on with fire; to expose to the action of fire (limestone, bricks), to make into by means of fire (to *burn* charcoal), to affect with a burning sensation; to apply a cautery to.—*To burn daylight*, to use artificial light before it is dark; to waste time. (*Shak*).—*v.i.* To be on fire, to flame, to suffer from or be injured by an excess of heat; to shine; to sparkle; to glow; to gleam; to be inflamed with passion or desire; to be affected with a sensation of heat (the cheeks *burn*), in certain games, to be near a concealed object which is sought; hence, to be nearly right in guessing (colloq.).—*n.* A hurt or injury of the flesh caused by the action of fire.—**burner**, bẽr′nẽr, *n.* A person who burns or sets fire to anything, the part of a lamp from which the flame issues; the part that holds the wick, the jet-piece from which a gasflame issues.—**burning**, bẽr′ning, *a.* Much heated; flaming; scorching; vehement; powerful; causing excitement, ardor, or enthusiasm (a *burning* question).—**burning glass**, *n.* A double-convex lens of glass, which, when exposed to the direct rays of the sun, collects them into a focus, where an intense heat is produced, so that combustible matter may be set on fire.

burn, bẽrn, *n.* [A.Sax. *burna*, a stream, a well; Icel. *brunnr*, D. *born*, Goth. *brunna*, G. *brunnen*, akin to verb to *burn*; comp. *torrent*, from L. *torreo*, to burn.] A rivulet; a brook. [Prov. E. and Sc.]

burnish, bẽr′nish, *v.t.* [O.Fr. *burnir*, *burnissant*, to polish, to embrown, from *brun*, O.H.G. *brun*, brown. BROWN.] To cause to glow or become resplendent; to polish and make shining by friction; to make smooth and lustrous.—*v.i.*† To grow bright or brilliant; to show conspicuously.—*n.*† Gloss; brightness; luster.—**burnisher**, bẽr′nish·ẽr, *n.* One who or that which burnishes or makes glossy.

burnoose, bẽr·nös′, *n.* [Fr. *burnous*, *bournous*, from Sp. *al-bornoz*, a kind of Moorish cloak. An Ar. word.] A white woolen mantle, with hood, woven in one piece, worn by the Arabs.

burr, burstone, bẽr, bẽr′stōn, *n.* A name given to certain siliceous or siliceocalcareous stones, whose dressed surfaces present a burr or keen-cutting texture, whence they are much used for millstones.

burro, bur′ō, *n.* A small donkey, used as a pack animal.

burrow, bur′ō, *n.* [The same word with *burgh*, *borough*, from A.Sax. *beorgan*, to protect, shelter.] A hole in the ground excavated by rabbits, hares, and some other animals, as a refuge and habitation.—*v.i.* To make a hole or burrow to lodge in; to work a way into or under something; to lodge in a burrow or in any deep or concealed place; to hide.—**burrower**, bur′ō·ẽr, *n.* One who burrows; an animal which excavates and inhabits burrows.

bursa, bẽr′sa, *n.* [L.] *Anat.* a kind of sac.—*Bursa mucosa*, a sac situated at a joint and containing the synovial fluid.

bursar, bẽr′sẽr, *n.* [BURSE.] A treasurer or cash keeper of a college or of a monastery; a purser; a student to whom a bursary is paid.

burse, bẽrs, *n.* [Fr. *bourse*, a purse, bursary, exchange, from L.L. *bursa*, a purse, a skin, leather. PURSE.] A purse to hold something valuable; one of the official insignia of the lord high chancellor of England.

bursitis, bẽr·sī′tis, *n.* [From *bursa* and Gr. *-itis*, inflammation.] Inflammation of a bursa.

burst, bẽrst, *v.i.—burst*, *bursting.* [A.Sax. *berstan*=Icel. *bersta*, Dan. *briste*, *bröste*, D. *bersten*, O.G. *bresten*, Mod. G. *bersten*, to burst; same root in Ir. *brisaim*, Gael. *bris*, *brisd*, to break.] To fly or break open from internal force and with sudden violence, to suffer a violent disruption; to explode; to become suddenly manifest; to rush; with prepositions, adverbs, and adverbial phrases (to *burst* out, to *burst* into life).—*v.t.* To break or rend by force or violence; to open suddenly (to *burst* one's bonds, to *burst* a cannon).—*n.* A sudden disruption; a violent rending; a sudden explosion or shooting forth; a rush; an outburst.

burthen. See BURDEN.

burton, bẽr′ton, *n.* A small tackle formed by two blocks or pulleys, used in ships to set up or tighten the topmost shrouds and for various other purposes.

bury, ber′i, *v.t.—buried*, *burying.* [A.Sax. *byrgan*, *byrigan*, to bury; allied to *beorgan*, to protect, and thus to *burgh*, *borough*, *burrow*, *barrow*, etc.] To cover with earth or other matter; to deposit in a grave when dead; to inter; to entomb; to hide; to conceal; to withdraw or conceal in retirement: used *refl.*; to hide in oblivion (to *bury* injuries, etc.).—**burying**, ber′i·ing, *n.* Burial; sepulture. (N.T.)—**burial**, ber′i·al, *n.* The act of burying, especially the act of burying a deceased person; sepulture; interment; the act of depositing a dead body in the earth, in a tomb or vault, or in the water.—**burier**, ber′i·ẽr, *n.* One who buries; that which buries or covers.

bus, bus, *n.* An abbreviation of *omnibus*, a public vehicle; a motor coach, a large public carriage.

busby, buz'bi, *n.* A military head-dress consisting of a fur hat with a bag, of the same color as the facings of the regiment, hanging from the top over the right side.

bush, bush, *n.* [Scandinavian: Dan. *busk.* Sw. *buske*, a bush = D. *bosch*, a grove; G. *busch*, a bush. The word passed from the Teutonic into the Romance languages, and *ambush*, *ambuscade*, *bosky*, *bouquet*, etc., are akin.] A shrub with branches; a thick shrub; a branch of a tree, properly of ivy, fixed or hung out as a tavern sign (*Shak.*), a stretch of shrubby vegetation; a district covered with brushwood, or shrubs, trees, etc.—*To beat about the bush*, to use circumlocution; to dilly-dally.—*v.i.* To grow thick or bushy.—*v.t.* To set bushes about; to support with bushes; to use a bush harrow on.—**bushiness**, bush'i·nes, *n.* The quality of being bushy.—**bushy**, bush'i, *a.* Full of bushes; overgrown with shrubs; resembling a bush; thick and spreading, like a bush.—**bushbuck**, bush'buk, *n.* [D. *bosch-bok*.] The name given to several species of South African antelopes.—**bushman**, bush'man, *n.* A woodsman; a settler in the bush or forest districts of a new country, as Australia; [*cap.*] an aboriginal of Bushmanland, near the Cape of Good Hope; a Bosjesman.—**bush-ranger**, *n.* In Australia, one who takes to the ' bush ', or woods, and lives by robbery.

bush, bush, *n.* [Parallel form of *box*, from D. *bus*, a box, a bush; G. *büchse*, a box, the bush of a wheel.] A lining of harder material let into an orifice (as for an axle) to guard against wearing by friction.—*v.t.* To furnish with a bush.

bushel, bush'el, *n.* [O.Fr. *bussel*, L.L. *bussellus*, a dim. form from *bussida*, for *buxida*, *pyxida*, from Gr. *pyxis*, a box.] A dry measure containing 8 gallons or 4 pecks. The standard bushel in the United States has a capacity of 2,150.42 cubic inches, and holds 77.627 lbs. avoirdupois of distilled water at the temperature of 39.2° Fahr.; a vessel of the capacity of a bushel.

business, biz'nes, *n.* [This word, though with the form of an ordinary abstract noun from *busy*, has lost the meaning of state of being busy, *busy-ness*.] A matter or affair that engages a person's time, care, and attention; that which one does for a livelihood; occupation; employment; mercantile concerns, or traffic in general; the proper duty; what belongs to one to do; task or object undertaken; concern; right of action or interposing; affair; point; matter.—*a.* Relating to or connected with business, traffic, trade, etc.

buskin, bus'kin, *n.* [For *broskin*, *bruskin*, a dim. from D. *broos*, a buskin, akin to *brogue*.] A kind of half-boot or high shoe covering the foot and leg to the middle of the calf; the high shoe worn by ancient tragic actors; the tragic drama as opposed to comedy.

bust, bust, *n.* [Fr. *buste*, It. and Sp. *busto*, L.L. *bustum*, from *busta*, a small box, L. *buxida*. BOX.] A sculptured figure of a person showing only the head, shoulders, and breast; the chest or thorax.

bustard, bus'tėrd, *n.* [O.Fr. *bistarde*, a corruption of L. *avis tarda*; lit. slow bird.] A bird belonging to the order of the runners, but approaching the waders. The great bustard is the largest European bird, the male often weighing 30 lbs.

bustle, bus'l, *v.i.*—*bustled*, *bustling*. [Same word as Icel. *bustla*, to bustle, to plash in water; *bustl*, *bustle*, a plash.] To display activity with a certain amount of noise or agitation; to be active and stirring.—*n.* Activity with noise and agitation; stir; hurry-scurry; tumult.

bustle, bus'l, *n.* [Perhaps for *buskle*, a dim. of *busk*, a support for a lady's stays.] A pad, cushion, or wire framework worn at one time, about 1880, beneath the skirt of a woman's dress, expanding and supporting it behind.

busy, biz'i, *a.* [O.E. *bisy*, A.Sax. *bysig*, *bisig* = D. *bezig*, L.G. *besig*, busy; further affinities doubtful.] Employed with constant attention; engaged about something that renders interruption inconvenient; occupied without cessation; constantly in motion; meddling with or prying into the affairs of others; officious; causing or spent in much employment (a *busy* day).—*v.t.*—*busied*, *busying.* To employ with constant attention; to keep engaged; to make or keep busy; often *refl.*—**busybody**, biz'i·bod·i, *n.* One who officiously concerns himself or herself with the affairs of others.—**busily**, biz'i·li, *adv.* In a busy manner; with constant occupation; importunately; officious-ly.

but, but. Originally a prep. and still often to be so regarded, though also an adv. and frequently a conj. [A.Sax. *butan*, without, out of, unless—*be*, by, and *utan*, out, without.] Except; besides; unless (all, none *but* one); save or excepting that; were it not (commonly followed by *that*); only; merely; simply (I do *but* jest); some-times equivalent to, that...not (who knows *but* or *but that* he may); as an adversative conj. equivalent to, on the contrary; on the other hand; yet; still; however; nevertheless.

butadiene, bū·ta·dī'ēn, *n.* A flam-mable colorless gas obtained from oil and carbon dioxide, used chiefly in making synthetic rubber.

butane, bū'tān, *n.* [From L. *buytrum*, Gr. *boutyron*, butter.] A hydrocarbon gas obtained from petroleum.

butcher, buch'ėr, *n.* [Fr. *boucher*, from *bouc*, a he-goat (from G. *bock*, a goat = E. *buck*), the males being killed for food, the females kept for milk.] One whose trade is to kill beasts for food; one who deals in meat; one who kills in a cruel or bloody manner.—*v.t.* To kill or slaughter for food or for market; to murder in a bloody or barbarous manner.—**butcherly**,‡ buch'ėr·li, *a.*

Cruel; savage; murderous. (*Shak.*)—**butchery**, buch'ėr·i, *n.* The business of slaughtering cattle for the table or for market; murder committed with unusual barbarity; great slaugh-ter.—**butcherbird**, *n.* A name given to the shrikes from their habit of suspending their prey, as a butcher does his meat, and then pulling it to pieces and devouring it at their leisure.—**butcher's-broom**, *n.* A stiff, erect, spiny-leaved shrub belonging to the lily family, often made into brooms for sweeping butchers' blocks.

butler, but'lėr, *n.* [O.E. *boteler*, from L.L. *botellarius*, a butler, from *botellus*, a bottle. BOTTLE.] A servant or officer in a house-hold whose prin-cipal business is to take charge of the liquors, silverware, etc.—**butlership**, but'lėr·ship, *n.* The office of a butler.

butt, but, *n.* [O.Fr. *bot*, *bout*, the end or extremity of a thing, Fr. *but*, an end, aim, goal, also *butte*, a butt used in shooting; from M.H.G. *bózen*, to strike, to beat, a word akin to E. *beat*.] The end or extremity of a thing, particularly the larger end of a thing, as of a piece of timber or of a felled tree; the thick end of a musket, fishing rod, whip handle, etc.; thickest and stoutest part of tanned ox hides; a mark to be shot at; the point where a mark is set or fixed to be shot at; the object of aim; the person at whom ridicule, jests, or contempt is directed; a goal; a bound (*Shak.*); *rifle-practice*, the hut, em-bankment, or other protection in which the marker sits.—**butt-end**, *n.* The largest, thickest, or blunt end of anything.—**butt shaft**,‡ *n.* An arrow. (*Shak.*)

butt, but, *v.t. & i.* [Fr. *bouter*, O.Fr. *boter*, to push, to butt. BUTT, an end.] To strike by thrusting the head against, as an ox or a ram; to have a habit of so striking.—*n.* [In the first sense directly from the verb; in second from Fr. *botte*, a pass or thrust in fencing.] A push or thrust given by the head of an animal; a thrust in fencing.

butt, but, *n.* [O.Fr. *boute*, Fr. *botte*, a boot, a butt, the two having a considerable resemblance. BOOT.] A large cask; a measure of 126 gallons of wine or 2 hogsheads.

butte, būt, *n.* [Fr.] A term applied to a detached hill or ridge of no great height rising abruptly.

butter, but'ėr, *n.* [A.Sax. *buter*, *butor*, from L. *butyrum*, from Gr. *boutyron*, butter, from *bous*, an ox, and *tyros*, cheese.] An oily or unctuous sub-stance obtained from cream or milk by churning; *old chem.* a term applied to certain anhydrous, metallic chlor-ides of buttery consistency and fusi-bility.—*Vegetable butters*, a name given to certain vegetable oils, from their resemblance to butter.—*Rock butter*, a peculiar mineral composed of alum combined with iron, of the consistence and appearance of soft butter, appearing as a pasty exuda-tion from aluminiferous rocks.—*v.t.* To smear with butter; to flatter grossly (vulgar).—**buttercup**, but'-ėr·kup, *n.* A name given to several species of Ranunculus, a common field plant with bright yellow flowers. —**butterfly,** but'ėr·flī, *n.* [The reason for the name is doubtful; probably it was originally given to a common yellow species.] The common name of all the diurnal lepidopterous insects (the nocturnal ones being moths), in their last and fully developed state, having four wings often decked with the most beautiful colors, and a suctorial mouth; *fig.* a person whose attention is given up to a variety of trifles of any kind; a showily dressed, vain and giddy person.—**buttermilk,** *n.* The milk that remains after the butter is separated from it.—**butternut,** *n.* The fruit of a North American tree akin to the walnut, so called from the oil it contains; also the fruit of one or two lofty hardwood trees growing in Guiana.—**butterscotch,** but'ėr·skoch, *n.* The name given to a kind of toffee containing a considerable admixture of butter.— **butter tree,** *n.* A species of African tree, the seeds of which yield a substance like butter, called shea butter.—**butterwort,** but'ėr·wėrt, *n.* A European plant growing in bogs or soft grounds, the leaves of which are covered with soft, pellucid, glandular hairs, which secrete a glutinous liquor that catches small insects.— **buttery,** but'ėr·i, *a.* Having the qualities or appearance of butter.

buttery, but'ėr·i, *n.* [Originally *botelerie,* a place for bottles, but altered to *buttery* from butter being also kept in it.] An apartment in a household, in which wines, liquors, and provisions are kept; in some colleges, a room where refreshments are kept for sale to the students.

buttock, but'ok, *n.* [Dim. of *butt.*] The rump, or the protuberant part of an animal behind.

button, but'n, *n.* [Fr. *bouton,* a button, a bud, from *bouter,* to push. BUTT, to thrust, BUTT, an end.] A small round or roundish object of bone, ivory, metal, wood, mother-of-pearl, etc., used for fastening the parts of dress, by being passed into a hole, slit, or loop, or sometimes attached as mere ornament; something resembling a button; a round knob or protuberance; the small disk at the end of fencing foils, etc. The plural used as a singular is a colloquial or slang term for a page boy, from the buttons on his jacket.—*v.t.* To attach a button or buttons to; to fasten with a button or buttons; to enclose or make secure with buttons.—*v.i.* To be capable of being buttoned (his coat will not *button*).—**buttonbush,** *n.* A North American shrub so called on account of its globular flower heads.— **buttonhole,** *n.* The hole or loop in which a button, or flower, is fastened. —*v.t.* To seize a man by the button or buttonhole and detain him in conversation against his will.—**buttonwood,** *n.* A common name in America for the western plane tree; also the same as *buttonbush.*

buttress, but'res, *n.* [O.E. *butrasse,*

boterase, etc., from Fr. *bouter,* to thrust (BUTT), or a modification of *brattice, bretèche.*] A projecting support of masonry built on to the exterior of a wall, especially common in churches in the Gothic style; *fig.* any prop or support (a *buttress* of the constitution).—*v.t.* To support by a buttress; to prop.

butyraceous, bū·ti·rā'shus, *a.* [From L. *butyrum,* butter. BUTTER.] Having the qualities of butter; resembling butter.—**butyric,** bū·tir'ik, *a.* Pertaining to or derived from butter; a term applied to an acid obtained from butter, and also occurring in perspiration.

buxom, buk'sum, *a.* [A.Sax. *buhsom,* compliant, obedient, from *búgan,* to bend, to *bow,* and term. *-som, -some,* as in *blithesome,* etc.; D. *buigzaam,* G. *biegsam,* flexible, tractable, are exactly similar.] Yielding to pressure‡; flexible or elastic (*Mil.*)‡; obedient‡; healthy and cheerful; brisk; jolly; lively and vigorous; applied especially to women.— **buxomly,** buk'sum·li, *adv.* In a buxom manner; briskly; vigorously. —**buxomness,** buk'sum·nes, *n.*

buy, bī, *v.t.—bought* (pret. & pp.), *buying.* [O.E. *bygge, bugge,* A.Sax. *bicgan, bycgan,* to buy; Goth. *bugjan,* to buy. Hence *aby.*] To acquire by paying a price to the satisfaction of the seller; to purchase: opposed to *sell ;* to get, acquire, or procure for any kind of equivalent (to *buy* favor with flattery); to bribe; to corrupt or pervert by paying a consideration. —*To buy in,* to buy for the owner at a public sale, especially when an insufficient price is offered.—*To buy off,* to release from military service by a payment; to get rid of the opposition of by paying; to purchase the non-intervention of.—*To buy out,* to purchase the share or shares of a person in a commercial concern, the purchaser thus taking the place of the seller.—*To buy over,* to detach by a bribe or consideration from one party and attach to the opposite party.—**buyer,** bī'ėr, *n.* One who buys; a purchaser.

buzz, buz, *v.i.* [Purely imitative of the sound. Comp. It. *buzzicare,* to buzz, whisper.] To make a low hissing sound, as that of bees; to whisper; to speak with a low hissing voice.— *v.t.* To whisper; to spread or report by whispers; to spread secretly.—*n.* A continuous humming sound, as of bees; a low whispering hum; a report circulated secretly and cautiously; a general confused conversation.— **buzzer,** buz'ėr, *n.* One who buzzes; a whisperer; one who is busy in telling tales secretly. (*Shak.*)

buzzard, buz'ėrd, *n.* [Fr. *busard, busard,* from *buse,* a buzzard, and term. *-ard, buse* being from L.L. *busio,* for L. *buteo,* a buzzard.] A name for several large raptorial birds of the falcon family, with short weak toes; a blockhead; a dunce.

by, bī, *prep.* [A.Sax. *bi, big,* by; O.Sax. O.Fris. *bi,* D. *bij,* G. *bei,* Goth. *bi.* Often as a prefix in form *be.*] Near; close to; near along with motion past;

through or with, denoting the author, producer, or agent, means, instrument, or cause; according to; by direction, authority; or example of (*by* his own account, ten *by* the clock, a rule to live *by*); at the rate of; in the ratio or proportion of (*by* the yard, *by* the dozen); to the amount or number of (larger *by* half, older *by* ten years); during the course of; within the compass or period of (*by* day); not later than (*by* this time, *by* two o'clock). In oaths or adjurations it comes before what is invoked or appealed to (*by* heaven).—*Two by two, day by day, piece by piece,* etc., each two, each day, each piece, taken separately or singly.—*Five feet by four,* measuring five feet one way and four the other.—*a.* Side; secondary: used only in composition, as *by*-path, *by*-play, *by*-street, etc.—*adv.* Near; in the same place with; at hand; aside (to stand *by,* to lay a thing *by*); so as to pass (to run *by*); so as to be past or over (the time went *by*).—*By and by,* in the near future; soon; presently.—**by, bye,** bī, *n.* A thing not directly aimed at; something not the immediate object of regard; as, by the *by,* or by the *bye,* that is, by the way, in passing; an odd or side run gained at cricket.—**by-blow,** *n.* A side or accidental blow (*Mil.*); an illegitimate child (vulgar).—**bygone,** bī'gon, *a.* Past; gone by.—*n.* What is gone by and past.—**byname,**‡ *n.* Nickname.—**bypast,** bī'past, *a.* Past; gone by. (*Shak.*)—**bypath, byroad, bystreet, byway,** *n.* A path, road, street, or way which is secondary to a main road, street, etc.; a lesser, private, or obscure way.—**byplay,** *n.* Action carried on aside, and commonly in dumb show, while the main action proceeds; action not intended to be observed by some of the persons present.—**by-product,** *n.* A secondary product; something obtained, as in a manufacturing process, in addition to the principal product or material.—**bystander,** *n.* One who stands by or near; an onlooker or spectator; one present but taking no part in what is going on.—**byword,** *n.* A common saying; a proverb.

bylaw, byelaw, bī'la, *n.* [From the Scand. *by,* a town, the termination in Whit-*by* and other names, and *law ;* Dan. *by-lov,* a municipal law; Sw. *by-lag,* a by-law.] A law made by an incorporated body, as a railroad company, for the regulation of its own affairs, or the affairs entrusted to its care.

byre, bīr, *n.* [A Scandinavian word= E. *bower.*] A cow house. [Scotch.]

byssus, bis'us, *n.* pl. **byssi,** bis'ī. [L. *byssus,* Gr. *byssos,* fine linen or cotton.] *Zool.* A long, lustrous, and silky bunch of filaments by which certain bivalve mollusks, as the oyster, are attached to fixed objects; *bot.* the stipe of certain fungi.

Byzantine, biz·an'tin or biz'an·tīn, *a.* Pertaining to *Byzantium,* at one time the capital of the Eastern Roman Empire, afterward Constantinople, now, Istanbul, the largest city and seaport of the Turkish Republic.

C

C, c, sē, the third letter in the English alphabet and the second of the consonants, originally having the sound of *k*, now having also the sharp sound of *s* (before *e, i,* and *y*); *music,* the name of the first or key note of the modern normal scale, answering to the *do* of the Italians and the *ut* of the French.

Caaba, kä′a·ba, *n.* [Ar. from *ka'b,* a cube.] An oblong stone building forming the great temple at Mecca, containing at the northwest corner the famous black stone (an aerolite), presented in Arab tradition by the angel Gabriel to Abraham.

cab, kab, *n.* [Heb.] A Hebrew dry measure containing according to one estimate 2 pints, according to another 4.

cab, kab, *n.* [Abbrev. of *cabriolet.*] A closed four-wheel vehicle, usually for public hire; a taxicab. The covered part of a locomotive.

cabal, ka·bal′, *n.* [Fr. *cabale,* the *cabala,* an intrigue, a cabal. CABALA.] Intrigue; secret artifices of a few persons united in some design; a number of persons united in some close design, usually to promote their private views in church or state by intrigue; a junto; specifically, a name given to a ministry of Charles II., consisting of Clifford, Ashley, Buckingham, Arlington, and Lauderdale, the initials of whose names happened to compose the word.—*v.i.*—*caballed, caballing.* To form a cabal; to intrigue; to unite in secret artifices to effect some design.

cabala, cabbala, kab′a·la, *n.* [Heb. *qabbâlâ,* reception, the cabala or mysterious doctrine received traditionally, from *qâbal,* to take or receive.] A mysterious kind of science or learning among Jewish rabbis, transmitted by oral tradition, serving for the interpretation of difficult passages of Scripture.—**cabalism,** kab′al·izm, *n.* The science of the cabalists.—**cabalist,** kab′al·ist, *n.* A Jewish doctor who professes the study of the cabala.—**cabalistic, cabalistical,** kab·al·ist′ik, kab·al·ist′-ik·al, *a.* Pertaining to the cabala; containing an occult meaning.

cabaret, kab′a·rā, *n.* [Fr.] A restaurant where dancers and singers entertain.

cabbage, kab′ij, *n.* [O.E. *cabbish, cabage,* from Fr. *cabus,* O.Fr. *choux cabus,* a large-headed cabbage—*cabus, cabuce,* large-headed, from L. *caput,* a head.] A well-known vegetable of several varieties, the kinds most cultivated being the common cabbage, the savoy, the broccoli, and the cauliflower; the common cabbage forms its leaves into dense rounded heads, the inner leaves being blanched.—*v.i.* To form a head like that of a cabbage in growing.

cabbage palm, cabbage tree, *n.* A West Indian palm, having a simple unbranched slender stem growing to a great height, and so called from the young unexpanded leaves being eaten as a vegetable.

cabbage, kab′ij, *v.t.*—*cabbaged, cabbaging.* [Fr. *cabasser,* to put in a *cabas* or basket; hence, to hoard, steal. CABAS.] To purloin, especially to purloin pieces of cloth after cutting out a garment.—*n.* A cant name for anything filched, more particularly, cloth purloined by one who cuts out garments.

cabbala, cabbalism, etc., *n.* See CABALA, CABALISM, etc.

cabby, kab′i, *n.* Driver of cab. (Colloq.)

caber, kā′ber, *n.* [Gael. *cabar,* a pole, a stake, a rafter.] In Highland games, a long undressed stem of a tree, used for tossing as a feat of strength.

cabin, kab′in, *n.* [From W. *caban,* a cabin, dim. of *cab,* a kind of hut; Ir. and Gael. *caban,* a cabin.] A small room or enclosed place; a cottage; a hut or small house or habitation, especially one that is poorly constructed; an apartment in a ship for officers or passengers—*v.i.* To live in a cabin; to lodge. (Shak.)—*v.t.* To confine as in a cabin. (Shak.)—**cabin boy,** *n.* A boy whose duty is to wait on the officers and passengers on board a ship.

cabinet, kab′in·et, *n.* [Fr. *cabinet,* a closet, receptacle of curiosities, etc., a dim. form, ultimately from the Celtic. CABIN.] A small room, closet, or retired apartment; a private room in which consultations are held; hence, the select or secret counsel of a prince or executive government; [*often cap.*] the collective body of ministers who direct the government of a nation or country: so called from the apartment in which the meetings were originally held; a piece of furniture consisting of a chest or box, with drawers and doors.—**cabinet-maker,** *n.* A man whose occupation is to make household furniture, such as cabinets, sideboards, tables, etc.

cable, kā′bl, *n.* [Fr. *câble,* a rope, from L.L. *capulum, caplum,* a rope, a halter, from L. *capio,* to take.] A large strong rope, usually of 3 or 4 strands of hemp, or a chain, such as is used to retain a vessel at anchor; a cablegram; *arch.* a molding with its surface cut in imitation of the twisting of a rope; also, a cylindrical molding in the flute of a column and partly filling it.—*Cable's length,* a United States nautical measure, 720 feet or 120 fathoms.—*Sub-marine,* or *electric telegraph cable,* a cable by which telegraphic messages are conveyed through the ocean, usually composed of a single wire of pure copper, or of several wires, embedded in a compound of gutta-percha and resinous substances, so as to be compacted into one solid strand, encircled by layers of gutta-percha or india rubber, hemp or jute padding, and coils of iron wire.—*v.t.*—*cabled, cabling.* To fasten with a cable; to send a message by electric cable; *arch.* to fill (the flutes of columns) with cables or cylindrical pieces.—**cablegram,** kā′bl·gram, *n.* A message by cable.

cabob, ka·bob′, *n.* [Per.] An oriental dish, consisting generally of a neck or loin of mutton cut in pieces and roasted, dressed with onions, eggs, spices, etc.

caboose, ka·bös′, *n.* [From D. *kabuis,* a caboose or ship's galley; Dan., Sw. *kabys, kabyssa,* a caboose. L.G. *kabuse, kabüse,* a little room or hut; probably from same root as *cabin.*] The cookroom or kitchen of a ship; last car of a freight train.

cabriole, kab′ri·ōl, *n.* [Fr. *cabriole,* a goat-leap; L.L. *capriolus,* a goat, from L. *caper,* a goat.] A leap or curvet of a horse; a capriole.—**cabriolet,** kab·rē·o·lā′, *n.* [Fr. *cabriolet,* dim. from *cabriole,* a goat-leap.] A one-horse carriage; a cab.

cacao, ka·kā′ō, *n.* [Fr. Sp. Pg. *cacao,* from Mexican *cacauatl, cacao.*] The chocolate tree, a small tree 16 to 18 feet high, a native of the West Indies, and much cultivated in the tropics of both hemispheres on account of its seeds, from which cocoa (a corruption of the word *cacao*) and chocolate are prepared.

cachalot, kash′a·lot or kash·a·lō, *n.* [Fr. *cachalot,* from Catalan *quichal,* a tooth, lit. therefore toothed whale.] A very large cetaceous mammal, the blunt-headed sperm whale, having a head of enormous size, containing a large receptacle filled with spermaceti; sperm oil and ambergris are also obtained from this animal.

cache, kash, *n.* [Fr.] A hole in the ground in which travelers hide and preserve provisions which it is inconvenient to carry.

cachet, ka·shā′, *n.* [Fr., from *cacher,* to conceal.] A seal.—*Lettre de cachet,* a private letter of state; a name given especially to letters bearing the private seal of the French kings, often employed as arbitrary warrants of imprisonment for an indefinite period.

cachexy, cachexia, ka·kek′si, ka·kek′si·a, *n.* [Gr. *kachexia,* from *kakos,* ill, and *hexis,* habit, from *echō,* to have.] A morbid state of the bodily system, the result of disease or of intemperate habits.—**cachectic, cachectical,** ka·kek′tik, ka·kek′tik·al, *a.* Having or pertaining to cachexy.

cachinnation, kak·in·nā′shon, *n.* [L. *cachinnatio,* from *cachinno,* to laugh; imitative of the sound.] Loud or immoderate laughter.

cachou, ka·shö′, *n.* [Fr. Same as *cashew.*] A sweetmeat generally in the form of a pill, and made of the extract of licorice, cashew nut, gum, etc., used to remove an offensive breath.

cachucha, ka·chö′cha, *n.* [Sp.] A Spanish dance similar to the bolero, a piece of music for it.

cacique, ka·sēk′, *n.* The native name of the princes or head chiefs of Haiti, Cuba, Peru, Mexico, and other regions of America, who were found reigning there when these countries were discovered.

cackle, kak′l, *v.i.*—*cackled, cackling.* [D. and L.G. *kakelen,* Sw. *kackla,* Dan. *kagle;* of imitative origin like *giggle, cachinnation,* etc.] To utter a noisy cry such as that often made by a goose or a hen; to laugh with a broken noise, like the cackling of a goose; to giggle; to prate; to prattle; to tattle.—*n.* The broken cry of a goose or hen; idle talk; silly prattle.—**cackler,** kak′lėr, *n.* A fowl that cackles; a telltale; a tattler.

cacodemon, cacodaemon, kak·o-dē′mon, *n.* [Gr. *kakos,* evil, and *daimōn,* a demon.] An evil spirit; a devil. (*Shak.*)

cacodyle, kak′o·dil, *n.* [Gr. *kakos,* bad, *odōdē,* smell, and *hylē,* matter.] A compound of hydrocarbon and arsenic; a clear liquid of an insupportably offensive smell and poisonous vapor.

cacoëthes, kak·ō·ē′thēz, *n.* [L. *cacoethes,* from Gr. *kakoēthes,* a bad habit, an itch for doing something—*kakos,* vicious, and *ēthos,* custom, habit.] A bad custom or habit.—*Cacoethes scribendi,* a diseased propensity for writing; an itch for authorship.

cacophony, ka·kof′o·ni, *n.* [Gr. *kakophōnia*—*kakos,* bad, and *phōnē,* sound, voice.] A disagreeable vocal sound; discord.—**cacophonous,** ka·kof′o·nus, *a.* Sounding harshly.

cactus, kak′tus, *n.* [L., from Gr, *kaktos,* a prickly plant.] A succulent. spiny, and usually leafless shrub of numerous species, natives of tropical America, the fruit of some being edible, and many being cultivated in conservatories for their showy flowers and curious stems.—**cactaceous,** kak·tā′shus, *a.* Relating to or resembling the cactus.

cad, kad, *n.* [An abbreviation of *cadet.*] A slang term applied originally to various classes of persons of a low grade, as hangers-on about inn yards, messengers or errand boys, etc.; now extended to any mean, vulgar fellow of whatever social rank.

cadastre, ka·das′tėr, *n.* [Fr. *cadastre,* a survey and valuation of property, from L.L. *capitastrum,* register for a poll tax, from L. *caput,* the head.] A detailed survey of a country, as the basis of an assessment for fiscal purposes, etc.

cadaver, ka·da′vėr, *n.* [L. *cadere,* to fall.] A dead body.—**cadaverous,** ka·dav′ėr·us, *a.* Of or like a cadaver; pale; sickly; especially, having the appearance or color of a dead human body; pale; wan; ghastly.—**cadaverously,** ka·dav′ėr·us·li, *adv.* In a cadaverous manner.—**cadaverousness,** ka·dav′ėr·us·nes, *n.*

caddice, caddis, kad′is, *n.* [From W. *cadach,* a rag, *cadas,* a kind of cloth, from the rough or ragged covering of the larva.] The larva of the caddice fly.—**caddice fly, caddis fly,** *n.* A neuropterous insect, called also the *May fly,* the larva or grub of which forms for itself a case of small roots, stalks, stones, shells, etc., and lives under water till ready to emerge from the pupa state.

caddie, caddy, kad′i, *n.* One who carries clubs for a golfer.—*v.i.* to serve as a caddie.—**caddy,** *n.* A small box for keeping tea.

cadence, kā′dens, *n.* [L.L. *cadentia,* a falling, from L. *cado,* to fall.] A decline; *Chance* is the same word.] A decline;

a state of falling or sinking; the general tone or modulation of the voice in reading or reciting; tone; sound; rhythm; measure; *mus.* a short succession of notes or chords at the close of a musical passage or phrase; also a shake or trill, run, or division, introduced as an ending or as a means of return to the first subject.—**cadent,**‡ kā′dent, *a.* Falling down; sinking. (*Shak.*)—**cadenza,** ka·den′za, *n.* [It.] *Mus.* an embellishment made at the end of a melody, either actually extempore or of an impromptu character; also, a running passage at the conclusion of a vocal piece.

cadet, ka·det′, *n.* [Fr. *cadet,* O.Fr. *capdet,* contr. from L.L. *capitettum,* dim. of L. *caput,* the head; lit. little head or chief.] A younger or youngest son; a junior male member of a noble family; a young man in training for the rank of an officer in the army or navy; cadets of the U. S. Naval Academy at Annapolis are officially called *midshipmen.*—**cadetship,** ka·det′ship, *n.* The state of being a cadet; the rank or office of a cadet.

cadge, kaj, *v.t.* and *i.* [Perhaps from noun *cadger.*] To carry about for sale; to hawk, go about begging.

cadger, kaj′ėr, *n.* [Perhaps from O.Fr. *cagier,* one who carried about falcons or other birds in a *cage* for sale.] An itinerant huckster or hawker.

cadi, käd′i or kā′di, *n.* [Turk.] A judge in civil affairs among the Turks; usually the judge of a town or village.

Cadmean, kad·mē′an, *a.* Relating to *Cadmus,* a legendary prince of ancient Greece, who is said to have introduced the sixteen simple letters of the Greek alphabet, thence called *Cadmean* letters.—*Cadmean victory,* a victory in which the victors suffer as much as the vanquished.

cadmium, kad′mi·um, *n.* [L. *cadmia,* Gr. *kadmia, kadmeia,* calamine.] A metallic element, malleable, ductile, and looking like tin. Symbol, Cd; at. no., 48; at. wt., 112.40.

cadre, kä′dr, *n.* [Fr. from L. *quadra,* a square.] The permanent skeleton or frame-work of a regiment, which may be filled up as need requires.

caduceus, ka·dū′sē·us, *n.* [L.] Mercury's rod represented as a winged rod entwisted by two serpents, in modern times used as a symbol of a physician.—**caducean,** ka·dū′sē·an, *a.* Belonging to the caduceus or wand of Mercury.

caducous, ka·dū′kus, *a.* [L. *caducus,* from *cado,* to fall.] Having a tendency to fall or decay; specifically applied to organs of animals and plants that early drop off, as branchiae, floral envelopes, etc.

caecum, sē′kum, *n.* pl. **caeca,** sē′ka. [L. *caecus,* blind.] The blind gut or intestine; a branch of an intestine with one end closed; mammals have generally only one caecum, birds usually two caeca, while in fishes they are often numerous.—**caecal,** sē′kal, *a.* Of or belonging to the caecum; having the form of a caecum; bagshaped.

Caesar, sē′zėr, *n.* A title, originally a surname of the Julian family at Rome, which, after being dignified in the person of the dictator C. Julius Caesar, was adopted by successive Roman emperors, and latterly came to be applied to the heir presumptive to the throne; personification of the civil power, the State.—**Caesarean,** sē·zâ′rē·an, *a.* Of or pertaining to Caesar.—*Caesarean operation,* the operation by which the fetus is taken out of the uterus by an incision through the abdomen and uterus, when delivery of a living child is otherwise impossible; said to be so named because Julius Caesar was brought into the world in this way.—**Caesarism,** sē′zėr·izm, *n.* Despotic sway exercised by one who has been raised to power by popular will; imperialism.

caesium, sē′zi·um, *n.* [L. *caesius,* blue.] A rare metal originally discovered in mineral waters, and so named because its spectrum exhibits two characteristic blue lines. It is always found in connection with rubidium.

caesura, sē·zū′ra, *n.* [L. *caesura,* a cutting, from *caedere, caesum,* to cut.] A pause or division in a verse; a separation, by the ending of a word or by a pause in the sense, of syllables rhythmically connected.

cafe, ka·fā′, *n.* [F. *café,* coffee.] A coffee house; a restaurant.—**cafeteria,** ka′fe·tēr″i·ä, *n.* A self-service restaurant.

caffeic, ka·fē′ik, *a.* Of or pertaining to coffee.—**caffeine,** ka·fē′in, *n.* A slightly bitter alkaloid found in coffee, tea, etc., which, when taken in large doses, is poisonous.

caftan. See KAFTAN.

cage, kāj, *n.* [Fr. *cage,* from L. *cavea,* a hollow, from *cavus,* hollow (whence E. *cave*).] A box, or enclosure, a large part of which consists of latticework of wood, wicker, wire, or iron bars, for confining birds or beasts; a prison or place of confinement for petty malefactors‡; a skeleton framework of various kinds; the framework of a hoisting apparatus, as the framework in which miners ascend and descend the shaft, and by which hutches are raised and lowered.—*v.t.*—**caged, caging.** To confine in a cage; to shut up or confine.—**cageling,** kāj′ling, *n.* A bird kept in a cage; a cage bird.

caiman, *n.* See CAYMAN.

Cain, kān, *n.* [Biblical.] Murderer, fratricide.

Cainozoic, kā·no·zō′ik, *a.* [Gr. *kainos,* recent, and *zōē,* life.] *Geol.* a term applied to the latest of the three divisions into which strata have been arranged, with reference to the age of the fossils they include, embracing the tertiary and posttertiary systems.

caïque, ka·ēk′, *n.* [Fr. from Turk. *kaik.*] A light skiff used in the Bosporus, where it almost monopolizes the boat traffic.

cairn, kârn, *n.* [Gael. Ir. W. *carn,* a heap, a cairn.] A heap of stones, common in Scotland and Wales, and generally of a conical form, erected as a sepulchral monument, to commemorate some event, as a landmark, etc.

cairngorm, Cairngorm stone, kärn'-gorm, *n.* A yellow or brown variety of rock crystal, found in great perfection on *Cairngorm* and the neighboring mountains in Scotland, and much used for brooches, seals, and other ornaments.

caisson, kās'son, *n.* [Fr., *caisson*, from *caisse*, a chest, a case, from L. *capsa*, a chest.] A wooden chest filled with explosives to be fired when approached by an enemy; also, an ammunition wagon, or an ammunition chest; a vessel in the form of a boat used as a floodgate in docks; a watertight structure or case filled with air and placed under sunken vessels to raise them; a kind of floating dock; a watertight box or cylindrical casing used in founding and building structures in water too deep for the cofferdam, such as piers of bridges, quays, etc.

caitiff, kā'tif, *n.* [O.Fr. *caitif*, captive, unfortunate; from L. *captivus*, a captive, from *capere*, to take.] A mean villain; a despicable knave; one who is both wicked and mean.—*a.* Belonging to a caitiff; servile; base.

cajeput, kaj'i·put, *n.* [Malay *kâyû*, a tree, and *putih*, white.] A pungent, volatile oil, having stimulant and antispasmodic properties, obtained from the cajeput tree of the Moluccas.

cajole, ka·jōl', *v.t.*—*cajoled*, *cajoling*. [Fr. *cajoler*, to cajole; O.Fr. *cageoler*, to sing or chatter like a bird in a cage, from *cage*.] To deceive or delude by flattery, specious promises, etc.; to wheedle; to coax.—**cajoler,** ka·jōl'ẽr, *n.* One who cajoles; a wheedler.—**cajolery,** ka·jōl'ẽr·i, *n.* The act of cajoling; coaxing language or tricks; a wheedling to delude.

cake, kāk, *n.* [Icel. and Sw. *kaka*, Dan. *kage*, D. *koeck*, G. *kuchen*, cake; probably from L. *coquere*, to cook. COOK.] A mass of fine light dough baked, and generally sweetened or flavored with various ingredients; something made or concreted in the form of a cake; a mass of matter in a solid form relatively thin and extended.—*To take the cake*, complete the victory, to surpass. (Colloq.) —*v.t.*—*caked*, *caking*. To form into a cake or mass.—*v.i.* To concrete or become formed into a hard mass, as dough in an oven, etc.

calabash, kal'a·bash, *n.* [Pg. *calabaca*, Sp. *calabaza*, from Ar. *qar*, a gourd, and *aibas*, dry.] A gourd shell dried; the fruit of the calabash tree; a vessel made of a dried gourd shell or of a similar shell, used for containing liquors or goods, as pitch, resin, and the like.—**calabash tree,** *n.* A name of several American trees bearing large gourdlike fruits, the hard shells of which are made into numerous domestic utensils, as basins, cups, spoons, bottles, etc.

calamander wood, kal·a·man'dẽr, *n.* [Supposed to be a corruption of *Coromandel*.] A beautiful species of wood, a kind of ebony obtained from a Ceylonese tree resembling rosewood, and so hard that it is worked with great difficulty.

calamint, kal'a·mint, *n.* [Gr. *kalaminthe*, *kalaminthos*.] A name for labiate plants akin to mint.

calamity, ka·lam'i·ti, *n.* [L. *calamitas*, *calamitatis*.] Any great misfortune or cause of misery; a disaster accompanied with extensive evils; misfortune; mishap; affliction; adversity.—**calamitous,** ka·lam'i·tus, *a.* [Fr. *calamiteux*, L. *calamitosus*.] Producing or resulting from calamity; making wretched; distressful; disastrous; miserable; baleful.—**calamitously,** ka·lam'i·tus·li, *adv.* In a calamitous manner.—**calamitousness,** ka·lam'i·tus·nes, *n.*

calamus, kal'a·mus, *n.* [L. *calamus*, a reed, a reed pen; same root as in E. *haulm*.] A reed or reedlike plant; a perennial tufted Indian grass, called also sweet-scented lemon grass, yielding an aromatic oil used in perfumery; the root of the sweet rush; the generic name of the palms yielding rattans.

calash, ka·lash', *n.* [Fr. *calèche*, from G. *kalesche*, a word of Slavonic origin: Bohem. *kolesa*, Pol. *kolaska*.] A light carriage with very low wheels and a folding top; the folding hood or top fitted to such a carriage; a kind of headdress worn by ladies, and consisting of a frame of cane or whalebone covered with silk.

calcaneum, kal·kā'nē·um, *n.* [L., the heel.] *Anat.* the largest bone of the tarsus; the bone that forms the heel.

calcar, kal'kär, *n.* [L. *calcar*, a spur, from *calx*, *calcis*, the heel.] *Bot.* a spur; a hollow projection from the base of a petal.—**calcarate,** kal'ka·rāt, *a. Bot.* furnished with a spur, as the corolla of larkspur.

calcar, kal'kär, *n.* [L. *calcaria*, a limekiln, from *calx*, lime.] A kind of oven or reverberating furnace, used in glassworks for the calcination of sand and salt of potash, and converting them into frit.

calcareous, kal·kā'rē·us, *a.* [L. *calcarius*, from *calx*, lime.] Partaking of the nature of, having the qualities of, containing calcium carbonate.

calceoralia, kal·sē·o·lā'ri·a, *n.* [L. *calceolus*, a slipper, from the shape of the inflated corolla resembling a shoe or slipper.] The generic name of a number of ornamental herbaceous or shrubby plants, natives of South America, and now very common in gardens, most having yellow flowers, some puce colored, and some with the two colors intermixed, while others are white.

calcic, kal'sik, *a.* [L. *calx*, *calcis*, lime.] Of or pertaining to lime; containing calcium. — **calciferous,** kal·sif'ẽr·us, *a.* [L. *calx*, and *fero*, to produce.] Producing or containing lime, especially when in considerable quantity (*calciferous* strata).—**calcification,** kal·si·fi·kā'shon, *n.* A changing into lime; the process of changing into a stony substance by the disposition of lime.—**calcify,** kal'si·fī, *v.i.*—*calcified*, *calcifying*. [L.

calx, and *facio*, to make.] To become gradually changed into a stony condition by the deposition or secretion of lime.—*v.t.* To make stony by depositing lime.—**calcimine,** kal'si·mīn, *n.* [From L. *calx*.] A superior kind of white or colored wash for the walls of rooms, ceilings, etc.—**calcine,** kal·sīn', *v t.*—*calcined*, *calcining*. [Fr. *calciner*, from L. *calx*.] To reduce to a powder or to a friable state by the action of heat, to free from volatile matter by the action of heat, as limestone from carbonic acid, iron ore from sulfur; to oxidize or reduce to a metallic calx.—*v.i.* To be converted into a powder or friable substance by the action of heat.—**calcination,** kal·si·na'shon, *n.* The act or operation of calcining.—**calcite,** kal'sīt, *n.* A term applied to various minerals, including limestone, all the white and most of the colored marbles, chalk, Iceland spar, etc.—**calcium,** kal'si·um, *n.* [From L. *calx*.] A silver-white metallic element occurring only in combination such as in limestone, milk, bones, etc. Symbol, Ca; at. no., 20; at. wt., 40.08.— *Calcium carbide*, a compound of calcium and carbon used in the preparation of acetylene.—*Calcium carbonate*, a mineral occurring in bones and teeth.—*Calcium chloride*, a compound of calcium and chloride used as a drying agent and in refrigeration.

calc-sinter, kalk'sin·tẽr, *n.* [L. *calx*, lime, and G. *sinter*; a stalactite.] A stalactitic calcium carbonate, a variety of calcite, consisting of deposits from springs holding calcium carbonate in solution.—**calc-spar,** kalk'-spär, *n.* Calcareous spar, or crystallized calcium carbonate.—**calc-tuff,** kalk'tuf, *n.* An alluvial formation of calcium carbonate.

calculate, kal'kū·lāt, *v.t.*—*calculated*, *calculating*. [L. *calculo*, *calculatum*, from *calculus*, a counter or pebble used in calculations, from *calx*, a small stone, a counter.] To ascertain by computation; to compute; to reckon up; to estimate (value, cost); to make the necessary or usual computations regarding (an eclipse, etc.); to fit or prepare by the adaptation of means to an end; to make suitable: generally in pp. in this sense=suited or suitable; adapted (a scheme *calculated* to do much mischief).—*v.i.* To make a computation; to weigh all the circumstances; to deliberate.—**calculable,** kal'kū·la·bl, *a.* Capable of being calculated or ascertained by calculation.—**calculating,** kal'kū·lāt·ing, *a.* Having the power or habit of making arithmetical calculations; given to forethought and calculation; deliberate and selfish; scheming (a *calculating* disposition).—**calculation,** kal·kū·lā'shon, *n.* The act of calculating; the art or practice of computing by numbers; reckoning; computation; a series of arithmetical processes set down in figures and bringing out a certain result; estimate formed by comparing the circumstances bearing on the matter in hand.—**calculative**, kal´kū·lā·tiv, *a.* Pertaining to calculation; tending to calculate.—**calculator**, kal´kū·lā·tėr, *n.* One who calculates.

calculus, kal´kū·lus, *n.* pl. **calculi**, kal´kū·lī. [L., a pebble used for calculating, from *calx*, a small stone, a counter.] A general term for hard concretions of various kinds formed in various parts of the body, the more important being those formed in the gall bladder, called *biliary calculi* or gallstones, and those formed by a deposition from the urine in the kidney or bladder, called *urinary calculi*; the stone; gravel; a method of mathematical computation using algebraic symbols.—**calculous**, kal´kū·lus, *a.* Stony; gritty; hard like stone; arising from calculi, or stones in the bladder.

caldron, **cauldron**, kal´dron, *n.* [O.Fr. *caldron* = Sp. *calderon*, It. *calderone*, from L. *caldus*, *calidus*, hot.] A large kettle or boiler of copper or other metal.

calefacient, kal·i·fā´shi·ent, *a.* [L. *calefacio*, to make warm, from *caleo*, to be warm, and *facio*, to make.] Warming; heating.—*n.* That which warms or heats; *med.* a substance which excites a degree of warmth in the part to which it is applied, as mustard, pepper, etc.—**calefaction**, kal·i·fak´shon, *n.* The act or operation of warming or heating; the state of being heated.—**calefactive**, **calefactory**, kal·i·fak´tiv, kal·i·fak´te·ri, *a.* Adapted to make warm or hot; communicating heat.

calendar, kal´en·dėr, *n.* [L. *calendarium*, an account book, a calendar, from *calendae*, the first day of each month, the calends; root in *calo*, Gr. *kalein*, to call.] A register of the year, in which the months, weeks, and days are set down in order, with the feasts observed by the church, etc.; an orderly table or enumeration of persons or things, as a list of criminal causes which stand for trial; a list; a catalogue; a register.—*v.t.* To enter or write in a calendar; to register.—**calends**, kal´endz, *n.* pl. [L. *calendæ*.] Among the Romans the first day of each month.—*The Greek calends*, a time that never occurred or never will occur, a phrase which originated in the fact that the Greeks had nothing corresponding to the Roman calends.

calender, kal´en·dėr, *n.* [Fr. *calandre*, L.L. *celendra*, a calender, from L. *cylindrus*, Gr. *kylindros*, a cylinder.] A machine consisting of two or more cylinders revolving so nearly in contact with each other that cloth or paper passing through between them is smoothed and glazed by their pressure.—*v.t.* To press or finish in a calender.—**calenderer**, kal´en·dėr·ėr, *n.* A person who calenders cloth.

calender, kal´en·dėr, *n.* [From the founder of the order.] One of an order of dervishes in Turkey and Persia, of not very strict morals,

nor held in very high esteem by the Mohammedans.

calenture, kal´en·tūr, *n.* [Fr. *calenture*, Sp. *calentura*, heat, a calenture, from *calentar*, to heat, from L. *caleo*, to be hot.] A kind of delirium caused within the tropics, especially on board ship, by exposure to excessive heat.

calescence, ka·les´ens, *n.* [From L. *calesco*, to grow warm, incept. of *caleo*, to be hot.] Growing warmth; growing heat.

calf, käf, *n.* pl. **calves**, kävz. [A.Sax. *cealf* = D. *kalf*, Icel. *kálfr*, Sw. *kalf*, Dan. *kalv*, G. *kalb*, a calf.] Properly the young of the cow or the bovine genus of quadrupeds, but applied also to the young of the marine mammalia, as the whale; an ignorant, stupid person; a dolt; a weak or cowardly man; leather made from the skin of a calf.—**calf love**, *n.* A youthful romantic passion or affection.—**calfskin**, *n.* The hide or skin of a calf; leather made of the skin.

calf, käf, *n.* [Icel. *kálfi*, the calf of the leg.] The thick fleshy part of the leg behind, below the knee.

caliber, **calibre**, kal´i·bėr, *n.* [Fr. *calibre*, possibly from Ar. *kâlib*, Pers. *kâlab*, a mould.] The diameter of a body, as of a column or a bullet; usually the diameter of the bore of a firearm; *fig.* compass or capacity of mind; the extent of one's intellectual endowments.—*Caliber-compasses*, *calibers*, or *callipers*, compasses made either with arched legs to measure the diameters of cylinders or globular bodies, or with straight legs and points turned outward to measure the interior diameter or bore of anything.—**calibrate**, kal´i·brāt, *v.t.* To ascertain the caliber of.—**calibration**, kal·i·brā´shon, *n.* The act or process of calibrating, especially of ascertaining the caliber of a thermometer tube, with the view of graduating it to a scale.

calico, kal´i·kō, *n.* [From *Calicut* in India, whence the cloth was first introduced.] A printed cotton cloth; originally, a white cotton cloth imported from India.

calif, **caliph**, kā´lif, *n.* [Fr. *calife*, from Ar. *khalîfa*, successor, from *khalafa*, to succeed.] A title given to the acknowledged successors of Mohammed, regarded among Mohammedans as being vested with supreme dignity and power in all matters relating to religion and civil policy. Written also *Kalif*, *Khalif*, etc.—**califate**, kal´i·fāt, *n.* The office or dignity of a calif; the government of a calif. Written also *Kalifate*, *Caliphate*.

californium, kal´i·for˝ni·um, *n.* [From California, the university and state where first identified.] A radioactive element. Symbol, Cf; at. no., 98.

caliginous, ka·lij´i·nus, *a.* [L. *caliginosus*, from *caligo*, *caliginis*, darkness.] Dim; obscure; dark.

calipash, kal´i·pash, *n.* [A form of *calabash*, with sense of *carapace*, the upper shell of the tortoise.] That part of a turtle which belongs to the

upper shield, consisting of a fatty, gelatinous substance of a dull, greenish color; spelled also *Callipash*.—**calipee**, kal´i·pē, *n.* That part of a turtle which belongs to the lower shield, of a light yellow color; spelled also *Callipee*.

caliph, **caliphate**, *n.* See CALIF, CALIFATE.

calisaya, kal·i·sā´a, *a.* A name for the yellow, or orange-yellow, febrifugal barks of several species of cinchona trees, consisting of the inner bark.

calisthenics, kal·is·then´iks, *n.* [Gr. *kalos*, beautiful, and *sthenos*, strength.] The art or practice of taking exercise for health, strength, or grace of movement.—**calisthenic**, kal·is·then´ik, *a.* Relating to calisthenics.

calk, **caulk**, kak, *v.t.* [O.E. *cauke*, O.Fr. *cauquer*, to tread, from L. *calcare*, to tread, to tread on, from *calx*, *calcis*, a heel.] To drive oakum into the seams of (a ship or other vessel), to prevent leaking, the seams being then smeared with melted pitch.—**calker**, **caulker**, ka´kėr, *n.* One who calks.

calk, kak, *n.* [Perhaps from L. *calcar*, a spur, from L. *calx*, the heel.] The prominent part of either extremity of a horseshoe, bent downward and brought to a sort of point; the semicircular ring of iron nailed on to the heel of a strong shoe or boot.—**calk**, kak, *v.t.* To furnish with a calker or calkin.

call, kal, *v.t.* [A.Sax. *ceallian* = Icel. and Sw. *kalla*, Dan. *kalde*, to call; D. *kallen*, to talk, to prattle; same root as Gr. *gēryō*, to cry; Skr. *gar*, to call.] To name; to denominate: with the name or appellation as well as the person or thing named; to pronounce the name of; to designate or characterize as; to affirm to be; to invite or command to come or assemble (a person, a cab, a meeting); to summon; to select or appoint, as for an office, duty, or employment; to invoke or appeal to; to arouse, as from sleep; to awaken; to proclaim or utter loudly.—*To call back*, to recall; to summon or bring back.—*To call forth*, to bring or summon to action (one's energies).—*To call in*, to collect (as debts or money); to draw from circulation (coin).—*To call names*, to use opprobrious epithets to.—*To call out*, to challenge to a duel; to summon into service or action (the military).—*To call over*, to go over by reading aloud name by name.—*To call to mind*, to recollect; to revive in memory.—*To call up*, to bring into view or recollection; to recall; to require payment of.—*v.i.* To utter a loud sound; or to draw a person's attention by name; often with *to*; to make a short stop or pay a short visit; often followed by *at*, *for*, or *on*.—*To call at*, to visit a place in passing; *to call for* (a person or thing) is to visit in order to obtain the company of the person to some other place, or to get the thing; also, to demand, require, claim (crime *calls for* punishment).—*To call on* or *upon*, to visit (a person); to demand from or appeal to; to invoke.—*To call out*, to utter in a loud voice; to bawl.—*n.* A summons or invitation made vocally or by an instrument; a demand; requisition; claim (the *calls* of justice or humanity; *calls* on one's time); divine vocation or summons; invitation or request to a clergyman by a congregation to become their minister; a short or passing visit paid to a person; the cry of a bird to its mate or young; a whistle or pipe used by a boatswain and his mate to summon sailors to their duty; a pipe to call birds by imitating their voice.—**callboy,** *n.* A boy whose duty it is to call actors on to the stage at the proper moment.—**caller,** kạl′ẽr, *n.* One who calls.—**calling,** kạl′ing, *n.* A vocation; profession; trade; usual occupation or employment; a collective name for persons following any profession; state of being divinely called (N.T.).

calligraphy, kal·lig′ra·fi, *n.* [Gr. *kalligraphia—kalos*, beautiful, and *graphō*, to write.] The art of beautiful writing; fair or elegant writing or penmanship.—**calligrapher, calligraphist,** kal·lig′ra·fẽr, kal·lig′ra·fist, *n.* One skilled in calligraphy.—**calligraphic,** kal·i·graf′ik, *a.* Relating to calligraphy.

calliope, ka·lī′o·pē, *n.* A set of musical whistles, played like an organ.

callipash, kal′i·pash. See CALIPASH.

callisthenic, callisthenics. See CALISTHENIC, CALISTHENICS.

callous, kal′us, *a.* [L. *callosus*, from *callus, callum*, hard thick skin. CALLID.] Hardened or thickened from continuous pressure or friction: said of the skin; having a hardened skin; hence, hardened in mind or feelings; insensible; unfeeling.—**callosity,** kal·los′i·ti, *n.* [L. *callositas*.] The state or quality of being hardened or indurated; any thickened or hardened part on the surface of the human body or that of any other animal; any part of a plant unusually hard.—**callously,** kal′us·li, *adv.* In a callous, hardened, or unfeeling manner.—**callousness,** kal′us·nes, *n.* The state or character of being callous; insensibility; apathy; indifference.—**callus,** kal′us, *n.* A callosity; a new growth of osseous matter between the extremities of fractured bones; any part of a plant unusually hard; the new formation over the end of a cutting before it sends forth rootlets.

callow, kal′ō, *a.* [A.Sax. *calu*, bald = D. *kaal*, Sw. *kal*, G. *kahl*, bald; cog. L. *calvus*, bald.] Destitute of feathers, as a young bird; naked; unfledged; pertaining to the condition of a young bird.

calm, käm, *a.* [Fr. *calme*, calm, from L.L. *cauma*, the heat of the sun, hence the hot part of the day, the time for rest; from Gr. *kauma*, heat, from *kaiō*, to burn.] Still; quiet; undisturbed; not agitated; not stormy: said of the weather, the sea, etc.;

undisturbed by passion; not agitated or excited in feeling; tranquil, as the mind, temper, etc.—*n.* Freedom from motion, agitation, or disturbance; stillness; tranquility; quiet; especially, a state or period at sea when there is neither wind nor waves.—*Region of calms* or *calm latitudes*, the tracts in the Atlantic and Pacific Oceans on the confines of the trade winds, where calms of long duration prevail.—*v.t.* To make calm; to still; to quiet; to appease, allay, or pacify (grief, anger, anxiety, etc.); to becalm (*Shak.*).—*v.i.* To become calm or serene.—**calmly,** käm′li, *adv.* In a calm manner; without agitation; quietly.—**calmness,** käm′nes, *n.* The state of being calm, quiet, or unruffled; quietness; stillness; tranquility.

calomel, kal′o·mel, *n.* [Gr. *kalos*, fair, good, and *melas*, black, perhaps because it was good for black bile.] A preparation of mercury, a compound of this metal and chlorine, usually in the form of a whitish powder, much used in medicine.

caloric, ka·lor′ik, *n.* [L. *calor*, heat.] In chemistry and physics, an obsolete term referring to the hypothetical fluid to which heat and combustion were attributed.—*Caloric engine*, an engine similar in principle to the steam engine, the motive power being the expansive force of heated air.—**calorie,** kal′o·rē, *n.* The quantity of heat, equivalent to 1/860 watthour, required to raise a gm. of water one degree C.; or the quantity required to raise a kg. of water the same amount (called a kilocalorie), used to express the heat-producing or energy value of food.—**calorific,** kal·o·rif′ik, *a.* Capable of producing heat; causing heat; heating.—*Calorific rays*, invisible rays emanating from the sun, manifested only by their effects on the thermometer.

calorimeter, kal·o·rim′e·tẽr, *n.* [L. *calor*, heat, and Gr. *metron*, measure.] An apparatus for measuring absolute quantities of heat.—**calorimetric,** ka·lor′i·met″rik, *a.* Of or belonging to the use of the calorimeter.—**calorimetry,** kal·o·rim′et·ri, *n.* The art or process of using the calorimeter.

calotte, ka·lot′, *n.* [Fr. *calotte*, a skull-cap, dim. of *cale*. CAUL.] A skull-cap worn by ecclesiastics, etc.

caloyer, kal′o·yẽr, *n.* [Fr. from Mod. Gr. *kalogeros*, from Gr. *kalos*, beautiful, and *gerōn*, Mod. Gr. *geros*, an old man.] One of a sect of monks of the Greek Church.

caltrop, kal′trop, *n.* [L.L. *calcitrapa*, from L. *calx, calcis*, a heel, and L.L. *trappa*, a snare.] *Milit.* an instrument with four iron points disposed in such a manner that any three of them being on the ground the other points upward, used as an obstacle to the advance of troops; *bot.* a term applied to several plants from the resemblance of their heads or fruits to the military instrument.

calumet, kal′u·met, *n.* [Fr. *calumet*, from L. *calamus*, a reed.] The

North American Indians' pipe of peace, the smoking of which was a pledge of amity and good faith.

calumniate, ka·lum′ni·āt, *v.t.*—*calumniated, calumniating.* [L. *calumnior, calumniatus*, to calumniate, from *calumnia*, calumny.] To speak evil of falsely; to cast aspersions on; to charge falsely and knowingly with some crime, offense, or something disreputable; to slander.—*v.i.* To propagate evil reports with a design to injure the reputation of another.—**calumniation,** ka·lum′ni·ā″shon, *n.* The act of calumniating; calumny.—**calumniator,** ka·lum′ni·ā″tẽr, *n.* One who calumniates or slanders.—**calumniatory, calumnious,** ka·lum′ni·ā″to·ri, ka·lum′ni·us, *a.* Using calumny; containing or implying calumny; injurious to reputation; slanderous.—**calumniously,** kalum′ni·us·li, *adv.* In a; calumnious manner; slanderously.—**calumny,** kal′um·ni, *n.* [L. *calumnia*.] False accusation of a crime or offense, knowingly or maliciously made or reported, to the injury of another; a defamatory or slanderous report; slander; defamation.

Calvary, kal′vâ·ri, *n.* [L. *calvaria*, a skull, from *calva*, a bare scalp.] Golgotha, the place where Christ was crucified, west of Jerusalem.

calve, käv, *v.i.*—*calved, calving.* [From *calf* = D. *kalven*, Dan. *kalve*, to calve.] To bring forth a calf or calves: used specifically of cows, whales, and seals.

Calvinism, kal′vin·izm, *n.* The theological tenets or doctrines of *Calvin*, the celebrated reformer, and his followers, among the distinguishing doctrines of whose system are, predestination, original sin, the irresponsible sovereignty of God, etc.—**Calvinist,** kal′vin·ist, *n.* A follower of Calvin; one who embraces the theological doctrines of Calvin.—**Calvinistic,** kal·vin·ist′ik, *a.* Pertaining to Calvin or to his opinions in theology.

calx, kalks, *n.* pl. **calxes, calces,** kalk′sēz, kal′sēz, [L. *calx*, limestone.] Lime or chalk; an old term for the substance of a metal or mineral which remains after being subjected to violent heat or calcination; an oxide; lime recently prepared by calcination; broken and refuse glass, which is restored to the pots in glassmaking.

calypso, ka·lip′sō, *n.* [Origin uncertain.] A type of improvised, often satirical folksong native to the West Indies.

calyptra, ka·lip′tra, *n.* [Gr. *kalyptra*, a veil or covering.] *Bot.* the hood of the theca or capsule of mosses.

calyx, kā′liks, *n.* pl. **calyces, calyxes,** kā′li·sēz, kā′lik·sez, [L. *calyx*, from Gr. *kalyx*, a calyx, a covering.] *Bot.* the exterior covering of a flower within the bracts and external to the corolla, which it encloses and supports, and consisting of several verticillate leaves called sepals, either united or distinct, usually of a green color and of a less delicate texture than the corolla.—**calycinal,**

ch, *chain*; *ch*, Sc. lo*ch*; g, *go*; j, *job*; ng, sing; TH, *then*; th, *thin*; w, *wig*; hw, *whig*; zh, azure.

calycine, ka·lis´i·nal, kal´i·sīn, *a.* *Bot.* pertaining to a calyx; situated on a calyx.—**calycle**, kal´ı·kl, *n.* [L. *calyculus*, dim. of *calyx*.] *Bot.* an outer accessory calyx, or set of leaflets or bracts looking like a calyx; *zool.* same as *Calice.*

cam, kam, *n.* [O.E. *camb*, a comb, a crest; comp. Dan. *kam-hiul*, G. *kamm-rad*, a cogweel, from *kam*, *kamm*, a comb.] *Mach.* A projecting part of a wheel or other revolving piece so placed as to give an alternating motion, especially in a rectilinear direction, to another piece (often a rod) that comes in contact with it and is free to move only in a certain direction. The eccentric is a kind of cam.

camaraderie, kam´a·räd·ėr·ē, *n.* [Fr.] Mutual good fellowship as comrades.

camarilla, kam·a·ril´a, Sp. pron. ka·ma·rēl´ya, *n.* [Sp., a small room, a dim. from *camara*, L. *camera*, *camara*, a vault. CHAMBER.] A company of secret counselors or advisers; a cabal; a clique.

camber, kam´bėr, *n.* [Fr. *cambrer*, to arch, to vault, from L. *camera*, a vault.] A convexity upon an upper surface, as a ship's deck, a bridge, a beam, a lintel; the curve of a ship's plank.—*Camber window*, a window arched at the top.—*v.t.* To arch; to bend; to curve ship planks.

cambist, kam´bist, *n.* [Fr. *cambiste*, from L. *cambio*, to exchange. CHANGE.] One who has to do with exchange, or is skilled in the science of exchange; one who deals in notes and bills of exchange; a banker.

cambium, kam´bi·um, *n.* [L. *cambio*, to exchange, from the alterations occurring in it.] The layer of soft tissue between the bark and the wood of vascular plants that produces new secondary growth.

Cambrian, kam´bri·an, *a.* Relating or pertaining to Wales or *Cambria.*— *n.* A Welshman; a series of strata on the base of the Paleozoic system of rocks.

cambric, kām´brik, *n.* A species of fine white linen fabric, said to be named from *Cambray* in Flanders.

came, kām, pret. of *come.*

camel, kam´el, *n.* [L. *camelus*, from Gr. *kamelos*, from Heb. *gâmâl*, camel.] A large hoofed quadruped of the ruminant class, with one or two humps on its back, used in Asia and Africa for carrying burdens, and for riding on; a watertight structure placed beneath a vessel in the water, being first filled with water and sunk, after which the water is pumped out, when the camel gradually rises, lifting the vessel with it.

camellia, ka·mel´i·a, or ka·mēl´ya, *n.* [After George Joseph *Kamel*, a Moravian Jesuit.] A genus of beautiful trees or shrubs belonging to the tea family, with showy flowers somewhat resembling the rose, and elegant dark-green, shining, laurel-like leaves.

camelopard, ka·mel´o·pärd or kam´-el·o·pard, *n.* [L. *camelus*, a camel, and *párdalis*, a leopard.] The giraffe.

cameo, kam´ē·ō, *n.* [It. *cameo*, *cammeo*, from L.L. *cammæus*, a word of uncertain origin.] A stone or shell composed of several different colored layers having a subject in relief cut upon one or more of the upper layers, an under layer of a different color forming the ground.

camera, kam´ėr·a, *n.* [L., a vault, a chamber, from Gr. *kamara*, anything arched. CHAMBER.] An apparatus that takes photographs by means of a light-proof enclosure fitted with a lens that focuses the image of an object on light-sensitive film or plates; the part of a television transmitter in which images to be televised are converted into electric impulses.—*Camera lucida* [L., lit. clear chamber], an optical instrument for facilitating the delineation of distant objects, by producing a reflected picture of them upon paper by means of a glass prism suitably mounted, and also for copying or reducing drawings.—*Camera obscura* [L., dark chamber], an apparatus in which the images of external objects, received through a double-convex lens, are exhibited in their natural colors, on a white surface placed at the focus of the lens.

camisade, kam·i·sād´, *n.* [Fr. *camisade*, Sp. *camisado*, O.Fr. *camise*, a shirt. CHEMISE.] A shirt worn by soldiers over their armor in a night attack to enable them to recognize each other; an attack by soldiers wearing the camisade; an attack made in the dark.

camisole, kam´i·sōl, *n.* [Fr. dim. or O.Fr. *camise*, L.L. *camisa*, a chemise.] A short light garment worn by ladies when dressed in *negligee*; strait jacket for lunatics or criminals condemned to the guillotine.

camlet, kam´let, *n.* [Fr. *camelot*, from *camel.*] A stuff originally made of camel's hair, now made sometimes of wool, sometimes of silk, sometimes of hair, especially that of goats, with wool or silk.

camomile, kam´o·mīl, *n.* Any plant of the genus *Anthemis*, especially *Matricaria chamomilla*. Foliage and flowers are strong-scented and contain essential oils of medicinal value.

camouflage, kam´ö·fläzh, *n.* [Fr.] The art of disguising; especially the art of disguising material in warfare. —*v.* To alter the appearance so as to mislead or render difficult to recognize.

camp, kamp, *n.* [Fr. *camp*, a camp, formerly a field, from L. *campus*, a plain. *Campaign*, *champion*, *de-camp*, *scamper*, are from same source.] The place where an army or other body of men is or has been encamped; the collection of tents or other erections for the accommodation of a number of men, particularly troops in a temporary station; an encampment.—*v.t.*† To put into or lodge in a camp, as an army; to encamp; to afford camping ground for (*Shak.*). *v.i.* To live in a camp, as an army; to encamp.— **camp follower**, *n.* One who follows

or attaches himself or herself to a camp or army without serving.— **camp meeting**, *n.* In *Amer.*- a religious meeting in the open air, where the frequenters encamp for some days for continuous devotion. —**campstool**, *n.* A stool with crossed legs, so made as to fold up when not used.

campaign, kam·pān´, *n.* [Fr. *campagne* country, open country, campaign, from L. *campania*, a level country, *campus*, a plain. CAMP.] An open field or open plain‡; the time, or the operations of an army during the time it keeps the field in one season.—*v.i.* To serve in a campaign; a political, commercial or other contest.—**campaigner**, kam-pān´er, *n.* One who has served in an army in several campaigns.

campanile, kam·pa·nē´la, or kam´-pa·nīl, *n.* pl. **campanili**, kam·pa-nē´lē. [It. *campanile*, from It. and L.L. *campana*, a bell.] *Arch.* a clock or bell tower; a term applied especially to detached buildings in some parts of Italy, erected for the purpose of containing bells.

campanology, kam·pa·nol´o·ji, *n.* [L.L. *campana*, a bell, and Gr. *logos*, discourse.] The art or principles of bell ringing; a treatise on the art.— **campanologist**, kam·pa·nol´o·jist, *n.* One skilled in the art of bell ringing or campanology.

campanula, kam·pan´ū·la, *n.* [L.L., a dim. of *campana*, a bell, from form of the corolla.] The bellflowers, a large genus of herbaceous plants, with bell-shaped flowers usually of a blue or white color.—**campanulate**, kam·pan´ū·lāt, *a.*

camphene, kam´fēn, *n.* The commercial term for purified oil of turpentine, obtained by distilling the oil over quicklime to free it from resin, and used in lamps.

camphor, kam´fėr, *n.* [L.L. *camphora*, L.Gr. *kaphoura*, from Ar. *kâfûr*, camphor, said to be from a Malay word signifying chalk.] A whitish translucent substance belonging to the class of vegetable oils, with a bitterish aromatic taste and a strong characteristic smell, found in many plants and sometimes secreted naturally in masses, obtained also by distillation of the wood, and used in medicine as a diaphoretic, antispasmodic, etc.—**camphorate**, kam´fėr·āt, *v.t.* To impregnate with camphor.—**camphoric**, kam·for´ik, *a.* Pertaining to or obtained from camphor, or partaking of its qualities.

campion, kam´pi·on, *n.* [Probably from L. *campus*, a field.] The popular name of certain English plants belonging to the genera *Lychnis* and *Silene*, such as bladder campion, sea campion, rose campion, etc.

campus, kam´pus, *n.* [L. field.] The grounds and buildings of a school or college.

can, kan, *v.i.*—pret. *could.* [A.Sax. *can*, pres. ind. of *cunnan*, to know, to know how to do, to be able; *could* = O.E. *coude* (with *l* erroneously inserted), A.Sax. *cúthe*, pret. of *cunnan*. Akin D. *kunnen*, to be able;

Sw. *kunna*, Dan. *kunde*, Icel. *kunna*, to know, to be able; G. *können*, to be able. The root is the same as that of *ken* and *know*. KNOW.] (A verb now used only as an auxiliary and in the indicative mood.) To be able, physically, mentally, morally, legally, or the like; to possess the qualities, qualifications, or resources necessary for the attainment of any end or the accomplishment of any purpose, the specific end or purpose being indicated by the verb with which *can* is joined.—*Can but*, can do no more than; can only (we *can but* fail).—*Cannot but*, cannot help doing or being; cannot refrain from (*cannot but* remember, *cannot but* acknowledge).

can, kan, *n.* [A.Sax. *canne*=D. *kan*, Icel. *kanna*, G. *kanne*, a can.] A rather indefinite term applied to various vessels of no great size, now more especially to vessels made of sheet metal, for containing liquids, preserves, etc.—*v.t.*—canned, canning. To put into a can (to *can* preserved meat, fruit, etc.).

Canaanite, kā′nan·īt, *n.* An inhabitant of the land of *Canaan*; specifically, one of the inhabitants before the return of the Israelites from Egypt.—**Canaanitish,** kā·nan·īt′ish, *a.* Of or pertaining to Canaan or the Canaanites.

Canadian, ka·nā′di·an, *a.* Pertaining to Canada.—*n.* An inhabitant or native of Canada.—*Canadian balsam, Canada balsam,* a fluid resin mixed with a volatile oil, obtained from fir trees, and much valued for optical purposes on account of its perfect transparency and its refractive power.—*Canada rice,* a plant growing in deep water in the northern states of America and Canada, the seeds of which form much of the food of the American Indians, and of the great flocks of waterfowl.

canaille, ka·nāl′ or ka·nä′ya, *n.* [Fr., from It. *canaglia*, a pack of dogs, from L. *canis*, a dog.] The lowest orders of the people; the rabble; the vulgar.

canal, ka·nal′, *n.* [Fr. *canal*, from L. *canalis*, a channel, from the same root as Skr. *khan*, to dig.] An artificial watercourse, particularly one constructed for the passage of boats or ships; *arch.* a channel; a groove or a flute; *anat.* any cylindrical or tubular cavity in the body through which solids, liquids, or certain organs pass; a duct; *zool.* a groove observed in different parts of certain univalve shells.—**canaliculate, canaliculated,** kan·a·lik′ū·lāt, kan·a·lik′ū·lāt·ed, *a.* [L. *canaliculatus* from *canaliculus*, a little pipe, from *canalis*.] Channelled; furrowed; grooved.—**canalize,** ka·nal′īz, *v.t.* To make a canal through (to *canalize* an isthmus); to make like a canal, to *canalize* a river.—**canalization,** ka·nal′i·zā′shon, *n.* The act of canalizing.

canard, kä·när′ or ka·närd′, *n.* [Fr., a duck, from L.L. *canardus*, a kind of boat, from G. *kahn*, a boat or skiff.] An absurd story which one attempts to impose on his hearers or readers; a false rumor set afloat by way of news.

canary, ka·nâ′ri, *n.* Wine made in the Canary Islands; an old dance introduced from the Canary Islands into Europe; a singing bird, belonging to the finch family, a native of those islands, and which has long been very common as a cage bird in various countries.—**canary grass,** *n.* A kind of grass, a native of the Canary Isles, the seeds of which are much used under the name of *Canary seed*, as food for cage birds.

canasta, ka·nas′ta, *n.* [Sp. basket.] A card game, similar to rummy, played with two decks of 52 cards and four jokers.

cancan, kan′kan, *n.* A kind of French dance performed by men and women, who indulge in extravagant postures and lascivious gestures.

cancel, kan′sel, *v.t.*—cancelled, cancelling. [Fr. *canceller*, to cancel; whence also *chancel*, *chancellor*.] To draw lines across (something written) so as to deface; to blot out or obliterate; to annul or destroy (an obligation, a debt); to throw aside as no longer useful (sheets of a printed book, etc.).—*n.* Latticework‡; that which is cancelled or thrown aside.—**cancellation,** kan·sel·lā′shon, The act of cancelling.

cancer, kan′sėr, *n.* [L., a crab, a cancer.] *Pathol.* a general term for any malignant growth, most tending to metastasize; any destructive condition; *astron.* [cap.] one of the twelve signs of the zodiac.—**cancerous,** kan′sėr·us, *a.* Like a cancer; having the qualities of a cancer; virulent.—**cancroid,** kang′kroid, *a.* Like cancer: applied to morbid growths somewhat like cancer, but not really cancerous.—*n.* A skin disease approaching in its nature to cancer.

candelabrum, kan·de·lä′brum, *n.* pl. **candelabra,** kan·de·lä′bra, [L., from *candela*, a candle.] A tall candlestick; a stand by which lamps were supported; a branched highly ornamental candlestick; a chandelier.

candent, kan′dent, *a.* [L. *candens*, *candentis*, from *candeo*, to be white or hot. CANDID.] Heated to whiteness; glowing with white heat.—**candescence,** kan·des′ens, *n.* [L. *candesco*, incept. of *candeo*.] A state of glowing; incandescence.

candid, kan′did, *a.* [L. *candidus*, white, bright, frank, sincere, from *candeo*, to be white; akin to *incense*, *incendiary*, etc.] White‡; honest and frank; open and sincere; ingenuous; outspoken; fair; just; impartial.—*A candid friend*, a person disposed to tell unpleasant truths or to say ill-natured things under the guise of candor.—**candid camera,** a small camera of hand size with powerful lens and quick shutter that permits the photographing of unposed pictures.—**candidly,** kan′did·li, *adv.* Openly; frankly.—**candid-ness,** kan′did·nes, *n.* Candor.—**candor,** kan′dėr, *n.* The quality or trait of being candid; readiness to make known anything relating to one's self; openness of heart; frankness; sincerity.

candidate, kan′di·dāt, *n.* [L. *candidatus*, from *candidus*, white; those who sought offices in Rome wearing a white robe during their candidature.] A person who aspires or is put forward by others as an aspirant to an office or honor.—**candidature, candidacy,** kan′di·dā·chėr, kan′di·da·si, *n.* The state of being, or act of standing as, a candidate.

candle, kan′dl, *n.* [L. *candela*, a candle, from *candere*, to shine. CANDID.] A taper; a cylindrical body of tallow, wax, spermaceti, or other fatty material, formed on a wick, and used for a portable light.—*Not fit to hold the candle to one*, not fit to act as a mere attendant; to be very inferior.—*The game is not worth the candle*, a phrase of French origin, indicating that an object is not worth the pains requisite for its attainment.—**candleberry, candlenut,** *n.* The fruit of the candleberry tree, a name given to several species of myrtle, especially the wax myrtle, a shrub common in North America, the berries of which are covered with a greenish-white wax, of which candles are made.—**candlefish,** *n.* A small sea fish of the salmon family, frequenting the northwestern shores of America, so extremely oily that it is used for making oil, and as a natural candle. whence its name.—**candle power,** *n.* The illuminating power of a candle, taken as a unit in estimating the luminosity of any illuminating agent (as gas), the standard usually employed being a spermaceti candle burning at the rate 120 grains of sperm per hour.—**Candlemas,** kan′dl·mas, *n.* [So named from the blessing or consecration of candles on this day, in the R. Cath. Ch.] An ecclesiastical festival held on the second day of February in honor of the purification of the Virgin Mary; in *Scot.* a quarterly money term.—**candlestick,** kan′dl·stik, *n.* An instrument to hold a candle when burning, made in different forms and of different materials.—**candlewood,** *n.* The wood of a West Indian resinous tree.

candor. See CANDID.

candy, kan′di, *n.* [It. *candi*, candy, from Ar. *qandi*, made of sugar, from *qand*, sugar.] A solid preparation of sugar or molasses, either alone or in combination with other substances, to flavor, color, or give it the desired consistency.—*v.t.*—candied, candying. To conserve with sugar so as to form a thick mass; to boil in sugar; to form into congelations or crystals.—*v.i.* To become incrusted by candied sugar; to become crystallized or congealed.—**candied,** kan′did, *p.* and *a.* Preserved or incrusted with sugar; *fig.* honeyed, flattering; glozing.

candytuft, kan′di·tuft, *n.* [From *Candia*, the ancient Crete.] The popular name of a tufted flower brought from the island of Candia.

cane, kān, *n.* [Old spelling also *canne*, from L. *canna*, Gr. *kanna*, a reed.] A term applied to the stems of some palms, grasses, and other plants, such as the bamboo, rattan, and sugarcane; a cane used as a walking stick.—*v.t.—caned, caning.* To beat with a cane or walking stick. to furnish or complete with cane (as chairs).—**canebrake,** *n.* A thicket of canes.—**cane sugar,** *n.* Sugar obtained from the sugarcane, as distinguished from beet root sugar, grape sugar, maple sugar, etc.

canella, ka·nel′la, *n.* [Dim. of L. *canna*, a reed, from the cylindrical form of the bark when peeled off.] A kind of aromatic bark, also called white cinnamon, brought from the West Indies and used as a tonic.

canescent, ka·nes′ent, *a.* [L. *canescens, canescentis,* ppr. of *canesco,* to grow white, from *caneo,* to be white.] Growing white or hoary; tending or approaching to white; whitish.

canine, kā′nīn, *a.* [L. *caninus,* from *canis,* a dog.] Pertaining to dogs; having the properties or qualities of a dog.—*Canine teeth,* or *canines,* two sharp pointed teeth in both jaws of man and other mammalia, one on each side, between the incisors and grinders, most highly developed in the Carnivora.

canister, kan′is·tėr, *n.* [L. *canistrum,* Gr. *kanastron,* from *kanna,* a reed.] A small basket‡; a small box or case, usually of tin, for tea, coffee, etc.; a case containing shot which bursts on being discharged; case shot.

canker, kang′kėr, *n.* [From L. *cancer,* properly pronounced *canker,* a crab, a cancer.] A kind of cancerous, gangrenous, or ulcerous sore or disease, whether in animals or plants; an eating, corroding, or other noxious agency producing ulceration, gangrene, rot, decay, and the like; anything that insidiously or persistently destroys, corrupts, or irritates, as care, trouble, annoyance, grief, pain, etc.; a kind of wild, worthless rose; the dog rose (*Shak.*).—*v.t.* To infect with canker either literally or figuratively; to eat into, corrode or corrupt; to render ill-conditioned, crabbed, or ill-natured.—*v.i.* To grow corrupt; to be infected with some poisonous or pernicious influence; to be or become malignant.—**cankerous,** kang′kėr·us, *a.* Corroding, destroying, or irritating like a cancer; cancerous.—**cankerworm,** *n.* A worm or larva destructive to trees or plants.

cannel coal, kan′el·kōl, *n.* A glistening grayish-black hard bituminous coal, so called because it burns with a bright flame like a candle; it is chiefly used in making gas.

cannery, kan′ėr·i, *n.* An establishment for canning or preserving meat, fish, or fruit in tins hermetically sealed.

cannibal, kan′i·bal, *n.* [Sp. *canibal,* a

cannibal, a corruption of *Caribal,* a Carib, the Caribs being reputed cannibals.] A human being that eats human flesh; a man-eater or anthropophagite; an animal that eats the flesh of its own or kindred species.—**cannibalism,** kan′i·bal··izm, *n.* The act or practice of eating human flesh by mankind; anthropophagy; murderous cruelty.

cannon, kan′un, *n. pl.* **Cannons** or **cannon.** [Fr. *canon,* a tube, barrel, cannon, from L. *canna,* Gr. *kanna,* a cane or reed. Akin *canister, canon, cane.*] A large military firearm for throwing balls and other missiles by the force of gunpowder; a big gun or piece of ordnance; *billiards,* the act of hitting your adversary's ball with your own, so that your ball flies off and strikes the red, or vice versa.—*v.i.* To make a cannon at billiards; to fly off or asunder from the force of collision.—**cannonade,** kan·un·ād′, *n.* The act of discharging cannon and throwing balls, for the purpose of destroying an army or battering a town, ship, or fort.—*v.t.* and *i.—cannonaded, cannonading.* To attack with ordnance or artillery; to batter with cannon.—**cannoneer,** kan·un·ēr′, *n.* A man who manages cannon.—**cannoneering,** kan·un·ēr′ing, *n.* The act or art of using cannons; practice with cannons.—**cannon bone,** *n.* (1) In horses, etc., the large metacarpal or metatarsal of the single digit. (2) In ruminants, the bone formed by fusion of third and fourth metacarpals or metatarsals. —**cannon shot,** *n.* A ball or shot for cannon; the range or distance a cannon will throw a ball.—**cannon ball,** *n.* A ball or solid projectile to be thrown from cannon.

cannot, kan′ot. *Can* and *not.* [These words are usually written as one word, being colloquially so pronounced.]

cannula, kan′ū·la, *n.* [L., dim. of *canna,* a reed.] A small tube used by surgeons for various purposes.—**cannular,** kan′ū·lėr, *a.* Having the form of a cannula or small tube.

canny, kan′i, *a.* [Akin to *can, ken.*] Cautious; prudent; wary; watchful; expert; not extortionate or severe; gentle; quiet in disposition; tractable; easy; comfortable.

canoe, ka·nö′, *n.* [Sp. *canoa,* from the native West Indian name.] A light narrow boat made by hollowing out and shaping the trunk of a tree, such as is used by savage tribes; any light boat narrow in the beam, and propelled by paddles.—**canoeist,** ka·nö′ist, *n.* One who uses a canoe.

canon, kan′on, *n.* [A.Sax. *canon,* from L. *canon,* Gr. *kanōn,* a straight rod, a rule or standard—from *kanē,* a form of *kanna, kannē,* a reed, a cane, whence also *cannon.*] A law or rule in general; a law or rule regarding ecclesiastical doctrine or discipline, especially one enacted by a council and duly confirmed; the books of the Holy Scriptures universally received as genuine by

Christian churches; the rules of a religious order; a dignitary who possesses a prebend or revenue allotted for the performance of divine service in a cathedral or collegiate church; the catalogue of saints acknowledged in the Roman Catholic Church; *mus.* a kind of perpetual fugue, in which the different parts, beginning one after another, repeat incessantly the same air; *printing,* one of the largest kinds of type or letter, supposed to be so named because it was used in the printing of canons.—**canoness,** kan′on·es, *n.* A female canon; a woman who enjoys a prebend without having to make religious vows.—**canonical,** ka·non′ik·al, *a.* Pertaining or according to a canon or rule, especially according to ecclesiastical canons or rules; belonging to the canon of Scripture.—*Canonical books,* those books of the Bible which are admitted to be of divine origin.—*Canonical hours,* hours appointed in Roman Catholic Church by canon law for the celebration of marriage, 8 a.m. to 3 p.m. Also the times, from midnight onward, at which certain parts of the daily service are recited. They are matins, prime, tierce, sext, nones, vespers, and compline (*Ps.* cxix. 164: 'Seven times a day do I praise thee').—**canonically,** ka·non′ik·al·li, *adv.* In a canonical manner; in accordance with a canon or canons.—**canonicals,** ka·non′ik·alz, *n. pl.* The dress or habit prescribed by canon to be worn by the clergy when they officiate; certain articles or appurtenances of dress sometimes worn by university men, English barristers, etc. —**canonicity,** kan·o·nis′i·ti, *n.* The quality of being canonical; the state of belonging to the canon or genuine books of Scripture.—**canonist,** kan′on·ist, *n.* A professor of canon law; one skilled in the study and practice of ecclesiastical law.—**canonistic,** kan·o·nis′tik, *a.* Pertaining to the canonists.—**canonization,** kan′on··i·zā″shon, *a.* The act of canonizing a person; the act of ranking a deceased person in the catalogue of saints, called a canon.—**canonize,** kan′on·īz, *v.t.—canonized, canonizing.* To declare a man a saint, and rank him in the catalogue or canon of saints, this act being in the power of the popes.—**canonry, canonship,** kan′on·ri, kan′on·ship, *n.* The benefice filled by a canon.—**canon law,** *n.* A collection of ecclesiastical constitutions for the regulation of a church; specifically those of the Roman Catholic Church.

canopy, kan′o·pi, *n.* [Fr. *canapé,* O.Fr. *conopé,* L. *conopeum,* Gr. *kōnōpeion,* lit. a net to keep off gnats, from *kōnōps,* a gnat.] A covering fixed at some distance above a throne or a bed; any somewhat similar covering; a covering held over a person's head in a procession or public ceremony; *arch.* a decoration, often richly sculptured, above a tomb, niche, pulpit, etc.— *v.t.—canopied, canopying.* To cover with a canopy, or as with a canopy.

canorous, ka·nō′rus, *a.* [L. *canorus*, from *cano*, to sing.] Musical; tuneful. —**canorousness,** ka·nō′rus·nes, *n.*

cant, kant, *v.i.* [From L. *canto*, freq. of *cano*, to sing.] To speak with a whining voice or in an affected, assumed, or supplicating tone (as a beggar); to make whining pretensions to goodness; to affect piety without sincerity; to sham holiness. —*n.* A whining manner of speech; the whining speech of beggars, as in asking alms; the language or jargon spoken by gypsies, thieves, professional beggars, etc.; a kind of slang; the words and phrases peculiar to or characteristic of a sect, party, or profession; a pretentious assumption of a religious character; a hypocritical addiction to the use of religious phrases, etc.; religious phrases hypocritically used.—*a.* Of the nature of cant or slang.— **canter,** kan′tėr, *n.* One who cants, whines, or uses an affected hypocritical style of speech.

cant, kant, *n.* [Same word as Dan. Sw. and D. *kant*, edge, border, margin, etc.; G. *kante*, a side, a border or brim; O.Fr. *cant*, corner, angle.] An external or salient angle; an inclination from a perpendicular or horizontal line; a toss, thrust, or push with a sudden jerk.—*v.t.* To turn about or over by a sudden push or thrust; to cause to assume an inclining position; to tilt; to toss; to cut off an angle from (a square block).

can't, kant. A colloquial contraction of *can not.*

Cantab, kan·tab′. An abbreviation of *Cantabrigian.* — **Cantabrigian,** kan·ta·brij′i·an, *n.* [L.L. *Cantabrigiensis*, pertaining to Cambridge.] A student or graduate of Cambridge University.

cantaloupe, kan′ta·lōp, *n.* [Fr. *canteloup*, from *Cantalupo*, Italian estate where grown.] A delicately flavored muskmelon.

cantankerous, kan·tang′kėr·us, *a.* [Comp. O.E. *contek, contak,* debate, strife.] Ill-natured; ill-conditioned; cross; waspish; contentious; disputatious. [Colloq.]—**cantankerously,** kan·tang′kėr·us·li, *adv.* In a cantankerous manner.—**cantankerousness,** kan·tang′kėr·us·nes, *n.*

cantata, kan·tä′tä, *n.* [It., from *cantare,* L. *cantare,* freq. of *cano,* to sing.] *Mus.* a short composition in the form of an oratorio, but without *dramatis personæ.*

canteen, kan·tēn′, *n.* [Fr. *cantine,* from It. *cantina,* a wine-cellar, a vault, from *canto,* an angle, a corner. CANT, an angle.] A shop in barracks, camps, garrisons, etc., where provisions, liquids, etc., are sold to noncommissioned officers and privates; a vessel used by soldiers, when on the march or in the field, for carrying liquid for drink; a box, fitted up with compartments, in which officers on foreign service pack bottles, knives, forks, etc.

canter, kan′tėr, *v.i.* [An abbrev. of *Canterbury Gallop,* the gallop of

pilgrims in olden times riding to Canterbury.] To move in a moderate gallop, raising the two forefeet nearly at the same time, with a leap or spring: said of horses.—*n.* A moderate gallop; a gallop by a winner at the end of an easy race.

Canterbury bell, *n.* A species of Campanula, so named because it is abundant around Canterbury.

cantharides, kan·thar′i·dēz, *n. pl.* [Gr. *kantharis, kantharidis,* a blistering fly.] Coleopterous insects of several species, the best known being the Spanish or blistering fly, which is, when bruised, extensively used as the active element in blistering plasters, having a very powerful effect.

canticle, kan′ti·kl, *n.* [L. *canticulum,* a little song, from *canto,* to sing. CANT.] A song, especially a little song; an unmetrical hymn taken from Scripture, arranged for chanting, and used in church service. [*cap.*] *pl.* The Song of Songs or Song of Solomon, one of the books of the Old Testament.

cantilever, kan′ti·lev·ėr, *n.* A beam or member projecting beyond a single support at one end; either of two beams projecting toward each other from piers to be joined to form the span of a cantilever bridge.

cantle, kan′tl, *n.* [O.Fr. *cantel,* cornerpiece, dim. of *cant.* CANT, an angle.] A corner; a fragment; a piece; a portion (*Shak.*); the protuberant part of a saddle behind; the hind-bow.—*v.t.*—*cantled, cantling.* To cut into pieces; to cut a piece out of.

canto, kan′tō, *n.* pl. **cantos,** kan′tōz, [It. *canto,* a song; L. *cantus.* CHANT, CANT.] A part or division of a poem of some length; *mus.* the highest voice part in concerted music.

canton, kan′ton, *n.* [Fr. *canton;* It. *cantone,* aug. of *canto,* a corner. CANT. CANTLE.] A distinct or separate portion or district of territory; one of the states of the Swiss republic; a distinct part or division, as of a painting or of a flag.—*v.t.* To divide into cantons or distinct portions; to separate off; to allot separate quarters to each regiment of.—**cantonal,** kan′ton·al, *a.* Pertaining to a canton or cantons.— **cantonment,** kan·ton′ment, *n.* A part or division of a town or village assigned to a particular regiment of troops; a permanent military station of a slighter character than barracks; military towns at some distance from any city, such as are formed in India.

cantor, kan′tor, *n.* [L. *cantor,* singer.] A leader of the singing in a cathedral or other church; a synagogue official in charge of music.

canvas, kan′vas, *n.* [Fr. *canevas,* Pr. *canabas,* It. *canavaccis,* L.L. *canabacius,* from L. *cannabis,* hemp.] A coarse cloth made of hemp or flax, used for tents, sails of ships, painting on, and other purposes; hence sails in general; a painting.— *Under canvas,* in a tent or tents;

with sails spread.—**canvasback,** *n.* A sea duck of North America, with delicate flesh: so called from the color of its back.

canvass, kan′vas, *v.t.* [From *canvas, canvas,* and formerly also a sieve, a strainer, because sieves were made of canvas; like O.Fr. *canabasser,* to examine, search, sift.] To examine; to scrutinize; to sift or examine by way of discussion; to discuss; to debate; to visit or apply to in order to obtain orders for goods, votes, or support for a candidate for an office or appointment, etc.— *v.i.* To seek or go about to solicit votes or interest, or to obtain mercantile orders.—*n.* The act of canvassing; close inspection; scrutiny; discussion; debate; a seeking; solicitation of votes, orders for goods, etc.—**canvasser,** kan′vas·ėr, *n.* One who canvasses or solicits votes, mercantile orders, etc.

canyon, cañon, kan′yun, kä·nyon′ *n.* [Sp. *cañon,* a canon, a tube, a canyon.] A narrow chasm with steep sides, formed by erosion.

canzonet, kan·zo·net′, *n.* [It. *canzonetta.*] *Mus.* a little or short song, shorter and less elaborate than airs of oratorio or opera; a short concerted air; a madrigal‡.

caoutchouc, kö′chök, *n.* [A South American word.] An elastic gummy substance, which is the inspissated juice of several tropical plants, much used in the industrial arts for covering fabrics to render them waterproof, making elastic webbing, flexible tubes, etc.: india rubber, gum elastic.

cap, kap, *n.* [A.Sax. *caeppe,* a cap, cope, cape, hood, from L.L. *capa, cappa* (of unknown origin), a cape, whence Sp. *capa,* It. *cappa,* Fr. *chape,* a cloak, cape, cover. *Cape* and *cope* are forms of the same word.] A part of dress made to cover the head, generally of softer material than a hat, and without a brim; an act of respect made by uncovering the head; the summit, top, or crown; anything resembling a cap in appearance, position, or use, as the inner case which covers the movement of some kinds of watches, etc.; a percussion cap (which see).—*v.t.*—*capped, capping.* To put a cap on; to cover with a cap or as with a cap; to cover the top or end of; to place a cap on the head of, when conferring official distinction, admitting to professional honors, etc.; to complete; to consummate; to crown; to follow up with something more remarkable than what has previously been done. —*To cap verses, texts,* or *proverbs,* to quote verses, texts, or proverbs alternately in emulation or contest.— *To set one's cap at,* to use measures to gain the affections of someone with a view to matrimony.

capable, kā′pa·bl, *a.* [Fr. *capable,* capable, able, sufficient L.L. *capabilis,* from L. *capio,* to take, which appears also in *captious, captive, accept, except, conception, susceptible, recipient, occupy,* etc.] Able to receive; open to influences; impressible; susceptible; admitting; with of (capable of pain, of being broken); having sufficient power, skill, ability: with of (capable of judging); able; competent; fit; duly qualified (a capable instructor).—**capability, capableness,** kā·pa·bil'i·ti, kā'pa·bl·nes, n. The state or quality of being capable.

capacious, ka·pā'shus, a. [L. capax, capacis, able to take in or contain, spacious, capable, from capio, to take. CAPABLE.] Capable of containing much, either in a physical or mental sense; large; wide; spacious; extensive; comprehensive.—**capaciously,** ka·pā'shus·li, adv. In a capacious manner or degree.—**capaciousness,** ka·pā'shus·nes, n. The state or quality of being capacious.— **capacitate,** ka·pas'i·tāt, v.t. —capacitated, capacitating. To make capable; to enable; to qualify.— **capacity,** ka·pas'i·ti, n. [L. capacitas, from capax, capacious.] The power of receiving or containing; specifically, the power of containing a certain quantity exactly; cubic contents; the extent or comprehensiveness of the mind; the power of receiving ideas or knowledge; the receptive faculty; active power; ability (a man with the capacity of judging); ability in a moral or legal sense; legal qualification (to attend a meeting in the capacity of an elector); character (to give advice in the capacity of a friend); used in phys. in various ways with the general notion of power of containing or receiving; in electrostatics, the capacity of a conductor is the quantity of electricity required to charge it to unit potential; in heat, the thermal capacity of a body of any mass is the quantity of heat required to raise its temperature one degree.

capacitor, ka·pas'i·tėr, n. Elect. a condenser.

cap-a-pie, kap·a·pē', adv. [O.Fr., lit. head to foot.] From head to foot; all over.

caparison, ka·par'i·son, n. [O.Fr. caparasson, from Sp. caparazon, a cover for a saddle, aug. of capa, a cover. CAP, CAPE.] A cloth or covering, more or less ornamented, laid over the saddle or furniture of a horse, especially a sumpter horse, or horse of state; hence, clothing, especially gay clothing.—v.t. To cover with a caparison; to adorn with rich dress.

cape, kāp, n. [O.Fr. cape, L.L. capa, a kind of covering for the shoulders. CAP.] The part of a garment hanging from the neck behind and over the shoulders; a loose cloak or garment, hung from the shoulders, and worn as a protection against rain, cold weather, etc.

cape, kāp, n. [Fr. cap, It. capo, a cape, from L. caput, the head.] A piece of land jutting into the sea or a lake beyond the rest of the coast line; a headland; a promontory; [usually cap.] by pre-eminence, the Cape of Good Hope, Cape Colony.

capeline, kap'e·lin, n. [Fr. capeline, hood, dim. from L. capa.] A kind of hood worn by ladies going to evening entertainments; a surgical bandage for the head.

caper, kā'pėr, n. [O.Fr. capriole, It. capriola, a caper, from L. caper, capra, a goat. Akin caprice, cab.] A leap; a skip; a spring, as in dancing or mirth, or in the frolic of a goat or lamb; a sportive or capricious action; a prank.—To cut capers; to leap or dance in a frolicsome manner; to act sportively or capriciously.— v.i. To cut capers; to skip or jump; to prance; to spring.—**caperer,** kā'pėr·ėr, n. One who capers.

caper, kā'pėr, n. [Fr. capre, O.Fr. cappre, L. capparis, Gr. kapparis, from Per. kabar, the caper.] The bud of a bush (the caperbush), pickled and used as a condiment; the plant itself, a low prickly shrub, growing in rocky or stony places in the countries bordering on the Mediterranean.—**caper tea,** n. A kind of black tea with a knotted curled leaf regarded as resembling the caper.

capercailzie, capercaillie, kā·pėr·kāl'yi, kā·pėr·kāl'ē, n. [Gael. capull-choile—capull, a horse, and coille, a wood—so named from its great size.] The wood grouse or cock of the woods, the largest of the gallinaceous birds of Europe.

Capetian, ka·pē'shan, a. Pertaining to the dynasty of the Capets, founded about the close of the tenth century, when Hugh Capet ascended the French throne.

capias, kā'pi·as, n. [L., you may take.] Law, a writ of various kinds authorizing a person or his goods to be laid hold of.

capillary, kap'il·la·ri or ka·pil'la·ri, a. [L. capillaris, from capillus, hair, from root of caput, the head.] Resembling a hair; fine, minute, small in diameter though long; filiform; as, a capillary tube, that is, a tube with a very minute bore; a capillary vessel in animal bodies (see the n.); pertaining to capillary tubes, or to the capillary vessels or capillaries in organic structures.—Capillary action, the spontaneous elevation or depression of liquids in fine hairlike tubes, or in bodies of a porous structure, when these are dipped in the liquid; the term capillary attraction being applied when the liquid rises, as the sap in trees, water in a sponge, etc.; and capillary repulsion when it sinks, as mercury does in a fine glass tube. —n. A tube with a small bore; a minute blood vessel constituting the termination of an artery or vein; one of the minute vessels which intervene between the terminal arteries and veins.—**capillarity,** kap·il·lar'i·ti, n. The state or condition of being capillary; capillary action.

capital, kap'i·tal, a. [L. capitalis, capital, deadly, also pre-eminent, from caput, capitis, the head, seen also in captain, chapter, chief, cadet, etc.] First in importance; chief; principal; notable; affecting the head or life (capital punishment); incurring the forfeiture of life (a capital

offense); punishable with death; excellent; very good; firstclass; splendid; a term applied to a type or letter of a certain form and a larger size than that generally used in the body of written or printed matter.—n. The uppermost part of a column, pillar, or pilaster, serving as the head or crowning, and placed immediately over the shaft and under the entablature; the chief city or town in a kingdom or state; a metropolis; a type or letter of a certain form, and of a larger size than that commonly used in the body of a piece of writing or printing; a capital letter; money or wealth in some shape employed in trade, in manufactures, or in any business; stock in trade, in money, goods, property, etc.; fig. stock of any kind, whether physical or moral; wealth; influence.—**capitalism,** kap'i·tal·izm, n. An economic system characterized by private ownership of natural resources and means of production.—**capitalist,** kap'i·tal·ist, n. One who owns or controls wealth; an advocate of capitalism.—**capitalistic,** kap'i·tal·is"tik, adj. Pertaining to capitalism or capitalists; based on or favoring capitalism.—**capitalization,** kap'i·tal·i·zā"shon, n. The act of capitalizing or being capitalized; the total investment in a business.— **capitalize,** kap'i·tal·īz, v.t.—capitalized, capitalizing. To write in capital letters; to convert into capital; to supply capital for; to turn to one's advantage.—**capitally,** kap'i·tal·li, adv. In a capital manner; excellently; so as to involve life; in a pre-eminent degree; excellently; finely.—**capitate,** kap'i·tāt, a. [L. capitatus.] Bot. growing in a head; having a rounded head; applied to a flower, etc.— **capitation,** kap·i·tā'shon, n. [L. capitatio.] Numeration by the head; a numbering of persons.—Capitation grant, a grant given to a certain number of persons, a certain amount being allowed for each individual among the number.—Capitation tax, a poll tax.

Capitol, kap'i·tol, n. [L. capitolium, from caput, the head.] In ancient Rome, the name of a hill crowned by a temple dedicated to Jupiter; the temple itself, in which the senate assembled; the edifice occupied by the United States Congress in their deliberations at Washington; [often not cap.] also, in some states the state house or house in which the legislature holds its sessions; a government house.—**Capitoline,** kap'i·tol·in, a. Pertaining to the Capitol in Rome.

capitular, capitulary, ka·pit'ū·lėr, ka·pit'ū·le·ri, n. [L.L. capitulare, from L. capitulum, a chapter, a capital. CAPITAL.] An act passed in a chapter, as of knights or canons; the body of laws or statutes of a chapter or of an ecclesiastical council; the member of a chapter.—**capitular,** ka·pit'ū·lėr, a. Belonging to a chapter; capitulary; bot. growing in a capitulum or head, as composite plants. —**capitularly,** ka·pit'ū·lėr·li, adv. In the form of an ecclesiastical chapter.

—**capitulary**, ka·pit′ū·la·ri, a. Relating to the chapter of a cathedral.
capitulate, ka·pit′ū·lāt, v.i.—capitulated, capitulating. [L.L. capitulo, capitulatum, to arrange in heads or chapters, from L. capitulum, a chapter, dim. of caput, the head.] To draw up articles of agreement; to arrange terms of agreement; to treat (Shak.); more usually to surrender, as an army or garrison, to an enemy on certain stipulated conditions.—**capitulation**, ka·pit′ū·lā′shon, n. The act of capitulating or surrendering to an enemy upon stipulated terms or conditions; the treaty or instrument containing the conditions of surrender; an article of agreement; formal agreement†.
capitulum, ka·pit′ū·lum, n. Bot. a close head of sessile flowers.
capon, kā′pon, n. [L. capo, Gr. kapōn—a capon, from a root seen in Gr. koptō, to cut.] A castrated cock; a cock-chicken castrated for the purpose of improving the flesh for table.—**caponize**, kā′pon·īz, v.t.—caponized, caponizing. To make a capon of.
capote, ka·pōt′, n. [Fr. capote, from cape, a hood or cape, L.L. capa. CAP.] A kind of long cloak. (Byron).
capreolate, kap′rē·ō·lāt, a. [From L. capreolus, a wild goat, a tendril of a vine, from caper, a goat.] Bot. having tendrils, or filiform spiral claspers, by which plants fasten themselves to other bodies, as in vines, etc.
capriccio, ka·prē′chō, n. [It., a caprice.] A caprice; a whim (Shak.); a musical piece in which the composer is guided more by fancy than by strict rule.
caprice, ka·prēs′, n. [Fr. caprice, It. capriccio, whim, freak, originally a fantastical goat leap, from L. caper, capra, a goat; akin caper, capriole.] A sudden start of the mind; a sudden change of opinion or humor; a whim or freak; capriciousness; fickleness.—**capricious**, ka·prish′us, a. Characterized by caprice; apt to change opinions suddenly, or to start from one's purpose; unsteady; changeable; fickle; subject to change or irregularity.—**capriciously**, ka·prish′us·li, adv. In a capricious manner.—**capriciousness**, ka·prish′us·nes, n. The quality of being capricious.
Capricorn, kap′ri·korn, n. [L. capricornus—caper, a goat, and cornu, a horn.] One of the twelve signs of the zodiac; the tenth sign, marking the winter solstice.
caprification, kap′ri·fi·kā′shon, n. [L. caprificatio, from caprificus, the wild figtree—caper, a goat, and ficus, a fig, from goats feeding on it.] A process intended to accelerate the ripening of the fig by causing a species of gall insect to spread over the plant, the supposed beneficial effect being produced by the insects either distributing the pollen of the male flowers or by puncturing the fruit.
capriole, kap′ri·ōl, n. [O.Fr. capriole, now cabriole, lit. a goat-leap, from L. capriolus, a wild goat, from caper, a goat.] A caper or leap, as in dancing; an active bound; a spring; a leap, accompanied with a jerking out of the hind legs, which a horse makes without advancing.—v.i. To execute a capriole.
capsicum, kap′si·kum, n. [From L. capsa, a box, from the shape of the fruit.] The generic name of some South American and Asiatic plants, many species of which are cultivated for their pods, used in cookery under the name of chillies, and when dried and ground called Cayenne pepper, to which the name capsicum is also sometimes given.—**capsaïcin**, kap′sā′e·sin, n. An alkaloid, the active principle of the capsules of Cayenne pepper.
capsize, kap·sīz′, v.i.—capsized, capsizing. [Origin doubtful; probably the first syllable means head or top, ultimately from L. caput.] To upset or overturn.—v.i. To be upset or overturned.
capstan, kap′stan, n. [Fr. cabestan, O.Fr. cabestron, from Latin capistrum. a halter.] An apparatus working on the principle of the wheel and axle, and consisting of a cylinder or barrel adjusted on an upright axis, the barrel being made to turn round by means of horizontal bars or levers, the ends of which are inserted in holes near the top of the barrel, so that a rope is thus wound round it and a weight, such as an anchor, raised or moved.
capsule, kap′sūl, n. [L. capsula, a little chest, dim. of capsa, a chest, from capio, to take.] Any membranous sac enclosing an organ of the body; a soluble case of gelatin for enclosing a dose of medicine; a sealed, detachable compartment of an airplane or spaceship; a dry fruit, containing seeds, and opening of itself by valves or pores when mature; chem. a small saucer used for roasting or melting ores, for evaporations, solutions, etc.; seal or cover for going over the cork or stopper of a bottle.—**capsular**, kap′sū·lėr, a. Hollow like a capsule; pertaining to a capsule.—**capsulate, capsulated**, kap′sū·lāt, kap′sū·lāt·ed, a. Enclosed in a capsule.
captain, kap′tn, n. [Fr. capitaine, O.Fr. capitain, from L.L. capitanus, from L. caput, the head.] One who is at the head of or has authority over others; a chief; a leader; a commander, especially in military affairs; more specifically, the military officer who commands a company, whether of infantry, cavalry, or artillery; an officer in the navy commanding a ship of war; the commander or master of a merchant vessel.—**captaincy**, kap′tn·si, n. The rank, post, or commission of a captain.—**captainship**, kap′tn·ship, n. The condition or post of a captain or chief commander; skill in military affairs.
caption, kap′shon, n. [L. captio, a taking, fraud, deceit, from capio, to seize.] The heading or title of a chapter, page, or article; the title or explanation under an illustration or picture.—v.t. To put a caption on.

—**captious**, kap′shus, a. [L. captiosus, from captio, a taking.] Apt to find fault or raise objections; apt to cavil; difficult to please; carping; cavilling; proceeding from a captious or cavilling disposition; fitted to ensnare or perplex (a captious question).—**captiously**, kap′shus·li, adv. In a captious manner.—**captiousness**, kap′shus·nes, n. The quality of being captious.
captive, kap′tiv, n. [From L. captivus, a captive, from capio, captus, to seize. Caitiff is the same word derived through the French.] One who is taken prisoner, especially a prisoner taken in war; one who is charmed or subdued by beauty or excellence; one whose affections are seized, or who is held by strong ties of love.—a. Made prisoner in war; kept in bondage or confinement; bound by the ties of love or admiration; captivated.—**captivate**, kap′ti·vāt, v.t.—captivated, captivating. [L. captivo, captivatum.] To capture or make prisoner‡; to overpower and gain with excellence or beauty; to charm; to engage the affections of; to fascinate, enslave, subdue, enchant.—**captivation**, kap·ti·vā′shon, n. The act of captivating; the act of gaining over or winning one's affections.—**captivity**, kap·tiv′i·ti, n. [L. captivitas.] The state of being a captive; subjection; a state of being under control; bondage; servitude.—**captor**, kap′tėr, n. [L. captor.] One who captures or takes by force, stratagem, etc.—**capture**, kap′chėr, n. [L. captura.] The act of one who captures; the act of making prize of something; seizure; arrest; the thing taken; a prize.—v.t.—captured, capturing. To take or seize by force, surprise, or stratagem, as an enemy or his property; to make a prize or prisoner of.
Capuchin, kap′ū·shin, n. [Fr. capuchon, capucine, from capuce, a hood or cowl, from cape, a cape.] A monk of the order of St. Francis, so called from the capuchon, a stuff cap or cowl, the distinguishing badge of the order; [not cap.] a garment for females, consisting of a cloak and hood in imitation of the dress of Capuchin monks.
capybara, kap·i·bä′ra, n. [The native Brazilian name.] A rodent quadruped, allied to the guinea pig, abounding in rivers of South America, feeding on vegetables and fish, over 3 feet in length, tailless, with a large head and blunted muzzle, and toes imperfectly webbed.
car, kär, n. [O.Fr. car (Mod.Fr. char), from L. carrus, a four-wheeled vehicle, from the Celtic Armor. carr, a chariot, W. car, Ir. and Gael. carr, a dray, wagon, etc. Akin carry, charge, cargo, etc.] A name applied to various kinds of wheeled vehicles, as railroad cars, freight cars, passenger cars, dining cars, sleeping cars, street cars, motor cars.
caracara, kä·ra·kä′ra, n. [From its hoarse cry.] American bird of prey of several species, akin to the eagles and vultures, and feeding on carrion.

---

ch, chain; ch, Sc. loch; g, go; j, job; ng, sing; TH, then; th, thin; w, wig; hw, whig; zh, azure.

caracole, kar′a·kōl, *n*. [Fr., from Sp. and Pg. *caracol*, a winding staircase, a caracole.] A half turn which a horseman makes, either to the right or left; *arch.* a spiral staircase.—*v.i.* —*caracoled, caracoling.* To move in a caracole; to wheel.

caracul, kar′a·kul, *n*. [From *karakul*.] A flat, glossy, curly fur made from the skin of newborn lambs; karakul sheep.

carafe, kar′af or ka·raf′, *n*. [Fr.] A glass water bottle or decanter.

carageen, caragheen, kar′a·gēn, *n*. See CARRAGEEN.

caramel, kar′a·mel, *n*. [Fr. *caramel*, caramel, from Sp. *caramelo*, a lozenge, of Ar. origin.] Anhydrous or burnt sugar, a product of the action of heat upon sugar; it dissolves readily in water, is of a brown color, and is used to color spirits and wines.

carapace, kar′a·pās, *n*. [Fr., from Sp. *carapacho*, a carapace or shell.] The shell which protects the body of chelonian reptiles; also the covering of the anterior upper surface of the crustaceans.

carat, kar′at, *n*. [Fr. *carat*, Ar. *qirrât*, a carat, from Gr. *keration*, lit. a little horn, also the seed of the carob-tree, used for a weight, a carat.] A weight, about 3 1/6 grains, used in weighing precious stones and pearls; a term used to express the proportionate fineness of gold, gold of twenty-four carats being pure gold, gold of sixteen (for instance) having eight parts of alloy.

caravan, kar′a·van, *n*. [Fr. *caravane*, from Sp. *caravana*, Ar. *qairawân*, Per. *kârwân*, a caravan.] A company of travelers who associate together in many parts of Asia and Africa that they may travel with greater security; a large close carriage for conveying traveling exhibitions or the like from place to place.—**caravansary, caravanserai**, kar·a·van′sa·ri, kar·a·van′se·rī, *n*. [Per. *kârwân*, a caravan, and *sarâi*, an inn.] In the East, a place appointed for receiving and lodging travelers.

caravel, carvel, kar′a·vel, kär′vel, *n*. [Sp. and It. *caravela*, a caravel, dim. of L. *carabus*, Gr. *karabos*, a light ship, a boat, also a crab.] A small galley-rigged ship formerly used by the Spanish and Portuguese; also a small fishing vessel.

caraway, kar′a·wä, *n*. [Sp. *al-carahweya*, from Ar. *karwiyâ, karawiyâ*, caraway; probably from Gr. *karon*, L. *careum*, caraway.] A biennial plant belonging to the carrot family, the seeds of which are used to flavor food.

carbide, kär′bīd, *n*. A compound of carbon with a metal; a carburet.

carbine, carabine, kär′bīn, kar′a·bīn, *n*. [Fr. *carabine*, a carabine; O.Fr. *carabin, calabrin*, a musketeer, from *calabre*, an engine of war, from L.L. *chadabula*, an engine for throwing stones, from Gr. *katabolē*, a throwing down—*kata*, down, and *ballo*, to throw.] A gun or firearm commonly used by cavalry, shorter in the barrel than the infantry musket or rifle.—**carbineer, carabineer**,

kär·bin·ēr′, kar′a·bin·ēr″, *n*. One armed with a carbine or carabine.

carbohydrate, kär·bo·hī′drāt, *n*. [L. *carbo*, charcoal, Gr. *hydōr*, water.] A chemical compound made of carbon, hydrogen, and oxygen, the two latter being commonly in the same proportion as in water (H_2O).

carbolic acid, kär·bol′ik as′id, *n*. [L. *carbo*, coal, *oleum*, oil, and *acid*.] An acid obtained from the distillation of coal tar, an oily, colorless liquid, with a burning taste, employed as an antiseptic and disinfectant and in industry.

carbon, kär′bon, *n*. [L. *carbo, carbonis*, a coal.] An element forming a constituent of all organic compounds, of carbonates, such as coal, and occurring in pure form in diamond. Symbol, C; at. no., 6; at. wt., 12.011—*Carbon-12*, the most common form of carbon and the standard for the atomic weights of elements.—*Carbon-14*, a radioactive isotope of carbon used as a tracer in biochemical studies and in archaeological and geological dating. Also called *radiocarbon.*—*Carbon cycle*, the process by which living organisms utilize carbon; the process by which hydrogen is converted into helium.—**carbonaceous**, kär·bo·nā′shus, *a*.—**carbonate**, kär′bon·āt, *n*. A salt or ester of carbonic acid.—*v.t.* To change into a carbonate; to charge with carbon dioxide.—**carbon dioxide**, *n*. A heavy, colorless, noncombustible gas present in the atmosphere and formed from the decay and combustion of organic substances.—**carbonic**, kär·bon′ik, *a*. —*Carbonic acid*, a weak acid formed when carbon dioxide is dissolved in water.—**carboniferous**, kär·bon·if′er·us, *a*. Containing or yielding carbon or coal; [*cap.*] pertaining to a geological period or system.— **carbon monoxide**, *n*. A poisonous gas that is the result of incomplete combustion of carbon.

carbonado, kär·bo·nā′dō, *n*. [From L. *carbo*, a coal.] An old name for a piece of meat, fowl, or game, cut across, seasoned, and broiled; a chop.

Carbonari, kär·bon·ä′rē, *n*. Members of a Neapolitan secret revolutionary society who took their name from the charcoal burners of the Abruzzi, among whom many of them were obliged to take refuge, and with whom they identified themselves.

carborundum, kär·bo·run′dum, *n*. [*Carbon* and *corundum*.] Silicon carbide, a very hard substance used as a substitute for emery.

carboxyl, karb·oks′il, *n*. [L. *carbo*, charcoal, Gr. *oxys*, acid.] The group CO . OH, typical of organic acids.

carboy, kär′boi, *n*. [Per. *karabâ*, a large vessel for containing wine.] A large, strong, glass bottle, protected by an outside covering.

carbuncle, kär′bung·kl, *n*. [L. *carbunculus*, a little coal, from *carbo*, a coal.] A beautiful gem of a deep red color, with a mixture of scarlet, found in the East Indies; an inflammatory tumor.

carburet, kär′bū·ret, *n*. Same as

Carbide.—**carburetor**, kär′bū·ret·ér, *n*. In an internal combustion engine the device for vaporizing gasoline or other fuel.—**carburize**. kär′bū·rīz, *v.t.* To combine with carbon or a compound of it.

carcajou, kär′ka·jö, *n*. [Fr. *carcajou*, from native name.] An American name for the wolverine or glutton, and erroneously for the badger and lynx.

carcanet, kär′ka·net, *n*. [Fr. *carcan*, a carcanet, from Armor. *kerchen*, the neck or bosom.] A necklace or collar of jewels.

carcass, carcase, kär′kas, *n*. [Fr. *carcasse*, the carcass, a framework, a kind of bomb, same word as *carquois*, a quiver, from L.L. *tarcasius*, a quiver, from Ar. and Per. *tarkash*, a quiver.] The body, usually the dead body, of an animal; a corpse; the decaying remains of a bulky thing; the frame or main parts of a thing unfinished; a kind of bomb or shell filled with combustible matter, and having apertures for the emission of flame, so as to set fire to buildings, etc.

carcinoma, kär·si·nō′ma, *n*. [Gr. *karkinōma*, from *karkinos*, a cancer.] A kind of cancer or cancerous growth.

card, kärd, *n*. [From Fr. *carte*, a card, from L. *charta*, paper, from Gr. *chartē, chartēs*, a layer of papyrus bark.] A rectangular piece of thick paper or pasteboard; such a piece with certain devices, marks, or figures, used for playing games; a piece having one's name, etc., written or printed on it, used in visiting; a larger piece written or printed, and conveying an invitation, or some intimation or statement; the dial or face of the mariner's compass.— **cardboard**, kärd′bōrd, *n*. A stiff kind of paper or pasteboard for making cards, etc.—**cardsharper**, *n*. One who cheats in playing cards; one who makes it a trade to fleece the unwary in games of cards.

card, kärd, *n*. [Fr. *carde*, from L.L. *cardus*, L. *carduus*, a thistle, from *carere*, to card—thistles having been used as cards.] An instrument for combing, opening, and breaking wool or flax, freeing it from the coarser parts and from extraneous matter.— *v.t. or i.* To comb or open wool, flax, hemp, etc., with a card.—**carder**, kär′dér, *n*. One who cards; the machine employed in carding.

cardamom, kär′da·mum, *n*. [L. *cardamomum*, Gr. *kardamōmon*.] The aromatic capsule of various plants of the ginger family, employed in medicine as well as an ingredient in sauces and curries.

cardiac, cardiacal, kär′di·ak, kär′di′ak·al, *a*. [L. *cardiacus*, Gr. *kardiakos*, from *kardia*, the heart.] Pertaining to the heart, exciting action in the heart through the medium of the stomach; having the quality of stimulating action in the system, invigorating the spirits, and giving strength and cheerfulness.—**cardiac**, *n*. A medicine which excites action in the stomach and animates the spirits; a cordial.—**cardiography,** kär·di·og′ra·fi, n. An anatomical description of the heart.—**cardialgia,** kär·di·al′ji·a, n. [Gr. *algos*, pain.] *Med.* heart burn.

cardigan, kär′di·gan, n. [After Earl of *Cardigan*.] A kind of knitted waistcoat worn over or instead of the waistcoat.

cardinal, kär′di·nal, a. [L. *cardinalis*, from *cardo*, a hinge.] Chief, principal, preeminent, or fundamental.—*Cardinal numbers*, the numbers *one, two, three*, etc., in distinction from *first, second, third*, etc., called ordinal numbers.—*Cardinal points*, north and south, east and west.—*Cardinal virtues*, justice, prudence, temperance, and fortitude.—n. An ecclesiastical prince in the Roman Catholic Church, next in rank to the pope, and having a distinguishing dress of a red color.—**cardinalate, cardinalship,** kär′di·nal·āt, kär′di·nal·ship, n. The office, rank, or dignity of a cardinal.—**cardinal bird,** n. A North American bird, with a fine red plumage, and a crest on the head.—**cardinal flower,** n. The name commonly given to a species of lobelia because of its large, very showy, and intensely red flowers.

cardiogram, kär′di·o·gram, n. [Gr. *kardia*, heart, and *gramma*, mark.] The tracing produced by a cardiograph.—**cardiograph,** kär′di·o·graf, n. [Gr. *kardia*, heart, and *graphō*, to write.] An instrument that registers the movement of the heart. —**cardiology,** kär·di·ol′o·ji, n. [Gr. *kardia*, heart, and *logos*, discourse.] The study of the heart and its diseases.—**cardiologist,** kär·di·ol′o·jist, n.—**cardiovascular,** kär·di·o·vas′ku·lar, a. Pertaining to the heart and blood vessels.

care, kâr, n. [A.Sax. *caru, cearu*, care, sorrow = O.Sax. *cara*, Icel. *kaeri*, complaint, Goth. *kara*, sorrow, O. H.G. *chara*, lamentation; from a root signifying to cry, seen also in E. *call*.] Some degree of pain in the mind from apprehension of evil; a painful load of thought; mental trouble; concern; anxiety; solicitude; attention or heed; a looking to; caution; regard; watchfulness; charge or oversight, implying concern for safety and prosperity; the object of care or watchful regard and attention. ∴*Care* denotes mental trouble regarding the present, the future, or even the past; *solicitude* and *concern* denote affections of the mind of a more active kind than *care*, and relate to the present and the future, while the latter may also be excited by something past.—v.i.—*cared, caring*. To be anxious or solicitous; to be concerned; to be inclined or disposed; to like.—**careful,** kâr′ful, a. Full of care; anxious; solicitous; attentive to support and protect; giving good heed; watchful, cautious; showing or done with care or attention: generally with *of* before the object.—**carefully,** kâr′ful·li, adv. In a careful manner.—**carefulness,** kâr′ful·nes, n. The state or quality of being careful.—**careless,** kâr′les, a.

Free from care or anxiety; heedless; negligent, unthinking, inattentive; regardless, unmindful, with *of* or *about* before an object, done or said without care; unconsidered.—**carelessly,** kâr′les·li, adv. In a careless manner or way.—**carelessness,** kâr′les·nes, n. The state or quality of being careless.—**careworn,** a. Worn, oppressed, or burdened with care; showing marks of care or anxiety.

careen, ka·rēn′, n. [Fr. *carener*, from *carène*, the side and keel of a ship, L. *carina*, a keel.] To heave or bring (a ship) to lie on one side for caulking, repairing, cleansing, or the like. —v.i. To incline to one side, as a ship under a press of sail, or a motor car turning a corner on two wheels.

career, ka·rēr′, n. [Fr. *carrière*, O.Fr. *cariere*, road, race-course, course, career, from L. *carrus*, a car. CAR.] A race or running, course of proceeding; a specific course of action or occupation forming the object of one's life.—v.i. To move or run rapidly (as a horse, a ship, etc.).

caress, ka·res′, n. [Fr. *caresse*, from It. *carezza*, L.L. *caritia* from L. *carus*, dear.] An act of endearment, any act or expression of affection.— v.t. To treat with caresses; to fondle; to embrace with tender affection.— **caressingly,** ka·res′ing·li, adv. In a caressing manner.

caret, ka′ret, n. [L. *caret*, there is (something) wanting, from *carere* to want.] In *writing*, a mark made thus, ∧ which shows that something, omitted in the line, is interlined above or inserted in the margin, and should be read in that place.

cargo, kär′gō, n. [Sp., from *cargar*, to load, L.L. *carricare*, to load, from L. *carrus*, a car. CAR, CHARGE.] The lading or freight of a ship.

Carib, kar′ib, n. One of a native race inhabiting certain portions of Central America, and formerly also the Caribbean Islands.

caribou, kar′i·bö, n. [Probably of Indian origin.] A North American variety of the reindeer.

caricature, kar′i·ka·chur″, n. [It. *caricatura*, an overloaded representation, from *caricare*, to load. CHARGE.] A representation, pictorial or descriptive, in which beauties are concealed and peculiarities or defects exaggerated so as to make the person or thing ridiculous, while a general likeness is retained.—v.t.—*caricatured, caricaturing*. To make or draw a caricature of; to represent in a ridiculous and exaggerated fashion. —**caricaturist,** kar′i·ka·chur″ist, n. One who caricatures others.

caries, kâ′ri·ēz, n. [L.] Ulceration of bony substance; the gangrenous eating away of a bone; decay of teeth.—**carious,** kâ′ri·us, a. Affected with caries; ulcerated: said of a bone.

carillon, kar′il·lon, n. [Fr., from L.L. *quadrilio*, from L. *quattuor*, four, because *carillons* were played formerly on four bells.] A chime of bells, properly tuned, and rung by means of finger keys like those of the pianoforte; a simple air adapted to

be performed on a set of bells.

carina, ka·rī′na, n. [L., the keel of a boat.] *Bot.* the two partially united lower petals of papilionaceous flowers; *zool.* a prominent median ridge or keel in the sternum or breastbone of all existing birds except the runners (ostrich, etc.).—**carinate, carinated,** kar′i·nāt, kar′i·nāt·ed, a. [L. *carinatus*.] Shaped like a keel; having a carina or keel; keeled; *bot.* having a longitudinal ridge like a keel; *zool.* applied to those birds whose sternum is keeled, or to their sternum.

cariole, kar′i·ōl, n. [Fr., from L. *carrus*, a car.] A small open carriage; a kind of calash; a covered cart.

carious. See CARIES.

carl, carle, kärl, n. [A Scandinavian word = Icel. Dan. Sw. *karl*, a man; A.Sax. *carl*, male, as in *carl-catt*, a he-cat.] A man; a robust, strong, or hardy man; an old man. [O.E. and Sc.] Hence **carline,** a woman.

carline, carling, kär′lin, kär′ling, n. [Fr. *carlingue* or *escarlingue*.] One of the fore-and-aft deck timbers in a ship.

Carlist, kär′list, n. A follower of Don *Carlos* of Spain, the heir to the crown but for the repeal of the Salic law; an adherent and supporter of the family of Don Carlos.—**Carlism,** kär′lizm, n. The principles of the Carlists.

Carlovingian, kär·lo·vin′ji·an, a. Pertaining to or descended from Charlemagne.

carmagnole, kär·ma·nyōl′, n. [Fr. *Carmagnole* in Piedmont.] A revolutionary dance and song in France during 1789-93 Revolution, from the street-dancing Savoyards; any bombastic harangue.

Carmelite, kär′mel·īt, n. A mendicant friar of the order of our Lady of Mount *Carmel;* a sort of pear; the White Friars founded at Mount Carmel; gray woolen stuff.

carminative, kär′mi·nā·tiv or kär·min′a·tiv, n. [L. *carmino, carminatum*, to card wool (hence to make fine or thin), from *carmen*, a card.] A medicine which tends to expel wind from the stomach and remedy flatulency.—a. Expelling wind from the stomach; antispasmodic.

carmine, kär′mīn, n. [Sp. *carmin*, from *carmesino*, carmine, crimson, from *carmes*, kermes (which see). *Crimson* has the same origin.] The pure coloring matter or principle of cochineal; a red or crimson pigment made from cochineal.

carnage, kär′nij, n. [Fr. *carnage*, slaughter, from L.L. *carnaticum*, from L. *caro, carnis*, flesh.] Slaughter; great destruction of men; butchery; massacre.

carnal, kär′nal, a. [L. *carnalis*, carnal, from *caro, carnis*, flesh.] Pertaining to the body, its passions and appetites; not spiritual; fleshly; sensual; lustful; impure.—**carnality,** kär·nal′i·ti, n. The state of being carnal; want of spirituality; fleshliness; fleshly lusts or desires, or the indulgence of those lusts; sensuality. —**carnally,** kär′nal·li, adv. In a carnal manner; according to the flesh; not spiritually.

carnallite, kär′nal·līt, n. [After a German called Von *Carnall*.] A pink-colored mineral obtained from the Stassfurt salt mines.

carnation, kär·nā′shon, n. [Fr. *carnation*, the naked part of a picture, flesh color; from L. *caro, carnis*, flesh.] Flesh color; the parts of a picture which exhibit the natural color of the flesh; the representation of flesh; a perennial plant found in many varieties, much prized for the beautiful colors of their sweet-scented double flowers.

carnauba, kär·nou′ba, n. The Brazilian name of a tall South American palm which has its leaves coated with small waxy scales, yielding a straw-colored wax by boiling. Also written *Carnahuba*.

carnelian, kär·nē′li·an, n. [More correctly *cornelian*, from Fr. *cornaline*, a carnelian, from L. *carnis*, flesh, from its fleshlike color.] A variety of chalcedony, of a deep red, flesh-red, or reddish-white color, tolerably hard, capable of a good polish.

carnival, kär′ni·val, n. [Fr. *carnaval*, It. *carnevale*, from L.L. *carnele-vamen*, for *carnis levamen*, solace of the body, permitted in anticipation of any fast—L. *caro*, flesh, and *levare*, to solace, to lighten.] The feast or season of rejoicing before Lent; feasting or revelry in general; an amusement place.

carnivorous, kär·niv′o·rus, a. [L. *caro, carnis*, flesh, and *voro*, to devour.] Eating or feeding on flesh: an epithet applied to animals which naturally seek flesh for food, as the lion, tiger, wolf, dog, etc.; also applied to some plants that can assimilate animal substances.—**Carnivora**, kär·niv′o·ra, n. pl. [L.] A term applicable to any creatures that feed on flesh or animal substances, but generally denoting an order of mammals which prey upon other animals.—**carnivore**, kär′ni·vōr, n. A carnivorous animal; one of the Carnivora.

carob, kar′ob, n. [O.Fr. *carobe*, from Ar. *kharrûb*, bean-pods.] A tree growing in the countries skirting the Mediterranean, the pods of which, known as locust beans, contain a sweet nutritious pulp.

carol, kar′ol, n. [O.Fr. *carole*, a kind of dance, also a Christmas song or carol; from the Celtic: Armor. *koroll*, a dance; W. *carol*, a carol, a song.] A song, especially one expressive of joy; a religious song or ballad in celebration of Christmas.—v.i.—*caroled, caroling.* To sing; to warble; to sing in joy or festivity.—v.t.—To praise or celebrate in song.

Carolingian, kar·ō·lin′ji·an, a. Same as *Carlovingian*.

carotic, ka·rot′ik, a. [Gr. *karos*, torpor, stupor.] Relating to stupor or carus; also same as carotid.—

carotid, ka·rot′id, a. [Gr. pl. *karō-tides*, the carotids, said to be from *karos*, a deep sleep, because the ancients believed that sleep was caused

by an increased flow of blood to the head through these arteries, or by the compression of these arteries.] Of or pertaining to the two great arteries, one on either side of the neck, which convey the blood from the aorta to the head and brain.—n. One of these arteries.

carouse, ka·rouz′, v.i.—*caroused, carousing.* [O.Fr. *carousser*, to quaff, to carouse, from *carous*, a carouse, a bumper, from G. *garaus!* quite out! that is, empty your glasses! an old German drinking exclamation.] To drink freely and with jollity; to quaff; to revel.—**carousal**, **carouse**, ka·rou′zal, ka·rouz′, n. A feast or festival; a noisy drinking bout or revelling.—**carouser**, ka·rouz′èr, n. One who carouses; a drinker; a toper; a noisy reveler or bacchanalian.

carp, kärp, v.i. [Formerly to speak, tell, from Icel. *karpa*, to boast, its modern sense being due to L. *carpo*, to seize, catch, pick.] To censure, cavil, or find fault, particularly without reason or petulantly: used absolutely or followed by *at*.—**carper**, kärp′èr, n. One who carps; a caviller.—**carping**, kärp′ing, a. Cavilling; captious; censorious.—**carpingly**, kärp′ing·li, adv. In a carping manner; captiously.

carp, kärp, n. [Same as D. *karper*, Dan. *karpe*, Sw. *karp*, a carp.] A fresh-water fish found in lakes, rivers, ponds, etc. The most noted species are the common carp and the gold fish. The carp has been introduced in America, where it has become so numerous as to be a pest.

carpal. See CARPUS.

carpel, kär′pel, n. [Mod. L. *carpellum*, dim. from Gr. *karpos*, fruit.] Bot. a single-celled ovary or seed vessel, or a single cell of an ovary or seed vessel together with what belongs to that cell.—**carpellary**, kär′pel·la·ri, a. Belonging to a carpel or carpels.

carpenter, kär′pen·tèr, n. [O.Fr. *carpentier* (Mod. Fr. *charpentier*); L.L. *carpentarius*, a carpenter, from L. *carpentum*, a chariot, a word of Celtic origin.] An artificer who works in timber; a framer and builder of houses and of ships.—**carpenter bee**, n. The common name of different species of bees, so called from their habit of excavating nests in decaying wood.—

carpentry, kär′pen·tri, n. The art of cutting, framing, and joining timber; an assemblage of pieces of timber connected by framing or letting them into each other.

carpet, kär′pet, n. [O.Fr. *carpite*, a carpet, from It. and L.L. *carpita*, a woolly cloth, from *carpere*, to tease wool, L. *carpo*, to pluck, to pull in pieces, etc.] A thick fabric used for covering floors, stairs, etc.; a covering resembling a carpet (a *carpet* of moss).—*To be on the carpet*, is to be under consideration; to be the subject of deliberation.—*Carpet knight*, a knight who has not known the hardships of the field.—v.t. To cover with or as

with a carpet; to spread with carpets.—**carpeting**, kär′pet·ing, n. Cloth for carpets; carpets in general. —**carpetbag**, n. A traveling bag made of the same material as carpets.—**carpetbagger**, n. A new comer to a place, having all his property in a carpet bag; a newcomer or political candidate, without possessing property in a community.

carpologist, kär·pol′o·jist, n. One who studies or treats of carpology.

carpology, kär·pol′o·ji, n. [Gr. *karpos*, fruit, *logos*, discourse.] The division of botany relating to the structure of seeds and seed vessels.

carpophore, kär′po·fōr, n. [L. *carpophorum*, from Gr. *karpos*, fruit, and *pherō*, to bear.] Bot. the prolongation of the floral axis which bears the pistil beyond the stamens.

carpus, kär′pus, n. [L., the wrist.] Anat. that part of the skeleton between the forearm and hand; the *wrist* in man and the corresponding bones in other animals.—**carpal**, kär′pal, a. Pertaining to the carpus.

carrageen, carragheen, kar′ra·gēn, n. [From *Carragheen*, near Waterford, Ireland, where it abounds.] A seaweed which, when dried, becomes whitish, and in this condition is known as Irish moss, being used for making soups, jellies, etc.

carriage, kar′ij, n. [O.Fr. *cariage*, from *carier*, to carry. CARRY.] The act of carrying, bearing, transporting, or conveying; the price or expense of carrying; the manner of carrying one's self; behavior; conduct; deportment; a wheeled vehicle for persons, especially a four-wheeled vehicle supported on springs and with a cover, belonging to a private person and not used for hire; in composition, a wheeled stand or support; as, a gun-*carriage*; *print.* the frame on rollers by which the bed carrying the types is run in and out from under the platen.

carrick bend, kar′ik, a kind of knot.—**carrick bitts**, supports for the windlass of a ship.

carrier. See CARRY.

carrion, kar′ri·on, n. [O.Fr. *caroigne*, from L.L. *caronia*, from L. *caro, carnis*, flesh.] The dead and putrefying body or flesh of animals; flesh so corrupted as to be unfit for food.—a. Pertaining to carrion; feeding on carrion.—**carrion crow**, n. The common crow, so called because it often feeds on carrion.

carronade, kar·on·ād′, n. [From *Carron* in Scotland, where it was first made.] A short piece of ordnance of confined range, formerly used in the navy.

carrot, kar′ot, n. [Fr. *carotte*; L.L. *carota*.] A plant having a long esculent root of a reddish color much used as a culinary vegetable and also for feeding cattle.—**carroty**, kar′ot·i, a. Like a carrot in color.

carry, kar′i, v.t.—*carried, carrying.* [O.E. *carie*, from O.Fr. *carier*, to convey in a car, from O.Fr. *car*, a cart or car. CAR.] To bear, convey, or transport by sustaining and moving with the thing carried; to drive, drag, or fetch (*carry* a person off prisoner); to transfer, as from one column, page, book, etc., to another; to convey or take with one generally (as a message, news, etc.); to urge, impel, lead, or draw, in a moral sense (anger *carried* him too far); to effect, accomplish, achieve, bring to a successful issue (a purpose, etc.); to gain; *milit.* to gain possession of by force; to capture (to *carry* a fortress); to extend or continue in any direction, in time, in space, or otherwise: commonly with such words as *up*, *back*, *forward*, etc. (to *carry* a history on to the present, to *carry* improvements far); to bear; to have in or on; to bear or bring as a result (words *carry* conviction); to import, contain, or comprise (the words *carry* a promise); to manage; to conduct (matters or affairs).—*To carry off*, to remove to a distance; to kill or cause to die (to be *carried off* by sickness or poison).—*To carry on*, to manage or prosecute; to continue to pursue (a business).—*To carry out*, *to carry through*, to sustain to the end; to continue to the end; to accomplish; to finish; to execute (a purpose, an undertaking).—*v.i.* To act as a bearer; to convey; to propel, as a gun.—*n.* Range or distance.—**carrier**, kär'i·ėr, *n.* One who or that which carries; a person or thing that transmits a disease; an underwriter or insurer; an aircraft carrier.—**carrier current** or **carrier wave**, *n.* An electric current, the modulations of which are used as radio or telegraphic signals.—**carrier pigeon**, *n.* A pigeon used to carry messages; a homing pigeon.

cart, kärt, *n.* [From W. *cart*, a cart or wagon, Ir. *cairt*. CAR.] A carriage usually without springs for the conveyance of heavy goods.—*v.t.* To carry or convey on a cart.—**cartage**, kär'tij, *n.* The act of carrying in a cart; the price for carting.—**carter**, kär'tėr, *n.* One who drives a cart. —**cart wheel**, *n.* The wheel of a cart; a large coin; a sideways handspring or somersault.

carte, kärt, *n.* [Fr., a card.] A card; a bill of fare at a tavern; a carte-de-visite photograph.—**carte blanche**, kärt blänsh', *n.* [Fr., white paper.] A blank paper; a paper duly authenticated with signature, etc., and intrusted to a person to be filled up as he pleases; hence, unconditional terms; unlimited power to decide.

cartel, kär'tel, *n.* [Fr., from L. *chartula*, dim. of *charta*, paper, a paper.] A writing or agreement between states at war, for the exchange of prisoners or for some mutual advantage. In Europe, an organization controlling the commercial policy of a number of independent companies, the equivalent of the American pool or trust.

Cartesian, kär·tē'zi·an, *a.* Pertaining to the philosopher René *Descartes*, or to his philosophy.—*n.* One who adopts the philosophy of Descartes.

—**Cartesianism**, kär·tē'zi·an·izm, *n.* The philosophy of Descartes.

Carthusian, kär·thu'zi·an, *n.* One of an order of monks, founded in 1086, under Benedictine rule, by St. Bruno, so called from *Chartreuse*, in France, the place of their institution; pupil of the Charterhouse School, founded on the site of the London monastery.

cartilage, kär'ti·lij, *n.* [Fr. *cartilage*, L. *cartilago*.] An elastic tissue occurring in vertebrate animals, and forming the tissue from which bone is formed by a process of calcification; gristle.—**cartilaginous**, kär·ti·laj'i·nus, *a.* Pertaining to or resembling a cartilage; gristly; consisting of cartilage; having cartilage only and not true bones (as many fishes).

cartography, kär·tog'ra·fi, *n.* [E. *chart*, L. *charta*, paper, and Gr. *graphē*, writing, description.] The making of maps or charts.—**cartographer**, kär·tog'ra·fėr, *n.*

carton, a box with cover made of various kinds of board, as pasteboard, fiberboard, for shipping light articles.

cartoon, kär·tön', *n.* [Fr. *carton*, pasteboard, a cartoon, from It. *cartone* (same sense), aug. of *carta*, L. *charta*, paper.] A pictorial design drawn on strong paper as a study for a picture intended to be painted of same size, and more especially for a picture to be painted in fresco; a caricature, often satirical, commenting on political and public events; a comic strip; a short, animated motion picture.—*v.t.* To represent by, or draw, cartoons.

cartouch, **cartouche**, kär·tösh', *n.* [Fr. *cartouche*, O.Fr. *cartoche*, from It. *cartoccio*, a cartridge, a roll of paper, from *carta*, L. *charta*, paper. *Cartridge* is a corruption of this.] A case of wood filled with shot to be fired from a cannon; a cartridge; a portable box for charges for firearms; on Egyptian monuments, papyri, etc., a group of hieroglyphics in a small oblong area; *arch.* a sculptured ornament in the form of a scroll unrolled.

cartridge, kär'trij, *n.* [Formerly also *cartrage*, a corruption of *cartouch*.] A case of pasteboard, parchment, copper, tin, etc., holding the exact charge of any firearm.—*Blank cartridge*, a cartridge without ball or shot.

cartulary, kär'chu̜·le·ri, *n.* Same as *Chartulary*.

caruncle, kar'ung·kl, *n.* [L. *caruncula*, dim. from *caro*, flesh.] A small fleshy excrescence; a fleshy excrescence on the head of a fowl, as a wattle or the like; *bot.* a protuberance surrounding the hilum of a seed.—**caruncular**, **carunculous**, ka·rung'ku̜·lėr, ka·rung'ku̜·lus, *a.* Pertaining to or in the form of a caruncle.—**carunculate**, **carunculated**, ka·rung'ku̜·lāt, ka·rung'ku̜·lāt·ed, *a.* Having a fleshy excrescence.

carve, kärv, *v.t.*—*carved*, *carving*. [A.Sax. *ceorfan*=D. *kerven*, Icel. *kyrfa*, to carve; Dan. *karve*, G. *kerven*, to notch or indent; same

root as *grave*.] To cut (some solid material) in order to produce the representation of an object or some decorative design; to make or shape by cutting; to form by cutting or hewing; to cut into, hew, or slash; to cut into small pieces or slices, as meat at table.—*v.i.* To exercise the trade of a carver; to engrave or cut figures; to cut up meat at table.—**carver**, kär'vėr, *n.* One who carves, as one who cuts ivory, wood, or the like, in a decorative way; one who cuts meat for use at table; a large tableknife for carving.—**carving**, kär'ving, *n.* A branch of sculpture usually limited to works in wood, ivory, etc.; the device or figure carved.

carvel, kär'vel, *n.* Same as *Caravel*.— **carvel-built**, *a.* A term applied to a ship or boat the planks of which are all flush and not overlapping, as in clincherbuilt boats.

caryatid, kar'i·at·id, *n. pl.* **caryatids**, **caryatides**, kar'i·at·idz, kar·i·at'i·dēz. [L., from Gr. *Karyatis*, name of a priestess of Diana.] Arch. a figure of a woman dressed in long robes, serving to support entablatures.

caryophyllaceous, kar'i·o·fil·lā″-shus, *a.* [Gr. *karyophyllon*, the clove-tree.] Pertaining or similar to the plants known as pinks, and their allies; applied to flowers having five petals with long claws in a tubular calyx.

caryopsis, kar·i·op'sis, *n.* [Gr. *karyon*, a nut, and *opsis*, an appearance.] *Bot.* a small, one-seeded, dry, indehiscent fruit, in which the seed adheres to the thin pericarp throughout, as in wheat and other grains.

cascade, kas·kād', *n.* [Fr. *cascade*, It. *cascata*, from *cascare*, to fall, from L. *cado*, *casum*, to fall.] A fall or flowing of water over a precipice in a river or other stream; a waterfall.—*v.i.* To fall in a cascade.—*v.t.* To cause to fall like a cascade.

cascara sagrada, kas·kâ'ra säg·rä'da, *n.* [Sp. sacred bark.] A purgative medicine obtained from the bark of an American tree.

cascarilla, kas·ka·ril'la, *n.* [Sp. dim. of *cascara*, peel, bark.] The aromatic bitter bark of a small tree chiefly in Eleuthera, one of the Bahamas, employed as a substitute for cinchona.

case, kās, *n.* [O.Fr. *casse* (now *caisse*), from *capio*, to take, receive, contain. *Cash* is really the same word.] A covering, envelope, box, frame, or sheath; that which encloses or contains; the skin of an animal‡; a case with its contents; hence, a certain quantity; *print.* a partitioned tray for types, from which the compositor gathers them and arranges them in lines and pages to print from.—*v.t.*—*cased*, *casing*. To cover with a case; to surround with any material that shall enclose or defend; to coat or cover over; to put in a case or box; to skin (*Shak.*).‡—**casing**, kās'ing, *n.* The act of putting a case on; a case or covering.—**caseharden**, *v.t.* To harden the outer part or surface of (iron tools, etc.) by converting it into steel.—**case history,** n. A record of facts of an individual's personal history for use in analyzing his case for treatment, compensation, etc.— **case knife,** n. A long knife kept in a case or sheath; a large table-knife.— **case law,** n. Law made by decided cases that serve as precedents; judge-made laws.—**case shot,** n. A collection of shot or small projectiles enclosed in cases to be discharged from cannon; an iron case holding a number of bullets.—**case-work,** n. A detailed study of persons in need of social assistance that can be used for diagnosis and treatment. —**caseworker,** n.

case, kās, n. [Fr. cas, a case, L. casus, a falling, from cado, casum, to fall.] The particular state, condition, or circumstances that befall a person, or in which he is placed; an individual occurrence or specific instance as of disease; a question or group of facts involving a question for discussion or decision; a cause or suit in court; a cause; one of the forms in the declension of a noun, pronoun, or adjective.—*In case,* in the event or contingency; if it should so fall out or happen.

casein, kā'sē·in, n. A white amorphous phosphoprotein contained in the milk of all mammals. Acids precipitate it as in souring milk. It is used for paints and glues, the coating of paper and, after treatment with formaldehyde, as artificial ivory; it is likewise the raw material in the manufacture of synthetic wool.

casemate, kās'māt, n. [Fr. casemate, from It. casamatta, a casemate, from casa, a house, and matto, obscure, dark.] *Fort.* a bomb-proof vault for the protection of the garrison, and sometimes used as a barrack or hospital; a loopholed gallery excavated in a bastion, from which the garrison could fire on an enemy in possession of the ditch.

casement, kās'ment, n. [From case, in the sense of a frame, as of a door, etc.]. A window frame, or portion of one made to turn and open on hinges; a compartment between the mullions of a window.

cash, kash, n. [O.Fr. casse, Mod. Fr. caisse, It cassa, a chest, box, coffer, from L. capsa, a box or case. CASE.] A receptacle for money‡; a money-box‡; money, primarily, ready money; money in chest or on hand, in bank or at command; Chinese copper coin of very small value, often strung on cord.—v.t. To turn into money, or to exchange for money (to cash a bank-note).—**cashier,** kash·ēr', n. One who has charge of cash; one who keeps an account of the monetary transactions of a commercial or trading establishment.—**cashier's check,** in the United States a check drawn by a bank upon itself and signed by its cashier.—**cashbook,** n. A book in which is kept a register or account of money received and paid.— **cash register,** n. A device recording

the amount of cash received. It contains an automatic adding machine and a money drawer.

cashew, ka·shö', n. [From native name.] The tree which produces cashew nuts, a native of tropical America.—**cashew nut,** n. The kidney-shaped fruit of an American tree, having a kernel abounding in a sweet milky juice; the inner layer of the shell contains a black acrid caustic oil.

cashier, kash·ēr', v.t. [Du. casseere, G. kassiren, from O.Fr. casser, to break, to cashier, from L. cassare, to annul, from cassus, void, empty.] To dismiss from an office, place of trust, or service for bad conduct; to discharge; to discard.

cashmere, kash'mēr, n. A fine costly shawl made of the downy wool of the Cashmere goat and the wild goat of Tibet, and so called from the country where first made.

casino, ka·sē'nō, n. [It., a small house, from L. casa, a cottage.] A building used for social meetings or public amusements, for dancing, gambling, etc.

cask, kask, n. [Sp. casco, helmet, winecask, skull, potsherd, peel or rind, from a L.L. quassicare, to break or burst, from L. quassare, to break, whence E. quash.] A closed vessel for containing liquors, formed by staves, heading, and hoops; a general term comprehending the pipe, hogshead, butt, barrel, etc.—v.t. To put into a cask.

casket, kas'ket, n. [In form a dim. of cask, but in meaning from Fr. cassette, a coffer or casket, dim. of casse, a box. CASH.] A small chest or box for jewels, etc.; a coffin. —v.t. To put in a casket.

casque, kask, n. [Fr., from Sp. casco, a helmet. CASK.] A helmet generally, but more precisely a headpiece wanting a visor, but furnished with cheek-pieces and earpieces, and frequently elaborately ornamented and embossed.

cassava, kas·sā'va or kas·sä'va, n. [Pg. cassave, Sp. casabe, cazabe, from Haytian name kasabi.] A slender erect shrub belonging to the spurge family extensively cultivated in tropical America and the West Indies on account of the nutritious starch obtained from the root, and formed into cakes (cassava-bread) and into tapioca.

casserole, kas'e·rōl, n. [Fr., of same origin as kettle.] A kind of stewpan or saucepan; a kind of stew; rice, potatoes, etc., formed into a cup to hold some other kind of food; a small dish with a handle, used for chemical operations.

cassia, kash'i·a, n. [L. cassia, Gr. kasia, kassia, from the Hebrew or Phoenician name.] A tropical leguminous plant of many species, consisting of trees, shrubs, or herbs, the leaflets of several of which constitute the drug called senna, while the pulp from the legumes of another species is used as a purgative.—**cassia bark,** n. The bark of a species of cinnamon, used

as a substitute for the true cinnamon.

cassimere, kas'si·mēr, n. [Fr. cassimir, same word as cashmere.] A twilled woolen cloth woven in imitation of Cashmere shawls; kerseymere.

Cassiopeia, kas'si·o·pē"ya, n. A constellation in the northern hemisphere with five of its stars forming a kind of W.

Cassiterite, kas'si·tėr·īt, n. [Gr. kassiteros, tin.] The most common ore of tin; it is a peroxide, consisting of tin 79, and oxygen 21.

cassock, kas'ok, n. [Fr. casaque, from It. casaca, from casa, a house, L. casa, a cottage.] A sort of long coat or tight-fitting garment worn by clergymen.

cassowary, kas'so·wa·ri, n. [Malay casuwaris.] A large cursorial bird inhabiting the islands of the Indian Archipelago, nearly as large as the ostrich, which it resembles; but its legs are thicker and stronger in proportion, and it has three toes on the foot; its head is surmounted by a large horny crest.

cast, kast, v.t.—cast, casting. [Dan. kaste, Sw. and Icel. kasta, to throw: a Scandinavian word.] To throw, fling, or send; to hurl; to shed or throw off (leaves, the skin); to discard, dismiss, or reject; to shed or impart (cast light); to turn or direct (a look, the eyes); to throw down (as in wrestling); to decide against at law; to condemn; to bring forth abortively (young); to form by pouring liquid metal, etc., into a mold; to compute, reckon, or calculate; to distribute (the parts of a drama) among the actors; to assign a part to, the work of the casting director in the movies. —*To cast aside,* to dismiss or reject.— *To cast away,* to reject; to lavish or waste by profusion; to wreck (a ship). —*To cast down,* to throw down; fig. to deject or depress.—*To cast forth,* to throw out or reject; to emit or send out.—*To cast a vote,* to enter a checkmark in the ballot for the candidate of one's choice.—*To cast off,* to discard or reject; to drive away; naut. to loosen from or let go. —*To cast out,* to reject or turn out.— *To cast up,* to compute; to reckon; to calculate; to eject; to vomit; to twit or upbraid with.—*To cast one's self on* or *upon,* to resign or yield one's self to the disposal of.—*To cast in one's lot with,* to share the fate or fortune of.—*To cast (something) in the teeth,* to upbraid (with something); to charge; to twit.—*v.i.* To throw or fling; to throw the line in angling, especially one with a fly; to work arithmetical calculations; to turn or revolve in the mind; to calculate; to consider; to warp or twist.—*n.* The act of casting; a throw; the distance passed by a thing thrown; motion or turn of the eye; direction, look, or glance; a throw of dice; the form or shape into which something is cast; anything formed in a mold, as a figure in bronze, plaster, etc.; fig. shape; mold; impression generally; a tinge or slight coloring or slight degree of a color

(a *cast* of green); manner; air; mien; style; the company of actors to whom the parts of a play are assigned.—*Cast in the eye*, squint.—**castaway,** kast′a·wā, *n.* One who or that which is cast away or shipwrecked; one ruined in fortune or character.—*a.* Thrown away; rejected; useless; abandoned.—**caster,** kas′tėr, *n.* One who or that which casts; specifically, one who makes castings; a founder; a small cruet or bottle for holding sauce, pepper, etc., for the table; spelled also *Castor ;* a small wheel attached by a vertical pivot to the legs of a chair, sofa, table, etc., to facilitate their being moved without lifting: spelled also *Castor.*—**casting,** kas′ting, *n.* The act of one who casts; that which is cast; especially, something cast or formed in a mold; something formed of cast-metal.—*a.* Throwing; sending; computing; turning; deciding; determining.—*Casting-vote*, a vote given by a president or chairman which decides when the votes are equally divided.—**cast iron, cast steel,** *n.* Iron, and steel melted and cast into pigs, ingots, or molds, which renders the metal hard and non-malleable.—**castoff,** *a.* Laid aside as worn out or useless; rejected.
Castalian, kas·tā′li·an, *a.* Pertaining to Castalia; the spring on Mount Parnassus, sacred to the Muses.
castanet, kas·ta·net′, *n.* [Sp. *castañeta,* from L. *castanea,* a chestnut, from resembling that fruit.] One of a pair of small concave pieces of ivory or hard wood, shaped like spoons, fastened to the thumb, and beat with the middle finger in certain Spanish dances.
caste, kast, *n.* [Fr. *caste,* Pg. *casta,* breed, race, caste.] One of the classes or distinct hereditary orders into which the Hindus are divided according to the religious law of Brahmanism; a class or order of the same kind prevailing in other countries; a rank or order of society; social position; in social insects, a set of similar individuals, e.g. the 'workers' in ants, bees, etc.
castellan, kas′tel·lan, *n.* [L.L. *castellanus,* from L. *castellum,* a castle. CASTLE.] A governor or constable of a castle.—**castellated,** kas′tel·lāt·ed, *a.* Furnished with turrets and battlements like a castle; built in the style of a castle.
castigate, kas′ti·gāt, *v.t.*—*castigated, castigating.* [L. *castigo, castigatum,* from *castus,* pure.] To chastise; to punish; to correct; to criticize for the purpose of correcting; to emend.—**castigation,** kas·ti·gā′shon, *n.* The act of castigating; punishment by whipping; correction; chastisement; discipline; critical scrutiny and emendation; correction of textual errors.—**castigator,** kas′ti·gā·tėr, *n.* One who castigates or corrects.
Castile soap, kas·tēl′, *n.* A kind of fine hard, white or mottled soap, originally from Castile, made with olive-oil and a solution of caustic soda.—**Castilian,** kas·til′i·an, *a.* Pertaining to Castile in Spain.—*n.* An

inhabitant or native of Castile; the language of Castile, the classic or literary language of Spain.
castle, kas′l, *n.* [L. *castellum,* dim. of *castrum,* a fort.] A building, or series of connected buildings, fortified for *defense* against an enemy; a house with towers, often surrounded by a wall and moat, and having a donjon or keep in the center; a fortified residence; a fortress; the house or mansion of a person of rank or wealth: somewhat vaguely applied, but usually to a large and more or less imposing building; a piece made in the form of a castle, used in the game of chess; the rook. —*Castle in the air*, a visionary project; a scheme that has no solid foundation. —*v.t.* or *i.* *Chess,* to move the king two squares to the right or left and bring up the castle to the square the king has passed over.—**castled,** cas′ld, *a.* Furnished with a castle or castles.
castor, kas′tėr, *n.* [L. *castor;* Gr. *kastōr,* a beaver.] A substance of a strong penetrating smell, secreted by special glands of the beaver, and used in medicine and perfumery; a beaver hat.—**castor oil,** *n.* [Probably from some resemblance to the substance *castor.*] The oil, used in medicine as a purgative, obtained from the seeds, or beans, of the castor-oil plant.
castrametation, kas′tra·mi·tā′′shon, *n.* [L. *castrametari,* to encamp— *castra,* camp, and *metior,* to measure.] The art or act of encamping; the marking or laying out of a camp.
castrate, kas′trāt, *v.t.*—*castrated, castrating.* [L. *castro, castratum,* to castrate.] To deprive of the testicles; to geld; to take the vigor or strength from; to emasculate; to remove something objectionable from, as obscene parts from a writing; to expurgate.—*n.* A man (as a eunuch) or male animal (as an ox) that has been castrated.—**castration,** kas·trā′shon, *n.* The act of castrating.
casual, kazh′ū·al, *a.* [L. *casualis,* from *casus,* a chance or accident, from *cado, casum,* to fall; akin *case, chance, accident,* etc.] Happening or coming to pass, without design in the person or persons affected, and without being foreseen or expected; accidental; fortuitous; coming by chance; not happening or coming regularly; occasional; incidental.—*n.* A person who receives relief or shelter for one night at the most in the workhouse of a parish or union to which he does not belong. —**casualist,** kazh′ū·al·ist, *n.* A believer in casualism.—**casually,** kazh′-ū·al·li, *adv.* In a casual manner; accidentally; fortuitously.—**casualness,** kazh′ū·al·nes, *n.* The fact of being casual.—**casualty,** kazh′ū·al·ti, *n.* Chance, or what happens by chance; accident; contingency; an unfortunate chance or accident, especially one resulting in death or bodily injury; loss suffered by a body of men from death, wounds, etc.
casuist, kaz′ū·ist, *n.* [Fr. *casuiste,* from L. *casus,* a case.] One versed in or

using casuistry; one who studies and resolves cases of conscience, or nice points regarding conduct.—**casuistic, casuistical,** kaz·ū·is′tik, kaz·ū·is′tik-·al, *a.* Pertaining to casuists or casuistry; partaking of casuistry.— **casuistically,** kaz·ū·is′tik·al·li, *adv.* In a casuistic manner.—**casuistry,** kaz′ū·ist·ri, *n.* The science, doctrine, or department of ethics dealing with cases of conscience; frequently used in a bad sense for quibbling in matters of morality, or making too nice moral distinctions.
cat, kat, *n.* [A.Sax. *cat, catt*=D. and Dan. *kat,* Sw. *katt,* Icel. *köttr,* G. *katze, kater,* O.Fr. *cat,* Mod. Fr. *chat,* Ir. *cat,* W. *cath,* Rus. and Pol. *kot,* Tur. *kedi,* Ar. *qitt*—a cat; origin unknown.] A name applied to certain species of carnivorous quadrupeds of the feline tribe; a strong tackle or combination of pulleys, to hook and draw an anchor perpendicularly up to the cat-head of a ship; a double tripod having six feet: so called because it always lands on its feet as a cat is proverbially said to do; an abbreviation of cat-o'-nine-tails (which see).—*To let the cat out of the bag*, to disclose a trick; to let out a secret.—**catamount, catamountain,** kat′a·mount, kat′a-·moun·tān, *n.* The cat of the mountain; the wild cat; the North American puma or cougar.—**catbird,** *n.* A North American singing bird, a species of thrush which utters a cry of alarm like the mew of a cat.— **catcall,** kat′kạl, *n.* A sound like the cry of a cat, such as that made by a dissatisfied audience in a theater; a small squeaking instrument for producing such a sound.—**catgut,** kat′gut, *n.* The intestines of sheep (sometimes of the horse or the ass) dried and twisted into strings for the violin and for other purposes: so called from a notion that the material was the gut or intestines of the cat.—**catkin,** kat′kin, *n.* The blossom of the willow, birch, hazel, etc., which resembles a kitten or cat's tail.—**catnip,** kat′nip, *n.* A plant resembling mint, having a strong odor and taste, and which cats are said to be fond of.—**cathead,** *n.* A strong beam projecting over a ship's bows, and furnished with a block and tackle to lift an anchor.— **cat-o'-nine-tails,** *n.* An instrument consisting generally of nine pieces of knotted cord, used to flog offenders on the bare back.—**cat's-eye,** *n.* A hard and semi-transparent variety of quartz, having an opalescent radiation or play of colors like a cat's eye.—**cat's-paw,** *n.* The instrument used by a person to accomplish his designs; a tool; a dupe: so called from the story of the monkey which, instead of using his own paw, used that of the cat to draw nuts from the fire.—**cat walk,** *n.* A narrow footpath.
catabolism, ka·ta′bo·lizm, *n.* [Gr. *katabolē,* throwing down.] Destructive metabolism.
catachresis, kat·a·krē′sis, *n.* [Gr. *katachrēsis,* abuse—*kata,* against, and

chraomai, to use.] The wresting of a word from its true signification; the employment of a word under a false form through misapprehension in regard to its origin (*crayfish* for example).—**catachrestic, catachrestical,** kat·a·kres′tik, kat·a·kres′tik·al, *a.* Belonging to catachresis; wrested from its natural sense, use, or form.—**catachrestically,** kat·a·kres′tik·al·li, *adv.* In a catachrestical manner.

cataclysm, kat′a·klizm, *n.* [Gr. *kataklysmos*, a deluge, from *kataklyzō*, to inundate—*kata*, down, and *klyzō*, to wash.] A deluge, flood, or inundation sweeping over a territory.—**cataclysmal, cataclysmic,** kat·a·kliz′mal, kat·a·kliz′mik, *a.* Of or belonging to a cataclysm.

catacomb, kat′a·kōm, *n.* [It. *catacomba*, L.L. *catacumba*, from Gr. *kata*, down, and *kumbe, kumbos,* a hollow or recess.] A cave or subterranean place for the burial of the dead, in which the bodies are deposited in recesses hollowed out of the sides of the cave, the most notable being those near Rome, supposed to be the cells and caves in which the primitive Christians concealed themselves, and in which were deposited the bodies of the martyrs.

catafalque, kat′a·falk, *n.* [Fr. *catafalque,* from It. *catafalco,* from *falco,* for O.H.G. *palcho* (G. *balke*), a beam, with *cata* (as in Sp. *catar,* to view) prefixed. *Scaffold* is the same word with French prefix es.] A temporary structure representing a tomb placed over the coffin of a distinguished person in churches or over the grave.

Catalan, kat′a·lan, *a.* Pertaining to Catalonia, a province of Spain.—*n.* A native of Catalonia; the language of Catalonia; an old Spanish literary dialect early cultivated.

catalectic, kat·a·lek′tik, *a.* [Gr. *katalēktikos,* from *katalēgo,* to leave off, to stop.] *Pros.* having the measure incomplete; ending abruptly, as a verse wanting a syllable of its proper length.

catalepsy, kat′a·lep·si, *n.* [Gr. *katalēpsis,* a seizing, from *katalambanō,* to seize.] A condition marked by loss of voluntary motion, muscular rigidity, and fixity of posture.—**cataleptic,** kat·a·lep′tik, *a.*

catalog, catalogue, kat′a·log, *n.* [Fr. *catalogue,* from Gr. *katalogos,* a counting up—*kata,* thoroughly, and *logos,* a reckoning.] A list or enumeration of the names of men or things disposed in a certain order, often in alphabetical order; a list; a register. —*v.t.*—*catalogued, cataloguing.* To make a catalogue of.—*Catalogue raisonné,* a catalogue of books, paintings, etc., classed according to their subjects.

catalysis, ka·tal′i·sis, *n.* [Gr. *kata,* down, an *lyō,* to loose.] A modification (usually increase) in the speed of a chemical reaction, induced by a catalyst.—**catalyst,** kat′a·list, *n.* An agent that induces catalysis but is not itself chemically changed.— **catalytic,** kat·a·lit′ik, *a.*

catamaran, kat′a·ma·ran″, *n.* [Said to be from a Tamil word signifying 'tied logs'.] A kind of float or raft used as a substitute for a surfboat, particularly in the East and West Indies, and consisting usually of three pieces of wood lashed together, the middle piece being longer than the others, and having one end turned up in the form of a bow.

catamenia, kat·a·mē′ni·a, *n. pl.* [Gr. *katamēnios*—*kata,* down, and *mēn,* a month.] The menstrual discharge of females.—**catamenial,** kat·a·mē′ni·al, *a.*

cataplasm, kat′a·plazm, *n.* [Gr. *kataplasma,* from *kataplasso,* to anoint or to spread as a plaster.] *Med.* a soft and moist substance to be applied to some part of the body; a poultice.

catapult, kat′a·pult, *n.* [L. *catapulta,* from Gr. *katapeltēs*—*kata,* against, and *pallō,* to brandish, hurl.] A military engine anciently used for discharging missiles against a besieged place; originally an engine of the nature of a powerful bow.

cataract, kat′a·rakt, *n.* [L. *cataracta,* Gr. *katarraktēs,* from *kata,* down, and *rhēgnymi,* to break.] A great fall of water over a precipice; a waterfall; any furious rush or downpour of water; a disease of the eye consisting in an opacity of the crystalline lens or its capsule, by which the pupil seems closed by an opaque body, usually whitish, vision being thus impaired or destroyed.

catarrh, ka·tär′, *n.* [From Gr. *katarrheō,* to flow down.] A discharge or increased secretion of mucus from the membranes of the nose, fauces, and bronchia, characteristic of the ailment commonly called a *cold* in the head.—**catarrhal, catarrhous,** ka·tär′ral, ka·tär′rus, *a.* Pertaining to catarrh, produced by it, or attending it (a *catarrhal* fever).

catastrophe, ka·tas′tro·fe, *n.* [Gr. *katastrophe,* an overthrowing, a sudden turn, from *katastrephō,* to subvert—*kata,* down, and *strephō,* to turn.] The unfolding and winding up of the plot, clearing up of difficulties, and closing of a dramatic piece; the dénouement; a notable event terminating a series; a finishing stroke or windup; an unfortunate conclusion; a calamity or disaster; a supposed change in the crust of the earth from sudden physical violence, causing elevation or subsidence of the solid parts; a cataclysm.—**catastrophic,** kat·as·trof′ik, *a.* Pertaining to a catastrophe or catastrophes; pertaining to the theory of great changes on the globe being due to violent and sudden physical action.

catatonia, ka·ta·tō″ni·a, *n.* [Gr. *kata,* down, and *tonos,* tension.] A mental disorder characterized by muscular inactivity and apparent, although not actual, insensitiveness to the outside world.— **catatonic,** ka′ta·ton″ik, *a.* and *n.*

Catawba, ka·tạ′ba, *n.* A variety of grape much cultivated in Ohio, discovered on the *Catawba* river; the wine made from the grape.

catch, kach, *v.t.* pret. & pp. *caught* (*catched* is obsolete or vulgar). [O.E. *cacche,* O.Fr. *cachier, chacier,* etc., to hunt (Mod. Fr. *chasser*), from L.L. *captiare,* from L. *captare,* from *capere,* to take (whence *capable, captious,* etc.). *Chase* is the same word.] To lay sudden hold on; to seize, especially with the hand; to grasp; to snatch; to perceive or apprehend; to seize, as in a snare or trap; to ensnare; to entangle; to get entangled with, or to come into contact or collision with (the branch *caught* his hat); to get; to receive (to *catch* the sunlight; especially, to take or receive as by sympathy, contagion, or infection; to take hold of; to communicate to; to fasten on (the flames *caught* the woodwork); to seize the affections of; to engage and attach; to charm; to captivate.—*To catch it,* to get a scolding, a beating, or other unpleasant treatment. (Colloq.)—*To catch hold of,* to take or lay hold of.—*To catch up,* to snatch; to take up suddenly; to lay hold suddenly of something said.—*v.i.* To take or receive something; to be entangled or impeded; to spread by or as by infection; to be eager to get, use, or adopt: with *at.*—*n.* The act of seizing; seizure; anything that seizes or takes hold, that checks motion or the like, as a hook, a ratchet, a pawl, a spring bolt for a door or lid, etc; a choking or stoppage of the breath; something caught or to be caught, especially anything valuable or desirable obtained or to be obtained; a gain or advantage; one desirable from wealth as a husband or wife (*colloq.*); *mus.* a kind of canon or round for three or four voices, the words written to which are so contrived that by the union of the voices a different meaning is given by the singers *catching* at each other's words.—**catcher,** kach′-er, *n.* One who or that which catches. —**catching,** kach′ing, *a.* Communicating, or liable to be communicated, by contagion; infectious; captivating; charming; attracting.—**catchment,** kach′ment, *n.* A surface of ground of which the drainage is capable of being directed into a common reservoir.—**catchpenny,** *n.* Something of little value got up to hit the popular taste, and thereby catch the popular penny; anything got up merely to sell.—**catchpoll,** *n.* [Med. L. *cacepollus,* Fr. *chacepol.*] A chaser *of fowls.* (L. *pullus.*) A sheriff's officer, bailiff, constable, or other person whose duty is to arrest persons.—**catchword,** *n.* The word formerly often, now rarely, placed at the bottom of each page, on the right hand under the last line, and forming the first word on the following page; in a play the last word of one actor to be caught up by another as a reminder that he is to speak next; cue; a word caught up and repeated for effect.— **catchy,** *a.* Attractive, infectious, easily picked up of tunes and songs.

catchup, kach′ip, *n.* Same as *Ketchup.*

cate, kāt, *n.* [O.E. *acates,* provisions purchased, from O.Fr. *acat,* buying. CATER.] Food, more particularly rich, luxuriant, or dainty food; a delicacy; a dainty: commonly used in the plural.

catechetic, catechetical, kat·e·ket'-ik, kat·e·ket'ik·al, *a.* [CATECHISE.] Relating to catechising, or one who catechises; consisting in asking questions and receiving answers, as in teaching pupils.

catechize, catechise, kat'e·kīz, *v.t.* —*catechized, catechised, catechizing, catechising,* [Gr. *katēchiso,* to catechize, from *katecheō,* to utter sound, to teach by the voice—*kata,* down, and *echeō,* to sound, whence *echo.*] To instruct by asking questions, receiving answers, and offering explanations and corrections; to question; to interrogate; to examine or try by questions, especially such questions as would implicate the answerer.—**catechizer,** kat'e·kīz·er, *n.* One who catechizes.—**catechism,** kat'e·kizm, *n.* [Gr. *katēchismos,* instruction.] A book containing a summary of principles in any science or art, but especially in religion, reduced to the form of questions and answers. —**catechist,** kat'e·kist, *n.* One who instructs question and answer; a catechizer.—**catechistic, catechistical,** kat·e·kist'ik, kat·e·kist'ik·al, *a.* Pertaining to a catechist or catechism.

catechu, kat'e·shū, *n.* [Tamil *katti,* tree, and *shu,* juice.] A name common to several astringent extracts prepared from the wood, bark, and fruits of various plants, especially from some species of acacia, and used in dyeing, tanning, and medicine.

catechumen, kat·e·kū'men, *n.* [Gr. *katēchoumenos,* instructed. CATE-CHISE.] One who is under instruction in the first rudiments of Christianity; a neophyte.

category, kat'e·gor·i, *n.* [Gr. *katēgoria,* a class or category, from *katēgoreō,* to accuse, show, demonstrate —*kata,* down, etc., and *agoreō,* to speak in an assembly, from *agora,* a forum or market.] One of the highest classes to which objects of thought can be referred; one of the most general heads under which everything that can be asserted of any subject may be arranged; in a popular sense, any class or order in which certain things are embraced.—**categorical,** kat·e·gor'ik·al, *a.* Pertaining to a category; absolute; positive; express; not relative or hypothetical (statement, answer).—**categorically,** kat·e·gor'ik·al·li, *adv.* In a categorical manner; absolutely; directly; expressly; positively.

catenary, catenarian, ka·tē'ne·ri or kat'ē·ne·ri, kat·e·nā'ri·an, *a.* [L. *catenarius,* from *catena,* a chain.] Relating to a chain; like a chain.—*Catenary curve,* that variety of curve which is formed by a rope or chain, of uniform density and thickness, when allowed to hang freely with its ends attached to two fixed points.—**catenate,** ‡ kat'e·nāt, *v.t.* To connect in a series of links or ties; to concatenate.—**catenation,**‡ kat·e·nā'shon, *n.* Connection of links; union of parts, as in a chain; regular connection;

concatenation.

cater, kā'ter, *v.i.* [From obs. *cater,* a caterer, O.Fr. *acateur, acator,* from *acater,* L.L. *accaptare,* to buy, from L. *ad,* to, and L. *captare,* intens. of *capere,* to take.] To buy or provide something for use, enjoyment, or entertainment; to purvey food, provisions, amusement, etc.: followed by *for.*—**caterer,** kā'ter·er, *n.* One who caters; a provider or purveyor of provisions; one who provides for any want or desire.—**cateress,** kā'ter·es, *n.* A woman who caters; a female provider. (*Mil.*)

cateran, kat'er·an, *n.* [Gael. and Ir. *ceatharnach,* a soldier.] A kern; a Highland or Irish irregular soldier; a Highland freebooter.

cater-cousin,† kā'ter·kuz·n, *n.* [*Cater*=Fr. *quatre,* four.] A distant cousin; a remote relation. (*Shak.*)

caterpillar, kat'er·pil·ler, *n.* [O.E. *catyrpel* (comp. *caterwaul*); from *cat,* and L. *pilosus,* hairy.] The hairy, wormlike larva or grub of the lepidopterous insects (butterflies and moths), but also sometimes applied to the larvae of other insects.

caterwaul, kat'er·wal, *v.i.* [From *cat,* and *waul,* in imitation of the sound made by a cat; O.E. *caterwawe.*] To utter noisy and disagreeable cries: said of cats; to make a disagreeable howling or screeching.

catharsis, ka·thär'sis, *n.* [Gr. *katharsis,* a cleansing.] Purgation; purging of the effects of emotional stress; discharge of repressed emotions or ideas.—**cathartic,** ka·thär'tik, *a.*—*n. Med.* a laxative or purgative.

cathedra, ka·thed'ra, *n.* [L. *cathedra,* a teacher's or professor's chair, a bishop's chair, Gr. *kathedra,* a chair or seat—*kata,* down, and *hedra,* a seat.] The throne or seat of a bishop in the cathedral or episcopal church of his diocese.—**cathedral,** ka·thē'dral, *n.* The principal church in a diocese, that which is specially the church of the bishop: so called from possessing the episcopal chair called *cathedra.*—*a.* Pertaining to the bishop's or head church of a diocese (a *cathedral* church).

catheter, kath'e·ter, *n.* [Gr. *kathetēr,* from *kathiēmi,* to thrust in—*kata,* down, and *hiēmi,* to send.] In *surg.* a tubular instrument, usually made of silver, to be introduced through the urethra into the bladder to draw off the urine when the natural discharge is arrested.—**catheterize,** kath'e·ter·īz, *v.t.* To operate on with a catheter.

cathode, kath'ōd, *n.* [Gr. *kata,* down, and *hodos,* a way.] The negative pole of an electric current, or that by which the current leaves: opposed to *anode.*—**cathode ray,** a stream of electrons projected from cathode to anode in a vacuum tube; the source of X rays.

catholic, kath'o·lik, *a.* [Gr. *katholikos* —*kata,* down, throughout, and *holos,* the whole; L. *catholicus,* Fr. *catholique.*] Universal or general; embracing all true Christians (the *catholic* church or faith); not narrowminded, partial, or bigoted; free from preju-

dice; liberal (*catholic* tastes or sympathies); [*cap.*] pertaining to or affecting the Roman Catholics.—*n.* A member of the universal Christian church; often restricted to members of the Church of Rome.—**catholicism,** ka·thol'i·sizm, *n.* The state of being catholic or universal; catholicity; [*cap.*] adherence to the Roman Catholic Church; the Roman Catholic faith.—**catholicity,** kath·o·lis'i·ti, *n.* The state or quality of being catholic or universal; catholic character or position; universality; the quality of being catholic or liberal-minded.—**catholicize,** ka·thol'i·sīz, *v.i.* To become a Catholic.—**catholicon,**‡ ka·thol'i·kon, *n.* [Gr. *katholikon iama,* universal remedy.] A remedy for all diseases; a panacea.

cation, kat'i·on, *n.* [Gr. *kata,* down, and *ion,* going.] A positive ion; the ion that moves toward the cathode in electrolysis.

catkin, *n.* See CAT.

catoptric, ka·top'trik, *a.* [Gr. *katoptrikos,* from *katoptron,* a mirror— *kata,* against, and *optomai,* to see.] Pertaining to incident and reflected light; pertaining to catoptrics.—**catoptrics,** ka·top'triks, *n.* That branch of optics which explains the properties of incident and reflected light, and particularly that which is reflected from mirrors or polished bodies.

catsup, *n.* See KETCHUP.

cattle, kat'l, *n. pl.* [O.E. *catel,* goods, cattle, from O.Fr. *catel, chatel,* property in general, from L.L. *capitale, captale,* property, capital, from L. *capitalis,* chief, capital, from *caput,* the head. *Cattle*=*chattel, capital.*] A term applied collectively to domestic quadrupeds, such as serve for tillage or other labor, or for food to man, including camels, horses, asses, cows, sheep, goats, and perhaps swine, but now chiefly restricted to domestic beasts of the cow kind.

catty, kat'i, *n.* A Chinese weight of 1⅓ lbs.

Caucasian, ka·kā'zi·an or ka·kā'zhi·-an, *a.* [From the Caucasus Mountains.] Pertaining to the Caucasus or its inhabitants; a designation of race; one of the races into which the human family has been divided.—*n.* An ethnological term applied to the highest type of the human family, including nearly all Europeans, the Circassians, Armenians, Persians, Indians, Jews, etc., being invented by Blumenbach, who regarded a skull he had got from Caucasus as representing the standard of perfection.

caucus, ka'kus, *n.* [Med. Gr. *kaukos,* a drinking cup, referring to convivial meetings of 18th-century U.S. political leaders in Boston and elsewhere.] A private meeting of citizens to agree upon candidates to be proposed for election to offices, or to concert measures for supporting a party.

caudal, ka'dal, *a.* [L. *cauda,* a tail.] Pertaining to a tail; of the nature of a tail; having the appearance of a tail. —**caudate, caudated,** ka'dāt, ka'dāt·ed, *a.* Having a tail or tail-like attachment: a term applied in *bot.* to seeds which have a taillike appendage.

ch, *chain;* ch, Sc. lo*ch;* g, *go;* j, *job;* ng, si*ng;* TH, *then;* th, *thin;* w, *wig;* hw, *whig;* zh, a*zure.*

caudex, kạ′deks, *n.* L. pl. **caudices,** kạ′di·sēz, E. pl. **caudexes,** kạ′deks·ez. [L.] In *bot.* the stem of a tree; specially the scaly trunk of palms and tree ferns.

caudle, kạ′dl, *n.* [O.Fr. *caudel, chaudel,* a dim. form from L.L. *calidum, caldum,* a kind of hot drink, from L. *calidus,* warm.] A kind of warm drink made of spiced and sugared wine or ale, given to sick persons, women in childbed, or the like.—*v.t.* To make into caudle; to refresh or make warm, as with caudle (*Shak.*).—**caudle cup,** *n.* A vessel or cup for holding caudle.

caught, kạt, pret. & pp. of *catch.*

caul, kạl, *n.* [From O.Fr. *cale,* a kind of little cap; from the Celtic; comp. Ir. *calla,* Gael. *call,* a veil, a hood.] A kind of head covering worn by females; a net enclosing the hair; the hinder part of a cap; a membrane investing some part of the viscera (O.T.); a portion of the amnion or membrane enveloping the fetus, sometimes encompassing the head of a child when born, and superstitiously supposed to be a preservative against drowning.

cauldron, kạl′dron. Same as *Caldron.*

caulescent, kạ·les′ent, *a.* [L. *caulis,* a stalk.] *Bot.* having a caulis or obvious stem rising above the ground.—**caulicle,** kạ′li·kl, *n.* [L. *cauliculus.*] *Bot.* a little or rudimentary stem.—**cauline,** kạ′lin, *a. Bot.* of or belonging to a stem (*cauline* leaves).—**caulis,** kạ′lis, *n. Bot.* the stem of a plant rising above the ground.

cauliflower, kol′i·flou·ėr, *n.* [Lit. cabbage-flower, from its appearance, from L. *caulis,* colewort, cabbage, and E. *flower;* comp. Fr. *choufleur* (*chou,* cabbage, *fleur,* flower), cauliflower.] A garden variety of cabbage, the inflorescence of which is condensed while young into a depressed fleshy head, which is highly esteemed as a table vegetable.

caulk, kạk. Same as *calk.*

cause, kạz, *n.* [Fr. *cause,* L. *causa,* a cause.] That which produces an effect; that which brings about a change; that from which anything proceeds, and without which it would not exist; the reason or motive that urges, moves, or impels the mind to act or decide; a suit or action in court; any legal process which a party institutes to obtain his demand, or by which he seeks his right; any subject of question or debate; case; interest; matter; affair; that object or side of a question to which the efforts of a person or party are directed.—*v.t.*—*caused, causing.* To be the cause of; to effect by agency; to bring about; to be the occasion of; to produce.—**causable,** kạ′za·bl, *a.* Capable of being caused, produced, or effected.—**causal,** kạ′zal, *a.* [L. *causalis.*] Relating to a cause or causes; implying, containing, or expressing a cause or causes.—*n.* A verb signifying to make to do something; as *fell,* to make to fall.—**causality,** kạ·zal′i·ti, *n.* The state of being causal; the fact of acting as a cause; the action or power of a cause, in producing its effect; the doctrine or

principle that every change implies the operation of a cause.—**causally,** kạ′zal·li, *adv.* In a causal manner; by tracing effects to causes; by acting as a cause.—**causation,** kạ·zā′shon, *n.* The act of causing or producing; the doctrines as to the connection of causes and effects.—**causative,** kạ′za·tiv, *a.* Effective as a cause or agent: often followed by *of; gram.* expressing a cause on reason; causal.—*n.* A word expressing a cause.—**causatively,** kạ′za·tiv·li, *adv.* In a causative manner.—**causeless,** kạz′les, *a.* Having no cause or producing agent; self-originated; uncreated; without just ground, reason, or motive.—**causer,** kạz′ér, *n.* One who or that which causes.

causerie, kōz·rē′, *n.* [Fr.] Newspaper light talk; literary conversation; an informal lecture.

causeway, kạz′wā, *n.* [Original spelling *causey,* from O.Fr. *caucis* (Mod. Fr. *chaussée*), a road in making which lime or mortar is used, from L. *calx, calcis,* lime (whence *chalk, calcareous*).] A road or path raised above the natural level of the ground by stones, earth timber, etc., serving as a passage over wet or marshy ground or the like; a raised and paved roadway.—*v.t.* To provide with a causeway; to pave, as a road or street, with blocks of stone.—**causey,** kạ′zi, *v.* and *n.* Causeway: a less common but more correct spelling.

caustic, kạs′tik, *a.* [Gr. *kaustikos,* from *kaiō, kausō,* to burn.] Capable of burning, corroding, or destroying the texture of animal substances; *fig.* severe; cutting; stinging; pungent; sarcastic.—*n. Med.* any substance which burns, corrodes, or disintegrates the textures of animal structures; an escharotic: sometimes popularly restricted to lunar caustic or nitrate of silver when cast into sticks for surgeons' use; *math.* the name given to the curve to which the rays of light reflected or refracted by another curve are tangents.—**caustically,** kạs′ti·kal·li, *adv.* In a caustic or severe manner.—**causticity,** kạs·tis′i·ti, *n.* The quality of being caustic or corrosive; *fig.* severity of language; pungency; sarcasm.

cauterize, kạ′tėr·īz, *v.t.*—*cauterized, cauterizing.* [L.L. *cauterizo,* from Gr. *kautēriazō,* from *kautērion, kautēr,* a burning or branding iron, from *kaiō,* to burn.] To burn or sear with fire or a hot iron or with caustics, as morbid flesh.—**cauterization,** kạ′tėr·iz·ā′shon, *n. Surg.* the act or the effect of cauterizing.—**cautery,** kạ′tėr·i, *n.* [L. *cauterium,* Gr. *kautērion.*] A burning or searing, as of morbid flesh, by a hot iron or by caustic substances; the instrument or drug employed in cauterizing.

caution, kạ′shon, *n.* [L. *cautio,* from *caveo, cautum,* to be on one's guard, beware.] Provident care; prudence in regard to danger; wariness; watchfulness, forethought, or vigilance; a measure taken for security; a security or guarantee‡; a warning or admonition.—*v.t.* To give notice of

danger to; to warn; to exhort to take heed.—**cautionary,** kạ′shon·ar·i, *a.* Containing caution, or warning to avoid danger; given as a pledge or in security.—**cautious,** kạ′shus, *a.* Possessing or exhibiting caution; attentive to examine probable effects and consequences of actions with a view to avoid danger or misfortune: prudent; circumspect; wary; watchful; vigilant; careful.—**cautiously,** kạ′shus·li, *adv.* In a cautious manner.—**cautiousness,** kạ′shus·nes, *n.* The quality of being cautious; caution.

cavalcade, kav′al·kād, *n.* [Fr. *cavalcade,* It. *cavalcata,* from L. *caballus,* a horse. CAVALIER, CAVALRY.] A procession of persons on horseback, or consisting mostly of persons on horseback.

cavalier, kav·a·lēr′, *n.* [Fr. *cavalier,* L.L. *caballarius,* from L. *caballus,* a horse, whence also *cavalry, chivalry, cavalcade,* etc. *Chevalier* is a parallel form.] A horseman, especially an armed horseman; a knight; [*cap.*] a partisan of Charles I, as opposed to a Roundhead or adherent to the Parliament; a gallant; *fort.* a work commonly situated within the bastion, and raised higher than the other works so as to command all the adjacent works and the surrounding country.—*a.* Gay; sprightly; easy; offhand; haughty; disdainful; supercilious (a *cavalier* answer).—**cavalierly,** kav·a·lēr′li, *adv.* In a cavalier manner; haughtily; arrogantly; disdainfully.—**cavalry,** kav′al·ri, *n.* [Fr. *cavalerie,* from It. *cavalleria,* from *cavallo,* L. *caballus,* a horse. *Chivalry* is a parallel form.] A body of troops, mounted on horseback or moving in motor vehicles.

cavatina, kav·a·tē′na, *n.* [It.] *Music,* a melody of short simple character, and without a second part and a return part.

cave, kāv, *n.* [Fr. *cave,* from L. *cavus,* hollow, whence also *cavity, cavern,* and *cage.*] A hollow place in the earth; a subterranean cavern; a den.—**cave,** *n.* A political party: desertion; seceders; applied by John Bright in 1866 to deserters, with reference to the Cave of Adullam, 1 *Sam.* xxii. 1-2—*v.t.* To make hollow.—*v.i.*† To dwell in a cave.—*To cave in,* to fall in and leave a hollow, as earth on the side of a well or pit or the roof of a subterranean passage.—**cave dweller, cave man,** *n.* One who dwells in caves, a name given to such of the earliest races of prehistoric man as dwelt in natural caves, subsisting on shellfish and wild animals.

caveat kā′vi·at, *n.* [L. *caveat,* let him beware, from *caveo,* to beware.] In *law,* a process in a court to stop proceedings; hence, an intimation of caution; hint; warning; admonition.—*v.i.* To enter a caveat.—**caveat emptor,** [L., let the buyer beware.] At the buyer's risk.

cavendish, kav′en·dish, *n.* Tobacco which has been softened and pressed into quadrangular cakes.

cavern, kav′ėrn, *n.* [L. *caverna,* from *cavus,* hollow. CAVE.] A deep hollow place in the earth; a cave.—**cavern-**

ous, kav´ėrn·us, *a.* [L. *cavernosus.* Hollow, or containing a cavern or caverns; filled with small cavities.

cavetto, ka·vet´tō, *n.* [It., from *cavo,* hollow, L. *cavus.*] *Arch.* a hollow member, or round concave molding, containing the quadrant of a circle.

caviar, kav´·i·är, *n.* [Fr. *caviar,* Turk *haviâr.*] A delicacy made from the salted roe of sturgeon and other large fish. —*Caviar to the general,* a delicacy beyond the reach of most; a reasoning beyond the popular grasp.

cavil, kav´il, *v.i.*—*cavilled, cavilling.* [O.Fr. *caviller,* from L. *cavillor,* to cavil, *cavilla,* a quibble, trick, shuffle.] To raise captious and frivolous objections; to find fault without good reason: frequently followed by *at.* —*n.* A captious or frivolous objection; captious or specious argument. —**caviller,** kav´il·ėr, *n.* One who cavils; one who is apt to raise captious objections; a captious disputant.— **cavilling,** kav´il·ling, *a.* Given to cavil or making captious objections.

cavity, kav´i·ti, *n.* [Fr. *cavité,* L. *cavitas,* from L. *cavus,* hollow. CAVE.] A hollow place; a hollow; a void or empty space in a body; an opening; a hollow part of the human body.

cavy, kā´vi, *n.* The name common to certain South American rodent animals, the most familiar species being the well-known guinea pig.

caw, ką, *v.i.* [Imitative of the sound; comp. Sc. *kae,* D. *kaauw,* Dan. *kaa,* a jackdaw.] To cry like a crow, rook, or raven.—*n.* The cry of the rook or crow.

cay, kā, *n.* [Sp. *cayo,* a rock, a shoal, an islet.] An islet; a range or reef of rocks lying near the surface of the water: used especially in the West Indies and sometimes written *Key.*

cayenne, kī·en´ or kā·en´. *n.* [From *Cayenne* in South America.] A kind of pepper, a powder made from the dried and ground fruits, and more especially the seeds, of various species of *Capsicum.*

cayman, kā´man, *n.* [Native Guiana name.] A name applied popularly to the alligator of the West Indies and South America.

cayuse, kī·ūs´, *n.* A small horse; an Indian pony: a bronco.

cease, sēs, *v.i.*—*ceased, ceasing.* [Fr. *cesser,* L. *cesso, cessare,* to cease, a freq. from *cedere,* to yield, to *cede.* CEDE.] To stop moving, acting, or speaking; to leave off; to give over; to desist: followed by *from* before a noun; to come to an end; to terminate; to become extinct; to pass away (the storm *ceases*).—*v.t.* To put a stop to; to put an end to; to desist from.—**ceaseless,** sēs´les, *a.* Without a stop or pause; incessant; continual; without intermission; enduring for ever; endless.

cedar, sē´dėr, *n.* [L. *cedrus,* Gr. *kedros,* a kind of juniper.] A coniferous evergreen tree which grows to a great size, and is remarkable for its durability, forming fine woods on the mountains of Syria and Asia Minor, and often called distinctively the cedar of Lebanon. The deodar cedar

is closely akin to it, and the name is also given to various other trees.—*a.* Made of cedar, belonging to cedar.— **cedarn,** sē´dėrn, *a.* Pertaining to the cedar; made of cedar. (*Tenn.*)

cede, sēd, *v.t.*—*ceded, ceding.* [L. *cedo, cessum,* to retire, yield, grant, give up, a word which appears also in *accede, concede, exceed, precede, recede, decease, abscess, antecedent, ancestor, predecessor, cease,* etc.] To yield; to surrender; to give up; to resign; to relinquish.—*v.i.* To yield; to submit; to pass over; to be transferred; to fall to; to lapse.

cedilla, si·dil´la, *n.* [Fr. *cédille,* It. *zediglia,* a dim. of *zeta,* the name of *z* in Greek; because formerly, in order to give *c* the sound of *s,* it was customary to write *cz:* thus *leczon,* for modern *leçon.*] A mark placed under the letter *c,* especially in French (thus *ç*), to show that it is to be sounded like *s.*

ceil, sēl, *v.t.* [O.E. *seile,* a canopy, from Fr. *ciel,* It. *cielo,* a canopy, heaven, from L. *cælum,* heaven, same root as Gr. *koilos,* hollow, and E. *hollow.*] To overlay or cover the inner roof of a room or building; to provide with a ceiling.—**ceiling,** sēl´ing, *n.* The inside lining of surface of an apartment above; the horizontal or curved surface of an apartment opposite the floor, usually finished with plastered work; maximum height to which an airplane can climb under certain conditions; the upper limit of wages, prices, etc.

celandine, sel´an-din, *n.* [O.Fr. *celidoine,* Fr. *chélidoine,* from L. *chelidonium,* Gr. *chelidonion,* swallowwort; from *chelidôn,* a swallow.] A name given to two plants belonging to the poppy family, which yield an acrid juice used in medicine.

Celanese, sel´an·ēz, *n.* A trademarked name for a type of rayon material.

celebrate, sel´e·brāt, *v.t.*—*celebrated, celebrating.* [L. *celebrare, celebratum,* to celebrate, from *celeber,* famous, frequented, populous.] To make known or mention often, especially with honor or praise; to extol; to distinguish by any kind of observance or ceremony (to *celebrate* a birthday). —**celebrant,** sel´e·brant, *n.* One who celebrates; one who performs a public religious rite.—**celebrated,** sel´e·brāt·ed, *a.* Having celebrity; distinguished; well known; famous.— **celebrator,** sel´e·brā·tėr, *n.* One who celebrates.—**celebration,** sel·e·brā´shon, *n.* The act of celebrating; the act of praising or extolling; honor or distinction bestowed; the act of observing with appropriate rites or ceremonies.—**celebrity,** se·leb´ri·ti, *n.* [L. *celebritas.*] The condition of being celebrated; fame; renown (the *celebrity* of the Duke of Wellington, of Homer, or of the Iliad); a person of distinction.

celerity, se·ler´i·ti, *n.* [L. *celeritas,* from *celer,* swift.] Rapidity of motion; swiftness; quickness; speed. ∴ As distinguished from *velocity, celerity* is now generally applied to the motions or actions of living beings, *velocity* to inanimate objects.

celery, sel´e·ri, *n.* [Fr. *céleri,* It. *seleri,* from Gr. *selinon,* parsley.] A plant indigenous to marshy places and long cultivated in gardens as a salad and culinary vegetable.

celestial, se·les´chel, *a.* [O.Fr. *celestial, celestiel,* L. *cælestis,* from *cælum,* heaven, whence also *ceiling.*] Heavenly; belonging or relating to heaven; dwelling in heaven; supremely excellent or delightful; belonging to the upper regions or visible heaven; pertaining to the heavens.—*Celestial Empire,* China, so called because the first emperors are fabled to have been deities.—*n.* An inhabitant of heaven; [*usually cap.*] a native of China, the so-called Celestial Empire.—**celestially,** se·les´chel·li, *adv.* In a celestial or heavenly manner.—**celestial navigation,** *n.* Navigation using celestial bodies for reference.

celibacy, sel´i·ba·si, *n.* [L. *cælibatus,* a single life, celibacy, from *cælebs,* unmarried.] The state of being celibate or unmarried; a single life.— **celibate,** sel´i·bāt, *n.* One who adheres to or practices celibacy.—*a.* Unmarried; single.

cell, sel, *n.* [L. *cella,* a cell, a small room, a hut, from same root as *celare,* whence *concelare,* to conceal. *Hole* and *hollow* are from same root.] A small apartment, as in a convent or a prison; a small or mean place of residence, such as a cave or hermitage; a small cavity or hollow place: variously applied (the *cells* of the brain, the *cells* of a honey comb, the *cells* of a galvanic battery); *eccles.* a lesser religious house, especially one subordinate to a greater; *arch.* the part of the interior of a temple where the image of a god stood; *biol.* a small, usually microscopic, mass of contractile protoplasm with a membranous envelope forming the most elementary constituent or the structural unit in the tissues of animals and plants.—**cellophane,** sel´lo·fān, *n.* Transparent moistureproof cellulose sheets or film, used extensively as coverings and wrappings for cigarettes, cigars, foodstuffs, and other kinds of merchandise.— **cellular,** sel´lū·lėr, *a.* [L. *cellula,* a little cell.] Consisting of cells, or containing cells.—**Celluloid,** sel´lū·loid, *n.* An artificial substance, chiefly composed of cellulose or vegetable fibrin, used as a substitute for ivory, bone, coral, etc.—**cellulose,** sel´lū·lōs, *a.* Containing cells.—*n. Bot.* the substance of which the permanent cell membranes of plants are always composed, in many respects allied to starch.—*n. Chem.* a chief constituent of wood, cotton, paper, etc.

cellar, sel´lėr, *n.* [L. *cellarium.* CELL.] A room in a house or other building, either wholly or partly under ground, used for storage purposes.—**cellarage,** sel´lėr·ij, *n.* The space occupied by cellars; cellars collectively; charge for storage in a cellar.—**cellarer,** sel´lėr·ėr, *n.* An officer in a monastery who has the care of the cellar; a butler; one who keeps wine or spirit cellars; a spirit-dealer.—**cellaret,** sel·lėr·et´, *n.* [Dim. of *cellar.*] A case of cabinet work for holding bottles of liquors.

Celt, selt, *n.* [L. *Celtæ,* Gr. *Keltoi, Keltai,* connected with W. *celt,* a covert or shade; Gael. *ceiltach,* an inhabitant of the forest.] One of a distinct group of men inhabiting many parts of ancient Europe; the Celts now speaking a distinctive language are the Bretons, Welsh, Scotch Highlanders, and a portion of the Irish. [The word with its derivaties is frequently written with an initial *K—Kelt, Keltic,* etc.]— **Celtic,** sel′tik, *a.* Pertaining to the Celts, or to their language.—*n.* The language or group of dialects spoken by the Celts.—**Celticism,** sel′ti·sizm, *n.* The manners and customs of the Celts; a Celtic expression or mode of expression.

cement, si·ment′, *n.* [O.Fr. *cement,* L. *cæmentum,* chips of stone made into cement, contr. from *cædimentum,* from *cædo,* to cut.] Any glutinous or other substance capable of uniting bodies in close cohesion; a kind of mortar consisting of those hydraulic limes which contain silica and therefore set quickly; *fig.* bond of union; that which unites persons firmly together.—*v.t.* To unite by cement or other matter that produces cohesion of bodies; *fig.* to unite firmly or closely.—*v.i.* To unite or become solid; to unite and cohere. —**cementation,** si·men·tā′shon, *n.* The act of cementing; the conversion of iron into steel by heating the iron in a mass of ground charcoal, and thus causing it to absorb a certain quantity of the latter.—**cementer,** si·men′tėr, *n.* The person or thing that cements.

cemetery, sem′e·te·ri, *n.* [L. *cœmeterium,* a burying place, from Gr. *koimētērion,* a sleeping place, afterward a burying place, from *koimaō,* to sleep.] A place set apart for interment; a graveyard; a necropolis.

cenobite, sen′o·bīt, *n.* [L. *cœnobita,* from Gr. *koinobios,* living in common, from *koinos,* common, and *bios,* life.] One of a religious order living in a convent or in community; in opposition to an anchorite or hermit, who lives in solitude.—**cenobitic,** sen·o·bit′ik, sen·o·bit′ik·al, *a.* Living in community, as men belonging to a convent.—**cenobitism,** sen′o·bīt·izm, *n.* The state of being a cenobite; the principles or practice of a cenobite.

cenotaph, sen′o·taf, *n.* [Gr. *kenotaphion—kenos,* empty, and *taphos,* a tomb.] A sepulchral monument erected to one who is buried elsewhere.

cense,† sens, *v.t.—censed, censing.* [Fr. *encenser.* INCENSE.] To perfume with incense.—*v.i.* To scatter incense.—**censer,** sen′sėr, *n.* [A shortened form for *incenser ;* Fr. *encensoir.*] A vase or pan in which incense is burned; a vessel for burning and wafting incense; a thurible.

censor, sen′sėr, *n.* [L. *censor,* from *censeo,* to value, enrol, tax.] An officer in ancient Rome whose business was to draw up a register of the citizens,

to keep watch over their morals, and to superintend the finances of the state; one empowered to examine all manuscripts, pamphlets, newspapers, and books before they are published, and to see that they contain nothing obnoxious; a war official employed to open, destroy, or revise correspondence, or sources of information calculated to instruct the enemy; one who censures, blames, or reproves.—**censor,** *v.t.* To revise in this sense.—**censorial,** sen·sō′ri·al, *a.* Belonging to a censor or to the correction of public morals; censorious.—**censorious,** sen·sō′ri·us, *a.* Addicted to censure; apt to blame or condemn; ready to pass severe remarks on a person's conduct; implying or expressing censure.— **censoriously,** sen·sō′ri·us·li, *adv.* In a censorious manner.—**censoriousness,** sen·sō′ri·us·nes, *n.* The quality of being censorious; disposition to blame and condemn.—**censorship,** sen′sėr·ship, *n.* The office or dignity of a censor; the period of his office.

censure, sen′shōr, *n.* [Fr. *censure ;* L. *censura,* an opinion or judgment; from *censere,* to value, to estimate, whence *censor, census.*] Judgment or opinion‡; the act of blaming or finding fault and condemning as wrong; expression of blame or disapprobation; faultfinding; condemnation; animadversion.—*v.t.—censured, censuring.* To find fault with and condemn as wrong; to blame; to express disapprobation of.—*v.i.†* To pass an opinion, especially a severe opinion. (*Shak.*)—**censurable,** sen′shōr·a·bl, *a.* Worthy of censure; blamable; culpable; reprehensible; blameworthy.—**censurably,** sen′shōr·a·bli, *adv.* In a censurable manner; in a manner worthy of blame.—**censurer,** sen′shōr·ėr, *n.* One who censures or expresses blame.

census, sen′sus, *n.* [L., from *censere,* to register, enroll, whence *census, censor.*] In ancient Rome a registered statement of the particulars of a person's property for taxation purposes; an enumeration and register of the Roman citizens and their property; in modern times, an enumeration of the inhabitants of a state or part of it, taken by order of its legislature; any official enumeration of population.—**censual,** sen′shō·al, *a.* [L. *censualis.*] Relating to or containing a census.

cent, sent, *n.* [Contr. of L. *centum,* a hundred.] A hundred, commonly used with *per ;* as, ten *per cent,* that is in the proportion of ten to the hundred; in various countries a coin equal to the hundredth part of the monetary unit; in the United States the hundredth part of the dollar.—**cental,** sen′tal, *n.* A weight of 100 lbs.—*a.* Pertaining to or consisting of a hundred; reckoned or proceeding by the hundred.—**centesimal,** sen·tes′i·mal, *a.* [L. *centesimus,* from *centum.*] Hundredth; by the hundred.—*n.* Hundredth part; the next step of progression after decimal.

centaur, sen′tạr, *n.* [L. *centaurus ;* Gr. *kentauros,* lit. bull-pricker; the Centaurs probably represented some race that hunted wild cattle and lived almost constantly on horseback.] *Greek myth,* a member of a race of fabulous beings supposed to be half man and half horse; [*cap.*] the name given to a constellation in the southern hemisphere.— **centaury,** sen′tạ·ri, *n.* [L. *centaurea,* Gr. *kentaurion,* after the *Centaur* Cheiron, because said to have cured a wound in his foot.] The popular name of various plants. Common centaury is an annual herb of the gentian family in high repute among the old herbalists for its medicinal properties.

centenary, sen′te·ne·ri, *n.* [L. *centenarius,* consisting of a hundred, relating to a hundred, from *centum,* a hundred.] What consists of or comprehends a hundred; the space of a hundred years; the commemoration of any event which occurred a hundred years before.—*a.* Relating to or consisting of a hundred; relating to a hundred years.— **centenarian,** sen·te·nâ′ri·an, *n.* A person a hundred years old or upward.—*a.* Of or pertaining to a centenary or centenarian.—**centennial,** sen·ten′ni·al, *a.* [L. *centum,* and *annus,* a year.] Consisting of or lasting a hundred years; aged a hundred years or upward; happening every hundred years.—*n.* The commemoration or celebration of any event which occurred a hundred years before.—**centennially,** sen·ten′ni·al·li, *adv.* Once in every hundred years.

center, sen′tėr, *n.* [Fr., from L. *centrum,* Gr. *kentron,* a prick or point, from *kenteō,* to prick.] That point of a line, plane figure, or solid body which is equally distant from the extremities; the middle point, portion, or place; the middle or central object; a point of concentration; the nucleus around which or into which things are collected (a *center* of attraction); the part of a target next the bull's-eye; the men of the moderate party in politics.— *Center of buoyancy,* in hydrostatics, the center of gravity of the liquid displaced by a floating body. It is the point through which the upward thrust of the liquid may be conceived to act.—*Center of gravity,* the point of a body about which all the parts of the body exactly balance each other, and which being supported, the whole body will remain at rest though acted on by gravity.—*Center of magnitude,* that point in a body which is equally distant from all the similar external parts of it. In the regular solids this point coincides with the center of gravity.— *Center of mass,* that point in a body through which the resultant of absolutely parallel forces exerted on its particles always acts, whatever the direction of the forces.—*Center of motion,* the point which remains at rest while all the other parts of a body move round it.—*Center of*

---

oscillation, the point of a body suspended, at which, if all the matter were concentrated, the oscillations would be performed in the same time.—*Center of pressure*, the point in a submerged plane area through which the resultant of the fluid-pressures upon it acts.—*v.t.*—*centered, centering.* To place on a center; to fix on a central point; to collect to a point.—*v.i.* To be placed in a center or in the middle; to be collected to one point; to be concentrated or united in one.—**central,** sen′tral, *a.* [L. *centralis.*] Relating or pertaining to the center; placed in the center or middle; constituting or containing the center; originating or proceeding from the center.—**centralism,** sen′tral·izm, *n.* The quality of being central; the combination of several parts into one whole; centralization.—**centralist,** sen′tral·ist, *n.* One who promotes centralization.—**centrality,** sen′tral′i·ti.—**centralization,** sen′tral·iz·ā′′shon, *n.* The act of centralizing or bringing to one center.—**centralize,** sen′tral·īz, *v.t.*—*centralized, centralizing.* To draw to a central point; to bring to a center; to render central; to concentrate in some particular part: often applied to the process of transferring local administration to the capital or seat of government of a country.—**centrally,** sen′tral·li, *adv.* In a central manner or position; with regard to the center.—**center bit,** *n.* A carpenter's tool for boring large circular holes, which turns on an axis or central point when in operation.—**centerboard,** *n.* A kind of movable keel in American yachts, capable of being raised and lowered in a well extending longitudinally amidships, to prevent leeway.—**centerpiece,** *n.* An ornament intended to be placed in the middle or center of something, as of a table.

centesimal, sen·tes′i·mal, *a.* [L. *centesimus,* hundredth.] Pertaining to division into a hundred parts.—**centesimally,** *adv.* By division into hundreds.

centigrade, sen′ti·grād, *a.* [From L. *centum,* a hundred, *gradus,* a degree.] Consisting of a hundred degrees; graduated into a hundred divisions or equal parts; pertaining to the scale which is divided into a hundred degrees.—*Centigrade thermometer,* a thermometer which divides the interval between the freezing and boiling points of water into 100 degrees, while in Fahrenheit's thermometer the same interval is divided into 180 degrees.

centime, sän·tēm′ or sän′tēm, *n.* [Fr.] French coin, the hundredth part of a franc.

centimeter, sen′ti·mē·tr, *n.* [Fr. *centimètre,* from L. *centum,* a hundred, and Gr. *metron,* measure.] A metric measure of length, the hundredth part of a meter; rather more than 0.39 of an inch.—**centimeter-gram-second,** *a.* Pertaining to a system of measurement in which the centimeter is the unit of length, the gram is the unit of mass, and the

second (1/86,400 of the mean solar day) is the unit of time.

centipede, sen′ti·pēd, *n.* [L. *centipeda*—*centum,* a hundred, and *pes, pedis,* a foot.] A term applied to various long, flatbodied animals having many feet, popularly called insects, but belonging to the Myriapoda.

Centner, sent′nėr, *n.* [G., from L. *centenarius,* from *centum,* a hundred.] A name in several European countries for a weight nearly equivalent to a hundredweight.

cento, sen′tō, *n.* [L. *cento,* patchwork, a poem made up of selections from different poems.] A composition (whether literary or musical) made up of selections from the works of various authors or composers.

centrifugal, sen·trif′ū·gal, *a.* [L. *centrum,* a center, and *fugio,* to flee.] Tending to recede from the center; acting by or depending on centrifugal force or action; *bot.* expanding first at the summit and later at the base, as an inflorescence.—*Centrifugal force,* that force by which all bodies moving round another body in a curve tend to fly off at any point of their motion in the direction of a tangent to the curve.—**centripetal,** sen·trip′e·tal, *a.* [L. *centrum,* a center, and *peto,* to seek.] Tending toward the center; progressing by changes from the exterior of an object to its center.—*Centripetal force* is that force which draws a body toward a center, and thereby acts as a counterpoise to the centrifugal force in circular motion.

centrosome, sen′tro·sōm, *n.* [L. *centrum,* centre, and *soma,* a body.] In cells, a minute particle outside the nucleus which plays an active part in indirect division.

centuple, sen′tū·pl, *a.* [L. *centuplus*—*centum,* a hundred, and root of *plica,* a fold.] Multiplied or increased a hundredfold.—*v.t.*—*centupled, centupling.* To multiply a hundredfold.—**centuplicate,** sen·tū′pli·kāt, *v.t.*—*centuplicated, centuplicating.* [L. *centum,* and *plicatus,* folded.] To make a hundredfold; to repeat a hundred times.

century, sen′tū·ri, *n.* [L. *centuria,* from *centum,* a hundred.] An aggregate of a hundred; anything consisting of a hundred in number; a period of a hundred years; often such a period reckoned from the birth of Christ.—**centurial,**†sen·tū′ri·al,*a.*[L. *centurialis.*] Relating to or occurring once in a century.—**centurion,** sen·tū′ri·on, *n.* [L. *centurio,* from *centum,* a hundred.] In ancient Rome a military officer who commanded a century or company of infantry consisting of a hundred men.

Cephalata, sef·a·lā′ta, *n. pl.* [Gr. *kephalē,* the head.] A division of mollusks which have a distinct head, with eyes, as the gasteropods, cuttlefishes, etc.—**cephalate,** sef′al·āt, *n.* A mollusk of the division Cephalata.

cephalic, se·fal′lik, *a.* [Gr. *kephalikos,* from *kephalē,* the head.] Pertaining to the head.—*n.* A medicine for headache or other disorder in the

head.—**cephalic index,** *n.* A number denoting the ratio of the transverse to the longitudinal (front to back) diameter of the skull, and according to which skulls and races of people are called brachycephalic or dolichocephalic.—**cephalitis,** sef·a·lī′tis, *n.* [The term. *-itis* signifies inflammation.] Inflammation of the brain.—**cephalous,** sef′a·lus, *a.* Having a head: applied specifically to the cephalates.

cephalopod, sef′a·lo·pod, *n.* [Gr. *kephalē,* a head, and *pous, podos,* a foot.] Any member of the class Cephalopoda.—**Cephalopoda,** sef·a·lop′o·da, *n. pl.* A class of mollusks, the highest in organization, characterized by having the organs of prehension and locomotion, called tentacles or arms, attached to the head, and including the cuttlefishes, squids, ammonites, etc.

cephalothorax, sef′a·lo·thō′′raks, *n.* [Gr. *kephalē,* the head, and *thōrax,* the thorax.] The anterior division of the body in crustaceans, spiders, scorpions, etc., which consists of the head and thorax blended together.

ceraceous, si·rā′shus, *a.* [L. *ceraceus,* waxy, from *cera,* wax.] *Bot.* waxy: a term applied to bodies which have the texture and color of new wax.

ceramic, se·ram′ik, *a.* [Gr. *keramikos,* from *keramos,* potter's clay, a piece of pottery.] Of or belonging to the fictile arts or pottery; pertaining to the manufacture of porcelain and earthenware.—**ceramics,** se·ram′iks, *n.* The art of the potter; pottery.

cerate, sē′rāt, *n.* [L. *ceratum,* from *cera,* wax.] A thick kind of ointment composed of wax, lard, or oil, with other ingredients, applied externally in various diseases.

ceratite, ser′a·tīt, *n.* [Gr. *keras, keratos,* a horn.] A genus of fossil cephalopods, allied to and resembling the ammonites.—**ceratodus,** se·rat′o·dus, *n.* [Gr. *keras,* horn, *odous,* tooth.] A fish of Australia, one of the few that have lungs, said to be able to leave the water for some time.

Cerberus, sėr′ber·us, *n.* [L.] *Class. myth.* the three-headed watchdog of the infernal regions; hence, any watchful and dreaded guardian.—**Cerberean,** sėr·bē′rē·an, *a.* Relating to Cerberus.

cere, sēr, *n.* [L. *cera,* wax; from its appearance.] The term applied to the space destitute of feathers, and having a waxy appearance, generally observed at the base of the bill in birds.

cereal, si′rē·al, *a.* [From *Ceres,* the goddess of corn.] Pertaining to edible grain, as wheat, rye, barley, oats, corn, rice, millet.—*n.* A grain plant, such as wheat, oats, barley, etc.

cerebellum, ser·e·bel′lum, *n.* [L. dim. of *cerebrum,* the brain.] The little brain; that portion of the brain in vertebrate animals which is posterior to and underlies the great cerebral mass or cerebrum.—**cerebellar,** ser·e·bel′lėr, *a.* Relating to the cerebellum.—**cerebral, cerebric,** ser′e·bral, se·rē′brik, *a.* Pertaining to the cerebrum or brain.—*Cerebral letters*, in *philol.* certain consonants in the Sanskrit alphabet, formed by bringing the tip of the tongue backward and applying its under surface against the roof of the mouth.—**cerebrate**, sĕr′e·brāt, *v.i.* To have the brain in action; to exhibit brain action.—**cerebration**, sĕr·e·brā′shon, *n.* Exertion or action of the brain, conscious or unconscious—**cerebrospinal**, se·rē′brō·spī′nal, *a.* Pertaining to the brain and spinal cord together; consisting in the brain and spinal cord.—**cerebrospinal meningitis**, men′in·jīt′′is, *n.* [Gr. *meninx, meningos*, a membrane, *-itis*, inflammation.] Spotted fever; a virulent bacterial disease, associated with inflammation of the membranes covering the brain and spinal cord.—**cerebrum**, sĕr′e·brum, *n.* [L.] The superior and chief portion of the brain, occupying the whole upper cavity of the skull.

cerecloth, cerement, sēr′kloth, sēr′ment, *n.* [L. *cera*, wax.] Cloth dipped in melted wax, with which dead bodies are enfolded when embalmed; hence, *pl.* graveclothes (poetical).

ceremony, sĕr′e·mo·ni, *n.* [Fr. *cérémonie*, from L. *cærimonia*, a rite or ceremony, veneration, sanctity; probably from same root as Skr. *kri, kar*, to do.] A religious or other rite or observance; a solemn or formal display or performance; a solemnity; a usage of politeness, or such usages collectively; formality; punctilio; punctiliousness.—*Master of ceremonies*, a person who regulates the forms to be observed by the company or attendants on a public occasion.—**ceremonial**, sĕr·e·mō′ni·al, *a.* [L. *cærimonialis.*] Relating to ceremonies or external forms or rites; ritual; pertaining to the forms and rites of the Jewish religion (the *ceremonial law*).—*n.* A system of rites; ceremonies or formalities to be observed on any occasion.—**ceremonialism,** sĕr·e·mō′ni·al·izm, *n.* Adherence to or fondness for ceremony.—**ceremonially,** sĕr·e·mō′ni·al·li, *adv.* In a ceremonial manner; according to rites and ceremonies.—**ceremonialness,** sĕr·e·mō′ni·al·nes, *n.*—**ceremonious,** sĕr·e·mō′ni·us, *a.* Full of ceremony; accompanied with rites; according to prescribed or customary formalities or punctilios; formally respectful or polite; observant of conventional forms; fond of using ceremony.—**ceremoniously,** sĕr·e·mō′ni·us·li, *adv.* In a ceremonious manner; formally; with due forms.—**ceremoniousness,** sĕr·e·mō′ni·us·nes, *n.* The quality of being ceremonious; the practice of much ceremony; formality.

Ceres, sē′rēz, *n.* A Roman goddess watching over the growth of grain and other plants; hence, grain; also a name of one of the asteroids or planetoids.

cerise, se·rēz′, *n.* [Fr., a cherry.] Cherry-color.—*a.* Of the color of cerise; cherry-colored.

cerium, sē′ri·um, *a.* [From the planet *Ceres*, discovered a year or two before.] A malleable, ductile, metallic element of the rare-earth series. Symbol, Ce; at. no., 58; at. wt., 140.12.—**cerite,** sē′rīt, *n.* A rare mineral, of a pale rose-red color, from which cerium was first obtained.

cermet, sėr′′met′, *n.* A strong heat-resistant alloy, for example, nickel and titanium.

cernuous, sėr′nū·us, *a.* [L. *cernuus.*] *Bot.* drooping; pendulous.

ceroplastic, sē·ro·plas′tik, *a.* [Gr. *kēros*, wax, and *plastikē (techné)*, the art of the modeler or carver.] Pertaining to the art of modeling in wax; modeled in wax.—*n.* The art of modeling or of forming models in wax.

certain, sėr′tin, *a.* [Fr. *certain*, as if from a L. adjective *certanus*, formed from *certus*, certain, by adding suffix *-anus*. *Certus* is connected with *cerno, certum*, to distinguish, discern.] Sure; undoubtedly true; established as a fact; undoubtedly existing or impending (death, danger); capable of being counted on or depended on; unfailing; infallible; of things (a sign, a remedy); capable of being counted upon or able to count on; of persons (he is *certain* to be there, you are *certain* to find him); assured in mind; free from doubt; having no doubt or suspicion regarding: often with *of*; stated; fixed; determinate; definite (a *certain* rate); not specifically named; indefinite; one or some (a *certain* person, a *certain* pleasure in something).—*For certain*, certainly.—**certainly,** sėr′tin·li, *adv.* Without doubt or question; in truth and fact; without fail; assuredly; of a certainty.—**certainty,** sėr′tin·ti, *n.* The fact of being certain; exemption from failure to happen or produce the natural result; a fact or truth certainly established; that which cannot be questioned; full assurance of mind; exemption from doubt.—**certify,** sėr′ti·fī, *v.t.*—*certified, certifying.* [Fr. *certifier*, from L.L. *certifico*, to certify—L. *certus*, certain, and *facio*, to make.] To assure or make certain; to give certain information *to* (a person); to give certain information *of*; to make clear or definite; to testify to in writing; to make known or establish as a fact.—**certificate,** sėr·tif′i·kit, *n.* [Fr. *certificat.*] A written testimony to the truth of a certain fact or facts; a testimonial; a legally authenticated voucher or testimony of certain facts; sometimes a kind of license.—*v.t.* To give a certificate to, as to one who has passed an examination; to attest or certify by certificate.—**certification,** sėr′ti·fi·kā′′shon, *n.* The act of certifying.—**certifier,** sėr′ti·fī·ėr, *n.* One who certifies.—**certiorari,** sėr′shi·o·râ′′rī, *n.* [Lit. to be informed of, L.L. *certioro*, to inform, from L. *certus*, certain.] *Law,* a writ to call up the records of an inferior court or remove a cause there depending, that it may be tried in a superior court.—**certitude,** sėr′ti·tūd, *n.* [L.L. *certitudo.*] Certainty; assurance; freedom from doubt.

cerulean, se·rö′lē·an, *a.* [L. *cæruleus*, azure, for *cæluleus*, sky-colored, from *cælum*, the sky.] Sky-colored; azure; blue.

cerumen, se·rö′men, *n.* [From L. *cera*, wax.] The wax or yellow matter secreted by certain glands lying in the external canal of the ear.—**ceruminous,** se·rö′mi·nus, *a.* Relating to or containing cerumen.

ceruse, sē′rös, *n.* [Fr., from L. *cerussa*, white lead, from *cera*, wax.] White lead, composed of hydroxide and carbonate of lead, produced by exposing the metal in thin plates to the vapor of vinegar. It is much used in painting, and a cosmetic is prepared from it.—*v.t.* To wash with ceruse; to apply ceruse to as a cosmetic.—**cerussite,** se′rus·īt, *n.* A native carbonate of lead; a common lead ore.

cervical, sėr′vi·kal, *a.* [L. *cervix, cervicis*, the neck.] Belonging to the neck.

cervine, sėr′vīn, *a.* [L. *cervinus*, from *cervus*, a deer.] Pertaining to the deer family.

Cesarean, Cesarian, si·zâ′rē·an, si·zā′ri·an, *n.* See CAESAREAN.

cesium, sē′zi·um, *n.* The most electropositive of the elements. Symbol, Cs; at. no., 55; at. wt., 132.905.

cespitose, ses′pi·tōs, *a.* [L. *caespes, cespitis*, turf.] Pertaining to turf; turfy; *bot.* growing in tufts.

cess, ses, *v.t.* [Shortened and corrupted from *assess.*] To impose a tax; to assess.—*n.* A rate or tax. (Colloq.)

cessation, ses·sā′shon, *n.* [L. *cessatio*, from *cesso*, from *cedo, cessum*, to cease. CEDE.] A ceasing; a stop; a rest; the act of discontinuing motion or action of any kind, whether temporary or final.

cession, sesh′on, *n.* [L. *cessio*, from L. *cedo, cessum.* CEDE.] The act of ceding, yielding, or surrendering, as of territory, property, or rights; a giving up, resignation, or surrender.

cesspool, ses′pōl, *n.* [The better spelling seems to be *sess-pool*, the word being from A.Sax. *sessian*, to settle; or from prov. *soss, suss*, a mess. filth; Gael. *sos.*] A cavity or well in a drain or privy to receive the sediment or filth.

cestoid, ses′toid, *a.* [L. *cestus*, a girdle, from their shape.] A term used to characterize certain intestinal worms, such as tapeworms.

cestus, ses′tus, *n.* [L. *cestus, cæstus*, from *cædo, cæsum*, to strike.] Among the Greeks and Romans, a kind of boxing glove, loaded with lead or iron, which boxers fastened on their hands and arms by leather thongs.

cesura. See CAESURA.

Cetacea, si·tā′sha, *n. pl.* [L. *cetus*, Gr. *kēto*, any large sea monster, a whale.] An order of marine mammals comprising the whales and dolphins.—**cetacean,** si·tā′shan, *n.* An animal of the order Cetacea.—**cetaceous,** si·tā′shus, *a.* Pertaining to the whale; belonging to the Cetacea or whale kind.

C.G.S. The standard contraction for the centimeter = gram = second system of units now in universal use for scientific purposes: named from the fundamental units of length, mass, and time.

Chablis, shab′lē, *n.* A celebrated white French wine, having good body and an exquisite perfume, so called from the town of that name near which it is produced.

chabouk, chabuk, cha·buk′, *n.* [Hind. *chabuk,* a horsewhip.] A long whip; the whip used in the East for inflicting corporal punishment.

chacma, chak′ma, *n.* A baboon found in South Africa.

chafe, chāf, *v.t.*—*chafed, chafing.* [O.E. *chaufe,* Fr. *chauffer,* O.Fr. *chaufer,* to warm, from L. *calefacere,* to warm, from *caleo,* to grow warm, and *facere,* to make.] To excite heat in (some part of the body) by friction: to stimulate to warmth by rubbing; to excite the passions of; to inflame; to anger; to excite violent action in; to cause to rage (the wind *chafes* the ocean); to fret and wear by rubbing (the rope was *chafed*).—*v.i.* To be excited or heated; to rage; to fret; to dash, as in anger; to rage or boil (as the sea); to be fretted and worn by rubbing.—*n.* A state of being angry or annoyed; heat; fret.—**chafer,** chā′fėr, *n.* One who or that which chafes; a chafing-dish.—**chafing dish,** *n.* A dish or vessel to hold coals for heating anything set on it or for cooking.

chafer, chā′fėr, *n.* [A.Sax. *ceafor,* a chafer: D. *kever,* G. *käfer,* a beetle.] A beetle: especially applied to such as are destructive to plants, and generally in compounds; as, cock-*chafer,* rose-*chafer,* bark-*chafer,* etc.

chaff, chaf, *n.* [A.Sax. *ceaf*=D. *kaf,* G. *kaff,* chaff.] The glumes or husks of corn and grasses, but more commonly restricted to the husks when separated from the corn by thrashing, sifting, or winnowing; worthless matter, especially that which is light and apt to be driven by the wind; refuse.—**chaffy,** chaf′i, *a.* Like chaff; full of chaff; light; frivolous; worthless.

chaff, chaf, *v.t.* and *i.* [A corruption of *chafe,* to irritate or annoy.] To assail with sarcastic banter or raillery; to banter; to make game of. (Colloq.)—*n.* Banter, especially slangy banter; sarcastic raillery. (Colloq.)—**chaffer,** chaf′ėr, *n.* One who employs chaff or slangy banter. (Colloq.)

chaffer, chaf′ėr, *v.i.* [O.E. *chapfare, chaffare,* bargaining, merchandise, from *chap,* A.Sax. *ceáp,* a bargain, and *fare,* procedure, journey, A.Sax. *faru,* a journey. Akin *cheap, cheapen.* CHEAP.] To treat about a purchase; to bargain; to haggle; to talk much and idly.—**chafferer,** chaf′ėr·ėr. *n.* One who chaffers; a bargainer; a buyer.

chaffinch, chaf′finsh, *n.* [Perhaps from its note; comp. *chiff-chaff,* the name of a British bird, from its cry.] A European bird of the finch family.

chagrin, sha·grin′, *n.* [Fr., said to be another form of *shagreen,* which from being used to polish wood, has come to be employed as a type

of grinding or gnawing care.] Ill humor, as from disappointment, wounded vanity, etc., vexation; peevishness; mortification, fretfulness. —*v.t.* To excite ill humor in; to vex; to mortify.

chain, chān, *n.* [Fr. *chaîne,* O.Fr. *chaene, cadene,* from L. *catena,* a chain.] A series of links or rings connected or fitted into one another, generally of some kind of metal, and used for various purposes; *fig.* that which binds, restrains, confines, or fetters; a bond; a fetter; bondage; slavery: in this sense often in the plural (the *chains* of evil habit); a series of things linked together; a series, line, or range of things connected or following in succession (*chain* of causes, events, etc.); *weaving,* the warp threads of a web, so called because they form a long series of links or loops; *pl. naut.* strong links or plates of iron bolted to a ship's sides, and forming part of the attachments of the shrouds; *surv.* a measuring instrument, generally consisting of 100 links, and having a total length of 66 feet.— *v.t.* To fasten, bind, restrain, or fetter with a chain or chains; to put in chains; to restrain; to hold in control; to unite firmly; to link.— **chain gang,** *n.* A gang of convicts chained together.—**chain mail,** *n.* Flexible armor of linked metal rings. —**chain reaction,** *n.* Any series of events each of which is initiated by a preceding one; *phys.* a nuclear reaction that continues automatically and becomes self-sustaining once started.—**chain saw,** *n.* A power saw that has teeth on a continuous band or chain.—**chain shot,** *n.* Two cannon balls connected by a chain, formerly much used in naval warfare for carrying away rigging.—**chain-stitch,** *n.* Sewing consisting of threads or cords linked together in the form of a chain; also, a kind of machine sewing, which consists in looping the upper thread into itself on the under side of the fabric, or in using a second thread to engage the loop of the upper thread: in contradistinction to *lock stitch.*

chair, châr, *n.* [Fr. *chaire,* O.Fr. *chayere,* L. *cathedra,* Gr. *kathedra,* a seat. CATHEDRAL. *Chaise* is a corruption of *chaire.*] A movable seat, with a back, for one person; a seat of office or authority; hence, the office itself, especially the office of a professor, and sometimes the person occupying the chair; a chairman or president; a sedan chair; one of the iron blocks which support and secure the rails in a railroad.— *v.t.* To place or carry in a chair; to carry publicly in a chair in triumph.— **chairman,** châr′man, *n.* The presiding officer of an assembly, association, or company, committee or public meeting; one whose business is to carry a sedan chair.—**chairmanship,** châr′man·ship, *n.* The office of a chairman.

chaise, shāz, *n.* [Fr., a corruption of *chaire,* a chair.] A two-wheeled

carriage drawn by one or more horses.—**chaise longue,** shāz′long, *n.* [Fr. long chair.] A long couchlike seat with a back at one end.

chalaza, ka·lā′za, *n.* [Gr. *chalaza,* a pimple.] *Bot.* that part of the ovule or seed where the integuments cohere with each other and with the nucleus; *zool.* one of the two membranous twisted cords which bind the yolk bag of an egg to the lining membrane at the two ends of the shell.

chalcedony, kal·sed′o·ni, *n.* [From *Chalcedon,* an ancient Greek town in Asia Minor.] A kind of quartz, resembling milk diluted with water, and more or less clouded or opaque, with veins, circles, and spots.

chalcography, kal·kog′ra·fi, *n.* [Gr. *chalkos,* copper, brass, and *graphō,* to engrave.] The art of engraving on copper or brass.—**chalcographer, chalcographist,** kal·kog′raf·ėr, kal·kog′raf·ist. *n.* An engraver on brass or copper.—**chalcographic,** kal·ko·graf′ik, *a.* Pertaining to chalcography.

Chaldaic, Chaldean, Chaldee, kal·dā′ik, kal·dē′an, kal′dē, *a.* Pertaining to Chaldea or Chaldæa, anciently a country on the Euphrates in Asia.— *n.* The language or dialect of the Chaldeans; Aramaic.

chalet, shal′ā, *n.* [Fr.; properly a Swiss word.] A cottage, cabin, or hut for sheltering the herdsmen and their cattle in the Swiss mountains; a small dwelling house built in a similar style.

chalice, chal′is, *n.* [Fr. *calice,* from L. *calix, calicis,* a cup or goblet.] A drinking cup or bowl, a cup used to administer the wine in the celebration of the Lord's supper.

chalk, chak, *n.* [A.Sax. *cealc,* from L. *calx,* lime, limestone.] A well-known earthy limestone, an impure carbonate of lime of an opaque white color, soft, and admitting no polish.— *v.t.* To rub with chalk; to mark with chalk; to trace out; to describe: from the use of chalk in making lines.—*Black chalk.* See under BLACK.—*Brown chalk,* a name for umber.—*Red chalk,* a natural clay containing 15 to 20 per cent of protoxide and carbonate of iron.— *French chalk,* steatite or soapstone.— **chalky,** cha′ki, *a.* Resembling chalk; consisting of or containing chalk.— **chalkstones,** *n.* Certain concretions in the joints of persons violently affected by the gout.

challenge, chal′lenj, *n.* [O.Fr. *chalenge, calenge, calonge,* etc., claim, accusation, dispute, from L. *calumnia,* a false accusation, a calumny. *Calumny* is thus the same word.] An invitation to a contest or trial of any kind; a calling or summons to fight in a single combat; the letter or message containing the summons to a contest; the calling in question or taking exception to something; the act of a sentry in demanding the countersign from any one who appears near his post; the claim of a party that certain jurors shall not sit in trial upon him or his cause, a right given both in civil and criminal trials when the impartiality of the jurors may be reasonably questioned.—*v.t.*—*challenged, challenging.* To address a challenge to; to call to a contest; to summon to fight, or to a duel; to demand the countersign or password from: said of a sentry; to claim as due, to demand as a right; *law*, to demand the removal of from among the jurymen; to object to (a person or thing); to take exception to; to call in question (a statement).—**challengeable,** chal'len·ja·bl, *a.* Capable of being challenged or called to an account.—**challenger,** chal'len·jėr, *n.* One who challenges; one who defies another to a contest; an objector; one who calls in question.

chalybeate, ka·lib'ē·āt, *a.* [From Gr. *chalyps, chalybos,* steel.] Impregnated with iron: applied to medicines containing iron, and especially to springs and waters impregnated with iron, or holding iron in solution.—*n.* Any water or other liquid into which iron enters.

cham,‡ kam, *n.* The sovereign prince of Tartary: now written *Khan.*

chamade, sha·mād' or sha·mäd', *n.* [Fr., from It. *chiamata,* a calling, *chiamare,* to call, from L. *clamare,* to call=E. *claim.*] The beat of a drum or sound of a trumpet inviting an enemy to a parley.

chamber, chām'bėr, *n.* [Fr. *chambre,* from L. *camera,* Gr. *kamara,* a vault or arched roof.] A room of a dwelling house; an apartment; a room where professional men, as lawyers, conduct their business; especially the room in which judges sit for the disposing of matters not sufficiently important to be heard in court; a hall or place where an assembly, association, or body of men meets; the assembly or body itself, as a *chamber* of commerce or of agriculture; a hollow or cavity in a thing, especially when of definite form and use; the part of a pump in which the bucket or plunger works; that part of a firearm where the powder lies.—*v.i.* To reside in or occupy as a chamber; to indulge in wantonness‡.— *v.t.* To shut up in, or as in, a chamber. (*Shak*).—**chambered,** chām'bėrd, *a.* Having or divided into a number of chambers or compartments.—**chamberer,** chām'bėr·ėr, *n.* One who intrigues or indulges in wantonness; a gallant. (*Shak*).—**chamberlain,** chām'bėr·lin, *n.* [O.Fr. *chamberlain,* from O.H.G. *chamarling, chamarlinc—chamar,* chamber, and suffix *-ling.*] A person charged with the direction and management of a chamber or chambers; specifically, an officer charged with the direction and management of the private apartments of a monarch or nobleman; the treasurer of a city, corporation, or the like.—**chambermaid,** *n.* A woman who has the care of chambers, making the beds and cleaning the rooms.—**chamber pot,** *n.* A vessel for urine and other

wastes, used in bedrooms.

chameleon, ka·mē'lē·on, *n.* [Gr. *chamaileōn—chamai,* on the ground, and *leōn,* lion; lit. ground-lion.] An insectivorous lizard, having a naked body, a prehensile tail, four feet suited for grasping branches, and the eye covered by a single circular eyelid with an aperture in the center. It has long been remarkable for its faculty of changing its color; and its powers of fasting and inflating itself gave rise to the notion that it lived on air.

chamfer, cham'fėr, *n.* [Fr. *chanfrein,* a chamfer.] A small gutter or furrow cut in wood or other hard material; a bevel or slope; the corner of anything originally right-angled cut aslope equally on the two sides which form it.—*v.t.* To cut a chamfer in or on; to flute; to channel; to cut or grind so as to form a bevel.

chamfron, cham'fron, *n.* [O.Fr. *chamfrein,* from *champ,* field, battle-field, and *frein,* L. *frenum,* a bridle.] The defensive armor for the fore part of the head of a war horse.

chamois, shäm·wä' or sham'i, *n.* [Fr.] A species of goatlike antelope inhabiting high inaccessible mountains in Europe and Western Asia, about the size of a wellgrown goat, and extremely agile; a kind of soft leather made from various skins dressed with fish oil; so called because first prepared from the skin of the chamois: in this sense often written *Shammy.*

champ, champ, *v.t.* [From O.Fr. *champayer,* to graze, from *champ,* L. *campus,* a field, or a modification of obsolete *cham,* to chew.] To bite with repeated action of the teeth and with a snapping noise; to bite into small pieces; to chew; to munch; to craunch.

champagne, sham·pān', *n.* A kind of light sparkling wine made chiefly in the department of Marne, in the former province of *Champagne,* in France.

champaign, sham·pān', *n.* [O.Fr. *champaigne,* from *champ,* L. *campus,* a field. CAMPAIGN.] A flat open country.—*a.* Level; open; having the character of a plain.

champignon, sham·pin'yon, *n.* [Fr., a mushroom, from L.L. *campinio,* what grows in fields, from L. *campus,* a field.] A name for two edible mushrooms, one the common mushroom, the other a species growing in fairy rings.

champion, cham'pi·on, *n.* [Fr. *champion,* L.L. *campio, campionis,* a champion, from L. *campus,* a field, later a combat, duel.] One who comes forward in defense of any cause; especially one who engages in single combat in the cause of another; more generally, a hero; a brave warrior; one who has acknowledged superiority in certain matters decided by public contest or competition; one open to contend with all comers, or otherwise required to resign the title.—*v.t.* To challenge to a combat; to come forward and maintain or support (a cause or a person).—

championship, cham'pi·on·ship, *n.* State of being a champion; support or maintenance of a cause.

chance, chans, *n.* [Fr. *chance,* chance, hazard, from L.L. *cadentia,* a falling (E. *cadence*), from L. *cadere,* to fall; in allusion to the falling of the dice.] A casual or fortuitous event; an accident; that which is regarded as determining the course of events in the absence of law, ordinary causation, or providence (to happen by *chance*); accident; what fortune may bring; fortune; possibility of an occurrence; opportunity (to lose a *chance*).—*v.i.* To happen; to fall out; to come or arrive without design or expectation.—*v.t.* To put under the influence of chance; to risk; to hazard.—*a.* Happening by chance; casual.—**chanceful,†** chans'ful, *a.* Full of chances or accidents; hazardous.—**chance-medley,** *n.* Originally, a casual affray or riot, without deliberate or premeditated malice; now, the killing of another in self-defense upon a sudden and unpremeditated encounter.

chancel, chan'sel, *n.* [So named from being railed off from the rest of the church by lattice-work—L. *cancelli.* CANCEL.] That part of the choir of a church between the altar or communion table and the balustrade or railing that encloses it, or that part where the altar is placed.—**chancellor,** chan'sel·ėr, *n.* [L.L. *cancellarius,* from L. *cancelli,* a lattice-work railing, from the chancellor formerly standing *ad cancellos* (at the latticed railing), to receive petitions, etc.] A state official in various European states, invested with judicial powers, and particularly with the superintendence of charters, letters, and other official writings of the government, varying in degree of political importance and responsibility. In the ecclesiastical sense, the chancellor of a cathedral is an official who superintends arrangements for religious ceremonies and services. The head of some universities; as the *chancellor* of McGill University, or of the University of Kansas. The usual title of university heads in the United States is *president.* In U. S. law courts, a judge in a court of chancery or equity; especially the presiding judge as distinguished from the vice-chancellors. — **chancellorship,** chan'sel·ėr·ship, *n.* The office of a chancellor.

chancery, chan'se·ri, *n.* [Modified from older *chancelry,* from Fr. *chancellerie.* CHANCELLOR.] A court or department of public affairs at the head of which is a chancellor; in England, formerly the highest court of justice next to parliament, but since 1873 a division of the High Court of Justice, which is itself one of the two departments of the Supreme Court of Judicature.

chancre, shang'kėr, *n.* [Fr.=*canker.*] A sore or ulcer which arises from the direct application of the venereal virus.—**chancrous,** shangk'rus, *a.* Having the qualities of a chancre; ulcerous; affected with ulcers.

---

fāte, fär, fâre, fat, fạll;   mē, met, hėr;   pīne, pin;   nōte, not, möve;   tūbe, tub, bụll;   oil, pound.

chandelier, shan·de·lēr′, *n.* [Fr. *chandelier,* a chandelier, from L. *candela,* a candle. CANDLE.] A stand with branches to hold a number of candles, to light up a room.

chandler, chand′lėr, *n.* [Fr. *chandelier,* a dealer in candles, from L. *candela,* a candle.] One who makes or sells candles; a dealer in general: the particular meaning of the term being determined by a prefix; as, tallow-*chandler;* ship-*chandler,* etc. —**chandlery,** chand′lėr·i, *n.* The commodities sold by a chandler; a chandler's warehouse; a storeroom for candles.

change, chānj, *v.t.*—*changed, changing.* [Fr. *changer,* to change, from L.L. *cambiare,* from L. *cambire,* to change, to barter.] To cause to turn or pass from one state to another; to vary in form or essence; to alter or make different; to substitute another thing or things for (to *change* the clothes); to shift; to give or procure another kind of money for (to *change* a bank note); to give away for a money equivalent of a different kind; to exchange (to *change* places with a person).—*v.i.* To suffer change; to be altered; to undergo variation; to be partially or wholly transformed; to begin a new revolution, or to pass from one phase to another, as the moon.—*n.* Any variation or alteration in form, state, quality, or essence; a passing from one state or form to another; a succession of one thing in the place of another (*change* of seasons); the passing from one phase of the moon to another; alteration in the order of a series; permutation; that which makes a variety or may be substituted for another (two *changes* of clothes); small money, which may be given for larger pieces; the balance of a sum of money returned when the price of goods is deducted; a place where merchants and others meet to transact business: in this sense an abbreviation for *Exchange,* and often written *Change.*—**changeable,** chān′ja·bl, *a.* Liable to change; subject to alteration; fickle; inconstant; mutable; variable. — **changeableness, changeability,** chān′ja·bl·nes, chān·ja·bil′i·ti, *n.* The quality of being changeable.—**changeably,** chān′ja·bli, *adv.* In a changeable manner.— **changeful,** chānj′ful, *a.* Full of change; inconstant; mutable; fickle; uncertain; subject to alteration.— **changefully,** chānj′ful·li, *adv.* In a changeful manner. — **changefulness,** chānj′ful·nes, *n.*—**changeless,** chānj′les, *a.* Constant; not admitting alteration.—**changeling,** chānj′ling, *n.* A child, often a deformed or stupid child supposed to be substituted by fairies for another.—**changer,** chānj′ėr, *n.* One who changes or alters the form of anything; one that is employed in changing and discounting money; a moneychanger; one given to change; one who is inconstant or fickle.

channel, chan′el, *n.* [From O.Fr. *chanel, canel,* L. *canalis,* a water pipe; whence also *canal* and *kennel,* a gutter.] The bed of a stream of water; the hollow or course in which a stream flows; the deeper part of an estuary, bay, etc., where the current flows, or which is most convenient for the track of a ship; a strait or narrow sea between two islands, two continents, or a continent and an island; that by which something passes or is transmitted (as news, information); means of passing, conveying, or transmitting; a furrow or groove.—*v.t.*—*channeled, channeling.* To form a channel in; to cut channels in; to groove. (*Shak.*)

channel, chan′el, *n.* [A corruption of *chain-wale.*] One of the pieces of plank projecting edgewise from a ship's sides and over which the shrouds are extended to keep them clear of the gunwale.

chant, chänt, *v.t.* [Fr. *chanter,* from L. *cantare,* aug. of *cano, cantum,* to sing. Akin *cant.*] To utter with a melodious voice; to warble; to sing; to celebrate in song; to repeat the words of, in a kind of intoning voice or in a style between air and recitative.—*v.i.* To sing; to make melody with the voice; to intone, or perform a chant.—*n.* A song or singing; melody; specifically, a short musical composition consisting generally of a long reciting note, on which an indefinite number of words may be intoned, and a melodic phrase or cadence.—**chanter,** chän′tėr, *n.* One who chants; a singer or songster; in bagpipes, the tube with finger holes for playing the melody.—**chanticleer,** chan′ti·klēr, *n.* [From *chant* and *clear.*] A cock, so called from the clearness or loudness of his voice in crowing.—**chantress,**† chänt′res, *n.* A female singer. (*Mil.*)—**chantry,** chän′tri, *n.* [O.Fr. *chanterie,* from *chant.*] A church or chapel endowed for the maintenance of one or more priests daily to sing or say mass for the souls of the donors or such as they appoint.

chanterelle, shan·trel′ or shan·tėr·el′, *n.* [Fr., perhaps from O.Fr. *chanterelle,* a small bell, from its shape, from *chanter,* to sing.] An English edible mushroom, having a bright orange color, a fragrant fruity smell, and being found frequently in woods under trees.

chaos, kā′os, *n.* [Gr. *chaos,* from a root *cha,* to gape, to yawn, whence also *chasm.*] That confusion or confused mass out of which the universe was created; a confused mixture of parts or elements; a scene of extreme confusion; disorder.—**chaotic,** kā·ot′ik, *a.* Resembling chaos; confused. —**chaotically,** kā·ot′ik·al·li, *adv.* In a chaotic state.

chap, chap or chop, *v.t.*—*chapped, chapping.* [Same word as *chop,* to cut.] To cause to cleave, split, crack, or open longitudinally, as the surface of the earth or the skin and flesh of the hand.—*v.i.* To crack; to open in long slits; to have the skin become cracked and sore, as from frost.—*n.* A crack in the surface of the hands or feet.

chap, chop, chop, *n.* [A form stand-ing for *chaf* or *chof,* and equivalent to Sc. *chäft,* Icel. *kjaptr,* Dan. *kjaeft,* Sw. *kaft,* a jaw, without the *t.*] The upper or lower part of the mouth; the jaw; either of the two planes or flat parts of a vise or pair of tongs or pliers, for holding anything fast.— **chapfallen,** chop′fạ·ln, *a.* Having the lower chap or jaw depressed; hence, dejected or dispirited; silenced.

chap, chap, *n.* [An abbrev. of *chapman;* as regards its modern use compare *customer,* in senses of regular purchaser and fellow or chap.] A buyer‡; a chapman (*Steele*)‡; a man or a boy; a youth: used familiarly and laxly, much as the word *fellow* is.—**chapbook,** *n.* A kind of small book or tract formerly much sold among the people by chapmen, containing generally lives of heroes, giants, etc., fairy lore, ghost and witch stories, ballads, songs, and the like.

chape, chāp, *n.* [Fr. *chape,* a catch, hook, chape, also a *cope;* same origin as *cape, cap.*] The part by which an object is attached, as the back piece by which a buckle is fixed on the article or garment; the transverse guard of a sword for a protection to the hand; the metal tip at the end of a scabbard, or at the end of a belt or girdle.

chapel, chap′el, *n.* [Fr. *chapelle,* from L.L. *capella,* dim. of *capa,* a cape, hood, canopy, covering of the altar, a recess or chapel attached to the altar. CAP, CAPE, CHAPLET.] A subordinate place of worship usually attached to a large church or cathedral, connected with a palace or private residence, or subsidiary to a parish church; a place of worship used by dissenters from the Church of England; a meetinghouse; a union or society formed by the workmen in a printing office; printing office, from Caxton's establishment in Westminster Abbey.

chaperon, shap′ėr·ōn or shap·ron, *n.* [Fr. *chaperon,* from *chape,* a cope. CHAPEL.] A kind of ancient hood or cap; a lady, especially a married lady, who attends a young lady to public places as a guide or protector.—*v.t.* To attend on as chaperon, guide, or the like.—**chaperonage,** shap′ėr·ōn·ij, *n.* The protection or countenance of a chaperon.

chapiter,‡ chap′i·tėr, *n.* [From O.Fr. *chapitel,* from L.L. *capitellum,* L. *capitulum,* dim. of *caput,* a head; *chapter* is the same word.] The upper part or capital of a column or pillar. (*O.T.*)

chaplain, chap′lin, *n.* [Fr. *chapelain;* L.L. *capellanus,* from *capella,* a chapel. CHAPEL.] An ecclesiastic who performs divine service in a chapel; more generally, an ecclesiastic who officiates at court, in the household of a nobleman, or in an army, garrison, ship, institution, etc.— **chaplaincy, chaplainship,** chap′lin·si, chap′lin·ship, *n.* The office or post of a chaplain.

chaplet, chap′let, *n.* [Fr. *chapelet,* a dim. of O.Fr. *chapel,* Mod.Fr. *chapeau,* a hat, from *chape,* L.L.

capa, a hood, a cape; akin *chapel*, *chape*, etc.] A garland or wreath to be worn on the head; a string of beads used by Roman Catholics, by which they count their prayers; a small rosary; *arch.* a small round molding, carved into beads, pearls, olives, or the like.

chaps, chaps, *n.* [From Mexican Spanish *chaparreras*, from *chaparro*, evergreen oak.] Leather trousers, usually open at the back, worn by cowboys as protection against thorns.

chapter, chap'tẽr, *n.* [Fr. *chapitre*, formerly *chapitle*, *capitel*, from L. *capitulum*, dim. of *caput*, the head, whence also *capital*, *cattle*, etc.] A division of a book or treatise; the council of a bishop, consisting of the canons or prebends and other clergymen attached to a collegiate or cathedral church, and presided over by a dean; the place in which the business of the chapter is conducted; a chapter house; the meeting of certain organized orders and societies; a branch of some society or brotherhood —**chapter house,** *n.* The building in which a chapter meets for the transaction of business.

char, charr, chär, *n.* [It. and Gael. *cear*, red; from its having a red belly.] A name given to at least two species of the salmon family, inhabiting lakes in many parts of the north of Europe.

char, chare, chär, chär, *n.* [From A.Sax. *cerr, cyrr,* a turn, time, occasion; *cerran, cyrran,* to turn = D. *keeren,* G. *kehren,* to turn, move or change. Hence *char*coal.] A turn of work; a single job or piece of work; household work.—*v.i.* To work at others' houses by the day without being a hired servant; to do small jobs.—**charwoman,** chär‧ or chär‧, *n.* A woman employed by the day on odd jobs about a house; one employed in the house of another to do occasional or miscellaneous work.

char, chär, *v.t.*—*charred, charring.* [O.E. *char,* to turn, from A.Sax. *cerran,* to turn, to *char* wood is to turn or change it; *char*coal is wood turned into coal. CHAR, a turn.] To burn with slight admission of air; to reduce to charcoal; to burn (wood) slightly or partially, and on the surface.—**charcoal,** chär′kōl, *n.* Coal made by charring wood; or more generally, the carbonaceous residue of vegetable, animal, or combustible mineral matter when they undergo smothered combustion. Wood-charcoal is much employed in the manufacture of gunpowder, and, like coke or *mineral charcoal,* as a more or less smokeless fuel; while *animal charcoal* from oils, fats, and bones, is the basis of lampblack and printer's ink.

character, kar′ak‧tẽr, *n.* [L. *character,* an engraved mark, from Gr. *charakter,* from *charattō, charaxō,* to cut, engrave.] A distinctive mark made by cutting, stamping, or engraving, as on stone, metal, or other hard material; a mark or figure, written

or printed, and used to form words and communicate ideas; a letter, figure, or sign; the peculiar form of letters, written or printed, used by a particular person or people (the Greek *character*); the peculiar qualities impressed by nature or habit on a person, which distinguish him from others; a distinctive quality assigned to a person by repute; reputation; sometimes restricted to good qualities or reputation; strongly marked distinctive qualities of any kind; an account or statement of qualities or peculiarities; especially, an oral or written account of a servant's or employee's character or qualifications; a person; a personage; especially applied to individuals represented in fiction or history, to persons of eminence, and to persons marked by some prominent trait.—*v.t.* To mark with or as with characters; to engrave; to inscribe.—**characteristic,** kar′ak‧tẽr‧is″tik, *a.* [Gr. *charakteristikos.*] Pertaining to or serving to constitute the character; exhibiting the peculiar qualities of a person or thing; peculiar; distinctive.—*n.* That which serves to constitute a character; that which characterizes; that which distinguishes a person or thing from another.—**characteristical,** kar′ak‧tẽr‧is″tik‧al, *a.* Characteristic.—**characteristically,** kar′ak‧tẽr‧is″tik‧al‧li, *adv.* In a characteristic manner.—**characterization,** kar′ak‧tẽr‧iz‧ā″shon, *n.* Act of characterizing.—**characterize,** kar′ak‧tẽr‧īz, *v.t.* [Gr. *charaktērizō.*] To give a special stamp or character to; to constitute a peculiar characteristic or the peculiar characteristics of; to stamp or distinguish (*characterized* by benevolence); to give a character or an account of the personal qualities of a man; to describe by peculiar qualities.—**characterless,** kar′ak‧tẽr‧les, *a.* Destitute of any peculiar character.

charade, sha‧rād′ or sha‧räd′, *n.* [Fr. Etymology unknown.] An enigma, the solution of which is a word of two or more syllables, each of which is separately significant, the word and its syllables being intended to be discovered from description, or in other cases from representation, when it is called an *acting charade.*

charcoal, *n.* See CHAR.

chard, chärd, *n.* [Fr. *charde,* from L. *carduus,* a thistle or artichoke.] The leaves of artichoke, covered with straw in order to blanch them, and to make them less bitter; the vegetable, Swiss chard.

chare, chär, *n.* and *v.* See CHAR.

charge, chärj, *v.t.*—*charged, charging.* [Fr. *charger,* from L.L. *carricare,* from L. *carrus,* a car, whence also *carry, cargo, caricature.*] To lay a load or burden on; to burden; to load; to fill; to occupy (to *charge* the memory); to impute or register as a debt; to put down to the debt of; to register as indebted or as forming a debt (to *charge* a person *for* a thing; to *charge* a thing *to* or *against* a person); to fix the price of: with *at* before the price or rate; to accuse;

to impeach (to *charge* a person *with* a crime); to lay to one's charge; to impute; to ascribe the responsibility of (to *charge* guilt *on* a person); to entrust; to commission (a person *with*); to command; to enjoin; to instruct; to urge earnestly; to exhort; to adjure; to give directions to (a jury, etc.); to instruct authoritatively; to make an onset on; to attack by rushing against violently. ∴ Syn. under ACCUSE.—*v.i.* To make an onset; to rush to an attack; to place the price of a thing to one's debit.—*n.* That which is laid on or in; in a general sense, any load or burden; the quantity of anything which an apparatus, as a gun, an electric battery, etc., is intended to receive and fitted to hold, or what is actually in as a load; an attack, onset, or rush; an order, injunction, mandate, or command; hence, a duty enjoined on or entrusted to one; care, custody, or oversight; the person or thing committed to another's custody, care, or management; a trust; instructions given by a judge to a jury, or an exhortation given by a bishop to his clergy; what is alleged or brought forward by way of accusation; accusation; the sum payable as the price of anything bought; cost; expense; rent, tax, or whatever constitutes a burden or duty.—**chargeable,** chärj′‧a‧bl, *a.* Capable of being charged; falling to be set, laid, or imposed, as a tax or duty; subject to a charge or tax, as goods; capable of being laid to one's charge; capable of being imputed to one; subject to accusation; liable to be accused; causing expense, and hence burdensome.—**charger,** chärj′ẽr, *n.* One who or that which charges; a large dish (N.T.); a war horse.

chargé d'affaires, shär‧zhä′ dä‧fâr′, *n.* [Fr., lit. charged with affairs.] One who transacts diplomatic business at a foreign court during the absence of his superior the ambassador, or at a court where no functionary so high as an ambassador is appointed.

charily, chariness. See CHARY.

chariot, char′i‧ot, *n.* [Fr. *chariot,* from *char,* a car. CAR.] A stately four-wheeled pleasure or state carriage with one seat; a two-wheeled car formerly used in war, in processions, and for racing, drawn by two or more horses.—*v.t.*† To convey in a chariot. (*Mil.*)—**charioteer,** char′i‧o‧tẽr″, *n.* The person who drives or conducts a chariot.

charity, char′i‧ti, *n.* [Fr. *charité,* O.Fr. *charitet, cariteit,* from L. *caritas, caritatis,* from *carus,* dear, whence also *caress.*] The good affection, love, or tenderness which men should feel toward their fellows, and which should induce them to do good to and think favorably of others; benevolence; liberality in thinking or judging; liberality in giving to the poor; whatever is bestowed gratuitously on the poor for their relief; alms; any act of kindness or benevolence; a charitable institution; a hospital.—**charitable,** char′it‧a‧bl, *a.* Pertaining to or characterized by charity; full of good will or tenderness; benevolent and kind; liberal in benefactions to the poor and in relieving them in distress; pertaining to almsgiving or relief to the poor; springing from charity or intended for charity; lenient in judging of others; not harsh; favorable.—**charitableness**, char′it·a·bl·nes, n. The quality of being charitable.—**charitably**, char′it·a·bli, adv. In a charitable manner.

charlatan, shär′la·tan, n. [Fr., from It. *ciarlatano*, a quack, from *ciarlare*, to prate, to chatter like birds.] One who prates much in his own favor and makes unwarrantable pretensions to skill; a quack; an empiric; a mountebank.—**charlatanic**, shär·la·tan′ik, a. Pertaining to or resembling a charlatan; quackish.—**charlatanism, charlatanry**, shär′la·tan·izm, shär′la·tan·ri, n. The behavior of a charlatan; undue pretensions to skill; quackery.

Charles's Wain, chärlz′iz·wān, n. [A corruption of *churl's* (that is farmer's or peasant's) *wain*.] The seven brightest stars in the constellation called Ursa Major or the Great Bear: known also as the *Plow*.

charlock, chär′lok, n. [A.Sax. *cerlic*; the termination is the same as in *garlic, hemlock*, and meant properly *leek*.] A weedy annual of the mustard family, with bright yellow flowers, occurring in cornfields.

charm, chärm, n. [Fr. *charme*, a charm, an enchantment, from L. *carmen*, a song, a verse, a charm.] A melody‡; a song‡ (*Mil.*); anything believed to possess some occult or supernatural power, such as an amulet or spell or some mystic observance; something which exerts an irresistible power to please and attract; fascination; allurement; attraction; a trinket, such as a locket, seal, etc., worn on a watch guard.—v.t. To subdue or control by incantation or magical or supernatural influence; to fortify or make invulnerable with charms; to subdue or soothe as if by magic; to allay or appease by what gives delight; to give exquisite pleasure to; to fascinate; to enchant.—v.i. To act as a charm or spell; to produce the effect of a charm.—**charmer**, chär′mer, n. One who charms, fascinates, enchants, allures, or attracts.—**charming**, chär′ming, a. Pleasing in the highest degree; delighting; fascinating; enchanting; alluring.—**charmingly**, chär′ming·li, adv. In a charming manner.

charnel, chär′nel, a. [Fr. *charnel*, O.Fr. *carnel*, carnal, from L. *carnalis*, from *caro, carnis*, flesh.] Containing dead bodies.—**charnel house**, n. A place under or near churches where the bones of the dead are deposited.

charqui, chär′kē, n. [The Chilian name, of which the term *jerked* beef is a corruption.] Jerked beef; beef cut into strips of about an inch thick and dried by exposure to the sun.

charr, n. A kind of fish, the char.

chart, chärt, n. [L. *charta*, paper, a leaf of paper. *Card* is the same word.] A sheet of any kind on which information is exhibited in a methodical or tabulated form; specifically, a marine map, with the coasts, islands, rocks, soundings, etc., to regulate the courses of ships.—v.t. To delineate, as on a chart; to map out.—**chartaceous**, kär·tā′shus, a. *Bot.* papery; resembling paper: applied to the paper-like texture of leaves, bark, etc.—**charter**, chär′ter, n. [O.Fr. *chartre*, from L. *chartarius*, from *charta*, paper.] A writing given as evidence of a grant, contract, etc.; any instrument executed with form and solemnity bestowing or granting powers, rights, and privileges; privilege; immunity; exemption.—v.t. To hire or let (a ship) by charter or contract; to establish by charter; to grant; to privilege.—**charterer**, chär′ter·er, n. One who charters.—**charter party**, n. [Fr. *charte-partie*, a divided charter, from the practice of cutting the instrument in two, and giving one part to each of the contractors.] *Com.* an agreement respecting the hire of a vessel and the freight, signed by the proprietor or master of the ship, and by the merchant who hires or freights it.—**Chartism**, chär′tizm, n. The political principles or opinions of the Chartists.—**Chartist**, chär′tist, n. One of a body of political reformers in England that sprung up about the year 1838, and advocated as their leading principles universal suffrage, no property qualification for a seat in parliament, annual parliaments, equal representation, payment of members, and vote by ballot, all which privileges they demanded as constituting the people's charter.

chartreuse, shär·trez′, n. A highly esteemed liqueur made with fine spirits and aromatic plants growing on the Alps, and so called from the monastery of the same name, where it used to be made.

chartulary, kär′chū·le·ri, n. [Fr. *cartulaire*, L.L. *cartularius*, from *chartula*, dim. of L. *charta*, paper.] A record or register, as of a monastery.

charwoman, chär′wum·an, n. [From A. Sax. *cerr, cyrr*, a turn, time, occasion; *cerran, cyrran*, to turn = D. *keeren*, G. *kehren*, to turn, move or change. CHORE.] A woman employed by the day on odd jobs about a house.

chary, châ′ri, a. [A.Sax. *cearig*, full of care, sad, from *cearu, caru*, care. CARE.] Careful; cautious; frugal; sparing: with *of* before an object.—**charily**, châ′ri·li, a. In a chary manner; carefully; sparingly.—**chariness**, châ′ri·nes, n.

chase, chās, v.t.—*chased, chasing*. [Also written *chace*, from O.Fr. *chacier*, Mod.Fr. *chasser*, to chase, a parallel form with *catch*, being like it from L.L. *captiare*. CATCH.] To pursue for the purpose of taking, as game; to hunt; to follow after or search for with eagerness; to pursue for any purpose; to follow with hostility; to drive off.—n. Pursuit; hunting; ardent search for or following after; that which is pursued or hunted; specifically, a vessel pursued by another; an open piece of ground or place well stored with game, and belonging to a private proprietor.—**chaser**, chās′er, n. One who or that which chases; a pursuer or hunter; a ship that pursues another; a chase-gun.—**chase gun**, n. In warships, a gun used in chasing an enemy or in defending a ship when chased.

chase, chās, n. [Fr. *châsse*, from L. *capsa*, box, case. *Case*, for holding things, is a form of the same word.] An iron frame used by printers to confine types when set in columns or pages; the part of a gun between the trunnions and the muzzle; a wide groove.

chase, chās, v.t. [Shortened from *enchase*.] To enchase; to cut a thread on, so as to make a screw.—**chaser**, chās′er, n. One who chases or enchases; an enchaser; a steel tool used for cutting or finishing the threads of screws.

chasm, kazm, n. [Gr. *chasma*, from root *cha*, as in *chaos*.] A gaping or yawning opening, as in the earth; an abyss; a wide and deep cleft; a fissure; a void space.—**chasmy**, kaz′mi, a. Abounding with chasms.

chasseur, shas·sėr′, n. [Fr., a huntsman.] One of a body of soldiers, light and active, both mounted and on foot, trained for rapid movements; a person dressed in a sort of military style in attendance upon persons of rank.

chassis, shä′sē, n. [Fr.] The framework of an automobile, carrying the body and other parts.

chaste, chāst, a. [Fr. *chaste*, from L. *castus*, chaste.] Pure from all unlawful sexual commerce; free from libidinous desires; continent; virtuous; free from obscenity or impurity in thought and language; as applied to literary style, free from barbarous words and phrases, affected or extravagant expressions, or the like; in art, free from meretricious ornament or affectation, not gaudy. — **chastely**, chāst′li, adv. In a chaste manner.—**chasteness**, chāst′nes, n. The state or quality of being chaste.—**chastity**, chas′ti·ti, n. The state or property of being chaste, pure, or undefiled; sexual purity; continence.

chasten, chās′n, v.t. [O.Fr. *chastier*, from L. *castigare*, to castigate or chastise, from *castus*, pure, whence *chaste*; comp. *chastise*.] To inflict pain, trouble, or affliction on for the purpose of reclaiming from evil; to correct; to chastise; to punish; not now used of corporal punishment, which is expressed by *chastise*; to purify, as the taste; to refine.—**chastener**, chās′n·er, n. One who chastens.

chastise, chas·tīz′, v.t.—*chastised, chastising*. [Same word as *chasten*, but with a different verbal termination; O.E. *chastie, chasty*, from O.Fr. *chastier*. CHASTEN.] To inflict pain on by stripes or in any other manner, for the purpose of punishing and recalling to duty; to correct by punishment; to free from faults or excesses; to correct; to restrain.—

chastisement, chas´tiz·ment, *n.* The act of chastising; pain inflicted for punishment and correction, either by stripes or otherwise.—**chastiser,** chas·tīz´ėr, *n.* One who chastises; a punisher; a corrector.

chasuble, chas´ū·bl, *n.* [Fr. *chasuble,* from L.L. *casubula,* from L. *casula,* a little cottage, a hooded garment, dim. of *casa,* a cottage.] A rich vestment or garment worn uppermost by a priest at the celebration of the eucharist.

chat, chat, *v.i.*—*chatted, chatting.* [An abbreviated form of *chatter.*] To talk idly or in a familiar manner; to talk without form or ceremony.—*n.* Free, familiar talk; idle talk; prate.—**chatty,** chat´i, *a.* Inclined to chat; talkative.

chat, chat, *n.* [From the chattering sound of its voice.] A name of several small, lively birds of the warbler family, species of which are found in Europe and America.

château, shä·tō´, *n.* pl. **châteaux,** shä·tōz´, Fr. tō. [Fr. *château,* O.Fr. *chastel,* a castle, from L. *castellum.* CASTLE.] A castle; a mansion in the country; a country seat.—**chatelaine,** shat´ė·lān, *n.* [Fr. *châtelaine,* lit. a female castellan or castle-keeper.] A female castellan; a bunch of chains worn at a lady's waist, having attached such articles as a key, thimble case, penknife, corkscrew, etc.

chatoyant, sha·toi´ant, *a.* [Fr., pp. of *chatoyer,* to change luster like the eye of a cat, from *chat,* a cat.] Having a changeable, undulating luster or color, like that of a cat's eye in the dark.

chattel, chat´el, *n.* [O.E. *chatel,* also *catel,* really the same word as *cattle* (which see).] An item or article of goods, specifically applied in law to goods movable or immovable, except such as have the nature of freehold.

chatter, chat´ėr, *v.i.* [Probably an imitative word, allied to D. *kwetteren,* Dan. *kviddre,* Sw. *kvittra,* to chirp, to chatter.] To utter sounds rapidly and indistinctly, as a magpie or a monkey; to make a noise by repeated rapid collisions of the teeth; to talk idly, carelessly, or rapidly; to jabber.—*v.t.* To utter as one who chatters.—*n.* Sounds like those of a magpie or monkey; idle talk.—**chatterbox,** *n.* One that talks incessantly: applied chiefly to children. (Colloq.)—**chatterer,** chat´ėr·ėr, *n.* One who chatters; a prater; an idle talker; the popular name of sundry insessorial birds, one of which is the waxwing, or Bohemian chatterer.

chauffer, cha´fėr, *n.* [Fr. *chauffer,* to heat. CHAFE.] A small portable furnace, usually of sheet iron, with a grating near the bottom.—**chauffeur,** shō·fėr´, *n.* [Fr.] The driver of a motor vehicle.

chauvin, shō·van´, *n.* [From Nich. *Chauvin,* an enthusiastic military adherent of Napoleon I.] Originally, one of the veterans of the first French Empire who professed, after the fall of Napoleon, a sort of adoration for his person and his acts; hence, anyone possessed by an absurdly exaggerated patriotism or military enthusiasm.—**chauvinism,** shō´vin·izm, *n.* The sentiments of a chauvin; absurdly exaggerated patriotism or military enthusiasm.

chaw, cha, *v.t.* To chew: an old form now vulgar.

chay, chā, *n.* An Indian root yielding a red dye.

cheap, chēp, *a.* [Strictly a noun, being = A.Sax. *ceáp,* price, bargain; from the use of the phrase *good cheap,* as to buy a thing *good cheap,* that is a good bargain, the noun came to be used as an adjective. Cog. D. *koop,* a purchase, *koopen,* to buy; Icel. *kaup,* a bargain; *kaupa,* to buy; G. *kaufen,* to buy; Goth. *kaufon,* to traffic. *Cheapen, chop, chaffer, chapman,* are akin.] Bearing a low price in market; capable of being purchased at a low price, either as compared with the usual price of the commodity, or with the real value, or more vaguely with the price of other commodities; being of small value; common; not respected.—**cheapen,** chē´pn, *v.t.* To ask the price of; to chaffer or bargain for; to beat down the price of; to lessen the value of; to depreciate.—**cheapener,** chē´pn·ėr, *n.* One who cheapens or bargains.—**cheaply,** chē´pli, *adv.* At a small price; at a low rate.—**cheapness,** chēp´nes, *n.* The state or quality of being cheap.

cheat, chēt, *v.t.* [Abbrev. of *escheat,* to act like an escheater, who held an office giving great opportunities of fraud. ESCHEAT.] To deceive and defraud; to impose upon; to trick (to *cheat* a person *of* or out *of* something); to illude; to deceive; to mislead.—*v.i.* To act dishonestly; to practice fraud or trickery.— *n.* A fraud committed by deception; a trick, imposition, or imposture; a person who cheats; a fraudulent person; a swindler.—**cheater,** chēt´-ėr, *n.* One who cheats; an escheater (*Shak.*)‡.—**cheatingly,** chēt´ing·li, *adv.* In a cheating manner.

check, chek, *n.* [From *chequer,* or *exchequer,* in old sense of banker's or moneychanger's office or counter; or from *check,* in sense of counterfoil.] An order for money drawn on a banker or bank, payable to the bearer.—**checkbook,** *n.* A book containing blank bankchecks.

check, chek, *n.* [Fr. *échec,* O.Fr. *eschec,* a check, a check at chess, lit. king, the call of king! in chess, from Per. *shâh,* king, the chief piece at chess. CHESS, CHEQUE, CHEQUER.] The act of suddenly stopping or restraining; a stop; hindrance; restraint; obstruction; a term or word of warning in chess when one party obliges the other either to move or guard his king; a reprimand; rebuke; censure; slight; a species of cloth, in which colored lines or stripes cross each other rectangularly, making a pattern resembling the squares of a chessboard; the pattern of such cloth; a mark put against names or items on going over a list; a duplicate, or counterpart, used for security or verification; a counterfoil; a ticket or token given for identification.—*v.t.* To stop or moderate the motion of; to restrain in action; to hinder; to curb; to rebuke; to chide or reprove; *chess,* to make a move which puts the adversary's king in check; to compare with a counterfoil or something similar, with a view to ascertain authenticity or accuracy.—*v.i.* To make a stop; to stop; to pause.—*a.* Made of check; chequered.—**checker,** chek´-ėr, *n.* One who checks.—**checkmate,** chek´māt, *n.* [From Per. *shâh mât,* the king is dead (*shâh,* the king, *mât,* he is dead).] *Chess,* the position of a king when he is in check, and cannot release himself, which brings the game to a close; hence, defeat, overthrow.—*v.t.*—*checkmated, checkmating.* To put in check, as an opponent's king in chess . —**check point,** *n.* A place where traffic is stopped for inspection and clearance; a geographical location on land or water used by a flier to determine his position.—**check up,** *n.* An examination; a thorough medical examination.

checker, chek´ėr, *n.* [O.Fr. *eschequier,* Mod. Fr. *échiquier,* a chessboard, an exchequer, from O.Fr. *eschecs,* chess. CHECK, CHESS.] Pl. a game for two players; one of the divisions of a pattern that consists of squares; the pattern itself.—*v.t.* To mark with little squares, like a chessboard, by lines or stripes of different colors; to mark with different colors; *fig.* to variegate with different qualities; to impart variety to (events that *checker* one's career).—**checkered, chequered,** chek´ėrd, *a.* Marked with or exhibiting squares of different colors; varied with a play of different colors; *fig.* variegated with different qualities, scenes, or events; crossed with good and bad fortune (a *checkered* life or narrative).—**checkerboard,** *n.* A board on which checkers or draughts are played.—**checkerwork,** *n.* Work exhibiting checkers or squares of varied color or materials.

cheddar, ched´ėr, *n.* A rich fine-flavored cheese made at *Cheddar* in Somersetshire, England; any cheese of similar character.

cheek, chēk, *n.* [A.Sax. *ceáce,* cheek; cog. D. *kaak,* Sw. *kek,* the jaw, *kak,* the cheek; probably same root as *chaw, jaw, chaps.*] The side of the face below the eyes on each side; something regarded as resembling the human cheek in position or otherwise; one of two pieces, as of an instrument, apparatus, framework, etc., which form corresponding sides or which are double and alike, as the *cheeks* of a vise, of a lathe, of a door, etc.; cool confidence; brazen-faced impudence; impudent or insulting talk (in these senses rather vulgar).

cheep, chēp, *v.i. & t.* [Imitative.] To pule or peep, as a chicken; to chirp; to squeak.—*n.* A chirp; a squeak.

cheer, chēr, *n.* [O.E. *chere,* face, look, mien, from O.Fr. *chere, chiere,* face, countenance, from L.L. *cara*, the face, from Gr. *kara*, the head.] Expression of countenance, as noting a greater or less degree of good spirits (*Shak.*); state or temper of the mind; state of feeling or spirits; a state of gladness or joy; gaiety; animation; that which makes cheerful or promotes good spirits; provisions for a feast; viands; fare; a shout of joy, encouragement, applause, or acclamation.—*v.t.* To gladden; to make cheerful; to encourage; to salute with shouts of joy or cheers; to applaud.—*v.i.* To grow cheerful; to become gladsome or joyous: often with *up*; to utter a cheer or shout of acclamation or joy.—**cheerer**, chēr′ėr, *n.* One who or that which cheers.—**cheerful**, chēr′- fųl, *a.* Of good cheer; having good spirits; gay; moderately joyful; associated with or expressive of agreeable feelings; lively; animated; promoting or causing cheerfulness; gladdening; animating; genial.— **cheerfully**, chēr′fųl·li, *adv.* In a cheerful manner; with alacrity or willingness; readily; with life, animation, or good spirits.—**cheerfulness**, chēr′fųl·nes, *n.* The state or quality of being cheerful.—**cheerily**, chē′- ri·li, *adv.* In a cheery manner.— **cheeriness**, chēr′i·nes, *n.* Quality or state of being cheery.—**cheerless**, chēr′les, *a.* Without joy, gladness, or comfort; gloomy; destitute of anything to enliven or animate the spirits.—**cheerlessly**, chēr′les·li, *adv.* In a cheerless manner; dolefully.— **cheerlessness**, chēr′les·nes, *n.* State of being cheerless.—**cheerly**, chēr′- li, *adv.* Cheerily; cheerfully; heartily; briskly. (*Shak.*)—**cheery**, chē′ri, *a.* Showing cheerfulness or good spirits; blithe; hearty; gay; sprightly; promoting cheerfulness.

cheese, chēz, *n.* [A.Sax. *cése, cyse*, cheese; derived like G. *käse*, D. *kaas*, from L. *caseus*, cheese.] An article of food consisting of the curd or casein of milk, coagulated by rennet or some acid, separated from the whey, and usually pressed into a solid mass in a mold.—**cheesy**, chē′zi, *a.* Having the qualities, taste, odor, or form of cheese; resembling or pertaining to cheese.—**cheesiness**, chē′zi·nes, *n.* The quality of being cheesy.—**cheesecake**, *n.* A cake filled with a jelly made of soft curds, sugar, and butter; a small cake made in various ways and with a variety of different ingredients.—**cheeseparing**, *a.* Meanly economical; parsimonious.

cheetah, chē′ta, *n.* [Native name, meaning spotted.] The hunting leopard, trained in India to hunt such game as deer, etc.

chef, shef, *n.* [Fr., lit. head, from L. *caput*.] Head or chief; specifically, the head cook of a great establishment, as a nobleman's household, a club, etc.—**chef-d'oeuvre**, shā·dė′·vr, *n. pl.* **chefs-d'oeuvre**, shā·dė′·vr. [Fr.] A masterpiece; a fine work in art, literature, etc.

chela, kē′la, *n. pl.* **chelae**, kē′lē. [Gr. *chēlē*, a claw.] One of the prehensile claws possessed by certain crustacea,

as the crab, lobster, etc.—**chelate**, **cheliferous**, kē′lāt, ki·lif′ėr·us, *a.* Furnished with chelae.—**cheliform**, kē′li·form, *a.* Having the form of a chela or prehensile claw.

chelonian, ki·lō′ni·an, *a.* [Gr. *chelōnē*, a tortoise.] Pertaining to or designating animals of the tortoise kind.—*n.* A tortoise or turtle.

chemise, she·mēz′, *n.* [Fr. *chemise*, L.L. *camisia*, a shirt, from Ar. *qamis*, a shirt, an undergarment of linen.] A shift or smock worn by females; a wall that lines the face of an earthwork; a breast wall.— **chemisette**, shem·i·zet′, *n.* [Fr.] A short undergarment worn on the breast over the chemise.

chemist, kem′ist, *n.* [Shortened from *alchemist*, from *alchemy*, O.Fr. *alchemie*, from Ar. *al*, the, and *qīmīā*, chemistry, from L. Gr. *chēmeia*, chemistry, from Gr. *cheō*, to pour, to drop.] A person versed in chemistry; one whose business is to make chemical examinations or investigations.—**chemistry**, kem′ist·ri, *n.* The science that investigates the composition of the various kinds of matter, the changes of composition that occur, the energy phenomena that accompany these changes, and the relationships involved; chemical properties, reactions, etc.—*Organic chemistry*, the study of carbon compounds.—*Inorganic chemistry*, the study of elements and compounds other than those of carbon.—**chemical**, kem′i·kal, *a.* Pertaining to chemistry.—*n.* A substance obtained by or used in a chemical process.— **chemically**, kem′i·kal·li, *adv.*—**chemical engineering**, *n.* A branch of chemistry that deals with the industrial uses of chemistry.—**chemical warfare**, *n.* Warfare with incendiary mixtures, poisonous gases, etc.

chemosmosis, kem·os·mō′sis, *n.* [*Chem-* in chemistry, and *osmosis*.] Chemical action acting through an intervening membrane, as parchment, etc.

chemotherapy, kem′o·ther″a·pi, *n.* Treatment of disease with chemicals having a specific destructive effect on the micro-organisms causing the disease.

chenille, she·nēl′, *n.* [Fr., a caterpillar.] A tufted cord of silk or worsted, somewhat resembling a caterpillar, used for making rugs, bedspreads, etc.

cherish, cher′ish, *v.t.* [O.Fr. *cherir*, *cherissant* (Fr. *chérir*), to hold dear, from *cher*, L. *carus*, dear, whence also *caress*.] To treat with tenderness and affection; to take care of; to foster; to hold as dear; to indulge and encourage in the mind; to harbor; to cling to.—**cherisher**, cher′- ish·ėr, *n.* One who cherishes; an encourager; a supporter.—**cherishingly**, cher′ish·ing·li, *adv.* In an affectionate or cherishing manner.

cheroot, she·röt′, *n.* [Tamil *shuruttu*, a roll.] A kind of cigar of a cylindrical or often somewhat tapering shape, with both ends cut square off.

cherry, cher′i, *n.* [O.E. *cheri, chiri*, from Fr. *cerise*, L. *cerasus*, from Gr.

kerasos, a cherry.] The fruit of a tree belonging to the plum family, consisting of a pulpy drupe inclosing a one-seeded smooth stone; the tree itself; also the name of other fruits.—*a.* Like a red cherry in color; red; ruddy; blooming.

chersonese, kėr′so·nēz, *n.* [Gr. *chersonēsos*—*chersos*, land, and *nēsos*, an isle.] A peninsula.

chert, chėrt, *n.* [Probably Celtic; comp. Ir. *ceart*, a pebble.] A variety of quartz, more or less translucent, less hard than common quartz, with a fracture usually conchoidal and dull, sometimes splintery.— **cherty**, chėr′ti, *a.* Like chert; full of chert; flinty.

cherub, cher′ub, *n. pl.* **cherubs**; Hebrew pl. **cherubim**, cher′ub·im. [Heb. *kerub*.] One of an order of angels; a beautiful child. [In the latter sense the plural is always *cherubs*.]—**cherubic**, che·rö′bik, *a.* Pertaining to or resembling cherubs; angelic.

chervil, chėr′vil, *n.* [A.Sax. *cerfille*, from L. *chœrophyllum*, from Gr. *chairephyllon*—*chairō*, to rejoice, and *phyllon*, leaf, from their agreeable odor.] A hairy herb of the carrot family, with longish grooved fruits, common in fields and waste places.— *Garden chervil*, an annual plant cultivated as an aromatic potherb.

chess, ches, *n.* [O.Fr. *eschecs*, Fr. *échecs*, chess, really a plural, meaning lit. kings, from Per. *shâh*, a king, the principal figure in the game, whence also *check*.] An ingenious game played by two persons or parties with different pieces on a checkered board, divided into sixty-four squares.—**chessboard**, *n.* The board used in the game of chess.— **chessman**, *n.* A piece used in playing the game of chess.

chest, chest, *n.* [A.Sax. *cyste*, from L. *cista*, Gr. *kistē*, a chest, a box.] A box of considerable size; *com.* a case in which certain kinds of goods, as tea, indigo, etc., are packed for transit; hence, the quantity such a chest contains; the trunk of the body from the neck to the belly; the thorax.—*Chest of drawers*, a piece of furniture with sliding boxes or drawers for holding various articles of dress, linen, etc.—*v.t.* To deposit in a chest; to hoard.

chestnut, ches′nut, *n.* [For *chesten-nut*, O.E. *chestrine, chesteyne*, from O.Fr. *chastaigne*, from L. *castanea*, the chestnut tree, from Gr. *kastanon*, from *Castana* in Pontus, where this tree abounded.] The seed or nut of a forest tree allied to the beech, inclosed in a prickly pericarp, containing two or more edible seeds; the tree itself or its timber; the color of the husk of a chestnut; a reddish-brown color; an old joke (colloq.).— *a.* Of the color of a chestnut; reddish-brown.

cheval-de-frise, she·val′de·frēz, *n. pl.* **chevaux-de-frise**, she·vō′de·frēz. [Fr. *cheval*, a horse, pl. *chevaux*, and *Frise*, Friesland, where first employed.] A horizontal piece of timber or iron with long spikes transversely through it, set on the ground to bar a passage, form an obstacle to the advance of cavalry, etc.

cheval glass, *n.* A swing looking glass mounted on a frame, and large enough to reflect the whole figure.

chevalier, shev•a•lēr′, *n.* [Fr., from *cheval,* a horse. CAVALRY, CAVALIER.] A horseman; a cavalier; a member of certain orders of knighthood.— *Chevalier d'industrie,* one who gains a living by dishonest means; a sharper; a swindler; a thief.

Cheviot, che′vi•ot, *n.* and *a.* A name for a variety of sheep, noted for their large carcass and valuable wool, so called from the Cheviot Hills between Scotland and England.

chevron, shev′run, *n.* [Fr., a rafter, from *chèvre,* L. *capra,* a goat, because rafters are reared on end like butting goats.] *Her.* a figure on a shield representing two rafters of a house meeting at the top; *arch.* a variety of fret ornament; a zigzag; *milit.* the distinguishing marks on the sleeves of noncommissioned officers' coats.

chew, chö, *v.t.* [From A.Sax. *ceówan,* to chew=D. *kaauwen,* to chew. *Jaw, jowl, chaps, chops* are from the same root.] To bite and grind with the teeth; to masticate.—*To chew the cud,* to ruminate, and *fig.* to ruminate or meditate on something.—*v.i.* To perform the act of chewing; to champ.—*n.* That which is chewed; a quid of tobacco.

chewing gum, *n.* Vegetable gum, usually chicle, sweetened and flavored, for chewing.

chi, kī, *n.* The twenty-second letter of the Greek alphabet, written as *ch* in English.

chiaroscuro, chiaro-oscuro, ki•ä′-rō•skö″rō, ki•ä′rō•os•kö″rō, *n.* [It., lit. clear-obscure, from L. *clarus,* clear, and *obscurus,* obscure; Fr. *clair-obscur.*] That department of painting which relates to light and shade; the art of judiciously distributing the lights and shadow in a picture.

chiasma, ki•az′ma, *n.* [Gr. *chiasma,* from the Greek letter χ.] *Anat.* the central body of nervous matter, where the optic nerves cross each other proceeding from the brain to the eyes; a cross arrangement [X] of clauses e.g. *I cannot sing, to laugh I would be ashamed.*

chibouque, chibouk, shi•bök′, *n.* [Turk.] A Turkish tobacco pipe.

chic, shēk, *n.* [Fr., from G. *schick,* due order, tact.] Easy elegance; smartness; adroitness; knowingness.—*a.* Smart.

chicane, chicanery shi•kān′, shi•kān′ér•i, *n.* [Fr. *chicane, chicanerie,* originally a kind of game and the maneuvers in playing it, from Per. *chaugan,* the game of golf played on horseback, polo.] The art of protracting a contest or discussion by the use of evasive stratagems or trickery; sophistry; artifice.—*v.t.* and *i.* To use chicane.

chickadee, chik′a•dē, *n.* [Amer. imitative of its call.] A small North American bird with black, white,

and gray feathers.

chicken, chik′en, *n.* [A.Sax. *cicen, cycen,* a chicken; cog. L.G. *kiken, küken,* Prov. G. *küchen.*] A young fowl; particularly a young domestic fowl; a person of tender years: generally used of females, as in the phrase, she is no *chicken.*—**chick,** chik, *n.* A chicken.—**chickenhearted,** *a.* Having no more courage than a chicken; timid; cowardly.—**chicken pox,** *n.* A mild contagious eruptive disease generally appearing in children.—**chickweed,** *n.* A common weed with small white blossoms much used for feeding cage birds.

chickling, chickling vetch, chik′-ling, *n.* [From Fr. *chiche,* It. *cece,* from L. *cicer,* the chick-pea.] A vetch or pea extensively cultivated in the south of Europe for its seed.— **chick-pea,** *n.* A plant cultivated for its seeds, which form an important article in French cookery.

chicle, chi′kl, *n.* [Mex.] Elastic gum of the sapodilla tree, usual base of chewing gum.

chicory, chik′o•ri, *n.* [Fr. *chicorée,* L. *cichorium,* from Gr. *kichōrion,* chicory.] The popular name of a composite plant common in Europe and America, with a fleshy tapering root which is extensively employed as a substitute for coffee, or to mix with coffee.

chide, chīd, *v.t.*—*chid* (pret.), *chid* or *chidden, chiding.* [A.Sax. *cidan,* to chide; connections unknown.] To scold; to reprove; to rebuke; to find fault with or take exception to (a thing); to strike by way of punishment or admonition (*Tenn.*). —*v.i.* To scold; to find fault; to contend in words of anger.—**chider,** chīd′ér, *n.* One who chides, reproves, or rebukes.—**chidingly,** chīd′-ing•li, *adv.* In a scolding or reproving manner.

chief, chēf, *a.* [O.Fr. *chef, chief* (Fr. *chef*), the head, top, chief; from L. *caput,* the head, whence also *capital, cattle, captain,* etc.] Highest in office, authority, or rank; principal or most eminent, in any quality or action; most important; at the head; leading; main.—*n.* The person highest in authority, the head or head man; a military commander; the person who heads an army; the principal person of a clan, tribe, family, etc.—**chiefly,** chēf′li, *adv.* Principally; above all; in the first place; for the most part; mostly. —**chief justice,** *n.* The presiding officer of a court.—**chief of state,** *n.* The formal or symbolic head of a country as distinguished from the head of government.

chieftain, chēf′tan, *n.* [O.Fr. *chevetaine, chieftaine,* etc.; from L.L. *capitanus,* from *caput,* the head; really the same word as *captain.*] A leader or commander; a chief; the head of a clan or family.— **chieftaincy, chieftainship,** chēf′tan•-si, chēf′tan•ship, *n.* The rank and dignity or office of a chieftain.

chiffonier, shif•o•nēr′, *n.* [Fr., a chiffonier, a rag-picker, from *chiffon,* a rag.] A kind of small sideboard;

a wooden stand with shelves.

chignon, shē•nyon′, *n.* [Fr., the nape of the neck, a chignon.] The term applied to ladies' back hair when raised and folded up, usually round a pad of artificial hair.

chigoe, chig′ō, *n.* [Of West Indian or South American origin.] An insect closely resembling the common flea, but of more minute size, found in the West Indies and South America, which burrows beneath the skin of the foot, and becoming distended with eggs produces a troublesome ulcer.

chihuahua, chi•wä′•wä, *n.* [Mexican Sp. from *Chihuahua,* Mexico.] A very small dog of ancient Mexican breed.

chilblain, chil′blān, *n.* [*Chill,* cold, and *blain.*] A blain or inflamed sore on the hands or feet produced by cold.—*v.t.* To afflict with chilblains; to produce chilblains in.

child, chīld, *n.* pl. **children,** chil′dren. [A.Sax. *cild,* a child, pl. *cildru,* afterward *cildre, childre,* to which *n* or *en* another plural termination was added. The root is the same as that of *kin, kind,* etc., G. *kind,* a child.] A son or a daughter of any age; a male or female descendant in the first degree; a very young person of either sex; one of crude or immature knowledge, experience, judgment, or attainments; *pl.* descendants; offspring.—*Child's play,* a trivial matter of any kind; anything easily accomplished or surmounted. —*With child,* pregnant.—**childhood,** chīld′hud, *n.* The state of a child; the time in which persons are still classed as children.—**childing,**† chīld′ing, *a.* Bearing children; productive; fruitful.—**childish,** chīld′ish, *a.* Of or belonging to a child or to childhood; like a child, or what is proper to childhood; with the disparaging senses of trifling, puerile, ignorant, silly, weak.—**childishly,** chīld′ish•li, *adv.* In a childish manner.—**childishness,** chīld′ish•nes, *n.* The state or quality of being childish. —**childless,** chīld′les, *a.* Destitute of children or offspring.—**childlessness,** chīld′les•nes, *n.* State of being without children.—**childlike,** chīld′-līk, *a.* Resembling a child or that which belongs to children; meek; submissive; dutiful; never used in a disparaging sense.—**childly,**† chīld′-li, *a.* Like a child; acquired or learned when a child. (*Tenn.*).— **childbearing,** *n.* The act of producing or bringing forth children; parturition.—**childbed,** *n.* The state of a woman who is lying-in or in labor.— **childbirth,** *n.* The act of bringing forth a child; travail; labor.— **Childermas,** chil′dér•mas, *n.* [*Childer,* pl. of *child,* and *mass.*] An anniversary of the Church of England, held on the 28th of December: Innocents Day.

chiliad, kil′i•ad, *n.* [Gr. *chilias,* from *chilioi,* a thousand.] A thousand; a collection or sum containing a thousand individuals or particulars; the period of a thousand years.— **chiliarch,** kil′i•ärk, *n.* [Gr. *archos,* a chief.] The military commander or chief of a thousand men.—**chiliasm,** kil'i·azm, n. A millennium.—**chiliast,** kil'i·ast, n. A millenarian.—**chiliastic,** kil·i·as'tik, a. Relating to the millennium; millenarian.

chill, chil, n. [A.Sax. cele, cyle, a cold, chill, from cól, cool; akin D. kill, chill, killen, to chill; Sw. kyla, to chill; same root as in L. gelidus, gelid. COOL.] A shivering with cold; a cold fit; sensation of cold in an animal body; chilliness; coldness or absence of heat in a substance; fig. the feeling of being damped or discouraged; a depressing influence. a. Cold; tending to cause shivering (chill winds); experiencing cold; shivering with cold; fig. depressing; discouraging; distant; formal; not warm (a chill reception).—v.t. To affect with chill; to make chilly; fig. to check in enthusiasm or warmth; to discourage; to dispirit; to depress; metal. to reduce suddenly the temperature of (a piece of castiron), with the view of hardening (a chilled shot).—**chiller,** chil'ėr, n. One who or that which chills.—**chillingly,** chil'ing·li, adv. In a chilling manner; coldly.—**chilly,** chil'i, a. [Chill, and term. -y.] Experiencing or causing the sensation of chillness; disagreeably cold; chilling.—adv., chil'li, [Chill, and term. -ly.] In a chill or chilly manner.—**chilliness,** chil'i·nes, n. The state or quality of being chilly.

chime, chīm, n. [O.E. chimbe, chymbe, a cymbal, a shortening of chymbale, A.Sax. cimbal, from L. cymbalum, a cymbal.] The harmonious sound of bells or musical instruments; a set of bells (properly five or more) tuned to a musical scale, and struck by hammers, not by the tongues.—v.i. To sound in consonance, rhythm, or harmony; to give out harmonious sounds; hence, to accord; to agree; to suit; to harmonize; to express agreement; often with in with (to chime in with one's sentiments or humor).—v.t. To cause to sound harmoniously, as a set of bells.—**chimer,** chīm'ėr, n. One who chimes.

chime, chimb, chīm, n. [D. kim, Sw. kim, kimb, the edge of a cask, G. kimme, edge, brim.] The edge or brim of a cask or tub, formed by the ends of the staves projecting beyond the head.

chimera, chimaera, ki·mē'ra, n. [L. chimæra, from Gr. chimaira, a chimaera.] Class. myth. a fire-breathing monster, the fore parts of whose body were those of a lion, the middle of a goat, and the hinder of a dragon; ornamental art. a fantastic assemblage of animal forms so combined as to produce one complete but unnatural design; hence, a vain or idle fancy; a mere phantasm of the imagination; also the name of a cartilaginous fish of extraordinary appearance inhabiting the northern seas, and sometimes called king of the herrings.—**chimeric, chimerical,** ki·mer'ik, ki·mer'ik·al, a. Merely imaginary; fanciful; fantastic; wildly or vainly

conceived.—**chimerically,** ki·mer'ik·al·li, adv. In a chimerical manner.

chimere, shi·mēr', n. [Fr. simarre, It. zimarra.] The upper robe, to which the lawn sleeves of a bishop are attached.

chimney, chim'ni, n. [Fr. cheminée, L.L. caminata, a chimney, from L. caminus, a furnace, a flue, from Gr. kaminos, an oven.] An erection, generally of stone or brick, containing a passage by which the smoke of a fire or furnace escapes to the open air; a chimney stack; a flue; the funnel of a steam engine; a tall glass to surround the flame of a lamp to protect it and promote combustion.—**chimney pot,** n. A pipe of earthenware or sheet metal placed on the top of chimneys to prevent smoking.—**chimney piece,** n. The assemblage of architectural dressings around the open recess constituting the fire place in a room. —**chimneysweep,** n. One whose occupation is to clean chinneys of the soot that adheres to their sides.

chimpanzee, chim·pan'zē or chim·pan·zē', n. [The native Guinea name.] A large West African ape belonging to the anthropoid or manlike monkeys, and most nearly related to the gorilla.

chin, chin, n. [A.Sax. cin=D. kin, G. kinn, the chin; Icel. kinn, Dan. kind, Goth. kinnus, the cheek; Cog. Armor. gen, the cheek; W. gen. the chin; L. gena, the cheek; Gr. genys, the jaw, the chin; Skr. hanu, the jaw.] The lower extremity of the face below the mouth.—v.t. To lift oneself up by the arms until the chin is level with the support.—v.i. To talk. (Slang).

china, chinaware, chī'na, chī'na·wâr, n. A species of earthenware made in China, or in imitation of that made there, and so called from the country; porcelain.—**China aster,** n. The common name of a hardy and free-flowering composite plant. —**China rose,** n. The name given to a number of varieties of garden rose, natives of China.

chinch, chinch, n. [Sp. chinche, a bug, from L. cimex.] The common bedbug; also the popular name of certain fetid American insects resembling the bedbug, very destructive to wheat, corn, etc.

chinchilla, chin·chil'la, n. [Spanish name.] A genus of rodent animals peculiar to the South American continent, one species of which produces a fine pearly-gray fur; the fur of the chinchilla.

chincough, chin'kof, n. [For chinkcough, chink being for kink, as in Sc. kinkhost (host, a cough), D. kinkhoest.] Whooping-cough.

chine, chīn, n. [Fr. échine, O.Fr. eschine, the spine.] The backbone or spine of an animal; a piece of the backbone of an animal, with the adjoining parts, cut for cooking.—v.t. To cut through the backbone, or into chine pieces.

Chinese, chī·nēz', a. Pertaining to China.—Chinese fire, a composition used in fireworks.—Chinese lantern,

a lantern made of colored paper used in illuminations.—Chinese white, the white oxide of zinc.—n. sing. and pl. A native or natives of China; the language of China.

chink, chingk, n. [Akin to O.E. chine, A.Sax. cinu, a chink, a fissure, cinan, to gape.] A narrow aperture; a cleft, rent, or fissure of greater length than breadth; a cranny, gap, or crack.—v.t. To cause to open or part and form a fissure; to make chinks in; to fill up chinks in.—v.i. To crack; to open.

chink, chingk, v.i. [Imitative; comp. jingle.] To make a small sharp metallic sound.—v.t. To cause to sound as by shaking coins or small pieces of metal.—n. A short, sharp, clear, metallic sound; a term for money (vulgar); the reed bunting.

chinquapin, ching'ka·pin, n. [Of Amer.-Indian origin.] The dwarf chestnut of the U.S. yielding edible nuts; also an American tree allied to the oak.

chintz, chints, n. [Hind. chint, Per. chinz, spotted, stained.] Cotton cloth or calico printed with flowers or other devices, generally glazed.

chip, chip, v.t.—chipped, chipping. [Closely connected with chop and chap; O.D. kippen, to knock to pieces; O.Sw. kippa, to chop; G. kippen, to clip or cut money.] To cut into small pieces; to diminish by cutting away a little at a time or in small pieces.—v.i. To break or fly off in small pieces.—n. A piece of wood, stone, or other substance separated from a body by a blow of an instrument; a flat counter used in games.

chipmunk, chip'mungk, n. The popular name of the ground squirrel.

chipper, chip'ėr, a. [Probably from North. E. kipper, lively.] Cheerful; sprightly.

Chippendale, chip'en·dāl, a. [Inventor's name.] A style of drawing-room furniture.

chirographer, kī·rog'ra·fėr, n. [Gr. cheir, the hand, graphō, to write.] One who exercises or professes the art of writing; one who tells fortunes by examining the hand.—**chirographic, chirographical,** kī·ro·graf'ik, kī·ro·graf'ik·al, a. Pertaining to chirography.—**chirography,** kī·rog'ra·fi, n. The art of writing; handwriting; the art of telling fortunes by examining the hand.

chiromancy, kī'ro·man·si, n. [Gr. cheir, the hand, and manteia, divination.] Divination by the hand; the art or practice of foretelling one's fortune by inspecting the lines and lineaments of his hand; palmistry.—**chiromancer,** kī'ro·man·sėr, n. One who practices chiromancy.

chiropodist, kī·rop'od·ist, n. [Gr. cheir, the hand, and pous, podos, the foot.] One who treats diseases of the feet.

chiropractic, kī·ro·prak'tik, n. [Gr. cheir, hand, and praktikos, practice.] Manipulation of the spine to cure disease.—**chiropractor,** kī'ro·prak·tėr, n. One who practices chiropractic by method of manipulation.

---

ch, chain; ch, Sc. loch; g, go; j, job; ng, sing; TH, then; th, thin; w, wig; hw, whig; zh, azure.

chiropter, kī·rop'tėr, n. [Gr. cheir, a hand, and pteron, a wing.] A bat. BAT.

chirp, cherp, v.i. [Akin to G. zirpen, tschirpen, schirpen, to chirp, chirrup being a lengthened form; the same root in D. kirren, to coo, L. garrio, to chatter.] To make a short sharp shrill sound, as is done by small birds or certain insects; to cheep.— n. A short, shrill note, as of certain birds or insects.

chirrup, chir'up, v.i. [A lengthened form of chirp.] To chirp.—n. A chirp.

chisel, chiz'el, n. [O.Fr. cisel (Fr. ciseau). L.L. cisellus, from L. cædo, cæsum, to cut.] An instrument of iron or steel, used in carpentry, joinery, cabinet work, masonry, sculpture, etc., for paring, hewing, or gouging.—v.t. chiseled, chiseling. To cut, pare, gouge, or engrave with a chisel (a statue chiseled out of marble); fig. to cut close, as in a bargain; to cheat (slang).—**chiseled**, chiz'eld, a. Worked with a chisel or as with a chisel; clear-cut; statuesque.

chit, chit, n. [A.Sax. cith, a shoot or twig.] A shoot or sprout; the first shoot of a seed or plant; a child or babe; a young and insignificant person.

chitchat, chit'chat, n. [A reduplication of chat.] Prattle; familiar or trifling talk.

chitin, kī'tin, n. [Gr. chitōn, a tunic.] The organic substance which forms the wing covers and integuments of insects and the carapaces of crustacea, having a somewhat horny character. —**chitinous**, kī'tin·us, a. Consisting of, or having the nature of chitin.

chiton, kī'ton, n. [Gr. chitōn, a tunic, a cuirass, a coat of mail.] The name of certain mollusks, the shell of which is formed of successive portions, often in contact and overlapping each other, but never truly articulated.

chitterling, chit'ėr·ling, n. Cookery, part of the small intestines, as of swine, fried for food: generally used in the plural.

chivalry, shiv'al·ri, n. [Fr. chevalerie, from chevalier, a knight or horseman, from cheval, a horse. CAVALRY.] Knighthood; the system to which knighthood with all its laws and usages belonged; the qualifications of a knight, as courtesy, valor, and dexterity in arms; knights or warriors collectively; any body of illustrious warriors, especially cavalry.— **chivalric, chivalrous**, shiv'al·rik, shiv'al·rus, a. Pertaining to chivalry or knight errantry; warlike; bold; gallant.—**chivalrously**, shiv'al·rus·li, adv. In a chivalrous manner or spirit.—**chivalrousness**, shiv'al·rus·nes, n. The quality of being chivalrous.

chive, chīv, n. [Fr. cive, L. cepa, an onion.] A small perennial plant of the same genus as the leek and onion, cultivated in kitchen gardens as a potherb.

chlamys, klā'mas, klă'mas, n. [L. chlamys, from Gr.] A short, oblong mantle usually clasped at the shoulder, worn by young men in ancient Greece.

chloral, klō'ral, n. [From chlor, the first part of chlorine, and al, the first syllable of alcohol.] An oily liquid with a pungent odor and slightly astringent taste, produced from chlorine and alcohol; also the name popularly applied to chloral hydrate, a white crystalline substance used in medicine for producing sleep.

chlorine, klō'rēn, n. [Gr. chlōros, greenish-yellow, from its color.] A gaseous element, yellowish green in color with a suffocating odor, used as a bleach and in industrial processes. Symbol, Cl; at. no., 17; at. wt., 35.453.—**chlorate**, klō'rāt, n. A salt of chloric acid.—**chloric**, klō'rik, a. Pertaining to or containing chlorine.—Chloric acid, a colorless unstable solution that has strong oxidizing properties.—**chloride**, klō'rīd, n. A compound of chlorine with another element.—Chloride of lime, chlorine and lime, used as a bleaching agent.—**chlorinate**, klō're·nāt, v.t. To treat or combine with chlorine.— **chlorination**, klō·re·nā'shon, n.— **chlorite**, klō'rīt, n. A green mineral silicate of aluminum.—**chlorous**, klō'rus, a.

chloroform, klo'ro·form, n. [Chlor-, from chloride or chlorine, and -form, from formic acid, from chemical connection.] A volatile colorless liquid, of an agreeable, fragrant, sweetish apple taste and smell, prepared by distilling together a mixture of alcohol, water, and chloride of lime, and much used as an anesthetic, for which purpose its vapor is inhaled.— v.t. To put under the influence of chloroform; to treat with chloroform.

chlorophyll, klō'ro·fil, n. [Gr. chlōros, green, and phyllon, a leaf.] The green coloring matter of plants, which is developed by the influence of light; hence arises the etiolation or blanching of plants by privation of light.

chlorosis, klo·rō'sis, n. [Gr. chlōros, greenish-yellow.] The greensickness, a peculiar form of anemia or bloodlessness which affects young females, and is characterized by a pale greenish hue of the skin.

chlorous. See CHLORINE.

chock-full, chok'ful, a. As full as possible; crammed.

chocolate, chok'o·lit, n. [Sp. chocolate; Mex. chocolatl—choco, cocoa, and latl, water.] A paste or cake composed of the kernels of the cacao nut ground and combined with sugar and vanilla, cinnamon, cloves, or other flavoring substance; the beverage made by dissolving chocolate in boiling water or milk.—a. Having the color of chocolate; of a dark, glossy brown.

choice, chois, n. [O.Fr. chois, a choice, from choisir, to choose; from the German. CHOOSE.] The act or power of choosing; a selecting or separating from two or more things that which is preferred; selection; election; option; preference; the thing chosen; the best part of anything.—a. Carefully selected; worthy of being preferred; select; precious.—**choicely**, chois'li, adv. In a choice manner or degree.—**choiceness**, chois'nes, n. The quality of being choice or select; excellence; value.

choir, kwir, n. [O.Fr. chœur, L. chorus, Gr. choros, a dance in a ring, a band; same word as chorus, quire.] A band of dancers‡; a collection of singers, especially in a church; that part of a church appropriated for the singers in cruciform churches; that part eastward of the nave, and separated from it usually by a screen of open work; a chancel.—v.t. and i. To sing in company.

choke, chōk, v.t.—choked, choking. [Akin to cough, and to Icel. koka, to gulp, kyka, to swallow; perhaps imitative of the convulsive sound made when the throat is impeded.] To deprive of the power of breathing by stopping the passage of the breath through the windpipe; to compress the windpipe; to strangle; to stop by filling (any passage); to obstruct; to block up; to hinder by obstruction or impediments (as plants from growing); to enrich the fuel mixture of an engine by decreasing the air supply.—v.i. To have the windpipe stopped; to have something stick in the throat.—n. The act of choking; the valve that chokes a gasoline engine.—**choker**, chōk'ėr, n. One who or that which chokes; a short necklace.

choler, kol'ėr, n. [O.Fr. cholere (Fr. colère), choler, anger, L. cholera, a bilious ailment, from Gr. cholera, from cholē, bile, anger.] The bile, the excess of which was formerly supposed to produce anger, etc.; hence, anger, wrath, irascibility.— **choleric**, kol'ėr·ik, a. Abounding with choler or bile; easily irritated; irascible; inclined to anger; proceeding from anger.

cholera, kol'ėr·a, n. [L. bile, a bilious complaint. CHOLER.] A serious gastrointestinal infection marked by diarrhea, vomiting, and dehydration.

cholesterol, ko·les'tėr·ōl, n. [Gr. cholē, bile, and stereos, solid.] A white crystalline solid found in all animal fats, gallstones, egg yolk, milk, etc.

chondrite, kon'drīt, n. [L. chondrus, a species of seaweed.] A fossil marine plant of the chalk and other formations resembling Irish moss.

chondrotomy, kon·drot'o·mi, n. [Gr. chondros, cartilage, and tome, a cutting.] A dissection of cartilages.

choose, chöz, v.t.—chose (pret.), chosen, choosing. [A.Sax. ceósan=D. kiezen, Icel. kjosa, G. kiesen, to choose, Goth. kiusan, to choose, to prove; from root seen in L. gustare, Gr. geuomai, to taste.] To take by preference; to make choice or selection of; to pick out; to select; to prefer; to wish; to be inclined or have an inclination for (colloq.).— v.i. To make a choice.—**chooser**, chöz'ėr, n. One that chooses; one that has the power or right of choosing.

chop, chop, v.t.—chopped, chopping. [Same word as chap, to split, with a slightly different form and meaning=D. and G. *kappen*, to chop, to mince, to cut; Dan. *kappe*, to cut, to lop.] To cut into pieces; to mince; to sever or separate by striking with a sharp instrument: usually with *off.*—*v.i.* To chap or crack, as the skin.—*n.* A piece chopped off; a slice, particularly of meat.—**chopper,** chop′ĕr, *n.* One who or that which chops; a tool for chopping or mincing meat; a cleaver.—**chophouse,** *n.* A house where meat chops are dressed ready for eating; an eating house.

chop, chop, *v.t.*—*chopped, chopping.* [Same origin as *cheap.*] To buy, or rather to barter; to truck or exchange.—*To chop logic,* to dispute or argue in a sophistical manner or with an affectation of logical terms or methods.—*v.i.* To bargain‡; to bandy words or dispute‡; to turn, vary, change, or shift suddenly: said of the wind.—*n.* A turn of fortune; change; vicissitude, especially in the phrase *chops and changes.*

chop, chop, *n.* The chap; the jaw; *pl.* the mouth or entrance to a channel. CHAP.—**chopfallen,** *a.* Dejected; chapfallen.

chop, chop, *n.* [Hind. *chhap,* stamp, print.] An eastern customhouse or other stamp on goods; hence, quality or brand (silk or tea of the first *chop*).

chopine, cho·pēn′, *n.* [From Sp. *chapin,* a clog or chopine.] A sort of very lofty clog or patten formerly worn.

choppy, chop′i, *a.* [From *chop,* change.] Showing short broken waves.

chopstick, chop′stik, *n.* One of two small sticks of wood, ivory, etc., used by the Chinese and Japanese for conveying food to the mouth.

choragus, kō·rā′gus, *n.* [Gr. *choragos—choros,* a chorus, and *agō,* to lead.] The leader or superintendent of a chorus or of a theatrical representation in ancient Greece; the person who had to provide at his own expense the choruses for dramatic representations and religious festivals.—**choragic,** kō·rā′jik, *a.* Pertaining to or connected with a choragus.

choral, etc. See CHORUS.

chord, kord, *n.* [L. *chorda,* from Gr. *chordē,* an intestine, of which strings were made. *Cord* is the same word.] The string of a musical instrument; *mus.* the simultaneous combination of different sounds, consonant or dissonant; *geom.* a straight line drawn or supposed to extend from one end of an arc of a circle to the other.—*v.t.* To furnish with chords or musical strings.

chore, chōr, *n.* [An alteration of E. *chare,* an odd job.] A task; a duty; a small odd job.

chorea, kō′rē·a or ko·rē′a, *n.* [Gr. *choreia,* a dance.] *Med.* St. Vitus's dance; convulsive motions of the limbs.

choreography, kŏr·ē·og′ra·fi, *n.* [Gr. *choreia,* dance, and *graphy, graphein,* to write.] The art of designing and arranging dances for a ballet.—**choreographer,** kŏr·ē·og′ra·fĕr, *n.*

choriamb, kō·ri·amb′, *n.* [Gr. *choreios,* a trochee, and *iambos,* iambus.]

Pros. a foot consisting of four syllables, the first two forming a trochee and the second two an iambus.

chorion, kō′ri·on, *n.* [Gr.] *Anat.* the external vascular membrane which invests the fetus in the womb; *bot.* the external membrane of the seeds of plants.—**choroid,** kor′oid, *a.* and *n.* A term applied to a membrane resembling the chorion, especially to one of the membranes of the eye of a very dark color.

chorister, etc. See CHORUS.

chorography, kō·rog′ra·fi, *n.* [Gr. *chōros,* a place or region, and *graphō,* to describe.] The art or practice of making maps of or of describing particular regions, countries, or districts. — **chorographer,** kō·rog′ra·fĕr, *n.* One skilled in chorography. —**chorographic, chorographical,** kō·ro·graf′ik, kō·ro·graf′ik·al, *a.* Pertaining to chorography; descriptive of particular regions or countries.

choroid. See CHORION.

chorus, kō′rus, *n.* [L. *chorus,* from Gr. *choros,* a dance in a ring, a chorus.] Originally a band of dancers accompanied by their own singing or that of others; the performers in a Greek play who were supposed to behold what passed in the acts, and sing their sentiments between the acts; the song between the acts; now, usually, verses of a song in which the company joins the singer, or the singing of the company with the singer; a union or chiming of voices in general (a *chorus* of laughter or ridicule); *mus.* a composition in parts sung by many voices; the whole body of vocalists other than soloists, whether in an oratorio, opera, or concert.—*v.t.* To sing or join in the chorus of; to exclaim or call out in concert.—**choral,** kō′ral, *a.* Belonging, relating, or pertaining to a chorus, choir, or concert.—**choral, chorale,** ko·ral′, ko·räl′, *n.* A psalm or hymn tune, often sung in unison by the congregation, the organ supplying the harmony.—**choric,** kō′rik, *a.* Pertaining to a chorus; choral. (*Tenn.*)—**chorister,** kor′ist·ĕr, *n.* A singer in a choir or chorus; a singer generally.

chose, chōz, pret. of *choose.*—**chosen,** chō′zn, pp. of *choose.* As an adjective, choice; select.

chough, chuf, *n.* [A.Sax. *ceó,* a chough or jackdaw; D. *haauw,* Dan. *kaa.*] A bird of the crow family, genus *Pyrrhocorax,* of a black color with red beak, legs, and toes.

chowchow, chou′chou, *n.* A Chinese term for any mixture, but in trade circles confined generally to mixed pickles.

chrestomathy, kres·tom′a·thi, *n.* [Gr. *chrēstos,* useful, and *mathein,* to learn.] A book of extracts from a foreign language, with notes, intended to be used in acquiring the language.

chrism, krizm, *n.* [Gr. *chrisma,* an unguent, from *chriō,* to anoint, whence also *Christ.*] Holy or consecrated oil or unguent used in the administration of baptism, confirmation, ordination, and extreme unc-

tion, more especially in the Latin and Greek churches; the baptismal cloth laid upon the head of a child newly baptized; the baptismal vesture; the chrisom.—**chrismal,** kriz′mal, *a.* Pertaining to chrism.—*n.* The vessel holding the consecrated oil or chrism; the white cloth laid over the head of one newly baptized, after the unction with chrism.—**chrisom,** kris′um, *n.* [A form of *chrism.*] A cloth anointed with chrism laid on a child's face at baptism; the white consecrated vesture put about a child when christened.—*Chrisom child,* a newly baptized infant; a child that dies within a month after christening.

Christ, krīst, *n.* [L. *Christus,* Gr. *Christos,* lit. anointed, from *chriō,* to anoint.] THE ANOINTED: an appellation given to the Saviour of the World, and synonymous with the Hebrew MESSIAH.—**christen,** kris′n, *v.t.* [A.Sax. *cristnian,* to christen, from *Cristen,* a Christian, from *Crist,* Christ.] To initiate into the visible church of Christ by the application of water; to name and baptize; to baptize; to name or denominate generally.—**Christendom,** kris′n·dum, *n.* [A.Sax. *cristendom—Cristen,* Christian, and term. *-dom.*] The territories, countries, or regions chiefly inhabited by Christians or those who profess to believe in the Christian religion; the whole body of Christians. — **Christian,** kris′chen, *n.* [L. *christianus,* from *Christus,* Christ.] One who believes, professes to believe, or who is assumed to believe, in the religion of Christ; a believer in Christ who is characterized by real piety.—*a.* Pertaining to Christ or to Christianity.—*Christian name,* the name given or announced at baptism, as distinguished from the family name.—*Christian era* or *period,* the period from the birth of Christ to the present time.—**Christianity,** kris·chi·an′i·ti, *n.* The religion of Christians, or the system of doctrines and precepts taught by Christ; conformity to the laws and precepts of the Christian religion. —**Christianization,** kris′chen·iz·ā″shon, *n.* The act or process of converting to Christianity.—**Christianize,** kris′chen·īz, *v.t.*—*christianized, christianizing.* To make Christian; to convert to Christianity.—**Christless,** krīst′les, *a.* Having no interest in Christ; without the spirit of Christ.—**Christmas,** kris′mas, *n.* [*Christ,* and *mass,* A.Sax. *mœssa,* a holy day or feast.] The festival of the Christian church observed annually on the 25th day of December, in memory of the birth of Christ; Christmas day or Christmastide.—**Christmas day,** *n.* The 25th day of December, when Christmas is celebrated.—**Christmas eve,** *n.* The evening of the day before Christmas.—**Christmastide,** *n.* The season of Christmas.—**Christmas tree,** *n.* A small evergreen tree set up by a family, etc., at Christmas, from which are hung ornaments and lights, with gifts placed underneath. —**Christ's thorn,** *n.* A deciduous

ch, *chain;* ch, Sc. *loch;* g, *go;* j, *job;* ng, *sing;* TH, *then;* th, *thin;* w, *wig;* hw, *whig;* zh, *azure.*

shrub with large hooked spines, a native of Palestine and the south of Europe: so named from a belief that it supplied the crown of thorns for Christ.

chromatic, krō·mat′ik, a. [Gr. *chromatikos,* from *chrōma,* color.] Relating to color, or to colored inks or pigments; *mus.* including notes not belonging to the diatonic scale.—*Chromatic scale,* a scale made up of thirteen successive semitones, that is, the eight diatonic tones and the five intermediate tones.—**chromatically,** krō·mat′ik·al·li, *adv.* In a chromatic manner.—**chromatics,** krō·mat′iks, *n.* The science of colors; that part of optics which treats of the properties of the colors of light and of natural bodies.—**chromatography,** krō·ma·tog′ra·fi, *n. Chem.* separation of closely related compounds by a method in which the compounds in solution are separately adsorbed in colored layers of an adsorbent.—**chromatology,** krō·ma·tol′o·ji, *n.* The doctrine of or a treatise on colors.—**chromatophore,** krō·mat′ō·fōr, *n.* [Gr. *chrōma,* and *pherein,* to bear.] One of the pigment cells in animals, well seen in the chameleons and cuttlefishes.

chromatin, krō′ma·tin, *n.* [Gr. *chroma, -atos,* color.] In cells, that part of the nucleus which can be deeply stained.

chrome, chromium, krōm, krō′mi·um, *n.* [Gr. *chrōma,* color.] A hard, grayish-white, metallic element, used as a plating and in chrome steel. Symbol, Cr; at. no., 24; at. wt., 51.996.—**chromic,** krōm′ik, *a.* Pertaining to chrome or obtained from it.—**chromite,** krō′mīt, *n.* A mineral containing chromium.

chromogen, krō′mo·jen, *n.* [Gr. *chroma,* color, and root *gen,* to produce.] A chemical compound containing color-forming groups; a substance that becomes a coloring matter.

chromolithography, krō′mo·li·thog′ra·fi, *n.* A method of producing colored lithographic pictures by using stones having different portions of the picture drawn upon them with inks of different colors, and so arranged as to blend into a complete picture.—**chromolithograph,** *n.* A picture obtained by means of chromolithography. — **chromolithographer,** *n.* One who practices chromolithography.—**chromolithographic,** *a.* Pertaining to chromolithography.

chromosome, krō′mo·sōm, *n.* [Gr. *chrōma,* color, and *sōma,* body.] Any of the small, elongated bodies in the cell nucleus that control the activity of the cell and play an important role in inheritance.

chromosphere, krō′mo·sfēr, *n.* [Gr. *chrōma,* color, and *sphaira,* a sphere.] The red layer of the sun's atmosphere, just beyond the solar disk, that is composed chiefly of hydrogen; a similar layer around any star.—**chromospheric,** krō·mo·sfer′ik, *a.*

chronic, kron′ik, *a.* [Gr. *chronikos,* from *chronos,* time, duration.] Pertaining to time; having reference to

time; continuing a long time, as a disease; continuing a long time, as a disease.

chronicle, kron′i·kl, *n.* [Fr. *chronique,* a chronicle.] An account of facts or events disposed in the order of time; a history, more especially one of a simple unpretentious character; *pl.* the title of two books of the Old Testament consisting mainly of the annals of the kingdom of Judah.—*v.t.* chronicled, chronicling. To record in history or chronicle; to record; to register.—**chronicler,** kron′i·klėr, *n.* One who chronicles; a writer of a chronicle.

chronogram, kron′o·gram, *n.* [Gr. *chronos,* time, and *gramma,* a letter or writing.] A word or words in which a date is expressed by the numeral letters occurring therein.—**chronogrammatic,** kron′o·gram·mat″ik, *a.* Belonging to a chronogram; containing a chronogram.

chronograph, kron′o·graf, *n.* [Gr. *chronos,* time, and *graphō,* to write.] A chronogram; a device of various kinds for measuring and registering very minute portions of time with extreme precision, generally consisting of a revolving hand, disk, or cylinder, moved by clockwork, the time of the event being indicated by a point or pen marking the disk or cylinder, such marking being controlled either by the observer himself or by electricity.

chronology, kro·nol′o·ji, *n.* [Gr. *chronologia*—*chronos,* time, and *logos,* discourse or doctrine.] The science of ascertaining the true periods or years when past events or transactions took place, and arranging them in their proper order according to their dates.—**chronologic, chronological,** kron·o·loj′ik, kron·o·loj′ik·al, *a.* Relating to chronology; containing an account of events in the order of time; according to the order of time.—**chronologically,** kron·o·loj′ik·al·li, *adv.* In a chronological manner.— **chronologist, chronologer,** kro·nol′o·jist, kro·nol′o·jėr, *n.* One versed in chronology; a person who investigates the dates of past events and transactions.

chronometer, kro·nom′et·ėr, *n.* [Gr. *chronos,* time, and *metron,* measure.] Any instrument that measures time, as a clock, watch, or dial; specifically, a timekeeper of great perfection of workmanship, made much on the principle of a watch, but rather larger, used (in conjunction with observations of the heavenly bodies) in determining the longitude at sea.—**chronometric, chronometrical,** kron·o·met′rik, kron·o·met′rik·al, *a.* Pertaining to a chronometer; measured by a chronometer.—**chronometry,** kro·nom′et·ri, *n.* The art of measuring time; the measuring of time by periods or divisions.

chronoscope, kron′o·skōp, *n.* [Gr. *chronos,* time, and *skopeō,* to observe.] An instrument for measuring the duration of extremely short-lived phenomena; more especially, the name given to instruments of various forms for measuring the velocity of projectiles.

chrysalis, chrysalid, kris′a·lis, kris′-

a·lid, *n.* [Gr. *chrysallis,* a grub, from *chrysos,* gold, from its golden color.] The form which butterflies, moths, and most other insects assume when they change from the state of larva or caterpillar and before they arrive at their winged or perfect state. Called also *Aurelia* and *Pupa.*

chrysanthemum, kri·san′the·mum, *n.* [Gr. *chrysos,* gold, and *anthemon,* a flower.] The generic and common name of numerous species of composite plants, some of which are common weeds, such as the ox-eye daisy, while the florists' chrysanthemum, in its numerous varieties, is equally well known.—**chryselephantine,** kris′el·e·fan″tin, *a.* [Gr. *elephas, elephantos,* ivory.] Composed or partly composed of gold and ivory: a term specially applied to statues overlaid with gold and ivory, as made among the ancient Greeks.—**chrysoberyl,** kris′o·ber·il, *n.* [Gr. *beryllion,* beryl.] A gem of a yellowish-green color, next to the sapphire in hardness, and employed in jewelry, being found in Ceylon, Peru, Siberia, Brazil, etc.—**chrysolite,** kris′ō·līt, *n.* [Gr. *lithos,* stone.] A greenish, sometimes transparent, gem, composed of silica, magnesium, and iron, not of great value.—**chrysoprase,** kris′o·prāz, *n.* [Gr. *prason,* a leek.] A translucent mineral of an apple-green color, a variety of chalcedony much esteemed as a gem.

chthonian, thon′i·an, *a.* [Gr. *chthonios,* from *chthōn,* the earth.] Pertaining to the earth; belonging to the underworld or divinities of subterranean regions, preceding the Olympian system.

chub, chub, *n.* [So called probably from its *chubbiness* or plumpness.] A river fish of the carp family, having the body oblong, nearly round; the head and back green, the sides silvery, and the belly white.

chubby, chub′i, *a.* [Akin to E. *chump;* Sw. dial. *kubbug,* plump, *kubb,* a lump, a block.] Having a round plump face or plump body; round and fat; plump.—**chubbiness,** chub′i·nes, *n.* The state of being chubby.

chuck, chuk, *n.* [Imitative; comp. *cluck.*] The voice or call of a hen and some other birds, or a sound resembling that.—*v.i.* To make the noise which a hen and some other birds make when they call their chickens.

chuck, chuk, *v.t.* [A modification of *shock.* Fr. *choquer,* and formerly written *chock.*] To strike, tap, or give a gentle blow; to throw, with quick motion, a short distance; to pitch.—*n.* A slight blow or tap under the chin; a toss; a short throw.

chuck, chuk, *n.* [Variant of *chock.*] A cut of beef between the neck and the shoulder; a device for holding a tool in a machine.—**chuck wagon,** *n.* A wagon that carries food and cooking equipment.

chuckle, chuk′l, *v.i.*—**chuckled, chuckling.** [A freq. and dim. from *chuck,* to cry like a hen; or connected with *choke.*] To laugh in a suppressed or broken manner; to feel inward triumph or exultation.

---

fāte, fär, fâre, fat, fạll; mē, met, hėr; pīne, pin; nōte, not, mŏve; tūbe, tub, bụll; oil, pound.

chuff,† chuf, *n.* [Perhaps from W. *cyff*, a stock or stump.] A coarse, heavy, dull, or surly fellow; a niggard; an old miser.

chum, chum, *n.* [Perhaps an abbrev. of *chamber-fellow*; or, a rather more probable suggestion, of *chimney-fellow.*] One who lodges or resides in the same room or rooms; hence, a close companion; a bosom friend; an intimate.—*v.i.* To occupy the same room or rooms with another; to be the chum of some one.

chump, chump, *n.* [Same as Icel. *kumbr*, a log, akin to *kubba*, to chop, and therefore allied to E. *chop, chub, chubby.*] A short, thick, heavy piece of wood; a blockhead.

chunk, chungk, *n.* Lump of bread, cheese, wood; a short, heavy-set person.

church, chèrch, *n.* [O.E. *chirche, cherche*, etc., A.Sax. *circe, cirice, cyrice* (the c's all hard), from Gr. *kyriakon*, a church, the Lord's house, from *Kyrios*, the Lord = Sc. *kirk*, D. *kerk*, Dan. *kirke*, G. *kirche*.] A house consecrated to the worship of God among Christians; in England often restricted to a place of public worship belonging to the Established Church (as opposed to *chapel* and *meeting-house*); the collective body of Christians; a particular body of Christians united under one form of ecclesiastical government, in one creed, and using the same ritual and ceremonies; ecclesiastical power or authority.—*v.t.* To perform with or for anyone the office of returning thanks in the church, as a mother after childbirth.—**churchgoer,** *n.* One who habitually attends church. —**churchgoing,** *a.* Usually attending church; summoning to church, as a bell.—**churchman,** chèrch′man, *n.* An ecclesiastic or clergyman; in England, a member of the Established Church.—**churchmanship,** chèrch′man·ship, *n.* State of being a churchman.—**churchwarden,** *n.* A functionary appointed by the minister, or elected by the parishioners, to superintend a church and its concerns, to represent the interests of the parish, etc.

churl, chèrl, *n.* [A.Sax. *ceorl*, a countryman of the lowest rank; Icel. Dan. Sw. *karl*, a man, a male; G. *kerl*, a fellow.] A rustic; a peasant; a countryman or laborer; a rude, surly, sullen, selfish, or rough-tempered man.—**churlish,** chèr′lish, *a.* Like or pertaining to a churl; rude; surly; sullen; unfeeling; uncivil; selfish; narrowminded; avaricious.— **churlishly,** chèr′lish·li, *adv.* In a churlish manner.—**churlishness,** chèr′lish·nes, *n.* The quality of being churlish.

churn, chèrn, *n.* [A.Sax. *cyrn*, Sc. *kirn*, Icel. *kirna*, Dan. *kierne*, a churn; probably from same root as *corn, kernel*, butter being as it were the kernel or best portion of the milk.] A vessel in which cream or milk is agitated for separating the oily parts from the caseous and serous parts, to make butter.—*v.t.* To stir or agitate (milk or cream) in order to make into butter; to make (butter) by the agitation of milk or cream; to shake or agitate with violence or continued motion.

chute, shöt, *n.* [Fr., a fall.] A riverfall or rapid over which timber is floated; an inclined trough or tube through which articles are passed from a higher to a lower level.

chutney, chutnee, chut′ni, chut′nē, *n.* An East Indian condiment compounded of ripe fruit, spices, sour herbs, cayenne, lemon juice, pounded and boiled together and bottled for use.

chyle, kīl, *n.* [Gr. *chylos*, juice, chyle, from *cheo*, to flow, whence also *chyme.*] A white or milky fluid separated from aliments while in the intestines, taken up by the lacteal vessels and finally entering the blood. —**chylous,** kī′lus, *a.* Consisting of, pertaining to, or resembling chyle.

chyme, kīm, *n.* [Gr. *chymos*, juice. CHYLE.] The pulpy mass of partially digested food before the chyle is extracted from it.—**chymous,** kīm′us, *a.* Pertaining to chyme.

cicada, si·kā′da, *n. pl.* **cicadae** or **cicadas,** si·kā′dē, si·kā′daz. [L.] The popular and generic name of certain insects, the males of which have on each side of the body an organ with which they can make a considerable noise.—**cicala,** si·kä′la; It. pron. chi·kä′la, *n.* [It., from L. *cicada.*] A cicada.

cicatrice, sik′a·tris, *n.* [Fr. *cicatrice*, L. *cicatrix.*] A scar; a little seam or elevation of flesh remaining after a wound or ulcer is healed. Also **cicatrix,** si·kā′triks, pl. **cicatrices,** sik·a·trī′sēz.—**cicatricle,** sik′a·tri·kl, *n.* [L. *cicatricula*, dim. of *cicatrix.*] The germinating point in the embryo of a seed; the point in the yolk of an egg at which development is first seen.—**cicatrize,** sik′a·trīz, *v.t.*—*cicatrized, cicatrizing.* To induce the formation of a cicatrice on; to heal up (a wound).—*v.i.* To become healed leaving a cicatrice; to skin over. —**cicatrization,** sik′a·tri·zā″shon, *n.* The process of healing or forming a cicatrice.

cicely, sis′e·li, *n.* [L. *seseli*, Gr. *seseli.*] Popular name applied to several umbelliferous plants, *sweet cicely*, or sweet chervil, being an aromatic plant with fine, fernlike foliage.

cicerone, sis·e·rō′ne; It. pron. chē·chā·rō′nā, *n.* [It., from *Cicero*, the Roman orator.] A name given by the Italians to the guides who show travelers the antiquities of the country; hence, in a general sense, one who explains the curiosities of a place; a guide.—**Ciceronian,** sis·e·rō′ni·an, *a.* Resembling the style of Cicero; eloquent.

cichoraceous, sik·o·rā′shus, *a.* [L. *cichorium*, chicory.] Having the qualities of or belonging to plants of the succory or chicory family.

cider, sī′dèr, *n.* [Fr. *cidre*, from L. *sicera*, Gr. *sikera*, strong drink, from Heb. *shakar*, to intoxicate.] The pressed juice of apples used as a beverage or for making a vinegar.

cigar, si·gär′, *n.* [Fr. *cigare*, Sp. *cigarro*, originally the name of a kind of tobacco in Cuba.] A small roll of tobacco leaf, with a pointed end for putting into the mouth, used for smoking.—**cigarette,** sig·a·ret′, *n.* [Fr. dim. of *cigare.*] A little cut tobacco rolled up in tissue paper, used for smoking.

cilia, sil′i·a, *n. pl.* [L. *cilium*, an eyelash.] The hairs which grow from the margin of the eyelids; eyelashes; hairs or bristles situated on the margin of a vegetable body; small, generally microscopic, hairlike vibratile processes which project from animal membranes, and have usually important functions.—**ciliary,** sil′i·a·ri, *a.* Belonging to the eyelids or eyelashes; pertaining to or performed by vibratile cilia (*ciliary* motion).— **ciliate, ciliated,** sil′i·āt, sil′i·āt·ed, *a.* Furnished with cilia; bearing cilia.

Cimmerian, sim·mē′ri·an, *a.* Pertaining to the *Cimmerii* or *Cimmerians*, a mythical people described as dwelling where the sun never shines, and perpetual darkness reigns; hence, very dark (*Mil.*).

cinch, sinch, *n.* [Sp. *cincha*, same as *cincture.*] A saddle girth, in United States; firm hold, a sure thing.

cinchona, sin·kō′na, *n.* [From the Countess of *Chinchon*, vice-queen of Peru, who was cured of fever by it in 1638, and assisted in spreading the remedy.] The name of a number of South American trees and shrubs, some of which yield the bark whence quinine is obtained; the bark of such trees, called also *Peruvian bark.*— **cinchonic,** sin·kon′ik, *a.* Of or belonging to cinchona; derived from cinchona; having the properties of cinchona.—**cinchonine,** sin′ko·nin, *n.* An alkaloid obtained from the bark of several species of cinchona, along with quinine, and one of the medicinal active principles of this bark, being valuable as a febrifuge.— **cinchonism,** sin′kon·izm, *n.* A disturbed condition of the system, the result of overdoses of cinchona or quinine.

cincture, singk′chèr, *n.* [L. *cinctura*, from *cingo, cinctum*, to gird, seen also in *precinct, succinct.*] A belt, girdle, or something similar; that which rings, encircles, or encloses; enclosure; *arch.* a ring round a column.

cinder, sin′dèr, *n.* [A.Sax. *sinder*, dross, cinder = Icel. *sindr*, Sw. *sinder*, Dan. *sinder, sinner*, a cinder; D. *sintel*, G. *sinter.*] A solid piece of matter remaining after having been subjected to combustion; especially, a piece of coal more or less completely burnt, but not reduced to ashes.— **Cinderella,** *n.* A dance ending at twelve at night, from the French fairy tale of that name; a household drudge.—**cindery,** sin′dèr·i, *a.* Resembling cinders; containing cinders, or composed of them.

cinematograph, sin·e·mat′o·graf, *n.* [Gr. *kinēma*, motion, and *-graph.*] *Brit.* A motion picture camera taking a large series of instantaneous pictures, at least sixteen images per second, to obtain consecutive, continuous, uninterrupted movement.

---

ch, *chain;* *ch,* Sc. lo*ch;* g, *go;* j, *job;* ng, *sing;* TH, *then;* th, *thin;* w, *wig;* hw, *whig;* zh, a*z*ure.

cinereous, si·nē′rē·us, a. [L. *cineraceus, cinereus,* from *cinis, cineris,* ashes.] Like ashes: having the color of the ashes of wood.—**cinerary,** sin′e·ra·ri, a. [L. *cinerarius.*] Pertaining to ashes; a term applied to the urns in which the ashes of bodies which had been burned were deposited.—**cineritious,** sin·e·ri′shus, a. [L. *cineritius.*] Having the color or consistence of ashes; ash-gray; *anat.* a term applied to the exterior or cortical part of the brain.

cinnabar, sin′na·bär, n. [L. *cinnabaris,* Gr. *kinnabari,* a word of Eastern origin; Per. *quinbâr.*] Red sulfide of mercury, which, when sublimed and used as a pigment, is called *vermilion;* a red resinous juice obtained from an East Indian tree formerly used as an astringent: called also *Dragon's-blood.*

cinnamon, sin′na·mon, n. [L. *cinnamomum;* from Gr. *kinnamōmon,* through Phœn. from Heb. *kinnamon.*] The inner bark of a tree of the laurel family, a native of Ceylon and other parts of tropical Asia, dried and having a fragrant smell, moderately pungent taste, with some degree of sweetness and astringency, being one of the best cordial, carminative, and restorative spices.—*White cinnamon.* CANELLA.—**cinnamic,** sin-nam′ik, a. Pertaining to or obtained from cinnamon.—**cinnamon stone,** n. A variety of garnet of a cinnamon color.

cinque, singk, n. [Fr., L. *quinque,* five.] A five: a word used in certain games.—**cinquefoil,** n. [L. *folium, a* leaf.] An ornament in the pointed style of architecture somewhat resembling five leaves about a common center, the apertures of circular windows being often in this form; the name of various plants having quinate leaves, as the five-bladed clover, etc.

cipher, sī′fèr, n. [O.Fr. *cifre,* Mod.Fr. *chiffre,* It. *cifra,* Ar. *sifr,* cipher, from Ar. *sifr,* empty.] The numerical character or figure 0 or nothing; any numerical character; some person or thing of no consequence, importance, or value; a monogram or literal device formed of the intertwined initials of a name; a kind of secret writing.—*v.i.* To use figures; to practice arithmetic. —*v.t.* To write in occult or secret characters.

Circean, sèr·sē′an, a. Pertaining to *Circe,* in Greek mythology a celebrated sorceress, who transformed the companions of Ulysses into swine by a magical beverage; hence, fascinating but brutifying or poisonous; magical.

circinate, sèr′si·nāt, a. [From L. *circinus,* a compass, a circle, from *circus,* a circle.] *Bot.* rolled up on itself like a shepherd's crook or bishop's crosier, as the fronds of ferns in a young state.

circle, sèr′kl, n. [L. *circulus,* dim. of *circus,* a circle.] A plane figure, comprehended by a single curve line, called its circumference, every part of which is equally distant from a point within it called the center; the line bounding or forming such a figure, or something in a similar form; a ring; a round body; compass; circuit; a series (as of actions) ending where it begins; an ending where one began; a number of particulars regarded as having a central point; a number of persons associated by some tie; a coterie; a set.—*v.t. circled, circling.* To encircle; to encompass; to surround; to enclose; to move round; to revolve round.— *v.i.* To move circularly; to circulate; to revolve.—*Great circle,* a circle on a sphere having as its center the center of the sphere: opposed to a *small* or *lesser circle.* The equator is a great circle; any parallel of latitude a small circle.—*Great circle sailing,* the manner of conducting a vessel between one place and another so that her track may always be along or nearly along the arc of a great circle. —*Polar circles,* the Arctic and the Antarctic circles 23½° from the respective poles.—**circlet,** sèr′klet, n. A little circle; a ring-shaped ornament for the head; a chaplet; a headband.

circuit, sèr′kit or sèr′kūt, n. [Fr. *circuit,* L. *circuitus—circum,* round, and *eo, itum,* to go.] The act of moving or passing round; a circular journey; a revolution; the distance round any space whether circular or otherwise; a boundary line encompassing an object; circumference; the journey of judges or other persons through certain appointed places for the purpose of holding courts or performing other stated duties; the district or portion of country in which a particular judge or judges hold courts and administer justice; the arrangement by which a current of electricity is kept up between the two poles of a galvanic battery; the path of a voltaic current.—**circuitous,** sèr·kū′it·us, a. Having a roundabout or devious course; not direct; roundabout.— **circuitously,** sèr·kū′it·us·li, adv. In a circuitous manner.—**circuitousness, circuity,** sèr·kū′it·us·nes, sèr·kū′i·ti, n. The character or condition of being circuitous.

circular, sèr′kū·lèr, a. [L. *circularis.* CIRCLE.] In the form of a circle; round; circumscribed by a circle; passing over or forming a circle, circuit, or round; addressed to a number of persons having a common interest (a *circular* letter).—*Circular note,* a note or letter of credit furnished by bankers to persons about to travel abroad, and which is payable at any one of a number of places.—*Circular numbers,* those whose powers terminate in the roots themselves, as 5 and 6, whose squares are 25 and 36. —*n.* A letter, notice, or intimation, generally printed or multiplied by some other rapid process, of which a copy is sent to several persons on some common business.—**circularity,** sèr·kū·lar′i·ti, n. The state or quality of being circular; a circular form.—**circulate,** sèr′kū·lāt, *v.i.— circulated, circulating.* [L. *circulo, circulatum.*] To move in a circle; to move round and return to the same point: to flow in the veins or channels of an organism; to pass from one person or place to another; to be diffused.—*v.t.* To cause to pass from place to place or from person to person; to put about; to spread. —*Circulating* or *recurring decimals,* interminate decimals in which two or more figures are continually repeated.—*Circulating library,* a library the books of which circulate among the subscribers.—**circulation,** sèr· kū·lā′shon, n. The act of circulating or moving in a course which brings or tends to bring the moving body to the point where its motion began; the act of flowing through the veins or channels of an organism; recurrence in a certain order or series; the act of passing from place to place or from person to person (as of money, news, etc.); the extent to which anything is circulated (a newspaper with a large *circulation*); currency; circulating coin, or notes, bills, etc., current and representing coin.—**circulative,** sèr′kū·lā·tiv, a. Circulating; causing circulation.— **circulator,** sèr′kū·lā·tèr, n. One who or that which circulates: specifically applied to a circulating decimal fraction.—**circulatory,**‡ sèr′kū· la·to·ri, a. Passing round a certain circuit; circular.

circumambient, sèr·kum·am′bi·ent, a. [L. *circum,* around, and *ambio,* to go about.] Surrounding; encompassing; enclosing or being on all sides, as the air about the earth.— **circumambiency,** sèr·kum·am′bi· en·si, n. The state or quality of being circumambient.

circumambulate, sèr·kum·am′bū· lāt, *v.i.* [L. *circum,* around, and *ambulo,* to walk.] To walk round about. —**circumambulation,** sèr·kum·am′· bū·la″shon, n. The act of circumambulating.

circumcise, sèr′kum·sīz, *v.t.—circumcised, circumcising.* [L. *circumcido, circumcisum—circum,* about, and *caedo,* to cut.] To cut off the prepuce or foreskin of, a ceremony or rite among the Jews, Mohammedans, and others.—**circumciser,** sèr′kum·sīz· èr, n. One who performs circumcision.—**circumcision,** sèr·kum·si′· zhon, n. The act of circumcising.

circumference, sèr·kum′fèr·ens, n. [L. *circumferentia—circum,* round, and *fero,* to carry.] The line that bounds a circle or any regular curvilinear figure; periphery; measure round a circular or spherical body.— **circumferential,** sèr·kum′fèr·en″shal, a. Pertaining to the circumference.

circumflect, sèr′kum·flekt, *v.t.* [L. *circum,* round, and *flecto, flexum,* to bend.] To bend round; to circumflex.—**circumflex,** sèr′kum·fleks, n. A wave of the voice, embracing both a rise and a fall on the same syllable; an accent placed only on long vowels, and indicating different things in different languages. In Greek it is marked by the signs ~ and ^, in French and some other languages by the sign ^.—*a.* Term for the above accent; *anat.* applied to several curved parts in the body.—*v.t.* To mark or pronounce with the circumflex; to curve or bend around.

circumfluence, sėr·kum'flu·ens, n. [L. *circumfluens—circum*, round, and *fluo*, to flow.] A flowing round on all sides; an enclosure of waters.— **circumfluent, circumfluous**, sėr·kum'flu·ent, sėr·kum'flu·us, a. Flowing round; surrounding as a fluid.

circumfuse, sėr·kum·fūz', v.t.—*circumfused, circumfusing*. [L. *circumfundo, circumfusus—circum*, round, and *fundo, fusus*, to pour.] To pour round; to spread round (*Mil.*).— **circumfusion**, sėr·kum·fū'zhon, n. The act of circumfusing.

circumgyrate, sėr·kum·jī'rāt, v.t. and i. [L. *circum*, round, and *gyro*, to turn, from *gyrus*, a circle.] To roll or turn round.—**circumgyration**, sėr·kum'jī·rā''shon, n. The act of circumgyrating; a circular motion.

circumjacent, sėr·kum·jā'sent, a. [L. *circumjacens—circum*, round, and *jaceo*, to lie.] Lying round; bordering on every side.

circumlocution, sėr·kum·lō·kū''shon, n. [L. *circum*, round, and *locutio*, a speaking, *loquor*, to speak.] A round-about way of speaking; the use of more words than necessary to express an idea; a periphrasis.—**circumlocutory**, sėr·kum·lok'ū·to·ri, a. Exhibiting circumlocution; periphrastic.

circumnavigate, sėr·kum·nav'i·gāt, v.t.—*circumnavigated, circumnavigating*. [L. *circumnavigo—circum*, round, and *navigo*, to sail, from *navis*, a ship.] To sail round; to pass round by water (the globe, an island, etc.)— **circumnavigable**, sėr·kum·nav'i·ga·bl, a. Capable of being circumnavigated or sailed round.—**circumnavigation**, sėr·kum·nav'i·gā''shon, n. The act of sailing round.—**circumnavigator**, sėr·kum·nav'i·gā·tėr, n. One who circumnavigates: generally applied to one who has sailed round the globe.

circumpolar, sėr·kum·pō'lėr, a. Surrounding either pole of the earth or heavens.

circumscissile, sėr·kum·sis'sil, n. [L. *circum*, round, and *scindo, scissum*, to cut.] *Bot.* opening or divided by a transverse circular line: a term applied to a mode of dehiscence in some fruits, as in the henbane, monkeypot, etc.

circumscribe, sėr'kum·skrīb, v.t.—*circumscribed, circumscribing*. [L. *circumscribo—circum*, round, and *scribo*, to write.] To inscribe or draw a line round; to mark out certain bounds or limits for; to enclose within certain limits; to limit, bound, confine, restrain (authority, etc.)—**circumscriber**, sėr·kum·skrīb'ėr, n. One who or that which circumscribes. —**circumscription**, sėr·kum·skrip'-shon, n. The act of circumscribing or state of being circumscribed; limitation; restriction; also a periphery or circumference. — **circumscriptive**, sėr·kum·skrip'tiv, a. Circumscribing or tending to circumscribe; limiting; restricting. (*Mil.*)

circumspect, sėr'kum·spekt, a. [L. *circumspectus—circum*, round, and *specio*, to look.] Examining carefully all the circumstances that may affect a determination; watchful on all sides;

wary; vigilant; prudent; cautious.— **circumspection**, sėr·kum·spek'shon, n. The quality of being circumspect; observation of the true position of circumstances; watchfulness; vigilance; wariness; caution.—**circumspective**,† sėr·kum·spek'tiv, a. Circumspect; cautious.—**circumspectly**, sėr'kum·spekt·li, adv. In a circumspect manner; cautiously; watchfully.—**circumspectness**, sėr'kum·spekt·nes, n. Circumspection.

circumstance, sėr'kum·stans, n. [L. *circumstantia*, from *circumstans*, standing about—*circum*, round, and *sto*, to stand.] Something attending, appendant, or relative to a fact or case; something incidental; some fact giving rise to a certain presumption, or tending to afford some evidence; detail; incident; event; *pl.* situation; surroundings; state of things; especially, condition in regard to worldly estate.—*v.t. circumstanced, circumstancing*. To place in a particular situation or in certain surroundings: usually in pp.—**circumstantial**, sėr·kum·stan'shal, a. Consisting in or pertaining to circumstances; attending; incidental; relating to, but not essential; exhibiting all the circumstances (account or recital); minute; particular; obtained or inferred from the circumstances of the case; not direct or positive (*circumstantial* evidence),—n. Something incidental and of subordinate importance: opposed to *essential*.—**circumstantiality**, sėr·kum·stan·shi·al'i·ti, n. The quality of being circumstantial; minuteness; fullness of detail;—**circumstantially**, sėr·kum·stan'shal·li, adv. In a circumstantial manner; minutely; in full detail; indirectly; not positively. —**circumstantiate**, sėr·kum·stan'-shi·āt, v.t. To confirm by circumstances; to describe circumstantially or in full detail.

circumvallate,† sėr·kum·val'lāt, v.t. [L. *circum*, round, and *vallum*, a rampart.] To surround with a rampart. —**circumvallation**, sėr·kum'val·lā''shon, n. The act of surrounding with a rampart; a line of field fortifications consisting of a rampart or parapet with a trench, surrounding a besieged place or a camp.

circumvent, sėr·kum·vent', v.t. [L. *circumvenio, circumventum—circum*, about, and *venio*, to come.] To gain advantage over by artfulness, stratagem, or deception; to defeat or get the better of by cunning; to outwit; to overreach.—**circumvention**, sėr·kum·ven'shon, n. The act of circumventing; outwitting or overreaching; stratagem. — **circumventive**, sėr·kum·vent'iv, a. Tending or designed to circumvent.—**circumventor**, sėr·kum·vent'ėr, n. One who circumvents.

circumvolve, sėr·kum·volv', v.t.— *circumvolved, circumvolving*. [L. *circum*, round, and *volvo, volutum*, to roll.] To turn or cause to roll round; to cause to revolve.—**circumvolution**, sėr·kum'vo·lū''shon, n. A rolling or being rolled round; one of the windings of a thing wound or twisted; a convolution; a roundabout procedure.

circus, sėr'kus, n. pl. **circuses**, sėr'-kus·ez. [L.] Among the ancient Romans a kind of theater or amphitheater adapted for horse races, the exhibition of athletic exercises, contests with wild beasts, etc.; in modern times, a place of amusement where feats of horsemanship and acrobatic displays form the principal entertainment.

cirque, sėrk, n. [Fr., a circle, a circus.] A kind of circular valley among mountains; an amphitheater.

cirrhosis, sir·rō'sis, n. [Gr. *kirrhos*, orange-tawny, from the appearance of the diseased liver.] A disease consisting of diminution and deformity of the liver, often seen in drunkards. —**cirrhotic**, sir·rot'ik, a. Affected with or having the character of cirrhosis.

cirribranch, sir'ri·brangk, a. [L. *cirrus*, a tendril, and *branchiæ*, gills.] Having tendril-like gills: a term applied to certain mollusks.—**cirriped**, sir'ri·ped, n. [L. *cirrus*, and *pes, pedis*, the foot.] A member of an order of lower crustaceous animals, so called from the cirri or filaments with which their transformed feet are fringed.—**cirrose, cirrous**, sir'-rōs, sir'rus, a. *Bot.* having a cirrus or tendril; resembling tendrils or coiling like them. Written also *Cirrhose, cirrhous*.—**cirrus**, sir'rus, n. pl. **cirri**, sir'rī. A tendril; a long thread-like organ by which a plant climbs; a soft curled filamentary appendage to parts serving as the feet of certain lower animals, as barnacles, and the jaws of certain fishes; one of the forms which clouds assume; a light fleecy cloud at a high elevation, *cirro-cumulus* and *cirro-stratus* being intermediate forms partaking partly of this character, partly of that of the cumulus and stratus.

cisalpine, sis·al'pīn, a. [L. *cis*, on this side, and *Alpes*, Alps.] On this side of the Alps, with regard to Rome; that is, on the south of the Alps.— **cismontane**, sis·mon'tān, a. Existing on this side of the mountains; specifically, on this side of the Alps: opposed to *Ultramontane*.—**cispadane**, sis'pa·dān, a. [L. *Padus*, the river Po.] On this side of the Po, with regard to Rome; that is, on the south side.

cist, sist, n. [L. *cista*, Gr. *kistē*, a chest. *Chest* is another form of this word.] A place of interment of an early or prehistoric period, consisting of a stone chest formed of two parallel rows of stones fixed on their ends, and covered by similar flat stones.

Cistercian, sis·tėr'shi·an, n. A member of a religious order, which takes its name from its original convent, *Cistercium* or Citeaux, near Dijon, where the society was founded in 1098.

cistern, sis'tėrn, n. [L. *cisterna*, from *cista*, a chest.] An artificial reservoir or receptacle for holding water, beer, or other liquor.

citadel, sit'a·del, n. [Fr. *citadelle*. Same origin as *city*.] A fortress or castle in or near a city, intended to keep the inhabitants in subjection, or, in case of a siege, to form a final point of defense.

cite, sīt, *v.t.*—*cited, citing.* [Fr. *citer,* from L. *cito, citare,* freq. of *cieo,* to call, to summon; seen also in *excite, incite, recite.*] To call upon officially or authoritatively to appear; to summon before a person or tribunal; to quote, adduce, or bring forward; to refer to in support, proof, or confirmation (to *cite* an authority).—**citable,** sīt′a‧bl. *a.* Capable of being cited or quoted.—**citation,** sī‧tā′shon, *n.* A summons; an official call or notice given to a person to appear, as in a court; the act of citing a passage from a book or person; the passage or words quoted; quotation.

cithara, sith′a‧ra, *n.* [L., from Gr. *kithara,* whence *gittern, guitar.*] An ancient stringed instrument resembling the more modern cittern or guitar.—**cithern, cittern,** sith′ern, sit′tern, *n.* An old instrument of the guitar kind, strung with wire instead of gut.

citizen, etc. See CITY.

citron, sit′ron, *n.* [Fr. *citron,* from L. *citreum,* from *citrus,* the lemon or citron.] The fruit of the citron tree, a large lemonlike fruit; the tree itself.—**citric acid,** sit′rik as′id, *n.* An organic acid obtained from citrus fruits or by fermentation of sugars.—*Citric acid cycle,* a series of chemical reactions occurring in the living organism, by which food is oxidized to create energy.—**citrus,** sit′rus, *n.* Any of a genus of trees or shrubs that bear citrons, lemons, grapefruit, etc.—*a.* Pertaining to such trees or shrubs.

cittern, sit′tern, *n.* See CITHARA.

city, sit′i, *n.* [Fr. *cité,* from L. *civitas, civitatis,* a city, state, from *civis,* a citizen, whence also *civil.*] In a general sense, a large and important town; in Great Britain, a town corporate that is or has been the seat of a bishop and of a cathedral church; in the United States an incorporated town governed by a mayor and aldermen; the inhabitants of a city collectively.—*a.* Pertaining to a city.—**citied,** sit′ēd, *a.* Belonging to a city; having the qualities of a city; covered with cities.—**citizen,** sit′i‧zen, *n.* [O.E. *citezein,* from O.Fr. *citeain, citeien,* etc. (Mod. Fr. *citoyen*), from *cité,* a city. The *z* is a corruption of the old symbol used for *y.*] The native of a city, or an inhabitant who enjoys the freedom and privileges of the city in which he resides; a member of a state with full political privileges.—*a.* Having the qualities of a citizen; townbred.—**citizenship,** sit′i‧zen‧ship, *n.* The state or principles of a citizen.

civet, siv′et, *n.* [Fr. *civette,* It. *zibetto,* from Ar. *zabad,* the substance civet.] A strong smelling substance taken from the anal glands of the civet cats, and yielding a perfume; the animal that yields this substance.—*v.t.* To scent with civet.—**civet cat,** *n.* The name of several carnivorous mammals natives of North Africa and Asia, having a gland near the anus containing the odoriferous substance civet.

civic, siv′ik, *a.* [L. *civicus,* from *civis,* a citizen; whence also *city.*] Pertaining to a city or citizen: relating to civil affairs or honors.—*Civic crown, Rom. antiq.* a crown of oak leaves given to a soldier who saved the life of a citizen in battle.—**civics,** siv′iks, *n.* The science of the rights and duties of citizens.—**civil,** siv′il, *a.* [L. *civilis,* from *civis.*] Relating to the community, or to the policy and government of the citizens and subjects of a state (*civil rights, government,* etc.); political; municipal or private, as opposed to criminal; not ecclesiastical or military; exhibiting some refinement of manners; civilized; courteous; obliging; well bred; affable; polite.—*Civil engineering,* that branch of engineering which relates to the forming of roads, bridges, railroads, canals, aqueducts, harbors, etc.—*Civil law,* law of a state, city, or country.—*Civil liberty,* the absence of arbitrary governmental restraint on individual freedom.—*Civil marriage,* marriage performed by a government official rather than a clergyman.—*Civil rights,* the legal and political rights enjoyed by the inhabitants of a country; especially the rights guaranteed by the United States Constitution and bills passed by Congress.—*Civil service,* that branch of the public service in which the nonmilitary employees of a government are engaged, or those persons collectively.—*Civil war,* a war between the people of the same state.—**civilly,** siv′il‧li, *adv.* In a civil manner; as regards civil rights or privileges; in a well-bred manner.—**civilian,** si‧vil′yen, *n.* One skilled in the Roman or civil law; one whose pursuits are those of civil life, not military or clerical.—**civility,** si‧vil′i‧ti, *n.* [L. *civilitas,* from *civilis.*] The state of being civilized‡; good breeding; politeness, or an act of politeness; courtesy; kind attention.—**civilizable,** siv′il‧iz‧a‧bl, *a.* Capable of being civilized.—**civilization,** siv′il‧iz‧ā″shon, *n.* The act of civilizing, or state of being civilized; the state of being refined in manners from the rudeness of savage life, and improved in arts and learning.—**civilize,** siv′il‧īz, *v.t.*—*civilized, civilizing.* [Fr. *civiliser,* formerly also *civilizer.*] To reclaim from a savage state; to introduce order and civic organization among; to refine and enlighten; to elevate in social life.

clack, klak, *v.i.* [An imitative word; comp. Fr. *claque,* a clap or clack; D. *klakken,* to clap; E. *clap, crack.*] To make a sudden sharp noise, as by striking or cracking; to rattle; to utter sounds or words rapidly and continually, or with sharpness and abruptness.—*v.t.* To cause to make a sharp, short sound; to clap; to speak without thought; to rattle out.—*n.* A sharp, abrupt sound, continually repeated; a kind of small windmill for frightening birds; continual talk; prattle.—**clacker,** klak′ėr, *n.* One who or that which clacks.—**clack valve,** *n.* A valve in pumps

with a single flap, hinged at one edge.

clad, klad, *pp.* Clothe.

claim, klām, *v.t.* [O.Fr. *claimer,* from L. *clamo, clamare,* to shout, whence also *clamor, acclaim, acclamation, exclaim, reclaim,* etc.] To ask or seek to obtain by virtue of authority, right, or supposed right; to assert a right to; to demand as due.—*v.i.* To be entitled to a thing; to have a right; to derive a right; to assert claims; to put forward claims.—*n.* A demand of a right or supposed right; a calling on another for something due or supposed to be due; a right to claim or demand; a title to anything; the thing claimed or demanded; specifically, in America, Australia, etc., a piece of land allotted to one.—**claimable,** klām′a‧bl, *a.* Capable of being claimed or demanded as due.—**claimant, claimer,** klām′ant, klām′ėr, *n.* A person who claims; one who demands anything as his right.

clairvoyance, klâr‧voi′ans, *n.* [Fr. *clair,* clear, and *voyant,* seeing, ppr. of *voir* (L. *videre*), to see.] A power attributed to persons in the mesmeric state, by which the person (called a clairvoyant or clairvoyante) discerns objects concealed from sight, tells what is happening at a distance, etc.—**clairvoyant,** klâr‧voi′ant, *a.* Of or pertaining to clairvoyance.—**clairvoyant,** klâr‧voi′ant, *n.* A man or woman in a certain stage of mesmerism, in which state the subject is said to see things not present to the senses.

clam,† klam, *v.t.*—*clammed, clamming.* [A.Sax. *clam,* mud, clay, that which is clammy; Dan. *klam,* clammy, *klamme,* to clog.] To clog with glutinous or viscous matter.—*v.i.*† To be glutinous or moist; to stick like clammy matter or moisture.—**clammy,** klam′mi, *a.* Viscous; adhesive; soft and sticky; glutinous; tenacious.—**clamminess,** klam′mi‧nes, *n.* The state of being clammy or viscous; viscosity; stickiness.

clam, klam, *n.* [Shortened from *clamp,* the former name, given from the firmness with which some of these animals adhere to rocks. CLAMP.] The popular name of certain bivalvular shellfish, of several genera and many species.

clamant, klam′ant, *a.* [CLAIM.] Clamorous; beseeching; pressing; urgent; crying.

clamber, klam′bėr, *v.i.* [O.E. *clamer, clammer,* akin to *clam,* to adhere, *clamp,* and *climb.*] To climb with difficulty or with hands and feet; to rise up steeply (*Tenn.*)†.—*v.t.*† To ascend by climbing; to climb with difficulty. (*Shak.*)—*n.* The act of clambering or climbing with difficulty.

clamor, klam′ėr, *n.* [L. *clamor,* an outcry, from *clamo,* to cry out, whence E. *claim.*] A great outcry; vociferation made by a loud human voice continued or repeated, or by a number of voices; loud complaint; urgent demand; loud and continued noise.—*v.t.* To utter in a loud voice;

---

fāte, fär, fâre, fat, f**ạ**ll;   mē, met, hėr;   pīne, pin;   nōte, not, mŏve;   tūbe, tub, b**ụ**ll;   oil, pound.

to shout.—*v.i.* To make a clamor; to utter loud sounds or outcries; to vociferate; to make importunate complaints or demands.—**clamorer,** klam′ẽr·ẽr, *n.* One who clamors.—**clamorous,** klam′ẽr·us, *a.* Making a clamor or outcry; noisy; vociferous; loud.—**clamorously,** klam′ẽr·us·li, *adv.* In a clamorous manner; with loud noise or words.—**clamorousness,** klam′ẽr·us·nes, *n.* State of being clamorous.

clamp, klamp, *n.* [Most closely connected with L.G. and D. *klamp,* Dan. *klampe,* G. *klampe,* a clamp; from root seen in E. *climb, clamber, clem* (to pinch with hunger), *clam.*] Something rigid that fastens or binds; a piece of wood or metal fastening two pieces together, or strengthening any framework; an instrument of wood or metal used by joiners, etc., for holding pieces of timber closely together until the glue hardens.—*v.t.* To fasten with clamps; to fix a clamp on.

clamp, klamp, *n.* [Imitative; comp. *clank, clink.*] A heavy footstep or tread; a tramp; a heap of turnips, potatoes, etc., covered over with straw earth for winter keeping; pile of bricks for burning.—*v.i.* To tread heavily. (*Thack.*)

clan, klan, *n.* [Gael. and Ir. *clann,* family, tribe.] A race; a family; a tribe; the common descendants of the same progenitor, under the patriarchal control of a chief; a clique, sect, society, or body of persons closely united by some common interest or pursuit.—**clannish,** klan′ish, *a.* Imbued with the feelings, sentiments, and prejudices peculiar to clans; blindly devoted to those of one's own clan, set, or locality, and illiberal toward others.—**clannishly,** klan′ish·li, *adv.* In a clannish manner.—**clannishness,** klan′ish·nes, *n.* The state or quality of being clannish.—**clansman,** klanz′-man, *n.* A member of a clan.

clandestine, klan·des′tin, *a.* [L. *clandestinus,* from *clam,* in secret.] Secret; private; hidden; withdrawn from public view; generally implying craft, deception, or evil design.—**clandestinely,** klan·des′tin·li, *adv.* In a clandestine manner; secretly; privately; in secret.—**clandestineness,**† klan·des′tin·nes, *n.* The state or quality of being clandestine.

clang, klang, *n.* [Imitative of sound, and akin to *clank, clink, clack*; G. *klingen,* to sound; Dan. Sw. G. *klang,* D. *klank,* a sound; L. *clangor,* Gr. *klanggē.*] A loud sound produced from solid bodies, especially that produced by the collision of metallic bodies; a clank; clangor.—*v.i.* To give out a clang; to clank; to resound —*v.t.* To cause to sound with a clang.—**clangorous,** klang′gẽr·us, *a.* Making a clangor; having a hard or ringing sound.—**clangor,** klang′gẽr, *n.* [Directly from L. *clangor.*] A sharp, hard, ringing sound as of a trumpet.

clank, klangk, *n.* [CLANG.] The loud sound made by collision of metallic or other similarly sounding bodies (as chains, iron armor, etc.): generally expressing a less resounding sound than *clang,* and a deeper and stronger sound than *clink.*—*v.t.* To cause to sound with a clank.—*v.i.* To sound with or give out a clank.

clap, klap, *v.t.*—*clapped* or *clapt* (pret. & pp.), *clapping.* [Same as Icel. and Sw. *klappa,* Dan. *klappe,* D. and L.G.*klappen,* to clap, to pat, etc.; perhaps imitative of sound.] To strike with a quick motion; to slap; to thrust; to drive together; to shut hastily; followed by *to* (to *clap to* the door); to place or put by a hasty or sudden motion (to *clap* the hand to the mouth, to *clap* spurs to a horse).—*To clap hands,* to strike the palms of the hands together, as a mark of applause or delight.—*To clap the wings,* to flap them, or to strike them together so as to make a noise.—*To clap hold of,* to seize roughly and suddenly.—*v.i.* To come together suddenly with noise; to clack; to strike the hands together in applause.—*n.* A collision of bodies with noise; a bang; a slap; a sudden act or motion (in phrase *at a clap,* that is at a blow, all at once); a burst or peal of thunder; a striking of hands to express approbation.—**clapper,** klap′ẽr, *n.* A person who claps or applauds by clapping; that which claps or strikes, as the tongue of a bell; a kind of small noisy windmill to scare birds.—**claptrap,** *n.* An artifice or device to elicit applause or gain popularity; high-flown sentiments or other rhetorical device by which a person panders to an audience; bunkum.—*a.* Designing or designed merely to catch applause.

claque, klak, *n.* [Fr., from *claquer,* to clap the hands, to applaud.] A name applied collectively to a set of men who in theaters (as in those of Paris) are regularly hired to applaud a piece or the actors.

clarabella, klärä·bel′a, *n.* An 8-foot organ stop with open wooden pipes, giving a soft sweet tone.

clarence, klar′ens, *n.* [After the Duke of *Clarence,* William IV.] A closed fourwheeled carriage, with inside seats for four.

clarendon type, klar′en·don, *n.* In printing, a style of type.

claret, klar′et, *n.* [Fr. *clairet,* from *clair,* clear; It. *claretto.*] The name given to the red wines of the Bordeaux district.—*a.* Having the color of claret wine.

clarify, klar′i·fī, *v.t.*—*clarified, clarifying.* [Fr. *clarifier,* from L. *clarificare*—*clarus,* clear, *facio,* to make.] To make clear, to purify from feculent matter; to defecate; to fine (liquor).—*v.i.* To grow or become clear or free from feculent matter; to become pure, as liquors.—**clarifier,** klar′i·fī·ẽr, *n.* One who or that which clarifies or purifies; a vessel in which liquor is clarified.—**clarification,** klar′i·fi·kā″shon, *n.* The act of clarifying; particularly the clearing or fining of liquid substances from all feculent matter.

clarinet, clarionet, klar′i·net, klar′i·- on·et, *n.* [Fr. *clarinette*—L. *clarus,* clear.] A wind instrument of music, made of wood, having finger holes and keys, and a fixed mouthpiece, containing a reed, forming the upper joint of the instrument.—**clarion,** klar′i·on, *n.* [L.L. *clario, clarionis,* a clarion, Fr. *clairon,* from L. *clarus,* clear, from its clear sound.] A kind of trumpet whose tube is narrower and tone more acute and shrill than that of the common trumpet.

clash, klash, *v.i.* [An imitative word; comp. D. *kletsen,* G. *klatschen,* Dan. *klatsche,* to clap.] To make a loud, harsh noise, as from violent or sudden collision; to dash against an object with a loud noise; to come into violent collision; *fig.* to act with opposite power or in a contrary direction; to meet in opposition (their opinions and their interests *clash* together).—*v.t.* To strike against with sound; to strike noisily together. —*n.* The noise made by the meeting of bodies with violence; a striking together with noise; collision or noisy collision of bodies; *fig.* opposition; contradiction, as between differing or contending interests.

clasp, klasp, *n.* [By metathesis for O.E. *clapse,* to clasp, *claps,* a clasp: allied to O.E. *clip,* to embrace, in the same way as *grasp,* to *grip,* and *gripe.*] A catch to hold something together; a hook for fastening, or for holding together the covers of a book, or the different parts of a garment, of a belt, etc.; a clinging, grasping, or embracing; a close embrace; bar on medal ribbon for additional service in a campaign.— *v.t.* To shut or fasten together with a clasp; to catch and hold by twining or embracing; to surround and cling to; to embrace closely; to catch with the arms or hands; to grasp.—*v.i.*† To cling. (*Shak.*)—**clasp knife,** *n.* A knife the blade of which folds into the handle.

class, klas, *n.* [L. *classis,* a class.] An order or rank of persons; a number of persons in society supposed to have some resemblance or equality in rank, education, property, talents, and the like; a number of pupils in a school, or students in a college, of the same standing or pursuing the same studies; *nat. hist.* a large group of plants or animals formed by the union or association of several orders.—*v.t.* To arrange in a class or classes; to rank together; to refer to a class or group; to classify.— *v.i.* To be arranged or classed.— **classible,** klas′i·bl, *a.* Capable of being classed.—**classic,** klas′ik, *n.* [L. *classicus,* pertaining to the first or highest of the classes or political divisions into which the Roman people were anciently divided, hence the use of the word in reference to writers.] An author of the first rank; a writer whose style is pure, correct, and refined: primarily, a Greek or Roman author of this character; a literary production of the first class or rank; *the classics,* specifically, the literature of ancient Greece and Rome.—*a.* Same as

---

ch, *ch*ain;   *ch,* Sc. lo*ch*;   g, *g*o;   j, *j*ob;   ng, si*ng*;   TH, *th*en;   th, *th*in;   w, *w*ig;   hw, *wh*ig;   zh, a*z*ure.

Classical.—**classical,** klas'ik·al, *a.* Pertaining to writers of the first rank; being of the first order; more specifically relating to Greek and Roman authors of the first rank or estimation; pertaining to ancient Greece or Rome; relating to localities associated with great ancient or modern authors, or to scenes of great historical events; pure, chaste, correct, or refined (taste, style, etc.). —*Classic orders,* arch. the Doric, Ionic, and Corinthian orders.— **classicalism,** klas'ik·al·izm, *n.* A classic idiom or style; classicism; *art,* close adherence to the rules of Greek or Roman art.—**classicalist,** klas'ik·al·ist, *n.* A devoted admirer of classicalism; one who scrupulously adheres to the canons of Greek or Roman art.—**classicality,** klas·i·kal'i·ti, *n.* The quality of being classical.—**classically,** klas'ik·al·li, *adv.* In a classical manner; according to the manner of classical authors. —**classicism,** klas·i·sizm, *n.* A classic idiom or style.—**classicist,** klas'i·sist, *n.* One versed in the classics.— **classify,** klas'i·fī, *v.t.*—*classified, classifying.* [L. *classis,* a class, and *facio,* to make.] To arrange in a class or classes; to arrange in sets.— **classifiable,** klas'i·fī·a·bl, *a.* Capable of being classified.—**classification,** klas'i·fi·kā''shon, *n.* The act of classifying or forming into a class or classes, so as to bring together those beings or things which most resemble each other, and to separate those that differ; distribution into sets, sorts, or ranks.—**classificatory,** klas'·i·fi·kā·to·ri, *a.* Belonging to classification; concerned with distribution into sets, sorts, or ranks.—**classified,** klas'i·fīd, *a.* Confidential, restricted; secret.—**classified ad,** *n.* A want ad. —**classifier,** klas'i·fī·ėr, *n.*—**classmate,** *n.* One of the same class at school or college.

clatter, klat'ėr, *v.i.* [From the sound. A.Sax. *clatrung,* a clattering, a rattle; D. *klater,* a rattle; *klateren,* to rattle.] To make rattling sounds; to make repeated sharp sounds, as when sonorous bodies strike or are struck rapidly together; to rattle.— *v.t.* To strike so as to produce a rattling noise from.—*n.* A rapid succession of abrupt, sharp sounds; rattling sounds; tumultuous and confused noise.—**clatterer,** klat'ėr·ėr, *n.* One who clatters; a babbler.

clause, kląz, *n.* [Fr. *clause,* from L.L. *clausa,* for L. *clausula,* a conclusion, a clause, from *claudo, clausum,* to close, whence *close, exclude,* etc.]. A member of a compound sentence containing both a subject and its predicate; a distinct part of a contract, will, agreement, charter, commission, or the like; a distinct stipulation, condition, proviso, etc.

claustral, kląs'tral, *a.* [L.L. *claustralis,* from L. *claustrum,* an inclosure, a cloister, from *claudo,* to shut.] Relating to a cloister; cloister-like; secluded.

claustrophobia, kląs''tro·fō'bē·a, *n.* [L. *claustrum,* an enclosure, Gr. *phōbōs,* fear.] Morbid fear of narrow spaces or closed rooms.

clavate, claviform, klā'vāt, klav'i·form, *a.* [L. *clava,* a club.] *Bot.* and *zool.* club-shaped; having the form of a club; growing gradually thicker toward the top, as certain parts of a plant.

clave, klāv, pret. of *cleave.*

clavichord, klav'i·kord, *n.* [L. *clavis,* a key, and *chorda,* a string.] An old stringed instrument, a precursor of the spinet and harpsichord.

clavicle, klav'i·kl, *n.* [L. *clavicula,* a little key or fastener, from *clavis,* a key.] The collarbone.—**clavicular,** kla·vik'ū·lėr, *a.* Pertaining to the collarbone or clavicle.

clavicorn, klav'i·korn, *n.* [L. *clava,* a club, and *cornu,* a horn.] A member of a family of beetles, so named from the antennae being thickened at the apex so as to terminate in a club-shaped enlargement.

clavier, klav'i·ėr, *n.* [Fr. *clavier,* from L. *clavis,* a key.] The key board of a pianoforte or other instrument whose keys are arranged similarly; the instrument itself.

claw, klą, *n.* [A.Sax. *cláwu, clá,* a claw=D. *klaauw,* Icel. *kló,* Dan. and Sw. *klo,* G. *klaue,* a claw; allied to *cleave,* to adhere.] The sharp hooked nail of a quadruped, bird, or other animal; the whole foot of an animal with hooked nails; a hooked extremity belonging to any animal member or appendage; anything shaped like the claw of an animal, as the crooked forked end of a hammer used for drawing nails; *bot.* the narrow base of a petal.—*v.t.* To tear, scratch, pull, or seize with claws or nails; to scratch.—**claw hammer,** *n.* A hammer furnished with two claws, for convenience of drawing nails out of wood; evening-dress coat, or coat with tails.

clay, klā, *n.* [A.Sax. *claeg*=Dan. *klaeg,* L.G. *klei,* D. *klai, klei,* G. *klei,* clay; same root as in *cleave, clog, glue.*] The name common to various earths, compounds of silica and alumina; earth which is stiff, viscid, and ductile when moistened, and many kinds of which are used in the arts, as pipe *clay,* porcelain *clay,* etc.; earth in general, especially as the material of the human body. —*a.* Formed or consisting of clay.— *v.t.* To cover or mingle with clay; to purify and whiten (sugar) with clay. —**clayey,** klā'i, *a.* Consisting of clay; abounding with clay; partaking of clay; like clay; bedaubed or besmeared with clay.

claymore, klā'mōr, *n.* [Gael. *claidheammor*—*claidheam,* a sword, and *mor,* great.] Formerly the large two-handed sword of the Scottish Highlanders; now a basket-hilted, double-edged broadsword.

clean, klēn, *a.* [A.Sax. *claene,* clean, pure, bright; cog. with W. *glain, glan,* Ir. and Gael. *glan,* clean, pure, radiant.] Clear of dirt or filth; having all impurities or foreign matter removed; pure, without fault, imperfection, or defect (timber, a copy); well-proportioned; shapely (*clean* limbs); not bungling; dexter-ous; adroit (a *clean* leap); complete or thorough; free from moral impurity, guilt, or blame; among the Jews, not defiled or polluted; not forbidden by the ceremonial law for use in sacrifice and for food.— *adv.* Quite; perfectly; wholly; entirely; fully.—*v.t.* To make clean; to remove all foreign matter from; to purify; to cleanse.—*To clean out,* to exhaust the pecuniary resources of. (Colloq.)—**cleaner,** klēn'ėr, *n.* One who or that which cleans.—**cleanly,** klen'li, *a.* Free from dirt, filth, or any foul matter; neat; carefully avoiding filth.—**cleanlily,**† klen'li·li, *adv.* In a cleanly manner.— **cleanliness,** klen'li·nes, *n.* The state or quality of being cleanly.—**cleanly,** klēn'li, *adv.* In a clean manner; neatly; without filth; adroitly; dexterously.—**cleanness,** klēn'nes, *n.* The state or quality of being clean. —**cleanhanded** *a.* Having clean hands; *fig.* free from moral taint or suspicion.—**clean-limbed,** *a.* Having well-proportioned limbs.

cleanse, klenz, *v.t.*—*cleansed, cleansing.* [A.Sax. *claensian,* from *claene,* clean.] To make clean; to free from filth, or whatever is unseemly, noxious, or offensive; to purify.— **cleanser,** klen'zėr, *n.* One who or that which cleanses.

clear, klēr, *a.* [O.Fr. *cleir* (Fr. *clair*), from L. *clarus,* clear; akin *claret, clarify, clarinet.*] Free from darkness or opacity; brilliant; light; luminous; unclouded; not obscured; free from what would dim transparency or bright color (*clear* water); free from anything that confuses or obscures; acute, sagacious, or discriminating (intellect, head); perspicuous; lucid (statement); evident; manifest; indisputable; undeniable; free from accusation, imputation, distress, imprisonment, or the like; followed by *of* or *from*; free from impediment or obstruction; unobstructed (a *clear* view); sounding distinctly; distinctly audible; in full; net (*clear* profit or gain),—*Clear days* (preceded by a numeral), days reckoned exclusively of those on which any proceeding is commenced or completed.—*adv.* Clearly; quite; entirely; clean; indicating entire separation.—*v.t.* To make or render clear; to free from whatever diminishes brightness, transparency, or purity of color; to free from obscurity, perplexity, or ambiguity: often followed by *up*; to free from any impediment or encumbrance, or from anything noxious or injurious; to remove; with *off, away,* etc.; to free from the imputation of guilt; to acquit; to make by way of gain or profit beyond all expenses and charges; to leap over or pass without touching or failure; *naut.* to pay the customs on or connected with; to obtain permission to sail for (a cargo, a ship).—*v.i.* To become free from clouds or fog; to become fair or serene; to pass away or disappear from the sky; often followed by *up, off,* or *away*; to exchange checks and bills and settle balances, as is done in clearing-houses; *naut.* to leave a port: often followed by *out* or *outward.*—**clearance,** klē′rans, *n.* The act of clearing.—**clearer,** klē′rėr, *n.* One who or that which clears.—**clearing,** klēr′ing, *n.* The act of one who clears; among *bankers,* the act of exchanging drafts on each other's houses and settling the differences; among *railroads,* the act of distributing among the different companies the proceeds of the through traffic passing over several railroads; a place or tract of land cleared of wood or cultivation.—**clearing-house,** *n.* An institution through which the claims of banks against one another are settled. These claims are represented in the form of bank checks in the case of bank clearing-houses. At the Stock Exchange and the Board of Trade similar clearing-houses exist for the facilitation of trading in stocks and in grain.—**clearly,** klēr′li, *adv.* In a clear manner; brightly; luminously; plainly; evidently.—**clearness,** klēr′nes, *n.* The state or quality of being clear.—**clearheaded,** *a.* Having a clear head or understanding; having acute discernment or keen intelligence.—**clearsighted,** *a.* Seeing with clearness; having acuteness of mental discernment; discerning; perspicacious.—**clear-sightedness,** *n.*—**clearstarch,** *v.t.* To stiffen and dress with clear or colorless starch.

cleat, klēt, *n.* [Allied to G. *klate, klatte,* a claw.] A piece of wood or iron used in a ship to fasten ropes upon; a piece of iron worn on a shoe; a piece of wood nailed on transversely to a piece of joinery for the purpose of securing it in its proper position, or for strengthening.—*v.t.* To strengthen with a cleat or cleats.

cleave, klēv, *v.i.*—pret. *clave* or *cleaved;* pp. *cleaved;* ppr. *cleaving.* [A.Sax. *clifian, cleofian,* pret. *clifode,* pp. *clifod* (*cleaved* is therefore historically the correct pret. and pp.); cog. D. and L.G. *kleven,* Dan. *klaebe,* G. *kleben,* to adhere, to cleave. *Climb* is akin.] To stick; to adhere; to be attached physically, or by affection or other tie.

cleave, klēv, *v.t.*—pret. *clove,* or *clave* (the latter antiquated), also *cleft;* pp. *cloven, cleft* or *cleaved;* ppr. *cleaving.* [A.Sax. *cleófan,* pret. *cleáf,* pp. *clofen,* (the historically correct conjugation is therefore *cleave, clave* or *clove, cloven*), to cleave or split; cog. D. *kloven,* Icel. *kljúfa,* Dan. *klóve,* G. *klieben.*] To part or divide by force; to split or rive; to sever forcibly; to hew; to cut.—*v.i.* To divide; to split; to open.—**cleavable,** klē′va·bl, *a.* Capable of being cleaved or divided.—**cleavage,** klē′vij, *n.* The act of cleaving or splitting; the manner in which rocks or mineral substances regularly cleave or split according to their natural joints, or regular structure; in animals, early divisions of fertilized egg cell.—**cleaver,** klē′vėr, *n.* One who or that which cleaves; a butcher's instrument for cutting carcasses into joints or pieces.

cleek, klēk, *n.* An iron club with a narrow face and a long shaft used as a golf club.

clef, klef, *n.* [Fr. *clef,* L. *clavis,* a key.] A character in music, placed at the beginning of a staff, to determine the degree of elevation to be given to the notes belonging to it as a whole.

cleft, kleft, pret. & pp. of *cleave,* to divide.—*n.* A space or opening made by splitting; a crack; a crevice.—**cleft palate,** *n.* A malformation in which more or less of the palate is wanting, so as to leave a longitudinal gap in the upper jaw, often an accompaniment of harelip.

cleistogamic, cleistogamous, klīs··to·gam′ik, klīs·tog′a·mus, *a.* [Gr. *kleiō,* to close or shut up, and *gamos,* marriage.] *Bot.* having minute, bud-like, self-fertilizing flowers as well as other flowers conspicuously colored.

clematis, klem′a·tis, *n.* [Gr. *klēmatis.*] The generic name of woody climbing plants of the crowfoot family having white or purple blossoms.

clemency, klem′en·si, *n.* [L. *clementia,* from *clemens, clementis,* merciful.] Mildness of temper as shown by a superior to an inferior; disposition to spare or forgive; mercy; leniency; softness or mildness of the elements.—**clement,** klem′ent, *a.* Mild in temper and disposition; gentle; lenient; merciful; kind; tender, compassionate.—**clemently,** klem′ent·li, *adv.* With mildness of temperature; mercifully.

clench, klench, *v.t.* [Shortened form = Sc. *clink,* Dan. *klinke,* Sw. *klinka,* to clinch, to rivet; akin *clink.*] To secure or fasten, as a nail, by beating down the point when it is driven through anything; to rivet; to establish, settle, or confirm (a denial, argument, etc.); to bring together and set firmly; to double up tightly (the teeth or the hands); to grasp firmly.—*n.* A catch; a grip; a persistent clutch; a clinch.

clepe, klēp, *v.t.*—pp. *yclept.* [A.Sax. *clipian, cleopian.*] To call or name. (*Shak.*)

clepsydra, klep′si·dra, *n.* [Gr. *klepsydra—kleptō,* to steal, to hide, and *hydōr,* water.] A name common to devices of various kinds for measuring time by the discharge of water; a water clock.

cleptomania, klep·to·mā′ni·a, *n.* See KLEPTOMANIA.

clergy, klėr′ji, *n.* [O.Fr. *clergie,* from L. *cleric,* Gr. *klērikos,* clerical, from *klēros,* a lot, an allotment, the clergy. Akin *clerical, clerk.*] The body of men set apart and consecrated, by due ordination, to the service of God in the Christian church; the body of ecclesiastics, in distinction from the laity; *law,* benefit of clergy.—*Benefit of clergy, law,* the exemption of clergymen from criminal process before a secular judge; in cases of felony, an immunity latterly extended to any person who could read, though laymen could only claim it once; abolished in 1827.—**clergyman,** klėr′ji·man, *n.* A man in holy orders;

the minister of a Christian church.

clerical, kler′ik·al, *a.* [L. *clericus,* Gr. *klērikos.* CLERGY, CLERK.] Relating or pertaining to the clergy; relating to a writer or copyist.—*Clerical error,* an error in the text of a document made by carelessness or inadvertence on the part of the writer or transcriber.—**cleric,** kler′ik, *n.* A clergyman or scholar.—**clericalism,** kler′ik·al·izm, *n.* Clerical power or influence; undue influence of the clergy; sacerdotalism.—**clerisy,**† kler′i·si, *n.* A body of clerks or learned men; the literati; the clergy, as opposed to the laity.

clerk, klėrk, *n.* [A.Sax. *clerc,* a priest; O.Fr. *clerc;* from L. *clericus.* Gr. *klērikos.* CLERGY.] A clergyman or ecclesiastic; a man in holy orders, especially in the Church of England; formerly also any man of education; the layman who leads in reading the responses in the service of the Anglican Church; one who is employed in keeping records or accounts; an officer attached to courts, municipal and other corporations, associations, etc., whose duty generally is to keep records of proceedings, and transact business under direction of the court, body, etc., by whom he is employed; in America, an assistant in a shop; a shopman.—*St. Nicholas' clerk,* a thief. (*Shak.*)—**clerkly,** klėrk′li, *a.* Pertaining to a clerk or to penmanship; scholarly.—*adv.*† In a scholarly manner. (*Shak.*)—**clerkship,** klėrk′ship, *n.* The office or business of a clerk or writer.

clever, klev′ėr, *a.* [Connected with O.E. *cliver,* a claw, and with *cleave,* to adhere.] Performing or acting with skill or address; possessing ability of any kind, especially such as involves quickness of intellect or mechanical dexterity; indicative of or exhibiting cleverness; dexterous; adroit; able.—**cleverish,** klev′ėr·ish, *a.* Tolerably clever.—**cleverly,** klev′ėr·li. *adv.* In a clever manner; dexterously; skillfully; ably.—**cleverness,** klev′ėr·nes, *n.* The quality of being clever; dexterity; adroitness; skill; ingenuity; smartness.

clew, *n.* or *v.t.* See CLUE.

cliché, klē·shā′, *n.* [Fr., from *clicher,* to stereotype, from older *cliquer,* to fasten, make firm, from root of *clinch, clench* (omitting the nasal).] Hackneyed jest or stereotyped phrase. A stereotype plate, especially one derived from an engraving.

click, klik, *v.i.* [An imitative word expressing a slighter sound than *clack;* comp. *clack, cluck, clink, clank;* D. *klikken,* Fr. *cliquer,* to click.] To make a small sharp sound, or a succession of small sharp sounds, as by a gentle striking; to tick.—*v.t.* To move with a clicking sound.—*n.* A small sharp sound; the cluck of the natives of South Africa; the piece that enters the teeth of a ratchet wheel; a detent or ratchet; the latch of a door.

client, klī′ent, *n.* [L. *cliens, clientis,* a client, from O.L. *cluo,* to hear.] An ancient Roman citizen who put himself under the protection of a

ch, *chain;* ch, Sc. *loch;* g, *go;* j, *job;* ng, *sing;* TH, *then;* th, *thin;* w, *wig;* hw, *whig;* zh, *azure.*

man of distinction and influence (his *patron*); one whose interests are represented by any professional man; especially one who applies to a lawyer, or commits his cause to his management.—**clientage**, kli′en·tij, *n.* The state or condition of being a client; a body of clients.—**cliental**, kli′en·tal, *a.* Pertaining to a client or clients.—**clientele**, **clientelage**, kli′en·tel, kli·en′tēl·ij, *n.* [L. *clientela.*] A body of clients or dependents; one's clients collectively.

cliff, klif, *n.* [A.Sax. *clif*, a rock. a cliff=D. *klif*, Icel. *klif*, a cliff; comp. also Dan. *klippe*, Sw. *klippa*, G. *klippe*, a crag.] A precipice; the steep and rugged face of a rocky mass; a steep rock; a headland.

climacteric, kli·mak′tėr·ik, *n.* [Gr. *klimakter*, the step of a ladder, from *klimax*, a ladder or scale. CLIMAX.] A critical period in human life, or a period in which some great change is supposed to take place in the human constitution; the *grand* or *great climacteric* being the 63d year. —*a.* Pertaining to a climacteric.

climate, kli′mit, *n.* [L. *clima*, Gr. *klima*, *klimatos*, a slope, a zone of the earth, a clime, from *klinō*, to bend, referring to the inclination of the earth from the equator to the pole.] The condition of a tract or region in relation to the various phenomena of the atmosphere, as temperature, wind, moisture, miasmata, etc., especially as they affect the life of animals or man.—**climatic**, kli·mat′ik, *a.* Pertaining to a climate or climates; limited by a climate.— **climatology**, kli′ma·tol′o·ji, *n.* The science of climates; an investigation of the causes on which the climate of a place depends.—**climatological**, kli′mat·o·loj″ik·al, *a.* Pertaining to climatology.—**clime**, klim, *n.* A tract or region of the earth. (Poetical.)

climax, kli′maks, *n.* [L., from Gr. *klimax*, a ladder, from *klinō*, to slope. CLIMATE, CLIMACTERIC.] A figure of speech or rhetorical device in which the language rises step by step in dignity, importance, and force; the highest point of anything; the culmination; acme.

climb, klim, *v.i.*—(*clomb* for pret. & pp. *climbed* is now only poetical). [A.Sax. *climban*, G. and D. *klimmen*; from same root as *cleave*, to adhere, *clip*, to embrace.] To mount or ascend anything steep with labor and difficulty; especially, to ascend by means of the hands and feet; of things, to rise with a slow motion, to ascend, as certain plants, by means of tendrils, etc.— *v.t.* To climb up.—**climbable**, klim′a·bl, *a.* Capable of being climbed.—**climber**, klim′ėr, *n.* One who climbs; a plant that rises by attaching itself to some support; one of an order of birds, including the parrots, woodpeckers, etc., so called from their climbing habits.

clime. See CLIMATE.

clinanthium, kli·nan′thi·um, *n.* [Gr. *klinē*, a bed, *anthos*, a flower.] *Bot.* a term for the receptacle of a composite plant.

clinch, klinsh, *v.t.* [A variant of CLENCH.] To secure a driven nail, bolt, etc. by flattening the protruding point; to fasten in this way; to settle a matter conclusively.—*v.i.* Boxing, to grasp firmly.—*n.* The act of clinching; a grasp; a grapple.— **clincher**, klinsh′ėr, *n.*

cling, kling, *v.i.*—*clung*, *clinging*. [A.Sax. *clingan*, to adhere, to dry up or wither; Dan. *klynge*, to grow in clusters; *klynge*, a heap, a cluster.] To adhere closely; to stick; to hold fast, especially by winding round or embracing.

clinic, klin′ik, *n.* [Gr. *klinikos*, from *klinē*, a bed, from *klinō*, to recline.] A medical institution in which a group of physicians jointly examine and treat patients; also, the examination and treatment of patients in the presence of medical students.— **clinical**, klin′i·kal, *adj.* Pertaining to a clinic or sickroom; pertaining to direct observation of a patient; analytical.—**clinically**, klin′ik·al·li, *adv.*

clink, klingk, *v.i.* [An imitative word, akin to *click* and *clank*; comp. D. *klinken*, to tinkle; Dan. *klinge*, to jingle; Icel. *klingja*, G. *klingen*, to ring, to chink.] To ring or jingle; to give out a small sharp sound or a succession of such sounds, as by striking small metallic bodies together; to rhyme.—*v.t.* To cause to produce a small sharp ringing sound. —*n.* A sharp sound made by the collision of sonorous bodies.—**clinker**, klingk′ėr, *a.* A partially vitrified brick; a kind of hard brick used for paving; a mass of incombustible slag which forms in grates and furnaces. —**clinkstone**, *n.* [From its sonorousness.] A feldspathic rock of the trachytic group with a slaty structure, sometimes used as roofing slates.

clinker-built, klingk′ėr, *a. Naut.* built with the planks of the side so disposed that the lower edge of each overlies the upper edge of the next below it, like slates on a roof.

clinometer, kli·nom′et·ėr, *n.* [Gr. *klinō*, to lean, and *metron*, measure.] An instrument for measuring the dip of rock strata.—**clinometric**, **clinometrical**, kli·no·met′rik, kli·no·met′rik·al, *a.* Of or pertaining to a clinometer; ascertained or determined by a clinometer; pertaining to crystals which have oblique angles between the axes.

Clio, kli′ō, *n.* The muse who was supposed to preside over history; the name of an asteroid; a genus of pteropodous mollusks.

clip, klip, *v.t.*—*clipped*, *clipt*; *clipping*. [Icel. *klippa*, to clip, to cut the hair; Dan. *klippe*, Sw. *klippa*, to clip or shear.] To cut off or sever with shears or scissors; to trim or make shorter (the hair) with scissors; to diminish (coin) by paring the edge; to curtail; to cut short (words); to pronounce shortly and indistinctly. —*n.* The quantity of wool shorn at a single shearing of sheep; a season's shearing; a clasp or spring holder for letters or papers.—**clipper**, klip′ėr, *n.* A full-rigged ship of a type devel-

oped in America about 1840, characterized by a sharp bow, graceful lines, tall masts and a large sail area.

clique, klēk, *n.* [Fr. *clique*, probably a mere variant of *claque*, with a somewhat different sense. CLAQUE.] A party; a set; a coterie: used generally in a bad sense.—**cliquish**, klēk′-ish, *a.* Relating to a clique or party; disposed to form cliques; having a petty party spirit.—**cliquishness**, klēk′ish·nes, *n.* The state or quality of being cliquish.

cloaca, klō·ā′ka, *n.* [L., a common sewer.] An underground conduit for drainage; a common sewer; the excrementory cavity in birds, reptiles, many fishes, and lower mammalia, formed by the extremity of the intestinal canal and the outlet of the urinary organs.—**cloacal**, klō·ā′kal, *a.* Pertaining to a cloaca.

cloak, klōk, *n.* [O. and Prov.Fr. *cloque*, L.L. *cloca*, *clocca*, a bell, a kind of horseman's cape of a bell-shape; same word as *clock*.] A loose outer garment worn over other clothes; *fig.* that which conceals; a disguise or pretext; an excuse.—*v.t.* To cover with a cloak; to hide; to conceal.

clock, klok, *n.* [Originally a bell. A.Sax. *clucga*, Icel. *klukka*, Dan. *klokke*, Sw. *klocka*, D. *klok*, G. *glocke*, a bell or clock; Ir. and Gael. *clog*, a bell or clock. *Cloak* is the same word.] A machine for measuring time, indicating the hours, minutes, and often seconds by means of hands moving over a dial plate, and generally marking the hours by the strokes of a hammer on a bell, the motion being kept up by weights or springs, and regulated by a pendulum or a balance wheel. ∴ *O'clock*, in such phrases as, 'it is one o'clock', is contracted from *of the clock.*— **clockwork**, *n.* The machinery of a clock; a complex mechanism of wheels producing regularity of movement.

clock, klok, *n.* [Possibly originally applied to a bell-shaped ornament or flower.] A figure or figured work embroidered on the side of a stocking.

clod, klod, *n.* [A slightly modified form of *clot*; comp. Dan. *klode*, a globe or ball, *klods*, a block or lump.] A lump or mass in general‡; a lump of earth, or earth and turf; a lump of clay; a dull, gross, stupid fellow; a dolt.—**cloddish**, klod′ish, *a.* Clownish; boorish; doltish; uncouth; ungainly.—**cloddy**, klod′i, *a.* Consisting of clods; abounding with clods; earthy; gross in sentiments or thoughts.—**clodhopper**, klod′hop·ėr, *n.* A clown; a dolt; a boor.— **clodpoll**, klod′pōl, *n.* [*Poll*=head.] A stupid fellow; a dolt; a blockhead.

clog, klog, *n.* [Comp. Sc. *clag*, a clog, an impediment, *clag*, to clog, as with something viscous or sticky, from A.Sax. *clæg*, clay. CLAY.] An encumbrance that hinders motion, or renders it difficult, as a piece of wood fastened to an animal's leg; hindrance; encumbrance; impediment; a sort of shoe with a wooden sole; a wooden shoe; a sabot; a patten.

—*v.t.*—*clogged, clogging.* To impede the movements of by a weight, or by something that sticks or adheres; to encumber, restrain, or hamper; to choke up (a tube, etc.); to obstruct so as to hinder passage through; to throw obstacles in the way of; to hinder; to burden; to trammel.—*v.i.* To become loaded or encumbered with extraneous matter.—**cloggy,** klog′i, *a.* Clogging or having power to clog; adhesive; viscous.—**clog dance,** *n.* A dance in which the feet, shod with clogs, are made to perform a noisy accompaniment to the music.

cloister, klois′tẽr, *n.* [O.Fr. *cloistre,* Fr. *cloître;* from L. *claustrum,* a bolt, enclosed place, from *claudo, clausum,* to shut. CLOSE.] An arched way or covered walk running round the walls of certain portions of monastic and collegiate buildings; a place of religious retirement; a monastery; a convent; any arcade or colonnade round an open court; a piazza.—*v.t.* To confine in a cloister or convent; to shut up in retirement from the world; to furnish with a cloister or cloisters.—**cloistral,** klois′tral, *a.* Of or pertaining to a cloister.—**cloistress,**† klois′tres, *n.* A nun; a woman who has vowed religious retirement. (*Shak.*)

cloke, klōk, *n.* and *v.* Same as *cloak.*

clonic, klon′ik, *a.* [From Gr. *klonos,* a shaking.] *Pathol.* convulsive, with alternate relaxation.—**Clonic spasm,** a spasm in which the muscles or muscular fibers rapidly contract and relax alternately, as in epilepsy: used in contradistinction to *tonic spasm.*

close, klōz, *v.t.*—*closed, closing.* [Fr. *clos,* pp. of *clore,* to shut up; from L. *claudo, clausum,* to shut; seen also in *conclude, exclude, include, seclude, cloister,* etc.] To bring together the parts of; to shut (a door, window, book, eyes, hands); make fast; to end, finish, conclude, complete; to fill or stop up; to consolidate: often followed by up; to encompass or enclose; to shut in.—*v.i.* To come together; to unite; to coalesce; to end, terminate, or come to a period; to engage in close encounter; to grapple; to accede or consent to (to *close with* terms); to come to an agreement (to *close with* a person). —*n.* Conclusion; termination; end; pause; cessation; a grapple, as in wrestling.—**closer,** klō′zẽr, *n.* One who or that which closes.—**closure,** klō′zhẽr, *n.* The act of closing; an end or conclusion; the act of bringing a parliamentary debate to an end, by special vote or otherwise.—**cloture,** klō′chẽr, *n.* The act of bringing a parliamentary debate to an end.

close, klōs, *a.* [Fr. *clos,* L. *clausus,* shut. CLOSE, *v.t.*] Shut fast; made fast so as to leave no opening; strictly confined; strictly watched (a *close* prisoner); retired; secluded; hidden; private; secret; having the habit or disposition to keep secrets; secretive; reticent; confined within narrow limits; narrow; without motion or ventilation; difficult to breathe; oppressive: of the air or weather; in direct contact or nearly so; adjoining; with little or no intervening distance in place or time; with little difference, as between antagonists or rival parties; almost evenly balanced (*close* contest); having the parts near each other; compact; dense; firmly attached; intimate; trusty; confidential (*close* friends); firmly fixed on a given object (*close* attention); keen and steady; not deviating from a model or original (a *close* translation); niggardly; stingy; penurious.—*n.* [Fr. *clos,* an inclosed place.] An enclosed place; any place surrounded by a fence; specifically, the precinct of a cathedral or abbey; a narrow passage or entry leading off a street.—*adv.* Tightly, so as to leave no opening; in strict confinement; in contact, or very near in space or time.—**closely,** klōs′li, *adv.* In a close manner.—**closeness,** klōs′nes, *n.*—**closed circuit,** *a.* Pertaining to television broadcasting that is limited to a specified group of interconnected receivers.—**closed shop,** *n.* A business in which an employer hires only members of labor unions.—**closefisted,** klōs′fis″ted, *a.* Stingy.—**close up,** *n.* A picture taken at close range; an intimate view.

closet, kloz′et, *n.* [O.Fr. *closet,* dim. of *clos,* an enclosure. CLOSE, *n.*] A small room or apartment for retirement; any room for privacy; a small side room or recess for storing utensils, furniture, provisions, etc.—*v.t.* To put in or admit into a closet, as for concealment or for private consultation: usually in pp. *closeted.*

closure, *n.* See CLOSE, *v.t.*

clot, klot, *n.* [Older form of *clod,* and formerly used in same sense; A.Sax. *clot,* a mass; D. *kloot,* a ball or globe; Sw. *klot,* a sphere; *klots,* a block; G. *kloss,* a clod, a lump, *klotz,* a block; akin *cloud.*] A coagulated mass of soft or fluid matter, as of blood, cream, etc.—*v.i.*—*clotted, clotting.* To coagulate, as soft or fluid matter, into a thick, inspissated mass. —*v.t.* To cause to coagulate; to make or form into clots.—**clotty,** klot′i, *a.* Full of clots; resembling a clot; coagulated.

cloth, kloth, *n.* [A.Sax. *cláth*=D. *cleed,* Icel. *klæthi,* Dan. and Sw. *klæde,* G. *kleid,* cloth.] A fabric of wool or hair, or of cotton, flax, hemp, etc., or of mineral filaments, formed by weaving; frequently, a fabric of wool in contradistinction to that made of other material; a piece of linen for covering a table at meals; a tablecloth; a professional dress, specifically that of a clergyman; hence, with the definite article or other defining word, the office of a clergyman; the members of the clerical profession.—**clothe,** klōTH, *v.t.*—*clothed* or *clad; clothing.* To put garments on; to dress; to furnish or supply with clothes or raiment; *fig.* to cover or spread over with anything; to invest; to put on or over.—**clothes,** klōTHz, *n. pl.* [A plural of *cloth,* though it cannot now be said to have a singular.] Garments for the human body; dress; vestments; vesture; the covering of a bed; bedclothes.—**clotheshorse,** *n.* A frame to hang clothes on.—**clothier,** klōTH′i·ẽr, *n.* A seller of cloth or of clothes.—**clothing,** klōTH′ing, *n.* Garments in general; clothes.

cloud, kloud, *n.* [Originally a mass or rounded mass in general; A.Sax. *clúd,* a rock, a hillock, the root being that seen in *clod;* so in O.D. *klot,* a clod, and *klote,* a cloud.] A collection of visible vapor or watery particles suspended in the atmosphere at some altitude, the principal forms being designated as the *cirrus,* the *cumulus,* and the *stratus* (see these words); something resembling a cloud, as a body of smoke or flying dust; a dark area of color in a lighter material; that which obscures, darkens, sullies, threatens, or the like; a multitude; a collection; a mass.— *v.t.* To overspread with a cloud or clouds: hence, to obscure; to darken; to render gloomy or sullen; to darken in spots; to variegate with colors. —*v i.* To grow cloudy; to become obscured with clouds.—**cloudberry,** kloud′be·ri, *n.* A plant of the bramble family, with large and white flowers and orange-red berries of an agreeable taste.—**cloudy,** kloud′i, *a.* Overcast with clouds; obscured with clouds, as the sky; consisting of a cloud or clouds; obscure; dark; not easily understood; having the appearance of gloom; indicating gloom, anxiety, sullenness, or ill-nature; not open or cheerful; marked with spots or areas of dark or various hues.—**cloudily,** kloud′i·li, *adv.* In a cloudy manner; with clouds; darkly; obscurely.— **cloudiness,** kloud′i·nes, *n.* The state of being cloudy.—**cloudless,** kloud′-les, *a.* Being without a cloud; unclouded; clear; bright.—**cloudlet,** kloud′let, *n.* A small cloud.—**cloudburst,** *n.* A tremendous downpour of rain over a limited area.

clout, klout, *n.* [A.Sax. *clút,* a clout, a patch; Dan. *klud,* Sw. *klut,* a clout; also W. *clwt,* Ir. and Gael. *clud,* a clout.] A patch or rag; a piece of cloth or the like used to mend something; any piece of cloth, especially a worthless piece; *archery,* the mark fixed in the center of a target; a hard blow, struck usually with the fist; in baseball, a long hard-hit ball; a dull or stupid person.

clout, clout nail, klout, klout′ nāl, *n.* [Fr. *clouet,* a dim. of *clou,* a nail.] A short, large-headed nail worn in the soles of shoes; also, a nail for securing small patches of iron, as on axle trees, etc.—*v.t.* To stud or fasten with nails.

clove, klōv, pret. of *cleave.*

clove, klōv, *n.* [Sp. *clavo,* a clove, a nail, from L. *clavus,* a nail, from its resemblance to a nail in shape.] The dried flower bud of an evergreen tree of the myrtle tribe, a native of the Molucca Islands, such buds forming a very pungent aromatic spice; the tree yielding cloves.

clove, klōv, *n.* [A.Sax. *clufe,* a bulb.] One of the small bulbs formed in the axils of the scales of a mother bulb, as in garlic; a denomination of weight of cheese, etc., being about 8 lbs.

cloven, klōv'n, pp. of *cleave.* Divided; parted.—**cloven footed,** *a.* Having the hoof divided into two parts, as the ox; bisulcate.

clover, klō'vėr, *n.* [A.Sax. *clæfre*=D. *klaver,* L.G. *klever,* Dan. *klover,* Sw. *klofver,* perhaps from root of *cleave,* from its trifid leaves.] A herbaceous leguminous plant of numerous species bearing three-lobed leaves and roundish heads or oblong spikes of small flowers, several species being widely cultivated for fodder.— *To be* or *to live in clover,* to be in most enjoyable circumstances; to live luxuriously or in abundance.

clown, kloun, *n.* [Icel. *klunni,* a clumsy, boorish fellow; Fris. *klonne,* a bumpkin; allied to Sw. *klunn,* a block.] An awkward country fellow; a peasant; a rustic; a man of coarse manners; a person without refinement; a boor; a lout; a churl; a jester, merryman, or buffoon, as in a theater, circus, or other place of entertainment.—*v.i.* To act as a clown; to play the clown.—**clownish,** kloun'ish, *a.* Of or pertaining to clowns or rustics; rude; coarse; awkward; ungainly; abounding in clowns.— **clownishly,** kloun'ish·li, *adv.* In a clownish manner. — **clownishness,** kloun'ish·nes, *n.* Boorishness; rusticity.

cloy, kloi, *v.t.* [O.Fr. *cloyer,* to stop up, equivalent to *clouer, cloer,* originally to fasten with a nail, O.Fr. *clo,* Fr. *clou,* from L. *clavus,* a nail.] To gratify to excess so as to cause loathing; to surfeit, satiate, or glut.

club, klub, *n.* [A Scandinavian word; Icel. *klubba, klumba,* Sw. *klubba,* Dan. *klub,* a club.] A stick or piece of wood. with one end thicker and heavier than the other, suitable for being wielded with the hand; a thick heavy stick used as a weapon; a cudgel; a staff with a crooked and heavy head for driving the ball in the game of golf, etc.; a card of the suit that is marked with trefoils; *pl.* the suit so marked; a select number of persons in the habit of meeting for the promotion of some common object, as social intercourse, literature, science, politics; a club house.—*v.i. clubbed, clubbing.* To form a club or combination for a common purpose; to combine to raise a sum of money; often with *for* before the object; to combine generally.—*v.t.* To beat with a club; to convert into a club; to use as a club by brandishing with the small end; to add together, each contributing a certain sum.—**clubbable,** klub'a·bl, *a.* Having the qualities that make a man fit to be a member of a club; social.—**clubfoot,** *n.* A short, distorted foot, generally of congenital origin.—**clubfooted,** *a.* Having a clubfoot or clubfeet.— **club moss,** *n.* A mosslike plant; a lycopod.

cluck, kluk, *v.i.* [A.Sax. *cloccian*=D. *klokken,* Dan. *klukke,* an imitative word like *clack, click,* etc.] To utter the call or cry of a brooding hen. —*n.* A sound uttered by a hen; a similar sound, or click, characteristic

of the languages of South Africa, especially the Kaffir and Hottentot.

clue, clew, klū, *n.* [A.Sax. *cliwe, cliwen,* a ball of thread=D. *kiuwen,* a clue; akin to L. *globus, glomus,* a mass.] A ball of thread; the thread that forms a ball; *fig.* anything that guides or directs one in an intricate case (there being sundry stories of persons being guided in intricate mazes or labyrinths by a clue of thread); *naut.* the lower corner of a square sail.

clump, klump, *n.* [Same as D. *klomp,* Dan. Sw. and G. *klump,* a lump, a clod; from same root as *clumsy, club,* etc.] A shapeless mass; a lump; a cluster of trees or shrubs.— **clumpy,** klump'i, *a.* Consisting of clumps; shapeless.

clumsy, klum'zi, *a.* [From old *clumsen, clomsen,* to benumb or stupefy; allied to Sw. *klummsen,* benumbed, Icel. *klumsa,* lockjaw, D. *kleumen,* to be benumbed; the root being same as in *clump,* etc.] Awkward; ungainly; without readiness, dexterity, or grace; ill-made; badly constructed; awkwardly done; unskillfully performed.—**clumsily,** klum'zi·li, *adv.* In a clumsy manner.—**clumsiness,** klum'zi·nes, *n.* The quality of being clumsy.

clung, klung, pret. & pp. of *cling.*

cluster, klus'tėr, *n.* [A. Sax. *cluster;* same root as Sw. and Dan. *klase,* Icel. *klasi,* a cluster.] A number of things, as fruits, growing naturally together; a bunch; a number of individuals of any kind collected or gathered into a body; an assemblage; a group; a swarm; a crowd.—*v.i.* To grow or be assembled in clusters or groups.—*v.t.* To collect into a cluster or group; to produce in a cluster or clusters.—*Clustered column,* *arch.* a column or pier which appears to consist of several columns or shafts clustered together.

clutch, kluch, *v.t.* [O.E. *clucche, cloche,* from *cloche,* a claw, a softened form of older *cloke,* a claw, Sc. *cluik, cluke,* a claw; allied to *claw.*] To seize, clasp, or grip with the hand; to close tightly; to clench.—*n.* A gripping or pinching with the fingers; seizure; grasp; a paw, talon, or grasping merciless hand; hence such phrases as, to fall into a person's *clutches; mach.* a contrivance for connecting shafts with each other or with wheels, so that they may be disengaged at pleasure.

clutch, klutch, *n.* [A form of *cluck,* cry of a brooding hen.] The eggs laid and hatched by a bird at one time.

clutter, klut'tėr, *n.* [A modification of *clatter.*] Confused noise; bustle; confusion; litter.—*v.t.* To put in a clutter; to crowd together in disorder. —*v.i.* To make a bustle or disturbance.

clypeate, clypeiform, klip'ē·āt, klip'ē·i·form, *a.* [L. *clypeus,* a shield.] Shaped like a round buckler; shield-shaped; scutate.

clyster, klis'tėr, *n.* [Gr. *klystēr,* from *klyzō,* to wash or cleanse.] A liquid substance injected into the lower

intestines to purge or cleanse them, or to relieve from costiveness; an injection.

coach, kōch, *n.* [Fr. *coche,* from Hung. *kocsi* (pron. ko-chi), from *Kocs,* in Hungary.] A vehicle drawn by horses and intended to carry passengers; more particularly a four-wheeled, closed vehicle of considerable size; a two-door automobile; a railroad passenger car; a private tutor, often one employed to prepare pupils for examination; an instructor in athletics, expecially an adviser and trainer for contests.—*v.t.* To carry in a coach; to prepare for an examination by private instruction; to train for an athletic contest; to direct the actions of a player (*Baseball*).— **coach dog,** *n.* A dog of Dalmatian breed, generally white spotted with black, kept to accompany carriages. —**coachman,** kōch'man, *n.* The person who drives a coach.—**coachmanship,** kōch'man·ship, *n.* Skill in coaching.

coact, kō·akt', *v.i.* [Prefix *co,* and *act.*] To act together.—**coactive,** kō·ak'tiv, *a.* Acting in concurrence; also forcing or compelling; compulsory (in this sense from L. *cogo, coactum,* to compel).

coadjutor, kō·ad·jū'tėr, *n.* [L. *coadjutor*—prefix *co, ad,* to, and *juvo, jutum,* to help.] One who aids another; an assistant; a fellow helper; an associate; a fellow worker; a colleague; the assistant of a bishop or other prelate.—**coadjutress, coadjutrix,** kō·ad·jū'tres, kō·ad·jū'triks, *n.* A female assistant or fellow helper.

coadunate, kō·ad'ū·nit, *a.* [L. *coadunatus*—prefix *co, ad,* to, *unus,* one.] United or joined together: especially used in *bot.* and applied to leaves united at the base.

coagulate, kō·ag'ū·lāt, *v.t.*—*coagulated, coagulating.* [L. *coagulo, coagulatum,* from *coagulum,* rennet—*con,* together, and *ago,* to bring, drive, etc.] To change from a fluid into a curdlike or inspissated solid mass; to curdle, congeal, or clot.—*v.i.* To curdle or congeal.—**coagulability,** kō·ag'ū·la·bil″i·ti, *n.* The capacity of being coagulated.—**coagulable,** kō·ag'ū·la·bl, *a.* Capable of becoming coagulated.—**coagulant,** kō·ag'ū·lant, *n.* That which produces coagulation. —**coagulation,** kō·ag·ū·lā″shon, *n.* The act of coagulating or clotting; the state of being coagulated; the substance formed by coagulation.—**coagulative,** kō·ag'ū·lā·tiv, *a.* Causing coagulation.—**coagulator,** kō·ag'ū·lā·tėr, *n.* That which causes coagulation.—**coagulum,** kō·ag'ū·lum, *n.* A coagulated mass, as curd, etc; *med.* a blood clot.

coal, kōl, *n.* [A.Sax. *col*=D. *kool,* Dan. *kul.* Icel. and Sw. *kol.* G. *kohle.*] A piece of wood or other combustible substance burning or charred; charcoal; a cinder; now, usually, a solid black substance found in the earth, largely employed as fuel, and formed from vast masses of vegetable matter deposited through the luxurious growth of plants in former epochs of the earth's history.—*v.t.* To supply with coal, as a steam vessel or locomotive engine.—*v.i.* To take in coals. —*To haul,* (*take,* etc.) *over the coals,* to call to a strict or severe account; to reprimand.—*To carry coals to Newcastle,* to take things where there are already plenty; to perform unnecessary labor.—**coalfish,** *n.* A species of cod, growing to the length of 2 feet or more, found on the northern coasts of Europe, and so named from the color of its back.—**coal gas,** *n.* A variety of carbureted hydrogen which produces the ordinary gaslight. GAS.—**coal heaver,** *n.* One who is employed in carrying coal, and especially in discharging it from coalships.—**coal measures,** *n. pl. Geol.* the upper division of the carboniferous system, consisting of alternate layers of sandstone with thinly laminated beds of clay, between which the coal seams occur.—**coal mine,** *n.* A mine or pit in which coal is dug. —**coal tar,** *n.* A thick, black, viscid, opaque liquid which condenses in the pipes when gas is distilled from coal.

coalesce, kō·a·les´, *v.t.*—*coalesced, coalescing.* [L. *coalesco*—prefix *co,* and *alesco,* to grow up, from *alo,* to nourish.] To unite by growth into one body; to grow together physically; to combine or be collected into one body or mass; to join or unite into one body, party, society, or the like.—**coalescence,** kō·a·les´ens, *n.* The act of coalescing or uniting; the state of being united or combined.—**coalescent,** kō·a·les´ent, *a.* Growing together; uniting.—**coalition,** kō·a·li´shon, *n.* Union in a body or mass; voluntary union of individual persons, parties, or states for a common object or cause.—**coalitionist,** kō·a·li´shon·ist, *n.* One who favors or joins a coalition.

coaming, kōm´ing, *n.* [For *combing,* from *comb.*] *Naut.* a raised border or edge round the hatches to keep out water.

coarse, kōrs, *a.* [The same word as *course,* a thing *of course,* or *in course,* being what is natural, ordinary, common.] Of ordinary or inferior quality; wanting in fineness of texture or structure, or in elegance of form; rude; rough; unrefined; gross; indelicate (*coarse* language).— **coarsely,** kōrs´li, *adv.* In a coarse manner; rudely; uncivilly; without art or polish; grossly.—**coarsen,†** kōr´sn, *v.t.* To render coarse or wanting in refinement; to make vulgar.— **coarseness,** kōrs´nes, *n.* The state or quality of being coarse.

coast, kōst, *n.* [O.Fr. *coste,* Fr. *côte,* rib, hill, shore, coast, from L. *costa,* a rib, side.] The exterior line, limit, or border of a country (O.T.); the edge or margin of the land next to the sea; the seashore.—*The coast is clear,* a phrase equivalent to danger is over; the enemies have gone.—*v.i.* To sail near a coast; to sail by or near the shore, or in sight of land; to slide down without using power. —**coaster,** kōs´tèr, *n.* One that coasts; a ship that trades between coastal ports; a sled; a tray or mat

to hold a glass or bottle.—**coaster brake,** *n.* A brake on the rear wheel of a bicycle, etc.—**coastwards,** kōst´- wèrdz, *adv.* Toward the coast.— **coastways, coastwise,** kōst´wāz, kōst´- wīz, *adv.* By way of or along the coast.—**Coast Guard,** *n.* That branch of the U. S. naval service detailed to ice patrol, lifesaving, and enforcement of customs, navigation and immigration laws.

coat, kōt, *n.* [O.Fr. *cote,* Fr. *cotte,* a coat, from L.L. *cota,* a coat, from O.G. *cotte,* a coarse mantle, G. *kutte,* a cowl: allied to *cot.*] An upper garment, in modern times generally applied to the outer garment worn by men on the upper part of the body; an external covering; a layer of one substance covering another; a coating.—*Coat of arms,* a representation of the armorial insignia which used to be depicted on a coat worn by knights over their armor; an escutcheon or shield of arms.— *Coat of mail,* armor worn on the upper part of the body, and consisting of a network of iron or steel rings, or of small plates, usually of tempered iron, laid over each other like the scales of a fish, and fastened to a strong linen or leather jacket.— *v.t.* To cover with a coat; to spread over with a coating or layer of any substance.—**coat card,** *n.* A card bearing a coated figure, as the king, queen, or knave: now corrupted into *Court-card.*—**coating,** kōt´ing, *n.* Any substance spread over for cover or protection; a thin external layer, as of paint or varnish; cloth for coats.

coax, kōks, *v.t.* [From O.E. *cokes,* a fool; to *coax* one being thus to make a *cokes,* or fool, of him.] To soothe, appease, or persuade by flattery and fondling; to wheedle; to cajole.—**coaxer,** kōk´sèr, *n.* One who coaxes; a wheedler.—**coaxingly,** kōk´sing·li, *adv.* In a coaxing manner.

coaxial, kō·ak´si·al, *a.* Having a common axis.

cob, kob, *n.* [Probably, in some of the meanings, from W. *cob,* a top, a tuft.] A roundish lump of anything; the receptacle on which the grains of corn grow in rows; a short-legged stout horse or pony; clay mixed with straw.—**cob coal,** *n.* A large round piece of coal.

cobalt, kō´balt, *n.* [G. *kobalt, kobolt,* the same word as *kobold,* a goblin, the demon of the mines.] A silverwhite metallic element occurring with iron and nickel. Symbol, Co; at. no., 27; at. wt., 58.9332; a blue pigment.—*Cobalt-60,* a radioactive isotope of cobalt used in medicine.

cobble, kob´l. *n.* [From *cob,* a lump.] A roundish stone; a stone rounded by the attrition of water; a boulder; a cobstone.

cobble, kob´l, *v.t.*—*cobbled, cobbling.* [O.Fr. *cobler,* to join or knit together; from L. *copulare,* to couple.] To make or mend coarsely (shoes); to botch; to make or do clumsily or unhandily.—*v.i.* To work as a cobbler; to do work badly.—**cobbler,** kob´lèr, *n.* One who cobbles; a

mender of boots and shoes; a clumsy workman; a cooling beverage, composed of wine, sugar, lemon, and finely pounded ice.

coble, kob´l, *n.* [W. *ceubal,* a coble.] A flattish-bottomed boat, clinkerbuilt, with a square stern.

cobra, cobra de capello, kōb´ra, kōb´ra de ka·pel´lō, *n.* [Pg., snake of the hood.] The hooded or spectacle snake, a reptile of the most venomous nature, found in different countries of Asia and Africa, especially in India.

cobweb, kob´web, *n.* [O.E., also *copweb,* A.Sax. *coppe,* a spider, seen in *attor-coppe,* a spider.] The network spun by a spider to catch its prey; something to entangle the weak or unwary; something flimsy and worthless; old musty rubbish. —**cobwebby,** kob´web·i, *a.* Covered with cobwebs; *bot.* covered with a thick interwoven pubescence.

coca, kō´ka, *n.* [Native name.] The dried leaf of a South American plant which is chewed by the inhabitants of countries on the Pacific side of South America, giving great power of enduring fatigue; the plant itself.

cocaine, kō·kān´ *n.* The active principle of coca, which has invigorating properties, and is also used as a local anesthetic in minor surgical operations.

coccus, kok´us, *n.* [Gr. *kokkos,* a berry.] In bacteria, a spheroidal type.

coccyx, kok´siks, *n.* [Gr. *kokkyx.*] An assemblage of small bones attached to the lower extremity of the backbone; the rump.—**coccygeal,** kok·- sij´ē·al, *a.* Of or belonging to the coccyx.

Cochin China, koch´in chī´na, *n.* and *a.* A term applied to a large variety of the domestic fowl, which was imported from Cochin China.

cochineal, koch´i·nēl, *n.* [Fr. *cochenille,* from Sp. *cochinilla,* a woodlouse, cochineal, dim. of *cochina,* a sow.] A dyestuff consisting of the dried bodies of a species of insect, a native of the warmer climates of America, found on the cochineal fig tree.—**cochineal fig,** *n.* A treelike cactaceous plant, a native of America, cultivated for the sake of the cochineal insect.

cochlea, kok´lē·a, *n.* [L., a snail or snail's shell.] A bony structure in the internal ear, so called from resembling a snail shell.—**cochleate, cochleated,** kok´lē·āt, kok´lē·āt·ed, *a.* Having a form like the spiral of a snail shell; spiral. Also *Cochleous,* kok´lē·us.

cock, kok, *n.* [A.Sax. *coc, cocc;* comp. O.Fr. *coc,* Fr. *coq,* a cock; probably like *cuckoo,* a word of onomatopoetic origin.] The male of birds, particularly of the gallinaceous, domestic or barn-door fowls: often used adjectively and occasionally to signify the male of certain animals other than birds (a *cock* lobster); a kind of faucet or turn valve, for permitting or arresting the flow of fluids through a pipe; a prominent portion of the lock of a firearm, the hammer; the act of cocking or setting up, or the

ch, *ch*ain; ch, Sc. lo*ch;* g, *go;* j, *j*ob; ng, si*ng;* TH, *th*en; th, *th*in; w, *w*ig; hw, *wh*ig; zh, a*z*ure.

effect or form produced by such an act (a *cock* of the head, nose, etc.).—*Cock of the wood*, the capercailzie.—*v.t.* [Probably from the strutting of the animal.] To set erect (the ears); to turn up with an air of pertness; to set or draw back the cock in order to fire (to *cock* a gun).—*v.i.* To hold up the head; to look big, pert, or menacing.—**cockerel**, kok′ér·el, *n.* A young cock.—**cock and bull**, *a.* [From some old tale about a cock and a bull; comp. Fr. *coq-à-l'âne* (cock-and-ass), a cock-and-bull story.] A term applied to idle or silly fictions, stories having no foundation; canards. (Colloq.)—**cockcrow, cock-crowing**, *n.* The time at which cocks crow; early morning.—**cockeye**, *n.* A squinting eye.—**cockeyed**, *a.* Having a squinting eye.—**cockfight, cockfighting**, *n.* A fight between gamecocks; the practice of fighting gamecocks.—**cockhorse**, *n.* A child's rocking horse: now commonly used in the adverbial phrase, *a-cock-horse*, on horseback; in an elevated position; on the high horse.—**cockloft**, *n.* [Lit. a loft for cocks to roost in.] A small loft in the top of a house; a small garret immediately under the roof.—**cockpit**, *n.* A pit or area where gamecocks fight; a space in the fuselage of an airplane for seating pilots or passengers.—**cockscomb**, koks′kōm, *n.* A cock's crest; an annual plant with feathery red or gold flowers.

cock, kok, *n.* [Dan. *kok*, a heap, a pile; Icel. *kökkr*, a lump.] A small conical pile of hay, so shaped for shedding rain.—*v.t.* To put into cocks or piles.

cock, kok, *n.* [O.Fr. *coque*, a kind of boat; Sp. *coca*, It. *cocca*, from L. *concha*, a kind of shell, a vessel.] A small boat. (*Shak.*)

cock, kok, *n.* [It. *cocca*, Fr. *coche*, a notch.] The notch of an arrow or crossbow.

cockade, ko·kād′, *n.* [Fr. *cocarde*, O.Fr. *coquarde*, from *coq*, a cock, from its resemblance to the comb of the cock.] A ribbon or knot of ribbon worn in the hat; a rosette of leather worn on the hat by gentlemen's servants.—*White Cock-ade*, white rosette, the emblem of the French and English Jacobites.—**cockaded**, ko·kā′ded, *a.* Wearing a cockade.

cockatoo, kok·a·tö′, *n.* [Malay *kaka-tûa*, from its cry.] A name common to numerous beautiful birds of the parrot kind, chiefly inhabiting Australia and the Indian islands, having crests composed of a tuft of elegant feathers, which they can raise or depress at pleasure.

cockatrice, kok′a·tris, *n.* [O.Fr. co-*catrice*, L.L. *cocatrix*, a crocodile, a cockatrice, a corrupted form of L. *crocodilus*, crocodile. In time the first syllable was thought = *cock*.] A fabulous monster said to be hatched by a serpent from a cock's egg, and represented as possessing characters belonging to both animals; a basilisk.

cockchafer, kok′chā·fér, *n.* [*Cock* is probably for *clock*, Prov. E. and Sc.

for a beetle.] A lamellicorn beetle, the larvae or caterpillars of which feed on the roots of corn, etc., and the insects in their winged state do much injury to trees.

cocker, kok′ér, *v.t.* [M.Dan. *kokre*, Norweg. *kokla*, to pet, pamper, fondle.] To fondle; to indulge; to treat with tenderness; to pamper.

cocker, kok′ér, *n.* A dog of the spaniel kind, used for raising woodcocks (whence probably the name) and snipes from their haunts.

cockle, kok′l, *n.* [A.Sax. *coccel*, tares; comp. Gael. *cogal*, Fr. *coquiole*, cockle.] A plant that grows among corn, the corn cockle.

cockle, kok′l, *n.* [Dim. from Fr. *coque*, a cockle, a shell, from L. *concha*, Gr. *kongchē*, a mussel or cockle.] A heart-shaped mollusk with wrinkled shells, common on the sandy shores of Europe and much used as food; a kind of stove, a stove in which the fuel chamber is surrounded by an open space.—*v.t.* and *i.*—**cockled, cockling**. [Perhaps from *cockle*, the shell, marked with wrinkles.] To wrinkle or ridge; to give or assume a wrinkled or ridged surface (as a piece of paper).

cockney, kok′ni, *n.* [Usually connected with the old term *Cockaigne*, land of abundance, perhaps from L. *coquo*, to cook.] A native or resident of London: used slightingly or by way of contempt.—*a.* Related to or like cockneys.—**cockneydom**, kok′ni·dum, *n.* The region or home of cockneys, a contemptuous or humorous name for London and its suburbs.—**cockneyfy**, kok′ni·fī, *v.t.* To make like a cockney.—**cockneyish**, kok′ni·ish, *a.* Relating to or like cockneys.—**cockneyism**, kok′ni·izm, *n.* The condition, qualities, manner, or dialect of the cockneys; a peculiarity of the dialect of the Londoners.

cockroach, kok′rōch, *n.* [Sp. *cucar-acha*, a wood louse, a cockroach.] An orthopterous insect, the so-called black beetle, very troublesome in houses, where they often multiply to a great extent, infesting kitchens and pantries.

cocksure, kok′shör, *a.* [Said to be derived from the *cock* of a musket, as being much more reliable than the match of the old matchlock.] Perfectly secure (*Shak.*)‡; confidently certain. (Colloq.)

cockswain, kok′swän or kok′sn, *n.* [*Cock*, a boat, and *swain*.] The person who steers a boat; a person on board a ship who has the care of a boat. Also *coxswain*.

coco, kō′kō, *n.* [Pg. *coco*, from *coco*, a bugbear, a distorted mask, from the monkey-like face at the base of the nut.] The coconut palm.—**coconut**, kō′kō·nut, *n.* The large, egg-shaped fruit of the coconut palm.—**coconut palm**, *n.* A tall, slender tropical tree.

cocoa, kō′kō, *n.* [Corruption of *cacao*.] Roasted and pulverized cacao seeds; a drink made from this powder.

cocoon, ko·kön′, *n.* [Fr. *cocon*, from

coque, a shell, from L. *concha*, a shell-fish.] The silky tissue or envelope which the larvae of many insects spin as a covering for themselves while they are in the chrysalis state.

cod, codfish, kod, kod′fish, *n.* [D. *kodde*, a club, from its large club-shaped head.] A species of fish of great commercial importance, inhabiting northern seas; used as food either fresh, salted, or dried, and yielding cod-liver oil.—**codling**, kod′-ling, *n.* A young cod.—**cod-liver oil**, *n.* An important medical oil obtained from the liver of the common cod.

cod, kod, *n.* [A.Sax. *cod, codd*, a small bag; Icel. *koddi*, a pillow; Sw. *kudde*, a cushion.] Any husk, envelope, or case containing the seeds of a plant; a pod.—*v.t.* To enclose in a cod.—**codling**, kod′ling, *n.* A term applied to several cultivated varieties of kitchen apple.—**codling moth**, *n.* A small moth, the larva of which feeds on the apple.

coda, kō′da, *n.* [It., from L. *cauda*, a tail.] *Music*, an adjunct to the close of a composition, for the purpose of enforcing the final character of the movement.

coddle, kod′l, *v.t.*—**coddled, coddling**. [O.Fr. *cadeler*, to cocker, pamper, make much of, *cadel*, an animal cast or born out of time, from L. *cado*, to fall.] To make effeminate by pampering; to make much of; to treat tenderly like an invalid; to pamper; to cocker.—*n.* An over-indulged, pampered being.

code, kōd, *n.* [Fr., from L. *codex*, the trunk of a tree, a tablet, a book.] A systematic collection or digest, of laws; any system or body of rules or laws relating to one subject; a system of signals or the like agreed upon; *teleg.* a set of words representing others for purposes of secrecy.—**codify**, kod′i·fī, *v.t.* To reduce to a code or digest, as laws.—**codification**, kod′i·fi·kā″shin, *n.* The act or process of codifying.—**codifier**, kod′i·fī·ér, *n.* One who codifies.—**codex**, kō′deks, *n.* pl. **codices**, kō′di·sēz. A manuscript volume, as of a Greek or Latin classic, or of the Scriptures.

codger, koj′ér, *n.* [Probably a form of *cadger* (which see).] A mean miserly man; a curious old fellow; an odd fish; a character; a familiar term of address. (Slang.)

codical, kod′i·kal, *a.* Relating to a codex or to a code.—**codicil**, kod′i·sil, *n.* [L. *codicillus*, dim. of *codex*.] A writing by way of supplement to a will, containing anything which the testator wishes to add, or any revocation or explanation of what the will contains.—**codicillary**, kod·-i·sil′la·ri, *a.* Of the nature of a codicil.

coed, kō′ed, *n.* [Short for *coeducational student*.] A female student in a coeducational institution.—**coeduca-tion**, kō′ed·ū·kā″shon, *n.* Joint education of both sexes in the same institution.—**coeducational**, kō′ed-ū·kā″shon·al, *a.*

coefficient, kō·ef·fish′ent, *a.* Cooperating, acting in union to the same end.—*n.* That which unites in action with something else to produce the same effect; *alg.* a number or known quantity put before letters or quantities, known or unknown, into which it is supposed to be multiplied.—*Coefficient of expansion*, in heat, for a given material a small fraction denoting the portion of its size by which it increases when heated through one degree of temperature.—*Coefficient of friction*, the constant ratio of the retarding force of friction between two surfaces to the mutual pressure between them. —*Coefficient of performance* (marine engineering), coefficient involving the efficiency of the engine and the efficiency of the screw, required in obtaining the speed of a ship in terms of engine power.—*Coefficient of restitution*, the radio of the relative velocity of two bodies after impact to their relative velocity before impact.

coelenterate, sē·len'tėr·āt, *n.* [Gr. *koilos*, hollow, *enteron*, an intestine.] Any of a group of aquatic invertebrates having a hollow saclike body but no head or segmentation, including corals, sea anemones, jellyfishes, etc.—**Coelenterata**, sē·len'tėr·ā"ta, *n. pl.* The coelenterate animals; the phylum consisting of the Hydrozoa, the Scyphozoa, and the Anthozoa.—**coelenteron**, sē·len'tėr·on, *n.* The digestive body cavity of coelenterates.

coeliac, celiac, sē'li·ak, *a.* [Gr. *koiliakos*, from *koilia*, the belly, *koilos*, hollow.] Pertaining to the cavity of the abdomen.

coelodont, sē'lo·dont, *a.* [Gr. *koilos*, hollow, *odous, odontos*, a tooth.] Having hollow teeth: said of certain lizard-like reptiles.—**coelom**, sē'lom, *n.* [Gr. *koilōma*, a cavity.] In animals, a secondary body cavity; the body cavity of metazoans.

coenesthesis, sē·nes·thē'sis, *n.* [Gr. *koinos*, common, and *aisthēsis*, perception.] The general sensibility of the system, as distinguished from the special sensations (sight, smell, etc.).

coenobite, sē'no·bīt. Same as *Cenobite*.

coequal, kō·ē'kwal, *a.* Equal with another person or thing; of the same rank, dignity, or power.—*n.* One who is equal to another.—**coequality**, kō·ē·kwol'i·ti, *n.* The state of being coequal.—**coequally**, kō·ē'kwal·li, *adv.* With joint equality.

coerce, kō·ėrs', *v.t.* [L. *coerceo*—prefix *co*, and *arcere*, to shut up, confine.] To restrain by force, particularly by moral force, as by law or authority; to repress; to compel to compliance; to constrain.—**coercible**, kō·ėr'si·bl, *a.* Capable of being coerced.—**coercion**, kō·ėr'shon, *n.* The act of coercing; restraint; compulsion; constraint.—**coercive**, kō·ėr'siv, *a.* Capable of coercing; restrictive; able to force into compliance.—*n.* That which coerces; that which constrains or restrains.—**coercively**, kō·ėr'siv·li,

adv. By constraint or coercion.

coessential, kō·es·sen'shal, *a.* Having the same essence.—**coessentiality**, kō·es·sen·shi·al"i·ti, *n.* The fact of having the same essence.

coetaneous,† kō·ē·tā'nē·us, *a.* [L. *coætaneus*—prefix *co*, and *ætas*, age.] Of the same age with another; beginning to exist at the same time; coeval.—**coetaneously**, kō·ē·tā'nē·us·li, *adv.* Of or from the same age or beginning.

coeternal, kō·ē·tėr'nal, *a.* Equally eternal with another.—**coeternally**, kō·ē·tėr'nal·li, *adv.* With coeternity or equal eternity.—**coeternity**, kō·ē·tėr'ni·ti, *n.* Existence from eternity equal with another eternal being; equal eternity.

coeval, kō·ē'val, *a.* [L. *coævus*—*con*, and *ævum*, age.] Of the same age; having lived for an equal period; existing at the same time, or of equal antiquity in general (*coeval with* a person).—*n.* One who is coeval; one who lives at the same time.

coexecutor, kō·ek·sek'ū·tėr, *n.* A joint executor.—**coexecutrix**, kō·ek·sek'ū·triks, *n.* A joint executrix.

coexist, kō·eg·zist', *v.i.* To exist at the same time with another (to *coexist with*).—**coexistence**, kō·eg·zis'tens, *n.* Existence at the same time with another; contemporary existence.—**coexistent**, kō·eg·zis'tent, *a.* Existing at the same time with another.

coextend, kō·eks·tend', *v.t. and i.* To extend through the same space or duration with another; to extend equally.—**coextension**, kō·eks·ten'shon, *n.* The fact or state of being equally extended with something else.—**coextensive**, kō·eks·ten'siv, *a.* Equally extensive; having equal scope or extent.—**coextensively**, kō·eks·ten'siv·li, *adv.* So as to exhibit coextension.

coffee, kof'i, *n.* [Fr. *café*, from Turk. *qahveh*, coffee.] The berries or the ground seeds of a tree, a native of Arabia and tropical Africa, but now extensively cultivated throughout tropical countries, each berry containing two seeds, commonly called coffee beans; a drink made from the roasted and ground seeds of the coffee tree, by infusion or decoction. —**coffee bean**, *n.* A coffee seed.— **coffeehouse** *n.* A house of entertainment where guests are supplied with coffee and other refreshments. —**coffeepot**, *n.* A covered pot in which the decoction or infusion of coffee is made, or in which it is brought upon the table for drinking. —**coffeeroom** *n.* A public room in an inn or hotel where guests are supplied with refreshments.— *n.* **coffee tree**, *n.* The tree which produces coffee.

coffer, kof'ėr, *n.* [Fr. *coffre*, O.Fr. *cofre, cofin*, a coffer, from L. *cophinus*, Gr. *kophinos*, a basket. *Coffin* is the same word.] A chest, trunk, or casket for holding jewels, money, or other valuables; a sunk panel or compartment in a ceiling of an ornamental character; a kind of

caisson or floating dock.—*v.t.* To deposit or lay up in a coffer.— **cofferdam**, *n.* A wooden enclosure formed in a river, etc., by driving two or more rows of piles close together, with clay packed in between the rows to exclude the water, and so obtain a firm and dry foundation for bridges, piers, etc.

coffin, kof'in, *n.* [O.Fr. *cofin*, a chest, L. *cophinus*, a basket. COFFER.] The chest or box in which a dead human body is buried or deposited in a vault; a casing of paste for a pie (*Shak.*)‡; the hollow part of a horse's hoof.—*v.i.* To put or enclose in a coffin.—**coffin bone**, *n.* A small spongy bone enclosed in the hoof of a horse.

cog, kog, *v.t.*—*cogged, cogging.* [W. *coegio, coegiaw*, to trick, from *coeg*, empty, vain.] To flatter; to wheedle; to draw from by flattery; to foist or palm: now hardly used except in regard to dice, *to cog a die* being to load it so as to direct its fall, for the purpose of cheating.—*v.i.* To cheat; to wheedle; to lie.—*n.* A trick or deception.

cog, kog, *n.* [Sw. *kugg, kugge*, a cog.] The tooth of a wheel, by which it drives another wheel or body, or any similar mechanical contrivance. —**cogwheel**, *n.* A wheel with cogs or teeth.—*v.t.*—*cogged, cogging.* To furnish with cogs.

cogent, kō'jent, *a.* [L. *cogens, cogentis*, forcing, compelling, from *cogo*—*con*, together, and *ago*, to lead or drive.] Compelling in a physical sense†; resistless†; convincing; having the power to compel conviction; powerful; not easily resisted; forcible; irresistible: of arguments, proofs reasoning, etc.—**cogently**, kō'jent·li, *adv.* In a cogent manner; powerfully; forcibly.—**cogency**, kō'jen·si, *n.* The quality of being cogent; power of moving the will or reason; power of compelling conviction; force; conclusiveness.

cogitate, koj'i·tāt, *v.i.*—*cogitated, cogitating.* [L. *cogito, cogitatum*—*co* for *con*, together, and *agito*, to shake, to agitate. AGITATE.] To think; to meditate; to ponder.—**cogitation**, koj·i·tā'shon, *n.* The act of cogitating or thinking; thought; meditation; contemplation.—**cogitative**, koj'i·tā·tiv, *a.* Thinking; having the power of cogitating; meditative; given to thought.—**cogitatively**, koj'i·tā·tiv·li, *adv.* In a cogitative or thinking manner.—**cogitable**, koj'i·ta·bl, *a.* Capable of being thought; capable of being conceived.—*n.* Anything capable of being the subject of thought.

cognac, kō·nyak', *n.* [Fr.] A kind of French brandy, so called from the town of the same name, where large quantities are made.

cognate, kog'nāt, *a.* [L. *cognatus*—prefix *co* for *con*, with, and *gnatus*, old form of *natus*, born.] Allied by blood; kindred by birth; *law*, connected by the mother's side; related in origin generally; proceeding from the same stock or root; of the same family (words, roots, languages);

allied in nature; having affinity of any kind (*cognate* sounds).—*n.* One connected with another by ties of kindred; *law*, a relation connected by the mother's side; anything related to another by origin or nature.—**cognation,** kog·nā´shon, *n.* [L. *cognatio.*] Relationship by descent from the same original; affinity; resemblance in nature or character.

cognition, kog·ni´shon, *n.* [L. *cognitio; cognosco, cognitus*—*co* for *con,* and *nosco,* anciently *gnosco,* to know.] Knowledge from personal view or experience; perception; a thing known.—**cognitive,** kog´ni·tiv, *a.* Knowing or apprehending by the understanding.—**cognizable,** kog´·niz·a·bl or kon´, *a.* Capable of falling under notice or observation; capable of being known, perceived, or apprehended; capable of falling under judicial notice.—**cognizably,** kog´niz·a·bli or kon´, *adv.* In a cognizable manner.—**cognizance,** kog´ni·zans or kon´, *n.* [O.Fr. *cognoissance, connoissance.*] Knowledge or notice; perception; observation; *law,* judicial or authoritative notice or knowledge, also right to try and determine causes; a crest; a badge; a badge worn by a retainer, soldier, etc., to indicate the person or party to which he belongs.—**cognizant,** kog´ni·zant or kon´, *a.* Acquainted with; having obtained knowledge of; competent to take legal or judicial notice.—**cognize,** kog·nīz´, *v.t.*—*cognized; cognizing.* To recognize as an object of thought; to perceive; to become conscious of; to know.

cognomen, kog·nō´men, *n.* [L. *cognomen*—prefix *co* for *con,* and *nomen,* formerly *gnomen,* a name.] Strictly the last of the three names by which a Roman of good family was known, indicating the family to which he belonged; hence a surname or distinguishing name in general.

cognoscible, kog·nos´i·bl, *a.* [From L. *cognosco.* COGNITION.] Capable of being known; subject to judicial investigation.—**cognoscibility,** kog·nos´i·bil´´i·ti, *n.* The quality of being cognoscible.

cohabit, kō·hab´it, *v.i.* [L. *cohabito,* from *eo,* with, and *habito,* to dwell.] To dwell or live together as husband and wife; often applied to persons not legally married, and suggesting sexual intercourse.—**cohabitation,** kō·hab´l·tä´shon, *n.* The state of living together as man and wife.

coheir, kō·ār´, *n.* A joint heir; one who succeeds to a share of an inheritance divided among two or more.—**coheiress,** kō´ār·es, *n.* A joint heiress.

cohere, kō·hēr´, *v.i.*—*cohered, cohering.* [L. *cohæro*—*co* for *con,* and *hæro,* to stick together.] To stick or cleave together; to be united; to keep in close contact as parts of the same mass, or as two substances that attract each other; to hang well together; to agree or be consistent (as parts of a discourse or an argument).—**coherence, coherency,** kō·hē´rens, kō·hē´ren·si, *n.* The

state of cohering; a cleaving together of bodies by means of attraction; suitable connection or dependence; due agreement as of ideas; consistency.—**coherent,** kō·hē´rent, *a.* Cohering or sticking together; united; having a due agreement of parts; hanging well together; consecutive; observing due agreement; consistent (a *coherent* argument or discourse, a *coherent* speaker).—**coherently,** kō·hē´rent·li, *adv.* In a coherent manner.—**coherer,** kō·hēr´ẽr, *n.* In wireless telegraphy, the essential part of the receiving instrument.—**cohesion,** kō·hē´zhon, *n.* [Fr. *cohésion.*] The act or state of cohering, uniting, or sticking together; logical connection; *physics,* the state in which, or the force by which, the particles of bodies of the same nature are kept in contact so as to form a continuous mass.—**cohesion,** kō·hē´zhun, *n.* [L. *cohæro, cohesum,* I stick to.] In flowers, the union of like parts, e.g. petals.—**cohesive,** kō·hē´siv, *a.* Causing cohesion.—**cohesively,** kō·hē´siv·li, *adv.* In a cohesive manner; with cohesion.—**cohesiveness,** kō·hē´siv·nes, *n.* The quality of being cohesive; the tendency to unite by cohesion.

cohort, kō´hort, *n.* [L. *cohors, cohortis.*] In Roman armies, the tenth part of a legion, a body of about 500 or 600 men; a band or body of warriors in general.

coif, koif, *n.* [Fr. *coiffe,* L.L. *cofia, cufia,* from M.H.G. *kuffe, kupfe,* a kind of cap.] A close-fitting cap or headdress worn usually by nuns, a hood without a cape; a cap of mail.—*v.t.* To cover with a coif.—**coiffure,** kwä·für´, *n.* A style of arranging the hair.

coign,‡ koin, *n.* A corner; a coin or quoin. (*Shak.*)

coil, koil, *v.t.* [O.Fr. *coillir, cueillir,* from L. *colligere,* to collect. COLLECT.] To gather (a rope, chain, etc.) into a series of rings above one another; to twist or wind spirally.—*v.i.* To form rings or spirals; to wind.—*n.* A ring or series of rings or spirals into which a rope or other pliant body is wound.

coin, koin, *n.* [Fr. *coin,* a wedge, the die with which money is stamped, a coin, a corner, from L. *cuneus,* a wedge.] A piece of metal, as gold, silver, copper, or some alloy, converted into money by impressing some stamp on it; such pieces collectively; metallic currency; money; also, a quoin.—*v.t.* To stamp and convert into money; to mint; to make, fabricate, or invent.—**coinage,** koi´nij, *n.* The stamping of money; coin; money coined; the act of inventing, forming, or producing; invention; fabrication; what is fabricated or produced.—**coiner,** koi´nẽr, *n.* One who coins; a maker of money; often a maker of base or counterfeit coin; an inventor or maker, as of words.

coincide, kō·in·sīd´, *v.i.*—*coincided, coinciding.* [L.L. *coincido,* from L. prefix *co,* with, and *incido,* to fall in—*in,* and *cado,* to fall.] To occupy

the same place in space, or the same position in a scale or series; to happen at the same point of time; to be exactly contemporaneous; to correspond exactly; to concur; to agree (to *coincide with* a person *in* an opinion).—**coincidence,**† kō·in´si·dens, *n.* The fact of coinciding; exact correspondence in position; a happening or agreeing in time; contemporaneousness; agreement in circumstance, character, etc.; exact correspondence generally, or a case of exact correspondence.—**coincident, coincidental,** kō·in´si·dent, kō·in·si·den´tal, *a.* Coinciding; happening at the same time; concurrent; exactly corresponding.—**coincidently,** kō·in´si·dent·li, *adv.* In a coincident manner; with coincidence.

coinheritance, kō·in·her´it·ans, *n.* Joint inheritance.—**coinheritor,** kō·in·her´it·ẽr, *n.* A joint heir; a coheir.

coir, koir, *n.* A species of yarn manufactured from the husk of cocoanuts, and formed into cordage, sailcloth, matting, etc.

coition, kō·i´shon, *n.* [L. *coitio*—*con,* and *eo, itum,* to go.] A coming together; copulation.

coke, kōk, *n.* [Perhaps from *cook* or *cake*; comp. *caking* coal.] Coal deprived of its bitumen, sulfur, or other extraneous or volatile matter by fire.—*v.t.*—*coked, coking.* To convert into coke; to deprive of volatile matter, as coal.

col, kol, *n.* [Fr., neck.] An elevated mountain pass between two higher summits; the most elevated part of a mountain pass.

colander, kul´an·dẽr or kol´an·dẽr, *n.* [From L. *colans, colantis,* ppr. of *colo,* to strain, from *colum,* a colander.] A vessel with a bottom perforated with little holes for straining liquids; a strainer.

colatitude, kō·lat´i·tūd, *n.* [Abbrev. of *complement* and *latitude.*] The complement of the latitude, or what it wants of 90°.

colchicum, kol´chi·kum, *n.* [L., a plant with a poisonous root, from *Colchis,* the native country of Medea, the famous sorceress.] A genus of liliaceous plants, the most familiar species being the meadow saffron, a plant with a solid bulblike rootstock and purple, crocus-like flowers, found in various parts of Europe.—**colchicine,** kol´chi·sin, *n.* An alkaloid obtained from colchicum bulbs, and used for the alleviation or cure of gout and rheumatism.

colcothar, kol´ko·thär, *n.* [Probably of Ar. origin.] The brownish-red peroxide of iron, used for polishing glass and other substances.

cold, kōld, *a.* [A.Sax. *cald, ceald, a,* and *n.*=Dan. *kold,* Icel. *kaldr,* Sw. *kall,* D. *koud,* Goth. *kaldo,* G. *kalt*; from root of *cool, chill,* which also appears in L. *gelidus,* gelid.] Not warm or hot; gelid; frigid; chilling; cooling; having the sensation of coolness; wanting warmth or animal heat; chill; wanting passion, zeal, or ardor; insensible; not animated or easily excited into action; not affectionate, cordial, or friendly;

unaffecting; not animated or animating; not able to excite feeling or interest; spiritless.—*In cold blood*, without excitement, emotion, or passion.—*To give, show, or turn the cold shoulder*, to treat a person with studied coldness, neglect, or contempt.—*n.* The relative absence or want of heat; the cause of the sensation of coolness; the sensation produced in animal bodies by the escape of heat; an indisposition occasioned by cold; a catarrh.—**coldly,** kōld′li, *adv.* In a cold manner; without warmth; without concern; without apparent passion, emotion, or feeling; with indifference or negligence; dispassionately; calmly.—**coldness,** kōld′nes, *n.* The state or quality of being cold; frigidity; indifference.—**cold-blooded,** *a.* Having cold blood; without sensibility or feeling; *zool.* a term applied to those animals the temperature of whose blood is a very little higher than that of their habitat.—**cold chisel,** *n.* A chisel for cutting metal in its cold state.—**cold cream,** *n.* A kind of cooling unguent for the skin, variously prepared.

cole, kōl, *n.* [From L. *colis, caulis*, a cabbage-stalk, a cabbage.] The general name of all sorts of cabbage.—**coleslaw,** kōl′slą. A salad made of sliced cabbage leaves.

colemanite, kōl′man·īt, *n.* A mineral.

Coleoptera, kol·ē·op′tėr·a, *n. pl.* [Gr. *koleos*, a sheath, and *pteron*, a wing.] An order of insects commonly known by the name of *beetles*, and characterized by having four wings, of which the two anterior, called elytra, are not suited for flight, but form a covering and protection to the two posterior, and are of a hard and horny or parchment-like nature.—**coleopteran,** kol·ē·op′tėr·an, *n.* A member of the order Coleoptera.—**coleopterous,** kol·ē·op′tėr·us, *a.* Pertaining or belonging to the Coleoptera.

coleorhiza, kol′ē·o·rī″za, *n.* [Gr. *koleos*, a sheath, and *rhiza*, a root.] *Bot.* the sheath which covers the young radicle of monocotyledonous plants.

colic, kol′ik, *n.* [L. *colicus*, Gr. *kōlikos*, from *kōlon*, the colon.] A painful spasmodic affection of the intestines.—**colicky,** kol′ik·i, *a.*

colin, kol′in, *n.* [Fr.] The Virginian quail or American partridge.

collaborate, kol·lab′o·rāt, *v.i.* [L. *collaboratus*, from *com*, together, and *labore*, to labor.] To work together, especially on scientific or literary efforts; to cooperate with the enemy.—**collaborator,** kol·lab′o·rā·tėr, *n.* [Fr. *collaborateur*—L. *col* for *con*. together, and *laboro*, to labor.] An assistant; an associate in labor, especially in literary or scientific pursuits.—**collaboration,** kol·lab′o·rā′shon, *n.*

collapse, kol·laps′, *v.i.*—*collapsed, collapsing.* [L. *collabor, collapsus*—*col* for *con*, and *labor, lapsus*, to slide or fall (whence *lapse*).] To fall in or together, as the two sides of a vessel; to close by falling together; hence, to come to nothing; to break down.—*n.* A falling in or together, as of the sides of a hollow vessel; a more or less sudden failure of the vital powers; a sudden and complete failure of any kind; a breakdown.—**collapsible,** kol·lap′si·bl, *a.* Capable of collapsing or being made to collapse.

collar, kol′ėr, *n.* [L. *collare*, Fr. *collier*, a collar, from L. *collum*, the neck.] Something worn round the neck, whether for use or ornament or both, or it may be for restraint; the necklace or chain worn by knights, and having the badge of the order appended to it; part of the harness of an animal used for draft; an article of dress or part of a garment going round the neck; something resembling a collar; anything in the form of a ring, especially at or near the end of something else.—*To slip the collar*, to escape or get free; to disentangle one's self.—*v.t.* To seize by the collar; to put a collar on; to roll up and bind with cord (a piece of meat) for keeping for a time.—**collarbone,** *n.* The clavicle; one of the two bones of the thorax in man and many quadrupeds joined at one end to the shoulder bone and at the other to the breastbone.

collate, kol·lāt′, *v.t.*—*collated, collating.* [L. *confero, collatum*, to bring together, compare, bestow—*col* for *con*, and *fero, latum*, to carry.] To bring together and compare; to examine critically, noting points of agreement and disagreement (manuscripts and books); to confer or bestow (a benefice) on (to *collate* a person *to* a church); to gather and place in order, as the sheets of a book for binding.—**collation,** kol·lā′shon, *n.* The act of collating; a comparison, especially the comparison of manuscripts or editions of books; the presentation of a clergyman to a benefice by a bishop who has the benefice in his own gift, or by neglect of the patron has acquired the patron's rights; the reading of passages in Scripture and in the Fathers, in Benedictine monasteries, followed by a discussion and light repast.—**collator,** kol·lā′tėr, *n.* One who collates.

collateral, kol·lat′ėr·al, *a.* [L.L. *collateralis*—*col* for *con*, and L. *lateralis*, from *latus*, a side.] At the side; belonging to the side or what is at the side; acting indirectly; acting through side channels; accompanying but subordinate; auxiliary; subsidiary; descending from the same ancestor, but not in a direct line, as distinguished from *lineal*.—*n.* Pertaining to an obligation or security attached to another to secure its performance; hence, guaranteed by security as in a loan.

colleague, kol′lēg, *n.* [L. *collega*, a colleague—*col* for *con*, and stem of *lego, legatum*, to send on a mission.] A partner or associate in the same office, employment, or commission, civil or ecclesiastical.—**colleagueship,** kol′lēg·ship, *n.* The state of being a

colleague in office or special work.

collect, kol·lekt′, *v.t.* [L. *colligo, collectum*—*col* for *con*, and *lego*, to gather, which appears also in *neglect, select, analect*, etc., also *coil, cull*.] To gather into one body or place; to assemble or bring together; to gather; to infer or conclude (in this sense now rare).—*To collect one's self*, to recover from surprise or a disconcerted state.—*v.i.* To run together; to accumulate.—*n.* (kol′lekt). A short comprehensive prayer; a form of prayer adapted to a particular day or occasion.—**collectanea,** kol·lek·tā′nē·a, *n. pl.* [L., things collected.] A selection of passages from various authors, usually made for the purpose of instruction; a miscellany.—**collected,** kol·lek′ted, *p.* and *a.* Gathered together; not disconcerted; cool; firm; prepared; self-possessed.—**collectedly,** kol·lek′ted·li, *adv.* In one view; together; in a cool, firm, or self-possessed manner.—**collectedness,** kol·lek′ted·nes, *n.* The state of being collected.—**collectible,** kol·lek′ti·bl, *a.* Capable of being collected.—**collection,** kol·lek′shon, *n.* The act or practice of collecting or of gathering; that which is collected or gathered together (as pictures or objects of interest); that which is collected for a charitable, religious, or other purpose; the jurisdiction of a collector; a collectorship; the act of deducing from premises, or that which is deduced (*Mil.*)‡—**collective,** kol·lek′tiv, *a.* [L. *collectivus*, Fr. *collectif*.] Formed by collecting; gathered into a mass, sum, or body; aggregate, *gram.* expressing a number or multitude united, though in the singular number (a *collective noun*).—*Collective note*, in *diplomacy* an official communication signed by the representatives of several governments.—*n. Gram.* a noun with a singular form comprehending in its meaning several individuals, such as *people, infantry, crowd*.—**collectively,** kol·lek′tiv·li, *adv.* In a collective manner; in a mass or body; in the aggregate; unitedly.—**collectivism,** kol·lek′tiv·izm, *n.* The socialistic doctrine that the land and means of production should belong to the people collectively. Also **collectivist.**—**collector,** kol·lek′tėr, *n.* One who collects; especially, one who collects objects of interest; an officer appointed to collect and receive customs, duties, taxes, etc., within a certain district.—**collectorship,** kol·lek′tėr·ship, *n.* The office or jurisdiction of a collector.

college, kol′ej, *n.* [L. *collegium*, a society, guild, or fraternity, from *collega*, a colleague. COLLEAGUE.] A society of men invested with certain powers and rights, performing certain duties, or engaged in some common pursuit, a guild, a corporation, especially a society or institution for purposes of instruction and scientific research in the higher branches of knowledge; the edifice belonging to a college.—**collegial,†**

kol·lē'ji·al, *a.* Pertaining to a college; collegiate.—**collegian**, kol·lē'ji·an, *n.* A member of a college, particularly of a literary institution so called; a student.—**collegiate**, kol·lē'ji·āt, *a.* Pertaining to a college (*collegiate* studies); constituted after the manner of a college.—*Collegiate church*, a church that has no cathedral, but does have a college of canons, or a dean, as Westminster Abbey; in the U. S., a church in an association of churches.

collenchyma, kol·len'ki·ma, *n.* [Gr. *kolla*, glue, and *enchyma*, an infusion.] *Bot.* the cellular matter in which pollen is generated.

collet, kol'et, *n.* [Fr. *collet*, a collar or necklace, from *col.* L. *collum*, the neck.] A band or collar; among jewelers, the horizontal face or plane at the bottom of brilliants, and the part of a ring containing the bezel in which the stone is set; *bot.* the neck or part of a plant from which spring the ascending and descending axes.

collide, kol·līd', *v.i.*—collided, colliding. [L. *collido*—col for *con*, and *lædo*, to strike.] To strike or dash against each other; to meet in shock; to meet in opposition or antagonism.—**collision**, kol·li'zhon, *n.* [L. *collisio*.] The act of striking or dashing together; the meeting and mutual striking of two or more moving bodies, or of a moving body with a stationary one; opposition; antagonism; interference.

collie, kol'i, *n.* [Origin doubtful.] A variety of dog especially common in Scotland, and much esteemed as a sheep dog.

collier, kol'yėr, *n.* [From *coal*; comp. *lawyer*, *sawyer*.] A digger of coal; one who works in a coal mine; a vessel employed in the coal trade.—**colliery**, kol'yėr·ri, *n.* The place where coal is dug; a coal mine or pit.

colligate, kol'li·gāt, *v.t.*—colligated, colligating. [L. *colligo*—col for *con*, and *ligo*, to bind.] To bind or fasten together; to connect by observing a certain relationship or similarity (to *colligate* phenomena).—**colligation**, kol·li·gā'shon, *n.* The act of colligating; that process by which many isolated facts are brought together under one general conception or observation.

collimation, kol·li·mā'shon, *n.* [From a fancied L. verb *collimare*, really a false reading for *collineare*—col, together, and *linea*, a line.] The act of leveling or of directing the sight to a fixed object.—*Line of collimation*, in an astronomical instrument, the straight line which passes through the center of the object glass, and intersects at right angles the fine wires which are fixed in the focus.—*Error of collimation*, the deviation of the actual line of sight in a telescope from the focus and center of the object glass, or from the proper position.—**collimate**, kol'li·māt, *v.t.* To adjust the line of collimation in.—**collimator**, kol·lim'ā·tėr, *n.* A small telescope used for adjusting the line of collimation.

collinear, kol·lin'ē·er, *a.* [L. *col* for *con*, and *linea*, a line.] Pertaining to or situated in a corresponding line.

collision. See COLLIDE.

collocate, kol'lo·kāt, *v.t.*—collocated, collocating. [L. *colloco*—col for *con*, together, and *loco*, to place, *locus*, a place.] To set or place; to set; to station.—**collocation**, kol·lo·kā'shon, *n.* [L. *collocatio*.] The act of collocating, placing, disposing, or arranging along with something else; the manner in which a thing is placed with regard to something else; disposition; arrangement.

collodion, kol·lō'di·on, *n.* [Gr. *kolla*, glue, and *eidos* resemblance.] A substance prepared by dissolving guncotton in ether, or in a mixture of ether and alcohol, used as a substitute for adhesive plaster in the case of slight wounds, and as the basis of a photographic process.—**colloid**, kol'loid, *a* Like glue or jelly; *chem.* applied to uncrystallizable liquids; *geol.* applied to partly amorphous minerals.—*n.* The name given to a transparent, viscid, yellowish, structureless or slightly granular matter, resembling liquid gelatine. CRYSTALLOID.—**colloidal**, kol·loi'dal, *a.* Of or pertaining to the nature of colloids.

collogue, ko·lōg', *v.i.* To plot together. (Colloq.)

collop, kol'op, *n.* [Perhaps lit. a piece of meat made tender by beating; Sw. *kollops*, G. *klopps*, meat that has been beaten; D. *kloppen*, G. *klopfen*, to beat; E. to *clap*.] A slice or lump of flesh.

colloquy, kol'lo·kwi, *n.* [L. *colloquium*—col, together, and *loquor*, to speak.] The mutual discourse of two or more; a conference; a dialogue; a conversation.—**colloquial**, kol·lō'kwi·al, *a.* Pertaining to conversation; peculiar to the place or usage of common conversation.—**colloquialism**, kol·lō'kwi·al·izm, *n.* A word or phrase peculiar to the language of common conversation.—**colloquially**, kol·lō'kwi·al·li, *adv.* In a colloquial or conversational manner; in colloquial language.

collotype, ko'lo·tīp, *n.* [Gr. *kolla*, glue.] Thin gelatinous plate etched by actinic rays and then printed from.

collude, kol·lūd', *v.i.*—colluded, colluding. [L. *colludo*—col, together, and *ludo*, to play, as in *allude*, *delude*.] To play into the hands of each other; to conspire in a fraud; to act in concert; to connive.—**colluder**, kol·lūd'ėr, *n.* One who colludes.—**collusion**, kol·lū'zhon, *n.* Secret agreement for a fraudulent purpose.—**collusive**, kol·lū'siv, *a.* Fraudulently concerted between two or more.—**collusively**, kol·lū'siv·li, *adv.* In a collusive manner; by collusion.—**collusiveness**, kol·lū'siv·nes, *n.* The quality of being collusive.

collyrium, kol·lir'i·um, *n.* [L.] Eye salve; eyewash.

colocynth, kol'o·sinth, *n.* [Gr. *kolokynthis*, a gourd or pumpkin.] A kind of cucumber, the fruit of the wild gourd, indigenous in the warmer parts of Asia, but now widely culti-

vated on account of its medicinal properties, being a purgative.

Cologne earth, ko·lōn', *n.* A kind of ochre of a deep-brown color, used in watercolor painting.—**Cologne water**, *n.* Eau de Cologne.

colon, kō'lon, *n.* [Gr. *kōlon*, the colon, a member or limb, a clause.] The largest portion of the human intestine, forming the middle section of the large intestine, and terminating in the rectum; a punctuation mark formed thus [:], used to mark a pause greater than that of a semicolon, but less than that of a period.

colonel, kėr'nel, *n.* [Formerly also *coronel*, which is an old French form and has given the modern pronunciation; Fr. *colonel*, O.Fr. *colonnel*, from It. *colonello*, a colonel, a little column, dim. of *colonna*, L. *columna*, a column; the name was originally given to the leading company in a regiment.] The chief commander of a regiment of troops, in any branch of service.—**colonelcy**, **colonelship**, kėr'nel·si, kėr'nel·ship, *n.* The office, rank, or commission of a colonel.

colonnade, kol·on·nād', *n.* [It *colonnata*, from *colonna*, a column. COLUMN.] *Arch.* any series or range of columns placed at certain intervals from each other, such intervals varying according to the rules of art and the order employed.

colony, kol'o·ni, *n.* [L. *colonia*, from *colo*, *cultum*, to till (hence *cultivate*, *culture*).] A body of people transplanted from their mother country to a remote province or country, and remaining subject to the jurisdiction of the parent state; a body of settlers or their descendants; the country planted or colonized; a number of animals or plants living or growing together.—**colonial**, ko·lō'ni·al, *a.* Pertaining to a colony.—*n.* A person belonging to a colony.—**colonist**, kol'on·ist, *n.* An inhabitant of or settler in a colony; a member of a colonizing expedition. — **colonize**, kol'on·īz, *v.t.*—colonized, colonizing. To plant or establish a colony in; to send a colony to; to migrate and settle in.—*v.i.* To move and settle in a distant country.—**colonization**, kol'on·iz·ā''shon, *n.* The act of colonizing or state of being colonized.—**colonizationist**, kol'on·iz·ā''shon·ist, *n.* An advocate for colonization.—**colonizer**, kol'on·īz·ėr, *n.* One who colonizes; one who establishes colonies.

colophon, kol'o·fon, *n.* [Gr. *kolophōn*, a summit, top, finishing.] A device, or printer's name, place of publication, and date, formerly put at the conclusion of a book; from the acme or finish of horsemanship displayed by the Ionians of Colophon.

colophony, kol'o·fo·ni, *n.* [Gr. *kolophōnia*, from *Colophōn*, a city of Ionia, whence the Greeks obtained it.] Black resin or turpentine boiled in water and dried.

coloquintida, kol·o·kwin'ti·da, *n.* The colocynth or bitter apple.

color, kul'ėr, *n.* [L. *color*, color.]

That in respect of which bodies have a different appearance to the eye independently of their form; any tint or hue distinguished from white; that which is used for coloring; a pigment; paint; the blood-red hue of the face; redness; complexion; false show; pretense; guise; *pl.* a flag, ensign, or standard borne in an army or fleet; a color used as a badge. —*Complementary colors*, colors which together make white; thus, any of the three primary colors is complementary to the other two.—*Primary colors*, red, green, and violet (or blue); or in a looser sense the colors into which white light is divided by a glass prism.—viz. red, orange, yellow, green, blue, indigo, and violet.—*v.t.* To impart color to; to dye; to tinge; to paint; to stain; *fig.* to clothe with an appearance different from the real; to give a specious appearance to; to make plausible.—*v.i.* To blush.—**colorable**, kul'ėr·a·bl, *a.* Specious; plausible; giving an appearance of right or justice (pretense, grounds); intended to deceive (a *colorable* imitation of a trademark). ∴ *Colorable*, having such an appearance as would not lead to the suspicion of anything underhand; *specious*, having a fair outside show, and likely to mislead thereby; *plausible*, apparently reasonable or satisfactory, though not convincing; *ostensible*, put forward as having a certain appearance but not really having it.—**colorableness**, kul'ėr·a·bl·nes, *n.* Speciousness.—**colorably**, kul'ėr·a·bli, *adv.* In a colorable manner.—**colored**, kul'ėrd, *p.* and *a.* Having a color; dyed, painted, or stained; having some other color than white or black; having a specious appearance; a term applied to the darker varieties of mankind; *bot.* applied to a leaf, calyx, seed, etc., to express any color except green. —**coloring**, kul'ėr·ing, *n.* The act or art of applying colors; color applied; tints or hues collectively, as in a picture; a specious appearance; show.—**colorist**, kul'ėr·ist, *n.* One who colors; a painter whose works are remarkable for beauty of color. —**colorless**, kul'ėr·les, *a.* Destitute of color.—**colorblind**, *a.* Incapable of accurately distinguishing colors; having an imperfect perception of colors.—**colorblindness**, *n.* Total or partial incapability of distinguishing colors, arising from some defect in the eye, though otherwise vision may be perfect.

colorate, kul'ėr·āt, *a.* [L. *coloratus*.] [*obs.*] Colored; dyed or tinged with some color.—**coloration**, kul·ėr·ā'shon, *n.* Coloring; the state of being colored; the tints of an object.— **colorific**, kul·ėr·if'ik, *a.* Having the quality of tingeing; able to give color or tint to other bodies.— **colorimeter**, kul·o·rim'et·ėr, *n.* An instrument for measuring the depth of color in a liquid by comparison with a standard liquid of the same tint.

colossus, ko·los'sus, *n.* pl. **colossi**, ko·los'sī, or rarely **colossuses**, ko··

los'sus·ez. [Gr. *kolossos*, a colossal statue.] A statue of a gigantic size or of size much greater than the natural, such as the statue of Apollo which anciently stood at the entrance to the port of Rhodes.— **colossal**, ko·los'sal, *a.* Like a colossus; much exceeding the size of nature; very large; huge; gigantic.

colostrum, ko·los'trum, *n.* [L.] The first milk secreted in the breasts after childbirth.

colporteur, kol'por·tėr, ė long, *n.* [Fr.—*col*, from L. *collum*, the neck, and *porteur*, a carrier, from L. *porto*, to carry.] A hawker of wares; a hawker of books and pamphlets, particularly a hawker of religious books and pamphlets.—**colportage**, kol'por·tij, *n.* The system of distributing religious books, tracts, etc., by colporteurs.

colt, kōlt, *n.* [A.Sax. *colt*, a young ass, a young camel; comp. Sw. *kult*, a young boar, a stout boy.] A young horse, or a young animal of the horse genus; commonly and distinctively applied to the male, *filly* being the female; a young camel or a young ass (O.T.)‡.—**coltish**, kōl'tish, *a.* Like a colt; wanton; frisky; gay. —**coltsfoot**, *n.* The popular name of a composite plant whose leaves were once much employed in medicine; *Tussilago*.

colubrine, kol'ū·brīn, *a.* [L. *colubrinus*, from *coluber*, a serpent.] Relating to serpents; cunning; crafty.

columbarium, kol·um·bā'ri·um, *n.* [L. *columba*, pigeon.] An ancient sepulchre with recesses for urns containing the ashes of the dead.

Columbian, ko·lum'bi·an, *a.* [From *Columbia*, a name sometimes given to the United States, after Christopher *Columbus*.] Pertaining to the United States or to America.

columbine, kol'um·bīn, *a.* [L. *columbinus*, from *columba*, a pigeon.] Like or pertaining to a pigeon or dove; of a dove color; resembling the neck of a dove in color.—*n.* [L. *columbina*.] A plant of the buttercup family, so called from the curved petals being in shape somewhat like pigeons, the sepals forming the wings; [*cap.*] the name of the mistress of Harlequin in pantomimes.

columbium, ko·lum'bi·um, *n.* [From *Columbia*, America.] A rare metal; niobium.—**columbite**, ko·lum'bīt, *n.* The ore of columbium.

columella, kol·ū·mel'a, *n.* [L. dim. of *columna*, column.] A name for various plants having column-like parts.

column, kol'um, *n.* [L. *columna*, a column, from root which appears in *collis*, a hill, *culmen*, a summit.] A solid body of considerably greater length than thickness, standing upright, and generally serving as a support to something resting on its top; a pillar; anything resembling a column in shape (a *column* of water, air, or mercury); *bot.* the united stamens and styles of plants when they form a solid central body, as in orchids; *milit.* a formation of troops, narrow in front, and deep

from front to rear; *naut.* a body of ships following each other; *printing* and *writing*, a division of a page; a perpendicular set of lines separated from another set by a line or blank space.—**columella**, kol·ū·mel'la, *n.* [L. *columella*, dim. of *columen* or *columna*, a column.] *Bot.* the central column in the capsule of mosses, from which the spores separate; the axis round which the parts of a fruit are arranged; *conch.* the upright pillar in the center of most of the univalve shells.—**columnar**, ko··lum'nėr, *a.* Formed in columns; like the shaft of a column.— **columned**, kol'umd, *a.* Furnished with columns; supported on or adorned by columns.—**columniation**, ko·lum'ni·ā''shon, *n. Arch.* the employment of columns in a design.

colure, kol'ūr, *n.* [Gr. *kolouros*, docktailed (with *grammē*, a line, understood)—*kolos*, stunted, and *oura*, a tail, because a part is always beneath the horizon.] Either of the two great circles supposed to intersect each other at right angles in the poles of the world, one of them passing through the solstitial and the other through the equinoctial points of the ecliptic, the points where they intercept the ecliptic being called cardinal points.

colza, kol'za, *n.* [Fr. *colza*, O.Fr. *colzat*, from D. *koolzaad*, lit. cabbage seed—*kool*, cabbage, and *zaad*, seed.] A variety of cabbage whose seeds afford an oil much employed for burning in lamps, and for many other purposes.

coma, kō'ma, *n.* [Gr. *kōma*, lethargy.] A state of more or less complete insensibility and loss of power of thought or motion; lethargy.— **comatose**, kō'ma·tōs, *a.* Pertaining to coma; drowsy; lethargic.

coma, kō'ma, *n.* [L., the hair.] *Bot.* the empty leaf or bract terminating the flowering stem of a plant, in a tuft or bush; also, the silky hairs at the end of some seeds; *astron.* the nebulous hairlike envelope surrounding the nucleus of a comet.—**comate**, kō'māt, *a.* [L. *comatus*.] Hairy; furnished with a coma.

comb, kōm, *n.* [A.Sax. *camb*, a comb, a crest=D. *kam*, Icel. *kambr*, a comb, a crest; Dan. *kam*, a comb, a cam; G. *kamm*, a comb.] An instrument with teeth for separating, cleansing, and adjusting hair, wool, or flax; also, an instrument used by women for keeping the hair in its place when dressed; the crest, caruncle, or red fleshy tuft growing on a cock's head; the top or crest of a wave; honeycomb.—*v.t.* To dress with a comb.—*v.i.* To roll over, as the top of a wave, or to break with a white foam.—**comber**, kōm'ėr, *n.* One who combs; one whose occupation is to comb wool, etc.

combat, kom'bat or kum'bat, *v.i.* [Fr. *combattre*—*com*, and *battre*, to beat. BATTER.] To fight; to struggle or contend.—*v.t.* To fight with; to oppose by force; to contend against; to resist: now chiefly *fig.* (he com-

bated their scruples.)—*n.* A fight; a struggle to resist, overthrow, or conquer; contest; engagement; battle.—*Single combat*, a fight between two individuals; a duel. ∴ Syn. under BATTLE.—**combatable**, kom·bat′a·bl, *a.* Capable of being combated, disputed, or opposed.—**combatant**, kom′ba·tant, *a.* Contending; disposed to combat or contend.—*n.* A person who combats; any person engaged in active war; a person who contends with another in argument or controversy.—**combative**, kom·bat′iv, *a.* Disposed to combat; showing such a disposition; pugnacious.—**combatively**, kom·bat′iv·li, *adv.* In a combative manner; pugnaciously.—**combativeness**, kom·bat′iv·nes, *n.* State of being combative; disposition to contend or fight.

combine, kom·bīn′, *v.t.*—*combined*, *combining*. [Fr. *combiner*, from the L.L. *combino*—*com*, and L. *binus*, two and two, or double.] To unite or join; to link closely together.—*v.i.* To unite, agree, or coalesce; to league together; to unite by affinity or chemical attraction.— kom′bīn, *n.* Group of persons or associations leagued together in a joint undertaking; a harvesting machine which cuts and threshes grain while traveling across a field.— **combinable**, kom·bī′na·bl, *a.*— **combination**, kom·bi·nā′shon, *n.* The act of combining; the act of joining, coming together, or uniting; union of particulars; concurrence; meeting; union or association of persons or things for effecting some object by joint operation; commixture; union of bodies or qualities in a mass or compound; chemical union; *math.* the union of a number of individuals in different groups, each containing a certain number of the individuals.—**combinative**, kom·bī′na·tiv, *a.* Tending to combine; uniting.—**combiner**, kom·bī′nėr, *n.* One who or that which combines.

combustible, kom·bus′ti·bl, *a.* [Fr. *combustible*, from L. *comburo*, *combustum*, to consume—*comb*, for *cum* or *con*, and *uro*, to burn; same root as Gr. *auein*, to kindle; Skr. *ush*, to burn.] Capable of taking fire and burning; flammable; *fig.* fiery or irascible; hot tempered.—*n.* A substance that will take fire and burn.— **combustibility**, **combustibleness**, kom·bus′ti·bil″i·ti, kom·bus′ti·bl·nes, *n.* The state or quality of being combustible.—**combustion**, kom·bus′chen, *n.* The operation of fire on flammable substances; burning; or, in chemical language, the union of a flammable substance with oxygen or some other supporter of combustion, attended with heat, and in most instances with light.— *Spontaneous combustion*, the ignition of a body by the internal development of heat without the application of an external flame.

come, kum, *v.i.*—*came* (pret.), *come* (pp.); *coming*. [A.Sax. *cuman* or *cwiman*=D. *komen*, Icel. *koma*, Dan.

komme, Sw. *komma*, G. *kommen*, Goth. *kwiman*: also from same root, L. *venio*, to come; Gr. *bainō*, to go.] To move hitherward; to advance nearer in any manner and from any distance; to approach the person speaking or writing, or the person addressed; opposed to *go*; to arrive; to take place; to reach a certain stage or point of progress; to arrive at: followed by an infinitive (I now *come* to consider the next subject); to get into a certain state or condition; especially followed by *to be*; to happen or fall out; to befall (*come* what will); to advance or move into view; to appear (color *comes* into the face); to accrue or result; to be formed (knowledge *comes*): frequently with *of* (this *comes* of not taking heed). *Come*, in the imperative, is used to excite attention, or to invite to motion or joint action; or it expresses earnestness, or haste, impatience, remonstrance, etc.—*To come and go*, to alternate; to appear and disappear. —*To come about*, to happen; to fall out (how did these things *come about*?).—*To come at*, to reach; to arrive within reach of; to gain.— *To come away*, to leave; to germinate; to sprout.—*To come by*, to pass near; to obtain, gain, acquire.—*To come down*, to descend; to be humbled or abased.—*To come home*, to come to one's dwelling; to touch nearly; to touch the feelings, interest, or reason.—*To come in*, to enter, as into an enclosure or a port; to become fashionable; to be brought into use.—*To come in for*, to get a share of; to get; to obtain.—*To come into*, to acquire by inheritance or bequest.—*To come near* or *nigh*, to approach in place; to approach in quality; to arrive at nearly the same degree.—*To come off*, to escape; to get free; to emerge (to *come off* with honor); to happen; to take place.— *To come on*, to advance; to progress; to thrive.—*To come out*, to remove from within; to become public; to be introduced to general society: said of a young lady; to appear after being obscured by clouds (the sun has *come out*); to result from calculation.—*To come out of*, to issue forth; to get clear of (he has *come out of* that affair very well).—*To come out with*, to give publicity to; to let out or disclose.—*To come over*, to pass above or across, or from one side to another.—*To come round*, to recover; to revive; to regain one's former state of health.—*To come short*, to fail; not to reach; to be inadequate.—*To come to*, to fall or be allotted to; to amount to.—*To come to one's self*, to get back one's consciousness; to recover.—*To come to pass*, to happen.—*To come true*, to be verified.—*To come up*, to ascend; to rise; to spring; to shoot or rise above the earth.—*To come up to*, to attain to; to equal; to amount to.—*To come up with*, to overtake in following or pursuit.— *Come your ways*, come along; come hither.—*To come*, future; in future

(time *to come*).—**comer**, kum′ėr, *n.* One that comes; one who has arrived and is present.—*All comers*, any one that may come; everybody, without exclusion.—**coming**, kum′ing, *p.* and *a.* Drawing nearer or nigh; approaching; moving toward; advancing; future; next in the future.

comedy, kom′e·di, *n.* [L. *comœdia*, Gr. *kōmōdia*, a comedy, from *kōmos*, a revel or feast, and *ōdē*, a song.] A dramatic composition of a light and amusing class, its characters being represented as in the circumstances or meeting with the incidents of ordinary life.—**comedian**, ko·mē′di·an, *n.* An actor or player in comedy; a player in general; a writer of comedy.

comely, kum′li, *a.* [A.Sax. *cymlic*, comely, from *cyme*, suitable, from *cuman*, to *come*.] Handsome; graceful; symmetrical; well proportioned; decent; suitable; proper; becoming. —**comeliness**, kum′li·nes, *n.* The quality of being comely.

comestible, ko·mes′ti·bl, *n.* [Fr. *comestible*, from L. *comedo*, *comesum* or *comestum*, to eat up—*com*, and *edo*, to eat.] An eatable; an article of solid food.

comet, kom′et, *n.* [L. *cometa*, from Gr. *komētēs*, long-haired, a comet, from *komē*, hair; from the appearance of its tail.] The name given to certain celestial bodies consisting of a star-like nucleus, surrounded by a luminous envelope, called the *coma*, and usually accompanied with a tail or train of light, appearing at irregular intervals, moving through the heavens in paths which seem to correspond with parabolic curves, or in a few instances in elliptical orbits of great eccentricity.—**cometic**, **cometary**, ko·met′ik, kom′et·a·ri, *a.* Pertaining to a comet.

comfit, kum′fit, *n.* [Fr. *confit*, pp. of *confire*, to preserve, to make into a sweetmeat, from L. *conficere*—*con*, together, and *facio*, to make.] A dry sweetmeat; any kind of fruit or root preserved with sugar and dried; a bonbon; a lollipop.

comfort, kum′fėrt, *v.t.* [O.E. *confort*, from O.Fr. *conforter*, to comfort, from L.L. *confortare*, to strengthen— *con*, intens., and L. *fortis*, brave.] To raise from depression; to soothe when in grief or trouble; to bring solace or consolation to; to console; to cheer; to hearten; to solace; to enliven.—*n.* Relief from affliction, sorrow, or trouble of any kind; solace; consolation; a state of quiet or moderate enjoyment, resulting from the possession of what satisfies bodily wants and freedom from all care or anxiety; a feeling or state of well-being, satisfaction, or content; that which furnishes moderate enjoyment or content.—**comfortable**, kum′fėrt·a·bl, *a.* Being in comfort or in a state of ease or moderate enjoyment; giving comfort; affording help, ease, or consolation.—**comfortableness**, kum′fėrt·a·bl·nes, *n.* The state of being comfortable.— **comfortably**, kum′fėrt·a·bli, *adv.* In a comfortable manner; in a manner

fāte, fär, fâre, fat, fǎll; mē, met, hėr; pīne, pin; nōte, not, möve; tūbe, tub, bṳll; oil, pound.

to give comfort or consolation.—
comforter, kum'fêrt·êr, n. One who
comforts; a knit woolen fabric for
tying round the neck in cold weather.
—**comfortless,** kum'fêrt·les, a. Without
comfort; without affording or
without being attended by any
comfort.

comfrey, kum'fri, n. [Fr. conferve,
L. conferva, from conferveo, to heal,
to grow together, from prefix con,
and ferveo, to boil, from the plant's
supposed healing power.] A name
given to several species of rough
herbaceous European and Asiatic
plants of the borage family.

comic, kom'ik, a. [L. comicus, Gr.
kōmikos. COMEDY.] Relating or belonging
to comedy, as distinct from
tragedy; also comical.—n. A comic
actor or singer.—**comical,** kom'ik·al,
a. Exciting mirth; ludicrous; laughable;
diverting; sportive; droll.—
comicality, kom·i·kal'i·ti, n. The
quality of being comical; ludicrousness;
that which is comical or ludicrous.—**comically,** kom'ik·al·li, adv.
In a comical manner; in a manner to
raise mirth; laughably; ludicrously.
—**comicalness,** kom'ik·al·nes, n.
The quality of being comical; comicality.

comitia, ko·mish'i·a, n. pl. [L.]
Legislative assemblies or meetings
among the ancient Romans.—
comitial, ko·mish'i·al, a. Pertaining
to the comitia.

comity, kom'i·ti, n. [L. comitas, from
comis, mild, affable.] Mildness and
suavity of manners; courtesy; civility;
good breeding.—Comity of nations
(comitas gentium), that kind
of courtesy by which the laws
and institutions of one state or
country are recognized and to some
extent given effect to by the government
of another within its territory.

comma, kom'ma, n. [Gr. komma, a
segment, from koptō, to cut off.]
A punctuation mark [,] denoting the
shortest pause in reading, and separating
a sentence into divisions
or members, according to the construction;
mus. an enharmonic interval,
being the difference between
a major and a minor tone.

command, kom·mand' or kom·mänd',
v.t. [Fr. commander, L. commendo,
to entrust, later to enjoin,
to command—com for con, and
mando, to commit to, to command.]
To order with authority; to lay
injunction upon; to direct; to charge;
to have or to exercise supreme
authority, especially military authority,
over; to have control over; to
dominate through position, often
specifically military position; to have
within the range of the eye; to overlook;
to exact or compel by moral
influence; to challenge (to command
respect); to have at one's disposal
and service (to command assistance).
—v.i. To act as or have the authority
of a commander; to exercise influence
or power.—n. The power of governing
with chief authority; supreme
power; control; exercise of authority;
a commandment; mandate; order;
power or control, as from holding an

advantageous military position; the
power of overlooking from elevated
position; a force under the command
of a particular officer.—**commandant,**
kom·man·dant', n. [Fr.] A
commander.—**commander,** kom·-
man'dêr, n. One who commands;
a chief; one who has supreme
authority; a leader; the chief officer
of an army or of any division of it;
a naval officer next in rank above
lieutenant and under the captain;
one on whom is bestowed a commandery.—Commander-in-chief, a supreme
military commander; the
highest staff appointment in the
British army.—**commandeer,** kom·-
mand·êr', v.t. [African-Dutch.] To
impress or force men or stores for military
purposes.—**commandership,**
kom·mand'dêr·ship, n. The office
of a commander.—**commandery,**
kom·man'dêr·i, n. [Fr. commanderie.]
Among several orders of knights,
and in certain religious orders, a
district under the control of a member
of the order called a commander
or preceptor; the office of such a
member; the official building of a
commandery.—**commanding,** kom·-
man'ding, a. Governing; bearing
rule; exercising supreme authority;
controlling by influence, authority,
or dignity (commanding eloquence);
dominating; overlooking a wide region
without obstruction (a commanding
eminence).—**commandingly,**
kom·man'ding·li, adv. In a commanding
manner.—**commandment,**
kom·mand'ment, n. A command; a
mandate; an order or injunction
given by authority; charge; precept;
a precept of the decalogue; authority;
power of commanding.—
commando, kom·man'dō, n. [D.
commando, lit. a command.] A body
of armed men raised for military
service among the Boers or other
whites of South Africa; a military
expedition undertaken by such a
body of men.

commeasure,† kom·mezh'ūr, v.t.
To coincide with; to be coextensive
with.—**commeasurable,**† kom·-
mezh'ūr·a·bl, a. Commensurate;
equal.

commemorate, kom·mem'or·āt. v.t.
—commemorated, commemorating. [L.
commemoro—com, and memoro, to
mention. MEMORY.] To preserve
the memory of by a solemn act; to
celebrate with honor and solemnity.
—**commemoration,** kom·mem'o·-
rā″shon, n. The act of commemorating
or calling to remembrance
by some solemnity; the act of honoring
the memory of some person or
event by solemn celebration.—**commemorative,**
kom·mem'or·āt·iv, a.
Tending to commemorate or preserve
the remembrance of something.—
commemorator, kom·mem'or·āt·-
êr, n. One who commemorates.

commence, kom·mens', v.i.—commenced,
commencing. [Fr. commencer,
from a (hypothetical) L.L. cominitiare—L.
prefix com, and initiare,
to begin. INITIATE.] To begin; to
take rise or origin; to have first
existence; to begin to be, as in a new

state or character.—v.t. To begin;
to enter upon; to perform the first
act of.—**commencement,** kom·-
mens'ment, n. The act or fact of
commencing; beginning; rise; origin;
first existence; the day when, or the
ceremonies at which, degrees are
conferred.

commend, kom·mend', v.t. [L. commendo,
to commit, to commend—
com, and mando, to commit to; the
same word as command with a
different signification.] To commit,
deliver, entrust, or give in charge
(N.T.); to represent as worthy of
confidence, notice, regard, or kindness;
to recommend; with reflexive
pronoun sometimes to call for notice
or attention (this subject commends
itself to our attention); to mention
with approbation; to mention by
way of keeping in memory; to send
greetings or compliments from
(Shak.).—v.i. To approve; to praise.
—**commendable,** kom·men'da·bl, a.
Capable or worthy of being commended
or praised; praiseworthy;
laudable. — **commendably,** kom·-
men'da·bli, adv. In a commendable
or praiseworthy manner.—**commendam,**
kom·men'dam, n. [L.L.] An
ecclesiastical benefice or living commended
to the care of a qualified
person to hold till a proper pastor
is provided. When a beneficed parson
was made a bishop, and was empowered
to retain his benefice, he
was said to hold it in commendam.—
commendation, kom·men·dā″shon,
n. [L. commendatio.] The act of commending;
praise; favorable representation
in words; declaration of esteem;
respects; greeting; message of love.—
commendatory, kom·men'da·to·ri,
a. Serving to commend; presenting
to favorable notice or reception;
containing praise; holding a benefice
in commendam.

commensal, kom·men'sal, n. [L.
com, with, and mensa, table.] One
that eats at the same table‡; one of
two animals or plants that are
always found together; an animal
which lives on or in another without
being parasitic.—a. Having the character
of a commensal.—**commensalism,**
kom·men'sal·izm, n. The
state of being commensal.

commensurable, kom·men'shu·ra·-
bl, a. [L. prefix com, and mensura,
measure. MEASURE.] Having a common
measure; reducible to a common
measure.—**commensurability,**
kom·men'shu·ra·bil″i·ti, n. The state
of being commensurable, or of having
a common measure. — **commensurably,**
kom·men'shu·ra·bli, adv. In a
commensurable manner.—**commensurate,**
kom·men'shu·rāt, a. Reducible
to a common measure; of equal
size; having the same boundaries;
corresponding in amount, degree, or
magnitude; adequate.—**commensurately,**
kom·men'shu·rāt·li, adv. In a
commensurate manner; so as to be
commensurate; correspondingly; adequately.—**commensuration,**
kom·-
men'shu·rā″shon, n. Proportion; a
state of being commensurate.

comment, kom·ment', v.i. [L. com-

mentor, from *commentus*, pp. of *comminiscor*, to reflect on—*com*, with, together with, and stem *min*, seen in *memini*, to remember, and in E. *mind*.] To make remarks or observations, either on a book or writing, or on actions, events, or opinions; to write notes on the works of an author, with a view to illustrate his meaning, or to explain particular passages; to make annotations.—*n.* (kom′ment). A remark or observation; a note intended to illustrate a difficult passage in an author; annotation; exposition; talk; discourse.—**commentary**, kom′men·ta·ri, *n.* A series or collection of comments or annotations; a historical narrative; a memoir of particular transactions (the *Commentaries* of Caesar).—**commentator**, kom′men·tā·tėr, *n.* One who writes a commentary; one who writes annotations; an annotator.

commerce, kom′mėrs, *n.* [Fr. *commerce*, L. *commercium*—*com*, together with, and *merx, mercis*, merchandise.] An interchange of goods, merchandise, or property of any kind between countries or communities; mercantile pursuits; trade; traffic; mutual dealings in common life; intercourse.—*v.i.* To carry on trade‡; to hold intercourse; to commune.—**commercial**, kom·mėr′shal, *a.* Pertaining to commerce or trade; dealing with or depending on commerce; carrying on commerce.—*Commercial announcement*, an announcement made over the radio concerning the product of the advertiser who sponsors the program.—**commercialism**, kom·mėr′shal·izm, *n.* The doctrines, tenets, or practices of commerce or of commercial men.

commination, kom·mi·nā′shon, *n.* [L. *comminatio*—*com*, and *minatio*, a threatening, from *minari*, to threaten. MENACE.] A threat or threatening; a denunciation of punishment or vengeance; an office in the liturgy of the Church of England, appointed to be read on Ash Wednesday or on the first day of Lent.—**comminatory**, kom·min′a·to·ri, *a.* Threatening; denouncing punishment.

commingle, kom·ming′gl, *v.t.* or *i.* —*commingled, commingling.* [Prefix *com*, and *mingle*.] To mix together; to mingle in one mass or intimately; to blend.

comminute, kom′mi·nūt, *v.t.*—*comminuted, comminuting.* [L. *comminuo, comminutum*, to make small—*com*, with, and *minuo*, to lessen; root *min*, as in *minor*, less.] To make small or fine; to reduce to minute particles or to a fine powder; to pulverize; to triturate; to levigate.—*a.* Divided into very small parts or particles.— **comminution**, kom·mi·nū′shon, *n.* The act of comminuting or reducing to a fine powder or to small particles; pulverization.

commiserate, kom·miz′ėr·āt, *v.t.*— *commiserated, commiserating.* [L. *commiseror*—*com*, and *miseror*, to pity. MISERABLE.] To feel sorrow, pain, or regret for, through sympathy; to compassionate; to pity.—**commiseration**, kom·miz′ėr·ā″shon, *n.* The

act of commiserating: a sympathetic suffering of pain or sorrow for the afflictions or distresses of another; pity; compassion.—**commiserative**, kom·miz′ėr·ā·tiv, *a.* Compassionate. —**commiseratively**, kom·miz′ėr·ā·tiv·li, *adv.*

commissar, kom′mis·sär, *n.* [Fr. *commissaire*, L.L. *commissarius*, one to whom something is entrusted.] A Communist party official in charge of teaching party doctrine; formerly, the head of a government department in Soviet Russia.

commissary, kom′mis·â·ri, *n.* [Fr. *commissaire*, L.L. *commissarius*, one to whom any trust or duty is delegated; L. *committo, commissum*, to commit.] In a general sense, a commissioner; one to whom is committed some charge, duty, or office by a superior; a representative; a store that supplies provisions, as in a camp; *Scots law*, the judge in a commissary-court; *milit.* a name given to officers or officials of various kinds, especially to officers of the commissariat department.—**commissarial**, kom·mis·sā′ri·al, *a.* Pertaining to a commissary.—**commissariat**, kom·mis·sā′ri·at, *n.* The department of an army whose duties consist in supplying transport, provisions, forage, camp equipage, etc., to the troops; also, the body of officers in that department; the office or employment of a commissary; the district or country over which the authority or jurisdiction of a commissary extends.

commission, kom·mish′on, *n.* [L. *commissio, commissionis.* COMMIT.] The act of committing; the act of doing something wrong; the act of perpetrating (the *commission* of a crime); the act of entrusting, as a charge or duty; the thing committed, entrusted, or delivered; a duty, office, charge, or piece of work entrusted to any one; the warrant by which any trust is held, or any authority exercised (as that of an officer in an army); mandate; authority given; a number of persons joined in an office or trust; commissioners; the state of acting in the purchase and sale of goods for another; position or business of an agent; agency; the allowance made to an agent for transacting business.—*Commission of the Justice of the Peace*, a warrant of authority issued by the state for the granting of certain powers to, and the appointment of, Justices of the Peace.—*To put a ship into commission*, to equip and man a vessel, and place it in service after it has been in dry dock for repairs.—*v.t.* To give a commission to; to give special powers and instructions for the accomplishment of an act; to empower or authorize by special commission; to send with a mandate or authority.—**commission merchant**, *n.* One who buys or sells goods for another on commission.—**commissionnaire**, kom·mēs·yon·âr′, *n.* [Fr.] At European hotels and terminals, a kind of messenger or light porter. —**commissioner**, kom·mish′on·ėr, *n.*

One who commissions; a person who has a commission or warrant from proper authority to perform some office or execute some business; an officer having charge of some department of the public service, which is put into commission; a steward or agent who manages affairs on a large estate.

commissure, kom·e·shur′, *n.* [Fr. *commissure*, from L. *commissura*, a joining together, joint, seam—*com*, together, and *mitto, missum*, to send.] A joint or seam; the place where two parts of a body meet and unite; a juncture; a suture: used chiefly in *anat.*—**commissural**, kom·mis·shu′ral, *a.* Belonging to a commissure.

commit, kom·mit′ *v.t.*—*committed, committing.* [L. *committo*, to make over in trust, to set to work, do wrong—*com*, together, and *mitto*, to send, whence also *admit, permit, dismiss, mission, missile*, etc.] To give in trust; to put into charge or keeping; to entrust; to surrender, give up, consign: with *to*; *refl.* to bind to a certain line of conduct, or to expose or endanger by a preliminary step or decision which cannot be recalled; to compromise; to order or send into confinement; to imprison (the magistrate *commits* a guilty person); to refer or entrust to a committee or select number of persons for their consideration and report; to do (generally something wrong); to perpetrate.—*To commit to memory*, to learn by heart.—**committable**, kom·mit′a·bl, *a.* Capable of being committed. —**commitment, committal**, kom·mit′ment, kom·mit′al, *n.* The act of committing; commission (but we do not say the *committal* or *commitment* of crimes, but the *commission*).—**committee**, kom·mit′tē, *n.* A body of persons elected or appointed to attend to any matter or business referred to them, often a section of a larger body.—*Committee of the whole house*, an arrangement by which matters are discussed in a particular manner in congress, the chair being occupied by the chairman of committee, and members being allowed to speak more than once on a question.—**committeeman**, *n.* A member of a committee, as of the national, state, county, and city district.

commix, kom·miks′, *v.t.* or *i.* [L. *commisceo, commixtus*—*com*, together, and *misceo*, to mix. MIX.] To mix or mingle; to blend.—**commixture**, kom·miks′chėr, *n.* The act of mixing; the state of being mingled; the mass formed by mingling; a compound.

commode, kom·mōd′, *n.* [Fr., from L. *commodus*, convenient. COMMODIOUS.] A kind of headdress formerly worn by ladies; a chest of drawers, often with shelves and other conveniences added; a night stool.

commodious, kom·mō′di·us, *a.* [L.L. *commodiosus*, from L. *commodus*, useful.—*com*, together, and *modus*, measure, mode.] Roomy and convenient; spacious and suitable; serviceable. —**commodiously**, kom·mō′di·us·li, *adv.* So as to be commodious.—**commodiousness**, kom·mō′di·us·nes, *n.*

The state or quality of being commodious.—**commodity**, kom·mod′i·ti, n. [Fr. commodité, convenience, commodity; L. commoditas, fitness, convenience.] Suitableness or convenience‡; what is useful; specifically, an article of merchandise; anything movable that is bought and sold, as goods, wares, produce of land and manufactures.

commodore, kom′mo·dōr, n. [From Sp. commendador, a commander, or from Pg. capitao mor, superior captain.] An officer who commands a detachment of ships in the absence of an admiral; a title given by courtesy to the senior captain when three or more ships of war are cruising in company, to the senior captain of a line of merchant vessels, and to the president of a yachting club; the leading ship in a fleet of merchantmen.

common, kom′on, a. [Fr. commun, L. communis—com, together, and munis, ready to be of service, obliging.] Belonging or pertaining equally to more than one, or to many indefinitely; belonging to all; general; universal; public; of frequent or usual occurrence; not extraordinary; frequent; usual; ordinary; habitual; not distinguished by rank or character; not of superior excellence; of low or mean rank or character; gram. applied to such nouns as are both masculine and feminine, and to those that are the names of all the objects possessing the attributes denoted by the noun (river, etc.).—Common council, the council of a city or corporate town, empowered to make bylaws for the government of the citizens.—Common law, the unwritten law, the law that receives its binding force from immemorial usage and universal reception, in distinction from the written or statute law.—Common measure, a number or quantity that divides two or more numbers or quantities without leaving a remainder.—Common Pleas, formerly one of the three superior courts of common law in England, now a division of the High Court of Justice.—Common Prayer, the liturgy or public form of prayer prescribed by the Church of England to be used in all churches and chapels.—Common seal, a seal used by a corporation as the symbol of their incorporation.—Common sense, sound practical judgment; the natural sagacity or understanding of mankind in general.—Common time, musical time or rhythm with two, four, or eight beats to a bar.—In common, equally with another or with others.—n. A tract of ground, the use of which is not appropriated to an individual, but belongs to the public or to a number; in all other senses pl.: the common people; the untitled; the vulgar, the lower house of the British Parliament, consisting of the representatives of cities, boroughs, and counties; food provided at a common table, as at colleges; food or fare in general.—Short commons, stinted allowance.—Extra commons, increased allowance.

—**commonage**, kom′on·ij, n. The right of pasturing on a common; the joint right of using anything in common with others.—**commonalty**, kom′on·al·ti, n. The common people; all below the rank of nobility.—**commoner**, kom′on·ėr, n. A person under the degree of nobility; a student of the second rank in the University of Oxford, not dependent on the foundation for support.—**commonly**, kom′on·li, adv. In a common manner; usually; generally; ordinarily; frequently; for the most part.—**commonness**, kom′on·nes, n. The state or fact of being common.—**commonplace**, kom′on·plās, a. Not new or extraordinary; common; trite.—n. A memorandum of something that is likely to be frequently referred to; a well-known or customary remark; a trite saying; a platitude.—**commonweal**, kom′on·wēl, n. A commonwealth; the body politic; a state.—**commonwealth**, kom′on·welth, n. [Here wealth means strictly well-being.] The body politic; the public; a republican state; the form of government which existed in England from the death of Charles I in 1649 to the abdication of Richard Cromwell in 1659.

commotion, kom·mō′shon, n. [L. commotio, from commoveo, commotum—com, with, and moveo, to move. MOVE.] Agitation; tumult of people; disturbance; perturbation; disorder of mind; excitement.—**commove**,† kom·mōv′, v.t.—commoved, commoving. [L. commoveo.] To put in motion; to disturb; to agitate; to unsettle.

commune, kom·mūn′, v.i.—communed, communing. [Fr. communier; L. communico, to communicate, from communis, common. COMMON.] To converse; to talk together familiarly; to impart sentiments mutually; to interchange ideas or feelings.—n. (kom′mūn). Familiar interchange of ideas or sentiments; communion; intercourse; friendly conversation (to hold commune, to be in commune).

commune, kom′mūn, n. [Fr., from commun, common.] A small territorial district in France and in some other countries, under the government of a mayor; the inhabitants of a commune; the members of a communal council.—The commune of Paris, a revolutionary committee which took the place of the municipality of Paris in the French revolution of 1789; also, a committee or body of communalists who in 1871 for a brief period ruled over Paris after the evacuation of the German troops.—**communal**, kom′mū·nal, a. Pertaining to a commune or to communalism.—**communalism**, kom′mū-nal·izm, n. The theory of governments by communes or other local self-governing bodies.—**communalist**, kom′mū·na·list, n. One who adheres to communalism.—**communalistic**, kom′mū·na·lis″tik, a. Pertaining to communalism.—**communism**, kom′mūn·izm, n. [Fr. communisme.] The system or theory which upholds the absorption of all proprietary rights in a common interest; the doctrine of a community of

property.—**communist**, kom′mūn·ist, n. One who holds the doctrines of communism.—**communistic**, kom·mū·nis′tik, a. Relating to communists or communism, according to the principles of communism.—**communistically**, kom·mū·nis′tik·al·li, adv. In accordance with communism; in a communistic way or form.

communicate, kom·mū′ni·kāt, v.t.—communicated, communicating. [L. communico, from communis, common.] To impart to another or others; to bestow or confer for joint possession, generally or always something intangible, as intelligence, news, opinions, or disease; with to before the receiver.—v.i. To share; to participate: followed by in; to have a communication or passage from one to another (one room communicates with another); to have or hold intercourse or interchange of thoughts; to partake of the Lord's supper or communion.—**communicability**, kom·mū′ni·ka·bil″i·ti, n. The quality of being communicable; capability of being imparted. — **communicable**, kom·mū′ni·ka·bl, a. Capable of being communicated or imparted from one to another; capable of being recounted; communicative; ready to impart information, news, etc.—**communicableness**, kom·mū′ni·ka·bl·nes, n. —**communicant**, kom·mū′ni·kant, n. One who communicates or partakes of the sacrament at the celebration of the Lord's supper.—**communication**, kom·mū′ni·kā″shon, n. The act of communicating; means of communicating; connecting passage; means of passing from place to place; that which is communicated or imparted; information or intelligence imparted by word or writing; a document or message imparting information.—**communicative**, kom·mū′ni·kā·tiv, a. Inclined to communicate; ready to impart to others; free in communicating; not reserved; open.—**communicatively**, kom·mū′ni·kā·tiv·li, adv. In a communicative manner; by communication.—**communicativeness**, kom·mū′ni·kā·tiv·nes, n. The state or quality of being communicative; readiness to impart to others; freedom from reserve.—**communicator**, kom·mū′ni·kā·tėr, n. One who or that which communicates.

communion, kom·mūn′yon, n. [L. communio, communionis, participation.] Participation of something in common; fellowship; concord; bond or association; intercourse between two or more persons; interchange of thoughts or acts; union in religious worship, or in doctrine and discipline; union with a church; a body of Christians who have one common faith and discipline; [cap.] the act of partaking in the sacrament of the eucharist; the celebration of the Lord's supper.—Communion elements, the bread and wine used in the sacrament of the Lord's supper.

communiqué, kom·mū·ni·kā′, n. [Fr.] An official communication, a statement given to the press.

communism, etc. See COMMUNE.

---

ch, chain; ch, Sc. loch; g, go; j, job; ng, sing; TH, then; th, thin; w, wig; hw, whig; zh, azure.

community, kom·mū′ni·ti, *n.* [L. *communitas.* COMMON.] Common possession or enjoyment (a *community* of goods); a society of people having common rights and privileges; a society of individuals of any kind; the body of people in a state; the public, or people in general: used in this sense always with the definite article; common character (individuals distinguished by *community* of descent).

commute, kom·mūt′, *v.t.*—commuted, *commuting.* [L. *commuto*—prefix *com*, and *muto*, to change. MUTABLE, MUTATION.] To exchange; to put one thing in the place of another; to give or receive one thing for another; to exchange, as one penalty or punishment for one of less severity; to pay in money instead of in kind or in duty; to travel back and forth daily between places, as to and from a city. —**commuter,** one who travels to and from a city daily.—**commutability,** kom·mūt′a·bil′i·ti, *n.* The quality of being commutable; interchangeableness.—**commutation,** kom·mū·tā′shon, *n.* [L. *commutatio.*] The act of commuting; the act of substituting one thing for another; the change of a penalty or punishment from a greater to a less.—*Commutation ticket.* A railroad ticket at a reduced rate for a number of trips, between stations.—**commutative,** kom·mūt′a·tiv, *a.* Relating to exchange; interchangeable; mutual.—**commutator,** kom′mū·tā·tẽr, *n.* [L. *commutatio*, a change.] *Elect.* A device for converting an alternating current into a direct one; the rotating terminal of the armature of an electric motor or generator.

comose, kō·mōs′, *a.* [L. *coma*, hair.] Hairy; comate.

compact, kom·pakt′, *a.* [L. *compactus*, pp. of *compingo*, *compactum*, to join or unite together—*com*, together and *pango*, to fix.] Closely and firmly united, as the parts or particles of solid bodies; having the parts or particles close; solid; dense; not diffuse; not verbose; concise; composed; made up: with *of* (*Shak.*).— *v.t.* To thrust, drive, or press closely together; to join firmly; to consolidate; to make close; to unite or connect firmly, as in a system.— **compactly,** kom·pakt′li, *adv.* In a compact or condensed manner; closely; concisely; briefly; tersely; neat. —**compactness,** kom·pakt′nes, *n.* State of being compact.

compact, kom′pakt, *n.* [L. *compactum*, a compact, from *compaciscor*, *compactus*, to make an agreement—*com*, together, and *paciscor*, to fix, settle, covenant.] An agreement; a contract, covenant, bargain, or settlement between parties.

companion, kom·pan′yon, *n.* [O.Fr. *compainon*, *companion*; Fr. *compagnon*—L. *com*, together, and *panis*, bread; lit. a sharer of one's bread; a mess fellow.] One with whom a person frequently associates and converses; a mate; a comrade; one who accompanies another; a person holding the lowest rank in an order of

knighthood (as of the Bath).—*a.* Accompanying; united with.—*v.t.* To be a companion to; to accompany, to put on the same level (*Shak.*)‡.— **companionable,** kom·pan′yon·a·bl, *a.* Fit for good fellowship; qualified to be agreeable in company; sociable.— **companionableness,** kom·pan′yon·a·bl·nes, *n.* The quality of being companionable; sociableness.—**companionably,** kom·pan′yon·a·bli, *adv.* In a companionable manner.—**companionless,** kom·pan′yon·les, *a.* Having no companion.—**companionship,** kom·pan′yon·ship, *n.* The state or fact of being a companion; fellowship; association.—**company,** kum′pa·ni, *n.* [Fr. *compagnie*; O.Fr. also *companie*.] The state of being along with; companionship; fellowship; society; any assemblage of persons; a collection of men or other animals, in a very indefinite sense; guests at a person's house; a number of persons united for performing or carrying on anything jointly, as some commercial enterprise, the term being applicable to private partnerships or to incorporated bodies; a firm (but this word usually implies fewer partners than *company*); the members of a firm whose names do not appear in the style or title of the firm: usually contracted when written (Messrs. Smith & *Co.*); a subdivision of an infantry regiment or battalion commanded by a captain; the crew of a ship, including the officers.—*To bear* or *keep* (a person) *company*, to accompany; to attend; to go with; to associate with.—*To be good company*, to be an entertaining companion.—*v.t.* and *i.*† To associate or associate with; to frequent the company of.

companion, kom·pan′yon, *n.* [Comp. O.Sp. *compaña*, an outhouse.] *Naut.* the framing and sash lights upon a quarter deck, through which light passes to the cabins below; a raised cover to the cabin stair of a merchant vessel.—*Companion ladder*, the steps or ladder between the main deck and the quarter deck.—*Companion way*, the staircase at the entrance to the cabin of a vessel.

compare, kom·pâr′ *v.t.*—compared, *comparing.* [L. *compaño*, to put together, unite, match, compare—*com*, together, and *par*, equal, whence *peer*, *pair*, *parity.* PAIR.] To set or bring together in fact or in contemplation, and examine the relations they bear to each other, especially with a view to ascertain agreement or disagreement, resemblances or differences (t⌐ *compare* one thing *with* another); to liken; to represent as similar for the purpose of illustration (to *compare* one thing *to* another); *gram.* to inflect by the degrees of comparison. —*v.i.* To hold or stand comparison; to contrast favorably.—*n.* Comparison; scope or room for comparison (rich beyond *compare*).—**comparable,** kom′pa·ra·bl, *a.* [L. *comparabilis.*] Capable of being compared; worthy of comparison; being of equal regard.—**comparableness,** kom′pa·ra·bl·nes, *n.* State of being compa-

rable.—**comparably,** kom′pa·ra·bli, *adv.* By comparison; so as to be compared.—**comparative,** kom·par′a·tiv, *a.* [L. *comparativus.*] Estimated by comparison; not positive or absolute; proceeding by comparison; founded on comparison, especially founded on the comparison of different things belonging to the same science or study (*comparative* anatomy, etc.); having the power of comparing different things (the *comparative* faculty; *gram.* expressing a greater degree; expressing more than the positive but less than the superlative: applied to forms of adjectives and adverbs.—*n. Gram.* the comparative degree.—**comparatively,** kom·par′a·tiv·li, *adv.* By comparison; according to estimate made by comparison; not positively, absolutely, or in itself.—**comparison,** kom·par′i·son, *n.* [Fr. *comparaison*, L. *comparatio.*] The act of comparing; the act of examining in order to discover how one thing stands with regard to another; the state of being compared; relation between things such as admits of their being compared; something with which another thing is compared; a similitude, or illustration by similitude; a parallel; *gram.* the inflection of an adjective or adverb to express degrees of the original quality.

compartment, kom·pärt′ment, *n.* [Fr. *compartiment*, L.L. *compartimentum*, from L. *compartior*, to divide, share, from *pars*, *partis*, a part.] A division or separate part of a general design, as of a building, railroad car, picture, plan, or the like.

compass, kum′pas, *n.* [Fr. *compas*, from L.L. *compassus*, a circuit—L. *com*, and *passus*, a step. PACE.] A passing round; a circular course; a circuit (to fetch a *compass*, that is, to make a circuit or round); limit or boundary; extent; range: applied to time, space, sound, etc.; moderate estimate; moderation; due limits (to keep within *compass*); an instrument consisting essentially of a magnet suspended so as to have as complete freedom of motion as possible, and used to indicate the magnetic meridian or the position of objects with respect to that meridian; a mathematical instrument for describing circles, measuring figures, distances between two points, etc.: often with the plural designation *compasses*, or a *pair of compasses.*—*v.t.* To stretch round; to encompass; to enclose, encircle, environ, surround; to go or walk about or round; to obtain; to attain to; to accomplish (to *compass* one's purposes); *law*, to plot; to contrive (a person's death).—**compassable,** kum′pas·a·bl, *a.* Capable of being compassed.—**compass plant,** *n.* A composite plant, common on the prairies of North America: so called from being disposed to present the edges of its leaves north and south.

compassion, kom·pa′shon, *n.* [Fr. *compassion*, L. *compassio.* PASSION.] A suffering with another; sympathy; pity; commiseration; an act of mercy (O.T.)‡.—**compassionate,** kom·pa′-

---

fāte, fär, fâre, fat, fạll; mē, met, hẽr; pīne, pin; nōte, not, mõve; tūbe, tub, bụll; oil, pound.

shon·it, *a.* Characterized by compassion; full of pity; tender-hearted. —*v.t.—compassionated, compassionating.* To pity; to commiserate; to have compassion for.—**compassionately,** kom·pa′shon·it·li, *adv.* In a compassionate manner; with compassion; mercifully.—**compassionateness,** kom·pa′shon·it·nes, *n.* The quality of being compassionate.

compatible, kom·pat′i·bl, *a.* [Fr. *compatible,* L.L. *compatibilis*—L. *com,* together, and *patior,* to suffer.] Capable of coexisting or being found together in the same subject; capable of existing together in harmony; suitable; agreeable; not incongruous (things *compatible* with one another). —**compatibility, compatibleness,** kom·pat′i·bil″i·ti, kom·pat′i·bl·nes, *n.* The quality of being compatible; consistency; suitableness. **compatibly,** kom·pat′i·bli, *adv.* In a compatible manner; fitly; suitably; consistently.

compatriot, kom·pā′tri·ot, *n.* [Fr. *compatriote.*] One of the same country.—*a.†* Of the same country; patriotic.

compeer, kom·pēr′, *n.* [L. *com,* and *par,* equal. PEER.] An equal; a companion; an associate; a mate.—*v.t.‡* To equal; to match. (*Shak.*)

compel, kom·pel′, *v.t.—compelled, compelling.* [L. *compello, compulsum,* to drive together—*com,* and *pello,* to drive; hence *compulsion, compulsory,* etc.] To drive or urge with force or irresistibly; to constrain; to oblige; to necessitate; to subject; to cause to submit; to take by force or violence (*Shak.*).—**compellable,** kom·pel′a·bl, *a.* Capable of being compelled or constrained.—**compeller,** kom·pel′ér, *n.* One who compels or constrains.—**compellingly,**— kom·pel′ing·li, *adv.* In a compelling or constraining manner; compulsively; in a way to force attention or obedience.

compellation, kom·pel·lā′shon, *n.* [L. *compellatio,* the act of accosting, from *compello, compellare,* to address.] Style or manner of address; word of salutation.

compendium, kom·pen′di·um, *n.* [L. *compendium,* a shortening, abbreviating—*com,* with, and *pendo,* to weigh.] A brief compilation or composition containing the principal heads or general principles of a larger work or system; an abridgment; a summary; an epitome. ∴ Syn. under ABRIDGMENT.—**compendious,** kom··pen′di·us, *a.* [L. *compendiosus.*] Containing the substance or general principles of a subject or work in a narrow compass; succinct; concise. —**compendiously,** kom·pen′di·us·li, *adv.* In a compendious manner; summarily; concisely; in epitome.— **compendiousness,** kom·pen′di·us··nes, *n.* The state of being compendious.

compensate, kom·pen′sāt or kom′·pen·sāt, *v.t.—compensated, compensating.* [L. *compenso, compensatum*— *com,* together, and *penso,* freq. of *pendo, pensum,* to weigh; lit. to weigh together, hence to balance, give an equivalent for.] To give equal value to; to recompense; to give an equivalent to (to *compensate* a laborer for his work); to make up for; to counterbalance; to make amends for (losses, defects, etc.).—*v.i.* To supply or serve as an equivalent: followed by *for;* to make amends.—**compensation,** kom·pen·sā′shon, *n.* The act of compensating; that which is given or serves as an equivalent for services, debt, want, loss, or suffering; amends; indemnity; recompense; that which supplies the place of something else or makes good a deficiency.—*Compensation Act for Workmen,* any of a number of state laws providing for the compensation of a workman by his employer in case of accident.—**compensative,** kom·pen′sa·tiv, *a.* Making amends or compensation.—*n.†* That which compensates; compensation.—**compensator,** kom′pen·sā·tér, *n.* One who or that which compensates.— **compensatory,** kom·pen′sa·to·ri, *a.* Serving for compensation; making amends.

compete, kom·pēt′, *v.i.—competed, competing.* [L. *competo,* to strive after—*com,* together, and *peto,* to seek.] To seek or strive for the same thing as another, to carry on a contest or rivalry for a common object; to vie (to *compete with* a person *for* a thing). —**competition,** kom·pe·ti′shon, *n.* [L.L. *competitio.*] The act of competing; mutual contest or striving for the same object; rivalry; a trial of skill proposed as a test of superiority or comparative fitness. ∴ In a *competition* the persons strive to attain a common end, and may have the most friendly feelings toward each other; in *rivalry* there is rather the desire of one to supplant or get before another, and usually a certain hostility.—**competitive,** kom·pet′i··tiv, *a.* Relating to competition; carried out by competition.—**competitor,** kom·pet′i·tér, *n.* [L. *competitor* (*i* long).] One who competes; one who endeavors to obtain what another seeks; one who claims what another claims; a rival.—**competitory,†** kom·· pet′i·to·ri, *a.* Acting in competition; rival.

competent, kom′pe·tent, *a.* [Fr. *compétent,* from *competer,* to be sufficient; L. *competo,* to be meet or suitable— *com,* together, and *peto,* to seek.] Answering all requirements; suitable; fit; sufficient or fit for the purpose; adequate; having legal capacity or power; rightfully or lawfully belonging.—**competently,** kom′pe·tent·li, *adv.* In a competent manner; sufficiently; adequately; suitably.—**competence, competency,** kom′pe·tens, kom′pe·ten·si, *n.* State of being competent; fitness; suitableness; adequateness; ability; sufficiency; such a quantity as is sufficient; especially, property or means of subsistence sufficient to furnish the necessaries and conveniences of life, without superfluity.

compile, kom·pīl′ *v.t.—compiled, compiling.* [L. *compilo,* to plunder, pillage—*com,* together, and *pilo,* to pillage.] To draw up, write out, or compose by collecting materials from various sources; to collect or put together by utilizing the writings of others,—**compilation,** kom·pi·lā′·shon, *n.* The act of compiling or collecting from written or printed documents or books; that which is compiled; a book or treatise drawn up by compiling.—**compiler,** kom··pil′ér, *n.* One who compiles.

complacent, kom·plā′sent, *a.* [L. *complacens, complacentis,* pleasing, ppr. of *complaceo,* to please—*com,* and *placeo,* to please (whence *pleasure*).] Accompanied with a sense of quiet enjoyment; displaying complacency; gratified; satisfied.—**complacence, complacency,** kom·plā′·sens, kom·plā′sen·si, *n.* A feeling of quiet pleasure; satisfaction; gratification; complaisance or civility‡.—**complacently,** kom·plā′sent·li,*adv.* In a complacent manner.

complain, kom·plān′, *v.i.* [Fr. *complaindre,* from L.L. *complangere*— L. *com,* together, and *plango,* to beat the breast in sorrow. PLAINT.] To utter expressions of grief, pain, uneasiness, censure, resentment, or the like; to lament; to murmur; to bewail; to make a formal accusation against a person; to make a charge: now regularly followed by *of* before the cause of grief or censure.— **complainant,** kom·plā′nant, *n.* One who complains or makes a complaint; a complainer; *law,* one who prosecutes by complaint, or commences a legal process against an offender; a plaintiff; a prosecutor.—**complainer,** kom·plā′nér, *n.* One who complains; one who finds fault; a murmurer.— **complainingly,** kom·plā·ning·li, *adv.* In a complaining manner; murmuringly.—**complaint,** kom·plānt′, *n.* [Fr. *complainte.*] Expression of grief, regret, pain, censure, or resentment; lamentation; murmuring; a finding fault; the cause or subject of complaint or murmuring; a malady; an ailment; a disease: usually applied to disorders not violent; a charge; a representation of injuries suffered; accusation.

complaisance, kom′plā·zans, *n.* [Fr. *complaisance,* from *complaisant,* ppr. of *complaire,* to please=L. *complacere.* COMPLACENT.] A pleasing deportment; affability; civility; courtesy; desire of pleasing; disposition to oblige.— **complaisant,** kom′plā··zant, *a.* Pleasing in manners; courteous; obliging; desirous to please; proceeding from an obliging disposition.

complected, kom·plek′ted, *a.* [L. prefix *com,* and *plecto,* to weave.] Woven together; interwoven.

complement, kom′ple·ment, *n.* [L. *complementum,* that which fills up or completes, from *compleo,* to complete. COMPLETE, *Compliment* is the same word.] Full quantity or number; full amount; what is wanted to complete or fill up some quantity or thing; difference; *math.* what is wanted in an arc or angle to make it up to 90°; outward show (*Shak.*)‡; courtesy or compliment (*Shak.*)‡.

—**complemental**, kom·ple·men'tal, a. Forming a complement; completing; complementary.—**complementary**, kom·ple·men'ta·ri, a. Completing; supplying a deficiency; complemental.—*Complementary colors.* COLOR.

complete, kom·plēt', a. [L. *completus*, pp. of *completo, completum*, to fill up—*com*, intens., and *pleo*, to fill; same root as E. *fill*.] Having no deficiency; wanting no part or element; perfect; thorough; consummate; in every respect; finished; ended; concluded. ∴ 'Nothing is *whole* that has anything taken from it; nothing is *entire* that is divided; nothing is *complete* that has not all its parts and those parts fully developed. *Complete* refers to the perfection of parts; *entire* to their unity; *whole* to their junction; *total* to their aggregate' (*Angus*).—*v.t.*—*completed, completing.* To make complete; to finish; to end; to perfect; to fulfill, to accomplish; to realize.—**completely**, kom·plēt'li, *adv.* In a complete manner; fully; perfectly; entirely; wholly; totally; utterly; thoroughly; quite.—**completeness**, kom·plēt'nes, *n.* The state of being complete.—**completion**, kom·plē'shon, *n.* Act of completing, finishing, or perfecting; state of being complete or completed; perfect state; fulfillment; accomplishment.—**completive**, kom·plē'tiv, *a.* Completing or tending to complete; making complete.

complex, kom'pleks, *a.* [L. *complexus*, pp. of *complector, complexus*, to fold or twine together—*com*, together, and stem *plec, plic*, to fold; seen also in *ply, apply, complicate, display*, etc.] Composed of various parts or things; including sundry particulars connected; composite; not simple (being, idea); involved; intricate; complicated; perplexed (process).—*n.* Assemblage of things related as parts of a system; *Psychoanalysis* (which see), a series of emotionally accentuated ideas in a repressed state.—**complexity, complexness**, kom·plek'si·ti, kom'pleks·nes, *n.* The state of being complex; anything complex; intricacy; involvement; entanglement.—**complexly**, kom'pleks·li, *adv.* In a complex manner; not simply.

complexion, kom·plek'shon, *n.* [L. *complexio, complexionis*, a combination, in L.L. physical constitution, from *complector, complexus.* COMPLEX.] The temperament, habitude, or natural disposition of the body or mind; physical character or nature‡; the color or hue of the skin, particularly of the face; the general appearance of anything; aspect (*Shak.*).—**complexioned**, kom·plek'shond, *a.* Having a complexion of this or that kind; having a certain hue, especially of the skin; used in composition.

compliance, etc. See COMPLY.

complicate, kom' pli·kāt, *v.t.*—*complicated, complicating.* [L. *complico*—*com*, and *plico*, to fold, weave, or knit. COMPLEX, PLY.] To intertwine;

to interweave; to render complex or intricate; to involve.—*a.* Composed of various parts intimately united; complex; involved; intricate; *bot.* folded together, as the valves of the glume or chaff in some grasses.—**complicated**, kom'pli·kāt·ed, *p.* and *a.* Complicate; involved; intricate.—**complicacy**, kom'pli·ka·si, *n.* A state of being complex or intricate.—**complication**, kom·pli·kā'shon, *n.* The act of complicating or state of being complicated; entanglement; complexity; something complicated; an aggregate of things involved, mixed up, or mutually united; what complicates or causes complication.

complice,‡ kom'plis, *n.* [Fr. *complice*, ACCOMPLICE.] An accomplice. (*Shak.*)—**complicity**, kom·plis'i·ti, *n.* The state of being an accomplice; partnership in crime.

compliment, kom'pli·ment, *n.* [Fr. *compliment*, It. *complimento*, from *complire*, to fill up, to satisfy, L. *compleo, complere*, to complete: same word as *complement*, which formerly was used in this sense.] An act or expression of civility, respect, or regard; delicate flattery; expression of commendation or admiration; praise.—*v.t.* To pay a compliment to; to flatter or gratify by expressions of approbation, esteem, or respect, or by acts implying the like.—**complimentary**, kom·pli·men'ta·ri, *a.* Full of or using compliments; intended to express or convey a compliment or compliments; expressive of civility, regard or praise.—**complimentarily**, kom·pli·men'ta·ri·li, *adv.* In a complimentary manner.

compline, kom'plin, *n.* [From Fr. *complie*, from L. *completae (horae)*, ' complete hours ': so called because this service completes the religious exercises of the day.] The last of the seven canonical hours in the Roman Catholic breviary; the last prayer at night, to be recited after sunset.

complot, kom'plot, *n.* [Fr. *complot*, a plot, from L. *complicitum.* COMPLICATE.] A plotting together; a plot; a conspiracy. (*Shak.*)—*v.t.* To plan together; to contrive; to plot.—*v.i.*—*complotted, complotting.* To plot together; to conspire; to form a plot.—**complotter**, kom·plot'er, *n.* One joined in a plot; a conspirator.

comply, kom·plī', *v.i.*—*complied, complying.* [From L. *complere*, to fill up, satisfy (whence *complete, compliment*), like *supply* from *supplere*—*com*, with, and *plere*, to fill. The meaning has been affected by *ply* and *pliant*.] To adopt a certain course of action at the desire of another; to yield; to acquiesce; to consent; to agree; used alone or followed by *with*.—**compliable**,‡ kom·plī'a·bl, *a.* Compliant. (*Mil.*)—**compliance**, kom·plī'ans, *n.* The act of complying; a yielding as to a request, wish, desire, etc; a disposition to yield to others; complaisance.—**compliancy**, kom·plī'an·si, *n.* A disposition to yield, or a habit of yielding to others.—**compliant**, kom·plī'ant, *a.* Given to

comply; yielding to request or desire; ready to accommodate; obliging.—**compliantly**, kom·plī'ant·li, *adv.* In a compliant or yielding manner.

component, kom·pō'nent, *a.* [L. *componens*—*com*, together, and *pono*, to place.] Composing; constituting; entering into as a part.—*n.* A constituent part.—**component**, kom·pō'nent, *n.* [L. *compono*, I construct.] The effective part of a force, velocity, etc., in a given direction; one of any number of constituent forces, velocities, etc., of which the given force, velocity, etc., is the resultant.

comport, kom·pōrt', *v.i.* [Fr. *comporter*, to admit of, allow, endure, from L. *comportare*, to bear or carry together—*com*, and *porto*, to carry.] To be suitable; agree; accord; fit; suit: with *with* (pride *comports* ill *with* poverty).—*v.t.* To behave; to conduct; used *refl.*—**comportment**, kom·pōrt'ment, *n.* Behavior; demeanor; deportment.

compose, kom·pōz', *v.t.*—*composed, composing.* [From Fr. *composer*, to compose, from prefix *com*, and *poser*, to place, L. *pausare* (see POSE), but early identified with L. *compono, compositum*, to compound, from *com*, and *pono*, to place; so also *dispose, expose*.] To form by uniting two or more things; to form, frame, or fashion; to form by being combined or united; to constitute; to make; to write, as an author; to become the author of (a book, a piece of music); to calm; to quiet; to appease; to settle; to adjust (differences, etc.); to place in proper form; to dispose; *fine arts*, to arrange the leading features of; *printing*, to set in proper order for printing, as types in a composing stick.—*v.i.* To practice literary, musical, or artistic composition.—**composed**, kom·pōzd', *a.* Free from disturbance or agitation; calm; sedate; quiet; tranquil.—**composedly**, kom·pō'zed·li, *adv.* In a composed manner; calmly; without agitation; sedately.—**composure**, composedness, kom·pō'zhėr, kom·pō'zed·nes, *n.* The state of being composed; a settled state of mind; sedateness; calmness; tranquillity.—**composer**, kom·pō'zėr, *n.* One who or that which composes; one who writes an original work; most commonly, one who composes musical pieces.—**composite**, kom'po·zit, *a.* [L. *compositus*, from *compono, compositum*, to compound.] Made up of distinct parts, elements, or substances; compounded; *arch.* a term applied to one of the orders because the capital belonging to it is *composed* out of those of the other orders, exhibiting leaves, volutes, etc.; *bot.* applied to plants forming a vast order, and having flowers forming dense heads composed of many florets, as in the daisy, dandelion, etc.—*Composite number*—A product of two or more integers each greater than 1.—*Composite ship*, a ship having a wooden skin on an iron framework.—*n.* Anything made up of parts or of different elements; a compound; a composition.—

composition, kom·po·zi'shon, n. [L. *compositio*, Fr. *composition*, in meaning akin partly to *compose*, partly to the verb *compound*.] The act of composing or compounding, or the state of being composed or compounded; the act of producing some literary or musical piece; what is composed, as a literary, musical, or artistic production; the act of writing for practice in English or a foreign language; the act of making a mutual agreement for the discharge of a debt, or the agreement itself; the amount or rate paid in compounding with creditors; *gram.* the act of forming compound words, the arrangement of parts in a whole; mode of arrangement; a material compounded of two or more ingredients; a compound; *printing*, the act of setting types or characters in the composing stick, to form lines, and of arranging the lines in a galley to make a column or page, and from this to make a form.—**compositor,** kom·poz'i·tẽr, n. *Printing*, one who sets types and makes up the pages and forms.—**composing stick,** n. A printer's instrument in which types are arranged into words and lines.

compost, kom'pōst, n. [O.Fr. *composte*, It. *composta*, a mixture, from L. *compositum*, from *compono*. COMPOUND.] A mixture or composition of various manuring substances for fertilizing land; a composition for plastering the exterior of houses.—*v.t.* To manure with compost; to plaster.

composure. See COMPOSE.

compotation, kom·pō·tā'shon, n. [L. *compotatio—com*, with, and *potatio*, from *poto*, to drink.] The act of drinking or tippling together.—**compotator,** kom·pō·tā'tẽr, n. One who drinks with another.

compote, kom'pōt, n. [Fr.] Fruit, generally stone fruit, stewed or preserved in syrup.

compound, kom'pound, a. [Originally a participle of O.E. *compoune*, *compone*, to compound. See the verb.] Composed of two or more elements, parts, or ingredients; not simple; *bot.* made up of smaller parts of like kind with or similar to the whole.—*Compound animals*, animals, such as coral polyps, in which individuals, distinct as regards many of the functions of life, are yet connected by some part of their frame so as to form a united whole.—*Compound fracture*, *surg.* a fracture in which a bone is broken and there is also laceration of the tissues.—*Compound interest*, that interest which arises from the principal with the interest added.—*Compound quantities*, *alg.* such quantities as are joined by the signs + and —, plus and minus; *arith.* quantities which consist of more than one denomination (as of dollars and cents); hence the operations of adding, subtracting, multiplying, and dividing such quantities are termed *compound addition, subtraction, multiplication,* and *division.*—*Compound word*, a word com-

posed of two or more words.—*n.* Something produced by compounding two or more ingredients, parts, or elements, as a substance or a word.—*v.t.* (kom·pound'). [O.E. *compone, compoune,* with *d* added (as in *expound, propound, sound,* vulgar *drownd,* etc.), from L. *compono—com,* together, and *pono, positum,* to set or put, whence *position.* COMPOSE.] To mix up or mingle together; to form by mingling two or more ingredients or elements into one; to combine; to settle amicably; to adjust by agreement (a controversy); to fail to prosecute (an offense) for a consideration; to discharge (a debt) by paying a part.—*v.i.* To agree upon concession; to come to terms of agreement; to arrange or make a settlement by compromise; especially, to settle with creditors by agreement, and discharge a debt by paying a part of its amount; or to make an agreement to pay a debt by means or in a manner different from that stipulated or required by law (to *compound with* a person, and *for* a debt).—**compoundable,** kom·poun'da·bl, *a.* Capable of being compounded.—**compounder,** kom·poun'dẽr, n. One who compounds.

compound, kom'pound, n. [From Malay *kampong,* a yard or court.] In the Orient, an enclosure containing European establishments; any large enclosed area; the enclosure in which isolated houses stand.

comprehend, kom·prē·hend' v.t. [L. *comprehendo—com,* together, *præ,* before, and an obs, *hendere,* to catch.] To take in or include within a certain scope; to include by implication or signification; to embrace; to comprise; to take into the mind; to grasp by the understanding; to possess or have in idea; to understand.—**comprehensible,** kom·prē·hen'si·bl, *a.* [L. *comprehensibilis.*] Capable of being comprehended; capable of being understood; conceivable by the mind; intelligible; also **comprehendible,** kom·prē·hen'di·bl.—**comprehensibility,** kom·prē·hen'si·bil''i·ti, n. The quality of being comprehensible; the capability of being understood.—**comprehensibly,** kom·prē·hen'si·bli·, *adv.* In a comprehensible manner; conceivably.—**comprehension,** kom·prē·hen'shon, n. [L. *comprehensio.*] The act of comprehending, including, or embracing; a comprising; inclusion; capacity of the mind to understand; power of the understanding to receive and contain ideas; capacity of knowing.—**comprehensive,** kom·prē·hen'siv, *a.* Having the quality of comprehending or embracing a great number or a wide extent; of extensive application; wide in scope; comprehending much in a comparatively small compass; having the power to comprehend or understand.—**comprehensively,** kom·prē·hen'siv·li, *adv.* In a comprehensive manner; with great extent of scope; so as to contain much in small compass.—**comprehensiveness,** kom·prē-

hen'siv·nes, n. The quality of being comprehensive.

compress, kom·pres', *v.t.* [L. *comprimo, compressum—com,* together, and *premo, pressum,* to press.] To press together; to force, urge, or drive into a smaller compass; to condense.—*n.* (kom'pres). In *surg.* a soft mass formed of tow, lint, or soft linen cloth, so contrived as by the aid of a bandage to make due pressure on any part.—**compressed,** kom·prest', *p.* and *a.* Pressed into narrow compass; condensed; *bot.* and *zool.* flattened laterally or lengthwise.—**compressibility,** kom·pres'i·bil''i·ti, n. The quality of being compressible, or yielding to pressure.—**compressible,** kom·pres'i·bl, *a.* Capable of being compressed or forced into a narrower compass, yielding to pressure; condensable.—**compression,** kom·presh'on, n. The act of compressing; the act of forcing into closer union or density; the state of being compressed; condensation.—**compressive,** kom·pres'iv, *a.* Having power to compress; tending to compress.—**compressor,** kom·pres'ẽr, n. [L.] One who or that which compresses.

comprise, kom·priz', *v.i.*—*comprised, comprising.* [Fr. *compris,* part. of *comprendre,* L. *comprehendo,* to comprehend. COMPREHEND.] To comprehend; to contain; to include (the United States *comprises* various states).—**comprisal,**† kom·pri'zal, n. The act of comprising; inclusion.

compromise, kom'pro·mīz, n. [Fr. *compromis,* a compromise, originally a mutual promise to refer to arbitration, from *compromettre,* L. *compromitto—com,* and *promitto, promissum,* to promise. PROMISE.] A settlement of differences by mutual concessions; a combination of two rival systems, principles, etc., in which a part of each is sacrificed to make the combination possible; what results from, or is founded on, such an agreement; a mutual concession.—*v.t.*—*compromised, compromising.* To adjust or combine by a compromise; to settle by mutual concessions; to put to risk or hazard, or expose to serious consequences, by some act or declaration which cannot be recalled; to put in jeopardy; to endanger the interests of: often *refl.* (he *compromised himself* by his rash statements).—*v.i.* To make a compromise.

Comptometer, komp·tom'e·tẽr, n. A name applied to a kind of calculating machine; hence, a machine bearing this trademark.

comptroller, kon·trōl'er, n. A controller; an officer who examines expenditures.—**comptrollership,** kon·trōl'ẽr·ship, n. The office of comptroller.

compulsion, kom·pul'shon, n. [L. *compulsio, compulsionis,* constraint, compulsion, from *compello, compulsum,* to compel. COMPEL.] The act of compelling or driving by force, physical or moral; an obsessive impulse.—**compulsive,** kom·pul'siv, Exercising compulsion; compulsory.—**compulsively,** kom·pul'siv·li, *adv.*

By or under compulsion; by force.—**compulsorily**, kom·pul'so·ri·li, *adv.* In a compulsory manner; by force or constraint.—**compulsory**, kom·pul'so·ri, *a.* Exercising compulsion; compelling; constraining; enforced; due to compulsion; obligatory (a *compulsory* contribution).

compunction, kom·pungk'shon, *n.* [L. *compunctio, compungo—com,* and *pungo,* to prick or sting. PUNGENT.] The stinging or pricking of the conscience; contrition; remorse.

compurgation, kom·pér·gā'shon, *n.* [L. *compurgo—com,* and *purgo,* to purge or purify.] An ancient mode of trial in England, where the accused was permitted to call a certain number of persons who joined their oaths to his in testimony to his innocence.

compute, kom·pūt', *v.t.—computed, computing.* [L. *computo,* to calculate—*com,* together, and *puto,* to reckon, esteem, whence also *dispute, impute.* To *count* is really the same as this word.] To determine by calculation; to count; to reckon; to calculate; to estimate.—*v.i.* To reckon.—**computability**, kom·pū'ta·bil'i·ti, *n.* The quality of being computable.—**computable**, kom·pū'ta·bl, *a.* Capable of being computed, numbered, or reckoned.—**computation**, kom·pū·tā'shon, *n.* [L. *computatio.*] The act or process of computing, reckoning, or estimating; calculation; the result of a computation.—**computer**, kom·pū'tér, *n.* One who computes; a reckoner; a calculator.

comrade, kom'rad, *n.* [O.E. *camarade, camerade,* from Sp. *camarada,* Fr. *camarade,* one who occupies the same chamber, from L. *camera,* a chamber.] An associate in occupation or friendship; a close companion; a mate.—**comradeship**, kom'rad·ship, *n.* The state or feeling of being a comrade; companionship; fellowship.

comsat, käm'sat, *n.* [From *communications* and *satellite.*] A satellite linked to a global communications network.

Comtism, kom'tizm, *n.* The philosophical system founded by Auguste *Comte;* positivism.—**Comtist**, kom'tist, *n.* A disciple of Comte; a positivist. Used also adjectively.

con, kon, *adv.* and *n.* [Abbrev. from L. *contra,* against.] Against, in the phrase *pro and con,* for and against, as a noun, a statement, argument, point, or consideration supporting the negative side of a question (to (discuss the *pros* and *cons*).

con, kon, *v.t.—conned, conning.* [A form of *can.*] To peruse carefully and attentively; to study over; to learn; to direct the steering of (a ship).—**conning tower,** a turret on a ship from which the vessel's movements are directed.

con, kon, *v.t.* [From *confidence.*] (Slang) To swindle.—*a.* Confidence.

conation, ko·nā'shon, *n.* [L. *conor, conatus,* to attempt.] *Metaph.* the faculty of voluntary agency, embracing desire and volition.—**conative**, kon'a·tiv, *a.* Relating to the faculty of conation.

concatenate, kon·kat'e·nāt, *v.t.—concatenated, concatenating.* [L. *concateno, concatenatum,* to link together—*con,* together, and *catena,* a chain. CHAIN.] To link together; to unite in a successive series or chain, as things depending on each other.—**concatenation**, kon·kat'e·nā''shon, *n.* The state of being concatenated or linked together; a series of links united.

concave, kon'kāv, *a.* [L. *concavus—con,* and *cavus,* hollow. CAVE.] Hollow and curved or rounded, as the inner surface of a spherical body; presenting a hollow or incurvation towards some direction expressed or understood; incurved.—*n.* A hollow; an arch or vault; a cavity.—*v.t.†—concaved, concaving.* To make hollow.—**concavely**, kon'kāv·li, *adv.* So as to be concave; in a concave manner.—**concaveness**, kon'kāv·nes, *n.* The state of being concave.—**concavity**, kon·kav'i·ti, *n.* Hollowness; a concave surface, or the space contained in it.—**concavo-concave**, kon·kā'vō·kon·kāv, *a.* Concave or hollow on both surfaces, as a lens.—**concavo-convex**, kon·kā'vō·kon·veks, *a.* Concave on one side and convex on the other.

conceal, kon·sēl', *v.t.* [From L. *concelo,* to conceal—*con,* together, and *celo,* to hide.] To hide; to withdraw from observation; to cover or keep from sight; to keep close or secret; to forbear to disclose; to withhold from utterance or declaration.—**concealable**, kon·sēl'a·bl, *a.* Capable of being concealed, hid, or kept close.—**concealment**, kon·sēl'ment, *n.* The act of concealing, hiding, or keeping secret; the state of being hid or concealed; privacy; shelter from observation; cover from sight.

concede, kon·sēd', *v.t.—conceded, conceding.* [L. *concedo, concessum,* to yield, grant—*con,* together, and *cedo,* to yield. CEDE.] To admit as true, just, or proper; to grant; to let pass undisputed; to grant as a privilege; to yield up; to allow; to surrender.—*v.i.* To make concession; to grant a request or petition; to yield.—**conceder**, kon·sē'dér, *n.* One who concedes.—**concession**, kon·sesh'on, *n.* [L. *concessio.*] The act of conceding, admitting, or granting; a yielding to demand or claim; the thing yielded; a grant; a grant empowering some scheme or work to be done.—**concessionary, concessionnaire**, kon·sesh'on·a·ri, kon·sesh'on·âr'', *n.* [Fr. *concessionnaire.*] A person to whom a concession for carrying out some scheme has been made; a member of a company to whom special powers have been granted by a government for carrying out some work.—**concessive**, kon·ses'iv, *a.* Implying or containing concession.

conceit, kon·sēt', *n.* [O.E. *conceipt,* O.Fr. *concept,* from L. *conceptus,* a conception, from *concipio,* to conceive—*con,* and *capio,* to take; comp. *deceit, receipt.*] Opinion, estimation, view, or belief (wise in one's own *conceit*); an ill-grounded opinion; a baseless fancy; a crotchety notion;

an ill-grounded opinion of one's own importance; self-conceit; vanity; a witty, happy, or ingenious thought or expression; a quaint or humorous fancy; now commonly a thought or expression intended to be striking or poetical, but rather farfetched, insipid, or pedantic.—*Out of conceit with,* not now having a favorable opinion of; no longer pleased with.—*v.t.* To imagine wrongly; to err in believing: used *refl.*—**conceited**, kon·sē'ted, *a.* Entertaining a flattering opinion of one's self; self-conceited; vain; egotistical.—**conceitedly**, kon·sē'ted·li, *adv.* In a conceited manner; with vanity or egotism.—**conceitedness**, kon·sē'ted·nes, *n.* The state of being conceited.

conceive, kon·sēv', *v.t.—conceived, conceiving.* [O.Fr. *concever, conceveir,* Fr. *concevoir,* from L. *concipere,* to conceive. CONCEIT.] To become pregnant with; to develop in the womb in an embryonic state; to form in the mind; to devise (an idea, a purpose); to realize in the mind; to form a conception of; to place distinctly before the thoughts; to comprehend; often used as a specific term in philosophy; to think; to imagine; to suppose possible.—*v.i.* To have a fetus formed in the womb; to become pregnant; to have or form a conception or idea; to think (to *conceive of* a thing).—**conceivable**, kon·sē'va·bl, *a.* Capable of being conceived, thought, imagined, or understood.—**conceivability, conceivableness**, kon·sē'va·bil'i·ti, kon·sē'va·bl·nes, *n.* The quality of being conceivable.—**conceivably**, kon·sē'va·bli, *adv.* In a conceivable or intelligible manner.—**conceiver**, kon·sē'vér, *n.* One that conceives.

concentrate, kon·sen'trāt, or kon', *v.t.—concentrated, concentrating.* [Fr. *concentrer—*L. *con,* together, and *centrum,* a center.] To bring to a common center or point of union; to cause to come together to one spot or point; to bring to bear on one point; to direct toward one object; in chemical manipulations, to intensify by removing nonessential matter; to reduce to a state of great strength and purity.—*v.i.* To approach or meet in a common point or center.—**concentration**, kon·sen·trā'shon, *n.* The act of concentrating; the act of collecting into a central point or of directing to one object; the state of being concentrated; the act of increasing the strength of fluids by volatilizing part of their water.—*Concentration camp.* Barracks with stockade, patrolled by the military, used for the detention and punishment of people politically, economically, or morally adverse to the policies of the government, esp., in Europe.—**concenter**, kon·sen'tér, *v.i.—concentered, concentering.* To converge to or meet in a common center; to combine or be united in one object.—*v.t.* To draw or direct to a common center; to concentrate.—**concentric, concentrical**, kon·sen'trik, kon·sen'tri·kal, *a.* [L. *concen-*

tricus.] Having a common center (circles, etc.).—**concentrically,** kon·sen'tri·kal·li, *adv.* In a concentric manner.—**concentricity,** kon·sen·tris'i·ti, *n.* State of being concentric.

concept, kon'sept, *n.* [L. *conceptum,* what is conceived, from *concipio.* CONCEIVE.] *Philos.* the subject of a conception; the object conceived by the mind; a notion.—**conceptacle,** kon·sep'ta·kl, *n.* [L. *conceptaculum.*] That in which anything is contained; a receptacle; *bot.* a hollow sac containing bodies connected with reproduction or fructification†.—**conception,** kon·sep'shon, *n.* [L. *conceptio.*] The act of conceiving; the first formation of the embryo of an animal; the act or power of conceiving in the mind; that which is conceived in the mind; product of the imaginative or inventive faculty; *philos.* that mental act or combination of acts by which an absent object of perception is brought before the mind by the imagination; the mental operation by which such notions or conceptions are formed; a general notion; that which constitutes the meaning of a general term; thought, notion, or idea in the loose sense (you have no *conception* how clever he is).—*Immaculate conception.* IMMACULATE.—**conceptional,** kon·sep'shon·al, *a.* Pertaining to or having the nature of a conception or notion. —**conceptive,** kon·sep'tiv, *a.* Capable of conceiving either physically or mentally.—**conceptual,** kon·sep'chū·al, *a.* Pertaining to conception, mental or physical.—**conceptualism,** kon·sep'chū·al·izm, *n.* The doctrine of the conceptualists, in some sense intermediate between realism and nominalism.—**conceptualist,** kon·sep'chū·al·ist, *n.* One who holds the doctrine that the mind has the power of assigning an independent existence to general conceptions.—**conceptualistic,** kon·sep'chū·a·lis"tik, *a.* Pertaining to conceptualism or conceptualists.

concern, kon·sèrn', *v.t.* [Fr. *concerner,* to concern, from L. *concerno,* to mix, as in a sieve—*con,* together, and *cerno,* to sift, akin to Gr. *krinō,* to separate. Akin *decree, discreet, secret,* etc.] To relate, pertain, or belong to; to affect the interest of; to be of importance to (that does not *concern* me); *refl.* to take or have an interest in, occupy or busy one's self; to disturb, make uneasy, or cause concern to: in this sense generally in pp.—*n.* That which relates or belongs to one; business; affair; matter of importance; that which affects one's welfare or happiness; solicitude; anxiety; agitation or uneasiness of mind; disturbed state of feeling; an establishment, such as a manufacturing or commercial establishment. ∴ *Syn.* under CARE.—**concerned,** kon·sèrnd', *p.* and *a.* Having concern; interested; engaged; anxious.—**concerning,** kon·sèr'ning, *prep.* In regard to; regarding; with relation to; about.—**concernment,** kon·sèrn'ment, *n.* A thing in which one is concerned or inter-

ested; concern; affair; business; interest; importance; participation; concern; solicitude.

concert, kon·sèrt', *v.t.* [Fr. *concerter,* from It. *concertare,* to concert, misspelled from L. *consero, consertus,* to join together—*con,* and *sero,* to join, from root of *series.*] To contrive and settle by mutual communication of opinions or propositions; to plan; to devise.—*n.* (kon'sèrt). [From above verb, but in musical meanings L. *concentus,* a singing together, seems to have had an influence.] Agreement of two or more in a design or plan; accordance in a scheme; cooperation; concord; the music of a company of players or singers, or of both united; a public or private musical entertainment, at which a number of vocalists or instrumentalists, or both, perform singly or combined.—**concerted,** kon·sèr'ted, *p.* and *a.* Mutually contrived or planned.— *Concerted piece,* in *music,* a composition in parts for several voices or instruments.—**concertina,** kon·sèr·tē'na, *n.* A musical instrument held between the hands in playing, and composed of a bellows, with two faces or ends, in which are the keys or stops by pressing which with the fingers air is admitted to the free metallic reeds producing the sounds.—**concerto,** kon·chär'tō, *n.* [It.] A musical composition, usually in a symphonic form, written for one principal instrument, with accompaniments for a full orchestra.

concession, etc. See CONCEDE.

conch, kongk, *n.* [L. *concha,* Gr. *kongchē,* Skr. *çankha,* a shell.] A marine shell, especially a large spiral shell of a trumpet shape, which may be blown like a trumpet; the external portion of the ear, more especially the hollow part of it.— **conchiferous,** kong·kif'ér·us, *a.* Belonging to the chonchifers.—**conchoidal,** kong·koi'dal, *a. Mineral,* having convex elevations and concave depressions like shells.—**conchological,** kong·ko·loj'ik·al, *a.* Pertaining to conchology.—**conchologist,** kong·kol'o·jist, *n.* One versed in conchology.—**conchology,** kong·kol'o·ji, *n.* That department of zoology which treats of the nature, formation, and classification of the shells with which the bodies of many Mollusca are protected, or of the animals themselves.

concierge, kon·syârzh', *n.* [Fr.] A doorkeeper to a hotel, house, prison, etc.; a janitor, male or female; a porter.

conciliar, kon·sil'i·ér, *a.* [From L. *concilium,* a council.] Pertaining or relating to a council.

conciliate, kon·sil'i·āt, *v.t.*—*conciliated, conciliating.* [L. *concilio, conciliatum,* to unite in thought or feeling, from *concilium,* plan, council. COUNCIL.] To bring to entertain a friendly feeling; to make friendly from being antagonistic; to pacify; to soothe; to win, gain, or engage (to *conciliate* one's affection or regard); to show to be compatible (statements, etc.).

—**conciliation,** kon·sil'i·ā"shon, *n.* The act of conciliating; the act of making friendly; the act of winning or gaining favor or esteem.—**conciliative,** kon·sil'i·ā·tiv, *a.* Tending to conciliate; conciliatory.—**conciliator,** kon·sil'i·ā·tèr, *n.* One who conciliates or reconciles.—**conciliatory,** kon·sil'i·a·to·ri, *a.* Tending to conciliate or bring to a friendly state of feeling; pacific.

concise, kon·sīs', *a.* [L. *concisus,* cut off, brief, from *concido*—*con,* and *caedo,* to cut.] Comprehending much in few words; brief and comprehensive; employing as few words as possible; succinct. ∴ *Concise* refers mainly to style or manner in speaking or writing; *succinct* refers rather to the result produced by conciseness; thus we speak of a *concise* style or phrase; a *succinct* narrative or account.— **concisely,** kon·sīs'li, *adv.* In a concise manner; briefly; in few words.— **conciseness,** kon·sīs'nes, *n.* The quality of being concise.

concision,‡ kon·si'zhon, *n.* Conciseness; a sect or faction; those in the apostles' time who laid too much stress on circumcision (N.T.).

conclave, kon'klāv, *n.* [L. *conclave,* a private room, a closet—*con,* together, and *clavis,* a key.] The assembly or meeting of the cardinals shut up for the election of a pope; hence, the body of cardinals; a private meeting; a close assembly.—**conclavist,** kon'klā·vist, *n.* An attendant whom a cardinal is allowed to take with him into the conclave for the choice of a pope.

conclude, kon·klūd', *v.t.*—*concluded, concluding.* [L. *concludo*—*con,* and *claudo,* to shut; whence also *clause, close.*] To shut up or enclose‡; to include or comprehend (N.T.)‡; to infer or arrive at by reasoning; to deduce, as from premises; to judge; to end, finish, bring to a conclusion; to settle or arrange finally (to *conclude* an agreement, a peace).—*v.i.* To infer; to form a final judgment; to come to a decision; to resolve; to determine; generally followed by an infinitive or a clause; to end; to make a finish.—**concluder,** kon·klū'dèr, *n.* One who concludes.— **conclusion,** kon·klū'zhon, *n.* [L. *conclusio.*] The end, close, or termination; the last part: often in the phrase *in conclusion*=finally, lastly, determination; final decision; inference; *logic,* the inference of a syllogism as drawn from the premises; an experiment (obsolete except in the phrase *to try conclusions*).—**conclusive,** kon·klū'siv, *a.* Putting an end to debate or argument; leading to a conclusion or determination; decisive; bringing out or leading to a regular logical conclusion.— **conclusively,** kon·klū'siv·li, *adv.* In a conclusive manner.—**conclusiveness,** kon·klū'siv·nes, *n.* The quality of being conclusive or decisive.

concoct, kon·kokt', *v.t.* [L. *concoquo, concoctum*—*con,* and *coquo,* to cook. COOK.] To digest by the stomach‡; to ripen or mature‡; to form and prepare in the mind; to devise; to plan; to plot (a scheme); to mix by combining different ingredients. —**concoction**, kon·kok′shon, n. [L. concoctio.] Digestion‡; the act of mixing ingredients, as for a dish in cookery.—**concoctive**, ‡ kon·kok′tiv, a. Maturing; ripening.

concomitant, kon·kom′i·tant, a. [From L. com, together, and comitor, to accompany, from comes, a companion.] Accompanying; conjoined with; concurrent; attending: of things, circumstances, etc.—n. A thing, that accompanies another; an accompaniment; an accessory. — **concomitance, concomitancy**, kon·kom′i·tans, kon·kom′i·tan·si, n. The state of being concomitant; a being together or in connection with another thing.—**concomitantly**, kon·kom′i·tant·li, adv. So as to be concomitant; concurrently; unitedly.

concord, kon′kord or kong′kord, n. [Fr. concorde, L. con, and cor, cordis, the heart. ACCORD.] Agreement or union in opinions, sentiments, views, or interests; harmony; agreement between things; suitableness; music, the pleasing combination of two or more sounds; the relation between two or more sounds which are agreeable to the ear; gram. agreement of words in construction.—**concordance**, kon·kor′dans, n. The state of being concordant; agreement; harmony; a book in which the principal words used in any work, as the Scriptures, Shakespeare, etc., are arranged alphabetically, and the book, chapter, verse, act, scene, line, or other subdivision in which each occurs are noted.—**concordant**, kon·kor′dant, a. [L. concordans, ppr. of concordare, to agree.] Agreeing; agreeable; correspondent; harmonious.—**concordantly**, kon·kor′dant·li, adv. In a concordant manner.—**concordat**, kon·kor′dat, n. [Fr.] An agreement; compact; convention; especially, a formal agreement between the see of Rome and any secular government.

concourse, kon′kōrs or kong′kōrs, n. [Fr. concours, from L. concursus, from concurro, to run together—con, and curro, to run.] A moving, flowing, or running together; confluence; a meeting or coming together of people; the people assembled; a throng; a crowd; an assemblage of things; agglomeration.

concrete, kon′krēt or kong′krēt, a. [L. concretus, from concresco, to grow together—con, and cresco, to grow; seen also in decrease, increase, crescent, etc.] Formed by union of separate particles in a mass; united in a solid form; logic, a term applied to an object as it exists in nature, invested with all its attributes, or to the notion or name of such an object. ABSTRACT.—n. A mass formed by concretion of separate particles of matter in one body; a compound; logic, a concrete term; a compact mass of gravel, coarse pebbles, or stone chippings cemented together by hydraulic or other mortar, employed extensively in building.—v.i. and t.—concreted, con-

creting. To coagulate; to congeal; to thicken.—**concretely**, kon·krēt′li, adv. In a concrete manner; not abstractly.—**concretion**, kon·krē′shon, n. The act of concreting or growing together so as to form one mass; the mass or solid matter formed by growing together; a clot; a lump; geol. a lump or nodule formed by molecular aggregation as distinct from crystallization.—Morbid concretions, hard substances which occasionally make their appearance in different parts of the body.—**concretionary**, kon·krē′sho·na·ri, a. Pertaining to concretion; formed by concretion; consisting of concretions.

concubine, kong′kū·bīn, n. [L. concubina, from concumbo, to lie together—con, and cumbo or cubo, to lie down.] A paramour, male or female‡; a woman who cohabits with a man without being legally married to him; a kept mistress; a wife of inferior condition, such as were allowed in ancient Greece and Rome; a lawful wife, but not united to the man by the usual ceremonies.—**concubinage**, kon′kū·bi·nij, n. The act or practice of having a concubine or concubines; the state of being a concubine; a living as man and wife without being married.—**concubinary**, kon·kū′bi·na·ri, a. Relating to concubinage; living in concubinage.

concupiscence, kon·kū′pi·sens, n. [L. concupiscentia, from concupisco, to lust after—con, and cupio, to desire.] Lustful feeling; lust; sinful desire.—**concupiscent**, kon·kū′pi·sent, a. Desirous of unlawful pleasure; libidinous; lustful.—**concupiscible**,† kon·kū′pis·i·bl, a. Concupiscent; lustful.

concur, kon·ker′, v.i.—concurred, concurring. [L. concurro, to run together —con, and curro, to run; seen also in course, current, incur, recur, etc.] To run or meet together‡; to agree, join, or unite, as in one action or opinion (to concur with a person in an opinion (to assent: with to (Mil.)†; to unite or be conjoined; to meet together; to be combined; to unite in contributing to a common object (causes that concur to an effect); to coincide or have points of agreement (Shak.).—**concurrence, concurrency**, kon·kur′ens, kon·kur′en·si, n. The act of concurring; conjunction; combination of agents, circumstances, or events; agreement in opinion; union or consent as to a design to be carried out; approbation; consent with joint aid or contribution of power or influence.— **concurrent**, kon·kur′ent, a. Concurring or acting in conjunction; agreeing in the same act; contributing to the same event or effect; operating with; conjoined; associate; concomitant; joint and equal; existing together and operating on the same objects (the concurrent jurisdiction of law courts).—n. One who concurs; one agreeing to or pursuing the same course of action; that which concurs; joint or contributory cause.—**concurrently**, kon·kur′ent-

li, adv. So as to be concurrent; in union or combination; unitedly.

concuss, kon·kus′, v.t. [L. concutio, concussum, to shake, and as a law term to extort—con, together, and quatio, quassum (in composition cutio, cussum), to shake. QUASH.] To shake or agitate†; to force by threats to do something, especially to give up something of value; to intimidate into a desired course of action; to coerce.—**concussive**, kon·kus′iv, a. Having the power or quality of shaking; agitating.—**concussion**, kon·kush′on, n. [L. concussio, concussionis, a shock, extortion.] The act of shaking, particularly by the stroke or impulse of another body; the shock occasioned by two bodies coming suddenly into collision; a shock; surg. applied to injuries sustained by the brain and other organs from falls, blows, etc.; the act of extorting by threats or force; extortion.

condemn, kon·dem′, v.t. [L. condemno—con, intens., and damno, to condemn, whence damn.] To pronounce to be utterly wrong; to utter a sentence of disapprobation against; to pronounce to be guilty; to sentence to punishment; to utter sentence against judicially: opposed to acquit or absolve; to judge or pronounce to be unfit for use or service, or to be forfeited.—Condemned cell or ward, in prisons, the cell in which a prisoner sentenced to death is detained till his execution.—**condemnable**, kon·dem′na·bl, a. Worthy of being condemned.— **condemnation**, kon·dem·nā′shon, n. [L. condemnatio.] The act of condemning; the state of being condemned; the cause or reason of a sentence of condemnation (N.T.).— **condemnatory**, kon·dem′na·to·ri a. Condemning; bearing condemnation or censure.—**condemner**, kon·dem′-ėr, n. One who condemns.

condense, kon·dens′, v.t.—condensed, condensing. [L. condenso—con, and denso, to make dense. DENSE.] To make more dense or compact; to reduce the volume or compass of; to bring into closer union of parts; to consolidate; to compress (to condense a substance, an argument, etc.); to reduce (a gas or vapor) to the condition of a liquid or solid.— v.i. To become close or more compact, as the particles of a body; to change from the vaporous to the liquid state.—**condensed**, kon·denst′, a. Made dense or close in texture or composition; compressed; compact (a condensed style of composition).—**condenser**, kon·den′sėr, n. One who or that which condenses; a pneumatic instrument or syringe in which air may be compressed; a vessel in which aqueous or spirituous vapors are reduced to a liquid form by coldness; a lens to gather and concentrate rays collected by a mirror and direct them upon an object; an instrument employed to collect and render sensible very small quantities of electricity.—**condensability**, kon·den′sa·bil″i·ti, n.

---

fāte, fär, fâre, fat, fạll; mē, met, hėr; pīne, pin; nōte, not, mŏve; tūbe, tub, bụll; oil, pound.

Quality of being condensable.—
condensable, condensible, kon·den'-
sa·bl, kon·den'si·bl, *a.* Capable of
being condensed; capable of being
compressed into a smaller compass,
or made more compact.—**conden-
sate,**† kon·den'sāt, *v.t.* and *i.*—*condensed, condensating.* To condense.
—**condensation,** kon·den·sā'shon, *n.*
[L. *condensatio.*] The act of condensing or making more dense or compact; the act of bringing into smaller
compass; consolidation; the act of
reducing a gas or vapor to a liquid
or solid form.
condescend, kon·dē·send', *v.i.* [Fr.
condescendre—L. *con,* with, and *des-
cendo.* DESCEND.] To descend voluntarily for a time to the level of an
inferior; to stoop; to lower one's
self intentionally: often followed by
the infinitive or a noun preceded
by *to.*—**condescending,** kon·dē·sen'-
ding, *a.* Marked or characterized
by condescension; stooping to the
level of one's inferiors.—**condes-
cendingly,** kon·dē·sen'ding·li, *adv.*
In a condescending manner.—**condescension,** kon·dē·sen'shon, *n.* The
act of condescending; the act of
voluntary stooping to an equality
with inferiors; affability on the part
of a superior.
condign, kon·dīn', *a.* [L. *condignus,*
well worthy—*con,* and *dignus,* worthy.
DIGNITY.] Well deserved; merited;
suitable: now always applied to
punishment or something equivalent.
—**condignly,** kon·dīn'li, *adv.* In a
condign manner.
condiment, kon'di·ment, *n.* [L. *con-
dimentum,* from *condio,* to season,
pickle.] Something used to give
relish to food, and to gratify the
taste; sauce; seasoning.
condisciple, kon·di·sī'pl, *n.* A comrade disciple or student associate;
a fellow learner; a schoolmate.
condition, kon·di'shon, *n.* [L. *con-
dicio, condicionis* (also *conditio*) situation, compact, etc.—*con,* and *dico,*
to declare. DICTION.] A particular
mode of being; situation; predicament; case; state; state with respect
to the orders or grades of society or
to property; rank in society; that
which is requisite to be done, happen,
exist, or be present in order to
something else being done, taking
effect, or happening; a clause in
a contract embodying some stipulation, provision, or essential point.
—*v.t.* To form the condition or
essential accompaniment of; to regulate or determine; to stipulate; to
arrange.—**conditional,** kon·di'shon··
al, *a.* Imposing conditions; containing or depending on a condition or
conditions; made with limitations;
not absolute; made or granted on
certain terms; *gram.* and *logic,*
expressing or involving a condition.
—**conditionality,** kon·di'sho·nal''i·-
ti, *n.* The quality of being conditional
or limited; limitation by certain
terms.—**conditionally,** kon·di'-
shon·al·li, *adv.* In a conditional
manner; with certain limitations;
on particular conditions, terms, or
stipulations.—**conditioned,** kon·di'-

shond, *a.* Having a certain state or
qualities, usually preceded by some
qualifying term, as *well conditioned,
ill conditioned; metaph.* placed or
cognized under conditions or relations.
condole, kon·dōl', *v.i.*—*condoled, condoling.* [L.L. *condoleo*—*con,* with,
and L. *doleo,* to grieve, whence
doleful, dolor.] To express pain or
grief at the distress or misfortunes
of another; to express sympathy
to one in grief or misfortune:
followed by *with.*—*v.t.*‡ To lament
or grieve over.—**condolence,** kon··
dō'lens, *n.* The act of condoling;
expression of sympathy with another's grief.—**condoler,** kon·dō'lėr,
n. One who condoles.
condominium, kon·do·min'i·um, *n.*
[L. *con,* and *dominium,* rule.] Joint
rule or control.
condone, kon·dōn', *v.t.*—*condoned,
condoning.* [L. *condonare,* to pardon—
con, and *donare,* to present, from
donum, a gift. DONATION.] To pardon;
to forgive; to overlook an offense
(never with a personal object); *law,*
to forgive, or to act so as to imply
forgiveness of a violation of the
marriage vow.—**condonation,** kon··
dō·nā'shon, *n.* [L. *condonatio.*] The
act of condoning or pardoning a
wrong act; *law,* an act or course of
conduct by which a husband or a
wife is held to have pardoned a
matrimonial offense committed by
the other, the party condoning being
thus barred from a remedy for that
offense.
condor, kon'dor, *n.* [Sp., from Peruv.
cuntur.] A south American bird, one
of the largest of the vulture tribe,
found most commonly in the Andes
at heights from 10,000 to 15,000
feet above the level of the sea.
conduce, kon·dūs', *v.i.*—*conduced,
conducing.* [L. *conduco,* to conduce—
con, and *duco,* to lead; *conduct* is
from the same verb.] To combine
with other things in bringing about
or tending to bring about a result;
to lead or tend; to contribute:
followed by the infinitive or a noun
preceded by *to.*—**conducible,**‡ kon··
dū'si·bl, *a.* [L. *conducibilis.*] Conducive.—**conducibleness,**‡ kon·dū'-
si·bl·nes, *n.* Conduciveness.—**conducive,** kon·dū'siv, *a.* Having the
quality of conducing, promoting,
or furthering; tending to advance
or bring about; followed by *to.*—
conduciveness, kon·dū'siv·nes, *n.*
The quality of being conducive.
conduct, kon'dukt, *n.* [L.L. *conductus,* L. *conductus,* pp. of *conduco.*
CONDUCE. DUKE.] The act of guiding
or commanding; mode of carrying
on or conducting; mode of handing
or wielding; administration; management; personal behavior; deportment: applied indifferently to a
good or bad course of action; the
act of convoying or guarding;
guidance or bringing along under
protection.—*v.t.* (kon·dukt'). To
accompany and show the way; to
guide; to lead; to escort; to lead,
as a commander; to direct; to
command; to manage (affairs, etc.);

refl. to behave; *physics,* to carry,
transmit, or propagate, as heat,
electricity, etc.; to lead or direct as
musical conductor.—*v.i.* To carry,
transmit, or propagate heat, electricity, sound, etc.; to act as musical
conductor.—**conductibility,** kon··
duk'ti·bil''i·ti, *n.* Capacity of being
conducted; conductivity.—**conduct-
ible,** kon·duk'ti·bl, *a.* Capable of
being conducted or conveyed.—
conduction, kon·duk'shon, *n. Physics,* the mode of transference of heat
through the substance of solids and
of electricity through any suitable
body called a *conductor.*—**conductive,**
kon·duk'tiv, *a. Physics,* having the
power or quality of conducting.—
conductivity, kon·duk·tiv'i·ti, *n.
Physics,* the power of conducting
heat, electricity, etc.; the quality
of being conductive; the quantity
of heat that flows in unit time
through unit area of a plate of
any substance of unit thickness,
with one degree of difference of
temperature between its faces.—
conductor, kon·duk'tėr, *n.* One who
conducts; a leader; a guide; a
commander; one who leads an army;
a director or manager; the director
of a chorus or orchestra; the person
who attends to the passengers in a
bus or a streetcar, or the like, as
contradistinguished from the driver;
physics, a body that receives and
transmits or communicates heat,
electricity, or force in any of its
forms; hence, specifically, a lightning rod.—**conductory,** kon·duk'-
to·ri, *a.* Having the property of
conducting.
conduit, kon'dit, or kon'duit, *n.* [Fr.
conduit, pp. of *conduire,* L. *conducere,
conductum,* to conduct.] A pipe, tube
or other channel for the conveyance
of fluids; a tube or pipe for protecting
electric wires or cables.
conduplicate, kon·dū'pli·kāt, *a.*
Doubled or folded over or together;
bot. applied to leaves in the bud when
they are folded down the middle,
so that the halves of the lamina are
applied together by their faces.
condyle, kon'dīl, *n.* [L. *condylus,* Gr.
kondylos, a knuckle, a joint.] *Anat.*
a protuberance on the end of a
bone serving to form an articulation
with another bone.—**condyloid,** kon'-
di·loid, *a. Anat.* resembling or
shaped like a condyle.
cone, kōn, *n.* [L. *conus,* Gr. *kōnos,*
a cone, from root seen in E. *hone,*
Skr. *co,* to sharpen.] A solid figure
rising from a circular base and
regularly tapering to a point; anything shaped like, or approaching the
shape of, a cone; one of the fruits
of fir trees, pines, etc.; a strobilus;
the name of certain molluscous
shells; the hill surrounding the
crater of a volcano, formed by the
gradual accumulation of ejected
material; a form of storm signal.—
conic, kon'ik, *a.* [L. *conicus,* Gr.
kōnikos.] Having the form of a
cone; conical; pertaining to a cone.—
Conic sections, the figures formed
by the outlines of the cut surfaces
when a cone is cut by a plane, more

ch, *chain;* ch, Sc. lo*ch;* g, *g*o; j, *j*ob; ng, si*ng;* TH, *th*en; th, *th*in; w, *w*ig; hw, *wh*ig; zh, a*z*ure.

especially the parabola, ellipse, and hyperbola, the first of which is seen when the section is made parallel to the slope of the cone.— *n.* A conic section.—**conical,** kon'- ik•al, *a.* Having the form of a cone; cone shaped.—**conically,** kon'ik•al•li, *adv.* In the form of a cone.—**conics,** kon'iks, *n.* That part of geometry which treats of the cone and the several curve lines arising from the sections of it.—**conifer,** kō'ni•fėr, *n.* [L. *conus,* and *fero,* to bear.] *Bot.* a plant producing cones, or hard, dry, scaly seed vessels of a conical figure, as the pine, fir, etc.—**coniferous,** kō•nif'ėr•us, *a.* Bearing cones; belonging or relating to the conifers.— **conoid,** kō'noid, *n. Geom.* a solid formed by the revolution of a conic section about its axis; *anat,* the pineal gland.—**conoid, conoidal,** kō'- noid, kō•noi'dal, *a.* Approaching to a conical form; nearly conical.

coney, *n.* See CONY.

confabulate, kon•fab'ū•lāt, *v.i.* [L. *confabulor—con,* and *fabulor,* to talk. FABLE.] To talk familiarly together; to chat; to prattle. This word is sometimes shortened colloquially to **confab,** kon•fab'.—**confabulation,** kon•fab'ū•lā″shon, *n.* [L. *confabulatio.*] A talking together; familiar talk; easy, unrestrained conversation. Often shortened to **confab,** kon'fab.

confect,‡ kon•fekt', *v.t.* [L. *conficio, confectum,* to prepare—*con,* and *facio,* to make. COMFIT.] To compose, mix, put together; to make into sweetmeats.—*n.*‡ (kon'fekt). A confection; a sweetmeat.—**confection,** kon•fek'shon, *n.* Anything prepared or preserved with sugar, as fruit; a sweetmeat; a composition or mixture‡.—**confectionary,**‡ kon•- fek'sho•ne•ri, *n.* A confectioner (O.T.).—*a.* Relating to confections. —**confectioner,** kon•fek'shon•ėr, *n.* One whose occupation is to make or sell sweetmeats or confections.— **confectionery,** kon•fek'sho•ne•ri, *n.* Sweetmeats; things prepared or sold by a confectioner; confections.

confederacy, kon•fed'ėr•a•si, *n.* [L. L. *confœderatio—con,* and L. *fœdus,* a league. FEDERAL.] A contract between two or more persons, bodies of men or states, combined in support of each other, in some act or enterprise; a league; compact; alliance; the persons, states, or nations united by a league.—**confederate,** kon•fed'ėr•āt, *a.* [L.L. *confœderatus.*] United in a league; allied by treaty; engaged in a confederacy; pertaining to a confederacy.—*Confederate States of America,* the alliance formed by eleven southern states after secession from the United States in 1860 and 1861.—**confederation,** kon•fed'ėr•ā″shon, *n.* A confederacy; a league; alliance; [*cap.*] the Government of the American Colonies from 1781-1789, previous to the adoption of the Constitution of the United States.—**confederative,** kon•fed'ėr•ā•tiv, *a.* Of or belonging to a confederation.

confer, kon•fėr', *v.t.*—*conferred, con-* ferring. [L. *confero,* to bring together, compare, bestow, consult, etc.—*con,* together, and *fero,* to bring.] To give or bestow: with *on* or *upon* before the recipient. ∴ *Confer* differs from *bestow,* inasmuch as it always implies a certain amount of condescension or superiority on the part of the giver.—*v.i.* To consult together on some special subject; to compare opinions; formerly often simply to discourse or talk, but *confer* now implies conversation on some serious or important subject.— **conferee,** kon•fėr•ē', *n.* One on whom something is conferred.— **conference,** kon'fėr•ens, *n.* [Fr. *conférence.*] The act of conferring or consulting together; a meeting for consultation, discussion, or instruction; a meeting of the representatives of different foreign countries in regard to some matter of importance to all; talk or conversation (*Shak.*)‡. —**conferrable,** kon•fėr'a•bl, *a.* Capable of being conferred or bestowed. —**conferrer,** kon•fėr'ėr, *n.* One who confers.

conferva, kon•fėr'va, *n.* pl. **confervae,** kon•fėr'vē. [L.] A name for various aquatic plants belonging to the algae, and chiefly composed of simple or branching filaments.—**confervoid,** kon•fėr'void, *a.* Resembling a conferva; partaking of the character of the confervae.

confess, kon•fes', *v.t.* [Fr. *confesser,* from L. *confiteor, confessum—con,* and *fateor,* to own or acknowledge.] To own, acknowledge, or avow, as a crime, a fault, a charge, a debt, or something that is against one's interest or reputation; to own to; to disclose; *eccles.* to disclose or recapitulate (sins) to a priest in private with a view to absolution: in this sense sometimes *refl.*; to hear or receive the confession of: said of the priest; to acknowledge as having a certain character or certain claims; to declare belief in; to grant, concede, admit; not to dispute, to attest, reveal, let be known (poet.). ∴ Syn. under ACKNOWLEDGE.—*v.i.* To make confession or avowal; to disclose faults; to make known one's sins to a priest.— **confessedly,** kon•fes'ed•li, *adv.* By general confession or admission; admittedly.—**confesser,** kon•fes'ėr, *n.* One who confesses.—**confession,** kon•fesh'on, *n.* The act of confessing; the act of making an avowal; profession (N.T.); a disclosing of sins or faults to a priest; the disburdening of the conscience privately to a confessor.—*Confession of Faith,* a formulary which comprises the articles of faith that a person, a church, etc., accepts as true.— **confessional,** kon•fesh'on•al, *n.* [Fr. *confessional,* L.L. *confessionale.*] A compartment or cell in which a priest sits to hear confession, having a small opening or hole at each side through which the penitent, kneeling without, makes confession.—*a.* Of or pertaining to a confession.— **confessionary,** kon•fesh'o•ne•ri, *a.* Pertaining to auricular confession.—

confessor, kon•fes'ėr, *n.* One who confesses; one who acknowledges a crime or fault; a priest who hears confession and assumes power to grant absolution; one who made a profession of his faith in the Christian religion, and adhered to it in the face of persecution.

confide, kon•fīd', *v.i.*—*confided, confiding.* [L. *confido—con,* and *fido,* to trust. FAITH.] To rely with full assurance of mind; to rest the mind firmly without anxiety; to trust; to believe: followed by *in.*—*v.t.*— *confided, confiding.* To entrust; to commit with full reliance on the party to whom the thing is committed (to *confide* a thing *to* a person). —**confidant,** kon'fi•dant, *n. masc.* —**confidante,** kon•fi•dant', *n. fem.* [O.Fr.] A person entrusted with the confidence of another; one to whom secrets are confided; a confidential friend.—**confidence,** kon'fi•dens, *n.* [L. *confidentia.*] Assurance of mind; firm belief; trust; reliance; reliance on one's own abilities, resources, or circumstances; self-reliance; assurance; boldness; courage; that in which trust is placed; ground of trust; a secret; a private or confidential communication (to exchange *confidences* together).—**confident,** kon'fi•dent, *a.* Full of confidence; having full belief; fully assured; relying on one's self; full of assurance; bold, sometimes overbold.— **confidential,** kon•fi•den'shal, *a.* Enjoying the confidence of another; entrusted with secrets or with private affairs; intended to be treated as private, or kept in confidence; spoken or written in confidence; secret.—**confidentially,** kon•fi•den'- shal•li, *adv.* In a confidential manner.—**confidently,** kon'fi•dent•li, *adv.* In a confident manner; with firm trust; with strong assurance; positively; dogmatically.—**confider,** kon•fī'dėr, *n.* One who confides; one who trusts in or entrusts to another. —**confiding,** kon•fī'ding, *p.* and *a.* Trusting; reposing confidence; trustful; credulous.—**confidingly,** kon•- fī'ding•li, *adv.* In a confiding manner; trustfully.

configure,† kon•fig'ūr, *v.t.*—*configured, configuring.* [L. *configuro—con,* and *figuro,* to form; *figura,* figure.] To form; to dispose in a certain form, figure, or shape.—**configuration,** kon•fig'ū•rā″shon, *n.* [L. *configuratio.*] External form, figure, or shape of a thing as resulting from the disposition and shape of its parts; external aspect or appearance; shape or form.

confine, kon'fīn, *n.* [L. *confinis,* bordering, adjoining, *confine,* a border—*con,* and *finis,* end, border, limit. FINE.] Border; boundary; frontier; the part of any territory which is at or near the end or extremity: generally in the plural and in regard to contiguous regions. —*v.t.* (kon•fīn')—*confined, confining.* [Fr. *confiner.*] To restrain within limits; to circumscribe; hence, to imprison; to immure; to shut up; to limit or restrain voluntarily in some act or practice (to *confine one's self* to a subject).—*To be confined*, to be in childbed.—**confinable**, kon·fī′na·bl, *a*. Capable of being confined or limited.—**confined**, kon·fīnd′, *p*. and *a*. Restrained within limits; limited; circumscribed; narrow (a *confined* scope or range).—**confinement**, kon·fīn′ment, *n*. The state of being confined; restraint within limits; any restraint of liberty by force or other obstacle or necessity; imprisonment; the lying-in of a woman.—**confiner**, kon·fī′nẽr, *n*. One who or that which confines.

confirm, kon·fẽrm′, *v.t.* [L. *con-firmo—con*, and *firmo*, to make firm, from *firmus*, firm.] To make firm or more firm; to add strength to; to strengthen; to settle or establish; to make certain; to put past doubt; to assure; to verify; to sanction; to ratify (an agreement, promise); to strengthen in resolution, purpose, or opinion; to administer the rite of confirmation to.—**confirmable**, kon·fẽr′ma·bl, *a*. Capable of being confirmed.—**confirmation**, kon·fẽr·mā′shon, *n*. The act of confirming; the act of establishing; establishment; corroboration; the act of rendering valid or ratifying; the ceremony of laying on hands by a bishop in the admission of baptized persons to the full enjoyment of Christian privileges, a rite of the Roman, Greek, and English churches; that which confirms; additional evidence; proof; convincing testimony.—**confirmative**, kon·fẽr′ma·tiv, *a*. Tending to confirm or establish; confirmatory.—**confirmatory**, kon·fẽr′ma·to·ri, *a*. Serving to confirm; giving additional strength, force, or stability, or additional assurance or evidence.—**confirmed**, kon·fẽrmd′, *p*. and *a*. Fixed; settled; settled in certain habits, state of health, etc. (a *confirmed* drunkard or invalid); having received the rite of confirmation.—**confirmedly**, con·fẽr′med·li, *adv*. In a confirmed manner.

confiscate, kon′fis·kāt or kon·fis′kāt, *v.t.*—*confiscated, confiscating*. [L. *con-fisco, confiscatum—con*, together, and *fiscus*, the state treasury.] To adjudge to be forfeited to the public treasury; to appropriate to public use by way of penalty; to appropriate under legal authority as forfeited.—*a*. Confiscated. (*Shak.*)—**confiscable**,† kon·fis′ka·bl, *a*. Capable of being confiscated; liable to forfeiture.—**confiscation**, kon·fis·kā′shon, *n*. The act of confiscating or appropriating as forfeited.—**confiscator**, kon′fis·kā·tẽr or kon·fis′, *n*. One who confiscates.—**confiscatory**, kon·fis′ka·to·ri, *a*. Confiscating; relating to confiscation.

conflagration, kon·fla·grā′shon, *n*. [L. *conflagratio—con*, with, and *flagro*, to burn, whence *flagrant*.] A great fire, or the burning of any great mass of combustibles.

conflict, kon′flikt, *n*. [L. *conflictus*, a conflict, from *confligo—con*, together, and *fligo*, to strike, to dash.] A fighting or struggle for mastery; a com-

bat; a striving to oppose or overcome; active opposition; contention; strife.—kon·flikt′, *v.i.* To meet in opposition or hostility; to contend; to strive or struggle; to be in opposition; to be contrary; to be incompatible or at variance.—**conflicting**, kon·flik′ting, a. Being in opposition; contrary; contradictory; incompatible.—**confliction**,† kon·flik′shon, *n*. Act of conflicting or clashing.

confluence, kon′flū·ens, *n*. [L. *confluentia*, from *confluo—con*, and *fluo*, to flow.] A flowing together; the meeting or junction of two or more streams of water; also, the place of meeting; the running together of people; a crowd; a concourse.—**confluent**, kon′flū·ent, *a*. [L. *confluens*.] Flowing together; meeting in their course, as two streams; meeting; running together; *bot*. united at some part.—*Confluent smallpox*, smallpox in which the pustules run together or unite.—*n*. A tributary stream.—**conflux**, kon′fluks, *n*. A flowing together; a crowd; a multitude collected.

conform, kon·form′, *v.t.* [L. *conformo—con*, and *forma*, form.] To make of the same form or character; to make like (to *conform* anything *to* a model); to bring into harmony or correspondence; to adapt; to submit: often *refl.*—*v.i.* To act in conformity or compliance; *eccles*. to comply with the usages of the Established Church.—*a*. [L. *conformis—con*, and *forma*, form.] Conformable.—**conformability**, kon·for·ma·bil″i·ti, *n*. The state or quality of being conformable.—**conformable**, kon·for′ma·bl, *a*. Corresponding in form, character, manners, opinions, etc.; in harmony or conformity; agreeable; suitable; consistent; adapted; compliant; submissive; disposed to obey; *geol*. lying in parallel or nearly parallel planes, and having the same dip and changes of dip: said of strata or groups of strata.—**conformableness**, kon·for′ma·bl·nes, *n*. State of being conformable.—**conformably**, kon·for′ma·bli, *adv*. In a conformable manner; in conformity; suitably; agreeably.—**conformation**, kon·for·mā′shon, *n*. The manner in which a body is formed; the particular disposition of the parts which compose it; configuration; form; structure.—**conformer**, kon·for′mẽr, *n*. One who conforms; one who complies with established forms or doctrines.—**conformist**, kon·for′mist, *n*. One who conforms or complies; one who complies with the worship of the Church of England as distinguished from a Dissenter or Non-conformist.—**conformity**, kon·form′i·ti, *n*. Correspondence in form or manner; agreement; congruity; likeness; harmony; correspondence with decrees or dictates; submission; accordance; compliance with the usages or principles of the English Church.

confound, kon·found′, *v.t.* [Fr. *confondre*, from L. *confundo—con*, together, and *fundo, fusum*, to pour out, whence *fuse, confuse, refuse*, etc.] To mingle confusedly together; to mix

in a mass or crowd so that individuals cannot be distinguished; to throw into disorder; to confuse; to mistake one for another; to make a mistake between; to throw into consternation; to perplex with terror, surprise, or astonishment; to astound; to abash; to overthrow, ruin, baffle, or bring to nought. ∴ Syn. under ABASH.—**confounded**, kon·foun′ded, *a*. Excessive; odious; detestable. (Colloq.)—**confoundedly**, kon·foun′ded·li, *adv*. Enormously; greatly; shamefully; odiously; detestably. (Colloq.)—**confounder**, kon·foun′dẽr, *n*. One who or that which confounds.

confraternity, kon·fra·tẽr′ni·ti, *n*. A fraternity or brotherhood.

confront, kon·frunt′, *v.t.* [Fr. *confronter—*L. *con*, together, and *frons, frontis*, the countenance or front.] To stand facing; to face; to stand in front of; to meet in hostility; to oppose; to set face to face; to bring into the presence of: followed by *with*.—**confrontation**,† **confrontment**,† kon·frun·tā′shon, kon·frunt′-ment, *n*. The act of confronting.—**confronter**, kon·frun′tẽr, *n*. One who confronts.

Confucian, Confucianist, kon·fū′-shi·an, kon·fū′shi·an·ist, *n*. A follower of Confucius, the famous Chinese philosopher. —**Confucianism**, kon·fū′shian·izm, *n*. The doctrines or system of morality taught by Confucius, which has been long adopted in China, and inculcates the practice of virtue but not the worship of any god.

confuse, kon·fūz′, *v.t.*—*confused, confusing*. [L. *confusus*, from *confundo*. CONFOUND.] To mix up without order or clearness; to throw together indiscriminately; to derange, disorder, jumble; to confound; to perplex or derange the mind or ideas of; to embarrass; to disconcert. ∴ Syn. under ABASH.—**confusedly**, kon·fū′zed·li, *adv*. In a confused manner; in a mixed mass; without order; indiscriminately; with agitation of mind.—**confusedness**, kon·fū′zed·nes, *n*. A state of being confused.—**confusion**, kon·fū′zhon, *n*. [L. *confusio*.] A state in which things are confused; an indiscriminate or disorderly mingling; disorder; tumultuous condition; perturbation of mind; embarrassment; distraction; abashment; disconcertment; overthrow; defeat; ruin.

confute, kon·fūt′, *v.t.*—*confuted, confuting*. [L. *confuto*, to cool down by cold water, to confute—*con*, together, and *futis*, a pitcher, from root of *fundo*, to pour.] To prove (an argument, statement, etc.) to be false, defective, or invalid; to disprove; to overthrow; to prove (a person) to be wrong; to convict of error by argument or proof.—**confutation**, kon·fū·tā′shon, *n*. The act of confuting, disproving, or proving to be false or invalid.—**confutative**, kon·fū′ta·tiv, *a*. Adapted or designed to confute.—**confuter**, kon·fū′tẽr, *n*. One who confutes.

congeal, kon·jēl′, *v.t.* [L. *congelare—*

con, together, and *gelare*, to freeze, from *gelu*, cold, whence also *gelid*, *jelly*.] To change from a fluid to a solid state by cold or a loss of heat; to freeze; to coagulate; to check the flow of; to make (the blood) run cold. —*v.i.* To pass from a fluid to a solid state by cold; to coagulate.— **congealable**, kon·jēl′a·bl, *a.* Capable of being congealed.—**congealment**, kon·jēl′ment, *n.* Congelation.—**congelation**, kon·je·lā′shon, *n.* [L. *congelatio*.] The act or process of congealing; the state of being congealed; what is congealed or solidified; a concretion.

congener, kon′jē·nẽr, *n.* [L.—*con*, together, and *genus, generis*, a kind or race.] A thing of the same kind or nearly allied; a plant or animal belonging to the same genus.— **congeneric**, kon·je·ner′ik, *a.* Being of the same kind or nature; belonging to the same genus.—**congenerous**, kon·jen′ẽr·us, *a.* Congeneric; *anat.* applied to muscles which concur in the same action.

congenial, kon·jē′ni·al, *a.* [L. *con*, and *genialis*, E. *genial*.] Partaking of the same nature or natural characteristics; kindred; sympathetic; suited for each other.—**congeniality**, kon·jē·ni·al″i·ti, *n.* The state of being congenial; natural affinity; suitableness.—**congenially**, kon·jē′ni·al·li, *adv.* In a congenial manner.

congenital, kon·jen′i·tal, *a.* [L. *congenitus*—*con*, and *genitus*, born, root *gen*, to produce.] Belonging or pertaining to an individual from birth (a *congenital* deformity).

conger, conger eel, kong′gẽr, *n.* [L. *conger*, a conger eel.] The sea eel, a large voracious species of eel, sometimes growing to the length of 10 feet, and weighing 100 lbs.

congeries, kon·jē′ri·ēz, *n. sing.* and *pl.* [L., from *congero*, to amass—*con*, and *gero*, to bear.] A collection of several particles or bodies in one mass or aggregate; an aggregate; a combination.

congest, kon·jest′, *v.t.* [L. *congero, congestum*—*con*, and *gero*, to bear.] To heap together‡; *med.* to cause an unnatural accumulation of blood in.— **congested**, kon·jes′ted, *a.* Med. containing an unnatural accumulation of blood; affected with congestion.— **congestion**, kon·jest′yon, *n.* [L. *congestio*.] Med. an excessive accumulation of blood in an organ, the functions of which are thereby disordered.—**congestive**, kon·jes′tiv, *a.* Pertaining to congestion; indicating an unnatural accumulation of blood in some part of the body.

conglobate, kon′glō·bāt, *a.* [L. *conglobatus*—*con*, and *globus*, a ball. GLOBE.] Formed or gathered into a ball or small spherical body; combined into one mass.—*v.t.*†—*conglobated, conglobating.* To collect or form into a ball; to combine into one mass.—*v.i.* To assume a round or globular form.—**conglobation**, kon·glō·bā′shon, *n.* The act of forming or gathering into a ball; a round body.—**conglobe**,† kon·glōb′, *v.t.* and *i.*—*conglobed, conglobing.* To

conglobate.

conglomerate, kon·glom′ẽr·āt, *a.* [L. *conglomero, conglomeratum*—*con*, and *glomus, glomeris*, a ball, a clew.] Gathered into a ball or round body; crowded together; clustered.—*v.t.*— *conglomerated, conglomerating.* To gather into a ball or round body; to collect into a round mass.—*n.* A kind of rock made up of rounded fragments of various rocks cemented together by a matrix of siliceous, calcareous, or other cement; gravel solidified by cement into a rock; pudding stone.—**conglomeration**, kon·glom′ẽr·ā″shon, *n.* The act of conglomerating; collection; accumulation; what is conglomerated; a mixed mass; a mixture.

conglutinate, kon·glü′ti·nāt, *v.t.*— *conglutinated, conglutinating.* [L. *conglutino*—*con*, and *glutino*, from *gluten*, glue. GLUE.] To glue together; to unite by some glutinous or tenacious substance; to reunite; to cement.— *v.i.* To coalesce; to unite by the intervention of some glutinous substance.—*a.* Glued together; *bot.* united by some adhesive substance, but not organically united.—**conglutination**, kon·glü′ti·nā″shon, *n.* The act of gluing together; a joining by means of some tenacious substance; union; coalescence.

congou, kong′gö, *n.* [Chinese *kung-fu*, labor.] The second lowest quality of black tea, being the third picking from a plant during the season.

congratulate, kon·grat′ū·lāt, *v.t.*— *congratulated, congratulating.*—[L. *congratulor*—*con*, and *gratulor*, from *gratus*, grateful, pleasing. GRACE.] To address with expressions of sympathetic pleasure on some piece of good fortune happening to the party addressed; to compliment upon an event deemed happy; to wish joy to; to felicitate; also *refl.* to have a lively sense of one's own good fortune; to consider one's self lucky.—**congratulant**, kon·grat′ū·lant, *a.* Congratulating; expressing pleasure in another's good fortune.—**congratulation**, kon·grat′ū·lā″shon, *n.* The act of congratulating; words used in congratulating; expression to a person of pleasure in his good fortune; felicitation.—**congratulator**, kon·grat′ū·lā·tẽr, *n.* One who congratulates.—**congratulatory**, kon·grat′ū·la·to·ri, *a.* Containing or expressing congratulation.

congregate, kong′grē·gāt, *v.t.*—*congregated, congregating.* [L. *congrego*—*con*, and *grex, gregis*, a herd. GREGARIOUS.] To collect into an assemblage; to assemble; to bring into one place or into a crowd or united body.—*v.i.* To come together; to assemble; to meet in a crowd.—*a.* Collected; compact; close.—**congregation**, kong′grē·gā′shon, *n.* The act of congregating; the act of bringing together or assembling; a collection or assemblage of persons or things; an assembly, especially an assembly of persons met for the worship of God; or a number of people organized as a body for the purpose of holding religious services

in common.—**congregational**, kong··grē·gā′shon·al, *a.* Pertaining to a congregation; [*cap.*] pertaining to the Independents or Congregationists, or to Congregationalism.— **congregationalism**, kong·gre·gā′shon·al·izm, *n.* A system of administering church affairs by which each congregation has the right of regulating the details of its worship, discipline, and government.—**Congregationalist**, kong·gre·gā′shon·al·ist, *n.* One who belongs to a Congregational church or society; an Independent.

congress, kong′gres, *n.* [L. *congressus*, a meeting, from *congredior, congressum*, to come together—*con*, and *gradior*, to go; *gradus*, a step, whence *grade, degree*, etc.] A meeting together of individuals; an assembly of envoys, commissioners, deputies, etc.; a meeting of sovereign princes or of the representatives of several courts, for the purpose of arranging international affairs; [*cap.*] the legislative assembly of the United States of America, consisting of the Senate and House of Representatives.— *v.i.*† To come together; to assemble; to meet.—**congressional**, kon·gresh′on·al, *a.* Pertaining to a congress or to the Congress of the United States. —**congressman**, *n.* A member of the United States Congress.

congrue, kon·grö′, *v.i.* [L. *congruo*, to suit, to be congruous.] [*obs.*] To be consistent; to agree. (*Shak.*)— **congruence, congruency**, kong′grū··ens, kong′grū·en·si, *n.* [L. *congruentia.*] Suitableness of one thing to another; agreement; consistency.— **congruent**, kong′grū·ent, *a.* Suitable; agreeing; corresponding.— **congruently**, kong′grū·ent·li, *adv.* In a congruent manner.—**congruity**, kong·grū′i·ti, kong′grū·us·nes, *n.* The state or quality of being congruous; agreement between things; suitableness; pertinence; consistency; propriety.— **congruous**, kong′grū·us, *a.* [L. *congruus*.] Accordant; harmonious; well adapted; appropriate; meet; fit.— **congruously**, kong′grū·us·li, *adv.* In a congruous manner; suitably; pertinently; agreeably; consistently.

conic, conifer, etc. See CONE.

conidium, -ia, kon·id′i·um, *n.* [Gr. dim. of *kōnis*, dust.] In fungi, a minute asexual spore.

coniine, kōn·i′ēn, *n.* [From *conium*, the hemlock.] An alkaloid poison contained in hemlock.

conjecture, kon·jek′chẽr, *n.* [Fr. *conjecture*, L. *conjectura*, a conjecture, lit. a throwing or putting of things together, from *conjicio*, to throw together—*con*, and *jacio*, to throw.] A guess or inference based on the supposed possibility or probability of a fact, or on slight evidence; an opinion formed on insufficient or presumptive evidence; surmise.— *v.t.*—*conjectured, conjecturing.* To judge by guess or conjecture; to guess.—*v.i.* To form conjectures.— **conjecturer**, kon·jek′chẽr·ẽr, *n.* One who conjectures; a guesser.—**conjecturable**, kon·jek′chẽr·a·bl, *a.* Capa-

---

fāte, fär, fâre, fat, fạll;   mē, met, hẽr;   pīne, pin;   nōte, not, mŏve;   tūbe, tub, bụll;   oil, pound.

ble of being guessed or conjectured.
—**conjectural,** kon·jek'chėr·al, *a.* Depending on conjecture; implying guess or conjecture.—**conjecturally,** kon·jek'chėr·al·li, *adv.* In a conjectural manner; by conjecture; by guess.

conjoin, kon·join', *v.t.* [*Con* and *join*; Fr. *conjoindre*.] To join together or in one; to unite; to associate or connect.—*v.i.* To unite; to join; to league.—**conjoint,** kon·joint', *a.* United; connected; associated.—**conjointly,** kon·joint'li, *adv.* In a conjoint manner; jointly; unitedly; in union; together.

conjugal, kon'jŭ·gal, *a.* [L. *conjugalis* —*con*, together, and *jugum*, a yoke, from *jug*, root of *jungo*, to join, seen also in E. *yoke*. YOKE.] Belonging to marriage or married persons; matrimonial; connubial.—**conjugally,** kon'jŭ·gal·li, *adv.* Matrimonially; connubially.

conjugate, kon'jŭ·gāt, *v.t.*—*conjugated, conjugating.* [L. *conjugo, conjugatus,* to couple—*con,* and *jugo,* to yoke. CONJUGAL.] *Gram.* to inflect (a verb) through its several voices, moods, tenses, numbers, and persons, or so many of them.—*a.* United in pairs; joined together; coupled; *bot.* applied to a pinnate leaf which has only one pair of leaflets; *chem.* containing two or more radicals acting the part of a single one; *gram.* applied to words from the same root, and having the same radical signification, but modified by the affix added, or to words which have the same form but are different parts of speech; *math.* applied to two points, lines, etc., when they are considered together, with regard to any property, in such a manner that they may be interchanged without altering the way of enunciating the property. —*Conjugate foci,* in a mirror or lens, are two points such that rays proceeding from either are reflected or refracted to the other.—*n.* What is conjugate; a conjugate word.—**conjugation,** kon·jŭ·gā'shon, *n.* [L. *conjugatio.*] The inflection of a verb in its different forms; a class of verbs conjugated in the same way; *biol.* the union of two sex cells (gametes) of similar appearance.—**conjugational,** kon·jŭ·gā'shon·al, *a.* Of or belonging to conjugation.

conjunct, kon·jungkt', *a.* [L. *conjunctus,* from *conjungo.* CONJOIN.] Conjoined; united; concurrent.—**conjunction,** kon·jungk'shon, *n.* [L. *conjunctio.*] Union; connection; association; *astron.* that position of a planet in which it is in a line with the earth or another planet and the sun; *gram.* an indeclinable particle, serving to unite words, sentences, or clauses of a sentence, and indicating their relation to one another.—**conjunctional,** kon·jungk'shon·al, *a.* Belonging or relating to a conjunction.—**conjunctionally,** kon·jungk'shon·al·li, *adv.* In a conjunctional manner.—**conjunctiva,** kon·jungk·tī'va, *n. Anat.* the mucous membrane which lines the inner surface of the eyelids, and is continued over the

fore part of the globe of the eye.— **conjunctive,** kon·jungk'tiv, *a.* [L. *conjunctivus.*] Uniting; serving to unite.—*Conjunctive mood, gram.* the mood which follows a conjunction or expresses some condition or contingency; the subjunctive.—**conjunctively,** kon·jungk'tiv·li, *adv.* In a conjunctive manner.—**conjunctivitis,** kon·junk·tiv·īt'is, *n.* [From *conjunctiva,* and Gr. *-itis,* inflammation.] Inflammation of the conjunctiva.—**conjunctly,** kon·jungkt'li, *adv.* In a conjunct manner; in union; jointly; together.—**conjuncture,** kon·jungk'chėr, *n.* Combination of circumstances or affairs; especially, a critical time, proceeding from a union of circumstances; a crisis of affairs.

conjure, *v.t.*—*conjured, conjuring.* [L. *conjuro,* to swear together, to conspire —*con,* with, and *juro,* to swear, whence also *jury, perjure.*] With pron. kon·jūr', to call on or summon by a sacred name or in a solemn manner; to implore with solemnity; to adjure: with pron. kun'jėr, to affect or effect by magic or enchantment; to bring about by affecting the arts of a conjurer.—*To conjure* (kun'jėr) *up,* to call up or bring into existence by conjuring or as if by conjuring.—*v.i.* (kun'jėr). To practice the arts of a conjurer; to use magic arts.— **conjuration,** kon·jŭ·rā'shon, *n.* The act of conjuring or imploring with solemnity; the act of binding by an oath; adjuration; an incantation; a spell.—**conjurer, conjuror,** kun'jėr·ėr, *n.* An enchanter; one who practices legerdemain; a juggler.

connascency, kon·nas'en·si, *n.* [L. *con,* and *nascor, natus,* to be born.] The common birth of two or more at the same time; the act of growing together or at the same time.— **connate,** kon'nāt, *a.* [L. *con,* and *natus,* born.] Belonging to from birth; implanted at birth: applied chiefly in *philos.* to ideas or principles; *bot.* united in origin; growing from one base, or united at their bases (a leaf, an anther); *med.* congenital.

connature, kon·nā'chėr, *n.* Likeness in nature; identity or similarity of character.—**connatural,** kon·nach'ė·rel, *a.* Connected by nature; united in nature; belonging to by nature.— **connaturally,** kon·nach'ė·rel·li, *adv.* In a connatural manner; by the act of nature; originally.

connect, kon·nekt' *v.t.* [L. *connecto, connexum*—*con,* and *necto,* to bind.] To fasten together; to join or unite; to conjoin; to combine; to associate. —*v.i.* To join, unite, or cohere.— **connectedly,** kon·nek'ted·li, *adv.* By connection; in a connected manner; conjointly.—**connection, connexion,** kon·nek'shon, *n.* [L. *connexio.*] The act of connecting or state of being connected; also that which connects; union by something physical or by relation of any kind; relationship by blood or marriage, but more specifically by marriage; a person connected with another by this relationship; circle of persons with whom

any one is brought into contact.— *In this connection,* in connection with what is now under consideration.— **connective,** kon·nek'tiv, *a.* Having the power of connecting; tending to connect; connecting.—*n.* That which connects; *gram.* a word that connects other words and sentences; a conjunction.—**connectively,** kon·nek'tiv·li, *adv.* In a connective manner; jointly.—**connector,** kon·nek'tėr, *n.* One who or that which connects.

conning tower, *n.* An armored structure on a warship from which the officer in charge issues his orders during the time the ship is in action.

connive, kon·nīv', *v.i.*—*connived, conniving.* [L. *conniveo,* to wink, to connive at—*con,* together, and *niveo,* to wink.] To wink or close and open the eyelids rapidly‡; *fig.* to close the eyes upon a fault or other act; to pretend ignorance or blindness; to forbear to see; to wink at or overlook a fault or other act and suffer it to pass unnoticed: followed by *at.*— **connivance,** kon·nī'vans, *n.* The act of conniving; voluntary blindness to an act.—**conniver,** kon·nī'vėr, *n.* One who connives.

connoisseur, kon'is·sėr, *n.* [O.Fr. *connoisseur,* Mod.Fr. *connaisseur,* from the verb *connoitre, connaître,* from L. *cognoscere,* to know. COGNIZANCE.] A critical judge; one competent to pass a critical judgment upon anything.

connote, connotate, kon·nōt', kon'ō·tāt, *v.t.*—*connoted, connoting; connotated, connotating.* [L. *con,* and *noto, notatum,* to mark. NOTE.] To include in the meaning; to comprise among the attributes expressed; to imply. ∴ *Connote* and *denote* are contrasted in logic. Thus the word 'horse' *connotes* the qualities that distinguish a horse from other animals, and *denotes* the class of animals which are characterized by having these qualities. 'Thames', however, *connotes* nothing, being simply the name of the particular river which it *denotes.*—*v.i.* To have a meaning or signification in connection with another word.—**connotation,** kon·ō·tā'shon, *n.* That which constitutes the meaning of a word; the attributes expressed by a word.—**connotative,** kon·no'ta·tiv, *a.* Connoting; significant.

connubial, kon·nū'bi·al, *a.* [L. *connubialis,* from *connubium,* marriage— *con,* and *nubo,* to marry.] Pertaining to marriage; nuptial; belonging to the state of husband and wife.— **connubiality,** kon·nū'bi·al'i·ti, *n.* The state of being connubial; anything pertaining to the state of husband and wife.—**connubially,** kon·nū'bi·al·li, *adv.* In a connubial manner; as man and wife.

conoid, conoidal, etc. See CONE.

conquer, kong'kėr, *v.t.* [O.Fr. *conquerre, conquerrer,* Mod.Fr. *conquérir,* from L. *conquiro,* to seek for, procure —*con,* and *quaero,* to seek (whence *quest* and *query*).] To overcome and bring to subjection in war; to reduce by physical force till resistance is no longer made; to vanquish; to gain by force; to overcome or surmount (obstacles, difficulties); to gain or obtain by effort. ∴ *Conquer* is wider and more general than *vanquish*, denoting usually a succession of struggles or conflicts; while *vanquish* refers more commonly to a single conflict, and has regularly a personal object. *Subdue* implies a continued process and a complete and thorough subjection.—*v.i.* To overcome; to gain the victory.—**conquerable,** kong′kėr·a·bl, *a.* Capable of being conquered, overcome, or subdued.—**conqueror,** kong′kėr·ėr, *n.* One who conquers or gains a victory.—*The Conqueror,* an epithet applied to William I of England, as expressing his conquest of the country.—**conquest,** kong′kwest, *n.* [O.Fr. *conquest,* Fr. *conquête.*] The act of conquering; the act of overcoming or vanquishing opposition by force, physical or moral; subjugation; that which is conquered; a possession gained by force.—*The Conquest,* by preeminence the conquest of England by William of Normandy.—**conquistador,** kong·kwis′ta·dŏr, *n.* [Sp.] A term applied to the early Spanish leaders who conquered Spanish America.

consanguinity, kon·sang·gwin′i·ti, *n.* [L. *consanguinitas*—prefix *con,* and *sanguis, sanguinis,* blood.] The relation of persons by blood, the relation or connection of persons descended from the same stock or common ancestor, in distinction from *affinity* or relation by marriage.—**consanguineous,** kon·sang·gwin′i·us, *a.* [L. *consanguineus.*] Of the same blood; related by birth; descended from the same parent or ancestor.

conscience, kon′shens, *n.* [L. *conscientia,* from *conscio,* to know, to be privy to—*con,* with, and *scio,* to know. SCIENCE.] Private or inward thoughts or real sentiments (*Shak.*); the faculty, power, or principle within us, which decides on the rightness or wrongness of our own actions and affections; the sense of right and wrong; the moral sense; morality; what a good conscience would approve.—*A bad conscience,* a reproving conscience.—*A good conscience,* an approving conscience.—*In all conscience,* to be reasonable, to keep within the bounds of moderation: a form of asseveration.—*Conscience clause,* a clause or article in an act or law which specially relieves persons having conscientious scruples in taking judicial oaths, or having their children present at school during the time of religious instruction or service.—**conscientious,** kon′shi·en′shus, *a.* Influenced by conscience; governed by a strict regard to the dictates of conscience, or by the known or supposed rules of right and wrong.—**conscientiously,** kon·shi·en′shus·li, *adv.* In a conscientious manner; according to the direction of conscience.—**conscientiousness,** kon·shi·en′shus·nes, *n.* The state or quality of being conscientious.

conscious, kon′shus, *a.* [L. *conscius—*

con, and *scio,* to know. CONSCIENCE.] Knowing what affects or what goes on in one's own mind; having direct knowledge of a thing; having such a knowledge as is conveyed by immediate sensation or perception; aware; sensible (*conscious of* something); having become the subject of consciousness; known to one's self (*conscious* guilt).—**consciously,** kon′shus·li, *adv.* In a conscious manner; with knowledge of one's own mental operations or actions.—**consciousness,** kon′shus·nes, *n.* The faculty of knowing what affects or what goes on in one's own mind; immediate knowledge, such as is given in sensation and perception; internal persuasion.

conscript, kon′skript, *a.* [L. *conscriptus,* from *conscribo,* to enroll—*con,* with, and *scribo,* to write.] Enrolled.—*Conscript fathers,* a title of the senators of Rome.—*n.* One who is compulsorily enrolled for military or naval service.—kon·skript′, *v.t.* to draft; to enroll by compulsion for military service.—**conscription,** kon··skrip′shon, *n.* [L. *conscriptio.*] A compulsory enrollment of individuals of a certain age, held liable to be drafted for military or naval service.

consecrate, kon′se·krāt, *v.t.*—*consecrated, consecrating.* [L. *consecro—con,* with, and *sacro,* to consecrate, from *sacer,* sacred. SACRED.] To make or declare to be sacred with certain ceremonies or rites; to appropriate to sacred uses; to enroll among deities or saints; to canonize; to give episcopal rank to; to dedicate with solemnity; to render venerable; to make respected; to hallow.—**consecrate,** kon′se·krāt, *a.* Sacred; consecrated; devoted; dedicated. [Obs. or poet.]—**consecration,** kon·se··krā′shon, *n.* The act or ceremony of consecrating or separating from a common to a sacred use; dedication of a person or thing to the service and worship of God, by certain rites or solemnities; dedication; the ceremony of elevating a priest to the dignity of a bishop; the giving of the bread and wine of the eucharist their sacred character in the mass or communion service.—**consecrator,** kon′se·krā·tėr, *n.* One who consecrates.

consecution, kon·se·kū′shon, *n.* [L. *consecutio—con,* and *sequor,* to follow (whence *sequence*); same root as *second.*] A following; a train or series; the state of being consecutive. —**consecutive,** kon·sek′ū·tiv, *a.* Uninterrupted in course or succession; succeeding one another in a regular order; successive; following; succeeding.—**consecutively,** kon·sek′ū·tiv·li, *adv.* In a consecutive manner; in regular succession; successively.—**consecutiveness,** kon·sek′ū·tiv·nes, *n.* State of being consecutive.

consent, kon·sent′, *v.i.* [L. *consentio,* to agree—*con,* with, and *sentio, sensum,* to feel, perceive, think; akin *sense, sentiment,* etc.] To agree; to accord; to yield, as to persuasion or entreaty; to comply; to acquiesce or accede.—*n.* Voluntary accordance

with what is done or proposed by another; a yielding of the mind or will to that which is proposed; acquiescence; concurrence; compliance; accord of minds; agreement in opinion or sentiment; *law,* intelligent concurrence in the terms of a contract or agreement, of such a nature as to bind the party consenting.—**consensual,** kon·sen′shū·al, *a.* *Law,* formed or existing by mere consent; *physiol.* excited or caused by sensation or sympathy and not by conscious volition.—**consensus,** kon·sen′sus, *n.* [L.] Unanimity; agreement; concord.—**consentaneous,** kon·sen·tā′ni·us, *a.* [L. *consentaneus.*] Accordant; agreeing; consistent; suitable.—**consentaneously,** kon·sen·tā′ni·us·li, *adv.* Agreeably; consistently; suitably.—**consentaneousness,** kon·sen·tā′ni·us·nes, *n.* Agreement; accordance; consistency.—**consenter,** kon·sen′tėr, *n.* One who consents.—**consentient,** kon·sen′shi·ent, *a.* Agreeing; accordant; unanimous.

consequence, kon′se·kwens, *n.* [L. *consequentia,* from *consequor.* CONSECUTION.] That which follows from any act, cause, principles, or series of actions; an event or effect produced by some preceding act or cause; inference; deduction; conclusion from premises; importance (a matter *of consequence,* a man *of* great *consequence*).—*In consequence of,* as the effect of; by reason of; through.—**consequent,** kon′se·kwent, *a.* [L. *consequens.*] Following as the natural effect: with *to* or *on.*—*n.* That which follows; *logic,* that member of a hypothetical proposition which contains the conclusion.—**consequential,** kon·se·kwen′shal, *a.* Following as the effect; produced by the connection of effects with causes; affecting airs of great self-importance, or characterized by such affectation; pompous.—*n.* An inference; a deduction; a conclusion.—**consequentially,** kon·se·kwen′shal·li, *adv.* In a consequential manner; with just deduction of consequences; with assumed importance; pompously.—**consequentialness,** kon··se·kwen′shal·nes, *n.* The quality of being consequential.—**consequently,** kon′se·kwent·li, *adv.* By consequence; by necessary connection of effects with their causes; in consequence of something.

conservatoire, kon·sâr·va·twär, *n.* [Fr., from It. *conservatorio.*] A name given to an establishment for promoting the study of any special branch, especially music.

conserve, kon·sėrv′, *v.t.*—*conserved, conserving.* [L. *conservo—con,* and *servo,* to preserve.] To keep in a safe or unimpaired state; to uphold and keep from decay, waste, or injury; to guard or defend from violation (institutions, customs, buildings, etc.); to preserve with sugar, etc., as fruits.—*n.* (kon′sėrv.) That which is conserved; a sweetmeat made of the inspissated juice of fruit boiled with sugar.—**conserver,** kon·sėr′vėr, *n.* One who conserves or preserves.—

---

fāte, fär, fâre, fat, fạll; mē, met, hėr; pīne, pin; nōte, not, möve; tūbe, tub, bụll; oil, pound.

conservable, kon·sėr′va·bl, *a.* That may be conserved.—**conservation**, kon·sėr·vā′shon, *n.* [L. *conservatio.*] The act of conserving, preserving, guarding, or protecting; preservation from loss, decay, injury, or violation. —*Conservation of energy*, the principle that energy or force is indestructible, the sum of all the energy in the universe being constant.— **conservational**, kon·sėr·vā′shon·al, *a.* Tending to preserve; preservative. —**conservatism**, kon·sėr′va·tizm, *n.* The political principles and opinions maintained by Conservatives; tendency to preserve what is established; opposition to change.—**conservative**, kon·sėr′va·tiv, *a.* Tending to conserve; traditional; cautious; inclining to keep up old institutions, customs, and the like; having a tendency to uphold and preserve entire the institutions of a country, both civil and ecclesiastical; opposed to radical changes or innovations; [*cap.*] pertaining to the Conservatives or their principles.—*n.* One who aims to preserve from ruin, innovation, injury, or radical change; [*cap.*] one of the political party the professed object of which is to support and preserve all that is good in the existing institutions of a country, and to oppose undesirable changes.— **conservator**, kon′sėr·vā·tėr or kon·sėr′ve·tėr, *n.* One who conserves; one who preserves from injury or violation; one appointed to conserve or watch over anything.—**conservatory**, kon·sėr′ve·to·ri, *a.* Having the quality of preserving from loss, decay, or injury.—*n.* A large greenhouse for preserving exotics and other tender plants.—Same as CONSERVATOIRE.

consider, kon·sid′ėr, *v.t.* [L. *considero*, to view attentively, to consider: originally (like *contemplor*) an augurial term—*con*, together, and *sidus, sideris*, a constellation.] To fix the mind on, with a view to a careful examination; to think on with care; to ponder; to study; to meditate on; to observe and examine; to regard with pity or sympathy, and hence relieve (the poor); to have regard or respect to; to respect; to take into view or account, or have regard to, in examination, or in forming an estimate; to judge to be; to reckon (to *consider* a man wise).—*v.i.* To think seriously, maturely, or carefully; to reflect.—**considerable**, kon·sid′ėr·a·bl, *a.* Worthy of consideration on account of its amount; more than a little; moderately large; somewhat important or valuable.—**considerably**, kon·sid′ėr·a·bli, *adv.* In a degree deserving notice; in a degree not trifling or unimportant.—**considerate**, kon·sid′ėr·it, *a.* [L. *consideratus.*] Given to consideration or to sober reflection; circumspect; discreet; prudent; characterized by consideration or regard for another's circumstances and feelings; thoughtful or mindful of others.—**considerately**, kon·sid′ėr·it·li, *adv.* In a considerate manner.—**considerateness**, kon·sid′ėr·it·nes, *n.* The state

or quality of being considerate.— **consideration**, kon·sid′ėr·ā″shon, *n.* [L. *consideratio.*] The act of considering; mental view; regard; notice; mature thought; serious deliberation; thoughtful, sympathetic, appreciative, or due regard or respect; contemplation; meditation; some degree of importance or claim to notice or regard; motive of action; ground of conduct; ground of concluding; reason; recompense or remuneration (colloq.).—*In consideration of*, in respect or regard of; in return for.— **considering**, kon·sid′ėr·ing, *prep.* Having regard to; taking into account; making allowance for.

consign, kon·sīn′, *v.t.* [L. *consigno*, to seal or sign—*con*, and *signum*, a sign, seal, or mark. SIGN.] To give or hand over; to transfer or deliver over into the possession of another or into a different state (to *consign* a body to the grave); to deliver or transfer in charge or trust; to entrust (as goods to a factor for sale); to commit for permanent preservation (to *consign* to writing).—**consignation,**† kon·sig·nā′shon, *n.* The act of consigning.—**consignee**, kon·si·nē′, *n.* The person to whom goods or other things are consigned for sale or superintendence; a factor.—**consigner, consignor**, kon·sī′nėr, kon·sī′nor, *n.* The person who consigns. —**consignment**, kon·sīn′ment, *n.* The act of consigning; the act of sending off goods to an agent for sale; goods sent or delivered to a factor for sale.

consist, kon·sist′, *v.i.* [L. *consisto*—*con*, and *sisto*, to stand.] To hold together or remain fixed‡; to be, exist, subsist‡; to stand or be; to be comprised or contained: followed by *in*; to be composed; to be made up: followed by *of*; to be compatible, consistent, or harmonious; to accord: followed by *with*.—**consistence, consistency**, kon·sis′tens, kon·sis′ten·si, *n.* An indefinite degree of density or viscosity; agreement or harmony of all parts of a complex thing among themselves, or of the same thing with itself at different times; congruity, agreement, or harmony.— **consistent**, kon·sis′tent, *a.* [L. *consistens.*] Having a certain substance or firmness; standing in agreement; compatible; congruous; not contradictory or opposed; not out of harmony with other acts or professions of the same person.—**consistently**, kon·sis′tent·li, *adv.* In a consistent manner; in agreement; suitably or agreeably to one's other acts or professions.

consistory, kon·sis′tor·i, *n.* [L. *consistorium*, a place of assembly, a council. CONSIST.] A spiritual or ecclesiastical court; the court of a bishop for the trial of ecclesiastical causes arising within the diocese; an assembly of prelates; the college of cardinals at Rome; a solemn assembly or council; in some Reformed churches, an assembly or council of ministers and elders.—**consistorial**, kon·sis·tō′ri·al, *a.* Pertaining or relating to a consistory.

console, kon·sōl′, *v.t.*—consoled, consoling. [L. *consolor*, to console—*con*, and *solor*, to comfort; akin *solace.*] To cheer the mind in distress or depression; to comfort; to soothe; to solace.—**consolable**, kon·sōl′a·bl, *a.* Capable of receiving consolation. —**consolation**, kon·sōl·ā′shon, *n.* [L. *consolatio.*] The act of consoling; alleviation of misery or distress of mind; a comparative degree of happiness in distress or misfortune, springing from any circumstance that abates the evil or supports and strengthens the mind, as hope, joy, courage, and the like; comfort of the mind; that which comforts or refreshes the spirits; the cause of comfort.—**consolatory**, kon·sōl′a·tor·i, *a.* Tending to console or give comfort; refreshing to the mind; assuaging grief.—**consoler**, kon·sōl′-ėr, *n.* One that consoles.—**consoling**, kon·sōl′ing, *a.* Adapted to console or comfort.

console, kon·sōl′, *n.* [Fr., from *consoler*, in sense of to support.] A variety of bracket, either useful or ornamental; an ornamental bracket projecting from a wall, employed to support a cornice, bust, vase, or the like; the desklike part of an organ containing keyboards, pedals, etc.

consolidate, kon·sol′id·āt, *v.t.*—consolidated, consolidating. [L. *consolido, consolidatum*—*con*, and *solidus*, solid.] To make solid or compact; to harden or make dense and firm; to bring together into one close mass or body; to make firm or establish (power).— *v.i.* To grow firm and hard; to unite and become solid.—*a.* Formed into a solid mass. (*Tenn.*).—**consolidation**, kon·sol′id·ā″shon, *n.* The act of consolidating; a making or process of becoming solid; the act of forming into a firm compact mass, body, or system.—**consols**, kon′solz, *n. pl.* [Contr. for *consolidated annuities.*] A term used to denote a considerable portion of the public debt of Britain, more correctly known as the three per cent consolidated annuities.

consonance, consonancy, kon′sō·nans, kon′sō·nan·si, *n.* [L. *consonantia*, from *consono*, to sound together—*con*, and *sono*, to sound. SOUND.] Accord or agreement of sounds; *mus.* an accord of sounds which produces an agreeable sensation in the ear, as the third, fifth, and octave; hence, agreement; accord; congruity; consistency; suitableness. —**consonant**, kon′so·nant, *a.* Like in sound; agreeing generally; according; congruous; consistent: followed by *to* or *with*.—*n.* A letter that receives its proper sound only in connection with a vowel; one of the closings or junctions of the organs of speech, which precede or follow the openings of the organs with which the vowels are uttered.—**consonantal**, kon·so·nant′al, *a.* Relating to or partaking of the nature of a consonant.— **consonantly**, kon′so·nant·li, *adv.* In a consonant manner; consistently; in agreement.

consort, kon′sort, *n.* [L. *consors*—*con*, and *sors*, a lot. SORT.] A partner;

an intimate associate; particularly, a wife or husband; *naut.* any vessel keeping company with another.— *Queen consort*, the wife of a king, as distinguished from a *queen regnant*, who rules alone, and a *queen dowager*, the widow of a king.—*v.i.* (kon·sort′). To associate; to unite in company; to keep company: followed by *with.—v.t.‡* To marry; to unite in company; to accompany.

conspectus, kon·spek′tus, *n.* [L.] A comprehensive view of a subject; an abstract or sketch.

conspicuous, kon·spik′ū·us, *a.* [L. *conspicuus*, from *conspicio*, to look or see—*con*, and *specio*, to see. SPECIES.] Obvious or prominent to the eye; easy to be seen; manifest; clearly or extensively known, perceived, or understood; eminent; distinguished (*conspicuous* abilities).— **conspicuously,** kon·spik′ū·us·li, *adv.* In a conspicuous manner; in a manner to be clearly seen; prominently; eminently; remarkably.—**conspicuousness,** kon·spik′ū·us·nes, *n.* The state of being conspicuous.

conspire, kon·spīr′, *v.i.*—*conspired, conspiring.* [L. *conspiro*, to plot—*con*, and *spiro*, to breathe; lit. to breathe together.] To agree by oath, covenant, or otherwise to commit a crime; to plot; to form a secret plot; to hatch treason; to agree, concur, or conduce to one end (circumstances *conspired* to defeat the plan).—*v.t.* To plot; to plan; to devise; to contrive; to concur to produce.—**conspiracy,** kon·spir′a·si, *n.* [L. *conspiratio*, from *conspiro.*] A secret combination of men for an evil purpose; an agreement or combination to commit some crime in concert; a plot; concerted treason.—**conspirator, conspirer,** kon·spir′at·ėr, kon·spī′rėr, *n.* One who conspires; one who engages in a plot to commit a crime, particularly treason.

constable, kun′sta·bl, *n.* [O.Fr. *conestable*, from L. *comes stabuli*, count of the stable.] An officer of high rank in several of the medieval monarchies; the keeper or governor of a castle belonging to the king or to a great baron; now usually a peace officer; a police officer.—**constableship,** kun′sta·bl·ship, *n.* The office of a constable.—**constabulary,** kon·stab′ū·le·ri, *a.* Pertaining to constables; consisting of constables.—*n.* The body of constables of a district, city, or country.

constant, kon′stant, *a.* [L. *constans*, pp. of *consto*—*con*, and *sto*, to stand.] Not undergoing change; continuing the same; permanent; immutable; fixed or firm in mind, purpose, or principle; not easily swayed; firm or unchanging in affection or duty; faithful; true; loyal.—*n.* That which is not subject to change; *math.* a quantity which remains the same throughout a problem.—**constantly,** kon′stant·li, *adv.* Firmly; steadily; invariably; continually; perseveringly.—**constancy,** kon′stan·si, *n.* [L. *constantia.*] Fixedness; a standing firm; immutability; steady, unshaken determination; fixedness or firmness

of mind under sufferings; steadiness in attachments; perseverance in enterprise.

constellation, kon·stel·lā′shon, *n.* [L. *constellatio—con*, together, and *stella*, a star.] A group of the fixed stars to which a definite name has been given; an assemblage of splendors or excellences (a *constellation* of poetic genius).

consternation, kon·stėr·nā′shon, *n.* [L. *consternatio*, from *consterno*, and *sterno*, to throw or strike down.] Astonishment; amazement or horror that confounds the faculties, and incapacitates a person for consultation and execution; excessive terror, wonder, or surprise.

constipate, kon′sti·pāt, *v.i.*—*constipated, constipating.* [L. *constipo, constipatum*, to crowd together—*con*, together, and *stipo*, to crowd, to cram.] To stop up by filling a passage‡; to make costive.— **constipation,** kon·sti·pā′shon, *n.* A state of the bowels in which the evacuations do not take place as frequently as usual, or are very hard and expelled with difficulty; costiveness.

constituent, kon·stit′ū·ent, *a.* [L. *constituens*, ppr. of *constituo—con*, and *statuo*, to set. STATUE, STATUTE.] Forming or existing as an essential component or ingredient; composing, or making up as an essential part; component, elementary (the *constituent* parts of water); having the power of constituting or appointing.—*n.* One who or that which establishes or determines; that which constitutes or composes, as a part, or an essential part; an essential ingredient; one who elects or assists in electing another as his representative in a deliberative or administrative assembly; one who empowers another to transact business for him.—**constituency,** kon·stit′ū·en·si, *n.* A body of constituents who appoint or elect persons to any office or employment, especially to state or national offices.

constitute, kon′sti·tūt, *v.t.*—*constituted, constituting.* [L. *constituo, constitutum—con*, and *statuo*, to set. STATUE, STATUTE.] To settle, fix, or enact; to establish; to form or compose: to make up; to make a thing what it is; to appoint, depute, or elect to an office or employment; to make and empower.—**constitution,** kon·sti·tū′shon, *n.* The act of constituting, enacting, establishing, or appointing; the peculiar structure and connection of parts which makes or characterizes a system or body; natural condition of the human body as regards general health or strength; the established form of government in a state; a system of fundamental rules, principles, and ordinances for the government of a state or nation. —*Constitution of the U. S.,* the document, ratified in 1789, creating the federal system of government, with twenty-two amendments, embodying the fundamental law.— **constitutional,** kon·sti·tū′shon·al, *a.* Pertaining to a constitution; connected with the constitution, or

natural condition of body or mind; consistent with the constitution of a state; authorized by the constitution or fundamental rules of a government.—*n.* A walk taken for health and exercise.—**constitutionalism,** kon·sti·tū′shon·al·izm, *n.* The theory or principle of constitutional rule or authority; constitutional principles; adherence to a constitution.— **constitutionalist,** kon·sti·tū′shon·al·ist, *n.* An adherent to the constitution of government; an upholder of the constitution of his country.— **constitutionality,** kon·sti·tū′shon·al″i·ti, *n.* The state of being constitutional.—**constitutionally,** kon·sti·tū′shon·al·li, *adv.* In a constitutional manner; in consistency with a national constitution; in accordance with the constitution of mind or body; naturally.—**constitutive,** kon′sti·tūt·iv, *a.* Forming, composing, enacting, or establishing; constituting; instituting. *Constitutively*, kon′sti·tūt·iv·li, *adv.* In a constitutive manner.

constrain, kon·strān′, *v.t.* [O.Fr. *constraindre*, Fr. *contraindre*, from L. *constringo*, to bind together—*con*, and *stringo*, to strain. STRAIN.] To compel or force; to urge with a power sufficient to produce the effect; to drive; to necessitate; to confine by force; to restrain, check, repress, confine, bind.—**constrainable,** kon·strā′na·bl, *a.* Capable of being constrained; liable to constraint or to restraint.—**constrainedly,** kon·strā′ned·li, *adv.* In a constrained manner; with constraint; by compulsion.— **constrainer,** kon·strā′nėr, *n.* One who constrains.—**constraint,** kon·strānt′, *n.* A constraining, compelling, or restraining; force; compulsion; restraint; confinement; feeling of reserve or being kept in check.

constrict, kon·strikt′, *v.t.* [L. *constringo, constrictum.* CONSTRAIN.] To draw together; to cramp; to contract or cause to shrink: said of canals, etc., of the body.—**constriction,** kon·strik′shon, *n.* The state of being constricted or drawn together as by some spasm, as distinguished from compression or the pressure of extraneous bodies.—**constrictive,** kon·strik′tiv, *a.* Tending to contract or compress.—**constrictor,** kon·strik′tėr, *n.* That which draws together or contracts; a muscle which draws together or closes an orifice of the body; one of the larger class of serpents which envelop and crush their prey in their folds.—**constringe,** kon·strinj′, *v.t.*—*constringed, constringing.* To strain into a narrow compass; to constrict.—**constringent,** kon·strin′jent, *a.* Having the quality of constringing.

construct, kon·strukt′, *v.t.* [L. *construo, constructum—con*, and *struo*, to pile up. STRUCTURE.] To put together the parts of in their proper place and order; to build up; to erect; to form; to form by the mind. —**constructer, constructor,** kon·struk′ter, *n.* One who constructs or frames.—**construction,** kon·struk′shon, *n.* [L. *constructio.*] The act of

---

fāte, fär, fâre, fat, fạll; mē, met, hėr; pīne, pin; nōte, not, mõve; tūbe, tub, bụll; oil, pound.

building, devising, or forming; fabrication; the form of building; the manner of putting together the parts; structure; conformation; the arrangement and connection of words in a sentence; syntactical arrangement; attributed sense or meaning to language; explanation; interpretation; the manner of describing a figure or problem in geometry for the purpose of any demonstration.—**constructional**, kon·struk′shon·al, *a.* Pertaining to construction; deduced from construction or interpretation. —**constructive**, kon·struk′tiv, *a.* Pertaining to construction or building; having ability to construct; created or deduced by construction or mode of interpretation.—**constructively**, kon·struk′tiv·li, *adv.* In a constructive manner, by way of construction or interpretation; by fair inference.— **constructiveness**, kon·struk′tiv·nes, *n.* State of being constructive; *phren.* a faculty supposed to produce constructive power.

construe, kon′strö, *v.t.*—construed, construing. [L. *construo.* CONSTRUCT.] To arrange words so that their grammatical bearing and meaning are apprehended; to analyze grammatically; as applied to a foreign language, to translate; to interpret or draw a certain meaning from; to explain (to *construe* actions wrongly).

consubstantial, consubstantiate, kon·sub·stan′shal, kon·sub·stan′shi·āt, *a.* [L. *consubstantialis—con* and *substantia.* SUBSTANCE.] Having the same substance or essence; coessential.—**consubstantiality**, kon·sub·stan′shi·al″i·ti, *n.* The quality of being consubstantial; the existence of more than one in the same substance; participation of the same nature.—**consubstantially**, kon·sub·stan′shi·al·li, *adv.* In a consubstantial manner.—**consubstantiate**,† kon·sub·stan′shi·āt, *v.t.* and *i.*—consubstantiated, consubstantiating. To unite in one common substance or nature, or regard as so united.—**consubstantiation**, kon·sub·stan′shi·ā″shon, *n.* The union of the body of the blessed Saviour with the sacramental elements; impanation.

consuetude,† kon′swi·tūd, *n.* [L. *consuetudo*, custom. CUSTOM.] Custom; usage.—**consuetudinary**, kon·swi·tūd′in·e·ri, *a.* Customary.—*Consuetudinary law*, in contradistinction to written or statutory law, is that law which is derived by immemorial custom from antiquity.

consul, kon′sul, *n.* [L. *consul—con*, together, and root seen also in *consulo, consultum*, to consult.] The title of the two chief magistrates of the ancient Roman republic, invested with legal authority for one year; the title given to the three supreme magistrates of the French republic after the dissolution of the Directory in 1799; a person commissioned by a sovereign or state to reside in a foreign country as an agent or representative, to protect the interests (especially the commercial interests) of his own country.—**consular**, kon′sul·ėr, *a.* Pertaining to a consul.—

consulate, kon′sul·it, *n.* [L. *consulatus.*] The office or jurisdiction of a consul; the official dwelling or residence of a consul; consular government.—**consulship**, kon′sul·ship, *n.* The office of a consul, or the term of his office.

consult, kon·sult′, *v.i.* [L. *consulto*, intens. from *consulo*, to consult.] To seek the opinion or advice of another; to take counsel together; to deliberate in common.—*v.t.* To ask advice of; to seek the opinion of as a guide to one's own judgment; to have recourse to for information or instruction; to regard or have reference or respect to, in judging or acting (to *consult* one's safety, one's means.) —**consultation**, kon·sul·tā′shon, *n.* The act of consulting; deliberation of two or more persons with a view to some decision; a meeting of experts, as physicians or counsel, to consult about a specific case.— **consultatory**, kon·sult′a·tō·ri,*a.* Having the privilege of consulting or deliberating; deliberative: often opposed to *executive*.—**consultant**, kon·sul′tent, *n.* One who consults.— **consulting**, kon·sult′ing, *a.* In the practice of giving advice; making the giving of advice one's business (a *consulting* attorney); used for consultations (*consulting* room).—**consultive**,† kon·sult′iv, *a.* Consultatory; advisory.

consume, kon·sūm′, *v.t.*—consumed, consuming. [L. *consumo*, to take wholly or completely—*con*, intens., and *sumo*, to take, seen also in *assume, resume*, etc.] To destroy by separating the component parts and annihilating the form of the substance, as by fire or by eating; to destroy by dissipating or by use; to expend; to waste; to spend; to pass (time); to waste slowly; to bring to ruin.—*v.i.* To waste away slowly; to be exhausted.—**consumable**, kon·sūm′a·bl, *a.* That may be consumed, destroyed, dissipated, or wasted.— **consumer**, kon·sūm′ėr, *n.* One who or that which consumes; *pol. econ.* one who uses commodities as distinguished from the producer of them.—**consumption**, kon·sum′shon, *n.* [L. *consumptio.*] The act of consuming, or state of being consumed; a progressive wasting of the body, especially from pulmonary tuberculosis; a decline; *pol. econ.* the use or expenditure of the products of industry, or of all things having an exchangeable value.—**consumptive**, kon·sum′tiv, *a.* Consuming, wasting, or exhausting; having the quality of consuming or dissipating; affected with or having a tendency to the disease consumption.—**consumptively**, kon·sum′tiv·li, *adv.* In a consumptive manner.—**consumptiveness**, kon·sum′tiv·nes, *n.* A state of being consumptive or a tendency to consumption.

consumedly, kon·sūm′ed·li, *adv.* [*Consumed* formerly had sense of deuced, confounded.] Greatly; hugely; deucedly.

consummate, kon′sum·āt, *v.t.*—consummated, consummating. [L. *con-*

summo, consummatus—con, and *summa*, sum. SUM.] To finish by completing what was intended; to perfect; to bring or carry to the utmost point or degree; to make complete.—*a.* (kon·sum′at). Complete; perfect; carried to the utmost extent or degree; thorough.—**consummately**,kon·sum′at·li, *adv.* Completely; perfectly.—**consummation**, kon·sum·ā′shon, *n.* [L. *consummatio.*] Completion; end; termination; perfection of a work, process, or scheme. —**consummative**, kon·sum′at·iv, *a.* Pertaining to consummation; consummating; final.

contact, kon′takt, *n.* [L. *contactus*, from *contingo, contactum*, to touch— *con*, and *tango* (root *tag*), to touch, whence also E. *tact, tangent*, etc.] A state or condition of touching; touch; proximity or association; connection; a junction of two electrical conductors through which current flows; a carrier of contagion. —*v.t.* To bring into contact; to get in touch with.—*v.i.* To be in contact.

contagion, kon·tā′jon, *n.* [L. *contagio —con*, and root *tag*. CONTACT.] The communication of a disease by contact; infection; that which propagates mischief (the *contagion* of vice); pestilential influence.—**contagium**, kon·tā′ji·um, *n.* That which carries the infectious element in diseases from one person to another. —**contagious**, kon·tā′jus, *a.* Containing or generating contagion; communicated by contagion or contact; catching; containing contagion; containing mischief that may be propagated; spreading from one to another, or exciting like affections in others (*contagious* fear).—**contagiously**, kon·tā′jus·li, *adv.* By contagion.—**contagiousness**, kon·tā′jus·nes, *n.*

contain, kon·tān′, *v.t.* [L. *contineo— con*, and *teneo*, to hold, seen also in *attain, retain, tenant, tempt*, etc.] To hold within fixed limits; to comprehend; to comprise; to include; to hold or be capable of holding; to comprise, as a writing; to have for contents; to keep in check an enemy's forces; to keep occupied, to hinder progress.—*To contain one's self*, to restrain one's feelings or prevent them showing themselves.— **containable**, kon·tā′na·bl, *a.* Capable of being contained or comprised.— **container**, kon·tā′nėr, *n.* One who, or that which, contains.

contaminate, kon·tam′in·āt, *v.t.*— contaminated, contaminating. [L. *contamino, contaminatum*, from *contamen*, contact, contamination contr. for *contagmen*, from root of *tango*, to touch. CONTAGION, CONTACT.] To defile; to pollute: usually in a figurative sense; to sully; to tarnish; to taint.—**contamination**, kon·tam′in·ā″shon, *n.* The act of contaminating, what contaminates; pollution; defilement; taint.

contemn, kon·tem′, *v.t.* [L. *contemno, contemptum*, to despise (whence also *contempt*)—*con*, intens., and *temno*, to despise.] To despise; to consider and treat as mean and despicable;

to scorn; to reject with disdain.—
contemner, kon·tem'ẽr, *n.* One who
contemns; a despiser; a scorner.
contemplate, kon'tem·plāt, *v.t.*—
contemplated, contemplating. [L. *contemplor, contemplatus,* to mark out a
templum, to view attentively, contemplate—*con,* and *templum,* the
space marked out by the augur as that
within which the omens should be
observed. TEMPLE.] To view or
consider with continued attention;
to study; to meditate on; to consider
or have in view in reference to a
future act or event; to intend.—*v.i.*
To think studiously; to study; to
muse; to mediate.—**contemplation,**
kon·tem·plā'shon, *n.* [L. *contem-
platio.*] The act of contemplating;
meditation; continued attention of
the mind to a particular subject; a
looking forward to the doing or
happening of something; expectation.—**contemplative,** kon·tem'plat·
iv, *a.* Given to contemplation, or
continued application of the mind to
a subject; thoughtful; meditative;
having the power of thought or
meditation (the *contemplative* faculty).—**contemplatively,** kon·tem'-
plat·iv·li, *adv.* With contemplation;
thoughtfully. —**contemplativeness,**
kon·tem'plat·iv·nes, *n.* State of being
contemplative.—**contemplator,** kon''-
tem·plā'tẽr, *n.* One who contem-
plates.
contemporary, kon·tem'po·re·ri, *a.*
[L. *con,* and *tempus, temporis,* time.]
Living, existing, or occurring at the
same time: of persons and things.—
n. One who lives at the same time
with another. —**contemporaneous,**
kon·tem·po·rā'nē·us, *a.* [L. *contem-
poraneus.*] Contemporary: most commonly of things.—**contemporaneously,** kon·tem·po·rā'ni·us·li, *adv.*
At the same time with some other
event.—**contemporaneousness,** kon·
tem'po·rā'ni·us·nes, *n.* Contempo-
raneity.
contempt, kon·temt', *n.* [L. *con-
temptus,* from *contemno.* CONTEMN.]
The feeling that causes us to consider
and treat something as mean, vile,
and worthless; disdain; scorn for
what is mean; the state of being
despised; *law,* disobedience to the
rules or orders of a court, or a
disturbance of its proceedings.—
contemptibility, kon·tem'ti·bil''i·ti,
n. Quality of being contemptible.—
contemptible, kon·tem'ti·bl, *a.* [L.
contemptibilis.] Worthy of contempt;
deserving scorn or disdain; despicable; mean; vile; despised or neglected from insignificance (a *contemptible* plant). ∴ Contemptible, deserving of being scorned or looked
down upon from meanness or worthlessness; *despicable,* implies a stronger feeling, scorn, and loathing, often
on moral grounds; *paltry* or *pitiful,*
too insignificant to waken any active
feeling.—**contemptibleness,** kon·
tem'ti·bl·nes, *n.* The state of being
contemptible.—**contemptibly,** kon·
tem'ti·bli, *adv.* In a contemptible
manner; meanly; in a manner deserving of contempt.—**contemptuous,**
kon·tem'tū·us, *a.* Manifesting or

expressing contempt or disdain;
scornful; apt to despise; haughty;
insolent.—**contemptuously,** kon··
tem'tū·us·li, *adv.* In a contemptuous
manner; with scorn or disdain;
despitefully. —**contemptuousness,**
kon·tem'tū·us·nes, *n.* Disposition to
contempt; scornfulness; haughtiness.
contend, kon·tend', *v.i.* [L. *contendo,*
to strive, contend—*con,* intens., and
tendo, stretch; whence E. *tend, tent,
attend, pretend;* root also in *tender.*]
To strive; to struggle in opposition;
absolutely, or with *against* or *with*
preceding an object; to use earnest
efforts to obtain, or to defend and
preserve: with *for* before the object.
—**contender,** kon·tend'ẽr, *n.* One
who contends; a combatant or rival.
—**contention,** kon·ten'shon, *n.* [L.
contentio.] The act of contending;
contest, struggle, or strife; strife in
words; debate; angry contest; quarrel; controversy; competition; emulation; a point that a person maintains, or the argument in support
of it.—**contentious,** kon·ten'shus, *a.*
[Fr. *contentieux.*] Apt to contend;
given to angry debate; quarrelsome;
perverse; relating to or characterized
by contention or strife; involving
contention.—**contentiously,** kon··
ten'shus·li, *adv.* In a contentious
manner.—**contentiousness,** kon·ten'-
shus·nes, *n.* The state or quality of
being contentious; a disposition to
contend; peevishness; quarrelsomeness.
content, kon·tent', *a.* [L. *contentus,*
from *contineo,* to contain—*con,* and
teneo, to hold. CONTAIN.] Having
a mind at peace; satisfied, so as not
to repine, object, or oppose; not
disturbed; contented; easy.—*v.t.* To
make content; to quiet, so as to stop
complaint or opposition; to appease;
to make easy in any situation; to
please or gratify.—*n.* The state of
being contented; contentment.—*n.*
(kon'tent' or kon'tent.) That which
is contained; the thing or things
held, included, or comprehended
within a limit or line; *geom.* the area
or quantity of matter or space included in certain lines. [Usually in
the pl.]—*Table of contents,* a summary or index of all the matters treated in a book.—**contented,** kon·tent'-
ed, *a.* Satisfied with what one has
or with one's circumstances; easy
in mind; not complaining, opposing,
or demanding more.—**contentedly,**
kon·tent'ed·li, *adv.* In a contented
manner; quietly; without concern.—
contentedness, kon·tent'ed·nes, *n.*
State of being contented.—**contentment,** kon·tent'ment, *n.* [Fr. *contente-
ment.*] The state or feeling of being
contented; content; a resting or
satisfaction of mind without disquiet
or craving for something else;
acquiescence in one's own circumstances. ∴ *Contentment* is passive,
satisfaction is active. The former
implies the absence of fretting or
craving, the latter an active feeling
of pleasure.
contention, etc. See CONTEND.
conterminous, kon·tẽr'min·us, *a.* [L.
conterminus—con, and *terminus,* a

border.] Terminating at a common
point; having common boundaries
or limits; touching at the boundary.
contest, kon·test', *v.t.* [Fr. *contester,*
from L. *contestari,* to call to witness,
to call witnesses—*con,* together, and
testis, a witness. DETEST.] To make
a subject of contention or dispute;
to enter into a struggle for; to
struggle to defend; to controvert:
to oppose; to call in question; to
dispute (statements).—*v.i.*† To strive;
to contend; followed by *with.*—*n.*
(kon'test.) A struggle for victory,
superiority, or in defense; struggle
in arms; dispute; debate; controversy; strife in argument.—**contestable,** kon·tes'ta·bl, *a.* Capable of
being disputed or debated; disputable; controvertible.—**contestant,**†
kon·tes'tant, *n.* One who contests.
context, kon'tekst, *n.* [L. *contextus,*
connection, from *contexo—con,* and
texo, to weave.] The parts of a book
or other writing which immediately
precede or follow a sentence quoted.
—**contexture,** kon·teks'chẽr, *n.* The
manner of interweaving several parts
into one body; the disposition and
union of the constituent parts of
a thing with respect to each other;
constitution.
contiguous, kon·tig'ū·us, *a.* [L. *con-
tiguus—con,* and *tango,* to touch.
CONTACT.] Situated so as to touch;
meeting or joining at the surface
or border; close together; neighboring; bordering or adjoining.—**contiguity.** kon·ti·gū'i·ti, *n.* The state
of being contiguous; closeness of
situation or place; a linking together,
as of a series of objects.—**contiguous-
ly,** kon·tig'ū·us·li, *adv.* In a contiguous manner; without intervening
space.—**contiguousness,** kon·tig'ū·
us·nes, *n.* The state or quality of
being contiguous; contiguity.
continence, continency, kon'ti·nens,
kon'ti·nen·si, *n.* [L. *continentia,* from
contineo, to hold or withhold. CON-
TAIN.] The restraint which a person
imposes upon his desires and passions; the restraint of the passion
for sexual enjoyment; forbearance
of lewd pleasures; chastity.—**continent,** kon'ti·nent, *a.* [L. *continens.*]
Refraining from sexual commerce;
chaste; also moderate or temperate
in general.—**continently,** kon'ti·
nent·li, *adv.* In a continent manner;
chastely.
continent, kon'ti·nent, *n.* [L. *continens,* a continent or mainland, lit.
land holding together.] An arbitrary
term applied to a connected tract
of land of great extent; one of the
great divisions of the land on the
globe.—**Continental,** kon·ti·nent'al,
a. Pertaining or relating to the
continent of Europe; pertaining to
the confederated colonies at the
time of the American Revolution;
a soldier in the Continental Army;
[*not cap.*] the least bit;—*not worth a
Continental*—from the low value of
Continental currency at the time.
contingency, kon·tin'jen·si, *n.* [L.
contingens, ppr. of *contingo—*to fall
or happen to—*con,* and *tango,* to
touch. CONTACT.] The quality of

being contingent; the possibility of happening or coming to pass; fortuitousness; something that may happen; a possible occurrence; a fortuitous event, or one which may occur. Also **contingence**, kon·tin′jens.—**contingent**, kon·tin′jent, *a.* Possibly occurring; liable to occur; not determinable by any certain rule; accidental; casual; dependent upon what is undetermined or unknown; dependent upon the happening of something else.—**contingent**, kon·tin′jent, *n.* A contingency‡; a quota or suitable proportion, as of troops furnished for some joint enterprise.—**contingently**, kon·tin′jent·li, *adv.* In a contingent manner.

continue, kon·tin′ū, *v.i.*—**continued**, **continuing**. [L. *continuo*, to carry on, to keep on, continue, from *continuus*, unbroken, continuous—*con*, together, and *teneo*, to hold. CONTAIN.] To remain in a state or place; to abide for any time indefinitely; to last; to endure; to be permanent; to persevere; to be steadfast or constant in any course.—*v.t.* To protract or lengthen out; not to cease from or to terminate; to extend; to make longer; to persevere in; not to ease to do or use; to suffer or cause to remain as before.—**continuable**, kon·tin′ū·a·bl, *a.* Capable of being continued—**continual**, kon·tin′ū·al, *a.* [Fr. *continuel*; L. *continuus*.] Proceeding without interruption or cessation; not intermitting; unceasing; of frequent recurrence; often repeated; incessant. ∴ Syn. under CONTINUOUS.—**continually**, kon·tin′ū·al·li, *adv.* Without pause or cessation; unceasingly; very often; in repeated succession; from time to time. Syn. under CONTINUOUSLY.—**continuance**, kon·tin′ū·ans, *n.* The state or continuing or remaining in a particular state or course; permanence, as of habits, condition, or abode; a state of lasting; constancy; perseverance; duration; the act of continuing; continuation. ∴ Syn. under CONTINUATION.—**continuation**, kon·tin′ū·a″shon, *n.* [L. *continuatio*.] The act of continuing or prolonging; extension or carrying on to a further point; the portion continued or extended; a prolongation or extension. ∴ *Continuation* is the act of continuing (also the part prolonged), *continuance* the state of continuing.—**continuative**, kon·tin′ū·āt·iv, *a.* Tending to continue, extend, prolong, or persist.—*n.* What is continuative.—**continuator, continuer**, kon·tin′ū·āt·ėr, kon·tin′ū·ėr, *n.* One who or that which continues; one who carries forward anything that had been begun by another.—**continued**, kon·tin′ūd, *p.* and *a.* Protracted or extended; proceeding without cessation; unceasing.—*Continued fraction*, one whose denominator is an integer with a fraction, which latter fraction has for its denominator an integer with a fraction, and so on.—**continuity**, kon·ti·nū′i·ti, *n.* [L. *continuitas*.] Connection uninter-

rupted; cohesion; close union of parts; unbroken texture.—**continuous**, kon·tin′ū·us, *a.* [L. *continuus*.] Joined without intervening space or time; proceeding from something else without interruption or without apparent interruption; uninterrupted; unbroken. ∴ *Continuous* means unbroken, uninterrupted; *continual* does not imply unceasing continuity, but the habitual or repeated renewals of an act, state, etc. *Perpetual* is *continuous* with the idea of lastingness.—**continuously**, kon·tin′ū·us·li, *adv.* In a continuous manner; in continuation; without interruption. ∴ *Continuously*, like its adjective, denotes unbroken continuity, *continually* close succession.—**continuousness**, kon·tin′ū·us·nes, *n.* State or quality of being continuous.

contort, kon·tort′, *v.t.* [L. *contorqueo, contortum*, to twist—*con*, intens., and *torqueo, tortum*, to twist, whence also *torture, torment, extort*, etc.] To twist together; to bend or curve in irregular forms; to writhe.—**contortion**, kon·tor′shon, *n.* [L. *contortio*.] The act of contorting, or state of being contorted; a twist or twisting; a writhing, especially spasmodic writhing; a wry motion or position; *med.* a twisting or wresting of a limb or member of the body out of its natural situation.—**contortionist**, kon·tor′shon·ist, *n.* An acrobat who practices contortions of the body.

contour, kon′tör, *n.* [Fr. *contour*—*con*, and *tour*, a turn, revolution, turner's lathe, from L. *tornus*, Gr. *tornos*, a lathe; hence also Fr. *tourner*, E. *turn*.] The outline of a figure or body; the line that defines or bounds a solid body; the periphery considered as distinct from the object.—*v.t.* To delineate or draw by the contour.

contraband, kon′tra·band, *a.* [Fr. *contrebande*—It. *contra*, against, and *bando*, a proclamation, a ban. BAN.] Prohibited or excluded by proclamation, law, or treaty.—*Contraband goods* are such as are prohibited to be imported or exported, either by the laws of a particular kingdom or state, or by the law of nations, or by special treaties.—*n.* Illegal or prohibited traffic; articles prohibited to be imported or exported.—**contrabandist**, kon′tra·band·ist, *n.* One who deals in contraband goods.—**contrabass**, kon′tra·bās, *n.* [It.] The largest of the violin species of instruments, of which it forms the lowest bass; usually called the double bass.

contract, kon·trakt′, *v.t.* [Fr. *contracter*, L. *contraho, contractum*—*con*, and *traho*, to draw, whence also *tract, treat. trace, train*, etc.] To draw together or closer; to draw into a less compass, either in length or breadth; to abridge, narrow, lessen; to wrinkle; to betroth or affiance; to bring on, incur, acquire (vicious habits, debts); to shorten by omission of a letter or syllable.—*v.i.* To be drawn together; to

become shorter or narrower; to shrink; to bargain; to make a mutual agreement as between two or more persons.—*n.* (kon′trakt). An agreement or mutual promise upon lawful consideration or cause which binds the parties to a performance; a bargain; a compact; the act by which a man and woman are betrothed each to the other; the writing which contains the agreement of parties.—**contractibility**, **contractibleness**, kon·trakt′i·bil″i·ti, kon·trakt′i·bl·nes, *n.* Quality of being contractible.—**contractible**, kon·trakt′i·bl, *a.* Capable of contraction.—**contractile**, kon·trakt′il, *a.* Tending to contract; having the power of shortening or of drawing into smaller dimensions.—**contractility**, kon·trakt·il′i·ti, *n.* The inherent quality or force by which bodies shrink or contract; *physiol.* that vital property which gives to certain parts the power of contracting.—**contraction**, kon·trak′shon, *n.* [L. *contractio*.] The act of contracting, drawing together, or shrinking; the act of shortening, narrowing, or lessening dimensions by causing the parts to approach nearer to each other; the state of being contracted; an abbreviation employed with the view of saving labor in writing, as *recd.* for *received*; the shortening of a word by the omission of one or more letters or syllables.—**contractive**, kon·trakt′iv, *a.* Tending to contract.—**contractor**, kon·trakt′ėr, *n.* One who contracts; one of the parties to a bargain; one who covenants to do anything for another; one who contracts to perform any work or service, or to furnish supplies, at a certain price or rate.

contradict, kon·tra·dikt′, *v.t.* [L. *contradico, contradictum*—*contra*, and *dico*, to speak, whence *diction*, etc.] To assert not to be so, or to assert to be the contrary to what has been asserted; to meet (a person, an assertion) with a statement quite different or opposite; to deny; to be directly contrary to.—**contradictable**, kon·tra·dik′ta·bl, *a.* Capable of being contradicted; deniable; disputable.—**contradicter**, kon·tra·dik′tėr, *n.* One who contradicts or denies.—**contradiction**, kon·tra·dik′shon, *n.* [L. *contradictio*.] The act of contradicting; an assertion of the contrary to what has been said or affirmed; denial; contrary declaration; direct opposition or repugnancy; inconsistency with itself; incongruity or contrariety of things, words, thoughts, or propositions; the person who, or thing that, contradicts or is inconsistent with him, her, or its self.—**contradictious**, kon·tra·dik′shus, *a.* Contradictory; given to contradict.—**contradictive**,† kon·tra·dik′tiv, *a.* Contradictory; inconsistent.—**contradictorily**, kon·tra·dik′tor·i·li, *adv.* In a contradictory way; in a manner inconsistent with itself.—**contradictoriness**, kon·tra·dik′tor·i·nes, *n.* The state or character of being contradictory; contrariety in assertion or effect.—**contradictory**, kon·tra·dik′tor·i, *a.* Contradicting; given to contradict; affirming the contrary; implying a denial of what has been asserted; inconsistent with one another; directly opposite.—*n.* A proposition which denies or opposes another in all its terms.

contradistinction, kon′tra·dis·tingk″shon, *n.* Distinction by opposite qualities or characteristics; a setting or bringing (terms, notions) into contrast or opposition.—**contradistinctive**, kon′tra·dis·tingkt″iv, *a.* Having the quality of, or characterized by, contradistinction; opposite in qualities.—*n.* A mark of contradistinction.—**contradistinguish**, kon′tra·dis·ting″gwish, *v.t.* To distinguish or set distinctly forward, not merely by different but by opposite qualities; used of ideas, terms, etc.

contraindicate, kon·tra·in′di·kāt, *v.t.* or *i.*—*contraindicated*, *contraindicating.* To indicate, suggest, or point to something contrary or opposite.—**contraindication**, kon·tra·in′di·kā″shon, *n.* What contraindicates.

contralto, kon·tral′tō, *n.* [It.] *Mus.* the lowest voice of a woman or boy, called also the *Alto*; generally a female voice below the mezzo soprano and soprano; also the countertenor; the person who sings with this voice.—*a.* Pertaining to, or possessed of the quality of, contralto.

contraposition, kon′tra·po·zi″shon, *n.* A placing over against; opposite position.

contrapuntal, kon·tra·punt′al, *a.* Pertaining to counterpoint.—**contrapuntist**, kon·tra·punt′ist, *n.* One skilled in counterpoint.

contrary, kon′tra·ri, *a.* [L. *contrarius*, from *contra*, against; Fr. *contraire*.] Opposite; adverse; moving against or in an opposite direction (*contrary* winds); contradictory; not merely different, but inconsistent or repugnant; perverse or froward (*colloq.*). [This adjective, in many phrases, is to be treated grammatically as an adverb, or as an adjective referring to a sentence or affirmation; as, this happened *contrary* to my expectations.]—*n.* A thing that is contrary or of opposite qualities; a proposition contrary to another, or fact contrary to what is alleged.—*On the contrary*, on the other hand; quite oppositely.—*To the contrary*, to an opposite purpose or fact.—**contrariety**, kon·tra·rī′e·ti, *n.* [L. *contrarietas*.] The state or quality of being contrary; opposition in fact, essence, quality, or principle; repugnance; inconsistency; quality or position destructive of its opposite.—**contrarily**, kon′tra·ri·li, *adv.* In a contrary manner; in opposition; on the other hand; in opposite ways.—**contrariness**, kon·trâr′i·nes, *n.* Contrariety; opposition.—**contrariwise**, kon′tra·ri·wīz, *adv.* On the contrary; oppositely; on the other hand (N.T.).

contrast, kon·trast′, *v.t.* [Fr. *contraster*, from L. *contra*, opposite, and *stare*, to stand.] To set in opposition so as to show the difference between, and to exhibit the excellence of the one and the defects of the other; to compare so as to point out dissimilarity.—*v.i.* To stand in contrast or opposition to something else; followed by *with*.—*n.* (kon′trast). The viewing or comparing of things together in order to render any difference between them more vividly marked; comparison by contrariety of qualities; opposition or dissimilitude of things or qualities.

contravallation, kon′tra·val·lā″shon, *n.* [Fr. *contrevallation*—L. *contra*, against, and *vallum*, a rampart.] *Fort.* a chain of redoubts and breastworks raised by the besiegers about a fortress to prevent sorties of the garrison.

contravene, kon·tra·vēn′, *v.t.*—*contravened*, *contravening.* [L. *contravenio*—*contra*, against, and *venio*, to come, as in *convene*, etc.] To come or be in conflict with; to obstruct in operation; to act so as to violate; to transgress.—**contravener**, kon·tra·vē′ner, *n.* One who contravenes.—**contravention**, kon·tra·ven′shon, *n.* The act of contravening, violating, or transgressing; violation; opposition.

contre-temps, kon·tre·täñ′, *n.* [Fr.] An unexpected and untoward accident; an embarrassing conjuncture; a hitch.

contribute, kon·trib′ūt, *v.t.*—*contributed*, *contributing.* [L. *contribuo*—*con*, and *tribuo*, to grant, assign, or impart. TRIBE, TRIBUTE.] To give or grant in common with others; to give to a common stock or for a common purpose; to pay as a share.—*v.i.* To give a part; to lend a portion of power, aid, or influence; to have a share in any act or effect; with *to*.—**contributable**, kon·trib′ūt·a·bl. *a.* Capable of being contributed.—**contribution**, kon·tri·bū′shon, *n.* The act of contributing; the payment of a share along with others; that which is given to a common stock or purpose, either by an individual or by many; the sum or thing contributed.—**contributive**, kon·trib′ūt·iv, *a.* Tending to contribute; contributing.—**contributor**, kon·trib′ūt·er, *n.* One who contributes, one who gives or pays money to a common fund; one who gives aid to a common purpose.—**contributory**, kon·trib′ū·to·ri, *a.* Contributing to the same stock or purpose; bringing assistance to some joint design, or increase to some common stock.—*n.* A contributor.

contrite, kon′trīt, *a.* [L. *contritus*, from *contero*, to break or bruise—*con*, and *tero*, to bruise. TRITE.] Brokenhearted for sin; deeply affected with grief and sorrow for sin; humble; penitent.—*n.* A contrite person; a penitent.—**contritely**, kon′trīt·li, *adv.* In a contrite manner; with penitence.—**contriteness**, **contrition**, kon′trīt·nes, kon·trish′on, *n.* [L. *contritio.*] Grief of heart for sin; sincere penitence.

contrive, kon·trīv′, *v.t.*—*contrived*, contriving. [O.Fr. *controver*, Fr. *controuver*, to invent, to fabricate—*con*, and *trouver*, to find.] To invent; to devise; to plan.—*v.i.* To form schemes or designs; to plan; to scheme.—**contrivable**, kon·trī′va·bl, *a.* Capable of being contrived, planned, invented, or devised.—**contrivance**, kon·trī′vans, *n.* The act of contriving, inventing, devising, or planning; the thing contrived; an artifice; scheme; invention.—**contriver**, kon·trī′ver, *n.* One who contrives, plans, or devises.

control, kon·trōl′, *n.* [Fr. *contrôle*, lit. counter-roll, from *contre*, against, and *rôle*, a roll, list. ROLL.] Restraining power or influence; check; restraint; power; authority; government; command.—*v.t.*—*controlled*, *controlling.* To exercise control over; to hold in restraint or check; to subject to authority; to regulate; to govern; to subjugate.—**controllable**, kon·trōl′a·bl, *a.* Capable of being controlled, checked, or restrained; subject to command.—**controller**, kon·trōl′er, *n.* One who controls; one that has the power or authority to govern or control; one who governs or regulates; an officer appointed to keep a counter register of accounts, or to oversee, control, or verify the accounts of other officers; a comptroller.—**controllership**, kon·trōl′er·ship, *n.* The office of a controller; comptrollership.—**controlment**, kon·trōl′ment, *n.* The power or act of controlling; control; restraint.

controvert, kon′tro·vert, *v.t.* [L. *contra*, against, and *verto*, *versum*, to turn.] To dispute; to oppose by reasoning; to contend against in words or writings; to deny and attempt to disprove or confute.—**controversial**, kon·tro·ver′shal, *a.* Relating to controversy.—**controversialist**, kon·tro·ver′shal·ist, *n.* One who carries on a controversy; a disputant.—**controversially**, kon·tro·ver′shal·li, *adv.* In a controversial manner.—**controversy**, kon′tro·ver·si, *n.* [L. *controversia.*] Debate; agitation of contrary opinions; a disputation or discussion between parties, particularly in writing; a litigation.—**controverter**, kon′tro·ver·ter, *n.* One who controverts; a controversial writer.—**controvertible**, kon·tro·ver′ti·bl, *a.* Capable of being controverted or disputed; disputable; not too evident to exclude difference of opinion.

contumacious, kon·tū·mā′shus, *a.* [L. *contumax*, *contumacis*—*con*, and *tumeo*, to swell, seen also in *tumid*, *tumult*, *contumely*.] Resisting legitimate authority; disobedient; froward or perverse; *law*, wilfully disobedient to the orders of a court.—**contumaciously**, kon·tū·mā′shus·li, *adv.* In a contumacious manner; obstinately; stubbornly; in disobedience of orders.—**contumaciousness**, kon·tū·mā′shus·nes, *n.* State of being contumacious; obstinacy; perverseness; contumacy.—**contumacy**, kon′tū·ma·si, *n.* [L. *contumacia.*] Contumacious conduct; character or state of being contumacious; willful and persistent resistance to legitimate authority; unyielding obstinacy; stubborn perverseness; *law*, wilful disregard of the orders of a court.

contumely, kon′tū·me·li, *n*. [L. *contumelia*, from *contumeo—con*, and *tumeo*. CONTUMACIOUS.] Haughtiness and contempt in language or behavior; contemptuous or insulting language; haughty insolence.—**contumelious**, kon·tū·mē′li·us, *a*. [L. *contumeliosus*.] Indicating or expressive of contumely; contemptuous; insolent; rude and sarcastic; disposed to utter reproach or insult; insolent; proudly rude.—**contumeliously**, kon·tū·mē′li·us·li, *adv*. In a contumelious manner; rudely; insolently.—**contumeliousness**, kon·tū·mē′li·us·nes, *n*. State of being contumelious.

contuse, kon·tūz′, *v.t.*—*contused, contusing*. [L. *contundo, contusum—con*, and *tundo*, to beat, same root as Skr. *tud*, to beat.] To wound or injure by bruising; to injure without breaking the flesh.—**contusion**, kon·tū′zhon, *n*. [L. *contusio*.] A severe bruise on the body; a hurt or injury as to the flesh or some part of the body without breaking of the skin, as by a blunt instrument or by a fall.

conundrum, ko·nun′drum, *n*. [Origin uncertain.] A sort of riddle, in which some odd resemblance is proposed for discovery between things quite unlike, the answer involving a pun.

convalescence, kon·va·les′ens, *n*. [L. *convalesco*, to grow stronger—*con*, and *valesco*, to get strength, *valeo*, to be strong. VALID, AVAIL.] The gradual recovery of health and strength after disease; the state of a person renewing his vigor after sickness or weakness.—**convalesce**, kon·va·les′, *v.i.*—*convalesced, convalescing*. To grow better after sickness; to recover health.—**convalescent**, kon·va·les′ent, *a*. Recovering health and strength after sickness or debility.—*n*. One who is recovering his health after sickness.

convection, kon·vek′shon, *n*. [L. *convectio*, from *conveho*, to convey.] The act of carrying or conveying; a process of transmission, as of heat or electricity by means of particles of matter affected by them.—**convective**, kon·vek′tiv, *a*. Resulting from or caused by convection.—**convectively**, kon·vek′tiv·li, *adv*. In a convective manner; by means of convection.

convene, kon·vēn′, *v.i.*—*convened, convening*. [L. *convenio—con*, and *venio, ventum*, to come: seen also in *intervene, advent, event, revenue*, etc.] To come together, to meet, to meet in the same place; to assemble: rarely said of things.—*v.t.* To cause to assemble; to call together; to convoke; to summon judicially to meet or appear.—**convener**, kon·vē′nėr, *n*. One who convenes or meets with others; one who convenes or calls a meeting.

convenience, conveniency, kon·vē′-ni·ens, kon·vē′ni·en·si, *n*. [L. *convenientia*, from *convenio*, to convene; lit. a coming together.] The state or quality of being convenient; freedom from discomfort or trouble; ease; comfort; that which gives ease or comfort; that which is suited to wants; opportune conjunction of affairs; opportunity.—**convenient**, kon·vē′ni·ent, *a*. Suitable or proper; giving certain facilities or accommodation; commodious; opportune; at hand or readily available (*colloq*.).—**conveniently**, kon·vē′ni·ent·li, *adv*. in a convenient manner or situation: suitably; with adaptation to the end or effect; with ease; without trouble or difficulty.

convent, kon′vent, *n*. [O.Fr. *convent*, from L. *conventus*, a meeting—*con*, together, and *venio, ventum*, to come. CONVENE.] A community of persons devoted to religion; a body of monks or nuns; a house for persons devoted to religion and celibacy; an abbey, monastery, or nunnery.—**conventual**, kon·ven′tū·al, *a*. Of or belonging to a convent; monastic.—**conventual**, kon·ven′tū·al, *n*. One who lives in a convent; a monk or nun.

conventicle, kon·ven′ti·kl, *n*. [L. *conventiculum*, dim. of *conventus*, a meeting. CONVENT.] An assembly or gathering, especially a secret assembly; a meeting of dissenters from the established church for religious worship; a secret meeting for religious worship held by the Scottish Covenanters.—**conventicler**, kon·ven′ti·klėr, *n*. One who supports or frequents conventicles.

convention, kon·ven′shon, *n*. [L. *conventio*. CONVENE.] The act of coming together; a meeting; an assembly; an assembly of delegates or representatives for consultation on important concerns, civil, political, or ecclesiastical; a special agreement or contract between two countries or parties; an agreement previous to a definitive treaty; conventionality†. — **conventional**, kon·ven′shon·al, *a*. [L. *conventionalis*.] Formed by agreement; tacitly understood; arising out of custom or tacit agreement; sanctioned by or depending on general concurrence and not on any principle; resting on mere usage.—**conventionalism**, kon·ven′shon·al·izm, *n*. That which is conventional; something received or established by convention or agreement; a conventional phrase, form, or ceremony; anything depending on conventional rules and precepts.—**conventionalist**, kon·ven′shon·al·ist, *n*. One who adheres to a convention or agreement.—**conventionality**, kon·ven′shon·al′i·ti, *n*. The character of being conventional; what is conventional; a conventional mode of living, acting or speaking, as opposed to what is natural.—**conventionalize**, kon·ven′tion·al·īz, *v.t.*—*conventionalized, conventionalizing*. To render conventional; to bring under the influence of conventional rules; to render observant of the conventional rules

of society.—**conventionally**, kon·ven′shon·al·li, *adv*. in a conventional manner.

conventual. See CONVENT.

converge, kon·vėrj′, *v.i.*—*converged, converging*. [L. *con*, together, and *vergo*, to incline. VERGE.] To tend to one point; to incline and approach nearer together in position; to approach in character.—**convergence, convergency**, kon·vėr′jens, kon·vėr′jen·si, *n*. The quality of converging; tendency to one point.—**convergent**, kon·vėr′jent, *a*. Converging; tending to one point; approaching each other.

converse, kon·vėrs′, *v.i.*—*conversed, conversing*. [Fr. *converser*; L. *conversor*, to associate with—*con*, and *versor*, to be engaged in anything, from *verto, versum*, to turn; seen also in *convert, reverse, verse, version*, etc. VERSE.] To associate, hold intercourse or communion; to talk familiarly; to have free intercourse in mutual communication of thoughts and opinions; to chat; to discourse.—*n*. (kon′vėrs). Acquaintance by frequent or customary intercourse; intercourse; communion; familiarity; free interchange of thoughts or opinions.—**conversable**, kon·vėr′sa·bl, *a*. [Fr. *conversable*.] Disposed to conversation; ready or inclined to mutual communication of thoughts; sociable; free in discourse.—**conversableness**, kon·vėr′sa·bl·nes, *n*. The quality of being conversable; disposition or readiness to converse; sociability.—**conversance, † conversancy**, † kon′vėr·sans, kon′vėr·san·si, *n*. The state of being conversant.—**conversant**, kon·vėr′sant, *a*. Keeping company; having frequent intercourse; intimately associating; followed by *with* or *among*; but the common meaning now is, acquainted by familiar use or study; having an intimate or thorough knowledge (of things); followed generally by *with*).—**conversantly**, kon·vėr′·sant·li, *adv*. In a conversant or familiar manner.—**conversation**, kon·vėr·sā′shon, *n*. [Fr. *conversation*, L. *conversatio*, intercourse.] Manners, behavior, or deportment, especially as respects morals; familiar discourse; general interchange of sentiments; chat; unrestrained talk, opposed to a formal conference (now the usual meaning); also sexual intercourse.—**conversational**, kon·vėr·sā′shon·al, *a*. Pertaining to conversation.—**conversationalist, conversationist**, kon·vėr·sā′shon·al·ist, kon·vėr·sā′shon·ist, *n*. One who excels in conversation.

converse, kon′vers, *a*. [L. *conversus*, turned round, *converto, conversum*, to turn round—*con*, and *verto, versum*, to turn. CONVERSE, *v.i.*] Turned so as to be transposed or inverted, put the opposite, reverse, or contrary way (*converse* statement, proposition, way).—*n*. Something forming a counterpart; what is contrary or opposite; a statement or proposition produced by inversion or interchange of terms; thus the *converse* of 'religion is true wisdom', is 'true

wisdom is religion '.—**conversely,** kon·vèrs´·li, *adv.* In a converse manner; with inversion of order; put the converse way.—**conversion,** kon·ver´zhon, *n.* [L. *conversio.*] The act of turning or changing from one state to another; the state of being so turned or changed; transmutation; the act of changing or state of being changed in opinions or conduct; a change of heart or dispositions, succeeded by a reformation of life; a change from heathenism or from irreligion to Christianity.—**convert,** kon·vert´, *v.t.* [L. *converto.*] To change or turn into another substance or form; to change from one state to another; to change or turn from one religion to another, or from one party or sect to another; to change from heathenism to Christianity; to turn from a bad life to a good, religious, and holy one; to turn from one use or destination to another; to interchange conversely.—*v.i.* To turn or be changed; to undergo a change.—*n.* (kon´vert). A person who turns from one opinion or practice to another: a person who renounces one creed, religious system, or party, and embraces another; one who is turned from sin to holiness. ∴ A *convert* is one who changes opinions, and thus goes over to another side, party, or religion; a *proselyte* is one who changes his religion; but proselytism does not, like conversion, necessarily imply conviction.—**converter,** kon·ver´tèr, *n.* One who converts; one who makes converts; that which converts, especially an iron retort used in the Bessemer process of steelmaking.—**convertibility, convertibleness,** kon·ver´ti·bil´i·ti, kon·ver´ti·bl·nes, *n.* The condition or quality of being convertible; the capability of being converted.—**convertible,** kon·ver´ti·bl, *a.* Capable of being converted; susceptible of change, transmutable; transformable; capable of being used the one for the other, as terms of similar signification; interchangeable. —**convertibly,** kon·ver´ti·bli, *adv.* In a convertible manner; with interchange of terms.
convex, kon´veks, *a.* [L. *convexus,* carried round, rounded—*con,* together, and *veho, vexum,* to carry; whence also *vehicle.*] Rising or swelling into a spherical or rounded form on the exterior surface: opposed to *concave.*—*n.* A convex part. —**convexly,** kon·veks´li, *adv.* In a convex form.—**convexity,** kon·vek´si·ti, *n.* State of being convex; the exterior surface of a convex body; roundness.—**convexo-concave,** *a.* Convex on one side and concave on the other: said of a lens. —**convexo-convex,** *a.* Convex on both sides: said of a lens.
convey, kon·vā´, *v.t.* [O.Fr. *conveier, convoyer,* L.L. *conviare,* to convey, to convoy—L. *con,* with, and *via,* a way; whence also *voyage, devious, deviate, obvious,* etc.] To carry, bear, or transport; to transmit, hand over, or transfer from one person to

another (rights, landed estate); to transmit or carry by any medium (air *conveys* sound, words *convey* meaning).—**conveyable,** kon·vā´a·bl, *a.* Capable of being conveyed or transferred.—**conveyance,** kon·vā´ans, *n.* The act of conveying; the act of bearing, carrying, or transporting; transmission; transference; the transmitting or transferring of property from one person to another; the document by which property is transferred; the means by which anything is conveyed, especially a vehicle or carriage of some kind. —**conveyancing,** kon·vā´ans·ing, *n.* The act or practice of drawing deeds, leases, or other writings for transferring the title to property from one person to another.—**conveyer,** kon·vā´èr, *n.* One who or that which conveys.
convict, kon·vikt´, *v.t.* [L. *convinco, convictum—con,* and *vinco,* to vanquish. CONVINCE.] To determine the truth of a charge against; to prove or find guilty of a crime charged; to determine or decide to be guilty: with *of* before the crime. —*n.* (kon´vikt). A person convicted or found guilty of a crime; a person undergoing penal servitude.—**conviction,** kon·vik´shon, *n.* The act of convicting or the state of being convicted; the act of a legal tribunal adjudging, finding, or determining a person to be guilty of an offense charged against him; strong belief on the ground of satisfactory evidence; settled persuasion. .. *Conviction* is assent founded on satisfactory proofs which appeal to the reason; *persuasion* is assent founded on what appeals to the feelings and imagination.—**convictive,**† kon·vik´tiv, *a.* Having the power to convince or convict.
convince, kon·vins´, *v.t.*—**convinced, convincing.** [L. *convinco, convictum—con,* and *vinco,* to vanquish, whence *victor, vanquish, evince.*] To persuade or satisfy by evidence; to bring to full belief or acquiescence by satisfactory proofs or arguments; to compel to yield assent; to convict or prove guilty (N.T.)‡; to overpower (*Shak.*)‡.—**convincible,** kon·vin´si·bl, *a.* Capable of conviction.—**convincingly,** kon·vin´sing·li, *adv.* In a convincing manner; in a manner to leave no room to doubt, or to compel assent.—**convincingness,** kon·vin´sing·nes, *n.* The power of convincing.
convivial, kon·viv´i·al, *a.* [L. *conviva,* a guest—*con,* and *vivo, victum,* to live, whence *victuals, vital, vivid,* etc.] Relating to a feast or entertainment; festal; social; jovial.—**conviviality,** kon·viv´i·al´´i·ti, *n.* The good humor or mirth indulged at an entertainment; a convivial spirit or disposition.—**convivially,** kon·viv´i·al·li, *adv.* In a spirit of conviviality; in a convivial manner; festively.
convoke, kon·vōk´, *v.t.*—**convoked, convoking.** [L. *convoco,* to convoke—*con,* and *voco,* to call. VOICE, VOCAL.] To call together; to summon to meet; to assemble by summons.—

convocation, kon·vo·kā´shon, *n.* The act of convoking or assembling by summons; an assembly; a convention; a congress; a council; in England, an assembly of the clergy, by their representatives, to consult on ecclesiastical affairs—a sort of ecclesiastical parliament.—**convocational,** kon·vo·kā´shon·al, *a.* Relating to a convocation.
convolve, kon·volv´, *v.t.*—**convolved, convolving.** [L. *convolvo—con,* and *volvo,* to roll, whence *involve, revolve, volume, vault.* WALLOW.] To roll or wind together; to roll one part on another; to coil up.—**convolute,** kon´vo·lūt, *a.* Rolled together, or one part on another; presenting convolutions.—**convolution,** kon·vo·lū´shon, *n.* [L. *convolutio, convolutionis.*] The act of rolling or winding together, or one thing on another; a winding motion; the state of being rolled round upon itself or rolled or wound together; a turn or winding; a twisted or tortuous part of something.
convolvulus, kon·vol´vū·lus, *n.* [L., from *convolvo,* to entwine, in reference to their twining habit.] Bindweed, a genus of plants consisting of slender twining herbs, with milky juice, and somewhat bell-shaped flowers, many of them beautiful.— **convolvulaceous,** kon·vol´vū·lā´´shus, *a.* Relating to the convolvulus or allied plants.
convoy, kon·voi´, *v.t.* [Fr. *convoyer. Convoy=convey.* CONVEY.] To accompany on the way for protection, either by sea or land; to escort, as a guard against enemies.—*n.* (kon´voi). A protecting force accompanying ships or property on their way from place to place either by sea or land; that which is conducted by such a force.
convulse, kon·vuls´, *v.t.* [L. *convello, convulsum—con,* and *vello,* to pull or pluck.] To draw together or contract spasmodically, as the muscular parts of an animal body; to affect by irregular spasms; to affect by violent irregular action; to agitate violently.—**convulsion,** kon·vul´shon, *n.* [L. *convulsio.*] A violent and involuntary contraction of the muscular parts of an animal body, with alternate relaxations; violent and irregular motion; a violent and far-reaching disturbance in nature or among peoples; turmoil; a violent commotion.—**convulsional,**† **convulsionary,**† kon·vul´shon·al, kon·vul´shon·e·ri, *a.* Pertaining to convulsion; of the nature of convulsion.—**convulsive,** kon·vul´siv, *a.* Producing or tending to produce convulsion; attended with, or characterized by, convulsion or spasms.—**convulsively,** kon·vul´siv·li, *adv.* In a convulsive manner; with convulsion.
cony, coney, kō´ni, *n.* [O.E. *coning, cunning,* perhaps from O.Fr. *conil, conin,* from L. *cuniculus,* a rabbit; comp. W. *cwning,* Gael. *coinean,* Ir. *coinin,* Manx *connee*—rabbit.] A rabbit; a rabbit-like animal found in Syria and Palestine; the hydrax, or daman, a small Old World mammal.

fāte, fär, fâre, fat, fạll; mē, met, hėr; pīne, pin; nōte, not, mōve; tūbe, tub, bụll; oil, pound.

coo, kö, *v.i.* [Imitative of the noise of doves; comp. D. *korren*, Icel. *kurra*, Fr. *roucouler*, to coo like a dove.] To cry or make the characteristic sound uttered by pigeons or doves; to act in a loving manner.

cooey, cooee, kö'i, *n.* [Imitative.] The cry or call of the Australian aborigines.—*v.t.* To cry or call like the aborigines of Australia.

cook, kụk, *v.t.* [A.Sax. *cóc*, a cock, borrowed, like Dan. *koge*, G. *kochen*, D. *kooken*, to boil, to cook, from L. *coquo*, to cook, *coquus*, a cook.] To prepare for the table by boiling, roasting, baking, broiling, etc.; to dress, as meat or vegetables, for eating; to dress up or give a color to for some special purpose, especially, to tamper with accounts so as to give them a more favorable aspect than they ought to have; to garble; to falsify.—*n.* One whose occupation is to cook or prepare victuals for the table.—**cookery,** kụk'ėr·i, *n.* The art or the practice of dressing and preparing victuals for the table.

cool, köl, *a.* [A.Sax. *col*=G. *kuhl*, cool; Icel. *kul*, D. *koel*, a cold blast; same root as in *chill, cold*, L. *gelu*, frost, *gelidus*.] Moderately cold; being of a temperature between hot and cold; not ardent or zealous; not excited by passion of any kind; not angry; not fond; indifferent; apathetic; chilling; frigid; deliberate; calm; quietly impudent and selfish: of persons and acts (*colloq.*).—*n.* A moderate state of cold; moderate temperature of the air between hot and cold (the *cool* of the day).—*v.t.* To make cool; to reduce the temperature of; to moderate or allay, as passion of any kind; to calm; to abate, as desire, zeal, or ardor; to render indifferent.—*v.i.* To become less hot; to lose heat; to lose the heat of excitement, passion, or emotion; to become less ardent, zealous, or affectionate.—**cooler,** köl'ėr, *n.* That which cools; a vessel in which liquids or other things are cooled.—**coolish,** köl'ish, *a.* Somewhat cool.—**coolly,** köl'li, *adv.* Without heat or sharp cold; in a cool or indifferent manner; without passion or ardor; without haste; calmly; deliberately. —**coolness,** köl'nes, *n.* The state or quality of being cool; a moderate degree of cold; a moderate degree or a want of passion; want of ardor or zeal; indifference; want of affection.

coolie, kö'li, *n.* An East Indian porter or carrier; an emigrant laborer from India, China, and other eastern countries.

coom, köm, *n.* [Perhaps from Fr. *écume*, foam, dross.] Soot; dirty refuse matter; the matter that works out of the naves or boxes of carriage wheels; coal dust.

coomb, comb, köm, kōm, *n.* [A.Sax. *cumb*, a liquid measure, a valley= Dan. and G. *kumme*, a bowl, a basin; D. *kom*, a trough, a chest.] An English dry measure of 4 bushels or half a quarter; a valley between hills (see COMB).

coon, kön, *n.* An abbreviation of *Raccoon.* A raccoon (colloq.).

coop, köp, *n.* [From L. *cupa*, a cask or vessel; akin *cup.*] A box of boards grated or barred on one side for keeping fowls in confinement; an enclosed place for small animals; a pen.—*v.t.* To put in a coop; to confine in a coop; to shut up or confine in a narrow compass: followed by *up, in,* or *within.*—**cooper,** kö'pėr, *n.* One whose occupation is to make barrels, tubs, etc.—*v.t.* and *i.* To do the work of a cooper.—**cooperage,** kö'pėr·ij, *n.* A place where coopers' work is done; the work or business of a cooper.—**coopery,** kö'pėr·i, *n.* The trade of a cooper; a cooper's workshop.

co-operate, kō·op'ėr·āt, *v.i.*—*co-operated, co-operating.* To act or operate jointly with another or others to the same end; to work or labor to promote a common object; to unite in producing the same effect.—**co-operation,** kō·op'ėr·ā"shon, *n.* The act of working or operating together to one end; joint operation; concurrent effort or labor.—**co-operative,** kō·op'ėr·ā·tiv, *a.* Operating jointly to the same end; established for the purpose of providing the members with goods at wholesale prices or at prime cost and cost of management (*co-operative* societies or stores).—**co-operator,** kō·op'ėr·ā·tėr, *n.* One who co-operates.

co-opt, kō·opt', *v.t.* [L. *co-opto.*] To elect by co-optation into some body of which the electors are members.

co-ordinate, kō·or'din·āt, *a.* [L. *co* for *con*, and *ordinatus*, from *ordo*, order. ORDER.] Being of equal order, or of the same rank or degree; not subordinate.—*v.t.*—*co-ordinated, co-ordinating.* To make co-ordinate; to arrange in due and relative order; to harmonize.—*n.* What is co-ordinate; *geom.* any straight line which, with another or others, serves to determine the position of certain points under consideration.—**co-ordinately,** kō·or'di·nāt·li, *adv.* In the same order or rank; without subordination.—**co-ordinateness,** kō·or'di·nāt·nes, *n.* The state of being co-ordinate.—**co-ordination,** kō·or'di·nā"shon, *n.* The act of making co-ordinate or state of being co-ordinated.—**co-ordinative,** kō·or'di·nā·tiv, *a.* Expressing or indicating co-ordination.

coot, köt, *n.* [Same as D. *koet*, a coot; comp. W. *cwta*, short-tailed.] A wading bird of the rail family, with a bald forehead, a black body, short tail, and lobated toes, and about 15 inches in length.

copaiba, kō·pā'ba, *n.* [Sp. and Pg.] A liquid resinous juice or balsam, flowing from incisions made in the stem of certain South American trees, used in medicine, especially in affections of the mucous membranes.

copal, kō'pal, *n.* [Mex. *copalli*, a generic name of resins.] A hard, shining, transparent, citron-colored, and odoriferous resinous substance, the product of several different trop-

ical trees: when dissolved and diluted with spirit of turpentine it forms a beautiful transparent varnish.

coparcener, kō·pär'sen·ėr, *n.* [Prefix *co*, and *parcener*, ultimately from L. *pars*, a part.] A coheir; one who has an equal portion of the inheritance of his or her ancestor with others.—**coparcenary,** kō·pär'sen·e·ri, *n.* Partnership in inheritance; joint heirship.

copartner, kō·pärt'nėr, *n.* A partner with others; one who is jointly concerned with one or more persons in carrying on trade or other business; a sharer; a partaker.—**copartnership,** kō·pärt'nėr·ship, *n.* The state of being a copartner; joint concern in business; the persons who have a joint concern.

cope, kōp, *n.* [A form of *cap* and *cape*, a hood.] An ecclesiastical vestment resembling a cloak, worn in processions, at vespers, at consecration, and other sacred functions; something spread or extended over the head; hence, the arch or concave of the sky, the roof or covering of a house, the arch over a door; a coping.—*v.t.*—*coped, coping.* To cover as with a cope.—**copestone,** *n.* A head or top stone, as on a wall or roof.—**coping,** kō'ping, *n.* The covering course of a wall, parapet, buttresses, etc.

cope, kōp, *v.i.*—*coped, coping.* [O.Fr. *coper*, to strike (Fr. *couper*, to cut), from *colp*, *cop* (Fr. *coup*), a blow. COPPICE.] To strive or contend on equal terms or with equal strength; to match; to oppose with success; to encounter: followed by *with.*

copeck, kō'pek, *n.* A Russian coin, the hundredth part of a silver rouble.

Copernican, kō·pėr'ni·kan, *a.* Pertaining to Copernicus, who taught the solar system now received, called the *Copernican* system.

coping. See COPE, *n.*

copious, kō'pi·us, *a.* [L. *copiosus*, from *copia*, plenty—*co*, and *ops, opis*, property.] Abundant; plentiful; in great quantities; furnishing abundant matter: rich in supplies.—**copiously,** kō'pi·us·li, *adv.* In a copious manner; abundantly; plentifully; in large quantities; fully; amply; diffusely.—**copiousness,** kō'pi·us·nes, *n.* The state or quality of being copious.

copper, kop'ėr, *n.* [L.L. *cuprum*, from L. *cyprium* (*aes*), Cyprian brass, from *Cyprus*, whence the Romans got their best copper.] A malleable, ductile metallic element, red in color and a good conductor; symbol, Cu; at. no., 29; at. wt., 63.546; vessel made of copper, particularly a large boiler; a coin made of copper or partly of copper; *pl.* the cast-iron apparatus used on board ship for cooking, and erected in the cook-house or galley.—*a.* Consisting of or resembling copper.—*v.t.* To cover or sheathe with sheets of copper; as, to *copper* a ship.—**copperhead,** *n.* [From its color.] A poisonous American serpent.—**copperplate,** *n.* A plate of polished copper on which some figure or design has been engraved, and from which an im-

---

ch, *ch*ain;   ch, Sc. lo*ch*;   g, *g*o;   j, *j*ob;   ng, si*ng*;   TH, *th*en;   th, *th*in;   w, *w*ig;   hw, *wh*ig;   zh, a*z*ure.

pression can be printed; a print or impression from such a plate.— **coppersmith,** n. One whose occupation is to manufacture copper utensils.—**coppery,** kop′ĕr·i, a. Mixed with or containing copper; like copper in taste, smell, or color.

copperas, kop′ĕr·as, n. [From L. *cuprirosa,* rose of copper, It. *copparosa,* Sp. Pg. *caparrosa,* Fr. *couperose.*] Sulfate of iron or green vitriol, a salt of a peculiar astringent taste and of various colors, but usually green.

coppice, copse, kop′is, kops, n. [O.Fr. *copeiz, coupiez,* wood newly cut, from *couper, coper,* to cut, from L.L. *colpus,* L. *colaphus,* Gr. *kolaphos,* a blow.] A wood of small growth, or consisting of underwood or brushwood; a wood cut at certain times for fuel or other purposes.

copra, kop′ra, n. The dried kernel of the coconut, from which the oil has yet to be expressed.

coprolite, kop′ro·līt, n. [Gr. *kopros,* dung, and *lithos,* a stone.] The petrified dung of extinct animals, such as lizards or sauroid fishes, found chiefly in the lias and coal measures.

coprophagous, kop·rof′a·gus, a. [Gr. *kopros,* dung, and *phâgo,* to eat.] Feeding upon dung or filth: a term particularly applied to certain insects.

copse, kops, n. See COPPICE.

Copt, kopt, n. A descendant of the ancient Egyptian race, and usually professing Christianity.—**Coptic,** kop′tik, a. Pertaining to the Copts.—n. The language of the Copts, an ancient Hamitic tongue, used in Egypt till superseded as a living language by Arabic.

copula, kop′ū·la, n. [L. *copula,* a band, a link, whence E. *couple.*] *Logic,* the word which unites the subject and predicate of a proposition; as in 'man is mortal,' where *is* is the copula.—**copulate,** kop′ū·lāt, v.i. —*copulated, copulating.* To unite in sexual embrace.—**copulation,** kop·ū·lā′shon, n. [L. *copulatio.*] The act of copulating; coition.—**copulative,** kop′ū·lā·tiv, a. Uniting or coupling. —*Copulative conjunction, gram.* a conjunction (such as *and*) which connects two or more subjects or predicates in an affirmative or negative proposition.—n. A copulative conjunction.—**copulatively,** kop′ū·lā·tiv·li, adv. In a copulative manner.

copy, kop′i, n. [Fr. *copie,* from L. *copia,* plenty.] A writing like another writing; a transcript from an original; a book printed according to the original; one of many books containing the same literary matter; what is produced by imitating; a thing made in close imitation of another; that which is to be imitated; a pattern; a model; an archetype; writing engraved or penned by a master to be imitated by a pupil; written or printed matter given to a printer to be put in type.—v.t.— *copied, copying.* To make a copy from; to write, print, engrave, construct, draw, paint, etc., according to an original; to transcribe; to imitate; to follow as in language,

style, manners, or course of life; take as one's model.—v.i. To make or produce a copy.—**copybook,** n. A book in which copies are written or printed for learners to imitate.— **copyhold,** kop′i·hōld, n. *English law,* a tenure for which the tenant has nothing to show except the copy of the rolls made on the tenant's being admitted to the possession of the subject; land held in copyhold.— **copyholder,** kop′i·hōl·dĕr, n. One who is possessed of land in copyhold; a device for holding copy; a proof-reader's assistant.—**copyright,** kop′i·rīt, n. The exclusive privilege which the law allows an author (or his assignee) of printing, reprinting, publishing, and selling his own original work; an author's exclusive right of property in his work for a certain time.—a. Relating to, or protected by the law of copyright.— v.t. To secure by copyright, as a book.

coquet, kō·ket′, v.t.—*coquetted, coquetting.* [Fr. *coqueter,* lit. to demean one's self as a cock amongst hens, to swagger, to strut, from *coq,* a cock.] To entertain with compliments and amorous tattle.—v.i. To act the lover from vanity; to endeavor to gain admirers.—**coquetry,** kōk′et·ri, n. [Fr. *coquetterie.*] The arts of a coquette; attempts to attract admiration, notice, or love, from vanity; affectation of amorous advances.— **coquette,** kō·ket′, n. [Fr. *coquette.*] A vain, airy, trifling girl, who endeavors to attract admiration and advances in love, from a desire to gratify vanity; a flirt.—**coquettish,** kō·ket′ish, a. Of or pertaining to coquetry; characterized by coquetry; practicing coquetry.—**coquettishly,** kō·ket′ish·li, adv. In a coquettish manner.

coquilla nut, ko·kēl′ya, n. The seed of one of the coconut palms, a native of Brazil, extensively used in turnery.

coracoid, kor′a·koid, a. [Gr. *korax, korakos,* a crow, and *eidos,* resemblance.] Shaped like a crow's beak.— *Coracoid process,* in *anat.* a small sharp process of the scapula in mammals; *coracoid bone,* a bone connecting the shoulder joint and sternum in birds.

coral, kor′al, n. [Fr. *corail* or *coral,* L. *corallium* or *corallum,* Gr. *korallion.*] A general term for the hard calcareous substance secreted by marine coelenterate polyps for their common support and habitation, exhibiting a great variety of forms and colors; a toy or plaything for an infant, made of coral; the unimpregnated eggs in the lobster, so called from being of a bright red color.— a. Made of coral; resembling coral.— **coralliferous, coralligerous,** kor·a·lif′ĕr·us, kor·a·lij′ĕr·us, a. Containing or consisting of coral; producing coral.—**coralline,** kor′al·in, a. Consisting of coral; like coral; containing coral.—n. One of the coral polyps or other zoophytes; a seaweed with calcareous fronds; an orange-red color.—**coralloid, coralloidal,** kor′al·oid, kor′al·oi·dal, a. Having the

form of coral; branching like coral.

corban, kor′ban, n. [Heb. *corbân,* an offering, sacrifice.] *Jewish antiq.* a solemn consecration of anything to God, as of one's self, one's services, or possessions; an alms basket; a treasury of the church.

corbeil, kor′bĕl, n. [Fr. *corbeille,* from L. *corbicula,* dim. of *corbis,* a basket.] *Fort.* a basket, to be filled with earth and set upon a parapet to shelter men; *arch.* a carved basket with sculptured flowers and fruits.— **corbel,** kor′bel, n. [L.L. *corbella,* a dim. from L. *corbis,* a basket.] *Arch.* a piece of stone, wood, or iron projecting from the vertical face of a wall to support some superincumbent object.—v.t. *corbelled, corbelling. Arch.* to support on a corbel or corbels; to provide with corbels.

cord, kord, n. [Fr. *corde,* from L. *chorda,* Gr. *chordē,* a string or gut, the string of a lyre.] A string or small rope composed of several strands twisted together; a quantity of wood, originally measured with a cord or line, containing 128 cubic feet, or a pile 8 feet long, 4 feet high, and 4 feet broad; *fig.* what, binds, restrains, draws, or otherwise in moral effects resembles a cord: corded cloth; corduroy.—v.t. To bind with a cord or rope; to pile up for measurement and sale by the cord.— **cordage,** kor′dij, n. Ropes or cords collectively; the ropes in the rigging of a ship.—**corded,** kor′ded, p. and a. Fastened with cords; made of cords (Shak.); striped or furrowed, as by cords (*corded* cloth).

cordate, kor′dāt, a. [L. *cor, cordis,* the heart.] Having the form of a heart; heart-shaped.—**cordately,** kor′dāt·li, adv. In a cordate form.—**cordiform,** kor′di·form, a. Heart-shaped.

Cordelier, kor′de·lēr, n. [Fr., from *corde,* a girdle or cord worn by the order.] A Franciscan friar under the strictest rules and wearing a girdle of knotted cord.

cordial, kor′di·al, a. [Fr. *cordial,* from L. *cor, cordis,* the heart; same root as E. *heart.*] Proceeding from the heart; hearty; sincere; not hypocritical; warm; affectionate; reviving the spirits; refreshing; invigorating (a *cordial* liquor).—n. Anything that strengthens, comforts, gladdens, or exhilarates; an exhilarating liquor; an aromatized and sweetened spirit employed as a beverage.—**cordiality, cordialness,** kor·di·al′i·ti, kor′di·al·nes, n. The state of being cordial; sincere affection and kindness; genial sincerity; hearty warmth of heart; heartiness.—**cordially,** kor′di·al·li, adv. In a cordial manner; heartily; sincerely; without hypocrisy; with real affection.

cordiform. See CORDATE.

cordillera, kor·del·yâ′ra, n. [Sp., from L. *chorda,* a string. CORD.] A ridge or chain of mountains; specifically, the mountain range of the Andes in South America.

cordite, kor′dīt, n. [From being made in *cord*-like forms.] A smokeless gunpowder, for use in ordnance.

cordon, kor′don, n. [Fr. and Sp.

cordon. CORD.] A line or series of military posts enclosing or guarding any particular place; a line of posts on the borders of a district infected with disease, to cut off communication; a ribbon worn across the breast by knights of the first class of an order.

cordovan, cordwain, kor′dō·van, kord′wān, n. [O.Fr. *cordouan*, Sp. *cordoban*, from *Cordova* or *Cordoba*, in Spain, where it is largely manufactured.] Spanish leather; goat skin tanned and dressed.—**cordwainer,** kord′wān·ėr, n. A shoemaker.

corduroy, kor·dū·roi′, n. [Fr. *corde du roy*, the king's cord.] A thick cotton stuff corded or ribbed on the surface.

core, kōr, n. [O.Fr. *cor, coer*, from L. *cor*, the heart, whence *cordial*.] The heart or inner part of a thing; particularly the central part of fruit containing the kernels or seeds; a center or central part, as the iron bar of an electromagnet round which is wound a coil of insulated wire, the conducting wires of a submarine telegraph cable, the interior part of a column, the internal mold which forms a hollow in the casting of metals; *fig.* the heart or deepest and most essential part of anything (the *core* of a question).—*v.t.* To remove the core of.

co-respondent, kō·ri·spon′dent, n. *Law*, a joint respondent, or one opposed, along with another or others, to the plaintiff; a person charged with adultery, and made a party to a suit for dissolution of marriage.

coriacoues, kō·ri·ā′shus, a. [L. *coriaceus*, from *corium*, leather.] Consisting of leather or resembling leather; tough and leathery.

coriander, kōr·i·an′dėr, n. [L. *coriandrum*, from Gr. *koriannon*, coriander, from *koris*, a bug, from the smell of its leaves.] An annual plant of the carrot family, the seeds of which have a strong smell, and are stomachic and carminative, being used in sweetmeats, in certain liqueurs, and also in cookery.

Corinthian, ko·rin′thi·an, a. Pertaining to *Corinth*, a celebrated city of Greece.—*Corinthian order*, an architectural order distinguished by fluted columns and capitals adorned with acanthus leaves.—n. An inhabitant of Corinth; a gay, fast, or spirited fellow.—**Corinthian,** kor·in′thi·an, n. A gentleman who does the work on his own or a friend's yacht, opposed to a paid hand; a gentleman jockey who rides his own horse; *pl.* two epistles written by St. Paul to the church of Corinth.

corium, kō′ri·um, n. [L., leather.] Leather body armor worn by the Roman soldiers; the innermost layer of the skin in mammals; the true skin.

cork, kork, n. [G. Dan. and Sw. *kork*, Sp. *corcho*, from L. *cortex, corticis*, bark.] The outer bark of a kind of oak (the cork oak or cork tree) growing in Spain and elsewhere, stripped off and made into such articles as

stoppers for bottles and casks; a stopper for a bottle or cask cut out of cork.—*v.t.* To stop or fit with cork; to confine or make fast with a cork.—**corkscrew,** kork′skrö, n. A screw to draw corks from bottles.—*v.t.* To direct or work along in a spiral; to wriggle forward.—**corky,** kor′ki, a. Consisting of cork; resembling cork.

corm, korm, n. [Gr. *kormos*, a stem.] *Bot.* a bulblike part of a plant, consisting of the dilated base of the stem, as in the crocus; a solid bulb.

cormorant, kor′mo·rant, n. [Fr. *cormoran*, from L. *corvus marinus*, sea raven.] A web-footed sea bird of the pelican family, of several species, catching fish by swimming and diving, and extremely voracious; *fig.* a greedy fellow; a glutton.

corn, korn, n. [A.Sax. *corn*, a word found throughout the Teutonic languages, of same root as L. *granum*, a seed. Akin *kernel, grain*.] A grain grown extensively in many parts of the United States, particularly the central west (corn belt) and southwest, and also throughout the world in most temperate zones. It is used as food for human consumption, but its principal use is for stock food. In Great Britain, corn means any of a variety of grains such as wheat, barley, etc.—*v.t.* To preserve and season with salt in grains; to sprinkle with salt (to *corn* beef.)—**corn cockle,** n. The common name of a plant with purple flowers, a frequent weed among grain crops.—**corn crake,** n. The crake or land rail, which frequents cornfields and is noted for its strange harsh cry.—**corn laws,** n. pl. In England, legislative enactments and restrictions relating to the exportation and importation of grain.—**corny,** kor′ni, a. Of the nature of, or furnished with, grains of corn; producing corn; containing corn; produced from corn; tasting of corn or malt.

corn, korn, n. [L. *cornu*, a horn.] A hard excrescence or induration of the skin on the toes or some other part of the feet, occasioned by the pressure of the shoes.

cornea, kor′ni·a, n. [L. *corneus*, horny, *cornu*, a horn.] The horny transparent membrane in the fore part of the eye through which the rays of light pass.

cornel, kor′nel, n. [L. *cornus*, from *cornu*, a horn, from the hardness of the wood.] A species of dogwood found in Europe and Northern Asia, which produces a small, red, acid, cherry-like fruit, used in preserves and confectionery. Sometimes called *Cornelian tree.*

cornelian, kor·nē′li·an, n. Same as *Carnelian.*

corneous, kor′ni·us, a. [L. *corneus*, from *cornu*, a horn.] Horny; like horn; consisting of a horny substance, or a substance resembling horn; hard.

corner, kor′nėr, n. [Fr. *cornière*, from L. *cornu*, a horn, projection.] The point where two converging lines or surfaces meet, or the space be-

tween; an angle; a secret or retired place; a nook or out-of-the-way place; any part (every *corner* of the forest); a combination to raise the price of goods in the market.—*v.t.* In trading, to secure a monopoly or sufficient quantity of any stock or commodity, so that prospective buyers will be forced to pay the seller's price.—**cornerstone,** n. The stone which forms the corner of the foundation of an edifice; hence, that which is of the greatest importance; that on which any system is founded.

cornet, kor′net, n. [Fr., dim. of *corne*, L. *cornu*, a horn.] A kind of brass wind instrument; a cornet-à-pistons; a troop of horse: said to be so called because each company had a cornet player; formerly the title of the officer who carried the ensign or colors in a troop of horse in the British army. — **cornet-à-pistons,** kor′net·a·pis″tonz, n. [Fr., cornet with pistons.] A brass or silver wind instrument, capable of producing the notes of the chromatic scale from the valves and pistons with which it is furnished.—**cornetcy,** kor′net·si, n. The commission or rank of a cornet.

cornice, kor′nis, n. [O.Fr. *cornice*, It. *cornice*, from Gr. *korōnis*, a summit, from *korōne*, a crown. CROWN.] *Arch.* any molded projection which crowns or finishes the part to which it is affixed; specifically, the highest part of an entablature resting on the frieze.

Cornish, korn′ish, a. Pertaining to Cornwall, in England.—*Cornish engine*, a single-acting steam engine used for pumping water.—n. The ancient language of Cornwall, a dialect of the Celtic.

cornucopia, kor·nū·kō′pi·a, n. [L. *cornucopiae*, the horn of plenty.] A wreathed horn, filled to overflowing with richest fruit, flowers, and grain, used in sculpture, etc., as a symbol of plenty, peace, and concord.

corolla, ko·rol′la, n. [L. *corolla*, dim. of *corona*, a crown.] *Bot.* the part of a flower inside the calyx, surrounding the parts of fructification, and composed of one or more petals, generally to be distinguished from the calyx by the fineness of its texture and the gayness of its colors.—**corollate, corollated,** kor′ol·āt, kor′ol·āt·ed, a. *Bot.* like a corolla; having corollas.

corollary, kor′ol·le·ri, n. [Fr. *corollaire*, from L. *corolla*, a little crown, from as it were crowning what it refers to.] That which follows over and above what is directly demonstrated in a mathematical proposition; any consequence necessarily concurrent with or following from the main one; an inference; a conclusion; a surplus (*Shak.*).‡

corona, ko·rō′na, n. [L., a crown. CROWN.] A technical term for various things supposed to have some resemblance to a crown; *astron.* a halo or luminous circle around one of the heavenly bodies; a luminous appearance observed during total eclipses of the sun, which lies outside the chromosphere; *arch.* the lower member or drip of a classical cornice having a broad vertical face, usually of considerable projection; *bot.* the circumference or margin of a radiated composite flower; also an appendage of the corolla or petals of a flower proceeding from the base of the limb.—**coronal,** ko·rō′nal, *a.* Pertaining to a corona†; belonging to the crown or top of the head: in this sense pron. kor′o·nal.—*n.* (kor′o·nal). A crown; wreath; garland.—**coronary,** kor′o·ne·ri, *a.* Relating to a crown; of or like a crown; pertaining to either or both of the two arteries of the heart. —*n.* A coronary artery; coronary thrombosis.—**coronary thrombosis,** *n.* Clotting of blood in one of the arteries of the heart.—**coronation,** kor·o·nā′shon, *n.* The act or solemnity of crowning a sovereign or investing him; the pomp attending on a coronation.—**coroner,** kor′o·nėr, *n.* [L.L. *coronator,* originally a crown officer of extensive powers, from L. *corona,* a crown.] An officer appointed to hold inquests on the bodies of such as either die, or are supposed to die, a violent death.—**coronet,** kor′o·net, *n.* An inferior crown worn by princes and noblemen, bearing crosses, fleurs-de-lis, strawberry leaves, pearls; the lower part of the pastern of a horse.—*v.t.* To adorn with a coronet or something similar.—**coroneted,** kor′o·net·ed, *a.* Wearing or entitled to wear a coronet.

coronach, kor′o·nach, *n.* [Gael. and Ir.] A dirge; a lamentation for the dead among the Highlanders and Irish.

corporal, kor′po·ral, *n.* [Corrupted from Fr. *caporal,* It. *caporale,* from *capo,* L. *caput,* the head.] The noncommissioned officer of a company of infantry next below a sergeant; in *ships-of-war,* a petty officer who attends to police matters.

corporal, kor′po·ral, *a.* [L. *corporalis,* from *corpus,* body.] Belonging or relating to the body; bodily; also material or not spiritual†. ∴ Syn. under BODILY.—**corporality,** kor··po·ral′i·ti, *n.* The state of being corporal; corporation; confraternity. —**corporally,** kor′po·ral·li, *adv.* Bodily; in or with the body (*corporally* present).—**corporate,** kor′po·rit, *a.* [L. *corporatus.*] United in a body, as a number of individuals who are empowered to transact business as an individual; formed into a body; united; collectively one (*Shak.*); belonging to a corporation.—**corporately,** kor′po·rit·li, *adv.* In a corporate capacity.—**corporation,** kor·po·rā′shon, *n.* A body corporate, formed and authorized by law to act as a single person; a society having the capacity of transacting business as an individual; the body or bodily frame of a man (*colloq.*).—**corporeal,** kor·pō′ri·al, *a.* Of or pertaining to a body; having a body; consisting of a material body; material; opposed to *spiritual* or *immaterial.* ∴ Syn. under BODILY.—**corporeality,** kor·pō′ri·al′i·ti, *n.* The state of being corporeal.—**corporeally,** kor·pō′ri·al·li, *adv.* In body;

in a bodily form or manner.—**corporeity,** kor·pō·re′i·ti, *n.* The state of having a body or of being embodied; materiality†.

corposant, kor′pō·zant, *n.* [It. *corpo santo,* holy body.] A name given to a ball of electric light often observed on dark tempestuous nights about the rigging; St. Elmo's light.

corps, kōr, *n.* pl. **corps,** kōrz. [Fr., from L. *corpus,* body.] A body of troops; any division of an army.— *Corps d'armée,* a large division of an army.—**corpse,** korps, *n.* The dead body of a human being.—**corpse-candle,** *n.* A local name for the will-o′-the-wisp.—**corpse gate,** *n.* A covered gateway at the entrance to churchyards, a lich gate.

corpulence, corpulency, kor′pū·lens, kor′pū·len·si, *n.* [L. *corpulentia,* from *corpulentus,* corpulent, *corpus,* a body.] Fleshiness or stoutness of body; excessive fatness.—**corpulent,** kor′pū·lent, *a.* Having a great bulk of body; stout; fat; obese.

corpus, kor′pus, *n.* A collected whole; a material substance; *anat.* a name for certain small bodies of various kinds.

Corpus Christi, kor′pus kris′ti, *n.* [L., body of Christ.] *R. Cath. Ch.* the host or eucharist; an annual festival in its honor.

corpuscle, kor′pus·l, *n.* [L. *corpusculum,* dim. of *corpus,* body.] A minute particle, molecule, or atom; a minute animal cell generally enclosing granular matter, and sometimes a spheroidal body called a nucleus. —**corpuscular,** kor·pus′kū·ler, *a.* Relating to corpuscles or small particles, supposed to be the constituent materials of all large bodies.— *Corpuscular theory,* a theory which supposes light to consist of minute particles emitted by luminous bodies, and traveling through space with immense rapidity till they reach the eye.

corral, kor·ral′, *n.* [Sp., from *corro,* a circle; Pg. *curral,* a cattle-pen.] A pen or enclosure for horses or cattle, and also an enclosure formed of wagons employed by emigrants as a means of defense [Amer.]; a strong stockade or enclosure for capturing wild elephants in Ceylon.—*v.t.* *corralled, corralling.* To form into a corral; to form a corral or enclosure by means of.

correct, kor·rekt′, *a.* [L. *correctus,* from *corrigo*—*con,* and *rego,* to set right. REGENT, RIGHT.] Set right or made straight; in accordance with a certain standard; conformable to truth, rectitude, or propriety; not faulty; free from error.—*v.t.* To make correct or right; to bring into accordance with a certain standard; to remove error or defect from; to amend or emend; to punish for faults or deviations from moral rectitude; to chastise; to discipline; to counteract or obviate, as by adding some new ingredient.—**correction,** ko·rek′shon, *n.* [L. *correctio.*] The act of correcting; the removal of faults or errors; something written to

point out an error, or substituted in the place of what is wrong; punishment; discipline; chastisement; critical notice; animadversion; the counteraction of what is inconvenient or hurtful in its effects.—*House of correction,* a house where disorderly persons are confined; a bridewell.— **correctional,** ko·rek′shon·al, *a* Tending to correction.—**corrective,** ko··rek′tiv, *a.* Having the power to correct; having the quality of removing or obviating what is wrong or injurious.—*n.* That which has the power of correcting; that which has the quality of altering or obviating what is wrong or injurious.— **correctly,** ko·rekt′li, *adv.* In a correct manner; according to a standard; in conformity with a copy or original; exactly; accurately; without fault or error.—**correctness,** ko·rekt′nes, *n.* The state of being correct; conformity to a standard or rule; exactness; accuracy.—**corrector,** ko·rek′tėr, *n.* One who corrects; one who amends faults; one who punishes for correction; that which corrects.

correlate, kor′e·lāt, *n.* [L. *cor* for *con,* and *relatus.* RELATE.] One who or that which stands in a reciprocal relation to something else, as father and son.—*v.i.*—*correlated, correlating.* To have a reciprocal relation; to be reciprocally related, as father and son.—*v.t.* To place in reciprocal relation; to determine the relations between, as between several objects or phenomena which bear a resemblance to one another.—**correlation,** kor·e·lā′shon, *n.* Reciprocal relation; corresponding similarity or parallelism of relation or law.—**correlative,** ko·rel′a·tiv, *a.* Having a reciprocal relation, so that the existence of one in a certain state depends on the existence of another; reciprocal.—*n.* That which is correlative; that of which the existence implies the existence of something else; one of two terms either of which calls up the notion of the other, as *husband* and *wife; gram.* the antecedent to a pronoun.— **correlatively,** ko·rel′a·tiv·li, *adv.* In a correlative relation.

correspond, kor·e·spond′, *v.i.* [*Cor* for *con,* and *respond.*] To be adapted or suitable; to have a due relation; to be adequate or proportionate; to accord; to agree; to answer; to fit: used absolutely or followed by *with* or *to;* to communicate or hold intercourse with a person by letters sent and received.—**correspondence,** kor·e·spon′dens, *n.* The state of corresponding or being correspondent; mutual adaptation of one thing or part to another; intercourse between persons by means of letters sent and received; the letters collectively which pass between correspondents; friendly intercourse; reciprocal exchange of offices or civilities.—**correspondency,** kor·e·spon′den·si, *n.* Correspondence, in sense of relation, congruity, adaptation, friendly intercourse.—**correspondent,** kor·e·spon′dent, *a.* Corresponding; suitable; duly related; congruous; agreeable; answerable; adapted.—*n.* One who corresponds; one with whom an intercourse is carried on by letters or messages; a person who sends regular communications to a newspaper from a distance.—**correspondently,** kor-e·spon'dent·li, *adv.* In a corresponding manner.—**corresponding,** kor-e·spon'ding, *a.* Answering; agreeing; suiting; correspondent.—**correspondingly,** kor·e·spon'ding·li, *adv.* In a corresponding manner.—**corresponsive,** kor·e·spon'siv, *a.* Answerable; adapted. (*Shak.*)

corridor, kor'i·dor, *n.* [It. *corridore,* from *correre,* L. *currere,* to run, CURRENT.] *Arch.* a passage in a building leading to several chambers at a distance from each other; a strip of land through foreign territory.

corrie, kor'i, *n.* [Gael.] A steep hollow in a hill.

corrigendum, kor·i·jen'dum, *n. pl.* **corrigenda,** kor·i·jen'da, [L.] A thing or word to be corrected or altered.

corrigible, kor'i·ji·bl, *a.* [Fr., from L. *corrigo,* to correct. CORRECT.] Capable of being corrected, amended or reformed; deserving punishment or correction; punishable.

corroborate, ko·rob'o·rāt, *v.t.*—**corroborated, corroborating.** [L. *corroboro, corroboratum—con,* and *roboro,* to strengthen, from *robur,* strength.] To strengthen or give additional strength to; to confirm; to make more certain; to add assurance to (to *corroborate* testimony, news).—**corroborant,** ko·rob'o·rant, *a.* Strengthening the body; having the power or quality of giving strength.—*n.* A medicine that strengthens the body when weak; a tonic.—**corroboration,** ko·rob'o·rā"shon, *n.* The act of corroborating; confirmation; that which corroborates.—**corroborative,** ko·rob'o·rā·tiv, *a.* Having the power of corroborating or confirming.—*n.* A medicine that strengthens; corroborant.—**corroboratory,** ko·rob'o·ra·to·ri, *a.* Corroborative.

corrode, ko·rōd', *v.t.*—**corroded, corroding.** [L. *corrodo—cor* for *con,* and *rodo,* to gnaw, whence also *rodent, erode.*] To eat away by degrees; to wear away or diminish by gradually separating small particles (nitric acid *corrodes* copper); *fig.* to gnaw or prey upon; to consume by slow degrees; to envenom or embitter; to poison, blight, canker.—**corrodible,** ko·rō'di·bl, *a.* That may be corroded.—**corrosion,** ko·rō'zhon, *n.* The action of corroding, eating, or wearing away by slow degrees, as by the action of acids on metals; *fig.* the act of cankering, fretting, vexing, envenoming, or blighting.—**corrosive,** ko·rō'siv, *a.* Having the power of corroding or eating into a substance; having the quality of fretting, envenoming, blighting.—*Corrosive sublimate,* a compound of chlorine and mercury, forming a white crystalline solid, an acrid poison of

great virulence, and a powerful antiseptic.—*n.* That which has the quality of eating or wearing gradually; anything which irritates, preys upon one, or frets.—**corrosively,** ko·rō'siv·li, *adv.* In a corrosive manner.—**corrosiveness,** ko·rō'siv·nes, *n.* The quality of being corrosive.

corrugate, ko'rū·gāt, *v.t.*—**corrugated, corrugating.** [L. *corrugo, corrugatum—cor* for *con,* and *rugo,* to wrinkle.] To wrinkle; to draw or contract into folds.—*a.* Wrinkled; showing wrinkles or furrows.—**corrugated,** ko'rū·gā·ted, *p.* and *a.* Wrinkled; furrowed or ridged.—*Corrugated iron,* common sheet iron or 'galvanized' iron, bent into a series of regular grooves and ridges by being passed between powerful rollers. Iron thus treated will resist a much greater strain than flat iron, each groove representing a half tube; it is used for roofing, etc.—**corrugation,** ko·ru·gā'shon, *n.* A wrinkling; contraction into wrinkles.

corrupt, ko·rupt', *v.t.* [L. *corrumpo, corruptum—con,* and *rumpo, ruptum,* to break; whence also *rupture, abrupt, disrupt,* etc.] To change from a sound to a putrid or putrescent state; to cause to rot; *fig.* to deprave; to pervert; to impair; to debase; to defile, taint, pollute, or infect; to bribe; to debase or render impure by alterations or innovations (language); to falsify (a text).—*v.i.* To become putrid; to putrefy; to rot; to become vitiated; to lose purity.—*a.* Changed from a sound to a putrid state; changed from the state of being correct, pure, or true to a worse state; vitiated; perverted; debased; impure; ready to be influenced by a bribe; infected with errors or mistakes (a *corrupt* text).—**corrupter,** ko·rup'tėr, *n.* One who or that which corrupts.—**corruptibility,** ko·rup'ti·bil"i·ti, *n.* The possibility of being corrupted.—**corruptible,** ko·rup'ti·bl, *a.* Capable of being made corrupt, putrid, or rotten; subject to decay and destruction, debasement, depravation, etc.—**corruptibleness,** ko·rup'ti·bl·nes, *n.*—**corruptibly,** ko·rup'ti·bli, *adv.* In such a manner as to be corrupted or vitiated.—**corruption,** ko·rup'shon, *n.* [L. *corruptio.*] The act of corrupting, or state of being corrupt, putrid, or rotten; putrid matter; pus; depravity; wickedness; loss of purity or integrity; debasement; impurity; depravation; pollution; defilement; vitiating influence, more specifically, bribery; *law,* an immediate consequence of attainder by which a person was formerly disabled from holding, inheriting, or transmitting lands.—**corruptive,** ko·rup'tiv, *a.* Having the power of corrupting, tainting, or vitiating.—**corruptly,** ko·rupt'li, *adv.* In a corrupt manner; with corruption; impurely; by bribery.—**corruptness,** ko·rupt'nes, *n.* Corrupt quality or state; putrid state.

corsage, kor·säzh', *n.* [Fr.] A small bouquet for a woman; the waist of a woman's dress.

corsair, kor'sâr, *n.* [Fr. *corsaire,* It. *corsare,* from *corsa,* a course, a cruise, from L. *cursus,* a course. COURSE.] A pirate; a sea robber; a rover; a piratical vessel.

corselet, kors'let, *n.* [Fr., a dim. of O.Fr. *cors,* L. *corpus,* the body.] A small cuirass, or armor to cover and protect the body; a type of lightly boned corset for women; that part of a winged insect to which the wings and legs are attached; the thorax.

corset, kor'set, *n.* [Dim. of O.Fr. *cors.*] A tight, boned undergarment, reaching from the bust to below the hips, worn by women, occasionally by men, to support and mold the body.

cortege, kor·tezh', *n.* [Fr., from It. *corteggio,* from *corte,* court.] A train of attendants to a great personage on a ceremonial occasion.

Cortes, kor'tez, *n. pl.* [Sp., pl. of *corte,* court.] The present legislative assembly of Portugal and formerly, the single legislative chamber of Republican Spain.

cortex, kor'teks, *n.* [L. *cortex, corticis,* bark; whence *cork.*] Bark, as of a tree; hence, an outer covering; *anat.* a membrane forming a covering or envelope for any part of the body. *Of brain,* external layer of cerebral hemispheres and cerebellum: that of cerebral hemispheres divided into *motor areas,* controlling muscles, and *sensory areas,* concerned with sensations.—**cortical,** kor'ti·kal, *a.* Belonging to, consisting of, or resembling bark or rind; external; belonging to the external covering.—**corticate, corticated,** kor'ti·kāt, kor'ti·kā·ted, *a.* [L. *corticatus.*] Resembling the bark or rind of a tree.—**corticose, corticous,** kor'ti·kōz, kor'ti·kus, *a.* Barky; full of bark.

cortisone, kor'ti·sōn, *n.* A compound extracted from the cortex of the adrenal gland of animals or produced synthetically and used in treatment of disease, as arthritis.

corundum, ko·run'dum, *n.* [Hind. *kurand.*] A mineral, next in hardness to the diamond, and consisting of nearly pure anhydrous alumina; the amethyst, ruby, sapphire, topaz, and emery are considered as varieties.

coruscate, kor'us·kāt, *v.i.*—**coruscated, coruscating.** [L. *corusco, coruscatum,* to flash.] To flash; to lighten; to gleam; to glitter.—**coruscation,** kor·us·kā'shon, *n.* [L. *coruscatio.*] A sudden burst of light in the clouds or atmosphere; a flash; glitter; a blaze.

corvette, kor·vet', *n.* [Fr. *corvette,* from L. *corbita,* a ship of burden, from *corbis,* a basket.] A flush-decked vessel, ship-rigged, but without a quarter-deck, and having only one tier of guns.

corvine, kor'vīn, *a.* [L. *corvus,* a crow.] Pertaining to the crow, or the crow family of birds.

Corybant, kor'i·bant, *n. pl.* **Corybants,** or **Corybantes,** kor·i·ban'tēz. [L. *corybas, corybantis,* Gr. *korybas.*] A priest of Cybele who celebrated the mysteries with mad dances to the

---

ch, *chain*; ch, Sc. *loch*; g, *go*; j, *job*; ng, *sing*; TH, *then*; th, *thin*; w, *wig*; hw, *whig*; zh, *azure.*

sound of drum and cymbal.—
Corybantic, kor·i·ban'tik, *a.* Madly agitated like the Corybantes.

corymb, ko'rimb, *n.* [L. *corymbus,* Gr. *korymbos,* a cluster of fruit or flowers.] *Bot.* an inflorescence in which the flowers or blossoms are so arranged as to form a mass of flowers with a convex or level top, as in the hawthorn, candytuft, etc.—**corymbose,** ko·rim'bōz, *a. Bot.* relating to or like a corymb.—**corymbous,** ko·rim'bus, *a.* Corymbose.

coryphaeus, kor·i·fē'us, *n.* [L. *coryphæus,* Gr. *koryphaios,* from *koryphē,* the head.] The chief of a chorus; the chief of a company.—**coryphee,** ko·ri·fā', *n.* [Fr.] A ballet dancer.

coryza, ko·rī'za, *n.* [Gr.] *Med.* a cold in the head.

cosecant, kō·sē'kant, *n.* [From *complement* and *secant.*] *Geom.* in a right-angle triangle, the cosecant of the base angle that is not 90° is the number obtained after dividing the hypotenuse by the perpendicular. Multiplied by the sine it equals one.

cosey, cosy, kō'zi. Same as *cozy.*

cosher, kosh'ér, *v.i.* [Ir. *coisir,* a feast.] To levy exactions in the shape of feasts and lodgings, as formerly Irish landlords with their trains did on their tenants.—*v.t.* To treat with dainties or delicacies; to fondle; to pet.

cosignatory, kō·sig'na·to·ri, *n.* One who signs a treaty or other agreement along with another or others. Also used as an adj.

cosine, kō'sīn, *n.* [*Complement* and *sine.*] *Geom.* in a right-angle triangle, the cosine of the base angle that is not 90° is the number obtained after dividing the base by the hypotenuse. Multiplied by the secant it equals one.

cosmetic, koz·met'ik, *a.* [Gr. *kosmētikos,* from *kosmos,* order, beauty.] Beautifying; improving beauty, particularly the beauty of the complexion.—*n.* Any preparation that renders the skin soft, pure, and white, or helps to beautify and improve the complexion.

cosmic, cosmical, koz'mik, koz'mi·kal, *a.* [Gr. *kosmikos,* from *kosmos,* the universe.] Relating to the universe and to the laws by which its order is maintained; hence, harmonious as the universe; orderly.—**cosmically,** koz'mi·kal·li, *adv.* In a cosmic manner; with the sun at rising or setting; said of a star.—**cosmic ray,** *n.* An electromagnetic ray of extremely high frequency and energy content that originates in outer space and bombards the earth, penetrating barriers impervious to all other radiation. Molecules of the earth's atmosphere are ionized upon impact with cosmic rays.

cosmogony, koz·mog'o·ni, *n.* [Gr. *kosmogonia—kosmos,* world, and root *gen,* to bring forth.] The origin or creation of the world or universe; the doctrine of the origin or formation of the universe.

cosmography, koz·mog'ra·fi, *n.* [Gr. *kosmographia—kosmos,* the world, and *graphō,* to describe.] A descrip-

tion of the world or universe; the science which treats of the construction of the universe.—**cosmographer,** koz·mog'ra·fér, *n.* One who describes the world or universe; one versed in cosmography.—**cosmographic, cosmographical,** koz·mo·graf'ik, koz·mo·graf'ik·al, *a.* Relating to cosmography.

cosmology, koz·mol'o·ji, *n.* [Gr. *kosmologia—kosmos,* the universe, and *logos,* discourse.] The science of the universe; a theory relating to the structure and laws of the universe; cosmogony.—**cosmological,** koz·mo·loj'ik·al, *a.* Pertaining to cosmology.—**cosmologist,** koz·mol'o·jist, *n.* One versed in cosmology.

cosmonaut, koz'mo·nat, *n.* Traveler in interplanetary space.—**cosmonette,** *n. fem.*

cosmopolitan, cosmopolite, koz·mo·pol'i·tan, koz·mop'o·lit, *n.* [Gr. *kosmos,* world, and *politēs,* a citizen.] A person who is nowhere a stranger, or who is at home in every place; a citizen of the world.—*a.* Free from local, provincial, or national prejudices or attachments; at home all over the world; common to all the world.—**cosmopolitanism, cosmopolitism,** koz·mo·pol'i·tan·izm, koz·mop'o·lit·izm, *n.* The state of being a cosmopolitan; disregard of local or national prejudices, attachments, or peculiarities.

cosmos, koz'mos, *n.* [Gr. *kosmos,* order, ornament, and hence the universe as an orderly and beautiful system.] The universe as an embodiment of order and harmony; the system of order and harmony combined in the universe.

Cossack, kos'ak, *n.* [Rus. *kosak,* Turk. *kazâk,* a robber.] One of a warlike people, very expert on horseback, inhabiting the steppes in the south of the Soviet Union.

cosset,‡ kos'et, *n.* [Comp. old *coss,* Icel. *koss,* a kiss.] A pet; a pet lamb.

cost, kost, *n.* [O.Fr. *cost,* from *coster, couster* (Mod.Fr. *coûter*), to cost, from L. *constare,* to cost—*con,* and *stare,* to stand. STATE.] The price, value, or equivalent of a thing purchased; amount in value expended or to be expended; charge; expense; *law.* the sum to be paid by the party losing in favor of the party prevailing, etc.; outlay, expense, or loss of any kind, as of time, labor, trouble, or the like; detriment: pain; suffering (he learned that to his *cost*).—*v.t.*—pret. and pp. *cost.* To require to be given or expended in order to purchase; to be bought for; to require to be undergone, borne, or suffered; often with two objects (to *cost* a person money or labor).—**costly,** kost'li, *a.* Of a high price; costing much; expensive; dear.—**costliness,** kost'li·nes, *n.* The state or quality of being costly, high in price, or expensive.

costal, kos'tal, *a.* [L. *costa,* a rib.] Pertaining to the side of the body or the ribs.—**costate,** kos'tāt, *a.* Ribbed; marked with elevated lines.

costard, kos'terd, *n.* [Lit. a *ribbed* apple, O.Fr. *coste,* L. *costa,* a rib.]

An apple; hence, humorously for the head. (*Shak.*)

costive, kos'tiv, *a.* [Contr. from It. *costipativo,* from L. *constipo,* to cram, to stuff. CONSTIPATE.] Suffering from a morbid retention of fecal matter in the bowels, in a hard and dry state; having the bowels bound; constipated. — **costively,** kos'tiv·li, *adv.* With costiveness.—**costiveness,** kos'tiv·nes, *n.* The state of being costive; constipation.

costmary, kost'ma·ri, *n.* [L. *costus,* Gr. *kostos,* an aromatic plant, and *Mary* (the Virgin).] A perennial composite plant, a native of the south of Europe, cultivated for the agreeable fragrance of the leaves.

costrel, kos'trel, *n.* [L. *costa,* O.Fr. *coste,* rib, side.] A small vessel, generally with ears for suspending at side, used by laborers in harvest time; a vessel for holding wine.

costume, kos'tūm, *n.* [Fr. *costume,* custom. CUSTOM.] An established mode of dress; the style of dress peculiar to a people or nation, to a particular period, or a particular class of people; a dress of a particular style.—**costumier, costumer,** kos·tū'mi·ér, kos'tūm·ér, *n.* One who prepares costumes, as for theaters, fancy balls, etc.; one who deals in costumes.

cosy, kō'zi, *a.* Same as *cozy.*

cot, kot, *n.* [A.Sax. *cot, cott,* a cot, chamber; Icel. and D. *kot,* a cot, G. *kot, kote,* a hut; *cote* is the same word. From this comes *cottage.*] A small house; a hut or cottage; a small bed or crib for a child to sleep in; *naut.* a sort of bed frame suspended from the beams.

cotangent, kō·tan'jent, *n.* [*Complement* and *tangent.*] In a right-angle triangle, the cotangent of the base angle that is not 90° is the number obtained after dividing the base by the perpendicular. Multiplied by the tangent it equals one.

cote, kōt, *n.* [COT.] A shelter or habitation for animals, as a dove-*cote*; a sheepfold; a cottage or hut.

cotemporaneous, cotemporary, kō·tem'po·rā'ni·us, kō·tem'po·re·ri. See CONTEMPORANEOUS, CONTEMPORARY.

cotenant, kō·ten'ant, *n.* A tenant in common.

coterie, kō'te·rē, *n.* [Fr., from L.L. *coteria,* an association of villagers, *cofa,* a cottage. COT.] A set or circle of friends who are in the habit of meeting for social or literary intercourse or other purposes; a clique.

coterminous, kō·tér'mi·nus, *a.* See CONTERMINOUS.

cothurnus, cothurn, kō·thér'nus, kō'thėrn, *n.* [L. *cothurnus.*] A buskin; a kind of high laced shoe, such as was anciently worn by tragic actors; hence, *fig.* tragedy.

cotidal, kō·tī'dal, *a.* Marking an equality of tides.

cotillion, cotillon, ko·til'yon, *n.* [Fr. *cotillon.*] A kind of brisk dance; a tune which regulates the dance.

Cotswold, kots'wōld, *n.* A large sheep of a breed belonging to the Cotswold Hills in Gloucestershire.

cottage, kot′ij, n, [From *cot*.] A cot or small dwelling house; a small country residence or detached suburban house, adapted to a moderate scale of living.—**cottager**, kot′ij·ėr, n. One who lives in a hut or cottage.—**cotter, cottier**, kot′ėr, kot′i·ėr, n. A cottager; one who inhabits a cot or cottage, dependent upon a farm, having sometimes a piece of land. Written also *cottar*.

cotton, kot′n, n. [Fr. *coton*, from Ar. *qoton*.] A soft downy substance resembling fine wool, growing in the pods or seed vessels of certain plants, being the material of a large proportion of cloth for apparel and furniture; cloth made of cotton.—*a.* Pertaining to cotton; made of cotton.—*v.i.* To fraternize; to agree or get on (with). (*Colloq.*)—**cottony**, kot′n·i, *a.* Downy or soft like cotton; pertaining to or resembling cotton.—**cotton gin**, *n.* A machine to separate the seeds from raw cotton. **cotton grass**, *n.* A name of plants of the sedge family with white cottony spikes.—**cottonwood**, *n.* A tree of the poplar genus, a native of North America.—**cotton wool**, *n.* A name sometimes given to raw cotton.

cotyledon, kot·i·lē′don, n. [Gr. *kotylēdōn*, from *kotylē*, a hollow.] *Bot.* the seed leaf; the first leaf or leaves of the embryo plant, forming, together with the radicle and plumule, the embryo, which exists in every seed capable of germination; *anat.* a tuft of vessels adhering to the chorion of some animals.—**cotyledonal**, kot·i·lē′do·nal, *a.* Belonging to a cotyledon; resembling a cotyledon.—**cotyledonary**, kot·i·lē′do·ne·ri, *a. Anat.* having the tuft called cotyledon (*cotyledonary placenta*).—**cotyledonous**, kot·i·lē′do·nus, *a.* Pertaining to cotyledons; having cotyledons.

couch, kouch, v.i. [Fr. *coucher*, O.Fr. *colcher*, Pr. *colcar*, It. *colcare*, from *collocare*, to lay, to place—*col* for *con*, and *locare*, to place.] To lie down, as on a bed or place of repose; to recline; to lie or crouch with body close to the ground, as a beast; to stoop; to bend the body or back (O.T.); to lie or be outspread (O.T.). —*v.t.* To lie down; to spread on a bed or floor (to *couch* malt); to express in obscure terms that imply what is to be understood: with *under*; to fix a spear in the rest in the posture of attack; *surg.* to cure of cataract in the eye by depressing the crystalline lens.—*n.* A bed; a seat for repose or on which one may lie down undressed; any place for repose, as the lair of a wild beast, etc.; a heap of steeped barley spread out on a floor to allow germination to take place, and so convert the grain into malt.—**couchant**, kouch′ant, *a.* Lying down; squatting. (*Tenn.*).

couch grass, kouch′gras, n. [A corruption of *quitch* or *quick grass*.] A species of grass which infests arable land, spreading over a field with great rapidity, being propagated both by seed and by its creeping rootstock.

cougar, kö′gär, n. [Native name modified.] A quadruped of the cat kind, 7 or 8 feet in length, one of the most destructive of all the animals of America, particularly in the warmer parts. Called also *puma* and *red tiger*.

cough, kof, n. [Imitative of the sound; like D. *kuch*, a cough; G. *keichen, keuchen*, to pant, cough.] A deep inspiration of air followed by a spasmodic and sonorous expiration, excited by the sensation of the presence of some irritating cause in the air passages.—*v.i.* To give a cough; to expel the air from the lungs suddenly with noise.—*v.t.* To expel from the lungs by a violent effort with noise; to expectorate; with *up* (to *cough up* phlegm).— *To cough down*, to put down an unpopular or too lengthy speaker by simulated coughs.—**cougher**, kof′ėr, n. One that coughs.

could, kud, v., pret. of *can*. [O.E. *coude*, A.Sax. *cúthe*, pret. of *cunnan*, to be able. See CAN. *L* has been improperly introduced through the influence of *would* and *should*.] Was able, capable, or susceptible.

coulee, kö′li, n. [Fr., from *couler*, to flow.] *Geol.* a stream of lava, whether flowing or consolidated.

coulisse, kö·lēs′, n. [Fr.] One of the side scenes of the stage in a theater or the space included between the side scenes.

coulomb, kö·lom′, n. [From *Coulomb*, the French physicist.] In *current elect.*, the practical unit of quantity, that transferred by a current of one ampere in one sec., equal to 1/10 of the absolute electromagnetic unit of quantity.

coulter, kōl′tėr, n. [L. *culter*, a knife, a coulter.] An iron blade or knife inserted into the beam of a plow for the purpose of cutting the ground and facilitating the separation of the furrow slice by the plow-share.

coumarine, kö′ma·rēn, n. [From *coumaron*, a tree of Guiana.] A vegetable principle obtained from the tonka bean, used in medicine and to give flavor to the Swiss cheese called schabzieger.

council, koun′sil, n. [Fr. *concile*, from L. *concilium*—*con*, together, and root *cal*, to summon; akin *conciliate, reconcile*. This word is often improperly confounded with *cousel*.] An assembly of men summoned for consultation, deliberation, and advice (a common *council*, an ecumenical *council*, the privy-*council*); act of deliberation; consultation, as of a council.—*Council of war*, an assembly of officers of high rank called to consult with the commander-in-chief of an army or admiral of a fleet on matters of supreme importance.—**councilor**, koun′sil·ėr, n. The member of a council; specifically, a member of a common council or of the privy-council.—**councilman**, n. A member of a city common council.

counsel, koun′sel, n. [Fr. *conseil*, from L. *consilium*, advice, from *consulo*, to consult, deliberate. Akin *consult*.] Opinion or advice, given upon request or otherwise, for directing the judgment or conduct of another; consultation; interchange of opinions; deliberation; the secrets entrusted in consultation; secret opinions or purposes (to keep one's *counsel*); intent or purpose; one who gives counsel in matters of law.— *v.t.*—*counseled, counseling.* To give advice or deliberate opinion to, for the government of conduct; to advise, exhort, warn, admonish, or instruct; to recommend or give an opinion in favor of.—**counselor**, koun′sel·ėr, n. Any person who gives counsel or advice; an adviser; one whose profession is to give advice in law, and manage causes for clients; a barrister. —**counselorship**, koun′sel·ėr·ship, the office of a counselor.

count, kount, v.t. [Fr. *conter, compter*, from L. *computare*, to compute. COMPUTE.] To tell or name one by one, or by small numbers, in order to ascertain the whole number of units in a collection; to reckon; to number; to compute; to esteem, account, think, judge or consider. *To count out*, to bring (a meeting) to a close by numbering the members and finding a quorum not present, as in the House of Commons, where this is done by the speaker.—*v.i.* To be added or reckoned in with others; to reckon; to rely; in this sense with *on* or *upon* (to *count on* assistance).—*n.* The act of numbering; reckoning; number; *law*, a particular charge in an indictment, or narration in pleading, setting forth the cause of complaint.—**countable**, koun′ta·bl, *a.* Capable of being counted or numbered.—**count down**, the count by seconds prior to the firing of a missile, with the precise moment of firing designated as zero.—**counter**, koun′tėr, n. One who counts, numbers, or reckons; that which is used to keep an account or reckoning, as in games, such as a small plate of metal, ivory, wood, etc.; a counterfeit or imitation of a coin; a registering apparatus or telltale; a table or board on which money is counted; a table in a store over which sales are made, and on which goods are exposed for sale.—**countless**, kount′-les, *a.* Not capable of being counted; innumerable.—**countinghouse**, n. A house or room appropriated by mercantile men to the business of keeping their books, accounts, etc.

count, kount, n. [Fr. *comte*, from L. *comes, comitis*, a companion, a companion of the emperor or a king— *com* for *con*, with, and stem of *eo, itum*, to go, seen also in *ambition, exit, transit, perish*, etc.] A title of foreign nobility, equivalent to the English *earl*, and whose domain is a *county*.—**countess**, koun′tes, n. The wife of an earl or count, or a lady possessed of the same dignity in her own right.

countenance, koun′te·nans, n. [Fr. *contenance*, demeanor, way of acting or holding one's self, from *contenir*, to contain. CONTAIN.] The whole form of the face; the features considered as a whole; the visage; the face; appearance or expression of the face; favor expressed toward a person; good will; support.—*In countenance*, in favor or estimation; free from shame or dismay.—*Out of countenance*, confounded; abashed; not bold or assured.—*v.t.* countenanced, countenancing. To favor; to encourage; to aid; to support; to abet.

counter, koun′tẽr, *adv.* [Fr. *contre*, from L. *contra*—*con*, and *tra*, denoting direction, as in *intra*, *extra*, *ultra*.] In an opposite direction; in opposition; contrariwise.—*n.* The opposite; a stiffener around the heel of a shoe.—*v.t.* To act in opposition to.—*v.i.* To make an opposing move.—*a.* Adverse; opposite; opposing.

counteract, koun·tẽr·akt′, *v.t.* To act in opposition to; to hinder, defeat, or frustrate by contrary agency; to oppose.—**counteraction,** koun′tẽr·ak·shon, *n.* Action in opposition; hindrance; resistance.—**counteractive,** koun′tẽr·ak·tiv, *a.* Tending to counteract.—*n.* One who or that which counteracts.

counterattraction, koun′tẽr·at·trak″shon, *n.* Opposite attraction.

counterbalance, koun·tẽr·bal′ans, *v.t.*—counterbalanced, counterbalancing. To weigh against with equal force; to counteract.—*n.* Weight, power, etc. balancing or counteracting another; counterpoise.

counterchange, koun′tẽr·chānj, *n.* Exchange; reciprocation. (*Shak.*)—*v.t.* To give and receive; to cause to make alternate changes; to alternate. (*Tenn.*)

countercharge, koun′tẽr·chärj, *n.* An opposite charge.

counterclockwise, koun′tẽr·klok″wīz, *adv.* and *a.* In a direction opposite to that in which the hands of a clock rotate.

countercurrent, koun′tẽr·kur·ent, *n.* A current in an opposite direction.

counterespionage, koun″tẽr·es′pi·o·nij, *n.* The measures taken by a nation to detect and defeat enemy espionage.

counterfeit, koun′tẽr·fit, *a.* [Fr. *contrefait*, made to correspond—*contre*, against, and *faire*, to make.] Made in imitation of something else, with a view to pass the false copy for genuine or original; forged; not genuine; base; assuming the appearance of something; false; spurious; hypocritical.—*n.* One who pretends to be what he is not; an impostor; a cheat; that which is made in imitation of something with a view to defraud by passing the false for the true.—*v.t.* To copy or imitate with a view to pass off as original or genuine; to make a likeness or resemblance of with a view to defraud; to forge; to imitate or copy generally; to sham or pretend.—*v.i.* To feign; to dissemble; to carry on a fiction or deception.—**counterfeiter,** koun′tẽr·fit·ẽr, *n.* One who counterfeits; a forger; one who assumes a false appearance, or

who makes false pretenses.

counterfoil, koun′tẽr·foil, *n.* [*Counter*, and *foil*, from L. *folium*, a leaf.] A portion of a document, such as a bank check or draft, which is retained by the person giving the other part, and on which is noted the main particulars contained in the principal document.

counterirritant, koun′tẽr·ir·i·tant, *n.* *Med.* an irritant substance employed to relieve another irritation or inflammation, as mustard, croton oil, Spanish flies.

countermand, koun·tẽr·mand′, *v.t.* [Fr. *contremander*—*contre*, and *mander*, L. *mando*, to command.] To revoke, as a former command; to order or direct in opposition to an order before given, thereby annulling it.—*n.* A contrary order; revocation of a former order or command by a subsequent order.

countermarch, koun·tẽr·märch′, *v.i.* To march back.—*n.* A marching back; a returning; a change of measures.

countermine, koun′tẽr·mīn, *n.* *Milit.* a mine sunk in search of the enemy's mine or till it meets it, to defeat its effect; *fig.* a stratagem or project to frustrate any contrivance; an opposing scheme or plot.—*v.t.* To mine so as to discover or destroy an enemy's mine; *fig.* to frustrate by secret and opposite measures.—*v.i.* To make a countermine; to counterplot.

counterpane, koun′tẽr·pān, *n.* [From older *counterpoint*, O.Fr. *contrepoinct*, corruptly derived from L.L. *culcita puncta*, lit. stitched quilt. QUILT, POINT.] A bedcover; a coverlet for a bed; a quilt.

counterpart, koun′tẽr·pärt, *n.* A part that answers to or resembles another, as the several parts or copies of an indenture corresponding to the original; a thing or person exactly resembling another; a copy; a duplicate; the thing that supplements another thing or completes it; a complement.

counterplot, koun′tẽr·plot, *v.t.* To oppose or frustrate by another plot or stratagem.—*n.* A plot or artifice set afoot in order to oppose another.

counterpoint, koun′tẽr·point, *n.* The art of writing music in several distinct parts or themes proceeding simultaneously, as distinguished from harmony, which depends more for its effects on the composition and progression of whole chords than on the melody of each separate part; so called because the points which formerly represented musical notes were written under or against each other on the lines; often used, but improperly, as equivalent to *harmony*.

counterpoise, koun′tẽr·poiz, *v.t.* To weigh against with equal weight; to equal in weight; to counterbalance; to act against with equal power or effect; to balance.—*n.* A weight equal to and acting in opposition to another weight; equal power or force acting in opposition; state of being in equilibrium by being bal-

anced by another weight or force.

counterrevolution, koun′tẽr·rev·o·lū·shon, *n.* A revolution opposed to a former one, and restoring a former state of things.

counterscarp, koun′tẽr·skärp, *n.* *Fort.* the slope of the ditch nearest the enemy and opposite the scarp; the face of the ditch sloping down from the covered way.

countersign, koun′tẽr·sīn, *v.t.* To sign (a document) formally or officially in proof of its genuineness; to attest or witness by signature.—*n.* A private signal, word, or phrase given to a guard with orders to let no man pass unless he first give that sign; a watchword; also, the signature of a subordinate to a writing signed by his superior, to attest its authenticity.—**countersignature,** koun′tẽr·sig″ne·chẽr, *n.* The name of a secretary or other subordinate officer countersigned to a writing.

countersink, koun′tẽr·singk, *v.t.* To form a cavity in timber or other materials so as to receive the head of a bolt, screw, etc., and make it flush with the surface; to sink below or even with a surface, as the head of a screw, bolt, etc., by making a depression for it in the material.—*n.* A drill or brace bit for countersinking; the cavity made by countersinking.

countertenor, koun′tẽr·ten·ẽr, *n.* *Mus.* the highest male adult voice, having about the same compass as the alto, with which term this is sometimes confounded; a singer with this voice.

countervail, koun′tẽr·vāl, *v.t.* [Fr. *contrevaloir*. AVAIL.] To act with equivalent force or effect against anything; to balance; to compensate; to equal.—*n.* Equal weight, strength, or value; compensation; requital.

counterview, koun′tẽr·vū, *n.* An opposite or opposing view; a posture in which two persons front each other; opposition; contrast.

counterweigh, koun′tẽr·wā, *v.t.* To weigh against; to counterbalance.—**counterweight,** koun′tẽr·wāt, *n.* A weight in the opposite scale; a counterpoise.

counterwork, koun′tẽr·wẽrk, *v.t.* To work in opposition to; to counteract; to hinder any effect by contrary operations.—*n.* A work in opposition or in answer to another.

country, kun′tri, *n.* [Fr. *contrée*, from L.L. *contrata*, country, from L. *contra*, against, opposite; *country* being thus literally the land opposite or before us. Akin *counter*, *adv.*, *encounter*.] A tract of land; a region; the land occupied by a particular race of people; a state; a person's native or adopted land.—*The country*, the rural parts of a region, as opposed to cities or towns; the inhabitants of a region; the people; the public; the parliamentary electors of a state, or the constituencies of a state, collectively.—*a.* Pertaining to the country or to a district at a distance from a city; rural; rustic.—**countrified,** kun′tri·fīd, *a.* Having the airs or manner of a rustic.—**countryman,**

kun′tri•man, *n*. One born in the same country with another; one who dwells in the country as opposed to the town; a rustic; an inhabitant or native of a region.—**countrywoman**, kun′tri•wu̥•man, *n*. A woman belonging to the country, as opposed to the town; a woman born in the same country; a female inhabitant or native of a region.—**country-dance**, *n*. [*Country* and *dance*; not from Fr. *contre-danse*, which is a kind of quadrille.] A dance in which the partners are arranged opposite to each other in lines.

county, koun′ti, *n*. [L.L. *comitatus*, from *comes, comitis*, a count. COUNT.] Originally, the district or territory of a count or earl; now, an administrative unit in various countries; in the United States, the political unit below a State; a shire (which see); a count; an earl or lord‡.—*a*. Pertaining to a county. —*County town*, the chief town of a county; that town where the various courts of a county are held.

coup, kö, *n*. A French term for stroke or blow, and used in various connections, to convey the idea of promptness, force, or violence.—*Coup d'état* (kö•dā•tä), a sudden decisive blow in politics; a stroke of policy; specifically, a daring or forcible alteration of the constitution of a country without the consent or concurrence of the people.—*Coup de grâce* (köd•gräs), the finishing stroke.—*Coup de main* (köd•maṅ), a sudden attack or enterprise.—*Coup d'œil* (kö•dė′i), glance of the eye; a comprehensive or rapid view.—*Coup de soleil* (köd•so•lā′i), sunstroke.

coupé, coupe, kö•pā, köp, *n*. [From Fr. *carosse coupé*, cut-off coach.] An enclosed carriage seating two inside and a driver outside; an enclosed two-door automobile, generally seating two but sometimes four persons.

couple, kup′l, *n*. [Fr. *couple*, from L. *copula*, a band, bond, connection.] Two of the same class or kind, connected or considered together; a brace; a pair; a male and female connected by marriage, betrothed, or otherwise allied; *mech*. two equal and parallel forces acting in opposite directions; *elect*. one of the pairs of plates of two metals which compose a battery, called a *galvanic* or *voltaic couple*; *carp*. one of a pair of opposite rafters in a roof, united at the top where they meet.—*v.t.*—**coupled**, **coupling**. To link, chain, or otherwise connect; to fasten together; to unite, as husband and wife; to marry.—*v.i.* To copulate.—**coupler**, kup′ler, *n*. One who or that which couples; specifically, the mechanism by which any two of the ranks of keys, or keys and pedals, of an organ are connected together.—**couplet**, kup′let, *n*. Two verses or lines of poetry, especially two that rhyme together; a pair of rhymes.—**coupling**, kup′ling, *n*. The act of one who couples; that which couples or connects; a coupler; a contrivance for connecting one portion of a system of shafting with

another; the chains or rods connecting the carriages, etc., of a train.

coupon, kö′pon, *n*. [Fr., from *couper*, to cut.] An interest certificate printed at the bottom of transferable bonds, and so called because it is cut off or detached and given up when a payment is made; hence, generally one of a series of tickets which binds the issuer to make certain payments, perform some service, or give value for certain amounts at different periods, in consideration of money received.

courage, kur′ij, *n*. [Fr. *courage*, from L. *cor*, the heart, whence also *cordial*, etc.] That quality of mind which enables men to encounter danger and difficulties with firmness, or without fear; bravery; intrepidity; valor; boldness; resolution; disposition or frame of mind (*Shak*.)‡.—**courageous**, ku•rā′jus, *a*. Possessing or characterized by courage; brave; bold; daring; intrepid.—**courageously**, ku•rā′jus•li, *adv*. In a courageous manner.—**courageousness**, ku•rā′jus•nes, *n*.

courier, kö′ri•er, *n*. [Fr. *courrier*, from *courir*, L. *curro*, to run.] A messenger sent express with letters or dispatches; an attendant on a party traveling abroad whose especial duty is to make all arrangements at hotels and on the journey.

course, kōrs, *n*. [Fr. *cours, course*, a course, a race, direction; way, etc.; from L. *cursus*, L.L. also *cursa*, from *curro, cursum*, to run (whence *current, incur, recur*, etc.).] A running, race, flight, career, a moving or motion forward in any direction; a continuous progression or advance; the direction of motion; the line in which a body moves; the ground or path marked out for a race; continuous or gradual advance; progress; order or succession; stated or orderly method of proceeding; customary or established sequence; series of successive and methodical proceedings; systematized order in arts or sciences for illustration or instruction (*course* of studies, etc.); way of life or conduct; line of behavior (to follow evil *courses*); the part of a meal served at one time; *arch*. a continued range of stones or bricks of the same height throughout the face or faces of a building; *naut*. one of the sails that hang from a ship's lowest yards; *pl*. the menstrual flux; catamenia.— *v.t.* coursed, coursing. To hunt; to pursue; to chase; to hunt (hares) with greyhounds; to drive with speed; to run through or over.—*v.i.* To move with speed; to run or move about.—*Of course*, by consequence; in regular or natural order; naturally; without special direction or provision.—**courser**, kōr′ser, *n*. One who courses; a swift horse; a war horse: used chiefly in poetry; a swift-footed cream-colored bird of the plover tribe; any bird of the cursorial order, or runners.

court, kōrt, *n*. [O.Fr. *cort, court* (Fr. *cour*), from L. *cors, cortis*, contracted from *cohors, cohortis*, a yard, a *court*—*co* for *con*, and *hor*,

a root seen in *hortus*, a garden, also in *garden, garth*.] An enclosed uncovered area, whether behind or in front of a house, or surrounded by buildings; a courtyard; an alley, lane, close, or narrow street; the place of residence of a king or sovereign prince; all the surroundings of a sovereign in his regal state; the collective body of persons who compose the retinue or council of a sovereign; a hall, chamber, or place where justice is administered; the persons or judges assembled for hearing and deciding causes, as distinguished from the counsel or jury; any judicial body, civil, military, or ecclesiastical; the sitting of a judicial assembly; attention directed to a person in power to gain favor; civility; flattery; address to gain favor (to pay *court* to a person).—*v.t.* To endeavor to gain the favor of or win over by attention and address; to flatter; to seek the affections or love of; to woo; to solicit for marriage; to attempt to gain by address; to solicit; to seek (to *court* applause); to hold out inducements to; to invite. —*v.i.* To pay one's addresses; to woo. —**courteous**, kėr′ti•us, *a*. Having courtly, refined, or elegant manners; characterized by courtesy; affable; condescending, polite.—**courteously**, kėr′ti•us•li, *adv*. In a courteous manner.—**courteousness**, kėrt′i•us•nes, *n*.—**courtesan, courtezan**, kōr′ti•zan, *n*. A prostitute.—**courtesy**, kėr′ti•si, *n*. Politeness of manners, combined with kindness; polished manners or urbanity shown in behavior toward others; an act of civility or respect; a curtsy (in this sense pronounced kėrt′si); favor or indulgence, as contradistinguished from right.—*Courtesy of England*, the husband's tenure of certain kinds of property after his wife's death.— *Courtesy title*, a title assumed or popularly accorded and to which the individual has no valid claim, as the title marquis to the eldest son of a duke, viscount to the eldest son of an earl, etc.—**courtier**, kōr′ti•er, *n*. One who attends or frequents the court of a sovereign; one who courts or flatters another with a view to obtain favor, etc.—**courtly**, kōrt′li, *a*. Relating or pertaining to a prince's court; refined and dignified; elegant; polite; courteous.—**courtliness**, kōrt′li•nes, *n*. The state or quality of being courtly.—**courtship**, kōrt′ship, *n*. The act of courting or soliciting favor; wooing.—**courtcard**, *a*. A corruption of *coat-card* (which see).—**court hand**, *n*. The old manner of writing used in records and judicial proceedings.—**courthouse**, *n*. A house in which established courts are held.—**court-martial**, *n*. pl. **courts-martial**. A court consisting of military or naval officers, for the trial of military or naval offenses.—**court plaster**, *n*. A fine kind of sticking plaster.—**courtyard**, *n*. A court or enclosure round a house or adjacent to it.

cousin, kuz′n, *n*. [Fr. *cousin*, from L.L. *cosinus*, for L. *consobrinus*, a

ch, *chain*; *ch*, Sc. loch; g, *go*; j, *job*; ng, *sing*; TH, *then*; th, *thin*; w, *wig*; hw, *whig*; zh, *azure*.

cousin—*con*, and *sobrinus*, akin to *soror*, a sister.] The son or daughter of an uncle or aunt; in a wider and now less usual sense, one collaterally related more remotely than a brother or sister; a kinsman or kinswoman; a blood-relation; a title given by a monarch to a nobleman.—**cousin-hood**, kuz'n·hu̯d, *n.* The state of being cousins; the individuals connected with a family regarded collectively.—**cousinly**, kuz'n·li, *a.* Like or becoming a cousin.—**cousinship**, kuz'n·ship, *n.* The state of being cousins; cousinhood.—**cousin-german**, *n.* A first or full cousin.

couvade, kö·väd, *n.* [Fr. *couver*, to hatch; L. *cubare*, to lie. COVEY.] A custom among primitive races (Basques, Corsicans, etc.) of men, by which, at the birth of a child, the father takes to bed and is attended by mother. Perhaps to prove paternity, by a survival from earlier days of promiscuity of intercourse.

cove, kōv, *n.* [A.Sax. *cófa*, a chamber, a cave; allied to Icel. *kofi*, Sw. *kofwa*, a hut.] A small inlet, creek, or bay; a sheltered recess in the seashore; *arch.* any kind of concave molding; the concavity of a vault.—*v.t.* coved, coving. To arch over.

covenant, kuv'e·nant, *n.* [O.Fr. *cove-nant*, for *convenant*, from L. *conve-nire*, to agree—*con*, and *venio*, to come. CONVENE.] A mutual consent or agreement of two or more persons to do or to forbear some act or thing; a contract; a compact; a bargain, arrangement, or stipulation; a writing containing the terms of agreement or contract between parties.—*v.i.* To enter into a formal agreement; to contract; to bind one's self by contract.—*v.t.* To grant or promise by covenant. [O.T.]—**cove-nantee**, kuv'e·nan·tē″, *n.* The person to whom a covenant is made.—**covenanter**, kuv'e·nan·tėr, *n.* One who makes a covenant; [*cap.*] a term specially applied to those who joined in the Solemn League and Covenant in Scotland, and in particular those who resisted the government of Charles II, and fought and suffered for adherence to their own form of worship.—**covenantor**, kuv'e·nan·tėr, *n. Law*, the person who makes a covenant and subjects himself to the penalty of its breach.

cover, kuv'ėr, *v.t.* [O.Fr. *covrir*, Fr. *couvrir*, from L. *cooperire*—*con*, intens., and *operire*, to cover.] To overspread the surface of with another substance; to lay or set over; to overspread so as to conceal; to envelop; to wrap up; to clothe; to shelter; to protect; to defend; to cloak; to screen; to invest with; to brood over; to be sufficient for; to include; to comprehend; to be equal to; to be coextensive with.—*n.* Anything which is laid, set, or spread over another thing; anything which veils or conceals; a screen; disguise; superficial appearance; shelter; defense; protection; concealment and protection; shrubbery, woods, underbrush, etc., which shelter and conceal game; the articles laid at table for

the use of one person.—plate, spoon, knife and fork, etc.—**coverer**, kuv'-ėr·ėr, *n.* One who or that which covers.—**covering**, kuv'ėr·ing, *n.* That which covers; anything spread or laid over another, whether for security, protection, shelter, or concealment; clothing; dress; wrapper; envelope.—**coverlet**, kuv'ėr·let, *n.* [O.Fr. *covre-lit*, *couvre-lit*, a bed-cover—*covrir*, to cover, and *lit*, L. *lectus*, a bed.] The upper covering of a bed.—**coverlid**, kuv'ėr·lid, *n.* A coverlet. (*Tenn.*)

covert, kuv'ėrt, *a.* [O.Fr. *covert*, part. of *covrir*, to cover.] Kept secret or concealed; not open (*covert* fraud or enmity); *law*, under cover, authority, or protection.—*n.* A place which covers and shelters; a shelter; a defense; a thicket; a shady place or a hiding place; *pl.* feathers covering the bases of the quills of the wing or tail of birds.—**covertly**, kuv'ėrt·li, *adv.* Secretly; in private; insidiously.—**coverture**, kuv'ėr·chėr, *n.* Covering; shelter; defense; *law*, the state of a married woman, who is considered as under the cover or power of her husband.

covet, kuv'et, *v.t.* [From O.Fr. *coveiter* (Fr. *convoiter*), from L. *cupidus*, desirous, *cupio*, to desire.] To desire or wish for with eagerness; to desire earnestly to obtain or possess; to desire inordinately; to desire with a greedy or envious longing; to long for; to hanker after.—*v.i.* To have or indulge inordinate desire.—**cov-etable**, kuv'e·ta·bl, *a.* That may be coveted.—**coveter**, kuv'e·tėr, *n.* One who covets.—**covetous**, kuv'e·tus, *a.* Very desirous; eager to obtain; inordinately desirous; excessively eager to obtain and possess; avaricious.—**covetously**, kuv'e·tus·li, *adv.* With a strong or inordinate desire; eagerly; avariciously.—**covetousness**, kuv'e·tus·nes, *n.* The state or quality of being covetous; avarice; cupidity; greediness; craving.

covey, kuv'i, *n.* [O.Fr. *covee*, Fr. *couvée*, a brood, from *couver*, *cover*, to sit on or brood, L. *cubare*, to lie; seen also in *incubate*.] A brood or hatch of birds; an old fowl with her brood of young; a small flock: usually confined to partridges.

cow, kou, *n.* pl. **cows**, kouz, old pl. **kine**, kīn. [A.Sax. *cú*, pl. *cý*; G. *kuh*, D. and Dan. *koe*, Icel. *kú*; the same root appears in Skr. *go*, nom. *gaus*, a cow, an ox., *Kine* is a double plural, the *en* form as in *oxen* being added to the older form.] The general term applied to the females of the bovine genus or ox, the most valuable to man of all the ruminating animals, on account of her milk, flesh, hide, etc.—**cowbane**, *n.* A kind of hemlock, water hemlock, highly poisonous, being sometimes fatal to cattle who eat its leaves.—**cowberry**, *n.* Red whortleberry.—**cowboy**, *n.* Boy who has charge of cows; a man who looks after cattle on a large stock farm and does this work on horseback.—**cow bunting**, *n.* An American bird belonging to the starling tribe, remarkable for drop-

ping its eggs into the nests of other birds to be hatched.—**cowcatcher**, *n.* A strong frame in front of locomotives for removing obstructions, such as strayed cattle, from the rails. —**cowhide**, *n.* The hide or skin of a cow, made or to be made into leather; a strong whip made of such leather.—*v.t.* To thrash or whip with a lash of cowhide.—**cowpea**, *n.* A kind of clover having bright red flowers.—**cowpox**, *n.* A disease which appears on the teats of the cow in the form of vesicles or blisters, the fluid or virus contained in which is capable of communicating the disease to the human subject, and of conferring, in the great majority of instances, security against smallpox.—**cowslip**, kou'slip, *n.* [A.Sax. *cu-slyppe*, *cu-sloppe*, the latter part of the name apparently meaning dung.] A perennial herb of the primrose family, growing in moist places in Britain. —*Cowslip wine*, a beverage made by fermenting cowslips with sugar, and used as a domestic soporific.

cow, kou, *v.t.* [Dan. *kue*, Icel. *kúga*, to depress, subdue, keep under.] To sink the spirits or courage of; to daunt, dishearten, intimidate, overawe.

coward, kou'ėrd, *n.* [Fr. *couard*, It. *codardo*, from L. *cauda*, a tail, the name being originally applied to the timid hare from its short tail.] A person who wants courage to meet danger; a poltroon; a craven; a dastard; a faint-hearted, timid, or pusillanimous man.—*a.* Destitute of courage; timid; of, proceeding from, or expressive of fear or timidity.—**cowardice**, kou'ėr·dis, *n.* [Fr. *couar-dise.*] Want of courage to face danger; timidity; pusillanimity; fear of exposing one's person to danger.—**cowardly**, kou'ėrd·li, *a.* Wanting courage to face danger; timid; timorous; pusillanimous; fainthearted; mean; base; proceeding from fear of danger; befitting a coward.—*adv.* In the manner of a coward.—**cowardliness**, kou'ėrd·li·nes, *n.* Cowardice.

cower, kou'ėr, *v.i.* [Same word as Sc. *curr*, to squat; Icel. *kúra*, Dan. *kure*, Sw. *kura*, to doze, to rest; G. *kauern*, to cower.] To squat; to stoop or sink downward, as from terror, discomfort, etc.

cowhage, **cowitch**, kou'ij, kou'ich, *n.* [Hind. *kawanch*, cowhage.] The short, brittle hairs of the pods of a leguminous plant, which easily penetrate the skin, and produce an intolerable itching; they are administered in honey or molasses as a vermifuge.

cowl, koul, *n.* [A.Sax. *cufle*, Icel. *kufl*, *kofl*, a cowl; comp. also O.Fr. *coule*, from L. *cucullus*, a cowl.] A hood, especially a monk's hood; a chimney covering designed to increase draft; the part of an automobile body on which the windshield and dashboard are mounted. —**cowled**, kould, *a.* Wearing a cowl; hooded in shape of a cowl (*cowled* leaf).

cowl, koul, *n.* [O.Fr. *cuvel*, dim. of *cuve*, a tub, from L. *cupa*. CUP.] A vessel to be carried on a pole betwixt two persons, for the conveyance of water.—**cowlstaff**, *n.* Same as *Colstaff.*

co-work, kō·wėrk', *v.i.* To work jointly; to co-operate.—**co-worker**, kō·wėr'kėr, *n.* One that works with another; a co-operator.

cowry, kou'ri, *n.* [Hind. *kauri.*] A small univalve shell used for coin on the coast of Guinea, and in many parts of Southern Asia.

coxa, kok'sa, *n.* [L.] *Anat.* the hip, haunch, or hip joint; *entom.* the joint of an insect's limb which is next the body.

coxcomb, koks'kōm, *n.* [*Cock's comb.*] The comb resembling that of a cock which licensed fools wore formerly in their caps; hence used often for the cap itself; the top of the head, or the head itself; a vain showy fellow; a superficial pretender to knowledge or accomplishments; a fop; a dandy.—**coxcombical**, koks·kom'i·kal, *a.* Like or indicating a coxcomb; conceited; foppish.—**coxcombry**, koks'kōm·ri, *n.* The manners of a coxcomb; foppishness.

coxswain, *n.* Same as *Cockswain.*

coy, koi, *a.* [O.Fr. *coi, coy, coit*, from L. *quietus*, quiet. QUIET.] Shrinking from familiarity; shy; modest; reserved; distant; backward; bashful.—**coyly**, koi'li, *adv.* In a coy manner; with disinclination to familiarity.—**coyness**, koi'nes, *n.* The quality of being coy; bashfulness; shyness; reserve; modesty.

coyote, koi·ōt', koi·ō'ti, *n.* [Sp. *coyote*, Mex. *coyotl.*] The American prairie wolf.

coypu, koi'pö, *n.* The native name of a South American rodent, beaverlike, semiaquatic mammal, valued for its fur.

cozen, kuz'n, *v.t.* [A form of *cousin*; Fr. *cousiner*, to sponge upon people (under pretext of relationship), from *cousin*, a cousin.] To cheat; to defraud; to deceive; to beguile.—*v.i.* To cheat; to act deceitfully.—**cozenage**, kuz'n·ij, *n.* Trickery; fraud; deceit.—**cozener**, kuz'n·ėr, *n.* One who cozens.

cozy, cosy, kō'zi, *a.* [Akin to Norse *koselig*, cosy, *kose sig*, to enjoy one's ease.] Well sheltered; snug; comfortable; social.—*n.* A kind of padded covering or cap put over a teapot to keep in the heat after the tea has been infused.—**cozily**, kō'zi·li, *adv.*

crab, krab, *n.* [A.Sax. *crabba*=D. *krab*, Icel. *krabbi*, Sw. *krabba*, G. *krabbe*, a crab; all perhaps from L. *carabus*, Gr. *karabos*, a kind of crab.] A popular name for all the ten-footed, short-tailed crustaceans, having the tail folded under the body, the two forefeet not used for locomotion, but furnished with strong claws or pincers, and several species being highly esteemed as food; Cancer, a sign in the zodiac; a name given to various machines, as a kind of portable windlass or machine for raising weights, etc.

crab, krab, *n.* [Sw. *krabbäple*, a crab apple, perhaps from *crab*, the animal, in allusion to its pinching or astringent juice.] A small, wild, very sour

apple; the tree producing the fruit; a sour-tempered, peevish, morose person‡.—**crab apple**, *n.* A wild apple.—**crabbed**, krab'ed, *a.* Rough or harsh as regards temper or disposition; sour; peevish; morose; difficult; perplexing; uninviting (a *crabbed* author).—**crabbedly**, krab'ed·li, *adv.* In a crabbed manner; peevishly; morosely.—**crabbedness**, krab'ednes, *n.* The state or quality of being crabbed.—**crabstick**, *n.* A walking stick made of the wood of the crab tree.—**crab tree**, *n.* The tree that bears crabs; the wild apple tree.

crack, krak, *v.t.* [An imitative word; A.Sax. *cracian*, to crack; G. *krachen*, to crack; D. *krak*, a crack; Gael. *knac*, a crack, as of a whip, etc.] To rend, break, or burst; to break partially; to break without an entire severance of the parts; to throw out or utter with smartness (to *crack* a joke); to snap; to cause to make a sharp sudden noise (a whip).—*v.i.* To break with a sharp sound; to burst; to open in chinks; to be fractured without quite separating into different parts; to give out a loud or sharp sudden sound; to boast or brag: with *of* (Shak.)‡.—*n.* A chink or fissure; a partial separation of the parts of a substance, with or without an opening; a burst of sound; a sharp or loud sound uttered suddenly; a violent report; injury or impairment to the intellect or to the character; flaw; blemish; an instant; a trice.—*a.* Having qualities to be proud of; first-rate; excellent (a *crack* regiment, a *crack* horse).—**cracked**, krakt, *p.* and *a.* Burst or split; rent; broken; impaired; crazy, as regards the mind.—**cracker**, krak'-ėr, *n.* One who or that which cracks; a noisy, boasting fellow (Shak.); a small kind of firework filled with powder, which explodes with a sharp crack or with a series of sharp cracks; a small hard biscuit.—**crackle**, krak'l, *v.i.*—**crackled, crackling.** [Dim. of *crack.*] To make slight cracks; to make small abrupt noises, rapidly or frequently repeated; to decrepitate.—**crackling**, krak'l·ing, *n.* A noise made up of small cracks or reports frequently repeated; the browned skin of roast pig; a kind of cake used for dog's food, made from the refuse of tallow melting.—**cracknel**, krak'nel, *n.* A hard brittle cake or biscuit.—**crackbrained**, *a.* Having a disordered intellect; insane; lunatic; mad.

cradle, krā'dl, *n.* [A.Sax. *cradel, cradal*; comp. G. *krätze*, a basket.] A small bed, crib, or cot in which an infant is rocked; hence, the place where any person or thing is nurtured in the earlier stage of existence; something resembling a cradle in construction or use, as a case in which a broken limb is placed after being set; a rocking machine in which gold is washed from the earth, etc., containing it; a vessel or basket attached to a line or lines between a wrecked ship and the shore for bringing off the crew or passengers, etc.—*v.t.*—**cradled, cradling.** To lay in a cradle; to rock in

a cradle; to compose or quiet by rocking; to nurse in infancy.—*v.i.* To lie or lodge as in a cradle. (*Shak.*)

craft, kraft, *n.* [A.Sax. *craeft*, craft, cunning, force, a craft=G. Sw. Icel. and Dan. *kraft*, D. *kracht*, power, faculty; from root of which *cramp* is a nasalized form, akin to Skr. *grabh.* to grasp.] Cunning art, or skill, in a bad sense; artifice; guile; dexterity in a particular manual occupation; hence, the occupation or employment itself; manual art; trade; the members of a trade collectively; *naut.* a vessel: often used in a collective sense for vessels of any kind.—**craftsman**, krafts'man, *n.* An artificer; a mechanic; one skilled in a manual occupation.—**craftsmanship**, krafts'man·ship, *n.* The skilled work of a craftsman.—**crafty**, kraf'ti, *a.* Characterized by, having, or using craft; cunning; wily; sly; deceitful; subtle; dexterous; skillful.—**craftily**, kraf'ti·li, *adv.* In a crafty manner; cunningly; slyly; deceitfully; skillfully; dexterously.—**craftiness**, kraf'-ti·nes, *n.* The state or quality of being crafty.

crag, krag, *n.* [Gael. *creag*, Ir. *craig*, W. *careg*, a rock, stone.] A steep, rugged rock; a rough broken rock, or point of a rock; a cliff; *geol.* shelly deposits in Norfolk and Suffolk, usually of gravel and sand, of the older pliocene period.—**cragged**, krag'ed, *a.* Full of crags or broken rocks; craggy.—**craggy**, krag'i, *a.* Full of crags; abounding with broken rocks; rugged with projecting points of rocks.—**cragginess**, krag'i·nes, *n.* The state of being craggy.—**cragsman**, kragz'man, *n.* One who is dexterous in climbing or descending rocks; one who takes seafowls or their eggs from crags.

crake, krāk, *n.* [Imitative of the bird's cry, like *croak, creak*; comp. L. *crex*, Gr. *krex*, a landrail; Icel. *kraka*, to croak, etc.] A grallatorial bird of various species belonging to the family of the rails, the best known species being the corncrake or land rail.

cram, kram, *v.t.*—**crammed, cramming.** [A.Sax. *crammian*, to cram; Dan. *kramme*, to crush; Sw. *krama*, to press; akin *cramp.*] To press or drive, particularly in filling or thrusting one thing into another; to stuff; to crowd; to fill to superfluity; to fill with food beyond satiety; to stuff; *fig.* to endeavor to qualify for an examination, in a comparatively short time, by storing the memory with only such knowledge as is likely to serve the occasion; to coach.—*v.i.* To eat greedily or beyond satiety; to stuff; to prepare for an examination by rapidly storing the memory with crude facts.—*n.* Information got up hurriedly for an examination or other special purpose.—**crammer**, kram'ėr, *n.* One who crams or stuffs; one who crams in study.

crambo, kram'bō, *n.* [Origin doubtful.] A game in which one person gives a word, to which another finds a rhyme; a word rhyming with another.

cramp, kramp, *n.* [Same as D. *kramp*,

Dan. *krampe*, Sw. *kramp, krampa,* G. *krampf, krampe,* cramp, a cramp-iron; from root seen in *cram, crimp, crumple.*] The contraction of a limb or some muscle of the body, attended with pain; spasm; a feeling of restraint; a piece of iron bent at the end, serving to hold together pieces of timber, stones, etc.; a cramp iron; a portable kind of iron screw press for closely compressing the joints of a timber framework.—*v.t.* To pain or affect with spasms or cramps; to confine, restrain, or hinder from action or expansion; to fasten, confine, or hold with a cramp or cramp iron.—*a.* Difficult; knotty.—**crampon,** kram′pon, *n.* [Fr. *crampon.*] *Bot.* an adventitious root which serves as a fulcrum or support in climbing, as in the ivy.—**crampoon,** kram′pön, *n.* An iron fastened to the shoes of a storming party, to assist them in climbing a rampart; an apparatus used in raising timber or stones for building, consisting of two hooked pieces of iron hinged together.

cranberry, kran′be·ri, *n.* [That is *craneberry,* perhaps because the berries are eaten by cranes.] The globose, dark red berry, about the size of a currant, produced by several species of small shrubs growing in peat bogs or swampy land in Europe and North America; the shrub producing this berry. Called also *Mossberry* and *Moorberry.*

crane, krān, *n.* [A.Sax. *cran;* cog. D. *kraan,* G. *krahn, kranich,* Icel. *trani,* Dan. *trane* (with *tr* for *kr*), W. *garan,* Gr. *geranos,* L. *grus,* the bird, also the lifting apparatus; from a root *gar,* seen in L. *garrio,* Gr. *geryō,* to call.] A large migratory grallatorial bird of several species, having long slender legs, a long neck, and powerful wings; a machine for raising great weights, and depositing them at some distance from their original place, the most common form consisting of a vertical shaft, with projecting arm or jib, at the outer end of which is a fixed pulley, carrying the rope or chain to receive the weight, which is raised by coiling the rope or chain round a cylinder; a movable iron arm or beam attached to the back or side of a fireplace for supporting a pot or kettle; a siphon or crooked pipe for drawing liquors out of a cask.—*v.i.—craned, craning.* To stretch out one's neck like a crane; hence, *hunting,* to look before one leaps; to pull up at a dangerous jump.—**crane fly,** *n.* A dipterous insect having very long legs, and lanceolate spreading wings; the daddy longlegs is a well-known species.—**crane's-bill,** *n.* The popular name given to the species of Geranium, from the long slender beak of their fruit.

cranium, krā′ni·um, *pl.* **crania,** krā′ni·a, *n.* [L.L. *cranium,* from Gr. *kranion,* a skull.] The bones which enclose the brain; the skull.—**cranial,** krā′ni·al, *a.* Relating to the cranium.—**craniofacial,** krā′ni·o·fā′shal, *a.* Pertaining to the cranium and face.—**craniology,** krā′ni·ol′o·ji, *n.* The knowledge of the cranium or skull; the art of determining the intellectual and moral peculiarities of individuals by the shape of their skulls; phrenology.—**craniological,** krā′ni·o·loj″ik·al, *a.* Pertaining to craniology.—**craniologist,** krā·ni·ol′o·jist, *n.* One who treats of or is versed in craniology.—**craniometer,** krā·ni·om′et·ėr, *n.* An instrument for measuring skulls.—**craniometrical,** krā′ni·o·met″ri·kal, *a.* Pertaining to craniometry.—**craniometry,** krā·ni·om′et·ri, *n.* The art of measuring skulls.

crank, krangk, *n.* [Allied to *cringe, crinkle;* D. *krinkel,* something bending, a curve, *krinkelen,* to bend.] An iron axis with the end bent like an elbow, serving as a handle for communicating circular motion (as in a grindstone), for changing circular motion into motion backward and forward or the reverse (steam engine), or for merely changing the direction of motion (as in bell hanging); any twisting or turning in speech; a whim; any perversity of action or manner; a crotchety or perverse person.—*v.t.* To bend into the shape of a crank; to furnish with a crank; to start by turning a crank.—*v.i.* To turn a crank.

crank, krangk, *a.* [A.Sax. *cranc,* weak, sick; D. and G. *krank,* Icel. *krankr,* sick, ill.] Liable to be overset, as a ship when she has not sufficient ballast to carry full sail; in a shaky or crazy condition; loose; disjointed.—**cranky,** krang′ki, *a.* Liable to overset; full of crotchets or whims; not to be depended on; unsteady; crazy.

cranny, kran′i, *n.* [Fr. *cran,* a notch, from L. *crena,* a notch; comp. G. *krinne,* a rent.] A small narrow opening, fissure, crevice, or chink, as in a wall or other substance.—*v.i.* To become intersected with or penetrated by crannies or clefts; to enter by crannies (*Shak.*).—**crannied,** kran′id, *p.* or *a.* Having chinks, fissures, or crannies.

crape, krāp, *n.* [Fr. *crêpe,* O.Fr. *crespe,* from L. *crispus,* curled. CRISP.] A thin transparent cloth with a crinkled surface; crepe; a band of black crepe worn in mourning.

crapulence, krap′ū·lens, *n.* [L. *crapulo,* intoxication.] Drunkenness; the sickness occasioned by intemperance.—**crapulent, crapulous,** krap′ū·lent, krap′ū·lus, *a.* Drunk; sick by intemperance; connected or associated with drunkenness.

crash, krash, *v.t.* [Imitative. Comp. *crack, clash, crush,* etc.] To break to pieces violently; to dash with tumult and violence.—*v.i.* To make the loud multifarious sound of a thing or things falling and breaking; or to make any similar noise.—*n.* The loud sound of a thing or things falling and breaking; a sound made by dashing; the collapse of a commercial undertaking; bankruptcy; failure.

crash, krash, *n.* [L. *crassus,* thick.] A coarse kind of linen cloth, mostly used for towels.

crasis, krā′sis, *n.* [Gr. *krasis,* a mixing.] *Med.* the mixture of the constituents of a fluid, as the blood; hence, temperament; constitution; *gram.* a figure by which two different letters are contracted into one long letter or into a diphthong: called also *Synaeresis.*

crass, kras, *a.* [L. *crassus.*] Gross; thick; coarse; not thin, nor fine: applied to fluids and solids; *fig.* gross; dense; stupid; obtuse.—**crassitude,** kras′i·tūd, *n.* Grossness; coarseness; thickness. — **crassness,** kras′nes, *n.* Grossness.

crate, krāt, *n.* [L. *crates,* wickerwork.] A kind of basket or hamper of wickerwork, used for the transportation of china, glass, etc.; also for fruit; framework made of wooden slats.—*v.t.* To pack in a crate.

crater, krā′tėr, *n.* [L. *crater,* from Gr. *kratēr,* a great cup, a mixing vessel, from *kerannymi,* to mix.] The orifice or mouth of a volcano; a hole made by a bomb or a meteorite.

craunch, kransh, *v.t.* [Imitative, same as *crunch, scranch.*] To crush with the teeth; to crunch.

cravat, kra·vat′, *n.* [Fr. *Cravate,* a Croat, and hence a cravat, because this piece of dress was adopted in the seventeenth century from the Croats who entered the French service.] A neckcloth; an article of muslin, silk, woolen, or other material worn by men about the neck.

crave, krāv, *v.t.—craved, craving.* [A.Sax. *crafian,* to ask—Icel. *krefja,* Sw. *kräfva,* Dan. *kraeve,* to crave, to ask.] To ask for with earnestness or importunity; to ask (a thing) with submission or humility; to beg, entreat, implore, solicit; to call for, as a gratification; to long for; to require or demand, as a passion or appetite.—*v.i.* To beg, ask, beseech, or implore; to long or hanker eagerly: with *for.*—**craver,** krā′vėr, *n.* One who craves.—**craving,** krā′ving, *n.* Vehement or inordinate desire; a longing.—*a.* Ardently or inordinately desirous or longing.

craven, krā′vn, *n.* [O.Fr. *cravanter,* to overthrow, from a L.L. *crepantare,* from L. *crepare,* to break; akin *crevice, crepitate.*] Formerly one vanquished in trial by battle, and yielding to the conqueror; hence, a recreant; a coward; a weak-hearted, spiritless fellow.—*a.* Cowardly; base.

craw, kra, *n.* [Of same origin as Dan. *kro,* D. *kraag,* G. *kragen,* the throat, craw.] The crop or first stomach of fowls; the stomach, in a general sense.

crawfish, *n.* The crayfish; also the spiny lobster, a marine crustacean.

crawl, kral, *v.i.* [Of same origin as Sw. *kråla,* also *krafla,* Icel. *krafla,* Dan. *kravle,* G. *krabbeln,* to crawl.] To move slowly by thrusting or drawing the body along the ground; to move on hands and knees; to move slowly or cautiously; to swarm with crawling things; to feel overrun by crawling things; to behave abjectly.—*n.* The act of crawling; a method of swimming consisting of double overarm strokes combined with fluttering leg movements; a creeping motion.—**crawler,** kra′lėr, *n.* One who or that which crawls;

a creeper; a reptile; a mean, cringing fellow.—**crawlingly,** krạ′ling‧li, *adv.* In a crawling manner.

crayfish, crawfish, krā′fish, krạ′fish, *n.* [A curious corruption of comparatively modern origin; formerly *crevise, creveys,* from O.Fr. *crevice,* O.H.G. *krebiz,* G. *krebs*—crab. CRAB.] The river lobster, a ten-footed crustacean found in streams, and resembling the lobster, but smaller, used as food; also the spiny lobster.

crayon, krā′on, *n.* [Fr. *crayon,* from *craie,* L. *creta,* chalk, whence *cretaceous.*] A pencil or cylinder of colored pipe clay, chalk, or charcoal, used in drawing upon paper; a composition pencil made of soap, resin, wax, and lampblack, used for drawing upon lithographic stones —*v.t.* To sketch with a crayon; hence, to sketch roughly.

craze, krāz, *v.t.*—*crazed, crazing.* [Same as Sw. *krasa,* to crush, break; Dan. *krase,* to crackle; from sound of crushing. Akin *crush, crash,* etc.] To break in pieces, grind or crush‡; to put out of order; to impair the natural force or energy of; to derange the intellect of; to render insane. —*v.i.* To become crazy or insane; to become shattered; to break down.— *n.* Craziness; an inordinate desire or longing; a passion; a wild fancy or notion.—**crazy,** krā′zi, *a.* Decrepit; feeble; shattered; unsound: of the body or any structure; disordered, deranged, weakened, or shattered in mind.—**crazily,** krā′zi‧li, *adv.* In a crazy manner.—**craziness,** krā′-zi‧nes, *n.* The state of being crazy; imbecility or weakness of intellect; derangement.

creak, krēk, *v.i.* [Imitative of a more acute and prolonged sound than *crack;* comp. Fr. *criquer,* to creak; W. *crecian,* to scream.] To make a sharp harsh grating sound of some continuance, as by the friction of hard substances.—*v.t.* To cause to make a harsh protracted noise.—*n.* A sharp, harsh, grating sound.

cream, krēm, *n.* [Fr. *crème,* from L.L. *cremum* (or *crema*), cream—a word suggested by L. *cremor,* thick juice or broth; It. Sp. and Pg. *crema,* cream.] Any part of a liquor that separates from the rest, rises, and collects on the surface; more particularly, the richer and butyraceous part of milk, which rises and forms a scum on the surface, as it is specifically lighter than the other part of the liquor; the best part of a thing; the choice part; a sweetmeat prepared from cream (as, ice *cream*).—*Cream of tartar,* the scum of a boiling solution of tartar; a salt obtained from the tartar of argol that forms on the inside of wine casks, frequently employed in medicine.—*v.t.* To skim; to take the cream off by skimming; to take off the best part of.—*v.i.* To gather cream; to gather a covering on the surface; to flower or mantle. (*Shak.*)—**creamy,** krē′mi, *a.* Full of cream; having the nature of or resembling cream.—**creaminess,** krē′mi‧nes, *n.* The state of being creamy.—**cream cheese,** *n.* A cheese

made with milk to which a certain quantity of cream is added.— **creamer,** krē′mėr, *n.* A pitcher for holding cream; a machine that separates cream from milk.—**creamery,** krē′mėr‧i, *n.* An establishment to which farmers send their milk to be made into butter and cheese.

crease, krēs, *n.* [Prob. related to O.Fr. *creast,* a line, ridge, or furrow.] A line or mark made by folding or doubling anything; hence, a similar mark, however produced; specifically, the name given to certain lines marking boundaries near the wickets in the game of cricket.—*v.t. creased, creasing.* To make a crease or mark in, as by folding or doubling.— **creasy,** krē′si, *a.* Full of creases; characterized by creases. (*Tenn.*)

crease, krēs, *n.* [Malay.] A Malay dagger.

creaser, krēs′ėr, *n.* A tool, or a sewing machine attachment for making creases on leather or cloth, as guides to see by; in *bookbinding,* a tool for making the band impression distinct on the back or for making blind lines or creases on covers.

create, krē‧āt′, *v.t.*—*created, creating.* [L. *creo, creatum,* to create; same root as Skr. *kri,* to make.] To originate or cause; to bring into being; to cause to exist; to make or form, by investing with a new character; to constitute; to appoint (to *create* a peer); to be the occasion of; to bring about; to cause; to produce (*create* a disturbance).—**creation,** krē‧ā′shon, *n.* The act of creating, producing, or causing to exist; especially, the act of bringing this world into existence; the act of investing with a new character; appointment; formation; the things created; that which is produced or caused to exist; the world; the universe.—**creational,** krē‧ā′shon‧al, *a.* Pertaining to creation.—**creative,** krē‧ā′tiv, *a.* Having the power to create, or exerting the act of creating. —**creator,** krē‧ā′tėr, *n.* [L.] One who, or that which, creates, produces, causes, or constitutes; [*cap.*] distinctively, the almighty Maker of all things.—**creatorship,** krē‧ā′tėr‧ship, *n.* The state or condition of a creator. —**creature,** krē′chėr, *n.* [O.Fr. *creature,* L.L. *creatura.*] Anything created‡; a thing‡; a created being: any living being; a human being, in contempt or endearment; a person who owes his rise and fortune to another; one who is entirely subject to the will or influence of another; a mere tool.—*a.* Of or belonging to the body (*creature* comforts).

creatic, krē‧at′ik, *a.* [Gr. *kreas, kreatos,* flesh.] Relating to flesh or animal food.—**creatin,** krē′a‧tin, *n.* Substances obtained from animal flesh by chemical processes.

creche, krāsh, *n.* [Fr. *crèche,* manger.] An institution or establishment where, for a small payment, children are fed and taken care of during the day, in cases where the mothers daily go from home to work; an asylum for foundlings; a representation of the manger and the Holy Family.

credence, krē′dens, *n.* [L.L. *credentia,* belief, from L. *credens, credentis,* pp. of *credo,* to believe. CREED.] Reliance on evidence derived from other sources than personal knowledge, as from the testimony of others; belief or credit (to give a story *credence*); the small table by the side of the altar or communion table, on which the bread and wine are placed before they are consecrated: called also *Credence-table.*—**credendum,** kri‧den′dum, *n.* pl. **credenda,** kri‧den′da. [L.] A thing to be believed; an article of faith.—**credent,**† krē′dent, *a.* Believing; giving credit; easy of belief; having credit; not to be questioned. (*Shak.*)—**credential,** kri‧den′shal, *n.* That which gives a title or claim to confidence†; *pl.* testimonials or documents given to a person as the warrant on which a belief, credit, or authority is claimed for him among strangers, such as the documents given to an ambassador when sent to a foreign court.

credible, kred′i‧bl, *a.* [L. *credibilis.*] Capable of being believed; such as one may believe; worthy of credit, reliance, or confidence as to truth and correctness: applied to persons and things.—**credibility, credibleness,** kred‧i‧bil′i‧ti, kred′i‧bl‧nes, *n.* The state or quality of being credible.—**credibly,** kred′i‧bli, *adv.* In a credible manner; so as to command belief (to be *credibly* informed).

credit, kred′it, *n.* [Fr. *crédit;* L. *creditum.* CREED.] Reliance on testimony; belief; faith; trust; good opinion founded on a belief of a man's veracity, integrity, abilities, and virtue; reputation derived from the confidence of others; esteem; honor; what brings some honor or estimation; reputation for commercial stability or solvency; the selling of goods or lending of money in confidence of future payment; trust; *bookkeeping,* the side of an account in which payment or other item lessening the claim against a debtor is entered: opposed to *debit;* the time given for payment for goods sold on trust.—*v.t.* To believe; to confide in the truth of; to sell, or lend in confidence of future payment; to trust; to enter upon the credit side of an account; to give credit for.— *Letter of credit,* an order given by bankers or others at one place to enable a specified person to receive money from their agents at another place.—**creditable,** kred′i‧ta‧bl, *a.* Accompanied with reputation and esteem; the cause of credit or honor; honorable; estimable.—**creditability,** kred′i‧ta‧bil′′i‧ti, *n.* The quality of being creditable.—**creditably,** kred′-i‧ta‧bli, *adv.* Reputably; with credit; without disgrace.—**creditor,** kred′-i‧tėr, *n.* [L.] One who gives goods or money on credit; one to whom money is due; one having a just claim for money; correlative to *debtor.*

credulous, kred′ū‧lus, *a.* [L. *credulus,* from *credo,* to believe.] Apt to believe without sufficient evidence; unsuspecting; easily deceived.—**credulously,** kred′ū‧lus‧li, *adv.* With credulity.—**credulousness, credulity,** kred′ū·lus·nes, kre·dū′li·ti, n. The state or quality of being credulous; disposition or readiness to believe without sufficient evidence.

creed, krēd, n. [A.Sax. *creda,* from L. *credo,* I believe, the first word of the Apostles' Creed, whence also *credence, credit, credible,* also *grant, recreant.*] A brief and authoritative summary of the articles of Christian faith; hence, a statement or profession of fundamental points of belief; a system of principles of any kind which are believed or professed.

creek, krēk, n. [O.E. *creke, cryke,* a creek, a bay; D. *kreek,* Icel. *kriki,* a crack, a corner; akin to *crook.*] A small inlet, bay, or cove; a recess in the shore of the sea or of a river; a stream of water smaller than a river but larger than a brook; a narrow winding passage.

creel, krēl, n, [Gael. *craidhleag;* same root as *cradle.*] An osier basket or pannier; specifically, a large deep fish basket for carrying on the back.

creep, krēp, v.i. pret. et pp. *crept.* [A.Sax. *creópan*—D. *kruipen,* Icel. *krjúpa,* Sw. *krypa,* Dan. *krybe,* to creep or crawl; akin *cripple, cramp.*] To move with the belly on the ground or any surface, as a reptile, or as many insects with feet and very short legs; to crawl; to move along a surface in growth (as a vine); to move slowly, feebly, or timorously; to move slowly and insensibly, as time; to move secretly or insidiously; to move or behave with extreme servility or humility; to cringe; to fawn; to have a sensation such as might be caused by worms or insects creeping on the skin.—**creeper,** krē′pėr, n. One who or that which creeps; a creeping plant, which moves along the surface of the earth, or attaches itself to some other body, as ivy; an instrument of iron with hooks or claws for dragging the bottom of a well, river, or harbor; a popular name of birds which resemble the woodpeckers in their habits of creeping on the stems of trees in quest of insect prey.—n. The act of creeping, or moving slowly and insensibly.

creese, krēs, n. A crease or Malay dagger.

cremate, kri·māt′, v.t.—*cremated, cremating.* [L. *cremo, crematum,* to burn.] To burn; to dispose of (a human body) by burning instead of interring.—**cremation,** kri·mā′shon, n. The act or custom of cremating; the burning of a dead body instead of burial.—**crematory,** krē′ma·to·ri, a. Connected with or employed in cremation.—n. A place for cremation.

Cremona, kri·mō′na, n. A general name given to the unrivalled violins made at *Cremona* in North Italy in the seventeenth and eighteenth centuries.

crenate, crenated, krē′nāt, kri′nā·ted, a. [L. *crenatus,* notched, *crena,* a notch.] Notched; intented; scalloped; *bot.* applied to a leaf having its margin cut into even and rounded notches or scallops.—**crenature,** kren′a·chėr, n. A tooth of a crenate leaf, or any other part that is crenate.

crenel, crenelle, kren′el, kre·nel′, n. [O.Fr. *crenel,* from L. *crena,* a notch.] An embrasure in an embattled parapet or breastwork to fire through; an indentation; a notch.—**crenelate,** kren′e·lāt, v.t. To furnish with crenels or similar openings; to embattle.—**crenelation,** krē·nel·lā′shon, n. The act of crenelating: a crenel or indentation.—**crenulate, crenulated,** kre′nū·lāt, kre′nū·lā·ted, a. Having the edge cut into very small scallops.

Creole, krē′ōl, n. [Fr. *créole,* Sp. *criollo;* said to be of Negro origin.] A white descendant of early French settlers in Louisiana; a Latin American descended from French or Spanish conquerors; [*often not cap.*] a person of mixed Spanish, French, and Negro ancestry.—a. Of or relating to Creoles.

creosote, krē′ō·sōt, n. A heavy, oily colorless liquid of strong odor obtained from wood tar, used as a powerful antiseptic.

crepe, krāp, n. [Fr. *crêpe.*] Thin crinkled fabric, often of silk, but also of other textiles; crape.—*Crepe paper,* paper resembling crepe.

crepitate, krep′i·tāt, v.i.—*crepitated, crepitating.* [L. *crepito, crepitatum,* freq. from *crepo,* to crackle (whence *crevice*).] To make a crackling noise; to rattle.—**crepitation,** krep′i·tā″shon, n.

crepuscular, kri·pus′kū·lėr, a. [L. *crepusculum,* twilight.] Pertaining to twilight; glimmering; flying or appearing in the twilight or evening, or before sunrise, as certain insects.

crescendo, kre·shen′dō. [It.] *Mus.* a term signifying that the notes of the passage are to be gradually swelled: usually written *Cres.,* and marked thus ‹.

crescent, kres′ent, a. [L. *crescens, crescentis,* from *cresco,* to grow, seen also in *increase, decrease, accrue, concrete,* etc.] Increasing; growing; waxing. (*Mil.*)—n. The increasing or new moon, which, when receding from the sun, shows a curving rim of light terminating in points or horns; anything shaped like a new moon, as a range of buildings whose fronts form a concave curve; the figure or likeness of the new moon, as that borne in the Turkish flag or national standard; the standard itself, and figuratively, the Turkish power.

cress, kres, n. [A.Sax. *caerse, cresse* —D. *kers,* G. *kresse,* Sw. *karse.*] The name of various plants, mostly cruciferous, in general use as a salad, such as water cress, common in streams, and having a pungent taste; garden cress, a dwarf cultivated species; Indian cress, a showy garden annual whose fruits are made into pickles.

cresset, kres′et, n. [O.Fr. *crusset, crasset;* akin to E. *cruse,* G. *kruse,* a jar.] A term most commonly applied to a lamp or firepan suspended on pivots and carried on a pole, or to a beacon light in a kind of iron basket; also a large lamp formerly hung in churches, etc.

crest, krest, n. [O.Fr. *creste,* L. *crista,* a crest.] A tuft or other excrescence upon the top of an animal's head, as the comb of a cock, etc.; anything resembling, suggestive of, or occupying the same relative position as a crest, as the plume or tuft of feathers, or the like, affixed to the top of the helmet; *her.* a figure placed upon a wreath, coronet, or cap of maintenance above both helmet and shield; the foamy, feather-like top of a wave; the highest part or summit of a hill, ridge, slope, or the like; the rising part of a horse's neck; *fig.* pride, high spirit, courage, daring (*Shak.*).—v.t. To furnish with a crest; to serve as a crest for; to adorn as with a plume or crest.—**crested,** kres′ted, a. Furnished with a crest or crests.—**crestless,** krest′les, a. Without a crest; without a family crest, and hence of low birth (*Shak.*).—**crestfallen,** a. Dejected; sunk; bowed; dispirited; spiritless.

cretaceous, kri·tā′shus, a. [L. *cretaceus,* from *creta,* chalk.] Composed of or having the qualities of chalk; like chalk; abounding with chalk; chalky.—*Cretaceous group,* in *geol.* the upper strata of the secondary series, immediately below the tertiary series, and superincumbent on the oölite system, containing immense chalk beds.

cretin, krē′tin, n. [Swiss dial. *crétin,* a Christian, a man, from L. *christianus.*] One afflicted with cretinism.—**cretinism,** krē′tin·izm, n. A congenital condition due to thyroid deficiency and characterized by physical and mental stunting.

cretonne, kri·ton′, n. [Fr.] A cotton cloth with various textures of surface printed with pictorial and other patterns, and used for curtains, covering furniture, etc.

crevasse, kre·vas′, n. [Fr. *crevasse.* CREVICE.] A fissure or rent: generally applied to a fissure across a glacier, and in the United States to a breach in the embankment of a river.

crevice, krev′is, n. [Fr. *crevasse,* from *crever,* L. *crepare,* to burst, to crack; akin *craven, crepitate, decrepit.*] A crack; a cleft; a fissure; a cranny; a rent.—v.t. To crack; to flaw.

crew, krū, n. [From O. Icel. *krú,* a swarm; or for old *accrue,* number added, company. ACCRUE.] A company of people; an assemblage; a crowd; a band; a gang; a herd; a horde; a company; the company of seamen who man a ship, vessel, or boat; the company belonging to a vessel.

crew, krū, pret. of *crow.*

crewel, krū′el, n. [From D. *krul,* a curl.] A kind of fine worsted or thread of silk or wool, used in embroidery and fancy work.

crib, krib, n. [A.Sax. *crib, cribb,* D. *kribbe,* Dan. *krybbe,* Icel. and Sw. *krubba,* G. *krippe,* a crib.] A small habitation or cottage; a hovel; the manger or rack of a stable or house for cattle; a feeding place for cattle; a small frame or bed for a child to sleep in; a theft, or the thing stolen (*colloq.*); a literal translation of a classic author for the use of students (*colloq.*); in the game of cribbage, a set of cards made up of two thrown from the hand of each player.—*v.t.* cribbed, cribbing. To shut or confine in a narrow habitation; to cage (*Shak.*), to pilfer or purloin (*colloq.*).—**cribbage**, krib´ij, *n.* A game at cards played with the whole pack by two, three, or four persons: so called because the dealer receives a *crib*, or additional hand partly drawn from the hands of his opponent or opponents.—*Cribbage board*, a board used for marking in the game of cribbage.

crick, krik, *n.* [Akin to *crook*.] A spasmodic affection of some part of the body, as of the neck or back, making motion of the part difficult.

cricket, krik´et, *n.* [O.Fr. *criquet*, from its sharp creaking sound; comp. D. *kriek*, a cricket, *krieken*, to chirp. Akin *creak*, *crack*.] An orthopterous insect of several species, nearly allied to the grasshoppers, noted for the chirping or creaking sound produced by the friction of the bases of its wing cases against each other.

cricket, krik´et, *n.* [Fr. *criquet*, a kind of game.] A favorite open-air game played in England, Australia, and other British possessions, generally by two sides of eleven each, with bats, ball, and wickets.—*v.i.* To engage in the game of cricket.

cricoid, krī´koid, *a.* [Gr. *krikos*, a ring, and *eidos*, appearance.] Ring-like: applied to a round ringlike cartilage of the larynx.

crier, krī´ėr, *n.* See CRY.

crime, krīm, *n.* [Fr. *crime*, L. *crimen*, an accusation, a crime; allied to *cerno*, to sift, *cribrum*, a sieve; Gr. *krinō*, to separate, judge, condemn.] A violation of a law whether human or divine; specifically, a gross violation of law, as distinguished from a misdemeanor, trespass, or other slight offense; any great wickedness or iniquity; a foul wrong; offense.—**criminal**, krim´i·nal, *a.* Guilty of a crime; culpable; wicked; iniquitous; atrocious; abandoned; villainous; felonious; nefarious; partaking of the nature of a crime; involving a crime; that violates public law, divine or human; relating to crime: opposed to *civil*.—*Criminal conversation*, in *law*, adultery; illicit intercourse with a married woman.—*n.* A person guilty of crime; a person indicted or charged with a public offense and found guilty; a culprit; a malefactor.—**criminality**, krim·i·nal´i·ti, *n.* The quality or state of being criminal; that which constitutes a crime; guiltiness.—**criminally**, krim´i·nal·li, *adv.* In a criminal or wicked manner.—**criminate**, krim´i·nāt, *v.t.*—criminated, criminating. [L. *criminor*, *criminatus*.] To accuse or charge with a crime; to involve in a crime or the consequences of a crime.—**crimination**, krim·i·nā´shon, *n.* The act of criminating; accusation; charge.—**criminative**, **criminatory**, krim´i·nā·tiv, krim´i·

na·to·ri, *a.* Relating to accusation; accusing.—**criminology**, krim´i·nol´´o·ji, *n.* The science of crime.

crimp, krimp, *v.t.* [A lighter form of *cramp*; D. *krimpen*, Dan. *krympe*, G. *krimpen*, to shrink; akin *crumple*.] To curl or crisp, as the hair; to flute or make regular ridges on, as on a frill; to crimple; to pinch and hold; to seize; hence, to decoy for service in the army or navy (see noun); *cookery*, to gash the flesh of a live fish with a knife, to give it greater hardness and make it more crisp.—*n.* One who decoys another into the naval or military service; one who decoys sailors by treating, advancing money, boarding and lodging, giving goods on credit, etc., and when he has them in his power, induces them to engage with a shipmaster whom it is the crimp's interest to serve.

crimson, krim´zn, *n.* [O.Fr. *cramoisin*, from L.L. *carmesinus*, from Ar. *kermez*, *qirmiz*, the kermes insect, which yields the dye; akin *carmine*.] A deep red color; a rich red slightly tinged with blue; a red color in general.—*a.* Of a deep red color. —*v.t.* To dye with crimson; to make red.—*v.i.* To become of a crimson color; to be tinged with red; to blush.

cringe, krinj, *v.i.* cringed, cringing. [A.Sax. *cringan*, *crincan*, to cringe, succumb, from root of *crank*, *crinkle*, etc.] To bend or crouch with servility; to fawn; to stoop or truckle. —*n.* A mean or fawning obeisance. —*v.t.*‡ To contract; to draw together; to distort.—**cringer**, krin´jėr, *n.* One who cringes or bows and flatters with servility.

cringle, kring´gl, *n.* [D. *kring*, *krinkel*, a curl, bend, ring; Icel. *kringla*, an orb, from *kringr*, a circle; A.Sax. *kring*, a ring. Akin *ring*, *cringe*.] A withe for fastening a gate; *naut.* an iron ring, or a short rope worked into the boltrope of a sail so as to form a ring or eye, etc.

crinite, krī´nīt, *a.* [L. *crinitus*, from *crinis*, hair.] Having the appearance of a tuft of hair†; *bot.* having tufts of long weak hairs on the surface.

crinkle, kring´kl, *v.i.*—crinkled, crinkling. [D. *krinkelen*, to turn or wind; akin *crank*.] To turn or wind; to bend; to wrinkle; to run in and out in little or short bends or turns; to curl.—*v.t.* To form with short turns or wrinkles; to make with many flexures.—*n.* A wrinkle; a winding or turn; sinuosity.

crinoid, krī´noid, *n.* [Gr. *krinon*, a lily, *eidos*, likeness.] A lily star or sea lily; one of an order of echinoderms having starshaped bodies, supported by a long, slender, calcareous jointed stem; most of the species are fossil.—**crinoid**, krī´noid, *a.* Containing or consisting of the fossil remains of crinoids.

crinoline, krin´o·lin, *n.* [Fr., from *crin*, L. *crinis*, hair, and *lin*, L. *linum*, flax.] A stiff fabric of horsehair, etc.; a skirt or petticoat stiffened by horsehair, hoops, etc.

criosphinx, krī´ō·sfingks, *n.* [Gr. *krios*, a ram, and *sphinx*, sphinx.] A

sphinx having the head of a ram.

cripple, krip´l, *n.* [A.Sax. *crypel*—G. *krüppel*, Icel. *kryppil*, a cripple, D. *kreupel*, lame; from stem of *creep*.] One who halts or limps; one who has lost or never enjoyed the use of his limbs; a lame person.—*a.* Lame.—*v.t.*—crippled, crippling. To disable by injuring the limbs, particularly the legs or feet; to lame; to deprive of the power of exertion; to disable (a *crippled* fleet).

crisis, krī´sis, *n.* pl. **crises**, krī´sēz. [L. *crisis*, Gr. *krisis*, from the root of *krinō*, to separate, to determine. CRIME.] The change of a disease which indicates recovery or death; the decisive state of things, or the point of time when an affair has reached its height, and must soon terminate or suffer a material change; turning point; conjuncture.

crisp, krisp, *a.* [A.Sax. *crisp*, *crips*, from L. *crispus*, curled, crisp.] Curling in small stiff or firm curls; indented or winding†; easily broken or crumbled; brittle; friable; possessing a certain degree of firmness and freshness; fresh; brisk, effervescing or foaming; sparkling.—*v.t.* To curl; to contract or form into ringlets; to wrinkle or curl into little undulations; to ripple.—*v.i.* To form little curls or undulations; to curl. (*Tenn.*) —**crisper**, kris´pėr, *n.* One who or that which crisps or curls; an instrument for friezing or crisping cloth. —**crisply**, krisp´li, *adv.* In a crisp manner.—**crispness**, krisp´nes, *n.* State of being crisp.—**crispy**, kris´pi, *a.* Curled; formed into ringlets; brittle; dried so as to break short.

cristate, cristated, kris´tāt, kris´tā·ted, *a.* [L. *cristatus*, from *crista*, a crest.] *Bot.* having an appendage like a crest or tuft, as some anthers and flowers; crested; tufted.

criterion, krī·tē´ri·on, *n.* pl. **criteria**, krī·tē´ri·a. [Gr. *kriterion*, from root of *krinō*, to judge. CRIME.] A standard of judging; any established law, rule, principle, or fact by which a correct judgment may be formed.

critic, krit´ik, *n.* [L. *criticus*, Gr. *kritikos*, from *kritēs*, a judge, from *krinō*, to judge. CRIME.] A person skilled in judging of the merit of literary works; a judge of merit or excellence in the fine arts generally; a writer whose chief function it is to pass judgment on matters of literature and art; a reviewer; one who judges with severity; one who censures or finds fault.—**critical**, krit´i·kal, *a.* Relating to criticism; belonging to the art of a critic; passing judgment upon literary and artistic matters; inclined to make nice distinctions; nicely judicious; exact; fastidious; inclined to find fault or to judge with severity: *med.* pertaining to the crisis or turning point of a disease; pertaining to any crisis; decisive; important, as regards consequences (a *critical* time or juncture); momentous; attended with danger or risk; dangerous; hazardous (a *critical* undertaking.—*Critical angle. Optics*, the angle of incidence of a ray passing from one medium into a less refracting

---

ch, *ch*ain; *ch*, Sc. lo*ch*; g, *g*o; j, *j*ob; ng, si*ng*; TH, *th*en; th, *th*in; w, *w*ig; hw, *wh*ig; zh, a*z*ure.

medium, when it emerges along the bounding surface.—*Critical temperature*, that temperature of a gas above which no pressure, however great, can liquefy it.—**critically,** kri'tik·al·li, *adv.* In a critical manner; with nice discernment or scrutiny; at the crisis: at the exact time; in a critical situation, place, or condition.—**criticalness,** krit'i·kal·nes, *n.* The state of being critical.—**criticaster,** krit'i·kas·tėr. *n.* A small or inferior critic.—**criticize,** krit'i·siz, *v.i.*—*criticized, criticizing.* To judge critically, estimating beauties and defects; to pick out faults; to utter censure.—*v.i.* To examine or judge critically; to notice beauties and blemishes or faults in; to pass judgment on with respect to merit or blame; to animadvert upon.—**criticizable,** krit'i·si·za·bl, *a.* Capable of being criticized.—**criticism,** krit'i·sizm, *n.* The art of judging with propriety of the beauties and faults of a literary performance or of any production in the fine arts; the art of judging on the merit of any performance; a critical judgment; a detailed critical examination; a critique.—**critique,** kri·tēk', *n.* [Fr.] A written estimate of the merits of a performance, especially of a literary or artistic performance; a criticism.

croak, krōk, *v.i.* [Purely imitative, like M.H.G. *krochzen,* G. *krächzen,* Fr. *croasser,* L. *crocire, crocitare,* Gr. *krōzein,* to croak.] To make a low, hoarse noise in the throat, as a frog, a raven, or crow; to produce any low harsh sound; to speak with a low, hollow voice; to forebode evil; to complain; to grumble.—*v.t.* To utter in a low hollow voice; to murmur out; to announce or herald by croaking.—*n.* The low, harsh sound uttered by a frog or a raven, or a like sound.—**croaker,** krō'kėr, *n.* One that croaks, murmurs, or grumbles; one who complains unreasonably; one who takes a desponding view of everything; an alarmist. —**croaky,** krō'ki, *a.* Having or uttering a low harsh sound; hoarse; grumbling.

crochet, krō·shā', *n.* [Fr., dim. of *croc,* a hook.] A species of knitting performed by means of a small hook, the material being worsted, cotton, or silk.—*v.t.* To knit in this style.

crocidolite, krō·sid'o·līt, *n.* [Gr. *krokis,* nap of cloth, *lithos,* stone.] A sort of fibrous quartz, made into trinkets, etc.

crock, krok, *n.* [A.Sax. *crocca*—D. *kruik,* Icel. *krukka,* Dan. *krukke,* G. *krug,* an earthen vessel, pitcher.] An earthen vessel; a pot or pitcher; the soot or smut from pots, kettles, etc.—**crockery,** krok'ėr·i, *n.* Earthenware; vessels formed of clay, glazed and baked.

crocket, krok'et, *n.* [Akin to *crochet* or to *crook.*] An architectural ornament, usually in imitation of curved and bent foliage, etc., placed on the angles of the inclined sides of pinnacles, canopies, gables, etc.; one of the terminal snags on a stag's horn.

crocodile, krok'o·dīl, *n.* [L. *crocodilus,* Gr. *krokodeilos.*] A large aquatic reptile of the lizard kind, sometimes reaching the length of 30 feet, and having a long and powerful tail flattened at the sides, the body covered with square bony plates, the jaws long, and the gape of enormous width; the best known species haunt the Nile.—*a.* Of or pertaining to or like a crocodile.— *Crocodile tears,* false or affected tears: in allusion to the old fiction that crocodiles shed tears over their victims.—**crocodilian,** krok·o·dil'i·an, *a.* Relating to the crocodile.— **crocodilian,** *n.* A reptile of the order (*Crocodilia*) which includes the true crocodile, the alligator, the gavial, etc.

crocus, krō'kus, *n.* [L. *crocus,* Gr. *krokos,* saffron, also the *crocus.*] A beautiful genus of plants of the iris family; deep yellow; saffron.

Cro-Magnon, krō·mag'non, *a.* [*Cro-Magnon,* a cave near Les Eyzies, France.] Pertaining to a group of tall, erect, prehistoric people who lived in southwestern Europe and used bone and stone implements.— *n.* One of this group.

cromlech, krom'lek, *n.* [W. *cromlech* —*crom,* bent, concave, and *llech,* a flat stone.] An ancient structure (probably a sepulchral monument) consisting of two or more large unhewn stones fixed upright in the ground supporting a large flat stone in a horizontal position.

crone, krōn, *n.* [Formerly *crony,* from D. *karonje,* a hussy, a slut, lit. a carrion. CARRION.] A contemptuous term for an old woman.—**crony,** krō'ni, *n.* A crone‡; an intimate companion; an associate.

crony, krō'ni, *n.* [Origin uncertain.] An intimate companion; an associate.

crook, kruk, *n.* [Same as Icel. *krókr,* Sw. *krok,* Dan. *krog,* a hook or crook; D. *kruk,* a crutch; comp. W. *crwg,* Gael. *crocan,* a crook, a hook. Akin *crutch, crouch.*] Any bend, turn, or curve; curvature; flexure; any bent or curved instrument; especially, a shepherd's staff, curving at the end, or the staff of a bishop or abbot, fashioned in the form of a shepherd's staff, as a symbol of his sway over and care for his flock; a pastoral staff; a small curved tube applied to a trumpet, horn, etc., to change its key; an artifice; a trick; a swindler, sharper.—*v.t.* To bend; to turn from a straight line; to make a curve or hook.— *v.i.* To bend or be bent; to be turned from a straight line. —**crooked,** kru̦'ked, *a.* Deviating from a straight line; bent, curved, or winding; wry or deformed; deviating from the path of rectitude; perverse, deceitful, devious, or froward.—**crookedly,** kru̦'ked·li, *adv.* In a crooked, curved, or perverse manner.—**crookedness,** kru̦'ked·nes, *n.* The state or quality of being crooked.

croon, krōn, *v.t.* and *i.* [Imitative of sound; D. *kreunen,* to groan, to lament.] To sing in a low humming tone; to hum; to utter a low, continued, plaintive sound.

crop, krop, *n.* [A.Sax. *crop,* top, bunch, craw of a bird; D. *krop,* G. *kropf,* a bird's crop; Icel. *kroppr,* a hump, bunch.] The first stomach of a fowl; the craw; that which is cropped, cut, or gathered from a single field; the quantity of a particular kind of grain, fruit, etc., obtained from a single field or in a single season; the corn or fruits of the earth collected; harvest; corn and other cultivated plants while growing; the act of cutting or clipping off, as hair.—*Hunting crop,* a riding whip with loop at end, with no lash.— *Neck and crop,* bodily; altogether; bag and baggage.—*v.t.*—*cropped, cropping.* To cut off the ends of; to eat off or browse; to pull off; to pluck; to mow: to reap; to cause to bear a crop; to raise crops on.—*v.i.* To yield harvest‡. (*Shak.*)—*To crop out,* to appear on the surface; to appear incidentally and undesignedly; to come to light.—**cropper,** krop'ėr, *n.* A breed of pigeons with a large crop; one who raises crops, generally receiving his wages in the form of shares of the crops. Known also as a *sharecropper.*

croquet, krō·kā', *n.* [Fr. *croquer,* to crack.] An open-air game played by two or more persons with mallets, balls, pegs or posts, and a series of iron hoops or arches, the object of each party being to drive their balls through the hoops and against the posts in a certain order before their opponents.

crore, krōr, *n.* In the East Indies, ten millions (a *crore* of rupees).

crosier, *n.* See CROZIER.

cross, kros, *n.* [Prov. *cros,* Fr. *croix,* from L. *crux, crucis,* a cross used as a gibbet, from same root as that of W. *crog,* a cross, *crwg,* a hook; Ir. *crohaim,* to hang; Gael. *crocan,* a hook.] An instrument on which malefactors were anciently put to death, consisting of two pieces of timber placed across each other, either in form of +, T, or ×, variously modified, such as [*cap.*] that on which Christ suffered; hence, the symbol of the Christian religion; and hence, *fig.* the religion itself; an ornament in the form of a cross; a monument with a cross upon it to excite devotion, such as were anciently set in market places; any figure, mark, or sign in the form of a cross, or formed by two lines crossing each other, such as the mark made instead of a signature by those who cannot write; anything that thwarts, obstructs, or perplexes; hindrance, vexation, misfortune, or opposition; a mixing of breeds; a hybrid.—*a.* Transverse; passing from side to side; falling athwart; adverse; thwarting; untoward; snappish; perverse; intractable; peevish; fretful; ill-humored; contrary; contradictory; perplexing; made or produced by the opposite party, as a *cross* question or examination.— *v.t.* To draw or run a line or lay a body across another; to erase by marking crosses on or over; to cancel; to make the sign of the cross upon; to pass from side to side of; to pass or move over; to thwart, obstruct, hinder, embarrass; to contradict; to counteract; to clash with; to be inconsistent with; to cause to interbreed; to mix the breed of.—*v.i.* To lie or be athwart; to move or pass across.—*To cross one's path*, to thwart or oppose one's interest, purpose, designs, etc.; to stand in one's way.—*Crossed check*, in Britain, a check crossed with two lines, between which may be written the name of a banking firm or the words ' and Co. ', such marks being made as an additional security that the sum shall be paid to the proper party.—**crossing**, kros'ing, *n.* The act of one who crosses; an intersection; a place specially set apart or adapted for passing across, as on a street or line of rails.—**crosslet**, kros'let, *n.* A little cross.—**crossly**, kros'li, *adv.* In a cross manner; athwart; transversely; *fig.* adversely; in opposition; unfortunately; peevishly; fretfully.—**crossness**, kros'nes, *n.* The state or quality of being cross; peevishness; ill-humor; fretfulness; perverseness.—**crosswise**, kros'wiz, *adv.* In the form of a cross; across.—**crossbill**, *n.* A bird of several species belonging to the finch family, the mandibles of whose bill curve opposite ways and cross each other at the points.—**crossbones**, *n. pl.* A symbol of death, consisting of two human thigh or arm bones placed crosswise, generally in conjunction with a skull.—**crossbow**, *n.* An ancient missile weapon formed by placing a bow athwart a stock.—**crossbred**, *a.* A term applied to an animal produced from a male and female of different breeds.—**crossbreed**, *n.* A breed produced from parents of different breeds.—**crossbreeding**, *n.* The system of breeding animals, such as horses, cattle, dogs, and sheep, from individuals of two different strains or varieties.—**crosscut**, *v.t.* To cut across.—*Crosscut saw*, a saw adapted for cutting timber across the grain.—**cross-examine**, *v.t.* To examine a witness of one party by the opposite party in the suit or his counsel.—**cross-examination**, *n.* The examination or interrogation of a witness called by one party by the opposite party or his counsel.—**cross-eye**, *n.* That sort of squint by which both eyes turn toward the nose.—**cross-fertilization**, *n. Bot.* the fertilization of the ovules of one plant by the pollen of another; the fecundation of a pistilliferous plant by a staminiferous one, which is effected by the agency of insects, the action of the wind, water, etc.—**cross fire**, *n. Milit.* a term used to denote that the lines of fire from two or more parts of a work cross one another.—**cross-grained**, *a.* Having the grain or fibers transverse or irregular, as timber; *fig.* perverse; intractable; crabbed.—**crosshatching**, *n.* Engraved lines which cross each other

regularly to increase or modify the depth of shadow.—**crosshead**, *n.* A beam or rod stretching across the end of the piston of a steam engine and moving between parallel guides.—**cross-pollination**, *n.* Same as *Cross-fertilization.*—**cross-purpose**, *n.* A contrary purpose; a misunderstanding; an inconsistency; *pl.* a sort of conversational game consisting in the mixing up of questions and answers.—*To be at cross-purposes*, to misunderstand each other, and so to act counter without intending it.—**cross-question**, *v.t.* To cross-examine.—**cross reference**, *n.* A reference from one part of a book to another where additional information on the subject is to be had.—**crossroad**, *n.* A road that crosses another, or the place where one road intersects another; a byroad. —**cross section**, *n.* Strictly, the cutting of any body at right angles to its length, but often used to denote the area of the surface thus exposed. —**crosstree**, *n. pl. Naut.* horizontal pieces of timber at the upper ends of the lower and top masts, to sustain the frame of the tops and extend the shrouds.

crotch, kroch, *n.* [Same as CRUTCH.] A fork or forking; the parting of two branches.

crotchet, kroch'et, *n.* [Fr. *crochet*, dim. from *croc*, a hook. CROCHET, CROOK.] A peculiar turn of the mind; a whim or fancy; a perverse conceit; *print.* a bracket; *music*, a black-faced note with a stem.— **crotchety**, kroch'e·ti, *a.* Full of crotchets; whimsical; fanciful; odd. —**crotchetiness**, kroch'e·ti·nes, *n.* The state of being crotchety.

croton, krō'ton, *n.* [Gr. *krotōn*, a tick, from the appearance of the seeds.] A genus of East Indian shrubs from the seeds of which is extracted an oil of active and dangerous purgative properties, and which, when applied externally, acts as an irritant and suppurative.

crouch, krouch, *v.i.* [A softened form of *crook*, with modification of meaning.] To bend down; to stoop low; to lie close to the ground, as an animal; to bend servilely; to stoop meanly; to fawn; to cringe.—*v.t.* To bend or cause to bend lowly.

croup, krōp, *n.* [Fr. *croupe*, the rump, croup. Same origin as *crop*.] The rump or buttocks of certain animals, especially of a horse; hence, the place behind the saddle.

croup, krōp, *n.* [Sc. *croup*, *roup*, hoarseness; allied to Goth. *hropjan*, to croak, to call; A.Sax. *hreópan*, to call.] A dangerous disease mostly attacking children, and consisting of inflammatory affection of the windpipe, accompanied with a short barking cough and difficult respiration, generally brought on by exposure to cold.

croupier, krō'pi·êr, *n.* [Fr. *croupier*, from *croupe*, the rump or hinder part.] One who superintends and collects and pays the money at a gaming table; one who at a public dinner party sits at the lower end

of the table as assistant chairman.

crow, krō, *n.* [A.Sax. *cráwe*, a crow, *cráwan*, to crow or croak, from the cry; like G. *krähe*, a crow, *krähen*, to crow; Goth. *kruk*, a croaking; L. *crocio*, Gr. *krazō*, to croak. Comp. *crake*, *croak*.] The general name of such conirostral birds as the raven, rook, jackdaw, carrion crow, hooded crow, etc.; usually of a black color, and having the voice harsh and croaking; the cry of the cock; a crowbar (which see).— *As the crow flies*, in a direction straight forward, resembling the flight of the crow.—*To have a crow to pluck with one*, to have something demanding explanation from one; to have some fault to find with one; to have a disagreeable matter to settle.—*v.i.* crowed or crew; pp. crowed. [A.Sax. *cráwan.*] To cry or make a noise as a cock in joy, gaiety, or defiance; to boast in triumph; to vaunt; to vapor; to swagger; to utter a sound expressive of pleasure, as a child.—**crowbar**, krō'bär, *n.* A bar of iron with a bent and sometimes forked end, used as a lever for forcing open doors or raising weights.—**crowfoot**, *n. Naut.* a complication of small cords spreading out from a long block, used to suspend the awnings, etc.; a popular name for the species of buttercups, from the leaf being supposed to have the shape of the foot of a crow.— **crow's-feet**, *n. pl.* The wrinkles brought on by age under and around the outer corners of the eyes.— **crow's-foot**, *n.* A caltrop (which see).—**crow's-nest**, *n.* A barrel or box fitted up on the main-topmast cross-trees of a vessel for the shelter of the lookout man.

crowd, kroud, *n.* [A.Sax. *crúdan*, to press; O.D. *cruden*, to press, to push; L.G. *krüden*, to oppress.] A number of persons or things collected or closely pressed together; a number of persons congregated without order; a throng; the lower orders of people; the populace; the vulgar; the mob.—*v.t.* To press into a crowd; to drive together; to fill by pressing numbers together without order; to fill to excess; to throng about; to press upon; to encumber or annoy by multitudes or excess of numbers.—*v.i.* To press in numbers; to swarm; to press or urge forward.

crown, kroun, *n.* [O.Fr. *corone*, Fr. *couronne*, L. *corona*—crown; Gr. *korōnē*, anything curved, a crown; akin W. *crwn*, Ir. *cruin*, round.] An ornament for the head, in the form of a wreath or garland, worn as a symbol of honor, victory, joy, etc.; a rich head covering of gold, gems, etc., worn by monarchs on state occasions as a badge of sovereignty; hence, regal power; royalty; kingly government or executive authority; the wearer of a crown; the sovereign, as head of the state; honorary distinction; reward; honor; completion; accomplishment; highest or most perfect state; acme; the top part of anything, as of the head, or

of a covering for the head, of a mountain or other elevated object; the portion of a tooth which appears above the gum; the end of the shank of an anchor, or the point from which the arms proceed; a coin anciently stamped with a crown (the English crown being a silver piece); paper of a particular size (15 by 20 inches), so called from formerly having the watermark of a crown.—*v.t.* To cover, decorate, or invest with, or as if with, a crown; hence, to invest with regal dignity and power; to honor; to reward; to dignify; to form the topmost or finishing part of; to terminate or finish; to complete; to consummate; to perfect.—*a.* Relating to, pertaining to, or connected with, the crown or government.—*Crown* or *demesne lands,* the lands, estate, or other real property belonging to the crown or sovereign.—**crown glass,** *n.* The finest sort of common window glass.—**crown prince,** *n.* The prince royal who is apparently successor to the crown.—**crown saw,** *n.* A species of circular saw formed by cutting the teeth round the edge of a cylinder, as the surgeon's trepan.
crownwork, *n. Fort.* an outwork running into the field, consisting of two demibastions at the extremes, and an entire bastion in the middle, with curtains.
crozier, crosier, krō′zhi·ėr, *n.* [O.E. *croisier, croysier,* from Fr. *crois,* a cross. CROSS.] A staff about 5 feet long, surmounted by an ornamental cross or crucifix, borne by or before an archbishop on solemn occasions; also (and more properly) a bishop's pastoral staff terminating in a crook.
crucial, krō′shi·al, *a.* [Fr. *crucial,* from L. *crux, crucis,* a cross. CROSS.] Relating to or like a cross; having the shape of a cross; transverse; intersecting; trying or searching, as if bringing to the cross; decisive (a *crucial* experiment).—**cruciate,†** krō′shi·āt, *v.t.* [L. *crucio, cruciatum,* to torture.] To torture; to torment; to afflict with extreme pain or distress.—*a.* Tormented†; *bot.* having four parts arranged like the arms of a cross; cruciform.—**crucifer,** krō′si·fėr, *n.* [L. *crux,* and *fero,* to bear.] A plant belonging to a very extensive order, all the members of which have flowers with six stamens, two of which are short, and four sepals and petals, the spreading limbs of which form a Maltese cross, whence the name.—**cruciform,** krō′si·form, *a.* Cross-shaped; disposed in the form of a cross.
crucible, krō′si·bl, *n.* [L.L. *crucibulum,* from the root seen in G. *kruse,* E. *cruse,* D. *kroes,* pitcher; akin *cresset.*] A chemical vessel or melting pot, made of earth, black lead, platina, etc., and so tempered and baked as to endure extreme heat without fusing; *fig.* a severe or searching test.
crucify, krō′si·fī, *v.t.*—*crucified, crucifying.* [Fr. *crucifier,* L. *crux,* cross, and *figo,* to fix. CROSS, FIX.] To nail to a cross; to put to death by

nailing the hands and feet to a cross or gibbet, sometimes anciently by fastening a criminal to a cross with cords; to subdue or mortify; also, to torture.—**crucifix,** krō′si·fiks, *n.* [L. *crucifixus,* crucified.] A cross with the figure of Christ crucified upon it.—**crucifixion,** krō·si·fik′shon, *n.* The act of nailing or fastening a person to a cross, for the purpose of putting him to death; death upon a cross; [*cap.*] the death of Christ.
crude, krōd, *a.* [L. *crudus,* raw, unripe; akin *crudelis,* cruel; from same root as E. *raw.* RAW.] Raw; not cooked; in its natural state; not digested in the stomach; not altered, refined, or prepared by any artificial process (*crude* salt or alum); unripe; not having reached its mature or perfect state; not brought to perfection; unfinished; immature; not matured; not well formed, arranged, or prepared in the intellect (notions, plan, theory).—**crudely,** krōd′li, *adv.* In a crude manner; without due preparation; without form or arrangement; without maturity or digestion.—**crudeness,** krōd·nes, *n.* The state or quality of being crude; rawness; unripeness; a state of being unformed or undigested; immatureness.—**crudity,** krō′di·ti,*n.* [L. *cruditas.*] Crudeness; that which is crude.
cruel, krō′el, *a.* [Fr. *cruel,* from L. *crudelis,* cruel. CRUDE.] Disposed to give pain to others in body or mind; destitute of pity, compassion, or kindness; hard-hearted: applied to persons; exhibiting or proceeding from cruelty; causing pain, grief, or distress; inhuman; tormenting, vexing, or afflicting (disposition, mood, manner, act, words, etc.).—**cruelly,** krō′el·li, *adv.* In a cruel manner; with cruelty; inhumanly; barbarously; painfully; with severe pain or torture; extremely (*colloq.*).—**cruelty,** krō′el·ti, *n.* [O.Fr. *cruelté,* L. *crudelitas.*] The state or character of being cruel; savage or barbarous disposition; any act which inflicts unnecessary pain; a wrong; an act of great injustice or oppression.
cruet, krō′et, *n.* [Contr. from Fr. *cruchette,* dim. of *cruche,* a pitcher. Akin *crock, cruse.*] A vial or small glass bottle for holding vinegar, oil, etc.
cruise, krōz, *v.i.*—*cruised, cruising.* [D. *kruisen,* to cross, to cruise, from *kruis,* a cross. CROSS.] To sail hither and thither, or to rove on the ocean in search of an enemy's ships for capture, for protecting commerce, for pleasure, or any other purpose.—*n.* A voyage made in various courses; a sailing to and fro, as in search of an enemy's ships, or for pleasure.—**cruiser,** krō′zėr, *n.* A person or a ship that cruises; an armed ship that sails to and fro for capturing an enemy's ships, for protecting commerce, or for plunder.
cruller, krul′ėr, *n.* [O.E. *crull,* curled; D. *krullen,* to curl.] A cake shaped in the form of a curl or twist, com-

posed of a rich batter, and fried crisp in deep fat.
crumb, krum, *n.* [A.Sax. *cruma*=D. *kruim,* Dan. *krumme,* G. *krume,* a crumb, from root of *crimp.*] A small fragment or piece; usually, a small piece of bread or other food, broken or cut off; the soft part of bread: opposed to *crust.*—*v.t.* To break into small pieces with the fingers; to cover (meat, etc.) with bread crumbs.—**crumble,** krum′bl, *v.t.*—*crumbled, crumbling.* [A dim. form from *crumb;* like D. *kruimelen,* G. *krümeln,* to crumble.] To break into crumbs or small pieces.—*v.i.* To fall into small pieces, as something friable; to molder; to become frittered away.—**crumbly,** krum′bli, *a.* Apt to crumble; brittle; friable.
crumpet, krum′pet, *n.* [Allied to *crimp,* brittle.] A sort of muffin or tea cake, very light and spongy.
crumple, krum′pl, *v.t.*—*crumpled, crumpling.* [Closely allied to *crimp* and *cramp.*] To draw or press into wrinkles or folds; to rumple.—*v.i.* To contract; to shrink; to shrivel.
crunch, krunsh, *v.t.* [See CRAUNCH.] To crush with the teeth; to chew with violence and noise.—*v.i.* To press with force and noise through a brittle obstacle.
crupper, krup′ėr, *n.* [Fr. *croupière,* from *croupe,* the buttocks. CROUP.] The buttocks of a horse; a strap of leather buckled to a saddle and passing under a horse's tail, to prevent the saddle from sliding forward on to the horse's neck.
crural, krō′ral, *a.* [L. *cruralis,* from *crus, cruris,* the leg.] Belonging to the leg.—*Crural arch,* the ligament of the thigh.
crusade, krō·sād′, *n.* [Fr. *croisade,* from L. *crux,* a cross.] [*often cap.*] A military expedition under the banner of the cross, undertaken by Christians in the eleventh, twelfth, and thirteenth centuries, for the recovery of the Holy Land from the power of infidels or Mohammedans; any enterprise undertaken through enthusiasm.—*v.i.*—*crusaded, crusading.* To engage in a crusade; to support or oppose any cause with zeal.—**crusader,** krō·sā′dėr, *n.* A person engaged in a crusade.
crusado, krō·sā′dō, *n.* A Portuguese coin, so called from having the cross stamped on it. (*Shak.*)
cruse, krōz, *n.* [Icel. *krús,* Dan. *krúus,* D. *kroes,* pot, mug; akin *cresset, crucible.*] A small cup; a bottle or cruet (O.T.).
crush, krush, *v.t.* [O.Fr. *cruisir, croissir,* to crack or crash, from the Teutonic; comp. Dan. *kryste,* Sw. *krysta,* Icel. *kreista,* to squeeze; Goth. *kriustan,* to gnash.] To press and bruise between two hard bodies; to squeeze so as to force out of the natural shape; to press with violence; to force together into a mass; to beat or force down, by an incumbent weight, with breaking or bruising; to bruise and break into fine particles by beating or grinding; to comminute; to subdue or conquer beyond resistance.—*v.i.* To press,

bruise, or squeeze.—*n.* A violent pressing or squeezing; the act or effect of anything that crushes; violent pressure caused by a crowd; a crowding or being crowded together.—**crusher,** krush′ėr, *n.* One who or that which crushes; a machine for crushing rocks, oilseeds or other materials; a worker who tends such a machine; a conclusive or overwhelming retort.

crust, krust, *n.* [O.Fr. *crouste,* L. *crusta.*] A hard or comparatively hard external coat or covering; a hard coating on a surface; the hard outside portion of a loaf; an incrustation; a deposit from wine, as it ripens, collected on the interior of bottles, etc.—*Crust of the earth,* the exterior portion of our globe which is so far accessible to our inspection and observation.—*v.t.* To cover with a crust; to spread over with hard matter; to incrust.—*v.i.* To gather or form into a crust.—**Crustacea,** krus·tā′shi·a, *n. pl.* [From their crusty covering or shell.] An important division of animals, comprising crabs, lobsters, crayfish, shrimp, etc., having an external calcareous skeleton or shell in many pieces, and capable of being molted or cast; a number of jointed limbs; head and thorax united into a single mass; abdomen often forming a kind of tail.—**crustacean,** krus·tā′shi·an, *n.* and *a.* One of, or pertaining to the crustaceans.—**crustaceous,** krus·tā′shus, *a.* Having a crustlike shell; belonging to the Crustacea; crustacean.—**crustily,** krus′ti·li, *adv.* In a crusty manner; peevishly; harshly; morosely.—**crustiness,** krus′ti·nes, *n.* The quality of being crusty; hardness; snappishness; surliness.—**crusty,** krus′ti, *a.* Like crust; of the nature of a crust; pertaining to a hard covering; hard; peevish; snappish; surly.

crutch, kruch, *n.* [A.Sax. *crycc, cricc,* a staff, a crutch; D. *kruk,* G. *krücke,* Dan. *krykke,* Sw. *krycka,* a crutch; same root as in *crook.*] A staff with a curving crosspiece at the head, to be placed under the arm or shoulder to support the lame in walking; any fixture or adjustment of similar form; used in various technical meanings.—*v.t.* To support on crutches; to prop or sustain with miserable helps.

crux, kruks, *n.* [L. *crux,* a cross.] Anything that puzzles greatly; a basic or essential point.

cry, krī, *v.i.*—*cried, crying.* [Fr. *crier,* from L. *quiritare,* to invoke the aid of the *Quirites,* or citizens.] To utter a loud voice; to speak, call, or exclaim with vehemence; to utter a loud voice by way of earnest request or prayer; to utter the voice of sorrow; to lament; to weep or shed tears; to utter a loud voice in giving public notice; to utter a loud inarticulate sound, as a dog or other animal.—*To cry out,* to exclaim; to vociferate; to clamor; to utter a loud voice; to utter lamentations.—*To cry out against,* to complain loudly against; to

blame or censure.—*I cry you mercy,*‡ I beg pardon.—*v.t.* To utter loudly; to sound abroad; to proclaim; to name loudly and publicly, so as to give notice regarding; to advertise by crying.—*To cry down,* to decry; to dispraise; to condemn.—*To cry up,* to praise; to applaud; to extol.—*n.* Any loud sound articulate or inarticulate uttered by the mouth of an animal; a loud or vehement sound uttered in weeping or lamentation; a fit of weeping; clamor; outcry; an object for which a party professes great earnestness; a political catchword or the like.—**crier,** krī′ėr, *n.* One who cries; especially, an officer whose duty it is to proclaim the orders or commands of a court, to keep silence, etc.—**crying,** krī′ing, *a.* Calling for vengeance and punishment; clamant; notorious; common; great (*crying* sins).

cryogenics, krī·o·jen′iks, *n.* [Gr. *kryos,* cold, and *gen,* to bring forth.] The physical science dealing with the phenomena of extreme cold.

cryolite, krī′o·līt, *n.* [Gr. *kryos,* cold, and *lithos,* stone—ice-stone.] A fluoride of sodium and aluminum.

crypt, kript, *n.* [L. *crypta,* Gr *cryptē,* from *kryptō,* to hide.] A subterranean cell or cave, especially one constructed for interment.—**cryptic, cryptical,** krip′tik, krip′ti·kal, *a.* Hidden; secret; occult.

cryptogam, krip′tō·gam, *n.* [Gr. *kryptos,* concealed, and *gamos,* marriage.] One of those plants forming a large division of the vegetable kingdom which do not bear true flowers consisting of stamens and pistils, and which are divided into cellular and vascular cryptogams, the former including algæ, fungi, lichens, mosses, etc., the latter the ferns, horsetails, lycopods, etc.—**cryptogamic, cryptogamous,** krip··to·gam′ik, krip·tog′a·mus, *a.*

cryptogram, krip′tō·gram, *n.* [Gr. *kryptos,* concealed, and *gramma,* a letter.] A message or writing in secret code or cipher.—**cryptogrammic,** krip·to·gram′ik, *a.*

cryptograph, krip′to·graf, *n.* [Gr. *kryptos,* concealed, and *graphō,* to write.] Something written in secret characters or cipher.—**cryptographer,** krip·tog′ra·fėr, *n.* One who writes in secret characters.—**cryptographic, cryptographical,** krip··to·graf′ik, krip·to·graf′i·kal, *a.* Written in secret characters or in cipher; pertaining to cryptography.—**cryptography,** krip·tog′ra·fi, *n.* The act or art of writing in secret characters; also, secret characters or cipher.

crystal, kris′tal, *n.* [L. *crystallus,* Gr. *krystallos,* from *kryos,* frost.] Quartz that is clear and transparent or nearly so; glass of superior quality; the transparent cover of a watch dial; *chem.* and *mineral.* a solid substance bounded by plane surfaces that show a symmetrical arrangement; anything made of, or similar to, such a substance; a natural or synthetic crystalline material used for rectification or frequency control. *Rock crystal,* a general name for all

the transparent crystals of quartz, particularly of limpid or colorless quartz.—*a.* Consisting of crystal, or like crystal; clear; transparent; pellucid.—**crystalline,** kris′tal·in, *a.* Consisting of crystal; relating or pertaining to crystals or crystallography; resembling crystal; pure; clear; transparent; pellucid.—*Crystalline lens,* a lens-shaped pellucid body situated in the anterior part of the eye, and serving to produce that refraction of the rays of light which is necessary to cause them to meet in the retina, and form a perfect image there.—**crystallizable,** kris′ta·līz·a·bl, *a.* Capable of being crystallized.—**crystallization,** kris′tal·i·zā″shon, *n.* The act of crystallizing or forming crystals; the act or process of becoming crystallized, so that crystals are produced with a determinate and regular form, according to the nature of the substance; a body formed by the process of crystallizing.—*Water of crystallization,* the water which unites chemically with many salts during the process of crystallizing.—**crystallize,** kris′ta·līz, *v.t.*—*crystallized, crystallizing.* To cause to form crystals.—*v.i.* To be converted into a crystal; to become solidified, as the separate particles of a substance into a determinate and regular shape.—**crystallographer,** kris·ta·log′ra·fėr, *n.* One who treats of crystallography, crystals, or the manner of their formation.—**crystallographic, crystallographical,** kris′·tal·o·graf″ik, kris′tal·o·graf″i·kal, *a.* Pertaining to crystallography.—**crystallographically,** kris′tal·o·graf″i·kal·li, *adv.* In the manner of crystallography.—**crystallography,** kris·ta·log′ra·fi, *n.* The doctrine or science of crystallization, teaching the principles of the process, and the forms and structure of crystals.—**crystalloid,** kris′tal·oid, *a.* Resembling a crystal.—*n.* The name given to a class of bodies which have the power, when in solution, of passing through membranes, as parchment-paper, easily: opposed to *colloids,* which have not this power; in *seeds,* etc., a minute crystal-shaped mass of albuminoid matter.

ctenoid, ten′oid, *a.* [Gr. *kteis, ktenos,* a comb, and *eidos,* form.] Comb-shaped; pectinated; having the posterior edge with teeth: said of the scales of certain fishes, those of the perch and flounder being of this kind; having scales of this kind.—*n.* A fish having ctenoid scales; one of an order of fishes, mostly fossil, having scales jagged or pectinated like the teeth of a comb.

cub, kub, *n.* [Etymology unknown.] The young of certain quadrupeds, as of the lion, bear, or fox; a whelp; a young boy or girl: in contempt; a junior member of the Boy Scouts.—*v.t.*—*cubbed, cubbing.* To bring forth a cub or cubs.

cubane, kū·bān, *n.* A molecule of boxlike structure.

cube, kūb, *n.* [Fr. *cube,* from L. *cubus,* Gr. *kybos,* a cube, a cubical die.] A solid body that is exactly square; a regular solid body with six equal sides, all squares, and containing equal angles; the product of a number multiplied into itself, and that product multiplied into the same number $(4 \times 4 = 16$, and $16 \times 4 = 64$, the cube of 4).—*Cube root*, the number or quantity which, multiplied into itself, and then into the product, produces the cube (thus 4 is the cube root of 64).—*v.t.*—*cubed, cubing*. To raise to the cube or third power by multiplying into itself twice.—**cubature**, kū′ba·chėr, *n*. The finding of the solid or cubic contents of a body.—**cubic, cubical**, kū′bik, kū′bi·kal, *a*. [L. *cubicus*.] Having the form or properties of a cube; pertaining to the measure of solids (a *cubic* foot, *cubic* contents).—**cubically**, kū′bi·kal·li, *adv*. In a cubical method.—**cubicalness**, kūb′i·kal·nes, *n*. The state or quality of being cubical.—**cubiform**, *a*. Having the form of a cube.—**cuboid, cuboidal**, kū′boid, kū·boi′dal, *a*. Having the form of a cube or differing little from it.

cubeb, kū′beb, *n*. [Ar. *kabâbah*.] The small spicy berry of a kind of pepper, a native of Java and other East India Isles.

cubicular, kū·bik′ū·lėr, *a*. [L. *cubiculum*, a sleeping room.] Belonging to a bedchamber.—**cubicule**,‡ kū′bi·kūl, *n*. A bedchamber; a chamber.

cubit, kū′bit, *n*. [L. *cubitus, cubitum*, the elbow, an ell or cubit, from root of L. *cubo*, to lie or recline.] *Anat*. the forearm; the ulna, a bone of the arm from the elbow to the wrist; a lineal measure, being the length of a man's arm from the elbow to the extremity of the middle finger: usually taken at 18 inches.

cucking stool, kuk′ing·stöl, *n*. [Icel. *kúka*, to ease one's self, *kúkr*, dung.] A chair in which an offender was placed, usually before her or his own door, to be hooted at or pelted by the mob; or it might be used for ducking its occupant.

cuckold, kuk′old, *n*. [Lit. one who is *cuckooed*, from O.Fr. *coucoul*, L. *cuculus*, a cuckoo; from the cuckoo's habit of depositing her eggs in the nests of other birds.] A man whose wife is false to his bed; the husband of an adulteress.—*v.t*. To make a cuckold of.—**cuckoldly**, kuk′old·li, *a*. Having the qualities of a cuckold. (*Shak*.)—**cuckoldry**, kuk′old·ri, *n*. The debauching of other men's wives; the state of being made a cuckold.

cuckoo, kụ′kö, *n*. [Fr. *coucou*, from L. *cuculus*, like G. *kukuk*, D. *koekoek*, Gr. *kokkux*, Skr. *kokila*, names derived from its cry.] A migratory bird remarkable for its striking call note and its habit of depositing its eggs in the nests of other birds; also the name of many allied birds in various parts of the world.—**cuckoo spit, cuckoo spittle**, *n*. A froth found on plants in summer, being a secretion formed by the larva of a small insect.

cucullate, cucullated, kū·kul′āt, kū-

kul′ā·ted, *a*. [L. *cucullatus*, from *cucullus*, a hood or cowl.] Hooded; cowled; covered as with a hood; having the shape or resemblance of a hood.

cucumber, kū′kum·bėr, *n*. [Fr. *concombre*, from L. *cucumis, cucumeris*, a cucumber.] An annual plant of the gourd family, extensively cultivated and prized as an esculent; in an unripe state used in pickles under the name of gherkins.—**cucumber tree**, *n*. A beautiful American tree, a species of *Magnolia*, abounding in the Alleghanies.—**cucumiform**, kū·kū′mi·form, *a*. Shaped like a cucumber.

cucurbit, kū·kėr′bit, *n*. [Fr. *cucurbite*, L. *cucurbita*, a gourd.] A chemical vessel originally in the shape of a gourd, but sometimes shallow, with a wide mouth, used in distillation.—**cucurbitaceous**, kū·kėr′bi·tā″shus, *a*. Resembling a gourd.

cud, kud, *n*. [A.Sax. *cud*, the cud, what is chewed, from *ceówan*, to chew.] The food which going into the first stomach of ruminating animals is afterward brought up and chewed at leisure; a portion of tobacco held in the mouth and chewed; a quid.—*To chew the cud* (*fig.*), to ponder; to reflect; to ruminate.

cuddle, kud′l, *v.i*.—*cuddled, cuddling*. [Origin doubtful; perhaps same as *coddle*.] To lie close or snug; to squat; to join in an embrace; to fondle.—*v.t*. To hug; to fondle; to press close, so as to keep warm.—*n*. A hug; an embrace.

cuddy, kud′i, *n*. [Probably a word of East Indian origin.] *Naut*. a room or cabin abaft and under the poop deck; also a sort of cabin or cook room in lighters, barges, etc.

cudgel, kuj′el, *n*. [A.Sax. *cycgel*, perh. from *cog*, a short piece of wood.] A short thick stick; a club.—*To take up the cudgels*, to stand boldly forth in defense.—*v.t*.—*cudgelled, cudgelling*. To beat with a cudgel or thick stick; to beat in general.—*To cudgel one's brains*, to reflect deeply and laboriously.

cue, kū, *n*. [Fr. *queue*, L. *cauda*, the tail; or partly from *Q*, the first letter of L. *quando*, when, which was marked on the actors' copies of the plays, to show when they were to enter and speak.] The end of a thing, as the long curl of a wig, or a long roll of hair; a queue; the last words of a speech which a player, who is to answer, catches and regards as an intimation to begin; a hint on which to act; the part which any man is to play in his turn; turn or temper of mind; the straight tapering rod used in playing billiards.

cuff, kuf, *n*. [Akin to Sw. *kuffa*, Hamburg dialect *kuffen*, to cuff.] A blow with the fist; a stroke; a box.—*v.t*. To strike with the fist, as a man; to buffet.—*v.i*. To fight; to scuffle.

cuff, kuf, *n*. [Perhaps from Fr. *coiffe*, It. *cuffia*, a coif, hence a covering for the hand.] The fold at the end of a sleeve; anything occupying the place of such a fold, as a loose band worn over the wristband of a shirt.

Cufic, kū′fik, *a*. [From *Cufa*, near

Bagdad.] Applied to the characters of the Arabic alphabet used in the time of Mohammed, and in which the Koran was written; Kufic.

cuirass, kwi·ras′, *n*. [Fr. *cuirasse*, from *cuir*, L. *corium*, leather. The cuirass was originally made of leather.] A breastplate; a piece of defensive armor made of iron plate, well hammered, and covering the body from the neck to the girdle.—**cuirassier**, kwi·ras·sēr′, *n*. A soldier armed with a cuirass or breastplate.

cuisine, kwē·zēn′, *n*. [Fr., from L. *coquina*, art of cooking, a kitchen, from *coquo*, to cook. COOK.] A kitchen; the cooking department; manner or style of cooking; cookery.

cul-de-sac, kul′de·sak, *n*. [Fr., lit. the bottom of a bag.] A place that has no thoroughfare; a blind alley; any natural cavity, bag, or tubular vessel, open only at one end.

culinary, kū′li·ne·ri, *a*. [L. *culinarius*, from *culina*, a kitchen.] Relating to the kitchen, or to the art of cooking; used in kitchens.

cull, kul, *v.t*. [Fr. *cueillir*, from L. *colligere*, to collect—*col*, and *legere*, to gather. COLLECT, COIL.] To pick out; to separate one or more things from others; to select from many; to pick up; to collect.

cullender, kul′en·dėr, *n*. A colander.

cullet, kul′et, *n*. Broken glass for melting up with fresh materials.

cullis, kul′is, *n*. [Fr. *coulisse*, a groove, from *couler*, to run.] *Arch*. a gutter in a roof.

culm, kulm, *n*. [L. *culmus*, a stalk.] *Bot*. the jointed stem of grasses, which is herbaceous in most, but woody and treelike in the bamboo.—**culmiferous**, kul·mif′ėr·us, *a*. Bearing culms.

culm, kulm, *n*. [Perhaps another spelling of *coom*; or akin to *coal*.] Anthracite shale, an impure shaly kind of coal.—**culmiferous**, kul·mif′ėr·us, *a*. Abounding in culm.

culmen, kul′men, *n*. [L.] Top; summit; highest ridge.—**culminant**, kul′mi·nant, *a*. Being vertical, or at the highest point of altitude; hence, predominating.—**culminate**, kul′mi·nāt, *v.i*.—*culminated, culminating*. To come or be in the meridian; to be in the highest point of altitude, as a planet; to reach the highest point, as of rank, power, size, numbers, or quality.—**culminating**, kul′mi·nāt·ing, *p*. or *a*. Being at the meridian; being at its highest point, as of rank, power, size, etc.—**culmination**, kul·mi·nā′shon, *n*. The transit of a heavenly body over the meridian, or highest point of altitude for the day; *fig*. the condition of any person or thing arrived at the most brilliant or important point of his or its progress.

culpable, kul′pa·bl, *a*. [L. *culpabilis*, from *culpa*, a fault.] Deserving censure; blamable; blameworthy; immoral: said of persons or their conduct.—**culpability, culpableness**, kul·pa·bil′i·ti, kul′pa·bl·nes, *n*. State of being culpable; blamableness; guilt.—**culpably**, kul′pa·bli, *adv*. In a culpable manner; blamably; in a faulty manner; criminally; immorally.

culprit, kul′prit, n. [Probably for *culpat*, from old law Latin *culpatus*, one accused, from L. *culpo*, to blame, accuse.] A person arraigned in court for a crime; a criminal; a malefactor.

cult, cult, n. [Fr. *culte*, L. *cultus*, worship, from *colo*, *cultum*, to till, worship.] Homage; worship; a system of religious belief and worship; the rites and ceremonies employed in worship.

cultch, kulch, n. The spawn of the oyster.

cultivate, kul′ti·vāt, v.t.—*cultivated*, *cultivating*. [L.L. *cultivare*, *cultivatum*, from L. *cultus*, pp. of *colo*, *cultum*, to till.] To till; to prepare for crops; to manure, blow, dress, sow, and reap; to raise or produce by tillage; to improve by labor or study; to refine and improve; to labor to promote and increase; to cherish; to foster (to *cultivate* a taste for poetry); to devote study, labor, or care to; to study (to *cultivate* literature); to study to conciliate or gain over; to labor to make better; to civilize.—**cultivable**, **cultivatable**, kul′ti·va·bl, kul′ti·vā·ta·bl, a. Capable of being tilled or cultivated.—**cultivation**, kul·ti·vā′shon, n. The act or practice of cultivating; husbandry; study, care, and practice directed to improvement or progress; the state of being cultivated or refined; culture; refinement.—**cultivator**, kul′ti·vā·tėr, n. One who cultivates; especially, a farmer or agriculturist; an agricultural implement used for the purpose of loosening the earth about the roots of growing crops.

culture, kul′chėr, n. [L. *cultura*, from *colo*, *cultum*, to till.] Tillage; cultivation; intellectual development; improvement by mental or physical training; education; refinement; the way of life of a people; growth of bacteria, fungi, etc. in a prepared medium.—v.t. To grow in a prepared medium.—**cultural**, kul′chėr·al, a.—**cultured**, kul′chėrd, a. Enlightened; cultivated; produced under artificial conditions.

culver, kul′vėr, n. [A.Sax. *culfre*.] A pigeon; a dove.

culverin, kul′vėr·in, n. [Fr. *couleuvrine*, from L. *coluber*, a serpent.] A long, slender piece of ordnance or artillery, serving to carry a ball to a great distance.

culvert, kul′vėrt, n. [O.Fr. *culvert*; Fr. *couvert*, a covered walk, from *couvrir*, to cover. COVER.] An arched drain of brickwork or masonry carried under a road, railroad, canal, etc., for the passage of water.

cumber, kum′bėr, v.t. [O.Fr. *combrer*, from L. *combrus*, *cumbrus*, a mass, from L. *cumulus*, a heap (whence also *cumulate*), by insertion of *b* (comp. *number*) and change of *l* to *r*.] To overload, to overburden; to check, stop, or retard, as by a load or weight; to make motion difficult; to obstruct; to perplex or embarrass; to distract or trouble; to cause trouble or obstruction in, as by anything useless.—**cumber**, kum′bėr, n. Hindrance; burdensomeness; embarrassment. —**cumbersome**,

kum′bėr·sum, a. Troublesome; burdensome; embarrassing; vexatious; unwieldy; unmanageable; not easily borne or managed.—**cumbersomely**, kum′bėr·sum·li, adv.—**cumbersomeness**, kum′bėr·sum·nes, n.—**cumbrance**, kum′brans, n. That which cumbers or encumbers; an encumbrance.—**cumbrous**, kum′brus, a. Serving to cumber or encumber; burdensome; troublesome; rendering action difficult or toilsome; unwieldy.—**cumbrously**, kum′brus·li, adv. In a cumbrous manner.—**cumbrousness**, kum′brus·nes, n.

cumin, **cummin**, kum′in, n. [L. *cuminum*, Gr. *kyminon*, Heb. *kamon*, cumin.] An annual umbelliferous plant found wild in Egypt and Syria, and cultivated for the sake of its agreeable aromatic seeds, which possess well-marked stimulating and carminative properties.

cummerbund, kum′ėr·bund, n. [Hind. *kamar*, the waist, and *bandhna*, to tie.] A girdle or waistband.

cumshaw, kum′shạ, n. [Chinese *komtsie*.] In the East, a present or bonus.

cumulate, kū′mū·lāt, v.t.—*cumulated*, *cumulating*. [L. *cumulo*, *cumulatum*, to heap up, from *cumulus*, a heap, seen also in *accumulate*; akin *cumber*.] To form a heap of; to heap together; to accumulate.—**cumulation**, kū·mū·lā′shon, n. The act of heaping together; a heap.—**cumulative**, kū′mū·lāt·iv, a. Forming a mass; aggregated; increasing in force, weight, or effect by successive additions (arguments, evidence).—*Cumulative system*, in elections, that system by which each voter has the same number of votes as there are persons to be elected, and can give them all to one candidate or distribute them as he pleases.—**cumulostratus**, kū′mū·lō·strā′tus, n. A species of cloud in which the cumulus at the top, mixed with cirri, overhangs a flattish stratum or base.—**cumulus**, kū′mū·lus, n. A species of cloud which assumes the form of dense convex or conical heaps, resting on a flattish base.

cuneal, kū′ni·al, a. [L. *cuneus*, a wedge, whence also *coin*.] Having the form of a wedge.—**cuneate**, **cuneated**, kū′ni·āt, kū′ni·āt·ed, a. Wedge-shaped; cuneiform.—**cuneiform**, **cuniform**, kū·nē′i·form, kū′ni·form, a. Having the shape or form of a wedge; wedge-shaped; the epithet applied to the arrow-headed inscriptions found on old Babylonian and Persian monuments, from the characters resembling a wedge.

cunning, kun′ing, a. [O.E. *cunnand*, from A.Sax. *cunnan*, Icel. *kunna*, Goth. *kunnan*, to know; akin *can*, *ken*, *know*.] Having skill or dexterity; skillful; wrought with skill; ingenious; shrewd; sly; crafty; astute; designing; subtle.—n. Knowledge‡; skill‡; artifice; artfulness; craft; deceitfulness or deceit; fraudulent skill or dexterity.—**cunningly**, kun′ing·li, adv. In a cunning manner; artfully; craftily; with subtlety; with fraudulent contrivance; skillfully; artis-

tically.—**cunningness**, kun′ing·nes, n. Cunning.

cup, kup, n. [A.Sax. *cuppe*, from L. *cupa*, a tub, a cask, in later times a cup.] A vessel of small capacity, used commonly to drink from; a chalice; the contents of a cup; the liquor contained in a cup, or that it may contain; anything formed like a cup (the *cup* of an acorn, of a flower).—*In his cups*, intoxicated; tipsy.—v.t.—*cupped*, *cupping*. To perform the operation of cupping upon.—**cupbearer**, n. An attendant at a feast who conveys wine or other liquors to the guests.—**cupboard**, kub′bėrd, n. Originally, a board or shelf for cups to stand on; now, a case or enclosure in a room with shelves to receive cups, plates, dishes, and the like.—**cupful**, kup′ful, n. As much as a cup holds.—**cupping**, kup′ing, n. Surg. a species of blood-letting performed by a scarificator and a glass called a cupping glass from which the air has been exhausted.

cupel, kū′pel, n. [L. *cupella*, dim. of *cupa*, a tub.] A small, shallow, porous, cuplike vessel: generally made of the residue of burned bones rammed into a mold, and used in refining metals.—**cupellation**, kū·pel·lā′shon, n. The refining of gold or silver by a cupel.

Cupid, kū′pid, n. [L. *Cupido*, from *cupido*, desire, from *cupio*, to desire.] The god of love, and *fig.* love.

cupidity, kū·pid′i·ti, n. [L. *cupiditas*, from *cupidus*, desirous, from *cupio*, to desire; akin *covet*.] An eager desire to possess something; inordinate or unlawful desire, especially of wealth or power; avarice; covetousness.

cupola, kū′po·la, n. [It. *cupola*, dim. of L. *cupa*, a cup. CUP.] Arch. a spherical vault on the top of an edifice; a dome, or the round top of a dome; the round top of any structure, as of a furnace; the furnace itself.

cupreous, kū′pri·us, a. [L. *cupreus*, from *cuprum*, copper.] Coppery; consisting of copper; resembling copper or partaking of its qualities.—**cupric**, **cuprous**, kū′prik, kū′prus, a. Of or belonging to copper.—**cupriferous**, kū·prif′ėr·us, a. Producing or affording copper.—**cuprite**, kū′prīt, n. The red oxide of copper; red copper ore.

cupule, kū′pūl, n. [From L. *cupa*. CUP.] Bot. a form of involucrum, occurring in the oak, the beech, and the hazel, and consisting of bracts cohering by their bases, and forming a kind of cup.—**cupuliferous**, kū·pū·lif′ėr·us, a. In bot. bearing cupules.

cur, kėr, n. [Sw. *kurre*, D. *korre*, a dog, from root of Icel. *kurra*, to grumble or mutter.] A degenerate dog; a worthless or contemptible man; a hound.—**currish**, kėr′ish, a. Like a cur; having the qualities of a cur; snappish; snarling; churlish; quarrelsome; malignant.—**currishly**, kėr′ish·li, adv. In a currish manner.

curable, kūr′a·bl, a. See CURE.

curaçao, kö·ra·sou′, n. A liquor or

cordial flavored with orange peel, cinnamon, and mace: so named from the island of *Curaçao* where it was first made.

curacy. See CURATE.

curari, curara, ku′rä·ri, ku′rä·rä, *n.* A brown-black resinous substance obtained from a small tree of the nux-vomica family; and forming a deadly poison; used by the South American Indians for poisoning arrows, especially for hunting, the animals killed by it being quite wholesome; a muscle relaxant.

curassow, kū·ras′sō, *n.* The name given to several species of gallinaceous birds found in the warmer parts of America, about the size of turkeys, and easily domesticated and raised.

curate, kū′rit, *n.* [L.L. *curatus,* one intrusted with the cure of souls, from L. *cura,* care.] One who has the cure of souls; a clergyman in Episcopal churches who is employed to perform divine service in the place of the incumbent, parson, or vicar.—**curacy,** kū′ra·si, *n.* The office or employment of a curate.—**curator,** kū·rā′tèr, *n.* [L., from *cura, curatum,* to take care of.] One who has the care and superintendence of anything, as a public library, museum, fine art collection, or the like; *Scots law,* a guardian.—**curatorship,** kū·rā′tèr·ship, *n.* The office of a curator. —**curé,** kū·rā, *n.* [Fr.] A curate; a parson.

curative, kū′ra·tiv, *a.* See CURE.

curb, kėrb, *v.t.* [Fr. *courber,* to bend or crook, from L. *curvare,* to curve, from *curvus,* curved.] To bend to one's will; to check, restrain, hold back; to keep in subjection; to restrain (a horse) with a curb; to guide and manage by the reins; to strengthen by a curbstone.—*n.* What checks, restrains, or holds back; restraint; check; hindrance; a chain or strap attached to a bridle, and passing under the horse's lower jaw, against which it is made to press tightly when the rein is pulled; the edge stone of a sidewalk or pavement; a curbstone.—**curb roof,** *n.* A roof formed with an upper and under set of rafters on each side, the under set being less inclined to the horizon than the upper; a mansard roof.— **curbstone,** *n.* A stone placed against earth or stonework to hold the work together; the outer edge of a foot pavement.

curd, kėrd, *n.* [Probably connected with W. *crwd,* a round lump, and perhaps with *crowd.*] The coagulated or thickened part of milk; the coagulated part of any liquid.—*v.t.* to cause to coagulate; to turn to curd; to curdle; to congeal.—*v.i.* To become curdled or coagulated; to become curd.—**curdle,** kėr′dl, *v.i. curdled, curdling.* To coagulate or concrete; to thicken or change into curd; to run slow with terror; to freeze; to congeal.—*v.t.* To change into curd; to coagulate; to congeal or make run slow.

cure, kūr, *n.* [O.Fr. *cure,* L. *cura,* care.] Care‡; a spiritual charge; care

of the spiritual welfare of people; the employment or office of a curate; curacy; remedial treatment of disease; method of medical treatment; remedy for disease; restorative; that which heals; a healing; restoration to health from disease and to soundness from a wound.—*v.t.*—*cured, curing.* To restore to health or to a sound state; to heal; to remove or put an end to by remedial means; to heal, as a disease; to remedy; to prepare for preservation, as by drying, salting, etc.—*v.i.* To effect a cure.—**curability,** kūr·a·bil′i·ti, *n.* The quality of being curable.— **curable,** kū′ra·bl, *a.* Capable of being healed or cured; admitting a remedy.—**curableness,** kūr′a·bl·nes, *n.* Possibility of being cured.— **curative,** kū′ra·tiv, *a.* Relating to the cure of diseases; tending to cure.— **cureless,** kūr′les, *a.* Incurable; not admitting of a remedy.—**curer,** kū′rėr, *n.* One who or that which cures or heals; a physician; one who preserves provisions, as beef, fish, and the like, from speedy putrefaction by means of salt, or in any other manner.

curé, *n.* See CURATE.

curfew, kėr′fū, *n.* [Fr. *couvre-feu,* coverfire, from L. *cooperire,* to cover, and *focus,* hearth, fireplace.] A bell formerly rung in the evening as a signal to the inhabitants to rake up their fires and retire to rest; a signal to withdraw from the streets; the time of such a signal.

curious, kū′ri·us, *a.* [L. *curiosus,* from *cura,* care, attention. CURE.] Eager to know things interesting; inquisitive; addicted to research or inquiry; wrought with care and art or with nice finish; singular; exciting surprise; awakening curiosity; odd or strange. —**curiosity,** kū·ri·os′i·ti, *n.* [L. *curiositas.*] The state or feeling of being curious; a strong desire to see something novel or to discover something unknown; a desire to see what is new or unusual, or to gratify the mind with new discoveries; inquisitiveness; a curious or singular object.—**curio,** kū′ri·ō, *n.* A curiosity; a small interesting article or object.—**curiously,** kū′ri·us·li, *adv.* In a curious manner; inquisitively; attentively; in a singular manner; unusually.—**curiousness,** kū′ri·us·nes, *n.*

curium, kū′ri·um, *n.* [From Pierre and Marie Curie.] A metallic element produced artificially by helium-ion bombardment of plutonium. Symbol, Cm; at. no., 96.

curl, kėrl, *v.t.* [Akin to D. *krullen,* Dan. *krölle,* to curl.] To bend or twist circularly; to bend or form into ringlets; to crisp (the hair); to writhe; to twist; to coil; to curve; to raise in breaking waves or undulations.—*v.i.* To bend or twist in curls or ringlets; to move in or form curves or spirals; to rise in waves; to writhe; to twist: to play at the game called curling.—*n.* A ringlet of hair or anything of a like form; something curled or bent round; a waving; sinuosity; flexure.—**curled,** kėrld, *a.*

Having the hair curled; curly.— **curler,** kėrl′ėr, *n.* One who or that which curls; one who engages in the amusement of curling.—**curliness,** kėrl′i·nes, *n.* State of being curly.— **curling,** kėrl′ing, *n.* A winter amusement on the ice (especially in Scotland), in which contending parties slide large smooth stones of a circular form from one mark to another, called the tee.—**curling irons, curling tongs,** *n.* An instrument for curling the hair.—**curling stone,** *n.* A stone shaped somewhat like a cheese with a handle in the upper side, used in the game of curling.—**curly,** kėr′li, *a.* Having or forming curls; tending to curl.

curlew, kėr′lū, *n.* [O.Fr. *corlieu;* imitative of the cry of the bird; Fr. *courlis.*] A bird allied to the snipe and woodcock, with a long, slender, curved bill, longish legs, and a short tail.

curmudgeon, kėr·muj′on, *n.* [Word of uncertain origin.] An avaricious churlish fellow; a miser; a niggard; a churl.—**curmudgeonly,** kėr·muj′on·li, *a.* Avaricious; covetous; niggardly; churlish.

currant, kur′ant, *n.* [From *Corinth,* whence it was probably first brought.] A small kind of dried grape, brought in large quantities from Greece; the name of several species of shrubs belonging to the gooseberry family, and of their fruits, as the red currant, the white currant, and the black currant.

current, kur′ent, *a.* [L. *currens, currentis,* ppr. of *curro,* to run, seen also in *concur, incur, occur, course, cursive,* etc.] Running†; passing from person to person, or from hand to hand (report, coin); circulating; common, general, or fashionable; generally received, adopted, or approved (opinions, beliefs, theories); popular; established by common estimation (the *current* value of coin); fitted for general acceptance or circulation (*Shak.*); now passing, or at present in its course (the *current* month; often in abbreviated expressions, such as, 20th *curt.*).—*Current coin,* coin in general circulation.—*n.* A flowing or passing; a stream; a body of water or air moving in a certain direction; course; progressive motion or movement; connected series; successive course (the *current* of events); general or main course (the *current* of opinion).—*Electric current,* the passage of electricity from one pole of an apparatus to the other.—**currency,** kur′en·si, *n.* The state of being current; a passing from person to person; a passing from mouth to mouth among the public; a continual passing from hand to hand, as coin or bills of credit; circulation; that which is in circulation, or is given and taken as having value, or as representing property; circulating medium (the *currency* of a country).—*Metallic currency,* the gold, silver, and copper in circulation in any country.—*Paper currency,* bank notes, or other documents serving as a substitute for money or a

fāte, fär, fâre, fat, fạll; mē, met, hèr; pīne, pin; nōte, not, mȯve; tūbe, tub, bụll; oil, pound.

representative of it.—**currently**, kur'ent·li, *adv*. Commonly; generally; popularly; with general acceptance. —**currentness**, kur'ent·nes, *n*. The state of being current; currency.

curricle, kur'i·kl, *n*. [L. *curriculum*, from *curro*, to run.] A chaise or carriage with two wheels, drawn by two horses abreast.

curriculum, ku·rik'ū·lum, *n*. [L.] A specified fixed course of study in a university, academy, school, or the like.

currish, kėr'ish, *a*. See CUR.

curry, kur'i, *v.t.*—**curried, currying**. [Fr. *courroyer, corroyer*, originally to prepare, put right, or make ready in general, from the prefix *con*, and the Germanic stem to which belong E. *ready, ray* in *array*.] To dress leather after it is tanned by scraping, cleansing, beating, and coloring; to rub and clean (a horse) with a comb; to beat, drub, or thrash (*colloq.*).—To *curry favor*, to seek favor by officiousness, kindness, flattery, caresses, and the like; the phrase being corrupted from 'to curry favel', from *favel*, an old name for a chestnut horse.—**currier**, kur'i·ėr, *n*. A man who curries leather or a horse.—**curriery**, kur'i·ėr·i, *n*. The trade of a currier or the place where the trade is carried on.—**currycomb**, *n*. An iron instrument or comb with very short teeth, for combing and cleaning horses.—*v.t.* To rub down or comb with a currycomb.

curry, currie, kur'i, *n*. [Per. *khur*, flavor, relish.] A kind of sauce much used in India, containing cayenne pepper, garlic, turmeric, coriander seed, ginger, and other strong spices; a dish of fish, fowl, etc., cooked with curry.—*v.t.*—**curried, currying**. To flavor with curry.— **curry powder**, *n*. A condiment used for making curry.

curse, kėrs, *v.t.*—**cursed, cursing**. [A. Sax. *cursian*, from *curs*, a curse—a word of doubtful connections.] To utter a wish of evil against one; to imprecate evil upon; to call for mischief or injury to fall upon; to execrate; to bring evil to or upon; to blast; to blight; to vex, harass, or torment with great calamities.—*v.i.* To utter imprecations; to use blasphemous or profane language; to swear.—*n*. A malediction; the expression of a wish of evil to another; an imprecation; evil solemnly or in passion invoked upon one; that which brings evil or severe affliction; torment; great vexation; condemnation or sentence of divine vengeance on sinners.—**cursed**, kėr'sed, *a*. Blasted by a curse; deserving a curse; execrable; hateful; detestable; abominable; wicked; vexatious; troublesome.—**cursedly**, kėr'sed·li, *adv*. In a cursed manner; miserably; in a manner to be cursed or detested.— **cursedness**, kėr'sed·nes, *n*. The state of being cursed.—**curst**, kėrst, *a*. Cursed; having a violent temper; snarling; peevish; forward.

cursive, kėr'siv, *a*. [L.L. *cursivus*, L. *cursus*, a running. COURSE, CURRENT.] Running; flowing: said of handwriting.—**cursively**, kėr'siv·li, *adv*. In a cursive manner.—**cursorial**, kėr·sō'ri·al, *a*. Adapted for running. —**cursorily**, kėr'so·ri·li, *adv*. In a cursory or hasty manner; slightly; hastily; without attention.—**cursoriness**, kėr'so·ri·nes, *n*. The state of being cursory.—**cursory**, kėr'so·ri, *a*. [L. *cursorius*.] Rapid or hurried, as if running; hasty; slight; superficial; careless; not exercising close attention (a *cursory* view, a *cursory* observer).

curst, *a*. See CURSE.

curt, kėrt, *a*. [L. *curtus*, short, docked.] Short; concise; brief and abrupt; short and sharp.—**curtly**, kėrt'li, *adv*. In a curt manner; briefly.— **curtness**, kėrt'nes, *n*. Shortness; conciseness; abruptness, as of manner.

curtail, kėr·tāl', *v.t.* [O.Fr. *courtault*, Mod.Fr. *courteau*, from *court*, L. *curtus*, short.] To cut off the end or a part of; to make shorter; to dock; hence, to shorten in any manner; to abridge; to diminish.— **curtailer**, kėr·tā'lėr, *n*. One who curtails.—**curtailment**, kėr·tāl'ment, *n*. The act of curtailing.

curtain, kėr'tin, *n*. [Fr. *curtine*, L.L. *cortina*, a little court, a curtain, from L. *cors, cortis*, an enclosure, a court. COURT.] A hanging cloth or screen before a window, around a bed, or elsewhere, that may be moved at pleasure so as to admit or exclude the light, conceal or show anything; the movable screen in a theater or like place serving to conceal the stage from the spectators; what resembles a curtain; *fort*. that part of a rampart which is between the flanks of two bastions, or between two gates.—*v.t.* To enclose or furnish with curtains. —**curtain lecture**, *n*. A lecture or reproof given behind the curtains or in bed by a wife to her husband.— **curtain raiser**, *n*. In the theater, a short piece, usually of one scene with few characters, used to open a performance.

curtsy, curtesy, kėrt'si, kėr'te·si, *n*. [A modification of *courtesy*.] An obeisance or gesture of respect by a woman, consisting in bending the knees and slightly dropping the body.—*v.i.*—**curtsied, curtsying**. To drop or make a curtsy.

curule, kū'röl, *a*. [L. *curulis*.] Rom. *antiq*. applied to a chair of state, something like a campstool, which belonged to certain of the magistrates of the republic in virtue of their office; hence, privileged to sit in such a chair.

curve, kėrv, *a*. [L. *curvus*, crooked. CURB.] Bending circularly, or so as in no part to be straight; having a bent form; crooked.—*n*. A bending in a circular form; a bend or flexure such that no part forms a straight line; *geom*. a line which may be cut by a straight line in more points than one; a line which changes its direction at every point.—*v.t.* curved, curving. To bend into the form of a curve; to crook.—*v.i.* To have a curved or bent form; to bend round.—**curvature**, kėr'va·chėr, *n*. A bending in a regular form; the manner or degree in which a thing is curved.

curvet, kėr'vet or kėr·vet', *n*. [It. *corvetta*, from L. *curvare*, to bend or curve.] The leap of a horse when he raises both forelegs at once, and as they are falling also his hind legs; a gambol; a leap.—*v.i.*—**curvetted, curvetting**. To make a curvet; to bound or leap; to prance; to frisk or gambol.—*v.t.* To cause to make a curvet.

curvicostate, kėr·vi·kos'tāt, *a*. [L. *curvus*, crooked, and *costa*, a rib.] Marked with small bent ribs.— **curvilinear, curvilineal**, kėr·vi·lin'i·ėr, kėr·vi·lin'i·al, *a*. [L. *linea*, a line.] Having the shape of a curved line; consisting of curved lines; bounded by curved lines.

cushat, kush'at, *n*. [A.Sax. *cusceote*.] The ring dove or wood pigeon.

cushion, kush'on, *n*. [Fr. *coussin*, It. *cuscino*; from a hypothetical *culcitinum*, dim. of L. *culcita*, a cushion, a quilt.] A pillow for a seat; a soft pad to be placed on a chair or attached to some kind of seat; any stuffed or padded appliance; the padded side or edge of a billiard table.—*v.t.* To furnish or fit with cushion or cushions.

cusk, kusk, *n*. A large edible marine fish, allied to the cod; the burbot.

cusp, kusp, *n*. [L. *cuspis*, a point, a spear.] A sharp projecting point; the point or horn of the crescent moon or other similar point; a prominence on a molar tooth; a projecting point formed by the meeting of curves, as in heads of Gothic windows and panels, etc.— **cusped**, kuspt, *a*. Furnished with a cusp or cusps; cusp-shaped.— **cuspidate, cuspidated**, ku'spi·dāt, kus'pi·dā·ted, *a*. Cusp-shaped or having cusps; terminating in a cusp or spine (as leaves).

cuspidor, kus'pi·dor, *n*. [Pg. from *cuspir*, to spit.] A spittoon.

custard, kus'tėrd, *n*. [Probably a corruption of old *crustade*, a kind of stew served up in a raised *crust*.] A composition of milk and eggs, sweetened, and baked or boiled, forming an agreeable kind of food.— **custard apple**, *n*. [From the yellowish pulp.] The large, dark-brown, roundish fruit of a West Indian tree, now cultivated in all tropical countries.

custody, kus'to·di, *n*. [L. *custodia*, from *custos, custodis*, a watchman, a keeper.] A keeping; a guarding; guardianship; care, watch, inspection, for keeping, preservation, or security; restraint of liberty; confinement; imprisonment.—**custodial**, kus·tō'di·al, *a*. Relating to custody or guardianship.—**custodian**, kus·tō'di·an, *n*. One who has the care or custody of anything, as of a library, some public building, etc.— **custodianship**, kus·tō'di·an·ship, *n*. The office or duty of a custodian.

custom, kus'tum, *n*. [O.Fr. *custume*, from L. *consuetudo, consuetudinis*, custom—*con*, with, and *sueo, suetum*, to be wont or accustomed. *Costume* is the same word.] Frequent or common use or practice; established manner; habitual practice; a practice or usage; an established and general mode of action, which obtains in a community; practice of frequenting a shop, manufactory, etc., and purchasing or giving orders; tribute, toll, or tax; *pl.* the duties imposed by law on merchandise imported or exported. *Custom* is the frequent repetition of the same act, *habit* being a custom continued so long as to develop a tendency or inclination to perform the customary act.—**customable,** kus'tum·a·bl, *a.* Subject to the payment of the duties called customs.—**customarily,** kus'tum·e·ri·li, *adv.* Habitually; commonly.—**customariness,** kus'tum·e·ri·nes, *n.* State of being customary; frequency; commonness.—**customary,** kus'tum·e·ri, *a.* According to custom or to established or common usage; wonted; usual; habitual; in common practice.—*n.* A book containing an account of the customs and municipal rights of a city, province, etc.—**customer,** kus'tum·er, *n.* A purchaser; a buyer; a dealer; one that a person has to deal with, or one that comes across a person; a queer fellow.—**customhouse,** *n.* An office where the customs on merchandise are paid or secured to be paid; the whole establishment by means of which the customs revenue is collected and its regulation enforced.

cut, kut, *v.t.*—**cut** (pret. & pp.), *cutting.* [Of Celtic origin; comp. W. *cwt,* a short piece, *cwtogi,* to curtail; Ir. *cut,* a short tail; *cutach,* bob-tailed.] To separate or divide the parts of by an edged instrument, or as an edged instrument does; to make an incision in; to sever; to sever and cause to fall for the purpose of removing; to fell, as wood; to mow or reap, as corn; to sever and remove, as the nails or hair; to fashion by, or as by, cutting or carving; to hew out; to carve; to wound the sensibilities of; to affect deeply; to intersect; to cross (one line *cuts* another); to have no longer anything to do with; to quit (*colloq.*); to shun the acquaintance of (*colloq.*).—*To cut down,* to cause to fall by severing; to reduce as by cutting; to retrench; to curtail (expenditure).—*To cut off,* to sever from the other parts; to bring to an untimely end; to separate; to interrupt; to stop (communication); to intercept; to hinder from return or union.—*To cut out,* to remove by cutting or carving; to shape or form by, or as by, cutting; to fashion; to take the preference or precedence of; *naut.* to seize and carry off, as a vessel from a harbor or from under the guns of the enemy.—*To cut short,* to hinder from proceeding by sudden interruption; to shorten; to abridge. —*To cut up,* to cut in pieces; to criticize severely; to censure; to wound the feelings deeply; to affect

greatly.—*To cut and run,* to cut the cable and set sail immediately; to be off; to be gone.—*To cut off with a penny;* to bequeath one's natural heir a penny; a practice adopted by a person dissatisfied with his heir, as a proof that the disinheritance was not the result of neglect—*To cut capers,* to leap or dance in a frolicsome manner.—*To cut a dash* or *figure,* to make a display. —*To cut a joke,* to joke; to crack a jest.—*To cut a knot,* to take short measures with anything; in allusion to the well-known story of Alexander the Great and the Gordian knot.—*To cut a pack of cards,* to divide it into portions before beginning to deal or for other purposes.—*To cut one's stick,* to move off; to be off at once. (*Slang.*)—*To cut the teeth,* to have the teeth pierce the gums.—*v.i.* To do the work of an edge tool; to serve in dividing or gashing; to admit of incision or severance; to use a knife or edge tool; to divide a pack of cards, to determine the deal or for any other purpose; to move off rapidly (*colloq.*).—*To cut across,* to pass over or through in the most direct way (*colloq.*).—*To cut in,* to join in suddenly and unceremoniously (*colloq.*).—*p.* and *a.* Gashed; carved; intersected; pierced; deeply affected. —*Cut and dry,* or *cut and dried,* prepared for use: a metaphor from hewn timber.—*Cut glass,* glass having the surface shaped or ornamented by grinding and polishing.— *Cut nail,* a nail manufactured by being cut from a rolled plate of iron by machinery.—*n.* The opening made by an edged instrument; a gash; a notch; a wound; a stroke or blow as with an edged instrument; a smart stroke or blow, as with a whip; anything that wounds one's feelings deeply, as a sarcasm, criticism, or act of discourtesy; a part cut off from the rest; a near passage, by which an angle is cut off; the block on which a picture is carved, and by which it is impressed; the impression from such a block; the act of dividing a pack of cards; manner in which a thing is cut; form; shape; fashion; the act of passing a person without recognizing him, or of avoiding him so as not to be recognized by him.—*To draw cuts,* to draw lots, as of paper, etc., cut of unequal lengths.—**cutter,** kut'er, *n.* One who or that which cuts; one who cuts out cloth for garments according to measurements; *naut.* a small boat used by ships of war; a vessel rigged nearly like a sloop, with one mast and a straight running bowsprit.—**cutting,** kut'ing, *a.* Penetrating or dividing by the edge; serving to penetrate or divide; sharp; piercing the heart; wounding the feelings; sarcastic; satirical; severe.—*n.* The act or operation of one who cuts; a piece cut off; a portion of a plant from which a new individual is propagated; an excavation made through a hill or rising ground in construct-

ing a road, railroad, canal, etc.— **cuttingly,** kut'ing·li, *adv.* In a cutting manner.—**cutpurse** *n.* One who cuts purses for the sake of stealing them or their contents; one who steals from the person; a thief; a robber.—**cutaway,** *n.* A coat, the skirts of which are rounded or cut away; used also adjectively.— **cutoff,** *n.* That which cuts off or shortens; that which is cut off; *steam engines,* a contrivance for economizing steam.—**cutthroat,** *n.* A murderer; an assassin; a ruffian.— *a.* Murderous; cruel; barbarous.— **cutwater,** *n.* The fore part of a ship's prow which cuts the water; the lower portion of the pier of a bridge formed with an angle or edge directed up stream.

cutaneous. See CUTICLE.

cutchery, kuch'er·i, *n.* In the East Indies, a court of justice or public office.

cute, kūt, *a.* [An abbrev. of *acute.*] Acute; clever; sharp.—**cuteness,** kūt'nes, *n.* The quality or character of being cute; attractive by reason of daintiness, usually with the idea of smallness, as a child.

cuticle, kū'ti·kl, *n.* [L. *cuticula,* dim. of *cutis,* skin.] *Anat.* the outermost thin transparent skin which covers the surface of the body; the epidermis or scarfskin; *bot.* the thin external covering of the bark of a plant; the outer pellicle of the epidermis.—**cutaneous,** kū·tā'ni·us, *a.* Belonging to the skin; existing on or affecting the skin.—**cutin,** kū'tin, *n.* A peculiar modification of cellulose, contained in the epidermis of leaves, petals, and fruits.— **cutis,** kū'tis, *n.* [L.] *Anat.* the dense resisting skin which forms the general envelope of body below the cuticle; the dermis or true skin.

cutlass, kut'las, *n.* [Fr. *coutelas,* from O.Fr. *coutel* (Fr. *couteau*), a knife; from L. *cultellus,* dim. of *culter,* a knife.] A broad curving sword used by cavalry, seamen, etc.

cutler, kut'lėr, *n.* [Fr. *coutelier,* from L. *culter,* a knife. CUTLASS.] One whose occupation is to make or deal in knives and other cutting instruments; one who sharpens or repairs cutlery; a knife grinder.—**cutlery,** kut'lėr·i, *n.* The business of a cutler; edged or cutting instruments.

cutlet, kut'let, *n.* [Fr. *côtelette,* lit. a little side or rib, from *côte,* side. COAST.} A piece of meat, especially veal or mutton, cut for cooking; generally cut from the short ribs or shank.

cuttle, cuttlefish, kut'l, *n.* [A.Sax. *cudele,* a cuttlefish; G. *kuttel-fisch.*] A two-gilled cephalopodous mollusk, having a body enclosed in a sac, eight arms or feet covered with suckers, used in locomotion and for seizing prey, a calcareous internal shell, and a bag or sac from which the animal has the power of ejecting a black inklike fluid (sepia) so as to darken the water and conceal it from pursuit.—**cuttlebone,** *n.* The internal calcareous plate of the cuttlefish, used for polishing wood, as also for pounce and tooth-powder.

cyanic, sī·an′ik, *a.* [Gr. *kyanos*, blue.] Of or pertaining to the color blue; *chem.* containing cyanogen.—**cyanide**, sī′an·id, *n.* A combination of cyanogen with a metallic base.—*Cyanide of potassium*, a poisonous substance used in photography and electrotyping.—**cyanogen**, sī·an′o·jen, *n.* A gas of a strong and peculiar odor composed of carbon and nitrogen.—**cyanosis**, sī·a·nō′sis, *n.* A condition in which the skin has a blue tint.

cybernetics, sī·bėr·net′iks, *n.* [Gr. *kybernetes*, helmsman, from *kybernan*, to steer. GOVERN.] The science that compares the communication and control systems in animals and machines.—**cybernetic**, sī·bėr·net′ik, *a.*—**cyberneticist**, sī·bėr·net′i·sist, *n.*

cycad, sī′kad, *n.* [Gr. *kykas*, a kind of plant.] One of a natural order of gymnospermous plants, resembling palms in their general appearance, inhabiting India, Australia, Cape of Good Hope, and tropical America.—**cycadaceous**, sī·ka·dā′shus, *a.* Belonging to the cycads.—**cycadiform**, sī·kad′i·form, *a.* Resembling in form the cycads.

cyclamen, sik′la·men, *n.* [From Gr. *kyklos*, a circle, referring to the roundshaped rootstock.] A genus of low-growing herbaceous plants, with fleshy rootstocks and very handsome flowers.

cycle, sī′kl, *n.* [Gr. *kyklos*, a circle or cycle.] A circle or orbit in the heavens; a circle or round of years, or a period of time, in which a certain succession of events or phenomena is completed; a long period of years; an age; the aggregate of legendary or traditional matter accumulated round some mythical or heroic event or character (as the siege of Troy or King Arthur); a bicycle or similar conveyance.—*v.i.* —*cycled, cycling.* To use a cycle; *bot.* a complete turn of leaves, etc., arranged spirally.—*Cycle of the moon*, or golden number, a period of nineteen years, after the lapse of which the new and full moons return on the same days of the month.—*Cycle of the sun* is a period of twenty-eight years, which having elapsed, the dominical or Sunday letters return to their former place according to the Julian calendar.—*v.i.* —*cycled, cycling.* To recur in cycles.—**cyclic**, sī′klik, *a.* Pertaining to or moving in a cycle or circle; connected with a cycle in the sense it has in literature.—*Cyclic poets*, Greek poets who wrote on matters and personages connected with the Trojan war.—**cyclical**, sī′kli·kal, *a.* Pertaining to a cycle; cyclic.—**cyclist**, sīk′list, *n.* One who uses a cycle.—**cycloid**, sī′kloid, *n.* A curve generated by a point in the circumference of a circle when the circle is rolled along a straight line and kept always in the same plane, that is, such a line as a nail in the circumference of a carriage wheel describes in the air while the wheel runs.—*a.* Having a circular form; belonging to the Cycloidians. —**cycloidal**, sī′kloi·dal, *a.* Of or pertaining to a cycloid.

cyclone, sī′klōn, *n.* [From Gr. *kyklos*, a circle.] A circular or rotary storm of immense force, revolving at an enormous rate round a calm center, and at the same time advancing at a rate varying from 20 to 40 miles an hour. In the northern hemisphere they rotate from right to left, and in the southern from left to right.—**cyclonic**, sī·klon·ik, *a.* Relating to a cyclone.

cyclopedia, **cyclopaedia**, sī·klo·pē′di·a, *n.* [Gr. *kyklos*, circle, and *paideia*, discipline.] A work containing definitions or accounts of the principal subjects in one or all branches of science, art, or learning; an encyclopedia.—**cyclopedic**, **cyclopaedic**, **cyclopedical**, **cyclopaedical**, sī·klo·pē′dik, sī·klo·pē′di·kal, *a.* Belonging to a cyclopedia.

Cyclops, sī′klops, *n. sing,* and *pl.* [Gr. *kyklōps*, a Cyclops, pl. *kyklōpes* —*kyklos*, a circle, and *ōps*, an eye.] *Class. myth.* a race of giants who had but one circular eye in the middle of the forehead.

cyclostome, sī′klo·stōm, *n.* [Gr. *kyklos*, a circle, and *stoma*, a mouth.] One of a family of cartilaginous fishes which have circular mouths, as the lamprey.—**cyclostomous**, sī·klos′to·mus, *a.* Having a circular mouth or aperture.

cyclotron, sī′klo·tron, *n. Phys.* an apparatus using electromagnetic and electrostatic means to cause electrified particles to move in circles at high speeds.

cygnet, sig′net, *n.* [Dim. of Fr. *cygne*, from L. *cygnus*, a swan.] A young swan.

cylinder, sil′in·dėr, *n.* [Gr. *kylindros*, from *kylindō*, to roll.] A body shaped like a roller; an elongated, round, solid body, of uniform diameter throughout its length, and terminating in two flat circular surfaces which are equal and parallel; that chamber of a steam engine in which the force of steam is exerted on the piston; in certain printing machines, a roller by which the impression is made, and on which stereotype plates may be secured.—**cylindric**, **cylindrical**, si·lin′drik, si·lin′dri·kal, *a.* Having the form of a cylinder, or partaking of its properties.—**cylindrically**, si·lin′dri·kal·li, *adv.* In the manner or shape of a cylinder.— **cylindroid**, sil′in·droid, *n.* A solid body resembling a cylinder, but having the bases elliptical.

cyma, sī′ma, *n.* [Gr. *kyma*, a wave, a sprout, from *kyō*, to swell.] *Arch.* a molding of a cornice, the profile of which is a double curve, concave joined to convex; an ogee molding; *bot.* a cyme.

cymar, si·mär′, *n.* [Fr. *simmare*.] Woman's light garment.

cymbal, sim′bal, *n.* [L. *cymbalum*, Gr. *kymbalon*, a cymbal, from *kymbos*, hollow.] A musical instru-ment, circular and hollow like a dish, made of brass or bronze, two of which are struck together, producing a sharp ringing sound.—**cymbalist**, sim′ba·list, *n.* One who plays the cymbals.

cyme, sīm, *n.* [Gr. *kyma*, a wave, a sprout. CYMA.] *Bot.* an inflorescence of the definite or determinate class, in which the flowers are in racemes, corymbs, or umbels, the successive central flowers expanding first.—**cymose**, sī′mōs, *a.* Containing a cyme; in the form of a cyme.

cymophane, sī′mō·fān, *n.* [Gr. *kyma*, a wave, and *phainō*, to show.] A siliceous gem of a yellowish-green color, the same as chrysoberyl.

Cymric, kim′rik, *a.* Of or pertaining to the Cymry (kim′ri), the name given to themselves by the Welsh; Welsh; pertaining to the ancient race to which the Welsh belong.—*n.* The language of the Cymry or ancient Britons; Welsh.

cynic, sin′ik, *n.* [L. *cynicus*, Gr. *kynikos*, from Gr. *kyōn*, *kynos*, a dog.] [*cap.*] One of an ancient sect of Greek philosophers who valued themselves on their contempt of riches, of arts, sciences, and amusements; a man of a currish temper; a surly or snarling man; a sneering faultfinder; a misanthrope.—**cynical**, sin′i·kal, *a.* surly; sneering; captious.—**cynically**, sin′i·kal·li, *adv.* In a cynical, sneering, captious, or morose manner.—**cynicalness**, sin′i·kal·nes, *n.* The state or character of being cynical.—**cynicism**, sin′i·sizm, *n.* The practice of a cynic; a morose contempt of the pleasures and arts of life.

cynosure, sī′no·shör, *n.* [Gr. *kyno-soura*, lit. dog's tail, the Little Bear— *kyōn*, *kynos*, a dog, and *oura*, tail.] [*cap.*] An old name of the constellation Ursa Minor or the Little Bear, which contains the polestar, and thus has long been noted by mariners and others; hence, anything that strongly attracts attention; a center of attraction.

cyperaceous, sī·pėr·ā′shus, *a.* [Gr. *kyperos*, an aromatic plant.] Belonging to the sedge family of plants; having the characters of the sedges.

cypher, sī′fėr, *n.* Same as *cipher*.

cypress, sī′pres, *n.* [O.Fr. *cypres*, Gr. *kyparissos*.] The popular name of a genus of coniferous trees, some species of which have attained much favor in shrubberies and gardens as ornamental evergreen trees, while the wood of others is highly valued for its durability; the emblem of mourning for the dead, cypress branches having been anciently used at funerals.

Cyprian, sip′ri·an, *a.* Belonging to the island of *Cyprus*; a term applied to a lewd woman, from the worship of Venus in Cyprus and women of this island having anciently had a bad character.—*n.* A native of Cyprus; a lewd woman; a courtesan; a strumpet.—**Cypriot**, sip′ri·ot, *n.* A native of Cyprus.

cypsela, sip′se·la, *n.* [Gr. *kypselē*, any hollow vessel.] *Bot.* the one-celled, one-seeded, indehiscent, inferior fruit of composite plants.

Cyrillic, si·ril′ik, *a.* [From St. *Cyril,* its reputed inventor.] The term applied to an alphabet adopted by all the Slavonic peoples belonging to the Eastern Church.

cyst, sist, *n.* [Gr. *kystis,* a bladder.] A close sac or bag of vegetable or animal nature; a bladder-like body; a hollow organ with thin walls (as the urinary bladder); a bladder-like bag or vesicle which includes morbid matter in animal bodies.—**cystic,** sis′tik, *a.* Pertaining to, or contained in, a cyst; having cysts; formed in, or shaped like, a cyst.—**cysticercus,** sis·te·ser′kus. [Gr. *kystis,* a bladder, *kerkos,* a tail.] In tapeworms, a simple cyst with only one head.—**cystitis,** sis·tī′tis, *n.* Inflammation of the bladder.—**cystocele,** sis′to·sēl, *n.* [Gr. *kelē,* a tumor.] A hernia or rupture formed by the protrusion of the urinary bladder. —**cystoscope,** sis′to·skōp. [Gr. *kystis,* a bladder, *skōpeō,* I look at.] An instrument for inspecting the interior of the bladder.—**cystotomy,** sis·tot′o·mi, *n.* The act or practice of opening encysted tumors; the operation of cutting into the bladder for the extraction of a calculus.

Cytherean, sith·e·rē′an, *a.* [From *Cythera,* now Cerigo, where Venus was specially worshiped.] Pertaining to Venus.

cytogenesis, sī·tō·jen′e·sis, *n.* [Gr. *kytos,* a cell, and *genesis,* origin.] *Biol.* the development of cells in animal and vegetable structures.— **cytogenetic,** sī′tō·je·net″ik, *a.* *Biol.* relating or pertaining to cell formation.—**cytology,** sī·tol′o·ji, *n.* The biological doctrine of cells; the study of cells.—**cytolysis,** sīt·ol′is·is. [Gr. *kytōs,* a cell, *lysis,* a loosing.] The dissolving of poisoned cells.— **cytoplasm,** sīt′o·plasm. [Gr. *kytōs,* a cell, *plasma,* anything formed.] Of a cell, the part of the protoplasm outside the nucleus.

czar, zär or tsär, *n.* [Perhaps a corruption of L. *Cæsar.*] A title of the Emperor of Russia.—**czarevna,** zä·rev′na, *n.* The wife of the czarevitch.—**czarina,** zä·rē′na, *n.* A title of the Empress of Russia.—**czarevitch,** zä′re·vich, *n.* The title of the eldest son of the Czar of Russia.

Czech, chech, *n.* A Bohemian; one of the Slavonic inhabitants of Bohemia; the language of the Czechs or Bohemians.

D

D, d, dē, in the English alphabet, is the fourth letter and the third consonant, representing a dental sound; as a numeral equivalent to 500; *mus.* the second note of the natural scale, answering to the French and Italian *re.*

dab, dab, *v.t.*—*dabbed, dabbing.* [Allied to O.D. *dabben,* to dabble,

probably also to *dub.*] To strike quickly but lightly with the hand or with some soft or moist substance.—*n.* A gentle blow with the hand or some soft substance; a quick but light blow; an expert (*colloq.*); a small lump or mass of anything soft or moist; a name common to many species of the flatfish, but especially to a kind of flounder which is found along the European and American coasts of the Atlantic Ocean.—**dabber,** dab′ér, *n.* One who dabs.

dabble, dab′l, *v.t.*—*dabbled, dabbling.* [A dim. and freq. from *dab.*] To wet; to moisten; to spatter; to sprinkle.—*v.i.* To play in water, as with the hands; to splash in mud or water; to do or engage in anything in a slight or superficial manner; to occupy one's self with slightly; to dip into; to meddle.—**dabbler,** dab′lér, *n.* One who dabbles in water or mud; one who partakes casually without going thoroughly into an activity; a superficial, casual participant, as one who *dabbles* in politics.

dabchick, dab′chik, *n.* [Dab, equivalent to *dip,* and *chick,* from its habit of dipping or diving below the water.] The little grebe, a small swimming bird of the diver family.

dace, dās, *n.* [O.Fr. *dars,* a dace, a dart; comp. also Fr. *vandoise,* the dace.] A small river fish resembling the roach, chiefly inhabiting the deep and clear waters of quiet streams.

dachshund, daks′hunt, *n.* [G. *dachs,* badger, *hund,* dog.] Badger dog; a long-bodied, short-legged dog, with pendulous ears and short hair, black with yellow extremities.

dacoit, dacoity. See DAKOIT, DAKOITY.

dactyl, dak′til, *n.* [Gr. *daktylos,* a finger, a dactyl, which, like a finger, consists of one long and two short members.] A poetical foot consisting of three syllables, the first long and the others short, or the first accented, the others not, as in hăppily.—**dactylic,** dak·til′ik, *a.* Pertaining to or consisting chiefly or wholly of dactyls.—*n.* A dactylic verse.—**dactylology,** dak·ti·lol′o·ji, *n.* The art of communicating ideas or thoughts by the fingers; the language of the deaf and dumb.

dad, daddy, dad, dad′i, *n.* [Comp. W. *tad,* Skr. *tata,* Hind. *dada,* Gypsy *dad, dada,* L. *tata,* Gr. *tata,* Lapp *dadda*—father.] A childish or pet name for father.—**daddy longlegs,** *n.* A kind of spider, called also *harvest-man.*

dado, dā′dō, *n.* [It., a die, a dado, same word as *die, n.*] That part of a pedestal which is between the base and the cornice; the finishing of the lower part of the walls in rooms, made somewhat to represent a continuous pedestal, and frequently formed by a lining of wood, by painting, or by a special wall paper.

daedal, dē′dal, *a.* [L. *Dædalus,* Gr. *Daidalos,* an ingenious artist.] Formed with art; showing artistic skill; ingenious; mazy; intricate.

daemon, dē′mon. Same as *Demon.*

daff,†‡ daf. *v.t.* [A form of *doff.*] To toss aside, to put off. (*Shak.*)

daffodil, daf′o·dil, *n.* [O.E. *affodille,* O.Fr. *asphodile,* Gr. *asphodelos.* ASPHODEL.] Common name of a plant of the amaryllis family with bright yellow bell-shaped flowers; a variety of narcissus; grows in woods and meadows; called also *Daffadowndilly, Daffadilly, Daffodilly.*

dag, dag, *n.* [Probably from same root as *dagger.*] A loose end, as of a lock of wool.

dagger, dag′ér, *n.* [W. *dagr,* Ir. *daigear,* Armor. *dager, dag.* a dagger or poniard; Gael. *daga,* a dagger, a pistol; Fr. *dague,* a dagger.] A weapon resembling a short sword, with usually a two-edged, sometimes a three-edged, sharp-pointed blade, used for stabbing at close quarters; *printing,* a mark of reference in the form of a dagger, thus†.—*At daggers drawn,* on hostile terms; at war.— *To look* or *speak daggers,* to look or speak fiercely, savagely.—*v.t.* To stab with a dagger.

daggle, dag′l, *v.t.*—*daggled, daggling.* [A freq. form of the obsolete verb *dag,* to bedew, from Icel. *dögg,* Sw. *dagg,* dew.] To make limp by passing through water; to trail in mud or wet grass; to befoul; to draggle.— *v.i.* To run through mud and water.

Dago, dā′gō, *n.* [Sp. *Diego,* James.] A name applied to Spanish, Portuguese, or Italian immigrants, often scornfully.

Dagon, dā′gon, *n.* [Heb. *dag,* a fish.] The national god of the Philistines, represented with the upper part of a man and the tail of a fish.

daguerreotype, da·gâr′ō·tīp, *n.* [From *Daguerre* of Paris, the inventor.] A photographic process by which the picture is fixed on a chemically coated metallic plate solely by the action of the sun's actinic or chemical rays; a picture produced by the process.

dahabeah, dä·ha·bē′ä, *n.* [Egyptian name.] A kind of boat in use on the Nile for the conveyance of travelers, and having one or two masts with a long yard supporting a triangular sail.

dahlia, däl′ya, *n.* [From *Dahl,* a Swedish botanist.] A genus of American composite plants, consisting of tuberous-rooted herbs, putting forth solitary terminal flowers, well known from the varieties of one species being florists' plants.

daily, dā′li, *a. adv.* and *n.* See DAY.

daimio, dī′mi·ō, *n.* [Japanese.] The title of a class of feudal lords in Japan, the greater number of whom, previous to 1871, exercised the authority of petty princes in their domains.

dainty, dān′ti, *a.* [From O.Fr. *daintie, daintē,* pleasantness, an agreeable thing, same word as *dignity,* or from W. *dantaidd, dantaeth,* a dainty, what is toothsome, from *dant,* a tooth.] Pleasing to the palate; of exquisite taste; delicious, as food; of acute sensibility; nice in selecting what is tender and good;

delicate; squeamish; luxurious, as the palate or taste; scrupulous; affectedly fine; nice; ceremonious; elegant; pretty and slight; tender; effeminately beautiful.—*n.* Something delicate to the taste; that which is delicious; a delicacy.—**daintily**, dān′ti•li, *adv.* In a dainty manner.—**daintiness**, dān′ti•nes, *n.* The state or quality of being dainty.

dairy, dâ′ri, *n.* [From O.E. *dey*, a dairymaid = Sw. *deja*, a dairymaid. Icel. *deigja*, a maid servant, a dairymaid.] The place where milk is processed and prepared for sale; a shop where milk, butter, etc., are sold; also used as an adj.—**dairying**, dâ′ri•ing, *n.* The business of conducting a dairy.—**dairymaid**, dâ′ri•mād, *n.* A female whose business is to milk cows and work in the dairy.—**dairyman**, dâ′ri•man, *n.*

dais, dā′is, *n.* [O.Fr. *dais*, *deis*, a dining table, from L. *discus*, a dish, a quoit. *Disk*, *desk*, are the same word.] The high table at the upper end of an ancient dining hall at which the chief persons sat; the raised floor on which the table stood; the chief seat at the high table; often with a canopy; a canopy.

daisy, dā′zi, *n.* [A.Sax. *daeges-eáge*, day's eye, because it opens and closes its flower with the daylight.] The popular name of a composite plant, one of the most common wild flowers, being found in all pastures and meadows, and several varieties being cultivated in gardens; also the name of several other plants having a somewhat similiar blossom. North Carolina's state flower.—**daisied**, dā′zid, *a.* Full of daisies; adorned with daisies.

dak, däk, *n.* See DAWK.

dakoit, da•koit′, *n.* An East Indian name for robbers who plunder in bands, but seldom take life.—**dakoity**, da•koi′ti, *n.* The system of robbing in bands.

dale, dāl, *n.* [A.Sax. *dael* = Icel. Sw. Goth. etc. *dal*, G. *thal*, a valley. *Dell* is akin; the root may be in *deal*.] A low place between hills; a vale or valley.—**dalesman**, dālz′man, *n.* One living in a dale or valley.

dally, dal′i, *v.i.*—dallied, dallying. [Probably allied to G. *dalen*, *dallen*, *tallen*, to speak or act childishly, to trifle, to toy; or perhaps E. *doll*.] To waste time in effeminate or voluptuous pleasures; to amuse one's self with idle play; to trifle; to linger; to delay; to toy and wanton; to interchange caresses; to fondle; to sport; to play; to frolic.—**dalliance**, dal′yans, *n.* The act of dallying, caressing, fondling, trifling, deferring, or delaying.—**dallier**, dal′i•ėr, *n.* One who dallies.

Dalmatian, dal•mā′shi•an, *a.* Of or pertaining to *Dalmatia*.—*Dalmatian dog*, a variety of dog of elegant shape, of a white color, thickly marked with black rounded spots; usually kept as a coach dog.—**dalmatic**, dal•mat′ik, *n.* The vestment used by the deacon at mass, and worn also by bishops under the chasuble, so called as coming originally from

Dalmatia, long, loose, and wide-sleeved.

Daltonism, dal′ton•izm, *n.* [From *Dalton*, the chemist, who suffered from this defect, and was the first to call attention to it.] Color blindness.

dam, dam, *n.* [A form of *dame*.] A female parent: used now only of quadrupeds, unless in contempt.

dam, dam, *n.* [Indian.] Name of a small Indian coin of slight value—*not worth a dam*. RAP.

dam, dam, *n.* [Same word as Sw. and G. *damm*, Dan. and D. *dam* (as in Amster*dam*, Rotter*dam*, etc.); Lith. *tama*, a dam.] A bank, mound of earth, wall, or other structure, built across a current of water, to raise its level for the purpose of driving millwheels, or for other purposes.—*v.t.*—dammed, damming. To obstruct by a dam; to confine by constructing a dam.

damage, dam′ij, *n.* O.Fr. *damage*; Fr. *dommage*, from L.L. *damnaticum*, from L. *damnum*, loss, injury. DAMN.] Any hurt, injury, or harm to person, property, character, or reputation; the value in money of what is injured, harmed, or lost; the estimated money equivalent for detriment or injury sustained: in this sense commonly in pl.—*v.t.*—damaged, damaging. To injure; to impair; to lessen the soundness, goodness, or value of.—*v.i.* To become injured or impaired in soundness or value.—**damageable**, dam′ij•a•bl, *a.* Capable of being injured or impaired; susceptible of damage.

daman, dā′man, *n.* A rabbit-like animal, the hyrax, or cony of Scripture.

damascene, dam′as•sēn, *n.* [L. *damascenus*, from *Damascus*.] A kind of plum; a damson.—*v.t.* To damask; to damaskeen.

damask, dam′ask, *a.* Of or belonging to *Damascus*; of the color of the rose so called; pink or rosy.—*Damask steel*, a fine steel chiefly from Damascus, used for sword blades.—*n.* The name given to textile fabrics of various materials, more especially silk and linen, ornamented with raised figures of flowers, etc.; a pink color, like that of the damask rose.—*v.t.* To form or imprint the figures of flowers upon, as upon cloth; to variegate; to diversify; to adorn with figures, as steelwork.—**damaskeen**, dam′as•kēn, *v.t.* [Fr. *damasquiner*.] To ornament (particularly iron and steel) with designs produced by inlaying or incrusting with another metal, as gold, silver, etc., by etching, and the like; to damask.—**damask rose**, *n.* A pink species of rose.

dame, dām, *n.* [Fr. *dame*, from L. *domina*, a mistress, fem. of *dominus*, a lord, whence *dominate*, *dominion*, *damsel*, etc.; same root as E. *tame*.] A woman in authority; a title equivalent to *Lady*, *Madam*, *Miss*, used as a form of address; a woman in general; particularly, a woman of mature years; an honor similar to knighthood bestowed on women.

dammar, dam′är, *n.* A gum or resin

used as a colorless varnish, and produced by various species of coniferous trees (dammar or dammara-pine) belonging to the South Asiatic islands and New Zealand, kauri gum being a variety.

damn, dam, *v.t.* [L. *damno*, to condemn, from *damnum*, damage, a fine, penalty, from root *da*, as in *dare*, to give.] To consign or send to punishment in a future state; to send to hell; to condemn, censure, reprobate severely; to condemn or destroy the success of by common consent, as by hissing in a theater or by criticisms in the press.—*n.* A profane oath; a curse or execration.—**damnable**, dam′na•bl, *a.* Liable to be damned or condemned; deserving damnation; odious, detestable, or pernicious.—**damnableness**, dam′na•bl•nes, *n.* The state or quality of being damnable.—**damnably**, dam′na•bli, *adv.* In a damnable manner; odiously; detestably; infernally.—**damnation**, dam•nā′shon, *n.* Sentence to punishment in a future state, or the state in which such punishment is undergone; eternal punishment; penalty inflicted for sin; condemnation.—**damnatory**, dam′na•to•ri, *a.* Containing a sentence of condemnation; condemning to damnation; condemnatory.—**damned**, damd, *p.* and *a.* Suffering punishment in hell; lost; hateful; detestable; abominable.—**damning**, dam′ning, dam′ing, *a.* Exposing to damnation; calling for damnation (a *damning* sin).

damp, damp, *a.* [Same word as D. and Dan. *damp*, G. *dampf*, steam, vapor, fog, smoke.] Being in a state between dry and wet; moderately wet; moist; humid; depressed or dejected.—*n.* Moist air; humidity; moisture; fog; dejection; depression of spirits; chill; a noxious exhalation issuing from the earth, and deleterious or fatal to animal life, such as exists in old disused wells, in mines and coal pits.—*v.t.* To make damp; to moisten; to chill, deaden, depress, or deject; to check or restrain; to discourage; to dispirit; to abate.—**dampen**, dam′pen, *v.t.* To make damp or moist.—*v.i.* To grow or become damp.—**damper**, dam′pėr, *n.* One who or that which damps; an iron plate sliding across a flue of a furnace, etc., to check or regulate the draft of air; a piece of mechanism in a pianoforte which, after the finger has left the key, checks a long-continued vibration of the strings; a cake made of flour and water without fermentation (a colonial word).—**dampish**, dam′pish, *a.* Moderately damp or moist.—**dampishness**, dam′pish•nes, *n.* The state of being dampish.—**dampness**, damp′nes, *n.* The state or condition of being damp; moistness; humidity.

damsel, dam′zel, *n.* [Fr. *demoiselle*, O.Fr. *damoisele*, *damisele*, from L.L. *dominicella*, dim. of L. *domina*, *domna*, a mistress. DAME.] A young unmarried woman; a maiden; a virgin.

damson, dam′zn, *n.* [Contr. from

damascene (which see).] A small black, dark-bluish, purple, or yellow plum.

Dan, dan, *n.* [O.Fr. *dan, dans,* a master, from L. *dominus.* DAME.] An old title of honor equivalent to *master, sir, don* ('*Dan* Chaucer').

dance, dans, *v.i.—danced, dancing.* [Fr. *danser,* from O.H.G. *danson,* to draw.] To leap or move with measured steps, regulated by music; to leap and frisk about; to move nimbly, as up and down, backward and forward.—*v.t.* To make to dance; to dandle.—*To dance attendance,* to be assiduous in attentions and officious civilities.—*n.* A leaping or stepping with motions of the body adjusted to the measure of a tune; the regular movements of one who dances; a tune by which dancing is regulated.—**dancer,** dan'sėr, *n.* One who dances.

dandelion, dan'di·li·un, *n.* [Fr. *dent de lion,* lion's tooth.] A well-known composite plant, having a naked stalk, with one large bright yellow flower, and a tapering milky perennial root of aperient and tonic properties.

dandle, dan'dl, *v.t.—dandled, dandling.* [Allied to G. *tand,* prattle, frivolity, *tändeln,* to trifle, to dandle.] To shake or jolt on the knee, as an infant; to fondle, amuse, or treat as a child; to pet.—**dandler,** dand'lėr, *n.* One who dandles.

dandruff, dan'druf, *n.* [Etym. unknown.] A scurf which forms on the head and comes off in small scales or particles.

dandy, dan'di, *n.* [Fr. *dandin,* a ninny, akin to E. *dandle.*] A man who pays excessive attention to dress; one who dresses with special finery; a fop; a coxcomb.—*a.* Finely or foppishly dressed; foppish; trim; gay.—**dandify,** dan'di·fī, *v.t.* To make, form, or dress out as a dandy or fop.—**dandyish,** dan'di·ish, *a.* Like a dandy.—**dandyism,** dan'di··izm, *n.* The manners and dress of a dandy; foppishness.

Dane, dān, *n.* A native or inhabitant of Denmark.—**Danegelt, Danegeld,** dān'gelt, dān'geld, *n.* [*Gelt, geld* = A.Sax. *geld, gild,* a payment.] An annual tax laid on the English nation in early times for maintaining forces to oppose the Danes, or to furnish tribute to procure peace.—**Danish,** dā'nish, *a.* Belonging to the Danes or Denmark.—*n.* The language of the Danes.

danger, dān'jėr, *n.* [Formerly control, power, Fr. *danger,* O.Fr. *dangier, dongier,* a feudal term for right to woods and waters, from L.L. *dominiarium,* from L. *dominus,* a lord; akin *dominion, dame, damsel,* etc.] Exposure to destruction, ruin, injury, loss, pain, or other evil; peril; risk; hazard; jeopardy.—**dangerous,** dān'jėr·us, *a.* Attended with danger; perilous; hazardous; unsafe; full of risk; creating danger, causing risk of evil.—**dangerously,** dān'jėr·us·li, *adv.* In a dangerous manner or condition.—**dangerousness,** dān'jėr·us··nes, *n.* The state or quality of being dangerous.

dangle, dang'gl, *v.i.—dangled, dangling.* [Allied to Dan. *dingle,* Sw. and Icel. *dingla,* to swing.] To hang loose, flowing, shaking, or waving; to hang and swing; to be a humble officious follower, or to hang about a person (with *about* or *after*).—*v.t.* To cause to dangle; to swing.—**dangler,** dang'glėr, *n.* One who dangles; a man who hangs about women.

dank, dangk, *a.* [Nasalized form allied to *daggle* and Sw. *dagg,* dew.] Damp; moist; humid.—*n.*‡ Moisture; humidity; the watery element. (*Mil.*)

danseuse, dän·sėz', *n.* [Fr.] A female stage dancer.

dap, dap, *v.i.* [Onomatopoeic.] To drop or let fall the bait gently into the water; an angling word.

dapper, dap'ėr, *a.* [Same word as D. *dapper,* Sw. and Dan. *tapper,* G. *tapfer,* brave.] Small and active; nimble; brisk; lively; neat.

dapple, dap'l, *a.* [Icel. *depill,* a spot; perhaps akin to *dip, deep.*] Marked with spots spotted; variegated with spots of different colors or shades of color.—*v.t.* *dappled, dappling.* To spot; to variegate with spots.

dare, dâr, *v.i.—*pret. *dared* or *durst;* pp. *dared;* ppr. *daring.* [A.Sax. *ic dear,* I dare, *he dear,* he dare, *we durran,* we dare; *ic dorste,* I durst; Goth. *daursan,* O.H.G. *turran;* cog. Gr. *tharsein,* Skr. *dharsh,* to be courageous.] To have courage for any purpose; to make up the mind to undertake something hazardous or dangerous; to be bold enough; to venture.—*v.t.—dared, daring.* To challenge, to provoke, to defy.—**daredevil,** *n.* A desperado; one who fears nothing and will attempt anything.—**daring,** dâ'ring, *a.* Bold; audacious; courageous; intrepid; adventurous.—*n.* Courage; boldness; fearlessness; audacity.—**daringly,** dâ'ring·li, *adv.* In a daring manner.—**daringness,** dâ'ring·nes, *n.* Boldness.

dare, dār, *v.t.* [A.Sax. *darian;* perhaps akin to Flemish *verdaren,* to amaze.] To stupefy by sudden terror; to daze.

dare, dār, *n.* See DACE.

dark, därk, *a.* [A.Sax. *deorc;* not found in the other Teutonic languages; comp. Gael. and Ir. *dorch,* dark, black.] Destitute of light; not radiating or reflecting light; wholly or partially black; having the quality opposite to white; gloomy; disheartening; not cheerful; concealed; secret; mysterious; not easily understood; not enlightened with knowledge; rude; ignorant (the *dark* ages); morally black; atrocious; wicked; sinister; keeping designs concealed; not fair; said of the complexion.—*n.* [Usually with *the.*] Darkness; the absence of light; a dark hue; a dark part; secrecy; obscurity; a state of ignorance.—**darken,** där'kn, *v.t.* To make dark or black; to deprive of light; to obscure, cloud, make dim; to deprive of vision; to render gloomy; to render ignorant or stupid; to render less clear or intelligible; to sully; to taint.—*v.i.* To grow dark or darker.—**dark horse,** *n.* A

contestant about whom little is known or who unexpectedly wins.—**darkish,** därk'ish, *a.* Somewhat dark. —**darkling,** därk'ling, *adv.* In the dark.—*a.* Dark; lowering; gloomy. (*Thack.*)—**darkly,** därk'li, *adv.* In a dark manner; with imperfect light, clearness, or knowledge; obscurely; dimly; blindly; uncertainly.—**darkness,** därk'nes, *n.* The state or quality of being dark; the want of physical light; gloom; obscurity; deepness of shade or color; physical, intellectual, or moral blindness. —**darkroom,** *n.* A room with no light, or with a dim, colored light, used in treating and handling photographic or other light-sensitive materials.—**darksome,** därk'sum, *a.* Poet. gloomy; dark.

darling, där'ling, *a.* [A.Sax. *deórling* —*deóre,* dear, and dim. term. *-ling* DEAR.] Dearly beloved; dear; favorite. —*n.* One much beloved; a favorite.

darn, därn, *v.t.* [W. and Armor. *darn,* Ir. *darne,* a piece, a patch.] To mend a rent or hole in, by imitating the texture of the cloth or stuff with yarn or thread and a needle; to sew or repair by crossing and recrossing the stitches.—*n.* A place mended by darning.

darnel, där'nel, *n.* [O.Fr. *darnelle;* same root as D. *door,* G. *thor,* a fool, Lith. *durnas,* foolish, mad; from its narcotic properties.] A troublesome weed in cornfields, with ryelike ears, which, when ground among corn, are said to be narcotic and stupefying.

dart, därt, *n.* [O.Fr. *dart,* Mod.Fr. *dard;* of Germanic origin = Sw. *dart,* A.Sax. *daroth,* O.H.G. *tart.*] A pointed missile weapon to be thrown by the hand; a short lance; anything which pierces and wounds; a sudden or rapid rush, leap, bound, spring, or flight.—*v.t.* To throw (a dart, etc.) with a sudden thrust; to throw swiftly; to shoot.—*v.i.* To fly, as a dart; to fly rapidly; to spring and run with velocity; to start suddenly and run.—**darter,** där'tėr, *n.* One that darts; a web-footed tropical bird of the pelican tribe, so called from darting after fish in the water.

Darwinian, där·win'i·an, *a.* Of or pertaining to Charles *Darwin,* the celebrated naturalist.—*n.* A believer in Darwinism.—**Darwinism,** där'-win·izm, *n.* The doctrine as to the origin and modifications of the species of animals and plants taught by Darwin, the principal points being that there is a tendency to variation in organic beings, so that descendants may differ ever widely from progenitors; that animals and plants tend naturally to multiply rapidly, so that if unchecked they would soon overstock the whole globe; that there is thus a continual struggle for existence among all organized beings; that the strongest and best fitted for particular surroundings naturally survive, and the others die out; that from a few forms (perhaps even one) sprang all existing species, genera, orders, etc., of animals and plants.

dash, dash, *v.t.* [A Scandinavian

word=Dan. *daske*, to slap, *dask*, a slap, Sw. *daska*, to beat.] To cause to strike or come against suddenly and with violence; to strike or throw violently or suddenly; to sprinkle or mix slightly; to disturb or frustrate (to *dash* courage); to confound, confuse, abash.—*To dash off*, to form or sketch out in haste carelessly; to execute hastily or with careless rapidity.—*v.i.* To rush with violence; to strike or be cast violently.—*n.* A violent striking together of two bodies; collision; something thrown into another substance; infusion; admixture; a sudden check; abashment; a rapid movement; a sudden onset; the capacity for unhesitating, prompt action; vigor in attack; a flourish or ostentatious parade; a mark or line [–] in writing or printing noting a break or pause.—**dasher,** dash′ẽr, *n.* One who or that which dashes; the float of a paddle wheel, the plunger of a churn, and the like; also a dashboard.—**dashing,** dash′-ing, *a.* Impetuous spirited; showy; brilliant.—**dashboard,** *n* A board or leathern apron on the fore part of a vehicle to intercept mud, etc.; a partition below the windshield of an automobile (instrument board).

dastard, das′tẽrd, *n.* [Icel. *daestr*, exhausted; akin to *daze*, the suffix being -*ard*.] A coward; a poltroon; one who meanly shrinks from danger. —*a.* Cowardly; meanly; shrinking from danger.—**dastardliness,** das′-tẽrd·li·nes, *n.* Cowardliness.—**dastardly,** das′tẽrd·li, *a.* Cowardly.

dasyure, dā′si·ūr, *n.* [Gr. *dasys*, hairy, and *oura*, a tail.] A carnivorous marsupial found in Australia.

data. See DATUM.

date, dāt, *n.* [Fr., from L. *datum*, given, used in a Roman letter as 'given' (at such a place and such a time).] That addition to a writing which specifies the year, month, and day when it was given or executed; the time when any event happened, when anything was transacted, or when anything is to be done; the period of time at or during which one has lived or anything has existed; an appointment made for a specified time; a social engagement with one of the opposite sex.—*Out of date,* obsolete; behind the times.—*Up to date,* modern; in the latest style.— *v.t.*—**dated, dating.** To write down the date on; to append the date to; to note or fix the time of; to make an appointment with a person of the opposite sex for a social engagement.—*v.i.* To reckon time; to begin at a certain date (to *date* from the 10th century) to have a certain date.—**dateless,** dāt′les, *a.* Having no date; undated; so old as to be beyond date; having no fixed limit; eternal.—**date line,** dāt′līn, *n.* A line in a newspaper, letter, etc., giving the date and place of origin; an imaginary line running north and south through the Pacific, approximately along the 180th meridian, where each calendar day begins.

date, dāt, *n.* [O.Fr. *date*, Fr. *datte*, from L. *dactylus*, Gr. *daktylos*, a finger, a date.] The fruit of the date palm, consisting of a soft fleshy drupe enclosing a hard seed and having a delicious flavor, used as food in North Africa and Western Asia, and imported into other countries.—**date palm,** *n.* A palm having a stem rising to the height of 50 or 60 feet, crowned with large feathery leaves, the female plant bearing 180 to 200 dates.

dative, dā′tiv, *a.* [L. *dativus*, from *do*, to give.] *Gram.* a term applied to the case of nouns which usually follows verbs that express giving, or the doing of something to or for.—*n.* The dative case.

datum, dā′tum, *n.* pl. **data,** dā′ta. [L.] Something given or admitted; some fact, proposition, quantity, or condition granted or known, from which other facts, propositions, etc., are to be deduced.—*Datum line, engin.* the base line of a section from which all the heights and depths are measured in the plans of a railroad, and so forth.

daub, dab, *v.t.* [O.Fr. *dauber*, to plaster, from L. *dealbare*, to whitewash—*de*, intens., and *albus*, white.] To smear with soft adhesive matter, as with mud or slime; to plaster; to soil; to defile; to besmear; to paint coarsely; to lay or put on without taste; to load with affected finery.—*n.* A smear or smearing; a coarse painting.—**dauber,** da′bẽr, *n.* One who daubs; a builder of walls with clay or mud mixed with straw; a coarse painter; a low and gross flatterer.—**dauby,** da′bi, *a.* Viscous; slimy; adhesive.

daughter, da′tẽr, *n.* [A.Sax. *dóhtor*= D. *dochter,* Dan. *dotter,* Icel. *dóttir,* G. *tochter,* Gr. *thygatẽr,* Per. *doktarah,* Skr. *duhitri,* Lith. *duktē,* —daughter.] A female child of any age; a female descendant, a title of affection given to a woman by a person whose age, position, or office entitles the speaker to respect or esteem; the female offspring of an animal or plant.—**daughter-in-law,** *n.* A son's wife.—**daughterly,** da′-tẽr·li, *a.* Becoming a daughter; dutiful.

dauk, dak, *n.* Same as *Dawk.*

daunt, dant, *v.t.* [O.Fr. *danter,* Fr. *dompter,* to tame, from L. *domitare,* a freq. of *domo,* to tame, from root of *dominus,* a lord. TAME.] To repress or subdue the courage of; to intimidate; to dishearten; to check by fear.—**dauntless,** dant′les, *a.* Bold; fearless; intrepid; not timid; not discouraged.—**dauntlessly,** dant′-les·li, *adv.* In a bold fearless manner. —**dauntlessness,** dant′les·nes, *n.* Fearlessness; intrepidity.

dauphin, da′fin, *n.* [Fr. *dauphin,* the title originally of the lords of *Dauphiny,* and afterwards attached to the French crown along with this province, from L. *delphinus,* a dolphin, the crest of the lords of Dauphiny.] The eldest son of the King of France prior to the revolution of 1830.— **dauphiness,** da′fin·es, *n.* The wife of the dauphin.

davit, da′vit, *n.* [Origin unknown.] *Naut.* either of the two projecting pieces of wood or iron on the side or stern of a vessel, used for suspending or lowering and hoisting the boats by means of pulleys.

Davy lamp, dā′vi lamp, *n.* A lamp whose flame is surrounded by wire, invented by Sir Humphry *Davy* to protect the miners from explosions of firedamp.

daw, da, *n.* [From cry.] A jackdaw.

dawdle, da′dl, *v.i.* [Akin to *daddle,* and probably to *dowdy,* a slattern.] To waste time; to trifle; to saunter.— *v.t.* To waste by trifling.—**dawdler,** da′dlẽr, *n.* One who dawdles; a trifler.

dawk, dak, *n.* [Hind.] In the East Indies, the post; a relay of men, as for carrying letters, despatches, etc., or travelers in palanquins.

dawn, dan, *v.i.* [A.Sax. *dagain,* to dawn or become day, from *daeg,* day.] To begin to grow light in the morning; to grow light; to begin to show intellectual light or knowledge; to begin to become visible or appear (the truth *dawns* upon me).—*n.* The break of day; the first appearance of light in the morning; first opening or expansion; beginning; rise; first appearance (the *dawn* of civilization, etc.).

day, dā, *n.* [A.Sax. *daeg*=D. Dan. and Sw. *dag,* Icel. *dagr,* Goth. *dags,* G. *tag;* not connected with L. *dies,* a day.] That space of time during which there continues to be light, in contradistinction to night; the time between the rising and setting of the sun; the period of one revolution of the earth on its axis, or twenty-four hours; light; sunshine (in the open *day*); any period of time distinguished from other time (the authors of that *day*); age; era; epoch; in the plural often=lifetime, earthly existence; the contest of a day or day of combat (to gain the *day*); an appointed or fixed time; time of commemorating an event; anniversary.—*Days of grace,* a certain number of days (usually three) allowed for the payment of a bill (not payable on demand) beyond the date marked on the face of it specifying when it becomes due.—*Astronomical, natural,* or *solar day,* the interval between the sun's leaving the meridian and its return to it.—*Mean solar day,* the mean of all the solar days in the year.—*Sidereal day,* the time of one apparent revolution of the fixed stars.—*Civil day,* the day beginning and ending at midnight.—*Jewish day,* the interval between sunset and sunset.—*Day's journey,* an indefinite measure of distance frequently mentioned in Scripture; the average distance one can travel in a day, say from 12 miles or more on foot, to 20 or over on horseback.—**daily,** dā′li, *a.* Happening, being, or appearing every day; done day by day; bestowed or enjoyed every day.— *adv.* Every day; day by day.—*n.* A newspaper published daily.—**day bed,** *n.* A bed used for rest during the day; a couch; a sofa. (*Shak.*)— **daybook,** *n.* A book in which are recorded the debts and credits or accounts of the day.—**daybreak,** dā'brāk, n. The dawn or first appearance of light in the morning.—**daydream,** dā'drēm, n. A visionary fancy indulged in when awake.—**daydreamer,** dā'drē·mėr, n.—**day laborer,** n. One who works by the day.—**daylight,** dā'līt, n. The light of the day; the light of the sun.—*Daylight saving time,* a method of reckoning time that provides more daylight for daytime activities by setting clocks ahead one or more hours in the spring and returning them to standard time in the fall.—**day lily,** n. A liliaceous plant, the flowers of which rarely last more than a day.—**day nursery,** n. A nursery for the care and training of small children during the day; a nursery school.—**daytime,** dā'tīm, n. The time of daylight.

daze, dāz, v.t. [The same word as Icel. *dasa,* to tire out; O.D. *daesen,* to be foolish; akin *doze, dizzy.*] To stun or stupefy, as with a blow, liquor, or excess of light; to blind by too strong a light.—n. The condition of being dazed.

dazzle, daz'l, v.t.—*dazzled, dazzling.* [Freq. of *daze.*] To overpower or blind with light; to dim by excess of light; *fig.* to overpower or confound by splendor or brilliancy, or with show or display of any kind.—v.i. To be overpoweringly bright or brilliant; to be overpowered or dimmed by light (as the eyes).—n. A dazzling light; glitter.—**dazzlingly,** daz'ling·li, adv.

DDT, n. [From dichloro-diphenyl-trichloro-ethane.] A symbol for a powerful water-soluble insecticide, $C_{14}H_9Cl_5$.

deacon, dē'kon, n. [L. *diaconus,* Gr. *diakonos,* a minister or servant.] In the Roman and Anglican churches, a member of the lowest of the three orders of priesthood (bishops, priests, and deacons); in Presbyterian churches, a functionary who attends to the secular interests of the church; among Congregationalists, Baptists and others, one who looks after the spiritual as well as temporal concerns of the congregation under the minister; in Scotland, the president of an incorporated trade.—**deaconess,** dē'kon·es, n. A female deacon in the primitive church.—**deaconry, deaconship,** dē'kon·ri, dē'kon·ship, n. The office of a deacon.

dead, ded, a. [A.Sax. *dedd*=D. *dood,* Dan. *dod,* Icel. *dauthr,* Goth. *dauths.* DEATH, DIE.] Deprived, devoid, or destitute of life; having lost the vital principle; lifeless; inanimate; hence, wanting animation, activity, spirit, vigor; numb; callous; void of perception; resembling death; deep and sound (a *dead* sleep); perfectly still or motionless (a *dead* calm); monotonous; unvarying or unbroken by apertures or projections (a *dead* level, or wall); unemployed; useless (*dead* capital or stock); unreverberating, dull, heavy (a *dead* sound); tasteless, vapid, spiritless, flat, as liquors; under; sure or

unerring as death (a *dead* shot); in a state of spiritual death; under the power of sin; cut off from the rights of a citizen; not communicating motion or power (*dead* steam); no longer spoken, or in common use by a people (a *dead* language); having no gloss, warmth, or brightness (a *dead* color).—*The dead* (*sing.*), the time when there is a remarkable stillness or gloom; the culminating point, as the midst of winter or of night; (*pl.*), those who are dead; the deceased; the departed.—adv. To a degree approaching death; to the last degree; thoroughly; completely (*dead* tired, *dead* drunk).—**deaden,** ded'n, v.t. To take away or lessen the vigor, force, feeling, etc., of; to make dull, flat, etc.; to soundproof. —v.i. To lose vigor, force, etc.— **deadly,** ded'li, a. Causing death; fatal; implacable; deathlike; intense. —**deadness,** ded'nes, n.—**dead-beat,** a. Tired out.—**deadbeat,** n. One who avoids paying his bills; a loafer.— **dead center, dead point,** n. A position in a link motion such as that when the crank and connecting rod of an engine are in a straight line.— **dead-end,** a. Closed at one end; leading nowhere.—**dead end,** n. An end, as of a street or pipe, that has no opening.—**deadeye,** n. A round block without a pulley pierced with three holes and used to extend the shrouds and stays, etc.—**deadhead,** ded'hed, n. A person who receives free tickets for theaters, or passes for conveyances.—v.t. To treat as a deadhead.—**dead heat,** n. The result, in a contest of speed, when two or more competitors finish at the same time so that no one is the winner.— **dead letter,** n. A letter which cannot be delivered from defect of address, and which is sent to the general post office to be opened and returned to the writer; anything, as a condition, treaty, etc., which has lost its force or authority, by lapse of time or any other cause, and has ceased to be acted on.—**deadlight,** n. *Naut.* a strong wooden shutter for protecting the windows of cabins, etc. — **deadline,** n. A line or limit that must not be crossed; the latest possible time for doing something. —**deadlock,** n. A complete standstill.—v.t. To bring to a deadlock. v.i. To come to a deadlock.—**dead reckoning,** n. The calculation of the position of a ship or airplane by log, compass, etc., when celestial observation is impossible; guesswork.— **dead weight,** n. The unrelieved weight of inert matter.—**dead wood,** n. Dead branches or trees; anything that is useless or unsatisfactory.

deaf, def, a. [A.Sax. *deaf*=D. *doof,* Dan. *dov,* Icel. *daufr,* G. *taub*—deaf; akin Sc. *daft,* stupid, Icel. *dofi,* torpor.] Wanting the sense of hearing, either wholly or in part; disinclined to hear; inattentive; unheeding; unconcerned.—**deafen,** def'n, v.t. To make deaf; to deprive of the power of hearing; to stun; to prevent the passage of sound.—**deafly,** def'li, adv. Without sense of sounds; ob-

scurely heard.—**deafness,** def'nes, n. The state of being deaf, or of being unable to hear sounds; want of hearing; unwillingness to hear; inattention.—**deaf-mute,** n. A person who is both deaf and dumb.

deal, dēl, n. [A.Sax. *dael,* a portion, a share=D. *deel,* a portion, a board or plank; Dan. *deel,* Sw. *del,* Goth. *dails,* G. *theil,* a part, a share. *Dole, dale* are akin.] A portion or part; an indefinite quantity, degree, or extent, generally implying that the amount is considerable (often qualified by *great* which hardly adds to the sense); the division or distribution of playing cards; a board or plank of fir, of some length and at least 7 inches wide; fir or pine timber.—v.t.—*dealt* (delt), *dealing.* [A.Sax. *daelan,* to divide.] To divide in portions; to give out; to part; to distribute; to scatter; to hurl (blows, destruction). —v.i. To distribute; to traffic; to trade; to negotiate; to transact; to have intercourse; to conduct one's self in relation to others; to act; to behave.—**dealer,** dēl'ėr, n. One who deals; one who has to do or has concern with others; a trader, merchant, or trafficker; one who distributes cards to the players.—**dealing,** dē'ling, n. Conduct; behavior; practice (double *dealing,* fair *dealing*); traffic; business; intercourse or business of friendship; concern:commonly in pl.—**dealfish,** n. [From *deal,* board.] A name for a fish with an extremely compressed body found in the northern seas.

dean, dēn, n. [O.Fr. *dean, deien,* Mod.Fr. *doyen,* from L. *decanus,* one set over ten persons, from *decem,* ten.] An ecclesiastical dignitary ranking next to the bishop; an administrative officer of a college or university, under the president, supervising students in regard to their choice of courses, heading the faculty of a division or college, or adviser to men or women; a senior member of a diplomatic corps; an acknowledged leader in a profession. —**deanery,** dē'nėr·i, n. The office or jurisdiction of a dean; the official residence of a dean.—**deanship,** dēn'ship, n. The office or title of a dean.

dear, dēr, a. [A.Sax. *deóre, dýre,* dear, beloved, high-priced; O.D. *dier,* Mod.D. *duur,* Icel. *dyrr,* Dan. and Sw. *dyr,* G. *theuer,* dear, beloved, high-priced, etc.] Bearing a high price in comparison with the usual price or the real value; high-priced: opposite to *cheap;* characterized by high prices resulting from scarcity (a *dear* year); greatly valued; beloved; precious; heartfelt‡; passionate or intense‡.—n. A darling; a term of affection or endearment.—adv. Dearly; tenderly; at a dear rate.— **dearly,** dēr'li, adv. At a high price; with great fondness; fondly; tenderly.—**dearness,** dēr'nes, n. The state or quality of being dear; high value in price, or estimation; preciousness; tender love.—**dearth,** dėrth, n. [Comp. *warm-th, heal-th, slo(w)-th,* etc.] Scarcity, which makes food dear; want, or time of want; famine; lack or absence.

death, deth, n. [A.Sax. *deáth*=Goth. *dauthus*, L.G. and D. *dood*, Sw. and Dan. *död*, G. *tod*—death. DEAD, DIE.] That state of a being, animal or vegetable, in which there is a total and permanent cessation of all the vital functions; the state of being dead; the state or manner of dying; cause, agent, or instrument of death; total loss or extinction (the *death* of one's faculties); capital punishment.—*Civil death*, deprivation of the rights of citizenship, as when a man is banished or becomes a monk. —**deathless,** deth′les, a. Not subject to death, destruction, or extinction; undying; immortal.—**deathly,** deth′li, a. and adv. Resembling death; cadaverously; wanly.—**deathbed,** n. The bed on which a person dies or is confined in his last sickness.— **deathblow,** n. A blow causing death; a mortal blow; any thing which extinguishes hope or blights one's prospects.—**death rate,** n. The proportion of deaths among the inhabitants of a town, country, etc.— **death rattle,** n. A peculiar rattling in the throat of a dying person.— **death's-head,** n. The skull of a human skeleton, or a figure representing one.—*Death's-head moth*, the largest lepidopterous insect having markings upon the back of the thorax very closely resembling a skull or death's-head.—**death warrant,** n. An order from the proper authority for the execution of a criminal.—**deathwatch,** n. A vigil kept over the dead or the dying; a small insect that makes a clicking noise.

debacle, di·bak′l, n. [Fr., from *débâcler*, to break up—*de*, not, and *bâcler*, to bar, from L. *baculus*, a bar.] A sudden breaking up of ice in a river; *geol.* a sudden outbreak of water; the complete collapse of an enterprise.

debar, di·bär′, v.t.—*debarred, debarring*. To bar or cut off from entrance; to preclude; to hinder from approach, entry, or enjoyment; to shut out or exclude.— **debarment,** di·bär′ment, n. The act of debarring.

debark, di·bärk′, v.t. and i. [Fr. *débarquer*—*de*, and *barque*, a boat or bark.] To land from a ship or boat; to disembark.—**debarkation,** di·bärk·ā′shon, n. The act of disembarking.

debase, di·bās′, v.t.—*debased, debasing*. To impart a certain baseness to; to reduce or lower in quality, dignity, character, etc.; to degrade; to vitiate; to adulterate; to abase.— **debasement,** di·bās′ment, n. The act of debasing, or state of being debased.—**debaser,** di·bā′ser, n. One who or that which debases.

debate, di·bāt′, n. [O.Fr. *debatre*, to debate—prefix *de*, and *batre*, to beat. BATTER, ABATE.] An argument or reasoning between persons of different opinions; dispute; controversy; quarrel; strife; contention.—v.t. *debated, debating*. To discuss by argu-

ments for and against; to dispute; to argue; to contest.—v.i. To discuss disputed points; to examine different arguments in the mind (to *debate* with one's self whether).—*Debating society*, a society for the purpose of debate and improvement in extemporaneous speaking.—**debatable,** dē·bā′ta·bl, a. Capable of being debated; disputable; subject to controversy and contention.—**debater,** di·bā′tėr, n. One who debates; a disputant.

debauch, di·bach′, v.t. [O.Fr. *desbaucher*, Fr. *débaucher*—*de, des*, and *bauche*, a workshop, a task; the original meaning would therefore be to draw one away from his work or duty.] To corrupt or vitiate (as principles, etc.); to corrupt with lewdness; to bring to be guilty of unchastity; to seduce; to lead astray from duty or allegiance.—n. Excess or a fit of excess in eating or drinking; intemperance; drunkenness.—**debauchedly,** di·bach′ed·li, adv. In a profligate manner.—**debauchee,** deb′o·shē, n. A man given to debauchery. —**debauchery,** di·ba′chėr·i, n. Excessive indulgence in sensual pleasures of any kind, as gluttony, intemperance, unlawful indulgence of lust.—**debauchment,** di·bach′ment, n. The act of debauching.

debenture, di·ben′chėr, n. [L. *debentur*, there are owing (certain things), a word used in old acknowledgments of debt. Akin *debt, debit*.] A deed or document charging certain property with the repayment of money lent by a person therein named, and with interest on the sum lent at a given rate; a certificate or drawback of customs duties on the exportation of certain goods.

debilitate, di·bil′i·tāt, v.t.—*debilitated, debilitating*. [L. *debilito, debilitatum*, to weaken, from *debilis*, weak.] To weaken; to impair the strength of; to enfeeble; to make faint or languid.—**debilitation,** di·bil′i·tā″shon, n. The act of weakening; relaxation.—**debility,** di·bil′i·ti, n. [L. *debilitas*.] A state of general bodily weakness; feebleness; languor of body; faintness.

debit, deb′it, n. [L. *debitum*, something owed, from *debeo*, to owe—*de*, from, and *habeo*, to have.] That which is entered in an account as a debt; a recorded item of debt; that part of an account in which is entered any article of goods furnished, or money paid to or on account of a person.—v.t. To charge with as a debt (to *debit* a person *for* or *with* goods); to enter on the debtor side of a book.

debonair, deb·o·när′, a. [Fr. *débonnaire*—*de*, from, *bon*, good, and *aire* (L. *area*), place, extraction.] Characterized by courtesy, affability, or gentleness; elegant; well-bred; winning; accomplished.—**debonairly,** deb·o·när′li, adv. In a debonair manner.—**debonairness,** deb·o·när′nes, n. The character of being debonair.

debouch, di·bösh′, v.i. [Fr. *déboucher*—*de*, from, and *bouche*, mouth, L. *bucca*, the cheek.] To issue or

march out of a narrow place, or from defiles, as troops.

debris, dā·brē′, n. [Fr., from *dé*, L. *dis*, asunder, apart, and *briser*, to break.] Fragments; rubbish; ruins; *geol.* any accumulation of broken and detached matter, as that which arises from the waste of rocks, and which is piled up at their base or swept away by water.

debt, det, n. [O.Fr. *debte* (now *dette*), L. *debita*, things due. DEBIT.] That which is due from one person to another; that which one person is bound to pay to or perform for another; what is incumbent on one to do or suffer; a due; an obligation; the state of owing something to another (to be in *debt*); a duty neglected or violated; a trespass; a sin (N.T.).—**debtor,** det′er, n. [L. *debitor*.] A person who owes another either money, goods, or services: the correlative of *creditor*; one who has received from another an advantage of any kind; one indebted or in debt.

debunk, di·bunk′, v.t. To show the error in false or high-flown statements. [*Colloq.*]

debut, dā·bü′, n. [Fr.—*de*, from, and *but*, mark, butt. Perhaps has its meaning from the bowl being brought from the butt on one commencing to play at bowls.] Entrance upon anything; first appearance before the public, as that of an actor or actress on the stage.— **debutant,** *fem.* **debutante,** dā·bü·tän′, dā·bü·tänt′, n. [Fr.] One who makes a debut or first appearance before the public.

decade, dek′ād, n. [L. *decas, decadis*, Gr. *dekas*, from *deka*, ten.] The sum or number of ten; an aggregate or group consisting of ten; specifically, an aggregate of ten years.

decadence, decadency, dek′a·dens, dek′a·den·si, n. [Fr. *décadence*, L.L. *decadentia*, from L. *de*, down, and *cado*, to fall.] Decay; a falling into a lower state.—**decadent,** dek′a·dent, a. In decadence; decaying; deteriorating.—n. An artist or writer of a morally weak fiber and style.

decagon, dek′a·gon, n. [Gr. *deka*, ten, and *gōnia*, a corner.] *Geom.* a plane figure having ten sides and ten angles.—**decagonal,** de·kag′o·nal, a. Of or belonging to a decagon.

decagram, decagramme, dek′a·gram, n. [Fr. *décagramme*, Gr. *deka*, ten, and Fr. *gramme*.] A French weight of 10 grams, equal to 5.644 drams avoirdupois.

decahedron, dek·a·hē′dron, n. [Gr. *deka*, ten, and *hedra*, a seat, a base.] *Geom.* a figure or body having ten sides.—**decahedral,** dek·a·hē′dral, a. Having ten sides.

decalcify, dē·kal′si·fī, v.t. [L. *de*, not, and *calx, calcis*, lime, chalk.] To deprive of lime, as bones of their hardening matter, so as to reduce them to gelatin.—**decalcification,** dē·kal′si·fi·kā″shon, n. The removal of calcareous matter, as from bones.

decalcomania, dē·kal′kō·mā″nia, n. [Fr. *decalcomanie*.] A process in printing which permits the transfer of the ink, forming a design or picture, from the paper on which it is printed to some object.

decaliter, decalitre, dek´a·lē·tėr, *n.* A metric measure of volume equal to ten liters.

Decalogue, dek´a·log, *n.* [Gr. *deka*, ten, and *logos*, a word.] The ten commandments.

decameter, decametre, dek´a·mē·tėr, *n.* A metric measure of length equal to ten meters.

decamp, di·kamp´, *v.i.* [Fr. *décamper* —*de*, from, and *camp*, a camp.] To remove or depart from a camp or camping ground; to march off; to depart; to take one's self off, especially in a secret or clandestine manner.—**decampment,** di·kamp´ment, *n.*

decant, dē·kant´, *v.t.* [Fr. *décanter*, to decant—*de*, and *canter*, from O.Fr. *cant*, a rim, an edge; lit. to pour out by canting or tilting. CANT.] To pour off gently, as liquor from its sediment, or from one vessel into another.—**decantation,** dē·kan·tā´shon, *n.* The act of decanting.—**decanter,** dē·kan´tėr, *n.* One who decants; a vessel used to decant liquors, or for receiving decanted liquors; a glass vessel or bottle used for holding wine or other liquors for filling drinking glasses.

decapitate, di·kap´i·tāt, *v.t.*—*decapitated, decapitating.* [L.L. *decapito, decapitatum,* to behead—L. *de,* and *caput,* head.] To behead; to cut off the head of.—**decapitation,** di·kap´i·tā´shon, *n.* The act of beheading.

decapod, dek´a·pod, *n.* [Gr. *deka,* ten, and *pous, podos,* a foot.] One of an order of crustaceans (crabs, lobsters) having ten feet; one of that division of the cuttlefishes which have ten prehensile arms.—*a.* Having ten feet; belonging to the decapods.

decarbonate, dē·kär´bo·nāt, *v.t.* To deprive of carbonic acid.—**decarbonization, decarburization,** dē·kär´bo·ni·zā´shon, dē·kär´bū·ri·zā´shon, *n.* The process of depriving of carbon.—**decarbonize, decarburize,** dē·kär´bo·nīz, dē·kär´bū·rīz, *v.t.* —*decarbonized, decarbonizing.* To deprive of carbon.

decasyllabic, dek´a·sil·lab˝ik, *a.* [Gr. *deka,* ten, and *syllabē,* a syllable.] Having ten syllables.

decathlon, di·kath´lon, *n.* [Prefix *deca,* ten, and Gr. *athlon,* contest.] An athletic contest having ten events.

decay, di·kā´, *v.i.* [O.Fr. *decaer* from L. *de,* down, and *cadere,* to fall; seen also in *cadence, chance, casual, incident,* etc.] To pass gradually from a sound, prosperous, or perfect state, to a less perfect state, or toward weakness, or dissolution; to become decomposed or corrupted; to rot; to be gradually impaired; to waste or molder away.—*v.t.* To impair.—*n.* The state or process of decaying.

decease, di·sēs´, *n.* [Fr. *décès* from L. *decessus,* departure—*de,* and *cedo, cessum,* to go. CEDE.] Departure from this life; death.—*v.i.* To depart

from this life; to die.—**deceased,** di·sēst´, *p.* Departed from life; dead; frequently used as a noun.

deceit, di·sēt´, *n.* [O.Fr. *deceit,* L. *deceptus,* from *decipio, deceptum,* to deceive, lit. to take down—*de,* down, and *capio,* to take. CAPABLE.] The quality or act of deceiving; guilefulness; the act of misleading a person; any artifice, stratagem, or practice, which misleads another, or causes him to believe what is false; act of fraud; cheat; fallacy. ∴ Syn. under FRAUD.—**deceitful,** di·sēt´ful, *a.* Given to deceive; full of deceit; tending to mislead, deceive, or ensnare; trickish; fraudulent; cheating.—**deceitfully,** di·sēt´ful·li, *adv.* In a deceitful manner.—**deceitfulness,** di·sēt´ful·nes, *n.* Disposition or tendency to mislead or deceive; the quality of being deceitful.—**deceive,** di·sēv´, *v.t.* and *i.*—*deceived, deceiving.* [Fr. *décevoir,* O.Fr. *decever.*] To mislead, especially intentionally; to cause to believe what is false, or disbelieve what is true; to cause to mistake; to impose on; to delude; to frustrate or disappoint (the hopes, etc.).—**deceiver,** di·sē´vėr, *n.*

decelerate, de·sel´ėr·āt, *v.t.* [Prefix *de,* not, and *accelerate.*] To decrease the velocity of.—*v.i.* To slow down. —**deceleration,** dē·sel·ėr·ā´shon, *n.* —**decelerator,** de·sel´ėr·ātėr, *n.*

December, di·sem´bėr, *n.* [L. from *decem,* ten, this being the tenth month among the early Romans, who began the year in March.] The twelfth and last month in the year, in which the sun is at his greatest distance south of the equator.

decemvir, di·sem´vėr, *n.* pl. **decemvirs, decemviri,** di·sem´vėrz, di·sem·vi·rī. [L. *decem,* ten, and *vir,* a man.] One of ten magistrates, who had absolute authority in ancient Rome, fro.n B.C. 449 to 447.— **decemviral,** di·sem´vėr·al, *a.* Pertaining to the decemvirs.—**decemvirate,** di·sem´vėr·āt, *n.* The office of the decemvirs; the decemvirs collectively.

decency. See DECENT.

decennary, di·sen´na·ri, *n.* [L. *decennium,* a period of ten years— *decem,* ten, and *annus,* a year.] A period of ten years.—**decennial,** di·sen´ni·al, *a.* Continuing for ten years; consisting of ten years; happening every ten years.

decent, dē´sent, *a.* [L. *decens, decentis,* ppr. of *decet,* it becomes; akin *decorate, decorum.*] Becoming; having a character or show that gains general approval; suitable, as to words, behavior, dress, and ceremony; seemly; decorous; free from immodesty; not obscene; modest; moderate, tolerable, passable, respectable *(colloq.).*—**decency,** dē´sen·si, *n.* [L. *decentia.*] The state or quality of being decent; propriety in actions or discourse; decorum; modesty; freedom from ribaldry or obscenity; a decent or becoming ceremony or rite.—**decently,** dē´sent·li, *adv.* In a decent or becoming manner; tolerably, passably, or fairly

(colloq.).—**decentness,** dē´sent·nes, *n.* The state of being decent; decency.

decentralize, dē·sen´tral·īz, *v.t.* To distribute what has been centralized; to remove from direct connection or dependence on a central authority. —**decentralization,** dē·sen´tra·lī·zā˝shon, *n.* The act of decentralizing; *politics,* the act of distributing among a number of places throughout a country the administration of its internal affairs.

deception, di·sep´shon, *n.* [L. *deceptio, deceptionis,* a deceiving. DECEIVE.] The act of deceiving or misleading; habit of deceiving; the state of being deceived or misled; that which deceives; artifice; cheat. ∴ Syn. under FRAUD.—**deceptive,** di·sep´tiv, *a.* Tending to deceive; having power to mislead or impress false opinions; misleading.—**deceptively,** di·sep´tiv·li, *adv.* In a manner to deceive.—**deceptiveness,** di·sep´tiv·nes, *n.* The state of being deceptive; tendency or aptness to deceive.

decibel, des´i·bel, *n.* [Prefix *deci,* ten, and *bel,* from A.G. *Bell.*] A unit for measuring the relative intensity of sound.

decide, di·sīd´, *v.t.*—*decided, deciding.* [L. *decido*—*de,* and *cædo,* to cut, seen also in *concise, precise, excision.*] To determine, as a question, controversy, or struggle, finally or authoritatively; to settle by giving the victory to one side or the other; to determine the issue or result of; to conclude; to end.—*v.t.* To determine; to form a definite opinion; to come to a conclusion; to pronounce a judgment.—**decidable,** di·sī´da·bl, *a.* Capable of being decided. —**decided,** di·sī´ded, *a.* Well marked; clear; unequivocal; that puts an end to doubt; free from ambiguity or uncertainty; unmistakable; resolute; determined; free from hesitation or wavering.—**decidedly,** dē·sī´ded·li, *adv.* In a decided or determined manner; in a manner to preclude doubt.

deciduous, di·sid´ū·us, *a.* [L. *deciduus, decido*—*de,* and *cado,* to fall; akin *decay.*] Not perennial or permanent; *bot.* applied to trees whose leaves fall in autumn and to leaves or other parts of the plant that fall; *zool.* applied to parts which fall off at a certain stage of an animal's existence, as hair, horns, teeth.—**decidua,** di·sid´ū·a, *n.* [For *decidua membrana,* the membrane that falls off.] A membrane arising from alteration of the upper layer of the mucous membrane of the uterus, after the reception into the latter of the impregnated ovum, the name being given to it because it is discharged at parturition.— **deciduousness,** di·sid´ū·us·nes, *n.* The quality of being deciduous.

decigram, decigramme, des´i·gram, *n.* A French weight of one-tenth of a gram.—**deciliter, decilitre,** des´i·lē·tėr, *n.* A French measure of capacity equal to one-tenth of a liter.

decillion, di·sil´yon, *n.* In English notation, the number denoted by a unit with 60 zeros annexed, while in the French and American notation, 33 zeros are annexed.—**decillionth,** de·sil′yonth, *a.* Being one of a decillion equal parts.—*n.* One such part.

decimal, des′i·mal, *a.* [L. *decimus,* tenth, from *decem,* ten.] Of or pertaining to tens; numbered or proceeding by tens; having a tenfold increase or decrease.—*Decimal fraction,* a fraction whose denominator is 10, or some number produced by the continued multiplication of 10 as a factor, such as 100, 1000, etc., but written with the denominator omitted, its value being indicated by a point placed to the left of as many figures of the numerator as there are ciphers in the denominator; thus 7/10, 3/1000, are written .7, .003.—*Decimal system,* a system of weights, measures, and moneys based on multiples of ten; the metric system; *in libraries,* a classification for books, dividing all knowledge into ten classes, indicating the specific subject of each book by a number ranging from .001 to 999.—*n.* A decimal fraction.

decimate, des′i·māt, *v.t.*—*decimated, decimating.* [L. *decimo, decimatum,* to select by lot every tenth man for punishment, from *decem,* ten.] To select by lot and punish with death every tenth man of, as was done by the Romans in punishing bodies of troops, etc.; hence, to destroy a great but indefinite number of.—**decimation,** des·i·mā′shon, *n.* A selection of every tenth by lot, as for punishment, etc.; the destruction of a great but indefinite proportion of people.—**decimator,** des′i·mā·tėr, *n.* One who or that which decimates.

decimeter, decimetre, des′i·mē·tėr, *n.* A French measure of length equal to the tenth part of a meter, or 3.9371 inches.

decipher, di·sī′fėr, *v.t.* To explain what is written in ciphers, by finding what each character or mark represents; to read what is written in obscure or badly formed characters; to discover or explain the meaning of, as of something difficult to be understood.—**decipherable,** di·sī′fėr·a·bl, *a.* That may be deciphered or interpreted.—**decipherment,** di·sī′fėr·ment, *n.* The act of deciphering.

decision, di·si′zhon, *n.* [L. *decisio, decisionis.* DECIDE.] The act of deciding; determination, as of a question or doubt; final judgment or opinion in a case which has been under deliberation or discussion; determination, as of a contest or event; arbitrament; the quality of being decided in character; unwavering firmness.—**decisive,** di·sī′siv, *a.* Having the power or quality of determining; final; conclusive; putting an end to controversy; marked by decision or prompt determination. —**decisively,** di·sī′siv·li, *adv.* In a decisive manner.—**decisiveness,** di·sī′siv·nes, *n.* The quality of being decisive; conclusiveness; decision of character.

deck, dek, *v.t.* [Same word as D. *dekken,* Dan. *dække,* G. *decken,* to cover, with the nouns, D. *dek,* Dan. *dæk,* a cover, a ship's deck, G. *decke,* a cover, *deck,* a deck; closely akin to E. *thatch* (Sc. *thack*), the root being that of L. *tego,* to cover. THATCH.] To clothe; to dress the person; but usually, to clothe with more than ordinary elegance; to array; to adorn; to embellish; to furnish with a deck, as a vessel or other structure.

deck, dek, *n.* [From D. *dek,* a covering; akin to D. *dekken,* G. *decken,* to cover. THATCH.] A platform that serves as a ship's flooring; any surface similar to a ship's deck; a pack of cards.—**decker,** dek′ėr, *n.* One or more decks (a double-*decker,* a three-*decker*).—**deck hand,** *n.* One whose duties are confined to the deck of a vessel, he being unfit for the work of a seaman properly so called.

deck, dek, *n.* [Origin unknown.] A pack of cards.

deckle, dek′l, *n.* [G. *deckel,* dim. of *decke,* cover.] A frame or rubber band upon a paper-making machine to limit the size of sheet.—**deckle edge,** *a.* Rough uncut edge.

declaim, di·klām′ *v.i.* [L. *declamo,* to practice speaking in public—*de,* and *clamo,* to cry out. CLAIM, CLAMOR.] To speak a set oration in public; to make a formal speech or oration; to harangue; to inveigh; to speak or write for rhetorical display.—*v.t.* To utter with rhetorical force; to deliver with inflation of tone.—**declaimer,** di·klā′mėr, *n.* One who declaims; one who habitually speaks for rhetorical display; one who speaks clamorously; an inveigher.—**declamation,** dek·la·mā′shon, *n.* [L. *declamatio.*] The act or art of declaiming or making a rhetorical harangue in public; the delivery of a speech or exercise in oratory, as by the students of a college, etc.; a display of showy rhetorical oratory; pretentious rhetorical language, with more sound than sense.—**declamatory,** di·klam′a·to·ri, *a.* [L. *declamatorius.*] Relating to the practice of declaiming; pertaining to declamation; merely rhetorical, without solid sense or argument.

declare, di·klâr′, *v.t.*—*declared, declaring.* [L. *declaro,* to declare—*de,* intens., and *claro,* to make clear, from *clarus,* clear. CLEAR.] To make known by words; to tell explicitly; to manifest or communicate plainly in any way; to exhibit; to publish; to proclaim; to assert; to affirm; to make a full statement of, as of goods on which duty falls to be paid to the customhouse.—*To declare one's self,* to throw off reserve and avow one's opinion; to show openly what one thinks, or which side he espouses.—*v.i.* To make a declaration; to make known explicitly some determination; to proclaim one's self; to pronounce adhesion in favor of a party, etc.: with *for* or *against.*—*To declare off,* to refuse to cooperate in any undertaking; to break off from one's party engage-

ments, etc.—**declarant,**† dē·klā′rant, *n.* One who declares.—**declaration,** dek·la·rā′shon, *n.* [L. *declaratio.*] The act of declaring, making known, or announcing; affirmation; explicit assertion; open expression; avowal; that which is declared; the document or instrument by which an announcement is authoritatively made; *law,* that part of the process or pleadings in which the plaintiff sets forth at large his cause of complaint; a simple affirmation substituted in lieu of an oath, solemn affirmation, or affidavit.—**declarative,** di·klâr′a·tiv, *a.* Making declaration, proclamation, or publication; declaratory.—**declaratory,** di·klâr′a·to·ri, *a.* Making declaration; distinctly expressive of opinions or intentions.

declension. See DECLINE.

decline, di·klīn′, *v.i.*—*declined, declining.* [L. *declino,* to bend down or aside—*de,* down, and a hypothetical *clino* = Gr. *klinō,* to bend. Root seen in L. *clivus,* sloping, and also in E. to *lean.*] To lean downward; to bend over; to hang down, as from weakness, despondency, submission, or the like; to sink to a lower level; to stoop, as to an unworthy object; to lean or deviate from rectitude (O.T.); to approach or draw toward the close (day *declines*); to avoid or shun; to refuse; not to comply; to tend to a less perfect state; to sink in character or value; to become diminished or impaired (as health, reputation); to fall; to decay.—*v.t.* To bend downward; to cause to bend; to depress; to shun or avoid; to refuse; not to accept or comply with; *gram.* to inflect, through cases and numbers; to change the termination of a word, for forming the oblique cases.—*n.* A falling off; a tendency to a worse state; diminution or decay; deterioration; a popular name for almost all chronic diseases in which the strength and plumpness of the body gradually decrease until the patient dies; consumption.—**decliner,** di·klī′nėr, *n.* One who declines.—**declinometer,** dek·li·nom′et·ėr, *n.* An instrument for measuring the declination of the magnetic needle, and for observing its variations.—**declension,** di·klen′shon, *n.* [L. *declinatio, declinationis,* in the grammatical sense it refers to the leaning away or differing of the other cases from the nominative; so *case* is lit. a falling.] The act of declining; declination; slope; a falling or declining toward a worse state; refusal; nonacceptance; *gram.* the inflection of nouns, adjectives, and pronouns by change of termination to form the oblique cases; the act of declining a word; a class of nouns declined on the same type. —**declinable,** di·klī′na·bl, *a.* Capable of being declined; having case inflections.—**declination,** dek·li·nā′shon, *n.* The act or state of declining; a bending down; inclination; a falling into a worse state; a falling away; deterioration; a deviation from a straight line; oblique motion;

deviation from rectitude in behavior or morals; the act of refusing; refusal; *astron.* the distance of a heavenly body from the celestial equator, measured on a great circle passing through the pole and also through the body; *physics,* the variation of the magnetic needle from the true meridian of a place—declination of the compass or magnetic declination.—**declinatory,** di·klī′na·to·ri, *a.* Of or pertaining to declination; characterized by declining; intimating declinature or refusal.—**declinature,** di·klī′na·chŭr, *n.* The act of declining or refusing; a refusal.

declivity, di·kliv′i·ti, *n.* [L. *declivitas,* a declivity, from *declivis,* sloping—*de,* and *clivus,* sloping; same root as in *decline.*] Slope or inclination downward; a slope or descent of the ground: opposed to *acclivity,* or ascent.—**declivitous,** di·kliv′i·tus, *a.* Sloping downward.

decoct, di·kokt′, *v.t.* [L. *decoquo, decoctum,* to boil down—*de,* and *coquo,* to cook, to boil. COOK.] To prepare by boiling; to extract the strength or flavor of by boiling; to heat up or excite (*Shak.*)†.—**decoction,** di·kok′shon, *n.* The act of decocting; an extract obtained by boiling a substance in water, for extracting its virtues; the water in which a substance has been thus boiled.

decode, dē·kōd′, *v.t.* To decipher a telegram by code. CODE.

decollate, di·kol′lāt, *v.t.*—decollated, decollating. [L. *decollo, decollatum,* to behead—*de,* from, and *collum,* the neck.] To behead.—**decollation,** dē·kol·lā′shon, *n.* The act of beheading.

decolleté, dā·kol·tā′, *a.* [Fr.] Low-necked style of dress.

decoloration, dē·kul′ér·ā″shon, *n.* [L. *decoloratio, decolorationis,* discoloring—*de,* from, and *color,* color.] The removal of color; abstraction or loss of color.—**decolorant,** dē·kul′ér·ant, *n.* A substance which removes color, or bleaches.—**decolorization,** dē·kul′ér·i·zā″shon, *n.* The process of depriving of color.—**decolorize, decolor,** dē·kul′ér·īz, dē·kul′ér, *v.t.* To deprive of color; to bleach.

decompose, dē·kom·pōz′, *v.t.*—decomposed, decomposing. [Fr. *decomposer*—*de,* from, and *composer,* to compose. COMPOSE.] To separate the constituent parts or elementary particles of; to resolve into original elements.—*v.i.* To become resolved into constituent elements; to decay, rot, or putrefy.—**decomposable,** dē·kom·pō′za·bl, *a.* Capable of being decomposed or resolved into constituent elements.—**decomposition,** dē·kom′pō·zi″shon, *n.* The act of decomposing; analysis; resolution; the state of being decomposed; disintegration; decay; putrescence.

decompound, dē·kom·pound′, *a.* [Prefix *de,* intens., and *compound.*] Composed of things or words already compounded; compounded a second time; *bot.* divided into a number of

compound divisions, as a leaf or panicle.—*n.* A decomposite.

décor, dā·kor′, *n.* [Fr. *décor,* from *décorer,* to decorate.] Decoration in general; stage scenery.

decorate, dek′o·rāt, *v.t.*—decorated, decorating. [L. *decoro, decoratum,* from *decus, decor,* comeliness, grace; akin *decent.*] To deck with something becoming or ornamental; to adorn; to beautify; to embellish; to make attractive the interiors of dwellings; to award a decoration of honor to.—*Decorated style, arch.* a style of Gothic architecture distinguished by the flowing or wavy lines of its tracery, and generally by profuse florid ornamentation.—**decoration,** dek·o·rā′shon, *n.* The act of adorning; ornamentation; that which decorates or adorns; ornament; any badge, as a medal, cross of honor, etc., bestowed for distinguished services.—**decorative,** dek′o·rā·tiv, *a.* Adorning; suited to embellish.—**decorativeness,** dek′o·rā·tiv·nes, *n.* Quality of being decorative.—**decorator,** dek′o·rā·tėr, *n.* One who decorates or embellishes.

decorous, dek′o·rus, *a.* [L. *decorus,* becoming.] Suitable to a character or to the time, place, and occasion; becoming; seemly; proper; befitting (speech, behavior, dress, etc.).—**decorously,** dek′o·rus·li, *adv.* In a becoming manner.—**decorousness,** dek′o·rus·nes, *n.* Decency or propriety of behavior.—**decorum,** di·kō′rum, *n.* [L., what is becoming.] Propriety of speech or behavior; seemliness; decency; opposed to rudeness, licentiousness, or levity.

decorticate, di·kor′ti·kāt, *v.t.*—decorticated, decorticating. [L. *decortico, decorticatum*—*de,* not, and *cortex,* bark.] To strip off the bark of; to peel; to husk.—**decortication,** di·kor′ti·kā″shon, *n.* The act of stripping off bark or husk.

decoy, di·koi′, *n.* [D. *eende-kooi,* a duck-cage.] A place into which wild fowls are enticed in order to be caught, being a structure of network covering in a piece of water; a fowl, or the likeness of one, employed to entice other fowl into a net or within range of shot; a thing or person intended to lead into a snare; a stratagem employed to mislead or lead into danger; a lure.—*v.t.* To lead or lure by artifice into a snare, with a view to catch; to entrap by any means which deceive; to allure, attract, or entice.

decrease, di·krēs′, *v.i.*—decreased, decreasing. [L. *decresco*—*de,* down, and *cresco,* to grow, seen also in *increase, crescent, accrue.*] To be diminished gradually in extent, bulk, quantity, or amount, or in strength, influence, or excellence; to become less.—*v.t.* To lessen; to make smaller in dimensions, amount, quality, or excellence, etc.; to diminish gradually or by small deductions.—*n.* A becoming less; gradual diminution; wane (as applied to the moon); decay.—**decreasingly,** di·krēs′ing·li, *adv.* By decreasing or diminishing.—**decrement,** dek′ri·ment, *n.* [L. *de-*

crementum.] Decrease; waste; the quantity lost by gradual diminution or waste; *math.* the small part by which a variable quantity becomes less and less: opposed to *increment.*—**decrescent,** di·kres′ent, *a.* [L. *decrescens, decrescentis.*] Decreasing; becoming less by gradual diminution.

decree, di·krē′, *n.* [L. *decretum,* from *decerno,* to judge—*de,* and *cerno,* to judge; also seen in *concern, discern, secret,* etc.] Judicial decision or determination of a litigated cause; the judgment or award of an umpire in a case submitted to him; an edict, law, or order by a superior authority as a rule to govern inferiors.—*Decree nisi* (decree unless), *law,* the order made by an English court of divorce, after satisfactory proof is given in support of a petition for dissolution of marriage; it remains conditional for at least six months, after which, *unless* sufficient cause is shown, it is made absolute, and the dissolution takes effect.—*v.t.*—decreed, decreeing. To determine judicially; to resolve by sentence; to determine or resolve legislatively; to fix or appoint; to determine or decide on.—*v.i.* To determine immutably; to make an edict; to appoint by edict.—**decretal,** di·krē′tal, *a.* Appertaining to a decree; containing a decree.—*n.* An authoritative order of decree; a letter of the pope determining some point or question in ecclesiastical law; *pl.* the second part of the canon law, so called because it contains the decrees of sundry popes.—**decretist,** di·krē′tist, *n.* One who studies or professes a knowledge of the decretals.—**decretive,** di·krē′tiv, *a.* Having the force of a decree; pertaining to a decree.—**decretory,** dek′ri·to·ri, *a.* Judicial; definitive; established by a decree.

decrepit, di·krep′it, *a.* [L. *decrepitus,* broken down, worn out—*de,* from and *crepare,* to make a noise, hence originally noiseless; akin *crevice, discrepant.*] Broken down or weakened with age; wasted or worn by the infirmities of old age; being in the last stage of decay.—**decrepitude,** di·krep′i·tūd, *n.* The state of being decrepit; the broken, crazy state of the body, produced by decay and the infirmities of age.

decrepitate, di·krep′i·tāt, *v.t.*—decrepitated, decrepitating. [L. *decrepo,* to break or burst, to crackle—*de* and *crepo.* DECREPIT.] To roast or calcine in a strong heat, with a continual bursting or crackling of the substance.—*v.i.* To crackle when roasting.—**decrepitation,** di·krep′i·tā″shon, *n.* The act of flying asunder with a crackling noise on being heated, or the crackling noise, attended with the flying asunder of their parts, made by several salts and minerals when heated.

decrescendo, dā·kre·shen′dō, *n.* [It.] *Mus.* a term which denotes the gradual weakening of the sound.

decry, di·krī′, *v.t.*—decried, decrying. [Fr. *décrier,* O.Fr. *descrier*—*des* (=L. *dis*). and *crier,* to cry.] To cry down;

to censure as faulty, mean, or worthless; to clamor against; to discredit by finding fault.—**decrial**, di·krī′al, n. The act of decrying or crying down.—**decrier**, di·krī′ėr, n. One who decries.

decuman, dek′ū·man, a. [L. *decumanus*, from *decimus*, tenth, from *decem*, ten.] Tenth; hence, from the ancient notion that every tenth wave was the largest in a series; large; immense. Sometimes used substantively for the tenth or largest wave.

decumbent, di·kum′bent, a. [L. *decumbens*, from *decumbo*, to lie down—*de*, and *cumbo*, for *cubo*, to lie.] Lying down; reclining; prostrate; recumbent; *bot.* declined or bending down, as a stem which rests on the earth and then rises again.—**decumbence, decumbency**, di·kum′bens, di·kum′ben·si, n. The state of being decumbent or of lying down; the posture of lying down.

decuple, dek′ū·pl, a. [L.L. *decuplus*, from L. *decem*, ten.] Tenfold; containing ten times as many.—n. A number ten times repeated.—v.t.—*decupled, decupling.* To increase to a tenfold proportion.

decurion, di·kū′ri·on, n. [L. *decurio*, from *decem*, ten.] An officer in the Roman army who commanded a *decuria*, that is, a body of ten soldiers.

decurrent, di·kėr′ent, a. [L. *decurrens, decurrentis*—*de*, and *curro*, to run.] *Bot.* applied to a sessile leaf having its base extended downward along the stem.—**decurrently**, di·kėr′ent·li, adv. In a decurrent manner.

decussate, di·kus′āt, v.t.—*decussated, decussating.* [L. *decusso*, to divide crosswise in the form of a ×, from *decussis*, the number 10, which the Romans represented by X.] To intersect so as to make acute angles, thus ×; to intersect; to cross, as lines, rays of light, leaves, or nerves in the body.—**decussate**, di·kus′it, a. Crossed; intersected; *bot.* arranged in pairs alternately crossing each other at regular angles.—**decussately**, di·kus′it·li, adv. In a decussate manner.—**decussation**, di·kus·ā′shon, n. The act of crossing at right or at acute angles; the crossing of two lines, rays, nerves, etc., which meet in a point and then proceed and diverge.

dedicate, ded′i·kāt, v.t.—*dedicated, dedicating.* [L. *dedico*—*de*, and *dico, dicare*, to devote, dedicate; akin *abdicate, diction, predict*, etc.] To set apart and consecrate to a divine Being, or to a sacred purpose; to appropriate to any person or purpose; to give wholly or earnestly up to (often *refl.*); to inscribe or address to a patron, friend, or public character (to *dedicate* a book).—a. Consecrated; devoted; appropriated.—**dedication**, ded·i·kā′shon, n. The act of dedicating; consecration or devotion to a sacred use; solemn appropriation; an address prefixed to a book, and inscribed to a friend of the author, some public character,

or other person, as a mark of esteem.—*Dedication day, dedication feast*, an annual festival commemorating the consecration of a church.—**dedicator**, ded′i·kā·tėr, n. One who dedicates.—**dedicatory**, ded′i·ka·to·ri, a. Serving to dedicate; serving as a dedication.

deduce, di·dūs′, v.t.—*deduced, deducing.* [L. *deduco*—*de*, and *duco*, to lead. DUKE.] To draw; to draw, bring out, or infer in reasoning; to attain or arrive at (a truth, opinion, or proposition), from premises; to infer from what precedes.—**deducible**, di·dū′si·bl, a. Capable of being deduced; inferable.—**deduct**, di·dukt′, v.t. To take away, separate, or remove, in numbering, estimating, or calculating; to subtract.—**deduction**, di·duk′shon, n. [L. *deductio, deductionis.*] The act of deducting or taking away; that which is deducted; sum or amount taken from another; abatement; the act or method of deducing from premises; that which is drawn from premises; inference; consequence drawn; conclusion.—**deductive**, di·duk′tiv, a. Deducible; pertaining to deduction; that is or may be deduced from premises.—*Deductive reasoning*, the process of deriving consequences from admitted or established premises, as distinguished from *inductive* reasoning, by which we arrive at general laws or axioms by an accumulation of facts.—**deductively**, di·duk′tiv·li, adv. By regular deduction; by deductive reasoning.

deed, dēd, n. [A.Sax. *daed*, a deed, from *dón*, to do = Icel. *dád*, D. and Dan. *daad*, Goth. *deds*, G. *that*, a deed. DO.] That which is done or performed; an act; a fact; anything that is done; an exploit; achievement; *law*, a writing containing some contract or agreement, and the evidence of its execution; particularly, an instrument conveying real estate to a purchaser or donee.—*In deed*, in fact, in reality; often united to form the single word *indeed.*

deem, dēm, v.t. [A.Sax. *déman*, to deem, to judge, from *dóm*, doom, judgment (same word as term. *-dom*); Icel. *dœma*, Dan. *dömme*, Goth. (*ga*)*domjan*, to judge; from root of *do.*] To think, judge, believe, or consider to be so or so.—v.i. To think or suppose.

deep, dēp, a. [A.Sax. *deóp* = D. *diep*, Dan. *dyb*, G. *tief*, deep; from root of *dip. dive.*] Extending or being far below the surface; descending far downward; profound: opposed to *shallow* (*deep* water, a *deep* pit); low in situation; being or descending far below the adjacent land (a *deep* valley); entering far (a *deep* wound); absorbed; engrossed; wholly occupied; not superficial or obvious; hidden; abstruse; hard to penetrate or understand; profoundly learned; having the power to enter far into a subject; penetrating; artful; concealing artifice; insidious; designing; grave in sound; great in degree; intense; profound (silence, grief, poverty); measured back from the

front.—n. Anything remarkable for depth; the sea; the abyss of waters; any abyss.—adv. Deeply; to a great depth; profoundly.—**deepen**, dē′pn, v.t. To make deep or deeper; to sink lower; to increase; to intensify; to make more grave (sound).—v.i. To become more deep, in all its senses.—**deeply**, dēp′li, adv. At or to a great depth; far below the surface; profoundly; thoroughly; to a great degree; intensely; gravely; with low or deep tone; with art or intricacy (a *deeply* laid plot).—**deepness**, dēp′nes, n.—**deep-freeze**, v.t.—*deep-froze, deep-frozen.* To put or store in a deep freeze.—**deep freeze**, n. A refrigerator that preserves food at freezing temperatures.—**deep-sea**, a. Of or in the deeper parts of the sea.

deer, dēr, n. *sing.* and *pl.* [A.Sax. *deór*, any wild animal, a deer = Goth. *dius*, D. *dier*, Dan. *dyr*, Icel. *dyr*, Sw. *diur*, G. *thier*, any animal or beast, especially a wild beast.] A name of many ruminant quadrupeds, distinguished by having solid branching horns which they shed every year, and eight cutting teeth in the lower jaw, and none in the upper; such as the red deer, fallow deer, roebuck, reindeer, moose, or elk, etc.—**deerhound**, n. A hound for hunting deer; a staghound.—**deerskin**, n. The skin of a deer; the leather made from it.—**deerstalker**, n. One who practices deerstalking.—**deerstalking**, n. The hunting of deer (especially the red deer) on foot by hiding and stealing within shot of them unawares.

deface, di·fās′, v.t.—*defaced, defacing.* To destroy or mar the face or surface of; to injure the beauty of; to disfigure; to erase or obliterate.—**defacement**, di·fās′ment, n. The act of defacing; injury to the surface or exterior; what mars or disfigures.—**defacer**, di·fā′sėr, n. One who defaces.

de facto, dē·fak′tō, a. and adv. [L.] In fact; actually existing.

defalcate, di·fal′kāt, v.i.—*defalcated, defalcating.* [L.L. *defalco, defalcatum*, to cut off with a sickle, hence to deduct—L. *de*, down, and *falx, falcis*, a sickle.] To take away or deduct, as money.—**defalcation**, di·fal·kā′shon, n. Deduction; abatement; a fraudulent deficiency in money matters.—**defalcator**, def′al·kā·tėr, n.

defame, di·fām′, v.t.—*defamed, defaming.* [L.L. *defamare*—*de*, not, and L. *fama*, fame.] To slander; to speak evil of; to calumniate; to libel; to bring into disrepute.—**defamation**, def·a·mā′shon, n. The uttering of slanderous words with a view to injure another's reputation; slander; calumny.—**defamatory**, di·fam′a·to·ri, a. Containing defamation; calumnious; slanderous.—**defamer**, di·fā′mer, n. One who defames; a slanderer; a calumniator.

default, di·falt′, n. [Fr. *défaut*, for *défault*, from *défaillir*, to fail—*de*, and *faillir*, to fail. FAIL, FAULT.] A failing or failure; an omission of that which ought to be done; *law*, a failure of appearance in court at a day assigned.

—*In default of*, in the absence or want of; hence, in place of; in lieu of.—*v.i.* To fail in fulfilling or satisfying an engagement, claim, contract, or agreement.—*v.t. Law,* to give judgment against on account of failing to appear and answer.—**defaulter,** di·fạl′tẽr, *n.* One who makes default; a delinquent; one who fails to meet his claims or to fulfill his engagements.

defeasance, di·fē′zans, *n.* [Fr. *défaisant,* from *défaire,* to undo—L. *dis,* and *facio,* to do.] A rendering null and void; *law,* a condition which being performed renders a deed null or void; the writing containing a defeasance.—**defeasible,** di·fē′zi·bl, *a.* Capable of being abrogated or annulled.—**defeasibleness,** di·fē′zi·bl·nes, *n.*

defeat, di·fēt′, *n.* [Fr. *défaite,* from *défaire,* to undo, O.Fr. *desfaire*—L. *dis,* and *facere,* to do.] An overthrow; loss of battle; check, rout, or destruction of an army by the victory of an enemy; a frustration by rendering null and void, or by prevention of success.—*v.t.* To overcome or vanquish; to overthrow; to frustrate; to prevent the success of; to disappoint; to render null and void.—**defeatism,** de·fē′tizm, *n.* An attitude of admitting defeat, as of one's own country, or of life itself, on the ground that failure is inevitable.

defecate, def′e·kāt, *v.t.*—*defecated, defecating.* [L. *defœco*—de, and *fæx,* dregs.] To clear from dregs or impurities; to clarify or purify; to void excrement.—*v.i.* To become clear or pure by depositing impurities; to clarify.—*a.* Purged from lees; defecated.—**defecation,** def·e·kā′shon, *n.* The act of defecating or separating from lees or dregs; purification.—**defecator,** def′e·kā·tẽr, *n.* One who or that which defecates.

defect, di·fekt′, *n.* [L. *defectus,* pp. of *deficio, defectum,* to fail—de, from, and *facio,* to make, to do.] Want or absence of something necessary or useful toward perfection; a fault; an imperfection; that which is wanting to make a perfect whole; blemish; deformity.—*v.i.* To desert a cause or party in order to support another.—**defector,** di·fek′tẽr, *n.*—**defection,** di·fek′shon, *n.* The act of abandoning a person or cause to which one is bound by allegiance or duty, or to which one has attached himself; a falling away; apostasy; backsliding.—**defective,** di·fek′tiv, *a.* [L. *defectivus,* imperfect.] Having some defect; wanting either in substance, quantity, or quality, or in anything necessary; imperfect; faulty; *gram.* wanting some of the usual forms of declension or conjugation (a *defective* noun or verb).—**defectively,** di·fek′tiv·li, *adv.* In a defective manner; imperfectly.—**defectiveness,** di·fek′tiv·nes, *n.* The state of being defective; faultiness.

defense, di·fens′, *n.* [Fr. *défense,* from L.L. *defensa,* defense, from L. *defendo, defensum,* to defend—de, and *fendo,* to strike, a verb used also in *offendo,* to offend.] The act of defend-ing, upholding, or maintaining; anything that opposes attack, violence, danger, or injury; fortification; guard; resistance against attack; protection; that which defends; means or methods of defense; the science or art of defending oneself, as in boxing, fencing, etc.; speech, action, etc. in favor of something; a defendant's answer to an accusation; a defendant and his legal advisors.—**defenseless,** di·fens′les, *a.*—**defenselessness,** di·fens′les·nes, *n.*—**defense mechanism,** *n.* An involuntary or subconscious process by which an individual copes with painful situations that are unacceptable at the conscious level.—**defensibility,** di·fen′si·bil′i·ti, *n.*— the state of being defensible. defensibleness.—**defensible,** di·fen′si·bl, *a.* Capable of being defended, vindicated, maintained, or justified. —**defensive,** di·fen′siv, *a.* [Fr. *défensif.*] Serving to defend; proper for or suited to defense; carried on in resisting attack or aggression; in distinction from *offensive.*—*n.* That which defends.—*To be on the defensive,* or *to stand on the defensive,* to be or stand in a state or posture of defense or resistance, in opposition to aggression or attack.—**defensively,** di·fen′siv·li, *adv.* In a defensive manner.—**defend,** di·fend′, *v.t.* To protect or support against any assault or attack; to ward off an attack upon; to protect by opposition or resistance; to vindicate, uphold, or maintain uninjured by force or by argument (rights and privileges); *law,* to come forward as defendant in (to *defend* an action).—*v.i.* To make opposition; to make defense.—**defendant,** di·fen′dant, *a.* Defensive (*Shak.*)‡; making defense.—*n.* One who defends; *law,* the party that opposes a complaint, demand, or charge.—**defender,** di·fen′dẽr, *n.* One who defends; a vindicator, either by arms or by arguments; a champion or an advocate.—*Defender of the Faith,* a title peculiar to the sovereigns of England, first conferred by Pope Leo X on Henry VIII in 1521, as a reward for writing against Luther.

defer, di·fẽr′, *v.t.*—*deferred, deferring* [O.Fr. *differre,* L. *differo,* to delay—*dis,* from, and *fero,* to carry.] To delay; to put off; to postpone to a future time.—*v.i.* To delay; to procrastinate.—**deferment,** di·fẽr′ment, *n.* The act of deferring; postponement or delay.—**deferrer,** di·fẽr′ẽr. *n.* One who defers or delays.

defer, di·fẽr′, *v.i.* [L. *defero,* to carry down or away, hand over, refer—de, down, and *fero,* to carry.] To yield to another's opinion; to submit or give way courteously or from respect (to *defer to* a friend's judgment).—**deference,** def′ẽr·ens, *n.* A yielding in opinion; submission of judgment to the opinion or judgment of another; respect; courteous consideration; obedience.—**deferential,** def·ẽr·en′shal, *a.* Expressing deference; accustomed to defer.—**deferentially,** def·ẽr·en′shal·li, *adv.* In a deferential manner; with deference.—**deferrer,**

di·fẽr′ẽr, *n.* One who defers in regard to opinion.

defiance, defiant, etc. See DEFY.

deficient, di·fish′ent, *a.* [L. *deficiens, deficientis,* ppr. of *deficio,* to fail—de, and *facio,* to do.] Wanting; defective; imperfect; not sufficient or adequate; not having a full or adequate supply: with *in* (*deficient in* strength).—**deficiency,** di·fish′en·si, *n.* The state of being deficient; a failing or falling short; want, either total or partial; defect; absence; something less than is necessary.—**deficiently,** di·fish′ent·li, *adv.* In a defective manner.—**deficit,** def′i·sit, *n.* [L., there is wanting.] A falling short of a requisite sum or amount; a deficiency (a *deficit* in revenue).

defier, di·fī′ẽr, *n.* See DEFY.

defilade, def′i·lād, *v.t.*—*defilated, defilading.* [Fr. *défilade.* DEFILE, *v.i.*] *Fort.* to surround by defensive works so as to protect the interior when in danger of being commanded by an enemy's guns.

defile, di·fīl′, *v.t.*—*defiled, defiling.* [L. prefix *de,* and A.Sax. *fýlan* (O.E. and Sc. *file,* to defile), from *ful,* foul. FOUL.] To make unclean; to render foul or dirty; to soil or sully; to tarnish, as reputation, etc.; to make ceremonially unclean; to pollute; to corrupt the chastity of; to debauch; to violate.—**defilement,** di·fīl′ment, *n.* The act of defiling, or state of being defiled.—**defiler,** di·fī′lẽr, *n.* One who or that which defiles.

defile, di·fīl′, *v.i.*—*defiled, defiling.* [Fr. *défiler*—de, and *file,* a row or line, from L. *filum,* a thread.] To march off in a line, or file by file; to file off.—*v.t. Fort.* to defilade.—*n.* A narrow passage or way, in which troops may march only in a file, or with a narrow front; a long narrow pass; as between hills, etc.

define, di·fīn′, *v.t.*—*defined, defining.* [L. *definio*—de, and *finio,* to limit, from *finis,* end, whence also *final, finish, finite,* etc.] To determine or set down the limits of; to determine with precision; to mark the limit of; to circumscribe, mark, or show the outlines of clearly; to determine the extent of the meaning of; to give or describe the signification of; to enunciate or explain the distinctive properties of.—*v.i.* To give a definition.—**definable,** di·fī′na·bl, *a.* Capable of being defined; capable of having the limits ascertained, fixed, and determined; capable of having its signification expressed with certainty or precision.—**definer,** di·fī′nẽr, *n.* One who defines.—**definite,** def′i·nit, *a.* [L. *definitus.*] Having fixed or marked limits; bounded with precision; determinate; having well-marked limits in signification; certain; precise; *gram.* defining; limiting; applied to particular things; *bot.* same as *centrifugal.*—The *definite article,* the article *the.*—**definitely,** def′i·nit·li, *adv.* In a definite manner.—**definiteness,** def′i·nit·nes, *n.* State or character of being definite.—**definition,** def·i·ni′shon, *n.* [L. *definitio, definitionis.*] The act of defining; a brief and precise description of a thing by its properties; an explanation of the signification of a word or term; the quality or power in a telescope or other optical instrument of showing distinctly the outlines or features of any object.—**definitive**, di·fin'i·tiv, a. [L. *definitivus*, definitive.] Limiting; determinate; positive; express; conclusive; final.—*n. Gram*, a word used to define or limit the extent of the signification of an appellative or common noun, as *this, the*, etc.—**definitively** di·fin'i·tiv·li, adv. In a definite manner; positively; expressly; finally; conclusively; unconditionally.

deflagrate, def'le·grāt, v.t.—*deflagrated, deflagrating*. [L. *deflagro, deflagratum*—*de*, intens., and *flagro*, to burn, whence *flagrant*.] To set fire to; to cause to burn rapidly; to consume.—*v.i*. To burn rapidly, or with violent combustion.—**deflagration**, def·le·grā'shon, n. The act or process of deflagrating; a rapid combustion of a mixture, attended with much evolution of flame and vapor; the process of oxidizing substances by means of niter; the rapid combustion of metals by the electric spark.

deflate, di·flāt', v.t. To reduce from an inflated state by releasing of the distending gas or air.—**deflation**, di·flā'shon, n. A deflating; a reduction in the volume of currency outstanding; a reduction in the volume of purchasing power.

deflect, di·flekt', v.i. [L. *deflecto*—*de*, from, and *flecto*, to turn or bend. FLEXIBLE.] To turn away or aside; to deviate from a true course or right line; to swerve.—*v.t*. To cause to turn aside; to turn or bend from a straight line.—**deflection**, di·flek'shon, n. [L. *deflecto*, I bend down.] The strain produced by a transverse stress, such as the bending of a horizontal beam under a load; also used to denote amount of deflection.—**deflection**, di·flek'shon, n. Deviation; a turning from a true line or the regular course.—**deflective**, di·flek'tiv, a. Causing deflection or deviation.—**deflector**, di·flek'tèr, n. A diaphragm in a lamp, stove, etc., by means of which air and gas are mingled, and made to burn completely.

deflower, di·flou'èr, v.t. [Fr. *déflorer*; L.L. *defloro*—L. *de*, from, and *flos, floris*, a flower.] To deprive of her viriginity; to violate, ravish, seduce.—**defloration**, di·flo·rā'shon, n. The act of deflowering or taking away a woman's virginity; rape.

defluxion, di·fluk'shon, n. [L. *defluxio, defluxionis*, from *defluo, defluxum*, to flow down—*de*, and *fluo*, to flow.] *Med*. a discharge, as from the nose or head in catarrh.

defoliate, di·fō'li·āt, a. [L. *de*, priv., and *folium*, a leaf.] Deprived of leaves.—**defoliation**, di·fō'li·ā''shon, n. The fall of the leaf or shedding of leaves.

deforce, di·fōrs', v.t.—*deforced, deforcing. Law*, to keep out of lawful possession of an estate; *Scots law*,

to resist (an officer of the law) in the execution of official duty.—**deforcement**, di·fōrs'ment, n. The act of deforcing.

deforest, dē·for'est, v.t. To clear of forests or trees.—**deforestation**, dē·for'es·ta''shon, n.

deform, di·form', v.t. [L. *deformo*—*de*, and *forma*, form.] To mar or injure the form of; to disfigure; to render ugly or unpleasing; to disfigure the moral beauty of (vices *deform* the character).—**deformation**, di·for·mā'shon, n. A disfiguring or defacing.—**deformed**, di·formd', p. and a. Disfigured; distorted; misshapen; ugly.—**deformedly**, di·for'med·li, adv. In a deformed manner.—**deformedness**, di·for'med·nes, n. The state or character of being deformed.—**deformity**, di·for'mi·ti, n. [L. *deformitas*.] The state of being deformed; some deformed or misshapen part of the body; distortion; irregularity of shape or features; ugliness; anything that destroys beauty, grace, or propriety.

defraud, di·frad', v.t. [L. *defraudo*—*de*, intens., and *fraudo*, to cheat; *fraus*, fraud.] To deprive of right, either by obtaining something by deception or artifice, or by taking something wrongfully without the knowledge or consent of the owner; to cheat; to keep out of just rights; with *of* before the thing.—**defraudation**, dē·fra·dā'shon, n. The act of defrauding.—**defrauder**, di·fra'dèr, n. One who defrauds; one who takes from another his right by deception, or withholds what is his due; a cheat.

defray, di·frā', v.t. [Fr. *defrayer*—*de*, and *frais*, expense, from L.L. *fractus* or *fractum*, expense, compensation, from L. *frango, fractum*, to break, whence *fraction, fragile*, etc.] To pay for; to disburse the amount of; to discharge or bear; with *cost, charge, expense* as the object.—**defrayal, defrayment**, di·frā'al, dē·frā'ment, n. The act of defraying.—**defrayer**, di·frā'èr, n. One who defrays or pays expenses.

defrost, dē·frost', v.t. To remove frost or ice from; to thaw.—**defroster**, dē·fros'tèr, n.

deft, deft, a. [A.Sax. *daeft*, fit, convenient from (*ge*)*dafam*, to become, to befit; Goth. *gadaban*, to befit.] Dexterous; clever; apt.—**deftly**, deft'li, adv.—**deftness**, deft'nes, n.

defunct, di·fungkt', a. [L. *defunctus*, having finished, discharged, or performed, from *defungor*, to perform—*de*, intens., and *fungor*, to perform.] Having finished the course of life; dead; deceased; used with reference to *defunct* periodicals, commercial organizations, or other enterprises.

defy, di·fī', v.t.—*defied, defying*. [Fr. *défier*, O.Fr. *desfier*, lit. to renounce faith or allegiance.—L. *dis*, apart, and *fides*, faith. FAITH.] To provoke to combat or strife, by appealing to the courage of another; to invite one to contest; to challenge; to dare; to brave; to set at nought; to despise or be regardless of.—*n.* A challenge.—**defiance**, di·fī'ans, n. [O.Fr.] The act of defying, daring, or challenging;

a challenge to fight; invitation to combat; a challenge to meet in any contest, or to make good any assertion; contempt of opposition or danger; daring that implies contempt for an adversary, or of any opposing power.—*To bid defiance to*, or *to set at defiance*, to defy; to brave.—**defiant**, di·fī'ant, a. Characterized by defiance, boldness, or insolence.—**defiantly**, di·fī'ant·li, adv. In a defiant manner; with defiance; daringly; insolently.—**defier**, di·fī'èr, n. One who defies; one who dares to combat or encounter; one who sets at nought.

degenerate, di·jen'ér·āt, v.i.—*degenerated, degenerating*. [L. *degenero, degeneratum*, to become unlike one's race, from *degener*, ignoble, base—*de*, from, and *genus, generis*, race.] To fall off from the qualities proper to the race or kind, to become of a lower type, physically or morally; to pass from a good to a worse state.—*a.* (di·jen'ér·et). Having degenerated; having declined in qualities from one's ancestors, or one's former self; having lower moral standards.—*n.* (di·jen'ér·et). One who has degenerated; a pervert.—**degeneracy**, di·jen'ér·a·si, n. The state of degenerating or of being degenerate; deterioration; lowness; meanness.—**degenerately**, di·jen'ér·āt·li, adv. In a degenerate or base manner; unworthily.—**degenerateness**, di·jen'ér·āt·nes, n. A degenerate state.—**degeneration**, di·jen'ér·ā''shon, n. The state or process of becoming degenerate; degeneracy; gradual deterioration from a state physiologically superior.—**degenerative**, di·jen'ér·ā·tiv, a. Tending to cause degeneration.

deglutition, dē·glū·ti'shon, n. [L. *deglutio, deglutitum*, to swallow—*de*, and *glutio*. GLUTTON.] The act or power of swallowing; the process by which animals swallow.

degrade, di·grād', v.t.—*degraded, degrading*. [Fr. *dégrader*—L. *de*, down, and *gradus*, a step, a degree. GRADE.] To reduce from a higher to a lower rank or degree; to strip of honors; to reduce in estimation; to lower or sink in morals or character; to debase.—*v.i.* To degenerate; to become lower in character.—**degradation**, deg·ra·dā'shon, n. The act of degrading; a depriving of rank, dignity, or office; the state of being reduced from an elevated or more honorable station to one that is meaner or humbler; a mean or abject state to which one has sunk; debasement; degeneracy; *geol.* the lessening or wearing down of higher lands, rocks, strata, etc., by the action of water, or other causes.—**degraded**, di·grā'ded, a. Sunk to an abject or vile state; exhibiting degradation; debased; low.—**degrading**, di·grā'ding, a. Dishonoring; disgracing the character; causing degradation.

degree, di·grē', n. [Fr. *degré*, from L. *de*, down, and *gradus*, a step. DEGRADE.] A step or single movement, upward or downward, toward any end; one of a series of progressive advances; measure, amount, or proportion (he is a *degree* worse); measure of advancement; relative position attained, rank; station (men of low *degree*); a certain distance or remove in the line of family descent, determining the proximity of blood (a relation in the third or fourth *degree*); the 360th part of the circumference of any circle, a *degree of latitude* being the 360th part of any meridian on the earth's surface, a *degree of longitude* the same part of any given parallel of latitude; an interval of musical sound, marked by a line on the scale; a division, space, or interval marked on a mathematical or other instrument, as a thermometer or barometer; in universities, a title of distinction (*bachelor, master, doctor*) conferred as a testimony of proficiency in arts and sciences, or merely as an honor.—*By degrees*, step by step; gradually; by moderate advances.—*To a degree*, to an extreme; exceedingly.

dehisce, dē·his′, *v.i.* [L. *dehisco*, to gape—*de*, intens., and *hisco*, to gape.] *Bot.* to open, as the capsules or seed vessels of plants.—**dehiscence,** dē·his′ens, *n. Bot.* the splitting of an organ in accordance with its structure, as the opening of the parts of a capsule or the cells of anthers, etc.—**dehiscent,** dē·his′ent, *a. Bot.* opening; dehiscing.

dehort, di·hort′, *v.t.* [L. *dehortor*—*de*, and *hortor*, to advise.] To dissuade; to exhort against.—**dehortation,** dē·hor·tā′shon, *n.* Dissuasion. —**dehortative,** di·hor′ta·tiv, *a.* Dissuasive; dehortatory.—**dehortatory,** dē·hor′ta·to·ri, *a.* Dissuading; belonging to dissuasion.—*n.* A dissuasive argument or reason.

dehumanize, dē·hū′man·īz, *v.t.* To deprive of the character of humanity.

dehumidify, dē·hū·mid′i·fī, *v.t.*— *dehumidified, dehumidifying.* To remove moisture from.

dehydrate, dē·hī′drāt, *v.t.*—*dehydrated, dehydrating.* To remove water or water elements from.—*v.i.* To lose water or moisture.—**dehydration,** dē·hī·drā′shon, *n.* The process of dehydrating; excessive loss of body fluids.

deicide,† dē′i·sīd, *n.* [Fr. *déicide*—L. *deus*, God, and *cædo*, to slay.] The act of putting to death Jesus Christ, the Saviour; one concerned in putting Christ to death.

deify, dē′i·fī, *v.t.*—*deified, deifying.* [L. *deus*, a god, and *facio*, to make.] To make a god of; to exalt to the rank of a deity; to enroll among deities; to treat as an object of supreme regard; to praise or revere as a deity; to make godlike.—**deification,** dē′if·i·kā′shon, *n.*

deign, dān, *v.i.* [Fr. *daigner*, from L. *dignor*, to think worthy, from *dignus*, worthy, whence *dignity*, etc.] To vouchsafe; to condescend: generally followed by an infinitive.—*v.t.* To grant or allow.

deism, dē′izm, *n.* [Fr. *déisme*, from L. *Deus*, God. DEITY.] The doctrine or creed of a deist.—**deist,** dē′ist, *n.* [Fr. *déiste.*] One who believes in the

existence of a God or supreme being but denies revealed religion, basing his belief on the light of nature and reason. ∴ The term *deist* generally implies a certain antagonism to Christianity; while the similar term *theist* is applied to Christians, Jews, Mohammedans, and all believers in one god, being opposed to *atheist* or *pantheist.*—**deistic, deistical,** dē·is′tik, dē·is′ti·kal, *a.* Pertaining to deism or to deists; embracing or containing deism.—**deistically,** dē·is′ti·kal·li, *adv.* In a deistical manner.

deity, dē′i·ti, *n.* [L.L. *deitas,* the Godhead, divine nature, from L. *Deus,* God, akin to Gr. *Zeus* (genit. *Dios*), the supreme divinity; L. *Diespiter, Jupiter,* and *dies,* a day; Skr. *deva,* a god; W. *Duw,* God, *dyw,* day; Gael. and Ir. *dia,* God; *Tiw,* the A.Sax. god whose name appears in *Tuesday*; all from a root implying brightness.] Godhead; divinity; the Supreme Being, or infinite self-existing Spirit; God; a fabulous god or goddess; a divinity.

deject, di·jekt′, *v.t.* [L. *dejicio, dejectum*—*de,* down, and *jacio,* to throw; seen also in *abject, eject, jet, jut,* etc.] To cast down; to depress the spirits of; to dispirit; discourage, dishearten.—**dejected,** di·jek′ted, *p.* and *a.* Downcast; depressed; sad; sorrowful.—**dejectedly,** di·jek′ted·li, *adv.* In a dejected manner; sadly; heavily.—**dejectedness,** di·jek′ted·nes, *n.* Dejection.—**dejection,** di·jek′shon, *n.* The state of being downcast; depression of mind; melancholy; lowness of spirits occasioned by grief or misfortune.—**dejecta,** di·jek′ta, *n. pl.* Droppings; castings; excrement.

delaine, de·lān′, *n.* [Fr. *de,* of, and *laine,* L. *lana,* wool.] A muslin made originally of wool, afterwards more commonly of a mixed fabric, generally cotton and wool, and used chiefly as a printing cloth.

delation, di·lā′shon, *n.* [L. *delatio,* from *de,* down, and *latus,* part. of *fero,* to bear.] *Law,* accusation; act of charging with a crime; information against.

delay, di·lā′, *v.t.* [Fr. *délai,* It. *dilata,* delay, from L. *dilatus,* put off—*dis,* apart, and *latus,* pp. of *fero,* to carry.] To prolong the time of doing or proceeding with; to put off; to defer; to retard; to stop, detain, or hinder for a time; to restrain the motion of.—*v.i.* To linger; to move slowly; to stop for a time.—*n.* A lingering; a putting off or deferring; procrastination; protraction; hindrance.—**delayer,** di·lā′er, *n.* One who delays.

delectable, di·lek′ta·bl, *a.* [L. *delectabilis,* from *delectare,* to delight. DELIGHT.] Delightful; highly pleasing; affording great joy or pleasure.— **delectableness,** di·lek′ta·bl·nes, *n.* Delightfulness.—**delectably,** di·lek′ta·bli, *adv.* In a delectable manner; delightfully.—**delectation,** dē·lek·tā′shon, *n.* A giving delight; delight.

delegate, del′e·gāt, *v.t.*—*delegated, delegating.* [L. *delego, delegatum*—*de,* and *lego,* to send as an ambassador.

LEGATE.] To depute; to send on an embassy; to send with power to act as a representative; to entrust, commit, or deliver to another's care and management (power, an affair).—*n.* A person appointed and sent by another or by others, with powers to transact business as his or their representative; a deputy; a commissioner; a representative.—**delegation,** del·e·gā′shon, *n.* The act of delegating; appointment to act as deputy; a person or body of persons deputed to act for another or for others.

delete, di·lēt′, *v.t.* [L. *deleo, deletum,* to blot out, to destroy.] To blot out; to erase; to strike or mark out, as with a pen, pencil, etc.—**deletion,** di·lē′shon, *n.* [L. *deletio.*] The act of deleting; an erasure; a passage deleted.

deleterious, del·e·ter′ē·us, *a.* [L.L. *deleterius,* from Gr. *dēlētērios,* noxious, from *dēleomai,* to injure.] Having the quality of destroying life; noxious; poisonous; injurious; pernicious.

delf, delft, delf, delft, *n.* Earthenware, covered with enamel or white glazing in imitation of chinaware or porcelain, made at *Delft,* in Holland; glazed earthenware dishes.

deliberate, di·lib′er·āt, *v.i.*—*deliberated, deliberating.* [L. *delibero, deliberatum*—*de,* and *libro,* to weigh, from *libra,* a balance; akin *level.*] To weigh consequences or results in the mind previous to action; to pause and consider; to ponder, reflect, cogitate, or debate with one's self.— **deliberate,** dē·lib′er·it, *a.* Weighing facts and arguments with a view to a choice or decision; carefully considering probable consequences; slow in determining; formed with deliberation; well advised or considered; not sudden or rash; not hasty.— **deliberately,** di·lib′er·it·li, *adv.* In a deliberate manner; with careful consideration; not hastily or rashly. —**deliberateness,** di·lib′er·it·nes, *n.* The state or quality of being deliberate.—**deliberation,** di·lib′er·ā′shon, *n.* [L. *deliberatio.*] The act of deliberating; careful consideration; mature reflection; mutual discussion and examination of the reasons for and against a measure; the act or habit of doing anything coolly or without hurry or excitement.— **deliberative,** di·lib′er·a·tiv, *a.* Pertaining to deliberation; proceeding or acting by deliberation or discussion; having or conveying a right or power to deliberate or discuss.— **deliberatively,** di·lib′er·a·tiv·li. *adv.* By deliberation.

delicate, del′i·kit, *a.* [Fr. *délicat,* L. *delicatus,* from *deliciæ,* delight, *delicio,* to allure—*de,* and *lacio,* to draw gently; akin *delight, delectable.*] Pleasing to a cultivated taste; refinedly agreeable; dainty; of a fine texture; fine; soft; smooth; tender; sensitive; easily injured; not capable of standing rough handling; nice; accurate; light or softly tinted; slender; minute; peculiarly sensitive to beauty, harmony, or their opposites; refined in manner; polite; nice.—**delicately,**

del′i·kit·li, *adv.* In a delicate manner; with nice regard to propriety and the feelings of others; tenderly; daintily; luxuriously.—**delicateness,** del′i·kit·nes, *n.* The state of being delicate.—**delicacy,** del′i·ka·si, *n.* The quality of being delicate or highly pleasing to the taste or some other sense; fineness; smoothness; softness; tenderness; slenderness; that which is pleasing to the senses; a luxury; refined taste or judgment; nicety.—**delicious,** di·lish′us, *a.* [Fr. *délicieux,* from L. *deliciæ,* delight.] Highly pleasing to the taste; most sweet or grateful to the senses; affording exquisite pleasure; charming; delightful; entrancing.—**deliciously,** di·lish′us·li, *adv.* In a delicious manner; exquisitely; delightfully.—**deliciousness,** di·lish′us·nes, *n.* The quality of being delicious.

delicatessen, del′i·ka·te″sen, *n.* [G. pl. of *delikatesse,* delicacy.] A shop that sells prepared foods such as cooked meat, smoked fish, salads, etc.

delight, di·līt′, *v.t.* [O.E. *delite,* from O.Fr. *deliter, deleiter,* from L. *delecto,* to delight, from *delicio,* to allure. DELICATE.] To affect with great pleasure; to please highly; to give or afford high satisfaction or joy.—*v.i.* To have or take great pleasure; to be greatly pleased or rejoiced (to *delight in* a thing).—*n.* A high degree of pleasure or satisfaction of mind; joy; rapture; that which gives great pleasure; the cause of joy; charm.—**delighted,** di·lī′ted, *a.* Experiencing delight; overjoyed.—**delightedly,** di·lī′ted·li, *adv.* In a delighted manner; with delight.—**delightful,** di·līt′ful, *a.* Giving delight; highly pleasing; charming; exquisite; delicious.—**delightfully,** di·līt′ful·li, *adv.* In a delightful manner; charmingly; exquisitely.—**delightfulness,** di·līt′ful·nes, *n.*

delimit, di·lim′it, *v.t.* To mark or settle distinctly the limits of.—**delimitation,** di·lim′i·tā″shon, *n.* The act of delimiting; the fixing or settling of limits or boundaries.

delineate, di·lin′ē·āt, *v.t.*—*delineated, delineating.* [L. *delineo, delineatum—de,* down, and *linea,* a line. LINE.] To draw the lines which exhibit the form of; to make a draught of; to sketch or design; to represent in a picture; to draw a likeness of; to portray to the mind or understanding; to depict, sketch, or describe.—**delineation,** di·lin′ē·ā″shon, *n.* The act or process of delineating; representation or portrayal, whether pictorially or in words; sketch; description.—**delineator,** di·lin′ē·ā·tėr, *n.* One who delineates.

delinquency, di·ling′kwen·si, *n.* [L. *delinquentia,* a fault, from *delinquo,* to abandon, fail, omit duty—*de,* out, and *linquo,* to leave.] Failure or omission of duty; a fault; a misdeed; an offense.—**delinquent,** di·ling′kwent, *a.* Failing in duty; offending by neglect of duty.—**delinquent,** di·ling′kwent, *n.* One who fails to perform his duty; one guilty of a

delinquency; an offender; a culprit; a malefactor.—**delinquently,** di·ling′kwent·li, *adv.* So as to fail in duty.

deliquesce, del·i·kwes′, *v.i.*—*deliquesced, deliquescing.* [L. *deliquesco—de,* and *liquesco,* to melt, from *liqueo,* to become liquid. LIQUID.] To melt gradually and become liquid by attracting and absorbing moisture from the air, as certain salts, acids, and alkalies.—**deliquescence,** del·i·kwes′ens, *n.* The process of deliquescing; a gradual melting or becoming liquid by absorption of moisture from the atmosphere.—**deliquescent,** del·i·kwes′ent, *a.* Liquefying in the air; deliquescing.

delirium, di·lir′i·um, *n.* [L., from *deliro,* to draw the furrow awry in plowing, to deviate from the straight line, hence to be crazy, to rave—*de,* from, and *lira,* a furrow.] A temporary disordered state of the mental faculties occurring during illness, either of a febrile or of an exhausting nature; violent excitement; wild enthusiasm; mad rapture.—*Delirium tremens* (trē′menz), an affection of the brain which arises from the inordinate and protracted use of ardent spirits.—**delirious,** di·lir′i·us, *a.* Affected with delirium; light-headed; disordered in intellect; crazy; raving; frenzied; characterized by, or proceeding from, delirium.—**deliriously,** di·lir′i·us·li, *adv.* In a delirious manner.—**deliriousness,** di·lir′i·us·nes, *n.* The state of being delirious; delirium.

deliver, di·liv′ėr, *v.t.* [Fr. *délivrer,* from L.L. *delibero,* to set free—L. *de,* from, *libero,* to free, from *liber,* free, whence also *liberal, liberate.*] To release, as from restraint; to set at liberty; to free; to rescue or save; to transfer, hand over, or commit (a letter, a person to enemies); to surrender, yield, give up, resign: often followed by *up;* to disburden of a child; to utter, pronounce, speak (a sermon, address, etc.); to direct, send forth, or discharge (a blow, a broadside).—**deliverable,** di·liv′ėr·a·bl, *a.* Capable of being delivered.—**deliverance,** di·liv′ėr·ans, *n.* The act of delivering; in modern usage most commonly release or rescue, as from captivity, oppression, danger, etc., *delivery* being used in other senses.—**deliverer,** di·liv′ėr·ėr, *n.* One who delivers; one who releases or rescues; a preserver; a savior.—**delivery,** di·liv′ėr·i, *n.* The act of delivering; release; rescue, as from slavery, restraint, oppression, or danger; the act of handing over or transferring; surrender; a giving up; a giving or passing from one to another; specifically, the distribution of letters, etc., from a post office to a district or districts; utterance; pronunciation, or manner of speaking; childbirth.

dell, del, *n.* [DALE.] A small narrow valley between hills or rising grounds; a ravine.

Delphian, Delphic, del′fi·an, del′fik, *a.* Relating to *Delphi,* a town in Greece, and to the celebrated oracle

of that place; hence, oracular; inspired.

delphinine, delf′in·in, *n.* [Gr. *delphinion,* larkspur.] A poisonous alkaloid used medicinally.

delphinium, del·fin′i·um, *n.* [Gr. *delphinion,* larkspur.] Larkspur.

delta, del′ta, *n.* The name of the Greek letter Δ, answering to the English D; the island formed by the alluvial deposits between the mouths of the Nile, from its resemblance in shape to this letter; any similar alluvial tract at the mouth of a river.—**deltaic,** del·tā′ik, *a.* Relating to or like a delta.—**deltoid,** del′toid, *a.* Resembling the Greek Δ; triangular.

delude, di·lūd′, *v.t.*—*deluded, deluding.* [L. *deludo—de,* and *ludo,* to play, *ludus,* sport, whence also *ludicrous, elude, illusion,* etc.] To cause to entertain foolish or erroneous notions; to impose on; to befool; to lead from truth or into error; to mislead; to beguile; to cheat: often *refl,* (to *delude one's self* with vain hopes).—**deluder,** di·lū′dėr, *n.* One who deludes; a deceiver; an impostor; one who holds out false pretenses.—**delusion,** di·lū′zhon, *n.* The act of deluding; a misleading of the mind; false impression or belief; illusion; error or mistake proceeding from false views; the state of being deluded or misled.—**delusive,** di·lū′siv, *a.* Apt to delude; tending to mislead the mind; deceptive; beguiling.—**delusively,** di·lū′siv·li, *adv.* In a delusive manner.—**delusiveness,** di·lū′siv·nes, *n.* The quality of being delusive.—**delusory,** di·lū′so·ri, *a.* Apt to deceive; deceptive.

deluge, del′ūj, *n.* [Fr. *déluge,* from L. *diluvium,* a flood, a deluge—*di* for *dis,* asunder, away, and *luo=lavo,* to wash; akin *lave, ablution,* etc.] An inundation; a flood; [*cap.*] but specifically, the great flood or overflowing of the earth by water in the days of Noah; anything resembling an inundation; anything that overwhelms, as a great calamity.—*v.t.*—*deluged, deluging.* To overflow, as with water; to inundate; to drown; to overwhelm.

de luxe, de·luks′, *a.* [Fr.] Elegant; of superior quality.

delve, delv, *v.t.*—*delved, delving.* [A.Sax. *delfan*=D. *delven,* to dig; probably connected with *dell,* a dale, Fris. *dollen,* to dig.] To turn up with a spade; to dig.—*v.i.* To dig; to labor with the spade.—**delver,** del′vėr, *n.* One who delves.

demagnetization, dē·mag′net·i·zā″shon, *n.* The act or process of depriving of magnetic or of mesmeric influence.—**demagnetize,** dē·mag′ne·tīz, *v.t.*

demagogue, dem′a·gog, *n.* [Gr. *dēmagōgos—demos,* the people, and *agōgos,* a leader, from *agō,* to lead.] A leader of the people; a person who sways the people by his oratory; generally, an unprincipled factious orator; one who acquires influence with the populace by pandering to their prejudices or playing on their ignorance.—**demagogic, demagogical,** dem·a·goj'ik, dem·a·goj'i·kal, *a.* Relating to or like a demagogue; factious.—**demagogism** dem'a·gog·izm, *n.* The practices and principles of a demagogue.

demand, di·mand' *v.t.* [Fr. *demander,* from L. *demando,* in its late sense of to demand, the opposite of *mando,* to commit to, lit. to put into one's hand, from *manus,* the hand, and *do,* to give; akin *mandate, command.*] To claim or seek as due by right (to *demand* a thing *of* a person); to ask or claim generally (a price, a reward); to ask (a thing) by authority; to question authoritatively (O.T.); to require as necessary or useful; to necessitate (a task *demands* industry).—*v.i.* To make a demand; to inquire; to ask.—*n.* An asking for or claim made by virtue of a right or supposed right to the thing sought; an asking or request with authority; the asking or requiring of a price for goods offered for sale; question; interrogation; the calling for in order to purchase (there is no *demand* for the goods).—*In demand,* in request; much sought after or courted (goods are *in demand,* his company is *in* great demand).—*On demand,* on being claimed; on presentation (a bill payable *on demand*).—**demander,** di·man'dér, *n.* One who demands.

demarcation, dē·mär·kā'shon, *n.* [Fr. *démarcation*—*de,* down, and *marquer,* to mark. MARK.] The act or process of marking off, or of defining the limits or boundaries of anything; separation; distinction. Also written *Demarkation.*—**demarcate,†** di·mär'kāt, *v.t.* To mark the limits or boundaries of.

dematerialize, dē·ma·tē'ri·al·īz, *v.t.* To divest of material qualities or characteristics.

deme, dēm, *n.* [Gr. *demos.*] A subdivision of ancient Attica and of modern Greece; a township.

demean, di·mēn', *v.t.* [Fr. *démener,* formerly to behave—*de,* intens., and *mener,* to lead, to manage, from L. *minare,* to drive with threats, from *mina,* a threat, whence also *menace, minatory.*] To behave; to carry; to conduct; used *refl.* From confusion with the adj. *mean* the word is also sometimes used in sense of to lower or degrade (one's self).—**demeanor,** di·mē'nér, *n.* Behavior, especially as regards air or carriage of the person, countenance, etc.; carriage; deportment; conduct.

demented, di·men'ted, *a.* [L. *demens, dementis,* out of one's mind—*de,* out of, and *mens,* the mind.] Infatuated; mad; insane; crazy.—**dementia,** di·men'shi·a, *n.* [L.] A form of insanity; in psychiatry, any condition of impaired mentality.—**dementia praecox,** prē'koks. Schizophrenia.

demerit, dē·me'rit, *n.* [Fr. *démérite*—*de,* and *mérite,* merit. MERIT.] Desert, or what one merits (*Shak.*)‡; the opposite or absence of *merit;* that which is blamable or punishable in moral conduct; vice or crime.

demesne, de·mān', *n.* [O.Fr. *demaine, domaine,* from L. *dominus,* a lord; akin *dame, damsel, dominate,* etc.] *Law,* possession of land as one's own; an estate in land; the land adjacent to a manorhouse or mansion kept in the proprietor's own hands, as distinguished from lands held by his tenants.

demi-, dem'i [Fr. *demi,* from L. *dimidius,* half—*di* for dis, and *medius,* the middle.] A prefix signifying half. The hyphen is not always inserted in all these words.—**demibastion,** dem'i·bas·ti·on, *n. Fort.* a bastion that has only one face and one flank. —**demigod,** dem'i·god, *n.* Half a god; an inferior deity; one partaking partly of the divine; partly of the human nature.—**demimonde,** dem'i·mond, *n.* [Fr. *monde,* the world, society.] Women of questionable reputation; courtesans; the society which these women frequent.—**demirep,** dem'i·rep, *n.* [A contr. for *demi-reputation.*] A woman of doubtful reputation, an adventuress.—**demisemiquaver,** dem'i·sem·i·kwā·vér, *n. Mus.* the half of a semiquaver, or one-fourth of a quaver.—**demitasse,** dem'i·täs, *n.* [Fr.] A small cup of, or for, black coffee.—**demivolt,** dem'i·vōlt, *n.* A kind of leap or curvet of a horse.

demijohn, dem'i·jon, *n.* [Fr. *dame-jeanne,* from Ar. *damagan,* from *Damaghan,* a town in Khorassan once famous for its glassworks.] A glass vessel or bottle with a large body and small neck, enclosed in wickerwork.

demise, di·mīz', *n.* [Lit. a laying off or aside, from Fr. *démettre*—*de,* L. *dis,* aside, and *mettre,* to put, L. *mitto,* to send.] The death of a person, especially of a person of distinction; decease: used with possessives; *law,* a conveyance or transfer of an estate by lease or will.—*v.t.*—*demised, demising. Law,* to transfer or convey, as an estate; to bequeath; to grant by will.—**demisable,** di·mīz'a·bl, *a.* Capable of being demised.

demit, di·mit', *v.t.*—*demitted, demitting.* [L. *demitto*—*de,* down, and *mitto,* to send.] To lay down formally, as an office; to resign; to relinquish; to transfer.—**demission,** di·mi'shon, *n.* The act of demitting; a laying down of office; resignation; transference.

demiurge, demiurgus, dem'i·érj, dem'i·ér''gus, *n.* [Gr. *demiourgos,* from *demos,* the people, and *ergon,* a work.] A maker or framer; the maker of the world; the Creator; specifically, the name given by the Gnostics to the creator or former of the world of sense.—**demiurgic,** demi·ér'jik, dem·i·er'ji·kal, *a.* Pertaining to a demiurge or to creative power.

demobilize, dē·mō'bi·līz, *v.t.*—*demobilized, demobilizing.* [L. *de,* not, and E. *mobilize.*] To disarm and dismiss (troops) home; to disband.—**demobilization,** dē·mō'bi·li·zā''shon, *n.* The act of demobilizing.

democracy, di·mok'ra·si, *n.* [Gr.

dēmokratia—*dēmos,* people, and *kratos,* strength, power.] That form of government in which the supreme power rests with the people, ruling themselves either directly, as in the New England town meetings, or indirectly, through representatives—aptly expressed by Abraham Lincoln's phrase, "*of the people, by the people, for the people.*" The modern concept of democracy assumes the political equality of all individuals, the right to private freedom, and to petition authority for redress of grievances; a country so governed.—**democrat,** dem'o·krat, *n.* One who adheres to principles of democracy; [*cap.*] a member of the Democratic party in the U.S.—**democratically,** dem·o·krat'i·kal·li, *adv.* In a democratical manner.—**democratize,†** di·mok'ra·tīz, *v.t.* To render democratic.

Demogorgon, dē·mo·gor'gon, *n.* [Gr. *daimōn,* a demon, and *gorgos,* terrible.] A mysterious divinity in classical or ancient mythology, viewed as an object of terror rather than of worship. (*Mil.*)

demography, di·mog'ra·fi, *n.* [Gr. *dēmos,* people, *graphō,* to write.] The description of peoples or communities in regard to their social relations and institutions, especially as compared with other communities; study of the size, density, composition, etc. of human populations.—**demographer,** di·mog'ra·fér, *n.*—**demographic,** di·mo·graf'ik, *a.*

demoiselle, dé·mwä·zel', *n.* [Fr. DAMSEL.] A young lady; a damsel; a bird, the Numidian crane, so called from its gracefulness and symmetry of form.

demolish, di·mol'ish, *v.t.* [Fr. *démolir, démolissant,* from L. *demolior*—*de,* not, and *molior,* to build, from *moles,* mass, whence *molecule.*] To throw or pull down; to raze; to destroy, as a structure or artificial construction; to ruin.—**demolisher,** di·mol'ish·ér, *n.* One who demolishes.—**demolition,** dem·o·lish'on, *n.* The act of demolishing; destruction; ruin.

demon, dē'mon, *n.* [L. *daemon,* from Gr. *daimōn,* a spirit, evil or good.] A spirit or immaterial being, holding a middle place between men and the celestial deities of the pagans; an evil or malignant spirit; a devil; a very wicked or cruel person.—**demoniac, demoniacal,** di·mō'ni·ak, di·mō·nī'a·kal, *a.* Pertaining to demons or evil spirits; influenced by demons; produced by demons or evil spirits; extremely wicked or cruel.—**demoniac,** di·mō'ni·ak, *n.* A human being possessed by a demon.—**demoniacally,** di·mō·nī'a·kal·li, *adv.* In a demoniacal manner.—**demonian,†** di·mō'ni·an, *a.* Having the characteristics of a demon. (*Mil.*)—**demonism,** dē'mon·izm, *n.* The belief in demons.—**demonist,** dē'mon·ist, *n.* A worshiper of or believer in demons.—**demonize,** dē'mon·īz, *v.t.* To render demoniacal or diabolical; to control by a demon.—**demonology,** dē-mon•ol′o•ji, *n.* A treatise on evil spirits and their agency, or beliefs regarding them.

demonetize, dē•mon′e•tīz, *v.t.* To deprive of standard value, as money; to withdraw from circulation.—**demonetization,** dē•mon′e•tī•zā″shon, *n.* The act of demonetizing.

demonstrate, dem′on•strāt, *v.t.*—*demonstrated, demonstrating.* [L. *demonstro—de,* intens., and *monstro,* to show, from *monstrum,* a portent, a monster.] To point out with perfect clearness; to show clearly; to make evident; to exhibit; to exhibit the merits and operation of; to show or prove to be certain; to prove beyond the possibility, of doubt.—**demonstrable,** di•mon′stra•bl, *a.* Capable of being demonstrated, proved, or exhibited.—**demonstrability,** di•mon′stra•bil″i•ti, *n.* The state or quality of being demonstrable.—**demonstrably,** di•mon′stra•bli, *adv.* In a manner so as to preclude doubt.—**demonstration,** dem•on•strā′shon, *n.* The act of demonstrating; an exhibition; the exhibition of parts dissected for the study of anatomy; *milit.* an operation, such as the massing of men at a certain point, performed for the purpose of deceiving the enemy respecting the measures which it is intended to employ against him.—**demonstrative,** di•mon′stra•tiv, *a.* Serving to demonstrate; showing or proving by certain evidence; invincibly conclusive; characterized by or given to the strong exhibition of any feeling; outwardly expressive of feelings or emotions.—*Demonstrative pronoun,* one that clearly indicates the object to which it refers, as *this* man, *that* book.—**demonstratively,** di•mon′stra•tiv•li, *adv.* In a demonstrative manner; by demonstration; with proof which cannot be questioned; with energetic outward exhibition of feeling.—**demonstrativeness,** di•mon′stra•tiv•nes, *n.* Quality of being demonstrative.—**demonstrator,** dem′on•strā•tėr, *n.* One who demonstrates or exhibits the merits or operation of something to the public, as a device or food product; an article or product used for purposes of demonstration, such as an automobile or radio.

demoralize, di•mor′a•līz, *v.t.*—*demoralized, demoralizing.* [Prefix *de,* not, and *moral.*] To corrupt or undermine the morals of; to destroy or lessen the effect of moral principles on; to render corrupt in morals; *milit.* to deprive (troops) of courage and self-reliance, to render them distrustful and hopeless.—**demoralization,** di•mor′a•li•zā″shon, *n.* The act of demoralizing; the state of being demoralized.

demote, di•mōt′, *v.t.* [Prefix *de,* and *mote,* from *promote.*] To reduce to a lower rank or class.—**demotion,** di•mō′shon, *n.*

demulcent, di•mul′sent, *a.* [L. *demulcens, demulcentis,* ppr. of *demulceo,* to stroke down—*de,* down, and *mulceo,* to stroke, to soften.]

Softening; mollifying; lenient.—*n.* Any medicine which lessens the effects of irritation, as gums and other mucilaginous substances.

demur, di•mėr′, *v.i.*—*demurred, demurring.* [Fr. *demeurer,* to delay, to stay, from L. *demorari—de,* and *mora,* delay.] To pause in uncertainty; to hesitate; to have or to state scruples or difficulties; to object hesitatingly; to take exceptions; *law—n.* Stop; pause; hesitation as to the propriety of proceeding; suspense of proceeding or decision; exception taken; objection stated.—**demurrage,** di•mėr′ij, *n.* The time during which any common carrier, such as a vessel, railroad car, or express truck, is detained beyond that originally stipulated for loading or unloading; the payment made for such detainment; the charge made for the storage of freight or luggage beyond the collection period.—**demurrer,** di•mėr′ėr, *n.* One who demurs; *law,* a pleading which claims that the contentions submitted by the opposing party are insufficient in law to warrant his justification in bringing action.

demure, di•mūr′, *a.* [From Fr. *de moeurs,* of manners, having manners, from L. *mores,* manners, whence *moral,* etc.] Affectedly modest or coy; making a show of gravity or decorousness; grave or reserved consciously and intentionally.—**demurely,** di•mūr′li, *adv.* In a demure manner; with a show of solemn gravity.—**demureness,** di•mūr′nes, *n.* The state or quality of being demure; gravity of countenance, real or affected.

den, den, *n.* [A.Sax. *denn,* a cave or lurking-place; akin *denu,* E. *dene,* a valley.] A cave or hollow place in the earth; a cave, pit, or subterranean recess, used for concealment, shelter, protection, or security; any squalid place of resort or residence; a dell, wooded hollow, or ravine; a quiet, private retreat, as a room for reading.

denarius, di•nâ′ri•us, *n.* [L., from *decem,* ten.] An ancient Roman silver coin originally worth 10 asses or 10 lbs. of copper.

denationalize, dē•na′shon•al•īz, *v.t.* To divest of national character or rights.—**denationalization,** dē•na′shon•al•i•zā″shon, *n.* The act of denationalizing.

denaturalize, dē•nat′ū•ra•līz, *v.t.* To render unnatural; to alienate from nature; to deprive of naturalization or acquired citizenship in a foreign country.—**denature,** dē•nā′chėr, *v.t.* To change the nature of; to render unfit for human consumption, without impairing usefulness for other purposes, as alcohol.

dendriform, den′dri•form, *a.* [Gr. *dendron,* a tree.] Having the form or appearance of a tree.—**dendrite,** den′drīt, *n.* A stone or mineral, on or in which are figures resembling shrubs, trees, or mosses, the appearance being due to arborescent crystallization, resembling the frost work on our windows.—**dendritic,**

dentritical, den•drit′ik, den•drit′i-kal, *a.* Resembling a tree; treelike; marked by figures resembling shrubs, moss, etc.—**dendroid, dendroidal,** den′droid, den•droi′dal, *a.* Resembling a small tree or shrub.—**dendrology,** den•drol′o•ji, *n.* The natural history of trees.—**dendrologist,** den•drol′o•jist, *n.* One versed in dendrology.

dengue, deng′gā, *n.* [Sp.] A febrile epidemic disease of the East and West Indies, with symptoms resembling those of scarlet fever and rheumatism combined.

denial, denier. See DENY.

denigrate, den′i•grāt, *v.t.* To blacken, to soil, or to defile; to defame.

denim, den′em, *n.* [Fr. *serge de Nîmes,* serge of Nîmes, France.] A heavy, twilled cotton fabric used for upholstery, overalls, sports clothes, etc.

denitrate, dē•nī′trāt, *v.t.* To set nitric acid free from.—**denitration,** dē•nī•trā′shon, *n.* A disengaging of nitric acid.—**denitrify,** dē•nī′tri•fī, *v.t.* To deprive of niter.

denitrification, dē•nī′tri•fi•kā″shon, [L. *de,* from, *facio,* I make (nitrogen)] Liberation of nitrogen from organic matter by the action of bacteria. Cp. NITRIFICATION.

denizen, den′i•zn, *n.* [O.Fr. *deinzein,* one living within a city, from *deins, dens,* Fr. *dans,* in, within, a contr. of L. *de inius,* from within, and thus opposed to *foreign.*] An alien who is admitted to the privileges of citizenship; one granted membership in a society or fellowship; hence, a stranger admitted to residence and certain rights in a foreign country; a citizen; a dweller; an inhabitant.—*v.t.* To make a denizen.

denominate, di•nom′i•nāt, *v.t.*—*denominated, denominating.* [L. *denomino—de,* intens., and *nomino,* to nominate.] To give a name or epithet to; to name, call, style, or designate.—**denomination,** di•nom′i•nā″shon, *n.* The act of naming; a name or appellation; a class, society, or collection of individuals called by the same name; a religious sect.—**denominational,** di•nom′i-nā″shon•al, *a.* Pertaining to or characterizing a denomination; pertaining to particular religious denominations or bodies.—**denominationalism,** di•nom′i•nā″shon•al•izm, *n.* A denominational or class spirit; adherence or devotion to a denomination; the principle or system of religious sects having each their own schools.—**denominationally,** di•nom′i•nā″shon•al•li, *adv.* By denomination or sect.—**denominative,** di•nom′i•nā•tiv, *a.* Giving or conferring a name or distinct appellation.—*n.* That which has the character of a denomination; *gram.* a verb formed from a noun or an adjective.—**denominatively,** di•nom′i•nā•tiv•li, *adv.* By denomination.—**denominator,** di•nom′i•nā•tėr, *n.* One who or that which denominates; the number placed below the line in vulgar fractions, showing into how many parts the integer is divided.

---

ch, *chain*; *ch*, Sc. loch; g, go; j, *job*; ng, *sing*; TH, *then*; th, *thin*; w, *wig*; hw, *whig*; zh, azure.

denote, di·nōt′, v.t.—denoted, denoting. [L. denoto, to mark, to point out, to denote—de, intens, and noto, to mark, from nota, a mark.] To signify by a visible sign; to indicate, mark, or stand for; to be the name of or express; to be the sign or symptom of; to show; to indicate. ∴ Syn. under CONNOTE.—**denotable**, di·nō′ta·bl, a. That may be denoted or marked.—**denotation**, dē·nō·tā′shon, n. [L. denotatio.] The act of denoting or marking off; what any word or sign denotes.—**denotative**, di·nō′ta·tiv, a. Having power to denote.

denouement, dā·nö·moṅ′, n. [Fr., from dénouer, to untie—de, not, and nouer, to tie, from L. nodus, a knot.] The winding up or catastrophe of a plot, as of a novel, drama, etc.; the solution of any mystery; the issue, as of any course of conduct; the event.

denounce, di·nouns′, v.t.—denounced, denouncing. [Fr. denoncer, L. denuntiare—de, and nuntiare, to declare, nuntius, a messenger; seen also in announce, pronounce, renounce.] To declare solemnly; to proclaim in a threatening manner; to announce or declare, as a threat; to threaten; to inform against; to accuse.—**denouncement**,† di·nouns′ment, n. The act of denouncing; denunciation.—**denouncer**, di·noun′sẽr, n. One who denounces.—**denunciate**,† di·nun′shi·āt, v.t. To denounce.—**denunciation**, di·nun′shi·ā″shon, n. The act of denouncing; proclamation of a threat; public menace.—**denunciative, denunciatory**, di·nun′shi·ā·tiv, di·nun′shi·a·to·ri, a. Relating to, containing, or implying denunciation; ready or prone to denounce.—**denunciator**, di·nun′shi·ā·tẽr, n. One who denounces, or solemnly and publicly threatens.

dense, dens, a. [Fr. dense, L. densus, thick, whence, condense.] Having its constituent parts closely united; close; compact; thick; crass; gross; crowded.—**densely**, dens′li, adv. In a dense manner; compactly.—**denseness**, dens′nes, n. Density.—**density**, den′si·ti, n. [L. densitas.] The quality of being dense, close, or compact; closeness of constituent parts; compactness; either the mass of unit volume of a substance (absolute density) or the ratio of the mass of a given volume of the substance to that of an equal volume of some standard substance (relative density). The standard for solids and liquids is water (see SPECIFIC GRAVITY); for gases, either air or (usually in chem.) hydrogen.

dent, dent, n. [A form of dint.] A mark made by a blow; especially, a hollow or depression made on the surface of a solid body.—v.t. To make a dent on or in.

dental, den′tal, a. [L. dentalis, dental, from dens, dentis, a tooth, a word akin to E. tooth.] Of or pertaining to the teeth; having the characteristic sound given by the teeth and tip of the tongue (d and t are

dental letters).—n. A dental letter, as d, t, and th.—Dental formula, a formula for showing briefly the number and kinds of teeth of an animal; thus the dental formula of cats is:

$$\text{I.}\ \frac{3-3}{3-3},\ \text{C.}\ \frac{1-1}{1-1},\ \text{P.M.}\ \frac{3-3}{2-2},\ \text{M.}\ \frac{1-1}{1-1} = 30;$$

which signifies that they have on each side of each jaw three incisors and one canine tooth, three premolars in the upper and two in the lower jaw on each side, and behind these one true molar.—**dentate**, den′tāt, a. [L. dentatus, toothed.] Toothed; having sharp teeth, with concave edges, as a leaf.—**denticle**, den′ti·kl, n. [L. denticulus.] A small tooth or projecting point.—**denticulate, denticulated**, den·tik′ū·lāt, den·tik′ū·lā·ted, a. Having small teeth, as a leaf, calyx, or seed.—**denticulation**, den·tik′ū·lā″shon, n. The state of being denticulate.—**dentiform**, den′ti·form, a. Having the form of a tooth.—**dentifrice**, den′ti·fris, n. [L. dens, and frico, to rub.] A powder, paste, or liquid, to be used in cleaning the teeth.—**dentil**, den′til, n. Arch. the name of the little cubes or square blocks often cut for ornament on Greek cornices.—**dentin**, den′tēn, n. The hard tissue lying below the enamel and constituting the body of the tooth.—**dentist**, den′tist, n. One who makes it his business to clean and extract teeth, repair them when diseased, and replace them when necessary by artificial ones.—**dentistry**, den′tist·ri, n. The art or profession of a dentist.—**dentition**, den·tish′on, n. [L. dentitio.] The breeding or cutting of teeth in infancy; the time of growing teeth; the system of teeth peculiar to an animal.—**denture**, den′chẽr, n. A dentist's term for one or more artificial teeth.

denude, di·nūd′, v.t.—denuded, denuding. [L. denudo—de, and nudus, naked.] To divest of all covering; to make bare or naked; to strip; to uncover or lay bare.

denunciate, denunciation, denunciator, etc. See DENOUNCE.

deny, di·nī′, v.t.—denied, denying. [Fr. dénier, from L. denego—de, intens., and nego, to say no, from nec, nor. NEGATION.] To declare not to be true; to affirm to be not so; to contradict; to gainsay; to refuse to grant; not to afford; to withhold (Providence denies us many things); to refuse or neglect to acknowledge; not to confess; to disavow; to disown; to reject.—To deny one's self, to decline the gratification of appetites or desires.—To deny one's self something, to abstain from it although desiring it.—v.i. To answer in the negative; to refuse; not to comply.—**denial**, di·nī′al, n. The act of denying; contradiction; a contradictory statement; refusal; rejection; disownment.—**deniable**, di·nī′a·bl, a. Capable of being denied.—**denier**, di·nī′ẽr, n. One who denies.

deodand, dē·ō·dand, n. [L. Deo dandus, to be given to God.] Law,

formerly a personal chattel which had been the immediate occasion of the death of a rational creature (as a horse that killed a man), and for that reason forfeited to the king to be applied to pious uses.

deodar, dē·ō·där, n. [Skr. devadāru, that is, divine tree.] A kind of Indian cedar, closely akin to the cedar of Lebanon, yielding valuable timber, and introduced into Europe and elsewhere as an ornamental tree.

deodorize, dē·ō′dẽr·īz, v.t.—deodorized, deodorizing. To deprive of odor or smell, especially of fetid odor resulting from impurities.—**deodorizer, deodorant**, dē·ō′dẽr·i·zẽr, dē·ō′dẽr·ant, n. That which deodorizes; a substance which has the power of destroying fetid effluvia, as chlorine, chloride of lime, etc.—**deodorization**, dē·ō′dẽr·i·zā″shon, n. The act or process of deodorizing.

deontology, dē·on·tol′o·gi, n. [Gr. deon, deontos, that which is binding or right, duty, and logos, discourse.] The science of duty; that doctrine of ethics which is founded on the principle of judging of actions by their tendency to promote happiness.—**deontological**, dē·on′to·loj″i·kal, a. Relating to deontology.—**deontologist**, dē·on·tol′o·jist, n. One versed in deontology.

deoxidize, dē·ok′si·dīz, v.t. [Prefix de, not, and oxide, or the first part of oxygen.] To deprive of oxygen, or reduce from the state of an oxide; also called deoxygenate (dē·ok′si·je·nāt).—**deoxidize**, dē·ok′si·dīz, v.t.—deoxidized, deoxidizing. To deoxidate.

depart, di·pärt′, v.i. [Fr. départir—de, and partir, to separate. PART.] To go or move away; to go elsewhere; to leave or desist, as from a practice; to forsake, abandon, deviate, not to adhere to or follow (commonly with from in these senses); to leave this world; to die; to decease.—v.t. To leave; to retire from; with ellipsis of from.—**departed**, di·pär′ted, p. and a. Gone; vanished; dead; with the definite article used as a noun for a dead person.—**department**, di·pärt′ment n. A separate branch of business; a distinct province, in which a class of duties are allotted to a particular person; a distinct branch, as of science, etc.; a division of territory, as in France; a district into which a country is formed for governmental or other purposes.—Department store, a store that sells a wide variety of goods arranged in different departments.—**departmental**, di·pärt·men′tal, a.—**departure**, di·pär′chẽr, n. The act of leaving a place; death; decease; a forsaking; abandonment; deviation, as from a standard, rule, or plan.

depasture, dē·pas′chẽr, v.t. To put out in order to graze or feed; to pasture; to graze; to eat up by cattle.—v.i. To feed or pasture; to graze.

depend, di·pend′, v.i. [L. dependeo, to hang down—de, down, and pendeo, to hang, seen also in pendant, *pendulum, pendulous, impend,* etc.] To be sustained by being fastened or attached to something above; to hang down; followed by *from*; to be related to anything in regard to existence, operation, or effects; to be contingent or conditioned: followed by *on* or *upon* (we *depend on* air for respiration); to rest with confidence; to trust, rely, or confide; to believe fully; with *on* or *upon*.— **dependable,** di·pen'da·bl, *a.* Capable of being depended on; trustworthy.— **dependability,** di·pen'da·bil''i·ti, *n.* Reliableness.— **dependent, dependant,** di·pen'dent, dē·pen'dant, *n.* One who is sustained by another, or who relies on another for support or favor; a retainer; a follower; a servant.—*a.* Hanging down; relying on something else for support; subject to the power of or at the disposal of another; not able to exist or sustain itself alone; relying for support or favor (*dependent on* another's bounty); in grammar, subordinate, as a *dependent* clause.— **dependence,** di·pen'dens, *n.* A state of being dependent; connection and support; mutual connection; interrelation; a state of relying on another for support or existence; a state of being subject to the operation of any other cause; reliance; confidence; trust; a resting on.— **dependency,** di·pen'den·si, *n.* The state of being dependent; dependence; now generally a territory remote from the kingdom or state to which it belongs, but subject to its dominion (Malta is a *dependency* of Britain).— **dependably,** di·pen'da·bli, *adv.* In a dependent manner.

depict, di·pikt', *v.t.* [L. *depingo, depictum*—*de,* and *pingo,* to paint. PAINT, PICTURE.] To form a likeness of in colors; to paint; to portray; to represent in words; to describe; to delineate.— **depicture,** di·pik'tūr, *v.t.* To depict; to picture; to imagine.

depilate, dep'i·lāt, *v.t.*—*depilated, depilating.* [L. *depilo, depilatum*—*de,* not, and *pilus,* hair.] To strip of hair.— **depilation,** dep·i·lā'shon, *n.* The removal of hair.— **depilatory,** di·pil'a·to·ri, *a.* Having the quality or power to remove hair from the skin.—*n.* An application which is used to remove hair without injuring the texture of the skin; a cosmetic employed to remove superfluous hairs from the human skin.

deplete, di·plēt', *v.t.*—*depleted, depleting.* [L. *depleo, depletum,* to empty out—*de,* not, and *pleo,* to fill, as in *complete,* etc.] To empty, reduce, or exhaust by draining away.— **depletion,** di·plē'shon, *n.* The act of depleting; *med.* the act of diminishing the quantity of blood in the vessels by bloodletting.— **depletive,** di·plē'tiv, *a.* Tending to deplete; producing depletion.—*n.* That which depletes; any medical agent of depletion.— **depletory,** di·plē'to·ri, *a.* Calculated to deplete or exhaust.

deplore, di·plōr', *v.t.*—*deplored, de-*

ploring. [L. *deploro*—*de,* intens., and *ploro,* to wail, to let tears flow (same root as *flow, flood*); seen also in *explore, implore.*] To feel or express deep and poignant grief for; to lament; to mourn; to grieve for, to bewail; to bemoan.— **deplorable,** di·plō'ra·bl, *a.* Lamentable; sad; calamitous; grievous; miserable; wretched; contemptible or pitiable.— **deplorably,** di·plō'ra·bli, *adv.* In a manner to be deplored; lamentably.

deploy, di·ploi', *v.t.* [Fr. *déployer*—*de,* not, and *ployer* (as in *employ*), equivalent to *plier,* to fold, from L. *plicare,* to fold. PLY.] *Milit.* to extend in a line of small depth, as a battalion which has been previously formed in one or more columns; to display; to open out.—*v.i.* To form a more extended front or line; to open out.— **deployment,** di·ploi'ment, *n.* The act of deploying.

deplume, di·plūm', *v.t.*—*deplumed, depluming.* [L.L. *deplumo*—L. *de,* not, and *pluma,* a feather.] To strip of feathers; to deprive of plumage.

depolarize, dē·pō'lėr·īz, *v.t.* To deprive of polarity.— **depolarization,** dē·pō'lėr·i·zā''shon, *n.* The act of depriving of polarity; the restoring of a ray of polarized light to its former state.

depone, di·pōn', *v.i.* [L. *depono*—*de,* down, and *pono, positum,* to place. POSITION.] To give testimony; to depose: chiefly a Scots law term.— **deponent,** di·pō'nent, *a.* Laying down.—*Deponent verb,* in *Latin gram.* a verb which has a passive termination, with an active signification.—*n.* One who depones; a deponent verb.

depopulate, dē·pop'ū·lāt, *v.t.*—*depopulated, depopulating.* [L. *de,* from, and *populus,* people.] To deprive of inhabitants, whether by death or by expulsion; to dispeople; to greatly diminish the inhabitants of.— **depopulation,** dē·pop'ū·lā''shon, *n.* The act of depopulating.— **depopulator,** dē·pop'ū·lā·tėr, *n.* One who or that which depopulates.

deport, di·pōrt', *v.t.* [Fr. *déporter,* to banish; O.Fr. *se deporter,* to amuse one's self; L. *deporto,* to banish—*de,* down, away, and *porto,* to carry.] To carry, demean, or behave: used *refl.*; also, to transport; to carry away; to eject undesirable aliens from a country, under compulsory edict. (*Mil.*)— **deportation,** dē·pōr·tā'shon, *n.* A removal from one country to another, or to a distant place; exile; banishment.— **deportment,** di·pōrt'ment, *n.* Manner of acting in relation to the duties of life; behavior; demeanor; carriage; conduct.

depose, di·pōz', *v.t.*—*deposed, deposing.* [Fr. *déposer*—*de,* from, and *poser,* to place. COMPOSE.] To remove from a throne or other high station; to dethrone; to divest of office; to give testimony on oath, especially in a court of law.— **deposable,** di·pō'za·bl, *a.* That may be deposed.— **deposal,** di·pō'zal, *n.* The act of deposing or divesting

of office.— **deposition,** dep'o·zish''un, *n.* The act of deposing or giving testimony under oath; the attested written testimony of a witness; declaration; the act of dethroning a king, or removing a person from an office or station. See also under DEPOSIT.

deposit, di·poz'it, *v.t.* [L. *depositum,* something deposited, a deposit, from *depono, depositum.* DEPONE, POSITION.] To lay down; to place; to put; to lay in a place for preservation; to lodge in the hands of a person for safekeeping or other purpose; to entrust; to commit as a pledge.—*n.* That which is laid down; any matter laid or thrown down, or lodged; matter that settles down and so is separated from a fluid, as (*geol.*) an accumulation of mud, gravel, stones, etc., lodged by the agency of water; anything entrusted to the care of another; a pledge; a thing given as security or for preservation; a sum of money lodged in a bank.— **depositary,** di·poz'i·te·ri, *n.* A person with whom anything is left or lodged in trust; a guardian.— **deposition,** dē·po·zish'on, *n.* [L. *depositio.*] The act of depositing, laying, or setting down; placing; that which is deposited, lodged, or thrown down. See also under DEPOSE.— **depositor,** di·poz'i·tėr, *n.* One who makes a deposit.— **depository,** di·poz'i·to·ri, *n.* A place where anything is lodged for safekeeping; a person to whom a thing is entrusted for safekeeping.

depot, dē'pō or dep'ō, *n.* [Fr. *dépôt,* O.Fr. *depost,* from L. *depono, depositum,* to deposit.] A place of deposit; a depository; a building for receiving goods for storage or sale; *milit.* the headquarters of a regiment; also a station where recruits for different regiments are received and drilled; a railroad station.

deprave, di·prāv', *v.t.*—*depraved, depraving.* [L. *depravo,* to make crooked, to -deprave—*de,* intens., and *pravus,* crooked, perverse, wicked.] To make bad or worse; to impair the good qualities of; to vitiate; to corrupt.— **depravation,** dep·ra·vā'shon, *n.* [L. *depravatio.*] The act of depraving or corrupting; the state of being depraved; corruption; deterioration.— **depraved,** di·prāvd', *p.* and *a.* Vitiated; tainted; corrupted (*depraved* taste); destitute of good principles; vicious; immoral; profligate; abandoned.— **depraver,** di·prā'vėr, *n.* One who depraves.— **depravity,** di·prav'i·ti, *n.* The state of being depraved; a vitiated state; especially, a state of corrupted morals; destitution of good principles; sinfulness; wickedness; vice; profligacy.

deprecate, dep're·kāt, *v.t.*—*deprecated, deprecating.* [L. *deprecor, deprecatus,* to pray against, to ward off by prayer—*de,* off, and *precor,* to pray.] To pray deliverance from, or that something may be averted; to plead or argue earnestly against; to urge reasons against; to express strong disapproval of (as of anger, a scheme, etc.).—**deprecatingly,** dep're·kā·ting·li, *adv.* In a deprecating manner.—**deprecation,** dep·re·kā'shon, *n.* The act of deprecating; a praying against; entreaty; disapproval; condemnation.—**deprecatory, deprecative,** dep're·ka·to·ri, dep're·kā·tiv, *a.* Serving to deprecate; having the character of deprecation.

depreciate, di·prē'shi·āt, *v.t.*—**depreciated, depreciating.** [L. *depretio,* to lower the price of—*de,* down, and *pretium,* price. PRICE.] To bring down the price or value of; to cause to be less valuable; to represent as of little value or merit, or of less value than is commonly supposed; to lower in estimation, undervalue, decry, disparage, or underrate.—*v.i.* To fall in value; to become of less worth.—**depreciation,** di·prē'shi·ā'shon, *n.* The act of depreciating; reduction in value or worth; a lowering or undervaluing in estimation; the state of being undervalued.—**depreciative, depreciatory,** di·prē'shi·a·tiv, di·prē'shi·a·to·ri, *a.* Tending to depreciate.—**depreciator,** di·prē'shi·a·ter, *n.* One who depreciates.

depredate, dep'ri·dāt, *v.t.*—**depredated, depredating.** [L. *depraedor,* to pillage—*de,* intens., and *praedor,* to plunder, from *praeda,* prey. PREY.] To plunder; to pillage; to waste; to spoil.—**depredation,** dep·ri·dā'shon, *n.* The act of depredating; a robbing; a pillaging by men or animals; a laying waste.—**depredator,** dep'ri·dā·ter, *n.* One who depredates; a spoiler; a waster.—**depredatory,** dep'ri·dā·to·ri, *a.* Consisting in pillaging.

depress, di·pres', *v.t.* [L. *deprimo, depressum,* to depress—*de,* and *premo, pressum,* to press. PRESS.] To press down; to let fall to a lower state or position; to lower; to render dull or languid; to deject or make sad; to humble, abase, bring into adversity; to lower in value.—**depressed,** di·prest', *p.* and *a.* Dejected; dispirited; discouraged; sad; humbled; languid; dull; *nat. hist.* flattened in shape; flattened as regards the under and upper surfaces.—**depressingly,** di·pres'ing·li, *adv.* In a depressing manner.—**depression,** di·presh'on, *n.* The act of pressing down or depressing; a sinking or falling in of a surface; a hollow; the state or feeling of being depressed in spirits; a sinking of the spirits; dejection; a low state of strength; a prolonged period of financial and commercial stagnation characterized by unemployment, restricted credit, low prices, and general social distress.—*Angle of depression. Astron.* The angle by which a straight line drawn from the eye to any object dips below the horizon.—**depressive,** di·pres'iv, *a.* Able or tending to depress or cast down.—**depressor,** di·pres'ẽr, *n.* One who or that which depresses; *anat.* a muscle which depresses or draws down the part to which it is attached.

deprive, di·prīv', *v.t.*—**deprived, de-**

priving. [L. *de,* intens., and *privo,* to take away. PRIVATE.] To take from; to dispossess; to despoil; to bereave of something possessed or enjoyed: followed by *of* (to *deprive* a person *of* a thing); to divest of an ecclesiastical preferment, dignity, or office.—**deprivation,** dep·ri·vā'shon, *n.* The act of depriving; a taking away; a state of being deprived; loss; want; bereavement; the act of divesting a clergyman of his spiritual promotion or dignity; the taking away of a preferment; deposition.

depth, depth, *n.* [From *deep;* comp. *width, breadth, length,* etc.] The distance or measure of a thing from the highest part, top, or surface to the lowest part or bottom, or to the extreme part downward or inward; the measure from the anterior to the posterior part; deepness: in a vertical direction opposed to *height;* a deep place; an abyss; a gulf; the inner, darker, or more concealed part of a thing; the middle, darkest, or stillest part (the *depth* of winter or of a wood); abstruseness; obscurity; immensity; infinity; intensity (the *depth* of despair or of love).—**depth charge,** *n.* A bomb designed to go off under water.

depurate, dep'ū·rāt, *v.t.*—**depurated, depurating.** [L.L. *depuro, depuratum,* to purify—L. *de,* intens., and *puro, puratum,* to purify, from *purus,* pure.] To free from impurities, heterogeneous matter, or feculence; to purify; to clarify.—**depuration,** dep'ū·rā'shon, *n.* The act of depurating; the cleansing of a wound.—**depurator,** dep'ū·rā·ter, *n.* One who or that which depurates.

depute, di·pūt', *v.t.*—**deputed, deputing.** [Fr. *députer,* from L. *deputo,* to destine, allot—*de,* and *puto,* to prune, set in order, reckon, as in *compute, dispute,* etc.] To appoint as a substitute or agent to act for another; to appoint and send with a special commission or authority to act for the sender.—*n.* (dep'ūt). A deputy; as, a sheriff-*depute.* (Scotch.)—**deputation,** dep·ū·tā'shon, *n.* The act of deputing or sending as a deputy; a special commission or authority to act as the substitute of another; the person or persons deputed to transact business for another.—**deputy,** dep'ū·ti, *n.* [Fr. *député.*] A person appointed or elected to act for another; a representative, delegate, agent, or substitute.

deracinate,† dē·ras'i·nāt, *v.t.* [Fr. *déraciner*—*de,* from, and *racine,* a root, from L. *radix,* a root.] To pluck up by the roots; to extirpate. (Shak.)

derange, di·rānj', *v.t.*—**deranged, deranging.** [Fr. *déranger*—*de,* not, and *ranger,* to set in order, to range. RANGE.] To put out of order; to throw into confusion; to disorder; to confuse; to disturb; to unsettle; to embarrass; to discompose.—**derangement,** di·rānj'ment, *n.* The act of deranging or state of being deranged; a putting out of order;

embarrassment; confusion; disorder; delirium; insanity; mental disorder.

derelict, der'e·likt, *a.* [L. *derelictus,* left behind, abandoned—*de,* intens., *re,* behind, and *linquo,* to leave.] Left; abandoned; especially abandoned at sea.—*n.* An article abandoned by the owner, especially a vessel abandoned at sea.—**dereliction,** der·e·lik'shon, *n.* The act of leaving with an intention not to reclaim; desertion; relinquishment; abandonment (a *dereliction* of duty).

deride, di·rīd', *v.t.*—**derided, deriding.** [L. *derideo*—*de,* intens., and *rideo,* to laugh.] To laugh at in contempt; to turn to ridicule or make sport of; to treat with scorn by laughter; to mock; to ridicule.—**derider,** dē·rī'dẽr, *n.* One who derides; a mocker; a scoffer.—**deridingly,** di·rī'ding·li, *adv.* By way of derision or mockery.—**derision,** di·rizh'on, *n.* [L. *derisio.*] The act of deriding, or the state of being derided; contempt manifested by laughter; mockery; ridicule; scorn.—**derisive,** di·rī'siv, *a.* Expressing or characterized by derision; mocking; ridiculing.—**derisively,** di·rī'siv·li, *adv.* With mockery or contempt.—**derisiveness,** di·rī'siv·nes, *n.* The state of being derisive.

derive, di·rīv', *v.t.*—**derived, deriving.** [L. *derivo,* to divert a stream from its channel, to derive—*de,* from, and *rivus,* a stream, whence also *rivulet, rival.*] To divert or turn aside from a natural course‡; to draw from, as in a regular course or channel; to receive from a source or as from a source or origin (to *derive* power, knowledge, facts); to deduce or draw from a root or primitive word; to trace the etymology of.—*Derived units.* Units based upon and determined by the FUNDAMENTAL UNITS (which see).—*v.i.*† To come or proceed. (*Tenn.*)—**derivable,** di·rī'va·bl, *a.* Capable of being derived.—**derivation,** der·i·vā'shon, *n.* The act of deriving, drawing, or receiving from a source; the drawing or tracing of a word from its root or origin; etymology.—**derivational,** der·i·vā'shon·al, *a.* Relating to derivation.—**derivative,** di·riv'a·tiv, *a.* Taken or having proceeded from another or something preceding; derived; secondary.—*n.* That which is derived; that which is deduced or comes by derivation from another; a word which takes its origin in another word, or is formed from it.—**derivatively,** di·riv'a·tiv·li, *adv.* In a derivative manner; by derivation.—**deriver,** di·rī'vẽr, *n.* One who derives.

derma, dermis, dẽr'ma, dẽr'mis, *n.* [Gr. *derma,* skin.] The true skin, or under layer of the skin, as distinguished from the cuticle, epidermis, or scarf skin.—**dermal,** dẽr'mal, *a.* Pertaining to skin; consisting of skin.—**dermatitis,** dẽr·ma·tīt'is. [Gr. *derma,* skin, *-itis,* inflammation.] Inflammation of the skin.—**dermatogen,** dẽr·mat'o·jen. [Gr. *derma, dermatos,* skin, *gen,* to produce.] A cellular layer at the tip of a root or stem from which the epidermis is produced.—**dermatologist,** dèr·ma·tol′o·jist, *n.* One versed in dermatology.—**dermatology,** dèr·ma·tol′o·ji, *n.* The branch of science which treats of the skin and its diseases.—**dermatophyte,** dèr′ma·to·fīt, *n.* [Gr. *phyton,* a plant.] A parasitic plant, infesting the cuticle and epidermis of men and animals, and giving rise to various forms of skin disease, as ringworm.—**dermic,** dèr′mik, *a.* Relating to the skin.

derogate, der′o·gāt, *v.t.*—**derogated, derogating.** [L. *derogo, derogatum,* to repeal part of a law, to restrict, to modify—*de,* not, and *rogo,* to ask, to propose.] To repeal, annul, or revoke partially, as a law: distinguished from *abrogate;* to lessen the worth of; to disparage‡.—*v.i.* To detract; to have the effect of lowering or diminishing, as in reputation; to lessen by taking away a part: with *from* (something *derogates* from a person's dignity).—**derogation,** der·o·gā′shon, *n.* The act of derogating; a taking away from, or limiting in extent or operation; a lessening of value or estimation; detraction; disparagement.—**derogatory,** di·rog′a·to·ri, *a.* Having the effect of derogating or detracting from; lessening the extent, effect, or value: with *to.*—**derogatoriness,** di·rog′a·to·ri·nes, *n.* The quality of being derogatory.—**derogatorily,** di·rog′a·to·ri·li, *adv.*

derrick, der′ik, *n.* [The name of a London hangman of the 17th century, applied first to the gallows, and hence to a contrivance resembling it.] An apparatus for hoisting heavy weights, usually consisting of a boom supported by a central post; a framework over an oil well, gas well, etc., that holds drilling and hoisting tackle.

derringer, der′in·jèr, *n.* [After the inventor, an American gunsmith.] A small pistol of large caliber.

dervish, dèr′vish, *n.* [Turkish *dervish,* Per. *darwesh,* poor, indigent, a dervish.] A Mohammedan friar or monk, who professes extreme poverty, and leads an austere life, partly in monasteries, partly itinerant.

descant, des′kant, *n.* [O.Fr. *deschant,* from L.L. *discantus*—L. *dis,* and *cantus,* singing, a song.] A discourse, discussion, or disputation; *mus.* an addition of a part or parts to a subject or melody; a song or tune with various modulations.—*v.i.* (des·kant′). To discourse, comment, or animadvert freely; to add a part or variation to a melody.

descend, di·send′, *v.i.* [Fr. *descendre* L. *descendere*—*de,* down, *scando,* to climb. SCAN.] To move from a higher to a lower place; to move, come, or go downward; to sink; to run or flow down; to invade or fall upon hostilely; to proceed from a source or origin; to be derived; to pass from one heir to another; to pass, as from general to particular considerations; to lower or degrade one's self; to stoop.—*v.t.* To walk,

move, or pass downward upon or along; to pass from the top to the bottom of.—**descendable,** di·sen′da·bl, *a.* Capable of descending by inheritance; descendible.—**descendant,** di·sen′dant, *n.* An individual proceeding from an ancestor in any degree, offspring.—**descendent,** di·sen′dent, *a.* Descending.—**descendible,** di·sen′di·bl, *a.* Capable of being descended or passed down; capable of descending from an ancestor to an heir.—**descent,** di·sent′, *n.* [Fr. *descente.*] The act of descending or passing from a higher to a lower place; inclination downward; slope; declivity; decline, as in station, virtue, quality, or the like; an incursion, invasion, or sudden attack on a country; transmission by succession or inheritance; a proceeding from a progenitor; extraction; lineage; pedigree; a generation; a single degree in the scale of genealogy; issue†; descendants†.

describe, di·skrīb′, *v.t.*—**described, describing.** [L. *describo,* to write down, to delineate—*de,* down, and *scribo,* to write, as in *ascribe, inscribe,* etc.; akin *scribe, scripture.*] To delineate or mark the form or figure of; to trace out; to form or trace by motion; to show or represent orally or by writing; to depict or portray in words.—*v.i.* To use the power of describing.—**describable,** di·skrī′ba·bl, *a.* Capable of being described.—**describer,** di·skrī′bèr, *n.* One who describes.—**description,** di·skrip′shon, *n.* [L. *descriptio, descriptionis.*] The act of describing; delineation; an account of the properties or appearance of a thing, so that another may form a just conception of it; the combination of qualities which constitute a class, species, or individual; hence, class, species, variety, kind (a person of this *description.*)—**descriptive,** di·skrip′tiv, *a.* Containing description; having the quality of representing.—**descriptively,** di·skrip′tiv·li, *adv.* In a descriptive manner.—**descriptiveness,** di·skrip′tiv·nes, *n.* State of being descriptive.

descry, di·skrī′, *v.t.*—**descried, descrying.** [O.Fr. *descrier,* to decry, to make an outcry on discovering something. DECRY.] To espy; to discover by the sight; to see or behold from a distance; to examine by the sight (O.T.).

desecrate, des′i·krāt, *v.t.*—**desecrated, desecrating.** [From L. *de,* from, away, and *sacer,* sacred, being thus the opposite of *consecrate.*] To divert from a sacred purpose or sacred character; to render unhallowed; to profane.—**desecration,** des·i·krā′shon, *n.* The act of desecrating; profanation.

desegregate, dē·seg′re·gāt, *v.t.* To abolish racial segregation.—**desegregation,** dē·seg′re·gā″shon, *n.*

desensitize, dē·sen′si·tīz, *v.t.* To make less sensitive; *photog.* to make less sensitive to light.

desert, dez′ért, *a.* [L. *desertus,* pp. of *desero, desertum,* to forsake—*de,* not, and *sero, sertum,* to unite, to join together, from root seen in *series.*]

Lying waste; uncultivated and uninhabited; in the natural state and unimproved by man; pertaining to a wilderness (the *desert* air).—*n.* An uninhabited tract of land; a wilderness; a solitude; often a vast sandy, stony, or rocky expanse, almost destitute of moisture and vegetation. *v.t.* (di·zèrt′). To forsake; to leave utterly; to abandon; to quit, leave, or depart from in defiance of duty. *v.i.* To quit a service or post without permission; to run away.—**deserter,** di·zèr′tèr, *n.* One who deserts; particularly, a soldier or seaman who quits the service without permission. —**desertion,** di·zèr′shon, *n.* The act of deserting; the state of being deserted or forsaken.

desert, di·zèrt′, *n.* [O.Fr. *deserte,* merit, from *deservir,* to deserve. DESERVE.] The quality of deserving either reward or punishment; merit or demerit; what is deserved on account of good or evil done; reward or punishment merited; due return.

deserve, di·zèrv′ *v.t.*—**deserved, deserving.** [O.Fr. *deservir, desservir,* from L. *deservio,* to serve diligently —*de,* intens., and *servio,* to serve.] To merit; to be worthy of, whether of good or evil; to merit by labor, services, or qualities; to be worthy of or call for on account of evil acts or qualities (actions that *deserve* censure).—*v.i.* To merit; to be worthy of or deserving (to *deserve* well of a person).—**deservedly,** di·zèr′ved·li, *adv.* According to desert, whether of good or evil; justly.—**deserver,** di·zèr′vèr, *n.* One who deserves or merits: used generally in a good sense.—**deserving,** di·zèr′ving, *a.* Worthy of reward or praise: meritorious.—**deservingly,** di·zèr′ving·li, *adv.* Meritoriously; with just desert.

deshabille, dez·a·bēl′, *n.* [Fr.—*des* = prefix *dis,* and *habiller,* to dress; akin *habiliment.*] The state of being in undress, or of not being properly or fully dressed.

desiccate, des′i·kāt, *v.t.*—**desiccated, desiccating.** [L. *desicco,* to dry up— *de,* intens., and *sicco,* to dry, from *siccus,* dry.] To exhaust of moisture; to exhale or remove moisture from; to dry.—*v.i.* To become dry.— **desiccant, desiccative,** des′ik·ant, de·sik′a·tiv, *a.* Drying.—*n.* A medicine or application that dries a sore. —**desiccation,** des·ik·kā′shon, *n.* The act of making dry; the state of being dried.

desiderate, di·sid′ér·āt, *v.t.* [L. *desidero, desideratum,* to long for, to feel the want of, whence also *desire.*] To feel the want of; to miss; to want; to desire.—**desiderative,** di·sid′ér·ā″tiv, *a.* Having or implying desire; expressing or denoting desire. —*n.* A verb formed from another verb and expressing a desire of doing the action implied in the primitive verb.—**desideratum,** di·sid′ér·ā″tum, *n. pl.* **desiderata,** di·sid′ér·ā″ta. [L.] That which is not possessed, but which is desirable; something much wanted.

design, di·zīn′, *v.t.* [L. *designo,*

to mark out, point out, contrive —*de*, and *signo*, to seal or stamp, from *signum*, a sign. SIGN.] To plan and delineate by drawing the outline or figure of; to sketch, as for a pattern or model; to project or plan; to contrive for a purpose; to form in idea (a scheme); to set apart in intention; to intend; to purpose.—*v.i.* To intend; to purpose. —*n.* A plan or representation of a thing by an outline; first idea represented by lines, as in painting or architecture; a sketch; a drawing; a tracing; a scheme or plan in the mind; purpose; intention; aim; the adaptation of means to a preconceived end; contrivance.—**designate,** dez′ig·nāt, *v.t.*—*designated, designating*. To mark out or indicate by visible lines, marks, description, etc.; to name and settle the identity of; to denominate; to select or distinguish for a particular purpose; to appoint, name, or assign.—**designation,** dez·ig·nā′shon, *n.* The act of designating; a distinguishing from others; indication; appointment; assignment; distinctive appellation.—**designative,** dez′ig·nā·tiv, *a.* Serving to designate or indicate.—**designator,** dez′ig·nā·tėr, *n.* One who designates or points out.—**designedly,** di·zī′ned·li, *adv.* By design; purposely; intentionally. —**designer,** di·zī′nėr, *n.* One who designs.—**designing,** di·zī′ning, *pp.* and *a.* Artful; insidious.

desire, di·zīr′, *v.t.*—*desired, desiring*. [Fr. *désirer*, from L. *desidero, desideratum*, to desire (*desiderate* being thus the same word)—prefix *de*, and *sidero*, as in *considero*. CONSIDER.] To wish for the possession or enjoyment of; to long for; to hanker after; to covet; to express a wish to obtain; to ask; to request; to petition.—*v.i.* To be in a state of desire or anxiety.—*n.* [Fr. *désir*, from the verb.] An emotion or excitement of the mind, directed to the attainment or possession of an object from which pleasure is expected; a wish, craving, or longing to obtain or enjoy; the object of desire; that which is desired.—**desirability, desirableness,** di·zī′ra·bil′i·ti, di·zī′ra·bl·nes, *n.* The state or quality of being desirable.—**desirable,** di·zī′ra·bl, *a.* Worthy of desire; calculated or fitted to excite a wish to possess.—**desirably,** di·zī′ra·bli, *adv.* In a desirable manner.—**desirous,** di·zī′rus, *a.* Filled with a desire; wishing to obtain; wishful; covetous: often with *of*.

desist, di·zist′, *v.i.* [L. *desisto*, to desist—*de*, away from, and *sisto*, to stand, as in *assist, consist, persist*, etc. STAND.] To cease to act or proceed; to forbear; to leave off; to discontinue; to cease.—**desistance, desistance,**† di·zis′tans, di·zis′tens, *n.* A ceasing to act or proceed; a stopping.

desk, desk, *n.* [A.Sax. *disc*, a table, a dish; L.L. *discus*, a desk, from L. *discus*, Gr. *diskos*, a disc, a quoit; *dais, dish, disk* are the same word.] A kind of table or piece of furniture for the use of writers and readers;

a frame or case to be placed on a table for the same purpose.

desolate, des′o·lit, *v.t.*—*desolated, desolating*. [L. *desolo, desolatum*, to leave alone, to forsake—*de*, intens., and *solo*, to lay waste, from *solus*, alone. SOLE, *a*.] To deprive of inhabitants; to make desert; to lay waste; to ruin; to ravage.—*a.* [L. *desolatus*, pp. of *desolo, desolatum*.] Destitute or deprived of inhabitants; desert; uninhabited; laid waste; in a ruinous condition; without a companion; solitary; forsaken; forlorn; lonely.—**desolately,** des′o·lit·li, *adv.* In a desolate manner.—**desolateness,** des′o·lit·nes, *n.* A state of being desolate.—**desolater, desolator,** des′o·lā·tėr, *n.* One who or that which desolates.—**desolation,** des·o·lā′shon, *n.* The act of desolating; devastation; havoc; ravage; a place depopulated, ravaged, or laid waste; the state of being desolate; gloominess; sadness; melancholy; destitution; ruin.

despair, di·spâr′, *v.i.* [O.Fr. *desperer* (now *desespérer*), from L. *despero*—*de*, not, and *spero*, to hope, allied to Skr. root *sprih*, to desire. *Prosper* is from same root.] To give up all hope or expectation: followed by *of*; to be sunk in utter want of hope. —*n.* The state of being without hope, combined with a dread of coming evil; hopelessness; desperation; that which causes despair; *theol.* loss of hope in the mercy of God.— **despairing,** di·spâr′ing, *a.* Indulging in despair; prone to despair; indicating despair.—**despairingly,** di·spâr′ing·li, *adv.* In a despairing manner.

desperado, des′pėr·ä″dō, des′pėr·ä″dō, *n.* A desperate fellow; one fearless or regardless of safety; a reckless ruffian.

desperate, des′pėr·it, *a.* [L. *desperatus*, pp. of *despero*, to despair. DESPAIR.] Without hope‡; regardless of safety; fearless of danger; reduced to extremity and reckless of consequences; frantic; proceeding from despair; reckless; beyond hope; irretrievable; past cure; hopeless (*desperate* disease, situation, undertaking).—**desperately,** des′pėr·it·li, *adv.* In a desperate manner; recklessly; violently; furiously; madly.—**desperateness,** des′pėr·it·nes, *n.* The state or quality of being desperate.— **desperation,** des·pėr·ā′shon, *n.* The state of being desperate; a giving up of hope; disregard of safety or danger; fury; rage; violence.

despicable, des′pi·ka·bl, *a.* [L.L. *despicabilis*, from L. *despicor, despicatus*, to despise, from *despicio*. DESPISE.] Deserving of being despised; contemptible; base; mean; vile; worthless. ∴ Syn. under CONTEMPTIBLE.—**despicableness,** des′pi·ka·bl·nes, *n.* The quality or state of being despicable.—**despicably,** des′pi·ka·bli, *adv.* In a despicable manner; basely; vilely.

despise, di·spīz′, *v.t.*—*despised, despising*. [O.Fr. *despire*, pp. of *despire*, to despise, from L. *despicere*, to despise—*de*, down, and *specio*, to look. SPECIES. Akin *despicable, des-*

pite.] To look down upon; to have the lowest opinion of; to contemn; to disdain; to scorn.

despite, di·spīt′, *n.* [O.Fr. *despit*, Mod. Fr. *dépit*, from L. *despectus*, a looking down upon, a despising, from *despicio*, to despise. DESPISE. Hence the shorter form *spite*.] Extreme malice; malignity; contemptuous hate; aversion; spite; defiance with contempt, or contempt of opposition; contemptuous defiance; an act of malice or contempt.—*v.t.*† To vex; to offend; to spite; to tease.— *prep.* In spite of; notwithstanding.— **despiteful,** di·spīt′fụl, *a.* Full of despite or spite; malicious; malignant. —**despitefully,** di·spīt′fụl·li, *adv.* With despite; maliciously; contemptuously.—**despitefulness,** di·spīt′fụl·nes, *n.*

despoil, di·spoil′, *v.t.* [O.Fr. *despoiller*, L. *despolio*, to rob, plunder—*de*, intens., and *spolio*, to spoil. SPOIL.] To take from by force; to rob; to strip; to divest; to deprive (to *despoil* a person *of* a thing).—**despoiler,** di·spoi′lėr, *n.* One who despoils; a plunderer.—**despoliation,** di·spō′li·ā″shon, *n.* The act of despoiling; a stripping.

despond, di·spond′, *v.i.* [L. *despondeo*, to promise in marriage, to promise away, to give up, to despond —*de*, away, and *spondeo, sponsum*, to promise solemnly, whence *sponsor, spouse, respond*.] To be quite cast down; to feel depressed or dejected in mind; to lose hope, heart, or resolution.—**despondency,** di·spon′den·si, *n.* The state or quality of being despondent.—**despondent,** di·spon′dent, *a.* Losing courage at the loss of hope; sinking into dejection. —**despondently, despondingly,** di·spon′dent·li, di·spon′ding·li, *adv.* In a despondent manner.

despot, des′pot, *n.* [Gr. *despotēs, potēs* being from same root as Gr. *posis*, Lith. and Skr. *patis*, lord, husband; L. *potior*, to be master of, *potis*, able, *potestas*, power; Slav. *hospodar, gospodar*, lord, master.] A sovereign or monarch ruling absolutely or without control; a tyrant; one who enforces his will regardless of the interests or feelings of others.—**despotic, despotical,** des·pot′ik, des·pot′i·kal, *a.* Absolute in power; unrestrained by constitution, laws, or men; arbitrary; tyrannical.—**despotically,** des·pot′i·kal·li, *adv.* In a despotic manner. —**despotism,** des′pot·izm, *n.* Absolute power; unlimited or uncontrolled authority; an arbitrary government; the rule of a despot; absolutism; autocracy; tyranny.

desquamate,† des′kwa·māt, *v.i.* [L. *desquamo, desquamatum*—*de*, off, and *squama*, a scale.] To scale off; to peel off.—**desquamation,** des·kwa·mā′shon, *n.* A scaling off.

dessert, di·zėrt′, *n.* [Fr. *dessert*, from *desservir*, to clear the table—*des* (=L. *dis*), and *servir*, to serve.] A service of fruits or sweetmeats at the close of a dinner or entertainment. —**dessertspoon,** *n.* A spoon intermediate in size between a tablespoon and teaspoon, used for dessert.

destine, des'tin, v.t.—destined, destining. [L. destino, to place down, to make firm or secure—de, and a root stan, a stronger form of sta, root of stare, to stand, E. stand, stay, being of the same root.] To set, ordain, or appoint to a use, purpose, state or place; to fix unalterably, as by a divine decree; to doom; to devote; to appoint inevitably.—**destination**, des·ti·nā'shon, n. [L. destinatio.] The act of destining; the purpose for which anything is intended or appointed; predetermined object or use; the place to which a thing is appointed; the predetermined end of a journey or voyage.—**destinist**, des'ti·nist, n. A believer in destiny.—**destiny**, des'ti·ni, n. A person's destined fate or lot; ultimate fate; doom; fortune; invincible necessity; fate; order of things fixed or established by divine decree, or by connection of causes and effects.—pl. [cap] the Fates.

destitute, des'ti·tūt, a. [L. destitutus, pp. of destituo, destitutum, to set down, to forsake—de, down, and statuo, to set. STATE, STATUE, etc.] Not having or possessing; wanting: with of; not possessing the necessaries of life; in abject poverty; entirely without the means of subsistence.—**destitution**, des·ti·tū'shon, n. The state of being destitute; a state of utter want; poverty; indigence; deprivation†.

destroy, di·stroi', v.t. [O.Fr. destruire (now détruire), from L. destruo, to destroy—de, not, and struo, to pile, to build. STRUCTURE.] To pull down; to knock to pieces; to demolish; to ruin; to annihilate; to put an end to; to cause to cease; to kill or slay; to ravage; to spoil.—**destroyer**, di·stroi'ér, n. One who or that which destroys; a swift class of vessel intended for the destruction of torpedo craft, and itself armed with guns and torpedoes.—**destructible**, di·struk'ti·bl, a. Liable to destruction; capable of being destroyed.—**destructibility**, di·struk'ti·bil″i·ti, n. The state of being destructible; —**destruction**, di·struk'-shon, n. [L. destructio.] The act of destroying; demolition; a pulling down; subversion; overthrow; ruin, by whatever means, extermination; death; murder; slaughter; the state of being destroyed; cause of destruction; a destroyer (O.T.).—**destructive**, di·struk'tiv, a. Causing destruction; having the quality of destroying; having a tendency to destroy; delighting in destruction; ruinous; mischievous; fatal; deadly: with of or to.—Destructive distillation, the distillation of organic products at high temperatures, by which the elements are separated or evolved in new forms, as in making gas from coal.—**destructively**, di·struk'tiv·li, adv. In a destructive manner.—**destructiveness**, di·struk'tiv·nes, n. The quality of being destructive; a propensity to destroy.—**destructor**, di·struk'tér, n. A destroyer; a furnace for burning refuse.

desuetude, des'wi·tūd, n. [L. desue-tudo—de, not, and suesco, to accustom one's self. CUSTOM.] A state of being no longer practiced or customary; disuse; discontinuance of practice, custom, or fashion.

desulfurate, desulfurize, dē·sul'fé·-rāt, dē·sul'fé·rīz, v.t. To deprive of sulfur.—**desulfuration, desulfurization**, dē·sul'fé·rā″shon, dē·sul'fé·ri·zā″shon, n. The act of depriving of sulfur.

desultory, des'ul·to·ri, a. [L. desultorius, pertaining to a desultor, or rider in the circus, from desilio, desultum, to leap down—de, down, and salio, to leap.] Leaping or hopping about‡; passing from one thing or subject to another without order or natural connection; rambling; unconnected; immethodical; inconstant; unsettled; hasty.—**desultorily**, des'ul·to·ri·li, adv. In a desultory manner; without method; loosely.—**desultoriness**, des'ul·to·ri·nes, n. The character of being desultory.

detach, di·tach', v.t. [Fr. detacher—de, not, and the root from which the English noun tack is derived TACK, ATTACH.] To separate or disunite; to disengage; to part from; to sever; to separate for a special purpose or service, especially some military purpose.—**detached**, di·tacht', a. Separated; disunited; standing apart or separately; drawn and sent on a separate service.—**detachment**, di·tach'ment, n. The act of detaching; a body of troops or number of vessels selected or taken from the main army or fleet and employed on some special service or expedition.

detail, di·tāl', v.t. [Fr. détailler, to cut in pieces—de, and tailler, L.L. taleare, taliare, to cut, from L. talea, a cutting. RETAIL, TAILOR.] To relate, report, or narrate in particulars; to recite the particulars of; to particularize; to relate minutely and distinctly; milit. to appoint to a particular service.—n. (dē'tāl). A fact, circumstance, or portion going along with others; an item; a particular; a minute account; a narrative or report of particulars; milit. an individual or small body; small detachment on special service.—In detail, circumstantially; item by item; individually; part by part.—**detailed**, di·tāld', p. and a. Related in particulars; minutely recited; exact; minute; particular.

detain, di·tān', v.t. [Fr. détenir, L. detineo, to detain—de, off, and teneo, to hold, as in contain, retain, etc., seen also in tenant, tenacious. TENANT.] To keep back or from; to withhold; to retain or keep what belongs to another; to keep or restrain from proceeding; to hinder; to stay or stop; to hold in custody.—**detainer**, di·tā'nér, n. One who detains; law, a holding or keeping possession of what belongs to another.—**detainment**, di·tān'ment, n. The act of detaining; detention.—**detent**, di'tent', n. [L. detentus, a keeping back.] A pin, stud, or lever forming a check in a clock, watch,

tumblerlock, or other machine; a click or pawl.—**detention**, di·ten'-shon, n. The act of detaining; a wrongful keeping of what belongs to another; state of being detained; confinement; restraint; delay from necessity or from accident.

detect, di·tekt', v.t. [L. detego, detectum, to uncover, expose—de, not, and tego, to cover. DECK.] To discover; to find out; to bring to light (an error, crime, criminal).—**detectable, detectible**, di·tek'ta·bl, di·tek'ti·bl, a. Capable of being or liable to be detected.—**detection**, di·tek'shon, n. The act of detecting; the finding out of what is concealed, hidden, or formerly unknown; discovery.—**detective**, di·tek'tiv, a. Fitted for or skilled in detecting; employed in detecting crime.—n. A species of police officer, having no specific beat nor uniform, whose special duty it is to detect offenses and to apprehend criminals; also a private person who engages to investigate cases, often of a delicate nature, for hire.—**detector**, di·tek'-tér, n. One who, or that which, detects or brings to light; a revealer; a discoverer.

detent, detention. See DETAIN.

deter, di·tér', v.t.—deterred, deterring. [L. deterreo, to frighten from, to prevent—de, from, and terreo, to frighten. TERROR.] To discourage and prevent from acting or proceeding, the preventing agency being something anticipated as difficult, dangerous, or unpleasant.—**deterrent**, di·tér'ent, n. and a. The act or cause of deterring; that which deters.

deterge, di·térj', v.t.—deterged, deterging. [L. detergeo—de, from, and tergeo, tersum, to wipe. TERSE.] To cleanse (a sore); to clear away foul or offending matter from.—**detergence, detergency**, di·tér'jens, di·tér'jen·si, n. The state or quality of being detergent; cleansing or purging power.—**detergent**, di·tér'jent, a. Cleansing; purging.—n. Anything that has a strong cleansing power.—**detersive**, di·tér'siv, a. Having power to cleanse; cleansing.—n. That which has the power of cleansing; a detergent.

deteriorate, di·tē'ri·o·rāt, v.i.—deteriorated, deteriorating. [L. deterioro, deterioratum, from deterior, worse, from de, as exterior from ex, interior from in.] To grow worse or inferior in quality; to be impaired in quality; to degenerate.—v.t. To make worse; to reduce in quality.—**deterioration**, di·tē'ri·o·rā″shon, n. The process or state of growing worse.

determine, di·tér'min, v.t.—determined, determining. [L. determino, to bound, to limit—de, intens., and terminus, a boundary, whence terminate, term.] To fix the bounds of; to set bounds or limits to; to mark off, settle, fix, establish; to end or settle conclusively, as by the decision of a doubtful or controverted point; to settle ultimately; to come to a fixed resolution and intention in respect of; to give a bent or direction to; to influence the choice of; to cause to come to a conclusion or resolution.—*v.i.* To resolve; to conclude; to decide; to settle on some line of conduct; to cease; to terminate.—**determinable**, di·tėr′mi·na·bl, *a.* Capable of being determined, ascertained, decided, brought to a conclusion.—**determinant**, di·tėr′mi·nant, *a.* Serving to determine; determinative.—*n.* That which determines or causes determination; *math.* the sum of a series of products of several numbers, these products being formed according to certain specified laws; a group of BIOPHORES (which see). —**determinate**, di·tėr′mi·nit, *a.* [L. *determinatus.*] Limited; fixed; definite; established; settled; positive; decisive; conclusive; fixed in purpose; resolute.—*Determinate inflorescence*, in *bot.* same as *centrifugal inflorescence.*—*v.t.*‡ To bring to an end; to terminate (*Shak.*).—**determinately**, di·tėr′mi·nit·li, *adv.* In a determinate manner; precisely; with exact specification; resolutely.—**determinateness**, di·tėr′mi·nit·nes, *n.* The state of being determinate.—**determination**, di·tėr′mi·nā″shon, *n.* The act of determining or deciding; decision in the mind; firm resolution; settled purpose; the mental habit of settling upon some line of action with a fixed purpose to adhere to it; adherence to aims or purposes; resoluteness; *chem.* the ascertainment of the exact proportion of any substance in a compound body; *med.* afflux; tendency of blood to flow to any part more copiously than is normal.—**determinative**, di·tėr′mi·nā·tiv, *a.* Having power to determine or direct to a certain end; directing; conclusive; limiting; bounding; having the power of ascertaining precisely; employed in determining.—**determined**, di·tėr′mind, *a.* Having a firm or fixed purpose; manifesting firmness or resolution; resolute.—**determinedly**, di·tėr′mind·li, *adv.* In a determined manner.—**determiner**, di·tėr′mi·nėr, *n.* One who decides or determines.—**determinism**, di·tėr′mi·nizm, *n.* A system of philosophy which denies liberty of action to man, holding that the will is not free, but is invincibly determined by motives.

deterrent. See DETER.

detersive, etc. See DETERGE.

detest, di·test′, *v.t.* [L. *detestor*, to invoke a deity in cursing, to detest—*de*, intens., and *testor*, to call to witness, from *testis*, a witness; so *attest, contest*, also *testify, testament.*] To abhor; to abominate; to hate extremely.—**detestable**, di·tes′ta·bl, *a.* Extremely hateful; abominable; very odious; deserving abhorrence. —**detestableness, detestability**, di·tes′ta·bl·nes, di·tes′ta·bil″i·ti, *n.* The state or quality of being detestable; extreme hatefulness.—**detestably**, di·tes′ta·bli, *adv.* In a detestable manner.—**detestation**, dē·tes·tā′shon, *n.* Extreme hatred; abhorrence; loathing.—**detester**, di·tes′-

tėr, *n.* One who detests.

dethrone, dē·thrōn′, *v.t.*—*dethroned, dethroning.* [Prefix *de*, from, and *throne.*] To remove or drive from a throne; to depose; to divest of royal authority and dignity; to divest of rule or power, or of supreme power.—**dethronement**, dē·thrōn′ment, *n.* Removal from a throne; deposition.—**dethroner**, dē·thrō′nėr, *n.* One who dethrones.

detonate, det′ō·nāt, *v.t.* and *i.*—*detonated, detonating.* [L. *detono, detonatum*, to thunder—*de*, and *tono*, to thunder.] To explode or cause to explode; to burn with a sudden report.—**detonation**, det·o·nā′shon, *n.* An explosion or sudden report made by the inflammation of certain combustible bodies.—**detonator**, det′o·nā·tėr, *n.* That which detonates; the device by which fulminate of mercury is made to explode the charge in a torpedo or submarine mine.

detour, de·tör′, *n.* [Fr. *détour*—prefix *de*, and *tour*=E. *turn.*] A roundabout or circuitous way; a going round instead of by a direct road or route.

detract, di·trakt′, *v.t.* [L. *detracto—de*, from, and *tracto*, to draw, from *traho, tractum*, to draw, whence *tract, trace*, etc.] To take away from a whole; to withdraw; to disparage†. —*v.i.* To take away a part; especially, to take away reputation; to derogate: followed by *from* (this *detracts from* his merit).—**detractor**, di·trak′tėr, *n.* One who detracts; a detractor.—**detraction**, di·trak′-shon, *n.* [L. *detractio.*] The act of detracting; an attempt, by calumny, or injurious or carping statements, to take something from the reputation of another; envious or malicious depreciation of a person, or denial of his merits.—**detractive**, di·trak′tiv, *a.* Having the quality or power to take away; having the character of detraction.—**detractor**, di·trak′tėr, *n.* One who uses detraction; one who tries to take somewhat from the reputation of another injuriously; a muscle that draws the part to which it is attached away from some other part.—**detractory**, di·trak′to·ri, *a.* Containing detraction; depreciatory.

detrain, dē·trān′, *v.t.* To remove from a railroad train; to cause to leave a train: said especially of bodies of men (to *detrain* troops).—*v.i.* To quit a railroad train.

detriment, det′ri·ment, *n.* [L. *detrimentum*, from *detero, detritum*, to rub off or down, to wear—*de*, down, and *tero*, to rub, whence *trite.*] A certain degree of loss, damage, or injury; injurious or prejudicial effect; harm; diminution.—**detrimental**, det·ri·men′tal, *a.*

detritus, di·trī′tus, *n.* [L. *detritus*, worn down. DETRIMENT.] *Geol.* a mass of substances worn off or detached from solid bodies by attrition; disintegrated materials of rocks.

detrude, di·tröd′, *v.t.*—*detruded, detruding.* [L. *detrudo—de*, down, and *trudo*, to thrust.] To thrust down;

to push down.—**detrusion**, di·-trö′zhon, *n.* The act of thrusting or driving down.

detruncate, di·trung′kāt, *v.t.*—*detruncated, detruncating.* [L. *detrunco—de*, and *trunco*, to maim, *truncus*, cut short. TRUNK.] To cut off; to lop; to shorten by cutting.—**detruncation**, di·trung·kā′shon, *n.* The act of detruncating.

deuce, dūs, *n.* [Fr. *deux*, two.] A playing card or a die with two spots; the two at dice, being the lowest throw.

deuce, dūs, *n.* [Perhaps from L. *deus*, God, used as an interjection; but comp. L.G. *duus*, G. *daus*, used similarly; Armor. *dus, teuz*, a goblin.] The devil; perdition: used only in exclamatory or interjectional phrases.

deuterium, dū·tėr′i·um, *n.* [N.L., from Gr. *deuteros*, second.] A nonradioactive isotope of hydrogen that has twice the mass of ordinary hydrogen.

deuterogamy, dū·tėr·og′a·mi, *n.* [Gr. *deuteros*, second, and *gamos*, marriage.] A second marriage after the death of the first husband or wife.—**deuterogamist**, dū·tėr·og′a·mist, *n.* One who marries a second time.

deuteron, dū′tėr·on, *n. Phys.* the nucleus of the deuterium atom; a particle with one positive charge.

Deuteronomy, dū·tėr·on′o·mi, *n.* [Gr. *deuteros*, second, and *nomos*, law.] Lit. the second law or second statement of the law, the fifth book of the Pentateuch.

deutoplasm, dū′to·plazm, *n. Biol.* that portion of the yolk of ova which furnishes nourishment for the embryo (the *protoplasm*).

devaluate, dē·val′ū·āt, *v.t.* [Prefix *de*, and *value.*] To reduce the value of; to fix a lower legal value on currency.—**devaluation**, dē·val·ū·ā′shon, *n.*—**devalue**, dē·val′ū, *v.t.* To devaluate.

devastate, dev′as·tāt, *v.t.*—*devastated, devastating.* [L. *devasto, devastatum*, to lay waste—*de*, intens., and *vasto*, to lay waste. WASTE.] To lay waste; to ravage; to desolate.—**devastation**, dev·as·tā′shon, *n.* [L. *devastatio.*] The act of devastating; the state of being devastated; ravage; havoc; desolation.—**devastator**, dev·as·tā′tėr, *n.*

develop, di·vel′up, *v.t.* [Fr. *développer* O.Fr. *desveloper*—prefix *des*, L. *dis*, apart.] To unfold gradually; to lay open part by part; to disclose or show all the ramifications of; *biol.* to make to pass through the process of natural evolution; in photography, to bring out the latent image on a sensitized surface by the action of chemical agents.—*v.i.* To be unfolded; to become manifest in all its parts; to advance from one stage to another by a process of natural or inherent evolution; to grow or expand by a natural process; to be evolved; to proceed or come forth naturally from some vivifying source. —**developable**, di·vel′up·a·bl, *a.* Capable of developing or of being developed.—**developer**, di·vel′up·ėr, *n.* One who or that which develops or unfolds.—**development**, di·vel′up·ment, n. The act or process of developing; unfolding; the unraveling of a plot; a gradual growth or advancement through progressive changes; the organic changes which take place in animal and vegetable bodies, from their embryo state until they arrive at maturity; *photog.* the process following exposure, by which the image on the plate is rendered visible.—*Development theory, biol.* the theory that plants and animals are capable of advancing, in successive generations and through an infinite variety of stages, from a lower to a higher state of existence, and that the more highly organized forms at present existing are the descendants of lower forms.

deviate, dē′vi·āt, v.i.—*deviated, deviating.* [L. *devio, deviatum*—*de,* from, and *via,* way; seen also in *convey, obvious, voyage,* etc.] To turn aside or wander from the common or right way, course, or line; to diverge; to err; to swerve; to vary from uniform state.—v.t. To cause to deviate.—**deviation,** dē·vi·ā′shon, n. A turning aside from the right way, course, or line; variation from a common or established rule or standard.—*Deviation of the compass,* the deviation of a ship's compass from the true magnetic meridian, caused by the near presence of iron.

device, di·vīs′, n. [O.Fr. *devise,* a device; Fr. *deviser,* to imagine, devise; from L. *divido, divisum,* to divide. DIVIDE.] That which is formed by design or invented; a scheme, contrivance, stratagem, project; invention or faculty of devising (*Shak.*); something fancifully conceived, as an ornamental design; an emblem or figure representative of a family, person, action, or quality, with or without a motto.

devil, dev′il, n. [A.Sax. *deófol,* from L. *diabolus,* Gr. *diabolos,* the accuser, from *diaballō,* to accuse.] An evil spirit or being; the evil one, represented in Scripture as the traducer, father of lies, tempter, etc.; a very wicked person; a ferocious marsupial animal of Tasmania; a printer's errand boy; a machine through which cotton or wool is first passed to prepare it for the carding machines; a teasing machine; a machine for cutting up rags and old cloth into flock and for other purposes; *cookery,* a dish, as a bone with some meat on it, grilled and seasoned with pepper.—*The devil,* is used as an expletive and also in various colloquial expressions, being equivalent to ruin or destruction, something very annoying or harassing, the deuce.—*Devil's advocate, R. Cath. Ch.* a person appointed to raise doubts against the claims of a candidate for canonization.—v.t.—*devilled, devilling.* To pepper or season excessively and broil; to tease or cut up by an instrument called a devil.—**devilish,** dev′il·ish, a. Partaking of the qualities of the devil; pertaining to the devil; diabolical; very evil and mischievous.—**dev-**

ilishly, dev′il·ish·li, adv. In a devilish manner.—**devilishness,** dev′il·ish·nes, n. The quality of being devilish.—**devilment,** dev′il·ment, n. Trickery; roguishness; devilry; prank. (*Colloq.*)—**devilry,** dev′il·ri, n. Devilment; extreme wickedness; wicked mischief.

devious, dē′vi·us, a. [L. *devius*—*de,* and *via,* way. DEVIATE.] Out of the common way or track; following circuitous or winding paths; rambling; erring; going astray.—**deviously,** dē′vi·us·li, adv. In a devious manner.—**deviousness,** dē′vi·us·nes, n. The character or state of being devious.

devise, di·vīz′, v.t.—*devised, devising.* [Fr. *deviser,* to devise or invent, to dispose of. See DEVICE.] To invent, contrive, or form in the mind; to strike out by thought; to plan; to scheme; to excogitate; *law,* to give or bequeath by will.—v.t. To consider; to contrive; to lay a plan; to form a scheme.—n. The act of bequeathing by will; a will or testament; a share of estate bequeathed.—**devisable,** di·vī′za·bl, a. Capable of being devised.—**devisee,** di·vi·zē′, n. The person to whom a devise is made.—**deviser,** di·vī′zėr, n. One who devises; a contriver; an inventor.—**devisor,** di·vī′zėr, n. One who gives by will.

devitalize, dē·vī′tal·īz, v.t. To deprive of vitality; to take away life from.

devitrify, dē·vit′ri·fī, v.t.—*devitrified, devitrifying.* To deprive of the character or appearance of glass.—**devitrification,** dē·vit′ri·fi·kā″shon, n. The act of devitrifying.

devoid, di·void′, a. [Prefix *de,* out, from, and *void.*] Destitute; not possessing: with *of* before the thing absent.

devoir, dev·wär′, n. [Fr., from L. *debere,* to owe, whence *debt.*] Service or duty; an act of civility or respect; respectful notice due to another.

devolution, dev·o·lū′shon, n. [L.L. *devolutio.*] The act of rolling down; the act of devolving, transferring, or handing over; a passing to or falling upon a successor.

devolve, di·volv′, v.t.—*devolved, devolving.* [L. *devolvo, devolutum*—*de,* and *volvo,* to roll, seen also in *revolve, convolve, volume, voluble,* etc.] To roll down; to move from one person to another; to deliver over, or from one possessor to a successor.—v.i. To roll down; hence, to pass from one to another; to fall by succession from one possessor to his successor.

Devonian, de·vō′ni·an, a. Of or pertaining to *Devonshire* in England; *geol.* a term applied to a great portion of the paleozoic strata of North and South Devon, lying between the Silurian and carboniferous rocks, and sometimes used as synonymous with ' old red sandstone '.

devote, di·vōt′, v.t.—*devoted, devoting.* [L. *devoveo, devotum,* to vow anything to a deity, to devote—*de,* intens., and *voveo,* to vow. VOW, VOTE.] To appropriate by vow;

to set apart or dedicate by a solemn act; to consecrate; to give up wholly; to direct the attention wholly or chiefly (to *devote* one's self or one's time to science); to give up; to doom; to consign over (to *devote* one to destruction).—**devoted,** di·vō′ted, a. Strongly attached to a person or cause; ardent; zealous.—**devotedness,** di·vō′ted·nes, n. The state of being devoted.—**devotee,** dev·ō·tē′, n. One who is wholly devoted; a votary; particularly, one who is superstitiously given to religious duties and ceremonies.—**devotement,** di·vōt′ment, n. The act of devoting.—**devoter,** di·vō′tėr, n. One that devotes.—**devotion,** di·vō′shun, n. The state of being devoted or set apart for a particular purpose; a yielding of the heart and affections to God, with reverence, faith, and piety, in religious duties, particularly in prayer and meditation; devoutness; performance of religious duties: now generally used in the plural; ardent attachment to a person or a cause; attachment manifested by constant attention; earnestness; ardor; eagerness.—**devotional,** di·vō′shon·al, a. Pertaining to devotion; used in devotion; suited to devotion.—**devotionally,** di·vō′shon·al·li, adv. In a devotional manner; toward devotion.

devour, di·vour′, v.t. [Fr. *dévorer,* L. *devorare*—*de,* intens., and *voro* to eat greedily, whence *voracious.*] To eat up; to eat with greediness; to eat ravenously; to destroy or consume; to waste.—v.i.† To act as a devourer; to consume (O.T.).—**devourer,** di·vou′rėr, n. One who devours.—**devouringly,** di·vou′ring·li, adv. In a devouring manner.

devout, di·vout′, a. [Fr. *dévot,* devout; L. *devotus.* DEVOTE.] Yielding a solemn and reverential devotion to God in religious exercises; pious; devoted to religion; religious; expressing devotion or piety; solemn; earnest.—**devoutly,** di·vout′li, adv. In a devout manner; piously; religiously; earnestly.—**devoutness,** di·vout′nes, n. The quality or state of being devout.

dew, dū, n. [A.Sax. *deáw,* D. *dauw,* Dan. *dug,* G. *thau*—dew.] The aqueous vapor or moisture which is deposited in small drops, especially during the night, from the atmosphere, on the surfaces of bodies when they have become colder than the surrounding atmosphere.—v.t. To wet with dew; to bedew.—**dewberry,** n. A species of bramble, the fruit of which is black, with a bluish bloom, and an agreeable acid taste.—**dewclaw,** n. The uppermost claw in a dog's foot, smaller than the rest, and not touching the ground.—**dewdrop,** dū·drop, n. A drop or spangle of dew.—**dewlap,** dū′lap, n. The fold of skin that hangs from the throat of oxen or cows, or a similar appendage in other animals.—**dewlapped,** dū′lapt, a. Furnished with a dewlap, or similar appendage. (*Shak.*)—**dew point,** n.

---

ch, *ch*ain; *ch,* Sc. lo*ch;* g, *g*o; j, *j*ob; ng, si*ng;* TH, *then;* th, *thin;* w, *w*ig; hw, *wh*ig; zh, a*z*ure.

The temperature when dew begins to be deposited, varying with the humidity of the atmosphere.—**dewy**, dū′i, *a.* Of or pertaining to dew; partaking of the nature or appearance of dew; like dew; moist with, or as with, dew; accompanied with dew; abounding in dew; falling gently, or refreshing, like dew (*dewy* sleep).

dexter, deks′tẽr, *a.* [L. *dexter*, right, on the right side, akin to Gr. *dexios*, Skr. *daksha*, on the right hand.] Pertaining to or situated on the right hand; right as opposed to left. —**dexterity**, deks·tẽr′i·ti, *n.* [L. *dexteritas*.] Ability to use the right hand more readily than the left†; righthandedness†; expertness; skill; that readiness in performing an action which proceeds from experience or practice, united with activity or quick motion; readiness of mind or mental faculties, as in contrivance, or inventing means to accomplish a purpose; promptness in devising expedients.—**dexterous**, deks′tẽr·us, *a.* Characterized by dexterity; skillful and active with the hands; adroit; prompt in contrivance and management; expert; quick at inventing expedients; skillful; done with dexterity. Sometimes written **dextrous**, deks′trus.—**dexterously**, deks′tẽr·us·li, *adv.* With dexterity; adroitly.—**dexterousness**, deks′tẽr·us·nes, *n.* Dexterity.—**dextral**, deks′tral, *a.* Right as opposed to left.—

dextrin, deks′trin, *n.* A carbohydrate formed when starch is decomposed by heat, acids, or enzymes.—**dextrorse**, deks·trors′, *a.* [L. *dextrorsum*, towards the right side—*dexter*, right, and *vorsum*, for *versum*, turned.] Turned towards the right; rising from left to right, as a spiral line, helix, or climbing plant.—**dextrose**, deks′trōs, *n.* A name for grape sugar, from its solution rotating the plane of polarization of a ray of light to the right.

dextran, deks′tran, *n.* A polymer of glucose, produced by enzyme action of *Leuconostoc* bacteria in sucrose; used as a blood-plasma substitute.

dey, dā, *n.* [Turk, *dâi*, an uncle.] The title of the old governors or sovereigns of Algiers, Tunis, and Tripoli, under the Sultan of Turkey.

dhole, dōl, *n.* The Singalese name for the wild dog of India.

dhow, dou, *n.* An Arab vessel, generally with one mast, from 150 to 250 tons burden, employed in mercantile trading, and also in carrying slaves.

diabetes, dī·a·bē′tez, *n.* [Gr. *diabanō*, —*dia*, and *bano*, to pass through.] An abnormal metabolic condition marked by an excessive discharge of urine.— *Diabetes insipidus*, a disorder of the pituitary gland, marked by excessive thirst.—*Diabetes mellitus*, a disorder of metabolism marked by excessive amounts of sugar in the blood.— **diabetic**, dī·a·bē′tik, *a.* Pertaining to diabetes.

diablerie, diablery, di·ab′lẽr·i, *n.* [Fr. *diablerie*, from *diable*, devil.]

Devilry; mischief; wickedness; sorcery; witchcraft.

diabolic, diabolical, dī·a·bol′ik, dī·a·bol′i·kal, *a.* [L. *diabolus*, the devil. DEVIL.] Devilish; pertaining to the devil; infernal; impious; atrocious.— **diabolically**, dī·a·bol′i·kal·li, *adv.* In a diabolical manner.—**diabolicalness**, dī·a·bol′i·kal·nes, *n.* The state or quality of being diabolical.

diacaustic, dī·a·kas̤′tik, *a.* [Gr. prefix *dia*, through, and E. *caustic*.] *Math.* belonging to a species of caustic curves formed by refraction.—*n. Math.* a diacaustic curve; *med.* cautery by a burning glass.

diachylon, diachylum, dī·ak′i·lon, dī·ak′i·lum, *n.* [Gr. *dia*, through, and *chylos*, juice.] *Med.* a plaster originally composed of the juices of herbs, now made of olive oil and finely pounded litharge.

diaconal, dī·ak′o·nal, *a.* [L. *diaconus*, Gr. *diakonos*, a deacon.] Pertaining to a deacon.—**diaconate**, dī·ak′o·nāt, *n.* The office or dignity of a deacon; a body of deacons.

diacritical, diacritic, dī·a·krit′i·kal, dī·a·krit′ik, *a.* [Gr. *diakritikos*—*dia*, and *krinō*, to separate.] Separating or distinguishing; distinctive.—*Diacritical mark*, a mark used in some languages to distinguish letters which are similar in form.

diactinic, dī·ak·tin′ik, *a.* [Gr. *dia*, through, and *aktis*, *aktinos*, a ray.] Capable of transmitting the actinic or chemical rays of the sun.

diadelph, dī′a·delf, *n.* [Gr. *di*, twice, and *adelphos*, a brother.] *Bot.* a plant the stamens of which are united into two bodies or bundles by their filaments.—**diadelphous**, dī·a·del′fus, *a. Bot.* having the stamens united in two bundles.

diadem, dī′a·dem, *n.* [Gr. *diadēma*—*dia*, and *deō*, to bind.] A head band or fillet formerly worn as a badge of royalty; anything worn on the head as a mark or badge of royalty; a crown; a coronet.—*v.t.*† To adorn with or as with a diadem; to crown.

diaeresis, dī·e′re·sis, *n.* [Gr. *diairesis*, from *diaireō*, to divide.] Separation of one syllable into two; a mark which signifies such a division, as in naïve, aërial.

diagnosis, dī·ag·nō′sis, *n.* [Gr. *diagnōsis*—*dia*, through, and *gignōskō*, to know.] Scientific discrimination of any kind; *med.* the discrimination of diseases by their distinctive marks or symptoms.—**diagnose**, dī·ag·nōs′, *v.t.*—*diagnosed, diagnosing.* To discriminate or ascertain from symptoms the true nature of.—**diagnostic**, dī·ag·nos′tik, *a.* Distinguishing; characteristic; indicating the nature of a disease.—*n.* A sign or symptom by which a disease is known.—*pl.* The department of medicine which treats of the diagnosis of diseases; symptomatology.

diagonal, dī·ag′o·nal, *a.* [Gr. *diagōnios*, from angle to angle—*dia*, and *gōnia*, an angle or corner.] Extending from one angle to the opposite of a quadrilateral figure, and dividing it into two triangles; lying in this direction.—*n.* A straight

line drawn between the opposite angles of a quadrilateral figure.— **diagonally**, dī·ag′o·nal·li, *adv.*

diagram, dī′a·gram, *n.* [Gr. *diagramma*—*dia*, and *graphō*, to write.] A figure or drawing for the purpose of demonstrating the properties of any geometrical figure, as a triangle, circle, etc.; any illustrative figure that explains something.—*v.t.*—*diagramed, diagrammed, diagraming, diagramming.* To represent by, or make, a diagram. —**diagrammatic**, dī′a·gram·mat″ik, *a.* Pertaining to or partaking of the nature of a diagram.—**diagrammatically**, dī′a·gram·mat″i·kal·li, *adv.*

dial, dī′al, *n.* [L.L. *dialis*, daily, from L. *dies*, a day, whence also *diary*, *diurnal*, *journal*, etc.] An instrument for showing the hour of the day from the shadow thrown by means of a *stile* or *gnomon* upon a surface; the face of a watch, clock, or other timekeeper; any somewhat similar plate or face on which a pointer or index moves, as in a gas meter or telegraphic instrument.—*v.t. dialed*, *dialing.* To use or measure with, or as with, a dial.—**dialing**, dī′al·ing, *n.* The art of constructing dials; the science which explains the principles of measuring time by the sundial.

dialect, dī′a·lekt, *n.* [Fr. *dialecte*, from Gr. *dialektos*—*dia*, and *legō*, to speak.] The form or idiom of a language peculiar to a province or to a limited region or people, as distinguished from the literary language of the whole people; language; speech or manner of speaking.— **dialectal**, dī·a·lek′tal, *a.* Pertaining to a dialect.—**dialectic, dialectical**, dī′a·lek′tik, dī·a·lek′ti·kal, *a.* Pertaining to a dialect or dialects; pertaining to dialectics.—**dialectically**, dī·a·lek′ti·kal·li, *adv.* In a dialectic manner.—**dialectician**, dī·a·lek·tish″an, *n.* One skilled in dialectics; a logician; a reasoner.— **dialectics**, dī·a·lek′tiks, *n.* [Gr. *dialektike* (*techne*), the art of discussing.] The art of reasoning or disputing; that branch of logic which teaches the rules and modes of reasoning, or of distinguishing truth from error; the art of using forms of reasoning so as to make fallacies pass for truth; wordfence. Also **dialectic**, in same sense.

diallage, dī′a·lij, *n.* [Gr. *diallage*, an interchange, difference.] A silicomagnesian mineral of a lamellar or foliated structure, akin to augite and exhibiting sometimes a beautiful green color, at other times brownish or yellowish; it includes bronzite and hypersthene.

dialogue, dī′a·log, *n.* [Fr. *dialogue*, from Gr. *dialogos*, dialogue, from *dialegomai*, to dispute—*dia*, and *legō*, to speak.] A conversation between two or more persons; a formal conversation in theatrical performances; a composition in which two or more persons are represented as conversing on some topic.—**dialogistic**, dī·al′o·jis″tik, *a.* Pertaining to, or partaking of the nature of, a dialogue; having the form of a dialogue.—**dialogist**, dī·al′o·jist, n. A speaker in a dialogue; a writer of dialogues.

dialysis, dī·al′i·sis, n. [Gr. dialysis, a separation—dia, and lyō, to dissolve.] Chem. the act or process of separating the crystalloid elements of a body from the colloid by diffusion through a parchment-paper septum; med. debility; also, a solution of continuity; in writing or printing, same as Diaeresis.—**dialyze**, dī′a·līz, v.t. To separate by a dialyzer.—**dialyzer**, dī′a·lī·zĕr, n. The parchment paper, or septum, stretched over a ring used in the operation of dialysis.—**dialytic**, dī·a·lit′ik, a. Pertaining to dialysis.

diamagnetic, dī′a·mag·net″ik, a. [Prefix dia, and magnetic.] Applied to a class of substances which, when under the influence of magnetism, and freely suspended, take a position at right angles to the magnetic meridian, that is, point east and west.—**diamagnetism**, dī·a·mag′ne·tizm, n. The characteristic phenomena of diamagnetic bodies.

diameter, dī·am′e·tĕr, n. [Gr. dia-metros—dia, and metron, measure.] A straight line passing through the center of a circle or other curvilinear figure, terminated by the circumference, and dividing the figure into two equal parts; a straight line through the center of any body; the measure transversely through a cylindrical body; thickness.—**diametric, diametrical, diametral**, dī·a·met′rik, dī·a·met′ri·kal, dī·a·met′ral, a. Of or pertaining to a diameter; directly opposed.—**diametrically**, dī·a·met′ri·kal·li, adv. In a diametrical direction or position.

diamond, dī′a·mond, n. [Fr. diamant, corrupted from adamant (which see).] A most valuable gem of extreme hardness, usually clear and transparent, but sometimes yellow, blue, green, black, etc., consisting of pure carbon; a small diamond fixed to a handle and used for cutting glass; a very small variety of printing type; a four-sided figure with the sides equal or nearly so, and having two obtuse and two acute angles, called also a lozenge or rhomb; one of a set of playing cards marked with one or more such figures in red.—Black diamond, a term applied colloquially to coal.—a. Resembling a diamond; consisting of diamonds; set with a diamond or diamonds.—**diamond type**, A kind of printing type.

diander, dī·an′dĕr, n. [Gr. di, twice, and anēr, andros, a male.] Bot. a plant having two stamens.—**diandrous**, dī·an′drus, a. Bot. having two stamens.

dianoetic, dī·a·nō·et″ik, a. [Gr. dianoētikos, from dia, and noeō, to revolve in the mind.] Capable of thought; thinking; intellectual.

diapason, dī·a·pā′zon, n. [Gr. diapasōn, lit. through all (notes).] Mus. an old Greek term for the octave; proportion in the constituent parts of an octave; harmony; the entire compass of a voice or an instrument;

a rule or scale by which the pipes of organs, the holes of flutes, etc., are correctly adjusted; a name of certain stops in the organ, given because they extend through the scales of the instrument.

diaper, dī′a·pĕr, n. [Fr. diapré, pp. of diaprer, to variegate with colors; from L.L. diasprus, a kind of precious cloth, from It. diaspro, jasper. JASPER.] A fabric, either linen or cotton, or a mixture of the two, upon the surface of which a figured pattern is produced; an infant's breechcloth.—v.i. To furnish with a diaper pattern; to put a diaper on.

diaphane, dī′a·fān, n. [Gr. dia, through, and phainō, to show.] A woven silk stuff with transparent and colorless figures.—**diaphanous**, dī·af′a·nus, a. Having power to transmit rays of light, as glass; pellucid; transparent; clear.—**diaphanously**, dī·af′a·nus·li, adv. In a diaphanous manner.

diaphoresis, dī′a·fo·rē″sis, n. [Gr. diaphorēsis, perspiration—dia, and phoreō, to carry.] Med. a greater degree of perspiration than is natural.—**diaphoretic**, dī′a·fo·ret″ik, a. Having the power to increase perspiration.—**diaphoretic**, n. A medicine which promotes perspiration; a sudorific.

diaphragm, dī′a·fram, n. [Gr. diaphragma, a partition—dia, and phrassō, I fence in, I enclose.] The midriff, a muscle separating the chest or thorax from the abdomen, a partition or dividing substance, as a circular ring used in telescopes, etc., to cut off marginal portions of a beam of light; a calcareous plate which divides the cavity of certain molluscous shells.—**diaphragmatic**, dī′a·frag·mat″ik, a. Appertaining to or having the character of a diaphragm.

diarchy, dī′är·ki, n. [Gr. di, double, and archē, rule.] A form of government in which the supreme power is invested in two persons.

diarrhea, dī·a·rē′a, n. [Gr. diarrhoia—dia, through, and rheō, to flow.] An ailment consisting in a morbidly frequent evacuation of the intestines.—**diarrhetic**, dī·a·rē′tik, a. Producing diarrhea.

diarthrosis, dī·är·thrō′sis, n. [Gr., from dia, through, asunder, and arthron, a joint.] Anat. a joint in which the bones revolve freely in every direction, as in the shoulder joint.

diary, dī′a·ri, n. [L. diarium, a daily allowance of food, a journal, from dies, a day, whence also dial, diurnal, journal.] A book in which daily events or transactions are noted; a journal; a blank book dated for the record of daily memoranda.—**diarist**, dī′a·rist, n. One who keeps a diary.

diastase, dī′as·tās, n. [Gr. diastasis, separation—dia, asunder, and root sta, to stand.] A substance existing in barley and oats after germination; so called because in solution it possesses the property of causing starch

to break up at 150° Fahr., transforming it first into dextrin and then into sugar.

diastole, dī·as′to·lē, n. [Gr. diastolē, a drawing asunder—dia, and stellō, to set.] Physiol. the dilatation of the heart with blood: opposed to systole, or contraction; gram. the lengthening of a syllable that is naturally short.—**diastolic**, dī·a·stol′ik, a. Pertaining to or produced by the diastole.

diatessaron, dī·a·tes′ar·on, n. [Gr. dia tessaron, by four.] A harmony of the four gospels.

diathermic, dī·a·thĕr′mik, a. [Gr. dia, and therme, heat.] Pertaining to diathermy.—**diathermy**, dī″a·thĕr′-mi, n. The application of electric current to produce heat in tissues below the skin for therapeutic purposes.

diathesis, dī·ath′e·sis, n. [Gr.] Med. particular disposition or habit of body, good or bad; predisposition to certain diseases rather than to others.—**diathetic**, dī·a·thet′ik, a. Pertaining to diathesis; constitutional.

diatom, dī′a·tom, n. [Gr. dia, through, and tomē, a cutting, from forming often loosely connected chains.] One of a natural order of microscopic vegetable organisms with siliceous coverings, found in fresh and salt water, and in moist places.—**diatomaceous**, dī′a·to·mā″shus, a. Pertaining to diatoms; containing or made up of the siliceous parts of diatoms.

diatomic, dī·a·tom′ik, a. [Gr. di, twice, and atomos, an atom.] Chem. consisting of two atoms.—**diatomite**, dī·at′o·mīt, n. A name for certain earthy deposits, consisting of the minute siliceous parts of diatoms, forming when dry a fine powder, and used in making dynamite, glaze for pottery, polishing, etc.

diatonic, dī·a·ton′ik, a. [Gr. dia, by or through, and tonos, sound.] Mus. applied to the major or minor scales, or to chords, intervals, and melodic progressions belonging to one scale.—**diatonically**, dī·a·ton′i·kal·li, adv. In a diatonic manner.

diatribe, dī′a·trib, n. [Gr. diatribē, a discussion, amusement, passing of time—dia, through, and tribō, to rub.] A continued disputation; a lengthy invective; a harangue in which a person inveighs against something.

dibasic, dī·bā′sik, a. [Gr. di, two and basis, base.] Containing two hydrogen atoms that can be replaced by basic atoms or radicals.

dibble, dib′l, n. [From dib, a form of dip.] A pointed instrument used in gardening and agriculture to make holes for planting seeds, bulbs, etc. Also called Dibber (dib′er).—v.t.—dibbled, dibbling. To plant with a dibble; to dig with a dibble.

dibranchiate, dī·brang′ki·āt, a. [Gr. di, double, and branchia, gills.] Having two gills.—n. A member of an order of cephalopods in which the branchiae are two in number, one situated on each side of the body.

dicast, dī′kast, n. [Gr. dikastēs, from

dikē justice.] *Greek antiq.* an officer answering nearly to the modern juryman.

dice, dīs, *n.* pl. of *die*, for gaming. DIE.—*v.i.—diced, dicing.* To play with dice.—**dicer,** dī'sėr, *n.* A player at dice.

dichogamy, dī·kog'a·mi, *n.* [Gr. *dicha,* in two parts, and *gamos,* marriage.] *Bot.* a provision in hermaphrodite flowers to prevent self-fertilization, as where the stamens and pistils within the same flower are not matured at the same time.— **dichogamous,** dī·kog'a·mus, *a. Bot.* exhibiting or characterized by dichogamy.

dichotomous, dī·kot'o·mus, *a.* [Gr. *dicha,* doubly, by pairs, and *temnō,* to cut.] *Bot.* regularly dividing by pairs from top to bottom.—**dichotomy,** dī·kot'o·mi, *n.*—A cutting in two‡; division‡; division or distribution of ideas by pairs; *bot.* a mode of branching by constant forking, as when the stem of a plant divides into two branches, each branch into two others, and so on.

dichroism, dī'krō·izm, *n.* [Gr. *di,* twice, and *chroa,* color.] *Optics,* a property possessed by several crystallized bodies of appearing under two distinct colors according to the direction in which light is transmitted through them.—**dichroic,** dī·krō'ik, *a.* Characterized by dichroism.— **dichroite,** dī'krō·īt, *n.* A mineral generally of a blue color, but exhibiting different colors in different positions.—**dichromatic,** dī·krō·mat'ik, *a.* [Gr. *di,* and *chrōma,* color.] Having or producing two colors.— **dichroscope,** dī'krō·skōp, *n.* [Gr. *di, chroa,* and *skopeō,* to see.] An instrument in which a prism of Iceland spar is used for testing the dichroism of crystals.—**dichroscopic,** dī·krō·skop'ik, *a.* Pertaining to the dichroscope.

dickens, dik'enz, *interj.* [Probably a fanciful euphemism for *devil*; comp. L.G. *duker, duks,* the deuce.] Devil; deuce: used interjectionally. (*Shak.*)

dicker, dik'ėr, *n.* [L.G. and Sw. *deker,* G. *decher,* ten hides, from L.L. *dacra, decara,* L. *decem,* ten.] The number or quantity of teń, particularly ten hides or skins.

dickey, dicky, dik'i, *n.* [Origin doubtful.] An article of dress like the front of a dress shirt, and worn instead.

diclinous, dī'kli·nus, *a.* [Gr. *di,* double, and *klinē,* a bed.] *Bot.* having the stamens in one flower and the pistil in another.

dicotyledon, dī'kot·i·lē″don, *n.* [Gr. *di,* and *kotylēdōn.*] A plant whose seeds contain a pair of cotyledons or seed leaves, which are always opposite to each other.—**dicotyledonous,** dī'kot·i·lē″do·nus, *a.* Having two cotyledons.

dictate, dik'tāt, *v.t.—dictated, dictating.* [L. *dicto, dictatum,* a freq. of *dico, dictum,* to say. DICTION.] To deliver or enounce with authority, as an order, command, or direction; to instruct to be said or written; to utter, so that another may write out; to direct by impulse on the mind

(an action *dictated* by fear); to instigate.—*n.* An order delivered; a command; a rule, maxim, or precept, delivered with authority; rule or direction suggested to the mind (the *dictates* of reason).—**dictation,** dik·tā'shon, *n.* The act of dictating; the act or practice of speaking or reading that another may write down what is spoken.—**dictator,** dik'tā·tėr, *n.* [L., a supreme magistrate appointed on special occasions with unlimited power.] One invested with absolute authority; a supreme leader or guide to direct the conduct or opinion of others.—**dictatorial,** dik·ta·tō'ri·al, *a.* Pertaining to a dictator; imperious; overbearing.—**dictatorially,** dik·ta·tō'ri·al·li, *adv.* In an imperious manner.—**dictatorship,** dik'tā·tėr·ship, *n.* The office of a dictator; authority; imperiousness.—**dictatress,** dik·tā'tres, *n.* A female dictator.

diction, dik'shon, *n.* [L. *dictio,* from *dico, dictum,* to speak, appearing in a great many English words, as *dictate, addict, contradict, edict, condition, preach,* etc.] A person's choice or selection of words in speaking or writing, general mode of expressing one's self; style. ∴ *Diction* refers chiefly to the words used; *phraseology* refers more to the manner of framing the phrases, clauses, and sentences; *style* includes both, referring to the thoughts as well as the words, and especially comprehends the niceties and beauties of a composition.— **dictionary,** dik'shon·e·ri, *n.* (L.L. *dictionarium.*) A book containing the words of a language arranged in alphabetical order, with explanations or definitions of their meanings; a lexicon; a word book; any work which communicates information on an entire subject or branch of a subject, under entries or heads arranged alphabetically.—*a.* Pertaining to, contained in, or given by a dictionary or dictionaries.—**dictum,** dik'tum, *n.* pl.—**dicta,** dik'ta. [L.] A positive assertion; an authoritative saying or decision.

did, did, *pret.* of *do.*

didactic, didactical, di·dak'tik, di·dak'ti·kal, *a.* [Gr. *didaktikos,* from *didaskō,* to teach.] Adapted to teach; containing doctrines, precepts, principles, or rules; intended to instruct. —**didactically,** di·dak'ti·kal·li, *adv.* In a didactic manner; in a form to teach.—**didactics,** di·dak'tiks, *n.* The art or science of teaching.

didapper, did'a·pėr, *n.* [For *divedapper* (*Shak.*), from *dive,* and *dap*≡*dip.* DABCHICK.] The dabchick or little grebe.

diddle, did'l, *v.t.* [A.Sax. *dyderian,* to deceive or delude, originally perhaps by rapid movements or sleight of hand.] To cheat or trick, especially in money matters (slang); to dandle (provincial).

didymium, di·dim'i·um, *n.* [Gr. *didymos,* double, twin.] A rare metal discovered in 1841 in the oxide of cerium, and so named from being, as it were, the twin brother of lanthanum, which was previously found in the same body.—**didymous,** did'i·-

mus, a. Bot. twin; growing double.

die, dī, *v.i.—died, dying.* [Not an A.Sax. word; closely allied to the O.Fris. *deja, deya,* Icel. *deya, deyja,* Dan. *dōe,* to die; A.Sax. *dedd,* dead, a kind of participial form, *deáth,* death.] To cease to live; to expire; to decease; to perish; to become dead; to lose life: said of both animals and plants; to come to an end; to cease to have influence or effect (his fame will not *die*); to sink; to faint (his heart *died* within him); to languish with pleasure, tenderness, affection, or the like; to become gradually less distinct or perceptible to the sight or hearing.

die, dī, *n.* [Fr. *dé,* O.Fr. *de,* from L. *datum,* something given, that which is thrown or laid on the table.] A small cube marked on its faces with numbers from one to six, used in gaming by being thrown from a box; a square body: in the above senses the plural is *dice*; *arch.* the cubical part of a pedestal between its base and cornice; a stamp used in coining money, in foundries, etc.: in the last two senses the plural is regular, *dies.—The die is cast,* everything is now put to hazard; all will depend upon fortune.—**diesinker,** *n.* An engraver of dies for stamping or embossing.—**diesinking,** *n.* The process of engraving dies.

dielectric, dī·e·lek'trik, *n.* [Gr. *dia,* through, and E. *electric.*] *Elect.* any medium through or across which electric induction takes place between two conductors.

dieresis, dī·e're·sis, *n.* Same as *Diaeresis.*

diesel, dē'zel, *n.* [From Rudolf *Diesel,* the inventor.] A type of internal-combustion engine, in which high pressure of air or fuel causes the ignition; also *diesel engine.*

diet, dī'et, *n.* [O.Fr. *diète,* L.L. *dieta,* Gr. *diaita,* a way of living, diet.] A person's regular food or victuals: manner of living as regards food and drink; course of food prescribed and limited in kind and quantity; allowance of provision.—*v.t.* To furnish diet or meals for; to prescribe a particular diet for.—*v.i.* To eat according to rules prescribed; to eat; to feed.—**dietary,** dī'e·te·ri, *a.* Pertaining to diet or the rules of diet. —*n.* A system or course of diet; allowance of food.—**dieter,** dī'et·ėr, *n.* One who diets; one who prescribes rules for eating. (*Shak.*)—**dietetic, dietetical,** dī·e·tet'ik, dī·e·tet'i·kal, *a.* Pertaining to diet, or to the rules for regulating diet.—**dietetically,** dī·e·tet'i·kal·li, *adv.* In a dietetical manner.—**dietetics,** dī·e·tet'iks, *n.* That department of medicine which relates to the regulation of diet.— **dietitian, dietician,** dī·e·ti'shon, *n.* One versed in dietetics; one who arranges diets.

diet, dī'et, *n.* [Fr. *diète,* from L.L. *dieta,* the space of a day, from L. *dies,* a day, whence also *dial, diary.*] A meeting, as of dignitaries or delegates, held from day to day for legislative, ecclesiastical, or other purposes; session; specifically [*often* *cap.*] the legislative or administrative assemblies, as the Japanese, etc.

differ, dif´ėr, *v.i.* [L. *differo*—prefix *dif, dis,* and *fero,* to bear, to carry, seen also in *confer, offer, refer, suffer, infer,* etc.; root also in *fertile.*] To be unlike, dissimilar, distinct, or various, in nature, condition, form, or qualities (men and things *differ* greatly; they *differ* from each other); to disagree; not to accord; to be of another opinion (we *differ with* or *from* a person); to contend; to be at variance; to dispute; to quarrel.— **difference,** dif´ėr·ens, *n.* The state or condition in virtue of which things differ from each other; a point or feature of disagreement; the being different; want of sameness; variation; dissimilarity; distinction; a dispute, contention, quarrel, controversy; the point in dispute; the remainder of a sum or quantity after a lesser sum or quantity is subtracted; the quantity by which one quantity differs from another.—*v.t.* —*differenced, differencing.* To cause a difference or distinction in; to distinguish; to discriminate.—**different,** dif´ėr·ent, *a.* Distinct; separate; not the same; various; of various natures, forms, or qualities; unlike; dissimilar.—**differential,** dif·ėr·en´shal, *a.* Making a difference; discriminating; distinguishing; *math.* an epithet applied to an infinitely small quantity by which two variable quantities differ; pertaining to mathematical processes in which such quantities are employed.—*Differential calculus,* an important branch of the higher mathematics which deals largely with the infinitely small differences of variable and mutually dependent quantities.—*Differential duties, pol. econ.* duties which are not levied equally upon the produce or manufactures of different countries, as when a heavier duty is laid on certain commodities from one country than on the same commodities from another country.—*n.* A coupling used to connect shafts, as in the driving axle of an automobile, so that a union is effected when moving straight, but allowing independent motion on a curve; *math.* an infinitesimal difference between two states of a variable quantity.—**differentiate,** dif·ėr·en´shi·āt, *v.t.* To produce, or lead to, a difference in or between; to mark or distinguish by a difference; to set aside for a definite or specific purpose; *math.* to obtain the differential of.—*v.i.* To acquire a distinct and separate character.— **differentiation,** dif·ėr·en·shi·ā´shon, *n.* The act of differentiating; the production or discrimination of differences or variations; the assignment of a specific agency to the discharge of a specific function; *biol.* the formation of different parts, organs, species, etc., by the production or acquisition of a diversity of new structures, through a process of evolution or development; *math.* the operation of finding the differential of any function.

difficulty, dif´i·kul·ti, *n.* [Fr. *diffi-*

culté; L. *difficultas,* from *difficilis,* difficult—*dis,* priv., and *facilis,* easy to be made or done.] Hardness to be done or accomplished; the state of anything which renders its performance laborious or perplexing: opposed to *easiness* or *facility*; that which is hard to be performed or surmounted; perplexity; embarrassment of affairs; trouble; objection; cavil; obstacle to belief; an embroilment; a falling out; a controversy; a quarrel.—**difficult,** dif´i·kult, *a.* Hard to make, do, or perform; not easy; attended with labor and pains; arduous; hard to understand.— **difficultly,** dif´i·kult·li, *adv.* Hardly; with difficulty.

diffidence, dif´i·dens, *n.* [L. *diffidentia, diffidens,* ppr. of *diffido,* to distrust—*dis,* not, and *fido,* to trust. FAITH.] Distrust; want of confidence; especially distrust of one's self; a doubt respecting some personal qualification; modest reserve.—**diffident,** dif´i·dent, *a.* Characterized by diffidence; distrustful of one's self; not confident; backward; bashful.— **diffidently,** dif´i·dent·li, *adv.* In a diffident manner.

diffract, dif·frakt´, *v.t.* [L. *diffringo, diffractum*—prefix *dif, dis,* and *frango,* to break.] To break; to bend from a straight line; to deflect.—**diffraction,** dif·frak´shon, *n. Optics,* the peculiar modifications which light undergoes when it passes by the edge of an opaque body; deflection.— **diffractive,** dif·frak´tiv, *a.* Causing diffraction.

diffuse, dif·fūz´, *v.t.*—*diffused, diffusing.* [L. *diffundo, diffusum*—prefix *dif, dis,* and *fundo, fusum,* to pour, whence *fusion.*] To pour out and spread, as a fluid; to cause to flow and spread; to send out or extend in all directions (light, information, happiness).—*a.* (dif·fūs´). Widely spread; using too many words to express meaning; wanting conciseness and due condensation; verbose; prolix; *bot.* spreading widely, horizontally, and irregularly.—**diffusely,** dif·fūs´li, *adv.* In a diffuse manner; widely; extensively; with too many words.—**diffuseness,** dif·fūs´nes, *n.* The quality of being diffuse; want of conciseness or due concentration in expressing one's meaning.—**diffuser,** dif·fū´zėr, *n.* One who or that which diffuses.—**diffusibility,** dif·fū·zi·bil´- i·ti, *n.* The quality of being diffusible. —**diffusible,** dif·fū´zi·bl, *a.* Capable of being diffused or spread in all directions.—**diffusion,** dif·fū´zhon, *n.* The act of diffusing or process of being diffused; a spreading abroad or scattering; dispersion; dissemination; extension; propagation; the tendency of two different gases to mix when separated by a porous partition.—**diffusive,** dif·fū´siv, *a.* Having the quality of diffusing or becoming diffused; extending in all directions; widely reaching (*diffusive* charity); diffuse as regards expression.—**diffusively,** dif·fū´siv·li, *adv.* In a diffusive manner; widely; extensively.—**diffusiveness,** dif·fū´siv·nes, *n.* The character of being diffusive.

dig, dig, *v.t.*—*digged* or *dug, digging.* [Probably connected with *dike* or *dyke, ditch*; A.Sax. *dic,* a dike or a ditch, *dician,* Dan. *dige,* to make a ditch.] To open and break, or turn up, with a spade or other sharp instrument; to excavate; to form in the ground by digging and removing the loose soil; to raise from the earth by digging (to *dig* coals, fossils, etc.).—*v.i.* To work with a spade or other similar instrument.— **digger,** dig´ėr, *n.* One who or that which digs; specifically, one who digs for gold.—**digging,** dig´ing, *n.* The act of one who digs; *pl.* a word applied to the different localities in California, Australia, New Zealand, etc., where gold is obtained by excavations in the earth.

digamma, dī´gam·ma, *n.* [Gr., lit. double gamma (gamma = E. *g* hard), because in form it resembled two gammas, the one set above the other, somewhat like our F.] A letter which once belonged to the alphabet of the Greeks, and appears to have had the force of *v* or *f.*

digastric, dī·gas´trik, *a.* [Gr. *di,* double, and *gastėr,* belly.] Having a double belly.—*Digastric muscle,* a double muscle that pulls the lower jaw downward and backward.

digest, di·jest´, *v.t.* [L. *digero, digestum,* to distribute, dispose, digest food—*di* for *dis,* asunder, and *gero, gestum,* to bear; also in *congest, suggest, gesture,* etc.] To arrange in suitable divisions or under proper heads or titles; to dispose in due method for being conveniently studied or consulted; to arrange methodically in the mind; to think out; to separate or dissolve in the stomach, preparing the nutritious elements for entering the system; *chem.* to soften and prepare by a heated liquid; *fig.* to bear with patience or with an effort; to brook; to put up with.— *v.i.* To undergo digestion, as food.— *n.* (dī´jest). A collection of Roman laws, digested or arranged under proper titles by order of the Emperor Justinian; any orderly or systematic summary, as of laws.—**digester,** di·jes´tėr, *n.* One who digests or disposes in order; that which assists the digestion of food; a vessel in which bones or other substances may be subjected to heat in water or other liquid.—**digestibility,** di·jes·ti·bil´i· ti, *n.* The quality of being digestible. —**digestible,** di·jes´ti·bl, *a.* Capable of being digested.—**digestion,** di· jes´chon, *n.* [L. *digestio.*] The act of methodizing or disposing in order; the process which food undergoes in the stomach, by which it is prepared for nourishing the body; *chem.* the operation of exposing bodies to heat in a liquid to prepare them for some action on each other; or the slow action of a solvent on any substance.—**digestive,** di·jes´tiv, *a.* Having the power to promote digestion in the stomach.—*n.* Any preparation or medicine which increases the tone of the stomach and aids digestion; a stomachic.

digger, digging, *n.* See DIG.

---

ch, *ch*ain; *ch,* Sc. lo*ch*; g, *g*o; j, *j*ob; ng, si*ng*; TH, *th*en; th, *th*in; w, *w*ig; hw, *wh*ig; zh, a*z*ure.

dight, dīt, *v.t.*—*dight*. [A.Sax. *dihtan*, from L. *dictare*, to dictate. DICTATE.] To put in order; to dress; to array. (Now only poet.)

digit, dij′it, *n.* [L. *digitus*, a finger; akin Gr. *daktylos*, a finger; root *dik*, to point out, as in Gr. *deiknymi*, to show, L. *dico*, to say.] A finger: sometimes used scientifically to signify toe, when speaking of animals; the measure of a finger's breadth or ¾ inch; *astron.* the twelfth part of the diameter of the sun or moon; *arith.* any integer under 10: so called from counting on the fingers.—**digital**, dij′i·tal, *a.* [L. *digitalis*.] Pertaining to the fingers or to digits.—*n.* One of the keys of instruments of the organ or piano class.—**digital computer**. A calculating machine with numbers expressed as digits.—**digitalin**, dij′i·ta·lin, *n.* A strong poison obtained from digitalis.—**digitalis**, dij·i·tā′lis, *n.* Any of a genus of Eurasian herbs of the figwort family; the dried and powdered leaf of the common foxglove, containing several important glucocides and serving as a powerful heart stimulant and a diuretic.—**digitately**, dij′i·tāt·li, *adv.* In a digitate manner. —**digitation**, dij·i·tā′shon, *n.* A division into finger-like processes.— **digitiform**, dij′i·ti·form, *a.* Formed like fingers.—**digitigrade**, dij′i·ti·grād, *n.* [L. *digitus*, and *gradior*, to go.] An animal that walks on its toes, as the lion, wolf, etc.—*a.* Walking on the toes.

dignify, dig′ni·fī, *v.t.*—*dignified, dignifying.* [Fr. *dignifier*—L. *dignus*, worthy, and *facere*, to make.] To invest with honor or dignity; to exalt in rank; to elevate to a high office; to honor; to make illustrious.— **dignified**, dig′ni·fīd, *p.* and *a.* Invested with dignity; honored; marked with dignity or loftiness; noble; stately in deportment.—**dignitary**, dig′ni·te·ri, *n.* One who holds an exalted rank or office.—**dignity**, dig′ni·ti, *n.* [L. *dignitas*.] Nobleness or elevation of mind; loftiness; honorable place or rank; degree of elevation; elevation of aspect; grandeur of mien; height or importance; an elevated office; one who holds high rank; a dignitary.

digraph, dī′graf, *n.* [Gr. *di*, twice, and *graphō*, to write.] A union of two vowels or of two consonants, representing a single sound of the voice (as *ea* in head).

digress, di·gres′, *v.i.* [L. *digredior, digressus*, to step apart—prefix *dis*, apart, and *gradior*, to step. GRADE.] To depart or wander from the main subject or tenor of a discourse, argument, or narration.—**digression**, di·gresh′on, *n.* [L. *digressio*.] The act of digressing; a departure from the main subject; the part or passage of a discourse, etc., which deviates from the main subject; transgression (*Shak.*)‡.—**digressional, digressive**, di·gresh′on·al, di·gres′iv, *a.* Pertaining to or consisting in digression.— **digressively**, di·gres′iv·li, *adv.* By way of digression.

dihedral, dī·hē′dral, *a.* [Gr. *di*, twice, and *hedra*, a seat or face.] Having two plane faces, as a crystal.

dike, dyke, dīk, *n.* [A.Sax. *dīc*, D, *dijk*, Dan. *dige*, a bank of earth, a ditch, the ditch being excavated and the bank formed by the same operation. *Ditch* is a softened form of this.] A ditch or channel for water; a barrier of earth, stones, or other materials, intended to prevent low lands from being inundated by the sea or a river; a low wall forming a fence; *geol.* a vein of igneous rock which has intruded in a melted state into rents or fissures of other rocks.— *v.t.*—*diked, diking.* To surround with a dike; to secure by a bank; to drain by one or more dikes or ditches.

dilacerate, di·las′ėr·āt, *v.t.* [L. *dilacero*—prefix *di* for *dis*, asunder, and *lacero*, to tear.] To tear; to rend asunder.—**dilaceration**, dī·las′ėr·ā″shon, *n.* The act of dilacerating.

dilapidate, di·lap′i·dāt, *v.i.*—*dilapidated, dilapidating.* [L. *dilapido, dilapidatum*—prefix *di* for *dis*, asunder, and *lapis, lapidis*, a stone.]—*v.t.* To suffer to go to ruin (buildings) by misuse or neglect; to waste; to squander.—*v.i.* To fall to ruin.— **dilapidated**, di·lap′i·dā·ted, *p.* and *a.* In a ruinous condition; suffered to go to ruin.—**dilapidation**, di·lap′i·dā″shon, *n.* The act of dilapidating; *eccles.* the ruinous neglect or actual wasting, by an incumbent, of any building or other property in his possession.

dilate, dī·lāt′, *v.t.*—*dilated, dilating.* [L. *dilato*, to make wider—*di* for *dis*, asunder, and *latus* broad.] To expand or swell out, especially by filling; to distend; to enlarge in all directions: opposed to *contract*; to tell copiously or diffusely (*Shak.*)‡.—*v.i.* To expand, swell, or extend in all directions; to speak largely and copiously; to dwell in narration; to descant: with *on* or *upon*.—**dilatability**, dī·lā′ta·bil′i·ti, *n.* The quality of being dilatable.—**dilatable**, dī·lā′ta·bl, *a.* Capable of being dilated; possessing elasticity; elastic.—**dilatation, dilation**, dī·lā·tā′shon, dī·lā′shon, *n.* The act of expanding, dilating, or state of being expanded or distended.— **dilater, dilator**, dī·lā′tėr, *n.* One who or that which dilates.—**dilative**, dī·lā′tiv, *a.* Tending to dilate.

dilatory, dil′a·to·ri, *a.* [Fr. *dilatoire*, L.L. *dilatorius*, from L. *differo, dilatum.* DELAY.] Marked with or given to procrastination or delay; making delay or resulting in delay; slow; tardy; not proceeding with diligence: of persons or things.— **dilatorily**, dil′a·to·ri·li, *adv.* In a dilatory manner; tardily.—**dilatoriness**, dil′a·to·ri·nes, *n.* The quality of being dilatory; delay in proceeding; tardiness.

dilemma, di·lem′ma, *n.* [Gr. *dilēmma*—prefix *di* for *dis*, double, and *lēmma*, an assumption, from *lambanō*, to take.] *Logic*, an argument in which the adversary is caught between two difficulties, by having two alternatives presented to him, each of which is equally conclusive against him; hence, a state of things in which evils or obstacles present themselves on every side, and it is difficult to determine what course to pursue.

dilettante, dil·e·tänt′, *n.* pl. **dilettanti**, dil·e·tan′tē. [It., from L. *delectare*, to delight. DELIGHT.] An admirer or lover of the fine arts; an amateur or trifler in art; one who pursues an art desultorily and for amusement. —**dilettantism**, dil·e·tan′tizm, *n.* The quality characteristic of a dilettante.

diligence, dil′i·jens, *n.* [L. *diligentia*, carefulness, diligence, from *diligo*, to love earnestly—*di* for *dis*, intens., and *lego*, to choose.] Steady application in business of any kind; constant effort to accomplish what is undertaken; due attention; industry; assiduity; care; heed; heedfulness; *Scots law*, a kind of warrant, and also a process by which persons or effects are attached.—**diligent**, dil′i·jent, *a.* [L. *diligens, diligentis*.] Steady in application to business; constant in effort to accomplish what is undertaken; assiduous; attentive; industrious; not idle or negligent: of persons or things.—**diligently**, dil′i·jent·li, *adv.* In a diligent manner.

diligence, dē·lē·zhäns′, *n.* [Fr.] A kind of four-wheeled stagecoach.

dill, dil, *n.* [A.Sax. *dil*, Sw. *dill*, G. *dill*; possibly from its soothing qualities in *dilling* or *dulling* pain. Comp. prov. E. *dill*, Icel. *dilla*, to lull a child.] A plant of the parsley family, seeds of which are moderately pungent and aromatic, and are used as a seasoning.

dillydally, dil′i·dal·i, *v.i.* [A reduplication of *dally*.] To loiter; to delay; to trifle.

dilute, di·lūt′, *v.t.*—*diluted, diluting.* [L. *diluo, dilutus*—prefix *di* for *dis*, and *luo*, to wash, as in *ablution*. DELUGE.] To render liquid or more liquid, especially by mixing with water; to weaken (spirit, acid, etc.) by an admixture of water.—*a.* Diluted; reduced in strength by intermixture.—**diluteness**, di·lūt′nes, *n.* The state or quality of being diluted. —**dilution**, di·lū′shon, *n.* The act of diluting.—**diluent**, dil′ū·ent, *a.* [L. *diluens, diluentis*.] Having the effect of diluting.—*n.* That which dilutes; *med.* a substance which increases the proportion of fluid in the blood.

diluvial, diluvian, di·lū′vi·al, di·lū′vi·an, *a.* [L. *diluvium*, a deluge, from *diluo.* DILUTE.] Pertaining to a flood or deluge, more especially to the deluge in Noah's days.—*Diluvial formation, geol.* a name of superficial deposits of gravel, clay, sand, etc., conveyed to their present sites by any unusual or extraordinary rush of water.

dim, dim, *a.* [A.Sax. *dim*, dark, obscure=O.Fris. *dim*, Icel. *dimmr*, dim; comp. Lith. *tamsa*, Skr. *tamas*, darkness.] Not seeing clearly; having the vision indistinct; not clearly seen; obscure; faint; vague; somewhat dark; not luminous; dull of apprehension; having the luster obscured; tarnished.—*v.t.*—*dimmed, dimming.* To render dim or less clear or distinct; to becloud; to obscure;

to tarnish or sully.—**dimly,** dim′li, *adv.* In a dim manner.—**dimness,** dim′nes, *n.* The state of being dim.

dime, dim, *n.* [Fr. *dîme,* a tenth, a tithe, O.Fr. *disme,* from L. *decimus,* tenth, from *decem,* ten.] A silver coin of the United States, value ten cents; the tenth of a dollar.

dimension, di·men′shon, *n.* [L. *dimensio,* from *dimetior,* to measure—*di* for *dis,* and *metior, mensus,* to mete. METE, MEASURE.] Extension in a single direction, as length, breadth, and thickness or depth, a solid body having thus three dimensions ; *pl.* measure, size, extent, capacity; *fig.* consequence; importance; *alg.* same as *degree.*

dimerous, dim′ér·us, *a.* [Gr. *di,* twice, and *meros,* part.] Having its parts in pairs; composed of two unrelated pieces or parts; *entom.* having the tarsi two-jointed.

dimeter, dim′e·tér, *a.* [Gr. *dimetros—di,* twice, and *metron,* a measure.] Having two poetical measures.—*n.* A verse of two measures.

dimidiate, di·mid′i·āt, *a.* [L. *dimidiatus,* from *dimidium,* half—*dis,* asunder, and *medius,* the middle.] Divided into two equal parts; halved; *bot.* applied to an organ when half of it is so much smaller than the other as to appear to be missing; *zool.* having the organs of one side of different functions from the corresponding organs on the other.

diminish, di·min′ish, *v.t.* [O.Fr. *demenuiser,* from L. *diminuo,* to lessen—*di* for *dis,* asunder, and *minuere,* to lessen, from root *min,* in *minor,* less.] To lessen; to make less or smaller by any means: opposed to *increase* and *augment*; to impair, degrade, or abase (O.T.).—*v.i.* To lessen; to become or appear less or smaller; decrease.—**diminishable,** di·min′ish·a·bl, *a.* Capable of being diminished.—**diminuendo,** di·min′ū·en″dō. [It.] *Mus.* an instruction to the performer to lessen the volume of sound from loud to soft: opposite of *crescendo.*—**diminution,** dim·i·nū′shon, *n.* [L. *diminutio.*] The act of diminishing; a making smaller; the state of becoming or appearing less; discredit; loss of dignity; degradation.—**diminutive,** di·min′ū·tiv, *a.* [Fr. *diminutif.*] Considerably smaller than the normal size; small; little.—*n.* Anything of very small size (*Shak.*)‡; *gram.* a word formed from another word to express a little thing of the kind (as *manikin,* a little man).—**diminutively,** di·min′ū·tiv·li, *adv.* In a diminutive manner.—**diminutiveness,** di·min′ū·tiv·nes, *n.* State of being diminutive; smallness; littleness.

dimissory, di·mis′o·ri, *a.* [L.L. *dimissorius.* DISMISS.] Sending away; dismissing to another jurisdiction; granting leave to depart.

dimity, dim′i·ti, *n.* [It. *dimito,* L.L. *dimitum,* from Gr. *dimitos,* dimity—*di,* double, and *mitos,* a thread.] A stout cotton fabric ornamented in the loom by raised stripes or fancy figures, rarely dyed, but usually employed white for beds, etc.

dimly, dimness. See DIM.

dimorphism, di·mor′fizm, *n.* [Gr. *di,* double, and *morphē,* form.] The property shown by some mineral bodies of crystallizing in two distinct forms not derivable from each other; the condition when analogous organs of plants of the same species appear under two very dissimilar forms; difference of form between animals of the same species.—**dimorphous, dimorphic,** di·mor′fus, di·mor′fik, *a.* Characterized by dimorphism.

dimple, dim′pl, *n.* [Probably a diminutive form connected with *dip* or *deep*; comp. G. *dümpel, tümpel,* a pool.] A small natural depression in the cheek or other part of the face, as the chin; a slight depression or indentation on any surface.—*v.i.*—**dimpled, dimpling.** To form dimples; to sink into depressions or little inequalities.—*v.i.* To mark with dimples.—**dimply,** dim′pli, *a.*

din, din, *n.* [A.Sax. *dyn, dyne,* noise, thunder; Icel. *dynr,* din, *dynia,* to resound; from same root as Skr. *dhvan,* to sound.] Noise; a clattering, or rumbling sound, long continued.—*v.t.* and *i.*—**dinned, dinning.** To strike with continued or confused sound; to stun with noise.

dine, dīn, *v.i.*—**dined, dining.** [Fr. *dîner,* O.Fr. *disner,* L.L. *disnare*—L. *de,* intens. (as in *devour*), and *cœnare,* to dine, from *cœna,* dinner.] To eat the chief meal of the day; to take dinner.—*To dine out,* to take dinner elsewhere than at one's own residence.—*v.t.* To give a dinner to; to supply with dinner; to afford convenience for dining.—**diner,** di′nėr, *n.* One who dines; a dining car; a restaurant shaped like a railroad car.—**dinette,** di·net′, *n.* A small dining room.—**dining car,** *n.* A railroad car in which meals are served.—**dining room,** *n.* A room used for dinner and other meals.—**dinner,** din′ėr, *n.* The chief meal of the day; a formal meal in honor of a person or an event.

ding, ding, *v.t.* and *i.*—**dung** or **dinged.** [Icel. *dengja,* Dan. *daenge,* Sw. *danga,* to knock, to beat.] To sound as a bell.—**dingdong,** ding′dong, *n.* The sound of bells, or any similar sound.

dinghy, dingey, ding′gi, *n.* [Hindi] An East Indian boat varying in size in different localities; a small boat used by a ship; a sailboat or yacht used in racing; a rubber life raft.

dingle, ding′gl, *n.* [Apparently a form of O.E. *dimble,* a dell or dingle, and *dimple.*] A narrow dale or valley between hills; a small secluded and embowered valley.

dingo, ding′gō, *n.* The wild Australian dog, or a wolflike appearance.

dingy, din′ji, *a.* [Probably connected with *dung.*] Of a dirty white or dusky color; soiled; sullied; dusky.—**dinginess,** din′ji·nes, *n.*

dinkey, dinky, dingk′i, *n.* [Amer.] A small locomotive used for hauling logs, shunting freight cars, etc.

dinky, dingk′i, *a.* [Sc. *dink,* neat.] Small; insignificant.

dinoceras, di·nos′e·ras, *n.* [Gr. *dei-nos,* terrible, *keras,* horn.] A fossil animal as large as an elephant, with three horns.

dinosaur, dinosaurian, di′no·sạr, di·nō·sạ′ri·an, *n.* [Gr. *deinos,* and *sauros,* a lizard.] One of a group of huge, terrestrial, fossil reptiles peculiar to the upper secondary formations, some of them carnivorous.—**dinothere,** di′nō·thėr, *n.* [Gr. *deinos,* and *thērion,* wild beast.] A gigantic extinct mammal allied to the elephant, occurring in the strata of the tertiary formation, with two tusks curving downward. These words are also spelled *Dei-.*

dint, dint, *n.* [A.Sax. *dynt,* a blow, O.E. and Sc. *dunt,* Icel. *dyntr,* a stroke; perhaps akin to *din* and *ding. Dent* is the same word.] A blow or stroke‡; the mark made by a blow; a cavity or impression made by a blow or by pressure on a substance; a dent.—*By dint of,* by the force or power of; by means of.—*v.t.* To make a dint in; to dent.

diocese, di′ō·sēs, *n.* [Gr. *dioikēsis,* administration, a province or jurisdiction—*dia,* and *oikēsis,* residence, from *oikeō,* to dwell, *oikos,* a house.] The circuit or extent of a bishop's jurisdiction; an ecclesiastical division of a state, subject to the authority of a bishop.—**diocesan,** di·os′es·an or di·ō·sē′san, *a.* Pertaining to a diocese.—*n.* A bishop as related to his own diocese; one in possession of a diocese, and having the ecclesiastical jurisdiction over it.

dioecious, di·ē′shus, *a. Bot.* having stamens on one plant and pistils on another; *zool.* having the germ cell or ovum produced by one individual (female), and the sperm cell, or spermatozoid, by another (male).

diopside, di·op′sid, *n.* [Gr. *dia,* through, and *opsis,* a view, from being sometimes transparent.] A variety of augite, of a vitreous luster and greenish or yellowish color.

dioptase, di·op′tās, *n.* [Gr. *dia,* through, and *optazō,* from *optomai,* to see.] Emerald copper ore, a translucent mineral of a beautiful green, occurring crystallized in six-sided prisms.

diopter, di·op′ter, *n.* [Gr. *diopter,* a spy.] In lenses, the unit of refractive power, being that of a lens with a focal length of one meter.—**dioptric, dioptrical,** di·op′trik, di·op′tri·kal, *a.* [Gr. *dioptrikos,* from *dia,* through, and the root *op,* to see.] Pertaining to dioptrics, or to the passing of light through instruments or substances.—*Dioptric system,* the mode of illuminating lighthouses in which the illumination is produced by a central lamp, sending its rays through a combination of lenses surrounding it.—**dioptrics,** di·op′triks, *n.* That part of optics which treats of the refractions of light passing through different mediums, as through air, water, or glass, and especially through lenses.

diorama, di·o·ra′ma, *n.* [Gr. *dia,* through, and *horama,* a view.] A painted scene in three dimensions, viewed through an aperture; a spectacular picture or scene of any size, with or without translucent features.

diorite, dī'o·rīt, n. [Gr. *dia*, through, and *horos*, boundary, the stone being formed of distinct portions.] A tough crystalline trap rock of a whitish color, speckled with black or greenish black.

dioxide, dī·ok'sīd, n. [Prefix *di*, double, and *oxide*.] An oxide consisting of one atom of a metal and two atoms of oxygen.

dip, dip, v.t.—*dipped* or *dipt, dipping*. [A.Sax. *dippan, dyppan*, to dip; Fris. *dippe*, D. *doopen*, G. *taufen*, to dip, to baptize, akin *deep, dive*.] To plunge or immerse in water or other liquid; to put into a fluid and withdraw; to lift with a ladle or other vessel; often with *out*; to baptize by immersion.—v.i. To plunge into a liquid and quickly emerge; to engage in a desultory way; to concern oneself to some little extent (to *dip* into a subject); to read passages here and there (to *dip* into a volume); to sink, as below the horizon; *geol.* to incline or slope.—n. An immersion in any liquid; a plunge; a bath; a candle made by dipping the wick in tallow; inclination or slope.—*Dip of the needle*, the angle which the magnetic needle makes with the plane of the horizon.—*The dip of strata*, in *geol.* the inclination or angle at which strata slope or dip.—**dipper,** dip'ẽr, n. One who or that which dips, especially, a kind of ladle or scoop; [cap.] either of two groups of seven stars in the Northern Hemisphere resembling a dipper.

diphtheria, dif·thē'ri·a, n. [Gr. *diphthera*, a membrane.] An epidemic inflammatory disease of the air passages, and especially of the throat, characterized by the formation of a false membrane.—**diphtheritic,** dif·the·rit'ik, a. Connected with, relating to, or formed by diphtheria.

diphthong, dif'thong or dip'thong, n. [Gr. *diphthongos—di*, twice, and *phthongos*, sound.] A union of two vowels pronounced in one syllable (as in *bound, oil*).—**diphthongization,** dif'thong·gi·zā'shon or dip-, n. The formation of a diphthong; the conversion of a simple vowel into a diphthong.—**diphthongize,** dif'thong·gīz or dip-, v.t. To form into a diphthong.

diphyllous, dī·fil'us, a. [Gr. *di*, twice, and *phyllon*, a leaf.] Bot. having two leaves, as a calyx, etc.

diplococcus, dip'lo·kok''us, n. [Gr. *diploos*, double, *kokkos*, a berry.] Of bacteria, a form consisting of a pair of cocci. See COCCUS.

diploma, di·plō'ma, n. [Gr. *diplōma*, a paper folded double, a license, from *diploō*, to fold, *diploos*, double.] A letter or writing, usually under seal and signed by competent authority, conferring some power, privilege, or honor, as that given to graduates of colleges on their receiving the usual degrees, to physicians who are

licensed to practice their profession, and the like.—v.t. To furnish with a diploma; to fortify by a diploma.—**diplomacy,** di·plō'ma·si, n. The science or art of conducting negotiations, arranging treaties, etc., between nations; the forms of international negotiations; dexterity or skill in managing negotiations of any kind; artful management or maneuvering with the view of securing advantages.—**diplomat,** dip'lo·mat, n. A diplomatist.—**diplomatic,** dip·lo·mat'ik, a. Pertaining to diplomacy or to the management of any negotiations; skillful in gaining one's ends by tact and cleverness; conferred by diploma; relating to diplomatics.—**diplomatically,** dip·lo·mat'i·kal·li, adv. In a diplomatic manner; artfully.—**diplomatics,** dip·lo·mat'iks, n. The science of deciphering old writings, to ascertain their authenticity, date, etc.; paleography.—**diplomatist,** di·plō'ma·tist, n. A person skilled in diplomacy; a diplomat.

diplopia, di·plō'pi·a, n. [Gr. *diploos*, double, and *ōps*, the eye.] A disease of the eye, in which the patient sees an object double or even triple.

dipper, dipping. See DIP.

dipsomania, dip·so·mā'ni·a, n. [Gr. *dipsa*, thirst, and *mania*, madness.] That morbid condition to which habitual drunkards of a nervous and sanguine temperament are liable to reduce themselves, and in which they manifest an uncontrollable craving for stimulants.—**dipsomaniac,** dip·so·mā'ni·ak, n. A victim of dipsomania.—**dipsomaniacal,** dip·so·mā'ni·a·kal, a. Pertaining to dipsomania.

dipteral, dip'tẽr·al, a. [Gr. *di*, double, and *pteron*, a wing.] Entom. having two wings only; dipterous; *arch.* a term applied to a temple having a double row of columns on each of its flanks.—n. Arch. a dipteral temple.—**dipteron,** dip'tẽr·an, n. A dipterous insect.—**dipterous,** dip'tẽr·us, a. Entom. having two wings. bot. a term applied to seeds which have their margins prolonged in the form of wings.

diptych, dip'tik, n. [Gr. *diptychos—di*, double, and *ptyssō*, to fold.] Anciently, a kind of register or list as of magistrates or bishops consisting usually of two leaves folded, a design, as a painting or carved work, on two folding compartments or tablets.

dire, dīr, a. [L. *dirus*, terrible.] Dreadful; dismal; horrible; terrible; evil in a great degree.—**direful,** dīr'ful, a. Same as *Dire.*—**direfully,** dīr'ful·li, adv. In a direful manner.—**direly,** dīr'li, adv. In a dire manner.—**direness,** dīr'nes, n. The state or quality of being dire. (Shak.)

direct, di·rekt', a. [L. *dirigo, directum*, to set in a straight line, to direct—*di* for *dis*. intens., and *rego, rectum*, to make straight. RIGHT, REGENT.] Straight; right; opposite to *crooked; circuitous, winding, oblique; astron.* appearing to move from west to east; opposed to *retrograde*; in the

line of father and son; opposed to *collateral*; straightforward; open; ingenuous; plain; not ambiguous,—v.t. To point or aim in a straight line toward something; to make to act or work, towards a certain end or object; to show the right road or course; to prescribe a course to; to order or instruct; to prescribe to; to inscribe (a letter) with the address.—v.i. To act as a guide; to point out a course.—n. Mus. the sign ⁓ placed at the end of a stave to direct the performer to the first note of the next stave.—**direct current,** *Elect.* A current flowing in one direction in a circuit; abbreviated D.C.—**direction,** di·rek'shon, n. The act of directing; the course or line in which anything is directed; a being directed toward a particular end; the line in which a body moves, or to which its position is referred; course; the act of governing; administration; management; guidance; superintendence; instruction in what manner to proceed; order; behest; the address on a letter, parcel, etc; a body or board of directors; directorate.—**directive,** di·rek'tiv, a Having the power of directing.—**directly,** di·rekt'li, adv. In a direct manner; in a straight line or course; straightway; immediately; instantly; soon; without delay; openly; expressly; without circumlocution or ambiguity.—**directness,** di·rekt'nes, n.—**direct object,** n. Gram. the person or thing that receives the action expressed by the verb.—**director,** di·rek'tẽr, n. One who or that which directs; one who superintends; specifically, one of a body appointed to direct, control, or superintend the affairs of a company.—**directorate,** di·rek'tẽr·it, n. The office of a director; a body of directors.—**directorship,** di·rek'tẽr·ship, n. The condition or office of a director.—**directory,** di·rek'te·ri, n. A rule to direct; a book containing directions for public worship or religious services; a book containing an alphabetical list of the inhabitants of a city, town, etc., with their places of business and abode; board of directors; directorate; [cap.] during the French Revolution, a body established by the Convention in 1795, and composed of five members.—**directress,** di·rek'tres, n. A female who directs or manages.—**directrix,** di·rek'triks, n. A directress; *geom.* a straight line of importance in the doctrine of conic sections.

direful. See DIRE.

dirge, dẽrj, n. [A contraction of L. *dirige* ('direct', imperative of *dirigere*, to direct), the first word in a psalm or hymn formerly sung at funerals.] A song or tune intended to express, grief, sorrow, and mourning.

dirigible, di'ri·ji·bl, a. That may be directed, turned, or guided in any direction.—n. A balloon or airship driven by motors whose course can be directed by means of steering or directing apparatus.

fāte, fär, fâre, fat, fȧll; mē, met, hẽr; pīne, pin; nōte, not, mȯve; tūbe, tub, bṳll; oil, pound.

dirk, dẻrk, *n.* [Origin doubtful.] A kind of dagger or poniard; a dagger worn as essential to complete the Highland costume.—*v.t.* To poniard; to stab.

dirt, dẻrt, *n.* [Icel. *drit*, dirt, excrement, *drita*, Sc. *drite*, A.Sax. *(ge) dritan*, to go to stool.] Any foul or filthy substance; as excrement, mud, mire, dust; whatever, adhering to anything, renders it foul or unclean; a gold-miner's name for the material, as earth, gravel, etc., put into his cradle to be washed.—*v.t.* To soil; to dirty.—**dirtily,** der′ti·li, *adv.* In a dirty manner; nastily; filthily; meanly; sordidly.—**dirtiness,** dẻr′ti·nes, *n.* The condition of being dirty; filthiness; foulness; nastiness.—**dirty,** dẻr′ti, *a.* Foul; nasty; filthy; not clean; impure; turbid; mean; base; despicable; sleety, rainy, or sloppy (weather).—*v.t.*—*dirtied, dirtying.* To defile; to make dirty or filthy; to soil.

disable, dis·ā′bl, *v.t.*—*disabled, disabling.* [Prefix *dis*, priv., and *able*.] To render unable; to deprive of competent strength or power, physical or mental; to injure so as to be no longer fit for duty or service; to deprive of adequate means, instruments, or resources; to impair; to deprive of legal qualifications; to incapacitate; to render incapable.—**disability,** dis·a·bil′i·ti, *n.* The state or quality of being disabled or unable; weakness; impotence; incapacity; inability; want of legal qualifications.—**disablement,**† dis·ā′bl·ment, *n.* The act of disabling; disability.

disabuse, dis·a·būz′, *v.t.*—*disabused, disabusing.* [Fr. *désabuser*, to disabuse.] To free from mistaken or erroneous notions or beliefs; to undeceive; to set right.

disaccustom, dis·ak·kus′tum, *v.t.* To destroy the force of habit in by disuse; to render unaccustomed.

disadvantage, dis·ad·van′tij, *n.* Absence or deprivation of advantage; that which prevents success or renders it difficult; any unfavorable circumstance or state, prejudice to interest, fame, credit, profit, or other good; loss; injury; harm; damage.—**disadvantageous,** dis·ad′van·tā″jus, *a.* Attended with disadvantage; unfavorable to success or prosperity; prejudicial.—**disadvantageously,** dis·ad′van·tā″jus·li, *adv.* In a disadvantageous manner.—**disadvantageousness,** dis·ad′van·tā″jus·nes, *n.*

disaffect, dis·af·fekt′, *v.t.* To alienate the affection of; to make less friendly or faithful, as to a person, party, or cause; to make discontented or unfriendly.—**disaffected,** dis·af·fek′ted, *p.* and *a.* Having the affections alienated; indisposed to favor or support; unfriendly; hostile to the governing power.—**disaffection,** dis·af·fek′shon, *n.* Alienation of affection, attachment, or good will; disloyalty.

disaffirm, dis·af·fẻrm′, *v.t.* To deny; to contradict; to annul, as a judicial decision, by a contrary judgment of a superior tribunal.

disafforest, dis·af·for′est, *v.t.* To reduce from the privileges of a forest to the state of common ground; to strip of forest laws and their oppressive privileges.

disagree, dis·a·grē′, *v.t.*—*disagreed, disagreeing.* To be not accordant or coincident; to be not exactly similar; to differ; to be of an opposite or different opinion; to be unsuitable to the stomach; to be in opposition; not to accord or harmonize; to become unfriendly; to quarrel.—**disagreeable,** dis·a·grē′a·bl, *a.* The reverse of agreeable; unpleasing; offensive to the mind or to the senses; repugnant; obnoxious.—**disagreeableness,** dis·a·grē′a·bl·nes, *n.* The state or quality of being disagreeable.—**disagreeably,** dis·a·grē′a·bli, *adv.* In a disagreeable manner; unpleasantly.—**disagreement,** dis·a·grē′ment, *n.* Want of agreement; difference, as of form or character; difference of opinion or sentiments; a falling out; a quarrel; discord.

disallow, dis·al·lou′, *v.t.* To refuse permission or sanction for; not to grant; not to authorize; to disapprove of; to reject, as being illegal, unnecessary, unauthorized, and the like.—**disallowance,** dis·al·lou′ans, *n.* Disapprobation; refusal; prohibition; rejection.

disannul, dis·an·nul′, *v.t.* To make void; to annul; to deprive of force or authority; to cancel. (*Shak.*)—**disannulment,** dis·an·nul′ment, *n.* Annulment.

disappear, dis·ap·pēr′, *v.i.* To cease to appear or to be perceived; to vanish from the sight; to go away or out of sight; to cease, or seem to cease, to be or exist.—**disappearance,** dis·ap·pē′rans, *n.* Act of disappearing; removal from sight.

disappoint, dis·ap·point′, *v.t.* [Fr. *désappointer*, originally to remove from an appointment or office.] To defeat of expectation, wish, hope, desire, or intention; to frustrate; to balk; to hinder from the possession or enjoyment of that which was hoped or expected (*disappointed of the expected legacy*).—**disappointed,** dis·ap·poin′ted, *p.* and *a.* Having suffered disappointment; balked; unprepared (*Shak.*)‡.—**disappointment,** dis·ap·point′ment, *n.* The act of disappointing or feeling of being disappointed; defeat or failure of expectation, hope, wish, desire, or intention.

disapprobation, dis·ap′ro·bā″shon, *n.* The reverse of approbation; disapproval; censure, expressed or unexpressed.—**disapprove,** dis·a·pröv′, *v.t.*—*disapproved, disapproving.* To censure; to regard as wrong or objectionable.—*v.i.* To express or feel disapproval: with *of* before the object.—**disapproval,** dis·a·prö′val, *n.* Disapprobation; dislike.—**disapprovingly,** dis·a·prö′ving·li, *adv.* In a disapproving manner.

disarm, dis·ärm′, *v.t.* To take the arms or weapons from, usually by force or authority; to reduce to a peace footing, as an army or navy; to deprive of means of attack or defense, or of annoyance, or power to terrify; to render harmless.—*v.i.* To lay down arms; to disband armed forces.—**disarmament,** dis·är′ma·ment, *n.* Act of disarming.

disarrange, dis·a·rānj′, *v.t.* To put out of order; to unsettle or disturb the order or due arrangement of.—**disarrangement,** dis·a·rānj′ment, *n.* The act of disarranging; disorder.

disarray, dis·a·rā′, *v.t.* To undress; to divest of clothes; to throw into disorder.—*n.* Disorder; confusion; disordered dress.

disaster, diz·as′tẻr, *n.* [Fr. *désastre—dis*, and L. *astrum*, a star; a word of astrological origin. Compare the adj. *disastrous* with *ill-starred*.] Any unfortunate event, especially a great and sudden misfortune; mishap; calamity; adversity; reverse.—**disastrous,** diz·as′trus, *a.* Occasioning or accompanied by disaster; calamitous.—**disastrously,** diz·as′trus·li, *adv.* In a disastrous manner.

disavow, dis·a·vou′, *v.t.* To deny to be true, as a fact or charge respecting one's self; to disown; to repudiate; to reject.—**disavowal,** dis·a·vou′al, *n.* Denial; repudiation.

disband, dis·band′, *v.t.* To dismiss from military service, to break up, as a band or body of men; to disperse.—*v.i.* To break up and retire from military service.—**disbandment,** dis·band′ment, *n.* The act of disbanding.

disbar, dis·bär′, *v.t.*—*disbarred, disbarring.* To expel from being a member of the bar; to remove from the list of lawyers.

disbelief, dis·bi·lēf′, *n.* Refusal of credit or faith; denial of belief; unbelief; infidelity; scepticism.—**disbelieve,** dis·bi·lēv′, *v.t.*—*disbelieved, disbelieving.* To refuse belief to; to hold not to be true or not to exist; to refuse to credit.—*v.i.* To deny the truth of any position; to refuse to believe.—**disbeliever,** dis·bi·lē′vẻr, *n.* One who disbelieves or refuses belief; an unbeliever.

disburden, dis·bẻr′den, *v.t.* To remove a burden from; to lay off or aside as oppressive; to get rid of.

disburse, dis·bẻrs′, *v.t.*—*disbursed, disbursing.* [O.Fr. *desbourser*—prefix *dis*, and L.L. *bursa*, a purse. PURSE.] To pay out, as money; to spend or lay out; to expend.—**disbursement,** dis·bẻrs′ment, *n.* The act of disbursing; a sum paid out.—**disburser,** dis·bẻr′sẻr, *n.* One who disburses.

disc. See DISK.

discard, dis·kärd′, *v.t.* and *i.* To throw out of the hand such cards as are not played in the course of the game; to dismiss from service or employment, or from society; to cast off.

discern, diz·zẻrn′, *v.t.* [L. *discerno—dis*, and *cerno*, to separate or distinguish, akin to Gr. *krinō*, to judge (whence *critic*); Skr. *kri*, to separate. CRIME.] To perceive or note as being different; to discriminate by the eye or the intellect; to distinguish or mark as being distinct; to dis-

---

ch, *chain*; *ch*, Sc. *loch*; g, *go*; j, *job*; ng, *sing*; TH, *then*; th, *thin*; w, *wig*; hw, *whig*; zh, *azure*.

cover by the eye; to see.—*v.i.* To see or understand differences; to make distinction; to have clearness of mental vision.—**discerner,** diz·zer′ner, *n.* One who discerns; a clearsighted observer; one who knows and judges; one who has the power of distinguishing.—**discernible,** diz·zer′ni·bl, *a.* Capable of being discerned; discoverable by the eye or the understanding; distinguishable.—**discernibleness,** diz·zer′ni·bl·nes, *n.*—**discernibly,** diz·zer′ni·bli, *adv.* So as to be discerned.—**discerning,** diz·zer′ning, *p.* and *a.* Having power to discern; capable of discriminating, knowing, and judging; sharp-sighted; acute.—**discerningly,** diz·zer′ning·li, *adv.* In a discerning manner.—**discernment,** diz·zern′ment, *n.* The act of discerning; the power or faculty of discerning by the mind; acuteness of judgment; power of perceiving differences of things or ideas, and their relations; penetration.

discharge, dis·chärj′, *v.t.*—*discharged, discharging.* To unload (a ship); to take out (a cargo); to free from any load or burden; to free of the missile with which anything is charged or loaded; to fire off; to let fly; to shoot; to emit or send out; to give vent to, *lit.* or *fig.*; to deliver the amount or value of to the person to whom it is owing; to pay (a debt); to free from an obligation, duty, or labor; to relieve (to *discharge* a person from a task); to clear from an accusation or crime; to acquit; to absolve; to set free; to perform or execute (a duty or office); to divest of an office or employment; to dismiss from service (a servant, a soldier, a jury); to release; to liberate from confinement. —*v.i.* To get rid of or let out a charge or contents.—*n.* The act of discharging, unloading or freeing from a charge; a flowing or issuing out, or a throwing out; emission; that which is thrown out; matter emitted; dismissal from office or service; release from obligation, debt, or penalty; absolution from a crime or accusation; ransom; price paid for deliverance; performance; execution, as of an office, trust, or duty; liberation; release from confinement; payment of a debt; a written acknowledgment of payment; a substance used in calico printing to remove color, and so form a pattern.—**discharger,** dis·chär′jer, *n.* One who or that which discharges.

disciple, dis·sī′pl, *n.* [L. *discipulus,* from *disco,* to learn.] One who receives instruction from another; a learner; a scholar; a pupil; a follower; an adherent.—**discipleship,** dis·sī′pl·ship, *n.* The state of being a disciple.

discipline, dis′si·plin, *n.* [L. *disciplina,* from *discipulus,* a disciple, from *disco,* to learn.] Training, education; instruction and the government of conduct or practice; the training to act in accordance with rules; drill; method of regu-

lating principles and practice; punishment inflicted by way of correction and training; instruction by means of misfortune, suffering, and the like; correction; chastisement. —*v.t.*—*disciplined, disciplining.* To subject to discipline; to apply discipline to; train; to teach rules and practice, and accustom to order and subordination; to drill; to correct, chastise, punish.—**discipliner,** dis′si·plin·er, *n.* One who disciplines.—**disciplinable,** dis′si·plin·a·bl, *a.* Capable of instruction and improvement in learning; capable of being made matter of discipline; subject or liable to discipline.—**disciplinarian,** dis′si·pli·nâ′ri·an, *n.* One who disciplines; one who instructs in military and naval tactics and maneuvers; one who enforces rigid discipline; a martinet.—*a.* Pertaining to discipline.—**disciplinary,** dis′si·pli·na·ri, *a.* Pertaining to discipline; intended for discipline; promoting discipline.

disclaim, dis·klām′, *v.t.* To deny or relinquish all claim to; to reject as not belonging to one's self; to renounce; to deny responsibility for or approval of; to disavow; to disown.—**disclaimer,** dis·klā′mer, *n.* A person who disclaims; an act of disclaiming; abnegation of pretensions or claims; *law,* a renunciation, abandonment, or giving up of a claim.

disclose, dis·klōz′, *v.t.*—*disclosed, disclosing.* To uncover and lay open to the view; to cause to appear; to allow to be seen; to bring to light; to make known, reveal, tell, utter.—**discloser,** dis·klō′zer, *n.* One who discloses.—**disclosure,** dis·klō′zher, *n.* The act of disclosing; exhibition; the act of making known or revealing; utterance of what was secret; a telling; that which is disclosed or made known.

discoid. See DISK.

discolor, dis·kul′er, *v.t.* To alter the hue or color of; to change to a different color or shade; to stain; to tinge.—**discoloration,** dis·kul′er·ā″shon, *n.* The act of discoloring; alteration of color; a discolored spot or marking.

discomfit, dis·kum′fit, *v.t.* [O.Fr. *disconfire, disconfit*—L. *dis,* not, and *conficere,* to achieve. COMFIT.] To rout, defeat, or scatter in flight; to cause to flee; to vanquish; to disconcert, foil, or frustrate the plans of.—*n.* A defeat; an overthrow. (*Mil.*)—**discomfiture,** dis·kum′fi·cher, *n.* Rout; defeat; overthrow; frustration; disappointment.

discomfort, dis·kum′fert, *n.* Absence or opposite of comfort or pleasure; uneasiness; disturbance of peace; pain, annoyance, or inquietude.— *v.t.* To disturb the peace or happiness of; to make uneasy; to pain.—**discomfortable,**† dis·kum′fer·ta·bl, *a.* Wanting in comfort; uncomfortable.

discommend,† dis·kom·mend′, *v.t.* To blame; to censure; to expose to censure or bad feeling.

discommode, dis·kom·mōd′, *v.t.*— *discommoded, discommoding.* To put

to inconvenience; to incommode.

discommon, dis·kom′on, *v.t.* To make to cease to be common land; to deprive of the right of a common.

discompose, dis·kom·pōz′, *v.t.*—*discomposed, discomposing.* To disorder, disturb, or disarrange; to disturb the peace and quietness of; to agitate, ruffle, fret, or vex.—**discomposure,** dis·kom·pō′zher, *n.* The state of being discomposed; a certain agitation or perturbation of mind.

disconcert, dis·kon·sert′, *v.t.* To throw into disorder or confusion; to undo, as a concerted scheme or plan; to defeat; to frustrate; to discompose or disturb the self-possession of; to confuse.—**disconcertion,** dis·kon·ser′shon, *n.* The act of disconcerting; the state of being disconcerted.

disconformable, dis·kon·for′ma·bl, *a.* Not conformable.—**disconformity,** dis·kon·for′mi·ti, *n.* Want of agreement or conformity; inconsistency.

disconnect, dis·kon·nekt′, *v.t.* To separate or sever the connection between; to disunite; to detach.— **disconnection,** dis·kon·nek′shon, *n.* The act of disconnecting; separation; want of union.

disconsolate, dis·kon′so·lit, *a.* [L. *dis,* not, and *consolatus,* pp. of *consolor,* to console, to be consoled. CONSOLE.] Destitute of consolation; hopeless; sad; dejected; melancholy; cheerless; saddening; gloomy.— **disconsolately,** dis·kon′so·lit·li, *adv.* In a disconsolate manner; without comfort.—**disconsolateness,** dis·kon′so·lit·nes, *n.*

discontent, dis·kon·tent′, *n.* Want of content; uneasiness or inquietude of mind; dissatisfaction; one who is discontented; a malcontent (*Shak.*). —*a.*‡ Uneasy; dissatisfied.—*v.t.* To make dissatisfied.—**discontented,** dis·kon·ten′ted, *a.* Not contented; dissatisfied; not pleased with one's circumstances; given to grumble.— **discontentedly,** dis·kon·ten′ted·li, *adv.* In a discontented manner or mood.—**discontentedness,** dis·kon·ten′ted·nes, *n.* The state of being discontented; dissatisfaction.—**discontentment,** dis·kon·tent′ment, *n.* The state of being discontented; discontent.

discontinue, dis·kon·tin′ū, *v.t.*—*discontinued, discontinuing.* [Prefix *dis,* neg., and *continue.*] To continue no longer; to leave off or break off; to give up, cease from, or abandon; to stop; to put an end to.—*v.i.* To cease; to stop.—**discontinuance,** dis·kon·tin′ū·ans, *n.* Want of continuance; breaking off; cessation; intermission; interruption.—**discontinuation,** dis·kon·tin′ū·ā″shon, *n.* Discontinuance.—**discontinuity,** dis·kon′ti·nū″i·ti, *n.* Want of continuity or uninterrupted connection; disunion of parts; want of cohesion.— **discontinuous,** dis·kon·tin′ū·us, *a.* Broken off; interrupted.

discord, dis′kord, *n.* [Fr. *discorde,* L. *discordia,* disagreement, from *discors,* discordant—*dis,* and *cor, cordis,* the heart, as in *concord, accord, cordial.*]

Want of concord or agreement; opposition of opinions; difference of qualities; disagreement; variance; contention; strife; *mus.* a union of sounds disagreeable or grating to the ear; dissonance; each of the *two* sounds forming a dissonance.—*v.i.* (dis-kord'). To disagree; to be out of harmony or concord; to clash.—**discordance, discordancy,** dis·kor'dans, dis·kor'dan·si, *n.* Disagreement; opposition; inconsistency.—**discordant,** dis·kor'dant, *a.* Disagreeing; incongruous; being at variance; dissonant; not in unison; not harmonious; not accordant; harsh; jarring.—**discordantly,** dis··kor'dant·li, *adv.* In a discordant manner.

discount, dis'kount, *n.* [Prefix *dis,* neg., and *count*; O.Fr. *descompte.*] A certain sum deducted from the credit price of goods sold on account of prompt payment, or any deduction from the customary price, or from a sum due or to be due at a future time; a charge made to cover the interest of money advanced on a bill or other document not presently due; the act of discounting.—*At a discount,* below par; hence, in low esteem; in disfavor.—*v.t.* (diskount'). To lend or advance the amount of (a bill or similar document), deducting the interest or other rate per cent from the principal; to leave out of account or disregard; to estimate or take into account beforehand; to enjoy or suffer by anticipation.—**discountable,** dis·koun'ta·bl, *a.* Capable of being discounted.—**discounter,** dis'koun·ter, *n.* One who discounts bills, etc.

discountenance, dis·koun'te·nans, *v.t.* To put out of countenance; to put to shame; to abash; to set one's countenance against; to discourage, check, or restrain by frowns, censure, arguments, cold treatment, etc.—*n.* Cold treatment; disapprobation.

discourage, dis·kur'ij, *v.t.*—*discouraged, discouraging.* To check the courage of; to dishearten; to deprive of self-confidence; to attempt to repress or prevent by pointing out difficulties, etc.; to dissuade.—**discouragement,** dis·kur'ij·ment, *n.* The act of discouraging; the act of deterring or dissuading from an undertaking; that which discourages or damps ardor or hope; the state of being discouraged.—**discourager,** dis·kur'i·jer, *n.* One who or that which discourages.—**discouraging,** dis·kur'i·jing, *a.* Tending to discourage or dishearten; disheartening. —**discouragingly,** dis·kur'i·jing·li, *adv.* In a discouraging manner.

discourse, dis'kors, *n.* [Fr. *discours,* from L. *discursus,* a running about, a conversation, from *discurro,* to ramble—*dis,* and *curro,* to run. CURRENT.] A running over a subject in speech; hence, a talking together or discussing; conversation; talk; speech; a treatise; a dissertation; a homily, sermon, or other production. —*v.i.* (dis-kors'),—*discoursing.* To communicate thoughts orally or in writing, especially in a formal

manner; to hold forth; to expatiate; to converse.—*v.t.* To talk over or discuss‡; to utter or give forth.— **discourser,** dis·kor'ser, *n.* One who discourses.

discourteous, dis·ker'te·us, *a.* Wanting in courtesy; uncivil; rude.— **discourteously,** dis·ker'te·us·li, *adv.* In a discourteous manner.—**discourteousness,** dis·ker'te·us·nes, *n.*—**discourtesy,** dis·ker'te·si, *n.* Want of courtesy; incivility; rudeness of manner; act of disrespect.

discover, dis·kuv'er, *v.t.* [Prefix *dis,* not, and *cover*; O.Fr. *descouvrir.*] To lay open to view; to disclose or reveal; to espy; to have the first sight of; to find out; to obtain the first knowledge of; to come to the knowledge of; to detect. ∴ We *discover* what before existed, though to us unknown; we *invent* what did not before exist.—**discoverable,** dis·kuv'er·a·bl, *a.* Capable of being discovered, brought to light, exposed, found out, or made known.—**discoverer,** dis·kuv'er·er, *n.* One who discovers; one who first sees or espies; one who finds out or first comes to the knowledge of something.—**discovery,** dis·kuv'er·i, *n.* The act of discovering; a disclosing or bringing to light; a revealing or making known; a finding out or bringing for the first time to sight or knowledge; what is discovered or found out.

discredit, dis·kred'it, *n.* Want of credit or good reputation; some degree of disgrace or reproach; disesteem; disrepute; want of belief, trust, or confidence; disbelief.—*v.t.* To give no credit to; not to credit or believe; to deprive of credit or good reputation; to bring into some degree of disgrace or disrepute; to deprive of credibility.—**discreditable,** dis·kred'i·ta·bl, *n.* Injurious to reputation; disgraceful; disreputable.— **discreditably,** dis·kred'i·ta·bli, *adv.* In a discreditable manner.

discreet, dis·krēt', *a.* [Fr. *discret,* from L. *discretus,* pp. of *discerno,* to discern. DISCERN.] Wise in avoiding errors or evil, and in selecting the best course or means; prudent in conduct; circumspect; cautious; heedful; guarded.—**discreetly,** dis··krēt'li, *adv.* In a discreet manner; prudently.—**discreetness,** dis·krēt'·nes, *n.* The quality of being discreet. —**discretion,** dis·kresh'on, *n.* [Fr. *discrétion,* L. *discretio.*] The quality or attribute of being discreet; discernment to judge critically of what is correct and proper, united with caution; prudence; sound judgment; circumspection; wariness; caution; liberty or power of acting without other control than one's own judgment (to leave an affair to one's *discretion,* to surrender at *discretion,* that is without stipulating for terms). —**discretionary,** dis·kresh'on·e·ri, *a.* Left to a person's own discretion or judgment; to be directed according to one's own discretion (*discretionary* powers).

discrepance, discrepancy, dis·krep'-ans, dis·krep'an·si, *n.* [L. *discrepantia,* from *discrepo,* to give a different

sound, to vary—*dis,* and *crepo,* to creak. CREPITATE.] A difference or inconsistency between facts, stories, theories, etc.; disagreement; divergence.—**discrepant,** dis·krep'ant, *a.* Differing or diverging; not agreeing or according; disagreeing; dissimilar.

discrete, dis·krēt', *a.* [L. *discretus,* separated, set apart. DISCREET.] Separate; distinct; disjunct; disjunctive.—*A discrete quantity,* quantity not continued in its parts, as any number, since a number consists of units.

discretion. See DISCREET.

discriminate, dis·krim'i·nāt, *v.t.*—*discriminated, discriminating.* [L. *discrimino, discriminatum,* to distinguish, from *discrimen,* difference—*dis,* a-sunder, and the root seen in *crimen,* accusation, *cerno,* to sift or separate. CRIME, DISCERN, DISCREET.] To distinguish from other things by observing differences; to perceive by a distinction; to discern; to separate; to select; to distinguish by some note or mark.—*v.i.* To make a difference or distinction; to observe or note a difference; to distinguish.— **discriminately,** dis·krim'i·nit·li, *adv.* With minute distinction; particularly.—**discriminating,** dis·krim'-i·nā·ting, *p.* and *a.* Serving to discriminate; distinguishing; distinctive; able to make nice distinctions.— **discrimination,** dis·krim'i·nā″shon, *n.* The act of discriminating; the faculty of distinguishing or discriminating; penetration; discernment; the state of being discriminated or set apart.—**discriminative,** dis·krim'-i·nā·tiv, *a.* Discriminating or tending to discriminate; forming the mark of distinction or difference; characteristic. — **discriminatively,** dis··krim'i·nā·tiv·li, *adv.* By discrimination.—**discriminatory,** dis·krim'i··na·to·ri, *a.* Discriminative.

discrown, dis·kroun', *v.t.* To deprive of a crown.

discursive, dis·ker'siv, *a.* [Fr. *discursif,* from L. *discursus.* DISCOURSE.] Passing rapidly from one subject to another; desultory; rambling; digressional; argumentative; reasoning; rational.—**discursively,** dis·ker'·siv·li, *adv.* In a discursive manner.— **discursiveness,** dis·ker'siv·nes, *n.*

discus, dis'kus, *n.* See DISK.

discuss, dis·kus', *v.t.* [L. *discutio, discussum,* to scatter, dissipate—*dis,* asunder, and *quatio,* to shake, as in concussion. QUASH.] To drive away, dissolve, or resolve (a tumor, etc.: a medical use); to agitate by argument; to examine by disputation; to reason on; to debate; to argue; to make an end of, by eating or drinking; to consume (*colloq.*).—**discussion,** dis·ku'shon, *n.* The act of discussing; debate; disquisition; the agitation of a point or subject with a view to elicit truth.

disdain, dis·dān', *v.t.* [O.Fr. *desdaigner,* Fr. *dédaigner,* from L. *dis,* not, and *dignor,* to deem worthy, from *dignus,* worthy. DEIGN.] To deem or regard as worthless; to consider to be unworthy of notice, care, regard, esteem, or unworthy of one's character; to scorn; to contemn.—*n.* A feeling of contempt, mingled with indignation; the looking upon anything as beneath one; haughtiness; contempt; scorn.—**disdainful**, dis·dān'fụl, *a.* Full of or expressing disdain; contemptuous; scornful; haughty.—**disdainfully**, dis·dān'fụl·li, *adv.* In a disdainful manner.—**disdainfulness**, dis·dān'fụl·nes, *n.* The quality of being disdainful; haughty scorn.

disease, di·zēz', *n.* Want or absence of ease‡; uneasiness, distress, or discomfort‡; any morbid state of the body, or of any particular organ or part of the body; ailment; distemper; malady; disorder; any morbid or depraved condition, moral, mental, social, political, etc.—**diseased**, di·zēzd', *a.* Affected with disease; having the vital functions deranged; disordered; deranged; distempered; sick.

disembark, dis·em·bärk', *v.t.* To remove from on board a ship to the land; to put on shore; to land.—*v.i.* To leave a ship and go on shore; to land.—**disembarkation, disembarkment**, dis·em'bär·kā″shon, dis·em·bärk'ment, *n.* The act of disembarking.

disembarrass, dis·em·bar'as, *v.t.* To free from embarrassment or perplexity; to clear; to extricate.—**disembarrassment**, dis·em·bar'as·ment, *n.* The act of disembarrassing.

disembody, dis·em·bod'i, *v.t.* To divest of the body (a *disembodied* spirit=a ghost); to set free from the flesh; to disband (*military*).—**disembodiment**, dis·em·bod'i·ment, *n.* The act of disembodying; the condition of being disembodied.

disembogue, dis·em·bōg', *v.t.* and *i.*—*disembogued, disemboguing.* To pour out or discharge at the mouth, as a stream; to discharge water into the ocean or a lake.—**disemboguement**, dis·em·bōg'ment, *n.* Discharge of waters by a stream.

disembowel, dis·em·bou'el, *v.t.*—*disemboweled, disemboweling.* To deprive of the bowels or of parts analogous to the bowels; to eviscerate; to gut.

disenchant, dis·en·chant', *v.t.* To free from enchantment; to deliver from the power of charms or spells; to free from fascination or pleasing delusion.—**disenchanter**, dis·en·chan'tẻr, *n.* One who or that which disenchants.—**disenchantment**, dis·en·chant'ment, *n.* Act of disenchanting.

disencumber, dis·en·kum'bẻr, *v.t.* To free from encumbrance, clogs, and impediments.

disendow, dis·en·dou', *v.t.* To deprive of an endowment or endowments, as a church or other institution.—**disendowment**, dis·en·dou'ment, *n.* The act of disendowing.

disenfranchise, dis·en·fran'chīz, *v.t.* To disfranchise.

disengage, dis·en·gāj', *v.t.*—*disengaged, disengaging.* To separate or set free from union or attachment; to detach; to disunite; to free; to disentangle; to extricate; to clear,

as from difficulties or perplexities; to free, as from anything that occupies the attention; to set free by dissolving an engagement.—**disengagement**, dis·en·gāj'ment, *n.* The act or process of disengaging; the state of being disengaged; freedom from engrossing occupation; leisure.

disentail, dis·en·tāl', *v.t.* To free from being entailed; to break the entail of.

disentangle, dis·en·tang'gl, *v.t.* To free from entanglements; to unravel; to extricate from perplexity or complications; to disengage.—**disentanglement**, dis·en·tang'gl·ment, *n.* Act of disentangling.

disenthrone, dis·en·thrōn', *v.t.* To dethrone; to depose from sovereign authority. (*Mil.*)

disentomb, dis·en·töm', *v.t.* To take out of a tomb; to disinter.

disestablish, dis·es·tab'lish, *v.t.* To cause to cease to be established; to withdraw (a church) from its connection with the state.—**disestablishment**, dis·es·tab'lish·ment, *n.* The act of disestablishing; the act of withdrawing a church from its connection with the state.

disesteem, dis·es·tēm', *n.* Want of esteem; slight dislike; disregard.—*v.t.* To dislike in a moderate degree; to regard as unworthy of esteem.

disfavor, dis·fā'vẻr, *n.* A feeling of some dislike or slight displeasure; unfavorable regard; disesteem; a state of being unacceptable, or not favored, patronized, or befriended; a disobliging act.—*v.t.* To withdraw or withhold favor, friendship, or support from.

disfigure, dis·fig'ūr, *v.t.*—*disfigured, disfiguring.* To mar the external figure of; to impair the shape or form of; to injure the beauty, symmetry, or excellence of; to deface; to deform.—**disfiguration**, dis·fig'-ū·rā″shon, *n.* The act of disfiguring; disfigurement.—**disfigurement**, dis·fig'ūr·ment, *n.* The act of disfiguring or state of being disfigured; that which disfigures.—**disfigurer**, dis·fig'ū·rẻr, *n.* One who disfigures.

disforest, dis·for'est, *v.t.* Same as *Disafforest.*

disfranchise, dis·fran'chīz, *v.t.*—*disfranchised, disfranchising.* To deprive of the rights and privileges of a free citizen; to deprive of any franchise, more especially of the right of voting in elections, etc.—**disfranchisement**, dis·fran'chiz·ment, *n.* The act of disfranchising, or state of being disfranchised.

disgorge, dis·gorj', *v.t.*—*disgorged, disgorging.* [O.Fr. *desgorger*, to vomit—*dis*, and *gorge.* GORGE.] To eject or discharge from, or as from, the stomach, throat, or mouth; to vomit; to belch; to discharge violently (a volcano *disgorges* lava); to yield up, as what has been taken wrongfully; to give up; to surrender.—*v.i.* To give up plunder or ill-gotten gains.

disgrace, dis·grās', *n.* A state of being out of favor; disfavor; state of ignominy; dishonor; shame; infamy; cause of shame.—*v.t.*—*disgraced, disgracing.* To bring into disgrace; to

put out of favor; to dismiss with dishonor; to treat ignominiously; to bring shame or reproach on; to humiliate or humble; to dishonor.—**disgraceful**, dis·grās'fụl, *a.* Entailing disgrace; shameful; infamous; dishonorable.—**disgracefully**, dis·grās'-fụl·li, *adv.* In a disgraceful manner.—**disgracefulness**, dis·grās'fụl·nes, *n.* The state or quality of being disgraceful.—**disgracer**, dis·grā'sẻr, *n.* One who disgraces.

disguise, dis·gīz', *v.t.*—*disguised, disguising.* [O.Fr. *desguiser*, Fr. *déguiser*—prefix *dis*, and *guise*, way, fancy, manner. GUISE.] To conceal the ordinary guise and appearance of by an unusual habit or mask; to hide by a counterfeit appearance; to cloak by a false show, false language, or an artificial manner (anger, intentions, etc.); to change in manners or behavior by the use of spirituous liquor; to intoxicate.—*n.* A counterfeit dress; a dress intended to conceal the identity of the person who wears it; a counterfeit show; artificial or assumed language or appearance intended to deceive.—**disguisedly**, dis·gī'zed·li, *adv.* With disguise.—**disguiser**, dis·gī'zẻr, *n.* One who disguises.

disgust, dis·gust', *n.* [O.Fr. *desgoust*, Fr. *dégoût*, from L. *dis*, not, and *gustus*, taste.] Aversion to the taste of food or drink; distaste; disrelish; nausea; aversion in the mind excited by something offensive in the manners, conduct, language, or opinions of others; loathing; repugnance; strong dislike.—*v.t.* To cause to feel disgust; to excite aversion in the stomach of; to offend the taste of; to stir up loathing or repugnance in.—**disgustful**, dis·gust'fụl, *a.* Exciting the feeling of disgust.—**disgusting**, dis·gus'ting, *a.* Producing or causing disgust; nauseous; loathsome; nasty.—**disgustingly**, dis·gus'ting·li, *adv.* In a disgusting manner.

dish, dish, *n.* [A.Sax. *disc*, a dish; like D. *disch*, G. *tisch*, a table, from L. *discus*, Gr. *diskos*, a quoit or disk. DESK, DISK.] A broad open vessel made of various materials, used for serving up meat and various kinds of food at the table; the meat or provisions served in a dish; hence, any particular kind of food; the concavity of certain wheels, as those of vehicles.—*v.t.* To put in a dish after being cooked; to make (a wheel) concave in the center; to damage, ruin, completely overthrow (*slang*).—**dishcloth, dishclout**, *n.* A cloth used for washing and wiping dishes.—**dishwater**, *n.* Water in which dishes are washed.

dishabille, dis'a·bẻl, *n.* Same as *Deshabille.*

dishearten, dis·här'tn, *v.t.* To discourage; to deprive of courage; to depress the spirits of; to deject; to dispirit.

dishevel, di·shev'el, *v.t.*—*disheveled, disheveling.* [O.Fr. *descheveler*, Fr. *décheveler*, to put the hair out of order—*des* for *dis*, not, and O.Fr. *chevel*, Fr. *cheveu*, hair, from L. *capillus*, the hair of the head.] To spread the locks or tresses of loosely and negligently; to suffer (the hair) to hang negligently and uncombed.

dishonest, dis·on′est, *a.* Void of honesty, probity, or integrity; not honest, fraudulent; inclined or apt to deceive, cheat, pilfer, embezzle, or defraud; proceeding from or marked by fraud; knavish; unchaste‡.— **dishonestly,** dis·on′est·li, *adv.* In a dishonest manner; fraudulently; knavishly.—**dishonesty,** dis·on′es·ti, *n.* The opposite of honesty; want of probity or integrity; a disposition to cheat, pilfer, embezzle, or defraud; violation of trust; fraud; treachery; deviation from probity or integrity; unchastity or incontinence‡.

dishonor, dis·on′ér, *n.* The opposite of honor; want of honor; disgrace; shame; anything that disgraces.—*v.t.* To disgrace; to bring shame on; to stain the character of; to lessen in reputation; to treat with indignity; to violate the chastity of; to debauch; to refuse or decline to accept or pay (a bill of exchange).—**dishonorable,** dis·on′ér·a·bl, *a.* Shameful; disgraceful; base; bringing shame; staining the character and lessening reputation; unhonored (*Shak.*).—**dishonorableness,** dis·on′ér·a·bl·nes, *n.* Quality of being dishonorable.—**dishonorably,** dis·on′ér·a·bli, *adv.* In a dishonorable manner.

disillusion, dis·il·lū′zhon, *v.t.* To disenchant; to free from illusion. —*n.* Disenchantment.—**disillusionment,** dis·il·lū′zhon·ment, *n.*

disincline, dis·in·klīn′, *v.t.* To excite slight aversion in; to make unwilling; to cause to hang back; to alienate.

disinfect, dis·in·fekt′, *v.t.* To cleanse from infection; to purify from contagious matter.—**disinfectant,** dis·in·fek′tant, *n.* A substance that disinfects, or is used for destroying the power or means of propagating diseases which spread by infection or contagion.—**disinfection,** dis·in·fek′shon, *n.* Purification from infecting matter.

disingenuous, dis·in·jen′ū·us, *a.* Not ingenuous; not open, frank, and candid; meanly artful; insincere; sly; uncandid.—**disingenuously,** dis·in·jen′ū·us·li, *adv.* In a disingenuous manner.—**disingenuousness,** dis·in·jen′ū·us·nes, *n.* The state or quality of being disingenuous.

disinherit, dis·in·her′it, *v.t.* To cut off from hereditary right; to deprive of the right to an inheritance.—**disinheritance,** dis·in·her′i·tans, *n.* Act of disinheriting.

disintegrate, dis·in′te·grāt, *v.t.* [L. *dis*, not, and *integer*, entire, whole.] To separate the component particles of; to reduce to powder or to fragments.—**disintegration,** dis·in′te·grā″shon, *n.* The act of separating the component particles of a substance; the gradual wearing down of rocks by atmospheric influence.

disinter, dis·in·tér′, *v.t.*—*disinterred, disinterring.* To take out of a grave or out of the earth; to take out, as from a grave; to bring from obscurity into view.—**disinterment,** dis·in·-

tér′ment, *n.* The act of disinterring; exhumation.

disinterested, dis·in′tér·es·ted, *a.* Free from self-interest; having no personal interest or private advantage in a question or affair; not influenced or dictated by private advantage; unselfish; uninterested.—**disinterestedly,** dis·in′tér·es·ted·li, *adv.* In a disinterested manner.—**disinterestedness,** dis·in′tér·es·ted·nes, *n.* The state or quality of being disinterested.

disjoin, dis·join′, *v.t.* To part asunder; to disunite; to separate; to detach; to sunder.—*v.i.* To be separated; to part.—**disjoint,** dis·joint′, *v.t.* To separate, as parts united by joints; to put out of joint; to dislocate; to break the natural order and relations of; to put out of order; to derange; to render incoherent.—*v.i.* To fall in pieces.—**disjointed,** dis·join′ted, *a.* Unconnected; incoherent; out of joint; out of order; ill-joined together.—**disjointedness,** dis·join′ted·nes, *n.* State of being disjointed.—**disjointly,** dis·joint′li, *adv.* In a disjointed manner or state.

disjunct, dis·jungkt′, *a.* [L. *disjunctus*, pp. of *disjungo—dis*, and *jungo*, to join.] Disjoined; separated.—**disjunction,** dis·jungk′shon, *n.* The act of disjoining, disunion; separation.—**disjunctive,** dis·jungk′tiv, *a.* Tending to disjoin or separate; *gram.* marking separation or opposition, a term applied to a word or particle which unites words or sentences in construction, but disjoins the sense (as *neither, nor*); *logic,* applied to a proposition in which the parts are opposed to each other by means of disjunctives.—*n. Gram.* a word that disjoins (as *or, nor, neither*); *logic,* a disjunctive proposition.—**disjunctively,** dis·jungk′tiv·li, *adv.* In a disjunctive manner.

disk, disc, disk, *n.* [L. *discus,* a quoit. DESK, DISH.] A kind of ancient quoit; any flat circular plate or surface, as of a piece of metal, the face of the sun, moon, or a planet as it appears to our sight, etc.; *bot.* the whole surface of a leaf; also, the central part of a radiate compound flower, the part surrounded by what is called the ray.—**discoid,** dis′koid, *a.* Shaped like a disk; resembling a disk.

dislike, dis·līk′, *n.* A feeling the opposite of liking; disinclination; aversion; distaste; antipathy; repugnance.—*v.t.*—*disliked, disliking.* To feel dislike toward; to regard with some aversion; to have a feeling against; to disrelish.—**dislikable,**† dis·lī′ka·bl, *a.* Worthy of, or liable to dislike; distasteful; disagreeable.

dislocate, dis′lo·kāt, *v.t.*—*dislocated, dislocating.* To displace; to shift from the original site; particularly, to put out of joint; to move (a bone) from its socket, cavity, or place of articulation.—**dislocation,** dis·lo·kā′shon, *n.* The act of dislocating; particularly, the act of removing or forcing a bone from its socket; luxation; *geol.* the displacement of parts of rocks, or portions of strata, from the situations which they originally occupied.

dislodge, dis·loj′, *v.t.*—*dislodged, dislodging.* To drive from the fixed position or place occupied; to drive (enemies) from any place of hiding or defense, or from a position seized.—*v.i.* To go from a place of rest.—**dislodgment,** dis·loj′ment, *n.* The act of dislodging.

disloyal, dis·loi′al, *a.* Not loyal or true to allegiance; false to a sovereign or country; faithless; false; perfidious; treacherous; not true to the marriage bed; false in love.—**disloyally,** dis·loi′al·li, *adv.* In a disloyal manner.—**disloyalty,** dis·loi′al·ti, *n.* The character of being disloyal; want of fidelity to a sovereign; violation of allegiance; want of fidelity in love.

dismal, diz′mal, *a.* [Etym. doubtful. According to one derivation, from L. *dies malus,* an evil day; according to another, from O.Fr. *dismal,* L. *decimalis, decem,* ten, referring to the day of paying tithes.] Dark, gloomy, or cheerless to look at; depressing; sorrowful; dire; horrid; melancholy; calamitous; unfortunate; frightful; horrible.—**dismally,** diz′mal·li, *adv.* In a dismal manner.—**dismalness,** diz′mal·nes, *n.* The state of being dismal; gloominess; horror.

dismantle, dis·man′tl, *v.t.*—*dismantled, dismantling.* [O.Fr. *desmanteler, desmanteller,* lit. to deprive of cloak or mantle.] To deprive of dress; to strip; to divest; more generally, to deprive or strip (a thing) of furniture, equipments, fortifications, and the like.

dismast, dis·mast′, *v.t.* To deprive of a mast or masts; to break and carry away the masts from.

dismay, dis·mā′, *v.t.* [Same word as Sp. and Pg. *desmayar,* to fall into a swoon, but no doubt directly from the French; from prefix *dis,* and O.H.G. *magan,* to be able (=E. *may*).] To deprive entirely of strength or firmness of mind; to discourage, with some feeling of dread or consternation; to confound; to daunt; to strike aghast.—*v.i.* To be daunted; to stand aghast. (*Shak.*)—*n.* A complete giving way of boldness or spirit; loss of courage together with consternation; a yielding to fear.

dismember, dis·mem′bér, *v.t.* To divide limb from limb; to separate the members of; to mutilate; to sever and distribute the parts of; to divide into separate portions (a kingdom, etc.).—**dismemberment,** dis·mem′bér·ment, *n.* The act of dismembering.

dismiss, dis·mis′, *v.t.* [From L. *dimitto, dimissum,* to dismiss—*di, dis,* and *mitto,* as in *admit, commit,* etc.] To send away; to permit to depart, implying authority in a person to retain or keep; to discard; to remove from office, service, or employment; *law,* to reject as unworthy of notice, or of being granted.—**dismissal,** dis·mis′al, *n.* The act of dismissing; dismission; discharge; liberation; manumission.— **dismission,** dis·mish′on, *n.* The act of dismissing or sending away; leave to depart; removal from office or employment; discharge; *law,* rejection of something as unworthy of notice or of being granted.

dismount, dis·mount´, *v.i.* To alight from a horse or other animal; to come or go down.—*v.t.* To throw or remove from a horse; to unhorse; to throw or remove (cannon or other artillery) from their carriages.

disobedience, dis·o·bē´di·ens, *n.* Neglect or refusal to obey; violation of a command or prohibition; the omission of that which is commanded to be done, or the doing of that which is forbidden.—**disobedient,** dis·o·bē´di·ent, *a.* Neglecting or refusing to obey; guilty of disobedience; not observant of duty or rules prescribed by authority.—**disobediently,** dis·o·bē´di·ent·li, *adv.* In a disobedient manner.—**disobey,** dis·o·bā´, *v.t.* To neglect or refuse to obey; to omit or refuse obedience to; to transgress or violate an order or injunction.—*v.i.* To refuse obedience; to disregard orders.

disoblige, dis·o·blīj´, *v.t.* To offend by acting counter to the will or desires of; to offend by failing to oblige or do a friendly service to; to be unaccommodating to.—**disobliging,** dis·o·blī´jing, *a.* Not obliging; not disposed to gratify the wishes of another; unaccommodating.

disorder, dis·or´dėr, *n.* Want of order or regular disposition; irregularity; immethodical distribution; confusion; tumult; disturbance of the peace of society; disturbance or interruption of the functions of the animal economy or of the mind; distemper; sickness; derangement.—*v.t.* To break the order of; to derange; to throw into confusion; to disturb or interrupt the natural functions of; to produce sickness or indisposition in; to disturb as regards the reason or judgment; to craze.—**disordered,** dis·or´dėrd, *p.* and *a.* Disorderly; irregular; deranged; crazed.—**disorderliness,** dis·or´dėr·li·nes, *n.* State of being disorderly.—**disorderly,** dis·or´dėr·li, *a.* Being without proper order; marked by disorder; confused; immethodical; irregular; tumultuous; unruly; violating law and good order.

disorganize, dis·or´ga·nīz, *v.t.* To disturb or destroy organic structure or connected system in; to throw out of regular system; to throw into confusion or disorder (a government, society, etc.).—**disorganization,** dis·or´ga·ni·zā´shon, *n.*

disorient, dis·ō´ri·ent, *v.t.* To cause to lose bearings; to confuse.—**disorientate,** dis·ō´ri·en·tāt, *v.t.* To disorient.—**disorientation,** dis·ō´ri·en·ta´shon, *n.*

disown, dis·ōn´, *v.t.* To refuse to acknowledge as belonging to one's self; to refuse to own; to deny; to repudiate.

disparage, dis·par´ij, *v.t.*—**disparaged, disparaging.** [O.Fr. *desparager,* to offer to a woman, or impose on her as husband, a man unfit or unworthy; to impose unworthy conditions—prefix *des* for *dis,* and *parage,* equality, from L. par, equal,

whence also *peer, pair.*] To dishonor by a comparison with something of less value or excellence; to treat with detraction or in a depreciatory manner; to undervalue; to decry; to vilify; to lower in estimation.—**disparagement,** dis·par´ij·ment, *n.* The act of disparaging; the act of undervaluing or depreciating; detraction; what lowers in value or esteem; disgrace; dishonor.—**disparager,** dis·par´i·jėr, *n.* One who disparages.—**disparagingly,** dis·par´i·jing·li, *adv.* In a manner to disparage.

disparate, dis´pa·rit, *a.* [L. *disparatus,* pp. of *disparo,* to part, separate—*dis,* asunder, and *paro,* to prepare.] Unequal; unlike; dissimilar.—*n.* One of two or more things so unequal or unlike that they cannot be compared with each other.

disparity, dis·par´i·ti, *n.* [Fr. *disparité,* from L. *dispar,* unequal—*dis,* and *par,* equal. DISPARAGE.] Inequality; difference in degree, in age, rank, condition, or excellence; dissimilitude; unlikeness.

dispart, dis·pärt´, *v.t.* To divide into parts; to separate, sever, burst, rend. —*v.i.* To separate; to open; to cleave.—*n.* (dis´pärt). The difference between the semi-diameter of the base ring at the breech of a gun, and that of the ring at the swell of the muzzle.

dispassionate, dis·pash´on·it, *a.* Free from passion; calm; composed; unmoved by feelings; not dictated by passion; not proceeding from temper or bias; impartial.—**dispassionately,** dis·pash´on·it·li, *adv.* Without passion; calmly; coolly.

dispatch, despatch, dis·pach´, des·pach´, *v.t.* [O.Fr. *despecher,* Fr. *dépêcher,* to despatch, to expedite, from L.L. *dispedico*—L. *dis,* apart, and *pedica,* a snare, or from a L.L. *dispactare,* from L. *dis,* and *pango, pactum,* to fasten, as in *compact, a.*] To send or send away; particularly applied to the sending of messengers, agents, and letters on special business, and often implying haste; to hasten; to expedite; to speed; to send out of the world; to put to death; to slay; to kill; to perform or execute speedily; to finish.—*n.* The act of dispatching; the getting rid of or doing away with something; dismissal; riddance; speedy performance; speed; haste; expedition; a letter sent or to be sent with expedition by a special messenger; a letter on some affair of state or of public concern; a letter, message, or document, sent by some public officer on public business.—**dispatcher,** dis·pach´ėr, *n.* One who dispatches.

dispel, dis·pel´, *v.t.*—**dispelled, dispelling.** [L. *dispello*—*dis,* asunder, and *pello,* to drive, as in *compel, repel,* etc.] To scatter by force; to disperse; to dissipate; to drive away (clouds, doubts, fears, etc.).—*v.i.* To be dispersed; to disappear.

dispense, dis·pens´, *v.t.*—**dispensed, dispensing.** [L. *dispenso,* to weigh out or pay, to manage, to act as steward—*dis,* distrib., and *penso,* freq. of *pendo,*

to weigh, whence *pension, poise, expend, spend.*] To deal or divide out in parts or portions; to distribute; to administer; to apply, as laws to particular cases; to grant dispensation to; to relieve, excuse, or set free from an obligation.—*v.i.* To bargain for, grant, or receive a dispensation; to compound.—*To dispense with,* to permit the neglect or omission of, as a ceremony, an oath, and the like; to give up or do without, as services, attendance, articles of dress, etc.—**dispenser,** dis·pen´sėr, *n.* One who or that which dispenses or distributes; one who administers.—**dispensable,** dis·pen´sa·bl, *a.* Capable of being dispensed or administered; capable of being spared or dispensed with.—**dispensableness,** dis·pen´sa·bl·nes, *n.* The capability of being dispensed with.—**dispensary,** dis·pen´se·ri, *n.* A shop in which medicines are compounded and sold; a house in which medicines are dispensed to the poor, and medical advice given gratis.—**dispensation,** dis·pen·sā´shon, *n.* The act of dispensing or dealing out; the distribution of good and evil in the divine government; system established by God settling the relations of man towards him as regards religion and morality (the Mosaic *dispensation*); the granting of a license, or the license itself, to do what is forbidden by laws or canons, or to omit something which is commanded.—**dispensator,** dis·pen·sā´tėr, *n.* [L.] A dispenser.—**dispensatory,** dis·pen´sa·to·ri, *a.* Having power to grant dispensations.—*n.* A book containing the method of preparing the various kinds of medicines used in pharmacy; a pharmacopoeia.

dispeople, dis·pē´pl, *v.t.* To depopulate; to empty of inhabitants.

disperse, dis·pėrs´ *v.t.*—**dispersed, dispersing.** [Fr. *disperser,* L. *dispersus,* from *dispergo*—*di* for *dis,* distrib., and *spargo,* to scatter, whence also *sparse.*] To scatter; to cause to separate and go far apart; to dissipate; to cause to vanish. ∴ *Dissipate* is said of things that vanish or are not afterwards collected: *disperse* and *scatter* are applied to things which do not necessarily vanish, and which may again be brought together.—*v.i.* To scatter; to separate or move apart; to break up; to vanish, as fog or vapors.—**dispersedly,** dis·pėr´sed·li, *adv.* In a dispersed manner; separately.—**disperser,** dis·pėr´sėr, *n.* One who disperses.—**dispersion, dispersal** dis·pėr´shon, dis·pėr´sal, *n.* The act of dispersing or scattering; the state of being scattered or separated into remote parts; *optics,* the separation of the different colored rays of a beam of light by means of a prism, prisms of different materials causing greater or less dispersion.—**dispersive,** dis·pėr´siv, *a.* Tending to scatter or dissipate.

dispirit, dis·pir´it, *v.t.* To depress the spirits of; to deprive of courage; to discourage; to dishearten; to deject; to cast down.—**dispirited,** dis·pir´i·ted, *p.* and *a.* Discouraged;

---

fāte, fär, fâre, fat, fȧll; mē, met, hėr; pīne, pin; nōte, not, mȯve; tūbe, tub, bṳll; oil, pound.

depressed in spirits; spiritless; tame.—**dispiritedly**, dis·pir'i·ted·li, adv. Dejectedly.—**dispiritedness**, dis··pir'i·ted·nes, n. Want of courage; depression of spirits.

displace, dis·plās', v.t.—displaced, displacing. To put out of the usual or proper place; to remove from its place; to remove from any state, condition, office, or dignity.—**displacement**, dis·plās'ment, n. The act of displacing; removal; the quantity of water displaced by a body floating at rest, as a ship.

display, dis·plā', v.t. [O.Fr. desployer, Fr. déployer—des, equal to L. dis, not, and ployer, same as plier, from L. plicare, to fold, as in deploy, employ.] To spread before the view; to set in view ostentatiously; to show; to exhibit to the eyes or to the mind; to make manifest.—v.i. To make a show or display.—n. An unfolding; an exhibition of anything to the view; ostentatious show; exhibition; parade.

displease, dis·plēz', v.t.—displeased, displeasing. To offend somewhat; to dissatisfy; to annoy; to make angry, usually in a slight degree; to excite aversion in; to be disagreeable to (the taste, the sense).—**displeasure**, dis·plezh'ūr, n. The feeling of one who is displeased; dissatisfaction; anger; vexation; annoyance; that which displeases; offense.

disport, dis·pōrt', n. [O.Fr. desport, Fr. déport, properly diversion resorted to in order to divert the thoughts—prefix dis, and L. porto, to carry (whence export, etc.). Sport is an abbrev. of disport.] Play; sport; pastime.—v.i. To play; to sport.

dispose, dis·pōz', v.t.—disposed, disposing. [Fr. disposer, to dispose, arrange—prefix dis, and poser, to place (E. pose). COMPOSE.] To arrange, place out, or distribute; to set in a particular order; to apply to a particular end or purpose; to set the mind of in a particular frame; to incline.—v.i. To regulate, determine, or settle; to bargain or make terms (Shak.).—To dispose of, to part with; to alienate; to sell; to put into another's hand or power; to bestow; to do with, make use of, use, or employ (one's self, one's time, etc.); to put away or get rid of.—**disposable**, dis·pō'za·bl, a. Subject to disposal; free to be used or employed as occasion may require.—**disposal**, dis·pō'zal, n. The act of disposing; a setting or arranging; power of ordering, arranging, or distributing; government; management; power or right of bestowing; the act of selling or parting with; alienation.—**disposer**, dis·pō'zėr, n. One who or that which disposes.—**disposition**, dis·po·zish'on, n. [L. dispositio, arrangement.] The act of disposing or state of being disposed; manner in which things or the parts of a complex body are placed or arranged; order; method; distribution; arrangement; natural fitness or tendency; temper or natural constitution of the mind; inclination; propensity; Scots law, disposal or

settlement of property or effects.—**disposure**,† dis·pō'zhur, n. Disposal; management; distribution; allotment.

dispossess, dis·poz·zes', v.t. To put out of possession; to deprive of the occupancy or ownership; to dislodge; with of before the thing taken away.—**dispossession**, dis·poz·zesh'on, n. The act of dispossessing.—**dispossessor**, dis·poz·zes'ėr, n. One who dispossesses.

dispraise, dis·prāz', n. The opposite of praise; blame; censure.—v.t. dispraised, dispraising. To blame; to censure.—**dispraiser**, dis·prā'zėr, n. One who dispraises.

disproof, dis·pröf', n. See DIS-PROVE.

disproportion, dis·pro·pōr'shon, n. Want of proportion of one thing to another, or between the parts of a thing; want of symmetry; want of proper quantity; according to rules prescribed; want of suitableness or adequacy; disparity; inequality.—v.t. To violate due proportion or symmetry in.—**disproportional, disproportionate**, dis·pro·pōr'shon·al, dis·pro·pōr'shon·it, a. Not having due proportion to something else; not having proportion or symmetry of parts; unequal; inadequate.—**disproportionateness**, dis·pro·pōr'shon·it·nes, n. Want of proportion or symmetry; unsuitableness in form, bulk, or value to something else.—**disproportionately**, dis·pro·pōr'shon·it·li, adv. With want of proportion or symmetry; unsuitably with respect to form, quantity, or value; inadequately; unequally.

disprove, dis·pröv', v.t.—disproved, disproving. To prove to be false or erroneous; to confute; to refute.—**disprovable**, dis·prö'va·bl, a. Capable of being disproved or refuted.—**disproof**, dis·pröf', n. Confutation; refutation; a proving to be false or erroneous.

dispute, dis·pūt', v.i.—disputed, disputing. [L. disputo, to compute, to weigh, examine, investigate, discuss—dis, asunder, apart, and puto, to clean, prune, clear up, reckon. COMPUTE.] To contend in argument; to reason or argue in opposition; to debate; to altercate; to wrangle; to contend in opposition to a competitor.—v.t. To attempt to disprove by arguments or statements; to attempt to overthrow by reasoning; to controvert (an assertion, a claim, etc.); to call in question; to strive to maintain; to contest (to dispute every inch of ground).—n. Strife or contest in words or by arguments; a difference of opinion vigorously maintained; controversy in words; a wordy war; contention; strife; contest.—**disputer**, dis·pū'tėr, n. One who disputes or who is given to disputes.—**disputable**, dis·pū'ta·bl, a. Capable of being disputed; liable to be called in question, controverted, or contested; controvertible; disputatious (Shak.).—**disputant**, dis·pū'tant, n. One who disputes; one who argues in opposition to another; a reasoner in opposition

—a. Disputing; engaged in controversy.—**disputation**, dis·pū·tā'shon, n. [L. disputatio.] The act of disputing; controversy; verbal contest respecting the truth of some fact, opinion, proposition, or argument.—**disputatious, disputative**, dis·pū·tā'shus, dis·pū'ta·tiv, a. Inclined to dispute; fond of arguing; characterized by disputes.—**disputatiously**, dis·pū·tā'shus·li, adv. In a disputatious manner.—**disputatiousness**, dis·pū·tā'shus·nes, n.

disqualify, dis·kwol'i·fī, v.t.—disqualified, disqualifying. To make unfit; to deprive of natural power, or the qualities or properties necessary for any purpose (weakness disqualifies a person for labor); to deprive of legal capacity, power, or right; to incapacitate.—**disqualification**, dis·kwol'i·fi·kā"shon, n. The act of disqualifying; the state of being disqualified; disability; legal disability or incapacity; that which disqualifies or incapacitates.

disquiet, dis·kwī'et, n. Want of quiet; uneasiness; anxiety.—v.t. To deprive of peace, rest, or tranquility; to make uneasy or restless; to disturb, harass, fret, or vex.—a. Unquiet; restless. (Shak.).—**disquieting**, dis·kwī'e·ting, a. Tending to disquiet; disturbing the mind.—**disquietly**, dis·kwī'et·li, adv. Unquietly; in a disquieting manner.—**disquietude**, dis·kwī'e·tūd, n. Want of peace or tranquility; uneasiness; disquiet.

disquisition, dis·kwi·zish'on, n. [L. disquisitio, from disquiro, disquisitum, to investigate—dis, distrib., and quaero, quaesitum, to ask, whence query, question, inquire, etc.] A formal or systematic inquiry into any subject, by discussion of the facts and circumstances bearing on it; an argumentative inquiry; a formal discussion or treatise on any matter; dissertation; essay.

disregard, dis·ri·gärd', n. Want of regard, notice, or attention; neglect; slight.—v.t. To omit to take notice of; to neglect to observe; to pay no heed to; to treat as unworthy of regard or notice.—**disregardful**, dis·ri·gärd'ful, a. Neglectful; heedless.

disrelish, dis·rel'ish, n. Distaste; dislike of the palate; some degree of disgust; dislike of the mind; aversion; antipathy.—v.t. To dislike the taste of; to feel some disgust at.

disrepair, dis·ri·pâr', n. A state of being not in repair or good condition; state of requiring to be repaired.

disreputable, dis·rep'ū·ta·bl, a. Not reputable; disgracing reputation; dishonorable; discreditable; low; mean.—**disreputability**, dis·rep'ū·ta·bil"i·ti, n. The state of being disreputable.—**disreputably**, dis·rep'ū·ta·bli, adv. In a disreputable manner.—**disrepute**, dis·ri·pūt', n. Loss or want of reputation; disesteem; discredit; dishonor.

disrespect, dis·ri·spekt', n. Want of respect or reverence; incivility, irreverence, or rudeness; a slight or neglect.—v.t. To have no respect or esteem for; to show disrespect to.—**disrespectability**, dis·ri·spek'-

ta·bil″i·ti, n. The state or quality of being disrespectable.—**disrespectable**, dis·ri·spek′ta·bl, a. Not respectable; unworthy of respect.—**disrespectful**, dis·re·spekt′ful, a. Wanting in respect; manifesting disrespect; irreverent; uncivil.—**disrespectfully**, dis·ri·spekt′ful·li, adv. In a disrespectful manner.—**disrespectfulness**, dis·ri·spekt′ful·nes, n.

disrobe, dis·rōb′, v.t.—disrobed, disrobing. To divest of a robe; to divest of garments; to undress; to strip of covering; to uncover.

disroot, dis·rōt′, v.t. To tear up the roots of, or by the roots; to uproot.

disrupt,† dis·rupt′, v.t. [L. disruptus, pp. of disrumpo (dirumpo), to break or burst asunder—dis, asunder, and rumpo, to burst, whence rupture, etc.] To tear or rive away; to rend; to sever; to break asunder.—**disruption**, dis·rup′shon, n. [L. disruptio.] The act of rending asunder; the act of bursting and separating; breach; rent; breakup; the rupture which took place in the Established Church of Scotland in 1843, resulting in the foundation of the Free Church.—**disruptive**, dis·rup′tiv, a. Causing, or tending to cause, disruption; produced by or following on disruption.

dissatisfaction, dis·sat′is·fak″shon, n. The feeling caused by want of satisfaction; discontent; uneasiness proceeding from the want of gratification, or from disappointed wishes and expectations.—**dissatisfactory**, dis·sat′is·fak″to·ri, a. Causing dissatisfaction; giving discontent; mortifying; displeasing.—**dissatisfy**, dis·sat′is·fī, v.t.—dissatisfied, dissatisfying. To fail to satisfy; to render discontented; to displease; to excite displeasure in by frustrating wishes or expectations.

dissect, dis·sekt′, v.t. [L. disseco, dissectum—dis, asunder, and seco, sectum, to cut, whence section, segment, intersect, etc.] To divide (an animal body) with a cutting instrument, by separating the joints; to cut up (an animal or vegetable) for the purpose of examining the structure and character of the several parts, or to observe morbid affections; to anatomize; fig. to analyze for the purpose of criticism; to describe with minute accuracy.—**dissection**, dis·sek′shon, n. The act or art of dissecting or anatomizing.—**dissector**, dis·sek′tėr, n. One who dissects; an anatomist.

disseize, dis·sēz′, v.t.—disseized, disseizing. [Prefix dis, neg., and seize; Fr. dessaisir, to dispossess.] Law, to dispossess wrongfully; to deprive of actual seizin or possession: with of before the thing.—**disseizee**, dis·sē·zē′, n. One who is disseized.—**disseizin**, dis·sē′zin, n. The act of disseizing.—**disseizor**, dis·sē·zėr′, n. One who dispossesses another.

dissemble, dis·sem′bl, v.t.—dissembled, dissembling. [O.Fr. dissembler (Fr. dissimuler), from L. dissimulo—dis, and simulo, to make like, to simulate, from similis, like.—ASSEMBLE, SIMILAR. Dissimulate is the

same word.] To hide under an assumed manner; to conceal or disguise by a false outward show; to hide by false pretenses (to dissemble love, hate, opinions, etc.).—v.i. To try to appear other than reality; to put on an assumed manner or outward show; to conceal the real fact, motives, intention, or sentiments under some pretense.—**dissembler**, dis·sem′blėr, n. One who dissembles; one who conceals his real thoughts or feelings.

disseminate, dis·sem′i·nāt, v.t.—disseminated, disseminating. [L. dissemino, disseminatum, to scatter seed—dis, and semen, seed.] To spread by diffusion or dispersion; to diffuse; to spread abroad among people; to cause to reach as many persons as possible (religious doctrines, knowledge, etc.).—**dissemination**, dis·sem′i·nā″shon, n. The act of disseminating.—**disseminative**, dis·sem′i·nā·tiv, a. Tending to disseminate or become disseminated.—**disseminator**, dis·sem′i·nā·tėr, n. One who disseminates.

dissent, dis·sent′, v.i. [L. dissentio, to think otherwise, to dissent—dis, asunder, and sentio, to perceive, as in consent, resent, etc. SENSE.] To disagree in opinion; to differ; to think in a different or contrary manner; with from; eccles. to differ from an established church in regard to doctrines, rites, or government.—n. Difference of opinion; disagreement; declaration of disagreement in opinion; eccles. separation from an established church.—**dissension**, dis·sen′shon, n. [L. dissensio.] Disagreement in opinion, usually a disagreement producing warm debates or angry words; strife; discord; quarrel; breach of friendship and union.—**dissentious**, dis·sen′shus, a. Disposed to dissension or discord.—**dissentaneous**, dis·sen·tā′nē·us, a. Disagreeing; inconsistent.—**dissenter**, dis·sen′tėr, n. One who dissents; one who differs in opinion, or one who declares his disagreement; eccles. one who separates from the service and worship of any established church.—**dissentient**, dis·sen′shi·ent, a. Disagreeing; declaring dissent; voting differently.—n. One who disagrees and declares his dissent.—**dissenting**, dis·sen′ting, p. and a. Disagreeing in opinion; having the character of dissent; belonging to or connected with a body of dissenters.

dissepiment, dis·sep′i·ment, n. [L. dissepimentum—dis, asunder, and sepio, to enclose, from sepes, a hedge.] A kind of small partition in certain hollow parts of animals and plants; one of the partitions in the ovary of some plants formed by the sides of cohering carpels.

dissertation, dis·sėr·tā′shon, n. [L. dissertatio, from disserto, a freq. of dissero, to argue, discuss—dis, asunder, and sero, to join, from root of series.] A formal discourse, intended to illustrate or elucidate a subject; a written essay, treatise, or disquisition.—**dissertator**, dis′sėr·

tā·tėr, n. One who writes dissertations.

disserve, dis·sėrv′, v.t. To do the reverse of a service to; to do an injury or ill turn to.—**disservice**, n. An ill turn or injury; something done to one's injury.

dissever, dis·sev′ėr, v.t. To part in two; to divide asunder; to separate; to disunite;—**disseverance, disseverment**, dis·sev′ėr·ans, dis·sev′ėr·ment, n. The act of dissevering; separation.

dissident, dis′si·dent, a. [L. dissidens, dissidentis, ppr. of dissideo, to disagree—dis, asunder, and sedeo, to sit; seen also in supersede, sedentary, session, etc.] Dissenting; specifically, dissenting from an established church.—n. One who dissents from others; a dissenter; one who separates from an established religion.—**dissidence**, dis′si·dens, n. Disagreement; dissent; nonconformity.

dissilient, dis·sil′i·ent, a. [L. dissilio, to leap asunder—dis, and salio, to leap, whence salient.] Starting asunder; bursting and opening with an elastic force, as the dry pod or capsule of a plant.

dissimilar, dis·sim′i·ler, a. Not similar; unlike, either in nature, properties, or external form.—**dissimilarity**, dis·sim′i·lar″i·ti, n. Want of similarity; unlikeness; want of resemblance.—**dissimilation**, dis·sim·i·lā·shon, n. The act or process of rendering dissimilar or different; philol. the change of a sound to another and a different sound when otherwise two similar sounds would come together or very close to each other.—**dissimilitude**, dis·si·mil′i·tūd, n. [L. dissimilitudo.] Unlikeness; want of resemblance.

dissimulation, dis·sim′ū·lā″shon, n. [L. dissimulatio, from dissimulo, dissimulatum, to feign that a thing is not what it is—dis, and simulo, to make like, from similis, like. DISSEMBLE.] The act or practice of dissembling, usually from a mean or unworthy motive; a hiding under a false appearance; false pretension; hypocrisy.—**dissimulate**, dis·sim′ū·lāt, v.i. To dissemble; to make pretense; to feign.—**dissimulator**, dis·sim′ū·lā″tėr, n. One who dissimulates or dissembles.

dissipate, dis′si·pāt, v.t.—dissipated, dissipating. [L. dissipo, dissipatum—dis, asunder, and the rare sipo, supo, to throw, allied probably to E. verb to sweep.] To scatter, to disperse, to drive away (mist, care, energy, etc.); to scatter in wasteful extravagance; to waste. ∴ Syn. under DISPERSE.—v.i. To scatter, disperse, separate into parts and disappear; to vanish; to be wasteful or dissolute in the pursuit of pleasure.—**dissipated**, dis′si·pā·ted, a. Given to extravagance in the expenditure of property; devoted to pleasure and vice; dissolute.—**dissipation**, dis·si·pā′shon, n. The act of dissipating; the insensible loss of the minute particles of a body, which fly off, so that the body is diminished or may altogether disappear; indulgence in dissolute and irregular courses; a reckless and vicious pursuit of pleasure; dissolute conduct.—*Dissipation of energy*, the running down of energy from higher to lower or less available forms, a process constantly going on in nature, and tending to the ultimate production of an earth uninhabitable by man as at present constituted.

dissociate, dis·sō'shi·āt, *v.t.*—*dissociated, dissociating*. [L. *dissocio, dissociatum*—*dis*, and *socio*, to unite, from *socius*, a companion. SOCIAL.] To separate or take apart; to disunite; to part.—**dissociable,**† dis·sō'shi·a·bl, *a.* Not well associated, united, or assorted; not sociable; incongruous; not reconcilable.—**dissocial**, dis·sō'shal, *a.* Disinclined to or unsuitable for society; not social.—**dissociation**, dis·sō·shi·ā"shon, *n.* The act of dissociating; a state of separation; disunion; *chem.* the decomposition of a compound substance into its primary elements.—**dissociative**, dis·sō'shi·ā·tiv, *a.* Tending to dissociate; *chem.* resolving or reducing a compound to its primary elements.

dissoluble, dis·sol'ū·bl, *a.* [L. *dissolubilis*. DISSOLVE.] Capable of being dissolved or melted; having its parts separable, as by heat or moisture; susceptible of decomposition or decay.—**dissolubility**, dis·sol'ū·bil'i·ti, *n.* The state or quality of being dissoluble.

dissolute, dis'so·lūt, *a.* [L. *dissolutus*, pp. of *dissolvo*. DISSOLVE.] Loose in behavior and morals; given to vice or profligacy; debauched; devoted to or occupied in dissipation.—**dissolutely**, dis'so·lūt·li, *adv.* In a dissolute manner; profligately; in dissipation or debauchery.—**dissoluteness**, dis'so·lūt·nes, *n.* The state or character of being dissolute; looseness of manners and morals, vicious indulgence in pleasure, as in intemperance and debauchery; dissipation.—**dissolution**, dis·so·lū'shon, *n.* [L. *dissolutio*, a breaking up, a loosening, from *dissolvo*.] The act of dissolving, liquefying, or changing from a solid to a fluid state by heat; liquefaction; the reduction of a body into its smallest parts, or into very minute parts; the separation of the parts of a body by natural decomposition; decomposition; death; the separation of the soul and body; the separation of the parts which compose a connected system or body; the breaking up of an assembly, or the putting an end to its existence.

dissolve, diz·zolv', *v.t.*—*dissolved, dissolving*. [L. *dissolvo*, to break up, to separate—*dis*, asunder, and *solvo, solutum*, to loose, to free, whence also *solve, soluble, solution, absolve*, etc.] To melt; to liquefy; to convert from a solid or fixed state to a fluid state, by means of heat or moisture; to disunite, break up, separate, or loosen; to destroy any connected system or body (parliament, a government); to break or make no longer binding (an alliance, etc.); to solve, explain, or resolve (doubts); to destroy the power of or

render ineffectual (a spell or enchantment); to destroy or consume (O.T.).—*v.i.* To melt; to be converted from a solid to a fluid state; to fall asunder; to crumble; to waste away; to be decomposed; to be dismissed; to separate; to break up; *motion pictures*, to fade out one shot while fading in the next, causing the two shots to overlap during the process.—*n. Motion pictures*, a scene made using the process of dissolving.—**dissolvable**, diz·zol'va·bl, *a.* Capable of being melted; capable of being converted into a fluid.—**dissolvent**, diz·zol'vent, *a.* Having power to melt or dissolve.—*n.* Anything that dissolves; a substance that has the power of converting a solid substance into a fluid, or of separating its parts so that they mix with a liquid.—**dissolver**, diz·zol'vėr, *n.* One who or that which dissolves.

dissonance, dis'so·nans, *n.* [Fr. *dissonance*, L. *dissonantia*, discordance—*dis*, asunder, and *sono*, to sound. SOUND.] Discord; a mixture or union of harsh, inharmonious sounds; incongruity; inconsistency.—**dissonant**, dis'so·nant, *a.* Discordant; harsh; jarring; unharmonious; unpleasant to the ear; disagreeing; incongruous.

dissuade, dis·swād', *v.t.*—*dissuaded, dissuading*. [L. *dissuadeo*, to advise against—*dis*, not, and *suadeo*, to advise.] To advise or exhort against; to attempt to draw or divert from a measure by reasons or offering motives; to divert by persuasion; to turn from a purpose by argument; to render averse; the opposite of *persuade*.—**dissuader**, dis·swā'dėr, *n.* One who dissuades.—**dissuasion**, dis·swā'zhon, *n.* Advice or exhortation in opposition to something; dehortation; the opposite of *persuasion*.—**dissuasive**, dis·swā'siv, *a.* Tending to dissuade.—*n.* Reason, argument, or counsel, employed to deter one from a measure or purpose; that which tends to dissuade.—**dissuasively**, dis·swā'siv·li, *adv.* In a dissuasive manner.

dissyllable, dis'sil·la·bl, *n.* [Gr. *dis*, twice, and *syllabe*, a syllable.] A word consisting of two syllables only.—**dissyllabic**, dis·sil·lab'ik, *a.* Consisting of two syllables only.

distaff, dis'taf, *n.* [A.Sax. *dist.f*, that is, *dis-* or *dise-staff*—*dis-*=O.E. *dise*, to put the flax on the distaff, allied to L.G. *diesse*, the flax on the distaff, G. *dusse*, tow, oakum.] The staff to which a bunch of flax or tow is tied, and from which the thread is drawn to be spun by the spindle; woman's work; woman or women.

distain, dis·tān', *v.t.* [O.Fr. *desteindre*, Fr. *déteindre*, to cause to lose color—*des* for L. *dis*, not, and *teindre*, from L. *tingere*, to stain.] To stain; to discolor; to sully, defile, tarnish.

distal, dis'tal, *a.* [From *distant*: formed on the type of *central*.] Applied to the end of a bone, limb, or organ in plants and animals farthest removed from the point of attach-

ment or insertion; situated away from or at the extremity most distant from the center.

distance, dis'tans, *n.* [Fr. *distance*, L. *distantia*, from *disto*, to stand apart—*dis*, apart, and *sto*, to stand. STATE, STATUE, etc.] An interval or space between two objects; the length of the shortest line which intervenes between things that are separate; remoteness of place; space of time, past or future; ideal space or separation, as between things that differ from each other; the remoteness or ceremonious avoidance of familiarity which respect requires; the remoteness or reserve which one assumes from being offended, from dislike, etc.; *mus.* the interval between two notes; *horse-racing*, a length of 240 yards from the winning post, marked by a post.—*v.t.*—*distanced, distancing*. To place at a distance or remote; to leave at a great distance; behind; to outdo or excel greatly.—**distant**, dis'tant, *a.* [L. *distans*, standing apart, ppr. of *disto*.] Separate or apart, the intervening space being of any indefinite extent; remote in place; in time, past or future; in a line of succession or descent; in natural connection or consanguinity; in kind or nature, etc.; as if remote or far off; hence, slight; faint (a *distant* resemblance); characterized by haughtiness, coldness, indifference, or disrespect; reserved; shy.—**distantly**, dis'tant·li, *adv.* Remotely; at a distance; with reserve.

distaste, dis·tāst', *n.* Aversion of the taste; dislike of food or drink; disrelish; disinclination; a want of liking (a *distaste* for rural sports).—**distasteful**, dis·tāst'ful, *a.* Causing distaste; unpleasant to the taste or liking; disagreeable; slightly repulsive.—**distastefully**, dis·tāst'ful·li, *adv.* In a distasteful manner.—**distastefulness**, dis·tāst'ful·nes, *n.* The state or character of being distasteful.

distemper, dis·tem'pėr, *n.* Any morbid state of an animal body or of any part of it; derangement of the animal economy; a disorder; malady; a disease of young dogs, commonly considered as a catarrhal disorder.—*v.t.* To derange the bodily functions of; to deprive of temper or moderation; to ruffle; to disturb; to make ill-humored.

distemper, dis·tem'pėr, *n.* [It. *distemperare*, to dissolve or mix with liquid.] *Painting*, a preparation of opaque color, ground with size and water; tempera; a kind of painting in which the pigments are mixed with size, and chiefly used for scene painting and interior decoration.

distend, dis·tend', *v.t.* [L. *distendo*—*dis*, asunder, and *tendo*, to tend, as in *extend, contend*. TENT.] To stretch or swell out by force acting from within; to dilate; to expand; to swell; to puff out (a bladder, the lungs).—*v.i.* To become inflated or distended; to swell.—**distensibility**, dis·ten'si·bil'i·ti, *n.* The quality or capacity of being distensible.—**distensible,** dis·ten′si·bl, *a.* Capable of being distended or dilated.—**distention, distension,** dis-ten′shon, *n.* [L. *distentio.*] The act of distending; the state of being distended; extent or space occupied by the thing distended.

distich, dis′tik, *n.* [Gr. *distichon—di,* twice, and *stichos,* a row, a line, a verse.] A couplet; a couple of verses or poetic lines making complete sense.—**distichous,** dis′ti·kus, *a.* Having two rows, or disposed in two rows, as the grains in an ear of barley.

distill, distil, dis·til′, *v.i.—distilled, distilling.* [Fr. *distiller,* from L. *destillo,* to trickle down—*de,* down, and *stillo,* to drop, from *stilla,* a drop.] To drop; to fall in drops or in a small stream; to trickle; to use a still; to practice distillation.—*v.t.* To yield or give forth in drops or a small stream; to let fall in drops; to drop; to obtain or extract by distillation; to subject to the process of distillation.—**distillable,** dis·til′a·bl, *a.* Capable of being distilled; fit for distillation.—**distillate,** dis′til·āt, *n.* A fluid distilled, and found in the receiver of a distilling apparatus.—**distillation,** dis·ti·lā′shon, *n.* The act of distilling or falling in drops; the volatilization and subsequent condensation of a liquid by means of an alembic, or still and refrigeratory, or of a retort and receiver; the operation of extracting spirit from a substance by evaporation and condensation.—**distiller,** dis·til′ẻr, *n.* One who distills; one whose occupation is to extract spirit by distillation.—**distillery,** dis·til′ẻr·i, *n.* The act or art of distilling; the building and works where distillation is carried on.

distinct, dis·tingkt′, *a.* [L. *distinctus,* pp. of *distinguo.* DISTINGUISH.] Separated or distinguished by some mark, note, or character; marked out; not the same in number or kind; different; having well-marked characteristics; standing clearly or boldly out; well defined; obvious; plain; unmistakable.—**distinction,** dis·tingk′shon, *n.* [L. *distinctio.*] The act of separating or distinguishing; that which distinguishes or marks as different; a note or mark of difference; distinguishing quality; eminence or superiority; elevation or honorable estimation; that which confers or marks eminence or superiority; a title or honor of some kind.—**distinctive,** dis·tingk′tiv, *a.* Marking or indicating distinction or difference.—**distinctively,** dis·tingk′tiv·li, *adv.* In a distinctive manner.—**distinctiveness,** dis·tingk′tiv·nes, *n.* The state or quality of being distinctive; distinctive character.—**distinctly,** dis·tingkt′li, *adv.* In a distinct manner; clearly; obviously; plainly; precisely.—**distinctness,** dis·tingkt′nes, *n.* The quality or state of being distinct; clearness; precision.

distinguish, dis·ting′gwish, *v.t.* [L. *distinguo,* to mark off, to distinguish—*di* for *dis,* asunder, and *stinguo,* to mark. STIGMA.] To mark or set apart as different or separate from others; to perceive or recognize the individuality of; to note as differing from something else by some mark or quality; to know or ascertain difference by the senses or the intellect; to classify or divide by any mark or quality which constitutes difference; to separate by definitions; to separate from others by some mark of honor or preference; to make eminent or known; to signalize.—*v.i.* To make a distinction; to find or show the difference.—**distinguishable,** dis-ting′gwish·a·bl, *a.* Capable of being distinguished or recognized; capable of being defined or classified; worthy of note or special regard.—**distinguishableness,** dis·ting′gwish·a·bl·nes, *n.* State of being distinguishable.—**distinguishably,** dis-ting′gwish·a·bli, *adv.* So as to be distinguished.—**distinguished,** dis-ting′gwisht, *p.* and *a.* Separated from others by superior or extraordinary qualities; eminent; extraordinary; transcendent; noted; famous; celebrated.—**distinguishing,** dis·ting′gwish·ing, *a.* Constituting difference or distinction from everything else; peculiar; characteristic.

distort, dis·tort′, *v.t.* [L. *distorqueo, distortum—dis,* asunder, and *torqueo,* to twist, as in *contort* (which see).] To twist out of natural or regular shape; to force or put out of the true bent or direction; to bias (the judgment); to wrest from the true meaning; to pervert.—**distorted,** dis·tor′ted, *p.* and *a.* Twisted out of natural or regular shape; shaped abnormally or awry.—**distortion,** dis·tor′shon, *n.* The act of distorting; a twisting or writhing motion; an unnatural direction of parts from whatever cause, as a curved spine, a wry mouth, squinting, etc.; a perversion of the true meaning of words.

distract, dis·trakt′, *v.t.* [L. *distraho, distractum,* to pull asunder, to perplex—*dis,* asunder, and *traho,* to draw; whence *tractable, trace,* etc.] To draw apart or pull separate‡; to turn or draw from any object or point; to divert toward various other objects (the attention); to perplex, confound, or harass (the mind); to disorder the reason of; to render insane or frantic.—**distracted,** dis·trak′ted, *p.* and *a.* Disordered in intellect; deranged; perplexed; crazy; frantic.—**distractedly,** dis·trak′ted·li, *adv.* In a distracted manner; insanely; wildly.—**distraction,** dis·trak′shon, *n.* The act of distracting; the state of being distracted; confusion from multiplicity of objects crowding on the mind and calling the attention different ways; perplexity; embarrassment; madness; frenzy; insanity; extreme folly; extreme perturbation or agony of mind, as from pain or grief; anything giving the mind a new and less onerous occupation; a diversion.—**distractive,** dis·trak′tiv, *a.* Causing perplexity.

distrain, dis·trān′, *v.t.* [O.Fr. *destraindre,* from L. *distringere,* to draw apart, bind, molest, later to exact a pledge—*dis,* asunder, and *stringere,* to strain (as in *constrain, restrain*). STRAIN. Akin *distress, district.*] To seize or take possession of (*Shak.*)‡; specifically, *law,* to seize, as goods and chattels, for debt.—**distrainable,** dis·trā′na·bl, *a.* Capable of being or liable to be distrained.—**distrainer, distrainor,** dis·trā′nẻr, *n.* He who seizes goods for debt or service.—**distraint,** dis·trānt′, *n.* A distress or distraining.

distrait, dis·trā′, *a.* [Fr.] Abstracted; absent minded; inattentive.

distraught, dis·trạt′, *a.* [Old pp. of *distract.*] Distracted; perplexed.

distress, dis·tres′, *n.* [O.Fr. *destresse, destrece,* oppression, from *destrecer,* to oppress, from a hypothetical L.L. *districtiare,* from L. *districtus,* pp. of *distringo,* to draw apart, hinder, molest. DISTRAIN.] Extreme pain; anguish of body or mind; that which causes suffering; affliction; calamity; adversity; misery; a state of danger; *law,* the act of distraining, the seizure of any personal chattel as a pledge for the payment of rent or debt, or the satisfaction of a claim.—*v.t.* To afflict with pain or anguish; to harass; to grieve; to perplex; to make miserable.—**distressful,** dis·tres′ful, *a.* Inflicting or bringing distress; calamitous; proceeding from pain or anguish; indicating distress.—**distressfully,** dis·tres′ful·li, *adv.* In a distressful manner.—**distressing,** dis·tres′ing, *a.* Very afflicting; affecting with severe pain.—**distressingly,** dis·tres′ing·li, *adv.* In a distressing manner; with great pain.

distribute, dis·trib′ūt, *v.t.—distributed, distributing.* [L. *distribuo, distributum,* to divide, distribute—*dis,* and *tribuo,* to give. TRIBUTE.] To divide among two or more; to deal out; to give or bestow in parts or portions; to dispense; to administer; to divide, as into classes, orders, genera; *printing,* to separate types and place them in their proper boxes or compartments in the cases.—**distributable,** dis·tri′bū·ta·bl, *a.* Capable of being distributed.—**distributer,** dis·trib′ū·tẻr, *n.* One who or that which distributes or deals out; a dispenser.—**distribution,** dis·tri·bū′shon, *n.* [L. *distributio.*] The act of distributing or dealing out; the act of dispensing or administering; the act of separating into distinct parts or classes; *printing,* the separating of the types and arranging of them in their proper places in the case; the manner of being distributed or spread over the earth (the *distribution* of animals or plants).—**distributive,** dis·trib′ū·tiv, *a.* Serving to distribute; expressing separation or division; specifically, *gram.* an epithet applied to certain words (as *each, every*) which denote the persons or things that make a number taken separately and singly.—*n. Gram.* a distributive word, as *each* and *every.*—**distributively,** dis·trib′ū·tiv·li, *adv.* In a distributive manner.

district, dis′trikt, *n.* [L.L. *districtum,*

a district subject to one jurisdiction, from L. *districtus*, pp. of *distringo*. DISTRAIN.] A part of a country, city, etc., distinctly defined or marked out; a portion of country without very definite limits; a tract; a region, locality, quarter.—**district attorney,** *n.* The prosecuting attorney of a judicial district.

distrust, dis·trust′, *v.t.* To doubt or suspect the truth, fidelity, firmness, sincerity, reality, sufficiency, or goodness of; to have no faith, reliance, or confidence in; to be suspicious of. —*n.* Doubt or suspicion; want of confidence, faith, or reliance.—**distrustful,** dis·trust′fụl, *a.* Apt to distrust; wanting confidence; suspicious; mistrustful; apprehensive; not confident; diffident; modest.—**distrustfully,** dis·trust′fụl·li, *adv.* In a distrustful manner.—**distrustfulness,** dis·trust′fụl·nes, *n.* The state or quality of being distrustful.

disturb, dis·tėrb′, *v.t.* [L. *disturbo*, to throw into disorder—*dis*, asunder, and *turbo*, to confuse, from *turba*, a crowd, tumult, whence also *turbid*, *turbulent*.] To excite from a state of rest or tranquillity; to stir; to move; to discompose; to agitate; to throw into confusion or disorder; to excite uneasiness in the mind of; to disquiet; to render uneasy; to ruffle; to move from any regular course, operation, or purpose; to make irregular; to interfere with; to interrupt.—**disturbance,** dis·tėr′bans, *n.* The act of disturbing; interruption of peace or quiet; interruption of a settled state of things; violent change; derangement; perturbation; agitation; disorder of thoughts; confusion; agitation in the body politic; a disorder; a tumult.—**disturber,** dis·tėr′bėr, *n.* One who disturbs; one who causes tumults or disorders.

disunion, dis·ūn′yon, *n.* A state of not being united; separation; disjunction; a breach of concord and its effect; contention; dissension.—**disunite,** dis·ū·nīt′, *v.t.* To separate; to disjoin; to part; to set at variance; to raise dissension between.—*v.i.* To fall asunder; to become separate.

disuse, dis·ūs′, *n.* Cessation of use, practice, or exercise.—*v.t.* (dis·ūz′). To cease to use; to neglect or omit to practice; to disaccustom.

disyoke, dis·yōk′, *v.t.* To unyoke; to free from any trammel. (*Tenn.*)

ditch, dich, *n.* [A softened form of *dike* (comp. *church* and *kirk*, etc.), both being formerly applied to the embankment as well as to the ditch. DIKE, DIG.] A trench in the earth made by digging, particularly a trench for draining wet land, or for making a fence to guard enclosures, or for preventing an enemy from approaching a town or fortress; any long artificial channel dug to contain water.—*v.i.* To dig or make a ditch or ditches.—*v.t.* To dig a ditch or ditches in; to drain by a ditch; to surround with a ditch.—**ditcher,** dich′ėr, *n.* One who digs ditches.

ditheism, dī′thē·izm, *n.* [Gr. *di*, double, and *theos*, a god.] The doctrine of the existence of two gods, especially that on which the old Persian religion was founded, or the opposition of the two (good and evil) principles; dualism; Manicheism.—**ditheist,** dī′thē·ist, *n.* One who believes in ditheism.—**ditheistic,** dī·thē·is′tik, *a.* Pertaining to ditheism.

dither, diTH′ėr, *n.* [Origin uncertain] Trembling; quivering; a state of great agitation; confusion. —*v.i.* To act hesitantly, irresolutely, or in a disturbed manner.

dithyramb, dith′i·ramb, *n.* [Gr. *dithyrambos*.] A hymn among the ancient Greeks, originally in honor of Bacchus, afterward of other gods, composed in an elevated or wildly enthusiastic style; hence, any poem of an impetuous and irregular character.—**dithyrambic,** *a.* Pertaining to or resembling a dithyramb; wild; enthusiastic.

dittany, dit′a·ni, *n.* [L. *dictamnus*, from growing abundantly on Mount *Dicte* in Crete.] A perennial plant found in the Mediterranean region, with large white or rose-colored flowers in terminal racemes, and having numerous glands containing a fragrant and very volatile oil.

ditto, dit′tō. [It. *ditto*, from L. *dictum*, something said. DICTION.] A word used chiefly in lists, accounts, etc., to save writing, equivalent to same as above, or aforesaid: often contracted into *Do*.; a symbol, (″).

ditty, dit′i, *n.* [O.Fr. *ditté*, story, poem, etc., from L. *dictatum*, pp. of *dictare*, to dictate. DICTION.] A song; a sonnet; a little poem to be sung.

diuretic, dī·ū·ret′ik, *a.* [Gr. *diourētikos*, from *dia*, through, and *ouron*, urine.] *Med.* having the power to excite the secretion of urine; tending to produce discharges of urine.—*n.* A medicine that excites the secretion of urine or increases its discharge.— **diuresis,** dī·ū·rē′sis, *n.* An excessive flow of urine.

diurnal, dī·ėr′nal, *a.* [L. *diurnalis*, from *diurnus*, daily, from *dies*, a day, whence also *dial*, *diary*, etc. *Journal* is the same word.] Relating to a day; pertaining to the daytime; happening daily.—**diurnally,** dī·ėr′nal·li, *adv.*

diva, dē′va, *n.* [It. from L. *diva*, goddess.] A great woman singer; a prima donna.

divan, di·van′, *n.* [Per. *divan*, a collection of writings, customhouse, council, raised seat.] Among the Turks and other orientals, a court of justice; a council; council chamber; a state or reception room; a kind of coffeehouse; a cushioned seat standing against the wall of a room; a collection of poems by one author.

divaricate, dī·var′i·kāt, *v.i.* [L. *divarico*, *divaricatum*, to spread asunder —*di* for *dis*, asunder, and *varico*, to straddle.] To fork; to part into two branches; *bot.* to diverge at an obtuse angle.—*v.t.* To divide into two branches; to cause to branch apart.— **divarication,** dī·var′i·kā″shon, *n.* A separation into two branches; a forking.

dive, dīv, *v.i.*—*dived*, *diving*. [A.Sax. *dȳfan*, to dive = Icel. *dȳfa*, to dip, to dive; akin *deep*, *dip*.] To descend or plunge into water head first; to go under water for the purpose of executing some work; to go deep into any subject; to plunge into any business or condition; to sink; to penetrate.—*n.* The act of diving; a plunge.—**diver,** dī′vėr, *n.* One who dives; one of a family of marine swimming birds, with short wings and tail, legs far back and toes completely webbed, preying upon fish, which they pursue under water. —**diving,** dī′ving, *n.* The act or practice of descending into water; especially, the art of descending below the surface of the water, and remaining there for some time, in order to remove objects from the bottom, etc.—**diving bell,** *n.* An apparatus, originally bell shaped, in which persons descend into the water and remain for a length of time, fresh air being pumped into the bell by assistants above.

diverge, di·vėrj′, *v.i.*—*diverged*, *diverging*. [L. *di* for *dis*, asunder, and *vergo*, to incline. VERGE.] To tend or proceed from a common point in different directions; to deviate from a given course or line: opposed to *converge*; to differ or vary.—**divergence, divergency,** di·vėr′jens, di·vėr′jen·si, *n.* The act of diverging; a receding from each other; a going farther apart.—**divergent,** di·vėr′jent, *a.* Diverging; separating or receding from each other, as lines which proceed from the same point.

divers, dī′vėrz, *a.* [Fr. *divers*, from L. *diversus*, diverse, turned away, from *di* for *dis*, asunder, and *verto*, *versum*, to turn. VERSE.] Different; various; several; sundry; more than one, but not a great number.— **diverse,** di·vėrs′ or dī′vėrs, *a.* [L. *diversus*.] Different; differing; unlike; not the same.—**diversely,** dī·vėrs′li, *adv.* In a diverse manner; in different directions.—**diversification,** di·vėr′si·fi·kā″shon, *n.* The act of diversifying; the state of being diversified.—**diversified,** di·vėr′si·fīd, *p.* and *a.* Distinguished by various forms, or by a variety of objects.— **diversiform,** di·vėr′si·form, *a.* Of a different form; of various forms.— **diversify,** di·vėr′si·fī, *v.t.*—*diversified*, *diversifying*. [Fr. *diversifier*—L. *diversus*, and *facio*, to make.] To make diverse or various in form or qualities; to give variety or diversity to; to variegate.—**diversion,** di·vėr′zhon, *n.* The act of diverting or turning aside from any course; that which diverts or turns the mind or thoughts away; what turns or draws the mind from care, business, or study, and thus relaxes and amuses; sport; play; pastime; a feint or other movement made to mislead an enemy as to the real point of attack.— **diversity,** di·vėr′si·ti, *n.* [L. *diversitas*.] The state of being diverse; difference; dissimilitude; unlikeness; multiplicity with difference; variety; distinctness or separateness of being, as opposed to *identity*.—**divert,** di·vėrt′, *v.t.* [L. *diverto*, *diversum*, to turn aside.] To turn off from any

ch, *chain*; *ch*, Sc. *loch*; g, *go*; j, *job*; ng, *sing*; TH, *then*; th, *thin*; w, *wig*; hw, *whig*; zh, *azure*.

course, direction, or intended application; to turn aside (to *divert* a stream, traffic, etc.); to turn from business or study; to turn from care or serious thoughts: hence, to please; to amuse; to entertain. ∴ Syn. under AMUSE.—**diverter**, di·vêr′têr, *n.* One who or that which diverts.—**diverting**, di·vêr′ting, *a.* Causing diversion; amusing; entertaining.—**divertingly**, di·vêr′ting·li, *adv.* In a diverting manner.

Dives, dī′vēz, *n.* [L. *dives*, rich.] Name in Biblical parable; type of the rich man.

divest, di·vest′, *v.t.* [O.Fr. *devestir*, from L. *devestio*, to undress—*de*, not, and *vestio*, to clothe, from *vestis*, a garment, whence also *vest*, *vesture*.] To strip; to strip of dress or of anything that surrounds or attends; to deprive: with *of* before the thing removed.

divide, di·vīd′, *v.t.*—*divided, dividing.* [L. *divido*, to divide—*di* for *dis*, asunder, and *vid*, a root signifying to cut or separate, akin to Skr. *vyadh*, to penetrate.] To part or separate into pieces; to cut or otherwise separate into two or more parts; to cause to be separate; to keep apart, as by a partition or by an imaginary line or limit; to make partition of among a number; to disunite in opinion or interest; to set at variance.—*v.i.* To become separated; to part; to open; to cleave; to vote by the division of a legislative house, as in the British Parliament, into two parts, that is, the "ayes" dividing from the "noes."—*n.* The watershed of a district or region.—**dividable**, di·vī′da·bl, *a.* Capable of being divided.—**divided**, di·vī′ded, *p.* and *a.* Parted, separated, or disunited; showing divisions; at variance in feeling.—**dividend**, div′i-dend, *n.* [L., lit. a thing to be divided.] A sum or a number to be divided; the profit or gain made by a corporation and which falls to be divided among the stockholders according to the stock of each; the sum that falls to the share of each; the share of the fund realized from the effects of a bankrupt, and apportioned according to the amount of the debt of each creditor; a share of surplus allocated by an insurance company to policy holders.—**divider**, di·vī′dêr, *n.* One who or that which divides; *pl.* an instrument for dividing lines, etc.; compasses.

divi-divi, div′i-div′i, *n.* The native and commercial name of a tropical American tree and its remarkably curled pods which yield tannic acid and gallic acid.

divine, di·vīn′, *a.* [L. *divinus*, divine, religious, divinely inspired, godlike, from *divus*, divine, a deity or divinity. DEITY.] Pertaining to God, or to a heathen deity or false god; partaking of the nature of God; godlike; heavenly; sacred; holy; excellent in the highest degree; apparently above what is human; relating to divinity or theology.—*Divine right*, the claim set up by sovereigns to the unqualified obedience of their subjects on the

assumption that they themselves were appointed by God to rule, and responsible to him only for their acts.—*n.* A minister of the gospel; a priest; a clergyman; a theologian.—*v.t.*—*divined, divining.* [L. *divino.*] To foretell; to predict; to prognosticate; to conjecture; to guess.—*v.i.* To use or practice divination; to utter presage s or prognostications; to bode; to guess.—**divination**, div·i·nā′shon, *n.* [L. *divinatio.*] The act of divining; a foretelling future events, or discovering things secret or obscure, by the aid of superior beings, or by certain rites, experiments, observations, etc.—**divinatory**, di·vin′a·to·ri, *a.* Professing or pertaining to divination.—**divinely**, di·vīn′li, *adv.* In a divine manner; in a manner resembling deity; by the agency or influence of God; in a supreme degree; excellently.—**divineness**, di·vīn′nes, *n.* The state or quality of being divine, likeness to God; sacredness; superexcellence.—**diviner**, di·vī′nêr, *n.* One who professes divination; a soothsayer; one who guesses or conjectures.—**divining rod**, *n.* A rod, usually of hazel, which, if carried slowly along in suspension by an adept, dips and points downwards, it is affirmed, when brought over the spot where water or treasure is to be found.—**divinity**, di·vin′i·ti, *n.* [L. *divinitas.*] The state of being divine; divineness; deity; godhead; divine element; divine nature; a celestial being; one of the deities belonging to a polytheistic religion; supernatural power or virtue; awe-inspiring character or influence; sacredness; the science of divine things; theology. [*Cap.*] God; Deity.

divisible, di·viz′i·bl, *a.* [L. *divisibilis*, from *divido.* DIVIDE.] Capable of division; that may be separated or disunited; separable.—**divisibility**, **divisibleness**, di·viz′i·bil′i·ti, di·viz′i·bl·nes, *n.* The quality of being divisible; that general property of bodies by which their parts or component particles are capable of separation.—**divisibly**, di·viz′i·bli, *adv.* In a divisible manner.—**division**, di·vizh′on, *n.* [L. *divisio.*] The act of dividing or separating into parts; the state of being divided; separation; a dividing line; a partition; the part separated from the rest, as by a partition, line, etc., real or imaginary; a distinct segment or section; a part or distinct portion; a certain section or portion of an organized whole, as an army, a fleet; disunion; discord; dissension; variance; difference; the separation of members in a legislative house in order to ascertain the vote; *arith.* one of the four fundamental rules, the object of which is to find how often one number is contained in another. —*Milit.* an administrative and tactical organization, smaller than a corps but larger than a brigade or regiment. —**divisional**, di·vizh′on·al, *a.* Pertaining to division; noting or making division; belonging to a division or district.—**divisive**, di·vī′ziv, *a.* Forming division; tending to divide; creat-

ing division or discord.—**divisor**, di·vī′zêr, *n. Arith.* the number by which the dividend is divided.

divorce, di·vōrs′, *n.* [Fr. *divorce*, from L. *divortium*, a separation, a divorce, from *divorto*, same as *diverto*, to turn away. DIVERT.] A legal dissolution of the bond of marriage; a legal separation between husband and wife, after which either is free to marry again; the sentence or writing by which marriage is dissolved; disunion of things closely united; separation.—*v.t.*—*divorced, divorcing.* To dissolve the marriage contract between; to separate from the condition of husband and wife; to separate or disunite from close connection; to force asunder; to put away.—**divorcee**, di·vōr·sē′, *n.* A person divorced.—**divorcement**, di·vōrs′ment, *n.* Divorce, (O.T.)—**divorcer**, di·vōr′sêr, *n.* One who or that which divorces.

divulge, di·vulj′, *v.t.*—*divulged, divulging.* [L. *divulgo*, to spread among the people— *di* for *dis*, distrib., and *vulgus*, the common people, whence also *vulgar.*] To tell or make known what was before private or secret; to reveal; to disclose; to let be known.—**divulgement**,† di·vulj′ment, *n.* The act of divulging.—**divulger**, di·vul′jêr, *n.* One who divulges.

divulsion, di·vul′shon, *n.* [L. *divulsio*, a tearing asunder, from *divello*, *divulsum*, to pluck or pull asunder—*di* for *dis*, asunder, and *vello*, to pull.] The act of pulling or plucking away; a rending asunder; violent separation; laceration.—**divulsive**, di·vul′siv, *a.* Tending or having power to pull asunder or rend.

dizzy, diz′i, *a.* [A.Sax. *dysig*, foolish; akin to L.G. *dusig*, *dösig*, O.D. *duyzigh*, Mod.D. *duizelig*, dizzy, Dan. *dosig*, drowsy. Allied are *daze*, *dazzle*, *dose.*] Having a sensation of whirling in the head with instability or proneness to fall; giddy; vertiginous; causing giddiness (a *dizzy* height); arising from, or caused by, giddiness; thoughtless; heedless; inconstant.— *v.t.*—*dizzied, dizzying.* To make dizzy or giddy; to confuse.—**dizzily**, diz′i·li, *adv.* In a dizzy manner.—**dizziness**, diz′i·nes, *n.* The state of being dizzy; giddiness; vertigo.

DNA, deoxyribonucleic acid, a nucleic acid constituting the genetic material of the chromosome. The molecule is a ladderlike helical chain in which purine bases determine the formation of RNA by a specific sequence.

do, dö, *v.t.* or *auxiliary*; pret., *did*; pp. *done*; ppr. *doing.* When transitive the present tense singular is, I *do*, thou *doest* or *dost* (dö′est, dust), he *does* or *doth* (duz, duth); when auxiliary, the second person is, thou *dost.* [A.Sax. *dón*, to do, *dó*, I do=D. *doen*, G. *thun*, to do, L. *do* in *abdo*, I put away, *condo*, I put together, Skr. *dhâ*, to place. From same stem are *deed, deem, doom.*] To perform; to execute; to carry into effect; to bring about, produce, effect; to give, confer, or pay (to *do* honor, reverence, etc.); to transact; to finish or complete; to hoax, cheat, swindle (colloq.); to inspect the sights or objects of interest in (colloq.); to prepare; to cook.—*To do away*, to remove; to put away; to annul; to put an end to.—*To do into*, to translate or render (in another language).—*To do over*, to perform again; to repeat; put a coating, as of paint, upon.—*To do up*, to put up, as a parcel; to tie up; to pack.—*To do with*, to dispose of; to employ; to occupy; to deal with; to get on with (as in what shall I *do with* it? I can *do* nothing *with* him, etc.).—*v.i.* [In this usage *do* is partly the intransitive form of the preceding verb, partly from A.Sax. *dugan*, to avail, be worth, same word as Icel. *duga*, Dan. *due*, D. *deugen*, Goth. *dugan*, G. *taugen*, to be worth, but the senses are so intermingled that it would be difficult to separate them.] To act or behave in any manner, well or ill; to conduct one's self; to fare; to be in a state with regard to sickness or health (how do you *do*?); to succeed; to accomplish a purpose; to serve an end; to suffice (will this plan *do*?); to find means; to contrive; to shift (how shall we *do* for money?).—*To do for*, to suit; to be adapted for; to answer in place of; to be sufficient for; to satisfy; to ruin; to put an end to (vulg.); attend on or do household duties for (colloq.).—*To do without*, to shift without; to put up without; to dispense with.—*To have done*, to have made an end; to have finished. —*To have done with*, to have finished; to cease to have part or interest in or connection with.—*Do* is often used for a verb to save the repetition of it; as, I shall probably come, but if I *do* not, you must not wait; that is, if I *come* not.—As an auxiliary it is used most commonly in forming negative and interrogative sentences; as, *do* you intend to go? *does* he wish me to come? *Do* is also used to express emphasis; as, I *do* love her. In the imperative, it expresses an urgent request or command; as, *do* come; help me, *do*; make haste, *do*. In the past tense it is sometimes used to convey the idea that what was once true is not true now. 'My lord, you once *did* love me.' (Shak.)—The past participle *done*, besides being used for all the ordinary meanings of the verb, has some colloquial or familiar uses; as *done!* an exclamation expressing agreement to a proposal, that is, it is agreed or I accept; *done up*, ruined in any manner, completely exhausted, very tired or fatigued.— **doable**, dö′a·bl, *a.* Capable of being done or executed.—**doer**, dö′ér, *n.* One who does, executes, performs, or acts; one who performs what is required: as opposed to a mere talker or theorizer.—**doings**, dö′ingz, *n. pl.* Things done; transactions; feats; actions, good or bad; behavior; conduct.

do, dō, *n.* Mus. the name given to the first of the syllables used in solmization; the first or key note of the scale.

docile, dō′sĭl or dos′il, *a.* [L. *docilis*, from *doceo*, to teach, whence also

doctor, document.] Teachable; easily instructed; ready to learn; tractable; easily managed.—**docility**, dō·sil′i·ti, *n.* The state or quality of being docile.

dock, dok, *n.* [A.Sax. *docce*, G. *docke*.] The common name of various species of perennial herbs, most of them troublesome weeds with stout rootstalks, erect stems, and broad leaves.

dock, dok, *n.* [Icel. *dockr*, a short tail; G. *docke*, a thick short piece; Fris. *dok*, a small bundle, bunch; comp. also W. *toc*, anything short, *tociaw*, to curtail.] The tail of a beast cut short; the stump of a tail; the solid part of the tail.—*v.t.* To cut off, as the end of a thing; to curtail; to cut short; to clip; to shorten.

dock, dok, *n.* [D. *dok*, G. *docke*, Sw. *docka*, a dock, Flem, *docke*, a kind of cage; perhaps from L. *doga*, a kind of vessel; from Gr. *dochē*, receptacle, from *dechomai*, to receive.] The place where a criminal stands in court; a place artificially formed on the side of a harbor or the bank of a river for the reception of ships, the entrance of which is generally closed by gates; a landing pier for boats, a wharf; an elevated platform for loading freight cars.—*Dry* or *graving dock*, a dock so constructed that the water may be excluded at pleasure, allowing the bottom of a vessel to be inspected and repaired.—*Wet dock*, a dock in which there is always water.—*Floating docks* are composed of large pontoons carrying along each side pumps on suitable stiff frames. When the pontoons are filled with water, they sink to the desired depth, *e.g.*, beneath a vessel, that is raised with them when the water is pumped out of the pontoons.—**dockage**, dok′ij, *n.* Charges for the use of docks.— **docker**, *n.* A worker at the wharves or a longshoreman.—**dockyard**, dok′-yärd, *n.* A yard or repository near a harbor for containing all kinds of naval stores and timber.

docket, dok′et, *n.* [A dim. of *dock*, anything curtailed or cut short.] A summary of a larger writing; a small piece of paper or parchment containing the heads of a writing; an alphabetical list of cases in a court of law; a ticket attached to goods, containing the name of the owner, the place to which they are to be sent, or specifying their measurement, etc.—*v.t.* To make an abstract of, and enter, or write it down; to mark the contents of papers on the back; to add a docket to.

doctor, dok′tėr, *n.* [L., from *doceo*, *doctum*, to teach. DOCILE.] A teacher‡; an instructor‡; a learned man; a person who has received the degree of this name from a university, being thus a *doctor* of divinity, laws, medicine, etc., and supposed capable of teaching the particular subject; a person duly licensed to practice medicine; a physician; one who cures diseases.—*v.t.* and *i.* To treat medically; to repair or patch up; to adulterate (in all senses colloq.).— **doctoral**, dok′tėr·al, *a.*—**doctorate**, dok′tėr·it, *n.* The university degree

of doctor.—**doctorship**, dok′tėr·ship, *n.* The degree of a doctor; doctorate.

doctrine, dok′trin, *n.* [L. *doctrina*, instruction, learning, from *doceo*, to teach, whence *doctor*, *docile*, etc.] In a general sense, whatever is taught; hence, a principle, view, or set of opinions maintained by any person or set of persons: whatever is laid down as true by an instructor or master; often instruction and confirmation in the truths of the gospel; one or more of the truths of the gospel.—**doctrinaire**, dok′tri·nâr″, *n.* [Fr., from L. *doctrina*; the name was originally given to certain French politicians after the restoration of 1815.] One who theorizes or advocates important changes in political or social matters without a sufficient regard to practical considerations; a political theorist.—**doctrinal**, dok′-tri·nal, *a.* Pertaining to doctrine; containing a doctrine; pertaining to the act or means of teaching.— **doctrinally**, dok′tri·nal·li, *adv.* In the form of doctrine or instruction; by way of teaching or positive direction.—**doctrinarianism**, dok·tri·nâ′-ri·an·izm, *n.* The principles or doctrines of doctrinaires.

document, dok′u·ment, *n.* [L. *documentum*, a lesson, a proof, from *doceo*, to teach. DOCTRINE.] Any official or authoritative paper containing instructions or proof, for information, establishment of facts, and the like. —*v.t.* To provide or support with documents.—**documental**, dok′u-men″tal, *a.*—**documentary**, dok′u-men″tė·ri, *a.* Certified in writing.— *n.* A documentary film.—**documentation**, dok′u·men·tā″shon, *n.* The act of authenticating with documents.

dodder, dod′ėr, *n.* [Dan. *dodder*, Sw. *dodra*, G. *dotter*, of unknown derivation.] The name of certain slender, twining, leafless pink or white parasitic plants, the common English species of which are found on nettles, vetches, furze, flax, etc.—**doddered**, dod′ėrd, *a.* Overgrown with dodder. —**doddered oak**, *a.* With the top branches blasted or withered.

dodecagon, dō·dek′a·gon, *n.* [Gr. *dōdeka*, twelve, and *gōnia*, an angle.] A regular figure or polygon, consisting of twelve equal sides and angles. —**dodecahedral**, dō·dek′a·hē″dral, *a.* Pertaining to a dodecahedron: consisting of twelve equal sides.— **dodecahedron**, dō·dek′a·hē″dron, *n.* [Gr. *hedra*, a base or side.] A regular solid contained under twelve equal and regular pentagons, or having twelve equal bases.

dodge, doj, *v.i.*—*dodged, dodging.* [Perhaps connected with *duck*, to stoop or bend down the head, G. *ducken*, to bow, to stoop.] To start suddenly aside; to follow the footsteps of a person, but so as to escape his notice (obs.); to play tricks; to play fast and loose; to quibble.—*v.t.* To evade by a sudden shift of place; to escape by starting aside; to pursue by rapid movements in varying directions; to baffle by shifts and pretexts; to overreach by tricky knavery.—*n.* A trick; an artifice;

an evasion.—**dodger,** doj'ẻr, *n.* One who dodges or evades; one who practices artful shifts or dodges.

dodo, dō'dō, *n.* [Pg. *doudo,* silly.] An extinct bird of Mauritius, having a massive, clumsy body, covered with down, short and extremely strong legs, and wings and tail so short as to be useless for flight.

doe, dō, *n.* [A.Sax. *dá,* Dan. *daa.*] The female of the fallow deer, the goat, the sheep, the hare, and the rabbit: corresponding to the masculine *buck.* —**doeskin,** *n.* The skin of a doe; a compact twilled woolen cloth.

doff, dof, *v.t.* [Contr. for *do off,* like *don* for *do on.*] To put, take, or lay off, as dress; to lay aside.—*v.i.* To lay off some article of dress; to take off the hat.

dog, dog, *n.* [A.Sax. *dogga* (very rare), a dog; same as D. *dog,* Dan. *dogge,* Sw. *dogg,* a large kind of dog. *Hound* (A.Sax. *hund*) was originally and long the common English word for dog.] A well-known domesticated carnivorous quadruped, closely allied to the wolf and the fox, noted for its sagacity, acute senses, and great attachment to man; a term of reproach or contempt given to a man; a mean, worthless fellow; a gay young man; a buck; a name applied to several tools, articles, etc., generally iron; as, an andiron, or kind of trestle to lay wood upon in a fireplace, an iron bar, with one or more sharp fangs or claws at one end, for fastening into a piece of wood or other heavy article, for the purpose of dragging or raising it, and the like. ∴ *Dog* is often used in composition for male; as, *dog*-fox, *dog*-otter, etc.; as also to denote meanness, degeneracy, or worthlessness; as, *dog*-Latin, *dog*-rose.—*To give* or *throw to the dogs,* to throw away as useless.—*To go to the dogs,* to go to ruin in life.—*v.t.*—**dogged,** *dogging.* To follow insidiously or indefatigably; to follow close; to hunt; to worry with importunity.—**dogged,** dog'ed, *a.* Having the bad qualities of a dog; sullen; sour; morose; surly; severe; obstinate.—**doggedly,** dog'ed·li, *adv.* In a dogged manner. —**doggedness,** dog'ed·nes, *n.* The quality of being dogged.—**doggish,** dog'ish, *a.* Snappish; surly; brutal.— **doggishness,** dog'ish·nes, *n.*—**dogbane,** *n.* A North American bitter plant used instead of ipecacuanha.— **dogberry,** *n.* The berry of the dogwood.—**dogcart,** *n.* A carriage with a box for holding sportsmen's dogs; a sort of double-seated gig, the occupants before and behind sitting back to back.—**dog days,** *n. pl.* The days when Sirius or the Dog Star (whence the term) rises and sets with the sun, extending from about July 3 to about August 11.—**dog-eared,** *a.* Having the corners of the leaves turned down from careless handling (a *dog-eared* book.)—**dogfight,** *n.* A fight, as of dogs; tenacious combat between fighter airplanes.—**dogfish,** *n.* A name given to several species of fishes closely allied to the sharks, but of no great size.—**dog Latin,** *n.*

Barbarous Latin; a jargon having a superficial resemblance to Latin.— **dog paddle,** *n.* A form of swimming in which the arms, remaining in the water, alternately reach forward while the legs kick.—**dog tag,** *n.* A metal identification disk worn around the neck.—**Dog Star,** *n.* Sirius, a star of the first magnitude, whose rising and setting with the sun gives name to the dog days. —**dog's-tooth violet,** *n.* A bulbous garden plant with spotted leaves and purple flowers.—**dog-tired,** *a.* Quite tired.—**dogtooth,** *n.* A sharp-pointed human tooth situated between the foreteeth and grinders; a canine tooth; an eyetooth.—**dog-trot,** *n.* A gentle trot like that of a dog.—**dogvane,** *n. Naut.* a small vane placed on the weather gunwale of a vessel to show the direction of the wind.—**dogwatch,** *n. Naut.* the name of the two watches of two hours each instead of four (between 4 and 8 p.m.) arranged so as to alter the watches kept from day to day by each portion of the crew, otherwise the same men would form the watch during the same hours for the whole voyage.—**dog-weary,** *a.* Quite tired; much fatigued.—**dogwood,** dog'wụd, *n.* A name of several trees or shrubs.

doge, dōj, *n.* [It.] The chief magistrate of the former republics of Venice (697-1797) and Genoa (1339-1797).

dogger, dog'ẻr, *n.* [D. *dogger-boot*— *dogger,* a codfish, and *boot,* a boat.] A Dutch fishing vessel having two masts, employed in the North Sea especially in the cod and herring fisheries.

doggerel, dog'ẻr·el, *a.* [Possibly from *dog.*] An epithet originally applied to a kind of loose irregular measure in burlesque poetry, but now more generally to mean verses defective in rhythm and sense.—*n.* Doggerel or mean verses.

dogma, dog'ma, *n.* [Gr. *dogma,* that which seems true, an opinion, from *dokeō,* to seem.] A settled opinion or belief; a tenet; an opinion or doctrine received on authority, as opposed to one obtained from experience or demonstration.—**dogmatic, dogmatical,** dog·mat'ik, dog·mat'i·kal, *a.* Pertaining to a dogma or dogmas; having the character of a dogma; disposed to assert opinions with overbearing or arrogance; dictatorial; arrogant; authoritative; positive.—**dogmatically,** dog·mat'i·kal·li, *adv.* In a dogmatic manner.— **dogmatics,** dog·mat'iks, *n.* Doctrinal theology; the essential doctrines of Christianity.—**dogmatism,** dog'ma·tizm, *n.* The quality of being dogmatic: arrogant assertion.—**dogmatist,** dog'ma·tist, *n.* One who is dogmatic; an upholder of dogmas; an arrogant advancer of principles or opinions.— **dogmatize,** dog'ma·tīz, *v.i.* To teach opinions with bold and undue confidence; to assert principles arrogantly or authoritatively.—**dogmatizer,** dog'ma·tī·zẻr, *n.* One who dogmatizes.

doily, doi'li, *n.* [Said to be named from the first maker.] A small orna-

mental mat used at table to put glasses on during dessert.

doit, doit, *n.* [D. *duit,* from Fr. *d'huit,* of eight, as the eighth part of a stiver.] A small Dutch copper coin, being the eighth part of a stiver, in value half a farthing; the ancient Scottish penny piece, of which twelve were equal to a penny sterling; any small piece of money; a trifle.

doldrums, dōl'drumz, *n. pl. Naut.* the parts of the ocean near the equator that abound in calms, squalls, and light baffling winds; low spirits; the dumps (*colloq.*).

dole, dōl, *n.* [DEAL.] That which is dealt out or distributed; a part, share, or portion; lot; fortune; that which is given in charity; gratuity; especially money distributed by the government during a financial depression.—*v.t.* To deal out; to distribute.

dole, dōl, *n.* [O.Fr. *dole,* Fr. *deuil,* mourning, from L. *doleo,* to grieve.] Grief; sorrow.—**doleful,** dōl'fụl, *a.* Full of dole or grief; sorrowful; expressing grief; mournful; melancholy; sad; dismal; gloomy.—**dolefully,** dōl'fụl·li, *adv.* In a doleful manner.—**dolefulness,** dōl'fụl·nes, *n.* The state or quality of being doleful.— **dolesome,**† dōl'sum, *a.* Doleful.

dolerite, dol'ẻr·īt, *n.* [Gr. *doleros,* deceptive.] A variety of traprock composed of augite and labradorite; so named from the difficulty of discriminating its component parts.

dolichocephalic, **dolichocephalous,** dol'i·kō·se·fal"ik, dol'i·kō·sef"a·lus, *a.* [Gr. *dolichos,* long, and *kephalē,* the head.] A term used in ethnology to denote skulls in which the diameter from side to side bears a less proportion to the diameter from front to back than 8 to 10, as seen in the West African negro tribes.—**dolichocephalism,** dol'i·kō·sef"a·lizm, *n.* The condition of being dolichocephalic.

doll, dol, *n.* [Of doubtful origin; perhaps for *Doll,* contr. of *Dorothy.*] A puppet or small image in the human form for the amusement of children; a girl or woman more remarkable for good looks than intelligence.

dollar, dol'ẻr, *n.* [D. Dan. and Sw. *daler,* from G. *thaler,* from *thal,* a dale, because first coined in Joachim's-*Thal,* in Bohemia, in 1519.] A silver coin of the United States, of the value of 100 cents.— *Dollar-diplomacy,* a diplomacy used to promote the financial or commercial interests of a country abroad.

dolly, dol'i, *n.* A child's name for a doll; a small, low platform on rollers, used for transporting heavy objects.

dolman, dol'man, *n.* [Fr. *dolman, doliman,* from Turk. *dōlāmān.*] A long outer robe, open in front, and having narrow sleeves buttoned at the wrist, worn by Turks; a kind of garment somewhat of the nature of a wide jacket, worn by ladies.

dolmen, dol'men, *n.* [Armor. *dolmen*; Gael. *tolmen—dol, tol,* a table, and *men,* a stone.] A rude ancient structure (probably of sepulchral origin) consisting of one large unhewn stone resting on two or more others placed erect; also applied to structures where several blocks are raised upon pillars so as to form a sort of gallery; a cromlech.

dolomite, dol′o·mīt, n. [After the French geologist *Dolomieu*.] A granular, crystalline, or schistose stone or rock, being a compound of carbonate of magnesia and carbonate of lime.

dolor, dolour, dō′lėr, n. [Fr. *douleur*, from L. *dolor, doloris*, grief, pain, from *doleo*, to grieve. Akin *dole*, *doleful*.] Grief; sorrow; lamentation. [Now only poetical.]—**dolorous,** dol′ėr·us, a. Sorrowful; doleful; exciting sorrow or grief; painful; expressing pain or grief.—**dolorously,** dol′ėr·us·li, adv. In a dolorous manner.—**dolorousness,** dol′ėr·us·nes, n. The state or quality of being dolorous.

dolphin, dol′fin, n. [O.Fr. *daulphin*, Mod. Fr. *dauphin*, a dolphin, the dauphin, from L. *delphinus*, a dolphin.] A name of several species of cetaceous mammals having numerous conical teeth in both jaws, as the dolphin proper, a peculiarly agile animal, the grampus, etc.; a fish about 5 feet long, celebrated for its swiftness and the brilliant and beautiful colors which it assumes in the act of dying; a spar or buoy made fast to an anchor, and usually supplied with a ring to enable vessels to ride by it; a mooring post placed at the entrance of a dock or along a quay or wharf.

dolt, dōlt, n. [Probably connected with E. *dull*, A.Sax. *dol*, dull, stupid; *dwelan*, to err, to be stupid.] A heavy, stupid fellow; a blockhead; a thickskull.—**doltish,** dōl′tish, a. Dull in intellect; stupid.—**doltishly,** dōl′tish·li, adv. In a doltish manner.—**doltishness,** dōl′tish·nes, n.

dom, dom, n. [L. *dominus*, lord.] Roman Catholic title of dignitaries of the Carthusian and Benedictine monks.

domain, dō·mān′, n. [Fr. *domaine*, from L.L. *domanium*, a form of L. *dominium*, ownership, property, from *dominus*, a lord.] The territory over which dominion is exercised; the territory ruled over; a dominion; an estate in land; the land about a mansion house and in the immediate occupancy of the owner; a demesne.

dome, dōm, n. [Fr. *dôme*, from Eccles, L. *dema*, a house, from Gr. *dōma*, a house, from *demō*, to build.] A roof rising up in the form of an inverted cup; a large cupola; the hemispherical roof of a building; anything shaped like a dome, as the steam chamber of a locomotive, rising above it with a rounded top, etc.—**domical,** dō′mi·kal, a. Shaped like a dome or cupola.

domestic, dō·mes′tik, a. [L. *domesticus*, from *domus*, a house; from root seen in Gr. *demō*, to build, and in E. *timber*; akin *domicile*.] Belonging to the house or home; pertaining to one's place of residence and to the family; devoted to home duties or pleasures; living in or about the habitations of man; kept for the use of man; tame; not wild; pertaining to one's own country; intestine; not foreign.—*Domestic economy*, the economical management of all household affairs; the art of managing domestic affairs in the best and thriftiest manner.—n. One who lives in the family of another, and is paid for some service; a household servant.—**domestically,** dō·mes′ti·kal·li, adv. In a domestic manner.—**domesticate,** dō·mes′ti·kāt, v.t.—*domesticated, domesticating.* To make domestic; to accustom to remain much at home; to accustom (animals) to live near the habitations of man; to tame; to reduce from a wild to a cultivated condition (plants).—**domestication,** dō·mes′ti·kā″shon, n. The act of domesticating; the state of being domesticated.—**domesticity,** dō·mes·tis′i·ti, n. State of being domestic.

domicile, dom′i·sīl, n. [L. *domicilium*, a mansion, from *domus*, a house, and root of *cella*, a cell. DOMESTIC.] A place of residence; a dwelling house; the place where one lives in opposition to the place where one only remains for a time.—v.t.—*domiciled, domiciling.* To establish in a fixed residence.—**domiciliary,** dom·i·sil′i·a·ri, a. Pertaining to a domicile.—*Domiciliary visit*, a visit to a private dwelling, particularly for the purpose of searching it under authority.—**domiciliate,** dom·i·sil′i·āt, v.t.—*domiciliated, domiciliating.* To domicile.

dominant, dom′i·nant, a. [L. *dominans, dominantis*, ppr. of *dominor*, to rule, from *dominus*, lord, master. DAME.] Ruling; prevailing; governing; predominant.—*Dominant chord, mus.* that which is formed by grouping three tones, rising gradually by intervals of a third from the dominant or fifth tone of the scale.—n. *Mus.* the fifth tone of the diatonic scale; thus G is the dominant of the scale of C, and D the dominant of the scale of G.—**dominance, dominancy,** dom′i·nans, dom′i·nan·si, n. Ascendency; rule; authority.—**dominate,** dom′i·nāt, v.t.—*dominated, dominating.* To have power or sway over; to govern; to prevail or predominate over.—v.i. To predominate.—**domination,** dom·i·nā′shon, n. The exercise of power in ruling; dominion; government; arbitrary authority; tyranny.—**dominations,** n. The fourth rank or order in the angelic hierarchy.—**dominative,** dom′i·nā·tiv, a. Presiding; governing; imperious; insolent.—**dominator,** dom′i·nā·tėr, n. One that dominates; a ruler or ruling power; the presiding or predominant power.—**domineer,** dom·i·nēr′, v.i. To rule with insolence or arbitrary sway; to bluster; to hector.—v.t. To govern harshly or overbearingly; to order or command insolently.—**domineering,** dom·i·nē′ring, p. and a. Given to domineer; overbearing.—**dominical,** dō·min′i·kal, a. [L.L. *dominicalis*, connected with Sunday, from L. *dominicus* (*dies dominica*, Sunday), pertaining to a lord or master, from *dominus*, lord. DOMINANT.] Noting or marking the Lord's day or Sunday; relating to our Lord.—*Dominical letter*, one of the seven letters, A, B, C, D, E, F, G, used in almanacs, etc., to mark the Sundays throughout the year.

Dominican, dō·min′i·kan, a. Of or pertaining to St. Dominic or the order founded by him.—n. A member of a religious order instituted in 1216 at Toulouse, by Dominic de Guzman (afterward St. *Dominic*) with the special purpose of combating the doctrines of the Albigenses: called also *Blackfriar*, from the color of the dress.

dominie, dom′i·ni, n. [From L. *domine*, vocative case of *dominus*, a lord or master.] A schoolmaster; a pedagogue. [Scotch.]

dominion, dō·min′yon, n. [L. *dominium*. See DOMAIN.] Sovereign or supreme authority; the power of governing and controlling; government; sway; rule; ascendency; predominance; territory under a government; country or district governed, or within the limits of the authority of a prince or state; *pl.* an order of angels (N.T.).

domino, dom′i·nō, n. pl. **dominoes,** dom′i·nōz. [Fr., a covering for the head worn by priests, from *dominus*, lord.] A masquerade dress, consisting of an ample cloak or mantle, with a cap and wide sleeves; frequently, though incorrectly, applied to a half mask worn by ladies as a partial disguise for the features; a person wearing a domino; *pl.* a game played with twenty-eight flat, oblong pieces of ivory or bone, dotted, after the manner of dice, with a certain number of points.

don, don. [From L. *dominus*, a lord. The feminine is *donna* or *doña*.] A title in Spain, formerly given to noblemen and gentlemen only, but now used much more widely; a fellow or one holding high office in an English college (*colloq.*).

don, don, v.t.—*donned, donning.* [To *do on*: opposed to *doff*.] To put on; to invest one's self with.

donation, dō·nā′shon, n. [L. *donatio*, an offering, from *dono*, to give; *donum*, a gift, from *do*, to give.] The act of giving or bestowing; that' which is gratuitously given; a grant; a gift.—**donative,** don′a·tiv, n. A gift; a largess; a gratuity; a present; a dole; *law*, a benefice given to a person by the founder or patron, without presentation, institution, or induction by the ordinary.—a. Vested or vesting by donation.—**donee,** dō·nē′, n. The recipient of a gift or grant.—**donor,** dō′nėr, n. One who gives, grants, or bestows; a giver.

done, dun, pp. of *do*.

donjon, don′jon, n. [Fr., from L.L. *domnio, domnionis*, for L. *dominio, dominion*.] The principal tower of a castle, which was usually situated in the innermost court, and into which the garrison could retreat in case of necessity, the lower part of it being commonly used as a prison: also called the *Keep*.

donkey, dong′ki, *n*. [Perh. a little *dun* animal, from *dun* and diminutive term. *-key*.] An ass; a stupid or obstinate and wrong-headed fellow. —**donkey engine**, *n*. A small steam engine used where no great power is required, and often to perform some subsidiary operation, as on board ships.

donna, don′na, *n*. [It., from L. *domina*, a lady or mistress.] A lady; as, *prima donna*, the first female singer in an opera, oratorio, etc.

donor. See DONATION.

dooly, doolie, dö′li, *n*. [Hind.] Light litter used in India.

doom, döm, *n*. [A.Sax. *dom*=O.Sax., O. Fris. *dom*, Goth. *doms*, Icel. *dómr*, the same word as the suffix *-dom* in king*dom*, etc., and derived probably from verb *to do*. Akin *deem*.] A judgment or judicial sentence; passing of sentence; the final judgment; the state to which one is doomed or destined; fate; fortune, generally evil; adverse issue; ruin; destruction.—*Crack of doom*, dissolution of nature.—*v.t.* To condemn to any punishment; to consign by a decree or sentence; to pronounce sentence or judgment on; to ordain as a penalty; to decree; to destine.—**doomsday**, dömz′dā, *n*. The day of doom or final judgment; a day of sentence or condemnation (*Shak.*).—*Doomsday Book*, a book compiled by order of William the Conqueror containing a survey of all the lands in England, giving the areas of estates, the amount of land under tillage, pasture, woods, etc., the number of villeins, etc.

door, dör, *n*. [A.Sax. *dór*, *dúru*= O.Sax. *dur*, *dor*, Icel. *dyr*, Goth. *daur*, G. *thür*, L. *fores*, Gr. *thura*, Ir. *dorus*, Skr. *dvâra*, door.] An opening or passage into a house or apartment by which persons enter; the frame of boards or other material that shuts such an opening, and usually turns on hinges; means of approach or access.—*To lie* or *be at one's door* (*fig.*), to be imputable or chargeable to one.—*Next door to* (*fig.*), near to; bordering on (*colloq.*). —*Out of door* or *doors*, out of the house; in the open air; abroad.—*In doors*, within the house; at home.— **doorkeeper**, *n*. A porter; one who guards the entrance of a house or apartment.—**doornail**, *n*. The nail on which, in ancient doors, the knocker struck.—**doorplate**, *n*. A plate upon a door bearing the name of the resident.—**doorstep**, *n*. The stone at the threshold.—**doorway**, dör′wā, *n*. The passage of a door; the entrance-way into a room or house.

dope, döp, *v.t.* To drug; to dose.—*n*. A narcotic; a dull or stupid person. (Slang.)

Doric, Dorian, dor′ik, dö′ri•an, *a*. Pertaining to the Dorians, a people of ancient Greece.—*Doric order*, *arch.* the oldest and simplest of the three orders of Grecian architecture,

characterized by the columns having no base, and the flutings few, large, and not deep, the capital of simple character.—*Dorian* or *Doric mode*, *mus.* a composition in which the second note of the normal scale acquires something of the dignity or force of a tonic, and upon it the melody closes.—*Doric*, *n*. The language of the Dorians, a Greek dialect characterized by broadness and hardness; hence, any dialect with similar characteristics, especially to the Scottish.

dorking, dor′king, *n*. A species of domestic fowl, distinguished by having five claws on each foot, so named because bred largely at *Dorking* in Surrey.

dormant, dor′mant, *a*. [Fr., from *dormir*, L. *dormio*, to sleep.] Sleeping; sunk in the winter sleep or torpid state of certain animals; at rest; not in action (*dormant energies*); neglected; not claimed, asserted, or insisted on (a *dormant* title or privileges); in *heraldry*, of beast with head on paws.—*Dormant partner*, a partner who takes no active part in a commercial concern.—**dormancy**, dor′man•si, *n*. State of being, dormant.—**dormer, dormer window**, dor′mėr, *n*. [Lit. the window of a sleeping apartment.] A window standing vertically on a sloping roof of a dwelling house, and so named because such windows are found chiefly in attic bedrooms.— **dormitory**, dor′mi•to•ri, *n*. [L. *dormitorium*.] A place, building, or room to sleep in.—**dormouse**, dor - mous, *n*. pl. **dormice**, dor′mīs. [Prov. E. *dorm*, to sleep, and *mouse*, lit. the sleeping-mouse.] A small rodent animal which passes the winter in a lethargic or torpid state, only occasionally waking and applying to its stock of provisions hoarded up for that season.

dorsal, dor′sal, *a*. [From L. *dorsum*, the back.] Of or pertaining to the back.—**dorsispinal**, *a*. Of or pertaining to the back and the spine.

dory, dö′ri, *n*. [Also called *John-Dory*, probably from Fr. *jaune dorée*, golden yellow, from its color.] A European fish of a beautiful yellow color, with a curious protrusible mouth, valued as food.

dory, dö′ri, *n*. A canoe or small boat.

dose, dös, *n*. [Fr., from Gr. *dosis*, a giving, from *didōmi*, to give]. The quantity of medicine given or prescribed to be taken at one time; anything given to be swallowed; as much as a man can take; a quantity in general.—*v.t.*—*dosed, dosing*. To form into suitable doses; to give a dose or doses to; to physic. —**dosage**, dö′sij, *n*. *Med.* act of dosing; administering of medicine by doses.

dosimeter, do•sim′e•tėr, *n*. An apparatus for measuring minute amounts of liquid.

dossal, dos′al, *n*. [L.L. *dorsale*, from L. *dorsum*, back.] An ornamental cloth hung at the back of an altar or a seat.

dossier, dos′e•ā, *n*. [Fr. word, from *dos*, back.] A collection of documents containing information about a person or incident.

dot, dot, *n*. [A.Sax. *dott*, a spot or speck (whence Sc. *dottle*, a small lump): comp. L.G. *dutte*, a plug, a stopper; D. *dot*, a small bundle.] A small point or spot made with a pen or other pointed instrument; a speck, used in marking a writing or other thing; a spot.—*v.t.*—*dotted, dotting*. To mark with dots; to mark or diversify with small detached objects (as clumps of trees).—*v.i.* To make dots or spots.

dotal, dö′tal, *a*. [Fr., from L. *dotalis*, from *dos*, dower. DOWER.] Pertaining to dower or a woman's marriage portion; constituting dower, or comprised in it.

dote, döt, *v.i.*—*doted, doting*. [The same word as O.D. *doten*, to dote; akin to D. *dut*, a nap, *dutten*, to take a nap; Icel. *dotta*, to nod with sleep.] To have the intellect impaired by age, so that the mind wanders or wavers; to be in a state of senile silliness; to be excessively in love; to love to excess or extravagance (to *dote on* a person).— **doter**, dö′tėr, *n*. One who dotes.— **dotage**, dö′tij, *n*. Feebleness or imbecility of understanding or mind, particularly in old age; childishness of old age; senility; weak and foolish affection.—**dotard**, dö′tėrd, *n*. A man whose intellect is impaired by age; one in his second childhood. —**dotingly**, dö′ting•li, *adv*. In a doting manner; foolishly; in a manner characterized by excessive fondness.—**dotterel, dottrel**, dot′ėr•el, dot′rel, *n*. [From the bird's supposed stupidity.] A species of plover, breeding in the highest latitudes of Asia and Europe, and migrating to the shores of the Mediterranean; a booby; a dupe; a gull.

double, dub′l, *a*. [Fr. *double*, from L. *duplus*, double—*duo*, two, and term. *-plus*, from root of *pleo*, to fill. FILL.] Forming a pair; consisting of two in a set together; coupled; composed of two corresponding parts; twofold; twice as much; multiplied by two (a *double* portion); acting two parts, one openly, the other in secret; deceitful; *bot.* having two or more rows of petals produced by cultivation from stamens and carpels.—*v.t.*—*doubled, doubling*. To make double or twofold; to fold one part upon another part of; to increase by adding an equal sum, value, or quantity; to contain twice as much as; to pass round or by; to march or sail round, so as to proceed along both sides of (to *double* a cape).—*v.i.* To increase or grow to twice as much; to turn back or wind in running.—*n*. Twice as much; a turn in running to escape pursuers; a trick; a shift; an artifice to deceive; something precisely equal or like; a counterpart; a duplicate; a copy; a person's apparition or likeness; a wraith; a fold or plait; *milit.* the quickest step in marching next to the run.—

fāte, fär, fåre, fat, fạll; mē, met, hėr; pīne, pin; nōte, not, möve; tūbe, tub, bụll; oil, pound.

double bass, *n.* The largest musical instrument of the viol kind.—**double-breasted,** *a.* Applied to a waistcoat or coat, either side of which may be made to lap over the other and button.—**double cross,** *n.* An act of deception or cheating.—**double-dealer,** *n.* One who deceitfully acts two different parts.—**double entry,** *n.* Mode of book-keeping in which two entries are made of every transaction, one on the Dr. side of one account, and the other on the Cr. side of another account, in order that the one may check the other.—**double-faced,** *a.* Deceitful; hypocritical; showing two faces.—**doubleheader,** *n.* Two games played consecutively on the same day.—**double-jointed,** *a.* Having joints that allow unusual freedom of motion.—**double-time,** *n. Milit.* the quickest step next to the run; a pace of 180 36-inch steps per minute; payment of twice one's normal wage.—**double star,** *n. Astron.* two stars so near each other that they are distinguishable only by the help of a telescope.—**doublet,** dub′let, *n.* [Dim. of *double.*] A close-fitting garment covering the body from the neck to a little below the waist; one of a pair; one of two (or more) words really the same but different in form (as *ant* and *emmet*).—**double-talk,** *n.* Purposely meaningless language that is made to appear sensible by mixing normal words with nonsense syllables; deliberately ambiguous language.

doubloon, dub·lŏn′, *n.* [Fr. *doublon,* Sp. *doblon.*] A coin of Spain and the Spanish American States.

doubt, dout, *v.i.* [O.Fr. *doubter,* from L. *dubitare,* to doubt, from same stem as *dubius,* doubtful, from *duo,* two. Akin *dubious, dual,* etc.] To waver or fluctuate in opinion; to be in uncertainty respecting the truth or fact; to be undetermined.—*v.t.* To question or hold questionable; to withhold assent from; to hesitate to believe; to suspect; to be inclined to think (governing clauses: I *doubt* you are wrong) (*Scot.*); to distrust; to be diffident of (to *doubt* a person's ability),—*n.* A fluctuation of mind respecting the truth or correctness of a statement or opinion, or the propriety of an action; uncertainty of mind; want of belief; unsettled state of opinion; suspicion; apprehension.—**doubtable,** dou′ta·bl, *a.* Liable to be doubted.—**doubter,** dou′tẽr, *n.* One who doubts.—**doubtful,** dout′-ful, *a.* Entertaining doubt; not settled in opinion; undetermined; wavering; dubious; ambiguous; not clear in its meaning; not obvious, clear, or certain; questionable; not without suspicion; not confident; not without fear; not certain or defined.—**doubtfully,** dout′ful·li, *adv.* In a doubtful manner.—**doubtfulness,** dout′ful·nes, *n.* The state or quality of being doubtful; uncertainty; suspense; ambiguity.—**doubtless,** dout′-les, *adv.* Without doubt or question; unquestionably.—**doubtlessly,** *adv.*

Unquestionably.

douche, dösh, *n.* [Fr.] A kind of bath consisting in a jet or current of water or vapor directed upon some part of the body.

dough, dō, *n.* [A.Sax. *dág, dáh*=D. *deeg,* Icel. and Dan. *deig,* Goth. *daigs,* G. *teig,* dough; akin Goth. *deigan,* to mold, to form.] Paste of bread; a mass composed of flour or meal moistened and kneaded but not baked.—**doughboy,** *n.* During World War I the nickname for an infantryman in the U.S. army.—**doughnut,** *n.* A small roundish cake, usually with a hole in the center.

doughty, dou′ti, *a.* [A.Sax. *dohtig, dyhtig,* from *dugan* (Sc. *dow*), to be able; Dan. *dygtig,* G. *tuchtig,* able, fit. Do, *v.i.*] Brave; valiant; noble; illustrious; now seldom used except in irony or burlesque.—**doughtily,** dou′ti·li, *adv.* With doughtiness.—**doughtiness,** dou′ti·nes, *n.* The character of being doughty; valor; bravery.

dour, dour, dụr, *a.* [L. *durus,* hard.] Sullen; gloomy; stern.—**dourly,** dour′li, dụr′li, *adv.*

douse, dous, *v.t.*—*doused, dousing.* [Origin doubtful; comp. Sw. *dunsa,* to plump; D. *doesen,* to strike.] To thrust or plunge into water; to immerse; to dip; *naut.* to strike or lower in haste; to slacken suddenly; to put out or extinguish (slang).—*v.i.* To fall or be plunged suddenly into water.

dove, duv, *n.* [A.Sax. *dúfa, dúfe,* from *dúfan,* to dive, to dip, probably from its habit of ducking the head, or from its manner of flight; D. *duif,* Dan. *due,* Sc. *doo,* G. *taube.*] A pigeon, some varieties being distinguished by an additional term prefixed, as *ring-dove, turtle-dove,* etc.; a word of endearment.—**dovecot, dovecote,** *n.* A small building or box in which domestic pigeons breed; a house for doves.—**dovetail,** *n. Carp.* a method of fastening the ends of boards together at right angles by letting one piece, cut into projections somewhat like a dove's tail spread, into corresponding cavities in another.—*v.t. Carp.* to unite by the above method; *fig.* to fit or adjust exactly and firmly.

dowager, dou′a·jẽr, *n.* [From a form *dowage,* from Fr. *douer,* to endow. DOWER.] A name given to the widow of a person of title, as a prince or nobleman, to distinguish her from the wife of her husband's heir bearing the same title; thus when a duke dies leaving a widow, and his successor in the title has a wife, the widow becomes the duchess-*dowager.*

dowdy, dou′di, *n.* [Akin to O.E. *dowde, dowd,* dull, sluggish; E. *dawdle,* L.G. *dödeln,* to be slow; Prov. E. *daw,* a sluggard.] An awkward, ill-dressed woman; a woman with no elegance or grace.—*a.* Awkward; illdressed; vulgar looking; applied to females.—**dowdyish,** dou′-di·ish, *a.* Like a dowdy.

dowel, dou′el, *n.* [Fr. *douille,* a groove or socket; L.L. *ductile,* a gutter, from L. *duco,* to lead.] A wooden or iron pin or tenon used in joining together two pieces of any substance edgewise (as the pieces of a barrel end); a piece of wood driven into a wall to receive nails of skirtings, etc.—*v.t.*—*dowelled, dowelling.* To fasten by means of dowels, as two boards together by pins inserted in the edges.—**dowel pin,** *n.* A pin inserted in the edges of boards to fasten them together.

dower, dou′ẽr, *n.* [Fr. *douaire,* from L.L. *dotarium,* from L. *doto, dotatum,* to endow, from *dos, dotis,* a dower, whence also *dotal, dowager.*] That with which one is endowed; the property which a woman brings to her husband in marriage; *law,* the right which a wife has in the third part of the real estate of which her husband died possessed — *v t.* To furnish with dower or a portion; to endow.—**dowry,** dou′ri, *n.* The money, goods, or estate which a woman brings to her husband in marriage; dower.

down, doun, *n.* [A.Sax. *dún,* a hill; L.G. *dünen,* Fris. *dunen,* D. *duin,* a dune; O.H.G. *dún, dúna,* promontory, Sw. dial. *dun,* a hill; also W., Ir., and Gael. *dun,* a hill, hillock.] A hill or rising ground; a low, rounded, grassy hill; a tract of naked, hilly land, used chiefly for pasturing sheep; a term commonly used in the south of England; also a dune or sand hill near the sea.

down, doun, *prep.* [A.Sax. *adúne, adown,* for *of-dúne,* off or down the hill. DOWN, a hill.] Along in descent; from a higher to a lower part of; toward the mouth of and in the direction of the current.—*adv.* In a descending direction; from a higher to a lower position, degree, or place in a series; from the metropolis of a country to the provinces, or from the main terminus of a railway to the subordinate stations; on the ground, or at the bottom; in a low condition; in humility, dejection, calamity, etc.; below the horizon (the sun is *down*); into disrepute or disgrace (to write *down* folly, vice, an author); from a larger to a less bulk (to boil *down*); from former to more recent times; extended or prostrate on the ground or on any flat surface; paid or handed over in ready money (a thousand dollars *down*). It is often used elliptically or interjectionally for go down, kneel down, etc. (*down!* dog, *down!*); also with *with,* in energetic commands; as, *down with* the sail, that is, take it down.—*Up and down,* here and there; everywhere.—*Down in the mouth,* dispirited; dejected. (*Colloq.*)—*To be down at heel,* to have the back part of the upper, or heel, turned down, or to have on shoes with the heel turned down; to be slipshod or slovenly.—*n.* A downward fluctuation (ups and *downs*).—**downcast,** doun′kast, *a.* Cast downward; directed to the ground (*downcast* eyes); in low spirits; dejected.—*n.*

Mining, the ventilating shaft down which the air passes in circulating through a mine.—**downfall,** doun'-fal, *n.* A falling down; a sudden descent or fall from a position of power, honor, wealth, fame, or the like; loss of rank, reputation, or fortune; loss of office; ruin; destruction.—**downfallen,** doun'fal'n, *a.* Fallen; ruined.—**downhearted,** doun'här·ted, *a.* Dejected in spirits. —**downhill,** doun'hil, *n.* A declivity; slope.—*a.* Sloping downwards; descending; sloping.—*adv.* Down a hill or slope.—**downpour,** doun'pōr, *n.* A pouring down; especially a heavy or continuous shower.— **downright,** doun'rīt, *adv.* Right down; perpendicularly; in plain terms; completely; thoroughly.—*a.* Directed straight or right down; coming down perpendicularly; directly to the point; plain; open; mere (*downright* nonsense); straightforward; unceremonious; blunt (a *downright* man).—**downrightly,** doun'rīt·li, *adv.* Plainly. — **downstairs,** *a.* Pertaining or relating to the lower floor of a house.— **down town,** *n.* The main part or business section of a town.—**downtown,** *a.* Pertaining to, or located in, the business section of a town.— *adv.* To or in the business section of a town.—**downtrodden, downtrod,** *a.* Trodden down; trampled upon; tyrannized over.—**downward, downwards,** doun'wėrd, doun'wėrdz, *adv.* From a higher place to a lower; in a descending course; in a course or direction from a spring or source; in a course of descent from an ancestor.—**downward,** *a.* Moving or extending from a higher to a lower place (a *downward* course); descending from a head, origin, or source; tending to a lower condition or state.

down, doun, *n.* [Same word as Icel. *dún,* Dan. *duun,* G. *daune,* down.] The fine soft covering of birds under the feathers, particularly on the breasts of waterfowl, as the duck and swan; the soft hair of the human face when beginning to appear; the pubescence of plants, a fine hairy substance; any fine feathery or hairy substance of vegetable growth.—*v.t.* To cover, stuff, or line with down.—**downiness,** dou'-ni·nes, *n.* The quality of being downy; knowingness or cuteness (slang).—**downy,** dou'ni, *a.* Covered with down or nap; covered with pubescence or soft hairs, as a plant; made of down; soft, calm, soothing (sleep); knowing, cunning, or artful (slang).

dowry, *n.* See DOWER.

doxology, dok·sol'o·ji, *n.* [Gr. *doxologia,* a praising—*doxa,* praise, glory, and *legō,* to speak.] A short hymn or form of words ascribing glory to God, and used in worship.—**doxological,** dok·so·loj'i·kal, *a.* Pertaining to doxology.

doxy, dok'si, *n.* [Comp. G. *docke,* Sw. *docka,* a doll, a plaything.] An old low term for a sweetheart or mistress.

doyley, doi'li, *n.* Same as *Doily.*

doze, dōz, *v.i.*—*dozed, dozing.* [Akin to Dan. *dōse,* to doze; *dōs,* drowsiness; G. *dōseln, doseln,* to doze; Prov. G. *dosen,* to slumber; allied to *dizzy* and to *daze.*] To slumber; to sleep lightly; to live in a state of drowsiness; to be dull or half asleep.—*v.t.* To pass or spend in drowsiness; to make dull; to stupefy.—*n.* A light sleep; a slumber.—**dozy,** dō'zi, *a.* Drowsy; heavy; inclined to sleep; sleepy.

dozen, duz'n, *n.* [Fr. *douzaine,* from *douze,* twelve, from L. *duodecim—duo,* two, and *decem,* ten.] A collection of twelve things of a like kind, or regarded as forming an aggregate for the time being; an indefinite or round number comprising more or less than twelve units, as the case may be.

drab, drab, *n.* [A Celtic word; Ir. *drabhog,* a slut, dregs, from *drab,* a spot, a stain; Gael. *drabach,* dirty, slovenly; *drabag,* a drab; akin to *draff.*] A strumpet; a prostitute; a low, sluttish woman; a slattern.— *v.i.* To associate with strumpets.— **drabble,** drab'l, *v.t.*—*drabbled, drabbling.* To draggle; to make dirty; to wet and befoul.

drab, drab, *n.* [Fr. *drap,* L.L. *drappus,* cloth, from a Teut. root seen in E. *trappings,* horse furniture.] A thick woolen cloth of a dun or dull-brown color; a dull brownish-yellow color.—*a.* Being of a dull brown or pale brown color; like the cloth so called.

drachma, drak'ma, *n.* [L. from Gr. *drachmē,* a drachm, from *drassomai,* to grasp with the hand. *Dram* is the same word.] An ancient Greek silver coin; the monetary unit of modern Greece; an ancient Greek unit of weight; a small modern weight, especially a *dram.*

Draconic, Draconian, drā·kon'ik, drā·kō'ni·an, *a.* Relating to *Draco,* the Athenian lawgiver; hence (applied to laws), extremely severe; sanguinary.

draff, draf, *n.* [Icel. *draf,* D. *draf,* also *drab,* Dan. *drav,* dregs, hog's-wash; allied to *drab,* a slut.] Refuse: dregs; hogwash; the refuse of malt which has been brewed or distilled from, given to swine and cows.— **draffy,** draf'i, *a.* Like, or consisting of draff; waste; worthless.

draft or, mainly *Brit.,* **draught,** draft, *n.* [From *draw, drag.*] The action of pulling or hauling; that which is hauled; an outline, drawing, sketch, map, or plan; a written order from one person to another, directing payment; a check; a demand or drain on anything; a selection of persons or things for a special purpose; the persons selected; a current of air; a device for regulating the flow of air; the drawing in of a net to catch fish; the quantity of fish caught; the depth of water required to float a ship, especially when loaded; the depth a ship sinks in water; the drawing of liquid from a keg, etc., when ordered; the act of drinking;

the amount taken in one drink; in the U.S., *draught* is sometimes the spelling for the fishing term, the drinking term, and air current.— *v.t.* To make a draft of; to make a rough sketch of; to outline; to select for a special purpose, as for military service.—**draftee,** draf'tē, *n.* One who is conscripted for military service.—**draftsman,** drafts'-man, *n.* One who makes drawings or diagrams, as of buildings or machinery.

drag, drag, *v.t.*—*dragged, dragging.* [A.Sax. *dragan,* to drag, to draw; Icel. *draga,* to drag, to carry; Goth. *dragan,* to draw, to carry; D. *dragen,* G. *tragen,* to carry, to bear. *Draw* is another form of the same word, *draggle* is a dim., and *drawl, dray, dredge,* are akin.] To pull; to haul; to draw along the ground by main force; to draw along slowly or heavily, as anything burdensome or troublesome; hence, to pass in pain or with difficulty; to search (a river, pond, etc.) with a net, hooked instrument, etc., for drowned persons, etc.—*To drag the anchor,* to draw or trail it along the bottom when it will not hold: said of a ship. —*v.i.* To be drawn along or trail on the ground, as a dress or as an anchor that does not hold; to move or proceed slowly, heavily, or laboriously; to move on lingeringly or with effort.—*n.* The act of dragging; any device used in dragging; that which is dragged; a sled for carrying heavy loads; a horse-drawn vehicle like a stage coach; an instrument for breaking up ground; anything that retards, hinders or obstructs; *aerodynamics,* the total force of the air acting parallel and opposite to an aircraft's direction of flight; a draw on a cigarette, etc.; a puff; an automobile race.—**dragnet,** *n.* A net drawn along the bottom of the water or along the ground to catch something; any system for catching or drawing in, as a police dragnet.

draggle, drag'l, *v.t.*—*draggled, draggling.* [Dim. from *drag,* or, as some think, a form of *drabble.*] To wet and dirty by drawing on damp ground or mud, or on wet grass; to drabble. —*v.i.* To be drawn on the ground; to become wet or dirty by being drawn on the mud or wet grass.

dragoman, drag'o·man, *n.* pl. **dragomans.** [Sp. *dragoman,* from Ar. *tarjuman,* an interpreter, from *tarjama,* to interpret; Chal. *targem,* to interpret.] An interpreter in Eastern countries.

dragon, drag'on, *n.* [Fr. *dragon,* from L. *draco,* Gr. *drakōn,* from root *drak* or *derk,* as in *derkomai,* to see; Skr. *darç,* to see; so called from its fiery eyes.] A fabulous animal, conceived as a sort of winged crocodile, with fiery eyes, crested head, and enormous claws, spouting fire, and often regarded as an embodiment of watchfulness; a kind of small lizard, having an expansion of the skin on each side, which forms a kind of wing, serving to sustain the animal when it leaps from branch to branch; a fiery, shooting meteor, or imaginary serpent (*Shak.*); a fierce, violent person, male or female; more generally now, a spiteful, watchful woman; a short carbine, carried by the original dragoons, having the representation of a dragon's head at the muzzle; a variety of carrier pigeons.—**dragonet,** drag'o·net, *n.* A little dragon; a small fish of the goby family.—**dragonfly,** *n.* The popular name of a family of insects, having large strongly reticulated wings, a large head with enormous eyes, a long body, and strong horny mandibles.—**dragon's blood,** *n.* The popular name of the inspissated juice of various plants, used for coloring spirit and turpentine varnishes, for tooth tinctures and powders, for staining marble, etc.—**dragon tree,** *n.* An evergreen tree of the Canary Islands, one of the plants that produce dragon's blood.

dragoon, dra·gön', *n.* [From *dragon*, the carbine carried by the original dragoons raised by Marshal Brissac in 1660, on the muzzle of which, from the old fable that the dragon spouts fire, the head of the monster was worked.] Originally a soldier serving both on foot and horseback; now a cavalry soldier, there being in the British army *heavy* and *light dragoons*, now nearly alike in weight of men, horses, and appointments.—*v.t.* To harass with or abandon to the rage of soldiers; to harass; to persecute; to compel to submit by violent measures.—**dragonnade,** drag·o··nād', *n.* A persecution of French Protestants in the reign of Louis XIV, from dragoons generally leading the persecuting force; a military attack upon civilians.

drain, drān, *v.t.* [Probably from A. Sax. *drehnigean*, to strain, and allied to *drag*.] To cause to pass through some porous substance; to filter; to exhaust any body of a liquid; to exhaust (land) of excessive moisture by causing it to flow off in channels; to exhaust; to deprive by drawing off gradually (to *drain* a country *of* men).—*v.i.* To flow off gradually; to be emptied or deprived of liquor by flowing or dropping.—*n.* The act of draining or drawing off, or of emptying by drawing off; gradual or continuous outflow or withdrawal; a channel through which water or other liquid flows off; a trench or ditch to convey water from wet land; a watercourse; a sewer; *pl.* the grain from the mash tub.—**drainage,** drā'nij, *n.* A draining; a gradual flowing off of any liquid; the system of drains and other works by which any town, surface, and the like, is freed from water; the mode in which the waters of a country pass off by its streams and rivers; the water carried away from a district by natural or other channels.—**drainer,** drā'nèr, *n.* One who or that which drains; one who constructs channels for draining land; *cookery*, a perforated plate for letting fluids escape.

drake, drāk, *n.* [Contr. from a form *enedrice*, *endrake* (Icel. *andrika*, O. H.G. *antrecho*, *antricho*), a hypo-

thetical masculine of A.Sax. *ened*, a duck, the termination *ric*, being the same as that in *bishopric*, and akin to Goth. *reiks*, ruling, G. *reich*, empire. *Ened* is cog. with L. *anas*, *anatis*, a duck.] The male of the duck kind; a species of fly used as bait in angling.

dram, dram, *n.* [Contr. from *drachma*.] *Apothecaries' weight*, a weight of the eighth part of an ounce, or 60 grains; *avoirdupois weight*, the sixteenth part of an ounce; as much spirituous liquor as is drunk at once. —**dramshop,** *n.* A shop where spirits are sold in small quantities.

drama, drä'ma, *n.* [Gr. *drama*, from *draō*, to do, to act.] A poem or composition representing a picture of human life, and accommodated to action, generally designed to be spoken in character and represented on the stage; a series of real events invested with dramatic unity and interest; dramatic composition or literature; dramatic representation and all that is connected with it.— **dramatic, dramatical,** dra·mat'ik, dra·mat'i·kal, *a.* Of or pertaining to the drama or plays represented on the stage; appropriate to or in the form of a drama; theatrical; characterized by the force and fidelity appropriate to the drama (a *dramatic* description); striking.—**dramatics,** dra·mat'iks, *n. sing.* The art of producing or acting plays; pl. amateur theatrical productions.—**dramatically,** dra·mat'i·kal·li, *adv.*— **dramatis personae,** dram'a·tis per·· sō'nē, *n. pl.* [L.] The characters in a play.—**dramatist,** dram'a·tist, *n.* A writer of plays.—**dramatize,** dram'a·tīz, *v.t.*—*dramatized*, *dramatizing*. To compose in the form of the drama; to adapt to the form of a play. —**dramaturgy,** dram'a·tèr·ji, *n.* [Gr. *dramatourgia*, dramatic composition —*drama*, and *ergon*, work.] The science which treats of the rules of composing dramas and representing them on the stage.—**dramaturgic,** dram·a·tèr'jik, *a.* Pertaining to dramaturgy; theatrical; hence, unreal.— **dramaturgist,** dram·a·tèr'jist, *n.* One skilled in dramaturgy.

drank, pret. of *drink*.

drape, drāp, *v.t.*—*draped*, *draping*. [Fr. *draper*, to drape, from *drap*, cloth. DRAB.] To cover or invest with clothing or cloth; to dispose drapery about for use or ornament.— **draperied,** drā'pèr·id, *a.* Furnished with drapery.—**drapery,** drā'pèr·i, *n.* [Fr. *draperie*.] Cloth or textile fabrics; the clothes or hangings with which any object is draped or hung.

drastic, dras'tik, *a.* [Gr. *drastikos*, from *draō*, to do, to act.] Acting with strength or violence; powerful; efficacious.—*n.* A strong purgative.

draught, draft, *n.* [From *draw*, *drag*.] The act of drawing; the capacity of being drawn (a cart or plough of easy *draught*); the drawing of liquor into the mouth and throat; the act of drinking; the quantity of liquor drunk at once.

Dravidian, dra·vid'i·an, *a.* Of or pertaining to *Dravida*, the name of an old province of India; applied to

a distinct family of tongues spoken in South India, Ceylon, etc.

draw, drą, *v.t.*—*drew* (drö), *drawn* (drąn), *drawing*. [A softened form of *drag* (which see).] To pull along after one; to haul; to cause to advance by force applied in front of the thing moved or at the fore end; to pull out; to unsheathe; to bring out from some receptacle (to *draw* water); to let run out; to extract (blood, wine); to attract; to cause to move or tend toward; to allure; to lead by persuasion or moral influence; to lead, as a motive; to induce to move; to inhale; to take into the lungs; to pull more closely together, or apart (to *draw* a curtain); to lengthen; to extend in length; to form by extension (to *draw* wire); to form (a line) between two points; to represent by lines drawn on a plain surface; to form a picture or image; to describe in words or to represent in fancy; to derive, deduce, have, or receive from some source; to receive from customers or patrons; to receive or take (to *draw* money from a bank); to extort; to force out (groans, tears); to write in due form; to form in writing; to take out of a box or wheel, as tickets in a lottery; to receive or gain by such drawing; to require (so many feet of water) for floating; to bend (to *draw* the bow); to eviscerate; to finish, as a game, battle, etc., so as neither party can claim the victory.—*To draw a badger, fox*, etc., to drag or force it from its cover.—*To draw in*, to contract; to pull back; to collect or bring together; to entice, or inveigle.—*To draw off*, to draw away; to withdraw; to abstract (the mind); to draw or take from; to cause to flow from.— *To draw on*, to allure; to entice; to occasion; to cause.—*To draw over*, to persuade or induce to revolt from an opposing party, and to join one's own party.—*To draw out*, to lengthen; to extend; to compose or form in writing; to cause to issue forth; to elicit, by questioning or address; to cause to be declared; to call forth. —*To draw together*, to collect or be collected.—*To draw up*, to raise; to lift; to form in order of battle; to array; to compose in due form, as a writing; to form in writing.—*v.i.* To pull; to exert strength in drawing; to act or have influence, as a weight; to shrink; to contract; to advance; to approach; to resort or betake one's self to; to unsheathe a sword; to use or practice the art of delineating figures; to form a picture; to make a draft or written demand for payment of a sum of money upon a person.—*To draw back*, to retire; to move back; to withdraw.—*To draw near* or *nigh*, to approach; to come near.—*To draw off*, to retire; to retreat.—*To draw on*, to advance; to approach.—*To draw up*, to form themselves in regular order (as troops); to assume a certain order or arrangement; to stop a horse by pulling the reins.—*n.* The act of drawing; the lot or chance drawn; a drawn game.—**drawback,** drą'bak, *n.* What detracts from profit or pleasure; a discouragement or hindrance; a disadvantage; a certain amount of duties or customs dues paid back or remitted, as duty on spirits when they are sent abroad.— **drawbridge**, drą'brij, *n.* A bridge which may be drawn up or let down or opened or shut horizontally, to admit or hinder communication, as before the gate of a town or castle, or over a navigable river.—**drawee**, drą·ē', *n.* The person on whom an order or bill of exchange is drawn.— **drawer**, drą'ėr, *n.* One who draws or pulls; one who takes water from a well; one who draws liquor from a cask; a waiter (*Shak.*); one who draws a bill of exchange or an order for the payment of money; a sliding box in a table, desk, etc., which is drawn out at pleasure; one of a set of such boxes in a case or bureau; *pl.* an under garment worn on the legs and lower part of the body by both sexes. CHEST.—**drawing**, drą'-ing, *n.* The act of one who draws; the representation or delineation of an object on a plain surface, by means of lines and shades, as with a pencil, crayon, pen. etc.; the amount of money taken for sales in a shop or other trading establishment.—**drawing room**, *n.* [For *withdrawing room*, a room to which the company withdraws from the dining room.] A room in a house appropriated for the reception of company; a room in which distinguished personages hold levees, or private persons receive parties; the formal reception of evening company at a royal court.—**drawn**, drąn, *p.* and *a.* Pulled, hauled, allured; unsheathed; extended; delineated, etc.; not decided, from both parties having equal advantage and neither a victory (a *drawn* battle).—**drawplate**, *n.* A stout plate of steel, pierced with a graduated series of conical holes, for drawing wire through in order to reduce and elongate it.

drawl, drąl, *v.t.* [A dim. form from *draw* or *drag*. DRAG.] To utter or pronounce in a slow lengthened tone; to while away in an indolent manner. —*v.i.* To speak with slow utterance. —*n.* A lengthened utterance of the voice.—**drawlingly**, drą'ling·li, *adv.* In a drawling manner.

dray, drā, *n.* [A.Sax. *dræge*, from *dragan*. DRAG, DRAW.] A low cart or carriage on heavy wheels, such as those used by brewers.—**drayage**, drā'ij, *n.* The use of a dray; charge for the use of a dray.—**drayman**, *n.* A man who attends a dray.

dread, dred, *n.* [A.Sax. *draedan, ondraedan*, to fear.] Great fear or apprehension of evil or danger; terror; awe; fear united with respect; the cause of fear; the person or the thing dreaded (O.T.).—*a.* Exciting great fear or apprehension; terrible; frightful; awful; venerable in the highest degree.—*v.t.* To fear in a great degree.—*v.i.* To be in great fear.—**dreadful**, dred'fųl, *a.* Impressing dread or great fear; terrible; formidable; awful; venerable.—*n.* A

printed work chiefly devoted to the narration of stories of criminal life, frightful accidents, etc. (*Colloq.*)— **dreadfully**, dred'fųl·li, *adv.* In a manner to be dreaded.—**dreadfulness**, dred'fųl·nes, *n.* The quality of being dreadful.—**dreadnought**, dred'nąt, *n.* A person that fears nothing; a thick cloth with a long pile, used for warm clothing or to keep off rain; a garment made of such cloth; general term for battleship of the highest class.

dream, drēm, *n.* [A.Sax. *dreám*, joy, melody; O.Fris. *drâm*, D. *droom*, G. *traum*, O.Sax. *drôm*, dream.] The thought or series of thoughts of a person in sleep; *Scrip.* impressions on the minds of sleeping persons made by divine agency; a matter which has only an imaginary reality; a visionary scheme or conceit; a vain fancy; an unfounded suspicion.— *v.i.*—*dreamed* or *dreamt* (dremt), *dreaming.* To have ideas or images in the mind in the state of sleep; with *of* before a noun; to think; to imagine; to think idly.—*v.t.* To see in a dream.—*To dream away*, to pass in reverie or inaction; to spend idly. —**dreamer**, drē'mėr, *n.* One who dreams; a visionary; one who forms or entertains vain schemes.—**dreamful**, drēm'fųl, *a.* Full of dreams. (*Tenn.*)—**dreaminess**, drē'mi·nes, *n.* State of being dreamy.—**dreamland**, drēm'land, *n.* The land of dreams; the region of fancy or imagination; the region of reverie.—**dreamless**, drēm'les, *a.* Free from dreams.— **dreamy**, drē'mi, *a.* Full of dreams; associated with dreams; giving rise to dreams; dreamlike.

dreary, drē'ri, *a.* [A.Sax. *dreórig*, bloody, sad, sorrowful, *dreór*, blood, from *dreósan* (Goth. *driusan*), to fall, with common conversion of *s* into *r*; akin to G. *traurig*, sad, *trauern*, to mourn.] Dismal; gloomy; waste and desolate; distressing; oppressively monotonous.—**drear**, drēr, *a.* Dismal; gloomy with solitude.—**drearily**, drē'ri·li, *adv.* Gloomily; dismally.— **dreariness**, drē'ri·nes, *n.* The state of being dreary.—**drearisome,**† drē'ri·sum, *a.* Very dreary.

dredge, drej, *n.* [From the stem of *drag*, the *g* being softened as in *bridge*, from older *brig*.] A dragnet for taking oysters, etc.; an apparatus for bringing up shells, plants, and other objects from the bottom of the sea for scientific investigation; a machine for clearing the beds of canals, rivers, harbors, etc.—*v.t.* *dredged, dredging.* To take, catch, or gather with a dredge; to remove sand, silt, etc., from by the use of a dredge.—**dredger**, drej'ėr, *n.* One who or that which dredges.—**dredging machine**, *n.* A machine used to take up mud or gravel from the bottoms of rivers, docks, etc.

dredge, drej, *n.* [Fr. *dragée*, mixed provender for horses and cattle; It. *treggéa*, from Gr. *tragémata*, dried fruits.] A mixture of oats and barley sown together.—*v.t.* To sprinkle flour on roast meat.—**dredger**, drej'-ėr, *n.* A utensil for scattering flour on meats when roasting.

dregs, dregz, *n. pl.* [Icel. *dregg*, Sw. *drägg*, dregs, lees; probably connected with *drag*, *drain*—the dregs being what remains after the liquor is drained off.] The sediment of liquors; lees; grounds; feculence; any foreign matter of liquors that subsides to the bottom of a vessel; dross; sweepings; refuse; hence, the most vile and worthless among men. *Dreg*, in the singular, is found in Spenser and Shakespeare.

drench, drensh, *v.t.* [A.Sax. *drencan, drencean*, to give to drink, to drench, from *drincan*, to drink. DRINK.] To wet thoroughly; to soak; to saturate; to purge violently (an animal) with medicine.—*n.* [A.Sax. *drenc*, a draught.] A draught; a dose of medicine for a beast, as a horse.—**drencher**, dren'shėr, *n.* One who drenches.

dress, dres, *v.t.*—*dressed* or *drest, dressing.* [Fr. *dresser*, to make right, prepare, from a L.L. verb *directiare, drictiare*, to make straight, from L. *directus*, straight. DIRECT.] To make straight or in a straight line (troops); to put to rights; to put in good order; to till or cultivate; to treat (a wound or sore) with remedies or curative appliances; to prepare, in a general sense; to make suitable or fit for something (leather, a lamp, etc.); to put clothes on; to invest with garments; to adorn; to deck.— *To dress up* or *out*, to clothe elaborately, pompously, or elegantly.— *v.i. Milit.* to arrange one's self in proper position in a line; to clothe one's self; to put on garments.—*n.* Clothes, garments, or apparel; collectively, a suit of clothes: a costume; a lady's gown.—**dress circle**, *n.* A portion of a theater, concert room; first gallery in a theater, etc. —**dress parade**, *n.* A ceremonial parade of soldiers or sailors in dress uniforms.—**dress rehearsal**, *n.* The final rehearsal of a play, etc., before the first performance.— **dresser**, dres'ėr, *n.* One who dresses; one employed in preparing, trimming, or adjusting anything; a hospital assistant, whose office is to dress wounds, ulcers, etc.—[Fr. *dressoir*.] A table or bench on which meat and other things are dressed or prepared for use; a kind of low cupboard for dishes and cooking utensils.—**dressing**, dres'ing, *n.* The act of one who dresses; what is used to dress; an application to a wound or sore; manure spread over land; gum, starch, paste, and the like, used in stiffening or preparing silk, linen, and other fabrics; *cookery*, the stuffing of fowls, pigs, etc., or the unctuous ingredients to complete a salad; *arch.* moldings round doors, windows, and other openings on an elevation.—**dressing gown**, *n.* A light gown or wide and flowing coat worn by a person while dressing, in the study, etc.—**dressing table**, *n.* A table provided with conveniences for the toilet; a toilet table.— **dressmaker**, dres'māk·ėr, *n.* A maker of ladies' dresses.—**dressy**, dres'i, *a.* Very attentive to dress; wearing rich or especially showy dresses.

drew, drö, v. pret. of *draw*.
dribble, drib'l, v.t.—*dribbled, dribbling*. [A dim. from *drip*, and properly *dripple*.] To give out or let fall in drops.—v.i. To fall in drops or small particles, or in a quick succession of drops.—**dribblet, driblet**, drib'let, n. One of a number of small pieces or parts; a small sum doled out as one of a series.
drier, drī'ėr, n. See DRY.
drift, drift, n. [From *drive*; A.Sax. *drifan* = Icel. *drift*, a snow drift; Dan. *drift*, impulse, drove; D. *drift*, drove, course. DRIVE, and comp. *rive, rift; shrive, shrift; thrive, thrift*.] A drove or flock‡; a heap of matter driven together by the wind or water (a snow *drift*); a driving or impulse; overbearing power or influence; course of anything; tendency; aim (the *drift* of one's remarks); intention; design; purpose; a name in South Africa for a ford; *milit*. the deflection of a shell to the right of its proper course, due to the resistance of the air and the right-hand spin or rotation imparted by the rifling; the deviation of an aircraft due to the wind; *mining*, a passage cut between shaft and shaft; *naut*. the distance which a vessel drives through wind or current when lying-to or hove-to during a gale; *geol*. earth and rocks which have been conveyed by icebergs and glaciers and deposited over a country while submerged.—*Drift of a current*, the rate at which it flows.—v.i. To accumulate in heaps by the force of wind; to be driven into heaps; to float or be driven along by a current of water or air; to be carried at random by the force of the wind or tide; *mining*, to make a drift; to search for metals or ores.—v.t. To drive into heaps.—a. Drifted by wind or currents (drift sand, drift ice).—**drifter**, drif'tėr, n. A boat that uses drift nets.—**driftwood**, n. Wood drifted or floated by water.—**drifty**, drif'ti, a. Forming or characterized by drifts, especially of snow.
drill, dril, v.t. [From D. *drillen*, to bore, to drill soldiers; G. *drillen*, to bore; from same root as *through, thrill, -tril* in *nostril*. (In the agricultural sense, however, perhaps of different origin.)] To pierce or perforate by turning a sharp-pointed instrument of a particular form; to bore and make a hole by turning an instrument; *agri*. to sow in rows, drills, or channels; to teach and train soldiers or others to their duty by frequent exercises; hence, to teach by repeated exercise or repetition of acts.—v.i. To go through the exercises prescribed to recruits, etc.—n. A pointed instrument used for boring holes, particularly in metals and other hard substances; the act of training soldiers, etc., to their duty, or the exercises by which they are trained; *agri*. a row of seeds deposited in the earth, or the trench or channel in which the seed is deposited; also a machine for sowing seeds in rows.—**drillmaster**, n. One who trains others; one who drills soldiers in marching.—**drill press**, n. A machine armed with one or more drills for boring holes in metal.
drill, drilling, dril, dril'ing, n. [G. *drillich*, from *drei*, three, a fabric in which the threads are divided in a threefold way.] A kind of coarse linen or cotton cloth.
drily. See DRY.
drink, dringk, v.i.—*drank* or *drunk* (pret.), *drunk* or *drunken* (pp.). [A. Sax. *drincan* = D. *drinken*, Icel. *drekka*, G. *trinken*, Goth. *drigkan*, to drink. Hence *drench* and *drown*.] To swallow liquor, for quenching thirst or other purpose; especially, to take intoxicating liquor; to be intemperate in the use of intoxicating liquors; to be an habitual drunkard.—*To drink to*, to salute in drinking; to drink in honor of; to wish well to, in taking the cup.—v.t. To swallow (liquids); to imbibe; to suck in; to absorb; to take in through the senses (to *drink* delight); to inhale.—*To drink down*, to take away thought or consideration of (care, etc.) by drinking.—*To drink off*, to drink the whole at a draught.—*To drink in*, to absorb; to take or receive into.—*To drink up*, to drink the whole.—*To drink the health*, or *to the health of*, to drink while expressing good wishes for; to signify good will to by drinking; to pledge.—n. Liquor to be swallowed; a draught of liquor; intoxicating liquors.—*In drink*, drunk; tipsy.—**drinkable**, dring'ka·bl, a. Fit or suitable for drink; potable.—n. A liquor that may be drunk.—**drinker**, dring'kėr, n. One who drinks, particularly one who practices drinking spirituous liquors to excess; a drunkard.
drip, drip, v.i.—*dripped, dripping*. [A.Sax. *drypan*, to drip, to drop = Dan. *dryppe*, Icel. *drjúpa*, D. *druipen*, G. *triefen*. Akin *drop*.] To fall in drops; to have any liquid falling from it in drops.—v.t. To let fall in drops.—n. A falling or letting fall in drops; a dripping; that which falls in drops; dripping, or melted fat from meat while roasting; the edge of a roof; the eaves; *arch*. a large flat member of the cornice projecting so as to throw off water; a dripstone.—**dripping**, drip'ing, n. The fat which falls from meat in roasting.
dripstone, n. *Arch*. a projecting molding or cornice over doorways, windows, etc., to throw off the rain.
drive, drīv, v.t.—*drove* (formerly *drave*); *driven, driving*. [A.Sax. *drifan* = Goth. *dreiban*, D. *drijven*, Dan. *drive*, G. *treiben*, to drive, to urge or carry on. *Drift* and *drove* are derivatives.] To impel or urge forward, or away from, by force; to force or move by physical means; to propel; to compel or urge by other means than absolute physical force, or by means that compel the will; to constrain; to press or carry to a great length (an argument); to chase or hunt; to keep horses or other animals moving onward while directing their course; to guide or regulate the course of an automobile or other vehicle; to guide or regulate a machine; to convey in a vehicle; to carry on, prosecute, engage in (a trade, a bargain); *mining*, to dig horizontally; to cut a horizontal gallery or tunnel.—v.i. To be forced along or impelled (a ship *drives* before the wind); to rush and press with violence (a storm *drives* against the house); to go in an automobile; to travel in a vehicle drawn by horses or other animals; to aim or tend; to aim a blow; to make a stroke.—n. A journey or airing in a vehicle; a course on which vehicles are driven; a road prepared for driving; a strong or sweeping blow or impulsion.—**drive-in**, a. A theater, restaurant, bank, etc., that caters to customers who remain in their automobiles.—**driver**, drī'vėr, n. One who or that which drives; the person who drives a vehicle, one who conducts a team; *naut*. a large fore-and-aft quadrilateral sail, called also the *Spanker*, on the mizzen mast; *mach*. the main wheel by which motion is communicated to a train of wheels; a driving wheel.—**driver ant**, n. A singular species of ant in West Africa, so named from its *driving* before it almost every animal that comes in its way.
drivel, driv'el, v.i.—*driveled, driveling*. [A modification of *dribble*, from root of *drib*.] To slaver; to let spittle drop or flow from the mouth, like a child, idiot, or dotard; to be weak or foolish; to dote.—n. Slaver; saliva flowing from the mouth; silly unmeaning talk; senseless twaddle.—**driveler**, driv'el·ėr, n. One who drivels; an idiot; a fool.
drizzle, driz'l, v.i.—*drizzled, drizzling*. [A dim. from A.Sax. *dreósan*, Goth. *driusan*, to fall; like Prov. G. *drieseln*, to drizzle. DREARY.] To rain in small drops; to fall from the clouds in very fine particles.—v.t. To shed in small drops or particles.—n. A small or fine rain; mizzle.—**drizzly**, driz'li, a. Shedding small rain, or small particles of snow.
droit, droit, n. [Fr., from L. *directus*.] Right; law; justice; a fiscal charge or duty.—*Droits of admiralty*, perquisites attached to the office of admiral of England, or lord high-admiral.
droll, drōl, a. [Same word as Fr. *drôle*, D. *drol*, G. *droll*, a thick, short person, a droll; Gael. *droll*, a slow, awkward person; perhaps from Icel. and Sw. *troll*, a kind of imp or hobgoblin.] Odd; merry; facetious; comical; ludicrous; queer; laughable; ridiculous.—n. One whose occupation or practice is to raise mirth by odd tricks; a jester; a buffoon; something exhibited to raise mirth or sport.—v.i. To jest; to play the buffoon.—**drollery**, drō'lėr·i, n. The quality of being droll; something done to raise mirth; sportive tricks; buffoonery; fun; comicalness; humor.
dromedary, drom'e·da·ri, n. [L. *dromedarius*, a dromedary, formed from Gr. *dromas, dromados*, running, from stem of *dramein*, to run.] A species of camel, called also the

Arabian camel, with one hump or protuberance on the back, in distinction from the Bactrian camel, which has two humps.

dromond, ‡drom′ond, n.[Gr. *dramein,* to run.] Fast-sailing ship of war.

drone, drōn, n. [A.Sax. *drán,* the dronebee; L.G. and Dan. *drone,* Sw. *dron, drönje,* G. *drohne,* from the sound it makes; comp. *humblebee,* G. *hummel,* and the verb *hum.*] The male of the honeybee; an idler; a sluggard; one who earns nothing by industry; a humming or low sound, or the instrument of humming; one of the largest tubes of the bagpipe, which emit a continued deep tone.—*v.i.*—droned, droning. [Dan. *dröne,* Sw. *dröna,* to drone; akin Goth. *drunjus,* a sound.] To give forth a low, heavy, dull sound; to hum; to snore; to make use of a dull monotonous tone; to live in idleness.—*v.t.* To read or speak in a dull, monotonous, droning manner.

drool, drōl, v.i. [Contraction of *drivel.*] To slaver; to drivel.

droop, drŏp, v.i. [A form of *drip, drop.*] To sink or hang down; to bend downward, as from weakness or exhaustion; to languish from grief or other cause; to fail or sink; to decline; to be dispirited; to come towards a close (*Tenn.*).—*v.t.* To let sink or hang down.—*n.* The act of drooping or of falling or hanging down; a drooping position or state.— **drooper,** drŏ′pèr, n. One who or that which droops.—**droopingly,** drŏ′ping·li, adv. In a drooping manner.

drop, drop, n. [A.Sax. *dropa,* O.Sax. *dropo,* Icel. *dropi,* D. *drop,* G. *tropfe,* a drop; akin *dribble, drip, droop.*] A small portion of any fluid in a spherical form, falling or pendant, as if about to fall; a small portion of water falling in rain; what resembles or hangs in the form of a drop, as a hanging diamond ornament, a glass pendant of a chandelier, etc.; a very small quantity of liquid; a small quantity of anything (a *drop* of pity: *Shak.*); that part of a gallows which sustains the criminal before he is executed, and which is suddenly dropped; also the distance which he has to fall; the curtain which conceals the stage of a theater from the audience; *pl.* a liquid medicine, the dose of which is regulated by a certain number of drops.—*v.t.*—dropped, dropping. [A.Sax. *dropian,* from the noun = D. *droppen,* G. *tropfen.*] To pour or let fall in drops; to let fall, lower, or let down (to *drop* the anchor); to let go, dismiss, lay aside, break off from; to quit, leave, omit; to utter (words) slightly, briefly, or casually; to send in an off-hand informal manner (*drop* me a few lines).—*v.i.* To fall in small portions, globules, or drops, as a liquid; to let drops fall; to drip; to discharge itself in drops; to fall; to descend suddenly or abruptly; to sink lower; to cease; to die suddenly; to fall, as in battle; to come to an end; to be allowed to cease; to be neglected and come to nothing;

to come unexpectedly: with *in* or *into.*—*To drop astern* (*naut.*), to slacken speed so as to let another vessel get ahead.—*To drop down,* to sail, row, or move down a river.— *Dropping fire* (*milit.*), a continuous irregular discharge of small arms.— **droplet,** drop′let, n. A little drop.— **dropper,** drop′èr, n. One who or that which drops.—**dropping,** drop′ing, n. The act of one who drops; a falling in drops; that which drops; *pl.* the dung of animals.—**drop kick,** n. A kick given to a football by dropping the ball and kicking it as it rises.—**dropout,** n. One who fails to complete a course, etc.

dropsy, drop′si, n. [Formerly *hydropsy,* from Gr. *hydrōps,* dropsy, from *hydōr,* water.] *Med.* an unnatural collection of water in any cavity of the body, or in the cellular tissue.—**dropsical,** drop′si·kal, a. Diseased with dropsy; inclined to dropsy; resembling or partaking of the nature of dropsy.—**dropsied,** drop′sid, a. Affected with dropsy; exhibiting an unhealthy inflation.

dropwort, drop′wèrt, n. A kind of spiraea or meadowsweet with fine-cut leaves.

drosky, dros′ki, n. [Rus. *drozhki.*] A kind of light four-wheeled carriage used in Russia and Prussia.

dross, dros, n. [A.Sax. *dros, drosn,* from *dreósan,* to fall; D. *droes,* Icel. *tros,* rubbish; Sc. *drush,* dregs; Dan. *drysse,* to fall. DREARY.] The refuse or impurities of metals; rust; waste matter; refuse; any worthless matter separated from the better part.— **drossy,** dros′i, a. Like dross; pertaining to dross; full of or abounding with refuse matter; worthless; foul; impure.

drought, drout, n. [Contr. from A.Sax. *drugath, drugoth,* from *drige, dryge,* dry; like D. *droogte,* from *droog,* dry. DRY.] Dry weather; want of rain; such a continuance of dry weather as affects the crops; aridness; thirst; want of drink; scarcity; lack.—**droughty,** drou′ti, a. Characterized by drought or the absence of rain or moisture; arid; thirsty.

drove, drōv, pret. of *drive.*

drove, drōv, n. [A.Sax. *dráf,* from *drifan,* to drive.] A number of animals, as oxen, sheep, or swine, driven in a body; a collection of animals moving forward; a crowd of people in motion; a flock.— **drover,** drō′vèr, n. One who drives cattle or sheep to market, or from one locality to another.

drown, droun, v.t. [From A.Sax. *druncnian,* to sink in water, to be drunk, from *druncen,* pp. of *drincan,* to drink; Dan. *drukne,* to drown. DRINK, DRENCH.] To deprive of life by immersion in water or other fluid; to overflow, overwhelm, or inundate; to put an end to, as if by drowning or overwhelming; to overpower (to *drown* care; to *drown* one's voice).— *v.i.* To be suffocated in water or other fluid; to perish in water.

drowse, drouz, v.i.—drowsed, drowsing. [A.Sax. *drúsan, drúsian,* to be

slow, to languish; allied to *dreósan* to fall, to droop; D. *droosen,* to doze, to slumber. DREARY.] To sleep imperfectly or unsoundly; to slumber; to be heavy with sleepiness; to be heavy or dull.—*v.t.* To make heavy with sleep; to make dull or stupid.—*n.* A slight sleep; a doze; slumber.—**drowsily,** drou′zi·li, adv. In a drowsy manner.—**drowsiness,** drou′zi·nes, n. State of being drowsy. —**drowsy,** drou′zi, a. Inclined to sleep; sleepy; heavy with sleepiness; lethargic; sluggish; stupid; disposing to sleep; lulling.

drub, drub, v.t.—drubbed, drubbing. [Prov. E. *drab;* akin to Icel. and Sw. *drabba,* to beat; G. *treffen* to hit.] To beat with a stick; to thrash; to cudgel.—*n.* A blow with a stick or cudgel; a thump; a knock.—**drubber,** drub′èr, n. One who drubs or beats. —**drubbing,** drub′ing, n. A cudgeling; a sound beating.

drudge, druj, v.i.—drudged, drudging. [Softened form of O.E. *drugge, drug,* to work laboriously; origin doubtful.] To work hard; to labor in mean offices; to labor with toil and fatigue. —*n.* One who labors hard in servile employments; a slave.—**drudgery,** druj′èr·i, n. Ignoble toil; hard work in servile occupations.

drug, drug, n. [Fr. *drogue;* Pr. Sp. Pg. It. *droga;* all from D. *droog,* the same word as A.Sax. *dryge,* dry— because the ancient medicines were chiefly dried herbs.] Any substance, vegetable, animal, or mineral, used in the composition or preparation of medicines; any commodity that lies on hand or is not saleable; an article of slow sale or in no demand in the market.—*v.i.*—drugged, drugging. To prescribe or administer drugs or medicines.—*v.t.* To mix with drugs; to introduce some narcotic into with the design of rendering the person who drinks the mixture insensible; to dose to excess with drugs or medicines; to administer narcotics to; to render insensible with a narcotic drug.—**druggist,** drug′ist, n. One who deals in drugs; a pharmacist.—**drugstore,** n. A store where drugs, medicines, meals, etc., are sold.

drugget, drug′et, n. [Fr. *droguet,* dim. of *drogue,* drug, trash. DRUG.] A cloth or thin stuff of wool, or of wool and thread, used for covering carpets, and also as an article of clothing.

druid, drū′id, n. [Ir. and Gael. *druidh,* W. *derwydd.*] [*often cap.*] A priest or minister of religion who superintended the affairs of religion and morality, and performed the office of judges among the ancient Celtic nations in Gaul, Britain, and Germany.—**druidess,** drū′i·des, n. A female druid.—**druidic, druidical,** drū·id′ik, drū·id′i·kal, a. Pertaining to the druids.—*Druidical stones,* the name popularly given to large upright stones, found in various localities and sometimes forming circles, from an uncertain assumption that they were druidical places of worship.— **druidism,** drū′i·dizm, n. The doctrines, rites, and ceremonies of the druids.

drum, drum, *n.* [Probably, like *drone*, a word of imitative origin; Dan. *tromme*, G. *trommel*, a drum, Dan. *drum*, a booming sound; Goth. *drunjus*, a sound.] An instrument of music commonly in the form of a hollow cylinder, covered at the ends with vellum, the ends being beaten with sticks to produce the sound; a mechanical contrivance resembling a drum in shape, and used in connection with machinery of various kinds, etc.; the tympanum or barrel of the ear; a quantity packed in the form of a drum; a round box containing figs; a tea before dinner; a kettledrum; a name formerly given to a fashionable and crowded evening party; a storm drum.—*v.i.*—*drummed, drumming.* To beat a drum; to beat with rapid movements of the fingers; to beat with a rapid succession of strokes; to throb; to resound dully.—*v.t.* To perform on a drum; to expel with beat of drum (he was *drummed out* of the regiment); to summon by beat of drum; to din.— *To drum up,* to assemble or call together by beat of drum.—**drumhead,** *n.* The head or top of a drum; a variety of cabbage having a large, rounded, or flattened head.—*Drumhead court-martial,* a court-martial called suddenly on the field.—*Drumhead service,* religious service on the field, at the front.—**drum major,** *n.* The chief or first drummer of a regiment; the leader of a band in marching.—**drumlin,** drum´lin. [Celtic name.] An elongated mound of glacial material sorted by water action.—**drummer,** drum´ėr, *n.* One who drums; one whose office is to beat the drum; commercial traveler. —**drumstick,** *n.* The stick with which a drum is beaten; what resembles a drumstick, as the upper joint of the leg of a turkey.

drunk, drungk, *a.* [From *drunken.* DRINK.] Intoxicated; inebriated; overcome, stupefied, or frenzied by alcoholic liquor.—**drunkard,** drung´kėrd, *n.* One given to an excessive use of strong liquor; a person who habitually or frequently is drunk.— **drunken,** drung´ken, *a.* [Part. of *drink,* but now used chiefly as an adjective.] Intoxicated; drunk; given to drunkenness; proceeding from intoxication; done in a state of drunkenness (a *drunken* quarrel).— **drunkenly,†** drung´ken·li, *adv.* In a drunken manner. (*Shak.*)—**drunkenness,** drung´ken·nes, *n.* The state of being drunk; the habit of indulging in intoxication; intoxication; inebriety.

drupe, dröp, *n.* [Fr. *drupe,* L. *drupa,* Gr. *dryppa,* an overripe olive.] *Bot.* a stone fruit, such as the cherry or plum; a fruit in which the outer part is fleshy while the inner hardens like a nut, forming a stone with a kernel.

dry, drī, *a.* [A.Sax. *dryge, drige, drie* (D. *droog,* G. *trocken*), dry, whence *dryan, drigan,* to dry. *Drought* and *drug* are derivatives.] Destitute of moisture; free from water or wetness;

free from juice, sap, or aqueous matter; not moist; arid; not giving milk; thirsty; craving drink; barren; jejune; plain; unembellished; destitute of interest; quietly sarcastic; caustic; discouraging; expressive of a degree of displeasure; cold and not friendly (a *dry* reception).—*Dry goods,* cloths, stuffs, silks, laces, ribbons, etc., in distinction from groceries.—*Dry steam,* superheated steam.—*Dry stone walls,* walls built of stone without mortar.—*Dry wines,* those in which no sweetness is perceptible.—*v.t.*—*dried, drying.* To make dry; to free from water or from moisture of any kind; to desiccate; to expose in order to evaporate moisture; to deprive of natural juice, sap, or greenness.—*To dry up,* to deprive wholly of water; to scorch or parch with thirst.—*v.i.* To grow dry; to lose moisture; to become free from moisture or juice; to evaporate wholly: sometimes with *up.*— **drier,** drī´ėr, *n.* One who or that which dries or makes dry; a desiccative; specifically a preparation to increase the hardening and drying properties of paint.—**dry cell,** *n.* An electric cell the contents of which are in the form of a paste.—**dryclean,** *v.t.* To clean textiles with solvents other than water.—**dry dock,** *n.* A dock from which water may be shut or pumped out, used in constructing or repairing ships.—**Dry Ice,** *n.* A trademark for solidified carbon dioxide used as a substitute for ice.—**drying,** drī´ing, *a.* Adapted to exhaust moisture; having the quality of rapidly becoming dry and hard.—**dryly, drily,** drī´li, *adv.* Without moisture; coldly; frigidly; without affection; severely; sarcastically; barrenly; without embellishment; without anything to enliven, enrich, or entertain.—**dryness,** drī´nes, *n.* The state or quality of being dry.— **dry measure,** *n.* Measure for dry commodities by quarts, etc.; in this system two pints make one quart, eight quarts make one peck, four pecks make one bushel.—**dry nurse,** *n.* A nurse who attends and feeds a child by hand.—*v.t.* To act as dry nurse to; to feed, attend, and bring up without the breast.—**dry point,** *n.* A sharp etching needle, used to cut fine lines in copper without the plate being covered with etching ground or the lines bit in by acid.—**dry rot,** drī´rot, *n.* A well-known disease affecting timber, occasioned by various species of fungi, the mycelium of which penetrates the timber, destroying it.—**dry run,** *n.* A trial; a practice session.—**dry-shod,** *a.* and *adv.* Without wetting the feet.

dryad, drī´ad, *n.* [Gr. *dryas, dryados,* from *drys,* an oak, a tree.] *Myth.* a deity or nymph of the woods; a nymph supposed to preside over woods.

dual, dū´al, *a.* [L. *dualis,* from *duo,* two; akin *duel, double, doubt, dubious,* etc.] Expressing the number two; existing as two; consisting of two; twofold; a term applied to a special form of a noun or verb used

in some languages when two persons or things are spoken of.—*n. Gram.* that number which is used when two persons or things are spoken of.— **dualism,** dū´a·lizm, *n.* A twofold division; *philos.* any system holding that all phenomena in the universe can be explained in terms of two fundamental and exclusive principles, such as mind and matter, being and nonbeing, etc.; *theol.* the doctrine that there are two distinct eternal principles, one good and the other evil; the belief that man embodies two irreducible elements such as body and soul; doctrine of those who maintain the existence of spirit and matter as distinct substances, in opposition to idealism, which maintains we have no knowledge or assurance of the existence of anything but our own ideas or sensations.—**dualist,** dū´a·list, *n.* One who holds the doctrine of dualism in any of its forms.—**dualistic,** dū·a·lis´tik, *a.* Pertaining to dualism; characterized by duality.—**duality,** dū·al´i·ti, *n.* The state of being two or of being divided into two.

dub, dub, *v.t.*—*dubbed, dubbing.* [A. Sax. *dubban,* to strike, to dub knight; Icel. *dubba,* to dub.] To strike with a sword and make a knight; to nickname; to make smooth by hammering; to make a blunder.—*n.* Something done poorly; a clumsy person.

dub, dub, *v.t.* [Shortening of *double.*] To insert music, dialogue, etc., into the sound track of a film.

dub, dub, *n.* [Probably of same root as *dip* and *deep.*] A puddle; a small pool of foul stagnant water.

dubious, dū´bi·us, *a.* [L. *dubius,* moving alternately in two opposite directions, from root of *duo,* two. DOUBT.] Doubtful; wavering or fluctuating in opinion; uncertain; not ascertained or known exactly; not clear or plain; occasioning or involving doubt; of uncertain event or issue.—**dubiously,** dū´bi·us·li, *adv.* In a dubious manner.—**dubiousness,** dū´bi·us·nes, *n.* The state of being dubious.—**dubiety,** dū·bī´e·ti, *n.* [L. *dubietas.*] Doubtfulness; a feeling of doubt.—**dubiosity,** dū·bi·os´i·ti, *n.* Dubiousness; doubtfulness.—**dubitable,†** dū´bi·ta·bl, *a.* [L. *dubito,* to waver in opinion.] Liable to be doubted; doubtful; uncertain.—**dubitation,†** dū·bi·tā´shon, *n.* [L. *dubitatio.*] The act of doubting or hesitating; doubt.

ducal, dū´kal, *a.* [L. *ducalis,* pertaining to a leader, from *dux, ducis,* a leader. DUKE.] Pertaining to a duke. —**ducally,** dū´kal·li, *adv.* After the manner of a duke; in relation with a duke or a ducal family.—**ducat,** duk´at, *n.* [Fr. *ducat,* It. *ducato,* from L.L. *ducatus,* a duchy (the particular duchy originating the name being uncertain), from L. *dux.* DUKE.] A gold coin.—**duchess,** duch´es, *n.* [Fr. *duchesse,* from *duc,* duke.] The consort or widow of a duke; a lady who has the sovereignty of a duchy. —**duchy,** duch´i, *n.* [Fr. *duché.*] The territory controlled or governed by a duke or duchess; a dukedom.

duck, duk, *n.* [Same word as D. *doek,* Sw. *duk,* G. *tuch,* cloth.] A species of coarse cloth or canvas, used for sails, sacking of beds, etc.

duck, duk, *n.* [Same word as Dan. *dukke,* G. *docke,* a baby or puppet; or the name of the bird used as a term of endearment.] A word of endearment or fondness.

duck, duk, *v.t.* [Akin to D. *duiken,* to bend the head, duck, dive, Dan. *dukke,* to dive, G. *tauchen,* to dip, to dive.] To dip or plunge in water and suddenly withdraw; to bow, stoop, or nod in order to escape a blow or the like.—*v.i.* To plunge into water and immediately withdraw; to dip; to plunge the head in water or other liquid; to drop the head suddenly; to bow; to cringe.— *n.* [From the verb to *duck.*] A name of various waterfowls akin to, but distinguished from swans and geese by having broader bills, a more waddling gait from their legs being placed further back, there being also a marked difference in the plumage of the sexes; a term of endearment (*colloq.*); an inclination of the head, resembling the motion of a duck in water.—*To make ducks and drakes,* to throw a flat stone, piece of slate, etc., along ·the surface of water so as to cause it to strike and rebound repeatedly; hence, *to make ducks and drakes of one's money,* to squander it in a foolish manner.—**duckbill,** *n.* A re-markable Australian animal with jaws which resemble the bill of a duck. ORNITHORHYNCHUS.—**ducker,** duk´ėr, *n.* One who ducks; a plunger; a diver; a cringer; a fawner.—**ducking stool,** *n.* A stool or chair in which common scolds were formerly tied and plunged into water.—**duckling,** duk´ling, *n.* A young duck.—**duckweed,** *n.* The popular name of several species of plants growing in ditches and shallow water, and floating on the surface, serving for food for ducks and geese.

duct, dukt *n.* [L. *ductus* a leading, conducting, from *duco, ductum,* to lead. DUKE.] Any tube or canal by which a fluid is conveyed, used especially of canals in the bodies of animals or in plants.—**ductile,** duk´til, *a.* [L. *ductilis.*] Easy to be led or influenced (persons); tractable; yielding to persuasion or instruction; capable of being drawn out into wire or threads (used of metals).— **ductility,** duk·til´i·ti, *n.* The prop-erty of solid bodies, particularly metals, which renders them capable of being extended by drawing, while their thickness or diameter is dimin-ished, without any actual separation of their parts; a yielding disposition of mind; ready compliance.—**ductless glands.** Structures of various use, superficially resembling glands, but devoid of ducts for carrying off a liquid secretion, e.g. thymus, thyroid, and spleen.

dude, dūd, *n.* A dandy; a fop. *Western slang,* an Easterner or city-bred person.

dude ranch, *n.* A ranch operated for, or accommodating tourists, where they may board and get a taste of ranching.

dudgeon, duj´on, *n.* [Origin un-known.] Anger; resentment; malice; ill will; discord.

due, dū, *a.* [O.Fr. *deu,* Fr. *dû,* pp. of *devoir,* from L. *debere,* to owe. DEBT.] Falling to be paid or done to another; owed by one to another, and by contract, justice, or propriety required to be paid; liable or meriting to be given or devoted; owing to (the attention *due* to one's studies); proper; fit; appropriate; suitable; becoming; seasonable; required by the circumstances (to behave with *due* gravity); exact; correct; owing origin or existence; to be attributed or assigned as causing (an effect *due* to the sun's attraction); that ought to have arrived or to be present; bound or stipulated to arrive (the mails are *due*).—*adv.* Directly; exact-ly (to sail *due* east).—*n.* What is owed or ought to be paid or done to another; that which justice, office, rank, or station, social re-lations or established rules of de-corum, require to be given, paid, or done; a toll, tribute, fee, or other legal exaction.—**duly,** dū´li, *adv.* In a due, fit, or proper manner; fitly; suitably; properly; at the proper time.

duel, dū´el, *n.* [Fr. *duel,* It. *duello,* from L. *duellum,* old form of *bellum,* war, from *duo,* two] A premeditated combat between two persons with deadly weapons for the purpose of deciding some private difference or quarrel; a single combat; a fight between two fortresses, two encamped armies, and the like, carried on without the tactics of a pitched battle or an assault —*v.i.*—**dueled, dueling.** To engage in a duel.—**dueling,** dū´-el·ing, *n.* The practice of engaging in duels.—**duelist,** dū´el·ist, *n.* One who engages in a duel or in duels.—**duello,** dū·el´lō, *n.* A duel; the art or practice of *dueling,* or the code of laws which regulate it (*Shak.*).

duenna, dū·en´na, *n.* [Sp. *duenna, dueña,* a form of *doña,* fem. of *don,* from L. *domina,* a mistress.] An elderly female appointed to take charge of the younger female mem-bers of Spanish and Portuguese families; an elderly woman who is kept to guard a younger.

duet, dū·et´, *n.* [It. *duetto,* from *duo,* two.] A musical composition for two voices or two instruments.

duffel, duffle, duf´el, duf´l, *n.* [From *Duffel,* a Belgian manufacturing town.] A kind of coarse woolen cloth having a thick nap; supplies as for camping.

duffer, duf´ėr, *n.* A peddler; a hawker of cheap, flashy articles; a hawker of sham jewelry; a person who is a sham; a useless character; a stupid person; a fogey (*colloq.*).

dug, dug, *n.* [Akin to Sw. *dägga,* Dan. *dægge,* to suckle; from root seen in Skr. *duh,* to milk.] The pap or nipple of a woman or (now generally) of an animal.

dug, dug, pret. & pp. of *dig.*

dugong, dū´gong, *n.* [Malayan.] A herbivorous mammal of the Indian Seas, allied to the manatee or sea cow.

dugout, dug´out, *n.* [Amer.] A boat made by hollowing out a large log; an underground shelter for troops in trenches; a shelter at the side of a baseball field containing the players' bench.

duke, dūk, *n.* [Fr. *duc,* from L. *dux, ducis,* a leader, from *duco,* to lead (seen also in *duct, ducat, conduct, produce, educate,* etc.); cog. A.Sax. *toga* a leader, E. *tug* and *tow.*] A chief, prince, or leader‡; in Great Britain, one of the highest order of nobility; a title of honor or nobility next below that of a prince; in some countries on the Continent, a sover-eign prince, the ruler of a state.— **dukedom,** dūk´dum, *n.* The seign-iory or possessions of a duke; the territory of a duke; the title or quality of a duke.

dulcet, dul´set, *a.* [O.Fr. *dolcet,* L. *dulcis,* sweet.] Sweet to the taste; luscious; exquisite; sweet to the ear; melodious; harmonious; agreeable to the mind.—**dulcification,** dul´si·fi·kā˝shon, *n.* The act of dulcifying.— **dulcify,** dul´si·fī, *v.t.*—*dulcified, dul-cifying.* [Fr. *dulcifier,* from L. *dulcis,* sweet, and *facio,* to make.] To sweeten; to free from acidity, salt-ness, or acrimony; to render more agreeable to the taste.

dulcimer, dul´si·mėr, *n.* [Sp. *dul-cemele,* It. *dolcimello,* from L. *dulcis,* sweet.] A musical instrument con-sisting in its modern form of a shallow quadrilateral box without a top, across which runs a series of wires, tuned by pegs at the sides, and played on by being struck by two cork-headed hammers.

dulia, dū´li·a, *n.* [Gr. *douleia,* service, from *doulos,* a slave.] An inferior kind of worship or adoration, as that paid to saints and angels in the Roman Catholic Church.

dull, dul, *a.* [A.Sax. *dol, dwol,* erring, dull, from *dwelan,* to be torpid or dull; akin Goth. *dvals,* foolish; Icel. *dul,* foolishness; D. *dol,* L.G. *dull,* G. *toll,* mad.] Stupid; doltish; slow of understanding; heavy; sluggish; without life or spirit; slow of motion; wanting sensibility or keenness in some of the senses (sight, hearing); not quick; sad; melancholy; depress-ing; dismal; gross; inanimate; in-sensible; not pleasing; not exhilarat-ing; cheerless; not bright or clear; tarnished; dim; obscure; blunt; ob-tuse; having a thick edge; cloudy; overcast.—*v.t.* To make dull; to stupefy; to blunt; to render less acute; to make less eager; to make sad or melancholy; to make insen-sible or slow to perceive; to render dim; to sully; to tarnish or cloud.— *v.i.* To become dull.—**dullard,** dul´-ėrd, *n.* A stupid person; a dolt; a blockhead; a dunce.—**dullish,** dul´-ish, *a.* Somewhat dull; somewhat stupid; tiresome.—**dully,** dul´i, *a.* Somewhat dull. (*Tenn.*)—*adv.* (dul´-li). Stupidly; slowly; sluggishly; without life or spirit.—**dullness,**

dulness, dul´nes, *n.* The state or character of being dull.

dulse, duls, *n.* [Gael. *duilliasg*, Ir. *duileasg*, dulse.] A kind of edible seaweed having a reddish-brown, or purple, frond, several inches long, found at low water.

Duma, dö´ma, *n.* The Russian parliament created in 1905, and overthrown by the Bolshevist revolution in 1917.

dumb, dum, *a.* [A.Sax. *dumb* = Goth. *dumbs*, Dan *dum*, G. *dumm*, dumb, stupid; allied to *dim*, and perhaps Goth. *daubs*, deaf.] Mute; silent; not speaking; destitute of the power of speech; unable to utter articulate sounds; not accompanied with speech; effected by signs (*dumb show*).—*To strike dumb*, to confound; to astonish; to render silent by astonishment.—*v.t.* To silence; to overpower with sound (*Shak.*).—**dumbly**, dum´li, *adv.* Mutely; silently; without words or speech.—**dumbness**, dum´nes, *n.* State of being dumb.—**dumbbells**, *n. pl.* Weights, usually consisting of two iron balls with a short piece for grasping between them, swung in the hands for developing the chest, the muscles of the arms, etc.—**dumb show**, *n.* A sort of dramatic representation performed pantomimically; gesture without words; pantomime. —**dumb-waiter**, *n.* A framework with shelves, made to move from floor to floor in a house for conveying food, etc.; a side table or other portable piece of furniture in a dining room, on which dessert, etc., is placed until required.—**dumfound**, **dumbfound**, dum·found´, *v.t.* To strike dumb; to confuse. (*Colloq.*)—**dumfounder**, dum·foun´dèr, *v.t.* To confuse; to stupefy; to strike dumb; to confound. (*Colloq.*)—**dummy**, dum´i, *n.* One who is dumb; the fourth or exposed hand during the play of bridge or whist; also when there are only three playing; a sham object doing service for a real one, as sham packages, etc.; a lay figure on which merchants display clothing. —*a.* Silent; mute; sham; fictitious.

dumdum, dum´dum, *n.* [Indian name of station with arsenal.] A soft-nosed bullet which expands and lacerates on striking.

dump, dump, *v.t.* [Akin to *bump*, *thump*.] To put or throw down with a bang; to deposit carelessly; to sell more cheaply abroad than in the home market.—*n.* A pile of refuse or other waste material; a place for dumping; *milit.* a temporary storehouse.

dump, dump, *n.* [Allied to *damp*; Dan. *dump*, dull; G. *dampf*, steam, vapor; comp. *dumps*, melancholy, with *vapors*, in the sense of nervousness or depression.] A dull gloomy state of the mind; sadness; melancholy; low spirits; heaviness of heart: generally in the plural, and now used only when a ludicrous effect is intended; a melancholy tune (*Shak.*).‡ —**dumpish**, dum´pish, *a.* Sad; melancholy; depressed in spirits.— **dumpishly**, dum´pish·li, *adv.* In a

moping manner. — **dumpishness**, dum´pish·nes, *n.* State of being dumpish.

dumpling, dump´ling, *n.* [Connected with Prov.E. *dump*, a clumsy leaden counter, a lump; also perhaps prov. *dump*, to knock.] A kind of pudding or mass of boiled paste, with or without fruit in it.—**dumpy**, dum´pi, *a.* Short and thick.—**dumpy level**, *n.* A spirit level having a short telescope with a large aperture, and a compass, used in surveying.

dun, dun, *a.* [A.Sax. *dunn*, perhaps from W. *dwn*, Gael. *donn*, dun.] Of a grayish-brown or dull-brown color; of a smoky color.—**dunnish**, dun´ish, *a.* Inclined to a dun color; somewhat dun.

dun, dun, *v.t.*—dunned, dunning. [A form of *din*.] To clamor for payment of a debt from; to demand a debt in a pressing manner from; to call on for payment repeatedly; to urge importunately.—*n.* One who duns.

dunce, duns, *n.* [From *Duns Scotus*, the leader of the Schoolmen of the fourteenth century, opposed to the revival of classical learning; hence this name was given to his followers in contempt by their opponents.] An ignoramus; a pupil too stupid to learn; a dullard; a thick-skull.

dunderhead, **dunderpate**, dun´dèr·hed, dun´dèr·pāt, *n.* [Comp. Dan. *dummerhoved*, a dunderhead, lit. stupid-head, from *dum*, stupid.] A dunce; a dull-head.—**dunderheaded**, dun´dèr·hed·ed, *a.* Stupid; thick-skulled.

dune, dūn, *n.* [A.Sax. *dún.* DOWN.] A low hill of sand accumulated on the sea-coast.

dung, dung, *n.* [A.Sax. *dung*, G. *dung.* Sw. *dynga*; connected with verb to *ding*.] The excrement of animals.— *v.t.* To manure with dung.—*v.i.* To void excrement.—**dunghill**, dung´hil, *n.* A heap of dung; the place where dung is kept collected; a mean or vile abode or situation.—*a.* Sprung from the dunghill; mean; low; vile.

dungaree, dun·ga·rē´, *n.* [Anglo-Indian, low, common, vulgar.] A coarse unbleached Indian calico, generally blue, worn by sailors.

dungeon, dun´jon, *n.* [Fr. *dongeon*, *donjon.* DONJON.] The innermost and strongest tower of a castle; the donjon; a close prison; a deep, dark place of confinement.—*v.t.* To confine in a dungeon.

duniewassal, dūn·i·was´sal, *n.* [Gael. *duin´ uasal*, from *duine*, a man, and *uasal*, gentle.] A gentleman of secondary rank among the Scottish Highlanders; a cadet of a family of rank.

dunk, dungk, *v.t. and i.* [Amer. from L.G. *dunken*, to dip.] To dip something into a liquid while eating.

Dunker, dung´kèr, *n.* A member of a sect of Baptists originating in Philadelphia.

dunlin, dun´lin, *n.* [From *dune* with dim. termination -*ling*; or from *dun*, adj.] A species of sandpiper, about eight inches in length, often occurring in vast flocks along sandy shores.

dunnage, dun´ij, *n.* [For *downage*, from *down*.] Faggots, boughs, or loose wood laid on the bottom of a ship to raise heavy goods above the bottom to prevent injury from water; also loose articles of lading wedged between parts of the cargo to hold them steady.

duo, dū´ō, *n.* [It. from L. *duo*, two.] *Mus.* a duet; a pair.

duodecimal, dū·o·des´i·mal, *a.* [L. *duodecim*, twelve.] Proceeding in computation by twelves, *n. pl.* An arithmetical method of ascertaining the number of square feet and square inches in a rectangular area or surface, whose sides are given in feet and inches.—**duodecimo**, dū·o·des´-i·mō, *a.* Having or consisting of twelve leaves to a sheet.—*n.* A book in which a sheet is folded into twelve leaves; the size of a book consisting of sheets so folded: usually indicated thus, 12mo.

duodenum, dū·o·dē´num, *n.* [From L. *duodeni*, twelve each, so called because its length is about twelve fingers' breadth.] The first portion of the small intestines; the twelve-inch intestine.—**duodenal**, dū·o·dē´-nal, *a.* Connected with or relating to the duodenum.—**duodenary**, dū·o·den´e·ri, *a.* [L. *duodenarius.*] Relating to the number twelve; twelve-fold; increasing by twelves.—*Duodenary arithmetic*, that system in which the local value of the figures increases twelvefold from right to left, instead of tenfold.

duologue, dū´o·log, *n.* [L. *duo*, two, -*logue*, from *dialogue.*] A dialogue between two.

dupe, dūp, *n.* [Fr. *dupe*, a name sometimes given to the hoopoe, and hence, from the bird being regarded as stupid, applied to a stupid person. Comp. *pigeon.*] A person who is deceived, or one easily led astray by his credulity.—*v.t.*—duped, duping. [Fr. *duper.*] To make a dupe of; to trick; to mislead by imposing on one's credulity.—**dupable**, dū´pa·bl, *a.* Liable to be or capable of being duped.—**duper**, dū´pèr, *n.* One who dupes; a cheat; a swindler.—**dupery**, dū´pèr·i, *n.* The art of duping.

duple, dū´pl, *a.* [L. *duplus*, double. DOUBLE.] Double.—*Duple ratio*, that of 2 to 1, 8 to 4, etc.—*Sub-duple ratio* is the reverse, or as 1 to 2, 4 to 8, etc.—*v.t.*† To double.—**duplex**, dū´pleks, *a.* [L.] Double; twofold; an apartment of rooms on two floors; a house with two apartments.

duplicate, dū´pli·kit, *a.* [L. *duplicatus*, from *duplico*, to double, from *duplex*, double, twofold—*duo*, two, and *plico*, to fold. DUAL, PLY.] Double; twofold.—*Duplicate proportion* or *ratio*, the proportion or ratio of squares.—*n.* Another corresponding to the first; a second thing of the same kind; another example or specimen of the same kind.—*v.t.* dū´pli·kāt.—duplicated, duplicating. To make an exact copy of; to repeat exactly.—**duplication**, dū·pli·kā´-shon, *n.* The act or process of duplicating; the state of being duplicated; a duplicate copy.—**dupli-**

cative, dū′pli•ka•tiv, *a.*—**duplicator,** dū′pli•kā•tẽr, *n.* One who duplicates; a machine for producing copies.

duplicity, dū•plis′i•ti, *n.* [F. *duplicité,* from LL. *duplicitas.*] The state of being double; doubleness; especially, doubleness of heart or speech; the act or practice of exhibiting a different or contrary conduct, or uttering different or contrary sentiments at different times in relation to the same thing; double-dealing; dissimulation; deceit.

durable, dū′ra•bl, *a.* [L. *durabilis,* from *duro,* to last, *durus,* hard.] Having the quality of lasting or continuing long in being without perishing or wearing out; not perishable or changeable.—**durability, durableness,** dū•ra•bil′i•ti, dū′ra•bl•nes, *n.* The quality of being durable.—**durably,** dū′ra•bli, *adv.* In a durable manner.

Duralumin, dūr•al′ū•min, *n.* A composite material consisting mainly of aluminum as strong as mild steel under proper heat treatment.

dura mater, dū′ra mā•tẽr. [L.; lit. hard mother: called *mother* as protecting the brain.] The outer membrane of the brain: so named from its hardness compared with the membrane which lies under it, called *pia mater* (pious mother), and which also surrounds the brain.

duramen, dū•rā′men, *n.* [L. *duramen,* hardness, *durus,* hard.] The central wood or heartwood in the trunk of an exogenous tree.

durance, dū′rans, *n.* [In the common sense apparently shortened from *endurance,* from the hardships of imprisonment; comp. *duress.*] Imprisonment; restraint of the person; custody; duration†.—**duration,** dū•rā′shon, *n.* Continuance in time; length or extension of existence, indefinitely; power of continuance.

durbar, dẽr′bär, *n.* [Hind. and Per. *darbâr*—Per. *dâr,* door. and *bâr,* court, assembly.] An audience room in the palaces of the native princes of India; state levee or audience held by the governor-general of India, or by a native prince; an official reception.

duress, dū′res, *n.* [O.Fr. *duresse,* hardship, constraint, from L. *duritia,* harshness, hardness, from *durus,* hard.] Imprisonment; restraint of liberty; *law,* also restraint or constraint by threats of personal injury.

durian, dū′ri•an, *n.* [The Malay name.] A tree of the Malayan Archipelago; also its fruit, which is extremely luscious and enticing to eat, but has an abominably offensive odor.

during, dū′ring. [From the L. phrase *vita durante,* while life lasts.] Continuing; lasting; in the time of; throughout the course of.

durmast, dẽr′mast, *n.* A highly valued species of oak, closely allied to the common oak.

durra, dur′a, *n.* [Ar.] A species of grain much cultivated in Africa, Asia, and the south of Europe; Indian millet; Guinea corn.

durst, dẽrst, *pret.* of *dare.*

dusk, dusk, *a.* [Probably akin to Sw. *dusk,* dull weather; Icel. *doska,* to dawdle; L.G. *dusken,* to slumber.] Tending to darkness, or moderately dark; tending to a dark or black color; moderately black; swarthy.—*n.* An approach to darkness; incipient or imperfect obscurity; a middle degree between light and darkness; twilight; darkness of color.—*v.t.†* To make dusky, or somewhat dark.—*v.i.†* To begin to lose light or whiteness; to grow dark; to cause a dusky appearance.—**dusken,** dus′kn, *v.i.* To grow dusk; to become dark.—*v.t.* To make dusk, or somewhat dark.—**duskily,** dus′ki•li, *adv.* In a dusky manner.—**duskiness,** dus′ki•nes, *n.* The state of being dusky.—**duskish,** dus′kish, *a.* Moderately dusky.—**dusky,** dus′ki, *a.* Partially dark or obscure; not luminous; tending to blackness in color; dark-colored; not bright; gloomy.

dust, dust, *n.* [A.Sax. *dust,* dust; same word as Icel. and L.D. *dust,* D. *duist,* dust; akin to G. *dunst,* vapor.] Fine dry particles of earth or other matter, so attenuated that they may be raised and wafted by the wind; hence, *fig.* commotion and confusion accompanying a struggle; earth or earthy matter as symbolic of mortality; the body when it has moldered in the grave; the grave; a low condition; money (*colloq.*).—*To throw dust in one's eyes,* to mislead; to blind as to the true character of something.—*v.t.* To free from dust; to brush, wipe, or sweep away dust; to beat; to sprinkle with dust.—**dust bowl,** *n.* An area subject to violent and frequent dust storms.—**duster,** dus′tẽr, *n.* One who or that which dusts; an overgarment that protects clothing from dust.—**dust jacket,** *n.* A paper cover for a book.—**dust storm,** *n.* A violent wind carrying masses of dust from or across a dry region.—**dusty,** dus′ti, *a.* Filled or sprinkled with dust; reduced to dust; like dust; of the color of dust.

Dutch, dutsh, *n.* [G. *deutsch,* German, Germanic, pertaining to the Germanic or Teutonic race; O.H.G. *diutisc,* from *diot,* A.Sax. *theod,* Goth. *thiuda,* people. The word has latterly been narrowed from its original meaning. The term *Low Dutch* means Dutch or Low German (*Plattdeutsch*), as opposed to *High Dutch* (*Hochdeutsch*), or German proper.] *Pl.* originally, the Germanic race; the German peoples generally; now only applied to the people of the Netherlands; *sing.* the language of the Netherlands.—*a.* Of or referring to the Netherlands or its inhabitants; pertaining to or characteristic of the Dutch.—*Dutch auction,* an auction at which the auctioneer starts with a high price, and comes down till he meets with a bidder; a mock auction.—*Dutch courage,* false or artificial courage; boldness inspired by intoxicating spirits.—*Dutch clover,* white clover, a valuable pasture plant.—*Dutch concert,* a concert in which a company join, each singing his own song at the same time as his neighbor, or in which each member sings a verse of a song, some well-known chorus being used as the burden after each verse.—*Dutch gold, Dutch metal,* an alloy of eleven parts of copper and two of zinc.—*Dutch leaf,* false gold leaf.—*Dutch mineral,* copper beaten out into very thin leaves.—*Dutch myrtle,* sweet gale; a fragrant shrub found in bogs and moors.—*Dutch oven,* a tin hanging screen for cooking before a kitchen range or ordinary fire grate; a metal utensil that opens in front, used for roasting before an open fire or on top of a stove; a heavy iron pot with a close-fitting cover; a brick oven in which the walls are preheated for cooking.—*Dutch treat,* a meal or treat at which each person pays for himself.—**Dutchman,** dutsh′man, *n.* A Netherlander.

duty, dū′ti, *n.* [From *due.*] That which a person is bound by any natural, moral, or legal obligation to do or perform; what has to be done as being due towards another; obligation to do something; obedience; submission; act of reverence or respect; any service, business, or office; particularly, military or similar service; a tax, toll, or impost; any sum of money required by government to be paid on the importation, exportation, or consumption of goods.—**duteous,** dū′tè•us, *a.* Performing that which is due, or that which law, justice, or propriety requires; dutiful; obedient; enjoined by duty (*Shak.*)†.—**duteously,** dū′tē•us•li *adv.* In a duteous manner.—**duteousness,** dū′tē•us•nes, *n.* Quality of being duteous. —**dutiable,** dū′ti•a•bl, *a.* Subject to the imposition of duty or customs.—**dutiful,** dū′ti•ful, *a.* Performing the duties or obligations required by law, justice, or propriety; obedient; submissive to superiors; expressive of respect or a sense of duty; respectful; reverential; required by duty.—**dutifully,** dū′ti•ful•li, *adv.* In a dutiful manner.—**dutifulness,** dū′ti•ful•nes, *n.* The state or character of being dutiful.

duvetyn, duvetine, dū′vè•tẽn, *n.* A soft fabric with a fine velvety nap, made of wool mixed with silk or cotton, or both.

dwarf, dwarf, *n.* [A.Sax. *dwerg, dweorg,* D. *dwerg,* Sw. *dwerg, dwerf,* L.G. *dwarf,* a dwarf.] A general name for an animal or plant which is much below the ordinary size of the species or kind; a very diminutive man or woman.—*v.t.* To hinder from growing to the natural size; to prevent the due development of; to stunt; to cause to look small or insignificant by comparison.—*v.i.* To become less; to become dwarfish or stunted.—**dwarfish,** dwarf′fish, *a.* Like a dwarf; below the common stature or size; very small; low; petty; despicable.—**dwarfishly,** dwarf′fish•li, *adv.* In a dwarfish manner.—**dwarfishness,** dwarf′fish•

nes, *n.* The state or quality of being dwarfish.

dwell, dwel, *v.i.*—*dwelled*, usually contracted into *dwelt*, *dwelling*. [From A.Sax. *dwellan*, to deceive, prevent, hinder; Icel. *dvelja*, to hinder, to delay; Dan. *dvaele*, to loiter, delay, dwell; akin *dull*.] To abide as a permanent resident; to live in a place; to have a habitation for some time or permanently; to be in any state or condition; to continue.— *To dwell on*, or *upon*, to keep the attention fixed on; to hang upon with fondness; to occupy a long time with; to be tedious over.— **dweller,** dwel′ẽr, *n.* One who dwells; an inhabitant.—**dwelling,** dwel′ing, *n.* Habitation; place of residence; abode; continuance; residence.

dwindle, dwin′dl, *v.i.*—*dwindled*, *dwindling*. [Freq. from O.R. and Sc. *dwine*; A.Sax. *dwinan*, to pine, waste away=D. *dwijnen*, Icel. *dvina*, Dan. *tvine*, to pine.] To diminish gradually; to become small and insignificant; to shrink; to waste or consume away; to degenerate.—*v.t.* To cause to dwindle.—*n.* The process of dwindling; decline.

dyad, di′ad, *n.* [Gr. *dyas*, *dyados*, from *dyo*, two.] Two units treated as one; a pair; a couple; *chem.* an elementary substance, each atom of which, in combining with other bodies, is equivalent to two atoms of hydrogen.—**dyadic,** di·ad′ik, *a.* Pertaining or relating to the number two, or to a dyad; consisting of two parts or elements.

dyarchy, di′är·ki, *n.* [Gr. *duo*, two, *archē*, rule.] The rule of two persons together.

dye, di, *v.t.*—*dyed*, *dyeing*. [A.Sax. *deâgan*, from *deâg*, dye, color.] To give a new and permanent color to: applied particularly to cloth or the materials of cloth, as wool, cotton, silk, and linen; also to hair, skins, etc.; to stain; to color; to tinge.—*n.* A coloring liquid; color; stain; tinge.—**dyer,** di′ẽr, *n.* One whose occupation is to dye cloth and the like.—**dyer's-weed,** *n.* Any of several dye-yielding plants, as the woodwaxen.—**dyestuff,** *n.* Materials used in dyeing.— **dyewood,** *n.* A general name for any wood from which dye is extracted.

dying, di′ing, *a.* Mortal; destined to death; given, uttered, or manifested just before death (*dying* words); pertaining to or associated with death (*dying* hour); drawing to a close; fading away.—*n.* The act of expiring; death.

dyke, *n.* and *v.* Same as *Dike*.

dynam, di′nam, *n.* [Gr. *dynamis*, power.] A term proposed to express a unit of work equal to a weight of 1 lb. raised through 1 foot in a second; a foot-pound.—**dynameter,** di·nam′e·tẽr, *n.* An instrument for determining the magnifying power of telescopes.—**dynamic, dynamical,** di·nam′ik, di·nam′i·kal, *a.* Pertaining to strength, power, or force; relating to dynamics; relating to the effects of the forces or moving agencies in

nature.—*Dynamical electricity*, current electricity.—**dynamically,** di·nam′i·kal·li, *adv.* In a dynamical manner.—**dynamics,** di·nam′iks, *n.* That area of mechanics that deals with forces and their effects on bodies in motion or at rest; patterns of change or growth in objects.—**dynamism,** di′na·mizm, *n.* The doctrine that all substance involves force.— **dynamite,** di′na·mit, *n.* An explosive substance consisting of a siliceous earth, and sometimes of charcoal, sawdust, etc., impregnated with nitroglycerin, and having a disruptive force estimated at about eight times that of gunpowder.— *v.t.* To shatter with dynamite.— **dynamiter,** din′a·mit·ẽr, *n.* One who uses dynamite for destroying public buildings or other criminal purposes.—**dynamo,** di′na·mō, *n.* A generator; a machine that transforms mechanical input into electrical output; a forceful, energetic person.— **dynamometer,** di′na·mom″e·tẽr, *n.* An instrument for measuring force or power, especially that of men, animals, machines, the strength of materials, etc.—**dynamotor,** di′na·mōt·ẽr, *n.* A machine combining the generator and the electric motor.— **dynamometric, dynamometrical,** di′na·mo·met″rik, di′na·mo·met″ri·kal, *a.*—**dynamoelectric,** di·nam′ō·ē·lek″trik, *a.* With *machine*, an electric generator or motor.

dynasty, din′as·ti, *n.* [Gr. *dynasteia*, sovereignty, from *dynastēs*, a lord or chief, from *dynamai*, to be strong, *dynamis*, power.] A race or succession of rulers of the same line or family, who govern a particular country; the period during which they rule.— **dynastic,** di·nas′tik, *a.* Relating to a dynasty or line of kings.

dyne, din, *n.* [Gr. *dynamis*, power.] *Physics*, a unit of force, being that force which, acting on a gram for one second, generates a velocity of a centimeter per second.

dyscrasia, dis·krā′si·a, *n.* [Gr. *dyskrasia*—*dys*, evil, and *krasis*, habit.] *Med.* a bad habit of body.

dysentery, dis′en·te·ri, *n.* [Gr. *dysenteria*—*dys*, bad, and *entera*, intestines.] An amoebic or bacillary inflammation of the mucous membrane of the large intestine, accompanied generally with much fever and great prostration, frequent stools, the discharges being mixed with blood and mucus.—**dysenteric,** dis·en·ter′ik, *a.*

dyslogistic, dis·lo·jis′tik, *a.* [Formed on the model of *eulogistic*, *dys* signifying ill, and the word having therefore the opposite signification of *eulogistic*.] Conveying censure, disapproval, or opprobrium; censorious; opprobrious.—**dyslogistically,** dis·lo·jis′ti·kal·li, *adv.* In a dyslogistic manner; so as to convey censure or disapproval.

dyspepsia, dyspepsy, dis·pep′si·a, dis·pep′si, *n.* [Gr. *dyspepsia*—*dys*, bad, and *peptō*, to concoct, to digest.] Indigestion, or difficulty of digestion; a state of the stomach in which its functions are disturbed, without the

presence of other diseases, or when, if they are present, they are but of minor importance.—**dyspeptic, dyspeptical,** dis·pep′tik, dis·pep′ti·kal, *a.* Afflicted with dyspepsia; pertaining to or consisting in dyspepsy. —**dyspeptic,** *n.* A person afflicted with dyspepsy.

dysphagia, dis·fā′ji·a, *n.* [Gr. *dys*, ill, and *phagō*, to eat.] *Med.* difficulty of swallowing.

dysphonia, dis·fō′ni·a, *n.* [Gr. *dys*, bad, and *phōnē*, voice.] *Med.* a difficulty of speaking occasioned by an ill disposition of the organs of speech.

dyspnea, disp·nē′a, *n.* [Gr. *dyspnoia* —*dys*, ill, and *pneō*, to breathe.] *Med.* difficulty of breathing.— **dyspneic,** disp·nē′ik, *a.* Affected with or resulting from dyspnea.

dysprosium, dis·prō′shi·um, *n.* A metallic element, highly magnetic, of the rare-earth series. Symbol, Dy; at. no., 66; at. wt., 162.50.

dysuria, dis·ū′ri·a, *n.* [Gr. *dysouria*— *dys*, ill, and *ouron*, urine.] *Med.* difficulty in discharging the urine, attended with pain and a sensation of heat.

E

E, e, ē, the second vowel and the fifth letter of the English alphabet, occurring more frequently than any other letter of the alphabet; *mus.* the third note or degree of the natural or diatonic scale.

each, ēch, *distrib. a.* and *pron.* [O.E. *eche*; *ech*, *ych*, *uch*, *elch*, *elc*, *ilk*; A.Sax. *aelc*, from *á*=*aye*, ever, and *lic*, like; similar to D. and L.G. *elk*, G. *jeglich*. Comp. *such* and *which*.] Every one of any number separately considered or treated; every one of two or more considered individually. With *other* it is used reciprocally; as, it is our duty to assist *each other* (that is, each to assist the other).

eager, ē′gẽr, *a.* [O.E. *egre*, O.Fr. *eigre*, Mod.Fr. *aigre*, eager, sharp, biting, from L. *acer*, *acris*, sharp, from root which appears in *acute* *acid*, *acrid*, etc.] Sharp, sour, acid (*Shak.*)‡; excited by ardent desire in the pursuit of any object; ardent to pursue, perform, or obtain; ardently wishing or longing; vehement; fervid; earnest; impetuous; keen.— **eagerly,** ē′gẽr·li, *adv.* In an eager manner.—**eagerness,** ē′gẽr·nes, *n.* The state or character of being eager; keenness; ardor; zeal.

eagle, ē′gl, *n.* [Fr. *aigle*, from L. *aquila*, an eagle, fem. of the rare adj. *aquilus*, dark-colored, swarthy.] A common name of many large birds of prey, characterized by a hooked beak and curved, sharp, and strong claws (talons), and by its great powers of flight and vision, often regarded as a symbol of royalty; the typical eagles constitute a genus (*Aquila*) in which the legs are feathered to the toes; a military standard

ch, *chain*; *ch*, Sc. lo*ch*; g, *go*; j, *job*; ng, si*ng*; TH, *then*; th, *thin*; w, *wig*; hw, *whig*; zh, azure.

having the figure of an eagle, such as that of ancient Rome and modern France; a gold coin of the United States, of the value of ten dollars, from the eagle on the reverse; a reading desk in churches in the form of an eagle with expanded wings; in golf, a score of two under par on any hole but a par-three hole.—**eaglet**, ē′glet, *n.* A small or young eagle.—**eaglestone**, *n.* A variety of argillaceous iron ore occurring in spherical, oval, or reniform masses varying from the size of a walnut to that of a man's head; so called from an ancient notion that they were often found in the nests of eagles.

eagre, ē′gėr, *n.* [A.Sax. *eágor, égor,* Icel. *ægir,* the sea.] A tidal wave moving up a river or estuary at spring tide; a bore.

ear, ēr, *n.* [A.Sax. *eáre*=D. *oor,* Icel. *eyra,* Dan. *öre,* G. *ohr,* L. *auris,* G. *ous.*] The organ of hearing, which in man and higher animals is composed of the external ear, a cartilaginous funnel for collecting the sound waves and directing them inward; the middle ear, tympanum or drum; and the internal ear or labyrinth; the sense of hearing; the power of distinguishing sounds; the power of nice perception of the differences of musical sounds; a favorable hearing; attention; heed; a part of any inanimate object resembling an ear; a projecting part from the side of anything; a handle of a tub, pitcher, etc.—*All ear,* all attention.—*To set by the ears,* to make strife between; to cause to quarrel.—*Up to the ears, over head and ears,* deeply absorbed or engrossed; overwhelmed. —**eared**, ērd, *a.* Having ears: usually in compounds, as *long-eared.*—**earache**, *n.* Pain in the ear.—**eardrop**, *n.* An ornamental pendant for the ear.—**eardrum**, *n.* The tympanum (which see).—**earmark**, *n.* A mark on the ear for distinguishing sheep, pigs, cattle, etc.; hence any mark for distinction or identification.—*v.t.* To distinguish by putting an earmark on; to set apart funds for an overdue purpose or estimate.— **ear phone**, *n.* A device worn over or in the ear that converts electrical energy into sound waves.—**earring**, *n.* An ornament that is worn in or on the lobe of the ear.—**ear shell**, *n.* One of a genus of gastropodous mollusks.—**earshot**, *n.* The distance the ear can perceive sound; hearing distance.—**earwax**, *n.* The waxy or viscous substance secreted by the ear; cerumen.—**earwig**, ēr′-wig, *n.* [A.Sax. *wicga,* a beetle.] One of a family of insects having a long narrow body and a pair of nippers at the extremity of the abdomen: so called from a popular delusion that they have a propensity to creep into the ear.

ear, ēr, *n.* [A.Sax. *ear,* D. *aar,* G. *ähre,* an ear.] A spike or head of corn or grain; that part of cereal plants which contains the flowers and seeds. —*v.i.* To shoot, as an ear; to form ears, as corn.

earl, ėrl, *n.* [A.Sax. *eorl,* Icel. Dan., and Sw. *jarl,* an earl.] In Britain a nobleman, the third in rank, being next below a marquis, and next above a viscount.—**earldom**, ėrl′-dum, *n.* The jurisdiction or dignity of an earl.—**earl marshal**, *n.* An officer of state in Great Britain, who, as the head of the College of Arms, determines all rival claims to arms, and grants armorial bearings, through the medium of the king-of-arms.

early, ėr′li, *a.* [A.Sax. *aerlice* (adv.), from *aer,* soon *lic,* like. ERE.] In advance of something else as regards time; sooner than ordinary; produced or happening before the usual time (*early* fruit, *early* maturity); forward; being at the beginning; first (in *early* manhood, *early* times). —*Early English architecture,* the style of architecture into which the Norman passed, the distinctive features of which are pointed arches, long, narrow, lancet-shaped windows without mullions, and a peculiar projecting ornament in the hollows of the moldings, called the dog-tooth ornament: called also the *First Pointed* or *Lancet Style.*—*Early Victorian,* of art, literature, or the state prevailing at the time, with a slight tinge of depreciation.—*adv.* Soon, or sooner than usual or than others; in good season; betimes.— **earliness**, ėr′li•nes, *n.* The state of being early.

earn, ėrn, *v.t.* [A.Sax. *earnian,* to earn, to reap the fruit of one's labors; O.D. *erne* G. *ernte* harvest.] To merit or deserve by labor or by any performance; to gain by labor, service, or performance; to deserve and receive as compensation.— **earnings**, ėr′ningz, *n. pl.* That which is earned; what is gained or deserved by labor, services, or performance; wages; reward; recompense.

earnest, ėr′nest, *a.* [A.Sax. *eornest,* earnestness, *eorneste* (adj.), earnest, serious; cog. D. and G. *ernst,* earnest, D. *ernsten,* to endeavor.] Ardent in the pursuit of an object; eager to obtain; having a longing desire; warmly engaged or incited; warm; zealous; intent; serious; grave. —*n.* Seriousness; a reality; a real event, as opposed to jesting or feigned appearance.—**earnestly**, ėr′-nest•li, *adv.* In an earnest manner.— **earnestness**, ėr′nest•nes, *n.* The state or quality of being earnest.

earnest, ėr′nest, *n.* [From W. *ernes,* earnest or pledge, from *ern,* a pledge.] Something given by way of token or pledge, to bind a bargain and prove a sale; a part paid or delivered beforehand, as a pledge and security for the whole, or as a token of more to come; *fig.* anything which gives assurance, promise, or indication of what is to follow; first fruits; token.—**earnest money**, *n.* Money paid as earnest to bind a bargain or ratify and prove a sale.

earth, ėrth, *n.* [A.Sax. *eorthe;* Goth. *airtha,* Icel. *jörth,* Sw. and Dan. *jord,* G. *erde,* allied to A.Sax. *eard,* soil, home, dwelling, and perhaps to Gr. *era,* Skr. *ira*—earth, and to L. *aro,* to plough.] The particles which compose the mass of the globe, but more particularly the particles which form the mold on the surface of the globe; the globe which we inhabit; the planet third in order from the sun; the world, as opposed to other scenes of existence; the inhabitants of the globe; dry land, as opposed to the sea; the ground; the hole in which a fox or other burrowing animal hides itself; *chem.* the name given to certain tasteless, inodorous, dry, and uninflammable substances, the most important of which are lime, baryta, strontia, magnesia, alumina, zirconia, glucina, yttria, and thoria.—*v.t.* To hide in the earth; to cover with earth or mold.—*v.i.* To retire under ground; to burrow.—*Earth currents,* in *elect.* strong irregular currents, which disturb telegraphic lines of considerable length, flowing from one part of the line to another, affecting the instruments and frequently interrupting telegraphic communication.—**earthen**, ėrth′n, *a.* Made of earth; composed of clay or other like substance.—**earthly**, ėrth′li, *a.* Pertaining to the earth or this world; worldly; temporal; gross; vile; carnal; mean; composed of earth; among the things of this earth; possible; conceivable.—**earthliness**, ėrth′li•nes, *n.* The state or quality of being earthly.—**earthling**, ėrth′-ling, *n.* An inhabitant of the earth; a mortal; a frail creature; one much attached to worldly affairs; a worldling.—**earthy**, ėr′thi, *a.* Of or pertaining to earth; composed of earth; partaking of the nature of earth; like earth or having some of its properties.—**earthborn**, *a.* Born of the earth; springing originally from the earth; relating to or occasioned by earthly objects; of low birth; meanly born.—**earth-bound**, *a.* Fastened by the pressure of the earth; firmly fixed in the earth.—**earthenware**, ėrth′n•wâr, *n.* Every sort of household utensil made of clay hardened in the fire; crockery; pottery.—**earthnut**, *n.* An umbelliferous plant common in woods and fields, producing a brown sweetish farinaceous tuber or nut about the size of a chestnut, formed 4 to 6 inches below the surface, and of which swine are fond; also a name given to the groundnut.—**earthquake**, ėrth′kwāk, *n.* A shaking, trembling, or concussion of the earth, sometimes a slight tremor, at other times a violent shaking or convulsion, in which vast chasms open, swallowing up sometimes whole cities; at other times a rocking or heaving of the earth: probably due to internal igneous forces.— **earthshine**, *n.* The illumination of the dark portion of the moon, due to the sunlight reflected from the earth.—**earthwork**, *n.* A term applied to all operations where earth has to be removed or collected together, as in cuttings, embankments, etc.; a fortification constructed of earth.— **earthworm**, *n.* An annelid worm, living in wet soil, that is characterized by a long cylindrical body tapering at each end, minute bristles used in movement, and the digesting of decayed organic material obtained from the soil; a mean sordid wretch.

ease, ēz, *n.* [Fr. *aise,* ease; O.Fr. *eise, ayse, aize,* ease; Pr. *aise,* It. *agio,* Ō.It. *asio,* ease; all words of very doubtful origin.] Freedom from labor or exertion, or from physical pain, disturbance, excitement, or annoyance; freedom from concern, anxiety, solicitude or anything that frets or ruffles the mind; tranquility; repose; freedom from difficulty or great labor; facility; freedom from constraint, formality, stiffness, harshness, forced expressions, or unnatural arrangement; unaffectedness.—*Chapel of ease,* a chapel taking off the burdens of a large parish, and having right to most part of ecclesiastical duties.—*v.t.*—*eased, easing.* To free from pain, suffering, anxiety, care, or any disquiet or annoyance; to relieve; to give rest to; to mitigate; to alleviate; to assuage; to allay; to abate or remove in part (to *ease* pain, grief, a burden, etc.); to render less difficult; to facilitate; to release from pressure or restraint by moving gently; to shift a little.—**easeful,** ēz′fu̇l, *a.* Giving ease. [Poet.]—**easement,** ēz′ment, *n.* Convenience; accommodation; that which gives ease or relief; *law,* a privilege without profit which one proprietor has in the estate of another proprietor, distinct from the ownership of the soil, as a way, watercourse, etc.; Scots law, *servitude* (q.v.).—**easy,** ē′zi, *a.* Being at rest; having ease; free from pain, disturbance, suffering, annoyance, care, trouble, concern, anxiety, or the like; quiet; tranquil; giving no pain or disturbance; requiring no great labor or exertion; not difficult; not steep, rough, or uneven; gentle; not unwilling; ready; not constrained, stiff, or formal; not rigid or strict; smooth; flowing; not straitened or restricted as regards money or means; affluent; comfortable.—**easily,** ē′zi•li, *adv.* In an easy manner.—**easiness,** ē′zi•nes, *n.* The state or quality of being easy.

easel, ē′zel, *n.* [G. *esel,* an ass, a wooden horse, or stand.] The wooden frame on which painters place pictures while at work upon them.

east, ēst, *n.* [A.Sax. *east*=D. *oost,* G. *ost,* Icel. *aust;* connected with L. *aurora* (anc. *ausosa*), Lith. *auszra,* the red of morning, Skr. *ushas,* the dawn, from a root *us,* to burn, as in L. *urere,* to burn.] One of the four cardinal points, being the point in the heavens where the sun is seen to rise at the equinox, or the corresponding point on the earth; that point of the horizon lying on the right hand when one's face is turned toward the north pole; [*cap.*] the regions or countries which lie east of Europe; the oriental countries.—*a.* Toward or in the direction of the rising sun; opposite from west.—

v.i. To move in the direction of the east; to veer from the north or south toward the east.—*adv.* In an easterly direction; eastward.—**easterling,** ēs′tėr•ling, *n.* An old name for a native of some country lying eastward of Britain, especially a trader from the shores of the Baltic.—**easterly,** ēs′tėr•li, *a.* Coming from the east; moving or directed eastward; situated or looking toward the east.—*adv.* On the east; in the direction of east.—**eastern,** ēs′tėrn, *a.* [A.Sax. *eastern.*] [*cap.*] Being or dwelling in the east; oriental; [not cap.] situated toward the east; on the east part; going toward the east, or in the direction of east.—*Eastern Church,* the Greek Church, established in Russia, into which it was introduced from Constantinople.—*Eastern Hemisphere,* the half of the earth east of the Atlantic Ocean, comprising the land masses of Africa, Asia, Australia, and Europe.—**eastward, eastwards,** ēst′wėrd, ēst′wėrdz, *adv.* Toward the east; in the direction of east from some point or place.—**eastward,** *a.* Facing, pointing, or having its direction toward the east.

Easter, ēs′tėr, *n.* [A.Sax. *eástre,* Easter, from A.Sax. *Eástre, Eóstre,* O.H.G. *Ostarâ,* a goddess of light or spring, in honor of whom a festival was celebrated in April, whence this month was called *easter-mônâth;* connected with *east.*] A movable festival of the Christian church observed in March or April in commemoration of the Saviour's resurrection. Easter is the first Sunday after the first full moon that falls on or next after the vernal equinox (March 21 in the Gregorian calendar); if the full moon happens on Sunday, Easter is celebrated one week later.

easy. See EASE.

eat, ēt, *v.i.* pret. eat or ate (et, āt); pp. eat or eaten (et, ē′tn). [A.Sax. *etan*=D. eten, Icel. eta, Dan. æde, Goth. *itan,* G. *essen;* from root seen also in L. edo, Gr. edō, Skr. ad, to eat.] To masticate and swallow; to partake of as food: said especially of solids; to corrode; to wear away; to gnaw into gradually.—*To eat one's heart,* to brood over one's sorrows or disappointments.—*To eat one's words,* to retract one's assertions.—*v.i.* To take food; to feed; to take a meal; to have a particular taste or character when eaten; to make way by corrosion; to gnaw; to enter by gradually wearing or separating the parts of a substance.—**eatable,** ē′ta•bl, *a.* Capable of being eaten; esculent.—*n.* Anything that may be eaten; that which is used as food; an edible or comestible.—**eater,** ē′tėr, *n.* One who eats; that which eats or corrodes.

Eau de Cologne, ō•dė•ko•lōn′, *n.* [Fr., from L. *aqua,* water.] A perfumed spirit, originally invented at *Cologne,* and consisting of spirits of wine flavored by a few drops of different essential oils blended so as to yield a fine fragrant scent.

eaves, ēvz, *n. pl.* [A.Sax. *efese, yfese* (sing.), the eave, the edge, whence *efesian,* to shave, to trim; same word as Goth. *ubizva,* O.H.G. *obisa,* a portico, a hall; from root of *over.*] That part of the roof of a building which projects beyond the wall and casts off the water that falls on the roof.—**eavesdrop,** *v.i.*—*eavesdropped, eaves-dropping.* To stand under the eaves, or near the windows of a house to listen and learn what is said within doors; to watch for an opportunity of hearing the private conversation of others.—*n.* The water which falls in drops from the eaves of a house.—**eavesdropper,** *n.* One who stands near the window or door of a house to catch what is said within doors; one who tries to hear private conversation.

ebb, eb, *n.* [A.Sax. *ebbe, ebba;* D. *eb, ebbe,* G. and Dan. *ebbe,* Sw. *ebb;* allied to E. *even,* G. *aben,* to fall off, to sink. EVENING.] The reflux of the tide; the return of tidewater toward the sea: opposed to *flood* or *flow;* a flowing backward or away; decline; decay (the *ebb* of prosperity or of life).—*v.i.* To flow back; to return, as the water of a tide toward the ocean: opposed to *flow;* to recede; to decrease; to decay; to decline.—**ebb tide,** *n.* The reflux of tidewater; the retiring tide.

ebony, eb′o•ni, *n.* [L. *ebenus,* Gr. *ebenos.*] A black colored wood of great hardness, heavier than water, and capable of taking on a fine polish, being much used in inlaid work and turnery; the most valuable variety is the heartwood of a large tree growing in Ceylon.—**ebon,** eb′on, *a.* Consisting of ebony; black like ebony; dark.—**ebonite,** eb′o•nīt, *n.* Same as *Vulcanite.*—**ebonize,** eb′-o•nīz, *v.t.* To make black or tawny; to tinge with the color of ebony.

ebracteate, ē•brak′tē•āt, *a.* [L. *e,* not, and *bractea,* a thin plate.] *Bot.* without bracts.

ebullition, eb•u̇•lish′on, *n.* [L. *ebullitio;* from *ebullio*—*e, ex,* out, up, and *bullio,* to boil, from *bulla,* a bubble. BOIL.] The operation or phenomenon of boiling; the bubbling up of a liquor by heat; the agitation produced in a fluid by the escape of a portion of it converted into an aeriform state by heat; effervescence; an outward display of feeling, as of anger; a sudden burst; a pouring forth; an overflowing.—**ebullience, ebulliency,** e•bu̇l′yens, e•bu̇l′yen•si, *n.* A boiling over; a bursting forth; overflow.—**ebullient,** e•bu̇l′yent, *a.* Boiling over; hence, over-enthusiastic; over-demonstrative.

écarté, ā•kär•tā′, *n.* [Fr., discarded.] A game of cards for two persons with thirty-two cards, the small cards from two to six being excluded: so called because the players may discard or exchange their cards for others.

eccentric, ek•sen′trik, *a.* [L. *eccentricus*—*ex,* from, and *centrum,* center.] Deviating or departing from the center; not having the same center; not concentric though sit-

uated one within the other; having the axis out of the center; deviating from usual practice; given to act in a way peculiar to one's self and different from other people; anomalous; singular; odd.—*n.* An eccentric person; a term applied to several mechanical contrivances for converting circular into reciprocating rectilinear motion, consisting of variously shaped disks, attached to a revolving shaft.—**eccentrically,** ek·sen′tri·kal·li, *adv.* With eccentricity; in an eccentric manner.—**eccentricity,** ek·sen·tris′i·ti, *n.* The state of having a center different from that of another related circle; the ratio, to the semi-major-axis, of the distance of the center of a planet's orbit (an ellipse) from the center of the sun (a focus); eccentric conduct; departure or deviation from what is regular or usual; oddity; whimsicalness.
ecclesiastic, ecclesiastical, ek·klē′zi·as″tik, ek·klē′zi·as″ti·kal, *a.* [Gr. *ekklēsiastikos,* from *ekklēsia,* an assembly, the church, from *ekkaleō,* to call forth or convoke—*ek,* and *kaleō,* to call.] Pertaining or relating to the church; not civil or secular.—**ecclesiastic,** *n.* A person in orders or consecrated to the services of the church and the ministry of religion.—**ecclesiastically,** ek·klē′zi·as″ti·kal·li, *adv.* In an ecclesiastical manner.—**Ecclesiastes,** ek·klē′zi·as″tēz, *n.* A canonical book of the Old Testament, placed between the book of Proverbs and the Song of Solomon; translation of *Koheleth,* the Preacher.—**ecclesiasticism,** ek·klē′zi·as″ti·sizm, *n.* Strong adherence to the principles of the Church, or to ecclesiastical observances, privileges, etc.—**Ecclesiasticus,** *n.* Book in the Apocrypha, but allowed for use in the Church.—**ecclesiology,** ek·klē′zi·ol″o·ji, *n.* [Gr. *ekklēsia,* the church, and *logos,* discourse.] The science of antiquities as applied to churches and other ecclesiastical foundations; the science and theory of church building and decoration.
ecdysis, ek′di·sis, *n.* [Gr., from *ekdyō,* to strip off—*ek,* out of, and *dyō,* to enter.] The act of shedding or casting an outer coat or integument, as in the case of serpents, certain insects, etc.
echelon, esh′e·lon, *n.* [Fr., from *échelle,* a ladder, from L. *scala,* a ladder.] *Milit.* the position of an army in the form of steps, or in parallel lines, each line being a little to the left or right of the preceding one.
echidna, e·kid′na, *n.* [Gr., an adder, a fabulous monster.] A burrowing mammal of Australia belonging to the Monotremata and resembling the hedgehog, except that the muzzle is protracted and slender, with a small aperture at the extremity for the protrusion of a long flexible tongue, by means of which it catches its insect prey; the porcupine anteater.—**echidnine,** e·kid′nin, *n.* Serpent poison; the secretion from the poison glands of the viper and

other serpents.
echinate, echinated, ek′i·nāt, ek′i·nā·ted, *a.* [L. *echinus,* Gr. *echinos,* a hedgehog, a sea-urchin.] Set with prickles; prickly, like a hedgehog; having sharp points.
echinoderm, e·kī′no·derm, *n.* [Gr. *echinos,* sea urchin, and *dermos,* skin.] Any marine animal of the phylum Echinodermata, having radial appendages, symmetrical body structure, and a spiny calcareous exoskeleton, such as the sea urchin, starfish, etc.—**echinus,** e·kī′nus, *n.* The generic name for the sea urchin; *arch.* a rounded molding at the top of a Doric column.—**echinoid,** e·kī′noid, *a.*
echo, ek′ō, *n.* pl. **echoes,** ek′ōz. [L. *echo,* from Gr. *ēchō,* an echo, a nymph, who, for love of Narcissus, pined away till nothing remained of her but her voice; a sound.] A sound reflected or reverberated from a distant surface; sound returned; repercussion of sound; repetition with assent; close imitation either in words or sentiments; a person who slavishly follows another in uttering sentiments.—*v.i.* To give forth an echo; to resound; to reflect sound; to be sounded back; to produce a sound that reverberates; to give out a loud sound.—*v.t.* To reverberate or send back the sound of; to repeat with assent.—**echolocation,** ek″ō·lō·kā′shon, *n.* A process by which the location or distance of an object is determined by the reflecting of sound waves off the object.
eclair, ā·klâr′, *n.* [Fr. *esclair,* lightning, and *esclairier,* to lighten.] An oblong pastry usually iced with chocolate and filled with custard.
éclat, ā·klä, *n.* [Fr., a splinter, noise, brightness, magnificence, from *éclater,* to split, to shiver, to glitter; from O.H.G. *skleizan,* G. *schleissen, schlitzen,* to split; E. *slit, slice, slate.*] A burst, as of applause; acclamation; approbation; brilliancy of success; splendor of effect; luster; renown; glory.
eclectic, ek·lek′tik, *a.* [Gr. *eklektikos*—*ek,* and *legō,* to choose.] Proceeding by the method of selection; choosing what seems best from others; not original nor following any one model or leader, but choosing at will from the doctrines, works, etc., of others; specifically applied to certain philosophers of antiquity who selected from the opinions and principles of various schools what they thought solid and good.—*n.* One who follows an eclectic method in philosophy, science, religion, and the like.—**eclectically,** ek·lek′ti·kal·li, *adv.* In an eclectic manner.—**eclecticism,** ek·lek′ti·sizm, *n.* The doctrine or practice of an eclectic.
eclipse, i·klips′, *n.* [L. *eclipsis,* from Gr. *ekleipsis,* defect, from *ekleipō,* to fail—*ek,* out and *leipō,* to leave.] An interception or obscuration of the light of the sun, moon, or other luminous body, by the intervention of some other body either between it and the eye or between the

luminous body and that illuminated by it; an eclipse of the moon, for instance, being caused by the earth coming between it and the sun; *fig.* a darkening or obscuring of splendor, brightness, or glory.—*v.t.*—*eclipsed, eclipsing.* To cause the eclipse or obscuration of; to cloud; to darken, obscure, throw into the shade; to cloud the glory of.—*v.i.* To suffer an eclipse.—**ecliptic,** i·klip′tik, *n.* [L. *linea ecliptica,* the ecliptic line, or line in which eclipses take place.] A great circle of the celestial sphere supposed to be drawn through the middle of the zodiac, making an angle with the equinoctial of about 23° 27′; the path which the sun, owing to the annual revolution of the earth, appears to describe among the fixed stars; a great circle on the terrestrial globe, answering to and falling within the plane of the celestial ecliptic.—*a.* Pertaining to or described by the ecliptic; pertaining to an eclipse.
eclogue, ek′log, *n.* [L. *ecloga,* Gr. *eklogē,* selection, from *eklegō,* to select. ECLECTIC.] A poetical composition in which shepherds are introduced conversing with each other; a bucolic.
ecology, ek·ol′o·jē, *n.* [Gr. *oikos,* a dwelling, *logos,* a discourse.] The branch of biology that deals with the relation between organisms and their natural environment.
economy, i·kon′o·mi, *n.* [L. *œconomia,* Gr. *oikonomia*—*oikos,* house, and *nomos,* law, rule.] The management, regulation, and government of a household; especially, the management of the pecuniary concerns of a household; hence, a frugal and judicious use of money; that management which expends money to advantage and incurs no waste; a prudent management of all the means by which property is saved or accumulated; a judicious application of time, of labor, and of the instruments of labor; the disposition or arrangement of any work or the system of rules and regulations which control it; the operations of nature in the generation, nutrition, and preservation of animals and plants; the regular, harmonious system in accordance with which the functions of living animals and plants are performed; the regulation and disposition of the internal affairs of a state or nation, or of any department of government.—**economic, economical,** ek·o·nom′ik, ek·o·nom′i·kal, *a.* Managing domestic or public pecuniary concerns with frugality; frugal; thrifty; relating to the science of economics, or the pecuniary and other productive resources of a country; relating to the means of living.—**economically,** ē·ko·nom′i·kal·li, *adv.*—**economics,** ē·ko·nom′iks, *n.* A social science that investigates the conditions and laws affecting the production, distribution, and consumption of the national wealth; formerly political economy.—**economist,** i·kon′o·mist, *n.*—One who

fāte, fär, fâre, fat, fạll; mē, met, hèr; pīne, pin; nōte, not, mŏve; tūb, tube, bụll; oil, pound.

manages domestic or other concerns with frugality; one who practices economy; one versed in economics or the science of political economy.—**economize,** i·kon′o·mīz, *v.i.*—*economized, economizing.* To manage pecuniary concerns with frugality; to make a prudent use of money, or of the means of having or acquiring property.—*v.t.* To use with prudence; to expend with frugality.

ecstasy, ek′sta·si, *n.* [Gr. *ekstasis,* a standing out, a displacement, distraction, astonishment—*ek,* out, and *histēmi,* to stand (from root of *stand*).] A state in which the mind is carried away as it were from the body; a state in which the functions of the senses are suspended by the contemplation of some extraordinary or supernatural object; a kind of trance; excessive joy; rapture; a degree of delight that arrests the whole mind; extreme delight; madness or distraction (*Shak.*)‡.—**ecstatic, ecstatical,** ek·stat′ik, ek·stat′i·kal, *a.* Pertaining to or resulting from ecstasy; suspending the senses; entrancing; rapturous; transporting; delightful beyond measure.—**ecstatically,** ek·stat′i·kal·li, *adv.* In an ecstatic manner.

ectoblast, ek′to·blast, *n.* [Gr. *ektos,* outside, and *blastos,* bud, germ.] *Physiol.* the membrane composing the walls of a cell, as distinguished from *mesoblast,* the nucleus, and *entoblast,* the nucleolus.

ectoderm, ek′to·dėrm, *n.* [Gr. *ecto,* outermost, and *dermos,* skin.] *Zool.* the outermost of the three primary germ layers of an embryo.—**ectodermal,** ek·to·dėrm′al, *a.* Belonging to the ectoderm.—**ectoparasite,** ek·to·par′a·sīt, *n.* A parasitic animal infesting the outside of animals; as opposed to *endoparasite,* which lives in the body.—**ectosarc,** ek′to·särk, *n.* [Gr. *sarx, sarkos,* flesh.] *Zool.* the outer transparent sarcode-layer of certain Protozoa, such as the amoeba.

ectoplasm, ek′to·plazm, *n.* [Gr. *ektos,* outside, and *plasma.* PLASM.] *Biol.* the exterior portion of a cell; matter forming a cell wall.

ectype, ek′tīp, *n.* [Gr. *ektypos,* worked in high relief—*ek,* out, and *typos,* type.] A reproduction of, or very close resemblance to, an original; opposed to *prototype;* a copy in relief or embossed.—**ectypal,** ek·tī′pal, *a.* Taken from the original; imitated.

ecumenic, ecumenical, ek·ū·men′ik, ek·ū·men′i·kal, *a.* [L. *œcumenicus,* Gr. *oikoumenē,* the habitable earth, from *oikos,* a habitation.] General; universal; specifically, an epithet applied to an ecclesiastical council regarded as representing the whole Christian Church, or the whole Catholic Church.

eczema, ek′zē·ma, *n.* [Gr., from *ekzeō,* to boil out—*ek,* out, and *zeō,* to boil.] An eruptive disease of the skin, characterized by minute vesicles which burst and discharge a thin acrid fluid, often giving rise to excoriation; one form is popularly known as grocers' itch.—**eczema-**

.**tous,** ek·zem′a·tus, *a.* Pertaining to or produced by eczema.

edacious, i·dā′shus, *a.* [L. *edax,* from *edo,* to eat.] Eating; given to eating; greedy; voracious.—**edacity,** i·das′i·ti, *n.* [L. *edacitas.*] Greediness; voracity; ravenousness; rapacity.

Edam cheese, ē′dam·chēz, *n.* [From the village of *Edam,* near Amsterdam.] A pressed, fine-flavored, yellow, Dutch cheese made in balls, weighing three to four pounds, and colored dark red on the outside.

Edda, ed′a, *n.* [Icel., great-grandmother; a name given to indicate that it is the mother of all Scandinavian poetry.] The name of two Scandinavian books, dating from the eleventh to the thirteenth century: first, the *Elder* or *Poetic Edda,* a collection of pagan poems or chants of a mythic, prophetic, mostly all of a religious character; second, the *Younger* or *Prose Edda,* a kind of prose synopsis of Scandinavian mythology.

eddy, ed′i, *n.* [From Icel. *itha,* an eddy, from prefix *ith,* Goth. *id,* A.Sax. *ed,* again, back.] A current of air or water turning round in a direction contrary to the main stream; a whirlpool; a current of water or air moving circularly.—*v.i.*—*eddied, eddying.* To move circularly, or as an eddy.—*v.t.* to cause to move in an eddy; to collect as into an eddy.

edelweiss, ā′dl·vīs, *n.* [G. *edel,* noble, *weiss,* white.] A composite plant inhabiting the Alps, and having a specially woolly foliage and involucre.

edema, i·dē′ma, *n.* [Gr. *oidēma,* a swelling, from *oideō,* to swell.] *Med.* a puffiness or swelling of parts arising from water collecting.—**edematous, edematose,** i·dē′ma·tus, i·dē′mā·tōs, *a.* Relating to edema.

Eden, ē′den, *n.* [Heb, and Chal, *eden,* delight, pleasure, a place of pleasure.] The garden in which Adam and Eve were placed by God; hence, a delightful region or residence.

edentate, ē·den′tāt, *a.* [L. *edentatus*—*e, ex,* out of, and *dens, dentis,* a tooth.] Destitute or deprived of teeth; pertaining to the Edentata.—*n.* An animal belonging to the order Edentata.

edge, ej, *n.* [A.Sax. *ecg,* edge, whence *ecgian, eggian,* to sharpen, to egg= D. *egge, egge,* Icel. and Sw. *egg,* G. *ecke,* edge, corner; from an Indo-European root *ak,* seen in L. *acies,* an edge, *acus,* a needle, *acuo,* to sharpen; akin *acid, acute,* eager.] The thin cutting side of an instrument; the abrupt border or margin of anything; the brink; the border or part adjacent to a line of division; the part nearest some limit; sharpness of mind or appetite; keenness; intenseness of desire; sharpness; acrimony.—*To set the teeth on edge,* to cause a tingling or grating sensation in the teeth.—*v.t.*—*edged, edging.* To sharpen; to furnish with an edge, fringe, or border; to exasperate; to embitter; to incite; to provoke; to insti-

gate; to move sideways; to move by little and little.—*v.i.* To move sideways or gradually; to advance or retire gradually.—**edgewise,** ej′wīz, *adv.* With the edge turned forward or toward a particular point; in the direction of the edge; sideways; with the side foremost.—**edging,** ej′ing, *n.* That which is added on the border or which forms the edge, as lace, fringe, trimming, added to a garment for ornament; a row of small plants set along the border of a flower bed.—**edgebone,** *n.* AITCH-BONE.—**edge tool,** *n.* An instrument having a sharp or cutting edge; *fig.* something dangerous to deal or sport with.—**edgy,** ej′ē, *a.* Having an edge; nervous or anxious; eager; impatient; snappish.—**edgily,** ej′i·li, *adv.*—**edginess,** ej′ē·nes, *n.* Nervousness; irritability.

edible, ed′i·bl, *a.* [L.L. *edibilis,* from L. *edo,* to eat.] Fit to be eaten as food; eatable; esculent.—*n.* Anything that may be eaten for food; an article of food; a comestible.—**edibility, edibleness,** ed·i·bil′i·ti, ed′i·bl·nes, *n.* The quality of being edible.

edict, ē′dikt, *n.* [L. *edictum,* from *edico,* utter or proclaim—*e,* out, and *dico,* to speak. DICTION.] An order issued by a prince to his subjects, as a rule or law requiring obedience; a proclamation of command or prohibition; a decree.—**edictal,** ē·dik′tal, *a.* Pertaining to an edict.

edify, ed′i·fī, *v.t.*—*edified, edifying.* [Fr. *édifier,* from L. *œdificare,* to build, erect, construct—*œdes,* a house and *facio,* to make.] To build or construct‡; to instruct and improve in knowledge generally, and particularly in moral and religious knowledge, or in faith and holiness. —*v.i.* To cause or tend to cause a moral or intellectual improvement.— **edifier,** ed′i·fī·ėr, *n.* One who edifies. —**edifying,** ed′i·fī·ing, *a.* Adapted to edify; having the effect of instructing and improving.—**edification,** ed′i·fi·kā′shon, *n.* The act of edifying; improvement and progress of the mind in knowledge, in morals or in faith and holiness.—**edifice,** ed′i·fis *n.* [L. *œdificium,* a building. EDIFY.] A building; a structure; a fabric: chiefly applied to houses and other large structures.—**edifical,** ed·i·fish′al, *a.* Pertaining to an edifice or structure; structural.

edile, ē′dil, *n.* [L. *œdilis,* from *œdes,* a building.] A magistrate of ancient Rome who had the superintendence of buildings of all kinds, especially public edifices, and also the care of the highways, public places, weights and measures, etc.

edit, ed′it, *v.t.* [L. *edo, editum,* to give forth, to publish—*e* forth, and *do, datum,* to give, whence *date, dative.*] To superintend the publication of; to prepare, as a book or paper, for the public eye, by writing, correcting, or selecting the matter; to conduct or manage as regards literary contents or matter; to publish.—**edition,**

i·dish′on, *n.* A literary work as bearing a special stamp or form when first published or subsequently; a work as characterized by editorial labors; the whole number of copies of a work published at once.—**editor,** ed′i·tẽr, *n.* One who edits; a person who superintends, revises, corrects, and prepares a book, newspaper, or magazine for publication.—**editorial,** ed·i·tõ′ri·al, *a.* Pertaining to, proceeding from, or written by an editor.—*n.* An article, as in a newspaper, written by the editor; a leading article.—**editorially,** ed·i·tõ′ri·al·li, *adv.* In the manner or character of an editor.—**editorship,** ed′i·tẽr·ship, *n.* The business of an editor; the care and superintendence of a publication.

educate, ed′ū·kāt, *v.t.*—*educated, educating.* [L. *educo, educatum,* from *educo, eductum,* to lead forth, to bring up a child—*e,* out, and *duco,* to lead. DUKE.] To inform and enlighten the understanding of; to cultivate and train the mental powers of; to qualify for the business and duties of life; to teach; to instruct; to train; to rear.—**education,** ed·ū·kā′shon, *n.* The act of educating, teaching, or training; the act or art of developing and cultivating the various physical, intellectual, aesthetic, and moral faculties; instruction and discipline; tuition; nurture; learning; erudition.—**educational,** ed·ū·kā′shon·al, *a.* Pertaining to education; derived from education.—**educationalist, educationist,** ed·ū·kā′shon·al·ist, ed·ū·kā′shon·ist, *n.* One who is versed in or who advocates or promotes education.—**educative,** ed′-ū·kā·tiv, *a.* Tending or having the power to educate.—**educator,** ed′-ū·kā·tẽr, *n.* One who or that which educates.

educe, i·dūs′, *v.t.*—*educed, educing.* [L. *educo, eductum*—*e,* out, and *duco,* to lead. EDUCATE.] To bring or draw out: to cause to appear; to extract.—**educible,** i·dū′si·bl, *a.* Capable of being educed.—**educt,** i′dukt, *n.* Extracted matter; a substance brought to light by separation, analysis, or decomposition; anything educed or drawn from another; an inference.—**eduction,** i·duk′shon, *n.* The act of educing, drawing out, or bringing into view.

edulcorate, i·dul′ko·rāt, *v.t.*—*edulcorated, edulcorating.* [L. *e,* out, and *dulcoro, dulcoratum,* to sweeten, from *dulcor,* sweetness, *dulcis,* sweet.] To remove acidity from; to sweeten†; *chem.* to free from acids, salts, or impurities by washing.—**edulcoration,** i·dul′ko·rā″shon, *n.* The act of sweetening by admixture of some saccharine substance†; *chem.* the act of freeing from acid or saline substances, or from any soluble impurities, by repeated affusions of water.—**edulcorative,** i·dul′ko·rā-tiv, *a.* Having the quality of sweetening or removing acidity.

eel, ēl, *n.* [A.Sax. *ael*=Dan. D. and G. *aal,* Icel. *all;* not connected with Gr. *echis,* Skr. *ahi,* a serpent; L.

anguilla, an eel, *anguis,* a snake.] A fish characterized by its slimy serpent-like elongated body, by the absence of ventral fins, and the continuity of the dorsal and anal fins round the extremity of the tail; some species are marine, some fresh-water; all are remarkable for their voracity and tenacity of life, many are considered excellent food.—**eelpout,** *n.* [A.Sax. *aele-puta.*] The name of two different species of fish—the viviparous blenny and the burbot.

e′en, ēn, *adv.* A contraction for *Even.*

e′er, âr, *adv.* A contraction for *Ever.*

eerie, ē′ri, *a.* [A.Sax. *earh,* timid.] Calculated to inspire fear; dreary; lonely; weird; superstitiously affected by fear, especially when lonely.—**eeriness,** ē′ri·nes, *n.* The state or quality of being eerie.

efface, ef·fās′, *v.t.*—*effaced, effacing.* [Fr. *effacer*—L. *e,* out, and *facies,* a face. Comp. *deface.*] To destroy, as a figure, on the surface of anything, so as to render it invisible or not distinguishable; to blot out; to erase, strike, or scratch out; to remove from the mind; to wear away.—**effaceable,** ef·fā′sa·bl, *a.* Capable of being effaced.—**effacement,** ef·fās′ment, *n.* Act of effacing; state of being effaced.

effect, ef·fekt′, *n.* [L. *effectus,* from *efficio*—*ex,* and *facio,* to make. FACT.] That which is produced by an operating agent or cause; the result or consequence of the action of a cause or agent; consequence; result: power to produce consequences or results; force, validity, or importance; purport, import, tenor, or general intent; reality and not mere appearance; fact: preceded by *in;* the impression produced on the mind, as by natural scenery, a picture, musical composition, or other work of art, by the object as a whole, before its details are examined; *pl.* goods; movables; personal estate.—*v.t.* To produce, as a cause or agent; to bring about or cause to be; to bring to pass; to achieve; to accomplish.—**effecter,** ef·fek′tẽr, *n.* One who effects, produces, causes, or brings about.—**effectible,**† ef·fek′ti·bl, *a.* Capable of being effected.—**effective,** ef·fek′-tiv, *a.* Having the power to cause or produce effect; efficacious; operative; active; efficient; having the power of active operation; fit for duty.—**effectively,** ef·fek′tiv·li, *adv.* In an effective manner.—**effectiveness,** ef·fek′tiv·nes, *n.* The quality of being effective.—**effectual,** ef·fek′chū·al, *a.* Producing an effect, or the effect desired or intended; having adequate power or force to produce the effect.—**effectually,** ef·fek′chū-al·li, *adv.* In an effectual manner.—**effectuate,** ef·fek′chū·āt, *v.t.*—*effectuated, effectuating.* [Fr. *effectuer.*] To bring to pass; to achieve; to accomplish; to fulfill.—**effectuation,** ef·fek′chū·ā″shon, *n.* Act of effectuating.

effeminate, ef·fem′i·nit, *a.* [L. *ef-*

feminatus, from *effeminor,* to grow or make womanish, from *ex,* out, and *femina,* a woman.] Having the qualities of a woman instead of those of a man; soft or delicate to an unmanly degree; weak and unmanly; womanish; voluptuous.—*v.t.* —*effeminated, effeminating.* To make womanish or effeminate.—*v.i.* To grow womanish or weak.—**effeminacy,** ef·fem′i·na·si, *n.* The state or character of being effeminate.

effendi, ef·fen′di, *n.* [Turk.] A title of respect frequently attached to the official title of certain Turkish officers, especially learned men and ecclesiastics.

efferent, ef′fẽr·ent, *a.* [L. *ef* for *ex,* out of, and *fero,* to carry.] *Physiol.* conveying outward or discharging.

effervesce, ef·fẽr·ves′, *v.i.*—*effervesced, effervescing.* [L. *effervesco*—*ef, ex,* out of, and *fervesco,* to begin boiling, from *ferveo,* to be hot. FERVENT.] To bubble and hiss or froth and sparkle, as fermenting liquors or any fluid when some part escapes in a gaseous form; to work, as new wine; *fig.* to exhibit signs of excitement; to exhibit feelings which cannot be suppressed.—**effervescence,** ef·fẽr-ves′ens, *n.* That commotion, bubbling, frothing, or sparkling of a fluid which takes place when some part of the mass flies off in a gaseous form, producing innumerable small bubbles; strong excitement or manifestation of feeling; flow of animal spirits.—**effervescent,** ef·fẽr·ves′ent, *a.* Effervescing.

effete, ef·fēt′, *a.* [L. *effetus,* exhausted, worn out by bearing—*ex,* and *fetus,* fruitful, pregnant.] Having the energies worn out or exhausted; having the vigor lost or dissipated; barren.

efficacious, ef·fi·kā′shus, *a.* [L. *efficax,* efficacious, from *efficio.* EFFECT.] Effectual; productive of effects; producing the effect intended; having power adequate to the purpose intended.—**efficaciously,** ef·fi-kā′shus·li, *adv.* In an efficacious manner.—**efficaciousness,** ef·fi·kā′-shus·nes, *n.* The quality of being efficacious.—**efficacy,** ef′fi·ka·si, *n.* [L. *efficacia,* efficacy.] Power to produce effects; production of the effect intended; effectiveness; efficiency; virtue; energy.—**efficiency,** ef·fish′-en·si, *n.* [L. *efficientia.*] The state or character of being efficient; effectual agency; power of producing the effect intended; active competent power; competence for one's duties; in any mechanical contrivance, the ratio of the useful work obtained to the energy expended.—**efficient,** ef·fish′ent *a.* Causing effects; causing anything to be what it is; efficacious; effectual; competent; able; operative. —*n.* One who is competent to perform the duties of a service.—**efficiently,** ef·fish′ent·li, *adv.* In an efficient manner.

effigy, ef′fi·ji, *n.* [L. *effigies,* from *effingo,* to fashion—*ef* for *ex,* and *fingo,* to form or devise. FEIGN.] The image, likeness, or representation of a person or thing; a likeness in sculpture, painting, or otherwise; an image; frequently applied to the figures on sepulchral monuments.—**effigial,**† ef·fij′i·al, *a.* Exhibiting or pertaining to an effigy.

effloresce, ef·flo·res′, *v.i.*—*effloresced, efflorescing.* [L. *effloresco*—*ef* for *ex*, and *floresco*, from *floreo*, to blossom, from *flos*, a flower. FLOWER.] To burst into bloom, as a flower; to break out into florid or excessive ornamentation; *chem.* to change over the surface or throughout to a whitish, mealy, or crystalline powder, from a gradual decomposition, on simple exposure to the air; to become covered with a whitish crust or light crystallization, from a slow chemical change.—**efflorescence,** ef·flo·res′ens, *n.* The act or process of efflorescing; *bot.* the time of flowering; the production of blossoms; *med.* a redness of the skin; eruption; *chem.* the formation of a whitish substance on the surface of certain bodies, as salts; the powder or crust thus formed.—**efflorescent,** ef·flo·res′ent, *a.* Showing efflorescence; incrusted or covered with efflorescence; liable to effloresce.

effluence, ef′flu·ens, *n.* [Fr. *effluence*, from L. *effluo*, to flow out—*e, ex*, and *fluo*, to flow.] The act of flowing out; that which flows out or issues; an emanation.—**effluent,** ef′flu·ent, *a.* Flowing out; emanating; emitted.—*n. Geog.* a stream that flows out of another stream or out of a lake.

effluvium, ef·flu′vi·um, *n.* pl. effluvia, ef·flu′vi·a. [L., from *effluo*, to flow out, FLOW.] Something flowing out in a subtle or invisible form; exhalation; emanation; especially applied to noxious or disagreeable exhalations.—**effluvial,** ef·flu′vi·al, *a.* Pertaining to or containing effluvia.

efflux, ef′fluks, *n.* [L. *effluo, effluxum*, to flow out. EFFLUENCE.] The act or state of flowing out or issuing in a stream; outflow; that which flows out; emanation.

effort, ef′fèrt, *n.* [Fr. *effort*—L. *ef* for *ex*, out, and *fortis*, strong.] An exertion of strength or power, whether physical or mental; strenuous exertion to accomplish an object; a straining to do something; endeavor.—**effortless,** ef′fèrt·les, *a.* Making no effort.

effrontery, ef·frun′tèr·i, *n.* [Fr. *effronterie*, from L. *effrons, effrontis*, barefaced, shameless—*ef* for *ex*, and *frons*, the forehead. FRONT.] Audacious impudence or boldness; assurance entirely unabashed; shamelessness; brazenness.

effulge, ef·fulj′, *v.i.*—*effulged, effulging.* [L. *effulgeo*—*ef* for *ex*, out, and *fulgeo*, to shine.] To send forth a flood of light; to shine with splendor.—**effulgence,** ef·ful′jens, *n.* A flood of light; a shining forth of light or glory; great luster or brightness; splendor.—**effulgent,** ef·ful′jent, *a.* Shining; bright; splendid; diffusing a flood of light.—**effulgently,** ef·ful′jent·li, *adv.* In a bright or splendid manner.

effuse, ef·fūz′, *v.t.*—*effused, effusing.* [L. *effundo, effusum*, to pour out—*ef* for *ex*, out, and *fundo, fusum*, to pour. FUSE.] To pour out, as a fluid; to spill; to shed.—*v.i.* To emanate; to come forth.—*a.* (ef′fūs). *Bot.* applied to a kind of panicle with a very loose one-sided arrangement; *conch.* applied to shells where the aperture is not whole behind, but the lips are separated by a gap or groove.—**effusion,** ef·fū′zhon, *n.* The act of pouring out; that which is poured out; *pathol.* the escape of any fluid out of the vessel containing it into another part; cordiality of manner; overflowing or demonstrative kindness.—**effusive,** ef·fū′siv, *a.* Pouring out; pouring forth largely; showing overflowing kindness or cordiality of manner.—**effusively,** ef·fū′siv·li, *adv.* In an effusive manner.—**effusiveness,** ef·fū′siv·nes, *n.*

eft, eft, *n.* [O.E. *evete, ewte*, A.Sax. *efete*. Newt is from *ewte*, the *n* of the art. *an* having adhered to the noun.] A newt.

egad, ē·gad′, *exclam.* [Probably a euphemistic corruption of ' by God '.] An exclamation expressing exultation or surprise.

egest, ē·jest′, *v.t.* [L. *egero, egestum*, to carry or bear out—*e*, out, and *gero*, to carry.] To cast or throw out; to void excrement.—**egestion,** ē·jest′yon, *n.* The act of voiding excrement.

egg, eg, *n.* [A.Sax. *æg*=Icel. *egg*, Dan. *æg*, Sw. *ägg*, G. and D. *ei*; allied in origin to L. *ovum*, Gr. *ōon*, Ir. *ugh*, Gael. *ubh*, an egg.] A roundish body covered with a shell or membrane, formed in a special organ of many female animals besides birds, and in which the development of the young animal takes place; an ovum. [Animals whose young do not leave the egg till after it is laid are called *oviparous*; those in which the eggs are retained within the parent body until they are hatched are called *ovoviviparous*.]—*Egg and anchor, egg and dart, egg and tongue, arch.* same as *Echinus*.—**egger,** eg′ér, *n.* Any of various moths (family Lasiocampidae) whose larvae feed on leaves.—**egghead,** *n.* An intellectual; highbrow.—**eggnog,** *n.* A drink of eggs beaten with sugar, milk, and sometimes whiskey.—**eggplant,** *n.* A plant of the potato family (*Solanum melongena*) with egg-shaped fruits, which are boiled, stewed in sauces, etc., and served as a vegetable.

egg, eg *v.t.* [A.Sax. *ecgian, eggian*, to incite, to sharpen; Icel. *eggja*, to egg. EDGE.] To incite or urge on; to stimulate; to instigate; to provoke.

egis, ē′jis, *n.* Same as *Aegis*.

eglantine, eg′lan·tīn, *n.* [Fr. *églantine*, O.Fr. *aiglent*, from a form *aculentus*, prickly, from L. *aculeus*, a spine, a prickle, *acus*, a needle. ACID.] An old and poetical name for the sweetbrier or wild rose.

ego, ē′gō, *n.* [L. *ego*, I.] The self; the self as distinguished from any other self; one's will; self-esteem; *philos.* the complete man comprising body and soul; *psych.* that part of man that experiences and reacts to the outside world.—**egocentric,** ē′gō·sen″trik, *a.* Concern with the individual rather than society; selfish.

egoism, ē′gō·izm, *n.* Evaluating experience only by one's personal interest; the doctine that all action is motivated by self-interest.—**egoist,** e′go·ist, *n.* A selfish or self-centered person; egotist; one holding the doctrine of egoism.—**egoistic, egoistical,** ē·gō·is′tik, ē·gō·is′ti·kal, *a.* Pertaining to egoism; addicted to or manifesting egoism; egotistic.—**egoistically,** ē·gō·is′ti·kal·li, *adv.* In an egoistic manner.—**egotism,** ē′go·tizm, *n.* The practice of too frequently using the word *I*; hence, a speaking or writing much of one's self; a passionate and exaggerated love of self, leading one to refer all things to one's self, and to judge of everything by its relation to one's interests or importance. ∴ *Egotism* and *self-conceit* are based on what we think of ourselves, the former being the more deep-seated and powerful; *vanity*, on what we believe others think of us.—**egotist,** ē′go·tist, *n.* One who repeats the word *I* very often in conversation or writing; one who speaks much of himself or magnifies his own achievements.—**egotistic, egotistical,** ē·go·tis′tik, ē·go·tis′ti·kal, *a.* Addicted to egotism; manifesting egotism.—**egotistically,** ē·go·tis′ti·kal·li, *adv.* In an egotistical or self-conceited manner.

egregious, i·grē′ji·us, *a.* [L. *egregius*, lit. out of the common flock or herd —*e* or *ex*, out, and *grex, gregis*, a flock (whence *gregarious*).] Extraordinary; remarkable; enormous: now mostly used in a bad or ironical sense (an *egregious* fool, blunder, impudence).—**egregiously,** i·grē′ji·us·li, *adv.* In an egregious manner.—**egregiousness,** i·grē′ji·us·nes, *n.*

egress, ē′gres, *n.* [L. *egressus*, from *egredior*—*e*, and *gradior*, to step. GRADE.] The act of going or issuing out; the power of departing from any enclosed or confined place; *astron.* the passing of an inferior planet from the disk of the sun in a transit.—*v.i.* (ē·gres′) To go out; to depart; to leave.—**egression,**† ē·gresh′on, *n.* [L. *egressio*.] Egress.—**egressor,** ē·gres′ér, *n.* One who goes out.

egret, ē′gret, *n.* [Fr. *aigrette*, a dim. from an old form *aigre*, from O.H.G. *heigro*, a heron, Sw. *häger*, Icel. *hegri*, a heron. *Heron* has the same origin.] A name of those species of herons which have the feathers on the lower part of the back lengthened and the barbs loose, so that this part of the plumage is very soft and flowing; the small white heron; a plume of heron's feathers, or of feathers, diamonds, etc.; an aigret.

Egyptian, i·jip′shan, *a.* [From *Egypt*, Gr. *Aigyptos*; akin *Gypsy*.] Pertaining to Egypt.—*Egyptian vulture*, a vulture, about the size of a raven, which frequents the streets of eastern towns, where it is protected on account of its services as a scavenger. Called also *Pharaoh's chicken*.—*n.* A native of Egypt; an old designation for a gypsy, so called because believed to have come from Egypt.—**Egyptologist,** ē·jip·tol′o·jist, *n.* One well acquainted with the antiquities of

Egypt, especially the hieroglyphic inscriptions and documents.—**Egyptological,** i·jip′to·loj″i·kal, a. Pertaining to Egyptology; devoted to the study of Egyptology.—**Egyptology,** ē·jip·tol′o·ji, n. The science of Egyptian antiquities; that branch of knowledge which treats of the ancient language, history, etc., of Egypt.

eider, eider duck, ī′dẽr, n. [G. eider, Sw. eider, Icel. ædr. Dan. eder.] A species of large duck, with down that is much valued for its warmth, lightness, and elasticity.

eidolon, ī·dō′lon, n. [IDOL.] An unreal or spectral form; a phantom.

eight, āt, a. [A.Sax. eahta=G. and D. acht, Icel. átta, Dan. aatte, L. octo, Gr. oktō, Ir. and Gael. achd, Skr. ashtan, ashtau.] One of the cardinal numeral adjectives; one more than seven and less than nine.—n. The number composed of seven and one; the symbol representing this number. —**eighteen,** ā′tēn, a. and n. Eight and ten; the sum of ten and eight; the symbol representing this sum.— **eighteenmo,** ā·tēn′mō, n. [From eighteen and -mo, in L. decimo, tenth.] The size of a book in which a sheet is folded into eighteen leaves: written often 18mo.—**eighteenth,** ā′tēnth, a. and n. Next in order after the seventeenth; one of eighteen equal parts of a thing.—**eightfold,** āt′fōld, a. Eight times the number or quantity. —**eighth,** ātth, a. and n. Next in order after the seventh; one of eight equal parts of anything; an octave.— **eighth note,** n. A musical note having one eighth the time value of a whole note; a quaver.—**eightieth,** ā′ti·eth, a. and n. Next in order to the seventy-ninth; one of eighty equal parts of anything.—**eighty,** ā′ti, a. and n. Eight times ten; fourscore.

einsteinium, īn·stī′ni·um, n. [From Albert Einstein.] A synthetic, radioactive, metallic element. Symbol, Es; at. no., 99.

Einstein theory, n. The theory of Relativity developed by Albert Einstein.

eisteddfod, ās·teTH′vŏd, n. [W.] A meeting of bards and minstrels in Wales; a periodical Welsh festival for the recitation of poems.

either, ē′THẽr or ī′THẽr; the former is more in accordance with analogy, a. or pron. [A.Sax. aegther; contracted from aeghwæther, compounded of a=aye, the augment ge, and hwæther. EACH, WHETHER.] One or the other; one of two things; each of two; the one and the other; both. —conj. A disjunctive conjunction always used as correlative to and preceding or (either the one or the other).

ejaculate, i·jak′ū·lāt, v.t.—ejaculated, ejaculating. [L. ejaculor, ejaculatus—e, out, and jaculum, a dart, from jacio, to throw, seen also in reject, project, etc.] To throw out, as an exclamation; to utter suddenly and briefly.—v.i.† To utter ejaculations.—**ejaculation,** i·jak′ū·lā″shon, n. The uttering of a short, sudden exclamation; the exclamation uttered; a prayer con-

sisting of a few words.—**ejaculatory,** i·jak′ū·la·to·ri, a. Of the nature of an ejaculation.

eject, i·jekt′, v.t. [L. ejicio, ejectum—e, and jacio, to throw, as in dejected, project, etc.] To throw out; to cast forth; to thrust out; to drive away; to expel; to dismiss from office; to turn out.—**ejection,** i·jek′shon, n. [L. ejectio.] The act of ejecting; dismissal; dispossession; expulsion; rejection.—**ejectment,** i·jekt′ment, n. A casting out; a dispossession; law, the removal of a person from the wrongful possession of land or tenements.—**ejector,** i·jek′tẽr, n. One who ejects.

eke, ēk, v.t.—eked, eking. [A.Sax. ēcan, to increase, to eke, Icel. auka, Goth. aukan, L. augeo (whence augment), Gr. auxanō, to increase.] To add to so as to make up for any deficiencies; to make a supply last by economy. ∴ Used with out, refers to the supply, not to the result of the addition.

elaborate, i·lab′o·rāt, v.t.—elaborated, elaborating. [L. elaboro, elaboratum—e, out, and laboro, to labor, from labor, labor.] To produce with labor; to work out or complete with great care; to work out fully or perfectly.—a. Wrought with labor; finished with great care; executed with exactness; highly finished.— **elaborately,** i·lab′o·rit·li, adv. In an elaborate manner.—**elaborateness,** i·lab′o·rit·nes, n. The quality of being elaborate.—**elaboration,** i·lab′o·rā″shon, n. The act of elaborating; careful or laborious finish bestowed; physiol. the process performed by the living organs in animals and plants by which something is produced (the elaboration of sap).—**elaborative,** i·lab′o·rā·tiv, a. Serving or tending to elaborate.—**elaborator,** i·lab′o·ra·tẽr, n. One who or that which elaborates.

eland, ē′land, n. [D. eland, an elk.] An African species of antelope, the largest of all antelopes; a name sometimes given to the moose.

elapse, i·laps′, v.i.—elapsed, elapsing. [L. elabor, elapsus, to slip away—e, out, and labor, lapsus, to glide. LAPSE.] To slip or glide away; to pass away silently: said of time.

elastic, i·las′tik, a. [Fr. élastique, L.L. elasticus, from Gr. elastos, beaten out, extensible, from elaunō, to drive, to beat out.] Having the power of returning to the form from which it is bent or extended; having the property of recovering its former figure or volume after being altered by pressure; rebounding; flying back; fig. possessing the power or quality of recovering from depression or exhaustion.—Elastic limit, for any material, is the maximum stress per unit area that can be applied without causing an appreciable permanent set.—**elastically,** i·las′ti·kal·li, adv. In an elastic manner; by elastic power.—**elasticity,** i·las·tis′i·ti, n.— **elastomer,** i·las′ta·mẽr, n. Any elastic substance having the physical qualities of natural rubber.

elate, i·lāt′, a. [L. elatus, pp. of

effero—e, out, and latus, borne or carried.] Raised or lifted up†; having the spirits lifted up; flushed, as with success; exultant; haughty.—v.t.— elated, elating. To raise; to exalt; to elevate with success; to cause to exult; to make proud.—**elatedly,** i·lā′ted·li, adv. With elation.— **elation,** i·lā′shon, n. Elevation of mind proceeding from self-approbation; haughtiness; pride of prosperity.

elater, el′a·tẽr, n. [Gr. elatēr, a driver.] An elastic spiral filament generated in tubes in certain liverworts and scale mosses, and supposed to assist in the dispersion of spores; a name of various small leaping beetles.

elaterium, el·a·tē′ri·um, n. [Gr. elatērion, from elatērios, driving, purgative, from elatēr, a driver, from elaunō, to drive.] A substance obtained from the fruit of the squirting cucumber, serving as a drastic purge.

elbow, el′bō, n. [A.Sax. elboga, elnboga—el, eln, forearm, an ell (akin to L. ulna, Gr. ōlenē, the forearm), and boga, a bow; D. elleboog, G. ellbogen, ellenbogen, Icel. alnbogi. ELL, BOW.] The outer angle made by the bend of the arm; the joint which unites the upper arm with the forearm; a flexure, angle, or part of a structure somewhat resembling an elbow, or which supports the arm or elbow, as the raised arm of a chair or sofa.— Out at elbows, having holes in the elbows of one's clothes; shabbily dressed.—v.t. To push or jostle with the elbow; to make or gain (a path through a crowd) by pushing with the elbows.—v.i. To jut into an elbow or angle; to push one's way. —**elbow grease,** n. Vigorous physical exertion.—**elbowroom,** n. Room to extend the elbows on each side, hence, ample room for motion or action.

elder, el′dẽr, a. [A.Sax. yldra, eldra, the compar. degree of eald old. OLD.] Having lived a longer time; of greater age; born, produced, or formed before something else; opposed to younger; prior in origin; senior; pertaining to earlier times; earlier.—n. [A.Sax. ealdor, an ancestor, a chief, a prince.] One who is older than another or others; an ancestor; a person advanced in life, and who, on account of his age, experience, and wisdom, is selected for office; a lay official in Presbyterian churches, who acts along with the minister in the administration of discipline and government, having an equal vote with the latter in all church courts.—**elderly,** el′dẽr·li a. Somewhat old; advanced beyond middle age; bordering on old age.— **eldership,** el′dẽr·ship, n. The office of an elder; elders collectively; order of elders.—**eldest,** el′dest, a. [A.Sax. yldest, superl. of eald, ald, old.] Oldest; most advanced in age; that was born before others.

elder, el′dẽr, n. [A.Sax. ellern, ellen; the d has been inserted in later times; D. elloorn, the elder; perhaps akin to alder.] Any tree or shrub of the honeysuckle family of rapid growth with white flowers and purple berries, and containing an unusual quantity of pith.—**elderberry,** *n.* The fruit of the elder.

El Dorado, el do·rä′dō or el do·rä′dō, *n.* [Sp. the golden—*el,* the, and *dorado,* gilt.] A country formerly reputed to exist in South America, and possessing immense stores of gold; hence; any region rich in gold or treasure of any kind.

Eleatic, el·i·at′ik *a.* Of or pertaining to *Elea,* an ancient Greek town in southern Italy, or to a sect of philosophers that originated there.— *n.* An adherent of the Eleatic philosophy.

elecampane, el′i·kam·pān″, *n.* [Fr. *énulecampane,* from L. *inula,* elecampane, and (probably) *campus,* a field.] A perennial plant with yellow-rayed flowers which grows in moist meadows and pastures, formerly regarded as expectorant; a coarse candy, professedly made from the root of the plant, but really composed of little else than colored sugar.

elect, i·lekt′, *v.t.* [L. *eligo, electum—e,* out, and *lego, lectum,* to pick, choose, as in *collect, select,* etc.; *legend, lecture,* etc., being also akin.] To pick out or select; especially, to select or take for an office or employment; to choose from among others; to appoint to an office by vote or designation; to choose; to determine in favor of (often with an infinitive; he *elected* to go).—*a.* Chosen or elected; especially, chosen, but not inaugurated, consecrated, or invested with office (bishop-*elect*); *theol.* chosen, selected, or designated to eternal life; predestinated in the divine counsels.—*n. sing.* or *pl.* One or several chosen or set apart; *theol.* those especially favored by God.— **election,** i·lek′shon, *n.* [L. *electio.*] The act of electing; the act of selecting one or more from others; the act of choosing a person to fill an office or employment, by any manifestation of preference, as by vote, uplifted hands, *viva voce,* or ballot; power of choosing or selecting; choice; voluntary preference; liberty to choose or act (it is at his *election* to accept or refuse); *theol.* predetermination of God, by which persons are distinguished as objects of mercy, become subjects of grace, are sanctified and prepared for heaven.—**electioneer,** i·lek′shon·ēr″, *v.i.* To work or exert one's self in any way to obtain the election of a candidate.—**electioneerer,** i·lek′shon·ē″rėr *n.* One who electioneers.— **elective,** i·lek′tiv, *a.* Chosen by election; dependent on choice; bestowed or passing by election; pertaining to or consisting in choice or right of choosing; exerting the power of choice.—**electively,** i·lek′tiv·lē, *adv.* By choice; with preference of one to another.—**elector,** i·lek′tėr, *n.* One who elects or has the right of electing; a person who has the right of voting for any functionary; specifically, one of the persons elected, by vote of the people, to the *electoral college,* whose function is to elect the

President and Vice-President of the United States.—**electoral,** i·lek′tėr-al, *a.* Pertaining to election or electors; consisting of electors.—**electorate,** i·lek′tėr·āt, *n.* A body of electors; the dignity or territory of an elector.

electric, electrical, i·lek′trik, i·lek′-tri·kal, *a.* [Fr. *électrique,* from L. *electrum,* Gr. *ēlektron,* amber, from the fact that the earliest electric phenomenon observed was the attraction of amber for light substances when rubbed.] Containing electricity, or capable of exhibiting it when excited by friction; pertaining to electricity; derived from or produced by electricity; conveying electricity; communicating a shock by electricity; *fig.* full of fire, spirit, or passion, and capable of communicating it to others.—*Electric battery,* a number of primary or secondary voltaic cells, connected with each other in one circuit.—*Electric charge,* a quantity of electricity existing on the surface of a body.—*Electric clock,* a clock in which the moving power, or the controlling power, is the action of a current of electricity.—*Electric condenser,* a system of two conducting surfaces, usually plane, facing each other across a narrow layer of air or other dielectric. A small difference of potential produces large charges on conductors so placed.—*Electric current,* a current or stream of electricity traversing a closed circuit formed of conducting substances, or passing by means of conductors from one body to another.—*Electric eel,* a fish which is capable of giving electric shocks.—*Electric eye,* a photoelectric cell.—*Electric lamp,* a lamp of any type depending on electricity, as the incandescent lamp, or the arc lamp.—*Electric light,* a light obtained by the conversion of electric energy into light energy. The usual method is to heat some material to incandescence by passing an electric current through it.—*Electric machine,* a machine for generating static electricity, by friction or by induction; the name is also given to the electric GENERATOR.—*Electric motor.* ELECTROMOTOR.—*Electric railway,* a railway on which electricity is the motor. —*Electric spark,* one of the forms in which accumulated electricity discharges itself.—*Electric telegraph.* TELEGRAPH.—**electrically,** i·lek′tri-kal·lē, *adv.* In the manner of electricity or by means of it.—**electrician,** i·lek·trish′an, *n.* One versed in the science of electricity; one who designs, sets up, repairs, or attends to electrical instruments and machinery. —**electricity,** i·lek·tris′i·tē, *n.* A phenomenon occurring in nature and based upon the imbalance of positive and negative charges.—*Static electricity,* electricity from the accumulation or deficiency of electrons (as manifest in lightning and the attraction of bodies electrified by friction).—*Current electricity,* electricity from the orderly movement of electrons through a circuit.—*Atmospheric electricity,* the electricity which is produced in the atmosphere, and which becomes

visible in the form of lightning.— **electrification,** i·lek′tri·fi·kā″shon, *n.* The act of electrifying, or state of being electrified.—**electrify,** i·lek′-tri·fī, *v.t.*—*electrified, electrifying.* To supply a community or region with electric power; to equip for the use of electric power; to charge with electricity; to affect by electricity; to give an electric shock to; *fig.* to give a sudden shock (as of surprise) to; to surprise with some sudden and brilliant effect; to thrill.—**electrocardiograph,** i·lek′trō·kärd″ē·o·graf, *n.* An instrument used to detect electrically the abnormal and irregular heartbeat.—**electrochemistry,** *n.* That branch of science which treats of, or is based upon, the relations between chemical and electrical phenomena.—**electrocute,** i·lek′trō·kūt, *v.t.* To execute by the agency of an electric current or shock.—**electrocution,** i·lek′trō·kū″shon, *n.*—**electrode,** i·lek′trōd, *n.* [-*ode* is from Gr. *hodos,* a way.] One of the conductors or terminals, either the cathode or anode, by which an electric current enters or leaves an electrolytic cell, vacuum tube, etc.—**electrodynamics,** i·lek′trō·dī·nam″iks, *n.* A science of mechanical actions exerted on one another by electric currents.—**electrodynamometer,** i·lek′-trō·dī·na·mom″e·tėr, *n.* An instrument for measuring electric currents. —**electroencephalograph,** i·lek′trō-en·sef″a·lō·graf, *n.* An instrument used in electrically detecting and recording brain waves.—**electrokinetics,** i·lek′trō·ki·net″iks, *n.* That science which treats of electricity in motion.—**electrokinetic,** *a.* Of or pertaining to electrokinetics or electricity in motion.—**electrolyze,** i·lek′-trō·līz, *v.t.* To decompose by direct action of the electric current.— **electrolyzation,** i·lek′trō·li·zā″shon, *n.* The act of electrolyzing.— **electrolysis,** i·lek·trol′i·sis, *n.* The resolution of compound bodies into their elements, or, in some cases, into groups of elements, under the action of a current of electricity.— **electrolyte,** i·lek′trō·līt, *n.* A compound which is decomposable, or is subjected to decomposition, by an electric current.—**electrolytic, electrolytical,** i·lek′trō·lit″ik, i·lek′trō·lit″i·kal, *a.* Pertaining to electrolysis. —**electromagnet,** *n.* A bar of soft iron rendered temporarily magnetic by a current of electricity having been caused to pass through a wire coiled round it.—**electromagnetic,** *a.* Having to do with the relations between electricity and magnetism. —*Electromagnetic units,* units employed in electrical measurement based upon the force exerted between two magnetic poles. The basis of the ordinary practical units.—**electrometallurgy,** *n* The art of depositing metals, as gold, silver, copper, etc., from solutions of their salts by electrolysis and of using the heating effects of the electric current—**electrometer,** i·lek·trom′e·ter, *n.* An instrument for measuring potential, or differences of electric potential between two conductors.—**electromotion**, *n.* The motion of electricity; mechanical motion produced by electricity.—**electromotive**, *a.* Causing or tending to cause an electric current.—*Electromotive force*, that which determines the flow of electricity along a conductor; proportional to difference of potential, and analogous to difference of level causing a flow in water, measured in volts.—**electromotor**, i·lek′trō·mō·tĕr, *n.* A machine for transforming the energy of the electric current into mechanical energy.—**electron**, i·lek′tron, *n.* The elementary, subatomic, negatively charged particle orbiting about the atom's nucleus.—**electronegative**, i·lek′trō·neg″a·tiv, *a.* Repelled by bodies negatively electrified, and attracted by those positively electrified.—**electronics**, i·lek′tron″iks, *n.* The science of phenomena related to the emission, behavior, and effects of electrons, as in vacuum tubes, and their application, as in radio and television.—**electrophoresis**, i·lek′trō·fo·rē″sis, *n.* The movement of particles suspended in a fluid under the influence of currents.—**electrophorus**, i·lek′trof′o·rus, *n.* An instrument for collecting electricity, and showing the phenomena of induction.—**electroplate**, *v.t.* To plate or give a coating of silver or other metal by means of electric currents.—*n.* Articles coated with silver or other metal by the process of electroplating.—**electroplater**, *n.* One who practices electroplating.—**electropositive**, *a.* Attracted by bodies negatively electrified or by the negative pole of the galvanic arrangement.—**electroscope**, i·lek′tro·skōp, *n.* An instrument for observing or detecting the existence of free electricity, and, in general, for determining its kind.—**electroscopic**, i·lek′tro·skop″ik, *a.* Of or belonging to the electroscope.—**electrostatics**, *n.* The science which treats of the phenomena occasioned by electricity at rest, and of the production and discharge of stationary charges of electricity.—*Electrostatic units*, units employed in electrical measurement, based upon Coulomb's law of attraction and repulsion between quantities of statical electricity. All electrical quantities may be expressed in either electrostatic or electromagnetic units but the dimensions in the two systems differ, the velocity of light entering into the difference.—**electrotherapy**, i·lek′trō·ther″a·pi, *n.* The treatment of disease by the use of certain electrical techniques that change the structure or function of the affected body tissue.—**electrotype**, i·lek′trō·tīp, *n.* The act of producing copies of types, woodcuts, medals, etc., by means of the electric deposition of copper upon a mold taken from the original; a copy thus produced.—*v.t.*—*electrotyped*, *electrotyping.* To stereotype or take copies of by electrotype.—**electrotypic**, i·lek′tro·ti″pik, *a.* Pertaining

to, or effected by means of, electrotype.—**electrotypist**, i·lek′trō·pist, *n.* One who practices electrotypy.—**electrotypy**, i·lek′tro·ti·pi, *n.* **electuary**, i·lek′tū·a·ri, *n.* [L.L. *electuarium*, a word of doubtful origin.] A medicine composed of powders or other ingredients, incorporated with some conserve, honey, or syrup.

eleemosynary, el·e·mos′i·ne·ri, *a.* [L.L. *eleemosynarius*, from Gr. *eleémosynē*, alms, from *eleeō*, to pity, *eleos*, compassion. ALMS.] Given in charity or alms, appropriated to charity; founded by charity (an *eleemosynary* institution); relating to charitable donations; supported by charity.—*n.* One who lives by receiving alms or charity.

elegance, el′e·gans *n.* [Fr. *élégance*, from L. *elegantia*, from *elegans*, for *eligens*, from *eligo*—*e*, *ex*, out, and *lego*, to pick, to choose. ELECT.] The quality of being elegant; beauty resulting from perfect propriety, or from the absence of anything calculated to produce a disagreeable sensation; refinement; an elegant characteristic of feature.—**elegancy**, el′e·gan·si, *n.* Elegance.—**elegant**, el′e·gant, *a.* [Fr. *élégant*, L. *elegans*.] Having beauty or a pleasing effect resulting from grace, refinement, or polish; pleasing to good taste; graceful; refined (a lady with an *elegant* figure); having the words or style polished and appropriate (an *elegant* speech); giving expression to thought with propriety and grace; pleasing to the eye by grace of form or delicacy of color; free from coarseness, blemish, or other defect; showing fine harmony or symmetry.—**elegantly**, el′e·gant·li, *adv.* In an elegant manner.

elegy, el′e·ji, *n.* [L. *elegia*, from Gr. *elegeia*, from *elegos*, a lament.] A mournful or plaintive poem, or a funeral song; a poem or a song expressive of sorrow and lamentation; a dirge; *class. poetry*, any poem written in elegiac verse.—**elegiac**, i·lē′ji·ak, *a.* Belonging to elegy; plaintive; expressing sorrow or lamentation; used in elegies: said especially of a style of verse commonly used by the Greek and Latin poets, and composed of couplets consisting of alternate hexameter and pentameter lines.—**elegist**, el′e·jist, *n.* A writer of elegies.—**elegize**, el′e·jīz, *v.t.* and *i.* To write or compose elegies; to celebrate or lament in an elegy; to bewail.

element, el′e·ment, *n.* [L. *elementum*, an element, a first principle; same root as *aliment*.] One of the simplest constituent principles, or parts, of which anything consists, or upon which its constitution is based; a fundamental or ultimate part or principle, by the combination or aggregation of which anything is composed; an ingredient; *chem.* any of over 100 substances that alone or in combination constitute all matter; *pl.* the first or simplest rules or principles of an art or science; rudiments; one of the four

constituents of the material world according to an old and still popular classification—fire, air, earth, water (hence such expressions as 'war of the *elements*' for a storm); the state or sphere natural to anything or suited to its existence (hence, *out of one's element*, out of one's natural sphere or position); a datum or value necessary to be taken into consideration in making a calculation or coming to a conclusion; *pl.* the bread and wine used in the Eucharist.—*v.t.* To constitute; to be an element in; to make a first principle.—**elemental**, el·e·men′tal, *a.* Pertaining to or produced by elements or primary ingredients; pertaining to the four so-called elements of the material world or some of them (hence 'elemental war,' applied to a tempest); arising from or pertaining to first principles; elementary†.—**elementally**, el·e·men′tal·li, *adv.* In an elemental manner; according to elements.—**elementariness**, el·e·men′te·ri·nes, *n.* The state of being elementary.—**elementary**, el·e·men′te·ri, *a.* Having the character of an element or primary substance; primary; simple; uncompounded; uncombined; initial; rudimentary; containing, teaching, or discussing first principles, rules, or rudiments.—*Elementary particle*, any subatomic particle that is thought to be irreducible into further components (such as the proton, electron, positron, etc.).

elemi, el′e·mi, *n.* The resinous exudation from various trees, used in plasters and ointments and the manufacture of varnish.

eleoptene, el·ē·op′tēn, *n.* [Gr. *elaion*, olive oil, and *ptēnos*, winged.] The liquid portion of volatile oils, as distinguished from the solid portion called *stearoptene*.

elephant, el′e·fant, *n.* [L. *elephas*, *elephantis*, from Gr. *elephas*, *elephantos*, an elephant; probably from Heb. *aleph*, an ox.] The name of two species of huge quadrupeds, one inhabiting India, the other Africa, and both remarkable for having their nose prolonged into a long proboscis or trunk with the nostrils at its extremity, and for their large tusks.—**elephantiasis**, el″e·fan·tī′a·sis, *n.* [Gr., from *elephas*, elephant.] *Med.* the massive swelling of the limbs caused by the obstruction of the lymphatic vessels by filarial worms.—**elephantine**, el·e·fan′tīn, *a.* Pertaining to the elephant; resembling an elephant.

Eleusinian, el·ū·sin′i·an, *a.* Relating to *Eleusis* in Greece; as, *Eleusinian mysteries* or *festivals*, the mysteries and festivals of Dēmētēr (Ceres), celebrated there.

elevate, el′e·vāt, *v.t.*—*elevated*, *elevating.* [L. *elevo*, *elevatum*, to lift up—*e*, out, up, and *levo*, to raise, from *levis*, light in weight, whence *levity*, *lever*, *levy*, etc.] To raise; in a literal sense, to raise from a low or deep place to a higher; to raise to a higher state or station; to improve, refine, or dignify; to raise from a low or common state, as by training or education; to exalt; to excite, cheer, animate; to augment or swell; to make louder.—**elevated**, el′e·vā·ted, a. Raised; exalted; dignified; raised above the natural pitch; somewhat loud.—**elevation**, el·e·vā′shon, n. [L. elevatio.] The act of elevating; the act of raising or conveying from a lower place or degree to a higher; the state of being raised or elevated; exaltation; that which is raised or elevated; an elevated place; a rising ground; height; degree of height; height above the surface of the earth; altitude; astron. altitude; gun. the angle which the axis of the bore of a firearm makes with the plane of the horizon; arch. a geometrical representation of a building in vertical section, as opposed to ground-plan.—**elevator**, el′e·vā·tėr, n. One who or that which elevates, raises, lifts, or exalts; a mechanical contrivance for raising passengers or goods from a lower place to a higher; an airfoil on the tail plane of an airplane for producing up-and-down motion.

eleven, i·lev′n, a. [A.Sax. endleofan, endlufon=Icel. ellifu, Dan. elleve, D. elf, Goth. ainlif; compounded of two elements meaning "one" and "left", or one left after ten.] Ten and one added.—n. The sum of ten and one; a symbol representing eleven units; football and cricket, the players selected to play as a team in a football game or cricket match.—**eleventh**, i·lev′nth, a. and n. Next in order after the tenth; one of eleven equal parts into which anything is divided.

elf, elf, n. pl. **elves**, elvz. [A.Sax. ælf, elf=L.G. elf, Dan. alf, Icel. álfr, O.H.G. alp, an elf. Original meaning a nightmare.] A kind of inferior spiritual being formerly believed in; a fairy; a goblin; a mischievous person; a pet name for a child.—**elfin**, el′fin, a. Relating or pertaining to elves.—n. A little elf; a little urchin.—**elfish**, el′fish, a. Of or pertaining to elves; resembling an elf; suggestive of elves.—**elflock**, n. A knot of hair twisted as if by elves.

elicit, i·lis′it, v.t. [L. elicio, elicitum—e, out, and lacere, to allure; akin delicate, delight.] To bring or draw out by reasoning, discussion, examination, or the like; to deduce or educe (as truth, facts, etc.).

elide, i·līd′, v.t. [L. elido—e, out, and lædo, to strike.] Gram. to cut off or suppress, as a syllable.—**elision**, i·lizh′on, n. Gram. the act of eliding; the cutting off or suppression of a vowel or syllable.

eligible, el′i·ji·bl, a. [Fr. éligible, from L. eligo—e, out; and lego, to choose. ELECT.] Fit to be chosen for some purpose or duty; worthy of choice; desirable; legally qualified to be chosen.—**eligibility**, el′i·ji·bil″-i·ti, n. The state or condition of

being eligible; capability of being chosen.—**eligibly**, el′i·ji·bli, adv. In a manner to be worthy of choice; suitably.

eliminate, i·lim′i·nāt, v.t.—eliminated, eliminating. [L. elimino, eliminatum—e, out, and limen, threshold.] To discharge or throw off (as a secretion of the human body); to take out or separate as not being an element of value or necessary; to set aside as unimportant or not to be considered; to leave out of consideration; alg. to cause to disappear from an equation; to deduce or elicit† (incorrect in this sense).—**elimination**, i·lim′i·nā″-shon, n. The act of eliminating.

elision. See ELIDE.

elite, ā·lēt′, n. pl. [Fr., lit. elected or select.] Those who are choice or select; the best; a type style.

elixir, i·lik′sėr, n. [Fr. elixir, from Sp. elixir, from Ar. el-iksir, the philosopher's stone, from Gr. xēros, dry.] A liquor sought for by the alchemists for transmuting metals into gold or prolonging life; quintessence; a cordial; med. a tincture composed of various substances held in solution by alcohol in some form.

Elizabethan, i·liz′a·beth″an, a. Pertaining to Queen Elizabeth I of England or her period.—Elizabethan architecture, the architectural style of the times of Elizabeth and James I, when the debased Gothic and Italian were combined, characterized by large windows, tall and highly decorated chimneys, and much ornament.

elk, elk, n. [Icel. elgr, O.H.G. elaho, Sw. elg; akin to L. alces, an elk.] In Europe and Asia, the largest member of the deer family, similar to the moose; in America, the wapiti, a member of the deer family, next in size to the moose.

ell, el, n. [A.Sax. eln; D. ell, elle, G. elle, O.H.G. elna, Sw. aln, Icel. alin, Goth. aleina; akin to L. ulna, Gr. ōlenē, the forearm, and hence, a measure of length. Comp. cubit.] A measure of different lengths in different countries, used chiefly for measuring cloth; the English ell being 45 inches, the Flemish ell 27, the Scotch 37.2, and the French 54.

ellipse, el·lips′, n. [Gr. elleipsis, an omission or defect, from elleipō, to leave out—ek, out, and leipō, to leave.] Geom. an oval figure produced when any cone is cut by a plane which passes through it, not parallel to nor cutting the base; a closed curve in which the distances of any point from two points called the foci have always the same sum.—**ellipsis**, el·lip′sis, n. Gram. the omission of one or more words which the hearer or reader may supply; printing, the marks,—or *** or . . ., denoting the omission or suppression of letters or words; geom. an ellipse‡.—**ellipsoid**, el·lip′-soid, n. Geom. a solid figure, all plane sections of which are ellipses

or circles.—**ellipsoidal**, el·lip·soi′dal, a. Pertaining to an ellipsoid; having the form of an ellipsoid.—**elliptic**, **elliptical**, el·lip′tik, el·lip′ti·kal, a. Pertaining to an ellipse; having the form of an ellipse; pertaining to ellipsis; having a word or words left out.—**elliptically**, el·lip′ti·kal·li, adv. According to the form of an ellipse; with a word or words left out.—**ellipticity**, el·lip·tis′i·ti n. The quality of being elliptical or having the form of an ellipse.

elm, elm, n. [A.Sax. elm, D. olm, Icel. álmr, Dan. ælm, alm; akin to L. ulmus, Bohem. gilm (pron. yilm), elm.] A valuable timber and shade tree, species of which are found in America and Europe.

elocution, el·o·kū′shon, n. [L. elocutio, from eloquor, elocutus, to speak out—e, out, and loquor, to speak, seen in colloquy, eloquent, loquacious, etc.] The art by which, in delivering a discourse before an audience, the speaker is enabled to render it effective and impressive; mode of utterance of delivery of an address, accompanied by gestures.—**elocutionary**, el·o·kū′shon·e·ri, a. Pertaining to elocution.—**elocutionist**, el·o·kū′shon·ist, n. One who is versed in elocution; a teacher of elocution.

Elohim, el·ō·hēm′, n. One of the Hebrew names of God of frequent occurrence in the Bible, used both of the true God and of false gods, while Jehovah is used only of the true God.—**Elohistic**, ē·lō·his′tik, a. A term applied to certain passages in Scripture, especially in the Pentateuch, in which the Almighty is always spoken of as Elohim.

elongate, i·long′gāt, v.t.—elongated, elongating. [L.L. elongo, elongatum—L. e, out, and longus, long.] To lengthen; to extend.—v.i. To recede apparently from the sun: said of a planet in its orbit.—**elongation**, i·long·gā′shon, n. The act of elongating or lengthening; the state of being stretched out or lengthened; astron. the angular distance of a planet from the sun, as it appears to the eye of a spectator on the earth.

elope, i·lōp′, v.i.—eloped, eloping. [From D. loopen, the same word as G. laufen, Goth. hlaupan, to run, to leap, E. leap, with prefix e, out, away.] To run away; to run away with a lover or paramour in defiance of duty or social restraints: said especially of a woman.—**elopement**, i·lōp′ment, n. The act of eloping; the running away of a woman, married or unmarried, with a lover.

eloquence, el′o·kwens, n. [Fr. éloquence, from L. eloquentia. ELOCUTION.] The art of expressing thoughts in such language and in such a way as to produce conviction or persuasion; oratory; that which is expressed with eloquence.—**eloquent**, el′o·kwent, a. Having the power of expressing strong emotions vividly and appropriately; adapted

---

ch, chain; ch, Sc. loch; g, go; j, job; ng, sing; TH, then; th, thin; w, wig; hw, whig; zh, azure.

to express strong emotion with fluency and power; characterized by eloquence.—**eloquently**, el′o‑kwent‑li, *adv.* In an eloquent manner.

else, els, *a.* or *adv.* [A.Sax. *elles*, else, otherwise; akin to O.H.G. *eli*, *ali*, Goth. *alis*; L. *alius* (see ALIEN), Gr. *allos*, another.] Other; besides; in addition; as in who *else*? nothing or nobody *else*, nowhere *else*.—*conj.* Otherwise; in the other case; if the fact were different; as, he was ill, *else* he would have come.—**else‑where**, els′hwâr, *adv.* In another place; somewhere else.

elucidate, i‑lū′si‑dāt, *v.t.*—*elucidated*, *elucidating*. [L.L. *elucido*, *elucidatum*—L. *e*, out, and *lucidus*, bright. LUCID.] To make clear or manifest; to explain; to remove obscurity from and render intelligible; to illustrate.—**elucidation**, i‑lū′si‑dā″shon, *n.* The act of elucidating; explanation; exposition; illustration.—**elucidative**, i‑lū′si‑dā‑tiv, *a.* Making or tending to elucidate; explanatory.—**elucidator**, i‑lū′si‑dā‑tėr, *n.* One who elucidates or explains.

elude, i‑lūd′, *vt*..—*eluded*, *eluding*. [L. *eludo*—*e*, and *ludo*, to play, as in *allude*, *collude*, *delude*, etc.] To evade; to avoid by artifice, stratagem, wiles, deceit, or dexterity; to remain unseen, undiscovered, or unexplained by (to *elude* scrutiny).—**elusion**, i‑lū′zhon, *n.* An escape by artifice or deception; an evasion.—**elusive**, i‑lū′siv, *a.* Practicing elusion; using arts to escape.—**elusively**, i‑lū′siv‑li, *adv.* With or by elusion.—**elusory**, i‑lū′so‑ri, *a.* Tending to elude; tending to deceive; evasive; fallacious.

Elul, el‑ōl′, *n.* [Heb.] The twelfth month of the Jewish civil year, corresponding nearly to our August.

elutriate, i‑lū′tri‑āt, *v.t.*—*elutriated*, *elutriating*. [L. *elutrio*, *elutriatum*, from *eluo*, *elutum*, to wash off—*e*, off, and *luo*, to wash.] To purify (ores) by washing and straining off or decanting the liquid from the substance washed, the lighter matters being then separated from the heavier.—**elutriation**, i‑lū′tri‑ā″shon, *n.* The operation of elutriating.

elves, elvz, *pl.* of *elf*.—**elvish**, el′vish, *a.* Pertaining to elves or fairies; mischievous, as if done by elves; elfish.

Elysium, i‑liz′i‑um, *n.* [L., from Gr. *ēlysion* (*pedion*), the Elysian fields.] *Myth.* a place assigned to happy souls after death; the seat of future happiness; hence, any place exquisitely delightful.—**Elysian**, i‑lizh′an, *a.* Pertaining to Elysium; exceedingly delightful.

elytron, **elytrum**, el′i‑tron, el′i‑trum, *n.* *pl.* **elytra**, el′i‑tra. [Gr., a cover, sheath, from *elyō*, to roll round.] The wing sheath or coriaceous membrane which forms the superior wing in certain insects, as beetles, serving to cover and protect the true wing.—**elytroid**, el′i‑troid, *a.* Like an elytron.

Elzevir, el′ze‑vėr, *a.* Of or belonging to the *Elzevir* family: applied to editions of the classics, etc., published by the Elzevir family at Amsterdam and Leyden, from about 1595 to 1680, and highly prized for their accuracy and elegance; a term applied to a variety of printing type consisting of tall thin letters.

em, em, *n. Print.* the unit of measurement, being a type whose breadth is equal to its depth.

emaciate, i‑mā′shi‑āt, *v.i.*—*emaciated*, *emaciating*. [L. *emacio*, *emaciatum*—*e*, intens., and *macies*, leanness.] To lose flesh gradually; to become lean from loss of appetite or other cause.—*v.t.* To cause to lose flesh gradually; to reduce to leanness.—*a.* Thin; wasted.—**emaciation**, i‑mā′shi‑ā′shon, *n.* The act of making or becoming lean or thin in flesh; the state of being reduced to leanness.

emanate, em′a‑nāt, *v.i.*—*emanated*, *emanating*. [L. *emano*, *emanatum*—*e*, out, and *mano*, to flow.] To flow forth or issue from a source: said of what is intangible, as light, heat, odor, power, etc.; to proceed from something as the source, fountain, or origin; to take origin; to arise; to spring.—**emanation**, em‑a‑nā′shon, *n.* The act of emanating; that which emanates, issues, flows, or proceeds from any source, substance, or body; efflux; effluvium; any person, power, or thing emanating or proceeding from the Divine Essence.—**emanative**,† em′a‑nā‑tiv, *a.* Tending to emanate.

emancipate, i‑man′si‑pāt, *v.t.*—*emancipated*, *emancipating*. [L. *emancipo*, *emancipatum*—*e*, out, *manus*, the hand, and *capio*, to take.] To set free from servitude or slavery by the voluntary act of the proprietor; to restore from bondage to freedom; to free from bondage, restriction, or restraint of any kind; to liberate from subjection, controlling power, or influence.—**emancipation**, i‑man′si‑pā″shon, *n.* The act of emancipating, deliverance from bondage or controlling influence, liberation.—**emancipator**, i‑man′si‑pā‑tėr, *n.* One who emancipates.

emarginate, **emarginated**, i‑mär′ji‑nāt, i‑mär′ji‑nā‑ted, *a.* [L. *emarginatus*—*e*, not, and *margo*, *marginis*, border, margin.] Having the margin or extremity taken away, having a blunt or obtuse notch in the margin; notched at the blunt apex; applied most commonly in *bot.* to a leaf, petal, etc.

emasculate, i‑mas′kū‑lāt, *v.t.*—*emasculated*, *emasculating*. [L. *e*, not, and *masculus*, dim. of *mas*, a male. MASCULINE.] To deprive of the properties of a male; to castrate; to geld; to deprive of masculine vigor; to render effeminate, to expurgate by removing coarse passages from (a book).—**emasculation**, i‑mas′kū‑lā″shon, *n.* The act of emasculating; the state of being emasculated.—**emasculatory**, i‑mas′kū‑la‑to‑ri, *a.* Serving to emasculate.

embalm, em‑bäm′, *v.t.* [Prefix *em*, and *balm*. balsam.] To preserve (a dead body) from decay by removing the intestines and filling their place with odoriferous and desiccative spices and drugs; to preserve from loss or decay; to cherish tenderly the memory of.—**embalmer**, em‑bä′mėr, *n.* One who embalms.

embank, em‑bangk′, *v.t.* [Prefix *em*, and *bank*.] To enclose with a bank, to defend by banks, mounds, or dikes; to bank up.—**embankment**, em‑bangk′ment, *n.* The act of surrounding or defending with a bank; a mound or bank raised to protect land from being overflowed by a river or the sea, or to enable a road or railway to be carried over a valley.

embarcation, *n.* See EMBARKATION.

embargo, em‑bar′gō, *n.* [Sp. *embargo*, an embargo, embarrassment, lit. what serves as a bar—prefix *em* for *in*, and L.L. *barra*, a bar; akin *embarrass*.] A restraint or prohibition imposed by the public authorities of a country on merchant vessels, or other ships, to prevent their entering or leaving its ports, sometimes amounting to an entire interdiction of commercial intercourse; a restraint or hindrance imposed on anything.—*v.t.* To put an embargo on; to subject to an embargo.

embark, em‑bärk′, *v.t.* [Fr. *embarquer*—*en*, in, and *barque*, a bark. BARQUE.] To put or cause to enter on board a ship or boat; to engage, invest, or make to enter on in any affair.—*v.i.* To go on board of a ship, boat, or vessel; to engage or take a share in any affair; to enlist.—**embarkation**, em‑bär‑kā′shon, *n.* The act of embarking; that which is embarked or put on board.

embarrass, em‑bar′as, *v.t.* [Fr. *embarrasser*, to embarrass, *embarras*, embarrassment—prefix *em*, and L.L. *barra*, a bar; akin *embargo*. BAR.] To derange, confuse, or entangle (affairs, business, etc.), so as to make a course of action difficult; to involve in pecuniary difficulties; to perplex, disconcert, or abash.—**embarrassing**, em‑bar′as‑ing, *a.* Perplexing; adapted to perplex or embarrass.—**embarrassingly**, em‑bar′as‑ing‑li, *adv.* In an embarrassing manner.—**embarrassment**, em‑bar′as‑ment, *n.* The state of being embarrassed; entanglement; perplexity arising from inability to pay one's debts; confusion of mind; abashment.

embassador, em‑bas′sa‑dor, *n.* An ambassador. [This spelling is not now used, though *embassy* and not *ambassy* is the correct form.]—**embassy**, em′bas‑si, *n.* [O.E. and Fr. *embassade*.] The mission of an ambassador; the charge or employment of an ambassador or envoy; the message of an ambassador; a message, especially a solemn or important message; the persons entrusted with ambassadorial functions; a legation; the business or official residence of an ambassador.

---

fāte, fär, fâre, fat, fạll;　mē, met, hėr;　pīne, pin;　nōte, not, mōve;　tūbe, tub, bụll;　oil, pound.

embattle, em·bat´l, v.t.—embattled, embattling. [Prefix em, and battle.] To arrange in order of battle; to array for battle; to furnish with battlements.—v.i. To be ranged in order of battle.

embay, em·bā´, v.t. [Prefix em, and bay.] To enclose in a bay or inlet; to landlock.—embayment, em·bā´ment, n. A portion of the sea closed in and sheltered by capes or promontories.

embed, em·bed´, v.t.—embedded, embedding. [Prefix em, and bed.] To lay in or as in a bed; to lay in surrounding matter.

embellish, em·bel´lish, v.t. [Fr. embellir—prefix em, and belle, L. bellus, pretty, beautiful.] To make beautiful; to adorn; to beautify; to decorate; to deck.—embellishment, em·bel´lish·ment, n. The act of embellishing or adorning, or state of being embellished; that which embellishes or adorns; that which renders anything pleasing to the eye or agreeable to the taste; adornment; ornament; decoration.

ember, em´bèr, n. [A.Sax. æmyrian, cinders; Dan. emmer, Icel. eimyrja, embers.] A small live coal, glowing piece of wood, etc.; used chiefly in the plural to signify live cinders or ashes; the smoldering remains of a fire.

Ember days, n. pl. [A.Sax. ymbrine, ymbren embren the circle or course of the year, from ymb or emb, round, and rinnan, to run.] Days returning at certain seasons, being the Wednesday, Friday, and Saturday after the first Sunday in Lent, after Whitsunday, after Holyrood-day (September 14) and after St. Lucia's day (December 13), appointed in the Church of England and the Roman Catholic Church for fasting and abstinence: called also Embering-days†.—Ember week, n. A week in which ember days occur.

embezzle, em·bez´l, v.t.—embezzled, embezzling. [O.Fr. embeasiler, to filch, besler, to deceive; origin doubtful.] To appropriate fraudulently to one's own use what is entrusted to one's care; to apply to one's private use by a breach of trust, as a clerk or servant who misappropriates his employer's money or valuables.—embezzlement, em·bez´l·ment, n. The act by which a clerk, servant, or person acting as such, fraudulently appropriates to his own use the money or goods entrusted to his care.—embezzler, em·bez´lèr, n. One who embezzles.

embitter, em·bit´èr, v.t. [Prefix em, and bitter.] To make bitter or more bitter; to make unhappy or grievous; to render distressing; to make more severe, poignant, or painful; to render more violent or malignant; to exasperate.—embitterment, em·bit´èr·ment, n. The act of embittering.

emblaze,‡ em·blāz´, v.t.—emblazed, emblazing. [Prefix em, and blaze.] To kindle; to set in a blaze; to make to glitter or shine; to display or set forth conspicuously or ostentatiously; to blazon.

emblazon, em·blā´zon, v.t. [Prefix em, and blazon.] To adorn with figures of heraldry or ensigns armorial; to depict or represent, as an armorial ensign on a shield; to set off with ornaments; to celebrate in laudatory terms; to sing the praises of.—emblazoner, em·blā´zon·èr, n. One that emblazons.—emblazonment, em·blā´zon·ment, n. The act of emblazoning; that which is emblazoned.—emblazonry, em·blā´zon·ri, n. The act or art of emblazoning; blazonry; heraldic decoration, as pictures or figures on shields, standards, etc.

emblem, em´blem, n. [Fr. emblême; Gr. emblēma, from emballō—em, in, and ballō, to cast.] A kind of inlaid work or mosaic‡; a picture, figure, or other work of art representing one thing to the eye and another to the understanding; any object or its figure whose predominant quality symbolizes something else, as another quality or state; a symbolic figure; a type; a symbol; a device, as a balance used to symbolize justice.—emblematic, emblematical, em·ble·mat´ik, em·ble·mat´i·kal, a. Pertaining to or comprising an emblem; serving as an emblem or symbolic figure; symbolic.—emblematically, em·ble·mat´i·kal·li adv. In an emblematic manner.—emblematize, em·blem´a·tīz v.t.—emblematized, emblematizing; emblemized, emblemizing. To represent by an emblem; to serve as the emblem of.

emblement, em´ble·ment n. [From O.Fr. embleer, to sow with corn—prefix em, and blé, bled, L.L. bladum, corn.] Law, the produce or fruits of land sown or planted; growing crops annually produced; used chiefly in the plural.

embody, em·bod´i, v.t.—embodied, embodying. [Prefix em, and body.] To lodge in a material body; to invest with a body; to incarnate; to clothe with a material form; to render obvious to the senses or mental perception (to embody thought in words); to form or collect into a body or united mass; to collect into a whole.—v.i. To unite into a body, mass, or collection; to coalesce.—embodiment, em·bod´i·ment, n. Act of embodying or investing with a body; the state of being embodied; bodily or material representation; the act of collecting or forming into a body or united whole.

embolden, em·bōl´dn, v.t. [Prefix em, and bold.] To give boldness or courage to; to encourage.

embolism, em´bol·izm, n. [Gr. embolismos, from emballō, to throw in, to insert.] The insertion of days, months, or years in an account of time, to produce regularity, intercalation; surg. the obstruction of a vessel by a clot of fibrin, a frequent cause of paralysis, and of gangrene of the part beyond the obstacle.—embolismic, em·bo·liz´mik, a. Pertaining to embolism or to intercalation; intercalated; inserted.

embolus, em´bo·lus, n. [Gr. embolos, wedge or plug.] Med. an abnormal particle circulating in the bloodstream, as an air bubble, blood clot, etc.

embosom, em·bu´zum, v.t. [Prefix em, and bosom.] To take into or hold in the bosom; to admit to the heart or affection; to cherish; to enclose in the midst; to surround.

emboss, em·bos´, v.t. [Prefix em, and boss.] To form bosses on; to fashion relief or raised work on; to represent in worked figures.—embosser, em·bos´èr, n. One who embosses.—embossment, em·bos´ment, n. The act of embossing; work in relief.

embouchure, om·bö·shür´, n. [Fr., from prefix em, and bouche, mouth.] A mouth of a river; the mouth hole of a wind instrument of music; the shaping of the lips to the mouth-piece.

embowel, em·bou´el, v.t.—emboweled, emboweling. [Prefix em, and bowel.] To take out the bowels or entrails of; to eviscerate; to take out the internal parts of; to sink or enclose in; to embed; to bury.

embower, em·bou´èr, v.i. [Prefix em, and bower.] To lodge or rest in a bower.—v.t. To cover with a bower; to shelter with, or as with, trees; to form a bower for.

embrace, em·brās´, v.t.—embraced, embracing. [Fr. embrasser, to embrace—em, in, and bras, the arm. BRACE.] To take, clasp, or enclose in the arms; to press to the bosom in token of affection; to enclose, encompass, or contain; to encircle; to seize eagerly, in a figurative sense; to accept with cordiality (doctrines, religion); to comprehend, include, or take in; to comprise; to submit to (Shak)‡.—v.i. To join in an embrace.—n. Enclosure or clasp with the arms; pressure to the bosom with the arms; sexual intercourse; conjugal endearment.—embracement, em·brās´ment, n. A clasp in the arms; a hug; embrace; sexual commerce (Shak.)‡.—embraceor, em·brā´sèr, n. Law, one who practices embracery.—embracer, em·brā´sèr, n. One who embraces.—embracery, em·brā´sèr·i, n. Law, an attempt to influence a jury corruptly to one side, by promises, persuasions, entreaties, money, entertainments, or the like.

embrasure, em·brā´zhur, n. [Fr., prefix em, and braser, to slope the edge of a stone.] Fort. an opening in a wall or parapet through which cannon are pointed and fired; the indent or crenelle of an embattlement; arch. the enlargement of the aperture of a door or window on the inside of the wall to give more room or admit more light.

embrocate, em´brō·kāt, v.t.—embrocated, embrocating. [L.L. embroco, embrocatum, from Gr. embrochē, a fomentation, from embrechō, to foment—prefix em for en, in, and brechō, to wet.] Med. to moisten and rub, as a diseased part, with a liquid substance, as with spirit, oil, etc.—**embrocation,** em·brō·kā'shon, n. The act of moistening and rubbing a diseased part with a cloth or sponge, dipped in some liquid substance, as spirit, oil, etc.; the liquid or lotion with which an affected part is rubbed or washed.

embroider, em·broi'dėr, v.t. [Prefix *em,* and *broider.* BROIDER.] To adorn with figures of needlework, often raised above the surface.—**embroiderer,** em·broi'dėr·ėr, n. One who embroiders.—**embroidery,** em·broi'dėr·i, n. Work in gold, silver, silk, or other fancy thread; elaboration with fictitious detail; anything pleasing but unimportant.

embroil, em·broil', v.t. [Prefix *em,* and *broil,* a noisy quarrel.] To mix up or entangle in a quarrel or disturbance; to intermix confusedly; to involve in contention or trouble.—**embroilment,** em·broil'ment, n. The act of embroiling; a state of contention, perplexity, or confusion.

embrown, em·broun', v.t. [Prefix *em,* and *brown.*] To make brown; to imbrown.

embrue, em·brö'. See IMBRUE.

embryo, em'bri·ō, n. [Gr. *embryon—em,* in, and *bryō,* to be full of anything.] The first rudiments of an animal in the womb, before the several members are distinctly formed, after which it is called a *fetus;* the rudimentary plant contained in the seed, produced by the action of the pollen on the ovule; the beginning or first state of anything, while yet in a rude and undeveloped condition; rudimentary state.—*Embryo buds,* spheroidal solid bodies formed in the bark of trees, and capable of developing into branches under favorable circumstances.—**embryogeny,** em·bri·oj'e·ni, n. [Gr. *embryon,* and root *gen,* to produce.] The formation and development of embryos; that department of science that treats of such formation and development.—**embryogenic,** em'bri·o·jen''ik, a. Pertaining to embryogeny.—**embryology,** em·bri·ol'o·ji, n. [Gr. *embryon,* and *logos,* discourse.] The doctrine of the development of embryos, whether in plants or animals.—**embryologic, embriological,** em'bri·o·loj''ik, em'·bri·o·loj''i·kal, a. Of or belonging to embryology.—**embryon,**‡ em'bri·on, n. An embryo. (*Mil.*).—**embryonal, embryonic,** em'bri·on·al, em·bri·on'ik, a. Of or pertaining to an embryo, or the embryo stage.

emcee, em·sē', v.t.—emceed, emceeing. [From the abbrev. *M.C.,* master of ceremonies.] To act as master of ceremonies of.—n. The master of ceremonies.

emend, e·mend', v.t. [L. *emendo,* to correct—*e,* not, and *menda,* a spot or blemish. *Amend* and *mend* are virtually the same as this.] To remove faults or blemishes from; to amend; especially to amend by criticism of the text; to improve the reading of (an *emended* text of

Vergil).—**emendation,** ē·men·dā'shon, n. The act of emending; removal of errors or corruptions from the text of a book or writing; a textual alteration or correction.—**emendator,** ē'men·dā·tėr, n. One who emends.—**emendatory,** ē·men'·da·to·ri, a. Contributing to emendation or correction.

emerald, em'e·rald, n. [Fr. *emeraude,* Sp. *esmeralda,* It. *smeraldo;* from L. *smaragdus,* Gr. *smaragdos,* an emerald.] A precious stone whose colors are a pure lively green, varying to a pale, yellowish, bluish, or grass green, akin to the beryl, found especially in South America; a variety of printing type intermediate between minion and nonpareil.—a. Of a bright green, like emerald; printed with the size of type known as emerald.—*Emerald green,* a durable pigment of a vivid light-green color, prepared from the arsenate of copper.—*Emerald Isle.* Ireland. From the green verdure of the grass, or from its being set like an emerald in the sea. First so named in song by Drennan, 1754-1820.

emerge, i·mėrj', v.i.—emerged, emerging. [L. *emergo, emersum—e,* out, and *mergo,* to plunge, as in *immerge, submerge.* MERGE.] To rise out of a fluid or other covering or surrounding substance; to issue or proceed from something; to reappear after being eclipsed; to leave the sphere of the obscuring object; to rise out of a state of depression or obscurity; to come to notice.—**emergence,** i·mėr'jens, n. The act of emerging.—**emergency,** i·mėr'jen·si, n. The act of emerging; sudden occasion; unexpected casualty; unforeseen occurrence; any event or combination of circumstances calling for immediate action; pressing necessity.—**emergent,** i·mėr'jent, a. Emerging; rising into view or notice; coming suddenly; unexpected; calling for immediate action; urgent; pressing.—**emersion,** i·mėr'shon, n. The act of emerging or rising out of a fluid or other substance; the act of coming forth to view; the reappearance of a heavenly body after an eclipse or occultation.

emeritus, i·mer'i·tus, a. [L. *emeritus,* having served out his time.—*e* out, and *mereor, meritus,* to merit, earn, serve.] Discharged from the performance of public duty with honor, on account of infirmity, age, or long service; as, a professor *emeritus.* Sometimes used as a noun.

emersion. See EMERGE.

emery, em'e·ri, n. [Fr. *émeri,* O.Fr. *esmeril,* from It. *smeriglio,* from Gr. *smyris, smiris, smēris,* from *smaō,* to rub.] A mineral substance, an amorphous variety of corundum and sapphire, varying in color from deep gray to bluish or blackish gray, sometimes brownish, used for grinding and polishing metals, hard stones, and glass.

emetic, i·met'ik, a. [Gr. *emetikos,* from *emeō,* to vomit.] *Med.* inducing to vomit; exciting the stomach to

discharge its contents by the mouth.—n. A medicine that provokes vomiting.—**emetin,** em'e·tin, n. The active principle of ipecacuanha.

emigrate, em'i·grāt, v.i.—emigrated, emigrating. [L. *emigro, emigratum,* to migrate, to emigrate—*e,* out, and *migro,* to migrate.] To quit one country, state, or region and settle in another; to remove from one country or state to another for the purpose of residence.—**emigrant,** em'i·grant, a. Emigrating; pertaining to emigration or emigrants.—**emigrant,** em'i·grant, n. One who emigrates.—**emigration,** em·i·grā'shon, n. The act of emigrating; departure of inhabitants from one country or state to another for the purpose of residence; a body of emigrants.

eminence, em'i·nens, n. [Fr. *éminence,* from L. *eminentia,* from *eminens, eminentis,* from *emineo—e,* out, and *mineo,* to project, to jut.] A rising ground; a hill of moderate elevation; a part rising or projecting beyond the rest or above the surface; a projection; a prominence; an elevated situation among men; station above men in general; rank; distinction; celebrity; conspicuousness; [*cap.*] a title of honor given to cardinals and others.—**eminency,**† em'i·nen·si, n. Same as *Eminence.*—**eminent,** em'i·nent, a. Standing out above other things‡; prominent‡; lofty‡; exalted in rank; high in office or public estimation; conspicuous; remarkable; distinguished.—**eminently,** em'i·nent·li, adv. In an eminent manner or position.

emir, em·ėr', n. [Ar. *amir,* a commander; from *amara,* Heb. *ámar,* to command.] The title given by Mohammedans to all independent chiefs, to the heads of certain departments, and to all the real or supposed descendants of Mohammed, through his daughter Fatimah.

emissary, em'is·se·ri, n. [L. *emissarius,* from *emitto, emissum,* to send out—*e,* out, and *mitto,* to send. EMIT.] A person sent on a mission; particularly, a secret agent, or one who carries on private negotiations or business; a spy; an outlet or channel by which water is drawn from a lake.—**emit,** i·mit', v.t.—emitted, emitting. [L. *emitto—e,* out, and *mitto, missum,* to send, whence *mission, missile, missive, message,* etc.] To throw or give out (light, heat, steam, etc.); to send forth; to vent; to cause or allow to issue or emanate.—**emission,** i·mish'on, n. [L. *emissio.*] The act of emitting or of sending or throwing out; that which is emitted, issued, sent, or thrown out.

emmenagogue, em·me'na·gog, n. [Gr. *emmena,* the menses—*em,* in, *mēn, mēnos,* month, and *agō,* to lead.] A medicine taken to promote the menstrual discharge.

emollient, i·mol'li·ent, a. [L. *emolliens, emollientis,* ppr. of *emollio.*] Softening; making supple; relaxing the solids.—n. A medicine which

fāte, fär, fâre, fat, fạll; mē, met, hėr; pīne, pin; nōte, not, mȯve; tūbe, tub, bụll; oil, pound.

softens and relaxes living tissues that are inflamed or too tense.

emolument, i·mol′ū·ment, n. [L. *emolumentum,* a working out, from *e,* and *molior,* to exert one's self, from *moles,* a heavy mass.] The profit arising from office or employment; compensation for services; remuneration; salary; income; profit; advantage or gain in general.

emotion, i·mō′shon, n. [L. *emotio,* from *emoveo, emotum—e,* out, up, and *moveo,* to move.] A moving of the mind or soul; a state of excited feeling of any kind, as pleasure, pain, grief, joy, astonishment; one of the three fundamental properties of the human mind, the other two being *volition* and *intellect.*—**emotional,** i·mō′shon·al, a. Pertaining to or characterized by emotion; attended by or producing emotion; liable to emotion.—**emotionalism,** i·mō′shon·al·izm, n. The character of being emotional; tendency to emotional excitement.—**emotive,**† i·mō′tiv, a. Emotional; indicating or exciting emotion.—**emotively,**† i·mō′tiv·li, adv. In an emotive manner.—**emotiveness,**† i·mō′tiv·nes, n. The state or quality of being emotive.

empanel, empanelment, em·pan′el, em·pan′el·ment. See IMPANEL.

empathy, em′pa·thē, n. [Gr. *empatheia,* from *em,* in, and *pathos,* suffering, passion.] The imaginative projection of one's consciousness into the feelings of another person or object; sympathetic understanding.

emperor, em′pėr·ėr, n. [Fr. *empereur,* from L. *imperator,* from *impero, imperatum,* to command—prefix *im,* and *paro,* to prepare, to order.] The sovereign or supreme monarch of an empire; a title of dignity superior to that of king.—**empress,** em′pres, n. The consort or spouse of an emperor; a woman who rules an empire.—**empery,** em′pe·ri, n. Empire; power.

emphasis, em′fa·sis, n. [Gr. *emphasis,* a setting forth, from *emphainō,* to indicate—*em,* in, and *phainō,* to show (whence *phenomenon*).] A particular stress of utterance or force of voice given to the words or parts of a discourse whose signification the speaker intends to impress specially upon his audience; a peculiar impressiveness of expression or weight of thought; impressiveness; vividness.—**emphasize,** em′fa·sīz, v.t.—*emphasized, emphasizing.* To utter or pronounce with emphasis; to lay particular stress upon; to render emphatic.—**emphatic,** em·fat′ik, a. Having emphasis.—**emphatically,** em·fat′i·kal·li, adv.

emphysema, em·fi·sē′ma, n. [Gr. *emphysēma,* from *emphysaō,* to inflate.] *Med.* the presence of air in the intra-alveolar tissue of the lung due to the rupturing and distention of the alveoli.

empire, em′pīr, n. [Fr. *empire,* from L. *imperium.* EMPEROR.] Supreme power in governing; supreme dominion; sovereignty; imperial power; the territory or countries under the dominion of an emperor or other powerful sovereign; usually a ter-

ritory of greater extent than a kingdom; supreme control; rule; sway.

empiric, em·pir′ik, n. [L. *empiricus,* from Gr. *empeirikos,* experienced—*en,* in, and *peira,* a trial.] One who relies only on experience and observation, as opposed to theory based on scientific conclusions; specifically, a physician who enters on practice without a regular professional education; an ignorant pretender to medical skill; a quack; a charlatan.—**empiric, empirical,** em·pir′i·kal, a. Pertaining to experiments or experience; depending altogether upon the observation of phenomena; depending upon experience or observation alone, without due regard to science and theory.—**empirically,** em·pir′i·kal·li, adv. In an empirical manner.—**empiricism,** em·pir′i·sizm, n. The quality or method of being empirical; the practice of an empiric; quackery.

emplacement, em·plās′ment, n. A position specially assigned to a gun or group of guns. A solid platform with accessories prepared for the support of a gun or guns.

employ, em·ploi′, v.t. [Fr. *employer,* from L. *implicare,* to infold, involve, engage—*in,* and *plicare,* to fold, seen also in *deploy, display.* PLY.] To occupy the time, attention, and labor of; to keep busy or at work; to make use of; to use as an instrument or means to, or as materials in forming anything; to engage in one's service; to use as an agent or substitute in transacting business; to apply or devote to an object; to occupy.—n. That in which one is employed; a state of being engaged by a master; occupation; employment.—**employable,** em·ploi′a·bl, a. Capable of being employed.—**employee,** em·ploi′ē, n. [The English form of the French *employé,* one who is employed, especially, a clerk.] One who works for an employer or master; a clerk, workman, or other person working for salary or wages.—**employer,** em·ploi′ėr, n. One who employs; one who uses; one who engages or keeps servants in employment.—**employment,** em·ploi′ment, n. The act of employing or using; the state of being employed; occupation; business; that which engages the head or hands; vocation; trade; profession; work.

empoison, em·poi′zn, v.t [Prefix *em,* and *poison.*] To poison; to taint with poison or venom; to embitter; to destroy all pleasure in.

emporium, em·pō′ri·um, n. [L., from Gr. *emporion,* an emporium or mart, from *emporos,* a merchant—*en,* in, and *poros,* a way, of same root as A.Sax. *faran,* to go, E. *fare.*] A town or city which is a center of commerce, or to which sellers and buyers resort from different countries; a commercial center; a department store.

empower, em·pou′ėr, v.t. [Prefix *em,* and *power.*] To give legal or moral power or authority to; to authorize, as by law, commission, letter of attorney, verbal license, etc.; to warrant; to license.

empress. n. See EMPEROR.

emprise, emprize, em·prīz′, n. [O. Fr. *emprise*—prefix *em,* and *prise,* a taking, from *prendre,* to take.] An undertaking; an enterprise; adventure. (*Poet.*)

empty, em′ti, a. [A.Sax. *aemti, aemtig, ǽmtig,* vacant, free, idle; *aemtian,* to be at leisure, to be vacant; from *aemta, ǽmta,* quiet, leisure.] Containing nothing, or nothing but air; void of contents or appropriate contents; destitute of solid matter; not filled; void; devoid; destitute of force or effect, or of sense or sincerity; wanting substance or solidity; wanting reality; unsatisfactory; not able to fill the mind or the desires; destitute of sense; knowledge, or judgment; vain; ignorant; unfruitful or producing nothing (O.T.); without effect (O.T.)‡.—n. An empty packing case or the like.—v.t. emptied, emptying. To remove the contents from; to discharge; to render void.—v.i. To pour out or discharge contents; to become empty.—**emptier,** em′ti·ėr, n. One who or that which empties.—**emptiness,** em′ti·nes, n. A state of being empty.

empyema, em·pi·ē′ma, n. [Gr. *empyēma,* from *em,* in and *pyon,* pus.] *Med.* a collection of pus, blood, or other fluid matter, in some cavity of the body, especially in the cavity of the chest.

empyreal, em·pir′ē·al, or em·pī·rē′al, a. [L.L. *empyrǽus,* from Gr. *empyros,* prepared by fire, fiery, scorched—*en,* and *pyr,* fire.] Formed of pure fire or light; refined beyond aerial substance; pertaining to the highest and purest region of heaven.—**empyrean,** em·pī·rē′an, a. Empyreal.—n. The highest heaven, where the pure element of fire was supposed by the ancients to exist.

emu, emeu, ē′mū, n. A large cursorial bird, closely allied to the ostrich and the cassowary, but differing from the former in having three toes, found in Australia.

emulate, em′ū·lāt, v.t.—*emulated, emulating.* [L. *ǽmulor, ǽmulatus,* to make one's self a rival, from *ǽmulus,* a rival.] To strive to equal or excel in qualities or actions; to vie with; to come forward as a rival of.—**emulation,** em·ū·lā′shon, n. The act of emulating; rivalry; desire of superiority, attended with effort to attain it; ambition to equal or excel; envy, jealousy, or malicious rivalry (*Shak.*).—**emulative,** em′ū·lā·tiv, a. Inclined to emulation; striving to emulate.—**emulatively,** em′ū·lā·tiv·li, adv. In an emulative manner.—**emulator,** em′ū·lā·tėr, n. One who emulates; a rival; a competitor.—**emulous,** em′ū·lus, a. Desirous or eager to imitate, equal, or excel another; desirous of like excellence with another (*emulous* of another's prowess); rivaling; engaged in competition; factious; contentious (*Shak.*)—**emulously,** em′ū·lus·li, adv. In an emulous manner.—**emulousness,** em′ū·lus·nes, n.

emulsion, ē·mul′shon, n. [From L. *emulgeo, emulsum,* to milk out—*e,* out, and *mulgeo*, to milk.] Any milky substance; *chem.* a mixture of two immiscible liquids, such as oil and water; a coating on photographic plates, paper, etc.—**emulsifier,** e‧mul′si‧fī‧ėr, *n.* That which promotes the formation and stabilization of an emulsion.—**emulsify,** i‧mul′si‧fī, *v.t.* —*emulsified, emulsifying.* To make or form an emulsion.—**emulsive,** i‧mul′siv, *a.* Softening; milklike; yielding oil by expression (*emulsive* seeds); producing a milklike substance.

emunctory, i‧mungk′to‧ri, *n.* [L. *emungo, emunctum,* to wipe.] *Anat.* any part of the body which serves to carry off excrementitious or waste matter; an excretory duct.

enable, en‧ā′bl, *v.t.*—*enabled, enabling.* [Prefix *en,* and *able.*] To make able; to supply with power, physical, moral, or legal; to furnish with sufficient power, ability, or authority; to render fit or competent; to authorize.

enact, en‧akt′, *v.t.* [Prefix *en,* and *act.*] To pass into an act or established law; to give sanction to (a bill or legislative proposal); to decree; to act or perform (*Shak.*)‡; to act the part on the stage (*Shak.*)‡.— **enactive,** en‧ak′tiv, *a.* Having power to enact, or establish as a law.— **enactment,** en‧akt′ment, *n.* The passing of a bill or legislative proposal into a law; a law enacted; a decree; an act.

enamel, en‧am′el, *n.* [Prefix *en,* and old *amel, ammel, amile,* enamel, from O.Fr. *esmail,* Mod.Fr. *émail,* enamel, from G. *schmelzen,* to smelt. SMELT.] A colored substance of the nature of glass, differing from it by a greater degree of fusibility or opacity, used as an ornamental coating for various articles; a smooth, glossy surface of various colors, resembling enamel; the smooth hard substance which covers the crown of a tooth, overlying the dentine.—*v.t.*—*enameled, enameling.* To lay enamel on; to paint in enamel; to form a glossy surface like enamel upon; to variegate or adorn with different colors.—*v.i.* To practice the use of enamel or the art of enameling.—**enameler, enamelist,** en‧am′el‧ėr, en‧am′el‧ist, *n.* One who enamels; one whose occupation is to lay on enamels.

enamor, en‧am′ėr, *v.t.* [O.Fr. *enamourer*—*en,* and *amour,* L. *amor,* love.] To inflame with love; to charm; to captivate: commonly in the past participle, and with *of* or *with* before the person or thing that captivates.

enarthrosis, en‧är‧thrō′sis, *n.* [Gr. *enarthrōsis*—*en,* in, and *arthron,* a joint.] *Anat.* a ball-and-socket joint; an articulation which consists in the insertion of the round end of a bone in the cuplike cavity of another.

encaenia, en‧sē′ni‧a, *n.* [Gr. *enkainia.*] Dedication, festival of commemoration.

encage, en‧kāj′, *v.i.*—*encaged, encaging.* [Prefix *en,* and *cage.*] To shut up or confine in a cage; to coop up.

encamp, en‧kamp′, *v.i.* [Prefix *en,* and *camp.*] To take up position in a camp; to make a camp.—*v.t.* To form into or place in a camp (*Shak.*)† —**encampment,** en‧kamp′ment, *n.* The act of encamping; the place where a body of men is encamped, together with the tents or other conveniences set in order for their accommodation; a camp.

encapsulate, in‧kap′su‧lāt, *v.t.* [L. *en,* and *capsula,* box.] To encase in a capsule.—*v.i.* To go into a capsule. —**encapsulation,** in‧kap′su‧lā″shon, *n.*

encaustic, en‧kas′tik, *a.* [Gr. *enkaustikos*—*en,* and *kaustikos,* caustic, from *kaiō,* to burn.] Pertaining to the art of enameling and to painting in colors that are fixed by burning.— *Encaustic painting,* a kind of painting in which, by heating or burning, the colors are rendered permanent in all their original splendor.—*Encaustic tiles,* decorated tiles of baked pottery, used in ornamental pavements, to cover parts of walls, etc.

encephalon, en‧sef′a‧lon, *n.* [Gr. *enkephalos,* within the head—*en,* in, and *kephalē,* the head.] The contents of the skull, consisting of the cerebrum, cerebellum, medulla oblongata, and membranes; the brain.—**encephalic,** en‧se‧fal′ik, *a.* Situated in the head; belonging to the head or brain.— **encephalalgia,** en′se‧fa‧lal″ji‧a, *n.* [Gr. *en, kephalē,* and *algos,* pain.] *Med.* headache, cephalalgy.—**encephalitis,** en‧sef′a‧lī″tis, *n.* Inflammation of the brain.

enchain, en‧chān′, *v.t.* [Prefix *en,* and *chain.*] To fasten with a chain; to bind or hold in chains; to hold in bondage; to hold fast, restrain, confine; to link together; to connect †.—**enchainment,** en‧chān′ment, *n.* The act of enchaining or state of being enchained; concatenation.

enchant, en‧chänt′, *v.t.* [Fr. *enchanter*—*en,* and *chanter,* to sing; L. *incanto*—*in,* and *canto,* freq. of *cano,* to sing. CHANT, CANT.] To practice sorcery or witchcraft on; to subdue by charms or spells; to hold as by a spell; to fascinate; to delight in a high degree; to charm, captivate, or enrapture.—**enchanter,** en‧chän′tėr, *n.* One who enchants; a sorcerer or magician; one who practices enchantment or pretends to perform surprising things by the agency of demons; one who charms or delights.—**enchanting,** en‧chän′ting, *a.* Charming; delighting; ravishing.—**enchantingly,** en‧chän′ting‧li, *adv.* In an enchanting manner.—**enchantment,** en‧chänt′ment, *n.* The act of enchanting; the use of magic arts, spells, or charms; incantation; that which enchants; an influence or power which fascinates or delights; overpowering influence of delight.— **enchantress,** en‧chänt′res, *n.* A female enchanter.

enchase, en‧chās′, *v.t.*—*enchased, enchasing.* [Fr. *enchâsser*—*en,* and *châsse,* a frame, from L. *capsa,* a chest, a case, from *capio,* to take or receive.] To incase or enclose in a border or rim; to surround with an ornamental setting, as a gem with gold; to adorn by embossed work; to beautify by some design or figure in low relief.

enchorial, enchoric, en‧kō′ri‧al, en‧kor′ik, *a.* [Gr. *enchōrios,* in or of the country—*en,* in, and *chōra,* a country.] Belonging to or used in a country; native; indigenous; demotic (which see).

encircle, en‧sėr′kl, *v.t.*—*encircled, encircling.*] To form a circle about; to enclose or surround; to encompass; to environ; to embrace.

enclasp, en‧klasp′, *v.t.* To clasp; to embrace.

enclave, en′klāv, *n.* [Fr.—*en,* in, and L. *clavis,* a key.] A place or country which is entirely surrounded by the territories of another power.

enclitic, en‧klit′ik, *a.* [Gr. *enklitikos,* inclined, from *enklinō,* to incline—*en,* in, and *klinō,* to lean.] *Gram.* subjoined, and as it were leaning: said of a word or particle which always follows another word, and is so closely connected with the preceding word as to seem to be a part of it.— **enclitic,** *n. Gram.* an enclitic word.

enclose, en‧klōz′, *v.t.*—*enclosed, enclosing.* [Prefix *en,* en, and *close.*] To surround, shut in, or confine on all sides; to shut up; to environ or encompass; to separate from common grounds by a fence (to *enclose* lands); to cover with a case, wrapper, or envelope.—**encloser,** en‧klō′zėr, *n.* One who encloses.—**enclosure,** en‧klō′zhėr, *n.* The act of enclosing; what is enclosed; a space enclosed or fenced; something enclosed along with a letter or the like.

encomium, en‧kō′mi‧um, *n.* [Gr. *enkōmion,* a laudatory ode, an encomium—*en,* in, and *kōmos,* a revel, a procession in honor.] A eulogy or commendation; a statement in praise of something or somebody; a panegyric.—**encomiast,** en‧kō′mi‧ast, *n.* [Gr. *enkōmiastēs.*] One who praises another; a panegyrist.—**encomiastic, encomiastical,** en‧kō′mi‧as″tik, en‧kō′mi‧as″ti‧kal, *a.* Bestowing praise; laudatory.

encompass, en‧kum′pas, *v.t.* To form a circle about; to encircle; to environ, enclose, or surround; to shut in; to go or sail round.—**encompassment,** en‧kum′pas‧ment, *n.* The act of encompassing or state of being encompassed.

encore, än′kōr, *adv.* [Fr., from L. (*in*) *hanc horam,* (to) this hour.] Again; once more: used by the auditors and spectators in calling for a repetition of a particular performance, song, or the like.—*v.t.*—*encored, encoring.* To call for a repetition of; to call upon to repeat.

encounter, en‧koun′tėr, *n.* [Fr. *encontre*—*en,* and *contre,* L. *contra,* against.] A meeting, particularly a sudden or accidental meeting of two or more persons; a meeting in contest; a fight; a conflict; a skirmish; a battle; an intellectual or moral conflict or contest; controversy; debate.—*v.t.* To meet face to face; to meet suddenly or unexpectedly; to meet in opposition or in a hostile manner; to engage with in battle; to come upon or light upon; to meet with; to meet and oppose; to resist.—

v.i. To meet face to face; to meet unexpectedly; to meet in hostile fashion; to come together in combat; to conflict.

encourage, in·kur′ij, *v.t.*—*encouraged, encouraging.* [Fr. *encourager—en,* and *courage.*] To give courage to; to inspire with courage; to embolden; to animate or inspirit; to help forward; to support or countenance.—**encouragement,** in·kur′ij·ment, *n.* The act of encouraging; that which encourages; incitement; incentive.—**encouraging,** in·kur′i·jing, *p.* and *a.* Exciting courage; furnishing ground to hope for success.—**encouragingly,** in·kur′i·jing·li, *adv.* In an encouraging manner.

encrinite, en′kri·nīt, *n.* [Gr. *en,* in, and *krinon,* a lily.] A crinoid, lily star, or stone lily; a common name for those fossil Echinodermata that have long many-jointed stalks supporting the somewhat flower-like animal.

encroach, en·krōch′, *v.i.* [Prefix *en,* and Fr. *crocher,* to hook on, from *croc,* a hook; E. *crook* (which see).] To trespass or intrude on the rights and possessions of another; to take possession of what belongs to another by gradual advances into his limits or jurisdiction (to *encroach on* one's privileges); to make inroads (the sea sometimes *encroaches* on the land); to assail gradually and stealthily.—**encroacher,** en·krō′chẽr, *n.* One who encroaches. — **encroachment,** en·krōch′ment, *n.* The act of encroaching; undue or unlawful trespass on the privileges, jurisdiction, etc., of another; that which is taken by encroaching.

encumber, en·kum′bẽr, *v.t.* [Prefix *en,* and *cumber;* Fr. *encombrer.*] To impede the motion of with a load, burden, or anything inconvenient; to clog; to load; to embarrass; to load, as an estate, with debts.—**encumbrance,** en·kum′brans, *n.* Anything that impedes action or renders it difficult and laborious; clog, load, burden, impediment; liability resting on an estate; a legal claim on an estate, for the discharge of which the estate is liable, as a mortgage, etc.

encyclical, en·sī′kli·kal, *a.* [Gr. *enkyklios—en,* in, and *kyklos,* a circle.] Sent to many persons or places; intended for many, or for a whole order of men.—*n.* A letter on some important occasion sent by the pope to the bishops.

encyclopedia, en·sī′klo·pē″di·a, *n.* [Gr. *enkyklopaideia—en,* in, *kyklos,* a circle, and *paideia,* instruction.] A work in which various branches of knowledge are discussed separately, and usually in alphabetical order; a kind of dictionary of things, not words; a cyclopedia; [*cap.*] specially of the great French encyclopedia projected by Diderot, D'Alembert, and others.—**encyclopedic, encyclopedical, encyclopedian,** en·sī′klo·pē″dik, en·sī′klo·pē″di·kal, en·sī′klo·pē″di·an, *a.* Pertaining to an encyclopedia; such as is embraced in an encyclopedia; universal as regards knowledge and information.—**ency-**

clopedism, en·sī′klo·pē·dizm, *n.* The making of encyclopedias; the possession of a wide range of information; extensive learning.—**encyclopedist,** en·sī′klo·pē·dist, *n.* The compiler of an encyclopedia, or one who assists in such compilation; a person whose knowledge is of a very wide range.

encyst, en·sist′, *v.t.* [Gr. *en,* in, and *kystis,* a bladder, a pouch.] To enclose in a cyst, sac, or vesicle.—**encystment,** en·sist′ment, *n.* A process undergone by certain Protozoa and Infusoria previous to fission, in which they become coated with a secretion of gelatinous matter, ultimately enclosing the body in a hard cyst.

end, end, *n.* [A.Sax. *ende*=Icel. *endi,* Dan. and G. *ende,* Goth. *andeis,* the end; Skr. *anta,* end, death.] The extreme point of a line, or of anything that has more length than breadth; the termination, conclusion, or last part of anything, as of a portion of time, of an action, of a state of things, of a quantity of materials; the close of life; death; consequence; issue; result; the ultimate point or thing at which one aims or directs his views; purpose intended; scope; aim; drift.—*On end,* resting on one end; upright; also, continuously; uninterruptedly.—*To make both ends meet,* to keep one's expenditure within one's income, or at least to keep them equal.—*v.t.* To put an end to or be the end of; to finish; to close, conclude, terminate; to destroy; to put to death.—*v.i.* To come to an end; to terminate; to close; to conclude; to cease.—**ender,** en′dẽr, *n.* One who or that which ends or finishes.—**ending,** en′ding, *n.* The act of putting or coming to an end; conclusion; termination; the last part; the final syllable or letter of a word.—**endless,** end′les, *a.* Without end; having no end or conclusion; applied to length and duration; perpetually recurring; interminable; incessant; continual; without object, purpose, or use; fruitless; forming a closed loop and working continuously round two wheels or pulleys in the same plane (an *endless* rope, chain, saw).—*Endless screw,* a screw on a revolving shaft, the thread of which gears into a wheel with skew teeth.—**endlessly,** end′les·li, *adv.* In an endless manner.—**endlessness,** end′les·nes, *n.* The state or quality of being endless.—**endlong,** end′long, *a.* or *adv.* With the end forward; lengthwise. — **endways, endwise,** end′wāz, end′wīz, *adv.* On the end; erectly; in an upright position; with the end forward.

endamage, en·dam′ij, *v.t.*—*endamaged, endamaging.* To bring loss or damage to; to damage; to harm; to injure.

endanger, en·dān′jẽr, *v.t.* To put in hazard; to bring into danger or peril; to expose to loss or injury.

endear, en·dēr′, *v.t.* To make dear; to make more beloved; to bind by ties of affection and love.—**endearment,** en·dēr′ment, *n.* The act of endearing; the state of being beloved;

tender affection; a caress (in this sense chiefly plural).

endeavor, en·dev′ẽr, *n.* [Fr. *en,* in, and *devoir,* duty, from the use of these words in such expressions as *se mettre en devoir,* to try to do, to set about; *devoir* (whence *due, duty*) is from L. *debere,* to owe; to be under obligation (whence *debt*).] An exertion of physical strength or the intellectual powers toward the attainment of an object; an effort; an essay; an attempt.—*v.i.* To labor or exert one's self for the accomplishment of an object; to strive; to try; to attempt; to essay.—*v.t.* To try to effect; to strive after: often governing an infinitive.—**endeavorer,** en·dev′-ẽr·ẽr, *n.* One who endeavors.

endemic, endemical, en·dem′ik, en·dem′i·kal, *a.* [Fr. *endémique,* from Gr. *endēmios—en,* in, among, and *dēmos,* people.] Peculiar to a people, locality, or region: a term applied to diseases to which the inhabitants of a particular country are peculiarly subject.—*n.* A disease of an endemic nature. — **endemically,** en·dem′i·kal·li, *adv.* In an endemic manner.

endermic, en·dẽr′mik, *a.* [Gr. *en,* and *derma,* skin.] *Med.* applied or effected by rubbing into the skin, especially after the cuticle has been removed, as by a blister.

endive, en′dīv, *n.* [Fr. *endive,* from L. *intybus;* probably from Ar. *hindeb.*] A composite herb used in salads; also called *escarole.*

endocardium, en·do·kär′di·um, *n.* [Gr. *endon,* within, and *kardia,* the heart.] *Anat.* a colorless transparent membrane which lines the interior of the heart.—**endocardiac,** en·do·kär′di·ak, *a.* Relating to the endocardium, or to the interior of the heart. —**endocarditis,** en′do·kär·dī″tis, *n.* An inflammatory disease of the internal parts of the heart, ending in the deposit of fibrin upon the valves.

endocarp, en′do·kärp, *n.* [Gr. *endon,* within, *karpos,* fruit.] *Bot.* the inner layer of the pericarp of fruits, when its texture differs from the outer layer, as the stone of a plum or the flesh of an orange.

endocrine, en′dō·krin, *a.* [L. *endon,* within, and *krinein,* separate.] Secreting internally; applied to those glands that secrete hormonal and metabolic substances into the blood or lymph.—*n.* An endocrine gland.

endoderm, en′dō·dẽrm, *n.* [Gr. *endon,* within, and *derma,* skin.] The innermost germ layer of an embryo from which is derived the epithelium of the digestive and respiratory tracts.—**endodermal,** en·dō·dẽrm′al, *a.*

endogamy, en·dog′a·mi, *n.* [Gr. *endon,* within, *gamos,* marriage.] A custom among some savage peoples of marrying only within their own tribe; opposite of *exogamy* (q.v.).—**endogamous,** en·dog′a·mus, *a.* Pertaining to, practicing, or characterized by endogamy.

endogenous, en·doj′e·nus, *a.* [Gr. *endon,* within, and *gen,* to produce.] Developing, originating from within. —**endogenously,** en·doj′e·nus·li, *adv.*

—endogenously, en·doj′e·nus·li, *adv.* In an endogenous manner; internally.

endolymph, en′do·limf, *n.* [Gr. *endon*, within, E. *lymph.*] *Anat.* a limpid fluid in the labyrinth of the ear.

endomorph, en′do·morf, *n.* [Gr. *endon*, within, *morphē*, form.] *Mineral.* a mineral enclosed in a crystal of another mineral.

endoparasite, en·do·par′a·sīt, *n.* [Gr. *endon*, within, and E. *parasite.*] A parasite living on the internal organs of animals, as opposed to an *ectoparasite.*

endoplasm, en′do·plazm, *n.* [Gr. *endon*, within, and *plasma.* PLASMA.] *Biol.* internal matter of a cell; internal protoplasm.

endorse, en·dors′, *v.t.*—*endorsed, endorsing.* [Prefix *en*, and L. *dorsum*, a back.] To write something on the back of, as one's name as payee on the back of (a check) in order to obtain the cash or credit represented on the face of the document; hence, to assign by writing one's name on the back; to assign or transfer by endorsement; to sanction, ratify, or approve; to acknowledge the receipt of (a sum specified) by one's signature.—**endorsable,** en·dors′a·bl, *a.* Capable of being endorsed.—**endorsement,** en·dors′ment, *n.* The act of endorsing; a note of the contents of any paper on its back; the signature of the holder of a note or bill of exchange written on its back; ratification, sanction, or approval; *insurance*, a provision added to an insurance contract whereby the scope of its coverage is restricted or enlarged.

endosarc, en′do·särk, *n.* [Gr. *endon*, within, *sarx*, flesh.] Endoplasm.

endoskeleton, en·do·skel′e·ton, *n.* [Gr. *endon*, within, and *skeleton.*] The internal bony structure of man and other animals, in contradistinction to *exoskeleton*, the outer hard covering of such animals as the crab, etc.

endosmosis, en·dos·mō′sis, *n.* [Gr. *endon*, within, *ōsmos*, impulsion, from *ōtheō*, to push.] The transmission of fluids or gases through porous septa or partitions, from the exterior to the interior.—**endosmotic,** en·dos·mot′ik, *a.* Of or pertaining to endosmosis; of the nature of or acting by endosmosis.

endosperm, en′do·spėrm, *n.* [Gr. *endon*, within, *sperma*, seed.] *Bot.* the albuminous tissue which surrounds the embryo in many seeds, and which contains the supply of food for the germinating embryo: called also *Albumen.*

endosteum, en·dos′ti·um, *n.* [Gr. *endon*, within, *osteon*, bone.] *Anat.* the lining membrane of the narrow cavity of a bone.

endothecium, en′di·thē″si·um, *n.* [Gr. *endon*, within, *thēkē*, a cell.] *Bot.* the fibrous cellular tissue lining an anther.

endothelium, en′do·thē″li·um, *n.* [Gr. *endon*, without, *thēlē*, a nipple.] A delicate cellular membrane lining blood vessels and cavities.

endothermic, en·do·ther′mik, *n.* [Gr. *endon*, within, *thermos*, heat.] Of a chemical reaction, involving absorption of heat; or of the compound so formed.

endow, en·dou′, *v.t.* [Prefix *en*, and Fr. *douer*, to endow, from L. *dos*, *dotis*, a dowry, from root seen in L. *do*, Gr. *didōmi*, to give.] To furnish with a portion of goods or estate, called *dower*; to settle a dower on; to furnish with a permanent fund or provision for support; to enrich or furnish with any gift, quality, or faculty.—**endowment,** en·dou′ment, *n.* The act of endowing; property, fund, or revenue permanently appropriated to any object; that which is given or bestowed on the person or mind; gift of nature; natural capacity.

endue, en·dū′, *v.t.*—*endued, enduing.* [L. *induo*, to put on. INDUE.] To invest; to clothe; to indue (as with virtue or other qualities).

endure, en·dūr′, *v.i.*—*endured, enduring.* [Fr. *endurer*, from *en*, and *durer*, L. *durare*, to last.] To continue in the same state without perishing; to last; to remain; to abide; to suffer without resistance or without yielding; to hold out; to bear; to suffer.—*v.t.* To bear, sustain, or support without breaking or yielding; to bear with patience; to bear without opposition or sinking under the pressure; to undergo, suffer, experience.—**endurable,** en·dū′ra·bl, *a.* Capable of being endured.—**endurance,** en·dū′rans, *n.* A state of lasting or duration; permanence; lastingness; continuance; a bearing or suffering; a continuing under pain or distress without sinking or yielding; sufferance; patience; fortitude.—**enduring,** en·dū′ring, *a.* Lasting long; permanent. — **enduringly,** en·dū′ring·li, *adv.* Lastingly; for a time.—**enduringness,** en·dū′ring·nes, *n.*

enema, en′e·ma or en·ē′ma, *n.* [Gr. *enema*, from *eniēmi*, to send in—*en*, in, and *hiēmi*, to send.] A liquid or gaseous substance injected into the rectum.

enemy, en′e·mi, *n.* [Fr. *ennemi*, from L. *inimicus*—*in*, neg., and *amicus*, a friend.] One hostile to another; one who hates another; a foe; an adversary; an antagonist; a hostile force, army, fleet, or the like.

energy, en′ėr·ji, *n.* [Gr. *energeia*—*en*, and *ergon*, work.] Internal or inherent power; the power of operating, whether exerted or not; power exerted; vigorous operation; force; vigor; effectual operation; efficacy; strength or force producing the effect; strength of expression; force of utterance; life; spirit; emphasis; *phys.* power to do work; it may be mechanical, electrical, thermal, chemical, etc.— *Conservation of energy.* CONSERVATION.—**energetic, energetical,** en·ėr·jet′ik, en·ėr·jet′i·kal, *a.* [Gr. *energētikos.*] Acting with or exhibiting energy; operating with force, vigor, and effect; forcible; powerful; efficacious; working; active; operative; vigorous.—**energetically,** en·ėr·jet′i·kal·li, *adv.* In an energetic manner;

with energy and effect.—**energize,** en′ėr·jīz, *v.i.*—*energized, energizing.* To act with energy or force; to act in producing an effect.—*v.t.* To give strength or force to; to give active vigor to.

enervate, en′ėr·vāt, *v.t.*—*enervated, enervating.* [L. *enervo, enervatum.*—*e*, out, away, and *nervus*, a nerve.] To deprive of nerve, force, or strength; to weaken; to render feeble; to debilitate.—*a.* Without strength or force; weakened; debilitated.—**enervation,** en′ėr·vā′shon, *n.* The act of enervating; the state of being enervated; effeminacy.

enfeeble, en·fē′bl, *v.t.*—*enfeebled, enfeebling.* To make feeble; to deprive of strength; to weaken; to debilitate or enervate.—**enfeeblement,** en·fē′bl·ment, *n.* The act of enfeebling or state of being enfeebled.

enfeoff, en·fef′, *v.t.* [Prefix *en*, and L.L. *feoffo*, to confer a fief or feud. FIEF.] *Law*, to give a fief or feud to; to invest with the fee of an estate; to give any corporeal hereditament to in fee.—**enfeoffment,** en·fef′ment, *n. Law*, the act of enfeoffing; the instrument or deed by which one is enfeoffed.

Enfield, en′fēld, *n.* [From *Enfield*, Government factory, as *Carronades* at Carron foundry.] A rifle.

enfilade, en·fi·lād′, *v.t.*—*enfiladed, enfilading.* [Fr. *en*, and *file*, a row, a rank, from *fil*, a thread, L. *filum.*] *Milit.* to rake or sweep with shot through the whole length of, as, through a work or line of troops: to fire in the flank of a line.—*n.* A firing in such a manner; the line of fire.

enforce, en·fōrs′, *v.t.*—*enforced, enforcing.* [Prefix *en*, and *force*; Fr. *enforcir.*] To give strength to; to add force, emphasis, or impressiveness to; to inculcate, urge, or press earnestly; to make or gain by force or compulsion; to force; to compel, constrain, or force; to put in execution; to cause to take effect (to *enforce* the laws).—**enforceable,** en·fōr′sa·bl, *a.* Capable of being enforced.—**enforcement,** en·fōrs′ment, *n.* The act of enforcing; compulsion; that which gives force, energy, or effect; sanction; that which urges or constrains; constraining power; a putting in execution (the *enforcement* of law).—**enforcer,** en·fōr′sėr, *n.* One who enforces.

enfranchise, en·fran′chīz, *v.t.*—*enfranchised, enfranchising.* To set free; to liberate from slavery; to free or release, as from custody, bad habits, or any restraining power; to confer the franchise on; to endow with the right of voting.—**enfranchisement,** en·fran′chiz·ment, *n.* The act of enfranchising or the state of being enfranchised.

engage, en·gāj′, *v.t.*—*engaged, engaging.* [Fr. *engager*—*en*, and *gager*, from *gage*, a pledge. GAGE.] To bind or bring under an obligation, as by oath, pledge, contract, or promise: generally with reflexive pron.; to pawn, stake, or pledge; to enlist; to bring into a party; to bespeak, as for service or the like; to win and attach (to *engage* one's affections); to attract and fix (attention); to occupy (to *engage* a person in conversation); to employ the attention or efforts of (to make to embark or take concern in); to enter into contest with; to bring to conflict (to *engage* an enemy).— *v.i.* To promise or pledge one's word; to become bound; to embark in any business; to take a concern in; to undertake; to attack in conflict; to begin mutually a hostile encounter.—**engaged**, en·gājd', *pp.* or *a.* Pledged; affianced; enlisted; attracted; occupied; earnestly employed.—*Engaged column, arch.* a column attached to a wall so that part of it is concealed.—**engagement**, en·gāj'ment, *n.* The act of engaging; obligation by agreement or contract; the act of betrothing or state of being betrothed; occupation; employment of the attention; affair of business; an appointment; a combat between bodies of troops or fleets; a fight; a conflict.— **engaging**, en·gā'jing, *a.* Winning; attractive; tending to draw the attention or the affections; pleasing. —**engagingly**, en·gā'jing·li, *adv.* In an engaging manner.

engender, en·jen'dėr, *v.t.* [Fr. *engendrer*, from L. *ingenero—in*, and *genero*, to beget, from *genus, generis*, birth, descent. GENUS.] To beget between the different sexes; more generally, to produce; to cause to exist; to cause, excite, stir up.— *v.i.* To be caused or produced; to meet in sexual embrace.

engine, en'jin, *n.* [Fr. *engin*, a machine, a tool, ingenuity, from L. *ingenium*, disposition, ability, invention—*in*, and root *gen*, to produce, as in *genius*. INGENIOUS.] Any instrument in any degree complicated; a tool, instrument, or appliance by which any effect is produced, as a musket, a cannon, the rack, a battering ram, etc.; a person regarded as a tool or instrument†; any mechanical instrument of complicated parts, which concur in producing an intended effect; a machine; especially, a machine for applying steam to drive machinery, to propel vessels, railway trains, etc.; a steam engine.—*v.t.* To furnish (a steam vessel) with an engine or engines.—**engineer**, en·ji·nēr', *n.* [Formed on type of *charioteer, musketeer*, etc.] Originally one who managed military engines or artillery; now one who manages an engine or has to do with the construction of engines and machinery; or a person skilled in the principles and practice of engineering, either civil or military.—*v.t.* To direct or superintend the making of in the capacity of engineer; to perform the office of an engineer in respect of (to *engineer* a canal).—**engineering**, en·ji·nē'ring, *n.* The art of constructing and using engines or machines; the art of executing such works as are the objects of civil and military architecture, in which machinery is in general extensively employed.—*Military engineering*,

that branch which relates to the construction and maintenance of fortifications, and the surveying of a country for the various operations of war.—*Civil engineering* relates to the forming of roads, bridges, and railroads, the formation of canals, aqueducts, harbors, drainage of a country, etc.—*Mechanical engineering* refers strictly to machinery. —*Electrical engineering* refers to electrical plant.—**enginery,†** en'jin·ri, *n.* Engines in general; artillery or instruments of war (*Mil.*); mechanism; machinery.

English, ing'glish, *a.* [A.Sax. *Englisc*, from the *Engle* or *Angles*, a North German tribe who settled in Britain.] Belonging to England or to its inhabitants.—*n.* One of the Low German group of languages, spoken by the people of England and the descendants of natives of that country, as the Americans, Canadian and Australian colonists, etc.; as a collective noun, the people of England; *print.* a size of type between great primer and pica.— *v.t.* To translate into the English language; to represent or render in English.—**Englishman**, ing'glish-man, *n.* A native or naturalized inhabitant of England.—**Englishry**, ing'glish·ri, *n.* A population of English descent; especially the persons of English descent in Ireland.

engorge, en·gorj', *v.t.*—*engorged, engorging.* [Fr. *engorger*—prefix *en*, and *gorge*, the throat.] To swallow; to gorge; to swallow with greediness or in large quantities.—*v.i.* To devour; to feed with eagerness or voracity.—**engorgement**, en·gorj'ment, *n.* The act of swallowing greedily; *med.* congestion.

engraft, en·graft', *v.t.* To ingraft.

engrail, en·grāl', *v.t.* [Fr. *engrêler*, to engrail, from *grêle, gresle*, hail.] To variegate; to spot, as with hail; to indent in curved lines.

engram, en'gram, *n.* [Gr. *gramma*, a picture.] *Biol.* the impression left on protoplasm by any physiological happening.

engrave, en·grāv', *v.t.*—*engraved*, pp. *engraved* or *engraven, engraving.* [Prefix *en*, and *grave*, to carve.] To cut figures, letters, or devices on, as on stone, metal, etc.; to delineate, copy, picture, or represent by incisions, as on stone, metal, wood, etc.; to imprint; to impress deeply; to infix.—**engraver**, en·grā'vėr, *n.* One who engraves; a cutter of letters, figures, or devices on stone, metal, or wood.—**engraving**, en·grā'ving, *n.* In its widest sense, the art of cutting designs, writing, etc., on any hard substance; specifically, the art of forming designs on the surface of metal plates or of blocks of wood for the purpose of taking off impressions or prints of these designs; that which is engraved; an engraved plate; an impression taken from an engraved plate; a print.

engross, en·grōs', *v.t.* [Fr. *en*, and *grossir*, to enlarge, from *gros*, big. GROSS.] To increase in bulk or

quantity (*Shak.*)‡; to seize, occupy, or take up the whole of (cares or duties *engross* one's time or attention); to purchase, with the purpose of making a profit by enhancing the price; to take or assume in undue quantity, proportion, or degree; to write a fair correct copy of in large and distinct legible characters (to *engross* a legal document).—*v.i.* To be employed in engrossing, or making fair copies of writings.—**engrosser**, en·grō'sėr, *n.* One who or that which engrosses; one who takes or assumes in undue quantity, proportion, or degree; one who copies a writing in large fair characters.

engulf, en·gulf', *v.t.* To swallow up in or as in a gulf or whirlpool; to overwhelm by swallowing.—**engulfment**, en·gulf'ment, *n.* The act of engulfing.

enhance, en·hans', *v.t.*—*enhanced, enhancing.* [Pr. *enanser*, to advance, enhance, from *enant, enans*, forward, from L. *in*, in, to, *ante*, before.] To heighten; to make greater; to increase (price, pleasure, difficulty, beauty, evil, or other nonphysical object).—*v.i.* To increase or grow larger.—**enhancement**, en·hans'ment, *n.* The act of enhancing or state of being enhanced; rise; augmentation; aggravation.

enharmonic, enharmonical, en·här·mon'ik, en·här·mon'i·kal, *a.* [Fr. *enharmonique*, Gr. *enarmonikos*, in harmony—*en*, in, and *harmonia*, harmony.] *Mus.* of or pertaining to that one of the three ancient Greek scales which consisted of quarter tones; pertaining to a scale of perfect intonation which recognizes intervals less than semitones. —**enharmonically**, en·här·mon'i·kal·li, *adv.* In the enharmonic style or system; with perfect intonation.

enigma, i·nig'ma, *n.* [L. *ænigma*, from Gr. *ainigma*, from *ainissomai*, to speak darkly, from *ainos*, a tale, a story.] A dark saying, in which something is concealed under obscure language; an obscure question; a riddle; something containing a hidden meaning which is proposed to be guessed; anything inexplicable to an observer, such as the means by which anything is effected, the motive for a course of conduct, the cause of any phenomenon, etc.; a person whose conduct or disposition is inexplicable.—**enigmatic, enigmatical**, i·nig·mat'ik, i·nig·mat'i·kal, *a.* Relating to or containing an enigma; obscure; darkly expressed; ambiguous.—**enigmatically**, i·nig·mat'i·kal·li, *adv.* In an enigmatic manner.

enjambment, en·jamb'ment, *n.* [Fr. *enjambement—en*, in, *jambe*, leg.] The prolongation of the words or sense beyond the second line of a couplet.

enjoin, en·join', *v.t.* [Fr. *enjoindre*, from L. *injungo—in*, and *jungo*, to join.] To prescribe or impose with some authority; to lay, as an order or command; to put by way of injunction; to order, direct, or urge

ch, *ch*ain;   *ch*, Sc. lo*ch*;   g, *g*o;   j, *j*ob;   ng, si*ng*;   TH, *th*en;   th, *th*in;   w, *w*ig;   hw, *wh*ig;   zh, a*z*ure.

(to *enjoin* submission or obedience *upon* a person; duties *enjoined* by law); to admonish or instruct with authority; to command.—**enjoiner,** en·joi'nêr, *n.* One who enjoins.

enjoy, en·joi', *v.t.* [O.Fr. *enjoier,* to receive with joy—prefix *en,* and *joie*=E. *joy.*] To feel or perceive with pleasure; to take pleasure or satisfaction in the possession or experience of; to have, possess, and use with satisfaction; to have, hold, or occupy, as a good or profitable thing, or as something desirable.—*To enjoy one's self,* to experience delight from the pleasures in which one partakes; to be happy. —**enjoyable,** en·joi'a·bl, *a.* Capable of being enjoyed; capable of yielding enjoyment.—**enjoyment,** en·joi'ment, *n.* The condition of enjoying; the possession or occupancy of anything with satisfaction or pleasure; that which gives pleasure or satisfaction in the possession; cause of joy or gratification; delight.

enkindle, en·kin'dl, *v.t.*—*enkindled, enkindling.* [Prefix *en,* and *kindle.*] To kindle; to set on fire; to inflame; to excite; to rouse into action.—*v.i.* To take fire.

enlace, en·lās', *v.t.*—*enlaced, enlacing.* To fasten with or as with a lace; to lace; to encircle.—**enlacement,** en·lās'ment, *n.* Act of enlacing; state of being enlaced; an encircling.

enlarge, en·lärj', *v.t.*—*enlarged, enlarging.* To make larger or greater in quantity or dimensions; to extend; to expand; to augment; to increase; to make more comprehensive (to *enlarge* the mind); to magnify to the eye; to set at liberty; to release from confinement or pressure.—*v.i.* To grow large or larger; to extend; to dilate; to expand; to expatiate in speaking or writing; to speak or write at length or in full detail.— **enlargement,** en·lärj'ment, *n.* The act of enlarging or state of being enlarged; augmentation; dilatation; expansion; something added on; an addition; expansion or extension, as applied to the mind or the intellectual powers; release from confinement; deliverance; a detailed discourse or argument.—**enlarger,** en·lär'jêr, *n.* One who or that which enlarges.

enlighten, en·lī'tn, *v.t.* [Prefix *en,* and *lighten,* to make light.] To shed light on; to give intellectual light to; to enable to see or comprehend.— **enlightenment,** en·lī'tn·ment, *n.* Act of enlightening; [*cap.*] a movement of the eighteenth century marked by the free use of reason and the rise of humanism.

enlist, en·list', *v.t.* [Prefix *en,* and *list.*] *Lit.* to enroll or enter on a list; to hire for the public service, especially military service, by entering the name in a register; to employ in advancing some interest; to engage the services of (to *enlist* a person in the cause of truth).— *v.i.* To engage in public service, especially military service, voluntarily; to enter heartily into a cause, as being devoted to its interests.—

enlistment, en·list'ment, *n.* The act of enlisting; the raising of soldiers by enlisting.

enliven, en·lī'vn, *v.t.* [Prefix *en,* and adj. *live.*] To give life, action, or motion to; to make vigorous or active; to stimulate; to give spirit or vivacity to; to animate; to make sprightly, gay, or cheerful.—**enlivener,** en·lī'vn·êr, *n.*

en masse, en·mas', *adv.* [Fr.] As a whole; altogether; in a body.

enmesh, in·mesh', *v.t.* [Prefix *en,* and *mesh.*] To catch in; to entangle.

enmity, en'mi·ti, *n.* [Fr. *inimitié,* O.Fr. *enemistie,* corresponding to a L. form *inimicitas,* from *inimicus,* unfriendly—*in,* not, and *amicus,* a friend.] The quality or state of being an enemy; hostile or unfriendly disposition; hostility; ill will.

ennead, en'e·ad, *n.* [Gr. *ennea,* nine, *ad,* as in *monad, triad, myriad.*] A collection of nine books, discourses, or accounts.

ennoble, en·nō'bl, *v.t.*—*ennobled, ennobling.* [Prefix *en,* and *noble;* Fr. *ennoblier.*] To make noble; to raise to nobility; to dignify; to exalt; to elevate in degree, qualities, or excellence.—**ennoblement,** en·nō'bl·ment, *n.* The act of ennobling; the state of being ennobled; exaltation; elevation.

ennui, än'wē, *n.* [Fr., O.Fr. *anui,* annoy, like O.Venet. *inodio,* from L. *in odio,* in hate, in disgust. ODIUM, ANNOY.] Languor of mind arising from lack of occupation; want of interest in present scenes and surrounding objects; listlessness; weariness; tedium.

enormous, i·nor'mus, *a.* [L. *enormis* —*e,* out of, and *norma,* a rule. NORMAL.] Great beyond or exceeding the common measure; excessively large; excessively wicked; flagitious; atrocious. ∴ *Enormous, lit.* out of rule, hence great, far beyond common: used especially of magnitude; *immense,* that cannot be measured: used especially of quantity, extent, and number; *excessive,* beyond bounds, beyond what is fit and right: said especially of degree.—**enormously,** i·nor'mus·li, *adv.* Excessively; beyond measure.—**enormousness,** i·nor'mus·nes, *n.* The state of being enormous.—**enormity,** i·nor'mi·ti, *n.* [L. *enormitas.*] The state or quality of being enormous, immoderate, or excessive; excessive degree; atrociousness; a very grave offense against order, right, or decency; an atrocious crime; an atrocity.

enough, i·nuf', *a.* [O.E. *inoh, enow,* A.Sax. *genóh, genóg*=D. *genoeg,* Icel. *gnógr,* O.Fris. *enoch,* Goth. *ganohs,* G. *genug,* enough, from a verb meaning to suffice.] Satisfying desire or giving content; meeting reasonable expectations; answering the purpose; adequate to want or demand. [*Enough* usually follows the noun with which it is connected.]—*n.* A sufficiency; a quantity of a thing which satisfies desire or is adequate to the wants; what is equal to the powers or abilities.—*Enough!* an exclamation denoting sufficiency.—

adv. Sufficiently; in a quantity or degree that satisfies or is equal to the desires or wants; fully; quite; denoting a slight augmentation of the positive degree (he was ready *enough* to embrace the offer); in a tolerable or passable degree (the performance is well *enough*).— **enow,** ē·nou'. An old form of *Enough.*

enounce, i·nouns', *v.t.*—*enounced, enouncing.* [Fr. *énoncer,* L. *enuncio*—*e,* out, and *nuncio,* to declare, as in *announce, denounce, renounce.*] To declare; to enunciate; to state, as a proposition or argument.

enquire, in·kwīr', *v.t.* and *i.* **enquirer,** in·kwī'rêr, *n.* **enquiry,** in·kwī'ri, *n.* Same as *Inquire, Inquirer, Inquiry.*

enrage, in·rāj', *v.t.*—*enraged, enraging.* To excite rage in; to exasperate; to provoke to fury or madness; to make furious.

enrapture, in·rap'chêr *v.t.*—*enraptured, enrapturing.* To transport with rapture; to delight beyond measure.

enravish, in·rav'ish, *v.t.* To transport with delight; to enrapture.

enrich, in·rich', *v.t.* To make rich, wealthy, or opulent; to supply with abundant property; to fertilize; to supply with an abundance of anything desirable; to fill or store; to supply with anything splendid or ornamental; to adorn.—**enrichment,** in·rich'ment, *n.* The act of enriching; something that enriches or adorns.

enrobe, en·rōb', *v.t.*—*enrobed, enrobing.* To clothe with attire; to attire; to invest.

enroll, in·rōl', *v.t.*—*enrolled, enrolling.* [O.Fr. *enroller*—*en,* and *rolle,* roll.] To write in a roll or register; to insert or enter the name of; to insert in records.—**enroller,** in·rōl'ér, *n.* One who enrolls or registers.—**enrollment,** en·rōl'ment, *n.*

en route, en·röt', *adv.* [Fr.] On the way; along the way.

ensanguine, en·sang'gwin, *v.t.*—*ensanguined, ensanguining.* [Prefix *en,* and L. *sanguis, sanguinis,* blood.] To stain or cover with blood; to smear with gore.

ensconce, en·skons', *v.t.*—*ensconced, ensconcing.* To cover or shelter, as with a sconce or fort; to protect; to hide securely; to take shelter behind something; to hide; with the reflexive pronoun.

ensemble, on·som'bl, *n.* [Fr., from L. *insimul,* at the same time—*in,* and *simul,* together.] All the parts of anything taken together so that each part is considered only in relation to the whole; the general effect of a whole work of art, as a picture, piece of music, drama, etc.

enshrine, in·shrīn', *v.t.*—*enshrined, enshrining.* To enclose in or as in a shrine or chest; to preserve with care and affection; to cherish.

enshroud, en·shroud', *v.i.* To cover with or as with a shroud; to envelop with anything which conceals from observation.

ensiform, en'si·form, *a.* [L. *ensiformis*—*ensis,* sword, and *forma,* form.] Having the shape of a sword;

sword-shaped: said of leaves of plants, also of a cartilage at the lower part of the human sternum or breastbone.

ensign, en'sīn, *n.* [Fr. *enseigne,* a sign, an ensign, from L. *insigne,* a sign, a badge—*in,* and *signum,* a mark, a sign. SIGN, SIGNAL.] A sign or token‡; a badge or mark of distinction, rank, or office; a symbol; a flag or standard; the flag or banner distinguishing a company of soldiers, an army, or vessel; the colors; *Military* (usually pronounced en'sin). The lowest commissioned officer in the United States Navy, ranking below a lieutenant, junior grade; formerly a commissioned officer of lowest rank in a British regiment of infantry, the equivalent rank now being that of second lieutenant.—**ensigncy, ensignship,** en'sin·si, en'sin·ship, *n.* The rank, office, or commission of an ensign.

ensilage, en'sil·ij, *n.* [Fr. *ensilage,* from Sp. *ensilar,* to store grain in an underground receptacle, from *en,* in, and *silo,* from L. *sirus,* a pit.] A mode of storing green fodder, vegetables, etc., by burying in pits or silos dug or built, the substance stored being pressed down with heavy weights, and undergoing a slight fermentation; the substance thus treated.—**ensile,** en·sīl', *v.t.* To store by this process.

enslave, en·slāv', *v.t.*—*enslaved, enslaving,* To make a slave of; to reduce to slavery or bondage; to subject to the dominant influence of; to master or overpower (*enslaved* by his passions).—**enslavement,** en·slāv'ment, *n.* The act of enslaving or state of being enslaved.—**enslaver,** en·slā'vėr, *n.* One who or that which enslaves.

ensnare, en·snâr', *v.t.*—*ensnared, ensnaring.* To take in a snare; to entrap; to insnare.

ensue, en·sū', *v.i.*—*ensued, ensuing.* [Prefix *en,* and *sue;* O.Fr. *ensuir,* from L. *insequor,* to follow upon.] To follow as a consequence; to follow in a train of events or course of time; to succeed; to come after. ∴ Syn. under FOLLOW.

ensure, in·shör', *v.t.*—*ensured, ensuring.* To make sure or secure; to make certain to turn out, arise, or follow (to *ensure* peace, to *ensure* a good crop).

entablature, en·tab'la·chėr, *n.* [O.Fr. *entablature*—*en,* and *table;* L. *tabula,* a board, plank.] The superstructure which lies horizontally upon the columns in *class. arch.,* and consists of three principal divisions, the architrave, the frieze, and the cornice.

entail, in·tāl', *n.* [Fr. *entaille,* a cutting, incision, from *entailler,* to cut in—*en,* and *tailler,* to cut, as in *detail, retail, tailor.*] *Law,* an estate or fee entailed or limited in descent to a particular heir or heirs, male or female; rule of descent settled for an estate.—*v.t. Law,* to settle the descent of (lands and tenements) by gift to a man and to certain heirs specified so that neither the donee nor any subsequent possessor can alienate or bequeath it; to transmit in an unalterable course; to devolve as a consequence or of necessity (crimes *entail* punishment).—**entailment,** in·tāl'ment, *n.* The act of entailing or state of being entailed.

entangle, in·tang'gl, *v.t.*—*entangled, entangling.* [TANGLE.] To interweave in such a manner as not to be easily separated; to make confused or disordered; to involve in anything complicated, and from which it is difficult to extricate one's self; to involve in difficulties or embarrassments; to puzzle; to perplex; to involve in contradictions; to hamper.—**entanglement,** in·tang'gl·ment, *n.* The act of entangling or state of being entangled.—**entangler,** in·tang'glėr, *n.* One who entangles.

entelechy, en·tel'e·ki, *n.* [Gr. *entelechia.*] The absoluteness, or actuality, of a thing, as opposed to simple capability or potentiality. A philosophic coinage by Aristotle, who styles the soul the *entelechy* of the body, that by which it actually is, though it had the capacity of existing before; actual, as opposed to virtual, or potential, power. In Rabelais, the kingdom of Queen Quintessence, the city of speculative science.

entellus, en·tel'lus, *n.* [Fr. *entelle,* from Gr. *entellō,* to command.] An East Indian species of monkey, the sacred monkey of the Hindus.

entente, än·tänt', *n.* [Fr. *entente.*] An understanding, a good feeling between two or more nations; *entente cordiale, triple entente.*

enter, en'tėr, *v.t.* [Fr. *entrer,* from L. *intrare,* to enter, from *intro,* into the inside—*in,* and root seen in *trans,* across (a common prefix), and in Skr. *tri,* to pass.] To come or go into in any manner whatever; to pierce; to penetrate; to begin or commence upon, as a new period or stage in the progress of life, a new state of things, etc.; to engage or become involved in; to join; to become a member of (an army, a profession, a college); to initiate into a business, service, society, method, etc.; to set down in a book or other record; to enroll; to inscribe; to report (a ship) at the customhouse on arrival in port, by delivering a manifest; *law,* to go in or upon and take possession of (lands); to place in regular form before a court.—*v.i.* To come in; to go or pass in; sometimes with *in;* to embark or enlist in an affair; to become a member.—*To enter into,* to get into the inside or interior of; to penetrate; to engage in (to *enter into* business); to deal with or treat by way of discussion, argument, and the like; to be an ingredient in; to form a constituent part in.—*To enter on* or *upon,* to begin; to commence; to treat or deal with; to discuss or talk of; to examine.

enteric, en·ter'ik, *a.* [Gr. *enterikos,* from *enteron,* intestine.] Belonging to the intestines.—*Enteric fever,* same as *Typhoid Fever.*—**enteritis,** en·te·rī'tis, *n. Med.* inflammation of the intestines.—**enterology,** en·te·rol'o·ji, *n.* A treatise or discourse on the viscera or internal parts of the body.—**enterotomy,** en·te·rot'o·mi, *n.* [Gr. *enteron,* and *tomē,* a cutting.] Dissection of the bowels or intestines; incision of the bowels for the removal of strangulation, etc.

enterprise, en'tėr·prīz, *n.* [Fr., from *entreprendre,* pp. *entrepris, entreprise*—*entre,* between, and *prendre,* to take, to lay hold of, from L. *prehendo, prendo,* as in *apprehend, comprehend.*] That which is undertaken or attempted to be performed; a project attempted; particularly, a bold, arduous, or hazardous undertaking; an active and enterprising spirit; readiness to engage in undertakings of difficulty, risk, or danger.—*v.t.*†—*enterprised, enterprising.* To undertake.—**enterpriser,** en'tėr·prī'zėr, *n.* An adventurer; one who engages in an enterprise.—**enterprising,** en'tėr·prī·zing, *a.* Having a disposition for or tendency to engage in enterprises; ready to start and carry on untried schemes.—**enterprisingly,** en'tėr·prī·zing·li, *adv.* In an enterprising manner.

entertain, en·tėr·tān', *v.t.* [Fr. *entretenir,* to maintain—*entre*=L. *inter,* between, and *tenir*=L. *tenere,* to hold.] To receive into the house and treat with hospitality; to receive as a host his guests; to engage the attention of agreeably; to amuse with anything that causes the time to pass pleasantly; to take into consideration; to hold or maintain in the mind with favor; to harbor; to cherish (to *entertain* charitable sentiments). ∴ Syn. under AMUSE.—*v.i.* To give entertainments; to receive company.—**entertainer,** en·tėr·tā'nėr, *n.* One who entertains.—**entertaining,** en·tėr·tā'ning, *a.* Affording entertainment; pleasing; amusing; diverting.—**entertainingly,** en·tėr·tā'ning·li, *adv.* In an amusing manner.—**entertainingness,** en·tėr·tā'ning·nes, *n.* The quality of being entertaining.—**entertainment,** en·tėr·tān'ment, *n.* The act of entertaining; the receiving and accommodating of guests; food, lodging, or other things required by a guest; a hospitable repast; the pleasure which the mind receives from anything interesting, and which holds or arrests the attention; that which entertains; that which serves for amusement, as a dramatic or other performance; reception; admission.

enthrall, en·thral', *v.t.* To reduce to the condition of a thrall; to enslave; to charm or to captivate; to hold spellbound.—**enthrallment,** en·thral'ment, *n.* The act of enthralling, or state of being enthralled.

enthrone, en·thrōn', *v.t.*—*enthroned, enthroning.* To place on a throne; to invest with sovereign authority; to exalt to an elevated place or seat; to induct or install (a bishop) into the powers and privileges of a vacant see.—**enthronement,** en·thrōn'ment, *n.* Act of enthroning, or

ch, *chain;* ch, Sc. lo*ch;* g, *go;* j, *job;* ng, si*ng;* TH, *then;* th, *thin;* w, *wig;* hw, *whig;* zh, a*z*ure.

state of being enthroned.—**enthron-ization,** en·thrō′ni·zā″shon, *n.* The act of enthroning; the placing of a bishop on his throne in his cathedral.

enthusiasm, en·thū′zi·azm, *n.* [Gr. *enthousiasmos,* from *enthousiazō,* to infuse a divine spirit, from *enthous, entheos,* inspired, divine—*en,* and *theos,* god (whence *theist*).] An ecstasy of mind, as if from inspiration or possession by a spiritual influence; complete possession of the mind by any subject; ardent zeal in pursuit of an object; predominance of the emotional over the intellectual powers; elevation of fancy; exaltation of ideas.—**enthusiast,** en·thū′zi·ast, *n.* [Gr. *enthousiastēs.*] One full of enthusiasm; one whose mind is completely possessed by any subject; one who is swayed to a great or undue extent by his feelings in any pursuit; a person of ardent zeal; one of elevated fancy; a highly imaginative person.—**enthusiastic, enthusiastical,** en·thū′zi·as″tik, en·thū′zi·as″ti·kal, *a.* Filled with or characterized by enthusiasm; prone to enthusiasm; ardent; devoted.—**enthusiastically,** en·thū′zi·as″ti·kal·li, *adv.* With enthusiasm.

enthymeme, en′thi·mēm, *n.* [Gr. *enthymēma*—*en,* and *thymos,* mind.] *Rhet.* an argument consisting of only two premises or propositions, a third proposition required to complete the syllogism being suppressed or kept in mind; as, 'we are dependent, therefore we should be humble'—the proposition omitted being 'all dependent creatures should be humble'.

entice, en·tīs′, *v.t.*—*enticed, enticing.* [O.Fr. *enticer, entiser*=Mod. Fr. *attiser,* from *tison,* L. *titio,* a firebrand.] To draw on by exciting hope or desire; to allure, attract, invite; to lead astray; to induce to evil.—**enticement,** en·tīs′ment, *n.* The act or means of enticing; allurement; attraction; seduction.—**enticer,** en·tī′sėr, *n.* One who or that which entices.—**enticing,** en··tī′sing, *p.* and *a.* Alluring; attracting; attractive.—**enticingly,** en·tī′sing·li, *adv.* In an enticing manner.

entire, en·tīr′, *a.* [Fr. *entier,* from L. *integer,* whole (whence *integer, integrity,* etc.).] Whole; unbroken; complete in its parts; perfect; not mutilated; not participated with others; mere; sheer. ∴ Syn. under COMPLETE.—*Entire horse,* an uncastrated horse; a stallion.—*n.* That kind of malt liquor known also as porter or stout: so called because it combined the qualities of various sorts of beer, and did not necessitate mixing.—**entirely,** en·tīr′li, *adv.* Wholly; completely; fully; altogether.—**entireness,** en·tīr′nes, *n.* Completeness; unbroken form or state.—**entirety,** en·tīr′ti, *n.* The state of being entire or whole; wholeness; completeness; the whole.

entitle, en·tī′tl, *v.t.*—*entitled, entitling.* [O.Fr. *entituler,* Fr. *intituler*—L. *in,* and *titulus,* a title.] To give a name or title to; to affix a name or appellation to; to designate; to denominate; to call; to name; to furnish with a title, right, or claim (a railway ticket *entitles* a person to travel).

entity, en′ti·ti, *n.* [L.L. *entitas,* from *ens, entis,* a thing. ENS.] Being; character of existence; essence; a being or species of being; an existing thing.

entomb, en·töm′, *v.t.* To deposit in a tomb; to bury; to inter.—**entombment,** en·töm′ment, *n.* The act of entombing; burial; sepulture.

entomology, en·to·mol′o·ji, *n.* [Gr. *entomon,* an insect, from *entomos,* cut in—*en,* in, and *temnō,* to cut; from the thorax being almost divided from the abdomen.] That branch of zoology which treats of the structure, habits, and classification of insects.—**entomologic, entomological,** en′to·mo·loj″ik, en′to·mo·loj″i·kal, *a.* Pertaining to entomology. —**entomologically,** en′to·mo·loj″i·kal·li, *adv.* In an entomological manner.—**entomologist,** en·to·mol′o·jist, *n.* One versed in entomology. —**entomophagous,** en·to·mof′a·gus, *a.* Feeding on insects; insectivorous.

entophyte, en′to·fīt, *n.* [Gr. *entos,* within, and *phyton,* a plant.] A plant growing in the interior of animal or vegetable structures; a plant growing on or in living animals. —**entophytic,** en·to·fit′ik, *a.* Pertaining to entophytes.

entourage, än·tu·räzh′, *n.* [Fr. *entour,* around—*en,* in, and *tour,* circuit.] The attendants to a person; one's associates; the surrounding environment.

entr'acte, än·träkt′, *n.* [Fr.] The interval between the acts of a drama; a short musical entertainment performed during such interval.

entrails, en′trālz, *n. pl.* [Fr. *entrailles*; from L.L. *intralia,* from L. *inter, within.*] The internal parts of animal bodies; the bowels; the viscera; the guts.

entrain, en·trān′, *v.t.* To put on board a railroad train; opposed to *detrain.*—*v.i.* To take places in a railroad train.

entrance, en′trans, *n.* [From *enter.*] The act of entering into a place; the power or liberty of entering; admission; the doorway or passage by which a place may be entered; initiation; beginning; the act of taking possession, as of property or an office.—**entrant,** en′trant, *n.* One who enters; one who begins a new course of life; one becoming a member for the first time of any association or body.

entrance, en·trans′, *v.t.* or *i.*— *entranced, entrancing.* To throw into a trance; to put into an ecstasy; to ravish with delight or wonder; to enrapture.—**entrancement,** en··trans′ment, *n.* The act of entrancing or state of being entranced.

entrap, en·trap′, *v.t.*—*entrapped, entrapping.* To catch as in a trap: to ensnare; to catch by artifices; to entangle.

entreat, en·trēt′, *v.t.* [Prefix *en,* and *treat*; O.Fr. *entraiter,* to treat of.] To ask earnestly (a person or a thing); to beseech; to supplicate; to solicit pressingly; to importune; to treat, handle, or deal with‡.— **entreatingly,** en·trē′ting·li, *adv.* In an entreating manner.—**entreaty,** en·trē′ti, *n.* Urgent prayer; earnest petition; pressing solicitation; supplication.

entree, än′trā, *n.* [Fr.] Entry; freedom of access; a dish served between courses at dinner, or a dish served as the main course.—**entremets,** än′-tr·mā, *n.* [Fr. *entre,* between, and *mets,* a dish.] A side dish or minor dish at table, as an omelet, a jelly, etc.

entrench, en·trensh′, *v.t.* [Prefix *en,* and *trench.*] To dig or cut a trench or trenches round, as in fortification; to fortify with a ditch and parapet; to lodge within or as within an entrenchment; to place in a strong position.—*v.i.* To invade; to encroach: with *on* or *upon.*—**entrenchment,** en·trensh′ment, *n.* The act of entrenching; *fort.* a work consisting of a trench or ditch and a parapet (the latter formed of the earth dug out of the ditch), constructed for a defense against an enemy; an inroad or encroachment on the rights of others.

entrepôt, än′tre·pō, *n.* [Fr., from L. *inter,* between, *positum,* placed.] A warehouse for the depositing of goods; an emporium or center for the distribution of merchandise.

entrepreneur, än′trä·pre·nür″, *n.*[Fr. *entreprendre,* to undertake.] The person who organizes, manages, and assumes the risks of a business; a successful businessman.

entresol, en′tėr·sol or än·tr·sol, *n.* [Fr.] *Arch.* a low story between two others of greater height.

entropy, en′trop·i, *n.* [Gr. *en,* in, *tropē*—transformation.] A measure of the unavailability of thermal energy for conversion into mechanical work.

entrust, en·trust′, *v.t.* [Fr. *en,* in, and E. *trust.*] To deliver in trust; to trust or confide to the care of; to commit with confidence (to *entrust* a thing *to* a person, or a person *with* a thing); consign; commit; confide.

entry, en′tri, *n.* [Fr. *entrée.* ENTER.] The act of entering; entrance; ingress; the act of recording in a book; any single item entered or set down; the passage into a house or other building or into a room; a beginning; a first attempt; the giving an account of a ship's cargo or exhibition of her papers, and obtaining permission to land goods; *law,* the act of taking possession of lands or tenements.

entwine, en·twin′, *v.t.* and *i.*—*en-twined, entwining.* [Prefix *en,* and *twine.*] To twist or become twisted round.

enumerate, i·nū′me·rāt, *v.t.*—*enu-merated, enumerating.* [L. *enumero, enumeratum*—*e,* out, and *numerus,* number.] To count or tell, number by number; to number; to count; to mention one by one; to recount.— **enumeration,** i·nū′me·rā″shon, *n.* The act of enumerating; an account of a number of things each by each.

—**enumerative,**† i·nū′me·rā·tiv, *a.* Counting; reckoning up.—**enumerator,** i·nū′me·rā·tẽr, *n.* One who enumerates.

enunciate, i·nun′shi·āt, *v.t.*—**enunciated, enunciating.** [L. *enuncio, enunciatum*—*e*, out, and *nuncio*, to tell. NUNCIO.] To utter, as words or syllables; to pronounce; to declare; to proclaim; to announce; to state.—*v.i.* To utter words or syllables.—**enunciable,** i·nun′shi·a·bl, *a.* Capable of being enunciated or expressed.—**enunciation,** i·nun′shi·ā″shon, *n.* The act of enunciating; declaration; expression; utterance; announcement; statement.—**enunciative,** i·nun′shi·ā·tiv, *a.* Pertaining to enunciation; declarative.—**enunciatively,** i·nun′shi·ā·tiv·li, *adv.* Declaratively.—**enunciator,** i·nun′shi·ā·tẽr, *n.* One who enunciates.—**enunciatory,** i·nun′shi·a·to·ri, *a.* Pertaining to enunciation or utterance.

enure, in·ūr′, *v.i.* [Same as *Inure*.] To take or have effect; to be available or of benefit.

enuresis, en·ū·rē′sis, *n.* [Gr. *en*, in, and *ouron*, urine.] *Pathol.* incontinence or involuntary discharge of urine.

envelop, en·vel′up, *v.t.* [Fr. *envelopper*, It. *invillupare*, to envelop—prefix *en*, in, and verb equivalent to E. *wrap*, an old form of which is *wlap*; so also *develop*.] To cover, as by wrapping or folding; to enwrap or wrap up; to surround entirely; to cover on all sides; to form a covering about; to lie around and conceal; to outflank or turn the enemy's line, so that it is partially surrounded.—**envelope,** en′ve·lōp, *n.* What is wrapped around or envelops something; a wrapper; an enclosing cover; an integument; *bot.* one of the parts of fructification surrounding the stamens and pistils; the outer covering of a balloon or airship distended by means of enclosed gas, usually a fabric into the construction of which a rubber enters.—**envelopment,** en·vel′up·ment, *n.* The act of enveloping; that which envelops.

envenom, en·ven′om, *v.t.* To taint or impregnate with venom; to poison; to imbue with bitterness or malice; to enrage; to exasperate.

enviable, envious, etc. See ENVY.

environ, en·vī′ron, *v.t.* [Fr. *environner*—*en*, and O.Fr. *vironner*, to veer, to environ, from *virer*, to veer. VEER.] To surround, encompass, or encircle; to hem in; to involve; to envelop.—**environment,** en·vī′ron·ment, *n.* Act of surrounding; state of being environed; that which environs; surroundings.—**environs,** en·vī′ronz, *n. pl.* The parts or places which surround another place, or lie in its neighborhood, on different sides.

envisage, en·viz′ij, *v.t.* [Fr. *envisager*—*en*, in, and *visage*, face.] To look in the face of; to face.

envoy, en′voi, *n.* [Fr. *envoyer*, to send—*en*, and *voie*, L. *via*, a way, as in *convoy, voyage*, etc. WAY.] One dispatched upon an errand or mission; a messenger; a person deputed to negotiate a treaty, or transact other business, with a foreign ruler or government; a diplomatic agent sent on a special occasion; short poem or stanzas addressed by the author to the reader, sending him 'on his way' with the book.

envy, en′vi, *n.* [Fr. *envie*, from L. *invidia*, envy, from *invidus*, envious—*in*, against, and root *vid*, to look. VISION.] Pain, uneasiness, mortification, or discontent excited by the sight of another's superiority or success; a feeling that makes a person begrudge another his good fortune; malice; object of envy.—*v.t.*—**envied, envying.** [Fr. *envier*.] To feel envy toward or on account of; to repine at; to regard with malice and longing; to desire earnestly.—*v.i.* To be affected with envy; to have envious feelings.—**enviable,** en′vi·a·bl, *a.* Exciting or capable of exciting envy.—**enviably,** en′vi·a·bli, *adv.* In an enviable manner.—**envious,** en′vi·us, *a.* [Fr. *envieux*.] Feeling or harboring envy; tinctured with envy; excited or directed by envy.—**enviously,** en′vi·us·li, *adv.* In an envious manner.—**enviousness,** en′vi·us·nes, *n.*

enwrap, en·rap′, *v.t.* To envelop; to inwrap.

enzootic, en·zō·ot′ik, *a.* [Gr. *en*, among, and *zōon*, an animal.] Limited to the animals of a district: said of diseases,—*n.* A disease affecting the animals of a district.

enzyme, en′zīm, *n.* [Gr. *en*, in, *zymē*, leaven.] *Physiol.* a very large class of protein substances that are produced by living cells and that are essential to life by acting as catalysts in the metabolism of the cell.

Eocene, ē′o·sēn, *a.* and *n.* [Gr. *eōs*, the dawn, and *kainos*, recent.] *Geol.* a term applied to strata at the base of the tertiary formations, having a small proportion of living species among the fossils.

Eolian, Eolic, ē·ō′li·an, ē·ol′ik, *a.* A name of one of the ancient Greek races.—*Eolian mode, mus.*, the fifth of the authentic Gregorian modes; it consists of the natural notes A B C D E F G.—*n.* The Eolian dialect; one of the Eolian race.

Eolian, ē·ō′li·an, *a.* Pertaining to *Aeolus*, the god of the winds.—*Eolian lyre* or *harp*, a simple instrument that sounds by the air sweeping across its strings.

eolith, ē′o·lith, *n.* [Gr. *eōs*, dawn, *lithos*, stone.] The oldest known type of prehistoric stone implements.

eolithic, ē·o·lith′ik, *a.* [Gr. *eos*, dawn, and *lithos*, stone.] *Archeol.* pertaining to the period 500,000 years ago during the use of the first stone tools.

eon, aeon, ē′on, *n.* [Gr. *aiōn*, age, duration, eternity.] A long indefinite space of time; an age; an era.

eosin, ē′o·sin, *n.* [Gr. *eōs*, dawn.] A dye obtained from coal-tar products, giving a rose-red color.

Eozoic, ē·o·zō′ik, *a.* [Gr. *eōs*, dawn, and *zōē*, life.] Of or pertaining to the oldest fossiliferous rocks, from their being supposed to contain the first or earliest traces of life in the stratified systems.

epact, ē′pakt, *n.* [Gr. *epaktos*, brought in or on—*epi*, on, and *agō*, to lead.] *Chron.* the excess of the solar month above the lunar synodical month, and of the solar year above the lunar year of twelve synodical months.

eparch, ep′ärk, *n.* [Gr. *eparchos*—*epi*, and *archē*, dominion.] In Greece, the governor of a province or eparchy.—**eparchy,** ep′är·ki, *n.* [Gr. *eparchia*.] The territory under the jurisdiction of an eparch.

epaule, e·pal′, *n.* [Fr. *épaule*, the shoulder, O.Fr. *espaule*, from L. *spatula, spathula*, a broad, flat thing; dim. of *spatha*, a broad blade; allied to *spade*.] *Fort.* the shoulder of a bastion, or the angle made by the face and flank.—**epaulet,** ep′e·let, *n.* [Fr. *épaulette*.] A shoulder piece; an ornamental badge worn on the shoulder, especially by military and naval officers.

epencephalon, ep·en·sef′a·lon, *n.* [Gr. *epi*, near, and *enkephalon*, the brain.] *Anat.* the hindmost of the four divisions or segments of the brain.—**epencephalic,** ep′en·se·fal″ik, *a. Anat.* of or belonging to the epencephalon.

epenthesis, e·pen′the·sis, *n.* [Gr. *epi*, on, *en*, in, and *tithēmi*, to put.] *Gram.* the insertion of a letter or syllable in the middle of a word.—**epenthetic,** ep·en·thet′ik, *a. Gram.* inserted in the middle of a word.

epergne, e·pẽrn′, *n.* [Apparently from Fr. *épargne*, thrift, economy.] An ornamental stand with a large dish and branches for the center of a table.

epexegesis, e·pek′se·jē″sis, *n.* [Gr. *epi*, and *exegesis.* EXEGESIS.] A full explanation or interpretation of something immediately preceding; exegesis.—**epexegetical,** e·pek′se·jet″i·kal, *a.* Explanatory; exegetical.

epha, ephah, ē′fä, *n.* [Heb.] A Hebrew measure of capacity, containing, according to one estimate, 8.6696 gallons; according to another, 4.4286.

ephemeral, e·fem′e·ral, *a.* [Gr. *ephemeros*, lasting but a day, short-lived—*epi*, and *hēmera*, a day.] Beginning and ending in a day; continuing or existing one day only; short-lived; fleeting.—**ephemera,** e·fem′e·ra, *n.* A small fly that lives but for a day or for a very short time; the day fly.—**ephemeris,** e·fem′e·ris, *n. pl.* **ephemerides,** e·fe·mer′i·dēz. [Gr., a diary.] A journal or account of daily transactions; a diary; *astron.* a publication exhibiting the places of the heavenly bodies throughout the year, and giving other information regarding them; an astronomical almanac; a collective name for reviews, magazines, and all kinds of periodical literature.—**ephemeron,** e·fem′e·ron, *n.*

Ephesian, e·fē′zhi·an, *a.* Pertaining to Ephesus in Asia Minor.

Ephesians, e·fē′zhanz, *n. pl.* construed as sing. [L. *Ephesius*.] In the New Testament, the Epistle of St. Paul, the Apostle to the Ephesians.

---

ch, *ch*ain;   *ch*, Sc. lo*ch*;   g, go;   j, *j*ob;   ng, si*ng*;   TH, *th*en;   th, *th*in;   w, *w*ig;   hw, *wh*ig;   zh, a*z*ure.

ephod, ef'od, n. [Heb., from *aphad*, to put on.] A species of vestment worn by the Jewish high priest over the second tunic, and consisting of two main pieces, one covering the back, the other the breast and upper part of the body.

ephor, ef'or, n. [Gr. *ephoros*.] A name of certain magistrates among the ancient Spartans.

epiblast, ep'i-blast, n. [Gr. *epi*, upon, and *blastos*, a bud.] *Bot.* a second cotyledon, consisting of a small transverse plate, found on some grasses; *anat.* the upper of the two layers of cells (the under being the *hypoblast*) forming the blastoderm.

epic, ep'ik, a. [L. *epicus*, from Gr. *epikos*, from *epos*, a word, a song.] Composed in a lofty narrative style of poetry; pertaining to such a style; narrative; heroic.—n. A narrative poem of elevated character, describing often the exploits of heroes.

epicalyx, ep'i-kā'liks, n. [Gr. *epi*, upon, and *calyx*.] *Bot.* the outer calyx in plants with two calyces, formed either of sepals or bracts.

epicarp, ep'i-kärp, n. [Gr. *epi*, upon, and *karpos*, fruit.] *Bot.* the outer skin of fruits, the fleshy substance or edible portion being termed the *mesocarp*, and the inner portion the *endocarp*.

epicene, ep'i-sēn, a. [Gr. *epikainos*, common to a number—*epi*, and *koinos*, common.] *Gram.* a term applied to nouns which have but one form of gender, either the masculine or feminine, to indicate animals of both sexes.

epicentrum, ep-i-sent'rum, n. [Gr. *epicentros*.] The point at which an earthquake breaks out.

epicotyl, ep'i-kot"il, n. [Gr. *epi*, above, *cotyl*(edon).] In seedlings, that part of the stem immediately above the seed leaves (cotyledons).

epicure, ep'i-kūr, n. [After *Epicurus*, a Greek philosopher who taught that pleasure and pain are the chief good and chief evil.] One devoted to sensual enjoyments; especially one who indulges in the luxuries of the table.—**Epicurean**, ep'i-kū-rē"an, a. Pertaining to Epicurus or his teaching; luxurious; given to luxury.—n. A follower of Epicurus; a man devoted to sensual pleasures or luxuries; an epicure.—**Epicureanism**, ep'i-kū-rē"an-izm, n. The principles or philosophical doctrines of Epicurus; attachment to luxurious habits.—**epicurism**, ep'i-kū-rizm, n. The practices of an epicure.

epicycle, ep'i-si-kl, n. [Gr. *epi*, and *kyklos*, a circle.] In old astronomy, a little circle, whose center moves round in the circumference of a greater circle.—**epicyclic**, ep'i-sī'-klik, a. Pertaining to an epicycle.—**epicycloid**, ep'i-sī'kloid, n. *Geom.* a curve generated by the movement of a curve upon the convex or concave side of another fixed curve. —**epicycloidal**, ep'i-sī-kloi"dal, a. Pertaining to the epicycloid, or having its properties.—*Epicycloidal wheel*, a fixed wheel or ring toothed on its inner side, and having in gear with

it another toothed wheel of half the diameter, fitted so as to revolve about the center of the larger.

epidemic, epidemical, ep-i-dem'ik, ep-i-dem'i-kal, a. [Gr. *epi*, upon, and *demos*, people.] Common to or affecting a whole people, or a great number in a community: said of diseases; prevalent; general; generally prevailing.—**epidemic**, n. A disease which, arising from a widespread cause, attacks many people at the same period and in the same country.— **epidemically**, ep-i-dem'i-kal-li, adv. In an epidemic manner.—**epidemiological**, ep-i-dē'mi-o-loj"i-kal, a. Pertaining to epidemiology.—**epidemiologist**, ep-i-dē'mi-ol"o-jist, n. One skilled in epidemiology.—**epidemiology**, ep-i-dē'mi-ol"o-ji, n. The doctrine of or method of investigating epidemic diseases.

epidermis, ep-i-dėr'mis, n. [Gr. *epidermis*—*epi*, and *derma*, skin.] *Anat.* the outermost layer of the skin; the cuticle or scarfskin of the body; a thin membrane covering the true skin of animals; *bot.* the cellular integument, or the exterior cellular coating of the leaf or stem of a plant. —**epidermal**, ep-i-dėr'mal, a. Relating to the epidermis; epidermic.— **epidermoid**, ep-i-dėr'moid, a. Resembling or pertaining to the epiderm. — **epidermic, epidermical**, ep-i-dėr'mik, ep-i-dėr'mi-kal, a. Pertaining to or like the epidermis.

epidote, ep'i-dōt, n. [Fr., from Gr. *epi*, over and above, and *didōmi*, to give, from the enlargement of the base of the primary in some of the secondary forms.] A mineral of a green or gray color, vitreous luster, and partial transparency, a member of the garnet family.

epigastric, ep-i-gas'trik, a. [Gr. *epi*, and *gastēr*, belly.] Pertaining to the upper and anterior part of the abdomen.—**epigastrium**, ep-i-gas'tri-um, n. The upper part of the abdomen.

epigene, ep'i-jēn, a. [Gr. *epi*, upon, and root *gen*, to produce.] *Geol.* formed or originating on the surface of the earth: opposed to *hypogene*.

epigenesis, ep-i-jen'e-sis, n. [Gr. *epi*, and *genesis*, generation.] The biological theory that organic bodies and parts are produced by superadded vital activity and not merely developed from pre-existing bodies. —**epigenetic**, ep'i-je-net"ik, a. Pertaining to or produced by epigenesis. —**epigenous**, ep-ij'e-nus, a. *Bot.* growing upon the surface of a part.

epigeous, ep-i-jē'us, a. [Gr. *epi*, upon, and *ge, gaia*, the earth.] *Bot.* growing on or close to the earth.

epiglottis, ep-i-glot'is, n. [Gr. *epiglōttis*—*epi*, upon, and *glōttis*.] *Anat.* a cartilaginous plate behind the tongue, which covers the glottis like a lid during the act of swallowing.

epigram, ep'i-gram, n. [Gr. *epigramma*, an inscription—*epi*, upon, and *gramma*, a writing, from *graphō*, to write.] A short poem usually keenly satirical, the last line of which generally contains the sting or pointed allusion; also an interesting

thought represented happily in a few words, whether verse or prose; a pointed or antithetical saying.— **epigrammatic, epigrammatical**, ep'-i-gram-mat"ik, ep'i-gram-mat"i-kal, a. Relating to, characterized by, or producing epigrams; like an epigram; antithetical; pointed.—**epigrammatically**, ep'i-gram-mat"i-kal-li, adv. In an epigrammatic manner or style; tersely and pointedly.— **epigrammatist**, ep-i-gram'ma-tist, n. One who composes epigrams or deals in them.—**epigrammatize**, ep-i-gram'ma-tīz, v.t. To represent or express by epigrams.

epigraph, ep'i-graf, n. [Gr. *epigraphē*—*epi*, and *graphō*, to write.] An inscription on a building, tomb, monument, statue, etc., denoting its use or appropriation; a quotation or motto at the commencement of a work, or at its separate divisions.— **epigraphic**, ep-i-graf'ik, a. Of or pertaining to an epigraph.—**epigraphy**, e-pig'ra-fi, n. That branch of knowledge which deals with the deciphering and explaining of inscriptions.— **epigraphist**, e-pig'ra-fist, n. One versed in epigraphics.

epigynous, e-pij'i-nus, a. [Gr. *epi*, upon, and *gyné*, female.] *Bot.* growing or appearing to grow upon the top of the ovary.

epilepsy, ep'i-lep-si, n. [Gr. *epilēpsia*, —*epi*, upon, and *lambanō*, *lēpsomai*, to take or seize.] A chronic nervous disease characterized by brief convulsive seizures and loss of consciousness.—**epileptic**, ep-i-lep'tik, a. Pertaining to, or affected with, epilepsy. —**epileptic**, n. One affected with epilepsy; a medicine for the cure of epilepsy.—**epileptoid**, ep-i-lep'toid, a. Of or pertaining to epilepsy; resembling epilepsy.

epilogue, ep'i-log, n. [L. *epilogus*, from Gr. *epilogos*, conclusion—*epi*, and *legō*, to speak.] A speech or short poem addressed to the spectators by one of the actors, after the conclusion of a drama.

epinasty, ep'i-nas-ti, n. [Gr. *epi*, on, *nastos*, pressed.] *Bot.* a bending downward of an organ owing to the more rapid growth of its upper than its under surface.

Epiphany, i-pif'a-nē, n. [Gr. *epiphaneia*, appearance, from *epiphainō*, to appear—*epi*, upon, and *phainō*, to show.] An appearance or a becoming manifest; specifically, a Christian festival celebrated on the sixth day of January in commemoration of the manifestation of the Saviour's birth to the wise men of the East.

epiphysis, i-pif'i-sis, n. [Gr. *epiphysis*—*epi*, upon, and *phyō*, to grow.] *Anat.* any portion of a bone separated from the body of the bone by a cartilage which becomes converted into bone by age.—**epiphyseal**, **epiphysial**, ep-i-fiz'ē-al, ep-i-fiz'i-al, a. Pertaining to or having the nature of an epiphysis.

epiphyte, ep'i-fīt, n. [Gr. *epi*, upon, and *phyton*, a plant.] A plant growing upon another plant, but not deriving its nourishment from it; an air plant. —**epiphytic, epiphytical**, ep-i-fit'ik, ep·i·fit′i·kal, *a.* Pertaining to or having the nature of an epiphyte.

episcopacy, i·pis′kō·pa·si, *n.* [L. *episcopatus*, from Gr. *episkopos*, a bishop. BISHOP.] That form of ecclesiastical government in which bishops are established, as distinct from and superior to priests or presbyters; the collective body of bishops.—**episcopal**, i·pis′ko·pl, *a.* Belonging to or vested in bishops or prelates; characteristic of or pertaining to a bishop or bishops.—**episcopalian,** i·pis′ko·pā′li·an, *a.* Pertaining to bishops or government by bishops; episcopal.—*n.* [*cap.*] One who belongs to an episcopal church or favors episcopacy.—**episcopalianism,** i·pis′ko·pā″li·an·izm, *n.* The system of episcopal religion, or government of the church by bishops.—**episcopally,** i·pis′ko·pal·li, *adv.* In an episcopal manner.—**episcopate,** i·pis′ko·pāt, *n.* A bishopric; the office and dignity of a bishop; the collective body of bishops.

episode, ep′i·sōd, *n.* [Gr. *epeisodion*, from *epi*, and *eisodos*, an entrance—*eis*, to, in, and *hodos*, a way.] A separate incident, story, or action, introduced for the purpose of giving a greater variety to the events related in a poem, romance, tale, etc.; an incident or action more or less connected with a complete series of events; that which follows on the entrance of the chorus into the orchestra.—*Greek play*, the part of the play or dialogue between two choral odes, incident.—**episodic, episodical,** ep·i·sod′ik, ep·i·sod′i·kal, *a.* Pertaining to an episode; contained in an episode or digression.—**episodically,** ep·i·sod′i·kal·li, *adv.* In an episodic manner.

epispastic, ep·i·spas′tik, *a.* [Gr. *epispaō*, to draw.] *Med.* drawing; blistering.—*n.* A vesicatory; a blister.

epistaxis, ep·i·stak′sis, *n.* [Gr. *epi*, upon, and *staxis*, a dropping.] Bleeding from the nose.

epistemology, i·pis′te·mol″o·jē, *n.* [Gr. *epistēmē*, knowledge, *logos*, discourse.] The theory of the method or ground of knowledge. ONTOLOGY.

episterna, ep·i·stér′na, *n. pl.* [Gr. *epi*, upon, and *sternon*, the breastbone.] The lateral pieces of the lower surface of the segment of a crustacean.—**episternal,** ep·i·stér′nal, *a. Anat.* a term applied to two bones forming part of the sternum, and situated upon its superior and lateral part.

epistle, i·pis′l, *n.* [L. *epistola*, Gr. *epistolē*, from *epistellō*, to send to—*epi*, on, and *stellō*, to send.] A writing, directed or sent, communicating intelligence to a distant person; a letter: applied particularly in dignified discourse or in speaking of the letters of the apostles or of the ancients.—**epistler,** i·pis′lér, *n.* A writer of epistles; one who reads the epistle in a church service.—**epistolary,** i·pis′to·la·ri, *a.* Pertaining to epistles or letters; suitable to letters; contained in or consisting of letters.

epitaph, ep′i·taf, *n.* [Gr. *epi*, upon, and *taphos* or *taphē*, a tomb.] An inscription on a tomb or monument in honor or memory of the dead; or a composition such as might be so used.—**epitaphic,** ep·i·taf′ik, *a.* Pertaining to an epitaph; of the nature of or serving as an epitaph.

epithalamium, ep′i·tha·lā″mi·um, *n.* [Gr. *epithalamion*—*epi*, upon, and *thalamos*, a bed-chamber.] A nuptial song or poem, in praise of a bride and bridegroom; a poem in honor of a newly married pair.

epithelioma, ep′i·thē·li·ō″ma, *n.* Cancer of the skin.

epithelium, ep·i·thē′li·um, *n.* [Gr. *epi*, upon, and *thēlē*, the nipple.] *Anat.* any thin cellular tissue that lines a cavity or covers a free surface and performs the functions of protection, secretion, and assimilation.—**epithelial,** ep·i·thē′li·al, *a.*

epithet, ep′i·thet, *n.* [Gr. *epitheton*, a name added, from *epi*, upon, and *tithēmi*, to place.] An adjective expressing some real quality of the thing to which it is applied, or some quality ascribed to it; any word or name implying a quality attached to a person or thing.—**epithetic, epithetical,** ep·i·thet′ik, ep·i·thet′i·kal, *a.* Pertaining to an epithet or epithets: containing or consisting of epithets; abounding with epithets.

epitome, i·pit′o·mi, *n.* [Gr. *epitome*, from *epi*, upon, and *tomē*, a cutting, from *temnō*, to cut, seen also in *anatomy, entomology*, etc.] A brief summary or abstract of any book or writing; a compendium; abridgement; a summary; *fig.* anything which represents another or others in a condensed form. ∴ Syn. under ABRIDGE.—**epitomize,** i·pit′o·mīz, *v.t.*—*epitomized, epitomizing.* To make an epitome of; to abstract, in a summary, the principal matters of.

epizoon, ep·i·zō′on, *n. pl.* **epizoa,** ep·i·zō′a. [Gr. *epi*, upon, and *zōon*, animal.] A term applied to those parasitic animals which live on or in the skin of other animals.—**epizootic,** ep′i·zō·ot″ik, *a.* Applied to any disease that is prevalent among many animals of the same kind at the same time.—*n.* An epizootic disease.

epoch, ep′ok, *n.* [L. *epocha*, from Gr. *epochē*, retention, delay, from *epechō*, to hold back—*epi*, upon, and *echō*, to hold.] A fixed point of time from which succeeding years are numbered; a point from which computation of years begins; any fixed time or period; a memorable term of years; era; age; date.—**epochal,** ep′ok·al, *a.* Belonging to an epoch; of the nature of an epoch.

epode, ep′ōd, *n.* [Gr. *epōdē*—*epi*, upon, and *ōdē*, a song, an ode.] The third or last part of the ode, the ancient ode being divided into strophe, antistrophe, and epode; a species of lyric poem in which a longer verse is followed by a shorter one.

eponym, ep′o·nim, *n.* [Gr. *epi*, upon, and *onoma*, a name.] A name of a place or people derived from that of a person; a name of a personage called into existence to account for the name of a country or people, as *Italus, Romulus,* for *Italy, Rome.*—**eponymic, eponymous,** ep·o·nim′ik, e·pon′i·mus, *a.* Of or relating to or connected with an eponym.—*Eponymous archon.* The chief magistrate of Athens among the archons, giving his name to the year as a date or point of time.

epopee, epopoeia, ep·o·pē′, ep·o·pē′ya, *n.* [Fr. *épopée*, Gr. *epopoiïa*—*epos*, a word, an epic poem, and *poieō*, to make.] An epic poem; the subject of an epic poem.—**epos,** ep′os, *n.* [Gr.] An epic poem or its subject; an epopee; epic poetry.

epoxy, ep·äkse′, *a.* [*epi*, and *oxy*, short for oxygen.] Containing oxygen attached to two different atoms, usually carbon, already united in a different manner.—**epoxy resin,** *n.* Any of various resins made by the polymerization of epoxy compounds and used as adhesives and coatings.

epsilon, ep′sä·län, *n.* [Gr. *e psilon*, simple e.] The fifth letter of the Greek alphabet, whose symbol is E.

Epsom salt, ep′som solt, *n.* The sulfate of magnesia, a cathartic producing watery discharges.

equable, ek′wa·bl, *a.* [L. *æquabilis*, from *æquo*, to make equal, from *æquus*, equal.] Characterized by uniformity, invariableness, or evenness; uniform in action or intensity; not varying; steady; even.—**equability, equableness,** ek·wa·bil′i·ti, ek′wa·bl·nes, *n.* State or quality of being equable.—**equably,** ek′wa·bli, *adv.* In an equable manner.

equal, ē′kwal, *a.* [L. *æqualis*, from *æquus*, equal (seen also in *equity, adequate, iniquity,* etc.); same root as Skr. *eka*, one, the same.] The same in size, value, qualities, or degree; neither inferior nor superior, greater nor less, better nor worse; uniform; not variable; being in just relation or proportion; of the same interest or importance; not unduly favorable to any party; just; equitable; fair; having competent power, ability, or means; adequate.—*n.* One not inferior or superior to another; a person having the same or a similar age, rank, station, office, talents, strength, etc.; a compeer.—*v.t.*—*equaled, equaling.* To make equal; to make of the same quantity or quality; to cause to be commensurate with or unsurpassed by; to equalize; to be equal to; to be adequate to; to be commensurate with; to rise to the same state, rank, estimation, or excellence with; to become equal to.—**equality,** i·kwol′i·ti, *n.* [L. *æqualitas*.] The state of being equal; likeness in size, number, quantity, value, qualities, or degree; the condition in which things or persons cannot be said to be inferior or superior, greater or less, one than another; parity; sameness in state or continued course.—**equalize,** ē′kwa·līz, *v.t.*—*equalized, equalizing.* To make equal; to cause to be equal in amount or degree; to adjust so that there shall be equality between.—

equalization, ē′kwal·i·zā″shon, *n.* The act of equalizing, or state of being equalized.—**equalizer**, ē′kwa·lī·zėr, *n.* One who or that which equalizes.—**equally**, ē′kwal·li, *adv.* In an equal manner or degree; in the same degree with another; alike; in equal shares or proportions; impartially.

equanimity, ek·wa·nim′i·ti, *n.* [L. *æquanimitas*—*æquus*, equal, and *animus*, mind.] Evenness of mind; that calm temper or firmness of mind which is not easily elated or depressed.

equate, i·kwāt′, *v.t.*—*equated*, *equating*. [L. *æquo*, *æquatum*, to make equal, from *æquus*, equal.] To make equal; to reduce to an average; to make such correction or allowance in as will reduce to a common standard of comparison, or will bring to a true result.—**equation**, i·kwā′shon, *n.* The act of equating; *alg.* a statement or expression asserting the equality of two quantities, equality being denoted by the sign = (equal to) between them; *astron.* a quantity which from some imperfect method has to be taken into account in order to give a true result.— *Equation of time*, the difference between mean and apparent time, or the difference between the time given by a dial and that given by a clock.— *Personal equation*, in astronomical observations the quantity of time by which a person is in the habit of noting a phenomenon wrongly.— **equator**, i·kwā′tėr, *n.* [L.L. *æquator*, from L. *æquo*, *æquatum*, to make equal.] That great circle of our globe which divides it into two hemispheres (the northern and southern), and every point of which is 90° from the poles, which are also its poles, its axis being also the axis of the earth; also, the equinoctial or celestial equator.—**equatorial**, ē·kwa·tō′ri·al, *a.* Pertaining to the equator.—*n.* An astronomical instrument, contrived for the purpose of directing a telescope upon any celestial object of which the right ascension and declination are known, and of keeping the object in view for any length of time, notwithstanding the diurnal motion.

equerry, ek′we·ri, *n.* [Fr. *écurie*, a stable, so that the word means really stable (man); from L.L. *scuria*, a stable; from O.H.G. *skiura*, a stable; Mod.G. *scheuer*, a barn or shed.] An officer of nobles or princes who has the care and management of their horses: in England, equerries are certain officers of the royal household in the department of the master of the horse.

equestrian, i·kwes′tri·an, *a.* [L. *equestris*, from *eques*, horseman, from *equus*, horse; akin Gr. *hippos*, Skr. *açva*, horse; Gr. *ōkys*, swift.] Pertaining to horses or horsemanship; consisting in or accompanied with performances on horseback; representing a person on horseback (an *equestrian* statue); pertaining to the class or rank of knights in ancient Rome.—*n.* A rider on horseback; one who earns his living by perform-

ing feats of agility and skill on horseback in a circus.—**equestrienne**, i·kwes′tri·en, *n.* [Spurious French form.] A female rider or performer on horseback.

equiangular, ē·kwi·ang′gū·lėr, *a. Geom.* consisting of or having the angles all equal.

equidistance, ē·kwi·dis′tans, *n.* Equal distance.—**equidistant**, ē·kwi·dis′tant, *a.* Being at an equal distance from some point or place.—**equidistantly**, ē·kwi·dis′tant·li, *adv.* At an equal distance.

equilateral, ē·kwi·lat′ėr·al, *a.* [L. *æquus*, equal, and *latus*, *lateris*, a side.] Having all the sides equal.

equilibrate, ē·kwi·lī′brāt, *v.t.*—*equilibrated*, *equilibrating*. [L. *æquus*, equal, and *libro*, to poise, from *libra*, a balance.] To balance equally; to keep in equipoise.—**equilibration**, ē′kwi·lī·brā″shon, *n.* Equipoise; the state of being equally balanced.— **equilibrist**, ē·kwil′i·brist, *n.* One that balances equally; one who keeps his balance in unnatural positions and hazardous movements, as a rope dancer.—**equilibrium**, ē·kwi·lib′ri·um, *n.* [L. *æquilibrium*.] Equality of weight or force; a state of rest produced by two or more weights or forces counterbalancing each other, as the state of the two ends of a balance when both are charged with equal weights, and they maintain an even or level position; a state of just poise; the state where an organism is normally oriented to its environment.

equine, ē′kwīn, *a.* [L. *equinus*, from *equus*, a horse. EQUESTRIAN.] Pertaining to or resembling a horse.

equinox, ē′kwi·noks, *n.* [L. *æquinoctium*, from *æquus*, equal, and *nox*, night.] The time when the sun reaches one of the two equinoctial points, or points in which the ecliptic and celestial equator intersect each other, the *vernal equinox* being about March 21, the *autumnal equinox* about September 23, the day and the night being then of equal length all over the world.— **equinoctial**, ē·kwi·nok′shal, *a.* Pertaining to the equinoxes; occurring or manifested about that time (*equinoctial* gales); pertaining to regions or climate under the equinoctial line or about the equator.— *Equinoctial points*, the two points of the heavens at which the equator and ecliptic intersect each other.—*n.* The celestial equator, so called because, when the sun is on it, the days and nights are of equal length in all parts of the world.

equip, i·kwip′, *v.t.*—*equipped*, *equipping*. [Fr. *équiper*, O.Fr. *esquiper*, to equip, to fit out a ship, from the Teut. stem *skip*, to provide, arrange, etc., as in Icel. *skipa*, to arrange, akin E. *ship*, shape.] To dress; to accouter; to prepare for some particular duty or service; specifically, to furnish with arms and munitions of war; to provide with everything necessary for an expedition or voyage; to fit out for sea, as a ship.—**equipage**, ek′wi·pij,

n. [Fr. *équipage*.] Materials with which a person or thing is equipped; accouterments; equipment; the furniture and supplies of an armed ship, or the necessary preparations for a voyage; a train of dependents accompanying or following a person; a carriage with the horse or horses, harness, etc.; retinue.—**equipment**, i·kwip′ment, *n.* The act of equipping or fitting out; anything that is used in equipping; necessaries for an expedition, a voyage, etc.; equipage.

equipoise, ek′wi·poiz, *n.* [L. *æquus*, equal, and E. *poise*.] Equality of weight or force; due balance; equilibrium; a state in which the two ends or sides of a thing are balanced.

equipollence, equipollency, ē·kwi·pol′lens, ē·kwi·pol′len·si, *n.* [Fr. *équipollence*—L. *æquus*, equal, and *polleo*, to be able.] Equality of power or force; *logic*, an equivalence between two or more propositions.— **equipollent**, ē·kwi·pol′lent, *a.* Having equal power, force, or signification; equivalent.

equiponderate, ē·kwi·pon′dėr·āt, *v.i.*—*equiponderated*, *equiponderating*. [L. *æquus*, equal, and *pondero*, to weigh, from *pondus*, *ponderis*, weight.] To be equal in weight; to weigh as much as another thing.—*v.t.* To weigh equally in an opposite scale; to counterbalance. — **equiponderance, equiponderancy**, ē·kwi·pon′dėr·ans, ē·kwi·pon′dėr·an·si, *n.* Equality of weight; equipoise.—**equiponderant**, ē·kwi·pon′dėr·ant, *a.*

equisetum, ek·wi·sē′tum, *n.* [L. *equus*, a horse, and *seta*, a bristle.] Any plant belonging to the genus *Equisetum*, popularly known as horsetails, having hollow jointed stems, leaves in the form of whorls of teeth terminating the joints, and growing in marshy places.

equitable, ek′wi·ta·bl, *a.* [Fr. *équitable*, from L. *æquitas*, equity, from *æquus*, equal.] Possessing or exhibiting equity; equal in regard to the rights of persons; giving each his due; just; fair; impartial; pertaining to a court of equity.—**equitableness**, ek′wi·ta·bl·nes, *n.* The quality of being equitable.—**equitably**, ek′wi·ta·bli, *adv.* In an equitable manner; justly; impartially.—**equity**, ek′wi·ti, *n.* [Fr. *équité*, L. *æquitas*.] The giving or disposition to give to each man his due; justice; impartiality; fairness; uprightness; *law*, a doing justice between parties where there is no guidance or remedy in strict law; more strictly, a system of supplemental law founded upon defined rules, recorded precedents, and established principles, the judges, however, liberally expounding and developing these to meet new exigencies.

equitant, ek′wi·tant, *a.* [L. *equitans*, ppr. of *equito*, to ride, from *eques*, *equitis*, a horseman, from *equus*, a horse.] *Bot.* a term applied to unexpanded leaves in a leaf bud, that overlap each other entirely without any involution, as in the iris.— **equitation**, ek·wi·tā′shon, *n.* The act or art of riding on horseback; horsemanship.

equivalent, i·kwiv′a·lent, *a.* [Fr. *équivalent*—L. *æquus*, equal, and *valens, valentis,* ppr. of *valeo,* to be worth (seen also in *avail, prevail,* etc.).] Equal in value, force, power, effect, excellence, import, or meaning; interchangeable.—*n.* Something that is equivalent; that which is equal in value, weight, dignity, or force with something else; something given as a fair exchange; compensation; *chem.* the quantity by weight in which an element combines with or replaces a unit of hydrogen; *geol.* a stratum or series of strata in one district formed contemporaneously with a stratum or series of a different character in a different region, and holding a similar place.—**equivalently,** i·kwiv′a·lent·li, *adv.* In an equivalent manner.—**equivalence,** i·kwiv′a·lens, *n.* The condition of being equivalent; equality of value, signification, or force.—**equivalency,** i·kwiv′a·len·si, *n.* Same as *Equivalence*; *chem.* the quality in chemical elements of combining with or displacing one another in certain definite proportions.

equivocal, i·kwiv′ō·kal, *a.* [L. *æquus,* equal, and *vox, vocis,* voice.] Being of doubtful signification; capable of being or liable to be understood in different senses; ambiguous; uncertain; dubious; unsatisfactory; deserving to be suspected; capable of being ascribed to different motives; doubtful; questionable.—**equivocally,** i·kwiv′ō·kal·li, *adv.* In an equivocal manner.—**equivocate,** i·kwiv′ō·kāt, *v.i.*—*equivocated, equivocating.* To use ambiguous expressions with a view to mislead; to prevaricate; to quibble.—**equivocation,** e·kwiv′ō·kā″shon, *n.* The act of equivocating; the use of words or expressions that are susceptible of a double signification, with a view to mislead; prevarication; quibbling. —**equivocator,** e·kwiv′ō·kā″tėr, *n.* One who equivocates; a prevaricator; a quibbler.—**equivoque, equivoke,** ek′wi·vōk, ē′kwi·vōk, *n.* [Fr. *équivoque.*] An ambiguous term or expression; a quirk; pun or punning.

era, ē′ra, *n.* [L.L. *æra,* a date, an item of an account, from L. *æra,* counters, pl. of *æs,* brass.] A fixed point of time, from which any number of years is begun to be counted; a succession of years proceeding from a fixed point, or comprehended between two fixed points; an age or period.

eradicate, i·rad′i·kāt, *v.t.*—*eradicated, eradicating.* [L. *eradico, eradicatum*—*e,* out, and *radix, radicis,* a root (whence *radical*).] To pull up by the roots; to destroy at the roots; to root out; to destroy thoroughly; to extirpate.—**eradicable,** i·rad′i·ka·bl, *a.* That may be eradicated. —**eradication,** i·rad′i·kā″shon, *n.* The act of eradicating.—**eradicative,** i·rad′i·kā·tiv, *a.* Serving to eradicate, uproot, extirpate, or destroy.

erase, i·rās′, *v.t.*—*erased, erasing.* [L. *erado, erasum*—*e,* out, and *rado,*

rasum, to scrape, to scratch. RAZE.] To rub or scrape out, as letters or characters written, engraved, or painted; to efface; to obliterate; to expunge; to remove or destroy, as by rubbing or blotting out.—**erasable,** i·rā′sa·bl, *a.* That may or can be erased.—**eraser,** i·rā′sėr, *n.* One who or that which erases; a sharp instrument, prepared caoutchouc and the like, used to erase writing, etc.—**erasure,** i·rā′zhėr, *n.* The act of erasing or scratching out; obliteration; the place where a word or letter has been erased.

Erastian, i·ras′ti·an, *n.* One whose opinions are the same or akin to those of Thomas *Erastus,* a German divine of the sixteenth century, who maintained the complete subordination of the ecclesiastical to the secular power.—*a.* Pertaining to the doctrines of Erastus or his followers.—**Erastianism,** i·ras′ti·an·izm, *n.* The doctrines or principles of Erastus or his followers; in a loose and inaccurate sense, the doctrine that an established church should be under the complete control of the state.

erbium, ėr′bi·um, *n.* [From *Ytterby,* in Sweden.] A metallic element of the rare-earth series. Symbol, Er; at. no., 68; at. wt., 167.26.

ere, âr, *adv.* or *conj.* [A.Sax. *aer*=D. *eer,* Icel. *ár,* Goth. *air,* before, sooner, earlier. It is the positive form, of which *erst* is the superlative.] Before; sooner than.—*prep.* Before, in respect of time.—**erelong,** âr·long′, *adv.* Before the lapse of a long time; before long; soon.—**erenow,** âr·nou′, *adv.* Before this time.—**erewhile,** âr′hwīl″, *adv.* Some time ago; a little time before.

Erebus, er′e·bus, *n.* [L. *erebus,* Gr. *erebos.*] According to the belief of the Greeks and Romans a dark and gloomy region under the earth, through which the shades passed into Hades.

erect, i·rekt′, *a.* [L. *erectus,* pp. of *erigo,* to erect—*e,* out, and *rego,* to straighten. REGENT.] In a perpendicular posture; upright; directed upward; raised; uplifted; firm; bold; unshaken.—*v.t.* To raise and set in an upright or perpendicular position, or nearly so; to set upright; to raise up; to construct; to set up; to build; to establish; to found; to form; to elevate; to exalt; to lift up; to encourage.— **erecter,** i·rek′tėr, *n.* One who or that which erects.—**erectile,** i·rek′til, *a.* Susceptible of erection.— **erectility,** i·rek·til′i·ti, *n.* The quality of being erectile.—**erection,** i·rek′shon, *n.* The act of erecting; a raising and setting perpendicular; a setting upright; the act of constructing or building; establishment; settlement; formation; anything erected; a building of any kind.— **erectly,** i·rekt′li, *adv.* In an erect posture.—**erectness,** i·rekt′nes, *n.* The state of being erect.—**erector,** i·rek′tėr, *n.* One who or that which erects.

eremite, er′e·mīt, *n.* [L. *eremita,* Late Gr. *erēmitēs,* from Gr. *erēmos,*

alone, desert.] One who lives in a wilderness or in retirement; a hermit.—**eremitic, eremitical,** er·ē·mit′ik, er·e·mit′i·kal, *a.* Relating to, having the character of, or like an eremite or hermit.

erethism, er′e·thizm, *n.* [Gr. *erethismos,* irritation, from *erethizō,* to stir.] *Med.* a morbid energy or excitement in any organ or tissue.

erg, ėrg, *n.* [Gr. *ergon,* work.] *Physics.* a unit of work, being the work done by a force which, acting for one second upon a mass of one gram (15.4 grains), produces a velocity of a centimeter (.3937 inch) per second.

ergot, ėr′got, *n.* [Fr. *ergot, argot,* a spur, ergot.] A diseased state of rye and other grasses, caused by the attack of a minute fungus on the seeds or grains; the diseased grain itself.—**ergotism,** ėr′go·tizm, *n.* An epidemic occurring in moist districts from the use of ergoted rye in food.

ericaceous, er·i·kā′shus, *a.* [L. *erica,* heath.] Of or belonging to the nat. order of heaths.

Erin, â′rin, *n.* [Uncertain origin.] Ireland.

eringo, e·ring′gō, *n.* Same as *Eryngo*.

Erinys, i·rin′is, *n.* pl. **Erinyes,** i·rin′i·ēz, *Greek myth.* one of the Furies; a goddess of discord.

eristic, eristical, ē·ris′tik, ē·ris′ti·kal, *a.* [Gr. *eristikos,* contentious, from *eris,* strife.] Pertaining to disputation or controversy; controversial; captious.

erlking, *n.* King of the elves, haunting the Black Forest, in poem by Goethe.

ermine, ėr′min, *n.* [O.Fr. *ermine,* Mod. Fr. *hermine,* from the Teut.; comp. Dan. Sw. and G. *hermelin,* O.G. *harm, harmo,* an ermine.] A quadruped of the weasel tribe found over temperate Europe, but common only in the north, much sought after in the winter on account of its fur, which is white at that season: known also as the *stoat;* the fur of the ermine, long considered as an emblem of purity; *fig.* the office or dignity of a judge, from his state robe being ornamented or bordered with ermine.—**ermined,** ėr′mind, *a.* Clothed or adorned with ermine.

erne, ėrn, *n.* [A.Sax. *earn*=Dan. and Sw. *ern,* an eagle, allied to G. *aar,* an eagle, and to Skr. *ara,* swift, from *ri,* to go.] A name sometimes given to the white-tailed sea eagle, the bald eagle, and other allied species.

erode, i·rōd′, *v.t.*—*eroded, eroding.* [L. *erodo*—*e,* and *rodo,* to gnaw, whence *rodent.*] To eat into or away; to corrode.—**erose,** i·rōs′, *a.* [L. *erosus.*] *Bot.* having small irregular sinuses in the margin, as if gnawed.—**erosion,** i·rō′zhon, *n.* [L. *erosio.*] The act or operation of eating or wearing away; *geol.* the wearing away of soil or rock by the influence of water and ice (especially in the form of glaciers).—**erosive,** i·rō′siv, *a.* Having the property of eating, corroding or wearing away.

ch, *chain;* *ch,* Sc. lo*ch;* g, *go;* j, *job;* ng, si*ng;* TH, *then;* th, *thin;* w, *wig;* hw, *whig;* zh, a*z*ure.

erotic, i·rot′ik, *a.* [Gr. *erōtikos,* from *erōs, erōtos,* love.] Pertaining to or prompted by love; treating of love.— *n.* An amorous composition or poem.

err, èr, *v.i.* [L. *erro, erratum,* to wander, to err; allied to G. *irren,* to wander, to go astray.] To wander from the right way; to go astray; to deviate from the path of duty; to fail morally; to transgress; to mistake in judgment or opinion; to blunder; to misapprehend.— **errant,** er′rant, *a.* [L. *errans, errantis,* ppr. of *erro,* to err.] Wandering; roving; rambling: applied particularly to the knights of yore who wandered about to seek adventures. —**errantry,** er′rant·ri, *n.* A wandering; a roving or rambling about; the condition or way of life of a knight-errant.—**erratic,** er·rat′ik, *a.* [L. *erraticus.*] Wandering; devious; having no certain course; irregular or peculiar in movements or actions; eccentric; peculiar; queer.—*Erratic blocks,* or *Erratics,* in *geol.* boulders or fragments of rocks which appear to have been transported from their original sites by ice in the pleistocene period, and carried often to great distances.—**erratically,** er·rat′i·kal·li, *adv.* In an erratic manner. —**erratum,** er·rä′tum, *n.* pl. **errata,** er·rä′ta, [L. *erratum,* a blunder.] An error or mistake in writing or printing.—**erroneous,** er·rō′ni·us, *a.* [L. *erroneus.*] Characterized by or containing error or errors; wrong; mistaken; false; inaccurate.—**erroneously,** er·rō′ni·us·li, *adv.* In an erroneous manner.—**erroneousness,** er·rō′ni·us·nes, *n.* The state of being erroneous.—**error,** er′rėr, *n.* [L. *error.*] An unintentional wandering or deviation from truth or what is right; a going wrong; a mistake; a misapprehension; a mistake made in writing, printing, calculation, or other performance; an inaccuracy; an oversight; a transgression of law or duty; a fault; a sin.

errand, er′rand, *n.* [A.Sax. *aerend, aerynd.* Dan. *aerrende,* Icel. *eyrendi, erendi,* O.G; *âranti, ârunti,* an errand, a message; Goth. *airus,* a message, a messenger.] A special business entrusted to a messenger; something to be told or done by one expressly sent.

Erse, èrs, *n.* [A variation of *Irish.*] The Celtic language spoken in the Highlands of Scotland, of Irish origin; Gaelic.

erubescence, er·u·bes′ens, *n.* [L. *erubesco,* to become red—*e,* and *ruber,* red (whence *rubric*).] A becoming red; redness of the skin or surface of anything; a blushing.— **erubescent,** er·u·bes′ent, *a.* Red or reddish; blushing.

eructate, i·ruk′tāt, *v.t.* [L. *eructo, eructatum—e,* out, and *ructo,* to belch.] To eject, as wind from the stomach; to belch.—**eructation,** i·ruk·tā′shon, *n.* [L. *eructatio.*] The act of belching wind from the stomach; a belch; a violent bursting forth or ejection of matter from the earth.

erudite, er′u·dīt, *a.* [L. *eruditus,* from *erudio,* to polish, to instruct—*e,* out, and *rudis,* rough, rude.] Fully instructed; learned; deeply read; characterized by erudition.—**eruditely,** er′u·dīt·li, *adv.* In an erudite manner.—**eruditeness,** er′u·dīt·nes, *n.* The quality of being erudite.— **erudition,** er·u·dish′on, *n.* Knowledge gained by study or from books and instruction; learning in literature, as distinct from the sciences; scholarship.

erupt, i·rupt′, *v.t.* [L. *erumpo, eruptum,* to break out—*e,* out, and *rumpo, ruptum,* to burst or break, as in *corrupt, disrupt,* etc.] To force out by internal action.—*v.i.* To become violent; to emit.—**eruption,** i·rup′shon, *n.* The act of breaking or bursting forth from enclosure or confinement; a violent emission of lava, etc.; the breaking out of a cutaneous disease; the rash, pustules, etc., accompanying the disease.—**eruptive,** i·rup′tiv, *a.*

erysipelas, er·i·sip′e·las, *n.* [Gr.— *erythros,* red, and *pella,* skin.] A contagious disease of the skin tissue, caused by a streptococcus and marked by inflammation of the infected area and high fever.

erythema, er·i·thē′ma, *n.* [Gr., from *erythros,* red.] A superficial redness of some portion of the skin without blisters and uninfectious.—**erythematic, erythematous,** er′i·thē′mat″ik, er·i·them′a·tus, *a.* Of the nature of erythema.

erythrite, e·rith′rīt, *n.* [Gr. *erythros,* red.] A mineral, a hydrous arsenate of cobalt; also a rose-red feldspar.

erythrocyte, i·rith′rä·sīt, *n.* [Gr. *erythro,* red, and *cyte,* hollow, vessel.] The red blood cell.

escalade, es·ka·lād′, *n.* [Fr., from L. *scala,* a ladder. SCALE.] A furious attack made by troops on a fortified place, in which ladders are used to pass a ditch or mount a rampart.— *v.t.*—*escaladed, escalading.* To climb up or over.—**escalate,** es′ka·lāt, *v.t.* To ascend slowly; to increase gradually the scope of a war, as calculated strategy, from the level of an incident to the level of nuclear warfare.— **escalation,** es′ka·lā′shon, *n.*—**escalator,** es″ka·lāt′ėr, *n.* A continuously ascending or descending stairway on an endless belt.

escalop, es·kal′op, *n.* [O.Fr. *escalope,* SCALLOP.] A kind of bivalve; a scallop.

escape, es·kāp′, *v.t.*—*escaped, escaping.* [O.Fr. *escaper,* Fr. *échapper,* Sp. Pg. Pr. *escapar,* to escape; from *ex,* out, and L.L. *cappa, capa,* a mantle (comp. *cape, cap*), lit. to slip out of one's mantle.] To flee from and avoid; to get out of the way of; to shun; to be unnoticed by.—*v.i.* To flee, shun, and be secure from danger; to be free, or get free, from any injury; to hasten or get away; to free one's self from custody or restraint; to regain one's liberty.—*n.* Flight to shun danger or injury; the act of fleeing from danger or imprisonment; the condition of being passed by without receiving injury, when danger threatens.—**escapable,**

es·kā′pa·bl, *a.*—**escapade,** es·ka·pād′, *n.* A freakish or mad prank; a wild adventure.—**escapement,** es·kāp′ment, *n.* The general contrivance in a timepiece by which the rotatory motion of the wheels gives rise to or maintains the vibratory motion of the pendulum or balance wheel.—**escapism,** es·kāp′izm, *n.* Continually diverting the mind to fantasy, as an escape from reality.—**escape mechanism,** *n.* A mode of thinking devised to avoid unpleasant situations.— **escape velocity,** *n.* The minimum speed a vehicle requires to escape the gravitational field of the earth or other planet.

escarp, es·kärp′, *v.t.* [Fr. *escarper,* to cut steep, as rocks or slopes. SCARP.] *Fort.* To slope; to form a slope to.—*n.* Same as *Scarp.*—**escarpment,** es·kärp′ment, *n. Fort.* ground cut away nearly vertically about a position in order to make it inaccessible to an enemy; also, the precipitous side of any hill or rock; a steep ridge of land; a cliff.

eschar, es·kär′, *n.* [Gr. *eschara,* a fireplace, a scab.] The crust or scab occasioned on the skin by burns or caustic applications. —**escharotic,** es·ka·rot′ik, *a.* Caustic; having the power of searing or destroying the flesh.—*n.* An application which sears or destroys flesh.

eschatology, es·ka·tol′o·ji, *n.* [Gr. *eschatos,* last, and *logos,* discourse.] The doctrine of the last or final things, as death, judgment, etc.

escheat, es·chēt′, *n.* [O.Fr. *eschet,* from *escheir, escheoir,* Mod. Fr. *échoir,* from L. *excadere—ex,* and *cadere,* to fall (whence *cadence, decay,* etc.). *Cheat* is shortened from this.] The resulting back or reverting of any land or tenements to the state or sovereign through failure of heirs, and formerly also by forfeiture or attainder; the property which falls to the state in this way.—*v.i.* To become an escheat.—*v.t.* To cause to be an escheat; to forfeit.—**escheatable,** es·chē′ta·bl, *a.*

eschew, es·chö′, *v.t.* [O.Fr. *eschever,* Fr. *esquiver,* to avoid, to shun, from O.G. *skiuhan,* G. *scheuen,* to avoid; akin to E. *shy.*] To flee from; to shun; to seek to avoid; to avoid.

escort, es′kort, *n.* [Fr. *escorte,* from It. *scorta,* a guard or guide, from *scorgere,* to guide, from L. *ex,* and *corrigere,* to correct.] Persons attending one as a mark of respect, honor, or attention; protection or safeguard on a journey or excursion. —*v.t.* es·kort′. To accompany as a guard or protector.

escrow, es′krō, *n.* [Fr. *escroue,* scroll.] *Law.* a written agreement, such as a bond, deed, etc., that is deposited with a person, and to be delivered by him to the grantee only upon the fulfillment of a condition.

escritoire, es·kri·twär′, *n.* [O.Fr. *escritoire,* from L. *scriptorium,* connected with writing, *scribo, scriptum,* to write. SCRIBE.] A desk or chest of drawers with an apartment for writing materials; a writing desk.

esculent, es′ku·lent, *a.* [L. *esculentus,*

from *esca*, food, from *edo*, to eat.] Capable of or fit for being used by man for food; edible.—*n.* Something that is eatable; an edible.

escutcheon, es·kuch'on, *n.* [O.Fr. *escusson*, from L. *scutum*, a shield. ESQUIRE.] The shield on which a coat of arms is represented; the shield of a family; a plate for protecting the keyhole of a door, or to which the handle is attached; a scutcheon.

esker, eskar, es'kêr, *n.* [Ir. *eiscir*.] In *geol.* a term for a long linear ridge of sand and gravel, common in regions where ice sheets have prevailed, and belonging to glacial phenomena.

Eskimo, es'ki·mō, *n.* pl. **eskimos,** es'ki·mōz. One of a race of men, generally short in stature, with broad oval faces and small oblique eyes, inhabiting the northern parts of North America and Greenland.

esophagus, ē·sof'a·gus, *n.* [Gr. *oisophagos*—*oisō*, I will bear, and *phagō*, to eat.] The gullet; the canal through which food and drink pass to the stomach.

esoteric, es·o·ter'ik, *a.* [Gr. *esōterikos*, from *esō*, within.] Taught only to a select number, and not intelligible to a general body of disciples; designed for, and understood only by, the initiated; private; opposed to *exoteric* or public.

espalier, es·pal'yêr, *n.* [Fr., from It. *spalliera*, a support for the shoulders, from *spalla*, a shoulder, L. *spathula*, *spatula*, a broad blade, dim. of *spatha*. EPAULET.] A broad piece of trellis work on which the branches of fruit trees or bushes are trained; a row of trees so trained.—*v.t.* To form an espalier of, or to train as an espalier.

esparto, es·pär'tō, *n.* [Sp., from L. *spartum*, Gr. *sparton*, *spartos*.] A name of two or three species of grass found in southern Spain and North Africa, and extensively exported to be used in the manufacture of paper, matting, baskets, etc.

especial, es·pesh'al, *a.* [O.Fr. *especial*, Fr. *spécial*, L. *specialis*, of particular sort or kind, special, from *species*, kind. SPECIES.] Of a distinct sort or kind; special; particular; marked; peculiar.—**especially,** es·pesh'al·li, *adv.* In an especial manner; particularly; specially; peculiarly.

Esperanto, es·per·ant'ō. A language formed for the purpose of enabling the inhabitants of all countries to converse with each other.

espial, espionage. See ESPY.

esplanade, es·pla·nād', *n.* [Fr., from the old verb *esplaner*, to make level, from L. *explanare*—*ex*, and *planus*, plain, level.] *Fort.* a wide open space between the glacis of a citadel and the first houses of the town; any open level space near a town, especially a kind of terrace along the seaside, for public walks or drives.

espouse, es·pouz', *v.t.*—*espoused, espousing.* [O.Fr. *espouser* (Fr. *épouser*), from L. *sponsare*, to betroth, to espouse, freq. of *spondeo, sponsum*, to pledge one's self, whence *despond, respond.*] To give or take in marriage; to promise, engage, or bestow in

marriage by contract or pledge; to betroth; to marry; to wed; to become a partisan in; to embrace or to adopt (a cause, a quarrel).—**espousal,** es·pou'zal, *n.* [O.Fr. *espousailles*, L. *sponsalia*, espousals, pl. n. of *sponsalis*, relating to betrothal.] The act of espousing or betrothing: frequently used in the plural; the adopting or taking up of a cause.—**espouser,** es·pou'zêr, *n.* One who espouses.

espy, es·pī', *v.t.*—*espied, espying.* [O.Fr. *espier*, It. *spiare*; same word as *spy*.] To see at a distance; to have the first sight of; to descry; to discover, as something concealed, or as if unexpectedly or unintentionally; to inspect; to spy.—**espial,** es·pī'al, *n.* The act of espying; observation; discovery.—**espionage,** es'pi·o·nij', *n.* The practice or employment of spies; the practice of watching the conduct and words of others as a spy.

esquire, es·kwīr' or es', *n.* [O.Fr. *escuyer*, Fr. *écuyer*, lit. a shield bearer, from L. *scutarius*, a soldier armed with a *scutum*, or shield, from root *sku*, to cover or protect.] Originally, a shield bearer or armor bearer; an attendant on a knight; hence, a title of dignity next in degree below a knight; a title properly given in Great Britain to the younger sons of noblemen, to justices of the peace, sheriffs, landed proprietors, etc. [*cap.*] A complimentary adjunct (usually abbreviated to *Esq.*) to a name in addressing letters, etc., to almost any person of respectable standing.

essay, es·sā', *v.t.* [Fr. *essayer*. ASSAY.] To exert one's power or faculties on; to make an effort to perform; to try; to attempt; to endeavor to do; to make experiment of.—*n.* (es'sā). An effort made for the performance of anything; a trial, attempt; or endeavor; a test or experiment; a literary composition intended to prove some particular point or illustrate a particular subject, not having the importance of a regular treatise; a short disquisition on a subject of taste, philosophy, or common life.—**essayer,** *n.* One who essays (pronounced es·sā'êr); one who writes essays; an essayist (pronounced es'sā·êr).†—**essayist,** es'sā·ist, *n.* A writer of an essay or of essays.

essence, es'sens, *n.* [Fr., from L. *essentia*, from *esse*, to be; akin *entity*.] That which constitutes the particular nature of a thing, and which distinguishes it from all others; that which makes a thing what it is; existence; a being having existence; constituent substance; the predominant elements or principles of any plant or drug extracted, refined, or rectified from grosser matter; an extract; perfume; odor; scent; the most important or fundamental doctrines, facts, ideas, or conclusions (the *essence* of a lecture, a statement).—*v.t.* To perfume; to scent.—**essential,** es·sen'shal, *a.* Being of or pertaining to the essence; necessary to the constitution or existence of a thing; constituting a thing what it is;

important in the highest degree; indispensable; volatile; diffusible (*essential* oils).—*n.* What is essential; fundamental or constituent principle; distinguishing characteristic.—**essentiality, essentialness,** es·sen''shi·al''i·ti, es·sen'shal·nes, *n.* The quality of being essential.—**essentially,** es·sen'shal·li, *adv.* In an essential manner; fundamentaly.

Essene, es·sēn', *n. pl.* [Gr. *Essēnoi*, L. *Esseni*.] Among the Jews, a member of a sect remarkable for their strictness and abstinence.

establish, es·tab'lish, *v.t.* [O.Fr. *establir* (Fr. *établir*), from L. *stabilio*, to make firm, to establish, from *sta*, root of *sto*, to stand. STAND.] To make steadfast, firm, or stable; to settle on a firm or permanent basis; to set or fix unalterably; to institute and ratify; to enact or decree authoritatively and for permanence; to ordain; to strengthen; to prove; to confirm; to originate and secure the permanent existence of; to found permanently; to set up in connection with the state and endow (a church); to set up in business.—**establisher,** es·tab'lish·êr, *n.* One who establishes.—**establishment,** es·tab'lish·ment, *n.* The act of establishing; the state of being established; settlement; fixed state; confirmation; a permanent civil or military force or organization, such as a fixed garrison or a local government; that form of doctrine and church government established by the legislature in any country; the place where a person is settled either for residence or for transacting business; a person's residence and everything connected with it, such as furniture, servants, carriages, etc.; an institution, whether public or private; the quota or number of men in an army, regiment, etc.

estafette, es·ta·fet', *n.* [Fr. *estafette*, from It. *staffetta*, a courier, from *staffa*, a stirrup, from O.H.G. *stapho* =E. *step*.] A military courier; an express of any kind.

estate, es·tāt', *n.* [O.Fr. *estat*, Fr. *état*, from L. *status*, a standing, state, from *sto, statum*, to stand. STAND.] Condition or circumstances of any person or thing; state; rank; quality; possessions; property; a piece of landed property; a definite portion of land in the ownership of some one; an order or class of men constituting a state; one of the classes of the nation invested with political rights, the *three estates of the realm*, in Britain, being the lords spiritual, the lords temporal, and the commons.—*The fourth estate*, the newspaper press; journalists.—*The Estates*, the old French and Scottish Parliament of nobles, clergy, burghers.—*The Third Estate—tiers état*, the commonalty.—*v.t.* To settle an estate upon (*Tenn.*)†; to bestow (*Shak.*)‡.

esteem, es·tēm', *v.t.* [Fr. *estimer*, L. *æstimare, estimatum*, from same root as Skr. *esha*, a wish, G. *heischen*, to desire. Akin *aim.*] To set a value on, whether high or low; to estimate;

to value; to set a high value on; to regard with reverence, respect, or friendship; to prize.—*n.* Opinion or judgment of merit or demerit; estimation; high value or estimation; great regard; favorable opinion, founded on supposed worth.—**esteemable,** es·tē′ma·bl, *a.* Worthy of esteem; estimable.—**estimable,** es′ti·ma·bl, *a.* Capable of being estimated or valued; worthy of esteem or respect; deserving our good opinion or regard.—**estimableness,** es′ti·ma·bl·nes, *n.* The quality of being estimable.—**estimably,** es′ti·ma·bli, *adv.* In an estimable manner. —**estimate,** es′ti·māt, *v.t.—estimated estimating.* [L. *æstimare, æstimatum.*] To form a judgment or opinion regarding; especially applied to value, size, weight, degree, extent, quantity, etc.; to rate by judgment, opinion, or a rough calculation; to fix the worth of; to compute; to calculate; to reckon.—*n.* A valuing or rating in the mind; an approximate judgment or opinion as to value, degree, extent, quantity, etc.—**estimation,** es·ti·mā′shon, *n.* [L. *æstimatio.*] The act of estimating; calculation; computation; an estimate; esteem; regard; favorable opinion; honor.—**estimative,** es′ti·ma·tiv, *a.* Having the power of estimating.—**estimator,** es′ti·mā·tėr, *n.* One who estimates or values.

ester, es′tėr, *n.* [G. *essigäther,* ethyl acetate—from *essig,* vinegar, and *äther,* ether.] A compound formed by the reaction of alchohol plus an acid with the elimination of water.

esthesia, es·thē′zha, *n.* [Gr. *aisthēsis,* perception, sensibility.] Perception; feeling; sensibility.—**esthesiology,** es·thē′zi·ol″o·ji, *n.* The doctrine or branch of knowledge concerned with the sensations.

esthesiometer, es·thē′zi·om″et·ėr, *n.* [Gr. *aisthēsis,* perception, and *metron,* a measure.] An instrument for testing the tactile sensibility of the human body in health and disease.

esthete, esthetic, etc. Same as *Aesthete.*

estival,† es′ti·val, *a.* [L. *æstivus,* from *æstas,* summer.] Pertaining to summer.—**estivate,**† es′ti·vāt, *v.i.* [L. *æstivo, æstivatum.*] To pass the summer.—**estivation, aestivation,** es·ti·vā′shon, *n. Bot.* the manner in which the parts of a flower bud are arranged with respect to each other before opening; the disposition of the petals within the flower bud— *vernation* being the disposition of leaves.

estop, es·top′, *v.t.—estopped, estopping.* [O.Fr. *estoper,* Fr. *étouper,* to stop with tow, from L. *stupa, stuppa,* tow.] *Law,* to impede or bar by one's own act.—**estoppel,** es·top′el, *n. Law,* a stop; a plea in bar, grounded on a man's own act.

estovers, es·tō′vėrz, *n. pl.* [O.Fr. *estoveir, estovoir,* to be needful.] *Law,* the right of taking the necessary amount of wood from an estate for fuel, fences, repairs, and other reasonable purposes.

estrange, es·trānj′, *v.t.—estranged,*

estranging. [O.Fr. *estranger,* from L.L. *extraneus,* foreign, strange. STRANGE.] To keep apart or out of friendly relations; to make to cease from being familiar; to alienate; to turn from kindness to indifference or malevolence; to apply to a purpose foreign from its original or customary one.—**estrangement,** es·trānj′ment, *n.* The act of estranging or state of being estranged.

estray, es·trā′, *n.* A stray, or animal that has strayed from the custody of its owner.

estreat, es·trēt′, *n.* [O.Fr. *estraite,* from L. *extraho, extractum,* to draw out.] *Law,* a true copy of an original writing, under which fines are to be levied.—*v.t. Law,* to levy (fines) under an estreat.

estrogen, es′trä·jen, *n.* [L. *estrus,* frenzy, and *gen,* producer.] Any compound acting as a female hormone, causing sexual receptivity and the development of secondary sex characteristics.

estuary, es′tū·a·ri, *n.* [L. *æstuarium,* from *æstuo,* to boil or foam, *æstus,* heat, tide.] The wide mouth of a river where the tide meets the currents, or flows and ebbs; a firth.

eta, āt′ä, *n.* [Gr. *eta;* akin to Heb. *heth.*] The seventh letter of the Greek alphabet, whose symbol is H.

et cetera, et·set′ėr·a. [L. *et,* and *cætera,* other things.] And others of the like kind: written also *Etcaetera, Etcetera,* and commonly contracted *etc., &c.*

etch, ech, *v.t.* and *i.* [From D. *etsen,* G. *ätzen,* to corrode by acids, to etch; lit. to bite into; O.H.G. *ezan,* to eat. EAT.] To produce figures or designs upon a plate of steel, copper, glass, or the like, by means of lines drawn through a thin coating or ground covering the plate and corroded or *bitten in* by some strong acid, which can only affect the plate where the coating has been removed by the etching instrument.—**etcher,** ech′ėr, *n.* One who etches.—**etching,** ech′ing, *n.* The art or operation of an etcher; a design or picture produced by an etcher.

eternal, i·tėr′nal, *a.* [Fr. *éternel;* L. *æternus, æviternus,* from *ævum,* an age, and adj. suffix *-ternus.* AGE.] Having no beginning or end of existence; everlasting; endless; continued without intermission; ceaseless; perpetual.—*The Eternal,* an appellation of God.—**eternally,** i·tėr′nal·li, *adv.* In an eternal manner; without beginning or end of duration; perpetually; unceasingly; continually.—**eternity,** i·tėr′ni·ti, *n.* The condition or quality of being eternal; duration or continuance without beginning or end; endless past time or endless future time; the state or condition which begins at death.— **eternize,** i·tėr′nīz, *v.t.—eternized, eternizing.* [Fr. *éterniser.*] To make eternal or endless; to perpetuate; to make for ever famous; to immortalize.

etesian, i·tē′zhan, *a.* [L. *etesius,* from Gr. *etēsios,* annual, from *etos,* a year.] [*often cap.*] Recurring every

year; blowing at stated times of the year: applied to the periodical winds in the Mediterranean.

ethane, eth′ān, *n.* A hydrocarbon (C_2H_6) allied to marsh gas (CH_4).

ether, ē′thėr, *n.* [L. *æther,* from Gr. *aithēr,* from *aithō,* to light up, to kindle, to burn or blaze; cog. L. *ætas,* summer heat, *Ætna,* Skr. *indh,* to set on fire, *iddhas,* bright.] The supposed subtle atmosphere in space beyond the earth's atmosphere; a hypothetical medium of extreme tenuity and elasticity supposed to be diffused throughout all space (as well as among the molecules of which solid bodies are composed), and to be the medium of the transmission of light and heat; a very light, volatile, and flammable fluid, obtained from alcohol, an excellent solvent of fats and resins, and used as a stimulant, antispasmodic, and anesthetic.—**ethereal,** i·thē′ri·al, *a.* Formed of ether or the fine atmosphere pervading all space; containing or filled with ether; belonging to the sky regions; heavenly; celestial.— **ethereality,** i·the′ri·al′i·ti, *n.* The state or quality of being ethereal.— **etherealize,** i·thē′ri·al·īz, *v.t.—etherealized, etherealizing.* To convert into ether; to purify and refine; to render spirit-like or ethereal.— **etherealization,** i·thē′ri·al·i·zā″shon, *n.* An ethereal or subtle spirit-like state or condition.—**ethereally,** i·thē′ri·al·li, *adv.* In an ethereal, celestial, or heavenly manner.— **etherification,** i·thē′ri·fi·kā″shon, *n.* The process of ether formation.— **etherization,** ē′thėr·i·zā″shon, *n.* The act of administering ether to a patient; the state of the system when under the influence of ether.— **etherize,** ē′thėr·īz, *v.t.—etherized, etherizing.* To convert into ether; to subject to the influence of ether.

ethic, ethical, eth′ik, eth′i·kal, *a.* [L. *ethicus,* from Gr. *ēthikos,* from *ēthos,* custom, habit.] Relating to morals; treating of morality; containing precepts of morality; moral. —**ethically,** eth′i·kal·li, *adv.* In an ethical manner.—**ethics,** eth′iks, *n.* The science which treats of the nature and grounds of moral obligation; moral philosophy, which teaches men their duty and the reasons of it; the science of duty.

Ethiop, Ethiopian, ē′thi·op, ē·thi·ō′pi·an, *n.* [Gr. *Aithiops—aithō,* to burn, and *ōps,* countenance.] A native of Ethiopia; a Negro or black man.—**Ethiopian,** *a.* Relating to Ethiopia or to its inhabitants.— **Ethiopic,** ē·thi·op′ik, *n.* The language of Ethiopia; the literary and ecclesiastical language of Abyssinia, one of the Semitic tongues.—*a.* Relating to Ethiopia.

ethmoid, ethmoidal, eth′moid, eth·moi′dal, *a.* [Gr. *ēthmos,* a sieve, and *eidos,* form.] Resembling a sieve.— *Ethmoid bone,* a light spongy bone situated between the orbital processes at the root of the nose, its pores forming passages for the olfactory nerves.

ethnic, ethnical, eth′nik, eth′ni·kal,

a. [L. *ethnicus*, from Gr. *ethnikos*, from *ethnos*, nation, pl. *ta ethnē*, the nations, heathens, gentiles.] Not Christian or Jewish; heathen; relating to a people, or race, with common physical and cultural traits.—**ethnically,** eth′ni·kal·li, *adv.*—**ethnocentric,** eth·nō′sen′trik, *a.* Having race as a main interest; believing that one's own race is superior.—**ethnographer,** eth·nog′ra·fėr, *n.* One who cultivates ethnography.—**ethnographic, ethnographical,** eth·no·graf′ik, eth·no·graf′i·kal, *a.*—**ethnographically,** eth·no·graf′i·kal·li, *adv.*—**ethnography,** eth·nog′ra·fi, *n.* That branch of science which has for its subject the description of the different races of men, or the manners, customs, religion, etc., peculiar to different nations.—**ethnologic, ethnological,** eth·no·loj′ik, eth·no·loj′i·kal, *a.* Relating to ethnology.—**ethnologist,** eth·nol′o·jist, *n.* One skilled in ethnology; a student of ethnology.—**ethnology,** eth·nol′o·ji, *n.* That branch of science which investigates the mental and physical differences of mankind and the organic laws on which they depend.

ethology, eth·ol′o·ji, *n.* [Gr. *ethos* or *ēthos*, manners, morals, and *logos*, discourse.] The science of ethics; the science of character.—**ethological,** eth·o·loj′i·kal, *a.*

ethos, ē′thäs, *n.* [Gr. *ethos*, character.] One's character and disposition; the fundamental spiritual characteristics of a culture.

ethyl, eth′il, *n.* [*Ether*, and Gr. *hylē*, matter.] A univalent hydrocarbon radical.—**ethylene,** eth′i·lēn, *n.* A colorless, highly flammable gas found in coal gas and used as an anesthetic and fuel.

etiolate, ē′ti·o·lāt, *v.i.*—*etiolated, etiolating.* [Fr. *étioler*, to blanch, from *éteule*, stubble, from L. *stipula*, a straw.] To grow white from absence of the normal amount of green coloring matter in the leaves or stalks; to be whitened by excluding the light of the sun, as plants.—*v.t.* To blanch or whiten by excluding the light or by disease.—**etiolation,** ē′ti·o·lā″shon, *n.* The act of etiolating or state of being etiolated or blanched.

etiology, ē·ti·ol′o·ji, *n.* [Gr. *aitia*, cause, and *logos*, discourse.] An account of the causes of anything, particularly of diseases.—**etiological,** ē′ti·o·loj″i·kal, *a.* Pertaining to etiology.

etiquette, et′i·ket, *n.* [Fr.; O.Fr. *estiquette*, a thing attached, a label, from G. *stecken*, to stick, to put. *Ticket* is same word.] Conventional forms of ceremony or decorum; the forms which are observed toward particular persons, or in particular places; social observances required by good breeding.

etna, et′na, *n.* [From *Etna*, the Sicilian volcano.] A table cooking utensil, heated by an alcohol lamp.

Etruscan, i·trus′kan, *a.* Relating to Etruria, an ancient country in Central Italy.—*n.* A native of ancient Etruria.

étude, ā·tūd′, *n.* [Fr.] A musical or artistic composition designed to serve as a study.

etui, etwee, et·wē′, *n.* [Fr. *étui.*] A pocket case for small articles, such as needles, pins, etc.; a ladies' reticule.

etymology, et·i·mol′o·ji, *n.* [Gr. *etymos*, true or real, *to etymon*, the true or literal signification of a word, its root, and *logos*, discourse.] That part of philology which explains the origin and derivation of words; derivation; that part of grammar which comprehends the various inflections and modifications of words.—**etymologic, etymological,** et′i·mo·loj″ik, et′i·mo·loj″i·kal, *a.* Pertaining to or treating of etymology or the derivation of words.—**etymologically,** et′i·mo·loj″i·kal·li, *adv.* In an etymological manner.—**etymologist,** et·i·mol′o·jist, *n.* One versed in etymology; one who searches into the origin of words.—**etymologize,** et·i·mol′o·jīz, *v.i.* To search into the origin of words.—*v.t.* To trace the etymology of; to give the etymology of.—**etymon,** et′i·mon, *n.* The root of a word.

eucaine, ū·kān′, *n.* A complex synthetic substance used as a local anesthetic.

eucalyptol, ū′ka·lip″tol, *n.* [From *eucalyptus*, and *oleum*, oil.] The oil of the blue gum tree (*Eucalyptus globulus*), used as a remedy for asthma and other ailments.—**eucalyptus,** ū·ka·lip′tus, *n.* [Gr. *eu*, well, and *kalypto*, to cover—referring to the cover of the flower bud.] The eucalyptus, a genus of very large trees of the myrtle order, natives of Australia, called gum trees, from the gum that exudes from them, also stringy bark, ironbark, etc.

eucharis, ū′ka·ris, *n.* [Gr. *eucharis*, pleasing.] South American plant of the bulbous kind, with white flowers of bell shape.

Eucharist, ū′ka·rist, *n.* [Gr. *eucharistia*, thanksgiving, the Lord's Supper, *eucharistos*, grateful—*eu*, well, good, and *charis*, grace, favor.] The sacrament of the Lord's Supper; the Communion; the consecrated elements, and especially the bread; thanksgiving.—**Eucharistic, Eucharistical,** ū·ka·ris′tik, ū·ka·ris′ti·kal, *a.* Pertaining to the Eucharist.

euchre, ū′kėr, *n.* [Origin unknown.] A game of cards, played by two, three, or four players with the thirty-two highest cards of the pack.

euclase, ū′klās, *n.* [Gr. *eu*, and *klao*, to break.] A mineral of the beryl family, of a pale-green color and very brittle.

eudemonism, ū·dē′mon·izm, *n.* [Gr. *eudaimōn*, happy.] The system of philosophy which makes human happiness the highest object, declaring that the production of happiness is the foundation of virtue.—**eudemonist,** ū·dē′mon·ist, *n.* A believer in eudemonism.

eudiometer, ū·di·om′e·tėr, *n.* [Gr. *eudios*, serene, and *metron*, measure.] An instrument usually in the form of a glass siphon with a graduated limb, originally designed for ascertaining the purity of the air, but now employed generally in the analysis of gases by the electric spark.—**eudiometric, eudiometrical,** ū′di·o·met″rik, ū′di·o·met″ri·kal, *a.* Pertaining to a eudiometer or to eudiometry.—**eudiometry,** ū·di·om′et·ri, *n.* The art or practice of using the eudiometer.

eugenics, ū·jen′iks, *n.* [Gr. *eu*, well, *genos*, race.] The science that deals with the improvement of the hereditary traits of a race.—**eugenic,** ū·jen′ik, *a.*—**eugenically,** ū·jen′i·kal·li, *adv.*—**eugenicist,** ū·jen′i·sist, *n.* A believer in eugenics.

euhemerism, ū·hem′ėr·izm, *n.* [After the Greek *Euēmeros*, who explained myths in this way.] That system of interpreting myths by which the gods are regarded as representing distinguished men who formerly lived, and so the myths are considered as founded on real histories.—**euhemerist,** ū·hem′ėr·ist, *n.* A believer in the doctrine of euhemerism.—**euhemeristic,** ū·hem′ėr·is″tik, *a.* Of or belonging to euhemerism.—**euhemerize,** ū·hem′ėr·īz, *v.t.* To treat or explain in the manner of Euemeros. Also written *Euemerism*, etc.

eulogy, ū′lo·ji, *n.* [Gr. *eulogia*—*eu*, well, and *logos*, speech, from *legō*, to speak.] Praise; encomium; panegyric; a speech or writing in commendation of a person on account of his valuable qualities or services.—**eulogically,** ū·loj′i·kal·li, *adv.* In a eulogic manner.—**eulogist,** ū·lo·jist, *n.* One who praises and commends another; one who pronounces a eulogy.—**eulogistic, eulogistical,** ū·lo·jis′tik, ū·lo·jis′ti·kal, *a.* Containing or pertaining to eulogy or praise; laudatory.—**eulogistically,** ū·lo·jis′ti·kal·li, *adv.* With commendation or eulogy.—**eulogium,** ū·lō′ji·um, *n.* A formal eulogy.—**eulogize,** ū′lo·jīz, *v.t.*—*eulogized, eulogizing.* To speak or write in commendation of another; to extol in speech or writing; to praise.

Eumenides, ū·men′i·dēz, *n. pl. Lit.* the gracious goddesses, a Greek name of the Furies, because it was considered unlawful and dangerous to name them under their true designation *Erinnyes*.

eunuch, ū′nuk, *n.* [Gr. *eunouchos*—*cunē*, a bed, and *echō*, to keep, to have charge of.] A castrated male of the human species; hence, from the employment to which eunuchs were commonly put, a chamberlain.

eupepsia, ū·pep′si·a, *n.* [Gr. *eupepsia*—*eu*, and *pepsis*, digestion, from *peptō*, to digest.] Good digestion; the opposite of dyspepsia.—**eupeptic,** ū·pep′tik, *a.* Having good digestion; easy of digestion.

euphemism, ū′fem·izm, *n.* [Gr. *euphēmismos*—*eu*, well, and *phēmi*, to speak.] A figure of speech in which a delicate word or expression is substituted for one which is offensive to good manners or to delicate ears.—**euphemistic, euphemistical,** ū·fem·is′tik, ū·fem·is′ti·kal, *a.* Pertaining to or containing euphemism.

—**euphemize,** ū′fem·īz, v.t. To express by a euphemism.

euphony, ū′fo·ni, n. [Gr. euphōnia—eu, well, and phōne, voice.] An agreeable sound; an easy, smooth enunciation of sounds; a pronunciation of letters, syllables, and words which is pleasing to the ear.—**euphonic, euphonical,** ū·fon′ik, ū·fon′i·kal, a. Of or pertaining to, or characterized by, euphony; agreeable in sound; pleasing to the ear.—**euphonious,** ū·fō′ni·us, a. Agreeable in sound; euphonic.—**euphoniously,** ū·fō′ni·us·li, adv. In a euphonious manner.—**euphonium,** ū·fō′ni·um, n. A brass bass instrument with three or four valves, used in military bands, and frequently in the orchestra as a substitute for the trombone. —**euphonize,** ū′fo·nīz, v.t. To make agreeable in sound.

euphorbia, ū·for′bi·a, n. [Gr. euphorbia, from the name of an ancient Greek physician.] A genus of exogenous plants, some of which are found in Britain, and are popularly called spurges, while the most remarkable are tropical shrubs or trees, often large, fleshy, and leafless, having the habit of a cactaceous plant.

euphoria, ū·fōr′i·a, n. [Gr. eu, well, phoreō, I possess.] Feeling of well-being.

euphrasy, ū′fra·si, a. [Gr. euphrasia, delight.] The herb popularly called eyebright, formerly a specific for diseases of the eye.

euphuism, ū′fū·izm, n. [From the name of the hero of two works by John Lyly, written in a strange and affected style, which became fashionable at the court of Elizabeth.— Euphues is the Gr. euphyēs, well-shaped—eu, well, and phyē, growth, stature.] Affectation of excessive elegance and refinement of language; high-flown artificial diction.—**euphuist,** ū′fū·ist, n. One addicted to euphuism: applied particularly to certain writers, at the head of which stood John Lyly.—**euphuistic,** ū·fū·is′tik, a. Belonging to the euphuists or to euphuism.

eupnea, ūp·nē′a, n. [Gr. eu, well, pneō, I breathe.] Easy, natural breathing.

Eurasian, ū·rā′zhi·an, n. [A contraction of European and Asian.] A person of mixed European and Asiatic descent.

eureka, ū·rē′ka. [Gr. (h)eurēka, I have found, perf. ind. act. of (h)euriskō, to find.] The exclamation of Archimedes, when, after long study, he discovered a method of detecting the amount of alloy in King Hiero's crown: hence, a discovery; especially, one made after long research; an expression of triumph at a discovery or supposed discovery.

eurhythmy, ū·rith′mi, n. Artistic harmony; proportion; harmonious movement. Med. regularity of the pulse.

European, ū·ro·pē′an, a. [L. Europa, Gr. Eurōpē, Europe.] Pertaining to Europe; native to Europe.—n. A native of Europe.—**Europeanize,** ū·- ro·pē′an·īz, v.t. To cause to become European; to assimilate to Europeans in manners, character, and usages.

europium, u·rō′pi·um, n. [From Europe.] A metallic element of the rare-earth series. Symbol, Eu; at. no., 63; at. wt., 151.96.

Eustachian, ū·stā′ki·an, a. Named after Eustachius or Eustachi, an Italian physician, who died 1574.— Eustachian tube, the tube which forms a communication between the internal ear and the back part of the mouth.—Eustachian valve, a valve which separates the right auricle of the heart from the inferior vena cava.

euthanasia, ū·tha·nā′zha, n. [Gr.— eu, well, and thanatos, death.] An easy death; a putting to death by painless means; a means of putting to a painless death.

evacuate, i·vak′ū·āt, v.t.—evacuated, evacuating. [L. evacuo, evacuatum—e, out, and vacuus, empty, from vaco, to be empty. VACANT.] To make empty; to make empty by removing one's self from (an army evacuates a town or a country); to void or discharge from the bowels.—**evacuant,** i·vak′ū·ant, a. Producing evacuation; purgative.—n. A medicine which promotes the natural secretions and excretions.—**evacuation,** i·vak′ū·ā″shon, n. The act of evacuating; that which is evacuated or discharged, especially from the bowels. —**evacuator,** i·vak′ū·ā·tėr, n. One who or that which evacuates.

evade, i·vād′, v.t.—evaded, evading. [L. evado—e, and vado, to go, as in invade, pervade; akin to E. wade. WADE.] To avoid, escape from, or elude in any way, as by dexterity, artifice, sophistry, address, or ingenuity: to slip away from; to elude; to escape the grasp or comprehension of; to baffle or foil.—v.i. To escape; to slip away; to practice artifice or sophistry for the purpose of eluding.—**evadible,** i·vā′di·bl, a. Capable of being evaded.—**evasion,** i·vā′zhon, n. [L. evasio.] The act of evading, eluding, avoiding, or escaping; shift; subterfuge; equivocation; prevarication; shuffling.— **evasive,** i·vā′siv, a. Using evasion or artifice to avoid; shuffling; equivocating; containing or characterized by evasion.—**evasively,** i·vā′siv·li, adv. In an evasive manner.—**evasiveness,** i·vā′siv·nes, n.

evaluate, i·val′ū·āt, v.t. [Back formation of evaluation; L. valere, be worth.] To appraise carefully; to judge as to worth or amount.— **evaluation,** i·val′ū·ā″shon, n. Exhaustive appraisement.

evanesce, ev·a·nes′, v.i.—evanesced, evanescing. [L. evanesco—e, and vanesco, to vanish, from vanus, vain, empty. VAIN.] To vanish, to disappear; to be dissipated, as vapor.— **evanescence,** ev·a·nes′ens, n. The state or character of being evanescent.—**evanescent,** ev·a·nes′ent, a. Vanishing; subject to vanishing, fleeting; passing away; liable to disappear or come to an end.— **evanescently,** ev·a·nes′ent·li, adv.

evangel, i·van′jel, n. [L. evangelium, the gospel; Gr. euangelion, good tidings, the gospel—eu, well, good, and angellō, to announce.] The gospel; one of the gospels or four New Testament books under the names of Matthew, Mark, Luke, and John.—**evangelical, evangelic,** i·van·jel′i·kal, i·van·jel′ik, a.[L.L. evangelicus.] According to the gospel, or religious truth taught in the New Testament; sound in the doctrines of the gospel; adhering closely to the letter of the gospel; fervent and devout; eccles. a term applied to a section in the Protestant churches who give special prominence to the doctrines of the corruption of man's nature by the fall, of his regeneration and redemption through the Saviour and of free and unmerited grace; applied in Germany to Protestants as distinguished from Roman Catholics, and more especially to the national Protestant church formed in Prussia in 1817 by a union of the Lutheran and Calvinistic churches.—**evangelicalism,** i·van·jel′i·kal·izm, n. Adherence to evangelical doctrines.— **evangelically,** i·van·jel′i·kal·i, adv. In an evangelical manner.—**evangelist,** i·van′jel·ist, n. [cap.] One of the four writers of the gospels. A layman engaged in preaching or missionary work.—**evangelistic,** i·van′jel·is″tik, a. Evangelical, tending or designed to evangelize.—**evangelization,** i·van′jel·i·zā″shon, n. The act of evangelizing.—**evangelize,** i·van′jel·īz, v.t.—evangelized, evangelizing. To instruct in the gospel; to preach the gospel to and convert.—v.i. To preach the gospel.

evanish,† i·van′ish, v.i. To vanish; to disappear.

evaporate, ē·vap′ėr·āt, v.i.—evaporated, evaporating. [L. evaporo, evaporatum—e, out, and vapor, vapor. VAPOR.] To pass off in vapor; to escape and be dissipated, either in visible vapor or in particles too minute to be visible; fig. to escape or pass off without effect; to be dissipated; to be wasted.—v.t. To convert or resolve into vapor; to cause to evaporate; to vaporize. —**evaporable,** ē·vap′ėr·a·bl, a. Capable of being converted into vapor or of being dissipated by evaporation.—**evaporation,** ē·vap′ėr·ā″shon, n. The act or process of evaporating; the conversion of a liquid by heat into vapor or steam, which becomes dissipated in the atmosphere in the manner of an elastic fluid; vaporization; the matter evaporated; vapor. —**evaporative,** i·vap′ėr·ā·tiv, a. Causing evaporation; pertaining to evaporation.—**evaporometer,** i·- vap′ėr·om″et·ėr, n. An instrument for ascertaining the quantity of a fluid evaporated in a given time; an atmometer.

evasion, evasive. See EVADE.

eve, ēv, n. [Short for even, evening.] The close of the day; the evening; the day or the latter part of the day before a church festival; the period just preceding some event (on the *eve* of a revolution).

even, ē'vn, *a.* [A.Sax. *efen,* even, level, equal=D. *even,* Dan. *jevn, jævn,* Icel. *jafn,* Goth. *ibns,* G. *eben,* even, level.] Level; smooth; flat; devoid of irregularities; straight or direct; uniform; equal; not easily ruffled; on a level or on the same level; in the same or in an equally favorable position; on a level in advantage; having accounts balanced; square; adjusted; fair; equitable; capable of being divided by 2 without a remainder: opposed to *odd.—v.t.* To make even; to level; to lay smooth; to place in an equal state; to balance.—*adv.* Expressing a level or equality; hence, just; exactly in consonance; according (*even as* he wished); expressing equality or sameness of time (I knew it *even then*); expressing, emphatically, identity of person (*even he did it*); expressing a strong assertion; not only this or so, but more, or but also.—**evenly,** ē'vn·li, *adv.* In an even manner; smoothly; equally; uniformly; impartially.—**evenness,** ē'vn·nes, *n.* The state or quality of being even.—**evenhanded,** *a.* Impartial; equitable; just.

even, ē'vn, *n.* [A.Sax. *aefen, efen.* EVENING.] Evening. (*Poet.*)—**evenfall,** ē'vn·fal, *n.* The fall of evening; early evening; twilight.—**evensong,** ē'vn·song, *n.* A form of worship for the evening; vespers.

evening, ēv'ning, *n.* [A.Sax. *aefnung,* verbal noun (like *morning*), from *aefen, efen,* evening; cog. G. *abend,* Sw. *afton,* Icel. *aftan,* Dan. *aften,* evening. The root meaning seems to be retiring, the word being akin to A.Sax. *af, of,* off; G. *ab, of,* from L. *ab,* Skr. *apa,* from.] The close of the day, and the beginning of darkness or night; the time from sunset until darkness; the latter part of the afternoon and the earlier part of the night; the decline or latter part of life: often used as an adjective.—**evening star,** *n.* Any planet visible in the western sky after sunset.

event, i·vent', *n.* [L. *eventus,* from *evenio, eventum,* to come out—*e,* out, and *venio,* to come, seen also in *advent, convene, prevent, venture,* etc.] That which happens or falls out; any incident good or bad; an occurrence; the consequence of anything; that in which an action, operation, or series of operations terminates; the issue, conclusion, end.—**eventful,** i·vent'ful, *a.* Full of events or incidents; characterized by great changes either in public or private affairs.—**eventual,** i·ven'tū·al, *a.* Coming or happening as a consequence or final result; consequential; final; ultimate.—**eventuality,** i·ven'tū·al"i·ti, *n.* That which eventuates or happens; a contingent result.—**eventually,** i·ven'tū·al·li, *adv.* In the event; in the final result or issue.—**eventuate,** i·ven'tū·āt, *v.i.* —*eventuated, eventuating.* To issue as an event or consequence; to fall out; to happen; to come to pass.

ever, ev'ėr, *adv.* [A.Sax. *aefre,* always; allied to Goth. *aivs,* time, *aiv,* ever; Icel. *æfi,* an age, the space of life; L. *ævum,* Gr. *aiōn,* Skr. *âyus,* an age. Akin *aye, every.*] At any time past or future; at all times; always; eternally; constantly; incessantly; continually; in any degree.—*For ever,* eternally; to perpetuity; sometimes with a repetition for the sake of emphasis (*for ever and ever*).—*Ever and anon,* now and then; again and again; time after time.—*Ever,* in *composition,* signifies always or continually, without intermission, or to eternity; as, *ever-active; ever-living.*—**evergreen,** ev'ėr·grēn, *a.* Always green; having verdant leaves throughout the year; *fig.* always fresh, vigorous, or in a good condition.—*n.* A plant that retains its verdure through all the seasons.—**everlasting,** ev·ėr·las'-ting, *a.* Lasting or enduring for ever; existing or continuing without beginning or end; eternal; perpetual; endless; continual.—*n.* Eternity; a plant whose flowers retain their form, color, and brightness for many months after being gathered.—*The Everlasting,* the Eternal Being; God.—**everlastingly,** ev·ėr·las'ting·li, *adv.* Eternally; perpetually; continually.—**everlastingness,** ev·ėr·las'ting·nes, *n.*—**evermore,** ev'ėr·mōr, *adv.* Always; for ever; at all times; continually.

evert, i·vėrt', *v.t.* [L. *everto, eversum* —*e,* and *verto,* to turn, as in *convert, invert, revert, verse,* etc.] To overturn; to overthrow; to turn outward, or inside out.—**eversion,** i·vėr'shon, *n.* The act of everting; an overthrowing; destruction.—*Eversion of the eyelids,* a disease in which the eyelids are turned outward so as to expose the red internal tunic.

every, ev'ri, *a.* [O.E. *everich, everilk,* from A.Sax. *aefre,* ever, and *ælc,* each. EVER, EACH.] Each individual of the whole number; each of a number singly or one by one.—**everybody,** ev'ri·bod·i, *n.* Every person.—**everyday,** ev'ri·dā, *a.* Used, occurring, or that may be seen or met with every day; common; usual; ordinary.—**everywhere,** ev'ri·hwâr, *adv.* In every place; in all places.

evict, i·vikt', *v.t.* [L. *evinco, evictum,* to vanquish utterly—*e,* intens., and *vinco,* to overcome, as in *convince, convict, evince.* VICTOR.] To dispossess by a judicial process or course of legal proceedings; to expel from lands or tenements by law.—**eviction,** i·vik'shon, *n.* The act of evicting; the expulsion of a tenant from lands or tenements by law.

evidence, ev'i·dens, *n.* [Fr. *évidence,* from L. *evidentia*—*e,* and *video, visum,* to see. VISION.] That which demonstrates or makes clear that a fact is so; that which makes evident or enables the mind to see truth; proof arising from our own perceptions by the senses, or from the testimony of others, or from inductions of reason; testimony; *law,*

that which is legally submitted to a competent tribunal as a means of ascertaining the truth of any alleged matter of fact under investigation.—*State's evidence,* evidence given by an accomplice, when the ordinary evidence is defective, on the understanding that he himself shall go free for his share of the crime.—*v.t.*—*evidenced, evidencing.* To render evident; to prove; to make clear to the mind.—**evident,** ev'i·dent, *a.* [L. *evidens.*] Open to be seen; clear to the mental or physical eye; manifest; obvious; plain.—**evidential,** ev·i·den'shal, *a.* Affording evidence; clearly proving.—**evidently,** ev'i·dent·li, *adv.* In an evident manner; clearly; manifestly.

evil, ē'vl, *a.* [A.Sax. *efel, yfel;* D. *euvel,* O.Fris. *evel,* G. *ubel,* Goth. *ubils.*] Having bad qualities of a natural kind; having qualities which tend to injury, or to produce mischief; injurious; pernicious; mischievous; having bad qualities of a moral kind; wicked; corrupt; perverse; wrong; vile; vicious; unfortunate; unpropitious; calamitous.—*The Evil One,* the devil.—*n.* Anything that causes injury, pain, or suffering; misfortune; calamity; mischief; injury; depravity; corruption of heart, or disposition to commit wickedness; malignity; the negation or contrary of good.—*adv.* Not well; ill.—**evildoer,** ē'vl·dö·ėr, *n.* One who does evil; one who commits sin, crime, or any moral wrong.—**evil eye,** *n.* A kind of influence superstitiously ascribed in former times to certain persons, their glance being supposed to injure.—**evil-minded,** *a.* Having evil dispositions or intentions; disposed to mischief or sin.—**evilness,** ē'vl·nes, *n.* Badness; viciousness; malignity of sin.

evince, i·vins', *v.t.*—*evinced, evincing.* [L. *evinco,* to vanquish, to prove or show. EVICT.] To show; to prove; to manifest; to make evident; to display as something belonging to one's own nature or character (to *evince* fear).—**evincible,** i·vin'si·bl, *a.* Capable of being evinced.

eviscerate, i·vis'ėr·āt, *v.t.*—*eviscerated, eviscerating.* [L. *eviscero*—*e,* and *viscera,* the bowels.] To take out the entrails of; to disembowel.—**evisceration,** i·vis'ėr·ā"shon, *n.* The act of eviscerating.

evoke, i·vōk', *v.t.*—*evoked, evoking.* [L. *evoco*—*e,* out, and *voco,* to call.] To call or summon forth.—**evocation,** ev·o·kā'shon, *n.* The act of evoking; a calling forth.

evolution, ev·o·lū'shon, *n.* [L. *evolutio,* from *evolvo, evolutum,* to unroll, to unfold. EVOLVE.] The act of unfolding, unrolling, or expanding; a gradual development or working out; the extraction of arithmetical or algebraic roots—the reverse of involution; a regulated or systematic series of movements which a body of troops, a fleet, or a ship makes when changing a previous formation or position; that theory which sees in the history of all things, organic and inorganic, a development from simplicity to complexity, a gradual advance from a simple or rudimentary condition to one that is more complex and of a higher character.—**evolutional, evolutionary,** ev·o·lū′shon·al, ev·o·lū′shon·e·ri, *a.* Of or pertaining to evolution; produced by or due to evolution.—**evolutionist,** ev·o·lū′shon·ist, *n.* One skilled in evolutions, specifically in military evolutions; a believer in the doctrine of evolution.

evolve, i·volv′, *v.t.*—*evolved, evolving.* [L. *evolvo*—*e*, and *volvo*, to roll, which is cog. with E. to *wallow*, and is seen also in *convolve, devolve, revolve, voluble, volume*, etc.] To unfold; to open and expand; to disentangle; to unravel; to develop; to cause to pass from a simple to a complex state.—*v.i.* To open or disclose itself.—**evolvement,†** i·volv′ment, *n.* Act of evolving.

ewe, ū, *n.* [A.Sax. *eowu*; allied to Fris. *ei*, O.H.G. *avi, ou*, Icel. *â*, L. *ovis*, Gr. *oïs*, Skr. *avi*, a sheep.] A female sheep.

ewer, ū′ėr, *n.* [From O.Fr. *ewe*, Mod. Fr. *eau*, water, from L. *aqua*, water (whence *aquatic*, etc.).] A large pitcher or jug with a wide spout, used to bring water for washing the hands; a sort of pitcher that accompanies a wash basin for holding the water.

exacerbate, ek·sas′ėr·bāt, *v.t.*—*exacerbated, exacerbating.* [L. *exacerbo, exacerbatum*—*ex*, intens., and *acerbus*, harsh, sharp, sour.] To irritate, exasperate, or inflame; to increase the malignant qualities of; to increase the violence of (a disease).—**exacerbation,** ek·sas′ėr·bā″shon, *n.* The act of exacerbating; increase of malignity; a periodical increase of violence in a disease.

exact, eg·zakt′, *a.* [L. *exactus*, pp. of *exigo*, to drive out, to measure—*ex*, out, and *ago*, to drive, to do, as in *agent, act, agitate*, etc.] Closely correct or regular; accurate; conformed to rule; precise; not different in the least; methodical; careful; observing strict method, rule, or order; punctual; strict.—*v.t.* [Fr. *exacter*, L.L. *exactare*.] To force or compel to be paid or yielded; to extort by means of authority or compulsion; to enforce a yielding of; to enjoin with pressing urgency.—**exacter,** eg·zak′tėr, *n.* One who exacts.—**exacting,** eg·zak′ting, *p.* and *a.* Demanding or disposed to demand without pity or justice; extorting; making unreasonable claims.—**exaction,** eg·zak′shon, *n.* The act of exacting; extortion; a wresting of contributions unjustly; that which is exacted; fees, rewards, or contributions levied with severity or injustice.—**exactitude,** eg·zak′ti·tūd, *n.* Exactness; accuracy; nicety.—**exactly,** eg·zakt′li, *adv.* In an exact manner.—**exactness,** eg·zakt′nes, *n.* The state or quality of being exact; accuracy; correctness; preciseness; regularity.—**exactor,** eg·zak′tėr, *n.* One who exacts.

exaggerate, eg·zaj′ėr·āt, *v.t.*—*exag-* gerated, exaggerating. [L. *exaggero, exaggeratum*—*ex*, intens., and *aggero*, to heap, from *agger*, a heap—*ad*, to, and *gero*, to carry.] To represent as greater than truth or justice will warrant; to heighten unduly; to magnify.—**exaggeration,** eg·zaj′ėr·ā″shon, *n.* The act of exaggerating; a representation of things beyond the truth or reality.—**exaggerative,** eg·zaj′ėr·ā·tiv, *a.* Having the tendency to exaggerate.—**exaggeratory,** eg·zaj′ėr·a·to·ri, *a.* Containing exaggeration.

exalt, eg·zalt′, *v.t.* [Fr. *exalter*, from L. *exaltare*—*ex*, and *altus*, high (whence *altitude, haughty*).] To raise high; to lift up; to elevate in power, wealth, rank, or dignity, character, and the like; to elevate with joy, pride, or confidence; to elate; to praise highly; to magnify; to extol; to elevate the tone of; to elevate in diction or sentiment.—**exaltation,** eg·zal·tā′shon, *n.* The act of exalting or state of being exalted; elevated state; state of greatness or dignity; a state of great elation; mental elevation.—**exaltedness,** eg·zal′ted·nes, *n.* The state of being exalted.—**exalter,** eg·zal′tėr, *n.* One who exalts.

examine, eg·zam′in, *v.t.*—*examined, examining.* [L. *examino, examinatum*, from *examen, examinis*, the tongue of a balance, for *exagmen*, from *ex*, out, and *ago*, to bring, to do (whence *agent*, etc.).] To inspect or observe carefully; to look into the state of; to view and consider in all its aspects; to question, as a witness or an accused person; to put judicial inquiries to; to inquire into the qualifications, capabilities, knowledge, or progress of, by interrogatories; to try or test.—**examinant,** eg·zam′i·nant, *n.* An examiner.—**examinee,** eg·zam′i·nē″, *n.* One who undergoes an examination.—**examiner,** eg·zam′i·nėr, *n.* One who examines; one who inspects; a person appointed to conduct an examination, as in a university.—**examinable,** eg·zam′i·na·bl, *a.* Capable of being examined.—**examen,†** eg·zam′en, *n.* An examination.—**examination,** eg·zam′i·nā″shon, *n.* The act of examining or state of being examined; a careful search or inquiry; careful and accurate inspection; a legal inquiry into facts by testimony; an attempt to ascertain truth by inquiries and interrogatories; a process for testing qualifications, knowledge, progress, of students, candidates, etc.; investigation; scrutiny; trial.

example, eg·zam′pl, *n.* [L. *exemplum*, from *eximo*, to take out or away—*ex*, out, and *emo, emptum*, to take, to purchase (as in *exempt*). *Sample* is the same word.] A sample or specimen; a pattern, in morals or manners, worthy of imitation; a copy or model; one who or that which is proposed or is proper to be imitated; a former instance, to be followed or avoided; one held out as a caution or warning to others; a particular case illustrating a general rule, position, or truth.

exanthema, ek·san·thē′ma, *n.* pl. **exanthemata,** ek·san·them′a·ta. [Gr. *exanthēma*, from *exantheō*, to blossom—*ex*, and *anthos*, a flower.] *Med.* an eruption or breaking out, as in measles, smallpox, etc.: frequently limited to such eruptions as are accompanied with fever.—**exanthematous, exanthematic,** ek·san·them′a·tus, ek·san′the·mat″ik, *a.* Of or pertaining to exanthema; eruptive.

exarch, ek′särk, *n.* [Gr. *exarchos*—*ex*, and *archos*, a chief.] A viceroy or governor of an Italian or African province under the Byzantine Empire.—**exarchate,** ek′sär·kāt, *n.* The office, dignity, or administration of an exarch.

exasperate, eg·zas′pėr·āt, *v.t.*—*exasperated, exasperating.* [L. *exaspero, exasperatum*, to irritate—*ex*, and *asper*, rough, harsh.] To irritate in a high degree; to provoke to rage; to enrage; to anger; to excite or inflame.—**exasperation,** eg·zas′pėr·ā″shon, *n.* The act of exasperating or state of being exasperated.

ex cathedra, eks·ka·thē′dra, *a.* [L. *ex*, from, and *cathedra*, Gr. *kathedra*, a chair (whence *cathedral*).] Lit. from the chair, as of authority or instruction; hence, applied to any decision, order, etc., given in an authoritative and dogmatic manner.

excavate, eks′ka·vāt, *v.t.*—*excavated, excavating.* [L. *excavo, excavatum*—*ex*, out, and *cavus*, hollow. CAVE.] To cut, scoop, dig, or wear out the inner part of anything and make it hollow; to hollow; to form by scooping or hollowing out.—**excavation,** eks·ka·vā′shon, *n.* The act of excavating; a hollow or a cavity formed by removing substance.—**excavator,** eks′ka·vā·tėr, *n.* One who or that which excavates; a machine for excavating.

exceed, ek·sēd′, *v.t.* [L. *excedo*—*ex*, out, and *cedo*, to go. CEDE.] To pass or go beyond; to proceed beyond the given or supposed limit, measure, or quantity of; to outgo; to surpass; to excel.—*v.i.* To go too far; to pass the proper bounds or limits.—**exceeding,** ek·sē′ding, *a.* Great in extent, quantity, degree, or duration; very large.—*adv.* In a very great degree; unusually. (O.T.)—**exceedingly,** ek·sē′ding·li, *adv.* In an exceeding manner or degree; very greatly; very much.

excel, ek·sel′, *v.t.*—*excelled, excelling.* [L. *excello*—*ex*, and root seen in Gr. *kellō*, to impel, L. *celsus*, raised high.] To surpass in good qualities or laudable deeds; to outdo in comparison; to surpass; to transcend; to exceed.—*v.i.* To be eminent or distinguished; to surpass others; to take a high rank.—**excellence,** ek′sel·lens, *n.* The state of excelling in anything; the state of possessing good qualities in an eminent or unusual degree; superiority; eminence; any valuable quality; anything highly laudable, meritorious, or esteemed; [*usually cap.*] a title of honor given to persons of high rank; excellency;—**excel-**

lency, ek′sel·len·si, *n.* Valuable quality; excellence; [*usually cap.*] a title of honor given to governors, ambassadors, ministers, and the like: with *your, his,* etc.—**excellent,** ek′sel·lent, *a.* Being of great virtue or worth; eminent or distinguished for what is amiable, valuable, or laudable; virtuous; good; worthy; excelling or surpassing in any quality, power, or attainment; being of great value or use; remarkable for good properties.—**excellently,** ek′sel·lent·li, *adv.* In an excellent manner; in an eminent degree.

excelsior, ik·sel′sē·ẽr, *n.* [L. lofty; the compar. of *excelsus.*] Fine curled wood shavings used in packaging for protection.

except, ek·sept′, *v.t.* [Fr. *excepter,* L. *excipio, exceptum*—*ex,* out, and *capio,* to take, seen also in *captious, capacious, capable, accept, conceive,* etc.] To take or leave out of any number specified; to exclude.—*v.i.* To object; to take exception: usually followed by *to.*—*prep.* Being excepted or left out; with exception of; excepting.—*conj.* excepting; unless.—**excepting,** ek·sep′ting, *ppr.* used as a *prep.* and *conj.* With exception of; excluding; unless; except.—**exception,** ek·sep′shon, *n.* The act of excepting or excluding from a number designated, or from a description; exclusion; that which is excepted or excluded; the person or thing specified as distinct or not included; an objection; that which is or may be offered in opposition to a rule, proposition, statement, or allegation; offense; slight anger or resentment (to *take exception at* a severe remark; to *take exception to* what was said).—**exceptionable,** ek·sep′shon·a·bl, *a.* Liable to exception or objection; objectionable.—**exceptional,** ek·sep′shon·al, *a.* Out of the ordinary course; relating to or forming an exception.—**exceptionally,** ek·sep′shon·al·li, *adv.* In an exceptional manner; unprecedentedly; extraordinarily; especially.—**exceptive,** ek·sep′tiv, *a.* Including an exception.

excerpt, ek·sẽrpt′, *v.t.* [L. *excerpo, excerptum*—*ex,* out, and *carpo,* to pick.] To pick out or extract from a book or other literary composition; to cull; to select; to cite.—*n.* ek′sẽrpt. An extract from a publication or from a writing of any kind.

excess, ek·ses′, *n.* [L. *excessus,* from *excedo,* to exceed. EXCEED.] That which exceeds any measure or limit; that which is beyond measure, proportion, or due quantity; superfluity; superabundance; any transgression of due limits; extravagance; wastefulness; riotous living; want of restraint in gratifying the desires; intemperance; overindulgence; the amount by which one number or quantity exceeds another.—**excessive,** ek·ses′iv, *a.* Beyond any given degree, measure, or limit, or beyond the common measure or proportion; immoderate; extravagant; extreme.—*Enormous, Excessive.* ∴ Syn. under ENORMOUS.—**excessively,** ek·ses′iv·li, *adv.* In an excessive manner or

degree; exceedingly; vehemently; violently.

exchange, eks·chānj′, *v.t.*—*exchanged, exchanging.* [O.Fr. *exchanger*—*ex,* and *changer,* to change. CHANGE.] To give or take in return for another thing; to barter; to lay aside, quit, or resign (a thing, state, or condition), and take something else; to give and receive reciprocally; to give and take; to interchange.—*v.i.* To make an exchange; to pass or to be taken as an equivalent.—*n.* The act of giving one thing or commodity for another; barter; traffic by interchange of commodities; the act of giving up or resigning one thing or state for another; the act of giving and receiving reciprocally; the thing given or the thing received in return; the place where the merchants, brokers, and bankers of a city meet to transact business; the difference of value in the respective currencies of different countries.—**exchangeable,** eks·chān′ja·bl, *a.* Capable of being exchanged; estimated by what may be procured in exchange.—**exchangeability,** eks·chān′ja·bil″i·ti, *n.* The quality or state of being exchangeable.

exchequer, eks·chek′ẽr, *n.* [O.Fr. *eschequier,* Fr. *échiquier,* a chessboard: the term was applied to a court of finance from its having at first held its meetings round a table covered with *checked* cloth, because accounts were taken by means of counters on the checks. CHECK, CHEQUER, CHESS.] A state treasury; hence, pecuniary property in general; a person's finances or pecuniary resources; [*often cap.*] an ancient English tribunal and court, founded chiefly for the collection and care of the royal revenues, now a division of the High Court of Justice.—*Exchequer bills,* bills for money, or bills of credit issued from the exchequer, and pledging the government to repay the sum with a certain rate of interest; a species of paper currency emitted under the authority of the government, and in Britain forming a principal part of the public unfunded debt.—*v.t.*† To institute a process against in the court of exchequer.

excipient, ek·sip′i·ent, *n.* [L. *excipiens, excipientis,* ppr. of *excipio,* to take out. EXCEPT.] *Med.* an inert or slightly active substance employed as the medium or vehicle for the administration of the active medicine, as bread crust, sugar, jelly, etc.

excise, ek·sīz′, *n.* [From O.D. *aksijs,* G. *accise,* excise, corruption of O.Fr. *assise,* an assize, a tax. ASSIZE.] A tax or duty imposed on certain commodities of home production and consumption, as beer, spirits, etc.; or levied on persons for licenses to pursue certain callings, deal in certain commodities, as well as use certain things (armorial bearings, carriages, plate, etc.), or the like; that branch of the civil service which is connected with the collecting of such duties.—*v.t.*—*excised, excising.*

To levy an excise on.—**excisable,** ek·sī′za·bl, *a.* Liable or subject to excise.—**exciseman,** ek·sīz′man, *n.* An inferior officer of the excise.

excise, ek·sīz′, *v.t.*—*excised, excising.* [From L. *excido, excisum*—*ex,* out, and *cædo,* to cut, as in *concise, circumcise.*] To cut out or off; to remove by cutting, as in surgery; to delete or expunge.—**excision,** ek·sizh′on, *n.* The act of cutting out; removal by cutting; amputation; deletion.

excite, ek·sīt′, *v.t.*—*excited, exciting.* [Fr. *exciter,* from L. *excito*—*ex,* and *cito* (as in *cite, incite, recite*), intens. of *cieo* or *cio,* to excite, call; akin to Gr. *kiō,* to go, *kineō,* to move.] To call into action; to animate; to rouse, provoke, or to stir up; to cause to act, as that which is dormant, sluggish, or inactive; to give new or increased action to; to stimulate; to call forth or increase the vital activity of; to raise, create, or set afoot.—**excitable,** ek·sī′ta·bl, *a.* Susceptible of excitement; capable of being excited; easily excited or stirred up; prone to or characterized by excitement.—**excitability, excitableness,** ek·sī′ta·bil″i·ti, ek·sī′ta·bl·nes, *n.* The state or quality of being excitable.—**excitant,** ek′si·tant, *n.* That which produces or may produce increased action in a living organism; an agent or influence which arouses the vital activity of the body or of any of the tissues or organs; a stimulant.—**excitation,** ek·si·tā′shon, *n.* The act of exciting; excitement.—**excitative, excitatory,** ek·sī′ta·tiv, ek·sī′ta·to·ri, *a.* Having power to excite; tending or serving to excite.—**excitement,** ek·sīt′ment, *n.* The act of exciting; stimulation; the state of being excited; agitation; sensation; commotion; a state of aroused or increased vital activity in the body or any of its tissues or organs; a vitiated and abnormal state of the actions and sensations, or both, produced by stimulants, irritants, or the like; that which excites or rouses; that which moves, stirs, or induces action.—**exciter,** ek·sī′tẽr, *n.* One who or that which excites.—**exciting,** ek·sī′ting, *p.* and *a.* Calling or rousing into action; producing excitement; deeply interesting; thrilling.—**excitingly,** ek·sī′ting·li, *adv.* So as to excite.

exclaim, eks·klām′, *v.i.* [L. *exclamo*—*ex,* and *clamo,* to call. CLAIM.] To utter with vehemence; to cry out; to shout; to declare with loud vociferation.—**exclaimer,** eks·klā′mẽr, *n.* One who exclaims.—**exclamation,** eks·kla·mā′shon, *n.* The act of exclaiming or making an outcry; noisy talk; vehement vociferation; clamor; an emphatical or passionate utterance; the mark or sign [!] in printing by which emphatical utterance or interjectional force is marked; *gram.* a word expressing outcry; an interjection.—**exclamatory,** eks·klam′a·to·ri, *a.* Pertaining to or characterized by exclamation; expressing exclamation.

exclude, eks·klūd′, *v.t.*—*excluded, ex-*

cluding. [L. *excludo*, to shut out—*ex*, out, and *claudo*, to shut, whence *clause, close*, etc.] To hinder from entering or from admission; to shut out; to hinder from participation or enjoyment; to debar; to except; not to comprehend or include in a privilege, grant, argument, description, etc.; to thrust out; to eject. —**exclusion**, eks·klū′zhon, *n.* The act of excluding, shutting out, debarring, expelling, excepting, or rejecting; the state of being excluded.—**exclusionism**, eks·klū′zhon·izm, *n.* Exclusive principles or practice.— **exclusionist**, eks·klū′zhon·ist, *n.* One who is in favor of exclusion.— **exclusive**, eks·klū′siv, *a.* Having the power or effect of excluding; possessed and enjoyed to the exclusion of others (an *exclusive* privilege); not taking into account something or certain individuals; not including or comprehending certain things (an *exclusive* estimate): often with *of* (500 men *exclusive of* officers); excluding from or chary in admitting to society or fellowship; fastidious as to the social rank of associates; illiberal; narrow.—*n.* One very fastidious as to the social position or breeding of his associates.— **exclusively**, eks·klū′siv·li, *adv.* Without admission of others; with the exclusion of all others; without comprehension in a number; not inclusively.—**exclusiveness**, eks·klū′siv·nes, *n.* State or quality of being exclusive.

excogitate, eks·koj′i·tāt, *v.t.*—*excogitated, excogitating.* [L. *excogito*—*ex*, out, and *cogito*, to think.] To strike out by thinking; to think out; to devise; to contrive.—**excogitation**, eks·koj′i·tā″shon, *n.* The act of excogitating.

excommunicate, eks·kom·mū′ni·kāt, *v.t.*—*excommunicated, excommunicating.* [L. *ex*, out, and *communico, communicatum*, to communicate, from *communis*, common.] To expel or eject from the communion of the church and deprive of spiritual advantages; hence, to expel from any association and deprive of the privileges of membership.—*n.* One who is excommunicated; one cut off from any privilege. — **excommunicable**, eks·kom·mū′ni·ka·bl, *a.* Liable or deserving to be excommunicated; punishable by excommunication.— **excommunication**, eks·kom·mū′ni·kā″shon, *n.* The act of excommunicating, or state of being excommunicated; expulsion from the communion of a church, and deprivation of its rights, privileges, and advantages.—**excommunicator**, eks·kom·mū′ni·kā·tėr, *n.* One who excommunicates.—**excommunicatory**, eks·kom·mū′ni·ka·tȯ·ri, *a.* Relating to or causing excommunication.

excoriate, eks·kō′ri·āt, *v.t.*—*excoriated, excoriating.* [L.L. *excorio*—L. *ex*, and *corium*, skin, hide.] To break or wear off the cuticle of; to abrade a part of the skin so as to reach the flesh; to gall.—**excoriation**, eks·kō′ri·ā″shon, *n.* The act of excoriating; a galling; abrasion.

excrement, eks′kre·ment, *n.* [L. *excrementum*, from *excerno, excretum*, to sift out—*ex*, out, and *cerno*, to separate. DISCERN.] Matter discharged from the animal body after digestion; alvine discharge.—**excremental**, **excrementitious**, eks·kre·men′tal, eks′kre·men·tish″us, *a.* Pertaining to or consisting of excrement; consisting of matter excreted from the animal body.

excrescence, excrescency, eks·kres′ens, eks·kres′en·si, *n.* [Fr. *excrescence*, from L. *excrescens*, pp. of *excresco*, to grow out—*ex*, out, and *cresco*, to grow (in *crescent, concrete, increase*, etc.).] Anything which grows out of something else and is useless or disfiguring (as a wart or tumor); a useless or troublesome outgrowth. —**excrescent**, eks·kres′ent, *a.*

excreta, eks·krē′tä, *n.* pl. [From L. *excrētus*, separated.] Matter excreted from the body, as sweat, feces, etc.

excrete, eks·krēt′, *v.t.*—*excreted, excreting.* [L. *excerno, excretum.* EXCREMENT.] To separate and throw off from the body by vital action; to discharge.—**excretion**, eks·krē′shon, *n.* A separation of some fluid from the blood by means of the glands; a discharge of animal fluids from the body; that which is discharged.— **excretory**, eks′krē·tȯ·ri, *a.* Having the quality of excreting or throwing off excrementitious matter.—*n. Anat.* a duct or vessel destined to receive secreted fluids and to excrete them.

excruciate, eks·krö′shi·āt, *v.t.*—*excruciated, excruciating.* [L. *excrucio, excruciatum*—*ex*, and *crucio*, to torment, from *crux*, a cross. CROSS.] To cause extreme pain or torture to; to torment; to inflict most severe pain on.—**excruciating**, eks·krö′shi·ā·ting, *p.* and *a.* Extremely painful; distressing; torturing; tormenting.— **excruciatingly**, eks·krö′shi·ā·ting·li, *adv.* In an excruciating manner.— **excruciation**, eks·krö′shi·ā″shon, *n.* The act of excruciating; torture; extreme pain; vexation.

exculpate, eks′kul·pāt, *v.t.*—*exculpated, exculpating.* [L.L. *exculpo, exculpatum*—L. *ex*, and *culpo, culpatum*, to blame, from *culpa*, a fault.] To clear from a charge or imputation of fault or guilt; to vindicate from a charge of fault or crime; to relieve of or free from blame; to regard as innocent; to exonerate; to absolve; to excuse.—**exculpation**, eks·kul·pā′shon, *n.* The act of exculpating; what exculpates; an excuse.—**exculpatory**, eks·kul′pa·tȯ·ri, *a.* Able to exculpate; containing excusatory evidence.

excurrent, eks·kur′ent, *a.* [L. *excurrens, excurrentis*, ppr. of *excurro*—*ex*, out, and *curro*, to run.] *Bot.* projecting or running beyond the edge or point, as when the midrib of a leaf projects beyond the apex.

excursion, eks·kėr′zhon, *n.* [L. *excursio*, from *excurro*—*ex*, out, and *curro*, to run.] Act of running out or forth; a deviation from a fixed or usual course; a wandering from a subject or main design; digression; a journey for pleasure or health, with the view

of return; a trip.—*Excursion train*, a railroad train specially put on for carrying passengers on a pleasure trip for a certain distance and at a low fare.—**excursionist**, eks·kėr′zhon·ist, *n.* One who makes an excursion; specifically, one who travels by an excursion train; one who professionally provides the public with facilities for making excursions. —**excursive**, eks·kėr′siv, *a.* Given to making excursions; rambling; wandering.—**excursively**, eks·kėr′siv·li, *adv.* In an excursive manner.— **excursiveness**, eks·kėr′siv·nes, *n.* The condition or character of being excursive.—**excursus**, eks·kėr′sus, *n.* [L.] A dissertation appended to a book, discussing some important point or topic more fully than could be done in the body of the work.

excuse, eks·kūz′, *v.t.*—*excused, excusing.* [L. *excuso*—*ex*, out, and *causa*, a cause, a suit.] To free from accusation or the imputation of fault or blame; to relieve from blame; to exculpate; to absolve; to justify; to pardon (a fault), to forgive, or to admit to be little censurable, and to overlook; to free from an obligation or duty; to release by favor.—*n.* (eks·kūs′). A plea offered in extenuation of a fault or irregular deportment; apology; that which extenuates or justifies a fault.—**excusable**, eks·kū′za·bl, *a.* Capable of being excused; pardonable; admitting of excuse.—**excusably**, eks·kū′za·bli, *adv.* In an excusable manner; pardonably. —**excusatory**, eks·kū′za·tȯ·ri, *a.* Making excuse; containing excuse or apology; apologetical.

execrate, ek′si·krāt, *v.t.*—*execrated, execrating.* [Fr. *exécrer*, from L. *execror*—*ex*, and *sacer*, consecrated or dedicated to a deity, accursed. SACRED.] To denounce evil against, or to imprecate evil on; to curse, hence, to detest utterly; to abhor; to abominate.—**execrable**, ek′si·kra·bl, *a.* Deserving to be execrated or cursed; very hateful; detestable; abominable.—**execrably**, ek′si·kra·bli, *adv.* In a manner deserving of execration; detestably.—**execration**, ek·si·krā′shon, *n.* The act of execrating; a curse pronounced; imprecation of evil; utter detestation; the object execrated.—**execrative**, **execratory**, ek′si·krā·tiv, ek′si·kra·tȯ·ri, *a.* Denouncing evil; cursing; vilifying.

execute, ek′si·kūt, *v.t.*—*executed, executing.* [Fr. *exécuter*, from L. *exsequor, exsecutus*, to follow to the end—*ex*, and *sequor*, to follow, as in *sequence, prosecute, persecute, pursue, ensue*, etc.] To follow out; to perform; to do; to carry into complete effect; to complete; to accomplish; to finish; to give effect to; to put in force (a law or measure); to inflict; to inflict capital punishment on; to put to death; to perform what is required to give validity to (a writing), as by signing and sealing; to perform (a piece of music) on an instrument or with the voice.— **executable**, ek·si·kū′ta·bl, *a.* Capable of being executed.—**executant**, eg·zek´ū·tant, *n.* One who executes or performs; a performer.—**executer,** ek´si·kū·ter, *n.* One who performs or carries into effect.—**execution,** ek·si·kū´shon, *n.* The act of executing; performance; the mode of producing or performing an artistic work, and the dexterity with which it is accomplished; the carrying out of the sentence of the law by putting a criminal to death; a case of the infliction of capital punishment; the carrying out of the sentence of a court by arresting the goods or body of a debtor.—*To do execution,* to cause great damage; to have a destructive effect (as a storm or a cannon ball).—**executioner,** ek·si·kū´shon·er, *n.* One who inflicts a capital punishment in pursuance of a legal warrant.—**executive,** eg·zek´ū·tiv, *a.* Having the quality of executing or performing; designed or fitted for execution, administering, or carrying into effect, laws; governing.—*n.* The person (or body of persons) who superintends the execution of the laws; the person or persons who administer the government.—**executor,** ek´se·kū·ter, *n.* One who executes or performs; a performer or doer; *law,* the person appointed by a testator to execute his will or to see it carried into effect; in this sense pronounced eg·zek´ū·ter.—**executorial,** eg·zek´ū·tō´´ri·al, *a.* Pertaining to an executor.—**executory,** eg·zek´ū·to·ri, *a.* Performing official duties; carrying laws into effect; executive.—**executrix,** eg·zek´ū·triks, *n.* A female executor; a woman appointed by a testator to execute his will.

exegesis, ek·se·jē´sis, *n.* [Gr. *exēgēsis,* from *exēgeomai,* to explain—*ex,* and *hēgeomai,* to lead, to guide.] The exposition or interpretation of any literary production, but more particularly the exposition or interpretation of Scripture; also the principles of the art of sacred interpretation; exegetics; hermeneutics.—**exegetic, exegetical,** ek·se·jet´ik, ek·se·jet´i·kal, *a.* Explanatory; tending to illustrate or unfold; expository.—**exegetically,** ek·se·jet´i·kal·li, *adv.* By way of exegesis or explanation.—**exegetics,** ek·se·jet´iks, *n.* The science which lays down the principles of the art of scriptural interpretation; exegesis; hermeneutics. — **exegete,** ek´se·jēt, *n.* One skilled in exegesis; an expounder or interpreter.

exemplar, eg·zem´plėr, *n.* [L. EXAMPLE.] A model, original, or pattern to be copied or imitated; a person who serves as a pattern.—**exemplary,** eg´zem·ple·ri, *a.* Serving for a pattern or model for imitation; worthy of imitation; such as may serve for a warning to others; such as may deter.—**exemplarily,** eg´zem·ple·ri·li, *adv.* In an exemplary manner.—**exemplariness,** eg´zem·ple·ri·nes, *n.* The state or quality of being exemplary.

exemplify, eg·zem´pli·fī, *v.t.*—*exemplified, exemplifying.* [L.L. *exemplifico,* to exemplify—L. *exemplum,* an example, and *facio,* to make.] To show or illustrate by example; to

serve as an example or instance of; to make an attested copy or transcript of.—**exemplification,** eg·zem´pli·fi·kā´shon, *n.* The act of exemplifying; a showing or illustrating by example; that which exemplifies.

exempt, ig·zemt´, *v.t.* [Fr. *exempter;* L. *eximo, exemptum,* to take out, to remove—*ex,* out, and *emo,* to buy, to take.] To free or permit to be free from any charge, burden, restraint, duty, etc., to which others are subject; to privilege; to grant immunity (no man is *exempted* from suffering).—*a.* Free from any service, charge, burden, tax, duty, requisition, or evil of any kind to which others are subject; not subject; not liable; not included; freed; free.—*n.* One who is exempted; one not subject.—**exemption,** ig·zem´shon, *n.* The act of exempting; the state of being exempt; immunity; privilege.

exequatur, ek·se·kwā´ter, *n.* [L., let him perform or execute.] A written recognition of a person in the character of consul or commercial agent; an official permission to perform some act.

exercise, ek´ser·sīz, *n.* [Fr. *exercice,* from L. *exercitium,* exercise, from *exerceo, exercitum,* to exercise—*ex,* out, and *arceo,* to inclose, to hinder.] A putting in action the powers or faculties of (the eyes, the limbs, the mind); use; employment; practice or performance; a carrying out in action, or performing the duties of anything (the *exercise* of an art, trade, occupation); exertion of the body as conducive to health; bodily exertion as a part of regimen; systematic exertion of the body for amusement or in order to acquire some art, dexterity, or grace; any such art or dexterity acquired by bodily training; training to acquire skill in the management of arms and in military evolutions; drill; moral training; discipline; a lesson or example for the practice of learners; a school task; puritan week-day service and sermon.—*v.t.*—*exercised, exercising.* To set in exercise or operation; to employ; to set or keep in a state of activity; to exert (the body, the mind) to put in practice; to carry out in action (to *exercise* authority); to train, discipline, or improve by practice; to task; to keep employed or busy; to cause to think earnestly and laboriously; to give anxiety to; to make uneasy; to task or try with something grievous; to pain or afflict.—*v.i.* To exercise one's self; to take exercise.—**exerciser,** ek´ser·sī·zer, *n.* One who or that which exercises.—**exercisable,** ek´ser·sī·za·bl, *a.* Capable of being exercised, enjoyed, or enforced.

exergue, ig·zerg´, *n.* [Gr. *ex,* out, and *ergon,* work.] The small space beneath the base line of a subject engraved on a coin or medal, left for the date, engraver's name, or something of minor importance.

exert, ig·zert´, *v.t.* [L. *exerto, exserto,* to stretch out, to thrust forth, freq. from *exsero, exsertum,* to thrust out

or forth—*ex,* out, and *sero,* to join. SERIES.] To put forth (strength, force, ability); to put in action; to bring into active operation (the mind, the bodily powers); *refl.* to use efforts; to strive; to put forth one's powers.—**exertion,** eg·zer´shon, *n.* The act of exerting; a putting forth of power; an effort; a striving or struggling; endeavor; trial.

exeunt. See EXIT.

exfoliate, eks·fō´li·āt, *v.i.*—*exfoliated, exfoliating.* [L. *exfolio, exfoliatum,* to strip of leaves—*ex,* and *folium,* a leaf.] To separate and come off in scales; to split into scales.—*v.t.* To free from scales or splinters.—**exfoliation,** eks·fō´li·ā´´shon, *n.* The process of exfoliating or separation in scales; desquamation; separation into scales or laminae, as in a mineral. —**exfoliative,** eks·fō´li·ā·tiv, *a.* Having the power of causing exfoliation.

exhale, egz·hāl´, *v.t.*—*exhaled, exhaling.* [L. *exhalo—ex,* out, and *halo,* to breathe.] To breathe or send out (something of a vaporous or gaseous character); to emit, as vapor; also, to cause to be emitted in vapor or minute particles.—*v.i.* To rise or pass off, as vapor; to vanish.—**exhalant,** egz·hā´lant, *a.* Having the quality of exhaling or evaporating.—**exhalation,** egz·ha·lā´shon, *n.* [L. *exhalatio.*] The act or process of exhaling; evaporation; that which is exhaled; that which is emitted or which rises in the form of vapor; emanation; effluvium.

exhaust, egz·zast´, *v.t.* [L. *exhaurio, exhaustum—ex,* out, up, and *haurio,* to draw, to draw water.] To draw out or drain off the whole of; to consume or use up; to empty by drawing out the contents; to use or expend the whole of by exertion; to wear out; to tire; to treat thoroughly; to leave nothing unsaid regarding.—*n.* Gaseous or other material exhausted, as from an internal combustion engine; also the muffler through which such material is passed.—**exhaustible,** eg·zas´ti·bl, *a.* Capable of being exhausted, drained off, consumed, or brought to an end. —**exhaustibility,** eg·zas´ti·bil´´i·ti, *n.* Capability of being exhausted; the state of being exhaustible.—**exhaustion,** eg·zast´shon, *n.* The act of exhausting; the state of being exhausted or emptied; the state of being deprived of strength or spirits; a state of complete fatigue and bodily weakness.—**exhaustive,** eg·zas´tiv, *a.* Causing exhaustion; tending to exhaust; treating of a subject in such a way as to leave no part of it unexamined; thorough.—**exhaustless,** eg·zast´les, *a.* Not to be exhausted; inexhaustible.

exhibit, eg·zib´it, *v.t.* [L. *exhibeo, exhibitum—ex,* out, and *habeo, habitum,* to hold, as in *prohibit,* etc. HABIT.] To hold out or present to view; to present for inspection; to show; to manifest publicly (to *exhibit* a noble example); *med.* to administer by way of medicine or remedy.—*v.i.* To show one's self in some particular capacity or character; to exhibit one's manufactures or productions at a public exhibition.—*n.* Anything exhibited, as at a public exhibition; a document or other thing shown to a witness when giving evidence, and referred to by him in his evidence.—**exhibitor, exhibiter,** ig‧zib′i‧tẽr, *n.* One who exhibits; one who presents a petition.—**exhibition,** eg′zi‧bish″on, *n.* [L. *exhibitio.*] The act of exhibiting; a showing or presenting to view; that which is exhibited; especially a public display, as of works of art, natural products, manufactures, feats of skill, and the like; formerly an allowance, pension, or salary; hence, a benefaction settled for the maintenance of scholars in English universities .—**exhibitionism,** eg′zi‧bish″on‧izm, *n.* The perversion of attaining gratification by indecent exposure; attempting to attract attention to oneself by boasting.

exhilarate, ig‧zil′a‧rāt, *v.t.*—**exhilarated, exhilarating.** [L. *exhilaro*—*ex,* and *hilaro,* to make merry, from *hilaris,* merry, jovial.] To make cheerful or merry; to inspire with hilarity; to make glad or joyous; to inspirit; to gladden; to cheer.—**exhilarant,** ig‧zil′a‧rant, *a.* Exhilarating.—*n.* That which exhilarates.—**exhilarating,** ig‧zil′a‧rā‧ting, *a.* Such as to exhilarate or make cheerful.—**exhilaration,** ig‧zil′a‧rā″shon, *n.* The act of exhilarating; cheerfulness; enlivenment; gladness; gaiety.

exhort, ig‧zort′, *v.t.* [L. *exhortor*—*ex,* and *hortor,* to encourage, to advise.] To incite by words or advice; to animate or urge by arguments to laudable conduct or course of action; to advise, warn, or caution; to admonish.—*v.i.* To use words or arguments to incite to good deeds.—**exhortation,** ig‧zor‧tā′shon, *n.* The act or practice of exhorting; language intended to incite and encourage; a persuasive discourse; a homily; an admonition.—**exhortative, exhortatory,** ig‧zor′ta‧tiv, ig‧zor′ta‧to‧ri, *a.* Containing exhortation; tending to exhort; serving for exhortation.—**exhorter,** ig‧zor′tẽr, *n.* One who exhorts or encourages.

exhume, eks‧hūm′, *v.t.*—**exhumed, exhuming.** [Fr. *exhumer,* to dig out of the ground—L. *ex,* out, and *humus,* earth, ground (akin *humble*).] To dig up after having been buried; to disinter.—**exhumation,** eks‧hū‧mā′shon, *n.* The act of exhuming.

exigence, exigency, ek′si‧jens, ek′‧si‧jen‧si, *n.* [Fr. *exigence,* from L. *exigo,* to drive out or forth, to demand, to exact. EXACT.] The state of being urgent or pressing; urgent demand; urgency; a pressing necessity; emergency.—**exigent,** ek′si‧jent, *a.* Pressing; requiring immediate aid or action.—**exigible,** ek′si‧ji‧bl, *a.* That may be exacted; demandable; requirable.

exiguous, ek‧sig′ū‧us, *a.* [L. *exiguus,* scanty.] Small; slender; minute; diminutive.—**exiguity,** ek‧si‧gū′i‧ti, *n.* [L. *exiguitas.*] Smallness; slenderness.

exile, eg′zīl, *n.* [Fr. *exil,* banishment,

exilé, an exiled person, from L. *exsilium,* banishment, *exsul,* a banished person—*ex,* out, and root of *salio,* to leap (whence *salient, sally*); Skr. *sar,* to go.] The state of being expelled from one's native country or place of residence by authority, and forbidden to return, either for a limited time or for perpetuity; banishment; a removal to a foreign country for residence; a separation from one's country and friends by distress or necessity; the person banished or expelled from his country, or who leaves his country and resides in another.—*v.t.*—*exiled, exiling.* To banish; to cause to be an exile.

exist, ig‧zist′, *v.i.* [Fr. *exister,* from L. *existo*—*ex,* and *sisto,* to stand, as in *assist, consist,* etc. STATE, STAND.] To have actual existence or being, whether in the form of matter or of spirit; to be; to live; to continue to have life or animation; to continue to be.—**existence,** ig‧zis′tens, *n.* The state of being or existing; continuance of being; that which exists; an entity.—**existent,** ig‧zis′tent, *a.* Having existence; being.—**existential,** eg‧zis‧ten′shal, *a.* Of or pertaining to, or consisting in existence.—**existentialism,** eg‧zis‧ten′shal‧izm, *n. Philos.* a twentieth-century movement that stresses the indescribable nature of the world and the volition of man.—**existentialist,** eg‧zis‧ten′shal‧ist, *n.*

exit, ek′sit, *n.* [L., he goes out, from *exeo,* to go out—*ex,* out, and *eo,* to go.] The departure of a player from the stage; a direction in a play to mark the time of an actor's quitting the stage; any departure; the act of quitting the stage of action; death; a way of departure; passage out of a place; a ramp by which an auto leaves a highway.—**exeunt,** ek′‧si‧unt. They go out: a common direction in plays, referring to more of the actors than one.

exocarp, ek′sō‧kärp, *n.* [Gr. *exō,* outside, *karpos,* fruit.] *Bot.* the outer layer of a pericarp.

exodus, ek′so‧dus, *n.* [Gr. *exodos*—*ex,* and *hodos,* way.] Departure from a place; especially, the emigration of large bodies of people from one country to another; [*cap.*] the second book of the Old Testament, which gives a history of the departure of the Israelites from Egypt.

ex officio, eks‧e‧fish′ē‧ō, *adv.* [L. from office.] By virtue of office or official position.—**ex-officio,** eks‧e‧‧fish′ē‧ō, *a.*

exogamy, ek‧sog′a‧mi, *n.* [Gr. *exō,* without, and *gamos,* marriage.] Marriage outside of a specific group; reproduction by unrelated organisms; custom among certain savage tribes which prohibits a man from marrying a woman of his own tribe, and so leads the men to capture their wives from among other tribes.—**exogamous,** ek‧sog′a‧mus, *a.* Of or belonging to exogamy; characterized by exogamy.

exonerate, ig‧zon′ẽr‧āt, *v.t.*—**exonerated, exonerating.** [L. *exonero, exone-*

ratum—*ex,* not, and *onus, oneris,* a load (whence also *onerous*).] To relieve of a charge or of blame; to clear of something that lies upon the character as an imputation; to discharge of responsibility, obligation, duty, or liability.—**exoneration,** ig‧zon′ẽr‧ā″shon, *n.* The act of exonerating.—**exonerative,** ig‧zon′ẽr‧ā‧tiv, *a.* Freeing from a burden, or obligation.

exorable, ek′so‧ra‧bl, *a.* [L. *exorabilis,* from *ex,* and *oro,* to pray.] That may be moved or persuaded by entreaty.

exorbitance, exorbitancy, ig‧zor′‧bi‧tans, ig‧zor′bi‧tan‧si, *n.* [L.L. *exorbitantia,* from *exorbito,* to go out of the track—L. *ex,* out, and *orbita,* a rut made by a wheel, from *orbis,* a circle. ORB.] A going beyond rule or ordinary limits; excess; extravagance (*exorbitance* of demands, of prices).—**exorbitant,** ig‧zor′bi‧tant, *a.* Going beyond the established limits of right or propriety; excessive; extravagant; enormous.—**exorbitantly,** ig‧zor′bi‧tant‧li, *adv.* In an exorbitant manner.

exorcise, ek′sor‧sīz, *v.t.*—**exorcised, exorcising.** [Fr. *exorciser,* from Gr. *exorkizō*—*ex,* intens., and *horkizō,* to bind by oath, from *horkos,* an oath.] To expel or cast out by conjurations, prayers, and ceremonies; to purify from unclean spirits by adjurations and ceremonies; to deliver from the influence or presence of malignant spirits or demons.—**exorciser, exorcist,** ek′sor‧sī‧zẽr, ek′‧sor‧sist, *n.* One who exorcises.—**exorcism,** ek′sor‧sizm, *n.* The act of exorcising; a prayer or charm used to expel evil spirits.

exordium, ig‧zor′di‧um, *n.* [L., from *exordior,* to begin a web, to lay the warp—*ex,* and *ordior,* to begin a web, to begin.] The beginning of anything; specifically, the introductory part of a discourse, which prepares the audience for the main subject.—**exordial,** ig‧zor′di‧al, *a.* Pertaining to an exordium; introductory; initial.

exoskeleton, ek′sō‧skel‧e‧ton, *n.* [Gr. *exō,* without, and *skeleton.*] The external skeleton; all those structures which are produced by the hardening of the integument, as the shells of the Crustacea, the scales and plates of fishes and reptiles; dermoskeleton.

exosmose, exosmosis, ek′sos‧mōs, ek‧sos‧mō′sis, *n.* [Gr. *exō,* outside, and *ōsmos,* impulsion, from *ōtheō,* to thrust, to push.] The passage of gases or liquids through membranes or porous media, from within outward, the reverse process being called *endosmose.*—**exosmotic,** ek‧sos‧mot′‧ik, *a.* Pertaining or relating to exosmose.

exosphere, ek′sō‧sfẽr, *n.* [Gr. *exo,* outside, and *sphaira,* globe.] The outermost region of the atmosphere.

exostosis, ek‧sos‧tō′sis, *n.* [Gr. *ex,* and *osteon,* a bone.] *Path.* Any protuberance or enlargement of a bone which is not natural; *bot.* a disease of trees, in which knots or large tumors are formed.

exoteric, ek·so·ter′ik, a. [Gr. *exōter-ikos*, external, from *exōteros*, exterior —*exō*, without.] Suitable to be imparted to the public; hence, capable of being readily or fully comprehended; public; opposed to *esoteric* or secret.

exothermic, eks·o·ther′mik, a. [Gr. *exō*, outside, *thermos*, heat.] Of chemical compounds or reactions, formed with or involving evolution of heat. See ENDOTHERMIC.

exotic, eg·zot′ik, a. [Gr. *exōtikos*, from *exō*, outward.] Introduced from a foreign country; not native; foreign; extraneous.—**exotic**, n. Anything of foreign origin, as a plant, tree, word, practice, introduced from a foreign country.

expand, iks·pand′, v.t. [L. *expando*—*ex*, and *pando*, to spread out, to extend, to open (seen also in *pace*, *pass*, etc.).] To spread out so as to give greater extent to; to open out; to cause the particles or parts of to spread or stand apart, thus increasing the bulk; to dilate; to enlarge in bulk; to distend; to widen or extend.—v.i. To become opened, spread apart, dilated, distended, or enlarged. —**expanse**, iks·pans′, n. [L. *expansum*.] A widely expanded surface or space; a wide extent of space.—**expansible**, iks·pan′si·bl, a. Capable of being expanded, extended, dilated, or diffused.—**expansile**, iks·pan′sil, a. Capable of expanding or of being dilated.—**expansion**, iks·pan′shon, n. The act of expanding or spreading out; the state of being expanded; the increase of bulk which a body undergoes by the recession of its particles from one another so that it occupies a greater space, its weight remaining still the same; enlargement; dilatation; distention; an expanse or extended surface; extension.—**expansive**, eks·pan′siv, a. Having the power of expanding or dilating; having the capacity of being expanded; embracing a large number of objects; wide extending.—**expansively**, eks·pan′siv·li, adv. In an expansive manner.—**expansiveness**, eks·pan′siv·nes, n.

ex parte, eks·pär′te, a. [L.] Proceeding only from one part or side of a matter in question; one-sided; partial; *law*, made or done by or on behalf of one party in a suit.

expatiate, iks·pā′shi·āt, v.i.—*expatiated, expatiating*. [L. *exspatior, exspatiatus*—*ex*, and *spatior*, to walk about, from *spatium*, space. SPACE.] To move at large; to rove without prescribed limits; to enlarge in discourse or writing; to be copious in argument or discussion.—**expatiation**, eks·pā′shi·ā″shon, n. Act of expatiating.

expatriate, iks·pā′tri·āt, v.t.—*expatriated, expatriating*. [L. *ex*, out, and *patria*, one's fatherland, from *patrius*, fatherly, from *pater*, a father.] To banish from one's native country; to exile: often *refl.*—**expatriation**, eks·pā′tri·ā″shon, n. The act of banishing or state of being banished; banishment; exile.

expect, iks·pekt′, v.t. [L. *exspecto*, *exspectatum*—*ex*, and *specto*, to behold, from *specio*, to look. SPECIES.] To wait for‡; to await‡; to look forward to in the future; to look for to happen; to entertain at least a slight belief in the happening of; to anticipate; to reckon or count upon.—**expectance**, **expectancy**, iks·pek′tans, iks·pek′tan·si, n. The act or state of expecting; expectation; something on which expectations or hopes are founded; the object of expectation or hope.—**expectant**, iks·pek′tant, a. Expecting; looking for.—n. One who waits in expectation; one held in dependence by his belief or hope of receiving some good.—**expectation**, eks·pek·tā′shon, n. The act of expecting or looking forward to an event as about to happen; the state of being expected or awaited; prospect of future possessions, wealth, or other good fortune; wealth in prospect: in this sense usually in the plural; the value of anything depending on the happening of some uncertain event; prospect of reaching a certain age.—**expectative**, iks·pek′ta·tiv, a. Giving rise to expectation; anticipatory.

expectorate, iks·pek′to·rāt, v.t.—*expectorated, expectorating*. [L. *expectoro, expectoratum*—*ex*, and *pectus, pectoris*, the breast (whence *pectoral*).] To eject from the trachea or lungs; to discharge, as phlegm or other matter, by coughing, hawking, and spitting; to spit out.—v.i. To eject matter by coughing and spitting; to spit.—**expectorant**, iks·pek′to·rant, a. Having the quality of promoting discharges from the mucous membrane of the lungs or trachea.—n. A medicine which promotes such discharges. — **expectoration**, iks·pek′to·rā″shon, n. The act of expectorating; the matter expectorated.

expediency, **expedience**, iks·pē′di·en·si, iks·pē′di·ens, n. [L. *expediens*, pp. of *expedio*, to set free. EXPEDITE.] Propriety under the particular circumstances of a case; advisability, all things being duly considered or taken into account; the seeking of immediate or selfish gain or advantage at the expense of genuine principle; time-servingness.—**expedient**, iks·pē′di·ent, a. Tending to promote the object proposed; proper under the circumstances; conducive or tending to selfish ends.—n. That which serves to promote or advance; any means which may be employed to accomplish an end; means devised or employed in an exigency; shift; contrivance; resort; plan; device.

expedite, eks′pi·dīt, v.t.—*expedited, expediting*. [L. *expedio, expeditum*, to free one caught by the feet in a snare—*ex*, out, and *pes, pedis*, the foot, seen also in *pedal, pedestal, pedestrian, despatch*, etc.] To free from impediments; to accelerate or facilitate the motion or progress of; to render quicker or easier in progress.—a. Clear of impediments; easy; expeditious.—**expedition**, eks·pi·dish′on, n. Promptness in action from being free from encumbrance; speed; quickness; dispatch; the march of an army or the voyage of a fleet to a distant place for hostile purposes; any important journey or voyage made by an organized body of men for some valuable end; such a body of men, together with their equipments, etc.—**expeditionary**, eks·pi·dish′on·e·ri, a. Pertaining to or composing an expedition.—**expeditious**, eks·pi·dish′us, a. Performed with expedition or celerity; quick; hasty; speedy; nimble; active; swift; acting with celerity.—**expeditiously**, eks·pi·dish′us·li, adv. In an expeditious manner.—**expeditiousness**, eks·pi·dish′us·nes, n. The quality of being expeditious.

expel, iks·pel′, v.t.—*expelled, expelling*. [L. *expello*—*ex*, out, and *pello*, to drive, as in *impel, repel, compel*, etc.] To drive or force out from any enclosed place, or from that within which anything is contained or situated; to cast or thrust out; to banish; to exclude; to drive out, as from any society or institution.—**expellable**, iks·pel′a·bl, a. That may be expelled or driven out.

expend, iks·pend′, v.t. [L. *expendo*—*ex*, out, and *pendo*, to weigh out, to pay. The same word takes another form in *spend*.] To lay out in paying, purchasing, etc.; to disburse; to spend; to deliver or distribute, either in payment or in donations; to use, employ, consume (time, labor, material).—**expenditure**, iks·pen′di·cher, n. The act of expending or laying out; disbursement; that which is expended; expense.—**expense**, iks·pens′, n. [L. *expensum*, from *expensus*, pp. of *expendo*.] A laying out or expending; that which is expended, laid out, or consumed; especially, money expended; cost; charge; cost, with the idea of loss, damage, or discredit (he did this at the *expense* of his character).—**expensive**, iks·pen′siv, a. Requiring much expense; costly; dear; extravagant; lavish.—**expensively**, iks·pen′siv·li, adv. In an expensive manner.—**expensiveness**, iks·pen′siv·nes, n. The quality of being expensive.

experience, iks·pē′ri·ens, n. [Fr. *expérience*, L. *experientia*, from *experior*, to try, to prove—*ex*, and a root *per*, to try, to pass through, same as in E. *ferry*, etc.] Personal trial, proof, or test; frequent trial; continued and varied observation; the knowledge gained by trial, or repeated trials, or observation; practical wisdom taught by the changes and trials of life.—v.t.—*experienced, experiencing*. To make practical acquaintance with; to try, or prove, by use, by suffering, or by enjoyment; to have happen to or befall.—**experienced**, iks·pē′ri·enst, p. and a. Taught by experience; skillful or wise by means of trials, use, or observation.—**experiential**, iks·pē′ri·en″shal, a. Relating to experience; derived from or based on experience, trial, or observation; empirical.

experiment, iks·per′i·ment, n. [L. *experimentum*, from *experior*. EXPERIENCE.] An act or operation designed to discover some unknown truth, principle, or effect, or to establish it when discovered; a trial.—*v.i.* To make trial; to make an experiment.—**experimental,** iks·per′i·men″tal, *a.* Pertaining to, derived from, founded on, or known by experiment; given to or skilled in experiment.—**experimentally,** iks·per′i·men″tal·li, *adv.* In an experimental manner; by experiment.—**experimentation,** iks·per′i·men·tā″shon, *n.* The act or practice of making experiments.—**experimenter,** iks·per′i·men·tėr, *n.* One who makes experiments.

expert, eks·pėrt′, *a.* [L. *experius,* having made trial, experienced, from *experior,* to try. EXPERIENCE.] Experienced; taught by use or practice; skillful; dexterous; adroit; having a facility of operation or performance from practice.—*n.* (eks′pėrt). A skillful or practiced person; a scientific or professional witness who gives evidence on matters connected with his profession.—**expertize,** ĕks′pėr·tīz, *v.i.* To give an expert opinion.—**expertly,** eks·pėrt′li, *adv.*—**expertness,** eks·pėrt′nes, *n.*

expiate, eks′pi·āt, *v.t.*—*expiated, expiating.* [L. *expio, expiatum,* to make satisfaction—*ex,* out, and *pio,* to appease, to propitiate, from *pius,* pious.] To atone for; to make satisfaction or reparation for.—**expiable,** eks′pi·a·bl, *a.* Capable of being expiated.—**expiator,** eks′pi·ā·tėr, *n.* One who expiates.—**expiatory,** eks′pi·a·to·ri, *a.* Having the power to make atonement or expiation.

expire, iks·pīr′, *v.t.*—*expired, expiring.* [L. *exspiro—ex,* out, and *spiro,* to breathe. SPIRIT.] To breathe out; to expel from the mouth or nostrils in the process of respiration: opposed to *inspire*; to emit in minute particles; to exhale.—*v.i.* To emit breath; to emit one's last breath; to die; to come to an end; to close or conclude, as a given period; to terminate; to end.—**expiration,** eks·pi·rā′shon, *n.* [L. *exspiratio.*] The act of breathing out, or forcing the air from the lungs; emission of breath; exhalation; close, end, conclusion, or termination; expiry.—**expiratory,** iks·pī′ra·to·ri, *a.* Pertaining to the emission or expiration of breath.—**expiry,** ik·spī′ri, *n.* Expiration; termination.

explain, iks·plān′, *v.t.* [L. *explano—ex,* and *plano,* to make plain, from *planus,* level, plain. PLAIN.] To make plain, manifest, or intelligible; to clear of obscurity; to make clear or evident; to expound; to give or show the meaning or reason of.—*v.i.* To give explanations.—**explainable,** iks·plā′na·bl, *a.* Capable of being explained.—**explanation,** iks·pla·nā′shon, *n.* [L. *explanatio.*] The act of explaining; a making clear or understood; exposition; interpretation; the clearing up of matters between parties who have been at variance.—**explanatory,** iks·plan′a·to·ri, *a.* Serving to explain; containing explanation.

expletive, eks′pli·tiv, *a.* [Fr. *explétif,*

from L. *expleo, expletum,* to fill full—*ex,* intens., and *pleo,* to fill (as in *complete,* etc.).] Added to fill a vacancy; superfluous: said of words.—*n.* A word or syllable inserted to fill a vacancy; an oath or a needless interjection.—**expletory,** eks′ple·to·ri, *a.* Expletive.

explicate, eks′pli·kāt, *v.t.*—*explicated, explicating.* [L. *explico, explicatum,* to unfold—*ex,* not, and *plico,* to fold, to complicate, implicate, apply,* etc. PLY.] To unfold the meaning or sense of; to explain; to interpret.—**explicable,** eks′pli·ka·bl, *a.* Capable of being explicated or explained.—**explication,** eks·pli·kā′shon, *n.* The act of explicating or explaining; explanation.—**explicative, explicatory,** eks′pli·kā·tiv, eks′pli·ka·to·ri, *a.* Serving to unfold or explain.

explicit, iks·plis′it, *a.* [L. *explicitus,* disentangled, from *explico, explicitum,* to unfold, to disentangle. EXPLICATE.] Not implied only, but distinctly stated; plain in language; open to the understanding; clear; not obscure or ambiguous; open; unreserved; outspoken.—**explicitly,** iks·plis′it·li, *adv.* In an explicit manner; expressly; plainly.—**explicitness,** iks·plis′it·nes, *n.* The quality of being explicit.

explode, iks·plōd′, *v.i.*—*exploded, exploding.* [L. *explodo,* to hoot off the stage, to cast out, reject—*ex,* and *plaudo,* to clap, as in *applaud, plaudit,* etc.] To burst with a loud report; to burst and expand with force and noise; to detonate; to burst into activity or into a passion.—*v.t.* To cause to explode or burst with a loud report; to drive from notice or practice and bring into disrepute; to cause to be no longer practiced, held, or believed in (generally in pp.; an *exploded* custom or theory).—**explodent,** iks·plō′dent, *n. Philol.* same as *explosive.*—**exploder,** iks·plō′dėr, *n.* One who or that which explodes.—**explosion,** iks·plō′zhon, *n.* [L. *explosio.*] The act of exploding; a bursting or sudden expansion of any elastic fluid with force and a loud report; a sudden and loud discharge caused by the application of fire, as of gunpowder or a flammable gas; *fig.* a violent outburst of feeling, as of rage, generally accompanied by excited language or by violent actions.—**explosive,** iks·plō′ziv, *a.* Causing explosion; readily exploding; *philol.* mute, forming a complete vocal stop: said of certain consonants.—*n.* Anything liable or with a tendency to explode, as gunpowder, dynamite, etc.; *philol.* a mute or noncontinuous consonant, as *k, t, b.*—**explosively,** iks·plō′ziv·li, *adv.* In an explosive manner.

exploit, eks′ploit, eks·ploit′, *n.* [Fr. *exploit,* O.Fr. *exploict,* from L. *explico, explicatum, explicitum,* to unfold, finish. EXPLICATE.] A deed or act of note; a heroic act; a deed of renown; a notable feat; a great or noble achievement.—*v.t.* eks·ploit′. [Fr. *exploiter.*] To utilize; to make use of basely for one's own advan-

tage.—**exploitation,** eks·ploi·tā′shon, *n.* [Fr.] Utilization; the successful application of industry on any object, as in the cultivation of land, the working of mines, etc.; now, esp., selfish or unfair utilization.

explore, iks·plōr′, *v.t.*—*explored, exploring.* [L. *exploro,* to cry aloud, to explore—*ex,* out, and *ploro,* to bewail, as in *deplore.*] To travel or range over with the view of making discovery, especially geographical discovery; to search by any means; to scrutinize; to inquire into with care; to examine closely with a view to discover truth.—**exploration,** iks·plo·rā′shon, *n.* The act of exploring; close search; strict or careful examination.—**explorative, exploratory,** iks·plō′ra·tiv, iks·plō′ra·to·ri, *a.* Serving or tending to explore; searching; examining.—**explorer,** iks·plō′rėr, *n.* One who explores.

explosion. See EXPLODE.

exponent, iks·pō′nent, *n.* [L. *exponens, exponentis,* ppr. of *expono,* to expose or set forth—*ex,* out, and *pono,* to place.] One who expounds or explains anything; one who stands forth to explain the principles or doctrines of a party; *alg.* a small number placed above a quantity at the right hand to denote to what power the quantity must be understood to be raised: thus a^2 denotes a raised to the second power.—**exponential,** eks·pō·nen′shal, *a.* Of or pertaining to an exponent or exponents.

export, eks·pōrt′, *v.t.* (often eks′pōrt, *esp. in contrast with import*). [Fr. *exporter,* from L. *exporto—ex,* out, and *porto,* to bear, to carry, as in *import, report, support, sport.*] To send for sale or consumption in foreign countries; to send or furnish for conveyance to distant places, either by water or land.—*n.* (eks′pōrt). The act of exporting; exportation; the gross quantity of goods exported; that which is exported; a commodity that is exported.—**exportable,** eks·pōr′ta·bl, *a.* Capable of being exported.—**exportation,** eks·pōr·tā′shon, *n.* The act of exporting; the act of conveying or sending abroad commodities in the course of commerce.—**exporter,** eks·pōr′tėr, *n.* (in contrast, eks′pōr·tėr). One who exports.

expose, iks·pōz′, *v.t.* [Fr. *exposer*—prefix *ex,* and *poser,* to set, to place. POSE; also COMPOSE, DEPOSE, etc.] To set out or leave in a place unprotected and uncared for; to abandon; to make bare; to uncover; to disclose; to put forward or place in a position to be seen; to exhibit; to set out to view; to lay open to examination; to subject or place in the way of something to be avoided (this *exposed* him to danger); to put in danger; to hold up to censure by disclosing the faults of; to show the folly or ignorance of.—**exposé,** eks·po·zā′, *n.* [Fr.] Exposure; the exposure of something which it was desirable to keep concealed.—**exposed,** iks·pōzd′, *p.* and *a.* Put in danger; unprotected; liable; subject;

open to the wind or the cold; unsheltered.—**exposer**, iks·pō′zẽr, n. One who exposes.—**exposition**, eks·po·zish′on, n. [Fr. *exposition*, L. *expositio*.] A laying open; a setting out to public view; explanation; interpretation; a laying open the sense or meaning; an exhibition or show.—**expositor**, iks·poz′i·tẽr, n. One who expounds or explains; an interpreter.—**expository**, iks·poz′i·to·ri, a. Serving to explain; tending to illustrate.—**exposure**, iks·pō′zhẽr, n. The act of exposing; abandonment; the state of being exposed; openness to view; openness or liability to danger, inconvenience, etc.; position in regard to the free access of light, air, etc.

ex post facto, eks·pōst·fak′tō, a. [L.] *Law*, done after another thing; after the deed is done; retrospective.

expostulate, iks·pos′che·lāt, v.i.—*expostulated, expostulating*. [L. *expostulo, expostulatum*—*ex*, and *postulo*, to demand vehemently, to find fault—*ex*, and *postulo*, to demand, from *posco*, to ask urgently, to beg. POSTULATE.] To reason earnestly with a person on some impropriety of his conduct; to remonstrate.—v.t.‡ To reason about; to discuss. (*Shak.*)—**expostulation**, iks·pos′che·lā″shon, n. The act of expostulating; the act of pressing on a person reasons or arguments against the impropriety of his conduct; an address containing expostulation.—**expostulator**, iks·pos′che·lā·tẽr, n. One who expostulates.—**expostulatory**, iks·pos′che·la·to·ri, a. Consisting of or containing expostulation.

exposure. See EXPOSE.

expound, iks·pound′, v.t. [O.Fr. *expondre*, from L. *exponere*, to set forth, to explain—*ex*, out, and *pono*, to place. *Compound* is similarly formed.] To explain; to lay open the meaning of; to clear of obscurity; to interpret.—**expounder**, iks·poun′dẽr, n. One who expounds.

express, iks·pres′, v.t. [O.Fr. *expresser*. L. *exprimo, expressum*—*ex*, out, and *premo*, to press. PRESS.] To press or squeeze out; to force out by pressure; to give utterance to or declare by words; to represent in words; to intimate; to indicate; to make known; to tell; to represent; to exhibit; to denote; to send or convey by special fast system; *refl.* to speak what one has got to speak.—a. Given in direct terms: not implied or left to inference; clearly expressed; not ambiguous; plain; explicit; intended or sent for a particular purpose or on a particular errand; traveling with special speed (an *express* train).—n. A messenger sent with haste on a particular errand or occasion; any regular provision made for the speedy transmission of parcels, money, goods; any vehicle or other conveyance sent on a special mission; a railroad train which travels at a specially high rate of speed; that sent by express.—**expression**, iks·presh′on, n. The act of expressing or forcing out by pressure, as juices and oils from plants; the act of

uttering, declaring, or representing; utterance; declaration; power of expressing one's thoughts, feelings, ideas, etc.; something uttered; a phrase or mode of speech; the peculiar manner of utterance suited to the subject and sentiment; cast of countenance, as indicative of character; play of features, as expressive of feeling or any emotion; the natural and lively representation of any state or condition, as in a picture by the pose of the figure, the conformation of the features, etc.; the power or quality in a picture or other work of art of suggesting an idea; *mus.* sound suited to any particular subject; *alg.* any algebraic quantity, simple or compound, as $3a$, $\sqrt{4a+b}$, etc.—**expressionism**, iks·presh′on·izm, n. *Art*, the depiction of subjective qualities by an artist.—**expressive**, iks·pres′iv, a. Serving to express, utter, or represent (words *expressive of* gratitude); full of expression; emphatic.—**expressively**, iks·pres′iv·li, adv.—**expressiveness**, iks·pres′iv·nes, n.—**expressly**, iks·pres′li, adv. In an express manner; of set purpose; in direct terms; plainly.—**expressway**, iks·pres′wā, n. A high-speed, nonstop highway.

expropriate, eks·prō′pri·āt, v.t. [L. *ex*, out of, from, and *proprius*, one's own. PROPER, PROPRIETY.] To disengage from appropriation; to give up a claim to the exclusive property of.—**expropriation**, eks·prō′pri·ā″shon, n. The act of expropriating; the act of dispossessing the owner of a property wholly or to a great extent of his proprietary rights.

expulsion, iks·pul′shon, n.[L. *expulsio*, a driving out, from *expello*, to expel.] The act of driving out or expelling; a driving away by violence; the state of being expelled, driven out, or away.—**expulsive**, iks·pul′siv, a. Having the power of expelling.

expunge, iks·punj′, v.t.—*expunged, expunging*. [L. *expungo*, to prick out, to cross or blot out—*ex*, out, and *pungo*, to prick. POINT.] To blot out, as with a pen; to rub out; to efface; to erase; to obliterate; to wipe out or destroy; to annihilate.

expurgate, eks′pẽr·gāt, v.t.—*expurgated, expurgating*. [L. *expurgo, expurgatum*—*ex*, and *purgo*, to purge. PURGE, PURE.] To purify from anything noxious, offensive, or erroneous; to purge; to cleanse; to strike obscene, coarse, or offensive passages out of (a book).—**expurgation**, eks·pẽr·gā′shon, n. The act of expurgating, purging, or cleansing; purification.—**expurgator**, eks·pẽr′gā·tẽr, n. One who expurgates.—**expurgatory**, iks·pẽr′ga·to·ri, a. Cleansing; purifying; serving to expurgate.

exquisite, eks′kwi·zit, a. [L. *exquisitus*, carefully sought out, exquisite, from *exquiro, exquisitum*—*ex*, out, and *quæro*, to seek, whence *question, quest, query*, etc.] Of great excellence or fineness; choice; select; consummate; perfect; of keen or delicate perception; keen; nice; refined; delicate; pleasurable or painful in the

highest degree; extreme.—n. One excessively nice in his dress; a dandy; a swell; a fop; a coxcomb.—**exquisitely**, eks′kwi·zit·li, adv. In an exquisite manner.—**exquisiteness**, eks′kwi·zit·nes, n.

exscind, ek·sind′, v.t. [L. *excsindo*, to cut out.] To cut out or off.

exsect, ek·sekt′, v.t. [L. *exseco*, to cut out.] To cut out or away.

exsert, exserted, ek·sẽrt′, ek·sẽr′ted, a. [L. *exsertus*, from *exsero*, to stretch out or forth. EXERT.] Standing out; projected beyond some other part.—**exsertile**, ek·sẽr′til, a. Capable of being protruded.

exsiccate, ek′sik·āt, v.t.—*exsiccated, exsiccating*. [L. *exsicco, exsiccatum*, to dry up—*ex*, intens., and *sicco*, to dry.] To exhaust of moisture; to dry up completely.—**exsiccation**, ek·sik·kā′shon, n. The act or operation of exsiccating or drying; dryness.—**exsiccator**, ek·sik′kā·tẽr, n. An apparatus or contrivance for drying moist substances.

exstipulate, eks·tip′ū·lāt, a. *Bot.* having no stipules.

extant, eks′tant, a. [L. *extans, exstans, extantis, exstantis*, ppr. of *exsto*, to stand out—*ex*, out, and *sto*, to stand. STATE.] Still existing; in being; now subsisting; not destroyed or lost.

extemporaneous, extemporary, iks·tem′po·rā″ni·us, iks·tem′po·ra·ri, a. [L. *extemporaneus*—*ex*, not, and *tempus, temporis*, time.] Performed, uttered, or made at the time without previous thought or study; unpremeditated; off-hand.—**extemporaneously, extemporarily**, iks·tem′po·rā″ni·us·li, iks·tem′po·ra·ri·li, adv. In an extemporaneous manner.—**extemporaneousness**,iks·tem′po·rā″ni·us·nes, n. The quality of being extemporaneous.—**extempore**, iks·tem′po·ri, adv. [L. phrase *ex tempore*, same meaning.] Without previous thought, study, or meditation; without preparation.—a. Extemporary; extemporaneous.—**extemporization**, iks·tem′po·ri·zā″shon, n. The act of extemporizing.—**extemporize**, iks·tem′po·rīz, v.i.—*extemporized, extemporizing*. To speak without previous thought, study, or preparation; to discourse without notes or written composition.—v.t. To make without forethought; to provide for the occasion; to prepare in great haste with the means within one's reach (to *extemporize* a speech or a dinner).—**extemporizer**, iks·tem′po·rī·zẽr, n. One who extemporizes.

extend, iks·tend′, v.t. [L. *extendo*, to stretch out—*ex*, out, and *tendo*, to stretch (as in *contend, pretend, tend*); same root as L. *tenuis*, thin, *tenax*, tenacious, E. *thin*.] To stretch in any direction; to carry forward or continue in length, as a line; to spread in breadth; to expand or dilate in size; to hold out or reach forth; to expand; to enlarge; to widen; to diffuse; to continue; to prolong; to communicate, bestow, or impart.—v.i. To stretch; to reach; to be continued in length, or breadth; to become larger or more comprehensive; to value land; to seize land for debt.—**extendedly,** eks·ten'ded··li, *adv.* In an extended manner.—**extendible,** iks·ten'di·bl, *a.* Capable of being extended.—**extensibility,** iks·ten'si·bil"i·ti, *n.* The quality of being extensible.—**extensible, extensile,** iks·ten'si·bl, iks·ten'sīl, *a.* Capable of being extended.—**extension,** iks·ten'shon, *n.* The act of extending; the state of being extended; enlargement; expansion; prolongation; that property of any body by which it occupies a portion of space, being one of the properties of matter; *logic,* the extent of the application of a general term, that is, the objects collectively which are included under it; compass.—**extensive,** iks·ten'siv, *a.* Having great or considerable extent; wide; large; embracing a wide area or a great number of objects; diffusive.—**extensively,** iks·ten'siv·li, *adv.* In an extensive manner.—**extensiveness,** iks·ten'siv·nes, *n.* The state or quality of being extensive.—**extensor,** iks·ten'sėr, *n. Anat.* a muscle which serves to extend or straighten any part of the body, as an arm or a finger: opposed to *flexor.*—**extent,** iks·tent', *n.* [L.L. *extentus,* a stretching out; L. *extentus,* extended.] Space or degree to which a thing is extended; extension; length; compass; bulk; size; valuation of land; seizure of land for debt.

extensometer, eks·ten·som'e·tėr, *n.* [L. *extensio,* stretching, Gr. *metron,* a measure.] An instrument of precision for measuring small lengths.

extenuate, iks·ten'ū·āt, *v.t.*—*extenuated, extenuating.* [L. *extenuo, extenuatum,* to make thin or small, to lessen—*ex,* and *tenuis,* thin, fine (whence *tenuity*); same root as E. *thin.*] To lessen or diminish; to weaken the import or force of; to palliate; to mitigate.—**extenuation,** iks·ten'ū·ā"shon, *n.* The act of extenuating; palliation; mitigation, as opposed to *aggravation.*—**extenuator,** iks·ten'ū·ā·tėr, *n.* One who extenuates.—**extenuatory,** iks·ten'ū·a·to·ri, *a.* Tending to extenuate.

exterior, iks·tē'ri·ėr, *a.* [L., compar. of *exter* or *exterus,* on the outside, outward, from *ex,* out of; akin *external, extreme, estrange, strange.*] External; outer; outward; bounding or limiting outwardly; situated beyond the limits of; on the outside; not arising or coming from within.—*n.* The outer surface; the outside; the external features.—**exteriorly,** iks·tē'ri·ėr·li, *adv.* In an exterior manner; outwardly; externally.

exterminate, iks·tėr'mi·nāt, *v.t.*—*exterminated, exterminating.* [L. *extermino, exterminatum,* to remove—*ex,* and *termino,* to terminate, from *terminus,* a limit. TERM.] To destroy utterly; to extirpate; to root out; to eradicate.—**extermination,** iks·tėr'mi·nā"shon, *n.* The act of exterminating; destruction; eradication; extirpation.—**exterminator,** iks·tėr'mi·nā·tėr, *n.* One who or that which exterminates.—**exterminatory,** iks·tėr'mi·na·to·ri, *a.* Tending to ex-

terminate; marked by extermination.

external, iks·tėr'nal, *a.* [L. *externus,* from *exter,* on the outside. EXTERIOR.] On the outside: opposite to *internal;* on the exterior; superficial; not being or arising within; outside of ourselves; relating to or connected with foreign nations; foreign.—*External-combustion engine,* an engine that derives its energy from the combustion of fuel outside the cylinder.—*n.* Something exterior; an outward rite or ceremony.—**externality,** iks·tėr·nal'i·ti, *n.* The state of being external; separation from the perceiving mind; exteriority.—**externalize,** iks·tėr'nal·īz, *v.t.* To embody in an outward form; to give shape and form to.—**externally,** iks·tėr'nal·li, *adv.* Outwardly; on the outside; apparently; exteriorly.

exterritorial, eks·ter'i·tō"ri·al, *a.* [Prefix *ex,* and *territorial.*] Beyond the jurisdiction of the laws of the country in which one resides.—**exterritoriality,** eks·ter'i·tō'ri·al"i·ti, *n.* Immunity from a country's laws, such as that enjoyed by an ambassador.

extinct, iks·tingkt', *a.* [L. *extinctus,* pp. of *extinguo, exstinguo.* EXTINGUISH.] Extinguished; quenched; having ceased; being at an end; no longer in existence; having died out (a family or race is *extinct*).—**extinction,** iks·tingk'shon, *n.* The act of putting out or quenching flame or fire; the state of being extinguished; a putting an end to, or a coming to an end.

extinguish, iks·ting'gwish, *v.t.* [L. *extinguo, exstinguo—ex,* and *stinguo,* to scratch out, as in *distinguish.*] To put out; to quench; to stifle; to put an end to; to suppress; to destroy; to crush; to eclipse.—**extinguishable,** iks·ting'gwish·a·bl, *a.* Capable of being quenched, destroyed, or suppressed.—**extinguisher,** iks·ting'gwish·ėr, *n.* One who or that which extinguishes; a hollow conical utensil to put on a candle or lamp to extinguish it.—**extinguishment,**† iks·ting'gwish·ment, *n.* The act of extinguishing; extinction.

extirpate, eks·tėr·pāt, *v.t.*—*extirpated, extirpating.* [L. *extirpo, exstirpo, exstirpatum—ex,* out, and *stirps,* the trunk of a tree.] To pull or pluck up by the roots; to root out; to eradicate; to destroy totally; to exterminate.—**extirpation,** eks·tėr·pā'shon, *n.* The act of rooting out; eradication; total destruction.—**extirpator,** eks·tėr'pā·tėr, *n.* One who or that which extirpates.

extol, iks·tōl', *v.t.*—*extolled, extolling.* [L. *extollo,* to raise up—*ex,* out, up, and *tollo,* to raise; from same root as in *tolero,* to endure, to tolerate.] To speak in laudatory terms of; to praise; to laud; to applaud; to eulogize; to magnify; to celebrate; to glorify.—**extoller,** iks·tōl'ėr, *n.* One who extols; a praiser or magnifier.

extort, iks·tort', *v.t.* [L. *extorqueo, extortum—ex,* and *torqueo,* to twist, seen in *contort, distort, retort, torture,* etc.] To obtain from a person

by force or compulsion; to wrest or wring by physical force, by menace, torture, or authority (to *extort* contributions, a confession, a promise, etc.).—**extorter,** iks·tor'tėr, *n.* One who extorts.—**extortion,** iks·tor'shon, *n.* The act of extorting; the act or practice of extorting or wringing money from people by any undue exercise of power; illegal compulsion to pay money; rapacity; that which is extorted.—**extortionary,** iks·tor'shon·e·ri, *a.* Practicing extortion; containing extortion.—**extortionate,** iks·tor'shon·at, *a.* Characterized by extortion; oppressive in exacting money.—**extortioner, extortionist,** iks·tor'shon·ėr, iks·tor'shon·ist, *n.*

extra, eks'tra, *a.* and *adv.* [Contr. from *extraordinary,* or directly from L. *extra,* beyond.] Beyond what is due, appointed, or expected; supplementary; additional.—*n.* Something in addition to what is due, expected, or usual; a special edition of a newspaper; one who plays small parts in a movie or stage show.

extract, iks·trakt', *v.t.* [L. *extractus,* from *extraho—ex,* and *traho,* to draw; seen also in *contract, detract, retract, trace, tract,* etc.] To draw out; to take out; to pull out or remove from a fixed position; to draw out by distillation or other chemical process; to select as a specimen or sample; to take (a passage or passages) from a book or writing; to ascertain the root of a number.—*n.* (eks'trakt). That which is extracted or drawn from something; a passage taken from a book or writing; an excerpt; a quotation; anything drawn from a substance by heat, distillation, or a chemical process, as an essence, a tincture, and the like.—**extractable, extractible,** iks·trak'ta·bl, iks·trak'ti·bl, *a.* Capable of being extracted.—**extraction,** iks·trak'shon, *n.* [L. *extractio.*] The act of extracting or drawing out; descent; lineage; derivation of persons from a stock or family; the stock or family from which one has descended; operation of finding the root of a given number or quantity.—**extractive,** iks·trak'tiv, *a.* Capable of being extracted; extracting.—*n.* That which is extracted or extractable.—**extractor,** iks·trak'tėr, *n.*

extracurricular, eks'tra·kėr·ik"ū·lėr, *a.* [Prefix *extra,* and *curriculum.*] Being outside one's routine activities; not being in the regular school curriculum, such as athletics, clubs, etc.

extradition, eks·tra·dish'on, *n.* [L. *ex,* and *traditio,* a giving up, surrender, from *trado, traditum,* to give up.] Delivery of a criminal or fugitive from one state or nation, usually under a treaty or statute, to another having jurisdiction to try the charge.—**extradite,** eks'tra·dīt, *v.t.* To deliver or give up for extradition.

extragalactic, eks'tra·gal·ăk"tik, *a.* [Prefix *extra,* and *galaxy.*] Lying outside or beyond a galaxy, especially the Milky Way.

extrajudicial, eks'tra·jū·dish"al, *a.* Out of the proper court, or the ordinary course of legal procedure.—

---

fāte, fär, fâre, fat, fạll; mē, met, hėr; pīne, pin; nōte, not, mȯve; tūbe, tub, bụll; oil, pound.

extrajudicially, eks·tra·jū·dish″al·li, *adv.* In an extrajudicial manner; out of court.

extramundane, eks·tra·mun′dān, *a.* Beyond the limit of the material world or mundane affairs.

extramural, eks·tra·mū′ral, *a.* [L. *extra*, beyond, and *murus*, a wall.] Without or beyond the walls, as of a fortified city or a university.

extraneous, eks·trā′ni·us, *a.* [L. *extraneus*, from *extra*, without, beyond; akin *strange*.] Foreign; not belonging to a thing; existing without; not intrinsic.—**extraneously,** eks·trā′ni·us·li, *adv.* In an extraneous manner.

extraofficial, eks′tra·of·fish″al, *a.* Not within the limits of official duty.

extraordinary, eks·tra·or′di·ne·ri, *a.* [L. *extraordinarius*—*extra*, and *ordo, ordinis*, order.] Beyond or out of the ordinary or common order or method; remarkable; uncommon; rare; wonderful; special; particular; sent for a special purpose or on a particular occasion (an ambassador *extraordinary*).—**extraordinarily,** eks·tra·or′di·ne·ri·li, *adv.*

extraphysical, eks·tra·fiz′i·kal, *a.* Not subject to physical laws or methods.

extrapolate, eks·trap′o·lāt, *v.t.* [L. *expolire*, to polish or refine—*extra*, beyond, and *polio*, polish. INTERPOLATE.] To project into an unknown field for the sake of knowledge by drawing parallelisms with a field that is known, under the assumption that they correspond.—**extrapolation,** eks·trap′o·lā″shon, *n.*

extraprofessional, eks′tra·pro·fesh″on·al, *a.* Not within the ordinary limits of professional duty or business.

extrasensory, eks·tra·sen″so·ri, *a.* [Prefix *extra*, and *sensory*.] Being beyond the ordinary sense perceptions; clairvoyant.

extraterritorial, eks′tra·ter′i·to″ri·al, *a.* [Prefix *extra*, and *territorial*.] Beyond the territorial limits of jurisdiction.—**extraterritoriality,** eks′·tra·ter′i·to′ri·al″i·ti, *n.* Immunity from a country's laws.

extravagance, extravagancy, iks·trav′a·gans, iks·trav′a·gan·si, *n.* [Fr. *extravagance*—L. *extra*, beyond, and *vagans*, ppr. of *vago, vagor*, to wander. VAGABOND.] Want of restraint; wildness; irregularity; unreasonableness; prodigality; lavish spending or waste; excess; profusion; bombast.—**extravagant,** iks·trav′a·gant, *a.* Exceeding due bounds; unreasonable; excessive; not within ordinary limits of truth or probability or other usual bounds; unrestrained; profuse in expenses.—**extravagantly,** iks·trav′·a·gant·li, *adv.*—**extravaganza,** iks·trav′a·gan″za, *n.* A literary or musical composition noted for its wildness and incoherence; a burlesque.

extravasate, iks·trav′a·sāt, *v.t.*—*extravasated, extravasating.* [L. *extra*, beyond, and *vas*, a vessel.] To force or let out of the proper vessels, as out of the blood vessels.—**extravasation,** iks·trav′a·sā″shon, *n.* The act of extravasating; the state of being forced or let out of the vessels or ducts of the body that contain it; effusion.—

extravascular, eks·tra·vas′kūlėr, *a.* Being out of the proper vessels.

extreme, iks·trēm′, *a.* [Fr. *extrême*, from L. *extremus*, superl. of *exter* or *exterus*, on the outside, external. EXTERIOR.] Outermost; furthest; at the utmost point, edge, or border; worst or best that can exist or be supposed; carrying principles to the uttermost; ultra.—*n.* The utmost point of a thing; extremity; utmost limit or degree that can be supposed or tolerated; height or extravagant pitch; *math.* the first or the last term of a proportion.—**extremely,** iks·trēm′li, *adv.*—**extremism,** iks·trēm′izm, *n.* The quality or state of being extreme.—**extremist,** iks·trēm′ist, *n.* A supporter of extreme doctrines or practice.—**extremity,** iks·trem′i·ti, *n.* [L. *extremitas*.] The utmost point or side; the verge; the highest degree; the most aggravated or intense form; extreme or utmost distress, straits, or difficulties; a limb or organ of locomotion.

extricate, eks′tri·kāt, *v.t.*—*extricated, extricating.* [L. *extrico, extricatum*—*ex*, and *tricæ*, trifles, perplexity. See INTRICATE.] To free, as from difficulties or perplexities; to disembarrass; to disengage; to disentangle; to clear; to relieve.—**extricable,** eks′tri·ka·bl, *a.* Capable of being extricated.—**extrication,** eks·tri·kā′shon, *n.* The act of extricating, disentangling, or setting free.

extrinsic, extrinsical, eks·trin′sik, eks·trin′si·kal, *a.* [L. *extrinsecus*, from without—*exter*, outward (as in *exterior*), and *secus*, by, along with.] External; outward; coming from without; not intrinsic; not contained in or belonging to a body.—**extrinsically,** eks·trin′si·kal·li, *adv.* In an extrinsic manner; from without.

extrorsal, extrorse, eks·tror′sal, eks·trors′, *a.* [Fr. *extrorse*, from L. *extra*, on the outside, and *verto, versum*, to turn.] *Bot.* turned or directed outward, or turned away from the axis: opposed to *introrse*.—**extroversion,** eks·trō·vėr′shon, *n. Path.* a malformation consisting in an organ being turned inside out, as the bladder.

extrovert, ek′strō·vėrt, *n.* [L. *extro*, extra, and *vertere*, to turn.] One whose attentions are turned toward that which is outside the self.—**extroversion,** ek′strō·vėr″zhun, *n.*

extrude, eks·tröd′, *v.t.*—*extruded, extruding.* [L. *extrudo*—*ex*, and *trudo*, to thrust, as in *intrude*.] To thrust out; to urge, force, or press out; to expel; to drive away; to displace. —**extrusion,** eks·trö′zhon, *n.* The act of extruding; expulsion.

exuberance, exuberancy, igz·ū′bėr·ans, igz·ū′bėr·an·si, *n.* [Fr. *exubérance*, from L. *exuberantia*—*ex*, intens., and *ubero*, to be fruitful, from *uber*, rich, fruitful.] The state of being exuberant; superfluous abundance; an overflowing quantity; richness; excess; redundance; copiousness.—**exuberant,** igz·ū′bėr·ant, *a.* [L. *exuberans, exuberantis*, ppr. of *exubero*.] Characterized by abundance, richness, or luxuriance; plenteous; rich; overflowing; over-abundant; superfluous.—**exuberantly,** igz·ū′bėr·ant·li, *adv.* In an exuberant manner.

exude, eks·ūd′, *v.t.*—*exuded, exuding.* [L. *exsudo*, to discharge by sweating—*ex*, and *sudo*, to sweat, from same root as E. *sweat*.] To discharge through the pores, as moisture or other liquid matter; to give out, like sweat or juice; to let ooze out.—*v.i.* To flow from a body through the pores; to ooze out like sweat.—**exudate,** eks′ū·dāt, *n.* [L. *exudare*, to sweat.] Material passing through the wall of a blood vessel into surrounding parts.—**exudation,** eks·ū′dā″shon, *n.* The act of exuding; that which is exuded.

exult, ig·zult′, *v.i.* [L. *exulto, exsulto*, to leap or jump about—*ex*, and *salio, saltum*, to leap, seen also in *insult, result, salient*, etc.] To rejoice in triumph; to rejoice exceedingly; to be glad above measure; to triumph.—**exultant,** ig·zul′tant, *a.* Rejoicing triumphantly.—**exultation,** eg·zul·tā′shon, *n.* The act of exulting; great gladness; rapturous delight; triumph.—**exultingly,** eg·zul′ting·li, *adv.* In an exulting manner.

exurb, ek′sėrb, *n.* [L. *ex*, outside, and *urb*, city.] A residential region located beyond the city and suburbs and usually inhabited by wealthy people.—**exurbanite,** ek·sėrb′an·īt, *n.*

exuviae, ig·zū′vi·ē, *n. pl.* [L., from *exuo*, to put off, to strip.] Cast skins, shells, or coverings of animals; any parts of animals which are shed or cast off, as the skins of serpents, etc.—**exuvial,** ig·zū′vi·al, *a.* Relating to or containing exuviae.—**exuviation,** ig·zū′vi·ā″shon, *n.* The rejection or casting off of exuviae.

eyas, ī′as, *n.* [Fr. *niais*, lit. a nestling falcon, from L.L. *nidax, nidacis*, still in the nest, L. *nidus*, a nest; with loss of n as in *adder*.] A young hawk just taken from the nest, not able to prey for itself. (*Shak.*)—*Eyas-musket*, a young sparrow hawk.

eye, ī, *n.* [O.E. *ye, eighe*, A.Sax. *eâge*, Dan. *öie*, D. *oog*, Icel. *auga*, G. *auge*, Goth. *augo*; cog. L. *oculus*, Skr. *akshi*—eye; from a root meaning sharp. ACID.] The nearly spherical hollow organ of sight filled with a vitreous fluid and located in a bony orbit in the anterior skull, consisting in man and the higher animals of the cornea, iris, pupil, lens, and retina that aid in transmitting, through the optic nerve, images to the brain; the faculty of seeing with the eye; delicate and accurate perception; anything resembling or suggesting an eye; the hole or aperture in a needle; the center of something; thus, the *eye* of a dome is the circular aperture at its apex.—*The wind's eye*, the direction right opposite to that of the wind.—*v.t. eyed, eying or eyeing.* To fix the eye on; to look on; to observe narrowly, or with fixed attention.—**eyed,** īd, *a.* Furnished with eyes; having eyes of this or that character.—**eyeless,** ī′les, *a.* Without eyes.—**eyeball,** ī′bạl, *n.* The ball, globe, or apple of the eye.—**eye-bright**, ī′brīt, *n*. A pretty little annual European herb common in meadows, heaths, etc., which formerly enjoyed a great reputation in diseases of the eyes.—**eyebrow**, ī′brou, *n*. The brow or hairy arch above the eye.—**eyeglass**, *n*. A glass to assist the sight; the lens of a telescope, microscope, etc., to which the eye is applied.—**eyelash**, ī′lash, *n*. One of the hairs that edge the eyelid.—**eyelet**, ī′let, *n*. A small hole or perforation to receive a lace or small rope or cord, or for other purposes.—**eyelid**, ī′lid, *n*. That portion of movable skin that serves as a cover for the eyeball.—**eye opener**, *n*. Startling news; a drink of liquor, particularly the first of the day (*Slang*). **eyepiece**, *n*. In an optical instrument the lens or combination of lenses to which the eye is applied.—**eyeservant**, *n*. A servant who attends to his duty only when watched.—**eyeservice**, *n*. Service performed only under inspection or the eye of an employer.—**eyesight**, ī′sīt, *n*. The sight of the eye; view; observation; the sense of seeing.—**eyesore**, ī′sōr, *n*. Something offensive to the eye or sight.—**eyetooth**, ī′töth, *n*. A tooth under the eye; a fang; a canine tooth.—**eyewash**, *n*. A lotion to cleanse or treat the eye.—**eyewitness**, *n*. One who sees a thing done; one who has ocular view of anything.

eyre, âr, *n*. [O.Fr. *erre*, *eirre*, a journey, from L. *iter*, *itineris*, a journey.] A journey or circuit of a court; a court of itinerant justices.—*Justices in eyre*, itinerant justices who formerly traveled to hold courts in the different English counties.

eyrie, **eyry**, â′ri, *n*. Same as *Aerie*.

F

F, f, ef, the sixth letter of the English alphabet, a consonant, formed by the passage of breath between the lower lip and the upper front teeth; *mus*. the fourth note of the diatonic scale.

fa, fä, *n*. *Mus*. the Italian name of the fourth note of the diatonic scale.

fabaceous, fa·bā′shus, *a*. [L. *faba*, a bean.] Having the nature of the bean; like the bean.

Fabian, fā′bi·an, *a*. Like the generalship of *Fabius* Maximus, who harassed the troops of Hannibal but took care to avoid a battle (*Fabian* strategy).

fable, fā′bl, *n*. [Fr. *fable*, L. *fabula*, from *fari*, to speak; akin *fate*.] A fictitious narration intended to enforce some useful truth or precept; a fabricated story; a fiction; the plot or connected series of events in an epic or dramatic poem; subject of talk (*Tenn*.).—*v.i.*—*fabled*, *fabling*, To tell fables or falsehoods. —*v.t.* To invent or fabricate; to speak of as true or real.—**fabled**,

fā′bld, *p*. and *a*. Celebrated in fables; fabulously imagined.—**fabler**, fā′blėr, *n*. One who fables; a writer of fables.—**fabliau**, fab′li·ō, *n*. pl. **fabliaux**, fab′li·ō. [Fr.] A kind of metrical tale common in French literature of the twelfth and thirteenth centuries.—**fabulist**, fab′ū·list, *n*. The inventor or writer of fables.—**fabulous**, fab′ū·lus, *a*. Having the nature of a fable; fictitious; invented; not real; mythical; hardly to be received as truth; incredible.—**fabulously**, fab′ū·lus·li, *adv*. In a fabulous manner.—**fabulousness**, fab′ū·lus·nes, *n*. The quality of being fabulous.

fabric, fab′rik, *n*. [Fr. *fabrique*, L. *fabrica*, from *faber*, a worker; same root as *facio*, to make. *Forge* is really the same word.] A structure; a building, edifice, or construction; the frame of a building; cloth manufactured; the structure of anything; the manner in which the parts are put together; texture.—**fabricant**, fab′ri·kant, *n*. [Fr.] A manufacturer.—**fabricate**, fab′ri·kāt, *v.t.*—*fabricated*, *fabricating*. [L. *fabrico*, *fabricatum*.] To frame, build, make, or construct; to form into a whole by connecting the parts; to form by art and labor; to invent and form; to forge; to devise falsely.—**fabrication**, fab·ri·kā′shon, *n*. The act of fabricating; construction; making; the act of devising falsely; forgery; that which is fabricated; a falsehood. —**fabricator**, fab′ri·kā·tėr, *n*. One who fabricates.

façade, fa·säd′ or fa·sād′, *n*. [Fr., from It., *faciata*, a façade, from *faccia*, L. *facies*, the face.] The face or front view or elevation of an edifice; exterior front or face.

face, fās, *n*. [Fr., from L. *facies*, face, figure, form, from *facio*, to make.] The front part of an animal's head, particularly of the human head, made up of the forehead, eyes, nose, mouth, cheeks, etc.; the visage; aspect or air of the face; cast of features; look; countenance; expression of the face; the surface of a thing, or the side which presents itself to the view of the spectator; the front; the forepart; a plane surface of a solid; one of the sides bounding a solid; appearance; aspect; effrontery; boldness; assurance; the dial of a clock, watch, compass card, or other indicator; the sole of a plane; operating edge or surface in certain implements.—*To make a face*, to distort the countenance; to make a grimace.—*To fly in the face of*, to act in direct opposition to or disregard of; to defy.—*Face to face*, both parties being present and confronting each other.—*v.t.*—*faced*, *facing*. To turn the face or front full toward; to meet in front; to stand up against in hostile encounter; to confront; to stand with the face or front toward; to finish or protect with a thin external covering over the front of; to smooth or dress the face of (a stone, etc.).—*To face down*, to oppose boldly or impudently.—*To face out*, to persist

in, especially to persist in an assertion which is not true; to brave (an accusation) with effrontery.—*To face tea*, to adulterate it by mixing it with coloring matter and other substances.—*v.i.* To turn the face (to *face* to the right or left).—**faced**, fāst, *a*. Having a face; marked with a face (as a court card).—**facial**, fā′shel, *a*. Of or pertaining to the face.—*Facial angle*, an angle formed by lines drawn from nose to ear, and from nose to forehead; an angle formed by lines drawn to show to what extent the jaws are protruding and the forehead receding.—**facing**, fās′ing, *n*. A covering in front for ornament, protection, defense, or other purposes; a mode of adulterating tea by mixing with coloring matter and other substances; the movement of soldiers in turning round to the left, right, etc.; *pl*. the distinctive trimmings on a regimental coat or jacket.—*Put through his facings*, to be cross questioned; to be examined.

facet, fas′et, *n*. [Fr. *facette*, dim. of *face*.] A small flat portion of a surface; one of the small smooth surfaces on a gem or crystal,—*v.t.* To cut a facet or facets on.—**faceted**, fas′et·ed, *a*. Having facets; formed into facets.

facetiae, fa·sē′shi·ē, *n. pl*. [L., from *facetus*, merry, elegant, from root of *facio*, to make.] Witty or humorous sayings; jests; witticisms.—**facetious**, fa·sē′shus, *a*. Merry; jocular; witty; full of pleasantry; playful; exciting laughter.—**facetiously**, fa·sē′shus·li, *adv*. In a facetious manner.—**facetiousness**, fa·sē′shus·nes, *n*. The quality of being facetious; pleasantry.

facial. See FACE.

facile, fas′il, *a*. [L. *facilis*, easy to be done or made, from *facio*, to make.] Easy to be done or performed; not difficult; easy to be dealt with; easy of access or converse; not haughty or distant; easily persuaded to good or bad; yielding; ductile to a fault; ready; dexterous (an artist's *facile* pencil).—**facileness**,† fas′il·nes, *n*. The state of being facile.—**facilitate**, fa·sil′i·tāt, *v.t.*—*facilitated*, *facilitating*. [Fr. *faciliter*, from L. *facilitas*, easiness.] To make easy or less difficult; to lessen the labor of.—**facilitation**, fa·sil′i·tā″-shon, *n*. The act of facilitating.—**facility**, fa·sil′i·ti, *n*. [Fr. *facilité*, L. *facilitas*.] Easiness to be performed; freedom from difficulty; ease; ease in performance; readiness proceeding from skill or use; dexterity; pliancy or ductility in character; easiness to be persuaded, usually implying a disposition to yield to solicitations to evil; the means by which the accomplishment of anything is rendered more easy: in this sense usually in the *pl*.

facsimile, fak·sim′i·li, *n*. [L. *facio*, to make, and *similis*, like.] An exact copy or likeness; an imitation of an original in all its proportions, traits, and peculiarities.

fact, fakt, *n*. [L. *factum*, a thing done,

---

fāte, fär, fâre, fat, fạll; mē, met, hėr; pīne, pin; nōte, not, mōve; tūbe, tub, bụll; oil, pound.

a deed, a fact, from *facio*, to do or make, a stem which appears in many words, as *affect, affair, counterfeit, defeat, difficult, faculty, profits,* etc.] Anything done or that comes to pass; something known to exist; a statement based upon objective reality.—**factual,** fak′chū·al, *a.*

faction, fak′shon, *n.* [L. *factio,* from *facio, factum,* to do. FACT.] A party combined or acting in union, in opposition to another party or a government; a party unscrupulously promoting their private ends at the expense of the public good; discord; dissension.—**factious,** fak′shus, *a.* Given to faction; prone to clamor against public measures or men; pertaining to faction; proceeding from faction.—**factiously,** fak′shus·li, *adv.* In a factious, turbulent, or disorderly manner.—**factiousness,** fak′shus·nes, *n.* The state or character of being factious; disposition to clamor and raise opposition; clamorousness for a party.

factitious, fak·tish′us, *a.* [L. *factitius,* made by art, from *facio,* to make. FACT.] Made by art, in distinction from what is produced by nature; artificial; conventional.—**factitiously,** fak·tish′us·li, *adv.* In a factitious manner.—**factitiousness,** fak·tish′us·nes, *n.*

factitive, fak′ti·tiv, *a.* [From L. *facio, factum,* to make. FACT.] Causative; tending to make or cause; *gram.* expressing the result of an action that produces a new condition in the object (in ‘ he struck him dead ’, *struck* is factitive).

factor, fak′tėr, *n.* [L., a maker, doer, from *facio, factum,* to do. FACT.] An agent employed by merchants residing in other places to buy and sell or transact other business on their account; in Scotland, a person appointed by a landholder or house proprietor to manage an estate, collect rents, etc.; *arith.* the multiplier or multiplicand, from the multiplication of which proceeds the product; *alg.* any expression considered as part of a product; hence, generally, one of several elements or influences which tend to the production of a result.—*Factor of safety,* the ratio of the breaking load to the working load in any structure.—**factorage,** fak′tėr·ij, *n.* The allowance to a factor for his services; commission.—**factorial,** fak·tō′ri·al, *a.* Of or pertaining to a factor or factors.—**factory,** fak′te·ri, *n.* A name given to establishments of merchants and factors resident in foreign countries; (contr. from *manufactory*) a building or collection of buildings appropriated to the manufacture of goods; a manufactory.

factotum, fak·tō′tum, *n.* [L. *facio,* to do, and *totum,* the whole.] A confidential agent that manages all kinds of matters for his employer.

faculae, fak′ū·lē, *n. pl.* [L. *facula,* a little torch, dim. of *fax,* a torch.] *Astron.* spots sometimes seen on the sun's disk, which appear brighter than the rest of its surface.

facultative, fak′ul·tā″tiv, *a.* [L. *facultas,* capability.] Of bacteria and parasites, able to adapt themselves to certain conditions of life.

faculty, fak′ul·ti, *n.* [Fr. *faculté,* L. *facultas,* from *facio,* to do, to make. FACT.] Any mental or bodily power; capacity for any action or function; skill derived from practice, or practice aided by nature; special power or endowment; a right or power granted to a person by favor or indulgence, to do what by law he may not do; the body of individuals constituting one of the learned professions, and more specifically the medical profession; the teachers and professors of the several departments of a university, or one of the departments themselves, a *Faculty* of Arts, Law, Medicine; the teaching staff of any institution of learning.

fad, fad, *n.* A passing whim, hobby, style or fancy, pursued for a time with undue zeal.—**faddist,** fad′ist, *n.* One who is enthusiastic over a fad.—**faddish,** fad′ish, *a.* Pertaining or given to fads, faddy.

fade, fād, *v.i.*—*faded, fading.* [O.E. *vade,* to fade; comp. Fr. *fade,* insipid, from L. *vapidus,* vapid.] To wither; to lose strength, health, or vigor gradually; to decay; to lose freshness, color, or brightness; to tend from a stronger or brighter color to a more faint shade of the same color, or to lose color entirely; to grow dim or indistinct to view.—*v.t.* To cause to wither; to deprive of freshness or vigor.—**fadeless,** fād′les, *a.* Unfading.

fadge, faj, *v.i.* [A.Sax. *fǣgian,* to fit, akin to *fæger,* fair; comp. G. *fügen,* D. *voegen,* Sw. *foga,* to fit.] To suit; to fit; to be found suitable or successful.

faecal, fē′kal, *a.* See FECES.

fag, fag, *v.i.*—*fagged, fagging.* [Probably from verb to *flag,* by omission of *l.*] To become weary; to fail in strength; to be faint with weariness; to labor hard or assiduously; to work till wearied; to act as a fag.—*v.t.* To use or treat as a fag or drudge; to exhaust.—*n.* A laborious drudge; in certain English schools, a boy who performs menial services for another boy who is in the highest or next highest form or class; a cigarette.—**fag end,** *n.* [The end which *flags* or hangs loose.] The end of a web of cloth; the latter or meaner part of anything.

fagaceous, fa·gā′shus, *a.* Pertaining to the beech family of shrubs and trees.

fagot, faggot, fag′ot, *n.* [Fr. *fagot,* It. *fagotto,* a faggot, from L. *fax, facis,* a faggot, a torch.] A bundle of sticks or small branches used for fuel, or for filling ditches, and other purposes in fortification; a fascine; a bundle of pieces of iron or steel in bars; a person formerly hired to take the place of another at the muster of a military company or to hide deficiency in its number; a term of contempt for a dry, shriveled old woman.—*v.t.* To bind in a

fagot or bundle; to collect promiscuously.

Fahrenheit, fa′ren·hīt, *a.* [After *Fahrenheit,* who first employed quicksilver in thermometers about 1720.] The name distinguishing that kind of thermometer in which the space between the freezing and the boiling points of water is divided into 180 degrees; the freezing point being marked 32°, and the boiling 212°.

faïence, fā·äns′ or fä·yäns′, *n.* [Fr.] A sort of fine pottery or earthenware glazed with a fine varnish, and painted in various designs, named from *Faenza* in Italy.

fail, fāl, *v.i.* [Fr. *faillir,* to fail, from L. *fallere,* to deceive, whence also *false, fallible, fault, falter.*] To become deficient; to be insufficient; to cease to be abundant for supply; to come short; not to have the due measure or degree; to decay, decline, sink, or diminished; to become weaker; to become extinct; to be entirely wanting; to be no longer produced, furnished, or supplied; not to produce the effect; to miscarry; to be unsuccessful; to be guilty of omission or neglect; to become insolvent or bankrupt.—*v.t.* To cease or to neglect or omit to afford aid or strength to; to be wanting to; to disappoint; to desert; not to be at hand when required.—*n.* Miscarriage; failure; deficiency; want.—*Without fail,* without omission to perform something; without doubt; certainly.—**failing,** fāl′ing, *n.* Imperfection; a weakness in character or disposition; foible; fault.—*Failing whom. Failing* used either as preposition or *abl. absol.* ‘ who failing ’.—**failingly,** fāl′ing·li, *adv.* By failing.—**failure,** fāl′yėr, *n.* A failing; deficiency; cessation of supply or total defect; omission; nonperformance; decay, or defect from decay; the act of failing or state of having failed to attain an object; want of success; a becoming insolvent or bankrupt.

faille, fāl or fī′y′, *n.* [Fr.] A heavy silk fabric of superior quality.

fain, fān, *a.* [A.Sax. *fægen,* joyful, *fægnian,* to rejoice; Goth. *faginon,* Icel. *fagna,* to be glad. *Fawn* (verb) is of same origin, and *fair* (adj.) is akin.] Glad or pleased under some kind of necessity; inclined; content to accept of or do something for want of better.—*adv.* Gladly; with joy or pleasure: with *would.*

fainéant, fā′ni·ent, *n.* [Fr. *faire,* do, *néant,* nothing.] An idler, a do-nothing, a puppet or phantom king in the Merovingian dynasty of the Franks.

faint, fānt, *v.i.* [O.Fr. *faint,* sluggish, negligent, pp. of *feindre,* L. *fingere,* to feign, whence also *feign, fiction,* etc.] To become feeble; to decline or fail in strength and vigor; to become temporarily unconscious, powerless, and motionless; to swoon; to sink into dejection; to lose courage or spirit; to become gradually weak or indistinct; to decay; to fade, disappear, or vanish.—*a.*

Weak; languid; feeble; exhausted; inclined to swoon; hardly perceptible by, or feebly striking, the senses; indistinct; wanting in brightness or vividness, loudness, sharpness, or force; not well defined; feeble; slight; imperfect; not carried on with vigor or energy; dejected; depressed; dispirited.—*n.* A fainting fit; a swoon; *pl.* the impure spirit which comes over first and last in the distillation of whisky.—**faint-hearted,** *a.* Cowardly; timorous; having lost courage; yielding to fear.—**faintheartedly,** *adv.* In a fainthearted manner.—**faintheartedness,** *n.* Want of courage.—**faintish,** fān′tish, *a.* Slightly faint.—**faintishness,** fān′tish·nes, *n.* A slight degree of faintness.—**faintly,** fānt′li, *adv.* In a faint, weak, feeble, or languid manner; without vigor or activity; without vividness or distinctness.—**faintness,** fānt′nes, *n.* The state of being faint.

fair, fār, *a.* [A.Sax. *fæger*, fair, pleasant, beautiful; Icel. *fagr*, Dan. *feir*, Sw. *fager*, Goth. *fagrs*, bright. FAIN.] Pleasing to the eye; beautiful; handsome; white or light colored in respect of skin or complexion; not dark or swarthy; not stormy or wet; not cloudy or overcast; clear (*fair* weather); free from obstruction, obstacle, or anything to impede (on the *fair* way to success); open, frank, or honest; not resorting to anything tricky or underhand; just; equitable; free from unfair or unfavorable circumstances or influences; civil, pleasing, or courteous (*fair* words); free from deletions, blots, and the like; perfectly or easily legible (a *fair* copy); free from stain or blemish; unspotted; untarnished (one's *fair* name); passably or moderately good; better than indifferent.—*Fair way*, the track or course that is clear of obstacles and is therefore taken by vessels in navigating a narrow bay, river, or harbor.—*adv.* Openly; frankly; civilly; complaisantly (especially in 'to speak a person *fair*'); on good terms (to keep *fair* with the world).—*To bid fair*, to promise well; to be in a fair way; to be likely.—*n.* Elliptically, a fair woman; a handsome female. (*Poet.*)—*The fair*, the female sex; specifically, the loveliest of that sex.—*v.t.* To make fair or beautiful.—**fairish,** fār′ish, *a.* Reasonably fair.—**fairly,** fār′li, *adv.* In a fair manner; beautifully; handsomely; honestly; justly; equitably; tolerably.—**fairness,** fār′nes, *n.* The quality or character of being fair; lightness of complexion, beauty; honesty; justice.—**fair-spoken,** *a.* Using fair speech; bland; civil, courteous, plausible.

fair, fār, *n.* [Fr. *foire*, a fair, market; It. *feria*; L. *feriæ*, holidays, festivals.] A stated market in a particular town or city; a stated meeting of buyers and sellers for trade.—**fairing,** fār′ing, *n.* A present given at a fair.

fairy, fā′ri, *n.* [O.Fr. *faerie*, Fr. *féerie*, the power of a fairy, enchantment;

from O.Fr. *fae*, Fr. *fée*, It. *fata*, a fairy, lit. a fate, from L. *fatum*, fate. FATE.] An imaginary being or spirit having a human form, though of a stature much below human and with sundry superhuman attributes; an elf or fay; any personage with superhuman power‡; fairyland‡.—*a.* Pertaining to or in some manner connected with fairies; coming from fairies; resembling a fairy.—*Fairy ring*, a ring (from a fungus) formed by the grass in certain places growing noticeably greener than that around, popularly supposed to be caused by fairies in their dances.—**fairyland,** *n.* The imaginary land or abode of fairies.—**fairy tale,** *n.* A tale relating to fairies.

faith, fāth, *n.* [O.E. *feid, feith,* O.Fr. *feid,* from L. *fides,* faith; akin *fidelity, confide, defy, infidel,* etc.] The assent of the mind to the truth of what is declared by another; firm and earnest belief on probable evidence of any kind; belief; belief in what is given forth as a revelation of man's relation to God and the infinite; a settled conviction in regard to religion; a system of religious belief; that which is believed on any subject, whether in science, politics, or religion; a doctrine or system of doctrines believed; faithfulness; fidelity; word or honor pledged; promise given.—*In good faith,* in real honesty; with perfect sincerity.—**faithful,** fāth′ful, *a.* Firm in faith; firmly adhering to religious or other duty; of true fidelity; loyal; true and constant to a person to whom one is bound; true to one's word; in conformity to the letter and spirit; conformable to truth; conformable to a prototype; true or exact; worthy of belief.—*The faithful,* those who adhere to the true faith, as contrasted with the adherents of another faith.—**faithfully,** fāth′ful·li, *adv.* In a faithful manner; sincerely; with strong assurance; earnestly; conformably to truth or fact; conformably to an example or prototype.—**faithfulness,** fāth′ful·nes, *n.* The quality or character of being faithful; fidelity; truth; loyalty; constancy.—**faithless,** fāth′les, *a.* Without faith; not adhering to allegiance, vows, or duty; disloyal; not observant of promises.—**faithlessly,** fāth′les·li, *adv.* In a faithless manner.—**faithlessness,** fāth′les·nes, *n.* State of being faithless.

fake, fāk, *n.* [A.Sax. *faec,* a space or interval.] One of the circles or windings of a rope as it lies in a coil.

fake, fāk. *v. t.* [E. dial., to patch, alter.] To impart a false character to; to deceive. *n.* A counterfeit or imitation offered as genuine; a fraud.

fakir, fä·kēr′, *n.* [Ar., lit. a poor man.] An oriental ascetic or begging monk.

falcate, fal′kāt, *a.* [L. *falcatus,* from *falx, falcis,* a sickle.] Hooked; in shape like a sickle or scythe.—**falciform,** fal′si·form, *a.* In the shape of a sickle or reaping hook.

falchion, fal′shon, *n.* [L. *falx, falcis,* a

sickle.] A broad short sword with a slightly curved point.

falcon, fal′kn, *n.* [O.Fr. *falcon,* Fr. *faucon,* L.L. *falco,* probably from L. *falx,* a reaping hook, from the curved claws and beak.] The common name of various raptorial birds inferior in size to the eagles and vultures, and remarkable for their elegant form and powers of flight; especially, one trained to hunt wild fowl or other game; a hawk. [The term falcon is by sportsmen restricted to the female, the male, which is smaller and less courageous, being called *tersel* or *tiercel*.] A small cannon. MUSKET.—**falconer,** fa′kn·ėr, *n.* A person who breeds and trains falcons or hawks for sport; one who follows the sport of fowling with hawks.—**falcon-gentle,** *n.* The female of the goshawk.—**falconry,** fa′kn·ri, *n.* The art of training falcons to attack wild birds or game; the sport of pursuing wild fowls or game by means of falcons or hawks.

faldstool, fald′stōl, *n.* [*Fald* or *fold,* and *stool*.] A folding stool similar to a campstool; a kind of stool at which the kings of England kneel at their coronation; a small desk at which in churches litany is said.

fall, fal, *v.i.*—**fell** (pret.), *fallen* (pp.). [A.Sax. *feallan*=D. *vallen,* Dan. *falde,* Icel. *falla,* G. *fallen,* to fall. *Fell* is the causal of this.] To sink from a higher to a lower position; to descend by the power of gravity; to drop down; to sink; to ebb; to drop from an erect posture; to empty, disembogue, or discharge itself; said of a stream; to depart from the faith or from rectitude; to sink into sin; to die, particularly by violence; to come to an end suddenly; to perish, be overthrown, or ruined; to sink into weakness; to become faint or feeble (our hopes *fall*); to sink into disrepute or disgrace; to decline in power, wealth, or glory; to pass into a new state, especially with suddenness or through inadvertence or ignorance (to *fall* asleep, to *fall* into error); to decrease; to be diminished in weight, size, value, or intensity (the price *falls,* the wind *falls*); to assume an expression of dejection, discontent, sorrow, shame, etc.; applied to the countenance; to happen; to befall; to take place; to pass or be transferred by lot, inheritance, or otherwise (something *falls* to one's share); to belong or appertain; to have to be reckoned to; to be dropped or uttered carelessly; to sink in tone or loudness.—*To fall among,* to come among or into the society of, accidentally or unexpectedly.—*To fall away,* to lose flesh; to become lean or emaciated; to renounce or desert allegiance, faith, or duty; to revolt or rebel; to apostatize; to decline gradually; to languish or become faint.—*To fall back,* to recede; to give way; to go from better to worse; to retrograde; to fail of performing a promise or purpose; not to fulfill.—*To fall* *back upon*, to have recourse to, generally to some support or expedient formerly tried.—*To fall down*, to prostrate one's self in worship or supplication; to sink; to come to the ground.—*To fall foul of*, to attack; to make an assault upon.—*To fall from*, to recede from; to depart; not to adhere to.—*To fall in*, to take one's place in an organized body of men, as soldiers; to terminate or lapse (an annuity *falls in* when the annuitant dies).—*To fall in with*, to meet casually; to happen to meet; to concur, agree, or comply with.—*To fall off*, to be broken or detached from something; to apostatize; to fall away; to get into disuse; to decline from former excellence; to become less valuable or interesting; to become less; to decrease; *naut.* to deviate from the course to which the head of the ship was before directed.—*To fall on* or *upon*, to begin suddenly and eagerly; to begin an attack on; to assault; to assail; to come upon, usually with some degree of suddenness and unexpectedness; to drop on; to light on; to come upon.—*To fall out*, to quarrel; to begin to contend; to happen; to befall; to chance; to turn out; to prove.—*To fall short*, to be deficient.—*To fall to*, to begin hastily and eagerly; to apply one's self to.—*To fall under*, to come under or within the limits of; to be subjected to; to become the subject of.—*n.* The act of one who or that which falls; a dropping or descending; descent; a tumble; death; destruction; overthrow; downfall; degradation; declension of greatness, power, or dominion; ruin; diminution; decrease of price or value; a sinking of tone; cadence; descent of water; a cascade or cataract; extent of descent; the distance through which anything falls or may fall; amount of slope; declivity; the season when leaves fall from trees; autumn; that which falls; a shower; a kind of ladies' veil; lapse or declension from innocence or goodness; [*cap.*] specifically the lapse into sin of our first parents Adam and Eve; *naut.* the part of a tackle to which the power is applied in hoisting.—*To try a fall*, to try a bout at wrestling.—**fallen**, fạl'en, *pp.* or *a.* Dropped; degraded; sunk in vice; lost to virtue; ruined; overthrown.—**fallout**, *n.* Particles of radioactive matter from nuclear explosions carried by air currents and dropped at a distance; the descent of such particles.—**falling sickness**, *n.* Epilepsy, a disease in which the patient suddenly loses his senses and falls.—**falling star**, *n.* A meteor appearing as a luminous point darting through the sky, and followed by a long train of light.—**fallacious**, fal·lā'shus, *a.* [Fr. *fallacieux*, from L. *fallax, fallacis*, deceitful, from *fallo*, to deceive. FAIL.] Pertaining to or embodying something deceptive or misleading; producing error or mistake; tending to

mislead. ∴ *Fallacious* reasoning consists of arguments that deceive or mislead one, though not necessarily purposely. *Sophistical* reasoning is intendedly false reasoning, consisting of arguments so subtle as not to be easily detected and controverted, advanced purposely to mislead.—**fallaciously**, fal·lā'shus·li, *adv.* In a fallacious manner; sophistically; with purpose or in a manner to deceive.—**fallaciousness**, fal·lā'shus·nes, *n.* State of being fallacious.—**fallacy**, fal'la·si, *n.* [L. *fallacia*, deceit.] A misleading or mistaken argument; an argument or proposition apparently sound but really containing some undetected error, and therefore misleading; any unsound but specious mode of arguing.

fallible, fal'i·bl, *a.* [L.L. *fallibilis*, from L. *fallo*, to deceive. FALLACIOUS, FAIL.] Liable to fail or mistake; liable to deceive or to be deceived; liable to error or going astray.—**fallibility**, fal·i·bil'i·ti, *n.* The state of being fallible; liableness to deceive or to be deceived.—**fallibly**, fal'i·bli, *adv.* In a fallible manner.

Fallopian tube, fá·lō'pē·en tūb, *n.* [From Gabriel *Fallopius*, a 16th—century Italian anatomist.] Either of the pair of tubes, arising from the uterus and each connected to an ovary, which conduct the egg into the uterus.

fallow, fal'ō, *a.* [O.E. *fealo, fealu*, pale yellow or dun; akin to G. *fahl*, pale, and Gr. *polios*, gray.] Of a pale yellow-brown; dun.—**fallow deer**, *n.* A small, pale yellow, European deer.

fallow, fal'ō, *a.* [O.E. *fealg, feahl*, plowed land.] Left to rest without a crop after plowing; untilled; uncultivated; neglected; unoccupied; unused.—*n.* Land that has lain a year or more untilled or unsown; land plowed without being sowed; the plowing of land, without sowing it, for a season.—*v.t.* To leave fallow or plowed but not sown in crop.

false, fols, *a.* [L. *falsus*, false, from *fallo, falsum*, to deceive. FAIL.] Not true; not conformable to fact; expressing what is contrary to that which exists, is done, said, or thought; intended to mislead; counterfeit; forged; not real or genuine; hypocritical; feigned; not agreeable to rule or propriety (*false* construction in language); not honest or just; fraudulent; not faithful or loyal; treacherous; perfidious; deceitful; unfaithful; inconstant; not well founded or based (*false* hopes); constructed for show or a subsidiary purpose (a *false* bottom, a *false* keel).—**falsehearted**, *a.* Treacherous; deceitful; perfidious.—**falsehood**, fols'·hȯd, *n.* Contrariety or want of conformity to fact or truth; falseness; want of truth or veracity; untruthfulness; what is false or untrue; a lie; an untrue assertion; want of honesty; deceitfulness; perfidy; imposture.—**falsely**, fols'li, *adv.* In a manner contrary to truth and fact; not truly; untruly.—**falseness**, fols'nes, *n.* The state or quality of being false; untruthfulness; want of verac-

ity; duplicity; deceit; unfaithfulness; perfidy.—**falsify**, fol'si·fī, *v.t.*—*falsified, falsifying.* [Fr. *falsifier*, from L. *falsus*, and *facio*, to make.] To represent falsely; to vitiate with false and misleading elements; to garble; to make not genuine; to disprove; to prove to be false; to cause to turn out false (to *falsify* a prediction); to violate or break by falsehood.—*v.i.* To violate the truth.—**falsification**, fol'si·fi·kā'shon, *n.* The act of falsifying; a counterfeiting; the giving to a thing an appearance of something which it is not.—**falsifier**, fol'si·fī·ėr, *n.* One who falsifies; one who counterfeits or gives to a thing a deceptive appearance.—**falsity**, fol'si·ti, *n.* The quality of being false; that which is false; a falsehood; a false assertion.

falsetto, fol·set'tō, *n.* [It., from L. *falsus*, false.] The tones above the natural compass of the voice.

falter, fol'tėr, *v.i.* [A freq. connected with *fault*, from a supposed Fr. verb corresponding to Sp. *faltar*, It. *faltare*, to fail, from L. *fallere*, to deceive. FAULT, FAIL.] To hesitate in the utterance of words; to speak with a broken or trembling utterance; to stammer; not to be firm and steady; to tremble.—*n.* The act of faltering; hesitation; trembling; quavering.—**faltering**, fol'tėr·ing, *a.* Trembling; hesitating.—**falteringly**, fol'tėr·ing·li, *adv.* With hesitation; with a trembling, broken voice.

fame, fām, *n.* [Fr. *fame*, from L. *fama*, fame, renown, from *fari*, to speak; whence also *fate*. FATE.] Public report or rumor; report or opinion widely diffused; renown; notoriety; celebrity.—**famed**, fāmd, *p.* and *a.* Much talked of; renowned; celebrated.—**famous**, fā'mus, *a.* [L. *famosus*, Fr. *fameux*.] Celebrated in fame or public report; renowned; much talked of; distinguished in story.—**famously**, fā'mus·li, *adv.* In a famous manner.—**famousness**,† fā'mus·nes, *n.* The state of being famous; renown; celebrity.

familiar, fa·mil'yėr, *a.* [L. *familiaris*, from *familia*, a household, the servants of a family, from *famulus*, a servant. FAMILY.] Well acquainted; closely intimate; well versed (in a subject of study); exhibiting the manner of an intimate friend; affable; accessible; characterized by ease or absence of stiffness of pedantry; easy; well known; well understood; of everyday occurrence or use.—*Familiar spirit*, a spirit or demon supposed to be constantly at the command of some person.—*n.* An intimate; a close companion; a familiar spirit; an officer of the Inquisition employed in apprehending and imprisoning persons accused.—**familiarity**, fa·mil'i·ar"i·ti, *n.* The state of being familiar; unconstrained intercourse; intimate acquaintance or knowledge; intimacy; *pl.* actions characterized by too much license; liberties.—**familiarization**, fa·mil'-yėr·i·zā'shon, *n.* Act or process of making or becoming familiar.—**familiarize**, fa·mil'yėr·īz, *v.t.*—*fa-*

miliarized, *familiarizing*. To make familiar or intimate; to habituate; to accustom; to make intimately acquainted; to render conversant or fully acquainted by practice or customary use, or by intercourse.— **familiarly**, fa·mil'yer·li, *adv.* In a familiar manner.

family, fam'i·li, *n.* [L. *familia*, a household, the slaves or servants of a house; from *famulus*, a servant, a slave, from Oscan *famel*, a servant, from *faama*, Skr. *dhâman*, a house.] The body of persons who live in one house and under one head; the parents and children alone; the children as distinguished from the parents; those who descend from one common progenitor; a tribe or race; kindred; lineage; line of ancestors; honorable descent; noble or respectable stock (a man of *family*); in scientific classifications, a group of individuals more comprehensive than a genus, and less so than an order.— **familial**, fä·mil'yäl, *a.* Of or pertaining to the family; hereditary .— *Family Compact*, the compact formed in 1733 between the divisions of the Bourbon family, Philip V of Spain and Louis XV of France, against British supremacy.—**family man**, *n.* One who has a family or household; a married man.

famine, fam'in, *n.* [Fr. *famine*, from L. *fames*, hunger.] Scarcity of food; dearth; a general want of provisions; destitution.—**famish**, fam'ish, *v.t.* [O.Fr. *famis*, starving, from L. *fames*.] To kill or destroy with hunger; to starve; to cause to suffer from hunger or thirst; to distress with hunger; to force or compel by famine.—*v.i.* To die of hunger; to suffer extreme hunger or thirst; to suffer by the deprivation of any necessary.

famous. See FAME.

fan, fan, *n.* [A.Sax. *fann*, *fan*, from L. *vannus*, a fan for winnowing; akin to L. *ventus*, wind, and E. *wind*, *winnow*.] The name of various instruments for exciting a current of air by the agitation of a broad surface, vanes or disks; a machine for winnowing grain; an instrument used by ladies to agitate the air and cool the face; anything resembling this; what fans or excites.—*v.t.—fanned*, *fanning.* To move or agitate as with a fan; to cool and refresh by moving the air with a fan; to winnow; to separate chaff from, and drive it away by a current of air; *fig.* to produce effects on analogous to those of a fan in exciting flame, to excite or stir up to activity; to stimulate.—**fanlight**, *n.* A fan-shaped window situated over a door in a circular-headed opening.—**fanner**, fan'er, *n.* One who fans; a rotatory contrivance with vanes for ventilating the interior of a chamber; an arrangement of vanes for blowing fires; *pl.* a fan or machine for winnowing grain.— **fantail**, *n.* A variety of the domestic pigeon; a form of gasburner.— **fanwindow**, *n.* A window having a semicircular outline and a sash formed of radial bars.

fanatic, fanatical, fa·nat'ik, fa·nat'i·kal, *a.* [L. *fanaticus*, inspired, enthusiastic, from *fanum*, a place dedicated to some deity, a temple.] Reckless and extravagant in opinions.—*n.* A person affected by excessive enthusiasm and devotion. —**fan**, fan, *n.* [From *fanatic*.] An admirer or devotee of someone or something.—**fanatically**, fa·nat'i·kal·li, *adv.*—**fanaticism**, fa·nat'i·sizm, *n.* The state or character of a fanatic; wild and extravagant notions of religion; religious frenzy; fervid zeal.—**fanaticize**, fa·nat'i·sīz, *v.t.* To make fanatic.

fancy, fan'si, *n.* [Contr. for *fantasy*, *phantasy*, from L. and Gr. *phantasia*, a fancy, from Gr. *phantazō*, to make visible, from *phainō*, to show; akin *phantom*, *phenomenon*.] A phase of the intellectual faculty of a lighter and less impressive cast than the imagination, or the active play of this lighter faculty; a new and pleasing thought or conception due to this faculty; the happy and poetical embodiment of such conception in words; a poetical illustration or ornament, as a simile, metaphor, and the like; an opinion or notion; an impression or supposition; a whim or conceit; inclination; liking; fondness; preference.—*The fancy*, a name for sporting characters, especially prize fighters.—*a.* Fine; elegant; ornamental (*fancy* goods); beyond intrinsic value; extravagant (a *fancy* price).—*v.i.—fancied*, *fancying.* To imagine; to figure to one's self; to believe or suppose without proof.— *v.t.* To form a conception of; to portray in the mind; to imagine; to like; to be pleased with.—**fancier**, fan'si·er, *n.* One who fancies; one who is influenced by his fancies.— **fanciful**, fan'si·ful, *a.* Guided by fancy rather than by reason and experience; subject to the influence of fancy; whimsical: applied to persons; dictated or produced by fancy; appealing to or pleasing the fancy; full of wild images; curiously shaped: applied to things.—**fancifully**, fan'si·ful·li, *adv.* In a fanciful manner.— **fancifulness**, fan'si·ful·nes, *n.* The quality of being fanciful.—**fanciless**, fan'si·les, *a.* Destitute of fancy.— **fancy ball**, *n.* A ball in which persons appear in fancy dresses, imitations of antique costumes, etc.—**fancy-free**, *a.* Free from the power of love.— **fancywork**, *n.* Ornamental knitting, embroidery, etc., performed by ladies.

fandango, fan·dang'gō, *n.* A lively Spanish dance borrowed from the Moors, danced by two persons, male and female, the music being in triple time.

fanfare, fan'fâr, *n.* [Fr.] A flourish of trumpets; a short tune of a cheerful cast, played with hunting horns; an ostentatious parade or boast; bravado.—**fanfaron**, fan'fa·ron, *n.* [Fr.] A bully; a hector; a swaggerer; an empty boaster.—**fanfaronade**, fan·far'o·nād", *n.* [Fr.] A swaggering; ostentation; bluster.

fang, fang, *n.* [A.Sax. *fang*, a taking,

grasp, from *fón* (for *fahan*), to seize (pret. *feng*, pp. *fangen*)=G. *fangen*, Goth. *fahan*, D. *vangen*, to take.] The tusk of a boar or other animal by which the prey is seized and held; a long pointed tooth; the hollow poison tooth of a serpent; a claw or talon; the catch of a pump.—*Off the fang*, out of sorts, listless.—*v.t.* To start a pump by pouring water on it.—**fanged**, fangd, *p.* and *a.* Furnished with fangs, tusks, or something resembling these.

fangled, fang'gld, *a.* [From old *fangle*, a gewgaw, something to catch the eye from old *fangen*, to catch.] Gaudy; showy; fond of finery. (Used by Shakespeare, but now only in the compound *new-fangled*.)

fanon, fan'on, *n.* [Fr. *fanon*, from Goth. *fana*, cloth, a banner.] *Eccles.* a kind of napkin or handkerchief used by the priest at mass; also an ornament attached to a priest's left arm.

fan palm, *n.* A name for the taliput and one or two other palms.

fantasia, fan·tä'zē·a, *n.* [It., lit. a fantasy or fancy, from L. and Gr. *phantasia*, a fancy, whence also E. *fancy*. FANCY.] A species of musical composition having no particular theme, but ranging amidst various airs and movements.—**fantasm**, fan'tazm, *n.* Same as *Phantasm*.—**fantast**, fan'tast, *n.* One whose mind is full of fantastic notions.—**fantastic, fantastical**, fan·tas'tik, fan·tas'ti·kal, *a.* [Fr. *fantastique*, from Gr. *phantastikos*, from *phantasia*, vision, fancy.] Fanciful; existing only in imagination; imaginary; chimerical; whimsical; capricious; indulging the vagaries of imagination; having oddness of figure or appearance; whimsically shaped; grotesque.—*n.* A whimsical person; a fop.—**fantasticality**, fan·tas'ti·kal"i·ti, *n.* Fantasticalness.—**fantastically**, fan·tas'ti·kal·li, *adv.* In a fantastic manner; capriciously; whimsically.—**fantasticalness**, fan·tas'ti·kal·nes, *n.* State of being fantastical.—**fantasy**, fan'ta·si, *n.* A mental image, especially of the unrestricted imagination; a daydream; a visionary idea; a caprice.

fantoccini, fan·to·chē'ni, *n. pl.* [It.] Puppets worked by concealed wires or strings; a puppet show; marionettes.

fantom, fan'tom, *n.* Same as *Phantom.*

far, fär, *a.* [A.Sax. *feor*; D. *ver*, Icel. *fjarri*, Goth. *fairra*, G. *fern*, far— allied to *fore*, *ferry*, *fare*; the root being same as that of L. *per*, through; G. *pera*, beyond; Skr. *para*, other.] Distant; separated by a wide space; hence, remote as regards wishes, feelings, affections; more distant of the two: applied to the right side of a horse.—*adv.* To a great extent or distance of space; to a remote period; in great part (the day *far* spent); in a great proportion; by many degrees; very much (*far* better or higher); to whatever point, degree, or distance (as *far* as).—*By far*, in a great degree; very much.—*From* *far*, from a great distance; from a remote place.—*Far other*, very different.—**far-fetched**, *p.* and *a.* Brought from a remote place; not easily or naturally introduced; elaborately strained (a *far-fetched* explanation).—**far-off**, *a.* Faraway; distant; remote in space or time.—**farsighted**, *a.* Seeing to a great distance; calculating carefully the distant results of present conduct or action; not capable of perceiving objects near at hand distinctly.—**farsightedness**, *n.* The state or quality of being farsighted.—**farther**, fär′THėr, *a. compar.* [Not the original compar. of *far*, which was *far-er* (*ferrer*), but assimilated to *further*.] More remote; more distant than something else; tending to a greater distance; additional.—*adv.* At or to a greater distance; more remotely; beyond; by way of progression in a subject; moreover.—**farthermost**, fär′THėr·mōst, *a. superl.* Being at the farthest distance; most remote.—**farthest**, fär′THest, *a. superl.* At the greatest distance either in time or place.—*adv.* At or to the greatest distance.

farad, far′ad, *n.* [In honor of *Faraday*.] The unit of electrical capacity in the practical system of units, being the capacity of a condenser which one coulomb of electricity raises to a potential of one volt.—**faradic**, fa·rad′ik, *a.* Applied to induction electricity.—**faradization**, **faradism**, far′a·di·zā″shon, far′ad·izm, *n.* The medical application of the magneto-electric currents which *Faraday* discovered in 1837.

farce, färs, *v.t.*—*farced, farcing.* [Fr. *farcir*, L. *farcio*, to stuff.] To stuff with forcemeat; to fill with mingled ingredients.—*n.* [Fr. *farce*, It. *farsa*, from L. *farcio*, to stuff, from being stuffed or crammed with humor.] A dramatic composition of a broadly comic character; a comedy full of extravagant drollery; ridiculous parade; empty pageantry; mere show.—**farcical**, fär′si·kal, *a.* Belonging to a farce; of the character of a farce; droll; ludicrous; ridiculous.—**farcically**, fär′si·kal·li, *adv.* In a farcical manner.

farcy, fär′si, *n.* A disease of horses intimately connected with glanders, the two diseases generally running into each other.—**farcy bud**, *n.* A tumor which appears early in the disease farcy.

fare, fâr, *v.i.*—*fared, faring.* [A.Sax. *faran*, to go = Icel. Sw. *fara*, Dan. *fare*, D. *varen*, G. *fahren*, to go, same root as L. *per*, through, *porta*, gate, Gr. *poros*, passage, *peirō*, to pierce; E. *far, ferry*, etc.] To go; to pass; to move forward; to travel; to be in any state, good or bad; to be in a certain condition as regards bodily or social comforts; to be entertained with food; to happen; to turn out or result; to be; with *it* impersonally.—*n.* The sum paid or due for conveying a person by land, air, or water; food; provisions of the table; condition; treatment by circumstances; fortune; the person

or persons conveyed in a vehicle.—**farewell**, fâr′wel, [From *fare*, in the imper., and *well*.] May you fare or prosper well; a wish of happiness to those who leave or those who are left: it sometimes has the pronoun inserted between its two elements; as *fare you well*. Sometimes it is an expression of mere separation (like 'good-bye' or 'adieu').—*n.* Good-bye; adieu; leave; departure; final look, reference, or attention.—*a.* Leave-taking; valedictory.

farina, fa·rē′na, *n.* [L. *farina*, flour, from *far*, a sort of grain.] Meal or flour; a soft, tasteless, and commonly white powder, obtained by trituration of the seeds of cereal and leguminous plants, and of some roots, as the potato.—**farinaceous**, far·i·nā′shus, *a.* Consisting or made of meal or flour; containing or yielding farina or flour; mealy.—**farinose**, far′i·nos, *a.* Yielding farina.

farm, färm, *n.* [A.Sax. *feorm, fyrm*, food, provisions, a feast, entertainment; hence, a piece of land that has to supply a certain quantity of provisions; from L.L. *firma* (from L. *firmus*, firm, established), farm rent, sum settled or fixed.] A tract of land cultivated by either the owner of the land or a tenant, and usually divided into fields.—*v.t.* To let to a tenant on condition of paying rent; to hold and cultivate either as tenant or as owner; to lease or let, as taxes or other duties, at a certain sum or a certain rate per cent.—*v.i.* To be employed in agriculture; to cultivate the soil.—**farmer**, fär′mėr, *n.* One who farms; one who cultivates a farm; an agriculturist; a husbandman; one who takes taxes, customs, excise, or other duties, to collect for a certain gross sum or a rate per cent.—**farmhouse**, färm′hous, *n.* A house attached to a farm for the residence of a farmer.—**farming**, fär′ming, *a.* Pertaining to agriculture.—*n.* The business of a farmer; husbandry.—**farmstead**, färm′sted, *n.* The system of buildings connected with a farm; a homestead.—**farmyard**, färm′yärd, *n.* The yard or enclosure surrounded by or connected with the farm buildings.

faro, fâ′rō, *n.* [Said to be from *Pharaoh* having formerly been depicted on one of the cards.] A game at cards in which a person plays against the bank.

farrago, fa·rā′gō, *n.* [L. from *far*, meal.] A mass composed of various materials confusedly mixed; a medley.—**farraginous**, fa·raj′i·nus, *a.* Formed of various materials mixed.

farrier, far′i·ėr, *n.* [O.Fr. *ferrier*, from *ferrer*, to shoe a horse, from L. *ferrum*, iron.] A shoer of horses; one who combines the art of horseshoeing with the profession of veterinary surgery.—*v.i.* To practice as a farrier.—**farriery**, far′i·ėr·i, *n.* The art of shoeing horses; the art of curing the diseases of horses, oxen, sheep, pigs, etc.; veterinary surgery.

farrow, far′ō, *n.* [A.Sax. *fearh*, a little pig; akin to O.H.G. *farah*, G.

ferkel, D. *varken*, a pig; L. *porcus*, a pig, being also allied.] A litter of pigs.—*v.t.* and *i.* To bring forth pigs.

farther. See FAR.

farthing, fär′THing, *n.* [A.Sax. *ferthing, feorthing*, the fourth part of a thing, from *feorth*, fourth, from *feówer*, four.] The fourth of a penny, a small copper coin of Britain, the fourth of a penny in value.

farthingale, fär′THing·gāl, *n.* [O.Fr. *vertugalle, vertugade*, from Sp. *verdugo*, a rod or shoot of a tree, hence a hoop.] A hoop petticoat formerly worn by ladies, or the circles of hoops used to extend the petticoat.

fasces, fas′sēz, *n. pl.* [L.] A bundle of rods, with an ax bound in along with them, anciently borne before the superior Roman magistrates as a badge of their power over life and limb; the symbol of the Fascist party in Italy.

fascia, fash′i·a, *n. pl.* **fasciae**, fash′i·ē. [L.] A band, sash, or fillet, or something resembling this in shape; a surgical bandage; *arch.* a long band of stone or brick forming a slight projection.—**fasciate**, fash′i·āt, *a.* Banded or bound together; fasciated.—**fasciated**, fash′i·ā·ted, *a.* Bound with a fillet, sash, or bandage; *bot.* applied to the peculiar flattened stems or branches which occur occasionally in trees.—**fasciation**, fash·i·ā′shon, *n.* The state of being fasciated; the act or manner of binding up diseased parts; bandage.

fascicle, fas′si·kl, *n.* [L. *fasciculus*, from *fascis*, a bundle.] A little bundle or collection; *bot.* a form of cyme in which the flowers are clustered together in a more or less compact bundle.—**fasciculate**, **fasciculated**, **fascicled**, **fascicular**, fas·sik′ū·lāt, fas·sik′ū·lā·ted, fas′si·kld, fas·sik′ū·lėr, *a. Bot.* growing in bundles or bunches from the same point: said of leaves, stems, roots, etc.—**fascicularly**, fas·sik′ū·lāt·li, *adv.* In a fasciculate manner.—**fascicule**, fas′si·kūl, *n.* A fascicle.—**fasciculus**, fas·sik′ū·lus, *n.* A fascicle; one of the separate divisions or numbers in which a book is published.

fascinate, fas′si·nāt, *v.t.*—*fascinated, fascinating.* [Fr. *fasciner*, L. *fascino, fascinatum*, to fascinate, bewitch.] To bewitch; to enchant; to operate on by some powerful or irresistible influence; to charm; to captivate; to allure irresistibly or powerfully.—*v.i.* To exercise a bewitching or captivating power.—**fascinating**, fas′si·nā·ting, *p.* and *a.* Bewitching; enchanting; charming; captivating.—**fascination**, fas·si·nā′shon, *n.* The act of fascinating, bewitching, or enchanting; enchantment; a charm.

fascism, fash′izm, *n.* A totalitarian form of government in Italy administered by the Fascisti (a political organization) which advocated the building of a highly nationalistic state, recognizing private ownership except when the state determined otherwise.—**Fascist**, fash′ist, *a.* Of or pertaining to fascism.—*n.* A member of the Fascisti.

fashion, fash′on, *n.* [O.Fr. *fachon*,

facion, from L. *factio*, a making, from *facio*, to make. FACT.] The make or form of anything; external form; shape; pattern; make according to the custom of the time; the prevailing mode of dress or ornament; manner, sort, way, or mode; custom; prevailing practice; genteel life or good breeding; genteel society.—*v.t.* To form; to give shape or figure to; to mold.— **fashionable**, fash'on·a·bl, *a.* Conforming to the fashion or established mode; taking the public taste and being in vogue; established by custom; current; prevailing; dressing or behaving according to the prevailing fashion; genteel; well-bred.—*n.* A person of fashion.— **fashionableness**, fash'on·a·bl·nes, *n.* The state of being fashionable.— **fashionably**, fash'on·a·bli, *adv.* In a manner according to fashion; according to the prevailing mode.— **fashioner**, fash'on·ėr, *n.* One who fashions.

fast, fast, *a.* [A.Sax. *fæst*, *fest*, fast, firm=D. *vast*, Icel. *fastr.* Dan. *fast*, G. *fest*, firm, solid. Hence *fast*, quick, and verb to *fast.*] Firmly fixed; close; tight; closely adhering; made close; strong against attack; firm in adherence; not easily alienated (a *fast* friend); steadfast; faithful; lasting; durable (a *fast* color).—*adv.* Firmly; immovably.— *To play fast and loose*, to act in an inconstant manner; to say one thing and do another.—**fasten**, fas'n, *v.t.* [A.Sax. *fæstnian*, to secure.] To fix firmly; to make fast or close; to secure, as by lock, bolt, or the like; to join in close union; to unite closely; to attach; to affix.—*v.i.* To fix one's self or itself, to become attached.—**fastener**, fas'n·ėr, *n.* One who or that which fastens.—**fastening**, fas'n·ing, *n.* Anything that fastens, binds, attaches, etc.—**fastness**, fast'nes, *n.* [A.Sax. *fæstnes*, firmness, a fortification.] The state of being fast, firm, or secure; strength; security; a stronghold; a fortified place; a castle; a fortress.

fast, fast, *a.* [The same word as *fast*, fixed firm or steadfast (one who runs fast runs steadfastly)=Icel. *fast*, rapidly, quickly, from *fastr*, firm.] Swift; moving rapidly; quick in motion; rapid; dissipated; devoted to pleasure; indulging in sensual vices: said of a man; imitating the manners or habits of a man: said of a female.—*adv.* In a fast or quick manner; swiftly; rapidly; with quick steps or progression; prodigally and wastefully; with dissipation.—**fastness**, fast'nes, *n.* The state or quality of being fast.

fast, fast, *v.i.* [A.Sax. *fæstan*, to fast; probably from *fæst*, firm, steadfast, the meaning being to be steadfast in abstaining=D. *vasten*, Dan. *faste*, Icel. and Sw. *fasta*, G. *fasten*, Goth. *fastan*, to fast.] To abstain from food beyond the usual time; to go hungry; to abstain from food, or particular kinds of food, voluntarily, especially for religious reasons.—*n.* Abstinence

from food; a withholding from the usual quantity of nourishment; voluntary abstinence from food as a religious mortification or humiliation; the time of fasting.

fastidious, fas·tid'i·us, *a.* [L. *fastidiosus*, from *fastidium*, loathing, fastidiousness, from *fastus*, haughtiness.] Hard or difficult to please; squeamish; delicate to a fault; overnice; difficult to suit.—**fastidiously**, fas·tid'i·us·li, *adv.* In a fastidious manner.—**fastidiousness**, fas·tid'i·us·nes, *n.*

fastigiate, **fastigiated**, fas·tij'i·āt, fas·tij'i·ā·ted, *a.* [L. *fastigiatus*, pointed, from *fastigium*, a top or peak.] Peaked or pointed at top; *bot.* tapering to a narrow point like a pyramid, as a plant when the branches become gradually shorter from the base to the apex.

fat, fat, *a.* [A.Sax. *fæt*=D. *vet*, Dan. *fed*, Icel. *feitr*, G. *fett*, fat. Hence, to *fatten*, *fatling*.] Fleshy; plump; obese; corpulent; the contrary to *lean*; oily; greasy; unctuous; coarse; heavy; dull; stupid (especially in such compounds as *fat*-brained, *fat*-witted); producing a large income; rich; fertile; nourishing.—*n.* A solid oily substance of whitish or yellow color, a compound of carbon, hydrogen, and oxygen, found in certain parts of animal bodies, lard and tallow being varieties of it; the best or richest part of a thing.—*v.t.*— *fatted, fatting.* To make fat; to fatten.—*v.i.* To grow fat.—**fatling**, fat'ling, *n.* Any young animal fattened for slaughter, as a lamb, kid, or the like. —**fatly**, fat'li, *adv.* In a fat manner; grossly; greasily.—**fatness**, fat'nes, *n.* The state or quality of being fat; corpulence; plumpness; unctuousness; oiliness; richness; fertility.— **fatten**, fat'n, *v.t.* To make fat; to feed for slaughter; to enrich; to make fertile.—*v.i.* To grow fat; to become plump or fleshy.—**fattener**, fat'n·ėr, *n.* One who or that which fattens; that which gives fatness, richness, or fertility.—**fatty**, fat'i, *a.* Having the nature or qualities of fat; greasy.—**fatty acid**, *n.* Any of numerous saturated or unsaturated, aliphatic, monocarboxylic, organic acids, such as palmetic acid and stearic acid, that naturally occur as esters in fat.

fatal, fā'tal, *a.* [L. *fatalis*, from *fatum*, fate. FATE.] Mortal; destructive; calamitous; disastrous.—**fatalism**, fā'tal·izm, *n.* The doctrine that all events take place by inevitable necessity, and man is powerless to change them; the belief in, or the attitude of mind determined by, such a doctrine.—**fatalist**, fā'tal·ist, *n.*—**fatalistic**, fā·ta·lis'tik, *a.* Pertaining to fatalism; implying fatalism.—**fatality**, fa·tal'i·ti, *n.* The state of being fatal; a fixed unalterable course of things; a fatal occurrence; a calamitous accident.— **fatally**, fā'tal·li, *adv.*

fata morgana, fä'ta mor·gä'na, *n.* [It., because supposed to be the work of a *fata* or fairy called *Morgana.*] A striking optical illusion

principally remarked in the Strait of Messina, between the coasts of Sicily and Calabria—a variety of mirage.

fate, fāt, *n.* [L. *fatum* (lit. that which has been spoken), destiny as pronounced by the gods, fate, from *fari*, to speak (whence also *fama*, fame, and *fanum*, a fane), from a root which appears also in Gr. *phanai*, to speak, and *phaos*, light; akin *fable*, *fairy*, *fay*, *affable*, etc.] A fixed decree or sentence, by which the order of things is prescribed; inevitable necessity settling how events are to befall; unavoidable concatenation and succession of events; destiny; predetermined lot; human destiny; the final fortune of anything; final event; death; destruction; [*cap.*] *pl.* (*myth.*) the Destinies or Parcae; [*cap.*] the three goddesses supposed to preside over the birth and life of men, called Clotho, Lachesis, and Atropos.—**fated**, fā'ted, *a.* Assigned or gifted with a certain fate; doomed; destined; regulated by fate.—**fateful**, fāt'ful, *a.* Bringing or deciding fate or destiny; fatal.

father, fä'тнėr, *n.* [A.Sax. *fæder*=D. *vader*, Icel. *fathir*, Dan. and Sw. *fader*, Goth. *fadar*, G. *vater*, L. *pater*, Gr. *patēr*, Per. *padar*, Skr. *pitri*—father; perhaps from a root *pa.* to feed.] He who begets a child; a male parent; a male ancestor more remote than a parent, especially the first ancestor; the founder of a race, family, or line; a respectful mode of address to an old man; one who exercises paternal care over another; a guardian, protector, or preserver; the first to practice any art; a distinguished example; a teacher; originator; cause; [*usually cap.*] the appellation of the first person in the Trinity; the title given to dignitaries of the church, confessors, and priests; the eldest member of a profession, or other body.—*Father of the House*, in England the member in the Commons who has sat the longest period of time—*Fathers of the Church*, the name given to the early teachers and expounders of Christianity, whose writings have thrown light upon the history, doctrines, and observances of the Christian church in the early ages.—*v.t* To beget as a father; to assume as one's own work; to profess or acknowledge one's self to be the author of; to ascribe or charge to one as his offspring or production (to *father* a book *on* a person).—**fatherhood**, fä'тнėr·hud, *n.* The state of being a father; the character or authority of a father.—**father-in-law**, *n.* The father of one's husband or wife.— **fatherland**, fä'тнėr·land, *n.* [A literal translation of the G. *Vaterland.*] One's native country; the country of one's fathers or ancestors.— **fatherless**, fä'тнėr·les, *a.* Destitute of a living father; without a known author.—**fatherliness**, fä'тнėr·li·nes, *n.* The state or quality of being fatherly; parental kindness, care, and tenderness.—**fatherly**, fä'тнėr·li, *a.* Like a father in affection and care; paternal; protecting; pertaining to a father.—*adv.* In the manner of a father.

fathom, faTH'um, *n.* [A.Sax. *fæthm*, the bosom, the space of both arms extended; Icel. *fathmr*, D. *vadem*, Sw. *famn*, G. *faden*, from a root meaning to stretch.] A measure of length containing 6 feet, being originally the space to which a man may extend his arms.—*v.t.* To try the depth of; to find the bottom or extent of; to sound; *fig.* to penetrate or comprehend.—**fathomable**, faTH'um·a·bl, *a.* Capable of being fathomed or comprehended.—**fathomless**, faTH'um·les, *a.* That of which no bottom can be found; bottomless; not to be penetrated or comprehended.

fatigue, fa·tēg', *v.t.*—*fatigued, fatiguing.* [Fr. *fatiguer*, from L. *fatigo*, to weary.] To weary with labor or any bodily or mental exertion; to harass with toil; to exhaust the strength by severe or long-continued exertion; to tire or wear out.—*n.* Weariness from bodily labor or mental exertion; lassitude or exhaustion of strength; the cause of weariness; labor undergone; toil; the labors of military men distinct from the use of arms.—**fatigue duty**, *n.* The work of soldiers distinct from the use of arms.

fatling, fatten, etc. See FAT.

fatuity, fa·tū'i·ti, *n.* [L. *fatuitas*, from *fatuus*, silly.] Weakness or imbecility of mind; feebleness of intellect; foolishness.—**fatuous**, fat'ū·us, *a.* [L. *fatuus.*] Feeble in mind; weak; idiotically silly; foolish.

fauces, fa̧'sēz, *n. pl.* [L., the throat, the gullet.] *Anat.* the gullet or windpipe; the posterior part of the mouth, terminated by the pharynx and larynx.—**faucal**, fa̧'kal, *a.* Pertaining to the fauces.

faucet, fa̧'set, *n.* [Fr. *fausset*, from L. *falsus*, false.] A spout fitted with a valve, for drawing liquids through a pipe; a spigot.

faugh, fa̧. Exclamation of contempt or abhorrence.

fault, folt, *n.* [O.Fr. *faulte*, Fr. *faute*, It. and Sp. *falta*, fault, defect, from a Romance verb (not recorded in French), from L. freq. *fallitare*, from *fallo*, to deceive. FAIL.] A slight offense; a neglect of duty or propriety; something worthy of some blame or censure; a defect; a blemish; a flaw; among *sportsmen*, the act of losing the scent; a lost scent; *geol.* and *mining*, a break or dislocation of strata; an interruption in the continuity of strata such that the strata on either side appear elevated or depressed.—*At fault*, puzzled; in some difficulty or perplexity; also, to blame; deserving censure.—*To find fault*, to express blame; to take exception.—*To find fault with*, to take exception to; to censure.—**faultily**, fol'ti·li, *adv.* In a faulty manner.—**faultiness**, fol'ti·nes, *n.* The state of being faulty, defective, or erroneous.—**faultless**, folt'les, *a.* Without fault; not defective or imperfect; free from blemish, vice, or offense; perfect.—**faultlessly**, folt'-

les·li, *adv.* In a faultless manner.—**faultlessness**, folt'les·nes, *n.* Freedom from faults or defects.—**faulty**, fol'ti, *a.* Containing faults, blemishes, or defects; defective; imperfect; guilty of a fault or of faults; blamable.—**faultfinder**, *n.* One who censures or objects.

faun, fa̧n, *n.* [L. *Faunus*, a deity of the woods and fields.] *Rom. myth.* one of a kind of demigods or rural deities, differing little from satyrs.

fauna, fa̧'na, *n.* [N.L. *Fauna*, sister of Faunus.] The animals peculiar to a region, epoch, or geological stratum; the animals adapted to a specific environment.

faveolate, fa·vē'o·lāt, *a.* [L. *favus*, a honeycomb.]. Formed like a honeycomb; alveolate; cellular.

favonian, fa·vō'ni·an, *a.* [L. *favonius*, the west wind.] Pertaining to the west wind.

favor, fā'ver, *n.* [Fr. *faveur*, from L. *favor, favoris*, from *faveo*, to favor, to befriend.] Kind regard; friendly disposition; a state of being looked on with good will or kindness; a kind act or office; kindness done or granted; an act of grace or good will; leave; good will; pardon; a token of love; a knot of ribbons worn at a marriage or on other festive occasions; something worn as a token of affection; convenience afforded for success (under *favor* of darkness); partiality; bias; aspect, look, or appearance (*Shak.*)‡.—*v.t.* To regard with favor or kindness; to support; to aid or have the disposition to aid; to be propitious to; to befriend; to show favor or partiality to; to afford advantages for success to; to render easier; to facilitate.—**favorable**, fā'ver·a·bl, *a.* Kind; propitious; friendly; affectionate; manifesting partiality; conducive; contributing; tending to promote; advantageous; affording facilities.—**favorableness**, fā'ver·a·bl·nes, *n.* The condition or quality of being favorable.—**favorably**, fā'ver·a·bli, *adv.* In a favorable manner.—**favored**, fā'verd, *a.* Regarded or treated with favor; having special advantages or facilities; featured, now only in the compounds *well-favored, ill-favored.*—**favorer**, fā'ver·er, *n.* One who favors.—**favorite**, fā'ver·it, *n.* A person or thing regarded with peculiar favor, preference, and affection; one greatly beloved; often one unduly favored; one treated with undue partiality.—*The favorite*, the horse favored by betting on a horse race.—*a.* Regarded with particular affection or preference.—**favoritism**, fā'ver·it·izm, *n.* The disposition to patronize favorites, or to promote the interest of a person or persons to the neglect of others having equal claims.

favus, fā'vus, *n.* [L., a honeycomb.] A kind of ringworm, a disease attacking the scalp, and characterized by yellowish dry incrustations somewhat resembling a honeycomb.

fawn, fa̧n, *n.* [Fr. *faon*, from a form *fetonus*, from L. *fetus*, progeny.] A young deer; a buck or doe of the first year.—*v.i.* To bring forth a

fawn.—*a.* Resembling a fawn in color; light brown.

fawn, fa̧n, *v.i.* [A.Sax. *fægnian*, Icel. *fagna*, to rejoice, flatter. FAIN.] To show a servile attachment; to court favor by low cringing, and the like; to flatter meanly; to cringe and bow to gain favor; to cringe and frisk about a person (as a dog).—*n.* A servile cringe or bow; mean flattery.—**fawner**, fa̧'ner, *n.* One who fawns.—**fawningly**, fa̧'ning·li, *adv.* In a fawning, servile way; with mean flattery.

fay, fā, *n.* [Fr. *fée*, L.L. *fata*, a fairy. FAIRY.] A fairy; an elf.

fay, fā, *v.t.* [A.Sax. *fægian*, to fit.] To fit two pieces of timber together so that they lie close and fair.

fayalite, fā'yal·it, *n.* [*Fayal*, one of the Azores, where it is found.] A black, greenish, or brownish mineral, consisting mainly of silicate of iron.

fealty, fē'al·ti, *n.* [O.Fr. *fealté, feauté*, fealty, from L. *fidelitas*, faithfulness, fidelity; it is thus the same word as *fidelity.*] Fidelity to a superior; faithful adherence of a tenant or vassal to the superior of whom he holds his lands; faithfulness of any person to another; faith.

fear, fēr, *n.* [A.Sax. *faer*, fear, peril; Icel. *far*, harm, mischief; O.H.G. *fára*, danger, fright; Mod.G. *gefahr*, danger; from root of E. *fare*, to travel; seen also in L. *periculum*, danger (E. *peril*).] A painful emotion excited by an expectation of evil or the apprehension of impending danger; anxiety; solicitude; holy awe and reverence for God and his laws; respect; due regard, as for persons of authority or worth.—*v.t.* To feel fear or a painful apprehension of; to be afraid of; to suspect; to doubt; to reverence; to have a reverential awe of; to venerate; to affright or to terrify (*Shak.*)‡.—*v.i.* To be in fear; to be in apprehension of evil; to be afraid.—**fearer**, fē'rer, *n.* One who fears.—**fearful**, fēr'ful, *a.* Affected by fear; apprehensive with solicitude; afraid; timorous; wanting courage; impressing fear; terrible; dreadful; awful.—**fearfully**, fēr'ful·li, *adv.* In a fearful manner.—**fearfulness**, fēr'ful·nes, *n.* The quality of being fearful.—**fearless**, fēr'les, *a.* Free from fear; bold; courageous; intrepid; undaunted.—**fearlessly**, fēr'les·li, *adv.* In a fearless manner.—**fearlessness**, fēr'les·nes, *n.* The state or quality of being fearless.—**fearsome**, fēr'sum, *a.* Alarming, terrible.

feasible, fē'zi·bl, *a.* [Fr. *faisible*, from *faire, faisant*, to do or make, L. *facere*, to do, to make. FACT.] Capable of being done, performed, executed, or effected; practicable.—**feasibility, feasibleness**, fē·zi·bil'i·ti, fē'zi·bl·nes, *n.* The quality of being feasible.—**feasibly**, fē'zi·bli, *adv.* In a feasible manner.

feast, fēst, *n.* [O.Fr. *feste* (Fr. *fête*), from L. *festum*, a holiday, a feast, from *festus*, solemn, festive.] A sumptuous repast or entertainment of which a number of guests partake; a banquet; a delicious meal; something particularly gratifying to the palate or the mind; a festival in commemoration of some great event, or in honor of some distinguished personage; a periodical or stated celebration of some event.—*v.i.* To take a meal of rich or sumptuous viands; to dine or sup on rich provisions; to be highly gratified or delighted.—*v.t.* To entertain with sumptuous food; to treat at the table magnificently; to pamper; to gratify luxuriously.—**feaster,** fēs'tėr, *n.* One who feasts.

feat, fēt, *n.* [Fr. *fait,* from L. *factum,* a deed, from *facio, factum,* to do. FACT.] An act; a deed; an exploit; in particular, any extraordinary act of strength, skill, or cunning.—*a.* [Fr. *fait,* made.] Neat; skillful; ingenious; deft. (*Shak.*)—**featly,** fēt'li, *adv.* Neatly; dexterously.

feather, feTH'ėr, *n.* [A.Sax. *fether* = D. *veder,* Sw. *fjäder,* Icel. *fjöthr,* G. *feder;* same root as L. *penna* (=*peina*), a feather: Skr. *pattra,* a wing, from root *pat,* to fly.] One of the growths which form the distinguishing covering of birds; a plume, consisting usually of a stem hollow at the lower part (called the quill), and having on each side of the upper part (called the shaft) the barbs, which with the shaft constitute the vane; something resembling a feather; a projection on the edge of a board which fits into a channel on the edge of another board.—*A feather in the cap,* an honor or mark of distinction.—*To be in high feather* to appear in high spirits; to be elated.—*To show the white feather* to give indications of cowardice (a white feather in the tail of a fighting cock showed that it was not of the true game breed).—*v.t.* To dress in feathers; to fit with feathers; to cover with feathers.—*To feather one's nest,* to collect wealth, particularly from emoluments derived from agencies for others.—*To feather an oar,* to turn the blade horizontally, with the upper edge pointing aft as it leaves the water, to lessen the resistance of the air upon it.—**feathered,** feTH'ėrd, *a.* Clothed or covered with feathers; fitted or furnished with feathers; furnished with wings; winged.—**featheredge,** *n. Carp.* the thinner edge of a board or plank.—**feather-edged,** *a.* Having one edge thinner than the other and overlapping.—**featherless,** feTH'ėr·les, *a.* Destitute of feathers; unfledged.—**feathery,** feTH'ėr·i, *a.* Clothed or covered with feathers; resembling feathers in appearance, softness, or lightness.—**feather grass,** *n.* A wiry grass whose flowers are produced in loose panicles, which, when dried and colored, form ornaments for rooms.—**feather star,** *n.* A beautiful crinoid, consisting of a central body or disk, from which spring slender radiating arms, furnished on both sides with processes that give a feather-like appearance.—**featherweight,** *n.* A weight as light as a feather; the lightest weight that is placed on a race horse; a weight classification in boxing, wrestling, etc.

feature, fē'chėr, *n.* [O.Fr. *faiture. faicture* from L. *factura,* a making, from *facio, factum,* to make. FACT.] The make, form, or cast of any part of the face; any single lineament; the make or form of any part of the surface of a thing, as of a country or landscape; the prominent part of something.—*v.t.* To depict; to delineate the characteristics of; to be a distinctive mark of; to give prominence to.—**featureless,** fē'chėr·les, *a.*

febricula, fe·brik'ū·la, *n.* [L., dim. of *febris,* fever.] A slight fever.—**febrifacient,** feb'ri·fā'shi·ent, *a.* [L. *febris,* and *facio,* to make.] Causing fever.—**febriferous,** fe·brif'ėr·us, *a.* [L. *febris,* and *fero,* to bring.] Producing fever.—**febrifuge,** feb'ri·fūj, *n.* [L. *febris,* and *fugo,* to drive away.] Any medicine that mitigates or removes fever.—*a.* Having the quality of mitigating or subduing fever.—**febrile,** fē'brīl, *a.* [L. *febrilis.*] Pertaining to fever; indicating fever, or derived from it.

February, feb'rụ·a·ri, *n.* [L. *februarius,* from *februa,* purification, because a great feast of purification was held on the 15th.] The second month in the year, consisting in common years of twenty-eight days, in leap-year of twenty-nine.

feces, fē'sēz, *n. pl.* [L. faeces.] Excrement; also, settlings; dregs; sediment. —**fecal,** fē'kal, *a.* Pertaining to feces.

feckless, fek'les, *a.* [Sc. for *effectless.*] Weak; impotent.

fecula, fek'ū·la, *n.* [L. *fæcula,* lees of wine, dim. of *fæx, fæcis,* dregs.] Powdery matter obtained from plants by crushing, washing with water, and subsidence; starch or farina.—**feculence,** fek'ū·lens, *n.* [L. *fæculentia.*] The quality or state of being feculent; sediment; dregs.—**feculent,** fek'ū·lent, *a.* [L. *fæculentus.*] Abounding with sediment, dregs, or impure and extraneous matter; dreggy; muddy; turbid; foul.

fecund, fē'kund, *a.* [L. *fecundus,* fruitful, from root *fe* (as in *fetus*), meaning to produce or bring forth.] Fruitful in children; prolific.—**fecundate,** fē'kun·dāt, *v.t.*—*fecundated, fecundating.* To make fruitful or prolific; to impregnate.—**fecundation,** fē·kun·dā'shon, *n.* The act of fecundating.—**fecundity,** fē·kun'di·ti, *n.* [L. *fæcunditas.*] The state or quality of being fecund or of bringing forth young abundantly; fertility; richness of invention.

fed, fed, pret. & pp. of *feed.*

federal, fed'ėr·al, *a.* [Fr. *fédéral,* from L. *foedus, foederis,* a league; seen also in *confederate.*] Pertaining to a league or contract, particularly between states, as the *federal* government of the United States is located in Washington, D.C.; united in a federation; founded on alliance between several states which unite for national or general purposes, each state retaining control of its home affairs, civil and criminal law, etc. of or relating to the central government of a federation; *hist.* applied to an early American political party

advocating strong federal government.—*n.* [cap.] A supporter of the United States government during the Civil War; a soldier of the northern army during the Civil War. —**federalism,** fed'ėr·al·izm, *n.* The principles of federal government; the upholding and strengthening of the central government in a federal republic.—**federalist,** fed'ėr·al·ist, *n.* One who upholds federalism; a member or supporter of the Federal party.—**federalize,** fed'ėr·al·īz, *v.t.* or *v.i.*—*federalized, federalizing.* To unite in a federal compact.—**federate,** fed'ėr·āt, *a.* Leagued; united by compact, as states or nations.— **federation,** fed'ėr·ā''shon, *n.* The act of uniting in a league; a federal government; a league.

fedora, fa·dō'ra, *n.* [From *Fédora,* drama by V. Sardou.] A soft felt hat with the crown creased lengthwise.

fee, fē, *n.* [A.Sax. *feoh, feó,* cattle, property, money=D. *vee,* Icel. *fé,* G. *vieh,* cattle; Goth. *faihu,* goods, money—allied to L. *pecus,* cattle (whence *pecuniary*). *Fief* is really the same word.] A reward or compensation for services; recompense: applied particularly to the reward of professional services; a fief or piece of land held of a superior on certain conditions; a feud; *law,* a freehold estate liable to alienation at the pleasure of the proprietor, who is absolute owner of the soil; hence, absolute property, possession, or ownership; an inherited or heritable estate.—*v.t.* **feed, feeing.** To give a fee to; to reward; to hire; to bribe. —**fee simple,** *n.* An estate in lands or tenements liable to alienation at the will of the owner: also called a *fee.*—**fee tail,** *n.* An estate limited to a man and the heirs of his body, or to himself and particular heirs of his body.

feeble, fē'bl, *a.* [Fr. *faible,* O.Fr. *fleble, floible, foible,* It. *flevole,* from L. *flebilis,* lamentable, from *fleo,* to weep.] Destitute of physical strength; infirm; debilitated; weak; wanting force, vigor, vividness, or energy.— **feebleness,** fē'bl·nes, *n.* The quality or condition of being feeble.— **feebly,** fē'bli, *adv.* In a feeble manner.—**feeble-minded,** *a.* Weak in mind; wanting firmness or constancy; irresolute.—**feeble-mindedness,** *n.*

feed, fēd, *v.t.*—pret. & pp. fed. [A.Sax. *fédan,* to feed, from *fóda,* food. FOOD.] To give food to; to supply with nourishment; *fig.* to entertain, indulge, delight (to *feed* one's self with hopes); to furnish with anything of which there is constant consumption, waste, use, or application for some purpose (to *feed* a lake, a fire); to supply.—*v.i.* To take food; to eat; to subsist by eating; to pasture; to graze; to satisfy a longing or craving.—*n.* That which is eaten; food; fodder; an allowance of provender given to a horse, cow, etc.; the material supplied at once to a machine or other contrivance to make it act.—**feeder,** fē'dėr, *n.* One who feeds; one who eats; that which supplies something.—**feedback,** fēd″bak′, n. Elect. a system in which part of the output of electric oscillation is returned and added to the input.—**feeding,** fē′ding, n. Food; that which furnishes food, especially for animals.

feel, fēl, v.t.—felt, feeling. [A.Sax. félan, D. voelen, G. fühlen, to feel; root and connections doubtful.] To perceive by the touch; to have sensation excited by contact with the body or limbs; to have a sense of; to be affected by; to be sensitive of (pain, pleasure, disgrace); to experience; to suffer; to examine by touching.—v.i. To have perception by the touch, or by the contact of any substance with the body; to have the sensibility or the passions moved or excited; to produce an impression on the nerves of sensation (iron feels cold); to perceive one's self to be (to feel sick or well); to know certainly or without misgiving.—n. The act of feeling; sensation or impression on being touched.—**feeler,** fē′lėr, n. One who feels; an organ of touch in insects and others of the lower animals, as antennae, palpi, etc.; any device for the purpose of ascertaining the designs, opinions, or sentiments of others.—**feeling,** fē′ling, a. Expressive of great sensibility; affecting; tending to excite the passions; possessing great sensibility; easily affected or moved.—n. The sense of touch; the sense by which we perceive external objects which come in contact with the body, and obtain ideas of their tangible qualities; the sensation conveyed by the sense of touch; physical sensation not due to sight, hearing, taste, or smell (a feeling of warmth, pain, or drowsiness); mental sensation or emotion; mental state or disposition; mental perception; consciousness; conviction; tenderness of heart; nice sensibility; the quality of exciting or expressing emotion; pl. the emotional part of our nature; sensitiveness; susceptibility.—**feelingly,** fē′ling·li, adv. In a feeling manner; tenderly; acutely; keenly.

feet, fēt, n. pl. of foot.

feign, fān, v.t. [Fr. feindre, from L. fingere, to shape, invent, feign, from root seen also in figment, figure, fiction, faint, etc.] To invent or imagine; to make a show of; to pretend; to assume a false appearance of; to counterfeit.—v.i. To represent falsely; to pretend.—**feigned,** fānd, p. and a. Devised; assumed; simulated; counterfeit.—**feint,** fānt, n. [Fr. feinte, from feindre.] A pretense; a mock attack; an appearance of aiming or thrusting at one part when another is intended to be struck.—v.i. To make a feint or mock attack.

feldspar, feld′spär, n. [G. feldspath—feld, field, and spath, spar.] A mineral, widely distributed, and usually of a foliated structure, consisting of silica and alumina, with potash, soda, or lime; it is a principal constituent in granite, gneiss, porphyry, etc. Called also felspar, feldspath.—**feldspathic, feldspathose,** feld·spath′ik,

feld′spath·ōs, a. Pertaining to feldspar or containing it: written also felspathic, felspathose.

felicitate, fe·lis′i·tāt, v.t.—felicitated, felicitating. [Fr. féliciter; L.L. felicito, from L. felix, felicis, happy.] To congratulate; to express joy or pleasure to another at his good fortune; refl. to congratulate one's self.—**felicitation,** fe·lis′i·tā″shun, n. The act of felicitating; expression of joy at another's good fortune.—**felicitous,** fe·lis′i·tus, a. Happy; extremely appropriate, suitable, or well expressed; managed with extreme skill and success.—**felicitously,** fe·lis′i·tus·li, adv. In a felicitous manner.—**felicitousness,** fe·lis′i·tus·nes, n. The state of being felicitous.—**felicity,** fe·lis′i·ti, n. [L. felicitas, from felix, happy.] The state of being happy or in extreme enjoyment; happiness; bliss; blissfulness; blessing; source of happiness; skillfulness; a skillful or happy turn; appropriateness.

feline, fē′līn, a. [L. felinus, from felis, a cat.] Pertaining to cats or to their species; like a cat; belonging to the family Felidae.

fell, fel, pret. of fall.

fell, fel, a. [A.Sax. fell, D. fel, O.Fr. fel, felle, sharp, fierce, cruel, a word perhaps of Celtic origin.] Cruel; barbarous; inhuman; fierce; savage; rancorous; bloody.—**fellness,** fel′nes, n. The state or quality of being fell; cruelty; ruthlessness.

fell, fel, n. [A.Sax. fell=Icel. fell, G. fell, D. vel, Goth. fill, skin. Cog. L. pellis, skin.] A skin or hide of an animal; a seam or hem sewed down level with the cloth.—v.t. To lay a seam or hem and sew it down level with the cloth.—**fellmonger,** fel′mung·gėr, n. One who deals in fells or hides.

fell, fel, v.t. [A.Sax. fellan, from feallan, to fall; causative form of fall. Comp. sit, set; lie, lay; rise, raise; etc.] To cause to fall; to bring to the ground, either by cutting or by striking; to hew down; to knock down.—**feller,** fel′ėr, n. One who fells or knocks or hews down.

fellah, fel′la, n. [Ar., a peasant; pl. fellahin.] An Egyptian peasant or agricultural laborer.

felloe, fel′ō. See FELLY.

fellow, fel′ō, n. [Icel. félagi, a partner, a sharer in goods, from félag, a community of goods (lit. a fee-laying), from fé, money, fee, and lag, partnership, a laying.] A companion; an associate; one of the same kind; an equal in rank, endowments, character, qualifications, etc.; a peer; a compeer; one of a pair, or of two things used together and suited to each other; an appellation of contempt for a man without good breeding or worth; an ignoble man; also, familiar for person, individual; in some universities and colleges, a member of the corporation or governing body; also a graduate appointed to a fellowship; a member of any incorporated society (as of the American College of Surgeons). [Used in composition to denote community in nature, station, or

employment; mutual association on equal or friendly terms: as, fellow-citizen, fellow-laborer; bed-fellow, school-fellow.]—**fellowship,** fel′ō·ship, n. The condition of being a fellow or associate; mutual association on equal and friendly terms; companionship; partnership; joint interest; an association of persons having the same tastes, occupations, or interests; a brotherhood; a foundation for the maintenance, under certain requirements, of a scholar called a fellow.—**fellow feeling,** n. Sympathy; a like feeling.

felly, fel′i, n. [A.Sax. felg, felge=Dan. fælge, D. velg, G. felge, a felly.] One of the curved pieces of wood which, joined together, form the circumference or circular rim of a wheel; the circular rim of a wheel. Written also felloe.

felon, fel′on, n. [Fr. félon, a traitor, from L.L. felo, a felon; origin doubtful.] A person who has committed felony; a person guilty of heinous crimes; a criminal; a malefactor; a whitlow.—a. Malignant; fierce; traitorous; disloyal.—**felonious,** fe·lō′ni·us, a. Villainous; traitorous; perfidious; law, done with the deliberate purpose to commit a crime.—**feloniously,** fe·lō′ni·us·li, adv. In a felonious manner.—**feloniousness,** fe·lō′ni·us·nes, n. The quality of being felonious.—**felony,** fel′o·ni, n. A serious crime, such as murder, burglary, etc., punishable by death or more than a year's imprisonment.

felsite, fel′sīt, n. [From the fels of feldspar (q.v.).] An eruptive rock, made up of quartz and orthoclase feldspar, and very hard.—**felsitic,** fel·sit′ik, a. Pertaining to or containing felsite.

felspar. See FELDSPAR.

felt, felt, pret. & pp. of feel.

felt, felt, n. [A.Sax. felt=D. vilt, G. filz, felt; allied to Gr. pilos, wool wrought into felt, and to L. pileus, a felt hat or cap. Akin filter.] A cloth or stuff made of wool, or wool and hair or fur, matted or wrought into a compact substance by rolling, beating, and pressure; a hat made of wool felted.—v.t. To make into felt; to cover with felt.—**felting,** fel′ting, n. The process by which felt is made; the materials of which felt is made, or the felt itself.

felucca, fe·luk′a, n. [It. felucca, feluca, from Ar. felûkah, from fulk, a ship.] A long, narrow vessel, once common in the Mediterranean, with two large lateen sails, and capable of being propelled by oars.

female, fē′māl, n. [Fr. femelle, L. femella, a young girl, from femina, a woman.] An animal of that sex which conceives and brings forth young; that plant which produces fruit; the flower that bears the pistil and receives the pollen of the male flowers.—a. Belonging to the sex which produces young; feminine; delicate; weak; bot. pistil-bearing; producing pistillate flowers.—Female rhymes, double rhymes, such as motion, notion, the second syllable being unstressed.—Female screw, a concave screw, corresponding to the convex or male screw which works in it.—**feminine**, fem'in·in, a. [L. *femininus*, feminine, from *femina*, a woman.] Pertaining to a woman or to women, or to the female sex; having the qualities belonging to a woman; womanly; effeminate; womanish; *gram*. denoting the gender of words which signify females, or the terminations of such words.—**femininely**, fem'in·in·li, adv. In a feminine manner.—**feminineness**, **femininity**, fem'in·in·nes, fem·in·in'i·ti, n. The quality of being feminine.

femoral, fem'o·ral, a. [L. *femoralis*, from *femur*, the thigh.] Belonging to the thigh.—**femur**, fē'mėr, n. [L.] The first bone of the leg or pelvic extremity; the thighbone.

fen, fen, n. [A.Sax. *fen*, *fenn*, marsh, mud, dirt; D. *veen*, G. *fenne*, Icel. *fen*, fen, peatbog, Goth. *fani*, mud, clay.] Low land covered wholly or partially with water, but producing sedge, coarse grasses, or other plants; boggy land; a marsh.—**fenny**, fen'i, a. Having the character of a fen; marshy; boggy; inhabiting or growing in fens.

fence, fens, n. [Abbrev. from *defence*.] A wall, hedge, bank, railing, or paling forming a boundary to or enclosing some area; that which defends; defense; the art of fencing; skill in fencing or swordsmanship; hence, skill in argument and repartee; receiver of, or place for receiving, stolen goods.—v.t.—**fenced**, **fencing**. To enclose with a fence; to secure by an enclosure; to guard; to hedge in; to ward off or parry by argument or reasoning.—v.i. To use a sword or foil for the purpose of learning the art of attack and defense; to practice fencing; to fight and defend by giving and avoiding blows or thrusts; to parry arguments; to equivocate; to prevaricate.—**fenced**, fenst, p. and a. Enclosed with a fence; guarded; fortified.—**fenceless**, fens'les, a. Without a fence; unenclosed; open.—**fencer**, fen'sėr, n. One who fences; one who teaches or practices the art of fencing with sword or foil.—**fencible**, fen'si·bl, n. A soldier for defense of the country against invasion, and not liable to serve abroad.—**fencing**, fen'sing, n. The art of using skillfully a sword or foil in attack or defense; material used in making fences; that which fences; a protection put round a dangerous piece of machinery.

fend, fend, v.t. [Contr. from *defend*, from *de*, and obs. L. *fendo*, to thrust, to strike; seen also in *offendo*, to offend.] To keep off; to ward off; to shut out: usually followed by *off* (to *fend off* blows).—**fender**, fen'dėr, n. One who or that which fends or wards off; a low metal screen in front of a fireplace to stop falling coals; the stamped, metal part covering the wheels of an automobile; a piece of timber, foam plastic, etc., hung from the side of a boat for protection in docking.

fenestra, fe·nes'tra, n. [L.] A window; an aperture; a foramen.—**fenestral**, fe·nes'tral, a. [L. *fenestralis*, from *fenestra*, a window.] Pertaining to a window.—**fenestrate**, fe·nes'trāt, a. Having windows or openings; *bot*. applied to leaves in which the cellular tissue does not completely fill up the interstices between the veins, thus leaving openings.—**fenestration**, fen·es·trā'shon, n. The series or arrangement of windows in a building.

Fenian, fē'ni·an, n. [A name assumed from Ir. *Fionna*, a race of superhuman heroes in Irish legendary history.] A person belonging to a secret society having for its principal object the erection of Ireland into an independent republic.—a. Of or belonging to the Fenians.—**Fenianism**, fē'ni·an·izm, n. The principles or politics of the Fenians.

fennec, fen'ek, n. [Moorish name.] A North African animal allied to the fox.

fennel, fen'el, n. [A.Sax. *finol*, *finugl*, like G. *fenchel*, borrowed from the L. *fœniculum*, fennel, dim. from *fœnum*, hay.] A fragrant, umbelliferous, perennial, cultivated plant, having seeds which are carminative, and frequently employed in medicine, and leaves that are used in sauces.

fenugreek, fen'ū·grēk, n. [L. *fœnum græcum*, Greek hay.] A leguminous annual plant resembling clover, and whose bitter and mucilaginous seeds are used in veterinary practice.

feod, **feodal**, **feodary**, fūd, fū'dal, fū'da·ri. Same as *Feud*, etc.

feoff, fef, n. [A form of *fief*.] A fief or fee.—**feoffee**, fef'fē, n. A person who is invested with land in fee.—**feoffer**, **feoffor**, fef'ėr, n. One who enfeoffs or grants a fee.—**feoffment**, fef'ment, n. The legal gift or transference to a person of a fee or freehold estate; the instrument or deed by which such property is conveyed.

feracious,† fe·rā'shus, a. [L. *ferax*, *feracis*, from *fero*, to bear.] Fruitful; producing abundantly.

feral, fē'ral, a. [L. *fera*, a wild beast.] Relating to, or having the nature of, a wild beast; uncultivated; undomesticated; barbarous; wild.

fer-de-lance, fâr·de·läns', n. [Fr., iron of a lance, lance-head.] The lance-headed viper, a very venomous serpent of tropical America.

feretory, fer'e·to·ri, n. [From L. *feretrum*, a bier or litter, from *fero*, to bear.] A shrine or repository for the relics of saints, variously adorned, and usually in the shape of a chest, with a roof-like top.

ferial, fē'ri·al, a. [L. *ferialis*, from *feriæ*, holidays.] Pertaining to holidays or days in which business is not transacted.

ferine, fē'rīn, a. [L. *ferinus*, from *fera*, a wild beast.] Relating to or resembling a wild beast; wild; untamed; savage.

Feringee, **Feringhee**, fe·ring'gē, n. [Probably a corruption of *Frank*.] The name given to Europeans by the Hindus.

ferment, fėr'ment, n. [L. *fermentum*, for *fervimentum*, from *fervo* or *ferveo*, to boil, to foam. FERVENT.] Any substance, as a yeast, whose presence in another body produces the peculiar effervescence and decomposition called fermentation; commotion; heat; tumult; agitation (as of a crowd, of the feelings, etc.).—v.t. (fėr·ment'). To cause fermentation in; to set in brisk motion or agitation; to warm; to excite.—v.i. To undergo fermentation; to work; to be in agitation or excited, as by violent emotions.—**fermentable**, fėr·men'ta·bl, a. Capable of fermentation.—**fermentation**, fėr·men·tā'shon, n. The act or process of fermenting; the decomposition or conversion of an organic substance into new compounds in presence of a ferment, generally indicated by a sensible internal motion, the development of heat, and the liberation of bubbles of gas; in common language, the process by which grape juice is converted into wine, and the wort of malt into beer; *fig*. the state of being in high activity or commotion; agitation; excitement.—**fermentative**, fėr·men'ta·tiv, a. Causing fermentation; consisting in or produced by fermentation.

fermium, fėr'mi·um, n. [After Enrico *Fermi*, American physicist.] A radioactive element. Symbol, Fm; at. no., 100.

fern, fėrn, n. [A.Sax. *fearn*=G. *farn*, *farren*, D. *varen*—fern; allied to Skr. *parna*, a wing or feather.] The name of many pteridophytes, consisting of herbaceous, shrubby, or arborescent plants, producing leaves called fronds, which are simple or more or less divided, and bear on their under surface or edge the capsules containing the minute spores.—**fernery**, fėr'nėr·i, n. A place where ferns are artificially grown —**fern seed**, n. The seed, or more correctly the spores, of fern, supposed to render the bearer invisible.—*To walk by fern seed*, to steal.—**ferny**, fėr'ni, a. Abounding or overgrown with fern.

ferocious, fe·rō'shus, a. [Fr. *féroce*; L. *ferox*, *ferocis*, fierce, allied to *ferus*, wild. FIERCE.] Fierce; savage; barbarous; ravenous; rapacious; indicating, or expressive of, ferocity.—**ferociously**, fe·rō'shus·li, adv. Fiercely; with savage cruelty.—**ferociousness**, fe·rō'shus·nes, n. State or quality of being ferocious; ferocity.—**ferocity**, fe·ros'i·ti, n. [Fr. *férocité*, L. *ferocitas*.] State of being ferocious; savage wildness or fierceness; fury; cruelty.

ferret, fer'et, n. [Fr. *furet*, It. *furetto*, a ferret, from L. *fur*, a thief.] A domesticated variety of the polecat, usually of a pale yellow color, with red eyes—used to drive rabbits out of their holes and to kill rats.—v.t. To hunt with ferrets; to drive out of a lurking place; (with *out*) to search out by perseverance and cunning.—**ferreter**, fer'e·tėr, n. One who ferrets.

ferret, fer'et, n. [Older *foret*, from It. *fioretti*, floss silk, from L. *flos, floris,* flower.] A kind of narrow tape, made of woolen thread, sometimes of cotton or silk.

Ferris wheel, fer'is·hwel, n. [G.W.G. *Ferris,* Amer. engineer and inventor.] A large, vertical, power-driven wheel used in amusement parks, having seats that remain in an upright position as it turns.

ferrite, fer'rit, n. [L. *ferrum,* iron.] Layers of pure iron seen in sections of steel.

ferro-, [From L. *ferrum,* iron.] A prefix in various words naming substances that contain iron or form compounds with this metal.—**ferro-concrete,** fer·rō·kon'krēt, n. Reinforced concrete.—**ferromanganese,** fer'rō·mang'ga·nēz, n. An alloy of iron and manganese. See FERROUS.

ferrous, fer'us, a. [L. *ferrum,* iron.] Pertaining to, obtained from, or containing iron.—**ferric,** fer'ik, a. *Chem.* pertaining to or extracted from iron (*ferric* acid and *ferric* oxide).—**ferriferous,** fe·rif'er·us, a. [L. *ferrum,* and *fero,* to produce.] Producing or yielding iron.—**ferrocyanic,** fer'ō·sī·an''ik, a. Pertaining to or derived from iron and cyanogen.—**ferrotype,** fer'ō·tīp, n. *Photog.* a term applied to some photographic processes in which the salts of iron are the principal agents; a photograph taken on japanned sheet iron by a collodion process.—**ferruginous, ferrugineous,** † fe·rūj'i·nus, fe·rū·jin'i·us, a. [L. *ferrugineus,* rusty, from *ferrugo, ferruginis,* iron rust, from *ferrum,* iron.] Partaking of iron; irony; of the color of the rust or oxide of iron.

ferrule, fer'ul, n. [Formerly *verril,* from Fr. *virole,* ferrule, from *virer,* to veer. VEER.] A ring of metal put round the end of a walking stick or other thing to strengthen it or prevent its splitting; a small cap or bushing placed in a joint to make it tight (as between pipes).

ferry, fer'i, v.t.—*ferried, ferrying.* [A.Sax. *ferian, farian,* to carry, to convey, causative of *faran,* to go. FARE.] To carry or transport over a river, strait, etc., in a boat or other conveyance.—*v.i.* To pass over a ferry.—*n.* The place or passage where boats pass over a narrow piece of water to convey passengers; the boat itself.—**ferryboat,** n. A boat that plies at a ferry.—**ferryman,** n. One who keeps a ferry.—**ferriage,** fer'i·ij, n. The price or fare to be paid at a ferry.

fertile, fer'til or fer'til, a. [Fr. *fertile,* from L. *fertilis,* from *fero,* to bear, to produce; same root as E. *bear* (BEAR); seen also in *confer, differ, refer,* etc.] Fruitful; producing fruit or crops in abundance; the opposite of barren; prolific or productive of anything, as of ideas, poetry, etc.; inventive; able to produce abundantly; *bot.* capable of producing fruit; fruit-bearing.—**fertilely,** fer'til·li, adv. In a fertile manner; fruitfully.—**fertileness,** fer'til·nes, n. Fertility.—**fertility,** fer·til'i·ti, n. [L.

fertilitas.] The state of being fertile or fruitful; fruitfulness; fecundity; productiveness; richness; fertile invention.—**fertilization,** fer'til·i·zā''shon, n. The act or process of rendering fertile; the act of impregnation, insemination, pollination, etc., whereby the union of two germ cells initiates the formation of a new individual; the application of fertilizer.—**fertilize,** fer'ti·līz, v.t.—*fertilized, fertilizing.* To make fertile or productive.—**fertilizer,** fer'ti·lī·zer, n. One who fertilizes; a chemical or organic compound used to enrich the soil.

ferula, fer'ū·la, n. [L.] A ferula, a genus of plants, members of which yield asafetida, galbanum, etc.

ferule, fer'ul, n. [L. *ferula,* a twig, a cane, a switch, from *ferio,* to strike.] A flat piece of wood used to punish children by striking them on the palm of the hand; a cane or rod for the same purpose.—*v.t.*—*feruled, feruling.* To punish with a ferule.

fervent, fer'vent, a. [L. *fervens, ferventis,* ppr. of *ferveo,* to boil, to ferment; akin *ferment.*] Hot; glowing; intensely warm; hot in temper; vehement; ardent; earnest; excited; animated; glowing with religious feeling; zealous.—**fervently,** fer'vent·li, adv. In a fervent manner or degree; earnestly; ardently; vehemently.—**fervency,** fer'ven·si, n. The state of being fervent; heat of mind; ardor; animated zeal; warmth of devotion.—**fervid,** fer'vid, a. [L. *fervidus,* from *ferveo.*] Very hot; burning; glowing; fervent; very warm in zeal; vehement; ardent.—**fervidly,** fer'vid·li, adv. Very hotly; with glowing warmth.—**fervidness,** fer'vid·nes, n. Glowing heat; ardor.—**fervor,** fer'ver, n. [L. *fervor,* heat.] Heat or warmth; intensity of feeling; ardor; burning zeal; extreme earnestness in religion, particularly in prayer.

Fescennine, fes'en·in, a. [From *Fescennia,* town in Etruria.] Sportive, ribald, licentious.

fescue, fes'kū, n. [O.E. *festue,* from O.Fr. *festu* (Fr. *fetu*), a straw; L. *festuca,* a shoot or twig.] A straw, wire, pin, or the like, used to point out letters to children; a kind of grass, some species being excellent meadow and pasture grasses.

fesse, fes, n. [O.Fr. *fesse,* Fr. *fasce,* L. *fascia,* a band.] *Her.* a band or girdle comprising the center third part of the escutcheon, which it crosses horizontally.

festal, fes'tal, a. [From L. *festum,* a feast. FEAST.] Pertaining to a feast; festive.—**festally,** fes'tal·li, adv. Joyfully; mirthfully.—**festival,** fes'ti·val, a. [L. *festivus.*] Pertaining to or befitting a feast; joyous; mirthful.—*n.* A time of feasting; an anniversary day of joy, civil or religious; a festive celebration.—**festive,** fes'tiv, a. [L. *festivus.*] Pertaining to or becoming a feast; joyous; gay; mirthful.—**festively,** fes'tiv·li, adv. In a festive manner.—**festivity,** fes·tiv'i·ti, n. [L. *festivitas.*] The con-

dition of being festive; social joy or exhilaration at an entertainment; something forming part of a festal celebration.

fester, fes'ter, v.i. [O.Fr. *festrir,* to fester.] To suppurate; to discharge or become full of pus or purulent matter; to rankle (passions, a sense of wrong, etc.).—*n.* Act of festering or rankling.

festinate,‡ fes'ti·nāt, a. [L. *festino, festinatum,* to hasten] Hasty; hurried. (Shak.)

festoon, fes·tön', n. [Fr. *feston,* lit. a festal garland; It. *festone,* from L. *festum,* a feast.] A string, chain, or garland of flowers, foliage, etc., suspended so as to form one or more depending curves; *arch.* a sculptured ornament in imitation of this.—*v.t.* To adorn with festoons; to connect by festoons.

fetal, a. **fetation,** n. See FETUS.

fetch, fech, v.t. [A.Sax. *feccan, gefeccan,* to fetch, to draw, to take, to seek; akin to O.Fris. *faka,* to prepare.] To go and bring; to bring; to bear toward the person speaking; to recall or bring back; to make or perform, with certain objects (to *fetch* a blow or stroke, to *fetch* a sigh); to bring or obtain as its price.—*To fetch out,* to bring or draw out.—*To fetch to,* to restore; to revive, as from a swoon; to bring up; to stop suddenly in any course; to overtake.—*v.i.* To bring things; to move or turn.—*To fetch and carry,* to perform menial services; to become a servile drudge.—*n.* A stratagem by which a thing is indirectly brought to pass; a trick; an artifice; the apparition of a living person; a wraith.—**fetcher,** fech'er, n. One who fetches.

fête, fāt, n. [Fr., from L. *festum,* a feast.] A feast; a holiday; a festival day.—*v.t.*—*fêted, fêting.* To entertain with a feast; to honor with a festive entertainment.

feticide, foeticide, fē'ti·sīd, n. See FETUS.

fetid, fē'tid, a. [L. *foetidus,* from *foeteo,* to stink.] Having an offensive smell; having a strong or rancid scent.—**fetidness,** fē'tid·nes, n. The quality of smelling offensively.—**fetor,** fē'ter, n. [L. *foetor.*] Any strong offensive smell; stench.

fetish, fē'tish, n. [Fr. *fétiche,* Pg. *feitiço,* sorcery, witchcraft, from L. *factitius,* artificial, from *facio,* to make. FACT.] Any object, animate or inanimate, natural or artificial, regarded by some uncivilized races with a feeling of awe, as having mysterious powers residing in it or as being the representative or habitation of a deity; hence, any object of exclusive devotion.—**fetishism,** fē'tish·izm, n. The worship of fetishes; emotional attachment to inanimate objects.—**fetishistic,** fē·tish·is'tik, a.

fetlock, fet'lok, n. [From *foot* or *feet* and *lock.*] A tuft of hair growing behind the pastern joint of horses; the joint on which the hair grows; an instrument fixed on the leg of a horse when put to pasture for the purpose of preventing him from running off.

fetor. See FETID.

fetter, fet′ėr, *n.* [A.Sax. *feter, fetor,* a fetter; O.G. *fezzera,* G. *fessel,* Icel. *fjöturr.* Probably connected with *foot.*] A chain for the feet; a chain by which a person or animal is confined by the foot; anything that confines or restrains from motion; a restraint.—*v.t.* To put fetters on; to bind; to confine; to restrain.

fettle, fet′l, *v.t.* [M. E. *fettlen,* to gird, fit, set in order.] To trim, put in order. *n.* Condition, state.

fetus, fē′tus, *n.* [L., from a root *fe,* implying fruitfulness, productiveness, as in *fecund.*] The young of viviparous animals in the womb, and of oviparous animals in the egg, after it is perfectly formed; before which time it is called *Embryo.*—**fetal,** fē′tal, *a.* Pertaining to a fetus.—**fetation,** fē·tā′shon, *n.* The formation of a fetus.—**feticide,** fē′ti·sīd, *n.* [L. *fetus,* and *cædo,* to kill.] The destruction of the fetus in the womb; the act by which criminal abortion is produced.

feud, fūd, *n.* [L.L. *feudum,* a fief; from O.Fr. or O.G., like *fief, feu, fee.*] A fief.—**feudal,** fū′dal, *a.* [L.L. *feudalis,* from *feudum.*] Pertaining to feuds or fiefs; founded upon or pertaining to the system of holding lands by military services.—*Feudal system,* a system according to which grants of land were made by the sovereign to the nobles, and by them to an inferior class, on the condition that the possessor should take an oath of fealty, and do military service.—**feudalism,** fū′dal·izm, *n.* An agricultural political organization developed in Europe during the early mediéval period, with vestiges remaining up to 1917 characterized by complete subservience of vassal to lord, and under which all lands owned by the lords were held in fief to the vassals who worked the land. —**feudalization,** fū′dal·i·zā″shon, *n.* The act of feudalizing.—**feudalize,** fū′dal·īz, *v.t.—feudalized, feudalizing.* To reduce to a feudal tenure; to conform to feudalism.—**feudally,** fū′dal·li, *adv.* In a feudal manner; by feudal tenure.—**feudary,** fū′da·ri, *a.* Held by or pertaining to feudal tenure.—*n.* A tenant who holds his lands by feudal service; a feudatory. —**feudatory,** fū′da·to·ri, *a.* Holding from another by feudal tenure.—*n.* A tenant or vassal holding his lands on condition of military service; the tenant of a feud or fief.

feud, fūd, *n.* [O.E. *feide,* from A.Sax. *faehth,* hostility, from *fáh,* hostile (whence *foe*); D. *veede,* G. *fehde,* Dan. *fejde,* a feud; the spelling being modified through confusion with L.L. *feudum,* a feud or fief. Akin *fiend.*] A contention or quarrel; hostility; often, hostility or declared warfare between families or parties in a state.

fever, fē′vėr, *n.* [A.Sax. *fefer,* from L. *febris,* a fever; or from O.Fr. *fevre,* Mod. Fr. *fièvre,* of same origin.] An increase in body temperature above the normal; any disease accompanied by an increase in temperature, diminished strength, and often with excessive thirst; agitation or excitement by anything that strongly affects the passions.—*v.t.* To put in a fever.—*v.i.* To be seized with fever.—**feverish,** fē′vėr·ish, *a.* Having fever; affected with fever, especially with a slight degree of fever; indicating or pertaining to fever.—**feverishly,** fē′vėr·ish·li, *adv.* In a feverish manner.—**feverishness,** fē′vėr·ish·nes, *n.* The state of being feverish; anxious, heated excitement.—**feverous,** fē′vėr·us, *a.* Affected with fever or ague; feverish.—**feverously,**† fē′vėr·us·li, *adv.* In a feverous manner.—**feverfew,** fē′vėr·fū, *n.* [A.Sax. *feferfuge,* from L. *febrifugia,* from *febris,* fever, and *fugo,* to drive away.] A European composite plant with much-divided leaves, and white flowers; once supposed to be a valuable febrifuge, hence the name.

few, fū, *a.* [A.Sax. *feáwa, feáwe,* Dan. *faa,* Goth. *favs,* pl. *favai,* little, few; of cognate origin with L. *paucus,* few, *paulus,* Gr. *pauros,* little.] Not many; small in number: used frequently, by ellipsis of a noun, for not many persons or things. *A few* is often used and generally means more than *few* alone.—**fewness,** fū′nes, *n.* The state of being few; paucity.

fey, fā; *a.* [A.Sax. *fæge,* Icel. *feigr,* near to death.] On the verge of a sudden or violent death; fated soon to die, and often showing this in some peculiar way.

fez, fez, *n.* [From *Fez,* the principal town in Morocco, where such caps are largely manufactured.] A red cap of fine cloth, fitting closely to the head, with a tassel of blue silk or wool at the crown, once worn in Turkey, on the shores of the Levant, in Egypt, and North Africa generally.

fiacre, fi·ä′kr, *n.* [Fr., from the Hotel St. *Fiacre,* where the inventor of these carriages established in 1640 an office for the hire of them.] A small four-wheeled carriage; a hackney, coach or similar vehicle plying for hire.—*v.* To convey pilgrims and others to the shrine of the Irish saint Fiachra.

fiancé, fiancée, fē·än·sā′, *n. masc.* and *fem.* [Fr.] An affianced or betrothed person.

fiasco, fi·as′kō, *n.* [It. *fiasco,* a flask or bottle, a cry in Italy when a singer fails to please, perhaps in allusion to the bursting of a bottle.] A failure in a musical performance; an ignominious and notorious failure generally; a conspicuous or chagrining frustration; a breakdown.

fiat, fī′at, *n.* [L. let it be done, 3rd pers. sing. subj. of *fio,* to be done.] A command to do something; a decisive or effective command.— **fiat money,** *n.* Paper currency issued by a government as money, which does not represent coin or bullion, but is made legal tender by law.— *Fiat in Bankruptcy,* an order in chancery allowing the institution of proceedings in bankruptcy.

fib, fib, *n.* [Probably an abbreviation and corruption from *fable.*] A lie or falsehood: a word used as a softer expression than lie.—*v.i. fibbed, fibbing.* To lie; to speak falsely.— **fibber, fibster,** fib′ėr, fib′stėr, *n.* One who tells lies or fibs.

fiber, fibre, fī′bėr, *n.* [Fr. *fibre,* L. *fibra,* allied to *filum,* a thread.] A thread or filament; one of the fine slender threadlike or hairlike bodies of which the tissues of animals and plants are partly constituted; the small slender root of a plant.— **fiber glass,** *n.* Fibrous glass that is used in woven or molded products.— **fibriform,** fī′bri·form, *a.* Like a fiber or fibers.—**fibril,** fī′bril, *n.* [Fr. *fibrille.*] A small fiber; the branch of a fiber; a very slender thread.— **fibrilla,** fī·bril′la, *n.* pl. **fibrillae,** fī·bril′lē. [Dim. of L. *fibra.*] One of the elements or components of fiber; *bot.* one of the hairs produced from the epidermis which covers the young roots of plants.—**fibrillation,** fī·bri·lā′shon, *n.* The state of being reduced to fibrils or fibrillae.— **fibrillose,** fī·bril′ōs, *a. Bot.* covered with or composed of little strings or fibers.—**fibrin,** fī′brin, *n.* A tough white fibrous protein formed from fibrinogen as the blood coagulates.— **fibrinogen,** fī·brin′ō·jen, *n.* A globulant that is present in blood plasma and formed in the kidneys.—**fibrinous,** fī′brin·us, *a.* Having fibrin present.—**fibroid,** fī′broid, *a.* [From L. *fibra,* fiber.] Of a fibrous character.—**fibrosis,** fī·brō′sis, *n. Pathol.* a morbid growth or development of fibrous matter.—**fibroma,** fī·brō′ma, *n. Pathol.* a tumor or growth of fibrous matter.—**fibrous,** fī′brus, *a.* Containing or consisting of fibers.— **fibrovascular,** fī·brō·vas′kū·lėr, *a. Bot.* consisting of wood fibers and vessels.

fibula, fib′ū·la, *n. pl.* **fibulae,** fib′ū·lē. [L. a clasp, a brace, a pin.] An ancient clasp or buckle; *anat.* the outer and lesser bone of the lower leg; *surgery,* a needle for sewing up wounds.—**fibular,** fib′ū·lėr, *a.* Of or pertaining to the fibula.

fichu, fi·shö′, *n.* [Fr.] A light piece of dress worn by ladies covering the neck, throat, and shoulders.

fickle, fik′l, *a.* [A.Sax. *ficol,* inconstant; akin to G. *ficken,* to move quickly to and fro.] Wavering; inconstant; unstable; of a changeable mind; irresolute; not firm in opinion or purpose; capricious; liable to change or vicissitude.—**fickleness,** fik′l·nes, *n.* The state or quality of being fickle; inconstancy; unsteadiness in opinion or purpose; changeableness.

fico, fē′kō, *n.* [It. from *ficus,* fig.] A fig. used in expressions of contempt or scorn, originally with obscene gesture. (*Shak.*)

fictile, fik′tīl, *a.* [L. *fictilis,* from *fingo, fictum,* to form. FEIGN.] Molded into form by art; manufactured by the potter; suitable for the potter; made of molded earth or clay.

fiction, fik'shon, *n.* [L. *fictio*, a shaping, a fashioning, from *fingo*, *fictum*, to fashion. FEIGN.] The act of inventing or imagining; that which is feigned, invented, or imagined; a feigned or invented story; a tale or story composed for amusement or entertainment; fictitious literature; prose narrative in the form of romances, novels, tales, and the like.—**fictional,** fik'shon·al, *a.* Pertaining to or characterized by fiction.—**fictionist,** fik'shon·ist, *n.* A writer of fiction.—**fictitious,** fik·tish'us, *a.* [L. *fictitius*.] Feigned; imaginary; not real; counterfeit; false; not genuine; invented to give literary pleasure; dealing with imaginary characters and events.—**fictitiously,** fik·tish'us·li, *adv.* In a fictitious manner; falsely.—**fictitiousness,** fik·tish'us·nes, *n.*—**fictive,** fik'tiv, *a.* Feigned; imaginary; hypothetical.

fid, fid, *n.* A bar or short piece of wood or metal, helping to support a topmast; a wooden pin for various purposes on board ship.

fiddle, fid'l, *n.* [A.Sax. *fithele*; L.G. *fidel*, Dan. *fiddel*, Icel. *fithla*, D. *vedel*; perhaps borrowed from L.L. *vidula*, a viol. VIOL.] A stringed instrument of music; a violin.—*v.i. fiddled, fiddling.* To play on a fiddle or violin; to trifle.—**fiddle-faddle,** *a.* Trifling; making a bustle about nothing. (*Colloq.*)—*v.i.* To trifle.—**fiddler,** fid'lėr, *n.* One who plays on a fiddle.—**fiddlestick,** *n.* A fiddle bow: used often as an interjection equivalent to nonsense! pshaw! etc.—**fiddlewood,** *n.* A tropical American timber tree which yields a hard wood valuable for carpenter work.—**fiddling,** fid'ling, *a.* Trifling; trivial; fussily busy with nothing.

fidelity, fi·del'i·ti, *n.* [L. *fidelitas*, from *fidelis*, faithful, from *fides*, trust, faith, *fido*, to trust. FAITH.] Faithfulness; careful and exact observance of duty or performance of obligations; firm adherence to a person or to a party; loyalty; honesty; veracity; adherence to truth.

fidget, fij'et, *v.i.* [Dim. of provincial *fidge*, *fike*, *fyke*, to be restless; akin to Icel. *fika*, to hasten; G. *ficken*, O.Sw. *fika*, to move quickly to and fro.] To move uneasily one way and the other; to move irregularly or in fits and starts.—*n.* Irregular motion; restlessness.—**fidgetiness,** fij'et·i·nes, *n.* The state or quality of being fidgety.—**fidgety,** fij'et·i, *a.* Given to fidget; restless; uneasy.

fiducial, fi·dū'shal, *a.* [L.L. *fiducialis*, from L. *fiducia*, trust, trustiness, from *fido*, to trust. FAITH.] Confident in trust or belief; undoubting; fiduciary.—**fiducially,** fi·dū'shal·li, *adv.* With confidence.

fiduciary, fi·dū'shi·er·i, *a.* [L. *fiduciarius*, held in trust.] Confident in belief; trustful; undoubting; having the nature of a trust; held in trust.—*n.* One who holds a thing in trust; a trustee.

fie, fī, *interj.* [Interjectional expression corresponding to Sc. *feigh*, Fr. *fi*, G. *pfui*, *fi*, Dan. *fy*, etc.] An exclamation denoting contempt, dislike, or impatience.

fief, fēf, *n.* [Fr. *fief*, from O.H.G. *fihu*, property, lit. cattle. FEE, FEUD.] An estate held of a superior on condition of military or other service; an estate held on feudal tenure.

field, fēld, *n.* [A.Sax. *feld*, a field=D. *veld*, Dan. *felt*, G. *feld*; allied to *fold*, an enclosure, *fell*, a hill; Dan. *falle*, greensward; Sc. *fale*, *feal*, a turf.] A piece of land suitable for tillage or pasture; a distinct or separate division of a farm; cleared land; cultivated ground; the open country; the ground where a battle is fought or military operations carried on; hence, a battle or action (the *field* is lost); area of activity, especially in sports; *phys.* an area where a given effect exists (magnetic *field*); subject of study; profession; scope; compass; extent; sphere (a wide *field* for conjecture); space on which figures are drawn; the general surface of a heraldic shield or escutcheon; *cricket*, the fielders collectively; *sporting*, those taking part in a hunt; all the horses, dogs, or the like, taking part in a race.—*Field of vision* or *view*, in a telescope or microscope, the space or range within which objects are visible to an eye looking through the instrument.—*To keep the field*, to continue active military operations in the field.—*To take the field*, to begin military operations.—*v.i.* To be one of the field whose duty is to watch and catch or recover the ball in baseball.—**fielder,** fēl'dėr, *n.* A player who fields at baseball.—**field artillery,** *n.* Light ordnance fitted for active operations in the field.—**field day,** *n.* A day when troops are drawn out for instruction in field exercises and evolutions; any day of unusual display.—**field glass,** *n.* A kind of binocular, telescope or opera glass for looking at objects at a considerable distance from the spectator.—**field gun,** *n.* A small cannon for use in the field, acting with infantry or cavalry. A common *field gun* is the 18-pounder quick-firing gun.—**field marshal,** *n.* The highest rank conferred on general officers in practically all armies.—**field mouse,** *n.* One of several species of rodent animals that live in the field, burrowing in banks, etc.—**fieldwork,** *n.* All the out-of-doors operations of a surveyor, engineer, geologist, etc.—**field work,** *n.* A temporary fortification thrown up.

fiend, fēnd, *n.* [A.Sax. *feónd*, *fynd*, a fiend, an enemy, from *feón*, to hate; like D. *vijand*, Icel. *fjandi*, Goth. *fijands*, G. *feind*, originally a present participle. Akin *foe*.] An infernal being; a demon; the devil; a person with devilish qualities; a wicked, cruel, or malicious person; one who is addicted to something.—**fiendish,** fēn'dish, *a.* Having the qualities of a fiend; infernal; excessively cruel; diabolic; devilish.—**fiendishly,** fēn'dish·li, *adv.* In a fiendish manner.—**fiendishness,** fēn'dish·nes, *n.* The quality of being fiendish.

fierce, fėrs, *a.* [O.Fr. *fers*, *fiers*, from L. *ferus*, wild, rude, cruel, whence *fera*, a wild beast; akin *feral* and *ferocious*.] Vehement; violent; furious; savage; ferocious; easily enraged; indicating ferocity or a ferocious disposition; very eager; vehement in anger or cruelty.—**fiercely,** fėrs'li, *adv.* In a fierce manner; furiously; with rage; with a fierce expression or aspect.—**fierceness,** fėrs'nes, *n.* The quality of being fierce, furious, or angry; violence; fury; ferocity; savageness.

fiery, fī'ėr·i, *a.* See FIRE.

fife, fīf, *n.* [Fr. *fifre*, a fife, from G. *pfeife*, (=E. *pipe*), a word of onomatopoeic origin. PIPE.] A small musical instrument of the flute kind, having but one key, and a compass of two octaves.—*v.i.* To play on a fife.—**fifer,** fī'fėr, *n.* One who plays on a fife; an inhabitant of the county of Fife.

fifteen, fif'tēn, *a.* [A.Sax. *fiftyne*, lit. five-ten.] Five and ten.—*n.* The number which consists of five and ten; a symbol representing this number, as 15 or xv.—*The Fifteen*, the old Scottish law court with its fifteen Lords of Session.—*The fifteen*, the '15, the Jacobite rebellion of 1715.—**fifteenth,** fif'tēnth, *a.* The fifth in order after the tenth; being one of fifteen equal parts into which a whole is divided.—*a.* A fifteenth part.—**fifth,** fifth, *a.* The ordinal of five; next after the fourth; being one of five equal parts of a whole.—*n.* One of five equal parts into which anything is divided; *mus.* an interval consisting of three tones and a semitone.—*Fifth-monarchy men*, believers in the last of the great monarchies of *Daniel*, ii. 44, expecting the advent of Christ, and denying all human organizations.—**fifth column,** *n.* The practice of sabotage and espionage by citizens of one country for the benefit of a foreign power; traitorous political activity.—**fifty,** fif'ti, *a.* [A.Sax. *fiftig*.] Five times ten.—*n.* The number which consists of five times ten; a symbol representing this number.—**fiftieth,** fif'ti·eth, *a.* and *n.*

fig, fig, *n.* [Fr. *figue*, like D. *vijg*, G. *feige*, from L. *ficus*, fig.] A fruit consisting of a hollow receptacle containing a great multitude of minute flowers, the ripe carpels of which, erroneously called the seed, are embedded in the pulp; the tree that bears this fruit; used also as a term of scorn or contempt (I do not care a *fig* for him; in this usage perhaps from O.Sp. *figo*, a motion denoting contempt.)

fig, fig, *n.* [A contr. for *figure*.] Dress; employed chiefly in the colloquial phrase *in full fig*, in full or official dress.

fight, fīt, *v.i.* pret. & pp. *fought*. [A.Sax. *feohtan*=G. *fechten*, D. *vechten*, Dan. *fegte*, Icel. *flkta*, to fight.] To contend for victory in battle or in single combat; to contend in arms or otherwise; to carry on active opposition; to strive or struggle to resist: with *with* or *against* before an object.—*To fight shy of,* to avoid from a feeling of dislike, fear, mistrust, etc.—*v.t.* To carry on or wage (a battle); to win or gain by struggle (to *fight* one's way); to contend with; to war against; to manage or maneuver in a fight (to *fight* one's ship).—*To fight it out,* to struggle till a decisive result is attained.—*n.* A contest; a battle; an engagement; a struggle for victory. Syn. under BATTLE.—**fighter,** fīt′ẽr, *n.* One that fights; a combatant.

figment, fig′ment, *n.* [L. *figmentum,* from *fingo,* to feign. FEIGN.] An invention; a fiction; something feigned or imagined.

figure, fig′ūr, *n.* [Fr. *figure,* from L. *figura,* figure, shape, from *fig,* root of *fingo,* to fashion, to shape; whence also *feign, fiction,* etc. FEIGN.] The form of anything as expressed by the outline or contour; shape; fashion; form; any form made by drawing, painting, carving, embroidering, etc.; especially the human body so represented; appearance or impression made by the conduct of a person (to cut a poor *figure*); *logic,* the form of a syllogism with respect to the relative position of the middle term; *arith.* a character denoting or standing for a number; hence, value, as expressed in numbers; price; *theol.* type or representative; *rhet.* a mode of speaking or writing in which words are deflected from their ordinary use or signification; a trope; a peculiar expression used for impressiveness as a metaphor, antithesis, etc.—*To cut a figure,* to make one's self celebrated or notorious; to appear to advantage or disadvantage.—*v.t.*—**figured, figuring.** To make a figure or likeness of; to represent by drawing, sculpture, carving, embroidery, etc.; to cover or adorn with figures or ornamental designs; to mark with figures; to represent by a typical or figurative resemblance; to typify; to imagine; to image in the mind.—*v.i.* To make a figure; to be a prominent figure or personage.—**figurant,** fig′ū•rant, *n. masc.*—**figurante,** fig′ū•rant, *n. fem.* [Fr.] One who dances at the opera in groups or figures; a character on the stage who figures in its scenes, but has nothing to say. —**figurate,** fig′ū•rāt, *a.* [L. *figuro, figuratum,* to form, to fashion.] Of a certain determinate form or shape.—*Figurate numbers,* such numbers as do or may represent some geometrical figure, being thus called triangular, square, pentagonal, etc., numbers.—**figuration,** fig•ū•rā′shon, *n.* The act of giving figure or determinate form.—**figurative,** fig′ū•rā•tiv, *a.* [Fr. *figuratif.*] Representing by means of a figure or type; typical; symbolical: used in a metaphorical sense; having the character of a figure or trope; metaphoric; not literal.—**figuratively,** fig′ū•re•tiv•li, *adv.* In a figurative manner; by a figure; in a sense different from that which words originally imply in a metaphorical sense.—**figurativeness,** fig′ū•re•tiv•nes, *n.* State of

being figurative.—**figured,** fig′ūrd, *a.* Adorned with figures.—**figurehead,** *n.* The ornamental figure on a ship immediately under the bowsprit.— **figurine,** fig•ū•rēn′, *n.* [Fr. dim. of *figure.*] A small ornamental figure or piece of statuary; a statuette.

filament, fil′a•ment, *n.* [L.L. *filamentum,* a slender thread, from L. *filum* a thread.] A fine single thread or fiber from flesh, roots, minerals, etc.; a thread-like metallic conductor made incandescent by the flow of electricity, as in an electric bulb or electron tube.—**filamentary,** fil•a•men′te•ri, *a.* Having the character of or formed by a filament.—**filamentous,** fil•a•men′tus, *a.* Like a thread; consisting of fine filaments; *bot.* bearing filaments.—**filar,** fī′lẽr, *a.* Pertaining to a thread: applied to a microscope, or other optical instrument, into whose construction one or more threads or fine wires are introduced.—**filature,** fil′a•chẽr, *n.* A forming into threads; the reeling off silk from cocoons; a filatory.—**filiform,** fil′i•form, *a.* Having the form of a thread or filament.—**filose,** fī′lōs, *a. Zool.* and *bot.* applied to a part when it ends in a threadlike process.

filbert, fil′bẽrt, *n.* [From St. *Philibert,* whose feast day is in the nutting season.] Either of two European hazels; the hazelnut.

filch, filch, *v.t.* [For *filk,* from O.E. *fele,* Icel. *fela,* to steal, like *talk* and *tell, stalk* (verb) and *steal.*] To steal, especially something of little value; to pilfer; to take in a thievish manner. —**filcher,** filch′ẽr, *n.* One who filches.

file, fīl, *n.* [Fr. *file,* from L. *filum,* a thread, string.] A collection of papers arranged for ready reference; a container in which records are kept in order; a row of soldiers arranged one behind another, from front to rear; hence, *rank and file* (*milit.*), the lines of soldiers from side to side, and from front to back; an old *file,* a sharper.—*v.t.*—**filed, filing.** To arrange or place in a file; to bring before a court by presenting the proper papers (to *file* a bill in chancery).—*v.i.* To march in a file or line; to register as a candidate in an election.

file, fīl, *n.* [A.Sax. *feol*=D. *vijl,* Dan. *viil,* G. *feile,* O.H.G. *vihila,* a file.] A steel instrument, having minute teeth upon the surface for cutting, abrading, and smoothing metal, ivory, wood, etc.—*v.t.*—**filed, filing.** To rub smooth, or cut with a file, or as with a file; to polish.—**filing,** fī′ling, *n.* A particle rubbed off by a file.

filet, fi•lā′, fē•lā′, *a.* Indicating a lace or net of square mesh.

filial, fil′i•al, *a.* [Fr. *filial,* from L.L. *filialis,* from L. *filius,* a son, *filia,* a daughter.] Pertaining to a son or daughter; becoming a child in relation to his parents; bearing the relation of a child.—**filially,** fil′i•al•li, *adv.* In a filial manner.—**filiate,** fil′i•āt, *v.t.* To adopt as a son or daughter.—**filiation,** fil•i•ā′shon, *n.* The relation of a child to a father; adoption; the fixing of the paternity of a child.

filibuster, fil′i•bus•tẽr, *n.* [Sp. *filibustero,* freebooter.] Any lawless adventurer who invades, with the view of occupying, a foreign country; an extreme stalling measure used to prevent action on, or to delay, legislation.—*v.i.* To engage in filibuster; to endeavor to defeat or to delay legislation by obstructionist tactics, as long speeches or motions.

filigree, fil′i•grē, *n.* [Formerly *filigrane,* from Fr. *filigrane,* It. *filigrana,* from L. *filum,* a thread, and *granum,* a grain: originally it is said to have had beads in it.] Ornamental open work executed in fine gold or silver wire, formed into flowers and arabesques.

fill, fil, *v.t.* [A.Sax. *fyllan,* to fill, from the adjective *ful,* full=Icel. and Sw. *fylla,* Goth. *fulljan,* G. *füllen,* D. *vullen,* to fill.] To make full; to cause to be occupied so that no space is left vacant; to put in so as to occupy a space; to occupy the whole space or capacity of; to repair cavities in teeth; to satisfy; to content; to glut; to press and dilate (a ship's sails); to supply with an occupant or holder; to possess and perform the duties of; to officiate in; to hold or occupy.—*To fill in,* to pour or put in for the purpose of filling something; to write in (items in a list).—*To fill out,* to distend or enlarge from within.—*To fill up,* to make quite full; to occupy or take up; to occupy the whole extent of; to engage or employ (time).—*v.i.* To grow or become full; to make something full.—*To fill out,* to become enlarged or distended.—*To fill up,* to grow or become full.—*n.* As much as fills or satisfies; material that fills a cavity or hole.—**filler,** fil′ẽr, *n.* One who or that which fills; a utensil for conveying a liquid into a bottle, cask, etc.—**filling,** fil′ing, *a.* Calculated to fill, satisfy, or satiate.—*n.* Materials used for occupying some vacant space, stopping up a hole, or the like.

fillet, fil′et, *n.* [Fr. *filet,* a thread, a band, the chine of an animal, etc., dim. of *fil,* thread, from L. *filum,* a thread. FILE.] A little band to tie about the head; a band or narrow strip; *cookery,* fi•lā′, a boneless piece of lean meat, sometimes rolled and tied; fillet of beef, a slice of tenderloin; fillet of veal, a slice from the fleshy part of the calf's thigh.—*Arch.* A small molding having the appearance of a narrow band, generally used to separate ornaments and moldings; also the ridge between the flutes of a column.—*v.t.* To bind or adorn with a fillet; to cut into fillets.

fillip, fil′ip, *v.t.* [Same as *flip.*] To strike with the fore or middle finger by jerking it away from the ball of the thumb; to strike with a smart stroke.—*n.* A jerk of the finger forced suddenly from the thumb; a smart blow or stroke; something which sharply rouses or stimulates.

fillister, fil′is•tẽr, *n.* A kind of plane used for grooving timber.

filly, fil'i, n. [A dim. form of foal= Icel. fylja, a filly, from foli, a foal. FOAL.] A young mare; a young girl.

film, film, n. [A.Sax. filmen, a skin; allied to fell, a skin.] A thin skin or membrane; a pellicle; a lamina; a thin layer for receiving a photographic negative; a motion picture. —v.t. To cover with a film; to take a motion picture of.—v.i. To become covered as with a film; to be suitable for photographing. —**filminess**, fil'mi·ness, n.—**film-strip**, film'strip, n. A strip of film, showing diagrams, charts, or photographs, for still projection.—**filmy**, fil'mi, a.

filose, a. See FILAMENT.

filter, fil'tėr, n. [Fr. filtre, from L.L. filtrum, feltrum, felt or fulled wool, used originally as a strainer. FELT.] A strainer; any substance or apparatus through which liquids or gases are passed to separate suspended matter; a device that selects certain wave frequencies to pass through it.—v.t. To remove by passing through a filter.—v.i. To pass through a filter.—**filtrate**, fil'trāt, v.t.—**filtrated**, **filtrating**. [L.L. filtro, filtratum.] To filter.—n. The liquid which has been passed through a filter.—**filtration**, fil·trā'shon, n. The act or process of filtering.

filth, filth, n. [A.Sax. fylth, from fúl, foul. FOUL.] Anything that soils or defiles; dirt; foul matter; nastiness; corruption; pollution.—**filthily**, filth'i·li, adv. In a filthy manner; foully.— **filthiness**, filth'i·nes, n. The state of being filthy; filth; foul matter; impurity.—**filthy**, filth'i, a. Dirty; foul; unclean; nasty; morally impure; licentious.

fimbriate, fim'bri·āt, a. [L. fimbriæ, threads, a fringe.] Fringed; having a sort of fringe or border; having the edge surrounded by fibers, hairs, or bristles.—v.t. To hem; to fringe.— **fimbriated**, fim'bri·ā·ted, a. Fimbriate.

fin, fin, n. [A.Sax. fin, finn, L.G. and Dan. finne, D. vin, Sw. fena; allied to L. pinna, penna, a feather.] One of the projecting winglike organs which enable fishes to balance themselves in an upright position, and assist in regulating their movements in the water.—**finless**, fin'les, a. Destitute of fins.—**finned**, find, a. Having a fin or fins or anything resembling a fin.—**finback**, fin'bak, n. A name given to several whales from their possessing a dorsal hump or fin.—**finny**, fin'i, a. Furnished with fins; relating to or abounding with fins.

final, fī'nal, a. [L. finalis, from finis, end; seen also in fine, adj. and noun, confine, define, affinity, finance, finish, etc.] Pertaining to the end or conclusion; last; ultimate; conclusive; decisive; respecting a purpose or ultimate end in view.—n. A final contest, test, etc.—**finale**, fē·nä'lā, n. Mus. the last part of a sonata, symphony, or opera; the closing part of any performance.—**finalist**, fī'nal·ist, n. One who is in a final contest. — **finality**, fī·nal'i·ti, n. The state of

being final; philos. the doctrine that nothing exists or was made except for a determinate end.—**finally**, fī'nal·li, adv. At the end or conclusion; ultimately; lastly; completely; beyond recovery.

finance, fi·nans', n. [Fr., from L.L. financia, a money payment, from finare, to pay a fine, from L. finis, end. FINE, n.] The system or science of public revenue and expenditure; pl. funds in the public treasury, or accruing to it; public resources of money.—v.t. and i. To raise or provide money for a charity or business; to provide on credit.—**financial**, fi·nan'shal, a. Pertaining to finance or public revenue; having to do with money matters.—**financially**, fi·nan'shal·li, adv. In relation to finances or public funds.—**financier**, fin·an·sēr', n. One who is skilled in financial matters or in the principles or system of public revenue.

finch, finsh, n. [A.Sax. finc=G. Dan. and Sw. fink, finke, Gr. spiza.] A large family (Fringillidae) of small song-birds, including the bunting, sparrow, and goldfinch, having a small conical beak adapted to cracking seeds.

find, fīnd, v.t.—pret. and pp. found. [A.Sax. findan, to find=D. vinden G. finden, Dan. finde, Icel. finna (for finda), Goth. finthan, to find. From same root as in L. peto, to aim at, to seek.] To discover; to gain first sight or knowledge of (something lost); to recover; to get; to meet; to come or light upon; to gain, acquire, or procure (leisure, happiness); to supply, provide, or furnish (to find money for a purpose); to catch; to detect; law, to determine and declare by verdict.—To find one's self, to fare in regard to ease or pain, health or sickness; to provide one's necessaries at one's own expense.—To find one in (something), to supply, furnish, or provide one with (something).—To find out, to detect; to discover, as something before unknown, a mystery, secret, trick, etc.; to solve.—To find fault with, to censure.—v.i. Law, to give judgment on the merits or facts of a case.—n. A discovery of anything valuable; the thing found.—**finder**, fīn'dėr, n. One who or that which finds; astron. a smaller telescope attached to a larger, for the purpose of finding an object more readily.—**finding**, fīn'ding, n. Discovery; that which is found; law, the return of a jury to a bill; a verdict.

fine, fīn, a. [Fr. fin, fine, delicate, etc.; G. fein, D. fijn, Dan. fiin, Sw. fin, Icel. finn, from L. finitus, finished, perfect, pp. of finio, to finish, from finis, an end. FINAL.] Slender; minute; very small; of very small diameter; not coarse; in very small grains or particles; thin; keen; sharp; made of fine threads or material; delicate; pure; of excellent quality; refined; elegant; perceiving or discerning minute beauties or deformities (fine taste); handsome; beautiful; accomplished (a fine gentleman); elegant; showy; splendid; free from

clouds or rain; sunshiny (fine weather); finically or affectedly elegant; aiming too much at show or effect.— Fine arts, the arts which depend chiefly on the labors of the mind or imagination, generally restricted to the imitative arts which appeal to us through the eye, such as painting and sculpture.—v.t.—fined, fining. To refine; to purify; to free from foreign matter.—**fine-draw**, fīn'draw, v.t. To sew up with so much nicety that the rent is not perceived.— **finely**, fīn'li, adv. In a fine or finished manner; admirably; beautifully; delicately.—**fineness**, fīn'nes, n. The state or quality of being fine.—**finery**, fī'nėr·i, n. Fineness; ornament; showy or excessive decoration; the forge in ironworks at which the iron is hammered into what is called a bloom or square bar.—**finespun**, fīn'spun, a. Drawn to a fine thread; minute, hence, overrefined; over-elaborated; subtile.

fine, fīn, n. [From L. finis, an end, and in later times and in a feudal sense, a final settlement of a claim by composition or agreement. FINANCE, FINAL.] A payment of money imposed upon a person as a punishment for an offense.—In fine, in conclusion; to conclude; to sum up all.—v.t.—fined, fining. To set a fine on by judgment of a court; to punish by fine.

finesse, fi·nes', n. [Fr., lit. fineness.] Artifice; stratagem; subtlety of contrivance to gain a point; in bridge, the attempt to win a trick by playing a low card while having a high card in reserve.—v.i. To use finesse.

finger, fing'gėr, n. [A.Sax. finger=D. vinger, G. Sw. and Dan. finger, Goth. figgrs; same root as in fang.] One of the five extreme members of the hand; any of them but the thumb; a digit; something resembling or serving the purpose of a finger; an index.—To have a finger in, to be concerned in.—To have at one's finger ends, to be quite familiar with; to be able to make available readily. —v.t. To touch with the fingers; to handle; to toy or meddle with; to touch or take thievishly; to apply the fingers to in order to produce musical effects.—v.i. To use the fingers in playing on an instrument. —**finger board**, n. The board at the neck of a violin, guitar, or the like, where the fingers act on the strings; also the whole range of keys of a piano, organ, etc; a. keyboard.— **fingerer**, fing'gėr·ėr, n. One who fingers or handles; a pilferer.— **fingering**, fing'gėr·ing, n. The act of touching lightly or handling; mus. the management of the fingers in playing on an instrument of music; the marking of the notes of a piece of music to guide the fingers in playing; a thick loose worsted used for knitting stockings.—**finger post**, n. A post set up to guide travelers, generally where roads cross or divide. —**fingerprint**, n. An impression made by fingers, often serving to identify the person.

finial, fin'i·al, n. [From L. finio, to

finish. FINAL.] The ornamental termination of a pinnacle, canopy, gable, or the like.

finical, fin′i·kal, *a.* [From *fine.*] Affecting great nicety or elegance; overnice; unduly particular about trifles.—**finicality,** fin·i·kal′i·ti, *n.* State of being finical; something finical.—**finically,** fin′i·kal·li, *adv.* In a finical manner.—**finicalness,** fin′i·kal·nes, *n.* Quality of being finical.—**finicking, finicky,** fin′i·king, fin′i·ki, *a.* [Equivalent to *finical.*] Precise in trifles; idly busy.

finis, fī′nis, *n.* [L.] An end; conclusion: often placed at the end of a book.

finish, fin′ish, *v.t.* [Fr. *finir,* ppr. *finissant,* from L. *finio, finitum,* to finish, from *finis,* end. FINAL.] To bring to an end; to make an end of; to arrive at the end of; to bestow the last required labor upon; to perfect; to polish to a high degree; to elaborate carefully.—*v.i.* To come to an end; to terminate; to expire.—*n.* The last touch to a work; polish; careful elaboration; a name for denatured alcohol.—**finished,** fin′isht, *p.* and *a.* Polished to the highest degree of excellence; complete; perfect.—**finisher,** fin′ish·ér, *n.* One who finishes; something that gives the finishing touch to or settles anything (*colloq.*).

finite, fī′nīt, *a.* [L. *finitus,* from *finio,* to finish, from *finis,* limit. FINAL.] Having a limit; limited; bounded: opposed to *infinite*; *gram.* a term applied to those moods of a verb which are limited by number and person, as the indicative, subjunctive, and imperative.—**finitely,** fī′nīt·li, *adv.* In a finite manner; limitedly; to a certain degree only.—**finiteness,** fī′nīt·nes, *n.* State of being finite.—**finitude,** fin′i·tūd, *n.* State of being finite; limitation.

Finn, fin, *n.* [O.E. *Finnas.*] A native of Finland; person of the same race.—**Finnish,** fin′ish, *a.* Relating to the Finns or Finland.—*n.* A language spoken by the Finns.

finnan haddie, fin′an had′i, *n.* [From river *Findhorn.*] A split and cured haddock.

fiord, fjord, fyord, *n.* [Dan. *fiord*; Icel. *fjörthr.* FIRTH.] An inlet from the sea, usually long, narrow, and very irregularly shaped, such as common on the coast of Norway.

fir, fér, *n.* [A.Sax. *furh*=Icel. Sw. *fura,* Dan. *fyr, fyrre,* G. *föhre. Fir* represents an ancient word, which appears in L. as *quercus,* an oak, and probably meant originally tree in general.] A general name for several species of coniferous trees, sometimes used as coextensive with the term pine (*Pinus*), but often restricted to trees of the genus *Abies,* which differ from the true pines in their leaves growing singly on the stem, and the scales of the cones being smooth, round, and thin.—**firry,** fér′i, *a.* Of or pertaining to firs; consisting of fir; abounding in firs.

fire, fīr, *n.* [A.Sax. *fyr*=Icel. *fyri,* Dan. and Sw. *fyr,* G. *feuer,* fire; cog.

Gr. *pyr,* fire; allied to Skr. *pu,* to purify, as fire is the great purifying element.] The evolution of heat and light during combustion; fuel in combustion; the burning of a house or town; a conflagration; the discharge of a number of firearms; a spark from hot iron accidentally lodged in the eye; light; luster; splendor; ardor of passion, whether of love, hate, anger, etc; consuming violence of temper; liveliness of imagination; vigor of fancy; animation; vivacity; force of sentiment or expression.—*On fire,* ignited; burning; hence, *fig.* eager; ardent.—*St. Anthony's fire,* erysipelas.—*v.t.* —*fired, firing.* To set on fire; to kindle; to inflame or irritate; to animate; to give life or spirit to; to cause to explode; to discharge (a gun, a shot).—*v.i.* To take fire; to be irritated or inflamed with passion; to discharge artillery or firearms.—*To fire away,* to begin; to go on. (*Colloq.*)—*Fireout,* to discharge or expel from office.—*To fire up,* to become irritated or angry; to fly into a passion. (*Colloq.*)—**fiery,** fī′ér·i, *a.* Consisting of fire; burning; flaming; blazing; highly flammable; hot; ardent; vehement; impetuous; passionate; irritable; fierce; like fire; bright; glaring.—*Fiery cross,* a light wooden cross, the extremities of which were set fire to and then extinguished in blood; used in ancient times in Scotland as a signal to assemble under arms.—**fierily,** fī′ér·i·li, *adv.* In a fiery manner.—**fieriness,** fī′ér·i·nes, *n.* The state or quality of being fiery.—**firing,** fī′ring, *n.* The act of discharging firearms; a setting on fire; material for burning; fuel.—**firearm,** fīr′ärm, *n.* A weapon whose charge is expelled by the combustion of powder, as cannon, pistols, muskets, etc.—**fireball,** fīr′bal, *n.* A ball filled with combustibles to be thrown among enemies; a meteor having the appearance of a globular mass of light.—**firebox,** *n.* The box (generally made of copper) in which the fire in a locomotive is placed.—**firebrand,** fīr′brand, *n.* A piece of wood kindled; an incendiary; one who inflames factions, or causes contention and mischief.—**firebrick,** *n.* A brick of clay that will sustain intense heat without fusion.—**firebug,** *n.* An arsonist.—**fire clay,** *n.* A kind of clay capable of sustaining intense heat, and used in making firebricks, gas retorts, crucibles, etc.—**firecracker,** *n.* A firework consisting of a paper cylinder enclosing powder, through which a fuse is passed, and exploding with a sharp report when ignited.—**firedamp,** *n.* Light carburetted hydrogen gas, sometimes very abundantly evolved in coal mines, and productive of the most dreadful results when brought into contact with a naked flame, being highly explosive.—**firedog,** *n.* An andiron.—**fire-eater,** *n.* A juggler who pretends to eat fire; a fighting character or duelist; a fireman (*Colloq.*).—**fire engine,** *n.* An engine,

acting on the force-pump principle, for throwing jets of water to extinguish fire and save buildings.—**fire escape,** *n.* An apparatus for escaping from the upper part of a building when on fire, a common form consisting of an arrangement of long ladders capable of being drawn out after the manner of a telescope.—**firefly,** fīr′flī, *n.* A name for any winged insect which possesses much luminosity.—**fireguard,** *n.* A framework of iron wire, to be placed in front of a fireplace to protect against fire.—**fire irons,** *n. pl.* Poker, tongs, and shovel.—**firelock,** fīr′lok, *n.* A musket or other gun with a lock furnished with a flint and steel.—**fireman,** fīr′man, *n.* A man whose business is to extinguish fires in towns; a member of a fire brigade; a man employed in tending fires, as of a steam engine.—**fireplace,** fīr′plās, *n.* The lower part of a chimney which opens into an apartment and in which fuel is burned; a hearth.—**fireplug,** *n.* A plug for drawing water from the pipes in the street to extinguish fire.—**fireproof,** fīr′pröf, *a.* Proof against fire; incombustible; rendered incombustible by some process.—**fire ship,** *n.* A vessel filled with combustibles to be set on fire for burning an enemy's ships.—**fireside,** fīr′sīd, *n.* The side of the fireplace; the hearth; home: often used adjectively.—**firestone,** fīr′stōn, *n.* Any kind of stone which resists the action of fire.—**fireweed,** *n.* A plant which appears abundantly on land over which a fire has passed.—**firewood,** fīr′wud, *n.* Wood for fuel.—**firework,** fīr′wérk, *n.* A preparation of gunpowder, sulfur, and other flammable materials to be let off for the purpose of making a show.

firkin, fér′kin, *n.* [From *four,* with dim. suffix *-kin,* being the fourth of a barrel.] An old measure of capacity equal to 7½ gallons; a small wooden vessel or cask.

firm, férm, *a.* [L. *firmus,* firm, seen also in *affirm, confirm, firmament, farm.*] Closely compressed; compact; hard; solid; fixed; steady; constant; stable; unshaken in purpose or will; resolute in mind; not easily moved; not giving way.—*n.* [Originally a signature by which a writing was *firmed* or rendered valid.] A partnership or association of two or more persons for carrying on a business; a commercial house; the name or title under which a company transacts business.—*v.t.* To make firm or solid; to solidify.—*v.i.* To become firm or solid.—**firmly,** férm′li, *adv.* In a firm manner.—**firmness,** férm′nes, *n.* The state or quality of being firm; compactness; solidity; solidity; steadfastness; resolution.—**firmament,** fér′ma·ment, *n.* [L. *firmamentum,* from *firmo, firmatum,* to make firm.] The region of the air; the sky or heavens.

firman, fér′man or fér·män′, *n.* [Per. *fermân, farmân,* a decree.] A decree, order, or grant of an Oriental sovereign, as of Turkey, etc., issued for various special purposes; a license or grant of privileges.

first, fėrst, *a.* [A superlative, of which *fore* may be regarded as the positive. A. Sax. *fyrst,* first, most to the fore. FORE.] The ordinal of *one;* preceding all others in a series; advanced before or further than any other in progression; foremost in place; preceding all others in time, rank, dignity, or excellence.—*n.* The beginning; number one in a series; the lowest forward gear.—*adv.* Before all others in place, time, etc.—*At first, at the first,* at the beginning or origin.—*First and last,* within the whole time or period; altogether.— *First or last,* at one time or another.—**firstling,** fėrst'ling, *n.* The first produce or offspring of a beast.—**firstly,** fėrst'li, *adv.* In the first place; first.—**first-born,** *a.* First brought forth; eldest.—**first-class,** *a.* First-rate; of the highest excellence or quality. (*Colloq.*).—**firsthand,** *a.* Obtained direct from the first source; obtained direct from the producer, maker, etc.—*At firsthand,* directly; without the intervention of an agent. —**first-rate,** *a.* Of the first class or rate; of the highest excellence.—*n.* A war ship of the first or most powerful class.—**first water,** *n.* The first or highest quality; purest luster: applied principally to diamonds and pearls.

firth, fėrth, *n.* [From Icel. *fjörthr,* Dan. *fiord,* N. *fjord,* a firth; same root as *fare, ferry.*] A name given to several estuaries or bays into which rivers discharge themselves in Scotland; a channel or arm of the sea (the Pentland *Firth*): written also *Frith.*

fiscal, fis'kal, *a.* [From L. *fiscus,* the state treasury.] Pertaining to the public treasury or revenue; financial. —*Fiscal year,* the twelve months for which a complete financial accounting is made.

fish, fish, *n.* pl. **fishes,** fish'ez, instead of which the sing. is often used collectively. [A.Sax. *fisc*=Icel. *fiskr,* Dan. and Sw. *fisk,* D. *visch,* G. *fisch,* Goth. *fisks;* cog. L. *piscis,* W. *pysg,* Gael. and Ir. *iasg,* fish.] A vertebrate animal that lives in water, breathes by gills, and has cold blood, with limbs in the form of fins; popularly applied also to whales and various other marine animals; a contemptuous or familiar term for a person (in such phrases as, a queer or strange *fish;* a loose *fish*); the flesh of fish used as food; *naut.* a purchase used to raise the flukes of an anchor up to the gunwale.—*Neither flesh nor fish,* neither one thing nor another; having no decided character or qualities; nondescript.—*v.i.* To employ one's self in catching fish; to endeavor to take fish by a rod and line or other means; to seek to obtain by artifice, or indirectly (to *fish* for compliments).—*v.t.* To catch or attempt to catch fish; to draw out or up, especially when in water; to search by dragging, raking, or sweeping; to strengthen or unite by a piece that extends on both sides of a joint or a crack.—**fish cake,** *n.* A small

ball of shredded fish, as codfish, mixed with potato, seasoned, and fried.—**fisher,** fish'ėr, *n.* One who fishes; one employed in catching fish. —**fisherman,** fish'ėr·man, *n.* One whose occupation is to catch fish.— **fishery,** fish'ėr·i, *n.* The business of catching fish; a place where fish are regularly caught, or other products of the sea or rivers are taken from the water.—**fishhook,** *n.* A hook for catching fish.—**fishing,** fish'ing, *n.* The art or practice of catching fish.— *a.* Used or employed in fishery or by fishermen.—**fish joint,** *n.* A railway contrivance for connecting two rails meeting end to end.—**fishtail,** fish'-tāl, *a.* Shaped like a fish's tail.— *Fishtail burner,* a gas burner whose jet takes the form of a fish's tail.— **fishy,** fish'i, *a.* Pertaining to fishes; consisting of fish; inhabited by fish; having the qualities of fish; as a slang term, worn out, as if by dissipation; seedy; applied to persons; equivocal; unsafe; unsound; applied to a project or speculation; dull; without luster (*fishy* eyes).

fissile, fis'sil, *a.* [L. *fissilis,* from *findo, fissum,* to split or cleave, whence also *fissure,* the root being same as in E. *bite.*] Capable of being split in the direction of the grain (like wood), or in certain planes; readily splitting in flakes or plates.—**fissility,** fis·sil'i·ti, *n.* The quality of being fissile.— **fission,** fish'on, *n.* [L. *fissio.*] The act of cleaving, splitting, or breaking up into parts; *biol.* a species of reproduction or multiplication by means of a process of self-division seen in animals of a low type, the body becoming divided into two parts, each of which then becomes a separate and independent individual.—*Nuclear fission, phys.* the splitting of an atomic nucleus, either spontaneously or by bombardment with neutrons, etc., to release energy.

fissirostral, fis·si·ros'tral, *a.* [L. *findo, fissum,* to divide, and *rostrum,* a beak.] Characterized by a deeply-cleft bill, as swallows, goat suckers, etc., in which the gape is extended beneath the eyes.

fissure, fish'ėr, *n.* [Fr., from L. *fissura,* from *findo,* to split. FISSILE.] A cleft; a crack; a narrow chasm made by the parting of any substance; a longitudinal opening; a separation or disagreement in thought.—*v.t.* and *i.*—*fissured, fissuring.* To cleave or make a fissure in; to crack or fracture.

fist, fist, *n.* [A.Sax. *fyst*=G. *faust,* D. *vuist,* Rus. *pjast;* same root as L. *pugnus,* Gr. *pygmē,* the fist.] The hand clenched; the hand with the fingers doubled into the palm.—*v.t.* To strike or grip with the fist. —**fistic,** fis'tik, *a.* Pertaining to boxing; pugilistic.—**fisticuffs,** fis'-ti·kufs, *n. pl.* Blows or a combat with the fists.—**fisty,** fis'ti, *a.* Pertaining to the fist or fists, or to pugilism.

fistula, fis'chu·la, *n.* [L., a pipe.] A musical pipe; *surg.* a channel excavated between an internal part (as the rectum) and the skin surface, show-

ing no tendency to heal, and generally arising from abscesses.—**fistular,** fis'-chu·lėr, *a.* Hollow, like a pipe or reed.—**fistulous,** fis'chu·lus, *a.* Formed like a fistula; fistular.

fit, fit, *n.* [Of doubtful origin; comp. A.Sax. *fit, fitt,* a fight, a struggle, Icel. *fet,* a pace, a step.] A sudden effort, activity, or motion followed by an interval of relaxation; a temporary but violent mental affection or attack; a paroxysm; a temporary attack of a disease or pain; particularly a sudden and violent attack, accompanied with convulsions and loss of consciousness, as in hysteria, apoplexy, etc.—**fitful,** fit'ful, *n.* Full of fits; varied by paroxysms; spasmodic; varied by events.—**fitfully,** fit'ful·li, *adv.* In a fitful manner; by fits; at intervals.—**fitfulness,** fit'ful·nes, *n.* The state of being fitful; impulsiveness; waywardness.

fit, fit, *a.* [Allied to Icel. *fitja,* to knit together, Goth. *fetjan,* to arrange, to adorn, E. *fettle;* or equivalent to *feat* (adj.), O.Fr. *feit,* L. *factum,* made.] Conformable to a standard of right, duty, taste, or propriety; of suitable kind; meet; becoming; appropriate; adapted to an end, object, or design; suitable; qualified; competent; prepared; ready.—*v.t.*— *fitted, fitting.* To make fit or suitable; to bring into some required form; to adapt; to suit; to furnish or accommodate with anything; to prepare; to put in order for; to qualify; to be properly fitted for or adjusted to; to suit; to become.—*To fit out,* to furnish; to equip; to supply with necessaries or means.—*To fit up,* to furnish (a house, etc.) with things suitable; to make proper for the reception or use of any person.—*v.i.* To be proper or becoming; to be adjusted to the shape intended; to suit or be suitable; to be adapted.—*n.* Nice adjustment; adaptation.—**fitly,** fit'li, *adv.* In a fit manner; suitably; properly.—**fitness,** fit'nes, *n.* The state or quality of being fit; suitableness; adaptation; preparation; qualification. The state of being fitted.— **fitter,** fit'ėr, *n.* One who fits; one who puts the parts of machinery together.—**fitting,** fit'ing, *a.* Fit or appropriate; suitable; proper.—*n.* Something fitted on or attached as subsidiary to another thing.—**fittingly,** fit'ing·li, *adv.* In a fitting manner; suitably.

fitch, fich, *n.* [O.D. *vitsche,* O.Fr. *fissau,* a polecat; akin *foist.*] The polecat; also its fur.—**fitchet, fitchew,** fich'et, fich'u, *n.* The polecat.

five, fīv, *a.* [A.Sax. *fif*=Goth. *fimf,* Icel. *fimm,* Sw. and Dan. *fem,* D. *vijf,* G. *fünf,* Lith. *penki,* W. *pump,* Gael. *coig,* L. *quinque,* Gr. *pempe, pente,* Skr. *panchan*—five.] Four and one added; the half of ten.—*n.* The number which consists of four and one; the number of the fingers and thumb of one hand; a symbol representing this number.—**fivefold,** fīv'fōld, *a.* Consisting of five in one; five times repeated; in fives.—**fives,** fīvz, *n.* A kind of play with a ball, originally called hand tennis: so named probably because the ball is struck with the hand or *five* fingers.

fix, fiks, *v.t.* [Fr. *fixer*, from L. *figo, fixum*, to fasten, seen also in *affix, prefix, suffix*.] To make stable, firm, or fast; to set or place permanently; to establish firmly or immovably; to fasten; to attach firmly; to direct steadily, as the eye, the mind, the attention, etc.; to make solid; to congeal; to deprive of volatility; to stop or keep from moving.—*v.i.* To become firm or stable.—*n.* A predicament; dilemma; the position of an object (as a ship) determined by radio signals, bearing, etc.—**fixate,** fiks'āt, *v.t.*—*fixated, fixating.* To make fixed; to focus intently upon. —*v.i.* To concentrate one's attention. —**fixation,** fiks·ā'shon, *n.* The act or state of being fixed; an obsessive preoccupation upon an object.— **fixative,** fiks'a·tiv, *n.* A substance that fixes or sets.—*Fixed stars*, such stars as always retain the same apparent position and distance with respect to each other, and are thus distinguished from planets.—**fixed-ly,** fik'sed·li, *adv.* In a fixed manner.—**fixedness,** fik'sed·nes, *n.* A state of being fixed.—**fixity,** fik'si·ti, *n.* State of being fixed; fixed character; fixedness; stability.— **fixture,** fiks'chėr, *n.* Anything placed in a firm or fixed position; that which is fixed to a building; any appendage or part of the furniture of a house which is fixed to it, as by nails, screws, etc.

fizz, fiz, *v.i.* [Imitative.] To make a hissing sound; effervesce.—*n.* A hissing sound.—**fizzle,** fiz'l, *n.* Fizz; a failure.—*v.i.* To fail after starting well.

flabby, flab'i, *a.* [Akin to *flap*, and to G. *flabbe*, Sw. *flabb*, Dan. *flab*, hanging lips.] Soft and yielding to the touch; easily moved or shaken; hanging loose by its own weight; flaccid: said especially of flesh.— **flabbily,** flab'i·li, *adv.* In a flabby manner.—**flabbiness,** flab'i·nes, *n.* State of being flabby.

flabellum, fla·bel'lum, *n.* [L.] A fan; specifically, an ecclesiastical fan anciently used to drive away flies from the chalice during the Eucharist.— **flabellate, flabelliform,** fla·bel'lāt, fla·bel'li·form, *a.* Fan shaped.

flaccid, flak'sid, *a.* [L. *flaccidus*, from *flaccus*, flabby; comp. W. *llac*, slack, loose; Ir. *fluich*, flabby.] Soft and weak; limber; lax; drooping; hanging down by its own weight.—**flaccidly,** flak'sid·li, *adv.* In a flaccid manner.— **flaccidity,** flak·sid'i·ti, *n.* The state of being flaccid.

flag, flag, *n.* [Not found in A.Sax.; same as D. *vlag*, Sw. *flagg, flagga*, Dan. *flag*, G. *flagge*, banner; connected with *flag*, to hang loose.] A cloth, usually bearing emblems or figures and employed as a symbol or signal; any material used like a flag; an indication on a musical note of less than a 1/4 beat; a deer's tail.—*Black flag*, a flag of a black color displayed on a piratical vessel as a sign that no mercy will be shown to the vanquished, or on a prison to indicate that an execution

has taken place.—*White flag*, a flag of truce.—*Yellow flag*, flag as sign of infection or disease on board a vessel.—*Flag of truce*, a white flag displayed as an invitation to the enemy to confer, and in the meantime as a notification that the fighting shall cease.—*v.t.* To signal with a flag; to signal to stop (to *flag* a train).—**Flag Day,** *n.* June 14, a day in commemoration of the United States flag.—**flag officer,** *n.* The title for an admiral of any grade. —**flagship,** *n.* The ship that bears the flag officer and displays his flag.— **flagpole,** *n.* A pole used to display the flag.

flag, flag, *v.i.*—*flagged, flagging.* [Formerly written *flack*, and connected with Icel. *flaka*, to hang loosely, G. *flacken*, to become languid, O.D. *flaggeren*, to be loose; akin also *flicker*.] To hang loose without stiffness; to be loose and yielding; to grow spiritless or dejected; to droop; to grow languid; to grow stale or vapid; to lose interest or relish.—**flaggingly,** flag'ing·li, *adv.* In a drooping or listless manner.

flag, flag, *n.* [From Icel. *flaga*, a flag, Sw. *flaga*, a flake or scale; allied to L.G. *flage*, a flat marshy place, and Gr. *plax*, a tablet.] A flat stone used for paving.—*v.t.*—*flagged, flagging.* To lay with flags or paving flat stones.—**flagstone,** *n.* Any fissile sandstone that splits up into flags; a large flat paving stone; a flag.

flag, flag, *n.* [Probably named from its broad leaves resembling flags or standards.] A popular name for many endogenous plants with sword-shaped leaves, mostly growing in moist situations; particularly appropriated to a species of iris.

flagellate, flaj'el·lāt, *v.t.* [L. *flagello, flagellatum*, to beat or whip, from *flagellum*, a whip or scourge, akin to *flail*.] To whip; to scourge.—*a.* Having flagella.—**flagellant,** flaj'el·lant, *n.*—One who whips himself, specifically, one of a fanatical sect founded in Italy A.D. 1260, who maintained that flagellation was of equal virtue with baptism and other sacraments.—**flagellation,** flaj·el·lā'shon, *n.* A flogging; the discipline of the scourge.—**flagelliform,** fla·jel'li·form, *a.* [L. *flagelliformis*.] Long, narrow, and flexible, like the thong of a whip.—**flagellum,** fla·jel'lum, *n.* pl. **flagella,** fla·jel'la. *Bot.* a runner or creeping branch sent out from the bottom of a stem, as in the strawberry; *zool.* the lashlike appendage exhibited by many infusoria.

flageolet, flaj·el·et', *n.* [Fr. *flageolet*, dim. of O.Fr. *flajol*, from L.L. *flauta, flautus*, flute. FLUTE.] A small wind instrument of music, played by a mouthpiece inserted in the bulb-shaped head of the pipe, which is holed and keyed like the flute.

flagitious, fla·jish'us, *a.* [L. *flagitiosus*, from *flagitium*, a shameful act, from *flagito*, to demand or urge hotly or violently, from root *flag*, whence *flagro*, to burn (as in *flagrant*).] Deeply criminal; grossly wicked;

vicious; abandoned; profligate; heinous; flagrant.—**flagitiously,** fla·jish'us·li, *adv.* In a flagitious manner. —**flagitiousness,** fla·jish'us·nes, *n.* The condition or quality of being flagitious.

flagon, flag'on, *n.* [Fr. *flacon, flascon*, L.L. *flasca*, a flask. FLASK.] A vessel with a narrow mouth, used for holding and conveying liquors.

flagrant, flā'grant, *a.* [L. *flagrans, flagrantis*, ppr. of *flagro*, to burn (seen in *conflagration*), the root being same as in *flamma*, flame, *flagitium*, a flagitious act.] Flaming into notice; glaring; notorious; enormous.—**flagrantly,** flā'grant·li, *adv.* In a flagrant manner.—**flagrancy,** flā'gran·si, *n.* The quality of being flagrant; heinousness; enormity.

flail, flāl, *n.* [O.Fr. *flael, flaiel, flaial*, from L. *flagellum*, a whip or scourge, whence also *flagellate*.] An instrument for thrashing or beating grain from the ear, consisting of the hand staff, which is held in the hand; the swiple, which strikes the grain; and a thong which connects the two.—*v.t.* and *i.* To beat as if with a flail.

flair, flâr, *n.* [O.Fr. odor, from L. *fragrare*.] Talent for discernment; taste and aptitude combined.

flak, also **flack,** flak, *n.* [From G. abbrev. of *flieger-abwehr-kanone*.] Anti-aircraft fire.

flake, flāk, *n.* [Allied to Icel. *flakna*, to flake off, *flyka*, a flake; E. *flag*, a stone for paving, and *flaw*; Sw. *flaga*, a flake.] A loose filmy or scale-like mass of anything; a scale; a small fleecy or feathery particle; a flock.—*v.t.* and *i.*—*flaked, flaking.* To break or separate in layers; to peel or scale off.—**flaky,** flā'ki, *a.*— **flakiness,** fla'ki·nes, *n.* The state of being flaky.

flambeau, flam'bō, *n.* pl. **flambeaux,** flam'bōz. [Fr., from *flambe*, a blaze, for *flamble*, from L. *flammula*, dim. of *flamma*, a flame.] A flaming torch; a light made of thick wicks covered with wax or other flammable material.—**flamboyant,** flam·boi'ant, *a.* [Fr., flaming.] Characterized by waving curves resembling flames, as in windows of French Gothic style of architecture; showy; ostentatious.— **flamboyance,** flam·boi'ance, *n.* Ostentation.

flame, flām, *n.* [Fr. *flamme*, from L. *flamma*, a flame, for *flagma*, from the root *flag*, whence *flagro*, to burn, to blaze, as in *flagrant, conflagration*; root also in Gr. *phlegō*, to burn.] A blaze; burning vapor or gas rising from matter in a state of visible combustion; fire in general; heat of passion; violent contention; passionate excitement or strife; a state of ardor; warmth of affection; the passion of love; one beloved.— *v.t.* and *i.*—*flamed, flaming.* To blaze; to make a flame or blaze; to send out a flame or blaze; to shine like burning gas or any other luminous body; to break out in violence of passion.— **flaming,** flā'ming, *a.* Of a bright red or yellow color; burning; ardent; violent;

vehement.—**flamingly,** flā′ming·li, *adv.* In a flaming manner.

flamen, flā′men, *n.* [L.] The name in ancient Rome for any priest devoted to the service of one particular deity.

flamingo, fla·ming′gō, *n.* [Sp. and Pg. *flamenco,* from L. *flamma,* flame, from its red color.] A web-footed tropical bird, with long neck and long slender legs, standing from 5 to 6 feet high, and having scarlet plumage.

flange, flanj, *n.* [A form of *flank.*] A projecting edge or rim on any object, as the rims by which cast-iron pipes are connected together, or those round the wheels of railroad carriages to keep them on the rails.—*v.t.*—*flanged, flanging.* To furnish with a flange; to make a flange on.

flank, flangk, *n.* [Fr. *flanc,* Sp. and Pg. *flanco,* It. *fianco,* the flank; of Germanic origin ultimately, same as O.H.G. *hlanca,* side, loin, flank; akin G. *gelenk,* joint.] The fleshy or muscular part of the side of an animal, between the ribs and the hip; the side of anything, particularly the extreme right or left of an army, brigade, regiment, etc.; the outer ships of a fleet, or the place occupied by such forces; any part of a fortified work defending another work by a fire along its face.—*v.t.* and *i.* To stand at the flank or side of; to place troops so as to command or attack the flank of; to pass round or turn the flank of.—**flanker,** flangk′ẽr, *n.* One who or that which flanks; one employed on the flank of an army.

flannel, flan′el, *n.* [O.E. and Sc. *flannen,* from W. *gwlanen.* from *gwlan,* wool.] A soft nappy woolen cloth of loose texture.—**flannelette,** flan·el·et′, *n.* A cotton cloth with a soft nap.

flap, flap, *n.* [Probably onomatopoetic, being imitative of a blow with a pliant flat surface; *flabby* is a kindred form.] Anything broad and flexible that hangs loose or is attached by one end or side and easily moved; a lappet, a lobe, a skirt or tail of a coat; the motion of anything broad and loose, or a stroke with it.—*v.t.*—*flapped, flapping.* To beat with or as with a flap; to move, as something broad or flaplike.—*v.i.* To move as wings, or as something broad or loose; to wave loosely or flutter.—**flapdragon,** *n.* A play in which the players snatch raisins out of burning brandy; snapdragon.—**flapjack,** *n.* A sort of broad, flat pancake; a fried cake.—**flapper,** flap′ẽr, *n.* One who or that which flaps; young women who manifested a freedom of conduct and dress during 10 years after World War I.—**flappy,** flap′ē, *a.* Likely to flap; slack.

flare, flâr, *v.i.*—*flared, flaring.* [Comp. Dan. *flagre,* G. *flackern* (freq. of *flacken*), to flicker, to flare; perhaps akin to *flash.*] To waver or flutter in burning; to burn with an unsteady light; hence, to flutter with gaudy show; to shine out with sudden and unsteady light or splendor; to give

out a dazzling light.—*To flare up,* to become suddenly angry or excited.—*n.* A bright unsteady light; a bright patch in the middle of a photographic print, caused by lens reflection; dazzling light used to signal.

flash, flash, *n.* [Comp. Icel. *flasa,* to rush, *flas,* a rush; also E. *flare.*] A sudden burst of light; a flood of light instantaneously appearing and disappearing; a gleam; a sudden burst of something regarded as resembling light, as wit, merriment, passion, etc.; a short and brilliant burst; momentary brightness or show; the time occupied by a flash of light; an instant.—*v.i.* To break or burst forth with a flash or flame; to give out a flash or gleam; to break forth into some new and dazzling condition; to burst out violently; to come, appear, or pass suddenly; to dart (a thought *flashes* through the mind).—*v.t.* To emit or send forth in a sudden flash or flashes; to convey or send instantaneously or startlingly.—*a.* Vulgarly showy or gaudy; forged; counterfeit (*flash* notes).—**flashy,** flash′i, *a.* Showy or gaudy; tawdry; fiery.—**flashily,** flash′i·li, *adv.*—**flashiness,** flash′i·nes, *n.*—**flash bulb,** *n.* Flash lamp that burns metal foil or wire to give momentary daylight brilliance in taking photographs.—**flash point,** flash point, *n.* Temperature at which vapor from oil or gaseous objects ignites.

flask, flask, *n.* [A.Sax. *flasc, flasca, flaxa,* Dan. *flaske,* Sw. *flasca;* ultimate origin doubtful; comp. O.Fr. *flasche, flascon;* Sp. *flasco,* It. *fiasco,* L.L. *flasco, flasca,* a flask; L. *vasculum,* dim. of *vas,* a vessel; also W. *fflasg,* a vessel of wickerwork, a basket.] A kind of bottle; a narrow-necked globular glass bottle; a metal or other pocket drambottle; a vessel for containing gunpowder, carried by sportsmen.—**flasket,** flas′ket, *n.* A vessel in which viands are served up; a long shallow basket.

flat, flat, *a.* [Not in A.Sax. = Icel. *flatr,* Sw. *flat,* Dan. *flad,* G. *flach,* flat; akin Gr. *platys,* Skr. *prithus,* broad.] Having an even and horizontal, or nearly horizontal surface, without elevations or depressions, hills or valleys; level without inclination; level with the ground; prostrate; fallen; laid low; tasteless; stale; vapid; insipid; depressed; without interest, point, or spirit; frigid; dull; peremptory; absolute; positive; downright (a *flat* denial); *mus.* below the natural or the true pitch; not sharp or shrill; not acute; *gram.* applied to consonants, in the enunciation of which voice (in contradistinction to breath) is heard; opposed to *sharp;* as, *b, d, g, z, v.*—*n.* A flat surface; a surface without relief or prominences; a level; a plain; a low tract of land; a shoal; a shallow; a sandbank under water; the flat part or side of anything (the *flat* of the hand, of a sword); *mus.* a mark (♭) placed on a line or in a space of the staff, which indicates that all notes on the same degree

(or their octaves) are lowered a semitone; a story or floor of a building; a foolish fellow; a flat section of theatrical scenery; a tire that has been punctured; a flat-bottomed boat.—*v.t.* and *v.i.*—*flatted, flatting.* To flatten.—**flatboat,** *n.* A flat-bottomed boat used to transport bulky materials on shallow waters.—**flatfish,** *n.* One of a group of fish, having a flattened body, that swim with the flattened side up and have both eyes on one side.—**flatiron,** *n.* An iron.—**flatly,** flat′li, *adv.* In a flat manner; horizontally; evenly; positively; plainly.—**flatness,** flat′nes, *n.*—**flatten,** flat′n, *v.t.* To make flat or level; to lay flat; *mus.* to lower in pitch; to render less acute or sharp.—*v.i.* To grow or become flat.—**flattop,** *n.* An aircraft carrier.—**flatwise,** flat′wīz, *a.* and *adv.* With the flat side downward or next to another thing.

flatter, flat′ẽr, *v.t.* [Fr. *flatter,* Pr. *flatar,* to pat, stroke, caress, flatter; perhaps from Icel. *flatr,* E. *flat;* comp. also Icel. *flathra,* to fawn or flatter, *flathr,* flattery.] To gratify by praise or obsequiousness; to please by applause, favorable notice, respectful attention, or anything that confirms one's good opinion of one's self; to encourage by favorable notice or by favorable representations or indications (to *flatter* hopes); to inspire with false hopes.—**flatterer,** flat′ẽr·ẽr, *n.* One who flatters; one who praises another with a view to please him, to gain his favor, or to accomplish some purpose.—**flatteringly,** flat′ẽr·ing·li, *adv.* In a flattering manner.—**flattery,** flat′ẽr·i, *n.* [Fr. *flatterie.*] The act of one who flatters; false, insincere, or venal praise; adulation; cajolery.

flatulent, flat′ū·lent, *a.* [L.L. *flatulentus,* from L. *flatus,* a blowing, from *flo, flatum,* to blow (as in *inflate*).] Affected with gases generated in the alimentary canal; generating or apt to generate wind in the stomach; windy.—**flatulence, flatulency,** flat′ū·lens, flat′ū·len·si, *n.* [L. L. *flatulentia.*] The state of being flatulent, or affected with an accumulation of gases in the alimentary canal.—**flatulently,** flat′ū·lent·li, *adv.* In a flatulent manner.

flaunt, flant, *v.i.* [Connected with prov. G. *flander,* a rag or tatter, *flandern,* to flutter, G. *flattern,* to flirt, to flutter.] To make an ostentatious display; to move or act ostentatiously; to be glaring or gaudy.—*v.t.* To display ostentatiously; to display impudently or offensively.—*n.* The act of flaunting; bold or impudent parade.—**flaunter,** flan′tẽr, *n.* One who flaunts.—**flauntingly,** flan′ting·li, *adv.* In a flaunting way.—**flaunty, flaunting,** flan′ti, flan′ting, *a.* Ostentatious; vulgarly or offensively showy; gaudy.

flautist, fla′tist, *n.* [It. *flauto,* a flute.] A player on the flute; a flutist.

flavescent, fla·ves′ent, *a.* [L. *flavesco,* to become yellow, from *flavus,* yellow.] *Bot.* yellowish or turning yellow.—**flavin**, flav'in, *n*. A yellow dye of vegetable origin.

flavor, flā'vẽr, *n*. [O. F. *flauor*, *flaveur*, *flaur*, *flair*, an odor; all used also in reference to taste.] The quality of any substance which affects the taste; that quality which gratifies the palate; relish; zest; the quality of a substance which affects the smell; odor; fragrance.—*v.t.* To communicate flavor or some quality of taste or smell to.—**flavoring**, flā'vẽr·ing, *n*. Any substance used for imparting flavor; seasoning.—**flavorless**, flā'vẽr·les, *a*. Without flavor; tasteless.—**flavorous**, flā'vẽr·us, *a*. Having a rich or pleasant flavor.

flaw, fḷạ, *n*. [A.Sax. *flóh*, that which has flown off, a fragment; Goth. *flaga*, a fragment; Sw. *flaga*, a flaw, *flaga sig*, to scale off, akin to *flake* and *flag*; comp. also W. *fflaw*, a splinter, *ffla*, a parting from.] A crack; a defect of continuity or cohesion; a gap or fissure; any blemish or imperfection; a defect; a fault; a sudden burst of wind; a sudden gust or blast of short duration.—*v.t.* To make or produce a flaw in.—**flawless**, fḷạ'les, *a*. Without flaw or defect.—**flawy**, fḷạ'i, *a*. Full of flaws; defective; faulty; subject to sudden gusts.

flax, flaks, *n*. [A.Sax. *fleax*=D. *vlas*, Fris. *flax*, G. *flachs*, flax; allied to Bohem. *vlas*, Rus. *volos*, Lith. *plaukas*, hair, from a root meaning to comb. weave, or twist, seen in L. *plecto*, Gr. *plekō*, to weave or plait.] A wiry, erect-stemmed annual plant, the fiber of which is used for making linen thread and cloth, lace, etc.; the fibrous part of the plant when broken and cleaned by scutching and hackling.—**flaxen**, flak'sn, *a*. Made of flax; resembling flax; of the color of flax; fair.

flay, flā, *v.t.* [A.Sax. *fleán*, to flay; O.D. *vlaegen*, *vlaen*, to flay; akin *flake*, *flaw*.] To skin; to strip off the skin of.—**flayer**, flā'ẽr, *n*. One who flays.

flea, flē, *n*. [A.Sax. *fleá*, from *fleôn*, *fleôgan*, to fly; D. *vloo*, Icel. *fló*, Sc. *flech*, G. *floh*, a flea.] A hardbodied, wingless insect, with remarkable powers of leaping, that feeds on warm-blooded animals.—*A flea in the ear*, an annoying, unexpected hint or reply.—*v.t.* To clean from fleas.—**fleabane**, flē'bān, *n*. A name popularly given to several composite plants from their supposed power of destroying or driving away fleas.—**fleabite**, flē'bīt, *n*. The bite of a flea; a trifling wound or pain; a slight inconvenience; a thing of no moment.

fleam, flēm, *n*. [D. *vlijm*, Fr. *flamme*, O.H.G. *fliedimā*, from L.L. *flevotomum*, *flebotomum*, from Gr. *phlebs*, *phlebos*, a vein, and *tomos*, a cutting. PHLEBOTOMY.] A sharp instrument used by farriers for opening veins for letting blood; a lancet.

flèche, flāsh, *n*. [Fr.] A slight fieldwork, with two faces forming an angle pointing forward. A spire at the intersection of the nave and transepts of a church.

fleck, flek, *n*. [Icel. *flekkr*, D. *vlek*, G. *fleck*, a spot; allied to *flick*.] A spot; a streak; a dapple; a stain.—*v.t.* To spot; to streak or stripe; to variegate; to dapple.

flection, flek'shon, *n*. [L. *flectio*.] The act of bending or state of being bent; inflection.

fled, fled, pret. & pp. of *flee*.

fledge, flej, *v.t.*—*fledged*, *fledging*. [Icel. *fleygr*, able to fly, from *fljúga*, to fly; comp. G. *flück*, *flügge*, feathered, from *fliegen*, to fly.] To furnish with feathers; to supply with the feathers necessary for flight: chiefly in pp.—**fledgling**, flej'ling, *n*. A young bird just fledged.

flee, flē, *v.i.* pret. and pp. *fled*; ppr., *fleeing*. [A.Sax. *fleón*, to flee, ic *fleó*, I flee; akin to *fleógan*, to fly, Icel. *flyja*, Dan. *flye*, Sw. *fly*, G. *fliehen*, to flee. FLY.] To hasten or run away, as from danger or evil; to resort to shelter; sometimes apparently transitive, *from* being omitted before the object.

fleece, flēs, *n*. [A.Sax. *fleós*, *flýs*, a fleece, wool=D. *vlies*, G. *fliess*; root meaning doubtful.] The coat of wool that covers a sheep or that is shorn from a sheep at one time; any covering resembling wool.—*Golden Fleece*, the object of the Argonauts under Jason.—*Order of Golden Fleece*, the Flemish and Spanish order, commemorating the wool trade of Flanders, a sheep suspended by ribbon from the neck.—*v.t.*—*fleeced*, *fleecing*. To deprive of the fleece; to strip of money or property; to rob or cheat heartlessly.—**fleecer**, flē'sẽr, *n*. One who fleeces or strips of money.—**fleecy**, flē'si, *a*. Covered with wool; woolly; resembling wool or a fleece.

fleer, flēr, *v.i.* [Comp. Dan. dial. *flire*, to laugh, to sneer, N. *flira*, to titter.] To make a wry face in contempt; to grin, sneer, mock, or gibe.—*v.t.* To mock; to flout at.—*n.* The act of one who fleers.

fleet, flēt, *n*. [A.Sax. *fleót*, *fliét*, a ship, from *fleótan*, to float; akin D. *vloot*, G. *flotte*, fleet. FLOAT.] A body or squadron of ships; a number of ships, trucks, etc., operating in company; old London prison, from the ditch or stream of the Fleet, giving its name to Fleet Street, crossing it at right angles, and entering the city by the *fleet-gate*, *flood-gate*.—**Fleet Street**, *n*. Newspaper headquarters in London.

fleet, flēt, *a*. [Icel. *fljótr*, A.Sax. *fleótig*. quick; allied to *flit*, and *float*. FLIT, FLOAT.] Swift of pace; moving or able to move with rapidity; nimble; light and quick in motion.—*v.i.* To fly swiftly; to hasten; to flit, as a light substance.—*v.t.* To skim over the surface; to pass over rapidly.—**fleeting**, flē'ting, *p*. and *a*. Passing rapidly; transient; not durable (the *fleeting* moments). ∴ Syn. under TRANSIENT.—**fleetly**, flēt'li, *adv*. In a fleet manner; rapidly; swiftly.—**fleetness**, flēt'nes, *n*. The quality of being fleet; swiftness; rapidity; velocity; celerity; speed.

Fleming, flem'ing, *n*. A native of Flanders.—**Flemish**, flem'ish, *a*. Pertaining to Flanders.—*n*. The language of the Flemings, closely akin to Dutch; *pl*. the people of Flanders.

flense, flens, *v.t.*—*flensed*, *flensing*. [Dan. *flense*; D. *vlensen*.] To cut up and obtain the blubber of a whale.

flesh, flesh, *n*. [A.Sax. *flaesc*=D. *vleesch*, G. *fleisch*, flesh; Icel. and Dan. *flesk*, bacon or pork; further connections are doubtful.] The substance which forms a large part of an animal, consisting of the softer solids, as distinguished from the bones, the skin, and the fluids; animal food, in distinction from vegetable; beasts and birds used as food, in distinction from fish; the body, as distinguished from the soul; the bodily frame; the human race; mankind; human nature; bodily appetite; kindred; family; the soft pulpy substance of fruit; also that part of a root, fruit, etc., which is fit to be eaten.—*v.t.* To initiate to the taste of flesh (as dogs used in hunting); to accustom to flesh; to imbrue a sword in blood for the first time.—**fleshed**, flesht, *p*. and *a*. Fat; fleshy; having flesh of a particular kind.—**flesher**, flesh'ẽr, *n*. A knife used for scraping flesh from hides.—**flesh fly**, *n*. Same as *Blowfly*.—**fleshiness**, flesh'i·nes, *n*. State of being fleshy; plumpness; corpulence.—**fleshing**, flesh'ing, *n*. [Generally in plural.] A kind of drawers worn by actors, dancers, etc., resembling the natural skin.—**fleshliness**, flesh'li·nes, *n*. State of being fleshly; carnal passions and appetites.—**fleshly**, flesh'li, *a*. Pertaining to the flesh; corporeal; carnal; lascivious; human.—**fleshpot**, flesh'pot, *n*. High living; a luxurious abundance.—**fleshy**, flesh'i, *a*. Full of flesh; pulpy, as fruit; plump; fat; corpulent; corporeal; human.

fleur-de-lis, flẽr·de·lē, *n*. [Fr., flower of the lily.] A heraldic figure representing either a lily or the head of a lance or some such weapon; the distinctive bearing of the kingdom of France; *bot*. the iris.

flew, flū, pret. of *fly*.

flex, fleks, *v.t.* [From L. *flecto*, *flexum*, to bend; seen also in *deflect*, *inflect*, *reflect*, etc.] To bend.—**flexed**, flekst, *p*. and *a*. Bent; having a bent shape. —**flexible**, flek'si·bl, *a*. [L. *flexibilis*, from *flecto*, *flexum*.] Capable of being flexed or bent; pliant; yielding to pressure; not stiff; capable of yielding to entreaties, arguments, or other moral force; manageable; tractable; easy and compliant; capable of being molded into different forms or styles; plastic; capable of being adapted or accommodated. —**flexibility**, flek·si·bil'i·ti, *n*. The quality of being flexible; pliancy; easiness to be persuaded; readiness to comply; facility.—**flexibly**, flek'si·bli, *adv*. In a flexible manner.— **flexile**, flek'sil, *a*. [L. *flexilis*.] Pliant; pliable; flexible.—**flexion**, flek'shon, *n*. [L. *flexio*.] The act of bending; the bending of a joint which brings the connected parts closer together;

a bending; a part bent; *gram.* an inflection.—**flexor,** flek'sẽr, *n. Anat.* a muscle whose office is to produce flexion.—**flexuous,** flek'sū•us, *a.* [L. *flexuosus.*] Winding or bending; having turns or windings; *bot.* changing its direction in a curve, from joint to joint, from bud to bud, or from flower to flower; in this sense written also *flexuose,* flek'shẽr, *n.* [L. *flexura.*] A bending; the form in which a thing is bent; part bent; a bend.

flick, flik, *n.* [Akin to *flip, flap.*] A sharp sudden stroke, as with a whip; a flip.—*v.t.* and *i.* To strike or move with a flick; to flip.

flicker, flik'ẽr, *v.t.* and *i.* [A.Sax. *flicerian,* to flutter or move the wings; G. *flackern,* to flare, to blaze, to flutter; D. *flikkeren,* to twinkle; Icel. *flaka,* to flap.] To flutter or flap the wings; to fluctuate or waver, as a flame in a current of air.—*n.* A wavering or fluctuating gleam, as of a candle; a flutter; North American woodpecker marked with red at the back of the neck and having speckled underparts.

flight, flīt, *n.* [A.Sax. *fligt,* from *fleógan,* to fly. FLY.] The act of fleeing; hasty or precipitate departure; the act or power of flying; volitation; the manner or mode of flying; a flock of birds flying in company; the birds produced in the same season; a discharge; a mounting or soaring; an extravagant excursion or sally, as of the imagination; scheduled airplane trip; basic unit of military air forces; series of steps or stairs from one platform or landing to another.—**flightily,** flī'ti•li, *adv.* In a flighty, wild, capricious, or imaginative manner.—**flightiness,** flī'ti•nes, *n.* The state of being flighty; extreme volatility.—**flighty,** flī'ti, *a.* Fleeting‡; indulging in flights or sallies of imagination, humor, caprice, etc.; volatile; giddy; fickle.

flimsy, flim'zi, *a.* [Origin doubtful.] Without strength or solid substance; of loose and unsubstantial structure; without reason or plausibility.—*n.* A thin sort of paper.—**flimsily,** flim'zi•li, *adv.* In a flimsy manner.—**flimsiness,** flim'zi•nes, *n.* State or quality of being flimsy.

flinch, flinsh, *v.i.* [Perhaps corrupted from *blench,* or from O.E. *flecche,* Fr. *fléchir,* L. *flectere,* to bend.] To draw back from pain or danger; to show signs of yielding or of suffering; to shrink; to wince.—**flincher,** flinsh'ẽr, *n.* One who flinches or fails.—**flinchingly,** flinsh'ing•li, *adv.* In a flinching manner.

flinder, *n.* Fragment; splinter.

fling, fling, *v.t.*—*flung, flinging.* [Akin to O.Sw. *flenga,* to strike or beat; Dan. *flenge,* to slash.] To cast, send, or throw; to hurl; to send or shed forth; to emit; to scatter; to throw to the ground; to prostrate.—*v.i.* To flounce; to throw out the legs violently; to start away with a sudden motion, as in token of displeasure; to rush away angrily.—*n.* A throw; a gibe; a sarcasm; a

severe or contemptuous remark; enjoyment of pleasure to the full extent of one's opportunities (to take one's *fling: colloq.*); a Scotch dance, the Highland *fling.*

flint, flint, *n.* [A.Sax. and Dan. *flint,* Sw. *flinta;* same root as Gr. *plinthos,* a brick.] A species of quartz, of a yellowish or bluish-gray or grayish-black color, very hard and used to form an ingredient in fine pottery; a piece of flint used to strike fire with steel or in a flintlock.—**flinty,** flin'ti, *a.* Consisting or composed of flint; containing flints; like flint; very hard; cruel; unmerciful.—**flintiness,** flin'ti•nes, *n.*—**flintlock,** *n.* A musket gunlock with flint fixed in the hammer to strike against steel and produce sparks which ignite the charge.

flip, flip, *n.* [A form of *flap.*] A smart blow, as with a whip; a flick; a drink.—*v.t.* To flick; to put into motion quickly so as to cause to turn over in the air, as to *flip* a coin.—*v.i.* To make a small, abrupt movement.

flippant, flip'ant, *a.* [Formed from *flip, flap;* comp. Icel. *fleipr,* tattle, *fleipinn,* pert, petulant.] Speaking fluently and confidently, without knowledge or consideration; heedlessly pert; showing undue levity.—**flippancy, flippantness,** flip'an•si, flip'ant•nes, *n.* The state or quality of being flippant.—**flippantly,** flip'ant•li, *adv.* In a flippant manner; volubly.

flipper, flip'ẽr, *n.* [Equivalent to *flapper,* from *flap.*] The paddle of a sea turtle; the broad fin of a fish; the arm of a seal; broad, flat, finlike rubber shoe used in skin diving.

flirt, flẽrt, *v.t.* [A.Sax. *fleard,* trifle; folly; *fleardian,* to trifle; comp. G. *flirren,* trifles, *flirren,* to make a confused noise.] To throw with a jerk or sudden effort or exertion; to fling suddenly; to move with short, quick movements; to make coquettish motions with (a fan).—*v.i.* To run and dart about; to act with levity or giddiness; to play the coquette.—*n.* A sudden jerk; a quick throw or cast; one who flirts; a woman who plays at courtship; a coquette.—**flirtation,** flẽr•tā'shon, *n.* A flirting; a playing at courtship; coquetry.—**flirtatious,**† flẽr•tā'shus, *a.* Given to flirtation.

flit, flit, *v.i.*—*flitted, flitting.* [Dan. *flytte,* Sw. *flytta,* to remove; akin to *flee, fleet, flutter,* etc.] To fly away with a rapid motion; to dart along, as a bird; to move with celerity through the air; to move rapidly about; to flutter; to migrate.—*n.* The act of one who flits.

flitch, flich, *n.* [A.Sax. *flicce,* a flitch of bacon; Icel. *flikki,* a flitch.] The side of a hog salted and cured; *carp.* a plank fastened side by side with others to form a compound beam.

float, flōt, *v.i.* [A.Sax. *flotian,* to float, *fleótan,* to fleet; *fleet, flow, flood* are closely allied. FLOW.] To rest or glide on the surface of a fluid; to swim or be buoyed up; to move

as if supported by a fluid; to move gently and easily through the air.—*v.t.* To cause to float; to cause to rest or be conveyed on the surface of a fluid; to flood; to inundate; to overflow.—*To float a scheme,* to bring it prominently before public notice; to raise funds for carrying it on.—*n.* That which floats on the surface of a fluid; a collection of timber fastened together and floated down a stream; a raft; a buoy; the cork or quill on an angling line, to support it and indicate the bite of a fish; a plasterer's tool for producing a plane surface; the float board of a water wheel or paddle wheel.—**floatage, flotage,** flō'tij, *n.* Anything that floats on the water.—**floatation,** flō•tā'shon, *n.* The science of floating bodies.—**floater,** flō'tẽr, *n.* One that floats.—**floating,** flō'ting, *p.* and *a.* Resting on and buoyed up by a fluid; circulating; not fixed or invested; opposed to *sunk* (*floating* capital; *floating* debt); disconnected; unattached (*floating* ribs in fishes); fluctuating; unsettled (a *floating* population).—*Floating dock.* Under DOCK.

floccose, flok•ōs', *a.* [L. *floccosus.*] *Bot.* composed of or bearing tufts of woolly, or long and soft, hairs.—**flocculence,** flok'ū•lens, *n.* The state of being flocculent; adhesion in small flakes.—**flocculent,** flok'ū•lent, *a.* Coalescing and adhering in locks or flakes.

flock, flok, *n.* [From O.Fr. *floc,* L. *floccus,* a lock of wool; comp. G. *flocke,* O.G. *floccho,* D. *vlok,* Sw. *flocka,* Dan. *flokke.*] A lock of wool or hair; the refuse of cotton and wool, or shreds of woolen goods, used for stuffing mattresses, etc.—**flocky,** flok'i, *a.* Abounding with flocks; floccose.

flock, flok, *n.* [A.Sax. *floc, flocc,* a flock, a company of men = Dan. *flok,* Sw. *flock,* Icel. *flokkr,* flock; perhaps same as *folk.*] A company or collection of living creatures, especially applied to birds and sheep; a Christian congregation in relation to their pastor, who takes charge of them in spiritual things.—*v.i.* To gather in flocks or crowds.

floe, flō, *n.* [Dan. *flage,* Sw. *flaga,* a floe; akin to *flake.*] A large mass of ice floating in the ocean.

flog, flog, *v.t.*—*flogged, flogging.* [Allied to Prov. E. *flack,* to beat; *flacket,* to flap about; perhaps also to *flap* or *flag.*] To beat or whip; to chastise with repeated blows.—*To flog a dead horse,* to try to revive interest in a stale subject.—**flogger,** flog'ẽr, *n.* One who flogs.

flood, flud, *n.* [A.Sax. *flód,* a flood = Fris. Dan. and Sw. *flod,* Icel. *flód,* D. *vloed;* from the root of *flow.*] A great flow of water; a body of water rising and overflowing the land; a river (*poet.*); the flowing in of the tide: opposed to *ebb;* a flow or stream of anything fluid; a great quantity; an overflowing; abundance; superabundance.—*The Flood,* the deluge in the days of Noah.—*v.t.* and *i.* To overflow; to inundate;

to cause to be covered with water.—
floodgate, *n.* A gate to be opened for letting water flow, or to be shut to prevent it.—**floodlight,** *n.* Lighting unit that casts a bright, broad beam.
floor, flōr, *n.* [A.Sax. *flór,* a floor = D. *vloer,* a floor; G. *flur,* a field, a floor; W. *llawr,* the ground, a floor.] That part of a building or room on which we walk; a platform; a story in a building; a suite of rooms on a level.—*v.t.* To furnish with a floor; to strike or knock down level with the floor (*colloq.*).—**floorer,** flō′rėr, *n.* One who or that which floors; a blow which floors a person (*colloq.*).—**flooring,** flō′ring, *n.* A floor; materials for floors.
flop, flop, *v.t.* [A form of *flap.*] To clap; to flap; to let fall or sink down suddenly.—*v.i.* To strike about with something broad and flat; to fail; to plump down suddenly.—*n.* A sudden sinking to the ground.—**floppy,** flop′i, *a.* Having a tendency to flop.
Flora, flō′ra, *n.* [L., from *flos, floris,* a flower (whence also *flower, flour, flourish,* etc.).] The Roman goddess of flowers; (*not. cap.*) a list of plants of a certain district or region; a collective term for the plants indigenous to any district, region, or period.—**floral,** flō′ral, *a.* Containing or belonging to the flower; pertaining to flowers in general; made of flowers.—**florally,** flō′ral·li, *adv.* In a floral manner.—**floriated,** flō′ri·ā·ted, *a.* Decorated with floral ornament; having florid ornaments.—**florescence,** flō·res′ens, *n.* [L. *florescens,* pp. of *floresco.*] *Bot.* a bursting into flower; the season when plants expand their flowers; inflorescence.—**florescent,** flō·res′ent, *a.* Bursting into flower; flowering.—**floret,** flō′ret, *n.* A single small flower in a compact inflorescence.—**floriculture,** flō′ri·kul·chėr, *n.* [L. *flos, floris,* and *cultura.*] The culture or cultivation of flowers or flowering plants.—**floricultural,** flō·ri·kul′chėr·al, *a.* Relating to floriculture.—**floriculturist,** flō·ri·kul′chėr·ist, *n.* One interested in floriculture.—**florid,** flor′id, *a.* [L. *floridus,* from *flos, floris.*] Flowery; bright in color; flushed with red; of a lively red color; embellished with profuse ornamentation, especially with flowers of rhetoric, or high-flown or elaborately elegant language.—**floridity, floridness,** flo·rid′i·ti, flor′id·nes, *n.* The quality or condition of being florid.—**floridly,** flor′id·li, *adv.* In a showy imposing way.—**floriferous,** flō·rif′ėr·us, *a.* Producing flowers.—**florist,** flor′ist, *n.* [Fr. *fleuriste,* a florist.] A cultivator of flowers; one who deals in flowers; one who writes a flora.
Florence, flor′ens, *n.* A kind of wine from *Florence* in Italy; a gold coin of the reign of Edward III. of Britain, value 6 shillings.—*Florence flask,* a globular bottle of thin transparent glass with a long neck.—**Florentine,** flor′en·tīn, *a.* Of or pertaining to Florence.—*n.* A native of Florence; a kind of silk cloth.

florin, flor′in, *n.* [Fr. *florin,* from It. *florino,* first applied to a Florentine coin, because stamped with a lily; It. *fiore,* a flower, from L. *flos, floris,* a flower.] A name given to different coins of gold or silver, of different values, and to moneys of account, in different countries; a British coin, value 2 shillings.
floss, flos, *n.* [It. *floscio, flosso,* soft, flaccid, from L. *fluxus,* flowing, loose.] A downy or silky substance in the husks of certain plants; untwisted filaments of the finest silk, etc.—**floss silk,** *n.* Floss; silk fibers broken off in unwinding cocoons, and used for coarser fabrics.
flotation. See FLOATATION, under FLOAT.
flotilla, flō·til′la, *n.* [Sp. dim. of *flota,* a fleet.] A little fleet; a fleet of small vessels.
flotsam, flot′sam, *n.* [From *float.*] Such a portion of the wreck of a ship and the cargo as continues floating on the surface of the water. JETSAM.
flounce, flouns, *v.i.*—*flounced, flouncing.* [Akin N. and O.Sw. *flunsa,* to plunge about in water.] To throw one's self about with jerks, as if in displeasure or agitation.—*n.* A sudden jerking motion of the body.
flounce, flouns, *n.* [Originally *frounce,* from Fr. *froncis,* a plait, from *froncer, fronser,* to wrinkle, from L. *frons, frontis,* the front or forehead. FRONT.] A strip of cloth sewed horizontally round a frock or gown, with the lower border loose and spreading.—*v.t.* To deck with a flounce or flounces.
flounder, floun′dėr, *n.* [Gr. *flunder,* Sw. *flundra,* Dan. *flynder,* flounder.] One of the most common of the flat fishes, found in the sea and near the mouths of rivers.
flounder, floun′dėr, *v.i.* [Akin to D. *flodderen,* to flap like a loose garment.] To fling arms and body in clumsy struggle to move, stand or swim; to struggle, as a fish on land.
flour, flour, *n.* [Fr. *fleur,* a flower, *fleur de farine,* flour, lit. 'flour of meal', the finest part of the meal; comp. *flowers of sulfur. Flower* is merely another form.] The finely ground meal of wheat or of any other grain; the finer part of meal separated by bolting; the fine and soft powder of any substance.—*v.t.* To convert into flour; to sprinkle with flour.—**floury,** flou′ri, *a.* Consisting of or resembling flour; covered with flour.
flourish, flur′ish, *v.i.* [Fr. *fleurir, fleurissant,* L. *florere,* to flower, to bloom, from *flos, floris,* a flower. FLORA.] To grow luxuriantly; to increase and enlarge; to thrive; to be prosperous; to increase in wealth, comfort, happiness, or honor; to prosper; to live at a certain period (said of authors, painters, etc.); to use florid language; to make ornamental strokes in writing; to move or be moved in fantastic irregular figures; to play a bold prelude or fanfare.—*v.t.* To adorn with flowers or beautiful figures; to ornament

with anything showy; to give a fair appearance to (*Shak.*); to make bold or irregular movements with; to hold in the hand and swing about; to brandish.—*n.* An ostentatious embellishment; parade of words and figures; show; a fanciful stroke of the pen or graver; a brandishing; the waving of a weapon or something held in the hand; the decorative notes which a singer or instrumental performer adds to a passage.—*Flourish of trumpets,* a trumpet call, fanfare, or prelude performed on the approach of any person of distinction; hence, any ostentatious preliminary sayings or doings.—**flourisher,** flur′ish·ėr, *n.* One who flourishes.—**flourishing,** flur′ish·ing, *p.* and *a.* Prosperous; thriving.—**flourishingly,** flur′ish·ing·li, *adv.* In a flourishing manner.
flout, flout, *v.t.* [D. *fluiten, fluyten,* to play on the flute, to whistle, to jeer, from *fluit,* a flute. FLUTE.] To mock or insult; to treat with contempt or disrespect; to jeer at; to jibe.—*v.i.* To behave with contempt: often with *at.*—*n.* A mock; an insult.—**flouter,** flou′tėr, *n.* One who flouts.
flow, flō, *v.i.* [A.Sax. *flówan,* to flow = D. *vloeijen,* to flow; Icel. *flóa,* to flood; O.H.G. *flawan,* to wash; from a root seen in L. *pluvius,* rain, Gr. *pleō,* to swim; Skr. *plu,* to flow. Akin are *flood, float, fleet,* etc.] To move along in the manner of liquids; to run like water; to melt; to proceed or issue as from a source; to abound; to have or be in abundance; to glide along smoothly, without harshness or roughness; to be smooth or pleasant to the ear; to be easily or smoothly uttered; to hang loose and waving; to rise, as the tide: opposed to *ebb.*—*v.t.* To cover with water; to overflow.—*n.* A stream of water or other fluid; a current; an outflow; the rise of the tide; abundance; copiousness; undisturbed and even movement.—**flowage,** flō′ij, *n.* Act of flowing; state of being flowed.—**flowingly,** flō′ing·li, *adv.* In a flowing manner.—**flowingness,** flō′ing·nes, *n.*
flower, flou′ėr, *n.* [O.Fr. *flour,* Mod. Fr. *fleur,* from L. *flos, floris,* a flower, whence also *floral, florid, florin,* etc. *Flour* is really the same word though it has taken a different signification and spelling.] The delicate and gaily-colored leaves or petals on a plant; a circle of leaves or leaflets of some other color than green; a bloom or blossom; more strictly, in *bot.* the organs of reproduction in a phenogamous plant, consisting of, when complete, stamens and pistils together with two sets of leaves which surround and protect them, the calyx and corolla; the early part of life or of manhood; the prime; youthful vigor; youth; the best or finest part; a figure of speech; an ornament of style; *pl.* a powdery or mealy substance (as *flowers* of sulfur); the menstrual discharge.—*v.i.* To blossom; to bloom; to flourish.—*v.t.* To embellish with figures of flowers; to adorn

with imitated flowers.—**flowerage,** flou′ẽr·ij, *n.* Flowers in general.—**floweret,** flou′ẽr·et, *n.* A small flower; a floret.—**flower head,** *n. Bot.* a capitulum or head of sessile flowers, as in the daisy.—**floweriness,** flou′ẽr·i·nes, *n.* The state of being flowery; floridness of speech.—**flowering,** flou′ẽr·ing, *p.* and *a.* Having or producing flowers.—**flowerless,** flou′ẽr·les, *a.* Having no flowers.—**flowerpot,** *n.* A pot in which flowering plants or other plants are grown.—**flowery,** flou′ẽr·i, *a.* Full of flowers; abounding with blossoms; richly embellished with figurative language; florid.

flu, flö, *n.* [Short for *influenza.*] Contagious respiratory ailment.

fluctuate, fluk′tū·āt, *v.i.*—*fluctuated, fluctuating.* [L. *fluctuo, fluctuatum,* from *fluctus,* a wave, from *fluo,* to flow, whence *fluent,* etc. FLUENT.] To move as a wave; to wave; to float backward and forward; to be in an unsettled state.—*v.t.* To put into a state of fluctuating or wavelike motion.—**fluctuant,** fluk′-chū·ant, *a.* [L. *fluctuans, fluctuantis.*] Moving like a wave; wavering; unsteady. —**fluctuation,** fluk·chū·ā′-shon, *n.* [L. *fluctuatio.*] A motion like that of waves; a moving in this and that direction; a rising and falling; a wavering; unsteadiness.

flue, flö, *n.* [Comp. O.Fr. *flue,* a flowing, from *fluer,* L. *fluere,* to flow.] A passage for smoke in a chimney; a pipe or tube for conveying heat, as in certain kinds of steam boilers, etc.

flue, flö, *n.* [FLUFF.] Downy matter; fluff.

fluent, flö′ent, *a.* [L. *fluens, fluentis,* ppr. of *fluo, fluxum,* to flow, as in *affluence, confluence, influence, flux,* etc.; akin Gr. *phlyō,* to bubble over.] Flowing; ready in the use of words; having words at command and uttering them with facility and smoothness; voluble; smooth.—*n. Math.* the variable or flowing quantity in fluxions which is continually increasing or decreasing.—**fluently,** flö′ent·li, *adv.* In a fluent manner.—**fluency,** flö′en·si, *n.* The quality of being fluent; readiness of utterance; volubility.

fluff, fluf, *n.* [Also *flue;* akin to *flock,* L.G. *flog, flok, flue.*] Light down or nap such as rises from beds, cotton, etc.; flue.—**fluffy,** fluf′i, *a.* Containing or resembling fluff; giving off fluff; fluey.

flugelman. Same as fugleman.

fluid, flö′id, *n.* [L. *fluidus,* from *fluo,* to flow. FLUENT.] Capable of flowing or moving like water; liquid or gaseous.—*n.* A fluid body or substance; a body whose particles on the slightest pressure move and change their relative position without separation.—**fluid dram,** flö′id dram, *n.* A unit equal to ¹⁄₈ fluid ounce.—**fluid ounce,** flö′id ounce, *n.* A unit of liquid capacity equal to ¹⁄₁₆ pint.—**fluidity,** flö·id′i·ti, *n.*

fluke, flök, *n.* [Akin to G. *flunk,* a wing, the fluke of an anchor; comp. also Sw. *flik,* Dan. *flig,* a flap or

lappet; Dan. *anker-flig,* anchor fluke.] The part of an anchor which catches in the ground; one of the two triangular divisions constituting the tail of a whale; *billiards,* an accidental successful stroke; hence, any unexpected or accidental advantage.—**fluky,** flö′ki, *a.*

fluke, flök, *n.* [A.Sax. *flóc,* a flatfish.] A flounder; a leaflike parasitic worm which infests the livers of sheep, cattle, etc.

flume, flöm, *n.* [Connected with *flow.*] The passage or channel for the water that drives a mill wheel; an artificial channel for gold washing.

flummery, flum′ẽr·i, *n.* [W. *llymru,* flummery, oatmeal steeped until sour, from *llymyr,* harsh, *llym,* sharp.] A sort of jelly made of flour or meal; flour from oats steeped in water until sour and then boiled; flattery; empty compliment; nonsense.

flunk, flungk, *v.t.* and *i.* [Colloq. U.S.] To fail, as in an examination or course of study.

flunky, flung′ki, *n.* [L.G. *flunkern,* to flaunt; D. *flonkeren, flinkeren,* to glitter; or from *flank,* one that keeps at his master's flank.] A male servant in livery; a toady.

fluorite, flö′or·īt, *n.* Fluorspar.

fluorspar, flö′or·spär, *n.* [L. *fluor,* a flowing (from *fluo,* to flow), and *spar.*] Calcium fluoride, a crystalline mineral sometimes colorless and transparent, but more frequently exhibiting tints of yellow, green, blue, and red, manufactured into various ornamental articles.

fluorescence, flö·o·res′ens, *n.* [From L. *fluor,* L. *flux,* fr. *fluere,* to flow.] Property of emitting electromagnetic radiation in the form of light as the result of (and only during) the absorption of light from another source.—**fluorescent,** flö·o·res′ent, *a.* —**fluorescent lamp,** flö·o·res′cent lamp, *n.* An electron tube, coated on the inside with phosphor and containing mercury vapors, that converts ultraviolet discharge into visible light.—**fluoroscope,** flö′ro·-sköp, *n.* A machine for examining the body internally by studying shadows cast on a fluorescent screen by structures through which X-rays are sent.

fluorine, flö′o·rin, *n.* [L. *fluor.*] A nonmetallic, gaseous element, yellow and corrosive. Symbol, F; at. no., 9; at. wt., 18.9984.—**fluoride,** flö′o·rīd, *n.* Fluorine combined with another element; salt of hydrofluoric acid.—**fluoridate,** flö′or·i·dāt, *v.t.* To add a fluoride to, as to drinking water.—**fluoridation,** flö·o·ri·dā′shon, *n.*

flurry, flur′i, *n.* [Of doubtful origin and connections; comp. Sw. *flurig,* disordered, *flur,* disordered hair.] A sudden blast or gust of wind; a short snowfall; agitation; commotion; bustle.—*v.t.* To put in agitation; to excite or alarm.

flush, flush, *v.i.* [Perhaps akin to *flash;* or from O.Fr. *flux,* a flowing, a flush at cards, from L. *fluxus.* FLUX.] To flow and spread suddenly, as the blood to the face; to become suf-

fused; to become suddenly red; to blush.—*v.t.* To cause to blush or redden suddenly; to elate; to excite; to animate with joy; to wash out by drenching with copious supplies of water; *sporting,* to cause to start up or fly off; to spring.—*n.* A sudden flow of blood to the face; the redness so produced; any warm coloring or glow; sudden thrill or shock of feeling; bloom; vigor; a rush or flow of water; a run of cards of the same suit.

flush, flush, *a.* [Origin doubtful.] Fresh; full of vigor; well supplied with money (*slang*); having the surface even or level with the adjacent surface.

fluster, flus′tẽr, *v.t.* [Icel. *flauster,* fluster, *flaustra,* to be in a fluster; Norweg. *flosa,* passion.] To make hot with drinking; to heat; to agitate; to confuse.—*n.* Heat; glow; agitation; confusion of mind.

flute, flöt, *n.* [Fr. *flûte,* O.Fr. *flaüte,* from *flaüter,* from a L.L. *flatuare* (giving *flautare* by metathesis), from L. *flatus,* a blowing, from L. *flo, flatum,* to blow (as in *inflate*); akin *flageolet.*] A musical wind instrument consisting of a tube with six holes for the fingers, and from one to fourteen keys which open other holes; a perpendicular furrow or channel cut along the shaft of a column or pilaster; any similar groove or channel in any material.—*v.i.*—*fluted, fluting.* To play on a flute.—*v.t.* To play or sing in notes resembling those of a flute; to form flutes or channels in.—**fluted,** flö′ted, *p.* and *a.* Channeled; furrowed; *mus.* clear and mellow; flutelike.—**fluter,** flö′tẽr, *n.* A flutist; one who makes grooves or flutes.—**fluting,** flö′ting, *n.* The act of forming a groove or flute; fluted work.—**flutist,** flö′tist, *n.* A performer on the flute.

flutter, flut′ẽr, *v.i.* [A.Sax. *floterian,* to fluctuate, from *flot,* the sea; allied to *float,* and to L.G. *fluttern,* G. *flattern,* to flutter.] To move or flap the wings rapidly, without flying, or with short flights; to move about with bustle; to move with quick vibrations or undulations; to be in agitation.—*v.t.* To agitate; to disorder; to throw into confusion. —*n.* Quick and irregular motion; vibration; agitation of the mind; confusion; disorder.—**flutterer,** flut′ẽr·ẽr, *n.* One who flutters.—**flutteringly,** flut′ẽr·ing·li, *adv.* In a fluttering manner.

fluvial, flö′vi·al, *a.* [L. *fluvialis, fluviaticus, fluviatilis,* from *fluvius,* a river, from *fluo,* to flow.] Belonging to rivers; produced by river action; growing or living in fresh-water rivers.—**fluviomarine,** flö′vi·ō·ma·-rēn″, *a. Geol.* formed or deposited in estuaries or on the bottom of the sea at the embouchure of a river.

flux, fluks, *n.* [Fr., from L. *fluxus,* from *fluo,* to flow. FLUENT.] The act of flowing; a flow; the flow of the tide, in opposition to the ebb; *med.* an extraordinary evacuation from the bowels or other part; that which flows or is discharged; *metal.* any

---

ch, *chain;* ch, Sc. loch; g, go; j, job; ng, sing; TH, then; th, thin; w, wig; hw, whig; zh, azure.

substance or mixture used to promote the fusion of metals or minerals; a liquid state from the operation of heat.—*v.t.* To melt or to fuse; make fluid.—*v.i.* To flow.—**fluxion,** *n.* A flux or flowing; a flow or determination of blood or other fluid toward any organ with greater force than natural; *math.* a differential, *fluxions* being an old method of mathematical analysis superseded by the differential calculus.—**fluxional, fluxionary,** fluk′shon‧al, fluk′shon‧‧e‧ri, *a.* Pertaining to fluxions; variable.

fly, flī, *v.i.*—pret. *flew,* pp. *flown,* ppr. *flying.* [A.Sax. *fleógan,* G. *fliegen,* Icel. *fljuga,* Dan. *flyue,* to fly; akin *flee, flight, fledge,* etc.] To move through air by the aid of wings; to move through the air by the force of wind or other impulse; to rise in air, as light substances; to run or pass with swiftness; to depart swiftly; to run away; to flee; to escape; to ride in or operate an airplane; to pass quickly from mouth to mouth; to burst in pieces; to flutter, vibrate, or play, as a flag in the wind.—*To fly at,* to rush on; to fall on suddenly.—*To fly in the face of,* to set at defiance; to act in direct opposition to.—*To fly open,* to open suddenly or with violence.—*To let fly,* to discharge; to throw or drive with violence.—*v.t.* To flee from; to shun; to avoid; to cause to fly or float in the air; to transport by airplane.—*n.* A winged insect whose distinguishing characteristics are that the wings are transparent and have no cases or covers; a fishhook dressed so as to resemble a fly; *baseball,* ball hit by batter and caught by defensive fielder before it hits ground, automatically putting the batter out; an arrangement of vanes upon a revolving axis or other contrivance to regulate the motion of machinery; a flier; one of the arms that revolve round the bobbin in a spinning frame, and twist the yarn as it is wound on the bobbin; a light carriage formed for rapid motion; a hackney coach; a cab; a gallery in a theater running along the side of the stage at a high level, where the ropes for drawing up parts of the scenes, etc., are worked.—**flier, flyer,** flī′ér, *n.* One that flies or flees; a runaway; a fugitive; a part of a machine which by moving rapidly equalizes and regulates the motion of the whole; a contrivance for taking off or delivering the sheets from a printing machine.—**flyblow,** flī′blō, *n.* The egg of a fly.—*v.t.* To deposit a fly's egg in; to taint with eggs which produce maggots.—**flyboat,** *n.* A large flat-bottomed Dutch vessel with a high stem; a long narrow passage boat, swifter than the cargo boats, formerly much used on canals.—**flycatcher,** *n.* One who or that which catches flies; especially, a name of various insessorial birds which feed on flies and other winged insects; the phoebe, bee-bird, or kingbird.—**fly-fishing,** *n.* The art or practice of angling for

fish with flies, natural or artificial.—**flyleaf,** *n.* A blank leaf at the beginning or end of a book, pamphlet, etc.—**flypaper,** *n.* A kind of porous paper impregnated with poison for destroying flies.—**flytrap,** *n.* A trap to catch or kill flies; an American sensitive plant, the leaves of which close upon and capture insects.—**flywheel,** *n.* A wheel with a heavy rim placed on the revolving shaft of any machinery put in motion by an irregular or intermittent force, for the purpose of rendering the motion equable and regular by means of its momentum.—**flying boat,** *n.* A seaplane supported on water by its hull.—**flying buttress,** *n.* A buttress springing from a solid mass of masonry, and abutting against and serving to support another part of the structure.—**flying fish,** *n.* One of those fishes which have the power of sustaining themselves for a time in the air by means of their large pectoral fins.—**flying fox,** *n.* A bat found in the islands of the Eastern Archipelago, so named from the resemblance of its head to that of a fox.—**Flying Dutchman,** *n.* A spectral or phantom ship seen off the Cape of Good Hope, believed to import foul weather or danger.—**flying jib,** *n. Naut.* A sail extended outside of the jib, upon a boom called the flying-jib boom.—**flying lemur,** *n.* An insectivorous mammal having the limbs connected by wide lateral folds of skin, which serve to bear it up when taking great leaps from tree to tree.—**flying phalanger,** *n.* A nocturnal marsupial. — **flying saucer,** *n.* Any of the unidentified flying objects, usually said to be saucer shaped, reported as seen in the sky.—**flying squirrel,** *n.* One of those squirrels that have a fold of skin extending between the fore and hind legs, so as to bear them up for a moment in the air, and enable them to make very great leaps; also a name of the flying phalanger.

foal, fōl, *n.* [A.Sax. *fola,* a foal; Icel. *foli,* Dan. *fole,* D. *veulen,* G. *fohlen, füllen;* Cog. Gr. *pōlos,* a foal; L. *pullus,* a young animal. *Filly* is a dim. from *foal.*] The young of the equine genus of quadrupeds, and of either sex; a colt; a filly.—*v.t.* To bring forth her young: said of a mare or a she-ass.—*v.i.* To bring forth a foal.

foam, fōm, *n.* [A.Sax. *fám* = G. *feim,* and dial. *faum,* foam; allied to L. *spuma,* foam, from *spuo,* to spit.] Froth; spume; the aggregation of bubbles which is formed on the surface of liquids by fermentation or violent agitation.—*v.i.* To gather foam; to froth; to be in a violent rage.—*v.t.* To cause to foam.—**foam rubber,** *n.* Fine-textured, spongy rubber used for mattresses, cushions, etc.—**foamy,** fō′mi, *a.* Covered with foam; frothy.

fob, fob, *n.* [Allied to Prov. G. *fuppe,* a pocket.] Small ornament or weight worn at the end of a watch chain.

fob, fob, *v.t.*—*fobbed, fobbing.* [Comp. G. *foppen,* to mock, to banter.] To

cheat; to trick; to impose on. (*Shak*).

focus, fō′kus, *n.* pl. **focuses,** fō′kus-ez, or **foci,** fō′sī. [L. *focus,* a fire, the hearth, whence also *fuel, fusil.*] A point of concentration; a central point; a center of special activity; *optics,* a point in which any number of rays of light meet after being reflected or refracted; *geom.* a name of two important points on the principal axis of the ellipse (which see).—*v.t.* and *i.* To bring to a focus; to adjust to a focus; to focalize.—**focal,** fō′kal, *a.*—**focalize,** fō′kal‧īz, *v.t.* To bring to a focus; to focus.

fodder, fod′ér, *n.* [A.Sax. *fódder, fóder,* from *fóda,* food = Icel. *fóthr,* L.G. *foder,* D. *voeder,* G. *futter,* fodder. FOOD.] Food for cattle, horses, and sheep consisting of entire plants, such as corn.—*v.t.* To feed with fodder.

foe, fō, *n.* [A.Sax. *fá, fáh,* an enemy, from same stem as *fiend.* FIEND, FEUD.] An enemy; one who entertains personal enmity; an enemy in war; a hostile or opposing army; an adversary; one who opposes anything (a *foe* to virtue).—**foeman,** fō′man, *n.* An enemy in war; a personal antagonist.

fog, fog, *n.* [Comp. Dan. *snee-fog,* a snow storm *fyge,* to drive with the wind, Dan. dial. *fuge,* to rain fine and blow, Icel. *fok,* snow storm.] A dense watery vapor exhaled from the earth or from rivers and lakes, or generated in the atmosphere near the earth; a state of mental confusion or uncertainty.—*v.t.* To envelop with or as with fog.—*v.i.* To obscure by enclosing in fog; confuse; perplex; befog.—**foggily,** fog′i‧li, *adv.* In a foggy manner.—**fogginess,** fog′i‧nes, *n.*—**foggy,** fog′i, *a.* Filled or abounding with fog; damp with humid vapors; misty; dull; stupid; beclouded.—**foghorn,** *n.* A horn to sound as a warning signal in foggy weather; a sounding instrument for warning vessels of their proximity to the coast during a fog.

fog, fog, *n.* [W. *ffwg,* dry grass.] Aftermath; a second growth of grass; long grass that remains on land through the winter.

fogey, fogy, fō′gi, *n.* [Lit. one who is in a *fog;* or from *fog,* after grass.] One who is behind the times; a dull fellow, usually with *old.*—**fogeyism, fogyism,** fō′gi‧izm, *n.* The habits or practices of a fogey.

foible, foi′bl, *n.* [O.Fr. weak. FEEBLE.] The weak part of a sword; opposed to *forte;* a particular moral weakness; a weak point; a fault of not a very serious character.

foil, foil, *v.t.* [Fr. *fouler,* to press, to crush, to oppress, from stem of L. *fullo,* a fuller.] To frustrate; to defeat; to render vain or nugatory, as an effort or attempt; to baffle; to balk.—*n.* Defeat; frustration; a blunt sword, or one that has a button at the end, used in fencing.

foil, foil, *n.* [Fr. *feuille,* L. *folium,* a leaf (whence *foliage*).] A leaf or thin plate of metal; a thin leaf of metal placed under precious stones to improve their appearance; any-

fāte, fär, fâre, fat, fạll; mē, met, hėr; pīne, pin; nōte, not, mȯve; tūbe, tub, bụll; oil, pound.

thing of a different character which serves to set off something else to advantage; that which, by comparison or contrast, sets off or shows more conspicuously the superiority of something else; *arch.* one of the small arcs or hollow curves in the tracery of a Gothic window, panel, etc.—**foiled,** foild, *a. Arch.* having foils (a *foiled* arch).

foist, foist, *v.t.* [D. *vuist,* fist; originally, it would appear, to insert by clever movements of the *fist;* compare to *palm off.*] To insert surreptitiously, or without warrant; to pass off as genuine, true, or worthy. —*n.* A trick; an imposition.

Fokker, fok'ėr, *n.* A type of airplane named after the designer.

fold, fōld, *n.* [A.Sax. *fald, feald,* a plait, a fold, *fealdan,* to fold; cog. Fris. *fald,* G. *falte,* Goth. *falths,* a doubling, a plait; Icel. *falda,* Dan. *folde,* Goth. *falthan,* to fold; same as *fold* in twofold, fivefold.] The doubling or double of any flexible substance, as cloth; a plait; one part turned or bent and laid on another; a clasp; an embrace (*Shak.*). [Often used following a numeral in compounds, and then signifying ' times ', as in two*fold,* four*fold,* ten*fold.*]—*v.t.* To lap or lay double or in plaits; to lay one part over another part of; to lay one over the other, as the hands or arms; to enfold; to embrace. —*v.i.* To become folded or doubled. —**folder,** fōld'ėr, *n.* An outer cover for loose papers; a brochure.

fold, fōld, *n.* [A.Sax. *fald*=Dan. *fold,* Sw. *falla,* a fold, a pen.] A pen or enclosure for sheep or like animals; a flock of sheep; hence, *Scrip.* the church, the flock of Christ.—*v.t.* To confine in a fold.

foliaceous, fō·li·ā'shus, *a.* [L. *foliaceus,* from *folium,* a leaf, akin to Gr. *phyllon,* a leaf.] Leafy; of the nature or form of a leaf; consisting of leaves or thin laminae.—**foliage,** fō'li·ij, *n.* Leaves collectively; the leaves of a plant; leafy growths represented by sculpture, etc.; the numbering of leaves in a book.—**foliate,** fō'li·āt, *v.t.* To beat into a leaf, thin plate, or lamina; to cover with tinfoil, etc.; furnish with leaves.—*v.i.* To form leaves.—**foliation,** fō'li·ā″shon,*n.* The leafing of plants; vernation; the act of beating metal into a thin plate or foil; the operation of spreading foil over a surface; the property in certain rocks of dividing into laminae or plates; the numbering of leaves in a book; *arch.* the foils, cusps, etc., in the tracery of Gothic windows.

folio, fō'li·ō, *n.* [Ablative case of L. *folium,* a leaf, short for *in folio.*] A book formed of sheets of paper folded once; a case for loose papers; *bookkeeping,* a page, or rather both the right and left hand pages, of an account book, expressed by the same figure; *printing,* the number appended to each page; *law,* a written page of a certain number of words.

folk, fōk, *n.* [A.Sax. *folc,* folk, a people or nation=L.G. Fris. Dan. and Sw. *folk;* Icel. *folk;* D. and G. *volk;* probably connected with E.

flock; Lith. *pulkas,* multitude, crowd; but further connections doubtful.] People in general; a separate class of people; though plural in signification it is frequently used with the plural form especially with a qualifying adjective (rich *folks*); group of people forming a nation.—**folk song,** *n.* A song that originates among the common people of a country.— **folk tale,** *n.* A legend begun by the common people of any land, handed down by word of mouth.—**folklore,** *n.* Rural superstitions, tales, traditions, or legends.—**folkway,** *n.* Any way of acting or thinking that is characteristic of a people or social group.—**folksy,** fōk'sy, *a.* Sociable; friendly.

follicle, fol'li·kl, *n.* [L. *folliculus,* dim. of *follis,* a bag or bellows.] A little bag or vesicle in animals and plants; a dry seed vessel or pod opening on one side only; a vessel distended with air; a gland; a minute secreting cavity.—**follicular,** fol·lik'ū·lėr, *a.* Pertaining to, or consisting of follicles.—**folliculated,** fol·lik'ū·lā·ted, *a.* Having follicles; follicular.

follow, fol'ō, *v.t.* [A.Sax. *folgian, fyligean*=G. *folgen,* Dan. *folge,* Icel. *fylgja,* to follow. By some regarded as connected with *folk, full,* etc.] To go or come after or behind; to move behind in the same direction; to pursue; to chase; to pursue as an object of desire; to go with (a leader); to be led or guided by; to accept as authority; to take as an example; to copy; to come after in order of time, rank, or office; to result from, as an effect from a cause or an inference from premises; to keep the attention fixed upon while in progress (a speech, piece of music, etc.); to understand the meaning, connection, or force of; to walk in (a road or course); to practice (a trade or calling).—*To follow suit,* in *card playing,* to play a card of the same suit as that first played; hence, to follow the line of conduct adopted by a predecessor. —*v.i.* To go or come after another; to be posterior in time; to result, as an effect or an inference. . . *Follow* and *succeed* are applied to persons or things; *ensue,* in modern literature, to things only. *Succeed* implies a coming into the place previously occupied by another; *ensue,* generally that which follows is an effect or result.—**follower,** fol'ō·ėr, *n.* One who follows; an adherent; a disciple; an imitator; a dependent.—**following,** fol'ō·ing, *n.* A body of followers or retainers.—*p.* Being next after; succeeding; related, described, or explained next after.

folly, fol'i, *n.* [Fr. *folie,* folly, from *fol,* a fool. FOOL.] Weakness of intellect; imbecility of mind; a weak or foolish act; foolish, weak, or light-minded conduct; criminal weakness.

foment, fō·ment', *v.t.* [Fr. *fomenter,* L. *fomento,* from *fomentum,* for *fovimentum,* a warm application, from *foveo,* to warm, to cherish.] To rouse; to instigate; to bathe with warm medicated liquids or warm water; to encourage; to abet, used especially

in a bad sense (to *foment* quarrels).— **fomentation,** fō·men·tā'shon, *n.* The act of fomenting; encouragement; what is used to foment; a warm lotion.—**fomenter,** fō·men'tėr, *n.* One who foments.

fond, fond, *a.* [O.E. *fonne,* to be foolish, fond, stupid; *fon,* a fool; akin to Icel. *fána,* to play the fool; Sw. *fane,* fatuous. The word is properly a past participle, whence the final *d.*] Foolish; indiscreet; imprudent; foolishly tender and loving; doting; relishing highly; loving ardently; delighted with: followed by *of;* foolishly or extravagantly prized (*Shak.*).—**fondle,** fon'dl, *v.t.* —*fondled, fondling.* To treat with tenderness; to caress.—**fondly,** fond'li, *adv.* In a fond manner; with indiscreet or excessive affection; affectionately; tenderly.—**fondness,** fond'nes, *n.* The state of being fond; great affection or liking.

font, font, *n.* [From L. *fons, fontis,* a fountain. FOUNT.] The vessel used in churches as the receptacle of the baptismal water.—**fontal,**† fon'tal, *a.* Pertaining to a fount, source, or origin.

font, font, *n.* [Fr. *fonte,* from *fondre,* to melt or found, from L. *fundo,* to pour out, whence also *found, foundry.*] A complete assortment of printing types of one size.

fontanel, fon'ta·nel, *n.* [Fr. *fontanelle,* lit. a little fountain, from L. *fons,* a fountain.] *Anat.* a vacancy in the infant cranium between the frontal and parietal bones, and also between the parietal and occipital.

food, fōd, *n.* [A.Sax. *fóda,* food, whence *fédan,* to feed; Dan. *fóde,* Sw. *foda,* food; from root meaning to feed, seen in L. *pasco,* to feed, *pastor,* a shepherd.] Whatever supplies nourishment to organic bodies; nutriment; aliment; victuals; provisions; whatever feeds, sustains, or nourishes.

fool, fōl, *n.* [Fr. *fol, fou,* foolish, a fool, from L.L. *follus,* from L. *folles,* bellows, cheeks puffed out, the *follus* or fool being originally one who made grimaces.] One who is destitute of reason or the common powers of understanding; an idiot; a natural; a person who acts absurdly, irrationally, or unwisely; one who does not exercise his reason; a professional jester or buffoon.—*To make a fool of,* to cause to appear ridiculous.—*v.i.* To act like a fool.—*v.t.* To make a fool of; to befool; to deceive; to impose on; to cheat.—*To fool away,* to waste or spend foolishly. —**foolery,** fōl'ér·i, *n.* Folly; the practice of folly; an act of folly; object of folly.—**foolhardiness,** fōl'- här·di·nes, *n.* Quality of being foolhardy; mad rashness.—**foolhardily,** fōl'här·di·li, *adv.* With foolhardiness. —**foolhardy,** fōl'här·di, *a.* [O.Fr. *fol-hardi.*] Daring without judgment; madly rash and adventurous; foolishly bold. ∴ Syn. under RASH.— **foolish,** fōl'ish, *a.* Characterized by or exhibiting folly; weak in intellect; unwise; silly; vain; trifling; ridiculous.—**foolishly,** fōl'ish·li, *adv.* In

ch, *ch*ain;   *ch,* Sc. lo*ch*;   g, *g*o;   j, *j*ob;   ng, si*ng*;   TH, *then*;   th, *thin*;   w, *w*ig;   hw, *wh*ig;   zh, a*z*ure.

a foolish manner.—**foolishness,** föl´-ish•nes, *n.* The quality or condition of being foolish; folly.—**foolscap,** fölz´-kap, *n.* Paper of the smallest regular size but one, its watermark in early times being the outline of a fool's head and cap.—**fool's errand,** *n.* An absurd or fruitless search or enterprise.—**fool's-parsley,** *n.* A British plant resembling parsley, commonly believed to be poisonous, but if so only in certain localities.

foot, fut, *n.* pl. **feet,** fēt. [A.Sax. *fót,* pl. *fét* = Icel. *fótr,* Sw. *fot,* Goth. *fotus,* G. *fuss;* the same word also as L. *pes, pedis,* Gr. *pous, podos,* Skr. *pâda,* a foot, from a root *pad,* to go.] The terminal part of the leg upon which the body rests while standing; the muscular organ of locomotion in mollusks; step; tread; footfall; the part of a stocking, boot, etc., which receives the foot; the lower end of anything that supports a body; the part opposite to the head or top; the bottom; soldiers who march and fight on foot; infantry, as distinguished from cavalry; a measure consisting of 12 inches, taken from the length of a man's foot; *pros.* a certain number of syllables forming a distinct part of a verse.—*Square foot,* a square whose side is one foot or any equivalent area; 144 square inches.—*Cubic foot,* a cube whose side is one foot, and which therefore contains 1728 cubic inches or any equivalent solid.—*By foot, on foot,* by walking.—*To set on foot,* to originate; to begin; to put in motion. —*To put one's best foot foremost,* to adopt all the means at command.— *Foot-and-mouth disease,* a highly contagious infection of cattle.—*v.i.* To dance; to walk: commonly followed by *it.*—*v.t.* To sum up; to pay (a bill); to tread; to add or make a foot to (to *foot* a stocking or boot). —**footage,** fut´aj, *n.* Length measurement expressed in feet.—**football,** fut´bal, *n.* An inflated oval ball made of a rubber bladder encased in pigskin; a field game in which each of two 11-member teams seeks to kick or carry the ball through or to the opposite goal line.—**footbridge,** fut´brij, *n.* A narrow bridge for foot passengers.—**footfall,** fut´fal, *n.* A footstep; tread of the foot.— **footgear,** fut´gēr, *n.* The covering of the feet; shoes or boots.— **foothill,** fut´hil, *n.* Any of the minor hills at the base of a mountain.— **foothold,** fut´hōld, *n.* That on which one may tread or rest securely; firm standing.—*Milit.* a position that provides a base for further advancement.—**footing,** fut´ing, *n.* Ground for the foot; established place; permanent settlement; foothold; basis; foundation; state (on a *footing* of equality).—**footlights,** *n. pl.* A row of lights in a theater on the front of the stage, and serving to light it up.—**footman,** fut´man, *n.* An infantry soldier; a male servant whose duties are to attend the door, the carriage, the table, etc.; a man in waiting.—**footmark,** fut´märk, *n.* A track; mark of a foot.—**footnote,**

n. A note of reference at the bottom of a page —**footpace,** *n.* A slow step, as in walking.—**footpad,** fut´pad, *n.* A highwayman that robs on foot.— **footpath,** fut´path, *n.* A narrow path for foot-passengers only.—**footpound,** *n.* In mechanics, a unit of work or energy; the work done in raising one pound of weight through a height of one foot against the force of gravity.—**footprint,** fut´-print, *n.* The mark of a foot.— **foot soldier,** *n.* A soldier that serves on foot.—**footsore,** *a.* Having the feet rendered sore or tender, as by much walking.—**footstalk,** fut´stak, *n. Bot.* a petiole; the stalk supporting a leaf; *zool.* a process resembling the footstalk in botany; a peduncle.— **footstep,** fut´step, *n.* The mark or impression of the foot; footprint; tread; footfall; sound of the step.— **footstool,** fut´stōl, *n.* A stool for the feet when sitting.—**footway,** fut´wā, *n.* A path for passengers on foot.—**footworn,** *p.* and *a.* Worn by the feet; footsore.

fop, fop, *n.* [D. *foppen,* to banter, to make a fool of, *fopper,* a wag.] A vain man of weak understanding and much ostentation; a gay, trifling man; a coxcomb; a dandy.—**foppery,** fop´ėr•i, *n.* The characteristics of a fop; showy folly; idle affectation; dandyism.—**foppish,** fop´ish, *a.* Pertaining to a fop; vain of dress; dressing in the extreme of fashion; affected in manners.—**foppishly,** fop´ish•li, *adv.* In a foppish manner. —**foppishness,** fop´ish•nes, *n.*

for, for, *prep.* [A.Sax. *for,* for, because of; D. *voor,* G. *für,* Goth. *faur,* for—allied to E. *fore, far, fare;* L. *pro,* for or in place of; Skr. *pra,* before: before, in advance, is the root-meaning. The prefix *for-* in *forbid,* etc., is different from this.] In the place of; instead of: indicating substitution or equivalence; corresponding to; accompanying (groan *for* groan); in the character of; as being (he took it *for* truth); toward; with the intention of going to; with a tendency to (an inclination *for* drink); conducive to; tending toward, in expectation of; with a view to obtain; in order to arrive at, get, or procure (to wait *for* money, he writes *for* money); suitable or proper to; against; with a tendency to resist and destroy (a remedy *for* the headache); because of; on account of; by reason of (*for* want of time) [in this usage *but* comes very often before the *for*]; on the part of; in relation to (easy *for* you, but difficult *for* me); in proportion to (tall *for* his age); through a certain space; during a certain time; according to; as far as; so far as concerns; notwithstanding (it may be so *for* anything I know); in favor of; on the part or side of (to vote *for* a person); desirous to have; willing to receive [in this sense often in interjections: O *for* revenge!]; to take up the part or character of (nature intended him *for* a usurer); having so much laid to

one's account; to the amount of (he failed *for* ten thousand). ∴. *For* was at one time common before the infinitives of verbs to denote purpose; but this usage is now vulgar.— *For all the world,* of everything else in the world; in every respect; exactly (an animal *for all the world* like a mouse).—*For ever.* EVER.— *conj.* For the cause or reason that; because: a word by which a reason is introduced of something before advanced, being really a preposition governing a clause.—*For as much as,* or *forasmuch as,* in consideration that; seeing that; since.

forage, for´ij, *n.* [Fr. *fourrage,* O.Fr. *forrage,* from *forre,* forage; from the old German or Scandinavian word equivalent to E. *fodder.*] Food of any kind for horses and cattle; the act of searching for provisions.— *v.i.*—*foraged, foraging.* To collect forage; to roam in search of food or provender.—*v.t.* To collect forage from; to supply with forage.— **forager,** for´i•jėr, *n.* One that forages.

foramen, fō•rā´men, *n.* pl. **foramina,** fō•ram´i•na. [L., from *foro,* to bore.] A small natural opening or perforation in parts of animals or plants; an opening by which nerves or blood vessels obtain a passage through bones.—**foraminifer,** fō•ra•min´i-fėr, *n.* [L. *foramen, foraminis,* a hole, and *fero,* to bear.] An individual of the Foraminifera.—**Foraminifera,** fō•ram´i•nif˝ėr•a, *n. pl.* An order of minute animals belonging to the protozoa, furnished with a shell, simple or complex, usually perforated by pores (whence the name).— **foraminiferal, foraminiferous,** fō•-ram´i•nif˝ėr•al, fō•ram´i•nif˝ėr•us, *a.* Belonging to the Foraminifera.

forasmuch, for•az•much´, *conj.* See FOR.

foray, for´ā, *v.i.* [A form of *forage.*] To ravage; to pillage.—*n.* The act of foraging; a predatory excursion; booty.—**forayer,** for´ā•ėr, *n.* One who takes part in a foray; a marauder.

forbade, for•bad´, *pret.* of *forbid.*

forbear, for•bār´, *v.i.*—*forbore* (pret.), *forborne* (pp.). [Prefix *for,* intens., and *bear;* A.Sax. *forberan, forbæran.*] To cease; to refrain from proceeding; to pause; to delay; to be patient; to restrain one's self from action or violence.—*v.t.* To avoid voluntarily; to abstain from; to omit; to avoid doing; to treat with indulgence‡.—**forbearance,** for•bār´ans, *n.* The act of forbearing; restraint of passions; longsuffering; indulgence toward those who injure us; lenity.—**forbearer,** for•bār´er, *n.* One who forbears.—**forbearing,** for•bār´-ing, *p.* and *a.* Having forbearance; long-suffering.

forbid, for•bid´, *v.t.*—pret. *forbade;* pp. *forbid, forbidden; forbidding.* [Prefix *for,* implying negation, and *bid.*] To prohibit; to interdict; to command to forbear or not to do; to refuse access; to command not to enter or approach; to oppose; to hinder; to obstruct (a river *forbids* approach).—**forbiddance,**† for•bid´-

ans, *n.* Prohibition; command or edict against a thing.—**forbidden,** for·bid′n, *p.* and *a.* Prohibited; interdicted.—**forbidder,** for·bid′ėr, *n.* One who forbids.—**forbidding,** for·bid′ing, *a.* Repelling approach; repulsive; raising abhorrence, aversion, or dislike.—**forbiddingly,** for··bid′ing·li, *adv.* In a forbidding manner; repulsively.—**forbiddingness,** for·bid′ing·nes, *n.*

force, fōrs, *n.* [Fr., from L.L. *forcia, fortia,* from L. *fortis,* strong; seen also in *fort, fortitude, fortress, comfort, effort,* etc.] Active power; vigor; might; strength; energy; that which is the source of all the active phenomena occurring in the material world; that which produces or tends to produce change; one of the modes or forms in which energy is exhibited in nature, as heat or electricity; momentum; the quantity of energy or power exerted by a moving body; violence; power exerted against will or consent; moral power to convince the mind; influence; validity; power to bind or hold (the *force* of an agreement); a military or naval armament; a body of troops; an army or navy; a body of men prepared for action in other ways (a police *force*).—*v.t.*—**forced,** *forcing.* To compel; to constrain to do or to forbear, by the exertion of a power not resistible; to impel; to press, drive, draw, or push by main strength; to compel by strength of evidence (to *force* conviction on the mind); to ravish; to violate (a female); to twist, wrest, or overstrain; to assume, or compel one's self to give utterance or expression to (to *force* a smile); to ripen or bring to maturity by heat artificially applied. In contract bridge, to demand a bid from one's partner, as by bidding one more of a suit than is required by the preceding bid, or by making an opening bid of two.—**forced,** fōrst, *p.* and *a.* Unnaturally assumed; constrained; affected; overstrained; unnatural. —**forceful,** fōrs′ful, *a.* Possessing force; powerful; driven with force; acting with power; impetuous (*Shak.*).—**forcefully,** fōrs′ful·li, *adv.* Violently or impetuously.—**force pump,** *n.* A pump which delivers the water by means of pressure or force directly applied, so as to eject it forcibly to a great elevation; in contradistinction to a pump that raises water by the pressure of the air simply.—**forcer,** fōr′sėr, *n.* One who or that which forces.—**forcible,** fōr′si·bl, *a.* Having force; exercising force; powerful; strong; marked by force or violence; violent.—**forcibleness,** fōr′si·bl·nes, *n.* The condition or quality of being forcible.

force, fōrs, *v.t.* [Same as *farce;* or perhaps from *force,* in old sense of season, *forcemeat* being thus highly seasoned meat.] *Obs.* To stuff; to farce.—**forcemeat,** fōrs′mēt, *n. Cookery,* meat chopped fine and seasoned, either served up alone or used as stuffing, *farced* meat, by corruption.

forceps, for′seps, *n.* [L., from *for* in *formus,* warm, and *capio,* to take.] A two-bladed instrument on the principle of pincers or tongs for holding anything difficult to be held by the hand: used by surgeons, dentists, jewelers, etc.

ford, fōrd, *n.* [A.Sax. *ford,* connected with *faran,* to go, to fare; comp. G. *furt,* a ford, *fahren,* to go; allied to Gr. *poros,* a passage; E. *ferry.*] A place in a river or other water where it may be passed by man or beast on foot or by wading.—*v.t.* To pass or cross (a stream) by wading; to wade through.—**fordable,** fōr′da·bl, *a.* Capable of being forded.

fordo, for·dö′, *v.t.*—*fordid* (pret.), *fordone* (pp.). [Prefix *for-,* intens., and *do.*] To exhaust, overpower, or overcome, as by toil.

fore, fōr, *a.* [A.Sax. *fore, foran,* before; D. *voor,* Dan. *for,* G. *vor,* before; Goth. *faura,* for; L. *præ,* before, *pro,* for, *por* (as in *porrigere,* to extend), Gr. *paros,* Skr. *pra, puras*—before. Akin *far, for, fare.* First and foremost are its superlatives.] Advanced, or, locally, in advance of something: opposed to *hind* or *hinder;* coming first in time: opposed to *after;* anterior; prior; antecedent; in front or toward the face; situated towards the stem of a ship.—*Fore and aft* (*naut.*), in a direction from stem to stern; *fore-and-aft* sail, a sail, such as a jib or spanker, that has a position more or less in this direction.—*n.* Toward the front as compared with another location; *golf,* warning cry to persons who may be in the path of a ball.

forearm, fōr·ärm′, *v.t.* To arm or prepare for attack or resistance before the time of need.

forearm, fōr·ärm′, *n.* That part of the arm which is between the elbow and the wrist.

forebear, fōr′bâr, *n.* [Prefix *fore,* and *beer,* be,-er.] Ancestor; forefather.

forebode, fōr·bōd′, *v.t.*—*foreboded, foreboding.* To feel a secret sense of a misfortune about to happen.—**foreboder,** fōr·bō′der, *n.*—**foreboding,** fōr·bō′ding, *n.* Presentiment of approaching evil.

forecast, fōr·kast′, *v.t.*—pret. & pp. *forecast.* To cast or scheme beforehand; to plan before execution; to calculate beforehand; to estimate in the future.—*v.i.* To form a scheme previously; to contrive beforehand.—*n.* (fōr′kast). Prediction (a weather *forecast*).—**forecaster,** fōr′kas′tėr, *n.* One who forecasts.

forecastle, fōr′kas·l; sailors' pronunciation, fōk′sl, *n.* A short raised deck in the forepart of a ship; the forepart of a vessel where the sailors live.

foreclose, fōr·klōz′, *v.t.*—*foreclosed, foreclosing.* [Fore for Fr. prefix *for* (as in *forfeit*), from L. *foris,* away, out of doors.] To preclude; to stop; to prevent.—*To foreclose a mortgage,* to compel the mortgager to pay the money due on it, or forfeit his right to the estate.—**foreclosure,** fōr·klō′zhėr, *n.* The act of foreclosing.

foredate, fōr·dāt′, *v.t.* To date before the true time; to antedate.

foredeck, fōr′dek, *n.* The forepart of a deck of a ship.

foredo, fōr·dö′, *v.t.*—*foredid* (pret.), *foredone* (pp.). To do beforehand.

foredoom, fōr·döm′, *v.t.* To doom beforehand; to predestinate.

forefather, fōr′fä·THėr, *n.* An ancestor.

forefend, fōr·fend′, *v.t.* To fend off; to avert; to prevent the approach of; to forbid or prohibit.

forefinger, fōr′fing·gėr, *n.* The finger next to the thumb; the index.

forefoot, fōr′fu̇t, *n.* One of the anterior feet of a quadruped or multiped.

forefront, fōr′frunt, *n.* The foremost part or place.

foregather, fōr·gaTH′ėr, *v.i.* Same as *Forgather.*

forego, fōr·gō′, *v.t.* To forgo (which see).

forego, fōr·gō′, *v.t.*—*forewent* (pret.), *foregone* (pp.). To go before; to precede.—**foregoer,** fōr·gō′ėr, *n.* One who goes before another; an ancestor; a progenitor.—**foregoing,** fōr·gō′ing or fōr′gō·ing, *p.* and *a.* Preceding; going before, in time or place; antecedent.—**foregone,** fōr·gon′ or fōr′gon, *p.* and *a.* Past; preceding; predetermined; made up beforehand.

foreground, fōr′ground, *n.* The part of a picture which is represented so as to appear nearest the eye of the observer.

forehand, fōr′hand, *n.* The part of a horse which is before the rider; *tennis,* etc., a stroke made with palm forward (by a righthanded player on his right).—*a.* Anticipative; referring to a forehand stroke.

forehead, fōr′hed or fōr′ed, *n.* The part of the face which extends from the usual line of hair on the top of the head to the eyes; the brow.

foreign, for′in, *a.* [Fr. *forain,* from L.L. *foraneus,* from L. *foras,* out of doors (also in *forest*)—same root as E. *door.* As in *sovereign* the g has been improperly inserted.] Belonging or relating to another nation or country; not of the country in which one resides; alien; extraneous; not our own; remote; not belonging; not connected; irrelevant; not to the purpose: with *to* or *from.*—**foreigner,** for′in·ėr, *n.* A person born in or belonging to a foreign country; an alien.—**foreignism,** for′in·izm, *n.* Foreignness; a foreign idiom or custom.—**foreignness,** for′in·nes, *n.* The quality of being foreign.

forejudge, fōr·juj′, *v.t.* To judge beforehand or before hearing the facts and proof; to prejudge.—**forejudgment,** fōr·juj′ment, *n.* Judgment previously formed.

foreknow, fōr·nō′, *v.t.*—*foreknew* (pret.), *foreknown* (pp.). To have previous knowledge of; to know beforehand.—**foreknowable,** fōr··nō′a·bl, *a.* Capable of being foreknown.—**foreknowledge,** fōr·nol′·ij, *n.* Knowledge of a thing before it takes place; prescience.

---

ch, *chain;*   *ch,* Sc. loch;   g, go;   j, *job;*   ng, sing;   TH, *then;*   th, *thin;*   w, *wig;*   hw, *whig;*   zh, azure.

foreland, fōr'land, *n.* A promontory or cape; a headland.

foreleg, fōr'leg, *n.* One of the front or anterior legs, as of an animal, a chair, etc.

forelock, fōr'lok, *n.* The lock or hair that grows from the forepart of the head.—*To take time by the forelock,* to make prompt use of anything; to let no opportunity escape.

foreman, fōr'man, *n.* The first or chief man; the chief man of a jury who acts as their speaker; a chief workman who superintends others.

foremast, fōr'mast, *n.* The mast of a ship or other vessel which is placed before the other or the others.

foremost, fōr'mōst or fōr'most, *a.* [Should have been *formest* (to correspond with *former*), being the A.Sax. *formest,* a double superlative, from *forma,* first, foremost (itself a superlative), and the *-est* of superlatives: the spelling has been modified by confusion with *most;* so also *hindmost, inmost, outmost.*] First in place, station, honor, or dignity; most advanced; first in time.

forename, fōr'nām, *n.* A name that precedes the family name or surname.—**forenamed,** fōr'nāmd, *a.* Named or mentioned before.

forenoon, fōr'nön, *n.* The part of the day that comes before noon; the part from morning to mid-day.

forensic, forensical, fō·ren'sik, fō·ren'si·kal, *a.* [From L. *forensis,* from *forum,* a court, a forum; akin *forest.*] Belonging to courts of justice or to public discussion and debate; used in courts or legal proceedings, or in public discussions.—*Forensic medicine,* medical jurisprudence.

foreordain, fōr'or·dān, *v.t.* To ordain or appoint beforehand; to preordain; to predestinate.—**foreordination,** fōr·or'di·nā'shon, *n.* Predetermination; predestination.

forepart, fōr'pärt, *n.* The most advanced part, or the first in time or place; the anterior part; the beginning.

forepeak, fōr'pēk, *n. Naut.* the part of a vessel in the angle of the bow.

forerun, fōr·run', *v.t.*—*foreran* (pret.), *forerun* (pp.), *forerunning* (ppr.). To run before; to come before, as an earnest of something to follow.—**forerunner,** fōr·run'er, *n.* A messenger sent before to give notice of the approach of others; a harbinger; a sign foreshowing something to follow.

foresaid, fōr'sed, *a.* Spoken of or mentioned before.

foresail, fōr'sāl, *n. Naut.* the principal sail set on the foremast.

foresee, fōr·sē', *v.t.*—*foresaw* (pret.), *foreseen* (pp.). To see beforehand; to see or know before it happens; to have prescience of; to foreknow.—*v.i.* To exercise foresight.—**foreseer,** fōr·sē'er, *n.* One who foresees.

foreshadow, fōr·shad'ō, *v.t.* To shadow or typify beforehand.

foreshore, fōr'shōr, *n.* The sloping part of a shore between high and low watermark.

foreshorten, fōr·shor'tn, *v.t. Persp.* to represent or depict (as an arm, a branch, directed towards the spectator) with the due impression of length, prominence, and relative position.

foreshow, fōr·shō', *v.t.*—*foreshowed,* (pret.), *foreshown* (pp.). To show, represent, or exhibit beforehand; to prognosticate; to foretell.

foreside, fōr'sīd, *n.* The front side.

foresight, fōr'sīt, *n.* The act or power of foreseeing; prescience; foreknowledge; provident care for the future; prudence in guarding against evil; wise forethought; the sight on the muzzle of a gun.—**foresighted,** fōr'sī·ted, *a.* Having foresight; prescient; provident.

foreskin, fōr'skin, *n.* The fold of skin that covers the anterior extremity of the male member of generation; the prepuce.

forest, for'est, *n.* [O.Fr. *forest,* Mod. Fr. *forêt,* from L.L. *foresta,* a forest, from L. *foris, foras,* out of doors, abroad; akin *foreign, forensic.*] An extensive wood, or a large tract of land covered with trees; a tract of mingled woodland and open uncultivated ground; *Eng. law.* a district wholly or chiefly devoted to hunting, and usually a royal domain.—*a.* Of or pertaining to a forest; sylvan; rustic.—*v.t.* To convert into a forest.—**forestation,** for'es·tā"shon, *n.* The act or process of planting a forest.—**forester,** for'es·ter, *n.* A person who possesses a knowledge of forestry, particularly one appointed to inspect and care for forests or trees; various moths; the giant kangaroo.—**forestry,** for'est·ri, *n.* The art of forming or of cultivating forests, or of managing growing timber.

forestall, fōr·stal', *v.t.* [A.Sax. *foresteall,* an intercepting; a placing before from *fore,* before, and *steall,* a place, a stall.] To take too early action regarding; to realize beforehand; to anticipate; to take possession of in advance of something or somebody else; to hinder by preoccupation or prevention.—*To forestall the market,* to buy up merchandise on its way to market with the intention of selling it again at a higher price; formerly an offense at law.—**forestaller,** fōr·stal'er, *n.* One who forestalls.

foretaste, fōr'tāst, *n.* A taste beforehand; anticipation; enjoyment in advance.—*v.t.* (fōr-tāst'). To taste before possession; to have a foretaste of.

foretell, fōr·tel', *v.t.*—*foretold* (pret. & pp.). To tell before happening; to predict; to prophesy; to foretoken or foreshow; to prognosticate.—*v.i.* To utter prediction or prophecy.—**foreteller,** fōr·tel'er, *n.* One who foretells.

forethought, fōr'that, *n.* A thinking beforehand; provident care; foresight.

foretoken, fōr·tō'kn, *v.t.* To betoken beforehand; to foreshow; to presignify; to prognosticate.

fore-tooth, fōr'töth, *n. pl.* **fore-teeth,** fōr'tēth. One of the teeth in the forepart of the mouth; an incisor.

foretop, fōr'top, *n.* Hair on the forepart of the head; *naut.* the platform erected at the head of the foremast.—**fore-topmast,** *n.* The mast above the foremast, and below the foretop-gallant mast.

forewarn, fōr·warn', *v.t.* To warn beforehand; to give previous notice to.

forewoman, fōr'wu·man, *n.* A woman who superintends others in a workshop or other establishment.

foreword, fōr'werd, *n.* A preface, an introduction to a book or reprint.

forfeit, for'fit, *v.t.* [Fr. *forfait,* a crime, misdeed, from *forfaire,* to transgress, L.L. *forisfacere,* to offend L. *foris,* out of doors, beyond (seen also in *foreclose, forest*), and *facere,* to do.] To lose the right to by some fault, crime, or neglect; to become by misdeed liable to be deprived of (an estate, one's life).—*n.* The act of forfeiting; that which is forfeited; a fine; a penalty; a sportive fine or penalty, whence the game of *forfeits.* —*p.* and *a.* Forfeited or subject to be forfeited; liable to deprivation or penal seizure.—**forfeitable,** for'fit·a·bl, *a.* Liable to be forfeited; subject to forfeiture.—**forfeiter,** for'fit·er, *n.* One who forfeits.—**forfeiture,** for'fi·cher, *n.* The act of forfeiting; the losing of some right, privilege, estate, honor, etc., by an offense, crime, breach of condition, or other act; that which is forfeited.

forfend, for·fend'. Same as *Forefend.*

forgather, for·gaTH'er, *v.i.* [For., intens., and *gather;* comp. O.Fris. *forgathera,* to assemble.] To meet; to convene; to come or meet together accidentally.

forgave, for·gāv', *pret.* of *forgive.*

forge, forj, *n.* [Fr. *forge,* It. *forgia,* from L. *fabrica,* a workshop, from *faber,* a workman, a smith. So that *forge=fabric.*] A furnace in which iron or other metal is heated to be hammered into form; a workshop for this purpose; a smithy.—*v.t.*—*forged, forging.* To work into shape in a forge; to form or shape out in any way; to invent; to produce, as that which is counterfeit or not genuine; to counterfeit, as a signature or document.—*v.i.* To commit forgery.—**forger,** for'jer, *n.* One who forges; especially, a person guilty of forgery.—**forgery,** for'jer·i, *n.* The act of forging, fabricating, or producing falsely; the crime of counterfeiting a person's signature on a document; that which is forged, fabricated, or counterfeited.

forge, forj, *v.i.*—*forged, forging.* [Perhaps from Icel. *farga,* to press.] *Naut.* to move on slowly and laboriously; to work one's way; usually with *ahead, off, past,* etc.

forget, for·get', *v.t.*—*forgot* (pret.), *forgot, forgotten* (pp.), *forgetting* (ppr.). [A.Sax. *forgitan*—*for,* not, or neg., and *gitan,* to get. GET.] To lose the remembrance of; to let go from the memory; to cease to have in mind; not to remember or think of; to slight; to neglect; *refl.* to be guilty of something unbecoming; to commit an oversight.—**forgettable,** for·get'a·bl, *a.* Capable of being forgotten.—**forgetful**, for·get′fu̇l, a. Apt to forget; easily losing remembrance; careless; neglectful; inattentive.—**forgetfully**, for·get′fu̇l·li, adv. In a forgetful manner.—**forgetfulness**, for·get′fu̇l·nes, n. The quality of being forgetful; a ceasing to remember; oblivion; neglect; negligence; inattention. — **forgetter**, for·get′ėr, n. One who forgets.—**forget-me-not**, n. A well-known plant, having bright blue flowers with a yellow eye, and considered to be the emblem of friendship and fidelity in many lands.

forgive, for·giv′, v.t.—**forgave** (pret.), **forgiven** (pp.), **forgiving** (ppr.). [A. Sax. forgifan—for, intens., and gifan, to give.] To give up resentment or claim to requital on account of; to remit, as an offense, debt, fine, or penalty; to pardon; to cease to feel resentment against; to free from a claim or the consequences of an injurious act or crime. Syn. under PARDON.—**forgivable**, for·giv′a·bl, a. Capable of being forgiven; pardonable.—**forgiveness**, for·giv′nes, n. The act of forgiving; disposition or willingness to forgive.—**forgiver**, for·giv′ėr, n. One who forgives.—**forgiving**, for·giv′ing, p. and a. Disposed to forgive; inclined to overlook offenses; mild; merciful; compassionate.—**forgivingness**, for·giv′ing·nes, n.

forgo, for·gō′, v.t.—**forwent** (pret.), **forgone** (pp.). [Also spelled less correctly forego; from prefix for, intens., or with sense of away, and go; A.Sax. forgán, to forgo, pass over. neglect.] To forbear to enjoy or possess; to voluntarily avoid enjoying or possessing; to give up, renounce, resign. —**forgoer**, for·gō′ėr, n. One who forgoes.

fork, fork, n. [A.Sax. forc, furc, from L. furca, a fork, which is also the parent of G. furke, D. vork, Fr. fourche.] An instrument, consisting of a handle with a shank, terminating in two or more parallel prongs, used for holding or lifting something; anything similar in shape; one of the parts into which anything is bifurcated; a prong.—Forks of a road or river, the point where a road parts into two, the point where two rivers meet and unite in one stream. —v.i. To divide into forks or branches.—v.t. To raise or pitch with a fork; to dig and break with a fork.— **forked**, forkt, a. Having prongs or divisions like a fork; opening into two or more prongs, points, or shoots; furcated.

forlorn, for·lorn′, a. [A.Sax. forloren, pp. of forleósan, to lose; prefix for, intens., leósan, to lose; comp. D. and G. verloren, forlorn, lost. LOSE.] Deserted; forsaken; abandoned; lost; helpless; wretched; solitary; bereft; destitute.—Forlorn hope. [D. verloren hoop—hoop, a troop.] A detachment of men appointed to lead in an assault, or perform other service attended with uncommon peril.— **forlornly**, for·lorn′li, adv. In a forlorn manner.—**forlornness**, for·lorn′nes, n.

form, form, n. [Fr. forme, form, shape, manner, bench, bed of a hare, from L. forma, form, whence conform, inform, reform, etc.] The shape or external appearance of a body, as distinguished from its material; the figure, as defined by lines and angles; appearance to the eye; configuration; a shape; a phantom; manner of arranging particulars; disposition of particular things (a form of words); general system or arrangement (a particular form of government); something on or after which things are fashioned; a model, draught, pattern; proper shape or trim; high condition or fitness for any undertaking; external appearance without the essential qualities; stated method; established practice; ceremony; a long seat; a bench; the bed of a hare; printing, the pages of type or stereotype plates arranged for printing a sheet, and fastened in an iron frame or chase.—v.t. To give form or shape to; to shape; to mold; to arrange; to combine in any particular manner; to model by instruction and discipline; to mold; to train; to devise; to contrive; to frame; to create; to be an element or constituent of; to combine to make up; to answer as; to take the shape of.—v.i. To take a form.—**formal**, for′mal, a. Given to outward forms, observances, or ceremonies; strictly ceremonious; done or made in due form or according to regular method; acting according to rule or established mode; having the form or appearance without the substance or essence; conventional; formative.—**formalism**, for′mal·izm, n. The quality of being formal or addicted to mere forms; outside and ceremonial religion.—**formalist**, for′mal·ist, n. One given to formalism.—**formality**, for·mal′i·ti, n. The condition or quality of being formal; form without substance; established order; rule of proceeding; mode; method; customary ceremony; ceremonial; conventionality.—**formalize**, for′mal·īz, v.t.—**formalized**, **formalizing**. To reduce to a form; to give a certain form to; to render formal.—**formally**, for′mal·li, adv. In a formal manner; ceremoniously; stiffly; precisely.—**format**, for′mat, n. [Fr.] Size of a book as regards length and breadth.—**formation**, for·mā′shon, n. The act of forming, making, creating, composing, shaping, etc.; production; the manner in which a thing is formed; geol. any series of rocks referred to a common origin or period; milit. an arrangement of troops, as in a square, column, etc.—**formative**, for′ma·tiv, a. Giving form; having the power of giving form; plastic; gram. serving to form; inflexional.—n. Gram. that which gives form to a word and is no part of the root.—**former**, for′mėr, n. One who forms.—**formless**, form′les, a. Wanting form or shape; shapeless.—**formlessness**, form′les·nes, n.

formaldehyde, form·al′de·hīd, n.

[FORMIC and ALDEHYDE.] A colorless gas, with a strong odor, used chiefly in solution, as a preservative and disinfectant.

former, for′mėr, a. compar. [A compar. from A.Sax. forma, first. FOREMOST.] Before or preceding another in time: opposed to latter; ancient; long past (former ages); preceding; earlier, as between two things mentioned together; first mentioned.—**formerly**, for′mėr·li, adv. In time past, either in time immediately preceding or at an indefinite distance; of old; heretofore. ∴ Formerly means before the present time; previously, before some particular event.

formic, for′mik, a. [L. formica, an act.] Pertaining to or produced by ants.—Formic acid, a pungent acid with a peculiar odor, and acting as a corrosive on the skin, originally obtained from ants.—**formicary**, for′mi·ka·ri, n. A colony of ants; an anthill.—**formicate**, for′mi·kāt, a. Pertaining to an ant.

formidable, for′mi·da·bl, a. [L. formidabilis, from formido, fear.] Exciting fear or apprehension; adapted to excite fear or deter from approach, encounter, or undertaking.—**formidableness**, for′mi·da·bl·nes, n. The quality of being formidable.—**formidably**, for′mi·da·bli, adv. In a formidable manner.

formula, for′mū·la, n. pl. **formulae**, for′mū·lē, or **formulas**, [L. formula, dim. of forma, a form.] A prescribed form; a prescribed form of words in which something is stated; med. a prescription; eccles. a written confession of faith; a formal enunciation of doctrines; math. a rule or principle expressed in algebraic symbols; chem. an expression by means of symbols and letters of the constituents of a compound.—**formularization**, for′mū·lėr·i·zā″shon, n. The act of formularizing.—**formularize**, for′mū·lėr·īz, v.t.—**formularized**, **formularizing**. To reduce to a formula; to formulate.—**formulary**, for′mū·le·ri, n. A book containing stated and prescribed forms; a book of precedents.—a. Prescribed; ritual. —**formulate**, for′mū·lāt, v.t.— **formulated**, **formulating**. To reduce to or express in a formula; to put into a precise and comprehensive statement; to state precisely.—**formulation**, for·mū·lā′shon, n. The act of formulating.—**formulization**, for′mū·li·zā″shon, n. The act of formulizing.—**formulize**, for′mū·līz, v.t. To reduce to a formula or formulas; to formulate.

fornicate, for′ni·kāt, v.i. [L. fornicor, fornicatus, from fornix, a vault, a brothel, brothels in Rome being generally in vaults or cellars.] To have unlawful sexual intercourse.— **fornication**, for·ni·kā′shon, n. [L. fornicatio.] The incontinence or lewdness of unmarried persons, male or female.—**fornicator**, for′ni·kā·tėr, n. One guilty of fornication.

forsake, for·sāk′, v.t.—**forsook** (pret.), **forsaken** (pp.), **forsaking** (ppr.). [A. Sax. forsacan, to oppose, to renounce;

prefix *for*, intens., and *sacan*, to contend; Dan. *forsage*, D. *vér-saken*, to deny. SAKE.] To quit or leave entirely, often to leave that to which we are bound by duty or natural affection; to desert; to abandon; to depart or withdraw from; to renounce; to reject.

forsooth, for·söth′, *adv.* [*For* and *sooth*, that is, for or in truth. A.Sax. *forsoth.*] In truth; in fact; certainly.

forswear, for·swâr′, *v.t.*—*forswore* (pret.), *forsworn* (pp.). [Prefix *for* with negative sense.] To reject or renounce upon oath; to renounce earnestly or with protestations; *refl.* to swear falsely; to perjure one's self.—*v.i.* To swear falsely.—**forswearer**, for·swa′rér, *n.*

forsythia, for·sith′·i·a, *n.* [After W. *Forsyth*, Brit. botanist.] Shrub of the oleaceous genus *Forsythia*, having bell-shaped yellow flowers that appear before the leaves in spring.

fort, fōrt, *n.* [Fr. *fort*, lit. strong place from *fort*, L. *fortis*, strong. FORCE.] A fortified place, usually small, occupied only by troops.—**forte**, fōr′tā, *a. Mus.* direction to sing or play with force of tone.—*adv.* Loudly, powerfully.—*n. Mus.* a passage played or sung powerfully.—**forte**, fōrt, *n.* [Fr. *fort*, strong part, also a person's forte (the final *e* being an English insertion).] The strong portion of a sword blade or rapier; peculiar talent or faculty a person has; a strong point; chief excellence.—**fortress**, fōrt′res, *n.* [Fr. *forteresse*, O.Fr. *fortelesse*: same word as *fortalice.*] A fortified place, especially one of considerable extent and complication; a stronghold; a place of security.

forth, fōrth, *adv.* [A.Sax. *forth*, from *fore*, before; G. *fort*, on, further; D. *voord*, forward. FORE.] Onward in time, place, or order (from that time *forth*); in advance from a given point; forward; out; abroad; from a state of concealment; from an interior; out into view.—**forthcoming**, fōrth′kum·ing, *a.* Ready to appear; making appearance.—**forthright**, fōrth′rit, *adv.* Straightforward; straightway.—*a.* Straightforward; direct; immediate.—*n.* A straight way; opposed to meanders. (*Shak.*)—**forthwith**, fōrth′with, *adv.* [*Forth* and *with*, forth along with that.] Immediately; without delay; directly.

fortify, for′ti·fī, *v.t.*—*fortified*, *fortifying*. [Fr. *fortifier*, from L.L. *forti-fico*—L. *fortis*, strong, and *facio*, to make.] To add strength to; to strengthen (an argument, resolution); to furnish with strength or means of resisting (to *fortify* one against cold); to surround, with a wall, ditch, palisades, or other works, with a view to defend against the attacks of an enemy; to increase the alcoholic strength of (wine) by means of adventitious spirit.—**fortification**, for′ti·fi·kā′shon, *n.* The act of fortifying; the art or science of strengthening military positions in such a way that they may be readily defended; the works constructed for the purpose of strengthening a position; a fortified place; a fort.—**fortifier**, for′ti·fī·ér, *n.* One who fortifies.

fortissimo, for·tis′sē·mō, *adv. Mus.* a direction to sing with the utmost strength or loudness.

fortitude, for′ti·tūd, *n.* [L. *fortitudo*, from *fortis*, strong. FORCE.] That strength or firmness of mind or soul which enables a person to encounter danger or to bear pain with coolness and courage; passive courage; resolute endurance.

fortnight, fort′nīt, *n.* [Contr. from *fourteen nights*, time being formerly often reckoned by nights. SE'N-NIGHT.] The space of fourteen days; two weeks.—**fortnightly**, fort′nīt·li, *adv.* Once a fortnight; every fortnight.—*a.* Occurring or appearing once a fortnight.

fortress. See FORT.

fortuitous, for·tū′i·tus, *a.* [L. *fortuitus*, from *fors*, *fortis*, chance. FORTUNE.] Accidental; happening by chance; occurring without any known cause.—**fortuitously**, for·tū′i·tus·li, *adv.* In a fortuitous manner; accidentally; by chance.—**fortuitousness**, for·tū′i·tus·nes, *n.*—**fortuity**, for·tū′i·ti, *n.* Accident; chance; casualty.

fortune, for′chen, *n.* [L. *fortuna*, a lengthened form from stem of *fors*, *fortis*, chance, hap, luck, from *fero*, to bring (as in *fertile*.)] Chance; accident; luck; fate; also, the personified or deified power regarded as determining the lots of life; the good or ill that befalls or may befall man; success, good or bad; what the future may bring; good success; prosperity; good luck; estate; possessions; especially, large estate; great wealth.—*v.i.* To befall; to fall out; to happen; to come casually to pass.—**fortunate**, for′che·nit, *a.* [L. *fortunatus.*] Coming by good fortune or favorable chance; bringing some unexpected good; having good fortune; lucky; successful. ∴ *Fortunate* refers to that which is deemed beyond our own control; *successful* denotes that effective effort has been made to gain the object; *prosperous* leaves both these notions out of account, simply conveying the fact of there being a flourishing state of matters.—**fortunately**, for′ché·nit·li, *adv.* In a fortunate manner; luckily; happily.—**fortunateness**, for′che·-nit·nes, *n.*—**fortune hunter**, *n.* A man who seeks to marry a woman with a large fortune, with a view to enrich himself.—**fortuneless**, for′-chen·les, *a.* Luckless; also, destitute of a fortune or wealth.—**fortune-teller**, *n.* One who pretends to tell people their fortune in life.—**fortunetelling**, *n.* The act or practice of telling fortunes.

forty, for′ti, *a.* [A.Sax. *feówertig*—*feówer*, four, and *tig*, ten. FOUR.] Four times ten; thirty-nine and one added.—*n.* The number which consists of four times ten; or a symbol expressing it.—*The roaring forties*, the stormy area of the Atlantic between 39° and 50° N. lat.—*The forty-five*, the Jacobite rebellion of 1745, following on the '15 of 1715.—*The forty thieves*, the tale of Ali Baba in the *Arabian Nights.*—*Forty winks*, short nap.—**fortieth**, for′ti·eth, *a.* Following the thirty-ninth; being one of forty equal parts into which anything is divided.—*n.* One of forty equal parts into which a whole is divided.

forum, fō′rum, *n.* [L., connected with *foris*, out of doors; hence *forensic.*] A public place in Rome where causes were judicially tried and orations delivered to the people; a tribunal; a court.

forward, for′wérd, *adv.* [A.Sax. *foreweard*—*fore*, before, and *weard*, used to signify direction. Comp. G. *vorwärts.*] Toward a part or place before or in front; onward; progressively; opposed to *backward.*—*a.* Being at the front; anterior; fore; ready; prompt; ardent; eager; over bold; self-assertive; pert; saucy; advanced beyond the usual degree; advanced for the season.—*n.* One in advance; a front player in a game, such as basketball.—*v.t.* To advance or help onward; to further, promote, accelerate, hasten; to send toward the place of destination; to transmit; *bookbinding*, to prepare for the finisher.—**forwarder**, for′wér·dér, *n.* One who forwards.—**forwardly**, for′-wérd·li, *adv.* In a forward manner; eagerly; pertly; saucily.—**forwardness**, for′wérd·nes, *n.* The quality of being forward; promptitude; pertness.—**forwards**, *adv.* Forward; toward the front.

fosse, foss, fos, *n.* [Fr. *fosse*, L. *fossa*, a ditch, a trench, from *fodio*, *fossum*, to dig, whence also *fossil.*] *Fort.* a ditch or moat, commonly full of water, outside the walls or rampart of a fortified place or post to be defended; *anat.* a kind of cavity in a bone with a large aperture.

fossil, fos′sil, *a.* [Fr. *fossile*, L. *fossilis*, from *fodio*, *fossum*, to dig. FOSSE.] Dug out of the earth; petrified and preserved in rocks.—*n.* Originally any substance dug out of the earth; now specifically applied to the petrified remains of plants and animals which occur in the strata that compose the surface of our globe; an antiquated person, a petrified fogey.—**fossiliferous**, fos·si·lif′ér·us, *a.* Producing or containing fossils.—**fossilization**, fos′sil·i·zā′shon, *n.* The act or process of fossilizing; the state of being fossilized.—**fossilize**, fos′sil·īz, *v.t.*—*fossilized*, *fossilizing.* To convert into a fossil; *fig.* to render permanently antiquated; to cause to be out of harmony with present time and circumstances.—*v.i.* To become a fossil; to become antiquated, rigid, and fixed.

fossorial fos·sō′ri·al, *a.* [L. *fossor*, a digger, from *fodio*, *fossum*, to dig.] Pertaining to animals which dig dwellings and seek their food in the earth; adapted for digging.

foster, fos′tér, *v.t.* [A.Sax. *fóstrian*, to nourish, from *fóster*, nourishment, from *fóda*, food. FOOD, FODDER.] To nourish or nurture; to bring up;

fāte, fär, fâre, fat, fall; mē, met, hér; pīne, pin; nōte, not, mōve; tūbe, tub, bull; oil, pound.

to cherish; to promote the growth of; to encourage; to sustain and promote.—**foster brother**, *n.* One who is a brother only by being nursed at the same breast.—**foster child**, *n.* A child nurtured by one who is not its mother or father.—**foster daughter**, *n.* One who is a daughter only by nursing.—**fosterer**, fos′tėr·ėr, *n.* One that fosters.—**foster father**, *n.* One who takes the place of a father in bringing up and educating a child.—**fosterling**, fos′tėr·ling, *n.* A foster child.—**foster mother**, *n.* A woman who takes the place of a mother in bringing up a child.—**foster parent**, *n.* A foster father or foster mother.—**foster sister**, *n.* A female, not a sister, nursed by the same person.—**foster son**, *n.* One brought up like a son, though not the person's son by birth.

foul, foul, *a.* [A.Sax. *fúl*, foul = Icel. *fúll*, Dan. *fuul*, D. *vuil*, G. *faul*, Goth. *fuls*, putrid, corrupt; same root as L. *puteo*, Skr. *púy*, to be putrid.] Covered with or containing extraneous matter, which is injurious, noxious, or offensive; filthy; dirty; not clean; turbid; muddy; scurrilous; obscene or profane; abusive; stormy, rainy, or tempestuous (*foul* weather); detestable; vile; shameful; odious; unfair; not lawful; *sports*, denoting, or pertaining to, an act committed contrary to the rules of the game; *naut.* entangled or in collision; opposed to *clear*.—*Foul ball*, *baseball*, a batted ball that falls or rolls outside the field of play bounded by two straight lines (*foul lines*) that extend from home plate past first base and third base to the boundary of the field.—*To run* or *fall foul of*, to rush upon; to attack; to run against; to stumble over or upon.—*v.t.* To make filthy; to defile; to dirty; to soil.—*v.i.* To become foul or dirty; to commit a foul; to hit a ball foul; *naut.* to come into collision; to become entangled or clogged.—*n.* The act of fouling; a colliding, or otherwise impeding due motion or progress.—**foully**, foul′li, *adv.* In a foul manner.—**foulness**, foul′nes, *n.* The quality or state of being foul or filthy.—**foulmouthed**, *a.* Using foul or vile language; uttering abuse, or profane or obscene words.

found, found, pret. & pp. of *find*.

found, found, *v.t.* [Fr. *fonder*, from L. *fundo*, to found, from *fundus*, the bottom of anything; hence also *fund*, *founder*.] To lay the basis of; to base; to establish on a basis literal or figurative; to take the first steps in erecting or building up; to originate.—*v.i.* To rest or rely; followed by *on* or *upon* (I *found upon* my own observation).—**foundation**, foun·dā′shon, *n.* The act of founding, establishing, or beginning to build; the masonry or the solid ground on which the walls of a building rest; the basis or groundwork of anything; that on which anything stands and is supported; fund invested for a benevolent purpose; endow-

ment; an endowed institution or charity.—**founder**, foun′dėr, *n.* One who founds; one who fixes, originates, or establishes.

found, found, *v.t.* [Fr. *fondre*, to melt, to cast, from L. *fundo*, *fusum*, to pour out (hence *fusc*, etc.).] To form by melting a metal and pouring it into a mold; to cast.—**founder**, foun′dėr, *n.* One who founds; one who casts metals in various forms.—**foundry**, foun′dri, *n.* [Fr. *fonderie*.] The art of casting metals; the buildings and works occupied for casting metals.

founder, foun′dėr, *v.i.* [O.Fr. *fondrer*, *afondrer*, to founder—*fond*, ground, bottom, from L. *fundus*, bottom. FOUND, to establish.] To fill or be filled and sink; to go down: said of a ship; to fail; to miscarry; to go lame: said of a horse.—*n.* Farriery, a lameness occasioned by inflammation within the hoof of a horse; an inflammatory fever or acute rheumatism.

foundling, found′ling, *n.* [Dim. formed from *found*, as *bantling* from *band*, *darling* from *dear*.] A child found without a parent or any one to take care of it.

fount, fount, *n.* [L. *fons*, *fontis*. FONT.] A spring of water; a fountain. —*Fount of types*. FONT, in this sense.—**fountain**, foun′ten, *n.* [Fr. *fontaine*, L.L. *fontana*, from L. *fons*, *fontis*.] A spring or natural source of water; the head or source of a river; an artificial spout, jet, or shower of water; a basin or other structure kept constantly supplied with water for use or for ornament; the origin or source of anything.—**fountainhead**, *n.* Primary source; origin.—**fountain pen**, *n.* A writing pen with a reservoir for furnishing a continuous supply of ink.

four, fōr, *a.* [A.Sax. *feówer* = Fris. *fiower*, Icel. *fjórir*, Dan. *fire*, G. and D. *vier*, Goth. *fidwor*, L. *quatuor*, Gr. *tettares*, Russ. *cetvero*, W. *pedwar*, Ir. *ceathair*, Skr. *chatvâr*.] Twice two; three and one.—*n.* The number consisting of twice two; the symbol representing this number.—**four-cycle**, *a.* A four-stroke cycle, as for an internal-combustion engine.—**fourflusher**, *n.* One who bluffs, boasts or deceives.—**fourfold**, fōr′fōld, *a.* Four times folded; quadruple.—**four-in-hand**, *n.* A vehicle drawn by four horses and guided by one driver holding all the reins; a necktie tied with a slipknot at the collar and hanging down the shirt front.—**fourpence**, **fourpenny**, fōr′pens, fōr′pen·i, *n.* A British silver coin of an earlier era; the sum of four British pennies.—**four-poster**, *n.* A large bed having four posts or pillars for the curtains.—**fourscore**, fōr′skōr, *a.* Four times twenty; eighty; often elliptically for fourscore years.—*n.* Twenty taken four times; eighty units.—**foursome**, fōr′sum, *n.* Game of golf between two pairs; dance or reel of two pairs. —**fourteen**, fōr′tēn, *n.* [A.Sax. *feówertýne*.] The number consisting of ten and four, or the symbol

representing it.—*a.* Four and ten; twice seven.—**fourteenth**, fōr′tēnth, *a.* The ordinal of fourteen; the fourth after the tenth.—*n.* One of fourteen equal parts in which a whole is divided.—**fourth**, fōrth, *a.* [A.Sax. *feórtha*.] The ordinal of four; the next after the third.—*n.* One of four equal parts into which a whole is divided; *mus.* an interval composed of two tones and a semitone.—*The Fourth of July*, in the U.S., the holiday celebrating the Declaration of Independence.—**fourth dimension**, *n.* The dimension that converts a three dimensional aggregate (length, breadth and thickness) into a space-time relationship; a thing outside the range of customary meaning.—**fourthly**, fōrth′li, *adv.*

fourchette, fōr·shet′, *n.* [Fr. dim. of *fourche*, fork. FORK.] A small fork-shaped piece or implement; the furculum, or wishbone, of a bird.

Fourierism, fō′ri·ėr·izm, *n.* A socialistic system or form of communism propounded by Charles *Fourier*, a Frenchman.—**Fourierist**, **Fourierite**, fō′ri·ėr·ist, fō′ri·ėr·īt, *n.* An adherent of this system.

foveate, **foveolate**, fō′vē·āt, fō′vē·ō·lāt, *a.* [L. *fovea*, a pit.] *Bot.* marked by little depressions or pits; pitted.

fowl, foul, *n.* [A.Sax. *fugel*, *fugol*, a fowl, a bird = D. and G. *vogel*, Icel. and Dan. *fugl*, Goth. *fugls*, a bird; can hardly be connected with *fly*.] A bird: often unchanged in the plural (the *fowl* of the air); now very commonly a cock or hen; a barnyard or domestic fowl.—*v.i.* To catch or kill wild fowls.—**fowler**, fou′lėr, *n.* A sportsman who pursues wild fowls.—**fowling piece**, *n.* A light gun for shooting fowls or birds of any kind.

fox, foks, *n.* [A.Sax. *fox*; G. *fuchs*, L.G. *voss*, *vos*, Prov. E. *faws*, Goth. *fauho*, fox. *Fixen* (E. *vixen*) was the A.Sax. for she-fox.] A carnivorous animal closely allied to the dog, remarkable for his cunning; a sly cunning fellow.—*v.t.* and *i.* To trick.—**foxglove**, foks′gluv, *n.* A common plant, conspicuous by its tall spike of large showy flowers in long one-sided racemes; digitalis.—**foxhound**, *n.* A hound for chasing foxes.—**foxtail grass**, *n.* Any of certain grasses with tail-like spikelets.—**fox terrier**, *n.* A small, smooth-haired or wire-haired dog, first bred to dig out foxes.—**fox trot**, *n.* A form of ballroom dance in four-four time.—**foxy**, foks′i, *a.* Wily, as of one who is cunning or sly as a fox.—**foxily**, foks′·i·li, *adv.* In a foxy manner.—**foxiness**, foks′·i·nes, *n.* Slyness.

foyer, fwä′yā, *n.* [Fr., L.L. *focarium*, a hearth, L. *focus*.] A lobby or anteroom in a public building, as a theater.

fracas, frä′kes, *n.* [Fr., from *fracasser*, to crash; It. *fracassare*, to break.] An uproar; a noisy quarrel; a disturbance.

fraction, frak′shon, *n.* [Fr. *fraction*, from L. *fractio*, a breaking, from *frango*, *fractum*, to break; akin *frail*,

fragile, fragment, fracture, infringe, etc.] A fragment; a portion; a very small part; *arith.* and *alg.* one or more of the equal parts into which a unit or whole number is divided or supposed to be divided (as $^2/_5$, $^1/_4$, .56, .004, decimal fractions); *chem.* one of several separable portions of a mixture or chemical compound.—*v.t.* To divide into fractions.—**fractional**, frak'shon·al, *a.*—*Fractional distillation*, the distillation of a mixture of liquids that have different boiling points, so that the most volatile comes over first, the others as more heat is applied, as in refining shale oil or petroleum.—**fractionary**, frak'shon·a·ri, *a.* Fractional; pertaining to a fraction or small portion of a thing.—**fractionize, fractionate**, frak·shon·īz', frak·shon'āt, *v.t.* To separate into fractions.
fractious, frak'shus, *a.* [From Prov. E. *fratch*, to quarrel or chide.] Apt to quarrel; cross; snappish; peevish; fretful.—**fractiously**, frak'shus·li, *adv.* In a fractious manner; snappishly.—**fractiousness**, frak'shus·nes, *n.* A fractious temper.
fracture, frak'tūr, *n.* [L. *fractura*, from *frango*, *fractum*, to break. FRACTION.] A breakage; a breach in a body, especially caused by violence; a crack; a rupture; *surg.* the breaking of a bone; *mineral.* the characteristic manner in which a mineral breaks, and by which its texture is displayed.—*v.t.*—*fractured*, *fracturing*. To cause fracture in; to break; to crack.—*v.i.* To undergo fracture or breaking.
fragile, fraj'il, *a.* [L. *fragilis*, from *frango*, to break. FRACTION. *Frail* is the same word.] Brittle; easily broken; easily destroyed; frail.—**fragilely**, fraj'il·li, *adv.* In a fragile manner.—**fragileness, fragility**, fraj'il·nes, fra·jil'i·ti, *n.* The condition or quality of being fragile; brittleness; delicacy of substance.
fragment, frag'ment, *n.* [L. *fragmentum*, from *frango*, to break. FRACTION.] A part broken off; a piece separated from anything by breaking; anything left uncompleted; a part separated from the rest.—**fragmental**, frag·men'tal, *a.* Consisting of fragments; fragmentary.—**fragmentarily**, frag'men·te·ri·li, *adv.* In a fragmentary manner; by piecemeal.—**fragmentariness**, frag'men·ta·ri·nes, *n.*—**fragmentary**, frag'men·te·ri, *a.* Composed of fragments or broken pieces.—**fragmentation**, frag·men·tā'shun, *n.* Separation into fragments; *biol.* mitosis or cell division, beginning with the nucleus.
fragrant, frā'grent, *a.* [L. *fragrans*, *fragrantis*, ppr. of *fragro*, to emit a scent.] Sweet of smell; affecting the olfactory nerves agreeably; having an agreeable perfume; odoriferous.—**fragrantly**, frā'grent·li, *adv.* With sweet scent.—**fragrance, fragrancy**, frā'grens, frā'gren·si, *n.* The quality of being fragrant; sweetness of smell; pleasing scent; perfume.
frail, frāl, *a.* [Fr. *frele*, O.Fr. *fraile*, L. *fragilis*, fragile. FRAGILE.] Easily broken; fragile; liable to fail and

decay; easily destroyed; perishable; not firm or durable; not strong against temptation to evil; liable to fall from virtue.—**frailly**, frāl'li, *adv.* In a frail manner; weakly.—**frailness**, frāl'nes, *n.* The condition or quality of being frail.—**frailty**, frāl'ti, *n.* The condition or quality of being frail; weakness of resolution; infirmity; liableness to be deceived or seduced; a fault proceeding from weakness; a foible.
frail, frāl, *n.* [O.Fr. *frael*, *frayel*.] A basket made of rushes, in which dried fruit is occasionally imported.
fraise, frāz, *n.* [Fr., same word as *frieze* (on a building).] *Fort.* a defense consisting of pointed stakes driven into the ramparts in a horizontal or inclined position.
framboesia, fram·bē'si·a, *n.* [Fr. *framboise*, a raspberry.] The yaws, a contagious disease prevalent in the Antilles and some parts of Africa, characterized by raspberry-like excrescences: whence the name.
frame, frām, *v.t.*—*framed*, *framing*. [A.Sax. *fremman*, to form, make, effect, from *fram*, *from*, strong, forward=*from*, prep.; O.Sax. *fremmian*, O.Fris. *frema*, Icel. *fremja*, to accomplish.] To construct by fitting and uniting together the several parts; to make, compose, contrive, devise, invent, fabricate; to fit, as for a specific end; to adjust, shape, conform; to surround or provide with a frame, as a picture.—*n.* Anything composed of parts fitted and united; fabric; structure; specifically, bodily structure; make or build of a person; the main timbers of a structure fitted and joined together for the purpose of supporting and strengthening the whole; framework; some kind of case or structure for admitting, enclosing, or supporting things; particular state, as of the mind; temper or disposition.—**frame house**, *n.* A house constructed with a wooden skeleton.—**framework**, frām'wėrk, *n.* A structure or fabric for supporting anything; a frame; fabric; structure. —**framing**, frā'ming, *n.* A framework or frame; a system of frames.
franc, frangk, *n.* [Fr., from the device *Francorum rex*, king of the French, on the coin when first struck by King John in 1360.] The French monetary unit, a silver coin worth 100 French centimes.
franchise, fran'chiz, *n.* [Fr., from *franc*, free. FRANK.] A particular privilege or right granted by a government, as the right to vote, to operate a railroad, or to form, and exercise the powers of, a corporate body.
Franciscan, fran·sis'kan, *n.* A mendicant of the order founded by St. Francis of Assisi about 1210, and also called *Minorites*, *Gray Friars*, from the former color of their habit, or *Black Friars*, from the color of the habit worn by the Conventuals.
francium, fran'si·um, *n.* An element of the alkali-metal series. Symbol, Fr; at. no., 87.

francolin, frang'ko·lin, *n.* [Dim. of Pg. *frango*, a hen.] A bird closely allied to the partridges, found throughout the warmer parts of Europe, as well as in Asia.
franc-tireur, frän'tē·rėr″, *n.* [Fr., lit. a free-shooter.] One of a body of irregular sharpshooters organized in France in the war of 1870, and employed in guerrilla warfare.
frangible, fran'ji·bl, *a.* [From L. *frango*, to break. FRACTION.] Capable of being broken; brittle.—**frangibility, frangibleness**, fran·ji·bil'i·ti, fran'ji·bl·nes, *n.* The state or quality of being frangible.
frangipani, fran·ji·pan'ni, *n.* A perfume prepared from, or imitating the odor of, the flower of a West Indian tree.
frank, frangk, *a.* [Fr. *franc*, free, originally free like the *Franks*, the word being from the name of this old Germanic tribe or nation.] Free in uttering real sentiments; not reserved.—*n.* The privilege granted by the federal government to its bureaus, legislators, and accredited representatives of foreign governments, of sending, postage free, mail concerned with official business.—*v.t.* To send by means of a frank; to transmit free of expense.—**frankly**, frangk'li, *adv.* In a frank manner; openly; candidly.—**frankness**, frangk'nes, *n.* The state or quality of being frank.—**frankpledge**, *n.* [A pledge given by free men.] An institution in early England by which the members of a tithing, composed of ten households, were made responsible for each other, so that if one committed an offense the others were bound to make reparation.
Frank, frangk, *n.* One of the Germanic race that entered the Roman Provinces and Gaul in A.D. 253, eventually establishing the Frankish Empire on the Rhine.—**Frankish**, frang'kish, *a.*
frankfurter, frangk'fėr·tėr, *n.* [From Frankfurt, German town.] Seasoned beef and pork sausage, linked and in casings.
frankincense, frangk'in·sens, *n.* [That is, pure, unadulterated incense.] A gum resin obtained from a tree inhabiting Africa and Asia, which, when burned, exudes a strong odor.
franklin, frangk'lin, *n.* [O.Fr. *frankeleyn*, *francheleyn*, from L.L. *franchilanus*, from *francus*, free. FRANK, *a.*] A freeholder; a yeoman; one whose estate was free of any feudal superior.
frantic, fran'tik, *a.* [Fr. *frénétique*, from L. *phreneticus*, from Gr. *phrenitis*, mental disorder, frenzy, from *phrēn*, the mind. FRENZY.] Mad; raving; furious; outrageous; distracted (a *frantic* person); characterized by violence, fury, and disorder (a *frantic* outburst).—**frantically, franticly**, fran'ti·kal·li, fran'tik·li, *adv.* In a frantic or furious manner.—**franticness**, fran'tik·nes, *n.*
frap, frap, *v.t.*—*frapped*, *frapping*.

[Fr. *frapper*, to strike, to frap, of Scandinavian origin.] *Naut.* to make fast or tight, as by passing ropes round a sail or a weakened vessel, or by binding tackle with yarn.

fraternal, fra·tėr′nal, *a.* [Fr. *fraternel*; L. *fraternus*, from *frater*, brother; a word cog. with E. *brother*.] Brotherly; pertaining to brothers; becoming or proceeding from brothers.—**fraternally**, fra·tėr′nal·li, *adv.* In a fraternal manner.—**fraternity**, fra·tėr′ni·ti, *n.* [Fr. *fraternité*; L. *fraternitas*.] The state or relationship of a brother; a body of men associated for their common interest, business, or pleasure; a brotherhood; a society; a class or profession of men.—**fraternization**, frat′ėr·ni·zā″shon, *n.* The act of fraternizing.—**fraternize**, frat′ėr·nīz, *v.i.* To associate or hold fellowship; to hold sympathetic intercourse; to have congenial sympathies and intercourse.—**fraternizer**, frat′ėr·nī·zėr, *n.* One who fraternizes.—**fratricide**, frat′ri·sīd, *n.* [L. *fratricidium*, the crime, *fratricida*, the criminal—*frater*, and *caedo*, to kill.] The crime of murdering a brother; one who murders or kills a brother.—**fratricidal**, frat·ri·sī′dal, *a.* Pertaining to or involving fratricide.

fraud, frad, *n.* [L. *fraus, fraudis*, Fr. *fraude*; hence *defraud*.] An act or course of deception deliberately practiced with the view of gaining an unlawful or unfair advantage; deceit; deception; imposition. ∴ *Deceit* is used of the mental process which underlies any proceeding intended to deceive; *deception* signifies the procedure by which deceit is carried out, and also that which deceives, misleads, or imposes on; while *fraud* is an act, or a series of acts of *deceit*, by which we attempt to benefit ourselves at the expense of another.—**fraudulence, fraudulency**, fra′dū·lens, fra′dū·len·si, *n.* [L. *fraudulentia*.] The quality of being fraudulent.—**fraudulent**, fra′dū·lent, *a.* [L. *fraudulentus*.] Using fraud in making bargains, contracts, etc.; given to using fraud; founded on fraud; proceeding from fraud.—**fraudulently**, fra′dū·lent·li, *adv.* In a fraudulent manner.

fraught, frat, *a.* [A participial form from old verb *fraught*, to load, a form of *freight*. FREIGHT.] Freighted‡; *fig.* filled, stored, charged, abounding, pregnant (a scheme *fraught* with mischief).—**fraughtage**, † fra′tij, *n.* Loading; cargo. (*Shak.*)

fray, frā, *n.* [Abbrev. of *affray*.] An affray; a broil, quarrel, or violent riot.—*v.t.* To fright; to terrify.

fray, frā, *v.t.* [Fr. *frayer*, from L. *fricare*, to rub (whence also *friction*).] To rub; to rub away the surface of; to fret, as cloth by wearing or the skin by friction.—*n.* A frayed or rubbed place.

freak, frēk, *n.* [A.Sax. *frec*, greedy, bold = Icel. *frekr*, greedy, exorbitant; Dan. *fraek*, bold, G. *frech*, saucy.] A sudden causeless change or turn of the mind; a whim or fancy;

a capricious prank; an odd, whimsical person.—**freakish**, frēk′ish, *a.* Addicted to freaks; whimsical; capricious; fanciful; grotesque.—**freakishly**, frēk′ish·li, *adv.* In a freakish manner.—**freakishness**, frēk′ish·nes, *n.* Capriciousness; whimsicalness.

freckle, frek′l, *n.* [O.E. *freckens, frekens*, freckles (akin to *freak*, to variegate); Icel. *freknur*, Dan. *fregner*, freckles; comp. G. *fleck*, a spot.] A spot of a yellowish color in the skin, particularly on the face, neck, and hands; any small spot or discoloration.—*v.t.* and *i.* To mark or become marked with freckles.—**freckled**, frek′ld, *pp.* and *a.* Marked with freckles.—**freckly**, frek′li, *a.* Covered with freckles.

free, frē, *a.* [A.Sax. *frí, freó* = Icel. *fri*, Dan. and Sw. *fri*, D. *vrij*, G. *frei*, Goth. *freis*, free; allied to *friend*, Goth. *frijon*, to love; Skr. *pri*, to love; perhaps also to L. *privus*, one's own, *privatus*, private.] Not being under necessity or restraint, physical or moral; exempt from subjection to the will of others; being at liberty; not in confinement; not under an arbitrary or despotic government; instituted by a free people; capable of being used, enjoyed, or taken advantage of without charge; unrestricted; open; not obstructed; going beyond due limits in speaking or acting; open; candid; frank; without care; unconcerned; liberal; not parsimonious; profuse; gratuitous; given with readiness or good will; clear; exempt; having got rid; not encumbered, affected, or oppressed; with *from*, and sometimes *of*; invested with or enjoying certain immunities; having certain privileges; with *of* (a man *free of* the city of London); *bot.* applied to parts which are not united together; *chem.* not chemically combined with any other body.—*Free agency*, the state of acting freely or without necessity or constraint of the will —*Free Church of Scotland*, that ecclesiastical body which seceded from the Established Church at the Disruption in 1843.—*Free labor*, labor performed by free persons in contradistinction to that of slaves.—*Free love*, the right to consort with those we have conceived a passion for, regardless of the shackles of matrimony.—*To make free with*, to intermeddle with; to use liberties with; to help one's self to.—*Free and easy*, unconstrained; regardless of conventionalities.—*v.t.* —*freed, freeing*. To remove from a thing any encumbrance or obstruction; to disentangle; to disengage; to rid; to strip; to clear; to set at liberty; to rescue or release from slavery, captivity, or confinement; to manumit; to loose; to exempt, as from some oppressive condition or duty.—**freeboard**, *n. Naut.* the part of a ship's side between the gunwale and the line of flotation.—**freebooter**, frē′bö·tėr, *n.* [D. *vrijbuiter*, G. *freibeuter*. BOOTY.] One who wanders about for booty or plunder; a robber; a pillager; a

plunderer.—**freeborn**, frē′born, *a.* Born free; not in vassalage; inheriting liberty.—**freedman**, frēd′man, *n.* A man who has been a slave and is manumitted.—**freedom**, frē′dum, *n.* The state of being free; exemption from slavery, servitude, confinement, or constraint; liberty; independence; frankness; openness; outspokenness; unrestrictedness.—*Freedom of the seas*, doctrine that merchant ships may traverse all waters, save those territorial, in both peace and war.—**free enterprise**, *n.* Economic system under which private businesses operate competitively to meet consumer demands and government limits its action to protecting rights of individuals.—**free fall**, *n.* Unconstrained fall of a body through air, as in a parachute jump.—**free-for-all**, *n.* An open competition; a promiscuous fight. (Colloq.)—**freehand**, frē′hand, *a.* Applied to drawing in which the hand is not assisted by any guiding or measuring instruments.—**freehanded**, *a.* Open-handed; liberal.—**freehearted**, *a.* Open; unreserved; liberal; charitable; generous.—**freehold**, frē′hōld, *n. Law*, an estate in real property, held either in fee simple or fee tail, or for life; the tenure by which such an estate is held.—**free lance**, *n.* One of the mercenary soldiers of the Middle Ages, who fought for any employer able to pay; one unattached to any political party; a writer (or artist or actor) not regularly employed by any one concern (*slang*).—**free liver**, frē′liv·ėr, *n.* One who eats and drinks abundantly; one who gives free indulgence to his appetites.—**freely**, frē′li, *adv.* In a free manner.—**freeman**, frē′man, *n.* A man who is free; one not a slave or vassal; one who enjoys or is entitled to a franchise or peculiar privilege.—**freemartin**, frē′mär·tin, *n.* A cow calf twinborn with a bull calf: generally barren.—**Freemason**, frē′mā·sn, *n.* A person belonging to a society or organization the members of which call themselves *free* and accepted *Masons.* — **Freemasonry**, frē′mā·sn·ri, *n.* The mysteries in which Freemasons are initiated.—**freeness**, frē′nes, *n.* The state or quality of being free.—**free port**, *n.* A port where ships may be unloaded and goods deposited without payment of customs.—**free-spoken**, frē′spō·kn, *a.* Outspoken.—**freestone**, frē′stōn, *n.* Any species of stone composed of sand or grit and easily cut or wrought; a kind of peach.—**freethinker**, frē′thingk·ėr, *n.* One whose opinions on religion are based on doubt and skepticism; a deist; an unbeliever; a sceptic.—**freethinking**, frē′thingk·ing, *n.—a.* Holding the principles of a freethinker.—**freethought**, frē′that, *a.* The beliefs or ways of thinking of freethinkers.—**free trade**, *n.* Trade or commerce free from restrictions, and in particular from customs duties levied on foreign commodities.—**free trader**, *n.* An advocate of free trade.—**free will**, *n.* The power

ch, *ch*ain; *ch*, Sc. lo*ch*; g, *g*o; j, *j*ob; ng, si*ng*; TH, *th*en; th, *th*in; w, *w*ig; hw, *wh*ig; zh, a*z*ure.

of directing our own actions without constraint by necessity or fate; voluntariness; spontaneousness.—*a.* Voluntary; spontaneous.

freeze, frēz, *v.i.*—*froze* (pret.), *frozen* or *froze* (pp.), *freezing* (ppr.). [A.Sax. *frysan, freosan*=D. *vriezen,* Icel. *frjósa,* Dan. *fryse,* G. *frieren;* same root as L. *pruina,* hoarfrost. Akin *frore, frost.*] To be congealed by cold; to be changed from a liquid to a solid state by the abstraction of heat; to be hardened into ice; to be of that degree of cold at which water congeals: used impersonally (it *freezes* hard); to become chilled in body with cold.—*v.t.* To congeal or cause to freeze; to harden into ice; to chill; to give the sensation of cold and shivering.—*n.* The act of freezing; frost. (*Colloq.*).—**freezer,** frē'zėr, *n.* One who or that which freezes.—**freezing point,** *n.* That degree of a thermometer at which a liquid begins to freeze; the temperature at which ordinarily water freezes. By the centigrade thermometer the freezing-point of water is $0°$ or zero; by Fahrenheit's thermometer $32°$ above zero.—**frozen,** frō'zn, *p.* and *a.* Congealed by cold; frosty; subject to severe frost; void of sympathy; wanting in feeling or interest; unsympathetic.

freight, frāt, *n.* [Formerly *fraht*=D. *vragt,* Dan. *fragt,* Sw. *frakt,* G. *fracht,* a freight or cargo. FRAUGHT.] A burden or load; goods laden for transportation by land, water, or air; the price charged or paid for the transportation of goods; transportation by common carrier, as opposed to express; a freight train.—*v.t.* To transport by freight; *fig. to pay the freight,* to bear the burden.—**freightage,** frā'tij, *n.* The act or process of freighting; money paid for freight; freight or lading (*Mil.*).—**freighter,** frā'tėr, *n.* One who freights; a ship mainly transporting freight.

French, frensh, *a.* [O.Fr. *franchois, françois,* Mod.Fr. *français,* from *France,* which received its name from the *Franks.*] Pertaining to France or its inhabitants.—*n.* The language spoken by the people of France; collectively the French people.—**French chalk,** *n.* A variety of talc resembling chalk, of a pearly white or grayish color.—**French horn,** *n.* A musical instrument of brass having several curves, and gradually widening from the mouthpiece to the other end.—**Frenchify,** frensh'i·fī, *v.t.* To make French; to imbue with French tastes or manners.—**Frenchman,** frensh'man, *n.* A man of the French nation; a native or naturalized inhabitant of France.

frenetic, frenetical, fre·net'ik, fre·net'i·kal, *a.* [Same word as *frantic.* FRENZY.] Frenzied; frantic.—**frenetically,** fre·net'i·kal·li, *adv.* In a frenetic or frenzied manner.

frenzy, fren'zi, *n.* [O.Fr. *frenaisie,* Mod.Fr. *phrénésie;* from Gr. *phrenēsis, phrenitis,* mental derangement, from *phren,* the mind. FRANTIC.] Distraction; delirium; madness; any

violent agitation of the mind approaching to distraction or temporary derangement of the mental faculties. —*v.t.*—*frenzied, frenzying.* To drive to madness; to render frenzied.— **frenzied,** fren'zid, *p.* and *a.* Affected with frenzy or madness; maddened; frantic.

frequent, frē'kwent, *a.* [Fr. *fréquent,* from L. *frequens, frequentis,* common, usual, full, crowded; same root as *farcio,* to cram (whence *farce*).] Often seen or done; often happening at short intervals; often repeated or occurring; doing a thing often; inclined to indulge in any practice.— *v.t.* (fri·kwent'). [L. *frequento;* Fr. *fréquenter.*] To visit often; to resort to often or habitually.—**frequence,**† frē'kwens, *n.* [L. *frequentia.*] A crowd; a throng; a concourse; an assembly.—**frequency,** frē'kwen·si, *n.* The state of being frequent; a frequent return or occurrence; the condition of being often repeated at short intervals.—**frequency modulation,** *Elect.* static-free broadcasting system in which the frequency of the transmitted waves is modulated in accordance with a signal.—**frequentation,** frē·kwen·tā'shon, *n.* The act or custom of frequenting.—**frequentative,** fri·kwen'ta·tiv, *a. Gram.* serving to express the frequent repetition of an action: applied to certain verbs.—*n.* A verb which denotes the frequent occurrence or repetition of an action.—**frequenter,** fri·kwen'tėr, *n.* One who frequents. —**frequently,** frē'kwent·li, *adv.* Often; many times, at short intervals; repeatedly; commonly.

fresco, fres'kō, *n.* pl. **frescoes** and **frescos,** fres'kōz. [It., fresh, from being executed on fresh plaster. FRESH.] A method of painting on walls with mineral and earthy pigments on fresh plaster, or on a wall laid with mortar not yet dry.—*v.t.* To paint in fresco, as walls.

fresh, fresh, *a.* [A.Sax. *fersc,* whence *fresh* by a common metathesis=D. *versch,* Icel. *ferskr, friskr,* Dan. *fersk, frisk,* G. *frisch;* hence It. Sp. and Pg. *fresco,* Fr. *frais, fraîche,* fresh. *Frisk* is a form of the same word.] Full of health and strength; vigorous; strong; brisk; lively; bright; not faded; undecayed; unimpaired by time; in good condition; not stale; not exhausted with labor or exertion; renewed in strength; re-invigorated; refreshing; health-giving: applied to pure cool water, and also to a rather strong wind; vivid; clearly remembered; new; recently grown, made, or obtained; not salt or salted.—*n.* A freshet; a spring of fresh water; a flood; an overflowing; an inundation.—**freshen,** fresh'n, *v.t.* To make fresh; to give a fresh appearance or character to; to make to feel fresh; to refresh; to revive.— *v.i.* To grow fresh; to grow strong (the wind *freshens*).—**freshet,** fresh'et, *n.* A small stream of fresh water; a flood or overflowing of a river, by means of heavy rains or melted snow.—**freshly,** fresh'li, *adv.* In a fresh manner.—**freshman,** fresh'-

man, *n.* A novice; a student of the first year in a university.—**freshness,** fresh'nes, *n.* The condition or quality of being fresh.—**fresh-water,** *a.* Pertaining to, produced by, or living in water that is fresh or not salt.

fret, fret, *v.t.*—*fretted, fretting.* [A. Sax. *fretan,* to eat, to gnaw, devour; D. *vreten,* G. *fressen,* O.H.G. *frezzan,* Goth. *fraïtan,* to eat, all from prefix =E. *for,* intens., and verb to *eat.*] To gnaw; to eat into; to rub or wear away; to fray; to chafe; to gall; to wear away so as to diminish; to impair; to agitate; to disturb (to *fret* the surface of the sea); *fig.* to chafe the mind of; to irritate; to tease; to make angry.—*v.i.* To become frayed or chafed; to be chafed or irritated; to become vexed or angry; to utter peevish expressions; to boil or work as angry feelings; to rankle.—*n.* A state of chafing or irritation; vexation; anger.—**fretful,** fret'ful, *a.* Disposed to fret; ill-humored; peevish; in a state of vexation.—**fretfully,** fret'ful·li, *adv.* In a fretful manner; peevishly.—**fretfulness,** fret'ful·nes, *n.* Peevishness; ill-humor.

fret, fret, *n.* [O.Fr. *freter,* to interlace, *frettes,* a grating; from L. *ferrum,* iron. Comp. also A.Sax. *fraetwe,* ornaments.] A kind of ornament formed of bands or fillets variously combined, but most frequently arranged in rectangular forms; a piece of perforated ornamental work; one of the small crossbars or ridges on the fingerboards of some stringed instruments, to regulate the pitch of the notes.—*v.t.* To ornament or furnish with frets; to variegate; to diversify.—**fretty,** fret'i, *a.* Adorned with fretwork.—**fretwork,** fret'werk, *n.* Ornamental work consisting of a series or combination of frets; designs cut through a thin plate of wood.—**fret saw,** *n.* A small saw for cutting fretwork.

friable, frī'a·bl, *a.* [L. *friabilis,* from *frio, friatum,* to crumble down.] Easily crumbled or pulverized; easily reduced to powder.—**friability, friableness,** frī·a·bil'i·ti, frī'a·bl·nes, *n.* The quality of being friable.

friar, frī'ėr, *n.* [Formerly *frere,* Fr. *frère,* O.Fr. *freire,* a brother, from L. *frater, fratris,* a brother. BROTHER.] A person belonging to one of the Roman Catholic mendicant religious orders or brotherhoods—Dominicans, Franciscans, Carmelites, Augustines, etc.; a monk.—**friar's lantern,** *n.* Will o' the wisp; marsh light.—**friary,** frī'ėr·i, *n.* A convent of friars; a monastery.

fribble, frib'l, *a.* [Perhaps corrupted from Fr. *frivole,* frivolous.] Frivolous; trifling; silly.—*n.* A frivolous, trifling, contemptible fellow.—*v.i.*— *fribbled, fribbling.* To act the fribble; to trifle.—**fribbler,** frib'lėr, *n.* A trifler; a coxcomb.—**fribbling,** frib'-ling, *a.* Frivolous; trifling.

fricandeau, frik·an·dō', *n.* [Fr., etymology doubtful.] A fricassee or other preparation of veal.

fricassee, frik·as·sē', *n.* [Fr. *fricassée,* from *fricasser,* to cook in this way: etymology doubtful.] A dish of food made by cutting chickens, veal, or other meat into pieces and stewing it in a gravy.—*v.t.*—*fricasseed, fricasseeing.* To dress in fricassee.

friction, frik'shon, *n.* [L. *frictio, frictionis,* from *frico, frictum,* to rub, to rub down.] The act of rubbing the surface of one body against that of another; attrition; *mech.* the effect of rubbing or the resistance which a moving body meets with from the surface on which it moves.—*Angle of friction,* the maximum angle at which one body will remain on another without sliding.—**fricative,** frik'a·tiv, *a.* A term applied to certain letters produced by the friction of the breath issuing through a narrow opening of the organs, as *f, v, s, z,* etc.—**frictional,** frik'shon·al, *a.* Relating to friction; moved by friction; produced by friction.—**friction clutch,** *n.* A species of loose coupling much used for connecting pieces in machines which require to be frequently engaged and disengaged. —**friction tape,** *elect.* a flat tape, both insulating and adhesive, used in repairs, etc.

Friday, frī'dā, *n.* [A.Sax. *Frige-dæg,* G. *Freytag,* the day sacred to *Frigga,* or *Freya,* the Teutonic goddess.] The sixth day of the week.—*Good Friday,* the Friday immediately preceding Easter, kept sacred as the day of Christ's crucifixion.

friend, frend, *n.* [A.Sax. *freónd,* virtually a pres. part. of *freón,* to love; like Goth. *frijonds,* from *frijon,* to love; D. *vriend,* Icel. *fraendi,* G. *freund,* a friend. *Fiend* is similarly formed. FREE.] One who is attached to another by affection; one who has esteem and regard for another and loves his society; one not hostile; one of the same nation, party, or kin; one who looks with favor upon a cause, institution, or the like; also a term of salutation or familiar address.—*Society of Friends,* the name assumed by the society of dissenters commonly called Quakers.—*To be friends with,* to feel as a friend toward; to be friendly toward: may be used when a single person is the friend of another.—*v.t.* To befriend; to support or aid.—**friendless,** frend'les, *a.* Destitute of friends.—**friendlessness,** frend'les·nes, *n.* The state of being friendless. — **friendlily,** frend'li·li, *adv.* In a friendly manner. —**friendliness,** frend'li·nes, *n.* The condition or quality of being friendly; a disposition to favor or befriend; good will; exercise of benevolence or kindness.—**friendly,** frend'li, *a.* Having the temper and disposition of a friend; disposed to promote the good of another; kind; amicable; befitting friends; not hostile; favorable; propitious.—*Friendly fire,* a fire kept within a container which has been provided for it, as a fire in a heater; opposed to *hostile fire,* a fire elsewhere than within a container provided for it. (*Fire Insurance.*) ∴ Syn. under AMICABLE.† In the manner of friends; amicably. (*Shak.*)— **friendship,** frend'ship, *n.* The feeling that subsists between friends or

binds them to one another; attachment to a person; mutual attachment; kind regard; intimacy between friends; kindness.

Friese, frēz, [*obs.*] *n.* The language of Friesland; Frisian.—**friesic,** frē'zik, *a.* Frisian.

frieze, frēz, *n.* [Fr. *frise*=It. *fregio,* Sp. *friso,* probably from Ar. *ifriz,* a ledge or a wall.] *Arch.* that part of the entablature of a column which is between the architrave and cornice; a band enriched with figures or other ornaments.

frieze, frēz, *n.* [Fr. *frise,* probably from *Friesland,* once the principal seat of its manufacture.] A coarse woolen cloth having a shaggy nap on one side.—*Chevaux de Frieze,* 'horses of Friesland', pointed stakes planted to keep off cavalry.—*v.t.*—*friezed, friezing.* To form a shaggy nap on; to frizzle; to curl.

frigate, frig'it, *n.* [Fr. *frégate,* It. *fregata;* Sp. and Pg. *fragata;* origin doubtful.] Formerly a light vessel propelled by sails and oars; later, a war vessel, rigged with sails; a U.S. warship of 5,000 to 7,000 tons, in between a destroyer and cruiser in size.—**frigate bird,** *n.* A tropical sea bird allied to the cormorants, remarkable for its powers of flight.

fright, frīt, *n.* [A.Sax. *fyrhtu, fyrhto,* fear; Dan. *frygt,* G. *furcht,* D. *vrucht,* fear. *Fear* is probably akin in origin.] Sudden and violent fear; a sudden fit of fear or dread; terror; a person of a shocking, disagreeable, or ridiculous appearance in person or dress. —*v.t.* To frighten; to affright; to scare.—**frighten,** frī'tn, *v.t.* To strike with fright; to terrify; to scare; to alarm suddenly.—**frightful,** frīt'ful, *a.* Causing fright; terrible; dreadful; awful; horrid; terrific.—**frightfully,** frīt'ful·li, *adv.* In a frightful manner; dreadfully; horribly; terribly; shockingly.—**frightfulness,** frīt'ful·nes, *n.* The quality of being frightful.

frigid, frij'id, *a.* [L. *frigidus,* from *frigeo,* to be cold, akin to *rigeo* to be numb or stiff; Gr. *rigos,* cold. *Frill* is of same origin.] Cold; wanting heat or warmth; of a very low temperature; cold in feeling or manner; wanting warmth of affection; wanting zeal, fire, energy, spirit, or animation; stiff; haughty; forbidding; lifeless.—*Frigid zones,* in geog. the two zones comprehended between the poles and the polar circles, which are about 23° 28' from the poles.—**frigidity,** fri·jid'i·ti, *n.* The state or quality of being frigid; coldness; want of warmth; coldness of feeling or manner; want of animation, ardor, or vivacity.—**frigidly,** frij'id·li, *adv.* In a frigid manner.— **frigidness,** frij'id·nes, *n.* The state of being frigid.—**frigorific, frigorifical,** frig·o·rif'ik, frig·o·rif'i·kal, *a.* [L. *frigorificus*—*frigus, frigoris,* cold, and *facio,* to make.] Causing cold.

frill, fril, *n.* [Flemish *frul,* frill, *frullen,* to have frills.] Something purely decorative; a crimped or ornamental edging of fine linen on the bosom of a shirt; a somewhat similar trimming on something else; a

ruffle; a fold of feathers or hair around the neck of a bird or beast. —*v.t.* To decorate with a frill.— **frilling,** fril'ing, *n.* Frills; ruffles.

fringe, frinj, *n.* [Fr. *frange,* fringe, It. *frangia,* from L. *fimbria,* fringe; akin to *fibra,* a fiber.] An ornament to the borders of garments, furniture, etc., consisting of threads attached at one end, the other hanging loose; something resembling a fringe; an edging; margin; extremity; *optics,* one of the colored bands of light in the phenomena of diffraction.—*v.t.* To adorn or border with or as with a fringe.—**fringed,** frinjd, *pp.* and *a.* Bordered or ornamented with a fringe or fringes.—**fringe tree,** *n.* A small American tree having snow-white flowers, which hang down like a fringe.

frippery, frip'ėr·i, *n.* [Fr. *friperie,* old clothes, from *friper,* to rumple, to spoil; from O.Fr. *frepe,* rag, tatter.] Old or castoff clothes; waste matter; useless things; trifles; traffic in old clothes; an old-clothes shop. (*Shak.*)—*a.* Trifling; contemptible.

Frisian, frizh'an, *a.* Belonging to Friesland.—*n.* A native of Friesland; the language of Friesland.

frisk, frisk, *v.i.* [O.Fr. *frisque,* brisk, lively, from the Germanic adjective corresponding to E. *fresh.* FRESH.] To leap, skip, dance, or gambol, as in gaiety or frolic; to frolic.—*v.t.* To search someone by running the hand over the clothing, also, to steal from in this manner.—*n.* A frisking; a gambol or romp.— **frisker,** fris'kėr, *n.* One who frisks.— **friskily,** fris'ki·li, *adv.* In a frisky manner.—**friskiness,** fris'ki·nes, *n.* The state or quality of being frisky.— **frisky,** fris'ki, *a.* Fond of frisking or capering; lively; frolicsome.

frit, frit, *n.* [Fr. *fritte,* from *frit,* fried. pp. of *frire,* from L. *frigo, frictum,* to roast. FRY.] The matter of which glass is made after it has been calcined or baked in a furnace.

frith, frith, *n.* Same as *Firth.*

fritillary, frit'il·la·ri, *n.* [L. *fritillus,* a dice box: from checkered markings.] The popular name of a genus of herbaceous bulbous plants.

fritter, frit'ėr, *n.* [Fr. *friture,* lit. a frying, fr. L. *frigere,* to fry.] A small amount of deep-fried batter, sometimes containing corn or fruit.

fritter, frit'ėr, *n.* [O.Fr. *freture, fraiture,* a breaking.] A fragment; a shred.—*v.t.* To break into fritters, meaning to scatter or fritter away; to waste piecemeal; to dwindle (away) little by little; to spend frivolously or in trifles.

frivolous, friv'o·lus, *a.* [L. *frivolus,* frivolous, silly, trifling; same root as *frico,* to rub (whence *friction*).] Of little weight, worth, or importance; not worth notice; trifling; trivial; given to trifling; characterized by unbecoming levity; silly; weak.— **frivolity,†** fri·vol'i·ti, *n.* The condition or quality of being frivolous or trifling; insignificance; also, the act or habit of trifling; unbecoming levity of mind or disposition.— **frivolously,** friv'o·lus·li, *adv.* In a frivolous manner. — **frivolousness,** friv′o·lus·nes, *n.* The quality of being frivolous.

friz, frizz, friz, *v.t.*—*frizzed, frizzing.* [Fr. *friser,* O.Fr. *frizer,* to curl, *frise,* frieze cloth. FRIEZE.] To curl; to crisp; to form into small curls or into little burs, as the nap of cloth.— *n.* That which is frizzed or curled.— **frizzle,** friz′l, *v.t.*—*frizzled, frizzling.* [Dim. from *frizz.*] To curl or crisp, as hair; to frizz.—*n.* A curl; a lock of hair crisped.—**frizzly, frizzy,** friz′-li, friz′i, *a.* Curly.

fro, frō, *adv.* [A.Sax. or Icel. *frá,* from; short form of *from.*] From; away; back or backward; as in the phrase *to and fro.*

frock, frok, *n.* [Fr. *froc,* a monk's habit; L.L. *frocus, flocus.*] Primarily, a woman's dress; a gown or habit worn by monks or friars; a sailor's woolen jersey.—**frock coat,** *n.* A coat with full skirts having the same length before and behind; a surcoat.

frog, frog, *n.* [A.Sax. *frocga, froga, frosc, frox;* D. *vorsch,* G. *frosch,* Dan. *frö,* Icel. *froskr.*]. The name of various amphibians, having four legs with four toes on the forefeet and five on the hind, more or less webbed, a naked body, no ribs, and no tail, and with great powers of leaping; a condition of the throat that causes hoarseness; a tender spot in the middle of the sole of a horse's foot.—**frogfish,** *n.* A fish with a wide and flattened head, larger than the body, a gaping mouth with many teeth, and spacious gill covers.— **froghopper,** *n.* A small leaping insect, the larvae of which are found on plants enclosed in a frothy liquid known as cuckoo spit.—**frog spit, frog spittle,** *n.* The frothy liquid of the larvae of the froghopper. —**frogman,** *n.* One who works underwater, usually for military reconnaissance.

frog, frog, *n.* A fastening for a frock or coat in the form of a tassel or large button passed through a loop on the breast; the loop of the scabbard of a bayonet or sword.—*v.t.*— *frogged, frogging.* To ornament or fasten with a frog.

frolic, frol′ik, *a.* [From D. *vrolijk,* from *vro*=O.Fris. *fro,* Dan. *fro,* glad, and *lijk*=E. *like;* so G. *fröhlich,* from *froh,* joyful, and *lich,* like.] Gay; merry; full of mirth; dancing, playing, or frisking about.—*n.* A wild or merry prank; a flight of levity or gaiety and mirth; a scene of gaiety and mirth; a merrymaking.— *v.i.*—*frolicked* (frol′ikt),*frolicking.* To play merry pranks; to play tricks of levity, mirth, and gaiety.— **frolicsome,** frol′ik·sum, *a.* Full of gaiety and mirth; given to frolics; sportive. — **frolicsomely,** frol′ik-sum·li, *adv.* In a frolicsome manner. —**frolicsomeness,** frol′ik·sum·nes, *n.*

from, from, *prep.* [A.Sax. *from, fram,* O.Sax. O.H.G. and Goth. *fram,* from; Icel. *fram,* forward, *frá,* from; Dan. *frem, fra,* from; cog. with L. *peren* in *perendie,* the day after tomorrow, Gr. *peran,* Skr. *param,* beyond. Allied to *far, forth,* etc.] Out of the neighborhood of; leaving

behind; by reason of; out of; by aid of; denoting source, beginning, distance, absence, privation, or departure, sometimes literally and sometimes figuratively; the antithesis and correlative of *from* is *to.*

frond, frond, *n.* [L. *frons, frondis,* a leaf.] *Bot.* a term used to designate the leaf of the sporophyte generation of the fern.

Fronde, frond, *n.* [Fr.] The party in opposition to Mazarin, the French prime minister, 1648-53, with civil war as result.

front, frunt, *n.* [Fr. *front,* L. *frons, frontis,* the forehead (allied to E. *brow*); seen also in *affront, confront,* etc.] The forehead, or part of the face above the eyes; the whole face; boldness of disposition; impudence; the part or side of anything which seems to look out or to be directed forward; the face or forepart; the foremost rank; position directly before the face of a person or the foremost part of anything; a set of false hair or curls for a lady; the van of war; the area of warfare in campaign; shirt front, real or false.—*To come to the front,* to take a high rank in one's profession, in society, etc.—*a.* Relating to the front or face; having a position in the front.—*v.t.* To oppose face to face; to stand in front of or over against; to face; to appear in the presence of; to confront; to supply with a front; to adorn in front.—*v.i.* To have the face or front in some direction.— **frontage,** frun′tij, *n.* The front part of any structure or object; extent of front.—**frontal,** frun′tal, *n.* Something worn on the forehead; a frontlet; an ornamental band for the hair; *arch.* a little pediment over a door or window.—*a.* Belonging to the forehead.—*Frontal attack,* attack on the front, opposed to flank or rear.—**frontal bone,** *a.* The bone forming the upper front part of the cranium.-**frontier,** frun′tėr, *n.* [Fr. *frontière,* a frontier, a border.] That part of a country which fronts or faces another country; the confines or extreme part of a country bordering on another country; an unsettled area or new idea that offers a challenge (as *The New Frontier.*)— **frontiersman,** frun·tėrz′man, *n.* A man living on the frontier.—**frontispiece,** frun′tis·pēs, *n.* An ornamental figure or engraving on the first page of a book or at the beginning. —**frontlet,** frunt′let, *n.* A fillet or band worn on the forehead.

frost, frost, *n.* [A.Sax. *frost, forst,* from *freósan,* to freeze; Icel. Dan. Sw. and G. *frost,* D. *vorst.* FREEZE.] That state or temperature of the air which occasions freezing or the congelation of water; freezing weather; frozen dew; rime; hoarfrost; coldness or severity of manner or feeling. —*v.t.* To injure by frost; to cover or ornament with anything resembling hoarfrost, as with white sugar; to furnish with frost nails.—*Frosted glass,* glass roughened on the surface, so as to destroy its transparency.— **frostbite,** *n.* A state of insensibility

or deadness with arrested circulation in any part of the body, such as the nose and ears, occasioned by exposure to severe frost.—*v.t.*—*frostbit* (pret.),*frostbitten, frostbit* (pp.); *frostbiting* (ppr.). To affect with frostbite. —**frostily,** fros′ti·li, *adv.* In a frosty manner; with frost or excessive cold; without warmth of affection; coldly.—**frostiness,** fros′ti·nes, *n.* The state or quality of being frosty. —**frosting,** fros′ting, *n.* A coating resembling frost; the composition resembling hoarfrost used to cover cake, etc.—**frostwork,** frost′wėrk, *n.* The beautiful covering of hoarfrost deposited on shrubs or other natural objects.—**frosty,** fros′ti, *a.* Attended with frost; of a freezing temperature; affected by frost; without warmth of affection or courage; resembling hoarfrost; grayhaired.

froth, froth, *n.* [A.Scandinavian word =Icel. *frotha, frauth,* Dan. *fraade,* froth, foam.] The bubbles caused in liquors by fermentation or agitation; spume; foam; empty talk; mere words without sense; light, unsubstantial matter.—*v.t.* To cause to foam or produce froth; to vent, or give expression to what is light, unsubstantial, or worthless.—*v.i.* To foam; to throw up or out froth.— **frothily,** froth′i·li, *adv.* In a frothy manner.—**frothiness,** froth′i·nes, *n.* The state or quality of being frothy. —**frothy,** froth′i, *a.* Full of or accompanied with froth; consisting of froth or light bubbles; foamy; light, empty, or unsubstantial; given to empty display.

frounce, frouns,*v.t.*—*frounced, frouncing.* [Fr. *froncer,* D. *fronssen,* to wrinkle, from a hypothetical L.L. *frontiare,* to wrinkle the brows, from L. *frons,* the forehead (whence *front*). *Flounce* (of a dress) is the same work.] To form into plaits or wrinkles; to adorn with fringes, plaits, etc.—*n.* A wrinkle, plait, or curl; a flounce.

frow, frō, *n.* A wedge-shaped tool with a handle used for splitting wood.

froward, frō′wėrd, *a.* [From *fro*= from, and *-ward,* denoting direction, being thus the reverse of *to-ward,* and nearly equivalent to *way-ward* (*awayward*); A. Sax. *fromweard,* turned away, about to depart.] Not willing to comply with what is right or reasonable; perverse; ungovernable; refractory; disobedient; peevish.—**frowardly,** frō′wėrd·li, *adv.* In a froward manner.—**frowardness,** frō′wėrd·nes, *n.* The quality of being froward.

frown, froun, *v.i.* [Fr. *frogner,* in *se refrogner,* to knit the brow, to frown; of doubtful origin.] To express displeasure, severity, or sternness by contracting the brow; to put on a stern look; to scowl; to show displeasure or disapprobation; to be ominous of evil; to lower (the clouds *frown*).—*n.* A contraction or wrinkling of the brow, or a severe or stern look expressive of displeasure; a scowl; frown.—**frowningly,** frou′-ning·li, *adv.* In a frowning manner.

frowzy, frowsy, frou′zi, *a.* [Comp. Prov. E. *froust*, a musty smell, also Prov. E. *frow*, a slattern, from D. *vrow*, G. *frau*, a woman.] Fetid; musty; rank; dingy; ill-colored; in a state of disorder; slovenly; slatternly.

froze, frozen, frōz, frō′zn. See FREEZE.

fructescence, fruk·tes′ens, *n.* [From L. *fructus*, fruit. FRUIT.] *Bot.* the time when the fruit of a plant arrives at maturity and its seeds are dispersed; the fruiting season.—**fructiferous,** fruk·tif′ėr·us, *a.* Bearing or producing fruit.—**fructification,** fruk′ti·fi·kā″shon, *n.* The act of forming or producing fruit; the act of fructifying or rendering productive of fruit; fecundation; the organs concerned in the production of the fruit of a plant.—**fructify,** fruk′ti·fī, *v.t.* [Fr. *fructifier*.] To make fruitful; to render productive; to fertilize.—*v.i.* To bear or produce fruit.—**fructose,** fruk′tōs, *n.* A variety of sugar from fruit.

frugal, frö′gal, *a.* [L. *frugalis*, from *frugi*, lit. fit for food, hence, worthy, temperate, dative case of *frux, frugis*, fruit; akin to *fruit*.] Economical in regard to expenditure; thrifty; sparing; not profuse, prodigal, or lavish; saving.—**frugality,** frö·gal′i·ti, *n.* The quality of being frugal; a prudent and sparing use of anything.—**frugally,** frö′gal·li, *adv.* In a frugal manner.—**frugalness,** frö′gal·nes, *n.* Frugality.

frugiferous, frö·jif′ėr·us, *a.* [L. *frugifer—frux, frugis*, fruit, and *fero*, to bear.] Producing fruit or crops; fruitful; fructiferous.—**frugivorous,** frö·jiv′ėr·us, *a.* [L. *frux, frugis*, and *voro*, to eat.] Feeding on fruits, seeds, or corn, as birds and other animals.

fruit, fröt, *n.* [Fr. *fruit*, from L. *fructus*, fruit, from *fruor, fructus*, to enjoy, from a root seen in E. verb to *brook*, originally to enjoy; akin *frugal, fruition*.] Whatever vegetable products the earth yields for the use of man and the lower animals (in this sense generally in the plural); in a more limited sense, the reproductive product of a tree or other plant; especially, the edible succulent products of certain plants, generally covering and including their seeds; such products collectively; *bot.* the seed of a plant, or the mature ovary, composed essentially of two parts, the pericarp and the seed; the produce of animals; offspring; young; something that results; effect, result, or consequence.—*v.i.* To produce or yield fruit.—**fruitage,** frö′tij, *n.* Fruit collectively; product or produce.—**fruitcake,** fröt′cake, *n.* A round or oblong loaf cake containing several varieties of spice and fruit; usually quite rich.—**fruitful,** fröt′ful, *a.* Producing fruit in abundance; very productive; prolific; bearing children; not barren; producing or presenting in abundance; productive (*fruitful* in expedients).—**fruitfully,** fröt′fu·li, *adv.* In a fruitful

manner; plenteously; abundantly.—**fruitfulness,** fröt′ful·nes, *n.* The state or quality of being fruitful; productiveness; fertility; fecundity.—**fruitless,** fröt′les, *a.* Not bearing fruit; destitute of fruit or offspring; productive of no advantage or good effect; vain.—**fruitlessly,** fröt′les·li, *adv.* In a fruitless manner.—**fruitlessness,** fröt′les·nes, *n.* The state or quality of being fruitless or unprofitable.—**fruity,** frö′ti, *a.* Resembling fruit; having the taste or flavor of fruit.

fruition, frö·ish′on, *n.* [From L. *fruor, fructus* or *fruitus*, to use or enjoy. FRUIT.] Use or possession of anything, especially when accompanied with pleasure; the pleasure derived from use of possession; enjoyment.

frumentaceous, frö·men·tā′shus, *a.* [L. *frumentaceus*, from *frumentum*, corn; same root as *fructus*, fruit. FRUIT.] Having the character of or resembling wheat or other cereal.—**frumenty,** frö′men·ti, *n.* [L. *frumentum*, wheat.] A dish made of hulled wheat boiled in milk and seasoned; furmenty.

frump, frump, *n.* [Connected with *frampold*, or with Prov. E. *frumple*, D. *frommelen*, to wrinkle or crumple.] A cross tempered, old-fashioned female.—**frumpish,** frump′ish, *a.* Cross-tempered; cross-grained; scornful; old fashioned as to dress.—**frumpy,** frump′i, *a.* Cross tempered; frumpish.

frustrate, frus′trāt, *v.t.*—*frustrated, frustrating.* [L. *frustror, frustratus*, from *frustra*, in vain, same root as *fraus*, fraud.] To make to be in vain or of no avail; to bring to nothing; to prevent from taking effect; to defeat; to balk.—**frustration,** frus·trā′shon, *n.* The act of frustrating.—**frustrative,** frus′tra·tiv, *a.* Tending to frustrate or defeat.

frustum, frus′tum, *n.* [L., a piece, same root as *frustra*, in vain, *fraus*, fraud, etc.] *Geom.* the part of a solid (as a cone or a pyramid) left by cutting off the top portion by a plane; a truncated solid.

frutescent, frö·tes′ent, *a.* [From L. *frutex, fruticis*, a shrub.] *Bot.* having the appearance or habit of a shrub; shrubby.—**fruticose,** frö′ti·kōs, *a.* [L. *fruticosus*.] Pertaining to shrubs; shrubby.

fry, frī, *v.t.*—*fried, frying.* [Fr. *frire*, to fry, from L. *frigo*, to fry, roast, or parch; Skr. *bhrij*, to parch.] To cook in a pan over a fire along with fat or butter.—*v.i.* To be cooked as above; to simmer; to be agitated or vexed.—*n.* A dish of anything fried; state of vexation or mental agitation.—**fryer, frier,** frī′ėr, *n.* One who or that which fries; a young chicken, suitable for frying.

fry, frī, *n.* [Icel. *frae, frjo*, spawn; Goth. *fraiv*, seed.] Young of fishes at a very early stage; a swarm of little fishes; a swarm of small animals, or of young people; small or insignificant objects collectively.

fuchsia, fū′shi·a, *n.* [From the discoverer Leonard *Fuchs*, a German

botanist.] A genus of beautiful flowering shrubs, natives of South America, Mexico, and New Zealand, having a funnel-shaped, colored, deciduous, four-parted calyx; a beautiful aniline color; magenta.

fuddle, fud′l, *v.t.*—*fuddled, fuddling.* [From a form *fuzzle*, akin to L.G. *fusslig*, G. *fusselig*, drunk.] To make foolish or stupid by drink; to make tipsy or intoxicated; to confuse or muddle.

fudge, fuj, *v.t.* and *i.*—*fudged, fudging.* [Origin unknown.] To make up or invent (a false story); to fabricate; to foist; to interpolate.—*n.* A made-up story; a creamy candy made of sugar, milk, and butter, often flavored with chocolate.

fuel, fū′el, *n.* [Norm. Fr. *fuayl, fouoyle, foualle*, from L.L. *focale*, from L. *focus*, a hearth, a fireplace. FOCUS.] Any matter used to produce heat or power; anything that feeds excitement.—*v.t.* and *i.*—*fueled, fueling.* To supply or get fuel.—**fuel cell,** fū′el sel, *n.* A device that produces electrical energy by direct conversion of chemical energy, combining hydrogen and oxygen to produce water and electricity.

fugacious, fū·gā′shus, *a.* [L. *fugax, fugacis*, from *fugio*, to flee.] Flying or disposed to fly; volatile; fleeting.—*Fugacious corolla, bot.* one that is soon shed.—**fugaciousness,** fū·gā′shus·nes, *n.* The quality of being fugacious.—**fugacity,** fū·gas′i·ti, *n.* The quality of being fugacious; fugaciousness; volatility; instability; transitoriness.—**fugitive,** fū′ji·tiv, *a.* [Fr. *fugitif*, L. *fugitivus*, from L. *fugio*, to flee.] Apt to flee away or be dissipated; volatile; staying or lasting but a short time; fleeting; not fixed or durable (*fugitive* dyes); fleeing or running from danger or pursuit, duty or service; as a literary term, applied to compositions which are short, unimportant, and published at intervals.—*n.* One who flees; a deserter; one who flees from danger or duty; one who flees for refuge.—**fugitively,** fū′ji·tiv·li, *adv.* In a fugitive manner.

fugleman, flugleman, fū′gl·man, flö′gl·man, *n.* † [G. *flügelmann*, a man at the head of a file or a wing, from *flügel*, a wing.] A soldier especially expert and well drilled, who takes his place in front of soldiers, as an example or model to the others in their exercises; a file leader; hence, any one who sets an example for others to follow.

fugue, fūg, *n.* [Fr., from L. *fuga*, a flight.] *Mus.* a composition in parts that do not all begin at once, but as it were, follow or pursue each other successively.

führer, fuehrer, fü′rėr, *n.* [G.] A leader or guide in Germany; the chancellor of the Third Reich.

fulcrum, ful′krum, *n.* pl. **fulcra, fulcrums,** [L., the post or foot of a couch, from *fulcio*, to support.] A prop or support; *mech.* the point about which a lever turns in lifting a body.

fulfill, fulfil, ful·fil′, *v.t.*—*fulfilled,*

fulfilling. [A compound of *full* and *fill*; A.Sax. *fulfyllan*.] To accomplish or carry into effect, as a prophecy, promise, intention, design, desire, prayer, bargain, etc.; to perform; to complete by performance; to complete (a term of years)‡.—**fulfiller**, fu̱l·fil′ėr, *n.* One that fulfills or accomplishes.—**fulfillment, fulfilment**, fu̱l·fil′ment, *n.* Execution; performance.

fulgent, ful′jent, *a.* [L. *fulgens, fulgentis*, from *fulgeo*, to shine.] Shining; dazzling; exquisitely bright.—**fulgently**, ful′jent·li, *adv.* In a fulgent manner; dazzlingly; glitteringly.

fulguration, ful·gū·rā′shon, *n.* [L. *fulguratio*, from *fulgur*, lightning.] The flashing of lightning; *assaying*, the sudden brightening of the melted globules of gold and silver in the cupel.—**fulgurite**, ful′gū·rīt, *n.* Any rocky substance that has been fused or vitrified by lightning.—**fulgurous**, ful′gū·rus, *a.* Flashing like lightning.

fuliginous, fū·lij′i·nus, *a.* [L. *fuliginosus*, from *fuligo*, soot.] Pertaining to soot; sooty; smoky; resembling smoke; dusky.—**fuliginously**, fū·lij′i·nus·li, *adv.* In a smoky manner; duskily.

full, fu̱l, *a.* [A.Sax. *ful* = Icel. *fullr*, Sw. *full*, Dan. *fuld*, Goth. *fulls*, G. *voll*; same root as L. *plenus*, full, *pleo*, to fill (as in *complete*). *Fill* is a derivative.] Having within its limits all that it can contain; replete; completely or largely supplied or furnished; abounding; supplied; occupied; not vacant; plump; filled out; inclined to be stout or corpulent; saturated; sated; abundant in quantity; plenteous; not defective or partial; entire; adequate; mature; perfect (*full* supply, accomplishment, age; a *full* stop); loud, clear, and distinct (voice); giving ample details or arguments; copious (a *full* account; the speech was *full*).—*Full brothers* or *sisters*, children of the same father and the same mother.—*Full cousin*, the son or daughter of an aunt or uncle.—*Full cry*, a term in *hunting* signifying that all the hounds have caught the scent and give tongue in chorus; hence, hot pursuit; hard chase.—*Full dress*, a dress which etiquette requires to be worn on occasions of ceremony and the like.—*Full moon*, the moon with its whole disk illuminated; also, the time when the moon is in this position.—*n.* The state of being full; complete measure; utmost extent; highest state or degree (fed to the *full*; the *full* of the moon).— *Written in full*, written without contractions; written in words, not in figures.—*adv.* Quite; fully; equally; completely; altogether; exactly (*full* in the center); directly; straight (he looked him *full* in the face); to satiety (to sup *full* of horrors). ∴ *Full* is often used, especially in poetry, to heighten or strengthen the signification of adjectives and adverbs (*full* sad), and is prefixed to other words, chiefly participles, to express utmost extent or degree (*full*-blown, *full*-

grown).—**fullback**, fu̱l′bak, *n.* In football, a back; originally the one standing farthest behind the line of scrimmage.—**full-blooded**, *a.* Having a full supply of blood; of pure blood or extraction; thoroughbred.—**full-blown** *a.* Fully expanded, as a blossom; mature (*full-blown* beauty). —**full house**, in poker, a hand containing three of a kind and a pair.—**fullness**, fu̱l′nes, *n.* The state or quality of being full or filled.—*In the fullness of time*, at the proper or destined time.—**fully**, fu̱l′li, *adv.* In a full manner; to the full extent; so as to be full; without lack or defect; completely; entirely.

full, fu̱l, *v.t.* [Partly from A.Sax. *fullian*, to whiten, *fullere*, a fuller, a bleacher, from L. *fullo*, a fuller; partly from Fr. *fouler*, to tread, to full or felt, from L.L. *fullare*, to full, also from L. *fullo*.] To thicken and condense the fibers of (woolen cloth) by wetting and beating; to scour, cleanse, and thicken in a mill.—*v.i.* To become fulled.—**fuller**, fu̱l′ėr, *n.* One who fulls; one whose occupation is to full cloth; one who bleaches or whitens (N.T.)‡.—**fuller's earth**, *n.* A variety of clay or marl, useful in scouring and cleansing cloth.

fulmar, fu̱l′mar, *n.* [Icel. *fúlmár*, lit. foul mew, from its feeding on putrid substances.] A marine swimming bird which inhabits the northern seas in prodigious numbers, and is valued for its feathers, down, and the oil it yields.

fulminate, ful′mi·nāt, *v.i.*—*fulminated, fulminating*. [L. *fulmino, fulminatum*, from *fulmen*, lightning, contr. for *fulgimen*, from *fulgeo*, to flash, whence *fulgent*.] To thunder; to explode with a loud noise; to detonate; to issue threats, denunciations, censures, and the like.—*v.t.* To cause to explode; to utter or hurl out (denunciation).—*n.* A kind of explosive compound.—**fulminant**, ful′mi·nant, *a.* [L. *fulminans, fulminantis*.] Thundering; making a loud noise.—**fulminating**, ful′mi·nā·ting, *p.* and *a.* Thundering; exploding; detonating.—*Fulminating powder*, a mixture of niter, sulfur, and potash.—**fulmination**, ful·mi·nā′shon, *n.* The act of fulminating; that which is fulminated or thundered forth, as a menace or censure. —**fulminatory**, ful′mi·na·to·ri, *a.* Sending forth thunders or fulminations.—**fulmine**, ful′min, *v.t.*—*fulmined, fulmining*. To fulminate or give utterance to in an authoritative or vehement manner.—*v.i.* To thunder; to fulminate or send forth denunciations, etc.—**fulminic**, ful·min′ik, *a.* Capable of detonation: applied to an acid.

fulsome, fu̱l′sum, *a.* [Partly from *full*, and term. *-some*, partly from old *ful*, foul.] Cloying‡; surfeiting‡; offensive from excess of praise; gross (flattery, compliments); nauseous; disgusting.—**fulsomely**, fu̱l′sum·li, *adv.* In a fulsome manner.—**fulsomeness**, fu̱l′sum·nes, *n.*

fulvous, ful′vus, *a.* [L. *fulvus*, yellow.]

Yellow; tawny; of a tawny yellow color.

fumarole, fū′ma·rōl, *n.* [It. *fumarola*, from L. *fumus*, smoke.] A hole from which smoke or gases issue (in a volcanic locality).

fumble, fum′bl, *v.t.* [From D. *fommelen*, L.G. *fummelen*, to fumble, Sw. *fumla*, to handle feebly.] To feel or grope about; to grope about in perplexity; to seek or search for something awkwardly; to employ the hands or fingers in an awkward fashion; in football, baseball, and other games, to drop the ball or fail to handle it properly.—*n.* A bungling try.—**fumbler**, fum′blėr, *n.*

fume, fūm, *n.* [L. *fumus*, smoke, vapor, fume; akin to Skr. *dhûma*, smoke, the root being that of E. *dust*.] Smoky or vaporous exhalation, especially if possessing narcotic or other remarkable properties; volatile matter arising from anything; exhalation, generally in the plural; mental agitation clouding or affecting the understanding; an idle conceit or vain imagination (*Shak.*).—*v.i.*—*fumed, fuming*. To yield fumes or exhalations; to pass off in vapors; with *away*; to be in a rage; to be hot with anger.—*v.t.* To fumigate; to perfume; to offer incense to.—

fumette, fū·met′, *n.* [Fr. *fumet*, from L. *fumus*.] The scent of meat, as venison or game when kept too long; the scent from meats cooking.—**fumigate**, fū′mi·gāt, *v.t.*—*fumigated, fumigating*. [L. *fumigo, fumigatum*.] To apply smoke to; to expose to fumes or vapors (as of sulfur) in cleansing infected apartments, clothing, etc.—**fumigation** fū·mi·gā′shon, *n.* The act of fumigating.

fumitory, fū′mi·to·ri, *n.* [O.E. *fumetere*, Fr. *fumeterre*, from L. *fumus*, smoke, and *terra*, the earth, because said to make the eyes water like smoke.] A common garden and field plant with much-divided leaves and purplish flowers, formerly much used in medicine.

fun, fun, *n.* [Perhaps connected with *fond*, O.E. *fon*, foolish, *fon, fonne*, to be foolish; or Ir. *fonn*, delight.] Sport; mirthful drollery; frolicsome amusement.—*To make fun of*, to turn into ridicule.—*Not to see the fun*, to be unwilling to regard something in the light of a joke.—**funnily**, fun′i·li, *adv.* In a funny, droll, or comical manner.—**funny**, fun′i, *a.* Making fun; droll; comical. —*n.* Comic strip.—**funny bone**, *n.* Crazy bone; the elbow joint, where the ulnar nerve rests.

funambulate, fū·nam′bū·lāt, *v.t.* [L. *funambulus*, a rope-walker, *funis*, rope, and *ambulo, ambulatum*, to walk on a rope.]—**funambulist**, fū·nam′bū·list, *n.* A rope walker or rope dancer.

function, fungk′shon, *n.* [Fr. *fonction*, L. *functio*, from *fungor, functus*, to perform; to execute; same root as Skr. *bhuj*, to enjoy; akin *defunct*.] Office, duty, or business belonging to a person in virtue of a particular station or character; what a person or body of persons has specially to perform in some capacity (the *functions* of a bishop, of a parent); the specific office or action which any organ or system of organs performs in the animal or vegetable economy, as the body, the mind, or a faculty of the mind (the *function* of memory, of nutrition); a formal or ceremonious meeting; *math.* a quantity so connected with another that no change can be made in the latter without producing a corresponding change in the former.—**functional,** fungk'shon·al, *a.* Pertaining to a function or functions: thus a *functional* disease is one in which some one or other of the animal functions is deranged, and is often opposed to an *organic* disease, in which an organ is directly affected.—**functionally,** fungk'shon·al·li, *adv.*—**functionary,** fungk'shon·a·ri, *n.* One who holds an office or trust.—**functionalism,** fungk'shon·al·izm, *n.* Any doctrine that stresses function, use and adaptation.

fund, fund, *n.* [Fr. *fond,* land, fund, a merchant's stock, from L. *fundus,* foundation, a piece of land, estate, whence also *found, founder, profound.*] A stock or capital; a sum of money appropriated as the foundation of some commercial or other operation; money which an individual may possess or can employ for carrying on trade; in England, money lent to government and constituting part of the national debt (used in plural); money set apart for any object more or less permanent; a store laid up from which one may draw at pleasure; stock; supply (a *fund* of amusement, of anecdote).—*Sinking fund,* a fund or stock set apart, generally at certain intervals, for the reduction of a debt of a government or corporation.—*Consolidated fund.* Under CONSOLIDATE.—*v.t.* To provide and appropriate a fund or permanent revenue for the payment of the interest of; to put into the form of bonds or stocks bearing regular interest; to place in a fund.—*Funded debt,* a debt existing in the form of bonds bearing regular interest; a debt forming part of the permanent debt of a country at a fixed rate of interest.

fundament, fun'da·ment, *n.* [L. *fundamentum,* a groundwork or foundation, from *fundo, fundatum,* found. FUND, FOUND.] The part of the body on which one sits; the anus.—**fundamental,** fun·da·men'tal, *a.* Pertaining to a groundwork, root, or basis; at the root or foundation of something; essential; elementary (a *fundamental* truth or principle).—*n.* A leading or primary principle, rule, law, or article; something essential.—**fundamentally,** fun·da·men'tal·li, *adv.* In a fundamental manner.

funeral, fū'nėr·al, *n.* [Fr. *funérailles,* from L. *funis, funeris,* a burial.] The ceremony of burying a dead human body; interment; burial; obsequies. —*a.* Pertaining to burial; used at the interment of the dead.—**funereal,**

fū·nē'ri·al, *a.* [L. *funereus.*] Suiting a funeral; pertaining to or calling up thoughts of death or the grave; dismal; mournful; gloomy.—**funereally,** fū·nē·ri'al·li, *adv.*

fungus, fung'gus, *n.* pl. **fungi,** fun'jī. [L. *fungus,* mushroom.] Any of the parasitic plants that lack chlorophyll, or plants that live on dead tissue, such as the mushrooms, molds, mildew, smut, rust, dry rot, etc.— **fungal,** fung'gal, *n.* A plant of the class of fungi and lichens.—*a.* Relating to fungi.—**fungivorous,** fun·jiv'ėr·us, *a.* [L. *fungus,* and *voro,* to devour.] Feeding on mushrooms or fungi.—**fungoid,** fung'goid, *a.* Having the appearance or character of a fungus.—**fungosity,** fung·gos'i·ti, *n.* The quality of being fungous; fungous excrescence.—**fungous,** fung'gus, *a.* Like a fungus; having the character of one of the fungi; hence, growing or springing up suddenly, but not substantial or durable.— **fungus,** fung'gus, *n.* A member of the fungi; *med.* a spongy morbid excrescence; a diseased state dependent on the growth of vegetable parasites.

funicle, fū'ni·kl, *n.* [L. *funiculus,* dim. of *funis,* a cord.] A small cord; a small ligament; *bot.* the little stalk by which a seed is attached to the placenta.

funicular, fū·nik'ū·lėr, *a.* [L. *funiculus,* dim. of *funis,* a cord.] Pertaining to a small cord; dependent upon the tension of a cord.—**funicular railway,** fū·nik'ū·lėr rāl'wā, *n.* A cable railway.

funk, fungk, *n.* Fear; cowardice.—*v.i.* To be in terror. (*Colloq.*)

funnel, fun'el, *n.* [Prov. Fr. *enfounil,* a funnel, from L. *infundibulum,* a funnel—*in,* into, and *fundo, fusum,* to pour, whence *fuse,* to melt. FUSE.] A utensil for conveying fluids into vessels with small openings, being a kind of hollow cone with a pipe issuing from its apex; the shaft or hollow channel of a chimney; a cylindrical iron chimney in steamships for the furnaces, rising above the deck.—**funneled, funnelled,** fun'eld, *a.* Having a funnel or funnels; funnel-shaped.

funny, fun'i, *a.* See FUN.

fur, fėr, *n.* [Fr. *fourrure,* fur, O.Fr. *forre, fuere,* a case or cover, from an old German word corresponding to modern G. *futter,* covering, case, lining, *fur* being so called from the skins of animals being used for lining or trimming clothes.] The short, fine, soft hair of certain animals growing thick on the skin, and distinguished from the hair, which is longer and coarser; the skin of certain wild animals with the fur; peltry; a coating regarded as resembling fur, as morbid matter collected on the tongue.—*a.* Made of fur.—*v.t.*—**furred, furring.** To line, face, or cover with fur.— **furrier,** fėr'i·ėr, *n.* A dealer in or dresser of furs.—**furriery,** fėr'i·ėr·i, *n.* Furs in general; the trade of a furrier.—**furry,** fėr'i, *a.* Covered with fur; dressed in fur; consisting

of fur or skins; resembling fur; coated with a deposit of morbid matter.

furbelow, fėr'bė·lō, *n.* [Fr. *falbala, farbala,* It. Sp. Pg. *falbala,* Sp. also *farfala,* flounce; origin unknown.] A kind of flounce; the plaited border of a petticoat or gown.

furbish, fėr'bish, *v.t.* [Fr. *fourbir,* from O.H.G. *furban,* to clean, to furbish, G. *fürben,* to sweep.] To rub or scour to brightness; to polish up; to burnish; *fig.* to clear from taint or stain; to brighten.—**furbisher,** fėr'bish·ėr, *n.* One who or that which furbishes.

furcate, fėr'kāt, *a.* [L. *furca,* a fork.] Forked; branching like the prongs of a fork.—**furcation,** fėr·kā'shon, *n.* A forking or branching.—**furcula,** fėr'kū·la, *n.* [L., dim. of *furca.*] The forked bone formed by the union of the collarbones in many birds; the wishbone.

furfur, fėr'fėr, *n.* [L.] Dandruff; scurf; scales like bran.—**furfuraceous,** fėr·fėr·ā'shus, *a.* [L. *furfuraceus.*] Branny; scurfy; like bran.

furious. See FURY.

furl, fėrl, *v.t.* [Fr. *ferler,* from *ferm, ferme,* firm, fast, and *lier,* to bind.] To roll up tightly, as a flag, or gather in firmly, as a sail.—*v.i.* To fold, as in being furled.—*n.* A furling.

furlong, fėr'long, *n.* [A.Sax. *furlang*— *furh,* a furrow, and *lang,* long.] A measure of length, being the eighth part of a mile; forty rods.

furlough, fėr'lō, *n.* [Dan. *forlov,* D. *verlof,* G. *verlaub,* leave, furlough, lit. leave off or away—*fur* being equivalent to *for-* in *forbear,* and *lough,* akin to *leave, lief.*] Leave or license given to a soldier to be absent from service for a certain time.—*v.t.* To furnish with a furlough.

furmenty, furmety, fėr'men·ti, fėr'me·ti, *n.* Same as *Frumenty.*

furnace, fėr'nes, *n.* [Fr. *fournaise,* from L. *fornax,* an oven.] An enclosed structure in which is kept up a strong fire for melting ores or metals, heating the boiler of a steam engine, and other such purposes; *fig.* an occasion of severe torture or trial.

furnish, fėr'nish, *v.t.* [Fr. *fournir,* to furnish; It. *fornire, frunire,* Pr. *formir, furmir,* to finish, perfect, to furnish; from O.H.G. *frumjan,* to perfect, of kindred origin with E. *frame.*] To supply with anything necessary or useful; to equip; to offer for use; to afford; to fit up; to supply with furniture.—**furnisher,** fėr'nish·ėr, *n.*—**furnishing,** fėr'nish·ing, *n.* Something that serves to equip or fit up; an appendage.— **furniture,** fėr'ni·chėr, *n.* That with which anything is furnished; equipment, specifically, the seats, tables, utensils, etc.; *print.* wood or metal bits smaller than type, placed between type to fill blank spaces or used with wedges to hold type in a metal frame (chase).

furor, fū'ror, *n.* See FURY.

furrier. See FUR.

furrow, fur'ō, *n.* [A.Sax. *furh*= O.H.G. *furich,* G. *furche,* furrow;

ch, chain; ch, Sc. *loch;* g, go; j, job; ng, sing; TH, *then;* th, *thin;* w, wig; hw, *whig;* zh, azure.

cog. with L. *porca*, a ridge between furrows.] A trench in the earth made by a plow; a narrow trench or channel; a groove; a wrinkle in the face.—*v.t.* To make furrows in; to plow; to mark with or as with wrinkles.

furry, fẽr′i, *a.* See FUR.

further, fẽr′THẽr, *adv.* [A.Sax. *furthor, furthur*, further, more, besides, compar. of *forth*, or of *fore*, before.] More in advance; still onward; moreover; besides; farther: this word can hardly be said to differ in meaning from *farther.*—*a.* More distant; farther.—*v.t.* To help forward; to promote; to forward or assist.—**furtherance**, fẽr′THẽr•ans, *n.* The act of furthering; promotion; advancement.—**furtherer**, fẽr′THẽr•ẽr, *n.* One who furthers; a promoter. —**furthermore**, fẽr′THẽr•mōr, *adv.* Moreover; besides; in addition to what has been said.—**furthest**, fẽr′THEST, *a.* Most distant; farthest.

furtive, fẽr′tiv, *a.* [L. *furtivus*, from *furtum*, theft, from *fur*, a thief.] Sly; accomplished by stealth; stealthy; thief-like.—**furtively**, fẽr′tiv•li, *adv.* In a furtive manner; stealthily.

fury, fū′ri, *n.* [Fr. *furie*, L. *furia*, fury, one of the three goddesses of vengeance, from *furo*, to rage.] Rage; a storm of anger; madness; turbulence; a violent rushing; impetuous motion; inspired or supernatural excitement of the mind; a virago; an enraged woman; *class. myth.* one of the avenging deities, the daughters of Earth or of Night, three in number, and called respectively Tisiphone, Alecto, and Megaera.—**furious**, fū′ri•us, *a.* [L. *furiosus.*] Exhibiting fury; raging; violent; transported with passion; mad; frenzied; rushing with impetuosity; violent; boisterous.—**furiously**, fū′ri•us•li, *adv.* In a furious manner.—**furiousness**, fū′ri•us•nes, *n.*—**furor**, fū′ror, *n.* [L.] Fury; rage; mania.—**furore**, fö•rō′rā, *n.* [It.] Rage; fury; great excitement; intense commotion; enthusiasm.

furze, fẽrz, *n.* [A.Sax. *fyrs.*] Whin or gorse; a spiny, almost leafless shrub, with yellow papilionaceous blossoms, growing abundantly in gravelly waste grounds in Western Europe.

fuscous, fus′kus, *a.* [L. *fuscus*, dark-colored.] Brown; of a dark color.

fuse, fūz, *v.t.*—*fused, fusing.* [L. *fundo, fusum*, to pour out, to melt, to cast; hence *found* (to cast), also *confound, confuse, diffuse, refuse*, etc.; akin also *futile.*] To melt or liquefy by heat; to render fluid; to dissolve; to blend or unite as if melted together.—*v.i.* To melt by heat; to become intermingled and blended.—**fusibility**, fū•zi•bil′i•ti, *n.* The quality of being fusible.—**fusible**, fū′zi•bl, *a.* Capable of being fused or melted.—*Fusible metal*, an alloy, usually of lead, tin, and bismuth, compounded in such definite proportions as to melt at a given temperature.—**fusil**, *fusile*, fū′zil. [Fr. *fusile*, L. *fusilis.*] Capable of being melted; fusible.—**fusion**, fū′zhon, *n.* [Fr. *fusion*, L. *fusio.*] The

act or operation of fusing; the state of being melted or dissolved by heat; the act or process of uniting or blending as if melted together; complete union; the combination of atomic nuclei of lighter elements to form a heavier nucleus, resulting in the release of enormous energy.

fuse, **fuze**, fūz, *n.* [From L. *fusus*, spindle.] A tube filled with combustible matter, used in blasting, or in discharging a shell, etc.; in an electric circuit, a piece of metal which melts when the load is too great, thus breaking the circuit and preventing possible damage; an electrical device used to set off torpedoes, etc.

fusee, fū•zē′, *n.* [Fr. *fusée*, a spindleful, from L.L. *fusata* (same sense), L. *fusus*, a spindle.] The cone or conical piece in a watch or clock round which is wound the chain or cord.—**fusiform** fū′zi•form, *a.* Shaped like a spindle.

fuselage, fū′zel•ij, *n.* [L. *fusus*, spindle.] The long, narrow, somewhat spindle-shaped body of an airplane.

fusel oil, fū′zel, *n.* [G. *fusel*, coarse spirits.] Amyl alcohol, a by-product of alcoholic fermentation, used as a solvent in making varnishes; a commercial pentyl alcohol.

fusil, fū′zil, *n.* [Fr. *fusil*, originally the part of the lock that struck fire, L.L. *focile*, from L. *focus*, a fire (whence also, *fuel*).] A light musket or firelock formerly used.—**fusilier**, **fusileer**, fū•zil•lẽr′, *n.* Properly, a soldier armed with a fusil; an infantry soldier who bore firearms, as distinguished from a pikeman and archer.—**fusillade**, fū′zi•lād, *n.* [Fr. from *fusil.*] A simultaneous discharge of musketry.—*v.t.*—*fusilladed, fusillading.* To shoot down by a fusillade.

fuss, fus, *n.* [From A.Sax. *fús*, quick, ready; Icel. *fúss*, eager.] A tumult; a bustle; unnecessary bustle in doing anything; much ado about nothing. —*v.t.* and *i.* To make much ado about trifles; to make a fuss; to worry.— **fussily**, fus′i•li, *adv.* In a fussy manner.—**fussiness**, fus′i•nes, *n.* The state of being fussy; needless bustle. —**fussy**, fus′i, *a.* Moving and acting with fuss; bustling; making more ado than is necessary.

fust, [*obs.*] fust, *n.* [O.Fr. *fusté*, tasting or smelling of the cask, *fust*, a cask, from L. *fustis*, a stick.] A strong musty smell.—*v.i.* To become moldy or musty; to smell ill.—**fustiness**, fus′ti•nes, *n.* State or quality of being fusty.—**fusty**, fus′ti, *a.* Moldy; musty; ill-smelling; rank; rancid.

fustian, fus′tyan, *a.* [O.Fr. *fustaine*, Fr. *futaine*, It. *fustagno*, from *Fostat*, the name of a suburb of Cairo, whence this fabric was first brought.] A coarse cotton stuff, or stuff of cotton and linen, with a pile like velvet, but shorter, such as corduroy, moleskin, etc.; an inflated style of writing; bombast.—*a.* Made of fustian; ridiculously tumid; bombastic. —**fustianist**, fus′tyan•ist, *n.* One who writes bombast.

fustic, fus′tik, *n.* [Fr. and Sp. *fustoc*, from Sp. *fuste*, wood, timber, from L. *fustis*, a stick, a staff.] The wood of a tree growing in the West Indies, extensively used as an ingredient in the dyeing of yellow.

fustigate,† fus′ti•gāt, *v.t.* [L. *fustigo*, from *fustis*, a stick.] To beat with a cudgel.

futile, fū′t′l *a.* [Fr. *futile*, from L. *futilis*, leaky, vain, worthless, from *fundo, fusum*, to pour. FUSE.] Serving no useful end; of no effect; answering no valuable purpose; worthless; trivial.—**futilely**, fū′til•li, *adv.* In a futile manner.—**futility**, fū•til′i•ti, *n.* The quality of being futile, or producing no valuable effect; triflingness; unimportance.—**futilitarian**, fū•til′i•tâ″ri•an, *a.* [Formed on the type of *utilitarian.*] Devoted to the belief that all human aims and hopes are futile; pessimistic.

futtock, fut′ok, *n.* [Corrupted from *foothook.*] *Naut.* one of those timbers raised over the keel which form the breadth of the ship.

future, fū′chẽr, *a.* [Fr. *futur*, from L. *futurus*, future part. of *sum, fui*, to be. BE.] That is to be or come hereafter; that will exist at any time after the present.—*Future tense*, that tense of a verb which expresses that something is yet to take place.—*n.* Time to come; time subsequent to the present; all that is to happen after the present time; the future tense.—**futurist**, fū′chẽr•ist, *n.* Member of the art, music and literature movement of about 1910 that rejected tradition and sought to express the energy and movement of mechanical processes.—**futurity**, fū•tū′ri•ti, *n.* Future state of time; future event.— *Futurity race*, a race for which horses are entered a long time in advance, often even before they are born.

fuze, fūz, *n.* See FUSE.

fuzz, fuz, *v.i.* [Comp. Prov.E. *fozy*, spongy, soft and woolly; D. *voos*, spongy.] To fly off in minute particles.—*n.* Fine, light particles; loose, light particles of fluff.—**fuzzy**, fuz′i, *a.* Covered with fuzz; indistinct, as fuzzy shapes or sounds.

fylfot, fil′fot, *n.* A rectangular cross with arms of equal lengths and each bent at right angles at the end.

G

G, g, jē, the seventh letter in the English alphabet, with two sounds, a hard (guttural), as in *good*; a soft (=j) as in *gem*, the former being the original sound; *mus.* the fifth note and dominant of the normal scale of C, called also *sol*.

G. [Initial letter of *gravity*.] The symbol always used to denote the acceleration with which any body falls freely to the earth in vacuo. It varies from place to place on the earth's surface, its value being about 32 feet per second per second.

gab, gab, *v.i.* [Icel. *gabb*, mockery, *gabba*, to mock; akin D. *gabberen*, to joke, to chatter; Fr. *gaber*, to deceive; E. *gabble*, *gape*.] To talk much; to prate; to talk idly. (*Colloq.*)—*n.* (Dan. *gab*, Sw. *gap*, the mouth.) The mouth; idle talk; chatter. (*Colloq.*)

gabardine, gab'ẽr·dēn", gab"ẽr·dēn', *n.* A wool or cotton cloth, like serge in appearance, but twilled on one side only.

gabble, gab'l, *v.i.*—*gabbled, gabbling.* [Freq. from *gab*; akin to *gobble*.] To talk noisily and rapidly, or without meaning; to prate; to utter rapid inarticulate sounds.—*n.* Loud or rapid talk without meaning; inarticulate sounds rapidly uttered, as of fowls.—**gabbler,** gab'lẽr, *n.* One who gabbles.

gabelle, ga·bel', *n.* [Fr. *gabelle*, O.It. *cabella.*] A tax or excise duty formerly imposed on salt in France.

gaberdine, gab'ẽr·dēn", gab"ẽr·dēn, *n.* A coarse frock or loose upper garment, worn in medieval times.

gabion, gā'bi·on, *n.* [Fr. *gabion*, It. *gabbione*, a large cage, from *gabbia*, a cage, from L.L. *gabia* (= L. *cavea*), a cage. CAGE.] *Fort.* a large basket of wickerwork, of a cylindrical form, but without a bottom, filled with earth, and serving to shelter men from an enemy's fire.—**gabionade,** gā'bi·on·ād, *n.* A work consisting of gabions.

gable, gā'bl, *n.* [O.Fr. *gable*, L.L. *gabulum*, from the Teut.; comp. Dan. *gavl*, D. *gevel*, Icel. *gafl*, G. *giebel*, Goth. *gibla*, a gable.] *Arch.* the triangular end of a house from the level of the eaves to the top; also the end wall of a house.—**gable window,** *n.* A window in the end or gable of a building.

gaby, gā'bi, *n.* [Akin to *gape*, *gab*.] A silly, foolish person; a dunce. (*Colloq.*)

gad, gad, *n.* [Icel. *gaddr*, Sw. *gadd*, Goth. *gazds*, a goad, a spike, a sting; akin to *goad*; comp. also Ir. *gada*, a bar or ingot of metal.] A spike, style, or other sharp thing; a wedge or ingot of steel or iron; a pointed wedgelike tool used by miners.—**gadfly,** gad'flī, *n.* [From *gad*, for *goad*, and *fly*.] A two-winged insect which stings cattle, and deposits its eggs in their skin; called also *Botfly* and *Breeze*; any fly that bites and annoys cattle; a person who purposely annoys or provokes others.

gad, gad, *v.i.*—*gadded, gadding.* [Probably from the restless running about of animals stung by the *gadfly*.] To rove or ramble idly or without any fixed purpose; to act or move without restraint; to wander, as in thought or speech.—**gadabout,** gad'a·bout, *n.* One who walks about idly; one who goes from one social entertainment to another.

gadget, gaj'et, *n.* A small object or device, usually of a mechanical nature; a part of a machine.

gadolinite, gad'ō·lin·īt, *n.* [From *Gadolin*, a Prussian chemist.] A blackish mineral, a silicate of yttrium and cerium.

gadolinium, gad'ō·lin"i·um, *n.* [From

J. *Gadolin*, Finnish chemist.] A metallic element of the rare-earth series. Symbol, Gd,; at. no., 64; at. wt., 157.25.

gadwall, gad'wạl, *n.* [Origin doubtful.] A duck belonging to Europe, Asia, and North America, not so large as the common wild duck.

Gaelic, gāl'ik, *a.* [Gael. *Gaidhealach*, Gaelic, from *Gaidheal*, a Gael.] Of or pertaining to the Gaels, a Celtic race inhabiting the Highlands of Scotland.—*n.* The language of the Celts, that is, the Scottish, Irish, and Manx Celts.—**Gael,** gāl, *n.* A Scottish Highlander.

gaff, gaf, *n.* [Fr. *gaffe*, Sp. and Pg. *gafa*, a hook; of Celtic origin.] A harpoon; a gaff hook; *naut.* a spar with a forked end used to extend the upper edge of some fore-and-aft sails; an ordeal or something difficult to endure (slang).—*v.t.* To strike or secure (a salmon) by means of a gaff hook.

gaffer, gaf'ẽr, *n.* [Contr. from *grandfather* or *good father*.] An old rustic; a word originally of respect, now rather of familiarity or contempt; (*Brit.*) the foreman of a squad of workmen; an overseer.

gag, gag, *v.t.*—*gagged, gagging.* [Perhaps from W. *cegiaw*, to choke, from *ceg*, a choking. Or it may be onomatopoetic; comp. *gaggle.*] To stop the mouth by thrusting something into it so as to hinder speaking but permit breathing; hence, to silence by authority or violence.—*n.* Something thrust into the mouth to hinder speaking; interpolations, additions by actors to their verbal parts; a joke or trick.

gage, gāj, *n.* [Fr. *gage*, from L.L. *gadium*, *vadium*, from Goth. *wadi*, pledge, G. *wette*, a bet; or from L. *vas*, *vadis*, a surety, a pledge. Akin *wage*.] Something laid down or given as a security for the performance of some act by the person giving the gage; a pledge; something thrown down as a token of challenge to combat.—*v.t.*—*gaged, gaging.*‡ To give or deposit as a pledge or security for some act; to pledge or pawn; to bind by pledge.

gage, gāj, *n.* and *v.t.* Same as GAUGE.

gage, gāj, *n.* [The name of the person who first introduced them.] A name of several varieties of plum.

gaggle, gag'l, *v.i.*—*gaggled, gaggling.* —[Imitative.] To cackle like a goose. —*n.* A flock of geese.

gaiety, gaily. See GAY.

gain, gān, *v.t.* [Fr. *gagner*, anciently, to earn profit from pasturage, hence, to gain; from O.H.G. *weidanjan*, to pasture; partly also from Icel. and Sw. *gagn*, gain, profit.] To obtain by industry or the employment of capital; to get as profit or advantage; to acquire: opposed to *lose*; to win or obtain by superiority or success (to *gain* a battle, a prize); to obtain in general; to procure (fame, favor); to win to one's side; to conciliate; to reach, attain to, arrive at (to *gain* a mountain top).—*To gain over*, to draw to another party or interest; to win over.—*To gain ground*, to

advance in any undertaking; to make progress.—*To gain time*, to obtain a longer time for a particular purpose.—*v.i.* To reap advantage or profit; to acquire gain.—*To gain on* or *upon*, to encroach on (the sea *gains on* the land); to advance nearer to, as in a race; to gain ground on.—*n.* Something obtained as an advantage; anything opposed to loss; profit; benefit derived.—**gainer,** gā'nẽr, *n.* One that gains or obtains profit or advantage.—**gainful,** gān'ful, *a.* Producing profit or advantage; profitable; advantageous; lucrative. —**gainfully,** gān'ful·li, *adv.* In a gainful manner.—**gainfulness,** gān'ful·nes, *n.* The state or quality of being gainful.—**gainless,** gān'les, *a.* Not producing gain; unprofitable.— **gainlessness,** gān'les·nes, *n.*

gainly, gān'li, *a.* Handsome: now only in the compound *ungainly* (which see).

gainsay, gān'sā, *v.t.*—*gainsaid, gainsaying.* [A.Sax. *gegn*, against (as in *again*), and E. *say*.] To contradict; to deny or declare not to be true; to controvert; to dispute.—*n.* Opposition in words; contradiction.— **gainsayer,** gān'sā·ẽr, *n.* One who gainsays.

'gainst, genst. Contr. for *Against*.

gait, gāt, *n.* [Akin Icel. *gata*, a way.] Walk; manner of walking or stepping; carriage.—**gaited,** gāt'ed, *a.* Having a particular gait: used in compounds (slow-*gaited*, heavy-*gaited*).

gaiter, gā'tẽr, *n.* [Fr. *guêtre*, a gaiter—origin unknown.] A covering of cloth for the leg, fitting over the shoe; a spatterdash.—*v.t.* To dress with gaiters.

gala, gäl'a or gā'la, *n.* [Fr., show, pomp; It. *gala*, finery; of Teut. origin; akin *gallant*. GALLANT.] An occasion of public festivity.

galactic, ga·lak'tik, *a.* [Gr. *galaktikos*, milky, from *gala*, *galaktos*, milk.] Of or belonging to milk; obtained from milk; lactic; *astron.* pertaining to the Galaxy or Milky Way.—**galactagogue,** ga·lak'ta·gog, *n.* [Gr. *gala*, and *agō*, to induce.] A medicine which promotes the secretion of milk.— **galactose,** ga·lak'tōz, *n.* [Gr. *gala*, *galaktos*, milk.] A sweet substance derived from milk sugar.

galangal, ga·lang'gal, *n.* [Fr. *galanga*, O.Fr. *garingal*; of Eastern origin.] A dried rhizome brought from China and used in medicine, being an aromatic stimulant of the nature of ginger.

galantine, gal·an·tēn', *n.* [Fr.] A dish of veal, chickens, or other white meat, freed from bones and served cold.

galaxy, gal'ak·si, *n.* [Fr. *galaxie*, from Gr. *galaxias* (*kyklos*, circle, being understood), from *gala*, *galaktos*, milk.] A multitude of stars, such as the Milky Way; a system of stars, including star clusters, nebulae, etc.; a brilliant or splendid assemblage of persons.

galbanum, gal'ba·num, *n.* [L., from Heb. *chelbnah*, galbanum, from *chelev*, fat.] A fetid gum resin brought from the Levant, Persia, and India, used in the arts, as in the manufacture of varnish, and also as a medicine.

gale, gāl, *n.* [Gael. and Ir. *gal,* a gale or puff of wind; or connected with Icel. *gol, gola,* a breeze.] A wind; a breeze; a wind between a breeze and a storm or tempest.

gale, gāl, *n.* [O.E. *gawl,* A.Sax. D. and G. *gagel,* wild-myrtle.] A small shrub with a pleasant aromatic odor found in bogs and wet heaths.

galea, gā′li·a, *n.* [L., a helmet.] *Bot.* parts of a calyx or corolla when with the form of a helmet.—**galeated, galeate,** gā′li·ā·ted, gā′li·āt, *a.* [L. *galeatus.*] Covered as with a helmet; shaped like a helmet.

galena, ga·lē′na, *n.* [Gr. *galēnē,* tranquillity—so named from its supposed effect upon diseases.] The principal ore of lead, of a lead-gray color, with a metallic luster, found massive, or sometimes granular or crystallized.

Galenic, Galenical, ga·len′ik, ga·len′i·kal, *a.* Relating to *Galen,* the celebrated Greek physician of the second century.—**Galenism,** gā′len·izm, *n.* The doctrines of Galen.—**Galenist,** gā′len·ist, *n.* A follower of Galen.

Galilean, gal·i·lē′an, *a.* Of or pertaining to, or invented by *Galileo,* the Italian astronomer.

galilee, gal′i·lē, *n.* [Named after the scriptural *Galilee*]. A portico or chapel annexed to some old churches, and used for various purposes.—**Galilean,** gal·i·lē′an, *n.* A native or inhabitant of Galilee, in Judea.—*a.* Relating to Galilee.

galimatias, gal·i·mā′shi·as, *n.* [Fr., origin doubtful.] Confused talk; nonsense; absurd mixture.

galiot, galliot, gal′i·ot, *n.* [Fr. *galiote,* dim. of *galie,* a galley. GALLEY.] A small galley, or sort of brigantine, moved both by sails and oars; a two-masted Dutch cargo vessel; with very rounded ribs and flattish bottom.

galipot, gal′i·pot, *n.* [Fr., perhaps from being sold in *gallipots.*] The French name for the resin which is obtained by incisions in the stems of the maritime pine.

gall, gal, *n.* [A.Sax. *gealla*=acel. *gall.* D. *gal,* G. *galle;* cog. with Gr. *cholē,* L. *fel,* bile.] A bitter fluid secreted in the liver of animals; bile; *fig.* bitterness of mind; rancor; malignity; the gall bladder; nerve, audacity, impudence, brazen assurance. (*Slang.*) —**gall bladder,** *n. Anat.* a small membranous sac shaped like a pear, which receives the gall or bile from the liver.—**gallstone,** *n.* A concretion formed in the gall bladder, or biliary passages.

gall, gal, *n.* [Fr. *gale,* It. *galla,* from L. *galla,* an oak gall, a gallnut.] A vegetable excrescence produced by the deposit of the egg of an insect in the bark or leaves of a plant, especially the oak, very extensively used in dyeing and in the manufacture of ink.—**gallfly,** *n.* An insect that punctures plants, and occasions

galls.—**gallic,** gal′ik, *a.* Belonging to galls; derived from galls.

gall, gal, *v.t.* [O.Fr. *galler,* to gall or fret, *galle,* an itching, scurf, perhaps L. *galla,* the diseased vegetable excrescence. Comp. also Armor. *gâl,* eruption.] To make a sore in the skin of by rubbing, fretting, and wearing away; to excoriate; to vex; to chagrin; to cause to have a feeling of bitterness or annoyance; to hurt the feelings of; to harass; to annoy (as by a musketry fire).—*n.* A sore place caused by rubbing.—**galling,** gal′ing, *n.* Adapted to fret or chagrin; vexing; harassing; annoying.—**gallingly,** gal′ing·li, *adv.* In a galling manner.

gallant, gal′ant, *a.* [Fr. *galant,* ppr. of O.Fr. verb *galer,* to rejoice, from the Teutonic; comp. G. *geil,* wanton, Goth. *gailjan,* to rejoice, A.Sax. *gál,* merry.] Gay, showy, or splendid in attire or outward appearance; handsome; fine; brave; high-spirited; courageous; magnanimous; noble; chivalrous; (in the following senses pron. also ga·lant′), courtly; polite and attentive to ladies; courteous.—*n.* A gay sprightly man; a high-spirited brave young fellow; a daring spirit; (in the following senses pron. also ga·lant′), a man who is polite and attentive to ladies; a wooer; a suitor.—*v.t.* (ga·lant′). To act the gallant toward; to wait on or be very attentive to (a lady).—**gallantly,** gal′ant·li, *adv.* In a gallant manner; gaily; splendidly; bravely; nobly.—**gallantry,** gal′ant·ri, *n.* [Fr. *galanterie.*] Show; ostentatious finery; bravery; dash; intrepidity; polite attention to ladies; court paid to females for the purpose of winning illicit favors.

galleass, gal′i·as, *n.* [Fr. *galeasse,* It. *galeazza;* akin to *galley.*] A large kind of galley formerly used in the Mediterranean.

galleon, gal′i·un, *n.* [Sp. *galeon,* It. *galeone,* augmentatives from L.L. *galea,* a galley.] A large ship formerly used by the Spaniards in their commerce with America.

gallery, gal′ėr·i, *n.* [Fr. *galerie,* It. *galleria,* L.L. *galeria,* perhaps from L.Gr. *galē,* a gallery.] An apartment of much greater length than breadth, serving as a passage of communication between different rooms of a building; a room or building for the exhibition of paintings, statues, and other works of art; a collection of paintings, statues, etc.; a platform projecting from the walls of a building, and overlooking a ground floor, as in a church, theater, and the like; *fort.* any communication covered in both above and at the sides; *mining,* a narrow passage; *naut.* a frame like a balcony projecting from the stern and quarters of a ship.

galley, gal′i, *n.* [O.Fr. *galie,* It. and L.L. *galea*—probably from Gr. *galē,* a kind of gallery, or *galeos, galē,* a sea fish, a kind of shark, which might suggest a swift-sailing vessel. Akin are *galleon, galleass, galiot.*] A low flat-built vessel with one deck, and navigated with sails and oars, once

commonly used in the Mediterranean; a ship of the ancient Greeks and Romans, propelled chiefly by oars; the boat of a warship appropriated for the captain's use; the cook room or kitchen on board ship; *printing,* a movable frame or tray on which the types are placed when composed.—*The galleys,* certain galleys on the Mediterranean which were worked by convicts; hence, a synonym for a place of forced and severe toil.—**galley slave,** *n.* A person condemned for a crime to work at the oar on board of a galley.

gallic, *a.* See GALL.

Gallic, Gallican, gal′ik, gal′i·kan, *a.* [L. *Gallicus,* from *Gallia,* Gaul, France.] Pertaining to Gaul or France (the *Gallican* church or clergy); in the days of Louis XIV and Bossuet, claiming liberty of action denied by the Papal or Ultramontane party.—**Gallicize,** gal′i·sīz, *v.t.*—*gallicized, gallicizing.* To render conformable to the French idiom or language.—**Gallicism,** gal′i·sizm, *n.* [Fr. *gallicisme.*] A mode of speech peculiar to the French nation; a custom or mode of thought peculiar to the French.

galligaskins, gal·i·gas′kinz, *n. pl.* [From Fr. *greguesques,* O.Fr. *guarguesques, garguesques,* from It. *grechesco,* Grecian (through such forms as *gleguesques, galligasks*).] Large open breeches; wide hose; leather guards worn on the legs by sportsmen.

gallimaufry, gal·i·ma′fri, *n.* [Fr. *galimafrée,* a ragout; of uncertain origin.] A hash; a medley; a hodgepodge.

gallinaceous, gal·i·nā′shus, *a.* [L. *gallinaceus,* from *gallina,* a hen, *gallus,* a cock.] Pertaining to the order of birds which includes the domestic fowls, pheasants, etc.—**gallinacean,** gal·i·nā′shen, *n.* One of the gallinaceous birds.—**gallinule,** gal′i·nūl, *n.* [L. *gallinula,* dim. of *gallina,* a hen.] A grallatorial bird closely allied to the coots; the water hen or moor hen.

gallipot, gal′i·pot, *n.* [Corrupted from O.D. *gleypot,* an earthen pot—*gley,* clay, and *pot.*] A small pot or vessel painted and glazed, used by druggists and apothecaries for containing medicines.

gallium, gal′i·um, *n.* [From *Gallia,* the Latin name for France.] A rare, widely distributed, metallic element of low melting point (29.7°C.). Symbol, Ga; at. no., 31; at. wt., 69.72.

gallivant, gal·i·vant′, *v.i.* [Probably a corrupt form of *gallant.*] To gad or run about; to flirt.

galliwasp, gal′i·wosp, *n.* A species of West Indian lizard, about 1 foot in length.

gallon, gal′un, *n.* [O.Fr. *galon, jalon;* Fr. *jale,* a jar, a bowl; origin unknown.] A measure of capacity equal to 4 quarts, dry or liquid, but usually the latter; the U.S. gallon contains 231 cu. in., the English imperial gallon, 277.42 cu. in.

galloon, ga·lön′, *n.* [Fr. and Sp. *galon;* It. *galone,* from *gala,* show.

GALA.] A kind of narrow close lace made of cotton, silk, gold, or silver threads, etc.—**gallooned**, ga·lönd′, *a.* Furnished or adorned with galloon.

gallop, gal′up, *v.i.* [Fr. *galoper*, from O.Flem. *walop*, a galop, an extension of *wallen*, A.Sax. *weallan*, to boil.] To move or run with leaps, as a horse; to run with speed; to ride a horse that is galloping; to ride at a rapid pace; to scamper.—*n.* The movement or pace of a horse, by springs or leaps.—**gallopade**, gal·up·ād′, *n.* [Fr. *galopade*.] A sidelong or curvetting kind of gallop; a sprightly kind of dance; a galop; the music adapted to it.—*v.i.*—*gallopaded, gallopading.* To gallop; to perform the dance called a gallopade.—**galloper**, gal′up·ėr, *n.* One who or that which gallops.

Galloway, gal′o·wā, *n.* A species of horses of small size but great endurance, first bred in *Galloway* in Scotland.—*Gallovidians, Galwegians,* inhabitants of Galloway.

gallowglass, **gallowglas**, gal′ō·glas, *n.* [Ir. *galloglach*—*gall*, a foreigner, an Englishman, and *oglach*, a youth; from being armed after the English model.] An ancient heavy-armed foot soldier of Ireland and the Western Isles.

gallows, gal′ōz, *n. sing.* or *pl.*; also **gallowses** in *pl.* [A plural form; A.Sax. *galga, gealga* (sing.), a gallows=Dan. and Sw. *galge,* Icel. *gálgi,* Goth. *galga,* G. *galgen,* gallows.] An upright wooden frame with crossbar, on which criminals are executed by hanging; also a pair of suspenders or braces.

galop, gal′op, *n.* [Fr. GALLOP.] A quick, lively kind of dance in 2=4 time, somewhat resembling a waltz; the music for this dance.

galore, ga·lōr′, *n.* [Ir. and Gael. *go leòr,* enough—*go,* to, and *leòr,* enough.] Abundance; plenty.—*adv.* In abundance; bountifully. (Colloq.)

galosh, **galoshe**, ga·losh′, *n.* [Fr. *galoche,* from L.L. *calopedia* (through the corruptions *calop′dia, calopdja*), from Gr. *kalopodion,* a wooden shoe —*kalon,* wood, and *pous, podos,* a foot.] A shoe to be worn over another shoe to keep the foot dry; also a kind of gaiter.

galvanic, **galvanical**,† gal·van′ik, gal·van′i·kal, *a.* [From *Galvani,* an Italian physiologist, an early investigator of galvanism.] Pertaining to galvanism; containing or exhibiting galvanism.—*Galvanic electricity,* electricity arising from chemical action. —*Galvanic pair* or *cell,* a combination of two substances in an exciting liquid which acts chemically upon one more than on the other.—*Galvanic battery,* an association of galvanic pairs for the production of current electricity.—**galvanism**, gal′van·izm, *n.* That branch of the science of electricity which treats of the electric currents arising from chemical action. *Current electricity, voltaic* are now used instead of *galvanism, galvanic.*—**galvanization**, gal′van·i·zā″shon, *n.* The act of affecting with galvanism; the state of being affected.—**galvanize**, gal′van·īz, *v.t.*—*galvanized, galvanizing.* To affect with galvanism; to electroplate by galvanism; to coat (sheets of iron) with tin or zinc in this way; to restore to consciousness by galvanic action, as from a state of suspended animation.—**galvanizer**, gal′van·i·zėr, *n.* One who or that which galvanizes.—**galvanometer**, gal·van·om′et·ėr, *n.* An instrument for detecting the existence and determining the strength and direction of an electric current. — **galvanometry**, gal·van·om′et·ri, *n.* The art or process of determining the force of electric or galvanic currents.—**galvanoscope**, gal′van·o·skōp, *n.* An instrument for detecting the existence and direction of an electric current.—**galvanoscopic**, gal′van·o·skop″ik, *a.* Of or pertaining to a galvanoscope.

gambeson, gam′bi·s'n, *n.* [O.Fr. *gambeson,* from O.H.G. *wamba,* A. Sax. *wambe,* womb, stomach; comp. G. *wams,* doublet.] A stuffed and quilted tunic, fitting the body, and formerly worn under the habergeon.

gambier, **gambir**, gam′bēr, gam′bir, *n.* [Malayan.] An earthy-looking substance of light-brown hue, procured from the leaves of a Malayan shrub, and used medicinally as an astringent, but far more extensively employed in tanning and dyeing.

gambit, gam′bit, *n.* [Fr., from It. *gambetto,* a tripping up of one's legs, from *gamba,* the leg.] Chess, the sacrifice of a pawn early in the game, for the purpose of taking up an attacking position.

gamble, gam′bl, *v.i.*—*gambled, gambling.* [Freq. of *game,* with *b* inserted, as in *number, humble.*] To play or game for money or other stake, especially to be in the habit of doing so.—*v.t.* To lose or squander by gaming: with *away.*—**gambler**, gam′bler, *n.* One who gambles.

gamboge, gam·bōj′, *n.* [From *Camboja, Cambodia,* a portion of the empire of Anam, in Asia.] The hardened juice or sap yielded by several species of trees, and used as a purgative in medicine, and also in the arts, chiefly in water-color painting.

gambol, gam′bol, *v.i.*—*gambolled, gambolling.* [O.E. *gambolde, gambaude,* from Fr. *gambade,* gambol, *gambiller,* to wag the leg or kick, O.Fr. *gambe,* It. *gamba,* the leg, Fr. *jambe.*] To dance and skip about in sport; to frisk; to leap; to play in frolic.—*n.* A skipping or leaping about in frolic; a skip, frisk, leap, prank.

gambrel, gam′brel, *n.* [From It. *gamba,* the leg.] The hind leg of a horse; a stick crooked like a horse's leg, used by butchers for suspending animals.—*Gambrel roof,* a hipped roof; a mansard roof.

game, gām, *n.* [A.Sax. *gamen,* joy, pleasure; Icel. *gaman,* Dan. *gammen,* delight, gratification; O.G. *gaman,* jest, sport. *Gamble* is a derivative, and *gammon,* humbug, is of same origin.] Sport of any kind; jest; play; some contrivance or arrangement for sport, recreation, testing skill, and the like (as baseball or football); a single contest in any such game; specifically (*pl.*), diversions or contests, as in wrestling, running, and other athletic exercises; a scheme pursued or measures planned; such animals, collectively, as are usually pursued or taken in the chase or in the sports of the field: in this sense without a plural; the animals enumerated in the game laws.—*To make game of,* to turn into ridicule; to delude or humbug.—*v.i.*—*gamed, gaming.* [A.Sax. *gamenian.*] To gamble; to play at cards, dice, billiards, etc., for money; to be in the habit of so doing.—*a.* Having the courageous spirit of a gamecock; courageous. (Colloq.)—*To die game,* to maintain a bold, resolute, courageous spirit to the last.—**gamebag**, *n.* A bag for holding the game killed by a sportsman.—**gamecock**, *n.* A cock bred or used to fight; a cock of a good fighting breed.—**gamekeeper**, *n.* One who has the care of game; one who is employed to look after animals kept for sport.—**game laws**, *n. pl.* Laws enacted with regard to, or for the preservation of, the animals called game.—**game** *n.* Cricket. *To play the game,* to play according to rule; to act straightforwardly.—**gamely**, gām′li, *adv.* In a game or courageous manner.—**gameness**, gām′nes, *n.*—**gamy**, gā′mi, *a.* Having the flavor of game.

gamete, ga·mēt′, *n.* [Gr. *gameō,* I marry.] *Biol.* a matured sex cell or germ cell; in lower plants, the similar sex cells of thallophytes, which unite to form a zygote; in animals and higher plants, the dissimilar cells, called sperm and egg, which unite to form an embryo.

gamin, gam′in, ga·man′, *n.* [Fr.] A neglected street boy; an Arab of the streets.

gamma, gam′mä, *n.* [M.E. from L.L. from Gr. of Sem. origin, akin to Heb. *gamel, gimel.*] The third letter of the Greek alphabet, equivalent to the English *g,* as in *go.*—**gamma rays**, *n. Phys.* rays similar to X-rays, emitted from radioactive materials and used in radiotherapy.

gammer, gam′ėr, *n.* [Contr. for *goodmother* or *grandmother.* Comp. *gaffer.*] An old wife; the correlative of *gaffer.*

gammon, gam′un, *n.* [O.Fr. *gambon,* It. *gambone,* a big leg, a gammon, from *gamba,* a leg.] The thigh of a hog, pickled and smoked or dried; a smoked ham.—*v.t.* To make into bacon; to pickle and dry in smoke.

gammon, gam′un, *n.* [Connected with *game;* comp. Dan. *gammen,* sport.] An imposition or hoax; humbug. (Colloq.)

gamogenesis, gam·o·jen′e·sis, *n.* [Gr. *gamos,* marriage, and *genesis.*] Generation by copulation of the sexes; sexual generation.—**gamogenetic**, gam′o·je·net″ik, *a.* Of or relating to gamogenesis.—**gamopetalous**, gam·o·pet′a·lus, *a.* [Gr. *gamos,* and *petalon,* a flower leaf.] *Bot.* monopetalous.

—**gamophyllous,** ga·mof′i·lus or gam·o·fil′lus, a. [Gr. gamos, and phyllon, a leaf.] Bot. having a single perianth whorl with coherent leaves.

—**gamosepalous,** gam·o·sep′a·lus, a. [Gr. gamos, and E. sepal.] Bot. monosepalous.

gamp, gamp, n. A clumsy umbrella, as carried by Mrs. Sairey Gamp, in Dickens. Fr. Robinson, from the umbrella of Robinson Crusoe.

gamut, gam′ut, n. [Gr. gamma, the letter G and gamma plus ut, the first note of Guido's music scale.] The series of recognized musical notes in a scale; an entire range or series; the compass of a voice or instrument.

gander, gan′der, n. [A.Sax. gandra, for ganra, from the root gan seen in G. gans, a goose, gänserich, a gander. GOOSE.] The male of the goose.

gang, gang, n. [A.Sax. gang, a way, a passage, genge, a gang, a company, from gangan, to go. GO.] A number going in company, hence, a company or number of persons associated for a particular purpose; contemptuous or disreputable persons.—v.i. To act in concert; to form a group.—v.t. To assemble or operate mechanical parts simultaneously; to attack in a gang.—**gangster,** gang′ster, n. One of a gang of toughs.—**gangway,** gang′-wā, n. A temporary means of access to some position, formed of planks or boards; a narrow framework or platform leading into or out of a ship, or from one part of a ship to another.—interj. Clear the way!

gangling, gan′gling, adj. [From Scottish, gang, to go.] Loosely built; lanky; spindly or awkwardly long.

ganglion, gang′gli·on, n. pl. **ganglia,** or **ganglions,** [Gr. ganglion, a sort of swelling or excrescence, a tumor under the skin.] Anat. an enlargement occurring somewhere in the course of a nerve; a mass of nervous matter containing nerve cells, and giving origin to nerve fibers; surg. an encysted tumor situated somewhere on a tendon.—**gangliated,** gang′gli·āt·ed, a. Having ganglions.—**ganglionic,** gang·gli·on′ik, a. Pertaining to a ganglion.

gangrene, gang′grēn, n. [L. gangræna, from Gr. gangraina, from graino, to gnaw.] The first stage of mortification of living flesh; bot. a disease ending in putrid decay.—v.t.—gangrened, gangrening. To produce a gangrene in; to mortify.—v.i. To become mortified.—**gangrenous,** gang′grē·nus, a. Attacked by gangrene; mortified; indicating mortification of living flesh.

gangue, gang, n. [G. gang, a vein.] The stony matrix of metallic ores.

gangway. See GANG.

ganister, gan′is·ter, n. A close-grained hard sandstone or grit found under certain coal beds in England.

gannet, gan′et, n. [A.Sax. ganet, ganot, a sea fowl, a gannet; allied to gander, goose.] The solan goose, an aquatic bird of the pelican family, 3 feet in length, common on insular rocks in the northern seas.

ganoid, gan′oid, a. [Gr. ganos, splend-or, and eidos, appearance.] Belonging to an order of fishes, the majority of them extinct, characterized by scales composed of horny or bony plates, covered with glossy enamel.—n. One of these fishes.

gantlet, gant′let, n. Same as Gauntlet.

gantlet, gant′let, n. [From Sw. gat-lopp, from gata, a street, a line of soldiers, and lopp, a course, akin to E. leap, D. loopen, to run.] A punishment in which the culprit was compelled to run between two ranks of men armed with rods, etc., receiving a blow from each; rail. a stretch of track where two lines overlap (as in a tunnel), eliminating the need for switching).

gantry, gan′tri, n. [O.F. gantier, chantier, from L. cantherius, from G. kanthelios, pack ass.] A framework raised on side supports and extended over something; a frame supporting a cask or barrel.

gap, gap, n. [Icel. and Sw. gap, a gap or hiatus; akin gape, gaby.] A break or opening, as in a fence, wall, or the like; a breach; a chasm; a hiatus.—v.t. To make a gap or gaps in; to notch or jag; to cut into teeth.

gape, gāp, v.i.—gaped, gaping. [A. Sax. geápan, to gape or open wide, from geáp, wide; Dan. gabe, Icel. gapa, to gaze with open mouth; D. gapen, G. gaffen, to gape; akin gap, gaby.] To open the mouth wide, as indicative of drowsiness, dullness, surprise, expectation, etc.; to stand open; to present a gap; to show a fissure or chasm.—To gape for or after, to crave; to desire or covet earnestly.—n. The act of gaping; zool. the width of the mouth when opened, as of birds, fishes, etc.; pl. a disease of young poultry attended with much gaping.—**gaper,** gā′per, n. One who gapes; a bivalve mollusk with a shell permanently open at the posterior end.

garage, ga·räzh′, n. [Fr.] A place for receiving or repairing motor vehicles.

garb, gärb, n. [O.Fr. garbe, a garb, appearance, comeliness, from O.H. G. garawi, garwi, attire; akin to A.Sax. gearwa, clothing; E. gear and yare.] Clothing; vesture; costume; habit; an official or other distinguishing dress; fashion or mode.—v.t. To dress; to clothe. (Tenn.)

garbage, gär′bij, n. [O.E. garbash, probably from garble, to sift; being thus what is sifted out, refuse.] Refuse or offal; refuse animal or vegetable matter; any worthless, offensive matter.

garble, gär′bl, v.t.—garbled, garbling. [O.Fr. garbeller, from Sp. garbillar, to sift garbillo, a coarse sieve; from Ar. gharbil, a sieve.] To sift or bolt‡; to examine for the purpose of separating the good from the bad‡; to falsify by leaving out parts; to mutilate so as to give a false impression (to garble historical documents); to sophisticate; to corrupt.—**garbler,** gär′bler, n. One who garbles; formerly an official in London who looked after the purity of drugs and spices.

garden, gär′dn, n. [O.Fr. gardin,

Mod.Fr. jardin, a word of Teutonic origin; comp. L.G. garden, G. garten, a garden; Goth. gards, A.Sax. geard, O.E. garth, an inclosed place, a yard. YARD.] A piece of ground appropriated to the cultivation of plants, fruits, flowers, or vegetables; a rich well-cultivated spot or tract of country.—v.i. To lay out or cultivate a garden.—**gardener,** gär′dn·ėr, n. One whose occupation is to keep a garden.—Garden city, a town laid out with many gardens and open spaces.—Garden party, a party held out of doors on the lawn or in the garden of a private residence.

gardenia, gär·dē′ni·a, n. [After Dr. Garden, an American botanist.] A name of certain plants of Asia and Africa with large white or yellowish fragrant flowers.

garfish, gär′fish, n. [A.Sax. gár, a dart.] A fish with a remarkably elongated body and a long, narrow, beaklike snout; seapike or sea needle.

Gargantua, gar·gan′tu·a, n. A gigantic hero of a satirical romance by Rabelais; **Gargantuan,** a. Gigantic; coarse.

gargle, gär′gl, v.t.—gargled, gargling. [A word akin to gargle, gorge, gargoil; Fr. gargouiller, to gargle; L. gurgulio, the gullet; Gr. gargarizō, to rinse the mouth; G. gurgel, the throat, gurgeln, to gargle.] To wash or rinse (the mouth or throat) with a liquid preparation.—n. Any liquid preparation for washing the mouth and throat.

gargoyle, gär′goil, n. [Fr. gargouille, a gargoil or spout. GARGLE.] Arch. a projecting spout for throwing the water from the gutters of a building, generally carved into a grotesque figure from whose mouth the water gushes.

garibaldi, gar·i·bold′i, n. A loose red blouse worn by women, named from the red-shirt troops of the Italian patriot Garibaldi.

garish, gâ′rish, a. [From O.E. gare, to stare, probably a form of gaze with change from z-sound to r, as in snore, snooze; frore, freeze, etc.] Gaudy; showy; staring; overbright; dazzling.—**garishly,** gâ′rish·ly, adv. In a garish manner.—**garishness,** gâ′rish·nes, n. The state or quality of being garish.

garland, gär′land, n. [O.E. girlond, gerlond, from Fr. guirlande, a garland, from O.H.G. wiera, a coronet, through a verb wierelen, to plait.] A wreath or chaplet made of leaves, twigs, flowers, or the like; a collection of little printed pieces; an anthology.—v.t. To deck with a garland or garlands.

garlic, gär′lik, n. [A.Sax. gárleác, from gár, a dart or lance—from the spear-shaped leaves—and leác, a leek, as in hemlock, charlock, etc.] A plant allied to the onion, leek, etc., having an acrid pungent taste and very strong odor, indigenous to the south of Europe, where it forms a favorite condiment.

garment, gär′ment, n. [Fr. garnement; O.Fr. garniment, from garnir, to garnish, to deck. GARNISH.] Any article of clothing or piece of dress, as a coat, a gown, etc.; a vestment.

garner, gär′nėr, *n.* [Fr. *grenier*, O.Fr. *gernier*, a cornloft, from L. *granaria*, a granary, from *granum*, grain. GRANARY.] A granary; a building or place where grain is stored for preservation.—*v.t.* To store in, or as in, a granary.

garnet, gär′net, *n.* [Fr. *grenat*, It. *granata*, from L. *granum*, grain, seed, and in later times the cochineal insect and the scarlet dye obtained from it, the stone being so called on account of its fine crimson color.] The name common to a group or family of precious stones, varying considerably in composition, the prevailing color being red of various shades, but often brown, and sometimes green, yellow, or black; *naut.* a sort of tackle fixed to a stay, and used to hoist in and out cargo.

garnish, gär′nish, *v.t.* [Fr. *garnir*, to provide or equip; It. *guarnire*, *guernire*, O.Sp. *guarnir*; from the German—comp. O.H.G. *warnôn*, G. *warnen*, A.Sax. *warnian*, to take care, to warn. WARN. Akin *garment*, *garrison*.] To adorn; to decorate with appendages; to set off; *cookery*, to ornament (a dish) with colorful trimming; *law*, to warn, or bring into court, by garnishment.—*n.* Something added for embellishment; ornament; decoration; *cookery*, something added to food as an embellishment.—**garnishee**, *v.t.* To obtain legal attachment on property or money.—*n.* The person subject to garnishment.—**garnisher**, gär′nish-ėr, *n.*—**garnishment**, gär′nish‧ment, *n.* Ornament; *law*, a legal notice commanding one to appear in court; the legal attachment of money for debt.

garotte, **garotter**. See GARROTE, GARROTTER.

garret, gar′et, *n.* [O.Fr. *garite*, a place of refuge or outlook, from *garer*, to beware, from O.H.G. *werjan*, Goth. *varjan*, to defend. Akin *ward*, *guard*, *wary*, *warn*.] That part of a house which is on the uppermost floor, immediately under the roof; a loft.

garrison, gar′i‧sn, *n.* [Fr. *garnison*, from *garnir*, to garnish. GARNISH.] A body of troops stationed in a fort or fortified town; a fort, castle, or fortified town furnished with troops.—*v.t.* To place a garrison in; to secure or defend by garrisons.

garrote, **garrotte**, ga‧rōt′, ga‧rot′, *n.* [Fr. *garrotte*, from Sp. *garrote*.] A mode of capital punishment in Spain by strangling the prisoner by means of an iron collar attached to a post; the instrument of this punishment.—**garrote**, **garrotte**, ga‧rōt′, ga‧rot′, *v.t.*—*garroted*, *garrotted*; *garroting*, *garrotting*. To strangle by means of the garrote; to rob by suddenly seizing a person and compressing his windpipe until he becomes insensible, or at least helpless, usually carried out by two or three accomplices.—**garroter**, ga‧rōt′ėr, *n.* One who commits the act of garroting.

garrulous, ga′rū‧lus, *a.* [L. *garrulus*, from *garrio*, to prate, to chatter; allied to Gr. *gēryō*, *garyō*, to cry; Ir. *gairim*, to bawl.] Talkative; prating; characterized by long prosy talk, with minuteness and frequent repetition in recording details.—**garrulity**, ga‧rū′li‧ti, *n.* The quality of being garrulous; talkativeness; loquacity.—**garrulously**, ga′rū‧lus‧li, *adv.* In a garrulous or talkative manner.—**garrulousness**, ga′rū‧lus‧nes, *n.* Talkativeness; garrulity.

garter, gär′tėr, *n.* [From O.Fr. *gartier* = Fr. *jarretière*, from *jarret*. O.Fr. *garret*, ham, hough, from the Celtic; Armor. *gar* or *garr*, W. *gar*, the leg, Gael. *gar*, in *gartan*, a garter.] A band or strip of elastic worn to hold up a stocking; [*usually cap.*] the badge of the highest order of knighthood in Great Britain, called *the Order of the Garter*; hence, also, the order itself, and the name given to the principal king-of-arms in England.—*v.t.* To bind with a garter.

gas, gas, *n.* [A word formed by the Dutch chemist Van Helmont, who died in 1644.] An elastic, airlike fluid; a substance, such as air, the particles of which tend to fly apart from each other, thus causing it to expand indefinitely; in common usage, any gaseous substance except air, as *acetylene gas*, which in combination with oxygen is used in welding; *coal gas*, distilled from coal and used for heating, cooking, and less frequently, lighting; *laughing gas* or nitrous oxide, employed in dentistry or surgery as an anesthetic; *natural gas*, found under the earth's crust and used as a fuel and illuminant; *poison gas*, such as chlorine, employed in warfare. Fuel gases, poison gases, and firedamp are often referred to simply as *gas*. Gasoline is colloquially termed *gas*.—*v.t.* To treat with gas, as in industrial processes; to poison with gas.—**gas burner**, a jet or series or jets where gas is burned as it issues out.—**gaselier**, gas′e‧lėr, *n.* A chandelier adapted for burning gas.—**gaseous**, gas′ē‧us, *a.* In the form of gas; of the nature of gas.—**gas fitter**, a workman who fixes pipes and fits burners and other appliances for gas.—**gasiform**, gas′i‧form, *a.* Gaseous; aeriform.—**gasify**, gas′i‧fī, *v.t.*—*gasified*, *gasifying*. To convert into gas.—**gaslight**, light produced by the combustion of coal gas; a gas jet.—**gas mask**, *n.* Covering for the face, worn as a protection against poison gas.—**gasoline**, gas′o‧lēn, *n.* Refined petroleum, a volatile liquid hydrocarbon, highly flammable and, when vaporized and mixed with air, explosive, used as a solvent and as a fuel in engines.—**gasometer**, gas‧om′e‧tėr, *n.* An instrument or apparatus intended to measure, collect, or mix gases.—**gas station**, *n.* Place where gasoline and oil are sold, chiefly for use in automobiles.—**gas turbine**, gas tėr′bin, *n.* An engine in which curved turbine blades are propelled by the forcing of compressed hot gases introduced

from the combustion chamber through the blades, creating a rotary work force.

Gascon, gas′kon, *n.* [Fr.; akin to *Basque*.] A native of Gascony in France; hence, a boaster, the Gascons being noted for boasting.—**gasconade**, gas‧ko‧nād′, *n.* [Fr.] A boast or boasting; a vaunt; a bravado; a bragging.—*v.i.*—*gasconaded*, *gasconading*. To boast; to brag; to vaunt; to bluster.

gash, gash, *n.* [Perhaps from O.Fr. *garser*, to scarify, to pierce with a lancet; L.L. *garsa*, scarification.] A deep and long cut, particularly in flesh.—*v.t.* To make a gash in.

gasket, gas′ket, *n.* [Fr. *garcette*, Sp. *garceta*, a gasket.] Anything used as a packing, such as a metal or rubber ring; a line used to bind a furled sail to the yard of a boat.

gasp, gasp, *v.i.* [Icel. *geispa*, to yawn; Dan. *gispe*, to gasp; L.G. *japen*, *japsen*; akin to E. *gape*.] To open the mouth wide in laborious respiration; to labor for breath; to respire convulsively; to pant violently.—*v.t.* To emit or utter with gaspings or pantings; with *away*, *forth*, *out*, etc.—*n.* A labored respiration; a short painful catching of the breath.

gastralgia, gas‧tral′ji‧a, *n.* [Gr. *gastēr*, *gastros*, the belly, and *algos*, pain.] Pain in the stomach or belly.

gastric, gas′trik, *a.* [From Gr. *gastēr*, *gastros*, the belly or stomach.] Of or pertaining to the belly or stomach.—*Gastric juice*, the digestive fluid containing enzymes and hydrochloric acid and secreted by stomach glands.—**gastritis**, gas‧trī′tis, *n.* Chronic inflammation of the stomach.—**gastroenteritis**, gas‧trō‧en‧te‧rīt′is, *n.* Inflammation of the stomach and intestines.—**gastrointestinal**, gas‧trō‧in‧tes′ti‧nul, *n.* Something that involves both stomach and intestines.—**gastronomy**, gas‧tron′o‧mi, *n.* The art or science of good living; the pleasures of the table; epicurism.—**gastronomic**, **gastronomical**, gas‧tro‧nom′ik, gas‧tro‧nom′i‧kal, *a.* Pertaining to gastronomy.—**gastronome**, **gastronomist**, gas′tro‧nōm, gas‧tron′o‧mist, *n.* One versed in gastronomy; a judge of the art of cookery; a gourmet; an epicure.—**gastroscopy**, gas‧tros′ko‧pi, *n.* [Gr. *skopeō*, to view.] *Med.* an examination of the abdomen in order to detect disease.—**gastrovascular**, *a.* Belonging to digestion and circulation (the *gastrovascular* body cavity of certain animals).

gastropod, **gasteropod**, gas′tro‧pod, gas′tėr‧o‧pod, *n.* [Gr. *gastēr*, the belly, and *pous*, *podos*, a foot.] One of a class of mollusks, consisting of snails, periwinkles, and other animals inhabiting a univalve shell (although some of them are destitute of a shell), the distinguishing characteristic being the *foot*, a broad muscular organ attached to the ventral surface.—**gastropodous**, gas‧trop′o‧dus, *a.* Belonging to the gastropods.

gastrula, gas′tru‧la, *n.* [A dim. of *gaster*, Gr. *gastēr*, belly.] A germ or embryonic form developed by invagination from a morula or blastula, and having the character of a doublewalled sac with an orifice leading into it.—**gastrulation**, *n*. The process by which a gastrula is produced.

gate, gāt, *n*. [A.Sax. *geat*, a gate or door.] A door or frame opening into an enclosing fence or wall; a movable barrier, often grated, that is raised or lowered to permit passage into an enclosure; a wooden barrier that is let down to block passage at a railroad crossing; the frame which shuts or stops a passage for water, as at the entrance to a dock.—**gate-leg table**, *n*. A table with folding leaves and movable legs.—**gateway**, gāt′wā, *n*. An opening which is or may be closed with a gate.

gather, gaTH′ẽr, *v.t.* [A.Sax. *gaderian*, *gadrian*, from *gador*, *geador*, together, seen also in *together*; comp. D. *gadern*, to gather, *te gader*, L.G. *to gader*, together.] To bring together; to collect into one place or one aggregate; to assemble; to congregate; to pick; to pluck; to accumulate; to amass; to draw together; to bring together in folds or plaits, as a garment; hence, to plait; to pucker; to acquire or gain, with or without effort (to *gather* strength); to deduce by inference; to conclude.—*To gather one's self together*, to collect all one's powers for a strong effort.—*To be gathered to one's fathers*, to be interred along with one's ancestors, or simply to die.—*v.i.* To collect; to become assembled; to congregate; to take origin and grow; to come to a head (as a boil).—*n*. A plait or fold in cloth held in position by a thread drawn through it; a pucker.—**gatherer**, gaTH′ẽr·ẽr, *n*. One who or that which gathers.—**gathering**, gaTH′ẽr·ing, *n*. The act of collecting or assembling; that which is gathered; a crowd; an assembly; a collection of pus; an abscess.

Gatling gun, gat′ling gun, *n*. A form of the mitrailleuse or repeating machine gun, so named from the inventor.

gauche, gōsh, *adj*. [Fr.] Tactless; lacking in the social graces.

gaucherie, gōsh·rē′, *n*. [Fr., from *gauche*, left-handed, awkward.] An awkward action; awkwardness.

Gaucho, gou′chō, *n*. A cowboy of the South American pampas, of mixed Spanish and Indian blood.

gaud, gad, *n*. [L. *gaudium*, joy, gladness; in later times something showy; akin *joy*, *jewel*.] Something worn for adorning the person; a piece of showy finery (*Shak.*).—**gaudery**,† ga′dẽr·i, *n*. Finery; fine things.—**gaudily**, ga′di·li, *adv*. In a gaudy manner.—**gaudiness**, ga′di·nes, *n*. The quality or condition of being gaudy.—**gaudy**, ga′di, *a*. Gay beyond the simplicity of nature or good taste; showy; tastelessly or glaringly adorned.

gauge, gage, gāj, *v.t.*—*gauged, gaged, gauging, gaging*. [O.Fr. *gauger*, perhaps of the same origin with *gallon*, and signifying to find the number of measures in a vessel.] To measure or to ascertain the contents or capacity of; to measure in respect to capability, power, character, etc.; to appraise; to estimate.—*n*. A standard of measure; an instrument to determine dimensions or capacity; a measure; means of estimating; the distance between the lines of rails of a railway, the standard distance being 4 feet 8½ inches; this is called *standard gauge*; *broad* or *wide gauge* and *narrow gauge* are respectively larger and smaller; *joinery*, a simple instrument made to strike a line parallel to the straight side of a board, etc.—**gauger**, gāj′ẽr, *n*. One who gauges; an officer whose business is to ascertain the contents of casks.

Gaul, gal, *n*. [L. *Gallus*, a Gaul, an inhabitant of *Gallia*, the country now called France.] An inhabitant of Gaul.—**Gaulish**, ga′lish, *a*. Pertaining to Gaul.

gaultheria, gal·thē′ri·a, *n*. [After M. Gaulthier, Canadian botanist.] A shrub of a large genus of plants of the heath family that includes the American wintergreen.—*gaultheria oil*, oil of wintergreen.

gaunt, gant, *a*. [Comp. N. *gand*, a slender stick, a thin man.] Attenuated, as with fasting or suffering; lean; meager; haggard; slender; forbidding; desolate, as of an abandoned and dilapidated building.—**gauntly**, gant′li, *adv*. Leanly; meagerly.—**gauntness**, *n*.

gauntlet, gant′let, *n*. [Fr. *gantelet*, dim. from *gant*, a glove, from the Teut.; D. *want*, Dan. *vante*, Icel. *vöttr* (for *vantr*), a glove.] A large iron glove with fingers covered with small plates, formerly worn as armor; a long glove for a lady, which envelops the hand and wrist. The gauntlet used to be thrown down in token of challenge; hence, *to throw down the gauntlet*, to challenge; *to take up the gauntlet*, to accept the challenge.—**gauntleted**, gant′let·ed, *a*. Wearing a gauntlet.

gauss, gous, *n*. [After the mathematician *Gauss*.] The unit of intensity of magnetic field, equal to the intensity produced by unit magnetic pole at a distance of one centimeter.

gauze, gaz, *n*. [Fr. *gaze*, Sp. *gasa*, from the town *Gaza*, whence it was first brought.] A very thin, slight, transparent stuff, of silk, linen, or cotton; any slight open material resembling this (wire *gauze*).—**gauzy**, ga′zi, *a*. Like gauze; thin as gauze.

gavel, gav′el, *n*. [Origin unknown.] The small mallet used by a presiding officer to rap for order or attention.—*v.t.* To force, through use of the gavel.

gavelkind, ga′vel·kind, *n*. [A.Sax. *gafol*, payment, *cynd*, kind, offspring.] An old land tenure in England, still prevailing in Kent, by which land descends to all the sons in equal shares.

gavial, gā′vi·al, *n*. [Indian name.] A crocodile found in India, with an extremely lengthened muzzle.

gavotte, ga·vot′, *n*. [Fr., from *Gavot*, a native of the Pays de *Gap* in the Hautes Alpes, where the dance originated.] A sort of French dance; the music to which the dance was performed, or a similar instrumental movement.

gawk, gak, *n*. [A.Sax. *geác*, Icel. *gaukr*, Sc. *gowk*, cuckoo, simpleton.] A clumsy, awkward person.—*v.i.* To stare; to act like a gawk.—**gawky**, ga′ki, *a*. Awkward; clownish.

gay, gā, *a*. [Fr. *gai*, of Teutonic origin; comp. O.H.G. *gâhi*, swift, excellent, G. *gähe*, *jähe*, quick. *Jay*, the bird, is akin.] Excited with merriment or delight; merry; sportive; frolicsome; fine; showy (a *gay* dress); given to pleasure, often to vicious pleasure; dissipated.—**gaiety**, gā′e·ti, *n*. The state of being gay; merriment; mirth; show.—**gaily, gayly**, gā′li, *adv*. In a gay manner.—**gayness**, gā′nes, *n*. The state or quality of being gay.

gaze, gāz, *v.i.*—*gazed, gazing*. [Sw. *gasa*, to gaze; allied to E. *agast*, Goth. *usgaisjan*, to terrify.] To fix the eyes and look steadily and earnestly; to look with eagerness or curiosity.—*v.t.* To view with fixed attention (*Mil.*).—*n*. A fixed look; a look of eagerness, wonder, or admiration.—**gazer**, gā′zẽr, *n*. One who gazes.

gazelle, ga·zel′, *n*. [Fr. *gazelle*, from Sp. *gazela*, from Ar. *ghazal*.] An antelope of Africa, central and southwest Asia, and India, about the size of a roebuck, of a graceful form, and with long slender limbs.

gazette, ga·zet′, *n*. [It. *gazzetta*, a gazette, from *gazzetta*, a small Venetian coin (from L. or rather Per. *gaza*, treasure), the price of the newspaper; or the name may have been equivalent to 'The Chatterer,' *gazzetta* being a dim. of *gazza*, a magpie.] A newspaper; especially an official or government newspaper containing public announcements, such as appointments to civil or military posts, the names of persons who have been declared bankrupt, etc.; hence, *to appear in the gazette* often means to be publicly announced there as a bankrupt.—*v.t.*—*gazetted, gazetting*. To insert or publish in a gazette; hence, *to be gazetted*, to have one's name announced in the gazette as appointed to some post or promoted to some rank.—**gazetteer**, gaz·et·tēr′, *n*. A manager of a gazette; more commonly a book containing geographical and topographical information alphabetically arranged; a geographical dictionary.

gean, gēn, *n*. [Fr. *guigne*, O.Fr. *guisne*, a word of Teutonic origin.] A kind of wild cherry tree common in England and Scotland, with fruit of an excellent flavor.

gear, gēr, *n*. [A.Sax. *gearwe*, habiliments, equipments, from *gearu*, *gearo*, prepared, ready, whence also *yare*, ready; akin *garb*, dress.] Whatever is prepared for use or wear; hence, dress; ornaments; the harness or furniture of domestic animals;

fāte, fär, fâre, fat, fạll; mē, met, hẽr; pīne, pin; nōte, not, mōve; tūbe, tub, bụll; oil, pound.

naut. the ropes, blocks, etc., belonging to any particular sail or spar; *mach.* a mechanism of toothed wheels and shafts that transmits or changes motion.—*v.t.* To put gear on; to harness; to put into gear.—*v.i.* To come into or be in gear; to fit exactly.—**gearing,** gē'ring, *n.* Harness; the parts by which motion is communicated from one portion of a machine to another.—**gearshift,** gēr'shift, *n.* A device by which transmission gears, as in an automobile, are engaged and disengaged.

geck, gek, *n.* [Comp. D. *gek,* G. *geck,* a silly person; also E. *gawk,* a simpleton.] A dupe; a gull. (*Shak.*)

gecko, gek'o, *n.* A name of various nocturnal lizards of the warm parts of both hemispheres.

geese, gēs, *n.* pl. of *goose.*

Gehenna, gi·hen'na, *n.* [L. *gehenna,* Gr. *geenna,* from the Heb. *ge-hinom,* the valley of Hinom at Jerusalem, where children were 'passed through the fire' to Moloch.] A term used in the New Testament as typical of the place of future punishment and translated hell, hell-fire.

Geiger counter, [After Hans *Geiger,* German physicist.] *Phys.* an instrument for detecting ionized particles, consisting of a metallic tube containing a gas into which projects a needle-like electrode.

geisha, gā'sha, *n.* One of the Japanese dancing and singing girls who perform at private parties and elsewhere.

gelatin, gelatine, jel'a·tin, *n.* [Fr. *gelatine,* It. and Sp. *gelatina,* from L. *gelo,* to congeal. GELID.] A substance obtained from various animal tissues, and employed in the arts and as human food, being known in its coarser forms as *glue, size,* and *isinglass;* a transparent color sheet stretched over a stage light to create a color spotlight. —**gelatination,** je·lat'i·nā'shon, *n.* The act or process of converting into gelatine.—**gelatinize,** je·lat'i·nīz, *v.t.* and *i.* To convert or be converted into gelatine. Also **gelatinate,** je·lat'i·nāt.—**gelatinous,** je·lat'i·nus, *a.* Of or pertaining to, or consisting of gelatine; resembling jelly; viscous.

geld, geld, *v.t.* [From Icel. *gelda,* Dan. *gilde,* G. *gelten,* to geld.] To castrate; to emasculate; to deprive of anything essential (*Shak.*). —**gelder,** gel'dèr, *n.* One who castrates.—**gelding,** gel'ding, *n.* A castrated animal; especially a castrated horse.

gelid, jel'id, *a.* [L. *gelidus,* from *gelo,* to freeze, seen also in *gelatine, congeal, jelly,* the root being that of *cool.*] Cold; very cold; icy or frosty.—**gelidity,** je·lid'i·ti, *n.* The state of being gelid; extreme cold.—**gelidly,** jel'id·li, *adv.* In a gelid manner.

gelsemium, jel·sē'mi·um, *n.* [It. *gelsomino,* jasmine.] A twining shrub, the yellow jasmine of the United States; a dangerous drug derived from this plant.

gem, jem, *n.* [L. *gemma,* a bud, a precious stone.] A precious stone of any kind, especially when cut or polished; a jewel; anything resembling a gem, or remarkable for beauty, rarity, or costliness.—*v.t.* *gemmed, gemming.* To adorn with gems or what resembles gems; to bespangle.

GEM. See AIR-CUSHION VEHICLE.

Gemara, ge·mä'ra, *n.* [Aramaic, completion.] A part of the Talmud, a commentary on the Mishna.

geminate,† jem'i·nāt, *v.t.* [L. *gemino, geminatum,* to double, from *geminus,* twin.] To double.—*a. Bot.* twin; combined in pairs; binate.—**gemination,** jem·i·nā'shon, *n.* A doubling; duplication; repetition.—**Gemini,** jem'i·nī, *n. pl.* [L., twin brothers, Castor and Pollux.] *Astron.* the third sign of the zodiac, so named from its two brightest stars, Castor and Pollux.

gemma, jem'a, *n.* pl. **gemmae,** jem'ē, [L., a bud. GEM.] *Bot.* a leaf bud as distinguished from a flower bud.—**gemmate,** jem'āt, *a.* [L. *gemmatus.*] *Bot.* having buds; reproducing by buds.—**gemmation,** jem·ā'shon, *n.* [L. *gemmatio.*] *Zool.* the process of reproduction by buds; the formation of a new individual by budding; *bot.* the act of budding; vernation.—**gemmiparous,** jem·ip'a·rus, *a.* [L. *pario,* to produce.] Producing buds; *zool.* reproducing by buds.—**gemmule,** jem'ūl, *n.* [L. *gemmula.*] *Bot.* the growing point of the embryo in plants; one of the buds of mosses; a reproductive spore of algae; *zool.* the ciliated embryo or reproductive body of some of the lowest animals.

gemsbok, gemz'bok, *n.* [D. *gemsbok,* G. *gemsbock,* the male chamois, from *gemse,* chamois, and *bock,* buck.] A fine large antelope inhabiting South Africa.

gendarme, zhän'därm, *n.* [Fr., from the pl. *gens d'armes,* men at arms.] A private in the armed police of France.—**gendarmery,** zhän·därm·rē', *n.* [Fr. *gendarmerie.*] The body of gendarmes.

gender, jen'dèr, *n.* [Fr. *genre,* from L. *genus, generis,* kind or sort, gender; with *d* inserted as in tender, adj. GENUS.] Kind or sort‡; a sex, male or female; *gram.* one of those classes or categories into which words are divided according to the sex, natural or metaphorical, of the beings or things they denote; a grammatical category in which words of similar termination are classed together; such a distinction in words. [In English grammar words expressing males are all said to be of the *masculine gender;* those expressing females, of the *feminine gender;* and words expressing things having no sex are of the *neuter gender;* but in other languages gender has a different basis, thus in French it has comparatively little to do with sex, all nouns being either masculine or feminine.]—*v.t.*† To beget; to engender.—*v.i.* To copulate.

gene, jēn, *n.* [From the Gr. root *genos,* born, of a certain kind.]

A unit of a chromosome that determines the character and activities of cells and transmits inherited traits.

genealogy, jē·ni·al'o·ji or jen·i·al'o·ji, *n.* [L. and Gr. *genealogia*—Gr. *genea,* family (root *gen,* to beget), and *logos,* discourse. GENUS.] An account or synopsis tracing the descent of a person or family from an ancestor; an enumeration or table of ancestors and their children in the order of succession; pedigree; lineage; the study of pedigrees or family history.—**genealogical,** jē·ni·a·loj"i·kal, *a.* Pertaining to genealogy; exhibiting or tracing genealogies.—*Genealogical tree,* the genealogy or lineage of a family drawn out under the form of a tree.—**genealogically,** jē·ni·a·loj"i·kal·li, *adv.* In a genealogical manner.—**genealogist,** jē·ni·al'o·jist, *n.* One who traces descents of persons or families.

genera, jen'ér·a, *n.* pl. of *genus.*

general, jen'ér·al, *a.* [Fr. *général,* from L. *generalis,* belonging to a genus, generic, general, from *genus, generis,* a kind. GENUS.] Relating to a whole genus, kind, class, or order; relating to, affecting, or comprehending the whole community; public; common to many or the greatest number; extensive, though not universal; common; usual; ordinary (a *general* opinion); not restrained or limited to a particular import; not specific (a *general* term); not directed to a single object; taken as a whole; regarded in the gross. ∴ This word affixed to another word is common in names expressive of rank or office, as *adjutant-general, attorney-general,* etc.—*General Assembly,* under ASSEMBLY. —*n.* The whole community‡; a general or comprehensive notion; a military officer of the highest rank; the commander of an army or of a division or brigade; the chief of an order of monks.—*In general,* in the main; for the most part; not always or universally; also in the aggregate, or as a whole.—**generalissimo,** jen'ér·a·lis"i·mō, *n.* [It.] The chief commander of an army or military force which consists of two or more grand divisions under separate commanders.—**generality,** jen·ér·al'i·ti, *n.* The state of being general; the quality of including species or particulars; a statement which is general or not specific, or which lacks application to any one case.—*The generality,* the main body; the bulk; the greatest part.—**generalization,** jen'ér·al·i·zā"shon, *n.* The act or process of generalizing; a general inference.—**generalize,** jen'ér·al·īz, *v.t.*—*generalized; generalizing.* To reduce or bring under a general law, rule, or statement; to bring into relation with a wider circle of facts; to deduce from the consideration of many particulars.—*v.i.* To form objects into classes; to bring or classify particulars under general heads or rules.—**generally,** jen'ér·al·li, *adv.* In general; commonly; ordinarily; extensively, though not universally; most frequently, but not without exceptions; without detail; leaving particular facts out of account; in the whole taken together.—**generalship,** jen'ér·al·ship. *n.* The office of a general; the discharge of the functions of a general; military skill exhibited in the judicious handling of troops; management or judicious tactics generally.

generate, jen'ér·āt, *v.t.*—generated, generating. [L. *genero, generatum,* to beget. GENUS.] To procreate (young); to produce; to cause to be; to bring into existence; to cause (heat, vibrations).—**generable,** jen'ér·a·bl, *a.* Capable of being generated.—**generation,** jen·ér·ā'shon, *n.* The act of generating; production formation; a single succession of the human race in natural descent, calculated at thirty years; the average period of time between one succession of children and the next following; people who are contemporary or living at the same time; a race; progeny; offspring.—*Equivocal* or *spontaneous generation,* in *biol.* the production of animals and plants without previously existing parents; abiogenesis.—*Alternate generation,* under ALTERNATE.—**generative,** jen'ér·ā·tiv, *a.* Having the power of generating; belonging to generation or the act of procreating.—**generator,** jen'ér·ā·tér, *n.* One who or that which begets, causes, or produces; *elec.* a device that changes mechanical energy into electrical energy; *chem.* an apparatus that causes vapor or gas to form.

generic, je·ner'ik, *a.* [Fr. *générique,* from L. *genus, generis,* kind. GENUS.] Pertaining to a genus; descriptive of, belonging to, or comprehending the genus, as distinct from the species or from another genus; referring to a large class.—**generically,** je·ner'i·kal·li, *adv.*

generous, jen'ér·us, *a.* [L. *generosus,* of honorable birth, generous, from *genus, generis,* birth, extraction, family. GENUS.] Noble; honorable; magnanimous (of persons or things); liberal; bountiful; munificent; free in giving; strong; full of spirit (*generous* wine).—**generously,** jen'ér·us·li, *adv.* In a generous manner.—**generosity,** jen·ér·os'i·ti, *n.* [L. *generositas.*] The quality of being generous; nobleness of soul; liberality of sentiment; a disposition to give liberally.—**generousness,** jen'ér·us·nes, *n.* The quality of being generous; generosity.

genesis, jen'e·sis, *n.* [Gr. *genesis,* from root *gen,* to beget. GENUS.] The act of producing or giving origin; a taking origin; generation; origination; [*cap.*] the first book of the Old Testament, containing the history of the creation of the world and of the human race.

genet, jen'et, *n.* [Fr. *genette,* Sp. *ginete,* from the name of a Berber tribe who supplied the Moorish sultans of Grenada with cavalry.] A small-sized, well-proportioned Spanish horse: spelled also *Jennet.*

genet, genette, jen'et, je·net', *n.* [Sp. *gineta,* from Ar. *jarnait.*] A carnivorous animal belonging to the civet family, a native of western Asia; the fur of the genet.

genetic, genetical, je·net'ik, je·net'i·kal, *a.* [From Gr. *genetēs,* a begetter, or *genesis,* generation.] Relating to genetics; pertaining to the origin of a thing or its mode of production.—**genetically,** je·net'i·kal·li, *adv.*—**genetics,** je·net'iks, *n.* The scientific study of heredity.

geneva, je·nē'va, *n.* [From L. *juniperus,* juniper; *gin* is a contraction of this.] A spirit distilled from grain or malt, with the addition of juniper berries; gin.

Genevan, je·nē'van, *a.* Pertaining to Geneva.—*n.* An inhabitant of Geneva; a Genevese; a Calvinist.

genial, jē'ni·al, *a.* [L. *genialis,* from *genius,* social disposition, genius, from root *gen.* GENUS.] Characterized by kindly warmth of disposition and manners such as promotes cheerfulness on the part of others; cordial; kindly; sympathetically cheerful; enlivening; warming; contributing to life and cheerfulness (the *genial* sun).—**geniality, genialness,** jē·ni·al'i·ti, jē'ni·al·nes, *n.* The state or quality of being genial; sympathetic cheerfulness or cordiality.—**genially,** jē'ni·al·li, *adv.* In a genial manner.

geniculate, je·nik'ū·lāt, *a.* [L. *geniculatus,* from *geniculum,* a knot or joint, from *genu,* the knee.] *Bot.* knee-jointed; having knots like knees. —**geniculation,** je·nik'ū·lā·shon, *n.* Knottiness; a knot or joint like a knee.

genie, jē'nē, *n.* pl. **genii,** je'nē·ī. [A form due to the influence of the word *genius.*] Same as *Jinni.*

genipap, jen'i·pap, *n.* [From *genipapo,* the name in Guiana.] The fruit of a South American and West Indian tree of the Madder family, about the size of an orange.

genital, jen'i·tal, *a.* [L. *genitalis,* from *gigno, genitum,* to beget. GENUS.] Relating to generation; of, or pertaining to, the sexual organs.—**genitals,** jen'i·talz, *n.* pl. The reproductive organs, especially the external sexual organs.—**genitalia,** jen·i·tāl'ia, *n.* pl. The genitals.

genitive, jen'i·tiv, *a.* [L. *genitivus,* relating to birth or origin, from *gigno, genitum,* to beget.] *Gram.* a term applied to a case in the declension of nouns, adjectives, pronouns, etc., in English called the possessive case.—*n. Gram.* the genitive case.—**genitival,** jen·i·ti'val, *a.* Relating to the genitive.

genius, jē'ni·us, *n.* [L., a genius or tutelary spirit, social disposition, wit or genius, from the root *gen,* to beget. GENUS.] A tutelary deity; an imaginary being ruling or protecting men, places, or things; a good or evil spirit supposed to be attached to a person; that disposition or bent of mind which is peculiar to every man, and which qualifies him for a particular employment; intellectual endowment of the high-

est kind, particularly, the power of invention or of producing original combinations; a man thus intellectually endowed; peculiar character or constitution; pervading spirit or influence from associations or otherwise (the special *genius* of a language). [Plural *Genii* meaning spirits, *Geniuses* meaning men.]

Genoese, jen'o·ēz, *a.* Relating to Genoa.—*n.* An inhabitant or the people of Genoa in Italy.

genocide, jen'o·sīd, *n.* [Gr. *genos,* race, plus *cide.*] The use of calculated, systematic means to bring about the extermination of a racial, cultural, or political group.

genre, zhänr, *n.* [Fr., from L. *genus, generis,* kind.] *Painting,* a term applied to paintings which depict scenes of ordinary life, as domestic, rural, or village scenes.

gent, jent. A vulgar abbreviation for *Gentleman.*

genteel, jen·tēl', *a.* [Fr. *gentil,* from L. *gentilis,* belonging to the same family or nation, not foreign, latterly also gentile or pagan, from *gens, gentis,* race, stock, family. GENUS. *Gentle* and *gentile* are doublets of this.] Having the manners of well-bred people; well-bred; refined; free from anything low or vulgar; of a station above the common people; furnishing a competence (a *genteel* allowance).—**genteelly,** jen·tēl'li, *adv.* In a genteel manner.—**genteelness,** jen·tēl'nes, *n.* The state or quality of being genteel.—**gentility,** jen·til'i·ti, *n.* The state or character of being genteel; the manners or circumstances of genteel people.

gentian, jen'shi·an, *n.* [L. *gentiana*— said to be named after *Gentius,* king of Illyria, who first experienced the virtue of gentian.] The name of certain bitter herbaceous plants with beautiful blue or yellow flowers, the roots of some species being highly valued as a tonic.

gentile, jen'til, *n.* [L. *gentilis,* from *gens, gentis,* nation, race. GENTEEL.] *Scrip.* any one belonging to the non-Jewish nations; any person not a Jew or a Christian; a heathen; applied by Mormons to those outside their sect.—*a.* Belonging to the non-Jewish nations; *gram.* denoting one's race or country (a *gentile* noun).—**gentilism,** jen'til·ism, *n.* Heathenism; paganism.

gentility. See GENTEEL.

gentle, jen'tl, *a.* [Fr. *gentil.* GENTEEL.] Well-born; of a good family; soft and refined in manners; mild; meek; not rough, harsh, or severe; not wild, turbulent, or refractory; placid; bland; not rude or violent.— *n.* A person of good birth; a gentleman.—**gentleness,** jen'tl·nes, *n.* The state or quality of being gentle.—**gently,** jen'tli, *adv.* In a gentle manner; mildly; meekly; placidly.— **gentlefolk,** jen'tl·fōk, *n.* Persons of good breeding and family: generally in plural, *gentlefolks.*—**gentleman,** jen'tl·man, *n.* [*Gentle,* that is, well-born, and *man;* Fr. *gentilhomme.* GENTEEL.] A man of good family or good social position; in a somewhat narrow and technical sense, any man above the rank of yeomen, including noblemen; in a more limited sense, a man who without a title bears a coat of arms; as commonly applied, any man whose education, occupation, or income raises him above menial service or an ordinary trade; a man of good breeding and politeness, as distinguished from the vulgar and clownish; a man of the highest honor, courtesy, and morality; often used almost as a polite equivalent for 'man': in the plural the appellation by which men are addressed in popular assemblies, whatever may be their condition or character.—**gentlemanly, gentlemanlike,** jen′tl‧men‧li, jen′tl‧men‧lĭk, a. Pertaining to or becoming a gentleman; like a gentleman.—**gentleman-at-arms,** n. One of forty gentlemen attached to the English court whose office it is to attend the sovereign to and from the chapel-royal, etc.—**gentlewoman,** jen′tl‧wu̧m‧an, n. A woman of good family or of good breeding; a woman above the vulgar; a woman who waits about the person of one of high rank.

gentry, jen′tri, n. [O.Fr. genterise, for gentilise, high birth, from gentil, L. gentilis. GENTEEL.] Rank or good birth (Shak.)‡; courtesy (Shak.)‡; pl. people of good position; wealthy or well-born people in general, of a rank below the nobility; also ironically applied to disreputable characters.

genuflect, jen′ū‧flekt, v.i. [L. genu, the knee, and flecto, to bend, as in inflect, reflect, etc.] To kneel, as in worship, to make a genuflection or genuflections.—**genuflection, genuflexion,** jen‧ū‧flek′shon, n. The act of bending the knee, particularly in worship.

genuine, jen′ū‧in, a. [L. genuinus, from root of gigno, to beget. GENUS.] Belonging to the original stock; hence, real; natural; true; pure; not spurious, false, or adulterated. ∴ Syn. under AUTHENTIC.—**genuinely,** jen′ū‧in‧li, adv. In a genuine manner.—**genuineness,** jen′ū‧in‧nes, n. The state of being genuine.

genus, jē′nus, n. pl. **genera** or **genuses,** jen′ẽr‧a, jē′nus‧ez. [L. genus, generis, a kind, class = Gr. genos, race, family; from root gen, Skr. jan, to beget, the same as in E. kin, kind. This root is seen in a great many words: generous, genesis, genial, genital, genuine, indigenous, ingenious, progeny, etc.] A kind, class, or sort; logic, a class of a greater extent than a species; a word which may be predicated of several things of different species; in scientific classifications, an assemblage of species possessing certain characters in common, by which they are distinguished: subordinate to phylum, class, order, family.

geocentric, geocentrical, jē‧ō‧sen′trik, jē‧ō‧sen′tri‧kal, a. [Gr. gē, earth, and kentron, center.] Astron. having reference to the earth for its center; seen from the earth: applied to the place of a planet as seen from the center of the earth.

geochemistry, jē‧ō‧kem′ist‧ri, n. [Gr. ge, earth, and E. chemistry (which see).]The chemical study of the earth; combining parts of geology and chemistry, a study of the elements in the earth, in its waters, and in its atmosphere.

geode, jē′ōd, n. [Gr. geōdes, earthy, from gē, earth.] Mineral, a roundish hollow lump of agate or other mineral, having the cavity frequently lined with crystals.

geodesy, jē‧od′e‧si, n. [Gr. geōdaisia —gē, the earth, and daiō, to divide.] That branch of applied mathematics which determines the figures and areas of large portions of the earth's surface, the general figure of the earth, and the variations of the intensity of gravity in different regions.—**geodesic,** jē‧o‧des′ik, a. Shaped like a dome from a basic framework of polygonal sections in tension.—n. The shortest line between any two points on a mathematically defined surface.—**geodesical,** jē‧o‧des′i‧kal, a.—**geodetic, geodetical,** jē‧o‧det′ik, jē‧o‧det′i‧kal, a. Of or pertaining to geodesy.

geognosy, jē‧og′no‧si, n. [Gr. gē, the earth, and gnōsis, knowledge.] That part of natural science which treats of the structure of the earth—a term nearly equivalent to geology, but having less to do with scientific reasoning and theory.

geography, jē‧og′ra‧fi, n. [Gr. geōgraphia—gē, the earth, and graphē, description.] The science or branch of knowledge which treats of the world and its inhabitants, describing more especially the external features of the world, and in its widest scope embracing mathematical geography, which deals with the figure and measurement of the earth, latitude and longitude, etc.; physical geography, which describes the earth's features and explains their relations to each other, treating also of climate, animals, and plants, and their distribution; the ocean and its phenomena, etc.; and political geography, which treats of the states and peoples of the earth and their political and social characteristics; a description of the earth or a certain portion of it; a book containing such a description. —**geographer,** jē‧og′ra‧fẽr, n. One who is versed in, or compiles a treatise on, geography.—**geographic, geographical,** jē‧o‧graf′ik, jē‧o‧graf′i‧kal, a. Relating to geography; containing information regarding geography.—**geographically,** jē‧o‧graf′i‧kal‧li, adv. In a geographical manner.

geology, jē‧ol′o‧ji, n. [Gr. gē, the earth, and logos, discourse.] The science which deals with the structure, especially the internal structure, of the crust of the globe, and of the substances which compose it; the science which treats of the minerals, rocks, earths, or other substances composing the globe, the relations which the several constituent masses bear to each other, their formation, structure, position, and history, together with the successive changes that have taken place in the organic and inorganic kingdoms of nature as illustrated by fossils or otherwise. —**geologic, geological,** jē‧o‧loj′ik, jē‧o‧loj′i‧kal, a. Pertaining to geology. —**geologically,** jē‧o‧loj′i‧kal‧li, adv. In a geological manner.—**geologist,** jē‧ol′o‧jist, n. One versed in geology. —**geologize,** jē‧ol′o‧jīz, v.i. To study geology; to make geological investigations.

geomancy, jē′o‧man‧si, n. [Gr. gē, the earth, and manteia, divination.] A kind of divination by means of figures or lines formed by little dots or points, originally on the earth and afterward on paper.—**geomancer,** jē′o‧man‧sẽr, n. One versed in or who practices geomancy.—**geomantic,** jē‧o‧man′tik, a. Of or pertaining to geomancy.

geometry, jē‧om′e‧tri, n. [Gr. geōmetria, gē, the earth, and metron, measure—the term being originally equivalent to landmeasuring or surveying.] The science of magnitude; that science which treats of the properties of lines, angles, surfaces, and solids; that branch of mathematics which treats of the properties and relations of magnitudes.— **geometric, geometrical,** jē‧ō‧met′rik, jē‧ō‧met′ri‧kal, a. [Gr. geōmetrikos.] Pertaining to geometry; according to the rules or principles of geometry; done or determined by geometry.—Geometrical elevation, a design for the front or side of a building drawn according to the rules of geometry, as opposed to perspective or natural elevation.— Geometrical progression, progression in which the terms increase or decrease by a common ratio, as 2, 4, 8, 16, etc.—Geometrical proportion, proportion involving equal ratios in the two parts—1:3::4:12.—**geometrically,** jē‧o‧met′ri‧kal‧li, adv. In a geometrical manner.—**geometrician, geometer,** jē‧om′e‧trish‧an, jē‧om′e‧tẽr, n. One skilled in geometry.

geophagism, jē‧of′a‧jizm, n. [Gr. gē, the earth, and phagō, to eat.] The act or practice of eating earth, as clay, chalk, etc.—**geophagist,** jē‧of′a‧jist, n. One who eats earth.

geophysics, jē‧o‧fiz″iks, n. The physics of the earth, particularly the use of instruments such as the seismograph and magnetometer to study the inaccessible portions of the earth.

geoponic, jē‧o‧pon′ik, a. [Gr. gē, the earth, and ponos, labor.] Pertaining to tillage or agriculture.—**geoponics,** jē‧o‧pon′iks, n. The art or science of cultivation.

George, jorj, n. [This proper name is from Gr. geōrgos, a husbandman—gē, the earth, and ergon, labor.] A figure of St. George on horseback encountering the dragon, worn pendent from the collar by knights of the Garter.—St. George, the patron saint of England, supposed to be martyred in A.D. 303 under Diocletian.— St. George's Cross, the English flag, a red cross on a white ground, opposed to the St. Andrew's Cross of Scotland, a silver saltire on a blue ground.—**Georgian,** jor′ji‧an, a. Be-

ch, chain; ch, Sc. loch; g, go; j, job; ng, sing; TH, then; th, thin; w, wig; hw, whig; zh, azure.

longing or relating to the reigns of the four *Georges*, kings of Great Britain; a native of Georgia in the United States, or of Georgia in the Caucasus.—**georgic**, jor′jik, *n.* [Gr. *geōrgikos*, rustic.] A rural poem; a poetical composition on the subject of husbandry.—**Georgics**, *n.* Poem in four books by Virgil.

geothermal, jē·o·thėr′mal, *a.* [Gr. *gē* plus *thermal.*] Of, or relating to, the heat of the earth's interior.

geotropism, jē·ot′ro·pizm, *n.* [Gr. *gē*, the earth, and *tropos*, a turning.] Disposition or tendency to turn or incline toward the earth, the characteristic exhibited in a young plant when deprived of light.—**geotropic**, jē·ō·trop′ik, *a.* Pertaining to or exhibiting geotropism.

gerah, gē′ra, *n.* [Heb.] The smallest piece of money among the ancient Jews, equal to about three half-pennies.

geranium, je·rā′ni·um, *n.* [L. *geranium*, Gr. *geranion*, from *geranos*, a crane—on account of the long projecting spike of the seed capsule.] The crane's-bill genus, a genus of herbaceous plants (rarely under-shrubs), natives of the temperate regions of the world, having flowers which are usually blue or red, and often handsome; the geraniums of gardens belong, however, to a different genus (*Pelargonium*).

gerbil, jėr′bil, *n.* [Fr. *gerbille*, from *gerbo*, the Arabic name.] A small burrowing rodent found in the sandy parts of Africa and Asia, one species, inhabiting Egypt, being about the size of a mouse.

gerfalcon, jėr′fạ·kn, *n.* See GYR-FALCON.

geriatrics, jer·i·at′riks, *n.* [Gr. *geras*, old age, and *iatrics*.] A field of medicine concerned with old age and its health problems.

germ, jėrm, *n.* [Fr. *germe*, L. *germen*, an offshoot, a sprout.] A microorgan-ism causing disease; *physiol.* the earliest form under which any organ-ism appears; the rudimentary or embryonic form of an organism; hence, that from which anything springs; origin; first principle.—**germ cell**, *n. Animal physiol.* the cell which results from the union of the spermatozoon with the germinal vesicle or its nucleus.—**germinal**, jėr′mi·nal, *a.* Pertaining to a germ or seed bud.—*Germinal vesicle, animal physiol.* a cell which floats in the yoke of an egg; *bot.* a cell contained in the embryo sac, from which the embryo is developed.—**germinal disk**, jėr′min·al disk, *n.* In large eggs full of nutritive matter (e.g., those of birds), the part which de-velops into the body of the embryo.—**germinate**, jėr′mi·nāt, *v.i.*—*ger-minated, germinating.* To sprout; to bud; to shoot; to begin to vegetate, as a plant or its seed.—*v.t.* To cause to sprout or bud.—**germi-nation**, jėr·mi·nā′shon, *n.*—**germi-native**, jėr′mi·nā·tiv, *a.*

german, jėr′man, *a.* [L. *germanus*, a brother, for *germinanus*, from *germen*, an offshoot. GERM.] Sprung from

the same father and mother or from members of the same family; ger-mane‡.—**germane**, jėr′mān, *a.* Close-ly akin; nearly related; allied; relevant; pertinent.

German, jėr′man, *n.* [L. *Germanus*, German, *Germani*, the Germans, not a native German appellation, but probably borrowed by the Romans from the Celts; of doubtful origin.] A native or inhabitant of Germany; the language of the higher and more southern districts of Germany, and the literary language of all Germany, called by the people themselves *Deutsch* (=*Dutch*), and also known as *High German*, to distinguish it from the *Low German*, or vernacular of the lowland or northern parts of Germany. See also DUTCH.—*a.* Be-longing to Germany.—**Germanic**, jėr·man′ik, *a.* Pertaining to Germany; a name of certain languages other-wise called *Teutonic.*—**Germanism**, jėr′man·izm, *n.* An idiom or phrase of the German language.—**German silver**, *n.* A white alloy of nickel, formed by fusing together 100 parts of copper, 60 of zinc, and 40 of nickel.—**German tinder**, *n.* Amadou.

germander, jėr·man′dėr, *n.* [Fr. *ger-mandrée*, corrupted from L. *chamæ-drys*, Gr. *chamaidrys*, germander—*chamai*, on the ground, and *drys*, an oak.] The common name of certain labiate plants, a few species of which are common in Britain.—*Germander speedwell.* SPEEDWELL.

germanium, jur·mā′ni·um, *n.* [From *Germany.*] A rare grayish-white me-tallic element. Symbol, Ge; at. no., 32; at. wt., 72.59.

germicide, jėr′mi·sīd, *n.* [E. *germ*, L. *cædo*, I kill.] A substance that destroys germs, especially disease germs.

germ plasm, jėrm′plazm, *n.* [From *germ* and Gr. *plasma*, anything formed.] A hypothetical constituent of the nucleus in a sex cell, by which hereditary characters are supposed to be transmitted.

gerontocracy, jer·on·tok′ra·si, *n.* [Gr. *gerōn, gerontos*, an old man, and *kratos*, power.] Government by old men.

gerrymander, ger′i·man″dėr, *v.i.* [From *Gerry*, governor of Mas-sachusetts.] To divide a state into election districts in an unfair way.

gerund, jer′und, *n.* [L. *gerundium*, from *gero*, to carry on or perform, the gerund expressing the doing or the necessity of doing something.] A part of the Latin verb, or a kind of verbal noun, used to express the meaning of the present infinitive active; a term adopted into other languages to indicate various forms or modifications of the verb, in English being applied to verbal nouns such as *teaching* in expres-sions like *fit for teaching boys.*—**gerundial**, je·run′di·al, *a.*—**gerun-dive**, je·run′div, *n.* A name given originally by Latin grammarians to the future participle passive, a form similar to the gerund, sometimes used in regard to other languages.

gestalt, ge·shtạlt′, *n.* [G. *gestalt*,

form.] An organized pattern of ex-periences or acts; *psychol.* the theory that acts or experiences do not occur through the sum-mation of separate elements, such as reflexes, but rather through the formed patterns or configurations of these called *Gestalten*, which operate individually or interact.

gestation, jes·tā′shon, *n.* [L. *gestatio*, from *gesto, gestatum*, freq. from *gero, gestum*, to carry, seen also in *gesture, gesticulate, congest, digest, suggestion*, etc.] The act of carrying young in the womb from conception to deliv-ery; pregnancy.—**gestic**,† jes′tik, *a.* [From old *gest*, a deed or exploit; L. *gestum*, from *gero.*] Pertaining to deeds or exploits. (Goldsmith.)

gesticulate, jes·tik′ū·lāt, *v.i.*—*gesticu-lated, gesticulating.* [L. *gesticulor, gesticulatus*, from *gero, gestum*, to bear or carry. GESTATION.] To make gestures or motions, as in speaking; to use postures.—*v.t.*† To represent by gesture.—**gesticulation**, jes·tik′-ū·lā′shon, *n.* [L. *gesticulatio.*] The act of gesticulating or making ges-tures; a gesture.—**gesticulator**, jes·-tik′ū·lā·tėr, *n.* One that gesticulates. —**gesticulatory**, jes·tik′ū·la·to·ri, *a.* Pertaining to gesticulation.

gesture, jes′chėr, *n.* [L.L. *gestura*, mode of acting, from L. *gestus*, posture, motion, from *gero, gestum*, to bear, to carry. GESTATION.] A motion or action intended to express an idea or feeling, or to enforce an argument or opinion; movement of the body or limbs.—*v.t.* gestured, gesturing. To express by gesture.—*v.i.* To make gestures.

get, get, *v.t.* pret. *got* (*gat*, obs.), pp. *got, gotten*, ppr. *getting.* [A.Sax. *gitan*, to obtain; Icel. *geta*, O.H.G. *gezan*, Goth. *gitan*; probably of same root as Gr. *chandanō*, to contain, L. (*pre*)*hendo*, to catch, as in *comprehend.* Hence *beget, forget.*] To procure; to obtain; to gain possession of by any means; to beget; to procreate; to commit to memory; to learn; to prevail on; to induce; to persuade; to procure or cause to be or occur (to *get* a letter sent, to *get* things together); *refl.* to carry or betake one's self.—*To get in*, to collect and bring under cover.—*To get off*, to put or be able to put off; to take off.—*To get on*, to be able to put on; to draw or pull on.—*To get out*, to draw or be able to draw forth.—*v.i.* To make acquisition; to gain; to arrive at any place or state; to become, followed by some modify-ing word, and sometimes implying difficulty or labor.—*To get above*, to surmount; to surpass.—*To get along*, to proceed; to advance.—*To get at*, to reach; to make way to; to come to.—*To get away*, to depart; to leave; to disengage one's self.—*To get back*, to arrive at the place from which one departed; to return.—*To get before*, to advance to the front or so as to be before.—*To get behind*, to fall in the rear; to lag.—*To get clear*, to disengage one's self; to be released.—*To get down*, to descend; to come from an elevation.—*To get* *drunk*, to become intoxicated.—*To get forward*, to proceed; to advance; also, to prosper.—*To get home*, to arrive at one's dwelling.—*To get in*, to obtain admission; to insinuate one's self.—*To get loose* or *free*, to disengage one's self; to be released from confinement.—*To get off*, to escape; to depart; to get clear; to alight or come down from a thing.—*To get on*, to proceed; to advance; to succeed; to prosper; to mount.—*To get out*, to depart from an enclosed place or from confinement; to escape; to free one's self from embarrassment.—*To get over*, to pass over; to surmount; to conquer; to recover from.—*To get quit of*, *to get rid of*, to shift off, or to disengage one's self from.—*To get through*, to pass through and reach a point beyond; also, to finish; to accomplish.—*To get to*; to reach; to arrive at.—*To get up*, to rise from a bed or a seat; to ascend; to climb; to originate and prepare or bring forward (to *get up* a concert); to dress; to equip (the actor was well *got up*).—**getter**, get′-ėr, *n.* One who gets; one who begets†.—**getting**, get′ing, *n.* The act of obtaining; acquisition.—**getup**, *n.* Equipment; dress and other accessories (an actor's *getup*); initiative.

gewgaw, gū′ga, *n.* [Origin unknown.] A showy trifle; a bauble.

geyser, gī′zẽr, *n.* [Icel. *geysir*, lit. the gusher, from *geysa*, to gush; allied to E. *gush*.] The name given to springs or fountains of hot water characterized by periodic eruptions, the water rising up in a column.

g-force, jē′fors, *n.* [*Gravity* and *force*.] *Phys.* gravitational pull equal to the force exerted on a body at rest, used to indicate the pull acting on a body when the body is accelerated.

ghastly, gast′li, *a.* [A.Sax. *gaestlic*, terrible, *gaest* being the same as *ghast* in *aghast*. AGHAST.] Terrible of countenance; deathlike; dismal; horrible; shocking; dreadful.—*adv.* In a ghastly manner; hideously.

ghat, ghaut, gät, gat, *n.* [Hind.] In the East Indies, a pass through a mountain; a range or chain of hills; a landing place or stairway to the rivers of India.—**ghat.** As at Cal*cutta*, Cali*cut*, to the shrines of the goddess *Kali*.

Gheber, Ghebre, gā′bėr, *n.* The name given by the Mohammedans to one belonging to the Persian fire worshipers, called in India, Parsees.

ghee, gē, *n.* [Hind.] In India, the butter made from the milk of the buffalo converted into a kind of oil.

gherkin, gėr′kin, *n.* [G. *gurke*, D. *agurkje*, Dan. *agurke*, from Ar. *al-khiyâr*, Per. *khiyâr*, cucumber.] A small-fruited variety of the cucumber used for pickling.

ghetto, get′to, *n.* [It. *borghetto*, *borgo*, borough.] Jewish pen or quarter, a Jewry; the quarter, closed and locked at night, in Italian and Rhine-valley towns, in which Jews lived.

ghost, gōst, *n.* [A.Sax. *gást*, a spirit, a ghost; D. *geest*, G. *geist*, a spirit; from a root seen in Icel. *geisa*, to chafe, to rage as fire; Sw. *gasa*, to

ferment; E. *yeast*.] The soul or spiritual part of man‡; the visible spirit of a dead person; a disembodied spirit; an apparition; shadow (not the *ghost* of a chance).—*To give up the ghost*, to yield up the spirit; to die.—*The Holy Ghost*, the third person in the Trinity.—**ghostlike**, gōst′līk, *a.* Like a ghost; spectral.—**ghostliness**, gōst′li·nes, *n.* The state or quality of being ghostly.—**ghostly**, gōst′li, *a.* Having to do with the soul or spirit; spiritual; not carnal or secular; pertaining to apparitions (a *ghostly* visitant); suggestive of ghosts (*ghostly* gloom).

ghoul, gōl, *n.* [Per. *ghûl*, a kind of demon supposed to devour men.] An imaginary evil being among eastern nations, which is supposed to prey upon human bodies.

ghyll, gil, *n.* Same as Gill, a ravine.

giant, jī′ant, *n.* [O.E. *geant*, Fr. *géant*, from L. *gigas*, *gigantis*, from Gr. *gigas*, *gigantos*, a giant, formed by reduplication of root *gan*, *gen*, to produce.] A man of extraordinary bulk and stature; a person of extraordinary strength or powers, bodily or intellectual.—*a.* Like a giant; extraordinary in size or strength.—**giantess**, jī′an·tes, *n.* A female giant.

gibber, jib′ėr, *v.i.* [Akin to *jabber* and *gabble*, perhaps also to *gibe*.] To speak rapidly and inarticulately; to gabble or jabber.—**gibberish**, jib′ėr·ish, *n.* Rapid and inarticulate talk; unintelligible language.

gibberellin, jib·er·el′in, *n.* [From *Gibberella*, genus name of *Gibberella fujikuroi* plus *in*.] A substance obtained from the fungus *Gibberella fujikuroi* and having plant growth-stimulating hormones.

gibbet, jib′et, *n.* [Fr. *gibet*, O.Fr. *gibbet*; comp. O.Fr. *gibet*, a large stick.] A kind of gallows; a gallows with a crossbeam or an arm projecting from the top, on which notorious malefactors were hanged; the projecting beam or jib of a crane.—*v.t.* To hang on a gibbet or gallows; to hold up to ridicule, scorn, infamy, etc.

gibbon, gib′on, *n.* A name of various apes of the Indian Archipelago, slender in form and with very long arms.

gibbous, gib′us, *a.* [L. *gibbosus*, from *gibbus*, humped, a hump.] Swelling out or protuberant; exhibiting a sort of hump or convex swelling; hunched: applied to the moon when more than half and less than full; *bot.* more convex or tumid in one place than another.—**gibbose**, gib·ōs′, *a.* Humped; having humps; gibbous. —**gibbosity**, gib·os′i·ti, *n.* The state of being gibbous or gibbose; a protuberance or round swelling prominence; convexity. — **gibbousness**, gib′us·nes, *n.*

gibe, jīb, *v.i.*—*gibed, gibing*. [From the same root as *gab*, the mouth, *gabble*, *jabber*, etc.; comp. Sw. *gipa*, to wry the mouth.] To utter taunting sarcastic words; to flout; to fleer.—*v.t.* To assail with contemptuous words; to mock; to flout; to treat with sarcastic reflections; to taunt.—*n.* A taunt or sarcastic remark; a

mocking jest; a scoff.—**giber**, jī′bėr, *n.* One who gibes.

giblets, jib′lets, *n. pl.* [O.Fr. *gibelet*, a dish of game.] The entrails of a goose or other fowl removed before roasting; rags or tatters†.

giddy, gid′i, *a.* [A.Sax. *gydig*, insane, from *god*, a god, a heathen deity.] Having in the head a sensation of a whirling or reeling about; affected with vertigo; dizzy; reeling; rendering giddy; inducing giddiness (a *giddy* height); suggestive of giddiness from its motion; whirling; inconstant; changeable; flighty; thoughtless; rendered wild by excitement; having the head turned.—*v.t.*—*giddied, giddying*. To make giddy.—*v.i.* To turn quickly; to reel.—**giddily**, gid′i·li, *adv.* In a giddy manner.—**giddiness**, gid′i·nes, *n.* The state of being giddy.

gier-eagle, gēr′ē·gl, *a.* [D. *gier*, G. *geier*, a vulture.] A kind of eagle. (O.T.)

gift, gift, *n.* [A.Sax. *gift*, from *gifan*, to give. GIVE.] That which is given or bestowed; a present; a donation; the act, right, or power of giving (it is not in his *gift*); a natural quality or endowment regarded as conferred; power; faculty; talent. *v.t.* To confer as a gift; to make a gift or present to; to endow.—**gifted**, gif′ted, *pp.* or *a.* Endowed by nature with any power or faculty; largely endowed with intellect or genius; talented.

gig, gig, *n.* [Origin doubtful; comp. *jig*.] Any little thing that is whirled round in play; a whirligig (*Shak.*); a light one-horse carriage with two wheels; a long narrow rowing boat; a ship's boat suited for rowing expeditiously, and generally furnished with sails; a machine for teazling woolen cloth; a kind of harpoon.

gigantic, jī·gan′tik, *a.* [L. *giganticus*, from *gigas*, a giant. GIANT.] Of the size or proportions of a giant; colossal; huge; enormous; immense. —**gigantically**, jī·gan′tik·a·li, *adv.*— **gigantism**, jī·gan′tizm, *n.* The state of being a giant; excessive largeness.

giggle, gig′l, *n.* [Imitative, like *cackle*; D. *gicken*, *gickelen*, to cackle; Swiss *gigelen*, to giggle.] A kind of laugh, with short catches of the voice or breath; a titter.—*v.i.*—*giggled, giggling*. To laugh with short catches of the breath or voice; to titter.—**giggler**, gig′lėr, *n.* One that giggles.—**giggling**, gig′ling, *a.* Characterized by giggles; tittering.—**giglet, giglot**, gig′let, gig′lot, *n.* [From *giggle*, or from *gig* with a diminutive termination.] A light giddy girl; a wanton.—*a.* Giddy; inconstant; wanton (*Shak.*).

gigot, jig′ot, *n.* [Fr., from O.Fr. *gigue*, the thigh, a fiddle, from O.G. *gîge*, G. *geige*, a violin, from its shape.] A leg of mutton.

gilbert, gil′bert, *n.* [After the natural philosopher *Gilbert*.] The C.G.S. unit of magnetomotive force.

gild, gild, *v.t.*—pret. and pp. *gilded* or *gilt*. [A.Sax. *gyldan*, from *gold*.] To overlay with gold, either in leaf or powder, or in amalgam with quicksilver; to give a golden hue to;

to illuminate; to brighten; to render bright; to give a fair and agreeable external appearance to.—**gilded,** *a.* *Gilded chamber*, the House of Lords. —*Gilded youth*, wealthy young people; fashionables. [Fr. *jeunesse dorée*.] **gilder,** gil′dẽr, *n.* One who gilds.—**gilding,** gil′ding, *n.* The art of a gilder; what is laid on by the gilder; a thin coating of gold leaf; *fig.* fair superficial show.

gild, gild, *n.* Same as *Guild*.

gilder, gil′dẽr, *n.* A Dutch coin; a guilder.

gill, gil, *n.* [Not in A.Sax. or German; a Scandinavian word: Dan. *giaelle*, Sw. *gäl*, *fisk-gel*, a fish gill; comp. Gael. *gial*, a jaw, a gill.] The respiratory organ of fishes and other animals which breathe the air that is mixed in water.—*Gill arches and clefts*, in fishes, etc., those visceral arches and clefts (which see) related to gills; *pl.* the flap that hangs below the beak of a fowl; the flesh under or about a person's chin; the radiating plates on the under side of a fungus.

gill, jil, *n.* [O.Fr. *gelle*, a wine measure; akin to *gallon*.] A measure of capacity containing the fourth part of a pint.

gill, gil, *n.* [Icel. *gil*, a ravine.] A ravine or chasm in a hill; a brook.

gillie, gil′i, *n.* [Gael. *gillie*, a boy, a gillie. In the Highlands an outdoor male servant, especially one who attends a person while hunting.

gillyflower, jil′i·flou·ẽr, *n.* [Formerly *gilofer*, from Fr. *giroflée*, from L. *caryophyllus*, Gr. *karyophyllon*, the clove tree—*karyon*, a nut, and *phyllon*, a leaf.] The popular name given to certain plants, as the pink or clove pink. CLOVE.

gilt, gilt, *pp.* of *gild*. Overlaid with gold.—*n.* Gold laid on the surface of a thing; gilding.—**gilt-edged securities.** Favored as safe by trustees, brokers, and bankers.—**gilt-head,** *n.* The name of two fishes.

gimbals, jim′bals, *n. pl.* [Formerly *gemmal*, *gimmal-ring*, from Fr. *gemelle*, from L. *gemellus*, twin, paired, double, from *geminus*, twin.] A contrivance consisting usually of two movable hoops or rings, supported upon horizontal pivots, the one moving within the other about two axes at right angles to each other and in the same plane; a contrivance such as supports the mariner's compass and causes it to assume a constantly vertical position.

gimcrack, jim′krak, *n.* [Probably from Prov.E. *gimp*, *gim*, neat, spruce, and old *crack*, a pert boy; originally applied to a boy.] A trivial piece of mechanism; a toy; a pretty thing.

gimlet, gim′let, *n.* [O.Fr. *guimbelet*, a bore.] A small instrument with a pointed screw at the end, for boring holes in wood by turning.—*v.t.* To use a gimlet upon.

gimmick, gim′ik, *n.* A device which can secretly and dishonestly be used to control a gambling apparatus; a novel idea or unconventional approach to a problem.—*v.t.* To alter by means of a gimmick.

gimp, gimp, *n.* [Origin unknown.] A narrow, ornamental twist of silk used for trimming dresses, furniture, etc.; a limping walk; a cripple.

gin, jin, *n.* [A contr. of *Geneva*.] Spirits distilled with juniper berries, etc.

gin, jin, *n.* [A contr. of *engine*.] A trap or snare; a contrivance for raising weights, consisting of three upright poles meeting at top with block and tackle; a machine for separating the seeds from cotton; a machine for driving piles.—*v.t.* *ginned*, *ginning*. To catch in a gin; to clear of seeds by the cotton gin.

ginger, jin′jẽr, *n.* [O.Fr. *gengibre*, Fr. *gingembre*, from L. *zingiber*, ultimately from Skr. *cringa-vêra*—*cringa*, horn, *vêra*, shape.] The rhizome or underground stem of a perennial herb cultivated in most tropical countries, used in medicine and largely as a condiment.—*v.t.* To put life and vigor into.—**ginger ale,** *n.* A carbonated beverage, amber colored, flavored with ginger.—**ginger beer,** *n.* A white carbonated, non-alcoholic beverage differing from ginger ale principally in that bitters are used in the brewing of it.— **gingerbread,** *n.* A plain cake flavored with ginger, and usually sweetened with molasses; gaudy ornamentation.—**gingersnap.** A small, thin cooky flavored with ginger and molasses.

gingerly, jin′jẽr·li, *adv.* [Connected with prov. *ging*, *gang*, to go.] Cautiously; daintily (to walk, to handle a thing gingerly).

gingham, ging′am, *n.* [From Malay *ginggang*, checkered cloth.] A kind of printed cotton cloth.

ginkgo, gingk′ō, *n.* [From Jap. *gingko*.] A tree with fan-shaped leaves and yellow fruit, native to eastern China and used as a temple tree.

ginseng, jin′seng, *n.* [Chinese name.] A name of two plants, the root of which is considered by the Chinese a panacea or remedy for all ailments.

gipsy, jip′si, *n.* See GYPSY.

giraffe, ji·raf′, *n.* [Fr. *girafe*, *giraffe*, Sp. *girafa*, from Ar. *zurafa*, said to mean longnecked.] The camelopard, a ruminant animal inhabiting Africa, the tallest of all animals (owing to the extraordinary length of the neck); a full-grown male reaching the height of 18 or 20 feet.

girandole, jir′an·dōl, *n.* [Fr., from It. *girandola*, from *girare*, to turn, from L. *gyrus*, a turn.] A chandelier; a kind of revolving firework.

girasole, jir′a·sōl, *n.* [Fr., from It. *girasole*—*girare*, to turn, L. *gyrus*, a turn, and *sole*, L. *sol*, the sun.] ARTICHOKE. *Jerusalem*. A plant, the European heliotrope or turnsole; a variety of opal showing a reddish color when turned toward the sun or any bright light.

gird, gẽrd, *n.* [A.Sax. *gyrd*, a rod (whence also E. *yard*, a measure); D. *garde*, G. *gerte*, a twig, a switch.] A stroke with a switch or whip; a jibe.—*v.t.* To gibe; to lash.—*v.i.* To gibe; to utter severe sarcasms with *at*.

gird, gẽrd, *v.t.* pret. & pp. *girded* or

girt. [A.Sax. *gyrdan*＝Goth. *gairdan*, Icel. *gyrtha*, Dan. *giorde*, G. *gûrten*, to gird; akin *garth*, *girth*, *yard*, an enclosure.] To bind by surrounding with any flexible substance; to make fast by binding; to tie round; usually with *on*; to clothe, invest, or surround; to encircle; to encompass.— **girder,** gẽr′dẽr, *n.* One who girds; a main beam, either of wood or iron, resting upon a wall or pier at each end, employed for supporting a superstructure or a superincumbent weight.—**girdle,** gẽr′dl, *n.* [A. Sax. *gyrdel*, from *gyrdan*, to gird; Sw. *gördel*, G. *gürtel*.] A band or belt for the waist; what girds or encloses. See GRIDDLE. (*Scottish*.)— *v.t.*—*girdled*, *girdling*. To bind with a girdle; to enclose or environ.

girl, gẽrl, *n.* [Formerly applied to both sexes, and probably connected with L.G. *gör*, *göre*, a child; Swiss *gurre*, *gurrli*, depreciatory term for girl.] A female child; a female not arrived at puberty; sweetheart (*colloq.*); a young woman.—**girlhood,** gẽrl′hud, *n.* The state of being a girl; the earlier stage of maidenhood. —**girlish,** gẽr′lish, *a.* Like or pertaining to a girl; befitting a girl.— **girlishly,** *adv.*—**girlishness,** *n.*—**Girl Scouts,** an organization for girls.

Girondist, ji·ron′dist, *n.* [Fr.] Member of the moderate Republican party formed in the French Legislative Assembly of 1791, and consisting of the Deputies for the Gironde district and their adherents.

girt, gẽrt, pret. & pp. of *gird*.

girth, gẽrth, *n.* [From *gird*, *v.t.*, or rather directly from Icel. *gerth*, *gjörth*, girth.] The band fastening the saddle on a horse's back; the measure round a person's body or anything cylindrical.—*v.t.* To bind with a girth.

gist, jist, *n.* [O.Fr. *giste*, a lying place, lodging, from *gesir*, L. *jacere*, to lie (as in *adjacent*).] The main point of a question or that on which it rests; the substance or pith of a matter.

gittern, git′ẽrn, *n.* [O.D. *ghiterne*, from L. *cithara*, Gr. *kithari*, a kind of lyre.] An instrument of the guitar kind strung with wire; a cittern.

give, giv, *v.t.*—*gave* (pret.), *given* (pp.), *giving* (ppr.). [A.Sax. *gifan*＝ Dan. *give*, Icel. *gefa*, D. *geven*, G. *geben*, Goth. *giban*, to give; probably causative from same root as L. *habeo*, to have (whence *habit*, etc.)＝to make to have.] To convey to another; to bestow; to communicate (an opinion, advice); to utter; to pronounce (a cry, the word of command); to grant; to cause or enable (he *gave* me to understand); to addict; often with *up*; to excite (to *give* offense); to pledge (one's word); to propose, as a toast; to ascribe; to pay; to yield, as a result or product.—*To give away*, to make over to another; to transfer.—*To give back*, to return; to restore.— *To give birth to*, to bring forth, as a child; to be the origin of.—*To give chase*, to pursue.—*To give ear*, to listen; to pay attention; to give heed.

—*To give forth*, to publish; to report publicly,—*To give ground*, to retire before an enemy; to yield.—*To give in*, to yield; to declare; to make known; to tender.—*To give the lie*, to charge with falsehood.—*To give over*, to leave; to cease; to abandon; to regard as past recovery.—*To give out*, to report; to decide, give the decision that the batsman is out; to proclaim; to publish; to issue; to declare or pretend to be; to emit; to distribute.—*To give place*, to retire so as to make room.—*To give tongue*, said of dogs, to bark.—*To give up*, to resign; to yield as hopeless; to surrender; to cede; to deliver or hand over.—*To give way*, to yield; to withdraw; to yield to force; to break or break down; *naut.* to row after ceasing, or to increase exertions.—*v.i.* To make gifts; to be liberal; to yield, as to pressure; to recede; to afford entrance or view; to face or be turned (as a house).—*To give in*, to give way; to yield; to confess one's self beaten.—*To give in to*, to yield assent to.—*To give out*, to cease from exertion; to yield.—*To give over*, to cease; to act no more.—**given**, giv′n, *p.* and *a.* Bestowed; conferred; admitted or supposed; addicted; disposed (much *given* to carping); *math.* supposed or held to be known.—**giver**, giv′ėr, *n.* One who gives.

gizzard, giz′ėrd, *n.* [Fr. *gésier*, O.Fr. *gezier*, from L. *gigeria*, entrails of poultry.] The second stomach of birds, having a thick, horny lining in which to grind food.

glabrous, glā′brus, *a.* [L. *glaber*, smooth.] Smooth; having a surface devoid of hair or pubescence.

glacial, glā′shi·al, *a.* [Fr., from L. *glacialis*, from *glacies*, ice.] Pertaining to ice or to the action of ice; pertaining to glaciers; icy; frozen; having a cold glassy look.—*Glacial period* or *epoch*, in *geol.* that interval of time in the later tertiary period during which both the arctic regions and a great part of the temperate regions were covered with a sheet of ice.—**glacialist**, glā′shi·al·ist, *n.* One who studies or writes on glacial phenomena.—**glaciate**, glā′shi·āt, *v.i.* To be converted into ice.—*v.t.* To convert into or cover with ice; to act upon by glaciers.—**glaciation**, glā′shi·ā′shon, *n.* The act of freezing; the process or result of glacial action on the earth's surface; the striation and smoothing of rock surfaces by glacial action.—**glacier**, glā′shi·ėr, *n.* [Fr., from *glace*, ice.] An immense accumulation of ice, or ice and snow, formed in lofty valleys above the line of perpetual congelation, and slowly moving downward into the lower valleys, reaching frequently to the borders of cultivation.—*Glacier snow*, the coarsely granular snow from which glaciers are formed; névé.—*Glacier tables*, large stones found on glaciers supported on pedestals of ice, formed by the melting away of the ice where it is not shaded from the

sun by the stone.—*Glacier theory*, a theory in regard to glaciers; the theory attributing important geological changes (as the erosion of valleys) to the action of glaciers.

glacis, glā′sis, *n.* [Fr., from *glace*, ice—from the smoothness of its surface.] *Fort.* a sloping bank so raised as to bring the enemy advancing over it into the most direct line of fire from the fort.

glad, glad, *a.* [A.Sax. *glaed*, glad= Dan. *glad*, glad, D. *glad*, Icel. *glathr*, smooth. polished, cheerful; G. *glatt*, smooth. Allied to *glide* and to *glow*.] Affected with pleasure or satisfaction; pleased; joyful; gratified; well contented: often followed by *of* or *at*; cheerful; bright; wearing the appearance of joy (a *glad* countenance).—*v.t.*—**gladded**, **gladding**. To make glad; to gladden. (*Poet.*)—**gladden**, glad′n, *v.t.* To make glad; to cheer; to please; to exhilarate.—*v.i.* To become glad; to rejoice.—**gladly**, glad′li, *adv.* With pleasure; joyfully; cheerfully.—**gladness**, glad′nes, *n.* The state or quality of being glad.—**gladsome**, glad′sum, *a.* Glad; cheerful; causing joy, pleasure, or cheerfulness. (*Poet.*)

glade, glād, *n.* [Lit. a light or bright place, a glad place; Icel. *glathr*, bright, glad. GLAD.] An opening or passage through a wood; a kind of avenue in a wood or forest covered with grass.

gladiate, glad′i·āt, *a.* [L. *gladius*, a sword.] Sword-shaped.—**gladiator**, glad′i·ā·tėr, *n.* [L., from *gladius*, a sword.] Among the ancient Romans one who fought with deadly weapons in the amphitheater and other places for the entertainment of the people; hence, a combatant in general; a prizefighter; a disputant.—**gladiatorial**, glad′i·a·tō″ri·al, *a.* Pertaining to gladiators; pertaining to combatants in general who fight singly, as to disputants.—**gladiolus**, gla·di′o·lus, glad·i·ō′lus, *n.* pl. **gladioli**, gla·di′o·li, glad·i·ō′li, [L. *gladiolus*, dim. of *gladius*, a sword, from their leaves.] An extensive and very beautiful genus of bulbous-rooted plants, found most abundantly in South Africa; sword lily.

glair, glâr, *n.* [Fr. *glaire*, from L. *clarus*, clear, the glair of an egg being the clear portion. CLEAR.] The white of an egg used as varnish to preserve paintings, and as a size in gilding; any similar substance.—*v.t.* To varnish or smear with glair.—**glairy**, glâ′ri, *a.*

glamour, glam′ėr, *n.* [A modified form of *glammar*—*grammar*—*gramarye*, having formerly meant learning, deep learning, magic.] A charm, as of manner, appearance and poise, endowing its owner with a mysterious, often illusory, fascination; a stirring attractiveness as of a person or a place.

glance, glans, *n.* [Same word as Sw. *glans*, Dan. *glands*, D. *glans*, G. *glanz*, luster, splendor; *glint*, *glitter*, *glisten*, *gleam*, etc., are connected.] A sudden dart or flash of light or splendor; a sudden look or darting

of sight; a rapid or momentary casting of the eye; a name given to some minerals which possess a metallic luster.—*v.i.*—**glanced**, **glancing**. To shoot or dart rays of light or splendor; to emit flashes or coruscations of light; to flash; to fly off in an oblique direction; to strike or graze; to dart aside; to look with a sudden cast of the eye.—*v.t.* To shoot or dart suddenly; to cast for a moment (to *glance* the eye).

gland, gland, *n.* [L. *glans*, *glandis*, an acorn.] *Anat.* a distinct soft body, formed by the convolution of a great number of vessels, different glands having specialized secretions; *bot.* a secreting organ occurring on the epidermis of plants; also, a kind of one-celled fruit, with a dry pericarp.—**glanders**, glan′dėrz, *n.* A very dangerous and highly contagious disease, chiefly seen in horses, but capable of being transmitted to man, which especially affects the glands (whence the name), the mucous membrane of the nose, the lungs, etc.—**glandered**, glan′dėrd, *p.* and *a.* Affected with glanders.—**glandular**, glan′dū·lėr, *a.* Consisting of a gland or glands; pertaining to glands.—**glandulous**, glan′dū·lus, *a.* [L. *glandulosus*.] Glandular.

glare, glâr, *n.* [Akin to A.Sax. *glaer*, amber; Dan. *glar*, Icel. *gler*, glass; L.G. *glaren*, to glow; E. *glass*, *glance*, *gleam*, etc.] A bright dazzling light; splendor that dazzles the eyes; a confusing and bewildering light; a fierce, piercing look.—*v.i.*—**glared**, **glaring**. To shine with a bright dazzling light; to look with fierce; piercing eyes; to have a dazzling effect; to be ostentatiously splendid.—*v.t.* To shoot out or emit, as a dazzling light.—**glaringness**, glâr′ing·nes, *n.* The state or quality of having a glaring appearance.—**glaring**, glâr′ing, *p.* and *a.* Shining with dazzling luster; excessively bright; vulgarly splendid; forcing one's notice; notorious; open; barefaced (a *glaring* crime).—**glaringly**, glâr′ing·li, *adv.* In a glaring manner.

glass, glas, *n.* [A.Sax. *glaes*; L.G. D.G. Sw. and Icel. *glas*: Icel. also *gler*; akin *glisten*, *glance*, *glare*, etc.] A hard, brittle, transparent artificial substance, formed by the fusion of siliceous matter (as powdered flint or fine sand) with some alkali; something made of glass; especially, a mirror or looking glass; a glass vessel filled with running sand for measuring time; a drinking vessel made of glass; the quantity which such a vessel holds (hence, *the glass*= strong drink); an optical instrument, such as a lens or a telescope; a barometer or thermometer; *pl.* spectacles.—*a.* Made of glass.—*v.t.* To reflect; to mirror; to cover with glass.—**glassful**, glas′fụl, *n.* As much as a glass will hold.—**glassily**, glas′i·li, *adv.* So as to resemble glass.—**glassiness**, glas′i·nes, *n.* The quality of being glassy.—**glassy**, glas′i, *a.* Made of glass; vitreous; resembling

ch, *chain*; ch, Sc. *loch*; g, *go*; j, *job*; ng, *sing*; TH, *then*; th, *thin*; w, *wig*; hw, *whig*; zh, *azure*.

glass; having a luster or surface like glass.—**glass blower,** *n.* One whose business it is to blow and fashion vessels of glass.—**glasshouse,** *n.* A manufactory of glass; a house built largely of glass, as a conservatory or greenhouse.—**glass snake,** *n.* A North American lizard, so called from its brittleness.—**glassware,** *n.* Articles made of glass.—**glasswork,** *n.* Articles of or in glass; an establishment where glass is made.—**glasswort,** glas´wẽrt, *n.* A name of various plants common on the Mediterranean coasts.

Glauber salt, glạ´bẽr sạlt, *n.* [After *Glauber* (died 1688), a German chemist, who first prepared it.] Sulfate of soda, a well-known cathartic.

glaucous, glạ´kus, *a.* [L. *glaucus,* from Gr. *glaukos,* bluish-green or sea-green.] Of a sea-green color; of a light green or bluish green; *bot.* covered with a fine bluish or greenish powder or bloom.—**glaucoma,** glạ·kō´ma, *n.* [Gr. *glaukōma,* from *glaukos,* sea-green.] A disease of the eye characterized by increased intraocular pressure and sudden or progressive loss of vision.—**glaucomatous,** glạ·kō´ma·tus, *a.* Pertaining to or resembling glaucoma.

glaze, glāz, *v.t.*—*glazed, glazing.* [From *glass.*] To furnish with glass or panes of glass; to encrust or overlay with glass or a vitreous coating; to give a glossy, or smooth, shining surface to.—*v.i.* To assume a dim, glassy luster; said of the eye.—*n.* That which is used in glazing.—**glazer,** glā´zẽr, *n.* One who or that which glazes.—**glazier,** glā´zhẽr, *n.* One whose business is to fix panes of glass in windows, etc. —**glazing,** glā´zing, *n.* The act or art of one who glazes; the substance with which anything is overlaid to give it a glassy appearance; enamel; glaze; *paint.* transparent or semitransparent colors passed thinly over other colors, to modify the effect.

gleam, glēm, *n.* [A.Sax. *glaem,* a glittering; comp. O.Sax. *glimo,* splendor, Sw. *glimma,* to flash; allied to *glimmer, glow, glance,* etc.] A beam or flash of light; a ray; a small stream of light; brightness.—*v.i.* To dart or throw rays of light; to glimmer.—**gleamy,** glē´mi, *a.*

glean, glēn, *v.t.* [Fr. *glaner,* from L.L. *glenare,* to glean, from W. *glain, glân,* clean; comp. A.Sax. *gilm,* a handful.] To gather after a reaper, or on a reaped cornfield, the ears of grain left ungathered, hence, to collect in scattered portions; to gather slowly and assiduously.—*v.i.* To gather ears of grain left by reapers; to go through carefully, as a book or written speech, in order to extract bits of information.—**gleaner,** glē´nẽr, *n.*

glebe, glēb, *n.* [Fr. *glèbe,* from L. *gleba,* a clod or lump of earth.] Soil; ground; earth; the land belonging to a parish church or ecclesiastical benefice.

glede, glēd, *n.* [A.Sax. *glida,* the kite, lit. glider, from its gliding flight. GLIDE.] A bird of prey.

glee, glē, *n.* [A.Sax. *gleo, gliw, glig,* music, sport; Icel. *gly,* laughter.] Joy; merriment; mirth; gaiety; a musical composition consisting of two or more contrasted movements, with the parts forming as it were a series of interwoven melodies.—**glee club.** A group organized for singing songs.—**gleeman,** glē´man, *n.* [A.Sax. *gleóman*] A minstrel or musician of former days.—**gleeful, gleesome,** glē´ful, glē´sum, *a.* Full of glee; merry; gay; joyous.

gleet, glēt, *n.* [O.Fr. *glette,* slime, phlegm; Sc. *glet, glit,* phlegm.] A transparent mucous discharge from the urethra, an effect of gonorrhea; a thin ichor running from a sore.

glen, glen, *n.* [Ir. and Gael. *gleann,* W. *glyn,* a glen.] A secluded narrow valley; a dale; a depression or space between hills.

Glengarry, *n.* Highland bonnet.

glenoid, glē´noid, *a.* [Gr. *glēnē,* the pupil, the eyeball.] *Anat.* a term applied to any shallow, articular cavity which receives the head of a bone.

glib, glib, *a.* [Comp. D. *glibberig,* smooth, slippery; *glibberen,* L.G. *glippen,* to slide; akin to *glide.*] Smooth; slippery; more commonly voluble; fluent; having words always ready.—**glibly,** glib´li, *adv.* In a glib manner; smoothly; volubly.—**glibness,** glib´nes, *n.*

glide, glīd, *v.i.*—*glided, gliding.* [A. Sax. *glidan*=Dan. *glide,* D. *glijden,* G. *gleiien,* to slide; allied to *glad.*] To flow gently; to move along silently and smoothly; to pass along without apparent effort (a river, a bird, a skater *glides*)—*v.i.* To fly on a descending path, when the aircraft is not under power.—*n.* A smooth, gliding step, as in dancing; act of moving smoothly or gliding.—**glider,** glī´dẽr, *n.* One who glides; a form of aircraft similar to an airplane but lacking an engine.—**glidingly,** glī´ding·li, *adv.* In a gliding manner.

glimmer, glim´ẽr, *v.i.* [A. freq. of *gleam*=Dan. *glimre,* to glitter, from *glimme,* to gleam; comp. G. *glimmer,* a faint light; *glimmen,* to shine.] To emit feeble or scattered rays of light; to shine faintly; to give a feeble light; to flicker.—*n.* A faint and unsteady light; feeble, scattered rays of light; glitter; twinkle; also, a name of mica.—**glimmering,** glim·ẽr·ing, *n.* A glimmer; a gleam; a faint indication; an inkling; a glimpse.

glimpse, glimps, *n.* [Formerly *glimse,* from the stem of *gleam, glimmer,* etc., the *p* being inserted as in *empty, sempstress,* etc. Comp. Swiss *glumsen,* to glow; D. *glimpen, glinsen,* to sparkle.] A gleam; a momentary flash; a short transitory view; a glance; a faint resemblance; a slight tinge.—*v.i.*—*glimpsed, glimpsing.* To appear by glimpses.—*v.t.* To see by a glimpse or glimpses.

glint, glint, *v.i.* [Of kindred origin with *glimpse, glimmer, glance,* etc.;

comp. Dan. *glimt,* a gleam, *glimte,* to flash.] To glance; to gleam; to give a flash of light.—*n.* A glance; a flash; a gleam.

glissade, glis·ād´, *n.* [Fr. *glissade;* from *glisser,* to glide or slide.] A sliding or gliding down a range.

glisten, glis´n, *v.i.* [A.Sax. *glisnian,* akin to G. *gleissen,* Icel. *glyssa,* O.G. *glizan,* to shine; same root as *glitter, gleam,* etc.] To shine; to sparkle with light; to shine with a scintillating light.—*n.*† Glitter; sparkle.—**glister,** glis´tẽr, *v.i.* To shine; to glitter.—*n.* Luster; glitter.

glitter, glit´ẽr, *v.i.* [A. freq. from stem *glit,* seen in A.Sax. *glitnian,* to glitter=Sw. *glittra,* Icel. *glitra* (from *glita,* to shine), G. *glitzern,* to shine; akin to *gleam, glance,* etc.] To shine with a broken and scattered light; to emit rapid flashes of light; to gleam; to sparkle; to glisten; to be showy or brilliant.—*n.* Bright sparkling light; brilliancy; splendor; luster.

gloaming, glōm´ing, *n.* [A.Sax. *glómung,* twilight, from *glóm,* E. *gloom.*] Fall of the evening; the twilight; closing period; decline. [Scotch; but adopted by English writers.]

gloat, glōt, *v.i.* [Allied to Sw. *glutta, glötta,* to look at with prying eyes; G. *glotzen,* to stare.] To gaze with admiration, eagerness, or desire; to contemplate with evil satisfaction.

globe, glōb, *n.* [L. *globus,* a ball; Fr. *globe,* Sp. and It. *globo.*] A round or spherical solid body; a ball; a sphere; the earth; an artificial sphere on whose convex surface is drawn a map or representation of the earth (*a terrestrial globe*) or of the heavens (*a celestial globe*).—*v.t.* To gather into a round mass; to conglobate.—**globate, globated,** glō´bāt, glō´bā·ted, *a.* [L. *globatus.*] Shaped like a globe; spherical.—**globose, globous,** glō·bōs, glō´bus, *a.* [L. *globosus.*] Spherical; globular.—**globosity,** glō·bos´i·ti, *n.* The quality of being globose.—**globular,** glob´-u·lẽr, *a.* Globe-shaped; having the form of a ball; world-wide.—**globule,** glob´ūl, *n.* A small particle of matter in spherical form; a round body or corpuscle found in the blood.

globe-trotter, glōb´trot·ẽr, *n.* One who travels to all parts of the globe.

globulin, glob´yä·lin, *n.* [Fr. from L. *globulus,* dimin. of *globus,* globe.] Proteins such as gamma globulin, characterized by their insolubility in water and solubility in a dilute salt solution.—**globefish,** *n.* The name of several fishes able to inflate themselves into a globular form.

glochidate, glō´kī·dāt, *a.* [Gr. *glōchis,* a point.] *Bot.* barbed at the point like a fishhook.

glomerate, glom´ẽr·āt, *v.t.* [L. *glomero, glomeratum,* from *glomus, glomeris,* a ball, as in *conglomerate.*] To gather or wind into a ball; to collect into a spherical form or mass.—*a.* Congregated; gathered into a round mass or dense cluster.—**glomeration,** glom·ẽr·ā´shon, *n.* The act of glomerating; conglomeration; an aggregate.—**glomerule**, glom′ẽr·ūl, *n. Bot.* a cluster of flower heads enclosed in a common involucre.

gloom, glöm, *n.* [A.Sax. *glóm*, gloom, twilight, *glómung*, gloaming; allied to *glum*, *glow*, *gleam*, *glimmer*, etc.] Obscurity; partial darkness; thick shade; dusk; cloudiness or heaviness of mind; heaviness, dejection, anger, sullenness; a depressing state of affairs; a dismal prospect.—*v.t.* To appear dimly; to be seen in an imperfect or waning light; to look gloomy, sad, or dismal; to frown; to lower.—*v.t.* To make gloomy or dark; to fill with gloom or sadness.—**gloomily**, glö′mi·li, *adv.* In a gloomy manner.—**gloominess**, glö′mi·nes, *n.* The condition or quality of being gloomy.—**gloomy**, glö′mi, *a.* Involved in gloom; imperfectly illuminated; dusky or dark; characterized by gloom; wearing the aspect of sorrow; dejected; heavy of heart; dismal; doleful.

glory, glō′ri, *n.* [L. *gloria*, fame, glory; allied to Gr. *kleos*, fame, *kleō*, to celebrate, *klyō*, to hear.] Praise, honor, admiration, or distinction, accorded by common consent to a person or thing; honorable fame; renown; celebrity; a state of greatness or renown; pomp; magnificence; brightness; luster; splendor; brilliancy; the happiness of heaven; celestial bliss; distinguished honor or ornament; an object of which one is or may be proud; *painting*, the radiation round the head or figure of a deity, saint, angel, etc.—*v.i.*—*gloried*, *glorying.* To exult with joy; to rejoice; to be boastful; to have pride.—**glorification**, glō′ri·fi·kā″shon, *n.* The act of glorifying or the state of being glorified.—**glorify**, glō′ri·fī, *v.t.*—*glorified*, *glorifying.* [Fr. *glorifier*, L. *gloria*, glory, and *facio*, to make.] To give or ascribe glory to; to praise; to magnify and honor; to honor; to extol; to make glorious; to exalt to glory.—**gloriole**, glō′ri·ōl, *n.* [Formed on type of *aureole*.] A circle, as of rays, in ancient paintings surrounding the heads of saints.—**glorious**, glō′ri·us, *a.* [Fr. *glorieux*, L. *gloriosus*, from *gloria.*] Characterized by attributes, qualities, or acts that are worthy of glory; of exalted excellence and splendor; noble; illustrious; renowned; celebrated; magnificent; grand; splendid; hilarious or elated (*colloq.*).—**gloriously**, glō′ri·us·li, *adv.* In a glorious manner.—**gloriousness**, glō′ri·us·nes, *n.*

gloss, glos, *n.* [Akin to Icel. *glossi*, flame, brightness, *glys*, finery, whence *glysligr*, showy or specious; Sw. *glossa*, to glow; G. *glotzen*, to shine, to glance; allied to *glass*, *glow*, *gloom*, *gleam*, etc.] Brightness or luster of a body proceeding from a smooth and generally a soft surface; polish; sheen (the *gloss* of silk); a specious appearance or representation; external show that may mislead. —*v.t.* To give gloss to; to give a superficial luster to; to make smooth and shining; hence, to give a specious appearance to; to render

specious and plausible; to palliate by specious representation.—**glosser**, glos′ẽr, *n.* One who glosses; one who palliates.—**glossily**, glos′i·li, *adv.* In a glossy manner.—**glossiness**, glos′i·nes, *n.* The state or character of being glossy; polish or luster of a surface.—**glossy**, glos′i, *a.* Having a gloss; having a soft, smooth, and shining surface; lustrous with softness to the touch; specious or plausible.

gloss, glos, *n.* [L. *glossa*, an obsolete or foreign word that requires explanation, from Gr. *glōssa*, the tongue, latterly also an obsolete or foreign word.] A marginal note or interlineation explaining the meaning of some word in a text; a remark intended to illustrate some point of difficulty in an author; comment; annotation; explanation.—*v.t.* To render clear by comments; to annotate; to illustrate.—**glossarial**, glos·sā′ri·al, *a.* Connected with, or consisting in a glossary.—**glossarist**, glos′a·rist, *n.* One who compiles a glossary.—**glossary**, glos′a·ri, *n.* [L. L. *glossarium*.] A vocabulary of words used by any author, especially by an old author, or one writing in a provincial dialect, or of words occurring in a special class of works, of technical terms, etc.—**glosser**, glos′ẽr, *n.* One who writes glosses.—**glossographer**, glos·og′ra·fẽr, *n.* A writer of glosses; a scholiast.—**glossological**, glos·o·loj′i·kal, *a.* Pertaining to glossology.—**glossologist**, glos·ol′o·jist, *n.* One who is versed in glossology.—**glossology**, glos·ol′o·ji, *n.* The definition and explanation of terms, as of a science; terminology; universal; grammar; glottology.—**glossotomy**, glos·ot′o·mi, *n. Anat.* dissection of the tongue.

glottis, glot′is, *n.* [Gr. *glōttis*, from *glōtta*, *glōssa*, the tongue, whence also *glossary*, etc.] The opening at the upper part of the windpipe, and between the vocal chords, which, by its dilatation and contraction, contributes to the modulation of the voice.—**glottal**, glot′al, *a.* Relating to the glottis.—**glottology**, glot·ol′o·ji, *n.* [Gr. *glōtta*, language, and *logos*, discourse.] The science of language; comparative philology; glossology.—**glottological**, **glottic**, glot·o·loj′i·kal, glot′ik, *a.* Pertaining to glottology.—**glottologist**, glot·ol′o·jist, *n.* One versed in glottology.

glove, gluv, *n.* [A.Sax. *glóf*; probably from prefix *ge*, and Goth. *lofa*, Sc. *loof*, Icel. *lófi*, the palm of the hand.] A cover for the hand, or for the hand and wrist, with a separate sheath for each finger.—*To throw down the glove.* Same as *to throw down the gantlet*, under GANTLET.—*v.t.*—*gloved*, *gloving.* To cover with or as with a glove.—**glover**, gluv′ẽr, *n.* One whose occupation is to make or sell gloves.

glow, glō, *v.i.* [A.Sax. *glówan*, to glow=D. *gloeijen*, G. *glühen*, to glow; Icel. *glóa*, to glitter; Sw. *gloa*, to sparkle; allied to *gloat*, *gleam*, *gloom*, *gloaming*, *gloss*, etc.] To burn

with an intense or white heat, and especially without flame; to give forth bright light and heat; to feel great heat of body; to be hot or flushed in person; to be bright or red, as with animation, blushes, or the like; to exhibit brightness of color; to feel the heat of passion; to be ardent; to burn or be vehement; to rage.—*n.* Shining heat, or white heat; incandescence; brightness of color; redness; vehemence of color; ardor; animation.—**glowing**, glō′ing, *p.* and *a.* Shining with intense heat; bright in color; red; ardent; vehement; fervid; heated; fiery.—**glowingly**, glō′ing·li, *adv.* In a glowing manner.—**glowworm**, glō′wẽrm, *n.* The wingless female of a kind of beetle, emitting a shining green light to attract the male.

glower, glou′ẽr, *v.i.* [M.L.G. *gluren* to watch, D. *glaren* to peep, Nor. dial. *glyra*.] To look intently; to stare angrily or with a scowling intentness.

gloxinia, glok·sin′i·a, *n.* [*Gloksin*, a German botanist.] A genus of almost stemless plants with fine bell-shaped flowers, natives of tropical America.

gloze, glōz, *v.i.*—*glozed*, *glozing.* [O.E. *glose*, a gloss or interpretation; the meaning being influenced by *gloss*, luster. GLOSS.] To comment or expound‡; to use specious words; to talk smoothly or flatteringly.—*v.t.* To gloss over; to extenuate.—*n.* Flattery; specious words.

glucose, glö′kōs, *n.* [From Gr. *glykys* or *glukus*, sweet, from its salts having a sweet taste.] Grape sugar, a variety of sugar, less sweet than cane sugar, produced from grapes, cane sugar, starch, etc.—**glucoside**, glö′kō·sīd, *n.* One of those substances that yield glucose.

glue, glö, *n.* [O.Fr. *glu*, from L.L. *glutis*, L. *gluten*, *glutinis*, glue; comp. W. *glyd*, viscous matter.] Common or impure gelatin, obtained by boiling animal substances, as the skins, hoofs, etc., of animals, with water; used for uniting pieces of wood or other materials.—*v.t.*—*glued*, *gluing.* To join with glue or other viscous substance; to hold together, as if by glue; to fix; to rivet.—**gluey**, glö′i, *a.*

glum, glum, *a.* [Akin to *gloom*, and Sc. *gloum*, a frown.] Frowning; sullen.—**glumly**, glum′li, *adv.*—**glumness**, glum′nes, *n.*

glume, glöm, *n.* [L. *gluma*, a husk, from *glubo*, to peel, akin to Gr. *glyphō*, to hollow out.] The husk or chaff of grain; the palea or pale.—**glumaceous**, glö·mā′shus, *a.* Having or bearing glumes; of or pertaining to the glumales.

glut, glut, *v.t.*—*glutted*, *glutting.* [L. *glutio*, *gluttio*, to swallow; whence also *englut*, *glutton.*] To swallow, or to swallow greedily (*Shak.*); to cloy, sate, or disgust; to feast or delight to satiety.—*To glut the market*, to furnish an oversupply of any article, so that there is no sale for it all.—*n.* Plenty even to loathing; superabundance; an oversupply of any commodity in the market.

gluteal, glö'ti·al, a. [Gr. *gloutos*, the buttock.] *Anat.* of or pertaining to certain parts connected with the buttocks.—**gluteus**, glö'tē·us, n. *Anat.* the three muscles of the buttocks.

gluten, glö'ten, n. [L. See GLUE.] A tough elastic substance of a grayish color, which becomes brown and brittle by drying, found in the flour of wheat and other grain.—**glutinous**, glö'ti·nus, a. [L. *glutinosus*.] Gluey; viscous; viscid; tenacious; resembling glue; *bot.* besmeared with a slippery moisture.—**glutinousness**, glö'ti·nus·nes, n. The quality of being glutinous.

glutton, glut'n, n. [Fr. *glouton*, from L. *gluto*, *glutto*, a glutton, from *glutio*, to swallow. GLUT.] One who indulges to excess in eating, or eating and drinking; a gormandizer; a carnivorous quadruped, 2½ feet long, yielding a valuable fur, and inhabiting Northern Europe and America, known also as the *Wolverine*.—**gluttonize**,† glut'n·īz, v.i. To eat gluttonously.—**gluttonous**, glut'n·us, a. Characterized by gluttony; given to excessive eating; insatiable.—**gluttonously**, glut'n·us·li, adv. In a gluttonous manner.—**gluttony**, glut'n·i, n. The act or practice of a glutton; excess in eating, or eating and drinking.

glycerin, glis'ér·in, n. [From Gr. *glykeros*, sweet.] A transparent, sirupy trihydric alcohol used as a solvent in cosmetics, explosives, etc., obtained from fatty acids and as a by-product in soapmaking.—**glycerol**, glis'ér·ōl, n. The same as glycerin.

glycogen, glī'ko·jen, n. [Gr. *glykys*, sweet, and root *gen*, to produce.] Animal starch, $(C_6H_{10}O_5)x$, a carbohydrate that serves as a sugar reserve for animals, formed in the liver and other organs.

glyph, glif, n. [Gr. *glyphē*, carving, from *glyphō*, to carve.] *Sculp.* and *arch.* a channel or cavity, usually vertical, intended as an ornament—**glyphic**, glif'ik, a. Of or pertaining to carving or sculpture.—**glyphograph**, glif'o·graf, n. A plate formed by glyphography.—**glyptic**, glip'tik, a. [Gr. *glyptikos*.] Pertaining to the art of sculpture or engraving.—**glyptographer**, glip·tog'ra·fér, n. An engraver on precious stones.—**glyptographic**, glip·to·graf'ik, a. Of or pertaining to glyptography.—**glyptography**, glip·tog'ra·fi, n. The art or process of engraving on precious stones.

gnarl, närl, n. [From old *gnar*, a knot, also *knarr*, *knurr*; akin to D. *knorre*, a knot, G. *knorren*, a lump.] A protuberance on the outside of a tree; a knot.—**gnarled**, närld, a. Having many knots or knotty protuberances; cross-grained; perverse.—**gnarly**, när'li, a. Having knots; knotty.

gnarl, närl, v.i. [O.E. *gnerr*, found in similar forms in the other Teut. languages, and probably imitative

of snarling.] To growl; to murmur; to snarl.

gnash, nash, v.t. [O.E. *gnaste*, *gnayste*, akin to Dan. *knaske*, D. *knarsen*, G. *knirschen*, Sw. *knastra*, *gnissta*, to gnash.] To strike together (the teeth), as in anger or pain.—v.i. To strike or dash the teeth together, as in rage or pain.

gnat, nat, n. [A.Sax. *gnaet*, L.G. *gnid*, a gnat; perhaps akin to G. *gnatze*, the itch.] A small two-winged fly whose mouth is furnished with bristly stings which inflict irritating wounds.

gnathic, nath'ik, a. [Gr. *gnathos*, jaw.] Pertaining to the jaw or jaws.

gnaw, naw, v.t. [A.Sax. *gnagan*=D. *knagen*, G. *gnagen*, Dan. *gnave*, *nage*, Icel. and Sw. *gnaga*, *naga*, to gnaw; akin verb to *nag*.] To bite by little and little; to wear away by biting; to nibble at; to bite in agony or rage; to fret; to corrode.—v.i. To use the teeth in biting; to bite with repeated efforts; to cause or be affected with steady annoying pain.—**gnawer**, naw'ér, n. One who or that which gnaws; a rodent.

gneiss, nīs, n. [G. *gneiss*, gneiss.] A kind of hard tough crystalline rock, having a structure exhibiting layers either straight or curved, and like granite composed in the main of quartz, feldspar, and mica.—**gneissoid**, nīs'oid, a. Resembling gneiss; having the characteristics of gneiss. Also **gneissic**, nīs'ik.

gnome, nōm, n. [Gr. *gnome*, formed from Gr. *gnōmē*, intelligence; see next art.] An imaginary being, fabled to inhabit the inner parts of the earth, and to be the guardian of mines, quarries, etc.; a goblin; a small misshapen person.

gnome, nōm, n. [Gr. *gnōmē*, a maxim, from stem of *gnōnai*, to know. KNOW.] A brief reflection or maxim; a saw; an aphorism.—**gnomic, gnomical**, nō'mik, nō'mi·kal, a. [Gr. *gnōmikos*.] Containing or dealing in maxims (the ancient Greek *gnomic* poets).

gnomon, nō'mon, n. [Gr. *gnōmōn*, an index, from stem of *gnōnai*, to know; whence also *gnome*, *Gnostic*.] The style or pin of a sun dial, which by its shadow shows the hour of the day; a style consisting of a pillar, pyramid, etc., erected perpendicular to the horizon, in order to find the altitudes, declinations, etc., of the sun and stars; the index of the hour circle of a globe.—**gnomonic, gnomonical**, nō·mon'ik, nō·mon'i·kal, a. Pertaining to the art of dialing; *bot.* bent at right angles.—*Gnomonic projection*, a projection of the surface of the sphere, in which the point of sight is taken at the center of the sphere.

Gnostic, nos'tik, n. [L. *gnosticus*, Gr. *gnōstikos*, from stem of *gnōnai*, to know, cog. with E. *know*.] One of several sects arising in the 2d century whose members claimed to have the only true knowledge of Christianity, actually basing their beliefs on a blend of several Christian and non-Christian doctrines.—**Gnosticism**,

nos'ti·sizm, n. The doctrines or principles of the Gnostics.

gnu, nū, n. [Hottentot *gnu* or *nju*.] A ruminant quadruped, partaking of the form of the antelope, ox, and horse, inhabiting South Africa.

go, gō, v.i.—pret. *went*, pp. *gone*. [A.Sax. *gán*, *gangan*, O. and Prov. E. and Sc. *gang*, to go; Dan. *gaae*, D. *gaan*, G. *gehen*, Goth. *gaggan* (that is *gangan*), Icel. *ganga*, O.H.G. *gangan*. *Went* though now used as the pret., is really the past tense of *wend*, A.Sax. *wendan*, to turn, to go.] To walk; to pass, proceed, move, or be in motion; to depart or move from a place; opposed to *come*; to have currency or use; to circulate (the story *goes*); to be reckoned or esteemed; to proceed or happen in a given manner; to have course; to turn out (the case *went* against him); to have recourse (to go to law); to be about to (in this usage a kind of auxiliary and usually in ppr.—*going* to say, *going* to begin); to be guided or regulated (to go by some rule); to be with young; to be pregnant; to be alienated, sold, or disposed of (it *went* for a trifle); to extend, reach, lead (this road *goes* to London); to extend in effect, meaning, or purport; to be of force or value; to proceed or tend toward a result or consequence; to contribute, conduce, concur (frequently with *to*, *towards*, etc.); to perish; to sink or die; to become (she has *gone* mad).—*To go about*, naut. to tack; to turn the head of a ship.—*To go about to*, to set one's self to; to take a circuitous way to.—*To go against*, to march to attack; to be in opposition; to be disagreeable.—*To go ahead*, to make rapid progress; to be enterprising. (*Colloq.*)—*To go between*, to interpose or mediate between; to attempt to reconcile.—*To go beyond*, to overreach.—*To go by*, to pass near and beyond (*by* being a prep.); to pass away unnoticed or disregarded (*by* adv.).—*To go down*, to descend; to come to nothing; to be received as true or correct.—*To go for nothing*, to have no value, weight, or efficacy. —*To go hard with*, to bring danger of a fatal issue to; to be all but ruinous for: used impersonally.—*To go in for*, to be in favor of; to make the object of acquirement or of attainment.—*To go in to* (*Scrip.*), to have sexual commerce with.—*To go off*, to leave a place; to die; to decease; to be discharged, as firearms; to explode; to be sold.—*To go on*, to proceed; to advance forward; to be put on, as a garment.—*To go out*, to issue forth; to go on an expedition; to become extinct, as light or life.—*To go over*, to read; to peruse; to examine; to view or review (*over* being the prep.); to change sides; to pass from one party to another (*over* adv.).—*To go through*, to pass or penetrate through; to accomplish; to perform thoroughly; to undergo; to sustain to the end.—*To go through with*, to execute effectually.—*To go upon*, to proceed as on a foundation; to take as a principle supposed or settled.—*To go with*, to accompany; to side with; to be in party or design with; to agree with; to suit.—*It goes ill* or *well with* a person, he has ill or good fortune.—*To go without*, to be or remain destitute.—*To go wrong*, to become unsound, as meat, fruit; to leave the paths of virtue; to take a wrong way.—*Go to!* come; move; begin; a phrase of exhortation; also a phrase of rebuke or reproof; tush; nonsense.—[In the following usages the verb may be construed as transitive.] To undertake (to *go* a journey, to *go* equal risks).—*To go one's way*, to set forth; to depart; to move on.—*To go an errand, to go a drive, to go circuit*, to go on an errand; to go upon or for a drive; to go upon circuit.—*n.* [As a noun the word is colloq. or slang.] The fashion or mode; a glass or other measure of liquor called in when drinking; stamina, bottom, or power of endurance; spirit; animation; fire.—*Great go, little go*, university cant terms for the examination for degrees and the previous or preliminary examination.—**goer,** gō'ér, *n.* One who or that which goes; one that has a gait good or bad; often applied to a horse, and to a watch or clock.—**going,** gō'ing, *n.* The act of moving in any manner; departure; procedure; behavior; or course of life: chiefly in the *pl.*—*Goings-on*, actions; conduct; used mostly in a bad sense.—**gone,** gon, *pp.* Passed; vanished away; consumed; finished; dead; lost or destroyed; worn out, exhausted, or overpowered.—**go-ahead,** *a.* Characterized by or disposed to progress; enterprising. (*Colloq.*)—**go-between,** *n.* An intermediary: often an agent in disreputable negotiations.—**gocart,** *n.* A framework on casters, to support children while learning to walk; a baby carriage with front wheels smaller than the rear.

goad, gōd, *n.* [A.Sax. *gád*, a point of a weapon, a goad. GAD.] A pointed instrument used to stimulate a beast to move faster; hence, anything that urges or stimulates.—*v.t.* To drive with a goad; hence, to incite; to stimulate; to instigate; to urge forward.

goal, gōl, *n.* [Fr. *gaule*, a pole, a word of Germanic origin, from Goth. *walus*, Fris. *walu*, Icel. *völr*, staff, rod.] The point set to bound a race; the space between the two upright posts in the game of football; also the act of driving the ball through between the posts; the end to which a design tends, or which a person aims to reach or accomplish.

goat, gōt, *n.* [A.Sax. *gát*=Icel. L.G., D., and Fris. *geit*, G. *geiss*, goat; cog. with L. *haedus*, a kid.] A well-known horned ruminant quadruped, nearly of the size of a sheep, but stronger, less timid, and more agile.—**goatee,** gō·tē', *n.* A beard that hangs down from the chin without whiskers.—**goatherd,** gōt'hėrd, *n.* One whose occupation is to tend goats.—**goatish,** gōt'ish, *a.* Resembling a goat in any quality, especially in smell or lustfulness.—**goatishly,** gōt'ish·li, *adv.* In a goatish manner; lustfully.—**goatishness,** gōt'ish·nes, *n.* The quality of being goatish; lustfulness.—**goat pepper,** *n.* A species of capsicum or Cayenne pepper.—**goatsbeard,** *n.* The name of herbaceous perennials, one species of which (*salsify*) is cultivated in gardens for its root.

gob, gob, *n.* [Origin unknown.] A sailor of the U.S. Navy.

gob, gob, *n.* [O.Fr. *gobe*.] A mass or lump.

gobbet, gob'et, *n.* [Fr. *gobet*, from O.Fr. *gob*, a mouthful.] A mouthful; a morsel; a lump.—**gobble,** gob'l, *v.t.* and *i.*—*gobbled, gobbling.* To swallow in large pieces; to swallow hastily.

gobble, gob'l, *v.i.* [Imitative.] To make a sound in the throat, as a turkey *gobbles.*—*n.* A noise made in the throat, as that made by the turkey cock.—**gobbler,** gob'lér, *n.* A turkey.

Gobelin, gob'e·lin, *a.* [From the *Gobelins* establishment in Paris, where tapestry, etc., is made, named from, and originally belonging to a family of dyers called *Gobelin.*] A term applied to a species of rich tapestry, also to a printed worsted cloth for covering chairs, sofas, etc., in imitation of tapestry.

goblet, gob'let, *n.* [Fr. *gobelet*, dim. of O.Fr. *gobel*, a drinking glass, from L.L. *gobellus*, from L. *cupa*, a tub, a cask. CUP.] A kind of cup or drinking vessel without a handle.

goblin, gob'lin, *n.* [Fr. *gobelin*, from L. *cobalus*, Gr. *kobalos*, a kind of malignant being or goblin; whence also G. *kobold.*] An evil or mischievous sprite; a gnome; an elf; a malicious fairy.

goby, gō'bi, *n.* [L. *gobius*, Gr. *kōbios*, the gudgeon.] A name given to various rather small fishes.

god, god, *n.* [A.Sax. *god*=D. *god*, Icel. *goth, guth*, Dan. and Sw. *gud*, Goth. *guth*, G. *gott*, God; root unknown; not connected with *good.*] A being conceived of as possessing divine power, and therefore to be propitiated by sacrifice, worship, and the like; a divinity; [*cap.*] the Supreme Being; Jehovah; the eternal Spirit, the Creator, and the Sovereign of the universe; any person or thing exalted too much in estimation, or deified and honored as the chief good.—**godchild,** god'child, *n.* A godson or goddaughter.—**goddaughter,** god'da·tér, *n.* A female for whom one becomes sponsor at baptism.—**goddess,** god'es, *n.* A female deity; a woman of superior charms or excellence.—**godfather,** god'fä·THér, *n.* In the Anglican, Roman Catholic, and several other churches, a man who at the baptism of a child makes a profession of the Christian faith in its name, and guarantees its religious education; a male sponsor.—*v.t.* To act as godfather to; to take under one's fostering care.—**godhead,** god'hed, *n.* [*God*, and suffix *-head*, same as *-hood.*] Godship; deity; divinity; divine nature or essence.—*The God-*

head, the Deity; God; the Supreme Being.—**godless,** god'les, *a.* Having or acknowledging no God; impious; ungodly; irreligious; wicked.—**godlessness,** god'les·nes, *n.* The state or quality of being godless.—**godlike,** god'lik, *a.* Resembling a god or God; divine; of superior excellence.—**godlikeness,** god'lik·nes, *n.* The state of being godlike.—**godlily,** god'li·li, *adv.* In a godly manner; piously; righteously.—**godliness,** god'li·nes, *n.* The condition or quality of being godly.—**godly,** god'li, *a.* Pious; reverencing God and his character and laws; devout; religious; righteous; conformed to or influenced by God's law.—*adv.* Piously; righteously.—**godmother,** god'muTH·ér, *n.* A woman who becomes sponsor for a child in baptism.—**godsend,** god'send, *n.* Something sent by God; an unlooked-for acquisition or piece of good fortune.—**godship,** god'ship, *n.* Deity; divinity; the rank or character of a god.—**godson,** god'sun, *n.* A male for whom one has been sponsor at baptism.—**Godspeed,** god'spēd, *n.* [A contraction of 'I wish that *God* may *speed* you.'] Success; prosperity; a prosperous journey: usually in phrase *to bid* a person *godspeed.*—**Godward, Godwards,** god'wérd, god'wérdz, *adv.* Toward God.—**God's acre,** *n.* The churchyard.

godwit, god'wit, *n.* [A.Sax. *god*, good, and *wiht*, creature, *wight*, from the excellence of their flesh.] A name of several grallatorial birds of no great size, the flesh of which is highly esteemed.

goffer, gof'ér, *v.t.* [GAUFFER.] To plait or flute; to gauffer.—**goffer,** gof'ér, *n.* An ornamental plaiting, used for the frills and borders of women's caps, etc.

goggle, gog'l, *v.t.* and *i.* [M.E. *gogelen*, to squint.] To stare or roll the eyes.—*a.* Prominent and rolling or staring: said of the eyes.—*n.* A strained or affected rolling of the eye; pl. a kind of spectacles with fixed plain glasses surrounded by leather for protecting the eyes from wind, debris, intense light.

goiter, goitre, goi'tér, *n.* [Fr. *goître*, from L. *guttur*, the throat.] An enlargement of the thyroid gland, forming a tumor or protuberance on the front part of the neck.—**goitrous,** goi'trus, *a.* Pertaining to goiter; affected with goiter.

gold, gōld, *n.* [A.Sax. *gold*=D. *goud*, Sc. *gowd*, Sw. *guld*, Icel. *gull*, Goth. *gulth*; from root of *yellow.* Hence *gild.*] A heavy yellow metallic element, the most malleable and ductile of all metals—symbol, Au (Latin, *aurum*); at. no., 79; at. wt., 196.967; sp. gr., 19.3—money; riches; wealth; a symbol of what is valuable or much prized; a bright yellow color, like that of the metal; *archery*, the exact center of the target, marked with gold, or of a gold color.—*a.* Made of gold; consisting of gold.—**goldbeater,** *n.* One whose occupation is to beat gold into thin leaves for gilding.—*Goldbeater's skin*, the prepared outside membrane of the large intestine of the ox, used by gold-beaters to lay between the leaves of the metal while they beat it.— **gold digger,** *n.* One who digs for gold; a woman whose relations with men are for selfish mercenary advantages.—**golden,** gōl'dn, *a.* Made of gold; of the color or luster of gold; yellow; shining; splendid; excellent; most valuable; precious; happy; marked by the happiness of mankind; pre-eminently favorable or auspicious (a *golden* opportunity).— *Golden age,* an early period in the history of the human race, fabled to have been one of primeval innocence and enjoyment; any period of great brilliancy or prosperity.—*Golden balls,* the three gilt balls placed in front of a pawnbroker's place of business; the arms of Lombardy, and the bankers settled in Lombard Street.—*Golden bull,* the edict issued in 1356, at Nuremberg, regulating the special form for election to the Holy Roman Empire.—*Golden calf* (*Exodus,* xxxii), money and its worship.—*Golden fleece,* an order of knighthood, the *toison d'or*; the order of Flanders and Spain, commemorating the wool trade of the Flemish towns; in *Greek myth.* the fleece of gold in quest of which Jason undertook the Argonautic expedition.— *Golden Horn,* the inlet of the Bosporus in European Turkey forming the harbor of Istanbul.—*Golden legend,* a collection of lives and legends of saints in high repute in the Middle Ages.—*Golden-mouthed,* eloquent, applied to John *Chrysostom* of Antioch, A.D. 347-407.—*Golden number,* in *chron.* a number showing the year of the moon's cycle.—*Golden wedding,* the fiftieth anniversary of a marriage, the seventy-fifth being the diamond wedding.—**goldeneye,** *n.* A species of duck; the garrot.—**golden pheasant,** *n.* A beautiful species of pheasant belonging to China.—**goldenrod,** *n.* A name of certain composite plants with rodlike stems and terminal spikes or racemes of small yellow flowers.—**goldfinch,** gōld'finsh, *n.* [A.Sax. *goldfinc.*] A songbird belonging to the finches, so named from the yellow markings on its wings.—**goldfish,** *n.* A species of carp, so named from its color, now largely bred in ponds, tanks, or glass vessels.—**gold leaf,** *n.* Gold beaten into an exceedingly thin sheet or leaf. —**goldsmith,** gōld'smith, *n.* An artisan who manufactures vessels and ornaments of gold.—**gold standard,** *n.* Monetary standard, in which the basic currency standard equals a specified amount of gold.—**gold-thread,** *n.* A thread formed of flattened gold laid over a thread of silk by twisting it.

golf, golf, *n.* [D. *kolf,* a club to drive balls with; Dan. and G. *kolbe,* a club.] A game played with clubs and balls, generally over large commons, downs, or links; the object being to drive the ball, with as few strokes as possible, into holes placed at considerable distances apart.—**golfer,** gol'fėr, *n.* One who plays golf.

Golgotha, gol'go·tha, *n.* [Heb.] A charnel house; scene of the Lord's crucifixion.

gollywog, go'li·wog, *n.* A black-faced, staring-eyed doll of hideous or whimsical appearance.

golosh, gō·losh', *n.* See GALOSH.

gomphosis, gom·fō'sis, *n.* [Gr., from *gomphos,* a nail.] *Anat.* an immovable articulation, as in the insertion of the teeth in their sockets.

gomuti, gō·mū'ti, *n.* The Malayan name for the sago palm, which yields a bristly useful fiber resembling black horsehair, known by the same name.

gonad, gon'ad, *n.* [Gr. *gonē,* that which generates.] *Anat.* a primary sex gland; ovary; testis.

gondola, gon'do·la, *n.* [It., origin unknown.] A flat-bottomed boat, very long and narrow, and having toward the center a curtained chamber for the passengers, used chiefly at Venice; a freight car, having sides and ends but no top, for carrying bulk loads.—**gondolier,** gon·do·lēr', *n.*

gone, gon, pp. of *go.*

gonfalon, gonfanon, gon'fa·lon, gon'fa·non, *n.* [Fr. *gonfalon,* O.Fr. *gonfanon,* from O.G. *guntfano—gunt,* a combat (=A.Sax. *gúth*), and *fano,* a banner.] An ensign or standard, the bearer of which in many of the medieval republican cities of Italy was often the chief personage in the state.—**gonfalonier,** gon'fal·o·nēr', *n.* One entrusted with a gonfalon; a chief magistrate in medieval Italian cities.

gong, gong, *n.* [Malay.] A Chinese percussion instrument, made of a mixed metal and shaped like a large round flat dish.

gonidia, go·nid'i·a, *n. pl.* [Gr. *gonē,* generation, and *eidos,* appearance.] *Bot.* the secondary, reproductive, green, spherical cells in the thallus of lichens.

goniometer, gō·ni·om'et·ėr, *n.* [Gr. *gōnia,* angle, and *metron,* measure.] An instrument for measuring solid angles, particularly the angles formed by the faces of mineral crystals.— **goniometric, goniometrical,** gō'ni·o·met"rik, gō'ni·o·met"ri·kal, *a.* Pertaining to or determined by a goniometer.—**goniometry,** gō·ni·om'et·ri, *n.* The art of measuring solid angles.

gonophore, gon'o·fōr, *n.* [Gr. *gonos,* seed, and *phoreō,* to bear.] *Bot.* the short stalk which bears the stamens and carpels in some plants; *zool.* one of the generative buds or receptacles of the reproductive elements in the Hydrozoa.

gonorrhea, gon·o·rē'a, *n.* [Gr. *gonorrhoia—gonos,* semen, and *rheō,* to flow.] An inflammatory infection of the male urethra or the female vagina, attended with secretion of mucus intermingled with pus.

good, gụd, *a.* [A.Sax. *gód,* good = D. *goed,* Dan. and Sw. *uod,* Icel. *gothr,* Goth. *gods,* G. *gut;* not connected with *god.*] The opposite of bad; conducive, in general, to any useful end or purpose; serviceable; advan-tageous; beneficial; wholesome; suitable; useful; fit; proper; right; possessing desirable or valuable physical or moral qualities; virtuous, righteous, dutiful, pious, or religious; excellent, valuable; precious; kind, benevolent, humane, merciful, or friendly; clever, skillful, or dexterous; adequate, sufficient, or competent; valid; of unimpaired credit; able to fulfill engagements; real, actual, serious (*good* earnest); considerable; more than a little; not deficient; full or complete; not blemished; unsullied; immaculate; honorable.—*Good Friday,* a feast of the Christian Church, in memory of the Saviour's crucifixion, kept on the Friday before Easter.—*In good time,* opportunely; not too soon nor too late; in proper time.—*To make good,* to perform; to fulfill; to verify or establish (an accusation); to supply deficiency in; to make up for defect; to maintain or carry out successfully.—*To stand good,* to be firm or valid.—*To think good, to see good,* to be pleased or satisfied; to think to be expedient.—*As good as his word,* equaling in fulfillment what was promised.—*n.* What is good, especially a result that is so (no *good* can come of it); what is serviceable, fit, excellent, kind, benevolent, or the like (to do *good*); benefit; advantage: opposed to *evil, ill, harm,* etc.; welfare or prosperity (the *good* of the state); a valuable possession or piece of property: almost always in the plural in this sense, and equivalent to wares, commodities, movables, household furniture, chattels, effects. —*For good, for good and all,* to close the whole business; for the last time; finally.—**good-by,** gụd·bi'. [Corruption of *God be with you.*] A form of salutation at parting; farewell.— **Good Conduct Medal,** gụd kon'dukt med'al, *n.* A medal given to a soldier as a reward for 'long service with irreproachable character and conduct'.—**good fellow,** *n.* A man esteemed for his companionable or social qualities; a good-natured pleasant person.—**good-fellowship,** *n.* Merry society; companionableness; friendliness.—**good humor,** *n.* A cheerful temper or state of mind.— **good-humored,** *a.* Characterized by good humor. — **good-humoredly,** *adv.* In a good-humored manner; in a cheerful way.—**goodish,** gụd'ish, *a.* Pretty good; tolerable; fair.— **goodliness,** gụd'li·nes, *n.* The quality of being goodly.—**goodly,** gụd'li, *a.* Being of a handsome form; fair to look on; beautiful; graceful; well-favored; pleasant; agreeable; large; considerable.—**goodman,** gụd'man, *n. Archaic.* A familiar appellation of civility; a husband; the head of a family.—**goodwife,** gụd'wīf, *n.* The mistress of a household: correlative to *goodman.*—**good nature,** *n.* Natural mildness and kindness of disposition. — **good-natured,** *a.* Having good-nature; naturally mild in temper.—**good-naturedly,** *adv.* In a good-natured manner. — **good-naturedness,** *n.* The quality of being good-natured.—**goodness,** gụd′nes, *n.* The state or quality of being good; a euphemism for God (thank *Goodness*).—**good-tempered,** *a.* Having a good temper; not easily irritated or annoyed.—**good will,** *n.* Benevolence; kindly feelings; heartiness; earnestness; zeal; *com.* the custom of any trade or business; the right to take up a trade or business connection, purchased of one who gives it up.—**goody,** gụd′i, *n.* [Probably contr. from *goodwife,* as *housewife, hussy.*] A term of civility applied to women in humble life.—**goody,** gụd′i, **goody-goody,** *a.* Affected with mawkish morality; excessively squeamish in morals.

goosander, gös′an·dėr, *n.* [Lit. goose-duck, from *goose,* and Icel. *andar,* genit. of *önd,* A.Sax. *ened,* a duck. DRAKE.] A swimming bird allied to the ducks and divers; the merganser. MERGANSER.

goose, gös, *n. pl.* **geese,** gēs. [A.Sax. *gós* (pl. *gés, gees*), a goose = Icel. *gás,* Dan. *gaas,* D. and G. *gans,* Rus. *gus*; cog. with L. *anser,* Gr. *chēn,* Skr. *hansa*; from a root meaning to gape, seen in E. *yawn.*] The name of several well-known swimming birds larger than ducks; a silly, stupid person, from the popular notion as to the stupidity of the goose; a tailor's smoothing iron; a game formerly common in England, played with dice on a card divided into small compartments, on certain of which a goose was figured.—*To cook one's goose,* to do for one; to finish a person (*slang*).—*v.t.* To hiss out; to condemn by hissing. (*Slang.*)—**goose flesh, goose skin,** *n.* A peculiar roughness of the human skin produced by cold, fear, and other depressing causes, as dyspepsia.—**gooseneck,** *n.* A pipe shaped like the letter S.—**goose-step,** *n.* The act of a soldier marking time by raising the feet alternately without advancing; the stiff German parade step.

gooseberry, gös′be·ri, *n.* [A corruption of *gossberry* for *gorseberry,* from prickles on the bush giving it a resemblance to gorse; or for *gooseberry,* from Fr. *groseille,* a gooseberry, from G. *kräusbeere, kräuselbeere,* a gooseberry—*kraus,* frizzled, curled, crisp, and *beere,* a berry.] The fruit of a prickly shrub either red, yellow, or green in color, and hairy or smooth on the surface, well known and much esteemed; also the shrub itself; a small ball of barbed wire.

gopher, gō′fėr, *n.* [Fr. *gaufre,* honeycomb.] The name given in America to several burrowing animals from their honeycombing the earth; also a species of burrowing tortoise of the Southern States.

gopherwood, gof′ėr, *n.* [Heb. *gopher.*] A species of wood used in the construction of Noah's ark, perhaps cypress.

gorbelly, gor′bel·li, *n.* [A.Sax. *gor,* dirt, dung, E. *gore,* and *belly.*] A prominent belly; a person having a big belly.—**gorbellied,** *a.* Big-bellied.—**gorcock,** gor′kok, *n.* [From its red color; or from *gorse,* furze.]

The red grouse.—**gorhen,** *n.* The female of the red grouse.

Gordian, gor′di·an, *a.* Pertaining to *Gordius,* king of Phrygia, or the knot tied by him, and which could not be untied, but which was ultimately cut by Alexander the Great; hence, the term *Gordian knot* is applied to any inextricable difficulty; and to *cut the Gordian knot* is to remove a difficulty by bold or unusual measures.

gore, gōr, *n.* [A.Sax. *gor,* gore, filth, Icel. and Dan. *gor,* Sw. *gorr.*] Blood that is shed; thick or clotted blood.—**gory,** gō′ri, *a.* Covered with gore; bloody.

gore, gōr, *n.* [A.Sax. *gára,* a point or corner of land, from *gár,* a spear; like Icel. *geiri,* a triangular piece, from *geirr,* a spear.] A triangular-shaped piece, as of cloth, let into or regarded as let into a larger piece; a gusset.—*v.t.* To cut a gore in; to piece with a gore.

gore, gōr, *v.t.*—*gored, goring.* [Directly from A.Sax. *gár,* a spear or dart; Icel. *geirr.*] To stab; to pierce with a pointed instrument, as a spear, or with the horns (as an ox).

gorge, gorj, *n.* [Fr. *gorge,* from It. *gorgia,* L. *gurges,* a whirlpool; akin *gargle, gurgle,* etc.] The throat or gullet; that which is swallowed; food caused to regurgitate through nausea or disgust; a narrow passage between hills or mountains; the entrance into a bastion or other outwork of a fort; *arch.* the narrowest part of the Tuscan and Doric capital; also, a cavetto.—*v.t.*—*gorged, gorging.* To swallow, especially with greediness or in large quantities; to fill the stomach of; to satiate: often *refl.*—*v.i.* To feed greedily; to stuff one's self.

gorgeous, gor′jus, *a.* [O.Fr. *gorgias,* gaudy, flaunting, from *gorgias,* a ruff for the neck, from *gorge,* the throat (which see).] Exceedingly showy; splendid; magnificent; glittering with gay colors.—**gorgeously,** gor′jus·li, *adv.* In a gorgeous manner.—**gorgeousness,** gor′jus·nes, *n.*

gorget, gor′jet, *n.* [Fr. *gorgette,* from *gorge,* the throat. GORGE.] A piece of armor for defending the throat or neck; a small crescent-shaped metallic ornament formerly worn by officers on the breast.

Gorgon, gor′gon, *n.* [Gr. *gorgō, gorgon,* from *gorgos,* fierce, grim.] *Greek myth.* one of several monsters of terrific aspect, the sight of which turned the beholder to stone; hence, some one like a Gorgon.—*a.* Very ugly or terrific.—**Gorgonian,** gor-**Gorgonian,** gor-gō′ni·an, *a.* [From Gr. *gorgos,* fierce, grim, and *Gorgon,* a Greek mythological monster.] Like a Gorgon; pertaining to Gorgons or monsters.—*a.* Very ugly.—**gorgonize,** gor′gō·nīz, *v.t.* To turn into stone; to petrify.

Gorgonzola, gor-gon·zō′la, *n.* A kind of Italian ewe-milk cheese made at Gorgonzola, a village near Milan.

gorilla, go·ril′la, *n.* [Originally an African name, found in use by the Phoenician navigator Hanno in the fifth century B.C.] The largest of the apes, very strong and fierce, found chiefly in the woody equatorial regions of Africa, sometimes living in trees, and feeding on vegetable substances.

gormand, gor′mand, *n.* [Fr. *gourmand.*] A gourmand.—**gormandism,** gor′man·dizm, *n.* Gluttony.—**gormandize,** gor′man·dīz, *v.i.*—*gormandized, gormandizing.* To eat greedily; to swallow voraciously.—**gormandizer,** gor′man·dī·zėr, *n.* A voracious eater.

goshawk, gos′hak, *n.* [A.Sax. *góshafoc,* goose-hawk—so called from being flown at geese.] A kind of large hawk, formerly much used in falconry.

gosling, goz′ling, *n.* [A.Sax. *gós,* goose, and the dim. term. *-ling.*] A young goose; a kind of catkin.

Gospel, gos′pel, *n.* [A.Sax. *godspell*—*gód,* good, and *spell,* history, narration—answering to the Gr. *euangelion,* L. *evangelium*; a good or joyful message, evangel; or compounded of A.Sax. *god,* God, and *spell*—lit. God's word.] The history of Jesus Christ; any of the four records of Christ's life left by his apostles; the whole scheme of salvation as revealed by Christ and his apostles; some portion of one of the Four Gospels appointed to be read in the service of the Anglican Church.—*a.* Accordant with the Gospel; relating to the Gospel; evangelical; [*not. cap.*] system of gospel doctrine or of religious truth; any general doctrine (a political *gospel*).—**gospeler,** gos′pel·ėr, *n.* An evangelist; the priest or minister who reads the gospel in the church service.

gossamer, gos′a·mėr, *n.* [A name apparently applied originally to the period at which gossamer is commonly observed, and equivalent to *goose-summer,* the term having perhaps arisen from geese being then driven out to the stubble and from their well-known connection with Michaelmas; comp. the German names for gossamer, 'our lady's summer', 'flying summer', 'old wives summer'.] A fine filmy substance, a kind of delicate cobwebs, floating in the air in calm clear weather, especially in autumn, formed by small species of spiders.—**gossamery,** gos′a·mėr·i, *a.* Like gossamer; flimsy; unsubstantial.

gossan, gos′an, *n. Mining,* an oxide of iron and quartz, a sure indication of ore at greater depth.

gossip, gos′sip, *n.* [From *God* and prov. E. *sib,* relation, related, lit. related in the service of God.] An idle tattler or carrier of tales; mere tattle; groundless rumor.—*v.i.* To prate; to chat; to tell idle tales.—**gossiper,** gos′sip·ėr, *n.* One who gossips; a gossip.—**gossipry,** gos′sip·ri, *n.* Idle talk or gossip.—**gossipy,** gos′sip·i, *a.* Full of gossip.

got, got, *pret.* of *get.*—**got, gotten,** got′n, *pp.* of *get.*

Goth, goth, *n.* [L. *Gothi,* Goths.] One of an ancient Teutonic race of people, first heard of as inhabiting the shores of the Baltic, and who afterward overran and took an important part in subverting the Roman empire; a barbarian; a rude ignorant person; one defective in taste.—**Gothic,** goth′ik, a. Pertaining to the Goths; rude; barbarous; the term applied to that style of architecture, the characteristic feature of which is the pointed arch and the subserviency of the other parts to this feature: originally used in a depreciatory sense.—n. The language of the Goths; printing, the name of a bold-faced type, used for titling and jobbing work; the Gothic style or order of architecture.—**Gothicism,** goth′i·sizm, n. A Gothic idiom; conformity to the Gothic style of architecture; rudeness of manners; barbarousness. —**Gothicize,** goth′i·sīz, v.t.—**Gothicized, Gothicizing.** To make Gothic; to bring back to barbarism.

gothamite, gŏt′am·it, n. A person deficient in wisdom, so called from Gotham, in Nottinghamshire, noted for some pleasant blunders; a term sportively applied to the inhabitants of New York, then pron. gō′tham·it.

gouge, gouj, n. [Fr. gouge, LL. guvia, a gouge; origin uncertain.] A chisel with a hollow or grooved blade, used to cut holes, channels, or grooves.— v.t.—**gouged, gouging.** To scoop out or turn with or as with a gouge.

gourd, gōrd, n. [Fr. gourde, O.Fr. gouorde, gougorde, from L. cucurbita, a gourd.] The popular name of the family of plants represented by the melon, cucumber, pumpkin, vegetable marrow, etc., or for their fruits.

gourmand, gōr′mand, n. [Fr., of Celtic origin; comp. W. gormant, that which tends to overfill; gormodd, excess, from gor, excess.] A glutton; a greedy feeder; a dainty feeder; an epicure; a gourmet.

gourmet, gōr′mā or gōr′met, n. [Fr., a wine taster, for groumet, from the O.D. word=E. groom.] A man of keen palate; a connoisseur in wines and meats; a nice feeder; an epicure.

gout, gout, n. [Fr. goutte, L. gutta, a drop, from the old medical theory that diseases were due to the deposition of drops of morbid humor in the part.] A disease giving rise to paroxysms of acute pain with inflammation, affecting the small joints, and generally the first joint of the great toe, and often accompanied by calculi or concretions at the joints; a drop; a clot or coagulation (Shak.). —**goutily,** gout′i·li, adv. In a gouty manner.—**goutiness,** gout′i·nes, n. The state of being gouty; gouty affections.—**gouty,** gout′i, a. Diseased with or subject to the gout; pertaining to the gout.

govern, guv′ern, v.t. [Fr. gouverner, from L. gubernare, to govern, a form of Gr. kybernaō, to govern.] To direct and control; to regulate by authority; to keep within the limits prescribed by law or sovereign will; to influence; to direct; to restrain; to keep in due subjection; to steer or regulate the course of; gram. to cause to be in a particular case, or

to require a particular case.—v.i. To exercise authority; to administer the laws; to maintain the superiority; to have the control.—**governable,** guv′ér·na·bl, a. Capable of being governed; submissive to law or rule.— **governance,** guv′ér·nans, n. Government; exercise of authority; control; management.—**governess,** guv′ér·nes, n. A female that governs; a lady who has the care of educating or teaching children in their homes.— **government,** guv′érn·ment, n. The act of governing; regulation; control; restraint; the exercise of authority; direction and restraint exercised over the actions of men in communities, societies, or states; the administration of public affairs; the system of polity in a state; the mode or system according to which the sovereign powers of a nation, the legislative, executive, and judicial powers, are vested and exercised; a body politic governed by one authority; a province or division of territory ruled by a governor; the persons or council who administer the laws of a kingdom or state; the administration; the executive power; gram. the influence of a word in regard to construction.—**governmental,** guv′érn·men·tal, a. Pertaining to government; made by government.—**governor,** guv′ér·nér, n. One who governs; the supreme executive magistrate of a state, community, corporation, etc.; a tutor to a boy at home; a contrivance in mills and machinery for maintaining a uniform velocity with a varying resistance; a contrivance in a steam engine which automatically regulates the admission of steam to the cylinder.—**governor general,** n. A governor who has under him subordinate or deputy governors; a viceroy.—**governorship,** guv′ér·nér·ship, n. The office of a governor.

gown, goun, n. [O.Fr. goune, L.L. gunna, furred robe, fur.] A woman's outer garment; a dress; a dressing gown or a nightgown; the official dress worn by members of certain professions, as divinity, medicine, law, by magistrates, university professors and students, etc.; sometimes used as the emblem of civil life, as the sword of military. 'Gowns not arms' (Milton, Sonnets, xvii); collectively, the students of a university or college (the town and gown).—v.t. Gowned, gowning. To put a gown on; to clothe or dress in a gown.—v.i. To put on a gown; to wear a gown or robe.—**gownsman,** gounz′man, n. One whose professional habit is a gown, as a lawyer, professor, or student of a university.

Graafian, grä′fi·an, a. [From Regnier de Graaf, a Dutch physician.] Applied to certain vesicles developed in the ovaries of mammals for the special purpose of expelling the ovum.

Graal, grāl, n. Same as Grail.

grab, grab, v.t.—**grabbed, grabbing.** [Sw. grabba, to grasp; D. grabbelen, to snatch; akin grapple, gripe, graip, grope, etc.] To seize; to snatch; to

grip suddenly. (Colloq.)—n. A sudden grasp or seizure; a catch; an advantage (colloq.); an implement for clutching objects.—**grabber,** grab′ér, n. One who or that which grabs.

grace, grās, n. [Fr., from L. gratia, favor, from gratus, pleasant (seen also in grateful, gratitude, agree, ingrate, etc.); from a root seen in Gr. chairō, to rejoice, Gael. gradh, love, and E. yearn.] Favor, goodwill, or kindness; disposition to oblige another; the love and favor of God; divine influence renewing the heart and restraining from sin; a state of reconciliation to God; virtuous or religious affection or disposition proceeding from divine influence; mercy; pardon; favor conferred; a license, dispensation, or peculiar privilege; a short prayer before or after meals acknowledging the grace or goodness of God; [usually cap.] (with possessive pronouns) a title used in addressing or speaking of a duke or duchess; that external element in acting or speaking which renders it appropriate and agreeable; elegance with appropriate dignity; a beauty or element in what pleases the eye; an embellishment; an affectation of elegance, dignity, or refinement (a person's airs and graces); dispensation by university authorities to take a degree; [cap.] Greek myth. beauty or elegance deified; one of three goddesses in whose gift were grace, loveliness, and favor; mus. a turn, trill, shake, etc., introduced for embellishment.—Days of grace, com. three days immediately following the day when a bill becomes due, which days are allowed to the debtor or payer to make payment in. —A person's good graces, a person's favor or friendly regard.—With a good grace, graciously; with at least an air of graciousness.—With a bad grace, ungracefully; ungraciously.— v.t.—**graced, gracing.** To lend or add grace to; to adorn; to serve to embellish or dignify; to honor.— **grace cup,** n. A final parting cup, after grace has been said.—**graceful,** grās′ful, a. Displaying grace in form or action; possessing a peculiar elegance or attraction in mien or appearance: used particularly of motion, looks, and speech.—**gracefully,** grās′ful·li, adv. In a graceful manner. —**gracefulness,** grās′ful·nes, n. The condition or quality of being graceful.—**graceless,** grās′les, a. Void of grace; somewhat careless in regard to religious matters; not at all devout; unregenerate; unsanctified.— **gracelessly,** grās′les·li, adv. In a graceless manner.—**gracelessness,** grās les·nes, n.—**grace note,** n. Mus. a note added by way of ornament, and printed or written in smaller characters; an appoggiatura.—**gracious,** grā′shus, a. [Fr. gracieux, L. gratiosus.] Favorable; benevolent; merciful; benign; kind; friendly; proceeding from, produced by, or associated with divine grace, virtuous; good; polite.—**graciously,** grā′shus·li, adv. In a gracious manner. —**graciousness,** grā′shus·nes, n.

gracile,† grăs′il, *a.* [L. *gracilis*, slender.] Slender.—**gracility,** gra·sil′i·ti, *n.* Slenderness.

grackle, grak′l, *n.* [L. *graculus*, a jackdaw, imitative of the cry.] Any of various birds of Asia and Africa of the starling family; any of certain blackbirds of the U.S., as the purple grackle.

grade, grād, *n.* [Fr. *grade*, from L. *gradus*, a step, from *gradior*, *gressus*, to go, seen also in *congress*, *degrade*, *degree*, *egress*, *ingredient*, *progress*, *retrograde*, etc.] A degree in any series, rank, or order, relative position or standing; one of the sections of a school system, as divided into years of work; the group of pupils in one of these sections; a mark rating a pupil's work; the rate of ascent or descent; the part of a road which slopes.—*v.t.*—*graded*, *grading.* To arrange in order according to size, quality, rank, degree of advancement, and the like; to reduce (the line of a railway, etc.) to such levels or degrees of inclination as may make it suitable for being used.—**gradation,** gra·dā′shon, *n.* [L. *gradatio.*] The act of grading; the state of being graded; arrangement by grades or ranks; a regular advance from step to step; a degree or relative position in any order or series; the gradual blending of one tint into another.—**gradational,** gra·dā′shon·al, *a.* Of or pertaining to, or according to gradation.—**gradient,** grā′di·ent, *a.* [L. *gradiens, gradientis,* ppr. of *gradior.*] Moving by steps†; walking†; rising or descending by regular degrees of inclination.—*n.* The degree of slope or inclination of the ground over which a railway, road, or canal passes; the rate of ascent or descent; the part of a road which slopes.—**gradual,** grad′ū·al, *a.* [Fr. *graduel.*] Proceeding by steps or degrees; advancing step by step; regular and slow; progressive.—*n.* An ancient servicebook of the church: also called *Grail*; [*cap.*] song sung between epistle and Gospel at the steps of the altar.—**gradually,** grad′ū·al·li, *adv.* In a gradual manner; by degrees; step by step; regularly.—**graduate,** grad′ū·āt, *v.t.*—*graduated, graduating.* [Fr. *graduer,* from L. *gradus.*] To mark with degrees, regular intervals, or divisions; to divide into small regular distances (to *graduate* a thermometer); to temper or modify by degrees; to characterize or mark with degrees or grades, as of intensity; to confer a university degree on; to reduce to a certain consistency by evaporation.—*v.i.* To receive a degree from a college or university; to pass by degrees; to change gradually; to shade off.—*n.* One who has been admitted to a degree in a college or university, or by some incorporated society; a vessel with graduated measurement marks.—*a.* Arranged by successive steps or degrees. — **graduation,** grad·ū·ā′shon, *n.* The act of graduating, or state of being graduated; the marks or lines made on an instrument to indicate degrees or other divisions.—**graduator,** grad′ū·ā·ter, *n.* One who or that which graduates; an instrument for graduating; a contrivance for accelerating evaporation.

graffiti, grä·fē′tē, *n. pl.* [Pl. of It. *graffito,* a scribbling, from *graffiare,* to scribble.] A class of rude scribblings or figures on the walls of Pompeii, the Catacombs etc., dating from ancient Roman times.

graft, graft, *n.* [O.Fr. *graffe,* Fr. *greffe,* a slip or shoot of a tree for grafting, originally a pointed instrument, from L. *graphium,* a style for writing on waxen tablets, from Gr. *graphō,* to write.] A small shoot or scion of a tree, inserted in another tree and becoming part of it, but retaining the characters of its own parent; *surg.* living tissue implanted, as in a lesion, to become an organic part; the act of grafting; corrupt gains or practices in politics.—*v.t.* To insert a graft on; to propagate by a graft; to incorporate after the manner of a graft.—*v.i.* To practice grafting or engage in corrupt but profitable pursuits.—**grafter,** graf′ter, *n.* One who grafts; one who gains money or material profit by graft.

graham flour, grā′am, wheat flour made from the whole kernel.

grail, grāl, *n.* [O.Fr. *graal, greal,* L.L. *gradalis, gradale,* etc., perhaps from *cratella,* dim. of L. *crater,* Gr. *kratēr,* a cup.] The holy vessel used by Christ in the Last Supper (called the Holy Grail), said to have been found by Joseph of Arimathea, who had caught the last drops of Christ's blood in it.

grain, grān, *n.* [Fr. *grain,* from L. *granum,* a grain, seed, kernel. Of same origin are *granite, grange, garner,* etc.] A single seed of a plant, particularly of those plants whose seeds are used for food of man or beast; used collectively for edible seeds in general, or the fruits of cereal plants, as wheat, rye, oats, etc., as also for the plants themselves; *pl.* the husks or remains of grain used in brewing or distilling; any small hard particle, as of sand, sugar, salt, etc.; a minute particle; a small amount (not a *grain* of sense); the twentieth part of the scruple in apothecaries' weight, and the twenty-fourth part of a pennyweight troy; the substance of a thing regarded with respect to the size, form, or direction of the constituent particles; the fibers of wood or other fibrous substance, with regard to their arrangement or direction; texture (stone or wood of a fine *grain*); formerly the scarlet dye made from the kermes or cochineal insects, from their round, seedlike form; hence, a red-colored dye; also, a permanent color of any kind.—*To dye in grain,* originally, to dye with kermes; then, to dye deeply or permanently; now usually to dye in the fiber or raw material.—*Grain side of leather,* the side from which the hair has been removed.—*Against the grain,* against the fibers of wood; hence, against the natural temper; unwillingly; unpleasantly; reluctantly.—*Grains of Paradise,* the pungent, somewhat aromatic seeds of a plant of the ginger family, a native of tropical Western Africa.—*v.t.* To form into grains, as powder, sugar, and the like; to paint so as to give the appearance of grains or fibers; *tan.* to give a granular appearance to the surface; to prepare the hairy side as the outer side.—*v.i.* To form grains or to assume a granular form, as the result of crystallization.—**grainer,** grā′ner, *n.* One who or that which grains; a peculiar brush or a toothed instrument used by painters.—**grainy,** grā′ni, *n.* Full of grains or corn; full of kernels.—**granary,** gran′a·ri, *n.* [L. *granarium,* from *granum.*] A storehouse for grain after it is threshed.—**graniform,** gran′i·form, *a.* *Bot.* formed like grains of corn.—**granivorous,** gra·niv′o·rus, *a.* [L. *granum,* and *voro,* to eat.] Eating grain; feeding or subsisting on seeds.

grain, grān, *n.* [Same word as Dan. *green,* a branch, a prong; Icel. *grein,* a branch; akin *groin.*] A tine, prong, or spike; *pl.* a kind of harpoon with four or more barbed points.

Grallatores, Grallae, gral·a·tō′rēz, gral′ē, *n. pl.* [L. *grallæ,* stilts, *grallator* (pl. *grallatores*), one who goes on stilts, from *gradior,* to go. GRADE.] An order of birds generally characterized by very long legs, long necks, and long bills, including the cranes, plovers, snipes, rails, coots, etc., etc.; the waders.—**grallatorial,** gral·a·tō′ri·al, *a.* Pertaining to the Grallatores.

gram, gram, *n.* The name of a chickpea extensively cultivated in the East Indies.

gram, gram, *n.* [Fr., from Gr. *gramma,* a letter, also the weight of a scruple, from *grapho,* to write.] The unit of weight in the metric system equivalent to a cubic centimeter of water.—**gram molecule,** gram mol′e·kūl, *n.* The quantity of a substance having a weight in grams numerically equal to its molecular weight; also **gram-molecular weight.**

gramineous, gra·min′i·us, *a.* [L. *gramineus,* from *gramen, graminis,* grass.] Like or pertaining to grass or to the tribe of grasses.

grammar, gram′mar, *n.* [Fr. *grammaire,* from a hypothetical L.L. form *grammaria,* from Gr. *gramma,* a letter, from *graphō,* to write (whence *graphic,* etc.). GRAVE, *v.t.*] The exposition of the principles which underlie the use of language; a system of general principles and of particular rules for speaking or writing a language; a book containing such principles and rules; language as regulated by rules or usage; propriety of speech (to violate *grammar*; *good* grammar, *bad* grammar, correct or incorrect language); a treatise on the elements or principles of any science; an outline of the principles of any subject.—*a.* Belonging to or contained in grammar.—**grammarian,** gram·mâ′ri·an, *n.* One versed in grammar.—**grammatical,** gram-·

mat′i·kal, *a.* Belonging to grammar; according to the rules of grammar.—**grammatically**, gram·mat′i·kal·li, *adv.* In a grammatical manner; according to the rules of grammar.—**grammar school**, *n.* A grade school; a school including the intermediate grades between the primary grades and high school; a school in which Latin and Greek are more especially taught.

grampus, gram′pus, *n.* [Sp. *gran pez*, from L. *grandis*, great, and *piscis*, a fish; comp. *porpoise, porpus*.] A marine mammal of the dolphin family, which grows to the length of 25 feet, and preys on fish; in secondary sense, a person who snores.

granadilla, gran·a·dil′la, *n.* [Sp., dim. of *granada*, a pomegranate.] The fruit of a species of passion flower much esteemed in tropical countries; also the plant.

granary. See GRAIN.

grand, grand, *a.* [Fr. *grand*, from L. *grandis*, great, grand, seen also in *aggrandize*.] Great; illustrious; high in power or dignity; noble; splendid; magnificent; principal or chief: used largely in composition (*grand* juror, *grand* master); conceived or expressed with great dignity; implying an additional or second generation, as in *grand*father, *grand*child, etc.—**grandam**, gran′dam, *n.* [*Grand* and *dame*] An old woman; a grandmother.—**grandaunt**, *n.* The aunt of one's father or mother.—**grandchild**, grand′child, *n.* A son's or daughter's child or offspring —**granddaughter**, grand′da̤·tĕr, *n.* The daughter of a son or daughter.—**grandfather**, grand′fä·THĕr, *n.* A father's or mother's father.—**grandmother**, grand′muTH·ĕr, *n.* A father's or mother's mother.—**grandnephew**, *n.* The grandson of a brother or sister.—**grandniece**, *n.* The granddaughter of a brother or sister.—**grandparent**, grand′pâ·rent, *n.* The parent of a parent.—**grandsire**, grand′sīr, *n.* A grandfather; any ancestor preceding a father.—**grandson**, grand′sun, *n.* The son of a son or daughter.—**granduncle**, *n.* The uncle of one's father or mother.—**grand duke**, the title of former sovereigns of certain German states; also applied to members of the former imperial family of Russia.—**grandee**, gran·dē′, *n.* [Sp. *grande*, a nobleman.] A Spanish nobleman of the first rank; hence a nobleman or man of high rank in general.—**grandeur**, grand′yĕr, *a.* [Fr.] The state or quality of being grand.—**grandiloquence**, gran·dil′o··kwens, *n.* The quality of being grandiloquent. — **grandiloquent**, gran·dil′o·kwent, *a.* [L. *grandiloquens* —*grandis*, and *loquor*, to speak.] Speaking in a lofty style; expressed in high-sounding words; bombastic; pompous.—**grandiose**, gran′di·ōs, *a.* [Fr.] Impressive from inherent grandeur; imposing; commonly, aiming at or affecting grandeur; grandiloquent; bombastic; turgid.—**grandiosity**, gran·di·os′i·ti, *n.* The quality of being grandiose.—**grand jury**,

jury whose duty is to examine into the grounds of accusation against offenders, and if they see just cause, to find a true bill against them.—**grandly**, grand′li, *adv.* In a grand or lofty manner.—**grandness**, grand′nes, *n.* Grandeur; greatness with beauty; magnificence.—**grand opera**, opera that compares with serious drama in characterization and plot and has a completely sung text.—**grandstand**, *n.* An elevated system of seats arranged one row above another at a racecourse or athletic field, usually with a roof, whence a good view can be obtained —**grand vizier**, the chief minister of the former Turkish Empire.

grange, grānj, *n.* [Fr. *grange*, a barn, from L.L. *granea, granica*, a barn, from L. *granum*, grain. GRAIN.] A farm, with the dwelling house, stables, barns, etc.; one of the local lodges of the secret farmers' organization called "The Patrons of Husbandry." Nationally, the Grange dates from 1867, and includes both men and women. Its social, fraternal, and educational aims were later expanded to become an effective influence in political and legislative matters, both state and national, in the interest of the farm population.

granite, gran′it, *n.* [Fr. *granit*, from It. *granito*, lit. grained stone, from L. *granum*, a grain. GRAIN.] An unstratified rock, one of the most abundant in the earth's crust, composed generally of grains or crystals of quartz, feldspar, and mica, united without regular arrangement.—**granitic**, gra·nit′ik, *a.* Of or pertaining to granite; having the nature of granite; consisting of granite.—**granitoid**, gran′i·toid, *a.* Resembling granite.—**graniteware**, *n.* Articles made of iron coated with vitreous enamel.

grant, grant, *v.t.* [From O.Fr. *graan-ter, graunter, craanter, creanter*, to promise, to agree, to guarantee, from (hypothetical) L.L. *credentare*, to make to believe or trust, from L. *credens*, pp. of *credo*, to believe. CREED.] To transfer the title or possession of; to convey, give, or make over; to bestow or confer, particularly in answer to prayer or request; to admit as true though not proved; to allow; to yield; to concede.—*v.i.* To make a grant; to consent (*Shak.*).—*n.* The act of granting, bestowing, or conferring; the thing granted or bestowed.—**grantable**, gran′ta·bl, *a.* Capable of being granted or conveyed.—**grantee**, gran·tē′, *n.* The person to whom a grant or conveyance is made.—**granter**, gran′tĕr, *n.* One who grants —**grantor**, gran′tor, *n.* *Law*, the person who makes a grant or conveyance.

granular, gran′ū·lĕr, *a.* [From L. *granum*, grain. GRAIN.] Consisting of or resembling granules or grains.—**granulate**, gran′ū·lāt, *v.t.*—*granulated, granulating.* [Fr. *granuler*.] To form into grains or small masses; to raise in granules or small asperities; to make rough on the surface.—*v.i.* To collect or be formed into grains;

to become granular.—**granulation**, gran·ū·lā′shon, *n.* The act of granulating; a reducing to the form of small grains; *surg.* a process by which little granular fleshy bodies form on sores when healing; the fleshy grains themselves —**granule**, gran′ūl, *n.* [Fr., dim. from L. *granum*, a grain.] A little grain; a small particle; a minute round body of vegetable or animal matter.

grape, grāp, *n.* [O.Fr. *grape*, grape, Mod.Fr. *grappe*, a bunch or cluster, originally a hook, from O.G. *krapfe*, a hook.] A smooth-skinned berry from a vine of the Vitaceae family, ranging in color from white to deep red and blue-black, eaten fresh or dried, as raisins, and used for making wine; *milit.* grapeshot.—*Sour grapes*, things professedly despised because they are beyond our reach: from Aesop's fable of 'The Fox and the Grapes'.—**grapery**, grā′pĕr·i, *n.* A place where grapes are grown; a vinery.—**grapefruit**, *n.* A large, yellow citrus fruit developed from the shaddock; the tree bearing this fruit.—**grapeshot**, *n.* Iron balls held in a frame and fired from a cannon.—**grapestone**, *n.* The stone or seed of the grape.—**grape sugar**, a variety of sugar from grapes; glucose.—**grapevine**, *n.* The vine that bears grapes; also some secret means of communicating rumor.

graph, graf, *n.* [Gr. *graphō*, I write.] A diagram representing the relation between two varying magnitudes by means of a curve referred to fixed axes.—**graphic, graphical**, graf′ik, graf′i·kal, *a.* Pertaining to the art of writing, engraving, or delineating; written; pictorial; describing with accuracy or vividly; vivid; portraying in vivid and expressive language.—*Graphic granite*, a variety of granite which when cut in one direction exhibits markings resembling Hebrew characters.—**graphically**, graf′i·kal·li, *adv.* In a graphic manner.—**graphite**, graf′īt, *n.* [Gr. *graphein*, to write.] One of the forms under which carbon occurs, made into pencils, and used as a moderator in atomic reactors.

grapnel, grap′nel, *n.* [Dim. from Fr. *grappin*, a grapnel; of same origin as *grape*.] A small anchor with four or five flukes or claws, used to hold boats or small vessels; a grappling iron.

grapple, grap′l, *v.t.*—*grappled, grappling*. [Directly from O.Fr. *grappil*, a grapnel; or from *grab* or *gripe*.] To lay fast hold on, either with the hands or with hooks; to seize and hold.—*v.i.* To contend in close fight, as wrestlers.—*To grapple with*, to contend with; to struggle with; to confront boldly.—*n.* A close seizure or hug; the wrestler's hold; close fight or encounter; a hook by which one ship fastens on another.—**grappling iron**. *n.* An instrument consisting of four or more iron claws for grappling and holding fast.

grasp, grasp, *v.t.* [From stem of *grope, gripe*, or *grab*; comp. G.

grapsen, to snatch, from O.G. *grappen*, *grabben*.] To seize and hold by the fingers or arms; to lay hold of; to take possession of; to seize by the intellect; to comprehend.—*v.i.* To make a clutch or catch; to gripe.—*To grasp at*, to catch at; to try to seize.—*n.* The grip or seizure of the hand; reach of the arms; hence, the power of seizing and holding; forcible possession; power of the intellect to seize and comprehend; wide-reaching power of intellect.—**grasper**, gras'pėr, *n.* One who or that which grasps.—**grasping**, gras'ping, *a.* Covetous; rapacious; avaricious; greedy; miserly.—**graspingly**, gras'ping·li, *adv.* In a grasping manner.

grass, gras, *n.* [A.Sax. *græs*, *gæs* = Goth. Icel. D. and G. *gras*, Dan. *græs*, Sw. *gräs*; probably akin to *grow* and *green*.] In common usage (and without a plural), herbage; the verdurous covering of the soil; also any plant of the family to which belong the grain-yielding and pasture plants.—*China grass*, a Chinese plant, of the nettle family, from the fiber of which grass cloth is made.—*Esparto grass*. ESPARTO. —*v.t.* To cover with grass; to furnish with grass; to bleach on the grass.—**grasshopper**, gras'hop·ėr, *n.* A leaping orthopterous insect allied to the locusts, commonly living among grass.—**grassiness**, gras'i·nes, *n.* The condition of being grassy.—**grassland**, *n.* Land kept under grass.—**grass roots**, gras rọts, *n.* The rural and farming districts regarded as a source of independent popular opinion.—*To get down to grass roots*, to get down to the fundamental part, close to, or emerging from, the people.—**grass widow**, *n.* Formerly, an unmarried woman who had a child: now applied to a wife separated from her husband.—**grassy**, gras'i, *a.*

grate, grāt, *n.* [It. *grata*, a grate, lattice, hurdle, from L.L. *grata*, *crata*, L. *crates*, a hurdle. CRATE.] A series of parallel or cross bars, with interstices; a kind of latticework; a grating; a metallic receptacle for holding burning fuel, and formed to a greater or less extent of bars.— *v.t.* To furnish with a grate or grates; to fill in or cover with crossbars.— **grating**, grā'ting, *n.* A partition or frame of parallel or cross bars.— **gratelike**, grāt'lik, *a.*

grate, grāt, *v.t.*—*grated, grating.* [O.Fr. *grater*, Fr. *gratter*, to scratch, to rub; from the Teutonic; comp. O.H.G. *chrazón*, G. *kratzen*, to scratch; Dan. *kratte*, *kradse*, to scratch; E. *scratch*.] To rub hard or roughly together, as a body with a rough surface against another body; to wear away in small particles by rubbing with anything rough or indented; to offend or irritate.—*v.i.* To rub roughly with the surface in contact (a body *grates* upon another); to have a galling or annoying effect (to *grate* upon the feelings); to make a harsh sound by friction; to sound disa-

greeably.—**grater**, grā'tėr, *n.* One who or that which grates.—**grating**, grā'ting, *p.* and *a.* Irritating; harsh.— *n.* The harsh sound or the feeling caused by strong attrition or rubbing.—**gratingly**, *adv.* In a grating manner.

grateful, grāt'fụl, *a.* [From O.Fr. *grat*. L. *gratus*, pleasing, and E. adjectival term, *ful*. GRACE.] Having a due sense of benefits; having kind feelings and thankfulness toward one from whom a favor has been received; expressing gratitude; indicative of gratitude; affording pleasure; agreeable; pleasing to the taste or the intellect; gratifying.—**gratefully**, grāt'fụl·li, *adv.* In a grateful manner.—**gratefulness**, grāt'fụl·nes, *n.* The state or quality of being grateful.—**gratitude**, grat'i·tūd, *n.* [L.L. *gratitudo*.] The feeling of one who is grateful; a warm and friendly emotion awakened by a favor received; thankfulness.

gratify, grat'i·fī, *v.t.*—*gratified, gratifying.* [Fr. *gratifier*, L. *gratificor*—*gratus*, pleasant, agreeable, and *facio*, to make. GRATEFUL.] To please; to give pleasure to; to indulge, delight, humor, satisfy.—**gratification**, grat'i·fi·kā″shon, *n.* [L. *gratificatio*.] The act of gratifying or pleasing; that which affords pleasure; enjoyment; satisfaction; delight.—**gratifier**, grat'i·fī·ėr, *n.* One who gratifies.

gratis, grā'tis, *adv.* [L., from *gratia*, favor. GRACE.] For nothing; freely; without recompense (to give a thing *gratis*).—*a.* Given or done for nothing.

gratitude. See GRATEFUL.

gratuitous, gra·tū'i·tus, *a.* [L. *gratuitus*, from *gratus*, pleasing, agreeable. GRATEFUL, GRACE.] Given without an equivalent or recompense; free; voluntary; not required, called for, or warranted by the circumstances; adopted or asserted without any good ground (a *gratuitous* assumption).—**gratuitously**, gra·tū'i·tus·li, *adv.* In a gratuitous manner.—**gratuitousness**, gra·tū'i·tus·nes, *n.*—**gratuity**, gra·tū'i·ti, *n.* A free gift; a present; a donation.

gratulate,† grat'ū·lāt, *v.t. gratulated, gratulating.* [L. *gratulor, gratulatus*, from *gratus*, pleasing, agreeable. GRACE.] To salute with declarations of joy; to congratulate.—**gratulant**, grat'ū·lant, *a.* Congratulatory.—**gratulation**, grat·ū·lā'shon, *n.* [L. *gratulatio*.] Congratulation.—**gratulatory**, grat'ū·la·to·ri, *a.* Congratulatory. —*n.* A congratulation.

gravamen, gra·vā'men, *n.* [L., from *gravo*, to weigh down, from *gravis*, heavy. GRAVE, *a.*] That part of an accusation which weighs most heavily against the accused; ground or burden of complaint in general.

grave, grāv, *v.t.*—*graved* (pret.), *graven* or *graved* (pp.), *graving* (ppr.). [A.Sax. *grafan*, to dig, to grave or carve = D. *graven* Dan. *grave*, Icel. *grafa*, G. *graben*, to dig, to engrave; cog. Ir. *grafaim*, to engrave, to scrape; Gr. *graphō*, to grave, to write.] To carve or cut; to form

or shape by cutting with a tool; to delineate by cutting; to engrave; hence, to impress deeply.—**graver**, grā'vėr, *n.* One who carves or engraves; an engraving tool; a burin.

grave, grāv, *n.* [A.Sax. *græf*, a grave, a trench, from stem of *grafan*, to dig or grave = Dan. *graf*, Icel. *gröf*, D. *graf*, G. *grab*, Rus. *grob*, a grave. GRAVE, to carve.] An excavation in the earth in which a dead human body is deposited; hence, any place of interment; a tomb; a sepulcher.— **graveclothes**, *n. pl.* The clothes in which the dead are interred.— **gravestone**, *n.* A stone placed at a grave as a monument to the dead.— **graveyard**, *n.* A yard or enclosure for the interment of the dead.

grave, grāv, *v.t.* [From the *graves* or dregs of melted tallow with which ships' hulls were formerly smeared.] To clean a ship's bottom of seaweeds, etc., and pay it over with pitch or tar.—**graving dock**, *n.* See DOCK.

grave, grāv, *a.* [Fr. *grave*, from L. *gravis*, heavy (whence also *grief*, *aggravate*, *gravid*, *gravitate*); allied to Gr. *barys*, heavy, *baros*, weight (in *barometer*); Skr. *guru*, heavy.] Solemn; serious; opposed to *light* or *jovial*; plain; not showy; important; momentous; having a serious and interesting import; *mus.* low; depressed; opposed to *sharp*, *acute*, or *high*.—**gravely**, grāv'li, *adv.* In a grave manner.—**graveness**, grāv'nes, *n.* The state or quality of being grave; gravity.

gravel, grav'el, *n.* [Fr. *gravele*, from O.Fr. *grave*, sand or gravel, from the Celtic; Armor. *grouan*, sand; W. *grou*, pebbles, coarse gravel.] Small stones or very small pebbles collectively; small stones, sand, etc., combined; *pathol.* small concretions or calculi in the kidneys or bladder; the disease occasioned by such concretions.—*v.t.*—*graveled, graveling*, or *gravelled, gravelling*. To cover with gravel; to cause to stick in the sand or gravel; hence, to perplex and bring to an intellectual standstill; to puzzle; to hurt the foot of (a horse) by gravel lodged under the shoe.—**gravel-blind**, *a.* [A mistaken coinage, as in Shak., *Merchant of Venice*, ii, 2, 38, on the supposed analogy of *sand-blind*.] More blind than sand-blind and less than stoneblind.—**gravelly**, grav'el·i, *a.* Abounding with gravel; consisting of gravel.

graven, grā'vn, *pp.* of *grave*, to carve.

gravid, grav'id, *a.* [L. *gravidus*, from *gravis*, heavy. GRAVE. *a.*] Being with child, pregnant.—**gravidity**, gra·vid'i·ti, *n.* pregnancy; impregnation.

gravimeter, gra·vim'et·ėr, *n.* [L. *gravis*, heavy, and Gr. *metron*, a measure.] An instrument for determining the specific gravities of bodies, whether liquid or solid, as a hydrometer.

graving dock, See GRAVE (to clean a ship's bottom) and DOCK.

gravitate, grav'i·tāt, *v.i.*—*gravitated, gravitating.* [Fr. *graviter*, from L.

gravitas, from *gravis*, heavy. GRAVE, a]. To be affected by gravitation; to move under the influence of gravitation; *fig.* to have a tendency toward some attracting influence.— **gravitation**, grav·i·tā'shon, *n.* The act of gravitating or tending to a center of attraction; the force by which bodies are drawn, or by which they tend toward the center of the earth or other center or the effect of that force.—**gravitative**, grav'i·tā·· tiv, *a.* Causing to gravitate or tend to a center.—**gravity**, grav'i·ti, *n.* The state or character of being grave; solemnity of deportment, character, or demeanor; seriousness; weight or weightiness; enormity (the *gravity* of an offense); the force which causes a mass of matter to tend toward a center of attraction, especially toward the center of the earth; the force by which the planets mutually attract each other and are attracted toward the sun; centripetal force.—*Specific gravity*, the relative gravity or weight of any body or substance considered with regard to the weight of an equal bulk of pure distilled water at a specific temperature.

gravy, grā'vi, *n.* [From *graves*, *greaves*, the dregs of melted tallow.] A sauce for meat, made chiefly from the juice that drips from meat in cooking, seasoned and thickened; (slang) something valuable offered or received over and above expectations.

gray, **grey**, grā, *a.* [A.Sax. *graeg*=D. *graauw*, Icel. *grār*, Dan. *graa*, G. *grau*, gray; other connections are unknown.] Of the color of hair whitened by age; hoary; white with a mixture of black; of the color of ashes; having gray hairs; old; mature (*gray* experience).—*n.* A gray color; a dull or neutral tint; an animal of a gray color, as a horse. —**grayback**, **greyback**, a whalebone whale.—**graybeard**, **greybeard**, *n.* A man with a gray beard; an old man; a large earthen jar or bottle for holding liquor.—**grayish**, grā'ish, *a.* Somewhat gray; gray in a moderate degree.—**grayling**, grā'ling, *n.* [From the silvery gray of its back and sides.] A game fish of the salmon family, 16 to 18 inches long, found in cold, swift streams.— **gray matter**, nerve tissue made up of both nerve cells and nerve fiber; hence, brains; intelligence.—**grayness**, **greyness**, grā'nes, *n.* The state or quality of being gray.— **gray owl**, the tawny owl; a large, arctic owl.—**gray squirrel**, a large, grayish-colored squirrel of the eastern U.S.—**graywacke**, **grauwacke**, grā·wak'e, grou·wak'e, *n.* [G. *grauwacke*—*grau*, gray, and *wacke*, a kind of rock.] A kind of sandstone in which grains or fragments of various minerals or rocks are embedded in an indurated matrix, which may be siliceous or argillaceous.

grayhound. See GREYHOUND.

graze, grāz, *v.t.*—*grazed*, *grazing.* [Perhaps from the combined influence of *grate*, to rub, and *rase*; or perhaps originally meaning to skim along the grass, from *grass*, like *graze*, to pasture.] To rub or touch lightly in passing, as a missile does; to brush lightly the surface of.—*v.i.* To pass so as to touch or rub lightly.—*n.* The act of grazing; a slight rub or brush.

graze, grāz, *v.t.*—*grazed*, *grazing.* [A.Sax. *grasian*, to graze or feed, from *græs*, grass; comp. D. *grazen*, to graze, and *gras*, grass, G. *grasen*, and *gras*.] To feed or supply with growing grass; to furnish pasture for; to feed on; to eat from the ground.—*v.i.* To eat grass; to feed on growing herbage.—*n.* The act of grazing or feeding on grass.—**grazer**, grā'zėr, *n.* One that grazes.—**grazier**, grā'zhėr, *n.* One who grazes or pastures cattle for the market; a farmer who raises and deals in cattle.—**grazing**, grā'zing, *n.* The act of feeding on grass; a pasture.

grease, grēs, *n.* [Fr. *graisse*, O.Fr. *gresse*, from L. *crassus*, fat, gross, whence E. *crass*; akin Gael. *creis*, fat.] Animal fat in a soft state; particularly the fatty matter of land animals, as distinguished from the oily matter of marine animals; *farriery*, a swelling and inflammation in a horse's legs attended with the secretion of oily matter and cracks in the skin.—*v.t.* (grēz or grēs).— *greased*, *greasing.* To smear, anoint or daub with grease or fat.—**greasily**, grē'zi·li, *adv.* In a greasy manner.— **greasiness**, grē'zi·nes, *n.* The quality or state of being greasy.—**greasy**, grē'zi, *a.* Composed of or characterized by grease; fatty; unctuous; having the appearance of fat or grease; seemingly unctuous to the touch, as some minerals; gross; indecent.

great, grāt, *a.* [A.Sax. *great*=L.G. and D. *groot*, G. *gross*, great; perhaps allied to L. *grandis*.] Large in bulk, surface, or linear dimensions; of wide extent; big; large in number; numerous; large, extensive, or unusual in degree; long continued; of long duration; important; weighty; involving important interests; holding an eminent or prominent position in respect of mental endowments or acquirements, virtue, or vice, rank, office, power, or the like; eminent; distinguished; celebrated; notorious; of elevated sentiments; generous; noble; on an extensive scale; sumptuous; magnificent; wonderful; sublime; grand; pregnant; teeming; filled; denoting a degree of consanguinity in the ascending or descending line (*great* grandfather).—*Great circle*, a circle formed on the surface of a sphere by its plane cutting through the center of the sphere.—*The great*, pl., the rich, the distinguished, persons of rank and position.—**Great Dane**, a dog of a breed noted for its great size and strength.—**Great Divide**, the Rocky Mountains, dividing continental drainage east and west.— **greathearted**, *a.* High-spirited; magnanimous.—**greatly**, grāt'li, *adv.* In

a great manner or degree.—**greatness**, grāt'nes, *n.* The state or quality of being great; magnitude; dignity; eminence; distinguished rank or position.

greave, grēv, *n.* [Fr. *grève*, armor for the leg; Sp. and Pg. *greba*, probably of Ar. origin.] Armor worn on the front of the lower part of the leg, across the back of which it was buckled.

grebe, grēb, *n.* [Fr. *grèbe*, from Armor. *krib*, W. *crib*, a comb, a crest, one variety having a crest.] An aquatic bird of various species, having no tail, toes separate, but broadly fringed by a membrane, and legs set so far back that on land it assumes the upright position of the penguin.

Grecian, grē'shan, *a.* [GREEK.] Pertaining to Greece; Greek.—*n.* A native of Greece; or a person of the Greek race; one versed in the Greek language.—**Grecism**, grē'sizm, *n.* An idiom of the Greek language.— **Grecize**, grē'siz, *v.t.*—*Grecized*, *Grecizing.* To render Grecian: to translate into Greek.—*v.i.* To speak the Greek language.

greedy, grē'di, *a.* [A.Sax. *grēdig*, *graedig*=Goth. *gredags*, Icel. *gráthugr*, Dan. *graadig*, D. *gretig*, greedy. Hence *greed*, which is quite a modern word in English=Icel. *gráthr*, Goth *gredus*, hunger.] Having a keen appetite for food or drink; ravenous; voracious; very fond of eating; gluttonous; having a keen desire for anything; covetous (*greedy* of gain).—**greed**, grēd, *n.* An eager desire or longing; greediness.— **greedily**, grē'di·li, *adv.* In a greedy manner; voraciously; eagerly.— **greediness**, grē'di·nes, *n.* The quality of being greedy.

Greek, grēk, *a.* [Fr. *grec*, L. *græcus*, Greek, from the *Graikoi*, an insignificant tribe of ancient northwestern Greece.] Pertaining to Greece.—*n.* A native of Greece; the language of Greece.—*Greek calends*, a supposed date, that never occurs, for payment, etc., there being calends only in the Roman calendar.—*Greek Church*, the established church in Greece; that part of the Christian church, more properly known as the Eastern Orthodox Church, that separated from the Roman (Western) Church in the eleventh century.— *Greek fire*, a combustible preparation, the constituents of which are supposed to have been asphalt, niter, and sulfur.—*Greek gift*, a gift presented in order to betray one.—*Greek-letter fraternity*, an organization, as in a university, designated by Greek letters.

green, grēn, *a.* [A.Sax. *grēne*=Dan. and Sw. *grön*, Icel. *grænn*, G. *grün*; akin to *grow*; L. *holus*, *olus*, green vegetables; Gr. *chloē*, a young shoot, *chlōros*, pale green; Skr. *hari*, green.] Of the color of grass or herbage and plants when growing; emerald; verdant; new; fresh; recent; fresh and vigorous; flourishing; undecayed (a *green* old age); containing its natural juices; not dry; not seasoned;

unripe, immature (*green* fruit); immature in age; young; raw; inexperienced; easily imposed upon.—*Green corn,* sweet Indian corn, grown for the table.—*Green tea,* tea of a greenish color from the mode in which the leaves are treated and having a peculiar flavor.—*Green turtle,* the turtle of which the soup is made.—*Green vitriol,* a name of sulfate of iron in a crystallized form. —*n.* A green color; a grassy plain or plat; a piece of ground covered with verdant herbage; a name of several pigments; *pl.* the leaves and stems of young plants used in cookery, especially certain plants of the cabbage kind.—*v.t.* To make green.—*v.i.* To grow green.—**greenback,** grēn'back, *n.* A note belonging to the paper money of the United States, first issued in 1862, from the back of the notes being of a green color.—**greenery,** grē'nėr·i, *n.* A mass of green foliage; the green hue of such a mass.—**green-eyed,** *a.* Having green eyes; seeing all things discolored or distorted; jaundiced.—**greenfinch,** *n.* A common European finch of a greenish color; the green linnet or grosbeak.— **greengage,** *n.* [After a person named *Gage,* who introduced it into England.] A species of plum having a juicy greenish pulp of an exquisite flavor.—**greengrocer,** *n.* A retailer of greens and other vegetables.— **greenheart,** *n.* See BEBEERU.—**greenhorn,** grēn'horn, *n.* A person easily imposed upon; a raw, inexperienced person.—**greenhouse,** grēn'hous, *n.* A building principally consisting of glazed frames or sashes for the purpose of cultivating exotic plants which are too tender to endure the open air: often artificially heated up.—**greening,** grēn'ing, *n.* A name given to certain varieties of apples green when ripe.—**greenish,** grēn'ish, *a.* Somewhat green; having a tinge of green; somewhat raw and inexperienced.—**greenness,** grēn'nes, *n.* The quality of being green.— **greenroom,** *n.* A room near the stage in a theater, to which actors retire during the intervals of their parts in the play.—**greensand,** *n.* A name given (from the color of some of the beds) to two groups of strata, the one (lower greensand) belonging to the lower cretaceous series, the other (upper greensand) to the upper cretaceous series.— **greenshank,** *n.* A well-known species of sandpiper with greenish legs.— **greensickness,** *n.* See CHLOROSIS.— **greenstone,** grēn'stōn, *n.* [From a tinge of green in the color.] A general designation for the hard granular crystalline varieties of trap.—**greensward,** *n.* Turf green with grass.— **greenth,** grēnth, *n.* The quality of being green; greenness.—**greenwood,** grēn'wud, *n.* A wood or forest when green, as in summer.—*a.* Pertaining to a greenwood.

greet, grēt, *v.t.* [A.Sax. *grétan,* to salute, hail, bid farewell=G. *grüssen,* D. *groeten,* to greet; comp. A.Sax. *grétan,* Prov. E. and Sc. *greet,* Goth.

gretan, Icel. *gráta,* to weep.] To address with salutations or expressions of kind wishes; to pay respects or compliments to; to salute; to hail.—*v.i.* To meet and salute each other.—**greeter,** grēt'ėr, *n.* One who greets.—**greeting,** grēt'ing, *n.* Expression of kindness or joy; salutation at meeting; compliment sent by one absent.

greet, grēt, *v.i.* [GREET, to salute.] To weep. (*Old English* and *Scotch.*)

gregarious, gri·gâ'ri·us, *a.* [L. *gregarius,* from *grex, gregis,* a flock or herd; seen also in *aggregate, congregate, egregious.*] Having the habit of assembling or living in a flock or herd; not habitually solitary or living alone.—**gregariously,** gri·gâ'ri·us·li, *adv.* In a gregarious manner. —**gregariousness,** gri·gâ'ri·us·nes, *n.* The state or quality of being gregarious.—**gregarine,** greg'a·rin, *n.* A name of certain minute animals of a low type, having no definite organs observable, found inhabiting the intestines of various animals.

Gregorian, gri·gō'ri·an, *a.* [From *Gregory.*] Relating to any pope named Gregory.—*Gregorian calendar,* the calendar as reformed by Pope Gregory XIII in 1582.—*Gregorian chant,* a choral melody introduced into the service of the Christian church by Pope Gregory I about the end of the sixth century.

gremlin, grem'lin, *n.* [Perhaps from E. *goblin,* Irish-Gaelic *gruaimin,* ill-humored little fellow.] A tiny mischievous gnome, whimsically said to be responsible for disordering equipment.

grenade, gre·nād', *n.* [Fr. *grenade,* Sp. *granada,* a pomegranate, a grenade (the missile somewhat resembling the fruit), from L. *granatum,* a pomegranate. GRAIN.] A hollow ball or shell of iron or other metal, or of annealed glass, filled with powder, fired by means of a fuse, and thrown among enemies.—**grenadier,** gren·a·dēr', *n.* Originally a soldier who threw hand grenades; a tall soldier.

grenadine, gren'a·dēn, *n.* [From *Granada.*] A thin gauzy fabric.

grenadine, gren'a·dēn, *n.* [GRENADE.] A red syrup used in mixed drinks.

gressorial, gres·sō'ri·al, *a.* [L. *gressus,* a going, step. GRADE.] *Ornith.* having three toes forward (two of them connected) and one behind.

grew, grö, *pret.* of *grow.*

grewsome. See GRUESOME.

grey, grā. See GRAY.

greyhound, grā'hound, *n.* [Icel. *greyhundr,* from *grey,* a greyhound, a bitch; Sc. *grew,* a greyhound; Ir. *grech,* a hound; the name has no reference to the color.] A dog kept for the chase, remarkable for its beauty of form and its great fleetness.

griddle, grid'l, *n.* [W. *greidell,* from *greidiaw,* to heat, to scorch; Ir. *greideal, greidaim,* to scorch.] A broad metal disk used for frying griddle cakes.—**griddlecake,** *n.* A batter cake browned on both sides.

gride, grīd, *v.i.* [Partly from O.E.

girden, to strike, pierce, cut, from *gerde,* a rod=*yard;* partly from O.E. *grede,* A.Sax. *graedan,* to cry.] To pierce; to cut through; to cut (*Mil.*); to give out a harsh creaking sound; to jar harshly (*Tenn.*)—*n.* A grating or harsh sound.

gridiron, grid'ī·ėrn, *n.* [From *grid-* of *griddle,* and *iron.*] A grated utensil for broiling flesh and fish over coals; anything likened to such a frame; a football field.

grief, grēf, *n.* [Fr. *grief,* grievance, what oppresses, from L. *gravis,* heavy. GRAVE. *a.*] Pain of mind, arising from any cause; sorrow; sadness; cause of sorrow or pain; that which afflicts; trial; grievance; bodily pain (*Shak.*)†.—*To come to grief,* to come to a bad end; to come to ruin; to meet with an accident. ∴ Syn. under AFFLICTION. —**grievance,** grē'vans, *n.* That which causes grief or uneasiness; wrong done and suffered; injury.—**grieve,** grēv, *v.t.*—*grieved, grieving.* [O.Fr. *griever.*] To cause to feel grief; to give pain of mind to; to make sorrowful; to afflict; to sorrow over; to deplore.—*v.i.* To feel grief; to sorrow; to mourn; followed by *at, for,* and *over.*—**griever,** grē'vėr, *n.* One who or that which grieves.— **grievingly,** grē'ving·li, *adv.* In a grieving manner.—**grievous,** grē'vus, *a.* Causing grief or sorrow; afflictive; hard to bear; heavy; severe; harmful; great; atrocious; aggravated; full of grief; indicating great grief or affliction.—**grievously,** grē'vus·li, *adv.* In a grievous manner.—**grievousness,** grē'vus·nes, *n.*

griffin, griffon, grif'in, grif'on, *n.* [Fr. *griffon,* It. *grifone,* from L. *gryps, gryphus,* griffin, from Gr. *gryps,* a griffon, from *grypos,* hook-beaked.] A mythical animal, in the fore part represented as an eagle, in the hinder part as a lion; a species of vulture found in the mountainous parts of Europe and in North Africa.

grig, grig, *n.* [Connected with *cricket;* in second sense with Sw. *kráka,* to creep.] A cricket; a grasshopper; the sand eel; a small eel of lively and incessant motion.

grill, gril, *v.t.* [From Fr. *griller,* to broil, from *gril,* a gridiron, *grille,* a grate; O.Fr. *graille,* from L.L. *graticula,* corrupted for L. *craticula,* a small gridiron, dim. of *crates,* a hurdle. GRATE, CRATE.] To broil on a gridiron or similar instrument. —*n.* A grated utensil for broiling meat, etc., over a fire; a gridiron.— **grillage,** gril'ij, *n.* [Fr., from *grille,* a grate, a railing.] A heavy framework of beams used to sustain foundations in soils of unequal compressibility.—**grille,** gril, *n.* [Fr.] A lattice or grating; a piece of grated work.

grilse, grils, *n.* [Probably a corruption of Sw. *grœ-lax,* gray salmon.] The young of the salmon on its first return from the sea to fresh water.

grim, grim, *a.* [A.Sax. *grim,* fierce, ferocious; akin to *grama,* fury; Icel. *grimmr,* savage, angry, *gramr,* wrath; Dan. *grim,* ugly; D. *gram,* angry, *grimmen,* to growl; Gr *grimm,* fu-

rious, *grimmen*, to rage; comp.
W. *grem*, a snarl, *gremiaw*, to snarl.]
Of a forbidding or fear-inspiring
aspect; fierce; stern; sullen; sour;
surly.—*v.t.* To make grim; to give
a forbidding or fear-inspiring aspect
to (*Carl.*).—**grimly**, grim′li, *a.* Having a grim, hideous, or stern look.—
adv. In a grim manner.—**grimness**,
grim′nes, *n.* The state or quality of
being grim.

grimace, gri·mās′, *n.* [Fr., a wry
face, from the Teutonic; comp. D.
grimmen, to snarl, to make faces.
GRIM.] A distortion of the countenance expressive of affectation, scorn,
disapprobation, self-satisfaction, or
the like; a smirk; a wry face.—*v.i.*
grimaced, *grimacing*. To make grimaces.

grimalkin, gri·mal′kin, *n.* [For *graymalkin*—gray, and *malkin*, that is
Mollkin, dim. from *Mary*; comp.
Tom-cat.] An old cat, especially a
female cat.

grime, grīm, *n.* [Same as Dan. *grime*,
a spot or streak, *grim*, soot, lampblack.] Foul matter; dirt; dirt deeply
ingrained.—*v.t.*—*grimed*, *griming*. To
sully or soil deeply; to dirt.—
grimily, grī′mi·li, *adv.* In a grimy
manner or condition; foully.—**griminess**, grī′mi·nes, *n.* The state or
quality of being grimy.—**grimy**,
grī′mi, *a.* Full of grime; foul;
dirty.

grin, grin, *v.i.*—*grinned*, *grinning*.
[A.Sax. *grinnian*, *grennian*, to grin=
Dan. *grine*, D. *grijnen*, G. *greinen*,
to grin, to cry, to weep; perhaps
allied to *groan*.] To snarl and show
the teeth, as a dog; to set the teeth
together and open the lips; to show
the teeth as in laughter, scorn, or
pain.—*v.t.* To show, set, or snap
(the teeth), in grinning; to express
by grinning.—*n.* The act of withdrawing the lips and showing the
teeth; a forced or sneering smile.—
grinner, grin′ėr, *n.* One who grins.—
grinningly, grin′ing·li, *adv.* In a
grinning manner.

grind, grīnd, *v.t.*—*ground* (pret. &
pp.), very rarely *grinded*. [A.Sax.
grindan, to grind; same root as Gr.
chriô, to graze or touch lightly;
Skr. *ghrish*, to grind. *Grist* and
ground (*n.*) are from this word.] To
break and reduce to fine particles
or powder by friction, as in a mill;
to comminute by attrition; to triturate; to wear down, smooth, or
sharpen by friction; to whet; to
oppress by severe exactions; to
harrass; to prepare for examination
in some subject of study, or to
study (in these senses university
slang).—*v.i.* To grind corn or other
matter; to be rubbed together, as
in the operation of grinding; to be
ground or pulverized; to drudge
or perform hard work; to study
hard, especially for an examination
(*slang*).—*n.* The act of one who
grinds; a spell of work.—**grinder**,
grin′dėr, *n.* One who or that which
grinds; a molar tooth.—**grindstone**,
grīnd′stōn, *n.* A revolving stone
used for grinding or sharpening
tools.—*To bring or hold a person's*

nose to the grindstone, to oppress
him; to punish him.

grip, grip, *n.* [Directly from Fr.
gripper, to grasp, which itself is
from a Germanic word=E. *gripe*.]
The act of grasping by the hand;
grasp; the grasp peculiar to any
secret fraternity as a means of
recognition; a fast hold; a hilt or
handle.—*v.t.*—*gripped*, *gripping*. To
grasp by the hand; to gripe; to
seize forcibly; to hold fast.—*v.i.*
To take hold; to hold fast.

gripe, grīp, *v.t.*—*griped*, *griping*.
[A.Sax. *grípan*, to gripe, to grasp=
Icel. *gripa*, D. *grijpen*, Goth. *greipan*,
G. *greifen*, to seize; same root as
grab, *grope*, *grasp*.] To catch with
the hand and clasp closely with
the fingers; to hold tight or close; to
clutch; to seize and hold fast; to
clench; to tighten; to give pain
in the bowels, as if by pressure
or contraction; to straiten or distress.—*v.i.* To take fast hold with
the hand; to clasp closely with the
fingers.—*n.* Grasp; seizure; grip;
oppression; affliction; pinching distress; a kind of brake to act on a
wheel; *pl.* a pinching intermittent
pain in the intestines, of the character of that which accompanies
diarrhea or colic.—**griper**, grī′pėr, *n.*
One who gripes.—**griping**, grī′ping,
a. Grasping; greedy; extortionate,
causing a pinching feeling in the
bowels.

grippe, grip, *n.* [Fr.] The influenza.

grisaille, gri·zāl′, *n.* [Fr., from *gris*,
gray.] A style of painting in various
gray tints employed to represent
solid bodies in relief, as friezes,
moldings, bas-reliefs, etc.

grisette, gri·zet′, *n.* [Fr. Originally, a
gray woolen fabric, much used for
dresses by women of the inferior
classes, from *gris*, gray.] A young
woman of the working class in
France; a belle of the working class
given to gaiety and gallantry.

grisly, griz′li, *a.* Gray; of a mixed
color; grizzled.

grisly, griz′li, *a.* [A.Sax. *grislic*,
from *grisan* or *ágrisan*, to dread,
to fear greatly; allied to G. *grässlich*,
horrible, *grausen*, horror; *grieseln*, to
shudder; E. *grewsome*.] Frightful;
horrible; terrible; grim.—**grisliness**,
griz′li·nes, *n.* Quality of being grisly.

grist, grist, *n.* [A.Sax. *grist*, a grinding, from *grindan*, to grind. GRIND.]
Corn ground in the mill or to be
ground; the grain carried to the mill
at one time, or the meal it produces.
—*To bring grist to the mill*, to be a
source of profit; to bring profitable
business into one's hands.—**gristmill**, *n.* A mill for grinding grain.

gristle, gris′l, *n.* [A.Sax. *gristel*,
gristle; akin to *grist*, being named
from the grinding or crunching it
requires; comp. A.Sax. *gristlung*, a
gnashing.] Cartilage.—**gristly**, gris′li, *a.* Consisting of or like gristle;
cartilaginous.

grit, grit, *n.* [A.Sax. *greót*, sand; akin
to E. *grits*, *grout*, *groats*; comp. Icel.
grjót, stones, rubble; G. *gries*, grit.]
Any hard sandstone; firmness of
character; structure of a stone in

regard to fineness and closeness of
texture.—*v.i.* To give forth a grating
sound, as sand beneath the shoes.
—*v.t.* To spread with grit or abrasive,
as marble before polishing; to clamp
one's teeth together, causing them
to grind.—**grittiness**, grit′i·nes, *n.*—
gritty, grit′i, *a.*

grits, grits, *n. pl.* [A.Sax. *grytta*,
gryttan, grits or groats.] Coarse
hominy (*U.S.*); grain hulled or
coarsely ground.

grivet, griv′et, *n.* A small green-gray
Abyssinian monkey.

grizzle, griz′l, *n.* [From Fr. *gris*,
gray, from O.G. *gris*, gray.] A gray
color; a mixture of white and black;
a mixture of white among dark
hairs.—*v.i.* To grow gray or grizzly;
to become gray-haired.—**grizzled**,
griz′ld, *a.* Of a grayish color.—
grizzly, griz′li, *a.* Somewhat gray;
grayish.—*Grizzly* or *grisly bear*, a
large and ferocious bear of Western
North America.

groan, grōn, *v.i.* [A.Sax. *gránian*, to
groan; perhaps imitative of the sound
made in groaning; comp. A.Sax.
grunan, to grunt; W. *grwn*, a groan.]
To utter a mournful voice, as in pain
or sorrow; to utter a deep, low-toned,
moaning sound.—*n.* A deep, mournful sound uttered in pain, sorrow,
or anguish; a deep sound uttered
in disapprobation or derision.—
groaner, grō′nėr, *n.* One who groans.

groat, grōt, *n.* [D. *groot*, G. *grot*, that
is, *great*, a great piece or coin: so
called because before this piece was
coined by Edward III (1351) the
English had no silver coin larger
than a penny.] An old English coin
and money of account, equal to
fourpence; hence, colloquially, in
England, fourpence, or a fourpenny
piece.

groats, grōts, *n. pl.* [A.Sax. *grátan*,
groats; akin *grits*, *grout*.] Oats or
wheat with the husks taken off.

grocer, grō′sėr, *n.* [Properly a *grosser*,
or one who sells things in the *gross*;
O.Fr. *grossier*, one who sells by
wholesale, from *gros*, great. GROSS.]
A merchant who deals in tea, sugar,
spices, coffee, fruits; a retail purveyor of foodstuffs.—**grocery**, grō′sėr·i, *n.* A grocer's shop; *pl.* the
commodities sold by grocers.

grog, grog, *n.* [From 'Old *Grog*', a
nickname given to Admiral Vernon,
who introduced the beverage, from
his wearing a *grogram* cloak in rough
weather.] A mixture of spirit and
water not sweetened; also used as
a general term for strong drink.—
grogginess, grog′i·nes, *n.* The state
of being groggy.—**groggy**, grog′i, *a.*
Overcome with grog; tipsy; *farriery*, moving in an uneasy, hobbling
manner, owing to tenderness of the
feet: said of a horse.—**grogshop**, *n.*
A dramshop.

grogram, grog′ram, *n.* [Fr. *grosgrain*,
coarse grain, of a coarse texture.
GROSS, GRAIN.] A kind of coarse stuff
made of silk and mohair; also, a kind
of strong, coarse silk.

groin, groin, *n.* [Icel. *grein*, a branch,
an arm of the sea, *greina*, to branch
off or separate; Sw. *gren*, a branch,

grena, to divide; Sc. *grain*, a branch, a prong of a fork.] The hollow of the human body in front at the junction of the thigh with the trunk; *arch.* the angular projecting curve made by the intersection of simple vaults crossing each other at any angle.— *v.t. Arch.* to form into groins; to ornament with groins.—**groined,** groind, *a. Arch.* having a groin or groins; formed of groins meeting in a point.—**groining,** groi′ning, *n. Arch.* the arrangement of groins; groins collectively.

grommet, grum′et, *n.* [Armor. *grom*, a curb.] *Naut.* a ring of rope; a metal eyelet, such as is used on canvas mailbags or the edge of a sail.

groom, gröm, *n.* [From A.Sax. *guma*, O.E. *gome,* man, with an inserted *r*; comp. O.D. *grom,* Icel. *gromr,* a youth. *Guma* (Goth. *guma,* O.H.G. *homo*) is the Teutonic word equivalent to L. *homo,* a man. Hence *bridegroom* (A.Sax. *brydguma*).] A man or boy who has the charge of horses; one who takes care of horses or the stable; one of several officers in the English royal household; a bridegroom.—*v.t.* To curry or care for a horse.—**groomsman,** grömz′man, *n.* One who acts as attendant on a bridegroom at his marriage.

groove, gröv, *n.* [From D. *groeve, groef,* a furrow, a ditch, a channel = G. *grube,* a pit, hole, grave; the stem being same as in E. *grave, v.t.*] A furrow or long hollow, such as is cut by a tool; a channel, usually an elongated narrow channel; the fixed routine of one's life.—*v.t.*—**grooved, grooving.** To cut a groove or channel in; to furrow.—**groover,** grö′vèr, *n.* One who or that which grooves.

grope, gröp, *v.i.*—**groped, groping.** [A.Sax. *grápian;* closely allied to *gripe, grab,* and *grasp.*] To search or attempt to find something in the dark, or as a blind person, by feeling; to feel one's way; to attempt anything blindly.—*v.t.* To search out by feeling in or as in the dark (to *grope* our way).—**groper,** grö′pèr, *n.* One who gropes.—**gropingly,** grö′ping·li, *adv.* In a groping manner.

grosbeak, *n.* See GROSS.

groschen, grö′shen, *n.* (*pl.* the same). [From L.L. *grossus,* thick—in opposition to ancient thin lead coins.] An old German coin; the ten-pfennig piece. (*Colloq.*)

gross, grös, *a.* [Fr. *gros,* big, thick, coarse; L.L. *grossus,* thick, crass; of doubtful origin. Hence *grocer.*] Coarse or rough; indelicate, obscene, or impure; sensual; great, palpable or enormous; shameful; flagrant (a *gross* mistake, *gross* injustice); dense; not attenuated; whole; entire; total; bulky‡; of some size‡.—*Gross weight,* the weight of merchandise or goods, with the bag, cask, chest, etc., in which they are contained.—*n.* Main body; chief part; bulk; the number of twelve dozen (being the *gross* or great hundred): has no plural form. —*A great gross,* twelve gross or 144 dozen.—*In the gross, in gross,* in the bulk, or the undivided whole; all parts taken together.—**grosbeak,**

grös′bēk, *n.* A name common to a group of finches distinguished by the thickness and strength of the bill.— **grossly,** grös′li, *adv.* In a gross manner.—**grossness,** grös′nes, *n.* The quality of being gross; obscenity; greatness.

grot, grot, *n.* See GROTTO. [Poet.]

grotesque, grö·tesk′, *a.* [Fr., from *grotte,* a grotto, from the style of the paintings found in the ancient crypts and grottos. GROTTO.] Having a wild, extraordinary, or extravagant form; of the utmost oddness; whimsical; extravagant.—*n.* A capricious variety of arabesque ornamentation; a whimsical figure or scenery.— **grotesquely,** grö·tesk′li, *adv.* In a grotesque manner.—**grotesqueness,** grö·tesk′nes, *n.*—**grotesquerie,** grö·tes′kèr·i, *n.* Grotesque whims or antics; grotesque conduct.

grotto, grot′tö, *n.* pl. **grottos,** or **grottoes,** grot′töz. [Fr. *grotte,* It. *grotta,* from L. *crypta,* Gr. *kryptē,* a cave, a vault, from *kryptö,* to conceal. CRYPT.] A cave or natural cavity in the earth, as in a mountain or rock; an artificial cavern decorated with rock work, shells, etc., constructed for coolness and pleasure.

grouch, grouch, *n.* [O.F. *groucher,* grumble.] (U.S. colloq.) A sulky or grumbling person.—*v.i.* To be morose; to grumble or sulk.

ground, ground, *n.* [A.Sax. *grund,* ground; G. Dan. and Sw. *grund,* D. *grond,* Icel. *grunnr,* ground.] The surface of the earth; the earth we tread on and subject to tillage, etc.; the soil; the soil of a particular country or person; land; estate; that on which anything may rest, rise, or originate; basis; foundation; support; *elect.,* a general term for the connection of an electrical conductor to the earth; *painting,* the first layer of color on which the others are wrought; the primary or predominating color; a foil or background that sets off anything; *etching,* a composition spread over the surface of the plate to be etched, to prevent the acid from eating into the plate, except where an opening is made with the point of the etching needle; *pl.* sediment at the bottom of liquors; dregs; lees.—*To break ground,* to penetrate the soil for the first time, as in cutting the first turf of a railway; hence, *fig.* to take the first step; to enter upon an undertaking.—*To fall to the ground,* to come to nought. —*To gain ground,* to advance; to obtain an advantage; to gain credit; to become more general or extensive. —*To lose ground,* to withdraw from the position taken; to lose advantage; to decline; to become less in force or extent.—*To give ground,* to recede; to yield advantage.—*To stand one's ground,* to stand firm; not to recede or yield.—*v.t.* To lay or set on or in the ground; to cause to run (a ship) aground; to settle or establish, as on a foundation or basis; to fix or settle firmly; to found; to base; to thoroughly instruct in elements or first principles; *elect.,* to connect an electrical conductor to the earth.—*v.i.*

To run aground; to strike the ground and remain fixed (the ship *grounded* in two fathoms of water).—**groundless,** ground′les, *a.* Wanting ground or foundation; wanting cause or reason; baseless; false.—**groundlessly,** ground′les·li, *adv.* In a groundless manner. — **groundling,** ‡ground′ling, *n.* A spectator who stood in the pit of the theater (*Shak.*) —**ground floor,** *n.* The floor of a house on a level, or nearly so, with the exterior ground.—**ground hog,** the woodchuck.—**ground-hog day,** February 2, when the woodchuck is supposed to rouse from its sleep to see if winter is over.—**ground ivy,** a trailing plant with purplish flowers and oval leaves; English ivy.— **groundnut,** *n.* The peanut; also see EARTHNUT.—**ground plan,** *n.* A plan showing the divisions of a building on the same level as the surface of the ground.—**ground rent,** *n.* Rent paid for the privilege of building on another man's land.— **ground squirrel,** *n.* The name of several animals allied to the true squirrels, but having cheek pouches, and living in holes.— **ground swell,** *n.* A drop swell or rolling of the sea, occasioned along the shore by a distant storm or gale. —**groundwork,** ground′werk, *n.* The work which forms the foundation of anything; that to which the rest is additional; the basis.

ground, ground, *pret. & pp.* of *grind.*

groundsel, ground′sel, *n.* [O.E. *groundswell,* Sc. *groundie-swallow,* A.Sax. *grundeswelge, grundswelige,* groundsel, lit. ground-swallowing, that is, entirely covering.] A common annual weed, much used as food for caged birds. Also *grunsel-edge* (Mil.).

group, gröp, *n.* [Fr. *groupe,* a group; allied to *croupe,* the buttocks of a horse; Icel. *croppr,* a hump or bunch. CROUP (rump) and CROP (craw of a bird.)] An assemblage, either of persons or things; a number collected; a cluster; an artistic combination of figures; in scientific classifications a number of individuals having some resemblance or common characteristic.—*v.t.* To form into a group; to arrange in a group or in groups.

grouper, gröp′èr, *n.* [Akin to Pg. *garoupa,* Sp. of Central America, *garopa,* the grouper.] A fish of warm seas of the genus *Epinephelus,* found chiefly off the Florida and West Indies coasts; also, the California rockfish.

grouse, grous, *n.* [Etym. doubtful.] The common name of a number of rasorial game birds with mottled plumage, more particularly applied to the red grouse and the ruffed grouse.

grout, grout, *n.* [A.Sax. *grút,* barley or wheat meal; Icel. *grautr,* porridge; akin to *groats, grits* (which see).] Coarse meal; pollard; a thin mortar used for pouring into the joints of masonry and brickwork; a kind of thick ale; lees; grounds; dregs.

grove, gröv, *n.* [A.Sax. *gróf,* a grove, from *grafan,* to dig, a grove being originally an alley cut out in a wood; akin *grave* (*v.* and *n.*).] A cluster of trees shading an avenue or walk;

an assemblage of growing trees of no great extent; a small wood.

grovel, grov'el, v.i.—groveled, groveling, or grovelled, grovelling. [Akin to O.E. grof, gruf, flat, with the face toward the earth; Icel. grufla, to grovel, grufl, a groveling; Sw. grufa, prone, with the face toward the earth.] To lie prone or move with the body prostrate on the earth; to have a tendency toward, or take pleasure in low or base things; to be low, abject, or mean.—**groveler,** grov'el·er, n. One who grovels.—**groveling,** grov'el·ing, p. and a. Indulging by preference in what is low or base.

grow, grō, v.i.—grew (pret.), grown (pp.). [A.Sax. grówan, past greów, pp. grówen=D. groeijen, Icel. gróa, Dan. groe, Sw. gro, to grow; allied to green.] To become enlarged in bulk or stature, by a natural and organic process: said of animals and vegetables; to increase in any way; to become larger and stronger; to be augmented; to wax; to advance; to extend; to swell (the wind grew to a hurricane); to be changed from one state to another; to result, as from a cause or reason; to become (to grow pale).—To grow out of, to issue from by growth; to result from, as an effect from a cause.—To grow up, to advance to full stature or maturity. —To grow together, to become united by growth.—v.t. To cause to grow; to cultivate; to produce; to raise.— **grower,** grō'er, n. One who or that which grows or increases; one who grows, raises, or produces; a cultivator.—**grown,** grōn, pp. of grow. Increased in growth; having arrived at full size or stature.—Grown over, covered by the growth of anything; overgrown.—Grown-up, full-grown; having attained man's or woman's estate.—**growth,** grōth, n. The process of growing; increase of bulk in animals and plants; gradual increase in any way, as in number, bulk, etc.; that which has grown; something produced by growing.

growl, groul, v.i. [Comp. D. grollen, to growl or grumble; G. grollen, to roar; perhaps imitative of sound.] To murmur or snarl, as a dog; to utter an angry, grumbling sound.— v.t. To express by growling; to utter in an angry or grumbling tone.—n. The angry snarl of a dog; the inarticulate grumble of a discontented or angry person.—**growler,** grou'ler, n. One who growls.

grub, grub, v.i. grubbed, grubbing. [O.E. grubbe, grobbe; akin to grope; comp. G. gruben, to dig.] To dig in or under the ground; to be occupied in digging.—v.t. To dig; to dig up by the roots; to root up by digging; generally followed by up or out.—n. [From grubbing in the ground, dirt, etc.] The larva of an insect, especially of beetles; food (slang).— **grubber,** grub'er, n. One who grubs; an instrument for grubbing out roots, weeds, etc.—**grub hoe,** an instrument for digging up trees, shrubs, etc., by the roots; a mattock.— **grubstake,** n. Food or equipment

given to a prospector in return for a share of what he may find.

grudge, gruj, v.t.—grudged, grudging. [Formerly grucche, grutche, groche etc., from O.Fr. groucher, grouchier, groucer, to grumble; of doubtful origin.] To permit or grant with reluctance; to begrudge.—v.i. To be envious; to cherish ill will.—n. Unwillingness to benefit; reluctance felt in giving; ill will from envy or sense of injury.—**grudger,** gruj'er, n. One that grudges. — **grudgingly,** gruj'ing·li, adv. With reluctance or discontent.

gruel, gru'el, n. [O.Fr. gruel, for grutel, from D. or L.G. grut=E. grout (which see).] A kind of broth made by boiling ingredients in water: usually made of the meal of oats.— **grueling,** grü'el·ing, a. Very tiring; wearisome to the point of exhaustion.

gruesome, grewsome, grö'sum, a. [D. gruwen, Dan. grue, G. grauen, to shudder.] Causing one to shudder; frightful; horrible.

gruff, gruf, a. [Same word as D. grof, Dan. grov, G. grob, coarse, blunt, rude.] Of a rough or stern manner, voice, or countenance; sour; surly.— **gruffly,** gruf'li, adv.—**gruffness,** n.

grum, grum, a. [Comp. A.Sax. grom, gram, severe.] Morose; severe of countenance; sour; surly; glum.

grumble, grum'bl, v.i.—grumbled, grumbling. [Perhaps same as D. grommelen, grommen, Fr. grommeler, to grumble; akin to A.Sax. grimman, to murmur, to rage; E. grim, grum. This, like other words such as grunt, growl, may have been partly affected by sound imitation.] To murmur with discontent; to utter in a low voice by way of complaint; to give vent to discontented expressions; to growl; to snarl; to rumble; to roar; to make a harsh and heavy sound.— v.t. To express or utter by grumbling.—**grumbler,** grum'bler, n. One who grumbles; a discontented man. —**grumblingly,** grum'bling·li, adv. With grumbling or complaint.

grume, gröm, n. [O.Fr. grume, Fr. grumeau, a clot; from L. grumus, a little heap.] A fluid of a thick, viscid consistence; a clot, as of blood.—**grumose,** grö'mōs, a. Bot. grumous.—**grumous,** grö'mus, a. Resembling or containing grume; thick; clotted; bot. formed of coarse grains, as some clustered tubercular roots.

grumpy, grum'pi, a. [Connected with grum, grumble.] Surly; angry; gruff.—**grumpily,** grum'pi·li, adv.

grunt, grunt, v.i. [Probably from an imitative root seen in A.Sax. grunan, E. groan, Dan. grynte, G. grunzen, to grunt; comp. also L. grunnio, Fr. grogner, to grunt; Gr. gru, the cry of a pig.] To snort or make a noise like a hog; to utter a short groan or a deep guttural sound, as of a hog.— n. A deep guttural sound, as of a hog.— **grunter,** grun'ter, n. One that grunts; a fish that makes a grunting sound.

Gruyère, gru·yār', n. A kind of cheese made from a mixture of goats' and ewes' milk, from Gruyère in Switzerland.

guacharo, gwa·chä'rō, n. [Sp.] A South American bird of the goatsucker family, valued for its fat.

guaiacum, gwä'ya·kum, n. [Native name.] A South American tree and the resin obtained from it, the latter, as well as the bark and wood, being of medicinal value.

guan, gwän, n. A South American gallinaceous bird, allied to the curassows.

guanaco, gwa·nä'kō, n. [Sp., Peruv. huanacu.] A quadruped closely allied to the llama and alpaca.

guano, gwä'nō, n. [Sp. guano, huano, from Peruv. huanu, dung.] A substance found on many small islands, especially in the Pacific Ocean and on the west coast of South America, chiefly composed of the excrement of sea fowl in a decomposed state, much used as a manure.—**guanine,** gū·ā'nēn, n. [From guano.] A nitrogenous waste product formed in the animal body.

guarantee, gar·an·tē', v.t.—guaranteed, guaranteeing. [O.Fr. guarantie, a form of warranty. WARRANT, etc.] To warrant; to pledge one's self for; to become bound that an article shall be as good or useful as it is represented; to secure the performance of; to undertake to secure to another (claims, rights, possessions); to undertake to uphold or maintain. —n. An undertaking that the engagement or promise of another shall be performed; a pledging of one's self as surety; one who binds himself to see the stipulations of another performed; a guarantor. — **guarantor,** gar·an·tor', n. A warrantor; one who gives a guarantee.—**guaranty,** same as Guarantee.

guard, gärd, v.t. [The form in which the Germanic equivalent of E. ward passed into English through the Norman; O.Fr. guarder, Fr. garder, to guard. WARD.] To secure against injury, loss, or attack; to defend; to keep in safety; to accompany for protection; to provide or secure against objections or attacks.—To guard one's self against, to be on one's guard against; to take pains to avoid doing or saying.—v.i. To watch by way of caution or defense; to be cautious; to be in a state of caution or defense (to guard against mistake). —n. A state of caution or vigilance, or the act of observing what passes in order to prevent surprise or attack; defense; attention; watch; heed; fencing or boxing, a posture of defense; the arms or weapon in such a posture; one who guards or keeps watch; one whose business is to defend or prevent attack or surprise; a brakeman or gateman on a railway; football, one of two players in the line on either side of center; in England, the body of troops that guards the king; that which guards or protects; any appliance or attachment designed to protect or secure against injury; an ornamental border on one's dress. —On guard, acting as a guard or sentinel.—To be on our (your, my, etc.) guard, to be in a watchful state.— **guarded,** gär'ded, p. and a. Protected; defended; cautious; circumspect (guarded in language); framed or uttered with caution.—**guardedly,** gär′ded·li, adv. In a guarded or cautious manner.—**guardedness,** gär′ded·nes, n.—**guardian,** gär′di·an, n. [Fr. gardien.] One who guards; one to whom anything is committed for preservation from injury; one who has the charge or custody of any person or thing.—a. Protecting; performing the office of a protector.—**guardianship,** gär′di·an·ship, n. The office of a guardian; protection; care; watch.—**guardhouse, guardroom,** n. A house or room for the accommodation of a guard of soldiers, and where military defaulters are confined.—**guardsman,** gärdz′man, n. A watchman; an officer or private in a regiment of guards.

guava, gwä′va, n. [The native name in Guiana.] A small tropical tree of the myrtle family, the fruit of which is made into a delicious jelly.

gubernatorial, gū′bėr·na·tō′ri·al, a. [L. gubernator, a governor. GOVERN.] Pertaining to government or to a governor.

gudgeon, guj′on, n. [Fr. goujon, from L. gobio, gobius, Gr. kōbios, a gudgeon.] A small fresh-water fish which is very easily caught; hence, a person easily cheated or ensnared.—v.t. To cheat; to impose on.

gudgeon, guj′on, n. [Fr. goujon; origin doubtful.] A metallic piece let into the end of a wooden shaft and forming a sort of axle to it; the bearing portion of a shaft.

guelder-rose, gel′dėr, n. [Brought from Guelderland in Holland.] A shrub of the woodbine family with handsome flowers.

Guelphs, Ghibellines, gwelfs, gib′el·ēns, n. The Welfs and Waiblings, names of German-Italian political parties in the early medieval times, favoring respectively the Pope and the Emperor; Papalists and Imperialists.

guerdon, gėr′don, n. [O.Fr. guerdon, It. guiderdone, from L.L. widerdonum, corrupted from O.G. widarlon (A.Sax. witherleán), a recompense, through the influence of the L. donum, a gift—from widar (G. wider), against, and lón, reward (=E. loan).] A reward; requital; recompense: used both in a good and bad sense (poet. or rhet.).—v.t. To give a guerdon to; to reward.

guernsey, gėrn′se, n. A sort of close-fitting woolen knitted shirt; [cap.] a breed of dairy cattle.

guerrilla, guerilla, ge·ril·lä: Sp. pron. ger·rēl′yä, n. [Sp. guerrilla, dim. of guerra, Fr. guerre, war, from O.H.G. werra, war.] One who engages in irregular warfare as a member of a small group, frequently harassing the regular army and committing other acts of sabotage.

guess, ges, v.t. [O.E. gesse=L.G. and D. gissen, Dan. gisse, Icel. giska, gizka, to guess, lit. to try to get. GET.] To form an opinion without good means of knowledge or sufficient evidence; to judge of at random; to suppose; to imagine: often

followed by a clause. [This verb is much used colloquially in the sense of to believe, to be sure.]—v.i. To form a conjecture; to judge at random, or without any strong evidence: with at.—n. A conjecture.—**guesser,** ges′ėr, n. One who guesses.—**guesswork,** ges′wėrk, n. Mere conjecture; the act of working by hazard.

guest, gest, n. [A.Sax. gaest, gest= Icel. gestr, Dan. giest, D. and G. gast, Goth. gasts, a guest, a stranger; cog. Armor. hostiz, Rus. gosty, a guest; L. hostis, an enemy (whence E, host, hostile).] A visitor or friend entertained in the house or at the table of another; a lodger at a hotel or lodginghouse.

guffaw, guf′fa, n. [Imitative.] A loud or sudden burst of laughter.—v.i. To burst into a loud or sudden laugh.

guggle, gug′l, v.i. [Imitative, suggested by gurgle.] To make a sound like that of a liquid passing through a narrow aperture; to gurgle.—n. A sound of this kind; a gurgle.

guide, gīd, v.t.—guided, guiding. [Fr. guider, It. guidare, Sp. guiar—of Teutonic origin, and akin to G. weisen, to show, to lead, Goth. witan, to watch over; A.Sax. witan, to know, to wit, with change of w to gu as in guile, guard. WIT.] To lead or direct in a way; to conduct in a course or path; to direct; to regulate; to influence in conduct or actions; to give direction to; to instruct and direct; to superintend.—n. [Fr. guide, It. guida, Sp. guia.] A person who guides; a leader or conductor; one who conducts travelers or tourists in particular localities; one who or that which directs another in his conduct or course of life; a director; a regulator; a guidebook; technology, applied to various contrivances intended to direct or keep to a fixed course or motion.—**guidable,** gī′da·bl, a. Capable of being guided.—**guidance,** gī′dans, n. The act of guiding; direction; government.—**guidebook,** n. A book for giving travelers or tourists information about the places they visit.—**guided missile.** A rocket or other missile (ballistic or air-breathing, solid or liquid-fueled) whose course is determined by self-contained instruments or radio signals.—**guidepost,** n. A post for directing travelers.

guidon, gī′don, n. [Fr., lit. a guiding flag.] The flag of a troop of cavalry; a flag used to signal with at sea, etc.

guild, gild, n. [A.Sax. gild, a payment, hence a society where payment was made for its protection and support, from gildan, to pay; D. gild, a guild. GUILT, YIELD.] An association or incorporation of men belonging to the same class or engaged in similar pursuits, formed for mutual aid and protection.

guile, gīl, n. [French form of E. wile (which see); O.Fr. guile, guile, from a Germanic form, with regular change of G. w into Romance gu (as in guide).] Craft; cunning; artifice; duplicity; deceit—**guileful,** gīl′ful, a. Full of guile; intended to

deceive; crafty; wily; deceitful; insidious; treacherous. — **guilefully,** gīl′ful·li, adv. In a guileful manner.—**guilefulness,** gīl′ful·nes, n. The state or quality of being guileful.—**guileless,** gīl′les, a. Free from guile.—**guilelessness,** gīl′les·nes, n.

guillemot, gil′li·mot, n. [Fr. guillemot, perhaps from Armor. gwéla, to weep, and O.Fr. moëtte, a gull.] A marine swimming bird allied to the auks and divers.

guillotine, gil·o·tēn′, n. [From Dr. Guillotin who introduced in the French Convention the motion for the use of the machine, first called Louisette, from inventor, Dr. Louis.] An engine for beheading persons by means of a steel blade loaded with a mass of lead, and sliding between two upright posts; a machine which consists of a knife descending between grooved posts, much used for cutting paper, straw, etc.—v.t.—guillotined, guillotining. To behead by the guillotine.

guilt, gilt, n. [A.Sax. gylt, a crime, from gildan, gyldan, to pay, to require; akin Icel. gjald, payment, retribution, gjalda, to pay, to yield; E. yield, guild.] Criminality; that state of a moral agent which results from his wilful or intentional commission of a crime or offense, knowing it to be a crime or violation of law—**guiltily,** gil′ti·li, adv. In a guilty manner.—**guiltiness,** gil′ti·nes, n. The state of being guilty; wickedness; criminality; guilt.—**guiltless,** gilt′les, a. Free from guilt, crime, or offense; innocent; not having experience; ignorant (with of; poet.).—**guiltlessly,** gilt′les·li, adv. In a guiltless manner.—**guiltlessness,** gilt′les·nes, n. State or quality of being guiltless.—**guilty,** gil′ti, a. Having incurred guilt; not innocent; criminal; morally delinquent: with of before the crime; pertaining to guilt; indicating guilt (a guilty look).

guinea, gin′ē, n. [Because first coined of gold brought from Guinea, in Africa.] A gold coin formerly current in Great Britain of the value of 21 shillings sterling; a sum of money of the same amount; also abbreviated form of guinea fowl.—**Guinea corn,** n. A kind of millet cultivated in Guinea and elsewhere.—**guinea fowl,** n. A fowl of the rasorial order, closely allied to the peacocks and pheasants, common in Guinea.— **Guinea pepper,** n. A kind of capsicum; a name of various kinds of pepper.—**guinea pig,** n. [Perhaps for Guianapig.] A tailless rodent mammal, about 7 inches in length, belonging to South America, and often used for medical experimentation.— **Guinea worm,** n. A worm common in hot countries, which often insinuates itself under the human skin, causing intense pain.

guipure, gē·pūr′, n. [Fr.] An imitation of antique lace; a kind of gimp.

guise, gīz, n. [Fr. guise, the equivalent of E. wise, mode, fashion, O.H.G. wisa, G. weise, with common change from w to gu- in words borrowed into French from the German; comp.

guile, wile.] External appearance: dress; garb; manner; mien; cast or behavior; custom; mode; practice.

guitar, gi·tär′, n. [Fr. guitare, It. chitarra, from L. cithara, Gr. kithara, a kind of lyre.] A musical stringed instrument having six strings, which are played by twitching with the fingers of the right hand, while the notes are stopped by the fingers of the left.

gular, gū′lẽr, a. [From L. gula, the throat or gullet.] Pertaining to the gullet.

gulch, gulch, n. [Allied to Sw. gölka, to swallow, D. gulzig, greedy.] A deep, abrupt ravine caused by the action of water; the dry bed of a torrent; a gully.

gulden, gŭl′den, n. The unit of the Netherlands coinage.

gules, gūlz, n. [Fr. gueules, from Per. gul, a rose.] Her. vertical, parallel lines in a shield indicating the color red.

gulf, gulf, n. [Fr. golfe, It. golfo, Mod.Gr. kolphos, from Gr. kolpos, a gulf or bay.] A large indentation on the coast line of a country and the sea embraced in it; a bay; a bight; an abyss, chasm, or deep opening in the earth; what gulfs or swallows; a wide interval, as in station, education, and the like.—v.t. To swallow up; to engulf; to refuse a degree with honors, but concede a pass.—**gulfweed,** n. A seaweed found abundantly in the Atlantic Ocean, where it covers vast areas; drift weed.

gull, gul, n. [In Old and Prov.E., a young unfledged bird, lit. a yellow bird, from the yellowness of the beak and plumage of young birds, from O.E. gul, yellow=Icel. gulr, Dan. gul, gaul, yellow. YELLOW. Comp. Fr. béjaune, yellow-beak, novice.] A young unfledged bird (Shak.); one easily cheated; a simpleton; a trick (Shak.).—v.t. To make a fool of; to mislead by deception; to trick.—**gullibility,** gul·i·bil′i·ti, n. The quality of being gullible.—**gullible,** gul′i·bl, a. Easily gulled or cheated.

gull, gul, n. [From the Celtic; W. gwylan, Armor. gwelan, Corn. gullan, a gull.] A name for many marine swimming birds found on the shores of all latitudes, and having large wings, slender legs, webbed feet, and a small or no hind toe.

gullet, gul′et, n. [Fr. goulet, from L. gula, the throat.] The passage in the neck of an animal by which food and liquid are taken into the stomach; the esophagus; something resembling this.

gully, gul′i, n. [Fr. goulet, a gullet, a channel for water. GULLET.] A channel or hollow worn in the earth by a current of water; a ravine; a ditch; a gutter; a large knife.—v.t. To wear into a gully or channel.

gulp, gulp, v.t. [M.E. gulpen, from Dan. gulpen, to drink heartily.] To swallow eagerly or in large draughts. —v.i. To catch the breath between swallows.—n. The act of taking a large swallow.

gum, gum, n. [A.Sax. góma, Icel.

gómr, G. gaum, palate, gum.] The fleshy substance on the jaws which envelops the neck of the teeth.— **gumboil,** n. A boil or small abscess on the gum.

gum, gum, n. [Fr. gomme, from L. gummi, Gr. kommi, gum.] A resinous substance extracted from trees or plants, soluble in water but hard when dry; chewing gum; the adhesive substance on the back of postage stamps.—v.t.—gummed, gumming. To smear with gum; to unite or stiffen by gum or a gumlike substance.—v.i. To exude or form gum.—**gum arabic,** n. The juice of various species of acacia.—**gumminess,** gum′i·nes, n. The state or quality of being gummy; viscousness. —**gummous,** gum′us, a. Of the nature or quality of gum; gummy.— **gummy,** gum′i, a. Consisting of gum; of the nature of gum; giving out gum; covered with gum or viscous matter.

gumbo, gum′bõ, n. A soup thickened with the mucilaginous seed pods of the okra, the plant okra or its seed pods; rich, black soil that becomes soapy or sticky when wet.

gumption, gump′shon, n. [Origin unknown.] Enterprise; initiative; shrewd common sense.

gun, gun, n. [From the name Gunnhildr, of fourteenth century. So Mons Meg, Brown Bess, Fat Bertha (Krupp), 1917.] A name applied to every species of firearm for throwing projectiles by the explosion of gunpowder or other explosive; any portable firearm, such as a rifle, pistol, shotgun, etc.; a discharge of a gun in signal or salute, as a 21-gun salute.—v.i. To hunt with a gun.— **gunboat,** n. A boat or small vessel fitted to carry one or more guns of heavy caliber, and from its light draught capable of running close inshore or up rivers.—**guncotton,** n. A highly explosive substance produced by soaking cotton or similar vegetable fiber in nitric and sulfuric acids, and then leaving it to dry.— **gunfire,** n. Milit. the hour at which the morning or evening gun is fired.—**gunflint,** n. A piece of shaped flint, fixed in the lock of a musket or pistol to fire the charge before the introduction of percussion caps. —**gun metal,** n. An alloy, generally of nine parts of copper and one part of tin, used for the manufacture of cannon, etc.—**gunner,** gun′ẽr, n. One who works a gun or cannon, either on land or sea; a warrant officer in the navy connected with the charge of the ordnance.—**gunnery,** gun′ẽr·i, n. The art of firing or managing guns; the science of artillery.—**gunpowder,** gun′pou·dẽr, n. An explosive mixture of saltpeter, sulfur, and charcoal, reduced to a fine powder, then granulated and dried.—Gunpowder tea, a fine species of green tea with a granular appearance.—**gunrunner,** n. One who runs or secretly conveys guns into a district.—**gunshot,** gun′shot, n. The firing of a gun; the distance to which shot can be

thrown so as to be effective.—a. Made by the shot of a gun (gunshot wounds).—**gunsmith,** gun′smith, n. One whose occupation is to make or repair small firearms.

gunny, gun′i, n. [Bengalee.] A strong coarse cloth manufactured of jute in Bengal, for making into bags, sacks, etc.

gunwale, gunnel, gun′el, n. [Gun and wale.] Naut. the upper edge of a ship's or boat's side.

guppy, gup′i, n. [After R. J. L. Guppy of Trinidad who first gave specimens of them to the British Museum.] The small minnow (Lebistes reticulatus) of Trinidad, Barbados and Venezuela, kept as an aquarium fish.

gurge,† gerj, n. [L. gurges, a whirlpool.] A whirlpool (Mil.).

gurgle, gẽr′gl, v.i.—gurgled, gurgling. [Probably imitative or connected with gorge; comp. G. gurgeln, It. gorgogliare, to gurgle. GARGLE.] To run or flow in an irregular, noisy current, as water from a bottle; to flow with a purling sound.—n. The sound made by a liquid flowing from the narrow mouth of a vessel, or generally through any narrow opening.

Gurkha, gụr′ka, n. A native of Nepal, in Hindustan. There are Gurkha regiments in the Indian army.

gurnard, gẽr′närd, n. [O.Fr. grougnaut, probably from grogner, L. grunnire, to grunt or grumble, from the sound these fishes make when taken from the water.] The name of certain marine fishes, having an angular head wholly covered with bony plates.

gush, gush, v.i. [Icel. gjosa, to gush, gusa, a gush, to gush; a Scandinavian word, allied to A.Sax. geótan, Goth. giutan, G. giessen, to pour; E. gut, gust (of wind), geyser.] To rush forth as a fluid from confinement; to flow suddenly or copiously; to be extravagantly and effusively sentimental.—v.t. To emit suddenly, copiously, or with violence.—n. A sudden and violent issue of a fluid; an emission of liquid in a large quantity and with force; an outpour; an effusive display of sentiment.— **gusher,** gush′ẽr, n. One that gushes; an oil well from which oil spurts freely.—**gushingly,** gush′ing·li, adv. In a gushing manner.

gusset, gus′et, n. [Fr. gousset, a gusset, from gousse, a husk or shell.] A triangular piece of cloth inserted in a garment for the purpose of strengthening or enlarging some part; something resembling such a piece of cloth in shape or function.

gust, gust, n. [L. gustus, taste; gusto, to taste (as in disgust); from root seen in choose.] The sense or pleasure of tasting; gratification of the appetite; relish; gusto; taste.—**gustable,** gus′ta·bl, a. Capable of being tasted; having a pleasant relish†.— **gustation,**† gus·tā′shon, n. [L. gustatio.] The act of tasting.—**gustatory,** gus′ta·to·ri, a. Pertaining to gust or taste.—**gusto,** gus′tõ, n. [It.] Nice appreciation or enjoyment; keen relish; taste; fancy.

gust, gust, *n.* [Icel. *gustr*, a blast of wind; allied to E. *gush*.] A violent blast of wind; a sudden rushing or driving of the wind, of short duration; a sudden violent burst of passion.—**gusty,** gus′ti, *a.* Subject to gusts or sudden blasts of wind; tempestuous; given to sudden bursts of passion.

gut, gut, *n.* [A.Sax. *gut, gutt,* gut, *guttas,* entrails; comp. Prov. E. *gut,* a water channel, a drain; O.E. *gote,* a drain; from stem of A.Sax. *geótan,* Goth. *giutan,* to pour out. GUSH.] The intestinal canal of an animal from the stomach to the anus; an intestine; *pl.* the stomach and digestive apparatus generally, the viscera or entrails; a preparation of the intestines of an animal used for various purposes, as for the strings of a fiddle; a channel or passage.—*v.t.*—*gutted, gutting.* To take out the entrails of; to eviscerate; to plunder of contents; to destroy or take out the interior of.

gutta, gut′ta, *n.* pl. **guttae,** gut′tē, [L.] A drop; specifically, *arch.* one of a series of pendent ornaments attached to the under side of the mutules and under the triglyphs of the Doric order.—**guttate,** gut′āt, *a. Bot.* spotted, as if discolored by drops.

gutta-percha, gut′ta pẽr′cha, *n.* [Malay *gutta,* gum, and *percha,* the tree.] The hardened milky juice of a large tree which grows in the Malayan Peninsula and in some of the islands of the Eastern Archipelago, resembling caoutchouc in many of its properties, but stronger, more soluble, and less elastic.

gutter, gut′ẽr, *n.* [Fr. *gouttière,* from *goutte,* L. *gutta,* a drop.] A channel at the side of a road, street, or the like, also at the eaves of, or on, a roof of a building for conveying away water.—*v.t.* To cut or form gutters in.—*v.i.* To become channeled.

guttle, gut′l, *v.i.* [A form of *guzzle*.] To swallow greedily; to gormandize. —**guttler,** gut′lẽr, *n.* A gormandizer.

guttural, gut′ẽr·al, *a.* [From L. *guttur,* the throat, whence also *goitre*.] Pertaining to the throat; uttered from the throat.—*n.* A letter or combination of letters pronounced in the throat; any guttural sound.—**gutturalize,** gut′ẽr·al·īz, *v.t.* To speak or enunciate gutturally.—**gutturally,** gut′ẽr·al·li, *adv.* In a guttural manner.—**gutturalness,** **gutturality,†** gut′ẽr·al·nes, gut·ẽr·al′i·ti, *n.* The quality of being guttural.

guy, gī, *n.* [Sp. *guia,* a guide, a small rope used on board ship. GUIDE.] A rope used to steady anything; a rope to steady an object which is being hoisted; a rope or rod to steady a suspension bridge.—*v.t.* To steady or direct by means of a guy.

guy, gī, *n.* A fright; a person of queer looks or dress: from the effigy of *Guy* Fawkes burned on November 5.

guzzle, guz′l, *v.i.* and *v.t.*—*guzzled, guzzling.* [O.Fr. *goziller,* to gulp down; connected with Fr. *gosier,* the throat.] To swallow liquor greedily; to swill; to drink much. *n.* A debauch, especially on drink. **guzzler,** guz′lẽr, *n.* One who guzzles.

gymkhana, jim·kä′na, *n.* [Of Anglo-Indian origin.] A meeting for athletic or other sport contests.

gymnasium, jim·nā′zi·um, *n.* pl. **gymnasiums, gymnasia.** [Gr. *gymnasion,* from *gymnos,* naked.] A place where athletic exercises are performed; in Europe, a school for the higher branches of education; a school preparatory to the universities.—**gymnast,** jim′nast, *n.* One who teaches or practices gymnastic exercises.—**gymnastic, gymnastical,** jim·nas′tik, jim·nas′ti·kal, *a.* [L. *gymnasticus;* Gr. *gymnastikos.*] Pertaining to athletic exercises.—**gymnastically,** jim·nas′ti·kal·li, *adv.* In a gymnastic manner.—**gymnastics,** jim·nas′tiks, *n.* The art of performing athletic exercises; athletic exercises; feats of skill or address.

gymnocarpous, jim·no·kär′pus, *a.* [Gr. *gymnos,* naked, and *karpos,* fruit.] *Bot.* having a naked fruit.—**gymnogynous,** jim·noj′i·nus, *a.* [Gr. *gynē,* female.] *Bot.* having a naked ovary.—**gymnosophist,** jim·nos′o·fist, *n.* [Gr. *sophistēs,* a philosopher.] One of a sect of ancient Hindu ascetics who lived solitarily, and wore little or no clothing.

gymnosperm, jim′no·spẽrm, *n.* [Gr. *gymnos,* and *sperma,* seed.] A plant that produces seeds not enclosed in an ovary.—**gymnospermous,** jim·no·spẽr′mus, *a.*

gynarchy, jin·är·ki, *n.* [Gr. *gynē,* woman, and *archē,* rule.] Government by a female or females.

gynecocracy, gynaecocracy, jin·e·kok′ra·si, *n.* [Gr. *gynē, gynaikos,* a woman, and *kratos,* power.] Government by a woman; female rule.—**gynecolatry,** jin·e·ol′a·tri, *n.* [Gr. *latreia,* worship.] The extravagant adoration or worship of woman.—**gynecology,** jin·e·kol′o·ji, *n.* The branch of medical science dealing with functions, diseases, and hygiene of women.—**gynecologist,** jin·e·kol′o·jist, *n.*

gynophore, jin′o·fōr, *n.* [Gr. *phoros,* bearing.] The stalk on which the ovary stands in certain flowers; *zool.* the generative bud of a hydrozoon containing ova.

gyp, jip, *n.* [Said to be a sportive application of Gr. *gyps,* a vulture, from their alleged rapacity.] A college servant (English usage).—*n., v.t.* and *i. U.S. slang,* to cheat; to swindle.

gypsum, jip′sum, *n.* [L. *gypsum,* from Gr. *gypsos,* chalk.] A mineral which is found in a compact and crystallized state, as alabaster, or in the form of a soft chalky stone which by heat becomes a fine white powder, extensively used under the name of plaster of Paris.—**gypseous,** jip′si·us, *a.* Of the nature of gypsum; resembling gypsum.—**gypsiferous,** jip·sif′ẽr·us, *a.* Producing gypsum.

gypsy, gipsy, jip′si, *n.* [For *Egyptian,* from the belief that the race are descendants of the ancient people of Egypt. Called by themselves *Romany,* perhaps indicative of their first reaching Europe by *Rumania.*] One of a peculiar wandering race deriving their origin from India; a name of slight or humorous reproach to a young woman; the language of the gypsies.—*a.* Pertaining to the gypsies.

gypsy moth, *n.* A European tussock moth, now found in the East, the caterpillars of which do much damage to trees.

gyrate, jī′rāt, *v.i.* [L. *gyro, gyratum,* from *gyrus,* Gr. *gyros,* a circle.] To turn round circularly; to revolve round a central point; to move spirally.—*a.* Winding or going round, as in a circle.—**gyration,** jī·rā′shon, *n.* A turning or whirling round; a circular motion.—**gyratory,** jī′ra·to·ri, *a.* Moving in a circle or spirally.—**gyre,** jīr, *n.* A circular motion, or a circle described by a moving body; a turn.—**gyrose,** jī′rōs, *a. Bot.* bent round like a crook.

gyrfalcon, jẽr′fạ·kn, *n.* [L.L. *gyrofalco,* from *gyrus,* a circle, so called from its flight.] A species of falcon, one of the boldest and most beautiful of the tribe.

gyrocompass, jī′rō·kum′pas, *n.* [From Gr. *gyros,* ring, and *compass.*] A compass which uses a steadily rotating gyroscope, instead of a magnetic needle, to determine the geographic north.

gyroscope, jī′ro·skōp, *n.* [Gr. *skopeō,* to view.] An apparatus, consisting of a pivoted disk rotating in different ways, for illustrating peculiarities of rotation; also used to increase steadiness of ships and airplanes.—**gyroplane,** jī′ro·plān, *n.* An airplane propelled by windmill-like wings revolving about a vertical axis.—**gyrostat,** jī′ro·stat, *n.* A kind of spinning top.

gyrus, jī′rus, pl. **gyri,** jī′ri, *n.* [Gr. *gyros,* a circle.] *Anat.* a name given to the ridges or raised convolutions on the surface of the brain.

gyve, jīv, *n.* [W. *gevyn;* Ir. *geibion,* from *geibhim,* to get; to hold; same root as L. *capio,* to take.] A shackle, usually for the legs; a fetter; commonly in the plural.—*v.t.*—*gyved, gyving.* To fetter; to shackle; to chain.

H

H, h, āch, the eighth letter of the English alphabet, a consonant often called the *aspirate,* as being a mere aspiration or breathing.

ha, hä. An exclamation, denoting surprise, wonder, joy, or other sudden emotion.

haaf, häf, *n.* [N. *haf,* high sea.] Deep-sea fishing ground.

habeas corpus, hā′bi·as kor′pus, [L., you may have the body.] *Law,* a common-law writ designed to safeguard citizens from unjust imprisonment, directed to any person who detains another in custody and commanding him to produce the body of this person with a statement of the day and cause of his apprehension and detention that the court may deal with him.

haberdasher, hab´er·dash·er, n. [Lit. a seller of *hapertas*, from O.Fr. *hapertas*, a kind of cloth.] The proprietor of a store which deals principally in men's furnishings; formerly a dealer in drapery goods, woolens, linens, silks, ribbons, etc.—**haberdashery,** hab´er·dash·er·i, n.

habergeon, ha·bėr´jon, n. [Fr. *haubergeon*, from *heuberc*, a hauberk. HAUBERK.] A short coat of mail or armor consisting of a jacket without sleeves.

habiliment, ha·bil´i·ment, n. [Fr. *habillement*, from *habiller*, to dress, from L. *habilis*, fit, proper. HABIT.] A garment; clothing: usually plural.—**habilitate,** ha·bil´i·tāt, v.t. To equip for operation, as a mine.

habit, hab´it, n. [Fr. *habit*, from L. *habitus*, state, dress, manner, condition, etc., from *habeo*, *habitum*, to have, to hold; of similar origin are *habiliment*, *habitation*, *inhabit*, *exhibit*, *prohibit*, also *able*, *debt*, *duty*, etc.] The ordinary state or condition of the body, either natural or acquired; tendency or capacity resulting from frequent repetition of the same acts; practice; usage; a way of acting; a peculiar practice or custom; a characteristic item of behavior; dress; garb; the outer dress worn by ladies while on horseback. ∴ *Syn.* under CUSTOM.—v.t. To dress; to clothe; to array.—**habited,** hab´it·ed, a. Clothed, as with a habit.—**habitual,** ha·bit´ū·al, a. [Fr. *habituel*.] Formed or acquired by habit, frequent use, or custom; constantly practiced; customary; regular; as a matter of course.—**habitually,** ha·bit´ū·al·li, adv. In a habitual manner.—**habitualness,** ha·bit´ū·al·nes, n. **habituate,** ha·bit´ū·āt, v.t.—*habituated*, *habituating*. [L. *habituo*, *habituatum*.] To accustom; to make familiar by frequent use or practice; to familiarize.—a. Formed by habit.—**habituation,** ha·bit´ū·ā˝shon, n. The act of habituating, or state of being habituated.—**habitude,** hab´i·tūd, n. [Fr. *habitude*, from L. *habitudo*.] Customary manner or mode of living, feeling, or acting; long custom; habit.—**habitué,** ha·bi´tū·ā, n. [Fr., pp. of *habituer*, to accustom.] A habitual frequenter of any place, especially one of amusement, recreation, and the like.

habitable, hab´i·ta·bl, a. [Fr., from L. *habitabilis*, from *habito*, to dwell, a freq. of *habeo*, to have.] Capable of being inhabited or dwelt in; capable of sustaining human beings.—**habitability, habitableness,** hab´i·ta·bil˝i·ti, hab´i·ta·bl·nes, n. State of being habitable; capacity of being inhabited.—**habitably,** hab´i·ta·bli, adv. So as to be habitable.—**habitant,** hab´i·tant, n. [L. *habitans*, *habitantis*, ppr. of *habito*.] An inhabitant; a dweller; a resident.—**habitat,** hab´i·tat, n. [L. *habitat*,

' it dwells'.] The natural abode or locality of a plant or animal.—**habitation,** hab·i·tā´shon, n. [L. *habitatio*.] Act of inhabiting; occupancy; place of abode; a settled dwelling; a house or other place in which man or any animal dwells.

habitude, habitué. See HABIT.

hachure, hä·shör´, n. [Fr., from *hacher*, to hack. HACK, v.t.] Short lines which mark half-tints and shadows in designing and engraving.—v.t. To cover with hachures.

hacienda, hä·sē·en´dä, n. [Sp.] In Spain, Spanish America, etc., a farmhouse; a farm.

hack, hak, v.t. and i. [A.Sax. *haccan* or *haccian*=E. *hatch* (in engraving), *hatchet*, *hash*.] To cut irregularly and into small pieces; to notch; to mangle; to chop; to cough in a short, dry manner.—n. A notch; a cut; a hacking cough.—**hack saw,** n. A fine-toothed saw fixed in a frame, used to cut metal.—**hacking,** hak´ing, a. Short and interrupted (a *hacking* cough).

hack, hak, n. [Short for *hackney*.] A horse kept for hire; a horse much worked; a worn-out horse; a person overworked; a writer employed in the drudgery and details of bookmaking.—a. Much used or worn, like a hired horse; hired.—v.t. To use as a hack; to let out for hire.

hackberry, hak´ber·ri, n. [Same as Prov. E. *hag-berry*, bird-cherry= *haw*-berry, *hedge*-berry.] A North American tree bearing sweet edible fruits as large as bird cherries.

hackbut, hak´but, n. Same as *arquebus*.

hackle, hak´l, n. [D. *hekel*, G. *hechel*, Dan. *hegle*, a hackle for flax or hemp; akin to *hook*. The secondary senses are from similarity to tufts of hackled fibers.] A hatchel, heckle, or comb for dressing flax; raw silk; any flimsy substance unspun; a long pointed feather on the neck of a fowl, or any similar feather.—v.t. To comb (flax or hemp); to hatchel or heckle.—**hackler,** hak´lėr, n. One who hackles.

hackmatack, hak´ma·tak, n. [Amer. Indian.] The American black larch.

hackney, hak´ni, n. [O.Fr. *haquenee*, a pacing horse, Sp. *hacanea*, a nag; probably from O.D. *heckeneye*, *hakkenei*, a hackney; lit. perhaps a hacked or dock-tailed nag.] A horse kept for riding or driving; a pad; a nag; a horse kept for hire; a hack; a person accustomed to drudgery, often literary drudgery.—a. Let out for hire; much used; common; trite.—v.t. To use as a hackney; to devote to common or vulgar use.—**hackney coach,** n. A coach kept for hire.—**hackneyed,** hak´nid, p. and a. Discussed or talked of without end; in everybody's mouth; trite; commonplace.

had, had, pret. & pp. of *have*.

haddock, had´ok, n. [Comp. O.Fr. *hadot*, *hadou*, Ir. *codog*, a haddock.] A well-known fish of the cod family, smaller than the cod, and having a dark spot on each side just behind the head.

hade, hād, n. [A.Sax. *heald*, inclined, bent; G. *halde*, declivity.] *Mining*, a slope or inclination; inclination of a vein or bed from a vertical direction.—v.i. To slope or incline from the vertical.

Hades, hā´dēz, n. [Gr. *Hadēs*, i.e. *aidēs*, invisible, unseen, from *a* not, and *idein*, to see.] The invisible abode of the dead; the place or state of departed souls; the world of spirits.

hadj, haj, n. [Ar.] The Mohammedan pilgrimage to Mecca and Medina.—**hadji,** haj´ē, n. A Mussulman who has performed his pilgrimage to Mecca.

haemal, hē´mal, a. [Gr. *haima*, *haimatos*, blood. Some of the words in which this forms part are spelled indifferently *he*- or *hæ*-; in others there is a preference. See also under HE.] Pertaining to the blood; connected with the blood vessels or circulation.—**haematite,** hē´ma·tīt, n. HEMATITE.—**haematocryal,** hē·ma·tok´ri·al, a. [Gr. *cryos*, cold.] *Zool.* applied to the cold-blooded vertebrates.—**haematothermal,** hē´ma·to·ther˝mal, a. [Gr. *thermos*, warm.] Of or pertaining to the warm-blooded vertebrates.—**haematoxylin,** hē·ma·tok´si·lin, HEMATOXYLIN.—**haematozoa,** hē´ma·to·zō˝a, n. pl. [Gr. *zōon*, an animal.] The entozoa which exist in the blood of mammals, birds, reptiles, etc.

hafnium, haf´ni·um, n.[From *Hafnia*, L. for Copenhagen.] A metallic element found in zirconium ores. Symbol, Hf; at. no., 72; at. wt., 178.49.

haft, haft, n. [A.Sax. *hæft*, a haft=D. and G. *heft*, a handle; Icel. *hepti* (=*hefti*), a haft, from the stem of *have* or *heave*.] A handle; that part of an instrument which is taken into the hand, and by which it is held and used.—v.t. To set in a haft; to furnish with a handle.

hag, hag, n. [Shortened from A.Sax. *hægtesse*; akin to G. *hexe*, D. *heks*, a witch; probably from A.Sax. *haga*, a hedge, G. *hag*, a wood (the meaning being woman of the woods).] An ugly old woman; a witch; a sorceress; a she-monster; an eel-shaped fish which eats into and devours other fishes.—**haggish,** hag´ish, a. Pertaining to or resembling a hag; ugly; horrid.

hagbut, hag´but, n. Same as *Arquebus*.

haggard, hag´ärd, a. [Fr. *haggard*, originally a wild falcon, from G. *hag*, a wood, and affix -*ard*. In secondary sense perhaps for *hagged*, that is *hag*-like. HEDGE, HAW.] Wild; intractable (a *haggard* hawk); having the expression of one wasted by want or suffering; having the face worn and pale; lean-faced; gaunt.—n. An untrained or refractory hawk.—**haggardly,** hag´ärd·li, adv. In a haggard manner.

haggis, hag´is, n. [From *hag*, to chop, a form of *hack*; comp. Fr. *hachis*, a hash.] A Scotch dish, commonly made in a sheep's stomach, of the heart, lungs, and liver of the animal minced with suet, onions, oatmeal, and seasoned with salt and pepper.

fāte, fär, fâre, fat, f̣all; mē, met, hėr; pīne, pin; nōte, not, mȯve; tūbe, tub, bu̟ll; oil, pound.

haggle, hag′l, v.t.—haggled, haggling. [Freq. of hag, for hack, to hack.] To cut into small pieces; to notch or cut in an unskillful manner; to mangle.—v.i. To be difficult in bargaining; to hesitate and cavil; to stick at small matters; to higgle.—**haggler,** hag′l·ėr, n. One who haggles.

Hagiographa, hā·gi·og′ra·fa, n. pl. [Gr. hagios, holy, and graphē, a writing.] The last of the three Jewish divisions of the Old Testament, comprehending Psalms, Proverbs, Job, Daniel, Ezra, Nehemiah, Ruth, Esther, Chronicles, Canticles, Lamentations, and Ecclesiastes.—**hagiography,** hā·gi·og′ra·fi, n. Sacred writing; the lives of the saints or holy men.—**hagiographic,** hā′gi·o·graf″ik, a. Pertaining to hagiography.—**hagiographer,** hā·gi·og′ra·fėr, n. One of the writers of the hagiography; a writer of lives of the saints.—**hagiologist,** hā·gi·ol′o·jist, n. One who writes or treats of the sacred writings; a writer of lives of the saints.—**hagiology,** hā·gi·ol′o·ji, n. [Gr. hagios, and logos.] Sacred literature; that branch of literature which has to do with the lives and legends of the saints.

ha-ha, hä′hä, n. [Reduplicated form of haw, a hedge.] A sunk fence or ditch; a hawhaw.

haiku, hī′kö, n. pl. **haiku.** [Japanese.] A 3-line unrhymed Japanese poem of 5, 7 and 5 syllables, respectively, containing a seasonal reference.

hail, hāl, n. [A.Sax. hagal, hagol = G., D., Dan. and Sw. hagel, Icel. hagl, hail; root doubtful.] The small masses of ice or frozen vapor falling from the clouds in showers or storms; frozen rain.—v.t. and i. To pour down hail.—**hailstone,** hāl′stōn, n. A single ball or pellet of hail.—**hailstorm,** n. A storm of hail.

hail, hāl, interj. [Same as hale, adj.; Icel. heill, Dan. heel, hale. HALE, HEALTH.] A term of greeting or salutation expressive of well-wishing. —v.t. To call to; to greet from a distance; to call to in order to arrest attention; to designate as; to salute or address as.—v.i. Used only in the phrase to hail from, originally used of a ship, which is said to hail from the port whence she comes; hence, to have as one's residence or birthplace; to belong to.—n. Call.—Within hail, within call; within reach of the sound of the voice.

hair, hâr, n. [A.Sax. haer, hér = Icel. hár, O.D. hair, D. Dan. and G. haar, hair; perhaps akin to Icel. hörr, flax, E. hards (which see).] A small filament issuing from the skin of an animal, and from a bulbous root; the collection or mass of filaments growing from the skin of an animal and forming an integument or covering; such filaments in the mass; a filament resembling a hair; bot. a species of down or pubescence.—To a hair, to a nicety.—To split hairs, to be unduly nice in making distinctions.—**hairbreadth, hairsbreadth,** n. The diameter or breadth of a hair; a

minute distance.—a. Of the breadth of a hair; very narrow (a hairbreadth escape).—**hairbrush,** n. A brush for dressing and smoothing the hair.—**haircloth,** n. A kind of cloth made of hair or in part of hair.—**hairdresser,** n. One who dresses or cuts people's hair; a barber.—**hairiness,** hā′ri·nes, n. The state of being hairy.—**hairless,** hâr′les, a. Destitute of hair; bald.—**hairline,** n. A line made of hair; a very slender line made in writing or drawing; a hair stroke.—**hairpin,** n. A pin used to keep the hair in a certain position; especially, a doubled pin or bent wire used by women.—**hair shirt,** n. Shirt or belt made of horsehair and worn by way of self-mortification.—**hair space,** n. The thinnest space used by printers.—**hairsplitting,** n. The act or practice of making minute distinctions in reasoning.—**hairsplitter,** n. One given to hair-splitting.—**hairspring,** n. The fine hairlike spring giving motion to the balance wheel of a watch.—**hair stroke,** n. The fine up-stroke in penmanship.—**hair trigger,** n. A trigger to a gunlock, so delicately adjusted that the slightest touch will discharge the piece.—**hairy,** hâ′ri, a. Overgrown with hair; covered with hair.

hake, hāk, n. [Prov. E. hake, a hook, from the hook-shaped jaw of the fish.] A fish of the cod family, one species of which is known as king of herrings, on which it preys.

hakim, hä·kēm′ n. [Ar.] An Oriental name for a physician.

halberd, halbert, hal′bėrd, hal′bėrt, n. [Fr. hallebarde, from O.G. helmparte, helmbarte, a halberd—helm, a handle, a helm, and parte, barte, an ax.] An ancient military weapon, a kind of combination of a spear and battle-ax, with a shaft about 6 feet long.—**halberdier,** hal·bėr·dėr′, n. One who is armed with a halberd.

halcyon, hal′si·on, n. [L. halcyon, from Gr. halkyōn, a kingfisher, said to be from hals, the sea, and kyō, to conceive.] An old or poetical name of the kingfisher, which was fabled to have the power of charming the winds and waves during the period of its incubation, so that the weather was then calm.—a. Pertaining to or connected with the halcyon; calm; quiet; peaceful.—Halcyon days, the seven days before and as many after the winter solstice, when the halcyon was believed to brood, and the weather was calm; hence, days of peace and tranquillity.

hale, hāl, a. [Same as Icel. heill, Dan. heel, Goth. hails, in good health, sound, etc. (hence, hail in salutations); closely akin to A.Sax. hál, whole, sound, whence E. whole; cog. with Gr. kalos, beautiful. Akin heal, health, hollow, holy.] Sound; healthy; robust; not impaired in health.

hale, hāl, v.t.—haled, haling. [HAUL.] To pull or draw with force; to haul.—n. A violent pull; a haul.

half, häf, n. pl. **halves,** hävz, [A.Sax.

half or healf = O.Fris., D., and Sw. half, Icel. halfr, Goth. halbs, G. halb, half.] One part of a thing which is divided into two equal parts, either in fact or in contemplation; a moiety (we usually say half a pound, half a mile, etc., omitting of). —To cry halves, to claim an equal share.—To go halves, to agree with another for the division of anything into equal parts.—adv. In an equal part or degree; by half; to some extent; much used in composition and often indefinite (half-learned, half-hatched).—a. Consisting of a moiety or half.—**half-and-half,** n. A mixture of two malt liquors, especially porter and sweet or bitter ale.—**halfback,** n. Player in football, immediately behind the forwards.—**half binding,** n. A style of binding books in which the back and corners are in leather and the sides in paper or cloth.—**half blood,** n. One born of the same mother but not the same father as another, or vice versâ; a half-breed.—**half-bound,** a. A term applied to a book in half binding.—**half-bred,** a. Imperfectly bred; mixed; mongrel; partially or imperfectly acquainted with the rules of good breeding.—**half-breed,** n. One born of parents of different races; specifically applied to the offspring of American Indians and whites.—**half brother,** n. A brother by one parent, but not by both.—**half-caste,** n. One born of a Hindu and a European; a halfblood or half-breed.—**half cock,** n. The position of the hammer of a gun when it is elevated only halfway and retained by the first notch.—**half crown,** n. A silver coin of Britain valued at 2s, 6d.—**half dollar,** n. A silver coin of the United States, value fifty cents.—**halfhearted,** a. Devoid of eagerness or enthusiasm; indifferent; lukewarm.—**half-hourly,** a. Occurring at intervals of half an hour.—**half life,** n. The time it takes one-half the atoms of a radioactive substance to disintegrate.—**halfmoon,** n. The moon at the quarters, when half its disk appears illuminated; anything in the shape of a half-moon.—**half note,** n. Mus. a minim, being half a semibreve; a semitone.—**half pay,** n. Half wages or salary; a reduced allowance paid to an officer in the army or navy when not in actual service.—a. Receiving or entitled to half pay.—**halfpenny,** hā′pen·i, n. pl. **halfpence,** häf′pens or hā′pens. A British copper coin of the value of half a penny or one cent.—a. Of the price or value of a halfpenny.—**half sister,** n. A sister by the father's side only, or by the mother's side only.—**half sovereign,** n. A British gold coin, value 10s.—**half tide,** n. The tide when halfway between the ebb and flood.—**half-timbered,** a. Built half of timber, as a dwelling.—**half tone,** n. A tone intermediate between the extreme lights and shades of a picture; a kind of photoengraving.—**halfway,** adv. In the middle; at half the distance.—a.

ch, chain; ch, Sc. loch; g, go; j, job; ng, sing; TH, then; th, thin; w, wig; hw, whig; zh, azure.

Midway; equidistant from the extremes.—**halfwitted,** *a.* Weak in intellect; silly; foolish.

halibut, holibut, hal'i·but, hol'i·but, *n.* [From *hali,* that is, holy, and *but* or *butt,* a flounder = D. *heilbot,* G. *heilbutt, heiligbutt.*] One of the largest of the flat-fish family, allied to the turbot, but much less broad comparatively, valuable as food.

halite, hal'īt, hā'līt, *n.* [Gr. *hals,* salt.] *Mineral.* native salt.

halitosis, hal·i·tō'sis, *n.* [L. *habitus,* breath, and *osis.*] Condition of having foul or offensive breath.

halitus, hal'i·tus, *n.* [L. from *halo,* to breathe out (in *exhale*).] *Physiol.* the breath or moisture of the breath; vapor exhaled from the body.

hall, hal, *n.* [A.Sax. *heal, heall* = Icel. *höll, hall,* Sw. *hall,* D. *hal,* from root signifying to cover, seen also in E. *hell.*] A large room, especially a large public room; a room or building devoted to public business, or in which meetings of the public or corporate bodies are held; a large room at the entrance of a house; lobby; a manor house.—**hallmark,** *n.* The official stamp affixed to articles of gold and silver; a distinguishing mark or characteristic.

hallelujah, halleluiah, hal·lē·lō'yä, *n.* and *interj.* See ALLELUIA.

halliard, hal'yård, *n.* See HALYARD.

halloo, hal·lö', *interj.* and *n.* [Comp. G. *halloh!* and Fr. *halle,* an exclamation used to cheer on dogs; *haller,* to encourage dogs.] An exclamation, used as a call to invite attention; also, a hunting cry to set a dog on the chase.—*v.i.* To call *halloo;* to shout; to cry, as after dogs.—*v.t.* To shout to.

hallow, hal'lō, *v.t.* [A.Sax. *hálgian,* to hallow, from *hálig,* holy. HOLY.] To make holy; to consecrate; to set apart for holy or religious use; to reverence; to honor as sacred.— **Halloween,** *n.* The eve or vigil of Allhallows or All Saints' Day. [Sc.] —**hallowmas,** hal'lō·mas, *n.* [A.Sax. *hálga,* a saint, and *mæsse,* mass, festival.] The feast of All Saints or the time at which it is held.

hallucination, hal·lū'si·nā"shon, *n.* [L. *hallucinatio,* from *hallucinor,* to wander in mind, to talk idly.] An unfounded and mistaken notion; an entire misconception; a mere dream or fancy. *med.* a morbid condition of the brain or nerves, in which objects are believed to be seen and sensations experienced; the object or sensation thus erroneously perceived.—**hallucinatory,** hal·lū'si·na·to·ri, *a.* Partaking of hallucination.

hallux, hal'uks, *n.* [Erroneous form, for L. *hallex,* the thumb or great toe.] The great toe or corresponding digit of an animal; the hind toe of a bird.

halm, ham, *n.* Same as *Haulm.*

halo, hā'lō, *n.* pl. **halos, haloes,** hā'lōz, [Gr. *halōs,* a round floor, the sun's disk, a halo.] A luminous ring, either white or colored, appearing round the sun or moon; any circle of light, as the glory round the head of saints; a colored circle round the nipple; an ideal glory investing an object (a *halo* of romance).—*v.i.,* To form itself into a halo.—*v.t.* To surround with a halo.

halogen, hal'o·jen, *n.* [Gr. *hals,* salt, and root *gen,* to produce.] *Chem.* a name given to substances (such as chlorine or iodine) which form compounds of a saline nature by their union with metals.—**halogenous,** ha·loj'e·nus, *a.* Having the nature of halogens.

haloid, hal'oid, *a.* [Gr. *hals,* sea-salt, and *eidos,* resemblance.] *Chem.* resembling common salt in composition; formed by the combination of a halogen and a metal; common salt is a *haloid salt.*—*n.* A haloid salt.

halophyte, hal'o·fīt, *n.* [Gr. *hals, halos,* the sea, salt, and *phyton,* a plant.] One of the plants which inhabit salt marshes, and by combustion yield barilla or Spanish soda.

halt, halt, *v.i.* [A.Sax. *healtian,* to be lame, *healt,* lame, from Icel. *haltr,* Dan. and Sw. *halt,* Goth. *halts,* lame; Dan. and Sw. *halte,* to limp. In sense of to stop in marching, probably of German origin, from *halten,* E. to *hold.*] To limp; to be lame; to limp or be defective in regard to meter, versification, or connection of ideas; to stop in marching or walking; to cease to advance; to stand in doubt whether to proceed or what to do; to hesitate. —*v.t.* To stop; to cause to cease marching.—*a.* Lame; not able to walk without limping.—*n.* Lameness; a limp; a stopping; a stop in walking or marching.—**halter,** hal'têr, *n.* One who halts or limps.— **haltingly,** hal'ting·li, *adv.* In a halting manner.

halter, hal'têr, *n.* [A.Sax. *hælfter,* headstall, noose = D.L.G. and G. *halfter;* origin doubtful.] A cord or strap forming a headstall for leading or confining a horse or other animal; a rope specially intended for hanging malefactors.—*v.t.* To put a halter on.

halteres, hal·tē'rēz, *n. pl.* [Gr. *haltēres,* weights held while leaping, from *hallomai,* to leap.] The balancers of insects; the aborted second pair of wings.

halve, häv, *v.t.*—*halved, halving.* [From *half.*] To divide into two halves or equal parts; to join (timbers) by lapping or letting into each other.—**halves,** hävz, *n. pl.* of *half.*

halyard, hal'yârd, *n.* [*Hale* or *haul,* and *yard.*] *Naut.* a rope or tackle for hoisting and lowering sails, yards, gaffs, etc.; halliard.

ham, ham, *n.* [A.Sax. *ham, hamm,* the ham = D. *ham,* Icel. *höm,* G. *hamme,* a ham.] The inner bend or hind part of the knee; the thigh of an animal, particularly of a hog, salted and cured; an unskilled actor; a showoff.—*v.t.* To overplay a scene in a play; overact (to *ham* it up.)

hamstring, ham'string, *n.* One of the tendons of the ham.—*v.t.* To lame or disable by cutting the tendons of the ham; to make ineffective.—**hamburger,** ham'bêr·

gêr, *n.* [From *Hamburg steak.*] Ground beef; a sandwich of cooked ground beef placed between halves of a bun.

hamadryad, ham'a·dri·ad, *n.* [Gr. *hamadryas,* from *hama,* together, and *drys,* a tree.] In classical mythology a wood nymph, fabled to live and die with the tree to which she was attached.

hamal, ham'al, *n.* A porter in the Orient.

hame, hām, *n.* [Same as D. *haam,* a hame.] One of two curved pieces of wood or metal in the harness of a draft horse, to which the traces are fastened, and which lie upon the collar or have pads attached to them fitting the horse's neck.

hamite, ham'īt, *n.* A descendant of *Ham;* an Ethiopian.—**hamitic,** ham·it'ik, *a.* Relating to *Ham* or his descendants; appellative of a class of African tongues, comprising Coptic, Ethiopian or Abyssinian, etc.

hamlet, ham'let, *n.* [Dim. of A.Sax. *ham,* dwelling, enclosure; akin *home.*] A small village; a little cluster of houses in the country.

hammer, ham'êr, *n.* [A.Sax. *hamor* = D. *hamer,* G. and Dan. *hammer,* Icel. *hamarr;* root doubtful.] An instrument for driving nails, beating metals, and the like, consisting usually of an iron head, fixed crosswise to a handle; a striking piece in the mechanism of a clock and a piano; that part in the lock of a gun, rifle, etc., which when the trigger is pulled falls with a smart blow, and causes the explosion of the detonating substance in connection with the powder.—*To bring to the hammer,* to sell by auction.—*v.t.* To beat, form, or forge, with a hammer; to contrive by intellectual labor; to excogitate: usually with *out;* to declare bankrupt or defaulting a member of the Stock Exchange.—*v.i.* To strike anything repeatedly, as with a hammer; to work; to labor in contrivance.—**hammerer,** ham'êr·êr, *n.* One who works with a hammer. —**hammerhead,** *n.* The iron head of a hammer; a genus of sharks with a head like a double-headed hammer.

hammock, ham'ok, *n.* [Sp. *hamaca,* a word of West Indian origin.] A kind of hanging bed, consisting of a piece of cloth suspended by cords and hooks.

hamper, ham'pêr, *n.* [Contr. from *hanaper* (which see).] A kind of rude basket or wickerwork receptacle, chiefly used as a case for packing articles.—*v.t.* To put into a hamper.

hamper, ham'pêr, *v.t.* [A nasalized form corresponding to D. *haperen,* to stammer, falter, stick fast; comp. Sc. *hamp,* to stammer; Goth. *hamfs, hanfs,* mutilated.] To impede in motion or progress, or to render progress difficult to; to shackle; to embarrass; to encumber.—*n.* Something that hampers or encumbers; a clog.

hamster, ham'stêr, *n.* [G.] A burrowing animal of the rat family common in Germany, having a short tail and large cheek pouches.

fāte, fär, fâre, fat, fall; mē, met, hêr; pīne, pin; nōte, not, mŏve; tūbe, tub, bull; oil, pound.

hamstring, *n.* and *v.t.* See HAM.

hamulus, ham′ū‧lus, *n.* [L., a little hook, dim. of *hamus*, a hook.] A little hook; a hooklike process in animals and plants.

hanaper, han′a‧pẽr, *n.* [L.L. *hanaperium*, lit. a receptacle for cups, from L.L. *hanapus*, a cup, from O.H.G. *hnap*, A. Sax. *hnaep*, a cup; hence *hamper*, *n.*] A kind of basket used in early days by the kings of England for holding and carrying with them their money; the king's treasury.—*Clerk of the hanaper.*

hand, hand, *n.* [Common in similar forms, to all the Teutonic tongues; allied to Goth. *hinthan*, to capture; O.E. *hent*, to seize; perhaps also *hunt. Handsel, handle, handy, handsome* are derivatives.] The extremity of the arm, consisting of the palm and fingers, connected with the arm at the wrist; the corresponding member in certain of the lower animals; a measure of 4 inches; a palm; applied chiefly to horses; side or direction, either right or left (on the one *hand* or the other); handiwork; style of penmanship; power of performance; skill; agency; part in performing (to have a *hand* in mischief); possession; power (in the *hands* of the owner); that which performs the office of the hand or of a finger in pointing (the *hands* of a clock); a male or female in relation to an employer; a person employed on board ship or in factories; a person with some special faculty or ability (a good *hand* at a speech); in *card playing*, the cards held by a single player; one of the players.— *At hand*, near in time or place; within reach or not far distant.—*At first hand*, from the producer or seller directly; *at second hand*, or simply *second hand*, from an intermediate purchaser; old or used.—*By hand*, with the hands and not by the instrumentality of tools, etc.—*For one's own hand*, on one's own account; for one's self.—*From hand to hand*, from one person to another.— *In hand*, in ready money; in possession; in the state of preparation or execution.—*Off hand*, without hesitation or difficulty; without previous preparation.—*Off one's hands*, out of one's care or attention; ended.— *On hand*, in present possession.— *On one's hands*, under one's care or management; as a burden upon one.—*Out of hand*, at once; directly; without delay or hesitation; off one's hands.—*To one's hand*, already prepared; ready to be received.—*Under one's hand*, with the proper writing or signature of the name.—*Hand in hand*, with hands mutually clasped: hence, in union; conjointly; unitedly.—*Hand to hand*, in close union; close fight.—*Hand to mouth*, as want requires; without making previous provision or having an abundant previous supply.—*Hands off!* keep off; forbear; refrain from blows.— *Clean hands*, innocence; freedom from guilt.—*To ask the hand of*, to ask in marriage.—*To be hand and glove with*, to be intimate and familiar, as

friends or associates.—*To bear a hand* (*naut.*), to give assistance quickly; to hasten.—*To change hands*, to change owners.—*To come to hand*, to be received; to come within one's reach.—*To have one's hands full*, to be fully occupied; to have a great deal to do.—*To lay hands on*, to seize; to assault.—*Laying on of hands*, a ceremony used in consecrating one to office.—*To lend a hand*, to give assistance.—*To set the hand to*, to engage in; to undertake.—*To shake hands*, to clasp the right hand mutually (with or without a shake), as a greeting or in token of friendship or reconciliation.—*To strike hands*, to . make a contract or to become surety for another's debt or good behavior (O.T.).—*To take by the hand*, to take under one's protection. —*To take in hand*, to attempt; to undertake; to seize and deal with (a person).—*To wash one's hands of*, to have nothing more to do with; to renounce all connection with or interest in.—*v.t.* To give or transmit with the hand (*hand* me a book); to lead, guide, and lift with the hand; to conduct.—*To hand down*, to transmit in succession, as from father to son, or from predecessor to successor.—*a.* Belonging to or used by the hand: much used in composition for that which is manageable or wrought by the hand.—**handbarrow,** *n.* A kind of litter or stretcher, with handles at each end, carried between two persons.—**handbill,** *n.* A printed paper or sheet to be circulated for the purpose of making some public announcement.—**handbook,** *n.* A small book or treatise such as may be easily held in the hand; an establishment where bets are accepted on horse races.—**handbreadth,** *n.* A space equal to the breadth of the hand; a palm.—**handcart,** *n.* A cart drawn or pushed by hand.— **handcuff,** hand′kuf, *n.* [Modified from A.Sax. *handcops—hand*, the hand, *cops*, a fetter.] A manacle or fastening for the hand.—*v.t.* To put a handcuff on; to manacle.—**handed,** han′ded, *a.* Having a hand possessed of any peculiar property: used especially in compounds (*right-handed*, *left-handed*, empty-*handed*, full-*handed*, etc.).—**handfasting,** *n.* An irregular marriage by agreement or mutual pledge.—**handful,** hand′ful, *n.* As much as the hand will grasp or contain; a small quantity or number.—**hand glass,** *n.* Hort. a glass used for placing over plants to protect them or forward growth.— **hand grenade,** *n.* A grenade to be thrown by the hand.—**handmade,** *a.* Manufactured by the hand and not by a machine.—**hand organ,** *n.* A portable or barrel organ.—**handrail,** hand′rāl, *n.* A rail or railing to hold by.—**handsaw,** *n.* A saw to be used with the hand.—**handspike,** hand′-spīk, *n.* A bar used as a lever for various purposes, as in raising weights, heaving about a windlass, etc.—**handwork,** *n.* Work done by the hands.—**handwrite,**† hand′rīt, *v.t.* To express in handwriting; to

write out.—**handwriting,** hand′rīt‧-ing, *n.* The cast of writing peculiar to each person; chirography; writing.

handicap, han′di‧kap, *n.* [For *hand i′ cap*, *hand in the cap*, the allusion being to drawing a lot out of a cap, from the fairness of both principles.] In sports, an advantage given to inferior competitors, or a disadvantage placed upon superior competitors, to equalize the chances of winning; a disadvantage that makes success more difficult.—*v.t.*—*handicapped, handicapping.* To place at a disadvantage; to assign handicaps to; to put a handicap on; to equalize by a handicap.—**handicapper,** han′di‧kap‧ẽr, *n.* One who handicaps.

handicraft, han′di‧kraft, *n.* [Equivalent to *hand-craft*, the *i* representing old prefix *ge*, as in *handiwork*.] Manual occupation; work performed by the hand.—**handicraftsman,** han′-di‧krafts‧man, *n.* A man employed in manual occupation; an artisan.

handiwork, han′di‧wẽrk, *n.* [A.Sax. *handgeweorc*, from *hand*, the hand, and *geweorc* = *weorc*, work, with prefix *ge*.] Work done by the hands; hence, the work or deed of any person.

handkerchief, hang′kẽr‧chẽf, *n.* [*Hand* and *kerchief.* KERCHIEF.] A piece of cloth, usually silk, linen, or cotton, carried about the person for wiping the face, hands, etc.; a similar piece worn round the neck.

handle, han′dl, *v.t.*—**handled,** *handling.* [A.Sax. *handlian*, to handle, a kind of freq. from *hand* = D. *handelen*, Dan. *handle*, Icel. *höndla*, G. *handeln*.] To bring the hand or hands in frequent contact with; to finger; to touch; to feel; to manage, ply, or wield; to treat of or deal with, as a person or a topic.—*v.i.* To use the hands; to feel with the hands.—*n.* That part of a thing which is intended to be grasped by the hand in using or moving it; the instrument or means of effecting a purpose.—*To give a handle*, to furnish an occasion. —*A handle to one's name*, a title (*colloq.*).—**handler,** han′dlẽr, *n.* One who handles.—**handling,** han′dling, *n.* A touching or using by the hand; a treating in discussion; dealing; action.

handsel, hansel, hand′sel, han′sel, *n.* [From *hand*, and stem *sell*, *sale*; Icel. *handsal* (from *hand*, and *sal*, sale), a bargain by shaking hands; Dan. *handsel*, hansel, earnest.] An earnest, or earnest penny; a sale, gift, or using, which is regarded as the first of a series; the first money received for the sale of goods.—*v.t.* To give a handsel to; to use or do for the first time.

handsome, hand′sum, *a.* [From *hand*, and term. *-some* = D. *handzaam*, tractable, serviceable, mild; G. *handsam*, convenient, favorable.] Possessing a form agreeable to the eye or to correct taste; having a certain share of beauty along with dignity; having symmetry of parts; well formed; shapely; becoming; appropriate; ample or large (a *handsome* fortune); characterized by or expressive of liberality or generosity.—**handsome-ly,** hand′sum•li, *adv.* In a handsome manner. — **handsomeness,** hand′-sum•nes, *n.*

handy, han′di, *a.* [From *hand*; comp. the D. and L.G. *handig*, handy.] Skilled to use the hands with ease; dexterous; ready; adroit; ready to the hand; near; convenient.—**hand-ily,** han′di•li, *adv.* In a handy manner.—**handiness,** han′di•nes, *n.*

hang, hang, *v.t.* pret. & pp. *hung* or *hanged* (the latter being obsolete except in sense to put to death by the rope). [A.Sax. *hangian*, to hang or be suspended, and *hón* (contracted for *hahan*), pret. *heng*, pp. *hangen*, to suspend; O.H.G. *hahan*, G. *hangen*, *hangen*, Dan. *hænge*, Icel. *hanga*, *hengja*. Goth. *hahan*, to suspend, to hang. Akin *hank*, *hanker*, *hinge*.] To suspend; to fasten to some elevated point without support from below: often with *up*; to put to death by suspending by the neck; to fit up so as to allow of free motion (a door, a gate, etc.); to cover, furnish, or decorate by anything suspended (to *hang* an apartment with curtains); to cause or suffer to assume a droop-ing attitude (to *hang* the head).—*To hang fire*, to be slow in communicat-ing fire through the vent to the charge: said of a gun; hence, to hesitate or be slow in acting; to be slow in execution.—*To hang out*, to suspend in open view; to display; to suspend in the open air.—*To hang up*, to suspend; to keep or suffer to remain undecided.—*v.i.* To be sus-pended; to be sustained wholly or partly by something above; to dangle; to depend; to bend forward or downward; to lean or incline; to be attached to or connected with in various ways; to hover; to impend (dangers *hang* over us); to linger, lounge, loiter; to incline; to have a steep declivity; to be put to death by suspension from the neck.—*To hang back*, to halt; to incline to retire; to go reluctantly forward.—*To hang on* or *upon*, to weigh upon; to drag; to rest; to continue (sleep *hung on* his eyelids); to be dependent on; to regard with the closest attention (he *hung* upon the speaker's words). —*To hang together*, to be closely united; to be self-consistent.—*n.* The way a thing hangs; slope or de-clivity; inclination, bent, or tenden-cy.—**hangdog,** *n.* A base and de-graded character, fit only to be the hangman of dogs.—*a.* Of or per-taining to a hangdog; having a low, degraded, or blackguard-like ap-pearance.—**hanger,** hang′er, *n.* One who hangs; a short broad sword, incurvated at the point, which was suspended from the girdle; that from which something is hung.— **hanger-on,** *n.* pl. **hangers-on.** One who hangs on or sticks to a person, a place, society, etc.; a parasite; a dependent.—**hanging,** hang′ing, *a.* Such as to incur punishment by the halter (a *hanging* matter).—*n.* Death by suspension; what is hung up to drape a room, as tapestry or the like: used chiefly in the plural.—

hangman, hang′man, *n.* One who hangs another.

hangar, hang′ar, *n.* [Fr. *hangar*, a shed.] A shed for housing airplanes.

hangnail, hang′nāl, *n.* [Corruption of *agnail*.] A tiny strip of skin peeling loose at the fingernail base.

hank, hangk, *n.* [Same as Icel. *hönk*, a hank or skein; Dan. *hank*, a hook, a clasp; Sw. *hank*, a band; akin to *hang*.] A parcel consisting of two or more skeins of yarn or thread tied together; *naut.* a ring of wood, rope, or iron, fixed to a stay to confine the staysails.

hanker, hang′ker, *v.i.* [Allied to D. *hunkeren*, to desire, to long after; probably to *hang*.] To long for; to be uneasily desirous.—**hankering,** hang′-ker•ing, *n.*

hanky-panky, hang′ki pang′ki, *n.* [From *hocus-pocus*, pretended incan-tation of jugglers.] Trickery; mis-chief; questionable activity.

Hansard, han′serd, *n.* The published debates of the British Parliament, originally issued by the Messrs. *Hansard.*

hanse, hans, *n.* [G. *hanse*, *hansa*, league.] A league; a confederacy.— **Hanse, Hanseatic,** han•sē•at′ik, *a.* Of or pertaining to a confederacy of commercial cities, associated together as early as the twelfth century; the name *Hanse towns* is still applied to Lübeck, Hamburg, and Bremen.

hansom, hansom cab, han′sum, *n.* A two-wheeled cab, so named after the inventor.

hap, hap, *n.* [Icel. *happ*, good fortune, luck; comp. A.Sax. *gehæp*, fit; D. *happen*, to snatch at; seen also in *mishap*, *perhaps*.] Chance; accident; casual event; vicissitude.—*v.i.* To happen; to befall; to come by chance. —**haphazard,** *n.* Chance; accident. —**hapless,** hap′les, *a.*—**happen,** hap′-n, *v.i.* [From *hap*.] To be or be brought about unexpectedly or by chance; to chance; to take place; to occur.—*To happen on*, to meet with; to fall or light upon.—**happily,** hap′-i•li, *adv.* In a happy manner, state, or circumstance.—**happiness,** hap′-i•nes, *n.* The state or quality of being happy; felicity; contentedness along with actual pleasure; good fortune.—**happy,** hap′i, *a.* [From *hap*.] Contented in mind; highly pleased; satisfied; fortunate; suc-cessful; secure of good; bringing or attended with good fortune; pros-perous; favorable; well suited for a purpose or occasion; well devised; felicitous; living in concord.

hara-kiri, hä′ra-kē′ri, *n.* [Jap. *hara*, belly, and *kiri*, cutting.] A traditional Japanese method of suicide, ceremo-nially performed by slashing across the abdomen with a dagger and then twisting it upward; simultaneously, the second, previously selected by the suicide, swings a sword on his friend's neck. Originally it was volun-tarily practiced by nobles defeated in battle, by men as a mark of loyalty to a deceased noble, by men who had lost face or prestige; and obligatorily practiced, as an honor-able way out, by men guilty of

treachery or disloyalty to the mikado. It is now practiced chiefly as a mark of protest against a national policy.

harangue, ha•rang′, *n.* [Fr. *harangue* =Pr. *arengua*, It. *aringa*, a harangue, lit. a speech made to a ring, or crowd, of people.] A loud address to a multitude; a popular oration; a bombastic or pompous address; a tirade or declamation.—*v.i.* ha-rangued, haranguing. To make a harangue; to make a bombastic or pretentious speech.—*v.t.* To address by a harangue.—**haranguer,** ha-rang′er, *n.* One who harangues.

harass, har′as, *v.t.* [Fr. *harasser*; probably connected with Fr. *harier*, to harry; vex; *harer*, to set a dog on.] To weary, fatigue, or tire with bodily labor; to weary with importunity, care, or perplexity; to perplex; to annoy by repeated attacks.—*n.*† Dis-tress; devastation.—**harasser,** har′-as•er, *n.* One who harasses.—**har-assment,** har′as•ment, *n.* The act of harassing or state of being harassed.

harbinger, här′bin•jer, *n.* [O.E. *har-begier*, *harbergeour*, *harbesher*, etc., one who provides harborage or lodg-ing, a harbinger; for the insertion of the *n* compare *messenger*, *passenger*. HARBOR.] One who went before to provide lodgings and other accom-modations; hence, a forerunner; a precursor; that which precedes and gives notice of the expected arrival of something else.—*v.t.* To precede as harbinger; to presage or prede-termine, as a harbinger.

harbor, här′ber, *n.* [Same as L.G. *harbarge*, D. *herberg*, Icel. *herbergi*, lit. army-shelter, the elements being the same as A.Sax. *here*, an army, and *beorgan*, *bergan*, to shelter or protect. BOROUGH.] A place of shelter, protection, or refuge; a port or haven for ships.—*v.t.* To shelter or take under protection; to protect; to entertain or cherish in the mind (to *harbor* malice).—*v.i.* To lodge or abide for a time for shelter or pro-tection; to take shelter.—**harborage,** här′ber•āj, *n.* State of being har-bored; shelter; lodgment.—**har-borer,** här′ber•er, *a.* One who harbors.—**harborless,** här′ber•les, *a.* Without a harbor; destitute of shel-ter.—**harbor master,** *n.* An officer who attends to the berthing, etc., of ships in a harbor.

hard, härd, *a.* [A.Sax. *heard*=Goth. *hardus*, Icel. *hardr*, Dan. *haard*, D. *hard*, G. *hart*; cog. Gr. *kratos*, *kartos*, strength (as in *aristocrat*, *democrat*, etc.). Hence *hardy*.] Not easily penetrated or separated into parts; not yielding to pressure; applied to material bodies, and opposed to *soft*; difficult to the understanding; not easy to the intellect; difficult of accomplishment; not easy to be done or executed; laborious; fatiguing; difficult to endure; oppressive; se-vere; cruel; distressing; painful; un-feeling; insensible; harsh; obdurate; exacting; avaricious; grasping; harsh or abusive (*hard* words); pinching with cold; rigorous (a *hard* winter); austere; rough; acid or sour (*hard* cider); forced; constrained; unnatural; coarse; unpalatable, or scanty (*hard* fare); *gram.* applied to the consonants (also called *surd*) *f*, *k*, *p*, *s*, *t*, and the sound of *th* in *thin*, and also to the sound of *c* as in *corn* and *g* as in *get*, as distinguished from the sounds in *city* and *gin*; applied to water not very suitable for washing from holding salts of lime or magnesia in solution.—*Hard cash*, gold or silver coin, as distinguished from paper money. (*Colloq.*)—*adv.* Close; near (*hard by*); with urgency; vehemently; vigorously; energetically; violently; with great force; with difficulty or labor.—*To die hard*, to die, as it were, reluctantly, and after a struggle for life; to die unrepentant. —*Hard up*, in want of money; needy; without resources.—*Hard up for*, having difficulty in getting anything; at a loss how to find.—*Hard a-weather! hard a-port!* etc., *naut.* a direction for the helm to be turned as much as possible to the weather-side, the port-side, etc.—**harden**, här'dn, *v.t.* To make hard or more hard; to confirm in effrontery, obstinacy, wickedness, opposition, or enmity; to make insensible or unfeeling; to make firm; to inure.—*v.i.* To become hard or more hard; to acquire solidity or mere compactness; to become unfeeling; to become inured.—**hardener**, här'dn·ér, *n.* One who or that which hardens.— **hard-featured**, *a.* Having a hard or stern face.—**hard-favored**, *a.* Having coarse features; harsh of countenance.—**hardfisted, hardhanded**, *a.* Having hard hands; closefisted; covetous. — **hardheaded**, *a.* Shrewd; clearheaded and firm.—**hardhearted**, *a.* Pitiless; unfeeling; inhuman; inexorable.—**hard landing**, *n.* The deliberate destruction of an experimental space capsule upon impact with a predetermined target.—**hardly**, härd'li, *adv.* Not easily; severely; harshly; scarcely; barely; not quite. —**hardness**, härd'nes, *n.* The state or quality of being hard; *mineral.*, the capacity of a substance to scratch another or be scratched by another. —**hardpan**, *n. Agri.* the name given to a hard stratum of earth below the soil proper.—**hardship**, härd'ship, *n.* Something hard, oppressive, toilsome, distressing; want or privation; grievance.—**hardtack**, härd'tak, *n.* A saltless biscuit made of flour and water.—**hardware**, härd·wâr, *n.* Articles of iron or other metal, as pots, kettles, saws, knives, etc.—**hardwood**, härd'wud, *n.* Any wood of a close and solid texture, as beech, oak, ash, maple, ebony, etc.

hards, härdz, *n. pl.* [Also written *hurds*; from A.Sax. *heordan* (pl.), hards, tow; Icel. *hörr*, flax; same root as L. *caro*, to card, *carduus*, thistle, *coma*, hair; perhaps E. *hair*.] The refuse or coarse part of flax or wool.

hardy, här'di, *a.* [Fr. *hardi*, bold, daring, properly the pp. of the old verb *hardir*, to make bold, from O.H.G. *hartjan*, from *hart* (E. *hard*), hard, bold. HARD.] Bold; brave; stout; daring; resolute; intrepid;

confident; full of assurance; inured to fatigue; proof against hardship; capable of bearing exposure to cold weather (a *hardy* plant).—**hardihood**, här'di·hud, *n.* Boldness; bravery; intrepidity; venturesomeness; audacity.—**hardily**, här'di·li, *adv.* In a hardy manner.—**hardiness**, här'di·nes, *n.* The state or quality of being hardy.

hare, hâr, *n.* [A.Sax. *hara* = Dan. and Sw. *hare*, Icel. *héri*, D. *haas*, G. *hase*; probably allied to Skr. *çaça*, a hare, from *çaç*, to jump.] A mammal of the genus *Lepus*, with long ears, a short tail, soft hair, a divided upper lip, and long hind legs, often hunted for sport or for its flesh, which is excellent food.—**harebell**, hâr'bel, *n.* A species of the campanula or bellflower, also termed the common bellflower and Scottish bluebell; also applied in many districts to the wild hyacinth.—**harebrained**, *a.* [Comp. 'mad as a March *hare*'.] Giddy; volatile; heedless.—**harelip**, *n.* A malformation of the lip consisting of a fissure or vertical division of one or both lips, sometimes extending also to the palate.

harem, hâ'rem, *n.* [Ar. *harām*, anything prohibited, from *hharram*, to prohibit.] In a Muslim household, a group of women who are the wives and concubines of one man; the apartments occupied by these women.

haricot, har'i·kō, *n.* [Fr., a ragout; O.Fr. *harigoter*, to mince, *harigote*, a morsel; *haricot*-bean = ragout-bean.] A kind of ragout of meat and roots; the kidney bean or French bean (in this sense short for haricot bean).

hark, härk, *v.i.* [Contr. from *hearken*.] To listen; to hearken: now only used in the imperative.—*Hark!* a hunting cry used with various adjuncts to stimulate or direct the hounds.—

harken, HEARKEN.

harl, härl, *n.* [Probably = *hardle*, from *hards*.] A filament, as of flax or hemp; a barb of one of the feathers from a peacock's tail, used in dressing fly hooks.

Harlequin, här'le·kwin, *n.* [Fr. *harlequin, arlequin*; O.Fr. *hellequin, hierlekin*, etc.; origin quite uncertain.] A performer in a pantomime, masked, dressed in tight particolored clothes, covered with spangles, and armed with a magic wand or sword; [*not. cap.*] a buffoon in general.— **harlequinade**, här'le·kwin·ād", *n.* The portion of a pantomime in which the harlequin and clown play the principal parts.

harlot, här'lot, *n.* [O.Fr. *harlot, herlot*, Pr. *arlot*, Sp. *arlote*, It. *arlotto*, a glutton, a lazy good-for-nothing, a word of uncertain origin; comp. W. *herlawd*, a stripling, *herlodes*, a damsel.] A woman who prostitutes her body for hire; a prostitute.—**harlotry**, här'lot·ri, *n.* A trade or practice of prostitution.

harm, härm, *n.* [A.Sax. *hearm*, harm, evil, grief = Dan., Sw., and G. *harm*, grief, offense; Icel. *harmr*; comp. Skr. *çram*, to weary.] Physical or material injury; hurt; damage; detriment; moral wrong; evil; mischief;

wickedness.—*v.t.* To hurt; to injure; to damage.—**harmful**, härm'ful, *a.* Full of harm; hurtful; injurious; noxious. — **harmfully**, härm'ful·li, *adv.* In a harmful manner.—**harmfulness**, härm'ful·nes, *n.*—**harmless**, härm'les, *a.* Free from harm; uninjured; free from power or disposition to harm; not injurious; innocuous; inoffensive.—**harmlessly**, härm'les·li, *adv.* In a harmless manner.—**harmlessness**, härm'les·nes, *n.*

harmattan, här·mat'tan, *n.* [Arabic name.] An extremely dry and hot wind which blows periodically from the interior parts of Africa toward the Atlantic Ocean.

harmony, här'mo·ni, *n.* [L. and Gr. *harmonia*, from Gr. *harmos*, a suiting or fitting together a joint, from *arō*, to fit, to adapt, the same root being seen in E. *ārm*.] The just adaptation of parts to each other, in any system or combination of things, or in things intended to form a connected whole; concord; consonance; concord or agreement in facts, views, sentiments, manners, interests, and the like; peace and friendship; *mus.* musical concord; the accordance of two or more sounds, or that union of different sounds which pleases the ear, or a succession of such sounds called chords; the science which treats of such sounds; the agreement or consistency of the accounts of the first three (synoptic) Gospels with the fourth by St. John.—**harmonic**, här·mon'ik, *a.* Relating to harmony or music; concordant; musical; harmonious.—*Acoustics*, a secondary tone heard along with a fundamental tone, produced by secondary or partial vibrations.—*Harmonical proportion*, *math.* the relation between four quantities when the first is to the fourth as the difference between the first and second is to the difference between the third and fourth; also a similar relation between three quantities.—*Harmonical series*, a series of numbers in continued harmonical proportion.—*Harmonic triad, mus.* the chord of a note consisting of its third and perfect fifth, or in other words, the common chord.—*n. Mus.* a secondary and less distinct tone which accompanies any principal and apparently simple tone.—**harmonica**, här·mon'i·ka, *n.* A collection of musical glass goblets; also an instrument, the tones of which are produced by striking rods or plates of glass or metal with hammers; a mouth organ.—**harmonically**, här·mon'i·kal·li, *adv.* In a harmonic manner.—**harmonicon**, här·mon'i·kon, *n.* A large barrel organ, containing, in addition to the common pipes, others to imitate the different wind instruments, and an apparatus to produce the effects of drums, triangles, cymbals, etc.; also, a toy musical instrument with free reeds blown by the mouth.—**harmonics**, här·mon'iks, *n.* The doctrine or science of musical sounds.—**harmonious**, här·mō'ni·us, *a.* Exhibiting or characterized by harmony.—**harmoniously**, här·mō'ni·us·li, *adv.* In a

ch, *chain*; *ch*, Sc. lo*ch*; g, *go*; j, *job*; ng, si*ng*; TH, *then*; th, *thin*; w, *wig*; hw, *whig*; zh, a*z*ure.

harmonious manner.—**harmoniousness**, här·mō′ni·us·nes, n.—**harmonist**, här′mon·ist n. One who harmonizes; one skilled in the principles of harmony; a writer of harmony.—**harmonium**, här·mō′ni·um, n. A musical instrument resembling a small organ, and much used as a substitute for it, the tones of which are produced by the forcing of air through free reeds.—**harmonization**, här′mon·i·zā″shon, n. The act of harmonizing. — **harmonize**, här′mon·īz, v.i.—harmonized, harmonizing. To unite harmoniously or in harmony; to be in peace and friendship; to agree in action, effect, sense, or purport; to be musically harmonious.—v.t. To bring to be harmonious; to cause to agree; to show the harmony or agreement of; to reconcile the contradictions between; mus. to combine according to the laws of counterpoint; to set accompanying parts to, as to an air or melody.—**harmonizer**, här′mon·i·zėr, n. One who harmonizes; a harmonist.

harness, här′nes, n. [W. harnais, haiarnaez, harness, from haiarn, iron. IRON.] A person's armor and military furniture; the gear or tackle by which a horse or other animal is yoked and made to work; the apparatus in a loom by which the sets of warp thread are shifted alternately.

harp, härp, n. [A.Sax. hearpe=D. harp, Icel. harpa, Dan. harpe, Gr. harfe, a harp; perhaps same root as L. carpo, to pluck or twitch.] A stringed musical instrument of great antiquity, now usually nearly triangular in form, with wire strings stretched from the upper part to one of the sides, played with both hands while standing upright, the strings being struck or pulled by fingers and thumb.—v.i. To play on the harp; to dwell on a subject tiresomely and vexatiously: usually with on or upon. —To harp on one string, to dwell too exclusively upon one subject, so as to weary or annoy the hearers.—**harper**, **harpist**, här′pėr, här′pist, n.

harpoon, här·pön′, n. [Fr. harpon, a harpoon, from harper, to clutch, from harpe, a claw, a hook, from Gr. harpagē, a hook, harpazō, to seize.] A spear or javelin used to strike and kill whales and large fish.—v.t. To strike with a harpoon.—**harpooner**, här·pö′nėr, n. One who uses a harpoon.

harpsichord, härp′si·kord, n. [From O.Fr. harpechorde, It. arpicordo—harp and chord.] A keyboard stringed instrument of the 15th century still used in concert, having strings which are plucked with quills.

harpy, här′pi, n. [Fr. harpie, from L. harpyia, Gr. harpuia, from root of harpazō, to seize.] [cap.] Class. mythol., the name given to three foul monsters having the face of a woman and the body of a bird, with feet and fingers armed with sharp claws, who were sent to punish Phineus for his cruelty to his children.—**harpy eagle**, n. A large and very powerful raptorial bird of Mexico and South America.

harquebus, harquebuse, harquebuss, här′kwē·bus. See ARQUEBUS.

harridan, har′i·dan, n. [Akin to Fr. haridelle, Prov. Fr. hardele, harin, a wornout horse, a jade.] A hag; an odious old woman; a vixenish woman; a trollop.

harrier, har′i·ėr, n. [From hare.] A small kind of dog of the hound species employed in hunting the hare; also, a cross-country runner.

harrier, har′i·ėr, n. [A.Sax. hergian, to afflict with an army, to ravage.] One who pillages; name for several species of hawks which strike their prey upon the ground and generally fly very low.

Harrovian, ha·rō′vi·an, a. Of or pertaining to Harrow, an exclusive boys' school in England.—n. One who attends, or is a graduate of, Harrow.

harrow, har′ō, n. [Same word as Dan. harve, Sw. harf, a harrow; akin to D. hark, G. harke, a rake.] An agricultural implement, usually formed of pieces of timber or metal crossing each other, and set with iron teeth, called tines, used for covering seed when sown, etc.—v.t. To draw a harrow over; fig. to lacerate (the feelings); to torment; to harass.—**harrower**, har′ō·ėr, n. One who harrows.—**harrowing**, har′ō·ing, a. Causing acute distress to the mind.

harry, har′i, v.t.—harried, harrying. [A.Sax. hergian, to ravage, from here (genit. herges), an army; Icel. herja, to lay waste, to oppress; Dan. hærge, hærje, G. (ver) heeren, to ravage. Akin herring, herald.] To pillage; to plunder; to rob; to harass‡.

harsh, härsh, a. [O.E. and Sc. harsk, harsh, acid; same as Dan. and O.Sw. harsk, rancid; G. harsch, harsh, rough; root doubtful; perhaps akin to hard.] Grating, either to the touch, to the taste, or to the ear; austere; crabbed; morose; rough; rude; rigorous; severe.—**harshen**, här′shn, v.t. To render harsh.—**harshly**, härsh′li, adv. In a harsh manner.—**harshness**, härsh′nes, n.

harslet, härs′let, n. See HASLET.

hart, härt, n. [A.Sax. heort=L.G. and D. hert, Dan. hiort, Sw. kjort, Icel. hjörtr, G. hirsch, stag; lit. horned animal; allied to Gr. keras, L. cornu, a horn. HORN.] A stag or male deer, especially when he has passed his fifth year, and the surroyal or crown antler is formed.—**hartshorn**, harts′horn, n. The horn of the hart or stag; an ammoniacal preparation obtained from the horn, and used medicinally; solution of ammonia.

hartal, här′täl, n. [Hindi, var. of hattāl.] An organized cessation of business to protest against government policy or action; noncooperation.

hartebeest, här′te·bēst, härt′bēst, n. [Dutch.] An antelope common in South Africa.

harum-scarum, hâ′rum·skâ′rum, a. [Perhaps from O.E. hare, to fright, or from hare, the animal, and scare.] Harebrained; unsettled; giddy; rash. —n. A giddy, harebrained, or rash person. (Colloq.)

haruspice, haruspicy. See ARUSPEX.

harvest, här′vest, n. [A.Sax. haerfest =O.Fris. harvest, G. herbst, D. herfst, Icel. haust, Sw. and Dan. höst, autumn, harvest; cognate with Gr. karpos, fruit, L. carpo, to pluck.] The season of gathering a crop of any kind; the time of reaping and gathering corn and other grain; that which is reaped and gathered in; the product of any labor; gain; result; effect; consequence.—v.t. To reap or gather (corn and fruits).—**harvest bug**, n. A species of tick which infests the skin in the autumn.—**harvester**, här′ves·tėr, n. One who or that which harvests; a mower; a reaper.—**harvest home**, n. The bringing home of the harvest; the harvest feast.—**harvest moon**, n. The full moon at the time of harvest, or about the autumnal equinox, when it rises nearly at the same hour for several days.

has, haz. The 3rd pers. sing. pres. of the verb have.—**has-been**, haz′-bin, n. One who has had his day; that which has passed its usefulness. (Colloq.)

hash, hash, v.t. [Fr. hacher, E. to hack. HACK.] To chop into small pieces; to talk over again a previous conversation (to hash it over).—n. Food previously cooked, as meat and potatoes, chopped up and cooked again; a restating of facts already well discussed (making a hash of them); a jumble; a hodgepodge.

hashish, hash′ēsh, n. A narcotic plant of Asia, similar to marijuana, the dried leaves of which are smoked in cigarettes.

haslet, has′let, n. [For hastelet, from Fr. hastille, the pluck of an animal, lit. a little roast, from haste, a spit, L. hasta, a spear.] The cooked heart, liver, etc., of a hog.

hasp, hasp, n. [A.Sax. hæpse, the hook of a hinge=Icel. hespa, G. haspe, häspe, a fastening; Dan. haspe, a hasp, a reel.] A clasp that passes over a staple to be fastened by a padlock; a metal hook for fastening a door; the fourth part of a spindle (of yarn).—v.t. To shut or fasten with a hasp.

hassle, has′l, n. An argument; a mix-up. (Slang)

hassock, has′ok, n. [Origin doubtful; comp. W. hesg, sedge, also Sw. hwass, rushes.] A thick mat or hard cushion on which persons kneel in church; a footstool stuffed with flock or other material.

hastate, has′tāt, a. [L. hastatus, from hasta, a spear.] Spear-shaped; resembling the head of a spear; triangular.

haste, hāst, n. [Same word as G.Sw. and Dan. hast, haste, whence O.Fr. haste, Mod. Fr. hâte, haste; akin to hate.] Celerity of motion; speed; swiftness; dispatch; expedition; applied only to voluntary beings, as men and animals; sudden excitement of passion; quickness; precipitance; the state of being pressed by business; hurry; urgency.—*To make haste*, to hasten; to proceed rapidly.—**haste**, hāst, hāst, hā'sn, *v.t.* [Sw. *hasta*, Dan. *haste*, G. *hasten*, to haste.] To drive or urge forward; to push on; to hurry; to expedite; with *me*, *him*, etc., to make haste; to be speedy or quick.—*v.i.* To move with celerity; to hurry.—**hastener**, hā'sn-ėr, *n.* One that hastens; a metal kitchen stand for keeping in the heat of the fire to a roast while cooking.—**hastily**, hās'-ti-li, *adv.* In a hasty manner.—**hastiness**, hās'ti-nes, *n.* The state or quality of being hasty.—**hasty**, hās'ti, *a.* Moving or acting with haste; quick; speedy: opposed to *slow*; precipitate; rash; inconsiderate; opposed to *deliberate*; irritable; easily excited to wrath; passionate; arising from or indicating passion (*hasty* words); early ripe (O.T.).—**hasty pudding**, *n.* A pudding made of milk and flour boiled quickly together; also, oatmeal and water boiled together; porridge.

hat, hat, *n.* [A.Sax. *hæt*=Dan. *hat* Sw. *hett*, Icel. *hattr*—hat, from a root meaning to cover.] A covering for the head; a headdress with a crown, sides, and continuous brim, made of different materials, and worn by men and women; the dignity of a cardinal: from the broad-brimmed scarlet hat which forms part of a cardinal's dress.—*To give one a hat*, to lift the hat to one.—**hatband**, *n.* A band round a hat.—**hatbox**, *n.* A box for a hat.—**hat tree**, *n.* A rack or stand of various forms furnished with pegs for hanging hats on.—**hatter**, hat'ėr, *n.*

hatch, hach, *v.t.* [Same word as Dan. *hække*, to hatch, or nidificate, from *hæk*, a hatching; Sw. *hächa*, to hatch; G. *hecken*, to hatch, *hecke*, the pairing of birds, a brood; connected with *hack*, from the chipping of the shell.] To produce young from eggs by incubation, or by artificial heat; to contrive or plot; to originate and produce (a scheme, mischief, etc.).—*v.i.* To perform or undergo the process of incubation.—*n.* A brood; as many young birds as are produced at once; the act of hatching.—**hatcher**, hach'ėr, *n.*—**hatchery**, hach'ėr·i, *n.* A place for hatching eggs, especially those of poultry and fish.

hatch, hach, *v.t.* [Fr. *hacher*, to hack, to shade by lines. HACK.] To shade by lines crossing each other in drawing and engraving.—**hatching**, hach'ing, *n.*

hatch, hach, *n.* [A.Sax. *hæc*, a grating; Dan. *hæk*, D. *hek*, a grating; G. *heck*, a fence of laths.] The frame of crossbars laid over the opening in a ship's deck; the cover or a hatchway; the opening in a ship's deck; the hatchway; a similar opening in a floor; a trap door; a half door or a door with an opening over it; a floodgate; a frame or weir in a river for catching fish.—*To be under hatches*, to be in the interior of a ship with the hatches

down.—*Naut.* dead, gone below, opposed to *gone aloft*.—*v.t.* To close with a hatch or hatches.—**hatchway**, hach'wā, *n.* A square or oblong opening in a ship's deck for communication with the interior.

hatchel, hach'el, *n.* [A form of *hackle* or *heckle*.] A hackle or heckle for flax.—*v.t.* To clean by drawing through the teeth of a hatchel; to hackle or heckle.

hatchet, hach'et, *n.* [Fr. *hachette*, from *hacher*, to cut, from G. *hacken*, to cut. HACK.] A small ax with a short handle, used with one hand. —*To take up the hatchet*, to make war; *to bury the hatchet*, to make peace; phrases derived from the customs of the American Indians.— **hatchet-faced**, *a.* Having a thin face with prominent features.

hatchment, hach'ment, *n.* [Corrupted from *achievement*.] The coat of arms of a dead person, placed on the front of a house, in a church, or elsewhere at funerals, notifying the death and the rank of the deceased. Also called *Achievement*.

hatchway, *n.* See HATCH, *n.*

hate, hāt, *v.t.*—*hated, hating.* [A.Sax. *hate*, *hete*, hate, hatred, *hatian*, to hate; D. *haat*, Sw. *hat*, Icel. *hatr*, Goth. *hatis*, hate; Goth. *hatan*, Icel. and Sw. *hata*, D. *haten*, G. *hassen*, to hate.] To dislike greatly or intensely; to have a great aversion to; to detest.—*n.* Great dislike or aversion; hatred.—**hatable, hateable**, hā'ta-bl, *a.* Capable or worthy of being hated; odious.—**hateful**, hāt'ful, *a.* Causing hate; exciting great dislike; odious; detestable; feeling hatred; malevolent.—**hatefully**, hāt'ful·li, *adv.* In a hateful manner.—**hatefulness**, hāt'ful·nes, *n.* The quality of being hateful.—**hater**, hā'tėr, *n.* One that hates.—**hatred**, hā'tred, *a.* [Hate, and suffix *-red*, as in *kindred*=A.Sax. *-raeden*, condition, state.] Great dislike or aversion; hate; detestation; active antipathy.

hauberk, ha'berk, *n.* [O.Fr. *hauberc*, from O.H.G. *halsberg*—*hals*, the throat, and *bergen*, to defend; A.Sax. *healsbeorga*, Icel. *hálsbjörg*, a gorget. *Habergeon* is a diminutive. HAWSE, BOROUGH.] A coat of mail without sleeves, formed of steel rings interwoven.

haughty, ha'ti, *a.* [O.Fr, *hautain*, haughty, from *haut*, *hault*, from L. *altus*, high (whence *altitude*, *exalt*); *gh* was inserted through influence of *high*.] Proud and disdainful; having a high opinion of one's self, with some contempt for others; lofty and arrogant; disdainful; supercilious.—**haughtily**, ha'ti-li, *adv.* In a haughty manner.—**haughtiness**, ha'ti-nes, *n.* The quality of being haughty.

haul, hal, *v.t.* [Same as D. *halen*, Icel. and Sw. *hala*, Dan. *hale*, to haul; G. *holen*, to fetch, to tow (whence Fr. *haler*, to haul); hence *halliard*, *halyard*.] To pull or draw with force; to transport by drawing; to drag; to tug.—*To haul over the coals*, to bring to a reckoning; to take to

task; to reprimand.—*v.i. Naut.* to change the direction of sailing: with *off*, *up*, etc.—*n.* A pulling with force; a violent pull; a draught of fish in a net; that which is caught by one haul; hence, that which is taken, gained, or received at once. —**haulage**, ha'lij, *n.* The act of hauling or drawing; the force expended in hauling; dues or charges for hauling or towing.—**hauler**, ha'-lėr, *n.* One who pulls or hauls.

haulm, halm, *n.* [A.Sax. *healm*=D. Dan. and Sw. *halm*, Icel. *hálmr*; cog. L. *calamus*, Gr. *kalamos*, a reed.] The stem or stalk of grain of all kinds, or of peas, beans, hops, etc.; dry stalks in general.

haunch, hansh, *n.* [Fr. *hanche*, the haunch, from the Teutonic; Fris. *hancke*, *hencke*, haunch; G. *hanke*, the haunch of a horse.] The hip; the bend of the thigh; part of the body of a man and of quadrupeds between the last ribs and the thigh; *arch.* the middle part between the vertex or crown and the springing of an arch; the flank.

haunt, hant, *v.t.* [Fr. *hanter*, to frequent, from Armor. *hent*, a way, *henti*, to frequent.] To frequent; to resort to much or often, or to be much about; to visit customarily; to appear in or about, as a specter; to be a frequent spectral visitant of. —*v.i.* To be much about a place; to make frequent resort.—*n.* A place to which one frequently resorts; a favorite resort; a common abiding place.

haustellum, has·tel'lum, *n.* [L., from *haurio*, *haustum*, to draw up.] The suctorial organ of certain insects, otherwise called the proboscis or antlia.—**haustellate**, has'tel·lāt, *a.* Provided with a haustellum or sucker; suctorial.

hautboy, hō'boi, *n.* [Fr. *hautbois*—*haut* (in E. *haughty*), high, and *bois* (E. *bush*), wood, from the high tone of the instrument.] An oboe; a wind instrument of wood, sounded through a double-reed.

hauteur, ō'tėr, *n.* [Fr. HAUGHTY.] Pride; haughtiness; insolent manner or spirit.

Havana, ha·van'a, *n.* A kind of cigar largely manufactured at *Havana*, the capital of Cuba.

have, hav, *v.t.*—pret. & pp. *had*, ppr. *having.* Ind. pres. I *have*, thou *hast*, he *has*; we, ye, they *have*. [A.Sax. *habban*, from *hafian* (*fi* becoming regularly *bb* between vowels)=Dan. *have*, Icel. *hafa*, Goth. *haban*, G. *haben*, to have; cog. L. *capio*, to take (whence *capable*, etc.). *Behave*, *haft*, *haven* are connected.] To possess; to hold; to be in close relation to (to *have* a son, a master, a servant); to accept; to take as husband or wife; to hold or regard (to *have* in honor); to maintain or hold in opinion; to be under necessity, or impelled by duty (to *have* to do it); to procure or make to be; to cause (he *had* him murdered); to gain, procure, receive, obtain; to bring forth (a child); to experience in any way, as to enjoy, to participate in,

---

ch, *chain*; *ch*, Sc. loch;   g, *go*;   j, *job*;   ng, *sing*;   TH, *then*;   th, *thin*;   w, *wig*;   hw, *whig*;   zh, *azure*.

to suffer from; to understand.—
I had as good, it would be as well for me; *I had better*, it would be better for me; *I had best*, it would be best for me; *I had as lief* or *lieve*, I would as willingly; *I had rather*, I should prefer.—*Have after!* pursue! let us pursue!—*Have at!* go at! assail! encounter! as *have at him!*—*Have with you!* come on! agreed!—*To have away*, to remove; to take away.—*To have in*, to contain.—*To have on*, to wear; to carry, as apparel or weapons.—*To have a care*, to take care; to be on guard, or to guard.—*To have a person out*, to meet him in a duel.—*To have it out of a person*, to punish him; to retaliate on him; to take him to task. [*Have* is used as an auxiliary verb to form certain compound tenses, as the perfect and pluperfect of both transitive and intransitive verbs.]

haven, hā′vn, *n.* [A.Sax. *hæfen*=D. and L.G. *haven*, Icel. *höfn*, Dan. *havn*, G. *hafen*; connected with *have*.] A harbor; a port; a bay, recess, or inlet which affords anchorage and a station for ships; a shelter, asylum, or place of safety.—*v.i.* To shelter, as in a haven.

haversack, hav′ėr·sak, *n.* [Fr. *havresac*, from D. *haverzak*, G. *hafersack*, a haversack, literally a sack for oats, from D. *haver*, G. *hafer*, Dan. *havre*, oats.] A bag of strong cloth worn over the shoulder by soldiers in marching order for carrying their provisions.

havoc, hav′ok, *n.* [From O.Fr. *havot*, pillage, plunder.] Devastation; wide and general destruction.—*v.t.* To destroy; to lay waste (*Mil.*).

haw, hą, *n.* [A.Sax. *haga*, an enclosure, a yard=Icel. *hagi*, Sw. *hage*, an enclosure, akin *hedge*, *haggard*.] A hedge; an enclosure; the hawthorn and its berry or seed.

haw, hą, *n.* [Origin unknown.] The nictitating membrane in the eye of a dog, horse, etc.

haw, hą, *v.i.* [Imitative.] To equivocate (to hem and *haw*).

hawk, hąk, *n.* [A.Sax. *hafoc*=D. *havik*, G. *habicht*, Icel. *haukr*, a hawk.] A rapacious bird of the falcon family; a falcon.—*v.t.* and *i.* To hunt by means of trained hawks or falcons; to practice falconry; to fly in the manner of the hawk.—**hawker,** hą′kėr, *n.* One who hawks; a falconer.—**hawk moth,** *n.* A moth, so called from its hovering motion.—**hawksbill,** *n.* A turtle with a mouth like the beak of a hawk.

hawk, hąk, *v.i.* [Probably imitative, Comp. D. *harke*, and W. *hochi*, to hawk.] To make an effort to force up phlegm with noise.—*v.t.* To raise by hawking.—*n.* An effort to force up phlegm by coughing.

hawk, hąk, *v.t.* [From D. *heukeren*, to retail, to huckster, *heuker*, a retailer; akin to G. *höken*, *höcken*, to retail, *höker*, *höcker*, a hawker, from *hocken*, *hucken*, to take upon the back, to squat. Akin *huckster*.] To sell, or try to sell, by offering the goods at people's doors; to convey through

town or country for sale.—**hawker,** hą′kėr, *n.* [D. *heuker*, a retailer.] One who travels selling wares; a peddler; a packman.

hawse, hąs, *n.* [O. and Prov. E. *halse*, the neck.] *Naut.* that part of a vessel's bow where the hawseholes are cut; the hole in the vessel's bow; the distance between a ship's head and her anchors.—**hawsehole,** *n.* A hole in a vessel's bow through which a cable passes.

hawser, hą′sėr, *n.* [M.E. *haucer*, from O.Fr. *haucier*, raise, from L. *altus*, high.] A large rope used in making a ship secure.

hawthorn, hą′thorn, *n.* [A.Sax. *hagathorn*, *hæg-thorn*, haw-thorn, lit. hedgethorn; like G. *hagedorn*, D. *haagedoorn*. HAW, HEDGE.] A kind of small tree, one species of which is an excellent hedge plant, while some of its varieties are very beautiful when in full blossom.

hay, hā, *n.* [A.Sax. *hig*=O.Fris. *hai*, Dan. *hö*, Icel. *hey*, Goth. *havi*, G. *heu*, hay; connected with verb to *hew*. HEW.] Grass cut and dried for fodder; a small sum of money; a reward.—**haycock,** *n.* A conical pile or heap of hay.—**hay fever,** *n.* A summer ailment caused by allergy to pollen and marked by sneezing and other symptoms of a cold.—**hayfork,** *n.* A two-pronged fork for turning or lifting hay, etc.—**haystack,** *n.* A large pile of hay in the open air, laid up for preservation.—**haywire,** *a.* Tangled; confused.

hazard, haz′ėrd, *n.* [Fr. *hasard*, from Sp. *azar*, an unlucky throw of the dice, from Ar. *az-zahr*, a die.] A fortuitous event; chance; danger; peril; risk; a game played with dice. —*v.t.* To expose to chance; to put in danger of loss or injury; to risk.—**hazardous,** haz′ėr·dus, *a.* Exposing to peril or danger of loss or evil; dangerous; risky.—**hazardously,** haz′ėr·dus·li, *adv.* In a hazardous manner.—**hazardousness,** haz′ėr·dus·nes.

haze, hāz, *n.* [Allied to A.Sax. *haso*, dusky, dark; Icel. *höss*, gray, dusky.] Fog; a grayish or dusky vapor in the air, hence, obscurity; dimness; mental fog.—**haze,** hāz, *v.t.* To make hazy.—*v.i.* To be hazy.—**hazy,** hā′zi, *a.* Foggy; misty; thick with haze; mentally obscure.

haze, hāz, *v.t.* [M.Fr. *haser*, to irritate, to vex.] To harass or annoy by practical jokes.

hazel, hā′zl, *n.* [A.Sax. *hæsel*, *hæsl*= Icel. *hasl*, Dan. *hassel*, G. *hasel*, hazel; cog. with L. *corylus*, for *cosylus*, a hazel.] A tree growing wild and yielding edible nuts, while the wood is employed for hoops, fishing rods, walking sticks, etc.—*a.* Of a light-brown color like the hazelnut.—**hazelly,** hā′zl·li, *a.*—**hazelnut,** *n.* The nut of the hazel.

H-bomb. See HYDROGEN BOMB.

he, hē, *pron.* possessive *his*, objective *him* (also dative). [A.Sax. *hé*, *heó*, *hit*, he, she, it; D. *hij*, Dan. and Sw. *han*, Icel. *haan*, he; akin *hence*, *her*, *here*, *hither*. She is of different origin.] The masc. sing. form of the pro-

noun of the 3rd person. It is sometimes used as a noun, being equivalent to man or male person, and is often prefixed to the names of animals to designate the male kind (a *he-goat*).—*n.* Male person or animal.

head, hed, *n.* [A.Sax. *heafod*=Dan. *hoved*, Icel. *höfuth*, G. *haupt*, Goth. *houbith*, head; cog. L. *caput* (whence *chief*), Gr. *kephalē*, head.] The name applied generally to the anterior part or extremity of animals; the part which forms the seat of the brain and mental faculties; hence, understanding, intellect, will or resolution, mind, an individual; a unit (a thousand *head* of sheep: used only in *sing.*); a chief; a leader; a commander; what gives a striking appearance to the head, as the hair, antlers of a deer, etc.; part of a thing resembling in position or otherwise the human head (the *head* of a spear, of a nail); the main point or part; the forepart (the *head* of a ship); the upper part (of a bed, etc.); the top; the principal source of a stream; the part most remote from the mouth or opening; a headland; promontory; the foremost place; crisis; height; pitch; division of discourse; title of a subdivision.—*Hydraulics*, the height of water or other fluid above a given level, regarded as producing pressure; *Head and ears*, deeply; wholly; completely.—*Head and shoulders*, by force; violently (to drag in a topic *head and shoulders*); by as much as the height of the head and shoulders.—*A broken head*, a flesh wound in the head.—*To make head against*, to resist with success.—*To give*, *to get*, etc., *the head*, used literally of a horse that is not held in by the reins, and hence figuratively *head* means license, freedom from check, control, or restraint.—*v.t.* To be or put one's self at the head of; to lead; to direct; to behead; to decapitate; to form a head to; to fit or furnish with a head; to go in front of, so as to keep from advancing (to *head* a drove of cattle). —*a.* Belonging to the head; chief; principal: often used in composition (*head* workman, a *head* master, etc.). —**headache,** hed′āk, *n.* Pain in the head.—**headband,** hed′band, *n.* A band for the head; the band at each end of a bound book.— **headcheese,** hed′chēz, *n.* A jellied mass or loaf consisting of parts of the head and feet of hogs, cut up, seasoned, cooked and cooled.— **headdress,** *n.* The dress of the head; the covering or ornaments of a woman's head.—**headed,** hed′ed, *p.* and *a.* Furnished with a head; used chiefly in composition (clear-*headed*, long*headed*, etc.).—**header,** hed′ėr, *n.* One who puts a head on anything; one who stands at the head of anything; a leader; a plunge or dive into water headforemost.— **headforemost,** *adv.* With the head first; rashly; precipitately.—**headily,** hed′i·li, *adv.* In a heady manner.— **headiness,** hed′i·nes, *n.* The quality of being heady.—**heading,** hed′ing, *n.* The act of one who heads; what stands at the head; a title of a section in a book; a compass direction used by ships or airplanes in aiming at a destination.—**headland,** hed′land, *n.* A cape; a promontory.—**headless,** hed′les, *a.* Having no head; destitute of a chief or leader.—**headline,** hed′-line, *n.* Title above a news story, summarizing its contents; *print.* the line at the top of the page that gives title, page number, etc.—*v.t.* To provide a headline for a news story.—**headlong,** hed′long, *adv.* With the head foremost; rashly; precipitately; without deliberation. —*a.* Precipitous; rash.—**headmaster,** *n.* The principal master of a school. —**headmost,** hed′most, *a.* Most advanced; first.—**headpiece,** *n.* A helmet; a morion; the head, especially the head as the seat of the understanding.—**headquarters,** *n. pl.* The quarters of the commander of an army; a center of authority or order; the place where one chiefly resides.—**headship,** hed′ship, *n.* The state or position of being a head or chief; authority; supreme power; government.—**headsman,** hedz′man, *n.* One that cuts off heads; an executioner.—**headstall,** *n.* That part of a bridle which encompasses the head.—**headstone,** *n.* The chief or corner stone; the keystone of an arch; the stone at the head of a grave.—**headstrong,** hed′-strong, *a.* Obstinate; ungovernable; bent on pursuing one's own course. —**headwater,** *n.* The part of a river near its source, or one of the streams that contribute to form it.—**headway,** hed′wā, *n.* The progress made by a ship in motion; hence, progress or success of any kind.—**headwind,** *n.* A wind directly opposed to a ship's course.—**headwork,** *n.* Mental or intellectual labor.—**heady,** hed′i, *a.* Rash; hasty; precipitate; headstrong; apt to affect the mental faculties; intoxicating; strong.

heal, hēl, *v.t.* [A.Sax. *haelan,* to heal, from *hál,* whole, sound (=E. *whole*). comp. the related words *hale, hail, whole, holy, health.*] To make hale, sound, or whole; to cure of a disease or wound and restore to soundness; to reconcile; as a breach or difference.—*v.i.* To grow sound; to return to a sound state; sometimes with *up* or *over.*—**healer,** he′lẻr, *n.* One who or that which heals.—**healingly,** hē′ling·li, *adv.* In a healing manner.

health, helth, *n.* [A.Sax. *haelth,* from *haelan,* to heal.] That state of a being in which all the parts and organs are sound and in proper condition; moral or intellectual soundness; salvation or divine favor or grace (O.T.). [It is often used in toasts, and hence sometimes means toast.]—**healthful,** helth′fụl, *a.* Full of health; free from disease; promoting health; wholesome.—**healthfully,** helth′fụl·li, *adv.* In a healthful manner.—**healthfulness,** helth′fụl·nes, *n.* The state of being healthful or healthy.—**healthily,** hel′thi·li, *adv.*

In a healthy manner or condition.— **healthy,** hel′thi, *a.* Being in health; enjoying health; hale; sound; conducive to health; wholesome; salubrious.—**healthiness,** hel′thi·nes, *n.* State of being healthy.

heap, hēp, *n.* [A.Sax. *heáp,* a pile, a crowd=D. *hoop,* Dan. *hob,* Icel. *hópr,* G. *haufe.* Akin *hip.*] A pile or mass; a collection of things piled up; a large quantity; a great number. —*v.t.* To lay in a heap; to pile; to amass; often with *up* or with *on*; to round or form into a heap.

hear, hēr *v.t.*—pret. & pp. *heard.* [A.Sax. *hýran, héran,* to hear= O.Fris. *hera, hora,* Icel. *heyra,* D. *hooren,* G. *hören,* Goth. *hausjan*; hence *hearken, hark.*] To perceive by the auditory sense; to take cognizance of by the ear; to give audience or allowance to speak; to listen to; to heed; to obey; to try judicially (a cause) in a court of justice; to listen to one repeating or going over, as a task or the like.—*v.i.* To enjoy the sense or faculty of perceiving sound; to listen; to hearken; to attend; to be told; to receive by report.—**hearer,** hē′rẻr, *n.* One who hears; an auditor; one who sits under the ministry of another. —**hearing,** hē′ring, *n.* The act of perceiving sound; the faculty or sense by which sound is perceived; audience; an opportunity to be heard; a judicial investigation before a court; reach of the ear; extent within which sound may be heard.— **hearsay,** hēr′sā, *n.* Report; rumor; common talk.—*Hearsay evidence,* evidence repeated at second hand by one who heard the actual witness relate or admit what he knew of the transaction or fact in question.

hearken, här′kn, *v.i.* [A.Sax. *heorcnian, hýrcnian,* from *hyran,* to hear. HEAR.] To listen; to lend the ear; to give heed to what is uttered; to hear with obedience or compliance. —*v.t.* To hear by listening; to hear with attention; to regard.

hearse, hẻrs, *n.* [O.Fr. *herce,* a harrow, a kind or portcullis, a *herse,* from L. *hirpex, hirpicis,* a harrow; hence *rehearse* (which see).] A bier; a bier with a coffin; a carriage for conveying the dead to the grave.— *v.t.* To put on or in a hearse.

heart, härt, *n.* [A.Sax. *heorte*=Goth. *hairto,* D. *hart,* Icel. *hjarta,* Dan. *hjerte,* G. *herz*; cog. Gael. *cridhe,* L. *cor, cordis,* Gr. *kardia,* Skr. *hrid,* heart; from a root meaning to leap.] A muscular organ, which is the propelling agent of the blood in the animal body, situated in the thorax of vertebrated animals; the mind, the soul, the consciousness; the thinking faculty; the seat of the affections and passions; the moral side of our nature in contradistinction to the intellectual; courage; spirit; the seat of the will or inclination; hence, disposition of mind; tendency; conscience, or sense of good and ill; the inner part of anything; the part nearest the middle or center; the vital or most essential part; the core; the very essence;

that which has the shape or form of a heart or is regarded as representing the figure of a heart; one of a suit of playing cards marked with such a figure.—*At heart,* in real character or disposition; at bottom; substantially; really (he is good *at heart*).—*To break the heart of,* to cause the deepest grief to; to kill by grief.—*To find in the heart,* to be willing or disposed.—*To get* or *learn by heart,* to commit to memory.—*To have in the heart,* to purpose; to have design or intention. —*To have the heart in the mouth,* to be terrified.—*To lay* or *take to heart,* to be much affected by; to be zealous, ardent, or solicitous about.— *To wear the heart upon the sleeve,* to expose one's feelings, wishes, or intentions to every one.—*v.i.* To form a close compact head, as a plant.—**heartache,** härt′āk, *n.* Anguish of mind.—**heartbreak,** *n.* Overwhelming sorrow or grief.— **heartbroken,** *a.* Deeply grieved; in despair.—**heartburn,** *n.* An uneasy burning sensation in the stomach from indigestion and excess of acidity.—**heartburning,** *a.* Causing discontent.—*n.* Discontent; secret enmity.—**hearted,** här′ted, *a.* Having a heart; frequently used in composition (hard-*hearted,* faint-*hearted,* etc.) —**hearten,** här′tn, *v.t.* To encourage; to incite or stimulate the courage of. —**heartfelt,** *a.* Deeply felt; deeply affecting.—**heartily,** här′ti·li, *adv.* In a hearty manner.—**heartiness,** här′ti·nes, *n.* The state of being hearty.—**heartless,** härt′les, *a.* Without a heart; destitute of feeling or affection; cruel.—**heartlessly,** härt′-les·li, *adv.* In a heartless manner.— **heartlessness,** härt′les·nes. *n.* The quality of being heartless.—**heart-rending,** *a.* Breaking the heart; overpowering with anguish; very distressing.—**heartsease,** *n.* Ease of heart; a plant of the violet genus; the pansy.—**heartsick,** *a.* Sick at heart; pained in mind; deeply depressed.—**heartsome,** härt′sum, *a.* Inspiring with heart or courage; exhilarating; cheerful; lively.—**heart-sore,** *a.* Sore at heart.—**heartstring,** *n.* A hypothetical nerve or tendon, supposed to brace and sustain the heart.—**heart-whole,** *a.* Not affected with love; having unbroken spirits or good courage.—**heartwood,** *n.* The central part of the wood of exogens; the duramen.—**hearty,** här′-ti, *a.* Having the heart engaged in anything; proceeding from the heart; sincere; warm; zealous; cordial; sound and healthy; large to satisfaction (a *hearty* meal); loud and unrestrained (a *hearty* laugh).

hearth, härth, *n.* [A.Sax. *heorth,* hearth=D. *haard,* G. *heerd, herd,* area, floor, hearth; root doubtful.] That portion of the floor of a room on which the fire stands, generally a pavement or floor of brick or stone below a chimney; the fireside; the domestic circle.—**hearthstone,** *n.* The stone forming the hearth.

heat, hēt, *n.* [A.Sax. *haetu, haete,* from *hát,* hot; root in Gr. *kaiō,* to burn (whence *caustic*).] A form of energy consisting of waves measuring 1 inch to 8½/1,000,000 of an inch; the sensation produced by bodies that are hot; the bodily feeling when one is exposed to fire, the sun's rays, etc.; the reverse of cold; high temperature, as distinguished from low; hot weather; a hot period; a single effort, as in a race; utmost ardor or violence; rage; vehemence; agitation of mind; inflammation or excitement; exasperation; animation in thought or discourse; fervency; sexual excitement in animals; fermentation.—*v.t.* To make hot; to communicate heat to; to cause to grow warm; to make feverish; to excite; to warm with passion or desire; to animate.—*v.i.* To grow warm or hot.—**heater**, hē'tėr, *n.* One who or that which heats.

heath, hēth, *n.* [A.Sax. *haeth*=L.G., D., Fris., and G. *heide*, the plant, also a moor; Goth. *haithi*, a field; Icel. *heithi*, *heithr*, a waste, a fell. Hence *heathen, heather*.] A name of numerous shrubby plants, many of them having beautiful flowers, and three species being common in Britain; a place overgrown with heath; a waste tract of land.—**heathberry**, *n.* The crowberry.—**heath cock**, *n.* The blackcock (under BLACK).—**heathy**, hē'thi, *a.* Of, pertaining to, or resembling heath; covered or abounding with heath.

heathen, hē'THen, *n.* [A.Sax. *haethen*, lit. one inhabiting a heath, from *haeth*, a heath, so that it is similar in meaning to the L. *paganus*, a pagan, originally a countryman.] One who worships idols or does not acknowledge the true God; a pagan; an idolater; a rude, barbarous, or irreligious person.—*a.* Gentile; pagan.—**heathendom**, hē'THen·dum, *n.* Those parts of the world in which heathenism prevails.—**heathenish**, hē'THen·ish, *a.* Belonging to heathens or their religions; barbarous; uncivilized; irreligious.—**heathenishness**, hē'THen·ish·nes, *n.* —**heathenism**, hē'THen·izm, *n.* The system of religion or the manners and morals of a heathen nation; paganism; barbarism.—**heathenize**, hē'THen·īz, *v.t.* To render heathenish—**heathenry**, hē'THen·ri, *n.* Heathenism; heathens collectively.

heather, heTH'ėr, *n.* [Formerly *hadder*; comp. G. *heiter*, gay.] Common heath, a low shrub with clusters of rose-colored flowers, covering immense tracts of waste land in Britain.—**heathery**, heTH'ėr·i, *a.* Abounding in heather; heathy.

heave, hēv, *v.t.*—*heaved* or *hove* (pret. and pp.), *heaving*. [A.Sax. *hebban*, pret. *hof*, pp. *hafen*=Goth. *hafjan*, O.Fris. *heva*, D. *heffen*, *heven*, Dan. *hæve*, Icel. *hefja*, G. *heben*, to lift; akin *heavy, heaven*.] To lift; to raise; to elevate; to raise or force from the breast (to *heave* a sigh); to throw; to cast; *naut.* to apply power to, as by means of a windlass, in order to pull or force in any direction.—*To heave to*, to bring

a ship's head to the wind and stop her motion.—*v.i.* To be thrown or raised up; to rise; to rise and fall with alternate motions; to swell up; to pant, as after severe labor or exertion; to make an effort to vomit; to retch.—*To heave in sight*, to appear; to make its first appearance, as a ship at sea. *n.* An upward motion; swell, as of the waves of the sea; an effort of the lungs, etc.; an effort to raise something; *pl.* a disease of horses, characterized by difficult and laborious respiration.—**heaver**, hē'vėr, *n.* One who or that which heaves.

heaven, hev'n, *n.* [A.Sax. *heofon*, heaven; O.Sax. *hevan*, L.G. *heben*, Icel. *hifinn*; from root of *heave*.] The blue expanse which surrounds the earth, and in which the sun, moon, and stars seem to be set; the sky; the upper regions; often in the plural; the final abode of the blessed; the place where God manifests himself to the blessed; [*cap.*] often used as equivalent to God or Providence; supreme felicity; bliss; a sublime or exalted condition.—**heavenliness**, hev'n·li·nes, *n.* The condition or quality of being heavenly.—**heavenly**, hev'n·li, *a.* Pertaining to heaven; inhabiting heaven; celestial; supremely blessed; supremely excellent.—*adv.* In a heavenly manner.—**heavenward**, hev'n·wėrd, *adv.* Toward heaven.

heavy, hev'i, *a.* [A.Sax. *hefig*, heavy, from the stem of *hebban*, to heave= Icel. *höfigr.* HEAVE.] That can be lifted only with labor; ponderous; weighty: the opposite of *light*; large in amount or quantity (a *heavy* rain, a *heavy* crop); not easily borne; hard to endure; burdensome; oppressive; severe; hard to accomplish; weighed or bowed down; burdened with sorrow, sleep, weariness, or the like; slow; sluggish; inactive; dull; lifeless; inanimate; impeding motion or action (*heavy* roads); acting or moving with violence (a *heavy* sea, cannonade; dark; gloomy; threatening; lowering (a *heavy* sky); not easily digested (food); deep and voluminous (sound).—**heavily**, hev'i·li, *adv.* In a heavy manner.—**heaviness**, hev'i·nes, *n.* The state or quality of being heavy; weight; severity; sadness; dullness or lifelessness.—**heavy spar**, *n.* The sulfate of barium, occurring in veins massive, fibrous, lamellar, and in prismatic crystals.—**heavyweight**, *n.* A boxer or wrestler, etc., of what is usually the heaviest class; one weighing not less than 175 pounds.

hebdomadal, heb·dom'a·dal, *a.* [Gr. *hebdomas*, the number seven, seven days, from *hepta*, seven.] Weekly; consisting of seven days, or occurring every seven days.

Hebe, hē'bē, *n.* The goddess of youth among the Greeks; hence, a beautiful young woman.

hebetate, heb'ē·tāt, *v.t.*—*hebetated*, *hebetating*. [L. *hebeto*, *hebetatum*, from *hebes*, dull.] To dull; to blunt; to stupefy.—**hebetude**, heb'ē·tūd, *n.* [L. *hebetudo*.] Dullness; stupidity.

Hebrew, hē'brö, *n.* [Fr. *hébreu*, L. *hebræus*, Gr. *hebraios*, from Heb.: supposed to mean a person *from beyond* (the Euphrates).] One of the descendants of Jacob; an Israelite; a Jew; the language of the Jews, one of the Semitic tongues.—*a.* Pertaining to the Hebrews.—**Hebraic** hē'brā·ik, *a.* Pertaining to the Hebrews or their language.—**Hebraism**, hē'brā·izm, *n.* A peculiarity of Hebrew or the Hebrews.—**Hebraist**, hē'brā·ist, *n.* One versed in the Hebrew language.—**Hebraize**, hē'brā·īz, *v.t.* —*hebraized, hebraizing.* To convert into the Hebrew idiom; to make Hebrew.—*v.i.* To conform to the Hebrew idiom, manners, etc.

hecatomb, hek'a·tom, *n.* [Gr. *hekatombē*—*hekaton*, a hundred, and *bous*, an ox.] A sacrifice of a hundred oxen or other beasts; hence, any great sacrifice of victims; a great number of persons or animals slaughtered.

heckle, hek'l, *n.* [Same as *hackle*.] A sort of comb for flax or hemp; a hackle or hatchel.—*v.t.* To dress with a heckle; *fig.* to tease or vex; to catechise severely.—**heckler**, hek'lėr, *n.* One who heckles.

hectare, hek'tär, *n.* [Fr.] A French measure containing 100 ares, or= 2.47 acres.

hectic, hek'tik, *a.* [Gr. *hektikos*, habitual, hectic or consumptive, from *hexis*, habit of body, from *echō*, future *hexō*, to have.] Relating to or affected with a fluctuating, but persistent, fever; characterized by excitement or feverish activity; restless.—*n.* A hectic fever.—**hectically**, hek'ti·kal·li, *adv.* In a hectic manner.

hectocotylus, hek·to·kot'i·lus, *n.* [Gr. *hekaton*, a hundred, and *kotylē*, a small cup, a sucker.] The reproductive arm of certain of the male cuttlefishes.

hectogram, hek'to·gram, *n.* [Fr., from Gr. *hekaton*, a hundred, and *gramma*, a gram.] A metric measure of weight containing 100 grams, or 3.527 ounces avoirdupois.—**hectoliter**, hek'to·lē·tėr, *n.* A metric measure for liquids, containing 100 liters, or 26.418 gallons.—**hectometer**, hec'to·mē·tėr, *n.* A metric measure of length containing 100 meters, or 109.36 yards.

hector, hek'tėr, *n.* [From *Hector*, the son of Priam, a brave Trojan warrior.] A bully; a blustering, turbulent, noisy fellow.—*v.t.* To treat with insolence; to bully.—*v.i.* To play the bully; to bluster; to be turbulent or insolent.

heddle, hed'l, *n.* [By metathesis for *heald*; perhaps from A.Sax. *heald*, hold.] *Weav.* one of the parallel double threads with a center loop or eye which raises the warp threads to form the shed and allow the shuttle to pass; a heald.

hedge, hej, *n.* [A.Sax. *hecg*, a hedge, closely akin to *haga*, an enclosure; Icel. *hagi*, an enclosed field; D. *hegge*, a hedge, *haag*, a hedge (whence the *Hague*); E. *hawthorn*, that is *hedgethorn*.] A fence formed by bushes or small trees growing close together; any line of shrubbery closely planted.

fāte, fär, fâre, fat, fạll; mē, met, hėr; pīne, pin; nōte, not, mȯve; tūbe, tub, bụll; oil, pound.

—*v.t.* *hedged, hedging*. To enclose or fence with a hedge; to obstruct with a barrier; to stop by any means; to surround for defense; to hem in.—*To hedge a bet*, to bet upon both sides, thus guarding one's self against great loss, whatever may be the result.—*v.i.* To hide in a hedge; to skulk (*Shak.*); to protect one's self from loss by cross bets.—**hedgehog,** hej′hog, *n.* An Old World insectivorous quadruped about 9 inches long, the upper part of whose body is covered with prickles or spines; in America, the porcupine; *elec.* a kind of transformer; *milit.* a kind of barbed wire entanglement.—**hedgehop,** hej′hop, *v.t. & i.* To fly an airplane at a very low altitude, just skimming the ground. (*Slang.*)—**hedge hyssop,** any of a number of herbs, as the goldenpert.—**hedger,** hej′ėr, *n.* One who makes or repairs hedges; one who hedges bets; one who evades.—**hedgerow,** hej′rō, *n.* A row or series of shrubs or trees forming a hedge between fields.—**hedge sparrow,** a red-brown European warbler.

hedonic, hē-don′ik, *a.* [Gr. *hēdonikos,* from *hēdonē,* pleasure.] Pertaining to pleasure; pursuing, or placing the chief good in, sensual pleasure.—**hedonics,** hē-don′iks, *n.* That branch of ethics which treats of active or positive pleasure or enjoyment.—**hedonism,** hē′don·izm, *n.* The doctrine that the chief good of man lies in the pursuit of pleasure.—**hedonist,** hē′don·ist, *n.* One who professes hedonism.

heed, hēd, *v.t.* [A.Sax. *hédan,* to heed; D. *hoeden,* to care for, *hoede,* care; G. *hüten,* to look after, from *hut,* protection; akin *hood.*] To regard with care; to take notice of; to attend to; to observe.—*n.* Care; attention; notice; observation; regard; usually with *give* or *take.*—**heedful,** hēd′ful, *a.* Full of heed; attentive; watchful; cautious; wary.—**heedfully,** hēd′ful·li, *adv.* In a heedful manner.—**heedfulness,** hēd′ful·nes, *n.* The quality of being heedful; attention; caution.—**heedless,** hēd′les, *a.* Without heed; inattentive; careless.—**heedlessly,** hēd′les·li, *adv.* In a heedless manner.—**heedlessness,** hēd′les·nes, *n.*

heel, hēl, *n.* [A.Sax. *hél*=Icel. *haell,* D. *hiel,* the heel; radically akin to L. *calx,* the heel (seen in *inculcate*).] The hinder part of the foot in man or quadrupeds; the hinder part of a covering for the foot; something shaped like the human heel, or that occupies a position corresponding to the heel; the latter or concluding part.—*To be at the heels,* to pursue closely; to follow hard; also, to attend closely.—*To be down at heel,* to be slipshod; hence, to be in decayed circumstances.—*To lay by the heels,* to fetter; to shackle; to confine.—*To show the heels,* to flee; to run away.—*To take to the heels,* to betake one's self to flight.—*v.t.* To perform by the use of the heels, as a dance (*Shak.*); to add a heel to.—**heelpiece,** *n.* A piece of leather on the heel of a shoe; armor for the heel.—

heeltap, *n.* A small piece of leather for the heel of a shoe; the small portion of liquor left in a glass when the main portion has been drunk.

heel, hēl, *v.i.* [Same as A.Sax. *heldan,* D. *hellen,* Dan. *helde,* Sw. *hälla,* to tilt.] To incline or cant over from a vertical position, as a ship.—*n.* The act of so inclining; a cant.

heft, heft, *n.* [From *heave,* to lift.] The act of heaving; violent strain or exertion; effort (*Shak.*).—**heft, hefty,** *a.* Vigorous, strong. (*Colloq.*)

Hegelian, he·gē′li·an, *a.* Pertaining to Hegel (hā′gl) or his system of philosophy.—*n.* A follower of Hegel.—**Hegelianism,** he·gē′li·an·izm, *n.* The system of philosophy of Hegel.

hegemony, hej′e·mo·ni or he·jem′o·ni, *n.* [Gr. *hēgemonia,* from *hegemōn,* guide, leader, from *hēgeomai,* to lead.] Leadership; predominance; preponderance of one state among others.—**hegemonic,** hej·e·mon′ik, *a.* Ruling; predominant; principal.

hegira, hej′i·ra, *n.* [Ar. *hijrah,* departure, from *hajara,* to remove.] [*Often cap.*] The flight of Mohammed from Mecca, adopted by the Mohammedans in reckoning their time, their era beginning July 16, 622, hence, [*not cap.*] any similar flight.

heifer, hef′ėr, *n.* [A.Sax. *heahfore;* origin doubtful.] A young cow.

heigh-ho! hī′hō. An exclamation usually expressing some degree of languor or uneasiness.

height, hīt, *n.* [For *highth,* as in *Milton;* A.Sax. *heáhtho, hyhtho,* from *heáh,* high. HIGH.] The condition of being high; the distance which anything rises above its foot, basis, or foundation, or above the earth; altitude; an eminence; a summit; a hill or mountain; elevation or pre-eminence among other persons; elevation in excellence of any kind; elevation or dignity, as of sentiment, expression, or the like; extent; degree; stage in progress or advancement: *the height,* the utmost degree in extent or violence.—**heighten,** hī′tn, *v.t.* To make high; to raise higher; to elevate; to increase; to augment; to intensify.—**heightener,** hī′tn·ėr, *n.* One who or that which heightens.

heinous, hā′nus, *a.* [Fr. *haineux,* from *haine,* malice, hate, from *haïr,* O.Fr. *hadir,* to hate, from Teut. verb=E. to hate.] Hateful; odious; hence, notorious; enormous; aggravated (sin or crime, sinner).—**heinously,** hā′nus·li, *adv.* In a heinous manner.—**heinousness,** hā′nus·nes, *n.* The condition or quality of being heinous.

heir, âr, *n.* [O.Fr. *heir,* L. *hæres,* an heir; whence *hereditary, heritage, inherit.*] One who succeeds or is to succeed another in the possession of property; an inheritor; one who receives any endowment from an ancestor.—*Heir apparent,* one whose right to inherit is unforfeitable, if he survives the ancestor.—*Heir presumptive,* one who will be the heir if the ancestor should die, but whose rights may be cut off by the birth of a nearer relative or some other contingency.—**heiress,** âr′es, *n.* A

female heir.—**heirloom,** âr′lōm, *n.* [*Heir* and *loom* in old sense of tool, implement, article.] A personal chattel that descends to an heir; any piece of personal property which has belonged to a family for a long time.—**heirship,** âr′ship, *n.* The state of an heir; right of inheriting.

hejira, hej′i·ra, *n.* Same as *Hegira.*

held, held, pret. & pp. of *hold.*

heliac, heliacal, hē′li·ak, hē·li′a·kal, *a.* [L. *heliacus,* from Gr. *hēlios,* the sun; akin L. *sol,* and W. *haul,* sun.] *Astron.* emerging from the light of the sun or passing into it; rising or setting at the same time, or nearly the same time, as the sun.—**heliacally,** hē·lī′a·kal·li, *adv.* In a heliacal manner.

helianthus, hē·li·an′thus, *n.* [Gr. *hēlios,* the sun, and *anthos,* a flower.] The sunflower; the Jerusalem artichoke genus.

helical, helicoid, helicoidal, etc. See HELIX.

Heliconian, hel·i·kō′ni·an, *a.* Pertaining to *Helicon,* the famous Grecian mountain, the residence of the muses.

helicopter, hel′i·kop·ter, *n.* [From Fr. *hélicoptère,* from Gr. *helix, -ikos,* spiral, plus *pteron,* wing.] A heavier-than-air craft, sustained in the air solely by propellers revolving around a vertical axis.—**heliport,** hel′i·port, *n.* A take-off and landing place for helicopters.

heliocentric, heliocentrical, hē′li·o·sen′trik, hē·li·o·sen′tri·kal, *a.* [Gr. *hēlios* (akin L. *sol,* W. *haul*), the sun, and *kentron,* center.] *Astron.* relating to the sun as a center; appearing as if seen from the sun's center.—**heliochrome,** hē′li·o·krōm, *n,* [Gr. *chrōma,* color.] A colored photograph.—**heliochromic,** hē′li·o·krōm′ik, *a.* Pertaining to heliochromy.—**heliograph,** hē′li·o·graf, *n.* [Gr. *graphō,* to write.] A photograph; an instrument for taking photographs of the sun; a sun telegraph; a heliostat.—*v.t.* and *i.* To convey or communicate by means of a heliostat or similar instrument.—**heliographic,** hē′li·o·graf′ik, *a.* Of or pertaining to heliography.—**heliography,** hē·li·og′ra·fi, *n.* Photography; also, the art or process of signaling by reflecting the sun's rays.—**heliogravure,** hē·li·o·grăv″ūr, *n.* [Gr. *helios,* sun, Fr. *gravure,* engraving.] A process by which a photographic print is mechanically etched on a copper plate, from which impressions are then taken.—**heliolater,** hē·li·ol′a·tėr, *n.* [Gr. *latrueō,* to worship.] A worshiper of the sun.—**heliolatry,** hē·li·ol′a·tri, *n.* The worship of the sun.

heliometer, hel·i·om′eter, *n.* [F. *heliometre.*] A double image micrometer used for measuring any short arc of the celestial sphere, but originally invented to measure the sun's diameter.

heliostat, hē′li·o·stat, *n.* [Gr. *statos,* fixed.] A name of various contrivances for reflecting the sun's light temporarily or continuously to an observer at a distance.

heliotrope, hē′li·o·trōp, *n.* [Gr. *tropē,*

a turning, *trepō*, to turn.] A heliostat; a variety of quartz, of a deep green color, with bright red spots; blood-stone; a name of plants, mostly natives of warm regions, one species of which is a favorite garden plant from the fragrance of its flowers.—**heliotropic**, hē′li·o·trop″-ik, *a.*—**heliotropism**, hē·li·ot′ro·pizm, *n.* The tendency of a plant to direct its growth toward the sun or toward light; a phototropism.—**helium**, hē′li·um, *n.* A nonflammable gaseous element, inert and colorless, the lightest gas next to hydrogen. Symbol, He; at. no., 2; at. wt., 4.0026.

helix, hē′liks, *n.* pl. **helices**, hel′i·sēz. [Gr. a winding, a spiral.] A spiral line, as of wire in a coil; something that is spiral; a circumvolution; *geom.* such a curve as is described by every point of a screw that is turned round in a fixed nut; *arch.* a small volute or twist under the abacus of the Corinthian capital; *anat.* the whole circuit of the external body of the ear; *zool.* a genus of mollusks, comprising the land shell snails.—**helical**, hel′i·kal, *a.* Of or pertaining to a helix; spiral.—**helically**, hel′i·kal·li, *adv.* In a helical manner.—**helicoid, helicoidal**, hel′-i·koid, hel′i·koi·dal, *a.* Spirally curved like the spire of a univalve shell.—**helicoid**, hel′i·koid, *n. Geom.* a spirally curved surface.

hell, hel, *n.* [A.Sax. *hel*, from *helan*, to cover, conceal, lit. a place of concealment = D. and Icel. *hel*, G. *hölle*, hell; same root as L. *celo*, to conceal. Akin *helmet*, perhaps *hole*.] The place of the dead, or of souls after death; the place or state of punishment for the wicked after death; the infernal powers; the domain of the devil; verbal castigation; unrestrained sportiveness (they raised *hell*); haunt of the vicious or depraved.—**hellish**, hel′ish, *a.* Pertaining to hell; infernal; malignant; wicked; detestable.—**hellishly**, hel′ish·li, *adv.* In a hellish manner.—**hellishness**, hel′ish·nes, *n.* The state or quality of being hellish.—**hell-fire**, *n.* The fire of hell; the torments of hell.—**hellhound**, *n.* A dog of hell; an agent of hell; a miscreant.

hellebore, hel′le·bōr, *n.* [L. *helleborus*, Gr. *helleboros*.] A name applied to plants of two very different genera, the black hellebore or Christmas rose, and the white hellebore; the powdered root of white hellebore used by gardeners for killing caterpillars.—**helleborin**, hel′le·bō·rin, *n.* A resin obtained from the root of black hellebore.

Hellenes, hel·lē′nez, *n. pl.* [Gr.] The inhabitants of Greece; the Greeks.—**Hellenic**, hel′len′ik, *a.* [Gr. *hellēnikos.*] Pertaining to the Hellenes; Greek; Grecian.—**Hellenism**, hel′len·izm, *n.* A Greek idiom; the type of character usually considered peculiar to the Greeks.—**Hellenist**, hel′len·ist, *n.* One who affiliates with Greeks; one skilled in the Greek language.—**Hellenistic, Hellenistical**, hel·len·is′tik, hel·len·is′ti·kal, *a.*

Pertaining to Hellenists.—**Hellenization**, hel′len·i·zā″shon, *n.* Act of Hellenizing.—**Hellenize**, hel′len·īz, *v.i.* To use the Greek language or adopt Greek manners.

hello, he·lo′, *interj.* [Apparently, a form of *hollo*, an exclamation.] A greeting or exclamation to call attention or show surprise, etc.

helm, helm, *n.* [A.Sax. *helma*, a helm; D. *helm*, a tiller; G. *helm*, a helve, a tiller; akin to *helve.*] The instrument by which a ship is steered, consisting of a rudder, a tiller, and in large vessels a wheel; in a narrower sense, the tiller; *fig.* the place or post of direction or management.—*v.t.*† To steer; to guide.—**helmsman**, helmz′man, *n.* The man at the helm or wheel who steers a ship.

helm, helm, *n.* [A.Sax. *helm*, what covers, a helmet, from *helan*, to cover; D. and G. *helm*, Goth. *hilms*, Icel. *hjálmr*, Dan. *hjelm*; *helmet* is a dim. form. HELL.] [*obs.*] A helmet. (*Poet.*)—*v.t.* To cover with a helmet.—**helmeted**, hel′met·ed, *a.* Furnished with a helmet.—**helmet**, hel′met, *n.* A defensive covering for the head; head armor composed of metal, leather, etc.; *bot.* the upper part of a ringent corolla.

helminthagogue, hel·min′tha·gog, *n.* [Gr. *helmins, helminthos,* a worm, and *agō*, to expel.] *Med.* a remedy against worms; an anthelmintic.—**helminthiasis**, hel·min·thī′a·sis, *n. Med.* the disease of worms in any part of the body.—**helminthic**, hel·min′thik, *a.* Relating to worms; expelling worms.—*n.* A medicine for expelling worms; a vermifuge.—**helminthology**, hel·min·thol′o·ji, *n.* The knowledge or natural history of worms.

Helot, hē′lot, *n.* [Gr. *heilōtēs.*] A slave in ancient Sparta; [*often not cap.*] hence, a slave in general.—**helotism**, hē′lot·izm, *n.* The condition of a Helot; slavery.—**helotry**, hē′lot·ri, *n.* Helots collectively; bondsmen.

help, help, *v.t.* [A.Sax. *helpan* = Goth. *hilpan*, D. *helpen*, Icel. *hjálpa*, Dan. *hjelpe*, G. *helfen*, to help—from same root as Skr. *kalp*, to suit, to be of service.] To give assistance or aid to; to aid; to assist; to succor, to relieve; to cure or mitigate (pain or disease); to avail against; to prevent; to remedy; to forbear; to avoid (to *help* doing something).—*To help forward*, to advance by assistance; to assist in making progress.—*To help on*, to forward; to aid.—*To help out*, to aid in delivering from difficulty, or to aid in completing a design.—*To help over*, to enable to surmount.—*To help* (a person) *to*, to supply with; to furnish with.—*v.i.* To lend aid; to be of use; to avail.—*n.* [A.Sax. *helpe*, Icel. *hjálp.*] Aid furnished; deliverance from difficulty or distress; assistance; that which gives assistance; one who or that which contributes to advance a purpose; remedy; relief; a domestic servant (U.S.).—**helper**, hel′pér, *n.* One that helps, aids, or assists; an assistant; an auxiliary.—**helpful**, help′ful, *a.* Furnishing help; useful.—**helpful-**

ness, help′ful·nes, *n.* The quality of being helpful.—**helpless**, help′les, *a.* Destitute of help or strength; needing help; feeble; weak; affording no help; beyond help. — **helplessly**, help′les·li, *adv.* In a helpless manner.—**helplessness**, help′les·nes, *n.* The state of being helpless.—**helpmate**, help′māt, *n.* An assistant; a helper; a partner; a consort; a wife.—**helpmeet**, help′mēt, *n.* A helpmate.

helter-skelter, hel′tér·skel′tér, *adv.* [A term formed to express hustle; comp. G. *holter-polter*, D. *hulter de bulter*, Sw. *huller om buller*, etc.] An expression denoting hurry and confusion.

helve, helv, *n.* [A.Sax. *helfe*, O.H.G. *halbe, helbe*; same root as *helm* (of a ship), *hilt.*] The handle of an ax or hatchet.—*v.t.*—**helved, helving.** To furnish with a helve, as an ax.

Helvetic, hel·vet′ik, *a.* [L. *Helveticus*, from *Helvetii*, the ancient inhabitants of Switzerland.] Of or pertaining to Switzerland.

hem, hem, *n.* [A.Sax. *hem*, a hem; akin to Icel. *hemja*, Dan. *hemme*, O.Fris. *hemma*, D. and G. *hemmen*, to stop, check, restrain.] The border of a garment, doubled and sewed to strengthen it; edge, border, margin.—*v.t.* **hemmed, hemming.** To form a hem or border on; to border; to edge.—*To hem in*, to enclose and confine; to surround closely; to environ.

hem, hem, *interj.* [Imitative and more correctly *hm*.] An exclamation consisting in a sort of half-cough, loud or subdued as the emotion may suggest; sometimes used as a noun.—*v.i.* To make the sound *hem*; hence, to hesitate or stammer in speaking.

hemachrome, hē′ma·krōm, *n.* Same as *Haemachrome*, some words of which Gr. *haima*, blood, forms the first part, being written *He* or *Hae*.—**hemastatics**, hē·ma·stat′iks, *n.* The doctrine as to the circulation of the blood.—**hemathermal**, hē·ma·thér′-mal, *a.* Warm-blooded.—**hematoxylin**, hē·ma·tok′si·lin, *n.* [Gr. *haima, haimatos,* and *xylon*, wood.] The coloring principle of logwood.

hematite, hē′ma·tīt, *n.* [Gr. *haimatitēs*, from *haima*, blood.] A name of two ores of iron, red hematite and brown hematite.—**hematitic**, hē·ma·tit′ik, *a.*

hematosis, hē·ma·tō′sis, *n.* [N.L. from Gr. *haimatōsis*, from *haimatoein*, to change into blood.] Arterialization of blood in the lungs; the formation of the blood.—**hematology**, hem·a·tol′o·gy, *n.* The science that deals with the blood.

hemicrania, hem·i·krā′ni·a, *n.* [Gr. *hēmi*, half, *cranion*, the skull.] A pain that affects only one side of the head.

hemicycle, hem′i·sī·kl, *n.* [Gr. *hēmi*, half, and *kyklos*, a circle.] A half circle; a semicircle; a semicircular area.

hemihedral, hem·i·hē′dral, *a.* [Gr. *hēmi*, half, and *hedra*, a face.] *Mineral*, applied to a crystal having only half the normal number of faces.—**hemihedrally**, hem·i·hē′dral·li, *adv.* In a hemihedral manner.

hemiplegia, hemiplegy, hem·i·plē′ji·a, hem′i·plej·i, n. [Gr. *hēmi*, half, and *plēgē*, a stroke.] Paralysis of one half of the body.—**hemiplegic,** hem·i·plej′ik, a. Relating to hemiplegia.

hemipter, he·mip′tẽr, n. [Gr. *hēmi*, half, and *pteron*, a wing.] One of an order of four-winged insects, so named because many of them have the outer wings leathery at the base and transparent toward the tips, including the locusts, bugs, plant lice, etc.—**hemipterous,** he·mip′tẽr·us, a. Pertaining to the hemipters.

hemisphere, hem′i·sfẽr, n. [Gr. *hēmisphairion*—*hēmi*, half, and *sphaira*, a globe.] A half sphere; one half of a sphere or globe; half the terrestrial or the celestial globe.—*Hemispheres of the brain*, the two parts, one on each side, which constitute great part of the brain.—**hemispheric, hemispherical,** hem·i·sfer′ik, hem·i·sfer′i·kal, a. Pertaining to a hemisphere.—**hemispheroid,** hem·i·sfer′oid, n. The half of a spheroid.

hemistich, hem′i·stik, n. [Gr. *hēmistichion*—*hēmi*, half, and *stichos*, a verse.] Half a poetic verse, or a verse not completed.—**hemistichal,** he·mis′ti·kal, a. Pertaining to or written in hemistichs.

hemlock, hem′lok, n. [A.Sax. *hemleác*.] A poisonous plant of the carrot family, with small white flowers; various evergreen trees native to North America.—*Ground hemlock*, the American yew.

hemoglobin, hē′mo·glō·bin, n. [Gr. *haima*, blood, and L. *globus*, globe.] Protein pigment of the red corpuscles of vertebrates, which contains iron and carries oxygen from the lungs to the body tissues.

hemophilia, hē·mo·fil′i·a, n. Med. A constitutional tendency, usually hereditary, to excessive bleeding.—**hemophiliac,** hē·mo·fil′i·ac, n. One afflicted with hemophilia.

hemoptysis, hē·mop′tis·is, n. [Gr. *ptysis*, a spitting.] The coughing up of blood.

hemorrhage, he′mor·ij, n. [Gr. *haimorrhagia*—*haima*, blood, and *rhēgnymi*, to break, to burst.] A discharge of blood from the blood vessels.—**hemorrhagic,** hē·mo·raj′ik, a. Pertaining to hemorrhage.

hemorrhoids, he′mor·oidz, n. pl. [Gr. *haimorrhois, haimorrhoïdos*, a gushing of blood—*haima*, blood, and *rhoos*, a flowing, from *rheō*, to flow.] Piles.

hemostat, hē′mo·stat, n. [Gr. *haima*, blood, and *stat*, from Gr. *statikos*, causing to stand.] An instrument that checks the flow of blood by compressing a bleeding blood vessel.

hemp, hemp, n. [A.Sax. *henep, hanep*; cog. L. *cannabis*, Gr. *kannabis*, Skr. *cana*, hemp.] An annual herbaceous plant, the prepared fiber of which, also called hemp, is made into sailcloth, ropes, etc.; the hangman's rope.—**hempen,** hem′pn, a.

hen, hen, n. [A.Sax. *hen, henn* = D. *hen*, Icel. *haena*, G. *henne*, hen—the feminines corresponding to A.Sax. and Goth. *hana*, D. *haan*, G. *hahn*, Icel. *hani*, a cock, the root being

same as in L. *cano*, to sing.] The female of any kind of bird; especially, the female of the domestic or barnyard fowl.—**henbane,** hen′bãn, n. A poisonous Old World plant found in waste ground, and sometimes fatal to domestic fowls, but yielding a juice that is used as a sedative and narcotic.—**hennery,** hen′ẽr·i, n. An enclosed place for hens.—**henpeck,** hen′pek, v.t. To govern or rule: said of a wife who has the upper hand of her husband.

hence, hens, adv. [O.E. *hennes*, a genit. form from older *henne*; A.Sax. *heonan*, hence; G. *hin*, Goth. *hina*, hence.] From this place; from this time (a week *hence*); as a consequence, inference, or deduction.—**henceforth, henceforward,** hens′forth, hens·for′wẽrd, adv. From this time forward.

henchman, hensh′man, n. [M.E. *henchemanne, henxtman*, probably meaning groom, apparently from O.E. *hengest*, stallion, and E. *mann*, man.] A trusted follower; a political follower, particularly one who desires personal gain.

hendecagon, hen·dek′a·gon, n. [Gr. *hendeka*, eleven, and *gōnia*, an angle.] Geom. a plane figure of eleven sides and as many angles.

hendecasyllable, hen·dek′a·sil·la·bl, n. [Gr. *hendeka*, eleven, and *syllabē*, a syllable.] A metrical line of eleven syllables.—**hendecasyllabic,** hen·dek′a·sil·lab″ik, a.

hendiadys, hen·dī′a·dis, n. [Gr. *hen dia dyoin*, one by two.] A figure of speech by which two nouns are used instead of one, or one and an adjective.

henna, hen′a, n. [Ar. *hinnâ-a*.] A tropical plant of the Old World, the leaves of which yield a rich reddish-orange dye; the color henna, a rich, brownish red.—v.t. To color with henna dye or paste.

henotheism, hen′o·thē·izm, n. [Gr. *heis, henos*, one, and *theos*, god.] The worship of one deity as supreme among others.

henry, n. The practical electrical unit of self-induction and mutual induction.

hepatic, hi·pat′ik, a. [L. *hepaticus*, Gr. *hepatikos*, from *hēpar, hēpatos*, the liver.] Pertaining to the liver.—n. A medicine that acts on the liver.—**hepatica,** hi·pat′i·ka, n. A species of anemone with trilobed leaves; any one of the genus of plants (*Hepatica*) allied to the mosses, and called liverworts.—**hepatitis,** hep·a·tī′tis, n. Inflammation of the liver.—**hepatization,** hep′a·tī·zā″shon, n. The state of being hepatized; the condensation of a texture so as to resemble the liver.—**hepatotomy,** hep′a·to″to·mi, n. [Gr. *tomē*, cutting.] The operation of cutting into the liver.

heptachord, hep′ta·kord, n. [Gr. *hepta*, seven, and *chordē*, chord.] Anc. mus. a diatonic octave without the upper note; an instrument with seven strings.

heptad, hep′tad, n. [Gr. *heptas, heptados*, from *hepta*, seven.] A sum of seven.

heptagon, hep′ta·gon, n. [Gr. *hepta*, seven, and *gōnia*, an angle.] Geom. a plane figure having seven sides and as many angles.—**heptagonal,** hep·tag′on·al, a. Having seven angles or sides.

heptamerous, hep·tam′ẽr·us, a. [Gr. *hepta*, seven, and *meros*, a part.] Bot. consisting of seven parts; having its parts in sevens.

heptarchy, hep′tär·ki, n. [Gr. *hepta*, seven, and *archē*, rule.] A government by seven persons, or the country governed by seven persons: usually applied to the seven Anglo-Saxon kingdoms into which England was once divided.

Heptateuch, hep′ta·tūk, n. [Gr. *hepta*, seven, and *teuchos*, book.] The first seven books of the Old Testament.

heptose, hep′tōs, n. [*Hept* and *ose*.] Any of several monosaccharides obtainable from lower sugars, containing 7 carbon atoms in the molecule.

her, hẽr, pron., a form answering to several cases of *she*. [O.E. *hire*, A.Sax. *hire, heore*, genit. and dat. case of the pronoun *heó*, she, the feminine of *hé*, he. HE.] The possessive case of *she* (*her* face); the dative case of *she* (give *her* that book); the objective case of *she* (I love *her*).—**hers,** hẽrz, pron. [From *her*, with *s* of the possessive case.] A possessive pronoun used instead of *her* and a noun, as subject, object, or predicate.—**herself,** hẽr·self′, pron. An emphasized or reflexive form of the third pers. pron. fem., used in the same way as *himself* (which see).

herald, her′ald, n. [O.Fr. *herault, herald*, Fr. *héraut*, from O.H.G. *hariwalt* (G. *herold*), an officer of an army—*hari, heri*, an army (akin E. *harry*), and *waltan*, to rule (E. *wield*).] An officer whose business was to denounce or proclaim war, to challenge to battle, to proclaim peace, to bear messages, etc.; an officer who marshals processions; a proclaimer; a forerunner.—v.t. To introduce or to give tidings of, as by a herald; to proclaim.—**heraldic,** he·ral′dik, a.—**heraldry,** her′ald·ri, n. The art or office of a herald; the art of blazoning arms or ensigns armorial, or the knowledge pertaining thereto.

herb, ẽrb or hẽrb, n. [Fr. *herbe*, L. *herba, herb*, from a root meaning to eat or nourish, seen in Gr. *phorbē*, pasture, fodder.] Any plant with a soft or succulent stem which dies to the root every year, as distinguished from a *tree* and a *shrub*, which have woody stems.—**herbaceous,** hẽr·bā′shus, a. [L. *herbaceus*.] Pertaining to herbs.—*Herbaceous plants*, plants which perish annually down to the root; soft, succulent vegetables.—**herbage,** ẽrb′ij or hẽrb′-ij, n. Herbs collectively; green food for beasts; grass; pasture.—**herbal,** hẽr′bal, n. A book containing the names and descriptions of plants; a collection of plants dried and preserved; a herbarium.—a. Pertaining to herbs.—**herbalist,** hẽr′bal·ist, n. A person who makes collections of plants;

a dealer in medicinal plants.—**herbarium**, hẽr·bā′ri·um, *n.* A collection of dried plants systematically arranged; a book or other contrivance for preserving dried specimens of plants.—**herbary**, hẽr′ba·ri, *n.* A garden of plants.—**herb bennet**, *n.* Common avens, an aromatic, tonic, and astringent plant.—**herbivore**, hẽr′bi·vōr, *n.* A herbivorous animal. —**herbivorous**, hẽr·biv′o·rus, *a.* [L. *herba*, and *voro*, to eat.] Eating herbs; subsisting on plants (a *herbivorous* animal).

herculean, hẽr·kū′li·an, *a.* Pertaining to *Hercules*; resembling Hercules in strength; very difficult or dangerous (a *Herculean* task).

herd, hẽrd, *n.* [A.Sax. *heord*, *herd*= Goth. *hairda*, D. *herde*, Dan. *hjord*, Icel. *hjörth*, G. *herde*, a herd, flock, drove, etc.] A number of beasts feeding or driven together; a company of men or people, in contempt or detestation; a crowd; a rabble.— *v.t.* and *i.* To form in a herd; to feed or run in herds; to associate; to unite in companies.—**herdsman**, hẽrdz′man,*n.* A man attending a herd.

herd, hẽrd, *n.* [A.Sax. *hirde*, a herdsman or shepherd, from *heord*, a flock or herd; Goth. *hairdeis*, Icel. *hirdi*, Dan. *hyrde*, G. *hirt*; same origin as the preceding.] A keeper of cattle or sheep: now mostly in composition, as shep*herd*, goat*herd*, swine*herd*.

here, hẽr, *adv.* [A.Sax. *hér*=Dan. and Goth. *her*, Icel. *hér*, G. and D. *hier*, here; based on the pronominal element seen in *he*.] In this place; in the place where the speaker is present: opposed to *there*; in the present life or state; to this place, hither (come *here*). *Here* in *Here's* for you, *Here* goes, etc., is a sort of exclamation to attract attention to something about to be done, the subject in familiar phrases having been dropped out.—*Neither here nor there*, neither in this place nor in that; hence, unconnected with the matter in hand; irrelevant; unimportant.—*Here and there*, in one place and another; thinly or irregularly dispersed.—**hereabout, hereabouts**, hẽr′a·bout, hẽr′a·bouts, *adv.* About this place; in this vicinity or neighborhood.—**hereafter**, hẽr·af′tẽr, *adv.* In time to come; in some future time or state.—*n.* A future state.—**hereat**, hẽr·at′, *adv.* At or by reason of this.—**hereby**, hẽr·bī′, *adv.* By this; by means of this; close by; very near.—**herein**, hẽr·in′, *adv.* In this.—**hereinafter**, hẽr·in·af′tẽr, *adv.* In this afterwards: applied to something afterwards to be named or described in a writing.—**hereinto**, hẽr·in′tö, *adv.* Into this.—**hereof**, hẽr·ov′, *adv.* Of this; concerning this; from this.—**hereon**, hẽr·on′, *adv.* On this.—**hereto**, hẽr·tö′, *adv.* To this. —**heretofore**, hẽr·tö·fōr′, *adv.* Before or up to this time; formerly.— **hereunto**, hẽr·un·tö′, *adv.* Unto this or this time; hereto.—**hereupon**, hẽr·up·on′, *adv.* Upon this; hereon. —**herewith**, hẽr·with′, *adv.* With this; by means of this.

hereditable, he·red′i·ta·bl, *a.*—[L.L. *hereditabilis*, from L. *hereditas*, *hereditatis*, the act of inheriting, from *heres*, *heredis*, an heir. HEIR.] Capable of being inherited.—**hereditability**, he·red′i·ta·bil′i·ti, *n.* State of being hereditable.—**hereditament**, he·re·dit′a·ment, *n.* [L.L. *hereditamentum*.] Any species of property that may be inherited.—**hereditarily**, he·red′i·te·ri·li, *adv.* By inheritance.—**hereditary**, he·red′i·te·ri, *a.* [L. *hereditarius*.] Descended by inheritance; descending from an ancestor to an heir; descendible to an heir-at-law; that is or may be transmitted from a parent to a child.—**heredity**, he·red′i·ti, *n.* [L. *hereditas*.] Hereditary transmission of qualities of like kind with those of the parent; the doctrine that the offspring inherits the characteristics of the parent or parents.

heresy, her′e·si, *n.* [Fr. *hérésie*, L. *hæresis*, from Gr. *hairesis*, a taking, a principle or set of principles, from *haireō*, to take.] A doctrine, principle, or set of principles at variance with established or generally received principles; especially an opinion or opinions contrary to the established religious faith, or what is regarded as the true faith; heterodoxy.—**heresiarch**, he·rē′si·ärk, *n.* [Gr. *hairesiarchos*, *hairesis*, heresy, and *archē*, rule.] A leader in heresy; a prominent or arch heretic.— **heretic**, her′e·tik, *n.* [L. *hæreticus*.] A person who holds heretical opinions; one who maintains heresy —**heretical**, he·ret′i·kal, *a.* Containing or pertaining to heresy.—**heretically**, he·ret′i·kal·li, *adv.* In a heretical manner.

heriot, her′i·ot, *n.* [A.Sax. *heregeatu*, military equipment, a heriot—*here*, an army, and *geatu*, equipment.] *Eng. law*, a chattel or payment given to the lord of a fee on the decease of the tenant or vassal.

heritable, her′i·ta·bl, *a.* [O.Fr. *héritable*, abbrev. from L.L. *hereditábilis*. HEREDITABLE.] Capable of being inherited; inheritable.—*Heritable property*, the name in Scotland for *real property*.—*Heritable security*, security constituted by heritable property.—**heritage**, her′i·tij, *n.* [Fr., from L. *hereditas*, heritage.] That which is inherited; inheritance; *Scots law*, heritable estate or realty.—**heritor**, her′i·tẽr, *n.* An inheritor; in Scotland, a proprietor or landholder in a parish.

hermaphrodite, hẽr·maf′ro·dīt, *n.* [From *Hermaphroditos* of Greek mythology, son of *Hermes* and *Aphrodite*, who became united into one body with a nymph.] An animal in which the characteristics of both sexes are either really or apparently combined; *bot.* a flower that contains both the stamen and the pistil, or the male and female organs. —*a.* Including or being of both sexes.—*Hermaphrodite brig*, a brig that is square-rigged forward and schooner-rigged aft.—**hermaphroditic, hermaphroditical**, hẽr·maf′ro·dit″ik, hẽr·maf′ro·dit″i·kal, *a.* Of

or pertaining to a hermaphrodite.— **hermaphroditically**, hẽr·maf′ro·dit″i·kal·li, *adv.* After the manner of hermaphrodites.—**hermaphroditism**, hẽr·maf′rod·it·izm, *n.* The state of being hermaphrodite.

hermeneutics, hẽr·mi·nū′tiks, *n.* [Gr. *hermēneutikos*, from *hermēneus*, an interpreter, from *Hermēs*, Mercury.] The art or science of interpretation; especially applied to the interpretation of the Scriptures; exegesis.—**hermeneutic, hermeneutical**, hẽr·mi·nū′tik, hẽr·mi·nū′ti·kal, *a.* Interpreting; explaining; exegetical; unfolding the signification.

hermetic, hermetical, hẽr·met′ik, hẽr·met′i·kal, *a.* [Fr. *hermétique*, from the ancient *Hermes Trismegistus*, who was regarded as skilled in alchemy and occult science.] Appellative of or pertaining to alchemy or the doctrines of the alchemists; effected by fusing together the edges of the mouth or aperture, as of a bottle or tube, so that no air, gas, or spirit can escape (the *hermetic* method of sealing).— **hermetically**, hẽr·met′i·kal·li, *adv.* In a hermetic manner; by fusing the edges together.

hermit, hẽr′mit, *n.* [Fr. *ermite*, O.Fr. *hermite*, Gr. *erēmitēs*, from *erēmos*, lonely, solitary, desert.] A person who retires from society and lives in solitude; a recluse; an anchorite.— **hermitage**, hẽr′mi·tij, *n.* The habitation of a hermit; a kind of French wine.—**hermit crab**, *n.* A species of crab which takes possession of and occupies the cast-off shells of various mollusks, carrying this habitation about with it, and changing it for a larger one as it increases in size.—**hermitical**, hẽr·mit′i·kal, *a.* Pertaining or suited to a hermit or to retired life.

hernia, hẽr′ni·a, *n.* [L.] *Surg.* a protrusion of some part from its natural cavity by an abnormal aperture; commonly the protrusion of viscera through an aperture in the wall of the abdomen; rupture.— **hernial**, hẽr′ni·al, *a.* Pertaining to hernia.

hero, hē′rō, *n.* pl. **heroes**, hē′rōz. [L. *heros*, from Gr. *hērōs*; akin to L. *vir* (seen in *virile*, *virtue*), A.Sax. *wer*, a man; Skr. *vira,* a hero.] A kind of demigod in ancient Greek mythology; hence, a man of distinguished valor or intrepidity; a prominent or central personage in any remarkable action or event; the principal personage in a poem, play, novel, etc.—**heroic**, he·rō′ik, *a.* [L. *heroicus*.] Pertaining to a hero; becoming a hero; characteristic of a hero; brave; magnanimous; intrepid and noble; reciting the achievements of heroes; epic.—*Heroic treatment, remedies*, *med.* treatment or remedies of a violent character.—*Heroic verse*, in English poetry, the iambic verse of ten syllables, in French the iambic of twelve, and in classical poetry the hexameter.—**heroically**, he·rō′i·kal·li, *adv.* In a heroic manner.—**heroine**, her′ō·in, *n.* [Fr. *héroïne*.] A female hero.—**heroism**,

he'rō·izm, *n.* The qualities of a hero; bravery; courage; intrepidity.

heroin, her'ō·in, *n.* [From *Heroin*, a trademark.] Diacetyl-morphine, a white crystalline drug used as a sedative, limited in distribution by law because it is habit-forming.

heron, her'un, *n.* [Fr. *heron*, O.Fr. *hairon*, from O.H.G. *heigro*, *heigero*, Icel. *hegri*, Sw. *häger*, a heron; hence also Fr. *aigre*, dim. *aigrette*, E. *egret*.] A grallatorial bird with a long bill cleft beneath the eyes, long slender legs and neck, formerly the special game pursued in falconry.—**heronry**, her'un·ri, *n.* A place where herons breed.

herpes, her'pēz, *n.* [Gr. *herpēs*, from *herpō*, to creep.] A skin disease characterized by the eruption of inflamed vesicles, such as shingles.—**herpetic**, her·pet'ik, *a.* Pertaining to or resembling herpes.

herpetology, her·pe·tol'o·ji, *n.* [Gr. *herpeton*, a reptile, from *herpō*, to creep, and *logos*, discourse.] A description of reptiles; the natural history of reptiles.—**herpetological**, her·pe·to·loj'i·kal, *a.* Pertaining to herpetology.—**herpetologist**, her··pe·tol'o·jist, *n.*

herring, her'ing, *n.* [A.Sax. *haering* = D. *haring*, G. *häring*, Icel. *haeringr*, herring; from A.Sax. *here*, G. *heer*, an army. HERALD.] A common fish, which is found in incredible numbers in the North Sea, the northern parts of the Atlantic, etc., of great importance as an article of food or commerce.—**herringbone**, *n.* A pattern made of rows of parallel lines, each with a reverse slant from the next, as in the spinal bones of the herring.—*v.t.* To produce a herringbone pattern, as in a fabric.—*v.i.* To climb a slope on skis, imprinting a *herringbone* pattern on the snow.

hers, herz, *pron.* See HER.

herse, hers, *n.* [Fr. *herse*, O.Fr. *herce*, a harrow, a portcullis; same as *hearse*.] A portcullis in the form of a harrow, set with iron spikes; a similar structure used for a cheval-de-frise; a framework whereon lighted candles were placed in some of the ceremonies of the church, and at the obsequies of distinguished persons; sometimes a hearse.

herself. See HER.

hertzian waves, hert'si·an wavz, *n.* [From Heinrich *Hertz*, G. physicist.] Long electromagnetic waves.

hesitate, hez'i·tāt, *v.i.*—hesitated, hesitating. [L. *hæsito*, *hæsitatum*, intens. from *hæreo*, *hæsum*, to stick, as in *adhere*, *cohere*, *inherent*.] To stop or pause respecting decision or action; to be doubtful as to fact, principle, or determination; to stammer; to stop in speaking.—**hesitatingly**, hez'i·tā·ting·li, *adv.*—**hesitation**, hez·i·tā'shon, *n.* The act of hesitating; stammering.—**hesitative**, hez'i·tā·tiv, *a.*—**hesitancy**, hez'i·tan··si, *n.*—**hesitant**, hez'i·tant, *a.*

Hesperian, hes·pē'ri·an, *a.* [L. *hesperius*, western, from Gr. *hesperos* (=L. *vesper*), the evening.] Western; situated at the west. (*Poet.*)—**Hesperides**, hes·per'i·dēz, *n. pl.* Greek *myth.* the daughters of Hesperus, possessors of the garden of golden fruit, watched over by a dragon, at the western extremities of the earth.

Hessian, hesh'n, *a.* Relating to *Hesse* in Germany.—*Hessian boot*, a kind of long boot originally worn by the Hessian troops.—*n.* A native of Hesse; a Hessian boot.—**Hessianfly**, *n.* A small two-winged fly nearly black, the larva of which is very destructive to young wheat.

hetaera, hetaira, he·tē'ra, he·tī'rā, *n.* [Gr. *hetarē*, *hetaira*.] A courtesan of the superior class.—**hetaerism, hetairism**, he·tēr'izm, he·tī'rizm, *n.* Concubinage; a supposed primitive social state, in which women of a tribe were held in common.

heterocercal, het'e·ro·ser·kal, *a.* [Gr. *heteros*, other, *kerkos*, a tail.] Having the vertebral column running to a point in the upper lobe of the tail, as in the sharks and sturgeons; contrasted with *homocercal*.

heteroclite, het'e·ro·klīt, *n.* [Gr. *heterokliton*—*heteros*, other, and *klinō*, to incline, to lean away from normal form.] A word which is irregular or anomalous either in declension or conjugation; something abnormal.

heterodox, het'e·ro·doks, *a.* [Gr. *heteros*, other, and *doxa*, opinion.] Contrary to established or generally received opinions; contrary to some recognized standard of opinion.—**heterodoxy**, het'e·ro·dok·si, *n.* The holding of heterodox opinions.

heterodyne, het'er·o·dīn, *n.* [Gr. *heteros*, other, and *dyne*, from Gr. *dynamis*, power.] The beating together in an electrical circuit of two frequencies, one of a signal-carrying current, and one of an uninterrupted current, to produce new frequencies.

heteroecism, het'er·ēs"ism, *n.* [Gr. *heteros*, different, *oikos*, a house.] In fungi, living on more than one kind of host in the course of the life history.

heterogamous, het·e·rog'a·mus, *a.* [Gr. *heteros*, other, *gamos*, marriage.] *Bot.* irregular in regard to the arrangement of the sexes; having florets of different sexes in the same flower head.—**heterogamy**, het·e··rog'a·mi, *n.*

heterogeneous, het'e·ro·jē"ni·us, *a.* [Gr. *heteros*, other, and *genos*, kind.] Differing in kind; composed of dissimilar or incongruous parts or elements: opposed to *homogeneous*.—**heterogeneously**, het'e·ro·jē"ni·us·li, *adv.*—**heterogeneousness, heterogeneity**, het'e·ro·jē"ni·us·nes, het'e·ro··ji"nē·i·ty, *n.*

heterogenesis, heterogeny, het'e··ro·jen"e·sis, het'e·roj'e·ni, *n.* [Gr. *heteros*, other, and *genesis*, generation.] *Biol.* spontaneous generation; also, same as *alternate generation.*

heterologous, het·e·rol'o·gus, *a.* [Gr. *heteros*, other, and *logos*, analogy, proportion.] Different; not analogous or homologous.—**heterology**, het·e·rol'o·ji, *n.* The state or quality of being heterologous; *biol.* want or absence of relation or analogy between parts.

heteromorphic, heteromorphous, het'e·ro·mor"fik, het'e·ro·mor"fus, *a.* [Gr. *heteros*, other, *morphē*, form.] Of an irregular or unusual form; having two or more diverse shapes.—**heteromorphism**, het'e·ro·mor"fizm, *n.* The state or quality of being heteromorphic; existence under different forms at different stages of development.

heteronomy, het·er·on'o·mi, *n.* [Gr. *heteronomie*, from Gr. *heteros*, and *nomos*, law.] Subjection to another's rule; not self-governed.

heteronym, het'er·o·nim, *n.* [Gr. *heteros*, other, *onoma*, name.] A word with the same spelling as another but a different pronunciation; a different name for the same thing.

heterophyllous, het·e·rof'i·lus or het·e·ro·fil"lus, *a.* [Gr. *heteros*, other, *phyllon*, leaf.] *Bot.* having two different kinds of leaves on the same stem.

heterosexual, het·er·o·seks'shu·al, *adj.* [Gr. *heteros*, other, and *sexual.*] Of or relating to relationships between persons of the opposite sex.

heterosphere, het'e·ro·sphere, *n.* [Gr. *heteros*, other, and *sphere.*] A layer of the atmosphere stretching about 22,000 miles.

heterosporous, het'er·o·spor"us, *a.* [Gr. *heteros*, different, *sporos*, seed.] With spores of different kinds.

heterotaxy, het'e·ro·tak"si, *n.* [Gr. *heteros*, other, and *taxis*, arrangement.] Arrangement other than normal; confused or abnormal arrangement or structure.

hetman, het'man, *n.* [Pol., from G. *hauptman*, head-man, chieftain.] The title of the head (general) of the Cossacks.

heuristic, hū·ris'tik, *a.* [Gr. *heuriskein*, to find out.] Aiding or leading on toward discovery or finding out.

hew, hū, *v.t.*—pret. *hewed*, pp. *hewed* or *hewn*. [A.Sax. *heáwan*, D. *houwen*, G. *hauen*, Icel. *höggva*, Dan. *hugge*, to hew; akin *hoe*, *hay*.] To cut or fell with an ax or other like instrument; to shape with a sharp instrument: often with *out*.—**hewer**, hū'er, *n.* One who hews.

hex, heks, *n.* [Gr. *hexe*, witch.] A spell or curse.—*v.t.* To put a curse on.

hexacord, hek'sa·kord, *n.* [Gr. *hex*, six, and *chordē*, a chord.] *Mus.* a series of six notes, each rising one degree over the other.

hexagon, hek'sa·gon, *n.* [Gr. *hex*, six, and *gōnia*, an angle.] *Geom.* a figure of six sides and six angles.—**hexagonal**, hek·sag'on·al, *a.*—**hexagonally**, hek·sag'on·al·li, *adv.*

hexahedron, hek·sa·hē'dron, *n.* [Gr. *hex*, six, and *hedra*, a base or seat.] A regular solid body of six sides; a cube.—**hexahedral**, hek·sa·hē'dral, *a.* Of the figure of a hexahedron.

hexameter, hek·sam'e·ter, *n.* [Gr. *hex*, six, and *metron*, measure.] *Pros.* a verse of six feet, the first four of which may be either dactyls or spondees, the fifth normally a dactyl, though sometimes a spondee, and the sixth always a spondee.

---

ch, *chain*; *ch*, Sc. *loch*; g, *go*; j, *job*; ng, *sing*; TH, *then*; th, *thin*; w, *wig*; hw, *whig*; zh, *azure*.

—a. Having six metrical feet.—
hexametric, hexametral, hek·sa·-
met′rik, hek·sam′et·ral, a. Consisting
of six metrical feet; forming a
hexameter.

hexangular, hek·sang′gū·lėr, a. [Gr.
hex, six, and E. angular.] Having
six angles.

hexapla, hek′sa·pla, n. pl. [Gr. he-
xaplous, sixfold—hex, six, and term.
as in double.] An edition of the
Holy Scriptures in six languages
or six versions in parallel columns.—
hexaplar, hek′sa·plėr, a. Pertaining
to a hexapla.

hexapod, hek′sa·pod, a. [Gr. hex, six,
and pous, podos, a foot.] Having six
feet.—n. An animal having six feet.

hexastich, hexastichon, hek′sa·stik,
hek·sas′ti·kon, n. [Gr. hex, six,
stichos, a verse.] A poem consisting
of six lines or verses.

hey, hā. [Comp. G. and D. hei.] An
exclamation of joy or to call attention.

heyday, hā′dā, interj. [Comp. G.
heyda, heidi, heia, huzzah! heyday!]
An exclamation of cheerfulness and
sometimes of wonder.

heyday, hā′dā, n. [Equivalent to
highday.] A frolic; the wildness, or
frolicsome period of youth.

hiatus, hi·ā′tus, n. [L., from hio, to
open or gape.] An opening; a gap;
a space from which something is
wanting; a lacuna; pros. the coming
together of two vowels in two
successive syllables or words.

hibernal, hi·bėr′nal, a. [L. hibernalis,
from hibernus, wintry, akin to hiems,
winter; Gr. chiōn, Skr. hima, snow.]
Belonging or relating to winter;
wintry.—**hibernate,** hi′bėr·nāt, v.i.
—hibernated, hibernating. [L. hiberno,
hibernatum.] To winter; to pass the
winter in sleep or seclusion, as
some animals.—**hibernation,** hi·bėr-
nā′shon, n. The act of hibernating.—
—**hibernaculum,** hi·bėr·nak′ū·lum,
n. The winter retreat of an animal.

Hibernian, hi·bėr′ni·an, a. [L. Hi-
bernia, Ireland.] Pertaining to Hi-
bernia, now Ireland; Irish.—n. A
native or inhabitant of Ireland.—
Hibernianism, Hibernicism, hi·-
bėr′ni·an·izm, hi·bėr′ni·sizm, n. An
idiom or mode of speech peculiar to
the Irish.

hibiscus, hi·bis′kus, n. [Gr. hibiskos.]
Any of a large genus (Hibiscus) of
herbs, shrubs or small trees of the
mallow family, having showy flowers.

hiccup, hiccough, hik′up, n. [Imi-
tative.] A spasmodic catching in the
breath with a sudden sound; a convulsive catch of the respiratory muscles repeated at short intervals.—v.t.
and i. To have, or say with, hiccups.

hickory, hik′o·ri, n. [North Amer.
Indian.] A North American tree
of the walnut family with pinnate
leaves, growing from 70 to 80 feet
high, the wood of which is heavy,
strong, tenacious, and very valuable.

hidalgo, hi·dal′gō, Sp. pron. ē·däl′gō,
n. [Sp., contr. for hijodalgo, hijo de
algo, son of somebody—hijo, from
L. filius, son, and algo, from L.
aliquod, something, somewhat.] In
Spain, a man belonging to the lower

nobility; a gentleman by birth.

hide, hid, v.t.—hid (pret.), hid, hidden
(pp.), hiding (ppr.). [A.Sax. hydan, to
hide; cog. W. cuddiaw, to cover,
cudd, darkness, Gr. keuthō, to hide;
akin hide, skin.] To withhold or
withdraw from sight or knowledge;
to keep secret; to conceal.—v.i. To
conceal one's self; to lie concealed.—
hid, hidden, hid, hid′n, p. and a.
Concealed; placed in secrecy; secret; unseen; mysterious.—**hider,**
hi′der, n. One who hides or conceals.

hide, hid, n. [A.Sax. hýd=D. huid,
Icel. huth, Dan. and Sw. hud, G.
haut, hide; cog. L. cutis, Gr. skutos,
the skin of a beast, from root
meaning to cover, as in hide, v.t.]
The skin of an animal; especially,
the undressed skin of the larger
domestic animals, as oxen, horses,
etc.; the human skin, in contempt.—
v.t. To beat; to flog. (Colloq.)—
hiding, hi′ding, n. A flogging or beating. (Colloq.)—**hidebound,** hid′-
bound, a. Having the skin tight on
the body, said of horses or cattle;
narrowminded; unyielding in opinion.

hide, hid, n. [A.Sax. hid, contr. from
higid, a hide; same root as hive.]
An old measure of land variously
estimated at 60, 80, and 100 acres.

hideous, hid′ē·us, a. [Fr. hideux,
O.Fr. hisdous, rough, shaggy, hideous, from L. hispidosus, for hispidus, rough, shaggy.] Frightful to
the sight; dreadful; shocking to the
eye; shocking in any way; detestable;
horrible.—**hideously,** hid′ē·us·li,adv.
In a hideous manner.—**hideousness,**
hid′ē·us·nes, n.

hideout, hid′out, n. A place of refuge
and concealment.

hie, hi, v.i.—hied, hieing. [A.Sax.
higian, to endeavor, to hasten; perhaps from hyge, hige, the mind,
thought; comp. D. hijgen, Dan.
hige, to covet.] To move or run with
haste; to go in haste (often with
him, me, etc., reflexively; as, he hied
him home).

hierarch, hi′ėr·ärk, n. [Gr. hieros,
sacred, and archē, rule.] One who
rules or has authority in sacred
things.—**hierarchic, hierarchical,**
hi·ėr·är′kik, hi·ėr·är′ki·kal, a. Pertaining to a hierarch or hierarchy.—
hierarchically, hi·ėr·är′ki·kal·li, adv.
In a hierarchic manner.—**hierarchy,**
hi′ėr·är·ki, n. Authority in sacred
things; a ranking of individuals, as
of officials according to their power
in government or in the church;
arrangement of scientific items according to their logical relationships.

hieratic, hieratical, hi·ėr·at′ik, hi·-
ėr·at′i·kal, a. [Gr. hieratikos, from
hieros, holy.] Consecrated to sacred
uses; pertaining to priests; sacred;
sacerdotal; especially applied to the
characters or mode of writing used
by the ancient Egyptian priests, a
development from the hieroglyphics.

hierocracy, hi·ėr·ok′ra·si, n. [Gr.
hieros, holy, and kratos, power.]
Government by ecclesiastics; hierarchy.

hieroglyph, hieroglyphic, hi′ėr·o·-
glif, hi′ėr·o·glif″ik, n. [Gr. hieros,
sacred, and glyphō, to carve.] The
figure of an animal, plant, or other
object intended to convey a meaning
or stand for an alphabetical character; a figure implying a word, an
idea, or a sound, such as those in use
among the ancient Egyptians; a
figure having a hidden or enigmatical
significance; a character difficult to
decipher.—**hieroglyphical,** hi′ėr·o·-
glif″i·kal, a. Forming a hieroglyphic;
consisting of hieroglyphics; expressive of meaning by hieroglyphics.—
hieroglyphically, hi′ėr·o·glif″i·kal·li,
adv. In a hieroglyphic manner.—
hieroglyphist, hi′ėr·o·glif·ist, n.
One versed in hieroglyphics.

hierology, hi·ėr·ol′o·ji, n. [Gr. hieros,
sacred, and logos, discourse.] Sacred
lore; knowledge of hieroglyphics or
sacred writing.

hierophant, hi′ėr·o·fant, n. [Gr.
hierophantēs — hieros, sacred, and
phainō, to show.] A priest; one
who teaches the mysteries and
duties of religion.—**hierophantic,**
hi′ėr·o·fan″tik, a. Belonging to hier-
ophants.

hi-fi, hi′fi, n. [Abbrev. for high
fidelity.] Life-like sound reproduction or high fidelity; the radio or
phonographic equipment that reproduces sound with comparatively
slight distortion.

higgle, hig′l, v.i.—higgled, higgling.
[A weaker form of haggle, to chaffer.]
To haggle.—**higgler,** hig′l·ėr, n.

high, hi, a. [A.Sax. heáh, héh=Goth.
hauhs, Icel. hár, Dan. hoi, D. hoog,
G. hoch, high; hence height.] Having
a great extent from base to summit;
rising much above the ground or
some other object; elevated, lofty,
tall; exalted, excellent, superior
(mind, attainments, art); elevated in
rank, condition, or office; difficult to
comprehend; abstruse; arrogant,
boastful, proud; loud, boisterous,
threatening, or angry (high words);
extreme, intense, strong, forcible;
exceeding the common measure or
degree (a high wind; high color);
full or complete (high time); dear;
of a great price, or greater price
than usual; remote from the equator
north or south (a high latitude);
mus. acute or elevated in tone;
capital; committed against the king,
sovereign, or state (high treason);
cook. tending towards putrefaction;
strong-scented (venison kept till
it is high). Used substantively for
people of rank or high station
(high and low).—On high, aloft; in a
lofty position.—High and dry, out
of the water; out of reach of the
current or waves.—High altar, the
chief altar in a church.—High
Church, that branch of the Church
of England known as the Anglo-
Catholic Church, in contradistinction to the Protestant Episcopal
Church.—High day, a festival or
gala day.—High day, high noon, the
time when the sun is in the meridian.
—High Dutch, High German. DUTCH,
GERMAN.—High life, the style of
living of the upper classes.—High

living, indulgence in rich or costly food and drink.—*High Mass*, principal Mass, a solemn ceremony in which the priest is assisted by a deacon and subdeacon.—*High place*, in Scrip. an eminence or mound on which sacrifices were offered, especially to heathen deities.—*High school*, the school next above a grammar or elementary school, usually public and offering a four-year course.—*To be on the high horse, to mount one's high horse*, to stand on one's dignity; to assume a lofty tone or manner; to take offense.—*adv.* In a high manner; to a great altitude; highly; richly; luxuriously.—**highball**, hī′bal, *n.* An iced alcoholic drink, made of spirits mixed with soda or ginger ale, etc., and served in a tall glass.—**highborn**, *a.* Being of noble birth.—**highbrow**, *n.* An intellectual. (*Slang*)—**high explosives**, *n.* Explosives of extremely powerful class, especially such as are based on nitroglycerine.—**high fidelity**. Sound reproduction by radio or phonograph to closely approximate the original; shortened form, hi-fi.—**highflier**, *n.* One who is extravagant in pretensions or manners. (*Colloq.*)—**high-flown**, *a.* Elevated; proud; turgid; extravagant. —**high frequency**, *adj.* Any frequency above the audible range, particularly a radio frequency.— **highhanded**, *a.* Oppressive; violent; arbitrary.—**highland**, hī′land, *n.* An elevated or mountainous region: [*cap.*] generally in plural (the *Highlands* of Scotland).—*a.* Pertaining to highlands, [*cap.*] especially the Highlands of Scotland.—**highlander**, hī′land·ėr, *n.* An inhabitant of highlands, [*cap.*] particularly the Highlands of Scotland.—**Highland fling**, *n.* A sort of dance peculiar to the Scottish Highlanders, danced by one person. —**high-hat**, *n.* A snob.—*v.t.* To snub someone.—**highly**, hī′li, *adv.* In a high manner or to a high degree; greatly; decidedly; markedly. —**high-minded**, *a.* Characterized by, or pertaining to, elevated principles and feelings.—**high-mindedness**, *n.* —**highness**, hī′nes, *n.* [*cap.*] A title of honor given to princes or other persons of rank: used with poss. pron. *his, her*, etc.—**high-pressure**, *a.* Having a pressure much greater than that of the normal pressure of the atmosphere; pressing, intense, urgent.—**high priest**, *n.* A chief priest.—**highroad**, *n.* A highway, hence, an easy way.—**high seas**, *n.* pl. The open sea or ocean; the ocean beyond the limit of 3 miles from the shore.—**high-sounding**, *a.* Pompous; ostentatious; bombastic.—**high-spirited**, *a.* Having a high spirit; bold; manly.—**high-strung**, *a.* Having some intense emotion.—**high tension**, *adj.* Having a high voltage; capable of operating under a voltage of 1,000 volts or more.—**high tide**, *n.* High water.—**high-toned**, *a.* High in tone or pitch; high-principled; dignified; chic.—**highway**, hī′wā, *n.* A public road; a way open to all travelers.— **highwayman**, hī′wā·man, *n.* One

who robs on the public road or highway.—**high-wrought**, *a.* Agitated to a high degree.

hike, hīk, *v.i.* [Perhaps from *hitch*.] To walk or tramp for some distance, usually in the country; to march, as a soldier; to raise, as a price. —*v.t.* To lift up with a jerk; to increase an amount suddenly.—*n.* A walk or tramp; a march.

hilarity, hi·lar′i·ti, *n.* [Fr. *hilarité*, from L. *hilaritas*, from *hilaris*, *hilarus*, Gr. *hilaros*, cheerful; hence *exhilarate*.] A pleasurable excitement of the animal spirits; mirth; merriment; gaiety.—*Hilary term*, a law term beginning near the festival of St. *Hilary*, which is January 13.— **hilarious**, hi·lâ′ri·us, *a.* Mirthful; merry.

hill, hil, *n.* [A.Sax. *hill, hyll*, a hill; O.D. *hille, hil*; same root as L. *collis*, a hill, *columna*, a column.] A natural elevation less than a mountain; an eminence rising above the level of the surrounding land; a heap (a mole*hill*),—**hillbilly**, *n.* One who lives in a rough, hilly region, such as the southern Appalachians or the Ozarks. (*Colloq.*)—**hilliness**, hil′i·nes, *n.*—**hillside**, hil′sīd, *n.* The side or declivity of a hill.—**hilltop**, hil′top, *n.* The top or summit of a hill.— **hilly**, hil′i, *a.* Consisting of hills.— **hillock**, hil′ok, *n.* [Dim. of *hill*.] A small hill.

hilt, hilt, *n.* [A.Sax. *hilt*, hilt = Icel. *hjalt*, Dan. *hjalte*, O.H.G. *helza*; same root as *helve*.] The handle of a sword, dagger, etc.

hilum, hī′lum, *n.* [L.] The mark or scar on a seed (as the black patch on a bean) produced by its separation from the placenta.

him, him, *pron.* [In A.Sax. the dative and instrumental of *he* and *hit*, he and it, afterwards used instead of *hine*, the real accusative sing. masc.; *m* is properly a dative suffix, as in *them, whom*.] The dative and objective case of *he*.—**himself**, him·self′, *pron.* An emphatic and reflexive form of the 3rd pers. pron. masc.; as, *himself*, he *himself*, the man *himself*, told me; it was *himself*, or he *himself*; he struck *himself*. It often implies that the person has command of himself, or is possessed of his natural frame or temper; as, he is not *himself* at all; he soon came to *himself*.—*By himself*, alone; unaccompanied.

Himyaritic, him·ya·rit′ik, *a.* [From *Himyar*, an ancient king of Yemen.] Pertaining to the ancient Arabic of Southeast Arabia.—*n.* The language of Southeast Arabia.

hin, hin, *n.* [Heb.] A Hebrew measure containing about 5 quarts.

hind, hīnd, *n.* [A.Sax. *hind* = G. and D. *hinde*, Icel., Dan., and Sw. *hind*.] The female of the red deer, the stag being the male.

hind, hīnd, *n.* [A.Sax. *hine, hina*, with *d* affixed, as in *lend, sound*; akin *hive*.] In England an agricultural laborer.

hind, hīnd, *a.* [A.Sax. *hind*, hind, *hindan*, behind; Goth. *hindana, hindar*, O.H.G. *hintar*, G. *hinten*,

behind, *hinter*, hind; hence to *hinder*.] Backward; pertaining to the part which follows or is behind; opposite of *fore*.—**hinder**, hin′dėr, *a.* In the rear; following; after.— **hindmost**, hīnd′mōst, *a.* [A.Sax. *hindema*, hindmost; the *-most* is a corruption as in *foremost* (which see).] Farthest behind; behind all others; last.—**hindsight**, hīnd′sīt, *n.* Rear sight on a gun; judgment of an incident after it has passed; opposite of *foresight*.

hinder, hin′dėr, *v.t.* [A.Sax. *hindrian*, to hinder, from *hinder*, compar. of *hind, a.* (which see).] To prevent from proceeding or from starting; to stop; to interrupt; to obstruct; to impede; to check or retard in progression or motion; to debar; to shut out; to balk; often with *from* and a verbal noun (to *hinder* him *from* going; the *from* is sometimes omitted).—*v.i.* To interpose obstacles or impediments.—**hinderer**, hin′dėr·ėr, *n.* One who hinders.— **hindrance**, hin′drans, *n.* The act of hindering; that which hinders; impediment; obstruction; obstacle.

Hindu, Hindoo, hin·dö′ or hin′dö, *n.* A disciple of Hinduism; an Asiatic Indian.—**Hinduism**, **hindooism**, hin′dö·izm, *n.* The doctrines and rites of the Hindus; Brahmanism.— **Hindustani**, hin·dö·stan′i, *n.* A language of Hindustan, akin to Sanskrit, but having a large admixture of Persian and Arabic words, spoken more or less throughout nearly the whole Peninsula.—**Hindi**, hin′di, *n.* A language of Northern India akin to Hindustani, but much more purely Sanskrit.

hinge, hinj, *n.* [Probably from *hang*, O. and Prov. E. and Sc. *hing*; comp. Prov. E. *hingle*, a small hinge; D. *hengsel*, a hinge.] The hook or joint on which a door, lid, gate, or shutter, and the like turns; the joint of a bivalve shell; *fig.* that on which anything depends or turns; a governing principle, rule, or point.— *v.t.* To furnish with hinges.—*v.i.*— *hinged, hinging.* To stand, depend, or turn, as on a hinge.

hint, hint, *n.* [Perhaps from O.E. *hente*, A.Sax. *hentan*, to seize; comp. also Icel. *ymtr*, a muttering.] A motive or occasion (*Shak.*); a distant allusion or slight mention; a word or two suggesting or insinuating something; a suggestion.—*v.t.* To bring to notice by a hint; to suggest indirectly. ∴ To *hint* is merely to make some reference or allusion that may or may not be apprehended; to *suggest* is to offer something definite for consideration.—*v.i.* To make or utter a hint.—*To hint at*, to allude to.—**hinter**, hin′tėr, *n.* One who hints.—**hintingly**, hin′ting·li, *adv.* In a hinting manner.

hinterland, hin′tėr·land, *n.* [G.] The outlying region, remote from any towns.

hip, hip, *n.* [A.Sax. *hype* = Icel. *huppr*, Dan. *hofte*, Goth. *hups*, D. *heup*, G. *hufte*; akin to *heap*, perhaps to *hump*.] The fleshy projecting part of the thigh; the haunch; *arch.* the

ch, *chain*; *ch*, Sc. lo*ch*; g, *go*; j, *job*; ng, si*ng*; TH, *then*; th, *thin*; w, *wig*, hw, *whig*; zh, azure.

external angle at the junction of two sloping roofs or sides of a roof.—*To have a person on the hip,* to have the advantage over him; to have got some catch on him.—*To smite hip and thigh,* to overthrow completely with great slaughter (O.T.).— *v.t.*—*hipped, hipping.* To sprain or dislocate the hip.—**hip joint,** *n.* The joint of the hip, a ball-and-socket joint.—**hip roof,** *n.* A roof, the ends of which slope inwards with the same inclination to the horizon as its two other sides.— **hipshot,** *a.* Having the hip dislocated; lame; awkward.

hip, hip, *n.* [A.Sax. *heope.*] The fruit of the dog rose or wild brier.

hip, hip, *n.* [Contr. of *hypochondria.*] Hypochondria.—*v.t.* To render hypochondriac or melancholy.— **hipped,** hipt, *p.* and *a.* Rendered melancholy; characterized by melancholy.—**hippish,** hip'ish, *a.* Somewhat melancholy or hypochondriac.

hip, hip, *interj.* An exclamation expressive of a call to any one or to arouse attention (*hip, hip, hip,* hurrah!).

hippocras, hip'o·kras, *n.* [Fr., lit. wine of *Hippocrates.*] A medicinal drink, composed of wine with an infusion of spices and other ingredients, used as a cordial.—**Hippocratic,** hip·o·krat'ik, *a.* Pertaining to Hippocrates, a Greek physician, born 460 B.C.—*Hippocratic oath,* pledge to a code of ethics taken by those entering upon medical practice.

Hippocrene, hip'o·krēn, *n.* [Gr. horse fount.] Fountain on Mount Helicon, the seat of the Muses in Boeotia, produced by the stamp of the foot of the winged horse Pegasus; source of poetic inspiration.

hippodrome, hip'o·drōm, *n.* [Gr. *hippodromos—hippos,* a horse, *dromos,* a course.] Anciently, a place in which horse races and chariot races were performed; a circus.

hippogriff, hippogryph, hip'o·grif, *n.* [Gr. *hippos,* a horse, and *gryps,* a griffon.] A fabulous monster, half horse and half griffon.

hippophagy, hip·pof'a·ji, *n.* [Gr. *hippos,* a horse, and *phagō,* to eat.] The act or practice of feeding on horse-flesh.—**hippophagous,** hip·pof'a·gus, *a.* Feeding on horse flesh.

hippopotamus, hip·o·pot'a·mus, *n.* pl. **hippopotamuses** or **hippopotami,** hip·o·pot'a·mus·ez, hip·o·pot'a·mi. [Gr. *hippos,* a horse, and *potamos,* a river.] A hoofed quadruped of great bulk inhabiting lakes and rivers in Africa, being an excellent swimmer and diver, and feeding on herbage.

hircine, hèr'sīn, *a.* [L. *hircinus,* from *hircus,* a goat.] Pertaining to or resembling a goat; having a strong, rank smell like a goat; goatish.

hire, hīr, *v.t.*—*hired, hiring.* [A.Sax. *hyrian,* from *hyr,* hire; Dan. *hyre,* to hire, *hyre,* wages, Sw. *hyra,* G. *heuer,* hire.] To procure from another person and for temporary use at a certain price or equivalent; to engage in service for a stipulated reward; to grant the temporary use or service of for compensation; to let: in this sense usually with *out,* and often reflexively.—*n.* The compensation given for the temporary use of anything; the reward or recompense paid for personal service; wages.—**hireling,** hīr'ling, *n.* [A.Sax. *hýreling.*] One who is hired or who serves for wages; a venal or mercenary person.—*a.* Venal; mercenary.—**hirer,** hī'rèr, *n.* One that hires.

hirsute, hèr·sūt', *a.* [L. *hirsutus,* shaggy, from *hirtus,* hairy, connected with *horrid.*] Rough with hair; hairy; shaggy.—**hirsuteness,** hèr·sūt'nes, *n.*

hirundine, hi·run'dīn, *a.* and *n.* [L. *hirundo,* a swallow.] Swallow-like; a swallow.

his, hiz, *pron.* [In A.Sax. the genit. sing. of *hé,* he, and of *hit,* it.] The possessive case singular of the personal pronoun *he;* of or belonging to him; formerly also used for *its.*

hispid, his'pid, *a.* [L. *hispidus,* rough, hairy. HIDEOUS.] Rough; shaggy; bristly; *bot.* beset with stiff bristles.—**hispidity,** his·pid'i·ti, *n.* The state of being hispid.— **hispidulous,** his·pid'ū·lus, *a. Bot.* having short stiff hairs.

hiss, his, *v.i.* [A.Sax. *hysian,* O.D. *hissen,* imitative of sound.] To make a sound like that of the letter *s,* in contempt or disapprobation; to emit a similar sound; said of serpents, of water thrown on hot metal, etc,—*v.t.* To condemn by hissing; to express disapproval of by hissing.—*n.* The sound made by propelling the breath between the tongue and upper teeth, as in pronouncing the letter *s,* especially as expressive of disapprobation; any similar sound.

hist, hist, *exclam.* [Origin unknown.] A word commanding silence, equivalent to *hush,* be silent.

histamine, his'tä·mēn, *n.* [*Hist*adine and *amine.*] A substance occurring in animal and vegetable tissues, used to dilate blood vessels and stimulate gastric secretions in treating certain diseases.

histological, his·to·loj'i·kal, *a.* [Gr. *histos,* tissue.] Pertaining to histology. —**histologist,** his·tol'o·jist, *n.*—**histology,** his·tol'o·ji, *n.* The science which deals with the microscopic structure of the tissues and organs.

history, his'to·ri, *n.* [L. *historia,* a history, from Gr. *historia,* a learning by inquiry, from G. *histor,* knowing, learned.] That branch of knowledge which deals with events that have taken place in the world's existence; the study or investigation of the past; a narrative or account of an event or series of events in the life of a nation, or that have marked the progress or existence of any community or institution; a verbal relation of facts or events; a narrative; an account of things that exist; a description; an account of an individual person.—**historian,** his·tō'ri·an, *n.* A writer or compiler of history; a historical writer.— **historic, historical,** his·tor'ik, his·tor'i·kal, *a.* [L. *historicus.*] Pertaining to or connected with history; containing or contained in, deduced from, suitable to, representing, etc., history.—**historically,** his·tor'i·kal·li, *adv.* In a historic manner.— **historied,**† his'to·rid, *a.* Recorded in history.—**historiographer,** his·tō'ri·og"ra·fèr, *n.* A historian; particularly, a professed or official historian.—**historiography,** his·tō'ri·og"ra·fi, *n.* The art or employment of a historian; the writing of history.

histrionic, histrionical, his·tri·on'ik, his·tri·on'i·kal, *a.* [L. *histrionicus,* from *histrio,* an actor; same root as Skr. *has,* to laugh at.] Pertaining to an actor or stage player; belonging to stage playing; theatrical; stagey; feigned for purposes of effect.— **histrionic,**† his·tri·on'ik, *n.* A dramatic performer.—**histrionically,** his·tri·on'i·kal·li, *adv.* In a histrionic manner.—**histrionics,** his·tri·on'iks, *n.* The art of theatrical representation.—**histrionism, histrionicism,** his'tri·on·izm, his·tri·on'i·sizm, *n.* Stage playing; theatrical or artificial manners or deportment.

hit, hit, *v.t.*—*hit, hitting.* [Same as Icel. *hitta,* Dan. *hitte,* to hit, to meet with.] To strike or touch with some degree of force; not to miss; to give a blow to; to reach or attain to an object desired; to light upon; to get hold of or come at (to *hit* a likeness); to suit; to agree with.—*v.i.* To strike; to meet; to clash: followed by *against* or *on;* to agree; suit.—*n.* The act of hitting; the blow which successfully strikes the target aimed at; a person or thing that is a noted success; *baseball,* a blow by which the ball is knocked, permitting the batter to get on base; an effective phrase or remark.—**hit-and-miss,** *a.* Sometimes effective, sometimes not; careless.—**hit-and-run,** *a.* Baseball, a play in which a runner starts for the next base, as the pitcher starts to pitch and the batter tries to hit the ball behind the runner; a term for motor vehicle drivers who leave the scene of an accident in which they are involved.—**hitter,** hit'er, *n.*

hitch, hich, *v.i.* [Comp. Prov. E. *hick,* to hop or spring; G. dial. *hiksen,* to limp; Sc. *hotch,* to move by jerks, to hobble; Prov. E. *huck,* to shrug.] To move by jerks or with stops; to become entangled; to be caught or hooked (the cord *hitched* on a branch); to be linked or yoked. —*v.t.* To fasten; to yoke; to make fast; to hook; to raise or pull up; to raise by jerks (to *hitch up* one's trousers).—*n.* A catch; an impediment; a breakdown, especially of a casual and temporary nature; a heave or pull up; temporary help or assistance (to give one a *hitch*); *naut.* a kind of knot or noose in a rope for fastening it to an object.— **hitchhike,** hich'hīk, *v.i.* To travel by getting free rides, especially in passing automobiles.—**hitchhiker,** hich'hīk·er, *n.*

hither, hiTH'ér, *adv.* [A.Sax. *hider,*

---

fāte, fär, fâre, fat, fạll;   mē, met, hėr;   pīne, pin;   nōte, not, mōve;   tūbe, tub, bụll;   oil, pound.

hither, Goth. *hidre*, Icel. *hethra*, hither, from stem of *he* with comparative suffix.] To this place; here: with verbs signifying motion.—*Hither and thither*, to this place and that.—*a.* On this side or in this direction; nearer.—**hitherto**, hiTH´er·tö, *adv.* To this time or place; until now.—**hitherward**, *adv.* Toward this place.

hive, hīv, *n.* [A.Sax. *hýf*, *hýfe*, *hýfi*, a hive; probably of same root as L. *cupa*, a cup, whence E. *cup*, *cupola*, *goblet*, etc.] A box or kind of basket for the reception and habitation of a swarm of honeybees; the bees inhabiting a hive; a place swarming with busy occupants.—*v.t.*—*hived*, *hiving*. To collect into a hive; to cause to enter a hive; to lay up in store for future use.—*v.i.* To take shelter together; to reside in a collective body.

hives, hīvz, *n.* [Perhaps akin to *heave*.] The eruption of urticaria.

ho, hoa, hō´ hō´a, *interj.* [Fr. *ho*, Icel. *hó*.] A cry or call to arrest attention.

hoar, hōr, *a.* [A.Sax. *hár*, hoary, grayhaired; Icel. *hárr*, hoar, *hœra*, gray hair, hoariness; comp. Sc. *haar*, a whitish mist.] White (hoarfrost); gray or grayish white; white with age; hoary.—*n.* Hoariness; antiquity.—*v.i.* To become moldy or musty.—**hoarfrost**, *n.* The white particles of frozen dew, rime.—**hoariness**, hō´ri·nes, *n.* The state of being hoary.—**hoary**, hō´ri, *a.* White or gray with age; hence, *fig.* remote in time past; *bot.* covered with short, dense, grayish-white hairs; canescent.

hoard, hōrd, *n.* [A.Sax. *hord*=O.Sax. and G. *hort*, Icel. *hodd*, Goth. *huzd*, hoard, treasure; from root of *house*, and of L. *custos*, a guardian.] A store, stock, or large quantity of anything accumulated or laid up; a hidden stock.—*v.t.* To collect and lay up in a hoard; to amass and deposit in secret: often followed by *up*.—*v.i.* To collect and form a hoard; to lay up store of money.—**hoarder**, hōr´dėr, *n.* One who hoards.

hoarding, hōr´ding, *n.* [O.Fr. *horde*, a barrier. HURDLE.] A timber enclosure round a building when the latter is in the course of erection or undergoing alteration or repair.

hoarse, hōrs, *a.* [A.Sax. *hás*, hoarse, husky=Icel. *háss*, Dan. *haes*, D. *heesch*, G. *heiser*, hoarse: the *r* is intrusive.] Having a harsh, rough, grating voice, as when affected with a cold; giving out a harsh, rough cry or sound.—**hoarsely**, hōrs´li, *adv.* In a hoarse manner.—**hoarsen**, hōr´sn, *v.t.* and *i.* To make or to grow hoarse.—**hoarseness**, hōrs´nes, *n.* The state or quality of being hoarse.

hoax, hōks, *n.* [For *hocus*.] Something done for deception or mockery; a trick played off in sport; a practical joke.—*v.t.* To play a trick upon for sport or without malice.—**hoaxer**, hōk´sėr, *n.* One that hoaxes.

hob, hob, *n.* [Same as *hub*; comp.

Dan. *hob*, a heap; *hump* is akin, and *hobnail* is a compound.] The part of a grate or fireplace on which things are placed in order to be kept warm.

hobble, hob´l, *v.i.*—*hobbled*, *hobbling*. [From or connected with *hop*; comp. D. *hobbelen*, to hobble, to stammer.] To walk lamely, bearing chiefly on one leg; to limp; to walk awkwardly; to wabble or wobble; *fig.* to halt or move irregularly in versification.—*v.t.* To hopple.—*n.* A halting gait; a difficulty; a scrape; a clog; a fetter.—**hobbler**, hob´lėr, *n.* One that hobbles.—**hobblingly**, hob´ling·li, *adv.*

hobbledehoy, hob´l·di·hoi, *n.* [Of uncertain origin.] A raw gawky youth approaching manhood.

hobby, hob´i, *n.* [Comp. Fr. *hoberau*, dim. of O.Fr. *hobe*, a little bird of prey.] A small but strong-winged Old World falcon.

hobby, hob´i, *n.* [M.E. *hoby*, *hobyn*, perhaps for *Hobbin*, nickname of Robert or Robin.] A favorite pursuit; an interest apart from one's regular work, as painting or gardening, enjoyed as a relaxation.

hobbyhorse, hob´i·hors, *n.* [Comp. D. *hoppe*, a mare.] A figure of a horse on which children ride.

hobgoblin, hob·gob´lin, *n.* [From *hob*, formerly a rustic, a clown, an elf; corruption of *Robin*, *Robert*.] A goblin; an elf; an imp.

hobnail, hob´nāl, *n.* [*Hob*, a projection, and *nail*.] A nail with a thick strong head used for shoeing horses, or for the soles of heavy boots.—**hobnailed**, hob´nāld, *a.* Set with hobnails; rough.

hobnob, hob´nob, *v.i.* [Lit., have or not have, drink if it please you—A.Sax. *habban*, to have, and *nabban*, for *ne habban*, not to have.] To drink familiarly; to clink glasses; to be boon or intimate companions.

hobo, hō´bō, *n.* [From *hey* and *beau*.] A migratory worker; a tramp.

hock, hok, *n.* [A.Sax. *hóh*, the heel; Icel. *ha*, D. *hak*.] The joint of an animal between the knee and the fetlock.

hock, hok, *v.t.* [D. *hok*, hovel, prison.] To hamstring; to pawn; to pledge.

hock, hok, *n.* [G. *Hochheimer*, from *Hochheim*, in Nassau, where it is produced.] A light sort of Rhenish wine which is either sparkling or still.

hockey, hok´i, *n.* [From *hook*.] A game played on ice (ice hockey) or in a field (field hockey) in which opposing teams try to send a rubber disk or a ball into each other's goal.—**hockey stick**, a club curved at the lower end, used in the game of hockey.

hocus, hō´kus, *v.t.*—*hocussed*, *hocussing*. [The *hocus* of *hocus-pocus*.] To impose upon; to cheat; to hoax; to stupefy with drugged liquor for the purpose of cheating or robbing; to drug for this purpose.—**hocus-pocus**, hō´kus·pō´kus, *n.* [An invented word imitative of Latin.] A juggler's trick; trickery used by conjurers.—*v.t.* and *i.* To cheat; to trick.

hod, hod, *n.* [Northern English for *hold*.] A kind of trough for carrying mortar and bricks to masons and bricklayers, fixed to the end of a pole, and borne on the shoulder.—**hod carrier, hodman**, a worker who carries bricks or mortar in a hod.

hodgepodge, hoj´poj, *n.* [Corruption of *hotchpot*.] A mixed mass; a medley of ingredients; in Scotland, a thick soup of vegetables boiled with beef or mutton (in this sense always *hotch-potch*).

hoe, hō, *n.* [O.Fr. *hoe*, Fr. *houe*, from the German; O.H.G. *houwa*, G. *haue*. HEW.] An instrument for cutting up weeds and loosening the earth in fields and gardens.—*v.t.*—*hoed*, *hoeing*. To cut, dig, scrape, or clean with a hoe.—*v.i.* To use a hoe.

hog, hog, *n.* [W. *hwch*, Corn. *hoch*, Armor. *houch* hoch, a sow, swine, hog.] A swine; a pig, or any animal of that species; a castrated boar; a sheep of a year old; a brutal fellow; one who is mean and filthy.—**hoggish**, hog´ish, *a.* Having the qualities of a hog; brutish; filthy.—**hoggishly**, hog´ish·li, *adv.* In a hoggish manner.—**hoggishness**, hog´ish·nes, *n.*—**hogwash**, *n.* The refuse of a kitchen or a brewery, or like matter given to swine; swill.

hogan, hō´gan, *n.* [From Navaho *qoghan*, a hut.] The dwelling of the Navaho Indian, a hut made of earth and branches.

hogmanay, hog´ma·nā, *n.* [Of French origin, and same as Norman *hoguinané*, O.Fr. *aguillanneuf*, a cry used in connection with New Year's gifts, and the last day of December, meaning perhaps 'to the mistletoe the New Year'.] The name given in Scotland to the last day of the year.

hogshead, hogz´hed, *n.* [Corrupted from D. *okshoofd*, Dan. *oxehoved*, the measure called a hogshead, and lit. ox's head; probably modified from some term of quite other meaning.] A large cask, especially a cask containing from 63 to 140 gallons; a liquid measure of 63 gallons or 238.5 liters; abbreviated to *hhd.*

hoiden, hoi´dn. See HOYDEN.

hoist, hoist, *v.t.* [O.E. *hoise*, Sc. *heese*=D. *hijsschen*, *hysen*, L.G. *hissen*, Dan. *heise*, *hisse*, to hoist; the *t* was added as in *against*, *amongst*.] To heave or raise; especially to raise by means of block and tackle.—*n.* The act of hoisting; that by which anything is hoisted; a machine for elevating goods, passengers, etc., in a warehouse, hotel, and the like; an elevator.—*pp.* Hoisted.

hoity-toity, hoi´ti·toi´ti. An exclamation denoting surprise or disapprobation, with some degree of contempt; equivalent to pshaw!—*a.* Elated; flighty; petulant.

hokum, hō´kum, *n.* [HOCUS-POCUS.] Material, especially speech, given a deliberate simulation of significance in order to excite interest and emotion; pleasing and effective nonsense; bunk; empty talk: claptrap.

ch, *ch*ain; *ch*, Sc. lo*ch*; g, go; j, job; ng, sing; TH, *th*en; th, *th*in; w, *w*ig; hw, *wh*ig; zh, azure.

hold, hōld, v.t. pret. & pp. held. [A.Sax. healdan=Dan. holde, D. houden, Icel. halda, Goth. haldan, G. halten, to hold; hence behold.] To have or grasp in the hand; to grasp and retain (to hold a sword, a pen, a candle); to bear, put, or keep in a certain position (to hold the hands up); to consider; to regard (I hold him in honor); to account (I hold it true); to contain, or to have capacity to receive and contain; to retain within itself; to keep from running or flowing out; to keep possession of; to maintain, uphold, preserve; not to lose; to be in possession of; to possess, occupy, own, keep; to have or to entertain (to hold enmity); to derive or deduce title to (he held lands of the king); to stop, restrain, withhold; to keep fixed, as to a certain line of action; to bind or oblige (to hold one to his promise); to keep in continuance or practice (to hold intercourse); to prosecute or carry on, observe, pursue (a course, an argument); to celebrate, solemnize, carry out (a feast, a meeting); to occupy or keep employed; to engage the attention of.—To hold in play, to keep occupied so as to withdraw from something else.—To hold water (fig.), to be logically sound or capable of standing investigation.—To hold in, to guide with a tight rein; hence, to restrain, check, repress.—To hold off, to keep off; to keep from touching.—To hold out, to extend; to stretch forth; hence, to propose; to offer.—To hold up, to raise; to keep in an erect position; to sustain, support, uphold; to show, exhibit, put prominently forward.—To hold one's own, to keep good one's present condition; not to lose ground.—To hold one's peace, to keep silence.—To hold the plow, to guide it in plowing.—v.i. To take or keep a thing in one's grasp; to maintain an attachment; to continue firm; not to give way or break; to adhere; to stand, be valid, apply (the argument holds good, this holds true); to stand one's ground; generally with out (the garrison held out); to refrain; to be dependent on for possessions, to derive right or title: with of, sometimes from; to stop, stay, or wait; to cease or give over: chiefly in the imperative. —To hold forth, to speak in public.— To hold off, to keep at a distance; to avoid connection.—To hold on, to continue; to keep fast hold; to cling; to proceed in a course.— To hold to, to cling or cleave to; to adhere.—To hold with, to side with; to stand up for.—To hold together, not to separate; to remain in union.—Hold on! hold hard! stop; cease.—n. A grasp, gripe, clutch (often in to take hold, to lay hold); fig. mental grasp; grasp on or influence working on the mind; something which may be seized for support; power of keeping; authority to seize or keep; claim; a place of confinement; a position of strength, a keep, stronghold;

the whole interior cavity of a ship between the bottom and deck or lowest deck (in this sense seems modified from D. hol, a hole, a ship's hold).—**holder,** hōl′dėr, n. One who or that which holds; a payee of a bill of exchange or a promissory note.—**holdfast,** hōld′- fast, n. Something used to secure and hold in place something else.— **holding,** hōl′ding, n. A tenure; a farm held of a superior; that which holds, binds, or influences. **hole,** hōl, n. [A.Sax. hol, hollow, hole; D. hol, Icel. hol, hola, a hollow, a cavity; G. hohl, hollow; of same root as A.Sax. helan, to cover, whence hell; or as Gr. koilos, hollow.] A hollow place or cavity in any solid body; a perforation, orifice, aperture, pit, rent, fissure, crevice, etc.; the excavated habitation of certain wild beasts; a mean habitation; a wretched abode.—v.i. holed, holing. To go into a hole.—v.t. To make a hole or holes in; to drive into a hole; mining, to undercut a coal seam.

holily, holiness. See HOLY.

holiday, hol′i·dā, n. [M.E. from O.E. haligdaeg, holy day.] Any day in which, by custom or law, ordinary business is suspended; a religious feast day; a day or several days exempt from labor;

holla, hollo, holloa, hol·lä′, hol·lō′. [Fr. holà—ho! ho! and là, there.] An exclamation to some one at a distance, in order to call attention or in answer to one that hails.— v.i. To call, shout, or cry aloud.

holland, hol′and, n. A kind of fine linen originally manufactured in Holland; also a coarser linen fabric used for covering furniture, carpets, etc.—**Hollander,** hol′an·dėr, n. A native of Holland.—**Hollands,** hol′- andz, n. A sort of gin imported from Holland.

hollow, hol′ō, a. [A.Sax. holg, holh, a hollow space, from hol, a hole. HOLE.] Containing an empty space within; having a vacant space within; not solid; concave; sunken (eye, cheek); sounding as if reverberated from a cavity; deep or low; not sincere or faithful; false; deceitful.— n. A depression or excavation below the general level or in the substance of anything; a cavity.—v.t. To make a hollow or cavity in, to excavate.— adv. Utterly; completely (in certain phrases, as he beat him hollow).— **hollowhearted,** a. Insincere; deceitful; not true.—**hollowly,** hol′ō·li, adv. In a hollow manner.—**hollow- ness,** hol′ō·nes, n. The state or quality of being hollow.

holly, hol′i, n. [O.E. holin, A.Sax. holegn, holen, holly, allied to W. celyn, Gael. cuilionn, holly.] An evergreen tree or shrub with in- dented thorny leaves, and which produces clusters of beautiful red berries; also a name sometimes given to the holm oak, an evergreen oak.— kneeholly, butcher's-broom.

hollyhock, hol′i·hok, n. [Lit. holy hock—hock being A.Sax. hoc, W. hocys, mallow; so called because

brought from the Holy Land.] A tall single-stemmed biennial plant of the mallow family, a frequent ornament of gardens.

holm, hōlm or hōm, n. [A.Sax. L.G., G., and Dan. holm, a small island in a river; Sw. holme, Icel. hólmr, an island.] A river island; a low flat tract of rich land by the side of a river.

holmium, hōl′mi·um, n. [From Stock- holm, Sweden.] A metallic element, one of the rare-earth series. Symbol, Ho; at. no., 67; at. wt., 164.930.

holm oak, hōlm or hōm, n. [Lit. hollyoak, holm being from A.Sax. holen, holly, the leaves resembling those of the holly. HOLLY.] The evergreen oak.

holoblast, hol′o·blast, n. [Gr. holos, whole, and blastos, a bud or germ.] Zool. an ovum consisting entirely of germinal matter. MEROBLAST.— **holoblastic,** hol′o·blas·tik, a. Per- taining to a holoblast; of fertilized ova from which the embryo is formed by complete division or cleavage.

holocaust, hol′o·kạst, n. [Gr. holos, whole, and kaustos, burned.] A burnt sacrifice or offering, the whole of which was consumed by fire; a great slaughter or sacrifice of life.

holograph, hol′o·graf, n. [Gr. holos, whole, and graphein, to write.] Any document, as a letter, deed, etc., wholly written by the person in whose name it appears. Used also as an adj.—**holographic, holograph- ical,** hol·o·graf′ik, hol·o·graf′i·kal, a. Being holograph; written by the grantor or testator himself.

holophotal, hol·o·fō′tal, a. [Gr. holos, whole, and phōs, phōtos, light.] Optics, reflecting the rays of light in one unbroken mass without perceptible loss.

holothurian, hol·o·thū′ri·an, n. [Gr. holothourion, a sea animal; origin doubtful.] One of the sea cucumbers or sea slugs.

Holstein, hōl′stīn, n. [From Holstein, a region in northwest Germany.] A breed of black and white dairy cattle that produces low-fat milk.

holster, hōl′stėr, n. [D. holster, a pistolcase=A.Sax. hoolster, a cover, a recess; Icel. hulster, Dan. hulster, a case; root seen in A.Sax. helad, to cover, whence also hell.] A leather case for a pistol, usually hung on a belt or saddle.

holus-bolus, hō′lus·bō′lus, adv. [From whole, and bolus, a pill.] All at a gulp; altogether; all at once. (Vulgar.)

holy, hō′li, a. [A.Sax. hálig, holy, from hál, whole; similarly D. and G. heilig, Icel. heilagr, Dan. hellig, holy; akin hale, heal, hallow, whole, etc., same root also in Gr. kalos, beauti- ful.] Free from sin and sinful affections; pure in heart; pious; godly; hallowed; consecrated or set apart to a sacred use.—**holily,** hō′li·li, adv. In a holy manner.— **holiness,** hō′li·nes, n. The state or quality of being holy or sinless; sanctity; godliness; sacredness; his holiness, a title of the pope.—Holy *of holies*, the innermost apartment of the Jewish tabernacle or temple, where the ark was kept.—*Holy Ghost* or *Holy Spirit*, the Divine Spirit; the third person in the Trinity.—*Holy Office*, the Inquisition.—*Holy Thursday*, Ascension Day; also Thursday in Holy Week.—*Holy Saturday*, Saturday in Holy Week.—*Holy water*, in the *Roman Catholic Church*, water consecrated by the priest, and used in various rites and ceremonies.—*Holy week*, the week before Easter (the last week of Lent).—*Holy Writ*, the sacred Scriptures.—**holystone**, *n.* A soft sandstone used by seamen for cleaning the decks of ships.—*v.t.* To scrub with holystone.

homage, hom′ij, *n.* [Fr. *hommage*, O.Fr. *homenage*, L.L. *hominaticum*, homage, from L. *homo, hominis*, a man, in late times a vassal. HUMAN.] Acknowledgment of vassalage made by a feudal tenant to his lord on receiving investiture of a fee; hence, obeisance; respect paid by external action; reverence directed to the Supreme Being; reverential worship; devout affection.—*v.t.* To pay homage to.—**homager**, hom′ij•ėr, *n.* One who does or is bound to do homage.

home, hōm, *n.* [A.Sax. *hám*, home, house, dwelling=L.G. and Fris. *ham*, D. and G. *heim*, Icel. *heimr*, Goth. *haims*, abode, village, etc.; cog. Gr. *kōmē*, a village, *keimai*, I rest; probably L. *quies*, quiet, etc.] One's own abode or dwelling; the abode of the family or household of which one forms a member; abiding place; one's own country; the seat (the *home* of war); an institute or establishment affording to the homeless, sick, or destitute the comforts of a home (a sailors′ *home*, an orphan′s *home*, etc.).—*At home*, in or about one's own house or abode; in one's own country.—*At home in* or *on a subject*, conversant, familiar, thoroughly acquainted with it.—*To make one's self at home*, to conduct one's self in another's house as unrestrainedly as if at home.—*a.* Connected with one's home; domestic; often opposed to *foreign*.—*Home economics*, the domestic science of making and caring for a home.—*adv.* To one's home or one's native country; often opposed to *abroad*; to one's self; to the point; to the mark aimed at; so as to produce an intended effect; effectively; thoroughly (to strike *home*).—**homebred**, hōm′bred, *a.* Bred at home; originating at home; not foreign; not polished by travel.—**homeless**, hōm′les, *a.* Destitute of a home.—**homelessness**, hōm′les•nes, *n.* The state of being homeless.—**homeliness**, hōm′li•nes, *n.* The state or quality of being homely.—**homely**, hōm′li, *a.* Pertaining to home; domestic‡; of plain features; not handsome; like that which is made for common domestic use; plain; coarse; not fine or elegant.—**homemade**, *a.* Made at home; of domestic manufacture.—**home plate**, a five-

sided plate of rubber, set in the ground, beside which the batter stands (*Baseball*).—**homer**, hō′mer, *n.* A *home run* (*Colloq.*)—**home rule**, government of a district, colony, territory, etc., by the inhabitants themselves, particularly with regard to local matters.—**home run**, a hit which, unaided by error, allows the batter to circle the bases and return to the home plate (*Baseball*).—**homesick**, *a.* Ill from being absent from home; affected with homesickness.—**homesickness**, *n.* Intense and uncontrolled grief at a separation from one's home or native land; nostalgia; longing for home.—**homespun**, hōm′spun, *a.* Spun or wrought at home; hence, plain; coarse; homely.—*n.* Cloth made at home.—**homestead**, hōm′sted, *n.* A house or mansion with the grounds and buildings immediately contiguous; a home.—**home stretch**, the section of a racecourse between the last curve and the finish.—**homeward**, **homewards**, hōm′wėrd, hōm′werdz, *adv.* Toward home; toward one's abode or native country.—*a.* Being in the direction of home.—**homework**, work to be done at home, especially that assigned by a teacher to students.—**homing**, hōm′ing, *a.* Coming home; a term applied to birds, such as the carrier pigeon.

homeopathy, hō•mē•op′a•thi, *n.* [Gr. *homoios*, like, *pathos*, feeling, suffering.] The system of treating disease by administering in minute quantities drugs which would, if given in larger doses, to a healthy person, produce symptoms similar to those of the disease.—**homeopathist**, hō•mē•op′a•thist, *n.* One who practices or supports homeopathy.

homer, hō′mėr, *n.* [Heb.] A Hebrew measure equivalent to about 75 gallons or to 11 bushels.

Homeric, hō•mer′ik, *a.* Pertaining to *Homer*, the great poet of Greece; resembling Homer's verse or style.

homicide, hom′i•sīd, *n.* [L. *homicidium*, the crime, *homicida*, the perpetrator—*homo*, man, and *cædo*, to strike, to kill.] The killing of one man or human being by another; a person who kills another; a manslayer.—**homicidal**, hom•i•sī′dal, *n.* Pertaining to homicide; murderous.

homily, hom′i•li, *n.* [Gr. *homilia*, intercourse or converse, instruction, a sermon, from *homilos*, a throng—*homos*, same (cog. with E. *same*), and *ilē*, a throng.] A discourse or sermon read or pronounced to an audience; a sermon; a serious discourse.—**homiletic**, **homiletical**, hom•i•let′ik, hom•i•let′i•kal, *a.* [Gr. *homilētikos*.] Relating to homilies or homiletics; hortatory.—*Homiletic theology*, homiletics.—**homiletics**, hom•i•let′iks, *n.* The art of preaching; that branch of practical theology which treats of sermons and the best mode of composing and delivering them.—**homilist**, hom′i•list, *n.* One that composes homilies; a preacher.

hominy, hom′i•ni, *n.* [Amer.-Indian *auhuminea*, parched corn.] Corn hulled and coarsely ground, prepared for food by being boiled with water.

homocentric, ho•mo•sen′trik, *a.* [Gr. *homos*, same, *kentron*, a center.] Having the same center; concentric.

homocercal, hō•mo•sėr′kal, *a.* [Gr. *homos*, same, *kerkos*, tail.] *Ichthyol.* having the lobes of the tail diverging symmetrically from the backbone, as in the cod, herring, etc. HETEROCERCAL.

homochromous, hō•mok′ro•mus, *a.* [Gr. *homos*, same, *chrōma*, color.] *Bot.* having all the florets of the same color.

homogamous, hō•mog′a•mus, *a.* [Gr. *homos*, same, *gamos*, marriage.] *Bot.* having all the florets of a flower head, or the florets of the spikelets in grasses, hermaphrodite.—**homogamy**, hō•mog′a•mi, *n.* The state of being homogamous.

homogeneous, ho•mō•jē′nē•us, *a.* [Gr. *homogenēs*—*homos*, like, and *genos*, kind; root *gen*, cog. with E. *kin*.] Of the same kind or nature; consisting of similar parts, or of elements of the like nature; opposite of *heterogeneous*.—**homogeneousness**, ho•mo•jē′nē•us•nes, *n.* The state or character of being homogeneous.—**homogenize**, ho•moj′e•nīz, *v.t.* To make homogeneous; to pass milk, cream, etc., through an apparatus that breaks up the fat globules to make the product the same throughout.

homogenesis, hō•mo•jen′e•sis, *n.* [Gr. *homos*, same, *genesis*, birth.] Sameness of origin; reproduction of offspring similar to their parents.

homograph, hō′mo•graf, *n.* [Gr. *homos*, same, *graphō*, to write.] A word which has exactly the same form as another, though of a different origin and signification; a homonym.—**homographic**, hō•mo•graf′ik, *a.* Relating to homographs.

Homoiousian, ho•moi•ō′si•an, *n.* [Gr. *homoios*, similar, and *ousia*, being.] A person holding the belief that the nature of Christ is not the same with, but only similar to, that of the Father. HOMOOUSIAN.

homologate, hō•mol′o•gāt, *v.t.*—*homologated, homologating.* [L.L. *homologo, homologatum*, from Gr. *homos*, same, and *logos*, discourse, from *legō*, to speak.] To approve; to express approval of or assent to; to ratify.

homologous, hō•mol′o•gus, *a.* [Gr. *homos*, same, and *logos*, proportion.] Having the same relative position, proportion, or structure; corresponding in use or general character; of similar type.—**homologue**, hō′mo•log, *n.* That which is homologous; an organ of an animal homologous with another organ.—**homology**, hō•mol′o•ji, *n.* The quality of being homologous; correspondence in character or relation; sameness or correspondence in organs of animals as regards general structure and type, thus the human arm corresponds to the foreleg of a quadruped and the

ch, *chain*; *ch*, Sc. lo*ch*; g, go; j, job; ng, si*ng*; TH, *then*; th, *thin*; w, wig; hw, whig; zh, azure.

wing of a bird.—**homological,** hō‐
mō·loj′i·kal, *a.* Pertaining to homol‐
ogy; having a structural affinity.—
homologically, hō·mo·loj′i·kal·li,
adv. In a homological manner.
homomorphous, homomorphic,
hō·mo·mor′fus, hō·mo·mor′fik, *a.*
[Gr. *homos,* same, *morphē,* shape.]
Having the same external appearance
or form.—**homomorphism,** hō·mo·
mor′fizm, *n.* The condition of being
homomorphous.
homonym, hō′mo·nim, *n.* [Gr. *ho‐
mos,* same, *onoma,* name.] A word
which agrees with another in sound,
and perhaps in spelling, but differs
from it in signification; a homograph;
as *fair, a.* and *fair, n.*—**homonymic,**
ho·mo·nim′ik, *a.* Relating to homon‐
ymy or to homonyms.—**homon‐
ymous,** hō·mon′i·mus, *a.* Having
the same sound or spelling.—**homon‐
ymy,** hō·mon′i·mi, *n.* Sameness
of name with a difference of mean‐
ing; ambiguity; equivocation.
Homoousian, hō·mō·ō′si·an, *n.* [Gr.
homos, same, and *ousia,* being.] A
person who maintains that the nature
of the Father and the Son is the
same, in opposition to the *Homo‐
iousians.*
homophone, hō′mo·fōn, *n.* [Gr.
homos, same, *phōnē,* sound.] A letter
or character expressing a like sound
with another; a word having the
same sound as another; a homonym.
—**homophonous,** hō·mof′o·nus, *a.*
Of like sound; agreeing in sound
but differing in sense.—**homophony,**
hō·mof′o·ni, *n.* Sameness of sound.
homoplasmy, hō′mo·plas·mi, *n.* [Gr.
homos, same, *plassō,* to form.] *Biol.*
resemblance in form or structure
with difference in origin.—**homo‐
plastic,** *a.* Similar in form or
structure.
Homo sapiens, hō′mō sā′pi·ens.
[From O.L. *hēmo,* man, and *sapio,*
wise.] Modern man, the surviving
species of the genus *Homo.*
homosexual, hō′mō·sek″shu·al, *a.*
[*Homo* and *sexual.*] Sexual attraction
toward those of the same sex.—*n.*
One who is attracted toward someone
of the same sex.
homotaxis, hō·mo·tak′sis, *n.* [Gr.
homos, same, *taxis,* arrangement.]
Agreement in arrangement; *geol.,*
agreement in the arrangement of
strata in different localities.
homuncule, homunculus, hō·
mung′kūl, hō·mung′kū·lus, *n.* [L.,
dim. of *homo,* a man.] A manikin;
a dwarf.
hone, hōn, *n.* [A.Sax. *hán,* Icel. *hein,*
Sw. *hen,* a hone, a whetstone; root
seen in Skr. *co,* to sharpen, and in L.
conus, a hone.] A stone of a fine grit,
used for sharpening instruments
that require a fine edge.—*v.t.* To
sharpen on a hone.
honest, on′est, *a.* [O.Fr. *honeste* (Fr.
honnête), from L. *honestus,* from
honor, honos, honor. HONOR.] Fair
in dealing with others; free from
trickishness, fraud, or theft; up‐
right; just; equitable; sincere, can‐
did, or unreserved; honorable; rep‐
utable; chaste or virtuous; pleasant‐
looking in features.—**honestly,** on′‐

est·li, *adv.* In an honest manner.—
honesty, on′es·ti, *n.* The state or
quality of being honest; integrity;
uprightness; fairness; candor.
honey, hun′i, *n.* [A.Sax. *hunig*=D.
and G. *honig,* Icel. *hunang,* honey.]
A sweet, viscid juice, collected from
flowers by several kinds of insects,
especially bees; *fig.* sweetness or
pleasantness; as a word of endear‐
ment, sweet one, darling.—*v.t.* To
become sweet; to become compli‐
mentary or fawning.—*v.i.* To become
tender and coaxing, also, to fawn
(to *honey* up a person).—**honeybee,**
n. A bee that produces honey; the
hive bee.—**honeycomb,** *n.* The waxy
structure formed by bees for the
reception of honey, and for the eggs
which produce their young.—**honey‐
dew,** *n.* A sweet saccharine sub‐
stance found on the leaves of trees
and other plants in small drops like
dew.—**honeydew melon,** a very
sweet muskmelon with a white,
smooth skin.—**honeyed, honied,**
hun′id, *p.* and *a.* Covered with or as
with honey; hence, sweet; full of
compliments or tender words.—
honeymoon, hun′i·mōn, *n.* The first
month after marriage; the interval
spent by a newly married pair
before settling down in a home of
their own.—**honeysuckle,** hun′i·
suk·l, *n.* [From children sucking
the honey out of the nectary.] The
popular name for a genus of upright
or climbing shrubs with fragrant
flowers of a tubular shape.
hong, hong, *n.* [Chinese *hong, hang.*]
The Chinese name for foreign
factories or mercantile houses.
honor, on′ėr, *n.* [O.Fr. *honor, honeur,*
Fr. *honneur,* from L. *honor, honos,*
honor, whence *honestus,* honest.]
Esteem paid to worth; high esti‐
mation; reverence; veneration; any
mark of respect or estimation by
words or actions; dignity; exalted
rank or place; distinction; repu‐
tation; good name; a nice sense of
what is right, just, and true; scorn
of meanness; a particular virtue,
as bravery or integrity in men and
chastity in females; one who or
that which is a source of glory or
esteem; he who or that which con‐
fers dignity (an *honor* to his country);
title or privilege of rank or birth;
one of the highest trump cards, as
the ace, king, queen, or knave, and,
in bridge, ten; a title of address or
respect now restricted, except among
the vulgar, to the holders of certain
offices (e.g. judges): with *his, your,*
etc.; (*pl.*) civilities paid, as at an
entertainment; (*pl.*) academic and
university distinction or pre-emi‐
nence.—*Honors of war,* distinctions
granted to a vanquished enemy, as
of marching out of a camp or in‐
trenchments armed and with colors
flying.—*An affair of honor,* a dispute
to be decided by a duel.—*Word
of honor,* a verbal promise or en‐
gagement which cannot be violated
without disgrace.—*Debt of honor,*
a debt, as a bet, for which no
security is required or given except
that implied by honorable dealing.—

Maid of honor, a lady whose duty
it is to attend a queen in public;
chief attendant, if unmarried, of a
bride at a wedding; if married,
matron of honor.—*v.t.* To regard
or treat with honor; to revere; to
respect; to reverence; to bestow
honor upon; to elevate in rank or
station; to exalt; to render illustrious;
com. to accept and pay when due
(to *honor* a bill of exchange).—
honorarium, on·ė·râ′ri·um, or hon′,
n. [L. *honorarium* (*donum,* gift).] A
fee to a professional man for profes‐
sional services.—**honorary,** on′ėr·
e·ri, *a.* [L. *honorarius.*] Done or
made in honor; indicative of honor;
intended merely to confer honor (an
honorary degree); possessing a title
or post without performing services,
or without receiving benefit or
reward (an *honorary* secretary or
treasurer).—**honorable,** on′ėr·a·bl,
a. Worthy of being honored; estim‐
able; illustrious or noble; actuated
by principles of honor; conferring
honor; consistent with honor or
reputation; regarded with esteem;
accompanied with marks of honor
or testimonies of esteem; upright
and laudable; directed to a just and
proper end; not base; a title of
distinction applied to certain mem‐
bers of noble families, persons in
high position, etc., *right honorable*
being a higher grade.—**honorable‐
ness,** on′ėr·a·bl·nes, *n.* The state of
being honorable.—**honorably,** on′‐
ėr·a·bli, *adv.* In an honorable man‐
ner.
hood, hud, *n.* [A.Sax. *hód*=D. *hoed,*
G. *hut,* a hat; allied to D. *heed;* G.
hüten, D. *hoeden,* to protect; Skr.
chad, to cover.] A soft covering for
the head worn by females and
children; the part of a monk's outer
garment with which he covers his
head; a cowl; a similar appendage
to a cloak or overcoat; an ornamental
fold at the back of an academic
gown; a covering for a hawk's head
or eyes, used in falconry; anything
that resembles a hood in form or use.
—*v.t.* To dress in a hood or cowl;
to put a hood on; to cover or hide.—
hooded, hud′ed, *p.* and *a.* —**hood‐
wink,** hud′wingk, *v.t.* To blind by
covering the eyes; to blindfold; to
deceive by external appearances.
hoodlum, höd′lum, *n.* A rowdy;
a rough. (*Colloq.*)
hoodoo, hö′dö, *n.* VOODOO. Some‐
thing which brings misfortune.—
v.t. To bring bad luck. (*Colloq.*)
hooey, hö′i, *n.* and *interj.* Nonsense.
(*Slang.*)
hoof, höf, *n.* pl. **hoofs,** rarely **hooves,**
hövz. [A.Sax. *hóf,* Icel. *hófr.* D.
hoef, Dan. *hov,* G. *huf,* a hoof.]
The horny substance that covers
the feet or the digits of the feet
of certain animals, as horses, oxen,
sheep, deer, etc.—**hoofbound,** *a.*
Farriery, having a dryness and con‐
traction of the hoof, which occa‐
sions pain and lameness.—**hoofed,**
höft, *a.* Furnished with hoofs.
hook, huk, *n.* [A.Sax. *hóc,* a hook, a
crook=D. *hoek,* Icel. *haki,* G.
haken, O.H.G. *hako,* a hook: same

root as *hang*.] A piece of iron or other metal bent into a curve for catching, holding, or sustaining anything; any similar appliance; *baseball*, a curve; *boxing*, a short, swinging blow delivered with elbow bent but rigid.—*By hook or by crook*, by some means or other.—*v.t.* To catch or fasten with a hook or hooks; to bend into the form of a hook; to furnish with hooks; to catch by artifice; to entrap.—*v.i.* To bend; to be curving; to catch into something.—**hookedness**, huk′ed·nes, *n.* —**hooker**, huk′ėr, *n.*

hookah, hö′kä, *n.* [Ar.] A tobacco pipe with a long pliable tube and water vase so constructed that the smoke passes through the water before being inhaled.

hooker, huk′ėr, *n.* [D. *hoeker*, *hoekboot*.] An Irish fishing smack.

hooky, huk′i, *n.* [Probably from M.E. *haken*, from *hak*, hook.] A word used in the phrase *to play hooky*, to play truant.

hooligan, hö′li·gan, *n.* [Irish personal name.] A street rough or rowdy.

hoop, höp, *n.* [A.Sax. *hóp*, Fris. *hop*, D. *hoep*; akin *hump*.] A band of wood or metal used to confine the staves of casks, tubs, etc., or for other similar purposes; a combination of circles of thin whalebone or other elastic material used to expand the skirts of ladies' dresses; a farthingale; a crinoline.—*v.t.* To bind or fasten with hoops.—**hooper**, hö′pėr, *n.*

hoopoe, hö′pö, *n.* [Fr. *huppe*, L. *upupa*, Gr. *epops*, hoopoe: names given from its cry.] A beautiful bird with a crest, which it can erect or depress at pleasure, and a long, sharp, curved bill, found in Europe and North Africa and named for its whooping cry.

hoosegow, hoosgow, hös′gou, *n.* [Sp. *juzgado*, a court.] A place of confinement; a jail. (Slang)

Hoosier, hö′zhėr, *n.* A person from the state of Indiana, which is nicknamed the *Hoosier State*.

hoot, höt, *v.i.* [From the sound; comp. Fr. *houter*, to call, to cry.] To cry out or shout in contempt; to cry as an owl.—*v.t.* To utter cries or shouts in contempt of; to utter contemptuous cries or shouts at.—*n.* A cry or shout in contempt; the cry of an owl.

hootenanny, höt′nan·i, *n.* [Origin unknown.] An informal folksinging party, sometimes with dancing.

hop, hop, *v.i.*—hopped, hopping. [A. Sax. *hoppian*=Icel. and Sw. *hoppa*, D. *huppen*, G. *hüpfen*, to hop; akin *hobble*, *hobby*.] To hop or leap; to leap or spring on one foot.—*v.t.* To move by successive leaps, as a frog.—*n.* A leap on one leg; a short trip; an informal dance.—**hopper**, hop′ėr, *n.* One who hops; a wooden trough through which grain, coal, etc., pass into a mill, so named from its moving or shaking; any similar contrivance; a box that holds legislative bills.—**hopscotch**, *n.* A children's game which consists in hopping over scores or scotches on the ground.

hop, hop, *n.* [D. *hop*, *hoppe*, G. *hopfen*, hop.] A climbing plant of the hemp family, whose female flowers are used to flavor malt liquors and make them keep.—*v.t.*—hopped, hopping. To mix hops with.—*v.i.* To pick or gather hops.

hope, hōp, *n.* [A.Sax. *hopa*=D. *hoop*, Sw. *hopp*, Dan. *haab*, hope; G. *hoffen*, to hope; possibly akin to L. *cupio*, to desire.] A desire of some good, accompanied with at least a slight expectation of obtaining it, or a belief that it is obtainable; expectation of something desirable; confidence in a future event; trust; that which gives hope; one in whom trust or confidence is placed; the object of hope; the thing hoped for.—*Forlorn hope*. Under FORLORN. —*v.i.*—hoped, hoping. [A.Sax. *hopian*. D. *hopen*, to hope.] To entertain or indulge hope; to have confidence; to trust.—*v.t.* To entertain hope for; to desire with expectation. —**hopeful**, hōp′ful, *a.* Full of or entertaining hope; having qualities which excite hope; promising.—*n.* A young person whose prospects are promising; one in whom another places hope.—**hopefully**, hōp′ful·li, *adv.*—**hopefulness**, hōp′ful·nes, *n.*— **hopeless**, hōp′les, *a.* Destitute of hope; giving no ground of hope.— **hopelessly**, hōp′les·li, *adv.*—**hopelessness**, hōp′les·nes, *n.*

hoplite, hop′līt, *n.* [Gr. *hoplitēs*, from *hoplon*, a weapon.] A heavy-armed soldier of ancient Greece.

hopple, hop′l, *v.t.* [From *hop*, to leap; also in form *hobble*.] To tie the feet of (a horse) near together to prevent leaping or running; to hobble.—*n.* A fetter for the legs of grazing horses or other animals.

horary, horal, hō′ra·ri, hō′ral, *a.* [L. *hora*, an hour.] Pertaining to the hours; occurring once an hour; hourly.

Horatian, ho·rā′shan, *a.* Relating to or resembling the Latin poet *Horace* (Horatius) or his poetry.

horde, hōrd, *n.* [Fr. *horde*, from Turk. and Per. *ordû*, court, camp, horde.] A tribe, clan, or race of Asiatic or other nomads; a wandering tribe; hence, a gang; a migratory crew; rabble.—*v.i.* To live in hordes; to huddle together.

horehound, hōr′hound, *a.* [A.Sax. *hárahune*—*hár*, hoar, and *hune*, the generic name of these plants.] The popular name of several plants of the mint family, one of which, white horehound, has an aromatic smell and bitter taste, and has been much in use for coughs and asthma. Written also *Hoarhound*.

horizon, ho·rī′zon, *n.* [Gr. *horizōn*, from *horizō*, to bound from *horos*, a limit; lit. that which bounds.] The circle which bounds that part of the earth's surface visible to a spectator from a given point; the apparent junction of the earth and sky; called the *visible* or *apparent* horizon; an imaginary great circle parallel to this whose plane passes through the center of the earth; called the *celestial horizon*.—*On the same horizon*, *geol.* said of fossils or strata which appear to be of the same age.—**horizontal**, hor·i·zon′tal, *a.* Pertaining to the horizon; on the same or a parallel plane with the horizon; on a level; measured or contained in the plane of the horizon (*horizontal* distance)—**horizontally**, hor·i·zon′tal·li, *adv.* In a horizontal direction or position.

hormone, hor′mōn, *n.* [Gr. *hormaō*, I excite.] An internal secretion of the endocrine glands, such as insulin, epinephrine, etc., carried by the blood to other organs, where it stimulates them to physiological activity; *bot.* similar substances operating in like manner in plants.— **hormonal**, hor·mōn′al, *a.*

horn, horn, *n.* [A.Sax. *horn*, a horn, a trumpet=Icel., Sw., Dan., and G. *horn*, D. *horen*, Goth. *haurn*; cog. W. and Armor. *corn*, L. *cornu*, Gr. *keras*—horn. *Hornet* is a derivative, and *hart* is akin.] A hard projecting appendage growing on the heads of certain animals, and particularly on cloven-hoofed quadrupeds; the material of which such horns are composed; a wind instrument of music, originally made of horn; a drinking cup of horn; a utensil for holding powder for immediate use, originally made of horn; a powder flask; something similar to a horn; the feeler of an insect, snail, etc.; an extremity of the moon when waxing or waning.—*Put to the horn*, to outlaw by three blasts on a horn at the Cross of Edinburgh for refusal to answer summons (in Scots law).—*To draw in the horns*, to repress one's ardor, or to restrain pride, in allusion to the habit of the snail withdrawing its feelers when startled.—**hornbeam**, horn′bēm, *n.* A small bushy tree of the oak family, with a hard white wood.—**hornbill**, horn′bil, *n.* A name of certain birds with very large bills surmounted by an extraordinary horny protuberance. —**hornblende**, horn′blend, *n.* [G. *horn*, horn, and *blende*, blende (from *blenden*, to dazzle), from its horny and glittering appearance.] A dark green or black lustrous mineral of several varieties, an important constituent of several rocks.—**hornblendic**, horn·blen′dik, *a.* Containing hornblende; resembling hornblende.—**hornbook**, horn′buk, *n.* In former times a child's alphabet book or primer, with a transparent sheet of horn placed over the single page of which it usually consisted, the whole being fixed to a wooden frame.—**horned**, hornd, *a.* Having horns or projections resembling them (the *horned* moon); wearing horns; made a cuckold.—**hornless**, horn′les, *a.* Having no horns.—**hornmad**, *a.* Outrageous; stark mad: in allusion to a mad bull.—**hornpipe**, horn′pīp, *n.* A musical instrument formerly popular in Wales; a lively dance tune; a sprightly dance, usually performed by one person.—**hornstone**, horn′stōn, *n.* A siliceous stone, a variety of quartz.—**horny**, hor′ni, *a.* Con-

ch, *chain*; *ch*, Sc. lo*ch*; g, *go*; j, *job*; ng, si*ng*; TH, *then*; th, *thin*; w, *wig*; hw, *whig*; zh, a*zure*.

sisting or composed of horn; resembling horn in appearance or composition; exhibiting hardened skin.—**horned toad**, horn'd töd, n. A small, harmless North American lizard of the genus *Phrynosoma*, having hornlike spikes.

hornet, hor'net, n. [A.Sax. *hyrnet*, from *horn*, a horn, from its antennae or horns, or because its buzzing is compared to the blowing of a horn; G. *horniss*, a hornet.] A large, powerful wasp, the sting of which is very painful; hence, anyone who gives particular annoyance.

horography, ho·rog'ra·fi, n. [Gr. *hōra*, hour, and *graphō*, to write.] An account of the art of constructing instruments for showing the hours; horology.—**horologe**, hō'ro·lōj, n. [Fr. *horologe*, L. *horologium*, Gr. *hōrologion*—*hōra*, hour, and *legō*, to tell.] A piece of mechanism for indicating the hours of the day; a timepiece of any kind.—**horologer, horologist**, hō·rol'o·jėr, hō·rol'o·jist, n. A maker or vender of clocks and watches; one versed in or who writes on horology. — **horologic, horological**, hō·ro·loj'ik, hō·ro·loj'i·kal, a. Pertaining to horology; *bot.* opening and closing at certain hours: said of flowers.—**horology**, hō·rol'o·ji, n. The science of measuring time; the art of constructing machines for measuring time, as clocks, watches, dials.—**horoscope**, hō'ro·skōp, n. [Gr. *hōroskopos*—*hōra*, hour, and *skopeō*, to view.] A scheme or figure of the heavens at a given time, used by astrologers to foretell future events and the fortunes of persons, according to the position of the stars at the time of their birth.—**horoscopy**, hō·ros'ko·pi, n. The predicting of future events by the disposition of the stars and planets.

horrible, hor'ri·bl, a. [L. *horribilis*, from *horreo*, to bristle or stand on end, to be terrified; akin to *hirtus*, shaggy, *hirsutus*, hirsute.] Exciting or tending to excite horror; dreadful; terrible; shocking; hideous.—**horrent**, hor'ent, a. [L. *horrens, horrentis*.] Bristling.—**horribleness**, hor'ri·bl·nes, n. The state or quality of being horrible.—**horribly**, hor'ri·bli, adv. In a horrible manner; excessively; very much.—**horrid**, hor'rid, a. [L. *horridus*, from *horreo*.] Fitted to excite horror; dreadful; hideous; shocking; very offensive (*colloq.*).—**horridly**, hor'rid·li, adv. In a horrid manner.—**horridness**, hor'rid·nes, n. The quality of being horrid.—**horrific**, hor·rif'ik, a. [L. *horrificus*.] Causing horror.—**horrify**, hor'ri·fī, v.t.—*horrified, horrifying*. [L. *horror*, and *facio*, to make.] To strike or impress with horror.—**horripilation**, hor·ri·pi·lā'shon, n. [L. *horreo*, to bristle, *pilus*, hair.] The bristling or standing on end of the hair.—**horror**, hor'rėr, n. [L., from *horreo*.] A powerful feeling of fear, dread, and abhorrence; a shuddering with terror and loathing; that which excites horror.

hors d'oeuvre, ar·dė'vr. [Fr.] An appetizer or relish (usually in pl.).

horse, hors, n. [A.Sax. *hors*=Icel. *hross, hors*, O.H.G. *hros*, G. *ross*, D. *ros*, allied to Skr. *hreca*, neighing, or to L. *curro*, to run.] A well-known quadruped, the most important to man of all animals that are used as beasts of burden and of draft; the male animal, in distinction from the female called a *mare*; cavalry; troops serving on horseback (in this sense no plural termination; a wooden frame with legs for supporting something; *naut.* a rope attached to a yard to support the sailors while they loose, reef, or furl the sails.—[*Horse*, in compounds, often implies largeness or coarseness; as *horse* chestnut, *horseplay*.]—*To take horse*, to mount or set out on horseback.—*v.t.*—*horsed, horsing*. To provide with a horse; to supply a horse or horses for; to sit astride; to bestride (*Shak.*).—**horseback**, hors'bak, n. The back of a horse; that part on which the rider sits: generally in the phrase *on horseback*, that is, mounted or riding on a horse.—**horse chestnut**, n. A well-known tree with beautiful flowers, often planted for ornament, the nuts of which have been used as food for animals.—**horsecloth**, n. A cloth to cover a horse.—**horseflesh**, hors'flesh, n. The flesh of a horse; horses generally; a species of mahogany.—**horsefly**, hors'flī, n. A large fly that sucks the blood of horses.—**Horse Guards**, n. *pl.* A body of cavalry for guards.—**horsefly**, hors'flī, n. A large fly that sucks the blood of horses.—**horsehair**, n. sing. and pl. The hair of horses, more particularly of the mane and tail.—**horse latitudes**, hors lat'i·tūdes, n. *Naut.* either of two belts of calms and light winds, 35° north and 35° south of the Equator.—**horselaugh**, n. A loud, coarse, boisterous laugh.—**horse mackerel**, n. A fish about the size of a mackerel, with oily rank flesh.—**horseman**, hors'man, n. A man who rides on horseback; one who uses and manages a horse; a soldier who serves on horseback.—**horsemanship**, hors'man·ship, n. The art of riding and managing horses; equestrian skill.—**horseplay**, n. Rough or rude practical jokes or the like; rude pranks.—**horsepower**, n. The power of a horse or its equivalent; the force with which a horse acts when drawing; the standard for estimating the power of a steam engine, each horsepower being estimated as equivalent to 33,000 lb. raised one foot high per minute.—**horse-radish**, n. A perennial plant of the cabbage family, white cylindrical root of which has a pungent taste, and is used as a condiment with roast beef.—**horseshoe**, n. A shoe for horses, commonly a piece of iron, in shape resembling the letter U, nailed to the horse's foot; anything shaped like a horseshoe.—*Horseshoe magnet*, an artificial steel magnet nearly in the form of a horseshoe.—**horsetail**, n. The tail of a horse; a standard of rank and honor among the Turks, consisting of one or more tails of horses mount-

ed on a lance; an equisetum (which see).—**horsewhip**, hors'hwip, n. A whip for driving or striking horses.—*v.t.*—*horsewhipped, horsewhipping*. To lash or strike with a horsewhip.—**horsewoman**, hors'wum·an, n. A woman who rides on horseback; an equestrienne.—**horsy**, hor'si, a. Connected with, fond of, or much taken up with horses.—**horsiness**, hor'si·nes, n. The quality of being horsy.

hortation, hor·tā'shon, n. [L. *hortatio*, from *hortor*, to exhort.] The act of exhorting; exhortation.—**hortative**, hor'ta·tiv, a. Giving exhortation.—n. A precept given to incite or encourage; exhortation.—**hortatory**, hor'ta·to·ri, a. Exhortative.

horticulture, hor'ti·kul·tūr, n. [L. *hortus*, a garden (same root as *garden, yard*), and *cultura*, culture.] The cultivation of a garden; the art of cultivating or managing gardens.—**horticultural**, hor·ti·kul'tūr·al, a. Pertaining to horticulture.—**horticulturist**, hor·ti·kul'tūr·ist, n. One who practices horticulture.—**hortus siccus**, hor'tus sik'kus, n. [L.] *Lit.* a dry garden; a collection of specimens of plants carefully dried and preserved; a herbarium.

hosanna, ho·zan'na, n. [Heb., save, I beseech you.] An exclamation of praise to God, or an invocation of blessings.

hose, hōz, n. [A.Sax. *hosa* (pl. *hosan*), a leg covering=D. *hoos*, Icel. *hosa*, G. and Dan. *hose*; comp. A.Sax. *hose*, Dan. *hase*, a husk; perhaps allied to *house*.] Stockings; socks (in these senses now used as a plural); close-fitting trousers or breeches reaching to the knee; covering for the lower part of the legs, including the feet; a flexible tube or pipe for conveying water or other fluid to any required point.—*v.t.* To apply water, etc., by means of a hose, as to *hose* a garden.—**hosiery**, hō'zhi·ėr·i, n. Stockings, or goods similarly knitted; also a place where knit goods are made or sold.

hospice, hos'pis, n. [Fr., from L. *hospitium*, hospitality, a lodging, an inn.] A place of refuge and entertainment for travelers on some difficult road or pass, as among the Alps.

hospitable, hos'pi·ta·bl, a. [Fr. *hospitable*, L. *hospitalis*, from *hospes, hospitis*, a host, a guest. HOST.] Receiving and entertaining strangers with kindness and without reward; kind to strangers and guests; pertaining to the liberal entertainment of guests.—**hospitably**, hos'pi·ta·bli, adv. In a hospitable manner.—**hospital**, hos'pi·tal, n. [O.Fr. *hospital*, L.L. *hospitale. Hotel, hostel* doublets of this.] An institution for the reception and treatment of the old, sick, etc., for the education and support of orphans, or for the benefit of any class of persons who are more or less dependent upon public help; an institution of medical service for the sick and injured, where medical and surgical treatment are given.—**hospitality**, hos·pi·tal'i·ti, n. The kind and generous reception of strangers or guests; hospitable treatment or disposition.—**hospitalization**, hos·pi·tal·i·zā′shon, n.—**hospitalize**, hos′pi·tal·iz, v.t. To place in a hospital for medical care.—**hospitaler**, hos′pi·tal·ér, n. A member of a religious body whose office it was to relieve the poor, the stranger, and the sick; one of an order of knights who built a hospital at Jerusalem in A.D. 1042 for pilgrims, called *Knights of St. John*, and, after their removal to Malta, *Knights of Malta.*

hospodar, hos·pō·där′, n. A Slavonic title formerly borne by the princes of Moldavia and Wallachia, etc.

host, hōst, n. [O.Fr. *hoste*, Fr. *hôte*; from L. *hospes, hospitis*, a host, for *hostipes*, from *hostis*, an enemy, a stranger (akin E. *guest*), and root *pa*, to protect, as in L. *pater*, a father, *potens*, powerful. From *hospes* are also derived *hospital, hostler, hotel*, etc.] One who receives and entertains another at his own house; a landlord: the correlative of *guest*; an animal or organism in or on whose organs a parasite exists.—**hostess**, hōs′tes, n. A female host.

host, hōst, n. [O.Fr. *host*, from L. *hostis*, a stranger, an enemy, in later usage an army; *guest* is cog. with *hostis*. See also HOST, above.] An army; a number of men embodied for war; any greater number or multitude.

host, hōst, n. [L. *hostia*, a sacrificial victim, from *hostire*, to strike.] The altar bread or wafer in the Eucharist, or in the Roman Catholic sacrament of the Mass.

hostage, hos′tij, n. [O.Fr. *hostage*, Fr. *otage*. L.L. *hostagius, obstagius, obsidaticus*, from L. *obses, obsidis*, hostage—*ob*, at, near, *sedeo*, to sit.] A person handed over to an enemy as a pledge for the performance of certain conditions.

hostel, hos′tel, n. [HOTEL.] An inn; a lodginghouse.

hostile, hos′tīl, a. [L. *hostilis*, from *hostis*, an enemy. See HOST, army.] Belonging to an enemy; holding the position of an enemy or enemies; showing ill will and malevolence.—**hostilely**, hos′til·li, adv. In a hostile manner.—**hostility**, hos·til′i·ti, n. [L. *hostilitas*.] State of being hostile; an act of an open enemy; an act of warfare (in this sense generally *pl.*).

hostler, hos′lér, n. [O.Fr. *hostelier*, from *hostel*, Mod. Fr. *hôtel*, an inn, from L.L. *hospitale*, a hospital. HOTEL.] The person who has the care of horses at an inn, formerly the innkeeper; a stableboy.

hot, hot, a. [A.Sax. *hát*=Sc. *het*. D. *heet*, Sw. *het*, Dan. *hed, heed*, Icel. *heitr*, G. *heiss*. HEAT.] Having much sensible heat; exciting the feeling of warmth in a great or powerful degree; very warm; ardent in temper; easily excited or exasperated; vehement; violent; furious; animated; brisk; keen; lustful; lewd; acrid; biting; stimulating; pungent; wanted by the police; *phys. and chem.* radioactive; electrically energized (*hot* wire).—**hotbed**, hot′bed, n. Hort. a bed of earth heated by fermenting substances, and covered with glass,

used for growing early or exotic plants; a place which favors rapid growth or development.—**hot-blooded**, a. Having hot blood; having warm passions; irritable.—**hot dog**, a hot frankfurter, usually served in a roll.—**hotheaded**, a. Violent; rash; impetuous.—**hothouse**, hot′hous, n. A greenhouse or house to shelter tender plants, artificially heated; a conservatory.—**hot war**, n. A shooting war.—**hotly**, hot′li, adv.—**hotness**, hot′nes, n. The condition or quality of being hot.

hotchpot, hoch′pot, n. [Fr. *hochepot*—*hocher*, to shake (from D. or Flem. *hotsen*), and *pot*, a pot or dish.] A hodgepodge or mixture; *law*, a commixture of property for equality of division.—**hotchpotch**, n. HODGEPODGE.

hotel, hō·tel′, n. [Fr. *hôtel*, O.Fr. *hostel*, an inn; same word as *hospital, hostel*.] A house for entertaining strangers or travelers; an inn; especially, one of some style and pretensions; a large town mansion (*French usage*).

Hottentot, hot′n·tot, n. [From D. *hot en tot, hot* and *tot*, syllables intended to imitate sounds frequent in their language.] A member of a primitive tribe or race of South Africa; the language of this people, characterized by curious clicking or clucking sounds.

hough, hok, n. [Written also *hock*, which see.] The hock of a horse; the back part of the human knee joint; the ham.—v.t. To hamstring; to disable by cutting the sinews of the ham. (O.T.)

hound, hound, n. [A.Sax. *hund*, a dog or hound=G. Dan. and Sw. *hund*, D. *hond*, Icel. *hundr*, Goth. *hunds*; cog. W. *cun*, Gael. *cù*, L. *canis*, Gr. *kyōn*, Skr. *çvan*, a dog.] A term restricted to particular breeds or varieties of dogs used in the chase, as in hunting the deer, the fox, the hare; sometimes used as a term of contempt for a man.—v.t. To set on the chase; to incite to pursuit of animals; hence, to urge, incite, or spur to action: usually with *on*.

hour, our, n. [O.Fr. *hore, houre*, from L. *hora*, from Gr. *hōra*, a season, an hour; seen also in *horologe, horoscope*.] The twenty-fourth part of a day; sixty minutes; the particular time of the day; a fixed or appointed time; a time, period, or season; *pl.* certain prayers in the Roman Catholic Church, to be repeated at stated times of the day.—*To keep good hours*, to be at home regularly in good season; or not after the usual hours of retiring to rest; *to keep bad hours*, the opposite.—*The small hours*, the early hours of the morning, as one, two, etc.—**hourglass**, n. A glass in two compartments connected by a narrow neck, for measuring time by the running of a quantity of sand from one compartment to the other.—**hourly**, our′li, a. Happening or done every hour; frequent; often repeated; continual.—adv. Every hour; frequently; continually.

houri, hou′ri or hö′ri, n. [Ar.] Among the Mohammedans, a nymph of paradise.

house, hous, n. pl. **houses**, hou′zez. [A.Sax. *hús*=Icel. *hús*, Dan. Sw. and Goth. *hus*, D. *huis*, G. *haus*; from root meaning to cover, as in *hide, hose, sky*, etc. Akin *husband, hussy*.] A building serving or intended to serve as an abode; a building for the habitation of man, or for his use or accommodation; a dwelling; an abode; a household; a family; a family regarded as consisting of ancestors, descendants, and kindred; especially a noble or illustrious family; a legislative body of men (the *House* of Representatives); a legislative quorum; the audience at a place of entertainment; a firm or commercial establishment; a twelfth part of the astrological heavens.—*House of Representatives*, the lower branch of the United States Congress.—*House organ*, a publication brought out by a business concern, etc., for its members.—*House party*, a social gathering, lasting one or more nights, usually at a country house.—*To bring down the house*, to draw forth a universal burst of applause, as in a theater.—*To keep house*, to maintain an independent family establishment.—v.t.—housed, housing (houz). To put or receive into a house; to provide with a dwelling or residence; to shelter; to cause to take shelter.—v.i. To take shelter or lodgings; to take up abode.—**houseboat**, n. A boat with a wooden house, for lodgings by river in summer.—**housebreaker**, n. One who breaks into a house with a felonious intent; a burglar.—**housebreaking**, n. Burglary.—**housecarl**, n. [*Hus-carl*.] A member of the bodyguard of king or nobleman, e.g., of Harold at Hastings.—**housefly**, n. A well-known two-winged fly common in dwelling houses.—**household**, hous′hōld, n. Those who dwell under the same roof and compose a family; those under the same domestic government; house; family.—a. Pertaining to the house and family; domestic.—*Household gods*, gods presiding over the house or family among the ancient Romans; hence, objects endeared to one from being associated with home.—*Household troops, Household brigade*, troops whose special duty it is to attend the sovereign and guard the metropolis.—**householder**, hous′hōl·dér, n. The chief of a household; the occupier of a house.—**housekeeper**, hous′kē·pér, n. A householder; a head female servant in a household; a female who looks after a person's household.—**housekeeping**, hous′kē·ping, n. The management of domestic concerns; the maintenance of a household.—**houseleek**, n. A well-known plant which grows on the tops of houses and on walls, and the fleshy leaves of which are applied to bruises and other sores.—**houseless**, hous′les, a. Destitute of a house or habitation; without shelter.—**housemaid**, hous′mād, n. A female servant employed to keep a house clean, etc.—**house-room**, hous'rōm, n. Room or accommodation in a house.—**housewarming**, n. A merrymaking at the time a family enters a new house.—**housewife**, hous'wīf, n. The mistress of a family; the wife of a householder; a female manager of domestic affairs; a little case for needles, thread, scissors, etc.—**housewifely**, hous'wīf·li, a. Pertaining to or like a housewife; thrifty.—**housewifery**, hous'wīf·ri, n. The business or management of a housewife.

housing, hou'zing, n. [HOUSE.] Act of sheltering; the providing of houses and other dwelling quarters, as by a government; a frame to support machinery, etc., or parts of a machine.

housing, hou'zing, n. [From Fr. housse, a covering, a horsecloth; from D. hulse, a husk or shell; akin holster, hull, husk.] A cloth laid over a saddle; a saddlecloth; a horsecloth.

hove, hōv, pret. of heave.

hovel, huv'el, n. [Dim. of A.Sax. hof, a house, a dwelling=Icel. hof, a hall, G. hof, a court, a farm.] A poor cottage; a small mean house.

hover, huv'er, v.i. [Perhaps from O.E. hove, to abide, to linger, same origin as hovel.] To hang fluttering in the air or upon the wing; to be in doubt or hesitation; to be irresolute; to move to and fro threateningly or watchingly (an army hovering on our borders).—**hoveringly**, huv'er·ing·li, adv. In a hovering manner.

how, hou, adv. [A.Sax. hú, hwú, hwý, instrumental case of hwá, hwæt, who, what; really the same word as why.] In what manner; by what means or method; to what degree or extent; by what measure or quantity (how long, how much better); in what state, condition, or plight. Besides being used as an interrogative, direct or indirect, it is sometimes used interjectionally, or even substantively (the how and why of it).—**howbeit**, hou·bē'it, adv. [How, be, and it.] However it be; be it as it may; nevertheless; however.—**however**, hou·ev'er, adv. In whatever manner or degree; in whatever state.—conj. Nevertheless; notwithstanding; yet; still; though.—**howsoever**, hou·sō··ev'er, adj. or conj. In what manner soever; however.

howdah, hou'da, n. [Hind. and Ar. haudah.] A seat erected on the back of an elephant for two or more persons to ride in: usually covered overhead.

howitzer, hou'it·sėr, n. [From G. haubitze, from Bohem. haufnice, originally a sling.] A short gun firing a heavy shell with a low velocity, fired at a high angle, reaching objects not to be reached with direct fire; it represents the old mortar.

howl, houl, v.i. [An imitative word = D. huilen, G. heulen, Dan. hyle, to howl; comp. L. ululo, Gr. ololyzō, to wail, to howl; akin owl, L. ulula, an owl.] To utter a loud, protracted, mournful cry, as that of a dog or wolf; to produce any similar sound, as the wind; to wail or lament (N.T.).

—v.t. To utter in a loud or mournful tone.—n. The cry of a dog or wolf or other like sound; a cry of distress.—**howler**, hou'lėr, n. One who howls; a name given to a monkey of South America from its cry; an error that cries aloud for correction.

hoy, hoi, n. [D. and G. heu (pron. hoi); Dan. höy.] A heavy barge; † a small coasting vessel.

hoyden, hoiden, hoi'dn, n. [O.D. heyden, a heathen, a gypsy, a vagabond. HEATHEN.] A rude, bold girl.—a. Romping, roistering.—v.i. To romp rudely; to act like a hoyden.

hub, hub, n. [HOB.] The central cylindrical part of a wheel in which the spokes are set; the nave; a block of wood for stopping a carriage wheel; a mark at which quoits, etc., are cast; the hilt of a weapon.

hubble-bubble, hub'l·bub'l, n. A kind of tobacco pipe so arranged that the smoke passes through water, making a bubbling noise—hence its name; a hookah.

hubbub, hub'ub, n. [Imitative of confused noise.] A noise of many confused voices; a tumult; uproar.

huckaback, huk'a·bak, n. [Originally linen hawked or huckstered by being carried on the back.] A kind of linen cloth with raised figures on it, used principally for towels.

huckle, huk'l, n. [Connected with hook; lit. a thing bent or hooked; akin huckster.] The hip; a bunch or part projecting like the hip.—**huckleberry**, huk'l·be·ri, n. [Corruption of whortleberry.] A name for North American plants allied to the whortleberry.—**hucklebone**, n. The hipbone.

huckster, huk'stėr, n. [Akin to hawker; the name was given from the bending of the back in carrying a pack; comp. D. hukken, to squat, heuker, a hawker; G. hocken, to take on the back; Dan. hökre, to huckster; huckle, hook, are also akin.] A retailer of small articles; a hawker; one who higgles.—v.i. To deal in small articles or in petty bargains; to higgle.—v.t. To hawk or peddle; to make a matter of bargain.

huddle, hud'l, v.i.—huddled, huddling. [Same word as G. hudeln, Dan. hutle, D. hoetelen, to bungle; akin hustle.] To crowd or press together without order or regularity; to hustle. —v.t. To crowd together without order; to produce in a hurried manner; to hunch one's body together, often with up.—n. A crowd or confused mass; a gathering of football players behind the line of scrimmage to receive instructions, etc.

hue, hū, n. [A.Sax. hiw, heow, appearance; Sw. hy, color: Goth. hiwi, shape, show.] Color, or shade of color; dye; tint; painting, a compound of one or more colors forming an intervenient shade.—**hued**, hūd, a. Having a hue or color.

hue, hū, n. [Fr. huer, to hoot, to shout; akin hoot.] A shouting or clamor: used only in the phrase hue and cry, which is the outcry raised, or public warning at once given, by a person who has been robbed,

or who knows that a felony has been committed.

huff, huf, n. [An imitative word meaning lit. to blow, to puff; comp. whiff.] A fit of peevishness or petulance; anger at some offense, real or fancied; one filled with a false opinion of his own importance.—To take huff, to take offense.—v.t. To swell or puff up‡; to treat with insolence; to bully; to make angry.—v.i. To swell up; to bluster; to take offense.—**huffiness**, huf'i·nes, n. The state of being huffy.—**huffish**, huf'-ish, a. Inclined to huff; insolent.—**huffishly**, huf'ish·li, adv. In a huffish manner.—**huffishness**, huf'ish·nes, n.—**huffy**, huf'i, a. Puffed up; swelled; arrogant or insolent; easily offended.

hug, hug, v.t.—hugged, hugging. [Origin doubtful; comp. Icel. hugga, to soothe, to comfort; D. hugen, to coax; Dan. huge, to squat.] To press closely with the arms; to embrace closely; to clasp to the breast; to grasp or gripe, as in wrestling; to cherish in the mind (to hug delusions); to keep close to (to hug the land in sailing); refl. to congratulate one's self.—v.i. To lie close; to crowd together (Shak.).—n. A close embrace; a clasp or gripe.—**hugger**, hug'ėr, n. One who hugs.

huge, hūj, a. [O.E. huge, also hogge; comp. O.Fr. ahuge, huge; origin unknown.] Having an immense bulk; very large or great; enormous; very great in any respect (a huge difference).—**hugely**, hūj'li, adv. In a huge manner.—**hugeness**, hūj'nes, n. The state of being huge.

huggermugger, hug'ėr·mug'ėr, n. [Comp. hug, to lie close; obsolete hugger, to lurk; N. mugg, secrecy.] †Concealment; privacy; secrecy.—a. Clandestine; sly; confused; slovenly.

Huguenot, hū'ge·not, n. [Fr.; probably corrupted from G. eidgenoss, a confederate, there being found various early forms, such as higuenot, eidguenot, enguenot, anguenot, etc.] A French Protestant of the period of the religious wars in France in the sixteenth century.—**Huguenotism**, hū'ge·not·izm, n. The religion of the Huguenots.

hulk, hulk, n. [Same word as D. hulk, G. hulk, holk, Sw. holk, a kind of ship, from L.L. hulca, olca, from Gr. holkas, a ship of burden, from helkō, to draw.] A heavy ship‡; the body of a ship; the body of an old ship laid by as unfit for service; something bulky or unwieldy.—The hulks, old or dismasted ships, formerly used as prisons.—**hulking, hulky**, hul'king, hul'ki, a. Large and clumsy of body; unwieldy; loutish.

hull, hul, n. [A.Sax. hulu, a hull or husk; akin G. hülle, a covering, Goth. huljan, to cover; same root as in hell, holster.] The outer covering of something, particularly of fruits, grain, etc.; the husk; the body of a ship, exclusive of her masts, yards, and rigging.—Hull down, said of a ship when so distant that her hull is below the horizon.—v.t. To deprive of the hull or hulls; to pierce the hull of,

as with a cannon ball.—' To hull on the flood', of the ark; drifting, or sinking in the flood (*Mil.*).—**huller,** hul´ėr, *n.* One who hulls; a machine for separating seeds from their hulls.
hullabaloo, hul´a·ba·lö″, *n.* [Imitative of confused noise; comp. *hurly-burly.*] Uproar; noisy confusion.
hullo, hul·lö´, *interj.* [Same as *Halloo.*] An exclamation to call attention.
hum, hum, *v.i.*—**hummed, humming.** [Imitative of sound; comp. G. *hummen, summen,* D. *hommelen,* to hum. *Humble-bee, humbug, humdrum* are connected.] To make a dull, prolonged sound, like that of a bee in flight; to drone; to murmur; to buzz; to give utterance to a similar sound with the mouth; to mumble; to make a drawling, inarticulate sound in speaking.—*v.t.* To sing in a low voice; to murmur without articulation.—*n.* The noise made by bees or any similar sound; a buzz; any inarticulate, low, murmuring, or buzzing sound; a murmur of applause; a low inarticulate sound uttered by a speaker.—*interj.* A sound with a pause, implying doubt and deliberation; ahem.—**humming,** hum´ing, *n.* The sound of that which hums; a buzzing; a low murmuring sound.—**hummingbird,** *n.* A name given to the individuals of a family of minute and beautiful birds, from the sound of their wings in flight.
human, hū´man, *a.* [Fr. *humain,* L. *humanus,* from *homo, hominis,* a man (whence also *homage*); akin to *humus,* the ground (whence *humilis,* E. *humble*); also to A.Sax. *guma,* a man (seen in *bridegroom*).] Belonging to a man or mankind; having the qualities or attributes of man.—*n.* A human being.—**humane,** hū·mān´, *a.* [Same word as *human.*] Human‡; having the feelings and dispositions proper to man; kind; benevolent; tender; merciful; tending to humanize or refine.—**humanely,** hū·mān´li, *adv.* In a humane manner.—**humaneness,** hū·mān´nes, *n.* The quality of being humane.—**humanism,** hū´man·izm, *n.* Classical learning; a philosophical system.—**humanist,** hū´man·ist, *n.* One who studies the humanities; one versed in the knowledge of human nature; one at the revival of letters devoted to the study of the ancient classics. So *Literæ Humaniores,* not rendering more humane, but as opposed to sacred studies.—**humanistic,** hū·man·is´tik, *a.* Of or pertaining to humanity.—**humanitarian,** hū·man´i·tâ´ri·an, *n.* One who has a great regard or love for humanity; a philanthropist; one who denies the divinity of Christ, and believes him to have been a mere man; one who maintains the perfectibility of human nature without the aid of grace.—**humanitarianism,** hū·man´i·tâ´ri·an·izm, *n.* The practices or beliefs of a humanitarian.—**humanity,** hū·man´i·ti, *n.* [Fr. *humanité,* L. *humanitas,* from *humanus.*] The quality of being human; humanness; mankind collectively; the human race; the quality of being humane; tenderness

and kindness toward all created beings: opposed to *cruelty*; classical and polite literature or a branch of such literature: in this sense generally plural and with the definite article—' *the humanities* ': but in the Scottish universities used in the singular and applied to Latin and Latin literature alone.—**humanization,** hū´man·i·zā″shon, *n.* The act of humanizing.—**humanize,** hū´man·īz, *v.t.*—**humanized, humanizing.** To render human or humane.—*v.i.* To become more humane; to become more civilized.—**humanizer,** hū´man·ī·zėr, *n.* One who humanizes.—**humankind,** hū´man·kīnd, *n.* The race of man; mankind; the human species.—**humanly,** hū´man·li, *adv.* In a human manner; after the manner of men.
humble, hum´bl, *a.* [Fr. *humble,* from L. *humilis,* from *humus,* the earth (seen also in *exhume*). HUMILIATE, HUMAN.] Of a low, mean, or unpretending character; not grand, lofty, noble, or splendid; having a low estimate of one's self; not proud, arrogant, or assuming; lowly; modest; meek; submissive.—*v.t.*—**humbled, humbling.** To render humble; to reduce the power, independence, or state of; to bring down; to abase; to lower; to bring down the pride or vanity of: often *refl.*—**humbleness,** hum´bl·nes, *n.* The state of being humble or low.—**humbler,** hum´blėr, *n.* One who or that which humbles.—**humbly,** hum´bli, *adv.* In a humble manner; meekly; submissively.
humblebee, hum´bl·bē, *n.* [From old *humble,* to hum, from *hum;* comp. G. *hummel,* Dan. *humle-bi,* Sw. *humla,* humblebee; from the humming sound it makes; whence also *bumblebee.* HUM.] The common name of various large wild bees; the bumblebee.
humble pie, *n.* A pie made of the *humbles,* or heart, liver, kidneys, etc., of the deer.—*To eat humble pie,* to have to take a humble tone; to come down from an assumed position; to apologize, or humiliate one's self, abjectly: the phrase arose from the humbles being allotted to the huntsmen and servants, the meaning being influenced by the adj. *humble.*
humbug, hum´bug, *n.* [From *hum* and *bug, hum* having its old sense of to deceive, and *bug* its old meaning of *bugbear;* hence = false alarm.] An imposition played off under fair pretenses; a hoax; spirit of deception or imposition; falseness; hollowness; a cheat; a trickish fellow.—*v.t.*—**humbugged, humbugging.** To impose on; to cajole or trick; to hoax.—**humbugger,** hum·bug´ėr, *n.* One who humbugs.—**humbuggery,** hum´bug·ėr·i, *n.* The practice of humbugging; quackery.
humdrum, hum´drum, *a.* [From *hum* and *drum;* originally droning, monotonous.] Commonplace; homely; dull; heavy.—*n.* A droning tone of voice; dull monotony.
humeral, hū´mėr·al, *a.* [L. *humerus,* the shoulder.] Belonging to

the shoulder.—**humerus,** hū´mėr·us, *n. Anat.* the long cylindrical bone of the arm, situated between the shoulder blade and the forearm; also the shoulder.
humid, hū´mid, *a.* [L. *humidus, umidus,* from *humeo, umeo,* to be moist.] Moist; damp; wet or watery.—**humidify,** hū·mid´i·fi, *v.t.* To moisten; to make humid, especially the atmosphere.—**humidity, humidness,** hū·mid´i·ti, hū´mid·nes, *n.* Moisture or dampness in the atmosphere.—**humidifier,** hū·mid´i·fī·ėr, *n.* A machine that keeps a specific amount of moisture in the air.—**relative humidity,** the ratio of the amount of aqueous vapor in the air to the amount that would saturate it at the same temperature, expressed as a percentage.—**humidor,** hū´mi·dōr, *n.* A box in which a suitable humidity is maintained, especially one for storing tobacco.
humiliate, hū·mil´i·āt, *v.t.*—**humiliated, humiliating.** [L. *humilio, humiliatum,* from *humilis,* humble. HUMBLE.] To reduce to a lower position in one's own estimation or the estimation of others; to humble; to depress.—**humiliating,** hū·mil´i·āt·ing, *p.* and *a.* Humbling; reducing self-confidence; mortifying. — **humiliation,** hū·mil·i·ā″shon, *n.* The act of humiliating; the state of being humiliated, humbled, or mortified.—**humility,** hū·mil´i·ti, *n.* [L. *humilitas.*] The state or quality of being humble; humbleness; lowliness of mind; a feeling of one's own insignificance.
hummock, hum´ok, *n.* [Probably a dim. form of *hump.*] A rounded knoll; a mound; a hillock; a protuberance on an ice field.—**hummocky,** hum´ok·i, *a.* Abounding in hummocks.
humor, humour, hū´mėr, ū´mėr, *n.* [Fr. *humeur;* L. *humor,* moisture, liquid, from *humeo,* to be moist. HUMID.] Moisture or moist matter; fluid matter in the human or an animal body, not blood (the vitreous *humor* of the eye); a morbid fluid collected; *old med.* a fluid, of which there were four—blood, phlegm, yellow bile, and black bile—on the conditions and proportions of which the bodily and mental health was supposed to depend; hence, turn or frame of mind; disposition, or a peculiarity of disposition, often temporary (not in the *humor* for reading); a caprice, whim, or fancy (*Shak.*); temper (as regards anger or annoyance or the opposite); that mental quality which gives to ideas a ludicrous or fantastic turn, and tends to excite laughter or mirth; a quality or faculty akin to wit, but depending for its effect rather on kindly human feeling than on point or brilliancy of expression.—*Bad humor,* feeling of irritation, annoyance, or displeasure.—*Good humor,* feeling of cheerfulness; good temper.—*Out of humor,* out of temper; displeased; annoyed.—*v.t.* To comply with the humor or inclination of; to soothe by compliance; to gratify; to indulge, to adapt one's self to.—**humoral,** hū´-

mĕr·al, *a.* Pertaining to or proceeding from the humors of the body (*humoral* pathology).—**humorist,** hū´-mĕr·ist, *n.* Formerly; a person who exhibited certain strong peculiarities of disposition or manner; one who indulged in whims or eccentricities; now, one that makes use of a humorous style in speaking or writing; one whose conversation or writings are full of humor; one who has a playful fancy or genius; a wag; also, one who attributes all diseases to a depraved state of the humors.—**humoristic,** hū·mĕr·is´tik, *a.* Pertaining to or like a humorist.—**humorous,** hū´mĕr·us, *a.* Moist or humid‡; full of humor; exciting laughter; jocular; governed by humor or caprice; capricious; whimsical. — **humorously,** hū´mĕr·us·li, *adv.* In a humorous manner; pleasantly; jocosely.—**humorousness,** hū´mĕr·us·nes, *n.* The state or quality of being humorous.

hump, hump, *n.* [A nasalized form of *hub* or *hob*=L.G. *hump,* heap; D. *homp,* a lump; akin *hunch, heap.*] A protuberance; especially the protuberance formed by a crooked back; a hunch.—**humpback,** hump´bak, *n.* A back with a hump; a person who has such a back; a whale that has a hump on the back.—**humpbacked,** hump´bakt, *a.* Having a crooked back.—**humped,** humpt, *a.* Having a hump.—**humpy,** hump´i, *a.* Full of humps.

humph, humf, *interj.* An exclamation expressive of disbelief, doubt, dissatisfaction, or the like.

humus, hū´mus, *n.* [L. *humus,* soil.] Vegetable mold; a dark-brown or blackish matter from decayed vegetable substances.—**humic,** hū´mik, *a.* Obtained from or pertaining to humus.

hunch, hunsh, *n.* [A form of *hump.*] A hump; a lump; a thick piece; a push or jerk with the fist or elbow.—*v.t.* To make a hunch on; to push with the elbow.—**hunchback,** hunsh´bak, *n.* A humpback; a humpbacked person. —**hunchbacked,** hunsh´bakt, *a.* Humpbacked.—**hunched,** hunsht, *a.* Having a hunch or hump.

hundred, hun´dred, *a.* [A.Sax. *hundred*=Icel. *hundrath,* Dan. *hundrede,* D. *honderd,* G. *hundert;* from *hund,* cog. with L. *centum,* Skr. *catam,* a hundred, and a termination akin to E. *read,* and to Goth. *garathjan,* to reckon.] Ten times ten; ninety and ten added.—*n.* The product of ten multiplied by ten; a collection of ten times ten individuals or units; a division of a county in England, supposed to have originally contained a *hundred* families or freemen.—**hundredfold,** *n.* A hundred times as much.—**hundredth,** hun´dredth, *a.* The ordinal of a hundred; one portion of a hundred equal parts into which anything is divided.—*n.* The one after the ninety-ninth; one of a hundred equal parts of a thing.—**hundredweight,** hun´dred·wāt, *n.* A weight, usually denoted by *cwt.,* containing 100 pounds in the United States; in England, 112 pounds.

hung, hung, *pret. & pp.* of *hang.*

Hungarian, hung·gā´ri·an, *n.* A native of Hungary; a Magyar; the language of the Hungarians; Magyar.—*a.* Pertaining to Hungary.

hunger, hung´gĕr, *n.* [A.Sax. *hunger, hungor*=G. Dan. and Sw. *hunger,* Icel. *hungr.* Goth. *huhrus,* hunger.] An uneasy sensation occasioned by the want of food; a craving for food; craving appetite; strong or eager desire.—*v.i.* To feel hunger; to crave food; to desire eagerly; to long.—**hungrily,** hung´gri·li, *adv.* In a hungry manner.—**hungry,** hung´gri, *a.* [A.Sax. *hungrig.*] Feeling hunger; having a keen appetite; eagerly desirous; proceeding from hunger.

hunk, hungk, *n.* [A form of *hunch.*] A large lump; a hunch.

hunky, hunky-dory, *a.* All right; satisfactory; comfortable. (*Slang.*)

hunt, hunt, *v.t.* [A.Sax. *huntian,* to hunt, akin to *hentan,* to seize; O.G. *hundjan,* Goth. *(fra)hinthan,* to catch; allied to E. *hand,* and to *hind* (female deer).] To chase, search for, or follow after (wild animals, particularly quadrupeds), for the purpose of catching or killing; to search after, pursue, follow closely; to pursue game or wild animals over (to *hunt* a district).—*To hunt up* or *out,* to seek for; to search for.—*To hunt down,* to pursue and kill or capture; to exterminate in a locality.—*v.i.* To follow the chase; to go in pursuit of game or other wild animals; to seek by close pursuit; to search: with *after* or *for.*—*n.* The chasing of wild animals; a pursuit; a chase; a pack of hounds; an association of huntsmen in a district.—**hunter,** hun´tĕr, *n.* One who hunts; a huntsman; a horse used in the chase; a watch whose glass is protected by a metal cover.—**hunting box, hunting lodge,** *n.* A residence occupied for the purpose of hunting.—**hunting watch,** *n.* See HUNTER.—**huntress,** hunt´res, *n.* A female that hunts or follows the chase.—**huntsman,** hunts´man, *n.* One who hunts or who practices hunting; a person whose office it is to manage the chase.—**hunt's-up,** *n.* The tune formerly played on the horn under the windows of sportsmen to awaken them, to show that the game was roused by the hounds, and the hunt was to begin.

hurdle, hĕr´dl, *n.* [A.Sax. *hyrdel,* a dim. corresponding to G. *horde,* *hürde,* a hurdle; Icel. *hurth,* Goth. *haurds,* a door; akin E. *hoarding.*] A movable frame made of interlaced twigs or sticks, or of bars or rods crossing each other, varying in form according to its use.—*v.t.*—*hurdled, hurdling.* To fence or provide with hurdles.—**hurdle race,** *n.* A race of men or horses over hurdles or fences.

hurds, hĕrdz, *n. pl.* [HARDS.] The coarse part of flax or hemp; hards.

hurdy-gurdy, hĕr´di·gĕr´di, *n.* [Intended to suggest its sound.] A stringed instrument, whose tones are produced by the friction of a wheel acting the part of a bow against four strings; various instruments, usually playing street music, operated by turning a handle.

hurl, hĕrl, *v.t.* [A contracted form of *hurtle,* influenced by *whirl.*] To send whirling or flying through the air; to throw or dash with violence; to emit or utter with vehemence.—*v.i.*† To move rapidly; to whirl.—*n.* The act of throwing with violence.—**hurler,** hĕr´lĕr, *n.* One who hurls.—**hurling,** hĕrl´ing, *n.* An old game of ball.

hurly, hurly-burly, hĕr´li, hĕr´li·bĕr´li, *n.* [Intended to express by its sound noise or confusion, suggested by *hurl* or *hurry;* comp. Dan. *hurlumhei,* hurry-scurry; Fr. *hurluberlu,* a hare-brained person.] Tumult; bustle; confusion.

hurrah, hurray, hu·rä´, hu·rā´ *interj.* [Comp. E. *huzza,* G. *hurrah,* Dan. and Sw. *hurra,* Pol. *hura.*] An exclamation expressive of joy, applause, or encouragement; also used as a noun.—*v.i.* To utter a hurrah.—*v.t.* To receive with hurrahs; to encourage by cheering.

hurricane, hur´i·kān, *n.* [Sp. *huracan,* Fr. *ouragan,* D. *orkaan,* G. *orkan,* all from a native American word.] An extremely violent tempest or storm of wind; anything resembling a violent tempest.—*Hurricane deck,* an elevated deck in steamboats, especially the deck above a saloon.

hurry, hur´i, *v.t.*—*hurried, hurrying.* [Akin to G. *hurren,* to move hastily; Icel. *hurr,* a confused noise; Dan. *hurre,* to buzz; Sw. *hurra,* to whirl; imitative like *whirr, hurlyburly,* etc.] To impel to greater speed or haste; to urge to act or proceed with precipitance; to cause to be performed with great or undue rapidity; to impel to violent or thoughtless action.—*v.i.* To move or act with haste; to proceed with precipitation; to make great haste in going.—*n.* The act of hurrying; urgency; bustle; confusion.—**hurried,** hur´id, *p.* and *a.* Done in a hurry; evidencing hurry.—**hurriedly,** hur´id·li, *adv.* In a hurried manner.—**hurriedness,** hur´id·nes, *n.* State of being hurried. —**hurry-skurry,** hur´i·skur´i, *adv.* [*Hurry* and *scurry.*] Confusedly; in a bustle.—*n.* Fluttering haste; great confusion.

hurt, hĕrt, *v.t. pret. & pp. hurt.* [O.Fr. *hurter,* Mod. Fr. *heurter,* to knock against; perhaps of Celtic origin; comp. W. *hwyrdd,* a push, a thrust, a blow. Hence *hurtle, hurl.*] To cause physical pain to; to wound or bruise painfully; to cause mental pain; to wound the feelings of; to cause injury, loss, or diminution to; to impair; to damage; to harm.—*n.* A wound, a bruise, or the like; injury; loss; damage; detriment.—**hurtful,** hĕrt´ful, *a.* Causing hurt; harmful; injurious; mischievous; detrimental.—**hurtfully,** hĕrt´ful·li, *adv.* In a hurtful manner.—**hurtfulness,** hĕrt´ful·nes, *n.* The quality of being hurtful.—**hurtless,** hĕrt´les,

a. Inflicting no injury; harmless; receiving no injury.—**hurtlessness,** hėrt′les·nes, *n.*

hurtle, hėr′tl, *v.i.*—*hurtled, hurtling.* [From *hurt.*] To clash or meet in shock; to make a sound suggestive of hostile clash; to clash; to sound threateningly; to resound.

hurtleberry, hėr′tl·be·ri, *n.* See WHORTLEBERRY.

husband, huz′band, *n.* [A.Sax. *hús-bonda,* the master of the house, from Icel. *húsbóndi* (*hús,* house, and *búandi,* dwelling in), Dan. *huusbond,* Sw. *husbonde,* the master of house; A.Sax. *búan,* Icel. *búa,* G. *bauen,* to inhabit, to cultivate. HOUSE, BOOR.] A man joined to a woman by marriage; the correlative of *wife.*—*Ship's husband,* an agent of the owners who sees that a ship is supplied with stores and properly repaired before she proceeds to sea.—*v.t.* To spend, apply, or use with economy; to keep from spending in view of an effort required.—**husbandman,** huz′band·man, *n.* A farmer; a cultivator; one engaged in agriculture.—**husbandry,** huz′band·ri, *n.* Domestic economy; good management; frugality; thrift; the business of a husbandman; agriculture.

hush, hush, *a.* [Akin to *hist, whist, hiss*; G. *hush,* Dan. *hys, hyst,* a sound made to enjoin silence.] Silent; still; quiet.—*v.t.* To silence; to make quiet; to repress the noise or clamor of.—*To hush up,* to suppress; to procure silence concerning; to keep concealed.—*v.i.* To be still; to be silent; used chiefly in the imperative; be still; make no noise.—*n.* Stillness; quiet.—**hush money,** *n.* A bribe to secure silence; money paid to prevent disclosure of facts.

husk, husk, *n.* [Akin to D. *hulze,* G. *hülse,* a husk; equivalent to E. *hull,* a husk, with *sk* as a termination. HULL.] The external covering of certain fruits or seeds of plants; glume; hull; rind; chaff.—*v.t.* To deprive of the husk.—**husker,** hus′kėr, *n.* One who or that which husks.—**husky,** hus′ki, *a.* Abounding with husks; consisting of husks; resembling husks.

husky, hus′ki, *a.* [Allied to *hoarse*; A. Sax. *hwósta,* Sc. *hoast,* a cough.] Rough in tone, as the voice; powerful; burly.—**huskily,** hus′ki·li, *adv.* In a husky manner.—**huskiness,** hus′ki·nes, *n.* The state of being husky; hoarseness; burliness.

hussar, hu̇·zär′, *n.* [Hung. *huszar,* from *husz,* twenty, because in the wars against the Turks every twenty families were bound to furnish one cavalry soldier.] Originally one of the national cavalry of Hungary; now a light cavalry soldier of European armies.

Hussite, hus′īt, *n.* A follower of John *Huss,* the Bohemian religious reformer, burned in 1415.

hussy, huz′i, *n.* [Contr. from *huswife, housewife.*] A bad or worthless woman or girl; a jade; a jilt; a forward girl; a pert, frolicsome wench; also a hussif. See HUSWIFE.

hustings, hus′tingz, *n. pl.* [A.Sax. *hústing,* from acel. *hús-thing.* an assembly, a council—*hús,* house, and *thing,* cause, council. THING.] *Eng.* the platform on which parliamentary candidates stood when addressing the electors; now, any such place; election campaign proceedings. *Hustings court,* a local court in Virginia.

hustle, hus′l, *v.t.* [From D. *hutselen, hutsen,* to jumble or shake together; Sw. *hutla,* to shuffle; akin *hotch*-pot.] To crowd upon so as to shove about roughly; to push or elbow out or about rudely; to jostle.—*v.i.* hustled, hustling. To push or crowd; to move in a confused crowd; to shamble hurriedly.

huswife, huz′if, *n.* A housewife.

hut, hut, *n.* [Same word as D. *hut,* G. *hütte,* Dan. *hytte,* Sw. *hydda,* a hut; comp. W. *cwt,* a hovel.] A small house, hovel, or cabin; a mean dwelling; a wooden house for troops in camp or for settlers in a wild country.—*v.t.*—*hutted, hutting.* To place in huts, as troops encamped in winter quarters.—*v.i.* To take lodgings in huts.

hutch, huch, *n.* [Fr. *huche,* a chest, from L.L. *hutica,* a chest; probably of Teutonic origin and akin to *hut.*] A chest, box, coffer, bin, or other receptable in which things may be stored or animals confined; a low wagon in which coal is drawn up out of the pit; a measure of two bushels.—*v.t.* To place in a hutch.

huzza, hu·zä′, *interj.* A form of *Hurrah.*

hyacinth, hī′a·sinth, *n.* [Gr. *Hyakinthos,* the name of a youth said to have been slain by Apollo, and changed into the flower.] A liliaceous bulbous plant, of which there are many varieties cultivated; a mineral; a variety of zircon, transparent or translucent, of a red color tinged with yellow or brown: the name is also given to varieties of the garnet, the sapphire, and the topaz.—**hyacinthine,** hī·a·sin′thīn, *a.* Made of hyacinth; resembling hyacinth.

Hyades, Hyads, hī′a·dēz, hī′adz, *n. pl.* [Gr. *hyades,* from *hyō,* to rain.] A cluster of seven stars supposed by the ancients to indicate the approach of rainy weather when they rose with the sun.

hyaline, hī′a·lēn, *n.* [L. *hyalinus,* from Gr. *hyalinos,* of glass.] Glassy, transparent, horny substance like that which forms the shell of insects (chitin), found in hydatid cysts.—**hyaline cartilage,** *n.* The horny substance covering the bone ends at the joint.—*a.* Glassy; crystalline; transparent.—**hyalite,** hī′al·īt, *n.* A pellucid variety of opal, resembling colorless gum or resin.—**hyaloid,** hī′al·oid, *a.* Resembling glass; vitriform; transparent.

hybrid, hī′brid or hib′rid, *n.* [From L. *hybrida, hibrida,* a hybrid; origin doubtful.] A crossbred animal or plant; an offspring of two different breeds, genera or varieties.—*a.* Derived or bred from heterogeneous sources.—**hybridism, hybridity,** hī′brid·izm, hib·rid′i·ti, *n.*—**hybridi-**

zation, hī′brid·i·zā″shon, *n.*—**hybridize,** hī′brid·īz, *v.t.* To bring into the condition of producing a hybrid; to render hybrid.—**hybridizer,** hī′-brid·īz·ėr, *n.*

hydatid, hīd′a·tid, *n.* [Gr. *hydatis,* a vesicle, from *hydōr,* water.] A term applied to larval forms of tapeworms, found in the bodies of men and certain animals, or to similar vesicular or cystlike bodies.

Hydra, hī′dra, *n.* [L. *hydra*; Gr. *hydra,* from *hydōr,* water.] A monster of Greek mythology destroyed by Hercules, and represented as having many heads, one of which, being cut off, was immediately succeeded by another, unless the wound was cauterized; [*not cap.*] hence, evil or misfortune arising from many sources and not easily to be surmounted; a genus of fresh-water polyps of a very low type of structure.—**hydroid,** hī′droid, *a.* Resembling the hydra polyp in character.

hydrangea, hī·dran′jē·a, *n.* [Gr. *hydōr,* water, and *angeion,* a vessel, from the shape of its capsules.] An Asiatic shrub cultivated in gardens for the beauty of its flowers.

hydrant, hī′drant, *n.* [Gr. *hydrainō,* to irrigate, from *hydōr,* water.] A pipe with suitable valves and a spout by which water is raised and discharged from a main pipe.

hydrargyrum, hī·drär′ji·rum, *n.* [L., from Gr. *hydōr,* water, and *argyros,* silver.] Quicksilver or mercury.

hydrate, hī′drāt, *n.* [Gr. *hydōr,* water.] A chemical compound in which water is a characteristic ingredient.—**hydrated,** hī′drā·ted, *a.* Formed into a hydrate.

hydraulic, hī·dra̧′lik, *a.* [Fr. *hydraulique,* L. *hydraulicus,* Gr. *hydraulikos,* from *hydraulis,* an instrument played by water—*hydōr,* water, and *aulos,* a pipe.] Pertaining to fluids in motion, or the action of water utilized for mechanical purposes.—*Hydraulic cement,* a cement having the property of becoming hard under water.—*Hydraulic press,* a machine for the application of great power by means of water.—*Hydraulic ram,* a machine by which descending water can be made to raise a portion of itself to a considerable height.—**hydraulics,** hī·dra̧′liks, *n.* That branch of science which treats of the motion of liquids, and deals with the application of water in machinery.

hydric, hī′drik, *a.* [Gr. *hydōr,* water.] Of or pertaining to hydrogen.

hydride, hī′drīd, *n.* [Gr. *hydōr,* water and *ide.*] *Chem.* a chemical compound of hydrogen and a metal, or some base.

hydrocarbon, hī·drō·kär′bon, *n.* A chemical compound of hydrogen and carbon.—*Hydrocarbon furnace, hydrocarbon stove,* one in which liquid fuel is used.

hydrocele, hī′dro·sēl, *n.* [Gr. *hydōr,* water, and *kēlē,* a tumor.] *Med.* a morbid collection of serous fluid in the scrotum or testicle.

hydrocephalus, hī′drō·sef″a·lus, *n.* [L. from Gr. *hydrokephalon,* from *hy-*

dōr, water, and *kephatē*, head.] *Med.* a condition in which an abnormal amount of cerebrospinal fluid accumulates in the brain's cavities (ventricles), exerting excessive pressure.

hydrochloric, hī·drŏ·klō′rik, *a.* *Chem.* pertaining to, or compounded of, chlorine and hydrogen.

hydrochloric acid, hī′drŏ·klō″rik as′id, *n.* [*Hydrogen* and *chlorine*.] A concentrated aqueous solution of hydrogen chloride, HCl, that is a strong corrosive acid.

hydrocyanic, hī′drŏ·sī·an″ik, *a.* [*Hydrogen* and *cyanogen*.] Derived from the combination of hydrogen and cyanogen.

hydrocyanic acid, hī′drŏ·sī·an″ik as′id, *n.* [*Hydrogen* and *cyanogen*.] An aqueous solution of hydrogen cyanide, HCN, that is a poisonous weak acid used in fumigating.

hydrodynamic, hī′drŏ·di·nam″ik, *a.* [Gr. *hydōr*, water, and *dynamis*, power.] Pertaining to the force or pressure of water.—**hydrodynamics**, hī′drŏ·di·nam″iks, *n.* That branch of science which treats of the application of forces to fluids, especially when producing motion in fluids.

hydroelectric, hī′drŏ·i·lek″trik, *a.* Pertaining to the production of electric current by water power; of a frictional electric machine worked by steam.

hydrofluoric, hī′drŏ·flū·or″ik, *a.* Consisting of fluorine and hydrogen (*hydrofluoric* acid, a most powerful corrosive.)

hydrofoil, hī″drŏ·foil′, *n.* [Gr. *hydōr*, water, and *foil*.] A surface, similar to an airfoil, that develops lift as it moves in water; a finlike submerged body, which, at high speeds, lifts a craft's hull above the surface of the water.

hydrogen, hī′drŏ·jen, *n.* [Gr. *hydōr*, water, and root *gen*, to generate.] A gaseous element, colorless, odorless, flammable, and lighter than any other element. Symbol, H; at. no., 1; at. wt., 1.00797.—**hydrogenate**, hī·droj′e·nāte, *v.t.* To treat with, or expose to, hydrogen; to combine with hydrogen.—**hydrogenous**, hī·droj′e·nus, *a.*—**hydrogen bomb**, *n.* A bomb which releases large quantities of atomic energy through the fusion of nuclei at high temperature and pressure.

hydrography, hī·drog′ra·fi, *n.* [Gr. *hydōr*, water, and *graphō*, to describe.] That branch of science which has for its object the measurement and description of the sea, lakes, rivers, and other waters, and includes marine surveying, the drawing of charts, etc.—**hydrographer**, hī·drog′ra·fèr, *n.* One who is proficient in hydrography.—**hydrographic**, **hydrographical**, hī·drŏ·graf′ik, hī·drŏ·graf′i·kal, *a.* Relating to or treating of hydrography.

hydroid. See HYDRA.

hydrokinetics, hī′drŏ·ki·net″iks, *n.* [Gr. *hydōr*, water, and *kinetics*.] Study of the effect of forces on fluids.

hydrology, hī·drol′o·ji, *n.* [Gr. *hydōr*, water, and *logos*, discourse.] The science that treats of water, its properties, laws, distribution, etc.—**hydrological**, hī·drŏ·loj′i·kal, *a.* Pertaining to hydrology.—**hydrologist**, hī·drol′o·jist, *n.* One skilled in hydrology.

hydrolysis, hī·drol′i·sis, *n.* [*Hydro* and *lysis*, N.L. from Gr., a loosing.] The chemical decomposition of organic compounds by water.

hydromancy, hī′drŏ·man·si, *n.* [Gr *hydōr*, water, and *manteia*, divination.] A method of divination by water.

hydromel, hī′drŏ·mel, *n.* [Fr., from Gr. *hydōr*, water, and *meli*, honey.] A liquor consisting of honey diluted in water; when fermented it forms mead.

hydrometallurgy, hī·drŏ·met′al·ėr·ji, *n.* The process of assaying or reducing ores by liquid reagents.

hydrometeorology, hī·drŏ·mē′tē·ėr·ol′o·ji, *n.* The branch of meteorology which concerns itself with water in the atmosphere in the form of rain, clouds, snow, etc.—**hydrometeorological**, hī·drŏ·mē′tē·ėr·o·loj″i·kal, *a.* Pertaining to this.

hydrometer, hī·drom′et·ėr, *n.* [Gr. *hydōr*, water, *metron*, a measure.] An instrument to measure the specific gravity or density of water and other fluids, and hence the strength of spirituous liquors and of various solutions.—**hydrometric**, **hydrometrical**, hī·drŏ·met′rik, hī·drŏ·met′ri·kal, *a.* Pertaining to a hydrometer or hydrometry.—**hydrometry**, hī·drom′et·ri, *n.* The art or operation of determining the specific gravity, density, force, etc., of fluids.

hydropathy, hī·drop′a·thi, *n.* [Gr. *hydōr*, water, and *pathos*, affection.] The treatment of disease by the use of cold water externally or internally; the water cure.—**hydropathic**, hī·drŏ·path′ik, *a.* Relating to hydropathy.—*n.* An establishment in which persons are boarded and receive the hydropathic treatment if they wish.—**hydropathist**, hī·drop′a·thist, *n.* One who practices or advocates hydropathy.

hydrophane, hī′drŏ·fān, *n.* [Gr. *hydōr*, water, and *phainō*, to show.] A variety of opal made transparent by immersion in water.

hydrophobia, hī·drŏ·fō′bi·a, *n.* [Gr. *hydōr*, water, *phobos*, fear.] A morbid unnatural dread of water; rabies.—**hydrophobic**, hī·drŏ·fob′ik, *a.*

hydrophone, hī′drŏ·fōn, *n.* [Gr. *hydōr*, water, and *phōnē*, sound.] An instrument used on ships for the detection of submarines.

hydrophyte, hī′drŏ·fīt, *n.* [Gr. *hydōr*, water, and *phyton*, a plant.] A plant which lives and grows in water.

hydropic, hydropical, hī·drop′ik, hī·drop′i·kal, *a.* [L. *hydropicus*, Gr. *hydrōpikos*, from *hydrōps*, dropsy—*hydōr*, water, and *ops*, the face.] Dropsical; pertaining to dropsy.

hydroplane, hī′drŏ·plān, *n.* [Gr. *hydōr*, water, and *plane*.] An airplane that can take off and land on water; a speedboat with hydrofoils.

hydroscope, hī′drŏ·skōp, *n.* [Gr. *hydōr*, water, and *skopeō*, to view.] An instrument to mark the presence of water in the air; a kind of ancient water clock.

hydrosoma, hydrosome, hī·drŏ·sō′ma, hī′drŏ·sōm, *n.* [*Hydra*, and Gr. *sōma*, body.] The entire organism of any hydrozoan.

hydrostatics, hī·drŏ·stat′iks, *n.* [Gr. *hydōr*, water, and *statics*.] The science which treats of the weight and equilibrium of fluids, particularly of water; that branch of science which treats of the properties of fluids at rest.

hydrotherapy, hī·drŏ·ther′a·pi, *n.* [*Hydro* and *therapy*.] The treatment of disease or injury with water, by immersion, etc.

hydrothermal, hī·drŏ·thėr′mal, *a.* [Gr. *hydōr*, water, and *thermos*, hot.] Of or relating to heated water.

hydrothorax, hī·drŏ·thō′raks, *n.* *Med.* dropsy in the thorax or chest.

hydrotropism, hīd′rŏ·trōp″ism, *n.* [Gr. *hydōr*, water, *trepō*, I turn.] *Bot.* curving toward or away from moisture.

hydrous, hī′drus, *a.* Containing water; watery.

hydroxide, hīd·roks′īd, *n.* [Gr. *hydōr*, water, *oxys*, acid.] A compound formed by the union of a metallic or basic radical with one or more hydroxyl groups.

hydroxyl, hīd·roks′il, *n.* [Gr. *hydōr*, water, and *oxys*, acid.] The univalent radical OH, consisting of an oxygen atom and a hydrogen atom linked together.

hydrozoan, hī·drŏ·zō′an, *n.* pl. **hydrozoa**, hī·drŏ·zō′a. [Gr. *hydra*, a hydra, and *zōon*, a living creature.] *Zool.* any one of a class of animals that belong to the phylum Coelenterata, consisting mostly of marine animals and including the jellyfish (or nettlefish), the sea anemone, the hydra (or fresh-water polyp), etc.

hyena, hī·ē′na, *n.* [L. *hyæna*, from Gr. *hyaina*, a hyena, from *hys*, a hog, from its hoglike back.] A digitigrade carnivorous animal of several species, belonging to Asia and Africa, strong and fierce, feeding chiefly on carrion, and of nocturnal habits.

hyetal, hī′e·tal, *a.* [Gr. *hyetos*, rain, from *hyō*, to rain.] Relating to rain, or its distribution with reference to different regions.—**hyetograph**, hī′e·to·graf, *n.* A chart showing the rainfall in different regions.—**hyetographic, hyetographical**, hī′e·to·graf″ik, hī′e·to·graf″i·kal, *a.* Pertaining to hyetography.—**hyetography**, hī·e·tog′ra·fi, *n.* The science of the distribution of rain.—**hyetology**, hī·e·tol′o·ji, *n.* That branch of meteorology which treats of the phenomena connected with rain.

hygeian, hī·jē′yan, *a.* [From Gr. *hygieia, hygeia*, health, from *hygiēs*, healthy.] Pertaining to health or its preservation.—**hygeist**, hī′jē·ist, *n.* One versed in hygiene.—**hygiene**, hī′ji·ēn, [Fr. *hygiène*, from Gr. *hygieinos*, healthy, wholesome.] A system of principles or rules designed for the promotion of health, especially the health of households or communities; sanitary science.—**hygienic**, hī·ji·en'ik, *a.* Relating to hygienic or sanitary matters.—**hygienically**, hī·ji·en'i·kal·li, *adv.* In a hygienic manner.—**hygienics**, hī·ji·en'iks, *n.* The science of health; hygiene; sanitary science.

hygrograph, hī'grō·graf, *n.* [Gr. *hygros*, moist, and *graphō*, I write.] An instrument which registers automatically the variations of the atmosphere as regards moistness.—**hygrometer**, hī·grom'et·ėr, *n.* An instrument for measuring the degree of moisture of the atmosphere.—**hygrometric**, hī·gro·met'rik, *a.* Pertaining to hygrometry; readily absorbing and retaining moisture.—**hygrometry**, hī·grom'et·ri, *n.* The determination of humidity, or of the moisture of the atmosphere.—**hygrophyte**, hī'gro·fīt, *n.* [Gr. *hygros*, moisture, *phyton*, a plant.] A land plant adapted to moist surroundings.—**hygroscope**, hī'gro·skōp, *n.* An instrument for indicating the presence of moisture in the atmosphere.—**hygroscopic**, hī·gro·skop'ik, *a.* Pertaining to the hygroscope; imbibing moisture from the atmosphere.

hylism, hī'lizm, *n.* [Gr. *hylē*, a wood, timber, matter.] A theory which regarded matter as the original principle of evil, in opposition to the good spirit.—**hylozoism**, hī·lo·zō'izm, *n.* [Gr. *zōe*, life.] The doctrine that matter possesses a species of life, or that life and matter are inseparably connected.—**hylozoist**, hī·lo·zō'ist, *n.* A believer in hylozoism.—**hylozoic**, hī·lo·zō'ik, *a.* Pertaining to hylozoism.

hymen, hī'men, *n.* [Gr. *hymēn*, a skin, a membrane; *Hymēn*, the God of marriage.] *Anat.* the virginal membrane, situated at the entrance of the vagina; *bot.* the fine pellicle which encloses a flower in the bud.—**hymeneal, hymenean**, hī·men·ē'al, hī·men·ē'an, *a.* Pertaining to marriage.—*n.* A marriage song.

hymenopter, hymenopteran, hī·men·op'tėr, hī·men·op'tėr·an, *n.* [Gr. *hymēn*, a membrane, and *pteron*, a wing.] A member of an order of insects, having four membranous wings, and including the bees, wasps, ants, etc.—**hymenopterous**, hī·men·op'tėr·us, *a.* Belonging or pertaining to the hymenopters.

hymn, him, *n.* [L. *hymnus*, from Gr. *hymnos*, a song, a song of praise.] A song or ode in honor of God, or in honor of some deity; a sacred lyric; a song of praise, adoration, or thanksgiving.—*v.t.* To praise or celebrate in hymn or song; to sing.—*v.i.* To sing in praise or adoration.—**hymnal, hymnbook**, him'nal, *n.* A collection of hymns, generally for use in public worship.—**hymnologist**, him·nol'o·jist, *n.* A composer of hymns.—**hymnology, hymnody**, him·nol'o·ji, him'no·di, *n.* A body of sacred lyrics composed by several authors of a particular period or country; hymns collectively.

hyoid, hī'oid, *a.* [Gr. *hyoeidēs*, shaped like the letter *u* or *y.*] Applied to a movable bone having somewhat the shape of the letter U, between the root of the tongue and the larynx.

hyoscyamine, hī·o·sī'am·in, *n.* [From *hyoscyamus.*] Alkaloid poisons occurring in henbane (*Hyoscyamus*).

hypaethral, hypethral, hī·pē'thral, *a.* [Gr. *hypaithros*, under the sky—*hypo* under, and *aithēr*, ether.] *Arch.* applied to a building not covered by a roof.

hypanthium, hī·pan'thi·um, *n.* [Gr. *hypo*, under, *anthos*, flower.] *Bot.* the fleshy enlarged hollow of the end of a flowerstalk, as in the rose.

hyperaemia, hī·per·ē'mi·a, *n.* [Gr. *hyper*, over or above, and *haima*, blood.] An excessive accumulation of blood in a part of the body.—**hyperaemic**, hī·pėr·ē'mik, *a.* Pertaining to or affected with hyperaemia.

hyperaesthesis, hyperaesthesia, hī'pėr·es·thē"sis, hī'pėr·es·thē"zi·a, *n.* [Gr. *over*, and *aisthēsis*, sensation.] Morbid excess of sensibility.

hyperbola, hī·pėr'bo·la, *n.* [Gr. *hyperbolē.* HYPERBOLE.] *Geom.* a curve formed by a plane that cuts a cone in a direction parallel to its axis, or so that the plane makes a greater angle with the base than the side of the cone makes.—**hyperbolic**, hī·pėr·bol'ik, *a.* Having the properties of the hyperbola.

hyperbole, hī·pėr'bo·lē, *n.* [Gr. *hyperbolē*, excess—*hyper*, beyond, *ballō*, to throw.] A figure of speech which expresses much more or less than the truth; an exaggerated statement; exaggeration.—**hyperbolic, hyperbolical**, hī·pėr·bol'ik, hī·pėr·bol'i·kal, *a.*—**hyperbolically**, hī·pėr·bol'i·kal·li, *adv.*—**hyperbolism**, hī·pėr'bol·izm, *n.*—**hyperbolize**, hī·pėr'bol·īz, *v.t.* and *i.* To speak or write with exaggeration; to exaggerate.

Hyperborean, hī·pėr·bō'rē·an, *a.* [Gr. *hyper*, beyond, *boreas*, the north.] Belonging to a region very far north; northern; arctic; frigid.—*n.* An inhabitant of the most northern region of the earth.

hypercatalectic, hī·pėr·kat'a·lek"tik, *a.* [Gr. *hyper*, beyond, and *katalēxis*, termination.] *Pros.* having a syllable or two beyond the regular measure.

hypercritic, hī·pėr·krit'ik, *n.* [Gr. *hyper*, beyond, and *kritikos*, critical. CRITIC.] One who is critical beyond measure or reason.—**hypercritical**, hī·pėr·krit'i·kal, *a.* Overcritical; critical beyond use or reason.—**hypercritically**, hī·pėr·krit'i·kal·li, *adv.* In a hypercritical manner.

hyperdulia, hī·pėr·dū'li·a, *n.* [Gr. *hyper*, beyond, and *douleia*, service.] The worship offered by Roman Catholics to the Virgin Mary, so called because higher than that given to saints (which is known as *dulia*).

hypergolic, hī·pėr·gol'ik, *adj.* [*Hypergol* and *ic.*] Capable of igniting itself on contact with an oxidizer, said of rocket fuel.

hyperkinesis, hī'pėr·ki·nē"sis, *n.* [Gr. *hyper*, beyond, and *kinēsis*, motion.] Abnormal increase of muscular move-

ment; spasmodic action.—**hyperkinetic**, hī'pėr·ki·net"ik, *a.*

hypermeter, hī·pėr'me·tėr, *n.* [Gr. *hyper*, beyond, and *metron*, measure.] A hypercatalectic verse; something beyond ordinary measure.—**hypermetrical**, hī·pėr·met'ri·kal, *a.*

hypermetropia, hypermetropy, hī'pėr·me·trō"pi·a, hī·pėr·met'ro·pi, *n.* [Gr. *hyper*, over, *metron*, measure, *ops*, the eye.] A defect of the eyesight in which the focus for all objects falls behind the retina, and which is corrected by convex glasses; long-sightedness.

hyperplasia, hī·pėr·plā'si·a, *n.* [Gr. *hyper*, beyond, *plassō*, to form.] *Pathol.* excessive growth of a part by multiplication of cells.

hyperpyrexia, hī'pėr·pi·rek"si·a, *n.* [Prefix *hyper* and *pyrexia.*] An excessive degree of fever.

hypersonic, hī·pėr·son'ik, *a.* [*Hyper* and *sonic*, from L. *sonus*, sound.] Of a speed five times or more faster than that of sound in air; capable of moving or using air currents that move at hypersonic speed.

hypersthene, hī·pėr'sthēn, *n.* [Gr. *hyper*, beyond, *sthenos*, strength; from its difficult frangibility as compared with hornblende.] A mineral of the hornblende group, a constituent of some rocks; also called *Labrador hornblende.*

hypertension, hī·pėr·ten'shon, *n.* [*Hyper* and *tension.*] Abnormally high arterial blood pressure.

hyperthyroidism, hī·pėr·thī'roid·ism, *n.* [*Hyper* and *thyroidism.*] *Med.* excessive activity of the thyroid gland.—**hyperthyroid**, hī·pėr·thī'roid, *n.* and *a.*

hypertrophy, hī·pėr'tro·fi, *n.* [Gr. *hyper*, above, and *trophē*, nutrition.] A morbid enlargement of a part of the body; excessive growth.—**hypertrophic**, hī·pėr·trof'ik, *a.*

hypha, hī'fa, *n.*; pl. **hyphae**, hī'fē. [Gr. *hyphē*, a web.] The thready or filamentous matter forming the mycelium of a fungus.—**hyphal**, hī'fal, *a.* Pertaining to a hypha.

hyphen, hī'fen, *n.* [Gr. *hyphen*, strictly *hyph'hen*, into or in one, together—*hypo*, under, and *hen*, one.] A mark or short line made between two words to show that they form a compound word, or used to connect the syllables of a divided word.—*v.t.* To join by a hyphen.

hypnosis, hip·nō'sis, *n.* The hypnotic state; a sort of sleep artificially induced, often by the person fixing his attention upon some bright object, being accompanied by more or less unconsciousness.—**hypnotist**, hip'no·tist, *n.* One who hypnotizes.

hypnotic, hip·not'ik, *a.* [Gr. *hypnos*, sleep; akin L. *sopor*, sleep, A.Sax. *swefen*, a dream.] Having the quality of producing sleep; tending to produce sleep; soporific.—*n.* A medicine that produces sleep; a soporific.—**hypnotism**, hip'no·tizm, *n.* A sleeplike condition brought on by artificial means.—**hypnotize**, hip'no·tīz, *v.t.* To affect with hypnotism.—**hypnologist**, hip·nol'o·jist, *n.* One versed in hypnology.—**hypnology,** hip·nol′o·ji, n. Facts relating to the phenomena of sleep.

hypoblast, hī′po·blast, n. [Gr. hypo, under, and blastos, a bud.] Bot. the flat dorsal cotyledon of a grass; anat. the lower of the two layers of cells forming the blastoderm, the upper being the epiblast.

hypocaust, hī′po·kạst, n. [Gr. hypokauston—hypo, under, and kaiō, to burn.] Anc. arch. an arched chamber in which a fire was kindled for the purpose of giving heat to the rooms above it; also a compartment of some modern stoves.

hypochondria, hī·po·kon′dri·a, n. [From the hypochondrium being regarded as the seat of the disease. See below.] Med. a disease characterized by exaggerated uneasiness and anxiety, mainly as to what concerns the health, etc.; spleen; vapors; low spirits.—**hypochondriac, hypochondriacal,** hī·po·kon′dri·ak, hī′po·kon·drī″a·kal, a. Pertaining to hypochondria or to the hypochondrium: affected with hypochondria.—**hypochondriac,** n. A person affected with hypochondria.—**hypochondriacally,** hī′po·kon·drī″a·kal·li, adv. In a hypochondriac manner.—**hypochondriasis,** hī′po·kon·drī″a·sis, n. Hypochondria.—**hypochondrium,** hī·po·kon′dri·um, n. pl. **hypochondria.** [Gr. hypochondrion, from hypo, under, and chondros, cartilage—from its situation.] Anat. the name of the two regions of the abdomen under the cartilages of the false ribs on the right and left side.

hypocotyl, hī′po·kot″il, n. [Gr. hypo, under, cotyl(edon).] In seedlings, that part of the stem below the seed leaves (cotyledons).

hypocrisy, hi·pok′ri·si, n. [Fr. hypocrisie, L. hypocrisis, Gr. hypokrisis, a playing a part on the stage, simulation, from hypokrinomai, to play a part, to feign—hypo, and krinō, to separate, discern. CRITIC.] The act or practice of simulating or feigning to be what one is not; especially, the assuming of a false appearance of piety and virtue; dissimulation; insincerity.—**hypocrite,** hip′o·krit, n. [Fr. hypocrite, Gr. hypokritēs.] One who practices hypocrisy.—**hypocritical,** hip·o·krit′i·kal, a. Pertaining to, or proceeding from, hypocrisy; characterized by hypocrisy; pretending goodness or religion; insincere.—**hypocritically,** hip·o·krit′i·kal·li, adv.

hypocycloid, hī·po·sī′kloid, n. [Gr. hypo, under, and E. cycloid.] A curve generated by the movement of a curve upon the concave side of a fixed curve.

hypodermic, hī·po·dėr′mik, a. [Gr. hypo, under, derma, the skin.] Pertaining to or relating to parts under the skin or to the introduction of medicines under the skin.—**hypodermic injection,** hī·po·dėr′mik in·jek′shon, n. Med. an injection made into the subcutaneous tissues.

hypogastrium, hī·po·gas′tri·um, n. [Gr. hypo, under, and gastēr, the belly.] Anat. the lower anterior region of the abdomen.—**hypogastric,** hī·po·gas′trik, a.

hypogeal, hypogeous, hī·po·jē′al, hī·po·jē′us, a. [Gr. hypo, beneath, gē, the earth.] Lit. subterranean; bot. a term applied to parts of plants which grow beneath the surface of the earth.

hypogene, hī′po·jēn, a. [Gr. hypo, under, and root gen, to produce.] Geol. formed or originating under the surface of the earth (as crystalline rocks).

hypoglossal, hī·po·glos′al, a. [Gr. hypo, under, glōssa, the tongue.] Anat. pertaining to the under side of the tongue.

hypogynous, hī·poj′i·nus, a. [Gr. hypo, under, gynē, a female.] Bot. placed below the ovary or seed vessel; having the corolla and stamens inserted below the ovary.

hyponasty, hī′po·nas·ti, n. [Gr. hypo, under, nastos, pressed.] Bot. excessive growth of the under surface of an organ, causing it to bend upward: as opposed to epinasty.

hypophosphite, hī′po·fos′fit, n. The name of certain bodies containing phosphorus, some of which are used medicinally.

hypostasis, hī·pos′ta·sis, n. pl. **hypostases,** hī·pos′ta·sēz. [Gr. hypostasis, substance, nature, essence, also sediment.] The sediment or deposit that settles at the bottom of a fluid; the essential nature of any thing or any person; the accumulation of blood in the lower parts of the body; theol. the distinct substance or subsistence of the Father, Son, and Holy Spirit in the Godhead.—**hypostatic, hypostatical,** hī·po·stat′ik, hī·po·stat′i·kal, a. Relating to hypostasis.—Hypostatic union, the union of the three persons in the Godhead, or the union of the divine and human nature in the person of Christ.—**hypostatize,** hī·pos′ta·tīz, v.t. To regard as a distinct substance.

hypostyle, hī′po·stīl, n. [Gr. hypo, under, stylos, a pillar.] Arch. a covered colonnade; a pillared hall.—a. Having the roof supported by pillars.

hyposulfite, hī·po·sul′fit, n. The name of certain substances containing sulfur, of which the hyposulfite of sodium is used in medicine and the arts.

hypotenuse, hypothenuse, hī·pot′e·nūs, n. [Gr. hypoteinousa—hypo, under, and teinō, to stretch.] Geom. the longest side of a right-angled triangle; the line that subtends the right angle.

hypothec, hī·poth′ek, n. [L. hypotheca, Gr. hypothēkē, a pledge, from hypotithēmi, to put under, to pledge.] Scots law, a lien such as that which a landlord has over the furniture or crops of his tenant in respect of the current rent.—**hypothecary,** hī·poth′e·ke·ri, a. Of or pertaining to hypothecation.—**hypothecate,** hī·poth′e·kāt, v.t.—**hypothecated, hypothecating.** To pledge in security for a debt, but without transfer; to mortgage.—**hypothecation,** hī·poth′e·kā″shon, n. The act of hypothecating.—**hypothecator,** hī·poth′e·kā·tėr, n. One who hypothecates.

hypothesis, hī·poth′e·sis, n. pl. **hypotheses,** hī·poth′e·sēz. [Gr. hypothesis, a supposition, from hypo, under, and tithēmi, to place.] A supposition; something not proved, but assumed for the purpose of argument; a theory imagined or assumed to account for what is not understood.—**hypothesize,** hī·poth′e·sīz, v.i. To form hypotheses.—**hypothetical,** hī·po·thet′i·kal, a.—**hypothetically,** hī·po·thet′i·kal·li, adv.

hypothyroid, hī·po·thī′roid, n. [Hypo and thyroid, Gr. thyreos, a shield, eidos, form.] One affected by a deficient thyroid gland.—**hypothyroidism,** hī·pō·thī′roid·izm, n. Med. the deficient activity of the thyroid gland; the resulting condition.

hypsometer, hip·som′et·ėr, n. [Gr. hypsos, height, metron, measure.] A special kind of barometer for measuring altitudes; an apparatus used for measuring heights by noting the boiling point of water.—**hypsometric, hypsometrical,** hip·so·met′rik, hip·so·met′ri·kal, a. Pertaining to hypsometry.—**hypsometrically,** hip·so·met′ri·kal·li, adv. According to hypsometry.—**hypsometry,** hip·som′et·ri, n. The art of measuring the heights of places upon the surface of the earth.

Hyrcanian, hėr·kā′ni·an, a. Pertaining to Hyrcania, which was an ancient province of the Persian Empire in Asia, somewhere southwest of the Caspian Sea. The Caspian Sea in literature is sometimes called the "Hyrcanian Sea."

hyrax, hī′raks, n. [Gr., a shrew mouse.] A small rabbit-like animal of Syria, believed to be the 'coney' of Scripture; a kindred species of South Africa.

hyson, hī′son, n. [Chinese hi-tshun, lit. first crop.] A species of green tea from China.

hyssop, his′op, n. [Gr. hyssōpos, hyssop.] The name of small bushy herbs of the mint family, the plants being aromatic and stimulating.

hysterectomy, his·tėr·ek′to·mē, n. [Gr. hystera, the uterus, ektomē, a cutting out or off.] In surgery, the excision, or removal, of the uterus.

hysteresis, his′te·rē″sis, n. [N.L. from Gr. hysterein, to be behind, to lag.] Any of several lagging effects resembling an internal friction which result when the forces acting on a body (such as magnetism, electricity and physical strain) are changed.

hysteria, hysterics, his·tē′ri·a, his·ter′iks, n. [L.L. hysteria, from Gr. hystera, the womb.] A nervous illness, marked by fits of laughing and crying.—**hysterical,** his·ter′i·kal, a.—**hysterically,** his·ter′i·kal·li, adv.

hysteron proteron, his′tėr·on prot″ėr·on, n. [Gr. hysteron, last, and proteron, first.] An inversion of the natural order in words; a putting first what should be last.

hysterotomy, his·tėr·ot′o·mi, n. [Gr. hystera, the uterus, tomē, a cutting.] The operation of cutting into the uterus to take out a fetus which cannot be expelled by the usual means.

I

I, i, ī, the ninth letter and the third vowel of the English alphabet, in which it represents not only several vowel sounds but also the consonantal sound of *y*.

I, ī, *pron.* pos. *my* or *mine*, dat. and obj. *me*; pl. nom. *we*, pos. *our* or *ours*, dat. and obj. *us*. [A.Sax. *ic*, D. *ik*, Goth. *ik*, Icel. *ek*, Dan. *jeg*, L. *ego*, Gr. *egō*, Skr. *aham*, W. *ym*, Armor. *em*—I.] The nominative case of the pronoun of the first person; the word by which a speaker or writer denotes himself: sometimes used as a noun; the ego.

iamb, iambus, ī′amb, ī·am′bus, *n.* pl.—**iambs, iambi,** ī′ambs, ī·am′bī. [Gr. *iambos*, from *iapto*, to assail.] *Pros.* a foot consisting of two syllables, the first short and the last long, or the first unaccented and the last accented, as in *delight*.—**iambic,** ī·am′bik, *a.* Pertaining to the iambus; composed of iambi.—*n.* An iambic foot; a verse consisting of iambi.

Iberian, ī·bē′ri·an, *n.* One of the primitive inhabitants of Spain; the language of the ancient Iberians, of which Basque is supposed to be the representative.

ibex, ī′beks, *n.* [L., a kind of goat.] An animal of the goat family found in the Alps and Pyrenees, with large horns directed backward and marked with transverse ridges in front.

ibis, ī′bis, *n.* [Gr. and L.] A name of certain grallatorial birds allied to the storks, the most remarkable species of which, the sacred ibis, was revered by the ancient Egyptians.

Icarian, ī·kâ′ri·an, *a.* [From *Icarus*, in Greek mythol., who, flying with a pair of artificial wings, soared so high that the sun melted the wax that cemented his wings, and caused him to fall into the sea.] Adventurous in flight; soaring too high for safety.

ICBM. See INTERCONTINENTAL.

ice, īs, *n.* [A.Sax. *is*=D. *ijs*, Dan. and Sw. *is*, Icel. *iss*, G. *eis*, referred along with *iron*, G. *eisen*, to a root meaning to shine or glance.] Water or other fluid congealed or in a solid state in consequence of the abstraction of the heat necessary to preserve its fluidity.—*To break the ice*, to make the first opening to any attempt; to open the way.—*v.t.*—**iced, icing.** To cover with ice; to convert into ice; to cool with ice; to freeze; to cover with concreted sugar.—**iceberg,** īs′bėrg, *n.* [D. *ijsberg*—*ijs*, ice, and *berg*, a mountain.] A vast body of ice floating on the ocean.—**iceboat,** *n.* A strong boat that can break a passage through ice; a boat for sailing with runners on the surface of ice.—**icebound,** īs′bound, *a.* Surrounded with ice so as to be immovable, or inaccessible.—**icebreaker,** *n.* A massive and powerful steamer that smashes and forces a way through ice.—**ice cream,** n. Cream variously flavored, and congealed by means of a freezing mixture.—**iced,** īst, *p.* Covered with ice;

cooled with ice; frosted.—**ice field,** *n.* A large sheet of sea ice whose limits cannot be seen.—**ice foot,** īs′fut, *n.* A belt or fringe of ice that forms round the shores in arctic regions.—**icehouse,** īs′hous, *n.* A repository for the preservation of ice during warm weather.—**ice plant,** *n.* A plant belonging to Greece, the Canaries, and the Cape, so called from being studded with pellucid watery vesicles which shine like pieces of ice.—**ice sheet,** *n.* A thick sheet of ice covering a land area and not limited to valleys.—**icicle,** ī′si·kl, *n.* [A.Sax. *is-gicel*, from *is*, and *gicel*, an icicle; akin to Icel. *jökull*, icicle, *jaki*, a piece of ice.] A pendent conical mass of ice formed by the freezing of water or other fluid as it drops from something.—**icily,** ī′si·li, *adv.* In an icy manner.—**iciness,** ī′si·nes, *n.* The state of being icy or very cold.—**icy,** ī′si, *a.* Pertaining to, composed of, produced by, resembling or abounding with ice; *fig.* characterized by coldness or coolness, as of manner, etc.; frigid; chilling; indifferent.

Icelander, īs′lan·dėr, *n.* A native of Iceland.—**Icelandic,** īs·lan′dik, *a.* Pertaining to Iceland.—*n.* The language of the Icelanders or of their literature, the oldest of the Scandinavian group of tongues.—**Iceland moss,** *n.* A species of lichen found in the arctic regions and on lofty mountains, used in medicine and as a nutritious article of diet.—**Iceland spar,** *n.* A transparent variety of calcareous spar, or carbonate of lime, valuable for experiments on the double refraction and polarization of light.

ichneumon, ik·nū′mon, *n.* [Gr., from *ichneuō*, to track out, from *ichnos*, a footstep—the animal searches out crocodiles' eggs.] A digitigrade carnivorous animal of Egypt, resembling a weasel, and feeding on crocodiles' eggs, snakes, etc.; a mongoose; a hymenopterous insect whose larvae are parasitic on other insects (called also *ichneumon fly*).

ichnite, ik′nīt, *n.* [Gr. *ichnos*, a footprint.] *Geol.* a fossil footprint; the footprint of an extinct animal marked on rocks.—**ichnology,** ik·nol′o·ji, *n.* The fossil footmarks of animals.

ichnography, ik·nog′ra·fi, *n.* [Gr. *ichnos*, a footstep, and *grapho*, to describe.] The horizontal section of a building or other object, showing its true dimensions according to a geometric scale; a ground plan.

ichor, ī′kor, *n.* [Gr.] An ethereal fluid that supplied the place of blood in the veins of the gods of the Greeks and Romans; *med.* a thin watery humor, like serum or whey; a thin watery acrid discharge from an ulcer, wound, etc.—**ichorous,** ī′ko·rus, *a.* Like ichor; thin; watery; serous.

ichthyic, ik′thi·ik, *a.* [Gr. *ichthys*, a fish.] Pertaining to fishes; fishlike.—**ichthyography,** ik·thi·og′ra·fi, *n.* The description of fishes.—**ichthyoid, ichthyoidal,** ik′thi·oid, ik·thi·oi′dal, *a.* More or less fishlike.—**ichthyologic, ichthyological,** ik′thi·o·loj″ik,

ik′thi·o·loj″i·kal, *a.* Pertaining to ichthyology.—**ichthyologist,** ik·thi·ol′o·jist, *n.* One versed in ichthyology.—**ichthyology,** ik·thi·ol′o·ji, *n.* The science of fishes; that branch of zoology which treats of fishes.—**ichthyophagous,** ik·thi·of′a·gus, *a.* Eating or subsisting on fish.—**ichthyophagy,** ik·thi·of′a·ji, *n.* The practice of eating fish.—**ichthyornis,** ik·thi·or′nis, *n.* [Gr. *ornis*, a bird.] A fossil bird with vertebrae like those of fishes, and with teeth set in sockets.—**ichthyosaurus, ichthyosaur,** ik″thi·o·sa̤′rus, ik″thi·o·sa̤r′, *n.* [Gr. *sauros*, a lizard.] A fishlike lizard; an immense fossil marine reptile, combining many of the characters of lizards and fishes.—**ichthyosis,** ik·thi·ō′sis, *n.* A disease of the skin, portions of which become hard and scaly, with a tendency to excrescences.

icon, ī′kon, *n.* [Gr. *eikōn*, an image, from *eikō*, to resemble.] An image or representation; a portrait; the holy picture or emblem regarded as sacred in the Greek and Russian Church.—**iconoclasm,** ī·kon′o·klazm, *n.* The act, principles, or proceedings of an iconoclast.—**iconoclast,** ī·kon′o·klast, *n.* [Gr. *eikōn*, and *klastēs*, a breaker, from *klaō*, to break.] A breaker of images; any destroyer or exposer of shams or superstitions; one who makes attacks upon cherished beliefs.—**iconoclastic,** ī·kon′o·klas″tik, *a.* Pertaining to an iconoclast.—**iconography,** ī·ko·nog′ra·fi, *n.* [Gr. *eikōn*, and *graphō*, to describe.] That branch of knowledge which treats of ancient statues, busts, paintings in fresco, mosaic works, engraving on gems or metals, and the like.—**iconographic,** ī·kon′o·graf″ik, *a.* Relating to iconography; representing by diagrams or pictures.—**iconolater,** ī·ko·nol′at·ėr, *n.* [Gr. *eikōn*, and *latreia*, service.] One that worships images.—**iconolatry,** ī·ko·nol′at·ri, *n.* The worship or adoration of images.—**iconology,** ī·ko·nol′o·ji, *n.* The doctrine of images or emblematical representations; iconography.

icosahedral, ī′kos·a·hē″dral, *a.* [Gr. *eikosi*, twenty, and *hedra*, seat, side.] Having twenty equal sides.—**icosahedron,** ī′kos·a·hē″dron, *n.* A solid of twenty equal sides.

icteric, icterical, ik·ter′ik, ik·ter′i·kal, *a.* [L. *icterus*, jaundice.] Affected with jaundice; curative of jaundice.

ictus, ik′tus, *n.* [L., from *ico*, to strike.] A stroke; the stress laid on an accented syllable.

id, id, *n.* [Gr. *idios*, distinct.] *Psych.* that part of the unconscious that harbors instinctive impulses and seeks pleasure.

idea, ī·dē′a, *n.* [L. *idea*, from Gr. *idea*, the form or appearance of a thing, kind or species, from *idein*, to see; same root as E. *wit*.] The form, image, or model of anything in the mind; that which is held or comprehended by the understanding or intellectual faculties; as a philosophical term, now generally used to designate subjective notions and representations, with or without objective validity; popularly it signifies notion, conception, thought, opinion, belief.—**ideal,** ĭ·dē′al, *a.* Existing in idea; existing in fancy or imagination only; visionary.—*n.* An imaginary model of perfection; a standard of perfection or beauty.—*Beau Ideal.* See BEAU.—**idealism,** ĭ·dē′al·izm, *n.* That system of philosophy according to which nothing exists but the mind itself and ideas perceived by the mind, or which maintains that we have no rational grounds for believing in the reality of anything but percipient minds and ideas.—**idealist,** ĭ·dē′al·ist, *n.* One who holds the doctrine of idealism; one who idealizes; one who indulges in flights of fancy or imagination; a visionary. —**idealistic,** ĭ·dē′al·is″tik, *a.* Pertaining to idealism or idealists.— **ideality,** ĭ·di·al′i·ti, *n.* The condition or quality of being ideal; capacity to form ideals of beauty and perfection. —**idealization,** ĭ·dē′al·i·zā″shon, *n.* The act of idealizing.—**idealize,** ĭ·dē′al·īz, *v.t.*—*idealized, idealizing.* To make ideal; to give form to in accordance with any preconceived ideal; to embody in an ideal form.— *v.i.* To form ideals.—**idealizer,** ĭ·dē′al·ī·zėr, *n.* One who idealizes; an idealist.—**ideally,** ĭ·dē′al·li, *adv.* In an ideal manner.—**ideation,** ĭ·di·ā′shon, *n.* The faculty of the mind for forming ideas; the establishment of a distinct mental representation or idea of an object.—**ideational,** ĭ·di·ā′shon·al, *a.* Pertaining to ideation.— **ideograph, ideogram,** id′i·ō·graf, id′i·ō·gram, *n.* In some systems of writing, a character, symbol, or figure which suggests the idea of an object without expressing its name; a hieroglyphic.—**ideographic, ideographical,** id′i·o·graf″ik, id′i·o·graf″i·kal, *a.* Representing ideas independently of sounds; pertaining to that mode of writing which, by means of symbols, figures, or hieroglyphics, suggests the ideas of objects.— **ideographically,** id′i·o·graf″i·kal·li, *adv.* In an ideographic manner.— **ideography,** id·i·og′ra·fi, *n.* Writing in ideographic characters or symbols. —**ideology,** id′i·ol″o·ji, *n.* The science of ideas or of their understanding; that system of mental philosophy which exclusively derives our knowledge from sensation.— **ideological,** id′i·o·loj″i·kal, *a.* Pertaining to ideology.—**ideologist,** id·i·ol′o·jist, *n.* One who treats of ideas; one who indulges in ideas or theories; a supporter of ideology. **identical, identic,** ĭ·den′ti·kal, ĭ·den′tik, *a.* [L.L. *identicus,* from L. *idem,* the same.] The same; not another or different.—*Identical proposition,* a proposition in which the terms of the subject and the predicate comprise the same idea, as that the whole is equal to its parts. **identically,** ĭ·den′ti·kal·li, *adv.* In an identical manner.—**identicalness,** ĭ·den′ti·kal·nes, *n.* Sameness.—**identification,** ĭ·den′ti·fi·kā″shon, *n.* The act of identifying.—*Identification tag.* A disk worn around the neck by both

officers and men in active military service, showing name, number, unit, etc.—**identify,** ĭ·den′ti·fī, *v.t.*— *identified, identifying.* [From *identi-,* in *identity,* and L. *facio,* to make.] To make to be the same; to unite or combine in such a manner as to make one; to determine or establish the identity of; to ascertain or prove to be the same with something described or claimed.—*v.i.* To become the same.—**identity,** ĭ·den′ti·ti, *n.* [L.L. *identitas,* from L. *idem,* same.] The state or fact of being identical; sameness, as distinguished from similitude and diversity.—*Personal identity,* our being the same persons from the commencement to the end of life while the matter of the body, the dispositions, habits, thoughts, etc., are continually changing.—*Principle of identity, philos.* the principle that a thing is what it is and not another. **ideograph, ideology,** etc. See IDEA. **ides,** īdz, *n. pl.* [L. *idus,* the ides, from *iduo,* to divide.] In the ancient Roman calendar the 13th of January, February, April, June, August, September, November, and December, and the 15th of March, May, July, and October. **idiocrasy,** id·i·ok′ra·si, *n.* [Gr. *idios,* peculiar, and *krasis,* mixture, temperament.] Peculiarity of constitution; temperament or constitution peculiar to a person; idiosyncrasy. **idiocy.** See IDIOT. **idioelectric,** id′i·ō·i·lek″trik, *a.* [Gr. *idios,* one's own, and E. *electric.*] Electric by virtue of its own peculiar properties. **idiom,** id′i·om, *n.* [Fr. *idiome,* L. *idioma,* from Gr. *idiōma,* from *idios,* proper, or peculiar to one's self.] A mode of expression peculiar to a language or to a person; a phrase or expression having a special meaning from usage, or a special grammatical character; the genius or peculiar cast of a language; a peculiar form or variety of language; a dialect.— **idiomatic, idiomatical,** id′i·o·mat″ik, id′i·o·mat″i·kal, *a.* Having the character of an idiom; pertaining to the particular modes of expression which belong to a language.— **idiomatically,** id′i·o·mat″i·kal·li, *adv.* In an idiomatic manner. **idiomorphic,** id′i·o·mor″fik, *a.* [Gr. *idios,* one's own, *morphē,* form.] Having a peculiar or distinctive form. **idiopathy,** id·i·op′a·thi, *n.* [Gr. *idios,* proper, peculiar, and *pathos,* suffering.] A morbid state or condition not preceded and occasioned by any other disease.—**idiopathic,** id′i·o·path″ik, *a.* Pertaining to idiopathy; not symptomatic. **idiosyncrasy,** id′i·o·sin″kra·si, *n.* [Gr. *idios,* proper, *syn,* with, and *krasis,* temperament.] A personal peculiarity of constitution or temperament; a mental or moral characteristic belonging to and distinguishing an individual; peculiar way of thinking or feeling.—**idiosyncratic,** id′i·o·sin·krat″ik, *a.* Relating to idiosyncrasy. **idiot,** id′i·ot, *n.* [L. *idiota,* from Gr.

idiōtēs, a private, vulgar, unskilled person, from *idios,* private, peculiar to one's self.] The lowest level of feeblemindedness in which an individual is possessed of a maximum mental age of two years, or an IQ of 25; a silly, foolish person.— *a.* Pertaining to an idiot; afflicted with idiocy.—**idiocy,** id′i·o·si, *n.*— **idiotic, idiotical,** id·i·ot′ik, id·i·ot′i·kal, *a.* Like or relating to an idiot; foolish; utterly absurd.—**idiotically,** id·i·ot′i·kal·li, *adv.* In an idiotic manner. **idle,** ī′dl, *a.* [A.Sax., *idel,* vain, empty, idle=D. *ijdel,* G. *eitel,* idle; Dan. *idel,* mere; from root meaning to shine (Skr. *idh,* Gr. *aithō,* to burn).] Not engaged in any occupation; unoccupied; doing nothing; slothful; averse to labor or employment; lazy; vacant, or not spent in work (*idle* hours); remaining unused; producing no effect; useless, vain, ineffectual, or fruitless (*idle* rage); trifling or irrelevant (an *idle* story).—*v.i.*— *idled, idling.* To lose or spend time in inaction or without being employed.—*v.t.* To spend in idleness: generally followed by *away.*—**idleness,** ī′dl·nes, *n.* The condition or quality of being idle.—**idler,** īd′lėr, *n.* One who idles.—**idle wheel,** *n.* In machinery, a wheel placed between two others for the purpose simply of transferring the motion from one axis to the other without change of direction.—**idly,** īd′li, *adv.* In an idle manner. **idocrase,** ī′dō·krās, *n.* [Gr. *eidos,* form, and *krasis,* mixture, from the mixture of forms its crystals display.] A mineral differing from garnet chiefly in form, occurring, variously colored, in the lavas of Vesuvius and elsewhere; pyramidal garnet or Vesuvian. **idol,** ī′dol, *n.* [Fr. *idole,* L. *idolum,* from Gr. *eidōlon,* an image, form, phantom, idol, from *eidos,* form; same root as in *idea.*] An image, representation, or symbol of a deity made or consecrated as an object of worship; any person or thing on which we strongly set our affections; that to which we are excessively, often improperly, attached.—**idolater,** ĭ·dol′a·tėr, *n.* [Fr. *idolatre,* L. *idololatre,* Gr. *eidōlolatrēs,* an idolworshiper. IDOLATRY.] A worshiper of idols; one who worships as a deity that which is not God; a pagan; an adorer; a great admirer.—**idolatress,** ĭ·dol′at·res, *n.* A female worshiper of idols.—**idolatrize,** ĭ·dol′at·rīz, *v.i.* To worship idols.—*v.t.* To adore; to worship.—**idolatrous,** ĭ·dol′at·rus, *a.* Pertaining to idolatry; partaking of the nature of idolatry; worshiping false gods; consisting in or partaking of an excessive attachment or reverence.—**idolatrously,** ĭ·dol′at·rus·li, *adv.* In an idolatrous manner.— **idolatry,** ĭ·dol′at·ri, *n.* [Fr. *idolatrie,* L. *idolatria,* from Gr. *eidōlolatreia* —*eidōlon,* idol, and *latreuō,* to worship.] The worship of idols, images, or anything made by hands, or which is not God; excessive attachment to or veneration for any person or thing.—**idolism,**† ī′dol·izm, *n.* The worship of idols.—**idolize,** ī′dol·īz, *v.t.*—*idolized, idolizing.* To worship as an idol; to make an idol of; to love to excess; to love or reverence to adoration.—**idolizer,** ī′dol·ī·zėr, *n.* One who idolizes.

idyl, idyll, ī′dil, *n.* [L. *idyllium,* Gr. *eidyllion,* from *eidos,* form.] A short highly wrought descriptive poem, consisting generally of scenes or events of pastoral life.—**idyllic,** ī·dil′ik, *a.* Of or belonging to idyls or pastoral poetry; pastoral.

if, if, *conj.* [A.Sax. *gif,* if; Icel. *ef,* if; akin O.G. *ibu,* G. *ob,* if, whether; Goth. *iba,* whether, *jabai,* if.] A particle used to introduce a conditional sentence, equal to—in case that, granting that, supposing that, allowing that; also, whether: in dependent clauses (I know not *if* he will).

igloo, ig′lö, *n.* [Eastern Eskimo *igdlu,* snow house.] A dome-shaped Eskimo dwelling made of square blocks of packed snow.

igneous, ig′ni·us, *a.* [L. *igneus,* from *ignis,* fire, allied to Skr. *agni,* fire.] Pertaining to, consisting of, or resembling fire; produced by or resulting from the action of fire.—**ignescent,** ig·nes′ent, *a.* [L. *ignescens.*] Emitting sparks of fire when struck, especially with steel.—*n.* A mineral that gives out sparks when struck.—**ignite,** ig·nīt′, *v.t.*—*ignited, igniting.* To kindle or set on fire; to communicate fire to.—*v.i.* To take fire; to become red with heat.—**ignition,** ig·nish′on, *n.* The act of igniting, or state of being ignited; the act or means of exploding the charge of gases in the cylinder of an internal-combustion engine.

ignoble, ig·nō′bl, *a.* [L. *ignobilis—in,* not, and *gnobilis,* or *nobilis,* noble. NOBLE.] Of low birth or family; not noble; not illustrious; mean; worthless; not honorable; base.—**ignobleness,** ig·nō′bl·nes, *n.* The condition or quality of being ignoble.—**ignobly,** ig·nō′bli, *adv.* In an ignoble manner.

ignominy, ig′no·min·i, *n.* [L. *ignominia—in,* not, and *gnomen, nomen,* name, from root seen in E. *know.*] Public disgrace; shame; dishonor; infamy.—**ignominious,** ig·no·min′i·us, *a.* [L. *ignominiosus.*] Marked with ignominy; shameful; dishonorable; infamous; despicable.—**ignominiously,** ig·no·min′i·us·ly, *adv.* In an ignominious manner.

ignoramus, ig·no·rā′mus, *n.* pl. **ignoramuses,** ig·no·rā′mus·ez. [1st pers. pl. pres. ind. of L. *ignoro*—lit. we are ignorant. IGNORE.] An ignorant person; a vain pretender to knowledge.

ignorant, ig′nė·rant, *a.* [L. *ignorans, ignorantis,* ppr. of *ignoro,* to be ignorant. IGNORE.] Destitute of knowledge; uninstructed or uninformed; untaught; unenlightened; unacquainted; unconscious.—**ignorantly,** ig′nė·rant·li, *adv.* In an ignorant manner.—**ignorance,** ig′nė·rans, *n.* [L. *ignorantia.*] The state of being ignorant; want of knowledge.

ignore, ig·nōr′, *v.t.*—*ignored, ignor-*

ing. [L. *ignoro,* to be ignorant of, from *ignarus,* not knowing—*in,* not, and *gnarus,* knowing, from root of *gnosco,* to know, and E. *know.*] To pass over or by without notice; to act as if one were unacquainted with; to shut the eyes to; to leave out of account; to disregard; to reject.

iguana, ig·wä′na, *n.* [Sp., from the Haytian language.] A reptile of the lizard family, with pendulous dewlaps, native of tropical America, some species of which are much esteemed as food.

iguanodon, ig·wä′no·don, *n.* [*Iguana* and Gr. *odous, odontos,* a tooth, from the character of its teeth.] A colossal fossil lizard found in the Wealden strata.

ileum, il′ē·um, *n.* [From Gr. *eilō,* to roll, from its convolutions; or from L. *ilia,* intestines. ILIAC.] *Anat.* the lower three-fifths of the small intestine in man.

ileus, ī′lē·us, *n.* [Gr. *ileos, eileos,* a severe pain in the intestines.] *Med.* colic; iliac passion.

iliac, il′i·ak, *a.* [L. *iliacus,* from *ilia,* the flank, the groin, the intestines.] Pertaining to the bowels, especially the lower bowels, or to the part of the abdomen containing them.—*Iliac region,* the side of the abdomen between the ribs and the hips.—*Iliac arteries,* the arteries formed by the bifurcation of the aorta near the last lumbar vertebra.—*Iliac passion,* a dangerous ailment, consisting in obstruction of the bowels, accompanied with severe griping pain, and often vomiting of fecal matter.—**ilium,** il′i·um, *n.* [Properly *os ilium,* bone of the ilia or flank.] *Anat.* a bone that forms the outer portion of the pelvis on either side; the hipbone.

ilk, ilk, *a.* [A.Sax. *ilc, ylc,* same.] Same. [Old E.]—*Of that ilk,* in Scot., a phrase sometimes used after the name of a landed gentleman to denote that his surname and the title of his estate are the same.

ill, il, *a.* [From the Scandinavian; Icel. *illr,* adj. ill; Icel. and Sw. *illa,* adv. *ill;* a contracted form of *evil.* Its comparative and superlative, *worse* and *worst,* are from a different root.] Bad or evil; the opposite of good; wicked; wrong: used of things rather than persons; producing evil or misfortune; calamitous or unfortunate (an *ill* end); cross, crabbed, surly, or peevish (*ill* nature, *ill* temper); suffering from disease or sickness; sick or indisposed; unwell (*ill* of a fever); not proper; rude or unpolished (*ill* manners, *ill* breeding).—*Ill turn,* an unkind or injurious act.—*n.* Wickedness; evil; misfortune; calamity; whatever annoys or impairs happiness or prevents success.—*adv.* Not well; not rightly or perfectly (*ill* at ease); not easily; with pain or difficulty (he is *ill* able to sustain the burden). [*Ill,* prefixed to participles, or adjectives having the form of participles, forms a great number of compound words the meaning of which is generally obvious.]—**illness,** il′nes, *n.* The state or condition of being ill; an ailment

or sickness.—**ill-advised,** *a.* Badly advised; resulting from bad advice or the want of good; injudicious.—**ill-bred,** *a.* Not well bred; badly educated or brought up; impolite.—**ill-fated,** *a.* Having an ill or evil fate; ill-starred; unfortunate.—**ill-favored,** *a.* Having ill features; ugly.—**ill-gotten,** *a.* Gained by unfair or improper means; dishonestly come by.—**ill-humor,** *n.* Ill temper, fretfulness.—**ill-judged,** *a.* Not well judged; injudicious; unwise.—**ill-mannered,** *a.* Uncivil; rude; impolite.—**ill-matched,** *a.* Badly assorted; not well suited.—**ill-nature,** *n.* Evil nature or disposition; bad temper; crossness; crabbedness.—**ill-natured,** *a.* Having ill-nature; of habitual bad temper; bad tempered.—**ill-naturedly,** *adv.* In an ill-natured manner; crossly.—**ill-omened,** *a.* Having unlucky omens; unfortunate.—**ill-starred,** *a.* Having an evil star presiding over one's destiny; hence, fated to be unfortunate; ill-fated.—**ill-tempered,** *a.* Of bad temper.—**ill will,** *n.* A desire that evil will befall a person; enmity.

illation, il·lā′shon, *n.* [L. *illatio—il* for *in,* in, on, and *latio,* a bearing, from *fero, latum,* to bear.] The act of inferring from premises or reasons; inference; an inference, deduction, or conclusion.—**illative,** il′la·tiv, *a.* Relating to illation; capable of being inferred or of inferring; denoting an inference (*then* or *therefore* is an *illative* word).—*n.* An illative word.

illaudable, il·la′da·bl, *a.* [Prefix *il* for *in,* not, and *laudable.*] Not laudable.

illegal, il·lē′gal, *a.* [Prefix *il* for *in,* not, and *legal.*] Not legal; contrary to law; unlawful; illicit.—**illegality,** il·lē·gal′i·ti, *n.* The condition or quality of being illegal.—**illegally,** il·lē′gal·li, *adv.* In an illegal manner.

illegible, il·lej′i·bl, *a.* [Prefix *il* for *in,* not, and *legible.*] Incapable of being read; obscure or defaced so that the words cannot be known.—**illegibility, illegibleness,** il·lej′i·bil″i·ti, il·lej′i·bl·nes, *n.* The state or quality of being illegible.—**illegibly,** il·lej′i·bli, *adv.* In an illegible manner.

illegitimate, il·li·jit′i·mit, *a.* [Prefix *il* for *in,* not, and *legitimate.*] Not legitimate; born out of wedlock; not in conformity with law; not authorized; not legitimately inferred or deduced; not warranted (an *illegitimate* inference).—*v.t.*—*illegitimated, illegitimating.* To render illegitimate; to bastardize.—**illegitimacy,** il·li·jit′i·me·si, *n.* The state of being illegitimate; bastardy.—**illegitimately,** il·li·jit′i·mit·li, *adv.* In an illegitimate manner.

illiberal, il·lib′ėr·al, *a.* [Prefix *il* for *in,* not, and *liberal.*] Not liberal; not free or generous; of narrow or contracted mind or opinions.—**illiberality, illiberalness,** il·lib′ėr·al″i·ti, il·lib′ėr·al·nes, *n.* The quality of being illiberal.—**illiberally,** il·lib′ėr·al·li, *adv.* In an illiberal manner.

illicit, il·lis′it, *a.* [L. *illicitus—il,* not, and *licitus,* lawful, from *liceo,* to be

ch, *chain;* ch, Sc. *loch;* g, *go;* j, *job;* ng, *sing;* TH, *then;* th, *thin;* w, *wig;* hw, *whig;* zh, *azure.*

allowed.] Not permitted, sanctioned, or allowed by law, rule or tradition; prohibited; unlawful.—**illicitly**, il··lis'it·li, *adv*. In an illicit manner.—**illicitness**, il·lis'it·nes, *n*. The state or quality of being illicit.

illimitable, il·lim'it·a·bl, *a*. [Prefix *il* for *in*, not, and *limitable*.] Incapable of being limited or bounded; boundless; immeasurable.—**illimitably**, il·lim'it·a·bli, *adv*. Without possibility of being bounded; without limits.—**illimitableness**, il·lim'it·a·bl·nes, *n*.

illiterate, il·lit'er·it, *a*. [L. *illiteratus*—*il* for *in*, not, and *literatus*, lettered, learned, from *litera*, a letter. LETTER.] Ignorant of letters or books; untaught; unlearned; ignorant.—**illiteracy**, il·lit'er·e·si, *n*. The state of being illiterate; a literary error†. — **illiterately**, il·lit'er·it·li, *adv*. In an illiterate manner.

illness. See ILL.

illogical, il·loj'i·kal, *a*. [Prefix *il* for *in*, not, and *logical*.] Ignorant or negligent of the rules of logic or correct reasoning; contrary to logic or sound reasoning.—**illogically**, il·loj'i·kal·li, *adv*. In an illogical manner.—**illogicalness**, il·loj'i·kal·nes, *n*. The quality of being illogical.

illuminate, il·lū'mi·nāt, *v.t*.—*illuminated*, *illuminating*. [L. *illumino*, *il*-*luminatum*—prefix *il* for *in*, in, and *lumen*, *luminis*, light. LUMINARY, LUCID.] To enlighten; to throw light on; to supply with light; to light up with festal lamps, bonfires, or the like; to adorn (a manuscript) with gilded and colored decorations or illustrations.—**illume**, il·lūm', *v.t*.—*illumed*, *illuming*. To illumine or illuminate. (*Poet*.)—**illuminable**, il·lū'mi·na·bl, *a*. Capable of being illuminated.—**illuminant**, il·lū'mi·nant, *n*. That which illuminates or affords light.—**illuminati**, il·lū'mi·nä"tī, *n. pl*. A term formerly applied to certain sects and secret societies, now applied to persons who affect to possess extraordinary knowledge whether justly or otherwise.—**illumination**, il·lū'mi·nā"shon, *n*. [L. *illuminatio*, *illuminationis*.] The act of illuminating, or state of being illuminated; a festive display of lights, etc.; an ornament or illustration in colors and gilding, such as those with which ancient manuscripts or books were embellished.—**illuminative**, il·lū'mi·nā·tiv, *a*. Having the power of illuminating; tending to throw light; illustrative.—**illuminator**, il·lū'mi·nā·tėr, *n*. One who or that which illuminates.—**illumine**, il·lū'min, *v.t*. To illuminate. (*Poet*.)

illusion, il·lū'zhon, *n*. [L. *illusio*, *illusionis*, from *illudo*. ILLUDE.] The act of deceiving or imposing upon; deception; mockery; a deceptive appearance; an unreal vision presented to the bodily or mental eye; hallucination.—**illusionist**, il··lū'zhon·ist, *n*. One given to illusion.—**illusive**, il·lū'siv, *a*. Deceiving by false show; illusory.—**illusively**, il·lū'siv·li, *adv*. In an illusive manner.—**illusiveness**, il·lū'siv·nes, *n*.—**illusory**, il·lū'so·ri, *a*.

[Fr. *illusoire*, from L. *illudo*, *illusum*.] Causing illusion; deceiving or tending to deceive by false appearances; false and deceptive; fallacious.

illustrate, il'us·trāt, *v.t*.—*illustrated*, *illustrating*. [L. *illustro*, *illustratum*, to light up, to illuminate—*il* for *in*, and *lustro*, to make light. LUSTER.] To illuminate‡; to glorify‡; to make bright or conspicuous‡; to make clear, intelligible, or obvious; to throw light on by examples, by comparisons, and the like; to ornament and elucidate by means of pictures, drawings, etc.—**illustration**, il·lus·trā'shon, *n*. The act of illustrating; that which illustrates; a particular case or example intended to throw light on one's meaning; a picture accompanying and illustrating the text of a book.—**illustrative**, il·lus'trā·tiv, *a*. Tending to illustrate.—**illustratively**, il·lus'trā·tiv·li, *adv*. By way of illustration or elucidation.—**illustrator**, il'lus·trā·tėr, *n*. One who illustrates.

illustrious, il·lus'tri·us, *a*. [From L. *illustris*, lighted up, clear, distinguished; probably contr. for *illucestris*—*il* for *in*, into, and *lux*, *lucis*, light. LUCID.] Distinguished by greatness, nobleness, or eminence among men; conspicuous for praiseworthy qualities; renowned; eminent; glorious; brilliant (an *illustrious* man, an *illustrious* action).—**illustriously**, il·lus'tri·us·li, *adv*. In an illustrious manner.—**illustriousness**, il·lus'tri·us·nes, *n*.

ilmenite, il'men·īt, *n*. A black ore of iron found in the *Ilmen* Mountains in Russia.

image, im'ij, *n*. [Fr., from L. *imago*, an image, likeness, apparition, etc., from stem of *imitor*, to imitate.] A representation of any person or thing, sculptured, painted, or otherwise made visible; a statue, picture, or stamped representation; an effigy; an idol; what forms a counterpart or likeness of something else; likeness; embodiment; a picture drawn by fancy; semblance; show; appearance; *optics*, the figure or appearance of an object made by reflection or refraction.—*v.t*.—*imaged*, *imaging*. To represent by an image; to reflect the image or likeness of; to mirror; to represent to the mental vision; to form a likeness of in the mind.—**imagery**, im'a·jėr·i, *n*. Images in general or collectively; forms of the fancy; imaginary phantasms; rhetorical figures collectively; comparisons, similes, etc., in discourse.

imagine, i·maj'in, *v.t*.—*imagined*, *imagining*. [Fr. *imaginer*, L. *imaginor*, *imaginatum*, to imagine, from *imago*, image. IMAGE.] To form a notion or idea of in the mind; to bring before the mind's eye; to produce by the imagination; to conceive in thought; to think, scheme, or devise (O.T.).—*v.i*. To conceive; to suppose; to fancy; to think.—**imaginable**, i·maj'i·na·bl, *a*. Capable of being imagined or conceived.—**imaginably**, i·maj'i·na·bli, *adv*. In an imaginable manner.—**imaginal**,† i·maj'i·nal, *a*. Characterized by ima-

gination; imaginative.—**imaginary**, i·maj'i·ne·ri, *a*. [L. *imaginarius*.] Existing only in imagination or fancy; conceived by the imagination, not real; fancied.—**imagination**, i·maj''i·nā'shon, *n*. [L. *imaginatio*, *imaginationis*.] The power or faculty of the mind by which it conceives and forms ideas of things from knowledge communicated to it by the organs of sense; the faculty by which we can bring absent objects and perceptions forcibly before the mind; the power or faculty which enables a person to produce a new, impressive, and artistic whole by selecting and working up ideas derived through observation and memory, and which thus includes a certain share of invention; an image or conception in the mind; idea; an unsolid or fanciful opinion.—**imaginative**, i·maj'i·nā·tiv, *a*. Endowed with imagination.—**imaginativeness**, i·maj'i·nā"tiv·nes. *n*.

imago, i·mā'gō, *n*. [L., an image.] The last or perfect state of an insect, usually that in which it has wings; *Psychoanalysis*, the childhood conception of the parent retained in the unconscious.

imam, imaum, i·mäm', i·mạm', *n*. [Ar. *imâm*, from *amma*, to walk before, to preside.] A minister or priest who performs the regular service of the mosque among the Mohammedans; a title given to the successors of Mohammed; one who has followers in law or theology.

imamate, i·mam'āt, *n*. The region that is ruled by an imam.

imbalance, im·bal'ans, *n*. [Prefix *im*, not, and *balance*.] A lack of balance; an unequal distribution; a disproportion; poor muscular or glandular functioning.

imbecile, imbecilic, im'be·sil, im·be·sil'ic, *a*. [L. *imbecillis*, *imbecillus*, feeble in body or mind—origin doubtful.] Having a mental capacity between idiocy and feeblemindedness, or a mental age of 2 to 7 years, or an IQ of 25 to 50.—*n*. One that is imbecile or impotent either in body or mind.—**imbecility**, im·be··sil'i·ti, *n*.

imbed, im·bed', *v.t*. To embed.

imbibe, im·bīb', *v.t*.—*imbibed*, *imbibing*. [L. *imbibo*—*im* for *in*, in, into, and *bibo*, to drink, whence also *beverage*.] To drink in; to absorb; to receive or admit into the mind and retain.—**imbiber**, im·bī'bėr, *n*. One who or that which imbibes.—**imbibition**, im·bi·bish'on, *n*. The act of imbibing.

imbitter, imbody, imbolden, imbosom, imbower. See EMBITTER, etc.

imbricate, imbricated, im'bri·kāt, im'bri·kā·ted, *a*. [L. *imbricatus*, from *imbrex*, *imbricis*, a hollow tile for a roof, from *imber*, a shower=Gr. *ombros*, rain.] Formed like a bent or hollow tile; lapping over each other, like tiles on a roof, scales of fishes, and reptiles. or leaves in a bud—**imbrication**, im·bri·kā'shon, *n*. State of being imbricate; a hollow like that of a roof tile.

imbroglio, im·brō'lyō, n. [It., from prefix *im* for *in*, and *brogliare,* to confound or mix together; akin *broil.*] An intricate and perplexing state of affairs; a misunderstanding between persons or nations of a complicated nature.

imbrown, im·broun', v.t. To make brown, to embrown.

imbrue, im·brö', v.t.—*imbrued, imbruing.* [O.Fr. *embruer, s'embruer,* to dabble one's self, from prefix *im* for *in,* in, and L. *bibere,* to drink; comp. Fr. *breuvage,* beverage, also from *bibere.*] To soak or drench in a fluid, as in blood.

imbrute, im·bröt', v.t.—*imbruted, imbruting.* To degrade to the state of a brute.—*v.i.* To sink to the state of a brute. (*Mil.*)

imbue, im·bū', v.t.—*imbued, imbuing.* [L. *imbuo,* allied to *imber,* a shower; Skr. *ambu,* water. IMBRICATE.] To soak, steep, or tinge deeply; *fig.* to inspire, impress, or impregnate (the mind); to cause to become impressed or penetrated.

imitate, im'i·tāt, v.t.—*imitated, imitating.* [L. *imitor, imitatus,* from a root which gives also *imago,* image.] To follow as a model, pattern, or example, to copy or endeavor to copy in acts, manners, or otherwise; to produce a likeness of in form, color, qualities, conduct, manners, and the like; to counterfeit.—**imitable,** im'i·ta·bl, a. Capable of being imitated or copied.—**imitation,** im·i·tā'shon, n. [L. *imitatio, imitationis.*] The act of imitating; that which is made or produced as a copy; a likeness; a copy; a counterfeit; *mus.* the repetition of the same melodic idea by different parts or voices in a composition.—**imitative,** im'i·tā·tiv, a. Inclined to imitate or copy; aiming at imitation; exhibiting an imitation of a pattern or model; formed after a model or original; intended to represent an actual sound by the sound of the letters (an *imitative* word).—**imitatively,** im'i·tā·tiv·li, adv. In an imitative manner.—**imitativeness,** im'i·tā·tiv·nes, n. Quality of being imitative.—**imitator,** im'i·tā·tėr, n. One who imitates.

immaculate, im·mak'ū·lit, a. [L. *immaculatus*—*im* for *in,* not, and *maculatus,* from *macula,* a spot.] Spotless, pure; unstained; undefiled; without blemish.—*Immaculate Conception,* the dogma of the Roman Catholic Church (settled in 1854), that the Virgin Mary was conceived and born without original sin.—**immaculately,** im·mak'ū·lit·li, adv. In an immaculate manner.—**immaculateness,** im·mak'ū·lit·nes, n. The condition or quality of being immaculate.

immanent, im'ma·nent, a. [L. *immanens, immanentis,* ppr. of *immaneo*—*im* for *in,* in, and *maneo,* to remain (as in *remain, mansion*).] Remaining in or within; hence, not passing out of the subject; inherent and indwelling; internal or subjective; opposed to *transitive.*—**immanence, immanency,** im'ma·

nens, im'ma·nen·si, n. The condition of being immanent.

Immanuel, im·man'ū·el, n. [Heb.—*im,* with, *anu,* us, and *El,* God.] God with us: an appellation of the Saviour.

immaterial, im·ma·tēr'i·al, a. [Prefix *im* for *in,* not, and *material.*] Not consisting of matter; incorporeal; spiritual; of no essential consequence; unimportant.—**immaterialism,** im·ma·tēr'i·al·izm, n. The doctrine that immaterial substances or spiritual beings exist or are possible; the doctrine that there is no material world, but that all exists only in the mind.—**immaterialist,** im·ma·tēr'i·al·ist, n. One who professes immaterialism.—**immateriality, immaterialness,** im·ma·tēr''i·al'i·ti, im·ma·tēr'i·al·nes, n. The quality of being immaterial or not consisting of matter; absence of matter.—**immaterialize,** im·ma·tēr'i·al·iz, v.t. To make immaterial or incorporeal.—**immaterially,** im·ma·tēr'i·al·li, adv. In an immaterial manner.

immature, im·ma·tūr', a. [L. *immaturus,* unripe—*im* for *in,* not, and *maturus,* ripe.] Not mature or ripe; unripe; not brought to a complete state; too early; premature.—**immaturely,** im·ma·tūr'li, adv. In an immature manner.—**immatureness, immaturity,** im·ma·tūr'nes, im·ma·tū'ri·ti, n. The state or quality of being immature; unripeness.

immeasurable, im·mezh'e·ra·bl, a. [Prefix *im* for *in,* not, and *measurable.*] Incapable of being measured.—**immeasurably,** im·mezh'e·ra·bli, adv. In an immeasurable manner; immensely; beyond all measure.

immediate, im·mē'di·it, a. [Prefix *im* for *in,* not, and *mediate.*] Not separated by anything intervening; placed in the closest relation; not separated by an interval of time; instant; acting without a medium, or without the intervention of another object as a cause, means, or condition; produced, acquired, or obtained without the intervention of a medium; direct.—**immediacy,** im·mē'di·e·si, n. The relation of being immediate; immediateness; proximity.—**immediately,** im·mē'di·it·li, adv. In an immediate manner; without the intervention of anything; directly; without delay; instantly; forthwith.—**immediateness,** im·mē'di·it·nes, n.

immemorial, im·me·mō'ri·al, a. [L. *im* for *in,* not, and *memoria,* memory.] Beyond memory; extending beyond the reach of record or tradition.—**immemorially,** im·me·mō'ri·al·li, adv. Beyond memory; from time out of mind.

immense, im·mens', a. [L. *immensus*—*im* for *in,* not, and *mensus,* measured, pp. of *metior, mensus,* to measure. MEASURE.] Vast in extent or bulk; very great; very large; boundless; huge; enormous. ∴ Syn. under ENORMOUS.—**immensely,** im·mens'li, adv. In an immense manner; vastly.—**immenseness,** im·mens'nes, n. The condition or quality of being

immense.—**immensity,** im·men'si·ti, n. [L. *immensitas.*] The condition or quality of being immense; that which is immense.

immensurable, im·men'sū·ra·bl, a. [L. *im* for *in,* not, and *mensurabilis,* from *mensura,* measure. MEASURE.] Not to be measured; immeasurable.

immerge, im·mėrj', v.t.—*immerged, immerging.* [L. *immergo*—*im* for *in,* into, and *mergo,* to plunge.] To plunge into or under anything, especially into or under a fluid.—*v.i.* To disappear by entering into any medium.

immerse, im·mėrs', v.t.—*immersed, immersing.* [L. *immergo, immersum*—*im* for *in,* into, and *mergo,* to plunge. MERGE.] To plunge into anything that covers or surrounds, as into a fluid; to dip; *fig.* to engage deeply; to involve (to be *immersed* in business).—**immersion,** im·mėr'shon, n. A baptism by total submersion in water; *astron.* the disappearance of a celestial body by passing either behind another or into its shadow: opposed to *emersion.*—**immersionist,** im·mėr'shon·ist, n. One who holds that immersion is essential to Christian baptism.

immethodical, im·me·thod'i·kal, a. [Prefix *im* for *in,* not, and *methodical.*] Not methodical; without system, order, or regularity.

immigrate, im'mi·grāt, v.i. [L. *immigro*—*im* for *in,* into, and *migro,* to migrate.] To remove into a country of which one is not a native for the purpose of permanent residence.—**immigrant,** the correlative of *emigrant.*—**immigration,** im·mi·grā'shon, n. The act of immigrating; the number of immigrants arriving in a certain country in a specific time.

imminent, im'mi·nent, a. [L. *imminens, imminentis,* ppr. of *immineo,* to hang over—*im* for *in,* on, and *mineo,* as in *eminent.*] Hanging over; threatening to fall or occur; impending; near at hand.—**imminence,** im'mi·nens, n.—**imminently,** im'mi·nent·li, adv.

immiscible, im·mis'i·bl, a. [Prefix *im,* not, and *miscible* from L. *miscere,* to mix.] Not capable of being intermingled.—**immiscibility,** im·mis'i·bil''i·ti, n.—**immiscibly,** im·mis'i·bli, adv.

immix, im·miks', v.t. [Prefix *im* for *in,* and *mix.*] To mix; to mingle.

immobile, im·mō'bil, a. [Prefix *im* for *in,* not, and *mobile;* L. *immobilis.*] Not mobile; immovable; fixed; stable.—**immobility,** im·mō·bil'i·ti, n.—**immobilize,** im·mō'bil·iz, v.t.—*immobilized, immobilizing.*—To make incapable of moving; to fix in place; *finance,* to employ currency as reserve by withholding it from circulation.—**immobilization,** im·mō'bi·li·za''shon, n.

immoderate, im·mod'e·rit, a. [Prefix *im,* not, and *moderate;* L. *immoderatus.*] Not moderate; exceeding just or usual bounds; excessive; extravagant; unreasonable. — **immoderately,** im·mod'e·rit·li, adv. In an immoderate manner.—**immod-**

erateness, **immoderacy, immod-eration,** im·mod′e·rit·nes, im·mod′-e·re·si, im·mod′e·rā″shon, *n.* The condition or quality of being immoderate.

immodest, im·mod′est, *a.* [Prefix *im* for *in*, not, and *modest*.] Not modest; wanting in the reserve or restraint which decency requires; indelicate; unchaste.—**immodestly,** im·mod′-est·li, *adv.* In an immodest manner. —**immodesty,** im·mod′es·ti. *n.* The quality of being immodest.

immolate, im′mo·lāt, *v.t.*—**immolated, immolating.** [L. *immolo, immolatum,* to sacrifice—*im* for *in*, on, and *mola,* meal, which was thrown on the head of the victim.] To sacrifice; to kill, as a victim offered in sacrifice; to offer in sacrifice.—**immolation,** im·mo·lā′shon, *n.* The act of immolating; a sacrifice offered.—**immolator,** im′mo·lā·tėr, *n.* One who immolates.

immoral, im·mor′al, *a.* [Prefix *im* for *in*, not, and *moral*.] Not moral; inconsistent with morality or rectitude; contrary to morals; wicked; unjust.—**immorality,** im·mo·ral′i·ti, *n.* The quality of being immoral; an immoral act or practice.—**immorally,** im·mor′al·li, *adv.* In an immoral manner.

immortal, im·mor′tal, *a.* [L. *immortalis*—*im*, for *in*, not, and *mortalis,* mortal.] Not mortal; having life that shall never end; undying; connected with immortality (*immortal* hopes); imperishable (*immortal* fame).—*n.* One who is immortal; often applied to the gods of classical mythology.—**immortality,** im·mor·tal′i·ti, *n.* [L. *immortalitas.*] The condition or quality of being immortal; exemption from death and annihilation; unending existence.—**immortalize,** im·mor′tal·īz, *v.t.*—**immortalized, immortalizing.** To render immortal; to make famous for ever.—**immortally,** im·mor′tal·li, *adv.* In an immortal manner.—**immortelle,** im·mor·tel′, *n.* A flower of the sort called *Everlasting,* or a wreath made of such flowers.

immovable, im·mö′va·bl, *a.* [Prefix *im* for *in*, not, and *movable*.] Not movable; incapable of being moved in place; firmly fixed; fast; not to be moved from a purpose; steadfast; unalterable; unchangeable; not impressible; unfeeling.—**immovability, immovableness,** im·mö′va·bil″i-ti, im·mö′va·bl·nes, *n.* The condition or quality of being immovable.—**immovably,** im·mö′va·bli, *adv.*

immunity, im·mū′ni·ti, *n.* [L. *immunitas,* from *immunis,* exempt—*im* for *in*, not, and *munis,* office, duty.] Exemption from obligation, duty, office, tax, etc.; a particular privilege; freedom or exemption in general. In medicine, the ability of the body to resist the growth and products of microörganisms.—**immune,** im·mūn′, *a.* Proof against disease or poison.

immunize, im′ū·nīz, *v.t.* To produce immunity.

immure, im·mūr′, *v.t.*—**immured,** im-

muring. [O.Fr. *emmurer*—L. *in,* and *murus,* a wall. MURAL.] To enclose or imprison within walls; to shut up; to confine.—**immurement,** im·mūr′ment, *n.* The act of immuring or state of being immured.

immutable, im·mū′ta·bl, *a.* [Prefix *im* for *in*, not, and *mutable*.] Not mutable; not subject to mutation; unchangeable; invariable; unalterable.

imp, imp, *n.* [Originally a shoot or scion; from L.L. *impotus,* a graft or scion, from Gr. *emphytos,* engrafted—*en,* in, and *phyō,* to grow, to produce; similarly Sw. *ymp,* Dan. *ympe,* twig, shoot, scion.] A scion or graft‡; a son, offspring, or progeny (*Shak.*)‡; a young or little devil; a little malignant spirit; hence, a mischievous child; also something added or united to another to repair or lengthen it out.—*v.t.* To graft; to strengthen or enlarge by something inserted or added; to mend a deficient wing by the insertion of a feather; to strengthen.—**impish,** imp′ish, *a.* Having the qualities of an imp; fiendish.—**impishly,** imp′-ish·li, *adv.* After the manner of an imp.

impact, im′pakt, *n.* [From L. *impingo, impactum,* to drive or strike. IMPINGE.] A forcible touch; a collision; a stroke; communicated force; *mech.* the shock or collision occasioned by the meeting of two bodies.

impair, im·pâr′, *v.t.* [Fr. *empirer,* from prefix, *em,* intens., *pire,* worse, from L. *pejor,* worse.] To make worse; to lessen in some good quality, as in quantity, value, excellence, strength; to deteriorate.—*v.i.* To become worse; to deteriorate.—**impairer,** im·pâ′rėr, *n.* One who or that which impairs.—**impairment,** im·pâr′ment, *n.* The act of impairing.

impale, im·pāl′, *v.t.*—**impaled, impaling.** [L. *im* for *in*, on, and *palus,* a pole, stake, pale.] To put to death by fixing on an upright sharp stake; to empale; *her.* to join, as two coats of arms, by an upright line.—**impalement,** im·pāl′ment, *n.* The act of impaling.

impalpable, im·pal′pa·bl, *a.* [Prefix *im* for *in*, not, and *palpable*.] Not to be felt; incapable of having its individual particles distinguished by the touch (an *impalpable* powder); not easily or readily apprehended or grasped by the mind.—**impalpably,** im·pal′pa·bli, *adv.* In an impalpable manner.—**impalpability,** im·pal′pa·bil″i·ti, *n.* The quality or state of being impalpable.

impanate, im·pā′nāt, *a.* [L. *in,* in, into, and *panis,* bread.] Embodied in the bread used in the Eucharist.—**impanation,** im·pa·nā′shon, *n.* The supposed real presence in, and union of the body and blood of Christ with the bread and wine, after consecration, in the Eucharist; consubstantiation: distinct from *transubstantiation,* which holds that there is a change of the elements into the real body and blood of Christ.

impanel, im·pan′el, *v.t.*—**impanelled,** im-

panelling. [Prefix *im* for *in*, and *panel*.] To form, complete, or enroll, the list of jurors in a court of justice.

imparidigitate, im·par′i·dij″i·tāt, *a.* [L. *impar,* unequal (*im,* not, *par,* equal), and *digitus,* a finger.] *Zool.* having an uneven number of fingers or toes.—**imparipinnate,** im·par′i-pin″āt, *a. Bot.* applied to a pinnate leaf when there is a terminal or odd leaflet at the end.

imparity, im·par′i·ti, *n.* [From L. *impar,* unequal—*im,* not, and *par,* equal. PAIR, PEER.] Inequality; disproportion; want of equality; disparity.

impart, im·pärt′, *v.t.* [O.Fr. *impartir,* from L. *impartio, impertio*—*im* for *in*, and *partio,* to divide, from *pars, partis,* a part.] To bestow a part, share, or portion of; to give, grant, confer, or communicate; to communicate the knowledge of; to make known; to show by words or tokens.—*v.i.* To give a part or share.—**impartation,** im·pär·tā′shon, *n.* The act of imparting.—**imparter,** im·pär′tėr, *n.* One who imparts.—**impartibility,** im·pär′ti·bil″i·ti, *n.* The quality of being impartible.—**impartible,** im·pär′ti·bl, *a.* Capable of being imparted.—**impartment,** im·pärt′ment, *n.* The act of imparting.

impartial, im·pär′shal, *a.* [Prefix *im* for *in*, not, and *partial*.] Not partial; not favoring one party more than another; unprejudiced; equitable; just.—**impartiality, impartialness,** im·pär′shi·al″i·ti, im·pär′shal·nes, *n.* The quality of being impartial.—**impartially,** im·pär′shal·li, *adv.* In an impartial manner; without bias; fairly.

impartible, im·pär′ti·bl, *a.* [Prefix *im* for *in*, not, and *partible*.] Not partible or subject to partition.—**impartibility,** im·pär′ti·bil″i·ti, *n.* The quality of being impartible.

impassable, im·pas′a·bl, *a.* [Prefix *im* for *in*, not, and *passable*.] Not passable; incapable of being passed. —**impassableness,** im·pas′a·bl·nes, *n.*

impasse, im·päs′, *n.* A blind alley; a cul-de-sac; a road having no way out; *fig.* a position from which there is no escape; a deadlock.

impassible, im·pas′i·bl, *a.* [L. *impassibilis*—*im* for *in*, not, and *passibilis,* capable of feeling, from *patior, passus,* to suffer. PATIENT.] Incapable of pain, passion, or suffering; not to be moved to passion or sympathy; without or not exhibiting feeling.—**impassibility, impassibleness,** im·pas′i·bil″i·ti, im·pas′i·bl·nes, *n.* The quality or condition of being impassible.

impassion, im·pash′on, *v.t.* [Prefix *im* for *in*, intens., and *passion*.] To move or affect strongly with passion.—**impassionate,** im·pash′-on·it, *a.* Strongly affected.—**impassioned,** im·pash′ond, *a.* Actuated or animated by passion, ardor, or warmth of feeling; animated; excited (an *impassioned* orator or discourse).

impassive, im·pas′iv, *a.* [Prefix *im* for *in*, intens., and *passive*.] Not susceptible of pain or suffering; impassible; not exhibiting feeling or sensibility.—**impassively,** im·pas′iv·li, *adv.* In an impassive manner.—**impassiveness, impassivity,** im·pas′iv·nes, im·pa·siv′i·ti, *n.* The state or quality of being impassive.

impaste, im·pāst′, *v.t.* [Prefix *im* for *in,* and *paste.*] To knead or make into paste; *painting,* to lay on (colors) thickly and boldly; *engrav.* to intermix lines and points on (a plate) so as to represent thickness of coloring.—**impastation,** im·pas·tā′shon, *n.* The act of impasting; a combination of materials of different colors and consistencies united by a cement and hardened.—**impasto,** im·pas′to, *n.* [It.] *Painting,* the thickness of the layer of pigment applied by the painter.

impatient, im·pā′shent, *a.* [Prefix *im* for *in,* not, and *patient.*] Not patient; uneasy under given conditions and eager for change; followed by *of, at, for, under*; prompted by impatience; exhibiting or expressing impatience (an *impatient* gesture).—**impatiently,** im·pā′shent·li, *adv.* In an impatient manner.—**impatience,** im·pā′shens, *n.* The condition or quality of being impatient.

impeach, im·pēch′, *v.t.* [Fr. *empêcher,* O.Fr. *empeechier,* Pr. *empedigar*; from L. *impedicare,* to entangle—*in,* and *pedica,* a snare, from *pes, pedis,* the foot. IMPEDE.] To charge with a crime or misdemeanor; to accuse; specifically, to exhibit charges of maladministration against, as against a minister of state or other high official, before a competent tribunal; to call in question (motives, sincerity); to disparage or detract from.—**impeachable,** im·pēch′a·bl, *a.* Liable to impeachment.—**impeacher,** im·pēch′ér, *n.* One who impeaches.—**impeachment,** im·pēch′ment, *n.* Impediment or obstruction‡; the act of impeaching, or state of being impeached.

impeccable, impeccant, im·pek′a·bl, im·pek′ant, *a.* [L. *impeccabilis*—prefix *im* for *in,* not, and *pecco,* to sin.] Not liable or subject to sin; exempt from the possibility of doing wrong.—*n.* A person exempt from the possibility of sinning.—**impeccability, impeccance, impeccancy,** im·pek′a·bil″i·ti, im·pek′ans, im·pek′an·si, *n.* The condition or quality of being impeccant or impeccable.

impecunious, im·pi·kū′ni·us, *a.* [Prefix *im* for *in,* not, and *pecunia,* money.] Not having money; hard-up; without funds.—**impecuniosity,** im·pi·kū′ni·os″i·ti, *n.* State of being impecunious.

impedance, im·pēd′ans, *n. Elect.* virtual resistance due to self-induction; opposed to true or ohmic resistance.

impede, im·pēd′, *v.t.*—*impeded, impeding.* [L. *impedio,* to entangle the feet of—*im* for *in,* and *pes, pedis,* the foot; seen also in *pedestrian, expedite, biped, pedestal, impeach,* etc.] To hinder; to stop or delay the

progress of; to obstruct.—**impediment,** im·ped′i·ment, *n.* [L. *impedimentum.*] That which impedes; obstruction; a voice defect.—**impedimenta,** [L.] Baggage.—**impedimental,** im·ped′i·men′tal, *a.* Of the nature of an impediment.—**impeditive,** im·ped′i·tiv, *a.* Impeding.

impel, im·pel′, *v.t.*—*impelled, impelling.* [L. *impello*—im for *in,* on, and *pello,* to drive (as in *compel, dispel, repel, pulse*).] To drive or urge forward; to press on; to excite to motion or action in any way.—**impellent,** im·pel′ent, *a.* Having the quality of impelling.—*n.* A power or force that impels.—**impeller,** im·pel′ér, *n.* One who or that which impels.

impend, im·pend′, *v.i.* [L. *impendeo*—*im* for *in,* in, on, over, and *pendeo,* to hang (as in *depend, pendant,* etc.).] To hang over; to threaten from near at hand; to be imminent.—**impendence, impendency,** im·pen′dens, im·pen′den·si, *n.* The state of being impendent.—**impendent,** im·pen′dent, *a.* Impending; imminent.

impenetrable, im·pen′i·tra·bl, *a.* [Prefix *im* for *in,* not, and *penetrable.*] Not penetrable; incapable of being penetrated or pierced; hence, incapable of intellectual or emotional impression; obtuse or unsympathetic; *phys.* preventing any other substance from occupying the same place at the same time.—**impenetrably,** im·pen′ē·tra·bli, *adv.* In an impenetrable manner.—**impenetrability, impenetrableness,** im·pen′i·tra·bil″i·ti, im·pen′i·tra·bl·nes, *n.* The quality of being impenetrable.

impenitent, im·pen′i·tent, *a.* [Prefix *im* for *in,* not, and *penitent.*] Not penitent; not repenting of sin; obdurate; of a hard heart.—*n.* One who does not repent; a hardened sinner.—**impenitence, impenitency,** im·pen′i·tens, im·pen′i·ten·si, *n.* The condition of being impenitent.—**impenitently,** im·pen′i·tent·li, *adv.*

impennate, im·pen′āt, *a.* [L. *im* for *in,* not, and *penna,* a feather.] *Ornithol.* having short wings covered with feathers resembling scales, as the penguins.

imperative, im·per′a·tiv, *a.* [L. *imperativus,* from *impero,* to command. EMPEROR.] Expressive of command; containing positive command; authoritative; not to be avoided or evaded; obligatory (*imperative* duty); *gram.* applied to the mood or form of a verb which expresses command, entreaty, advice, or exhortation (*go, write, attend*); in this sense often used substantively.—**imperatively,** im·per′a·tiv·li, *adv.* In an imperative manner; also, by way of, or as, the imperative mood.—**imperatorial,** im·per·a·tō′ri·al, *a.* [From L. *imperator,* a commander.] Pertaining to a commander or emperor; commanding; imperial.

imperceptible, im·pér·sep′ti·bl, *a.* [Prefix *im* for *in,* not, and *perceptible.*] Not perceptible; not to be perceived; not discernible; not easily apprehended. —**imperceptibility, imperceptibleness,** im·pér·sep′ti-

bil″i·ti, im·pér·sep′ti·bl·nes, *n.* The state or quality of being imperceptible.—**imperceptibly,** im·pér·sep′ti·bli, *adv.* In an imperceptible manner.—**imperceptive,** im·pér·sep′tiv, *a.* Not perceiving.

imperfect, im·pér′fekt, *a.* [Prefix *im* for *in,* not, and *perfect*; L. *imperfectus.*] Not perfect; not complete in all parts; wanting something necessary to completeness; defective; not reaching a certain standard or ideal; morally deficient or defective; not completely good.—*Imperfect tense, gram.* a tense expressing an uncompleted action or state, especially in time past.—*n.* An imperfect tense.—**imperfection,** im·pér·fek′shon, *n.* The condition or quality of being imperfect; defect; flaw; blemish.—**imperfectly,** im·pér′fekt·li, *adv.* In an imperfect manner or degree; defectively; faultily.—**imperfectness,** im·pér′fekt·nes, *n.* The state or quality of being imperfect.

imperforate, im·pér′fo·rit, *a.* [Prefix *im* for *in,* not, and *perforate.*] Not perforated or pierced; having no opening or pores.

imperial, im·pér′i·al, *a.* [L. *imperialis,* from *imperium,* empire, supreme command, from *impero,* to command. EMPEROR.] Pertaining to an empire or to an emperor; pertaining to supreme authority or to one who wields it; sovereign; supreme; suitable for an emperor; of superior excellence.—*n.* A tuft of hair on a man's lower lip (the style of beard made fashionable by Napoleon III); a trade term for an article of unusual size or excellence, as a large decanter, etc.; a size of paper measuring 23 by 31 inches.—**imperialism,** im·pér′i·al·izm, *n.* Imperial state or authority; the spirit of empire.—**imperialist,** im·pér′i·al·ist, *n.* A subject or soldier of an emperor; one favorable to empire or imperial government.—**imperially,** im·pē′ri·al·li, *adv.* In an imperial manner.

imperil, im·per′il, *v.t.*—*imperilled, imperilling.* [Prefix *im* for *in,* into, and *peril.*] To bring into peril; to endanger.

imperious, im·pēr′i·us, *a.* [L. *imperiosus,* from *imperium,* empire. IMPERIAL.] Giving orders or commands in an arbitrary or absolute manner; dictatorial; haughty; arrogant; domineering; urgent, pressing, or overmastering (*imperious* necessity).—**imperiously,** im·pēr′i·us·li, *adv.* In an imperious manner.—**imperiousness,** im·pēr′i·us·nes, *n.*

imperishable, im·per′ish·a·bl, *a.* [Prefix *im* for *in,* not, and *perishable.*] Not perishable; not subject to decay; indestructible; enduring permanently.—**imperishableness, imperishability,** im·per′ish·a·bl·nes, im·per′ish·a·bil″i·ti, *n.* The quality of being imperishable.—**imperishably,** im·per′ish·a·bli, *adv.*

impermeable, im·per′mi·a·bl, *a.* [Prefix *im* for *in,* not, and *permeable.*] Not permeable; impervious.—**impermeability, impermeableness,** im·pér′mi·a·bil″i·ti, im·pér′mi·a·bl-nes, n.—**impermeably**, im·pėr′mi·a·bli, adv.

impersonal, im·pėr′son·al, a. [Prefix im for in, not, and personal.] Not having personal existence; not endued with personality.—Impersonal verb, gram. a verb (such as it rains, it becomes us to be modest) which is used only with an impersonal nominative or subject.—n. That which wants personality; an impersonal verb.—**impersonality**, im·pėr′so·nal″i·ti, n. The condition of being impersonal.—**impersonally**, im·pėr′son·al·li, adv. In an impersonal manner.

impersonate, im·pėr′son·āt, v.t.—impersonated, impersonating. [Prefix im for in, in (or in intens.), and personate.] To invest with personality; to assume the person or character of; to represent in character (as on the stage).—**impersonation**, im·pėr′so·nā″shon, n. The act of impersonating.—**impersonator**, im·pėr′son·ā·tėr, n. One who impersonates.

impertinent, im·pėr′ti·nent, a. [Prefix im for in, not, and pertinent.] Not pertinent or pertaining to the matter in hand; having no bearing on the subject; not to the point; irrelevant; unbecoming in speech or action; meddling with matters in which one has no concern; petulant and rude; uncivil.—n. One who acts impertinently.—**impertinently**, im·pėr′ti·nent·li, adv. In an impertinent manner; irrelevantly; in a rude, saucy manner.—**impertinence, impertinency**, im·pėr′ti·nens, im·pėr′ti·nen·si, n. The quality of being impertinent; that which is impertinent; impertinent conduct or language.

imperturbable, im·pėr·tėr′ba·bl, a. [Prefix im for in, not, and perturb.] Incapable of being perturbed or agitated; unmoved; calm; cool.—**imperturbability**, im·pėr·tėr′ba·bil″i·ti, n. Quality of being imperturbable.—**imperturbation**, im·pėr′tėr·bā″shon, n. Freedom from agitation of mind.

impervious, im·pėr′vi·us, a. [Prefix im for in, not, and pervious.] Not pervious; not admitting entrance or passage; incapable of being passed through.—**imperviously**, im·pėr′vi·us·li, adv. In an impervious manner.—**imperviousness**, im·pėr′vi·us·nes, n.

impetigo, im·pe·tī′gō, n. [L., from impeto, to assail. IMPETUOUS.] Med. an eruption of itching pustules in clusters on the skin.—**impetiginous**, im·pe·tij′i·nus, a. Pertaining to impetigo.

impetrate, im′pe·trāt, v.t.—impetrated, impetrating. [L. impetro, impetratum, to obtain—prefix im for in, intens., and patro, to bring to pass.] To obtain by prayer or petition.—**impetration**, im·pe·trā′shon, n. The act of impetrating; formerly specifically applied to the obtaining from the Roman see of benefices belonging to lay patrons.—**impetrative**, im′pe·trā·tiv, a. Containing or expressing entreaty.

impetuous, im·pet′ū·us, a. [L. impetuosus, from impetus, an attack—im, in, and peto, to assail (whence petition, compete).] Rushing with force and violence; furious in motion; forcible; fierce; raging; vehement in feeling; passionate; violent.—**impetuously**, im·pet′ū·us·li, adv. In an impetuous manner.—**impetuosity, impetuousness**, im·pet′ū·os″i·ti, im·pet′ū·us·nes, n. The quality of being impetuous; fury; vehemence. —**impetus**, im′pe·tus, n. [L.] Force of motion; the force with which any body is driven or impelled; momentum.

impi, im′pi, n. A brigade or large body of Kaffir soldiers.

impignorate,† im·pig′no·rāt, v.t. [L. in, in, and pignus, pignoris, a pledge.] To pledge or pawn, to transfer as security.

impinge, im·pinj′, v.i. [L. impingo, impactum—im for in, on, and pango, to strike. PACT.] To strike, knock, or dash against; to clash upon; to strike; to hit.—**impingement**, im·pinj′ment, n. Act of impinging.

impious, im′pi·us, a. [L. impius—im for in, not, and pius, pious.] The reverse of pious; irreverent toward the Supreme Being; wanting in veneration for God and His authority; irreligious; irreverent; profane (impious men, deeds, words).—**impiously**, im′pi·us·li, adv. In an impious manner.—**impiousness**, im′pi·us·nes, n. Impiety.—**impiety**, im·pī′e·ti, n. [L. impietas.] The condition or quality of being impious; an act of wickedness or irreligion: in this latter sense with a plural.

impish, impishly. See IMP.

implacable, im·plā′ka·bl, a. [Prefix im for in, not, and placable.] Not placable; not to be appeased or pacified; inexorable; stubborn or constant in enmity.—**implacability, implacableness**, im·plā′ka·bil″i·ti, im·plā′ka·bl·nes, n. The quality of being implacable.—**implacably**, im·plā′ka·bli, adv. In an implacable manner.

implacental, im′pla·sen″tal, a. [Prefix im for in, not, and placental.] Destitute of a placenta, as marsupials and monotremes.—n. A mammal destitute of a placenta.

implant, im·plant′, v.t. [Prefix im for in, in, into, and plant.] To plant; to set in soil (lit. or fig.); to insert; to sow (to implant truths, principles, virtue, etc.).—**implantation**, im·plan·tā′shon, n. The act of implanting.

implead, im·plēd′, v.t. [Prefix im for in, and plead.] To institute and prosecute a suit against in court; to sue at law.—**impleader**, im·plē′dėr, n. One who impleads; an accuser.

implement, im′ple·ment, n. [L.L. implementum, lit. what accomplishes, from L. impleo, to fill up—im for in, and pleo, to fill, as in complete, replete, etc., the root being in E. full.] An instrument, tool, or utensil; an article assisting in carrying on manual labors. ∴ Syn. under TOOL. —v.t. To fulfill or satisfy the conditions of; to fulfill or perform; to carry into effect (to implement a bargain). —**implemental**, im·ple·-

men′tal, a. Pertaining to implements; characterized by the use of implements (implemental stage in civilization).

implicate, im′pli·kāt, v.t.—implicated, implicating. [L. implico, implicatum—im for in, in, into, and plico, to fold. PLY.] To entangle to a certain extent in some affair; to show or prove to be connected or concerned; to involve (implicated in a conspiracy. ∴. Implicate is a less strong word than involve, a person who is implicated being connected only to a small extent, while one who is involved is deeply concerned or entangled.—**implication**, im·pli·kā′shon, n. The act of implicating or state of being implicated; an implying, or that which is implied but not expressed; an inference, or something which may fairly be understood though not expressed in words.—**implicative**, im′pli·kā·tiv, a. Tending to implicate.—**implicatively**, im′pli·kā·tiv·li, adv. By implication.

implicit, im·plis′it, a. [L. implicitus, from implico, implicitum, and implicatum, to infold. IMPLICATE.] Fairly to be understood, though not expressed in words; implied (an implicit promise); entirely depending or resting on something or someone else; hence, free from doubt or questioning; settled; deep rooted (implicit faith in one's word).—**implicitly**, im·plis′it·li, adv. In an implicit manner.—**implicitness**, im·plis′it·nes, n.

implore, im·plōr′, v.t.—implored, imploring. [L. imploro—im for in, on, upon, and ploro, to cry out (as in deplore, explore).] To call upon or for, in supplication; to beseech; to pray earnestly; to entreat; to beg (to implore forgiveness, to implore a person to forgive).—v.i. To entreat; to beg.—**imploration**, im·plo·rā′shon, n. The act of imploring; earnest supplication.—**imploratory**, im·plōr′a·to·ri, a. Earnestly supplicating; imploring; entreating.—**implorer**, im·plōr′ėr, n. One who implores.—**imploringly**, im·plōr′ing·li, adv. In an imploring manner.

imply, im·plī′, v.t.—implied, implying. [From L. implico—in, and plico, to fold, whence also implicate (which see); comp. apply, reply, ply.] To involve or contain by fair inference; to contain by implication or as a consequence; to include virtually (words imply a promise; an effect implies a cause).—**impliedly**, im·plīd′li, adv. In an implied manner; by implication.

impolite, im·po·līt′, a. [Prefix im for in, not, and polite.] Not polite; unpolite; uncivil; rude.—**impolitely**, im·po·līt′li, adv. In an impolite manner.—**impoliteness**, im·po·līt′nes, n.

impolitic, im·pol′i·tik, a. [Prefix im for in, not, and politic.] Not politic; wanting policy or prudent management; unwise; imprudent; indiscreet; injudicious.—**impolicy**, im·pol′i·si, n. The quality of being impolitic; inadvisability.—**impoliticly**, im·pol′i·tik·li, adv.—**impoliticness**, im·pol′i·tik·nes, n.

imponderable, im·pon′dėr·a·bl, *a.* Not ponderable; without sensible weight.—*n.* A thing which has no appreciable weight.—**imponderability, imponderableness,** im·pon′dėr··a·bil′i·ti, im·pon′dėr·a·bl·nes, *n.* The quality of being imponderable.

import, im·pōrt′, *v.t.* [Fr. *importer,* to bring from abroad, to matter or be of consequence, L. *importo,* to bring in, to cause—*im* for *in,* and *porto,* to bring or carry, whence *port,* a person's bearing, *porter.* PORT.] To bring into a place from abroad; to bring into one's own country: opposed to *export;* to bear or carry as a signification; to mean; to signify; to imply; to be of importance, moment, or consequence to; to matter to.—*n.* (im′pōrt). That which is imported or brought into a country from abroad; that which a word bears as its signification; purport; meaning; the application or interpretation of an action, of events, etc.; bearing; importance, weight, or consequence.—**importable,** im·pōr′ta·bl, *a.* Capable of being imported.—**importation,** im·pōr·tā′shon, *n.* The act or practice of importing; a quantity imported.—**importer,** im·pōr′tėr, *n.* One who imports.

important, im·por′tant, *a.* [Fr. *important,* lit. being of great import or moment. IMPORT.] Full of or bearing import, weight, or consequence; momentous; weighty; material; influential; grave.—**importantly,** im·por′tant·li, *adv.* In an important manner.—**importance,** im·por′tans, *n.* The quality of being important; weight; consequence; moment.

importune, im·por·tūn′, sometimes im·por′tūn, *v.t.*—*importuned, importuning.* [Fr. *importuner,* to importune, pester, from L. *importunus,* distressing, rude—*im* for *in,* not, and *portus,* a port or harbor, access.] To press with solicitation; to solicit or urge with frequent or unceasing application; to annoy with unremitting demands.—*v.i.* To solicit earnestly and repeatedly.—**importunate,** im·por′tū·nit, *a.* Troublesome by frequent demands; incessant in solicitation; urgent; unreasonable.—**importunately,** im·por′tū·nit·li, *adv.* In an importunate manner.—**importuner,** im·por·tū′nėr, *n.* One who importunes.—**importunity, importunacy, importunateness,** im·por·tū′ni·ti, im·por·tū′ni·si, im·por′tū·net·nes, *n.* The quality of being importunate; application urged with troublesome pertinacity.

impose, im·pōz′, *v.t.*—*imposed, imposing.* [Fr. *imposer—im* for *in,* on, upon, and *poser,* to place. COMPOSE, POSE.] To lay, set, or place on (to *impose* the hands); to lay or enjoin as a burden, tax, penalty, command, law, etc.; to palm or pass off; *printing,* to arrange and adjust (pages) and fasten into a chase.—*v.i.* Used in phrase *to impose on* or *upon,* to pass or put a trick or deceit on; to deceive; to victimize.—**imposer,** im·pōz′ėr, *n.* One who imposes; one who enjoins.—**imposing,** im·pōz′ing, *a.* Impressive in appearance; com-manding; stately; majestic.—**imposingly,** im·pō′zing·li, *adv.* In an imposing manner.—**imposing stone, imposing table,** *n. Printing,* a table of stone or metal on which the pages or columns of type are imposed or made into forms.—**imposition,** im··po·zish′on, *n.* The act of imposing or laying on; that which is imposed, levied, inflicted, enjoined, and the like; the act of tricking or deceiving; a trick or deception; a fraud; an imposture; an exercise enjoined on students as a punishment.

impossible, im·pos′i·bl, *a.* [L. *impossibilis—im* for *in,* not, and *possibilis,* possible. POSSIBLE.] Not possible; not capable of being or being done; incapable of being accomplished, thought, endured, etc.—**impossibly,** im·pos′i·bli, *adv.* Not possibly.—**impossibility,** im·pos′i·bil′i·ti, *n.* The state or quality of being impossible; that which is impossible.

impost, im′pōst, *n.* [O.Fr. *impost,* Fr. *impôt,* L. *impositum,* from *impono, impositum,* to lay upon—*in,* on, and *pono,* to place.] That which is imposed or levied; a tax, tribute, or duty; *arch.* the point where an arch rests on a wall or column.

impostor, im·pos′tėr, *n.* [L. *impostor,* from *impono—in,* on, and *pono,* to place.] One who imposes on others; a person who assumes a character for the purpose of deception; a deceiver under a false character.—**imposture,** im·pos′chėr, *n.* [L. *impostura,* from *impono, impositum.*] The act or conduct of an impostor; fraud or imposition.

impotent, im′po·tent, *a.* [L. *impotens, impotentis—im* for *in,* not, and *potens,* able, *potent.*] Entirely wanting power, strength, or vigor of body or mind; deficient in capacity; weak; feeble; destitute of the power of sexual intercourse or of begetting children.—**impotently,** im′po·tent·li, *adv.* In an impotent manner.—**impotence, impotency,** im′po·tens, im′po·ten·si, *n.* The condition or quality of being impotent.

impound, im·pound′, *v.t.* [Prefix *im* for *in,* and *pound.*] To put in a pound (as a straying animal); to confine; to take possession of, as of a document, for use when necessary.—**impoundage,** im·poun′dij, *n.* The act of impounding.—**impounder,** im·poun′dėr, *n.* One who impounds.

impoverish, im·pov′ėr·ish, *v.t.* [Prefix *im,* intens., and Fr. *pauvre,* poor. POOR.] To make poor; to reduce to poverty or indigence; to exhaust the strength, richness, or fertility of (to *impoverish* land).—**impoverisher,** im·pov′ėr·ish·ėr, *n.* One who or that which impoverishes.—**impoverishment,** im·pov′ėr·ish·ment, *n.* The act of impoverishing.

impower, im·pou′ėr, *v.t.* To empower.

impracticable, im·prak′ti·ka·bl, *a.* Not practicable; not to be performed or effected by human means or by the means at command; not to be dealt with or managed; unmanageable; incapable of being passed or traveled (an *impracticable* road).—**impracticably,** im·prak′ti·ka·bli, *adv.* In an impracticable manner.—**impracticability, impracticableness,** im·prak′ti·ka·bil′i·ti, im·prak′ti·ka·bl·nes, *n.* The state or quality of being impracticable.—**impractical,** im·prak′ti·kal, *a.* Not practical; not taking a common-sense view of things; full of theories.

imprecate, im′pri·kāt, *v.t.*—*imprecated, imprecating.* [L. *imprecor, imprecatus—im* for *in,* on, and *precor,* to pray. PRAY.] To call down, as a curse, calamity, or punishment, by prayer; to invoke (a curse or some evil).—**imprecation,** im·pri·kā′shon, *n.* [L. *imprecatio.*] The act of imprecating; a prayer that a curse or calamity may fall on anyone; a curse.—**imprecatory,** im′pri·kā·to·ri, *a.* Of the nature of or containing an imprecation.

impregnable, im·preg′na·bl, *a.* [O. Fr. *imprenable* (the *g* being inserted as in *pregnable*)—*im* for *in,* not, and *prendre,* to take.] Not to be taken; incapable of being reduced by force (an *impregnable* fortress); not to be moved, impressed, or shaken.—**impregnability, impregnableness,** im·preg′na·bil′i·ti, im·preg′na·bl·nes, *n.* State of being impregnable.—**impregnably,** im·preg′na·bli, *adv.*

impregnate, im·preg′nāt, *v.t.*—*impregnated, impregnating.* [L.L. *impraegno, impraegnatum*—L. *im* for *in,* in, and *praegnans,* pregnant. PREGNANT.] To make pregnant or with young; to cause to conceive; to transmit or infuse an active principle into; to imbue; to communicate qualities to by mixture.—**impregnation,** im·preg·nā′shon, *n.* The act of impregnating.

impresario, im·pres·ä′ri·o, *n.* [It.] One who organizes, manages, or conducts a company of concert or opera performers.

imprescriptible, im·pri·skrip′ti·bl, *a.* [Prefix *im* for *in,* not, and *prescriptible.*] Incapable of being lost by neglect to use, or by the claims of another founded on prescription.—**imprescriptibility,** im·pri·skrip′ti·bil′i·ti, *n.* State of being imprescriptible.

impress, im·pres′, *v.t.* [L. *imprimo, impressum—im* for *in,* on, upon, and *premo,* to press. PRESS.] To press or stamp in or upon; to mark by pressure; to make a mark or figure upon; to stamp (to *impress* a design on; to *impress* with a design); to stamp on the mind; to inculcate (truth, facts, etc.); to affect deeply the feelings or sentiments.—*n.* (im′pres). A mark or figure made by pressure, or as by pressure; stamp; impression.—**impressibility,** im·pres′i·bil′i·ti, *n.* The quality of being impressible.—**impressible,** im·pres′i·bl, *a.* Capable of being impressed; susceptible of impression; easily affected; susceptive.—**impression,** im·presh′on, *n.* [L. *impressio, impressionis.*] The act of impressing; that which is impressed, printed, or stamped; a copy taken by pressure from type, from an engraved plate, and the like; the aggregate of copies taken at one time; edition; effect or influence on the senses, on the mind, feelings, or sentiments; an indistinct notion, remembrance or belief.—**impressionability, impressionableness,** im·presh′on·a·bil″i·ti, im·presh′on·a·bl·nes, *n.*—**impressionable,** im·presh′on·a·bl, *a.* Having the mind or feelings easily affected.—**impressionist,** im·presh′on·ist, *n.*—**impressionism,** im·presh′on·izm, *n.* A type of art which strives to create a sensation or evoke a mood; *paint.* a 19th-century French school of painting that emphasized quick visual impression and painting directly from nature; *mus.* a style of orchestral composition that invokes mood through associations.—**impressionistic,** im·presh′on·ist″ic, *a.*—**impressive,** im·pres′iv, *a.* Making or tending to make an impression; having the power of affecting or of exciting attention and feeling.—**impressively,** im·pres′iv·li, *adv.* In an impressive manner.—**impressiveness,** im·pres′iv·nes, *a.*

impress, im·pres′, *v.t.* [Influenced by *press*, but originally meaning to hire by ready money, from O.E. *prest*, ready money; O.Fr. *prester*, to give, to lend; L. *præsto*, in readiness (*præ*, before, and *sto*, to stand).] To compel to enter into public service, as a seaman; to seize and take into service by compulsion; to take for public use.—*n.* The act of impressing; compulsion to serve.—**impressment,** im·pres′ment, *n.* The act of impressing.

imprimatur, im·pri·mā′tėr, *n.* [L., let it be printed.] A license to print a book, etc.; hence, a mark of approval in general.

imprint, im·print′, *v.t.* [O.E. *emprent*, Fr. *empreint*, pp. of *empreindre*, to imprint, L. *imprimere*, to impress. PRINT.] To mark by pressure; to stamp; to print; to fix indelibly or permanently, as on the mind or memory; to impress.—*n.* (im′print). Whatever is impressed or printed; especially, the name of the printer or publisher of a book, with the place and often the time of publication.

imprison, im·priz′on, *v.t.* [Prefix *im* for *in*, in, and *prison*.] To put into a prison; to incarcerate; to confine.—**imprisoner,** im·priz′on·ėr, *n.* One who imprisons.—**imprisonment,** im·priz′on·ment, *n.* The act of imprisoning or state of being imprisoned.

improbable, im·prob′a·bl, *a.* [Prefix *im* for *in*, not, and *probable*.] Not probable; not likely to be true; unlikely.—**improbability, improbableness,** im·prob′a·bil″i·ti, im·prob′a·bl·nes, *n.* The quality of being improbable.—**improbably,** im·prob′a·bli, *adv.* In an improbable manner.

improbity, im·prob′i·ti, *n.* [L. *improbitas*—*im* for *in*, not, and *probitas*, probity.] Want of probity; want of integrity or rectitude of principle; dishonesty.

impromptu, im·promp′tū, *adv.* [L. *in promptu*, in readiness, from *promp-*

tus, readiness. PROMPT.] Off hand; without previous study.—*n.* A saying, poem, epigram, or the like made offhand, or without previous study; an extemporaneous effusion. —*a.* Offhand; extempore.

improper, im·prop′ėr, *a.* [Prefix *im* for *in*, not, and *proper*.] Not proper; not suitable, adapted, or suited; unbecoming; indecent.—*Improper fraction*, a fraction whose numerator is equal to or greater than its denominator.—**improperly,** im·prop′ėr·li, *adv.* In an improper manner.—**impropriety,** im·prō·prī′e·ti, *n.* [Fr. *impropriété*, from L. *improprius*, improper.] The quality of being improper; that which is improper; an unsuitable act, expression, and the like.

impropriate, im·prō′pri·āt, *v.t.*—*impropriated, impropriating.* [L. *im* for *in*, and *proprio, propriatum*, to appropriate, from *proprius*, one's own. PROPER.] To appropriate; *eccles.* to place the profits or revenue of in the hands of a layman; to put in the possession of a layman or lay corporation.—*a.* Devolved into the hands of a layman.—**impropriation,** im·prō′pri·ā″shon, *n.* The act of impropriating; that which is impropriated.—**impropriator,** im·prō′pri·ā·tėr, *n.* One who impropriates.

impropriety. See IMPROPER.

improve, im·prōv′, *v.t.*—*improved, improving.* [Prefix *im* for *in*, intens., and O.Fr. *prover*, to test, to show to be sufficient. PROVE.] To make better; to increase the value, worth, or good qualities of; to use or employ to good purpose; to turn to profitable account (to *improve* the time).—*v.i.* To grow or become better; to advance in goodness, knowledge, wisdom, or anything else desirable.—*To improve* on or *upon*, to make additions or amendments to; to make an advance in; to bring nearer to perfection. ∴ Syn. under AMEND.—**improvability, improvableness,** im·prō′va·bil″i·ti, im·prō′va·bl·nes, *n.* The state or quality of being improvable.—**improvable,** im·prō′va·bl, *a.* Capable of being improved.—**improvement,** im·prōv′ment, *n.* The act of improving, or state of being improved; that which improves; that by which the value of anything is increased, its excellence enhanced, and the like; a beneficial or valuable addition or alteration.—**improver,** im·prō′vėr, *n.* One who improves.—**improvingly,** im·prō′ving·li, *adv.* In an improving manner.

improvident, im·prov′i·dent, *a.* [Prefix *im* for *in*, not, and *provident*.] Not provident; wanting forecast; wanting care to make provision for future exigencies; thriftless; thoughtless.—**improvidence,** im·prov′i·dens, *n.* The quality of being improvident.—**improvidently,** im·prov′i·dent·li, *adv.* In an improvident manner; thriftlessly.

improvise, im′pro·vīz, *v.t.*—*improvised, improvising.* [Fr. *improviser*, It. *improvvisare*, to sing in extempore rhymes, from L. *in*, not, *pro*, before,

and *visus*, seen.] To compose and recite or sing without premeditation; to speak extempore, especially in verse; to do or form on the spur of the moment for a special occasion; to bring about in an offhand way.—*v.i.* To recite or sing compositions without previous preparation.—**improvisation,** im·prov′i·zā″shon, *n.* The act or faculty of improvising; a song or other poem which is improvised.—**improviser, improvisator,** im·pro·vī′zėr, im·prov′i·zā·tėr, *n.* One who improvisates or improvises. —**improvisatory,** im·pro·viz′a·tõ·ri, *a.* Relating to improvisation or improvisers.

imprudent, im·prö′dent, *a.* [L. *imprudens*—*im* for *in*, not, and *prudent*.] Not prudent; wanting prudence or discretion; indiscreet; injudicious; rash; heedless.—**imprudence,** im·prö′dens, *n.* The quality of being imprudent; an imprudent act or course of conduct.—**imprudently,** im·prö′dent·li, *adv.* In an imprudent manner.

impudent, im′pū·dent, *a.* [L. *impudens, impudentis,* without shame—*in*, not, and *pudens*, from *pudeo*, to be ashamed.] Offensively forward in behavior; intentionally treating others without due respect; wanting modesty; shameless; impertinent.—**impudently,** im′pū·dent·li, *adv.* In an impudent manner.—**impudence,** im′pū·dens, *n.* The quality of being impudent; impudent language or behavior; offensive forwardness.

impugn, im·pūn′, *v.t.* [Fr. *impugner*; L. *impugno*—*im* for *in*, against, and *pugno*, to fight or resist (akin *pugnacious, repugnant, pugilism*.] To attack (a statement, truthfulness, etc.) by words or arguments; to contradict; to call in question; to gainsay.—**impugnable,** im·pū′na·bl, *a.* Capable of being impugned.—**impugner,** im·pū′nėr, *n.* One who impugns.

impulse, im′puls, *n.* [L. *impulsus,* from *impello, impulsum,* to drive on. IMPEL.] Force communicated suddenly; motion produced by suddenly communicated force; thrust; push; influence acting on the mind suddenly or unexpectedly; sudden thought or determination; a force of infinitely large magnitude acting for an infinitely short time so as to produce a finite change of momentum.—**impulsion,** im·pul′shon, *n.* [L. *impulsio, impulsionis.*] The act of impelling or state of being impelled; instigation; impulse.—**impulsive,** im·pul′siv, *a.* [Fr. *impulsif.*] Having the power of impelling; impellant; actuated or liable to be actuated by impulses; under the sway of one's emotions.—**impulsively,** im·pul′siv·li, *adv.* In an impulsive manner.—**impulsiveness,** im·pul′siv·nes, *n.*

impunity, im·pū′ni·ti, *n.* [Fr. *impunité*, from L. *impunitas*, from *impunis*, unpunished—*im* for *in*, not, and *punio*, to punish. PUNISH.] Exemption from punishment or penalty; freedom or exemption from injury, suffering, or loss.

impure, im·pur′, *a.* [Fr. *impur*, from

L. *impurus*—*im* for *in*, not, and *purus*, pure.] Not pure; mixed or impregnated with foul or extraneous substance; foul; obscene; unchaste; lewd; unclean; defiled by sin or guilt; unhallowed or unholy.—**impurely**, im·pūr′li, *adv.* In an impure manner. —**impureness**, im·pūr′nes, *n.* The quality or condition of being impure. —**impurity**, im·pū′ri·ti, *n.* [L. *impuritas.*] The condition or quality of being impure; foulness; that which is impure; foul matter.

impute, im·pūt′, *v.t.* [L. *imputo*—*in* into, and *puto*, think, consider, reckon (as in *compute, repute, putative*).] To charge, attribute, or ascribe; to set to the account of; *theol.* to reckon or set down to the account of one what does not belong to him. —**imputability, imputableness**, im·pū″ta·bil″i·ti, im·pū′ta·bl·nes, *n.* The quality of being imputable.—**imputable**, im·pū′ta·bl, *a.* Capable of being imputed.—**imputation**, im·pū·tā′shon, *n.* [L. *imputatio, imputationis.*] The act of imputing; that which is imputed or charged; charge, as of evil; censure; reproach; *theol.* the charging or reckoning to the account of one, something which properly attaches to another.—**imputative**, im·pū′ta·tiv, *a.* Coming by imputation; imputed.—**imputatively**, im·pū′ta·tiv·li, *adv.* By imputation.—**imputer**, im·pū′tėr, *n.* One that imputes.

in, in, *prep.* [A.Sax. *in* = D. and Goth. *in*, Icel. *inn, i*, Dan. *ind, i*, G. *in, ein*, forms corresponding to L. *in*, Gr. *en*, W. *yn*, Armor. *enn*; akin to *on*.] Within; inside of; surrounded by; indicating presence or situation within limits, whether of place, time, or circumstances (*in* the house, *in* the year, *in* sickness); or existence as a part, constituent, or quality of (evil *in* a man's disposition); or a certain state (a vehicle *in* motion, to put *in* operation).—*In as much as*, or *inasmuch as*, seeing that; considering that; since.—*In that*, because; for the reason that.—*In name of*, by way of; as (a sum paid *in name of* damages).—*In the name of*, in behalf of; on the part of; by the authority of.— *adv.* In or within some place; in some state, affair, or circumstances; not out (he is *in*, that is, in the house; the party is *in*, that is, in office; the ship is *in*, that is, in port); into some place or state, implying motion or change (come *in*, that is, into the house).—*To breed in and in*, to breed among members of the same family.—*To keep one's hand in*, to keep up one's acquirements; to maintain one's skill by practice.— Sometimes used substantively, as in the phrase '*ins* and outs', nooks and corners; all the details and intricacies of a matter.

inability, in·a·bil′i·ti, *n.* [Prefix *in*, not, and *ability*.] The state of being unable; want of the necessary power or ability.

inaccessible, in·ak·ses′i·bl, *n.* [Prefix *in*, not, and *accessible*.] Not accessible; not to be reached, obtained, or approached.—**inaccessibly**, in·ak-

ses′i·bli, *adv.* In an inaccessible manner.—**inaccessibility**, **inaccessibleness**, in·ak·ses′i·bil″i·ti, in·ak·ses′i·bl·nes, *n.* The quality or state of being inaccessible.

inaccurate, in·ak′kū·rāt, *a.* [Prefix *in*, not, and *accurate*.] Not accurate, exact, or correct; making or containing incorrect statements; not according to truth; erroneous.— **inaccurately**, in·ak′kū·rāt·li, *adv.* In an inaccurate manner.—**inaccuracy**, in·ak′kū·ra·si, *n.* The state of being inaccurate; an inaccurate statement; a mistake in a statement; an error.

inaction, in·ak′shon, *n.* [Prefix *in*, not, and *action*.] Want of action; state of being inactive; idleness; rest. —**inactive**, in·ak′tiv, *a.* [Prefix *in*, not, and *active*.] Not active; inert; having no power to move; not engaged in action or effort; idle; indolent; sluggish; *chem.* and *med.* inoperative.—Syn. see INERT.—**inactively**, in·ak′tiv·li, *adv.* In an inactive manner.—**inactivity**, in·ak·tiv′i·ti, *n.* The quality or condition of being inactive.

inadequate, in·ad′i·kwit, *a.* [Prefix *in*, not, and *adequate*.] Not adequate; not equal to the purpose; insufficient; defective.—**inadequacy**, **inadequateness**, in·ad′i·kwi·si, in·ad′i·kwit·nes, *n.* The state or quality of being inadequate.—**inadequately** in·ad′i·kwit·li, *adv.*

inadmissible, in·ad·mis′i·bl, *a.* [Prefix *in*, not, and *admissible*.] Not admissible; not proper to be admitted, allowed, or received.— **inadmissibly**, in·ad·mis′i·bli, *adv.* In a manner not admissible.— **inadmissibility**, in·ad·mis′i·bil″i·ti, *n.* The quality of being inadmissible.

inadvertent, in·ad·vėr′tent, *a.* [L. prefix *in*, not, and *advertens, advertentis*, ppr. of *adverto*, to attend to. ADVERT.] Not paying strict attention; failing to notice or observe; heedless; unwary.—**inadvertently**, in·ad·vėr′tent·li, *adv.* In an inadvertent manner.—**inadvertence**, **inadvertency**, in·ad·vėr′tens, in·ad·vėr′ten·si, *n.* The quality of being inadvertent; an oversight, mistake, or fault which proceeds from some degree of heedlessness.

inalienable, in·āl′yen·a·bl, *a.* [Prefix *in*, not, and *alienable*.] Incapable of being alienated or transferred to another.—**inalienability**, in·āl′yen·a·bil″i·ti, *n.* The state or quality of being inalienable.—**inalienably**, in·āl′yen·a·bli, *adv.* In a manner that forbids alienation.

inalterable, in·al′tėr·a·bl, *n.* [Prefix *in*, not, and *alterable*.] Not alterable; unalterable.

inamorato, in·ä′mō·rä″tō, *n.* [It. *innamorato*, fem. *innamorata*, from L. *in*, in, *amor*, love.] A male lover.— **inamorata**, in·ä′mō·rä″ta, *n.* A female in love; a mistress.

inane, in·ān′, *a.* [L. *inanis*, empty.] Empty; void; frivolous; worthless; void of sense or intelligence.—*n.* That which is void or empty; infinite void space. (*Tenn.*)—**inanition**, in·a·nish′on, *n.* The condition of being inane; exhaustion from want of food.

—**inanity**, in·an′i·ti, *n.* The state of being inane; mental vacuity; silliness.

inanimate, in·an′i·mit, *a.* [Prefix *in*, not, and *animate*.] Not animate; destitute of life or animation; without vivacity or briskness; dull; inactive; sluggish. — **inanimateness**, in·an′i·mit·nes, *n.*

inappetence, **inappetency**, in·ap′pe·tens, in·ap′pe·ten·si, *n.* [Prefix *in*, not, and *appetence, appetency*.] Want of appetence, desire, or inclination.

inapplicable, in·ap′pli·ka·bl, *a.* [Prefix *in*, not, and *applicable*.] Not applicable; incapable of being applied; not suited or suitable to the purpose. —**inapplicability, inapplicableness**, in·ap′pli·ka·bil″i·ti, in·ap′pli·ka·bl·nes, *n.*—**inapplicably**, in·ap′pli·ka·bli, *adv.*

inapposite, in·ap′po·zit, *a.* [Prefix *in*, not, and *apposite*.] Not apposite, fit, or suitable; not pertinent.

inappreciable, in·ap·prē′shi·a·bl, *a.* [Prefix *in*, not, and *appreciable*.] Not appreciable; so small as hardly to be noticed or estimated.

inapproachable, in·ap·prōch′a·bl, *a.* [Prefix *in*, not, and *approachable*.] Not approachable; inaccessible; that cannot be equaled; unrivaled.

inappropriate, in·ap·prō′pri·it, *a.* [Prefix *in*, not, and *appropriate*.] Not appropriate; unsuited; unsuitable; not proper.—**inappropriately**, in·ap·prō′pri·it·li, *adv.* In an inappropriate manner.—**inappropriateness**, in·ap·prō′pri·it·nes, *n.*

inapt, in·apt′, *a.* [Prefix, *in*, not, and *apt*.] Unapt; not apt; unsuitable; unfit.—**inaptitude, inaptness**, in·ap′ti·tūd, in·apt′nes, *n.* Unfitness; unsuitableness.—**inaptly**, in·apt′li, *adv.* Unfitly; unsuitably.

inarch, in·ärch′, *v.t.* [Prefix *in*, into, and *arch*.] To graft by uniting to the stock without separating (for a time) the scion from its parent tree.

inarticulate, in·är·tik′ū·lit, *a.* [Prefix *in*, not, and *articulate*.] Not articulate; not uttered with distinctness of sounds or syllables; *zool.* not jointed or articulated.—**inarticulately**, in·är·tik′ū·lit·li, *adv.* In an inarticulate manner.—**inarticulateness**, in·är·tik′ū·lit·nes, *n.* The state or quality of being inarticulate.

inartificial, in·är′ti·fish″al, *a.* [Prefix *in*, not, and *artificial*.] Not artificial; formed without art; simple; artless. —**inartificially**, in·är′ti·fish″al·li, *adv.* In an inartificial manner.

inasmuch, in·az·much′, *adv.* See IN.

inattention, in·at·ten′shon, *n.* [Prefix *in*, not, and *attention*.] Want of attention; heedlessness.—**inattentive**, in·at·ten′tiv, *a.* Not attentive; not fixing the mind on an object; heedless.— **inattentively**, in·at·ten′tiv·li, *adv.* Carelessly; heedlessly.—**inattentiveness**, in·at·ten′tiv·nes, *n.*

inaudible, in·a′di·bl, *a.* [Prefix *in*, not, and *audible*.] Not audible; incapable of being heard.—**inaudibly**, in·a′di·bli, *adv.* In an inaudible manner.—**inaudibility, inaudibleness**, in·a′di·bil″i·ti, in·a′di·bl·nes, *n.* The quality of being inaudible.

inaugurate, in·a′gū·rāt, *v.t.*—*inaugurated, inaugurating.* [L. *inauguro*, *inauguratum*, to inaugurate, to install —*in*, into, and *augur*, an augur.] To introduce or induct into an office with solemnity or suitable ceremonies; to invest in a formal manner; to begin or set in progress with formality or some degree of solemnity, pomp, or ceremony; to initiate; to perform in public initiatory ceremonies in connection with; to celebrate the completion of.—**inaugural,** in·a̱′gū·ral, *a.* Having to do with an inauguration.—*n.* An address given at the inception of a term of office.—**inauguration,** in·a̱′gū·rā″shon, *n.* —**inaugurator,** in·a̱′gū·rā·tėr, *n.*

inauspicious, in·a·spish′us, *a.* [Prefix *in*, not, and *auspicious*.] Not auspicious; ill-omened; unlucky; unfavorable.—**inauspiciously,** in·a·spish′us·li, *adv.* In an inauspicious manner. —**inauspiciousness,** in·a·spish′us·nes, *n.*

inboard, in′bōrd, *a.* Within a ship or other vessel (an *inboard* cargo).—*adv.* Within the hold of a vessel; on board of a vessel.

inborn, in′born, *a.* Innate; implanted by nature.

inbreathe, in·brēTH′, *v.t.* To breathe in, or infuse by breathing.

inbred, in′bred, *a.* Bred within; innate; natural.—**inbreed,** in·brēd′, *v.t.* To produce or generate within; to cross or mate closely related individuals.

Inca, ing′ka, *n.* A king or prince of Peru before the Spanish conquest; the dominant group of Indians in Peru at that time.

incalculable, in·kal′kū·la·bl, *a.* [Prefix *in*, not, and *calculable*.] Not calculable; beyond calculation; very great.—**incalculableness,** in·kal′kū·la·bl·nes, *n.*—**incalculably,** in·kal′·kū·la·bli, *adv.*

incalescent, in·ka·les′ent, *a.* [L. *incalesco*, to grow warm—*in*, and *calesco*, to grow warm, *caleo*, to be warm. CALID.] Growing warm; increasing in heat.—**incalescence,** in·ka·les′ens, *n.* The state of being incalescent.

incandescent, in·kan·des′ent, *a.* [L. *incandesco*, to become warm—*in*, intens., and *candesco*, to begin to glow.] White or glowing with heat; luminous; radiant.—**incandescent lamp,** *n.* A lamp whose light is produced by the action of electric current on some specially prepared material.—**incandescence,** in·kan·des′ens, *n.*

incantation, in·kan·tā′shon, *n.* [L. *incantatio, incantationis*, from *incanto*, to chant a magic formula over one—*in*, on, and *canto*, to sing. CHANT.] The act of using certain words and ceremonies for the purpose of raising spirits or performing magical actions; the form of words so used; a magical spell, charm, or ceremony.

incapable, in·kā′pa·bl, *a.* [Prefix *in*, not, and *capable*.] Not capable; possessing inadequate power; not admitting; not susceptible; not equal to anything; unable; unqualified or disqualified: generally followed by *of*. ∴ *Incapable* properly denotes a want of passive power, and is applicable particularly to the mind, or

said of something inanimate; *unable* denotes the want of active power or power of performing, and is applicable to the body or mind.—*n.* One physically or mentally unable to act with effect; an inefficient or silly person.—**incapability, incapableness,** in·kā′pa·bil″i·ti, in·kā′pa·bl·nes, *n.* The quality of being incapable.—**incapably,** in·kā′pa·bli, *adv.* In an incapable manner.

incapacitate, in·ka·pas′i·tāt, *v.t.*—*incapacitated, incapacitating.* [Prefix *in*, not, and *capacitate*.] To deprive of capacity or natural power; to render or make unable or unfit; to disqualify or render incompetent.—**incapacitation,** in·ka·pas′i·tā″shon, *n.* The act of incapacitating.—**incapacity,** in·ka·pas′i·ti, *n.* Want of capacity, power, or ability; inability; incompetency.

incarcerate, in·kär′sėr·āt, *v.t.*—*incarcerated, incarcerating.* [L. *in*, into, and *carcer*, a prison.] To imprison; to confine in a jail; to shut up or enclose.—**incarceration,** in·kär′sėr·ā″shon, *n.* The act of incarcerating; imprisonment.—**incarcerator,** in·kär′sėr·ā·tėr, *n.* One who incarcerates.

incarnadine, in·kär′na·din, *v.t.* [Fr. *incarnadin*, flesh-colored—L. *in*, and *caro, carnis*, flesh.] To tinge with the color of flesh; to dye red.

incarnate, in·kär′nāt, *v.t.*—*incarnated, incarnating.* [L.L. *incarno, incarnatum*—L. *in*, into, and *caro, carnis*, flesh (whence also *carnage, carnal, carnation*).] To clothe with flesh; to embody in flesh.—*a.* Invested with flesh; embodied in flesh or a human body.—**incarnation,** in·kär·nā′shon, *n.* The act of assuming flesh or taking a human body and the nature of man; the state of being incarnated; a visible embodiment; a vivid exemplification in person or act (he is the *incarnation* of wickedness).

incase, in·kās′, *v.t.*—*incased, incasing.* To enclose in, or as in, a case.

incautious, in·ka̱′shus, *a.* [Prefix *in*, not, and *cautious*.] Not cautious; unwary; heedless.—**incautiously,** in·ka̱′shus·li, *adv.* In an incautious manner.—**incautiousness,** in·ka̱′shus·nes, *n.*

incendiary, in·sen′di·e·ri, *n.* [L. *incendiarius*, from *incendo*, to burn—*in*, and *candeo*, to shine or be on fire. CANDID.] A person who willfully and maliciously sets fire to a building, etc.; one who sets fire to another's property; one who is guilty of arson; one who excites or inflames factions and promotes quarrels.—*a.* Pertaining to willful and malicious fire raising; tending to excite or inflame factions, sedition, or quarrel.—**incendiarism,** in·sen′di·er·izm, *n.* The act or practice of an incendiary.

incense, in′sens, *n.* [Fr. *encens*, from L. *incensum*, what is set on fire, from *incensus*, pp. of *incendo*, to burn. INCENDIARY.] The odors of spices and gums, burned in religious rites, or as an offering to some deity; the materials burned for making perfumes.—*v.t.—incensed, incensing.* To perfume with incense.

incense, in·sens′, *v.t.—incensed, incensing.* [L. *incensus*, provoked, inflamed; same word as *Incense*, above.] To enkindle or inflame to violent anger; to excite to angry passions; to provoke, irritate, exasperate.

incentive, in·sen′tiv, *a.* [L. *incentivus*, striking up or leading a melody—*in*, on, and *cano*, to sing. CHANT.] Inciting; encouraging or stirring up.—*n.* That which incites or has a tendency to incite to determination or action; what prompts to good or ill; motive; spur.

inception, in·sep′shon, *n.* [L. *inceptio, inceptionis*, from *incipio*, to begin—prefix *in*, and *capio*, to take. CAPABLE.] The act of beginning; a beginning; commencement; first stage.—**inceptive,** in·sep′tiv, *a.* [L. *inceptivus*.] Pertaining to inception; beginning; applied to a verb which expresses the beginning of an action.—*n.* An inceptive verb.—**inceptor,** in·sep′tėr, *n.* A beginner; one who is on the point of taking the degree of Master of Arts at an English university.

incertitude, in·sėr′ti·tūd, *n.* [Prefix *in*, not, and *certitude*.] Uncertainty; doubtfulness; doubt.

incessant, in·ses′ant, *a.* [L. prefix *in*, not, and *cessans, cessantis*, ppr. of *cesso*, to cease. CEASE.] Continuing without interruption; unceasing; unintermitted; uninterrupted; continual; ceaseless.—**incessantly,** in·ses′ant·li, *adv.* In an incessant manner; continually.

incest, in′sest, *n.* [Fr. *inceste*, L. *incestum*, unchastity, incest, from *incestus*, unchaste—*in*, not, and *castus*, chaste (whence *chaste*).] The offense of sexual commerce between persons related within the degrees wherein marriage is prohibited by law.—**incestuous,** in·ses′tū·us, *a.* Guilty of incest; involving the crime of incest.—**incestuously,** in·ses′tū·us·li, *adv.* In an incestuous manner.

inch, insh, *n.* [A.Sax. *ince, ynce*, an inch, the twelfth part of a foot; from L. *uncia*, a twelfth part. *Ounce* is the same word.] A lineal measure, being the twelfth part of a foot; proverbially, a small quantity or degree.—*By inches*, by slow degrees; gradually.—*a.* Measuring an inch: used in composition (two-*inch*, four-*inch*).

inchoate,† in′kō·āt, *v.t.* [L. *inchoa, inchoatum*, to begin.] To begin.—*a.* Recently or just begun; incipient; rudimentary; incomplete.—**inchoately,** in′kō·āt·li, *adv.* In an inchoate state.—**inchoation,** in·kō·ā′shon, *n.* The act of beginning; inception.—**inchoative,** in′kō·ā·tiv, *a.* Expressing or indicating beginning; inceptive.—*n.* That which serves to begin; *gram.* an inceptive verb.

incidence, in′si·dens, *n.* [L.L. *incidentia*, from E. *incido*, to fall upon—*in*, into, upon, and *cado*, to fall (whence *cadence, chance, case*, etc.).] A falling or occurring; the manner of falling (the *incidence* of taxation in a state); *physics*, the direction in which a body, or a ray of light, heat, etc., falls upon any surface, this direction, as regards the surface on which the body or ray falls, being called the *line of incidence.*—*Angle of incidence,* the angle formed by the line of incidence, and a line drawn from the point of contact, perpendicular to the surface.—*Point of incidence,* the point where an incident ray meets a surface.—**incident,** in′·si·dent, *a.* [L. *incidens, incidentis,* ppr. of *incido.*] Falling or striking, as a ray of light upon a surface; liable to happen; apt to occur; hence, naturally happening or appertaining (ills *incident to* human life).—*n.* What falls out, happens, or takes place; an event; an appertaining fact; *law,* a thing appertaining to, or passing with another or principal thing.—**incidental,** in·si·den′tal, *a.* Happening as an occasional event forming an incident; casual; not necessary to the chief purpose; appertaining and subsidiary.—**incidentally,** in·si·den′tal·li, *adv.* In an incidental manner.

incinerate, in·sin′·ėr·āt, *v.t.* [L. *in,* into, and *cinis, cineris,* ashes.] To burn to ashes.—**incineration,** in·sin′ėr·ā″shon, *n.* The act of incinerating.

incipient, in·sip′i·ent, *a.* [L. *incipiens, incipientis,* ppr. of *incipio,* to begin—*in,* and *capio,* to take. CAPABLE.] Beginning; commencing; beginning to show itself.—**incipience, incipiency,** in·sip′i·ens, in·sip′i·en·si, *n.* The condition of being incipient.—**incipiently,** in·sip′i·ent·li, *adv.* In an incipient manner.

incise, in·sīz′, *v.t.*—*incised, incising.* [Fr. *inciser,* from L. *incido, incisum—in,* into, and *cædo,* to cut, as in *concise, decide, excision,* etc.] To cut into; to make a deep cut in; to carve.—**incised,** in·sīzd′, *p.* and *a.* Cut; made by cutting.—**incision,** in·sizh′on, *n.* The act of cutting into a substance; that which is produced by incising; a cut; a gash; *fig.* sharpness; trenchancy.—**incisive,** in·sī′siv, *a.* [Fr. *incisif,* incisive.] Cutting in; sharply and clearly expressive; trenchant (*incisive* language or style).—**incisor,** in·sī′zėr, *n. Zool.* a foretooth; one of those teeth, the special task of which is to cut or separate.—**incisory,** in·sī′ze·ri, *a.* Having the quality of cutting.

incite, in·sīt′, *v.t.*—*incited, inciting.* [L. *incito—in,* on, and *cito,* to urge, to rouse. CITE.] To move to action; to stir up; to stimulate, urge, provoke, spur on.—**incitement, incitation,** in·sīt′ment, in·si·tā′shon, *n.* The act of inciting; that which incites or moves to action; incentive; impulse; spur; stimulus.—**inciter,** in·sī′tėr, *n.* One who incites.

incivil, in·siv′il, *a.* [Prefix *in,* not, and *civil.*] [*obs.*] Not civil; rude; unpolite. —**incivility,** in·si·vil′i·ti, *n.* Want of courtesy; rudeness; impoliteness.

incivism, in·siv′izm, *n.* In French Revolution the charge of lack of patriotism, of bad performance of civic duties; disaffection.

inclement, in·klem′ent, *a.* [Prefix *in,* not, and *clement.*] Not clement; unmerciful, severe, or harsh; tempestuous, rough, stormy, boisterous,

or otherwise hard to bear (weather). —**inclemency,** in·klem′en·si, *n.* The condition or quality of being inclement.

incline, in·klīn′, *v.i.*—*inclined, inclining.* [L. *inclino,* to incline—*in,* in, on, and *clino,* Gr. *klinō,* to bend. DECLINE.] To deviate from a direction which is regarded as normal; to bend, lean, tend; to tend, as toward an opinion, course of action, etc.—*v.t.* To cause to deviate from a line, position, or direction; to give a leaning to; to give a tendency or propensity to; to dispose; to bend, stoop, or bow (the body, the head).—*n.* (in′klīn). An ascent or descent, as in a road; a slope.—**inclinable,** in·klī′na·bl, *a.* [L. *inclinabilis,* from *inclino.*] Tending; inclined; somewhat disposed.—**inclination,** in·kli·nā′shon, *n.* [L. *inclinatio, inclinationis.*] The act of inclining, leaning, or bending; deviation from a direction regarded as the normal one; *geom.* the approach or leaning of two lines or planes toward each other, so as to make an angle at the point where they meet, or where their lines of direction meet; a disposition more favorable to one thing or person than to another; leaning; feeling in favor; propensity. —*Inclination of an orbit, astron.* the angle which the plane of an orbit makes with the ecliptic. DIP.—**inclinatory,** in·klī′na·to·ri, *a.* Having the quality of inclining.—**inclined,** in·klīnd′, *p.* and *a.* Having a leaning or tendency; disposed.—*Inclined plane,* a plane inclined to the horizon, or forming with a horizontal plane any angle whatever excepting a right angle: it is one of the mechanical powers.

include, in·klūd′, *v.t.*—*included, including.* [L. *includo—in,* in, and *claudo,* to shut up, as in *conclude, exclude,* etc. CLOSE.] To confine, hold, or contain; to comprise; to comprehend; to embrace or involve. —*Included style, included stamens, bot.* a style or stamens which do not project beyond the mouth of the corolla.—**includible,** in·klu′di·bl, *a.* Capable of being included.—**inclusion,** in·klū′zhon, *n.* [L. *inclusio.*] The act of including.—**inclusive,** in·klū′siv, *a.* [Fr. *inclusif,* from L. *includo.*] Enclosing; encircling; comprehended in the number or sum; comprehending the stated limit or extremes.—**inclusively,** in·klū′siv·li, *adv.* In an inclusive manner.

incogitable, in·koj′i·ta·bl, *a.* [Prefix *in,* not, and *cogitable.* COGITATE.] Not cogitable; incapable of being made the object of thought.—**incogitant,** in·koj′i·tant, *a.* Not thinking; thoughtless.

incognito, in·kog′ni·tō, *a.* or *adv.* [It., Sp., and Fr., from L. *incognitus,* unknown—*in,* not, and *cognitus,* known. COGNITION.] In disguise; in an assumed character and under an assumed name.—*n.,* the fem. being **incognita,** in·kog′ni·ta. One unknown, or in disguise, or passing under an assumed name; assumption of a disguised or feigned character.—

incog, in·kog′, *a., adv.* & *n.* Incognito. (*Colloq.*)

incognizable, in·kog′ni·za·bl or in·kon′i·za·bl, *a.* [Prefix *in,* not, and *cognizable.*] Not cognizable; incapable of being recognized, known, or distinguished.—**incognizance,** in·kog′ni·zans or in·kon′i·zans, *n.* Failure to recognize, know, or apprehend.—**incognizant,** in·kog′ni·zant or in·kon′i·zant, *a.* Not cognizant; unacquainted with.

incoherent, in·kō·hē′rent, *a.* [Prefix *in,* not, and *coherent.*] Not coherent; not cohering or attached together; unconnected (*incoherent* particles); wanting coherence or rational connection (ideas, language, etc.); rambling and unintelligible.—**incoherence, incoherency,** in·kō·hē′rens, in·kō·hē′ren·si, *n.* The quality of being incoherent.—**incoherently,** in·kō·hē′rent·li, *adv.* In an incoherent manner.

incombustible, in·kom·bus′ti·bl, *a.* [Prefix *in,* not, and *combustible.*] Not combustible; incapable of being burned or consumed by fire.—**incombustibility, incombustibleness,** in·com·bus′ti·bil″i·ti, in·kom·bus′ti·bl·nes, *n.* The quality of being incombustible.—**incombustibly,** in·kom·bus′ti·bli, *adv.* So as to resist combustion.

income, in′kum, *n.* [From *in* and *come,* lit. that which comes in: comp. *outcome.*] Receipts or benefits (usually in the form of money) regularly accruing from labor, business, or property (as, his annual *income* is $1,000); revenue.—**income tax,** *n.* A tax levied on incomes according to their amount.—**incomer,** in′kum·ėr, *n.* One who comes in; a stranger, not a native.—**incoming,** in′kum·ing, *a.* Coming in, as an occupant (an *incoming* tenant).—*n.* The act of coming in.

incommensurable, in·kom·men′shū·ra·bl, *a.* [Prefix *in,* not, and *commensurable.*] Not commensurable; having no common measure.—*n.* One of two or more quantities which have no common measure.—**incommensurability, incommensurableness,** in·kom·men′shū·ra·bil″i·ti, in·kom·men′shū·ra·bl·nes, *n.*—**incommensurably,** in·kom·men′shū·ra·bli, *adv.* —**incommensurate,** in·kom·men′shū·rāt, *a.* [Prefix *in,* not, and *commensurate.*] Not commensurate; not adequate or of sufficient amount.—**incommensurately,** in·kom·men′shū·rāt·li, *adv.* Not in due measure or proportion; inadequately.

incommode, in·kom·mōd′, *v.t.*—*incommoded, incommoding.* [Fr. *incommoder,* from L. *incommodo,* to be troublesome to—*in,* not, *commodus,* convenient.—COMMODIOUS.] To give inconvenience to; to inconvenience; to put about; to trouble.—**incommodious,** in·kom·mō′di·us, *a.* [Prefix *in,* not, and *commodious.*] Not commodious; inconvenient; tending to incommode.—**incommodiously,** in·kom·mō′di·us·li, *adv.* In an incommodious manner.—**incommodiousness,** in·kom·mō′di·us·nes, *n.*

incommunicable, in·kom·mū′ni·ka·bl, a. [Prefix *in*, not, and *communicable*.] Not communicable; incapable of being communicated, told, or imparted to others.—**incommunicability, incommunicableness,** in·kom·mū′ni·ka·bil′i·ti, in·kom·mū′ni·ka·bl·nes, n.—**incommunicably,** in·kom·mū′ni·ka·bli, adv.—**incommunicative,** in·kom·mū′ni·kā·tiv, a. [Prefix *in*, not, and *communicative*.] Not communicative; not inclined to impart information to others; not disposed to hold communion or intercourse.—**incommunicativeness,** in·kom·mū′ni·kā·tiv·nes, n.

incommunicado, in·ko·mū′ni·kä″dō, a. [Sp. *in*, in, and *comunicar*, to communicate.] Held without communication with others; in solitary confinement.

incommutable, in·kom·mū′ta·bl, a. [Prefix *in*, not, and *commutable*.] Not commutable; incapable of being exchanged.—**incommutability, incommutableness,** in·kom·mū′ta·bil′i·ti, in·kom·mū′ta·bl·nes, n.

incomparable, in·kom′pa·ra·bl, a. [Prefix *in*, not, and *comparable*.] Not comparable; without a match, rival, or peer; unequaled; transcendent.—**incomparableness,** in·kom′pa·ra·bl·nes, n.—**incomparably,** in·kom′pa·ra·bli, adv.

incompatible, in·kom·pat′i·bl, a. [Prefix *in*, not, and *compatible*.] Not compatible; incapable of subsisting, being possessed, or being made to accord with something else; incapable of harmonizing (feelings or tempers *incompatible with* each other).—n. A thing that is incompatible.—**incompatibility, incompatibleness,** in·kom·pat′i·bil′i·ti, in·kom·pat′i·bl·nes, n. The quality or condition of being incompatible.—**incompatibly,** in·kom·pat′i·bli, adv.

incompetent, in·kom′pe·tent, a. [Prefix *in*, not, and *competent*.] Not competent; wanting adequate strength, power, capacity, means, qualifications, etc.; unable; incapable; inadequate; wanting necessary legal or constitutional qualifications (an *incompetent* witness in a court); not permissible or admissible (an *incompetent* defense).—**incompetence, incompetency,** in·kom′pe·tens, in·kom′pe·ten·si, n. The condition or quality of being incompetent.—**incompetently,** in·kom′pe·tent·li, adv. In an incompetent manner.

incomplete, in·kom·plēt′, a. [Prefix *in*, not, and *complete*.] Not complete; not finished; imperfect; defective.—**incompletely,** in·kom·plēt′li, adv. In an incomplete manner.—**incompleteness, incompletion,** in·kom·plēt′nes, in·kom·plē′shon, n. The state of being incomplete.

incompliant, in·kom·plī′ant, a. [Prefix *in*, not, and *compliant*.] Not compliant; not disposed to comply.—**incompliance,** in·kom·plī′ans, n. The quality of being incompliant.—**incompliantly,** in·kom·plī′ant·li, adv. In an incompliant manner.

incomprehensible, in·kom′pri·hen″si·bl, a. [Prefix *in*, not, and *comprehensible*.] Not comprehensible; inca-pable of being comprehended or understood; beyond the reach of human intellect; inconceivable; *theol.* as in Athanasian Creed; illimitable; infinite; not comprehended in or bounded by space.—**incomprehensibility, incomprehensibleness,** in·kom′pri·hen′si·bil″i·ti, in·kom′pri·hen″si·bl·nes, n. The quality of being incomprehensible. — **incomprehensibly,** in·kom′pri·hen″si·bli, adv. In an incomprehensible manner.—**incomprehensive,** in·kom′pri·hen″siv, a. Not comprehensive; not extensive; limited.—**incomprehensiveness,** in·kom′pri·hen″siv·nes, n.

incompressible, in·kom·pres′i·bl, a. [Prefix *in*, not, and *compressible*.] Not compressible; resisting compression.—**incompressibility, incompressibleness,** in·kom·pres′i·bil″i·ti, in·kom·pres′i·bl·nes, n. The quality of being incompressible.

incomputable, in·kom·pū′ta·bl, a. [Prefix *in*, not, and *computable*.] Not computable; incapable of being computed or reckoned.

inconceivable, in·kon·sē′va·bl, a. [Prefix *in*, not, and *conceivable*.] Not conceivable; incapable of being conceived or thought of; incomprehensible.—**inconceivability, inconceivableness,** in·kon·sē′va·bil″i·ti, in·kon·sē′va·bl·nes, n. The quality of being inconceivable.—**inconceivably,** in·kon·sē′va·bli, adv. In an inconceivable manner; beyond conception.

inconclusive, in·kon·klū′siv, a. [Prefix *in*, not, and *conclusive*.] Not conclusive; not producing a conclusion; not settling a point in debate or a doubtful question.—**inconclusively,** in·kon·klū′siv·li, adv. In an inconclusive manner.—**inconclusiveness,** in·kon·klū′siv·nes, n. The quality of being inconclusive.

incondensable, incondensible, in·kon·den′sa·bl, in·kon·den′si·bl, a. [Prefix *in*, not, and *condensable*.] Not condensable; incapable of being condensed.—**incondensability, incondensibility,** in·kon·den′sa·bil″i·ti, in·kon·den′si·bil″i·ti, n.

incondite, in·kon′dit, a. [L. *inconditus*, confused, rude—*in*, not, and *conditus*, pp. of *condo*, to put together, to join.] Rude; unpolished: said of literary compositions.

inconformity, in·kon·for′mi·ti, n. [Prefix *in*, not, and *conformity*.] Non-conformity; lack of conformity.

incongruous, incongruent, in·kong′gru·us, in·kong′gru·ent, a. [L. *incongruus*—*in*, not, and *congruus*, congruous.] Not congruous; not of a kind or character to mingle well together; not such as to make a harmonious whole; not suiting each other; inharmonious; inconsistent (*incongruous* parts, elements, mixtures).—**incongruity, incongruence,** in·kon·gru′i·ti, in·kong′gru·ens, n. The quality of being incongruous; that which is incongruent; something exhibiting a want of congruity.—**incongruously,** in·kong′gru·us·li, adv. In an incongruous manner.—**incongruousness,** in·kong′gru·us·nes, n. The state or quality of being incongruous.

inconsequent, in·kon′si·kwent, a. [Prefix *in*, not, and *consequent*; L. *inconsequens*.] Not following from the premises; not in accordance with logical method; inconclusive.—**inconsequence,** in·kon′si·kwens, n. [L. *inconsequentia*.] The condition or quality of being inconsequent; want of logical sequence.—**inconsequential,** in·kon′si·kwen″shal, a. [Prefix *in*, not, and *consequential*.] Not consequential; inconsequent; not of consequence or importance; of little moment.—**inconsequentiality,** in·kon′si·kwen″shi·al″i·ti, n. State of being inconsequential.—**inconsequentially,** in·kon′si·kwen″shal·li, adv. In an inconsequential manner.

inconsiderable, in·kon·sid′ėr·a·bl, a. [Prefix *in*, not, and *considerable*.] Not worthy of consideration or notice; unimportant; small; trivial; insignificant.—**inconsiderably,** in·kon·sid′ėr·a·bli, adv. In an inconsiderable manner or degree.

inconsiderate, in·kon·sid′ėr·it, a. [Prefix *in*, not, and *considerate*; L. *inconsideratus*.] Not considerate; not acting with due consideration; hasty; imprudent; thoughtless; heedless.—**inconsiderately,** in·kon·sid′ėr·it·li, adv. In an inconsiderate manner.—**inconsiderateness,** in·kon·sid′ėr·it·nes, n. The condition or quality of being inconsiderate.—**inconsideration,** in·kon·sid′ėr·ā″shon, n. Want of due consideration.

inconsistent, in·kon·sis′tent, a. [Prefix *in*, not, and *consistent*.] Not consistent; irreconcilable in conception or in fact; contrary; contradictory; incompatible; incongruous; not exhibiting uniformity of sentiment or conduct, steadiness to principle or the like.—**inconsistently,** in·kon·sis′tent·li, adv. In an inconsistent manner.—**inconsistency, inconsistence,** in·kon·sis′ten·si, in·kon·sis′tens, n. The condition or quality of being inconsistent; opposition or disagreement of particulars; self-contradiction; incongruity in action or conduct.

inconsolable, in·kon·sōl′a·bl, a. [Prefix *in*, not, and *consolable*.] Incapable of being consoled; grieved beyond consolation.—**inconsolableness,** in·kon·sōl′a·bl·nes, n. State of being inconsolable. — **inconsolably,** in·kon·sōl′a·bli, adv. So as to be inconsolable.

inconsonant, in·kon′so·nant, a. [Prefix *in*, not, and *consonant*.] Not consonant or agreeing; inconsistent; discordant.—**inconsonantly,** in·kon′so·nant·li, adv. In an inconsonant manner.—**inconsonance,** in·kon′so·nans, n. Want of harmony; discordance.

inconspicuous, in·kon·spik′ū·us, a. [Prefix *in*, not, and *conspicuous*.] Not conspicuous or readily noticed; not to be easily perceived.—**inconspicuously,** in·kon·spik′ū·us·li, adv. In an inconspicuous manner.—**inconspicuousness,** in·kon·spik′ū·us·nes, n. Want of conspicuousness.

inconstant, in·kon′stant, a. [Prefix *in*, not, and *constant*; L. *inconstans*, Fr. *inconstant*.] Not constant; subject to change of opinion, inclination, or purpose; not firm in resolution; unsteady; fickle; capricious: said of persons; mutable, changeable, or variable: said of things.—*n.* A thing which is not constant; a variable.—**inconstantly**, in·kon′stant·li, *adv.* In an inconstant manner.—**inconstancy**, in·kon′stan·si, *n.* [L. *inconstantia.*] The quality of being inconstant.

inconsumable, in·kon·sū′ma·bl, *a.* [Prefix *in*, not, and *consumable.*] Not consumable; incapable of being consumed.

incontestable, in·kon·tes′ta·bl, *a.* [Prefix *in*, not and *contestable.*] Not contestable; not to be disputed; too clear to be controverted; incontrovertible.—**incontestability**, in·kon·tes′ta·bil″i·ti, *n.* The state or quality of being incontestable.—**incontestably**, in·con·tes′ta·bli, *adv.* In an incontestable manner; incontrovertibly; indubitably.

incontinent, in·kon′ti·nent, *a.* [Prefix *in*, not, and *continent*; L. *incontinens*; Fr. *incontinent*, incontinent, and (as adv.) forthwith, immediately.] Not continent; not restraining the passions or appetites, particularly the sexual appetite; unchaste; lewd; *med.* unable to restrain natural discharges or evacuations.—**incontinence**, in·kon′ti·nens, *n.* [L. *incontinentia*, Fr. *incontinence.*] The condition or quality of being incontinent.—**incontinently**, in·kon′ti·nent·li, *adv.* In an incontinent manner; immediately; instantly; forthwith; at once.

incontrovertible, in·kon′tro·vėr″ti·bl, *a.* [Prefix *in*, not, and *controvertible.*] Not controvertible; too clear or certain to admit of dispute or controversy.—**incontrovertibility**, **incontrovertibleness**, in·kon′tro·vėr″ti·bil″i·ti, in·kon′tro·vėr″ti·bl·nes, *n.* State of being incontrovertible.—**incontrovertibly**, in·kon′trō·vėr″ti·bli, *adv.* In an incontrovertible manner; incontestably.

inconvenient, in·kon·vē′ni·ent, *a.* [Prefix *in*, not, and *convenient.*] Not convenient; incommodious; giving some trouble; wanting due facilities; causing embarrassment; inopportune.—**inconveniently**, in·kon·vē′ni·ent·li, *adv.* In an inconvenient manner.—**inconvenience**, **inconveniency**, in·kon·vē′ni·ens, in·kon·vē′ni·en·si, *n.* The quality of being inconvenient; something that incommodes or gives trouble or uneasiness.—**inconvenience**, in·kon·vē′ni·ens, *v.t.*—*inconvenienced, inconveniencing.* To put to inconvenience; to incommode.

inconvertible, in·kon·vėr′ti·bl, *a.* [Prefix *in*, not, and *convertible.*] Not convertible; incapable of being converted into or exchanged for something else.—**inconvertibility**, **inconvertibleness**, in·kon·vėr′ti·bil″i·ti, in·kon·vėr′ti·bl·nes, *n.* The quality of being inconvertible.

inconvincible, in·kon·vin′si·bl, *a.* [Prefix *in*, not, and *convincible.*] Incapable of being convinced.

incorporate, in·kor′po·rāt, *v.t.*—*incorporated, incorporating.* [L. *incor-poro, incorporatum*—*in*, into, and *corpus, corporis*, a body.] To form into one body; to combine or mix into one mass; to unite with another body or substance; to combine or unite intimately (to *incorporate* things together or one thing *with* another); to embody or give material form to; to form into a corporation or body of individuals that can act as one.—*v.i.* To unite so as to form a part of another body; to be mixed or blended; to grow into; usually followed by *with.*—*a.* Incorporated; united in one body.—**incorporated**, in·kor′po·rā·ted, *p.* and *a.* Mixed or united in one body; associated so as to form a corporation; united in a legal body.—**incorporation**, in·kor′po·rā″shon, *n.* The act of incorporating or state of being incorporated; that which is incorporated; a society or body formed by the union of individuals and authorized by law to act as a single person.—**incorporative**, in·kor′po·rā·tiv, *a.* Tending to incorporate; incorporating; *philol.* tending to combine many elements into one long word.

incorporeal, in·kor·pō′ri·al, *a.* [Prefix *in*, not, and *corporeal.*] Not corporeal; not consisting of matter; not having a material body; immaterial; intangible.—**incorporeally**, in·kor·pō′ri·al·li, *adv.* In an incorporeal manner; immaterially.—**incorporeity**, in·kor′pō·rē″i·ti, *n.* The quality of being incorporeal.

incorrect, in·ko·rekt′, *a.* [Prefix *in*, not, and *correct.*] Not correct; not exact; inexact; erroneous; faulty; not according to fact.—**incorrectly**, in·ko·rekt′li, *adv.* In an incorrect manner.—**incorrectness**, in·ko·rekt′nes, *n.*

incorrigible, in·kor′i·ji·bl, *a.* [Prefix *in*, not, and *corrigible.*] Incapable of being corrected or amended; bad beyond correction or reform.—*n.* One who is bad beyond correction or reform.—**incorrigibility**, **incorrigibleness**, in·kor′i·ji·bil″i·ti, in·kor′i·ji·bl·nes, *n.* The condition or quality of being incorrigible.—**incorrigibly**, in·kor′i·ji·bli, *adv.* In an incorrigible manner.

incorrupt, in·ko·rupt′, *a.* [Prefix *in*, not, and *corrupt*; L. *incorruptus.*] Not corrupt or corrupted; not suffering from corruption or decay; not depraved; pure; untainted; above the influence of corruption or bribery.—**incorruptibility**, **incorruptibleness**, in·ko·rup′ti·bil″i·ti, in·ko·rup′ti·bl·nes, *n.* The condition of being incorruptible.—**incorruptible**, in·ko·rup′ti·bl, *a.* Incapable of corruption, decay, or dissolution; incapable of being corrupted or bribed; inflexibly upright.—**incorruptibly**, in·ko·rup′ti·bli, *adv.* In an incorruptible manner.—**incorruption**, in·ko·rup′shon, *n.* Absence of or exemption from corruption or decay.—**incorruptly**, in·ko·rupt′li, *adv.* In an incorrupt manner; without corruption.—**incorruptness**, in·ko·rupt′-nes, *n.* The condition or quality of being incorrupt; probity; integrity.

incrassate, in·kras′āt, *v.t.*—*incras-sated, incrassating.* [L. *incrasso, in-crassatum*—*in*, intens., and *crassus*, thick, crass.] To make thick or thicker; to make less fluid; to inspissate; to thicken.—**incrassation**, in·kras·ā′shon, *n.* The act of thickening; inspissation.

increase, in·krēs′, *v.i.*—*increased, increasing.* [Prefix *in* or *en*, and O.Fr. *creser*, L. *crescere*, to grow, allied to *creare*, to create—similarly *decrease.*] To become greater; to grow; to augment; to advance; to multiply by the production of young; *astron.* to show a gradually enlarging luminous surface; to wax (the moon *increases*).—*v.t.* To make greater or larger; to augment in bulk, quantity, amount, or degree; to add to.—*n.* (in′krēs). Augmentation; a growing greater or larger; enlargement; extension; the amount by which anything is augmented; increment; interest of money; produce; issue or offspring (O.T.); *astron.* the period of waxing, as of the moon.—**increasable**, in·krēs′a·bl, *a.* Capable of being increased.—**increaser**, in·krēs′ėr, *n.* One who or that which increases.—**increasingly**, in·krēs′ing·li, *adv.* In the way of increase; by continual increase.

incredible, in·kred′i·bl, *a.* [Prefix *in*, not, and *credible.*] Not credible; impossible to be believed; too extraordinary and improbable to admit of belief.—**incredibility**, in·kred′i·bil″i·ti, *n.* The quality of being incredible; that which is incredible.—**incredibleness**, in·kred′i·bl·nes, *n.* The quality of being incredible.—**incredibly**, in·kred′i·bli, *adv.* In an incredible manner.

incredulous, in·kred′ū·lus, *a.* [Prefix *in*, not, and *credulous.*] Not credulous; not given to believe readily; refusing or withholding belief; skeptical.—**incredulity**, **incredulousness**, in·krē·dū′li·ti, in·kred′ū·lus·nes, *n.* The quality of being incredulous.—**incredulously**, in·kred′ū·lus·li, *adv.* In an incredulous manner.

increment, in′kre·ment, *n.* [L. *incrementum*, from *incresco*, to increase. INCREASE.] Act or process of increasing; augmentation or growth; something added; increase; *math.* the increase of a quantity from its present value to its next ascending value; *rhet.* an amplification without necessarily involving a true climax.

increscent, in·kres′ent, *a.* [L. *increscens, increscentis*, ppr. of *incresco*, to increase.] Increasing; growing; augmenting; swelling.

incriminate, in·krim′i·nāt, *v.t.*—*incriminated, incriminating.* [L.L. *incrimino, incriminatum*—L. *in*, and *crimino*, to accuse one of a crime, from *crimen, criminis*, a charge.] To charge with a crime or fault; to accuse; to criminate.—**incriminatory**, in·krim′-i·na·to·ri, *a.* Accusatory; tending to criminate.

incrust, in·krust′, *v.t.* [L. *incrusto*—*in*, in, on, and *crusta*, crust.] To cover with a crust or with a hard coat; to form a crust on the surface of.—**incrustation**, in·krus·tā′shon, *n.* The act of incrusting; a crust or hard coating on the surface of a body; a covering or inlaying.

incubate, in'kū·bāt, *v.i.* [L. *incubo, incubatum,* to lie in or upon—prefix *in,* in, on, and *cubo,* to lie, seen also in *incubus, incumbent, covey.*] To care for in such a way as to induce hatching (of eggs) or promote development (of embryos, etc.)—*v.i.* To be incubated; to brood.—**incubation,** in·kū·bā'shon, *n.* Act of incubating; *pathol.* the period of maturation, without visible symptoms, of a contagious disease.—**incubative,** in''kū·bā'tiv, *a.*—**incubator,** in''kū·bā'tẽr, *n.* An apparatus for hatching eggs by artificial heat; an apparatus for maintaining proper body temperature in babies born prematurely or otherwise physically subnormal; an apparatus for incubating bacteriological cultures, etc.

incubus, in'kū·bus, *n.* pl. **incubuses, incubi,** in'kū·bus·ez, in'kū·bī. [L., from *incubo,* to lie on. INCUBATE.] Nightmare; an imaginary being or demon, formerly supposed to be the cause of nightmare; hence something that weighs heavily on the mind or feelings; an encumbrance of any kind; a dead weight.

inculcate, in·kul'kāt, *v.t.*—*inculcated, inculcating.* [L. *inculco, inculcatum—in,* in, and *calco,* to tread; akin *calx,* the heel.] To impress by frequent admonitions; to teach and enforce by frequent repetitions; to urge on the mind.—**inculcation,** in·kul·kā'shon, *n.* The act of inculcating.—**inculcator,** in·kul'kā·tẽr, *n.* One who inculcates.

inculpable, in·kul'pa·bl, *a.* [Prefix *in,* not, and *culpable.*] Not culpable; not to be accused; blameless.

inculpate, in·kul'pāt, *v.t.*—*inculpated, inculpating.* [L.L. *inculpo, inculpatum*—L. *in,* into, and *culpa,* a fault; akin *culpable, culprit.*] To show to be in fault; to accuse of crime; to impute guilt to; to incriminate: opposed to *exculpate.*—**inculpation,** in·kul·pā'shon, *n.* The act of inculpating.—**inculpatory,** in·kul'pa·to·ri, *a.* Tending to inculpate or criminate.

incult, in·kult', *a.* [L. *incultus*—prefix *in,* not, and *cultus,* pp. of *colo,* to cultivate.] Uncultivated; rude; not polished or refined.

incumbent, in·kum'bent, *a.* [L. *incumbens, incumbentis,* ppr. of *incumbo,* to lie—*in,* on, and *cumbo,* to lie down. INCUBATE.] Lying or resting upon; resting upon a person as a duty or obligation to be performed; imposed and calling for performance. —*n.* A person in possession of an ecclesiastical benefice or other office. —**incumbently,** in·kum'bent·li, *adv.* In an incumbent manner.—**incumbency,** in·kum'ben·si, *n.* The state of being incumbent; what is incumbent; *eccles.* the state of holding or being in possession of a benefice.

incumber, in·kum'bẽr, *v.t.* Same as *Encumber.*

incunabulum, in·kū·nab'ū·lum, *n.* pl. **incunabula,** in·kū·nab'ū·la. [L. *incunabula,* swaddling clothes, birthplace, origin—prefix *in,* and *cuna-*

bula, from *cunæ,* a cradle.] A book printed in the early times of printing; generally, a book printed before the year 1500.

incur, in·kẽr', *v.t.*—*incurred, incurring.* [L. *incurro,* to run against—*in,* and *curro,* to run. CURRENT.] To run in danger of or liability to; to expose one's self to; to become liable to; to become subject to (to *incur* danger, inconvenience, etc.); to contract (to *incur* a debt).—**incurrence,** in·kẽr'ens, *n.* The act of incurring.

incurable, in·kū'ra·bl, *a.* [Prefix *in,* not, and *curable.*] Not curable; beyond the power of skill and medicine; not admitting remedy.—*n.* A person diseased beyond the reach of cure.—**incurability, incurableness,** in·kū·ra·bil''i·ti, in·kū'ra·bl·nes, *n.* The state of being incurable.—**incurably,** in·kū'ra·bli, *adv.* In an incurable manner.

incurious, in·kū'ri·us, *a.* [Prefix *in,* not, and *curious.*] Not curious or inquisitive; destitute of curiosity.—**incuriously,** in·kū'ri·us·li, *adv.* In an incurious manner.—**incuriosity, incuriousness,** in·kū'ri·os''i·ti, in·kū'ri·us·nes, *n.* The quality of being incurious.

incursion, in·kẽr'zhon, *n.* [L. *incursio, incursionis,* from *incurro.* INCUR.] An entering into a territory with hostile intention; an invasion not followed by continued occupation; an inroad.—**incursive,** in·kẽr'siv, *a.* Making an attack or incursion; aggressive.

incurvate, incurve, in·kẽr'vāt, in·kẽrv', *v.t.*—*incurvated, incurvating; incurved, incurving.* [L. *incurvo, incurvatum*—*in,* in, and *curvo,* to bend. CURVE.] To curve inward; to make curved; to bend; to crook.—**incurvate,** *a.* Curved inward or upward.—**incurvation,** in·kẽr·vā'shon, *n.* The act of incurvating; a bending or bend.

incus, ing'kus, *n.* [L., an anvil.] A bone of the internal ear, so called from its shape.

incuse,† in·kūz', *v.t.* [L. *incudo, incusum,* to forge.] To impress by striking or stamping.

indagate,† in'da·gāt, *v.t.* [L. *indago, indagaium.*] To seek or search out.

indebted, in·det'ed, *a.* [Prefix *in,* in, and *debt.*] Being under a debt; having incurred a debt; held to payment or requital; obliged by something received, for which restitution or gratitude is due.—**indebtedness,** in·det'ed·nes, *n.* The state of being indebted; the amount of debt owed.

indecent, in·dē'sent, *a.* [Prefix *in,* not, and *decent;* L. *indecens,* unseemly.] Offending against decency; unfit to be seen or heard; offensive to modesty and delicacy; immodest; unseemly.—**indecently,** in·dē'sent·li, *adv.* In an indecent manner.—**indecency,** in·dē'sen·si, *n.* The quality of being indecent; what is indecent in language, actions, or manners; grossness in speech or behavior; immodesty.

indeciduate, in·di·sid'u·āt, *a.* [Prefix *in,* not, and *deciduate.*] Not deciduate; not having a decidua.

indeciduous, in·di·sid'ū·us, *a.* [Prefix *in,* not, and *deciduous.*] Not deciduous; evergreen.

indecipherable, in·di·sī'fẽr·a·bl, *a.* [Prefix *in,* not, and *decipherable.*] Not decipherable; incapable of being deciphered.

indecision, in·di·sizh'on, *n.* [Prefix *in,* not, and *decision.*] Want of decision or settled purpose; a wavering of mind; irresolution.—**indecisive,** in·di·sī'siv, *a.* [Prefix *in,* not, and *decisive.*] Not decisive; not bringing to a final close or ultimate issue; not having come to a decision; irresolute; vacillating; hesitating.—**indecisively,** in·di·sī'siv·li, *adv.* In an indecisive manner.—**indecisiveness,** in·di·sī'siv·nes, *n.*

indeclinable, in·di·klī'na·bl, *a.* [Prefix *in,* not, and *declinable.*] *Gram.* not declinable; not varied by terminations.—*n. Gram.* a word that is not declined.

indecomposable, in·dē'kom·pō''za·bl, *a.* [Prefix *in,* not, and *decomposable.*] Not decomposable; incapable of decomposition.—**indecomposableness,** in·dē'kom·pō''za·bl·nes, *n.*

indecorous, in·dek'o·rus, *a.* [Prefix *in,* not, and *decorous.*] Not decorous; violating decorum or propriety; unseemly; unbecoming.—**indecorously,** in·dek'o·rus·li, *adv.* In an indecorous manner.—**indecorousness,** in·dek'o·rus·nes, *n.* The quality of being indecorous.—**indecorum,** in·de·kō'rum, *n.* Want of decorum; impropriety of behavior.

indeed, in·dēd', *adv.* [Prep. *in,* and *deed.*] In reality; in truth; in fact: sometimes used as intimating a concession or admission; sometimes interjectionally, as an expression of surprise, or for the purpose of obtaining confirmation.

indefatigable, in·di·fat'i·ga·bl, *a.* [L. *indefatigabilis,* from *in,* not, and *defatigo,* to tire completely—*de,* intens., and *fatigo,* to fatigue.] Incapable of being fatigued; not yielding to fatigue; unremitting in labor or effort; unwearied; untiring.—**indefatigably,** in·di·fat'i·ga·bli, *adv.* In an indefatigable manner; unremittingly; sedulously.—**indefatigability, indefatigableness,** in·di·fat'i·ga·bil''i·ti, in·di·fat'i·ga·bl·nes, *n.* The quality of being indefatigable.

indefeasible, in·di·fē'zi·bl, *a.* [Prefix *in,* not, and *defeasible.*] Not defeasible; not to be defeated or made void (right, claim, or title).—**indefeasibly,** in·di·fē'zi·bli, *adv.* In an indefeasible manner.—**indefeasibility,** in·di·fē'zi·bil''i·ti, *n.* The quality of being indefeasible.

indefensible, in·di·fen'si·bl, *a.* [Prefix *in,* not, and *defensible.*] Not defensible; incapable of being defended, vindicated, or justified.—**indefensibility,** in·di·fen'si·bil''i·ti, *n.* The quality or state of being indefensible.—**indefensibly,** in·di·fen'si·bli, *adv.* In an indefensible manner.

indefinable, in·di·fī'na·bl, *a.* [Prefix *in,* not, and *definable.*] Incapable of being defined; unsusceptible of definition; not to be clearly explained by words.—**indefinably**, in·di·fī′na·bli, *adv.* In an indefinable manner.

indefinite, in·def′i·nit, *a.* [Prefix *in*, not, and *definite*.] Not definite; not limited or defined; not precise or certain; having no determinate or certain limits; *bot.* too numerous or various to make a particular enumeration important: said of the parts of a flower.—*Indefinite inflorescence*, *bot.* one in which the flowers all arise from axiliary buds, the stem growing indefinitely.—**indefinite article**, *Gram.*, *a* or *an.*—**indefinitely**, in·def′i·nit·li, *adv.*—**indefiniteness**, in·def′i·nit·nes, *n.*

indehiscent, in·di·his′ent, *a.* [Prefix *in*, not, and *dehiscent*.] *Bot.* not dehiscent; not opening spontaneously when ripe, as a capsule.—**indehiscence**, in·di·his′ens, *n. Bot.* the property of being indehiscent.

indelible, in·del′i·bl, *a.* [L. *indelebilis*—*in*, not, and *deleo*, to delete.] Not to be blotted out; incapable of being effaced, canceled, or obliterated.—**indelibility, indelibleness**, in·del′i·bil″i·ti, in·del′i·bl·nes, *n.* Quality of being indelible.—**indelibly**, in·del′i·bli, *adv.* In an indelible manner; ineffaceably.

indelicate, in·del′i·kit, *a.* [Prefix *in*, not, and *delicate*.] Wanting delicacy; offensive to modesty or purity of mind; tending toward indecency or grossness; somewhat immodest.—**indelicately**, in·del′i·kit·li, *adv.* In an indelicate manner.—**indelicacy**, in·del′i·ka·si, *n.* The condition or quality of being indelicate; a certain want of modesty or purity of mind.

indemnify, in·dem′ni·fi, *v.t.*—*indemnified, indemnifying.* [L. *indemnis*, free from loss or injury, and *facio*, to make. INDEMNITY.] To save harmless; to secure against loss, damage, or penalty; to reimburse for expenditure made.—**indemnification**, in·dem′ni·fi·kā″shon, *n.* The act of indemnifying; that which indemnifies.

indemnity, in·dem′ni·ti, *n.* [Fr. *indemnité*, from L. *indemnitas*, from *indemnis*, uninjured—prefix *in*, not, and *damnum*, loss, damage. DAMN.] Security or exemption from damage, loss, injury, or punishment; compensation or equivalent for loss, damage, or injury sustained.

indent, in·dent′, *v.t.* [L.L. *indenture*, O.Fr. *endenter*, from L. *in*, in, and *dens, dentis*, a tooth. DENTAL.] To notch, jag, or cut into points or inequalities, like a row of teeth; to indenture; *printing*, to begin (a line) farther in from the margin than the rest of the paragraph.—*n.* A notch in a margin; an indentation; *printing*, the blank space at the beginning of a paragraph; *com.*, an order for goods.—**indentation**, in·den·tā′shon, *n.* The act of indenting; a cut or notch in a margin; an angular recess or depression like a notch in any border.—**indented**, in·den′ted, *p.* and *a.* Having notches or points like teeth on the margin; toothed; bound by indenture.—**indenture**, in·den′chėr, *n.* The act of indenting; an

indentation; *law*, a deed under seal, entered into between two or more parties, each party having a duplicate: so called from the duplicates having originally been written on one skin, which was divided by a jagged cut, so that the correspondence of the two halves was at once manifest.—*v.i.*—*indentured, indenturing.* To indent; to bind by indentures, as in apprenticeship.

independent, in·di·pen′dent, *a.* [Prefix *in*, not, and *dependent*.] Not dependent; not subject to the control of others; not relying on others; with *of* before an object; not subordinate; moderately wealthy, as an *independent* fortune; acting and thinking for one's self; not swayed by bias or influence; self-directing; proceeding from or expressive of a spirit of independence in air or manner; [*cap.*] in England, pertaining to the Independents or Congregationalists.—*adv.* Irrespective; without taking note or regard; not to make mention: with *of.*—*n.* In politics, one not bound by party; *eccles.* one who maintains that every congregation forms a church or independent religious society in itself.—*Independent clause, gram.*, a clause not dependent on other words of a sentence.—**independence, independency,**† in·di·pen′dens, in·di·pen′den·si, *n.* The state of being independent; that which renders one independent; property or income sufficient to make one independent of others or of his own exertions.—**Independence Day**, the 4th of July, an annual holiday in the United States, commemorative of the adoption of the Declaration of Independence in 1776.—**independently**, in·di·pen′dent·li, *adv.* In an independent manner; leaving out of consideration (he is richer *independently of* that).

indescribable, in·di·skrī′ba·bl, *a.* [Prefix *in*, not, and *describable*.] Not describable; incapable of being described.

indestructible, in·di·struk′ti·bl, *a.* [Prefix *in*, not, and *destructible*.] Not destructible; incapable of being destroyed.—**indestructibility**, in·di·struk′ti·bil″i·ti, *n.* The quality of being indestructible. — **indestructibly**, in·di·struk′ti·bli, *adv.* In an indestructible manner.

indeterminate, in·di·tėr′mi·nāt, *a.* [Prefix *in*, not, and *determinate*.] Not determinate; not settled or fixed; not definite; uncertain; not precise; *math.* applied to problems which have an indefinite number of solutions, not arbitrary but correlated; of a sentence, one making the imprisonment or release of the prisoner dependent on his conduct and amendment.—*Indeterminate inflorescence.* Same as *indefinite inflorescence.*—**indeterminable**, in·di·tėr′mi·na·bl, *a.* [Prefix *in*, not, and *determinable*.] Incapable of being determined, ascertained, or fixed; not to be determined or ended; interminable.—**indeterminately**, in·di·tėr′mi·nāt·li, *adv.* In an indeterminate manner.—**indeterminate**-

ness, in·di·tėr′mi·nāt·nes, *n.* The state or quality of being indeterminate.—**indetermination**, in·di·tėr′mi·nā″shon, *n.* Want of determination; an unsettled or wavering state, as of the mind.—**indeterminism**, *n.* The philosophic theory maintaining that not all our actions are determined or conditioned by motives; the opposite of rigid determinism.

indevout, in·di·vout′, *a.* [Prefix *in*, not, and *devout*.] Not devout; not having devout affections.

index, in′deks, *n.* pl. **indexes**, in′dek·sez, or **indices**, in′di·sez. [L., one who or that which points out, a table of contents—*in*, in, and stem of *dico*, to say (DICTION); seen in Skr. *diç*, Gr. *deiknymi*, to show.] Something that points out, shows, indicates, or manifests; a pointer or hand that points or directs to anything; the hand ☞ used by printers, etc., to call attention; a table of the contents of a book in alphabetical order; *anat.* the forefinger; *math.* the figure or letter which shows to what power any quantity is evolved; the exponent.—*Index of refraction, optics*, the ratio of the sine of the angle of incidence to the sine of the angle of refraction when a ray passes from one medium into another (*relative index*), or from a vacuum into a medium (*absolute index*).—*Index Expurgatorius* (Index Expurgatory), *Index Prohibitorius* (Index Prohibitory), or more fully *Index Librorum Prohibitorum* (Index of Prohibited Books), a catalogue of books which are forbidden by the Roman Catholic Church to be read by the faithful.—*v.t.* To provide with an index; to place in an index.—**indexer**, in′dek·sėr, *n.* One who makes an index.—**index finger**, *n.* The forefinger.—**indexical**, in·dek′si·kal, *a.* Having the form of an index; pertaining to an index.

India, in′di·a, *n.* [From *Indus*, the name of a river in Asia; akin Skr. *sindhu*, a river, *syand*, to flow.] A republic in Asia, formerly part of the British Empire; a color darker than cream and lighter than tan.—*India ink*, a black writing fluid used chiefly by draftsmen.—*Indiaman*, a large ship formerly employed in the India trade.—*India paper*, a thin opaque paper used in printing.—*India rubber*, caoutchouc; a soft variety of rubber.—**Indian**, *a.* Of or pertaining to either of the Indies, East or West, or to the aborigines of America, so called by Columbus who mistook his discovery of America for the finding of a new route to India; made of maize or India corn.—*Department of Indian Affairs*, a division of the Department of the Interior with jurisdiction over affairs between the Indians and the Federal government.—*Indian club*, a wooden club used in calisthenics.—*Indian corn*, a native American plant and its ripened ears.—*Indian file*, single file.—*Indian red*, a species of ocher; a very fine purple earth used in both oil and watercolor painting.—

Indian summer, summer-like weather, with calm and absence of rain, occurring in autumn.—*Indian turnip*, Jack-in-the-pulpit.—*Indian yellow*, a bright yellow pigment.—*n.* An East Indian, West Indian or Anglo-Indian; one of the aborigines of America; a Red Indian.—**Indic**, in′dik, *a.* Applied to that branch of the Indo-European languages of India which includes Hindustani, Prakrit, Pali, and Sanskrit.

indican, in′di·kan, *n.* [From *indigo.*] A substance which is present in the indigo plant, and is the source of indigo blue.

indicate, in′di·kāt, *v.t.*—*indicated, indicating.* [L. *indico, indicatum,* from *index, indicis.* INDEX.] To point out; to direct the mind to a knowledge of; to show; to intimate. —**indicant**, in′di·kant, *a.* [L. *indicans, indicantis.*] Serving to point out; indicating.—**indication**, in·di·kā′shon, *n.* The act of indicating or pointing out; what serves to indicate or point out; intimation; mark; token; sign; symptom.— **indicative**, in·dik′a·tiv, *a.* [L. *indicativus.*] Pointing out or indicating; serving as an indication; giving intimation or knowledge of (movements *indicative of* uneasiness); *gram.* applied to that mood of the verb that declares directly or that asks questions.—*n. Gram.* the indicative mood.—**indicatively**, in·dik′a·tiv·li, *adv.* In an indicative manner. —**indicator**, in′di·kā·tėr, *n.* One who or that which indicates, an instrument for ascertaining and recording the pressure of steam in the cylinder of a steam engine; a recording instrument of various kinds; a South African cuckoo that by its movements indicates the presence of the nests of wild bees.—*Indicator diagram*, the diagram traced by the indicator in a steam engine. It represents the pressures at all stages of the piston stroke, and its area gives the work done by the piston during the stroke.—**indicatory**, in′di·ka·to·ri, *a.* Serving to indicate.

indict, in·dīt′, *v.t.* [O.Fr. *inditer, indicter,* from L. *indico, indictum,* to declare publicly—*in*, and *dico,* to say, to speak. INDEX.] To accuse or charge with a crime or misdemeanor in due form of law.— **indictable**, in·dī′ta·bl, *a.* Capable of being or liable to be indicted; that may bring an indictment on one (an *indictable* offense).—**indictment**, in·dīt′ment, *n.* The act of indicting; a formal accusation or charge against a person; a written accusation.—**indicter, indictor**, in·dī′tėr, *n.* One who indicts.—**indiction**, in·dik′shon, *n. Chron.* a cycle of fifteen years.

indifferent, in·dif′ėr·ent, *a.* [L. *indifferens, indifferentis*—*in*, not, and *differens*, ppr. of *differo,* to differ. DIFFER.] Impartial; unbiased; uninterested; unconcerned; careless; having no preference; of no account or moment; neither very good nor very bad, but rather bad than good; middling; tolerable.—Formerly used adverbially (*indifferent* honest).— **indifference**, in·dif′ėr·ens, *n.* The state or quality of being indifferent; absence of feeling or interest; unconcern; apathy; mediocrity or some degree of badness.—**indifferentism**, in·dif′ėr·ent·izm, *n.* Systematic indifference; reasoned disregard; want of zeal.—**indifferently**, in·dif′ėr·ent·li, *adv.* In an indifferent manner; impartially; no more than passably.

indigene, in′di·jēn, *n.* [L. *indigena*—*indu,* old form of *in,* and *gen,* root of *gigno,* to beget. GENUS.] One born in a country; a native animal or plant.—**indigenous**, in·dij′en·us, *a.* Originating or produced naturally in a country or climate; native, not foreign or exotic.

indigent, in′di·jent, *a.* [L. *indigens, indigentis,* from *indigeo,* to want— *ind,* a form of *in,* and *egeo,* to be in want.] Destitute of the means of comfortable subsistence; needy; poor.—**indigence**, in′di·jens, *n.* The condition of being indigent; penury; poverty.

indigested, in·di·jes′ted, *a.* [Prefix *in,* not, and *digested.*] Not digested; undigested; not reduced to due form; not methodized; crude; not prepared or softened by heat, as chemical substances.—**indigestibility, indigestibleness**, in·di·jes′ti·bil″i·ti, in·di·jes′ti·bl·nes, *n.* The quality of being indigestible.—**indigestible**, in·di·jes′ti·bl, *a.* [Prefix *in,* not, and *digestible.*] Not digestible; digested with difficulty.— **indigestion**, in·di·jest′yon, *n.* [Prefix *in,* not, and *digestion.*] Incapability of or difficulty in digesting food; dyspepsia.

indignant, in·dig′nant, *a.* [L. *indignans, indignantis,* ppr. of *indignor,* to consider as unworthy, to disdain— *in,* not, and *dignor,* to deem worthy, from *dignus,* worthy (whence *dignity, deign*).] Displeased at what is unworthy or base; affected with indignation.—**indignantly**, in·dig′nant·li, *adv.* In an indignant manner. —**indignation**, in·dig·nā′shon, *n.* [L. *indignatio, indignationis.*] A feeling of displeasure at what is unworthy or base; anger, mingled with contempt, disgust, or abhorrence; violent displeasure.—**indignity**, in·dig′ni·ti, *n.* [L. *indignitas.*] Any action toward another which manifests contempt for him or design to lower his dignity; an insult; an affront; an outrage.

indigo, in′di·gō, *n.* [Sp. and It. *indigo,* from L. *indicum,* indigo, from *Indicus,* Indian, from *India.*] A deep, slightly reddish blue, one of the seven chief colors of the spectrum, as named by Newton; a blue dye, extensively employed, now usually synthesized from amino compounds, but originally obtained from various plants native to the East and West Indies.—**indigo blue**, the color indigo; the substance indigotin.— **indigo bunting**, a small bird of the eastern United States.—**indigoid**, in′di·goid, *a.* Referring to a class of dyes, similar in structure to indigo.—**indigo plant**, a plant yielding indigo.—**indigotin**, in·dig′o·tin, *n.* A powder, the coloring principle of indigo.

indirect, in·di·rekt′, *a.* [Prefix *in,* not, and *direct.*] Not direct; deviating from a direct line or course; circuitous; not tending directly to an aim or end; roundabout; not open and straightforward; not resulting directly; having something mediate or interposed.—**indirection**, *n.* Roundabout methods; deceit. (*Shak.*) —**indirectly**, in·di·rekt′li, *adv.* In an indirect manner.— **indirectness**, in·di·rekt′nes, *n.*

indiscernible, in·diz·zėr′ni·bl, *a.* [Prefix *in,* not, and *discernible.*] Incapable of being discerned; undiscernible.

indiscoverable, in·dis·kuv′ėr·a·bl, *a.* [Prefix *in,* not, and *discoverable.*] Incapable of being discovered; undiscoverable.

indiscreet, in·dis·krēt′, *a.* [Prefix *in,* not, and *discreet.*] Not discreet; wanting in discretion or sound judgment; injudicious; inconsiderate.—**indiscreetly**, in·dis·krēt′li, *adv.* In an indiscreet manner.—**indiscreetness**, in·dis·krēt′nes, *n.* The quality of being indiscreet.—**indiscretion**, *n.* The condition or quality of being indiscreet; want of discretion; an indiscreet act; an ill-judged act.

indiscriminate, in·dis·krim′i·nit, *a.* [Prefix *in,* not, and *discriminate.*] Without discrimination or distinction; not making any distinction; confused; promiscuous.—**indiscriminately**, in·dis·krim′i·nit·li, *adv.* In an indiscriminate manner.—**indiscriminating**, in·dis·krim′i·nāt·ing, *p.* and *a.* Not discriminating; not making any distinction.—**indiscrimination**, in·dis·krim′i·nā″shon, *n.* Want of discrimination.

indispensable, in·dis·pen′sa·bl, *a.* [Prefix *in,* not, and *dispensable.*] Incapable of being dispensed with; absolutely necessary or requisite.— **indispensability, indispensableness**, in·dis·pen′sa·bil″i·ti, in·dis·pen′sa·bl·nes, *n.* The quality of being indispensable.—**indispensably**, in·dis·pen′sa·bli, *adv.* In an indispensable manner; absolutely.

indispose, in·dis·pōz′, *v.t.*—*indisposed, indisposing.* [Fr. *indisposer*— prefix *in,* not, and *disposer,* to dispose. DISPOSE.] To disincline; to render averse or unfavorable; to render unfit or unsuited; to disqualify; to affect with indisposition.—**indisposed**, in·dis·pōzd′, *p.* and *a.* Not disposed; disinclined; averse; slightly disordered in health, somewhat ill.—**indisposition**, in·dis′po·zish″on, *n.* The state of being indisposed; disinclination; want of tendency; slight ailment or disorder of the health.

indisputable, in·dis·pū′ta·bl, *a.* [Prefix *in,* not, and *disputable.*] Incapable of being disputed; incontrovertible; incontestable.—**indisputability, indisputableness**, in·dis·pū′ta·bil″i·ti, in·dis·pū′ta·bl·nes, *n.* The state or quality of being indisputable.— **indisputably**, in·dis·pū′ta·bli, *adv.*

In an indisputable manner; incontrovertibly.

indissoluble, in·dis·sol′ū·bl, *a.* [Prefix *in*, not, and *dissoluble*; L. *indissolubilis*.] Not capable of being dissolved; not capable of being broken or rightfully violated; perpetually binding or obligatory (agreement, ties, etc.); firm; stable.—**indissolubility, indissolubleness,** in·dis·sol′ū·bil′i·ti, in·dis·sol′ū·bl·nes, *n.* The quality of being indissoluble.—**indissolubly,** in·dis·sol′ū·bli, *adv.* In an indissoluble manner.

indistinct, in·dis·tingkt′, *a.* [Prefix *in*, not, and *distinct*; L. *indistinctus*.] Not distinct; not readily distinguishable; faint to the sight; obscure to the mind; not clear; confused; imperfect or dim (*indistinct* vision).—**indistinctly,** in·dis·tingkt′li, *adv.* In an indistinct manner; not clearly; dimly or obscurely.—**indistinctness,** in·dis·tingkt′nes, *n.* The quality or condition of being indistinct.

indistinguishable, in·dis·ting′gwish·a·bl, *a.* [Prefix *in*, not, and *distinguishable*.] Incapable of being distinguished; undistinguishable.—**indistinguishably,** in·dis·ting′gwish·a·bli, *adv.* So as not to be distinguishable.

indite, in·dīt′, *v.t.*—*indited, inditing.* [O.Fr. *inditer.* INDICT.] To compose or write; to direct, prompt, or dictate.—*v.i.* To compose; to write; to pen.—**inditement,** in·dīt′ment, *n.* The act of inditing.—**inditer,** in·dī′tėr, *n.* One who indites.

indium, in′di·um, *n.* [From the *indigo* lines in its spectrum.] A rare metallic element, white, malleable, and easily fusible, found in various ores. Symbol, In; at. no., 49; at. wt., 114.82.

individual, in·di·vid′ū·al, *a.* [Fr. *individuel*, from L. *individuus*, indivisible—*in*, not, and *dividuus*, divisible. DIVIDE.] Subsisting as one indivisible entity or distinct being; single; one; pertaining to one only; peculiar to or characteristic of a single person or thing.—*n.* A being or thing forming one of its kind; a single person, animal, or thing; especially, a human being; a person.—**individualism,** in·di·vid′ū·al·izm, *n.* The quality of being individual; individuality; self-interest; a system or condition in which each individual works for his own ends, in either social, political, or religious matters.—**individualistic,** in·di·vid′ū·al·is″tik, *a.* Pertaining to or characterized by individualism.—**individuality,** in·di·vid′ū·al′i·ti, *n.* The condition of being individual; existence as an individual; oneness; the sum of the characteristics or traits peculiar to an individual.—**individualization,** in·di·vid′ū·al·ī·zā″shon, *n.* The act of individualizing.—**individualize,** in·di·vid′ū·al·īz, *v.t.*—*individualized, individualizing.* To mark as an individual; to distinguish by peculiar or distinctive characters.—**individually,** in·di·vid′ū·al·li, *adv.* In an individual manner; separately; each by itself.—**individuate,** in·di·vid′ū·āt, *v.t.*—*individ-*

uated, individuating. To give the character of individuality to; to individualize.—*v.i.* To become individual.—**individuation,** in′di·vid·ū·ā″shon, *n.* The act of individuating, or state of being.

indivisible, in·di·viz′i·bl, *a.* [Prefix *in*, not, and *divisible*.] Not divisible; not separable into parts.—*n.* That which is indivisible.—**indivisibility, indivisibleness,** in·di·viz′i·bil″i·ti, in·di·viz′i·bl·nes, *n.* The state or property of being indivisible.—**indivisibly,** in·di·viz′i·bli, *adv.* In an indivisible manner.

indocile, in·dos′il or in·dō′sīl, *a.* [Prefix *in*, not, and *docile*; L. *indocilis*, unteachable.] Not docile or teachable; intractable.—**indocility,** in·dō·sil′i·ti, *n.* The quality of being indocile.

indoctrinate, in·dok′tri·nāt, *v.t.*—*indoctrinated, indoctrinating.* [L. *in*, in, and *doctrina*, learning. DOCTRINE.] To instruct in any doctrine; to imbue or cause to imbibe certain principles; to instruct.—**indoctrination,** in·dok′tri·nā″shon, *n.* The act of indoctrinating; instruction.

Indo-European, *a.* A term applied to that family of languages which includes the Sanskrit and the kindred tongues of India and Persia, Greek, Latin, and the Romance tongues, the Teutonic, Celtic, and Slavonic tongues.—*n.* An Aryan.

Indo-Germanic, *a.* A term sometimes used as equivalent to *Indo-European* or *Aryan*.

indolent, in′do·lent, *a.* [Fr. *indolent*—L. *in*, not, and *dolens, dolentis,* ppr. of *doleo*, to feel pain (whence *dolor, dole*).] Habitually idle or indisposed to labor; lazy; slothful; sluggish; idle (person, life); *med.* causing little or no pain (an *indolent* tumor)—**indolently,** in′do·lent·li, *adv.* In an indolent manner.—**indolence,** in·do′lens, *n.* The condition or quality of being indolent; laziness; sloth.

indomitable, in·dom′i·ta·bl, *a.* [L. prefix *in*, not, and *domito*, freq. of *domo, domitum*, to tame. DAUNT, TAME.] Not to be tamed or subdued; unconquerable; untamable.—**indomitably,** in·dom′i·ta·bli, *adv.* In an indomitable manner.

indoor, in′dōr, *a.* Being within doors; domestic (an *indoor* servant).—**indoors,** in′dōrz, *adv.* Within doors; inside a house.

indorse, in·dors′, *v.t.* Same as *Endorse*.

indri, in′dri, *n.* [Native name, signifying 'man of the woods'.] A tailless quadrumanous animal of the lemur family, a native of Madagascar, about the size of a cat.

indubitable, in·dū′bi·ta·bl, *a.* Prefix *in*, not, and *dubitable*; L. *indubitabilis*.] Not dubitable; too plain to admit of doubt; incontestable; unquestionable. —**indubitableness,** in·dū′bi·ta·bl·nes, *n.* State of being indubitable.—**indubitably,** in·dū′bi·ta·bli, *adv.* In an indubitable manner; undoubtedly; unquestionably.

induce, in·dūs′, *v.t.*—*induced, inducing.* [L. *induco, inductum*—*in*, in,

and *duco*, to lead. DUKE.] To lead by persuasion or argument; to prevail on; to draw by motives; to impel; to bring on, produce, cause (an ailment *induced* by overstudy); to establish a theory from observation of situations or given facts. —*Induced current*, an electric current excited by the presence of a primary current.—*Induced magnetism*, magnetism produced in soft iron when a magnet is held near, or a wire through which an electric current is passing is coiled round it.—**inducement,** in·dūs′ment, *n.* The act of inducing; that which induces or leads one to act; a motive; a consideration that leads to action.—**inducer,** in·dū′sėr, *n.* One who or that which induces.—**inducible,** in·dū′si·bl, *a.* Capable of being induced; capable of being inferred.

induct, in·dukt′, *v.t.* [L. *inductus*, pp. of *inducere*, to lead in, introduce, induce.] To bring into; to introduce; to install in office; to call into military service.—**inductance,** in·duk′tans, *n.* That in a circuit or circuit element that resists changes in the flow of current, therefore causing changes in current to lag behind changes in voltage.—**inductee,** in·duk·tee′, *n.* One called into military service.—**induction,** in·duk′shon, *n.* The act of inducting; introduction; installation in office or benefice; *logic*, the method of reasoning from particulars to generals; the deriving of a general principle or conclusion from particular facts; the conclusion or inference thus drawn or arrived at; *phys.* the property by which one body, having electrical, galvanic, or magnetic polarity, causes or induces it in another body without direct contact.—*Induction coil*, an apparatus for producing electric currents by induction and for utilizing them.—**inductive,** in·duk′tiv, *a.* Proceeding by induction; employed in drawing conclusions by induction; *elect.* able to produce electricity by induction; operating by induction; facilitating induction.—**inductively,** in·duk′tiv·li, *adv.*—**inductor,** in·duk′tėr, *n.* A device possessing inductance.

inductile, in·duk′til, *a.* [Prefix *in*, not and *ductile*.] Not ductile.—**inductility,** in·duk·til′i·ti, *n.* The quality of being inductile.

indue, in·dū′, *v.t.*—*indued, induing.* [L. *induo*, from *indu*, old form of *in*, in, and verbal stem seen also in *exuo*, to put off (whence *exuviæ*).] To put on, as clothes; to clothe or invest; hence, to furnish; to supply; to endow.

indulge, in·dulj′, *v.t.*—*indulged, indulging.* [L. *indulgeo*, to indulge or give one's self up to; origin doubtful.] To give one's self up to; not to restrain or oppose; to give free course to (to *indulge* the passions); to gratify by compliance; to humor to excess (to *indulge* children).—*v.i.* To indulge one's self; to practice indulgence; to be self-indulgent (to *indulge* in pleasure).—**indulgence,** in·dul′jens, *n.* [L. *indulgentia*.] The act or practice of indulging; an indulgent act; favor granted; intemperance in eating and drinking; readiness to forgive faults; tolerance; *R. Cath. Ch.* remission, by church authority, to a repentant sinner, of the penance attached to certain sins.—*The Declaration of Indulgence*, illegal declarations or proclamations by Charles II in 1672, and by James II in 1687, dispensing with penal laws against Roman Catholics and Dissenters.—**indulgent**, in·dul′jent, *a.* [L. *indulgens*, *indulgentis*, ppr. of *indulgeo*.] Prone to indulge or humor; overcompliant; not strict.—**indulgently**, in·dul′jent·li, *adv.* In an indulgent manner.—**indulger**, in·dul′jėr, *n.* One who indulges.

induplicate, in·dū′pli·kāt, *a.* [L. *in*, in, and *duplicatus*, doubled.] *Bot.* having the edges bent or rolled inward, as petals or leaves in the bud.

indurate, in′dū·rāt, *v.i.* [L. *induro*, *induratum*—prefix *in*, intens., and *duro*, to harden, from *durus*, hard, whence also *durable*, *durance*, etc.] To grow hard; to harden or become hard.—*v.t.*—**indurated**, **indurating**. To make hard; to harden; to make unfeeling; to render obdurate.—**induration**, in·dū·rā′shon, *n.* The act of hardening or process of growing hard; the state of being indurated.

indusium, in·dū′zi·um, *n.* pl. **indusia**, in·dū′zi·a. [L., a woman's undergarment, from *induo*, to put on. INDUE.] *Bot.* United hairs forming a sort of cup enclosing the stigma of a flower; the covering of the capsules or spore cases in ferns; *zool.* the case or covering of a larva; *anat.* the amnion.—**indusial**, in·dū′zi·al, *a.* Pertaining to an indusium; composed of or containing indusia or the cases of larvae (*indusial* limestone).

industrious, in·dus′tri·us, *a.* [L. *industrius*, from *indu*, old form of *in*, and *struo*, to fabricate. STRUCTURE.] Given to or characterized by industry; diligent in business or study; always working at something.—**industriously**, in·dus′tri·us·li, *adv.* In an industrious manner.—**industrial**, in·dus′tri·al, *a.* Pertaining to, involving, or characterized by industry (arts, establishment, capacity).—*Industrial exhibition*, *industrial museum*, an exhibition, museum of industrial products. — *Industrial school*, a school for training youth in the industrial arts and in habits of industry.—**industrialism**, in·dus′tri·al·izm, *n.* Devotion to or employment in industrial pursuits.—**industrialist**, in·dus′tri·al·ist, *n.* One engaged in industry, usually as promoter or director.—**industrialize**, in·dus′tri·al·ize, *v.t.* To make industrial.—**industrially**, in·dus′tri·al·li, *adv.* In an industrial manner.—**industry**, in′dus·tri, *n.* [L. *industria*, from *industrius*.] Diligence in employment; steady attention to work or business; assiduity; the industrial arts generally, or any one of them;

any productive occupation, especially one in which numbers of people are employed.

indwell, in·dwel′, *v.t.* To abide within; to occupy.—*v.i.* To dwell or exist in or within some place.—**indweller**, in′dwel·ėr, *n.* One who dwells in a place; an inhabitant.

inebriate, in·ē′bri·āt, *v.t.*—**inebriated**, **inebriating**. [L. *inebrio*, *inebriatum*—*in*, intens., and *ebrio*, to intoxicate, from *ebrius*, drunk, whence also *ebriety*: akin *sober*.] To make drunk; to intoxicate; to disorder the senses of; to turn the head of.—*n.* An habitual drunkard.—**inebriation**, in′ē·bri·ā″shon, *n.* The act of inebriating or state of being inebriated.—**inebriety**, in·ē·brī′e·ti, *n.* Drunkenness; intoxication.—**inebriant**, in·ē′bri·ant, *a.* [L. *inebrians*, *inebriantis*, ppr. of *inebrio*.] Intoxicating. —*n.* Anything that intoxicates.

inedible, in·ed′i·bl, *a.* Not edible.

inedited, in·ed′it·ed, *a.* [Prefix *in*, not, and *edited*.] Not edited; unpublished.

ineffable, in·ef′a·bl, *a.* [L. *ineffabilis*—prefix *in*, not, and *effabilis*, speakable, from *effor*, to speak—*ef* for *ex*, out, and *for*, *fari*, to speak. FATE.] Incapable of being expressed in words.—**ineffability**, **ineffableness**, in·ef′a·bil″i·ti, in·ef′a·bl·nes, *n.* The quality of being ineffable or unutterable.—**ineffably**, in·ef′a·bli, *adv.* In an ineffable manner; unutterably.

ineffaceable, in·ef·fā′sa·bl, *a.* [Prefix *in*, not, and *effaceable*.] Incapable of being effaced.—**ineffaceably**, in·ef·fā′sa·bli, *adv.* So as not to be effaceable; indelibly.

ineffective, in·ef·fek′tiv, *a.* [Prefix *in*, not and *effective*.] Incapable of producing any effect, or the effect intended; inefficient; useless; impotent; wanting energy.—**ineffectively**, in·ef·fek′tiv·li, *adv.* In an ineffective manner.—**ineffectiveness**, in·ef·fek′tiv·nes, *n.* Quality of being ineffective.—**ineffectual**, in·ef·fek′chū·al, *a.* [Prefix *in*, not, and *effectual*.] Not effectual; inefficient; weak.—**ineffectually**, in·ef·fek′chū·al·li, *adv.* In an ineffectual manner.—**ineffectualness**, in·ef·fek′chū·al·nes, *n.*

inefficacious, in·ef′fi·kā″shus, *a.* [Prefix *in*, not, and *efficacious*.] Not efficacious; not producing the effect desired; of inadequate power.—**inefficaciously**, in·ef′fi·kā″shus·li, *adv.* In an inefficacious manner.—**inefficaciousness**, **inefficacy**, in·ef′fi·kā″shus·nes, in·ef′fi·ka·si, *n.* Want of efficacy; ineffectualness; failure of effect.

inefficient, in·if·fish′ent, *a.* [Prefix *in*, not, and *efficient*.] Not efficient; not producing the required effect; incapable of effective action; incompetent.—*n.* One who is incompetent to perform the duties of a service.—**inefficiency**, in·if·fish′en·si, *n.* The condition or quality of being inefficient.—**inefficiently** in·if·fish′ent·li, *adv.* In an inefficient manner.

inelastic, in·ē·las′tik, *a.* [Prefix *in*, not, and *elastic*.] Not elastic; wanting

elasticity; unelastic.—**inelasticity**, in·i′las·tis″i·ti, *n.* Want of elasticity.

inelegant, in·el′e·gant, *a.* [Prefix *in*, not, and *elegant*; L. *inelegans*, *inelegantis*, inelegant.] Not elegant; wanting in elegance; wanting in anything which correct taste requires.—**elegance, inelegancy**, in·el′e·gans, in·el′e·gan·si, *n.* [L. *inelegantia*; Fr. *inélégance*.] The condition or quality of being inelegant; an inelegant point or feature.—**inelegantly**, in·el′e·gant·li, *adv.* In an inelegant manner.

ineligible, in·el′i·ji·bl, *a.* [Prefix *in*, not, and *eligible*.] Not eligible; not capable of or fit for being elected or adopted; not worthy to be chosen or preferred.—**ineligibility**, in·el′i·ji·bil″i·ti, *n.* Condition of being ineligible.—**ineligibly**, in·el′i·ji·bli, *adv.* In an ineligible manner.

ineloquent, in·el′o·kwent, *a.* [Prefix *in*, not, and *eloquent*.] Not eloquent; wanting in eloquence; not eloquently written or delivered.—**ineloquently**, in·el′o·kwent·li, *adv.* In an ineloquent manner.—**ineloquence**, in·el′o·kwens, *n.* The quality of being ineloquent.

inept, in·ept′, *a.* [L. *ineptus*—prefix *in*, not, and *aptus*, fit, apt. APT.] Unsuitable; improper; foolish; silly; nonsensical.—**ineptitude, ineptness**, in·ep′ti·tūd, in·ept′nes, *n.* [L. *ineptitudo*.] The condition or quality of being inept; unfitness; inaptitude; foolishness.—**ineptly**, in·ept′li, *adv.* In an inept manner.

inequal, in·ē′kwal, *a.* [Prefix *in*, not, and *equal*; L. *inæqualis*.] Not equal; unequal; uneven; varying.—**inequality**, in·ē·kwol′i·ti, *n.* [L. *inæqualitas*.] The condition or quality of being inequal or unequal; disparity; unevenness; want of levelness; an elevation or a depression of a surface.

inequitable, in·ek′wi·ta·bl, *a.* [Prefix *in*, not, and *equitable*.] Not equitable; not just or fair.—**inequity**, in·ek′wi·ti, *n.* Unfairness; injustice.

ineradicable, in·i·rad′i·ka·bl, *a.* [Prefix *in*, not, and *eradicable*.] Incapable of being eradicated.—**ineradicably**, in·i·rad′i·ka·bli, *adv.* So as not to be eradicated.

inert, in·ėrt′, *a.* [L. *iners*, *inertis*, unskilled, inactive—*in*, not, and *ars*, acquired skill, art. ART.] Destitute of the power of moving itself; not moving or acting; indisposed to move or act; sluggish; inactive. ∴ *Inert* refers rather to the external manifestation of a habit which may be either natural or induced; *inactive*, not exhibiting activity, often refers to a temporary, perhaps voluntary, state.—**inertia**, in·ėr′shi·a, *n.* Passiveness; inactivity; inertness; sluggishness; *phys.* the property of matter by which it retains its state of rest or of uniform rectilinear motion so long as no foreign cause occurs to change that state.—*Inertial guidance*, navigation of a missile or other aircraft through self-contained governors which respond to inertial forces.—**inertly**, in·ėrt′li, *adv.*—**inertness**, in·ėrt′nes, *n.*

inessential, in·es·sen'shal, *a.* [Prefix *in*, not, and *essential*,] Not essential; unessential.

inestimable, in·es'ti·ma·bl, *a.* [Prefix *in*, not, and *estimable*; L. *inæstimabilis*.] Incapable of being estimated or computed; too valuable or excellent to be rated or fully appreciated; incalculable.—**inestimably**, in·es'ti·ma·bli, *adv.* In a manner not to be estimated.

inevitable, in·ev'i·ta·bl, *a.* [L. *inevitabilis*, from *in*, not, and *evito*, to avoid—*e*, out, and *vito*, to shun.] Incapable of being avoided; unavoidable; admitting of no escape or evasion; certain to befall.—**inevitability, inevitableness**, in·ev'i·ta·bil''i·ti, in·ev'i·ta·bl·nes, *n.* Unavoidableness; certainty.—**inevitably**, in·ev'i·ta·bli, *adv.* Unavoidably; certainly.

inexact, in·ig·zakt', *a.* [Prefix *in*, not, and *exact*.] Not exact; not precisely correct or true.—**inexactness**, in·ig·zakt'nes, *n.* The state of being inexact; incorrectness.

inexcusable, in·iks·kū'za·bl, *a.* [Prefix *in*, not, and *excusable*.] Incapable of being excused or justified; unpardonable; indefensible.—**inexcusableness**, in·iks·kū'za·bl·nes, *n.* The condition or quality of being inexcusable.—**inexcusably**, in·eks·kū'za·bli, *adv.* In an inexcusable manner; without excuse.

inexhaustible, in·igz·as'ti·bl, *a.* [Prefix *in*, not, and *exhaustible*.] Not exhaustible; incapable of being exhausted or spent; unfailing.—**inexhaustibility**, in·igz·as'ti·bil''i·ti, *n.* The state of being inexhaustible.—**inexhaustibly**, in·igz·as'ti·bli, *adv.* In an inexhaustible manner or degree.

inexorable, in·ek'so·ra·bl, *a.* [Prefix *in*, not, and *exorable*.] Incapable of being moved by entreaty or prayer; too firm and determined to yield to supplication; unyielding; unbending; implacable.—**inexorability, inexorableness**, in·ek'so·ra·bil''i·ti, in·ek'so·ra·bl·nes, *n.* The state or quality of being inexorable.—**inexorably**, in·ek'so·ra·bli, *adv.* In an inexorable manner.

inexpedient, in·eks·pē'di·ent, *a.* [Prefix *in*, not, and *expedient*.] Not expedient; inappropriate; unsuitable to time and place; not advisable.—**inexpedience, inexpediency**, in·eks·pē'di·ens, in·eks·pē'di·en·si, *n.* The condition or quality of being inexpedient.—**inexpediently**, in·eks·pē'di·ent·li, *adv.* In an inexpedient manner.

inexpensive, in·iks·pen'siv, *a.* [Prefix *in*, not, and *expensive*.] Not expensive.

inexperience, in·iks·pē'ri·ens, *n.* [Prefix *in*, not, and *experience*.] Want of experience.—**inexperienced**, in·iks·pē'ri·enst, *a.* Not having experience.

inexpert, in·iks·pėrt', *a.* [Prefix *in*, not, and *expert*.] Not expert; not skilled.—**inexpertness**, in·iks·pėrt'nes, *n.*

inexpiable, in·eks'pi·a·bl, *a.* [Prefix *in*, not, and *expiable*; L. *inexpiabilis*.]

Incapable of being expiated; not to be atoned for; unpardonable.—**inexpiableness**, in·eks'pi·a·bl·nes, *n.*—**inexpiably**, in·eks'pi·a·bli, *adv.*

inexplicable, in·eks'pli·ka·bl, *a.* [Prefix *in*, not, and *explicable*; L. *inexplicabilis*,] Incapable of being explained or interpreted; unaccountable; mysterious.—**inexplicability, inexplicableness**, in·eks'pli·ka·bil''i·ti, in·eks'pli·ka·bl·nes, *n.* The quality of being inexplicable.—**inexplicably**, in·eks'pli·ka·bli, *adv.* In an inexplicable manner; unaccountably.

inexplicit, in·iks·plis'it, *a.* [Prefix *in*, not, and *explicit*.] Not explicit; not clear in statement; not clearly stated.

inexpressible, in·iks·pres'i·bl, *a.* [Prefix *in*, not, and *expressible*.] Not expressible; not to be uttered; unspeakable; unutterable.—**inexpressibles**, in·iks·pres'i·blz, *n. pl.* A colloquial euphemism for trousers.—**inexpressibly**, in·iks·pres'i·bli, *adv.* In an inexpressible manner.—**inexpressive**, in·iks·pres'iv, *a.* Not expressive; wanting in expression; inexpressible; ineffable.—**inexpressiveness**, in·iks·pres'iv·nes, *n.*

inextinguishable, in·iks·ting'gwish·a·bl, *a.* [Prefix *in*, not, and *extinguishable*.] Incapable of being extinguished; unquenchable (flame, thirst, desire).—**inextinguishably**, in·iks·ting'gwish·a·bli, *adv.* In an inextinguishable manner.

inextricable, in·eks'tri·ka·bl, *a.* [Prefix *in*, not, and *extricable*; L. *inextricabilis*.] Incapable of being extricated or disentangled; not permitting extrication.—**inextricableness**, in·eks'tri·ka·bl·nes, *n.*—**inextricably**, in·eks'tri·ka·bli, *adv.*

infallible, in·fal'i·bl, *a.* [Prefix *in*, not, and *fallible*.] Not fallible; not capable of erring or falling into error; not leading into error; perfectly reliable; certain (*infallible* testimony).—**infallibly**, in·fal'i·bli, *adv.* In an infallible manner.—**infallibility**, in·fal'i·bil''i·ti, *n.* The quality of being infallible.—*Infallibility of the pope*, the dogma established as an article of faith in 1870, that the pope, when speaking as pope upon matters of faith or morals, is infallible.

infamy, in'fa·mi, *n.* [L. *infamia*, ill fame, ill report, from *infamis*, infamous—*in*, not, and *fama*, fame.] Total loss of reputation; public disgrace; bad or disgraceful repute; shamefulness; disgracefulness; scandalousness; extreme baseness or vileness.—**infamous**, in'fa·mus, *a.* Having a reputation of the worst kind; scandalous; notoriously vile; shameful; branded with infamy.—**infamously**, in'fa·mus·li, *adv.* Scandalously; disgracefully; shamefully.

infant, in'fant, *n.* [L. *infans, infantis*, that cannot speak, an infant—prefix *in*, not, and *fari*, to speak. FAME.] A child in the first two or three years of life; *law*, a person not of legal age.—*a.* Pertaining to infancy.—**infancy**, in'fan·si, *n.* [L. *infantia*.] The state of being an infant; earliest period of life; *law*, the period

from birth to twenty-one; nonage; minority; the first age of anything.—**infanta**, in·fan'tä, *n., fem.*; **infante**, in·fan'tā, *n., m.* Formerly in Spain and Portugal, children of the king except the eldest son.—**infanticide**, in·fan'ti·sīd, *n.* [L. *infanticidium*, the crime, *infanticida*, the perpetrator—*infans*, and *cædo*, to kill.] The murder and murderer of an infant: child murder.—**infantile**, in'fan·til, *a.* Pertaining to or characteristic of infancy or an infant.—**infantile paralysis**, *n.* Poliomyelitis.—**infantilism**, in·fan'ti·lizm, *n.* Childlike speech patterns; retarded anatomical, physiological, and psychological development in adults.

infantry, in'fant·ri, *n.* [Fr. *infanterie*, It. *infanteria*, infantry (lit. a band of youths), from *infante*, a young person, originally an infant.] The soldiers or troops that serve on foot, as distinguished from *cavalry*.

infatuate, in·fat'ū·āt, *v.t.*—**infatuated, infatuating**. [L. *infatuo, infatuatum*, to make foolish—prefix *in*, intens., and *fatuus*, foolish (whence *fatuous*).] To make foolish; to inspire with folly; to inspire with an extravagant passion that cannot be controlled.—**infatuated**, in·fat'ū·ā·ted, *p.* and *a.* Affected with folly; besotted; inspired with foolish passion.—**infatuation**, in·fat'ū·ā''shon, *n.* The act of infatuating or state of being infatuated; extreme folly; foolish passion.

infeasible, in·fē'zi·bl, *a.* [Prefix *in*, not, and *feasible*.] Not feasible; impracticable.

infect, in·fekt', *v.t.* [Fr. *infecter*, from L. *inficio, infectum*, to put in, to stain—*in*, into, and *facio*, to do. FACT.] To communicate disease to; to contaminate with germs or bacteria; to affect with one's mood, opinion, or beliefs; to impart qualities to (usually unfavorable); *law*, to place in danger of penalty or forfeiture.—**infector**, in·fek'tėr, *n.* —**infection**, in·fek'shon, *n.* The act or process of infecting; the state of being infected; a disease communicated from one organism to another; the imparting of qualities or mood or belief by means of example, teaching, etc.—**infectious**, in·fek'shus, *a.*—**infective**, in·fek'shus, in·fek'tiv, *a.*—**infectiously**, in·fek'shus·li, *adv.*—**infectiousness**, in·fek'shus·nes, *n.*

infecund, in·fē'kund, *a.* [Prefix *in*, not, and *fecund*: L. *infecundus*.] Not fecund; unfruitful; barren.—**infecundity**, in·fi·kun'di·ti, *n.* State of being infecund.

infelicity, in·fē·lis'i·ti, *n.* [Prefix *in*, not, and *felicity*; L. *infelicitas*.] The state of being unhappy; unhappiness; misery; unfavorableness.—**infelicitous**, in·fē·lis'i·tus, *a.* Not felicitous; unhappy; unfortunate.

infelt, in'felt, *a.* [Prefix *in*, within, and *felt*.] Felt within or deeply; heartfelt.

infer, in·fėr', *v.t.*—**inferred, inferring**. [L. *infero*, to bring in or on, to conclude—*in*, upon, and *fero*, to bear. FERTILE.] To gather or derive either by induction or deduction; to deduce, as a fact or consequence; to conclude or arrive at by reasoning.—**inferable,** in·fẽr´a·bl, *a.* Capable of being inferred; inferrible.—**inference,** in´fẽr·ens, *n.* The act of inferring; conclusion drawn or inferred; deduction; consequence.—**inferential,** in·fẽr·en´shal, *a.* Of or pertaining to an inference.—**inferentially,** in·fẽr·en´shal·li, *adv.* In an inferential manner; by way of inference.—**inferrible,** in·fẽr´i·bl, *a.* Such as may be inferred; to be gathered or concluded by reasoning.

inferior, in·fē´ri·ẽr, *a.* [L. compar. from *inferus,* low; akin *infernal.*] Lower in place, station, rank, value, importance; subordinate; *bot.* growing below some other organ; *astron.* situated between earth and sun (the *inferior* planets).—*n.* One lower in station, rank, intellect, than others.—**inferiority,** in·fē´ri·or´´i·ti, *n.* The state of being inferior.—*Inferiority complex,* a feeling of personal inferiority (real or imaginary).—**inferiorly,** in·fē´ri·ẽr·li, *adv.* In an inferior manner.

infernal, in·fẽr´nal, *a.* [L. *infernalis,* from *infernus,* infernal; akin *inferior.*] Pertaining to the lower regions, or regions of the dead; pertaining to hell; inhabiting hell; characteristic or worthy of hell or the inhabitants of hell; hellish; diabolical; wicked and detestable.—*Infernal machine,* a machine or apparatus of an explosive nature, contrived for the purposes of assassination or other mischief.—**infernally,** in·fẽr´nal·li, *adv.* In an infernal manner.—**inferno,** *n.* A hell upon earth, with general reference to the poem of Dante, the first part of his *Divine Comedy.*

infertile, in·fẽr´til or in·fẽr´til, *a.* [Prefix *in,* not, and *fertile.*] Not fertile; not fruitful or productive; barren.—**infertility,** in·fẽr·til´i·ti, *n.* Unproductiveness; barrenness.

infest, in·fest´, *v.t.* [Fr. *infester;* L. *infestare,* to attack, to molest, from *infestus,* hostile—*in,* in, and same root as *fendo* in *offendo, defendo,* to offend, defend.] To make hostile attacks or depredations on; to harass, torment, disturb, annoy.—**infestation,** in·fes·tā´shon, *n.* [L. *infestatio.*] The act of infesting.—**infester,** in·fes´tẽr, *n.* One who infests.

infidel, in´fi·del, *n.* [L. *infidelis,* faithless, unbelieving—prefix *in,* not, and *fidelis,* faithful. FIDELITY.] A disbeliever; one who has no religious faith; an atheist; not holding the true faith.—*a.* Unbelieving.—**infidelity,** in·fi·del´i·ti, *n.* [Fr. *infidélité;* L. *infidelitas.*] Want of faith or belief; atheism or disbelief in God or religion; skepticism; unfaithfulness in married persons; adultery; unfaithfulness to a charge or moral obligation; treachery; deceit.

infield, in´fēld, *n.* Baseball, the square or diamond portion of a playing field marked off by four bases; collectively, the shortstop and three basemen.—**infielder,** in´fēl´dẽr, *n.* One member of the infield; a base-man or the shortstop.

infiltrate, in·fil´trāt, *v.t.* and *i.* [Prefix *in,* and *filtrate.*] To enter by penetrating the pores or interstices of a substance; to pass through or pervade, as by filtering; to enter inconspicuously or secretly in small groups (troops *infiltrating* enemy territory).—**infiltration,** in·fil·trā´shon, *n.*

infinite, in´fi·nit, *a.* [Prefix *in,* not, and *finite;* L. *infinitus.*] Not finite; without limits; not limited or circumscribed: applied to time, space, and the Supreme Being and his attributes; exceedingly great in excellence, degree, capacity, and the like; boundless; limitless; immeasurable.—*n.* That which is infinite; an infinite space or extent; the infinite being; the Almighty.—**infinitely,** in´fi·nit·li, *adv.* In an infinite manner.—**infiniteness,** in´fi·nit·nes, *n.* The state of being infinite.—**infinitesimal,** in´fin·i·tes´´i·mal, *a.* [Fr. *infinitésimal.*] Infinitely or indefinitely small; less than any assignable quantity.—*n. Math.* an infinitely small quantity, or one less than any assignable quantity.—**infinitesimally,** in´fin·i·tes´´i·mal·li, *adv.* To an infinitesimal extent or in an infinitesimal degree.—**infinitive,** in·fin´i·tiv, *a.* [L. *infinitivus,* unlimited, indefinite.] Not limiting or restricting: a grammatical term applied to that mood of a verb which expresses the action of the verb, without limitation of person or number.—*n.* The infinitive mood.—**infinitival,** in·fin´i·ti·val, *a. Gram.* of or belonging to the infinitive mood.—**infinitude,** in·fin´i·tūd, *n.* The quality or state of being infinite; infinite extent; infinity; immensity; boundless number.—**infinity,** in·fin´i·ti, *n.* [L. *infinitas.*] Unlimited extent of time, space, quantity, excellence.

infirm, in·fẽrm´, *a.* [Prefix *in,* not, and *firm;* L. *infirmus,* not strong, weak, feeble.] Not firm or sound; weak as regards the body; feeble; not steadfast; irresolute; not solid or stable.—**infirmary,** in·fẽr´ma·ri, *n.* A place where the infirm or sick, or those suffering from accidents, are lodged and nursed, or have their ailments attended to.—**infirmity,** in·fẽr´mi·ti, *n.* [L. *infirmitas.*] The state of being infirm; an unsound or unhealthy state of the body; a disease; a malady; an ailment, weakness, failing, defect, foible.

infix, in·fiks´, *v.t.* [L. *infigo, infixum—in,* in, into, and *figo,* to fix.] To fix or fasten in; to cause to remain or adhere, as in the mind; to implant or fix, as principles, thoughts, etc.—*n.* A part of a word similar to a prefix or suffix, but inserted in the body of a word.

inflame, in·flām´, *v.t.*—*inflamed, inflaming.* [L. *inflammo—in,* and *flammo,* to inflame, from *flamma,* flame. FLAME.] To set on fire; to kindle; to redden or make fiery (the eyes, the face); to excite or increase, as passion or appetite; to enkindle into violent action; to enrage or exasperate; *med.* to make morbidly red and swollen.—

v.i. To take fire; to grow angry; to grow hot and painful.—**inflamer,** in·flā´mẽr, *n.* One who or that which inflames.—**inflammability, inflammableness,** in·flam´a·bil´´i·ti, in·flam´a·bl·nes, *n.* The state or quality of being inflammable.—**inflammable,** in·flam´a·bl, *a.* Capable of being set on fire; easily kindled; combustible.—**inflammably,** in·flam´a·bli, *adv.* In an inflammable manner.—**inflammation,** in·fla·mā´shon, *n.* [L. *inflammatio.*] The act of inflaming; *med.* a redness and swelling of any part of an animal body, attended with heat, pain, and febrile symptoms.—**inflammatory,** in·flam´a·to·ri, *a.* Tending to inflame; tending to excite inflammation; accompanied with great heat and excitement of arterial action; tending to excite anger, animosity, or the like.

inflate, in·flāt´, *v.t.*—*inflated, inflating.* [L. *inflo, inflatum—in,* into, and *flo,* to blow. FLATULENT.] To swell or distend by injecting air; to puff up; to elate, as with pride; to raise above the real value or value according to sound commercial principles (*inflated* prices).—**inflatable,** in·flā´ta·bl, *a.* Capable of being inflated.—**inflated,** in·flā´ted, *p.* and *a.* Distended with air; puffed up; turgid; tumid; bombastic (an *inflated* style of writing.)—**inflation,** in·flā´shon, *n.* [L. *inflatio, inflationis.*] The act of inflating; the state of being inflated; sharp increase in amount of money and credit causing advances in the price level.—**inflationist,** in·flā´shon·ist, *n.* One who causes or believes in manipulated expansion of prices.

inflect, in·flekt´, *v.t.* [L. *inflecto—in,* intens., and *flecto,* to bend. FLEX.] To bend; to turn from a direct line or course; to modulate (the voice); *gram.,* to go over the inflections of; to decline or conjugate.—**inflection, inflexion,** in·flek´shon, *n.* [L. *inflexio, inflexionis.*] The act of inflecting, or the state of being inflected; modulation or rise and fall of the voice; *optics,* deflection or diffraction; *gram.* the variation of nouns, etc., by declension, and of verbs by conjugation.—**inflectional,** in·flek´shon·al, *a.* Pertaining to or having inflection.—**inflective,** in·flek´tiv, *a.* Having the power of inflecting.—**inflexed,** in·flekst´, *a.* [L. *inflexus,* pp. of *inflecto.*] Curved; bent.—*Inflexed leaf, bot.* a leaf curved or bent upward and inward at the apex.—**inflexibility,** in·flek´si·bil´´i·ti, *n.* The quality of being inflexible.—**inflexible,** in·flek´si·bl, *a.* [L. *inflexibilis,* that cannot be bent.] Incapable of being bent; firm in purpose; not to be prevailed on; incapable of being turned from a purpose; inexorable; unalterable.—**inflexibleness,** in·flek´si·bl·nes, *n.* Inflexibility.—**inflexibly,** in·flek´si·bli, *adv.* In an inflexible manner; firmly; inexorably.

inflict, in·flikt´, *v.t.* [L. *infligo, inflictum—in,* upon, and *fligo,* to strike, as in *afflict, conflict.*] To cause to bear or suffer from; to cause to feel or experience; to impose (pain, disgrace, punishment).—**inflicter,** in·flik′tèr, *n.* One who inflicts.—**infliction,** in·flik′shon, *n.* [L. *inflictio, inflictionis.*] The act of inflicting or imposing; that which is inflicted.—**inflictive,** in·flik′tiv, *a.* Tending to inflict.

inflorescence, in·flō·res′ens, *n.* [From L. *inflorescens,* ppr. of *infloresco,* to begin to blossom—*in,* intens., and *floresco,* to begin to blossom. FLOURISH.] A flowering; the unfolding of blossoms; *bot.* a mode of flowering or the manner in which blossoms are arranged and supported on their footstalks or peduncles.

influence, in′flụ·ens, *n.* [Fr. *influence,* from L. *influens, influentis,* ppr. of *influo,* to flow in—*in,* in, *fluo,* to flow. FLUENT.] Agency or power serving to affect, modify, or sway in some way; ability or power sufficient to produce some effect; sway; effect; power or authority arising from elevated station, wealth, and the like; acknowledged ascendancy with people in power.—*v.t.*—**influenced,** *influencing.* To exercise influence on; to modify or affect in some way; to act on; to bias; to sway.—**influent,** in′flụ·ent, *a.* [L. *influens, influentis,* ppr.] Flowing in.—**influential,** in·flụ·en′shal, *a.* Exerting influence.

influenza, in·flụ·en′za, *n.* [It. *influenza,* lit. influence. INFLUENCE.] An acute, infectious, and highly contagious disease affecting the respiratory tract, and producing symptoms not unlike a severe cold; pneumonia is a frequent complication, particularly when the disease is epidemic; intestinal, or abdominal, influenza attacks the digestive system

influx, in′fluks, *n.* [L. *influxus,* a flowing in, from *influo.* INFLUENCE.] The act of flowing in; infusion; inflow; a coming in; introduction; importation in abundance (an *influx* of money); the point at which one stream runs into another or into the sea.

infold, in·fōld′, *v.i.* To fold in; to wrap up or inwrap; to clasp with the arms; to embrace.

inform, in·form′, *v.t.* [Fr. *informer,* to apprise, L. *informo,* to shape, to describe—*in,* intens., and *formo,* to form, from *forma,* form.] To give form or shape to; to inspire and give life to; to actuate with vitality; to animate; to communicate knowledge to; to instruct, to tell, acquaint, apprise (to *inform* a person *of* something).—*v.i.* To give information.—*To inform against,* to communicate facts by way of accusation against.—**informant,** in·for′mant, *n.* One who informs; an informer.—**information,** in·for·mā′shon, *n.* [L. *informatio.*] The act of informing; news or intelligence communicated by word or writing; intelligence; knowledge derived from reading or instruction, or gathered in any way; a statement of facts laid before a court of justice.—**informative,** in·for′ma·tiv, *a.* Affording knowledge or information; instructive.—**in-**

former, in·for′mèr, *n.* One who informs; an accomplice who in order to escape punishment gives evidence against another or others; one who makes a business of informing against others.

informal, in·for′mal, *a.* [Prefix *in,* not, and *formal.*] Not in the regular or usual form; not in accordance with official, conventional, or customary forms; without ceremony.—**informality,** in·for·mal′i·ti, *n.* The state of being informal; want of formality.—**informally,** in·for′mal·li, *adv.* In an informal manner.

infraction, in·frak′shon, *n.* [L. *infractio, infractionis,* a breaking in pieces, from *infringo, infractum.* INFRINGE.] The act of infringing; breach; violation; infringement.

infralapsarian, in′fra·lap·sâ′ri·an, *a.* and *n.* The doctrine of the sect holding that God's election or predestination of some was consequent on his prescience of the fall, and contemplated man as already fallen. Modifications are *sublapsarian, supralapsarian.*

infrangible, in·fran′ji·bl, *a.* [Prefix *in,* not, and *frangible.*] Not capable of being broken; not to be violated or infringed.—**infrangibility, infrangibleness,** in·fran′ji·bil″i·ti, in·fran′ji·bl·nes, *n.* State or quality of being infrangible.

infrared, in·fra·red′, *a.* Pertaining to rays beyond the visible red of the spectrum.

infrasonic, in·fra·so′nik, *a.* [Prefix, *infra,* below, and *sonic,* from L. *sonus,* sound.] Beneath the range of human hearing.

infrequent, in·frē′kwent, *a.* [L. *infrequens—in,* not, and *frequens,* frequent.] Not frequent; seldom; rare. —**infrequency,** in·frē′kwen·si, *n.*—**infrequently,** in·frē′kwent·li, *adv.* Not frequently; seldom.

infringe, in·frinj′, *v.t.*—*infringed, infringing.* [L. *infringo—in,* intens., and *frango,* to break. FRACTION.] To break, as laws or contracts; to violate; to contravene; to impair or encroach on.—*v.i.* To encroach: followed by *on* or *upon.*—**infringement,** in·frinj′ment, *n.* Act of infringing or violating.—**infringer,** in·frin′jèr, *n.* One who infringes; a violator.

infundibular, infundibulate, infundibuliform, in·fun·dib′ū·lèr, in·fun·dib′ū·lāt, in·fun·dib′ū·li·form, *a.* [From *infundibulum,* a funnel—*in,* in, and *fundo,* to pour. FUSE.] Having the form of a funnel.

infuriate, in·fū′ri·āt, *v.t.*—*infuriated, infuriating.* [L.L. *infurio, infuriatum*—L. *in,* intens., and *furia,* rage, madness.] To render furious or mad; to enrage.—*a.* Enraged; mad; raging.

infuse, in·fūz′, *v.t.*—*infused, infusing.* [Fr. *infuser,* from L. *infundo, infusum,* to pour into—*in,* into, and *fundo,* to pour. FUSE.] To pour in, as a liquid; to pour; to shed; to instill, as principles or qualities; to introduce; to diffuse; to steep in liquor without boiling, in order to extract medicinal or other qualities. —**infuser,** in·fū′zèr, *n.* One who infuses.—**infusibility,** in·fū′zi·bil″i-

ti, *n.* The capability of being infused. —**infusible,** in·fū′zi·bl, *a.* Capable of being infused.—**infusion,** in·fū′zhon, *n.* The act or process of infusing; that which is infused or instilled; liquor obtained by infusing or steeping.—**infusive,** in·fū′siv, *a.* Having the power of infusion.

infusorian, in·fū·sō′ri·an, *n.* [L.] One of a group of minute, mostly microscopic animals, belonging to the class Infusoria of the protozoa.— **infusorial,** in·fū·sō′ri·al, *a.*

infusible, in·fū′zi·bl, *a.* [Prefix *in,* not, and *fusible.*] Not fusible; incapable of fusion.—**infusibility,** in·fū′zi·bil″i·ti, *n.* Absence of fusibility.

ingeminate, in·jem′i·nāt, *v.t.* [L. *ingemino, ingeminatum—in,* intens., and *gemino,* to double. GEMINATE.] To double or repeat.—*a.* Redoubled; repeated.—**ingemination,** in·jem′i·nā″shon, *n.* Repetition; reduplication.

ingenerate, in·jen′èr·āt, *v.t.* [L. *ingenero, ingeneratum—in,* and *genero,* to generate.] To generate or produce within.—*a.* Generated within; inborn; innate; inbred.

ingenious, in·jē′ni·us, *a.* [L. *ingeniosus,* able, ingenious, from *ingenium,* ability, cleverness—*in,* in, and root *gen,* to beget. GENUS.] Possessed of cleverness or ability†; having the faculty of invention; skillful or prompt to invent; apt in contriving or forming new combinations of ideas; contrived with ingenuity; of curious design, structure, or mechanism; witty or well conceived (an *ingenious* compliment).—**ingeniously,** in·jē′ni·us·li, *adv.* In an ingenious manner.—**ingeniousness,** in·jē′ni·us·nes, *n.* Ingenuity.—**ingenuity,** in·jen·ū′i·ti, *n.* [Fr. *ingénuité,* L. *ingenuitas,* from *ingenuus.* INGENUOUS.] Ingenuousness‡; the quality or power of being ingenious; ready invention; skill in contrivance. [In form, though not in meaning, this word belongs to the next entry.]

ingenuous, in·jen′ū·us, *a.* [L. *ingenuus,* inborn, freeborn, ingenuous— *in,* and root *gen,* to produce. GENUS.] Honorable, noble, or generous‡; open, frank, or candid; free from reserve, disguise, equivocation, or dissimulation; of persons or things. —**ingenuously,** in·jen′ū·us·li, *adv.* In an ingenuous manner; openly; candidly.—**ingenuousness,** in·jen′ū·us·nes, *n.* The condition or quality of being ingenuous; openness of heart; frankness.—**ingénue,** aṅ·zhā·nū′, *n.* An ingenuous, artless, naïve girl or young woman: used often of female parts in plays; also, an actress who plays such parts.

ingest, in·jest′, *v.t.* [L. *ingero, ingestum—in,* into, and *gero,* to bear. GESTURE.] To take into the stomach. —**ingestion,** in·jest′shon, *n.* The act of taking into the stomach.— **ingesta,** in·jes′ta, *n. pl.* [*Lit.* things carried in. INGEST.] Substances absorbed by an organism, or entering the alimentary canal; things taken into the mind.

inglorious, in·glō′ri·us, *a.* [Prefix *in,* not, and *glorious;* L. *inglorius.*] Not glorious; without renown; obscure; bringing disgrace rather than glory; disgraceful; ignominious.—**ingloriously**, in·glō'ri·us·li, *adv.* In an inglorious manner. — **ingloriousness**, in·glō'ri·us·nes, *n.*

ingoing, in'gō·ing, *n.* The act of entering; entrance.—*a.* Going in; entering, as on an office.

ingot, in'got, *n.* [From *in*, and A.Sax. *geótan*, D. *gieten*, to pour; originally meaning a mass of molten metal. GUSH.] A mass or wedge of gold or silver cast in a mold; a mass of unwrought metal.

ingraft, in·graft', *v.t.* [*In* and *graft*.] To graft; to attach by grafting; hence, to insert; to introduce; to set or fix deeply and firmly.

ingrain, in·grān', *v.t.* To dye with grain or kermes; hence, from the permanence and excellence of this dye, to dye in any deep, permanent, or enduring color; to dye deep; to incorporate with the grain or texture of anything; to paint in imitation of the grain of wood; to grain.

ingrate, in'grāt, *n.* [Fr. *ingrat*, from L. *ingratus*, ungrateful—*in*, not, and *gratus*, grateful.] An ungrateful person.

ingratiate, in·grā'shi·āt, *v.t.*—*ingratiated*, *ingratiating*. [L. *in*, into, and *gratia*, favor. GRACE.] To introduce or commend to another's good will, confidence, or kindness: always *refl.*

ingratitude, in·grat'i·tūd, *n.* [Prefix *in*, not, and *gratitude*.] Want of gratitude; insensibility to favors, and want of a disposition to repay them; unthankfulness.

ingredient, in·grē'di·ent, *n.* [L. *ingrediens*, *ingredientis*, ppr. of *ingredior*, to go in—*in*, into, and *gradior*, to go. GRADE.] That which enters into a compound or is a component part of any compound or mixture; an element, component, or constituent.

ingress, in'gres, *n.* [L. *ingressus*, a going into, from *ingredior*. INGREDIENT.] Entrance; *astron.* the entrance of the moon into the shadow of the earth in eclipses, the sun's entrance into a sign, etc.; power or liberty of entrance; means of entering.—*v.i.* (in·gres'). To go in or enter.—**ingression**, in·gresh'on, *n.* [L. *ingressio*.] The act of entering; entrance.

inguinal, in'gwi·nal, *a.* [L. *inguinalis*, from *inguen*, *inguinis*, the groin.] Pertaining to the groin.

ingulf, in·gulf', *v.t.* Same as *Engulf*.

ingurgitate, in·gėr'ji·tāt, *v.t.*—*ingurgitated*, *ingurgitating*. [L. *ingurgito*, *ingurgitatum*, to gorge—*in*, into, and *gurges*, a gulf. GORGE.] To swallow eagerly or in great quantity.—*v.i.* to drink largely; to swill.—**ingurgitation**, in·gėr'ji·tā'shon, *n.* The act of ingurgitating.

inhabit, in·hab'it, *v.t.* [L. *inhabito—in*, and *habito*, to dwell. HABIT.] To live or dwell in; to occupy as a place of settled residence.—*v.i.* To dwell; to live; to abide.—**inhabitable**, in·hab'i·ta·bl, *a.* Capable of being inhabited; habitable.—**inhabitancy**, in·hab'i·tan·si, *n.* The condition of an inhabitant; habitancy.—**inhabitant**,

in·hab'i·tant, *n.* [L. *inhabitans*, *inhabitantis*, ppr. of *inhabita*.] One who inhabits; one who dwells or resides permanently in a place, as distinguished from an occasional visitor.—**inhabitation**, in·hab'i·tā'shon, *n.* The act of inhabiting; an abode.—**inhabiter**, in·hab'i·tėr, *n.* One who inhabits; an inhabitant (N.T.).

inhale, in·hāl', *v.t.*—*inhaled*, *inhaling*. [L. *inhalo—in*, in, into, and *halo*, to breathe, as in *exhale*.] To draw into the lungs; to inspire; to suck in.—**inhaler**, in·hā'lėr, *n.* One who inhales; *med.* an apparatus for inhaling vapors and volatile substances, as steam of hot water, vapor of chloroform, iodine, etc.; a respirator.—**inhalant**, in·hā'lant, *a.* Inhaling.—**inhalation**, in·ha·lā'shon, *n.* The act of inhaling.

inharmonic, **inharmonical**, in·här·mon'ik, in·här·mon'i·kal, *a.* Not harmonic; inharmonious; discordant. —**inharmonious**, in·här·mō'ni·us, *a.* Not harmonious; discordant.—**inharmoniously**, in·här·mō'ni·us·li, *adv.* In an inharmonious manner. —**inharmoniousness**, in·här·mō'ni·us·nes, *n.* Want of harmony; discord.

inhere, in·hēr', *v.i.*—*inhered*, *inhering*. [L. *inhæreo*, *inhæsum—in*, and *hæreo*, to stick, as in *adhere*, *cohere*, *hesitate*.] To exist or be fixed in; to belong, as attributes or qualities, to a subject; to be innate.—**inherence**, **inherency**, in·hē'rens, in·hē'ren·si, *n.* The state of inhering; existence in something.—**inherent**, in·hē'rent, *a.* [L. *inhærens*, *inhærentis*, ppr. of *inhæreo*.] Inhering; inseparable; naturally pertaining; inborn; innate.—**inherently**, in·hē'rent·li, *adv.* In an inherent manner.

inherit, in·her'it, *v.t.* [O.Fr. *enheriter*, L. *inhæredito*, to inherit, from *hæres*, *hæredis*, an heir. HEIR.] To receive or obtain by descent from an ancestor; to take by being the heir; to receive from a progenitor as part of one's nature; to come into possession of; to hold as belonging to one's lot.—*v.i.* To take an inheritance; to take the position of heir or heirs.—**inheritability**, in·her'i·ta·bil'i·ti, *n.* The quality of being inheritable.—**inheritable**, in·her'i·ta·bl, *a.* Capable of being inherited; capable of being transmitted from parent to child.—**inheritance**, in·her'i·tans, *n.* That which is or may be inherited; an estate derived or to be derived from an ancestor to his heir; a possession received by gift or without purchase. —**inheritor**, in·her'i·tėr, *n.* One who inherits or may inherit; an heir.—**inheritress**, **inheritrix**, in·her'it·res, in·her'it·riks, *n.* An heiress.

inhibit, in·hib'it, *v.t.* [L. *inhibeo*, *inhibitum*, to restrain—*in*, in, and *habeo*, to have. HABIT.] To restrain by command or interdict; to hinder; to forbid, prohibit, or interdict.—**inhibiter**, in·hib'i·tėr, *n.*—**inhibition**, in·hi·bish'on, *n.* The act of inhibiting; *physiol.* the restraining of an action by stimulating an antagonistic action; *psych.* restraint of spontaneous activity by psychological

impediments or social or cultural controls; suppressive interaction between two or more processes.—**inhibitory**, in·hib'i·to·ri, *a.*

inhospitable, in·hos'pi·ta·bl, *a.* [Prefix *in*, not, and *hospitable*.] Not hospitable; wanting in hospitality; hence, affording no subsistence or shelter to strangers (*inhospitable* shores).—**inhospitality**, **inhospitableness**, in·hos'pi·tal'i·ti, in·hos'pi·ta·bl·nes, *n.* The quality of being inhospitable.—**inhospitably**, in·hos'pi·ta·bli, *adv.* In an inhospitable manner.

inhuman, in·hū'man, *a.* [Prefix *in*, not, and *human*; L. *inhumanus*.] Destitute of the kindness and tenderness that belong to human beings; cruel; barbarous; savage; unfeeling. —**inhumanity**, in·hū·man'i·ti, *n.*—**inhumanly**, in·hū'man·li, *adv.*

inhume, in·hūm', *v.t.*—*inhumed*, *inhuming*. [Fr. *inhumer*, L. *inhumo*, *inhumatum—in*, in, and *humus*, the ground. HUMBLE.] To deposit in the earth; to bury; to inter (a dead body).—**inhumation**, in·hū·mā'shon, *n.* The act of burying; interment.

inimical, in·im'i·kal, *a.* [L. *inimicus* —*in*, not, and *amicus*, friendly. AMICABLE.] Unfriendly; hostile; adverse; hurtful (*inimical* to commerce). —**inimically**, in·im'i·kal·li, *adv.* In an inimical manner.

inimitable, in·im'i·ta·bl, *a.* [Prefix *in*, not, and *imitable*.] Incapable of being imitated or copied; surpassing imitation.—**inimitability**, **inimitableness**, in·im'i·ta·bil'i·ti, in·im'i·ta·bl·nes, *n.* The quality of being inimitable.—**inimitably**, in·im'i·ta·bli, *adv.* In an inimitable manner.

inion, in'i·on, *n.* [Gr. *inion*, the nape.] *Anat.* the ridge of the occiput; the nape.

iniquity, in·ik'wi·ti, *n.* [L. *iniquitas*, from *iniquus*, unequal, from *in*, not, and *æquus*, equal. EQUAL.] Want of equity; a deviation from rectitude; unrighteousness; a sin or crime; wickedness; an act of injustice.—**iniquitous**, in·ik'wi·tus, *a.* Characterized by iniquity; unjust; wicked; unrighteous.—**iniquitously**, in·ik'wi·tus·li, *adv.* In an iniquitous manner.

initial, in·ish'al, *a.* [L. *initialis*, from *initium*, beginning, from *ineo*, *initum*, to go in—*in*, in, and *eo*, *itum*, to go, present also in *ambition*, *exit*, *circuit*, *issue*, *transient*, etc. AMBITION.] Placed at the beginning (an *initial* letter); of or pertaining to the beginning; beginning; incipient.—*n.* The first letter of a word: a person's *initials* are the first letters in proper order of the words composing his name.—*v.t.*—*initialed*, *initialing.* To put one's initials on or to; to sign or mark by initials.—**initially**, in·ish'al·li, *adv.* In an initial manner; by way of beginning.—**initiate**, in·ish'i·āt, *v.t.* —*initiated*, *initiating.* [L. *initio*, *initiatum*, from *initium*.] To begin or enter upon; to set afoot; to be the first to practice or bring in; to guide or direct by instruction in rudiments or principles; to let into secrets; to indoctrinate; to introduce into a society or organization; to admit.— *a.* Initiated; introduced to the knowledge of something.—**initiation,** in··ish′i·ā″shon, *n.* The act or process of initiating.—**initiative,** in·ish′i·a·tiv, *a.* Serving to initiate; initiatory.—*n.* An introductory act or step; the first active procedure in any enterprise; power of taking the lead or of originating.—**initiatory,** in·ish′i·a·to·ri, *a.* Pertaining to initiation or introduction; introductory; initiating or serving to initiate.

inject, in·jekt′, *v.t.* [L. *injicio, injectum—in,* into, and *jacio,* to throw, as in *abject, eject, reject,* etc. DEJECT, JET.] To throw in; to cast in or into. —**injection,** in·jek′shon, *n.* The act of injecting; the throwing of a liquid medicine into a cavity of the body by a syringe or pipe; that which is injected.—**injector,** in·jek′tėr, *n.* One who or that which injects; an apparatus for supplying the boilers of steam engines with water.

injudicious, in·ju·dish′us, *a.* [Prefix *in,* not, and *judicious.*] Not judicious; acting without judgment; not according to sound judgment or discretion; unwise; indiscreet; inconsiderate.—**injudiciously,** in·ju·dish′us·li, *adv.* In an injudicious manner.—**injudiciousness,** in·ju·dish′us·nes, *n.*

injunction, in·jungk′shon, *n.* [L. *injunctio, injunctionis,* from *injungo,* to enjoin—*in,* and *jungo,* to join. JOIN.] The act of enjoining or directing; that which is enjoined; a command, order, precept; *law,* a writ requiring a person to do or refrain from doing certain acts.

injure, in′jur, *v.t.*—*injured, injuring.* [Fr. *injurier,* L. *injurior, injuriari,* from *injuria,* injury, *injurius,* injurious, from *in,* not, and *jus, juris,* right, justice. JURY.] To do harm or injury to; to impair the excellence, value, strength, etc., of; to hurt; to damage.—**injurer,** in′jur·ėr, *n.* One who or that which injures.—**injurious,** in·ju′ri·us, *a.* [L. *injurius.*] Tending to injure; hurtful; harmful; prejudicial.—**injuriously,** in·ju′ri·us·li, *adv.* In an injurious or hurtful manner.—**injuriousness,** in·ju′ri·us·nes, *n.* The quality of being injurious.—**injury,** in′ju·ri, *n.* [L. *injuria,* from *injurius.*] The doing of harm; harm or damage occasioned; a wrong or loss received; mischief; detriment.

injustice, in·jus′tis, *n.* [L. *injustitia—in,* not, and *justitia,* justice.] Want of justice or equity; any violation of another's rights; iniquity; wrong.

ink, ingk, *n.* [O.E. *enke, inke,* O.Fr. *enque,* Fr. *encre,* Pr. *encaut,* from L. *encaustum,* purple ink used by the Roman emperors, from Gr. *enkaustos,* burned in—*en,* in, and *kaiō,* to burn (whence *caustic, encaustic, calm*).] A colored liquid, usually black, used for writing, printing, and the like; a pigment, as China or India *ink* (under INDIAN).—*v.t.* To blacken, color, or daub with ink.— **inkhorn,** ingk′horn, *n.* [From horns being formerly used for holding ink.] A small vessel used to hold ink on a writing table or desk, or for carrying it about the person.—**inkstand,** ingk′stand, *n.* A vessel for holding ink and other writing utensils.— **inkwell,** *n.* An ink bottle fitted into a hole in the top of a writing-desk.— **inky,** ingk′i, *a.* Consisting of ink; containing ink; smeared with ink; resembling ink; black.

inkle, ingk′l, *n.* [Formerly *lingle,* then, by loss of *l, ingle, inkle,* from Fr. *ligneul, lignol,* strong thread used by shoemakers, L. *linum,* flax (whence *linen*).] Formerly, a kind of crewel or worsted; afterward a sort of broad linen tape.

inkling, ingk′ling, *n.* [M. E. *inclen,* to hint.] A hint or whisper; an intimation; inclination; desire.

inlaid, in·lād′, *pp.* of *inlay.*

inland, in′land, *a.* [That is, *in the land* or interior as opposed to the coast.] Interior; remote from the sea; carried on within a country; domestic, not foreign; confined to a country; drawn and payable in the same country (an *inland* bill of exchange).—*adv.* In or toward the interior of a country.—*n.* The interior part of a country.—**inlander,** in′lan·dėr, *n.* One who lives in the interior of a country.

inlay, in·lā′, *v.t.*—*pret. & pp. inlaid.* [*In* and *lay.*] To lay or insert in; to ornament or diversify by inserting precious stones, metals, fine woods, ivory, etc., in a groundwork of some other material.—*n.* Pieces inlaid and forming a pattern.—**inlayer,** in·lā′ėr, *n.* One who inlays.

inlet, in′let, *n.* [Something *let in.*] A passage or opening by which an enclosed place may be entered; place of ingress; entrance; a creek or narrow recess in a shore.

inlier, in·lī′ėr, *n. Geol.* a portion of one formation lying in and completely surrounded by another formation: opposed to *outlier.*

inly, in′li, *adv.* [Adv. *in,* and suffix *-ly.*] Internally; in the heart; secretly.

inmate, in′māt, *n.* [*In* or *inn,* and *mate.*] A person who lodges or dwells in the same house with another; one of the occupants of hospitals, asylums, prisons, etc.

inmesh, in·mesh′, *v.t.* Same as *Enmesh.* To involve in meshes, as of a net; to entangle or ensnare.

inmost, in′mōst, *a.* [A.Sax. *innemest,* a double superlative of the prep. or adv. *in,* altered erroneously like *foremost.* FOREMOST.] Farthest within; remotest from the surface or external part.

inn, in, *n.* [A.Sax. *inn,* a chamber, a house, an inn; Icel. *inni,* a house; from the prep. *in.*] A house for the lodging and entertainment of travelers; a college of law professors and students.—*Inns of Court,* certain colleges or corporate societies in London; they are now four, the Inner Temple, the Middle Temple, Lincoln's Inn, and Gray's Inn.— **innkeeper,** in′kē·pėr, *n.* The keeper of an inn.

innate, in·nāt′, *a.* [L. *innatus—in,* in, and *natus,* born. NATAL.] Inborn; belonging to the body or mind by nature; natural; derived from the constitution of the mind, as opposed to being derived from experience (*innate* ideas).—**innately,** in·nāt′li, *adv.* In an innate manner.—**innateness,** in·nāt′nes, *n.* The quality of being innate.

inner, in′ėr, *a.* [A.Sax. *innera,* compar. of *in.*] Interior; farther inward than something else; internal; not outward (the *inner* man); not obvious; esoteric.—*n.* The center, or that part of a rifle target next to the bull's-eye; a shot that strikes the center.—**innermost,** in′ėr·mōst, *a.* Farthest inward.

innerve, in·nėrv′, *v.t.* [Prefix *in,* in, and *nerve.*] To give nerve to; to invigorate; to strengthen.—**innervation,** in·nėr·vā′shon, *n.* Act of innerving or strengthening; *physiol.* the properties or functions of the nervous system; a special activity in any part of the nervous system.

inning, in′ing, *n.* [Lit. the state of being *in*; a sort of verbal noun.] *Baseball, Cricket,* etc. A team's turn at bat and to score; opposing teams each having innings in a game of baseball; a turn or opportunity in other ways.

innocent, in′no·sent, *a.* [L. *innocens, innocentis,* harmless—*in,* not, and *nocens,* ppr. of *noceo,* to hurt. NOXIOUS.] Not noxious or hurtful; free from guilt; not having done wrong or violated any law; guiltless; sinless; pure; upright; free from the guilt of a particular crime or evil action.—*n.* One free from guilt or harm; an innocent person; a natural or simpleton.—**innocently,** in′no·sent·li, *adv.* In an innocent manner. —**innocence, innocency,** in′no·sens, in′no·sen·si, *n.* [L. *innocentia.*] The quality of being innocent; harmlessness; freedom from crime, guilt, or sin; freedom from the guilt of a particular crime.

innocuous, in·nok′ū·us, *a.* [L. *innocuus—in,* not, and *nocuus,* hurtful, from *noceo,* to hurt. INNOCENT.] Harmless; producing no ill effect.— **innocuously,** in·nok′ū·us·li, *adv.* In an innocuous manner.—**innocuousness,** in·nok′ū·us·nes, *n.*

innominable, in·nom′i·na·bl, *a.* [L. *innominabilis—in,* not, and *nomen,* a name.] Not to be named.— **innominate,** in·nom′i·nāt, *a.* [L. *innominatus.*] Having no name.— *Innominate bone,* the bony mass forming either side of the pelvis and consisting of three bones that have grown together.

innovate, in′no·vāt, *v.t.*‡—*innovated, innovating.* [L. *innovo, innovatum,* to renew—*in,* intens., and *novus,* new (whence *novel*). NEW.] To change or alter by introducing something new.—*v.i.* To introduce novelties; to make changes in anything established: with *on* or *in* (to *innovate on* established customs). —**innovation,** in·no·vā′shon, *n.* The act of innovating; change made in established laws, customs, rites, and practices by the introduction of something new.—**innovator,** in′no·vā·tėr, *n.* One who innovates.—

innovationist, in·no·vā′shon·ist, *n.* One who favors or introduces innovations.—**innovative,** in′no·vā·tiv, *a.* Introducing or tending to introduce innovations.

innuendo, in·nü·en′dō, *n.* [L. *innuendo* (ablative of gerund), by giving a nod, *innuo,* to give a nod—*in,* and *nuo,* Gr. *neuō,* to nod.] An oblique hint; a remote intimation; an insinuation.

innumerable, in·nū′mėr·a·bl, *a.* [L. *innumerabilis—in,* not, and *numerabilis,* from *numero,* to number.] Incapable of being enumerated or numbered for multitude; hence, extremely numerous; countless.—**innumerably,** in·nū′mėr·a·bli, *adv.* Without number.—**innumerous,**† in·nū′mėr·us, *a.* [L. *innumerus.*] Innumerable. [*Mil.*]—**innumerableness,** in·nū′mėr·a·bl·nes, *n.*

innutrition, in·nu·trish′on, *n.* [Prefix *in,* not, and *nutrition.*] Want of nutrition or nourishment.—**innutritious,** in·nū·trish′us, *a.* Not nutritious; not nourishing.

inobservable, in·ob·zėr′va·bl, *a.* [Prefix *in,* not, and *observable.*] Incapable of being seen, perceived, or observed.—**inobservance,** in·ob·zėr′vans, *n.* Want of observance; disobedience.—**inobservant,** in·ob·zėr′vant, *a.* [Prefix *in,* not, and *observant.*] Not taking notice; not quick or keen in observation; heedless; disobedient.

inoculate, in·ok′ū·lāt, *v.t.*—*inoculated, inoculating.* [L. *inoculo, inoculatum,* to ingraft an eye or bud of one tree into another—*in,* into, and *oculus,* an eye (whence *ocular*).] To graft by inserting a bud; to bud; *med.* to communicate a disease to by introducing its germs or virus into the tissues; to communicate a disease to a healthy body in order to produce immunity through a mild form of the disease.—*v.i.* To practice inoculation.—**inoculation,** in·ok′ū·lā″shon, *n.* The act or practice of inoculating.—**inoculator,** in·ok′ū·lā·tėr, *n.* One who inoculates.

inoffensive, in·of·fen′siv, *a.* [Prefix *in,* and *offensive.*] Giving no offense or provocation; harmless; doing no injury or mischief.—**inoffensively,** in·of·fen′siv·li, *adv.* In an inoffensive manner.—**inoffensiveness,** in·of·fen′siv·nes, *n.*

inoperative, in·op′e·rā·tiv, *a.* [Prefix *in,* not, and *operative.*] Not operative; producing no effect.

inopportune, in·op′por·tūn, *a.* [Prefix *in,* not, and *opportune;* L. *inopportunus.*] Not opportune; inconvenient; unseasonable.—**inopportunely,** in·op′por·tūn·li, *adv.* In an inopportune manner.

inordinate, in·or′di·nāt, *a.* [L. *inordinatus—in,* not, and *ordinatus,* well-ordered. ORDER.] Excessive; immoderate; not limited by rules prescribed or to usual bounds.—**inordinateness,** in·or′di·nāt·nes, *n.* The state or quality of being inordinate.—**inordinately,** in·or′di·nāt·li, *adv.* In an inordinate manner; excessively.

inorganic, in·or·gan′ik, *a.* [Prefix *in,* not, and *organic.*] Having no organs;

devoid of an organized structure, or the structure of a living being; pertaining to or embracing the department of unorganized substances (*inorganic* chemistry).

inosculate, in·os′kū·lāt, *v.i.*—*inosculated, inosculating.* [L. *in,* and *osculor, osculatus,* to kiss. OSCULATION.] To unite by apposition or contact, as arteries, nerves, geometrical curves, etc.; to anastomose; to run into one another.—*v.t.*—*inosculated, inosculating.* To cause to unite in this way.—**inosculation,** in·os′kū·lā″shon, *n.*

inosite, ī′no·sit, *n.* [Gr. *is, inos,* strength, nerve.] A saccharine substance found in the human body and also in plants.

inpatient, *n.* A patient who is lodged, fed, and treated in hospital or infirmary.

inphase, in′fāz, *a. Elec.* In the same phase.

input, in′put, *n.* Something put in; power or energy introduced into a machine or circuit to operate it or be converted; the terminal for such power or energy; data supplied to a computer; an ingredient in production.

inquest, in′kwest, *n.* [O.Fr. *enquesis,* from L. *inquiro,* to seek after. INQUIRE.] Act of inquiring; inquiry; search; *law,* a judicial inquiry, especially before a jury; the jury itself.—*Coroner's inquest,* an inquest held by a coroner on bodies of such as die a violent death.

inquietude, in·kwī′e·tūd, *n.* [L. *inquietudo—in,* not, and *quietudo, quietude.*] Want of quiet; restlessness; uneasiness, either of body or mind.

inquire, in·kwīr′, *v.i.*—*inquired, inquiring.* [L. *inquiro,* to seek after—*in,* into, and *quæro,* to seek. QUERY, QUEST.] To ask a question or questions; to seek for information by asking questions; to seek for truth by argument or the discussion of questions, or by investigation (to *inquire* of a person, *after, concerning, into,* etc., a thing).—*v.t.* To ask about; to seek by asking (to *inquire* the way of a person).—**inquirer,** in·kwī′rėr, *n.* One who inquires; an investigator.—**inquiringly,** in·kwī′ring·li, *adv.* In an inquiring manner; by way of inquiry.—**inquiry,** in·kwī′ri, *n.* [From *inquire,* like *expiry* from *expire.*] The act of inquiring; a question or interrogation; search for information or knowledge; research; investigation.

inquisition, in·kwi·zish′on, *n.* [L. *inquisitio, inquisitionis,* from *inquiro, inquisitum,* to seek after. INQUIRE.] The act of inquiring; inquiry; investigation; a judicial inquiry; an inquest; [cap.] a former Roman Catholic court or tribunal established for the examination and punishment of heretics; any attempt to suppress nonconformity.—**inquisitional,** in·kwi·zish′on·al, *a.* Relating to inquisition or inquiry; relating to the Inquisition.—**inquisitive,** in·kwiz′i·tiv, *a.* Addicted to inquiry; inclined to seek information; given to pry into

anything; troublesomely curious; prying.—**inquisitively,** in·kwiz′i·tiv·li, *adv.* In an inquisitive manner.—**inquisitiveness,** in·kwiz′i·tiv·nes, *n.* The quality of being inquisitive.—**inquisitor,** in·kwiz′i·tėr, *n.* One whose official duty it is to inquire and examine; a member of the Inquisition.—**inquisitorial,** in·kwiz′i·tō″ri·al, *a.* Pertaining to inquisition, especially to the Court of Inquisition; making strict or searching inquiry.—**inquisitorially,** in·kwiz′i·tō″ri·a·li, *adv.* In an inquisitorial manner.

inroad, in′rōd, *n.* [A *road* or rather a *raid* or riding into a country.] The hostile entrance of an enemy into a country; a sudden incursion or invasion; an encroachment; loss or impairment (to make *inroads* on one's health).

insalivation, in·sal′i·vā″shon, *n.* The blending of the saliva with the food in eating.

insalubrious, in·sa·lū′bri·us, *a.* [Prefix *in,* not, and *salubrious.*] Not salubrious; unfavorable to health; unhealthy.—**insalubrity,** in·sa·lū′bri·ti, *n.* The state or quality of being insalubrious; unhealthiness.

insane, in·sān′, *a.* [Prefix *in,* not, and *sane;* L. *insanus.*] Not sane; unsound or deranged in mind or intellect; mad; crazy; delirious; distracted; intended for insane persons.—**insanely,** in·sān′li, *adv.* In an insane manner.—**insanity, insaneness,** in·san′i·ti, in·sān′nes, *n.* The state of being insane or of unsound mind; madness; lunacy.

insanitary, in·san′i·ta·ri, *n.* [Prefix *in,* not, and *sanitary.*] Not sanitary; injurious to health.

insatiable, in·sā′shi·a·bl, *a.* [Prefix *in,* not, and *satiable;* L. *insatiabilis.*] Incapable of being satiated, satisfied, or appeased.—**insatiability, insatiableness,** in·sā′shi·a·bil′i·ti, in·sā′shi·a·bl·nes, *n.* The quality of being insatiable.—**insatiably,** in·sā′shi·a·bli, *adv.* In an insatiable manner.—**insatiate,** in·sā′shi·āt, *a.* [L. *insatiatus.*] Not satisfied; insatiable.

inscribe, in·skrīb′, *v.t.*—*inscribed, inscribing.* [L. *inscribo, inscriptum—in,* and *scribo,* to write. DESCRIBE.] To write down or engrave; to mark down (to *inscribe* a motto); to mark with characters or words (to *inscribe* a monument); to assign, address, or dedicate (to *inscribe* a poem to a person); to imprint deeply; to impress; *geom.* to draw or delineate within another figure so that the boundaries of the two are in contact at certain points.—**inscriber,** in·skrī′bėr, *n.* One who inscribes.—**inscription,** in·skrip′shon, *n.* [L. *inscriptio, inscriptionis.*] The act of inscribing; any words or writing engraved on stone, metal, or other hard substance for public inspection; an address of a book, poem, etc., to a person as a mark of respect, less formal than a dedication; *numis.* the words placed in the middle of the reverse side of some coins and medals.—**inscriptive,** in·skrip′tiv, *a.*

Of the character of an inscription. **inscrutable**, in·skrö′ta·bl, a. [Fr. *inscrutable*, L. *inscrutabilis—in*, not, and *scrutor*, to search. SCRUTINY.] Incapable of being searched into and understood; incapable of being penetrated or understood by human reason; not to be satisfactorily accounted for or explained.—**inscrutably**, in·skrö′ta·bli, adv. In an inscrutable manner.—**inscrutability**, **inscrutableness**, in·skrö′ta·bil″i·ti, in·skrö′ta·bl·nes, n.

insculp,† in·skulp′, v.t. [L. *insculpo—in*, and *sculpo*, to engrave.] To engrave; to carve.

insect, in′sekt, n. [L. *insectum*, something cut in (from their shape), from *inseco, insectum*, to cut into—*in*, into, and *seco*, to cut. DISSECT.] One of a class of small animals that in their mature state have the three divisions of the body—the head, thorax, and abdomen—always distinct from one another, and usually have three pairs of legs and two pairs of wings, as the numerous creatures known as flies, beetles, bees, etc.; a puny contemptible person.—a. Pertaining to insects; resembling an insect.—**insecticide**, in·sek′ti·sīd, n. That which kills insects.—**insectivore**, in·sek′ti·vŏr, n. A member of the Insectivora, nocturnal terrestrial mammals which feed on insects; an insect-eating animal or plant.—**insectivorous**, in·sek·tiv′ŏ·rus, a. Feeding or subsisting on insects.

insecure, in·si·kūr′, a. [Prefix *in*, not, and *secure*.] Not secure; not confident of safety; not sufficiently strong or guarded; unsafe.—**insecurity**, in·si·kū′ri·ti, n. The state of being insecure; want of security.

inseminate, in·sem′i·nāt, v.t.—*inseminated, inseminating*. [L. *inseminatus*, pp. of *inseminare*, to sow.] To implant seed; to inject (the female genital tract) with sperm; to imbed ideas, etc.—**insemination**, in·sem′i·nā″shon, n.—*Artificial insemination*, injection of semen into the female by artificial means, used in animal breeding.

insensate, in·sen′sāt, a. [L.L. *insensatus*—L. *in*, not, and *sensus*, sensation, sense. SENSE.] Destitute of sense or sensation; wanting sensibility; stupid.—**insensateness**, in·sen′sāt·nes, n. The state of being insensate.

insensible, in·sen′si·bl, a. [L. *insensibilis*—prefix *in*, not, and *sensibilis*, sensible.] Not apprehended by the senses; imperceptible; incapable of being felt or perceived; so slow or gradual that the stages are not noted; destitute of the power of feeling or perceiving; numb or dead to pain; not susceptible of emotion or passion; void of feeling; unfeeling; callous; apathetic; indifferent.—**insensibly**, in·sen′si·bli, adv. In an insensible manner; imperceptibly; by slow degrees.—**insensibility**, in·sen′si·bil″i·ti, n. The condition or quality of being insensible; dullness; apathy; numbness; torpor.—**insensitive**, in·sen′si·tiv, a. Not sensi-

tive; having little sensibility.—**insentient**, in·sen′shi·ent, a. Not sentient; inanimate.

inseparable, in·sep′a·ra·bl, a. [Prefix *in*, not, and *separable*; L. *inseparabilis*.] Incapable of being separated or disjoined; not to be parted; always together.—**inseparably**, in·sep′a·ra·bli, adv. In an inseparable manner.—**inseparability**, in·sep′a·ra·bil″i·ti, n.

insert, in·sért′, v.t. [L. *insero, insertum—in*, and *sero*, to put (as in *assert, exert, concert*). SERIES.] To set in or among; to put or thrust in; to introduce.—**insertion**, in·sér′shon, n. [L. *insertio*.] The act of inserting; something inserted; *bot.* the place or mode of attachment of an organ to its support; of a muscle, the end attached to a relatively movable part.

Insessores, in·ses·sō′rēz, n. pl. [Pl. of L. *insessor*, one that sits—*in*, and *sedeo*, to sit.] In old classifications an order of perchers or passerine birds, comprehending all those which live habitually among trees, with the exception of the birds of prey and climbing birds.—**insessorial**, in·ses·sō′ri·al, a. Belonging to the Insessores or perching birds.

inset, in·set′, v.t. To set in; to infix or implant.—n. (in′set). That which is set in; insertion.

insheathe, in·shēTH′, v.t. To hide or cover in a sheath.

inshore, in′shōr, a. or adv. Near the shore.

inside, in′sīd, a. [Lit., within the sides.] Being within; interior; internal.—n. That which is within; specifically, the entrails or bowels; an inside passenger in a vehicle.—prep. In the interior of; within.

insidious, in·sid′i·us, a. [L. *insidiosus*, from *insidiæ*, an ambush, from *insideo*, to sit upon—*in*, upon, and *sedeo*, to sit. SIT.] Characterized by treachery or stealthy and guileful acts; treacherous; guileful; working evil secretly (an *insidious* person, plot, disease).—**insidiously**, in·sid′i·us·li, adv. In an insidious manner.—**insidiousness**, in·sid′i·us·nes, n.

insight, in′sīt, n. [Prefix *in*, and *sight*.] Deep inspection or view; thorough knowledge; power of observation; discernment; penetration.

insignia, in·sig′ni·a, n. pl. [L., pl. of *insigne*, a mark, neut. of *insignis*, remarkable—*in*, intens., and *signum*, a mark. SIGN.] Badges or distinguishing marks of office or honor; any characteristic marks or signs.

insignificant, in·sig·nif′i·kant, a. [Prefix *in*, not, and *significant*.] Void of signification; having no weight or effect; unimportant; trivial or trifling; without weight of character; mean; contemptible.—**insignificantly**, in·sig·nif′i·kant·li, adv. In an insignificant manner. —**insignificance, insignificancy**, in·sig·nif′i·kans, in·sig·nif′i·kan·si, n. The condition or quality of being insignificant.

insincere, in·sin·sēr′, a. [Prefix *in*, not, and *sincere*; L. *insincerus*.] Not

sincere; dissembling; hypocritical; false; deceitful; of persons, statements, etc.—**insincerely**, in·sin·sēr′li, adv. In an insincere manner.—**insincerity**, in·sin·ser′i·ti, n. The quality of being insincere.

insinuate, in·sin′ū·āt, v.t.—*insinuated, insinuating*. [L. *insinuo, insinuatum—in*, and *sinuo*, to wind, from *sinus*, a bending, curve, bosom.] To introduce gently, or as by a winding or narrow passage; hence, *refl.* to push or work gradually into favor; to introduce one's self by slow or artful means; to infuse gently or artfully; to instill (to *insinuate* a doubt); to hint or suggest.—v.i. To creep or wind; to act by insinuation; to make an insinuation; to wheedle.—**insinuating**, in·sin′ū·āt·ing, p. and a. Given to or characterized by insinuation; wheedling; insensibly winning favor and confidence.—**insinuatingly**, in·sin′ū·āt·ing·li, adv. In an insinuating manner.—**insinuation**, in·sin′ū·ā″shon, n. [L. *insinuatio, insinuationis*.] The act of insinuating; a wheedling manner; a suggestion, hint, or innuendo.—**insinuative**, in·sin′ū·ā·tiv, a. Insinuating; stealing on the affections.—**insinuator**, in·sin′ū·ā·tér, n. One who insinuates.

insipid, in·sip′id, a. [L. *insipidus—in*, not, and *sapidus*, savory, from *sapio*, to taste. SAVOR.] Tasteless; destitute of taste; vapid; wanting interest, spirit, life, or animation; dull, heavy, or uninteresting.—**insipidity**, **insipidness**, in·si·pid′i·ti, in·sip′id·nes, n. The quality of being insipid.—**insipidly**, in·sip′id·li, adv. In an insipid manner.

insist, in·sist′, v.i. [L. *insisto—in*, and *sisto*, to stand, as in *consist, desist, persist, resist*, etc. STATE.] To rest, dwell, or dilate upon as a matter of special moment; to be persistent, urgent, peremptory, or pressing; usually with *on* or *upon*.—**insistence**, in·sis′tens, n. Act of insisting; persistency; urgency.

insociable, in·sō′shi·a·bl, a. [Prefix *in*, not, and *sociable*.] Not sociable; unsociable; taciturn.—**insociably**, in·sō′shi·a·bli, adv. In an unsociable manner; unsociably.—**insociability**, in·sō′shi·a·bil″i·ti, a. The quality of being insociable.

insolate, in′sō·lāt, v.t.—*insolated, insolating*. [L. *insolo, insolatum—in*, and *sol*, the sun (whence *solar*).] To dry or prepare in the sun's rays; to expose to the heat of the sun.—**insolation**, in·sō·lā′shon, n. [L. *insolatio, insolationis*.] The act of exposing, or condition of being exposed, to the rays of the sun; sunstroke.

insolent, in′so·lent, a. [L. *insolens, insolentis*, contrary to custom, immoderate, haughty, insolent—*in*, not, and *solens*, ppr. of *soleo*, to be wont.] Showing haughty disregard of others; using rude and haughty or defiant language; overbearing; saucy; proceeding from insolence.—**insolently**, in′so·lent·li, adv. In an insolent manner.—**insolence**, in′so·lens, n. [L. *insolentia*, from *insolens*.] Haughtiness manifested in contemptuous and overbearing treatment of others; insolent language.

insoluble, in·sol′ū·bl, a. [Prefix *in*, not, and *soluble*.] Incapable of being dissolved, particularly by a liquid; not to be solved or explained.— **insolubility, insolubleness**, in·sol′ū·bil′i·ti, in·sol′ū·bl·nes, n. The quality of being insoluble.

insolvable, in·sol′va·bl, a. [Prefix *in*, not, and *solvable*.] Not solvable; not to be solved or explained; not admitting solution.

insolvent, in·sol′vent, a. [Prefix *in*, not, and *solvent*.] Not solvent; not having money, goods, or estate sufficient to pay all debts.—*n*. A debtor unable to pay his debts.— **insolvency**, in·sol′ven·si, n. The condition of being insolvent; inability of a person to pay all his debts.

insomnious, in·som′ni·us, a. [L. *insomniosus*, from *insomnia*, sleeplessness—*in*, not, and *somnus*, sleep.] Restless in sleep, or being without sleep.—**insomnia**, in·som′ni·a, n. [L.] Want of sleep; morbid or unnatural sleeplessness.

insomuch, in·sō·much′, adv. [*In*, so, and *much*.] To such a degree; in such wise; so: followed by *that*, sometimes *as*.

insouciant, an·sö·syän′, a. [Fr.—*in*, not, and *soucier*, to care, *souci*, care, from L. *sollicitus*, uneasy, solicitous.] Careless; heedless; regardless; unconcerned.—**insouciance**, an·sö·syäns′, n. The quality of being insouciant.

inspan, in·span′, v.t. [D. *inspannen*—*in*, in, and *spannen*, to yoke.] To yoke, as draft oxen: correlative of *outspan*. [South African.]

inspect, in·spekt′, v.t. [L. *inspicio*, *inspectum*—*in*, and *specio*, to view. SPECIES.] To view or examine for the purpose of ascertaining the quality or condition, discovering errors, etc.; to examine officially.—**inspection**, in·spek′shon, n. [L. *inspectio*.] The act of inspecting; official view or examination.—**inspector**, in·spek′tėr, n. One who inspects or oversees. —**inspectorate**, in·spek′tėr·at, n. A body of inspectors or overseers; inspectorship.

inspire, in·spīr′, v.i.—*inspired, inspiring*. [L. *inspiro*—*in*, and *spiro*, to breathe, whence *spirit*, *expire*, *respire*.] To draw in breath; to inhale air into the lungs.—*v.t.* To breathe in; to draw into the lungs; to infuse by or as if by breathing; to instill; to communicate divine instructions to the mind of; to animate by supernatural infusion; to rouse or animate in general.— **inspirer**, in·spī′rėr, n. One who inspires.—**inspirable**, in·spī′ra·bl, a. Capable of being inspired; inhalable. —**inspiration**, in·spi·rā′shon, n. [L. *inspiratio*.] The act of inspiring; the divine influence by which the sacred writers were instructed; influence emanating from any object, giving rise to new and elevated thoughts or emotions; the state of being inspired; something conveyed

to the mind when under extraordinary influence.—*Verbal*, *plenary inspiration*, the doctrine maintaining that the very words were inspired, as opposed to general inspiration by the Spirit; textual inerrancy.— **inspirational**, in·spi·rā′shon·al, a. Pertaining to inspiration.—**inspiratory**, in·spīr′a·to·ri, a. Pertaining to or assisting in inspiration (the *inspiratory* muscles).

inspirit, in·spir′it, v.i. [Prefix *in*, and *spirit*.] To infuse or excite spirit in; to enliven, animate, encourage, invigorate.

inspissate, in·spis′āt, v.t.—*inspissated, inspissating*. [L. *inspisso*, *inspissatum*—*in*, intens., and *spissus*, thick.] To thicken by boiling so as to evaporate the water; to bring to greater thickness by evaporation.— *a.* Thick; inspissated.—**inspissation**, in·spis·ā′shon, n. The act or operation of inspissating.

instable, in·stā′bl, a. [L. *instabilis*— *in*, not, and *stabilis*, stable.] Not stable; unstable.—**instability**, in·sta·bil′i·ti, n. Want of stability; inconstancy; want of firmness in construction.

install, in·stal′, v.t. [Fr. *installer*—*in*, in, and O.H.G. *stal*, a place, E. *stall*. STALL.] To place in an office or post; to invest formally with a charge, office, or rank; to set up or establish for use (as a heating system).—**installation**, in·sta·lā′shon, n. Act of installing; something installed. —**installment**, in·stal′ment, n. Installation; a part of a whole (especially a novel) produced at stated periods; one part of a sum to be paid at stated intervals.

instance, in′stans, n. [L. *instantia*, a standing near, importunity, urgency —*in*, on, and *sto*, to stand. STATE.] The act or state of being instant or urgent; urgency; a case occurring; a case offered as an exemplification or precedent; an example; an occurrence.—*v.t.*—*instanced, instancing*. To mention as an instance, example, or case in point.—**instant**, in′stant, a. [E. *instans, instantis*.] Pressing, urgent, importunate, or earnest (N.T.); immediate; without intervening time (send him to *instant* execution); quick; making no delay; present or current: usually abbreviated to *inst.*, as 10th *inst.*, that is, 10th day of the present month.—*n*. A point in duration; a moment; a part of duration that occupies the time of a single thought.— **instantaneousness**, in·stan·tā′ni·us·nes, n. The quality of being instantaneous.—**instantaneous**, in·stan·tā′ni·us, a. [Made on the model of *contemporaneous*.] Done in an instant; occurring without any perceptible lapse of time.—**instantaneously**, in·stan·tā′ni·us·li, adv. In an instant; in a moment.—**instanter**, in·stan′tėr, adv. [L., from *instans*.] Immediately; forthwith; on the moment.—**instantly**, in′stant·li, adv. With urgency; earnestly; immediately; forthwith; at once.

instate, in·stāt′, v.t.—*instated, instating*. [Prefix *in*, and *state*.] To

establish, as in a rank or condition; to install.

instead, in·sted′, adv. [From *in*, and *stead*, place; *stead* retaining its character of a noun, and being followed by *of*.] In the place or room. [When *instead* is used without *of* following, there is an ellipsis of a word or words that would otherwise follow the *of*.]

instep, in′step, n. [Formerly *instop*, *instup*, perhaps from *in* and *stoop*, lit. the bend in.] The forepart of the upper side of the human foot, near its junction with the leg; part of the hind leg of a horse from the ham to the pastern joint.

instigate, in′sti·gāt, v.t.—*instigated, instigating*. [L. *instigo*, *instigatum*— *in*, on, and root *stig*, to prick. INSTINCT, STIGMA.] To incite; to set on; to provoke; to urge; used chiefly or wholly in a bad sense.— **instigation**, in·sti·gā′shon, n. [L. *instigatio*.] act of instigating; incitement, as to evil or wickedness.— **instigator**, in′sti·gā·tėr, n. One who instigates.

instill, instil, in·stil′, v.t.—*instilled, instilling*. [L. *instillo*—*in*, and *stillo*, to drop. DISTILL.] To pour in by drops; hence, to infuse slowly or by degrees into the mind; to cause to be imbibed; to insinuate imperceptibly.—**instillation**, in·stil·ā′shon, n. The act of instilling.—**instillatory**, in·stil′a·to·ri, a. Relating to instillation.—**instiller**, in·stil′ėr, n. One who instills.—**instillment**, in·stil′ment, n. The act of instilling.

instinct, in′stingkt, n. [L. *instinctus*, instigation, impulse, from *instinguo*, *instinctum*, to impel—*in*, on, and root meaning to prick, as in *stimulus*, *sting*.] An impulse to a particular kind of action which the being needs to perform as an individual, but which it could not possibly learn to perform before it needs to act; as a general term it includes all original impulses and that apparent knowledge and skill which animals have without experience; hence, natural feeling or sense of what is correct or effective in artistic matters or the like.—*a.* (in·stingkt′). Animated or stimulated from within; inspired; fully suffused and breathing out (a portrait *instinct* with life).—**instinctive**, in·stingk′tiv, a. Prompted by or proceeding from instinct; determined by natural impulse or propensity; spontaneous.— **instinctively**, in·stingk′tiv·li, adv. In an instinctive manner.

institute, in′sti·tūt, v.t.—*instituted, instituting*. [L. *instituo*, *institutum*— *in*, and *statuo*, to set, place, from *sto, statum*, to stand. STATE.] To set up or establish; to ordain; to originate; to found; to set in operation; to begin (an investigation, etc.). —*n*. That which is instituted or formally established; an established law, precept, or principle; a society established according to certain laws or regulations for the furtherance of some particular object (a philosophic *institute*, a literary *institute*, a mechanics *institute*); *pl*. a book of elements or principles, particularly a work containing the principles of a system of jurisprudence.—**institution**, in·sti·tū´shon, n. [L. *institutio*.] The act of instituting; something instituted or established; a permanent rule of conduct or of government; something forming a prominent or established feature in social or national life; a society established or body organized for promoting any object, public or social.—**institutional**, in·sti·tū´shon·al, a. Relating to institutions; instituted by authority; relating to elementary knowledge.—**institutionary**, in·sti·tū´shon·e·ri, a. Relating to an institution or to institutions.—**institutive**, in´sti·tū·tiv, a. Tending or intended to institute or establish.—**institutor**, in´sti·tū·tèr, n. [L.] One who institutes.

instruct, in·strukt´, v.t. [L. *instruo*, *instructum*—*in*, and *struo*, to join together, to pile up. STRUCTURE.] To teach; to educate; to impart knowledge or information to; to enlighten; to direct or command; to furnish with orders; to order or enjoin.—**instruction**, in·struk´shon, n. [L. *instructio*.] The act of instructing; that which is communicated for instructing; that with which one is instructed; information; order, mandate, or direction.—**instructional**, in·struk´shon·al, a. Relating to instruction; educational.—**instructive**, in·struk´tiv, a. Conveying knowledge; serving to instruct or inform.—**instructively**, in·struk´tiv·li, adv. In an instructive manner.—**instructiveness**, in·struk´tiv·nes, n.— **instructor**, in·struk´tèr, n. [L.] One who instructs; a teacher.

instrument, in´stru·ment, n. [L. *instrumentum*, from *instruo*, to prepare. INSTRUCT.] That by which work is performed or anything is effected; a tool; a utensil; an implement; one who or that which is subservient to the execution of a plan or purpose; means used or contributing to an effect; any contrivance from which music is produced, as an organ, harp, violin, flute, etc.; *law*, a writing instructing one in regard to something that has been agreed upon.—**instrumental**, in·stru·men´tal, a. Conducive as an instrument or means to some end; pertaining to instruments, especially musical instruments.—**instrumentalist**, in·stru·men´tal·ist, n. One who plays upon a musical instrument.—**instrumentality**, in´stru·men·tal´i·ti, n. The condition of being instrumental; subordinate or auxiliary agency; agency as means to an end.—**instrumentally**, in·stru·men´tal·li, adv. By way of an instrument; as means to an end; with instruments of music.—**instrumentation**, in´stru·men·tā´shon, n. The art of arranging music for a number of instruments; the music for a number of instruments; execution of music on an instrument.

insubordinate, in·sub·or´di·nāt, a. [Prefix *in*, not, and *subordinate*.] Not submitting to authority; mutinous; riotous.—n. One who is unruly.—**insubordination**, in·sub·or´di·nā˝shon, n. The quality of being insubordinate.

insubstantial, in·sub·stan´shal, a. [Prefix *in*, not, and *substantial*.] Unsubstantial.

insufferable, in·suf´fèr·a·bl, a. [Prefix *in*, not, and *sufferable*.] Not to be suffered, borne, or endured; intolerable; unendurable.—**insufferably**, in·suf´fèr·a·bli, adv.

insufficient, in·suf·fish´ent, a. [Prefix *in*, not, and *sufficient*.] Not sufficient; inadequate to any need, use, or purpose.—**insufficiency**, in·suf·fish´en·si, n. The condition or quality of being insufficient.—**insufficiently**, in·suf·fish´ent·li, adv. In an insufficient manner.

insular, in´sū·lèr, a. [L. *insularis*, from *insula*, an island.] Of or pertaining to an island or the opinions or views of islanders; hence, narrow-minded (*insular* prejudices); contracted.—**insularity**, in·sū·lar´i·ti, n. The state of being insular.—**insulate**, in´sū·lāt, v.t.—*insulated*, *insulating*. To make an island of; to isolate; to separate, as an electrified or heated body, from other bodies by inserting nonconductors; to free from combination with other substances, as a chemical substance.—**insulation**, in·sū·lā´shon, n. The act of insulating, or state of being insulated; materials for insulating.—**insulator**, in´sū·lā·tèr, n. One who or that which insulates; *elec.* a nonconducting piece, as of glass, used to insulate wires, etc.

insulin, in´sū·lin, n. [L. *insula*, island, and *in*.] A secretion of the islands of Langerhans in the pancreas which controls the use of sugar in the body; a trademark for a similar hormone extracted from the pancreas of some animals.

insult, in´sult, n. [Fr. *insulte*; L. *insultus*, from *insilio*, *insultum*, to leap on—*in*, and *salio*, to leap.] Any gross affront offered to another, either by words or actions; act or speech of insolence or contempt.—v.t. (in·sult´). To treat with insult, gross abuse, insolence, or contempt.—v.i. To behave with insolent triumph.—**insulter**, in·sult´èr, n. One who insults.—**insulting**, in·sult´ing, a. Containing or conveying insult.—**insultingly**, in·sult´ing·li, adv. In an insulting manner; so as to insult.

insuperable, in·sū´pér·a·bl, a. [L. *insuperabilis*—*in*, not, and *supero*, to overcome. SUPERIOR.] Incapable of being overcome or surmounted; insurmountable (difficulties, objections, obstacles, etc.).—**insuperability**, in·sū´pér·a·bil´i·ti, n. The quality of being insuperable.—**insuperably**, in·sū´pér·a·bli, adv. In an insuperable manner.

insupportable, in·sup·pōr´ta·bl, a. [Prefix *in*, not, and *supportable*.] Not to be supported or borne; insufferable; intolerable.—**insupportably**, in·sup·pōr´ta·bli, adv.

insuppressible, in·sup·pres´i·bl, a. [Prefix *in*, not, and *suppressible*.] Incapable of being suppressed or concealed.—**insuppressibly**, in·sup·pres´i·bli, adv. So as not to be suppressed.

insure, in·shōr´, v.t.—*insured*, *insuring*. [Prefix *in*, intens., and *sure*.] To make sure; to ensure (which is the word now commonly used in this general sense); to contract for the payment of a certain sum in the event of loss or damage happening to, or at the death or termination of (to *insure* a house against fire, a ship against damage, to *insure* one's life); to make a subject of insurance.—**insurer**, in·shō´rer, n. One who insures.—**insurable**, in·shō´ra·bl, a. Capable of being insured.—**insurance**, in·shō´rans, n. The act of insuring; a contract by which a person or company, in consideration of a sum of money or percentage (technically called a *premium*), becomes bound to indemnify the insured or his representatives against loss by certain risks; the premium paid for insuring property or life.—*Marine insurance* is the term used for the insurance on ships, goods, etc., at sea.—*Fire insurance* is for the insuring of property on shore from fire.—*Life insurance* is for securing the payment of a certain sum at the death of the individual insured, or when he reaches a given age, or of an annuity.—*Social insurance*, a type of insurance which provides benefits for unemployment, sickness, old age, etc., obtained from funds into which usually the worker, employer, and government contribute.—*Insurance policy*, the document by which the insurance is ratified.

insurgent, in·sér´jent, a. [L. *insurgens*, *insurgentis*, ppr. of *insurgo*, to rise against—*in*, on, and *surgo*, to rise, whence *surge*, *source*, etc.] Rising in opposition to lawful civil or political authority; rebellious.—n. A person who rises in opposition to civil or political authority. ∴ An *insurgent* differs from a *rebel* in holding a less pronounced position of antagonism, and may or may not develop into a rebel. INSURRECTION.—**insurgency**, in·sér´jen·si, n. The condition of being insurgent.

insurmountable, in·sér·moun´ta·bl, a. [Prefix *in*, not, and *surmountable*.] Incapable of being surmounted, passed over, or overcome.—**insurmountably**, in·sér·moun´ta·bli, adv.

insurrection, in·sér·rek´shon, n. [L. *insurrectio*, *insurrectionis*, from *insurgo*, *insurrectum*. INSURGENT.] The open and active opposition of a number of persons to the civil or political authorities of a city or country, in defiance of law and order; a revolt by a number of persons against constituted authorities. ∴ An *insurrection* is less serious than a *rebellion*, for the latter attempts to overthrow the government, to establish a different one, or to place the country under another jurisdiction; a *mutiny* is a movement of revolt against minor institutions, or against the authorities in the army or navy;

a *revolt* is a less strong form of a rebellion.—**insurrectional, insurrectionary,** in·sėr·rek'shon·al, in··sėr·rek'shon·a·ri, *a.* Pertaining to insurrection.—**insurrectionist,** in·sėr·rek'shon·ist, *n.* One who favors insurrection.

insusceptible, in·sus·sep'ti·bl, *a.* [Prefix *in*, not, and *susceptible*.] Not susceptible; not capable of being affected or impressed (a heart *insusceptible of* pity).—**insusceptibility,** in·sus·sep'ti·bil"i·ti, *n.* The quality of being insusceptible.

intact, in·takt', *a.* [L. *intactus*—prefix *in*, not, and *tactus*, touched, pp. of *tango*, to touch; whence also *tangent*, *tact*, etc.] Untouched by anything that harms or defiles; uninjured; unimpaired; left complete, whole, or unharmed.

intaglio, in·tal'yō, *n.* [It., from *intagliare*, to carve—*in*, and *tagliare*, to cut, Fr. *tailler* (whence *tailor*).] Any figure engraved or cut into a substance so as to form a hollow; a gem with a figure or design that is sunk below the surface; the reverse of *cameo*, which has the figure in relief.

intake, in'tāk, *n.* A point where a water supply is diverted from a main stream; amount taken in (hourly *intake*).

intangible, in·tan'ji·bl, *a.* [Prefix *in*, not, and *tangible*.] Not tangible; incapable of being touched; not perceptible to the touch.—**intangibleness, intangibility,** in·tan'ij·bl·nes, in·tan'ji·bil"i·ti, *n.*—**intangibly,** in·tan'ji·bli, *adv.*

integer, in'te·jėr, *n.* [L. *integer*, whole, entire—*in*, not, and *tag*, root of *tango*, to touch. ENTIRE, TANGENT.] *Arith.* a whole number, in contradistinction to a fraction.—**integral,** in'te·gral, *a.* Whole; entire; complete; belonging to, or forming a necessary part of, a whole; *math.* pertaining to a whole number or undivided quantity; not fractional; pertaining to integration.—*n.* A whole; an entire thing.—**integrally,** in'ti·gral·li, *adv.*—**integrant,** in'ti·grant, *a.*

integrate, in'ti·grāt, *v.t.*—*integrated, integrating.* [L. *integratus*, pp. of *integrare*, to make whole.] To make entire; to form into one whole; to perfect; to give the sum or total of.—**integration,** in·ti·grā'shon, *n.* The act of integrating; incorporation of diverse groups or individuals into a well-ordered community or society whose behavior is based on similar standards; *math.* the determination of a function from its differential or its differential coefficient.—**integrationist,** in·ti·grā'shon·ist, *n.*—**integrator,** in'ti·grā·tėr, *n.*

integrity, in·teg'ri·ti, *n.* [F. *integrité*, from L. *integritas*, from *integer*, entire.] Behavior in accordance with a strict code of values, moral, artistic, etc.; honesty; entirety; the quality of wholeness; something without mark or stain; soundness.

integument, in·teg'ū·ment, *n.* [L. *integumentum*, *intego*, to cover—*in*, intens., and *tego*, to cover (same root

as E. *thatch*).] *Anat.* the skin, membrane, or shell which covers any part; *bot.* the cellular skin of seed, leaf, or stem.—**integumentary,** in·teg'ū·men"te·ri, *a.* Belonging to or composed of integument.

intellect, in'tel·lekt, *n.* [L. *intellectus*, from *intelligo*, to understand—*inter*, between, and *lego*, to choose or pick, to read; seen also in *collect*, *elect*, *select*, *legend*, *lesson*, *lecture*, etc.] That faculty of the human mind which receives or comprehends ideas, as distinguished from the power to feel and to will; the understanding faculty; also, the capacity for higher forms of knowledge.—**intellection,** in·tel·lek'shon, *n.* The act of understanding; simple apprehension.—**intellective,** in·tel·lek'tiv, *a.* Pertaining to the intellect; perceivable by the understanding only, not by the senses.—**intellectively,** in·tel·lek'tiv·li, *adv.* In an intellective manner.—**intellectual,** in·tel·lek'chū·al, *a.* Relating to the intellect or understanding; appealing to or perceived by the intellect; existing in the understanding; ideal; having or characterized by intellect.—**intellectualism,** in·tel·lek'chū·al·izm, *n.* Intellectuality; the doctrine that knowledge is derived from pure reason.—**intellectualist,** in·tel·lek'chū·al·ist, *n.* One who overrates intellectualism.—**intellectuality,** in·tel·lek'chū·al"li·ti, *n.* The state of being intellectual; intellectual power.—**intellectualize,** in·tel·lek'chū·al·īz, *v.t.* To endow with intellect; to give an intellectual or ideal character to.—**intellectually,** in·tel·lek'chū·al·li, *adv.* In an intellectual manner.—**intelligence,** in·tel'i·jens, *n.* [L. *intelligentia*.] Intellectual power; knowledge imparted or acquired; general information; information communicated; news or notice; an intelligent or spiritual being.—*Intelligence quotient,* Abbr. *I. Q.,* mental rating found by test. (Divide age into mental age shown.) *Intelligence test,* a psychological test used to show comparative mental capacity.—**intelligencer,** in·tel'i·jen·sėr, *n.* One who conveys intelligence; a messenger or spy.—**intelligent,** in·tel'i·jent, *a.* [L. *intelligens, intelligentis*, ppr. of *intelligo*.] Endowed with the faculty of understanding or reason; endowed with a good intellect; having superior intellectual capacities; well informed.—**intelligently,** in·tel'i·jent·li, *adv.* In an intelligent manner. — **intelligibility,** in·tel'i·ji·bil"i·ti, *n.* The quality or state of being intelligible.—**intelligible,** in·tel'i·ji·bl, *a.* [L. *intelligibilis*.] Capable of being understood or comprehended; comprehensible; clear. —**intelligibly,** in·tel'i·gi·bli, *adv.*

intelligentsia, in·tel·li·jen'si·a, *n. pl.* Intellectuals; the broadly educated.

intemperance, in·tem'pėr·ans, *n.* [Prefix *in*, not, and *temperance*; L. *intemperantia*, want of moderation. TEMPER.] Want of moderation or due restraint; excess of any kind; specifically, habitual indulgence in the use of alcoholic liquors, especially with intoxication.—**intemperate,** in··

tem'pėr·it, *a.* [L. *intemperatus*, immoderate.] Not exercising due moderation or restraint; addicted to an excessive or habitual use of alcoholic liquors; excessive, immoderate, or inordinate (*intemperate* language).—*n.* One who is not temperate.—**intemperately,** in··tem'pėr·it·li, *adv.* In an intemperate manner.—**intemperateness,** in·tem'pėr·it·nes, *n.* State of being intemperate.

intend, in·tend', *v.t.* [L. *intendo*, to stretch forth, to intend—*in*, and *tendo*, to stretch (as in *attend*, *contend*, etc.). TEND.] To fix the mind upon, as the object to be effected or attained; to mean; to design; to purpose.—**intendancy,** in·ten'dan·si, *n.* The office, employment, or district committed to the charge of an intendant.—**intendant,** in·ten'dant, *n.* [Fr., from L. *intendo*.] One who has the charge or management of some public business; a superintendent.—**intended,** in·ten'ded, *p.* and *a.* Betrothed; engaged.—*n.* A person engaged to be married to another; an affianced lover.

intense, in·tens', *a.* [L. *intensus*, stretched, tight, pp. of *intendo*, to stretch. INTEND.] Closely strained; kept on the stretch (study, thought, etc.); extreme in degree; vehement; violent; severe (pain, cold, etc.).—**intensely,** in·tens'li, *adv.* In an intense manner.—**intenseness,** in·tens'nes, *n.* The state of being intense.—**intensification,†** in·ten'si·fi·kā"shon, *n.* The act of intensifying or making more intense.—**intensifier,** in·ten'si·fī·ėr, *n.* One who or that which intensifies.—**intensify,** in·ten'si·fī, *v.t.*—*intensified, intensifying.* To render intense or more intense.—*v.i.* To become intense or more intense. —**intension,** in·ten'shon, *n.* [L. *intensio, intensionis*.] Act of straining or intensifying; the state of being strained: opposed to *remission* or *relaxation*.—**intensity,** in·ten'si·ti, *n.* The state of being intense; relative degree, vigor, or activity; keenness (of feeling, etc.); *phys.,* the amount of energy with which a force operates or a cause acts.—*Intensity of field,* the force experienced by a unit pole when placed in a field of magnetic force.—*Intensity of magnetization,* in a uniformly magnetized mass, is the quotient of the moment (q.v.) of the magnet by its volume.—*Intensity of pressure,* where the pressure is uniform over an area, is the total pressure divided by the area; measured in dynes or grams per square centimeter or pounds per square inch.—**intensive,** in·ten'siv, *a.* Serving to give force or emphasis (an *intensive* particle or prefix.)—*Intensive cultivation,* thorough cultivation of the soil by free use of stimulating manures, etc.—*Intensive drill,* a method of drill especially adopted for particular purposes of attack by shock or storm troops in war. (*Recent.*)—**intensively,** in·ten'siv·li, *adv.* In an intensive manner.—**intensiveness,** in·ten'siv·nes, *n.* The quality of being intensive.—**intent,** in·tent', *a.* [L.

intentus, pp. of *intendo*.] Having the mind strained or bent on an object; sedulously applied; eager in pursuit of an object; anxiously diligent: with *on* before a noun.—*n.* Design, purpose, or intention; meaning; drift; aim.—*To all intents and purposes*, in all applications or senses; practically; really.—**intention**, in·ten'shon, *n.* [L. *intentio*, attention, design.] Determination to act in a particular manner; purpose; design; end; aim; the state of being strained or intensified; intension; *logic*, any mental apprehension of an object.—**intentional**, in·ten'shon·al, *a.* Done with intention, design, or purpose; intended; designed.—**intentionally**, in·ten'shon·al·li, *adv.* With intention; by design; of purpose.—**intently**, in·tent'li, *adv.* In an intent manner.—**intentness**, in·tent'nes, *n.* The state of being intent.

inter, in·ter', *v.t.*—*interred, interring.* [Fr. *enterrer*—*en*, and *terre*, L. *terra*, the earth (whence *terrace, terrestrial*, etc.).] To bury; to inhume.—**interment**, in·ter'ment, *n.* The act of interring; burial.

interact, in'ter·akt, *n.* [Prefix *inter*, and *act*.] The interval between two acts of a drama; an interlude; any intermediate employment of time.—*v.i.* To act reciprocally; to act on each other.—**interaction**, in·ter·ak'shon, *n.* Intermediate action; mutual or reciprocal action.

interblend, in·ter·blend', *v.t.* and *i.* [Prefix *inter*, and *blend*.] To blend or mingle together.

interbreed, in·ter·brēd', *v.t.* and *i.* [Prefix *inter*, and *breed*.] To breed by crossing one kind of animal or plant with another.

intercalary, in·ter'ka·le·ri, *a.* [L. *intercalarius*—*inter*, between, and *calo*, to call or proclaim, seen also in *calendar, council*.] Inserted or introduced among others, as the odd day (February 29th) inserted in leap year.—**intercalate**, in·ter'ka·lāt, *v.t.*—*intercalated, intercalating.* [L. *intercalo*.] To insert between others; *chron.* to insert between other days or other portions of time; *geol.* to insert, as a layer or series of layers, between the regular series of the strata.—**intercalation**, in·ter'ka·lā"shon, *n.* [L. *intercalatio*.] The act of intercalating.—**intercalative**, in·ter'ka·lā·tiv, *a.* Tending to intercalate; intercalating.

intercede, in·ter·sēd', *v.i.*—*interceded, interceding.* [L. *intercedo*—*inter*, between, and *cedo*, to go; *lit.* to pass between. CEDE.] To act between parties with a view to reconcile those who differ or contend; to plead in favor of another; to interpose; to mediate or make intercession.—**interceder**, in·ter·sē'der, *n.* One who intercedes.—**intercession**, in·ter·sesh'on, *n.* [L. *intercessio*.] The act of interceding; mediation.—**intercessional**, in·ter·sesh'on·al, *a.* Pertaining to or containing intercession.—**intercessor**, in·ter·ses·sér, *n.* One who intercedes.—**intercessory**, in·ter·ses'se·ri, *a.* Containing intercession; interceding.

intercellular, in·ter·sel'lū·lér, *a.* [Prefix *inter*, between, and *cellular*.] *Bot.* and *zool.* lying between cells or cellules.

intercept, in·ter·sept', *v.t.* [Fr. *intercepter*; L. *intercipio, interceptum*, to intercept—*inter*, between, and *capio*, to take. CAPABLE.] To stop or interrupt the journey or the progress of.—**interceptor**, in·ter·sep'tér, *n.* A fighter plane equipped for fast climb and high speeds, used for intercepting enemy aircraft.—**interception**, in·ter·sep'shon, *n.*—**interceptive**, in·ter·sep'tiv, *n.*

interchange, in·ter·chānj', *v.t.*—*interchanged, interchanging.* [Prefix *inter*, and *change*.] To change reciprocally; to put each in the place of the other.—*v.i.* To change reciprocally; to succeed alternately.—*n.* in'ter·chānj. The act or process of mutually giving and receiving; a junction of highways where bridges and underpasses separate the roads in levels so as to accommodate change from one roadway to another without stopping traffic.—**interchangeable**, in·ter·chān'ja·bl, *a.*—**interchangeability, interchangeableness**, in·ter·chān'ja·bil'i·ti, in·ter·chān'ja·bl·nes, *n.*—**interchangeably**, in·ter·chān'ja·bli, *adv.*

interclavicle, in·ter·klav'i·kl, *n.* [Prefix *inter*, and *clavicle*.] A bone between the clavicles or in front of the breastbone in many vertebrates.

intercolonial, in·ter·ko·lō'ni·al, *a.* [Prefix *inter*, between, among, and *colonial*.] Subsisting between different colonies.

intercolumniation, in'ter·ko·lum'ni·ā"shon, *n.* [Prefix *inter*, between, and *column*.] *Arch.* the space between two columns measured at the lowest part of their shafts.

intercom, in'ter·kom, *n.* [INTERCOMMUNICATE.] An intercommunication system with a microphone and speaker at each end for local communication.

intercommunicate, in'ter·kom·mū"ni·kāt, *v.i.* and *t.* [Prefix *inter*, and *communicate*.] To communicate mutually; to hold mutual communication.—**intercommunication**, in'ter·kom·mū'ni·kā"shon, *n.*

intercommunion, in'ter·kom·mūn"yon, *n.* [Prefix *inter*, and *communion*.] Mutual communion; mutual intercourse.—**intercommunity**, in'ter·kom·mū"ni·ti, *n.* A mutual communication or community.

interconnect, in'ter·kon·nekt", *v.t.* [Prefix *inter*, and *connect*.] To connect or unite closely or by various bonds.—**interconnection**, in'ter·kon·nek"shon, *n.*

intercontinental, in'ter·kon·ti·nen"tal, *a.* [Prefix *inter*, and *continent*.] Subsisting between different continents.—*Intercontinental ballistic missile*, a ballistic missile capable of traveling from one continent to another, its minimum range being 5,000 miles. Abbrev. ICBM.

intercostal, in·ter·kos'tal, *a.* [L. *inter*, between, and *costa*, a rib.] *Anat.* placed or lying between the ribs.

intercourse, in'ter·kōrs, *n.* [Prefix *inter*, between, and *course*; L. *inter-cursus*.] Reciprocal dealings between persons or nations; interchange of thought and feeling; copulation.

intercross, in·ter·kros', *v.t.* and *i.* [Prefix *inter*, and *cross*.] To cross mutually; to cross one another, as lines; to interbreed.

intercurrent, in·ter·kur'ent, *a.* [Prefix *inter*, between, and *current*; L. *intercurrens, intercurrentis*.] Running between or among; intervening; *med.* applied to diseases which occur sporadically during the prevalence of other diseases.

interdenominational, in'ter·di·nom'i·nā"shon·al, *a.* [Prefix *inter*, and *denomination*.] Between or among diverse religious denominations.

interdependence, interdependency, in'ter·dē·pen'dens, in'ter·dē·pen"den·si, *n.* [Prefix *inter*, and *depend*.] Reciprocal dependence; dependence each upon the others reciprocally.—**interdependent**, in'ter·dē·pen"dent, *a.* Reciprocally dependent.

interdict, in·ter·dikt', *v.t.* [L. *interdico, interdictum*—*inter*, between, and *dico*, to speak. DICTION.] To debar, forbid, or prohibit; to restrain by an interdict.—*n.* in'ter·dikt. A prohibition; a prohibiting order or decree; a papal prohibition of the performance of divine service and the administration of religious rites.—**interdiction**, in·ter·dik'shon, *n.*—**interdictive, interdictory**, in·ter·dik'tiv, in·ter·dik'te·ri, *a.*

interest, in'ter·est, *n.* [O.Fr. *interest*, Fr. *intérêt*, from L. *interest*, it concerns, it is of importance, from L. *interesse*—*inter*, between, and *esse*, to be (whence also *essence, entity*).] The profit per cent derived from money lent or invested; a share of an investment or business or other value; heed or curiosity paid to something; advantage; benefit; the situation in which one is or is not affected by something; something in addition to a mere equivalent (to repay injury with *interest*); influence with a person, especially with persons in power (to get a post by *interest*); a collective name for those interested in any particular business (the landed *interest*, the shipping *interest*).—*Simple interest* is that which arises from the principal sum only.—*Compound interest* is that which arises from the principal with the interest of one year added together to form a new principal for the next year, and so on successively.—*v.t.* To engage the attention of; to awaken interest or concern in.—**interested**, in'ter·es·ted, *p.* and *a.* Having an interest or share; affected; moved; having attention roused; concerned in a cause or in consequences; liable to be biased by personal considerations; chiefly concerned for one's own private advantage.—**interestedness**, in'ter·es·ted·nes, *n.*—**interesting**, in'ter·es·ting, *a.* Engaging the attention or curiosity; exciting or adapted to excite attention and sympathy.—**interestingly**, in'ter·es·ting·li, *adv.* In an interesting manner.—**interestingness**, in'ter·es·ting·nes, *n.*

interface, in'ter·fās, *n.* [Prefix *inter*,

and *face*.) The line or surface between two facing bodies.—**interfacial**, in·tėr·fā'shi·al, *a*.

interfere, in·tėr·fēr', *v.i.*—*interfered, interfering*. [O.Fr. *entreferir*, to exchange blows—L. *inter*, between, and *ferio*, to strike (whence *ferule*).] To interpose; to intermeddle; to enter into or take a part in the concerns of others; to clash, come in collision, or be in opposition; *phys*. to act reciprocally upon each other so as to modify the effect of each; *sports*, to prevent an opposing player's movement by some illegal means.—**interference**, in·tėr·fē'rens, *n*. The act of interfering or intermeddling; *phys*. the mutual action of waves of any kind (water, sound, heat, or light) upon each other, by which the vibrations and their effects are increased, diminished, or neutralized; *sports*, illegal prevention of the opposition's action; defense of one's team members by blocking of the opposition.—**interferer**, in·tėr·fē'rėr, *n*.—**interferingly**, in·tėr·fēr'ing·li, *adv*.

interfuse, in·tėr·fūz', *v.t.*—*interfused, interfusing*. [L. *interfusus*, pp. of *interfundo*—*inter*, between, and *fundo*, to pour. FUSE.] To pour or spread between or among; to mix up together; to make interdependent.—**interfusion**, in·tėr·fū'zhon, *n*.

intergalactic, in·tėr·gė·läk'tik, *a*. [Prefix *inter*, and *galactic*.] Existing or happening in the large areas between galaxies.

interglacial, in·tėr·glā'shi·al, *a*. [Prefix *inter*, and *glacial*.] *Geol*. formed or occurring between two periods of glacial action.

interim, in'tėr·im, *n*. [L., in the meantime.] The meantime; time intervening.—*a*. Belonging to an intervening time; belonging to the meantime; temporary.

interior, in·tē'ri·ėr, *a*. [L., inner, interior, compar. of *interus*, internal, itself a compar. from *in*. Akin *entrails*, *internal*, *intestine*.] Internal; being within any limits, enclosure, or substance: opposed to *exterior* or *superficial*; inland; remote from the frontiers or shore.—*Interior angles*, *geom*. the angles made within any figure by the sides of it.—*Interior planets*, *astron*. the planets between the earth's orbit and the sun; inferior planets.—*Interior screw*, a screw cut on the interior surface of anything hollow.—*n*. The internal part of a thing; the inside; the inland part of a country; the department of a government having charge of home affairs.—**interiority**, in·tē'ri·or''i·ti, *n*. The quality of being interior.—**interiorly**, in·tē'ri·or·li, *adv*. Internally; inwardly.

interjacent, in·tėr·jā'sent, *a*. [L. *interjacens*, ppr. of *interjaceo*—*inter*, between, and *jaceo*, to lie, as in *adjacent*, *subjacent*, etc.] Lying or being between; intervening.

interject, in·tėr·jekt', *v.t.* [L. *interjicio*, *interjectum*—*inter*, between, and *jacio*, to throw. JET.] To throw between; to throw in between other words.—**interjection**, in·tėr·jek'shon,

n. [L. *interjectio*.] The act of throwing between; a word thrown in between words connected in construction, to express some emotion or passion, as exclamations of joy, grief, astonishment, etc.—**interjectional**, in·tėr·jek'shon·al, *a*. Thrown in between other words; partaking of the character of an interjection.—**interjectionally**, in·tėr·jek'shon·al·li, *adv*. In an interjectional manner.

interknit, in·tėr·nit', *v.t.* [Prefix *inter*, and *knit*.] To knit together closely.

interlace, in·tėr·lās', *v.t.*—*interlaced, interlacing*. [Prefix *inter*, and *lace*; Fr. *entrelacer*.] To weave or twine together; to entangle or interweave one thing with another.—*v.i.* To be intertwined or interwoven; to have parts crossing or intersecting.—**interlacement**, in·tėr·lās'ment, *n*. The act or state of interlacing.

interlard, in·tėr·lärd', *v.t.* [Prefix *inter*, and *lard*.] Primarily, to mix fat with lean; hence, to mix by something frequently occurring; to diversify by mixture (talk *interlarded* with oaths).

interleave, in·tėr·lēv', *v.t.*—*interleaved, interleaving*. [Prefix *inter*, and *leaf*.] To insert a blank leaf or blank leaves in; to insert between the other leaves of (a book).

interline, in·tėr·līn', *v.t.*—*interlined, interlining*. [Prefix *inter*, and *line*.] To write or print in alternate lines; to write or print between the lines of.—**interlineal, interlinear**, in·tėr·lin'i·al, in·tėr·lin'i·ėr, *a*. Written or printed between lines before written or printed.—**interlineation**, in·tėr·lin'i·ā''shon, *n*. The act of interlining; that which is interlined.

interlock, in·tėr·lok', *v.i.* [Prefix *inter*, and *lock*.] To unite or be locked together by a series of connections.—*v.t.* To lock one in another firmly.

interlocution, in·tėr·lō·kū''shon, *n*. [L. *interlocutio*, from *interloquor*—*inter*, between, and *loquor*, to speak (in *loquacious*, *elocution*, etc.).] Dialogue; interchange of speech; *law*, an intermediate act or decree before final decision.—**interlocutor**, in·tėr·lok'ū·tėr, *n*. One who speaks in a dialogue or conversation; *Scots law*, the term, judgment, or order of any court of record.—**interlocutory**, in·tėr·lok'ū·to·ri, *a*. Consisting of dialogue or conversation.

interlope, in·tėr·lōp', *v.i.*—*interloped, interloping*. [From the noun, which is from D. *enterlooper*, a smuggler or smuggling vessel—Fr. *entre*, between, and D. *loopen*, to leap, to run=E. to *leap*. LEAP.] To traffic without a proper license; to run into a matter in which one has no right.—**interloper**, in·tėr·lō'pėr, *n*. One who unwarrantably intrudes or thrusts himself into a business, position, or matter.

interlude, in'tėr·lūd, *n*. [L.L. *interludium*, an interlude—L. *inter*, between, and *ludus*, a play. DELUDE.] A short lively entertainment performed between the acts of a play, or between the play and the afterpiece; a piece of music played between the verses of a canticle or

hymn, or between certain portions of a church service.

interlunar, in·tėr·lū'nėr, *a*. [L. *inter*, between, and *luna*, the moon.] Belonging to the time when the moon is invisible.

intermarry, in·tėr·mar'i, *v.i.*—*intermarried, intermarrying*. [Prefix *inter*, and *marry*.] To marry together; to become connected by marriage, as two families, ranks, tribes, or the like.—**intermarriage**, in·tėr·mar'ij, *n*. Marriage between two families, tribes, or nations.

intermeddle, in·tėr·med'l, *v.i.*—*intermeddled, intermeddling*. [Prefix *inter*, and *meddle*.] To meddle in affairs in which one has no concern; to meddle officiously; to interfere.—**intermeddler**, in·tėr·med'lėr, *n*. One who intermeddles.

intermediate, in·tėr·mē'di·it, *a*. [Fr. *intermédiat*, L. *intermedius*—*inter*, between, and *medius*, middle (whence *medium, mediate*, etc.).] Lying or being between; in the middle place or degree between two extremes; intervening; interposed. Also **intermediary**, in·tėr·mē'di·a·ri, in same sense.—**intermediately**, in·tėr·mē'di·it·li, *adv*. In an intermediate position.—**intermediation**, in·tėr·mē'di·ā''shon, *n*. Intervention; interposition.—**intermediary**, in·tėr·mē'di·e·ri, *n*. One who or that which interposes or is intermediate; an intervening agent.—**intermediator**, in·tėr·mē'di·a·tėr, *n*. A mediator between parties.

interment. See INTER.

intermezzo, in·tėr·met'zō, *n*. [It.] *Mus*. a short composition, generally of a light sparkling character, played between more important pieces; an interlude.

intermigration, in'tėr·mi·grā''shon, *n*. [Prefix *inter*, and *migration*.] Reciprocal migration.

interminable, in·tėr'mi·na·bl, *a*. [L. *interminabilis*—*in*, not, and *terminus*, a bound or limit. TERM.] Boundless; endless; admitting no limit; wearisomely spun out or protracted.—**interminably**, in·tėr'mi·na·bli, *adv*. In an interminable manner; endlessly.

intermingle, in·tėr·ming'gl, *v.t.*—*intermingled, intermingling*. [Prefix *inter*, and *mingle*.] To mingle or mix together; to mix up; to intermix.—*v.i.* To be mixed or incorporated.

intermission. See INTERMIT.

intermit, in·tėr·mit', *v.t.*—*intermitted, intermitting*. [L. *intermitto*, to let go between, to interrupt—*inter*, and *mitto*, to send. MISSION.] To cause to cease for a time; to interrupt; to suspend or delay.—*v.i.* To cease for a time; to cease or relax at intervals, as a fever.—**intermittence**, in·tėr·mit'ens, *n*. The act or state of intermitting; intermission.—**intermittent**, in·tėr·mit'ent, *a*. Ceasing at intervals.—*Intermittent* or *intermitting spring*, a spring which flows for some time and then ceases, again flows and again ceases, and so on, usually having a siphon-shaped channel of outflow.—*n*. A fever which entirely subsides or ceases at certain intervals.

—**intermission,** in·tẽr·mish′on, *n.* [L. *intermissio.*] The act or state of intermitting; cessation for a time; pause; the temporary subsidence of a fever.—**intermissive,** in·tẽr·mis′iv, *a.* Intermittent.

intermix, in·tẽr·miks′, *v.t.* [Prefix *inter,* and *mix.*] To mix together; to intermingle.—*v.i.* To be mixed or intermingled.—**intermixture,** in·tẽr·miks′chẽr, *n.* A mass formed by mixture; a mass of ingredients mixed; admixture.

intermundane, in·tẽr·mun′dān, *a.* [L. *inter,* between, *mundus,* a world.] Being between worlds or between orb and orb (*intermundane* spaces).

intermural, in·tẽr·mū′ral, *a.* [L. *inter,* between, *murus,* a wall.] Between walls.

intern, interne, in′tẽrn, *n.* [Fr. *interne.*] A graduated physician serving in a hospital for experience.—**internship,** in′tẽrn·ship, *n.* A period of service for the purpose of gaining experience.

intern, in·tẽrn′, *v.t.* [Fr. *interner,* from L. *internus,* internal.] To send to or cause to remain in the interior of a country without permission to leave it; to disarm and quarter in some place, as a defeated body of troops.—**internment,** in·tẽrn′ment, *n.* The act of interning; the state of being interned.

internal, in·tẽr′nal, *a.* [L. *internus,* internal. INTERIOR.] Inward; interior; being within any limit or surface; not external; pertaining to the mind or thoughts, or to one's inner being; pertaining to itself, its own affairs, or home interests: said of a country; domestic; not foreign.—*Internal-combustion engine,* an engine which is propelled into motion by the combustion of a fuel-air mixture within the cylinders.—*Internal revenue,* taxes derived from levies on certain domestic transactions.—**internality,** in·tẽr·nal′i·ti, *n.*—**internally,** in·tẽr′nal·li, *adv.*

international, in·tẽr·nash′on·al, *a.* [Prefix *inter,* and *national.*] Pertaining to or reciprocally affecting nations; regulating the mutual intercourse between different nations.—*International law,* the law of nations; those maxims or rules that regulate states in their conduct toward one another.—[*cap.*] **International,** *n.* The International Congress of Socialistic Workers.—**internationalism,** in·tẽr·na′shon·al·izm, *n.* The principle of cooperation among nations for their common good; an international as opposed to a national policy.—**internationally,** in·tẽr·nash′on·al·li, *adv.*

internecine, in·tẽr·nē′sin, *a.* [L. *internecinus,* deadly, murderous—*inter,* between, among, and *neco,* to kill.] Marked by destructive hostilities or much slaughter; causing great slaughter, as between fellow citizens (*internecine* war).

internode, in′tẽr·nōd, *n.* [L. *inter,* between, and *nodus,* knot.] *Bot.* the space which intervenes between two nodes or leafbuds.

internuncio, in·tẽr·nun′shi·ō, *n.* [L. *internuncius*—*inter,* between, and *nuncius,* a messenger.] A messenger between two parties; an envoy of the pope, sent to small states and republics while a nuncio is sent to emperors and kings.

interoceanic, in·tẽr·ō′shē·an″ik, *a.* [Prefix *inter,* and *ocean.*] Between oceans (*interoceanic* railway, canal, etc.).

interosculate, in·tẽr·os′kū·lāt, *v.i.* [Prefix *inter,* and *osculate.*] To touch or run into one another at various points; to form a connecting link between objects or groups by having characters in common.

interpellate, in·tẽr′pel·lāt, *v.t.*—*interpellated, interpellating.* [L. *interpello, interpellatum,* to interrupt in speaking—*inter,* between, and *pello,* to drive (seen in *appeal, compel, pulse,* etc.).] To question, especially to question imperatively; to interrupt by a question.—**interpellation,** in·tẽr·pel·lā″shon, *n.* [L. *interpellatio.*] The act of interrupting; an interruption by speaking; a question put by a member of a legislative assembly to a minister or member of the government.

interpenetrate, in·tẽr·pen′e·trāt, *v.t.* and *i.*—*interpenetrated, interpenetrating.* [Prefix, *inter,* and *penetrate.*] To penetrate between or within; to penetrate mutually.—**interpenetration,** in·tẽr·pen′e·trā″shon, *n.* The act of interpenetrating.

interplanetary, in·tẽr·plan′e·te·ri, *a.* [Prefix *inter,* and *planetary.*] Situated or existing between the planets; carried on between planets.

interplead, in·tẽr·plēd′, *v.i.* [Prefix *inter,* and *plead.*] *Law,* to proceed by interpleader.—**interpleader,** in·tẽr·plē′dẽr, *n. Law,* one who interpleads; a legal process by which a person threatened with a suit in which he has no real interest gets the proper parties to plead in the matter.

interpolate, in·tẽr′po·lāt, *v.t.*—*interpolated, interpolating.* [L. *interpolo, interpolatum,* to interpolate or falsify, from *interpolus,* vamped up, falsified—*inter,* between, and *polio,* to polish.] To foist in; to insert, as a spurious word or passage in a manuscript or book; to corrupt or vitiate by the insertion of new matter; *math.* and *phys.,* to fill up intermediate terms of, as of a series, according to the law of the series.—**interpolation,** in·tẽr′po·lā″shon, *n.* [L. *interpolatio.*] The act of interpolating; that which is interpolated or inserted; a spurious word or passage inserted.—**interpolater,** in·tẽr′po·lā·tẽr, *n.* One who interpolates.

interpose, in·tẽr·pōz′, *v.t.*—*interposed, interposing.* [Fr. *interposer*—*inter,* between, and *poser,* to place. POSE, COMPOSE.] To place between; *fig.* or *lit.* to present or bring forward by way of interruption or for some service (to *interpose* one's hand, one's self, one's aid or services).—*v.i.* To step in between parties at variance; to mediate; to interfere; to put in or make a remark by way of interruption.—**interposer,** in·tẽr-

pō′zẽr, *n.* One who interposes.—**interposition,** in·tẽr′po·zish″on or in′tẽr·po·zish″on, *n.* The act of interposing; a coming between; mediation; intervention.

interpret, in·tẽr′pret, *v.t.* [L. *interpretor,* from *interpres, interpretis,* an interpreter—*inter,* between, and root seen in (*pre*)*paro,* to prepare.] To explain the meaning of; to expound; to translate from an unknown to a known language, or into intelligible or familiar words; to free from mystery or obscurity; to make clear; to unravel; to represent artistically.—**interpretable,** in·tẽr′pre·ta·bl, *a.*—**interpretation,** in·tẽr′pre·tā″shon, *n.* [L. *interpretatio.*] The act of interpreting; translation; explanation; the sense given by an interpreter; conception and representation of a character on the stage.—**interpretative,** in·tẽr′pre·tā·tiv, *a.* Designed or fitted to explain; explanatory.—**interpretatively,** in·tẽr′pre·tā·tiv·li, *adv.* In an interpretative manner.—**interpreter,** in·tẽr′pre·tẽr, *n.* One who or that which interprets.

interracial, in·tẽr·rā′shi·al, *a.* [Prefix *inter,* and *racial.*] Concerning two or more races; intended for members of two or more races.

interregnum, in·tẽr·reg′num, *n.* [L. from *inter,* between, and *regnum,* reign.] The time between the death or abdication of a king and the accession of his successor; the interval between the cessation of one government and the establishment of another.

interrelation, in′tẽr·ri·lā″shon, *n.* [Prefix *inter,* and *relation.*] Mutual; reciprocal, or corresponding relation; correlation.

interrogate, in·tẽr′o·gāt, *v.t.* [L. *interrogo, interrogatum*—*inter,* between, and *rogo,* to ask (as in *abrogate, arrogant, derogate, prorogue,* etc.).] To question; to examine by asking questions.—**interrogation,** in·tẽr′o·gā″shon, *n.* [L. *interrogatio.*] The act of questioning; a question put; the sign ?, indicating that the sentence immediately preceding it is a question, or used to express doubt or to mark a query.—**interrogative,** in·tẽr·rog′a·tiv, *a.* [L. *interrogativus.*] Denoting a question; expressed in the form of a question.—*n. gram.* a word used in asking questions; as *who? what? which?*—**interrogatively,** in·tẽr·rog′a·tiv·li, *adv.* In an interrogative manner.—**interrogator,** in·tẽr′o·gā·tẽr, *n.* One who interrogates or asks questions.—**interrogatory,** in·tẽr·rog′a·to·ri, *n.* [L. *interrogatorius.*] A question; an interrogation.—*a.* Containing a question; expressing a question.

interrupt, in·tẽr·rupt′, *v.t.* [L. *interrumpo, interruptum*—*inter,* between, and *rumpo,* to break. RUPTURE.] To stop or hinder by breaking in upon the course or progress of; to break the current or motion of; to cause to stop in speaking; to cause to be delayed or given over; to break the uniformity of.—**interrupter,** in·tẽr·rup′tẽr, *n.* One that interrupts.—**interruption,** in·tẽr·rup′shon, *n.* [L.

interruptio.] The act of interrupting or breaking in upon; a break or breach; intervention; interposition; obstruction or hindrance; cause of stoppage.—**interruptive**, in·tẽr·rup′tiv, a. Tending to interrupt; interrupting.

intersect, in·tẽr·sekt′, v.t. [L. interseco, intersectum—inter, between, and seco, to cut. SECTION.] To cut into or between; to cut or cross mutually; to divide into parts by crossing or cutting.—v.i. To cut into another; to meet and cross each other.—**intersection**, in·tẽr·sek′shon, n. [L. intersectio.] The act or state of intersecting; the point or line in which two lines or two surfaces cut each other.—**intersectional**, in·tẽr·sek′shon·al, a. Relating to or formed by an intersection.

intersperse, in·tẽr·spẽrs′, v.t.—interspersed, interspersing. [L. interspergo, interspersum—inter, between, and spargo, to scatter.] To scatter or set here and there among other things; to diversify by scattering objects.—**interspersion**, in·tẽr·spẽr′zhon, n. The act of interspersing.

interspinal, interspinous, in·tẽr·spī′nal, in·tẽr·spī′nus, a. [Prefix inter, and spine.] Anat. lying between the processes of the spine, as muscles, nerves, etc.

interstate, in·tẽr·stāt′, a. Relations of or between states, as interstate commerce. Interstate Commerce Commission (I.C.C.), established by the U.S. in 1887 to regulate commerce between the states, especially railroads and express companies, or rail and water transport when combined. It passes on rates, financing, building and abandonment of railroads.

interstellar, in·tẽr·stel′ẽr, a. [Prefix inter, and stellar.] Situated among the stars.

interstice, in·tẽr′stis, n. [Fr., from L. interstitium—inter, between, and sto, to stand. STATE.] A narrow or small space between things close together, or between the component parts of a body; a chink, crevice, or cranny.—**interstitial**, in·tẽr·stish′al, a. Of or containing interstices.

interstratify, in·tẽr·strat′i·fī, v.t. [Prefix inter, and stratify.] Geol. to cause to occupy a position between other strata; to intermix as to strata. —v.i. To assume a position between other strata.—**interstratification**, in·tẽr·strat′i·fi·kā″shon, n. The condition of being interstratified.

intertexture, in·tẽr·teks′chẽr, n. [Prefix inter, and texture.] The act of interweaving; state of things interwoven; what is interwoven.

intertropical, in·tẽr·trop′i·kal, a. [Prefix inter, and tropic.] Situated between or within the tropics.

intertwine, in·tẽr·twīn′, v.t.—intertwined, intertwining. [Prefix inter, and twine.] To unite by twining or twisting one with another; to interlace.—v.i. To be mutually interwoven.

intertwist, in·tẽr·twist′, v.t. [Prefix inter, and twist.] To twist one with another; to interweave or interlace.

interurban, in·tẽr·ẽr′ban, a. [Prefix inter, and urban.] Between cities.—n. A train or car which commutes between two cities.

interval, in′tẽr·val, n. [L. intervallum, the space between the rampart—inter, between and vallum, an earthen rampart. WALL.] A space or distance between things; space of time between two definite points or events; the lateral space between units having the same alignment or frontage; mus. the difference in pitch between two sounds, sounded successively (melodic) or simultaneously (harmonic).

intervene, in·tẽr·vēn′, v.i.—intervened, intervening. [L. intervenio—inter, between, and venio, to come, as in advene, convene, etc. VENTURE.] To come or be between persons or things; to be situated between; to occur, fall, or come between points of time or events; to come in the way.—**intervener, interventionist**, in·tẽr·vē′nẽr, in·tẽr·ven′shon·ist, n. One who intervenes or advocates intervention.—**intervention**, in·tẽr·ven′shon, n. [L. interventio.] Act of intervening; a coming between.

interview, in′tẽr·vū, n. [Prefix inter, and view; Fr. entrevue.] A meeting between two or more persons face to face for the purpose of obtaining information as to aptitude, skills, etc.; the conversation, published or aired over television or radio, between a writer or reporter and a person of importance or notoriety from whom he is seeking information.—v.t. To have an interview with.—**interviewer**, in′tẽr·vū·ẽr, n.

interweave, in·tẽr·wēv′, v.t.—interwove (pret.); interwoven (pp.); interweaving (ppr.). To weave together; to intermingle as if by weaving; to unite intimately; to interlace.

intestate, in·tes′tāt, a. [L. intestatus—in, not, and testatus, having made a will, pp. of testor, to make a will. TESTAMENT.] Dying without having made a will; not disposed of by will; not devised or bequeathed.—n. A person who dies without making a will, or a valid will.—**intestacy**, in·tes′ta·si, n. The state of being intestate.

intestine, in·tes′tin, a. [L. intestinus, inward, intestinum, an intestine, from intus, within, from in, in; akin interior.] Internal with regard to a state or country; domestic; not foreign.—n. The canal or tube that extends with convolutions from the stomach to the anus; pl. entrails or viscera in general.—**intestinal**, in·tes′ti·nal, a. Pertaining to the intestines of an animal body.—Intestinal canal, the intestine or tube through which food passes in being digested.

inthrall, inthral, in·thral′, v.t. To enthrall.

inthrone, in·thrōn′, v.t. To enthrone.

intimate, in′ti·mit, a. [Fr. intime, L. intimus, inmost, superl. of obs. interus, internal. INTERIOR.] Inward or internal‡; close in friendship; on very familiar terms (also refers to illicit sex relationship); very close as regards connection or relation (an

intimate union).—n. An intimate friend; a close associate.—**intimacy**, in′ti·ma·si, n. The state of being intimate.—**intimately**, in′ti·mit·li, adv. In an intimate manner.

intimate, in′ti·māt, v.t.—intimated, intimating. [L. intimo, intimatum, to publish or make known, from intimus, inmost. INTIMATE.] a. To hint, indicate, or suggest‡; to announce; to make known.—**intimation**, in·ti·mā′shon, n. [L. intimatio.] The act of intimating; a hint; an explicit announcement or notification.

intimidate, in·tim′i·dāt, v.t.—intimidated, intimidating. [L.L. intimido, intimidatum—L. in, intens., and timidus, timid.] To inspire with fear; to dishearten; to cow; to deter by threats.—**intimidation**, in·tim′i·dā″shon, n. The act of intimidating; the deterring of a person by threats or otherwise.

intitle, in·tī′tl. See ENTITLE.

into, in′tö, prep. [A.Sax. in tó, in being the adv. and tó the prep.] A compound preposition expressing motion or direction toward the inside of, whether literally or figuratively; or expressing a change of condition (to go into a house, to fall into a fever).

intolerable, in·tol′ẽr·a·bl, a. [L. intolerabilis—in, not, and tolerabilis, bearable, from tolero, to bear. TOLERATE.] Not to be borne or endured; unendurable; insufferable.—**intolerableness, intolerability**, in·tol′ẽr·a·bl·nes, in·tol′ẽr·a·bil″i·ti, n. The state or quality of being intolerable.—**intolerably**, in·tol′ẽr·a·bli, adv. In an intolerable manner; unendurably.—**intolerant**, in·tol′ẽr·ant, a. [L. intolerans, intolerantis—in, not, and tolero, to bear.] Not enduring; not able to endure (an animal intolerant of cold); refusing to tolerate others in the enjoyment of their opinions, rights, or worship; unduly impatient of difference of opinion on the part of others.—**intolerantly**, in·tol′ẽr·ant·li, adv. In an intolerant manner.—**intolerance**, in·tol′ẽr·ans, n. The quality of being intolerant; want of toleration; want of capacity to endure.

intomb, in·töm′, v.t. To entomb.

intonate, in′to·nāt, v.i. [L. in, in, and tonus, tone.] To modulate the voice; to sound the notes of the musical scale.—v.t. to pronounce with a certain tone or modulation.—**intonation**, in·to·nā′shon, n. The act or manner of intonating; modulation of the voice musically as in reading; the act of intoning; utterance with a special tone.—**intone**, in·tōn′, v.i. To use a musical monotone in pronouncing or repeating; to chant. —v.t. To pronounce with a musical tone; to chant.

intort, in·tort′, v.t. [L. intorqueo, intortum—in, and torqueo, to twist. TORTURE.] To twist inward; to wreathe.—**intortion**, in·tor′shon, n. A winding or twisting inward.

intoxicate, in·tok′si·kāt, v.t.—intoxicated, intoxicating. [L.L. intoxico, intoxicatum—L. in, and toxicum, poison=Gr. toxikon, a poison in which arrows were dipped, from *toxon*, a bow.] To inebriate; to make drunk, as with spirituous liquor; *fig.* to excite the spirits of to a very high pitch; to elate to enthusiasm, frenzy, or madness. *v.i.* To have the power of intoxicating, or making drunk.—**intoxicant**, in·tok′si·kant, *n.* That which intoxicates; an intoxicating liquor or substance.—**intoxication**, in·tok′si·kā″shon, *n.* The act of intoxicating; the state of being intoxicated; inebriation; drunkenness.

intracellular, in·tra·sel′lū·ler, [L. *intra*, within, *cellula*, a little cell.] Within a cell.

intractable, in·trak′ta·bl, *a.* [Prefix *in*, not, and *tractable*; L. *intractabilis*.] Not tractable; not to be governed or managed; perverse; refractory; indocile.—**intractableness, intractability**, in·trak′ta·bl·nes, in·trak″ta·bil′i·ti, *n.* The quality of being intractable.—**intractably**, in·trak′ta·bli, *adv.* In an intractable manner.

intrados, in·trā′dos, *n.* [Fr., from L. *intra*, within, and *dorsum*, back.] *Arch.* the interior and lower line or curve of an arch.　EXTRADOS.

intramundane, in·tra·mun′dān, *a.* [Prefix *intra*, and *mundane*.] Being within the world; belonging to the material world.

intramural, in·tra·mū′ral, *a.* [Prefix *intra*, and *mural*.] Being within the walls or boundaries, as of a university, city, or town; of activities carried on within the confines of a college, company, etc.; *athletics*, games between various teams formed within a university, company, etc.

intransigent, in·tran′si·jent, *a.* [Fr. *intransigeant*, from L. *in*, not, and *transigo*, to transact; to come to a settlement.] Refusing to agree or come to a settlement; irreconcilable. —*n.* An irreconcilable person.

intransitive, in·tran′si·tiv, *a.* [Prefix *in*, not, and *transitive*.] *Gram.* expressing an action or state that is limited to the subject; not having an object (an *intransitive* verb).— **intransitively**, in·tran′si·tiv·li, *adv.* In an intransitive manner.

intrant, in′trant, *a.* [L. *intrans, intrantis*, ppr. of *intro*, to go into, to enter.] Entering.—*n.* One who makes an entrance; one who enters upon public duty or office.

intrastate, in′tra·stāte, *a.* Within a state, as intrastate shipping of goods.

intravenous, in′tra·vē″nus, *a.* [Prefix *intra*, and *venous*.] Introduced within the veins.

intrepid, in·trep′id, *a.* [L. *intrepidus* —*in*, not, and *trepidus*, alarmed. TREPIDATION.] Fearless; bold; brave; undaunted.—**intrepidity**, in·tre·pid′i·ti, *n.* Fearlessness; fearless bravery in danger; undaunted courage. —**intrepidly**, in·trep′id·li, *adv.* In an intrepid manner.

intricacy. See INTRICATE.

intricate, in′tri·kit, *a.* [L. *intricatus*, pp. of *intrico*, to entangle—*in*, into, and *tricoe*, trifles, hindrances, as in *extricate*; akin *intrigue*.] Entangled; involved; difficult to unravel or

follow out in all the windings; complicated.—**intricately**, in′tri·kit·li, *adv.* In an intricate manner.— **intricacy**, in′tri·ka·si, *n.* The state of being intricate or entangled; a winding or complicated arrangement; entanglement; complication.

intrigue, in·trēg′ or in′trēg, *n.* [Fr. *intriguer*, from L. *intrico*, to entangle. INTRICATE.] A plot or scheme of a complicated nature, and especially political in character; the plot of a play, poem, or romance; an illicit intimacy between two persons of different sexes; a liaison.—*v.i.*— intrigued, intriguing. To form an intrigue; to engage in an intrigue; to carry on a liaison.—**intriguer**, in·trē′ger, *n.* One who intrigues.— **intriguing**, in·trēg′ing, *p.* and *a.* Addicted to intrigue.—**intriguingly**, in·trēg′ing·li, *adv.* In an intriguing manner.

intrinsic, intrinsical, in·trin′sik, in·trin′si·kal, *a.* [L. *intrinsecus*—*intra*, inward, *in*, in, and *secus*, beside, from root of *sequor*, to follow (whence *sequence*).] Inherent; essential; belonging to the thing in itself; not extrinsic or accidental (the *intrinsic* value of gold or silver, *intrinsic* merit).—**intrinsically**, in·trin′si·kal·li, *adv.* By intrinsic character; in its nature; essentially; inherently.

introduce, in·tro·dūs′, *v.t.*—introduced, introducing. [L. *introduco*— *intro*, within, and *duco*, to lead. DUKE.] To lead or bring in; to conduct or usher in; to pass in; to put in; to insert; to make known by stating one's name; often used of the action of a third party with regard to two others; to bring to be acquainted; to present (to *introduce* one person, one's self, to another); to bring into use or practice (a fashion, custom, etc.); to bring before the public; to bring into a country; to bring forward (a topic) with preliminary or preparatory matter.—**introducer**, in·tro·dū′ser, *n.* One who introduces.—**introduction**, in·tro·duk′shon, *n.* [L. *introductio*.] The act of introducing, bringing in, making persons acquainted, etc.; the part of a book or discourse which precedes the main work, and which gives some general account of its design and subject; a preface or preliminary discourse; a treatise introductory to more elaborate works on the same subject.—**introductive**, in·tro·duk′tiv, *a.* Serving to introduce.— **introductory**, in·tro·duk′to·ri, *a.* Serving to introduce something else; serving as or given by way of an introduction; prefatory; preliminary.

introit, in·trō′it, *n.* [L. *introitus*, an entrance, from *intro*, within, and *eo*, to go. INITIAL.] *R. Cath. Ch.* the beginning of the mass; a piece sung or chanted while the priest proceeds to the altar to celebrate mass; a musical composition designed for opening the church service.

intromit, in·tro·mit′, *v.t.*—intromitted, intromitting. [L. *intromitto*—

intro, within, and *mitto, missum*, to send.] To send in, put in, or let in.— *v.i. Scots law*, to intermeddle with the effects, of another.—**intromittent**, in·tro·mit′ent, *a.* Letting or conveying into or within.—**intromitter**, in·tro·mit′er, *n.* One who intromits.—**intromission**, in·tro·mish′on, *n.* The act of sending or letting in; admission; *Scots law*, the transactions of an agent or subordinate with the money of his superior.

introrse, in·trors′, *a.* [L. *introrsum*, inward—*intro*, within, and *versus*, pp. of *verto*, to turn.] Turned or facing inward; turned toward the axis to which they appertain, as the anthers in plants.

introspect, in·tro·spekt′, *v.t.* [L. *introspicio, introspectum*—*intro*, within, and *specio*, to look.] To examine in depth; to look inside of.—*v.i.* To look inward; to contemplate one's thoughts or feeling.—**introspection**, in·trō·spek′shun, *n.*—**introspective**, in·trō·spek′tiv, *a.*

introvert, in·tro·vert′, *v.t.* [L. *intro*, within, and *verto*, to turn.] To turn inward; to turn thought on oneself.— *n.* in′tro·vert. That which can be introverted; *psych.* one inclined to introversion.—**introversion**, in′tro·ver″shon, *n.* Turning inward; *psych.* interest directed inward.

intrude, in·tröd′, *v.i.*—intruded, intruding. [L. *intrudo*—*in*, into, and *trudo*, to thrust, as in *detrude, obtrude, protrude, abstruse*.] To thrust one's self forwardly or unwarrantably into any place or position; to force one's self upon others; to encroach; to enter unwelcome or uninvited into company; *geol.* to penetrate, as into fissures or between the layers of rocks.—*v.t.* To thrust in, or cause to enter without right or welcome: often with the reflexive pronoun.— **intruder**, in·trö′der, *n.* One who intrudes.—**intrusion**, in·trö′zhon, *n.* The act of intruding; unwarrantable entrance; *law*, an unlawful entry into lands and tenements void of a possessor by a person who has no right to the same; *geol.* the penetrating of one rock, while in a melted state, into fissures, etc., of other rocks.—**intrusive**, in·trö′siv, *a.* Characterized by intrusion; apt to intrude; of the nature of an intrusion.—**intrusively**, in·trö′siv·li, *adv.* In an intrusive manner.— **intrusiveness**, *n.*

intrust, in·trust′, *n.* See ENTRUST.

intubation, in·tūb·ā′shon, *n.* [L. *in*, in, *tuba*, tube.] The process of inserting a tube into a body organ to keep it open.

intuition, in·tū·ish′on, *n.* [From L. *intueor, intuitus*, to look upon, to contemplate—*in*, in, upon, and *tueor*, to look (whence *tutor, tuition*).] *Philos.* the act by which the mind perceives the agreement or disagreement of two ideas, or the truth of things immediately, and without reasoning and deduction; a truth discerned by the mind directly and necessarily as so; a truth that cannot be acquired by, but is assumed in experience.—**intuitional,** in·tū·ish′on·al, *a.* Pertaining to, derived from, or characterized by intuition; intuitive.—**intuitionalism,** in·tū·ish′on·al·izm, *n.* The doctrine that the perception of truth is from intuition.—**intuitive,** in·tū′i·tiv, *a.* Perceived by the mind immediately without the intervention of reasoning; based on intuition; received or obtained by intuition; having the power of discovering truth without reasoning.—**intuitively,** in·tū′i·tiv·li, *adv.* In an intuitive manner; by intuition.

intumesce, in·tū·mes′, *v.i.*—*intumesced, intumescing.* [L. *intumesco—in,* and *tumesco,* to begin to swell, incept. of *tumeo,* to swell. TUMID.] To enlarge or expand with heat; to swell out in bulk.—**intumescence,** in·tū·mes′ens, *n.* The state or process of intumescing.

intussuscept, in′tus·sṳ·sept″ *v.t.* [L. *intus,* within, and *suscipio,* to take or receive. SUSCEPTIBLE.] To take into the interior; to receive by intussusception. — **intussusception,** in′tṳs·sṳs·sep″shon, *n.* The reception of one part within another; the descent or doubling in of a higher portion of intestine into a lower one; the act of taking foreign matter into the substance of a living body; the process by which nutriment is absorbed into and goes to form part of the system.

intwine, in·twīn′, *v.t.*—*intwined, intwining.* To twine or twist in or together; to wreathe; to entwine.

inunction, in·ungk′shon, *n.* [L. *in-unctio, inunctionis,* from *inungo, inunctum,* to anoint.] The action of anointing; unction.

inundate, in′un·dāt or in·un′dāt, *v.t.* *inundated, inundating.* [L. *inundo, inundatum—in,* and *undo,* to overflow (also in *abound*), from *unda,* a wave. UNDULATE.] To spread or flow over; to overflow; to deluge; to flood; to submerge; to fill with an overflowing abundance or superfluity.—**inundation,** in·un·dā′shon, *n.* [L. *inundatio.*] The act of inundating or state of being inundated; a flood; a rising and spreading of waters over low grounds.—**inundant,** in·un′dant, *a.* Overflowing; inundating.

inure, in·ūr′, *v.t.*—*inured, inuring.* [Prefix *in,* in, and obsol. *ure,* operation, work, from O.Fr. *eure,* Mod. Fr. *œuvre,* from L. *opera,* work. The *-ure* of this word therefore = *ure* of *manure.* OPERATE.] To apply or expose in use or practice till use gives little or no pain or inconvenience, or makes little impression; to habituate; to accustom (to toil or hardships).—**inurement,** in·ūr′ment, *n.* The act or process of inuring.

inurn, in·ėrn′, *v.t.* [Prefix *in,* and *urn.*] To put in an urn, especially a funeral urn; hence, to bury; to entomb. (*Poet.*)

inutility, in·ū·til′i·ti, *n.* [Prefix *in,* not, and *utility*; L. *inutilitas.*] The quality of being useless or unprofitable; uselessness; unprofitableness.

invade, in·vād′, *v.t.*—*invaded, in-* vading. [L. *invado—in,* into, and *vado,* to go, seen also in *evade, pervade*; akin *wade.*] To enter with hostile intentions; to enter as an enemy, with a view to conquest or plunder; to enter by force; to make an inroad or incursion on; to intrude upon; to infringe, encroach on, or violate (rights or privileges).— *v.i.* To make an invasion.—**invader,** in·vā′dėr, *n.* One who invades.— **invasion,** in·vā′zhon, *n.* [L. *invasio,* from *invado.*] The act of invading; a hostile entrance into the country or possessions of another; an attack on the rights of another.—**invasive,** in·vā′siv, *a.* Tending to invade; aggressive.

invaginate, in·vaj′i·nāt, *v.i.* [L. *in,* in, into, and *vagino,* a sheath.] To enter as into a sheath; to enter by intussusception into another part.— **invagination,** in·vaj′i·nā″shon, *n.* *Anat.* the reception of one part within another by being doubled backward; intussusception.

invalid, in·val′id, *a.* [Prefix *in,* not, and *valid*; L. *invalidus.*] Not valid; of no force, weight, or cogency; weak (an *invalid* argument); *law,* having no force, effect, or efficacy; void; null.—*n.* (in′va·lid). [Directly from Fr. *invalide.*] A person who is weak and infirm; a sufferer from ill health; one who is disabled for active service, especially a soldier or seaman worn out in service.— *a.* In ill health; infirm; disabled for active service.—*v.t.* To render an invalid; to enroll on the list of invalids in the military or naval service.—**invalidate,** in·val′i·dāt, *v.t.* —*invalidated, invalidating.* To render invalid or not valid; to render of no legal force or effect.— **invalidation,** in·val′i·dā″shon, *n.* Act of invalidating.—**invalidism,** in′va·lid·izm, *n.* The condition of being an invalid.—**invalidity,** in·va·lid′i·ti, *n.* Want of validity; want of cogency; want of legal force or efficacy.

invaluable, in·val′ū·a·bl, *a.* [Prefix *in,* not, and *valuable.*] Precious above estimation; so valuable that its worth cannot be estimated; inestimable.—**invaluably,** in·val′ū·a·bli, *adv.* Inestimably.

invar, in′var, *n.* [From *invariable.*] An alloy of nickel and steel which is practically unaffected by extremes of temperature.

invariable, in·vâ′ri·a·bl, *a.* [Prefix *in,* not, and *variable.*] Not variable; constant in the same state; always uniform; never varying.—*n. Math.* an invariable quantity; a constant.— **invariableness, invariability,** in·vâ′ri·a·bl·nes, in·vâ′ri·a·bil″i·ti, *n.* State of not varying.—**invariably,** in·vâ′ri·a·bli, *adv.* Constantly; uniformly; always.

invasion, invasive. See INVADE.

invective, in·vek′tiv, *n.* [Fr., from L. *invectivus,* abusive, from *inveho,* to inveigh. INVEIGH.] A severe or violent utterance of censure or reproach; something uttered or written intended to cast opprobrium, censure, or reproach on another; railing language; vituperation.—*a.* Contain- ing invectives; abusive; vituperative. —**invectively,** in·vek′tiv·li, *adv.* In an invective manner; abusively.— **invectiveness,** in·vek′tiv·nes, *n.* The quality of being invective or vituperative.

inveigh, in·vā′, *v.i.* [L. *invehor,* to attack with words, to inveigh against —*in,* into, against, and *veho,* to carry. VEHICLE.] To utter invectives; to exclaim or rail against a person or thing; to utter censorious or opprobrious words; with *against.* —**inveigher,** in·vā′ėr, *n.* One who inveighs or rails; a railer.

inveigle, in·vē′gl, *v.t.* [Norm. *enveogler,* to inveigle, to blind, for Fr. *aveugler,* to blind, from *aveugle,* blind—L. *ab,* not, and *oculus,* the eye. OCULAR.] To persuade to something evil by deceptive arts or flattery; to cajole into wrongdoing; to entice; to seduce.—**inveiglement,** in·vē′gl·ment, *n.* The act of inveigling.—**inveigler,** in·vē′gl·ėr, *n.* One who inveigles.

invent, in·vent′, *v.t.* [Fr. *inventer,* from L. *invenio, inventum,* to come upon, to find—*in,* upon, and *venio,* to come, as in *advent, convent, convene, prevent*; etc. VENTURE.] To contrive and produce; to devise, make, or construct as the originator of something that did not before exist; to frame by the imagination; to excogitate; to concoct; to fabricate. ∴ Syn. under DISCOVER.— **inventible,** in·ven′ti·bl, *a.* Capable of being invented.—**invention,** in·ven′shon, *n.* [L. *inventio, inventionis.*] The act of inventing; the contrivance of that which did not before exist; origination; something invented or contrived; a contrivance; the power of inventing; that skill or ingenuity which is or may be employed in contriving anything new; that faculty by which a poet or novelist produces plots, incidents, and characters, etc.—**inventive,** in·ven′tiv, *a.* Able to invent; quick at invention or contrivance; ready at expedients.—**inventively,** in·ven′tiv·li, *adv.* By the power of invention. —**inventiveness,** in·ven′tiv·nes, *n.* The faculty of inventing.—**inventor, inventer,** in·ven′tor, in·vent′ėr, *n.* One who invents or creates some new contrivance or device.

inventory, in′ven·tō·ri, *n.* [L. *inventarium,* an inventory, lit. a list of goods *found* in a place, from *invenio.* INVENT.] A list containing a description, with the values, of goods and chattels, made on various occasions, as on the sale of goods, or at decease of a person; any catalogue of goods or wares; a catalogue or account of particular things.—*v.t.—inventoried, inventorying.* To make an inventory, list, catalogue, or schedule of; to insert or register in an account of goods.—**inventorial,** in·ven·tō′ri·al, *a.* Of or pertaining to an inventory.—**inventorially,** in·ven·tō′ri·al·li, *adv.* In the manner of an inventory.

inverse, in·vėrs′, *a.* [L. *inversus,* pp. of *inverto—in,* on, to, and *verto,* to turn, as in *advert, convert, revert,* *subvert*, etc. VERSE.] Opposite in order or relation; inverted; having what usually is or should be after placed before; proceeding the backward or reverse way; *math.* opposite in nature and effect; thus, subtraction is *inverse* to addition, division to multiplication.—*Inverse proportion*, proportion such that one thing is greater or less as another is less or greater.—**inversely,** in·vėrs´li, *adv.* In an inverse order or manner; in inverse proportion.—**inversion,** in·vėr´zhon, *n.* [L. *inversio, inversionis*, from *inverto, inversum*.] The act of inverting or the state of being inverted; a change of order or position so that what was after is now before, and *vice versa*; a making inverse in order; *gram.* and *rhet.* transposition of words so that they are out of their natural order ('wise was Solomon' for 'Solomon was wise'); *mus.* change of position, as of an interval or a chord; *math.* a change in the order of the terms of a proportion, so that the second takes the place of the first, and the fourth of the third.

invert, in·vėrt´, *v.t.* [L. *invertere, inversum*, from *in*, in, and *vertere*, to turn.] To turn upside down; to place in a contrary order or position; to put in inverse order or position.—*n.* in´vėrt. A homosexual; something inverted.—**inverted,** in··vėr´ted, *p.* and *a.* Turned to a contrary direction; turned upside down; changed in order; *bot.* having the apex in an opposite direction to that which is normal.—*Inverted arch*, an arch with its curve turned downward, as in a sewer, in foundations, etc.—*Inverted commas*, commas turned upside down to mark the beginning of a quotation, the end being indicated by apostrophes.—**invertible,** in·vėr´ti·bl, *a.*

invertebrate, in·vėr´te·brit, *a.* [Prefix *in*, not, and *vertebrate*. VERTEBRA.] Destitute of a backbone or vertebral column; morally or mentally without stamina or backbone.—**invertebrate,** in·vėr´te·brāt, *n.* An animal belonging to a major division of the animal kingdom, including all animals that have no vertebral column or spine.

invest, in·vest´, *v.t.* [L. *investio*—*in*, and *vestio*, to clothe, from *vestis*, a garment. VEST.] To put garments on; to clothe, to dress, to array: usually followed by *with*, sometimes by *in*, before the thing put on; to clothe, as with office or authority; to place in possession of an office, rank, or dignity; *milit.* to enclose or surround for the purpose of besieging; to lay siege to; to lay out (money or capital) on some species of property, usually of a permanent nature, and with the purpose of getting a return (to *invest* money *in* bank shares).—*v.i.* To make an investment.—**investiture,** in·ves´ti·chėr, *n.* The act of investing; the act or right of giving possession of an office, dignity, etc.; that which invests or clothes; clothing; covering (*poet.* in this sense); the long medieval contest between Kings and the Papacy for the right of investing bishops and others with ecclesiastical or feudal dignities and rights.—**investment,** in·vest´ment, *n.* The act of investing; the act of besieging by an armed force; the laying out of money in the purchase of some species of property; money laid out for profit; that in which money is invested.—**investor,** in·ves´tėr, *n.* One who invests.

investigate, in·ves´ti·gāt, *v.t.*—*investigated, investigating.* [L. *investigo, investigatum*—*in*, and *vestigo*, to follow a track, to search, from *vestigium*, a track. VESTIGE.] To search into; to inquire and examine into with care and accuracy; to make careful research or examination into.—**investigable,** in·ves´ti·ga·bl, *a.* Capable of being investigated.—**investigation,** in·ves´ti·gā˝shon, *n.* [L. *investigatio, investigationis*.] The act of investigating; the process of inquiring into a subject; research; inquiry.—**investigative,** in·ves´ti·gā·tiv, *a.* Given to or concerned with investigation.—**investigator,** in··ves´ti·gā·tėr, *n.* One who investigates.

inveterate, in·vet´ėr·it, *a.* [L. *inveteratus*, pp. of *invetero*, to render old—*in*, in, and *vetus, veteris*, old. VETERAN.] Firmly established by long continuance; deep-rooted or ingrained in a person's nature or constitution; firmly fixed by time or habit (*inveterate* disease, custom); confirmed in any habit by practice (an *inveterate* liar).—**inveterately,** in·vet´ėr·it·li, *adv.* In an inveterate manner.—**inveteracy,** in·vet´ėr·a·si, *n.* The state or quality of being inveterate; obstinacy confirmed by time.

invidious, in·vid´i·us, *a.* [L. *invidiosus*, from *invidia*, envy, *invidus*, envious. ENVY.] Envious‡; likely to bring on envy, ill will, or hatred; likely to provoke envy; entailing odium (*invidious* distinctions, preference, position).—**invidiously,** in·vid´i·us·li, *adv.* In an invidious manner.—**invidiousness,** in·vid´i·us·nes, *n.* The quality of being invidious.

invigorate, in·vig´or·āt, *v.t.*—*invigorated, invigorating.* [L. *in*, intens., and *vigor*, strength. VIGOR.] To give vigor to; to cause to feel fresh and vigorous; to strengthen; to give life and energy to.—**invigoration,** in·vig´o·rā˝shon, *n.* Act of invigorating; state of being invigorated.

invincible, in·vin´si·bl, *a.* [L. *invincibilis*—*in*, not, and *vincibilis*, conquerable, from *vinco*, to conquer. VICTOR.] Incapable of being conquered or subdued; incapable of being overcome; unconquerable; insuperable.—*n.* One who is invincible.—**invincibility, invincibleness,** in··vin´si·bil˝i·ti, in·vin´si·bl·nes, *n.* The quality of being invincible.—**invincibly,** in·vin´si·bli, *adv.* In an invincible manner; unconquerably; insuperably.

inviolable, in·vī´o·la·bl, *a.* [L. *inviolabilis*—*in*, not, and *violabilis*, that may be violated, from *violo*, to violate. VIOLATE.] Not to be violated or profaned; not to be polluted or treated with irreverence; not to be broken or infringed (agreement, secrecy); not to be injured or tarnished (chastity, honor); not susceptible of hurt or wound (*Mil.*).—**inviolably,** in·vī´o·la·bli, *adv.* In an inviolable manner; without violation or profanation.—**inviolability, inviolableness,** in·vī´o·la·bil˝i·ti, in·vī´o·la·bl·nes, *n.* The state or quality of being inviolable.—**inviolate,** in·vī´o·lāt, *a.* [L. *inviolatus*.] Not violated; unprofaned; unpolluted; unbroken; inviolable.—**inviolately,** in·vī´o·lāt·li, *adv.* In an inviolate manner.—**inviolateness,** in·vi´o·lāt·nes, *n.*

invisible, in·viz´i·bl, *a.* [Prefix *in*, not, and *visible*; L. *invisibilis*.] Incapable of being seen; imperceptible by the sight.—*Invisible green*, a shade of green so dark as scarcely to be distinguishable from black.—**invisibleness, invisibility,** in·viz´i·bl·nes, in·viz´i·bil˝i·ti, *n.* The state of being invisible; imperceptibleness to the sight.—**invisibly,** in·viz´i·bli, *adv.* In an invisible manner; imperceptibly to the eye.

invite, in·vīt´, *v.t.*—*invited, inviting.* [L. *invito*, to invite, perhaps for *invicto, invecto*—*in*, and root of *vox*, voice.] To ask, request, bid, or call upon to do something; to summon; to ask to an entertainment or to pay a visit; to allure or attract; to tempt to come.—*v.i.* To give invitation; to allure or entice.—*n.* An invitation. (*Genteel slang.*)—**invitation,** in·vi·tā´shon, *n.* [L. *invitatio, invitationis*.] The act of inviting; solicitation; the requesting of a person's company as to an entertainment, on a visit, or the like.—**invitatory,** in·vī´ta·to·ri, *a.* Using or containing invitations.—**inviter,** in·vī´tėr, *n.* One who invites.—**inviting,** in·vī´ting, *p.* and *a.* Alluring; tempting; attractive (an *inviting* prospect).—**invitingly,** in·vī´ting·li, *adv.* In an inviting manner; attractively.—**invitingness,** in·vī´ting·nes, *n.* Attractiveness.

invocate, in´vō·kāt, *v.i.*—*invocated, invocating.* [L. *invoco, invocatum*—*in*, and *voco*, to call, *vox*, voice. VOICE, VOCAL.] To invoke; to call on in supplication; to implore; to address in prayer.—**invocation,** in·vo·kā´shon, *n.* [L. *invocatio, invocationis*.] The act of invoking or addressing in prayer; the form or act of calling for the assistance or presence of any being, particularly of some divinity.—**invocatory,** in·vō´ka·to·ri, *a.* Making invocation; invoking.

invoice, in´vois, *n.* [Fr. *envois*, things sent, goods forwarded, pl. of *envoi*, a sending, a thing sent, from *envoyer*, to send—L. *in*, and *via*, a way. ENVOY.] A written account of the particulars of merchandise sent to a purchaser, consignee, factor, etc., with the value or prices and charges annexed.—*v.t.*—*invoiced, invoicing.* To write or enter in an invoice.

invoke, in·vōk´, *v.t.*—*invoked, invoking.* [Fr. *invoquer*, L. *invocare*. INVOCATE.] To address in prayer; to call on for assistance and protection; to call for solemnly or with earnestness.

involucre, involucrum, in·vo·lū´kẽr, in·vo·lū´krum, n. [L. *involucrum*, a wrapper or envelope, from *involvo*, to involve or wrap round—*in*, and *volvo*, to roll. INVOLVE.] *Bot.* any collection of bracts round a cluster of flowers; *anat.* a membrane which surrounds or encloses a part, as the pericardium.—**involucral,** in·vo·lū´kral, a. Pertaining to or having an involucre.—**involucrate,** in·vo·lū´krāt, a. *Bot.* having an involucre, as umbels, etc.—**involucel,** in·vol´ū·sel, n. [Dim. of *involucre, involucrum*.] *Bot.* the secondary involucrum or small bracts surrounding an umbellule of an umbelliferous flower.

involuntary, in·vol´un·te·ri, n. [Prefix *in*, not, and *voluntary*.] Not voluntary; not able to act or not acting according to will or choice (an *involuntary* agent); independent of will or choice (an *involuntary* movement); not proceeding from choice; not done willingly; unwilling.—**involuntarily,** in·vol´un·te·ri·li, adv. In an involuntary manner.—**involuntariness,** in·vol´un·te·ri·nes, n.

involute, involuted, in´vo·lūt, in´vo·lū·ted, a. [L. *involutus*, pp. of *involvo.* INVOLVE.] Involved; twisted; confusedly mingled; *bot.* rolled inward from the edges: said of leaves and petals in vernation and estivation; *zool.* turned inward at the margin: said of the shells of mollusks.—n. A curve traced by any point of a tense string when it is unwrapped from a given curve.—v.i., in·vo·lūt´, *involuted, involuting.* To curl up; return to normal.—**involution,** in·vo·lū´shon, n. The action of infolding; the state of being entangled or of being folded in; complication; *arith.* and *alg.* the raising of a quantity from its root to any power assigned; *biol.*, the reverse growing process; degeneration; *physiol.* the aging process.

involve, in·volv´, v.t.—*involved, involving.* [L. *involvo*—*in*, into, and *volvo*, to roll, as in *convolve, devolve, evolve, revolve, voluble*, etc. WALLOW.] To roll or wrap up; to envelop in folds; to entwine; to envelop; to cover with surrounding matter (*involved* in darkness); to imply or comprise, as a logical consequence (a statement that *involves* a contradiction); to connect by way of natural result or consequence; to entangle; to implicate; to complicate; to blend; to mingle confusedly; *arith.* and *alg.* to raise to any assigned power. ∴ Syn. under IMPLICATE.—**involved,** in·volvd´, p. and a. Complicated; entangled; intricate.—**involvement,** in·volv´ment, n. Act of involving.

invulnerable, in·vul´nẽr·a·bl, a. [Prefix *in*, not, and *vulnerable*; L. *invulnerabilis*.] Not vulnerable; incapable of being wounded or of receiving injury; unassailable, as an argument; able to reply to all arguments.—**invulnerability, invulnerableness,** in·vul´nẽr·a·bil´i·ti, in·vul´nẽr·a·bl·nes, n. The quality or state of being invulnerable.—**invulnerably,** in·vul´nẽr·a·bli, adv. In an invulnerable manner.

inward, in´wẽrd, a. [A.Sax. *inneweard*—prep. *in*, and suffix *-ward*, as in *backward, toward*, etc.] Internal; interior; placed or being within; in or connected with the mind, thoughts, soul, or feelings.—adv. also **inwards** (in´wẽrdz). Toward the inside; toward the center or interior; into the mind or thoughts.—n. pl. the inner parts of an animal; the viscera.—**inwardly,** in´wẽrd·li, adv. In an inward manner; internally; mentally; privately.—**inwardness,** in´wẽrd·nes, n. The state of being inward or internal.

inweave, in·wēv´, v.t.—*inwove* (pret.), *inwoven* (pp.), *inweaving* (ppr.). To weave together.

inwreathe, in·rēTH´, v.t.—*inwreathed, inwreathing.* [Prefix *in*, and *wreathe*.] To surround or twine, as with a wreath; to infold or involve.

inwrought, in´rąt, p. and a. [Prefix *in*, and *wrought*.] Wrought or worked in or among other things.

iodine, i´o·dīn, n. [Gr. *iōdēs*, resembling a violet (from its color)—*ion*, a violet, and *eidos*, resemblance.] A nonmetallic element occurring as a grayish-black crystalline solid; used in medicine. Symbol, I; at. no., 53; at. wt., 126.9044.—**iodic,** i·od´ik, a. Pertaining to or containing iodine (*iodic* silver).—*Iodic acid,* an acid formed by the action of oxidizing agents on iodine in presence of water or alkalies.—**iodide,** i´o·dīd, n. A compound of iodine and another element; a salt of hydriodic acid.—**iodism,** i´o·dizm, n. *Pathol.* a peculiar morbid state produced by the use of iodine.—**iodize,** i´o·dīz, v.t.—*iodized, iodizing.* To treat with iodine; to impregnate or affect with iodine.—**iodoform,** i·od´o·form, n. A compound of carbon, hydrogen, and iodine, analogous to chloroform.

iodol, i´od·ōl. [From *iodine*.] An antiseptic derived from coal tar.

iolite, i´o·līt, n. [Gr. *ion*, a violet, and *lithos*, stone.] A mineral of a violet blue color; dichroite.

ion, i´on, n. [Gr. *ion*, from *eimi*, go.] An atom or group of atoms having either a positive or a negative charge from having lost or gained one or more electrons.—*Ion exchange,* a reversible transfer of ions between a solid and a solution without a substantial change in the make-up of the solid.—**ionize,** i´on·īz, v.t.—*ionized, ionizing.* To convert into ions; to cause ions in.—v.i. To become conductors, by being changed into the form of ions.—**ionization,** i´on·i·zā´shon, n. The conversion into ions.—*Ionization chamber,* an enclosure where ionized gases are studied; a device for the calculation of the radioactivity of a substance by measuring the current resulting from the ionization of its escaping vapor.—**ionosphere,** i·on´o·sfēr, n. That part of the earth's atmosphere which lies beyond the stratosphere, approximately 65 miles up.

Ionic, i·on´ik, a. Relating to *Ionia*, or to the Ionian Greeks.—*Ionic order,* one of the five orders of architecture, the distinguishing characteristic of which consists in the volutes of its capital.—*Ionic dialect,* a dialect of the ancient Greek language.

iota, i·ō´ta, n. [Gr. *iōta*; hence *jot*.] Primarily the name of the Greek letter *i*, which in certain cases is indicated by a sort of dot under another letter (as φ); hence, a very small quantity; a tittle; a jot.

I O U, i´ō´ū, n. [A phonetic equivalent of *I owe you.*] A paper addressed to a person having on it these letters, followed by a sum, and duly signed; serving as an acknowledgment of a debt.

ipecac, ipecacuanha, ip´i·kak, i´pi·kak·ū·an˝a, n. [Tupi, *ipekaaguene*, from *ipeh* low *kaa*, leaves, and *guene*, vomit.] A South American shrub from whose root a powerful emetic or expectorant is extracted; the drug itself.

iracund,† i´ra·kund, a. [L. *iracundus*, angry, from *ira*, anger; whence *ire, irate*, etc.] Angry; passionate. (*Carl.*)

irade, i·rä´di, n. [Turk.] A decree or proclamation of the Sultan of Turkey.

Iranian, i·rā´ni·an, a. Pertaining to *Iran*, the native name of Persia; applied to certain languages, including Persian, Zend, and cognate tongues.

irascible, i·ras´i·bl, a. [L. *irascibilis*, from *irascor*, to be angry, from *ira*, anger, whence also *ire, irate*.] Readily made angry; easily provoked; apt to get into a passion; irritable.—**irascibility, irascibleness,** i·ras´i·bil˝i·ti, i·ras´i·bl·nes, n. The quality of being irascible.—**irascibly,** i·ras´i·bli, adv. In an irascible manner.

irate, i·rāt´, a. [L. *iratus*, angry, from *irascor*, to be angry. IRASCIBLE.] Angry; enraged; incensed.

ire, īr, n. [O.Fr., from L. *ira*, wrath.] Anger; wrath; keen resentment.—**ireful,** īr´ful, a. Full of ire; angry; wroth.—**irefully,** īr´ful·li, adv.

iridescent, ir·i·des´ent, a. [L. *iris, iridis*, the rainbow.] Giving out colors like those of the rainbow; gleaming or shimmering with rainbow colors.—**iridescence,** ir·i·des´ens, n.

iridium, i·rid´i·um, n. [L. *iris*, the rainbow.] A metallic element resembling platinum; one of the heaviest substances known. Symbol, Ir; at. no., 77; at. wt., 192.2.—**iridosmine, iridosmium,** ir·i·dos´min, ir·i·dos´mi·um, n. A native compound of iridium and osmium used for pointing gold pens.

iris, i´ris, n. pl. **irises,** i´ris·ez, **irides,** i´ri·dēz (especially of the eye). [L. *iris, iridis*, Gr. *iris, iridos*, the rainbow, the plant iris, the iris of the eye.] The rainbow; an appearance resembling the rainbow; a kind of muscular curtain stretched vertically in the anterior part of the eye, forming its colored part, and perforated by the pupil for the transmission of light; the fleur-de-lis, or flag flower, a plant of various species.

Irish, i´rish, a. Pertaining to Ireland or its inhabitants; Erse.—n. The Irish language; with plural signification, the people of Ireland.—*Irish moss*, a seaweed of the Atlantic Ocean which, when dried and bleached, is used to keep solids in suspension, and as a thickening in some cooking.—*Irish setter*, a russet-colored hunting dog taught to stand rigid and point upon finding game.

irk, ėrk, *v.t.* [The same word as Sw. *yrka*, to urge, enforce, press, from root of *work*, *wreak*, and *urge*.] To weary; to give annoyance or uneasiness to; to be distressingly tiresome to; to annoy: used chiefly or only impersonally (it *irks* me).—**irksome,** ėrk′sum, *a.* Wearisome; burdensome; vexatious; giving uneasiness (*irksome* labor, delay, etc.).—**irksomely,** ėrk′sum·li, *adv.* In an irksome manner.—**irksomeness,** ėrk′sum·nes, *n.*

iron, ī′ėrn, *n.* [A.Sax. *iren, isen,* Goth. *eisarn,* D. *ijzer;* comp. Skr. *ayas,* W. *haiarn.*] A metallic element, silver white, malleable, and ductile, widely found in combination, strongly attracted by magnets, and easily oxidized. Symbol, Fe (Latin *ferrum*); at. no., 26; at. wt., 55.847.—An instrument or utensil made of iron; an instrument that when heated is used for smoothing cloth; *pl.* fetters; chains; manacles; handcuffs.—*To have many irons in the fire,* to be engaged in many undertakings. [*Cast iron* is iron direct from the smelting furnace (blast furnace), also called *pig iron; wrought* or *malleable iron* has to undergo the further process of puddling; *steel* is a variety of iron containing more carbon than malleable iron and less than cast iron.]—*a.* Made of iron; consisting of iron; resembling iron, either really or metaphorically; hence, harsh, rude, severe; capable of great endurance; firm; robust; inflexible.—*v.t.* To smooth with an iron; to fetter or handcuff; to furnish or arm with iron. —**Iron Age,** that cultural epoch chiefly distinguished by the use of iron; roughly, the last thousand years B. C.—**ironbark,** ī′ėrn·bärk, *n.* Certain Australian eucalypti with hard bark.—**ironbound,** *a.* Bound with iron; faced or surrounded with rocks; rugged (an *ironbound* coast).— **ironclad,** *a.* Covered or clothed with iron plates; armor-plated.—*n.* A vessel prepared for naval warfare by being cased or covered, wholly or partially, with thick iron plates. —**iron curtain,** *n.* A barrier of strict censorship and restriction of freedom, as the boundary between Soviet-held territory and the free world.—**ironer,** ī′rėn·ėr, *n.*—**iron horse,** a locomotive. (Colloq.)—**iron lung,** *n.* A device for forcing air into and out of the lungs by means of rhythmically changing pressure in a chamber surrounding the lungs.— **iron pyrites.** PYRITES.—**ironsmith,** ī′ėrn·smith, *n.* A worker in iron, as a blacksmith, locksmith, etc.— **ironstone,** *n.* A general name applied to the ores of iron containing oxygen and silica.—**ironware,** ī′ėrn·wâr, *n.* Utensils, tools, and various light

articles of iron.—**ironweed,** ī·ėrn·wēd, *n.* A plant of the genus *Vernonia* found in the eastern U.S.—**ironwood,** *n.* The popular name given to several very hard and very heavy woods in different countries.—**ironwork,** ī′ėrn·wėrk, *n.* A general name of the parts of a building, vessel, bridge, etc., which consist of iron; a work or establishment where iron is manufactured.—**irony,** ī′ėrn·i, *a.* Pertaining to or resembling iron in any qualities.

irony, ī′ron·i, *n.* [Fr. *ironie,* L. *ironia,* from Gr. *eirōneia,* from *eirōn,* a dissembler in speech, from *eirō,* to speak.] A mode of speech by which words express a sense contrary to that really intended; sarcasm, in which apparent praise really conveys disapprobation.—**ironical, ironic,** ī·ron′i·kal, ī·ron′ik, *a.* Relating to or containing irony; addicted to irony; using irony.—**ironically,** ī·ron′i·kal·li, *adv.* In an ironical manner.— **ironicalness,** *n.*

Iroquois, ir′o·kwoi, *n.* sing., pl. An early Indian confederation of New York state, composed of Cayugas, Mohawks, Oneidas, Onondagas, Senecas and later the Tuscaroras, referred to as the Five Nations; a member of one of these tribes.

irradiate, ir·rā′di·āt, *v.t.*—**irradiated,** *irradiating.* [L. *irradio, irradiatum— in,* in or on, and *radius,* a ray.] To illuminate or shed a light upon; to cast splendor or brilliancy upon; to illuminate; to penetrate by radiation; to treat for healing by radiation, as by that of X rays or ultraviolet rays. —*v.i.* To emit rays; to shine.— **irradiance, irradiancy,** ir·rā′di·ans, ir·rā′di·an·si, *n.* Emission of rays of light on an object; luster; splendor. —**irradiant,** ir·rā′di·ant, *a.*—**irradiation,** ir·rā′di·ā″shon, *n.* Exposure to rays of all types; use of X-rays in therapy; emission of radiant energy; use of radiation to induce chemical change.

irrational, ir·rash′on·al, *a.* [Prefix *ir* for *in,* not, and *rational.*] Not rational; void of reason or understanding; contrary to reason; absurd; *math.* not capable of being exactly expressed by an integral number or by a vulgar fraction; surd.— **irrationality, irrationalness,** ir·rash′on·al″i·ti, ir·rash′on·al·nes, *n.* The condition or quality of being irrational.—**irrationally,** ir·rash′on·al·li, *adv.* In an irrational manner.

irreclaimable, ir·ri·klā′ma·bl, *a.* [Prefix *ir* for *in,* not, and *reclaimable.*] Incapable of being reclaimed or recalled from error or vice; incapable of being reformed; incorrigible.— **irreclaimably,** ir·ri·klā′ma·bli, *adv.*

irreconcilable, ir·rek′on·sī″la·bl, *a.* [Prefix *ir* for *in,* not, and *reconcilable.*] Not reconcilable; not to be reconciled; implacable (an enemy, enmity); incapable of being made to agree or be consistent; inconsistent. —*n.* One who is not to be reconciled; especially, a member of a political body who will not work in harmony with his co-members.— **irreconcilability, irreconcilableness,**

ir·rek′on·sī″la·bil″i·ti, ir·rek′on·sī″la·bl·nes, *n.* The quality of being irreconcilable.—**irreconcilably,** ir·rek′on·sī″la·bli, *adv.* So as to preclude reconciliation.

irrecoverable, ir·ri·kuv′ėr·a·bl, *a.* [Prefix *ir* for *in,* not, and *recoverable.*] Incapable of being recovered or regained; not capable of being restored, remedied, or made good.— **irrecoverableness,** ir·ri·kuv′ėr·a·bl·nes, *n.* The state of being irrecoverable.—**irrecoverably,** ir·ri·kuv′ėr·a·bli, *adv.* In an irrecoverable manner; beyond recovery.

irredeemable, ir·ri·dē′ma·bl, *a.* [Prefix *ir* for *in,* not, and *redeemable.*] Not redeemable; not subject to be paid at its nominal value: specifically applied to a depreciated paper currency.—**irredeemably,** ir·ri·dē′ma·bli, *adv.* So as not to be redeemed.

irreducible, ir·ri·dū′si·bl, *a.* [Prefix *ir* for *in,* not, and *reducible.*] Not reducible; incapable of being reduced.

irrefragable, ir·ref′ra·ga·bl, *a.* [Prefix *ir* for *in,* not, and L. *refragor,* to withstand or gainsay—*re,* back, and root of *frango,* to break. FRACTION.] Incapable of being refuted or overthrown; incontestable; undeniable; incontrovertible. —**irrefragability,** ir·ref′ra·ga·bil″i·ti, *n.* The quality of being irrefragable.—**irrefragably,** ir·ref′ra·ga·bli, *adv.* In an irrefragable manner; incontestably.

irrefutable, ir·ref′ū·ta·bl or ir·ri·fū′ta·bl, *a.* [Prefix *ir* for *in,* not, and *refutable.*] Not refutable; incapable of being refuted or disproved.— **irrefutably,** ir·ri·fū′ta·bli or ir·ref′ū·ta·bli, *adv.* In an irrefutable manner.

irregular, ir·reg′ū·lėr, *a.* [Prefix *ir* for *in,* and *regular.*] Not regular; not according to rules, established principles, or customs; not conformable to the usual operation of natural laws; deviating from the rules of moral rectitude; vicious; not straight or uniform; *gram.* deviating from the common form in respect to the inflectional terminations; *geom.* applied to a figure whose sides as well as angles are not all equal and similar among themselves; *bot.* not having the parts of the same size or form, or arranged with symmetry.—*n.* One not conforming to settled rule; especially, a soldier not in regular service. —**irregularity,** ir·reg′ū·lar″i·ti, *n.* State or character of being irregular; want of regularity; that which is irregular; a part exhibiting or causing something to be irregular or impairing uniformity; an action or behavior constituting a breach of morality; vicious conduct.—**irregularly,** ir·reg′ū·lėr·li, *adv.* In an irregular manner.

irrelative, ir·rel′a·tiv, *a.* [Prefix *ir* for *in,* not, and *relative.*] Not relative; without mutual relations.—**irrelatively,** ir·rel′a·tiv·li, *adv.*

irrelevant, ir·rel′e·vant, *a.* [Prefix *ir* for *in,* not. and *relevant.*] Not relevant; not applicable or pertinent; not bearing on the case in point or matter in hand.—**irrelevantly,** ir··

rel′e·vant·li, *adv*. In an irrelevant manner.—**irrelevance, irrelevancy,** ir·rel′e·vans, ir·rel′e·van·si, *n*. The quality of being irrelevant.

irreligion, ir·ri·lij′on, *n*. [Prefix *ir* for *in*, not, and *religion*.] Want of religion or contempt of it; impiety.—**irreligious,** ir·ri·lij′us, *a*. Characterized by irreligion; disregarding or contemning religion; contrary to religion; profane; impious; ungodly.—**irreligiously,** ir·ri·lij′us·li, *adv*. In an irreligious manner.

irremeable,† ir·re·mi′a·bl, *a*. [L. *irremeabilis*—*ir* for *in*, not, *re*, back, and *meo*, to go.] Not permitting of a person's return.

irremediable, ir·ri·mē′di·a·bl, *a*. [Prefix *ir* for *in*, not, and *remediable*.] Incapable of being remedied or cured; not to be corrected or redressed; incurable; irreparable.—**irremediableness,** ir·ri·mē′di·a·bl·nes, *n*.—**irremediably,** ir·ri·mē′di·a·bli, *adv*.

irremissible, ir·ri·mis′i·bl, *a*. [Prefix *ir* for *in*, not, and *remissible*.] Not remissible; unpardonable; not capable of being remitted.—**irremissibly,** ir·ri·mis′i·bli, *adv*.

irremovable, ir·ri·mö′va·bl, *a*. [Prefix *ir* for *in*, not, and *removable*.] Not removable; immovable; inflexible.—**irremovably,** ir·ri·mö′va·bli, *adv*. In an irremovable manner.—**irremovability,** ir·ri·mö′va·bil″i·ti, *n*. The quality or state of being irremovable.

irreparable, ir·rep′a·ra·bl, *a*. [Prefix *ir* for *in*, not, and *reparable*.] Not reparable; incapable of being repaired; irremediable.—**irreparability, irreparableness,** ir·rep′a·ra·bil″i·ti, ir·rep′a·ra·bl·nes, *n*. State of being irreparable.—**irreparably,** ir·rep′a·ra·bli, *adv*. In an irreparable manner; irrecoverably.

irrepressible, ir·ri·pres′i·bl, *a*. [Prefix *ir* for *in*, not, and *repressible*.] Not repressible; incapable of being repressed, restrained, or kept under control.—**irrepressibly,** ir·ri·pres′i·bli, *adv*. In a manner or degree precluding repression.

irreproachable, ir·ri·prōch′a·bl, *a*. [Prefix *ir* for *in*, not, and *reproachable*.] Incapable of being reproached; not occasioning reproach; upright; innocent; faultless; unblemished.—**irreproachableness,** ir·ri·prōch′a·bl·nes, *n*. The quality or state of being irreproachable.—**irreproachably,** ir·ri·prōch′a·bli, *adv*. In an irreproachable manner; faultlessly; blamelessly.

irresistance, ir·ri·zis′tans, *n*. [Prefix *ir* for *in*, not, and *resist*.] Forbearance to resist; nonresistance.—**irresistible,** ir·ri·zis′ti·bl, *a*. Not resistible; incapable of being successfully resisted or opposed; resistless; invincible.—**irresistibility,** ir·ri·zis′ti·bil″i·ti, *n*. The quality of being irresistible.—**irresistibly,** ir·ri·zis′ti·bli, *adv*. In an irresistible manner; resistlessly.

irresoluble,† ir·rez′o·lū·bl, *a*. [Prefix *ir* for *in*, not, and *resoluble*.] Incapable of resolution into parts; indissoluble.—**irresolubleness,** ir·rez′o·lū·bl·nes, *n*.

irresolute, ir·rez′o·lūt, *a*. [Prefix *ir*

for *in*, not, and *resolute*.] Not resolute; not firm or constant in purpose; undecided; wavering; given to doubt or hesitation; vacillating.—**irresolutely,** ir·rez′o·lūt·li, *adv*. In an irresolute manner.—**irresoluteness,** ir·rez′o·lūt·nes, *n*. The quality of being irresolute.—**irresolution,** ir·rez′o·lū″shon, *n*. Want of resolution or decision; a fluctuation of mind; vacillation.

irresolvable, ir·ri·zol′va·bl, *a*. [Prefix *ir* for *in*, not, and *resolvable*.] Incapable of being resolved.

irrespective, ir·ri·spek′tiv, *a*. [Prefix *ir* for *in*, not, and *respective*.] Having no respect to particular circumstances: generally used in the prepositional phrase *irrespective of*, that is, leaving out of account.—**irrespectively,** ir·ri·spek′tiv·li, *adv*. Without regard to certain circumstances (*irrespectively of* these matters).

irrespirable, ir·ri·spī′ra·bl, *a*. [Prefix *ir* for *in*, not, and *respirable*.] Not respirable; unfit for respiration.

irresponsible, ir·ri·spon′si·bl, *a*. [Prefix *ir* for *in*, not, and *responsible*.] Not responsible; not liable to answer for consequences. —**irresponsibly,** ir·ri·spon′si·bli, *adv*. In an irresponsible manner.—**irresponsibility,** ir·ri·spon′si·bil″i·ti, *n*. Want of responsibility.

irresponsive, ir·ri·spon′siv, *a*. [Prefix *ir* for *in*, not, and *responsive*.] Not responsive.

irretraceable, ir·ri·trā′sa·bl, *a*. [Prefix *ir* for *in*, not, and *retraceable*.] Not retraceable.

irretrievable, ir·ri·trē′va·bl, *a*. [Prefix *ir* for *in*, not, and *retrievable*.] Not retrievable; irrecoverable; irreparable.—**irretrievably,** ir·ri·trē′va·bli, *adv*. In an irretrievable manner; irrecoverably.

irreverence, ir·rev′er·ens, *n*. [Prefix *ir* for *in*, not, and *reverence*; L. *irreverentia*.] Want of reverence or veneration; want of a due regard to the authority and character of a superior; irreverent conduct or an irreverent action.—**irreverent,** ir·rev′er·ent, *a*. [L. *irreverens*.] Exhibiting or marked by irreverence (person, conduct, words); wanting in respect to superiors.—**irreverently,** ir·rev′er·ent·li, *adv*. In an irreverent manner; with want of reverence; disrespectfully.

irreversible, ir·ri·vėr′si·bl, *a*. [Prefix *ir* for *in*, not, and *reversible*.] Not reversible; incapable of being reversed.—**irreversibly,** ir·ri·vėr′si·bli, *adv*. In an irreversible manner; so as not to be reversed; immutably.

irrevocable, ir·rev′o·ka·bl, *a*. [Prefix *ir* for *in*, not, and *revocable*.] Not to be recalled or revoked; incapable of being reversed, repealed, or annulled; irreversible (fate, decree, etc.).—**irrevocability, irrevocableness,** ir·rev′o·ka·bil″i·ti, ir·rev′o·ka·bl·nes, *n*. State of being irrevocable.—**irrevocably,** ir·rev′o·ka·bli, *adv*. In an irrevocable manner; irreversibly; immutably.

irrigate, ir′ri·gāt, *v.t.*—**irrigated, irrigating.** [L. *irrigo, irrigatum*—*ir* for *in*,

and *rigo*, to water. RAIN.] To bedew or sprinkle; to water (land) by causing a stream to flow upon it and spread over it; to water by various artificial channels for water.—**irrigation,** ir·ri·gā′shon, *n*. [L. *irrigatio*.] The act or operation of irrigating.—**irriguous,** ir·rig′ū·us, *a*. [L. *irriguus*.] Having many streams; well watered. (*Mil.*)

irritant, ir′ri·tant, *a*. [L. *irrito*, to make void, from *in*, not, and *ratus*, ratified.] *Scots law*, rendering null and void.—**irritancy,** ir′ri·tan·si, *n*. The state of being irritant or null and void.

irritate, ir′ri·tāt, *v.t.* [L. *irrito, irritatum*, to incite, stir up, provoke; perhaps from *hirrire*, to snarl.] To excite anger in; to provoke; to tease; to exasperate; to excite heat and redness in, as in the skin or flesh; to inflame; to fret; *physiol.* to excite by certain stimuli; to cause to exhibit irritation.—**irritation,** ir·ri·tā′shon, *n*. [L. *irritatio, irritationis*.] The act of irritating or state of being irritated; provocation; exasperation; angry feeling; feeling of heat and pain in a part of the body; *physiol.* the change or action which takes place in muscles or organs when a nerve or nerves are affected by the application of external bodies.—**irritative,** ir′ri·tā·tiv, *a*. Serving to excite or irritate.—**irritable,** ir′ri·ta·bl, *a*. [L. *irritabilis*.] Capable or susceptible of being irritated; readily provoked or exasperated; of a fiery temper; *physiol.* susceptible of responding to or being acted upon by stimuli.—**irritability, irritableness,** ir′ri·ta·bil″i·ti, ir′ri·ta·bl·nes, *n*. The state or quality of being irritable.—**irritably,** ir′ri·ta·bli, *adv*. In an irritable manner.—**irritant,** ir′ri·tant, *a*. [L. *irritans, irritantis*, ppr. of *irrito*.] Irritating; producing pain, heat, or tension; producing inflammation (an *irritant* poison).—*n*. That which excites or irritates; a medical application that causes pain or heat (as a fly blister); an irritant poison.

irruption, ir·rup′shon, *n*. [L. *irruptio, irruptionis*, from *irrumpo, irruptum*—*in*, in, and *rumpo*, to break. RUPTURE.] A bursting in; a breaking, or sudden, violent rushing into a place; a sudden invasion or incursion.—**irruptive,** ir·rup′tiv, *a*. Rushing in or upon.

is, iz, [A.Sax. is=Goth. *ist*, L. *est*, Gr. *esti*, Skr. *asti*, is. AM.] The 3rd, pers. sing. of the verb *to be*. BE.

isagogic, i·sa·goj′ik, *a*. [Gr. *eisagōgikos*, from *eisagó*, to introduce—*eis*, in, into, and *agó*, to lead.] Introductory; especially, introductory to the study of theology.—**isagogics,** i·sa·goj′iks, *n*. The department of theological study introductory to exegesis.

ischiadic, is·ki·ad′ik, *a*. [L. *ischiadicus*, from *ischias*, sciatica, from *ischium*, Gr. *ischion*, the hip.] Pertaining to sciatica.—*Ischiadic passion* or *disease*, sciatica.—**ischial,** is′ki·al, *a*. Belonging to the ischium or hipbone.—**ischiatic,** is·ki·at′ik, *a*. Per-

taining to the ischium of the hip.—
ischium, is′ki•um, *n.* [Gr. *ischion.*]
Anat. the posterior and inferior
part of the pelvic arch at the hip
joint.
Ishmaelite, ish′mi•el•it, *n.* [From
Ishmael: Gen. xvi. 12.] A descendant of Ishmael; one resembling
Ishmael, whose hand was against
every man and every man's hand
against him; one at war with society.
Ishmaelitish, ish′mi•el•it•ish, *a.*
Like Ishmael or an Ishmaelite.
isinglass, i′zing•glas, *n.* [Corrupted
from D. *huizenblas*—*huizen*, a sturgeon, and *blas*, a vesicle, a bladder
(akin to *blow, bladder*).] A gelatinous
substance from air bladders of certain fishes, particularly species of
sturgeon found in the rivers of
Russia, used in clarifying liquors,
as a cement, etc.; also thin sheets
of mica.
Isis, i′sis, *n.* One of the chief deities
in the Egyptian mythology, regarded
as the sister or sister-wife of Osiris.
Islam, iz′lam, *n.* [Ar., from *salama*,
to be free, safe, or devoted to God.]
The religion of Mohammed, and
also the whole body of those who
profess it throughout the world.—
Islamic, iz•lam′ik, *a.*—**Islamism,** iz′-
lam•izm, *n.*—**Islamite,** iz′lam•it, *n.*
A Mohammedan.—**Islamize,** iz′lam•-
iz, *v.t.* or *i.* To conform to Islamism;
to Mohammedanize.
island, i′land, *n.* [From A.Sax. *igland*,
lit. island-land, from *ig*, an island,
and *land*, land; the *s* is due to
erroneous connection with L. *insula*,
O.Fr. *isle*. ISLE.] A tract of land
surrounded by water, whether of the
sea, a river, or a lake; anything
resembling an island; a safety zone
in the middle of a street; the raised
area located next to the flight deck
on the starboard side of an aircraft
carrier.—*v.t.* To cause to become
or appear like an island; to isolate;
to dot, as with islands.—**islander,**
i′lan•der, *n.*
isle, il, *n.* [O.Fr. *isle*, Fr. *ile*, Prov.
isla, from L. *insula*, an island.
INSULATE.] An island. [Chiefly poet.]
—*v.t.*—**isled, isling.** To cause to
become or appear like an isle; to
isolate; to island.—**islet,** il′et, *n.*
[Dim. of *isle*.] A little isle or something similar.
isobar, i′so•bär, *n.* [Gr. *isos*, equal,
and *baros*, weight.] A line drawn
on a map connecting places at which
the mean height of the barometer at
sea level is the same; isotopes of
different chemical elements which
have equal atomic masses but
different atomic numbers.—**isobaric,**
i•so•bar′ik, *a.*
isocheim, i′so•kim, *n.* [Gr. *isos*,
equal, and *cheima, cheimōn*, winter.]
A line drawn on a map through
places which have the same mean
winter temperature.—**isocheimal,
isochimal,** i•so•ki′mal, *a.* Of the
same mean winter temperature;
marking places with the same mean
winter temperature.—*Isocheimal line.*
Same as Isocheim.
isochromatic, i′so•krō•mat′ik, *a.* [Gr.
isos, equal, and *chrōma*, color.]

Having the same color; marking
correspondence in tint as colored
light passes through biaxial crystals.
isochronal, isochronous, i•sok′ron•-
al, i•sok′ron•us, *a.* [Gr. *isos*, equal,
and *chronos*, time.] Uniform in time;
of equal time; performed in equal
times (as oscillations of pendulums).
—**isochronally,** i•sok′ron•al•li, *adv.*
So as to be isochronal.—**isochron-
ism,** i•sok′ron•izm, *n.* State or quality
of being isochronous.
isoclinal, isoclinic, i•so•kli′nal, i•so-
klin′ik, *a.* [Gr. *isos*, equal, and
klinō, to incline.] Of equal inclination or dip.
isodynamic, i′so•di•nam″ik, *a.* [Gr.
isos, equal, and *dynamis*, power.]
Having equal power or force.
isogeotherm, i•so•jē′o•thėrm, *n.* [Gr.
isos, equal, *gē*, the earth, and *thermē*,
heat.] An imaginary line or plane
under the earth's surface passing
through points having the same
mean temperature.—**isogeothermal,**
i•so•jē′o•thėr″mal, *a.* Pertaining to
isogeotherms.
isogonic, i•so•gon′ik, *a.* [Gr. *isos*,
equal, and *gōnia*, an angle.] Having
equal angles.—*Isogonic lines,* lines
connecting those places where the
deviation of the magnetic needle
from the true north is the same.
isohel, i′so•hel, *n.* [Gr. *helios*, sun.]
A line drawn on a map through
places having the same amount of
bright sunshine.
isolate, i′so•lāt or is′o•lāt, *v.t.*—*isolated, isolating.* [Fr. *isoler*, It. *isolare*,
from *isola*=L. *insula*, an island.
INSULATE.] To place or leave in a
detached situation; to place apart;
elect. to insulate; *chem.* to obtain
(a substance) free from all its combinations.—**isolation,** i•so•lā′shon,
n. State of being isolated or alone.—
isolable, i′so•la•bl, *a.*
isomerism, i•som′ėr•izm, *n.* [Gr. *isos*,
equal, and *meros*, a part.] *Chem.*
identity or close similarity of
elements in weight, but with differences in structure, and therefore
in properties; *phys.* and *chem.*
elements of the same atomic number
and mass number but having
different properties.—**isomeric,** i•so-
mėr′ik, *a.*—**isomerous,** i•som′ėr•us,
a. Bot. having organs composed each
of an equal number of parts.
isometric, isometrical, i•so•met′-
rik, i•so•met′ri•kal, *a.* [Gr. *isos*,
equal, *metron*, measure.] Pertaining
to, or characterized by, equality of
measure.—*Isometrical perspective* or
projection, a method of drawing
plans whereby the elevation and
ground plan are represented in
one view.—**isometrics,** i•so•met′riks,
n. Physiol. a series of physical exercises, employing opposing forces,
such as in pushing against the
body itself or against an immovable
object.
isomorphism, i•so•mor′fizm, *n.* [Gr.
isos, like, and *morphē*, form.] A
similarity of crystalline form in
minerals.—**isomorphous,** i•so•mor′-
fus, *a.* Exhibiting the property of
isomorphism.
isonomy, i•son′o•mi, *n.* [Gr. *isos*,

equal, and *nomos*, law.] Equal law;
equal distribution of rights and
privileges.
isopod, i′so•pod, *n.* [Gr. *isos*, equal,
and *pous, podos*, the foot.] One
of an order of crustaceans, comprehending those whose feet are of
equal size and move in the same
direction; the wood lice, and slaters
are examples.
isopyre, i′so•pir, *n.* [Gr. *isos*, like,
and *pyr*, fire.] A variety of opal mixed
with impurities.
isosceles, i•sos′se•lēz, *a.* [Gr. *isos-
kelēs*—*isos*, equal, and *skelos*, leg.]
Having two legs or sides only that
are equal (an *isosceles* triangle).
isoseismal, isoseismic, i•so•sis′-
mal, i•so•sis′mik, *a.* [Gr. *isos*, equal,
and *seismos*, an earthquake, from
seiō, to shake.] Marking equal earthquake disturbance on the earth's
surface.
isothere, i′so•thėr, *n.* [Gr. *isos*, equal,
and *theros*, summer.] An imaginary
line on the earth's surface passing
through points having the same
mean summer temperature.—**isoth-
eral,** i•soth′ėr•al, *a.* Pertaining to
or marked by isotheres.
isotherm, i′so•thėrm, *n.* [Gr. *isos*,
equal, proper, and *therme*, heat.]
An imaginary line on the earth's
surface passing through places having
a corresponding temperature either
throughout the year or at any particular period.—**isothermal,** i•so•-
thėr′mal, *a.* Pertaining to an isotherm or isotherms; marking correspondence in temperature.—*Isothermal line,* an isotherm.
isotonic, i•so•ton′ik, *a.* [Gr. *isos*,
equal, and *tonos*, tone.] Having or
indicating equal tones.
isotope, i′so•tōp, *n.* [Gr. *isos*, equal,
and *topos*, place.] Any of two or
more forms of a chemical element
having the same atomic number
but different atomic weights.
isotropic, i•so•trop′ik, *a.* [Gr. *isos*,
equal, and *tropē*, a turning, from
trepō, to turn.] *Phys.* pertaining
to bodies whose properties are the
same in all directions; *biol.* without
predetermined axes, as some eggs.
Israelite, iz′ri•el•it, *n.* A descendant
of *Israel*, or Jacob; a Jew.—**Israelitic,
Israelitish,** iz′ri•el•it″ik, iz′ri•el•it″-
ish, *a.* Pertaining to Israel; Jewish;
Hebrew.
issue, ish′ū, *n.* [Fr. *issue*, issue,
outlet, event, from O.Fr. *issir*, to
go out, to flow forth, and that from
L. *exeo, exire*, to go out—*ex*, out,
and *eo*, to go (in *circuit, exit, initial*,
etc). ITINERANT.] The act of passing
or flowing out; a moving out of any
enclosed place; the act of sending
out; delivery (of commands, money,
etc.); the whole quantity sent forth
or issued at one time (an *issue* of
paper money; yesterday's *issue* of
the *Times*); what happens or turns
out; event; consequence; progeny;
a child or children; offspring; all
persons descended from a common
ancestor; a flux of blood (*N.T.*);
surg. an artificial ulcer made in
some part of the body to promote
a secretion of pus; *law*, the close

---

ch, *chain*;   ch, Sc. lo*ch*;   g, *go*;   j, *job*;   ng, si*ng*;   TH, *then*;   th, *thin*;   w, *wig*;   hw, *whig*;   zh, a*z*ure.

or result of pleadings; the point or matter depending in a suit on which two parties join and put their cause to trial; hence, a material point turning up in any argument or debate, when one party takes the negative, the other the positive side on an important point.—*At issue*, in controversy; disputed; opposing or contesting.—*To join issue, to take issue*, said of two parties who take up a positive and negative position respectively on a point in debate.—*v.i.*—*issued,issuing*. To pass, flow, or run out, as from any enclosed place; to proceed, as from a source; to rush out; to proceed, as progeny; to be produced, as an effect or result; to close, end, terminate.—*v.t.* To send out; to deliver for use; to deliver authoritatively (orders, etc.); to put (notes, coin, newspapers) into circulation.—**issuable**, ish′ū·a·bl, *a.* Capable of being issued; admitting of issue being taken upon it.—**issuance**, ish′ū·ans, *n.* The act of issuing or giving out.—**issuer**, ish′ū·er, *n.* One who issues or emits.

isthmus, is′mus, *n.* [L., from Gr. *isthmos*, a neck of land or narrow passage.] A neck or narrow slip of land by which two continents are connected, or by which a peninsula is united to the mainland.—**isthmian**, is′mi·an, *a.* Of or pertaining to an isthmus.—*Isthmian games*, ancient Greek games celebrated at the Isthmus of Corinth, in the first and third year of each olympiad, in honor of Poseidon.

it, it, *pron*, [A.Sax. nom. *hit*, neut. corresponding to *hé*, he, genit. or pos. *his*, dat. and instrumental *him*; Goth. *ita*, D. *het*, O.H.G. *iz*, G. *es*. HE.] A pronoun of the neuter gender corresponding with the masculine *he* and the feminine *she*, having the same plural *they*. Besides standing in place of neuter nouns *it* is used (1) as the nominative to impersonal verbs (*it* rains; *it* snows); (2) to introduce a sentence, preceding a verb as a nominative, but referring to a clause or distinct member of the sentence following (*it* is well ascertained that the figure of the earth is an oblate spheroid); (3) for a preceding clause of a sentence (we have been defeated for the present, *it* is true); (4) to begin a sentence when a personal pronoun, or the name of a person, or a masculine or feminine noun follows, where it may represent any one of the three persons or of the three genders (as, *it* is I; *it* was they); (5) for state of matters, condition of affairs, or the like (has *it* come to this?); (6) after intransitive verbs very indefinitely (to walk *it*, to run *it*). ∴ The possessive case *its* does not appear till a year or two before 1600, *his* being used both for the masculine and the neuter possessive.

Italian, i·tal′yan, *a.* Pertaining to *Italy*.—*n.* A native of Italy; the language used in Italy or by the Italians.—*Italian iron*, a smoothing iron, consisting essentially of a

metal tube with a closed rounded end heated by a metal bolt; used for fluting or gauffering.—*Italian warehouse*, a name in England for shops where groceries, including some Italian products, are sold.—*Italian handwriting*, the method of penmanship, practically the copperplate hand of clear lettering, adopted from Italy, opposed to the old Gothic script.—**Italianism, Italicism**, i·tal′yan·izm, i·tal′i·sism, *n.* An Italian expression, manner, or custom.—**Italianize**, i·tal′yan·īz, *v.t.* To give an Italian color or character to.—**Italic**, i·tal′ik, *a.* Pertaining to Italy; [*not cap.*] the name of a printing type sloping toward the right, invented about A.D. 1500 by Aldus Manutius, a Venetian printer. —*n.* [*not cap.*] An italic letter or type.—**italicize**, i·tal′i·sīz, *v.t.*—*italicized, italicizing*. To write or print in italic characters; to distinguish by italics.

itch, ich, *n.* [O.E. *ichyn, gykin*, A.Sax. *giccan*, to itch; G. *jucken*, to itch; D. *jeuking, jeukte*, Sc. *yuik*, itch.] A sensation in the skin causing a great desire to scratch or rub; a cutaneous disease due to a minute species of mite; a constant teasing desire (an *itch* for praise).—*v.i.* To feel an itch; to have an uneasy or teasing sensation impelling to something.—**itch mite**, *n.* The microscopic animal which produces itch. —**itchy**, ich′i, *a.* Infected with or having the sensation as if suffering from itch.

item, ī′tem, *n.* [L. *item*, also.] A separate article; a particular; a piece of information; one thing in a list; a scrap of news.—**itemize**, ī′tem·īz, *v.t.* To list or state the items, to particularize.

iterate, it′ér·āt, *v.t.*—*iterated, iterating*. [L. *itero, iteratum*, to do again, to repeat, from *iterum*, again, from *id*, it, with the comparative suffix; akin Skr. *itara*, another.] To utter or do a second time; to repeat.— **iteration**, it·ér·ā′shon, *n.* [L. *iteratio, iterationis*.] Repetition; recital or performance a second time.—**iterative**, it′ér·ā·tiv, *a.* Repeating.

itinerant, ī·tin′ér·ant, *a.* [L.L. *itinerans, itinerantis*, traveling, from L. *iter, itineris*, a way or journey; from root *i*, to go, seen also in *circuit, exit, transit, ambition, initial, issue, perish*, etc.] Passing or traveling about a country or district; wandering; not settled; strolling.—*n.* One who travels from place to place.— **itinerary**, ī·tin′ér·a·si, *n.* Practice of itinerating.—**itinerancy**, ī·tin′ér·an·si, *n.* A passing from place to place; the passing from place to place in the discharge of official duty.—**itinerantly**, ī·tin′ér·ant·li, *adv.* In an itinerant, unsettled, or wandering manner.—**itinerary**, ī·tin′ér·a·ri, *n.* [L.L. *itinerarium*.] A work containing notices of the places and stations; route of a journey or trip; the outline of a prospective route to be taken in making a journey; the course of an official tour of royal or distinguished visitors.—*a.*

Pertaining to a travel route.— **itinerate**, ī·tin′ér·āt, *v.i.*—*itinerated, itinerating*. To travel from place to place, particularly for the purpose of preaching.

its, its. Possessive case of the pronoun it.—**itself**, it·self′, *pron.* The neuter pronoun corresponding to *himself, herself*.

ivory, ī′vo·ri, *n.* [O.Fr. *ivurie*, Fr. *ivoire*, from L. *eboreus*, made of ivory, from *ebur*, ivory; akin Skr. *ibha*, an elephant.] The substance of elephant tusks; a similar substance obtained from the tusks of the walrus, the hippopotamus, the narwhal, etc.; a color, like ivory. *pl.* Articles made of ivory, such as piano keys or dice.—*a.* Consisting or made of ivory.—**ivory black**, *n.* A fine black pigment, prepared from ivory dust by calcination.— **ivory nut**, *n.* The seed of a South American palm, about as large as a hen's egg, and resembling ivory in texture and color; vegetable ivory.— **ivory palm**, *n.* The tree which bears the ivory nut.

ivy, ī′vi, *n.* [A.Sax. *ifig*; akin to G. *epheu*. O.G. *ebeheu, ebah*, ivy.] An evergreen climbing plant, growing in hedges, woods, on old buildings, rocks, and trunks of trees.

ixtle, iks′tle, *n.* A name for a kind of fiber obtained in Mexico from a species of agave.

J

J, j, jā, Tenth letter in the English alphabet, the seventh consonant, sounding like *g* in *genius*.

jab, jab, *v.t.* and *i.* [Imitative.] To stab, as with a sharp stick.—*n.* A poke or quick thrust with something sharp.

jabber, jab′ér, *v.i.* [A form equivalent to *gabble*, Sc. *gabber*, freq. of *gab*, to talk much or pertly, GAB.] To talk rapidly, indistinctly, or nonsensically; to chatter.—*v.t.* To utter rapidly (to *jabber* French).—*n.* Rapid, indistinct utterance.—**jabberer**, jab′ér·ér, *n.* One who jabbers.

jabiru, jab′i·rö, *n.* [Brazilian name.] A tall wading bird resembling the stork, a native of Africa and America.

jaborandi, jab·o·ran′di, *n.* [Brazilian.] A drug obtained from a Brazilian plant of the rue family, causing increase of saliva and profuse perspiration.

jaçana, zhä′se·nä″, *n.* The name of sundry tropical grallatorial birds, having very long toes, so that they can easily walk on the leaves of aquatic plants.

jacaranda, jak·a·ran′da, *n.* The name of several Brazilian trees yielding fancy woods.

jacinth, ja′sinth, *n.* The gem also called *Hyacinth*.

jack, jak, *n.* [From Fr. *Jacques*, L. *Jacobus*, James; it came to be used as a familiar substitute for the common name *John*, instead of for *James*.] [*cap.*] A sailor; a name of various contrivances or implements; an implement to assist a person in pulling off his boots; a bootjack; a contrivance for raising great weights by the action of screws; a contrivance for turning a spit; a blackjack; a small bowl thrown out for a mark to the players in the game of bowls; a flag displayed from a staff on the end of a bowsprit; male of certain animals, as the ass; the fish more commonly called the pike; a young pike; any of the knaves in a pack of cards; pl. a game played with a half dozen small six-pointed metal pieces and a rubber ball; the metal pieces themselves; a receptacle with connections to electric circuits, into which a plug can be inserted.—**jackanapes**, jak′a·nāpes, n. An impertinent or presumptuous fellow.—**jack-in-the-box**, n.—A toy made of a box, out of which, when the lid is opened, a figure springs.—**jack-o′-lantern**, n. A lantern made from a hollowed pumpkin carved to resemble a face.—**jackass**, jak′ass, n. The male of the ass; an ignorant or stupid person.—**jack boot**, n. A kind of large boot reaching up over the knee.—**jackdaw**, jak′dạ, n. A small species of crow.—**jack-of-all-trades**, n. A man handy with tools; a man possessing a superficial skill in several trades, hence, *Jack-of-all-trades, and master of none.*—**jackknife**, n. A large strong clasp knife for the pocket.—**jack-in-the-pulpit**, n. An American flowering herb of the Arum family (*Arisaema atrorubens*), its upright spadix arched over by a green and purple spathe.—**jackpot**, n. *Poker,* the pool which is opened when one player has a pair of jacks or something higher; unexpected success or winnings.—**jack rabbit**, n. One of the large hares, several species of which have long ears and long hind legs, destructive to crops in the middle west and west.—**jackscrew**, n. A jack for lifting heavy objects.—**jacksnipe**, n. A small species of snipe.—**jackstone**, n. A children's game, played with small stones or metal pieces.—**jackstraw**, n. A figure of a man made of straw; pl. a game played with straws or strips of wood, etc.—**jack towel**, n. A coarse towel for general use, hanging from a roller.

jackal, jak′ạl, n. [Fr. *chacal*, Turk. *chakal*, Per. *shaghái, shagál*, a jackal.] A carnivorous animal closely allied to the dog and the wolf; from an erroneous notion that the jackal hunted up prey for the king of beasts, he was often called the lion's provider, hence, a person who performs a similar office for another.

jacket, jak′et, n. [Fr. *jaquette*, dim. of *jaque*, a coat of mail, a jacket.] A short outer garment extending downward to the hips; an outer casing of cloth, felt, wood, etc.; a general term for an outside covering (a potato *jacket*); the outside covering of a book.—v.t. To cover or furnish with a jacket.

Jacobean, ja·kō·bē·an, a. [L. *Jacobus*, James, from Heb. *Jacob*.] *Arch.*

the term sometimes applied to the later style of Elizabethan architecture prevailing in the age of James I.—**Jacobin**, jak′o·bin, n. [Fr., from L. *Jacobus*, James.] A Gray or Dominican Friar, from these friars having first established themselves in Paris in the Rue St. Jacques (Saint James Street); a member of a club of violent republicans in France during the revolution of 1789; a politician of similar character; [*not cap.*] a variety of pigeon whose neck feathers form a hood.—**Jacobinic, Jacobinical**, jak·o·bin′ik, jak·o·bin′i·kal, a. Pertaining to or resembling the Jacobins of France.—**Jacobinism**, jak′o·bin·izm, n. The principles of Jacobins.—**Jacobinize**, jak′o·bin·īz, v.t.—*jacobinized, jacobinizing.* To taint with Jacobinism.—**Jacobite**, jak′o·bīt, n. [From L. *Jacobus*, James.] A partisan or adherent of James II of England after he abdicated the throne, and of his descendants.—a. Pertaining to the Jacobites.—**Jacobitical**, jak·o·bit′i·kal, a. Pertaining to the Jacobites.—**Jacobitism**, jak′o·bit·ism, n. The principles of the Jacobites.—**Jacob's-ladder**, n. A garden plant with handsome blue (sometimes white) flowers; *naut.* a rope ladder with wooden steps or spokes.

Jacquard loom, jak·kärd′, n. [From *Jacquard* of Lyons, who died in 1834.] An ingenious loom for weaving figured goods.

jactitation, jak·ti·tā′shon, n. [L. *jactito*, freq. from *jacto*, freq. of *jacio*, to throw. JET.] A frequent tossing of the body; restlessness; also, vain boasting; bragging.

jaculate, jak′ū·lāt, v.t. [L. *jaculatus*, to throw the javelin, from *jaculum*, javelin, *jacio*, to throw.] To dart; to throw out.

jade, jād, n. [Sc. *yaud, jaud*, an old mare; Icel. *jalda*, Prov. Sw. *jälda*, a mare.] A mean or poor horse; a worthless nag; a mean or vile woman; a hussy, used opprobriously; a young woman, used in humor or slight contempt.—v.t.—*jaded, jading.* To ride or drive severely; to overdrive; to weary or fatigue.—v.i. To become weary; to lose spirit.—**jaded**, jā′ded, p. and a. Wearied out; fatigued; harassed.—**jadish**, jā′dish, a. Like or pertaining to a jade.

jade, jād, n. [Fr. *jade* from Sp. *ijada*, colic stone.] A kind of hard, tenacious gem or stone of a color more or less green, of a resinous or oily aspect when polished, capable of being carved, and used, especially by the Chinese, for ornaments.

jag, jag, v.t.—*jagged, jagging.* [Origin doubtful; comp. W. and Gael. *gag*, a cleft or chink; Gael. *gag*, to notch.] To notch; to cut into notches or teeth like those of a saw.—n. A notch or denticulation; a sharp protuberance or indentation; state of inebriation (*slang*).—**jagged**, jag′ed, p. and a. Having notches or teeth; cleft; divided; laciniate.—**jaggedness**, jag′ed·nes, n.—**jagger**, jag′ẽr, n. One who or that which jags.

jaggery, jag′ẽr·i, n. [Hind *jâgri*.] In the East Indies sugar in its coarse state; imperfectly granulated sugar; also, the inspissated juice of the palmyra tree.

jaguar, jag·wär′, n. [Brazilian *jaguara*.] The American tiger; a powerful, spotted member of the cat family found mostly in South America.

Jahve, yä′ve, n. [Heb.] Jehovah.

jail, jāl, n. [Fr. *geole*, O.Fr. *gaiole*, a prison; L.L. *gabiola*, from L. *cavea*, a cage, coop, den, from *cavus*, hollow. CAVE.] A prison; a building or place for the confinement of persons arrested for crime; a lockup.—v.t. To put in prison; to imprison.—**jailbird**, jāl′bẽrd, n. One who has been confined in jail.

Jain, Jaina, jān, jā′na, n. One of a Hindu religious sect believing doctrines similar to those of Buddhism.—**Jainism**, jān′izm, n. The doctrines of the Jains.

jalap, jal′ap, n. [Fr. *jalap*; Sp. *jalapa*, from *Jalapa* in Mexico.] A purgative medicine, principally obtained from the tuberous roots of a climbing plant of the convolvulus family, a native of Mexico.

jalopy, ja·lop′i, n. [Origin unknown.] A neglected or run-down automobile or airplane. (Slang)

jalousie, zhäl·ö·zē′, n. [Fr., from *jaloux*, jealous. JEALOUS.] A wooden frame or blind for shading from the sunshine, much used in hot countries; a venetian blind.

jam, jam, n. [Probably from *jam*, v.t.; related to *champ*.] A conserve of fruits boiled with sugar and water.

jam, jam, v.t.—*jammed, jamming.* [Perhaps from *jamb*, pressing between two uprights or jambs.] To squeeze or press into a close or tight position; to become unworkable, as a machine, because parts are wedged together; to apply suddenly with force (*jam* on the brakes).—n. Act of jamming; a crush of people.—**jamming**, jam′ing, n. *Radio,* blocking radio messages by broadcasting noises, etc. on the same wavelength.—**jam session**, n. A meeting of jazz musicians for the purpose of improvising together.

jamb, jam, n. [Fr. *jambe*, a leg, a jamb.] The side or vertical piece of any opening in a wall, such as a door or window.

jamboree, jam·bo·rē′, n. A boy scout assembly; a noisy gathering.

jangle, jang′gl, v.i.—*jangled, jangling.* [O.Fr. *jangler, gangler*, from L.G. and D. *jangelen*, to brawl; imitative of sound.] To sound discordantly or harshly; to quarrel in words; to altercate; to bicker; to wrangle.—v.t. To cause to sound harshly or inharmoniously; to utter in a discordant manner.—n. Discordant sound; prate; babble.

janitor, jan′i·tẽr, n. [L., from *janua*, a door.] A caretaker of a building.

Janizary, jan′i·ze·ri, n. [Turk. *yeni*, new, and *tcheri*, militia, soldiers.] [*often not cap.*] A soldier of the Turkish footguards, a body originally composed of Christian slaves, but suppressed after a terrible struggle in 1826.

Jansenist, jan′sen·ist, n. A follower of *Jansen*, R. Catholic bishop of Ypres in Flanders, who leaned to the doctrine of irresistible grace as maintained by Calvin.—**Jansenism**, jan′sen·izm, n. The doctrine of the Jansenists.

January, jan′ū·e·ri, n. [L. *januarius*, the month consecrated to the god *Janus*, a deity represented with two faces looking opposite ways.] The first month of the year according to the present computation.—**Janus-faced**, a. Having two faces; double-dealing; deceitful.

japan, ja·pan′, n. [From the country so called.] Work varnished and figured in the manner practiced by the natives of Japan; the varnish employed in japanning articles; Japan lacquer.—v.t.—*japanned, japanning*. To varnish or cover with Japan lacquer.—*Japanned leather*, a species of enameled or varnished leather.—**Japanese**, jap′a·nēz, a. Pertaining to Japan or its inhabitants.— n. A native or natives of Japan; the language of the inhabitants of Japan. —**Japan lacquer**, n. A valuable black hard varnish used in japanning.

jape, jāp, n. A merry jest, or joke.

Japhetic, ja·fet′ik, a. Pertaining to *Japheth*, one of the sons of Noah (the *Japhetic* nations).

japonica, ja·pon′i·ka, n. [From *Japan*.] Japanese species of pear or quince.

jar, jär, v.i.—*jarred, jarring*. [Also found in forms *chur, jur*, and imitative of sound.] To strike together with a short rattle or tremulous sound; to give out a harsh sound; to sound discordantly; to be inconsistent; to clash or interfere; to quarrel; to dispute.—v.t. To cause a short tremulous motion to; to cause to shake or tremble.—n. A rattling vibration of sound; a harsh sound; clash of interest or opinions; collision; discord.

jar, jär, n. [Fr. *jarre*, Sp. *jarra*, a jar, from Ar. *jarra*, a water-pot.] A vessel of earthenware or glass, of various shapes and dimensions; the contents of a jar.

jardiniere, zhär·dēn·yâr′, n. [Fr., a female gardener, a gardener's wife.] An ornamental stand for plants and flowers.

jargon, jär′gon, n. [Fr.; origin doubtful. JAR. v.i.] Confused; unintelligible talk or language; gabble; gibberish; phraseology peculiar to a sect, profession, or the like; professional slang.—v.i. To utter unintelligible sounds.—**jargonize**, jär′gon·īz, v.i. To utter jargon.

jargon, jargoon, jär′gon, jär·gön′, n. [Fr. *jargon*, from It. *giargone*, properly a yellow stone, from Pers. *zargun*, gold-colored.] A variety of zircon, colorless or colored, the colorless forms resembling the diamond.—**jargonelle**, jär·go·nel′, n. [Fr., from *jargon*, the mineral.] A variety of early pear.

jasmine, jasmin, jas′min, n. [Fr. *jāsmin*; Ar. and ultimately Pers. *yāsemin*, jasmine.] The name of several elegant erect or climbing shrubs, with white or yellow flowers, from some of which delicious perfumes are extracted.

jasper, jas′pėr, n. [O.Fr. *jaspre*, Fr. *jaspe*, L., Gr. *iaspis*, Ar. *yashb*, Heb. *yashpheh*; hence *diaper*.] An impure opaque colored quartz, which admits of an elegant polish, and is used for vases, seals, etc.

jaundice, jan′dis, n. [O.E. *jaunes, jaunis*, Fr. *jaunisse*, from *jaune*, O.Fr. *jalne*, L. *galbanus, galbinus*, yellowish, *galbus*, yellow; same root as *yellow*.] A disease characterized by suppression and alteration of the liver functions, yellowness of the eyes and skin, with loss of appetite and general languor and lassitude; any feeling or emotion disordering the judgment.—v.t.—*jaundiced, jaundicing*. To affect with jaundice; to affect with prejudice.

jaunt, jant, v.i. [Formerly *jaunce*, from O.Fr. *jancer*; of doubtful origin.] To wander here and there; to make an excursion or trip; to ramble. —n. An excursion; a ramble; a short journey.—**jaunting car**, n. A light car used in Ireland in which the passengers ride back to back on folding-down seats placed at right angles to the axle.

jaunty, jan′ti, a. [O.E. *gent*, Sc. *genty* elegant, pretty; from *gentle*, genteel, but modified by *jaunt*.] Gay and easy in manner or actions; airy; sprightly.—**jauntily**, jan′ti·li, adv.—**jauntiness**, jän′ti·nes, n.

Java, jä′va, n. Indonesian island; a variety of coffee; slang for coffee.— **Javanese**, jäv′a·nēz, a. Relating to Java.—n. A native of, or the language of Java.

javelin, jav′lin, n. [Fr. *javeline*, It. *giavelina*, Sp. *jabalina*.] A light spear of wood, 8½ feet long, thrown by hand as a weapon in war; a wooden spear thrown for distance in athletic competition.—v.t. To strike or wound with a javelin.

jaw, ja, n. [O.E. *chaw*, that which *chaws* or *chews*. CHEW.] The bones of the mouth in which the teeth are fixed; the upper or lower bony portion of the mouth; anything resembling a jaw in form or use (the *jaws* of a vise); loquacity or talk (a vulgar usage).—v.i. To talk or gossip; also, to scold (vulgar).—v.t. To use impudent language toward (vulgar). —**jawbone**, n. The bone of the jaw in which the teeth are fixed.

jay, jā, n. [Fr. *geai*, O.Fr. *gai*, Pr. *gai, jai*, Sp. *gayo*; same origin as adjective *gay*; lit. the gay or lively bird.] A bird allied to the crows, and one species of which, a beautiful bird with a crest of erectile feathers, is a native of Britain, another (the blue jay) is a native of North America.

jaywalk, jā′wak, v.i. To cross a street carelessly amid traffic and away from a regular crossing place.

jazz, jaz, n. [Originally from Creole *jazz*, for *jass*, to speed things up.] *Mus.* American music derived from Negro spirituals and ragtime, characterized by syncopated dance rhythms and spontaneous and inventive harmonies improvised on melodic themes.—v.t. To play a musical instrument in jazz style.—v.i. To dance to jazz.—(Slang) To enliven or speed up a performance.—**jazzy**, jaz′ē, a. Something lively or suggestive of jazz.

jealous, jel′us, a. [O.Fr. *jalous*, Fr. *jaloux*, It. *geloso*, from L.L. *zelosus*— L. *zelus*, Gr. *zēlos*, zeal. Another form of *zealous*.] Uneasy through fear of, or on account of, preference given to another; suspicious in love; apprehensive of rivalry; zealous.— **jealously**, jel′us·li, adv.—**jealousness**, jel′us·nes, n.—**jealousy**, jel′us·i, n.

jean, jēn, n. [Probably from *Genoa*.] A twilled cotton cloth; pl. trousers of this material.

jeep, jēp, n. [After *G.P.*, for *General Purpose* (Vehicle).] A multipurpose motor vehicle of ¼ ton capacity used by the U.S. military.

jeer, jēr, v.i. [Perhaps from O.Fr. *girer*.] To utter severe sarcastic reflections; to scoff; to make a mock of some person or thing (to *jeer at* a person).—v.t. To treat with scoffs or derision.—n. A scoff; a taunt.— **jeerer**, jē′rėr, n.—**jeeringly**, jē′ring·li, adv.

Jeffersonian, jef·fer·sō′ni·an, a. Of Thomas Jefferson (third U. S. president, 1801-9) or his political teachings, advocating broad rights of the states.

Jehovah, ji·hō′va, n. A Scripture name of the Supreme Being, the proper form of which, according to most scholars, should be *Yahveh* or *Yahweh*.—**Jehovist**, ji·hō′vist, n. The supposed author or authors of the *Jehovistic* portions of the Old Testament. ELOHIST.—**Jehovistic**, ji·hō·vis′tik, a. Pertaining to those passages in the Old Testament, especially of the Pentateuch, in which the Supreme Being is spoken of under the name *Jehovah*.

jehu, jē′hū, n. [From *Jehu*, the son of Nimshi, 2 Ki. ix. 20.] A slang name for a coachman or one fond of driving.

jejune, ji·jūn′, a. [L. *jejunus*, hungry, dry, barren.] Devoid of interesting matter, or attractiveness of any kind: said especially of literary productions; bare; meager; barren; unprofitable.—**jejunely**, ji·jūn′li, adv.

jejunum, ji·jū′num, n. [L., from *jejunus*, hungry or empty.] *Anat.* the second portion of the small intestine comprised between the duodenum and ileum.

jelly, jel′i, n. [Fr. *gelée*, from *geler*, L. *gelo*, to freeze; so *gelatine, congeal*.] A food preparation of fruit juice boiled down with sugar, which achieves its soft elasticity through the presence of pectin.—v.t. To bring to the consistency of jelly.— v.i. To become jelly.—**jellyfish**, n. Popular name for various marine coelenterates having a soft, gelatinous body and long tentacles; a medusa.

jemadar, jem·a·där′, n. [Hind. *jamadâr*, from *jama*, a number or body, and *dâr*, a holder.] In India, a native officer in a sepoy government corresponding in rank to a lieutenant.

jenny, jen′i, n. [For *ginny*, from *gin*, short for *engine*, influenced by its resemblance to a common female name.] A machine for spinning, moved by water or steam.

jeopardy, jep′ẽr·di, n. [O.E. *jupartie*, from Fr. *jeu parti*, lit. a divided game; L.L. *jocus partitus*, an even chance. JOKE, PART.] Exposure to death, loss, or injury; hazard; danger; peril.—v.t.†—*jeopardied*, *jeopardying*. To jeopardize.—**jeopard**, jep′ẽrd, v.t. To put in danger; to hazard.—**jeopardize**, jep′ẽr·dīz, v.t. To expose to loss or injury; to jeopard.—**jeopardous**, jep′ẽr·dus, a. Perilous; hazardous.

jerboa, jẽr·bō′a, n. [Ar. *yerbôa*, *yerbûa*.] A name of certain small rodents mainly characterized by the disproportionate length of the hind limbs.

jereed, jerid, je·rēd′, n. A wooden javelin used in Persia and Turkey, especially in mock fights.

jerk, jẽrk, v.t. [Comp. O.E. and Sc. *yerk*, a quick, smart lash or blow; prov. *girk*, a rod; perhaps same as *gird* (n.).] To thrust with a sudden effort; to give a sudden pull, twitch, thrust, or push to; to throw with a quick smart motion.—v.i. To make a sudden motion; to give a start.—n. A short sudden thrust, push, or twitch; a jolt; a sudden spring; a start; a leap or bound.—**jerky**, jẽr′ki, a. Moving by or exhibiting jerks.

jerk, jẽrk, v.t. [Chilian, *charqui*.] To cut (beef) into long thin pieces, and dry in the sun, as is done in S. America. CHARQUI.

jerkin, jẽr′kin, n. [Dim. of D. *jurk*, a frock.] A jacket; a short coat; a close waistcoat.

jeroboam, jer·a·bō′am, n. [After *Jeroboam*, first King of Israel.] A large wine bottle that holds ⅕ of a gallon; a large bowl.

jerry-builder, je′ri·bil″dẽr, n. [Origin dubious.] One who builds with cheap, flimsy materials.

jersey, jẽr′zi, n. [From the island so called.] Fine yarn of wool; a kind of close-fitting knitted woolen upper shirt or similar article of dress; [*cap.*] a species of dairy cow developed on the island and noted for its rich milk.

Jerusalem artichoke, ji·rū′sa·lem, n. [*Jerusalem* is here a corruption of the Italian *girasole*. GIRASOLE.] A well-known plant, the tubers of which are of a sweetish farinaceous nature, somewhat akin to the potato.

jess, jes, n. [O.Fr. *ges, gest, get*, etc., from L.L. *jactus*, a jess, from L. *jacio, jactum*, to throw. JET.] A short strap of leather fastened round each of the legs of a hawk, to which the leash tied round the falconer's hand was attached.—**jessed**, jest, a. Having jesses.

jessamine, jes′a·min, n. Jasmine.

jesse, jes′sē, n. [From its resemblance to the genealogical tree of *Jesse*, the father of David, of which a picture used to be hung up in churches.] A large brass candlestick branched into many sconces, used in churches.—*Jesse tree*, alluding to Isaiah. xi. 1: 'A rod out of the stem of Jesse'.

jest, jest, n. [O.E. *geste*, a jest, a tale, from L. *gestum*, something done, a deed, a feat, from *gero*, to do, whence *gesture*, etc.] A joke; something ludicrous uttered and meant only to excite laughter; the object of laughter; a laughingstock.—*In jest*, for mere sport or diversion; not in truth and reality; not in earnest.—v.i. To make merriment by words or actions; to utter jests; to talk jokingly; to joke.—**jester**, jes′tẽr, n. One who jests; a person given to jesting; a buffoon; a merry-andrew; a person formerly retained by persons of rank to make sport for them.—**jestingly**, jes′ting·li, adv. In a jesting manner; not in earnest.

Jesuit, jez′ū·it, n. [One of the order or Society of *Jesus*.] One of a religious order belonging to the Roman Catholic church, founded by Saint Ignatius of Loyola in 1534, and approved by Pope Paul III in 1540.—**Jesuitic, Jesuitical**, jez·ū·it′ik, jez·ū·it′i·kal, a.—**Jesuitically**, jez·ū·it′i·kal·li, adv.—**Jesuitism**, jez′ū·it·izm, n.

Jesus, jē′zus, n. [Gr. *Iesous*, from Heb. *Jeshuah, Jehosuah*, 'help of Jehovah'.] The Son of God; the Saviour of men; frequently conjoined with Christ (which see).

jet, jet, n. [Old forms *jeat, jayet*, O.Fr. *jayet, gayet*, from Gr. *gagatēs*, from *Gagæ*, a town and river in Lycia, where it was obtained.] A highly compact species of coal susceptible of a good polish, deep black and glossy, wrought into buttons and ornaments of various kinds.—**jet-black**, a. Of the deepest black, the color of jet.

jet, jet, n. [Fr. *jet*, a throw, a jet, a fountain, from L. *jactus*, a throwing, from *jacio*, to throw.] A shooting forth or spouting; what issues or streams forth from an orifice, as water or other fluid, gas or flame.—v.i.—*jetted, jetting*. To issue in a jet. —v.t. To emit; to spout forth.—**jet airplane**, n. An airplane propelled by one or more jet engines.—**jet engine**, n. A reaction engine driven by jet propulsion, having one or more combustion chambers and exhaust nozzles for discharging a mixture of hot, gaseous air.—**jet-propelled**, a. Propelled by one or more jet engines; high-powered and suggestive of speed and force (a *jet-propelled* career).—**jet propulsion**, A method of producing forward motion of a vehicle by the rearward discharge of a high-speed jet, usually of hot gases.

jetsam, jet′sam, n. [See JETTISON.] Goods cast overboard to lighten a ship in distress.

jettison, jet′i·sun, n. [O.Fr. *getaison*, L. *jactatio*, a throwing, from *jacio*, to throw.] The throwing of goods overboard to lighten a ship in distress.—v.t. To throw overboard.

jetty, jet′i, n. [O.Fr. *jettée*, Fr. *jetée*, from O.Fr. *jetter*, to throw. JET.] A projecting portion of a building; a projecting structure (generally of piles), affording a convenient landing place for vessels or boats; a kind of small pier.

Jewish, jū′ish, a. [O. Fr. *Juis*; L. *Judaeus*, from *Judaea*, so named from *Judah*.] Pertaining to the Jews or Hebrews.—**Jewry**, jū′ri, n. Judaea; also a city quarter inhabited by Jews.—**jew's-harp**, n. An instrument of music which is held between the teeth and by means of a thin bent metal tongue, struck by the finger, gives out a sound.

jewel, jū′el, n. [O.Fr. *jouel, joiel, joel* (Fr. *joyau*), either from L.L. *jocale*, a jewel, from L. *jocare*, to jest, *jocus*, a jest (whence *joke*), or from L.L. *gaudiale*, from L. *gaudium*, joy (whence *joy*).] A personal ornament in which precious stones form a principal part; a precious stone; anything of exceeding value or excellence.—v.t.—*jeweled, jeweling*. To dress or adorn with jewels; to fit or provide with a jewel (as a watch); to deck or adorn as with jewels.—**jeweler**, jū′el·ẽr, n. One who makes or deals in jewels and other ornaments.—**jewelry**, jū′el·ri, n. The trade or occupation of a jeweler; jewels in general.

Jezebel, jez′e·bel, n. [From *Jezebel*, the infamous wife of Ahab, king of Israel.] An unscrupulous, daring, vicious woman.

jib, jib, n. [From Dan. *gibbe*, D. *gijpen*, to turn suddenly, said of sails.] The foremost sail of a ship, triangular in shape and extended from the outer end of a jib boom toward the foretopmast-head; in sloops, a sail on the bowsprit.—**jibe**, jīb, v.t.—*jibed, jibing*. *Naut.* to shift (a fore-and-aft sail) from one side to the other.—**jib boom**, n. A spar run out from the extremity of the bowsprit, and which serves as a continuation of it.

jib, jib, v.i.—*jibbed, jibbing*. [O.Fr. *giber*, to struggle; *regibber*, to kick.] To balk, as a horse; to move restively sideways or backward.—**jibber**, jib′ẽr, n.

jibe, jīb, v.t. To jeer. GIBE.

jibe, jīb, v.i. [Origin unknown.] To be in accord. (Colloq.)

jiffy, jif′i, n. [Prov.E. *jiffle*, to be restless; comp. *jib*, to turn suddenly.] A moment; an instant. (Colloq.)

jig, jig, n. [O.Fr. *gigue, gige*, a stringed instrument; the same word as *gig*.] A lively step dance in triple rhythm; a hook or group of hooks which can be jerked up and down through water, as in ice fishing.—*mech.* a device for guiding a drill, etc., so that machined pieces will be uniform.—**jigsaw**, n. A saw with a vertical motion, moved by a vibrating lever or crank rod.—v.i.—*jigged, jigging*. To dance a jig; to move with a light jolting motion; to fish with a jig.—v.t. To sing in the style of a jig, or in *jig* time; to work with the mechanical aid of a *jig*.—**jigger**, jig′ẽr, n. *Mining*, a man who cleans ores by means of a wirebottom sieve; the sieve itself; a kind of light tackle used in ships; a potter's wheel by which earthenware vessels are shaped; 1½-ounce glass measure.

jigger, jig′ẽr, n. [CHIGOE.] The chigoe.

jiggle, jig′l, v.t.—*jiggled, jiggling*.

[From *jig*.] To move up and down or back and forth in quick little jerks. —*n.* The motion of jiggling.

jilt, jilt, *n.* [Contr. from *jillet*, a dim. of *jill, gill,* a young woman, a giddy girl. GILL.] A woman who gives her lover hopes and capriciously disappoints him.—*v.t.* To treat as a jilt does her lover.

jimmy, jim'i, *n.* [Nickname for *James*.] A short crowbar used by burglars.— *v.t.* To force open with a jimmy.

Jimson weed, *n.* [From *Jamestown weed,* for Jamestown, Va.] A poisonous datura (*Datura stramonium*) with large white flowers and rank-smelling foliage.

jingle, jing'gl, *v.i.*—*jingled, jingling.* [Probably imitative, like *jangle, chink, tinkle,* G. *klingeln*.] To sound with a tinkling metallic sound.—*v.t.* To cause to give a tinkling metallic sound.—*n.* A rattling or clinking sound, as of metal; something that jingles; a brief musical advertisement on television or radio.

jingo, jing'gō, *n.* An expletive used as a mild oath (*By jingo!*); a person exaggeratedly patriotic and clamorous for war.—**jingoism,** jing'gō·izm, *n.* Exaggerated and bellicose patriotism.—**jingoist,** jing'gō·ist, *n.* & *a.* —**jingoistic,** jing'gō·is″tic, *a.*

jinks, jingks, *n.* [Chiefly in *high jinks*.] Frolics; pranks.

jinni, jinnee, ji·nē′, *n.* pl. **jinn,** jin. [From Ar. *jinn,* a demon.] *Mohammedan mythology,* one of a class of good or evil spirits (angels or demons) inhabiting the earth, capable of assuming various forms and of exercising magical powers.

jinrikisha, jin·rik′shä, *n.* [Japanese.] A small, two-wheeled vehicle, drawn by one or more men.

jinx, jingks, *n.* & *v.* [From *jynx,* bird, the wryneck used in witchcraft.] Some thing which brings bad luck; a hoodoo. (Slang)

jitney, jit′ni, *n.* [Origin doubtful.] A nickel; five cents; a bus or taxicab having a low fare. (Slang)

jitter, jit′ẽr, *v.i.* [CHATTER.] To behave nervously.—**jitterbug,** jit′ẽr·bug, *n.* A dance to swing music; a dancer who does the jitterbug.—**jitters,** jit′ẽrz, *n.* pl. Nervousness. (Slang)

jiujitsu, jiujutsu. See JUJITSU.

job, job, *n.* [A form of Prov.E. *gob,* a lump, a portion; akin *gobbet*.] A piece of work undertaken; employment; position; a public transaction made for private profit; a task; something that has to be done with great labor; a robbery. (Slang)—*v.t. jobbed, jobbing.* To sublet work (*job* a contract); to buy in large quantities and sell in smaller lots.—*v.i.* To work at chance jobs; to deal in the public stocks; to buy and sell as a broker; to put some public undertaking to private advantage.—*a.* Applied to goods bought and sold under special circumstances, and generally under the ordinary trade price.—**jobber,** job′ẽr, *n.* One who deals in goods as middle man; one who deals or dabbles in stocks; a stockjobber.— **jobbery,** job′ẽr·i, *n.*—**jobless,** job′les, *a.*—**job lot,** *n.* A miscellaneous

collection sold.—**job printer,** *n.* A printer who does miscellaneous work, as bills, circulars, etc.

Job's comforter, jōb, *n.* [From *Job* of Scripture.] One who pretends to sympathize with you, but attributes your misfortunes to your own misconduct.

jockey, jok′i, *n.* [For *Jackey,* dim. of *Jack,* for *John; Jockey* and *Jock* being Northern English forms. JACK.] A man whose profession it is to ride horses in horse races.—*v.t.*— *jockeyed* or *jockied, jockeying.* To ride in a race; to maneuver (to *jockey* for position); to jostle by riding against; to cheat; to trick; to deceive in trade.

jocose, jō·kōs′, *a.* [L. *jocosus,* from *jocus,* a joke. JOKE.] Given to jokes and jesting; merry; waggish; containing a joke; sportive; merry.— **jocosely,** jō·kōs′li, *adv.* In a jocose manner.—**jocoseness,** jō·kōs′nes. *n.* The quality of being jocose.— **jocosity,** jō·kos′i·ti, *n.* Jocularity; merriment; waggery; a jocose act or saying.—**jocular,** jok′ū·lẽr, *a.* [L. *jocularis,* from *jocus*.] Given to jesting; jocose; merry; waggish; containing jokes; facetious.—**jocularity,** jok·ū·lar′i·ti, *n.* The quality of being jocular.—**jocularly,** jok′ū·lẽr·li, *adv.* In a jocular manner.

jocund, jok′und, *a.* [L. *jocundus, jucundus,* connected with *juvenis,* a young man, *juvare,* to assist (as in *adjutant, coadjutor*); E. *young*.] Merry; cheerful; blithe; gleeful; gay; sprightly; sportive; lighthearted.— **jocundity,** jō·kun′di·ti, *n.* State of being jocund.—**jocundly,** jok′und·li, *adv.*

jodhpurs, jōd′pörs, *n.* pl. [From Jodhpur, India.] Riding breeches that fit tightly from the knees to the ankles.

jog, jog, *v.t.*—*jogged, jogging.* [Perhaps a form of *jag,* or allied to W. *gogi,* to shake.] To push or shake with the elbow or hand; to give notice or excite attention by a slight push.— *v.i.* To move at a slow trot; to walk or travel idly or slowly; to move along with but little progress: generally followed by *on*—*n.* A push; a slight shake; a shake or push intended to give notice or awaken attention; *carp.* and *masonry,* a square notch.—**joggle,** jog′l, *v.t.*—*joggled, joggling.* [Freq. of *jog*.] To shake slightly; to give a sudden but slight push; *carp.* to join or match by jogs or notches so as to prevent sliding apart.—*v.i.* To push; to shake; to totter.—*n.* A joint made by means of jogs or notches; a joint held in place by means of pieces of stone or metal introduced into it; the piece of metal or stone used in such a joint.—**jog trot,** *n.* A slow, easy trot; hence, a slow routine of daily duty to which one pertinaciously adheres. —*a.* Monotonous; easygoing; humdrum.

John, jon, *n.* [L. *Johannes, Joannes,* Gr. *Ioannēs,* from Heb.] A proper name of men.—*John Bull,* a humorous designation of the English people, first used in Arbuthnot's

satire *The History of John Bull.*— **John Doe,** *n. Law.* Name used for an unknown person.—**John Dory,** *n.* DORY.—**John Hancock,** han′kok, *n.* One's signature, from the exceptionally legible writing of John Hancock. —**johnnycake,** jon′i, *n.* Bread or cake made of corn meal, salt, water, and shortening.—**Johnny-jump-up,** *n.* The wild pansy.

Johnsonese, jon·son·ēz′, *n.* The style or language of Dr. Johnson, or an imitation of it; a pompous inflated style.

join, join, *v.t.* [Fr. *joindre,* from L. *jungere, junctum,* to join, seen in many E. words, as *junction, juncture, adjoin, conjoin, enjoin, rejoin, conjugal, conjugate,* etc.; same root as Skr. *yuj,* to join; E. *yoke*.] To connect or bring together, physically or otherwise; to place in contiguity; to couple; to combine; to associate; to engage in (to *join* the fray); to make one's self a party in; to become connected with; to unite with; to enter or become a member of; to merge in (to *join* the army, one river joins another).—*To join battle,* to engage in battle.—*To join issue.* Under ISSUE.—*v.i.* To be contiguous or in contact; to form a physical union; to coalesce; to unite or become associated, as in marriage, league, partnership, society; to confederate; to associate; to league.—**joiner,** joi′nẽr, *n.* One who joins; a mechanic who does the woodwork of houses; a carpenter.—**joinery,** joi′nẽr·i, *n.* The art of a joiner; carpentry.

joint, joint, *n.* [Fr. *joint,* from *joindre,* pp. *joint,* to join. JOIN.] The place or part at which two separate things are joined or united; the mode of connection of two things; junction; articulation; *anat.* the joining of two or more bones, as in the elbow, the knee, or the knuckle; *bot.* a node or knot; also, the part between two nodes; an internode; *geol.* a fissure or line of parting in rocks at any angle to the plane of stratification; *building,* the surface of contact between two bodies that are held firmly together by means of cement, mortar, etc., or by a superincumbent weight; the place where or the mode in which one piece of timber is connected with another. DOVETAIL, SCARF, MITER, MORTISE, TENON.— *Universal joint,* a mechanical arrangement by which one part may be made to move freely in all directions in relation to another connected part. —*Out of joint,* dislocated, as when the head of a bone is displaced from its socket; hence, figuratively, confused; disordered.—*a.* Shared by two or more (*joint* property); having an interest in the same thing (*joint* owner); united; combined; acting in concert (a *joint* force, *joint* efforts).— *v.t.* To form with a joint or joints; to articulate; to unite by a joint or joints; to fit together; to cut or divide into joints or pieces.—*v.i.* To coalesce by joints.—**jointed,** join′ted, *p.* and *a.* Provided with joints; formed with knots or nodes.—**jointer,** join′-tẽr, *n.* One who or that which joints.

—jointly, joint′li, *adv.* In a joint manner; together; unitedly; in concert.—**joint stock,** *n.* Stock held in common.—*Joint stock company,* an association of a number of individuals who jointly contribute funds for the purpose of carrying on a specified business or undertaking, of which the shares are transferable by each owner without the consent of the other partners.—**jointure,** join′chẽr, *n.* Property settled on a woman in consideration of marriage, and which she is to enjoy after her husband's decease.

joist, joist, *n.* [O.Fr. *giste,* Fr. *gîte,* a bed, a place to lie on, L.L. *gista,* from L. *jacitum,* pp. of *jacere,* to lie. JET, GIST.] One of the stout pieces of timber to which the boards of a floor or the laths of a ceiling are nailed, and which are supported by the walls or on girders.—*v.t.* To fit or furnish with joists.

joke, jōk, *n.* [L. *jocus,* Fr. *jeu,* It. *giuoco, gioca,* a jest; same root as *jacio,* to throw (JET). Akin *jocose, jocular, juggler, jeopardy.*] Something said for the sake of exciting a laugh; something witty or sportive; a jest; what is not in earnest or actually meant.—*A practical joke,* a trick played on one, usually to the injury or annoyance of his person.—*In joke,* in jest; with no serious intention.—*v.i.*—*joked, joking.* To jest; to utter jokes; to jest in words or actions.—*v.t.* To cast jokes at; to make merry with; to rally.—**joker,** jōk′ẽr, *n.* A jester; a merry fellow; in a legal document, a seemingly harmless clause which greatly alters the apparent meaning; an extra playing card which, when used, as in poker or euchre, has special privileges.—**jokingly,** *adv.*

jole, jōl, *n.†* [JOWL, Hence *jolt.*] The jowl; the head.

jolly, jol′i, *a.* [O.Fr. *joli, jolif,* Fr. *joli,* gay, merry, from the Scand., and originally referring to the festivities of Christmas; from Icel. *jól,* Sw. and Dan. *jul,* E. *yule,* Christmas. YULE.] Merry; gay; lively; full of life and mirth; jovial; expressing mirth; exciting mirth or gaiety; plump; in excellent condition of body.—**jollification,** jol′i·fi·kā″shon, *n.* A scene of merriment, mirth, or festivity; a carouse; merrymaking.—**jollily,** jol′i·li, *adv.* In a jolly manner.—**jolliness,** jol′i·nes, *n.* The quality or condition of being jolly.—**jollity,** jol′i·ti, *n.* The quality of being jolly; mirth; gaiety; festivity; joviality.

jolly boat, *n.* [*Jolly* here is same as Dan. *jolli,* D. *jol,* a yawl, a jollyboat.] One of a ship's boats, about 12 feet in length, with a bluff bow; a yawl.

jolt, jolt, *v.i.* [From *joll,* obs. of *jowl,* and obs. *jot,* to bump.] To jar or jounce with light bumping motions, as a car traveling on a rough road; to shock by speech (a remark to *jolt* you); to jar with a hard blow, as in boxing.—*n.* A sudden sharp blow; a jar or shock.—**jolter,** jol′tẽr, *n.*

Jonathan, jo′na·than, *n.* Son of Saul, friend of David; a variety of apple.

jongleur, jong′glẽr, *n.* [Fr.] A juggler; a medieval wandering minstrel; akin to *juggler, jingler.*

jonquil, jon′kwil, *a.* [Fr. *jonquille*; It. *giunchiglia,* dim. from L. *juncus,* a rush.] A species of narcissus or daffodil, with rush-like leaves and flowers that yield a fine perfume.

jorum, jō′rum, *n.* [Perhaps a corruption of *jordan,* a vessel in which pilgrims brought home water from the *Jordan.*] A colloquial term for a bowl or drinking vessel with liquor in it.

joseph, jō′zef, *n.* [Probably in allusion to *Joseph's* coat of many colors.] A riding coat or habit for women, formerly much in use.

josh, josh, *v.t.* [Origin unknown.] To tease or make fun of lightly.—*v.i.* To banter good-naturedly.—*n.* A good-humored joking.

joss, jos, *n.* [Chin. *joss,* a deity, from Pg. *deos,* from L. *deus,* a god.] A Chinese idol.—**joss house,** *n.* A Chinese temple.—**joss stick,** *n.* In China, a small reed covered with dust of odoriferous woods, and burned before an idol.

jostle, jos′l, *v.t.*—*jostled, jostling.* [A dim. from *joust.*] To push against; to crowd against; to elbow; to hustle.—*v.i.* To hustle; to shove about as in a crowd.—*n.* A crowding or pushing together.

jot, jot, *n.* [From *iōta,* the smallest letter in the Greek alphabet. IOTA.] An iota; the least quantity assignable.—*v.t.*—*jotted, jotting.* To make a memorandum of.—*jotting,* jot′ing, *n.*

joule, jōl, *n.* [*Joule,* scientist.] The unit of electric energy, equal to the work done in maintaining for one second a current of 1 ampere against a resistance of 1 ohm; equal to 10^7 ergs.

journal, jẽr′nal, *n.* [Fr., from L. *diurnalis,* diurnal, from *dies,* a day. DIURNAL, DIAL, DIARY.] A diary; an account of daily transactions and events, or the book containing such account; a newspaper or other periodical published daily; a periodical; *bookkeeping,* a book in which every particular article or charge is entered under each day's date, or in groups at longer periods; *naut.* a daily register of the ship's course and distance, the winds, weather, and other occurrences; a log book; *mach.* that part of an axle or shaft which rests and moves in the bearings.—**journalism,** jẽr′nal·izm, *n.* The trade or occupation of publishing, writing in, or conducting a journal.—**journalist,** jẽr′nal·ist, *n.* The conductor of or writer in a public journal; a newspaper editor or regular contributor.—**journalistic,** jẽr·nal·is′tik, *a.* Pertaining to journalism.—**journalize,** jẽr′nal·īz, *v.t.*—*journalized, journalizing.* To enter in a journal; to give the form of a journal to.—**journalese,** jẽr·nal·ēs′, *n.* Choice of language considered to be typical of newspapers. (Colloq.)

journey, jẽr′ni, *n.* [Fr. *journée,* a day, a day's work, a day's journey, from L. *diurnus,* daily, from *dies,* a day. JOURNAL.] Travel from one place to another; a passage made between places; a distance traveled at a time.—*v.i.* To travel from place to place; to pass from home to a distance.—**journeyer,** jẽr′ni·ẽr, *n.*—**journeyman,** jẽr′ni·man, *n.* Strictly, a man hired to work by the day, but in fact, any experienced mechanic or workman.

joust, joust, just, *n.* [O.Fr. *juste, jouste, joste,* jousting, from O.Fr. *juster, jouster, joster,* to tilt; from L. *juxta,* near to, nigh.] An encounter with spears on horseback for trial of skill; a combat between two knights at a tournament for sport or for exercise.—*v.i.* To engage in a mock fight on horseback; to tilt.—**jouster,** joust′ẽr, jus′tẽr, *n.* One who jousts.

Jove, jōv, *n.* [L. *Jovis, Diovis,* the old name of *Jupiter* (that is Jove-father), latterly appearing only in the oblique cases; same root as *deus,* a god. See DEITY.] The chief divinity of the Romans; Jupiter; the planet Jupiter.—**jovial,** jō′vi·al, *a.* [L.L. *Jovialis,* because the planet Jupiter was believed to make those born under it of a jovial temperament.] Gay; merry; joyous; jolly.—**joviality, jovialness,** jō·vi·al′i·ti, jō′vi·al·nes, *n.* The state or quality of being jovial.—**jovially,** jō′vi·al·li, *adv.*—**Jovian,** jō′vi·an, *a.* Pertaining to Jupiter.

jowl, jōl, *n.* [Also in forms *jole, joll, chowl,* from A.Sax. *ceafl,* jaw, snout. Akin *jolt.*] The hanging flesh of the jaw, as in a fat person; the wattle of a fowl; the dewlap of cattle.

joy, joi, *n.* [O.Fr. *joye, joie, goie,* Fr. *joie,* It. *gioja,* from L. *gaudium,* joy, *gaudere,* to rejoice; seen also in *gaudy, rejoice, jewel.*] Excitement of pleasurable feeling caused by the acquisition or expectation of good; gladness; pleasure; delight; exultation; exhilaration of spirits; the cause of joy or happiness.—*v.i.* To rejoice; to be glad; to exult.—*v.t.* To give joy to; to gladden. (Shak.)—**joyance,** joi′ans, *n.* [O.Fr. *joiant,* joyful.] Enjoyment; happiness; delight. (*Poet.*)—**joyful,** joi′ful, *a.* Full of joy; very glad; exulting; joyous; gleeful.—**joyfully,** joi′ful·li, *adv.* In a joyful manner.—**joyfulness,** joi′ful·nes, *n.* The state of being joyful.—**joyless,** joi′les, *a.* Destitute of joy; wanting joy; giving no joy or pleasure.—**joylessly,** joi′les·li, *adv.* In a joyless manner.—**joylessness,** joi′les·nes, *n.* State of being joyless.—**joyous,** joi′us, *a.* [O.Fr. *joyous*; Fr. *joyeux*; from L. *gaudiosus,* from *gaudium.*] Glad; gay; merry; joyful; giving joy.—**joyously,** joi′us·li, *adv.* In a joyous manner.—**joyousness,** joi′us·nes, *n.* The state of being joyous.

jubilant, jū′bi·lant, *a.* [L. *jubilans,* ppr. of *jubilo,* to shout for joy, from *jubilum,* a shout of joy; not connected with *jubilee.*] Uttering songs of triumph; rejoicing; shouting or singing with joy.—**jubilate,** jū′bi·lāt, *v.i.* To rejoice; to exult; to triumph.—**jubilation,** jū·bi·lā′shon, *n.* [L. *jubilatio.*] A rejoicing; a triumph; exultation; a joyful or festive celebration.

jubilee, jū′bi·li, *n.* [Fr. *jubilé,* L. *jubilæus,* jubilee, from Heb. *yôbēl,* a ram's horn.] Among the Jews, every fiftieth year, at which time there was a general release of all debtors and slaves, hence, a season of great public joy and festivity; any occasion of rejoicing or joy; a celebration of a marriage, pastorate, or the like, after it has lasted fifty years; Negro spiritual saluting a future happy time; the sound of jubilation.

Judaic, Judaical, jū·dā′ik, jū·dā′i·kal, *a.* [L. *Judaicus,* from *Judæa.* JEW.] Pertaining to the Jews.—**Judaism,** jū′dä·izm, *n.* The religious doctrines and rites of the Jews, as enjoined in the laws of Moses; conformity to the Jewish rites and ceremonies.—**Judaist,** jū′dä·ist, *n.* An adherent to Judaism.—**Judaistic,** jū·dä·is′tik, *a.* Relating or pertaining to Judaism.—**Judaize,** jū′dä·īz, *v.i.*—*judaized, judaizing.* To conform to the religious doctrines and rites of the Jews; to assume the manners or customs of the Jews.—*v.t.* To bring into conformity with what is Jewish.—**Judaizer,** jū′dä·ī·zėr, *n.* One who judaizes.—**Judean,** jū·dē′an, *n.* A native or inhabitant of Judaea.—*a.* Relating to Judaea.

Judas, jö′das, *n.* [After the false apostle.] A treacherous person; one who betrays under the semblance of friendship.

judge, juj, *n.* [Fr. *juge,* from L. *judex, judicis,* a judge, from *jus, juris,* law or right, and *dico,* to pronounce (JURY, DICTION). This word appears in *adjudge, judicature, judicial, judicious,* etc.] A civil officer invested with power to hear and determine causes, civil and criminal, and to administer justice between parties in courts held for the purpose; one who has skill to decide on the merits of a question or on the value of anything; a critic; a connoisseur; *Jewish hist.* a chief magistrate with civil and military powers; hence, *pl.* the name of the seventh book of the Old Testament.—*v.i.*—*judged, judging.* [Fr. *juger,* L. *judicare,* to judge.] To hear and determine, as in causes on trial; to pass judgment upon any matter; to sit in judgment; to compare facts, ideas, or propositions, and perceive their agreement or disagreement; to form an opinion; to express censorious opinions; to determine; to estimate; to discern.—*v.t.* To hear and determine authoritatively, as a cause or controversy; to examine into and decide; to examine and pass sentence on; to try; to be censorious toward; to esteem, think, reckon.—**judgeship,** juj′ship, *n.* The office of a judge.—**judgment,** juj′ment, *n.* [Fr. *jugement.*] The act of judging; the act of deciding or passing decision on something; the act or faculty of judging truly, wisely, or skillfully; good sense; discernment; understanding; opinion or notion formed by judging or considering; the act or mental faculty by which man compares ideas and ascertains the relations of terms and propositions; a

determination of the mind so formed, producing when expressed in words a proposition; *law,* the sentence pronounced in a cause by the judge or court by which it is tried; hence, a calamity regarded as inflicted by God for the punishment of sinners; the final trial of the human race.—*Judgment of God,* a term formerly applied to trials of crimes by single combat, by ordeal, etc.—**judgment day,** *n.* The last day, when final judgment will be pronounced on men.

judicable, jū′di·ka·bl, *a.* [L. *judicabilis,* from *judico,* to judge, from *judex,* a judge. JUDGE.] Capable of being tried or decided.—**judicative,** jū′di·kā·tiv, *a.* Having power to judge.—**judicatory,** jū′di·ka·to·ri, *a.* [L. *judicatorius.*] Pertaining to the passing of judgment; belonging to the administration of justice; dispensing justice.—*n.* A court of justice.—**judicature,** jū′di·kā·chėr, *n.* The power of distributing justice; a court of justice; a judicatory; extent of jurisdiction of a judge or court.

judicial, jū·dish′al, *a.* [L. *judicialis,* from *judicium,* a trial, a judicial inquiry, judgment, discernment, from *judex, judicis,* a judge. JUDGE.] Pertaining or appropriate to courts of justice or to a judge thereof; proceeding from, issued or ordered by, a court of justice; inflicted as a penalty or in judgment; enacted by law or statute.—**judicially,** jū·dish′al·li, *adv.* In a judicial manner.—**judiciary,** jū·dish′i·a·ri, *a.* [L. *judiciarius.*] Pertaining to the courts of judicature or legal tribunals; judicial.—*n.* The system of courts of justice in a government; the judges taken collectively.—**judicious,** jū·dish′us, *a.* [Fr. *judicieux,* from L. *judicium,* judgment.] According to sound judgment; adapted to obtain a good end by the best means; well considered; said of things; acting according to sound judgment; possessing sound judgment; directed by reason and wisdom: said of persons.—**judiciously,** jū·dish′us·li, *adv.* In a judicious manner.—**judiciousness,** jū·dish′us·nes, *n.* The quality of being judicious.

judo, jū′dō, *n.* [Japanese *jūdō.*] A modern form of jujitsu.

jug, jug, *n.* [From *Jug* or *Judge,* an old familiar form or *Joan* or *Jenny,* the name being jocularly given to the vessel, like *jack, black-jack.*] A vessel, usually of earthenware, metal, or glass, of various sizes and shapes, and generally with a handle or ear, used for holding and conveying liquors; a drinking vessel; a mug.

jugate, jugated, jū′gāt, jū′gā·ted, *a.* [L. *jugum,* a yoke, a ridge or summit.] *Bot.* coupled together, as the pairs of leaflets in compound leaves.

Juggernaut, jug′ėr·nat, *n.* [Properly *Jagannâtha,* lord of the world.] The famous idol to which people in India used to sacrifice themselves at festivals. [*not cap.*] Any idea, custom, fashion, or the like, to which

one either devotes himself or is blindly or ruthlessly sacrificed.

juggle, jug′l, *v.i.*—*juggled, juggling.* [O.Fr. *jogler,* Fr. *jongler,* It. *giocolare,* from L. *joculor,* to jest or joke, from L. *jocus,* a jest. JOKE.] To play tricks by sleight of hand; to practice artifice or imposture; to toss and catch articles, keeping several continuously in the air.—**juggler,** jug′lėr, *n.* [O.Fr. *jugleor, jogleor,* from L. *joculator,* one who jokes.] One who juggles.—**jugglery,** jug′lėr·i, *n.* The art or performances of a juggler; legerdemain; trickery; imposture.

jugular, ju′gū·lėr, *a.* [L. *jugulum,* the collarbone, the neck, from root of *jungo,* to join. JOIN.] *Anat.* pertaining to the neck or throat.—*Jugular vein,* one of the large trunks (two on each side) by which the greater part of the blood that has circulated in the head, face, and neck is returned to the heart.

juice, jūs, *n.* [O.E. *jows,* Fr. *jus,* from L. *jus,* broth, soup; cog. Skr. *yûsha,* broth.] The sap or watery part of vegetables, especially of fruits; also, the fluid part of animal substances; electricity. (*Slang.*)—**juiceless,** jūs′les, *a.*—**juiciness,** jū′si·nes, *n.* The state of being juicy—**juicy,** jū′si, *a.* Abounding with juice; succulent; also, interesting; amusing.

jujitsu, jö·jit′sö, *n.* [Japan.] A style of Japanese wrestling resting on a knowledge of muscular action.

jujube, jö′jöb, *n.* [Fr. *jujube,* a jujube, from L. *zizyphum,* Gr. *zizyphon,* Ar. *zizuf,* the jujube tree.] The fruit of a spiny shrub or small tree of lands about the Mediterranean sea; the tree itself; a confection made of gelatin, sweetened and flavored to resemble the jujube fruit.

julep, jū′lep, *n.* [Fr. *julep,* Ar. *julâb,* from Per. *gulâb,* rose-water—*gul,* rose, and *âb,* water.] A sweet drink; a sweetened mixture serving as a vehicle to some form of medicine; a drink composed of spirituous liquor, as bourbon whisky, sugar, crushed ice, and mint leaves.

Julian, jū′li·an, *a.* Pertaining to or derived from *Julius* Caesar.—*Julian calendar,* the calendar as adjusted by Julius Caesar.

julienne, jö·li·en′, *n.* [Fr.] A kind of soup made with various herbs or vegetables cut in very small pieces.

July, jū·lī′, *n.* The seventh month of the year, during which the sun enters the sign Leo; so called from *Julius* Caesar, who was born in this month, and by whom the calendar was reformed.

jumble, jum′bl, *v.t.*—*jumbled, jumbling.* [O.E. *jombre, jumbre, jumpre,* to agitate, to shake together; akin to *jump,* and to Dan. *gumpe,* to jolt.] To mix in a confused mass; to put or throw together without order; often followed by *together* or *up.*—*v.i.* To meet, mix, or unite in a confused manner.—*n.* Confused mixture, mass, or collection without order; disorder; confusion; medley.

jump, jump, *v.i.* [Akin Dan. *gumpe,* Prov. G. *gumpen,* to jolt or jump; Icel. *goppa,* to jump or skip; also *jumble.*] To throw one's self in any direction by lifting the feet wholly from the ground and again alighting upon them; to leap; to spring; to cause a price to rise swiftly; to make a sudden verbal attack on (to *jump on* someone).—*To jump at,* to embrace or accept (an offer) with eagerness (colloq.).—*v.t.* To increase sharply, as an admission price; to pounce upon; to seize another's rights, as a mining claim; to pass by a leap; to pass over eagerly or hastily; to skip over; to leap.—*n.* The act of jumping; a leap; a spring; a bound; an advantage, as in time (he got the *jump* on me); one in a series of moves (a *jump* ahead).—**jumper,** jump'er, *n.* One who or that which jumps; a horse trained to jump, as for a horse show; a woman's sleeveless, one-piece dress, worn with a blouse; *elec.* a piece of wire across a broken circuit.—**jumpy,** jump'i, *a.*

juncaceous, jung·kā'shus, *a.* [L. *juncus,* a rush.] *Bot.* pertaining to or resembling the order of plants of which the rush is the type.

junco, jun'kō, *n.* A snowbird; a genus of American finches.

junction, jungk'shon, *n.* [From L. *junctio,* from *jungo,* to join. JOIN.] The act or operation of joining; the state of being joined; the place or point of union; joint; juncture; the place where two or more railroads meet.—**juncture,** jung'chèr, *n.* [L. *junctura.*] The line or point at which two bodies are joined; a point of time; particularly, a point rendered critical or important by a concurrence of circumstances.

June, jūn, *n.* [L. *Junius,* perhaps after L. *Junius* Brutus.] The sixth month of the Gregorian calendar, having 30 days.—**June bug** or **beetle,** *n.* Any of the large, brown, winged beetles that appear about June and feed on grass and plant roots.

jungle, jung'gl, *n.* [Hind. *jangal,* forest, jungle.] Land covered with forest trees, thick, impenetrable brushwood, or any coarse, rank vegetation; any tangled mass of seemingly impenetrable material, as objects, words, etc.—**jungle fowl,** *n.* A name given to two birds, the one a native of Australia, the other of India.

junior, jū'ni·ėr, *a.* [L., contracted from *juvenior,* comp. of *juvenis,* young. JUVENILE, YOUNG.] Younger; not as old as another; applied to distinguish the younger of two persons bearing the same name: opposed to *senior;* lower or younger in standing, as in a profession.—*n.* A person younger than another; one of inferior standing in his profession to another.—**junior college,** *n.* An educational institution offering the first two years of college study.—**junior high school,** *n.* A school offering the upper elementary grades and one or more years of high school.

juniper, jū'ni·pėr, *n.* [L. *juniperus*—akin to L. *juncus,* a rush or reed. JONQUIL.] A coniferous shrub whose berries are used in the preparation of gin, varnish, etc., and in medicine as a powerful diuretic.

junk, jungk, *n.* [Fr. *jonc,* L. *juncus,* a bulrush, of which ropes were made in early ages. JUNKET.] Pieces of old cable or old cordage; waste material; salt beef supplied to vessels for long voyages.

junk, jungk, *n.* [Fr. *jonque,* Sp. and Pg. *junco,* from Malay *ajong,* a large ship.] A flat-bottomed ship used in China and Japan, often of large dimensions.

junket, jung'ket, *n.* [Formerly written *juncate,* from It. *giuncata,* cream cheese brought to market in rushes, from L. *juncus,* a rush. JUNK (rope).] Curds mixed with cream, sweetened and flavored; a gay entertainment of any kind; a trip taken for pleasure; a business trip. —*v.i.* To go on a junket; to feast; to banquet; to take part in a gay entertainment.—*v.t.* To entertain; to feast.

Juno, jū'nō, *n.* [L.; the root is the same as that of *Jove.*] The highest divinity of the Latin races in Italy, next to Jupiter, of whom she was the sister and wife, the equivalent of the Greek Hera.

junta, jun'tä, hun'tä, *n.* [Sp. *junta,* a meeting or council, *junto,* united, from L. *junctus,* joined. JOIN.] A meeting; a council; persons controlling a government after a revolutionary seizure.—**junto,** jun'to, hon'to, *n.* A select council or assembly which deliberates in secret on any affair of government; a faction; a cabal.

Jupiter, jū'pi·tėr, *n.* [L., equivalent to *Jovis pater,* lit. Jove-father. JOVE.] The supreme deity among the Latin races in Italy, the equivalent of the Greek Zeus; one of the superior planets, remarkable for its size and brightness.

jupon, ju·pon', *n.* [Fr. from Sp. *jupon,* from Ar. *jubbah,* an outer garment.] A tight-fitting military garment without sleeves, formerly worn over the armor; a petticoat.

Jurassic, jū·ras'ik, *a.* *Geol.* of or belonging to the formation of the *Jura* mountains between France and Switzerland.—*Jura limestone,* the limestone rocks of the Jura corresponding to the oölite formation.— *Jurassic system,* the system of rocks of the Mesozoic era between the Triassic and the Cretaceous.

jurat, jū'rat, *n.* [Fr., from L. *juratus,* sworn, from *juro,* to swear. JURY.] A person under oath; specifically, a magistrate in some corporations; an alderman, or an assistant to a bailiff.

juridical, juridic, jū·rid'i·kal, jū·rid'ik, *a.* [L. *juridicus*—*jus, juris,* law, and *dico,* to pronounce. JURISDICTION.] Acting in the distribution of justice; pertaining to a judge, or the administration of justice; used in courts of law or tribunals of justice.—**juridically,** jū·rid'i·kal·li, *adv.*

In a juridical manner.

jurisconsult, jū'ris·kon·sult, *n.* [L. *juris consultus*—*jus, juris,* law, and *consultus,* from *consulo,* to consult.] One who gives his opinion in cases of law; anyone learned in jurisprudence; a jurist.

jurisdiction, jū·ris·dik'shon, *n.* [L. *jurisdictio*—*jus, juris,* law, and *dictio,* from *dico,* to pronounce. JURY, DICTION.] The extent of the authority which a court has to decide matters tried before it; the right of exercising authority; the extent of the authority of a government, an officer, etc., to execute justice; the district or limit within which power may be exercised. —**jurisdictional,** jū·ris·dik'shon·al, *a.* Pertaining to jurisdiction.

jurisprudence, jū·ris·prō'dens, *n.* [L. *jurisprudentia*—*jus, juris,* law, and *prudentia,* skill. JURY, PRUDENT.] The science of law; the knowledge of the laws, customs, and rights of men in a state or community, necessary for the due administration of justice.—**jurisprudent,** jū·ris·prō'dent, *n.* A jurist.—**jurisprudential,** jū'ris·prō·den''shal, *a.*

jurist, jū'rist, *n.* [Fr. *juriste;* from L. *jus, juris,* law. JURY.] A man who professes the science of law.— **juristic, juristical,** jū·ris'tik, jū·ris'-ti·kal, *a.*

juror, jū'rėr, *n.* [O.Fr. *jureur,* a sworn witness, from *jurer,* to swear. JURY.] One that serves on a jury; a member of a jury; a juryman.

jury, jū'ri, *n.* [O.Fr. *jurie,* an assize, from Fr. *jurer,* L. *jurare,* to swear; same origin as *jus, juris,* right, law (whence *jurist,* etc.), *justus,* just, from root meaning to bind, seen in *jungo,* to join (see JOIN), and in E. *yoke.*] A certain number of men selected according to law and sworn to inquire into or to determine facts, and to declare the truth according to the evidence legally adduced; a body of men selected to adjudge prizes, etc., at a public exhibition.— **juryman,** jū'ri·man, *n.* One who is impaneled on a jury, or who serves as a juror.

jury, jū'ri, *a.* [The origin of this term is quite uncertain; perhaps from Pg. *ajuda,* help.] *Naut.* a term applied to a thing employed to serve temporarily in room of something lost, as a *jury* mast, a *jury* rudder.

jussive, jus'iv, *a.* [From L. *jussum,* an order, from *jubeo, jussi,* to command.] Conveying or containing a command or order.

just, just, *a.* [Fr. *juste,* L. *justus,* what is according to *jus,* the rights of man. JURY.] Acting or disposed to act conformably to what is right; rendering or disposed to render to each one his due; equitable in the distribution of justice; upright; impartial; fair; blameless; righteous; conformed to rules or principles of justice; equitable; due; merited (*just* reward or punishment); rightful; proper; conformed to fact; exact.—*adv.* Exactly or nearly in time (*just* at that moment, *just* now); closely in place (*just* by, *just* behind him); exactly; nicely; accurately (*just* as they were);

narrowly; barely; only.—**justly,** just′li, *adv.* In a just manner.— **justness,** just′nes, *n.* The quality of being just.—**justice,** jus′tis, *n.* [L. *justitia,* from *justus,* just.] The quality of being just; justness; propriety; correctness; rightfulness; just treatment; vindication of right; requital of desert; merited reward or punishment; a judge holding a special office; used as an element in various titles, as Chief-*Justice* and the eight associate *justices* of the U. S. Supreme Court.—*Justices of the peace,* local judges or magistrates appointed to keep the peace, to inquire into felonies and misdemeanors, and to discharge numerous other functions. —**justiciable,** jus·tish′a·bl, *a.* Proper to be brought before a court of justice.—**justiciary, justiciar,** jus·tish′i·a·ri, jus·tish′i·ér, *n.* [L. *justiciarius.*] An administrator of justice; in England, a lord chiefjustice.—*High Court of Justiciary,* the supreme criminal tribunal of Scotland.

justify, jus′ti·fī, *v.t.*—*justified, justifying.* [Fr. *justifier;* L. *justus,* just, and *facio,* to make.] To prove or show to be just or comfortable to law, right, justice, propriety, or duty; to defend or maintain; to vindicate as right; to absolve or clear from guilt or blame; to prove by evidence; to verify; to make exact; to cause to fit, as the parts of a complex object; to adjust, as lines and words in printing; *theol.* to pardon and clear from guilt; to treat as just, though guilty and deserving punishment.—*v.i.* To form an even surface or true line with something else.— **justifiable,** jus′ti·fī·a·bl, *a.* Capable of being justified; defensible; vindicable; warrantable; excusable.— **justifiableness,** jus′ti·fī·a·bl·ness. *n.* The quality of being justifiable.— **justifiably,** jus′ti·fī·a·bli, *adv.* In a manner that admits of justification; defensibly; excusably.—**justification,** jus′ti·fi·kā″shon, *n.* The act of justifying or state of being justified; *theol.* acceptance of a sinner as righteous through the merits of Christ.— **justificative,** jus′ti·fi·kā·tiv, *a.* Justifying; justificatory.—**justificatory,** jus·tif′i·ka·to·ri, *a.* Vindicatory; defensory.—**justifier,** jus′ti·fī·ér, *n.* One who justifies.

justle, jus′l, *v.i.* See JOSTLE.

jut, jut, *v.i.*—*jutted, jutting.* [A different spelling of *jet.*] To shoot out or to project beyond the main body.— *n.* That which juts; a projection.— **jutty,** jut′i, *n.* A jetty.

jute, jūt, *n.* [Hind. *jût.*] A fibrous substance resembling hemp, obtained from an Indian plant of the linden family, and used in the manufacture of carpets, bagging, etc.; the plant itself.

juvenile, jū′ve·nil, *a.* [L. *juvenilis,* from *juvenis,* young; cog. Skr. *yuvan,* young, E. *young.*] Young; youthful; pertaining or suited to youth.—*n.* A young person or youth.—*Juvenile delinquent,* a youth who violates a U.S. law not punishable by death; a youth guilty of antisocial behavior

(truancy, etc.) outside the range of parental control.—**juvenility,** jū·ve·nil′i·ti, *n.*—**juvenescent,** jū·ve·nes′ent, *a.* Becoming young.—**juvenescence,** jū·ve·nes′ens, *n.*

juxtapose, juks·ta·pōz′, *v.t.* [L. *juxta,* near, and E. *pose.*] To place near or next; place side by side.—**juxtaposition,** juks′ta·po·zish″on, *n.* The act of juxtaposing, or state of being juxtaposed; proximity.

K

K, k, kā, the eleventh letter and the eighth consonant of the English alphabet; in Anglo-Saxon represented by *c.*

Kaaba, kä′a·ba, *n.* See CAABA.

kab, kab, *n.* A Hebrew measure. CAB.

kabala, kab′a·la, *n.* Cabala.

Kabyle, ka·bēl′, *n.* [Ar. *k'bila,* a league.] One belonging to a race of Berbers inhabiting Algeria and Tunis.

kadi, käd′i or kā′di, *n.* See CADI.

Kaffir, Kafir, kaf′ér, *n.* [Ar. *Kâfir,* an unbeliever, an infidel.] One of a group of Bantu people; the language of the Kafirs.—*a.* Of or belonging to the Kafirs.—**kafir corn,** *n.* A kind of millet (sorghum) cultivated in parts of Africa.

kaftan, kaf′tan, *n.* [Per.] A garment worn in Turkey, Egypt, etc., consisting of a kind of long vest tied round at the waist with a girdle and having sleeves longer than the arms.

kainite, kī′nīt, *n.* [Gr. *kainos,* recent.] A mineral (hydrated magnesium sulfate and potassium chloride) occurring in the upper layers of Stassfurt salt deposits in Germany and used as a fertilizer and a source of potassium and magnesium.

kaiser, kī′zer, *n.* [G.] An emperor. CAESAR.

kaka, kä′kä, *n.* [From its cry.] A New Zealand parrot of the same genus as the kea, which latter attacks sheep and tears out portions of flesh from their backs.

kakapo, kak′a·po, *n.* [Native name.] The owl parrot, a New Zealand parrot resembling an owl.

kale, kāl, *n.* [Icel. *kal,* Dan. *kaal.* COLE.] Cabbage having curled or wrinkled leaves, but not a close head; colewort.

kaleidoscope, ka·lī′do·skōp, *n.* [Gr. *kalos,* beautiful, *eidos,* form, and *skopeō,* to view.] An optical instrument which exhibits, by reflection, a variety of beautiful colors and symmetrical forms, consisting in its simplest form of a tube containing two reflecting surfaces inclined to each other at a suitable angle, with loose pieces of colored glass, etc., inside. —**kaleidoscopic, kaleidoscopical,** ka·lī′do·skop″ik, ka·lī′do·skop″i·kal, *a.* Relating to the kaleidoscope.

kalendar, kal′en·dér. See CALENDAR.

kali, kā′li, *n.* [Ar. *qali.* ALKALI.] Glasswort, a plant, the ashes of which are used in making glass.

kalif, kā′lif. See CALIPH.

kalmia, kal′mi·a, *n.* [From Peter *Kalm,* a botanist.] A genus of American evergreen shrubs of the heath family, with showy flowers in corymbs.

Kalmuk, Kalmuck, kal′muk, *n.* Calmuck.

kalong, kā′long, *n.* [Native name.] A name given to several species of fox bats.

kamala, kam′a·la, *n.* [Of Asiatic origin.] A drug obtained from an Asiatic tree, used as a vermifuge and a dyestuff.

kangaroo, kang′ga·rö, *n.* The native name of certain marsupials of Australia, with long and powerful hind legs for leaping, and small and short forelegs.—**kangaroo rat,** *n.* A small jumping rodent.—**kangaroo court,** *n.* An unauthorized court which mocks or disregards legal procedure.

Kantianism, kant′i·a·nizm, *n.* The philosophic system of Immanuel Kant.

kaolin, kā′o·lin, *n.* [Chinese *kau-ling,* high ridge, the name of a hill where it is found.] A fine variety of clay, resulting from the decomposition of the feldspar of a granitic rock under the influence of the weather; porcelain or China clay.

kappa, kap′ä, *n.* [Gr.] The tenth letter of the Greek alphabet, *k.*

kaput, kä·put′, *a.* [G. *kaput,* broken.] Finished; done for; ruined.

karma, kär′ma, *n.* [Skr., act, fate.] In the Buddhist religion, the quality belonging to actions in virtue of which they entail on the actor a certain fate or condition in a future state of existence; a term also used in theosophy.

karroo, karoo, ka·rö′, *n.* [Hottentot *karusa,* hard, from the hardness of their soil under drought.] The name given to the immense arid tracts of clayey tablelands of South Africa, which are covered with verdure only in the wet season.

karyokinesis, kar′i·ō·ki·nē″sis, *n.* [Gr. *karyon,* a nut, *kinēsis,* movement.] Indirect cell division.

katabolism, ka·tab′ol·ism, *n.* [Gr. *katabolē,* a casting down.] Downbreaking chemical changes in living bodies.

katalysis. See CATALYSIS.

kathode, kath′ōd, *n.* See CATHODE.

kation, kat′i·on, *n.* See CATION.

katydid, kā′ti·did, *n.* A species of grasshopper found in the United States: it gives out a loud sound which its name is intended to imitate.

kauri, kou′ri, *n.* [Native name.] A coniferous tree of New Zealand, yielding gum-damar, damar-resin, or kauri-gum, and having a tall straight stem, rising to a height of 150 to 200 ft., yielding valuable timber.

kava, kā′vä, *n.* A Polynesian shrub of the pepper family, and beverage made from it.

kayak, kī′ak, *n.* [Eskimo name.] A light boat, made of sealskins stretched round a wooden frame, with an opening in the middle.

kea, kē′a, *n.* See KAKA.

keck, kek, *v.i.* To vomit.

kedge, kej, *n.* [Softened form of *keg*, Icel. *kaggi*, a keg, a cask fastened as a float to an anchor, hence, the anchor itself.] A small anchor used to keep a ship steady when riding in a harbor or river, or to assist in warping her.—*v.t.* kedged, kedging. To warp (a ship) by means of a rope attached to a kedge.

keel, kēl, *n.* [From Icel. *kjölr*, Dan. *kjöl*, Sw. *köl*, a keel of a vessel; D. *kiel*, a keel; in sense of barge, from Icel. *kjöll*, a barge=A.Sax. *ceól*, barge, O.H.G. *kiol*, a ship.] The principal timber in a ship, extending from stem to stern at the bottom, and supporting the whole frame; the corresponding part in iron vessels; *fig.* the whole ship; a projecting ridge on a surface; a low, flat-bottomed vessel used in the river Tyne for loading the colliers; a coal barge; *bot.* the lower petal of a papilionaceous corolla, enclosing the stamens and pistil.—*v.i.* To turn up the keel; to capsize.—**keelhaul**, kēl′hal, *v.t.* To punish by dropping into the sea on one side of a ship and hauling up on the other.—**keelson**, kēl′sun or kel′sun, *n.* [Dan. *kjölsviin*, Sw. *kölsvin*, G. *kielschwein*, lit. *keelswine*; comp. *pig* of lead.] An internal keel laid on the middle of the floor timbers over the keel.

keen, kēn, *a.* [A.Sax. *céne, cén*=Icel. *kænn*, wise, clever; D. *koen*, G. *kühn*, keen, bold; same root as *ken*.] Acute of mind; penetrating; quick-witted; eager; vehement; full of relish or zest; sharp (a *keen* appetite); having a very fine edge (a *keen* razor); piercing; penetrating; severe (cold or wind); bitter, acrimonious (*keen* satire).—**keenly**, kēn′li, *adv.* In a keen manner.—**keenness**, kēn′nes, *n.* The state or quality of being keen; acuteness; eagerness.

keen, kēn, *v.i.* [Ir. *caoinim*.] To lament in a wailing tone.

keep, kēp, *v.t.* pret. & pp. *kept*. [A.Sax. *cépan*, to keep, observe, regard; Fris. *kijpen*, to look.] To hold; to retain in one's power or possession; not to lose or part with; to have in custody for security or preservation; to preserve; to protect; to guard; to restrain; to detain or delay; to tend or have the care of; to maintain, as an establishment, institution, etc.; to manage; to hold in any state; to continue or maintain, as a state, course, or action (to *keep* silence; to *keep* the same pace; to *keep* step); to remain confined to; not to quit (the house, one's bed); to observe in practice; not to neglect or violate; to fulfill; to observe or solemnize; to board, maintain, supply with necessaries of life; to have in the house; to entertain (to *keep* lodgers, company); to be in the habit of selling; to have a supply of for sale.—*To keep back*, to reserve; to withhold; not to disclose or communicate; to restrain; to prevent from advancing; not to deliver.—*To keep down*, to prevent from rising; to hold in subjection; to restrain.—*To keep house*, to maintain a separate residence for one's self, or for one's self and family; to remain in the house; to be confined to the house.—*To keep in*, to prevent from escape; to hold in confinement; not to tell or disclose; to restrain; to curb, as a horse.—*To keep off*, to hinder from approach or attack.—*To keep on foot*, to maintain, as a standing army.—*To keep one's self to one's self*, to shun society; to keep one's own counsel; to keep aloof from others.—*To keep out*, to hinder from entering or taking possession.—*To keep under*, to hold in subjection.—*To keep up*, to maintain; to prevent from falling or diminution; to continue; to hinder from ceasing.—*v.i.* To remain in any position or state; to continue; to abide; to stay; not to be impaired; to continue fresh or wholesome; not to become spoiled.—*To keep at it*, to continue hard at work. (*Colloq.*)—*To keep from*, to abstain from; to refrain from.—*To keep on*, to proceed; to continue to advance.—*To keep to*, to adhere strictly to; not to neglect or deviate from.—*To keep up*, to retain one's spirits; to be yet active or not to be confined to one's bed.—*n.* Guard, care, or heed; the state of being kept; the means by which one is kept; subsistence; provisions; the stronghold of an ancient castle; a donjon.—**keeper**, kēp′ėr, *n.* One who keeps; one who has the care of a prison and the custody of prisoners; one who has the charge of animals in a zoological garden; one who has the care, custody, or superintendence of anything; something that keeps or holds safe.—**keeping**, kēp′ing, *n.* A holding; custody; guard; maintenance; support; food; just proportion; consistency; harmony. — *To be in keeping with*, to accord or harmonize with; to be consistent with.—**keepsake**, kēp′sāk, *n.* Anything kept or given to be kept for the sake of the giver; a token of friendship.

keg, keg, *n.* [Formerly *kag*; Icel. *kaggi*, Sw. *kagge*, a keg. KEDGE.] A small cask or barrel.

kelp, kelp, *n.* [Origin unknown.] The alkaline substance yielded by seaweeds when burned, containing soda and iodine; any member of the order or large brown seaweed called Laminariaceae and Fucaceae.

kelpie, kelpy, kel′pi, *n.* [Perhaps connected with *yelp*, from his bellowing.] In Scotland, a malignant spirit of the waters, generally seen in the form of a horse.

kelson, kel′son, *n.* Same as *Keelson*.

kelt, keltic, kelt, kel′tik. See CELT, CELTIC.

kelter, kilter, kel′tėr, kil′tėr, *n.* [Comp. *kilt*, to tuck up the clothes.] Regular or proper state. (*Colloq.*)

ken, ken, *v.t.*—*kenned*, *kenning*. [Icel. *kenna*, D. and G. *kennen*, A.Sax. *cunnan*, to ken, to know; allied are *can*, *cunning*, *known*. KNOW.] To know; to take cognizance of; to see at a distance; to descry; to recognize. (Now only provincial and poetical.) —*n.* Cognizance; reach of sight or knowledge.

kennel, ken′el, *n.* [Norm. Fr., from *ken*, Fr. *chien*, a dog, from L. *canis*, a dog.] A shelter for dogs; a dog-house; a place where dogs are bred; a pack of dogs.—*v.i.*—kenneled, kenneling, or kennelled, kennelling. To live in, as a dog.—*v.t.* To keep or confine in a kennel.

kennel, ken′el, *n.* [A form of *channel*, *canal*.] The watercourse of a street; a gutter.

kenosis, ken′ō·sis, *n.* [Gr. *kenōsis*, emptying.] The renunciation for a time of the divine nature by Christ during the incarnation.

kentledge, kent′lej, *n.* Pig iron for ballast laid on the floor of a ship.

Kentucky bluegrass, ken·tuk′i, *n.* [From its jointed, bluish-green stem.] A perennial, rough-stalked pasture grass of the U. S., Europe, and Asia, grown in its finest state in the limestone regions of Kentucky and Tennessee. Kentucky is called the *Bluegrass State*.

kepi, kep′i, *n.* A military cap.

kept, kept, pret. & pp. of *keep*.

keramic, ke·ram′ik, *a.* Ceramic.

keratin, ker′a·tin, *n.* [Gr. *keras, keratos*, horn.] The complex compound of which horny substances (*e.g.* hair and nails) are mainly composed.

keratode, keratose, ker′a·tōd, ker′a·tōs, *n.* [Gr. *keras, keratos*, horn.] The horny substance of which the skeleton of many sponges is composed.

kerbstone. See CURB.

kerchief, kėr′chēf, *n.* [O.E. *coverchief*, O.Fr. *couvrechief*, *couvrechef*—Fr. *couvrir*, to cover, and *chef*, the head. COVER, CHIEF.] A cloth to dress or cover the head; hence, any loose cloth used in dress.—**kerchiefed, kerchieft**, kėr′chēft, *a.* Dressed or covered with a kerchief.

kerf, kėrf, *n.* [A.Sax. *cyrf*, a cutting off, from *ceorfan*, *cearfan*, to cut, to carve. CARVE.] The cut or way made through wood by a saw or other cutting instrument.

kermes, kėr′mēz, *n.* [Ar. and Per. *kermes*, *kirmis*, from Skr. *krimi*, a worm; *crimson*, *carmine*, are derivatives.] A scarlet dyestuff consisting of the dried bodies of the females of certain insects found on various species of oak round the Mediterranean.

kern, kerne, kėrn, *n.* [O.Gael. and Ir. *cearn*, a man.] A light-armed foot soldier of ancient Ireland and the Highlands of Scotland: opposed to *gallowglass*.

kern, kėrn, *n.* [Probably from L. *crena*, notch.] *Printing*, that part of a type which hangs over the body or shank.

kernel, kėr′nel, *n.* [A.Sax. *cyrnel*, a little corn, a kernel, dim. of *corn*, a grain. CORN, GRAIN.] The edible substance contained in the shell of a nut or the stone of a fruit; anything enclosed in a shell, husk, or integument; a grain of corn; the seed of pulpy fruit; a small mass around which other matter is concreted; a nucleus; *fig.* the main or essential point, as opposed to matters of less import; the core; the gist.—*v.i.* To harden or ripen into kernels, as the seeds of plants.

kerosene, ker′o·sēn, *n.* [Gr. *kēros*, wax.] A liquid hydrocarbon distilled from coals, bitumen, petroleum, etc., extensively used in lamps, stoves, etc.

kersey, kĕr′zi, *n.* [Said to be from *Kersey*, in Suffolk.] A species of coarse woolen cloth, usually ribbed, made from long wool.—*a.* Consisting of kersey; hence, homespun; homely.

kerseymere, kĕr′zi·mēr, *n.* [CASSIMERE.] A thin twilled stuff woven from the finest wools, used for men's garments; cassimere.

kestrel, kes′trel, *n.* [Fr. *quercerelle, cresserelle,* kestrel; L. *querquedula,* a teal.] A common British species of falcon, 13 to 15 inches in length, capable of hovering against the wind.

ketch, kech, *n.* [Perhaps akin to *catch.*] A fore-and-aft rigged vessel with a mainmast and a mizzenmast, the latter being forward of the rudder post.

ketchup, catchup, catsup, kech′up, *n.* [Malay *kechap,* a kind of East Indian pickles.] A sauce for meat and fish, made from mushrooms, unripe walnuts, tomatoes, etc.; usually, a thick, seasoned tomato sauce.

ketone, kē′tōn, [G. *keton,* from F. *acétone.*] An organic compound of the general formula R-CO-R′, in which the radicals (R and R′) may be identical or different alkyl or aryl groups, as in CH_3COCH_3, acetone.

kettle, ket′l, *n.* [A. Sax. *cetel*=D. *ketel,* Icel. *ketill,* kettle; from L. *catillus,* dim. of *catinus,* a deep bowl, a vessel for cooking food.] A vessel of iron or other metal, of various shapes and dimensions, used for heating and boiling water or other liquor.— **kettledrum,** *n.* A drum consisting of a copper vessel, usually hemispherical, covered with parchment.

kevel, kev′el, *n.* [Dan. *kievle,* a peg, a rolling-pin.] *Naut.* a piece of timber serving to belay great ropes to.—**kevelhead,** *n. Naut.* the end of one of the top timbers used as a kevel.

key, kē, *n.* [A.Sax. *caeg, caege,* Fris. *kai, kei,* a key; affinities doubtful.] An instrument for shutting or opening a lock; that whereby any mystery is disclosed or anything difficult explained; a guide; a solution; an explanation; a tone or pitch; a legend, as on a map or a puzzle; something that fastens, keeps tight, prevents movement, or the like; a movable piece in a musical instrument, struck or pressed by the fingers in playing to produce the notes; the keynote.—*a.* Of basic importance; main.—*v.t.* To furnish or fasten with a key; to fasten or secure firmly; to make a legend to aid understanding; to make nervous, with *up.*—**keyboard,** *n.* The series of levers in a keyed musical instrument, as a pianoforte, organ, or in a type-

writer or typesetting machine, on which the fingers press.—**keyhole,** *n.* A hole in a door or lock for receiving a key.—**keynote,** *n.* The main idea; *mus.,* the first note, or "do" tone, of a scale.—*Keynote address,* a speech, as at a political convention, to arouse enthusiasm and present the basic issues.—**keystone,** kē′stōn, *n.* The stone at the apex of an arch which, when put in, keys or locks the whole.

key, kē, *n.* CAY.

khaki, kä·kē, *n.* [Hind., from *khâk;* dust.] A light-brown thin material used for uniforms.

khalif, kā′lif, *n.* Calif.

khamsin, kam′sin, *n.* [Ar. *khamsin,* fifty, because it blows about fifty days.] A hot southerly wind in Egypt; the simoom.

khan, kän, *n.* [Tartar and Turk. *khân.*] In Asia, a governor; a king; a prince; a chief.—**khanate,** kan′āt, *n.* The dominion or jurisdiction of a khan.

khan, kän, *n.* [Per. *khân,* a house, a tent.] An eastern inn; a caravansary.

khedive, ke·dēv′, *n.* A Turkish title formerly applied to the Pasha or governor of Egypt, implying a rank or authority superior to a prince or viceroy, but inferior to an independent sovereign.

khitmutgar, kit·mut′gär, *n.* [Hind. *khidmat-gâr—khidmat,* service, duty, and *gâr,* a doer.] In India, a waiter at table; an under butler.

kibe, kīb, *n.* [W. *cibwst—cib,* cup, and *gwst,* moist, fluid.] A chilblain.

kibitzer, kib′it·sĕr, *n.* [Yiddish, from G. *kiebitzen,* to look on, from *kiebitz,* a bothersome spectator.] One who gives unwanted advice, especially such a one looking on at a card game. —**kibitz,** kib′its, *v.i.* To behave as a kibitzer; to meddle.

kibosh, ki·bosh′, kī′bosh, *n.* [Origin doubtful.] Nonsense.—*Put the kibosh on,* squelch; stop. (Slang)

kick, kik, *v.t.* [W. *ciciaw,* to kick, *cic,* the foot.] To strike with the foot; to strike in recoiling, as a gun; *football,* to win a goal by kicking.— *To kick up a row or a dust,* to create a disturbance. (Colloq.)—*v.i.* To strike with the foot or feet; to be in the habit of so striking; to manifest repugnance to restraint; to be recalcitrant; to recoil, as a firearm.— *n.* A blow with the foot or feet; a striking or thrust of the foot; the recoil of a firearm; a measurable feeling; a thrill.—**kicker,** kik′ĕr, *n.*— **kickback,** kik′bak, *n.* An unofficial and sometimes illegal return of a portion of wages or dividends, etc., to the payer.—**kickoff,** kik′af, *n. Football,* a place kick at or near the center of the field to begin play; the opening or beginning of a campaign or event.—**kickup,** kik′up, *n.* A disturbance; a row.

kickshaw, kik′sha, *n.* [Originally *kickshaws,* as a singular noun, from Fr. *quelque chose,* something.] Something fantastical or uncommon; a light, unsubstantial dish.

kid, kid, *n.* [Dan. and Sw. *kid,* Icel.

kith, G. *kitz, kitze,* a kid; akin *chit, child.*] A young goat; leather made from the skin of a kid, or in imitation of it; a child or youngster.—*v.t.* and *i.*—**kidded, kidding.** To bring forth a young goat; to tease; to joke.

kid, kid, *n.* [A form of *kit.*] A small wooden tub or vessel.

Kidderminster, kid′ĕr·min·stĕr, *n.* A carpeting, so named from the town where formerly it was principally manufactured.

kidnap, kid′nap, *v.t.*—**kidnaped, kidnaping.** [Slang E *kid* a child, and *nap* for *nab,* to steal.] To forcibly abduct or steal a human being, to seize and forcibly carry away.— **kidnaper,** kid′nap·ĕr, *n.*

kidney, kid′ni, *n.* [O.E. *kidnere*=Sc. *kite,* A.Sax. *cwith,* Icel. *kvithr,* Sw. *qued,* the belly, and Sc. *neer,* Icel. *nyra,* G. *niere,* a kidney.] Either of the two oblong, flattened, bean-shaped glands which secrete the urine, situated in the belly on either side of the backbone; constitution, character, or temper.—**kidney bean,** *n.* The English term for the common string bean; in France the haricot bean.

kilderkin, kil′der·kin, *n.* [O.D. *kindeken, kinneken.*] A small barrel; an old liquid measure containing the eighth part of a hogshead or 18 gallons.

kill, kil, *v.t.* [O.E. *kylle, kulle, culle,* to strike.] To deprive of life by any means; to render inanimate; to put to death; to slay; to deprive of active qualities; to deaden (pain); to overpower; to stop; to cause to waste (to *kill* time).—*n.* The act of killing; the game killed in a hunt. —**killer,** kil′ĕr, *n.* A murderer; that which kills, as a beast of prey.— **killjoy,** kil′joi, *n.* One who ruins the fun or enjoyment for others.— **killingly,** kil′ing·li, *adv.*

killdeer, kil′dēr, *n.* [From its clear, plaintive cry.] An American plover, a shore bird with a grayish-brown back and a white breast.

kiln, kil, *n.* [A.Sax. *cylene, cyln,* perhaps from L. *culina,* a kitchen (whence *culinary*).] An oven of brick or stone which may be heated for the purpose of hardening, burning, or drying anything placed in it.

kilocycle, kil′o·si·kl, *n.* A thousand cycles; *radio,* a thousand cycles per second.

kilogram, kil′o·gram, *n.* [Fr. *kilogramme* from Gr. *chilioi,* a thousand, and Fr. *gramme.*] A measure of weight, being 1,000 grams.—**kilogram-meter,** *n.* A unit of work, or the amount taken to raise one kilogram one meter (almost 7¼ foot-pounds).—**kiloliter,** kil′o·lē·tĕr, *n.* 1,000 liters.

kilometer, ki·lom′e·tĕr, *n.* 1,000 meters.—**kilowatt,** kil′o·wot, *n.* An electric unit of power, equivalent to 1,000 watts, or to 1.34 horsepower. —**kilowatt hour,** *n.* A unit of energy equal to that expended by one kilowatt acting for one hour.

kilt, kilt, *n.* [A Scandinavian word; comp. Icel. *kilting,* a skirt, *kjalta,* a person's lap; Dan. *kilte*, to tuck up or kilt.] A kind of short petticoat worn by men as an article of dress in lieu of trousers; regarded as peculiarly the national dress of the Highlanders of Scotland; the filibeg. —*v.t.* To tuck up like a kilt for greater freedom of movement.

kimono, ki·mo′no, *n.* [Jap.] A loose, robe-like garment, usually made of silk, worn by both Japanese men and women; a similar garment worn indoors by occidental women; a dressing gown.

kin, kin, *n.* [A.Sax. *cynn, cyn*, Icel. *kyn*, Goth. *kuni*, O.H.G. *chunni*, kin, kind, family, race; akin are *kind, n.* and *a., king*; D. and G. *kind*, a child; L. *genus*, Gr. *genos*, race, offspring. GENUS.] Relationship; consanguinity or affinity; connection by blood; relatives collectively; kindred; used in this sense with a verb in the plural. *a.* Of the same nature or kind; kindred; congenial.—**kinsfolk,** kinz′-fōk, *n. pl.* Relations kindred.—**kinship,** kin′ship, *n.* Relationship; consanguinity.—**kinsman,** kinz′man, *n.* A man of the same race or family, one related by blood.—**kinswoman,** kinz′wum·an, *n.* A female relation.

kind, kīnd, *n.* [A.Sax. *cynde, gecynde*, nature, kind, race, generation, from same root as *cyn*, offspring. KIN.] Race genus; generic class; sort; variety; nature; style; manner; character.—*In kind*, with produce or commodities, as opposed to *in money* (to pay one *in kind*).

kind, kīnd, *a.* [A.Sax. *cynde, gecynde*, natural harmonious; closely akin to *kind, n.* KIN.] Disposed to do good to others, and to make them happy; having tenderness or goodness of nature; benevolent; benignant; friendly; proceeding from or dictated by tenderness or goodness of heart.—**kindhearted,** *a.* Having much kindness of nature; characterized by kindness of heart.—**kindheartedness,** *n.* Kindness of heart.—**kindliness,** kīnd′li·nes, *n.* The quality of being kindly.—**kindly,** kīnd′li, *adv.* In a kind manner.—*a.* Of a kind disposition or character; sympathetic; congenial; benevolent favorable; refreshing (*kindly* showers).—**kindness,** kīnd′nes, *n.* The state or quality of being kind; good will; benevolence; a kind act; an act of good will.

kindergarten, kin′dèr·gär·ten, *n.* [G.; lit. children's garden. CHILD, GARDEN.] A kind of infants' school, intermediate between the nursery and the primary school, in which systematically arranged amusements are combined with a certain amount of instruction.

kindle, kin′dl, *v.t.*—**kindled, kindling.** [Allied to or derived from Icel. *kynda*, to kindle, *kyndill*, a torch or candle; perhaps from L. *candela*, E. *candle*.] To set on fire; to cause to burn with flame; to light; to inflame, as the passions; to rouse; to provoke; to excite to action.—*v.i.* To take fire; to grow warm or animated; to be roused or exasperated.—**kindling,** kind′ling, *n.* The act of one who kindles; materials for lighting a fire.

kindred, kind′red, *n.* [O.E. *kinrede*, kindred, from *kin*, and term. *-red*, as in hat*red* (which see): the *d* is inserted, as in gen*der*, thun*der*. KIN.] Relationship by birth or marriage; consanguinity; kin; in plural sense, relatives by blood or marriage, more properly the former; relations or relatives.—*a.* Related; congenial; allied.

kinematics, ki·ne·mat′iks, *n.* [Gr. *kinēma*, movement, from *kineō*, to move.] That branch of the science of mechanics which treats of motion, without reference to the forces producing it.—**kinematic, kinematical,** ki·ne·mat′ik, ki·ne·mat′i·kal, *a.* Of or belonging to kinematics.—*Kinematic viscosity*, the relation of absolute viscosity to density; air being fourteen times as kinematically viscous as water.—**kinetic,** ki·net′ik, *a.* Causing motion; motory: applied to force actually exerted.—*Kinetic energy*, energy of motion, equal (in absolute measure) to $\frac{1}{2} mv^2$, where *m* represents the mass and *v* the velocity of the moving body; in gravitational measure it is $mv^2/2\,g$.—**kinetics,** ki·net′iks, *n.* That branch of the science of dynamics which treats of forces causing or changing motion in bodies. DYNAMICS.—**kinematograph,** ki·ne·mat′o·graf (popularly, sin·e·mat′o·graf), *n.* A method of casting upon a screen a series of instantaneous photographs, producing the effect of motion.

king, king, *n.* [A.Sax. *cyning*, from *cyn*, kin, race, and term. *-ing*, one of, descendant (as in *atheling*); D. *koning*, Icel. *konungr*, Dan. *konge*, G. *könig*, king. KIN.] The sovereign of a nation; a man invested with supreme authority over a nation, tribe, or country; a monarch; a prince; a ruler; a playing card having the picture of a king; the chief piece in the game of chess; a crowned man in the game of checkers; [*cap.*] *pl.* title of two books in the Old Testament, relating particularly to the Jewish kings.—*v.t.* To rule over as king.—*v.i.* To act like a king.—*a.* Most important; main: often in combination (*king* post).—**kingbird,** *n.* Certain of the various birds of the fly-catcher family.—**kingcrab,** *n.* A kind of crustacean with a carapace of horseshoe shape, and a long tail spine.—**kingcraft,** king′kraft, *n.* The art of governing; royal polity or policy.—**kingdom,** king′dum, *n.* The power or authority of a king (*Shak.*); the territory or country subject to a king; the dominion of a king or monarch; domain or realm in a general sense; *nat. hist.* one of the most extensive divisions into which natural objects are classified (the animal, vegetable, and mineral *kingdoms*).—**kingfisher,** king′fish·èr, *n.* A crested and bright-colored bird with a short tail and long sharp-pointed bill. It frequents the banks of rivers and dives for fish.—**kinglet,** king′let, *n.* A little king; a tiny bird, similar to the warbler, the golden-crowned or ruby-crowned kinglet.—

kingliness, king′li·nes, *n.* State of being kingly.—**kingly,** king′li, *a.* Belonging or pertaining to a king or to kings; royal; monarchical; becoming a king; august; splendid. ∴ Syn. under ROYAL.—*adv.* With an air of royalty; as becoming a king.—**kingpin,** *n. Bowling*, the number-one pin; the leader; the chief person.—**king post,** *n.* The middle post standing at the apex of a pair of rafters, and having its lower end fastened to the middle of the tie beam.—**king's evil,** *n.* A disease of the scrofulous kind, formerly believed curable by the touch of a king.—**kingship,** king′ship, *n.* Royalty; the state, office, or dignity of a king; royal government.—**king truss,** *n.* A truss for a roof framed with a king post.—**kingwood,** *n.* A Brazilian wood beautifully streaked with violet tints, and used in cabinetwork.

kink, kingk, *n.* [D., G., and Sw. *kink*, a twist or coil in a cable.] A twist in a rope or thread such as prevents it running freely; an unreasonable and obstinate notion; a crotchet.—*v.i.* To get into a kink; to twist or run into knots.

kinkajou, king′ka·jö, *n.* A plantigrade carnivorous mammal of South America, resembling the lemurs in structure and aspect, but allied to the bear.

kino, kī′nō, *n.* [An East Indian word.] An astringent extract resembling catechu, obtained from various tropical trees.

kinsfolk, kinship, kinsman, kinswoman. See KIN.

kiosk, ki·osk′, *n.* A Turkish word signifying a kind of open pavilion or summer house; a similar lightweight structure used as an open-air newsstand, bandstand, etc.; a roadside telephone booth.

kipper, kip′ér, *n.* [O.E. *cypera*, spawning salmon, prob. from *coper*, copper, the color.] A salmon at, or directly after, the spawning season; a fish, as a salmon or herring, split open, salted, and dried or smoked. —*v.t.* To cure (salmon) by splitting open, salting, and drying.

kirk, kirk, *n.* [The old form of *church*; A.Sax. *cyrc*. CHURCH.] A church: still in common use in Scotland.

kirsch, kérsh, *n.* [G., from *kirsche*, cherry.] An alcoholic liquor distilled from the fermented juice of the small black cherry.

kirtle, kér′tl, *n.* [A.Sax. *cyrtel*, Icel. *kyrtill*, Dan. *kjortel*; akin to *short*.] A kind of short gown; a petticoat. —*v.t.* To tuck up so as to give the appearance of a kirtle to.—**kirtled,** kér′tld, *a.* Wearing a kirtle.

kismet, kis′met, *n.* [Per. *kusmut*.] A Mohammedan expression for fate or destiny.

kiss, kis, *v.t.* [A.Sax. *cyssan*, from *coss*, a kiss; Icel. and Sw. *kyssa*, Dan. *kysse*, G. *kussen*, to kiss; the corresponding nouns being Icel. *koss*, Dan. *kys*, G. *kuss*.] To touch with the lips in salutation or as a mark of affection; to caress by joining lips; to touch gently, as if with

---

ch, *ch*ain; *ch*, Sc. lo*ch*; g, *g*o; j, *j*ob; ng, si*ng*; TH, *th*en; th, *th*in; w, *w*ig; hw, *wh*ig; zh, a*z*ure.

fondness.—*v.i.* To join lips in love or respect; to meet or come in contact (as curved lines, etc.).—*n.* A salute given with the lips; a kind of confection.—**kisser**, kis´ér, *n.* (Slang) The mouth or face.

kit, kit, *n.* [D. *kit*, a large bottle; O.D. *kitte*, a beaker, decanter.] A large bottle; a kind of wooden tub for holding fish, butter, etc.; that which contains necessaries or tools, and hence the necessaries and tools themselves; something to be assembled (airplane *kit*); a collection of related materials (a convention *kit*).

kit, kit, *n.* [Probably an abbreviated form of *guitar, gittern, cittern.*] A diminutive fiddle, used generally by dancing masters.

kitchen, kich´en, *n.* [A.Sax. *cycene*, from L. *coquina*, kitchen, from *coquo*, to cook. COOK.] The room of a house appropriated to cookery; style of cooking or of food prepared.— **kitchener**, kich´en·ér, *n.* A servant in the kitchen; a cookstove.— **kitchenette, kitchenet**, *n.* A small room or recess compactly furnished as a kitchen.—**kitchen garden**, a garden in which vegetables are grown for the table.—**kitchenmidden**, *n.* [Dan. *kjokkenmodding.*] A refuse heap of a prehistoric people. —**kitchenware**, *n.* Utensils used in a kitchen.

kite, kīt, *n.* [A.Sax. *cyta*, a kite.] A bird of the falcon family having a somewhat long forked tail, long wings, and comparatively weak bill and talons; a light frame of wood and paper constructed for flying in the air for amusement.

kith, kith, *n.* [A.Sax. *cytth*, knowledge, relationship, native country, from *cúth*, known, pp. of *cunnan*, to know. CAN.] Acquaintances or friends collectively.—*Kith and kin*, friends and relatives.

kitten, kit´n, *n.* [Dim. of *cat*.] A young cat.—*v.i.* To bring forth young, as a cat.—**kittenish**, kit´n·ish, *a.* Like a kitten; fond of playing.—**kitty**, kit´i, *n.* A kitten.

kittiwake, kit´i·wāk, *n.* [From its cry.] A species of gull found in great abundance in the northern parts of the world.

kitty, kit´i, *n.* [From *kit*.] A pool or common fund into which participants contribute for a particular purpose.

kiwi, kē´wē, *n.* [Maori.] An apteryx, a flightless bird of New Zealand.

kleptomania, klep·tō·mā´ni·a, *n.* [Gr. *kleptō*, to steal, and *mania*, madness.] A form of neurosis marked by an irresistible impluse to steal, usually for no economic reason.—**kleptomaniac**, klep·tō·mā´ni·ak, *n.* One affected with kleptomania.

knack, nak, *n.* [Imitative of sound, like D. *knak*, Dan. *knaek*, G. *knack*, a crack, a snap; originally a snap of the fingers, then a trick or way of doing a thing as if with a snap.] Readiness; habitual facility of performance; dexterity; adroitness; a knickknack or toy (*Shak.*).

knacker, nak´ér, *n.* [From Icel.

hnakkr, a saddle: originally it meant a saddler and harness maker.] One whose occupation is to slaughter diseased or useless horses.

knap, nap, *v.t.*—**knapped, knapping.** [Same as D. *knappen*, to crack, to munch, to lay hold of; G. *knappen*, to crack, to snap.] To bite; to bite off; to break short; to snap; to make a short sharp sound.—*n.* A short sharp noise; a snap.

knapsack, nap´sak, *n.* [L.G. *knappsack*, D. *knapzak*, G. and D. *knappen*, to snap, to eat, and *sack*—lit. a provision sack.] A bag of leather or strong cloth for carrying a soldier's necessaries, strapped to the back between the shoulders; any similar bag, such as those used by tourists and others for carrying light personal luggage.

knar, när, *n.* [GNARL.] A knot in wood.—**knarred**, närd, *a* Gnarled; knotty.—**knarry**, när´i, *a.* Knotty; stubby.

knave, nāv, *n.* [A.Sax *cnapa*. or *cnafa*, a boy, a youth, a son; D. *knaap*, G. *knabe*, a boy or young man, Icel. *knapi*, a servant boy; root doubtful; comp. *knight*.] A boy‡; a male servant‡; a false deceitful fellow; a dishonest man or boy; a rascal; in a pack of playing cards, a card with a soldier or servant painted on it: a jack.—**knavery**, nā´vér·i, *n.* The conduct of a knave; dishonesty; deception in traffic; trickery; petty villainy; fraud.—**knavish**, nā´vish, *a.* Acting like or belonging to a knave; dishonest; fraudulent; mischievous‡. —**knavishly**, nā´vish·li, *adv.* In a knavish manner.—**knavishness**, nā´vish·nes, *n.* The quality or habit of being knavish.

knead, nēd, *v.t.* [A.Sax. *cnedan, cnaedan;* D. *knedan*, G. *kneten*, Icel. *knotha*, to knead; akin Slav. *gneta, gnesti*, to press, to knead.] To work and press into a mass; particularly, to work into a well-mixed mass, as the materials of bread, cake, or paste; to beat or pommel.—**kneader**, nē´dér, *n.* One who kneads.

knee, nē, *n.* [A.Sax. *cneó, cneów*=Icel. *kné*, Dan. *knae*, D. and G. *knie*, Goth. *kniu;* cognate with L. *genu*, Gr. *gonu*, Skr. *jânu*, knee.] The joint connecting the two principal parts of the leg; the articulation of the thigh and bones of the lower leg; something resembling or suggestive of this; a piece of bent timber or iron used to connect the beams of a ship with her sides or timbers.—**knee action**, *n.* In an automobile, independent front wheel suspension.— **kneecap**, *n.* The movable bone covering the knee joint in front; the kneepan; the patella; a leather cap or covering for the knee of a horse.— **kneed**, nēd, *a.* Having knees: chiefly in composition (in-*kneed*, out-*kneed*); *bot.* geniculated.—**knee-deep**, *a.* as deep as would come to the knee. —*adv.* so as to be up to the knees in something.—**kneepan**, *n.* The bone covering the knee joint; the kneecap.

kneel, nēl, *v.i.*—pret. & pp. *kneeled, knelt.* [O.E. *kneole, kneoli*, from *knee*

corresponding to D. *knielen*, Dan. *knaele*, to kneel. Comp. *handle*, from *hand.*] To bend the knee; to fall on the knees.—**kneeler**, nēl´ér, *n.* One who kneels or worships by kneeling.

knell, nel, *n.* [A.Sax. *cnyll*, a sound of a bell; *cnyallan*, to sound a bell; comp. G. *knellen, knallen*, to make a loud noise; G. and D. *knal*, Sw. *knall*, a loud sound; Icel. *knylla*, to beat, *gnella*, to scream; imitative of sound; *knoll* is akin.] The sound of a bell rung at a funeral; a passing bell; a death signal in general.—*v.i.* To sound as a funeral knell; to sound as an omen or warning of coming evil.—*v.t.* To summon by, or as by, a knell.

knelt, nelt, pret. & pp. of *kneel.*

knew, nū, pret. of *know.*

knickerbockers, nik´ér·bok·érz, *n. pl.* [Properly Dutch breeches, after Washington Irving's character Diedrich *Knickerbocker*, as representative of a Dutchman.] A kind of loose breeches reaching just below the knee, where they are gathered in so as to clasp the leg.—**knickers**, *n. pl.* A short form for *Knickerbockers.*

knickknack, nik´nak, *n.* [A reduplication of *knack*; comp. *click-clack, tip-top, ding-dong*, etc.] A trifle or toy; any small article more for ornament than use.

knife, nīf, *n. pl.* **knives**, nīvz. [A.Sax. *cnif*=D. *knijf*, Icel. *knifr*, Dan. *kniv*, Sw. *knif;* akin to *nip.* NIP.] A cutting instrument consisting of a sharp-edged blade of small or moderate size attached to a handle.—*War to the knife*, a war carried on to the utmost extremity; mortal combat.— **knife-edge**, *n.* A piece of steel with a fine edge, serving to support with the least friction an oscillating body, as the beam of a pair of scales.

knight, nīt, *n.* [A.Sax. *cniht*, a boy, a servant, a military follower; D. and G. *knecht*, a male servant, Dan. *knegt*, a fellow, the knave at cards: perhaps from root of *kin* or of *knave.*] In feudal times, a man admitted to a certain military rank, with special ceremonies; in the British Empire, one holding a dignity conferred by the sovereign and entitling the possessor to have the title of *Sir* prefixed to his Christian name, but not hereditary like the dignity of baronet; a member of an order of chivalry; a champion; one of the pieces in the game of chess, usually the figure of a horse's head.—*Knight of the shire*, a county member of the British Parliament.— *v.t.* To dub or create a knight; to confer the honor of knighthood upon, the accolade or blow of a sword being commonly a part of the ceremony.—**knight-errant**, *n.* A knight who traveled in search of adventures and to exhibit his prowess.—**knight-errantry**, *n.* The role, character, or practice of a knight-errant.—**knighthood**, nīt´hud *n.* The character or dignity of a knight; the rank or honor accompanying the title of knight; knights collectively.—*Order of Knighthood*, in

England, an organized and duly constituted body of knights, as those of the Garter or the Bath.—**knightliness**, nīt′li•nes, *n.* The character or quality of being knightly.—**knightly**, nīt′li, *a.* Pertaining to a knight; becoming a knight; chivalrous.—*adv.* In a manner becoming a knight.—**Knights of Columbus**, a Roman Catholic society.—**Knight Templar**, member of a branch of Freemasonry.

knit, nit, *v.t.*—*knit* or *knitted, knitting*. [A.Sax. *cnyattan*, to knit, to tie, from *cnotta*, a knot; Icel. *knyta*, from *knutr*, a knot; Dan. *knytte*, to knit, to knot. KNOT.] To tie together; to tie with a knot; to fasten by tying; to weave or form by looping or knotting a continuous thread by means of wires or needles; to cause to grow together; to join closely; to contract into folds or wrinkles (to *knit* the brows).—*v.i.* To make a fabric by interlooping yarn or thread by means of needles, etc.; to unite closely; to grow together.—**knitter**, nit′ėr, *n.* One that knits; a knitting machine.

knives, nīvz, *n.* pl. of *knife.*

knob, nob, *n.* [Older form *knop*; comp. A.Sax. *cnæp*, a top, a knob, D. *knop, knoop*, G. *knopf*, Icel. *knappr*, Dan. *knop, knap*, a knob, button, bud, etc.; also W., Ir., and Gael. *cnap*, a knob.] A hard protuberance; a hard swelling or rising; a round ball at the end of anything; the more or less ball-shaped handle for a door, drawer, or the like; a boss; a knot; a bunch of foliage carved or cast for ornament.—*v.i.*—*knobbed, knobbing.* To grow into knobs; to bunch.—**knobbed**, nobd, *a.* Containing knobs; full of knobs.—**knobby**, nob′i, *a.* Full of knobs or hard protuberances.

knock, nok, *v.i.* [A.Sax. *cnocian, cnucian*, to knock; to beat; Icel. *knoka*, Sw. *knacka*, to knock; also seen in Gael. and Ir. *cnag*, a knock; W. *cnociaw*, to knock; akin *knack, knag, knuckle*, etc.] To strike or beat with something thick, hard, or heavy; to drive or be driven so as to come in collision with something; to strike against; to clash; to criticize, belittle, or disparage. *(Colloq.)* —*To knock about*, to wander here and there; to move about in the world. *(Colloq.)*— *To knock off*, to cease from labor; to stop work. *(Colloq.)*—*To knock under*, to yield; to submit; to acknowledge one's self conquered. *(Colloq.)*—*v.t.* To dash; to drive; to cause to collide; to drive or force by a succession of blows.—*To knock down*, to strike down; to fell; to prostrate by a blow; at *auctions*, to assign to a bidder, generally by a blow with a hammer.—*To knock on the head*, to stun or kill by a blow or blows on the head; hence, to frustrate, as a project or scheme; to render abortive. *(Colloq.)*—*n.* A blow; a stroke with something thick, hard, or heavy; a stroke on a door, intended as a request for admittance; a rap.—**knocker**, nok′ėr, *n.* One that knocks;

a contrivance fastened to a door to knock for admittance.—**knock-kneed**, *a.* Having the legs so much curved inward that they touch or knock together in walking; hence, feeble (a *knock-kneed* argument).—**knockout**, *n.* A person or thing strikingly attractive *(slang)*; *boxing*, a blow which fells an opponent for a minimum period of ten seconds.

knoll, nol, *n.* [A.Sax. *cnoll*, a knoll, a summit; N. *knoll*, Dan. *knold*, a knoll; G. *knolle, knollen*, a lump; comp. W. *cnol*, the top, a round hillock.] The top or crown of a hill; a small or low round hill; a small elevation of earth.

knop, nop, *n.* [KNOB.] A knob; a boss; a bunch. (O.T.)

knot, not, *n.* [A.Sax. *cnotta*, a knot = D. *knot*, Icel. *knútr*, Sw. *knut*, G. *knoten*, a knot; cog. L. *nodus*, that is, *gnodus* (whence *node*). KNIT.] A complication of a thread, cord, or rope, or of two or more, by tying, knitting, or entangling; a fastening made by looping a cord or thread on itself; a tie; a figure with interlaced lines; a bond of association; a union (the nuptial *knot*); a cluster, collection, group; a difficulty or perplexity; something not easily solved; a hard part in timber caused by the shooting out of a branch; a protuberance; a nodule; a bunch; a knob; *naut.* a division of the log line, forming the same fraction of a mile as half a minute is of an hour, that is, the hundred and twentieth part of a nautical mile; so that the number of knots run off the reel in half a minute shows the vessel's speed per hour in miles; hence, a nautical mile or 6080 feet.—*v.t.*—*knotted, knotting.* To tie in a knot or knots; to form a knot on; to entangle; to unite closely.—*v.i.* To become knotted; to form knots or joints, as in plants.—**knotgrass**, *n.* A common, low weed, with branched trailing stems and knotted joints.—**knotted**, not′ed, *a.* Full of knots; having knots; *bot.* having knobs or enlargements as on a stem.—**knottiness**, not′i•nes, *n.* The quality of being knotty.—**knotty**, not′i, *a.* Full of knots; having many knots; difficult; intricate; involved; hard to unravel (a *knotty* question or point).—**knotweed**, *n.* Knotgrass.

knot, not, *n.* [Said to be named after king *Canute* (*Cnut*), who was very fond of it.] A small grallatorial bird, closely allied to the snipe.

knout, nout, *n.* [Russ. *knute*.] An instrument of punishment used in Russia consisting of a handle 2 feet long, a leather thong 4 feet, with a metal ring at the end to which the striking part, a flat tongue of hardened hide 2 feet long is attached; the punishment inflicted with the knout.—*v.i.* To punish with the knout.

know, nō, *v.t.*—*knew* (pret.), *known* (pp.). [A.Sax. *cnáwan*, pret. *cneów*, pp. *cnáwen*, to know; Icel. *kná*, to be able; comp. the allied words E. *can*, to be able, *ken*, to know, Icel. *kunna*, used in both senses; G.

kŏnnen, to be able (*ich kann*, I can), *kennen*, to know; from a root *gna*, *gan*, to know, seen also in *name*, *noble, narrate* (these words have lost *g* before the *n*, as in *ignoble, ignorant*), *uncouth*; L. *gnosco, nosco*, Gr. *gignŏskō*, to know.] To perceive with certainty; to understand clearly; to be convinced or satisfied regarding the truth or reality of; to be assured of; to be aware of; to distinguish (to *know* a star from a planet); to be familiar or acquainted with (a person, a topic, etc.); to have experience of.—*v.i.* To have clear and certain perception; not to be doubtful; to be informed.—**knowable**, nō′a•bl, *a.* Capable of being known.—**knower**, nō′ėr, *n.* One who knows.—**knowing**, nō′ing, *a.* Well-informed; well-instructed; intelligent; sagacious; conscious; expressive of knowledge or cunning (a *knowing* look).—**knowingly**, nō′ing•li, *adv.* In a knowing manner.—**knowingness**, nō′ing•nes, *n.*—**knowledge**, nol′ij, *n.* [O.E. *knowleche*, from *know*, and term. seen in Icel. *kunnleikr*, knowledge, and in E. *wedlock*, and which is derived from A.Sax. *lác*, Icel. *leikr*, Goth. *laiks*, sport, play, gift.] The clear and certain perception of that which exists, or of truth and fact; indubitable apprehension; cognizance; learning; erudition; information; skill in anything; familiarity gained by actual experience; acquaintance with any fact or person.—**known**, nōn, *p.* and *a.* Perceived; understood; recognized; familiar.

knuckle, nuk′l, *n.* [A.Sax. *cnucel*, D. *knokkel, kneukel*, Dan. *knokkel*, G. *knŏchel*, a knuckle, *knochen*, a bone; comp. W. *cnwc*, a knob or knot; allied are probably *knock, knag, knack.*] The joint of a finger, particularly when protuberant by the closing of the fingers; the knee joint of a calf or pig (a *knuckle* of veal).—*v.t.*—*knuckled, knuckling.* To strike with the knuckles; to pommel. —*v.i.* Only used in the colloquial phrases *to knuckle down, to knuckle under*, to yield; to submit; to acknowledge one's self beaten; phrases of doubtful origin.—**knuckle-duster**, *n.* An iron instrument with knobs or points projecting, contrived to cover the knuckles, and which renders a blow struck more powerful.—**knuckle joint**, *n.* Mach. any flexible joint formed by two abutting links.

knur, knurl, nėr, nėrl, *n.* Same as GNARL.

koala, kō•ä′la, *n.* [Native name.] A marsupial animal of Australia, arboreal in habit.

kobold, kō′bold, *n.* [GOBLIN.] A domestic spirit or elf in German mythology; a kind of goblin.

Kodak, kō′dak, *n.* Trade name of a photographic camera.

Kohinoor, kō′i•nŏr, *n.* [Per. *koh-i-nur*, mountain of light.] The great Indian diamond of the Deccan, owned first by the Mogul kings, and finally, in 1849, the property of the British Crown; anything of supreme excellence.

---

ch, *ch*ain;   *ch*, Sc. lo*ch*;   g, *g*o;   j, *j*ob;   ng, si*ng*;   TH, *th*en;   th, *th*in;   w, *w*ig;   hw, *wh*ig;   zh, a*z*ure.

kohl, kōl, *n.* A black pigment used by Eastern women as a cosmetic.

kohlrabi, kōl·rä′bē, *n.* [G., from *kohl*, kale, and L. *rapa*, a turnip; kale or cabbage turnip.] A variety of cabbage distinguished by a globular swelling immediately above the ground, which is the part used.

koodoo, kö′dö, *n.* See KUDU.

kopeck, kopek, kō′pek, *n.* A small Russian coin, one hundredth part of a ruble, worth about half a cent.

Koran, kō′ran or ko·rän′, *n.* See ALKORAN.

kos, kos, *n.* A Jewish measure of capacity equal to about 4 cubic inches.

kosher, kōsh′ĕr, *a.* [Heb. *kasher*, right.] Designating food prepared in the way prescribed by Jewish ceremonial rites; right; proper.

kowtow, kou·tou′, *n.* [Chinese.] Prostrating one's self and touching the ground with the forehead; showing deference and submissiveness.—*v.i.* To perform the kowtow; to show honor and respect.

kraal, kräl, *n.* [Pg. *curral*, a pen for animals, akin *corral*.] A native village or collection of huts in South Africa; a pen for livestock in Africa.

kraken, krä′ken, *n.* A supposed enormous sea monster, said to have been seen at different times off the coast of Norway.

Kremlin, krem′lin. [Rus. *kreml*.] The citadel of Moscow, including within it the Soviet government.

kreutzer, kreuzer, kroit′sĕr, *n.* [G. *kreuzer*, from *kreuz*, a cross, because formerly stamped with a cross.] An old South German copper coin, the sixtieth part of the gulden or florin; an Austrian coin equal to the hundredth part of a florin.

kriegspiel, krēg′spēl, *n.* [G., game of war—*krieg*, war, and *spiel*, game.] A game of German origin, played by means of pieces representing troops on a map exhibiting all the features of a country.

kris, krēs, *n.* A Malay dagger; a creese.

krone, krō′ne, *n.* [Dan., a crown.] A Scandinavian monetary unit.

kruller, krul′ĕr, *n.* [O.E. *crult*, curled; D. *krullen*, to curl.] See CRULLER.

krypton, krip′ton, *n.* A rare gaseous element. Symbol, Kr; at. no., 36; at. wt., 83.80.

Kshatriya, kshat′ri·a, *n.* A member of the second or military caste in the social system of the Brahmanical Hindus.

kudos, kū′dos, *n.* [Gr.] Glory; fame; renown.

kudu, kö′dö, *n.* [Native name.] A striped antelope of South Africa, the male having long and twisted horn.

Kufic, *a.* See CUFIC.

kumiss, kö′mis, *n.* [Of Tartar origin.] A liquor made from mare's milk fermented and distilled; fermented milk used by the Tartars.

kümmel, kṳm′l or kim′l, *n.* [G. *kümmel*, caraway.] A liqueur, flavored with caraway seeds.

kumquat, kum′kwot, *n.* [Chinese (Cantonese) *kam*, golden, and *kwat*, orange.] A small citrus fruit, used chiefly in preserves.

Kurd, kĕrd, *n.* An inhabitant of Kurdistan.—**Kurdish,** kĕr′dish, *a.* Of or relating to Kurdistan or the Kurds.

kyanite, kī′an·ĭt, *n.* [Gr. *kyanos*, blue.] A gem of the garnet family of a blue color, somewhat resembling sapphire.

kymograph, kī′mo·graf, *n.* [Gr. *kyma*, a wave, *graphō*, I write.] An instrument for graphically recording variations in blood pressure.

Kyrie eleison, kir″ē·e′ e·lā″i·s'n, *n.* [Gr. *kyrie*, Lord, *eleēson*, have mercy.] A form of invocation in ancient Greek, liturgies and still used in the Roman Catholic service.

L

L, l, el, the twelfth letter and ninth consonant of the English alphabet.

la, lä, *Mus.* the sixth of the seven syllables that represent the seven sounds in the diatonic scale.

laager, lä′gĕr, *n.* [D., a camp.] In South Africa, an encampment; a temporary defensive enclosure, formed of wagons.—*v.i.* To encamp; to form a temporary defense by means of wagons.

labarum, lab′a·rum, *n.* [L. *labarum*, *labōrum*, Gr. *labaron*, *labōron*; etym, doubtful.] The standard adopted by Constantine the Great after his conversion to Christianity; a banner bearing the Greek letters X P (that is, *Chr*), conjoined so as to form a monogram of the name of Christ.

labdanum, lab′da·num. See LADANUM.

labefaction, lab·e·fak′shon, *n.* [L. *labefactio*, from *labefacio*—*labo*, to totter, and *facio*, to make.] A weakening; decay; downfall.

label, lā′bl, *n.* [O.Fr. *label*, *lambel*, a rag, a tatter, a shred; of Germanic or Celtic origin.] A slip of paper, parchment, or other material, containing a name, title, address, statement of contents, nature, or the like, affixed to anything; a narrow slip affixed to diplomas, deeds, or writings to hold the appended seal; *arch.* a projecting tablet or molding over doors, windows, etc.—*v.t.*—*labeled, labeling.* To affix a label to; to classify and name.—**labeler, labeller,** lā′bl·ĕr, *n.* One who labels.

labellum, la·bel′lum, *n.* [L., a little lip, dim. of *labrum*, a lip.] *Bot.* one of the three pieces forming the corolla in orchidaceous plants, usually turned downward.

labial, lā′bi·al, *a.* [From L. *labium*, a lip. LIP.] Pertaining to the lips; uttered by the lips; owing its special character to the lips (a *labial* consonant).—*n.* A vowel or consonant formed chiefly by the lips, as *b*, *m*, *p*, *o*.—**labialize,** lā′bi·al·īz, *v.t.* To give a labial sound or character to; to utter labially.—**labiate,** lā′bi·āt, *a.* [L.L. *labiatus*, from L. *labium*, lip.] *Bot.* applied to an irregular gamopetalous corolla, the limb or expanded portion cleft so as to present an upper and lower lip.—**labiodental,** lā′bi·o·den·tal, *a.* and *n.* [L. *labium*, a lip, and *dens*, a tooth.] Formed or pronounced by the cooperation of the lips and teeth; a sound thus formed (*f* and *v*).

labium, lā′bi·um, *n.* [L.] One of the lip-like folds of the vulva, *Labia majora*, the two outer folds, and *Labia minora*, the two inner folds; the lower lip of insects.

labor, labour, lā′bĕr, *n.* [O.Fr. *labour*, Fr. *labeur*, L. *labor*, *laboris*, labor.] Exertion, physical or mental, or both, undergone in the performance of some task or work; particularly, the exertion of the body in occupations by which subsistence is obtained; the performance of work; toil; work done or to be done; laborers or producers in the aggregate (the claims or rights of *labor*); travail; the pangs and efforts of childbirth.—*v.i.* To engage in labor; to work; to toil; to exert the body or mind, or both, in the prosecution of any design; to proceed or act with difficulty; to be burdened; to suffer (to *labor* under a disease); *naut.* to pitch and roll heavily, as a ship in a turbulent sea.—*v.t.* To till; to cultivate; to prosecute with effort.—*Labor Day*, in the U.S., the first Monday in September, observed as a legal holiday in honor of the working classes.—*Labor Party*, a party claiming to represent the interests of the working classes. *Labor union*, a trade union; an organization of wage earners designed to advance the economic interests and general working conditions of its members.—**labored,** lā′bĕrd, *p.* and *a.* Produced with labor; bearing the marks of constraint and effort; opposed to *easy* or *natural* (a *labored* speech).—**laborer,** lā′bĕr·ĕr, *n.* One who labors; a man who does work that requires little skill or special training, as distinguished from an artisan.—**laborsaving,** *a.* Saving labor; adapted to supersede or diminish the labor of men.—**laborious,** la·bō′ri·us, *a.* [L. *laboriosus.*] Requiring labor; toilsome; not easy; diligent in work or service; industrious; assiduous.—**laboriously,** la·bō′ri·us·li, *adv.* In a laborious manner.—**laboriousness,** la·bō′ri·us·nes, *n.*

laboratory, lab′o·ra·to·ri, *n.* [L.L. *laboratorium*, from L. *labor*, labor. LABOR.] A building or room designed for investigation and experiment in chemistry, physics, or other subject; a chemist's workroom; the shop of a druggist.

laborite, lā′bĕr·īte, *n.* One who upholds the theories and practices of labor organizations.

labradorite, lab′ra·dor·īt, *n.* A mineral, a kind of feldspar, found on the coast of Labrador, distinguished by its splendent changeability of color; called also *Labrador feldspar.*

labret, lab′ret, *n.* [L. *labrum*, lip.] A lip ornament worn by certain savage peoples, consisting of a piece of bone, wood, or the like, inserted in an artificial opening.

labrum, lā′brum, n. [L.] An upper or outer lip, LABIUM.—**labrose,** lā′brōs, a. Having thick lips.

laburnum, la-bér′num, n. [L.] A leguminose tree, well known for the beauty of its pendulous racemes of yellow pea-shaped flowers, and having wood which is much valued for turnery work.

labyrinth, lab′i-rinth, n. [L. labyrinthus; Gr. labyrinthos.] A structure having numerous intricate winding passages; a place full of inextricable windings; an ornamental maze or wilderness in gardens; an intricate arrangement of bands or lines used for ornamentation; any intricate matter or business; anat. that part of the internal ear which lies behind the tympanum; metal. a series of troughs attached to a stamping mill, through which a current of water passes so as to carry off and deposit in certain places the ground ore.—**labyrinthian,** lab·i·rinth′i·an, a. Labyrinthine.—Also **labyrinthic,** lab·i·rinth′ik, **labyrinthical,** lab·i·rinth′i·kal.—**labyrinthine,** lab·i·rinth′in, a. Pertaining to or like a labyrinth; full of windings; intricate; mazy.

lac, lak, n. [Per. lak, Skr. lâkshâ, and râkshâ, the lac insect, from ranj, to dye; hence lacquer, lake (color).] A resinous substance produced mainly upon the banyan tree, by the puncture of a small insect, and used in preparing lacquers, varnishes, etc.—Stick lac is the substance in its natural state, incrusting small twigs; when broken off and washed with water it is called seed lac; when melted and reduced to a thin crust it is called shell-lac, shellac.—Lac dye and lac lake, scarlet coloring matters obtained from stick lac.

lac, lakh, lak, n. [Hind. lakh, Skr. laksha.] In the East Indies a word used to denote 100,000.

LACE. See LIQUID.

lace, lās, n. [O.Fr. las, from L. laqueus, a noose, a snare; akin lasso, latchet.] A string or cord used for fastening boots or some other part of the dress, or plaited and otherwise ornamented and used for decoration; a delicate kind of network, used for the ornamenting of female dresses, etc.—v.t.—laced, lacing. To fasten with a lace or string through eyelet holes; to adorn with lace, or as with a lace; to strengthen beer, tea, with some alcoholic flavoring.—v.i. To be fastened or tied by a lace; to have a lace.—**lacing,** lās′ing, n. The act of fastening with a lace; a cord used in drawing tight or fastening.

lacerate, las′ėr·āt, v.t.—lacerated, lacerating. [L. lacero, laceratum, to tear, from lacer, mangled, torn.] To tear; to rend; to make a ragged wound or gash in by violence or tearing; fig. to torture; to harrow.—**lacerate, lacerated,** las′ėr·āt, las′ėr·ā·ted, p. and a. Rent; torn; bot. having the appearance of being

torn.—**laceration** las·ėr·ā′shon, n. The act of lacerating; the breach made by rending.

lacertian, lacertilian, la-sér′shi·an, las·ėr·til′i·an, a. [L. lacerta, a lizard.] Belonging to the family of lizards.

laches, lach′es or lash′ez, n. [Norm. Fr. lachesse, remissness, lit. looseness, from O.Fr. lasche, from L. laxus, lax, slow.] Law, neglect; negligence; remissness; inexcusable delay.

lachrymal, lak′ri·mal, a. [L. lachryma, lacryma, lacrima, a tear; cog. with Gr. dakry, a tear, and E. tear.] Pertaining to tears; generating or secreting tears (the lachrymal gland); conveying tears (lachrymal canal).—**lachrymatory,** lak′ri·ma·to·ri, n. A vessel found in sepulchres of the ancients, in which it has been supposed the tears of a deceased person's friends were collected and preserved with the ashes and urn. Also called Lachrymal.—**lachrymose,** lak′ri·mōs, a. Generating or shedding tears; appearing as if shedding or given to shed tears; tears; tearful.—**lachrymosely,** lak′ri·mōs·li, adv. In a lachrymose manner.

lacing. See LACE.

laciniate, laciniated, la-sin′i·āt, la-sin′i·ā·ted, a. [L. lacinia, a lappet, fringe, or border.] Adorned with fringes; bot. jagged; applied to leaves or petals which are divided by deep tapering incisions.

lack, lak, v.t. [Same as D. laken, to blame, O.D. laecken, to fail, to decrease; Dan. lak, fault, want; Icel. lakr, defective; perhaps connected with leak.] To be destitute of; not to have or possess; to want; to need; to require.—v.i. To be in want; to be wanting.—n. Want; destitution; need; failure.—**lackluster,** a. Wanting luster or brightness.

lackaday, lak·a·dā′, [Contr. for alack, the-day.] Exclamation of sorrow or regret; alas!—alas! the day.—**lackadaisical,** lak·a·dā′zi·kal, a. Affectedly pensive; listless; maudlinly sentimental.

lackey, lak′i, n. [Fr. laquais, from Sp. and Pg. lacayo, alacay, possibly from Ar. lakiyy, attached to some one.] An attending male servant; a footboy or footman; any servile follower.—v.t. To wait on as a lackey; to attend servilely.—v.i. To act as a lackey; to pay servile attendance on some person.

laconic, la-kon′ik, a. [Fr. laconique, L. laconicus, from Lacones, the Spartans.] Short; brief; pithy; sententious; expressing much in few words, after the manner of the Spartans, who were Laconians.—**laconically,** la-kon′i·kal·li, adv. In a laconic manner; concisely; in few words.—**laconism,** lak′on·izm, n. [L. laconismus.] A concise style; a brief sententious phrase or expression.

lacquer, lak′ėr, n. [Pg. lacre, from laca, lac. LAC.] A solution of shellac (sometimes sandarach, mastic, etc.) in alcohol; sap of the Japanese or Chinese sumac or any of the synthetic varnishes used to

give a highly lustrous coating to wood or metals; an item coated with lacquer.—v.t. To varnish with lacquer.

lacrosse, la-kros′, n. [Fr.] A game which originated with the North American Indians, played with two opposing teams of twelve men each, the object of the game being to score by throwing a hard-rubber ball about the size of a baseball into the opponents' goal with a crosse or lacrosse stick.

lactarene, lactarine, lak′ta·rēn, lak′ta·rin, n. [L. lac, lactis, milk; cog. with Gr. gala, galaktos, Ir. laith, milk.] A preparation of the casein of milk, extensively used by calico printers.—**lactary,** lak′ta·ri, a. [L. lacterius, milky.] Milky; full of white juice like milk.—**lactate,** lak′tāt, n. Chem. a salt or ester of lactic acid.—v.i. To produce milk.—**lactation,** lak·tā′shon, n. The function of secreting and excreting milk.—**lactase,** lak′tās, n. An enzyme capable of reducing lactose to dextrose and galactose.—**lacteal,** lak′ti·al, a. Pertaining to or resembling milk; milky; conveying chyle.—n. Anat. one of numerous minute tubes which absorb or take up the chyle or milk-like fluid from the alimentary canal and convey it to the thoracic duct.—**lacteous,** lak′ti·us, a. [L. lacteus.] Milky; lacteal.—**lactescence,** lak·tes′ens, n. The state of being lactescent; milkiness or milky color; the milky liquor which flows from a plant when wounded.—**lactescent,** lak·tes′ent, a. [L. lactescens, ppr. of lactesco, to become milky.] Becoming milky; having a milky appearance or consistence.—**lactic,** lak′tik, a. [Fr. lactique.] Pertaining to milk or produced from sour milk or whey (lactic acid).—Lactic acid, a sirupy acid, $CH_3CH(OH)CO_2H$.—**lactiferous,** lak·tif′ėr·us, a. Producing or conveying milk or milky juice.—**lactose,** lak′tōs, n. Sugar of milk, a crystalline deposit, $C_{12}H_{22}O_{11}$, left after milk has been evaporated.

lacuna, la-kū′na, n. pl. **lacunae,** la-kū′nē. [L., a hollow.] A pit or depression on a surface; a small blank space; a gap; a hiatus; one of the spaces left among the tissues of the lower animals, serving in place of vessels for the circulation of the fluids.—**lacunal,** la-cū′nal, a. Pertaining to or having lacunae.—**lacunar,** la-kū′nėr, n. pl. **lacunars, lacunaria,** la-kū′nėrz, lak·u·nâ′ri·a. [L.] Arch. one of the sunk compartments or panels in ceilings, etc.—**lacunose,** la-kū′nōs, a. [L. lacunosus.] Having lacunae; furrowed or pitted.

lacustrine, lacustral, la-kus′trin, la-kus′tral, a. [From L. lacus, a lake.] Pertaining to a lake.—Lacustrine or lake dwellings, the name given to ancient habitations built on small islands in lakes, or on platforms supported by piles near the shores of lakes.

lad, lad, n. [Of doubtful origin; comp. W. llawd, Ir. lath, a lad, a youth; lass is the feminine corresponding.] A young man or boy; a stripling; a familiar term applied to grown men; fellow; comrade.

ladanum, lad′a·num, *n.* [Gr. *ladanon,* from Per. *lâdan,* the shrub.] The resinous juice which exudes from several species of cistus growing in Spain and Portugal, Crete, Syria, etc., formerly used in plasters, etc.

ladder, lad′ėr, *n.* [A.Sax. *hlaedder*= O.Fris. *hladder,* D. *ladder,* O.H.G. *hleitra, hleitara,* Mod.G. *leiter,* a ladder; cog. L. *clathri,* a trellis or grate.] An article of wood, metal, or rope, consisting of two long side-pieces connected by crosspieces at suitable distances, forming steps by which persons may ascend a building etc.; *fig.* a means of rising to eminence.

lade, lād, *v.t.*—pret. *laded,* pp. *laded laden* (the former always in second sense), ppr. *lading.* [A.Sax. *hladan,* to load, to lade water; O.Sax. and O.H.G. *hladan,* Icel. *hlatha,* Goth. *hlathan,* D. *laden,* G. *(be)laden,* to load. *Load* is almost the same word, and *ladle* is a derivative.] To load; to put a load or cargo on or in; to lift or throw in or out (a fluid) with some utensil; to lave.—**laden,** lā′dn, *p.* and *a.* [Pp. of *lade* in first sense.] Loaded; charged with a burden or freight; *fig.* oppressed; burdened.—**lading,** lā′ding, *n.* That which constitutes a load or cargo; freight; burden.—*Bill of lading.* See BILL.

ladle, lā′dl, *n.* [A.Sax. *hlaedel,* from *hladan,* to draw water. LADE, *v.*] A sort of dish with a long handle, used for lifting or serving out liquids from a vessel; the receptacle of a mill wheel which receives the water that moves it; *founding,* an iron vessel in which liquid metal is carried from the furnace to the mold.—*v.t.*—*ladled, ladling.* To lift or deal out with a ladle; to lade.

lady, lā′di, *n.* [A.Sax. *hlaefdige, hlaef-die,* lit. bread kneader, from *hlâf,* bread, loaf, and -*dige,* kneader. LORD.] A woman of rank or distinction; correlative to *lord;* in the British Empire, the proper title of any woman whose husband is above the rank of a baronet or knight, or who is the daughter of a nobleman not lower than an earl, though often the wife of a baronet or a knight is called by this title; a term applied by courtesy to any woman; one of the fair sex; specifically, a woman of good breeding, education, and refinement of mind: the correlative to *gentleman;* the wife of a gentleman or man in good position; the mistress or possessor of an estate; an apparatus in the stomach of a lobster for grinding its food.—*Our Lady,* the Virgin Mary.—**ladies' man, lady's man,** *n.* One who much affects the society of ladies; a beau.—**ladybird, ladybug, ladybeetle,** *n.* A small beetle, the larva of which feeds on aphids or plant lice.—**Lady chapel,** *n.* A chapel dedicated to the Virgin Mary, frequently attached to large churches.—**Lady Day,** *n.* The day of the annunciation of the Virgin

Mary, March 25.—**ladyfinger,** *n.* A kind of finger-shaped spongecake. —**lady-killer,** *n.* A man whose fascinations are irresistible among the ladies; a general lover.—**lady-killing,** *n.* Act or practice of a lady-killer; gallantry.—**ladylike,** lā′-di·līk, *a.* Like a lady in any respect.— **ladylove,** *n.* A female sweetheart; a lady who is loved.—**ladyship,** lā′di·ship, *n.* The condition or rank of a lady; employed as a title (with *her, your,* etc.)—**lady's maid,** *n.* A female attendant upon a lady.—**lady's-slipper,** *n.* An orchid having flowers resembling a slipper; in the U. S., the garden balsam.

lag, lag, *a.* [Of Celtic origin; W. *llag,* weak; akin L. *laxus,* loose; lax; *languidus,* languid.] Coming after or behind (*lag* end of my life).— *n.* The quantity of retardation of some movement (the *lag* of the valve of a steam engine, the *lag* of the tide); a comparative retardation of movement or progress (a cultural *lag*).—*v.i.*—*lagged, lagging.* To walk or move slowly; to loiter; to stay behind.—**laggard,** lag′ėrd, *a.* [*Lag.* and suffix -*ard.*] Slow; sluggish; backward.—*n.* One who lags; a loiterer; a lazy, slack fellow.—**lagger,** lag′ėr, *n.* One who lags or loiters.— **laggingly,** lag′ing·li, *adv.* Loiteringly.

lagan, lag′an, *n.* Same as *Ligan.*

lager beer, lä′gėr bēr, *n.* [G. *lagerbier*—*lager,* a storehouse, and *bier,* beer.] A beer, so called from its being stored for some months before use.

lagniappe, lagnappe, lan·yap′, *n.* [Creole, *la,* the, Sp. *ñapa, llapa,* lagniappe.] A small present given by a storekeeper to a customer.

lagoon, lagune, la·gön′, la·gün′, *n.* [It. and Sp. *laguna,* from L. *lacuna,* from *lacus,* a lake. LAKE.] A shallow lake or sheet of water connected with the sea or a river.

laic, laical, lā′ik, lā′i·kal, *a.* [L. *laicus,* from Gr. *laikos,* from *laos,* people. LAY, *a.*] Belonging to the laity or people, in distinction from the clergy.—*n.* A layman.—**laically,** lā′i·kal·li, *adv.* In a laic manner.

laid, lād, pret. & pp. of *lay;* so written for *Layed.*—*Laid paper,* writing paper with a slightly ribbed surface, called *cream-laid, blue-laid,* etc., according to color.

lain, lān, pp. of *lie.*

lair, lâr, *n.* [A.Sax. *leger,* a bed, a couch, a grave, from the root of *lay, lie*=D. *leger,* G. *lager.* LAY.] A place to lie or rest; especially the resting place of a wild beast, etc.; in Scotland, a portion of a burying-ground sufficient for one grave.

laird, lârd, *n.* [A form of *lord.*] In Scotland, a land owner or house proprietor.

laissez-faire, laisser-faire, les′ā·fâr″, *n.* [Fr. *laisser,* leave, let, *faire,* to do.] A letting alone; non-interference; a term especially used in regard to the interference of a government with social, commercial or other matters.

laity. See LAY, *a.*

lake, lāk, *n.* [Fr. *lac,* from L. *lacus,*

lake; cog. *loch.*] A sheet or body of water wholly surrounded by land, and having no direct communication with the sea, or having so only by means of rivers.—**lake dwelling,** *n.* See LACUSTRINE.—**laky,** lā′ki, *a.* Pertaining to a lake or lakes.

lake, lāk, *n.* [Fr. *laque.* LAC.] A pigment consisting of an earthy substance impregnated with red coloring matter of certain animal and vegetable substances, there being thus cochineal and lac lakes, madder lake, etc.

lallation, lal·lā′shon, *n.* [Fr. *lallation,* from the letter *l.*] The imperfect pronunciation of the letter *r,* which is made to sound like *l.*

lama, lä′mä, *n.* [Tibetan.] A priest or ecclesiastic belonging to that variety of Buddhism which is known as Lamaism, and prevails in Tibet and Mongolia.—**Lamaism,** lä′mä·izm, *n.* A variety of Buddhism chiefly prevailing in Tibet and Mongolia.— **Lamaist,** lä′mä·ist, *n.* One belonging to the religion of Lamaism.—**Lamaistic,** lä·mä·is′tik, *a.* Pertaining to lamaism.—**lamasery,** lä′mä·sėr·i, *n.* A monastery of lamas.

Lamarckian, la·mark′i·an, *a.* [*Lamark,* French zoologist.] The theory of organic evolution by inherited modifications of the individual through habit or other causes.

lamb, lam, *n.* [A.Sax., O.Sax., Goth., Icel., and O.H.G. *lamb;* D. and Dan. *lam,* G. *lamm,* lamb.] The young of sheep; a person as gentle or innocent as a lamb.—*The Lamb, The Lamb of God,* the Saviour Jesus Christ.—*v.i.* To bring forth a lamb or lambs.—**lambkin,** lam′kin, *n.* A small lamb; one fondly cherished.— **lamblike,** lam′līk, *a.*—**lambskin,** lam′skin, *n.* The skin of a lamb dressed with the fleece on, or made into leather.

lambda, lam′dä, *n.* [Gr.] The eleventh letter of the Greek alphabet, corresponding to the English letter L, l.

lambdoidal, lam′doi·dal, *a.* [Gr. *lambdoeidēs*—*lambda* (Λ), and *eidos,* resemblance.] In the form of the Greek letter lambda (Λ).

lambent, lam′bent, *a.* [L. *lambens, lambentis,* ppr. of *lambo,* to lick, a nasalized form akin to *lap.*] Licking; playing about; touching lightly; gliding over (a *lambent* flame); gleaming; twinkling; flickering.

lame, lām, *a.* [A.Sax. *lama*=D. Dan. and Sw. *lam,* G. *lahm,* lame; Icel. *lama,* a lame person; akin prov. E. *lam,* to beat.] Crippled or disabled in one or more of the limbs; crippled; disabled (a *lame* arm); imperfect, defective, not sound or unassailable (a *lame* excuse).—*v.t.*—*lamed, laming.* To make lame; to cripple or disable; to render imperfect.—**lame duck,** *n.* A slang term for a defaulter on the stock exchange; a Congressman not reelected and serving the last session of his term.—**lamely,** lām′li, *adv.* In a lame or imperfect manner.— **lameness,** lām′nes, *n.* The condition of being lame, crippled or disabled.

fāte, fär, fâre, fat, fạll; mē, met, hėr; pīne, pin; nōte, not, möve; tūbe, tub, bụll; oil, pound.

lamella, la·mel′la, *n.* pl. **lamellae,** la·mel′lē. [Dim. of *lamina.*] A thin plate or scale; one of an aggregate of thin plates; one of the thin plates which compose the gills of certain mollusks; one of the gills forming the hymenium of an agaric.— **lamellar,** la·mel′lėr, *a.* Composed of thin plates or lamellae; disposed in thin plates or scales.—**lamellate, lamellated,** lam′el·lāt, lam′el·lā·ted, *a.* Formed in thin plates or lamellae, or covered with them; furnished with lamellae.—**lamellibranchiate,** la·mel′li·brang″ki·āt, *a.* [L. *lamella,* a thin plate, and *branchiae,* gills.] Having lamellar gills, especially having lamellar gills and bivalve shells as the mollusks of the class or order (Lamellibranchiata) of which mussels, cockles, and oysters are familiar examples. Also used as a noun.— **lamellicorn,** la·mel′li·korn, *a.* [L. *lamella,* a plate, and *cornu,* a horn.] Having lamellar antennae; having antennae the three last joints of which are plate-like and disposed somewhat like the teeth of a comb: said of beetles, such as the cockchafers, etc. Used also as *n.*—**lamellirostral,** la·mel′li·ros″tral, *a.* [L. *rostrum,* a beak.] Having a beak furnished along its margins with numerous lamellae or dental plates as the ducks, geese, swans, etc.—**lamellose,** la·mel′lōs, *a.* Covered with or in the form of lamellae.

lament, la·ment′, *v.i.* [L. *lamentor,* to wail, from *lamentum,* a wail; same root as *latrare,* to bark, an onomatopoetic word.] To mourn; to weep or wail; to express sorrow; to regret deeply; to grieve.—*v.t.* To bewail; to mourn for; to bemoan.—*n.* .Lamentation; an elegy or mournful ballad or air.—**lamentable,** lam′en·ta·bl, *a.* [L. *lamentabilis.*] To be lamented; exciting or calling for sorrow; grievous; mournful; miserable; pitiful; wretched.—**lamentably,** lam′en·ta·bli, *adv.* In a lamentable manner.—**lamentation,** lam·en·tā′shon, *n.* [L. *lamentatio.*] The act of lamenting; a wailing; expression of sorrow; cries or words expressive of grief; [*cap.*] *pl.* a book of Scripture containing the Lamentations of Jeremiah.

lamia, lā′mi·a, *n.* [Gr.] *Greek myth.* A female monster sucking the blood of infants.

lamina, lam′i·na, *n.* pl. **laminae,** lam′i·nē. [L., a thin plate or lamina.] A thin plate or scale; a layer or coat lying over another: applied to the plates of minerals, bones, etc.; *bot.* the upper broad part of the petal in a polypetalous corolla; the blade of a leaf.—**laminable,** lam′i·na·bl, *a.* Capable of being formed into thin plates.—**laminar,** lam′i·nėr, *a.* Formed of laminae or plates; consisting of thin plates or layers.—**laminate,** lam′i·nāt, *a.*—**laminate,** lam′i·nāt, *v.i.*—*laminated, laminating.* To separate or split up into thin plates or layers.—*v.t.* To divide in thin sheets; to form into thin layers by beating or rolling; to compress layers of material into a hard, durable

substance by means of heat and chemicals; to overlay with laminae. —**lamination,** lam·i·nā′shon, *n.*

Lammas, lam′as, *n.* [A.Sax. *hláf-mæsse,* that is *loaf mass,* bread feast, so called because on this day offerings were formerly made of the first fruits of harvest.] The first day of August.—**Lammastide,** *n.* The time of Lammas.

lammergeier, laemmergeyer, lam′-mėr·gī·ėr, lem′mėr·gī·ėr, *n.* [G. *lämmergeier*—*lämmer,* pl. of *lamm,* a lamb, and *geier,* a vulture.] The bearded vulture, the largest European bird of prey, inhabiting the Alps, as well as Asia and Africa.

lamp, lamp, *n.* [Fr. *lampe,* L. and Gr. *lampas,* from Gr. *lampō,* to shine; akin *lantern.*] A vessel for containing oil or other liquid inflammable substance, to be burned by means of a wick; any contrivance adapted to contain an artificial light; something metaphorically communicating light.—**lampblack,** lamp′-blak, *n.* A fine soot formed by the condensation of the smoke of burning oil, pitch, or resinous substances, used as a pigment.—**lamplighter,** *n.* A man employed to light street or other public lamps.

lampas, lam′pas, *n.* [Fr. *lampas.*] A swelling in the roof of a horse's mouth immediately behind the fore-teeth.

lampoon, lam·pön′, *n.* [Fr. *lampon,* a drinking or scurrilous song, from *lamper,* to drink, to guzzle; akin *lap,* to lick.] A personal satire in writing; a satiric or abusive attack in prose or verse.—*v.t.* To write a lampoon against; to assail in a lampoon.— **lampooner,** lam·pön′ėr, *n.* The writer of a lampoon.—**lampoonry,** lam·pön′ri, *n.* The act of lampooning; the matter in a lampoon.

lamprey, lam′pri, *n.* [Fr. *lamproie,* It. *lampreda,* from L.L. *lampetra*— L. *lambo,* to lick, and *petra,* a stone, from their habit of attaching themselves to stones by their mouths.] The name of several marsipobranchiate, eel-like, scaleless fishes, with suctorial mouths, inhabiting both fresh and salt water.

lanate, lā′nāt, *a.* [L. *lanatus.*] Woolly; covered with a growth or substance resembling wool.

lance, lans, *n.* [Fr. *lance,* from L. *lancea,* a lance.] An offensive weapon consisting of a long wooden shaft with a sharp-pointed head of steel or other metal, used in war by both ancient and modern nations; a spear.—*v.t.*—*lanced, lancing.* To pierce with a lance or other pointed instrument; to open with a lancet or other sharp instrument.— **lance corporal,** *n.* A private soldier performing the duties of a corporal with a temporary rank as such.— **lancelet,** lans′let, *n.* A small worm-like transparent fish of very anomalous structure.—**lanceolate,** lan′-sē·o·lāt, *a.* [L. *lanceola,* dim. of *lancea,* a lance.] Shaped like a lance head.—**lancer,** lan′sėr, *n.* One who lances; one who carries a lance; a

cavalry soldier armed with a lance.— **lancet,** lan′set, *n.* [Fr. *lancette,* dim. of *lance.*] A small surgical instrument, sharp-pointed and generally two-edged, used in opening veins, tumors, abscesses, etc.—**lancet window,** *n.* A high and narrow window pointed like a lancet.— **lancet arch,** *n.* An arch whose head is shaped like the point of a lancet: generally used in lancet windows.— **lancewood,** *n.* [So named from its being suitable for making the shafts of lances.] The wood of several trees of the custard-apple family, natives of Guiana and the West Indies, which possesses great toughness and elasticity, and is much used for rods, etc.

lancinate, lan′si·nāt, *v.t.* [L. *lancino, lancinatum*; akin to *lance, lacerate.*] To tear; to lacerate.—**lancinating,** lan′si·nā·ting, *a.* Piercing: applied to a sudden sharp shooting pain, as in cancer.—**lancination,** lan·si·nā′-shon, *n.* A sudden, sharp, shooting pain; laceration; wounding.

land, land, *n.* [A.Sax. D. Dan. Icel. Sw. Goth. and G. *land*; connections very doubtful.] The solid or fixed part of the surface of the globe, in distinction from the sea or other waters, which constitute the fluid or movable part; a definite portion of the solid surface of the globe as set apart or belonging to an individual or a people, as a country, estate, or farm (to travel in all *lands,* his *land* adjoins mine); the people of a country or region; ground or soil (good *land,* poor *land*); in Scotland, a building including houses occupied by different families.—*To make the land,* or *to make land* (*naut.*), to discover land from the sea as the ship approaches it.—*v.t.* To set on shore; to disembark; to bring to or put in a certain place or condition; to catch, as a fish.—*v.i.* To bring an aircraft to rest on the ground or on water; to go on shore from a ship or boat; to disembark; to arrive; to reach.—**landed,** lan′ded, *a.* Having an estate in land; consisting in real estate or land (*landed* property).—**landfall,** land′fal, *n.* The first land discovered after a voyage; a landslide.—**landgrant school,** in the U. S., a college or university which received federal aid by the Morrill Act of 1862 for teaching vocational subjects, as agriculture, etc.— **landholder,** *n.* A holder, owner, or proprietor of land.—**landing,** land′-ing, *n.* The level part of anything, especially on a staircase, used for resting; the act of going or setting on land; a place where persons land or where goods are set on shore; the act of alighting, as an aircraft on a field.—*Landing gear,* the understructure of an aircraft, consisting of wheels, or of floats, and their supporting frame.—*Landing net,* a small bag-shaped net used to take the fish from the water after being hooked.— *Landing stage,* a stage or platform, frequently so constructed as to rise and fall with the tide, for the convenience of landing or shipping pas-

---

ch, *ch*ain; ch, Sc. lo*ch*;   g, *g*o;   j, *j*ob;   ng, si*ng*;   TH, *th*en;   th, *th*in;   w, *w*ig;   hw, *wh*ig;   zh, a*z*ure.

sengers and goods.—**landlady** land'-lā·di, *n.* A woman who has tenants under her; the mistress of an inn or of a lodginghouse; correlative to *landlord*.—**landless**, land'les, *a.* Destitute of land; having no property in land.—**landlocked**, land'lokt, *pp.* Enclosed or encompassed by land.—**landloper**, land'lō·per (Scottish *land louper*), *n.* [*Land*, and *loper*, as in *interloper*.] A vagabond or vagrant; one who has no settled habitation.—**landlord**, land'lord, *n.* The owner of land or of houses who has tenants under him; the master of an inn, tavern, lodginghouse; a host.—**landlubber**, land'lub·er, *n.* A contemptuous term among seamen for a landsman.—**landmark**, land'märk, *n.* A mark to designate the boundary of land; any mark or fixed object by which the limits of a portion of territory may be known and preserved; any prominent and distinguishing feature of a locality; some elevated object on land that serves as a guide to seamen; what marks a stage in any course of development; any striking historical event to which others may be referred.—**land measure**, *n.* The system of quantities used in computing the area of pieces of land.—**land office**, *n.* A government office in which the sales of public lands are recorded.—**land-office business**, a rushing, profitable business (*colloq.*).—**land-owner**, *n.* A proprietor of land.—**land-poor**, *a.* Financially embarrassed by having too much money invested in land, or by too much expense for upkeep of land.—**landscape**, land'skāp, *n.* [D. *landschap*, Dan. *landskab*, equivalent to *land-shape*.] A picture representing a tract of country with the various objects it contains; such pictures in general, or the painting of such pictures; a natural scene that might form the subject of such a picture.—**landslide**, land'slīd, *n.* The slipping or sliding down of a considerable portion of land or earth from a higher to a lower level; the earth which so slides or slips.—**landsman**, landz'man, *n.* One who lives on the land: opposed to *seaman*.—**Landsturm**, länt'stürm, *n.* [G., lit. land-storm.] A former local militia of Germany, called in case of actual invasion.—**landward**, land'-werd, *adv.* Toward the land.—*a.* Lying toward the land, or toward the interior, or away from the seacoast; situated in or forming part of the country, as opposed to the town; rural.—**Landwehr**, länt'vâr, *n.* [G.—*land*, country, and *wehr*, defense (E. *ware*, *beware*).] Formerly that portion of the military forces of some European nations who in time of peace followed their occupations, excepting when called out to complete compulsory training.

landau, lan·da̱', *n.* [From *Landau*, a town in Germany, where first made.] A kind of carriage with an openable top; an automobile of similar design.

landgrave, land'grāv, *n.* [G. *landgraf*, D. *landgraaf*—*land*, land, and *graf*,

graaf, an earl or count.] In Germany, originally, the title of district or provincial governors; later, the title of three princes of the empire, whose territories were called landgravates.—**landgravate**, land'gra·vāt, *n.* The territory or office of a landgrave.—**landgravine**, land'gra·vēn, *n.* The wife of a landgrave.

lane, lān, *n.* [A.Sax. *lane*, a lane; D. *laan*, alley; Fris. *lona*, *lana*, a lane.] A narrow way or passage, as between hedges or buildings; a narrow street; an alley; a narrow pass; one division of a road used for a single line of traffic; prescribed routes for shipping or air traffic so as to avoid collisions.

langrage, **langrel**, lang'grij, lang'-grel, *n.* Old bolts, nails, and pieces of iron bound together and fired from a ship's guns.

langsyne, lang·sīn', *n.* [Sc. *lang*, long, and *syne*, since.] The time long ago. (*Scotch*.)

language, lang'gwij, *n.* [Fr. *langage*, from *langue*, L. *lingua*, the tongue; which is cog. with E. *tongue* (*l* corresponding to *t*, as in L. *lacrima*, E. *tear*).] Human speech; the expression of thoughts by words or articulate sounds; the aggregate of the words employed by any community for intercommunication; the speech peculiar to a nation; words appropriate to or especially employed in any branch of knowledge (the *language* of chemistry); general style or manner of expression; the expression of thought in any way articulate or inarticulate (the *language* of the eyes, of flowers, etc.).

languid, lang'gwid, *a.* [L. *languidus*, from *langueo*, to droop or flag. LANGUISH.] Flagging; drooping; weak; heavy; dull; indisposed to exertion; slow; tardy; without animation.—**languidly**, lang'gwid·li, *adv.* In a languid manner.—**languidness**, lang'gwid·nes, *n.* The state or quality of being languid.

languish, lang'gwish, *v.i.* [Fr. *languir*, ppr. *languissant*, from L. *langueo*, to languish; akin to *lax*, *lag*, *slack*.] To lose strength or animation; to be or become dull, feeble, or spiritless; to pine; to be or to grow heavy; to droop; to wither; to fade; to be no longer active and vigorous.—*n.* Act of pining; also, a soft and tender look or appearance.—**languisher**, lang'gwish·er, *n.* One who languishes.—**languishing**, lang'gwish·-ing, *p.* and *a.* Losing strength; becoming feeble; pining; having a soft and tender expression (a *languishing* eye).—**languishingly**, lang'-gwish·ing·li, *adv.* In a languishing manner. —**languishment**, lang'-gwish·ment, *n.* The state of languishing or pining; softness of look or mien.—**languor**, lang'gwer, *n.* [L. *languor.*] The state of body induced by exhaustion of strength; feebleness; faintness; lassitude of body; dullness of intellect; listlessness; an agreeable listless or dreamy state.—**languorous**, lang'gwer·us, *a.* Characterized by languor.

laniard, lan'yerd, *n.* See LANYARD.

laniary, lan'i·e·ri, *n.* [L. *laniarius*,

pertaining to a butcher, from *lanius*, a butcher.] Shambles‡; a place of slaughter‡; one of the canine teeth of the carnivorous animals.—*a.* Used for lacerating or tearing flesh (*laniary* teeth).

lank, langk, *a.* [A.Sax. *hlanc*; connections doubtful.] Loose or lax and easily yielding to pressure‡; languid or drooping‡; not distended; not plump; of a thin or slender habit of body.—**lankly**, langk'li, *adv.* In a lank manner; loosely; laxly.—**lankness**, langk'nes, *n.* The state or quality of being lank.—**lanky**, lang'-ki, *a.* Lank.

lanner, lan'er, *n.* [Fr. *lanier*, L. *laniarius*, *lanius*, a butcher.] A species of hawk, especially the female of the species, found in the south and east of Europe.—**lanneret**, lan'er·et, *n.* The male of the lanner.

lanolin, lan'o·lin, *n.* [L. *lana*, wool, *oleum*, oil.] An oily or greasy substance obtained from unwashed wool, used as a basis of many ointments, lotions, etc.

lansquenet, lans'ke·net, *n.* [Originally a foot soldier, from G. *lands-knecht*, a foot soldier—*land*, country, *knecht*, a servant, a *knight*.] An old game at cards.

lantern, lan'tern, *n.* [Fr. *lanterne*, L. *lanterna*, from Gr. *lamptēr*, a light, a beacon, from *lampō*, to shine, whence also *lamp*.] A case enclosing a light and protecting it from wind and rain, sometimes portable and sometimes fixed; *arch.* an erection on the top of a dome, the roof of an apartment, etc., to give light, for ventilation, or for ornament; a tower which has the whole or a considerable portion of the interior open to view; a light open erection on the top of a tower; the upper part of a lighthouse where the light is shown.—*Chinese lantern.* See CHINESE.—*Dark lantern*, one with a single opening, which may be closed so as to conceal the light.—*Magic lantern.* See MAGIC. —**lantern fly**, *n.* A hemipterous insect of South America which emits a strong light in the dark.—**lantern-jawed**, *n.* Having lantern-jaws; having a long thin visage. (*Colloq.*)

lanthanum, lan'tha·num, *n.* [Gr. *lanthanō*, I lie hid, because its existence long remained unknown.] A metallic element of the rare-earth series, allied to aluminum. Symbol, La; at. no., 57; at. wt., 138.91.

lanthorn, lan'tern, *n.* An old and erroneous spelling of *Lantern*, due to the fact that lanterns used to have *horn* sides.

lanuginous, **lanuginose**, la·nū'ji·-nus, la·nū'ji·nōs, *a.* [L. *lanuginosus*, from *lanugo*, down, from *lana*, wool.] Downy; covered with down or fine soft hair.

lanyard, lan'yerd, *n.* [Also written *lanier*, *laniard*, from Fr. *lanière*, a thong, strap, originally a woolen band, from L. *lana*, wool.] *Naut.* a short piece of rope or line used for fastening something in ships; *milit.* a piece of strong twine with an iron hook at one end, used in firing cannon with a friction tube.

---

fāte, fär, fâre, fat, fall; mē, met, her; pīne, pin; nōte, not, möve; tūbe, tub, bull; oil, pound.

Laodicean, la·od′i·sē″an, *a.* Like the Christians of Laodicea; lukewarm in religion.

lap, lap, *n.* [A.Sax. *læppa*; D. and Dan. *lap*, Sw. *lapp*, G. *lappen*, a lap, a loose flap, *lappen*, to hang loose; akin to *label*, *lobe*, *limp* (*a*.), *lapse*; *lapel*, *lappet*, are derivatives.] The lower part of a garment that hangs loosely; the part of clothes that lies on the knees when a person sits down; hence, the upper part of the legs in this position; the part of one body which lies on and covers a part of another (as a slate in roofing); the last part or round in a race.— **lapboard,** *n.* A board resting on the lap, employed by tailors for cutting out or ironing work upon.—**lap dog,** lap′dog, *n.* A small dog fondled in the lap, a pet dog.—**lapful,** lap′fůl, *n.* As much as the lap can contain.

lap, lap, *v.t.*—*lapped, lapping.* [From O.E. *wlap*, to wrap, a form of *wrap* (which see).] To wrap or twist round; to fold; to double over; to lay partly above; to overlap ideas; *racing*, to win or be ahead of by at least one circuit of the racetrack; to cuddle.—*v.i.* To be spread or laid; to be turned over; to lie over something in part (as slates on a roof).—**lapper,** lap′ér, *n.*

lap, lap, *v.i.*—*lapped, lapping.* [A.Sax. *lapian, lappian*, acel. *lepja*, O.D. *lappen, lapen*, L.G. *lappen*, to lap or lick up; allied to L. *lambo*, Gr. *laptō*—to lap or lick.] To take up liquor or food with the tongue; to feed or drink by licking up; to make a sound like that produced by taking up water by the tongue.—*v.t.* To take into the mouth with the tongue; to lick up.—*n.* A lick, as with the tongue; a sound made in this way; a sound as of water rippling against the beach.—**lapper,** lap′ér, *n.* One who laps or takes up with the tongue.

lap, lap, *n.* [Short for *lapidary* wheel.] A wheel or revolving disk of soft metal, which by means of a polishing powder is used in cutting glass, gems, etc.

laparectomy, lap′ar·ek″to·mi, *n.* [Gr. *lapara*, flanks, *ektomē*, cutting out.] The excision of intestines at the side.

laparotomy, lap′ar·ot″o·mi, *n.* Cutting of the abdominal walls.

lapel, la·pel′, *n.* [Dim. from *lap*, part of a garment.] That part of a garment which is made to lap or fold over; the part in the front of a coat or waistcoat that is folded back.

lapidary, lap′i·de·ri, *n.* [L. *lapidarius*, from *lapsis, lapidis*, a stone; akin Gr. *lepas*, a rock.] An artificer who cuts, polishes, and engraves gems or precious stones; a dealer in precious stones.—*a.* Of or pertaining to the art of polishing and engraving precious stones.—*Lapidary style*, pompous style of language adopted on monuments; sonorous Latinity.— **lapidification,** la·pid′i·fi·kā″shon, *n.* The act of lapidifying or converting into stone; the state of being lapidified.—**lapidify,** la·pid′i·fī, *v.t.*—*lapidified, lapidifying.* To form into

stone.—*v.i.* To turn into stone; to become stone.

lapilli, la·pil′lī, *n. pl.* [L. *lapillus*, a little stone, contr. of *lapidulus*, dim. of *lapis*, a stone. LAPIDARY.] Volcanic ashes which consist of small angular fragments or particles.

lapis lazuli, la′pis laz′ū·li, *n.* [L. *lapis*, a stone, and L.L. *lazulum*, this mineral; same origin as *azure*.] An aluminous mineral of a rich blue color, used in mosaic work and other kinds of ornament, and when powdered yielding ultramarine.

lappet, lap′et, *n.* [Dim. of *lap*, a loose part, etc.] A little lap or flap, as on a dress, especially on a headdress; a cotton fabric with imitation of embroidery on surface.

Lapps, *n.* The natives of Lapland, in northern Scandinavia.

lapse, laps, *n.* [L. *lapsus*, from *labi, lapsus*, to slide, to fall (as in *collapse, elapse, relapse*, etc.); akin *lap* (*n*.), *lobe*, etc. LAP.] A gliding, slipping, or gradually falling; an unobserved or very gradual advance; an unnoticed passing away (of time); a slip or error; a failing in duty; a deviation from truth or rectitude; *eccles. law*, the omission of a patron to present a clerk to a benefice within six months after it becomes void.—*v.i.*—*lapsed, lapsing.* To pass slowly, silently, or by degrees; to glide away; to fall gradually; to slip in moral conduct; to fail in duty; to commit a fault; to fall or pass from one person to another, through some omission or negligence; *law*, to become ineffectual or void.

lapwing, lap′wing, *n.* [O.E. *lapwinke*, A.Sax. *hleápewince*, equivalent to *leapwink*; from its leaping or jerking mode of flight.] A well-known and handsome bird belonging to the plover family, about the size of a pigeon, often called the *pee-wit* from its cry.

lar, lär, *n. pl.* **lares,** lâ′rēz. [Related to L. *larva*, a specter.] A household deity among the ancient Romans, regarded as the spirit of a deceased ancestor.

larboard, lär′bōrd, *n.* [Perhaps from M.E. *ladeborde*, the loading side.] *Naut.* the left-hand or port side of a ship, a term now given up in favor of *port*, the latter being shorter and more distinctive in sound : opposite of *starboard*.

larceny, lär′se·ni, *n.* [Contr. for *latrociny*, from L. *latrocinium*, from *latro*, a robber.] The unlawful taking and carrying away of any article or piece of goods with intent to deprive the right owner of the same; theft.— **larcener, larcenist,** lär′sen·ér, lär′sen·ist, *n.* One who commits larceny; a thief.—**larcenous,** lär′sen·us, *a.* Pertaining to or having the character of larceny; guilty of or inclined to larceny.

larch, lärch, *n.* [L. and G. *larix*, the larch.] A well-known coniferous tree remarkable for the elegance of its form and the durability and value of its wood.

lard, lärd, *n.* [Fr. *lard*, L. *lardum, laridum*, allied to Gr. *larinos*, fat, from *laros*, dainty.] The fat of swine

after being melted and separated from the flesh.—*v.t.* To mix with lard or bacon; to stuff with pieces of bacon (as in cooking a fowl); to fatten; to mix with something by way of improvement.—*v.i.* To grow fat.—**larder,** lär′dér, *n.* A room, house, box, or the like, where meat and other food are kept.—**lardon,** lär-don, *n.* A strip of pork or bacon used to lard meat.

lares, *n. pl.* of *Lar*.

large, lärj, *a.* [Fr. *large*, L. *largus*, abundant, large.] Being of great size; having great dimensions; big; bulky; great; containing or consisting of a great quantity or number; abundant; plentiful; numerous; liberal, many-sided, comprehensive (a *large* mind); generous, noble, sympathetic (a *large* heart).—*At large*, without restraint or confinement; diffusely; fully; with all details; elected at large (by the whole state), as congressman-*at-large*.—**largehearted,** *a.* Having a large heart; generous, magnanimous; sympathetic.—**largeheartedness,** *n.* Largeness of heart.—**largely,** lärj′li, *adv.* In a large manner; to a large or great degree or extent; widely; extensively.

largess, lär′jes, *n.* [Fr. *largesse*, from L. *largitio*, a bounty, from *largiri*, to bestow, from *largus*, large.] A present; a gift or donation; a bounty bestowed.

larghetto, lär·get′to. [It.] *Mus.* somewhat slowly, but not so slowly as *largo*.—**largo,** lär′gō. [It.] *Mus.* slowly; slowly, with breadth and dignity.

lariat, la′ri·at, *n.* [Sp. *lariata*.] The lasso; a long cord or thong of leather with a noose used in catching wild horses, etc.

lark, lärk, *n.* [A.Sax. *láwerce, láferce*, O. and Prov.E. *lavrock, laverock*= D. *leeuwerik, leeuwrik*, Dan. *lærke*, Icel. *lævirki*, G. *lerche*—a lark; the Icel. *lævirki* seems to literally mean *craft-worker*.] One of a genus of perching birds characterized by having a long straight hind claw, and of which there are various species, as the skylark, wood lark, shore lark, etc., the skylark being celebrated for its song.—**larkspur,** lärk′spér, *n.* [From the long spur of one of the sepals.] The common name of a genus of plants, several species of which are common in gardens.

lark, lärk, *n.* [From A.Sax. *lác*, Icel. *leikr*, Goth. *laiks*, sport, play.] Sport; frolic; a piece of merriment. (*Slang* or *colloq.*)—*v.i.* and *t.* To sport; to make sport. (*Slang* or *colloq.*)

larrikin, lar′i·kin, *n.* Australian hooligan; street-corner rough.

larrup, lar′up, *v.t.* To whip or flog.

larva, lär′va, *n. pl.* **larvae,** lär′vē. [L. *larva*, a mask, a specter.] The early form of any animal which during its development is unlike its parent; an insect in the caterpillar or grub state, that is, the first stage after the egg, preceding the chrysalis and the perfect insect.—**larval,** lär′val, *a.* Pertaining to a larva.

larynx, lar′ingks, *n.* [Gr.] *Anat.* the upper part of the windpipe or trachea, a cartilaginous cavity which plays an important part in the utterance of articulate sounds.—**laryngeal,** lar·in·ji'al, *a.* Pertaining to the larynx.—**laryngitis,** la·rin·ji'tis, *n.* [Term. -*itis* denotes inflammation.] An inflammation of the larynx of any sort.—**laryngoscope,** la·ring'go·skōp, *n.* A reflecting contrivance for examining the larynx and commencement of the trachea.—**laryngoscopic,** la·ring'go·skop"ik, *a.* Pertaining to the inspection of the larynx.—**laryngotomy,** lar·in·got'o·mi, *n.* [Gr. *tomē,* a cutting.] The making of an incision into the larynx for assisting respiration when obstructed, for removing foreign bodies, or for other reasons.

lascar, las'kar, *n.* In the East Indies, properly, a camp follower; but by Europeans applied to a native sailor.

lascivious, las·siv'i·us, *a.* [L. *lascivia,* lewdness, *lascivus,* wanton, allied to Skr. *las,* to embrace, *lash,* to desire, Gr. *lilaiomai,* to desire.] Wanton; lewd; lustful; exciting voluptuous emotions.—**lasciviously,** las·siv'i·us·li, *adv.* In a lascivious manner.—**lasciviousness,** las·siv'i·us·nes, *n.* The state or quality of being lascivious.

laser, lā'zėr, *n.* [*l*ight *a*mplification by *s*timulated *e*mission of *r*adiation.] A microwave amplifier that produces an intense beam of light by the stimulation of high-energy atoms in the visible spectrum.

lash, lash, *n.* [Akin to G. *lasche,* a flap, a thong, a latchet, also a scarf joint; D. *lasch,* a piece joined on, a joining; Dan. *laske,* Sw. *laska,* to scarf.] The thong or cord at the point of a whip; any thong, cord, or the like for flogging; a whip; a scourge; a stroke with a whip or anything pliant and tough; a stroke of satire; a sarcasm or cutting remark.—*v.t.* To strike with a lash or anything pliant; to scourge; to beat, as with something loose; to dash against (as waves); to satirize; to censure with severity.—*v.i.* To ply the whip; to aim sarcasms; to hit.—*To lash out,* to make a sharp verbal attack; to kick.

lash, lash, *v.t.* [O.Fr. *lachier,* form of *lacier,* to lace.] To bind, lace, or tie with a rope.—**lashing,** lash'ing, *n.* A piece of rope binding or making fast one thing to another.

lass, las, *n.* [A contr. for *ladess,* fem. of *lad,* or a contr. of W. *llodes,* a lass. LAD.] A young woman; a girl: in familiar language often applied to a woman of any age.—**lassie,** las'i, *n.* [Dim. of *lass.*] A young girl; a term of endearment for a young woman. (*Colloq.*)

lassitude, las'i·tūd, *n.* [L. *lassitudo,* from *lassus,* weary; same root as *late.*] The state of having the energies weakened; weakness; weariness; languor of body or mind; enervation.

lasso, las'sō, *n.* [Sp. *lazo,* Pg. *laço,* from *laqueus,* a noose. LACE.] A lariat, rope or cord, with a noose, used for catching wild horses and other animals.—*v.t.* To catch with a lasso.

last, last, *a.* [A.Sax. *last,* a contr. for *latost,* latest; comp. *best* for *betst.* LATE.] Coming after all the others; latest; hindmost; closing; final; next before the present; most recent; utmost; extreme; lowest; meanest; farthest of all from possessing a given quality, character, use, or the like; most unlikely (you are the *last* man I should consult).—*At last,* formerly *at the last,* at the end; in the conclusion.—*To the last,* to the end; till the conclusion.—*adv.* On the last occasion; the time before the present; after all others; lastly; finally.

last, last, *v.i.* [A.Sax. *laestan,* to follow, to observe or perform, to last, to endure; Goth. *laistjan,* to trace footsteps, to follow, from A. Sax. *last,* Goth. *laists,* a footstep. See LAST, for shoes.] To continue in time; to endure; to remain in existence; to hold out and be sufficient in quantity (provisions to *last* a week); to continue unimpaired; not to decay or perish.—**lasting,** las'ting, *p.* and *a.* Such as will or can continue or endure; durable; of long continuance (*lasting* good, evil, impression).—*n.* A species of stiff and very durable woolen stuff, used for making shoes and other purposes.—**lastingly,** las'ting·li, *adv.* In a lasting manner.—**lastingness,** las'ting·nes, *n.* The state or quality of being lasting.—**lastly,** last'li, *adv.* In the last place; at last; finally.

last, last, *n.* [A.Sax. *hlæst,* from *hladan,* to lade; D., Dan., and G. *last,* Icel. *lest,* a load. LADE.] A load; hence, a certain weight or measure, which varies in different articles, but is generally estimated at 4000 lb.; the burden of a ship.

last, last, *n.* [A.Sax. *lást,* *laest,* D. *leest,* Dan. *læst,* a last; Goth. *laists,* footstep; Icel. *leistr,* the foot below the ankle, a short sock. LAST, *v.i.*] A mold or form of the human foot, made of wood, on which boots and shoes are formed.—*v.t.* To form on or by a last.

Latakia, lät·a·kē'a, *n.* A fine variety of Turkish tobacco, so named from *Latakia* (anciently *Laodicea*), near which it is produced.

latch, lach, *n.* [From O.E. *lacche,* *latche,* A.Sax. *læccan,* to seize, to take hold of.] A simple contrivance or catch for fastening a door.—*v.t.* To fasten with a latch; to catch hold of; to attach oneself to.—**latchkey,** *n.* A key used to raise the latch of a door.

latchet, lach'et, *n.* [Fr. *lacet,* a lace or string. LACE.] The string or thong that fastens a shoe or sandal.

late, lāt, *a.* [A.Sax. *læt,* D. *laat,* Icel. *latr,* Dan. *lad,* Sw. *lat,* late, slow, tardy; Goth. *lats,* sluggish; G. *lass,* wearied; akin L. *lassus* (for *ladtus*); the root is that of *let.* This adjective is compared by *later,* *latter,* *latest* or *last.*] Coming after the usual time; slow; tardy; long delayed; far advanced toward the end or close (a *late* hour of the day); existing not long ago, but not now; deceased; departed; last or recently in any place, office, or character.—*adv.* After the usual time, or the time appointed; after delay; not long ago; lately; far in the night, day, week, or other particular period.—*Of late,* lately, in time not long past, or near the present.—**lately,** lāt'li, *adv.* Not long ago; recently.—**lateness,** lāt'nes, *n.* The state of being late; tardiness; far advanced period.—**latish,** lāt'ish, *a.* Somewhat late.

lateen, la·tēn', *a.* [Fr. *voile latine,* lit. Latin sail.] A term applied to a triangular sail having its foremost edge fastened to a yard which hoists obliquely to the mast: used in xebecs, feluccas, etc., in the Mediterranean.

latent, lā'tent, *a.* [L. *latens, latentis,* from *lateo,* to lurk; allied to Gr. *lanthanō, lathein,* to escape notice.] Not visible or apparent; not seen; not manifested; under the surface of what outwardly appears.—*Latent heat,* that portion of heat which exists in any body without producing any effect upon another, or upon the thermometer.—**latently,** lā'tent·li, *adv.* In a latent manner.—**latency,** lā'ten·si, *n.* The state of being latent.

lateral, lat'ėr·al, *a.* [L. *lateralis,* from *latus, lateris,* a side, as in *collateral, equilateral.*] Pertaining to the side; directed to the side; proceeding from the side; situated on the side. —**laterally,** lat'ėr·al·li, *adv.*

laterite, lat'ėr·ît, *n.* [L. *later,* a brick or tile.] An argillaceous sandstone of a reddish color.

latescent,† la·tes'ent, *a.* [L. *latesco,* to hide one's self. LATENT.] Lying hid; latent.—**latescence,**† la·tes'ens, *n.* The quality or condition of being latescent.

latex, lā'teks, *n.* [L., a fluid juice.] *Bot.* the white milky sap of some seed plants which coagulates on exposure to air and from which rubber, gutta-percha, chicle, etc., are produced.

lath, lath, *n.* [A.Sax. *lætta,* D. and G. *latte,* whence Fr. *latte.* It. *latta,* a lath, a pole, etc. Akin *lattice, latten.*] A thin narrow board or slip of wood that is nailed to the rafters of a building to support the tiles or covering; a thin narrow slip of wood, perforated metal, or wire mesh that is nailed to a wall to support the plastering; such materials collectively; any similar piece of wood.—*v.t.* To cover or line with laths.—**lather,** *n.* One who applies laths.—**lathing,** *n.* Lath materials; lath work on a wall; work of putting on lath materials.

lathe, lāтн, *n.* [Icel. *löth,* Dan. *lad,* a lathe, *dreielad,* a turning lathe; in second sense it corresponds with Sw. and G. *lade,* a lay or lathe in a loom.] An apparatus for turning and polishing wood, ivory, metals, etc., by supporting and causing the article to revolve while being operated on; the part of a loom to which the reed is fixed, and by the movements of which the weft-threads are driven home in weaving; called also *lay.*

lather, laтн'ėr, *n.* [A.Sax. *leáthor;* akin to Icel. *lauthr, löthr,* froth of sea water, also a kind of soap; Sw. *lodder*, soap; from root meaning to wash, seen also in *lave*.] Foam or froth made by soap and water; foam or froth from profuse sweat, as of a horse.—*v.i.* To form a foam with soap and water; to become frothy.—*v.t.* To spread over with lather.

laticiferous, lat·i·sif′ẽr·us, *a.* [L. *latex*, sap, and *fero*, to bear.] *Bot.* bearing or containing latex or elaborated sap.

latifoliate, latifolious, lā·ti·fō′li·āt, lā·ti·fō′li·us, *a.* [L. *latus*, broad, and *folium*, a leaf.] Broad-leaved, as a plant.

Latin, lat′in, *a.* [L. *Latinus*, from *Latium*, the district of Italy in which Rome was built.] Pertaining to the Latins, a people of Latium in Italy; Roman; pertaining to or composed in the language spoken by the Latins or Romans.—*Latin Church*, the Western Church; the Church of Rome, as distinct from the Greek or Eastern Church.—*Latin races*, the Italian, French, Spanish, etc., whose language is based on the Latin, and among whose ancestors were Roman colonists.—*n.* The language of the ancient Romans.—*v.t.* To turn into Latin.—**Latinism**, lat′in·izm, *n.* A Latin idiom; a mode of speech peculiar to the Latins.—**Latinist**, lat′in·ist, *n.* One skilled in Latin.—**Latinity**, la·tin′i·ti, *n.* Latin style or idiom; purity of Latin style.—**Latinization**, lat′in·i·zā″shon, *n.* The act of rendering into Latin.—**Latinize**, lat′in·īz, *v.t.*—*latinized, latinizing.* To translate into Latin; to give Latin terminations or forms to, as to foreign words.—*v.i.* To use words or phrases borrowed from the Latin.

latitude, lat′i·tūd, *n.* [L. *latitudo*, lit. breadth, from *latus*, broad, wide; as applied in geography this term was adopted because ancient geographers thought the breadth (latitude) of the earth from north to south was much less than its length (longitude) from east to west.] Extent from side to side; breadth; width; room or scope; comprehensiveness or looseness of application; extent of deviation from a standard; freedom from rules or limits; laxity; extent; amplitude; distance north or south of the equator, measured on a meridian and expressed in degrees, minutes, and seconds, the greatest possible latitude being 90° north or south, and any latitude approaching this being a *high* latitude, the opposite being a *low* latitude; *astron.* the distance of a star north or south of the ecliptic, measured on a circle at right angles to the ecliptic and passing through the body.—*Parallels of latitude*, circles parallel to the equator, used in measuring latitude. —**latitudinal**, lat·i·tū′di·nal, *a.* Pertaining to latitude; in the direction of latitude.—**latitudinarian**, lat′i·tū·di·nā″ri·an, *a.* Embracing a wide circle or range; having a wide scope; characterized by freedom, independence, or want of respect for the

usual standards of belief or opinion; lax in religious principles or views; freethinking; liberal.—*n.* One who is liberal or loose in his notions; one who has no respect for commonly accepted doctrines or opinions; one who indulges a latitude of thinking and is careless of orthodoxy.—**latitudinarianism**, lat′i·tū·di·nā″ri·an·izm, *n.* The principles of latitudinarians; freedom of opinion, particularly in theology.

latria, la·trī′a, *n.* [L., from Gr. *latreia*, service.] The highest kind of worship, or that paid to God, distinguished by Roman Catholics from *dulia*, or the inferior worship paid to saints.

latrine, la·trēn′, *n.* [L. *latrina*, a bath, a water closet, from *lavo*, to wash.] A privy; a water closet.

latten, lat′en, *n.* [O.Fr. *laton*, Fr. *laiton*, brass; It. *latta*, tin-plate; akin to *lath*; so called from the material being used in flat pieces or plates. LATH.] A fine kind of brass or bronze anciently used for crosses, candlesticks, brasses of sepulchral monuments, etc.; as a modern commercial term, metal in sheets or strips, especially sheet or plate brass or thin plates of mixed metal.

latter, lat′ẽr, *a.* [An irregular comparative of *late*. LATE.] More late or recent; the second of two; opposed to *former*; mentioned the last of two; modern; lately past (in these *latter* ages).—**Latter-day Saint**, *n.* MORMON.—**latterly**, lat′ẽr·li, *adv.* Of late; in time not long past; lately; ultimately; at last.

lattice, lat′is, *n.* [Fr. *lattis*, from *latte*, lath. LATH.] A structure of wood or iron made by crossing laths, rods, or bars, and forming open checkered or reticulated work; a window made of laths or strips of iron which cross one another like network, so as to leave open interstices.—*v.t.*—*latticed, latticing.* To give the form or appearance of a lattice to; to furnish with a lattice. —**lattice girder**, *n.* A girder of which the side consists of diagonal pieces arranged like lattice work.

laud, lạd, *v.t.* [L. *laudo*, to praise, from *laus, laudis*, praise; *allow* is a derivative.] To praise in words alone, or with words and singing; to extol; to celebrate.—*n.* Praise; a song or hymn of praise; *pl.* a service of the church comprising psalms of praise, and generally included in matins.—**laudability**,† **laudableness**, lạ·da·bil′i·ti, lạ′da·bl·nes, *n.* The quality of being laudable.—**laudable**, lạ′da·bl, *a.* [L. *laudabilis*.] Praiseworthy; commendable.—**laudably**, lạ′da·bli, *adv.* In a laudable or commendable manner.— **laudation**, lạ·dā′shon, *n.* Praise; commendation.—**laudatory**, lạ′da·to·ri, *a.* Containing or expressing praise; tending to praise.—*n.* That which contains or expresses praise.— **lauder**, lạ′dẽr, *n.* One who lauds or praises.

laudanum, lạ′da·num, *n.* [From L. *ladanum*, a resinous juice. LADA-

NUM.] Opium prepared in spirit of wine by maceration, straining, and filtering; tincture of opium.

laugh, läf, *v.i.* [A.Sax. *hlehhan, hlihhan*, to laugh; comp. Goth. *hlahjan*, O.H.G. *hlahhan*, Icel. *hlæja*, D. *lagchen*, G. *lachen*, to laugh; imitative of sound made in laughing.] To make that convulsive or chuckling noise which sudden merriment excites; when said of things, to appear gay, bright, or brilliant.—*To laugh at*, to ridicule; to treat with some degree of contempt.—*To laugh in the sleeve*, to laugh to one's self or so as not to be observed, especially when apparently maintaining a demure countenance.—*To laugh on the wrong side of the mouth*, to weep or cry; to be made to feel vexation or disappointment after exhibiting a boastful or exultant spirit.—*n.* The inarticulate expression of sudden mirth peculiar to man.—*v.t.* To express by laughing; to ridicule or deride; with *out* or *down*.—*To laugh to scorn*, to deride; to treat with mockery, contempt, and scorn.—**laughable**, läf′a·bl, *a.* That may justly excite laughter; comical; ludicrous.—**laughableness**, läf′a·bl·nes, *n.* The quality of being laughable.—**laughably**, läf′a·bli, *adv.* In a manner to excite laughter.— **laugher**, läf′ẽr, *n.* One who laughs or is fond of merriment.—**laughing gas**, *n.* Nitrous oxide, or protoxide of nitrogen: so called because, when inhaled, it usually produces exhilaration.—**laughingly**, läf′ing·li, *adv.* In a laughing or merry way; with laughter.—**laughingstock**, *n.* A person or thing that is an object of ridicule; a butt for laughter or jokes. —**laughter**, läf′tẽr, *n.* [A.Sax. *hleahtor*, Icel. *hlair*, O.H.G. *hlahtar*.] The act or sound of laughing; an expression of mirth, manifested chiefly in certain convulsive and partly involuntary actions of the muscles of respiration, which produce a succession of short abrupt sounds, with certain movements of the muscles of the face, and often of other parts of the body.

launce, läns, *n.* A name of two species of sand eels, from their lancelike form.

launch, länsh, *v.t.* [Fr. *lancer*, O.Fr. *lanchier*, to throw or dart.] To throw, as a lance; to dart; to let fly; to set afloat (to *launch* a ship); to catapult or send off (to *launch* a rocket); *fig.* to put out into another sphere of duty, another field of activity, or the like.—*v.i.* To glide forward, as a ship into the water; to enter upon a new field of activity; to enter upon a new topic (to *launch* into a discussion).—*n.* The setting afloat of a ship or boat.—**launcher**, län′shẽr, *n.*—**launching pad**, *n.* A nonflammable platform from which a rocket or missile can be launched.

launch, länsh, *n.* [Sp. and Pg. *lancha*, boat.] A kind of boat, longer, lower, and more flat-bottomed than a long boat; the largest boat carried by a man-of-war.

launder, län′dẽr, *n.* [Contr. from

O.E. *lavander*, from Fr. *lavandier*, *lavandière*, from *laver*, L. *lavo*, to wash. LAVE.] A washerwoman; a long trough used by miners for washing ore.—*v.t.‡* To wash; to wet.—**launderer**, län′dėr·ėr, *n.* A man who follows the business of washing clothes.—**laundress**, län′dres, *n.* A female whose employment is the washing and the ironing of underclothing, table linen, etc.—**laundry**, län′dri, *n.* [Contr. for *lavendery*.] The place or room where clothes are washed.

laureate, lạ′ri·āt, *a.* [L. *laureatus*, from *laurea*, a laurel, from *laurus*, a laurel. LAUREL.] Decked or invested with laurel.—*Poet laureate*, in Great Britain, an officer belonging in virtue of his office to the royal household, who was formerly required to compose an ode annually for the sovereign's birthday, for a great national victory, and the like—a requirement discontinued since the reign of George III, the post being now a sinecure.—*n.* One crowned with laurel; a poet laureate.—*v.t.*—*laureated, laureating.* To honor with a wreath of laurel; to invest with the office of poet laureate.—**laureateship**, lạ′ri·āt·ship, *n.* Office of a laureate; the post of a poet laureate.

laurel, lạ′rel, *n.* [O.E. *laurer, lorer*, Fr. *laurier*, Sp. Pr. *laurel*, from L. *laurus*, a laurel, for *daurus*, being akin to Gr. *drys*, W. *derw*, an oak, E. *tree*.] The sweet bay, a native of the North of Africa and south of Europe, cultivated in gardens from its elegant appearance and the aromatic fragrance of its evergreen leaves; a name also given to several other shrubs botanically very different, but somewhat similar in their evergreen foliage, as the cherry laurel and Portugal laurel, both of the cherry genus; *pl.* a crown of laurel, formerly bestowed as a distinction on poets, heroes, etc.; hence, honor, fame, distinction.—**laureled**, lạ′reld, *a.* Crowned or decorated with laurel, or with a laurel wreath; laureate.

laurustine, lạ′rus·tīn, *n.* [L. *laurus*, laurel, and *tinus*, this plant.] A popular garden evergreen shrub or tree, native of the south of Europe, with pinkish or white flowers.

lava, lä′va, *n.* [It., from L. *lavo*, to wash. LAVE.] The general term for all rock-matter that flows in a molten state from volcanoes.—*Lava ware*, a kind of coarse ware resembling lava made from iron slag.

lavaliere, lavalier, lav′ä·lēr″, *n.* [Fr. *la valliere, lavalliere*, a kind of necktie with a bow, prob. from Louise de *La Valliere*, mistress of Louis XIV.] A pendant necklace, usually jeweled.

lave, lāv, *v.t.*—*laved, laving.* [Fr. *laver*, L. *lavo*, to wash; to bathe; akin to *luo*, Gr. *louō*, to wash; connected are *laundress, lavender, lava, ablution, alluvial, deluge, lotion.*] To wash; to bathe.—*v.i.* To wash one's self; to bathe; to wash, as the sea on the beach.—**lavation**, la·vā′shon, *n.* [L.

lavatio.] A washing or cleansing.—**lavatory**, lav′a·to·ri, *a.* Washing or cleansing by washing.—*n.* A room or place for washing or personal ablutions; a wash or lotion.—**laver**, lā′vėr, *n.* A vessel for washing; a large basin; in *Script. hist.* a basin placed in the court of the Jewish tabernacle, where the officiating priests washed their hands and feet.

lavender, lav′en·dėr, *n.* [L.L. *lavendula, lavandula*, It. *lavandola*, *lavanda*, Fr. *lavande*, G. *lavandel*, lavender.] An aromatic plant of the mint family, the flower spikes of which are used to perfume clothes, and afford by distillation a valuable essential oil; a pale blue color with a slight mixture of red.

lavish, lav′ish, *v.t.* [Irregularly formed from E. *lave*, to pour out.] To expend or bestow with profusion; to expend without necessity or use; to waste; to squander.—*a.* Expending or bestowing with profusion; profuse; liberal to a fault; wasteful; being overflowing or in profusion; superabundant; superfluous.—**lavisher**, lav′ish·ėr, *n.* One who lavishes.—**lavishly**, lav′ish·li, *adv.* In a lavish manner.—**lavishness**, lav′ish·nes, *n.*

law, lạ, *n.* [A.Sax. *lagu*, from same root as *lie, lay, low*; cog. Sw. *lag.* Icel. *lag, lög*, Dan. *lov*, a law; the root is also in L. *lex*, a law (whence *legal*). LIE.] A rule of action or conduct laid down or prescribed by authority; an edict or decree of a ruler or a government; a general command or order expressly laid down; such rules, edicts, or decrees collectively; the whole body of rules regulating and controlling the individuals of a state or community (to break the *law*, a violation of *law*, a father-in-*law*); legal procedure; litigation; the science dealing with legal enactments and procedure; jurisprudence; rights established by law; justice; one of the rules or principles by which any matter or proceeding is regulated (the *laws* of versification, of horse racing); an allowance in distance or time granted to a weaker competitor in a race or the like; a theoretical principle deduced from practice or observation; a formal statement of facts invariably observed in natural phenomena (the *law* of gravitation).—*The law, theol.* the code of Moses, or the books containing it; the preceptive part of revelation in contradistinction to the doctrinal, that is, to *the gospel.*—*Law French*, the Norman dialect or old French, still employed in certain formal state proceedings.—*Law language*, the language used in legal writings and forms.—*Law Latin*, corrupt Latin used in law and legal documents.—*Law merchant*, mercantile or commercial law; international law regulating commerce. See also under CIVIL, COMMERCIAL, COMMON, CRIMINAL, ECCLESIASTICAL, etc.—**law-abiding**, *a.* Observant of the law; obeying the law.—**lawbreaker**, *n.* One who violates the

law.—**lawful**, lạ′ful, *a.* Agreeable or conformable to law; allowed by law; legitimate; permissible (*lawful* but not expedient); competent; free from objection; rightful (*lawful* owner).—**lawfully**, lạ′ful·li, *adv.* In a lawful manner; legitimately; legally.—**lawfulness**, lạ′ful·nes, *n.* The quality of being lawful.—**lawless**, lạ′les, *a.* Not obedient or conforming to law; unrestrained by the law of morality or of society; contrary to or unauthorized by law; illegal; apparently uncontrolled by any law; capricious.—**lawlessly**, lạ′les·li, *adv.* In a lawless manner.—**lawlessness**, lạ′les·nes, *n.* Illegality; disregard of law; arbitrariness; violence.—**lawmaker**, *n.* A legislator; a lawgiver.—**law of nations**, international law.—**lawsuit**, lạ′sūt, *n.* A suit in law for the recovery of a supposed right; an action before a court instituted by a party to compel another to do him justice.—**lawyer**, lạ′yėr, *n.* [From *law*; comp. *bowyer, sawyer.*] One versed in the laws; or a practitioner of law; one whose profession is to institute suits in courts of law, or to prosecute or defend the cause of clients.

lawn, lạn, *n.* [O.E. *laund, lawnde*, a clear space in a forest, a wild shrubby or woody tract, from W. *llan*, an enclosed space, or from Fr. *lande*, a heath or wild tract.] A glade in a forest; a vista through trees; a space of ground covered with grass, and kept smoothly mown, generally in front of or around a mansion.—**lawn mower**, *n.* machine for mowing lawns.

lawn, lạn, *n.* [Perhaps same as preceding word, and so called from its transparency, being seen through as we see through a lawn or vista, but more probably, derived from the earlier term *laune lynen*, i. e., lawn linen, from *Laon*, a town in France.] A fabric of linen or cotton, sheer, fine, and plain woven, thinner than cambric, employed in handkerchiefs, dresses, etc.—**lawny**, lạn′i, *a.*

lawrencium, lạ·ren′sē·um, *n.* [After Ernest Lawrence.] A radioactive metallic element of the actinoid series; symbol Lw; at. no. 103.

lax, laks, *a.* [L. *laxus*, loose, from same root as *langueo*, to languish, and probably E. *slack*; hence *relax, lease, leash, release.*] Loose; flabby; soft; not tense, firm, or rigid; not tightly stretched or drawn; not rigidly exact or precise; vague; equivocal; not sufficiently strict or rigorous; remiss; having too frequent discharges from the bowels.—**laxation**, lak·sā′shon, *n.* [L. *laxatio.*] The act of loosening or slackening.—**laxative**, lak′sa·tiv, *a.* [Fr. *laxatif.*] Having the power or quality of loosening or opening the intestines and relieving from constipation.—*n.* A medicine that acts as a gentle purgative.—**laxity**, lak′si·ti, *n.* [L. *laxitas.*] The state or quality of being lax; looseness; want of strictness; remissness.—**laxly**, laks′li, *adv.* In a lax manner; loosely; with-

out exactness; remissly; flabbily.
lay, lā, pret. of *lie.*

lay, lā, *v.t.*—pret. & pp. laid; ppr. *laying.* [A.Sax. *lecgan* (pret. *legde, léde,* pp. *gelegd, geled*), a causal corresponding to *lie,* A.Sax. *licgan;* similarly Goth. *lagjan,* Icel. *laggja,* Dan. *lœgga,* D. *leggen,* G. *legen,* to lay, from corresponding intrans. verbs. [LIE.] To place in a lying position; to cause to lie; to prostrate; to put, set, or place in general; to impose (taxes, commands, blame, etc.); to bring into a certain state; with various adjectives (to *lay* bare; to *lay* open, etc.); to settle (dust); to still (the wind); to allay (pain); to dispose with regularity in building or in other technical operations; to place at hazard; to wager; to stake; to contrive, scheme, plan (a plot); to place before a court of justice (an indictment, damages).— *To lay aside,* to put off or away; not to retain; to abandon.—*To lay away,* to reposit in store; to put aside for preservation.—*To lay before,* to exhibit or show to; to present to the view of.—*To lay by,* to reserve for future use; to put off.—*To lay by the heels,* to put in the stocks; to confine; to put in prison.—*To lay claim,* to claim; to advance or bring forward a claim.—*To lay down,* to give up or resign; to declare (to *lay down* a proposition or principle); to delineate on paper; to stake, or deposit as a pledge, equivalent, or satisfaction.— *To lay down the law,* to assert dictatorially what the speaker holds to be right.—*To lay eggs,* to produce them naturally from the body, as a bird or reptile.—*To lay hold of, to lay hold on,* to seize; to catch; to apprehend.—*To lay in,* to collect and store; to provide previously.— *To lay it on,* to do something to excess, as to charge an exorbitant price.—*To lay on,* to apply with force; to supply, as water, gas, etc., to houses by means of pipes leading from a main reservoir.—*To lay one's self open to,* to expose one's self to.— *To lay one's self out for,* to be ready to take part in; to put one's self in the way of.—*To lay one's hand on a thing,* to find it when wanted.— *To lay open,* to open; to make bare; to uncover; also, to show; to expose; to reveal.—*To lay out,* to expend; to plan or dispose in order the several parts of (to *lay out* a garden); to dress in graveclothes and place in a decent posture (to *lay out* a corpse). —*To lay to heart,* to consider seriously and intently; to feel deeply or keenly.—*To lay to one's charge,* to accuse him of.—*To lay up,* to store; to treasure; to reposit for future use; to confine to the bed or chamber; *naut.* to dismantle (a ship) and put in a dock or other place of security.—*To lay siege to,* to besiege; to importune; to annoy with constant solicitations.—*To lay wait,* to lie in ambush.—*To lay waste,* to devastate; to desolate.—*v.i.* To bring forth or produce eggs; *betting,* to wager; to bet; to stake money.—*To lay about one,* to strike on all sides; to

act with vigor.—*To lay at,* to endeavor to strike.—*To lay on,* to deal blows with vehemence. [*To lay* is sometimes erroneously used, even by good writers, for *to lie,* but this should be carefully avoided. See under LIE.]—*n.* A stratum; the direction or lie in which the different strands of a rope are twisted.—**layoff,** lā′af, *n.* Discharge, as of workmen; a period of closing down; the act of laying off.—**layout,** lā′out, *n.* Floor plan, such as of a house; the equipment, as of an office or shop; a rough sketch to show how a proposed arrangement of photographs and type will look in print (an artist's *layout*).—**layover,** lā′ō·vėr, *n.* A wait between stages of a journey; a stopover in a place.
lay, lā, *a.* [Fr. *lai,* from L. *laicus,* Gr. *laikos,* from *laos,* people.] Pertaining to the people, as distinct from the clergy; not clerical; not professional; not appertaining to one who has professional knowledge.—*Lay brother,* a person received into a convent of monks, under vows, but not in holy orders.—*Lay clerk,* in the *English Ch.* a person not in orders who leads the people in their responses.—*Lay sister,* one received into a convent of nuns, under vows, but who does not perform any sacred office.—**laity,** lā′i·ti, *n.* Collectively all people who do not belong to the clergy; people outside of any profession as distinguished from those in it.—**layman,** lā′man, *n.* Any man not a clergyman; one of the laity; a man not professionally or specially devoted to a pursuit.
lay, lā, *n.* [O.Fr. *lai,* from the Celtic; Ir. and Gael. *laoi,* a verse, hymn, poem; same root as in G. *lied,* a song.] A song; a ballad; a narrative poem.
layer, lā′ėr, *n.* [From the verb *lay.*] One who or that which lays; a stratum; a coat, as of paint; a row or course of masonry, brickwork, or the like; a shoot or twig of a plant, not detached from the stock, partly laid under ground for growth or propagation.—*v.t. Gardening,* to propagate by bending the shoot of a living stem into the soil, the shoot striking root while being fed by the parent plant.
layette, lā·et′, *n.* [Fr.] Clothing, blankets, etc., for a new-born child.
lay figure, layman, lā′fig·ur, lā′man, *n.* [D. *leeman,* lit. joint-man, *lee* being for *lede,* from *leden,* pl. of *lid* (A.Sax. *lith,* Dan. *lid.* Goth. *lithus*), a joint.] A jointed figure used by painters in imitation of the human body, and which can be placed in any attitude so as to serve when clothed as a model for draperies, etc.
lazar, lā′zėr, *n.* [O.Fr. *lazare,* from *Lazarus* of the New Testament (Luke, xvi. 20).] A leper; any person infected with a nauseous and pestilential disease.—**lazaretto, lazaret,** laz·a·ret′tō, laz′a·ret, *n.* A hospital for the reception of diseased persons, particularly those affected with contagious diseases; at seaports often a vessel used for this purpose; a

hospital for quarantine.
lazuli, laz′ū·lī, *n.* Lapis lazuli.— **lazulite,** laz′ū·līt, *n.* Blue spar, a phosphate of aluminum, magnesium and iron.
lazy, lā′zi, *a.* [Origin doubtful; perhaps for *late-sy* (from *late*), with term, as in *tricksy, tipsy;* or O.Fr. *lasche,* lax, slow, remiss, from L. *laxus.*] Disinclined to action or exertion; sluggish; indolent; averse to labor; heavy in motion; moving slowly or apparently with labor.— **lazily,** lā′zi·li, *adv.* In a lazy manner. —**laziness,** lā′zi·nes, *n.* The state or quality of being lazy; indolence; sloth.—**lazybones,** lā′zi·bōnz, *n.* A lazy fellow; an idler.
lea, lē, *n.* [Also written *lay,* from A.Sax. *leáh,* untilled land, pasture; Dan. dialect *lei,* fallow; D. *leeg,* empty, fallow.] A meadow or grassy plain; land under grass or pasturage.
leach, lēch, *n. Naut.* the side edge of a sail. LEECH.
leach, lēch, *v.t. and i.* To remove soluble parts by percolating a liquid through something.
lead, led, *n.* [A.Sax. *leád;* akin D. *lood,* Sw. and Dan. *lod,* G. *loth,* a plummet, the lead for taking soundings.] A heavy metallic element, pliable and soft and of a grayish-blue color, its chief ore being sulfide galena—symbol, Pb (Latin *plumbum*); at. no., 82; at. wt., 207.19; a plummet or mass of lead used in sounding at sea; *print.* a thin plate of metal used to give space between lines; a neutral gray color of medium brilliance; bullets (a shower of *lead*); a small piece of black lead, or plumbago, used in pencils.—*Black lead,* a name of graphite or plumbago. See GRAPHIC.—*White lead,* carbonate of lead, forming a white, quick-drying substance much used in painting. —*v.t.* To cover or line with lead; to fit with lead; *print.* to widen the space between (lines) by inserting a lead or thin plate of type metal.— **leaden,** led′n, *a.* Made of lead; resembling lead (a *leaden* sky); dull; gloomy.—**lead pencil,** *n.* An instrument for drawing or writing, usually made by enclosing a slip of plumbago, or graphite (black lead), in a casing of wood.—**leadsman,** ledz′man, *n. Naut.* the man who heaves the lead.
lead, lēd, *v.t.* pret. & pp. led. [A.Sax. *laeden,* to lead, from *lad,* a course, from *lithan,* to go or travel; D. *leiden;* akin *lode, lodestone.*] To guide by the hand; to guide or conduct by showing the way; to direct; to conduct, as a chief or commander; to head; to direct and govern; to precede; to hold the first place in rank or dignity among; to show the method of attaining an object; to direct, as in an investigation; to draw, entice, allure; to induce; to prevail on; to influence; to pass or spend (to *lead* a life of gaiety); to cause to spend or endure (he *led* his wife a sad life); *card playing,* to commence a round or trick with.— *To lead captive,* to carry into captivity.—*To lead one a dance* or *a fine dance,* to cause one more exertion

or trouble than necessary or expected.—*To lead the way*, to go before and show the way.—*v.i.* To go before and show the way; to have precedence or pre-eminence; to take the first place; to have a position of authority; to be chief, commander, or director; to conduct, bring, draw, induce (gambling *leads* to other evils); *card playing*, to play the first card of a round or trick.— *To lead off* or *out*, to begin.—*n.* A going before; guidance; act of leading; precedence; the right of playing the first card in a round or trick.—**leader**, lē′dėr, *n.* One that leads or conducts; a guide; a conductor; a chief; a commander; the chief of a party, faction, or any body of people; a musical performer who leads a band or choir; one of the front horses in a team.— **leadership**, lē′dėr•ship, *n.* The office of a leader; guidance.—**leading**, lē′-ding, *p.* and *a.* Guiding; conducting; chief; principal; most influential.— *Leading question*, a question which suggests the answer.—**leading strings**, *n. pl.* Strings by which children are supported when beginning to walk; hence, *to be in leading strings*, to be a mere puppet in the hands of others.

leaf, lēf, *n.* pl. **leaves**, lēvz. [A.Sax. *leáf*=O.Sax. *lôf*, Goth. *laufs*, Icel. *lauf*, Dan. *löv*, D. *loof*, G. *laub*, a leaf; allied to Lith. *lapas*, a leaf; Gr. *lepis*, a scale.] One of the external parts of a plant, usually shooting from the sides of the stem and branches, and ordinarily green in color; something resembling a leaf; the part of a book or folded sheet containing two pages; a side, division, or part of a flat body, the parts of which move on hinges, as folding doors, window shutters, a fire screen, etc.; the part of a table which can be raised or lowered at pleasure; a very thin plate of metal (gold-*leaf*); the brim of a soft hat.—*To turn over a new leaf*, to adopt a different and better line of conduct. —*v.i.* To shoot out leaves; to produce leaves.—**leafage**, lēf′ij, *n.* Leaves collectively; abundance of leaves; foliage.—**leafless**, lēf′les, *a.* Destitute of leaves.—**leaflet**, lēf′let, *n.* A little leaf; a small printed folder; *bot.* one of the divisions of a compound leaf; a foliole.—**leafstalk**, *n.* The petiole or stalk which supports a leaf.—**leafy**, lē′fi, *a.* Full of leaves; abounding with leaves.— **leave**, lēv, *v.i.* To produce leaves; to leaf.—**leaved**, lēvd, *a.* With leaves; and compounded, as two-*leaved*.

league, lēg, *n.* [Fr. *ligue*, It. *lega*, L.L. *liga*, from L. *ligo*, to bind (in *ligament*, *ligature*, *ally*, etc.).] A combination of parties for promotion of their mutual interests, or for executing any design in concert, as of states for military aid or defense.— *League of Nations*, a group of nations formed after the World War (1920) to cooperate in world affairs. It assigned mandates of surrendered territories and planned arbitration in disputes between nations.—*Base-*

ball, *National League* (organized 1876), *American League* (1900), of ten teams each in major cities.

league, lēg, *n.* [O.Fr. *legue*, Fr. *lieue*, from L.L. *leuca*, *leuga*, etc., and that from the Celtic.] A measure of length varying in different countries, the English land league being 3 statute miles, the nautical league nearly 3½.

leaguer, lē′gėr, *n.* [D. *leger*, G. *lager*, a bed, a couch, a camp; allied to *lair*, *lie*, *lay*.] A camp; the camp of a besieging army; a siege.

leak, lēk, *n.* [Icel. *leki*, a leak; *lekr*, leaky; D. *lek*, Dan. *laek*, G. *leck*, a leak, leaky. See the verb.] A crack, fissure, or hole in a vessel that admits water, or permits a fluid to escape; the passing of liquid through such a crack or aperture.— *To spring a leak*, to open or crack so as to let in water; to begin to let in water.—*v.i.* [Icel. *leka*, Dan. *laekke*, D. *lekken*, to leak; allied to A.Sax. *leccan*, to wet, to moisten, and to E. *lack*.] To let water or other liquor in or out through a hole or crevice (the vessel *leaks*); to ooze or pass, as water or other fluid, through a crack, fissure, or aperture in a vessel.—*To leak out*, to find vent; to find publicity in a clandestine or irregular way.— **leakage**, lēk′ij, *n.* A leaking; the quantity of a liquor that enters or issues by leaking; *com.* a certain allowance for the leaking of casks, or the waste of liquors by leaking.— **leakiness**, lēk′i•nes, *n.* State of being leaky.—**leaky**, lēk′i, *a.* Letting water or other liquid pass in or out.

lean, lēn, *v.i.*—pret. & pp. *leaned* or *leant* (lent). [A.Sax. *hlinian*, to lean; O.H.G. *hlinen*, cog. with Gr. *klinō*, to make to bend, and L. *clino*, *inclino*, to bend, to *incline*.] To slope or incline from a straight or perpendicular position or line; to slant; to incline in feeling or opinion; to tend toward; to rest as for support, hence, to depend for consolation, comfort, and the like, usually with *against*, *on*, or *upon*.—*v.t.* To cause to lean; to incline; to support or rest.—**lean-to**, lēn′tö, *a.* Having rafters pitched against or leaning on another building or a wall.—*n.*, *n. pl.* **lean-tos**, lēn′töz, *Arch.* a building addition having a lean-to roof; a shed built against trees or posts or another building.

lean, lēn, *a.* [A.Sax. *hlaene*, L.G. *leen*, lean; allied to *lean*, v.] Wanting flesh or fat on the body; meager; not fat; not rich, fertile, or productive; barren of thought; jejune.— *n.* That part of flesh which consists of muscle without fat.—*Lean mixture*, a compound of air and gas or vapor without a combustible component.

leap, lēp, *v.i.*—*leaped*, pret. & pp., rarely *leapt* (lept). [A.Sax. *hleápan*, to leap, to run, pret. *hleóp*; Sc. *loup*, Goth. *hlaupan*, G. *laufen*; allied to Gr. *kraipnos*, *karpalimos*, swift.] To spring or rise from the ground with feet in the air; to move with springs or bounds; to jump, vault, bound, skip; to make a sudden transition.—

v.t. To pass over by leaping; to spring or bound from one side to the other of; to cause (one's horse) to take a leap; to make to pass by leaping.—*n.* The act of leaping; the space passed over or cleared in leaping; a jump; a spring; a bound; a sudden transition.—**leapfrog**, *n.* A game in which one player, by placing his hands on the back or shoulders of another in a stooping posture, leaps over his head.— **leap year**, *n.* Bissextile; every fourth year, in which February has an additional day, and there are thus 366 days in all: so called because after February the days of the week *leap* an extra day as compared with other years.

learn, lėrn, *v.t.*—*learned*, *learnt* (lėrnd, lėrnt), pret. & pp. [A.Sax. *leornian*, to learn, to teach; akin to *laeran*, to teach, *lár*, learning, lore; comp. G. *lernen*, to learn, *lehren*, to teach; D. *leeren*, Icel. *laera*, to teach, to learn; Goth. *laisjan*, to teach; allied to A.Sax. *lesan*, Icel. *lesa*, to gather.] To gain or acquire knowledge of or skill in; to acquire by study; to teach (*Shak.*).—*v.i.* To gain or receive knowledge, information, or intelligence; to receive instruction; to be taught.—**learned**, lėr′ned, *a.* Possessing knowledge; having a great store of information obtained by study; erudite; well acquainted; having much experience; skillful; often with *in* (*learned in* martial arts); containing or indicative of learning (a *learned* book).— **learnedly**, lėr′ned•li, *adv.* In a learned manner.—**learner**, lėr′nėr, *n.* A person who learns; one who is taught; a scholar; a pupil.—**learning**, lėr′ning, *n.* Acquired knowledge in any branch of science or literature; knowledge acquired by the study of literary productions; erudition.

lease, lēs, *n.* [Norm. *lees*, *leez*, a lease, L.L. *lessa*; from L. *laxare*, to loosen, relax, from *laxus*, lax. LAX.] A letting of lands, tenements, etc., to a person for a specified rent or compensation; the written contract for such letting; any tenure by grant or permission; the time for which such a tenure holds good.—*v.t.*— *leased*, *leasing*. To grant by lease; to let for a specified rent; to let; to occupy in terms of a lease.— **leasehold**, lēs′hōld, *a.* Held by lease. —*n.* A tenure by lease.—**leaseholder**, lēs′hōl•dėr, *n.* A tenant under a lease.

leash, lēsh, *n.* [Fr. *laisse*, O.Fr. *lesse*, a leash, from L.L. *laxa*, a loose cord, from L. *laxus*, loose. LAX.] A thong or line by which a dog (or two or three dogs) is held in hunting; a line holding in a hawk; three creatures of any kind, especially greyhounds, foxes, bucks, and hares; hence, three things in general.—*v.t.* To hold or fasten by a leash.

least, lēst, *a.* [A.Sax. *laest*, *laesast*, superl. of *laessa*, less.] Smallest; little beyond others, either in size, degree, value, worth, importance, or the like.—*adv.* In the smallest or lowest degree.—*At least*, *at the least*, to say no more; at the lowest degree; on the lowest estimate.—**leastways, leastwise,** lēst'wāz, lēst'wīz, *adv.* At least; however. (*Vulgar.*)

leather, leTH'ẽr, *n.* [A.Sax. *lether* = L.G. *ledder, lier,* Icel. *lethr,* Dan. *læder, lær,* G. and D. *leder;* root unknown.] The skin of animals dressed and prepared for use by tanning, tawing, or other processes; tanned hide.—*a.* Consisting of leather.—*v.i.* To furnish with leather; to beat as with a thong of leather. (*Vulgar*)—**leatherneck,** *n.* A marine, from the stock once worn around the neck.—**leatherette,** leTH·ẽr·et', *n.* A kind of imitation leather.—**leathery,** leTH'-ẽr·i, *a.* Pertaining to or resembling leather; tough.

leave, lēv, *n.* [A.Sax. *leáf, geleaf,* leave, permission; same as the -*lieve* in *believe;* akin D. -*lof* in *oorlof,* permission; Icel. *leyfi,* permission, *lof,* praise, permission; G. (*er*)*lauben,* to permit; allied also to E. *love, lief;* L. *libet,* it is pleasing.] Liberty granted to act; permission; allowance; a formal parting of friends or acquaintances; farewell: used chiefly in the phrase to *take leave.* ∴ *Leave* is usually employed on familiar or unimportant occasions; *liberty* in relation to more important matters. —**leave-taking,** *n.* The act of taking leave; a bidding good-bye.

leave, lēv, *v.t.*—*left* (pret. & pp.), *leaving.* [A.Sax. *laefan,* to leave, to cause to remain, from *lifian,* to remain; Icel. *leifa,* O.Fris. *leva,* O.H.G. *bi-liban,* Mod.G. *b-leiben,* to remain; same stem as *live.*] To suffer to remain; not to take or remove; to have remaining at death; to commit or trust to, as a deposit; to bequeath; to give by will; to withdraw or depart from; to forsake, desert, abandon; to relinquish, resign, renounce; to refer; to commit for decision; to let remain without further discussion.—*To be left to one's self,* to be left alone; to be permitted to follow one's own opinions or desires.—*To leave off,* to desist from; to forbear; to cease wearing or practicing.—*To leave out,* to omit.—*v.i.* To set out; to take one's departure; to desist.—*To leave off,* to cease; to desist; to stop.— **leavings,** lēv'ings, *n.* Residue; that which is left; remains.

leaven, lev'n, *n.* [Fr. *levain,* from *lever,* L. *levare,* to raise; akin *levity, lever, relieve,* etc.] A substance that produces fermentation, as in dough; fermenting dough; what resembles leaven in its effects.—*v.t.* To mix with leaven; to impregnate or imbue with a modifying influence.—**leavening,** lev'en·ing, *n.*

lebensraum, lā'bens·roum, *n.* [G. *leben,* life, living, and *raum,* space.] A term used by Germans to indicate area in Europe which they considered vital to their national existence.

lecher, lech'ẽr, *n.* [O.Fr. *lecheor,* gourmand, parasite, libertine; Fr. *lécher,* to lick; from G. *lecken,* O.H. G. *leccôn,* to lick. LICK, LICKERISH.] A man given to lewdness.—*v.i.* To practice lewdness.—**lecherous,** lech'-ẽr·us, *a.* Addicted to lewdness; prone to indulge lust; lustful; lewd. —**lecherously,** lech'ẽr·us·li, *adv.* In a lecherous manner.—**lecherousness,** lech'ẽr·us·nes, *n.*—**lechery,** lech'ẽr·i, *n.* [O.Fr. *lecherie.*] Lewdness; free indulgence or practice of lust.

lecithin, les'ith·in, *n.* [Gr. *lekithos,* egg yolk.] A complex fatty compound containing nitrogen and phosphates, and widely distributed through the animal body.

lectern, lek'tẽrn, *n.* [O.Fr. *lectrin;* L.L. *lectrinum,* from *lectrum,* pulpit, Gr. *lektron,* a couch.] A desk or reading stand, especially in churches, from which scripture is read.

lection, lek'shon, *n.* [L. *lectio,* from *lego,* to read. LECTURE.] The act of reading; a difference or variety in copies of a manuscript or book; a reading; a lesson or portion of Scripture read in divine service.— **lectionary,** lek'shon·e·ri, *n.* A book containing portions of Scripture to be read for particular days.—**lector,** lek'tẽr, *n.* [L.] A person in the Church of Rome whose office it is to read the lessons in church.

lecture, lek'chẽr, *n.* [Fr. *lecture,* from L. *lectura,* a reading, from *lego,* to read, whence also *legend, lesson, legible,* etc. LEGEND.] A discourse on some subject read or delivered before an audience; a formal or methodical discourse intended for instruction; a reprimand, as from a superior; a formal reproof.—*v.t.*—*lectured, lecturing.* To give a lecture to; to speak to dogmatically or authoritatively; to reprimand; to reprove.—*v.i.* To read or deliver a formal discourse; to deliver lectures for instruction.— **lecturer,** lek'chẽr·ẽr, *n.* One who lectures; a professor or instructor who delivers formal discourses to students.—**lectureship,** lek'chẽr·-ship, *n.* The office of a lecturer.

led, led, pret. and pp. of *lead.*

ledge, lej, *n.* [From stem of *lie;* comp. Sc. *leggin,* Icel. *lögg,* the ledge or rim at the bottom of a cask.] A shelf on which articles may be placed; anything which resembles such a shelf; a part rising or projecting beyond the rest; a ridge or shelf of rocks; *arch.* a small molding; also, a string course; *joinery,* a piece against which something rests.

ledger, lej'ẽr, *n.* [Perhaps lit. a book that rests on a *ledge* or shelf; in any case from the same stem; comp. old *leger, ledger,* resting in a place; D. *legger,* one that lies; akin *lie* (to rest).] The principal book of accounts among merchants and others, so arranged as to exhibit on one side all the sum at the debit of the accounts and on the other all those at the credit; *arch.* a flat slab of stone, such as is laid horizontally over a grave; the covering slab of an altar tomb.—**ledger line,** *n. Mus.* a short line added above or below the staff for the reception of a note too high or too low to be placed on the staff.

lee, lē, *n.* [Icel. *hlé,* Dan. *lae;* D. *lij,* G. *lee,* lee; akin A.Sax. *hleó,* a shade, a shelter, Goth. *hlija,* a tent.] The quarter toward which the wind blows, as opposed to that from which it proceeds; the shelter caused by an object interposed, and keeping off the wind: almost exclusively a nautical term.—*Under the lee of,* on that side of which is sheltered from the wind; protected from the wind by; opposed to on the *weather* side of.— *a. Naut.* of or pertaining to the part or side toward which the wind blows; opposite to *weather.*—*Lee shore,* the shore under the lee of a ship, or that toward which the wind blows.—*Lee tide,* a tide running in the same direction as the wind is blowing.—**leeboard,** *n.* A long flat piece of wood attached to each side of a flat-bottomed vessel (as a Dutch galiot), intended to prevent her from drifting fast to leeward.— **leeward,** lē'wẽrd or lū'wẽrd, *a.* Pertaining to the part toward which the wind blows.—*n.* The quarter or direction toward the lee.—**leeway,** lē'wā, *n.* The drifting of a ship to the leeward of her course; the deviation from her true course which a vessel makes by drifting to leeward; extra time, space, etc.; a degree of freedom or choice; tolerance.

leech, lēch, *n.* [A.Sax. *laece,* a physician; Goth. *leikeis,* Icel. *læknari,* Sw. *läkare,* a physician.] The common name of several bloodsucking wormlike animals, some of which are used in medicine; a hanger-on; a parasite.—*v.t.* To bleed by the use of leeches; to exhaust.— *v.i.* To attach like a leech.

leech, lēch, *n.* [L.G. *leik,* Icel. *lik,* Sw. *lik,* Dan. *lig,* leech-line, boltrope.] *Naut.* the border or edge of a sail which is sloping or perpendicular.

leek, lēk, *n.* [A.Sax. *leác,* an herb, a leek = L.G. and D. *look,* Icel. *laukr,* Sw. *lök,* Dan. *lög,* G. *lauch,* Rus. *luk;* this gives the term. in *garlic, hemlock.*] A plant of the lily family, *Allium Porrum,* similar to the onion in form and use, but having flat, succulent leaves.

leer, lẽr, *n.* [A.Sax. *hleór,* O.E. *lere, lire,* O.Sax. *hlear,* Icel. *hlyr,* face, cheek.] A side glance expressive of malignity, amorousness, or some unworthy feeling; an arch or affected glance or cast of countenance.—*v.i.* To cast a look expressive of contempt, malignity, or amorousness; to cast a sly or amorous look.—*v.t.* To allure with a leer.—**leeringly,** lē'ring·li, *adv.* In a leering manner.

leery, lẽr'i, *a.* [E. dial. *lear,* from E. *lore,* learning.] Suspicious, knowing, wary.

lees, lēz, *n. pl.* [Fr. *lie,* Walloon *lizi,* L.L. *liæ;* origin unknown.] The grosser parts of any liquor which have settled on the bottom of a vessel; dregs; sediment.

leet, lēt, *n.* [Icel. *leiti,* a share or part.] In Scotland, a list of candidates for any office.

leeward, leeway. See LEE.

left, left, pret. & pp. of *leave.*— **left-off,** *a.* Laid aside; no longer worn (*left-off* clothes).

left, left, *a.* [A.Sax. *left,* worthless; O.E. *lift, luft,* O.D. *lucht, luft,* left; probably allied to A.Sax. *lef,* O.Sax. *lef,* weak, infirm.] Denoting the part opposed to the *right* of the body; belonging to the side next which the heart is situated (the *left* hand, arm, or side); in a political sense, a party or individuals opposed to conservatism; espousing progressive and advanced liberal policies and legislation.—*The left bank of a river,* that which would be on the left hand of a person whose face is turned down stream.—*n.* The side opposite to the right; that part which is on the left side; a liberal or radical political group.—**left-handed,** *a.* Having the left hand more capable of being used than the right; clumsy; turned toward the left hand.—*Left-handed marriage.* MORGANATIC.—**left-handedness,** *a.*—**leftist,** lef'tist, *n.* A member of the left; a radical.—*a.* Of or pertaining to the left.—**leftover,** *n.* The part remaining, as of a meal.—**left wing,** *n.* The most liberal or radical elements of a political or social group.—*a.* Of or pertaining to the left wing.—**left-winger,** *n.*

leg, leg, *n.* [A Scandinavian word: Icel. *leggr,* a leg, hollow bone, stem or trunk; Dan. *laeg,* Sw. *lägg,* the calf or shin.] The limb of an animal, used in supporting the body and in walking and running; in a narrower sense, that part of the limb from the knee to the foot; a long slender support, as the *leg* of a chair or table; one of the sides of a triangle as opposed to the base; the part of a stocking or other article of dress that covers the leg; *cricket,* the part of the field that lies to the left and behind the batsman as he faces the bowler; the fielder who acts in that part of the field.—*To put one's best leg foremost,* to do one's utmost endeavor.—*To have not a leg to stand on,* to have exhausted all one's strength or resources.—*On one's legs,* standing, especially to speak.—**legged,** legd, *a.* Having legs: used in composition (bandy-*legged,* two-*legged*).—**legging,** leg'ing, *n.* A covering for the leg, usually worn over the trousers and reaching to the knees; a long gaiter.—**legless,** leg'les, *a.*

legacy, leg'a·si, *n.* [From L. *legatum,* a legacy, from *lego,* to bequeath, to appoint. LEGATE.] A bequest; a particular thing or certain sum of money given by last will or testament; anything handed down by an ancestor or predecessor.

legal, lē'gal, *a.* [Fr. *légal,* from L. *legalis,* from *lex, legis,* law (also in *alloy, legitimate, legislator,* etc.); akin to *legare,* to delegate (as in *legate*); root same as in E. *lay, lie. Loyal* is the same word.] According to law; in conformity with law; permitted by law; pertaining to law; created by law.—**legalism,** lē'gal·izm, *n.* Strict adherence to law; a legal doctrine; inclination to the doctrine of works as opposed to grace.—**legalist,** lē'gal·ist, *n.* A stickler for adherence to law.—**legality,** li·gal'-

i·ti, *n.* The state or quality of being legal.—**legalization,** lē'gal·iz·ā"shon, *n.* The act of legalizing.—**legalize,** lē'gal·īz, *v.t.*—*legalized, legalizing.* To make legal or lawful; to render conformable to law.—**legally,** lē'gal·li, *adv.* In a legal manner; by permission of or in conformity with law.

legate, leg'it, *n.* [L. *legatus,* from *lego,* to send, to delegate. LEGAL.] An ambassador; especially, the pope's ambassador to a foreign prince or state.—**legateship,** leg'it·ship, *n.* The office of a legate.—**legatine,** leg'a·tin, *a.* Pertaining to a legate; made by or proceeding from a legate.—**legation,** li·gā'shon, *n.* [L. *legatio.*] A person or persons sent as envoys or ambassadors to a foreign court; an embassy; a diplomatic minister and his suite; a district ruled by a papal legate.

legatee, leg·a·tē', *n.* [From L. *legatum,* a legacy. LEGACY.] One to whom a legacy is bequeathed.

legato, li·gä'tō. [It., tied, from L. *ligare,* to tie.] *Mus.* played or sung in an even, smooth, gliding manner.

legend, lej'end, *n.* [Fr. *légende,* from L. *legenda,* lit. things to be read from *lego,* to read; originally applied to lives of the saints that had to be read as a religious duty. *Lego,* to read, originally to gather, appears in a great many English words, as in *lecture, lesson, coil, cull, collect, intellect, neglect, diligent, elegant,* etc.] A story generally of a marvelous character told respecting a saint; hence, any marvelous story handed down from early times; a tradition; a nonhistorical narrative; an inscription; *numismatics,* the words arranged circularly on a medal or coin, as distinguished from the inscription, which is across it.—**legendary,** lej'en·de·ri, *a.* Consisting of legends; like a legend; fabulous.

legerdemain, lej'èr·di·mān", *n.* [Fr. *léger de main,* light of hand—*léger,* L.L. *leviarius,* from L. *levis,* light (whence *levity*), and *main,* L. *manus,* hand.] Sleight of hand; a deceptive performance which depends on dexterity of hand; trickery or deception generally.—**legerdemainist,** lej'èr·di·mān"ist, *n.* One who practices legerdemain; a juggler.

leghorn, leg'orn, *n.* A kind of straw plait for bonnets and hats imported from Leghorn; a hat made of that material. [*cap.*] A Mediterranean breed of domesticated fowl.

legible, lej'i·bl, *a.* [L. *legibilis,* from *lego,* to read. LEGEND.] Capable of being read; consisting of letters or figures that may be distinguished by the eye.—**legibility,** lej·i·bil'i·ti, *n.* The quality of being legible.—**legibly,** lej'i·bli, *adv.* In a legible manner.

legion, lē'jon, *n.* [L. *legio,* from *lego,* to collect. LEGEND.] A body of ancient Roman infantry consisting at different periods of from 3000 to above 6000, often with a complement of cavalry; hence, a body of troops in general; a great number.—*Legion of honor,* an order instituted in France

by Napoleon I, as a reward for merit, both civil and military, now greatly altered in character.—*American Legion,* veterans of World War I and World War II, organized Nov. 8, 1919, in the interests of fellowship, world peace, justice, freedom, democracy. Has state and national bodies.—*v.t.* To enroll or form into a legion.—**legionary,** lē'jon·a·ri, *a.* Belonging to a legion or legions.—*n.* One of a legion; a Roman soldier belonging to a legion.

legislate, lej'is·lāt, *v.i.*—*legislated, legislating.* [L. *lex, legis,* law, and *fero, latum,* to give, pass, or enact. LEGAL.] To make or enact a law or laws.—**legislation,** lej·is·lā'shon, *n.* The act of legislating or enacting laws; laws when enacted.—**legislative,** lej'is·lā·tiv, *a.* Enacting laws; having power or authority to enact laws; pertaining to the enacting of laws.—*n.* The branch of government which makes and repeals laws.—**legislatively,** lej'is·lā·tiv·li, *adv.* In a legislative manner.—**legislator,** lej'is·lā·tèr, *n.* A law giver; one who frames or establishes the laws and polity of a state or kingdom; a member of a national or supreme legislative assembly.—**legislature,** lej'is·lā·chèr, *n.* The body of men in a state or kingdom invested with power to make and repeal laws; the supreme legislating power of a state.—**legist,** lē'jist, *n.* One skilled in the laws.

legitimate, li·jit'i·mit, *a.* [L.L. *legitimatus,* from *legitimare,* to legitimate, from L. *legitimus,* lawful, from *lex,* law. LEGAL.] Lawfully begotten or born; born in wedlock; genuine; not false or spurious; following by logical or natural sequence; allowable (a *legitimate* argument or influence); rightful; *politics,* according to law or established usage; in a narrower sense, according to the doctrine of divine right.—*Legitimate drama,* drama or plays performed on the stage, as opposed to motion picture, vaudeville, or radio performances.—*v.t.*—*legitimated, legitimating.* To make lawful (*Mil.*); to render legitimate.—**legitimately,** li·jit'i·mit·li, *adv.* In a legitimate manner.—**legitimacy,** li·jit'i·ma·si, *n.* The state or quality of being legitimate.—**legitimation,** li·jit'i·mā"shon, *n.* The act of making or rendering legitimate.—**legitimatize,** li·jit'i·ma·tīz, *v.t.* To make legitimate.—**legitimism,** li·jit'im·izm, *n.* The principles of the legitimists.—**legitimist,** li·jit'i·mist, *n.* One who supports legitimate authority; one who believes in the sacredness of hereditary monarchies or the doctrine of divine right.—**legitimize,** li·jit'i·mīz, *v.t.*—*legitimized, legitimizing.* To legitimate.

legume, leg'ūm, *n.* [L. *legumen,* pulse—said to be from *lego,* to gather, because gathered and not cut. LEGEND.] *Bot.* a seed vessel of two valves, like the pod of a pea, in which the seeds are fixed to the ventral suture only; *pl.* the fruit of leguminous plants of the pea kind;

pulse.—**legumin**, leg´ū·min, _n._ A nitrogenous substance obtained from peas; vegetable casein.—**leguminous**, le·gū´mi·nus, _a. bot._, bearing legumes.

lei, lā´i, lā, _n._ pl. **leis**, lā´ēz. [Hawaiian.] A wreath of leaves and flowers, etc., worn about the neck or head.

leister, lēs´tér, _n._ [Icel. _ljóstr_, Sw. _ljustra_, a leister.] A pronged and barbed instrument for striking and taking fish; a salmon spear. (Scotch.)

leisure, lē´zhér or lezh´ér, _n._ [O.E. _leisere_, _leiser_, etc., Fr. _loisir_, from O.Fr. _leisir_, _loisir_ (infin.), from L. _licere_, to be allowed, to be lawful; comp. _pleasure_, which is similarly formed. Akin _license_.] Freedom from occupation or business; vacant time; time free from employment; time which may be appropriated to any specific object.—_At leisure_, free from occupation; not engaged.—_At one's leisure_, at one's ease or convenience. —_a._ Not used or spent in labor or business; vacant: said of time.—**leisurely**, lē´zhér·li or lezh´ér·li, _adv._ Not in haste or hurry; slowly; at leisure.—_a._ Done at leisure; not hasty; deliberate.

leitmotiv, leitmotif, līt˝mō·tēf´, _n._ [G. _leitmotiv_, leading motive.] _Musical drama_, a theme or musical passage which signifies a particular character and recurs with his every appearance.

lemma, lem´ma, _n._ [Gr. _lemma_, from _lambanō_, to receive.] _Math._ a preliminary or preparatory proposition laid down and demonstrated for the purpose of facilitating something more important that follows.

lemming, lem´ing, _n._ [Dan.] A rodent mammal found in Norway, Lapland, Siberia, etc., vast hordes of which periodically migrate toward the sea, destroying all vegetation in their path.

lemon, lem´on, _n._ [Sp. _limon_, It. _limone_, Ar. _laymum_, Hind. _limu_, _limbu_.] A fruit resembling the orange, but having a much more acid pulp, and furnishing a cooling acid juice; the tree that produces lemons; a failure or dud.—_a._ Possessing the color of a lemon.—**lemonade**, lem·on·ād´, _n._ A liquid consisting of lemon juice mixed with water and sweetened.—**lemon yellow**, _n._ A beautiful, vivid, light yellow color.

lemur, lē´mér, _n._ [L., a spectre: so called from its nocturnal habits and stealthy step.] A name of certain small, arboreal, nocturnal mammals, family Lemuroidea, inhabiting Madagascar, allied to monkeys, insectivores, and rodents.—**lemures**, lem´ū·rēz, _n._ The ghosts or spirits of the dead, regarded as mischievous. —**lemuroid**, lem´ū·roid, _a._ Resembling the lemurs; belonging to the family or group of the lemurs.

lend, lend, _v.t._—pret. & pp. _lent_. [A.Sax. _laenan_, to lend, from _laen_, a loan; Icel. _lana_, to lend. LOAN.] To grant to another for temporary use on condition of the thing or its equivalent in kind being returned; to afford, grant, or furnish in general (assistance, an ear to a discourse, etc.);

refl. to accommodate; to give up so as to be of assistance (he _lent himself_ to the scheme); to make a loan to be returned with interest over a period of time.—_v.i._ To make a loan or loans.—**lender**, len´dér, _n._

length, length, _n._ [A.Sax. _length_, from _lang_, long; comp. _strength_, from _strong_. LONG.] The longest measure of any object, in distinction from _depth_, _thickness_, _breadth_, or _width_; extent from end to end; one of the three dimensions of space; distance to a place; a portion of space considered as measured longwise; some definite long measure (to cut a rope into _lengths_); long continuance; duration of any extent in time; detail or amplification in language; extent, degree, height, as in conduct or action (to go to great _lengths_); extent of progress; one of the three fundamental conceptions (corresponding to space) represented by a fundamental unit. United States and British scientific unit, the foot; French, the centimeter.—_At length_, at or in the fullest extent; with amplitude of detail; at last; after a long period; at the end or conclusion. —**lengthen**, leng´thn, _v.t._ To make long or longer; to extend in length (often followed by _out_).—_v.i._ To grow longer.—**lengthily**, leng´thi·li, _adv._ In a lengthy manner.—**lengthiness**, leng´thi·nes, _n._ The state of being lengthy.—**lengthwise**, length´wīz, _adv._ In the direction of the length; in a longitudinal direction.—**lengthy**, leng´thi, _a._ Long or moderately long; protracted, as a _lengthy_ discourse.

lenient, lē´ni·ent, _a._ [L. _leniens_, from _lenio_, to soften, from _lenis_, soft, mild; akin _lentus_, slow (in _relent_).] Softening‡; mitigating‡; acting without rigor or severity; gentle; merciful; clement.—**leniently**, lē´ni·ent·li, _adv._ In a lenient manner.—**lenience**, **leniency**, lē´ni·ens, lē´ni·en·si, _n._ The quality of being lenient; clemency.—**lenitive**, len´i·tiv, _a._ Having the quality of softening or mitigating, as pain; assuasive; emollient.—_n._ A medicine or application of this kind.—**lenity**, len´i·ti, _n._ [L. _lenitas_.] Gentleness; clemency; tenderness; mercy.

lens, lenz, _n._ pl. **lenses**, len´zez. [L. _lens_, a lentil—a convex lens somewhat resembles a lentil seed.] A transparent substance, usually glass, with one or both sides curved so that rays of light passing through it are made to change their direction, and thus cause objects to appear magnified or diminished in size; one of the glasses of a telescope, microscope, etc.; a part of the eye which focuses light rays.

lent, lent, pret. and pp. of _lend_.

Lent, lent, _n._ [A.Sax. _lencten_, spring, _lencten-faesten_, spring fast, Lent; D. _lente_, G. _lenz_, spring; perhaps connected with _long_, the days becoming longer in spring.] A fast of forty days, beginning at Ash Wednesday and continuing till Easter, observed in the Christian Church in commemoration of the forty days' fast of Christ.—**Lenten**, len´ten, _a._ Pertain-

ing to Lent; as meager as the fasting diet of Lent; hence, spare; plain (_lenten_ fare).

lenticel, len´ti·sel, _n._ [Fr. _lenticelle_, L. _lenticula_, dim. of _lens_, _lentis_, a lentil. LENS.] _Bot._ one of the small oval spots found on the surface of young stems; a small lens-shaped gland on the under side of some leaves.—**lenticular**, len·tik´ū·lér, _a._ [L. _lenticularis_.] Resembling a lentil in size or form; having the form of a double-convex lens.—**lentoid**, len´toid, _a._ Of the form of a lens; lenticular.

lentigo, len·tī´gō, _n._ [L. _lentigo_, a freckle, from L. _lens_, _lentis_, a lentil.] _Med._ a freckly eruption on the skin. —**lentiginous**, len·tij´i·nus, _a._ Pertaining to lentigo; freckly; scurfy.

lentil, len´til, _n._ [Fr. _lentille_, from L. _lens_, _lentil_, a lentil. LENS.] An annual pea-like leguminous plant cultivated in Egypt and Palestine from remote antiquity, having seeds used in soups, etc., and forming a very nutritious diet.

lento, len´tō. [It., from L. _lentus_, slow.] _Mus._ a direction that the music is to be performed slowly.

l'envoi, l'envoy, len´voi, _n._ [Fr. ENVOY.] A sort of postscript appended to literary compositions.

Leo, lē´ō, _n._ [L., a lion.] The Lion, the fifth sign of the zodiac.—**Leonides**, lē·on´i·dēz, _n. pl._ A name for the group of meteors observed annually in November, which seem to radiate from the constellation _Leo_.—**leonine**, lē´o·nīn, _a._ [L. _leoninus_.] Belonging to a lion; resembling a lion or partaking of his qualities.—**leoninely**, lē´o·nīn·li, _adv._ In a leonine manner; like a lion.

Leonine, lē´o·nīn, _a._ [From _Leon_ or _Leoninus_, an ecclesiastic of the twelfth century, who wrote largely in this measure.] A term applied to a certain Latin measure popular in the middle ages, consisting of hexameter and pentameter verses, rhyming at the middle and end.

leopard, lep´érd, _n._ [L. _leo_, lion, and _pardus_, a panther.] A carnivorous animal of the cat genus, inhabiting Africa, Iran, China, and India, of a yellowish-fawn color variegated with dark spots.

leotard, lē´o·tärd, _n._ [From _Léotard_, a French aerial gymnast.] A close-fitting garment with or without sleeves worn by acrobats, dancers, etc.; tights.

leper, lep´ér, _n._ [Fr. _lepre_, L. _lepra_, from Gr. _lepra_, leprosy, from _lepros_, scaly, connected with _lepos_, a husk.] A person affected with leprosy; a social outcast.—**leprosy**, lep´ro·si, _n._ An infectious disease characterized by dusky red or livid tubercules on the face, ears, and extremities, thickened or rugose state of the skin, loss of fingers and toes, etc., eventually causing death.—**leprous**, lep´rus, _a._

lepidolite, lep´i·do·līt, _n._ [Gr. _lepis_, _lepidos_, a scale, and _lithos_, a stone.] A mineral found in scaly masses, ordinarily of a violet or lilac color, allied to mica.

lepidopterous, lepidopteral, lep·-

i·dop′tèr·us, lep·i·dop′tèr·al, a. [Gr. *lepis*, a scale, and *pteron*, a wing.] Of or belonging to the order of insects called Lepidoptera (lep·i·dop′tèr·a), comprising the butterflies and moths.

lepidosiren, lep′i·do·sī″ren, n. [Gr. *lepis, lepidos*, a scale, and *seirēn*, a siren.] A fish found in western Africa and South America, having both gills and lungs, and being thus enabled to lie packed in the mud of their native rivers during the dry season. Called also *mudfish*.

lepidote, lep′i·dōt, a. [Gr. *lepidōtos*, scaly, from *lepis*, a scale.] Bot. covered with scurfy scaly spots.

leporine, lep′o·rīn, a. [L. *leporinus*, from *lepus, leporis*, a hare.] Pertaining to a hare; having the qualities of the hare.

lepra, lep′ra, n. [L., leprosy.] Med. a non-contagious skin disease, in which scales occur, generally on the limbs.—**leprose,** lep′rōs, a. Bot. having a scurfy appearance.

leprechaun, lep′ri·kon, n. [Ir. *luprecān, lugharcān*, from Ir. *luchrupān*, from *lu*, little, and *corpān*, dim. of *corp*, body, from L. *corpus*.] *Irish folklore*, a small fairy, thought of as a sly tricky old man who, if caught, will point out a treasure.

leprosy, leprous, etc. See LEPER.

leptodactylous, lep·tō·dak′ti·lus, a. [Gr. *leptos*, slender, *daktylos*, a digit.] Having slender toes.

Lesbian, les′bi·an, a. [Gr. Island of Lesbos.] Addicted to the unnatural vice attributed to Sappho.

lese-majesty, lēz′maj·is·ti, n. [Fr. *lèsemajesté*, high treason, from L. *laesa majestas, laesed, laesum*, to injure, and *majestas*, majesty.] Any crime committed against the sovereign power in a state; treason.

lesion, lē′zhon, n. [L. *laesio*, from *laedo*, to hurt; seen also in *collide, elide*.] Med. injury; a morbid change in the texture or substance of organs.

less, les, a. serving as the comparative of *little*. [A.Sax. *læs, læssa*; O.Fris. *lessa*; allied to Goth. *lasiws*, weak, Icel. *lasinn*, feeble; the superl. *least*. *Little* is from a different root. Hence *lest*.] Smaller; not so large or great.—*adv*. In a smaller or lower degree.—*n*. Not so much; a quantity not so great as another quantity; what is below a certain standard.—*No less*, nothing of inferior consequence or moment; nothing else.—**lessen,** les′n, *v.t*. To make less or smaller; to diminish; to reduce; to reduce in dignity; to depreciate; to disparage.—*v.i*. To become less or smaller; to decrease or diminish.—**lesser,** les′ér, a. [A double compar. from *less*.] Less; smaller; especially common with the definite article, and where there is opposition to *greater*: not used in comparisons with *than*.—*adv*. Less. (*Shak*.)

lessee, les·sē′, n. [LEASE.] The person to whom a lease is given.—**lessor,** les′sor′, n. One who leases or lets to a tenant for a term of years.

lesson, les′n, n. [Fr. *leçon*, from L. *lectio, lectionis*, from L. *lego, lectum*, to read. LEGEND.] Anything read

or recited to a teacher by a pupil or learner; what is assigned by a preceptor to a pupil to be learned at one time; something to be learned; piece of instruction conveyed; what is learned or may be learned from experience; a portion of Scripture read in divine service; a doctrine or notion inculcated; a precept; a reproof or rebuke.

lessor. See LESSEE.

lest, lest, conj. [O.E. *leste*, for *les the*, shortened from A.Sax. *thý, læs the*, the, less that, lest—*thý*, by that (=*the* in the more, etc.), *læs*=less, *the*, indeclinable relative.] For fear that; in case; that . . . not.

let, let, v.t.—*let* (pret. & pp.), *letting*. [A.Sax. *laetan, létan*=D. *laten*, Icel. *láta*, Goth. *letan*, G. *lassen*; allied to E. *late*, and L. *lassus*, weary.] To permit; to allow; to suffer; to give leave; not to prevent; to lease; to grant possession and use of for a compensation.—In such phrases as *let us go, let* often expresses merely a suggestion for mutual action, in *let him go*, etc., it often has the force of a command. (When *let* governs an infinitive the latter never takes *to*.)—*To let alone*, to leave untouched; to suffer to remain without intermeddling.—*To let be*, to suffer to be as at present; to let alone.—*To let blood*, to open a vein and suffer the blood to flow.—*To let down*, to permit to sink or fall; to lower.—*To let drive* or *let fly*, to send forth or discharge with violence, as an arrow, stone, etc.—*To let go*, to allow or suffer to go; to relax hold of anything.—*To let in* or *into*, to permit or suffer to enter; to admit; to place in as an insertion.—*To let loose*, to free from restraint; to permit to wander at large.—*To let off*, to allow to escape; to release, as from a penalty or an engagement; to discharge, as an arrow; to fire, as a gun.—*To let out*, to allow to issue; to suffer to escape; to extend; to lease or let on hire.—*To let slip*, to let go from one's hold; to let loose; to lose (an opportunity) by negligence.—*To let well alone*, to forbear trying to improve what is already satisfactory.—*v.i*. To yield a certain rent by being hired out; to be taken on hire.—*To let in*, to leak; to admit water.

lethal, lē′thal, a. [L. *lethalis, letalis*, mortal, from *letum*, death.] Deadly; mortal; fatal.

lethargy, leth′är·ji, n. [L. *lethargia*, from Gr. *lēthargia*, oblivion, *lēthargos*, forgetful, from *lēthē*, oblivion.] Unnatural sleepiness; morbid drowsiness; profound sleep, from which a person can scarcely be awaked; dullness; inaction; inattention.—**lethargic, lethargical,** le·thär′jik, le·thär′ji·kal, a. Affected with lethargy; morbidly inclined to sleep; dull; heavy; pertaining to lethargy.—**lethargically,** le·thär′ji·kal·li, adv. In a lethargic manner.—**lethargize,** leth′èr·jīz, v.t. To render lethargic.

Lethe, lē′thē, n. [Gr. *lēthē*, forgetfulness; akin L. *lateo*, to lie hid.]

Greek myth. the river of oblivion; one of the streams of the infernal regions; hence, oblivion; a draft of oblivion.—**Lethean,** lē·thē′an, a. Pertaining to the river Lethe; inducing forgetfulness or oblivion.

Lett, let, n. A member of a race inhabiting the Baltic provinces of Russia.—**Lettish, Lettic,** let′ish, let′ik, a. Pertaining to the Letts.—*n*. The language spoken by the Letts, one of the Aryan tongues.

letter, let′ér, n. [Fr. *lettre*, from L. *litera*, a letter.] A mark or character used as the representative of a sound; a character standing for a vowel or a consonant; a written or printed message; an epistle; *printing*, a single type or character; also types collectively; *pl*. learning; erudition (a man of *letters*).—*The letter*, neither more nor less than what words literally express; the literal or verbal meaning.—*v.t*. To impress or form letters on (to *letter* a book).—**letter carrier,** n. A man who carries about and delivers letters; a postman.—**letterhead,** n. A heading engraved on stationery; paper having such engraving.—**lettering,** let′ér·ing, n. The act of impressing letters; the letters impressed.—**letterpress,** n. Words impressed by types; print.

Lettish, Lettic, a. and n. See LETT.

lettuce, let′is, n. [From L. *lactuca*, a lettuce; from *lac, lactis*, milk (as in *lacteal*).] The popular name of several species of annual composite plants, the leaves of some of which are used as salads.

leucine, leucin, lū′sin, n. [Gr. *leukos*, white.] A white pulverulent substance obtained by treating muscular fiber with sulfuric acid, and afterward with alcohol.—**leucite,** lū′sīt, n. A mineral, so called from its whiteness, found among volcanic products.

leucocyte, lūk′o·sīt, n. [Gr. *leukos*, white, *kytos*, a cell.] A white or colorless blood corpuscle.—**leucocytosis,** lūk′o·sīt·ō″sis, n. [Gr. *leukos, kytos*.] An increase in the number of leucocytes in the blood, esp. as in certain pathologic conditions: fevers, anemia, etc.—**leukemia,** lū·kē′mia, n. [Gr. *leukos*, white, *kytos*, a cell, and *haima*, blood.] Med. A fatal disease in which there is a pronounced increase in the number of leucocytes, attended by progressive anemia and complications.

leucoma, lū·kō′ma, n. [Gr. *leukōma*, from *leukos*, white.] A white opacity of the cornea of the eye, the result of acute inflammation.

leucorrhea, lū·ko·rē′a, n. [Gr. *leukos*, and *rheo*, to flow.] Med. a morbid discharge of a white or yellowish mucus from the female genital organs; the whites.

Levant, le·vant′, n. [It. *levante*, the east, the direction of sunrise, from L. *levare*, to raise, *se levare*, to rise. LEVITY.] The eastern portion of the Mediterranean and its seaboard or the contiguous countries, as Syria, Asia Minor, Egypt, etc.—**Levanter,** le·van′tèr, n. A wind in the Mediterranean from the direction of the

Levant.—**Levantine,** le·van'tin or lev'an·tīn, _a._ Pertaining to the Levant.—_n._ A native of the Levant; [_not cap._] a particular kind of silk cloth.

levant, le·vant', _v.i._ [Sp. _levantar,_ to raise, to remove; _levantar la casa,_ to break up house—from L. _levare,_ to raise. See above.] To run away; to decamp; to run away without paying debts.—**levanter,** le·van'tẽr, _n._ One who levants.

levator, le·vā'tẽr, _n._ [L., what raises, from _levo,_ to raise.] _Anat._ a name applied to many muscles, such as raise the lips, eyelids, etc.; a surgical instrument used to raise a depressed part of the skull.

levee, lev'ē, _n._ [Fr. _lever,_ a rising, a levee or reception; _levée,_ a levy, an embankment. from _lever,_ L. _levare,_ to raise, from _levis,_ light. LEVITY.] A morning reception of visitors held by a prince or great personage; any similar assemblage; in America, an embankment on the margin of a river, to confine it within its natural channel.

level, lev'el, _n._ [O.Fr. _level, livel_ (now _niveau_), from L. _libella,_ dim. of _libra,_ a level, a balance; akin _deliberate, equilibrium._] An instrument by which to find or draw a straight line parallel to the plane of the horizon; a line or surface which coincides with the plane of the horizon; a surface without inequalities; usual elevation; customary height; equal elevation with something else; a state of equality; natural position; position to which anything is entitled; _mining,_ a horizontal gallery in a mine.—_a._ Horizontal; coinciding with the plane of the horizon, or parallel to it; not having one part higher than another; even; flat; on the same line or plane; equal in rank or degree; having no degree of superiority; well-balanced; steady; honest; fair in dealings; trustworthy. —_v.t._—_leveled, leveling._ To make level; to remove inequalities of surface in; to bring to ground level; to reduce to equality of condition, state, or degree; to point, in taking aim; to aim; to direct or point at.— _v.i._ To bring to a level; to deal frankly with.—_v.i._ To point a gun or the like at the mark; to aim.— **leveler,** lev'el·ẽr, _n._ One who levels; one who would destroy social and political distinctions, in advocating equality.—**level-headed,** _a._ Of sound judgment.—**leveling,** lev'el·ing, _n._ The act of one who levels; the art or operation of ascertaining the different elevations of objects on the surface of the earth, as in surveying. —**leveling pole, leveling rod, leveling staff,** _n._ An instrument used in leveling in conjunction with a spirit level and telescope.—**levelly,** lev'el·li, _adv._ In a level manner; evenly.—**levelness,** lev'el·nes, _n._ The condition of being level; evenness.

lever, lē'vẽr, _n._ [Fr. _levier,_ from _lever,_ L. _levare,_ to raise. LEVITY.] A bar of metal, wood, or other substance turning on a support called the fulcrum or prop, and used to over-

come a certain resistance (called the weight), encountered at one part of the bar, by means of a force (called the power) applied at another part; a watch having a vibrating lever to connect the action of the escape wheel with that of the balance.—**leverage,** lē'vẽr·ij, _n._ The action of a lever; lever power; the mechanical advantage or power gained by using a lever.

leveret, lev'ẽr·et, _n._ [Fr. _levrette,_ dim. of O.Fr. _levre_ (now _lièvre_), a hare, from L. _lepus, leporis,_ a hare.] A hare in the first year of its age.

leviable. See LEVY.

leviathan, le·vī'a·than, _n._ [Heb. _livyāthān,_ a long jointed monster.] An aquatic animal described in the book of Job, ch. xli; a fabulous sea monster of immense size; a large political state run by a totalitarian bureaucracy and the machinery of coercion; something large and formidable.

levigate, lev'i·gāt, _v.t._—_levigated, levigating._ [L. _lævigo,_ from _lævis,_ smooth.] To make smooth; to polish; to rub or grind to a fine impalpable powder, especially with the use of a liquid.—**levigation,** lev·i·gā'shon, _n._ The operation of grinding or rubbing a solid substance to a fine impalpable powder.

levirate, leviratical, lev'i·rāt, lev·i·rat'i·kal, _a._ [L. _levir,_ a husband's brother; akin Gr. _daēr._] Pertaining to marriage with a husband's brother; applied to the Jewish law according to which a woman whose husband died without issue was to be married to the husband's brother. —**leviration,** lev·i·rā'shon, _n._ Marriage according to the levirate law.

levitate, lev'i·tāt, _v.t._ [L. _levitas,_ lightness, from _levis,_ light.] To cause to become buoyant in the atmosphere; to cause to float in the air.— **levitation,** lev·i·tā'shon, _n._ The act of making light or buoyant; lightness; buoyancy.

Levite, lē'vīt, _n._ [From _Levi,_ one of the sons of Jacob.] In _Jewish history,_ one of the tribe or family of Levi; a descendant of Levi; more particularly, an inferior or subordinate priest.—**Levitical,** le·vit'i·kal, _a._ Belonging to or connected with the Levites; priestly.—_Levitical degrees,_ degrees of kindred within which persons are prohibited (in the book of Leviticus) to marry.—**Leviticus,** le·vit'i·kus, _n._ A book of the Old Testament containing the ceremonial law or the laws and regulations relating to the priests and Levites and to offerings.

levity, lev'i·ti, _n._ [L. _levitas,_ from _levis,_ light; akin to E. _light,_ G. _leicht,_ easy, slight, Gr. _elachys,_ small. L. _levis_ gives _lever, levy, elevate, alleviate, relieve,_ etc.] Lightness; especially lightness of temper or conduct; want of seriousness; disposition to trifle; fickleness; capriciousness; volatility.

levogyrate, lē·vo·jī'rāt, _a._ [L. _lævus,_ left, _gyro,_ to turn. GYRE.] Turning rays to the left in the polarization of light: said of crystals; opposite of

dextrogyrate.

levulose, lev'ū·lōs, _n._ [L. _lævus,_ left, and _ule_ and _ose._] Fructose; fruit sugar, $C_6H_{12}O_6$, obtained from honey and most sweet fruits.

levy, lev'i, _n._ [Fr. _levée,_ from _lever,_ L. _levare,_ to raise. LEVITY, LEVEE.] The act of raising, collecting, or enlisting troops; the raising of taxes; that which is levied; a body of troops raised.—_v.t._—_levied, levying._ To raise or enlist (troops); to collect (taxes).—_To levy war,_ to raise or begin war; to raise troops for attack. —**leviable,** lev'i·a·bl, _a._ Capable of being levied.—**levier,** lev'i·ẽr, _a._ One who levies.

lewd, lūd, _a._ [O.E. _lewed,_ A.Sax. _laewed,_ lay, ignorant, pp. of _laewan,_ to weaken, to betray; akin Icel. _læ,_ Goth. _lew,_ craft.] Vile, despicable, profligate, or wicked (_N.T._); given or pertaining to the unlawful indulgence of lust; lustful; libidinous; lascivious.—**lewdly,** lūd'li, _adv._ In a lewd manner.—**lewdness,** lūd'nes, _n._ The state or quality of being lewd; lechery; lasciviousness.

Lewis machine gun, lū'is ma·shēn' gun, _n._ An automatic rifle, gas-operated and air-cooled, capable of firing forty-seven rounds without reloading.

lexicon, lek'si·kon, _n._ [Gr. _lexicon,_ from _lexis,_ a speaking, speech, a word, from _lego,_ to speak. LEGEND.] A dictionary; a book containing an alphabetical arrangement of the words in a language, with the definition or an explanation of the meaning of each; usually applied to dictionaries of the Greek or Hebrew tongues.—**lexical,** lek'si·kal, _a._ Pertaining to a lexicon.—**lexicographer,** lek·si·kog'ra·fẽr, _n._ The author or compiler of a lexicon or dictionary.— **lexicographic, lexicographical,** lek'si·ko·graf"ik, lek'si·ko·graf"i·kal, _a._ Pertaining to lexicons or lexicography.—**lexicography,** lek·si·kog'ra·fi, _n._ The act or art of compiling a lexicon or dictionary; the occupation of composing dictionaries.—**lexigraphic, lexigraphical,** lek·si·graf'ik, lek·si·graf'i·kal, _a._ Pertaining to lexigraphy.

Leyden jar, lī'dn, _n._ [So named from having been invented at _Leyden,_ Holland.] A glass phial or jar coated inside and outside, usually with tinfoil, to within a third of the top, that it may be readily charged with electricity.

leze majesty, lez'maj·is·ti, _n._ See LESE-MAJESTY.

liable, lī'a·bl, _a._ [Either from the verb to _lie,_ with the sense of lying open or subject to, or from Fr. _lier,_ to bind, and hence akin to _ally, lien._ Comp. _rely_ and _reliable._] Answerable for consequences; bound to make good a loss; responsible; apt or not unlikely to incur something undesirable; subject; exposed; with _to._ ∴_Liable_ is used chiefly with regard to what may befall; _subject_ to what is likely to do so, and does so customarily.—**liability,** lī·a·bil'i·ti, _n._ The state of being liable; that for which one is liable; _pl._ sums or amounts which one is under obligation to pay; debts.—*Limited Liability.*—See LIMITED.

liaison, lē·ā·zoń′, n. [Fr., from L. *ligatio,* a binding, from L. *ligare,* to bind. LIGAMENT.] A bond of union; an entanglement; commonly, an illicit intimacy between a man and a woman.—*Liaison officer,* an officer employed in linking up troops under different commands.

liana, li·ä′na, n. [Fr. *liane,* from *lier,* L. *ligare,* to bind; akin *lien.* LIAISON.] A term applied to the larger climbing and twining plants in tropical forests.

liar, lī′ėr, n. See LIE.

Lias, lī′as, n. [Fr. *liais,* O.Fr. *liois,* Arm. *liach,* Gael. *leac,* a stone.] *Geol.* that series of strata, consisting principally of thin layers of limestone embedded in thick masses of blue argillaceous clay, lying at the basis of the oölitic series, and above the triassic or new red sandstone.

libation, li·bā′shon, n. [L. *libatio, libationis,* from *libō,* to taste, to make libation; Gr. *leibō;* same root as *liquid.*] The act of pouring a liquid, usually wine, either on the ground or on a victim in sacrifice, in honor of some deity; a portion of wine or other liquor poured out in honor of a deity by the person who is to drink.

libel, lī′bel, n. [Fr. *libelle,* L. *libellus,* a libel or lampoon, lit. a little book, dim. of *liber,* the inner bark or rind of a tree used for paper, and hence a book; akin *library.*] A defamatory writing; a malicious publication containing representations tending to bring a person into contempt, or expose him to public hatred or derision; *law,* the writ commencing a suit and containing the plaintiff's allegations.—*v.t.*—**libeled,** **libeling.** To publish a libel against; to defame by libel; to lampoon.—**libelant,** lī′bel·ant, n. One who brings a libel in a court.—**libeler,** lī′bel·ėr, n. One who libels; a lampooner.—**libelous,** lī′bel·us, a. Containing matter of the nature of a libel; defamatory.—**libelously,** lī′bel·us·li. adv. In a libelous manner.

liberal, lib′ėr·al, a. [L. *liberalis,* from *liber,* free; akin to *libet, lubet,* it pleases, it is agreeable, Skr. *lubh,* to desire. L. *liber* gives also *liberate, liberty, libertine, livery, deliver.*] Befitting a freeman or one wellborn (the *liberal* arts, a *liberal* education); of a free heart; bountiful; generous; giving largely, ample, large, abundant, profuse (donation, supply, etc.); not characterized by selfish, narrow, or contracted ideas or feelings; favorable to civil, political, and religious liberty; favorable to reform or progress, and in politics often opposed to *conservative;* not too literal or strict; free. It is used in various self-explanatory compounds; as, *liberal*-hearted; *liberal*-minded; *liberal*-souled.—n. An advocate of freedom from restraint, especially in politics and religion; a member of that party which advocates progressive reform.—*Lib-*

eral Arts, the modern curriculum of an undergraduate academic or collegiate education, as distinguished from professional training; the languages, science, history and philosophy which are the requisites for a baccalaureate degree.—**liberalism,** lib′ėr·al·izm, n. Liberal principles; the principles or practice of Liberals.—**liberality,** lib·ėr·al′i·ti, n. [L. *liberalitas;* Fr. *liberalité.*] The quality of being liberal; largeness of mind or view; disposition to give largely; munificence; generosity; a particular act of generosity (in this sense with a plural).—**liberalize,** lib′ėr·al·īz, v.t. —*liberalized, liberalizing.* To render liberal; to free from narrow views or prejudices.—**liberally,** lib′ėr·al·li, adv. In a liberal manner.

liberate, lib′ėr·āt, v.t.—*liberated, liberating.* [L. *libero, liberatum,* from *liber,* free. LIBERAL.] To release from restraint or bondage; to set at liberty; to free; to deliver; to disengage.—**liberation,** lib·ėr·ā·shon, n. [L. *liberatio.*] The act of liberating.—**liberator,** lib′ėr·ā·tėr, n. One who liberates.

libertarian. See LIBERTY.

liberticide, lib′ėr·ti·sīd, n. [*Liberty,* and L. *cædo,* to kill.] Destruction of liberty; a destroyer of liberty.

libertine, lib′ėr·tēn, n. [L. *libertinus,* a freedman, from *liber,* free. LIBERAL.] A freedman or manumitted slave (N.T.); one unconfined; one free from restraint (Shak.); one who indulges his lust without restraint; one who leads a dissolute, licentious life; a rake.—a. Licentious; dissolute.—**libertinism,** lib′ėr·tin·izm, n. The conduct of a libertine or rake.

liberty, lib′ėr·ti, n. [Fr. *liberté,* L. *libertas,* from *liber,* free. LIBERAL.] The state or condition of one who is free; exemption from restraint; power of acting as one pleases; freedom; permission granted to do something; leave; immunity enjoyed; a special privilege or exemption; a place or district within which certain exclusive privileges may be exercised; freedom of action or speech beyond the ordinary bounds of civility or decorum; freedom from occupation or engagements; state of being disengaged.—*Liberty of the press,* the free power of publishing what one pleases, subject only to punishment for publishing what is mischievous to the public or injurious to individuals. —*Cap of liberty,* a cap or hat used as a symbol of liberty; a red cap worn by French revolutionaries. ∴ Syn. See LEAVE.—**libertarian,** lib·ėr·tā′ri·an, a. Pertaining to the doctrine of free will, as opposed to the doctrine of necessity.—n. One who holds the doctrine of the freedom of the will.—**libertarianism,** lib·ėr·tā′ri·an·izm, n. The principles or doctrines of libertarians.

libidinous, li·bid′i·nus, a. [L. *libidinosus,* from *libido, lubido,* lust, from *libet, lubet,* it pleases. LIBERAL.] Characterized by lust or lewdness; having an eager appetite for sexual indulgence; fitted to excite lustful

desire; lustful; lewd.—**libidinously,** li·bid′i·nus·li, adv. In a libidinous manner.—**libidinousness,** li·bid′i·nus·nes, n. The quality of being libidinous; lustfulness.

Libra, lī′bra, n. [L., a balance.] The Balance, the seventh sign in the zodiac, which the sun enters at the autumnal equinox in September.

library, lī′bra·ri, n. [L. *librarium,* a bookcase, *libraria,* a bookseller's shop, from *liber,* a book. LIBEL.] A collection of books belonging to a private person or to a public institution, etc.; an apartment, suite of apartments, or a whole building appropriated to the keeping of a collection of books.—**librarian,** lī·brā′ri·an, n. The keeper of a library.

librate, lī′brāt, v.t.—*librated, librating.* [L. *libro, libratum,* from *libra,* a balance, a level. LEVEL.] To hold in equipoise; to poise; to balance.—*v.i.* To balance; to be poised.—**libration,** lī·brā′shon, n. The act of balancing; a state of equipoise; *astron.* a real or apparent motion like that of a balance before coming to rest; an apparent irregularity of the moon's motion, whereby those parts very near the border of the lunar disk alternately become visible and invisible.—**libratory,** lī′bra·to·ri, a.

libretto, lē·bret′tō, n. [It., a little book. LIBEL, LIBRARY.] A book containing the words of an extended musical composition, as an opera; the musical text itself.—**librettist,** li·bret′ist, n.

lice, līs, n. pl. of louse.

license, lī′sens, n. [Fr. *license,* from L. *licentia,* from *licet,* it is permitted (seen also in *illicit, leisure*); akin to *linquo,* to leave.] Authority given to act in a particular way; power conferred upon a person by proper authority, to do particular acts, practice in professions, conduct certain trades, etc.; the document containing such authority; excess of liberty; undue freedom; freedom abused or used in contempt of law or decorum; deviation from an artistic standard.—**license,** v.t.—*licensed, licensing.* To permit or empower by license; to grant a license to.—**licensee,** lī·sen·sē′, n. One to whom a license is granted.—**licenser,** lī′sen·sėr, n. One who licenses.—**licentiate,** li·sen′shi·āt, n. One who has a license to practice some profession; a person licensed in medicine or theology; in Scottish church, one licensed but not ordained to a charge; a probationer; corresponding largely to the French *abbé.*—**licentious,** li·sen′shus, a. [L. *licentiosus.*] Characterized by license; overpassing due bounds; loose in behavior; profligate; dissolute; libidinous.—**licentiously,** li·sen′shus·li, adv. In a licentious manner.—**licentiousness,** li·sen′shus·nes, n.

lichen, lī′ken, n. [Gr. *leichēn,* the plant, the disease, from *leichō,* to lick.] *Bot.* one of the group of thallophyte plants, a fungus and alga in symbiotic association, growing on the bark of trees, etc., and including

---

fāte, fär, fâre, fat, fäll; mē, met, hėr; pīne, pin; nōte, not, mōve; tūbe, tub, bụll; oil, pound.

rock moss, tree moss, etc.; *med.* an eruption of small pimples, of a red or white color, clustered together or spread over the surface of the skin.—**lichenous,** lī′ken•us or lich′-en•us, *a.* Relating to or covered with lichens; pertaining to the disease called lichen.

lich gate, lich′gāt, *n.* [Lit. corpsegate, from A.Sax. *lic,* Icel. *lik,* Goth. *leik,* form, body; G. *leiche,* a corpse. Akin *like.*] A church-yard gate, with a porch under which a bier might stand while the introductory part of the service was read.

licit,† lis′it, *a.* [L. *licitus,* lawful, from *liceo,* to be permitted. LICENSE.] Lawful.—**licitly,**† lis′it•li, *adv.* Lawfully.

lick, lik, *v.t.* [A.Sax. *liccian*=D. *likken,* Dan. *likke,* G. *lecken,* Goth. *laigon* (in *bilaigon*); cog. Ir. *lighim,* L. *lingo,* Gr. *leichō,* Skr. *lih,* to lick. Akin *lecher, lickerish.*] To pass or draw the tongue over the surface of; to lap; to take in by the tongue; to flog, beat, or conquer (*colloq.*).— *To lick up,* to devour; to consume entirely (O.T.).—*To lick the dust,* to be slain; to perish in battle; to act abjectly and servilely.—*To lick into shape,* to give form or method to, from the old notion that the young bear is born shapeless and its mother licks it into shape.—*n.* A rubbing or drawing of the tongue over anything; a slight smear or coat, as of paint; a blow or stroke (*colloq.*).—**lickspit,** lik′spit, *n.* A flatterer or parasite of the most abject character.

lickerish, lik′ėr•ish, *a.* [From the stem *lick,* and akin to *lecher, lecherous*; comp. G. *lecker,* lickerish, dainty, delicate.] Nice in the choice of food; dainty; eager to taste or enjoy; appetizing.—**lickerishness,** lik′ėr•ish•nes, *n.* The quality of being lickerish.

licorice, lik′or•is, *n.* [Fr. *liquerice,* [L.L. *liquiritia,* from Gr. *glykyr-rhiza*—*glykys,* sweet, and *rhiza,* root.] A perennial plant of the bean family, the roots of which supply a sweet juice.

lictor, lik′tor, *n.* [L., from *ligare,* to bind.] A Roman officer whose ensigns of office were an ax and fasces, and who attended the chief magistrates in public.

lid, lid, *n.* [A.Sax. *hlid,* lid, cover, protection; D. *lid,* O.Fris. *hlid, lid,* G. *lied,* as in *augen-lied,* an eyelid; Icel. *hlith,* a gate, gateway, interval; allied to L. *claudo,* to shut.] A movable cover for the opening of a vessel, box, etc.; the cover of the eye; the eyelid.—**lidless,** lid′les, *a.* Having no lid.

lie, lī, *v.i.*—*lied, lying.* [A.Sax. *leógan* =D. *liegen,* Goth. *liugan,* Icel. *ljúga,* G. *lügen,* to lie; comp. Gael. *leog,* idle talk.] To utter falsehood with an intention to deceive; to knowingly utter untruth.—*n.* [A. Sax. *lige, lyge,* a lie, from *leógan,* to lie; acel. *lygi,* D. *logen,* G. *lüge,* a lie.] A falsehood uttered for the purpose of deception; an intentional violation of truth.—*To give the lie to,*

to charge with falsehood; to prove to be false; to belie.—**liar,** lī′ėr, *n.* One who lies or tells lies; a person who knowingly utters falsehood; one who declares to be a fact what he knows is not.

lie, lī, *v.i.*—*pret. lay; pp. lain* (*lien,* obsolete); *ppr. lying.* [A.Sax. *licgan,* to lie (of which *lecgan,* to lay, is a causative)=Goth. *ligan,* D. *liggen,* Dan. *ligge,* acel. *liggja,* G. *liegen,* to lie; same root as L. *lectus,* Gr. *lechos,* a bed, also seen in L. *lex,* E. *law; ledge, layer, lair,* etc., being also akin.] To occupy a horizontal or nearly horizontal position; to rest lengthwise, or be flat upon the surface of anything; to be placed and remain without motion; to lay or place one's self in a horizontal or nearly horizontal position: often with *down;* to be in bed; to sleep or pass the night; to lean or recline; to be situated; to have place or position (Ireland *lies* west of England); to be posted or encamped, as an army; to remain or be in some condition : with words denoting the particular condition (to *lie* waste, to *lie* fallow, to *lie* open, to *lie* hid, etc.); to be present or contained; to be found; to exist; to depend (it does not *lie in* my power; success *lies* in vigilance); to weigh or press; to be sustainable in law; to be capable of being maintained (an action will not *lie*).—*To lie at one's heart,* to be an object of affection, desire, or anxiety.—*To lie by,* to rest untouched or unnoticed.—*To lie hard* or *heavy,* to press; to oppress; to burden.—*To lie in,* to be in childbed.—*To lie in the way,* to be an obstacle or impediment.— *To lie in wait,* to wait in ambush or concealment.—*To lie on* or *upon,* to be incumbent on; to be a matter of obligation or duty; to depend on. —*To lie on hand, to lie on one's hands,* to be or remain unsold or undisposed of.—*To lie over,* to remain for future attention; to be deferred to some future occasion, as a motion or resolution in a deliberate assembly.—*To lie to, naut.* to stop in her course and remain stationary, as a ship.—*To lie under,* to be subject to; to suffer; to be oppressed by.—*To lie with,* to lodge or sleep with; to have carnal knowledge of; to belong to (it *lies with* you to make amends). [The trans. verb *to lay* is often erroneously used for *to lie.* This is a gross blunder which should be carefully avoided, and may easily be so by attending to the meaning and conjugation of the two verbs. *To lay* is always transitive, and has for its preterit *laid*; as, he told me to *lay* it down, and I *laid* it down. Hence it is utterly wrong to say, we must know how the land *lays*; I went and *laid* down for a little.]—*n.* The relative position of one object with regard to another or to a point of the compass; general bearing or direction; position or state of an affair; *geol.* the manner in which strata are disposed.

lied, lēt, lēd, *n.* pl. **lieder,** lē′dėr. [G.] A German song, lyric, or lay.

liege, lēj, *a.* [Fr. *lige,* Pr. *litje,* It. *ligio,* L.L. *ligius, legius*; origin uncertain; perhaps O.G. *lidic* (G. *ledig*), free.] Connected by loyalty or duty; bound by or resting on feudal ties (a *liege* lord, *liege* vassalage).—*n.* A vassal or person owing duties to his feudal lord; a lord or superior; a sovereign; a law-abiding citizen or citizen in general (in this sense usually in the *pl.*).—**liege man,** lēj′man, *n.* A vassal; a liege.

lien, lē′en, *n.* [Fr. *lien,* from L. *ligamen,* from *ligo,* to bind. LIGA-MENT.] *Law,* a legal claim; a right in one man to retain the property of another until some claim of the former is paid or satisfied.

lientery, lī′en•tėr•i, *n.* [Gr. *leienteria* —*leios,* smooth, and *enteron,* an intestine.] *Med.* a species of diarrhea, in which the food is discharged undigested.—**lienteric,** lī•en•tėr′ik, *a.* Pertaining to a lientery.

lieu, lū, *n.* [Fr., from L. *locus,* place.] Place; room; stead; preceded by *in* (to give goods *in lieu* of wages).

lieutenant, lū•ten′ant, *n.* [Fr., composed of *lieu,* L. *locus,* place, and *tenant,* L. *tenens,* holding.] An officer, civil or military, who supplies the place of a superior in his absence; a commissioned officer in the army, ranking next below a captain; in the navy the ranking is: ensign, lieutenant junior grade, lieutenant, lieutenant commander, commander.— **lieutenancy,** lū•ten′an•si, *n.* The office or commission of a lieutenant. —**lieutenant colonel,** *n.* An army officer next in rank below a colonel.— **lieutenant general,** *n.* An army officer next in rank below a general. —**lieutenant governor,** *n.* An officer ranking next below a governor.

life, līf, *n.* pl. **lives,** līvz. [A.Sax. *lif,* acel. *lif,* Dan. *liv,* D. *lijf,* Goth. *libains,* life. LIVE.] That state of an animal or a plant in which its organs are capable of performing their functions, or in which the performance of functions has not permanently ceased; animate existence; vitality; the time during which such a state continues; the period during which anything continues to exist; outward manifestation of life; a person's condition or circumstances; mode, manner, or course of living, as morally good or bad; social surroundings and characteristics (high or low *life*); that which makes alive; animating or inspiring principle; animation; vivacity; energy; the living form, or nature itself, in opposition to a copy or imitation; a living person (many *lives* were sacrificed); collectively, human beings in any number (a great loss of *life*); animated beings in the aggregate (the abundance of *life* on the globe); narrative of a person's life; a biography or memoir; human affairs; course of things in the world; happiness in the favor of God; eternal felicity; phase or aspect of a creature's existence (adult *life,* sex *life*); the period of existence of a thing (*life* of a car); one inspiring animation and vigor (the *life* of the party).—*For life*, for the whole term of one's existence. —**lifeblood,** *n.* The blood necessary to life; vital blood; that which is essential to existence or strength.— **lifeboat,** *n.* A boat for saving shipwrecked people; a small boat carried by ships for emergency use.—**life buoy,** *n.* See BUOY.—**life cycle,** *n.* A series of activities including development, changes of environment, dormancy and return to original status, experienced by various organisms.—**life expectancy,** *n.* The probable life span of an individual or class of persons, determined by a study of their heredity and environment.—**lifeguard,** *n.* A skilled swimmer employed at a beach to save bathers from drowning.—**life history,** *n.* Account of the activity and environment of an individual from birth to death.—**lifeless,** *lif´les, a.* Deprived of life; dead; inanimate; inorganic; destitute of life or spirit; spiritless; dull; heavy; inactive.— **lifelessly,** *lif´les·li, adv.*—**lifelessness,** *lif´les·nes, n.*—**lifelike,** *lif´lik, a.* Like a living person; true to the life.— **lifeline,** *n.* A rope projected to a foundering ship, or to a drowning person; a line by which a diver is kept in touch with the surface; an indispensable sea, land, or air transportation route.—**lifelong,** *lif´long, a.* Lasting or continuing through life. —**life preserver,** *n.* A buoyant jacket, belt, or similar device worn to prevent drowning.—**lifesaver,** *n.* One who saves a life; a lifeguard; a life preserver.—**lifesaving,** *n.*—**lifetime,** *lif´tim, n.* The time that life continues; duration of life; *phys.* the average time between the appearance and disappearance of an ion or subatomic particle.

lift, lift, *v.t.* [From O.E. *lift,* A.Sax. *lyft,* air, sky; comp. Icel. *lypta* (pron. *lifta*), from *lopt* (pron. *loft*), air; Sw. *lyfta,* Dan. *löfte,* G. *lüften,* to lift, from Sw. Dan. and G. *luft,* air, atmosphere. LURE.] To bring from a lower to a higher position or place; to raise, elevate, upheave; to elevate, exalt, or improve, as in fortune, estimation, dignity, or rank; to elate; often with *up*; to take and carry away; to remove by stealing (to *lift* cattle).— *To lift up the eyes,* to look; to raise the eyes in order to look.—*To lift the hand,* to raise the hand for the purpose of striking; to strike or threaten to strike.—*To lift the hand against,* to strike; to assail; to injure; to oppress.—*To lift up the voice,* to cry aloud; to call out, either in grief or joy.—*v.i.* To raise or try to raise; to rise, or to be raised or elevated (the fog *lifts*).—*n.* The act or manner of raising or lifting; elevation; the act of stealing; *aeronautics,* the component of the force exerted by the air on an airfoil, being opposite the force of gravity and causing an aircraft to stay in the air; a conveyor that carries people up a mountain (a ski *lift*); an elevating

influence.—**lifter,** lif´tėr, *n.*—**lift-off,** *n.* A take-off by an aircraft or a missile.

ligament, lig´a·ment, *n.* [L. *ligamentum,* from *ligo,* to bind (whence also *ligation, ligature, lien, league, -ly* in *ally,* etc.).] What ties or unites one thing or part to another; a band; a bond; a strong flexible fastening; *anat.* a strong, compact, tendinous substance, serving to bind one bone to another.—**ligamentous,** lig·a·men´tus, *a.* Of the nature of a ligament.

ligan, li´gan, *n.* [Contr. for *ligamen,* a band, from *ligo,* to bind.] Goods sunk in the sea, but having something buoyant attached to mark their position.

ligation, li´ga´shon, *n.* [L. *ligatio, ligationis.* LIGAMENT.] The act of binding; a bond; a ligature.— **ligature,** lig´a·chėr, *n.* [L. *ligatura.*] Something that binds; a cord, thong, band, or bandage; a ligament; the act of binding; *mus.* a line connecting notes; *printing,* a type consisting of two or more letters or characters cast on the same body, as *fi, fl; surg.* a cord or string for tying blood vessels to prevent hemorrhage.

light, lit, *n.* [A.Sax. *leóht,* bright, shining, *leóht, liht,* a light; D. and G. *licht,* Icel. *ljos,* Dan. *lys,* Goth. *liuhath;* allied to L. *lux, lumen,* light, *luceo,* to shine, *luna,* the moon; Gr. *leukos,* white, *leassō,* to see; W. *llug,* Gael. *leus,* light. LUCID.] That agent or force by the action of which upon the organs of sight objects from which it proceeds are rendered visible; that phenomenon which makes vision possible, traveling 186,326 miles per second; a radiant body, as the sun, the moon, a candle, etc.; mental or spiritual illumination; knowledge; information; a person who is conspicuous or eminent in any study; a model or example; the phenomenon constituting day, hence, open view, public observation, publicity; a compartment of a window; the illuminated part of an object or picture; the point of view or position in which or from which anything is looked at or considered; aspect.—*Northern lights,* the aurora borealis. See AURORA.—*To stand in one's own light,* to be the means of preventing one's own good, or frustrating one's own purposes.—*To bring to light,* to bring to knowledge, detection, or discovery.—*To come to light,* to be detected; to be discovered or found. —*a.* Bright; clear; not dark or obscure; white or whitish; not intense or deep, as a color; not dark in hue.—*v.t.*—pret. & pp. *lighted,* sometimes *lit.* To set fire to; to kindle; to ignite; to set burning; to give light to; to fill or spread over with light; to show the way to by means of a light; to illuminate.—**lighten,** li´tn, *v.i.* To exhibit the phenomenon of lightning; to give out flashes; to flash; to become lighter; to become less dark or gloomy; to clear.—*v.t.* To make

light or clear; to dissipate darkness from; to illuminate; to enlighten; to flash forth.†—**lighter,** li´tėr, *n.* One who or that which lights.— **lighthouse,** lit´hous, *n.* A tower or other lofty structure with a powerful light at top, erected as a guide or warning of danger to navigators at night.—**lighting,** lit´ing, *n.* Illumination; the disposition of light in a work of art, as a painting or a play; artificial light, either direct or indirect; the fixture supplying light. —**lightless,** lit´les, *a.*—**lightness,** lit´nes, *n.*—**lightning,** lit´ning, *n.* A flash of light, the result of a discharge of atmospheric electricity.—**lightning bug,** *n.* A firefly.—**lightning rod,** *n.* A metallic rod attached to buildings or vessels to protect them from lightning by conducting it into the earth or water.—**lightship,** *n.* A ship anchored and hoisting a strong light to serve as a lighthouse.—**lightsome,** lit´sum, *a.* Bright; light; gay; cheering.—**lightsomely,** lit´sum·li, *adv.*— **lightsomeness,** lit´sum·nes, *n.*—**light year,** *n.* The distance light can travel in a year, about 5,880,000,000,000 miles, used to measure stellar distances.

light, lit, *a.* [A.Sax. *leóht,* D. *ligt,* G. *leicht,* Icel. *léttr,* Dan. *let,* light; allied to L. *levis* (whence *levity*), Gr. *elachys,* Skr. *laghu,* light. Hence *alight, lighter* (boat), *lights.*] Not heavy; having little weight; not burdensome; easy to be lifted, borne, or carried; not oppressive; easy to be suffered or endured; easy to be performed; not difficult; easy to be digested; not oppressive to the stomach; not heavily armed, or armed with light weapons; swift; nimble; not dense or gross; not strong; not copious or vehement (a *light* rain); inconsiderable; easily influenced by trifling considerations; unsteady; volatile; trifling; gay; airy; wanton; unchaste; not of legal weight (*light* coin); loose; sandy; easily pulverized (a *light* soil); having a sensation of giddiness; employed in light work (a *light* porter).—*To set light by,* to slight; to treat as of no importance.—*To make light of,* to treat as of little consequence; to slight; to disregard.—**lighten,** li´tn, *v.t.* To make lighter or less heavy; to relieve of a certain amount of weight; to make less burdensome or oppressive; to alleviate.—**lighter,** li´tėr, *n.* A large open flat-bottomed barge, often used in lightening or unloading and loading ships.—**lightfingered,** *a.* Thievish; addicted to petty thefts; often applied to pickpockets.—**light-footed,** *a.* Nimble in running or dancing; active.— **lightheaded,** *a.* Having dizziness or giddiness in the head; dizzy; delirious; thoughtless; heedless; weak; volatile; unsteady,—**lightheadedness,** *n.*—**lighthearted,** *a.* Free from grief or anxiety; gay; cheerful; merry.—**lightheartedness,** *n.*—**lightly,** lit´li, *adv.*—**lightness,** lit´nes, *n.*— **light opera,** *n.* An opera with a gay, popular musical score and trivial, entertaining plot.—**lightweight,** *n.*

Sporting, a man weighing not more than 135 pounds.

light, lĭt, *v.i.*—pret. & pp. *lighted*, sometimes *lit*. [A.Sax. *lihtan*, to descend, alight, from *leóht*, light, not heavy: to *alight* from horseback or a vehicle is to make it lighter by relieving it of weight.] To descend, as from a horse or carriage (with *down, off, from*); to fly or fall and settle; to come to rest; to fall or come by chance; to happen to find: with *on* or *upon*.

ligneous, lĭg´nĭ·us, *a.* [L. *ligneus*, from *lignum*, wood.] Made of wood; consisting of wood; resembling wood; woody; wooden.—**lignifi-cation,** lĭg´nĭ·fĭ·kā˝shon, *n.* The act of lignifying, or the state of being lignified.—**ligniform,** lĭg´nĭ·form, *a.* Like wood; resembling wood.—**lignify,** lĭg´nĭ·fĭ, *v.t.*—*lignified, lignifying*. [L. *lignum*, and *facio*, to make.] To convert into wood.—*v.i.* To become wood.—**lignin,** lĭg´nĭn, *n.* A modification of cellulose; vegetable fiber.—**lignite,** lĭg´nīt, *n.* Fossil wood, wood coal, or brown coal, a combustible substance mineralized to a certain degree, but retaining distinctly its woody texture.—**lignitic,** lĭg·nĭt´ĭk, *a.* Containing lignite; resembling lignite.—**lignose,** lĭg´nōs, *a.* Ligneous.—**lignum vitae,** lĭg´num vī´tē, *n.* [L., wood of life, from its hardness and durability.] The popular name of a small West Indian and South American tree, the wood of which is valued for its extreme hardness.

ligroine, lĭg´rō·in, *n.* An oil of medium density distilled from crude petroleum.

ligula, ligule, lĭg´ū·la, lĭg´ūl, *n.* [L. *ligula*, a strap, from *ligo*, to bind. LIGAMENT.] *Bot.* a strap-shaped petal of composite flowers; the membrane at the base of a grass leaf.—**ligulate,** lĭg´ū·lāt, *a.* Like a bandage or strap; *bot.* having the form of a ligula: applied especially to the ray florets of composite flowers.

ligure, lĭg´ūr, *n.* [Gr. *linggourion, ligurion*.] A kind of precious stone (O.T.).

like, lĭk, *a.* [A.Sax. *lic, gelic*=D. *lijk, gelijk*, Icel. *likr, glikr*, G. *gleich*, Goth. *leiks, galeiks*, like. From A.Sax. *lic*, form, body (see LICH GATE). Hence the termination in *each, such, which*, and the *-ly* of adjectives and adverbs, as also the verb *to like*.] Equal; exactly corresponding; of the same kind; similar; resembling (*like* passions); probable; likely (it is *like* he will); feeling equal or disposed to.—*Had like*, was like; had nearly; came little short of. *Like* is frequently suffixed to nouns to form adjectives denoting resemblance, as *childlike*, etc.—*n.* Some person or thing resembling another; an exact counterpart.—*adv.* In the same or a similar manner; similarly; likely; probably.—**likelihood,** lĭk´lĭ·hud, *n.* Likeliness; probability.—**likely,** lĭk´-li, *a.* Like the truth; credible; probable (a *likely* story); giving a probability of something (I am *likely* to be away from home tonight); suit-

able, well adapted, or convenient for some purpose.—*adv.* Probably; as may be expected or reasonably thought.—**liken,** lī´kn, *v.t.* To make like; to cause to resemble; to compare; to represent as resembling.—**likeness,** līk´nes, *n.* The condition or quality of being like; similarity; what exactly resembles something else, especially, a portrait.—**likewise,** līk´wīz, *conj.* and *adv.* In like manner; also; moreover; too.

like, lĭk, *v.t.*—*liked, liking*. [A.Sax. *lician, gelician*, to please, to suit, lit. to be *like* one's tastes; originally impersonal; D. *lijken*, to suit; Icel. *lika*, to please, to like; from the adjective (which see).] To please or suit: used impersonally‡; to be pleased with in a moderate degree; to approve; to take satisfaction in; to enjoy.—*v.i.* To be pleased; to choose.—*n.* A liking; a fancy: used chiefly in the phrase *likes and dislikes*.—**likeable,** lĭk´a·bl, *a.* Such as to attract liking; lovable.—**likeableness,** lĭk´a·bl·nes, *n.* Quality of being likeable.—**liking,** lĭk´ing, *n.* Inclination; desire; satisfaction: often with *for* or *to* (an amusement to your *liking*).

lilac, lī´lak, *n.* [Sp. *lilac*, Ar. *lilak*, lilac; Per. *lilaj*; from a word meaning blue.] A beautiful flowering shrub of the genus *Syringa* with flowers generally pink, white, bluish, or lavender.

Lilliputian, lil·i·pū´shan, *n.* A member of the diminutive race of beings described in Swift's imaginary kingdom of *Lilliput* in *Gulliver's Travels*; a person of very small size.—*a.* Very small.

lilt, lilt, *v.t.* and *i.* [Akin to *lull*.] To sing, especially in a cheerful manner; to give musical or harmonious utterance. (*Tenn.*)—*n.* A song; a tune.

lily, lil´i, *n* [A.Sax. *lilie*, from L. *lilium*, Gr. *leirion*.] The popular name of many bulbous plants with showy and fragant flowers, as the white lily, orange lily, tiger lily, scarlet lily, etc.—*Lily of the valley*, a perennial plant with small white bell-shaped flowers.—**liliaceous,** lil·i·ā´shus, *a* Pertaining to the order of lilies; lilylike.—**lily-livered,** *a.* White-livered; cowardly. (*Shak.*)

limb, lim, *n.* [A.Sax. *lim*, Icel. *limr*, Dan. and Sw. *lem*, a limb. The *b* is added as in crum*b*, thum*b*, etc.] One of the jointed members of the human body or of any animal; an arm or leg, more especially the latter; a pretty large or main branch of a tree.—*v.t.* To supply with limbs; to dismember; to tear the limbs from.—**limbed,** limd, *a.* Having limbs: mostly in composition (large-*limbed*, short-*limbed*).

limb, lim, *n.* [L. *limbus*, a border, edging, or fringe.] *Astron.* the border or outermost edge of the sun or moon; the graduated edge of a circle or other astronomical or surveying instrument, etc.; *bot.* the border or upper spreading part of a monopetalous corolla, or of a petal or sepal.—**limbate,** lim´bāt, *a.* *Bot.* bordered, as when one color is surrounded by an edging of another.

limber, lim´ber, *a.* [Closely allied to *limp*, pliant, flaccid.] Easily bent; flexible; pliant.—*v.t.* To render limber or pliant.—**limberness,** lim´ber·nes, *n.* The quality of being limber.

limber, lim´ber, *n.* [Really a plural form from Icel. *limar*, limbs, branches of a tree; akin to *limb*.] *Artill.* a carriage on two wheels with the ammunition boxes and shafts for the horses, attached to the gun carriage, properly so called, of a field gun or cannon; *pl.* thills; shafts of a carriage (*local*).—*v.t.* To attach the limber to.

limbo, lim´bō, *n.* [It., from L. *limbus*, a hem or edge.] A supposed region where souls of the innocent are detained till the final judgment; any similar region apart from this world; a prison or other place of confinement (*colloq.*).

Limburger, lim´berg·er, *n.* A soft cheese with a characteristic odor.

lime, lim, *n.* [A.Sax. *lim*, glue, cement =D. *lijm*, acel. *lim*, G. *leim*, glue; allied to *loam*, L. *limus*, slime, Skr. *li*, to be viscous.] A viscous substance for catching birds; birdlime; calcium oxide, prepared by heating limestone or shells; quicklime, as used in mortar, in industry, and to counteract acidity in soil.—*v.t. limed, liming*. To smear with birdlime; to entangle; to ensnare; to manure with lime; to cement or glue (*Shak.*).—**limekiln,** lim´kil, *n.* A kiln in which limestone is exposed to a strong heat and reduced to lime.—**limelight,** *n.* A powerful light produced by an oxyhydrogen flame on a piece of lime; on the stage, a spotlight; *fig.* center of public interest.—**limestone,** lim´stōn, *n.* A kind of stone consisting of varieties of carbonate of lime.—**limewater,** *n.* A water solution of calcium hydroxide, used in medicine as an antacid, and in the chemical industry; natural water containing calcium carbonate or calcium sulfate.—**limy,** li´mi, *a.*

lime, lim, *n.* [Formerly *line*, from A.Sax. *lind*, D. and G. *linde*, Dan. Sw. Icel. *lind*, the tree.] The linden tree.

lime, lim, *n.* [Fr. *lime*, from Per. *limû, limûn*, whence also *lemon*.] A species of tree cultivated in southern Europe, the U. S., etc., and producing small, greenish-yellow fruit used for flavoring punch, sherbet, etc.

limerick, lim´er·ik, *n.* A jingling verse form of five lines, with lines 1, 2, and 5 rhyming, as do lines 3 and 4, popularized by Edward Lear (1812-88) in his *Book of Nonsense*, 1846.

liminal, lim´in·al, *a.* [L. *limen*, threshold.] Belonging to the lowest limit (or threshold) of perception.

limit, lim´it, *n.* [Fr. *limite*, from L. *limes, limitis*, a bound or limit; allied to *limen*, a threshold; akin *lintel, eliminate*.] That which terminates, circumscribes, or confines; bound, border, utmost extent; *math.* a determinate quantity to which a variable one continually approaches, but can never exceed.—*v.t.* To set limits or bounds to; to bound; to confine within certain bounds; to circumscribe; to restrain; to narrow or confine the signification of; to apply exclusively (words or conceptions).—**limitable**, lim′i·ta·bl, a. Capable of being limited.—**limitary**, lim′i·te·ri, a. Circumscribed or bounded in power or authority.—**limitation**, lim·i·tā′shon, n. The act of limiting, bounding, or circumscribing; the condition of being so limited; that which limits; limiting circumstance; restriction; qualification.—**limited**, lim′i·ted, p. and a. Confined within limits; narrow; circumscribed.—*Limited monarchy*, a monarchy in which the monarch shares the supreme power with a class of nobles, with a popular body, or with both.—**limitedly**, lim′i·ted·li, adv. In a limited manner or degree.—**limiter**, lim′i·tėr, n. One who limits.—**limitless**, lim′it·les, a. Having no limits; unbounded; boundless; infinite.

limn, lim, v.t. [Fr. *enluminer*, from L. *illumino*, to illuminate.] To draw or paint; to make a portrait or likeness of.—**limner**, lim′nėr, n. One who limns; a painter of portraits or miniatures.

limonene, li′mo·nēn, n. [Fr. *limon*, a lemon.] A hydrocarbon in oil of lemon.

limonite, li′mon·īt, n. [Gr. *leimōn*, meadow.] An important ore of iron, a variety of which is brown hematite.

limousine, lim′o·zēn″, n. [From *Limousin*, an old French province.] A closed automobile with the driver partitioned off from the passengers.

limp, limp, v.i. [A.Sax. *limp-halt*, *lemp-healt*, limping-halt, lame; comp. L.G. *lumpen*, to limp; Icel. *limpa*, weakness; allied to *limp*, *limber*, and probably to *lame*.] To halt or walk lamely.—n. The act of limping; a halt in one's gait; the Jacobite toast, with a limping motion, from the initial letters of Louis XIV, James, Mary (of Modena, wife of James II), Prince (the old Pretender).

limp, limp, a. [Akin to *limp*, the verb, and to *limber*; comp. Skr. *lamb*, to hang.] Easily bent; flexible; pliant; lacking stiffness; flaccid.

limpet, lim′pet, n. [O.Fr. *limpine*, a limpet.] A univalve mollusk with a conical shell, found adhering to rocks; a person who clings to something; an explosive designed to adhere to the side of a ship.

limpid, lim′pid, a. [L. *limpidus*, allied to Gr. *lampō*, to shine, hence akin to *lamp*.] Characterized by clearness or transparency; clear and bright; translucent; transparent: said of water.—**limpidity, limpidness**, lim·pid′i·ti, lim′pid·nes, n. The state of being limpid.

limy, a. See LIME.

linage, līn′ij, n. The number of printed lines on a page; measure of space sold for advertising; alignment.

linchpin, linsh′pin, n. [Lit. axle-pin, from A.Sax. *lynis*, an axletree; D. *luns, lens*, G. *lünse*, a linchpin.] A pin used to prevent the wheel of a carriage or other vehicle from sliding off the axletree; an axle pin.

linden, lin′den, n. [An adj. form from A.Sax. *lind*, the linden.] The basswood tree.

line, līn, n. [A.Sax. *line*, a cord or line, from L. *linea*, a linen thread, a string, a line or stroke, from *lineus*, flaxen, *linum*, flax; Fr. *ligne*, a line. LINEN.] A small rope or cord; a thread-like marking, as with a pen, pencil, etc.; a stroke or score; a marking or furrow upon the hands or face; a mark traced or imagined to show latitude, longitude, temperature, or the like on a map or the globe; a row of things; a straight row of soldiers drawn up with an extended front; a similar disposition of ships in preparation for an engagement; a straight row of words or figures between two margins (a page of thirty *lines*); the words which form a certain number of poetical feet; a verse; an outline, contour, lineament (a statue of fine *lines*); a short epistle; course of thought, conduct, occupation, policy, or the like; a continuous or connected series, as of descendants from a common progenitor; a series of public conveyances, as buses, steamships, airplanes, etc., passing between places with regularity; *fort.* (pl.) works made to cover extended positions; (pl.) words of a character in a drama; *football*, offensive or defensive players that take their positions near the scrimmage; a source of communication.—*Line engraving, photoengraving*, an engraving, usually on zinc, without a screen (*line cut*).—*Line of defense, mil.* fortifications or trenches used as protective barriers; the standing army.—*Line drive*, in baseball, a low-hit ball which approximately parallels the ground the greater part of its course.—*Meridian line*, a line drawn at any station to show the directions of true north and south.—*Fraunhofer's lines*, the dark lines observed crossing a spectrum at right angles to its length.—**streamline**, n. The design of form which permits passage through the air or water with a minimum of resistance, as in the shape of an airplane or boat.—v.t.—**lined, lining**. To draw lines upon; to mark with lines or thread-like strokes; cross out; form in lines; place at intervals.—**linage**, līn′ij, n. The number of printed lines on a page; measure of space sold for advertising.—**liner**, līn′ėr, n. One of a line of oceangoing ships.—**lineman**, n. A repair man who works on electric light, power, telephone or telegraph lines; *football*, one who plays forward.—**linesman**, n. A referee in football or tennis.—**line-up**, n. Arrangement of players in football or baseball; a line of persons to be inspected (a police *line-up*).

line, līn, v.t.—**lined, lining**. [O.E. *line*, to double a garment with *linen*.] To cover on the inside; to protect by a layer on the inside (to *line* a garment).—**lining**, līn′ing, n. The covering of the inner surface of anything, as a coat lining.—**liner**, līn′ėr, n. Something used as a lining; one who lines.

lineage, lin′i·ij, n. [Fr. *lignage*, from *ligne*, L. *linea*, a line. LINE.] Descendants in a line from a common progenitor; line of descent from an ancestor; race; progeny.—**lineal**, lin′i·al, a. [L. *linealis*.] Composed of lines; in a direct line from an ancestor; hereditary; pertaining to or ascertained by a line or lines (*lineal* measure).—**lineally**, lin′i·al·li, adv. In a lineal manner; in a direct line of descent.—**lineament**, lin′i·a·ment, n. [L. *lineamentum*.] The outline or contour of a body or figure, particularly of the face; a line of form or feature.—**linear**, lin′i·ėr, a. [L. *linearis*.] Pertaining to a line; consisting of lines; lineal; in *bot.* like a line in form; long and slender.—*Linear perspective*, that which regards only the positions, magnitudes, and forms of the objects delineated.—**lineate, lineated, lineolate**, lin′i·āt, lin′i·ā·ted, lin′i·o·lāt, a. Bot. marked longitudinally with depressed parallel lines.

linen, lin′en, n. [Properly an adj. signifying made of flax, from A.Sax. *lin*, flax, L. *linum*, Gr. *linon*, flax; comp. Armor. *lin*, W. *llin*, flax.] Cloth made of flax; a flaxen fabric or material; underclothing in general, because chiefly made of linen or similar materials.—a. Made of flax, or yarn from flax.

ling, ling, n. [D. *ling*; Dan. and N. *lange*; G. *leng, langfisch*, so named from being *long*.] A fish of the cod family, rather long in proportion to its thickness, found in the North Atlantic Ocean, and when salted and dried, is used as food.

ling, ling, n. [Icel. and Dan. *lyng*, heather.] Common heather.

linger, ling′gėr, v.i. [From A.Sax. *lengra*, compar. of *lang*, long; comp. the verb *lower*, from compar. of *low*.] To delay; to loiter; to lag or hang behind; to be slow to move or act; to hesitate; to remain long (the disease *lingers*).—v.t. To spend in a wearisome manner: with *out* or *away*.—**lingerer**, ling′gėr·ėr, n. One who lingers.

lingerie, län′zhe·rē, n. [Fr.] Linen articles, especially women's underwear. Now used for feminine intimate apparel.

lingo, ling′gō, n. [L. *lingua*, the tongue.] Language; speech; a contemptuous term for language one does not understand. (*Vulgar*.)

lingua franca. A compound or mongrel language in the Levant, made up of words from French, Italian, Spanish, and modern Greek, serving as a common medium of communication.

lingual, ling′gwal, a. [L. *lingua*, the tongue, originally *dingua*; cog. with E. *tongue* (comp. L. *lacrima*, E. *tear*).] Pertaining to the tongue; pronounced chiefly by means of the tongue.—n. A letter pronounced chiefly by means of the tongue, as *l*, *r*.—**linguiform**, ling′gwi·form, n. Having the form or shape of a tongue.—**linguist**, ling′gwist, n. A person skilled in languages; one who knows several languages.—**linguistic**, ling·gwis′tik,

a. Relating to language or to the affinities of language; philological.— **linguistics,** ling'gwis'tiks, *n.* The science of language, or of the origin, significations, affinities, and application of words; comparative philology. —**lingulate,** ling'gū·lāt, *a.* Shaped like the tongue or a strap; ligulate.
liniment, lin'i·ment, *n.* [L. *linimentum,* from *lino,* to anoint.] *Med.* a species of soft ointment, of a stimulating or soothing character, to be rubbed into the skin.
lining, *n.* See LINE.
link, lingk, *n.* [A.Sax. *hlence,* Sw. *länk,* Dan. *lænke,* Icel. *hlekkr,* a link; G. *gelenk,* a joint, a link (from *lenken,* to bend).] A single ring or division of a chain; anything doubled and closed like a link; something that serves to connect one thing or part with another; any constituent part of a connected series; *land measuring,* a division of Gunter's chain, having a length of 7.92 inches; *mach.* any straight rod connecting two rotating pieces by flexible joints.—*v.t.* To connect by, or as if by, a link or links; to unite or join.—*v.i.* To be joined or connected : with *together* or *in.*—**linkage,** lingk'ij, *n.* The act of linking; the state of being linked; *biol.* the inclination of certain genes to remain correlated in inheritance; *elec.* the product of the magnetic flux through a coil by its number of turns; *mech.* a combination of bars or pieces linked so as to pivot about each other in parallel planes.
link, lingk, *n.* [Origin uncertain; perhaps equivalent to *lint,* the first part of *linstock.*] A torch made of tow or other materials, with tar or pitch.—**linkboy,** *n.* A boy or man that carries a link.
links, lingks, *n.* pl. [A.Sax. *hlinc,* rising ground; same root as L. *clivus,* sloping. DECLINE.] A golf course.
Linnaean, Linnean, lin·nē'an, *a.* Pertaining to Linnaeus, the celebrated botanist.
linnet, lin'et, *n.* [A.Sax. *linet;* Fr. *linot, linotte,* from L. *linum,* flax.] One of the commonest of Old World singing birds, frequenting open places.
linoleum, li·nō'li·um, *n.* [L. *linum,* flax, and *oleum,* oil.] A preparation of linseed oil with chloride of sulfur, which when mixed with ground cork and pressed upon canvas forms floor-cloth; the floor-cloth thus produced.
Linotype, *n.* [A 'line o'type'.] In printing, a machine for setting and casting lines of type by the operation of a keyboard.
linseed, lin'sēd, *n.* [O.E. *lin,* flax. LINE.] The seed of flax.—**linseed oil,** *n.* An oil procured by pressure from the seed of flax.—**linsey-woolsey,** lin'si·wul·si, *n.* A fabric made of linen and wool; an incongruous mixture (*Shak.*)—*a.* Made of linen and wool mixed; of different and unsuitable ingredients.
linstock, lin'stok, *n.* [For *lintstock, luntstock,* from D. *lont,* Dan. *lunte,* a match, and *stock,* a stick.] A staff with a crotch or fork at one end to

hold a lighted match, used in firing cannon.
lint, lint, *n.* [A.Sax. *linet,* L. *linteum, linteus,* from *linum,* flax. LINE.] Flax; linen scraped into a soft substance; bits of thread or fuzz from yarn or fabrics; cottonseed wool.
lintel, lin'tel, *n.* [O.Fr. *lintel,* Fr. *linteau,* from L.L. *limitellus,* dim. from L. *limes, limitis,* a limit. LIMIT.] The horizontal piece of timber or stone supporting the load above a window, door, or other opening.
lion, lī'on, *n.* [Fr. *lion,* from L. *leo, leonis,* a lion; Gr. *leōn.*] A well-known carnivorous animal, of a tawny color, having a full-flowing mane in the male, and a tufted tail; a sign of the zodiac; Leo; an object of interest and curiosity (the *lion* of the day; to visit the *lions* of the place), a usage derived from the time when the lions kept in the Tower of London were one of the chief sights to which strangers were taken.—*Lion's provider,* a popular name for the jackal.—*Lion's share,* the whole or a very disproportionate share in advantages.—**lionel, lionet,** lī'on·el, lī'on·et, *n.* A lion's whelp; a young lion.—**lioness,** lī'on·es, *n.* The female of the lion.—**lionism,** lī'on·izm, *n.* The attracting of notice as a lion; the treating of a person as an object of curiosity.—**lionize,** lī'on·īz, *v.t.* To visit, as the objects of curiosity in a place; to treat as a lion or object of curiosity and interest.
lip, lip, *n.* [A.Sax. *lippe* = D. *lip,* Dan. and G. *lippe;* allied to verb to *lap;* Lith. *lupa,* Per. *lab,* Hind. *lub,* L. *labium,* lip; *lambo,* to lap.] The name of the two fleshy or muscular parts (upper and lower) covering the front teeth in man and many other animals; something similar; the edge or border of something hollow (as a vessel, a wound); brink or margin; back talk (slang).—*v.t.* and *i.* To touch, as with the lip; to kiss.—**lipreading,** *n.* Understanding what one says from the movement of his lips : used in communicating with the deaf.—**lip service,** *n.* A mere verbal profession of service.
lipase, lī'pās, lip'ās, *n.* [Gr. *lipos,* fat, and *ase.*] A fat-digesting enzyme; an enzyme secreted by the pancreas and other organs of the digestive system which converts fats to fatty acids and glycerol.
lipoma, lip·ō'ma, *n.* [Gr. *lipos,* fat, *oma,* a tumor.] A fatty tumor.
liquate, lī'kwāt, *v.i.* and *t.*—*liquated, liquating.* [L. *liquo, liquatum.* LIQUID.] To melt; to liquefy; *metal.* to separate from a less fusible metal, by applying just sufficient heat to melt the more easily liquefiable.—**liquation,** lī'kwā'shon, *n.* The act or operation of liquating.—**liquefacient,** lik·wi·fā'shi·ent, *n.* That which causes to melt.—**liquefaction,** lik·wi·fak'shon, *n.* [L. *liqueo,* to be fluid, and *facio,* to make.] The act or operation of melting or dissolving; a becoming liquid; the state of being melted.—**liquefiable,** lik'wi·fī·a·bl, *a.* Capable of being liquefied.— **liquefy,** lik'wi·fī, *v.t.*—*liquefied, li-*

quefying. To convert from a solid form to that of a liquid; to melt by heat.—*v.i.* To be melted; to become liquid.—**liquescency,** li·kwes'en·si, *n.* The condition of being liquescent. —**liquescent,** li·kwes'ent, *a.* [L. *liquesco,* to melt.] Melting; becoming fluid.
liqueur, li·kėr' or li·kūr', *n.* [Fr. lit. liquor.] A sweet, alcoholic beverage with some infusion or extract from fruits, spices, or various aromatic substances, usually served after dinner.
liquid, lik'wid, *a.* [L. *liquidus,* from *liqueo,* to melt, from root seen also in *lino,* to smear (whence *liniment*).] Composed of particles that move freely among each other on the slightest pressure and do not separate as in a gas; fluid; not solid; flowing smoothly or easily to the ear; devoid of harshness; pronounced with a slight contraction of the organs of articulation.—*n.* Fluid; investments that may be quickly be converted to cash; a letter pronounced with a smooth flowing sound, as *l* and *r.*—**liquid air,** *n.* Air in its liquid state, prepared by subjection to great pressure and cooling.— **liquid-air-cycle-engine** (LACE), *n.* A bi-propellant rocket engine that produces its own oxidizer.—**liquidambar,** lik'wid·am·bėr, *n.* A kind of fragrant gum or resin from several trees.—**liquidate,** lik'wi·dāt, *v.t.*—*liquidated, liquidating.* To make liquid; to decide the precise amount of something by agreement; to adjust, dissolve or clear off debts; to distribute the assets and liabilities and clear up the accounts of a business or estate when terminating it; to dispose of secretly; to do away with.—*v.i.* To close out one's debts or accounts. —**liquidation,** lik·wi·dā'shon, *n.*—**liquidator,** lik·wi·dā'tėr, *n.*—**liquidity,** lik·wid'i·ti, *n.*—**liquidly,** lik'wid·li, *adv.*—**liquidness,** lik'wid·nes, *n.*— **liquor,** lik'ėr, *n.* A liquid or fluid substance, often specifically an intoxicating beverage; drink.—*v.t.* To moisten; to drench.—*v.i.* To drink, especially intoxicating liquor. (Colloq.)
liquorice, lik'ėr·is, *n.* See LICORICE.
lira, lē'ra, *n.* pl. *lire,* lē'rā. [From L. *libra,* a pound, whence also Fr. *livre.*] An Italian silver coin.
lisle, līl, *n.* A kind of thread made of linen, or linen and cotton; material made of lisle.
lisp, lisp, *v.i.* [A.Sax. *wlisp, wlips,* lisping; D. *lispen,* Dan. *laespe,* Sw. *läspa,* to lisp; G. *lispeln,* to whisper, to lisp.] To pronounce the sibilant letters *s* and *z* imperfectly, as by giving the sound of *th* or *dh;* to speak imperfectly, as a child.—*v.t.* To pronounce with a lisp or imperfectly.—*n.* The habit or act of lisping; the habitual utterance of *th* for *s.*—**lisper,** lis'pėr, *n.* One who lisps.
lissom, lissome, lis'um, *a.* [Fr. *lithesome.* LITHE.] Supple; flexible; lithe; nimble; active.—**lissomeness,** lis'um·nes, *n.* State of being lissome.
list, list, *n.* [A.Sax. *list,* selvedge =

Icel. *listi*, Sw. *list*, Dan. *liste*, a fillet, a selvedge; G. *leiste*, a strip, a border; D. *lijst*, border, margin, catalogue.] The edge or selvage woven on cloth; a strip of cloth; a fillet; a record or register of names or items; pl. the ground or field enclosed for a combat or competition.—**list price**, *n. Bus.* a price given in a catalogue; the common or retail price of an item.—*v.t.* To enroll; to enlist; to fit or cover with list; to put an edge or border on.—*v.i.* To enlist, as in the army.

list, list, *v.i.* [A.Sax. *lystan*, to wish (used impers.), from *lust*, pleasure; so Icel. *lysta*. LUST.] To desire or choose; to be disposed; to please.

list, list, *n.* [Origin unknown.] *Naut.* an inclination to one side (the ship has a *list* to port).—*v.t.* To cause to list.—*v.i.* To lean to one side (said of a ship); to careen.

listen, lis'n, *v.i.* [A.Sax. *hlystan*, from *hlyst*, hearing.] To pay attention with the ear; to hear and attend to; to take advice.—**listener,** lis'n·ẽr, *n.*

listless, list'les, *a.* [O.E. *list*, A.Sax. *lyst*, desire, pleasure. See LIST, to desire.] Indifferent to or taking no pleasure in what is passing; languid and indifferent; uninterested; vacant.—**listlessly,** list'les·li, *adv.* In a listless manner.—**listlessness,** list'les·nes, *n.* The state of being listless.

lit, lit, pret. & pp. of *light*, to kindle; also sometimes of *light*, to alight, to chance.

litany, lit'a·ni, *n.* [Fr. *litanie*; Gr. *litaneia*, from *litaneuō*, to pray, *litē*, a prayer.] A solemn supplication used in public worship; [*cap.*, with *The*] a collection of short supplications in the *Book of Common Prayer*, uttered by the priest and people alternately.

litchi, lēch'ē, *n.* A delicious fruit yielded by a tree belonging to China and the Malayan Archipelago.

liter, lē'tẽr, *n.* [From Gr. *litra*, a pound.] Metric measure of capacity, a cubic decimeter, or 61.025 cu. in., or 1.0567 U. S. liquid quarts.

literal, lit'ẽr·al, *a.* [L. *literalis*, from *litera*, a letter. LETTER.] According to the letter or verbal expression; not figurative or metaphorical; following the letter or exact words; not free (a *literal* translation); consisting of or expressed by letters.—**literalism,** lit'ẽr·al·izm, *n.* The act of adhering to the letter; a mode of interpreting literally.—**literalist,** lit'ẽr·al·ist, *n.* One who practices literalism; an interpreter according to the letter.—**literally,** lit'ẽr·al·li, *adv.* In a literal manner or sense; according to the primary and natural import of words; not figuratively.—**literalness,** lit'ẽr·al·nes, *n.* The state or quality of being literal.—**literary,** lit'er·e·ri, *a.* [L. *literarius.*] Pertaining to letters or literature; treating of or dealing with learning or learned men; engaged in literature; consisting in written or printed compositions (*literary* property).—**literate,** lit'ẽr·it, *a.* [L. *literatus.*] Instructed; learned; lettered.—*n.* One who has received a certain university

education, but was not graduated; a literary man.—**literati,** lit·ẽr·ä'tī. [It. *litterato*] Literary men.—**literator.**† lit'ẽr·ā·tẽr, *n.* [L.] A literary man; a litterateur, lit'ẽr·a·chẽr, *n.* [L. *litteratura.*] Learning; literary knowledge; literary productions collectively; the literary productions upon a given subject, or a particular branch of knowledge; the collective writings of a country or period; the class of writings in which beauty of style is a characteristic feature; the calling of authors of books; etc.

lith, lith, *n.* [A.Sax. *lith*=D. *lid*, Dan. *led*, Icel. *lithr*, Goth. *lithus*, limb, joint.] A limb; a joint; a symmetrical part or division; a member.

litharge, lith'ärj, *n.* [Gr. *lithargyros*—*lithos*, stone, *argyros*, silver.] An oxide of lead, much used in assaying as a flux, and entering into the composition of the glaze of common earthenware.

lithe, līth, *a.* [A.Sax. *lithe*, gentle; G. *linde*, *gelind*, Dan. *lind*, Icel. *linr*, soft, mild; allied to L. *lentus*, pliant, *lenis*, mild (whence *lenity*). Hence *lissome*.] That may be easily bent; pliant; flexible; limber.—**litheness,** līth'nes, *n.* Pliancy; flexibility; limberness.—**lithesome,** līth'sum, *a.* Pliant; lissome.

lithia, lith'i·a, *n.* [From Gr. *lithos*, a stone.] The oxide of the metal lithium, of a white color, acrid and caustic; *med.* the formation of stone or concretions in the human body.—**lithic,** lith'ik, *a.* Pertaining to or consisting of stone; pertaining to stone in the bladder.

lithium, lith'i·um, *n.* [N.L. from Gr. *lithos*, stone.] A metallic element, soft and silver white, the lightest metal known. Symbol, Li; at. no., 3; at. wt., 6.939.—**lithia water,** *n.* A mineral water containing lithium salts.

lithograph, lith'o·graf, *v.t.* [Gr. *lithos*, a stone, and *grapho*, to write.] To engrave or trace on stone and transfer to paper, etc., by printing.—*n.* A print from a drawing on stone.—**lithographer,** li·thog'ra·fẽr, *n.* One who practices lithography.—**lithographic, lithographical,** lith·o·graf'ik, lith·o·graf'i·kal, *a.* Pertaining to lithography; engraved upon or printed from stone.—*Lithographic stone, lithographic slate,* a slaty compact limestone, of a yellowish color and fine grain, used for receiving the designs in lithography.—**lithographically,** lith·o·graf'i·kal·li, *adv.* By the lithographic art.—**lithography,** li·thog'ra·fi, *n.* The art of writing or drawing with special pigments on a peculiar kind of stone, and of producing impressions from it on paper.

lithoid, lithoidal, lith'oid, li·thoi'dal, *a.* [Gr. *lithos*, a stone.] Resembling a stone; of a stony structure.

lithologic, lithological, lith·o·loj'ik, lith·o·loj'i·kal, *a.* [Gr. *lithos*, a stone, and *logos*, discourse.] Of or pertaining to lithology or the science of stones.—**lithologist,** li·thol'o·jist, *n.* A person skilled in the science of stones.—**lithology,** li·thol'o·ji, *n.* The

science or natural history of stones; the study of the mineral structure of rocks.

lithomarge, lith'o·märj, *n.* [Gr. *lithos*, stone, L. *marga*, marl.] A term applied to varieties of clay of great fineness and capable of being fused into a soft slag.

lithophyte, lith'o·fīt, *n.* [Gr. *lithos*, stone, *phyton*, a plant.] A polyp whose substance is stony or horny.

lithosphere, lith'o·sfẽr, *n.* [Prefix *litho*, and *sphere.*] The solid part of the earth.

lithotome, lith'o·tōm, *n.* [Gr. *lithos*, stone, and *temnō*, to cut.] A surgical instrument for cutting into the bladder in operations for the stone.—**lithotomic, lithotomical,** lith·o·tom'ik, lith·o·tom'i·kal, *a.* Pertaining to or performed by lithotomy.—**lithotomy,** li·thot'o·mi, *n.* The operation, art, or practice of cutting for the stone in the bladder.

lithotrity, li·thot'ri·ti, *n.* [Gr. *lithos*, a stone, and L. *tero*, *tritum*, to grind.] The operation of crushing to pieces a stone in the bladder by means of an instrument called a lithotritor.

litigate, lit'i·gāt, *v.t.*—*litigated*, *litigating.* [L. *litigo, litigatum*—*lis, litis*, strife, dispute, and *ago*, to carry on.] To make the subject of a lawsuit; to bring before a court of law for decision.—*v.i.* To carry on a suit by judicial process.—**litigable,** lit'i·ga·bl, *a.* Capable of being litigated or defended at law.—**litigant,** lit'i·gant, *a.* Disposed to litigate; contending in law; engaged in a lawsuit.—*n.* A person engaged in a lawsuit.—**litigation,** lit·i·gā'shon, *n.* The act or process of litigating; the proceedings in a suit at law; a lawsuit.—**litigator,** lit'i·gā·tẽr, *n.* One who litigates.—**litigious,** li·tij'us, *a.* [L. *litigiosus*, from *litigium*, a dispute.] Inclined to go to law; fond of litigation; given to bringing lawsuits; contentious.—**litigiously,** li·tij'us·li, *adv.* In a litigious manner.—**litigiousness,** li·tij'us·nes, *n.*

litmus, lit'mus, *n.* [From G. *lackmus*, D. *lakmoes*—*lack*, lacker, and *mus*, *moes*, pulp, pap.] A coloring matter procured from certain lichens, used as a test for acids, paper tinged blue with it turning red with acids, and blue again with alkalies.

litotes, lī'to·tēz, *n.* [Gr. *litotēs*, plainness, simplicity.] *Rhet.* a figure which expresses less than what is intended to be conveyed. Thus. 'a citizen of no mean city,' means of an illustrious or important city.

litter, lit'ẽr, *n.* [Fr. *litière*, from L.L. *lectaria*, from L. *lectus*, a bed; same root as *lie*, *lay*.] A kind of frame for supporting a bed, in which a person may be borne by men or by a horse; straw, hay, or other soft substance, used as a bed for horses and other animals; articles scattered in a slovenly manner; scattered rubbish; a condition of disorder.—*v.t.* To furnish (animals) with litter or bedding; to spread straw, etc., for; to scatter in a careless or slovenly manner.—*v.i.* To lie or sleep in litter.

litter, lit′ėr, n. [Comp. Icel. látr, the place where animals lay their young, from lag, a laying; Sc. lachter, the quantity of eggs a hen lays.] The young produced at a birth by a quadruped which brings forth several at a birth; a birth or bringing forth, as of pigs, kittens, rabbits, puppies, etc.—v.t. To bring forth or give birth to: said of such quadrupeds as the sow, cat, rabbit.—v.i. To bring forth a litter.

litterateur, lit′ėr·a·tėr, n. [Fr. littérateur. LITERAL.] A literary man; one who adopts literature as a profession.

little, lit′l, a.—comparative less, superlative least (both from a different root); superlative very rarely littlest. [A.Sax. lytel, D. luttel, Icel. litill, Sw. liten, Dan. liden, lille, Goth. leitile, little; same root as lout.] Small in size or extent; not great or large; short in duration; small dignity, power, or importance; of small force or weight; slight; inconsiderable; small in mind; petty; mean; narrow.—n. That which is little; a small quantity, space, etc; small degree or scale; miniature.—A little, somewhat; to or in a small degree; to a limited extent.—Little by little, by slow degrees; gradually.—adv. In a small quantity or degree.—littleness, lit′l·nes, n. The state or quality of being little.

littoral, lit′o·ral, a. [L. littoralis, from littus, littoris, the shore.] Pertaining to a shore; inhabiting the seashore.—n. The shore of a sea, or other water, and the country lying near it.—Littoral zone, the interval or zone on a seacoast between high and low water mark; a coast strip or district (the Red Sea littoral).

liturgy, lit′ėr·ji, n. [Gr. leitourgia—leitos, public, from laos, leōs, the people, and ergon, work.] The ritual or established formulas for public worship in those churches which use prescribed forms.—**liturgic, liturgical**, li·tėr′jik, li·tėr′ji·kal, a. Pertaining to a liturgy or to public prayer and worship.—**liturgics**, li·tėr′jiks, n. The doctrine or theory of liturgies.

live, liv, v.i.—lived, living. [A.Sax. lifian, to live or dwell; L.G. and D. leven, Icel. lifa, Dan. leve, G. leben, Goth. liban, to live; akin life; same root as leave, the original meaning being to be left, to survive.] To have life; to be capable of performing the vital functions; to continue; to remain still effective; not to perish; to pass or spend life in a particular manner; to conduct one's self in life; to regulate one's life; to abide, dwell, reside; to feed; subsist; be nourished and supported (to live on grass or insects); to acquire a livelihood; Scrip. to be exempt from spiritual death.—v.t. To pass or spend (to live a life of ease).—To live down, to live so as to subdue or give the lie to; to prove false by the course of one's life (to live down a calumny).—**liver**, liv′ėr, n. One who lives; one who resides; a resident; one who lives

in a certain manner (the manner being expressed by an adjective).—**living**, liv′ing, p. and a. Having life; not dead; producing action, animation, and vigor; quickening.—Living force, in physics, the force of a body in motion.—Living rock, rock in its natural place and condition.—The living, those who are alive.—Living wage, sufficient to live by, enough for bare life.—n. Means of subsistence; livelihood; power of continuing life; manner of life.—**living room**, n. The parlor; a centralized, general room.

live, liv, a. [Short for alive, that is, 'in life'.] Having life; alive; not dead; exhibiting or containing force (a live wire, a live ball, or a live bomb); of, involving, or before real people at the time of production (live audience, live broadcast); ignited; not extinct (a live coal), vivid, as color.—Live salesman, a person whose business it is to sell livestock.—Livestock, the quadrupeds and other animals employed or reared on a farm.—**lived**, livd, a. Having a life; existing; used in composition (long-lived, short-lived).—**livelihood**, līv′li·hud, n. [Corrupted from O.E. liflode, livelode, A. Sax. lif-láde, lit. life-leading, lead or course of life; from lif, life, and lád, a leading, as in lode, lodestone.] Means of maintaining life; support of life; maintenance.—**livelily**, līv′li·li, adv. In a lively manner.—**liveliness**, līv′li·nes, n. The quality or state of being lively or animated.—**livelong**, liv′long, a. That endures long; lasting; durable.—Livelong day, day throughout its whole length; entire day; with undercurrent of joy or lassitude; originally lefe (LIEF) long.—**lively**, līv′li, a. Brisk; vivacious; active; animated; spirited; living; strong, energetic, keen (a lively faith or hope); fresh; bright: said of colors.—adv. In a lively manner.—**live oak**, n. An evergreen oak of the Southern United States yielding valuable timber.—**live wire**, n. A fun-loving, energetic person.

liver, liv′ėr, n. [A.Sax. lifer, D. and Dan. lever, Icel. lifr, G. leber; root doubtful.] The glandular organ which in animals secretes the bile, in man placed in the right upper side and toward the front of the abdominal cavity.—**liverwort**, liv′ėr·wėrt, n. [From the appearance of the plants.] The Hepaticae, a class of the byrophytes allied to the scale mosses.

livery, liv′ėr·i, n. [Fr. livrée, a giving out, something given out or delivered over, from livré, pp. of livrer, to deliver, from L. libero, to liberate. LIBERAL.] Release‡; deliverance (Mil.)‡; an allowance of food statedly given out, as to a family, to servants, to horses, etc.‡; hence, the state of a horse that is kept and fed at a certain rate (to keep horses at livery); a distinctive dress in which the male servants of some person of position are clad; a distinctive garb worn by any body or association of persons; the body or association of persons wearing such

a garb; characteristic covering or outward appearance (the livery of May, of grief).—v.t. To clothe in, or as in, livery.—**livery company**, n. A company of London liverymen.—**liveryman**, liv′ėr·i·man, n. One who wears a livery; one who keeps horses for hire; keeper of a livery stable.—**livery stable**, n. A stable where horses are kept for hire.

livid, liv′id, a. [L. lividus, from liveo, to be black and blue.] Black and blue; of a lead color; discolored, as flesh by contusion.—**lividity, lividness**, li·vid′i·ti, liv′id·nes, n. The state of being livid.

livre, lē·vr, n. [Fr., from L. libra, a pound.] An old French money of account, superseded by the franc.

lixivial, lixivious, lik·siv′i·al, lik·siv′i·us, a. [L. lixivius, made into lye, lixivium, lye, from lix, ashes.] Pertaining to lye or the water impregnated with alkaline salt extracted from wood ashes; of the nature of lye; obtained by lixiviation.—**lixiviate**, lik·siv′i·āt, v.t. To subject to the process of lixiviation.—**lixiviation**, lik·siv·i·ā″shon, n. The process of extracting alkaline salts from ashes by pouring water on them, the water passing through them taking up the salts and thus forming lye.—**lixivium**, lik·siv′i·um, n. Lye, that is, water impregnated with alkaline salts taken up from wood ashes.

lizard, liz′ėrd, n. [Fr. lézard, from L. lacerta, a lizard.] The popular name of many four-footed, tailed reptiles; naut. a piece of rope with one or more iron thimbles in it for ropes to lead through.

llama, lä′mä or lyä′mä, n. [A Peruvian word.] A hoofed ruminating quadruped of South America, allied to the camel, but smaller and not having a hump.

llanos, lan′ōz or lyä′nōz, n. pl. [Sp., from L. planus, level.] Vast and almost entirely level grassy plains in the northern part of South America.

Lloyd's, loidz, n. [Because the headquarters of the underwriters were originally (from 1716) Lloyd's coffee-house.] A society of underwriters and others in London, Eng., for the collection and diffusion of maritime intelligence, the insurance, classification, and certification of vessels, and the transaction of business of various kinds connected with shipping.—Lloyd's numbers, numbers selected to designate the size of various parts of ships.—Lloyd's Register, an annual register of ships, their size, classification, etc.

lo, lō, interj. [A.Sax. lá.] Look; see; behold; observe.

loach, lōch, n. [Fr. loche, a loach, origin unknown.] A small, fresh-water fish of the Old World, related to the carp family.

load, lōd, n. [O.E. lode, a load, from A.Sax. hladan, to load, pret. hlód. LADE.] What is laid on or put in anything for conveyance; a burden; as much as can be carried at one time by any conveyance; a grievous weight; an encumbrance; something that burdens or oppresses the mind or spirits; in building construction, the external forces acting upon a structure and the weight of the structure itself.—*Dead load*, one gradually applied and remaining steady.—*Live load*, one suddenly applied and accompanied by shock or vibration.—*Load line*, a line drawn on the side of a vessel to show the depth to which she may safely sink in the water.—*v.t.* To charge with a load; to lay a burden on; to weigh down, oppress, encumber; to bestow or confer in great abundance; to fill; to stuff; to make heavier for some purpose by adding special weight; to charge; as a gun with powder, or with powder and ball or shot.—*To load a cane* or *a whip*, to make it serve as a weapon by weighting it with lead or iron.—*To load dice*, to make one side heavier than the other, so as to cause the opposite to come regularly up.—*To load wine*, to drug or hocus wine.—**loader**, lō′dẽr, *n.* One who loads.

loadstar, lodestar, lōd′stär, *n.* [*Lode*, *load*, is from A.Sax. *lád*, course, way (the termination of *livelihood*), from *lithan*, to go (akin to lead).] A star that leads or serves to guide; especially the pole star.—**loadstone, lodestone**, lōd′stōn, *n.* An ore of iron; the magnetic oxide of iron, which possesses the property of attracting iron, and the power of communicating this property to iron and steel, thus forming artificial magnets; hence, a magnet.

loaf, lōf, *n.* pl. **loaves**, lōvz. [A.Sax. *hláf*; Icel. *hleifr*, Goth. *hlaibs, hlaifs*, O.H.G. *hlaib*, G. *laib, leib*, allied to Rus. *chljeb*, Pol. *chleb*, bread, loaf. This word forms part of *lord, lady,* and *lammas*.] A regularly shaped or molded mass of bread of some size; a conical lump of sugar.

loaf, lōf, *v.i.* [The verb is from the noun *loafer*, G. *läufer*, D. *looper*, one that runs or gads about. Akin *leap*.] To lounge; to idle away one's time.—*v.t.* To pass or spend in idleness, as time; to spend lazily.—**loafer**, lō′fẽr, *n.* A lazy or disreputable lounger; a lazy fellow who picks up a living anyhow.

loam, lōm, *n.* [A.Sax. *lám*; D. *leem*, G. *lehm*, loam, clay, allied to E. *lime*, and probably L. *limus*, slime, mud.] A rich soil compounded of sand, clay, vegetable mold, etc.; a mixture of sand, clay, etc., used for molding in iron founding.—*v.t.* To cover with loam; to clay.—**loamy**, lō′mi, *a.* Consisting of loam; partaking of the nature of loam.

loan, lōn, *n.* [A.Sax. *lan* (?), *laen*, a loan, from *lihan*, to lend; Icel. *lán*, Dan. *laan*, D. *leen*, a loan; same root as L. *linguo*, to leave (whence *relinquish*). LEND.] The act of lending or condition of being lent; a lending; that which is lent; especially a sum of money lent at interest.—*v.t.* and *i.* To lend.—**loan shark**, *n.* One who lends money at an excessive rate of interest.

loath, lōth, *a.* [A.Sax. *lath*, hateful, odious; O.H.G. *leit*, odious.] Filled with disgust or aversion; unwilling; reluctant; averse.—**loathe**, lōth, *v.t.* —*loathed, loathing.* To feel disgust at; to have an extreme aversion of the appetite toward; to dislike greatly; to abhor.—**loathful**, lōth′fựl, *a.*—**loathing**, lōth′ing, *n.* Extreme disgust.—**loathly**, lōth′li, *a.*—**loathsome**, lōth′sum, *a.* Causing to loathe; exciting disgust.—**loathsomely**, lōth′sum·li, *adv.*—**loathsomeness**, lōth′sum·nes, *n.*

lob, lob, *v.t.*—*lobbed, lobbing.* [M.L.G. *lobbe*, short, fat person, akin Fris. *lob, lobbe*, hanging mass of flesh.] To throw or toss slowly and heavily.—*n.* An unhurried toss.

lobar, lō′bẽr, *a.* Pertaining to a lobe, as of the liver or brain.—*Lobar pneumonia*, inflammation of a whole lobe of the lungs, as distinguished from *lobular pneumonia*, which attacks the lungs in patches.

lobate, lobated. See LOBE.

lobby, lob′i, *n.* [L.L. *lobia, lobium*, etc., a portico, from O.H.G. *laubja*, G. *laube*, an arbor, from *laub*, a leaf, foliage. LEAF. *Lodge* is another form of this word.] An entrance hall, especially one used as a waiting room; a large public room in a hotel, where guests register and check out, etc.; a foyer, an open room or hallway at a theater entrance; in politics, a group of people who endeavor by personal persuasion to influence legislators.—*v.i.* To persuade by lobbying.—*v.t.* To accomplish by lobbying.

lobe, lōb, *n.* [Fr. *lobe*, L.L. *lobus*, from Fr. *lobos*, a lobe.] A round projecting part of an organ, as of the liver, lungs, brain, etc., the lower soft part of the ear; *bot.* a rounded projection or division of a leaf.—**lobate, lobated**, lō′bāt, lō′bā·ted, *a.* Consisting of or having lobes; applied to the foot of a bird furnished at the side with a broad-lobed membrane.—**lobed**, lōbd, *a.* Lobate.—**lobular**, lob′ū·lẽr, *a.* Having the character of a lobule.—**lobule**, lob′ūl, *n.* [Dim. of *lobe*.] A small lobe.

lobelia, lō·bē′li·a, *n.* [From Matthew *Lobel*, physician and botanist to James I.] A genus of beautiful plants belonging to the bell-flower family, a blue species being common in gardens.

lobscouse, lob′skous, *n.* [For *lobscourse*, from *lob* and *course*, that is, course or dish for lubbers.] *Naut.* a hash of meat, biscuit, etc., baked.

lobster, lob′stẽr, *n.* [A.Sax. *loppestere, lopystre*, corrupted from L. *locusta*, a lobster, a locust.] The name of certain long-tailed (macrurous), ten-footed crustaceans with large claws, allied to the crabs, and used for food.

lobular, lobule. See LOBE.

lobworm, lob′wẽrm, *n.* The lugworm.

local, lō′kal, *a.* [L. *localis*, from *locus*, a place, seen also in *lieu, lieutenant, allocate, collocate, couch, allow*, etc.] Pertaining to a particular place;

limited or confined to a spot, place, or definite district, *med.* confined to a particular part or organ.—*Local option* the principle by which the inhabitants of a locality vote directly on the sale there of intoxicants.—*n.* A local item of news; a local railroad train. (*Colloq.*)—**local color**, *n. Lit.* the distinctive features and peculiarities of a people or an area, used for interest and realism in writing.—**locale**, lō·kal′, *n.* A locality.—**localism**, lō′kal·izm, *n.* The state of being local; a local idiom or peculiarity of speech.—**locality**, lō·kal′i·ti, *n.* Position, situation, place, district; geographical place or situation.—**localization**, lō′kal·i·zā″shon, *n.* The act of localizing.—**localize**, lō′kal·īz, *v.t.*—*localized, localizing.* To fix in or assign to a particular place to discover or detect the place of.—**locally**, lō′kal·li, *adv.* With respect to place; in place.—**locate**, lō′kāt, *v.t.*—*located, locating.* [L. *loco, locatum*.] To set in a particular spot or position; to place; to settle.—*v.i.* To reside; to adopt a fixed residence.—**location**, lō·kā′shon, *n.* The act of locating; situation with respect to place; place.—**locative**, lō′ka·tiv, *a. Gram.* indicating place (a *locative* adjective; a *locative* case).—*n.* The locative case; a case expressing position.

loch, loch, *n.* [Gael.; allied to *lake*.] A lake; an arm of the sea running into the land, especially if narrow or to some extent landlocked.

lock, lok, *n.* [A.Sax. *loca, loc*, a lock; Icel. *lok*, a cover, shutter; *luka*, to shut; Dan. *lukke*, a lock, *lukke*, to lock; D. *luiken*, to shut.] An appliance used for fastening doors, chests, drawers, etc., its main feature being a bolt moved with a key; the mechanism by which a firearm is discharged; a fastening together; a state of being closely entangled; a grapple in wrestling; an enclosure in a canal, with gates at each end, used in raising or lowering boats as they pass from one level to another.—*v.t.* To fasten with a lock and key; to fasten so as to impede motion (to *lock* a wheel); to shut up or confine with, or as with, a lock, or in an enclosed place; to close fast; to seal; to join or unite firmly, as by intertwining or infolding; to embrace closely.—*To lock out*, to close the doors of an industrial establishment against the operatives; to throw out of employment, so as to bring workmen to the master's terms.—*To lock up*, to close or fasten with a lock; to confine; to restrain.—*v.i.* To become fast; to unite closely by mutual insertion of parts.—**lockage**, lok′ij, *n.* Works which form the locks on a canal; toll paid for passing the locks.—**locker**, lok′ẽr, *n.* A closed receptacle, as a drawer or small cupboard in a ship, that may be closed with a lock.—**locket**, lok′et, *n.* [Dim. from *lock*.] A little case worn as an ornament, often pendent to a necklace.—**lock nut**, *n.* A nut, usually of metal, so constructed that it cannot work itself loose when properly applied.—**lock-jaw**, *n. Med.* a form of tetanus consisting in spasmodic rigidity of the under jaw, so that the mouth cannot be opened.—**lockout**, *n.* The closing of a place of work against the workmen on the part of the employers, in order to bring the men to their terms as to hours, wages, etc.—**locksmith**, lok′smith, *n.* A mechanic whose occupation is to make or repair locks.—**lock step**, step used by a file of men keeping as close as possible to one another.—**lock stitch**, stitch formed by the locking of two threads.—**lockup**, *n.* A room or place in which persons under arrest are temporarily confined.

lock, lok, *n.* [A.Sax. *locc*=D. and Dan. *lok*, Icel. *lokkr*, G. *locke*, a curl or ringlet.] A tuft of hair or wool; a tress; a ringlet; a tuft of hay or other like substance.

locomotion, lō·ko·mō′shon, *n.* [L. *locus*, place, and *motio*, motion. LOCAL.] The act or power of moving from place to place.—**locomotive**, lō·ko·mō′tiv, *a.* Pertaining to locomotion; moving from place to place.—*n.* A self-driven vehicle, used for hauling passenger or freight cars, that runs on rails.

locomotor ataxia, lō·ko·mō′tèr ä·tak′si·ä, *n.* [L.] *Med.* difficulty in walking and coordination caused by the effects of syphilis on the nervous system.

locoweed, lō′kō·wēd, *n.* [Prefix Sp. *loco*, crazy, and *weed*.] Any of the herbs of the genera *Astragalus* and *Oxytropis*, common in the southwestern U.S.

locum tenens, lō′kum tē′nenz, *n.* [L.] One who temporarily acts for another; a deputy or substitute.

locus, lō′kus, *n.* pl. **loci**, lō′sī. [L. LOCAL.] A place; specifically, *geom.* the line traversed by a point which is constrained to move in accordance with certain determinate conditions.—*Locus classicus*, the classical or all-important passage in an author or book dealing with a specific point.—*Locus standi*, recognized place or position; the right of a party to appear and be heard on the question before any tribunal.

locust, lō′kust, *n.* [L. *locusta* (whence *lobster*).] The name of several large insects allied to the grasshoppers and crickets, and some of which appear in immense multitudes and eat up every green thing; the locust tree.

locution, lō·kū′shon, *n.* [L. *locutio*, *locutionis*, from *loquor*, to speak. LOQUACIOUS.] A mode of speech; a phrase.

lode, lōd, *n.* [A.Sax. *lád*, a way, a course, same as *load* in *loadstar*, *loadstone*.] An open ditch; a straight water channel; *mining*, a metallic vein, or any regular mineral vein.

lodestar, *n.* Same as *Loadstar*.

lodestone, *n.* Same as *Loadstone*.

lodge, loj, *n.* [Fr. *loge*, It. *loggia*, from L.L. *lobia*. LOBBY.] A small house in a park, forest, or domain; a small country residence; a temporary ha-

bitation; a hut; a small house connected with a larger (a porter's *lodge*); a place where a society or branch of a society, as freemasons, holds its meetings; the body of members who meet at such a place.—*v.t.*—*lodged, lodging*. To furnish with temporary house accommodation; to provide with a temporary place of abode; to set, lay, or deposit for keeping (to *lodge* money in a bank); to plant, fix, or settle (to *lodge* an arrow in one's breast); to beat down or lay flat (growing crops).—*v.i.* To have a temporary abode; to dwell at someone else's house; to be deposited or fixed; to settle; to reside; to dwell or have a fixed position.—**lodging**, loj′ing, *n.* A place of temporary rest or residence; a room or rooms hired for residence by a person in the house of another: often in this sense spoken of as plural.—**lodginghouse**, *n.* A house in which lodgers are accommodated.—**lodgment**, loj′ment, *n.* The act of lodging; accumulation of something deposited; deposition; *milit.* the occupation of a position, as in a siege, by the besieging party.

lodicule, lō′di·kūl, *n.* [L. *lodicula*, a coverlet.] *Bot.* one of the scales which occur at the base of the fruit of grasses.

loess, lės, *n.* [G. *löss*, from *lösen*, to pour or dissolve.] An unstratified yellowish-brown loam or alluvial deposit found in North America, Europe and Asia.

loft, loft, *n.* [Dan. *loft*, a ceiling, loft; Icel. *lopt*, air, sky.] The room or space below the rafters; also a gallery in a church, hall, etc.; upper rooms in a factory or barn; the act of lofting.—*v.t.*—*lofted, lofting*. To furnish with a loft; to place in a loft (to *loft* hay); *golf*, to slant the face of the club; to hit the ball so it rises well; to clear an obstacle.—*v.i. Golf*, to loft the ball.—**loftily**, lof′ti·li, *adv.*—**loftiness**, lof′ti·nes, *n.*—**lofty**, lof′ti, *a.* [From *loft, aloft*.] Much elevated in place; high; tall; elevated in condition or character; dignified; indicative of pride or haughtiness; proud; haughty; elevated in language or style; sublime; stately.

log, log, *n.* [Icel. *lág*, a felled tree; D. Dan. and G. *log*, the nautical log; akin *lie*, *lay*.] A bulky piece of timber unhewed; a large lump or piece of wood not shaped for any purpose; *naut.* a contrivance for measuring the rate of a ship's velocity through the water, consisting essentially in a piece of board in form of a quadrant of a circle, loaded so as to float upright, which, being thrown from a ship, drags on the line to which it is attached and causes it to unwind at a rate corresponding to the ship's velocity; the record of a ship's progress; a logbook.—**logbook**, *n. Naut.* a book in which are entered all particulars relating to the weather, winds, courses, etc., with any other matters relating to the vessel's voyage that are considered worthy of being

registered; a book for memoranda kept by a public teacher.—**log chip**, **log ship**, *n.* The log or board attached to the log line.—**log line**, *n.* —**log-rolling**, *n.* The lumbermen's water sport of treading floating logs; the political practice of legislators' combining forces to aid one another.—**logroller**, *n.*

log, log, *n.* A Hebrew measure of liquids, containing three-quarters or five-sixths of a pint.

loganberry, *n.* A cross between a blackberry and a raspberry.

logarithm, log′a·riTHm, *n.* [Gr. *logos*, ratio, and *arithmos*, number.] *Math.* the exponent of the power to which a given invariable number (or base) must be raised in order to produce another given number. Thus, in the common system of logarithms, in which the base is 10, the logarithm of 1000 is 3, because 10 raised to the third power is 1000. Many calculations are greatly facilitated by the use of logarithms, but for this special tables are required.—**logarithmic, logarithmical**, log·a·riTH′mik, log·a·riTH′mi·kal, *a.* Pertaining to logarithms; consisting of logarithms.—**logarithmically**, log·a·riTH′mi·kal·li, *adv.* By the use or aid of logarithms.

loggerhead, log′ér·hed, *n.* [From *log* and *head*; comp. *blockhead*.] A blockhead; a dunce; a dolt; a species of turtle found in the south seas.—*To be at loggerheads*, to be engaged in a fight; to be involved in a dispute.—*To come to loggerheads*, to come to a quarrel.

loggia, loj′a, *n.* pl. **loggias**, loj′az [It. LODGE.] *Italian arch.* a term applied to a gallery or arcade in a building running along the front or part of the front and open on one side to the air, on which side are a series of pillars or slender piers.

logic, loj′ik, *n.* [Fr. *logique*; L. *logica*; Gr. *logikē* (*technē*, art, understood), from *logos*, reason.] The science of reasoning; the science of the operations of the understanding subservient to the estimation of evidence; the science whose chief end is to ascertain the principles on which all valid reasoning depends, and which may be applied to test the legitimacy of every conclusion that is drawn from premises; the art or practice of reasoning.—**logical**, loj′i·kal, *a.* Pertaining to logic; used in logic; according to the rules or principles of logic; skilled in logic; discriminating.—**logicality**, loj·i·kal′i·ti, *n.* The state or quality of being logical.—**logically**, loj′i·kal·li, *adv.* In a logical manner.—**logician**, lō·jish′an, *n.* A person skilled in logic.—**logistic, logistical**, lō·jis′tik, lō·jis′ti·kal, *a.* [Gr. *logistikos*, from *logizomai*, to calculate or reckon.] Pertaining to judging, estimating, or calculating.

logogram, log′o·gram, *n.* [Gr. *logos*, a word, and *gramma*, a letter.] A single printing type that forms a word; a phonogramic symbol that, for the sake of brevity, represents a word.—**logographic, logo-**

graphical, lo·go·graf′ik, lo·go·graf′i-·kal, *a.* Pertaining to logography.—**logography,** lō·gog′ra·fi, *n.* A method of printing, in which a type forms a word, instead of forming a letter.

logomachy, lō·gom′a·ki, *n.* [Gr. *logos,* word, and *machē,* contest.] A contention about words; a war of words.—**logomachist,** lō·gom′a·kist, *n.* One who contends about words.

Logos, lŏg′os, *n.* [Gr., word, speech, reason, from *legō,* to speak.] The Word; the Divine Word; Christ.

logotype, log′o·tīp, *n.* A word or group of words cast together, as the name of a magazine, or the masthead of a paper, as opposed to a *ligature,* two or three letters united and cast together, as *æ, ffl.*

logwood, log′wụd, *n.* [From being imported in *logs.*] A dark-red dyewood, imported from Central America and the West Indies, much employed in dyeing and in calico printing to give a black or brown color.

loin, loin, *n.* [O.Fr. *logne* (Fr. *longe*), from L. *lumbus,* the loin.] The part of an animal on either side between the false ribs and the haunch bone; the part on either side of the trunk from the ribs to the lower limbs.

loiter, loi′tẽr, *v.i.* [Allied to D. *leuteren,* to waggle or waver; perhaps to *late,* like Icel. *lötra,* to linger, from *latr,* late; comp. E. *linger,* from *long.*] To be slow in moving; to delay; to spend time idly; to hang about.—*v.t.* To consume in trifles; to waste carelessly; used with *away.*—**loiterer,** loi′tẽr·ẽr, *n.* One who loiters.

Loki, lō′ki, *n.* [Icel. *loki.*] *Scandinavian myth.* the evil deity, the author of all calamities.

loll, lol, *v.i.* [Akin to Icel. *lulla,* to loll, *lalla,* to toddle as a child.] To lie at ease; to lie in a careless attitude; to recline; to hang extended from the mouth, as the tongue of a dog when heated from exertion; to move in a lax, lazy manner.—*v.t.* To suffer to hang out, as the tongue.

Lollard, lol′ẽrd, *n.* [L.G. and D. *lollen, lullen,* to sing, from the practice of the original Lollards of singing dirges at funerals.] A member of a society for the care of the sick and the burial of the dead, originating at Antwerp about 1300, and blamed for holding heretical opinions; one of the followers of Wickliffe in England.

lollipop, lol′i·pop, *n.* [From *loll,* to protrude the tongue, and *pop,* probably same as *pap,* infants' food.] Candy; usually a hard candy that is sucked rather than chewed, and so each piece is on a short stick, for easy handling; a sucker. (*Colloq.*)

Lombard, lom′bärd, *n.* [L.L. *Longobardi,* lit. 'long beards', being a latinized form of the German words for *long* and *beard.*] A native of Lombardy in Italy; an old name for a banker or money lender. Hence—*Lombard Street,* in London, where a large number of the principal bankers, moneybrokers, and bullion dealers have their offices.—*a.*

Of or pertaining to Lombardy or the Lombards.—**Lombardic,** *a.*

Lombardy poplar, lom′bär·di, *n.* A variety of *Populus nigra italicus,* or black poplar, whose branches lie close to the upright, tapering tree trunk, used for beauty in landscaping rather than for shade.

loment, lomentum, lō′ment, lō-·men′tum, *n. Bot.* an indehiscent legume which separates spontaneously by a transverse division between every two seeds.—**lomentaceous,** lō·men·tā′shus, *a.* Bearing loments; pertaining to a loment.

lone, lōn, *a.* [A contr. from *alone.*] Solitary; retired; unfrequented; without any companion or fellow; not having others near; single; unmarried, or in widowhood.—**loneliness,** lōn′li·nes, *n.* The condition of being lonely.—**lonely,** lōn′li, *a.* Unfrequented by man; retired; sequestered; not having others near; apart from fellows or companions; sad from want of companionship or sympathy.—**lonesome,** lōn′sum, *a.* Dreary from want of company or animation.

long, long, *a.* [A.Sax. *lang, long=* D., Dan., and G. *lang,* Icel. *langr,* Goth. *laggs* (*langs*); same as (but not borrowed from) L. *longus,* long. Hence verb to *long, along, belong, length, ling, linger,* etc.] Drawn out in a line or in the direction of length: opposed to *short,* and contradistinguished from *broad* or *wide*; drawn out or extended in time; lasting during a considerable time; continued or protracted; extended to any specified measure; having certain linear extent (a yard *long*; a mile *long*); occurring after a protracted interval; late; containing much verbal matter (a *long* speech or book). *Long home,* the grave or death. (O.T.)—*In the long run,* in the ultimate result.—*Long cloth,* a kind of fine cotton or calico fabric.—*Long clothes,* a baby's dress, which stretches much below the feet.—*Long firm,* a fictitious or pretended firm, consisting of swindlers who order goods without any intention of paying.—*Long ton,* the weight of 2240 pounds avoirdupois.—*n.* Something that is long.—*The long and the short,* or *the short and the long,* the sum of a matter in a few words; the whole.—*adv.* To a great extent in time; at a time far distant, either prior or posterior (not *long* before or after); throughout; without intermission (in such phrases as all my life *long,* forty years *long*).—**longboat,** *n.* The largest and strongest boat carried by a ship.—**longbow,** *n.* The old English archer's weapon, measuring about 6 feet long.—**long distance,** *a.* Being far away; placed at a great distance; over a great distance (*long-distance* running).—*n.* Telephone communication between two points widely separated.—**long dozen,** *n.* Thirteen. —**longhair,** *n.* One seriously interested in the arts; a lover of classical music.—**longhand,** long′hand, *n.* Ordinary written characters; handwriting.—**longheaded,** *a.* Having a

long head; dolichocephalic; shrewd; far-seeing; discerning.—**longhorn,** *n.* A type of cattle so called because of their very long horns and, in the U. S., found mostly in Texas.—**long-lived,** long′līvd, *n.* Having a long life or existence; lasting long. —**long-range,** *a.* Involving a long period of time; at a great distance; designed to cover a long distance.—**long shot,** *n.* Something involving great risk but promising equally great rewards if successful; an entry (in a horse race) having little chance of winning.—**longshoreman,** *n.* A stevedore; a dock laborer employed at loading cargo, etc.—**long-suffering,** *a.* Bearing injuries or provocation for a long time; patient; not easily provoked.—*n.* Long endurance; patience of offense.—**longways, longwise,** long′wāz, long′wīz, *adv.* Lengthwise.—**long-winded,** *a.* Tedious in speaking, argument, or narration.

long, long, *v.i.* [A.Sax. *langian,* to lengthen, to long, from *lang,* long; similarly Icel. *langa,* G. *verlangen,* to wish for.] To desire earnestly or eagerly; usually followed by the infinitive, or *for* or *after*; to have an eager appetite; to have a morbid craving; usually followed by *for.*—**longing,** long′ing, *n.* An eager desire; a craving or morbid appetite. —**longingly,** long′ing·li, *adv.*

longevous, lon·jē′vus, *a.* [L. *longus,* long, and *ævum,* age.] Long-lived.—**longevity,** lon·jev′i·ti, *n.* [L. *longævitas.*] Length or duration of life; more generally, great length of life.

longing, longingly. See LONG, *v.i.*

longitude, lon′ji·tūd, *n.* [L. *longitudo,* from *longus,* long. LONG.] Length; measure along the longest line; *geog.* distance (in degrees, minutes, and seconds, or in miles) on the surface of the globe measured on an arc of the Equator or parallel of latitude, the meridian of Greenwich being selected as a starting point, and called the first meridian, and longitude being called *east* or *west* accordingly; *astron.* distance measured on the ecliptic from the first point of Aries.—**longitudinal,** lon-·ji·tū′di·nal, *a.* Pertaining to longitude; running lengthwise, as distinguished from *transverse* or *across.*—*Longitudinal vibrations,* vibrations executed in the same line as that in which the undulation advances, as in the transmission of sound waves through air.—**longitudinally,** lon·ji·tū′di·nal·li, *adv.*

loo, lö *n.* [Originally called *lanterloo,* Fr. *lanturlu,* the meaningless refrain of a famous song.] A game at cards, formerly played with five cards, now commonly with three.

looby, lö′bi, *n.* [Allied to *lob, lubber.* W. *llabi,* a looby; *llab,* a blockhead.] An awkward, clumsy fellow; a lubber.

look, lụk, *v.i.* [A.Sax. *lócian,* to look; akin Prov. G. *lugen,* O.H.G. *luogen, luoken,* to look, G. *loch,* a hole.] To direct the eye toward an object; to gaze; to apply the mind or understanding; to consider; to have expectation or anticipation; to expect; to take heed or care; to mind; to have a particular direction or situation; to face; to front; to appear; to have a particular aspect; to give certain indications; to have or assume any air or manner.—*To look about*, to look on all sides or in different directions.—*To look after*, to tend; to take care of; to seek; to search for.—*To look down on* or *upon*, to regard as an inferior; to regard with contempt; to despise.—*To look for*, to expect (*to look for news*); to seek or search for.—*To look into*, to inspect closely; to examine.—*To look on*, to regard; to consider; to think or judge.—*To look over*, to examine one by one.—*To look out*, to be on the watch.—*To look to*, to watch; to take care of; to depend on for fulfilling some expectation.—*To look through*, to see through; to penetrate with the eye or with the understanding; to take a view of the contents of.—*v.t.* To express or manifest by a look.—*To look out*, to search for and discover.—*To look up*, to search for till found; to pay a visit to. (*Colloq.*)—*n.* Cast of countenance; air of the face; aspect; the act of looking or seeing.—**looker**, lụk'ẽr, *n.* One who looks.—*A looker on*, a mere spectator.—**looking glass**, *n.* A glass silvered on the back and intended to show by reflection the person looking on it; a mirror.—**lookout**, *n.* A careful looking or watching for any object or event; a place from which such observation is made; the person or party watching.

loom, lōm, *n.* [O.E. *lome*, A.Sax. *lóma*, tool, utensil, vessel; connections unknown. Hence *heir-loom*.] A frame or machine by means of which thread is worked into cloth being either driven by the person weaving (a *hand loom*) or driven and worked by steam or other motive power (a *power loom*); that part of an oar which is within the boat when used in rowing.

loom, lōm, *v.i.* [Icel. *ljóma*, to shine, *ljómi*, a ray; A.Sax. *leómian*, *leóma*, a ray or beam.] To appear larger than the real dimensions and indistinctly; to show large in darkness or fog: said of distant objects; to appear to the mind faintly or as at a distance.—*n.* The indistinct and magnified appearance of objects in darkness, fog, mist, etc.

loon, lön, *n.* [Same word as O.D. *loen*, a stupid man.] A crazy person; an idler.

loon, lön, *n.* [O.E. *loom*, Dan. *loom*, Icel. *lómr*, G. *lohme*, *lomme*, a loon.] A bird, the great northern diver.

loony, lö'ni, *a.* [From *lunatic*.] Crazy; daft.—*n.* One who is crazy.

loop, löp, *n.* [Ir. *lup*, Gael. *lub*, *luib*, loop, noose, thong, etc.] The doubled part of a string, rope, chain, etc.; a noose; a bight; anything resembling a loop, as the bend of a river; *elec.* a complete electric or magnetic circuit; *phys.* the part of a string

or column between two nodes.—*v.t.* To form into a loop or loops; *avi.* to make a complete circle vertically in the air.

loop, löp, *n.* [G. *luppe*, a loop, akin *lupp*, rennet; same root as E. *leap*, D. *loopen*, to run; comp. *run*, in sense of melting.] A mass of half-melted iron taken from the furnace in a pasty state for the forge or hammer.

loophole, löp'hōl, *n.* [D. *luipen*, to peep.] A small aperture in the wall of a fortification through which small arms are fired at an enemy; a hole that gives a passage or the means of escape; *fig.* an underhand or unfair opportunity of escape or evasion.

loose, lös, *a.* [A.Sax. *leás*, D. and G. *los*, Dan. Sw. *lös*, Icel. *laus*, loose; Goth. *laus*, empty; same as term. *-less. Lose*, *loss*, are closely allied.] Not attached together or to something fixed; untied; not fastened or confined; *fig.* free from ties; not tight or close (a *loose* garment); not dense, close, or compact (*loose* texture); not precise or exact; vague; indeterminate; lax; careless; unconnected; rambling; having lax bowels; dissolute; unchaste.—*To break loose*, to escape from confinement; to gain liberty by violence; *fig.* to cast off moral restraint.—*To let* or *set loose*, to free from restraint or confinement. Used substantively in the phrases.—*On the loose*, escaped from restraint; leading a loose life.—*To give a loose*, to give free vent. (*Thack.*)—*v.t.*—*loosed*, *loosing*. [Partly from the adj., partly from the allied A.Sax. *losian*, to set free.] To untie or unbind; to free from any fastening; to set free; to liberate; to relax; to loosen; to free from obligation, burden, or the like.—**loosely**, lös'li, *adv.* In a loose manner; laxly; slackly; carelessly; negligently; dissolutely.—**loosen**, lös'n, *v.t.* To make loose; to untie; to unfix or unsettle; to free from restraint, tightness, tension, firmness, or fixedness.—*v.i.* To become loose.—**loosener**, lös'n·ẽr, *n.* One who or that which loosens.—**looseness**, lös'nes, *n.* The state of being loose or relaxed; slackness; laxity; dissoluteness.

loot, löt, *n.* [Hind. *lūt*, plunder.] Booty; plunder, especially such as is taken in a sacked city.—*v.t. and i.* To plunder, as a sacked city; to ransack.—**looter**, lö'tẽr, *n.*

lop, lop, *v.t. and i.*—*lopped*, *lopping*. [Akin O.D. *luppen*, to maim.] To cut off, as the top or extreme part of anything or superfluous parts; to trim by cutting.—*n.* That which is lopped off.—**lopper**, lop'ẽr, *n.*

lop, lop, *v.t. and i.* [Allied to *lap*.] To be pendulous.—**lop-eared**, *a.* Having pendulous ears.—**loppy**, lop'i, *a.*—**lopsided**, *a.* Heavier at one side than the other; lying to one side.

lope, lōp, *v.i.* [O.N. *hlaupa*, to leap.] To move or run with a long, easy stride.—*v.t.* To cause to lope.—*n.* An easy gait which may be maintained a long while.

lophobranchiate, lō·fo·brang'ki·āt, *a.* [Gr. *lophos*, a crest or tuft, and *branchia*, gills.] Having the gills disposed in tufts along the branchial arches, as in the pipefish and hippocampus.

loquacious, lo·kwā'shus, *a.* [L. *loquax*, *loquacis*, from *loquor*, to speak; Skr. *lap*, to speak, to talk; seen also in *locution*, *colloquy*, *eloquent*, *obloquy*, etc.] Talkative; given to continual talking; prating.—**loquaciously**, lo·kwā'shus·li, *adv.* In a loquacious manner.—**loquacity**, lo·kwas'i·ti, *n.* The quality of being loquacious; talkativeness.

loquat, lō'kwät, *n.* A Chinese and Japanese evergreen tree of the apple family, yielding a fruit the size of a large gooseberry, with the flavor of an apple.

loran, lō'ran, la'ran, *n.* [*Long-range navigation*.] A device for determining a ship's position by means of pulsed signals sent out by two known radio stations.

lord, lord, *n.* [O.E. *laverd*, *lowerd*, etc., A.Sax. *hlaford*, a lord, from *hláf*, bread, a loaf, and *weard*, E. *ward*, that is, breadward.] A master; a person possessing supreme power and authority; a lady's husband; a ruler, governor, monarch; the proprietor of a manor; a nobleman; a title in Britain given to those who are noble by birth or creation, being thus applied to peers of the realm (dukes, marquises, earls, viscounts, and barons), and by courtesy to the sons of dukes and marquises, and to the eldest sons of earls; an honorary title of certain official personages, generally as part of a designation (*Lord* chancellor, *Lord*-mayor, *Lord*-provost); [cap.] the Supreme Being; Jehovah; Christ.—to Christ, especially in the expression *our Lord*.—*The Lord's Supper*, the sacrament of the Eucharist.—*Lords of Session*, the judges of the Court of Session in Scotland.—*Lords temporal*, those lay peers who have seats in the House of Lords.—*Lords spiritual*, the archbishops and bishops who have seats in the House of Lords.—*House of Lords*, that branch of the British legislature which consists of the lords spiritual and temporal assembled in one house.—*v.i.* To domineer; to rule with arbitrary or despotic sway: often followed by *over* and an indefinite *it* (to *lord it over* us).—**lordliness**, lord'li·nes, *n.* The state or quality of being lordly.—**lordly**, lord'li, *a.* Pertaining to, befitting, or suitable for a lord; large; liberal; haughty; imperious.—*adv.* Proudly; imperiously; despotically.—**Lord's day, the**, *n.* The first day of the week; Sunday.—**lordship**, lord'ship, *n.* The state or quality of being a lord; (with *his*, *your*, *their*) a title given to a lord; the territory over which a lord holds jurisdiction.

lordosis, lor·dō'sis, *n.* [N.L., from Gr. *lordōsis*, from *lordos*, bent so as to be convex in front.] *Med.* forward curvature of the spine.

lore, lōr, *n.* [A.Sax. *lár*, from stem of

laeran, to teach; D. *leer*, Dan. *laere*, G. *lehre*, lore. LEARN.] The store of knowledge which exists regarding anything; learning; erudition.—*Folklore*, the study of customs and legendary institutions.

lore, lōr, *n.* [L. *lorum*, a strap.] *Ornith.* the space between the bill and the eye of a bird; *entom.* a horny process observed in the mouth of some insects.

lorgnette, lorn•yet′, *n.* [Fr., from *lorgner*, to spy or peep.] An opera glass with folding handle; eyeglasses with hollow handle, into which they fold.

lorica, lo•rī′ka, *n.* [L., originally a corselet of leather thongs, from *lorum*, a thong.] An ancient Roman cuirass or corselet; a kind of lute or clay with which vessels are coated before they are exposed to the fire, as in chemical processes; *zool.* the protective case with which certain infusoria are provided.—**loricate**, lor′i•kāt, *v.t.*—**loricated**, *loricating*. To cover with some protective coating or crust.—**loricate**, **loricated**, lor′i•kā•ted, *pp.* Covered or plated over; covered as with plates of mail.

lorikeet, lor′i•kēt, *n.* [A dim. of *lory*, formed on the type of *parrakeet*.] The name of certain small Australian birds belonging to the parrot tribe.

loris, lō′ris, *n.* [Native name.] A quadrumanous mammal allied to the lemurs.

lorn, lorn, *a.* [An old or poetic pp. of *loss*. FORLORN.] Undone; forsaken; forlorn.

lorry, lor′i, *n.* [Comp. Prov. E. *lurry*, to pull or drag.] A four-wheeled truck or railroad car for heavy or bulky loads, with or without sides; a low, flat, motor-driven or horse-drawn truck.

lory, lō′ri, *n.* [Malay *luri*.] A name of certain Oriental birds of the parrot family with brilliant plumage.

lose, lōz, *v.t.*—*lost* (pret. & pp.), *losing*. [A.Sax. *losian*, to become loose, to lose, from *los*, loss, also *leósan*, to lose, usually in the compound form *forleósan*, like Goth. *fraliusan*, Dan. *forlise*, D. *verliezen*, G. *verlieren*. The old pp. was *loren*, hence E. *lorn*.] To cease to have in possession, as through accident; to become dispossessed or rid of unintentionally; to cease to possess; to forfeit, as by unsuccessful contest; not to gain or win; to wander from and not be able to find; to miss; to cease to perceive, as from distance or darkness; to cease or fail to see or hear.—*To lose one's self*, to lose one's way; to be bewildered.—*To lose one's temper*, to become angry.—*To lose sight of*, to cease to see; to overlook; to omit to take into calculation.—*v.i.* To forfeit anything in contest; to fail in a competition; not to win; to suffer by comparison.—**loser**, lō′zėr, *n.* One who loses, or is deprived of anything by defeat, forfeiture, or the like.—**losing**, lō′zing, *a.* Causing or incurring loss.—**loss**, los, *n.* [A.Sax. *los*,

damage.] The act of losing something; privation from something being lost; deprivation; forfeiture; failure to win or gain; that which is lost; quantity or amount lost; defeat; overthrow; ruin; misuse; failure to utilize (*loss* of time).—*To bear a loss*, to make it good; also, to sustain it without sinking under it.—*To be at a loss*, to be puzzled; to be unable to determine; to be in a state of uncertainty.—**lost**, lost, *p.* and *a.* Parted with; not to be found; no longer held or possessed; missing (a *lost* book or sheep); forfeited (as in an unsuccessful contest; not gained (a *lost* prize, a *lost* battle); not employed or enjoyed; misspent; squandered; wasted; having wandered from the way, bewildered; perplexed; ruined; quite undone; wrecked or drowned at sea; hardened beyond sensibility or recovery (*lost* to shame); no longer perceptible to the senses; not visible (a person *lost* in a crowd).—*The lost*, those who are doomed to misery in a future state.

lot, lot, *n.* [A.Sax. *hlot*, from *hleótan*, to get by lot; D. *lot*, Dan. *lod*, Icel. *hlutr*, G. *loos*, Goth. *hlauts*, lot. Hence *allot*; akin *lottery*.] Something selected by or falling to a person by chance, and adopted to determine his fate, portion, or conduct; the part, fate, or fortune which falls to one by chance; part in life allotted to a person; a distinct portion or parcel (a *lot* of goods); a large or considerable quantity or number (a *lot* of people): often in plural in same sense (he has *lots* of money).—*To cast in one's lot with*, to connect one's fortunes with.—*To cast lots*, to throw dice or use similarly some other contrivance to settle a matter as by previous agreement determined.—*To draw lots*, to determine an event by drawing so many lots from a number whose marks are concealed from the drawers.—*v.t.*—*lotted*, *lotting*. To allot; to assign; to distribute; to sort; to catalogue; to portion.

loth, lōth, *a.* [See LOATH.] Unwilling; not inclined; reluctant; loath.

Lothario, lō•thā′ri•ō, *n.* [From *Lothario*, one of the characters in Rowe's *Fair Penitent*.] A gay libertine; a seducer of female virtue; a gay deceiver: as *Lovelace*, the character in Richardson's *Clarissa*.

lotion, lō′shon, *n.* [L. *lotio*, from *lavo*, to wash. LAVE.] A wash or fluid preparation for improving the complexion, etc.; a fluid applied externally in cutaneous diseases to relieve pain, and the like.

lottery, lot′ėr•i, *n.* [Fr. *loterie*. LOT.] Allotment or distribution by lots or chance; a procedure or scheme for the distribution of prizes by lot; the drawing of lots.

lotto, lot′ō, *n.* [It. *lotto*, lottery.] A game of chance, played with a series of balls or knobs, numbering from one to ninety, with a set of cards or counters having corresponding numbers.

lotus, lō′tus, *n.* [Gr. *lōtos*.] A name

vaguely applied to a number of different plants famous in mythology and tradition; especially, a tree, the fruit of which was fabled among the ancient Greeks to have the property of making people forget their country and friends and to remain idle in the lotus-land; a name also applied to the Egyptian water lily and other plants.—**lotuseater**, *n.* in the *Odyssey*, one of a fabulous people who ate lotus fruit, which induced languor and forgetfulness of home.

loud, loud, *a.* [A.Sax. *hlud*, loud; O.Sax. O.Fris. *hlud*, D. *luid*, G. *laut*, loud; Icel. *hljóth*, G. *laut*, sound; akin *listen*; cog. Gr. *klyó*, to hear, *klytos*, famous; L. (*in*)*clytus*, famous; *laus*, praise, whence E. *laud*.] Strong or powerful in sound; high-sounding; making use of high words; clamorous; vehement; flashy; showy: colloquially applied to dress or manner.—*adv.* Loudly.—**loudly**, loud′li, *adv.* In a loud manner; with great sound or noise; noisily; clamorously;vehemently.—**loudness**, loud′nes, *n.* The quality of being loud; noise; clamor.

louis d'or, lö•i•dor, *n.* [Fr., a Louis of gold, as *Napoleon*, *Daric* (Darius), *Philip*, *Jacobus*.] A gold coin of France, first struck in 1640, in the reign of *Louis* XIII.

lounge, lounj, *v.i.*—*lounged*, *lounging*. [O.E. *lungis*, an awkward, slow-moving fellow, from O.Fr. *lóngis*, *longin*, a lout, from *long*, L. *longus*, long.] To dawdle or loiter; to spend the time in idly moving about; to recline in a lazy manner; to loll.—*n.* A sauntering or strolling; the act of reclining at ease or lolling; a place which idlers frequent; a kind of couch or sofa.—**lounger**, loun′jėr, *n.* One who lounges.

louse, lous, *n.* pl. **lice**, līs, [A.Sax. *lús*, pl. *lys*=D. *luis*, Dan. *lus*, Icel. *lús*, G. *laus*, perhaps from root of *lose*.] The common name of various wingless insects, parasitic on man and other animals.—*v.t.* (louz)—*loused*, *lousing*. To clean from lice.—**lousily**, lou′zi•li, *adv.* In a lousy manner.—**lousiness**, lou′zi•nes, *n.* The state of being lousy.—**lousy**, lou′zi, *a.* Swarming with lice; infested with lice.

lout, lout, *v.i.* [A.Sax. *lútan*, to bow or stoop; Icel. *lúta*, Dan. *lude*, to stoop; same root as *little*.] To bend, bow, or stoop down.—*n.* A mean awkward fellow; a bumpkin; a clown.—**loutish**, lout′ish, *a.* Clownish; rude; awkward.—**loutishly**, lout′ish•li, *adv.* In a loutish manner.—**loutishness**, lout′ish•nes, *n.*

louver, lö′vėr, *n.* [Fr. *lover*, *lovier*, a louver; a word of which the origin is unknown.] A dome or turret rising out of the roof of a hall or other apartment, formerly open at the sides, and intended to allow the smoke to escape.—*Louver window*, a window partially closed by sloping boards or bars called *louver boards* (corrupted into *luffer* or *lever boards*), placed across so as to admit air, but exclude rain.

lovage, luv′ij, n. [By corruption from L. *ligusticum*, lovage, from *Ligusticus*, Ligurian.] A name of certain stout, umbelliferous plants of Europe, one of them specially known as Scottish lovage.

love, luv, v.t.—*loved, loving.* [A.Sax. *lufian*, from *lufu*, love; D. *lieven*, G. *lieben*, to love, *liebe*, love; allied to *lief*, dear, *leave*, permission, believe; L. *libido*, desire, *liber*, free (whence *liberal*); *libeo, lubeo*, to please; Skr. *lubh*, to desire.] To regard with a strong feeling of affection; to have a devoted attachment to; to regard with the characteristic feelings of one sex toward the other; to like; to be pleased with; to delight in.—*v.i.* To be in love; to love each other; to be tenderly attached.—*n.* A strong feeling of affection; devoted attachment to a person; especially, devoted attachment to a person of the opposite sex; courtship (as in the phrase to *make love to*, that is, to court, to woo); fondness; strong liking (*love* of home, of art, etc.); the object beloved; a sweetheart; a representation or personification of love; a Cupid.—*Love* is the first element in a great number of compound words of obvious signification.—**lovable, loveable,** luv′a‑bl, a. Worthy of love; amiable.—**love apple,** n. The tomato.—**love-bird,** n. A name of a diminutive bird belonging to the parrot family, so called from the great attachment shown to each other by the male and female.—**love feast,** n. AGAPE.—**Love-in-idleness,** n. A plant, the heart's-ease.—**love knot,** n. A complicated knot, or a figure representing such; so called from being symbolic of love.—**loveless,** luv′les, a. Void of love.—**lovelily,**† luv′li·li, adv. In a lovely manner.—**loveliness,** luv′li·nes, n. The state or quality of being lovely; great beauty.—**lovelock,** n. A particular curl or lock of hair hanging by itself or so as to appear prominently.—**lovelorn,** a. Forsaken by one's love; pining or suffering from love.—**lovely,** luv′li, a. Fitted to attract or excite love; exciting admiration through beauty; extremely beautiful.—**love-making,** n. Courtship; paying one's addresses to a lady.—**lover,** luv′ér, n. One who loves or is attached to another; a person in love; a man who loves a woman; one who likes or has a fondness for anything (a *lover* of books).—**lovesick,** a. Sick or languishing with love.—**loving,** luv′ing, p. and a. Fond; affectionate; expressing love or kindness.—**loving cup,** n. A large cup containing liquor passed from guest to guest at banquets, especially those of a ceremonious character.—**loving-kindness,** luv′‑ing·kĭnd′nes, n. Tender regard; mercy; favor; a scriptural word.—**lovingly,** luv′ing·li, adv. In a loving manner; affectionately.—**lovingness,** luv′ing·nes, n.

low, lō, a. [O.E. *law, lagh,* etc.; not in A.Sax.=Icel. *lágr,* Dan. *lav.* D. *laag,* akin to *lie,* and to *law.*] Not rising to any great elevation; of little height: the opposite of *high*; not of the usual height; much below the adjacent ground; not much above sea level; below the usual rate or amount (*low* wages; a *low* estimate); not loud; grave; depressed in the scale of sounds; indicative of a numerical smallness (a *low* number); near or not very distant from the Equator (a *low* latitude, as opposed to a *high* latitude); dejected; depressed; humble in rank; groveling; base; dishonorable; feeble; having little vital energy (a *low* pulse, a *low* state of health); not excessive or intense; not violent (a *low* temperature); plain; not rich, high-seasoned, or nourishing (a *low* diet); in a prone position.—*Low Church,* the party in the *Ch.* of *Eng.* which believes in evangelical doctrine.—*Low Countries,* n. The land region near the North Sea corresponding to the Netherlands, Belgium and Luxembourg.—*Low Sunday,* the Sunday next after Easter.—*Low water, low tide,* the lowest point of the ebb or receding tide.—*adv.* Not aloft or on high; near the ground; under the usual price; in a mean condition.—**low-born,** a. Of mean or lowly birth.—**lowbrow,** a. Pertaining to those of uncultivated tastes.—*n.* One who is unable to appreciate intellectual influences.—**lower case,** n. *Print.* the case of boxes that contains the small letters of printing type, hence, small letters of printing type.—**low-down,** a. Mean; sneaking; treacherous.—*n.* The facts in the case; the truth of the matter.—**lowland,** lō′land, n. Land which is low with respect to the neighboring country; a low or level country.—*The Lowlands,* applies to the southern parts of Scotland.—**lowliness,** lō′li·nes, n.—**lowly,** lō′li, a. Low or humble in position of life; not lofty or exalted; meek; free from pride.—*adv.* In a low manner or condition.—**lowness,** lō′nes, n. Want of elevation; depression; dejection; meanness.—**low-pressure,** a. Having a low degree of expansive force, and consequently exerting a low degree of pressure; applied to steam or steam engines.—**low-spirited,** a. Cast down in spirit; dejected; depressed.

low, lō, v.i. [A.Sax. *hlówan*=D. *loeijen,* Icel. *hlóa,* O.H.G. *hlojan,* to low.] To bellow, as an ox or cow.—*n.* The sound uttered by a bovine animal, as a bull, ox, cow; a moo.—**lowing,** lō′ing, n. The bellowing or cry of cattle.

lower, lō′ér, v.t. [From *lower,* compar. of *low;* comp. *linger,* from *long,* adj.] To make lower in position; to let down; to take or bring down; to reduce or humble; to make less high or haughty; to reduce, as value or amount.

lower, lou′ér, v.i. [Same word as D. *loeren,* to frown; L.G. *luren,* to look sullen; akin to *leer.*] To frown; to look sullen; to appear dark or gloomy; to be clouded; to threaten a storm.—**lowering,** lou′ér·ing, p. and a. Threatening a storm; cloudy; overcast.—**loweringly,** lou′ér·ing·li, adv. In a lowering manner.—**lowery,** lou′ér·i, a. Cloudy; gloomy.

lown, loun, n. A low fellow; a loon. (*Shak.*)

lox, loks, n. [Yiddish, *laks,* from M.H.G. *lahs,* salmon.] A kind of smoked salmon.

lox, loks, n. Liquid oxygen, a colloq. abbreviation.

loxodromic, lok·so·drom′ik, a. [Gr. *loxos,* oblique, and *dromos,* a course.] Pertaining to oblique sailing, or sailing by the rhumb.—*Loxodromic curve,* or *line,* or *spiral,* the path of a ship when her course is directed constantly toward the same point of the compass, so as to cut all the meridians at equal angles.—**loxodromics, loxodromy,** lok·so·drom′‑iks, lok·sod′ro·mi, n.

loyal, loi′al, a. [Fr. *loyal,* O.Fr. *loial, leial, leal,* from L. *legalis,* legal, from *lex, legis,* a law. *Leal* is another form. LEGAL.] True or faithful in allegiance; faithful to the lawful government, to a prince or superior; true to plighted faith, duty, or love; not treacherous; constant.—**loyalist,** loi′al·ist, n. A person who adheres to his sovereign or to constituted authority.—**loyally,** loi′al·li, adv. In a loyal manner; faithfully.—**loyalism,** loi′al·izm, n. Loyalty.—**loyalty,** loi′al·ti, n. The state or quality of being loyal; fidelity; constancy.

lozenge, loz′enj, n. [Fr. *losange,* probably from Sp. *losa,* a slate or flat stone for paving.] A rectilineal figure with four equal sides, having two acute and two obtuse angles: called also a *diamond*; a small medicated candy in the form of a lozenge.

LSD-25. See LYSERGIC ACID DIETHYL-AMIDE.

luau, lū′ou, n. [Hawaiian.] A Hawaiian dinner of many courses served outdoors.

lubber, lub′ér, n. [Allied to *looby, lob,* W. *llob, llabi,* a lubber.] A clumsy or awkward fellow; a term applied by sailors to one who does not know seamanship.—*Lubber's point,* a black vertical mark drawn on the inside of the case of the mariner's compass in a line with the ship's head, as a guide to show the vessel's course.—*Lubber's hole,* the hole in the top or platform at the head of a lower mast through which sailors may mount without going over the rim by the futtock shrouds.—**lubberly,** lub′ér·li, a. Like a lubber; clumsy; clownish.

lubricate, lū′bri·kāt, v.t.—*lubricated, lubricating.* [L. *lubrico,* from *lubricus,* slippery.] To soften with an emollient or mucilaginous substance; to rub or supply with an oily or greasy substance, for diminishing friction.—**lubricant,** lū′bri·kant, a. Lubricating.—*n.* That which lubricates.—**lubrication,** lū·bri·kā′shon, n. The act of lubricating.—**lubricator,** lū′‑bri·kā·tér, n. One who or that which lubricates; an oil cup attached to a machine.—**lubricity,** lū·bris′i·ti, n. Smoothness or slipperiness; instability; shiftiness; lasciviousness.

lucarne, lū′kärn, n. [Fr. *lucarne,* L.

lucerna, a lamp, from *luceo,* to shine.] A dormer or garret window.

luce, lūs, *n.* [L. *lucius.*] The fish called the pike.

lucent, lū′sent, *a.* [L. *lucens, lucentis,* ppr. of *luceo,* to shine. LUCID.] Shining; bright; resplendent.—**lucency,** lū′sen·si, *n.* The state or quality of being lucent.

lucerne, lucern, lū′sėrn, *n.* [Fr. *luzerne, luserne;* origin unknown.] A leguminous plant cultivated for fodder in the U. S. and Europe; also called alfalfa.

lucid, lū′sid, *a.* [L. *lucidus,* akin to L. *lucere,* to shine.] Bright; clear; easily understandable; rational or sane.—**lucidity,** lū·sid′i·ti, *n.*

Lucifer, lū′si·fėr, *n.* [L. *lux, lucis,* light, and *fero,* to bring.] The morning star; Satan (from an erroneous interpretation of the term as applied by Isaiah); a person of Satanic attributes; [*not cap.*] a match ignitible by friction; called also *lucifer-match.*—**luciferous,** lū·cif′er·us, *a.* Light-giving.

luciferin, lū·cif′er·in, *n.* A substance generated by luminescent fishes and insects which causes their luminosity.

luck, luk, *n.* [O.Fris. *luk,* D. *luk, geluk,* G. *glück,* fortune, prosperity; allied to D. *lokken,* Dan. *lokke,* G. *locken,* to entice.] What is regarded as happening by chance; what chance or fortune sends; fortune; chance; accident; hap; good fortune; success.—**luckily,** luk′i·li, *adv.* In a lucky manner.—**luckiness,** luk′i·nes, *n.* The state or quality of being lucky.—**luckless,** luk′les, *a.* Without luck; ill-fated; unfortunate.—**lucklessly,** luk′les·li, *adv.* In a luckless manner.—**lucky,** luk′i, *a.* Favored by luck; fortunate; meeting with good success; sent by good luck; favorable; auspicious.

lucrative, lū′kra·tiv, *a.* [Fr. *lucratif,* from L. *lucrativus,* from *lucror,* to profit, from *lucrum,* gain; same root as G. *lohn,* reward.] Yielding lucre or gain; gainful; profitable.—**lucratively,** lū′kra·tiv·li, *adv.* In a lucrative manner.—**lucre,** lū′kėr, *n.* [Fr. *lucre,* L. *lucrum.*] Gain in money; profit; pelf: often in sense of base or unworthy gain.

lucubrate, lū′kū·brāt, *v.i.* [L. *lucubro, lucubratum,* to study by candlelight, from obs. adj. *lucuber,* bringing light, from *lux,* light.] To study by candlelight or a lamp; to study by night.—*v.t.* To elaborate, as by laborious night study.—**lucubration,** lū·kū·brā′shon, *n.* Nocturnal study; what is composed, or supposed to be composed, by night; a literary composition of any kind.—**lucubrator,** lū′kū·brā·tėr, *n.* One who makes lucubrations.

luculent, lū′kū·lent, *a.* [L. *luculentus,* from *luceo,* to shine.] Lucid; bright; evident; unmistakable.

Lucullan, lū·kul′len, *a.* [From the Roman consul *Lucullus,* who was famous for luxurious living.] Bountiful; voluptuous.

Luddite, lud′īt, *n.* In 18th Century England, one of the rioters against the displacement of factory workers by machinery. (From a leader, Ned Lud.)

ludicrous, lū′dik·rus, *a.* [L. *ludicrus,* from *ludus,* sport or game; seen also in *allude, delude, elude, illusion, prelude.*] Adapted to raise good-humored laughter; very ridiculous; comical; droll.—**ludicrously,** lū′dik·rus·li, *adv.* In a ludicrous manner.—**ludicrousness,** lū′dik·rus·nes, *n.*

lues, lū′ēz, *n.* [L.] A poison or pestilence; a plague.—*Lues venerea,* the venereal disease.

luff, luf, *n.* [Formerly *loof,* from D. *loef,* Dan. *luv,* G. *luf,* weather gauge.] *Naut.* the weather gauge; the weather part of a fore-and-aft sail.—*v.t.* and *i.* To turn the head of a ship toward the wind.

lug, lug, *v.t.*—*lugged, lugging.* [A.Sax. *geluggian,* to lug; N. *lugga,* to haul by the hair.] To haul; to drag; to pull along or carry, as something heavy and moved with difficulty; to introduce laboriously (to *lug* a story into the conversation.)—*v.i.* To pull or tug.—*n.* The ear; a projecting part of an object resembling the human ear, as the handle of a vessel.—**luggage,** lug′ij, *n.* That which is lugged; baggage; collectively, the containers for a traveler's belongings.—**lugger,** lug′ėr, *n.* A vessel carrying either two or three lugsails.—**lugsail,** *n.* A square sail bent upon a yard that hangs obliquely to the mast at one-third of its length.

lugubrious, lū·gū′bri·us, *a.* [L. *lugubris,* mournful, from *lugeo,* to weep; akin Gr. *lygros,* sad.] Mournful; indicating or expressive of sorrow; doleful.—**lugubriously,** lū·gū′bri·us·li, *adv.* In a lugubrious manner.—**lugubriousness,** lū·gū′bri·us·nes, *n.* The quality of being lugubrious.

lugworm, lug′wėrm, *n.* [Sw. *lugg,* tuft of hair, the forelock; it has tufts and bristles along its sides.] An annelid or worm which burrows in the muddy sand of the shore, and is much esteemed for bait. Also called *Lobworm.*

lukewarm, lūk′wạrm, *a.* [O.E. *luke,* lukewarm, D. *leuk,* G. *lau,* lukewarm.] Moderately warm; tepid; not ardent; not zealous; cool; indifferent.—**lukewarmly,** lūk′wạrm·li, *adv.*—**lukewarmness,** lūk′wạrm·nes, *n.*

lull, lul, *v.t.* [Dan. *lulle,* Sw. *lulla,* G. *lullen;* probably an imitation of the sound.] To sing to in order to induce to sleep; to cause to rest by gentle, soothing means; to quiet; to compose.—*v.i.* To subside; to cease; to become calm (the wind *lulls*).—*n.* A season of temporary quiet after storm, tumult, or confusion.—**lullaby,** lul′a·bī, *n.* A song to lull or quiet babes.

lumbago, lum·bā′gō, *n.* [L., from *lumbus,* loin.] Rheumatism or rheumatic pains affecting the lumbar region.—**lumbar,** lum′bėr, *a.* [L. *lumbus,* a loin. LOIN.] Pertaining to the loins.—*Lumbar region,* the portion of the body between the false ribs and the upper part of the hip bone; the small of the back.

lumber, lum′bėr, *n.* [Originally a pawnbroking establishment, from the *Lombards,* who were famed as pawnbrokers or moneylenders.] Things bulky and thrown aside as of no use; old furniture, discarded utensils, or the like; timber sawed or split for use as beams, boards, planks, etc.—*v.t.* To heap together in disorder; to fill with lumber.—*v.i.* To move heavily, as a vehicle; to cut timber in the forest and prepare it for the market.—**lumbering,** *n.* Logging; cutting and removing timber for commercial purposes.—*a.* Clumsy; awkward.—**lumberjack,** *n.* A timber cutter. (*Colloq.*)

lumbrical, lum′bri·kal, *a.* [L. *lumbricus,* a worm.] Pertaining to or resembling a worm.—*n.* A worm-like muscle of the fingers and toes.

lumen, lö′men, *n.* [L. for *light.*] The cavity of a blood vessel or other tube; a unit of light, being the light emitted by a source of one international candle intensity per unit space angle in a second.

luminary, lū′mi·na·ri, *n.* [Fr. *luminaire,* L. *luminare,* from *lumen, luminis,* light, for *lucmen,* from *luceo,* to shine. LUCID.] Any body that gives light, but chiefly one of the heavenly bodies; a person who enlightens mankind.—**luminescence,** *n.* The emission of light by certain bodies that have been exposed to light or radiant energy, or self-generated light, as in fireflies and certain deep-sea fishes.—**luminiferous,** lū·mi·nif′ėr·us, *a.* Producing light; yielding light; serving as the medium for conveying light (the *luminiferous* ether).—**luminosity, luminousness,** lū·mi·nos′i·ti, lū′mi·nus·nes, *n.* The quality of being luminous; brightness; clearness.—**luminous,** lū′mi·nus, *a.* [L. *luminosus.*] Shining; emitting light; bright; brilliant; giving mental light; clear (a *luminous* essay or argument).

lummox, lum′uks, *n.* A dull-witted, awkward person.

lump, lump, *n.* [O.D. *lompe,* Sw. *lump,* N. *lump,* piece, mass; allied to *lubber, lunch.*] A small mass of matter, of no definite shape; a mass of things blended or thrown together without order or distinction.—*In the lump,* the whole together; in gross.—*v.t.* To throw into a mass; to take in the gross.—**lumpfish,** lump′fish, *n.* A fish of the northern seas, having the ventral fins modified into a sucker, by means of which it adheres to bodies.—**lumpy,** lump′i, *a.* Full of lumps or small compact masses.

lump, lump, *v.t.* [Origin unknown.] To put up with (something disagreeable) (like it or *lump* it).

lunacy, lū′na·si, *n.* [From L. *lunaticus,* lunatic, moon-struck, from *luna,* the moon (lunatics being at one time supposed to be affected by the moon), for *lucna,* from root of *luceo,* to shine. LUCID.] The state or quality of being lunatic; insanity; properly the kind of insanity which is broken by intervals of reason; the height of folly.—**lunatic,** lū′na·tik, *a.* Affected by lunacy; mad; insane.—

n. A person affected by lunacy; an insane person.—*Lunatic asylum*, a house or hospital established for the reception of lunatics.

luna moth, *n.* A large American moth (*Tropaea luna*) having long tails on the hind wings and greenish coloring.

lunar, lū′nẽr, *a.* [L. *lunaris*, from *luna*, the moon. LUNACY.] Pertaining to the moon; measured by the revolutions of the moon (*lunar* days or years).—*Lunar caustic*, nitrate of silver (silver being called *Luna* by the alchemists).—*Lunar month*, the period of a complete revolution of the moon, 29½ days.—**lunate, lunated,** lū′nāt, lū′nā·ted. *a.* Crescent-shaped.—**lunation,** lū·nā′shon, *n.* The time from one new moon to the following.

lunch, lunsh, *n.* [A form of *lump*, as *hunch* of *hump*, *bunch* of *bump*.] A luncheon.—*v.i.* To eat a lunch.— **luncheon,** lunsh′on, *n.* [A longer form of *lunch*, perhaps for *lunching*.] A slight repast or meal between breakfast and dinner.—**luncheonette,** lunsh·on·et′, *n.* A lunchroom where light lunches are served.—**lunchroom,** u. A restaurant where quick meals are served.

lune, lūn, *n.* [L. *luna*, the moon. LUNACY.] Anything in the shape of a crescent or half-moon; a geometrical figure in shape of a crescent. —**lunette,** lū·net′, *n.* [Fr. *lunette*, dim. from L. *luna*.] *Fort.* a work in the form of a redan with flanks, used as an advanced work; *arch.* an aperture for the admission of light in a concave ceiling; *archaeol.* a crescent-shaped ornament for the neck.—**luniform,** lū′ni·form, *a.* Resembling the moon.

lung, lung, *n.* [A.Sax. *lunge*, pl. *lungan*, Icel. *lunga*, D. *long*, D. and G. *lunge*, a lung; same root as *light*, from their lightness (comp. the name *lights*).] One of the two organs of respiration in air-breathing animals, light and spongy and full of air cells; a similar saclike respiratory organ found in certain air-breathing invertebrates; an underwater device that enables persons leaving a submarine to rise to the surface; a device used to introduce, mechanically, fresh air into the lungs.— **lungwort,** lung′wẽrt, *n.* A common garden flower, having leaves speckled like lungs.—**lungfish,** *n.* One of a group of fishes (Dipnoi) breathing by means of lungs as well as gills.

lunge, lunj, *n.* [Formerly *longe*, *allonge*, from Fr. *allonger*, to lengthen, to thrust—L. *ad*, to, *longus*, long.] A sudden thrust or pass, as with a sword.—*v.i.*—*lunged, lunging*. To make a thrust or pass, as with a sword or rapier.—*v.t.* To exercise (a horse) by making him run round in a ring while held by a *long* rein.

lunisolar, lū·ni·sō′lẽr, *a.* [L. *luna*, moon, and *sol*, sun.] Compounded of the revolutions of the sun and moon; resulting from the united action of the sun and moon.— **lunula, lunule,** lū′nū·la, lū′nūl, *n.* [Dim. of L. *luna*, the moon.] Some-

thing in the shape of a little moon or crescent.—**lunulate, lunulated,** lū′nū·lāt, lū′nū·lā·ted, *a.* Resembling a small crescent.

Lupercal, lū·pẽr′kal or lū′pẽr·kal, *a.* Pertaining to the Lupercalia, or feasts of the Romans in honor of Lupercus or Pan.—*n.* pl. **Lupercalia,** lū·pẽr·kā′li·a. An ancient Roman feast in honor of Pan.

lupine, lū′pīn, *a.* [L. *lupus*, a wolf; cog. with E. *wolf*.] Like a wolf; wolfish; ravenous.—**lupine,** lū′pin, *n.* [Fr. *lupin*; L. *lupinus*, in allusion to its destroying or exhausting land.] The name of various leguminous plants, some of which are commonly cultivated in gardens for the sake of their gaily-colored flowers.

lupulin, lupuline, lū′pū·lin, *n.* [L. *lupulus*, hops.] The peculiar bitter aromatic principle of the hop; the fine yellow powder of hops, which contains the bitter principle, largely used in medicine.

lupus, lū′pus, *n.* [L., a wolf.] A disease which eats away the flesh, producing ragged ulcerations of the nose, cheeks, forehead, eyelids, and lips.

lurch, lẽrch, *n.* [O.Fr. *lourche*, It. *lurcio*, G. *lurz*, *lurtsch*, a lurch at cribbage.] A term in the game of cribbage, denoting the position of a player who has not made his thirty-first hole when his opponent has pegged his sixty-first. Hence, *to leave in the lurch*, to leave in a difficult situation or in embarrassment; to leave in a forlorn state or without help.

lurch, lẽrch, *v.i.* [A form of *lurk*, as *church* of *kirk*, *birch* of *birk*, etc. LURK.] To lie in ambush or in secret; to lie close; to lurk; to shift or to play tricks (*Shak.*); to roll suddenly to one side, as a ship in a heavy sea; to stagger to one side, as a tipsy man.—*n.* A sudden roll of a ship; a roll or stagger of a person.—**lurcher,** lẽrch′ẽr, *n.* One that lies in wait or lurks; a dog that lies in wait for game.

lurdan, lurdane, lẽr′dan, lẽr′dān, *a.* [O.Fr. *lourdin*, *lourdein*, from *lourd*, heavy, dull.] Blockish; stupid; clownish; lazy and useless. (*Tenn.*)

lure, lūr, *n.* [Fr. *leurre*, from M.H.G. *luodar*, a lure, G. *luder*, carrion, a bait for wild beasts.] Any artificial bait, usually imitating the appearance of insects or small fish, used in angling; any enticement; that which invites by the prospect of advantage or pleasure.—*v.t.*—*lured, luring*. To attract by a lure or to a lure; to entice; to attract; to invite.

lurid, lū′rid, *a.* [L. *luridus*.] Pale yellow, as flame; ghastly pale. Also vivid; violent; harshly terrible; as a *lurid* crime or *lurid* story.

lurk, lẽrk, *v.i.* [Akin to N. *luska*, Dan. *luske*, to lurk, to skulk; Dan. *lur*, G. *lauer*, an ambush or watching.] To lie hid; to lie in wait; to lie concealed or unperceived.—**lurker,** lẽr′kẽr, *n.* One that lurks.

luscious, lush′us, *a.* [Perhaps for *lustious*, from *lusty*.] Very sweet; delicious; delightful; sweet to ex-

cess, hence, unctuous; fulsome.— **lusciously,** lush′us·li, *adv.* In a luscious manner. —**lusciousness,** lush′us·nes, *n.* The state or quality of being luscious.

lush, lush, *a.* [Shortened from *luscious*.] Fresh, luxuriant, and juicy; succulent.

lush, lush, *n.* [Origin unknown.] A habitual drunkard; liquor.

lust, lust, *n.* [A.Sax., D., G., and Sw. *lust*, Icel. and Dan. *lyst*, desire.] Longing desire; eagerness to possess or enjoy; depraved affection or desire; more especially, sexual appetite; unlawful desire of sexual pleasure; concupiscence.—*v.i.* To desire eagerly; to long; to have carnal desire: with *after*.—**lustful,** lust′ful, *a.* Inspired by lust or the sexual appetite; provoking to sensuality.—**lustfully,** lust′ful·li, *adv.* In a lustful manner.—**lustfulness,** lust′ful·nes, *n.* The state of being lustful.

luster, lustre, lus′tẽr, *n.* [Fr. *lustre*, from L. *lustrum*, purificatory sacrifice (see LUSTRAL), or from stem of *luceo*, to shine (see LUCID).] Brightness; splendor; brilliance; sheen; *mineral.* a variation in the nature of the reflecting surface of minerals; the splendor of birth, of deeds, or of fame; renown; distinction; a branched chandelier ornamented with drops or pendants of cut glass; a fabric for ladies' dresses, consisting of cotton warp and woolen weft.— **lustring,** lus′tring, *n.* A species of glossy silk cloth.—**lustrous,** lus′trus, *a.* Characterized by luster; bright; shining; luminous.—**lustrously,** lus′trus·li, *adv.* Brilliantly; luminously.

lustily, lustiness. See LUSTY.

lustral, lus′tral, *a.* [L. *lustralis*, from *lustro*, to purify, from *lustrum*, a purificatory sacrifice, from stem of *luo*, *lavo*, to wash. LAVE.] Used in purification; pertaining to purification.—**lustrate,** lus′trāt, *v.t.* [L. *lustro*, *lustratum*, to cleanse.] To purify as by water.—**lustration,** lus·trā′shon, *n.* A cleansing or purifying. —**lustrum,** lus′trum, *n.* pl. **lustrums** or **lustra,** lus′trumz, lus′tra. [L.] In ancient Rome, the purification of the whole people performed at the end of every five years; hence a period of five years.

lusty, lus′ti, *a.* [From *lust*=D. and G. *lustig*, D. *lystig*, merry, jovial.] Characterized by life, spirit, vigor, health, or the like; stout; vigorous; robust; healthful; bulky; large; lustful; hot-blooded.—**lustihood,** lus′ti·hud, *n.* The quality of being lusty; vigor of body. (*Tenn.*)—**lustily,** lus′ti·li, *adv.* In a lusty manner; vigorously; stoutly.—**lustiness,** lus′ti·nes, *n.* The state of being lusty.

lute, lūt, *n.* [Fr. *luth*, *lut*, Sp. *laud*, from Ar. *al ûd*, the wood (*al* being the definite article).] A stringed musical instrument of the guitar kind, formerly very popular in Europe.—*v.t.* To play on a lute.— **lutanist, lutist,** lū′tan·ist, lū′ten·ist, lūt′ist, *n.* A performer on the lute.

lute, luting, lūt, lūt′ing, *n.* [L. *lutum*, mud, clay, from *luo*, to wash.] *Chem.* a composition of clay or other substance used for stopping the juncture of vessels so closely as to prevent the escape or entrance of air, or applied as a coating to glass retorts in order that they may support a high temperature.—**lute**, v.t.—*luted, luting.* To close or coat with lute.

lutetium, lu·te'shi·um, n. [L. *Lutetia*, Paris.] A metallic element of the rare-earth series. Symbol, Lu; at. no., 71; at. wt., 174.97.

Lutheran, lū'thėr·an, a. Pertaining to Martin *Luther*, the reformer.—n. A disciple or follower of Luther; one who adheres to the doctrines of Luther.—**lutheranism,** lū'thėr·an·-izm, n. The doctrines of religion as taught by Luther.

luxate, luk'sāt, v.t.—*luxated, luxating.* [L. *luxo, luxatum*, from *luxus*, dislocated, Gr. *loxos*, slanting.] To put out of joint, as a limb; to dislocate.—**luxation,** luk'sā·shon, n. The act of luxating; a dislocation.

luxuriant, lug·zhū'ri·ant, a. [L. *luxurians*, from *luxurio*, to luxuriate, from *luxuria*, luxury, *luxus*, excess.] Exuberant in growth; rank; abundant; growing to excess; excessive or superfluous.—**luxuriantly,** lug·zhū'-ri·ant·li, adv. In a luxuriant manner or degree.—**luxuriance, luxuriancy,** lug·zhū'ri·ans, lug·zhū'ri·an·si, n. The state of being luxuriant.—**luxuriate,** lug·zhū'ri·āt, v.i.—*luxuriated, luxuriating.* [L. *luxurio*, to be rank or luxurious, to be wanton.] To grow rankly or exuberantly; to feed or live luxuriously; *fig.* to indulge or revel without restraint.—**luxuriation,** lug·zhū'ri·ā"shon, n. The act of luxuriating.—**luxurious,** lug·zhū'ri·us, a. [L. *luxuriosus.*] Characterized by indulgence in luxury; given to luxury; voluptuous; administering to luxury; furnished with luxuries.—**luxuriously,** lug·zhū'ri·us·li, adv. In a luxurious manner.—**luxuriousness,** lug·-zhū'ri·us·nes, n. The state or quality of being luxurious.—**luxury,** lug'-zhū·ri, n. [L. *luxuria.*] A free or extravagant indulgence in the pleasures of the table, or in costly dress and equipage; that which is delightful to the senses, the feelings, etc.; that which gratifies a nice and fastidious appetite; anything not necessary, but used for personal gratification.

lycanthrope, lī'kan·thrōp, n. [Gr. *lykos*, a wolf, and *anthrōpos*, a man.] Formerly a man believed to be transformed into a wolf; a werwolf; now, a person affected with lycanthropy.—**lycanthropy,** lī·kan'thro·pi, n. A kind of insanity in which the patient supposes himself to be a wolf.

lyceum, lī·sē'um, n. [L. *Lyceum*, Gr. *Lykeion*, from a temple dedicated to Apollo *lykeios.*] Apollo the wolf-slayer, from *lykos*, a wolf.] A building at ancient Athens where Aristotle taught; hence a building appropriated to instruction by lectures; a literary institute; a cultural association which provides lectures, concerts, etc.

lycopod, lī'kō·pod, n. [Gr. *lykos*, a wolf, and *pous, podos*, a foot.] A plant belonging to an order inter-

mediate between mosses and ferns, and in some respects allied to the conifers.—**lycopodium,** lī·kō·pō'di·-um, n. A genus of lycopods.

lyddite, lid'īt, n. [From *Lydd*, in Kent.] An explosive prepared from picric acid.

Lydian, lid'i·an, a. Pertaining to ancient *Lydia* in Asia Minor; a term applied to one of the ancient Greek modes of music of a soft pleasing character.—*Lydian stone*, a jasper-like siliceous rock used by the ancients as a touchstone.

lye, lī, n. [A.Sax. *leáh*, G. *lauge*, D. *loog*, lye; allied to L. *lavo*, to wash.] Water impregnated with alkaline salt imbibed from the ashes of wood; a solution of an alkali used for cleaning purposes.

lymph, limf, n. [Fr. *lymphe*, L. *lympha*, water.] A fluid in animal bodies contained in certain vessels called *lymphatics*, which differs from the blood in its corpuscles being all of the colorless kind.—**lymphatic,** lim·fat'ik, a. Pertaining to lymph; phlegmatic; sluggish.—n. A vessel or duct in an animal body containing lymph.—**lymph gland,** n. Gland-like bodies occurring in the lymphatic vessels from which come lympho-cytes.—**lymphocyte,** lim'fō·cit, n. A white or colorless blood cell derived from lymphoid tissue.—**lymphoid,** lim'foid, a. Of, pertaining to, or resembling lymph; of or pertaining to tissue characteristic of the lymph glands.

lynch, linsh, v.t. [Said to be from a Virginian farmer of the name of *Lynch*, noted for taking the law into his own hand.] To inflict punishment upon, without the forms of law, as by a mob or by unauthorized persons.—**lynch law,** n. The practice of punishing men by unauthorized persons without a legal trial.

lynx, lingks, n. [L. and G. *lynx*; same root as in L. *lux*, light, from its bright eyes.] A name given to several carnivorous mammals of the cat family, long famed for their sharp sight.—**lynx-eyed,** a. Having extremely acute sight.

lyonnaise, lī·o·nāz', a. [From French *Lyonnais*, Lyon.] Prepared with onions (*lyonnaise* potatoes).

lyre, līr, n. [Fr. *lyre*, L. and Gr. *lyra*; etymology uncertain.] One of the most ancient stringed musical instruments of the harp family, used by the Greeks.—**lyrate, lyrated,** lī'rāt, lī'rā·ted, a. Shaped like a lyre.—**lyrebird,** n. An Australian bird somewhat smaller than a pheasant, having erect tail feathers in form resembling an ancient lyre.—**lyric, lyrical,** lir'ik, lir'i·kal, a. Pertaining to a lyre or harp; *poetry*, exhibiting the poet's own thoughts and feelings.—**lyric,** n. A lyric poem; pl. the words of a song.—a. Suitable to be set to music or sung.—**lyricism,** lir'i·sizm, n. Lyric composition; a lyrical form of language.—**lyricist,** lir'i·sist, n.—**lyrist,** lir'ist, n. A musician who plays on the lyre.

lysis, lī'sis, n. [Gr., a solution, from *lyō*, to dissolve.] *Med.* the gradual

ending of a disease, without critical symptoms.

lysergic acid diethylamide, lī'sėr·-jik as'id dī'ethl·a·mīd, n. A drug causing hallucinations and other simulated mental disorders, used in psychological experimentation. Abbrev. LSD-25.

M

M, m, em, is the thirteenth letter and tenth consonant of the English alphabet, representing a labial and nasal articulation.

ma'am, mam, n. A colloquial contraction for *Madam*.

macabre, macaber, ma·kä'bėr, a. [Fr. *Danse macabre*, dance of death.] Ghastly; hideous; gruesome; representing death.

macadamize, mak·ad'am·īz, v.i.—*macadamized, macadamizing.* [From J. L. McAdam, the inventor.] To cover, as a road, with small broken stones, which, when consolidated, form a firm surface.—**macadamization,** mak·ad'am·i·zā"shon, n.—**macadam,** mak·ad'am, n. Macadamized pavement or roadway; the broken stone used in the process.

macaque, ma·kāk', n. [Fr.] An Old World monkey with short tail and prominent eyebrows.

macaroni, mak·a·rō'ni, n. pl. [Fr. and Prov. It. *macaroni*, It. *mac-cheroni*, originally a mixture of flour, cheese, and butter.] A dough of fine wheaten flour made into a tubular or pipe form, a favorite food among the Italians; a medley; a sort of droll or fool; a name formerly given to fops or dandies; a confused mixture of things; a macaronic verse or poem.

macaroon, mak·a·rön', n. A small sweet cake, with egg white and sugar basis, containing almond meal or shredded coconut.

macaw, ma·ka', n. [Native name in the Antilles.] One of a genus of beautiful birds of the parrot family, having cheeks destitute of feathers, and long tail feathers.

Maccabean, mak·ka·bē'an, a. Pertaining to the Jewish princes called *Maccabees*.—**Maccabees,** mak'ka·-bēz, n. pl. Two books treating of Jewish history under the Maccabean princes, included in the Apocrypha.

mace, mās, n. [O.Fr. *mace*, Fr. *masse*, It. *mazza*, a club; from L. *matea* (only found in the dim. *mateola*), a kind of mallet.] A weapon of war consisting of a staff with a heavy metal head frequently in the form of a spiked ball, used for breaking armor; an ornamental staff of metal borne before a dignitary as a symbol of his authority.—**mace-bearer,** n. A person who carries a mace before public functionaries.—**macer,** mās'-ėr, n. A mace-bearer; an officer attending several Scottish courts.

mace, mās, n. [Fr. *macis*, It. *mace*, L. *macis, macir*, Gr. *maker*, an Indian spice.] A spice, the dried aril or covering of the seed of the nutmeg, chiefly used in cooking or in pickles.

macédoine, mas•e•dwän′, n. [Fr., early meaning, Macedonian parsley.] A combination or mixture; used to designate a sauce or jellied salad containing mixed small or diced vegetables.

macerate, mas′er•āt, v.t.—*macerated, macerating*. [L. *macero, maceratum,* to make soft: same root as *mass,* a lump.] To steep almost to solution; to soften and separate the parts of by steeping in a fluid, or by the digestive process; to mortify‡.—*v.i.* To become macerated; to waste away.—**maceration,** mas•er•ā′shon, n. The act of macerating.

machete, mä•chä′tä, n. [Sp.] A kind of large knife or cutlass used in South America and the West Indies as a tool or a weapon.

Machiavelian, mak′i•a•vel′yan, a. Pertaining to *Machiavelli,* an Italian writer, secretary and historiographer to the Republic of Florence (died 1527); in conformity with Machiavelli's principles; cunning in political management; crafty.—*n.* One who adopts the principles of Machiavelli.

machicolation, ma•chik′o•lā″shon, n. [Fr. *mâchicoulis, mâchecoulis*; origin doubtful.] *Milit. arch.* a vertical opening in the floor of a projecting gallery, parapet, etc., for hurling missiles or pouring boiling lead, pitch, etc., upon the enemy; a part thus projecting, as at the top of a tower, without any such opening.—**machicolate,** ma•chik′o•lāt, v.t. To form with machicolations.

machinate, mak′i•nāt, v.t. and i.—*machinated, machinating*. [L. *machinor, machinatus,* from *machina.* MACHINE.] To plan; to contrive; to form, as a plot or scheme.—**machination,** mak•i•nā″shon, n. The act of machinating; a plot; an artful design or scheme formed with deliberation.—**machinator,** mak′i•nā•tėr, n. One who machinates or plots with evil designs.

machine, ma•shēn′, n. [Fr. *machine,* L. *machina,* from Gr. *mēchanē,* machine, device, contrivance, from *mechos,* means, expedient.] Any appliance which serves to increase or regulate the effect of a given force or to produce motion (*simple machines* or mechanical powers being such as the lever, pulley, etc.); a complex structure, consisting of a combination or peculiar modification of the mechanical powers; a term of contempt applied to a person whose actions do not appear to be under his own control, but to be directed by some external agency; a mere tool or creature; a term formerly applied to a coach or cart, now particularly to an automobile, airplane, etc.—*v.t.* To apply machinery to; to produce by machinery.—**machine gun,** n. A piece of ordnance that is loaded and fired mechanically, and can discharge a number of projectiles in rapid succession, having usually two or more barrels, as

in the case of the Gatling gun, the mitrailleuse, etc.—**machinery,** ma•shēn′ėr•i, n. A complicated apparatus, or combination of mechanical powers, designed to increase, regulate, or apply motion and force; machines in general; any complex system of means and appliances designed to carry on any particular work or effect a specific purpose.—**machine shop,** n. A workshop in which machines are made.—**machine tool,** n. An adjustable machine for cutting metals into any required shape.—**machinist,** ma•shēn′ist, n. A constructor of machines; one who tends or works a machine.

Mach number, mäk, n. [After Ernest *Mach,* an Austrian physicist.] A number indicating the ratio of the air speed of an object to the speed of sound in the atmosphere.

mackerel, mak′ėr•el, n. [O.Fr. *maquerel,* Fr. *maquereau,* from L.L. *macarellus.*] A well-known food fish (*Scomber scombrus*) of the North Atlantic, a spiny-finned swift swimmer 18 inches long sporting blue bars on his back, and silver bars below.—*Mackerel sky,* a sky in which the clouds have the form called *cirro-cumulus.*

macle, mak′l, n. [Fr.; L. *macula,* a spot, the mesh of a net.] A double crystal, particularly a flat, double crystal of diamond.

macramé, mak•ra•mā′, n. [Ar. *miqramah,* emboidered veil, Turk, *maqramah,* kerchief.] Fringe or heavy lace of knotted thread, usually in geometrical patterns.

macrobiotic, mak′ro•bī•ot″ik, a. [Gr. *makros,* long, and *bios,* life.] Long-lived.—**macrocosm,** mak′ro•kozm, n. [Gr. *kosmos,* world.] The great world; the universe, regarded as analogous to the *microcosm,* or little world constituted by man.—**macron,** mak′ron, n. [Gr. *makros,* long.] A mark placed over a vowel to show that it is long, as fāte, mē, nōte, tūbe.—**macroscopic,** mak•ro•skop′ik, a. [Gr. *makros* long, *skopeo,* I see.] Visible to the naked eye; opposed to *microscopic.*—**macrospore,** mak′ro•spōr, n. [Gr. *makros,* long, *sporos,* seed.] *Bot.* a large (female) spore.

Macrura, mak•rụ′ra, [Gr. *makros,* long, and *oura,* a tail.] A family of stalk-eyed decapod crustaceans, including the lobster, prawn, shrimp, so called in contrast to the Brachyura (crabs), because their flexible abdomen extends straight backward, and is used in swimming.—**macrural, macrurous,** mak•rụ′ral, mak•rụ′rus, a. Belonging to the Macrura.—**macruran,** mak•rụ′ran, n. One of the Macrura.

macula, mak′ụ•la, n. pl. **maculae,** mak′ụ•lē. [L. *macula,* a spot; hence, *mackerel, mail* (armour).] A spot, as on the skin.—**maculate,** mak′ụ•lāt, v.t. [L. *maculo.*] To spot; to stain; to blur.—*a.* Marked with spots; blotted; hence, defiled; impure.—**maculation,** mak•ụ•lā′shon, n. The act of spotting; a spot; a stain.—**macule,** mak′ụl, n. A spot; *printing,*

a blur causing the impression of a page to appear double.

mad, mad, a. [O.E. *maad,* A.Sax. *mád, gemaed,* mad; allied to Goth. *gamaids,* injured; O.H.G. *gameit,* blunt, dull; Icel. *meitha,* to hurt.] Disordered in intellect; deprived of reason; distracted; crazy; insane; beside one's self; frantic; furious; wildly frolicsome; infatuated; furious from disease or otherwise; said of animals.—*Like mad,* madly; furiously. (*Colloq.*)—*v.t.—madded, madding.* To make mad; to madden.—*Madding crowd,* distracting (*v.t.*) or raving madly (*v.i.*) (?) Gray's 'madding crowd's ignoble strife', taken by him from Drummond of Hawthornden's 'madding worldling's hoarse discords', apparently *v.i.*—**madcap,** mad′kap, n. A person of wild or eccentric behavior; a flighty or hare-brained person; one who indulges in frolics.—*a.* Pertaining to a madcap.—**madden,** mad′n, v.t. To make mad; to craze; to excite with violent passion; to enrage.—*v.i.* To become mad; to act as if mad.—**madding,** mad′ing, a. Raging; furious; wild.—**madhouse,** mad′hous, n. A house where insane persons are confined; a lunatic asylum.—**madly,** mad′li, adv. In a mad or frenzied manner; frantically; furiously.—**madman,** mad′man, n. A lunatic; a crazy person; one inflamed with extravagant passion, and acting contrary to reason.—**madness,** mad′nes, n. The state or quality of being mad; lunacy; insanity; frenzy; extreme folly.

madam, mad′am, n. [Fr. *ma,* my, and *dame,* lady, from L. *mea domina,* in same sense.] *Lit.* my lady; a term of compliment used in address to ladies, chiefly to married and elderly ladies; sometimes used with a slight shade of disrespect (a proud *madam*). Pl. **mesdames,** mā′damz.

madder, mad′ėr, n. [A.Sax. *maeddere,* madder.] A climbing perennial plant, largely cultivated in Southern Europe, the root of which furnishes several valuable dyes and pigments, such as *madder-red, madder-lake, madder-yellow.*—*v.t. and i.* To dye with madder.

made, mād, *pret. and pp.* of *make.* The pp. besides being used in the senses of the verb is often equivalent to destined, fitted, suitable ('a place *made* for murders', Shak.).

Madeira, ma•dē′ra, n. A rich wine made in the island of Madeira.

Madonna, ma•don′a, n. [It. *madonna,* from L. *mea domina,* my lady. MADAM.] An Italian form of address equivalent to *Madam*; the Virgin Mary, pictures of whom are called *madonnas.*

madras, ma•dras′, n. A cotton cloth of fine thread and close weave much used for men's shirts; a large cotton kerchief.

madrepore, mad′ri•pōr, n. [Fr. *madrépore,* from It. *madrepora,* from *madre,* mother, and Gr. *pōros,* a kind of stone.] A common variety of reef coral, of a stony hardness and of a spreading or branching

ch, *chain*; ch, Sc. loch; g, go; j, job; ng, sing; TH, then; th, thin; w, wig; hw, whig; zh, azure.

form; the coral-building polyp itself.

madrigal, mad′ri·gal, *n.* [Fr. *madrigal*; It. *madrigale*, older It. *mandriale*, from L. and Gr. *mandra*, a sheepfold; originally a shepherd's song.] A little amorous poem, consisting of not less than three or four stanzas, and containing some tender and delicate, though simple thought, suitably expressed; a vocal composition, now commonly of two or more movements, and in five or six parts.

Maecenas, me·sē′nas, *n.* A munificent patron of art or literature, after Horace's friend.

Maelstrom, māl′strom, *n.* [Dutch *malen*, to grind, *stroom*, a stream.] A great whirlpool off the coast of Norway. Hence, [*not cap.*] a vortex or gulf; some dangerous movement or current in social life.

maenad, mē′nad, *n.* [Gr. *mainas*, *mainados*, from *mainomai*, to rave.] A votaress of Bacchus; hence, a raving, frenzied woman.

maestro, mīs′trō, *n.* [It. from L. *magister*, a master.] A master of any art; specifically, a master in music; a musical composer.—**maestoso,** mī·stō′sō, *a.* Majestic; stately, a direction in music.

Maffia, Mafia, mäf′fē·ä, *n.* A secret organization in Sicily which disregards or flouts laws and legal restrictions; branch organizations in other countries where the members are lawless and defiant toward all government.

magazine, mag′a·zēn′, *n.* [Fr. *magasin*, a storehouse, Sp. *magacen*, *almagacen*, from Ar. *al-makhzen*, a warehouse, from *khazana*, to store.] A receptacle in which anything is stored; a warehouse; a storehouse; a building or chamber constructed for storing in security large quantities of gunpowder or other explosive substances; a publication issued in a series of numbers or parts and containing papers of an entertaining or instructive character; a lighttight chamber for storing motion picture film.—**magazinist,** mag·a·zēn′ist, *n.* One who writes for a magazine.

magdalen, mag′da·len, *n.* [From Mary *Magdalene*, erroneously supposed to be the woman mentioned in St. Luke vii. 36-50.] A reformed prostitute; a house into which prostitutes are received with a view to their reformation.

Magellanic, maj·el·lan′ik, *a.* Pertaining to *Magellan*, the celebrated navigator.—*Magellanic clouds*, two conspicuous whitish nebulae, of a cloud-like appearance, near the South Pole.

magenta, ma·jen′ta, *n.* [Discovered in 1859, the year of the battle of *Magenta*.] A brilliant blue-red color derived from coal tar.

maggot, mag′ot, *n.* [W. *magiad*, a maggot or grub, from *magu*, to breed.] The larva of a fly or other insect; a grub; a whim; an odd fancy; a crotchet.—**maggotiness,** mag′ot·i·nes, *n.* The state of being maggoty.—**maggoty,** mag′o·ti, *a.* Full of or infested with maggots;

capricious; whimsical.

Magi, mā′jī, *n. pl.* [L. *magus*, from Gr. *magos*, a Magian, from Per. *mag*, a priest, same root as L. *magnus*, great.] The caste of priests among the ancient Medes and Persians; hence holy men or sages of the East.—**Magian,** mā′ji·an, *a.* Pertaining to the Magi.—*n.* One of the Magi; a priest of the Zoroastrian religion.

magic, maj′ik, *n.* [L. *magicus*, pertaining to sorcery, from *magia*, Gr. *mageia*, the theology of the Magians, magic. MAGI.] The art of producing effects by superhuman means, as by spiritual beings or the occult powers of nature; sorcery; enchantment; necromancy; power or influence similar to that of enchantment.— *Natural magic*, the art of applying natural causes, whose operation is secret, to produce surprising effects. —*a.* Pertaining to magic; used in magic; working or worked by or as if by magic.—*Magic square*, a square figure formed by a series of numbers disposed in parallel and equal ranks, and such that the sums of each row or line taken perpendicularly, horizontally, or diagonally are equal. *Magic lantern*, a kind of lantern by means of which small pictures are represented on the wall of a dark room, or on a white sheet, magnified to any size at pleasure.—**magical,** maj′i·kal, *a.* Pertaining to magic; proceeding from magic; having supernatural qualities; acting or produced as if by magic. ∴ *Magical* differs from *magic*, chiefly in the fact that the latter is not used predicatively; thus we do not say 'the effect was *magic*'.—**magically,** maj′i·kal·li, *adv.* In a magical manner.— **magician,** ma·jish′an, *n.* One skilled in magic; an enchanter; a necromancer.

magilp, magilph, ma·gilp′, ma·gilf′, *n.* See MEGILP.

magisterial, maj′is·tē′ri·al, *a.* [L. *magisterius*, from *magister*, a master. MASTER.] Belonging to a master or ruler; pertaining to a magistrate or his office; authoritative; arrogant; imperious; domineering.—**magisterially,** maj·is·tē′ri·al·li, *adv.* In a magisterial manner.—**magistral,** maj′is·tral, *a.* Imperious; authoritative; *phar.* specially prepared.

magistrate, maj′is·trāt, *n.* [L. *magistratus*, a magistrate, from *magister*, a master.] A public civil officer invested with the executive government or some branch of it; a justice of the peace; a person who dispenses justice in police courts, etc.—**magistracy,** maj′is·tra·si, *n.* The office or dignity of a magistrate; the body of magistrates.

magma, mag′ma, *n.* [Gr., a mass, dregs, from *massō*, to knead. MASS.] A mixture of mineral or other matters in a pasty state; a thick residuum separated from a fluid.

magna cum laude, mag′na cum lou′dā, *a.* [L.] With great praise, the second highest honors awarded at graduation.

magnanimous, mag·nan′i·mus, *a.*

[L. *magnanimus*—*magnus*, great (MAGNITUDE), and *animus*, mind (ANIMAL).] Great of mind; elevated in soul or in sentiment; raised above what is low, mean, or ungenerous: said of persons; exhibiting nobleness of soul: said of actions, etc.— **magnanimously,** mag·nan′i·mus·li, *adv.* In a magnanimous manner.— **magnanimity,** mag·na·nim′i·ti, *n.* The quality of being magnanimous; greatness of mind; elevation, nobility, or dignity of soul; lofty generosity.

magnate, mag′nāt, *n.* [L. *magnates* (pl.), powerful persons, the great, from *magnus*, great. MAGNITUDE.] A person of rank; a noble or grandee; a person of note or distinction in any sphere.

magnesia, mag·nē′shi·a, *n.* [From *Magnesia* in Asia Minor, whence also *magnet*.] Oxide of magnesium, a white tasteless earthy substance, possessing alkaline properties.—*Sulfate of magnesia*, Epsom salts.— **magnesian,** mag·nē′shi·an, *a.* Pertaining to magnesia; containing or resembling magnesia.—*Magnesian limestone*, a rock composed of carbonates of lime and magnesia, more or less useful for building or ornamental purposes; dolomite.—**magnesium,** mag·nē′shi·um, *n.* A light, malleable, ductile, silver-white metallic element that burns with a dazzling light, used in lightweight alloys. Symbol, Mg; at. no., 12; at. wt., 24.312.—*Magnesium light*, a dazzlingly bright light produced by burning magnesium.

magnet, mag′net, *n.* [L. *magnes*, *magnetis*, from Gr. *magnēs*, from *Magnesia* in Asia Minor, whence the stone was first brought.] The loadstone; also a bar or mass of iron or steel to which the peculiar properties of the loadstone have been imparted, either by contact or by other means. ELECTROMAGNET, HORSESHOE MAGNET.—**magnetic,** mag·net′ik, *a.* Pertaining to the magnet or magnetism; possessing the properties of the magnet, or corresponding properties; pertaining to the earth's magnetism; attractive, as if magnetic.—*Magnetic amplitude, azimuth*, etc., *navig.* the amplitude, azimuth, etc., indicated by the compass.—*Magnetic battery*, a kind of battery formed of several magnets (usually horseshoe magnets) combined together with all their poles similarly disposed.—*Magnetic compensator*, a contrivance connected with a ship's compass for compensating or neutralizing the effects upon the needle of the iron of the ship.—*Magnetic dip*. See DIP.—*Magnetic elements*, for any place, are the intensity of the earth's attraction, the DIP (which see), and the DECLINATION (which see).—*Magnetic equator*, a line passing round the globe near its equator, in every part of which the dip of the needle is nothing.—*Magnetic field*, the space in the vicinity of a magnet through which magnetic forces act. —*Magnetic meridian*, a great circle, the plane of, which at any place corresponds with the direction of the magnetic needle at that place.—*Magnetic needle*, any small magnetized iron or steel rod turning on a pivot, such as the needle of the mariner's compass.—*Magnetic north*, that point of the horizon which is indicated by the direction of the magnetic needle.—*Magnetic oxide of iron*, magnetite.—*Magnetic poles*, nearly opposite points on the earth's surface where the dip of the needle is 90°, at some distance from the earth's poles.—*Magnetic reluctance.* See RELUCTANCE.—*Magnetic susceptibility.* See SUSCEPTIBILITY.— *Magnetic storm*, a violent disturbance in the earth's magnetism; a sudden alteration in the magnetic elements of a place.—**magnetical**, mag·net′i·kal, *a.* Magnetic.—**magnetically**, mag·net′i·kal·li, *adv.* In a magnetic manner; by magnetism.—**magnetism**, mag′net·izm, *n.* A peculiar property possessed by certain bodies, whereby, under certain circumstances, they naturally attract or repel one another according to determinate laws; that branch of science which treats of the properties of the magnet, and magnetic phenomena in general; power of attraction.—*Animal magnetism.* MESMERISM.—*Terrestrial magnetism*, the magnetic force exerted by the earth.—**magnetite**, mag′net·īt, *n.* A black oxide of iron, which sometimes possesses polarity, and is highly magnetic; magnetic iron ore.—**magnetizable**, mag·net·ī′za·bl, *a.* Capable of being magnetized.—**magnetization**, mag′net·i·zā″shon, *n.* The act of magnetizing, or state of being magnetized. —**magnetize**, mag′net·īz, *v.t.*—*magnetized, magnetizing.* To communicate magnetic properties to; to attract or repel one another according to determinate laws.—**magneto**, mag·nē′tō, *n.* A small machine or generator having permanent magnets for poles, used to generate current. —**magnetoelectric, magnetoelectrical,** *a.* Pertaining to magnetoelectricity.—**magnetoelectricity**, *n.* Electricity evolved by the action of magnets; the science which treats of phenomena connected with both magnetism and electricity.—**magnetometer**, mag·net·om′et·ėr, *n.* An instrument for measuring any of the terrestrial magnetic elements, as the dip, inclination, and intensity, especially the latter.—*Magnetomotive force*, the magnetizing influence to which a magnetic substance is subjected in a magnetic field; its unit is the GILBERT (which see).— **magnetron**, mag′ne·tron, *n.* A vacuum tube in which the flow of electrons from cathode to a heated anode is under the influence of an external magnetic field; used for generation of ultrashort radio waves. —**magnetosphere**, mag·nē′tō·sfėr, *n.* A belt of highly charged particles, trapped in the earth's magnetic field, which extends to an altitude of over 40,000 miles at the Equator. **Magnificat**, mag·nif′i·kat, *n.* Canticle

of the Virgin Mary in Luke, i. 46-55: 'My soul doth magnify (L. *magnificat*) the Lord'.
magnificent, mag·nif′i·sent, *a.* [L. *magnificens—magnus*, great, *facio*, to make. MAGNITUDE.] Grand in appearance; splendid; fond of splendor; showy; stately.—**magnificently**, mag·nif′i·sent·li, *adv.* In a magnificent manner.—**magnific, magnifical**, mag·nif′ik, mag·nif′i·kal, *a.* [L. *magnificus*, noble, splendid.] Grand; splendid; illustrious.—**magnificence**, mag·nif′i·sens, *n.* [L. *magnificentia*.] The condition or quality of being magnificent.—**magnifico**, mag·nif′i·kō, *n. pl.* **magnificoes**, A grandee; a magnate.—**magnifier**, mag′ni·fī·ėr, *n.* One who or that which magnifies.—**magnify**, mag′ni·fī, *v.t.*—*magnified, magnifying.* [Fr. *magnifier*, L. *magnificare*.] To make great or greater; to increase the apparent dimensions of; to enlarge; to augment; to exalt; to represent as greater than reality; to exaggerate.— *v.i.* To possess the quality of causing objects to appear larger than reality. —*Magnifying glass*, a plano-convex or double-convex lens.—**magnification**, mag′ni·fi·kā″shon, *n.* Exaltation; praise; the seeming enlargement of an object by means of optics.
magniloquence, mag·nil′o·kwens, *n.* [L. *magniloquentia—magnus*, great (MAGNITUDE), and *loquens*, speaking (LOCUTION).] A lofty manner of speaking or writing; tumidity; pompous words or style; grandiloquence; bombast.—**magniloquent**, mag·nil′o·kwent, *a.* Big in words; speaking loftily or pompously; tumid; grandiloquent.—**magniloquently**, mag·nil′o·kwent·li, *adv.* In a magniloquent manner.
magnitude, mag′ni·tūd, *n.* [L. *magnitudo*, from *magnus*, great; same root as Gr. *megas*, great, E. *may*, *might*, *much*, *more*, etc. More or less akin are *magnate*, *majesty*, *master*, etc.] Greatness; the comparative extent, bulk, size, quantity, or amount of anything that can be measured; any quantity that can be expressed in terms of a quantity of the same kind taken as a unit; *geom.* that which has one or more of the three dimensions, length, breadth, and thickness; consequence (an affair of *magnitude*); a star's brightness according to a 100 logarithmic numbering system, as *first* magnitude, etc.
magnolia, mag·nō′li·a, *n.* [After Pierre *Magnol*, professor of botany at Montpellier.] A genus of trees and shrubs, chiefly natives of North America, India, China, Japan, etc., much admired for their flowers and foliage.
magnum, mag′num, *n.* [L., a large thing. MAGNITUDE.] A bottle holding two quarts.—**magnum opus**, *n.* [L.] Literally, a great work; the major production of an author or artist.
magpie; mag′pī, *n.* [*Mag*, for *Margaret*, and *pie*, a magpie, from L. *pica*, a pie or magpie; comp. *Jenny-wren*, *Robin*-red-breast, etc.] A well-

known bird of the crow family, about 18 inches in length, plumage black and white, tail very long; a person who chats like a magpie.
Magyar, mag′yär; Hung. pron. mod′-yor, *n.* A Hungarian of Asiatic race, allied to the Turks and Finns; the language of the Hungarians, belonging to the Turanian class of tongues.
maharajah, mä′ha·rä″ja, *n.* [Skr. *mahä*, great, and *räjä*, a prince or king.] The title assumed by some Indian princes ruling over a considerable extent of territory.—**maharani, maharanee**, mä′ha·rä″nē, *n.* [Skr., great queen or princess.] A female Indian ruler.
mahatma, ma·hät′ma, *n.* [Skr. *maha*, great, *âtmâ*, mind, soul.] A name among theosophists for certain Asiatic chiefs of their faith, said to be able to communicate by occult or nonmaterial means with other persons at any distance.
Mahdi, mä′di, *n.* [Ar., the director.] A name assumed by some of the successors of Mohammed; a descendant of Mohammed who is to arise and at the head of the faithful spread Mohammedanism over the world.
mahlstick, mal′stik *n.* See MAULSTICK.
mahogany, ma·hog′an·i, *n.* [*Mahagoni*, native American name.] A valuable timber tree, the wood of which is of a reddish color, very hard, and susceptible of a fine polish; a dinner table or table in general (over the *mahogany*).
Mahometan, ma·hom′e·tan. See MOHAMMEDAN, etc.
Mahound, ma·hound′, *n.* An old corruption of Mohammed; also applied to the devil or other evil spirit.
mahout, ma·hout′, *n.* [Hind.] In the East Indies, an elephant driver or keeper.
Mahratta, ma·rat′ta, *n.* One of a race of Hindus inhabiting central India.
maid, mād, *n.* [Short for *maiden*, A.Sax. *mægden*, dim of *mægeth*, a maiden, Goth. *magaths*, G. *magd*, maid; akin A.Sax. *magu*, Goth. *magus*, Icel. *mögr*, a boy, a son; allied to Gael. *mac*, a son.] A young unmarried woman; a virgin; an unmarried woman who has preserved her chastity; a female servant; a female skate.—*Maid of all work*, a female servant who does housework of every kind.—**maid of honor**, an unmarried woman who accompanies a bride to the altar.—**maiden**, mā′dn, *n.* A young unmarried woman; a virgin or maid; an instrument of capital punishment; a race horse that has not yet won a race.—*a.* Pertaining to a maiden or virgin; consisting of virgins; like a maiden; fresh; unpolluted; unused.—*Maiden fortress*, one hitherto impregnable to assaults from the enemy; uncaptured.—*Maiden over* (cricket), one during whose delivery no runs are made.—*Maiden speech*, a person's first public speech.—*Maiden sword*,

a sword hitherto unused and unstained with blood.—**maidenhair,** mā′dn·hār, *n.* An elegant fern found growing on rocks and walls.—**maidenhead,** mā′dn·hed, *n.* [Maiden, and term. -*head.*] Virgin purity; virginity.—**maidenhood,** mā′dn·hụd, *n.* The state of being a maid or maiden; the state of an unmarried female; virginity.—**maidenliness,** mā′dn·li·nes, *n.* Behavior that becomes a maid; modesty.—**maidenly,** mā′dn·li, *a.* and *adv.* Like a maid; modest.—**maidhood,** mād′hụd, *n.* Virginity.—**maidservant,** *n.* A female servant; a female domestic.

maieutic, mā·ū′tik, *a.* [Gr. *maieutikos,* pertaining to midwifery, from *maia,* a midwife.] Serving to assist or accelerate childbirth; pertaining to the obstetric art; aiding in bringing forth, in a metaphorical sense.

maigre, mā′gr, *a.* [Fr., lean, spare, meager.] *Cookery,* a term applied to a preparation cooked merely with butter.—*Maigre dishes, maigre food,* dishes used by Roman Catholics on the days when their church forbids flesh-meats.

mail, māl, *n.* [Fr. *maille,* the mesh of a net, a link of mail; from L. *macula,* a spot, a mesh. MACULA.] Armor; a defensive covering for warriors, and sometimes their steeds; any defensive covering, as the shell of a lobster.—*v.t.* To put on mail or armor; to arm defensively.—**mail-clad,** *a.* Clad with a coat of mail.—**mailed,** māld, *p.* and *a.* Covered with mail or armor; *zool.* protected by an external covering of scales or hard substance.

mail, māl, *n.* [Fr. *malle,* O.Fr. *male,* a bag, a mail; either from Armor. *mal,* Ir. and Gael. *mala,* a bag. or from O.H.G. *malaha,* a wallet; Icel. *malr,* a knapsack.] Originally a bag; hence, a bag for the conveyance of letters and papers; the letters, papers, etc., conveyed in such a bag; the person or conveyance by which the mail is conveyed.—*v.t.* To put in the mail.—**mailable,** māl′a·bl, *a.* Capable of being carried in the mail.—**mailbag,** *n.* A bag in which the public mail is carried.—**mailer,** *n.* A machine for addressing mail.—**mailman,** *n.* A postman.—**mail order,** *n.* An order sent by mail for goods to be shipped to the buyer.

maim, mām, *v.t.* [O.E. *main,* to hurt or maim; from O.Fr. *mechaigner,* Pr. *maganhar,* at. *magagnare,* to maim; origin doubtful.] To deprive of the use of a limb; to mutilate; to cripple; to disable.—*n.* An injury by which a person is maimed or mutilated.

main, mān, *a.* [Icel. *megn, meginn,* main, strong, mighty; *megin,* might, main, main part; A.Sax. *maegn, maegen,* power, strength; same root as *may, might.*] Principal, chief, or most important among other things; most to be regarded or considered; first in size, rank, importance, etc. (the *main* branch of a river, the *main* timbers of an edifice, the *main* consideration); mighty; vast (the *main* ocean); directly applied; used with all one's might (*main* strength).—*Main body,* the corps of an army which marches between the advance and rear guard. —*The main chance,* the chance of making gain; one's own interests generally.—*n.* All one's strength; violent effort (in the phrase 'with might and *main*'); the chief or main portion; the gross, bulk, greater part; the ocean, the great sea, the high sea; a principal gas or water pipe in a street, as distinguished from the smaller ones supplied by it.—*In the main,* for the most part; speaking generally.—**mainland,** mān′land, *n.* The continent; territory of great extent as compared with an island near it.—**mainly,** mān′li, *adv.* In the main; chiefly; principally.—**mainmast,** *n.* Naut. the principal mast in a ship or other vessel; the middle lower mast of a ship.—**mainsail,** *n.* Naut. the principal sail in a ship; the chief sail on the mainmast bent on the main yard.— **mainsheet,** *n.* Naut. a rope at one or both of the lower corners of a mainsail to keep it properly extended. —**mainspring,** mān′spring, *n.* The principal spring of any piece of mechanism, as in a watch; *fig.* the main cause of any action.—**mainstay,** *n.* Naut. the stay extending from the top of the mainmast to the deck; hence, *fig.* chief support.— **maintop,** *n.* Naut. a platform placed at the head of the main mast.— **mainyard,** *n.* Naut. the yard on which the mainsail is extended.

maintain, mān·tān′, *v.t.* [Fr. *maintenir*—*main,* L. *manus,* the hand, and Fr. *tenir,* L. *teneo,* to hold.] To preserve or keep in any particular state or condition; to support; to keep possession of; not to lose or surrender; to continue (a conversation); to support with food, clothing, etc.; to uphold; to vindicate or justify (one's right or cause); to assert.—**maintainable,** mān·tā′na·bl, *a.*—**maintainer,** mān·tā′nėr, *n.*—**maintenance,** mān′ten·ans, *n.* The act of maintaining, upholding, or keeping up; that which maintains or supports; *law,* intermeddling in a suit in which the person has no interest, by assisting either party with money or means to prosecute or defend it.

maître d'hôtel, mā′tre dō·tel′, *n.* [Fr. master of the house.] The chief steward or servant of a house or hotel; a kind of sauce prepared with melted butter, chopped parsley, and vinegar or lemon juice.

maize, māz, *n.* [Sp. *maíz,* from Taino *mahiz, mayz.*] Indian corn.

majesty, maj′es·ti, *n.* [L. *majestas,* from *majus,* compar. form of *magnus,* great. MAGNITUDE.] Grandeur or dignity of rank, character, or manner; imposing loftiness of person or mien; stateliness; sublimity; a title of emperors, kings, and queens; generally with a possessive pronoun (may it please your *majesty*).— **majestic,** ma·jes′tik, *a.* Possessing majesty; having dignity of appearance; august; splendid; grand; sub- lime; stately.—**majestical,** ma·jes′ti·kal, *a.* Majestic.—**majestically,** ma·jes′ti·kal·li, *adv.* In a majestic manner.

majolica, ma·jol′i·ka, *n.* [It. *Maiolica* or *Maiorica,* for *Majorca.*] A kind of earth used for making dishes, vases, etc., afterward applied to the ware itself.

major, mā′jėr, *a.* [L., compar. of *magnus,* great. MAGNITUDE.] The greater in number, quantity, extent, or dignity; the more important; *mus.* applied to the modes in which the third is four semitones above the tonic, or keynote, and to intervals consisting of four semitones; pertaining to a subject in one's special field of study or research.—*Major tone* or *interval,* an interval represented by the ratio of 8 to 9, while a minor tone is represented by the ratio of 9 to 10.— *Major term* of a syllogism, in *logic,* the predicate of the conclusion; the *major premise* is that which contains the major term.—*n.* An officer in the army next in rank above a captain and below a lieutenant-colonel; the lowest field officer; *law,* a person of full age to manage his own concerns; *logic,* the first proposition of a regular syllogism, containing the major term.—**majordomo,** mā·jėr·dō′mō, *n.* [It. *maggiordomo*—L. *major,* greater, and *domus,* a house.] A man who takes charge of the management of a large household; a steward; a chief minister or great officer of a palace.— **major general,** *n.* A military officer the next in rank below a lieutenant-general.—**major-generalship,** *n.* The office of a major general.— **majority,** ma·jor′i·ti, *n.* [Fr. *majorité.*] The state of being major or greater; the greater number; more than half; the number by which one quantity which can be counted exceeds another; full age; the age at which the law permits a young person to manage his own affairs; the office, rank, or commission of a major.—*To join the majority,* to pass over to the dead.

majuscule, ma·jus′kŭl, *n.* [L. *majuscala* (*litera,* letter, understood), from *majusculus,* somewhat great, dim. from *major, majus,* greater.] A capital letter; opposed to *minuscule.*— *Majuscule writing,* writing composed entirely of capital letters, as in ancient manuscripts.

make, māk, *v.t.* pret. & pp. *made;* ppr. *making.* [A.Sax. *macian,* L.G. and D. *maken,* G. *machen,* to make: same root as *may,* and L. *magnus,* great.] To cause to exist as a distinct thing; to create, frame, fashion, fabricate; to produce or effect, as agent or cause (money *makes* friends); to cause to be or become: with words expressive of the result or condition of the object (to *make* a matter public; to *make* a man king); to constrain, compel, cause, occasion, with infinitives after the object (to *make* a person laugh: *to* the sign of the infinitive, being omitted); to gain, acquire (money, profit, etc.); to get or ascertain, as the result of computation or calculation; to pass over in sailing or traveling; to put in a desired or desirable position or condition; to prepare for use (a bed, a fire); to compose, as parts united in a whole; to constitute; to serve or answer for (she *makes* a good wife); to complete, as by being added to a sum; *naut.* to arrive at; to have within sight (to *make* a port, land).—*Make* is often used periphrastically with substantives, the two together being thus equal to a single verb; thus to *make complaint*=to complain; to *make answer*=to answer; to *make haste*=to hasten, etc.—*To make believe*, to pretend.—*To make good*, to maintain; to establish (to *make good* one's footing); to accomplish (to *make good* one's word); to supply an equivalent for (to *make good* a loss).—*To make love to*, to court.—*To make out*, to discover; to decipher; to prove or establish by evidence or argument; to find to the full; as, he was not able to *make out* the whole sum.—*To make over*, to transfer the title of; to convey; as, he *made over* his estate in trust.—*To make sail* (*naut.*), to increase the quantity of sail already set.—*To make shift*, to contrive or manage with such means or appliances as are available.—*To make up*, to make full or complete; to collect into a sum or mass; to compose, as ingredients or parts; to constitute; to compensate for or make good (to *make up* a loss); to reconcile, settle, adjust (quarrels, etc.); to bring to a definite conclusion (to *make up* one's mind).—*To make water*, to leak, as a ship; to void the urine.—*To make way*, to make progress; to open a passage; to clear the way.—*v.i.* To act or do: often with adjectives to express the manner of acting (to *make bold*, etc.); to interfere; to proceed, move, direct one's course (he *made* toward home; he *made* after the boy); to rise or flow toward land: said of the tide.—*To make against*, to tend to injure; to be adverse to; to form an argument against; to tend to disprove.—*To make as if*, to act as if; to pretend that.—*To make at*, to make a hostile movement against.—*To make away with*, to take away and put out of reach; to remove by killing; to murder secretly.—*To make bold*, to venture; to take leave or liberty (to *make bold*, to say).—*To make for*, to contribute toward; to be of service to; to favor (this *makes for* the argument).—*To make free with*, to treat with freedom or without ceremony; to make free use of.—*To make light of*, to regard as trifling or of no consequence; to belittle.—*To make out*, to succeed and no more.—*To make sure*, to ascertain with certainty.—*To make sure of*, to consider as certain; to secure to one's self.—*To make up*, to dress, etc., as an actor.—*To make up to*, to approach; to court.—*To make*

up for, to serve as compensation for.—*n.* Structure; construction; shape; form (a man of slender *make*).—**make-believe**, *n.* Making believe or pretending; pretense; pretext; sham.—*a.* Unreal; sham.—**maker**, mā′kėr, *n.* One who makes: [*cap.*] the Creator;—**makeshift**, *n.* Something to serve a present purpose; a temporary substitute.—**make up**, *v.t.* To compose something; to settle in one's mind; to shuffle (a deck) for dealing; to bring up to; to concoct (a story); to arrange, prepare, adjust, assume a guise, compensate or reconcile; in printing, to arrange the type in columns or pages; in the theater and motion pictures, to apply cosmetics, dress, or accessories for a part; in education, to remove a deficiency.—*v.i.* To put on cosmetics for a performance; to resume friendship after an argument; to compensate.—**make-up**, *n.* The ingredients of a thing; cosmetics used to accentuate and highlight facial features; the mental or physical constitution of a person.
Malacca, ma·lak′ka, *a.* Pertaining to Malacca, in the Malay Peninsula.—*Malacca cane*, a cane made of the brown mottled or clouded stem of a kind of palm.
malachite, mal′a·kīt, *n.* [Fr. *malachite*, from Gr. *malachē*, a mallow, from its color resembling that of the leaves of mallow.] A mineral; a carbonate of copper found in solid masses of a beautiful green color, the green carbonate of copper, used for many ornamental purposes.
malacology, mal·a·kol′o·ji, *n.* [Gr. *malakos*, soft, and *logos*, discourse.] The branch of zoology that treats of the Mollusca or soft-bodied animals.—**malacologist**, mal·a·kol′o·jist, *n.* One versed in malacology.
malacopterygian, mal·a·kop′tėr·ij″i·an, *a.* [Gr. *malakos*, soft, and *pterygion*, a fin, a little wing, from *pteryx*, a wing.] A term applied to those osseous fishes that have all the rays of the fins soft.—**malacostracan**, mal·a·kos′tra·kan, *n.* [Gr. *ostrakon*, a shell.] A division of crustaceans, including the shrimps, lobsters, etc.—**malacostracan, malacostracous**, mal·a·kos′tra·kus, *a.*
maladjustment, mal·ad·just′ment, *n.* [Prefix *mal*, bad.] A bad or wrong adjustment: *psychology*, a lack of harmony between an individual's desires or capacities and his mode of living.
maladministration, mal·ad·min′is·trā″shon, *n.* [Prefix *mal*, bad.] Faulty administration; bad management of public affairs.
maladroit, mal·a·droit′, *a.* [Prefix *mal*, bad.] Not adroit or dexterous; awkward.—**maladroitly**, mal·a·droit′li, *adv.* Clumsily; awkwardly.—**maladroitness**, mal·a·droit′nes, *n.* Clumsiness; awkwardness.
malady, mal′a·di, *n.* [Fr. *maladie*, from *malade*, O.Fr. *malabde*, ill, from L. *male*, *habitus*, in bad condition. HABIT.] Any disease of the human body; an ailment; an indisposition; moral or mental disorder.

Malaga, mal′a·ga, *n.* A wine imported from Malaga in Spain; the white grape from which the wine is made, grown also in California.
Malagasy, mal′a·gas·i, *a.* and *n.* The language of Madagascar.
malaise, mal·āz′, *n.* [Fr., from *mal*, bad, and *aise*, ease.] State of being ill at ease; morbid and indefinite feeling of uneasiness.
malanders, mal′an·dėrz, *n.* [Fr. *malandres*, L. *malandria*.] A dry scab or scurfy eruption on the hock of a horse or at the bend of the knee.
malapert, mal′a·pėrt, *a.* [O.Fr. *malappert*, over-ready—prefix *mal*, badly, and O.Fr. *appert*, ready, prompt, from L. *apertus*, open. PERT.] Pert; saucy; impudent; forward.—*n.* A pert, saucy person.—**malapertly**, mal′a·pėrt·li, *adv.* Saucily; with impudence.—**malapertness**, mal′a·pėrt·nes, *n.* Sauciness; impudent pertness.
malapropos, mal·ap′rō·pō″, *a.* and *adv.* [Prefix *mal*, badly, and *apropos*.] The opposite of apropos; ill to the purpose.—**malapropism**, mal′a·prop·izm, *n.* The blundering use of words characteristic of Mrs. *Malaprop* in Sheridan's *Rivals*, e.g. 'an allegory on the banks of the Nile'.
malar, mā′lėr, *a.* [From L. *mala*, the cheek bone, the jaw.] Pertaining to the cheek or cheek bone.—*n. Anat.* the cheek bone.
malaria, ma·lā′ri·a, *n.* [It. *mala aria*, bad air, from L. *malus*, bad, and *aer*, air.] An infectious febrile disease formerly believed contracted from air tainted by deleterious emanations from animal or vegetable matter, but now known to be caused by a blood parasite transmitted by the bite of certain mosquitoes.—**malarial, malarian, malarious**, *a.*
malassimilation, mal′as·sim·i·lā″shon, *n.* [Prefix *mal*, bad.] Imperfect or morbid assimilation or nutrition; faulty digestion.
Malay, Malayan, ma·lā′, ma·lā′yan, *n.* A native of the Malay Peninsula; the language of the Malays.—*a.* Belonging to the Malays or to their country.
malcontent, mal′kon·tent, *n.* [Prefix *mal*, ill.] A discontented person; a discontented subject of a government.—**malcontent**, *a.* Discontented with the government.
mal de mer, mal· dä· mâr′, *n.* [Fr.] Seasickness.
male, māl, *a.* [Fr. *mâle*, O.Fr. *masle*, from L. *masculus*, male, from *mas*, *maris*, a male. MASCULINE.] Pertaining to the sex that begets young, as distinguished from the *female*; masculine; *bot.* having fecundating organs, but not fruit-bearing.—*Male rhymes*, rhymes in which only the final syllables correspond.—*Male screw*, the screw whose threads enter the grooves of the female screw.—*n.* One of the sex which begets young; *bot.* a plant which bears stamens.
malediction, mal·e·dik′shon, *n.* [L. *maledictio, maledictionis—male*, evil, and *dico*, to speak. DICTION.] Evil speaking; a curse or execration; an imprecation; the act of slandering.

malefactor, mal·e·fak′tėr, *n.* [L., evildoer—*male*, ill, and *facio*, to do.] One who commits a crime; a criminal. —**malefaction,** mal·e·fak′shon, *n.* An offense; an evil or criminal deed.

malefic, ma·lef′ik, *a.* [L. *maleficus*, that does ill—*male*, ill, and *facio*, to do.] Doing mischief.—**maleficence,** ma·lef′i·sens, *n.*—**maleficent,** ma·lef′i·sent, *a.* Doing evil; harmful.

malevolent, ma·lev′o·lent, *a.* [L. *malevolens, malevolentis*—*male*, ill, and *volens*, willing or disposed. VOLITION.] Having an evil disposition toward another or others; malicious; spiteful.—**malevolently,** ma·lev′o·lent·li, *adv.*—**malevolence,** ma·lev′o·lens, *n.*

malfeasance, mal·fē′zans, *n.* [Fr. *malfaisance*—*mal*, ill, and *faire*, L. *facere*, to do.] *Law*, doing what a person ought not to do; illegal deed.

malformation, mal·fòr·mā′shon, *n.* Ill or wrong formation; a deviation from the normal structure of an organ.

malfunction, mal·funk′shon, *v.t.* (Prefix *mal*, bad, and *function*.) To operate or function badly; to misfire. —*n.* The act or state of functioning badly.

malic, mā′lik, *a.* [L. *malum*, an apple.] Pertaining to apples; obtained from the juice of apples.— *Malic acid*, an acid found in many fruits, particularly in the apple.

malice, mal′is, *n.* [Fr. *malice*, L. *malitia*, from *malus*, evil; cog. Gr. *melas*, black; Skr. *malam*, filth; Ir. *maile*, evil. *Malus* is seen also in *malady, malign, malignant*, etc.] Enmity of heart; a disposition to injure others for mere personal gratification, or from a spirit of revenge; spite; ill-will; *law*, a formed design of doing mischief to another; called also *malice prepense* or *aforethought*. ∴ *Malice* is a deeper and more abiding feeling than *malevolence*, *malevolence* being of a more casual and temporary character. *Malignity* is malice intensified, proceeding from an innate love of doing harm to others.—**malicious,** ma·lish′us, *a.* [L. *malitiosus*.] Indulging malice; harboring ill-will without provocation; proceeding from ill-will; dictated by malice.—*Malicious mischief*, an injury to property from sheer malice, in some instances a felony, in others a misdemeanor.—*Malicious prosecution*, a prosecution preferred without reasonable cause.—**maliciously,** ma·lish′us·li, *adv.* In a malicious manner.—**maliciousness,** ma·lish′us·nes, *n.*

malign, ma·lin′, *a.* [L. *malignus* for *maligenus*, of an evil nature—*malus*, bad, and *genus*, kind (MALICE, GENUS). Comp. *benign*, with exactly the opposite sense.] Of an evil nature, disposition, or character; malicious; pernicious; tending to injure or produce evil effects.—*v.t.* To speak evil of; to traduce, defame, vilify.— **malignance, malignancy,** ma·lig′nans, ma·lig′nan·si, *n.* The quality of being malignant; extreme malevolence; bitter enmity; *med.* viru-

lence.—**malignant,** ma·lig′nant, *a.* [L. *malignans*, from *maligno*, to act maliciously.] Having extreme malevolence or enmity; virulently inimical; malicious; exerting pernicious influence; *med.* threatening a fatal issue; virulent (a *malignant* ulcer); extremely heinous. ∴ Syn. under MALICE.—*n. English history*, one of the adherents of Charles I and his son: so called by the Roundheads.— **malignantly,** ma·lig′nant·li, *adv.* In a malignant manner.—**maligner,** ma·lin′ėr, *n.* One who maligns.— **malignity,** ma·lig′ni·ti, *n.* [L. *malignitas*.] The state or quality of being malignant; evil disposition of heart toward another; malice without provocation; rancor; virulence.

malinger, ma·ling′gėr, *v.i.* [Fr. *malingre*, sickly, weakly; from *mal*, ill, and O.Fr. *hingre, heingre*, feeble, nasalized form of L. *aeger*, sick.] *Milit.* to feign illness in order to avoid duty.—**malingerer,** ma·ling′gėr·ėr, *n.* A soldier who feigns himself ill.

malison, mal′i·zn, *n.* [O.Fr. *malison, maleïcon*, contr. from *malediction*. Comp. *benison*, for *benediction*.] A malediction; curse; execration.

mall, mal, *n.* [Fr. *mail*, It. *maglio, malleo*, L. *malleus*, a hammer. MALLEABLE.] A heavy wooden beetle or hammer; (originally an alley where the game of *pall-mall* was played with *malls* and balls) a public walk; a level shaded walk.

mallard, mal′ėrd, *n.* [O.Fr. *malard*, Prov. Fr. *maillard*, from *maille* (L. *macula*), a spot on a bird's feather, from the iridescent spot on the wing.] The common wild duck.

malleable, mal′lē·a·bl, *a.* [Fr. *malléable*, from L.L. *malleo*, to beat with a hammer, from L. *malleus*, a hammer (akin *mallet, maul*).] Capable of being shaped or extended by beating with the hammer: said of metals.— **malleability, malleableness,** mal′lē·a·bil″i·ti, mal′lē·a·bl·nes, *n.* The quality of being malleable.

mallee, mal′lē, *n.* Kind of dwarf eucalyptus.

malleolus, mal′lē·o·lus, *n.* [L., dim. of *malleus*, a hammer.] One of the two projections of the leg bones at the ankle.—**malleolar,** mal′lē·o·lėr, *a. Anat.* pertaining to the ankle.

mallet, mal′et, *n.* [Dim. of *mall*.] A wooden hammer, used chiefly by stonecutters, joiners, etc.

malleus, mal′ē·us, *n.* [L., a mallet.] *Anat.* one of the chain of small bones in the ear; *zool.* a hammer-shaped body forming part of the masticatory apparatus in some microscopic animals.

mallow, mal′ō, *n.* [A.Sax. *malwe*, G. *malve*, from L. *malva*, mallow, allied to Gr. *malachē*, mallow, *malakos*, soft—from its emollient properties.] The common name of a number of plants, chiefly herbaceous or annual, some of them valuable for medicinal properties. Also called *mallows*, as a singular.

malm, mäm, *n.* [A.Sax. *mealm*, Goth. *malma*, sand; akin to *meal*, from root meaning to grind.] A soft, grayish

limestone, easily crumbled; *Eng.* marl; a soil containing clay and chalk.

malmsey, mäm′zi, *n.* [O.E. *malvesie*, Fr. *malvoisie*; from Napoli di *Malvasia*, in the Morea; the white and red wines produced there first received the name.] A kind of grape; a strong sweet white wine made in Madeira.

malnutrition, mal·nū·trish″un, *n.* Insufficient or otherwise faulty nutrition.

malodor, malodour, mal·ō′dėr, *n.* [Prefix *mal*, bad.] An offensive odor. —**malodorous,** mal·ō′dėr·us, *a.* Having a bad or offensive odor.

Malpighian, mal·pig′i·an, *a.* [After *Malpighi*, an eminent Italian anatomist and botanist.] *Anat.* applied to certain small round bodies in the cortical substance of the kidney, and to corpuscles in the spleen.

malposition, mal·po·zish′on, *n.* [Prefix *mal*, bad.] A wrong position.

malpractice, mal·prak′tis, *n.* [*Mal* and *practice*.] Professional malfeasance or improper and careless performance of duty, as of a physician or lawyer.

malt, malt, *n.* [A.Sax. *mealt* G. *malz*, malt, from *meltan*, to melt.] Grain, usually barley, steeped in water and made to germinate and used in brewing and distilling; liquor produced from malt; beer.—*v.t.* To make into malt.—*v.i.* To be converted into malt.—**malted milk,** *n.* A beverage prepared by whipping a combination of flavored malt, ice cream, and milk.— **maltster,** malt′stėr, *n.* A man who makes malt.

maltase, mal′tās, *n.* [*Malt* and *ase*.] *Chem.* an enzyme found in plants, animals, bacteria, yeast, etc., which speeds the hydrolysis of maltose to glucose.

Maltese, mal′tēz, *n. sing.* and *pl.* A native or natives of Malta.—*a.* Belonging to Malta.

maltha, mal′tha, *n.* [Gr., a mixture for caulking ships.] A variety of bitumen like pitch, intermediate between liquid petroleum and solid asphalt.

Malthusian, mal·thū′zi·an, *a.* Relating to the theory of the Rev. T. R. *Malthus*, that population, when unchecked, goes on increasing in a higher ratio than the means of subsistence can be made to increase. —*n.* One who holds the doctrines of Malthus.

maltose, malt′ōz, *n.* [From *malt*.] Malt sugar; a white crystalline sugar, $C_{12}H_{22}O_{11}$-H_2O, formed by the action of amylase on starch.

maltreat, mal·trēt′, *v.t.* [*Mal* and *treat*.] To treat ill.—**maltreatment,** mal·trēt′ment, *n.*

malvaceous, mal·vā′shus, *a.* [L. *malva*, mallow.] Pertaining to the plants of the mallow family.

malversation, mal·vėr·sā′shon, *n.* [Fr. *malversation*—L. *male*, badly, and *versor*, to occupy one's self, from *verto, versum*, to turn. VERSE.] Evil conduct; fraudulent tricks; misbehavior in an office or employment, as fraud, breach of trust, etc.

Mameluke, mam′e·lūk, mam′a·lūk,

n. [Ar. *mamlúk*, that which is possessed, a slave, from *malak*, to possess.] One of the former mounted soldiery of Egypt, a powerful body broken up and massacred in 1811.

mamma, mama, mä′mä, *n.* [A repetition of the infantile utterance *ma, ma.*] Mother; a word of tenderness and familiarity, used chiefly by young persons in addressing, or reference to, mother.

mamma, mam′ma, *n.* pl. **mammae,** mam′mē. [L., the female breast, from root meaning to swell, to swell with juice.] The breast; the organ in females that secretes the milk.— **mammal,** mam′mal, *n.* An animal of the class Mammalia.—**Mammalia,** mam·mā′li·a, *n. pl.* [Lit. breast-animals.] The highest class in the animal kingdom, whose distinctive characteristic is that the female suckles the young.—**mammalian,** mam··mā′li·an, *a.* Pertaining to the mammals.—**mammalogy,** mam·mal′o·ji, *n.* The science of mammals.— **mammary,** mam′ma·ri, *a.* Pertaining to the female breasts or paps.— **mammiferous,** mam·mif′ėr·us, *a.* Having the distinguishing characteristics of a mammifer.—**mammilla,** mam·mil′la, *n.* [L. *mamilla,* a little breast.] A little breast; something of this form.—**mammillary,** mam′-mil·a·ri, *a.* Pertaining to or resembling a nipple or pap; *anat.* applied to two small protuberances like nipples in the brain; *mineral.* studded with mammiform protuberances.— **mammillate, mammillated,** mam′-mil·āt, mam′mil·ā·ted, *a.* In the form of a pap or nipple; having small protuberances like nipples.

mammee, mam·mē′, *n.* An American tree yielding a large and nourishing fruit.—**mammee sapota,** mam-mē′sa·pō′ta, *n.* A large tree of the West Indies and tropical America, yielding a fruit which is called natural marmalade.

mammon, mam′mon, *n.* [L. *mammona,* Gr. *mammōnas,* mammon, riches, from Chal. *mammōn, māmōn.*] The Syrian god of riches, mentioned in the New Testament as a personification of worldliness; hence, riches; [*cap.*] wealth.—**mammonism,** mam′mon·izm, *n.* Devotion to the service of Mammon or the pursuit of wealth.—**mammonist, mammonite,** mam′mon·ist, mam′mon·īt, *n.* A person entirely devoted to the acquisition of wealth.

mammoth, mam′moth, *n.* [Rus. *mamant, mamont,* from Tart. *mamma,* the earth, because their remains being found in the earth the natives believed that they burrowed like moles.] An extinct species of elephant with long tusks and covered with dense, shaggy hair, the remains of which are found in Siberia and elsewhere.—*a.* Resembling the mammoth in size; very large; gigantic.— **mammoth tree,** *n.* The giant sequoia tree of California, specimens having reached more than 325 feet with a diameter of 25 feet.

man, man, *n.* pl. **men,** men. [A.Sax. *man, mann,* man, person = D., O.

H.G., and Sw. *man,* G. *mann,* Icel. *mathr, mannr,* Dan. *mand,* Goth. *manna;* from root *man,* to think, seen in Skr. *man,* to think, *manas,* mind, *manushya,* man, and also in E. *mean,* to intend, *mind,* L. *mens,* the mind (whence *mental*).] A human being; a person; particularly, a male adult of the human race; the human race; mankind: in this sense without article or plural (*man* is born to trouble); a male servant; an adult male in some person's employment or under his direction; a piece with which a game, as chess or checkers, is played.—*Man of straw,* a man of no substantial character, influence, or means; in commercial language, a person destitute of capital put forward by way of decoy.—*v.t.* **manned, manning.** To supply with men; to furnish with a sufficient force or complement of men; to infuse courage into.—**man-at-arms,** *n.* A term applied to a fully equipped or heavily armed soldier of the Middle Ages.— **man-eater,** *n.* A cannibal; one of those tigers which have acquired a special preference for human flesh. —**manful,** man′ful, *a.* Manly; bold; brave.—**manfully,** man′ful·li, *adv.* In a manful manner.—**manfulness,** man′ful·nes, *n.* The quality of being manful.—**manhole,** man′hōl, *n.* A hole through which a man may creep into a drain, cesspool, steam boiler, etc., for cleaning or repairing.— **manhood,** man′hud, *n.* The state of being a man; the qualities of or becoming a man.—**manikin,** man′i·-kin, *n.* A little man; a dwarf; an anatomic model of the human body. —**mankind,** man·kīnd′ or man′kīnd, *n.* The human race; man taken collectively; the males of the human race.—**manlike,** man′līk, *a.* Resembling a man; having the qualities proper to a man.—**manliness,** man′-li·nes, *n.* The quality of being manly.—**manly,** man′li, *a.* Pertaining to or becoming a man; having the nobler attributes of a man; self-reliant; brave.—**mannish,** man′ish, *a.* Characteristic of or resembling a man; as applied to a woman, masculine; unwomanly.—**mannishly,** man′-ish·li, *adv.* In a mannish manner.— **mannishness,** man′ish·nes, *n.*—**man-power,** *n.* The amount of power provided by human effort; a nation's strength as determined by the number of men and women available for the armed services and civil defense.—**man-of-war,** *n.* A government vessel employed for the purposes of war.—**manservant,** *n.* A male servant.—**manslaughter,** *n.* The unlawful killing of a man, without malice.

manacle, man′a·kl, *n.* [Fr. *manicle,* L. *manicula,* dim. of *manica,* a manacle, from *manus,* the hand. MANAGE.] An instrument of iron for fastening the hands; handcuff; shackle: generally in plural.—*v.t.* **manacled, manacling.** To put handcuffs or other fastening upon; to shackle.

manage, man′ij, *v.t.*—**managed, managing.** [Fr. *manège,* the management of a horse; It. *maneggiare,* to handle,

to manage; from L. *manus,* the hand, whence also *manacle, manual,* etc. MANUAL.] To have under control and direction; to conduct, carry on, guide, administer; to make tractable, or get under due control; to wield; to move or use in the manner desired (tools or the like); to treat (a person) with caution or judgment; to govern with address.—*v.i.* To direct or conduct affairs; to carry on concerns or business.—**manageability,** man′-ij·a·bil″i·ti, *n.* State of being manageable.—**manageable,** man′ij·a·bl, *a.* Capable of being managed; easily made subservient to one's views or designs.—**manageableness,** man′ij·-a·bl·nes, *n.* The quality of being manageable.—**manageably,** man′ij·-a·bli, *adv.* In a manageable manner. —**management,** man′ij·ment, *n.* The act of managing; the manner of treating, directing, carrying on, or using for a purpose; conduct; administration; cautious handling or treatment; the body of directors or managers of any undertaking, concern, or interest collectively.— **manager,** man′ij·ėr, *n.* One who manages; one who has the guidance or direction of anything; one who is directly at the head of an undertaking.—**managerial,** man·a·jē′ri·al, *a.* Of or belonging to a manager.— **managership,** man′ij·ėr·ship, *n.* The office of a manager.

manakin, man′a·kin, *n.* [Dim. of *man,* as applied to birds, originally the name of a species with a beard-like tuft of feathers on the chin.] A manikin; a name for certain small tropical American birds.

manatee, man·a·tē′, *n.* [Haitian.] The sea cow, an aquatic herbivorous mammal allied to the cetaceans, and found on the coasts of South America, Africa, and Australia.

manchet, man′shet, *n.* [Comp. Fr. *miche, michette,* a manchet or small loaf.] A small loaf of fine bread; fine white bread.—*a.* Fine and white: said of bread or flour.

manchineel, man·chi·nēl′, *n.* [It. *mancinello,* Fr. *manzanille,* Sp. *manzanillo,* from *manzana,* an apple, from L. *malum Matianum,* a kind of apple, from *Matius,* a Roman name.] A tree of the West Indies and Central America, abounding in acrid and highly poisonous juice, the wood being valuable for cabinet work.

Manchu, man·chö′, *n.* A native of Manchuria, or one of the same race; one of the reigning dynasty in China; the language of the Manchus; the court language of China.

manciple, man′si·pl, *n.* [O.Fr. *man-cipe,* L. *manceps,* one who purchases anything at a public sale—*manus,* the hand, and *capio,* to take.] A steward; a purveyor, particularly of a college or inn of court.

mandamus, man·dā′mus, *n.* [L., lit. we command.] *Law,* a command or writ issuing from a superior court, directed to any person, corporation, or inferior court, requiring them to do some specified act.

mandarin, man·da·rin′, *n.* [Pg. *man-*

darim, from Skr. *mantrin*, a counsellor, a minister, from *mantra*, counsel.] The general name given by Europeans to Chinese magistrates or public officials, whether civil or military; a northern dialect of China; a miniature orange tree from which our mandarin orange comes.

mandate, man'dāt, *n.* [L. *mandatum*, an order, from *mando*, to command (from *manus*, the hand, and *do*, to give), seen also in *command*, *commend*, *demand*, *remand*, *recommend*, etc.] A command; an order, precept, or injunction; written authority by one person to another to act for him.—**mandatory**, man'da·to·ri, *n.* [Fr. *mandataire*.] One to whom a mandate or charge is given; one who receives special written authority to act for another.—**mandatory**, *a.* Containing a command; directory.

mandible, man'di·bl, *n.* [L. *mandibulum*, the jaw, from *mando*, to chew.] An animal's jaw, particularly the under jaw of a mammal; the upper or lower jaw of a bird; one of the upper or anterior pair of jaws of an insect or other articulate animal.—**mandibular**, man·dib'ū·lėr, *a.* Belonging to a mandible.—**mandibulate**, man·dib'ū·lāt, *a.* Provided with mandibles, as many insects.

mandolin, man'do·lin, *n.* [Fr. *mandoline*, from It. *mandola*, *mandora*, *pandora*, a species of lute. BANDORE.] A musical instrument of the guitar kind.

mandragora, man·drag'o·ra, *n.* [L. and Gr. *mandragoras*, the mandrake.] Mandrakes.—**mandrake**, man'drāk, *n.* A plant of the Mediterranean region, with large thick roots, and possessing strong purgative and narcotic properties, formerly the subject of various superstitions.

mandrel, mandril, man'drel, man'dril, *n.* [Fr. *mandrin*, from Gr. *mandra*, an enclosed space, the bed in which the stone of a ring is set.] A bar of iron on which an article is fitted to be turned on a lathe; any straight bar upon which a tube or ring is welded.

mandrill, man'dril, *n.* [Fr. *mandrille*, from the West African name.] The great blue-faced or rib-nosed baboon, the largest and most hideous of the baboons.

manducate, man'dū·kāt, *v.t.*—*manducated*, *manducating*. [L. *manduco*, *manducatum*, from *mando*, to chew; akin *mandible*, *manger*.] To masticate; to chew.

mane, mān, *n.* [O.D. *mane*, D. *manen*, Dan. *man*, Icel. *mön*, O.H.G. *mana*, G. *mähne*; allied to W. *mwng*, a mane, *mwn*, the neck.] The long hair on the upper side of the neck of some animals, as the horse, lion, etc., usually hanging down on one side.—**maned**, mānd, *a.* Having a mane.

manège, ma·nezh', *n.* [Fr. *manège*, from It. *maneggio*, management. MANAGE.] A school for training horses and teaching horsemanship; the art of breaking, training, and riding horses; the art of horsemanship.

manes, mā'nēz, *n. pl.* [L., from O.L. *manus*, good, benevolent.] [*often cap.*]

Among the Romans the ghosts, shades, or souls of deceased persons; the deified shades of the dead.

maneuver, manoeuvre, ma·nö'vėr, or ma·nū'vėr, *n.* [Fr. *manœuvre*—*main*, L. *manus*, the hand, and *œuvre*, L. *opera*, work. *Manure* is the same word.] A regulated dexterous movement, particularly in an army or navy; any movement of troops, ships, etc., for attack on or defense against an enemy; management with address or artful design; an adroit procedure; intrigue; stratagem.—*v.i.* —*maneuvered*, *maneuvering*. To perform maneuvers, especially military or naval maneuvers; to employ intrigue or stratagem to effect a purpose.—*v.t.* To make to perform maneuvers or evolutions.—**maneuverer**, ma·nö'vėr·ėr, or ma·nū'vėr·ėr, *n.* One who maneuvers.

manful, etc. See MAN.

manganese, man'ga·nēz, *n.* [By metathesis from *magnesium*, the name first given to it.] A grayish-white metallic element used as an alloying agent to give steel toughness. Symbol, Mn; at. no., 25; at. wt., 54.9380. —**manganic**, man·gan'ik, *a.*—**manganite**, man'gan·īt, *n.* One of the ores of manganese, used in the manufacture of glass.

mange, mānj, *n.* [O.Fr. *mangeson*, Fr. *démangeaison*, an itching, from *manger*, L. *manduco*, to eat. MANDUCATE.] A cutaneous disease very similar to itch, and to which horses, cattle, dogs, and other beasts are subject.—**mangily**, mān'ji·li, *adv.* In a mangy manner.—**manginess**, mān'ji·nes, *n.* The quality or condition of being mangy.—**mangy**, mān'ji, *a.* Infected with the mange; scabby; mean.

mangel-wurzel, mang'gl·wėr'zl, *n.* [G., lit. want-root, but the proper form is *mangold-wurzel*—G. *mangold*, beet, and *wurzel*, root=beet-root.] A variety of beet, extensively cultivated as food for cattle.

manger, mān'jėr, *n.* [Fr. *mangeoire*, from *manger*, from L. *manducare*, to eat. MANDUCATE.] A trough or box in which fodder is laid for horses or cattle; the receptacle from which horses or cattle eat in a stable or cow house.

mangle, mang'gl, *v.t.*—*mangled*, *mangling*. [Perhaps from L. *mancus*, maimed, through L.L. *mangulare*, to mangle; comp. A.Sax. *bemancian*, to maim; L.G. *mank*, mutilated; D. *mank*, lame; G. *mangel*, a defect; *mangeln*, to be wanting.] To cut by repeated blows, making a ragged or torn wound, or covering with wounds; to cut in a bungling manner; to hack; to lacerate; applied chiefly to the cutting of flesh; *fig.* to destroy the symmetry or completeness of; to mutilate.—**mangler**, mang'glėr, *n.* One who mangles; one who mutilates.

mangle, mang'gl, *n.* [D. and G. *mangel*, from O.Fr. *mangonel*, Gr. *manganon*, a war engine, the axis of a pulley.] A well-known machine for smoothing tablecloths, sheets, and other articles of linen or cotton.

—*v.t.* To smooth cloth with a mangle.—**mangler**, mang'glėr, *n.* One who uses a mangle.

mango, mang'gō, *n.* [Malay.] The fruit of the mango tree, a native of tropical Asia, but widely cultivated throughout the tropics; a fruit highly valued for dessert.

mangonel, man'go·nel, *n.* [O.Fr. *mangonel*, It. *manganello*, *mangano*, from Gr. *manganon*. MANGLE, *n.*] An engine formerly used for throwing stones and battering walls.

mangosteen, mang'go·stēn, *n.* [Malay *mangusta*.] A tree of the East Indies, the fruit of which is about the size of an orange, and most delicious.

mangrove, man'grōv, *n.* [Malay *manggi-manggi*.] A tropical tree growing on the banks of rivers and on the seacoast, remarkable for giving off adventitious roots from the stem and branches.

mania, mā'ni·a, *n.* [L., from Gr.; allied to Gr. *menos*, the mind; E. *mind* and *man*.] Madness; also rage or eager desire for anything; insane or morbid craving; mental disorder characterized by high, uncontrolled excitement; excitement and frenzy. —**maniac**, mā'ni·ak, *a.* Raving with madness; proceeding from disordered intellect; mad; excited; frenzied. —*n.* A madman; one who has an ungovernable enthusiasm for something.—**maniacal**, ma·nī'a·kal, *a.*— **manic depressive**, *n.* One who has a type of mental disorder alternating between periods of acute excitement and periods of acute depression.

Manichaean, Manichean, man·i·kē'an, *n.* [From the founder *Manes* or *Manichaeus*, who lived in the third century.] One of a sect in Persia who maintained that there are two supreme principles, the one good, the other evil, which produce all the happiness and calamities of the world.—**Manichaean**, *a.* Pertaining to the Manichaeans or their doctrines.—**Manichaeanism**, *n.*

manicure, man'i·kūr, *n.* [L. *manus*, hand, *cura*, care.] The care of the nails and the hands; a person whose occupation is to trim the nails and improve the condition of the hands. —*v.t. & i.* To trim or care for the nails.—**manicurist**, *n.*

manifest, man'i·fest, *a.* [L. *manifestus*, lit. that may be laid hold of by the hand—*manus*, the hand, and root seen in obs. *fendo*, to dash against (as in *offend*).] Clearly visible to the eye or obvious to the understanding; not obscure or difficult to be seen or understood; evident; plain.—*n.* A document signed by the master of a vessel at the place of lading, to be exhibited at the customhouse, containing a description of the ship and her cargo, the destination of the ship and the goods, etc.—*v.t.* To disclose to the eye or to the understanding; to show plainly; to display; to exhibit.— **manifestation**, man'i·fes·tā'shon, *n.* The act of manifesting; a making evident to the eye or to the understanding; the exhibition of anything by clear evidence; display; what is the means of displaying.—**manifestly,** man'i·fest·li, *adv.* In a manifest manner; clearly; evidently; plainly.—**manifesto,** man·i·fes'to, *n.* [It.] A public declaration, usually of a sovereign or government.

manifold, man'i·fōld, *a.* [*Many* and *fold.*] Numerous and various in kind or quality; exhibiting or embracing many points, features, or characteristics (the *manifold* wisdom of God); operating several parts at once.—*v.t.* To multiply impressions of, as of a letter.—*n.* A copy made by manifolding; a whole having many different parts; *mech.* that part of an internal-combustion engine which distributes a fuel-air mixture to the various cylinders; a pipe to which several other pipes are attached.—**manifoldly,** man'i·fōld·li, *adv.*—**manifoldness,** man'i·fōld·nes, *n.*

manikin, man'i·kin, *n.* [D. *manneken,* dim. of *man,* man.] A little man; a dwarf; an anatomic model of the human body.

Manila hemp, *n.* A fibrous material from a plant which grows in the Philippine Islands, etc.—**Manila paper,** *n.* A paper of strong fiber made from Manila hemp.

manioc, man'i·ok, *n.* [Pg. and Brazil *mandioca.*] A plant cultivated in tropical America and the West Indies, from the large fleshy root of which tapioca and cassava are prepared.

maniple, man'i·pl, *n.* [L. *manipulus, maniplus,* a handful, a company of soldiers—*manus,* the hand, and root of *plenus,* full (as in *plenary,* etc.).] *Rom. antiq.* a company of soldiers consisting of sixty common soldiers, two centurions, and a standard-bearer; in the Latin Ch., originally a handkerchief, now only a symbolical ornament attached to the left arm of the celebrant at mass.—**manipular,** ma·nip'ū·lėr, *a.* Pertaining to a maniple.—**manipulate,** ma·nip'ū·lāt, *v.t.*—*manipulated, manipulating.* [L.L. *manipulo, manipulatum.*] To handle or operate on with the hands, as in artistic or mechanical operations; to subject to certain processes; to operate upon for the purpose of giving a false appearance to (to *manipulate* accounts).—*v.i.* To use the hands, as in artistic processes, mechanical operations, or the like.—**manipulation,** ma·nip'ū·lā'shon, *n.* The art or mode of manipulating or working by hand; the act of operating upon skillfully, for the purpose of giving a false appearance to.—**manipulative, manipulatory,** ma·nip'ū·lā·tiv, ma·nip'-ū·lā·to·ri, *a.* Pertaining to or performed by manipulation.—**manipulator,** ma·nip'ū·lā·ter, *n.* One who manipulates.

manito, manitou, man'i·tō, man'-i·tö, *n.* Among North American Indians, a good or evil spirit or a fetish.

mankind, manly, etc. See MAN.

manna, man'na, *n.* [Generally derived from the Heb. *man hu,* what is it?] A substance miraculously furnished as food for the Israelites in their journey through the wilderness of Arabia; the sweet solidified juice which is obtained by incisions made in the stem of a species of ash.—**mannite,** man'īt, *n.* A peculiar variety of sugar obtained from manna.

mannequin, man'e·kin, *n.* [A corruption of *manikin.*] An artist's model fashioned of wood or wax; a woman who serves as a model by wearing clothes for display.

manner, man'ėr, *n.* [From Fr. *manière,* manner, O.Fr. *manier,* belonging to the hand, from L. *manus* the hand—properly, the method of handling a thing. MANAGE, MANUAL.] The mode in which anything is done; the way of performing or effecting anything; a person's peculiar or habitual way of carriage; bearing or conduct; deportment; *pl.* carriage or behavior, considered as decorous or indecorous, polite or impolite, pleasing or displeasing; ceremonious behavior; polite or becoming deportment (he has no *manners*); sort; kind; in this use having often the sense of a plural = sorts, kinds (all *manner* of things).—*In a manner,* in a certain degree or measure: to a certain extent (it is *in a manner* done already.)—**mannered,** man'ėrd, *a.* Having manners of this or that kind; exhibiting the peculiar style of an author or artist, more particularly in its objectionable form.—**mannerism,** man'-ėr·izm, *n.* Excessive adherence to a characteristic, mode or manner of action or treatment; a personal and prominent peculiarity of style, as in a writer or an artist.—**mannerist,** man'ėr·ist, *n.* One addicted to mannerism.—**mannerliness,** man-ėr·li·nes, *n.* The quality of being mannerly.—**mannerly,** man'ėr·li, *a.* Showing good manners; correct in deportment; polite; not rude or vulgar.—*adv.* With good manners; without rudeness.

mannish, etc. See MAN.

mannite. See MANNA.

mannose, man'ōs, *n.* [From *manna.*] A kind of sugar related to glucose.

man-of-war. See MAN.

manometer, ma·nom'e·ter, *n.* An instrument for measuring the pressure of gases and vapors.—**manometric, manometrical,** man'o·met'-rik, man·o·met'ri·kal, *a.* Pertaining to the manometer.

manor, man'or, *n.* [O.Fr. *manoir, maneir, maner,* L.L. *manerium,* a dwelling-place, a mansion, from L. *maneo,* to stay, to dwell. MANSION.] The land belonging to a lord or nobleman, or so much land as a lord formerly kept in his own hands for the use and subsistence of his family; a residence with a certain portion of land annexed to it.—**manor house,** *n.* The mansion belonging to a manor.—**manorial,** ma·nō'ri·al, *a.* Pertaining to a manor.

mansard roof, *n.* [From Francois Mansard, a French architect, the inventor, who died in 1666.] A curb roof, or roof of two slopes, the lower being steeper than the upper slope.

manse, mans, *n.* [L.L. *mansus, mansum,* a residence, from L. *mansum,* to stay, to dwell. MANSION.] The dwelling-house of a clergyman.

manservant. See MAN.

mansion, man'shon, *n.* [L. *mansio, mansionis,* from *maneo, mansum,* to dwell (seen also in *manor, menial, remain, remnant,* etc.).] A dwelling or residence, especially one of considerable size and pretension; a habitation; an abode.

mantel, man'tel, *n.* [O.Fr. *mantel,* Fr. *manteau,* mantle.] The supporting beam for the masonry above a fireplace.—**mantelpiece,** *n.* The shelf of a mantel.

mantelet, mantlet, man'tel·et, mant'let, *n.* [Dim. of *mantle.*] A small cloak worn by women; *fort.* a kind of movable parapet or penthouse set on wheels for protecting sappers from musketry fire.

mantic,† man'tik, *a.* [Gr. *mantikos,* from *mantis,* a prophet.] Relating to prophecy or divination; prophetic.

mantilla, man·til'la, *n.* [Sp.; same origin as *mantle.*] A hood; a Spanish head covering for women, which falls down upon the shoulders and may be used as a veil; a light cloak thrown over the dress of a lady.

mantis, man'tis, *n.* [Gr., a prophet, the mantis.] A genus of orthopterous insects, frequently resembling twigs and leaves, the praying mantis being so called from the position of the anterior legs resembling that of a person's hands at prayer.

mantissa, man·tis'a, *n.* [L., addition, increase.] The decimal part of a logarithm following the integral part.

mantle, man'tl, *n.* [O.Fr. *mantel,* Fr. *manteau,* It. *mantello,* from L. *mantellum, mantelum,* a mantle, a napkin.] Hence *mantel.*] A kind of cloak or loose garment to be worn over other garments; a covering; something that covers and conceals; *zool.* the external fold of the skin in most mollusks. Sometimes used in same sense as *mantel.*—*v.t.*—*mantled, mantling.* To cloak or cover.—*v.i.* To be expanded or spread out like a mantle; to become covered with a coating, as a liquid; to send up froth or scum; to cream; to display superficial changes of hue.

mantlet, *n.* See MANTELET.

mantua, man'tū·a, *n.* [Either a corruption of Fr. *manteau,* a mantle, or from *Mantua* in Italy (comp. *milliner,* from *Milan*).] A lady's gown.

manual, man'ū·al, *a.* [L. *manualis,* pertaining to the hand, from *manus,* the hand (root *ma,* to measure), seen also in *manacle, manage, manifest, manner, manure, maintain,* etc.] Performed or done by the hand; such as to require bodily exertion (*manual* labor); used or made by the hand.—*Manual training,* training in handicraft, as the work of carpenters, plumbers, or machinists.—*n.* A small book, such as may be carried in the hand or conveniently handled; any book of instructions or orders; the keyboard of an organ or the like.—**manually,** *adv.*

manubrium, ma·nū′bri·um, n. [L., a handle, from *manus*, the hand.] *Anat.* the upper bone of the sternum.

manufactory, man·ū·fak′to·ri, n. [L. *manus*, the hand, and *factura*, a making, from *facio*, to make.] A building in which goods are manufactured; a factory.—**manufacture,** man·ū·fak′chėr, n. The operation of making wares of any kind; the operation of reducing raw materials into a form suitable for use, by more or less complicated operations; an article made from raw materials.—*v.t.*—*manufactured, manufacturing*.To make or fabricate from raw materials, and work into forms convenient for use, especially by more or less complicated processes.—*v.i.*—To be occupied in manufactures.—**manufacturer,** man·ū·fak′chėr·ėr n. One who manufactures; one who employs workmen for manufacturing; the owner of a manufactory.—**manufacturing,** man·ū·fak′chėr·ing, pp. and a. Employed in making goods; pertaining to manufactures.

manumit, man·ū·mit′, v.t.—*manumitted, manumitting*. [L. *manumitto*—*manus*, hand, and *mitto*, to send.] To release from slavery; to free, as a slave; to emancipate.—**manumission,** man·ū·mish′on, n. [L. *manumissio*.] The act of manumitting; emancipation.

manure, ma·nūr′, v.t.—*manured, manuring*. [Originally to work by manual labor or by the hand, the same word as *manœuvre*.] To cultivate by manual labor;‡ to enrich (soils) with fertilizing substances; to treat with manure.—n. Any matter or substance added to the soil with the view of fertilizing it, or of accelerating vegetation and increasing the production of the crops, such as guano, dung, bone dust, the drainage from a dung heap (liquid *manure*), etc.—**manurer,** ma·nū′rėr, n. One that manures lands.

manus, mā′nus, n. [L., the hand.] The hand; the part of an animal's fore limb corresponding to the hand in man.

manuscript, man′ū·skript, n. [L. *manuscriptum*, written with the hand —*manus*, the hand, and *scribo, scriptum*, to write.] A book or paper written with the hand or pen; a writing of any kind, in contradistinction to what is printed; often contracted to *MS.*, pl. *MSS.*—a. Written with the hand; not printed.

Manx, mangks, n. The native language of the inhabitants of the Isle of Man; pl. the natives of Man.—a. Belonging to the Isle of Man or its language.

many, men′i, a. [A.Sax. *manig, maenig, monig*; D. *menig*, Dan. *mange*, Goth. *manags*, O.H.G. *manac*, G. *manch*, many.] Numerous; forming or comprising a great number (*many* men); always followed by *an* or *a* before a noun in the singular number (*many* a man), and then with more of a distributive force.— *The many*, the great majority of people; the crowd; the common herd.—*So many*, the same number

of; a certain number indefinitely.— *Too many*, too strong; too powerful; too able (*colloq.*). [*Many* is prefixed to a great number of adjectives forming compounds which explain themselves (*many*-colored, *many*-cornered, *many*-eyed, etc.).]—**many-sided,** a. Having many sides; showing mental or moral activity in many different directions; exhibiting many phases.

Maori, mä′o·ri, n. [A New Zealand word signifying native or indigenous.] One of the native inhabitants of New Zealand.—a. Of or belonging to the native inhabitants of New Zealand.

map, map, n. [L. *mappa*, a napkin— *mappa mundi*, a map of the world; akin are *apron, napery*.] A representation of the surface of the earth or of any part of it, or of the whole or any part of the celestial sphere, usually on paper or other material.—*v.t.*—*mapped, mapping*. To delineate in a map, as the figure of any portion of land; to represent in detail.

maple, mā′pl, n. [A.Sax. *maepel*.] The name given to any tree of the genus *Acer*, the wood of which is valuable.—*Sugar maple*, a maple of North America, the juice of which, obtained in early spring by tapping, is converted into sugar.

mar, mär, v.t.—*marred, marring*. [A.Sax. *myrran, merran, amyrran, amerran*, to hinder, to spoil; D. *marren*, to retard; Icel. *merja*, to crush; O.H.G. *marrjan*, to hinder. Akin to *moor* (verb).] To injure in any way; to spoil, impair, deface, deform.—**marplot,** mär′plot, n. One who, by his officious interference, mars or defeats a design or plot.

marabou, mar′a·bö, n. [Fr. *marabout*, orig. a Mohammedan hermit.] The name of two large storks, the delicate white feathers beneath the wing and tail of which form the marabou feathers, used in millinery.

maraschino, mar·as·kē′nō, n. [It., from *marasca, amarasca*, a kind of sour cherry, from L. *amarus*, bitter.] A kind of liqueur made in Dalmatia from cherries.

marasmus, ma·ras′mus, n. [Gr. *marasmos*, from *marainō*, to cause to pine or waste away.] A wasting of flesh without fever or apparent disease; atrophy.

marathon, mar′a·thon, n. [From the Battle of *Marathon*, 490 B.C.] A long-distance race; a 26-mile foot race; an endurance test.

maraud, ma·rad′, v.i. [Fr. *marauder*.] To rove in quest of plunder.—*v.t.* To raid for plunder.—**marauder,** ma·rad′dėr, n.

maravedi, mar·a·vā′di, n. [Sp., from *Márabitin*, an Arabian dynasty which reigned in Spain.] A very small copper coin formerly used in Spain.

marble, mär′bl, n. [Fr. *marbre*, from L. *marmor*, marble, Gr. *marmaros*, any stone or rock which sparkles in the light, from *marmairō*, to flash, to gleam.] The popular name of any species of calcareous stone, of a compact texture and of

a beautiful appearance, susceptible of a good polish; a column, tablet, or the like, of marble, remarkable for some inscription or sculpture; a little ball of marble, of other stone, or of baked clay, used by children in play.—a. Composed of marble; stained or veined like marble; *fig.* hard or insensible like marble (*marble*-hearted, *marble*-breasted).—*v.t.*—*marbled, marbling*. To give an appearance of marble to; to stain or vein like marble.— **marbling,** mär′bling, n. Imitation of marble; any marking resembling that of veined marble.

marc, märk, n. [Fr.] The refuse matter which remains after the pressure of fruit, as of grapes, olives, etc.

marcasite, mär′ka·sīt, n. [Fr. *marcassite*, a word of Arabic origin.] Iron pyrites or bisulfide of iron, nearly of the color of tin, used for industrial or ornamental purposes.

marcescent, mär·ses′ent, a. [L. *marcescens, marcescentis*, ppr. of *marcesco*, to fade.] Withering; fading; decaying; specifically, *bot.* withering, but not falling off till the part bearing it is perfected.

march, märch, n. [A.Sax. *mearc*, a mark, sign, boundary; Icel. *mark*, O.H.G. *marcha* (whence Fr. *marche*, boundary). MARK.] A frontier or boundary of a territory; most common in pl., and especially applied to the boundaries or confines of political divisions; in Scotland the boundary line of conterminous estates or lands, whether large or small.—*v.i.* To be contiguous; to be situated next, with a boundary line between.

march, märch, v.i. [Fr. *marcher*; It. *marciare*; either from Fr. *marche*, a boundary (MARCH, a frontier), through such usages as in 'aller de *marche* en *marche*', to wander from boundary to boundary; or from L. *marcus*, a hammer, through L.L. *marcare*, to beat the ground with the feet, to march.] To move by steps and in order, as soldiers; to move in a military manner; to walk with a steady, regular tread.— *Marching regiment*, a colloquial term for an infantry regiment of the line.— *v.t.* To cause to march.—n. The measured and uniform walk of a body of men, as soldiers, moving simultaneously and in order; stately and deliberate walk; steady or labored progression; an advance of soldiers from one halting place to another; the distance passed over; progressive advancement; progress (the *march* of intellect); a musical composition designed to accompany and regulate the movement of troops or other bodies of men.—*March past*, a march past the reviewing officer or some high dignitary on parade.

March, märch, n. [O.Fr. *march*, from L. *Martius*, pertaining to Mars, the god of war; *Martius mensis*, Mars' month.] The third month of the year.—*Mad as a March hare*, quite mad or crazy, from March being the rutting month of hares, during which they are in an excited state.

marchioness, mär′shun·es, *n*. [A fem. from L.L. *marchio*, a marquis. MARQUIS.] The wife or widow of a marquis; a female having the rank of a marquis.

marchpane, märch′pān, *n*. [O.Fr. *marcepain*, It. *marzapane*, L.Gr. *maza*, a barleycake, and L. *panis*, bread.] A kind of sweet bread or cracker containing almonds.

marconigram, mär·kō′ni·gram, *n*. A message sent by Marconi's system of wireless telegraphy.

mare, mâr, *n*. [A.Sax. *mere, miere*, a mare, fem. of *mear, mearh*, a horse; Icel. *mar*, a horse, *merr*, a mare, G. *mähre*, a mare, O.H.G. *marah, march*, a horse; allied to Ir. *marc*, W. *march*, a horse.] The female of the horse.—*Mare's nest*, a discovery that is no discovery, and that a person merely fancies he has made.— **mare's-tail,** *n*. A common marsh plant somewhat resembling in appearance the equisetum or horsetail, but quite distinct.

mare, mâr, *n*. pl. **maria**, ma·rē′ä, [N.L. from L. *mare*, sea.] Any of the dark sections of the surface of the moon or Mars.

maremma, ma·rem′ma, *n*. pl. **maremme**, ma·rem′me. [It.] Marshy and malarious tracts of country in middle Italy.

margaric, mär·gar′ik, *a*. [L. *margarita*, Gr. *margarites*, pearl, from Per. *mervarid*, a pearl.] Pertaining to pearl; having a pearly appearance.— *Margaric acid*, a so-called acid, a mixture of palmitic and stearic acid obtained from oils and fats, and often in the form of pearly scales.

margarine, mär′je·rin, *n*. [Fr. from Gr. *margaron* and *ine*.] A mixture of artificially prepared edible fats, extracted from animal fats and vegetable oils, sold as a substitute for butter.

margay, mär′gā, *n*. A Brazilian carnivorous animal about the size of a cat.

margin, mär′jin, *n*.; poetically **marge,** märj. [Formerly *margine*, or *margent*, Fr. *marge*, It. *margine*, from L. *margo, marginis*, a brink, a margin.] A border; edge; brink; verge (of a river, etc.); the edge of the leaf or page of a book, left blank or partly occupied by notes; a sum or quantity reserved to meet contingencies in addition to what is known to be necessary; the difference between the cost of an article and its selling price; *bot*. the edge or border of a leaf or other organ of a plant; *fig*. a certain latitude to go and come upon.—**marginal,** mär′ji·nal, *a*. Pertaining to a margin; written or printed in the margin of a page.—**marginalia,** mär·ji·nā′li·a, *n. pl*. Notes written on the margins of books.—**marginally,** mär′ji·nal·li, *adv*. In the margin of a book.— **marginated,** mär′ji·nā·ted, mär′ji·nāt, *a*. Having a margin.

margrave, mär′grāv, *n*. [Fr. *margrave*, from D. *markgraaf*, G. mark-

graf—mark, a march or border, and *graf*, an earl or count.] Originally, like marquis, a lord or keeper of the marches or borders; a title of nobility in Germany, etc.—**margravate, margraviate,** mär′gra·vāt, mär·grā′vi·āt, *n*. The territory or jurisdiction of a margrave.—**margravine,** mär′gra·vēn, *n*. [Fr. *margravine*, G. *markgräfin*.] The wife of a margrave.

marigold, mar′i·gōld, *n*. [*Mary*, that is, the Virgin Mary, and *gold*.] The popular name applied to several composite plants bearing bright yellow flowers.

marijuana, marihuana, mä·ri·wä′nä, *n*. [Am. Sp., native word, from *Maria Juana*, Mary Jane.] Indian hemp (*Cannabis sativa*); a narcotic derived from the dried leaves and flowers of the hemp.

marinade, mar·i·nād′, *n*. [Fr., from *marin*, marine, L. *mare*, the sea.] A compound liquor, generally of wine and vinegar, with herbs and spices, in which fish or meats are steeped before dressing to improve their flavor.—*v.t*. To salt or pickle (fish); to let stand in oil and vinegar. Also **marinate.**

marine, ma·rēn′, *a*. [L. *marinus*, from *mare*, the sea; allied to W. *mór*, the sea, A.Sax. *mere*, a lake, and E. *marsh*; the root being same as in L. *mors*, death (dead or stagnant water).] Pertaining to or in some way connected with the sea; found or formed in the sea; inhabiting the sea (*marine* forms of life); used at sea; suited for use at sea (a *marine* engine); naval; maritime (a *marine* officer; *marine* forces).—*n*. The entire navy of a kingdom or state; the collective shipping of a country.— *Marines*, troops serving on a war vessel or at shore-stations, as a separate unit of the Navy to supplement naval activities. They are used primarily as landing forces in wartime, and to guard American lives and property abroad.—**mariner,** mar′i·nėr, *n*. [Fr. *marinier*.] A seaman or sailor; one whose occupation is to assist in navigating ships.—*Mariner's compass*, a navigator's device consisting of a magnetic needle and a card marking directions.

Mariolatry, mâ·ri·ol′a·tri, *n*. [L. *Maria*, Mary, the Virgin Mary, and Gr. *latreia*, service, worship.] The adoration of the Virgin Mary.

marionette, mar′i·o·net″, *n*. [Fr., for *Mariolette*, a dim. of *Mariole*, a little figure of the Virgin *Mary*.] A puppet moved by strings.

marish,† mar′ish, *n*. A fen; a marsh.

marital, mar′i·tal, *a*. [L. *maritalis*, from *maritus*, marriage.] Of or pertaining to a marriage.

maritime, mar′i·tīm, *a*. [L. *maritimus*, from *mare*, the sea. MARINE.] Relating or pertaining to navigation or commerce by sea; connected or belonging to shipping; naval; having a navy and commerce by sea (*maritime* powers); bordering on the sea; situated near the sea (a *maritime* town).

marjoram, mär′jo·ram, *n*. [G. *marjoran*, It. *marjorana*, L.L. *marjoraca*,

from L. *amaracus*, Gr. *amarakos*, marjoram.] A perennial plant of the mint family, of several species; the sweet marjoram is aromatic and fragrant, and used in cookery.

mark, märk, *n*. [A.Sax. *mearc*, mark, sign, limit, boundary = Goth. *marka*, a boundary; L. *margo*, edge or border; G. *mark*, a boundary, a district.] A visible sign or impression on something, as a dot, line, streak, stamp, figure, or the like; any sign by which a thing can be distinguished; a certain sign which a merchant puts upon his goods in order to distinguish them from others; a trademark; pre-eminence, distinction, importance, eminent position (a man of *mark*); respectful attention or regard; heed; anything to which a missile may be directed; the point to be reached; the proper standard; the extreme estimate or allowance (below or within the *mark*); a character, generally in the form of a cross, made by a person who cannot write his name, and intended as a substitute for it; a mark in paper (a water *mark*); a target or focal point (hit the *mark*); the point at which one begins a race (on your *mark...*); a postmark; a grade given a student.—*To make one's mark*, to gain a place of influence and distinction.—*v.t*. To make a mark on; to single out, point out, stamp, or characterize; to denote; often with *out*, to take particular observation of; to take note of; to trace or chart a route; to set off boundaries (used with *off*); to indicate; to register, as an instrument; to trace with marks. —*To mark time, milit*. to lift and bring down the feet alternately at the same rate as in marching; to stall progress for a time.—*v.i*. To note; to observe critically; to remark.— **markdown,** märk′doun, *n*. A reduction in price.—**marker,** mär′kėr, *n*. One who marks; something used to make a mark.—**marking,** mär′king, *n*. The act of impressing a mark; a mark or series of marks upon something; characteristic arrangement of natural coloring (the *markings* on a bird's egg).—**marksman,** märks′man, *n*. One who is skillful to hit a mark; one who shoots well.— **marksmanship,** märks′man·ship, *n*.

mark, märk, *n*. [A.Sax. *marc*; G. *mark*.] A German monetary unit and coin; formerly a European weight for gold and silver, about 8 oz.

market, mär′ket, *n*. [O.Fr. *markiet*, It. *marcato*, L. *mercatus*, from *mercor*, to buy, from *merx, mercis*, merchandise. MERCANTILE.] An occasion on which goods are publicly exposed for sale and buyers assemble to purchase; a fair; a public place in a city or town where goods are exposed for sale, whether a building or an open space; country or place of sale (the U.S. *market*, the foreign *market*); purchase or sale, or rate of purchase and sale; demand for commodities.—*v.i*. To deal in a market; to make bargains for provisions or goods.—*v.t*. To offer for sale in a market; to vend; to sell.—

ch, *chain*; ch, Sc. lo*ch*; g, *go*; j, *job*; ng, si*ng*; TH, *then*; th, *thin*; w, *wig*; hw, *whig*; zh, a*z*ure.

marketable, mär′ket·a·bl, a. Capable of being sold; salable; fit for the market; current in the market.—**market price**, n. The price at which anything is currently sold; current value.

marking, marksman, etc. See MARK.

markka, mär′kä, n. [A.Sax. marc; G. mark.] A monetary unit of Finland.

marl, märl, n. [O.Fr. marle, D., Dan. Sw., and G. mergel, L.L. margila, from L. marga, marl—a word of Celtic origin.] A mixture of calcareous and argillaceous earth found at various depths under the soil, and extensively used for the improvement of land, there being several varieties of it, as clay marl, shell marl, etc.—v.t. To overspread or manure with marl.—**marlite**, mär′lit, n. A variety of marl.—**marlitic**, mär·lit′ik, a. Partaking of the qualities of marlite.—**marly**, mär′li, a. Resembling marl; abounding with marl.

marlin, mär′lin, n. [From marlinspike.] A large oceanic game fish, having a spiked snout, which appears in the Atlantic and Pacific oceans.

marline, mär′lin, n. [D. marling, marlijn—marren, to tie, to moor, and lijn, a line, a cord. MOOR, LINE.] Naut. a small line composed of two strands loosely twisted, used for winding around ropes to prevent their being chafed.—v.t. Naut. to wind marline round, as a rope.—**marline-spike, marlinspike**, mär′lin·spik, n. A sort of iron spike with an eye or hole on one end, used to separate the strands of a rope in splicing.

marmalade, mär′ma·lad, n. [Fr. marmelade; Pg. marmēlada, from marmelo, a quince; from L. melimelum, Gr. melimēlon, lit. a sweet apple—meli, honey, and mēlon, an apple, peach, orange.] A name applied to preserves made from various fruits, especially bitter and acid fruits, such as the orange, lemon, etc.

marmoreal, marmorean, mär·mō′ri·al, mär·mō′ri·an, a. Pertaining to marble; made of marble.

marmoset, mär′mo·zet, n. [O.Fr. marmoset, Fr. marmouset, originally a small grotesque figure, from L.L. marmoretum, a small marble figure, from L. marmor, marble.] A beautiful American monkey with long tail, long fur, and tufted ears.

marmot, mär′mot, n. [Fr. marmotte; It. marmotta, marmontana, from L. mus (muris) montanus, mountain mouse.] A rodent quadruped, an inhabitant of northern latitudes, living in colonies, in extensive burrows, and hibernating in winter.

maroon, ma·rön′, n. [Fr. marron, runaway, from Sp. cimarron, wild, unruly, from cima, the top of a hill.] A name once given to fugitive slaves living on the mountains in the West Indies and Guyana.—v.t. To put ashore and leave on a desolate island, by way of punishment, as was done by the buccaneers, etc.

maroon, ma·rön′, a. [Fr. marron, It. marrone, a chestnut.] Brownish-crimson; of a color resembling claret.—n. A brownish-crimson or claret color.

marque, märk, n. [Fr. marque, a boundary; letters of marque originally empowered the receivers to cross the boundaries or marches of an enemy. MARK, MARCH (a frontier).] A license granted to a private vessel to make attacks on the ships or belongings of a public enemy, usually in the phrase letters of marque or letters of marque and reprisal, which constitute a vessel a privateer.

marquee, mär·kē′, n. [Fr. marquise, a marchioness, a marquee.] A large tent erected for a temporary purpose; a roof-like projection above the entrance to a theater or hotel, etc.

marquess, n. See MARQUIS.

marquetry, mär′ket·ri, n. [Fr. marqueterie, from marqueter, to spot, to inlay, from marque, a mark. MARK.] Inlaid work, often consisting of thin pieces of fine woods of different colors, arranged on a ground so as to form various patterns.

marquis, marquess, mär′kwis, mär′kwes, n. [Fr. marquis, It. marchese, L.L. marchisus, marchensis, a prefect of the marches or border territories. MARK and MARCH, a boundary.] A title of dignity in Britain next in rank to that of duke, and hence the second of the five orders of English nobility.—**marquisate**, mär′kwis·āt, n. The seigniory, dignity, or lordship of a marquis.—**marquise**, mär′kēz, n. [Fr.] The wife of a marquis; a marchioness.

marriage, mar′ij, n. [Fr. mariage, L.L. maritaticum, marriage, from L. maritus, a husband, from mas, maris, a male. MASCULINE.] The act of marrying; the legal union of a man and woman for life; the ceremony by which they are so united; a wedding.—Marriage portion, dower given by a father to his daughter at her marriage. Marriage settlement, an arrangement made before marriage whereby a jointure is secured to the wife, and portions to children, in the event of the husband's death. ∴ Marriage, the union, or the act of forming or entering into the union; wedding, the ceremonies celebrating the union; nuptials, a more dignified word for wedding; matrimony, the married state; wedlock, the vernacular English word for matrimony.—**marriageable**, mar′ij·a·bl, a. Of an age suitable for marriage.—**marriageableness**, mar′ij·a·bl·nes, n. State of being marriageable.—**married**, mar′id, p. and a. Formed or constituted by marriage; conjugal; connubial (the married state).—**marry**, mar′i, v.t.—married, marrying. [Fr. marier, L. maritare, to marry, from maritus, a husband.] To unite in wedlock or matrimony; to constitute man and wife (the clergyman marries a couple); to dispose of in wedlock (as a father his daughter); to take for husband or wife; to wed; fig. to unite by some close bond of connection.—v.i. To enter into a con-

jugal state; to take a husband or a wife.

marrow, mar′ō, n. [A.Sax. mearh, mearg = D. marg, merg, Dan. marv, Icel. mergr, G. mark, marrow; comp. A.Sax. mearu, D. murw, tender, soft.] The fat contained in the osseous tubes and cells of the bones; fig. the essence; the best part; a kind of gourd yielding an oblong fruit used as a vegetable, also called vegetable marrow.—Spinal marrow, the spinal cord or cord of nervous matter extending through the spine.—**marrowbone**, n. A bone containing marrow.—To go down on one's marrowbones, to assume a kneeling position. [Humorous.]—**marrowfat**, n. A kind of rich pea.—**marrow squash**, n. Another name for the vegetable marrow.

marry, mar′i. interj. Indeed; forsooth: a term of asserveration derived from the practice of swearing by the Virgin Mary.

Mars, märz, n. A Latin deity, the god of war, identified at an early period by the Latins themselves with the Greek Ares; the fourth planet from the sun or the first outside of the earth's orbit.

Marseillaise, mär·sā·yāz′, n. The national song of the French Republic, dating from the first revolution, being written in 1792, and first sung in Paris by revolutionaries from Marseilles.

marsh, märsh, n. [A.Sax. mersc, for merisc (mere, pool, isc, ish), a bog; L.G. marsch, O.D. maersche, meersch; allied to L. mare, the sea. MARINE.] A tract of low and very wet land; a fen, swamp, morass.—**marsh gas**, Same as METHANE.—**marshiness**, märsh′i·nes, n. State of being marshy.—**marsh marigold**, n. A marsh plant of the ranunculus family with a bright yellow flower.—**marshy**, märsh′i, a. Partaking of the nature of a marsh or swamp; swampy; fenny; produced in marshes.

marshal, mär′shal, n. [O.F. mareschal, Fr. maréchal, L.L. mariscalcus, from O.H.G. marahscalc—O.G. marah, a horse, and scalc (Mod.G. schalk), a servant. MARE.] Formerly an officer whose duty was to regulate tournaments or combats in the lists; one who regulates rank and order at a feast or any other assembly, directs the order of procession, and the like; in France, the highest rank of military officer; in other countries of Europe, a military officer of high rank, called in full field-marshal; in U. S., a civil officer in each judicial district, to execute court orders, and with other duties paralleling those of sheriff.—v.t.—marshaled, marshaling. To dispose in due order (an army, troops); to arrange in a suitable or most effective order (arguments, evidence, etc.).

marshmallow, marsh′mal·ō, n. [O.E. merscmealwe; see MARSH and MALLOW.] A plant, Althaea officinalis, of the hollyhock genus, growing naturally in marshes.—**marshmallow**, marsh″mel′ō, n. A soothing confection obtained from marsh mallow, a medicinal root; a corn sirup and gelatin confection, sometimes with beaten egg whites.

marsupial, mär·sū′pi·al, *a.* [L. *marsupium*, Gr. *marsupion*, a pouch.] Having an external abdominal pouch; belonging to the order of marsupials.—*n.* One of an extensive group of mammalia characterized by the absence of a placenta, and the consequent premature production of the fetus, which immediately on its birth is placed by the mother in an external abdominal pouch, in which are the teats, and there nurtured until fully developed.—**marsupium,** mär·sū′pi·um, *n.* The pouch of the marsupials.

mart, märt, *n.* [Contr. from *market*.] A place of sale or traffic, where buying and selling are active; an emporium, a center; as Furniture Mart or Merchandise Mart.

martello tower, mär·tel′lō·tou·ėr, *n.* [From *Mortella* in Corsica, where a tower of this kind made a strong resistance to an English naval force in 1794.] A small circular fort, with very thick walls, built chiefly to defend the seaboard.

marten, mär′ten, *n.* [Older *martern*, Fr. *martre*, from D. *marter*, G. *marder*, a marten.] A carnivorous quadruped of the weasel family, very destructive to game, poultry, and eggs; the pelt of a marten, frequently called *sable* by fur traders.

martial, mär′shal, *a.* [L. *martialis*, from *Mars, Martis,* the god õf war.] Pertaining to war; suited to war; military; given to war; warlike.—*Martial law,* an arbitrary kind of law, proceeding directly from the military power, and proclaimed in times of war, insurrection, rebellion, or other great emergency.—**martially,** mär′shal·li, *adv.* In a martial manner.

Martian, mär′shan, *a.* Pertaining to Mars, god of war, or to the planet Mars or its supposed inhabitants.

martin, mär′tin, *n.* [From the proper name *Martin*; comp. *robin*-redbreast, etc.] A general name applied to various species of swallows, the best-known being the sand martin and the purple martin.

martinet, mär′ti·net, *n.* [From General *Martinet*, a very strict French officer in the reign of Louis XIV.] A military or naval officer who is an excessively strict disciplinarian; one who lays stress on a rigid adherence to the details of discipline, dress, etc.

martingale, mär′tin·gāl, *n.* [Fr. *martingale*, Sp. *martingala*, a martingale, old kind of breeches; from *Martigal*, an inhabitant of *Martigues*, in Provence.] A strap from a horse's head to the girth under his belly and passing between the forelegs, to prevent him from rearing; *naut.* a short perpendicular spar under the bowsprit.

martini, mar·tē′nē, *n.* [From name *Martini*.] An alcoholic beverage made from gin and dry vermouth.

Martinmas, mär′tin·mas, *n.* [*Martin* and *mass*.] The feast of St. Martin, the 11th of November, a Scotch term-day, on which rents are paid, servants hired, etc.

martlet, märt′let, *n.* [Dim. of *martin*.] The martin, a kind of swallow. (*Shak.*)

martyr, mär′tėr, *n.* [Gr. *martyr*, a martyr, a form of *martys*, a witness.] One who by his death bears witness to the truth; one who suffers death rather than renounce his religious opinions; one who suffers death or persecution in defense of any cause.—*v.t.* To persecute as a martyr; to torment or torture.—**martyrdom,** mär′tėr·dom, *n.* The state of being a martyr; the death of a martyr.—**martyrize,** mär′tėr·īz, *v.t.* To devote to martyrdom. —**martyrological,** mär·tėr·o·loj″i·kal, *a.* Pertaining to martyrology.—**martyrologist,** mär·tėr·ol′o·jist, *n.* A writer of a martyrology.—**martyrology,** mär·tėr·ol′o·ji, *n.* A history or account of martyrs with their sufferings; a register of martyrs.

marvel, mär′vel, *n.* [Fr. *merveille*; It. *maraviglia*; from L. *mirabilia*, wonderful things, from *mirabilis*, wonderful, from *mirar*, to wonder. MIRACLE.] A wonder; an object of great astonishment.—*v.i.*—**marveled, marveling.** To be struck with surprise or astonishment; to wonder.—*v.t.* To wonder at (with clause as object); to be curious about.—**marvelous,** mär′vel·us, *a.* Exciting wonder; astonishing; partaking of the miraculous or supernatural.—**marvelously,** mär′vel·us·li, *adv.*—**marvelousness,** mär′vel·us·nes, *n.*

Marxism, märks′izm, *n.* [After Karl *Marx*.] Communism; the theories of Marx and Engels, in which class struggle is the key to world history and will eventually destroy barriers and cause a classless society.—**Marxist,** märks′ist, *n.* Advocate of the theories of Marx.—**Marxian,** märks′i·an, *a.*

marzipan, mär′zi·pan, *n.* [G.] Same as *marchpane* (which see).

mascara, mas·kâr′ä, *n.* [Sp. *máscara*, a mask.] A coloring for the eyelashes.

mascle, mas′kl, *n.* [O.Fr. *mascle*, Fr. *macle*, from L. *macula*, a spot, the mesh of a net.] *Armor,* a lozenge-shaped plate or scale.

mascot, mas′kot, *n.* [Fr. *mascotte*.] A thing or person supposed to bring good luck.

masculine, mas′kū·lin, *a.* [L. *masculinus*, from *masculus*, male, from *mas, maris,* a male.] Of the male sex; strong; robust; powerful; manly; *gram.* denoting or pertaining to the gender of words which are especially applied to male beings or things regarded grammatically as male.—*Masculine rhymes,* rhymes in which only the last, accented syllable agrees, as *contain, domain.*—*n. Gram.* the masculine gender; a word of this gender.—**masculinely,** mas′kū·lin·li, *adv.* — **masculineness, masculinity,** mas′kū·lin·nes, mas·kū·lin′i·ti, *n.*

maser, mā′zėr, *n.* [microwave amplification by stimulated emission of radiation.] A device that produces highly stable electromagnetic waves by harnessing the natural oscillations of an atomic or molecular system.

mash, mash, *n.* [Akin to Dan. *mask,* a mash, Sw. *mäska,* to mash; Sc. *mask,* to infuse, as tea, G. *meisch,* mash (of malt), *meischen,* to mash, mix; E. *mess,* a mixture.] A mixture of ingredients beaten or blended together in a promiscuous manner; especially, a mixture for feeding horses; *brewing,* a mixture of ground malt and warm water yielding wort. —*v.t.* To beat into a confused mass; to crush by beating or pressure; to mix (malt) and steep in warm water for brewing.—**masher,** mash′ėr, *n.* [From being supposed to *mash* the hearts of the fair sex.] An affected fop who dresses in the extremest fashion, and lounges about fashionable resorts; a weak, would-be gallant. (*Slang.*)

mask, mask, *n.* [Fr. *masque,* from Sp. and Pg. *mascara,* a mask, from Ar. *maskharat,* a buffoon, jeer, laugh, from *sakhira,* to ridicule.] A cover for the face, often intended to conceal identity; a disguise, pretense, or subterfuge; a masquerade; a protective covering for the face; a grotesque representation of a face. —*v.t.* To cover the face with a mask; to disguise for concealment; to conceal from an enemy, as by camouflage.—*v.i.* To wear a mask; to disguise oneself.—**masker,** mas′kėr, *n.*

masochism, ma′zō·kizm, *n.* [From Leopold von Sacher-*Masoch,* Austrian novelist who portrayed it.] A pleasure derived from being abused or humiliated; *psych.* the dependence on pain, suffering, and humiliation for sexual gratification.—**masochist,** ma′zō·kist, *n.*—**masochistic,** ma′zō·kis″tic, *a.*

mason, mā′sn, *n.* [Fr. *maçon*; L.L. *macio, machio, machionis,* from root seen in L. *maceria,* a wall.] A builder in stone or brick; one who constructs the walls of buildings, etc.; [*cap.*] a member of the fraternity of Freemasons.—**Masonic,** ma·son′ik, *a.* Pertaining to the craft or mysteries of Freemasons.—**masonry,** mā′sn·ri, *n.* [Fr. *maçonnerie.*] The art or occupation of a mason; the work produced by a mason; [*cap.*] the mysteries, principles, and practices of Freemasons.

Masonite, mā′sn·īt, *n.* A fiberboard made from steam-exploded wood fiber pressed into sheets.

Mason jar, mā′sn jär, *n.* A preserve glass with porcelain-insert metal top.

Masoretic, mas·o·ret′ik, *a.* Relating to the Jewish interpretation of the Masora, the great traditional body of Biblical information.

masque, mask, *n.* A kind of theatrical spectacle. MASK.—**masquerade,** mas′kėr·ād, *n.* [Fr. *masquerade.*] An assembly of persons wearing masks, and amusing themselves with various diversions, as dancing, walking in procession, etc.; a disguise.—*v.i.* —*masqueraded, masquerading.* To wear a mask; to take part in a masquerade; to go in disguise.—**masquerader,** mas·kėr·ā′dėr, *n.* A person taking part in a masquerade; one that appears in masquerade.

ch, *chain*; *ch,* Sc. loch; g, *go*; j, *job*; ng, si*ng*; TH, *then*; th, *thin*; w, *wig*; hw, *whig*; zh, a*zure*.

mass, mas, *n.* [Fr. *masse*, L. *massa*, a lump, from Gr. *maza*, a barley-cake, from *massō*, to knead; akin *macerate*.] A body of matter collected into a lump; a lump; a collective body of fluid matter; a great quantity collected; an assemblage (a *mass* of foliage); bulk; magnitude; the main body of things collectively; the generality; the bulk (the *mass* of the people); *phys.* a measure of the amount of matter in a body as determined by comparing the changes in the speeds resulting from impact between the body and a standard body: *mass* is the quotient resulting from dividing the weight of a body by the acceleration due to gravity.— *The masses*, the great body of the people.—*a.* Of, pertaining to, or characteristic of the mass or masses; of a large number.—*v.t.* and *i.* To form a mass; to collect into masses. —**massive,** mas'iv, *a.* Forming or consisting of a large mass; having great size and weight; ponderous; *mineral.* having a crystalline structure, but not a regular form as a whole.—**massively,** mas'iv·li, *adv.* —**massiveness,** mas'iv·nes, *n.*—**mass meeting,** *n.* A large or general meeting called for some specific purpose. —**mass number,** *n. Phys.* and *chem.* an integer most nearly expressive of the mass of an isotope.—**mass production,** *n.* The rapid production by machinery of large quantities of goods.

mass, mas, *n.* [A.Sax. *maesse*, Fr. *messe*, Dan. and G. *messe*, L.L. *missa*, mass, from the proclamation— Ite, *missa* est; 'Go, the assembly is dismissed' (L. *missus*, pp. of *mitto*, to send)—made in the ancient churches when the catechumens were dismissed after a portion of the service, whereupon followed the communion. MISSION.] The service of the Eucharist in the Roman Catholic and Greek Churches; the Roman Catholic communion service; the elaborate musical setting of certain portions of the service of the mass.—*High mass*, a mass performed on solemn occasions, by a priest or prelate, attended by a deacon and subdeacon, with choral music.—*Low mass*, the ordinary mass performed by the priest, assisted by one altar servant only.

massacre, mas'a·kėr, *n.* [Fr. *massacre*, probably from such a German word as L.G. *matsken, matschkern*, to cut in pieces, or G. *metzger*, a butcher, *metzeln*, to cut to pieces; O.G. *meizan*, to cut down.] The indiscriminate killing of human beings, especially without authority or necessity, and without forms civil or military; a great slaughter.— *v.t.*—*massacred, massacring*. To kill with indiscriminate violence; to butcher; to slaughter.—**massacrer,** mas'a·krėr, *n.*

massage, ma·säzh' or mas'aj, *n.* [Fr., from Gr. *massō*, to knead.] The process of kneading, rubbing, pressing, slapping, etc., parts of the body of a person for remedial or hygienic purposes.—*v.t.* To rub,

knead, push, or slap parts of a living body for healthful purposes. —**masseur,** ma·sūr', *n.* A man who gives massages.—**masseuse,** ma·sėz', *n.* A woman who practices massage.

masseter, mas'se·tėr, mas·sē'ter, *n.* [Gr. *masētēr, massētēr*, lit. a chewer, from *massaomai*, to chew.] Either of the pair of muscles which raise the under jaw.

massicot, mas'i·kot, *n.* [Fr. *massicot*.] Protoxide of lead or yellow oxide of lead of a deep yellow color and used as a pigment.

mast, mast, *n.* [A.Sax. *maest*=D., G., Sw., and Dan. *mast*, a mast.] A long, round piece of timber or a hollow pillar of iron or steel standing upright in a vessel, and supporting the yards, sails, and rigging in general.—*v.t.* To fix a mast or masts in; to erect the masts of.— **masted,** mas'ted, *a.* Having a mast or masts: chiefly in compounds.— **master,** mas'tėr, *n.* Having a mast or masts: in compounds (a three-*master*).—**masthead,** *v.t.* To send to the top of a mast and cause to remain there for a time by way of punishment.

mast, mast, *n.* (no pl.). [A.Sax. *maest*, G. *mast*, mast; akin to *meat*.] The fruit of the oak and beech or other forest trees; nuts; acorns.

master, mas'ter, *n.* [O.E. *maister, maistre*, O.Fr. *maïstre*, from L. *magister*, master, from root *mag*, seen in L. *magnus*, great (MAGNITUDE): same root as *may, might, much*.] One who rules, governs, or directs; one who has others under his immediate control; an employer; correlative to *slave, servant*, etc. (often in compounds, as, *master-printer, master-builder*, etc.); one who has possession and the power of controlling or using at pleasure; the owner; proprietor; a chief, principal, head, leader; the person entrusted with the care and navigation of a merchant ship: otherwise the *captain*; an artist, a sculptor, an architect, whose accomplishments rank far above those of their contemporaries, a Raphael, a Michelangelo, a Brunelleschi; a man so well trained in his profession as to be able to follow it alone; in the *navy*, formerly an officer who navigated the ship under the direction of the captain; the head of, or a teacher in, a school; a man eminently skilled in any pursuit, accomplishment, art, or science; a proficient or adept (a *master* of the violin; a *master* of sarcasm); a civil or respectful title of address used before a person's name, and when the person is grown up always pronounced mis'tėr and written *Mr.* (*Mr.* John Smith); when applied to a boy or young gentleman, however, written in full and pronounced mas'tėr; a title of dignity; a degree in colleges and universities (*Master* of Arts); the title of the head of some societies or corporations; the title of certain high legal or other functionaries (*Master* in chancery). —*The old masters*, ancient painters of

eminence.—*To be master of one's self*, to have the command or control of one's own passions.—*v.t.* To become the master of; to overpower; to subdue; to make one's self master of.—*a.* Belonging to a master; chief; principal: often used as the first element in a compound word; as *master*-piece, *master*-mind, etc.— **masterbuilder,** *n.* A chief builder; one who employs workmen in building.—**masterful,** mas'tėr·ful, *a.* Inclined to exercise mastery; imperious; arbitrary; headstrong.—**masterfully,** mas'tėr·ful·li, *adv.* In a masterful manner.—**masterfulness,** mas'tėr·ful·nes, *n.* The quality of being masterful.—**masterless,** mas'-tėr·les, *a.* Destitute of a master or owner; ungovernable; beyond control.—**masterliness,** mas'tėr·li·nes, *n.* The quality of being masterly; masterly skill.—**masterly,** mas'tėr·li, *a.* Formed or executed with superior skill; suitable to a master; most able or skillful (a *masterly* design or performance).—*adv.* With the skill of a master.—**masterpiece,** *n.* Something superior to any other performance of the same person; anything done or made with superior skill.— **mastership,** mas'tėr·ship, *n.* The state or office of a master; pre-eminence; mastery.—**mastersinger,** *n.* One of a society of German poets of the fifteenth and sixteenth centuries.—**master stroke,** *n.* A masterly achievement.—**masterwork,** *n.* Principal performance; chef-d'œuvre.—**mastery,** mas'tėr·i, *n.* The act of mastering; dominion or command over something; superiority in competition; pre-eminence; victory in war; eminent skill.

mastic, mas'tik, *n.* [Fr. *mastic*, L. *mastiche, mastichum*, Gr. *mastichē*, from *mastax*, the jaws: so named because chewed in the East.] A resin exuding from a tree of Southern Europe, etc., yielding a varnish; the tree itself; a kind of mortar or cement for plastering walls.

masticate, mas'ti·kāt, *v.t.*—*masticated, masticating*. [L. *mastico, masticatum*, from G. *mastichaō*, to gnash the teeth. MASTIC.] To grind with the teeth and prepare for swallowing and digestion; to chew.—**mastication,** mas·ti·kā'shon, *n.* The act of masticating.—**masticator,** mas'-ti·kā·tėr, *n.* One who or that which masticates; a machine for cutting up meat for persons unable to chew properly, also for kneading up raw India rubber or gutta-percha.— **masticatory,** mas'ti·kā·to·ri, *a.* Adapted to perform the office of chewing.—*n. Med.* a substance to be chewed to increase the saliva.

mastiff, mas'tif, *n.* [From a hypothetical Fr. *mastif*, from G. *masten*, to fatten, O.H.G. *mastjan*, to feed, from *mast*, food, mast (acorns, etc.).] A variety of dog of old English breed, large and very stoutly built, and with deep and pendulous lips.

mastitis, mas·tī'tis, *n.* [Gr. *mastos*, the breast, and term. *-itis*, denoting inflammation.] Inflammation of the breast.

mastodon, mas′to·don, *n.* [Gr. *mastos*, breast, and Gr. *odous*, *odontos*, tooth.] A genus of extinct fossil quadrupeds resembling the elephant, but larger.

mastoid, mas′toid, *a.* [Gr. *mastos*, breast, and *oid*.] Resembling a nipple or breast; a process or projection of certain bones behind the ear.—**mastoiditis,** mas′toid·i″tis, *n.* An inflammation of the mastoid or the mastoid cells.

masturbate, mas′tėr·bāt. *v.t.*—*marturbated, masturbating.* [L. *masturbari*, to practice self-gratification.] To artificially stimulate the genitals for sexual self-gratification.—*v.i.* To practice masturbation.—**masturbation,** mas′tėr·bā″shon, *n.*

mat, mat, *n.* [A.Sax. *meatta*, G. *matte*, D. *mat*, Dan. *matte*, Ir. *mata*, all from L. *matta*, a mat made of rushes.] An article of interwoven material to be laid down for cleaning the boots and shoes; some kind of coarse fabric used for covering floors, etc.; an article put below dishes on the table; anything growing thickly or closely interwoven so as to resemble a mat in form or texture (a *mat* of hair).—*v.t.*—*matted, matting.* To cover or lay with mats; to interweave like a mat; to entangle.—*v.i.* To grow thick together.—**matting,** mat′ing, *n.* Materials for mats; matwork.

mat, matte, mat, *a.* [O.Fr. *mat*, downcast, afflicted, from L. *mattus*, a hangover from drinking.] Without luster; dull in surface; lusterless.—*n.* A dull, flat finish; a border of gold, white, or colored paper between the frame and a painting; *print.* a matrix. —*v.t.* To render mat, as glass or metal; to border a picture with a mat.

matador, mat′a·dôr, *n.* [Sp., lit. a killer, from *matar*, L. *mactare*, to kill, to sacrifice.] The man appointed to kill the bull in bullfights.

match, mach, *n.* [Fr. *mèche*, Pr. *mecha*, from L. *myxus*, a wick, Gr. *myxa*, the nozzle of a lamp.] A small slip of wood with a composition on one end that ignites with friction. —**matchlock,** mach′lok, *n.* Originally, the lock of a musket containing a match for firing, hence, a musket fired by means of a match.

match, mach, *n.* [O.E. *make*, a mate, A.S. *maecca, maca*, a mate, a wife. MATE.] A person equal to another; one who is able to mate or cope with another; an equal; a mate; the coming together of two parties suited to one another, as for a trial of strength or skill, or the like; a contest; union by marriage; one to be married or gained in marriage.—*v.t.* To be a match or mate for; to be able to compete with; to equal; to show an equal to; to place in competition or comparison with; to oppose as equal; to suit; to make to correspond; to marry; to give in marriage; to join in any way, combine, couple.—*v.i.* To be united in marriage; to be of equal size or quality; to tally, suit, correspond. —**matchless,** mach′les, *a.* Having no match or equal; unequaled; unrivaled.—**matchlessly,** mach′les·li,

adv. In a matchless manner.—**matchlessness,** mach′les·nes, *n.* The state or quality of being matchless.—**matchmaker,** *n.* One who contrives or effects a union by marriage. —**matchmaking,** *a.* and *n.* Working to bring about marriages.

mate, māt, *n.* [A form of old *make*, a mate, and also of *match* (an equal); O.D. *maet*, D. *maat*, companion, mate; same root as *mete*, to measure.] One who customarily associates with another; a companion; an equal; a match; an officer in a ship whose duty is to assist the master or commander; a husband or wife; one of a pair of animals which associate for propagation and the care of their young.—*v.t.*—*mated, mating.* To match; to marry; to match one's self against; to cope with; to equal.

mate, māt, *v.t.* [Fr. *mater*, to enfeeble, from *mat*, worn out or exhausted, from the chess term, Per. *shâh mât*=E. *checkmate*.] To confound; to subdue; to crush; *chess*, to checkmate.—*n.* Same as *Checkmate.*

maté, mä′tā, *n.* [Sp.] Paraguay tea, a shrub whose leaves are used in South America as a substitute for tea.

materfamilias, mä′tėr·fa·mil″i·as, *n.* [L.] The mother of a family: correlative of *paterfamilias.*

material, ma·tē′ri·al, *a.* [L. *materialis*, material, from *materia*, matter. MATTER.] Pertaining to matter; consisting of matter; not spiritual; not mental; pertaining to the physical nature of man, or to the bodily wants, interests, and comforts; important; weighty; momentous; more or less necessary; *logic*, pertaining to the matter of a thing and not to the form.—*n.* What is composed of matter; the substance or matter of which anything is made.—*Raw material*, unmanufactured material; material in its natural state.—**materialism,** ma·tē′ri·al·izm, *n.* The doctrine which denies the existence of spirit or anything but matter; due care of our material nature.—**materialist,** ma·tē′ri·al·ist, *n.* One who holds the doctrine of materialism.—**materialistic,** ma·tē′ri·al·is″tik, *a.* Relating to or partaking of materialism.—**materiality,** ma·tē′ri·al″i·ti, *n.* The quality of being material; material, as opposed to spiritual existence; importance.—**materialization,** ma·tē′ri·al·i·zā″shon, *n.* The act of materializing; among spiritualists, the alleged assumption by a spirit of a material or bodily form.—**materialize,** ma·tē′ri·al·īz, *v.t.*—*materialized, materializing.* To invest with matter; to make material; to regard as matter; to explain by the laws appropriate to matter.—**materializing,** ma·tē′ri·al·īz·ing, *a.* Directed toward materialism.—**materially,** ma·tē′ri·al·li, *adv.* In a material manner; in the state of matter; substantially; in an important manner or degree; essentially.—**materia medica,** ma·tē′ri·a med′i·ka, *n.* [L.] That branch of medical science which treats of the drugs, etc., employed in medicine; collectively, all the curative

substances employed in medicine.— **matériel,** ma·tā·rē·el, *n.* [Fr.] Material or instruments employed, as the baggage, etc., of an army, in distinction from the *personnel*, or the men; or the buildings, etc., of a college, in distinction from its officers.

maternal, ma·tėr′nal, *a.* [L. *maternus*, from *mater*, mother (which is cog. with E. *mother*); akin *matrimony, matriculate, matron*, etc.] Pertaining to a mother; becoming a mother; motherly. — **maternally,** ma·tėr′nal·li, *adv.* In a maternal manner.—**maternity,** ma·tėr′ni·ti, *n.* The state, character, or relation of a mother.

mathematics, math·e·mat′iks, *n.* [L. *mathematica*, Gr. *mathematikē* (*technē*, art, understood), from stem of *manthanō, mathēsomai*, to learn.] The science that treats of the properties and relations of quantities, comprising *pure mathematics*, which considers quantity abstractly, as arithmetic, geometry, algebra, trigonometry; and *mixed*, which treats of magnitude as subsisting in material bodies, and is consequently interwoven with physical considerations (astronomy, optics, etc.).—**mathematical, mathematic,** math·e·mat′i·kal, math·e·mat′ik, *a.* [L. *mathematicus*.] Pertaining to mathematics, according to the principles of mathematics.—**mathematically,** math·e·mat′i·kal·li, *adv.* In a mathematical manner.—**mathematician,** math′e·ma·tish″an, *n.* One versed in mathematics.

matin, mat′in, *a.* [Fr. *matin*, from L. *matutinus*, pertaining to the morning; same root as *mature*.] Pertaining to the morning; used in the morning. —*n. pl.* Morning worship or service; morning prayers or songs; time of morning service; the first canonical hour in the Roman Church.— **matinal,** mat′in·al, *a.* Relating to the morning or to matins.—**matinee,** mat·i·nā′, *n.* [Fr.] An entertainment or reception held early in the day.

matrass, mat′ras, *n.* [Fr. *matras*, a mattrass.] A chemical vessel with a tapering neck used for digestion, evaporation, etc.

matriarchy, mā′tri·är·ki, *n.* [Gr. *matēr*, mother, *archē*, rule.] The rule or predominance of the mother in a family; the principle of determining descent and inheritance on the mother's side and not on the father's, as is done by certain primitive tribes. —**matriarchal,** mā·tri·är′kal, *a.* Pertaining to matriarchy.

matricide, mat′ri·sīd, *n.* [L. *matricidium*, the crime, *matricida*, the perpetrator—*mater, matris*, mother, and *caedo*, to slay.] The killing or murder of one's mother; the killer or murderer of one's mother.— **matricidal,** mat′ri·sī·dal, *a.* Pertaining to matricide.

matriculate, ma·trik′ū·lāt, *v.t.*—*matriculated, matriculating.* [L. *matricula*, a public register, dim. of *matrix*, a womb, a parent stem, a register, from *mater*, a mother. MATERNAL.] To enter in a register;

to enroll: especially, to admit to membership in a college or university, by enrolling the name in a register.—*v.i.* To be entered as a member of a society.—*a.* Matriculated; enrolled.—*n.* One who is matriculated.—**matriculation,** ma‧‧trik′ū‧lā″shon, *n.* The act of matriculating.

matrimony, mat′ri‧mō‧ni, *n.* [L. *matrimonium,* from *mater, matris,* a mother. MATERNAL.] Marriage; the nuptial state. ∴ Syn. under marriage.—**matrimonial,** mat‧ri‧mō′ni‧al, *a.* [L. *matrimonialis.*] Pertaining to matrimony or marriage; connubial.—**matrimonially,** mat‧ri‧mō′ni‧al‧li, *adv.* In a matrimonial manner.

matrix, mā′triks, *n.* pl. **matrices,** mā′tri‧sēz. [L. *matrix,* from *mater,* mother.] The womb; that which encloses anything or gives origin to anything, like a womb; the form or mold in which something is shaped; the rock or main substance in which a crystal, mineral, or fossil is embedded; *type founding,* a metal plate engraved to serve as a mold for the type; that part of the cutis which occurs under the nail.

matron, mā′tron, *n.* [Fr. *matrone,* L. *matrona,* from *mater,* mother. MATERNAL.] A married woman, especially an elderly married woman; the mother of a family; a head nurse in a hospital.—**matronage,** mā′tron‧ij, *n.* The state of a matron; matrons collectively.—**matronal,** mā′tron‧al, *a.* [L. *matronalis.*] Pertaining to a matron.—**matronize,** mā′tron‧īz, *v.t.* To render matronlike; to act as a mother to; to chaperon.—**matronly,** mā′tron‧li, *a.* Becoming a wife or matron; sedate.

matter, mat′ėr, *n.* [O.Fr. *matere,* Fr. *matière,* from L. *materia,* matter, from root of *mother.*] That which occupies space and which becomes known to us by our senses; that of which the whole sensible universe is composed; body; substance; not mind; the substance of any speech or writing; the ideas or facts as distinct from the words; the meaning; *logic* and *metaph.,* that which forms the subject of any mental operation, as distinguished from the *form;* good sense; substance, as opposed to empty verbosity or frivolous jesting; thing treated; that about which we think, write, or speak; affair or business (thus the *matter* ended); cause or occasion of trouble, disturbance, etc. (as in the phrase, what is the *matter?*); import; consequence; moment (as in 'no *matter* which'); indefinite amount or quantity (a *matter* of 7 miles); substance excreted from living animal bodies; that which is discharged in a tumor, boil, or abscess; pus.—*Matter of fact,* a reality, as distinguished from what is fanciful.—*v.i.* To be of importance; to signify (in such phrases as, it does not *matter;* what does it *matter?*).—**matter-of-fact,** *a.* Treating of facts or realities; not fanciful, imaginative, or ideal; adhering to facts; not given to wandering beyond

realities; prosaic.

matting. See MAT.

mattock, mat′ok, *n.* [A.Sax. *mattoc,* a mattock.] A pickax with one or both of its ends broad instead of pointed.

mattoid, mat′oid, *n.* [G. *matt,* dull.] A kind of stupid monomaniac.

mattress, mat′tres, *n.* [O.Fr. *materas,* Fr. *matelas,* It. *materasso,* from Ar. *ma′tra′h,* a quilted cushion.] A manufactured pad stuffed with sponge rubber, cotton matting, etc., and supported on springs and a bedstead.

maturate, mat′ū‧rāt, *v.t.—maturated, maturating.* [L. *maturo, maturatum,* to make ripe, from *maturus,* ripe, same root as *mater,* mother.] To bring to ripeness or maturity; to mature; *med.* to promote perfect suppuration in.—*v.i.* To ripen; to come to or toward maturity.—**maturation,** mat‧ū‧rā′shon, *n.* [L. *maturatio.*] The process of maturing or ripening; *med.* a beginning to suppurate.—**maturative,** ma‧tū′ra‧tiv, *a.* Ripening; conducing to suppuration.—*n. Med.* anything that promotes suppuration. — **mature,** ma‧tūr′, *a.* [L. *maturus,* ripe.] Ripe; perfected by time or natural growth; brought by natural process to a complete state of development; ripe or ready to be put in action; *med.* in a state of perfect suppuration; *com.* become payable; having reached the time fixed for payment.—*v.t.—matured, maturing.* [L. *maturo.*] To make mature; to ripen; to make ripe or ready for any special use; *med.* to maturate.—*v.i.* To advance toward ripeness, to become mature or ripe; *com.* to reach the time fixed for payment; *med.* to maturate.—**maturely,** ma‧tūr′li, *adv.* In a mature manner; with ripeness; with full deliberation.—**matureness,** ma‧tūr′nes, *n.* The state of being mature; maturity.—**maturity,** ma‧tū′ri‧ti, *n.* The state or quality of being mature; ripeness; a state of perfection or completeness; *com.* the time when a note or bill of exchange becomes due.

matutinal, mat‧ū′ti‧nal, *a.* [L. *matutinus,* pertaining to the morning. MATIN.] Pertaining to the morning; early in the day.

matzo, mät′zō, *n.* pl. **matzoth,** mät′soth. [Heb. *matstsah,* unleavened.] The unleavened bread which the Jews eat at the Feast of Passover.

maud, mᶐd, *n.* A plaid of undyed brown wool; a gray woolen plaid worn by shepherds in Scotland.

maudlin, mᶐd′lin, *a.* [From *Maudlin,* Mary *Magdalen,* who is drawn by painters with eyes swollen and red with weeping.] Approaching intoxication; overemotional; sickly sentimental.

maul, mᶐl, *n.* [Same as *Mall.*] A kind of large hammer or mallet.—*v.t.* To beat with a maul, or as with a maul; to maltreat severely.

maulstick, mᶐl′stik, *n.* [G. and D. *malen,* to paint, and E. *stick.*] A stick used by painters to steady and support the hand in working.

maund, mᶐnd, *n.* In the East Indies,

a measure of weight, differing according to locality from 25 to about 82 pounds.

maund, mᶐnd, *n.* [A.Sax. *mand,* mond, D. *mand,* a basket.] A handbasket. (*Shak.*)—**maunder,** mᶐn′dėr, *v.i.* [From old *maunder,* a beggar, one who carries a *maund.*] To speak with a beggar's whine; to grumble; to wander in talking like a drunk or silly old person; to drivel.—**maunderer,** mᶐn′dėr‧ėr, *n.* One who maunders.

Maundy Thursday, mᶐn′di, *n.* [O.E. *maundee,* a command, Fr. *mandé,* from L. *mandatum*—the first word used in the Vulgate to render the words of the Saviour, when, after supper, he washed his apostles' feet: '*Mandatum* novum do vobis,' a new commandment I give unto you.] The Thursday before Good Friday, on which the sovereign of England distributes alms to a certain number of poor persons at Whitehall.— *Maundy money,* small silver coins (including twopenny and penny pieces) struck for this distribution.

Mauser, mou′zėr, *n.* [Inventor's name.] A kind of rifle.

mausoleum, mᶐ‧so‧lē′um, *n.* [Gr. *mausōleion,* from *Mausolus,* king of Caria, to whom Artemisia, his widow, erected a stately monument so called.] A magnificent tomb or stately sepulchral monument.

mauve, mōv, *n.* [Fr., mallow, L. *malva,* a mallow—its petals having purple markings.] One of the coal-tar colors, a purple dye obtained from aniline.

maverick, mav′ėr‧ik, *n.* [From S.A. *Maverick,* Texas cattle owner who didn't brand his cattle.] An unbranded animal; a calf parted from his mother; one who breaks away from group conformity and forges a new course.

mavis, mā′vis, *n.* [Fr. *mauvis,* Sp. *malvis,* from the Celtic; comp. Armor. *milvid,* a mavis.] The throstle or song thrush.

maw, mᶐ, *n.* [A.Sax. *maga*=D. *maag,* Icel. *magi,* O.H.G. *mago,* G. *magen,* the stomach.] The stomach of carnivores; the crop of fowls.

mawkish, mᶐk′ish, *a.* [From old *mawk, mauk,* a maggot; Icel. *mathkr,* N. *makk.*] Apt to cause satiety or loathing; sickly; nauseous.—**mawkishly,** mᶐk′ish‧li, *adv.*—**mawkishness,** mᶐk′ish‧nes, *n.*

maxilla, mak‧sil′la, *n.* pl. **maxillae,** mak‧sil′lē. [L., a jaw, dim. of *mala,* a jaw, from root of *macerate.*] A term applied to each of the bones supporting the teeth of either jaw: often restricted to the upper jaw of the inferior vertebrates.—**maxillary,** mak′sil‧la‧ri, *a.*

maxim, mak′sim, *n.* [Fr. *maxime,* from L. *maxima* (*sententia,* opinion, understood), the greatest or chief opinion, *maximus,* superlative of *magnus,* great. MAGNITUDE.] An established principle; a principle or formula embodying a rule of conduct.

maximize, mak′sim‧īz, *v.t.* To make as great as possible; to raise to the maximum.—*v.i.* To give a constitution or duty, etc., the broadest interpretation.—**maximal**, mak′si•mal, *a.* Highest; greatest amount or degree. —**maximum**, mak′si•mum, *n.* The greatest quantity or degree attainable or attained in any given case.—*a.* Greatest.

Maxim gun, mak′sim, *n.* A quick-firing machine gun, single-barreled, with water casing to keep the parts cool, so called from Sir Hiram *Maxim*, the inventor.

may, mā, *n.* [Fr. *mai*, Pr. *mai*, May, from L. *Maius*, from the goddess *Maia*, a goddess of growth or increase, from root of L. *magnus*, great, and E. *may*, the auxiliary.] [*cap.*] The fifth month of the year; *fig.* the early part of life; hawthorn blossom, so named because the hawthorn blooms in this month.—*v.i.* To celebrate the festivities of May Day: used only as a participial noun in such phrases as *to go a Maying*, etc.— **May Day**, *n.* The first day of May, on which various festivities were, and in some places still are, observed.— **Mayflower**, *n.* The trailing arbutus; the name of the ship that brought the Pilgrims to America in 1620.— **may fly**, *n.* A neuropterous insect that appears first in May.—**Maypole**, *n.* A pole wreathed with flowers and set up to be danced round on May Day.—**May queen**, *n.* A young woman honored as queen on May Day.

may, mā, *verb auxiliary*; pret. *might.* Used similarly to *can*, *could*. [A.Sax. *mugan*, *magan* = L.G. and D. *mogen*, Goth. and O.H.G. *magan*, G. *mögen*, Icel. *mega*, Dan. *maa*, to be able; from same root are *much*, *maid*, L. *magnus*, Gr. *megas*, Skr. *mahâ*, great.] Formerly often used in sense of *can*, implying personal power or ability; now to imply possibility with contingency (it *may* be so, the king *may* be killed); opportunity; moral power; permission granted (you *may* now go); desire, as in prayer, aspiration, imprecation, benediction, etc. (*may* he perish miserably!); frequently used to form the compound tenses of the potential mood (you *might* have gone had you pleased).— **maybe**, mā′bē, *adv.* [That is, 'it *may* be'.] Perhaps; possibly; probably. (*Colloq.*)—*n.* A possibility; a probability.—**mayhap**, mā•hap′, *adv.* Peradventure; it may happen; perhaps.

Maya, mä′ya, *n.* An Indian belonging to a great pre-Columbian civilization, whose descendants live in Yucatan and Central America; also, the language spoken by those people. —**Mayan**, mä′yan, *a.*

mayhem, mā′hem, *n. Law*, the act of maiming a man. MAIM.

mayonnaise, mā•on•āz′, *n.* [Fr.] A dish composed of yolks of eggs and salad oil beaten together, used as a sauce for salads, lobster, salmon, etc.

mayor, mā′ẽr, *n.* [Fr. *maire*, Sp. *mayor*, from L. *major*, greater, compar. of *magnus*, great. MAGNITUDE.] The chief magistrate of a city or borough; the chief officer of a municipal corporation.—*Mayor of*

the Palace, the chief official in the palaces of the Merovingian kings, wielding and controlling all power, rendering the kings *fainéants* or idle puppets in his hands.—**mayoralty**, mā′ẽr•al•ti, *n.* The office of a mayor, and the time of his service.— **mayoress**, mā′ẽr•es, *n.* The wife of a mayor; a woman mayor.

Mazdean, maz′di•an, *a.* [From *Ahura-Mazda*, the chief deity of the ancient Persians, the Ormuzd of English writers.] Pertaining or relating to Mazdeism.—**Mazdeism**, maz′-de•izm, *n.* The religion of the ancient Persians; the worship of Ormuzd.

maze, māz, *n.* [Akin to Prov.E. *mazle*, to wander as if stupefied; Icel. *masa*, to chatter or prattle; Dan. *mase*, to have trouble; comp. also W. *masu*, to swoon. *Amaze* is from this.] A confusing network of paths or passages; a winding and turning; an intricacy; a labyrinth; confusion of thought; perplexity.—*v.t.*—*mazed*, *mazing.* To confound; to stupefy; to bewilder.—**mazily**, mā′zi•li, *adv.* In a mazy manner.—**maziness**, mā′zi•nes, *n.* The state of being mazy.— **mazy**, mā′zi, *a.* Having the character of a maze; intricate; perplexed.

mazer,‡ mā′zẽr, *n.* [Originally a cup made of maple or spotted wood, from O.Fr. *mazre*, spotted wood, or A.Sax. *maser*, a maple (from being spotted); O.H.G. *masar*, G. *maser*, a knur, a spot in wood, G. *mase*, a spot; akin *measles*.] A cup or large goblet, generally of valuable material.

mazurka, ma•zur′ka, *n.* A lively Polish round dance in 3-8 or 3-4 time; the music written for this dance.

me, mē, *pron. pers.* [A.Sax. *mé*, *mec* (accusative), *mé* (dat.), G. *mich* (acc.), *mir* (dat.), Icel. *mik*, *mér*, Goth. *mik*, *mis*, L. *me*, *mihi*, Gr. *eme*, *emoi*, Skr. *mâm*, *mahyam*, me, to me.] The objective or accusative, as also the dative, of *I*, the pronoun of the first person. It stands as a dative in *methinks*; woe is *me*; give *me* a drink, and the like.

mead, mēd, *n.* [A.Sax. *medu* = D. *mede*, Icel. *mjöthr*, Dan. *miöd*, Sw. *mjöd*, W. *medd*, Ir. *meadh*, mead; Gr. *methy*, wine; Lith. *medus*, Rus. *med*, Skr. *madhu*, honey.] A fermented liquor made from honey and water flavored with spices.

meadow, med′ō, *n.*; poetical, **mead**, mēd. [A.Sax. *maedu*, a meadow, shorter form *maed*, a mead, allied to *math* (after-*math*) and *mow*.] A low, level tract of land under grass, and generally mown annually or oftener for hay; a piece of grassland in general.—*a.* Belonging to or growing in a meadow.—**meadow grass**, *n.* Variety known as June grass or Kentucky blue in U. S.—**meadow lark**, *n.* The American genus *Sturnella* with clear, but melancholy note. It is as large as a robin; its plumage is brown, with yellow breast.—**meadowsweet**, *n.* The plant genus *Spiraea*, containing many beautiful herbs and low deciduous shrubs.

meager, meagre, mē′gẽr, *a.* [Fr. *maigre*, from L. *macer*, lean.] Having little flesh; thin; lean; wanting richness, fertility, strength, etc.; scanty; *mineral*, dry and harsh to the touch, as chalk.—**meagerly, meagrely**, mē′gẽr•li, *adv.* Poorly; thinly; sparely; feebly.—**meagerness, meagreness**, mē′gẽr•nes, *n.* The condition of being meager.

meal, mēl, *n.* [A.Sax. *mael*, time, portion, repast; D. and Dan. *maal*, G. *mahl*, *mal*, Icel. *mál*, part, repast, time; from root seen in *measure*, *mete*, *moon*. It is the termination seen in *piecemeal*, etc.] A portion of food taken at one of the regular times for eating; occasion of taking food; a repast.—**mealtime**, *n.* The usual time of eating meals.

meal, mēl, *n.* [A.Sax. *melu*, *melo* = Icel. Sw. *mjöl*, D. Dan. *meel*, G. *mehl*, meal; from the verbal stem seen in Icel. *mala*, Goth. *malan*, G. *mahlen*, L. *molo*, to grind. MILL, MOLAR, MELLOW, MOLLIFY.] The edible part of wheat, oats, rye, barley, etc., ground into flour or a powdery state.—**mealies**, mē′liz, *n. pl.* A name given in South Africa to maize or Indian corn.—**mealiness**, mēl′i•nes, *n.* The quality of being mealy.—**mealy**, mēl′i, *a.* Having the qualities of meal, or resembling meal; powdery like meal; overspread with something that resembles meal.— **mealymouthed**, *a.* Unwilling or hesitating to tell the truth in plain language; inclined to speak of anything in softer terms than the truth will warrant.

mean, mēn, *a.* [A.Sax. *maene*, mean, false, bad, from *mán*, evil, wickedness; Icel. *meinn*, mean; comp. D. and Dan. *gemeen*, Goth. *gamains*, G. *gemein*, common.] Low in rank or birth; ignoble; humble; low-minded; base; spiritless; of little value; contemptible; despicable.—**meanly**, mēn′li, *adv.* In a mean manner; in a low condition; poorly; sordidly.— **meanness**, mēn′nes, *n.* The state or quality of being mean; want of dignity or rank; want of spirit or honor; mean or base conduct or action.

mean, mēn, *a.* [O.Fr. *meien*, *moien*, Fr. *moyen*, Pr. *meian*, from L. *medianus*, middle, from *medius*, middle. MEDIUM, MID.] Occupying a middle position; middle; midway between extremes; intermediate; *math.* having an intermediate value between two extremes (*mean* distance, *mean* motion).—*Mean proportional*, the second of any three quantities in continued proportion.—*Mean time*, the time according to an ordinary clock, which makes every day of exactly the same length, though if days are measured by the sun they are not so.—*n.* What is midway or intermediate between two extremes; the middle or average rate or degree; medium; *math.* a quantity having an intermediate value between several others, the simple average formed by adding the quantities together and dividing by their number being called an *arithmetical mean*, while a

ch, *chain*; *ch*, Sc. lo*ch*; g, *go*; j, *job*; ng, si*ng*; TH, *then*; th, *thin*; w, *wig*; hw, *whig*; zh, a*z*ure.

géometrical mean is the square root of the product of the quantities; *pl.* the medium or what is used to effect an object; measure or measures adopted; agency; instrumentality (though pl. in form generally used as sing.; by *this means, a means* to an end); income, revenue, resources, estate (his *means* were large).—*By all means*, certainly; on every consideration.—*By no means*, not at all; certainly not.—**meantime,** mēn′tīm, *adv.* During the interval; in the interval between one specified period and another.—*n.* The interval between one specified period and another.—**meanwhile,** mēn′whīl, *adv.* and *n.* Meantime.

mean, mēn, *v.t.*—pret. & pp. *meant* (ment). [A.Sax. *maenan*, to mean, to intend; D. *meenen*, Dan. *mene*, G. *meinen*, to think, to mean; same root as *man, mind, mental*, Skr. *man*, to think.] To have in the mind, view, or contemplation; to intend; to purpose; to design; to signify or be intended to signify (what does the word *mean*?); to import; to denote. —*v.i.* To be minded or disposed; to have such and such intentions (he *means* well).—**meaning,** mēn′ing, *p.* and *a.* Significant; intended to convey some idea (a *meaning* look).—*n.* That which a person means; aim or purpose; intent; what is to be understood, whether by act or language; the sense of words; signification; import; force.—**meaningless,** mēn′ing‧les, *a.* Having no meaning.— **meaningly,** mēn′ing‧li, *adv.* In a meaning manner; so as to hint at something indirectly; significantly.

meander, mē‧an′dėr, *n.* [L. *Maeander*, Gr. *Maiandros*, a river in Phrygia proverbial for its windings.] The winding of a river; a winding course; a maze; a labyrinth; a kind of ornamental or decorative design having a labyrinthine character.—*v.t.* To wind or flow over.—*v.i.* To wind or turn; to have an intricate or winding course.

meanly, meanness, etc. See MEAN (low).

meantime, meanwhile. See MEAN (intermediate).

measles, mē′zlz, *n.* [Lit. the spots or spotted sickness; D. *mazelen*, G. *masern*, pl. of *maser* (also *mase, masel*), O.G. *mása, masar*, a spot. MAZER.] A contagious disease of the human body, usually characterized by a crimson rash upon the skin; rubeola; a disease of swine, characterized by reddish watery pustules on the skin.—**measly, measled,** mēz′li, mē′zld, *a.* Infected with measles or eruptions like measles.

measure, mezh′ėr, *n.* [Fr. *mesure*, from L. *mensura*, from *metior, mensus*, to measure (seen also in *immense, dimension, commensurate*); from root *ma*, to measure, whence also *moon, mete*, etc.] The extent of a thing in length, breadth, and thickness, in circumference, capacity, or in any other respect; a standard of measurement; a fixed unit of capacity or extent; the instrument by which extent or capacity is ascertained; a

measuring rod or line; a certain definite quantity (a *measure* of wine); that which is allotted or dealt out to one; moderation; just degree: in such phrases as, *beyond* measure, *within measure*; indefinite quantity or degree (in some *measure* erroneous); action or proceeding directed to an end; something done with a view to the accomplishment of purpose; *music*, that division by which the time of dwelling on each note is regulated; musical time; *poetry*, the metrical arrangement of the syllables in each line with respect to quantity or accent; a grave solemn dance with slow and measured steps, like the minuet; *geol.* beds; strata; used in the term *coal-measures*.— *Measure of a number or quantity*, *math.* a number or quantity contained in the other a certain number of times exactly.—*Greatest common measure of numbers*, the greatest number which divides them all without a remainder.—*v.t.*—*measured, measuring*. To ascertain the extent, dimensions, or capacity of; to judge of the greatness of; to appreciate; to value; to pass through or over; to proportion; to allot or distribute by measure (often with *out*).—*To measure one's (own) length*, to fall or be thrown down.—*To measure strength*, to ascertain by trial which of two parties is the stronger.—*To measure swords*, to fight with swords. —*v.i.* To take a measurement or measurements; to result or turn out on being measured; to be in extent.— **measurable,** mezh′ūr‧a‧bl, *a.* That may be measured; not beyond measure.—**measurableness,** mezh′ūr‧a‧bl‧nes, *n.* The quality of being measurable.—**measurably,** mezh′ūr‧a‧bli, *adv.* In a measurable manner or degree; moderately.— **measured,** mezh′ūrd, *p.* and *a.* Deliberate and uniform; slow and steady; stately; formal; restricted; within bounds; moderate.—**measureless,** mezh′ūr‧les, *a.* Without measure; immeasurable.—**measurement,** mezh′ūr‧ment, *n.* The act of measuring; the amount ascertained by measuring.—**measurer,** mezh′‧ūr‧ėr, *n.* One who measures; one whose occupation or duty is to measure work or commodities.

meat, mēt, *n.* [A.Sax. *mete*=D. *met*, Icel. *matr*. D. *mad*, Sw. *mat*, Goth. *mats*, food; further connections doubtful.] Food in general; anything eaten as nourishment; the flesh of animals used as food; the edible portion of something (the *meat* of an egg).—*The meat of a* discourse, book or article, its underlying thoughts or argument.—**meaty,** mēt′i, *n.* Abounding in meat; resembling meat.

meatus, mi‧ā′tus, *n.* [L., from *meo*, to go.] A passage: applied to various ducts and passages of the body; as, *meatus auditorius*, the passage of the ear.

mechanic, me‧kan′ik, *n.* [L. *mēchanicus*, Gr. *mēchanikos*, from *mēchanē*, a machine. MACHINE.] An artisan; an artificer; one who follows a

handicraft for his living: sometimes restricted to those employed in making and repairing machinery.— *a.*, Same as *mechanical*, but not so common.—**mechanical,** me‧kan′i‧kal, *a.* Pertaining to or in accordance with the laws of mechanics; resembling a machine; hence, acting without thought or independence of judgment; done as if by a machine, that is, by the mere force of habit (a *mechanical* motion of the hand); pertaining to artisans or mechanics or their employments; acting by or resulting from weight or momentum (*mechanical* pressure); physical; opposed to *chemical* (a *mechanical* mixture, that is, one in which the ingredients do not lose their identity).—*Mechanical equivalent of heat*, the number of units of mechanical work equivalent to one unit of heat : 778 foot-pounds per pound-degree F., or 1400 foot-pounds per pound-degree C., or 41.9 million ergs per gram-degree C—*Mechanical drawing*, the sketching or drawing of machinery by means of scales, rulers, compasses, etc.—*Mechanical philosophy*, that which explains the phenomena of nature on the principles of mechanics.—*Mechanical powers*, the simple elements of which every machine, however, complicated, must be constructed; they are the lever, the wheel and axle, the pulley, the inclined plane, the wedge, and the screw.—*Mechanical solution of a problem*, a solution by any art or contrivance not strictly geometrical, as by means of the ruler and compasses or other instruments.—**mechanically,** me‧kan′i‧kal‧li, *adv.* In a mechanical manner; by the mere force of habit.—**mechanician,** mek‧an‧ish′an, *n.*—**mechanics,** me‧kan′iks, *n.* The science which treats of motion and force; the technical aspects of something (*mechanics* of poetry).—**mechanism,** mek′an‧izm, *n.* The parts, collectively, of a machine or machinery; *phys.* and *biol.* a natural process believed to be mechanically determined and possibly explained by means of physics and chemistry; an automatic natural process; automatic action.— **mechanist,** mek′an‧ist, *n.* One skilled in the use of machinery; an adherent of mechanical philosophy.—**mechanistic,** mek′an‧is″tik, *a.*—**mechanize,** mek′an‧iz, *v.t.*—*mechanized, mechanizing*. To make mechanical or automatic; *milit.* to equip an army with motorized weapons and armored vehicles.—**mechanization,** mek′an‧i‧zā″shon, *n.*

Mechlin, mek′lin, *n.* A species of fine lace made at *Mechlin* or Malines in Belgium.

medal, med′al, *n.* [Fr. *médaille*, It. *medaglia*, from L. *metallum*, Gr. *metallon*, metal. METAL.] A coin, or a piece of metal in the form of a coin, stamped with some figure or device, often issued to commemorate a noteworthy event or as a reward of merit.—**medalist, medallist,** med′al‧ist, *n.* An engraver, stamper, or molder of medals; a person skilled in medals; one who has gained a medal as a reward of merit; in golf tournament the one who qualifies with the lowest score.—**medallion**, me·dal′yun, n. [Fr. *médaillon*.] A large antique medal, usually of gold or silver; anything resembling such a piece of metal, as a circular or oval tablet, bearing on it objects represented in relief.

meddle, med′l, v.i.—*meddled*, *meddling*. [O.E. *medlen*, to mix, from O.Fr. *medler*, *mesler* (Fr. *méler*), to mix, *se mesler de*, to mix one's self up with; from L.L. *misculare*, from L. *misceo*, to mix. MEDLEY, MIX.] To mix one's self; to deal, treat, tamper (followed by *with*); to interfere; to take part in another person's affairs in an officious, impertinent, or offensive manner (often followed by *with* or *in*).—**meddler**, med′lėr, n. One that meddles; a busybody.—**meddlesome**, med′l·sum, a. Given to meddling; officiously intrusive.—**meddlesomeness**, med′l·sum·nes, n.

Mede, mēd, n. A native or inhabitant of *Media*, an ancient kingdom of Asia.

media, n. pl. See MEDIUM.

medial, mē′di·al, a. [L. *medialis*, from *medius*, middle, (akin to *mid*), seen also in *mediate*, *medium*, *medieval*, *mediocre*, *meridian*, *moiety*, etc.] Mean; pertaining to a mean or average.—**median**, mē′di·an, a. [L. *medianus*.] Situated in the middle; passing through or along the middle.—*Median line*, *anat.* a vertical line, supposed to divide the body longitudinally into two equal parts.—**mediant**, mē′di·ant, n. [It. *mediante*.] *Mus.* an appellation given to the third above the keynote.

mediastinum, mē′di·as·ti″num, n. [L. *mediastinus*, in the middle, from *medius*, middle.] The division of the chest from the sternum backward between the lungs, dividing the cavity into two parts.

mediate, mē′di·it, a. [L. *medio*, *mediatum*, to be in the middle, from *medius*, middle. MEDIAL.] Being between two extremes; middle; acting as a means or medium; not direct or immediately; effected by the intervention of a medium.—v.i. mē′di·āt, *mediated*, *mediating*. To interpose between parties as the equal friend of each; to negotiate between persons at variance with a view to reconciliation.—v.t. To effect by mediation or interposition between parties (to *mediate* a peace).—**mediately**, mē′di·it·li, adv. In a mediate manner; indirectly.—**mediation**, mē′di·ā′shon, n. The act of mediating; entreaty for another; intercession; interposition; intervention.—**mediative**, mē′di·ā·tiv, a. Of or belonging to a mediator; mediatorial.—**mediatize**, mē′di·at·īz, v.t. —*mediatized*, *mediatizing*. To render mediately dependent.—**mediatization**, mē′di·at·i·zā″shon, n. The act of mediating; the term applied to the annexation of the smaller German sovereignties to larger contiguous states, when they were made

mediately, instead of immediately, dependent on the empire.—**mediator**, mē′di·ā·tėr, n. One that mediates or interposes between parties at variance for the purpose of reconciling them: by way of eminence, Christ is called THE MEDIATOR, being our intercessor with God.—**mediatorial**, mē′di·a·tō″ri·al, a. Belonging to a mediator.—**mediatress**, **mediatrix**, mē′di·āt·res, mē′di·āt·riks, n. A female mediator.

medic, med′ik, n. [Gr. *mēdikē*, lit. a plant of *Media*.] A name of certain leguminous plants yielding fodder and allied to clover; alfalfa.

medical, med′i·kal, a. [L.L. *medicalis*, from L. *medicus*, medical, *medeor*, to heal, to cure; allied to *meditor*, to meditate; Gr. *mēdos*, care.] Pertaining to or connected with medicine or the art of healing diseases; medicinal; tending to cure; intended or instituted to teach medical science.—*Medical jurisprudence*. See JURISPRUDENCE.—**medically**, med′i·kal·li, adv. In a medical manner; according to the rules of the healing art.—**medicament**, me·dik′a·ment, n. [L. *medicamentum*.] Anything used for healing diseases or wounds; a healing application.—**medicate**, med′i·kāt, v.t.—*medicated*, *medicating*. [L. *medico*, *medicatum*.] To imbue with healing substances.—**medication**, med·i·kā′shon, n. The act or process of medicating.—**medicative**, med′i·kā·tiv, a. Tending to cure or heal.—**medicinal**, me·dis′i·nal, a. [L. *medicinalis*.] Having the property of healing or of mitigating disease; containing healing ingredients (*medicinal* springs): pertaining to medicine.—**medicinally**, me·dis′i·nal·li, adv. In a medicinal manner.—**medicine**, med′i·sin, n. [Fr. *médecine*, L. *medecina*, from *medicus*, healing.] Any substance used as a remedy for disease; a drug; physic; the science and art of preventing, curing, or alleviating disease.—**medicine man**, n. Among the American Indians and other savage tribes any man whom they suppose to possess mysterious or supernatural powers.

medieval, **mediaeval**, med·i·ē′val, a. [L. *medius*, middle, and *ævum*, age.] Relating to the Middle Ages or the period between the eighth and the middle of the fifteenth century, A.D.—**medievalism**, **mediaevalism**, med·i·ē′val·izm, n. The spirit or principles of the Middle Ages.—**medievalist**, **mediaevalist**, med·i·ē′val·ist, n. One versed in the history of the Middle Ages.

mediocre, mē′di·ō·kėr, a. [Fr. *médiocre*, from L. *mediocris*, middling. MEDIAL.] Of moderate degree or quality; of middle rate; middling.—**mediocrity**, mē·di·ok′ri·ti, n. [L. *mediocritas*.] The quality or state of being mediocre; a middle state or degree; a person of mediocre talents or abilities of any kind.

meditate, med′i·tāt, v.i.—*meditated*, *meditating*. [L. *meditor*, *meditatus*, to meditate. MEDICAL.] To dwell on anything in thought; to cogitate;

to turn or revolve any subject in the mind.—v.t. To plan by revolving in the mind; to intend; to think on.—**meditation**, med·i·tā′shon, n. [L. *meditatio*.] The act of meditating; close or continued thought; the revolving of a subject in the mind.—**meditative**, med′i·tā·tiv, a. Addicted to meditation; pertaining to meditation.—**meditatively**, med′i·tā·tiv·li, adv. In a meditative manner.

mediterranean, med′i·te·rā″ni·an, a. [L. *mediterraneus*—*medius*, middle, and *terra*, land.] Surrounded by or in the midst of land; inland: now applied exclusively to the *Mediterranean* Sea between Europe and Africa; [cap.] pertaining to, situated on or near the Mediterranean Sea.

medium, mē′di·um, n. pl. **media** or **mediums**, mē′di·a, mē′di·umz. [L. *medium*, the middle, midst, a means. MEDIAL.] Something placed or ranked between other things; a mean between two extremes; a state of moderation; something serving as a means of transmission of communication; necessary means of motion or action; agency of transmission; that by or through which anything is accomplished, conveyed, or carried on; agency; instrumentality; a person through whom spiritual manifestations are claimed to be made by believers in spiritualism, or who is said to be capable of holding intercourse with the spirits of the deceased; the liquid vehicle with which dry colors are ground and prepared for painting.—*Circulating medium*, coin and bills, or paper convertible into money on demand.—a. Middle; middling.

medlar, med′lėr, n. [O.Fr. *meslier*, *mesler*, *medler*, from L. *mespilus*, Gr. *mespilon*, medlar.] A tree found wild in Central Europe, and cultivated in gardens for its fruit.

medley, med′li, n. [O.Fr. *medlée*, *meslée* (Fr. *mêlee*), from *medler*, *mesler*, to mix. MEDDLE.] A mingled and confused mass of ingredients; a jumble; a hodge-podge; a kind of song made up of scraps of different songs.

Medoc, mā·dok′, mā′dok, n. An excellent red French wine. from *Médoc*, in the department of Gironde.

medulla, mi·dul′a, n. [L., marrow, from *medius*, middle.] *Anat.* the fat substance or marrow which fills the cavity of the bones; *bot.* pith.—*Medulla oblongata*, the upper enlarged portion of the spinal cord and the base of the brain.—*Medulla spinalis*, the spinal marrow or cord.—**medullary**, med″u·ler′i, a. [L. *medullaris*.] Consisting of or resembling marrow; relating to the pith of plants.—*Medullary sheath*, *bot.* a thin layer of spiral vessels formed immediately over the pith.—*Medullary rays*, the vertical plates of cellular tissue which connect the pith of exogenous plants with the bark.—*Medullary substance*, that which is the white substance composing the greater part of the brain, spinal marrow, and nerve fibers.

Medusa, me·dū′sa, *n*. [Gr. *Medousa*, originally the fem. of *medōn*, a ruler.] *Myth.* one of the three Gorgons who had her hair changed into serpents by Athene; *zool.* (pl. **medusae**), in zoophytes, a free-swimming sexual stage (jellyfish).—**medusoid**, me·du′soid, *a.* Pertaining to a medusa.

meed, mēd, *n*. [A.Sax. *méd, meord* = L.G. *mede*, D. *miede*, G. *miethe*, Goth. *mizdo*, reward, recompense; allied to Gr. *misthos*, pay, hire.] That which is bestowed in consideration of merit; reward; recompense; a gift.

meek, mēk, *a.* [Same as Sw. *miuk*, Icel. *mjúkr*, soft, meek; Dan. *myg*, pliant, supple; Goth. *muks*, soft, meek.] Mild of temper; gentle; submissive; not easily provoked or irritated; marked by meekness.—**meekly**, mēk′li, *adv.* In a meek manner; gently; submissively.—**meekness**, mēk′nes, *n.* The quality of being meek; mildness; gentleness; forbearance under injuries and provocations.

meerschaum, mēr′shum, *n.* [G., lit. seafoam—*meer*, the sea, and *schaum*, foam; from having been found on the seashore in lumps resembling petrified sea foam. MERE (*n.*), SCUM.] A silicate of magnesium occurring as a fine white clay, and largely made into tobacco pipes; a tobacco pipe made of meerschaum.

meet, mēt, *a.* [A.Sax. *gemet*, fit, proper, from *metan*, to measure; Icel. *maetr*, meet, worthy. METE.] Fit; suitable; proper; appropriate.—**meetly**, mēt′li, *adv.* In a meet manner; fitly.

meet, mēt, *v.t.*—pret. & pp. met. [A.Sax. *métan*, to meet, from *mót*, a meeting; Dan. *mōde*, Sw. *mōta*, Icel. *maeta*, Goth. *motjan, gamotjan*, to meet; akin *moot*.] To come face to face with; to come in contact with; to come to be in company with; to come in hostile contact with; to encounter; to join battle with; to find; to light on; to get, gain, or receive; to satisfy, gratify, answer (to *meet* a demand, one's views or wishes).—*To meet the ear*, to strike the ear; to be heard.—*To meet the eye*, to come into notice; to become visible.—*v.i.* To come together by mutual approach; to come together in hostility; to encounter; to assemble; to come together by being extended; to join.—*To meet with*, to light on; to find; to suffer; to suffer unexpectedly (to *meet with* a loss, an accident).—*n.* A meeting as of huntsmen.—**meeting**, mēt′ing, *n.* A coming together; an interview; an assembly; a hostile encounter; a duel.

megacephalous, meg·a·sef′a·lus, *a.* [Gr. *megas*, great, and *kephalē*, the head.] Large-headed; having a large head.

megacycle, meg″a·sī′kl, *n.* [Gr. *megas*, great, and *kyklos*, circle.] *Phys.* a million cycles.

megalith, meg′a·lith, *n.* [Gr. *megas*, great, *lithos*, stone.] A huge stone, such as those in cromlechs, dol-

mens, the Cyclopean architecture of the Greeks, etc.—**megalithic**, meg-·a·lith′ik, *a.* Pertaining to such stones or structures.

megalomania, meg′a·lo·mā″ni·a, *n.* [Gr. *megalē*, great, and *mania*.] Over-estimation of one's importance and abilities; a mania for great things.

megalopolis, meg·a·lop′a·lis, *n.* [Gr. *megal*, large, and *polis*, city.] A large urban region, often consisting of several adjoining cities and suburbs.—**megalopolitan**, meg′a·lō·pol″i·tan, *n.*

megalosaur, meg′a·lō·sar, *n.* [Gr. *megas, megalē*, great, and *sauros*, a lizard.] A fossil carnivorous reptile found in the oölite and Wealden strata, 40 to 50 feet long.

megaphone, me′ga·fōn, *n.* [Gr. *megalē*, great, and *phone*.] A funnel-shaped device for magnifying sound.—**megaton**, me′ga·ton, *n.* [Prefix *mega*, and *ton*.] 1,000,000 tons.

megas, megasse, me·gäs′. Same as *Bagasse*.

megilp, megilph, me·gilp′, me·gilf′, *n.* A mixture of linseed oil and mastic varnish which artists employ as a vehicle for colors.

megrim, mē′grim, *n.* [Fr. *migraine*, corrupted from Gr. *hemicrania*, half the head—*hēmi*, half, and *kranion*, the head.] A neuralgic pain in the side of the head, also called *migraine*, *pl.* low spirits; whims or fancies.

meiosis, mī·ō′sis, *n.* [Gr., a lessening, from *meton*, less.] *Biol.* a process in which, through two cell divisions, one cell with the regular (diploid) number of chromosomes becomes four cells, each with half the (haploid) number of chromosomes.

melancholy, mel′an·kol·i, *n.* [Gr. *melancholia*, excess of black bile, melancholy madness—*melas, melaina* black, and *cholē*, bile.] Depression of spirits induced by grief; dejection; sadness.—*a.* Gloomy; depressed in spirits; dejected.—**melancholia**, mel-·an·kō′li·a, *n.* A variety of mental alienation characterized by excessive depression; a manic-depressive psychosis.—**melancholic**, mel·an·kol′-ik, *a.*

mélange, mā·länzh′, *n.* [Fr., from *mêler*, to mix. MEDDLE.] A mixture; a medley.

melanic, me·lan′ik, *a.* [Gr. *melas, melan*, black.] Of or pertaining to melanism.—**melanism**, mel′an·izm, *n.* An undue development of coloring material in the skin and its appendages: the opposite of *albinism*.—**melanin**, mel·a′nin, *n. Biol.* a dark pigment present in man and some animals, as in dark-skinned peoples, also produced by certain diseases.

melanite, mel′an·īt, *n.* A mineral, a variety of garnet, of a velvet-black or grayish-black color.

melaphyre, mel′a·fīr, *n.* A compact black or blackish-gray trap-rock, consisting of a matrix of labradorite and augite, with embedded crystals of the same minerals.

melee, mā′lā, *n.* [Fr., a participial substantive, from *mêler*, to mix. MEDDLE.] A fight in which the combatants are mingled in confused mass; an affray.

melic, mel′ik, *a.* [Gr. *melikos*, from *melos*, a song.] Relating to song; lyric.

meliceris, mel·i·sē′ris, *n.* [Gr. *meli-kēris—meli*, honey, and *kēros*, wax.] *Pathol.* an encysted tumor, the contents of which resemble wax or honey in consistence.

melilot, mel′i·lot, *n.* [Gr. *melilōton, melilōtos—meli*, honey, and *lōtos*, lotus.] A leguminous annual or biennial plant allied to the clovers, and cultivated for fodder; hart's-clover.

melinite, mel′in·īt, *n.* A French explosive, the basis or chief ingredient of which is picric acid.

meliorate, mēl′yor·āt, *v.t.*—**meliorated, meliorating.** [L. *melioro, melioratum*, from *melior*, better, compar. of *bonus*, good.] To make better; to improve; to ameliorate.—*v.i.* To grow better.—**meliorater, meliorator**, mēl′yor·ā·tėr, *n.* One who meliorates.—**melioration**, mēl′yor·ā′shon, *n.* Improvement; amelioration.—**meliorism**, mēl′yor·izm, *n.* The doctrine or opinion that everything in nature is so ordered as to produce a progressive improvement.

meliphagous, me·lif′a·gus, *a.* [Gr. *meli*, honey, *phagein*, to eat.] Feeding upon honey.

mellay, melley, mel′lā, *n.* A melee; a conflict.

melliferous, mel·lif′ėr·us, *a.* [L. *mellifer—mel, mellis*, honey, and *fero*, to bear.] Producing honey.—**mellification**, mel·lif′i·kā″shon, *n.* [L. *mellifico—mel*, and *facio*, to make.] The making or production of honey.—**mellifluence**, mel·lif′lū·ens, *n.* [L. *mel*, and *fluo*, to flow.] The quality of being mellifluent; a flow of sweetness, or a sweet smooth flow.—**mellifluent, mellifluous**, mel·lif′lū·ent, mel·lif′lū·us, *a.* Flowing as with honey; sweetly flowing.—**mellifluently, mellifluously**, *adv.* In a mellifluent manner.

mellow, mel′ō, *a.* [Allied to Prov. G. *möll*, soft, ripe, *mölich*, mellow, *mollig*, soft, L. *mollis*, Gr. *malakos*, Skr. *mridu*, tender, soft, and to E. *meal*, from root *mar*, to grind or crush.] Soft with ripeness; soft to the senses; rich or delicate to the eye, ear, palate, etc., as color, sound, flavor, and the like; toned down by the lapse of time; softened or matured by length of years; rendered good-humored by liquor; half-tipsy.—*v.t.* To render mellow; to soften by ripeness or age; to give richness, flavor, or delicacy; to tone or smooth down; to soften in character; to mature.—*v.i.* To become mellow; to soften in character; to become toned down.—**mellowly**, mel′ō·li, *adv.* In a mellow manner.—**mellowness**, mel′ō·nes, *n.* The state or quality of being mellow.

melodeon, me·lō′di·on, *n.* [From *melody*, Gr. *melōdia*.] A wind instrument furnished with metallic free reeds and a keyboard; a variety of the harmonium.

melodrama, mel·o·drä′ma, *n.* [Gr. *melos*, a song, and *drama*, drama.] A romantic play, generally of a serious character, in which effect is sought by startling incidents, striking situations, and exaggerated sentiment, aided by splendid decoration and music.—**melodramatic**, mel´o‧dra‧mat˝ik, a. Pertaining to, suitable for, or having the character of a melodrama.—**melodramatically**, mel´o‧dra‧mat˝i‧kal‧li, adv. In a melodramatic manner; in an affected and exaggerated manner.—**melodramatist**, mel‧o‧dram´a‧tist, n. One who acts in melodramas or who writes them.

melody, mel´o‧di, n. [Gr. melōdia, a tune, a choral song—melos, a limb, a part, and ōdē, a song, an ode.] An agreeable succession of sounds; sweetness of sound; sound highly pleasing to the ear; mus. a succession of tones produced by a single voice or instrument, and so arranged as to please the ear or to express some kind of sentiment; the particular air or tune of a musical piece.—**melodic**, me‧lod´ik, a. Of the nature of melody; relating to melody.—**melodics**, me‧lod´iks, n. That branch of music which investigates the laws of melody.—**melodious**, me‧lō´di‧us, a. Containing or characterized by melody; musical; agreeable to the ear by a sweet succession of sounds.—**melodiously**, me‧lō´di‧us‧li, adv. In a melodious manner.—**melodiousness**, me‧lō´di‧us‧nes, n. The quality of being melodious.—**melodist**, mel´o‧dist, n. A composer or singer of melodies.—**melodize**, mel´o‧dīz, v.t.—melodized, melodizing. To make melodious.

melon, mel´on, n. [Fr. melon, L. melo, an apple-shaped melon, from Gr. mēlon, an apple or apple-shaped fruit.] A climbing or trailing annual plant and its fruit, which is large and fleshy, especially the muskmelon or cantaloupe, and the watermelon.

Melpomene, mel‧pom´e‧nē, n. [Gr. Melpomenē, from melpomai, to sing.] The muse of tragedy; also a small asteroid.

melt, melt, v.t. [A.Sax. meltan, allied to malt, mellow, etc.; Gr. meldō, to liquefy; probably also in smelt.] To reduce from a solid to a liquid or flowing state by heat; to liquefy; to dissolve; to fuse; fig. to soften; to render gentle or susceptible to mild influences.—v.i. To become liquid; to dissolve; to pass by imperceptible degrees; to blend; to shade; to become tender, mild, or gentle.—**meltable**, mel´ta‧bl, a.—**melter**, mel´tėr, n.—**melting point**, n. The degree of heat at which a solid will melt or fuse.—**melting pot**, n. A crucible; a society containing many cultures and races.

melton, mel´tn, n. [From Melton Mowbray, Eng.] A smooth strong wool having a short nap.

member, mem´bėr, n. [L. membrum, a limb, a member of the body; comp. Skr. marman, a joint.] A part of an animal body capable of performing a distinct office; an organ; a limb; part of an aggregate or a whole; one of the persons composing a society, community, or the like;

a representative in a legislative body.—Member of Congress, a representative elected by the voters of a congressional district to that branch of Congress called the House of Representatives.—**membership**, mem´bėr‧ship, n. The state of being a member; the members of a body regarded collectively.

membrane, mem´brān, n. [L. membrana, a thin skin, parchment, from membrum, a limb.] A thin tissue of the animal body which covers organs, lines the interior of cavities, takes part in the formation of the walls of canals, etc.; a similar texture in vegetables.—**membranaceous**, mem‧bra‧nā´shus, a. Membranous; bot. thin, like membrane, and translucent.—**membranous**, mem´bra‧nus, a. Belonging to a membrane; consisting of membranes; resembling a membrane.

memento, mi‧men´tō, n. [L., remember, be mindful, from memini, to remember.] A suggestion, notice, or memorial to awaken memory; something that reminds.

memoir, mem´wär, mem´wạr, n. [Fr. mémoire, from L. memoria, memory, from memor, mindful; same root as Skr. smar, to remember.] A notice of something remembered or deemed noteworthy; an account of transactions or events written familiarly; a biographical notice; recollections of one's life (in this sense usually in the pl.); a biography or autobiography; a communication to a scientific society on some subject of scientific interest.—**memorabilia**, mem´or‧a‧bil˝i‧a, n. pl. [L.] Things remarkable and worthy of remembrance or record.—**memorable**, mem´or‧a‧bl, a. [L. memorabilis.] Worthy to be remembered; illustrious; remarkable; distinguished.—**memorability**, mem´or‧a‧bil˝i‧ti, n. The quality of being memorable.—**memorably**, mem´or‧a‧bli, adv. In a manner worthy to be remembered.—**memorandum**, mem‧or‧an´dum, n. pl. **memoranda**, mem‧or‧an´da, less commonly now **memorandums**. [L., something to be remembered.] A note to help the memory; a brief entry in a diary; diplomacy, a summary of the state of a question, or a justification of a decision adopted.—**memorial**, me‧mō´ri‧al, a. [L. memorialis.] Preservative of memory; serving as a memorial; contained in the memory.—n. That which serves to perpetuate the memory of something; a monument; a written representation of facts made to a legislative or other body or to some person; a species of informal state paper much used in diplomatic negotiations.—**memorialist**, me‧mō´ri‧al‧ist, n. One who writes or presents a memorial or memorials.—**memorialize**, me‧mō´ri‧al‧īz, v.t.—memorialized, memorializing. To present a memorial to; to petition by memorial.—**memorize**, mem´or‧īz, v.t.—memorized, memorizing. To cause to be remembered; to record; to hand down to memory by writing.—**memory**, mem´o‧ri, n.

[L. memoria, memory, from memor, mindful.] The power, capacity, or faculty of the mind by which it retains the knowledge of past events or ideas; that faculty which enables us to treasure up and preserve for future use the knowledge which we acquire; remembrance; the state of being remembered; that which is remembered about a person or event; the time within which a person may remember what is past. ∴ Memory is the faculty or capacity of retaining in the mind and recalling what is past; recollection and remembrance are exercises of the faculty, the former being a calling to mind, the latter a holding in mind; while reminiscence always, and recollection often, are used of the thing remembered.

Memphian, mem´fi‧an, a. [From Memphis, the ancient metropolis of Egypt.] Pertaining to Memphis; Egyptian (Memphian darkness).

men, men, pl. of man.

menace, men´as, v.t.—menaced, menacing. [Fr. menacer, from L. minax, threatening, mina, a threat, from root min, seen in mineo, to project (in prominent, eminent); akin mien, demean, amenable, etc.] To threaten; to show a disposition to inflict punishment or other evil on: followed by with before the evil threatened (threatened him with death); to hold out threats of (to threaten revenge).—n. A threat or threatening; the indication of a probable evil or catastrophe to come.—**menacingly**, men´as‧ing‧li, adv. In a menacing manner.

ménage, men‧äzh´, n. [Fr. ménage, a household; O.Fr. mesnage, L.L. mansionaticum, from L. mansio, a dwelling. MANSION.] A household; housekeeping; household management.—**menagerie**, me‧naj´ėr‧i, n. [Fr. ménagerie.] A collection of wild animals, especially of wild or foreign animals kept for exhibition.

mend, mend, v.t. [Shorter form of amend.] To repair, as something broken, rent, decayed, or the like; to restore to a sound state; to patch up; to alter for the better; to improve (to mend one's manners); to better; to improve upon (to mend one's pace).—v.i. To advance to a better state; to improve; to act or behave better.—**mender**, men´dėr, n. One who mends.

mendacious, men‧dā´shus, a. [L. mendax, mendacis, lying, from stem of mentior, to lie: same root as mens, mind (whence mental).] Lying; false; given to telling untruths.—**mendacity**, men‧das´i‧ti, n. The quality of being mendacious; lying; falsehood; a lie.

mendelevium, men´de‧lē˝vi‧um, n. A synthetic radioactive element. Symbol, Mv; at. no., 101.

Mendelism, men´del‧izm, n. [From Mendel, an Austrian abbot.] A set of laws of heredity advanced by Mendel, which show that traits are inherited in definite predictable combinations involving dominant and recessive genes.

---

ch, chain; ch, Sc. loch; g, go; j, job; ng, sing; TH, then; th, thin; w, wig; hw, whig; zh, azure.

mendicant, men′di•kant, a. [L. *mendicans, mendicantis*, ppr. of *mendico*, to beg, from *mendicus*, a beggar (akin to *menda*, a fault).] Practicing beggary; poor to a state of beggary; begging as part of religious discipline (a *mendicant* friar).—*n.* A beggar; a member of a begging order or fraternity; a begging friar.—**mendicancy**, men′di•kan•si, *n.* Beggary; a state of begging.—**mendicity**, men•dis′i•ti, *n.* [L. *mendicitas*.] The state or practice of begging; the life of a beggar.

menhaden, men•hā′den, *n.* [American Indian.] A salt-water fish of the herring family, abounding on the shores of New England.

menhir, men′hir, *n.* [W. *maen*, a stone, and *hir*, long.] A name for tall, rude, or sculptured stones of unknown antiquity, standing singly or in groups.

menial, mē′ni•al, *a.* [O.E. *meyneal*, etc., O.Fr. *meignial*, from *meignee, maisgnee*, a household, L.L. *masnata*; same origin as *mansion*.] Pertaining to household or domestic servants; servile.—*n.* A domestic servant, especially one of a train of servants, mostly as a term of disparagement.

meninges, me•nin′jēz, *n. pl.* [Gr. *mēningx, mēningos*, a membrane.] *Anat.* the three membranes that envelop the brain, the *dura mater, pia mater*, and *arachnoid membrane*.—**meningeal**, me•nin′jē•al, *a.* Relating to the meninges.—**meningitis**, men•in•jī′tis, *n.* Inflammation of the membranes of the brain or spinal cord.

meniscus, me•nis′kus, *n. pl.* **menisci**, me•nis′si, or **meniscuses**. [Gr. *mēniskos*, a little moon, from *mēn, mēnos*, the moon.] A lens, convex on one side and concave on the other, and in which the two surfaces meet, or would meet if continued, so that it resembles a crescent.

Mennonite, men′non•īt, *n.* [From Simon *Menno*, the founder, 1496-1561.] One of a sect of Anabaptists who do not believe in original sin, and object to taking oaths, making war, or going to law.

menology, mē•nol′o•ji, *n.* [Gr. *mēn*, a month, *logos*, account.] A register or calendar of events according to the days of the months; a calendar of saints and martyrs with their feasts throughout the year.

menopause, men′o•paz, *n.* [Gr. *mēn*, month, *pausis*, a stopping.] The cessation of menstruation at the change of life in woman.

menorrhagia, men•or•rā′ji•a, *n.* [Gr. *mēn, mēnos*, a month, and *rheō*, to flow.] *Med.* an immoderate menstrual discharge; hemorrhage from the uterus.

mensal, men′sal, *a.* [L. *mensis*, a month; same root as Gr. *mēn*, a month. MONTH.] Occurring once a month; monthly.—**menses**, men′sēz, *n. pl.* The catamenial or monthly discharge of a woman.—**menstrual**, men′strö•al, *a.* [L. *menstrualis*, monthly; pertaining to the menses of females; menstruous.]—**menstruate**, men′strö•āt, *v.i.*—**menstruated**, *menstruating*. To discharge the menses.—

menstruation, men•strö•ā′shon, *n.* The act of menstruating; the period of menstruating.—**menstruous**, men′strö•us, *a.* [L. *menstruus*.] Pertaining to the monthy flow of females.

menstruum, men′strö•um, *n. pl.* **menstrua, menstruums**. [From L. *menstruus*, monthly, from *mensis*, a month; from some old belief of the alchemists about the influence of the moon.] Any fluid which dissolves a solid; a solvent.

mensurable, men′shu•ra•bl, *a.* [L. *mensurabilis*, from *mensuro*, to measure, from *mensura*, measure. MEASURE.] Capable of being measured; measurable.—**mensurability**, men′shu•ra•bil′i•ti, *n.* Quality of being mensurable.—**mensural**, men′shu•ral, *a.* Pertaining to measure.—**mensuration**, men•shu•rā′shon, *n.* The act or art of measuring or taking the dimensions of anything; the process of finding any dimension of a figure, or its area or solid content, by means of the most simple measurements possible.

mental, men′tal, *a.* [Fr. *mental*, from L. *mens, mentis*, mind. MENTION.] Pertaining to the mind or intellect; affected with mental disorder (*mental* patient); of or pertaining to telepathic or occult power; performed by or present in the mind.—**mental deficiency**, *n.* A lack of intellectual capacity which sets one apart from his peers, the most extreme form being idiocy, and the mildest form being moronity.—**mentally**, men′tal•li, *adv.*—**mentality**, men•tal′i•ti, *n.* Intellectual capacity and ability.

menthol, men′thol, *n.* [L. *mentha*, mint, *oleum*, oil.] A white crystalline substance obtained from oil of peppermint.—**mentholated**, men′tho•lā•ted, *a.* Treated with menthol.

mention, men′shon, *n.* [L. *mentio, mentionis*, from same root as *mens*, mind, Skr. *man*, to think. MAN.] A brief notice or remark in regard to something; a cursory speaking of anything; often in the phrase *to make mention of*, to name or say something in regard to.—*v.t.* To make mention of.—**mentionable**, men′shon•a•bl, *a.* That can or may be mentioned.

mentor, men′tor, *n.* [From *Mentor*, the counselor of Telemachus, according to Homer.] A wise or faithful adviser or monitor.

menu, men′yū, *n.* [Fr., lit. minute or detailed list, from L. *minutus*, minute.] A list of the dishes, etc., to be served at a dinner, supper, or the like; a bill of fare.

Mephistophelean, mef′i•sto•fē′li•an, *a.* Resembling the character of Mephistopheles, the diabolic spirit of Goethe's Faust and the Faust legend generally; diabolical; sardonic.

mephitis, me•fī′tis, *n.* [L. *mephitis*, a pestilential exhalation.] Noxious exhalations from decomposing substances, filth, or other source.—**mephitic**, me•fit′ik, *a.* Pertaining to mephitis; offensive to the smell; noxious; pestilential.

mercantile, mėr′kan•tīl, *a.* [Fr. *mercantile*, from L. *mercans, mercantis*. MERCHANT.] Pertaining to merchants, or their traffic; pertaining to trade or commerce; commercial.—**mercantilism**, mėr′kan•til•izm, *n.* The economic program which superseded that of medieval feudalism and advocated that each nation seek to establish a favorable balance of trade and so accumulate bullion.

Mercator's projection, mėr•kā′tėr. [From Gerard *Mercator*, a Flemish geographer.] A projection or map of the earth's surface, with the meridians and parallels of latitude all straight lines.

mercenary, mėr′se•ne•ri, *a.* [Fr. *mercenaire*, L. *mercenarius*, from *merces*, reward, wages. MERCHANT.] Hired; obtained by hire (services, troops); that may be hired; moved by the love of money; greedy of gain; venal; sordid; entered into from motives of gain (a *mercenary* marriage).—*n.* One who is hired; a soldier that is hired into foreign service.

mercerize, mėr′sėr•īz, *v.t.* [From John *Mercer*, the originator.] To subject to treatment with certain chemical agents, as caustic soda, sulfuric acid, zinc chloride, etc., in order to produce desired results on textile fabrics.

merchant, mėr′chant, *n.* [O.Fr. *marchant*, from L. *mercans, mercantis*, ppr. of *mercor, mercatus*, to barter, to deal, from *merx*, merchandise; akin *mercer, mercenary, mercantile, mercy*, etc.; same root as *merit*.] One who carries on trade on a large scale, especially, a man who exports and imports goods and sells them at wholesale.—*a.* Relating to trade or commerce; commercial.—**merchantable**, mėr′chant•a•bl, *a.* Fit for market; such as is usually sold in market.—**merchantman**, mėr′chant•man, *n.* A ship engaged in commerce, as distinguished from a ship of war; a trading vessel.—**merchant marine**, the commercial vessels belonging to a nation.—**merchandise**, mėr′chan•dīz, *n.* [Fr. *marchandise*, from *marchand*, a merchant.] The objects of commerce; wares; goods.

mercury, mėr′kū•ri, *n.* [L. *Mercurius*, from root of *merces*, wares. MERCHANT.] A heavy silver-white metallic element, the only element that is fluid at ordinary temperatures; quicksilver—symbol, Hg (hydrargyrum); at. no., 80; at. wt., 200.59; [cap.] name of a Roman divinity, identified in later times with the Greek Hermes; [cap.] *astron.* the planet that is closest to the sun.—*Mercury-vapor lamp*, a lamp in which an electric discharge, passing through mercury vapor, produces ultraviolet and actinic radiation.—**mercurial**, mėr•kū′ri•al, *a.* [L. *mercurialis*.] Like the god Mercury or what belongs to him; light-hearted; gay; sprightly; flighty; fickle; pertaining to quicksilver; containing or consisting of quicksilver or mercury.—*n.* A preparation of mercury used as a drug.—**mercurially**, mėr•kū′ri•al•li, *adv.* In a mercurial manner.—**mercuric**,

mercurous, mėr·kū´rik, mėr´kū·rus, *a.* Containing mercury; terms used as part of the name of certain chemical compounds, the former indicating that they contain a smaller proportion of mercury than the latter.

mercy, mėr´si, *n.* [Fr. *merci*, from L. *merces, mercedis*, pay, recompense, in L.L. mercy, from stem of *mereo*, to deserve (whence *merit*); akin *mercantile, merchant, market, amerce*, etc.] That benevolence, mildness, or tenderness of heart which disposes a person to overlook injuries; the disposition that tempers justice and leads to the infliction of a lighter punishment than law or justice will warrant; clemency; an act or exercise of mercy or favor; a blessing; compassion; pity; unrestrained exercise of will or authority: often in the phrase *at one's mercy*, that is, completely in one's power.—*To cry mercy*, to beg pardon.—*Sisters of Mercy*, members of female religious communities founded for the purpose of nursing the sick and the performance of similar works of charity and mercy.—**mercy seat,** *n.* The place of mercy or forgiveness; the covering of the ark of the covenant among the Jews.—**merciful,** mėr´si·ful, *a.* Full of mercy; unwilling to punish for injuries; compassionate; tender; not cruel.—**mercifully,** mėr´si·ful·li, *adv.* In a merciful manner.—**mercifulness,** mėr´si·ful·nes, *n.*—**merciless,** mėr´si·les, *a.* Destitute of mercy; pitiless; hard-hearted.—**mercilessly,** mėr´si·les·li, *adv.* In a merciless manner.—**mercilessness,** mėr si·les·nes, *n.*

mere, mēr, *a.* [O.Fr. *mier*, L. *merus*, pure, unmixed.] This or that and nothing else; simple; absolute, entire, utter (*mere* folly).—**merely,** mēr´li, *adv.* Solely; simply; only; for this and no other purpose.

mere, mēr, *n.* [A.Sax. *maere, gemaere*, O.D. *meer*, a boundary; Icel. *moerr*, borderland.] A boundary; a boundary stone.

meretricious, mer·e·trish´us, *a.* [L. *meretricius*, from *meretrix, meretricis*, a prostitute, from *mereo*, to earn. MERIT, MERCY.] Pertaining to prostitutes; alluring by false show; having a gaudy but deceitful appearance; showy, but in bad taste.—**meretriciously,** mer·e·trish´us·li, *adv.* In a meretricious manner.—**meretriciousness,** mer·e·trish´us·nes, *n.*

merganser, mėr·gan´sėr, *n.* [L. *mergo*, to dive, and *anser*, a goose.] A diving duck having a narrow bill and subsisting on fish.

merge, mėrj, *v.t.*—merged, merging. [L. *mergo*, to dip, to dive; seen also in *emerge, immerge, immersion, submerge*.] To cause to be swallowed up, absorbed, or incorporated; to sink; to bury; chiefly figurative (the smaller grief was *merged* in the greater).—*v.i.* To be sunk, swallowed, incorporated, or absorbed.—**merger,** mėrj´ėr, *n.* The absorption of one estate, contract, or interest, in another.

meridian, me·rid´i·an, *a.* [L. *meridianus*, from *meridies*, for *medidies*,

mid-day—*medius*, middle, and *dies*, day.] Pertaining to midday or noon, when the sun is on the meridian.—*Meridian altitude of the sun* or *stars*, their altitude when on the meridian of the place where they are observed.—*n.* Midday; noon; *fig.* the culmination; the point of greatest splendor; one of the innumerable imaginary circles or lines on the surface of the earth passing through both poles, and through any other given place, and used in denoting the longitudes of places; a similar imaginary line in the heavens passing through the poles of the heavens and the zenith of any place (often called a *celestial meridian*), noon therefore occurring at all places directly under this line when the sun is on it.—*First meridian*, that from which all the others are counted eastward and westward, and from which longitudes are reckoned, usually the meridian of Greenwich.—*Meridian of a globe*, the brazen circle in which it turns, and by which it is supported.—*Magnetic meridian*, one of the great circles which pass through the magnetic poles.—**meridional,** me·rid´i·on·al, *a.* Pertaining to the meridian; hence, southern; having a southern aspect.—*Meridional distance, navig.* the distance or departure from the meridian, the easting or westing.—**meridionally,** me·rid´i·on·al·li, *adv.* In the direction of the meridian.

meringue, me·rang´, *n.* A light delicacy made of powdered sugar and the beaten whites of eggs.

merino, me·rē´nō, *n.* [Sp. *merino*.] A breed of sheep with long, fine wool; a soft, twilled fabric.

meristem, me·ris´tem, *n.* [Gr. *merizō*, I divide.] *Bot.* embryonic plant tissue that reproduces similar cells or differentiates to produce the organs and tissue.

merit, mer´it, *n.* [Fr. *mérite*, L. *meritum*, what is deserved, from *mereo*, to earn or deserve. MERCY.] Desert of good or evil; excellence entitling to honor or reward; worth; reward deserved or merited; pl. the rights of a case or question; the essential points or circumstances.—*v.t.* To deserve, in a good sense; to have a right to claim, as a reward, regard, honor.—**meritorious,** mer·i·tō´ri·us, *a.* Deserving reward or praise; praiseworthy.—**meritoriously,** mer·i·tō´ri·us·li, *adv.*—**meritoriousness,** mer·i·tō´ri·us·nes, *n.*—**merit system,** *n.* The system whereby government employees receive appointment and promotion on the basis of ability rather than by political pressure.

merl, mėrl, *n.* [Fr. *merle*, a blackbird.] The European blackbird.—**merlin,** mėr´lin, *n.* [Fr. *émerillon*, from L. *merula*, a blackbird, meaning blackbird hawk.] A courageous species of hawk about the size of a blackbird.

merlon, mėr´lon, *n.* [Fr. *merlon*; comp. L. *moerus*, for *murus*, a wall.] *Fort.* the part of an embattled parapet which lies between two embrasures.

mermaid, mėr´mād, *n.* [*Mer* is same as *mere*, a lake.] A fabled marine creature, having the upper part like a woman and the lower like a fish.—**merman,** mėr´man, *n.* The male corresponding to *mermaid*; a man of the sea, with the tail of a fish instead of legs.

meroblast, mer´o·blast, *n.* [Gr. *meros*, a part, and *blastos*, a sprout.] *Biol.* an ovum consisting both of a protoplasmic or germinal portion and an albuminous or nutritive one, as contradistinguished from *holoblast*, an ovum entirely germinal.—**meroblastic,** mer·o·blas´tik, *a.* Pertaining to a meroblast.

Merovingian, mer·o·vinj´i·an, *a.* Of or relating to the Merovingian line of Franks founded by Clovis, and lasting from A.D. 500 to 750.

merry, mer´i, *a.* [O.E. *myrie, murie*, A.Sax. *merg, mirig*, perhaps from root of *mearo*, tender; comp. Ir. and Gael, *maer*, Gael. *mir*, merry.] Gay and noisy; in overflowing good spirits; hilarious; mirthful; sportive.—*To make merry*, to be jovial; to indulge in hilarity.—**merrily,** mer´i·li, *adv.*—**merriment,** mer´i·ment, *n.* Gaiety with laughter or noise; mirth; hilarity.—**merriness,** mer´i·nes, *n.*—**merry-go-round,** *n.* A circular frame, made to revolve, and on which children are treated to a ride.—**merrymaking,** *n.* A convivial entertainment; a festival.

mesa, mā´sa, *n.* [Sp., from L. *mensa*, a table.] A tableland of small extent rising abruptly from a surrounding plain.

mésalliance, mā·zal´i·ans, *n.* [Fr.] A marriage to a person of an inferior social rank.

mescal, mes·kal´, *n.* [Sp. *mezcal*, from Nahuatl *mexcalli*, a drink.] A cactus (*Lophophora Williamsii* or *L. Lewinii*) of Mexico and Texas, the buttonlike tips of which are dried and used as a stimulant and antispasmodic (by the Indians); a potent liquor distilled from pulque, the fermented juice of the cactus; a cactus yielding such liquor, as the maguey.

meseems, mē·sēmz´, *v. impersonal*—pret. *meseemed*. [Not properly a simple verb, being really an impersonal verb preceded by a pronoun in the dative = it seems to me. Comp. *methinks*.] It seems to me.

mesencephalon, mes·en·sef´a·lon, *n.* [Gr. *mesos*, middle, and *enkephalos*, the brain.] The middle or central portion of the brain.

mesentery, mes´en·ter·i, *n.* [Gr. *mesenterion*—*mesos*, middle, and *enteron*, intestine.] A membrane in the cavity of the abdomen, the use of which is to retain the intestines and their appendages in a proper position.—**mesenteric,** mes·en·ter´ik, *a.* Pertaining to the mesentery.—**mesenteritis,** mes´en·ter·i´tis, *n.* Inflammation of the mesentery.

mesh, mesh, *n.* [A.Sax. *masc, max*, a noose, *mæscre*, a mesh, a net; D. *maas*, Dan. *maske*, Icel. *möskvi*, G. *masche*, a mesh; W. *masg*, a mesh, Lith. *megsti*, to knit, are allied.] The opening or space between the threads of a net; geared wheels.—*v.t.* To catch in a net; to ensnare.—**mesh-work**, *n.* Network.

mesial, mē′zi·al, *a.* [Gr. *mesos*, middle.] Middle; median.—*Mesial line, mesial plane*, an imaginary line and plane dividing the body longitudinally into symmetrical halves, one toward the right and the other toward the left.

mesmerism, mez′mẽr·izm, *n.* [After *Mesmer*, a German physician, who propounded the doctrine in 1778.] The doctrine that one person can exercise influence over the will and nervous system of another by virtue of a supposed emanation proceeding from him, or simply by the domination of his will over that of the person operated on; the influence itself, now called hypnotism.—**mesmeric**, mez·mer′ik, *a.* Pertaining to mesmerism.—**mesmerist**, mez′mẽr·ist, *n.* One who practices or believes in mesmerism.—**mesmerize**, mez′-mẽr·īz, *v.t.*—*mesmerized, mesmerizing*. To bring into a state of mesmeric sleep.—**mesmerizer**, mez′-mẽr·īz·ẽr, *n.* One who mesmerizes.

mesne, mēn, *a.* [Norm. *mesne*, middle, from L. *medianus*, middle. MEAN, *a.*, middle.] *Law*, middle, intervening; as, a *mesne* lord, *i.e.* a lord who holds land of a superior but grants a part of it to another person.

mesoblast, mes′o·blast, *n.* [Gr. *mesos*, middle, and *blastos*, a bud.] *Physiol.* the layer between the epiblast and hypoblast, the two primary layers of the embryo.

mesocaecum, mes′o·sē·kum, *n.* [Gr. *mesos*, middle, and L. *caecum*.] That part of the peritoneum which embraces the caecum and its appendages.

mesocarp, mes′o·kärp, *n.* [Gr. *mesos*, middle, and *karpos*, fruit.] *Bot.* the middle part or layer of the pericarp, immediately under the epicarp.

mesocephalic, mes′o·se·fal′ik, *a.* [Gr. *mesos*, middle, and *kephalē*, the head.] A term applied to the human skull when it is of medium breadth.

mesoderm, mes′o·dẽrm, *n.* [Gr. *mesos*, middle, and *derma*, skin.] *Zool.* the middle layer of tissue between the ectoderm and the endoderm.

mesogastric, mes·o·gas′trik, *a.* [Gr. *mesos*, middle, *gastēr*, the belly.] *Anat.* applied to the membrane which sustains the stomach, and by which it is attached to the abdomen.—**mesogastrium**, mes·o·gas′tri·um, *n. Anat.* the umbilical region of the abdomen.

mesogloea, me·so·glē′a, *n.* [Gr. *mesos*, middle, *gloios*, a jelly.] In zoophytes, a middle layer of the body, often jelly-like.

mesognathous, me·sog′na·thus, *a.* [Gr. *mesos*, middle, *gnathos*, jaw.] *Anthropol.* intermediate between prognathous and orthognathous.

meson, mes′on, *n. Phys.* a particle having a mass of the order of 200 times that of an electron and with a unit positive or negative charge, found in cosmic rays and in high-energy X-rays.

mesonephros, mes′o·nef″ros, *n.* [Gr. *mesos*, middle, *nephros*, a kidney.] In vertebrates, the second of three successive renal organs.

mesosphere, mez′o·sfẽr, *n.* [Prefix *meso*, and *sphere*.] An atmospheric layer located above the ionosphere, about 250 miles above the earth's crust.

mesothorax, mes·o·thō′raks, *n.* [Gr. *mesos*, middle, and *thōrax*, the chest.] *Entom.* the middle ring of the thorax.

mesotron, mez′o·tron, *n.* [Prefix *meso*, and *tron*.] A meson.

Mesozoic, mes·o·zō′ik, *a.* [Gr. *mesos*, middle, and *zōē*, life.] *Geol.* pertaining to the secondary age, between the Paleozoic and Cenozoic.

mesquite, mes′kēt, *n.* [Sp. *mezquite*, probably of American origin.] A leguminous shrub of southwestern U. S. and Mexico.

mess, mes, *n.* [O.Fr. *mes*, a dish, a course of dishes at table; It. *messo*; properly that which is sent, from L. *missus*, pp. of *mitto*, to send. MISSION.] A dish or quantity of food set on a table at one time; food for a person at one meal; a number of persons who eat together at the same table, especially in the army or navy. —*v.i.* To take meals in common with others, as one of a mess; to associate at the same table.

mess, mes, *n.* [Formerly *mesh*, which is same as *mash*, lit. a mixture.] A disorderly mixture; a state of dirt and disorder; *fig.* a situation of confusion or embarrassment; a muddle.

message, mes′ij, *n.* [Fr. *message*, It. *messaggio*, L.L. *missaticum*, message, from L. *mitto*, *missum*, to send. MISSION.] Any communication, written or verbal, sent from one person to another; an official communication delivered by a messenger.—**messenger**, mes′en·jẽr, *n.* [O.E. *messager*, Fr. *messager*. The *n* has intruded as in *passenger*.] One who delivers a message or performs an errand; one who conveys dispatches from one government to another; an envoy; an emissary; a harbinger; a herald.

Messiah, mes·sī′a, *n.* [Heb. *mäshiach*, anointed, from *māshach*, to anoint.] The deliverer and savior promised to the Hebrews; Christ, the Anointed; the Saviour of the world.—**Messiahship**, mes·sī′a·ship, *n.* The office of the Saviour.—**Messianic**, mes·si·an′ik, *a.* Relating to the Messiah.

messieurs, mes′ẽrz, *n.* [Fr. pl. of *Monsieur* (which see).] Sirs; gentlemen; the plural of *Mr.*, employed in addressing firms or companies of several persons, and generally contracted into *Messrs.*

messuage, mes′wij, *n.* [O.Fr. *messuage*, *mesnage*, L.L. *messuagium*, *mansionaticum*, from L. *mansio*, a dwelling. MANSION.] *Law*, a dwelling house, with the adjacent buildings, etc., appropriated to the use of the household; a manor house.

mestizo, mes·tē′zō, *n.* [Sp. *mestizo*, from L. *mixtus*, *pp.* of *misceo*, to mix.] The offspring of a Caucasian

and American Indian; an individual of mixed breed.

metabolic, met·a·bol′ik, *a.* [Gr. *metabolē*, change.] Pertaining to metabolism.—**metabolism**, me·tab′o·lizm, *n. Physiol.* the sum total of the build-up and destruction of cell tissue; the chemical cellular changes providing the energies for the life processes and the elimination of waste materials.—**metabolize**, me·tab′o·līz, *v.t.* To subject to metabolism; transform by metabolism.

metacarpus, met·a·kär′pus, *n.* [Gr. *meta*, beyond, *karpos*, the wrist.] *Anat.* the part of the hand between the wrist and the fingers.—**metacarpal**, met·a·kär′pal, *a.* Pertaining to the metacarpus.

metacenter, met·a·sen′tẽr, *n.* [Gr. *meta*, beyond, and *kentron*, center.] *Physics*, that point in a floating body on the position of which its stability depends, and which must be above the center of gravity to prevent the body from turning over.

metage, mēt′ij, *n.* [From *mete*.] Measurement of coal; charge for measuring.

metagenesis, met·a·jen′e·sis, *n.* [Gr. *meta*, after, change, and *genesis*.] *Zool.* the changes of form which the representative of a species undergoes in passing, by a series of successively generated individuals, from the ovum or egg to the perfect state; alternation of generation.—**metagenetic, metagenic**, met′a·je·net″ik, met·a·jen′ik, *a.* Pertaining to metagenesis.

metal, met′al, *n.* [L. *metallum*, from Gr. *metallon*, a mine, a metal—*meta*, after, and root meaning to go or search.] A name given to certain substances of which gold, silver, iron, lead, are examples, having a luster and generally fusible by heat; the name given by workers in glass, pottery, etc., to the material on which they operate when in a state of fusion.—**metallic**, me·tal′ik, *a.* [L. *metallicus*.] Pertaining to metals; consisting of metal; like a metal.—*Metallic oxide*, a compound of metal and oxygen.—*Metallic paper*, paper the surface of which is washed over with a solution of whiting, lime, and size, and which is written on with a pewter pencil.—**metalliferous**, met·al·if′ẽr·us, *a.* Producing metal; yielding metal.—**metalline**, met′al·in, *a.* Consisting of or containing metal.—**metallize**, met′al·īz, *v.t.*—*metalized, metalizing*. To form into metal; to give its proper metallic properties to (an ore).—**metallography**, met·al·og′ra·fi, *n.* The science or description of metals; the study of metals by the microscope.—**metalloid**, met′al·oid, *n.* A metallic base of a fixed alkali or alkaline earth; any non-metallic elementary substance.—*a.* Like metal; having the form or appearance of a metal.—**metallurgy**, met′al·ẽr·ji, *n.* [Gr. *ergon*, work.] The art of working metals; the process of separating them from other matters in the ore, smelting, refining, etc.—**metallurgic, metallurgical**, met·al·ẽr′jik, met·al·ẽr′ji·kal, *a.* Pertaining to metallurgy.—**metallurgist**, met'al·ėr·jist, *n.* One engaged in metallurgy.

metalloid, metallurgy, etc. See METAL.

metamere, met'a·mēr, *n.* [Gr. *meta*, with or among; and *meros*, a part.] *Compar. anat.* one of a series of similar parts; in segmented animals, one of the segments.—**metamerism,** me·tam'ėr·izm, *n. Chem.* the character in certain compound bodies, differing in chemical properties, of having the same elements combined in the same proportion and with the same molecular weight.

metamorphosis, met·a·mor'fō·sis, *n.* [Gr. *metamorphōsis—meta*, denoting change, and *morphē*, form, shape.] Change of form, shape, or structure; transformation; *zool.* the alterations which an animal undergoes after its exclusion from the egg, and which alter extensively the general form and life of the individual; such changes as those from the caterpillar to the perfect butterfly.—**metamorphic,** met·a·mor'fik, *a.* Pertaining to or producing metamorphosis.—*Metamorphic rocks, geol.* stratified rocks of any age whose texture has been rendered less or more crystalline by subterranean heat, pressure, or chemical agency; the lowest and non-fossiliferous stratified rocks, originally deposited from water and crystallized by subsequent agencies.—**metamorphism,** met·a·mor'fizm, *n.* The process of metamorphosing; the change undergone by stratified rocks under the influence of heat and chemical or mechanical agents.—**metamorphose,** met·a·mor'fōz, *v.t.—metamorphosed, metamorphosing.* To change into a different form; to change the shape or character of; to transform.—**Metamorphoses,** *n. pl.* The poem by Ovid dealing with the various changes of human beings and others into different characters.

metanephros, met'a·nef'ros, *n.* [Gr. *meta*, after, *nephros*, a kidney.] In vertebrates, the third of three successive renal organs. The definitive kidney of mammals, birds, and reptiles.

metaphor, met'a·fėr, *n.* [Gr. *metaphora*, from *metapherō*, to transfer—*meta*, over, and *pherō*, to carry.] A figure of speech founded on resemblance, by which a word is transferred from an object to which it properly belongs to another in such a manner that a comparison is implied though not formally expressed. Thus, 'that man is a fox', is a metaphor; but 'that man is like a fox', is a simile or comparison.—**metaphoric, metaphorical,** met·a·for'ik, met·a·for'i·kal, *a.* Pertaining to metaphor; comprising a metaphor; not literal; figurative.—**metaphorically,** met·a·for'i·kal·li, *adv.* In a metaphorical manner; not literally.

metaphrase, met'a·frāz, *n.* [Gr. *metaphrasis—meta*, according to or with, and *phrasis*, phrase.] A verbal translation of one language into another, word for word: opposed to *paraphrase.*—**metaphrast,** met'a·frast, *n.* A literal translator.

metaphysics, met·a·fiz'iks, *n.* [L. *metaphysica*, pl. neut. from Gr. *meta*, after, and *physica*, physics, from *physis*, nature, the science of natural bodies or *physics* being regarded as properly first in the order of studies, and the science of mind or intelligence to be the second.] That science which seeks to trace the branches of human knowledge to their first principles in the constitution of our nature, or to find what is the nature of the human mind and its relations to the external world; the science that seeks to know the ultimate grounds of being or what it is that really exists, embracing both psychology and ontology.—**metaphysic,** met·a·fiz'ik, *n.* Metaphysics.—**metaphysic, metaphysical,** met·a·fiz'i·kal, *a.* Pertaining to metaphysics; according to rules or principles of metaphysics.—**metaphysically,** met·a·fiz'i·kal·li, *adv.* In a metaphysical manner.—**metaphysician,** met·a·fi·zish'an, *n.* One who is versed in metaphysics.

metaplasm, met'a·plazm, *n.* [Gr. *metaplasmos*, transformation—*meta*, over, and *plassō*, to form.] *Gram.* a change in a word by adding, transposing, or retrenching a syllable or letter.

metastasis, me·tas'ta·sis, *n.* [Gr. *metastasis—meta*, over, and *stasis*, position.] *Med.* a translation or removal of a disease from one part to another.—**metastatic,** met·a·stat'ik, *a.* Relating to metastasis.

metatarsus, met·a·tär'sus, *n.* [Gr. *meta*, beyond, and *tarsos*, tarsus.] The middle of the foot, or part between the ankle and the toes.—**metatarsal,** met·a·tär'sal, *a.* Belonging to the metatarsus.—*n.* A bone of the metatarsus.

metathesis, me·tath'e·sis, *n.* [Gr. *metathesis—meta*, over, and *tithēmi*, to set.] *Gram.* transposition of the letters, sounds, or syllables of a word.—**metathetic, metathetical,** met·a·thet'ik, met·a·thet'i·kal, *a.* Relating to metathesis.

metathorax, met·a·thō'raks, *n.* [Gr. *meta*, after, and *thōrax*, the chest.] *Entom.* the third and last segment of the thorax.

métayer, me·tā'yėr, *n.* [Fr. *métayer*, L.L. *medietarius*, from L. *medietas*, middle state, from *medius*, middle.] A cultivator who tills the soil on condition of receiving a share of its produce, the owner furnishing the whole or part of the stock, tools, etc.

Metazoa, met·a·zō'a, *n. pl.* [Gr. *meta*, after, *zoon*, animal.] The subkingdom of animals comprising all except the Protozoa, characterized by two cell layers differentiated into tissues, organs and a digestive cavity.—**metazoan,** met·a·zō'an, *a. and n.*

mete, mēt, *v.t.—meted, meting.* [A. Sax. *metan*=D. *meten*, Goth. *mitan*, G. *messen*, to measure; Icel. *meta*, to value; from root of L., *modus* a measure (whence *mode*); Gr. *metron*, a measure; Skr. *mâ*, to measure.] To measure; to ascertain the quantity, dimensions, or capacity of by any rule or standard.

metempirical, met·em·pir'i·kal, *a.* [Gr. *meta*, beyond, and *empeiria*, experience, from *en*, in, and *peira*, trial, experiment.] *Metaph.* beyond or outside of experience; not based on experience; transcendental; a priori: opposed to *empirical* or *experiential.*—**metempiric,** met·em·pir'ik, *n.* One who believes in the transcendental philosophy.

metempsychosis, me·tem'si·kō"sis, *n.* [Gr. *meta*, denoting change, *en*, in, and *psyche*, soul.] Transmigration; the passing of the soul of a man after death into some other animal body.

meteor, mē'tē·ėr, *n.* [From Gr. *meteōros*, raised on high—*meta*, beyond, and *aeirō*, to raise.] A transient celestial body that enters the earth's atmosphere with terrific velocity, white with heat generated by the resistance of the air.—**meteoric,** mē·tē·or'ik, *a.* Pertaining to a meteor or meteors; *fig.* transiently or irregularly brilliant.—*Meteoric iron,* iron as found in meteoric stones.—*Meteoric stones,* those aerolites which fall from the heavens on the surface of the earth, and usually consist of metallic iron and certain silicates.—*Meteoric showers,* showers of shooting stars occurring periodically.—**meteorite,** mē'tē·ėr·īt, *n.* A meteoric stone; an aerolite; especially a meteor which has reached the earth's crust without being completely consumed.—**meteorograph,** mē'tē·ėr·o·graf, *n.* An instrument or apparatus for registering meteorological phenomena.—**meteorology,** mē'tē·ėr·ol''o·ji, *n.* [Gr. *meteorologia*.] The science which treats of atmospheric phenomena, more especially as connected with or in relation to weather and climate.—**meteorologic, meteorological,** mē'tē·ėr·o·loj''ik, mē'tē·ėr·o·loj''i·kal, *a.* Pertaining to meteorology or to the atmosphere and its phenomena.—**meteorologist,** mē'tē·ėr·ol''o·jist, *n.* A person skilled in meteorology.

meter, mē'tėr, *n.* [Fr. *mètre*, L. *metrum*, meter, Gr. *metron*, meter, a measure; same root as in *measure, mete*.] Rhythmical arrangement of syllables into verses, stanzas, strophes, etc.; rhythm; measure; verse.—**metric, metrical,** met'rik, met'ri·kal, *a.* Pertaining to rhythm or meter; consisting of verse.—**metrically** met'ri·kal·li, *adv.* In a metrical manner; according to poetic measure.—**metrist,** mē'trist, *n.* A composer of verses.

meter, mē'tėr: Fr. pron. mā·tr, *n.* [Fr. *mètre*, from Gr. *metron*, a measure. See above.] A basic measure of length, equal to 39.37 inches, the standard of linear measure.—**metric,** met'rik, *a.* Pertaining to a system of weights, measures, and moneys, first adopted in France—the decimal system. See DECIMAL.—**metrical,** met'ri·kal, *a.* Pertaining to or employed in measuring.—**metrology,** mi·trol'o·ji, *n.* An account of weights and measures; the art and science of mensuration.—**metronome,** met'ro·nōm, *n.* [Gr.

nomos, a law.] An instrument, consisting of a pendulum set in motion by clockwork, that determines the quickness or slowness of musical compositions.

meter, mē′tẽr, *n.* [From *mete.*] One who or that which measures; an instrument that measures and records automatically, as a gas meter, water meter, etc.

methane, me′thān, *n.* Marsh gas (CH_4), the simplest hydrocarbon.

methanol, meth′ä·nol, *n.* [*Methane* and *ol.*] A pungent, flammable, poisonous liquid alcohol (CH_3 OH), formerly distilled from wood, now made synthetically, used as an antifreeze, solvent, etc.

metheglin, mi·theg′lin, *n.* [W. *meddyglyn—medd*, mead, and *llyn*, liquor.] A Welsh variety of the liquor mead.

method, meth′od, *n.* [Fr. *méthode*, L. *methodus*, from Gr. *methodos—meta*, after, and *hodos*, a way.] A way or mode by which we proceed to the attainment of some aim; mode or manner of procedure; logical or scientific arrangement or mode of acting; systematic or orderly procedure; system; *nat. hist.* principle of classification (the Linnaean *method*). —**methodic, methodical,** me·thod′ik, me·thod′i·kal, *a.*—**methodically,** me·thod′i·kal·li, *adv.*—**methodism,** meth′od·izm, *n.* The doctrines and worship of the *Methodists.*—**methodist,** meth′od·ist, *n.* [cap.] One characterized by strict adherence to method; one of a sect of Christians founded by John Wesley, so called from the regularity of their lives and the strictness of their observance of religious duties.—**methodistic,** meth·o·dis′tik, *a.*—**methodize,** meth′od·īz, *v.t.—methodized, methodizing,* To reduce to method.—**methodology,** meth·od·ol′o·ji, *n.* The science of methods, rules, procedures, etc., as it is applied by a science or art.

methyl, meth′il, *n.* [Gr. *meta*, after, with, and *hylē*, wood.] A univalent hydrocarbon radical (CH_3).—**methylamine,** me·thil′a·min, *n.* A colorless gas having a strong ammoniacal odor, and resembling ammonia in many of its reactions.—**methylated,** meth′i·lā·ted, *a.* Impregnated or mixed with methyl.—*Methylated spirit*, ordinary, or ethyl, alcohol denatured with wood alcohol, which renders it unfit for drinking.—**methylic,** me·thil′ik, *a.* Pertaining to methyl.

meticulous, me·tik′ū·lus, *a.* [Fr. *méticuleux*, L. *metus*, fear.] Timidly scrupulous; too careful or fastidious.

métier, mā′tyā, *n.* [Fr. *métier*, trade, business.] A calling, business, to which one is peculiarly suited.

metis, mā′tis, *n.* [Fr. on analogy of *mestizo* (q.v.).] A child of white and American Indian parents (*Canada*); an octoroon (*U.S.*).

Metonic cycle, me·ton′ik. [After *Meton*, an ancient astronomer.] The cycle or period of nineteen years, in which the phases of the moon return to the same days of the month.

metonymy, me·ton′i·mi, *n.* [Gr. *metōnymia—meta*, denoting change, and *onoma*, a name.] *Rhet.* a figure by which one word is put for another on account of some actual relation between the things signified, as when we say. 'We read *Virgil*', that is, his *poems* or *writings.*—**metonymic, metonymical,** met·o·nim′ik, met·o·nim′i·kal, *a.*

metope, met′o·pē, *n.* [Gr. *metopē—meta*, between, and *opē*, an aperture.] *Arch.* the space between the triglyphs of the Doric frieze.

metronymic, met·ro·nim′ik, *n.* and *a.* [Gr. *mētrōnymikos—mētēr*, *mētros*, a mother, and *onoma*, a name.] A term applied to a name derived from a mother, as opposed to *patronymic.*

metropolis, me·trop′o·lis, *n.* [Gr. *mētropolis—mētēr*, *mētros*, a mother, and *polis*, a city.] The chief city or capital of a kingdom, state, or country; the see or seat of a metropolitan bishop.—**metropolitan,** met·ro·pol′i·tan, *a.* Belonging to a metropolis; *eccles.* having the authority of a metropolitan; proceeding from a metropolitan.—*n.* A resident of a metropolis or one who is urbane in manners; *eccles.* a bishop having authority over the other bishops of a province.

mettle, met′l, *n.* [Merely an altered spelling of *metal.*] Spirit; constitutional ardor; courage; fire.—*To put a man on* or *to his mettle*, to stimulate a man to do his uttermost.—**mettlesome,** met′l·sum, *a.* Brisk; fiery.

mew, mū, *n.* [A.Sax. *maew*, a gull or mew—Sc. *maw*, D. *meeuw*, G. *mōve*, Icel. *már*, a mew.] A sea mew; a gull.

mew, mū, *n.* [Fr. *mue*, a molting, a mew or cage, from L.L. *muta*, a mew, from L. *mutare*, to change. MUTABLE.] The molting of a hawk; a cage for hawks or other birds while molting; a coop for fowls; a place of confinement in general.—*v.t.* To shed or cast; to molt; to shut up, enclose, confine, as in a cage or other enclosure.—*v.i.* To cast the feathers; to molt.—**mews,** mūz, *n. pl.* The royal stables in London, England, so called because built where the king's hawks were once *mewed* or confined; hence (with verbs, etc., in *sing.*), a place where carriage horses are kept in large towns; a lane or alley in which stables or mews are situated.

mew, mū, *v.i.* [Imitative, and also written *meaw, miaw*, etc.; comp. W. *mewian*, G. *miauen*, to mew.] To cry as a cat.—*n.* The cry of a cat.

mewl, mūl, *v.i.* [Imitative; comp. *miaul*, Fr. *miauler.*] To cry or squall, as a child.

Mexican, mex′i·can, *a.* Of or pertaining to Mexico, a country in North America.

mezereon, mi·zē′ri·on, *n.* [Fr. *mézereon*, Sp. *mezereon*, from Ar. and Per. *māzariyūn*, the camellia.] A common garden shrub whose fragrant pink flowers appear in spring before the leaves expand.

mezzanine, mez′za·nēn, *n.* [It. *mezzanino*, from *mezzo*, middle. MEZZO.] *Arch.* an entresol or low story be-

tween two higher ones.

mezzo, med′zō or met′zō, *a.* [It., from L. *medius*, middle.]—*Mus.* middle; mean.—*Mezzo soprano*, a treble voice of medium range, lower than soprano and higher than contralto.—**mezzo-relievo,** med′zō·ri·lē″vō, *n.* Middle relief.—**mezzotint, mezzotinto,** med′zo·tint, med·zo·tin′tō, *n.* [It. *mezzo*, middle, *tinto*, tint.] A manner of engraving on copper or steel in imitation of drawing in India ink, the lights being scraped and burnished out of a prepared dark ground.

mi, mē, *n.* The third note in the musical scale, between *re* and *fa.*

miasma, mī·az′ma, *n. pl.* **miasmata,** mī·az′ma·ta. [Gr. *miasma, miasmatos*, from *miainō*, to stain, sully.] Evil-smelling vapor, formerly supposed to be the effluvia or fine particles of any putrefying bodies, rising and floating in the atmosphere, and considered to be noxious to health; noxious emanation.—**miasmal,** mī·az′mal, *a.* Containing miasma; miasmatic.—**miasmatic, miasmatical,** mī·az·mat′ik, mī·az·mat′i·kal, *a.* Pertaining to miasma.

miaul, myạl, *v.i.* [MEW.] To cry as a cat or kitten; to mew.

mica, mī′ka, *n.* [L. *mico*, to glitter.] A mineral of a foliated structure, consisting of thin flexible laminae or scales, having a shining and almost metallic luster.—*Mica schist, mica slate*, a metamorphic rock composed of mica and quartz, highly fissile and passing by insensible gradations into clay slate.—**micaceous,** mī·kā′shus, *a.* Pertaining to or containing mica; resembling mica or partaking of its properties.—*Micaceous rocks*, rocks of which mica is the chief ingredient, as mica slate.—*Micaceous schist*, mica schist.

mice, mīs, *n. pl.* of *mouse.*

Michaelmas, mik′el·mas, *n.* [*Michael*, and *mass*, a feast.] The feast of St. *Michael*, the archangel, which falls on the 29th of September.

microanalysis, mī′kro·a·nal′i·sis, *n. Chem.* analysis of extremely minute amounts of material.

microbe, mī′krōb, *n.* [Gr. *mikros*, small, *bios*, life.] A microscopic organism such as a bacillus or bacterium.

microbiology, mī′kro·bī·ol′o·ji, *n.* The study and use of microscopic and submicroscopic organisms.

microcephalous, mī·kro·sef′a·lus, *a.* [Gr. *mikros*, small, and *kephalē*, the head.] Having a very small skull.

microchemistry, mī′kro·kem″is·tri, *n.* Chemistry concerned with microscopic objects or amounts.

micrococcus, mī·kro·kok′us, *n.* [Gr. *mikros*, small, and *kokkos*, a berry.] *Zool.* a microscopic organism of a round form.

microcopy, mī′kro·kop·i, *n.* [Gr. *mikros*, small, and *copy.*] A photographic copy of printed matter or photographs, etc., reduced in size and put on film.

microcosm, mī′kro·kozm, *n.* [Gr. *mikros*, small, and *kosmos*, world.] *Lit.* a little world or cosmos, applied to man, as supposed to be an epitome of the universe or great world (the *macrocosm*); a community or unity that epitomizes a larger unit. **microcosmic**, mĭ·kro·koz′mik, *a.*

microfarad, mī′kro·far·ad, *n.* [Gr. *mikros*, small, and E. *farad*.] The millionth part of a farad.

microfilm, mī′kro·film, *n.* [Gr. *mikros*, small, and E. *film*.] The film of printed matter, etc., that has been reduced in size.—*v.t.* and *i.* To photograph on microfilm.

microgeology, mī′kro·jē·ol″o·ji, *n.* [From *microscope* and *geology*.] That department of the science of geology whose facts are ascertained by the use of the microscope.

micrography, mī·krog′ra·fi, *n.* [Gr. *mikros*, small, and *graphō*, to describe.] The description of objects too small to be discerned without the aid of a microscope.—**micrographic**, mī·kro·graf′ik, *a.* Connected with or relating to micrography.

microhm, mī′krōm, *n.* [Gr. *mikros*, small, and E. *ohm*.] The millionth part of an ohm.

micrology, mī·krol′o·ji, *n.* [Gr. *mikros*, small, and *logos*, description.] That part of science dependent on microscopic investigations; micrography.

micrometer, mī·krom′et·ėr, *n.* [Gr. *mikros*, small, and *metron*, a measure.] An instrument or appliance fitted to a telescope or microscope, for measuring very small distances, or the apparent diameters of objects which subtend very small angles.—**micrometry**, mī·krom′et·ri, *n.* The art of measuring with a micrometer.

micromillimeter (mµ), mī′krō·mil″li·mē·tėr, *n.* [Gr. *mikros*, small, and *millimetre*.] 1/1000000 millimeter; the unit of microscopical measurement.

micron (µ), mī′kron, *n.* [Gr. *mikron*, small.] A unit of length equal to one millionth part of a meter.

micro-organism, mī·krō-or′gan·izm, *n.* [Gr. *mikros*, small, and E. *organism*.] A microscopic organism, as a bacterium or bacillus.

microphone, mī′kro·fōn, *n.* [Gr. *mikros*, small, and *phōnē*, sound.] An instrument for transmitting or intensifying sounds by means of electricity; an instrument for converting sound waves into electrical waves, used especially in radiobroadcasting; often referred to as a *mike*.

microphotography, mī′kro·fo·tog″ra·fi, *n.* [Gr. *mikros*, small, and E. *photography*.] A photographic representation of microscopic size; the photography of microscopic objects.

micropyle, mī′kro·pīl, *n.* [Gr. *mikros*, small, *pylē*, gate.] *Bot.* the opening by which a pollen tube enters the ovule; *zool.* an opening by which the spermatozoa fertilize an ovum.

microscope, mī′kro·skōp, *n.* [Gr. *mikros*, small, and *skopeō*, to view.] An optical instrument consisting of a lens or combination of lenses for rendering minute objects distinctly visible.—**microscopic, microscopical**, mī·kro·skop′ik, mī·kro·skop′i·kal, *a.* Pertaining to the microscope;

made by the aid of a microscope (*microscopic* observations); resembling a microscope; capable of seeing small objects; visible only by the aid of a microscope.—**microscopically**, mī·kro·skop′i·kal·li, *adv.* In a microscopic manner; by the microscope.—**microscopist**, mī′kro·skō·pist or mī·kros′ko·pist, *n.* One skilled or versed in microscopy.—**microscopy**, mī·kros′ko·pi, *n.* The use of the microscope; investigation with the microscope.

microspore, mik′ro·spōr, *n.* [Gr. *mikros*, small, *sporos*, seed.] *Bot.* a small (male) spore.

microtome, mī′kro·tōm, *n.* [Gr. *mikros*, small, and *tomos*, a cutting.] An instrument for making very fine sections or slices of objects for the microscope.

microwave, mī′kro·wave, *n.* [Gr. *mikros*, small, and E. *wave*.] Short electromagnetic waves, between 30 centimeters and 1 millimeter in wave length.

micturition, mik·tū·rish′on, *n.* [L. *micturio*, to desire to make water.] The desire of making water; a morbid frequency in the passage of urine.

mid, mid, *a.*; no compar.; superl. *midmost*. [A.Sax. *mid*, mid, in the middle; Goth. *midjis*, Icel. *midr* (*mithr*); cog. L. *medius* (see MEDIAL); Gr. *mesos*, Skr. *madhyas*, middle.] Middle; at equal distance from extremes; intervening.—**mid-channel**, *n.* The middle of a channel.—**midday**, *n.* The middle of the day; noon.—*a.* Pertaining to noon; meridional.—**midland**, mid′land, *a.* Being in the interior country; distant from the coast or seashore; inland.—*n.* The interior of a country.—**midmost**, mid′mōst, *a.* In the very middle.—**midnight**, mid′nīt, *n.* The middle of the night; twelve o'clock at night.—*a.* Being or occurring in the middle of the night; dark as midnight; very dark. —**midnoon**, *n.* The middle of the day; noon. (*Tenn.*)—**midrib**, mid′rib, *n. Bot.* a continuation of the petiole extending from the base to the apex of the lamina of a leaf.—**midship**, mid′ship, *a.* Being or belonging to the middle of a ship.—**midshipman**, mid′ship·man, *n.* [From his rank being between that of a superior officer and a common seaman.] An officer in training in the navy, occupying the rank below ensign.—**midsummer**, mid′sum·ėr, *n.* The middle of summer; the summer solstice, about the 21st of June.—**midway**, mid′wā, *n.* A middle way or the middle of the way.—*a.* Being in the middle of the way or distance.—*adv.* In the middle of the way or distance; halfway.—**midwinter**, *n.* The middle of winter, or the winter solstice, December 21.

midden, mid′n, *n.* [A.Sax. *midding*, same word as Dan. *mödding*, *mögdynge*, from *mög*, dung, and *dynge*, a heap.] A dunghill. [Prov.E. and Scot.]—*Kitchen-midden*. See KITCHEN.

middle, mid′l, *a.*; no compar.; superl.

middlemost. [From *mid*; A.Sax., D., and Dan. *middel*, G. *mittel*, middle. MID.] Equally distant from the extremes; forming a mean; intermediate; intervening.—*Middle Ages*, the period in Europe from the fifth to the middle of the fifteenth century of the Christian era.—*n.* Middle point or part; middle part of the body; an intervening point or part in space, time, or order; something intermediate; a mean.—**middle-aged**, *a.* Being about the middle of the ordinary human life span.—**middle class.** Originally, people having a social position between wage earners and the leisure class; now including many wage earners, such as clerks and office workers.—**middle C**, *n.* The musical note C, represented by the first ledger line below the treble staff, and the first above the bass staff.—**middle ear**, *n. Anat.* the tympanum.—**middleman**, *n.* An intermediary between two parties; a jobber.—**middlemost**, mid′l·mōst, *a.* Midmost.—**middleweight**, mid′l·wāt, *n.* A person of average weight; in boxing, a fighter whose weight lies between that of a welterweight and a light heavyweight, at about 160 pounds.—**middling**, mid′ling, *a.* Of middle state, size, or quality; moderate; mediocre; second-rate.

midge, mij, *n.* [A.Sax. *micge*, a midge=D. *mug*, Dan. *myg*, G. *mücke*; allied to Gr. *myia*, a fly.] The common name of numerous minute species of gnats or flies.—**midget**, mij′et, *n.* [Dim. of *midge*.] A very small creature.

midriff, mid′rif, *n.* [A.Sax. *midhrif*—*mid*, and *hrif*, belly.] The diaphragm; the respiratory muscle dividing the cavity of the thorax from that of the abdomen.

midst, midst, *n.* [From old *middes* (with *t* appended, as in *against*, *amongst*), the genit. of *mid*, middle.] The middle; in the central part of a place; the position of a thing surrounded by other things.—*In the midst (of)*, in the middle part of, in the middle stage.—*prep.* Amidst.

midwife, mid′wīf, *n.* [From O.E. and A.Sax. *mid*, with, together with (G. *mit*), and *wife*; comp. Sp. and Pg. *comadre*, a midwife, *co*=L. *cum*, with, and *madre*, a mother.] A practical nurse, as distinguished from a registered nurse, who assists a mother in childbirth.—**midwifery**, mid′wīf·ri, *n.* The art or practice of a midwife; obstetrics.

mien, mēn, *n.* [Fr. *mine*, air, mien; It. *mina*, course, behavior, L.L. *minare*, to lead, conduct, properly to drive with threats, from L. *mina*, a threat. MENACE. Or from Arm. *mîn*, face.] External air or manner of a person; look; bearing; appearance; carriage.

miff, mif, *n.* [Comp. Prov.G. *muff*, sullenness.] A slight quarrel. (*Colloq.*)

might, mīt, *n.* [A.Sax. *miht*, also *meaht*, might, from stem of *may*, to be able; D. Sw. and Dan. *magt*, G. *macht*, might. MAY.] Strength; force; power; often bodily strength or physical power; but also mental power; power of will; political power.—*With might and main*, with the utmost strength or bodily exertion.—**mightily**, mīt′i•li, *adv.* Powerfully; vehemently; greatly; highly.—**mightiness**, mīt′i•nes, *n.* State or attribute of being mighty: also, with possessives, a title of dignity.—**mighty**, mīt′i, *a.* [A.Sax. *mihtig.*] Having great power or dominion; strong; powerful: often an epithet of honor (most *mighty* prince); very great; vast; eminent in intellect or acquirements; displaying great power; performed with great power (*mighty* works).—*adv.* In a great degree; very (*mighty* wise; *mighty* thoughtful). (*Colloq.*)

might, mīt, past tense of *may.*

mignonette, min′yon•et, *n.* [Fr. *mignonnette*, a dim. of *mignon*, darling. MINION.] An annual plant, a native of Egypt, but universally cultivated in gardens on account of the sweet scent of its flowers.

migraine, mī′grān, *n.* [Gr. *hemikrania*, from *hemi*, half, and *kranion*, skull.] A recurring headache, usually on one side of the head, accompanied by nausea and often by sensory disturbances.

migrate, mī′grāt, *v.i.*—*migrated, migrating.* [L. *migro, migratum*, to migrate.] To move from one place of residence to another; changing from one geographic area to another.—**migrant**, mī′grant, *a.* Migratory.—*n.* One who migrates; a migratory bird or other animal.—**migration**, mī•grā′shon, *n.*—**migratory**, mī′gra•to•ri, *a.* Given to migration; migrating at certain seasons (as birds); roving or wandering.

mikado, mi•kä′dō, *n.* [Japanese, lit. the Venerable.] [*often cap.*] The emperor of Japan.

mil, mil, *n.* [From L. *mille*, thousand.] A unit of 0.001 inch, used in measuring the diameter of wire.

milanese, mil•an•ēz′, *n. sing.* and *pl.* A citizen or citizens of *Milan.*—*a.* Of or belonging to Milan or the people of Milan.

milch, milch, *a.* [A.Sax. *melc*, milch, giving milk; comp. L.G. *melke*, Icel. *milkr*, G. *melk*, milch, but L.G. *melk*, *mjólk*, G. *milch*, milk. MILK.] Giving milk; applied only to beasts (a *milch* cow).

mild, mīld, *a.* [A.Sax. *milde*=D. Dan. Sw. and G. *mild*, Icel. *mildr*, Goth. *milds*; from a root meaning to grind or crush, and hence allied to *mellow*, *meal*, *mould*, L. *mollis*, soft (whence *mollify*).] Tender and gentle in temper or disposition; not severe or cruel; not fierce, rough, or angry; placid; not stern; not frowning; gently and pleasantly affecting the senses; not violent; soft; bland; gentle (a *mild* temperature); not acrid, pungent, corrosive, or drastic; moderately sweet or pleasant to the taste (*mild* fruit).—**milden**, mīl′den, *v.t.* To render mild; to soften; to make less severe, stringent, or intense.—*v.i.* To become mild; to soften.—**mildly**, mīld′li, *adv.* In a mild manner.—**mildness**, mīld′nes,

n. The state or quality of being mild; gentleness; softness; clemency; blandness; tenderness.

mildew, mil′dū, *n.* [A.Sax. *mildeáw, meledeáw*; O.H.G. *militou*, G. *mehlthau*; probably = 'honey-dew'; comp. L. *mel*, honey.] Decay produced in living and dead vegetable matter, and in some manufactured products of vegetable matter, by very minute parasitical fungi; a sort of blight; the minute fungi causing this condition.—*v.t.* To affect with mildew.—*v.i.* To become affected with mildew.—**mildewy**, mil′dū•i, *a.* Abounding in mildew; moldy; resembling mildew.

mile, mīl, *n.* [A.Sax. *mil*, like D. *mijl*, Dan. *miil*, G. *meile*, a mile, from L. *mille*, a thousand, used shortly for *mille passus* (or *passuum*), a thousand paces, a Roman mile. Akin *million, milliard*, etc.] A land measure of distance used in the United States and Great Britain, and equal to 1,760 yards, or 5280 feet: the nautical or sea mile, in the United States, is equal to 6,080.20 feet.—*Last mile*, the last walk of a condemned man to the execution chamber. (*Slang.*)—**mileage**, mīl′ij, *n.* A fee or allowance paid for travel by the mile; the aggregate of miles in a railway, canal, etc.; aggregate of miles gone over by vehicles such as automobiles, railroad trains, etc.—

milestone, mīl′stōn, *n.* A stone or post set up on the side of a road or highway to mark the miles.

milesian, mi•lē′zhi•an, *n.* A native of Ireland, whose inhabitants, according to Irish legend, are descended from *Milesius*, a king of Spain.—*a.* Pertaining to the ancient Irish race.

milfoil, mil′foil, *n.* [Fr. *mille-feuille*, from L. *millefolium*, lit. thousand-leaf.] The yarrow.

miliary, mil′i•e•ri, *a.* [L. *miliarius*, from *milium*, millet.] Resembling millet seeds; accompanied with an eruption like millet seeds (a *miliary* fever).

milieu, mē•lyu′, *n.* [Fr., from Old Fr. *mi*, middle, and *lieu*, place.] Environmental setting.

militant, mil′i•tant, *a.* [L. *militans, militantis*, ppr. of *milito*, to fight, from *miles, militis*, a soldier; perhaps connected with *mille*, a thousand.] Fighting; serving as a soldier.—*Church militant*, the Christian church on earth, which is supposed to be engaged in constant warfare and struggle: as distinguished from the *church triumphant*, or in heaven.—**militantly**, mil′i•tant•li, *adv.* In a militant or warlike manner.—**militancy**, mil′i•tan•si, *n.* Warfare; militarism.—**militarily**, mil′i•te•ri•li, *adv.* In a military or soldierly manner.—**militarism**, mil′i•te•rizm, *n.* [Fr. *militarisme.*] The system that leads a nation to pay excessive attention to military affairs; the keeping up of great armies.—**militarist**, mil′i•te•rist, *n.* A military man; one proficient in the art of war (*Shak.*); one in favor of militarism; one who favors a warlike policy.—

military, mil′i•te•ri, *a.* [L. *militaris.*] Pertaining to soldiers or the profession of a soldier; becoming the profession of a soldier; pertaining to war; warlike; martial.—*Military attaché*, an army officer, resident abroad with his nation's diplomatic representative, whose duty it is to observe and report on the military developments of a foreign power.—*Military brush*, a hair brush without a handle.—*Military hospital*, a hospital for the treatment of sick and wounded soldiers.—*Military police*, that part of the army which performs police duty among soldiers.—**militate**, mil′i•tāt, *v.i.* [L. *milito, militatum*, to fight.] To stand opposed; to have weight or influence on the opposite side: said of arguments, considerations, etc., and followed by *against* (another fact *militated against* that theory).—**militia**, mi•lish′a, *n.* [L., military service, soldiery.] A body of men enrolled and trained as military reserves for the defense of a nation in time of war; the organized militia of the individual states is called the National Guard.—**militiaman**, *n.* One who belongs to the militia.

milk, milk, *n.* [A.Sax. *meolc, milc*, milk=D. Dan. and L.G. *melk*, Icel. *mjólk*, Sw. *mjölk*, Goth. *miluks*, G. *milch*, milk; also Rus. *moloko*, Pol. and Bohem. *mleko*, milk; root also in L. *mulgeo*, Gr. *amelgō*, to milk.] A whitish fluid secreted by the mammary glands of females of the class Mammalia, including the human species, and drawn from the breasts for the nourishment of their young; the white juice of certain plants; an emulsion of which juice expressed from seeds is one of the constituents (the *milk* of almonds).—*v.t.* To draw milk from the breasts or udder of by the hand (to *milk* a cow).—**milk-and-water**, *a.* Tasteless; insipid; characterless; wishy-washy (*Colloq.*).—**milker**, milk′er, *n.* One who or that which milks; a cow or other animal giving milk.

milk fever, *n.* A fever which sometimes accompanies the first secretion of milk in females after childbirth.—**milkiness**, milk′i•nes, *n.* State of being milky; qualities like those of milk.—**milk-livered**, *a.* Cowardly; timorous (*Shak.*).—**milkmaid**, milk′mād, *n.* A woman that milks or is employed in the dairy.—**milkman**, milk′man, *n.* A man that sells milk or carries milk to market.—**milk of magnesia**, *n. Phar.* a solution of magnesium hydroxide, $Mg(OH)_2$ suspended in water, used as an antacid or a laxative.—**milk shake**, *n.* A foamy drink made of cold milk, flavoring and, usually, ice cream, shaken together.—**milksop**, *n.* An effeminate man.—**milk sugar**, *n.* Lactose.—**milk tooth**, *n.* One of the first teeth in the temporary set in young animals and children.—**milkweed**, *n.* Any plant of the family Asclepiadaceae, so named for its milky fluid, or latex.—**milky**, milk′i, *a.*—**Milky Way**, *n.* See GALAXY.

mill, mil, *n.* [L. *mille*, a thousand.]

A money of account of the United States, value the thousandth of a dollar, or one-tenth of a cent.

mill, mil, *n.* [O.E. *miln,* A.Sax. *mylen, myln,* from L. *molina,* a mill, from *mola,* a mill or millstone, from *molo,* to grind—root same as in *meal, mould,* etc.] A machine for grinding and reducing to fine particles grain, fruit, or other substance; applied also to many machines for grinding or polishing by circular motion, or to complicated machinery for working up raw material, etc.; the building where grinding or some process of manufacturing is carried on; *calico printing,* a copper printing cylinder; a pugilistic contest; a fight with the fists (*slang*).—*v.t.* To grind in a mill; to pass through a mill; to stamp in a coining press; especially to stamp so as to make a transversely grooved edge round; to throw, as silk; to full, as cloth.—**millboard,** *n.* A stout kind of pasteboard made in a paper mill.—**milldam,** *n.* A dam crossing a watercourse and raising the water to a height sufficient to turn a mill wheel; in Scotland, a millpond.—**milled,** mild, *p.* and *a.* Having undergone the operation of a mill; having the edge transversely grooved, as a dime or the head of a screw that is to be turned by the fingers; fulled, as cloth.—**miller,** mil′ėr, *n.* One who keeps or attends a mill, especially a flour mill.—**miller's-thumb,** *n.* A small fish found in streams, the bull head.—**millpond,** *n.* A pond or reservoir of water for driving a mill wheel.—**millrace,** *n.* The stream of water that drives a mill wheel, or the channel in which it runs.—**millstone,** mil′stōn, *n.* One of the stones for grinding the grain in a mill; stone or rock from which such stones are made.—*Millstone grit,* a siliceous conglomerate rock used for millstones, building, etc., forming one of the members of the carboniferous group of strata underlying the true coal measures.—*To see into or through a millstone,* to see with acuteness or to penetrate into abstruse subjects.—**mill wheel,** *n.* A wheel used to drive a mill; a water wheel.—**millwright,** *n.* A mechanic or wright whose occupation it is to construct the machinery of mills.

millenarian, mil·le·nā′ri·an, *a.* [L. *millenarius,* containing a thousand, from *mille,* a thousand. MILE.] Consisting of a thousand; especially consisting of a thousand years; pertaining to the millennium.—*n.* One who believes in the millennium.—**millenary,** mil′le·ne·ri, *a.* Consisting of a thousand.—*Millenary Petition,* the petition presented by the Puritan and Conformist parties to James I in 1603, signed by a thousand ministers, complaining that they were overburdened with the human rites and ceremonies in the Prayer Book. —*n.* The space of a thousand years; a thousandth anniversary.—**millennial,** mil·len′i·al, *a.* Pertaining to the millennium, or to a thousand years. —**millennium,** mil·len′i·um, *n.* [L.

mille, a thousand, and *annus,* year.] An aggregate of a thousand years; the thousand years mentioned in Rev. xx. 1-5, during which millenarians believe Christ will reign on earth with his saints.

millepede, millipede, mil′e·pēd, mil′i·pēd, *n.* [L. *mille,* a thousand, and *pes,* a foot.] A name common to worm-like articulated animals, from the number of their feet; a myriapod.

millepore, mil′le·pōr, *n.* [L. *mille,* a thousand, and *porus,* a pore.] One of the reef-building corals, so named from their numerous minute cells or pores.

millesimal, mil·les′i·mal, *a.* [L. *millesimus,* from *mille,* a thousand.] Thousandth.

millet, mil′et, *n.* [Fr. *millet,* dim. of *mil,* from L. *milium,* millet; from root meaning to grind as in *mill.*] A common name for various species of small grain cultivated largely in many parts of Europe, Asia, and Africa as food for men; various forage grasses; the seed of any of these grains and grasses.

milliard, mil·yärd, *n.* [Fr.] A thousand millions, usually called a *billion* in America.

milliary, mil′i·e·ri, *a.* [L. *milliarius,* from *mille,* a thousand.] Pertaining to the ancient Roman mile of a thousand paces or five thousand feet; denoting a mile.

millibar, mil′i·bär, *n.* [L. *mille,* thousand, and Gr. *baros,* weight.] *Meteor.* one thousand dynes per square centimeter, used in measuring atmospheric pressure.

milligram, mil′i·gram, *n.* [L. *mille,* thousand, and *gram,* a small weight.] The thousandth part of a gram; equal to a cubic millimeter of water.

milliliter, mil″i·lē′tėr, *n.* [Fr. *milli-litre*—L. *mille,* thousand, and Fr. *litre,* an old measure.] A unit of capacity in the metric system equal to 1/1,000 liter.—**millimeter,** mil″i·mē′tėr, *n.* The thousandth part of a meter.—**millimicron,** mil″i·mī′kron, *n.* The millionth part of a millimeter, or thousandth part of a micron.

milliner, mil′i·nėr, *n.* [Supposed to be for *Milaner,* from *Milan,* in Italy, famous for its silks and ribbons.] A person, now usually a woman, who makes and sells hats for females. —**millinery,** mil′i·ner·i, *n.* The business or occupation of a milliner; the articles made or sold by milliners.

million, mil′yon, *n.* [Fr. *million,* from L. *mille,* a thousand. MILE.] The number of ten hundred thousand, or a thousand thousand; with the definite article, the great body of the people; the multitude; the public; the masses.—**millionaire, million-naire,** mil′yon·âr, *n.* [Fr. *million-naire.*] A man worth a million of money; a man of great wealth.— **millionth,** mil′yonth, *a.* Ten hundred thousandth; constituting one of a million.—*n.* One of a million parts; a ten hundred thousandth part.

milreis, mil′rās, *n.* [Pg. *mil,* a thousand, and *reis,* pl. of *real,* a small

denomination of money.] A Brazilian money of account, written 1$000; an old Portuguese coin.

milt, milt, *n.* [A.Sax. *milte,* Dan. *milt,* Icel. *milti,* G. *milz,* the spleen; D. *milt,* the spleen, the milt of fishes; same root as *melt.*] The soft roe of fishes, or the spermatic organ of the males.—**milter,** milt′ėr, *n.* A male fish, or one having a milt.

mime, mīm, *n.* [L. *mimus,* from Gr. *mimos,* an actor, a mime.] A species of ancient dramatic entertainment in which gestures and mimicry predominated; an actor in such performances.—**mimesis,** mi·mē′sis, *n. Rhet.* imitation of the voice or gestures of another; *nat. hist.* same as *Mimicry.*—**mimetic,** mi·met′ik, *a.* Apt to imitate; given to aping or mimicry; *nat. hist.* characterized by mimicry.—**mimic,** mim′ik, *a.* Imitative; inclined to imitate or ape; imitating; consisting of or made in imitation (*mimic gestures*).—*n.* One who imitates or mimics; one who attempts to excite laughter or derision by acting or speaking in the manner of another.—*v.t.*—*mimicked, mimicking.* To imitate; to ridicule by imitation.—**mimicker,** mim′ik·ėr, *n.* —**mimicry,** mim′ik·ri, *n. Nat. hist.* the close resemblance presented by certain plants and animals to certain other plants or animals, or to the natural objects among which they live, this resemblance serving for protection.

mimeograph, mim″e·ō·graf′, *n.* [From the former trademark.] A device capable of making many copies of typewritten material by means of a stencil.

mimosa, mi·mō′sa, *n.* [From Gr. *mimos,* a mimic, from their sensitive leaves.] A genus of plants, some of which are remarkable for the irritability of their leaves, hence their name *sensitive-plants.*

mina, mī′na, *n.* Among the Greeks, a weight of 100 drachmae; also, a piece of money valued at 100 drachmae.

minacious, mi·nā′shus, *a.* [L. *minax, minacis,* threatening, MENACE.] Threatening; menacing.—**minacity,†** mi·nas′i·ti, *n.* Disposition to threaten.

minaret, min′a·ret, *n.* [Fr. *minaret,* Sp. *minarete,* from Ar. *menâra,* a lighthouse, a minaret, from *nâr,* to shine.] A slender lofty turret rising by different stages or stories, surrounded by one or more projecting balconies, common in mosques in Mohammedan countries, and used for summoning the people to prayers.

minatory, min′a·to·ri, *a.* [L. *minatorius,* from *minator,* a threatener, *mina,* a threat. MENACE.] Threatening; menacing.—**minatorily,** min′-a·to·ri·li, *adv.* In a minatory manner.

mince, mins, *v.t.*—*minced, mincing.* [A.Sax. *minsian,* from *min,* small; also O.Fr. *mincer,* from *mince,* fine, small; root same as that of *minor, minister.*] To cut or chop into very small pieces (to *mince* meat); to diminish in speaking; to extenuate; to palliate (to *mince* the matter, to *mince* matters); to pronounce with affected elegance.—*v.i.* To walk with short steps; to affect delicacy in manner; to speak with affected elegance.—**mincemeat,** : *n.* Meat chopped fine; chopped mixture of raisins, apples, other fruit, spices, suet, etc.—**mince pie,** *n.* A pie made of mincemeat.—**mincer,** mins′ėr, *n.* One who minces; a detractor.—**mincing,** mins′ing, *p.* and *a.* Speaking or walking affectedly.—**mincingly,** mins′ing·li, *adv.* With a mincing manner.

mind, mīnd, *n.* [A.Sax. *mynd, gemynd,* mind, thought, intention; Dan. *minde,* Icel. *minni,* memory; from root *man,* to think, seen also in *mean,* to intend; L. *mens, mentis,* mind (whence *mental*); Gr. *menos,* mind. MAN, MEAN.] The intellectual power in man; the understanding (not in one's right *mind*); cast of thought and feeling; opinion (of the same *mind*); intention; purpose; memory; remembrance (to call to *mind,* to keep in *mind*).—*To be in two minds* about a thing, to be in doubt.—*v.t.* To attend to; to fix the thoughts on; to heed; to notice; to pay attention to; to attend with submission; to obey.—**minder,** mīn′dėr, *n.* One who minds.—**mindful,** mīnd′ful, *a.* Attentive; bearing in mind; heedful.—**mindfully,** mīnd′ful·li, *adv.*—**mindfulness,** mīnd′ful·nes, *n.*—**mindless,** mīnd′les, *a.* Destitute of mind; inattentive; heedless.—**mind reader,** *n.* One who discerns the thoughts of others without the customary means of communication.

mine, mīn, *pronominal adjective.* [A.Sax. *min,* genit. or adj. corresponding to *me*=Dan. and Sw. *min,* Icel. *minn,* Goth. *meina,* D. *mijn,* G. *mein. My* is a shortened form. Comp. *thy, thine.*] My; belonging to me: once regularly used before nouns beginning with a vowel, now generally used similarly to *thine, hers, ours, yours, theirs,* as equivalent to *my* followed by a noun, and serving either for a nominative or an objective.

mine, mīn, *n.* [Fr. *mine,* a mine, *miner,* to form a mine. Of Celtic origin. Comp. Ir. *meinn,* mine, ore, vein of metal, *mianach,* abounding in ore, W. *Mwn,* mine.] A pit or excavation in the earth, from which coal, metallic ores, or other mineral substances are taken by digging; a contrivance floating on, or near, the surface of the sea to destroy ships by explosion; *milit.* an underground gallery or passage dug under a fortification, in which a quantity of powder or other explosive may be lodged for blowing up the works; *fig.* a rich source or store of wealth or anything highly valued.—*v.i.*—*mined, mining.* To dig a mine; to burrow.—*v.t.* To dig away the foundation from; to undermine; to sap.—**mine sweeping,** *n.* The 'sweeping' of the sea to clear an area of hostile mines.—**mining,** mīn′ing, *p.* and *a.* Of burrowing

habits; insidious.—**miner,** mīn′ėr *n.* One who mines; one who digs or works in a mine for metals or other minerals.

mineral, min′ėr·al, *n.* [Fr. *minéral,* from *miner,* to mine. MINE.] Any ingredient in the earth's crust; an inorganic body with a definite chemical composition, and which naturally exists within the earth or at its surface.—*a.* Pertaining to minerals; consisting of minerals; impregnated with minerals or mineral matter (*mineral* waters).—*Mineral acids,* a name given to sulfuric, nitric, and hydrochloric acids.—*Mineral caoutchouc,* a variety of bitumen, much resembling India rubber in its softness and elasticity.—*Mineral charcoal,* a fibrous variety of non-bituminous mineral coal.—*Mineral green,* carbonate of copper.—*Mineral kingdom,* that grand division of natural objects which includes all minerals, and of which mineralogy is the science.—*Mineral oil.* PETROLEUM.—*Mineral pitch,* a solid softish bitumen.—*Mineral tar,* bitumen of a tarry consistence.—*Mineral waters,* a term applied to certain waters, either naturally or artificially impregnated with gases, carbonates, sulfates, iron, etc.—*Mineral wax,* ozocerite.—**mineralization,** min′ėr·al·i·zā″shon, *n.* The act or process of mineralizing; the process of being converted into a mineral.—**mineralize,** min′ėr·al·īz, *v.t.*—*mineralized, mineralizing.* To convert into a mineral; to impregnate with mineral substance.—**mineralizer,** min′ėr·al·īz·ėr, *n.* A substance or agent that mineralizes.—**mineralogy,** min′ėr·al′o·ji, *n.* The science which treats of the properties of mineral substances, and teaches us to characterize, distinguish, and classify them according to their properties.—**mineralogical,** min′ėr·a·loj″i·kal, *a.* Pertaining to mineralogy.—**mineralogically,** min′ėr·a·loj″i·kal·li, *adv.* According to the principles of mineralogy.—**mineralogist,** min·ėr·al′o·jist, *n.*

Minerva, mi·nėr′va, *n.* [L., from root of *mens,* mind. MIND, MENTAL.] One of the chief divinities of the Romans, the goddess of wisdom, of war, and of the liberal arts.

minestrone, min·e·strō′nė, *n.* [From It. *minestra,* soup, from *minestrare,* from L. *ministrāre.*] A thick soup made from meat broth, containing vegetables, herbs, etc.

mingle, ming′gl, *v.t.*—*mingled, mingling.* [From A.Sax. *mengan,* to mix, with freq. term. *-le;* D. *mengen,* G. *mengen,* to mingle.] To mix up together so as to form one whole; to blend; to join in mutual intercourse or in society; to debase by mixture.—*v.i.* To become mixed; to become united in the same whole; to join (to *mingle with* or *in* a crowd).—**mingler,** ming′glėr, *n.* One that mingles.

miniature, min′ye·chėr, *n.* [It. *miniatura,* originally a design such as drawn on the margins of old manuscripts, from *miniare,* to write

with *minium* or red lead, this pigment being much used in the ornamenting of old manuscripts.] A painting of very small dimensions, usually executed in watercolors, on ivory, vellum, etc.; anything represented on a greatly reduced scale; a small scale (shown in *miniature*).—*a.* On a small scale.

minify, min′i·fī, *v.t.* [L. *minus,* less, and *facio,* to make.] To make little or less; opposite of magnify; to lessen; to diminish; to slight; to depreciate.

minikin,† min′i·kin, *n.* [O.D. *minneken,* darling, from *minne,* love; akin *minion.*] A darling; a favorite.—*a.* Small; diminutive.

minim, min′im, *n.* [Fr. *minime,* L. *minimus,* least, superlative corresponding to *minor,* small. MINOR.] A note in music, equal in time to half a semibreve or two crotchets; the smallest liquid measure, generally regarded as about equal to one drop, the fluid drachm being divided into sixty minims.—**minimum,** min′i·mum, *n.* [L.] The smallest amount or degree; least quantity assignable in a given case: opposed to *maximum.*—**minimize,** min′i·mīz, *v.t.* To reduce to a minimum.

minion, min′yon, *n.* [Fr. *mignon,* a darling, from O.G. *minne,* love.] An unworthy favorite; a servile dependent.

miniskirt, min′i·skėrt, *n.* [*Miniature* and *skirt.*] A woman's skirt of abbreviated length, usually several inches above the knee.

minister, min′is·tėr, *n.* [L. *minister,* from stem of *minor, minus,* less.] One who acts under the authority of another; a servant; an attendant; one authorized to conduct Christian worship, as a priest or clergyman; one to whom the executive head of a government entrusts the direction of affairs of state; one engaged in the administration of government.—*v.t.* To give; to supply.—*v.i.* To act as a minister or attendant; to perform service; to afford supplies; to give things needful; to supply the means of relief; to furnish (to *minister to* one's necessities).—**ministerial,** min·is·tē′ri·al, *a.* Pertaining to ministry or the performance of service; pertaining to a ministry or to ministers of state; pertaining to ministers of the gospel.—**ministerialist,** min·is·tē′ri·al·ist, *n. Politics,* a supporter of the ministry in office.—**ministerially,** min·is·tē′ri·al·li, *adv.* In a ministerial manner or character.—**ministrant,** min′is·trant, *a.* [L. *ministrans, ministrantis.*] Performing service; acting as minister or attendant; attendant on service.—**ministration,** min·is·trā′shon, *n.* [L. *ministratio.*] The act of ministering or performing service; service or attendance given; ecclesiastical function.—**ministrative,** min′is·trā·tiv, *a.* Affording service; assisting.—**ministry,** min′is·tri, *n.* [L. *ministerium.*] The act of ministering; service; aid; instrumentality; the office or functions of a minister of the gospel; the body of ministers of state or the chief officials of the executive government; duration of the office of a minister, civil or ecclesiastical.

minium, min′i·um, n. [L. Hence *miniature*.] Red oxide of lead; red lead.

miniver, min′i·vėr, n. [O.Fr. *menuveir, menuvair*, a grayish fur—*menu* [L. *minutus*), small, and *vair*, fur.] The fur of the Siberian squirrel; a fine white fur.

mink, mingk, n. An American and European quadruped, allied to the polecat and weasel, yielding a fur of some value.

minnesinger, min′ne·sing·ėr, n. [O. G. *minne*, love (MINION), and *singer*, a singer.] One of a class of German lyric poets of the twelfth and thirteenth centuries, so called from love being their chief theme.

minnow, min′ō, n. [A.Sax. *myne*, a minnow.] Any of various small fishes of the carp family; loosely, any of several other small fishes.

Minoan, mi·nō′an, a. [L. *Minous*, from Gr. *Minōs*, a King of Crete.] Pertaining to the ancient, advanced culture of Crete, existing about 3000 B.C. to 1100 B.C.

minor, mī′nor, a. [L. *minor*, smaller (without a positive), from a root *min*, small, seen also in A.Sax. *min*, small; Dan., Sw., *mindre*, Icel. *minni*, G. *minder*, less; Ir. and Gael. *min*, small, fine. Akin *minute, minister, minish*, etc.] Lesser; smaller; used relatively, and opposed to *major*; absolutely small; petty; *music*, less by a lesser semitone, as applied to an interval; having a tone and semitone between the keynote and its third: applied to a scale.—*Minor term, logic*, the subject of the conclusion of a categorical syllogism.—*Minor premise*, that which contains the minor term.—*n.* A person of either sex under full age (not yet twenty-one years); one under the authority of his parents or guardians; *logic*, the minor term or premise; *music*, the minor key.—**Minorite,** mī′nor·īt, n. A Franciscan friar.—**minority,** mi·nor′i·ti, n. [Fr. *minorité*.] The state of being a minor or not yet come of age; the period or interval before one is of full age, generally the period from birth until twenty-one years of age; the smaller number out of a whole divided into two: opposed to *majority*; a race, religion or political group that is subject to a larger controlling group.

Minotaur, min′ō·taur, n. [Gr.] Mythical monster, reputed half man, half bull, offspring of Pasiphaë, wife of Minos, the ancient King of Crete, and connected with the legend of Theseus.

minster, min′stėr, n. [A.Sax. *mynster* (like G. *münster*, D. *monster*), from L. *monasterium*, a monastery. MONASTERY.] Originally, a monastery; afterward the church of a monastery; latterly, a cathedral church.

minstrel, min′strel, n. [O.Fr. *menestrel*, from L.L. *ministrellus*, a harper, one who ministered to the amusement of the rich by music or jesting; a dim. from L. *minister*, a servant.] A singer or musical performer; in the Middle Ages, one of a class of men who subsisted by the arts of poetry and music.—**minstrel show,** a performance of jokes, melodies, etc., given by comedians usually made up as Negroes.—**minstrelsy,** min′strel·si, n. A group of minstrels; the art or occupation of minstrels; music; a body of songs or ballads.

mint, mint, n. [A.Sax. *mynet*, from L. *moneta*, the mint, money, from *Moneta*, a surname of *Juno*, in whose temple at Rome money was coined, from *moneo*, to remind (whence *monition, monitor*).] The place where money is coined by public authority; a great supply or store that may be drawn on (a *mint* of reasons).—*v.t.* To coin; to make and stamp into money; to invent; to fabricate.—**mintage,** mint′ij, n. That which is coined or stamped; the duty paid for coining.—**minter,** mint′ėr, n. A coiner.

mint, mint, n. [A.Sax. *minte*, from L. *mentha*, Gr. *mintha, minthē*, mint.] The name of several herbaceous aromatic plants which partake largely of the tonic properties found in all labiate plants; a mint-flavored confection. *Spearmint* and *peppermint* are the popular names of two well-known species.—**mint julep,** n. A drink made of whisky, usually Bourbon, with sugar, cracked ice, and mint leaves.

minuend, min′ū·end, n. [L. *minuendus*, to be lessened, *minuo*, to lessen. MINOR.] *Arith.* the number from which another number is to be subtracted.

minuet, min′ū·et, n. [Fr. *menuet*, from *menu*, small, from L. *minutus*, minute—on account of the small steps of the dance.] A slow graceful dance and the tune or air for it.

minus, mī′nus, a. [Neut. of L. *minor*, less. MINOR.] Involving subtraction, as the *minus* sign; not positive, as a *minus* quality.—*prep.* Decreased by the subtraction of (five *minus* three).

minuscule, mi·nus′kūl, a. [L. *minusculus*, small, minute.] Very small.

minute, mi·nūt′, a. [L. *minutus*, pp. of *minuo*, to lessen, from root *min*, small. MINOR.] Very small; characterized by attention to small things or details; precise; attentive to the smallest particulars.—**minutely,** mi·nūt′li, adv. With minuteness; exactly; nicely.—**minuteness,** mi·nūt′nes, n. Extreme smallness; critical exactness.

minute, min′it, n. [Fr. *minute*, from L. *minuta*, a minute portion. MINUTE, *a*.] A small portion of time, strictly the sixtieth part of an hour; sixty seconds; *geom.* the sixtieth part of a degree of a circle; *arch.* the sixtieth part of the diameter of a column at the base; a short sketch of any agreement or other subject, taken in writing; a note to preserve the memory of anything.—*v.t.*—*minuted, minuting.* To set down in a short sketch or note.—**min-**

utely, min′it·li, adv. Every minute; with very little time intervening.—**minutebook,** n. A book in which minutes are recorded.—**minute gun,** n. A gun discharged at intervals of a minute as a signal from a vessel in distress.—**minute hand,** n. The hand that points to the minutes on a clock or watch.

minutia, mi·nū′shi·a, n.; generally in pl.—**minutiae,** mi·nū′shi·ē. [L. from *minutus*, small. MINUTE, *a*.] Small, minor, or unimportant particulars or details,

minx, mingks, n. [Perhaps a sort of abbrev. form of *minikin*.] A pert, wanton girl; a hussy; a shepuppy.

Miocene, mī′o·sēn, a. [Gr. *meiōn*, less, and *kainos*, recent.] *Geol.* the name given to the middle subdivision of the tertiary strata, being applied to those strata which overlie the Ocene and are below the Pliocene.—*n. Geol.* the Miocene strata.

miracle, mir′a·kl, n. [Fr. *miracle*, from L. *miraculum*, something wonderful, from *miror*, to wonder; akin *marvel, mirror, mirage, admire*, etc.] A wonder or wonderful thing; something that excites astonishment; a sensible deviation from the known laws of nature, held to be wrought by a supernatural being; a supernatural event.—*To a miracle*, wonderfully; astonishingly.—**miracle play,** n. Formerly a dramatic representation exhibiting the lives of the saints, or other sacred subjects.—**miraculous,** mi·rak′ū·lus, a. Of the nature of a miracle; effected by the direct agency of almighty power; exceedingly surprising or wonderful.—**miraculously,** mi·rak′ū·lus·li, adv. In a miraculous manner; by miracle; supernaturally; wonderfully.—**miraculousness,** mi·rak′ū·lus·nes, n.

mirage, mi·räzh′, n. [Fr., from *mirer*, to look; *se mirer*, to be reflected. MIRACLE, MIRROR.] The name given to a natural optical illusion, consisting in an apparent elevation or approximation of coasts, mountains, ships, etc., accompanied by inverted images; in deserts often causing a plain to assume the appearance of a lake.

mire, mīr, n. [Same as Icel. *mýrr, mýri*, Sw. *myra*, N. *myre*, a swamp, fen; same root as *moor, marsh*.] Wet, clayey soil; mud.—*v.t.—mired, miring*. To fix or sink in mire (as a carriage); to soil or daub with mud.—*v.i.* To sink in mud, so as to be unable to advance.—**miry,** mī′ri, a. Full of or covered with mire or mud.

mirror, mir′ėr, n. [Fr. *miroir*, a mirror, from *mirer*, to look at, from L. *miror*, to admire. MIRACLE.] A looking glass; any polished substance that forms images by the reflection of rays of light; a pattern; an exemplar.—*v.t.* To furnish with mirrors; to reflect as in a mirror.

mirth, mėrth, n. [A.Sax. *myrgth, mirhth*, etc., from *mirig, merg*, merry. MERRY.] The feeling of being merry; merriment; noisy gaiety; glee; hilarity.—**mirthful,** mėrth´ful, *a.* Merry; jovial; causing or provoking mirth.—**mirthfully,** mėrth´ful·li, *adv.* In a mirthful manner.—**mirthfulness,** mėrth´ful·nes, *n.* Mirth; merriment.—**mirthless,** mėrth´les, *a.* Without mirth; joyless.

mirza, mėr´za, *n.* [Persian, for *emirzadeh,* son of the prince—*emir,* prince, and *zadeh,* son.] A common title of honor in Persia.

misadventure, mis·ad·ven´chėr, *n.* A mischance; ill luck; an unlucky accident.

misadvise, mis·ad·vīz´, *v.t.* To give bad advice to.

misalliance, mis·al·lī´ans, *n.* [MESALLIANCE.] Any improper alliance or association; specifically, an improper connection by marriage.

misanthrope, misanthropist, mis´an·thrōp, mis·an´thrōp·ist, *n.* [Gr. *misanthrōpos*—*miseō,* to hate, and *anthrōpos,* man.] A hater of mankind.—**misanthropic, misanthropical,** mis·an·throp´ik, mis·an·throp´i·kal, *a.*—**misanthropy,** mis·an´thro·pi, *n.* Hatred or dislike of mankind.

misapply, mis·ap·plī´, *v.t.* To apply to a wrong purpose.—**misapplication,** mis·ap´pli·kā˝shon, *n.* The act of misapplying.

misapprehend, mis·ap´pri·hend˝, *v.t.* To misunderstand; to take in a wrong sense.—**misapprehension,** mis·ap´pri·hen˝shon, *n.* A mistaking; wrong apprehension of one's meaning or of a fact.

misappropriate, mis·ap·prō´pri·āt, *v.t.* To appropriate wrongly; to put to a wrong purpose.—**misappropriation,** mis·ap·prō´pri·ā˝shon, *n.* Wrong appropriation.

misarrange, mis·a·rānj´, *v.t.* To arrange in a wrong order.—**misarrangement,** mis·a·rānj´ment; *n.* Disorderly arrangement.

misbecome, mis·bi·kum´, *v.t.*—pret. *misbecame,* ppr. *misbecoming,* pp. *misbecome* or *misbecomed.* Not to become; to suit ill; not to befit.—**misbecoming,** mis·bi·kum´ing, *p.* and *a.* Unbecoming; unseemly.

misbegot, misbegotten, mis·bi·got´, mis·bi·got´n, *p.* and *a.* Unlawfully or irregularly begotten; used also as a general epithet of opprobrium.

misbehave, mis·bi·hāv´, *v.i.* To behave ill; to conduct one's self improperly; often used with the reflexive pronouns.—**misbehavior,** mis·bi·hāv´yėr, *n.* Improper, rude, or uncivil behavior.

misbelief, mis·bi·lēf´, *n.* Erroneous belief; false religion; unbelief.—**misbeliever,** mis·bi·lē´vėr, *n.* One who holds a false religion.

miscalculate, mis·kal´kū·lāt, *v.t.* To calculate erroneously; to make a wrong guess or estimate of.—**miscalculation,** mis·kal´kū·lā˝shon, *n.* Erroneous calculation or estimate.

miscall, mis·kal´, *v.t.* To call by a wrong name; to name improperly; to give a bad name or character to†.

miscarriage, mis·kar´ij, *n.* Unfortunate issue or result of an undertaking; *med.* expulsion of the human

fetus prematurely, before it is capable of living outside the womb; abortion.—**miscarry,** mis·kar´i, *v.i.* To fail of the intended effect; to bring forth young before the proper time.

miscast, mis·cast´, *v.t.* [From prefix *mis,* and *cast.*] To place in an unsuitable role.

miscegenation, mis´si·je·nā˝shon, *n.* [L. *misceo,* to mix, and *genus,* a race.] Mixture or amalgamation of races.

miscellaneous, mis·sel·lā´ni·us, *a.* [L. *miscellaneus,* from *misceo,* to mix. MEDDLE.] Consisting of several kinds or things mingled; diversified.—**miscellaneously,** mis·sel·lā´ni·us·li, *adv.*—**miscellaneousness,** mis·sel·lā´ni·us·nes, *n.*—**miscellanist,** mis·sel´la·nist, *n.*—**miscellany,** mis´sel·a·ni, *n.* A mixture of various kinds; a collection of written compositions on various subjects.

mischance, mis·chans´, *n.* Ill luck; misfortune; mishap; misadventure.

mischief, mis´chif, *n.* [O.Fr. *mescheif, meschef,* mischief; from Fr. *mes,* Sp. and Pg. *menos*=L. *minus,* less, and *chef*=L. *caput,* the head. MINOR, CHIEF.] Harm; hurt; injury; damage; evil, whether intended or not; source of vexation, trouble, or annoyance; troublesome or annoying conduct; conduct causing injury; wrong-doing.—**mischief-maker,** *n.* One who makes mischief; one who excites or instigates quarrels or enmity.—**mischief-making,** *a.* Causing harm; exciting enmity or quarrels.—**mischievous,** mis´chi·vus, *a.* Harmful; injurious; fond of mischief; annoying or troublesome in conduct.—**mischievously,** mis´chi·vus·li, *adv.* In a mischievous manner.—**mischievousness,** mis´chi·vus·nes, *n.* The quality of being mischievous.

miscible, mis´i·bl, *a.* [Fr. *miscible,* from L. *misceo,* to mix. MEDDLE.] Capable of being mixed.—**miscibility,** mis·i·bil´i·ti, *n.* State of being miscible.

misconceive, mis·kon·sēv´, *v.t.* or *i.* To receive a false notion or opinion of anything; to misjudge; to have an erroneous understanding of anything.—**misconceiver,** mis·kon·sē´vėr, *n.* One who misconceives.

misconception, mis·kon·sep´shon, *n.* Erroneous conception; false opinion; wrong notion or understanding of a thing.

misconduct, mis·kon´dukt, *n.* Wrong or bad conduct; misbehavior.—*v.t.* (mis-kon-dukt´). To conduct amiss; *refl.* to misbehave.

misconstrue, mis·kon´strö, *v.t.* To construe or interpret erroneously; to take in a wrong sense; to misjudge; to misunderstand.—**misconstruction,** mis·kon·struk´shon, *n.* The act of misconstruing.

miscount, mis·kount´, *v.t.* To count erroneously; to misjudge.—*v.i.* To make a wrong reckoning.—*n.* An erroneous counting or numbering.

miscreant, mis´kri·ant, *n.* [O.Fr. *mescreant*—*mes,* prefix, from L. *minus,* less, and *creant,* believing, from L. *credo,* to believe. MINOR, CREED.]

An infidel, or one who embraces a false faith‡; a vile wretch; a scoundrel; a detestable villain.

miscredit, mis·kred´it, *v.t.* To give no credit or belief to; to disbelieve. (*Carl.*)

miscue, mis·kū´, *v.i.* [From prefix *mis,* and *cue.*] *Dram.* to make a mistake on stage because of a missed signal; to miss one's cue.—*n. Billiards,* a stroke in which the cue fails to hit the ball; a slip; a mistake. (Slang)

misdate, mis·dāt´, *v.t.* To date erroneously.

misdeal, mis·dēl´, *n. Card playing,* a wrong deal; a deal in which each player does not receive his proper cards.—*v.t.* or *i.* To divide cards wrongly or unfairly.

misdeed, mis·dēd´, *n.* An evil deed; a wicked action.

misdeem, mis·dēm´, *v.t.* To judge erroneously; to misjudge; to mistake in judging.

misdemean, mis·di·mēn´, *v.t.* To behave ill; used *refl.*—**misdemeanant,** mis·di·mē´nant, *n.* One who commits a misdemeanor.—**misdemeanor,** mis·di·mē´nėr, *n.* Ill behavior; evil conduct; a fault or transgression; *law,* an offense of a less atrocious nature than a crime.

misdirect, mis·di·rekt´, *v.t.* To give a wrong direction to; to direct into a wrong course; to direct to a wrong person or place.—**misdirection,** mis·di·rek´shon, *n.* A wrong direction.

misdo, mis·dö´, *v.t.* or *i.* To do wrong; to do amiss; to commit a crime or fault.—**misdoer,** mis·dö´ėr, *n.* One who does wrong; one who commits a fault or crime.—**misdoing,** mis·dö´ing, *n.* A wrong done; a fault or crime; an offense.

misdoubt, mis·dout´, *n.* Suspicion of crime or danger.—*v.t.* To suspect of deceit or danger.

misemploy, mis·em·ploi´, *v.t.* To employ to no purpose, or to a bad purpose.

miser, mī´zėr, *n.* [L. *miser,* wretched, akin to *mæstus,* sorrowful, and Gr. *misos,* hatred.] One wretched or afflicted (*Shak.*)‡; a sordid wretch; a niggard; one who in wealth makes himself miserable by the fear of poverty.—**miserly,** mī´zėr·li, *a.* Like a miser in habits; pertaining to a miser; penurious; sordid; niggardly.

miserable, miz´ėr·a·bl, *a.* [Fr. *misérable,* L. *miserabilis,* from *miser,* wretched. MISER.] Very unhappy; suffering misery; wretched; filled with misery; abounding in misery; causing misery; very poor or mean; worthless; despicable.—**miserableness,** miz´ėr·a·bl·nes, *n.* The state or quality of being miserable.—**miserably,** miz´ėr·a·bli, *adv.* In a miserable manner.—**Miserere,** miz·e·rē´re, *n.* The name given to the 50th Psalm in the Vulgate, corresponding to the 51st Psalm in the English version, beginning '*Miserere mei,* Domine' ('Pity me, O Lord'); a piece of music composed to this psalm.—**misery,** miz´ėr·i, *n.* [L. *miseria,* from *miser,* wretched.] Great unhappiness; extreme distress;

wretchedness; calamity; misfortune; cause of misery.

misfeasance, mis·fē′zans, n. [Fr. mes, wrong (L. minus), and faisance, from faire, to do.] Law, a trespass; a wrong done.

misfit, mis·fit′, n. A wrong or bad fit; a bad match,—v.t. To make (a garment, etc.) of a wrong size; to supply with something that does not fit, or is not suitable.

misform, mis·form′, v.t. To make of an ill form.—**misformation,** mis·for·mā′shon, n. An irregularity of formation.

misfortune, mis·for′chun, n. Ill fortune; ill luck; calamity; some accident that prejudicially affects one's condition in life.

misgive, mis·giv′, v.t. To fill with doubt; to deprive of confidence; to fail; usually with 'heart' or 'mind', etc., as subject, and a pronoun as object.—**misgiving,** mis·giv′ing, n. A failing of confidence; doubt; distrust.

misgovern, mis·guv′ern, v.t. To govern ill; to administer unfaithfully.—**misgovernment,** mis·guv′ern·ment, n. The act of misgoverning; bad administration or management of public or private affairs; irregularity in conduct.

misguide, mis·gīd′, v.t. To lead or guide into error; to direct ill; to direct to a wrong purpose or end.—**misguidance,** mis·gī′dans, n. Wrong direction; guidance into error.

mishap, mis·hap′, n. Mischance; evil accident; ill luck; misfortune.

Mishna, mish′na, n. [Heb. shanah, to repeat.] The collection of precepts that constitute the basis of the Talmud.

misinform, mis·in·form′, v.t. To give erroneous information to; to communicate an incorrect statement of facts to.—**misinformation,** mis′in·for·mā′shon, n. Wrong information.

misinterpret, mis·in·tèr′pret , v.t. To interpret erroneously; to understand or explain in a wrong sense.—**misinterpretation,** mis·in·tèr′pre·tā″shon, n. The act of interpreting erroneously.

misjudge, mis·juj′, v.t. To mistake in judging of; to judge erroneously.—v.i. To err in judgment; to form false opinions or notions.—**misjudgment,** mis·juj′ment, n. A wrong or unjust determination.

mislay, mis·lā′, v.t. To lay in a wrong place; to lay wrongly; to lay in a place not recollected.

mislead, mis·lēd′, v.t. To lead astray; to guide into error; to deceive.—**misleading,** mis·lēd′ing, p. and a. Leading astray; leading into error; causing mistake.

mislike, mis·līk′, v.t. To dislike; to disapprove; to have aversion to.

mismanage, mis·man′ij, v.t. To manage ill; to administer improperly.—**mismanagement,** mis·man′ij·ment, n. Ill or improper management.

mismate, mis·māt′, v.t. To mate or match amiss or unsuitably. [Tenn.]

misname, mis·nām′, v.t. To call by the wrong name.

misnomer, mis·nō′mèr, n. [Prefix mis, from Fr. prefix mes, wrong (L. minus, less), and nommer, to name, nom, L. nomen, a name.] A mistaken or inapplicable name or designation; a misapplied term.

misogamist, mi·sog′am·ist, n. [Gr. miseō, to hate, and gamos, marriage.] A hater of marriage.—**misogamy,** mi·sog′a·mi, n. Hatred of marriage.

misogynist, mi·soj′i·nist, n. [Gr. miseō, to hate, and gynē, woman.] A woman-hater.—**misogyny,** mi·soj′i·ni, n. Hatred of the female sex.

mispickel, mis′pik·el, n. [G.] Arsenical pyrites; an ore of arsenic, containing this metal in combination with iron.

misplace, mis·plās′, v.t. To put in a wrong place; to set on an improper object.—**misplacement,** mis·plās′ment, n. The act of misplacing or putting in the wrong place.

misprint, mis·print′, v.t. To mistake in printing; to print wrong.—n. A mistake in printing; a deviation from the copy.

misprision, mis·prizh′on, n. [From Fr. prefix mes (=L. minus, less), and L. prehensio, a taking, from prehendo, to take.] Mistake; misconception; law, any high offense under the degree of capital, but nearly bordering thereon.—Misprision of treason, a bare knowledge and concealment of treason, without assenting to it.

misprize, misprise, mis·prīz′, v.t. [O.Fr. mespriser (Fr. mépriser), to despise—prefix mes, mis=L. minus, less, and priser=L. pretiare, to prize, from pretium, price. PRICE.] To slight or undervalue.

mispronounce, mis·pro·nouns′, v.t. or i. To pronounce erroneously.—**mispronunciation,** mis·pro·nun′si·ā″shon, n. A wrong or improper pronunciation.

misproportion, mis·pro·pōr′shon, v.t. To err in proportioning one thing to another; to join without due proportion.

misquote, mis·kwōt′, v.t. or i. To quote erroneously; to cite incorrectly.—**misquotation,** mis·kwō·tā′shon, n. An erroneous quotation; the act of quoting wrong.

misread, mis·rēd′, v.t. To read amiss; to mistake the sense of.

misreckon, mis·rek′n, v.t. To reckon or compute wrong.

misreport, mis·ri·pōrt′, v.t. To report erroneously; to give an incorrect account of.—n. An erroneous report; a false or incorrect account given.

misrepresent, mis·rep′ri·zent″, v.t. To represent falsely or incorrectly; to give a false or erroneous representation of.—**misrepresentation,** mis·rep′ri·zen·tā″shon, n. The act of misrepresenting; a false or incorrect representation.

misrule, mis·röl′, n. Bad rule; disorder; confusion.—v.t. To rule amiss; to govern badly or oppressively.

miss, mis, n. [Contr. from mistress.] An unmarried female; a young unmarried lady; a girl; a title or

address prefixed to the name of an unmarried female; a kept mistress; a concubine.

miss, mis, v.t. [A.Sax. missan, to miss=D. and G. missen, Icel. missa, Dan. miste, to miss; closely akin to Teut. prefix mis; same root as A.Sax. mithan, to conceal, avoid; G. meiden, to avoid.] To fail in hitting, reaching, obtaining, finding, seeing, and the like; to discover the absence of; to feel or perceive the want of; to mourn the loss of; to omit; to let slip; to pass over.—v.i. To fail to hit or strike what is aimed at.—n. A failure to hit, reach, obtain, etc.; loss; want.—**missing link,** n. A unit or part needed to complete a series; a hypothetical form of animal connecting the anthropoid apes with man.

missal, mis′al, n. [L.L. missale, liber missalis, from missa, the mass. MASS.] The Roman Catholic mass-book or book containing the office of the mass.

missel, missel thrush, mis′el, n. [From its feeding on the mistletoe; comp. G. mistel-drossel, mistletoe thrush.] A common British thrush rather larger than the common thrush.

misshape, mis·shāp′, v.t. To shape ill; to give an ill form to; to deform. —**misshapen,** mis·shā′pn, a. Ill formed; deformed; malformed; distorted.

missile, mis′il, a. [L. missilis, from mitto, missum, to send, to throw. MISSION.] Capable of being thrown or projected from the hand or from any instrument or engine.—n. A weapon or projectile thrown or to be thrown; an unmanned, self-propelled projectile, as a rocket.—**missileman,** n. One who helps to design, build, or operate a guided missile.—**missilery, missilry,** mis′il·rē, n. The science of designing, launching, and controlling guided missiles.

mission, mish′on, n. [L. missio, a sending, from mitto, missum, to send, which enters into a great many English words; as admit, commit, permit, remit, dismiss, remiss, promise, message, mess, etc.] A sending or delegating; duty on which one is sent; a commission; an errand; persons sent by authority to perform any service; particularly, persons sent on some political business or to propagate religion; a station of missionaries; the persons connected with such a station.—**missionary,** mish′on·e·ri, n. One who is sent upon a religious mission; one who is sent to propagate religion.—a. Pertaining to missions.

missive, mis′iv, n. [Fr. missive, a letter, from L. missus, sent. MISSION.] That which is sent; a message; a letter sent.—a. Sent or proceeding from some authoritative or official source; intended to be thrown, hurled, or ejected; missile.

misspell, mis·spel′, v.t. To spell wrong.

misspend, mis·spend′, v.t. To spend amiss, to no purpose, or to a bad one; to waste; to spend for wrong uses.

ch, chain; ch, Sc. loch; g, go; j, job; ng, sing; TH, then; th, thin; w, wig; hw, whig; zh, azure.

misstate, mis·stāt', v.t. To state wrongly; to make an erroneous statement of.

mist, mist, n. [A.Sax. mist, gloom, cloud=L.G., D., and Sw. mist, Icel. mistr, mist; akin G. mist, dung; from root seen in Skr. mih, to sprinkle.] Visible watery vapor suspended in the atmosphere at or near the surface of the earth; aqueous vapor falling in numerous but separately almost imperceptible drops; cloudy matter; something which dims or darkens, and obscures or intercepts vision.—v.t. To cover with mist; to cloud. (Shak.)—v.i. To be misty or drizzling.—**mistily**, mis'ti·li, adv. In a vague or misty manner; obscurely.—**mistiness**, mis'ti·nes, n. The state of being misty.—**misty**, mis'ti, a. Accompanied or characterized by mist; overspread with mist; dim; fig. obscure; not perspicuous.

mistake, mis·tāk', v.t.—pret. mistook, pp. mistaken, ppr. mistaking. To take in error; to select wrongly; to conceive or understand erroneously; to regard otherwise than as the facts warrant; to misjudge; to take for a certain other person or thing; to regard as one when really another.—v.i. To be under a misapprehension or misconception; to be in error.—To be mistaken, to be misunderstood or misapprehended; to make or have made a mistake; to be in error.—n. An error in opinion or judgment; misapprehension; misunderstanding; a slip; a fault; a wrong act done unintentionally.—**mistakable**, mis··tāk'a·bl, a. Capable of being mistaken or misconceived.—**mistaken**, mis··tā'kn, p. and a. Erroneous; incorrect; having made, or laboring under, a mistake; wrong.—**mistakenly**, mis·tā'kn·li, adv. By mistake.

misteach, mis·tēch', v.t. To teach wrongly; to instruct erroneously.

Mister, mis'tėr, n. [See MASTER.] The title of respect for a man, usually abbrev. Mr., prefixed to the name, as Mr. Jones, prefixed also to certain official designations, as Mr. President.

mistime, mis·tīm', v.t. To time wrongly; not to adapt to the time.

mistletoe, mis'l·tō, n. [A.Sax. misteltán, Icel. mistel-teinn; tán, teinn, meaning a twig or sprout; meaning of mistel, doubtful.] A European evergreen plant growing parasitically on trees, with oblong leaves, yellowish-green flowers, and in winter white berries; a similar American plant.

mistral, mis'tral, n. [Pr. from L. magistralis, lit. the master-wind.] A violent cold northwest wind experienced in Southern France.

mistreat, mis·trēt', v.t. To treat amiss; to maltreat.—**mistreatment**, mis·trēt'ment, n. Wrong treatment; abuse.

mistress, mis'tres, n. [O.Fr. maistresse (Fr. maîtresse), fem. corresponding to maistre, L. magister, a master. MASTER.] The female appellation corresponding to master; a woman who is chief or head in a certain sphere; a woman who has

authority, command, ownership, etc.; the female head of some establishment, as a family, school, etc.; a female who is well skilled in anything, or has mastered it; a female sweetheart; a woman filling the place but without the rights of a wife; a concubine; a title of address or term of courtesy pretty nearly equivalent to madam: now applied only to married or matronly women, and written in the abbreviated form Mrs., which is pronounced mis'is, and used before personal names.

mistrust, mis·trust', n. Want of confidence or trust; suspicion.—v.t. To suspect; to doubt; to regard with jealousy or suspicion.—**mistrustful**, mis·trust'ful, a. Suspicious; doubting; wanting confidence.—**mistrustfully**, mis·trust'ful·li, adv. In a mistrustful manner.—**mistrustfulness**, mis·trust'ful·nes, n. The state or quality of being mistrustful.—**mistrustingly**, mis·trust'ing·li, adv. With distrust or suspicion.

misty. See MIST.

misunderstand, mis·un'dėr·stand", v.t. To misconceive; to mistake; to take in a wrong sense.—**misunderstanding**, mis·un'dėr·stand"ing, n. Misconception; mistake of meaning; error; disagreement; dissension.

misuse, mis·ūz', v.t. To treat or use improperly; to use to a bad purpose; to abuse; to maltreat.—n. (mis·ūs'). Improper use; employment in a wrong way or to a bad purpose; abuse; ill-treatment.—**misusage**, mis·ū'zij, n. Ill usage; abuse.—**misuser**, mis·ū'zėr, n. One who misuses.

mite, mīt, n. [A.Sax. mite=D. mijt, L.G. mite, Dan. mide, G. miete—mite; from root seen in Icel. meita, Goth. maita, to cut.] A name common to numerous small, in some cases microscopic, animals, of the class Arachnida (cheese-mite, sugar-mite, itch-mite, etc.).

mite, mīt, n. [D. mijt, a small coin; perhaps lit. something cut small, origin being same as mite, a small insect.] A small coin formerly current; anything proverbially very small; a very little particle or quantity.

miter, **mitre**, mī'tėr, n. [Fr. mitre, L. mitra, from Gr. mitra, headband, turban.] The headdress anciently worn by the inhabitants of Asia Minor; a sort of cap pointed and cleft at the top worn on the head by bishops and archbishops (including the pope), cardinals, and in some instances by abbots, upon solemn occasions, as also by a Jewish high priest.—v.t.—mitered, mitred; mitering, mitring. To adorn with a miter; to raise to a rank which entitles to a miter; to unite or join by a miter joint.—**mitral**, mī'tral, a. Pertaining to a miter; resembling a miter.—**miter joint**, n. Carp. and masonry, a joint connecting two pieces of wood, stone, etc., at right angles, the line of the joint making an acute angle, or an angle of 45° with both pieces.

mithridate, mith'ri·dāt, n. [From

Mithridates, king of Pontus, who was celebrated for his knowledge of poisons and antidotes.] An antidote against poisons.

mitigate, mit'i·gāt, v.t. and i.—mitigated, mitigating. [L. mitigatum, to mitigate, from mitis, mild.] To alleviate or render less painful, rigorous, intense, or severe; to assuage, lessen, abate, moderate.—**mitigable**, mit'i·ga·bl, a.—**mitigant**, mit'i·gant, a.—**mitigation**, mit'i·gā'shon, n.—**mitigative**, mit'i·gā·tiv, a.—**mitigator**, mit'i·gā'tėr, n.—**mitigatory**, mit'i·ge·to·ri, a.

mitosis, mī·tō'sis, n. [Gr. mitos, thread.] Ordinary cell division resulting when the chromatin of the nucleus forms into a threadlike segment (chromosomes), which gradually develops, then divides longitudinally into two parts, each having a set of chromosomes similar to that of the original cell.

mitrailleuse, me·trä·yėz', n. [Fr. mitraille, small missiles, case shot, as in mite.] A breech-loading machine gun discharging small missiles at one time or in quick succession.

mitten, mit'n, n. [Fr. mitaine, from G. mitte, the middle, O.H.G. mittamo, half, the mitten being a kind of half or half-divided glove (akin mid).] A covering for the hand, differing from a glove in not having a separate cover for each finger, the thumb only being separate.—To handle without mittens, to treat roughly.—**mitt**, mit, n. [Abbrev. of mitten.] A mitten; also a covering for the hand and wrist only, and not for the fingers. In baseball, a glove, heavily padded on the palm side.

mittimus, mit'i·mus, n. [L., we send.] Law, a warrant of commitment to prison; a writ for removing records from one court to another.

mix, miks, v.t. [A.Sax. miscan; cog. L. misceo, mixtum (MEDLEY, MEDDLE), Gr. mignymi, misgō, to mix.] To unite or blend promiscuously, as various ingredients, into one mass or compound; to mingle; to blend; to join; to associate; to unite with in company; to produce by blending different ingredients.—v.i. To become united or blended promiscuously in a mass or compound; to be joined or associated: to mingle.—n. The act of mixing; a mixture.—**mixer**, mik'sėr, n.—**mixed number**, n. Math. the sum of a whole number and a fraction, as 2½.—**mix-up**, miks'-up, n. A confused state of affairs; a tangle; a fight. (Colloq.).

mixture, miks'tūr, n. [L. mixtura, from misceo, to mix. MIX.] The act of mixing, or state of being mixed; a mass or compound, consisting of different ingredients blended without order; a liquid medicine formed by mixing several ingredients together.

mizzen, **mizen**, miz'n, n. [Fr. misaine, from It. mezzana, mizzen, from mezzano, middle, from mezzo, middle: originally a large lateen sail on a middle mast. MEZZO, MEDIAL.] Naut. a fore-and-aft sail on the mast of a ship or barque next the stern; called also Spanker.—a. Naut.

belonging to the mizzen: applied to the mast supporting the mizzen, and the rigging and shrouds connected with it.

mizzle, miz′l, *v.i.* [For *mistle, misle,* a dim. and freq. from *mist.*] To rain in very fine drops; to drizzle.

mnemonics, ni·mon′iks, *n.* [Gr. *mnēmonikos,* pertaining to memory, from *mnēmōn,* mindful, *mnaomai,* to remember; same root as in E. *mind.*] The art of improving the memory. —**mnemonic,** ni·mon′ik, *a.* Pertaining to mnemonics; assisting or training the memory.

moa, mō′a, *n.* [Maori.] Any of the various extinct New Zealand birds of the family Dinornithidae.

moan, mōn, *v.i.* [O.E. *mone, moone,* etc., A.Sax. *maenan,* to moan.] To utter a low dull sound under the influence of grief or pain; to make lamentations; to utter a groan.—*v.t.* To bemoan or lament.—*n.* A low dull sound due to grief or pain; any sound that resembles a moan.

moat, mōt, *n.* [Fr. *mote,* L.L. *mota,* the mound of earth dug from a trench, a hill or mound on which a castle was built; origin unknown.] A ditch or deep trench round the rampart of a castle or other fortified place to serve as a defense, often filled with water.—*v.t.* To surround with a ditch for defense.

mob, mob, *n.* [Abbreviated from L. *mobile vulgus,* the fickle crowd, from *mobilis,* movable, fickle, from *moveo,* to move. MOVE, VULGAR.] A crowd; a promiscuous multitude of people, rude and disorderly; a rabble; a riotous assembly. — *v.t.* — *mobbed, mobbing.* To crowd round and annoy. —**mobbish,** mob′ish, *a.* Pertaining to a mob; tumultuous.—**mobocracy,** mob·ok′ra·si, *n.* [Mob, and Gr. *kratos,* power.] The rule or ascendancy of the mob.

mob, mob, *n.* [Comp. D. *mop,* a pug-dog, *mopmuts,* a mobcap.] A mobcap.—**mobcap,** *n.* A plain cap for females.

mobile, mō′bil, *a.* [Fr. *mobile,* L. *mobilis,* fickle, mobile, movable, from *moveo,* to move. MOVE.] Capable of being easily moved; readily liable to change (*mobile* features); changeable; fickle; readily adaptable.—*n.* mō′bēl. A sculpture of movable parts of wire, paper, etc., which can be set in motion by a current of air.—**mobilize,** mōb′il·iz, *v.t.*— *mobilized, mobilizing. Milit.* to put in a state of readiness for active service.—*v.i.* To be assembled for war.—**mobilization,** mob′il·i·zā″shon, *n.*—**mobility,** mō·bil′i·ti, *n.*

moccasin, mok′a·sin, *n.* [Spelled *mawcahsuns* in old glossary of North American Indian words.] A kind of shoe made of deerskin or other soft leather, without a stiff sole, worn by the North American Indians; a venomous snake, genus *Agkistrodon,* found in North America.

mocha, mō′kä, *n.* [From the seaport, *Mocha,* in Yemen, Arabia.] A choice variety of coffee; coffee flavoring; a fine glove leather.

mock, mok, *v.t.* [Fr. *moquer,* in se

moquer, to mock, flout; origin doubtful; comp. It. *mocca,* a grimace; also Gr. *mōkos,* mockery.] To imitate or mimic; to deride or flout; to ridicule; to fool, tantalize, disappoint, deceive; to set at naught; to defy.—*v.i.* To use ridicule; to gibe or jeer.—*n.* An object of scorn; an act of ridicule; something jeered at.—*a.* False; counterfeit; assumed: often in compounds.—**mocker,** mok′ér, *n.*— **mockery,** mok′ér·i, *n.* The act of mocking; derision; ridicule; sportive insult; sport; subject of laughter; imitation; counterfeit appearance; false show; vain effort.—**mock-heroic,** *a.* Burlesquing the heroic in poetry, action, character, etc.— **mockingly,** mok′ing·li, *adv.*—**mockingbird,** *n.* An American bird of the thrush family remarkable for its wonderful faculty of imitating sounds. —**mock orange,** *n.* A common shrub with creamy white flowers having an odor which at a distance resembles that of orange flowers; the syringa. —**mock turtle,** *n.* A soup prepared from calf's head, in imitation of real turtle soup.—**mock-up,** mok′up, *n.* [From *mock,* imitate, and *up.*] A structural model, built to scale in cardboard, canvas, paper, etc., for use in testing and in study (a *mock-up* of a rocket).

mode, mōd, *n.* [Fr. *mode,* from L. *modus,* mode, manner, measure, etc.: same root as *mete.* Akin are *modify, modest, moderate; mood* (in gram.) is same word.] Manner; method; way (of speaking, acting, etc.); fashion; custom; *the mode,* the prevailing fashion or style; *gram.* and *logic,* same as *mood; mus.* a species of scale of which modern musicians recognize only two, the *major* and the *minor, modes.* MAJOR, MINOR.— **modal,** mō′dal, *a.* Relating to a mode or mood; pertaining to the mode, manner, or form, not to the essence. —*Modal proposition,* in *logic,* one which affirms or denies with a qualification or limitation.—**modality,** mō·dal′i·ti, *n.* The quality of being modal; *philos.* that quality of propositions in respect of which they express possibility or impossibility, existence or non-existence, necessity or contingency.—**modally,** mō′dal·li, *adv.* In a manner or relation expressing or indicating a mode.

model, mod′el, *n.* [Fr. *modèle,* O.Fr. *modelle,* from It. *modello,* a model, lit. 'a little measure', dim. from L. *modus,* measure. MODE.] A pattern of something to be made; a form in miniature of something to be made on a larger scale; a copy, in miniature, of something already made or existing; an image, copy, facsimile; standard; that by which a thing is to be measured; anything serving or worthy of serving as a pattern; an example; a person, male or female, from whom a painter or sculptor studies his proportions, details, postures, etc.—*v.t.*—*modeled, modelled, modeling, modelling.* To plan or form after some model; to form in order to serve as a model; to mold; to shape.—*v.i.* To make

a model; *sculp.* to form a work of some plastic material, as clay.— **modeler, modeller,** mod′el·ér, *n.* One who models in clay, wax, etc.

moderate, mod′ér·āt, *v.t.*—*moderated, moderating.* [L. *modero* and *moderor, moderatus,* to limit, moderate, from *modus,* a measure. MODE.] To restrain from excess of any kind; to reduce in intensity (rage, passion, desire, joy, etc.); to qualify; to temper; to lessen; to allay.—*v.i.* To become less violent or intense; to preside as a moderator.—*To moderate in a call,* in Presbyterian churches, to preside at a meeting at which a call is addressed to a minister.—*a.* [L. *moderatus.*] Applied to persons, not going to extremes; temperate in opinions or views; applied to things, not extreme or excessive; not very great; mediocre.—*n.* A member of a party in the Church of Scotland which claimed the character of moderation in doctrine, discipline, and church government.—**moderately,** mod′ér·it·li, *adv.* In a moderate manner or degree; not excessively.— **moderateness,** mod′ér·it·nes, *n.* State of being moderate.—**moderation,** mod′ér·ā′shon, *n.* [L. *moderatio.*] The act of moderating, tempering, or repressing; the state or quality of being moderate; the keeping of a due mean between extremes; freedom from excess; due restraint; the act of presiding as a moderator. *Moderations,* at Oxford University, the first public examination for degrees.—**moderator,** mod′ér·ā·tér, *n.* One who or that which moderates or restrains; the person who presides at a meeting or discussion: now chiefly applied to the chairman of meetings or courts in Presbyterian churches; substance, such as graphite, etc., used to slow down neutrons in a nuclear reactor.—**moderatorship,** mod′ér·ā·tér·ship, *n.*

moderato, mod·er·ä′tō, *a.* [It.] *Mus.* moderate; used as a direction indicating *moderate* time.

modern, mod′érn, *a.* [Fr. *moderne,* from L.L. *modernus,* modern, belonging to the present mode, from L. *modus,* mode, manner. MODE.] Pertaining to the present time, or time not long past; recent; not ancient.—*n.* A person of modern times: opposed to *ancient.*—**modernism,** mod′érn·izm, *n.* The state of being modern; deviation from ancient manner, practice, or mode of expression, notably in literature and the arts; a tendency in churches toward rationalistic interpretation of doctrine.—**modernist,** mod′érn·ist, *n.* One who admires what is modern. —**modernistic,** mod·érn·is′tic, *a.* Having modern appearance or characteristics.—**modernize,** mod′érn·īz, *v.t.*—*modernized, modernizing.* To give a modern character to; to adapt to modern times; to cause to conform to modern ideas or style.— **modernizer,** mod′érn·i·zér, *n.* One who renders modern or modernizes. —**modernization,** mod′érn·i·zā″shon, *n.* The act of modernizing; what is produced by modernizing.

ch, *ch*ain; ch, Sc. lo*ch*; g, *g*o; j, *j*ob; ng, si*ng*; TH, *th*en; th, *th*in; w, *w*ig; hw, *wh*ig; zh, a*z*ure.

modest, mod′est, a. [Fr. modeste, L. modestus, from modus, a limit. MODE.] Restrained by a sense of propriety; not forward or bold; unpretending; bashful; diffident; free from anything suggestive of sexual impurity; pure; moderate; not excessive, extreme, or extravagant.— **modestly,** mod′est·li, adv. In a modest manner; with modesty; diffidently; bashfully; not wantonly; not excessively.—**modesty,** mod′es·ti, n. [L. modestia.] The state or quality of being modest; absence of tendency to forwardness, pretense, or presumption; bashful reserve; absence of anything suggestive of sexual impurity; chastity; moderation; freedom from excess.

modicum, mod′i·kum, n. [L., a small or moderate quantity, from modicus, moderate, from modus, measure. MODE.] A little; a small quantity; a scanty allowance or allotment.

modify, mod′i·fī, v.t.—modified, modifying. [Fr. modifier, from L. modifico—modus, limit, manner, and facio, to make. MODE, FACT.] To change the external qualities of; to give a new form or external character to; to vary; to alter in some respect.— **modifier,** mod′i·fī·ėr, n. One who or that which modifies.—**modifiable,** mod′i·fī·a·bl, a. Capable of being modified.—**modification,** mod′i·fi·kā″shon, n. The act of modifying; the state of being modified; some alteration in form, appearance, or character; a particular form or manner of being; a mode.—**modificatory,** mod′i·fi·kā·to·ri, a. Tending to modify or produce change.

modillion, mō·dil′yon, n. [Fr. modillon, from L. modulus, a model, dim. of modus, a measure. MODE.] Arch. a block carved into the form of an enriched bracket used in cornices of buildings.

modish, mōd′ish, a. [From mode.] According to the mode or fashion; affectedly fashionable.—**modishly,** mōd′ish·li, adv. In a modish manner. —**modishness,** mod′ish·nes, n. The quality of being modish; affectation of the fashion.—**modiste,** mō·dēst′, n. [Fr. modiste, a milliner, from mode, fashion.] A female who deals in articles of ladies' dress; particularly, a milliner or dressmaker.

modulate, mod′ū·lāt, v.t.—modulated, modulating. [L. modulor, modulatus, from modus, limit, measure, mode. MODE.] To proportion; to adjust; to vary or inflect the sound of in such a manner as to give expressiveness to what is uttered; to vary (the voice) in tone; music, to change the key or mode of in the course of composition; to transfer from one key to another.—v.i. Music, to pass from one key into another.— **modulation,** mod·ū·lā′shon, n. The act of modulating; adjustment; the act of inflecting the voice or any instrument musically; melodious sound; music, the change from one scale or mode to another in the course of a composition.—**modulator,** mod′ū·lā·tėr, n. One who, or

that which modulates; in the tonic sol-fa system of music, a sort of map of musical sounds representing the relative intervals of the notes of a scale, its chromatics, and its more closely related scales.

module, mod′ūl, n. [Fr., from L. modulus, dim. of modus, a measure. MODE.] Arch. a measure taken to regulate the proportions of an order or the disposition of the whole building.—**modulus,** mod′ū·lus, n. pl. **moduli,** Math. and physics. a term for some constant multiplier or quantity required to be used in certain calculations.—Modulus of elasticity, the quotient of a stress (in units of force per unit area) by the resulting strain.—**modular,** mod′ū·lėr, a. Pertaining to a module or modulus.—**modus,** mō′dus, n. Mode, manner, or method; law, a fixed payment by way of tithe.— Modus vivendi, lit. way of living; a temporary arrangement between parties pending the final settlement of matters in dispute.

mogul, moghul, mō·gul′, n. [From Ar. and Per. Mughul, Mongol.] One of the Mongolian conquerors of India; a person prominent in a particular field or business.

mohair, mō′hâr, n. [From Ar. mokhayyar, a kind of camlet or haircloth = Fr. moire.] The hair of the Angora goat; cloth made of this hair; camlet; a wool-and-cotton cloth made in imitation of real mohair.

Mohammedan, mō·ham′med·an, a. Pertaining to Mohammed, or the religion founded by him.—n. A follower of Mohammed; one who professes Mohammedanism.—**Mohammedanism,** mō·ham′med·an·izm, n. The religion of Mohammed, contained in the Koran.

Mohawk, mō′hak, n. A tribe of North American Indians in what is now New York State, one of the Five Nations confederacy; a member of the tribe; the language of the tribe.

mohole, mō′hōl, n. [From moho, or Mohorovicic discontinuity.] A projected hole to the line (moho) between the earth's crust and mantle.

moiety, moi′e·ti, n. [Fr. moitié, from L. medietas, from medius, middle. MEDIAL.] The half; one of two equal parts; a portion or share in general.

moil, moil, v.i. [From O.Fr. moiller, Fr. mouiller, to wet, to soften, from L. mollis, soft. MOLLIFY.] To labor; to toil; to work with painful efforts.

moire, mwär, mōr, n. [Fr. from E. mohair.] A watered mohair or other textile fabric.

moiré, mwä·rā′, mōr′ā, a. [Fr. pp. of moirer, to water.] Watered; having a watered appearance, as silk, etc. —n. A wavelike design on fabrics or metallic surfaces.

moist, moist, a. [O.Fr. moiste, from L. musteus, fresh.] Moderately wet; damp; not dry; humid.—**moisten,** mois′n, v.t. To make moist or damp. —v.i. To become moist.—**moisture,** mois′chėr, n. Diffused wetness.

molar, mō′lėr, a. [L. molaris, from mola, a mill; same root as meal.

MILL.] Serving to bruise or grind the food in eating; grinding.—n. A grinding tooth; a tooth having a flattened, triturating surface.

molar, mō′lėr, a. [L. moles, a mass.] Pertaining to a mass as a whole.

molasses, mō·las′ez, n. [Also melasses, a better spelling, being from Fr. mélasse, Sp. melaza, L. mellaceus, resembling honey, from mel, mellis, honey.] The uncrystallized sirup produced from sugar in the process of making.

mold, mōld, n. [A.Sax. molde, mold, earth, from root seen in Goth. malan.] Fine, soft earth; dust from incipient decay.—**molder,** mōl′der, v.i. To turn to dust by natural decay.—v.t. To cause to molder.

mold, mōld, n. [M.E. moul, perhaps confused with mold, earth.] A minute fungus, indicative of decay, appearing as a furry growth or film on animal and vegetable tissues, especially where exposed to dampness; a film of fungoid growth.—v.t. To cause to contract mold.—v.i. To become moldy.—**moldiness,** mōl′di·nes, n.—**moldy,** mōl′di, a.

mold, mōld, n. [Fr. modle, from L. modulus, dim. of modus, a measure. MODE.] The matrix in which anything is cast and receives its form; a hollow tool for producing a form by percussion or compression; cast; form; shape; character.—v.t. To form into a particular shape; to shape; to model; to fashion.— **moldboard,** n. The curved board or metal plate in a plow, which serves to turn over the furrow.— **molder,** mōl′dėr, n.—**molding,** mōl′ding, n. Something cast in a mold; arch. a general term applied to the varieties of outline or contour given to cornices, bases, door or window jambs, lintels, etc.

molder, mōl′dėr, v.i. [From mold, earth, mustiness; lit. to turn to mold.] To turn to dust by natural decay; to waste away by a gradual separation of the component particles; to crumble; to perish.

moldwarp, mōld′wärp, n. The mole.

mole, mōl, n. [Same word as mold, earth, being abbreviated from the fuller name moldwarp, mouldwarp, lit. earth-caster, from mold, and warp, to cast.] An insectivorous animal which forms burrows just under the surface of the ground, throwing up the excavated soil into little hills; a kind of plow for making drains.—**molehill,** n. A heap of earth thrown up by a mole; something insignificant as contrasted with something important.—**moleskin,** mōl′skin, n. A strong twilled fustian or cotton cloth, so called from its being soft like the skin of a mole.

mole, mōl, n. [A.Sax. mál, a blot, a spot=O.D. mael, Dan. maal, G. mal, a spot; cog. L. macula, a spot.] A spot, or small discolored protuberance on the human body.

mole, mōl, n. [Fr., from L. moles, a mass, a dam, a mole; same root as magnus, great.] A mound or breakwater formed so as to partially enclose a harbor or anchorage, and protect it from the waves.

molecule, mol'e·kūl, n. [Fr. *molécule*, dim. of L. *moles*, a mass. MOLE.] The smallest unit of matter capable of existing independently while retaining its chemical properties.—**molecular,** mo·lek'ū·lėr, a. Pertaining to, or consisting of, molecules.— *Molecular attraction*, that force which acts between the molecules or particles of a body, keeping them together in one mass. It is distinct from gravitational attraction and is of much greater magnitude.—**molecular weight,** n. The weight of any molecule, obtained by adding the weights of the atoms it contains.

molest, mo·lest', v.t. [Fr. *molester*, from L. *molestus*, troublesome, from *moles*, trouble, a great mass. MOLECULE.] To annoy; to disturb; to vex. —**molestation,** mol·es·tā'shon, n. The act of molesting; disturbance; annoyance.

moll, mol, n. [Probably from *Moll*, a nickname for Mary.] A gangster's girl friend; a wench; a prostitute.

mollify, mol'i·fī, v.t.—*mollified, mollifying.* [O.Fr. *mollifier,* L. *mollificare*—*mollis*, soft, and *facio*, to make. MEAL, MELLOW.] To assuage, as pain or irritation; to pacify; to reduce in harshness; to tone down.— **mollification,** mol'i·fi·kā"shon, n. The act of mollifying; mitigation; pacification.—**mollities,** mol·lish'i·ēz, n. [L., softness.] *Med.* diseased softening of an organ.

mollusk, mol'usk, n. [Fr. *mollusque*, from N.L. *mollusca*, soft, from *mollis*, soft.] One of a large phylum of invertebrates including the snails, mussels, bivalves, cuttlefish, etc., having usually a calcareous shell protecting a soft, unsegmented body, gills, and a muscular foot for digging and creeping.—**molluscan,** mol·lus'kan, n.—**molluscous,** mol·lus'kus, a. —**molluscoid,** mol·lus'koid, n.

mollycoddle, mol'i·kod·l, n. [From *Molly*, as general name for a female, and *coddle*.] An effeminate person. (*Slang*.)

Moloch, mō'lok, n. [Heb. *molech*, king.] The chief god of the Phoenicians and of the Ammonites, whose worship consisted chiefly of human sacrifices, ordeals by fire, mutilation, etc.; a genus of lizards of repulsive appearance found in Australia.

molt, mōlt, v.i. [O.E. *moute, mowte* (the *l* having intruded as in *could*), like D. *muiten*, O.L.G. *muton*, from L. *muto, mutare*, to change. MEW.] To shed or cast the feathers, hair, skin, horns, etc., as birds and other animals do; most commonly used of birds, but also of crabs, serpents, etc. —v.t. To shed or cast, as feathers, hair, skin, etc.—The act of molting; the shedding or changing of feathers.

molten, mōl'tn, p. and a. Melted.

molto, mōl'tō, adv. [It. from L. *multum*, much.] *Mus.* much; very: used in directions.

moly, mō'li, n. [Gr. *mōly*.] A fabulous herb of magic power spoken of by Homer.

molybdenum, mol·ib'dē·num, n. [N.L. from L. *molybdaena*, from Gr. *molybdaina*, galena (lead ore).] A whitish metallic element mainly used in alloy steel. Symbol, Mo; at. no., 42; at. wt., 95.94.—**molybdic,** mo·lib'dik, a.

moment, mō'ment, n. [L. *momentum*, movement, impulse, brief space of time, importance, contr. for *movimentum*, from *moveo*, to move. MOVE.] A minute portion of time; an instant; importance; consequence. In *phys*. the moment (or importance) of a force round a point is the product of the magnitude of the force into the perpendicular distance of the point from its line of action.— *The moment of a couple* is the product of either force into the arm.—*The moment of a magnet* is the strength of either pole multiplied by the distance between the poles.—*Moment of inertia*, of a body or system of bodies round an axis, is the sum of the products of each small element of mass by the square of its distance from the axis; similarly with reference to a point and a plane.— *Momentum*, the product of a moving mass into its velocity.—**momentarily,** mō'men·te·ri·li, adv. Every moment; from moment to moment.— **momentary,** mō'men·ta·ri, a. Lasting but a moment or a very short time; fleeting.—**momently,** mō'ment·li, adv. From moment to moment; every moment.—**momentous,** mō·men'tus, a. Of moment or importance; weighty; of great consequence.—**momentously,** mō·men'tus·li, adv. Weightily; importantly.— **momentum,** mō·men'tum, n. The force possessed by a body in motion; the product of the mass and velocity of a body; impetus.

Momus, mō'mus, n. [Gr. *mōmos*, derision.] *Greek myth.* the god of raillery and ridicule.

monachal, mon'a·kal, a. [L. *monachus*, Gr. *monachos*, a monk, from *monos*, alone. MONK.] Pertaining to monks or a monastic life; monastic. —**monachism,** mon'ak·izm, n. [Fr. *monachisme*.] The monastic life or system; monkery; monkishness.

monad, mon'ad, n. [Gr. *monas, monados*, unity, from *monos*, alone.] An ultimate atom or simple substance without parts; *zool*. a microscopical organism of an extremely simple character developed in organic infusions; *chem*. a univalent element, such as hydrogen, chlorine, etc.; an imaginary entity in the philosophy of Leibnitz.—**monadic, monadical,** mo·nad'ik, mo·nad'i·kal, a. Having the nature or character of a monad.

monadelph, mon'a·delf, n. [Gr. *monos*, sole, and *adelphos*, brother.] *Bot.* a plant whose stamens are united in one body by the filaments; *zool.* a mammal in which the uterus is single.—**monadelphous,** mon·a·del'fus, a. Belonging to the monadelphs.

monander, mon·an'dėr, n. [Gr. *monos*, single, and *anēr, andros*, a male.] *Bot.* a monoclinous plant having one stamen only.—**monandrous,** mon·an'drus, a. *Bot.* monoclinous, and having one stamen only.—

monandry, mon·an'ri, n. Marriage to one husband only: as opposed to *polyandry*.

monanthous, mon·an'thus, a. [Gr. *monos*, single, *anthos*, flower.] *Bot.* producing but one flower.

monarch, mon'ėrk, n. [L. *monarcha*, from Gr. *monarchēs*, a monarch, *monarchos*, ruling alone—*monos*, alone, and *archē*, rule.] A sole ruler; the hereditary ruler of a state; a sovereign, as an emperor, king, queen, prince, etc.; one who is superior to others of the same kind (an oak is called the *monarch* of the forest).—**monarchal,** mon·är'kal, a. Pertaining to a monarch; sovereign. —**monarchic, monarchical,** mon·är'kik, mon·är'ki·kal, a. Vested in a monarch or single ruler; pertaining to a monarchy.—**monarchically,** mon·är'ki·kal·li, adv. In a monarchical manner.—**monarchism,** mon'ėrk·izm, n. The principles of monarchy; love or preference of monarchy.—**monarchist,** mon'ėrk·ist, n. An advocate of monarchy.—**monarchy,** mon'ėr·ky, n. [Gr. *monarchia*.] A state or country in which the supreme power is either actually or nominally lodged in the hands of a single person; the system of government in which the supreme power is vested in a single person; the territory ruled by a monarch; a kingdom; an empire.

monastery, mon'as·tėr·i, n. [L.L. *monasterium*, from Gr. *monastērion*, from *monastēs*, a solitary, *monazō*, to be alone, from *monos*, alone, sole.] A house of religious retirement, or of seclusion from ordinary temporal concerns, whether an abbey, a priory, a nunnery, or convent; usually applied to the houses for monks.— **monasterial,** mon·as·tē'ri·al. a. Pertaining to a monastery.—**monastic, monastical,** mon·as'tik, mon·as'ti·kal, a. [Gr. *monastikos*.] Pertaining to monasteries; pertaining to religious or other seclusion.—**monastic,** n. A member of a monastery; a monk.—**monastically,** mon·as'ti·kal·li, adv. In a monastic manner; reclusely.—**monasticism,** mon·as'ti·sizm, n. Monastic life; the monastic system or condition.

monatomic, mon·a·tom'ik, a. *Chem.* said of an element the molecule of which contains only one atom; in older use＝univalent.

monaural. See MONOPHONIC.

Monday, mun'dā, n. [A.Sax. *mónandaeg*—*mónan*, genit. of *móna*, the moon, and *daeg*, day.] The second day of the week.

monetary, mon'e·te·ri, a. [L. *moneta*, money. MONEY.] Pertaining to money or consisting in money.— *Monetary unit*, the standard of currency.—**monetize,** mon'e·tīz, v.t. To form into coin or money.—**monetization,** mon'et·i·zā"shon, n. The act of monetizing.

money, mun'i, n. pl. **moneys** or **monies,** mun'iz. [O.Fr. *moneie, monnoie,* Fr. *monnaie,* from L. *moneta*, the mint, money, originally a surname of Juno (lit. the warner or admonisher, from *moneo*, to admonish), in whose temple at Rome money was coined; whence also *mint.* MONITION.] Coin; gold, silver, or other metal, stamped by public authority and used as the medium of exchange; in a wider sense, any equivalent for commodities, and for which individuals readily exchange their goods or services; a circulating medium; wealth; affluence (a man of *money*); The plural is used in the sense of sums of money or denominations of money.—*A money of account*, a denomination used merely for convenience in keeping accounts, and not represented by any coin.—*To make money*, to gain money; to be in the way of becoming rich.—*Paper money*, bank notes, bills, etc., representing value and passing current as so.—**moneyed**, mun´id, *a.* Rich.—**money-making**, *n.* The process of accumulating money.—*a.* Lucrative; profitable.—**money order**, *n.* An order granted upon payment of a sum and a small commission, by one post office or express or telegraph company, and payable at another.

monger, mung´gėr, *n.* [A.Sax. *mangere*, a dealer, from *mangian*, to traffic; perhaps from L. *mango*, dealer.] A trader; a dealer: now only or chiefly in compounds.

Mongol, Mongolian, mon´gol, mongō´li·an, *n.* [*Mongol*, Mongol, from MOGUL.] A native of Mongolia.—*a.* Belonging to Mongolia; one of the great divisions of the human family, having a thick fold of skin over the inner eye, high cheek bones, and straight black hair.—**mongolism**, mon´gol·ism, *n.* A congenital idiocy of unknown cause, producing a broad, flattened skull and slanting eyes.

mongoose, mon´gös, *n.* [East Indian name.] An Indian mammal, quick-eyed and agile, having a long, thick tail, and feeding on snakes, rats, etc.

mongrel, mung´grel, *a.* [From A. Sax. *mang*, mixture, with dim. suffix as in *cockerel*; akin *mingle*, *among*.] Of a mixed breed; of mingled origins; hybrid.—*n.* A cross between two plants or animals, (breeds, races). Usually fertile, e.g. crosses between varieties of apple or breeds of sheep. Cp. HYBRID.

moniker, monicker, mon´i·kėr, *n.* [Origin unknown.] A name or nickname.

moniliform, mō·nil´i·form, *a.* [L. *monile*, a necklace.] Like a necklace; like a series or string of beads: used especially in natural history.

monism, mon´izm, *n.* [Gr. *monos*, alone, single.] The doctrine which holds that in the universe there is only a single element or principle from which everything is developed, this single principle being either mind (*idealistic monism*) or matter (*materialistic monism*).—**monistic**, mon·is´tik, *a.* Pertaining to monism; pertaining to or derived from a single source.

monition, mo·nish´on, *n.* [L. *monitio, monitionis*, from *moneo*, to admon-

ish (hence *moneta*, E. *money*); root in *monstrum*, a monster, *monstrare*, to show (*demonstrate*); *mens*, mind (whence *mental*), E. *mind*.] Admonition; warning; advice by way of caution; indication; intimation.—**monitor**, mon´i·tėr, *n.* One who admonishes or warns of faults and informs of duty; an admonisher; a senior pupil in a school appointed to instruct and look after juniors; a genus of large lizards; something used for monitoring, especially a receiver used to view or pick up what is transmitted; a name for a class of shallow, heavily armed, iron-clad steam vessels sunk deeply in the water: so called from the name of the first vessel of the kind.—*v.t. and i.* To tap on to a transmitter of a telephone, television, etc., to be certain it operates properly, without interfering with the transmission; to watch or check for a particular purpose; to keep track of.—**monitory**, mon´i·to·ri, *a.* Giving admonition; admonitory.—**monitress**, mon´i·tres, *n.* A female monitor.

monk, mungk, *n.* [A.Sax. *monec, munec*, from L.L. *monachus*, Gr. *monachos*, one who lives alone, from *monos*, alone.] One of a community of males inhabiting a monastery, and bound by vows to celibacy and religious exercises.—**monkhood**, mungk´hud, *n.* Character or condition of a monk.—**monkish**, mungk-ish, *a.* Like a monk, or pertaining to monks; monastic.—**monkishness**, mungk´ish·nes, *n.* The quality of being monkish.

monkey, mung´ki, *n.* [O.Fr. *monne*, a monkey, It. *monna*, a female ape, properly dame, mistress, a contr. of *madonna*, the term -*key* being diminutive, as in *donkey*.] A name used in its wider sense to include all the quadrumana except the lemurs and their allies; but in a more restricted sense designating the long-tailed members of the order as distinguished from the apes and baboons; a term applied to a boy or girl either in real or pretended disapproval; a pile-driving apparatus: a sort of powerhammer; a comical person.—**monkey bread**, *n.* BAOBAB.—**monkey jacket**, *n.* A close-fitting jacket, generally of some stout material.—**monkeypot**, *n.* The fruit of a gigantic Brazilian tree consisting of a capsule furnished with a lid, containing nuts of which monkeys are fond.—**monkey wrench**, *n.* A screw key with a movable jaw, which can be adjusted by a screw.

monobasic, mon·o·bās´ik, *a.* [Gr. *monos*, single, and *basis*, a base.] *Chem.* having only one hydrogen atom replaceable by a basic atom or radical, said of acids.

monocarp, mon´o·kärp, *n.* [Gr. *monos*, single, and *karpos*, fruit.] *Bot.* a plant that perishes after having once borne fruit; an annual plant.—**monocarpous, monocarpic**, mon·o·kär´pus, mon·o·kär´pik, *a. Bot.* a term applied to annual plants.

monochord, mon´o·kord, *n.* [Gr. *monos*, sole, and *chordē*, a chord.]

Mus. a single string stretched across a soundboard, and having under it a movable bridge, used to show the lengths of string required to produce the notes of the scale, etc.

monochromatic, mon´o·krō·mat˝-ik, *a.* [Gr. *monos*, sole, and *chrōma*, color.] Consisting of one color, or presenting rays of light of one color only.—**monochrome**, mon´o·krōm, *n.* A painting in one color, but relieved by light and shade.

monocle, mon´o·kl, *n.* [MONOCULAR.] A single eyeglass.

monoclinal, mon·o·klī´nal, *a.* [Gr. *monos*, single, and *klinō*, to bend.] *Geol.* applied to strata that dip for an indefinite length in one direction.—**monoclinic**, mon·o·klin´ik, *a. Mineral.* having three unequal axes, two intersecting at an oblique angle, and cut by the third at right angles.—**monoclinous**, mon·ok´li·nus, *a. Bot.* having both stamens and pistils in the same flower; *geol.* monoclinal.

monocotyledon, mon´ö·kot·i·lē˝don, *n.* A plant with one cotyledon only; a monocotyledonous plant.—**monocotyledonous**, mon´o·kot·i·lē˝do·nus, *a. Bot.* Having only one seed lobe or cotyledon, as endogenous plants have.

monocracy, mon·ok´ra·si, *n.* [Gr. *monos*, sole, and *kratos*, rule.] Government or rule by a single person; autocracy.—**monocrat**, mon´o·krat, *n.* One who governs alone.

monocular, mon·ok´ū·lėr, *a.* [Gr. *monos*, sole, and L. *oculus*, an eye.] Having one eye only; adapted to be used with one eye only, a *monocular* microscope.

monodactylous, mon·o·dak´til·us, *a.* [Gr. *monos*, single, and *daktylos*, finger.] Having one finger or toe only.

monodrama, mon´o·drä·ma, *n.* [Gr. *monos*, single, and *drama*, a drama.] A dramatic performance by a single person.

monody, mon´o·di, *n.* [Gr. *monōdia*—*monos*, single, and *ōdē*, a song.] A mournful kind of song, in which a single mourner is supposed to give vent to his grief.—**monodical**, mon·od´i·kal, *a.* Pertaining to a monody.—**monodist**, mon´od·ist, *n.* One who writes or sings a monody.

monoecious, mo·nē´shus, *a.* [Gr. *monos*, one, and *oikos*, a house.] *Bot.* having male and female flowers on the same plant; *zool.* having male and female organs of reproduction in the same individual.

monogamic, mon·o·gam´ik, *a.* [Gr. *monos*, sole, and *gamos*, marriage.] *Bot.* having flowers distinct from each other, and not collected in a head; monogamous.—**monogamist**, mo·nog´a·mist, *n.* One who practices or upholds monogamy, as opposed to a *bigamist* or *polygamist*.—**monogamous**, mo·nog´a·mus, *a.* Upholding or practicing monogamy; *zool.* having only one mate; *bot.* monogamic.—**monogamy**, mo·nog´a·mi, *n.* The practice or principle of marrying only once; the marrying of only one at a time; *zool.* the pairing with but a single mate at a time.

monogenesis, mon·o·jen′e·sis, *n.* [Gr. *monos*, single, and *genesis*, origin.] *Biol.* direct development of an embryo from a parent similar to itself; descent of an individual from one parent form; development of all the beings in the universe from a single cell.—**monogenetic**, mon′o·je·net″ik, *a.* Of or relating to monogenesis.—**monogenist**, mo·noj′e·nist, *n.* One who maintains the doctrine of monogeny.—**monogeny**, mo·noj′e·ni, *n.* Origin from a single species; the unity of the human species.

monogram, mon′o·gram, *n.* [Gr. *monos*, sole, and *gramma*, letter.] A character or cipher composed of one, two, or more letters interwoven, being an abbreviation of a name, used for instance on seals, letter-paper and envelopes, etc.—**monogrammatic**, mon′o·gram·mat″ik, *a.* In the style or manner of a monogram; pertaining to monograms.

monograph, mon′o·graf, *n.* [Gr. *monos*, single, and *graphē*, description.] An account or description of a single thing or class of things; the only book written by some distinguished writer on a topic.—**monographer**, mon·og′ra·fer, *n.* A writer of monographs.—**monographic**, mon·o·graf′ik, *a.* Pertaining to a monograph.

monogyny, mo·noj′i·ni, *n.* Marriage to one woman only; the state of having but one wife at a time.

monolith, mon′o·lith, *n.* [Gr. *monos*, single, and *lithos*, a stone.] A pillar, column, and the like formed of a single stone, generally applied to such only as are noted for their magnitude.—**monolithic**, mon·o·lith′ik, *a.* Formed of a single stone; consisting of monoliths.

monologue, mon′o·log, *n.* [Fr. *monologue*, from Gr. *monos*, sole, and *logos*, speech.] That which is spoken by one person alone; a dramatic soliloquy; a long speech or dissertation, uttered by one person in company.—**monologist**, mo·nol′o·jist, *n.* One who soliloquizes; one who monopolizes conversation.

monomania, mon·o·mā′ni·a, *n.* [Gr. *monos*, single, and *mania*, madness.] That form of mania in which the mind of the patient is absorbed by one idea, or is irrational on one subject only.—**monomaniac**, mon·o·mā′ni·ak, *n.* A person affected by monomania.—**monomaniac, monomaniacal**, mon·o·mā′ni·ak, mon·o·mā·nī″a·kal, *a.* Affected with, pertaining to, or resulting from monomania.

monometallism, mon·o·met′al·izm, *n.* [Gr. *monos*, single, E. *metal*.] The fact of having only one metal as a standard in the coinage of a country; the theory of a single metallic standard.—**monometallic**, mon·o·me·tal′ik, *a.* Pertaining to monometallism.

monomial, mo·nō′mi·al, *n.* [Gr. *monos*, sole, and *onoma*, a name.] *Alg.* an expression or quantity consisting of a single term.—*a. Alg.* consisting of only one term or letter.

monomorphic, monomorphous, mon·o·mor′fik, mon·o·mor′fus, *a.* [Gr. *monos*, single, and *morphē*, form.] *Biol.* retaining the same form throughout the various stages of development.

mononucleosis, mon′ō·nū″klē·o″sis, *n.* [N.L. *mono*, one, and *nuclear*, nucleus, and suffix *osis*, condition, state.] A disease in which an abnormally large number of mononuclear leukocytes are present in the blood.

monopetalous, mon·o·pet′al·us, *n.* [Gr. *monos*, single, and *petalon*.] *Bot.* having the petals united together into one piece by their edges; gamopetalous.

monophonic, mon·ō·fon′ik, *a.* [Gr. *monos*, one, and *phōnē*, sound.] Having a single melodic line with little or no accompaniment; in sound transmission, using recording techniques that result in a single transmission path.

monophthong, mon′of·thong, *n.* [Gr. *monos*, sole, and *phthongos*, sound.] A simple vowel sound; two or more written vowels pronounced as one.—**monophthongal**, mon·of·thong′gal, *a.* Consisting of a simple vowel sound.

monophyletic, mon′o·fi·let″ik, *a.* [Gr. *monos*, single, *phylē*, a tribe.] Pertaining to a single family or tribe.

monophyllous, mo·nof′il·us, *a.* [Gr. *monos*, sole, and *phyllon*, leaf.] *Bot.* having one leaf only, or formed of one leaf.

Monophysite, mo·nof′i·sīt, *n.* [Gr. *monos*, single, and *physis*, nature.] One who maintains that Jesus Christ had but one nature. Used also as adj.

monoplane, mon′o·plān, *n.* A flying apparatus with its wings or carrying surfaces arranged in the same plane. AIRPLANE.

monopoly, mo·nop′o·li, *n.* [Fr. *monopole*, L. *monopolium*, Gr. *monopōlion*—*monos*, single, and *pōleō*, to sell.] An exclusive trading privilege; the sole right or power of selling something, or full command over the sale of it; that which is the subject of a monopoly; the possession or assumption of anything to the exclusion of others.—**monopolist, monopolizer**, mo·nop′o·list, mo·nop′o·lī·zer, *n.*—**monopolize**, mo·nop′o·līz, *v.t.*—monopolized, monopolizing. To obtain a monopoly of; to obtain or engross the whole of.

monorail, mon′o·rāl, *n.* [Gr. *monos*, one, and *rail*.] A system of vehicular propulsion requiring only one rail.

monosepalous, mon·o·sep′al·us, *a.* [Gr. *monos*, one, and E. *sepal*.] *Bot.* composed of sepals which are united by their edges; gamosepalous.

monosperm, mon′o·sperm, *n.* [Gr. *monos*, single, and *sperma*, seed.] A plant of one seed only.—**monospermous**, mon·o·sper′mus, *a. Bot.* having one seed only.

monostich, mon′o·stik, *n.* [Gr. *monos*, single, and *stichos*, a verse.] A poem consisting of one verse only.

monostrophe, mo·nos′tro·fi, *n.* [Gr. *monos*, single, and *strophē*, strophe.] A metrical composition having only one strophe.—**monostrophic**, mon·o·strof′ik, *a.* Having one strophe only; written in unvaried measure.

monosyllabic, mon′o·sil·ab″ik, *a.* [Gr. *monos*, single, and *syllabē*, a syllable.] Consisting of one syllable; consisting of words of one syllable.—*Monosyllabic languages*, a class of languages in which each word is a simple uninflected root.—**monosyllable**, mon′o·sil·a·bl, *n.* A word of one syllable.

monotheism, mon′o·thē·izm, *n.* [Gr. *monos*, single, and *theos*, God.] The doctrine or belief of the existence of one God only.—**monotheist**, mon′o·thē·ist, *n.*—**monotheistic**, mon′o·thē·is″tik, *a.*

monotone, mon′o·tōn, *n.* [Gr. *monos*, single, and *tonos*, tone, sound.] A sameness of sound, or the utterance of successive syllables on one unvaried key, without inflection or cadence; sameness of style in writing or speaking.—**monotonous**, mo·not′o·nus, *a.*—**monotonously**, mo·not′o·nus·li, *adv.*—**monotonousness**, mo·not′o·nus·nes, *n.*—**monotony**, mo·not′o·ni, *n.* Uniformity of tone or sound; tiresome sameness; want of variety.

monotrematous, mon·o·trem′a·tus, *a.* [Gr. *monos*, single, *trēma*, aperture.] Characteristic of the Monotremata, the lowest order of mammals, oviparous, and with a single outlet for the feces and the products of the urinary and generative organs, comprising only the ornithorhynchus and echidna.—**monotreme**, mon′o·trēm, *n.* One of the Monotremata.

monotypic, mon·o·tip′ik, *a.* [Gr. *monos*, single and *typos*, a type.] Of one type.—**monotype**, mon′ō·tīp, *n.* In printing, a mechanical method of setting and casting type in single letters.

monovalent, mon′o·vā″lent, *n.* [Gr. *monos*, single, and L. *valens*, *valentis*, ppr. of *valeo*, to be worth.] *Chem.* having a valence of one, as the cuprous ion (Cu^1).

monoxide, mon·ox′īd, *n.* [Gr. *monos*, one, and Fr. *oxide*, *oxyde*, from *oxygène*, oxygen, and *acide*, acid.] *Chem.* an oxide containing a single atom of oxygen in the molecule.

Monroe Doctrine. The doctrine formulated by President Monroe of the United States that any attempt at colonizing by a European power within the American area constitutes an unfriendly act, leading to war.

monseigneur, mon·sen·yer′, *n.* pl. **messeigneurs**, mā·sen·yer′. [Fr. *mon*, my, and *seigneur*, lord. SENIOR.] A French title of honor given to princes, bishops, and other high dignitaries.—**monsieur**, mos′yė, *n.* pl. **messieurs**, mes′yė. [Fr., contr. of *monseigneur*.] The common title of courtesy and respect in France, answering to the English *Sir* and *Mr.*; abbreviated *Mons.*, *M.*; plural *Messrs.*, *MM.*

monsoon, mon·sön′, *n.* [Fr. *monson*,

mousson, Sp. *monzon,* Pg. *mousão,* from Ar. *mausim,* a time, a season, the favorable season for sailing to India.] The trade wind of the Arabian and Indian seas, for six months (November to March) blowing from about N.E.; and for the next six months (April to October) from about S.W.; an alternating wind in any region.

monster, mon′stėr, *n.* [Fr. *monstre,* from L. *monstrum,* a marvel, a monster, from *moneo,* to admonish. MONITION.] A plant or animal of abnormal structure or greatly different from the usual type; an animal exhibiting malformation in important parts; a person looked upon with horror on account of extraordinary crimes, deformity, or power to do harm; an imaginary creature, such as the sphinx, mermaid, etc.—*a.* Of inordinate size or numbers (a *monster* meeting).—**monstrosity,** mon·stros′i·ti, *n.* The state of being monstrous; that which is monstrous; an unnatural production.—**monstrous,** mon′strus, *a.* [L. *monstrosus.*] Unnatural in form; out of the common course of nature; enormous; huge; extraordinary; shocking; frightful; horrible.—*adv.* Exceedingly; very much (now vulgar or colloquial).—**monstrously,** mon′strus·li, *adv.* In a monstrous manner.—**monstrousness,** mon′strus·nes, *n.*

monstrance, mon′strans, *n.* [L.L. *monstrantia,* from L. *monstro,* to show.] *R. Cath. Ch.* the transparent or glass-faced shrine in which the consecrated host is presented for the adoration of the people.

montage, mon·täj′, *n.* [Fr. *montage,* mounting, putting together.] The art of combining several pictures into one distinct picture; the showing of a series of brief film scenes in rapid succession to present a series of interconnected ideas.

monte, mon′tā, *n.* [Sp., the stock of cards which remain after each player has received his share, from L. *mons,* a mountain.] A Spanish gambling game played with dice or cards.

Montessorian, Mon·tes·so′ri·an, *a.* [After Dr. Maria *Montessori* (1870-1952) of Italy.] A training for children aged three to six, based on methods of scientific pedagogy.

month, munth, *n.* [A.Sax. *mónath, mónth,* from *móna,* the moon=Icel. *mánathr,* Dan. *maaned,* D. *maand,* G. *monath;* allied to Gr. *mēn,* a month. MOON.] One of the twelve parts of the calendar year, consisting unequally of 30 or 31 days, except February, which has 28, and in leap year 29 days: called distinctively a *calendar month;* the period between change and change of the moon, reckoned as twenty-eight days.—**monthly,** munth′li, *a.* Continued a month or performed in a month; happening once a month, or every month.—*adv.* Once a month; in every month.—*n.* A magazine or other literary periodical published once a month.—**month's mind,** *n.*

A celebration in remembrance of a deceased person held a month after the death.

monticule, mon′ti·kūl, *n.* [L. *monticulus,* dim. of *mons, montis,* a mountain.] A little mount; a hillock.

monument, mon′ū·ment, *n.* [L. *monumentum,* from *moneo,* to remind, to warn. MONITION.] Anything by which the memory of a person, period, or event is perpetuated; a memorial; especially something built or erected in memory of events, actions, or persons; any enduring evidence or example; a singular or notable instance.—**monumental,** mon·ū·men′tal, *a.* Pertaining to a monument; serving as a monument; memorial; preserving memory.—**monumentally,** mon·ū·men′tal·li, *adv.* By way of monument or memorial; by means of monuments.

moo, mö, *v.i.* [Imitative.] To low, as a cow.—*n.* The low of a cow.

mood, möd, *n.* [Fr. *mode,* L. *modus;* merely a different spelling of *mode.*] *Gram.* a special form of verbs expressive of certainty, contingency, possibility, or the like; *logic,* the determination of propositions according to their quantity and quality, that is, whether universal, affirmative, etc.

mood, möd, *n.* [A.Sax. *mód,* mind, passion, disposition=D. *moed,* Icel. *módr (móthr),* Dan. and Sw. *mod,* Goth. *mods,* G. *muth,* mood, spirit, passion, courage, etc.; root doubtful.] Temper of mind; state of the mind in regard to passion or feeling; temporary disposition; humor; a fit of temper or sullenness.—**moodily,** möd′i·li, *adv.* In a moody manner.—**moodiness,** möd′i·nes, *n.* The state or quality of being moody.—**moody,** möd′i, *a.* [A.Sax. *módig,* angry.] Subject to or indulging in moods or humors; fretful; out of humor; gloomy; sullen; melancholy.

moon, mön, *n.* [A.Sax. *móna,* (masc.) =Icel. *máni,* Dan. *maane,* D. *maan,* G. *mond,* Goth. *mena,* Lith. *menu,* Gr. *mēnē,* Skr. *más;* from root *ma,* to measure.] The earth's satellite, revolving around the earth and accompanying it on its annual revolution around the sun, having a diameter of 2,163 miles, and a mean distance from earth of 238,857 miles; a satellite of any planet (the *moons* of Jupiter); the period of a revolution of the moon; a month (poetical); something in the shape of a moon or crescent.—*v.i.* To wander or gaze idly or moodily as if moonstruck (colloq.).—**moonbeam,** *n.* A ray of light from the moon.—**mooncalf,** *n.* A stupid fellow.—**moonish,** mön′ish, *a.* Variable, as the moon; fickle.—**moonlight,** mön′līt, *n.* The light afforded by the moon.—**moonlighter,** mön′līt·ėr, *n.* A person who holds a second job after his day's work is done.—**moonlighting,** mön′līt·ing, *n.* Holding a second job.—**moonlit,** *a.* Lit or illuminated by the moon.—**moonshine,** mön′shīn, *n.* The light

of the moon; pretense; empty show; illegal liquor.—**moonstone,** mön′stōn, *n.* A pearly white, translucent fedspar, used as a gem.—**moonstruck,** mön′struk, *a.* Crazed; lunatic.—**moony,** mön′i, *a.* Bewildered or silly.

moor, mör, *n.* [A.Sax. *mór*=Icel. *mór,* a heath; D. *moer,* a morass; Dan. *mor,* a moor, a marsh; G. *moor,* a marsh, a moor; same root as *mire; morass* is a derivative.] A tract of waste land, especially when covered with heath; a tract of ground on which game is preserved for sport. (*Brit.*)—**moor cock, moorfowl,** *n.* The red grouse. GROUSE.—**moor hen,** *n.* The gallinule or water hen; also the female of the red grouse.

Moor, mör, *n.* [Fr. *Maure,* from L. *Maurus,* Gr. *Mauros,* a Moor; comp. Gr. *mauros,* black or dark-colored.] A Moslem of the northern coast of Africa.—**moorish,** mö′rish, *a.*

moor, mör, *v.t.* [D. *marren, maren,* to tie, to moor; same word as E. *mar,* A.Sax. *merran,* to hinder, to mar, O.H.G. *marrjan,* to stop.] To confine or secure (a ship) in a particular station, as by cables and anchors, or by chains; to fix firmly.—**mooring,** mör′ing, *n. Naut.* the act of one who moors; that by which a ship is moored; *pl.* the place where a ship is moored.

moose, mös, *n.* [American Indian name.] A large animal of the deer family, with broadly palmated antlers, found in Canada and northern U. S.

moot, möt, *v.t.* [A.Sax. *mótian,* to meet for deliberation, to discuss, from *mót,* a meeting, whence *métan,* to meet. MEET.] To bring forward and discuss.—*n.* A debate on a hypothetical legal case by way of practice.—*a.* Debatable.

mop, mop, *n.* [A Celtic word: W. *mop,* a mop; Gael. *mob,* a tuft, tassel, mop.] A piece of cloth or coarse yarn fastened to a long handle and used for cleaning floors; something likened to a mop, as a tangle of hair, etc.—*v.t.*—**mopped, mopping.** To rub or wipe with a mop.—**mop-up,** *n.* Act of cleaning up or disposing of.—**mop up,** *v.t.* To clear out, especially where enemy resistance still remains.—*v.i.* To complete a project.

mop, mop, *n.* [Comp. D. *moppen,* to pout, to make a sulky face. MOPE.] A wry mouth; a grimace.

mope, mōp, *v.i.*—**moped, moping.** [Connected with *mop,* a wry mouth; D. *moppen,* to pout.] To show a dull, downcast, or listless air; to be spiritless or gloomy.—*v.t.* To make listless or dejected.—*n.* One who mopes.—**mopish,** mōp′ish, *a.*

moppet, mop′et, *n.* [Dim. from M.E. *mop, moppe,* rag doll, baby.] Young child, youngster. (Colloq.)

moraine, mō·rān′, *n.* [Fr., akin to It. *mora,* a heap of stones.] An accumulation of stones or other debris on the surface of glaciers or in the valleys at their foot, a regular feature in glacier phenomena.

moral, mor'al, *a.* [Fr. *moral*, from L. *moralis*, from *mos, moris,* manner, *mores,* manners, morals (seen also in *demoralize, demure, morose*).] Relating to right and wrong as determined by duty; relating to morality or morals; ethical; capable of distinguishing between right and wrong; governed by the laws of right and wrong; appealing to man as engaged in the practical concerns of life; sufficient for practical purposes (*moral* evidence, certainty); sexually virtuous; conforming to the rules of right conduct.—*Moral law,* the law prescribing moral duties and teaching right and wrong.—*Moral philosophy,* the science which treats of the nature and grounds of moral obligation; ethics.—*Moral sense,* the capacity to perceive what is right and wrong, and to approve or disapprove; conscience.—*n.* The practical lesson inculcated by any story; *pl.* general conduct or behavior as right or wrong; principles and mode of life; also moral philosophy or ethics.—**morale,** mō·räl', *n.* [An erroneous spelling of Fr. *moral,* used in same sense.] Mental condition of soldiers, etc., as regards courage, good cheer, and determination to do one's duty well, despite privation; the attitude of good will and devotion to duty existing among members of a group for its honor.—**moralist,** mor'al·ist, *n.* One who teaches morals; a writer or lecturer on ethics; one who inculcates or practices moral duties.—**morality,** mō·ral'i·ti, *n.* The doctrine of moral duties; morals; ethics; the practice of the moral duties; the quality of an action, as estimated by a standard of right and wrong.—**morality play,** mō·ral'i·ti plā, *n.* An allegorical dramatic form of the 14th to 18th centuries.—**moralize,** mor'al·īz, *v.t.* *moralized, moralizing.* To apply to a moral purpose; to draw a moral from.—*v.i.* To make moral reflections; to draw practical lessons from the facts of life.—**moralizer,** mor'al·ī·zėr, *n.*—**morally,** mor'al·li, *adv.*

morass, mō·ras', *n.* [Same as D. *moeras,* from *moer,* a moor.] A tract of low, soft, wet ground; a marsh.

moratorium, mor·a·tō'ri·um, *n.* [L. *moratorius,* from *mora,* delay.] A special period of delay granted by law to debtors.

Moravian, mō·rā'vi·an, *a.* Pertaining to Moravia or the Moravians.—*n.* A native of Moravia; one of a religious sect, also called United Brethren, tracing its origin to John Huss, and holding evangelical principles.

moray, mō·rā', mō·rā', *n.* [Pg. *moreia,* from L. *muraena.*] Any of numerous voracious eels of the family Muraenidae, found in the Mediterranean and other warm seas.

morbid, mor'bid, *a.* [L. *morbidus,* from *morbus,* a disease. MORTAL.] Gloomy; gruesome; not sound and healthful; relating to disease.—**morbidity, morbidness,** mor·bid'i·ti, mor'bid·nes, *n.*—**morbidly,** mor'bid·li, *adv.*

mordacious, mor·dā'shus, *a.* [L.

mordax, mordacis, from *mordeo,* to bite. MORSEL.] Biting; sarcastic.—**mordacity,** mor·das'i·ti, *n.* [L. *mordacitas.*] The quality of biting; readiness to bite.—**mordant,** mor'dant, *n.* [Fr. *mordant,* from L. *mordeo* to bite.] A substance employed in the process of dyeing which serves to fix the colors; sticky matter by which gold leaf is made to adhere.—*a.* Biting; caustic; severe.

more, mōr, *a.* Serving as the comparative of *much* and *many,* the superlative being *most.* [A.Sax. *mára,* D. *meer,* Dan. *meer, meere,* G. *mehr,* Icel. *meiri, meirr,* Goth. *mais, maiza,* more; from same root as L. *magnus,* great, E. *may.*] With singular nouns (as comparative of *much*): greater in amount, extent, degree, etc. (*more* land, *more* light); with plural nouns (as comparative of *many*): greater in number; in greater numbers (*more* men); added to some former number; additional (one day *more,* or one *more* day).—*adv.* In a greater degree, extent, or quantity; in addition; besides; again (once *more,* no *more*).—*To be no more,* to be destroyed or dead; to have perished. ∴ *More* is used to modify an adjective (or adverb) and form the comparative degree, having the same force and effect as the termination *er* in comparatives; as *more* wise (=*wiser*); *more* wisely; *more* illustrious (*more* illustriously).—*n.* What is more or greater; something farther or in addition.

moreen, mo·rēn', *n.* [Connected with *mohair,* Fr. *moire.*] A watered woolen, or woolen and cotton fabric used for curtains, heavy dresses, etc.

morel, mo·rel', *n.* [Fr. *morelle,* nightshade, from L.L. *morellus,* dark-colored, L. *morulus,* dark. So also the morel cherry is a dark-colored cherry.] Garden nightshade; a kind of cherry. MORELLO.

morel, mo·rel', *n.* [Fr. *morille,* from O.H.G. *morilla,* G. *morchel,* Sw. *murkla.*] A kind of edible fungus.

morello, mo·rel'lō, *n.* [It. *morello,* dark-colored. MOREL.] A kind of cherry with a dark-red skin.

moreover, mōr·ō'vėr, *adv.* [*More* and *over.*] Beyond what has been said; further; besides.

mores, mō'rēz, *n.* pl. [L.] Customs and conventions or folk ways containing the moral views of a people and having the force of law through long use.

Moresque, mō·resk', *a.* [Fr., from It. *moresco,* from *Moro,* L. *Maurus,* a Moor.] Moorish; after the manner of the Moors.—*n.* A style of ornamentation for flat surfaces; same as *Arabesque.*

morganatic, mor·ga·nat'ik, *a.* [L.L. *morganatica,* a kind of dowry paid on the morning before or after marriage, a dowry accepted in lieu of other claims; corrupted from G. *morgen-gabe,* lit. morning gift (A. Sax. *morgen-gifu*).] Said of a kind of marriage between a monarch, or one of the highest nobility, and a lady of inferior rank; called also a *left-handed marriage,* the offspring of

which do not inherit the father's rank or possessions, but are considered legitimate in most other respects.—**morganatically,** mor·ga·nat'i·kal·li, *adv.* In the manner of a morganatic marriage.

morgue, morg, *n.* [Fr. Origin unknown.] A place where the bodies of persons found dead are exposed that they may be claimed by their friends; reference files in a newspaper office.

moribund, mor'i·bund, *a.* [L. *moribundus,* from *morior,* to die. MORTAL.] In a dying state.

morion, mor'i·on, *n.* [Fr. *morion,* from Sp. *morrion,* a morion; origin doubtful.] A kind of helmet of iron, steel, or brass, somewhat like a hat in shape, and without beaver or visor.

Morisco, mo·ris'kō, *n.* [Sp. *morisco,* Moorish, from *Moro,* a Moor.] A name applied to the ancient Moorish population of Spain and to their language; a morris dance.

Mormon, mor'mon, *n.* [From the Book of *Mormon,* accepted by them as of divine origin, and said to have been made known to Joseph Smith by an angel.] A term generally applied to a member of that religious body properly known as the Church of Jesus Christ of Latter-day Saints.—**Mormonism,** mor'mon·izm, *n.* The religion or doctrines of the Mormons.

morn, morn, *n.* [Contr. from O.E. *morwen,* A.Sax. *morgen,* morning, whence also *morrow.*] The first part of the day; the morning: used chiefly in poetry.—**morning,** morn'ing, *n.* [O.E. *morwening,* from A.Sax. *morgen* (D., Dan., and G. *morgen,* Icel. *morginn,* Goth. *maurgins*) by common change of *g* to *w,* with the *-ing* of verbal nouns. (Comp. *even, evening, dawn, dawning.*) The root is seen in Lith. *mirgu,* to glimmer, to gleam.] The first part of the day, beginning at twelve o'clock at night and extending to twelve at noon; in a more limited sense, the time beginning at break of day and extending to the hour of breakfast and of beginning the labors of the day or considerably later; *fig.* the first or early part (as of life). It is often used adjectively.—**morning-glory,** *n.* A name given to several climbing plants of the convolvulus family, with handsome flowers.—**morning star,** *n.* Any of the planets, Venus, Jupiter, Mars, Mercury, Saturn, when it rises before the sun.

morocco, mo·rok'ō, *n.* A fine leather made from the skins of goats, first imported from Morocco, and extensively used in the binding of books, upholstering furniture, making ladies' shoes, etc.

moron, mō'ron, *n.* [Gr. *mōros,* sluggish.] A person having the mental age of 8 to 12 years.

morose, mo·rōs', *a.* [L. *morosus,* wayward, peevish, morose, from *mos, moris,* a custom, habit. MORAL.] Of a sour temper; severe; sullen and austere.—**morosely,** mo·rōs'li, *adv.* In a morose manner; sourly; with sullen austerity.—**moroseness,** mo•rōs'nes, *n.* The quality of being morose; sourness of temper; sullenness.

morpheme, mor'fēme, *n.* [Fr. *morphème,* from Gr. *morphē.*] A word such as *wait,* or a part of a word, as *ed* in wait*ed,* not further divisible into a meaningful part.—**morphemics,** mor'fē•miks, *n.* The study and analysis of morphemes.

Morpheus, mor'fi•us, *n.* [Gr. from *morphē,* form, from the forms he causes to appear to people in their dreams.] *Greek myth.* the god of sleep and dreams.

morphia, morphine, mor'fi•a, mor'-fēn, *n.* [Gr. *Morpheus,* the god of sleep.] The narcotic principle of opium, a vegetable alkaloid of a bitter taste, of medicinal value as an anodyne.

morphology, mor•fol'o•ji, *n.* [Gr. *morphē,* form, and *logos,* description.] That department of science which treats of the form and arrangement of the structures of plants and animals; the science of form in the organic world.—**morphologic, morphological,** mor•fo•loj'ik, mor•fo•loj'i•kal, *a.* Pertaining to morphology.—**morphologically,** mor•fo•loj'-i•kal•li, *adv.* In a morphological manner.—**morphologist,** mor•fol'o•jist, *n.* One versed in morphology.

morris, mor'is, *n.* **morris dance,** [Fr. *moresque,* from Sp. *morisco,* from *Moro,* a Moor.] A dance borrowed from the Moors, or in imitation of their dances; a fantastic dance formerly practiced in England, as in the May games.

Morris chair, a comfortable armchair having an adjustable back.

Morris Plan, a method for making small loans employed by an industrial bank in the United States.

morrow, mor'ō, *n.* [MORNING.] The day next after the present or after any day specified.—*Good morrow,* good morning, a term of salutation. —*To-morrow,* on the morrow; next day.

Morse code. [After its inventor, Professor *Morse,* of Massachusetts.] A system of symbols, consisting of dashes and dots, to be used in transmitting messages either audibly or visually.

morsel, mor'sel, *n.* [O.Fr. *morcel* (Fr. *morceau*), from L.L. *morcellum,* a dim. from L. *morsus,* a bite, from *mordeo,* to bite.] A bite; a mouthful; a small piece of food; a fragment; a little piece in general.

mort, mort, *n.* [Fr. *mort,* death. MORTAL.] A flourish sounded at the death of game.

mortal, mor'tal, *a.* [L. *mortalis,* from *mors, mortis,* death: same root as Skr. *mri,* to die, *mrita,* dead; this root meaning to crush or grind, and being also that of *meal, mild, murder,* etc.] Subject to death; destined to die; deadly; destructive to life; causing death; fatal; incurring the penalty of death or divine condemnation; not venial (*mortal* sin); human; belonging to man, who is

mortal. Colloquially applied to periods of time felt to be long or tedious (ten *mortal* hours).—*n.* A being subject to death; a man; a human being.—**mortally,** mor'tal•li, *adv.* In the manner of a mortal; in a deadly manner or manner that must cause death.—**mortality,** mor•-tal'i•ti, *n.* [L. *mortalitas.*] The state of being mortal; death; frequency of death; death of numbers in proportion to a population; humanity; human nature; the human race.— *Bills of mortality,* abstracts showing the numbers that have died during certain periods of time.—*Tables of mortality,* tables showing how many out of a certain number of persons of a given age will probably die successively in each year till the whole are dead.

mortar, mor'ter, *n.* [From L. *mortarium,* a mortar in which things are pounded.] A vessel, usually in form of an inverted bell, in which substances are pulverized or pounded with a pestle; a short piece of ordnance, thick and wide, used for throwing shells, etc., and named from its resemblance to the above utensil; a mixture of lime and sand with water, used as a cement for stones and bricks in walls.—**mortarboard,** mor'ter•bôrd, *n.* A board for holding mortar; a square-topped academic cap.

mortgage, mor'gij, *n.* [Fr. *mort,* dead, and *gage,* pledge—the estate pledged becomes *dead* or entirely lost by failure to pay.] An assignment or conveyance of land or house property to a person as security for the payment of a debt due to him, and on the condition that if the money shall be paid according to contract the grant shall be void; the deed by which this conveyance is effected.—*v.t.*—**mortgaged, mortgaging.** To grant or assign on mortgage; to pledge; to make liable to the payment of any debt.—**mortgagee,** mor•gi•jē', *n.* The person to whom an estate is mortgaged.—**mortgagor,** mor'gij•ėr, *n.* The person who mortgages.

mortician, mor•tish'an, *n.* [L. *mors, mortis,* death.] An undertaker.

mortify, mor'ti•fī, *v.t.*—**mortified, mortifying.** [Fr. *mortifier.*—L. *mors, mortis,* death, and *facio,* to make. MORTAL.] To affect with gangrene or mortification; to subdue or bring into subjection by abstinence or rigorous severities; to humiliate.— *v.i.* To practice mortification; to become gangrenous.—**mortification,** mor'ti•fi•ka″shon, *n. Med.* the death of a part of an animal body while the rest is alive; gangrene; the subduing of the passions and appetites by penance, abstinence, etc.; humiliation or slight vexation; chagrin.

mortise, mor'tis, *n.* [Fr. *mortaise,* a mortise; origin unknown.] A hole cut in one piece of material to receive a corresponding projecting piece called a *tenon,* on another piece, in order to fix the two together.— *v.t.*—**mortised, mortising.** To cut a

mortise in; to join by tenon and mortise.

mortmain, mort'mān, *n.* [Fr. *mort,* dead, and *main,* hand.] *Law,* possession of lands or tenements in dead hands, or hands that cannot alienate, as those of a corporation; the holding of property more particularly by religious houses, which has been restricted by various statutes.

mortuary, mor'chū•e•ri,*n.* [L.L.*mortuarium,* from L. *mortuus,* dead, from *mori,* to die. MORTAL.] A place for the temporary reception of the dead; a dead-house. *a.* Pertaining to the burial of the dead.

morula, mor'ū•la, *n.* [Dim. of L. *morum,* mulberry, from the appearance of the mass of cells.] *Physiol.* a roundish mass of cells (called blastomeres) resulting from the division or segmentation of an ovum or its yolk in the process of development.

Mosaic, Mosaical, mō•zā'ik, mō-zā'i•kal, *a.* Relating to *Moses,* the Hebrew lawgiver, or his writings and institutions.

mosaic, mō•zā'ik, *a.* [Fr. *mosaïque,* from It. *mosaico, musaico,* from L. Gr. *mousaikos,* belonging to the Muses, from *Mousa,* a Muse.] A term applied to inlaid work formed by little pieces of enamel, glass, marble, precious stones, etc., of various colors, cut and disposed on a ground of cement in such a manner as to form designs, and to imitate the colors and gradations of painting. —*n.* Mosaic or inlaid work.—*Mosaic gold,* an alloy of copper and zinc, called also *ormolu.*—**mosaicist,** mō•-zā'i•sist, *n.* One who makes mosaics.

moschatel, mos'ka•tel, *n.* [Fr. *moscatelle,* from L.L. *muscatus,* having the odor of musk. MUSK.] A plant of the temperate regions, with pale green flowers which smell like musk.

Moselle, mo•zel', *n.* A species of white French and German wine, so named from the river *Moselle.*

Moslem, moz'lem, *n.* [Ar. *moslem, muslim,* a true believer, from *salama,* to resign one's self to God.] A Mussulman or Mohammedan.—*a.* Mohammedan.

mosque, mosk, *n.* [Fr. *mosquée,* It. *moschea,* Sp. *mezquita,* from Ar. *mesjid,* the place of adoration, from *sajad,* to adore.] A Mohammedan temple or place of religious worship.

mosquito, mos•kē'tō, *n.* [Sp. and Pg. *mosquito,* dim. from *mosca,* L. *musca,* a fly.] A name applied to several species of gnatlike flies, common in many regions, and which are very annoying from their severe bites.— *Mosquito nets* or *curtains,* of gauze, are often used to ward off attacks by mosquitoes upon persons reposing or asleep.

moss, mos, *n.* [D., O.G., and Dan. *mos,* Sw. *mossa,* Icel. *mosi,* A.Sax. *meós,* G. *moos,* moss, a bog. Cog. L. *muscus,* moss; Gr. *moschos,* a sprout or tender shoot.] A name common to many cryptogamic plants of small size with simple branching stems and numerous, generally narrow leaves; also a name of various lichens; a bog; a place where peat is found.—*v.t.* To cover with moss. —**mossy**, mos′i, *a.* Overgrown with moss; abounding with moss; like moss.—**mossiness**, mos′i·nes, *n.* The state of being mossy, or overgrown with moss.—**moss agate**, *n.* A kind of agate having internally a moss-like appearance.—**moss-grown**, *a.* Overgrown with moss.—**moss rose**, *n.* A beautiful variety of rose, so named from the calyx being covered with a moss-like growth.—**mosstrooper**, *n.* One of the marauders upon the borders of England and Scotland previous to the union of the crowns, from the mosses so common on the borders.

most, mōst, *a.* superl. of *more.* [A.Sax. *maest*, for *má-est*, superl. of old positive *má*, more; Goth. *maists*, Icel. *mestr*, D. and Dan. *meest*, G. *meist.* MORE.] Greatest in any way: with singular nouns (*most* wisdom, need, etc.); greatest in number; amounting to a considerable majority; with plurals (*most* men; *most* sorts of learning).—*adv.* In the greatest or highest, or in a very great or high degree, quantity, or extent; mostly; chiefly: often used before adjectives and adverbs to form the superlative degree, as *more* is to form the comparative.—*The Most High*, the Almighty.—*n.* The greatest or greater number; the majority: in this case plural; greatest amount or advantage; utmost extent, degree, effect, etc.: often with *the*, and in this sense singular.—*At most* or *at the most*, at furthest; at the utmost extent.—**mostly**, mōst′li, *adv.* For the most part; chiefly; mainly.

mot, mō, *n.* [Fr. *mot*, a word, a motto, L.L. *muttum*, from L. *muttio*, to mutter.] A pithy or witty saying; a bon-mot.

mote, mōt, *n.* [A.Sax. *mot*, a mote; comp. D. *mot*, dust, sweepings.] A small particle; a mere atom; anything proverbially small.

motel, mō·tel′, *n.* [From *motorists′* ho*tel.*] A lodging for motorists along the highway with accommodations for automobiles.

motet, mo·tet′, *n.* [Fr. *motet*, from It. *mottetto*, a dim. of *motto.* MOTTO.] *Mus.* a sacred cantata; a choral composition, usually of a sacred character.

moth, moth, *n.* [A.Sax. *moththe*; D. *mot*, Icel. *motti*, G. *motte*, Sw. *mott*, a moth.] The name of numerous lepidopterous insects allied to the butterflies, but seldom seen on the wing except in the evening or at night; the clothes-moth, the caterpillar of which is notoriously destructive to woolen materials, furs, skins, etc.—**mothy**, moth′i, *a.* Full of moths; eaten by moths.—**moth-eat**, *v.t.* To eat or prey upon, as a moth eats a garment.—**moth-eaten**, *a.* Eaten by moths or rather their larvae.

mother, muTH′ėr, *n.* [A.Sax. *módor*, D. *moeder*, Dan. and Sw. *moder*, Icel. *móthir*, G. *mutter*, Ir. *matair*, Gael. *mathair*, L. *mater*, Gr. *mētēr*, Skr. *mâtâ*, *mâtar*, Per. *mâder*; from root *ma* to bring forth, the term., as in *father*, denoting an agent.] A female parent, especially one of the human race; a woman who has borne a child; that which has produced anything; source of anything; generatrix; a familiar term of address to elderly females; an abbess or other female holding an important position in religious or semi-religious institutions.—*Mother Carey′s chicken*, a name given by sailors to the stormy petrel.—*a.* Native; natural (*mother* wit); giving birth or origin; originating (*mother* country).—**motherhood**, muTH′ėr·hud, *n.* The state of being a mother.—**mother-in-law**, *n.* The mother of one′s husband or wife.—**motherless**, muTH′ėr·les, *a.* Destitute of a mother; having lost a mother.—**motherliness**, muTH′ėr·li·nes, *n.* Quality of being motherly.—**motherly**, muTH′ėr·li, *a.* Pertaining to a mother; becoming a mother; tender and affectionate.—**mother-of-pearl**, *n.* The hard silvery brilliant internal layer of several kinds of shells extensively used in the arts. Called also *Nacre.*—**mother tongue**, *n.* One′s native language; a language to which other languages owe their origin.—**mother wit**, *n.* Native wit; common sense.

mother, muTH′ėr, *n.* [L.G. *moder*, D. *modder*, Dan. *mudder*, G. *mutter* —dregs, mud, slime, etc.; allied to *mud.*] A thick slimy substance that gathers in liquors, particularly vinegar.—*v.i.* To become mothery.

motif, mō·tēf′, *n.* [Fr.] A passage or theme that reappears in varying form throughout a musical composition; the prevailing idea an artist or writer has endeavored to express.

motific, mō·tif′ik, *a.* [L. *motus*, motion, and *facio*, to make.] Producing motion.—**motile**, mō′til, *a.* Having inherent power of motion, as certain organs of plants.—**motility**, mō·til′i·ti, *n.* Capability of motion.

motion, mō′shon, *n.* [L. *motio*, *motionis*, from *moveo*, *motum*, to move. MOVE.] The act or process of changing place; the passing of a body from one place to another; opposed to *rest*; the power of moving; a single act of motion; a movement; movement of the mind or soul; internal impulse; proposal made; a proposition made in a deliberative assembly; the proposing of any matter for the consideration of an assembly or meeting; *med.*, evacuation of the intestine; alvine discharge. —*v.t.* and *i.* To make a significant motion or gesture for guidance, as with the hand or head.—**motionless**, mō′shon·les, *a.* Wanting motion; being at rest.—**motion picture**, A form of drama produced by means of a series of photographs projected upon a screen to give an illusion of continuous, lifelike motion; any series of pictures photographed and presented in this way.

motivate, mō′ti·vāt, *v.t.* Motivated, motivating. To furnish with a motive; to be the motive of; to impel; to induce.

motive, mō′tiv, *n.* [Fr. *motif*, a motive, L.L. *motivus*, moving, from L. *moveo*, *motum*, to move. MOVE.] That which incites to action; that which determines the choice or moves the will; cause; object; inducement; prevailing design; the theme or leading subject in a piece of music; the prevailing idea in the mind of an artist, to which he endeavors to give expression in his work.—*a.* Causing motion.—*Motive power* or *force*, the power or force acting upon any body or quantity of matter to move it.—*v.t.* To supply a motive to or for; to prompt.— **motivity**, mō·tiv′i·ti, *n.* The power of producing motion.

motley, mot′li, *a.* [W. *mudliw*, a changing color, a motley color— *mud*, change, and *lliw*, a stain, a hue; or akin to *mottle.*] Consisting of different colors; parti-colored (a *motley* coat); exhibiting a combination of discordant elements; heterogeneous (a *motley* style); of a dress of various colors, or the usual dress of a domestic fool.

motor, mō′tėr, *n.* [L., A mover, from *moveo*, to move.] That which imparts motion; a prime mover, especially a machine which develops power through rotary action, as an electric motor or an internal-combustion engine; an automobile.—*a.* Imparting motion; equipped with a motor; designating or pertaining to a nerve which stimulates the movement of a muscle or the secretory activity of glands.—*v.i.* To travel in, or drive, an automobile or other automotive vehicle.—**motorboat**, *n.* A boat propelled by an internal-combustion engine or by electricity. —**motorbus**, **motor coach**, *n.* A public vehicle propelled by an internal-combustion engine.—**motorcycle**, *n.* A two-wheeled vehicle propelled by an internal-combustion engine.—**motordrome**, *n.* An enclosed, circular track where motorcycles or automobiles are raced or tested.—**motoring**, *n.* The recreation or act of driving, or traveling in, an automobile.—**motorist**, *n.* A person who drives, or travels in, an automobile.—**motorize**, *motorized*, *motorizing*, *v.t.* To provide with a motor or with motor-powered equipment.—**motorman**, *n.* A man who operates a motor-powered vehicle, as a streetcar or electric locomotive.—**motor ship**, *n.* A ship propelled by internal-combustion (usually Diesel) engines.

mottle, mot′l, *n.* [O.Fr. *mattelé*, clotted, curdled; probably from the German; comp. Prov. G. *matte*, curds.] A blotched or spotted sort of surface as seen in woods employed in cabinet work when polished.—*v.t.* To mark with spots or blotches as if mottled.—**mottled**, mot′ld, *p.* and *a.* Spotted; marked with blotches of color, as some kinds of cabinet wood.

motto, mot′tō, *n.* [It. *motto*, Fr. *mot*, a word, from L.L. *muttum*, a word, from L. *muttio*, to mutter.] A short pithy sentence or phrase, or even a single word, adopted as expressive of one's guiding idea or principle, appended to a coat of arms, or otherwise put prominently forward.

moufflon, mouflon, möf′lon, n. [Fr. *mouflon.*] An animal of the sheep kind inhabiting Corsica, Sardinia, and Greece.

mouillé, mü·yā′, a. [Fr., wet.] Given a softened, liquid sound, usually caused by a succeeding *y*-sound, as *l* in *William.*

moulin, mö′laṅ, n. [Fr. *moulin,* L.L. *molinus,* from L. *mola,* a mill.] A deep cylindrical hole in a glacier, formed by a rill on its surface draining into it.

mound, mound, n. [A.Sax. and G. *mund,* a defense; same root as *mount.*] An elevation of earth, generally artificial; a rampart; a hillock or knoll; *baseball,* the slight elevation on which the pitcher stands while pitching.—v.t. To heap up in a mound.—**Mound Builder,** n. An Indian of any of the various groups that once lived in the Mississippi River and Great Lakes regions and built earthworks.

mount, mount, n. [A.Sax. *munt,* Fr. *mont,* from L. *mons, montis,* a hill, from root seen in *eminent, prominent.*] A hill; a mountain; now chiefly poetical, or used in proper names, as *Mount* Vesuvius, *Mount* Sinai; a bulwark for offense or defense (O.T.); the cardboard or other material on which a picture or drawing is mounted or fixed; the setting of a gem or something similar; the opportunity or means of riding on horseback.—v.i. [Fr. *monter,* from *mont,* a hill.] To rise on high; to go up; to ascend; to be built to a great altitude; to get on or upon anything, specifically, to get on horseback; to amount; to reach in value.—v.t. To raise aloft; to ascend; to climb up to or upon; to place one's self upon (a throne or the like); to furnish with a horse or horses; to put on or cover with something necessary, useful, or ornamental (to *mount* a map on cloth); to prepare for use; to carry or be furnished with (a fort *mounts* a hundred cannon).—*To mount guard,* to take the station and do the duty of a sentinel.—**mountable,** moun′ta·bl, a. Capable of being mounted.—**mounter,** moun′tėr, n. One that mounts.—**mounting,** moun′ting, n. The act of ascending; that with which an article is mounted or set off, or finished for use, as the setting of a gem; the furnishings of a sword, of harness; cardboard on which a picture is pasted, etc.

mountain, moun′tin, n. [O.Fr. *muntaine, montaigne,* Fr. *montagne,* from L.L. *montaneus,* mountainous, from L. *mons, montis,* a mountain. MOUNT.] A huge mass of earth and rock rising above the common level of the earth or adjacent land; an elevated mass higher than a hill; something very large or great.—*Chain of mountains,* a group of mountains linked together, thus forming a series, a system, or a chain, as the Allegheny Mountains which range over four states.—*The*

Mountain, the extremists of the revolutionary party during the first French Revolution who occupied the highest benches in the National Convention.—a. Of, or pertaining to, a mountain.—**mountain ash,** n. A genus of trees found in the United States and Europe, having ash-colored leaves, white corymbose flowers and scarlet fruit; in Europe, called the rowan tree.—**mountaineer,** moun′tin·ēr″, n. An inhabitant of a mountainous district; a climber of mountains.—v.i. To climb mountains.—**mountain goat,** n. A goat native to the mountainous regions of the northwestern United States and Canada.—**mountain lion,** n. A puma, also called cougar, panther or cata-mount, largest American species of the cat kind.—**mountainous,** moun′tin·us, a. Full of mountains; large as a mountain; huge.

mountebank, moun′ti·bangk, n. [It. *montimbanco, montambanco*—*montare,* to mount, and *banco,* bench.] One who mounts a bench or stage in the market or other public place, and vends medicines which he pretends are infallible remedies; a quack doctor; any boastful and false pretender; a charlatan.—v.t. To gull (*Shak.*).

mourn, mōrn, v.i. [A.Sax. *murnan*= Icel. *morna,* O.H.G. *mornan,* Goth. *maurnan,* to grieve; root same as *murmur.*] To express grief or sorrow; to grieve; to be sorrowful; to lament; to wear the dress or appearance of grief.—v.t. To grieve for; to lament; to deplore; to bewail.—**mourner,** mōr′nėr, n. One that mourns; one that follows a funeral in the habit of mourning.—**mournful,** mōrn′ful, a. Expressing sorrow; exhibiting the appearance of grief; doleful; causing sorrow; sad; calamitous; sorrowful; feeling grief.—**mournfully,** mōrn′ful·li, adv. In a mournful manner; dolefully; sorrowfully; sadly.—**mournfulness,** mōrn′ful·nes, n. The state or character of being mournful.—**mourning,** mōr′ning, n. The act of expressing grief; lamentation; the dress or customary habit worn by mourners.—a. Employed to express grief (a mourning ring).—**mourning cloak,** n. A handsome purplish brown butterfly with wings bordered with yellow, brown and blue. It is found from the arctic south, in both Europe and America.—**mourning dove,** a small wild dove found in the United States, having a lamenting cry.

mouse, mous, n. pl. **mice,** mīs. [A.Sax. *mús,* pl. *mýs* (like *lús, lýs,* louse, lice); Icel. *mús,* Dan. *muus,* D. *muis,* G. *maus;* cog. L. *mus,* Gr. *mys,* Per. *mûsh,* Skr. *mûsha,* mouse.] A well-known small rodent quadruped that infests dwelling-houses, granaries, fields, etc.; a name of various allied animals; a term of endearment.—v.i. (mouz)—*moused, mousing.* To hunt for or catch mice.—**mouse-ear,** n. Any of various plants, so named from their soft, hairy leaves which seem to resemble in shape the ear of a mouse; the

blue or white flowered forget-me-not, symbolic of fidelity.—**mouser,** mou′zer, n. A cat good at catching mice; one who snoops about; a detective (*slang*).

mousse, mös, n. [Fr. froth, foam.] A frozen dessert of whipped cream, sweetened and flavored, sometimes made firm with gelatin.

mouth, mouth, n. pl. **mouths,** mouᴛʜz. [A.Sax. *múth*=Icel. *muthr, munnr,* Sw. *mun,* Dan. and G. *mund,* D. *mond,* Goth. *munths*—mouth. Like *tooth, sooth,* etc., this word has lost an *n* before the *th.*] The aperture in the head of an animal through which food is received and voice uttered; the aperture between the lips or the portion of the face formed by the lips; the cavity within the lips; the opening of anything hollow, as of a pitcher or other vessel; the entrance to a cave, pit, or den, the opening of a well, etc.; the part of a river, creek, etc., by which it joins with the ocean or any large body of water.—*To make a mouth* or *to make mouths,* to distort the mouth; to make a wry face, as in derision.—*Down in the mouth,* chapfallen; dejected; mortified.—*To give mouth to,* to utter, to express.—v.t. (mouᴛʜ). To utter with a voice affectedly big or swelling; to seize or shake with the mouth.—v.i. To speak with a full, round, or loud, affected voice; to vociferate; to rant; to make wry faces, to grimace (*Tenn.*).—**mouthed,** mouᴛʜd, a. Having a mouth of this or that kind: used in composition (foul-mouthed).—**mouther,** mou′ᴛʜėr, n. One who mouths; an affected declaimer.—**mouthful,** mouth′ful, n. As much as the mouth contains at once; a small quantity.—**mouthpiece,** mouth′pēs, n. The part of a musical instrument that is applied to the mouth; a tube by which a cigar is held in the mouth while being smoked; one who speaks on behalf of others.

mouton, mö′ton, n. [Fr. sheep, from M.Fr. *mouton,* ram.] A sheepskin that is sheared and dyed and treated to be used as fur similar to otter and sealskin.

move, möv, v.t.—*moved, moving.* [O. Fr. *mover, mouver,* Mod.Fr. *mouvoir,* from L. *movere, motum,* to move.] To carry, convey, or draw from one place to another; to cause to change place or posture; to set in motion; to stir; to excite into action; to influence; to prevail on; to rouse or excite the feelings of; to cause the bowels to move; to affect with tender feelings; to touch; to offer formally, as a motion for consideration by a deliberative assembly; *chess, checkers,* etc., to change the position of (a piece) in the regular course of play.—v.i. To change place or posture; to stir; to pass or go; to walk; to carry or bear one's self; to change residence; to take action; to begin to act.—n. Proceeding; action taken; the moving of a piece in playing chess, etc.; a change of residence; the act of moving; an advance or step.—

To be on the move, to be stirring about.—**movable, moveable**, möv′-a·bl, *a.* Capable of being moved; changing from one date to another. —*n.* Any part of a man's goods capable of being moved.—**movableness, moveableness, movability**, möv′a·bl·nes, möv·a·bil′i·ti, *n.*—**movably, moveably**, möv′a·bli, *adv.* —**movement**, möv′ment, *n.* Act of moving; course or process of change; motion; an individual act of motion; a gesture; an agitation set on foot by one or more persons for the purpose of bringing about some result desired; *mus.* motion or progression in time, also a detached and independent portion of a composition; the train of wheelwork in a watch or clock; *milit.* part of a maneuver; *art*, a trend in style, technique, or subject matter followed by a sufficient number of artists to introduce a significant change.—**mover**, möv′ér, *n.* One who or that which gives motion.—**moving**, möv′ing, *a.* Causing to move or act; impelling; exciting the feelings; touching; pathetic.—**movingly**, möv′ing·li, *adv.*— **moving picture**, *n.* See MOTION PICTURE.—**movie**, möv′ē, *n.* A motion picture.

mow, mō, *v.t.*—*mowed* (pret.) *mowed* or *mown* (*pp.*) [A.Sax. *máwan*; akin. Icel. *múgr, múgi*, a swathe; Dan. *meie*, D. *maaijen*, G. *mähen*, to mow; allied to L. *meto*, Gr. *amaō*, to mow. *Meadow* is from this root.] To cut down with a scythe or mowing machine (to *mow* grass); to cut the grass from (to *mow* a meadow); to cut down (men, etc.) indiscriminately, or in great numbers or quantity.—*v.i.* To cut grass; to use the scythe or mowing machine.—**mower**, mō′ér, *n.* One who mows; a mowing machine.—**mowing machine**, *n.* An agricultural machine employed to cut down grass, clover, grain, etc.

mow, mou, *n.* [A.Sax. *muga*, a heap, a mow, N. *muga, mua*, a heap of hay.] A pile of hay or sheaves of grain deposited in a barn; the part of a barn where they are packed.— *v.t.* To put or pile in a mow.

moxa, mok′sa, *n.* [Chinese.] A soft downy substance prepared in China and Japan from the young leaves of certain plants, used for the gout, etc., by burning it on the skin; any substance used in this way as a counterirritant.

mu, mū, mö, *n.* [Gr. *my*.] The twelfth letter of the Greek alphabet, corresponding to the English *M*.

much, much, *a.*; *more* and *most* serve as its comparative and superlative. [Shortened form of old *mochel, muchel, micel*, much, from A.Sax. *mycel, micel*, much, great, many; akin Icel. *mjög, mjōk*, much, *mikill*, great; Goth. *mikils*, O.H.G. *mihil*; same root as L. *magnus*, great, E. *may*. MAGNITUDE, MAY.] Great in quantity or amount; abundant: used with singular nouns (*much* food, seed, water, money, etc.).—*adv.* In a great degree; to a great amount or extent; greatly: used especially with comparatives and past participles (*much*

better, larger, sooner, surprised, etc.); nearly (*much* as it was).— *Much about the same*, nearly equal.— *n.* A great quantity; a great deal; equivalent to an adjective with a noun omitted, and often qualified by *too, as*, and *so*.—**muchness**, much′-nes, *n.* State of being much; quantity.

mucilage, mū′si·lij, *n.* [L. *mucilago*, from *mucus*, slime, mucus.] A gummy vegetable matter contained in gum tragacanth, many seeds, roots, etc.; a solution in water of gummy matter of any kind.—**mucilaginous**, mū·si·laj′i·nus, *a.* Pertaining to or secreting mucilage; slimy; ropy; soft, and slightly viscid.

muck, muk, *n.* [From Icel. *myki*, Dan. *mög*, dung (whence *mödding*, midden).] Dung in a moist state, or a mass of dung and rotten vegetable matter; something mean, vile, or filthy.—*v.t.* To manure with muck; to remove muck from.— **mucker**, muk′ér, *n.* A dishonorable and impolite person; an impudent boor. (*Slang*).—**muck rake**, muk′rāk, *n.* A rake for removing muck.— **muckrake**, *v.i.* To accuse of bad faith or broadcast accusation of corruption, especially if unjustly.

mucous, mucosity. See MUCUS.

mucronate, mū′kro·nāt, *a.* [L. *mucronatus*, from *mucro*, a sharp point.] *Bot.* and *zool.* narrowed to a point; terminating in a sharp point.

mucus, mū′kus, *n.* [L., mucus from the nose; akin *mungo*, to wipe the nose; *mucilage*.] A viscid fluid secreted by the mucous membrane of animals, which it serves to moisten and defend; *bot.* gummy matter soluble in water.—**mucous**, mū′kus, *a.* [L. *mucosus*.] Pertaining to or resembling mucus; slimy; ropy; secreting a slimy substance.—*Mucous membrane*, a membrane that lines all the cavities of the body which open externally (such as the mouth, nose, intestines), and secretes mucus.— **mucosity**, mū·kos′i·ti, *n.* The state of being mucous; sliminess.

mud, mud, *n.* [Allied to L.G. *mod, mudde*, D. *modder*, Dan. *mudder*, Sw. *modd*, mud, mire; Icel. *mod*, dust; E. *mother*, slimy sediment. *Muddle* is a derivative.] Wet and soft earth or earthy matter as in a puddle; sediment from turbid waters; mire. —*Mud wall*, a wall built of mud or clay, rendered firm by drying.—*v.t.* —*mudded, mudding.* To soil with mud; to muddy.—**muddily**, mud′-i·li, *adv.* In a muddy manner; turbidly; obscurely; confusedly.— **muddiness**, mud′i·nes, *n.* The quality or condition of being muddy.— **muddy**, mud′i, *a.* Abounding in mud; foul with mud; turbid; miry; cloudy in mind; confused; stupid; obscure; wanting in perspicuity.— *v.t.*—*muddied, muddying.* To soil with mud; to dirty; to make turbid; to cloud or make dull.—**mudguard**, *n.* A cover over the wheel of a conveyance to stop flying mud.— **mud hen**, *n.* One of several species of waterfowl.—**mud puppy**, *n.* A kind of salamander.—**mudsill**, *n.* The base or lowest sill of a structure,

as of a bridge, at the bottom of a river, etc.—**mud turtle**, *n.* A name of the soft tortoises and terrapins.

muddle, mud′l, *v.t.*—*muddled, muddling.* [Freq. from *mud*.] To make foul, turbid, or muddy; to intoxicate partially; to cloud or stupefy, particularly with liquor; to bring into a state of confusion; to make a mess of.—*v.i.* To become muddy; to be in a confused state.—*n.* A mess; dirty confusion; intellectual confusion; bewilderment.—**muddled**, mud′ld, *p.* and *a.* Made turbid or muddy; stupefied; confused.— **muddleheaded**, *a.* Having the brains muddled; stupidly confused or dull; doltish.

muezzin, mu̯·ez′zin, mö·ez′in, *n.* [A *muezzin*, from *azzana*, to inform, from *azana*, to hear.] A Mohammedan crier attached to a mosque, whose duty it is to proclaim from the balcony of a minaret the summons to prayers five times a day.

muff, muf, *n.* [Dan. *muffe*, D. *mof*, L.G. *muffe*, *muff*, G. *muff*, a muff, akin to O.H.G. *mouwa*, D. *mouw*, a long sleeve; comp. also D. *mof*, a clown, *muf*, musty, silly, doting. Hence *muffle*.] A cylindrical cover, usually made of fur, into which both hands may be thrust in order to keep them warm; a soft, useless fellow; a mean, poor-spirited person (*colloq.*); in various games, an unsuccessful attempt to hold a caught ball.—*v.t.* To bungle; to miss a chance; in games, to fail to hold a caught ball.

muffin, muf′in, *n.* A quick bread baked in individual cup-shaped molds; a drop biscuit.

muffle, muf′l, *v.t.*—*muffled, muffling.* [O.E. also *muffle*, akin to *muff*; comp. D. *muffel*, a muff; Fr. *moufle*, a mitten.] To enfold or wrap up so as to conceal from view or protect from the weather; to wrap up or cover close, particularly the neck and face; to deaden the sound of (to *muffle* an oar or a drum); to restrain from speaking by wrapping up the head; to put to silence; *fig.* to wrap up or envelop; to involve.—*n.* [Fr. *moufle*, a kind of glove, a chemical vessel.] An arched vessel, resisting the strongest fire, and made to be placed over cupels in the operation of assaying, to preserve them from coming in contact with fuel, smoke, or ashes; a pulley block containing several sheaves.—**muffled**, muf′ld, *p.* and *a.* Wrapped up closely, especially about the face; treated so as to deaden the sound (as when an oar is wrapped with a mat at the rowlock).—**muffler**, muf′ler, *n.* A wrapper for muffling or enveloping the neck; something that deadens noise, especially on a car.

muffle, muf′l, *n.* [Fr. *mufle*, from G. *muffel*, an animal with large hanging lips.] The tumid and naked portion of the upper lip and nose of ruminants and rodents.

mufti, muf′ti, *n.* [Ar. *mufti*, from *āftā*, to judge, to give a decision.] The chief of the ecclesiastical order among the Mohammedans; a doctor of Mohammedan law; an Anglo-Indian term for plain dress worn by officers off duty; civilian dress.

mug, mug, *n.* [N. *mugge,* a ewer, a mug; Sw. *mugg,* an earthen cup; Ir. *mugan,* a mug.] A familiar name for an earthen or metal vessel for drinking from; the face (slang); a tough person (slang).—*v.t.* To photograph, especially a criminal; to assault from behind.—*v.i.* To make faces.—**mugger,** mug'ėr, *n.*

muggy, mug'i, *a.* [Prov. E. *mug,* mist; Icel. *mugga,* mugginess, drizzle; comp. Gael. *mugach,* cloudy; W. *mwg,* smoke.] Damp and close: said of the atmosphere or weather; warm and humid; moist; moldy.

mugwump, mug'wump, *n.* [Algonkin, a great man, a chief.] A person who takes an independent position in politics; a highly superior person in his own eyes.

mukluk, muk'luk, *n.* [Alaskan Eskimo *makliak, muklok, makluk,* large seal.] A variety of sealskin boot worn by Eskimos.

mulatto, mū·lat'tō, *n.* [Sp. *mulato,* from *mulo,* a mule. MULE.] The offspring of a Caucasian and a Negro; loosely, any individual of mixed Caucasian and Negro blood.

mulberry, mul'be·ri, *n.* [For *murberry;* A.Sax. *múrberie,* a mulberry, also *múr, mór,* from L. *morus,* a mulberry tree.] The berry or fruit of a well-known tree, and also the tree itself cultivated from a remote period for silk-worm rearing.—**mulberry-faced,** *a.* Having the face spotted as if with mulberry stains.

mulch, mulsh, *n.* [Akin to *mols* in A.Sax. *molsnian,* to rot, G. *mulsch, molsch,* rotten; D. *molsemen,* to molder.] Strawy dung in a somewhat moist state, but not rotten, used for protecting the roots of newly planted shrubs or trees, etc.—*v.t.* To cover with mulch.

mulct, mulkt, *n.* [L. *mulcta, multa,* a fine.] A fine or penalty.—*v.t.* To punish by fine or forfeiture; to punish by depriving; to deprive (to *mulct* a person *of* $300).

mule, mūl, *n.* [A.Sax. *múl,* Fr. *mule,* from L. *mulus,* a mule.] A quadruped of a mongrel breed, the offspring of an ass and a mare, or a horse and a she-ass; also any animal produced by a mixture of different species; a hybrid; a hybrid plant; a spinning machine invented by Crompton in 1775, so called from being a combination of the drawing rollers of Arkwright and the jenny of Hargreaves.—**mule skinner,** *n.* A driver of mules. (*Colloq.*)—**muleteer,** mū·le·tēr', *n.* [Fr. *muletier.*] A muledriver.—**mulish,** mūl'ish, *a.* Like a mule; sullen; stubborn. —**mulishly,** mūl'ish·li, *adv.* In a mulish manner.—**mulishness,** mūl'ish·nes, *n.* Obstinacy or stubbornness.

mule, mūl, *n.* [Fr. from D. *muil,* from L. *mulleus,* a red leather shoe.] A backless slipper.

muliebrity, mū·li·eb'ri·ti, *n.* [L. *muliebritas,* from *muliebris,* womanly, womanish, from *mulier,* a woman.]

Womanhood; puberty in a female; womanishness; effeminacy; softness.

mull, mul, *v.t.* [From the spurious participle *mulled* in *mulled ale,* equivalent to *mold-ale,* that is funeral ale, from *mold,* earth, the earth of the grave.] To heat, sweeten, and flavor with spices (to *mull* wine).

mull, mul, *v.i. & t.* To cogitate; to contemplate thoughtfully. (*Colloq.*)

mull, mul, *n.* [Hind. *mul-mul,* muslin.] A thin, soft kind of muslin.

mullein, mullen, mul'en, *n.* [A.Sax. *molegn;* comp. Dan. *mól,* a moth: one species is used to drive away moths.] The common name of a genus of wild plants used in domestic medicine.

muller, mul'ėr, *n.* [O.Fr. *moulleur,* from *moulre, mouldre* (Fr. *moudre*), L. *molere,* to grind, from *mola,* a millstone.] A sort of flat-bottomed pestle used for grinding pigments, etc.

mullet, mul'et, *n.* [Fr. *mulet,* from L. *mullus,* the surmullet.] A name common to spiny-rayed fishes of two somewhat widely separate families, the gray mullets and the red mullets, or surmullets.

mulligan, mul'i·gan, *n.* A stew of meat and vegetables. (*Slang.*)

mulligatawny, mul'i·ga·tạ'ni, *n.* [Tamil *milagutannir,* lit. pepper water.] An East Indian curry soup.

mullion, mul'yon, *n.* [For *munnion,* a word equivalent to Fr. *moignon,* Sp. *muñon,* a stump, the mullion of a window being the stump below the tracery.] *Arch.* a vertical division between the lights of windows, screens, etc., in Gothic architecture; also a division between the panels in wainscoting.

multangular, mul·tang'gū·lėr, *a.* [L. *multus,* many, and *angulus,* angle.] Having many angles; polygonal.

multicostate, mul·ti·kos'tāt, *a.* [L. *multus,* many, *costa,* a rib.] Having many ribs; *bot.* having two or more diverging ribs: said of leaves.

multidentate, mul·ti·den'tāt, *a.* [L. *multus,* many, and *dens,* a tooth.] Having many teeth or teeth-like processes.

multifarious, mul·ti·fā'ri·us, *a.* [L. *multifarius,* manifold—*multus,* many.] Having great multiplicity; having great diversity or variety; made up of many differing parts.—**multifariously,** mul·ti·fā'ri·us·li, *adv.* In a multifarious way.—**multifariousness,** mul·ti·fā'ri·us·nes, *n.*

multifid, mul'ti·fid, *a.* [L. *multifidus* —*multus,* many, and *findo,* to divide.] Cleft or cut by many divisions; *bot.* divided into several parts by clefts extending to about the middle (a *multifid* leaf).

multiflorous, mul·ti·flō'rus, *a.* [L. *multus,* many, *flos, floris,* a flower.] Many-flowered; having many flowers.

multiform, mul'ti·form, *a.* [L. *multiformis*—*multus,* many, and *forma,* form.] Having many forms, shapes, or appearances.—**multiformity,** mul·ti·for'mi·ti, *n.* The state of being multiform.

multilateral, mul·ti·lat'ėr·al, *a.* [L.

multus, many, and *latus,* side.] Having many sides; polygonal; something involving more than two nations (*multilateral* conference).

multilineal, multilinear, mul·ti·lin'ē·al, mul·ti·lin'ē·ėr, *a.* [L. *multus,* many, and *linea,* a line.] Having many lines.

multilocular, mul·ti·lok'ū·lėr, *a.* [L. *multus,* many, *loculus,* a cell.] Having many cells, loculi, or compartments.

multimillionaire, mul·ti·mil·yon·âr', *n.* [L. *multus,* many, and *millionaire.*] One whose wealth is measured in millions.

multiparous, mul·tip'a·rus, *a.* [L. *multus,* many, *pario,* to bear.] Producing many at a birth.

multipartite, mul'ti·pär·tīt, *a.* [L. *multus,* many, and *partitus,* divided— *pars,* a part.] Divided into several or many parts; *bot.* more deeply cleft than *multifid.*

multipede, multiped, mul'ti·pēd, *n.* [L. *multus,* many, *pes, pedis,* a foot.] An animal that has many feet, as a centipede.

multiphase, mul'ti·fās, *a.* [L. *multus,* many, *phasis,* phase.] Showing many phases.

multiple, mul'ti·pl, *a.* [Fr. *multiple,* from L.L. *multiplus—multus,* many, and term. as in *triple.*] Manifold; having many parts or divisions.—*n.* A number which contains another an exact number of times without a remainder (thus 24 is a *multiple* of three).—*Multiple sclerosis,* a disease in which tissue of the brain or spinal cord hardens, causing headache, partial paralysis, jerking muscle tremor, etc.

multiplex, mul'ti·pleks, *a.* [L. *multiplex—multus,* many, and stem of *plico,* to fold. PLY.] Manifold; complex; *bot.* having petals lying over each other in folds.—**multipliable,** mul'ti·plī·a·bl, *a.* Capable of being multiplied.—**multiplicable,** mul'ti·pli·ka·bl, *a.* Multipliable.—**multiplicand,** mul'ti·pli·kand, *n.* [L. *multiplicandus.*] *Arith.* the number to be multiplied by another, which is called the multiplier.—**multiplicate,** mul'ti·pli·kāt, *a.* [L. *multiplicatus.*] Multiplex.—**multiplication,** mul'ti·pli·kā''shon, *n.* [L. *multiplicatio, multiplicationis.*] The act or process of multiplying; the state of being multiplied; *arith.* and *alg.* the operation by which any given number or quantity may be added to itself any number of times proposed.— *Multiplication table,* a table containing the product of all the simple digits multiplied into each other, and onward, to some assumed limit, as to 12 times 12.—**multiplicative,** mul'ti·pli·kā''tiv, *a.* Tending to multiply; having the power to multiply.—**multiplicity,** mul·ti·plis'i·ti, *n.* [L. *multiplicitas,* from *multiplex.*] The state of being multiplex, numerous, or various; an extensive aggregate of individuals of the same kind; a great number.— **multiplier,** mul'ti·pli·ėr, *n.* One who or that which multiplies; the number in arithmetic by which another is multiplied; *teleg.* an instrument for increasing by repetition the strength of an electric current.—**multiply,** mul'ti·plī, *v.t.*—*multiplied, multiplying.* [Fr. *multiplier,* from L. *multiplicare,* from *multiplex.*] To increase in number; to make more by natural reproduction or by addition; to make more numerous; *arith.* to add to itself any given number of times. —*v.i.* To grow or increase in number, or to become more numerous by reproduction; to extend; to spread.

multisonous, mul·tis'ō·nus, *a.* [L. *multus,* many, *sonus,* sound.] Having many sounds, or sounding much.

multispiral, mul·ti·spī'ral, *a.* [L. *multus,* many, *spira,* a coil.] Having many spiral coils or convolutions.

multistriate, mul·ti·strī'āt, *a.* [L. *multus,* many, *stria,* a streak.] Marked with many streaks or striae.

multitubular, mul·ti·tū'bū·lėr, *a.* [L. *multus,* many, and E. *tubular.*] Having many tubes (a *multitubular* boiler).

multitude, mul'ti·tūd, *n.* [L. *multitudo,* from *multus,* much, many.] The state of being many; a great number, collectively; a great many, indefinitely; a crowd or throng; a gathering of people.—*The multitude,* the populace, or the mass of men without reference to an assemblage. —**multitudinous,** mul·ti·tū'di·nus, *a.* Pertaining or belonging to a multitude; consisting of a multitude. —**multitudinously,** mul·ti·tū'di·nus·li, *adv.* In a multitudinous manner.—**multitudinousness,** mul·ti·tū'di·nus·nes, *n.*

multivalent, mul·ti·vā'lent, *a.* [Prefix *multi,* and *valent.*] *Chem.* having a valence of three or more.

multivalve, mul'ti·valv, *a.* [L. *multus,* many, and E. *valve.*] Having many valves (a *multivalve* shell).— *n.* An animal which has a shell of many valves or pieces.

mum, mum, *a.* [Imitative of a low sound made with the lips closed, like L. and Gr. *mu;* akin *mumble.*] Silent; not speaking. Often used as an exclamation=be silent; hush.

mum, mum, *n.* [G. *mumme,* from Christian *Mumme,* who first brewed it at Brunswick in 1492.] A species of malt liquor used in Germany, made of wheat malt.

mum, mumm, mum, *v.i.* [Of Dutch or German origin; comp. G. *mummen,* to mask, *mumme,* a mask, *mummel,* a bugbear; D. *mommen,* to mask, *mom,* a mask, whence O.Fr. *momer,* to mask, *momerie,* mummery; originally perhaps to cover the face and cry *mum,* or similar sound.] To sport or make diversion in a mask or disguise.—**mummer,** mum'ėr, *n.* A masker; a masked buffoon.—**mummery,** mum'ėr·i, *n.* A masking or masquerade; buffoonery; farcical show; hypocritical disguise and parade.

mumble, mum'bl, *v.i.*—*mumbled, mumbling.* [Freq. from *mum;* like D. *mommelen,* Dan. *mumle,* G. *mummeln,* to mumble.] To mutter; to speak so as to render the sounds inarticulate and imperfect; to chew

or bite softly; to eat with the lips closed.—*v.t.* To utter with a low inarticulate voice; to chew gently, or to eat with a muttering sound.— **mumbler,** mum'blėr, *n.* One who mumbles.—**mumblingly,** mum'bling·li, *adv.* In a mumbling manner.

mumblety-peg, mumble-the-peg, mum'bl·ti·peg, mum'bl·THi·peg, *n.* [From *mumble the peg,* the phrase said to the game's loser who had to snatch, with his teeth, a peg driven in the ground.] A game in which the players, from several positions, must toss or throw a knife, making it stick in the ground.

Mumbo Jumbo, mum'bō jum·bō, *n.* A god of certain Negro tribes; any senseless object of popular idolatry.

mummy, mum'i, *n.* [Fr. *mumie, momie,* Sp. *momia,* It. *mummia,* from Ar. *mûmia,* from *mûm,* wax.] A dead human body embalmed and dried after the manner of those taken from Egyptian tombs; a human body dried up and preserved, either artificially or by accident; a sort of wax used in grafting and planting trees; a sort of brown bituminous pigment.—*To beat to a mummy,* to beat soundly, or till senseless.—*v.t.* To embalm.— **mummify,** mum'i·fī, *v.t.* To make into a mummy; to embalm and dry, as a mummy.—**mummification,** mum'i·fi·kā"shon, *n.* The act of mummifying; the process of becoming a mummy.

mump, mump, *v.i.* [An imitative word, allied to *mumble* and *munch.*] To mumble or mutter, as in sulkiness; to move the lips with the mouth closed; to nibble; to chew; to munch; to grin or make mouths; to implore alms; to play the beggar. —*v.t.* To munch or chew.

mumps, mumps, *n. pl.* [From *mump,* sullenness.] A disease consisting in an inflammation of the salivary glands, with swelling along the neck; parotitis.

munch, munsh, *v.t. and i.* [Imitative of sound; akin *mumble, mump.*] To chew audibly; to mump; to nibble.— **muncher,** munsh'er, *n.* One who munches.

mundane, mun'dān, *a.* [L. *mundanus,* from *mundus,* the world.] Belonging to this world; worldly; terrestrial; earthly.—**mundanely,** mun'dān·li, *adv.* In a mundane manner; with reference to worldly things.

mungo, mung'gō, *n.* [Perhaps from some person of this name.] Artificial short-staple wool formed by tearing to pieces and disintegrating old woolen fabrics; akin to shoddy.

municipal, mū·nis'i·pal, *a.* [L. *municipalis,* from *municipium,* a town governed by its own laws—*munia,* official duties, and *capio,* to take.] Pertaining to local self-government; pertaining to the corporation of a town or city, or to the citizens of a state.—*Municipal bond,* a bond issued by a municipal government to provide funds for a public undertaking. —*Municipal law,* the law which pertains to the citizens of a state in their private capacity.—**municipalism,** mū·nis'i·pal·izm, *n.* Municipal

state or condition.—**municipality,** mū·nis'i·pal"i·ti, *n.* A town or city possessed of local self-government; a community under municipal jurisdiction.

munificence, mū·nif'i·sens, *n.* [L. *munificentia*—*munus,* a gift or favor, and *facio,* to make.] The quality of being munificent; a giving with great liberality; bounty; liberality. —**munificent,** mū·nif'i·sent, *a.* Liberal in giving or bestowing; bounteous; generous.—**munificently,** mū·nif'i·sent·li, *adv.* In a munificent manner; liberally.

muniment, mū'ni·ment, *n.* [L. *munimentum,* a defense, from *munio,* to fortify, from *mœnia,* walls.] A fortification; a stronghold; support; defense; a writing by which claims and rights are defended or maintained; a title-deed, charter, record, etc.—*Muniment house, Muniment room,* a house or room for keeping deeds, charters, etc.

munition, mū·nish'on, *n.* [L. *munitio, munitionis,* from *munio,* to fortify; hence *ammunition.*] Materials used in war; military stores; ammunition.

mural, mū'ral, *a.* [L. *muralis,* from *murus,* a wall; same root as *munio,* to fortify. MUNITION.] Pertaining to a wall; resembling a wall; perpendicular or steep.—*Mural circle,* an astronomical instrument for measuring angular distances in the meridian, permanently fixed exactly perpendicular in the plane of the meridian.—*Mural crown,* a golden crown bestowed among the ancient Romans on him who mounted the wall of a besieged place and lodged a standard.—*Mural literature,* placards or posters on walls by political parties during elections.—*Mural painting,* a painting upon the surface of a wall.

murder, mėr'dėr, *n.* [A.Sax. *morthor, morther,* from *morth,* death; Goth. *maurthr,* D. *moord,* Dan., Sw., and G. *mord,* Icel. *morth;* L. *mors,* death (E. *mortal*); Skr. *mri,* to die.] The act of unlawfully killing a human being with premeditated malice; something difficult to do.—*v.t.* To kill (a human being) with premeditated malice; to slay feloniously; *fig.* to abuse or violate grossly (to *murder* the king's English).—*v.i.* To commit murder.—**murderer,** mėr'dėr·ėr, *n.* —**murderess,** mėr'dėr·es, *n.* A female who commits murder.—**murderous,** mėr'dėr·us, *a.*—**murderously,** mėr'dėr·us·li, *adv.*

murex, mū'reks, *n. pl.* **murices,** mū'ri·sēz. [L.] A mollusk resembling the whelk, in esteem from the earliest ages on account of the purple dye that some of them yielded; the dye itself.

muriate, mū'ri·āt, *n.* [L. *muria,* brine.] The old name for *Chloride.*— **muriatic,** mū·ri·at'ik, *a.* Pertaining to or obtained from brine or sea salt.—*Muriatic acid,* the older name of *Hydrochloric acid.*

muricate, muricated, mū'ri·kāt, mū'ri·kā·ted, *a.* [L. *muricatus,* from *murex,* the point of a rock.] Full of sharp points; armed with prickles.

murine, mū′rīn, a. [L. *murinus*, from *mus, muris*, a mouse.] Pertaining to a mouse or to mice.

murk, mėrk, n. [A.Sax *murc, mirce*, dark, Icel. *myrkr*, Dan. and Sw. *mörk*, dark.] Darkness or gloom. (*Shak*.)—**murky**, mėr′ki, a. Dark; obscure; gloomy.—**murkily**, mėr′ki·li, adv. In a murky manner; darkly.—**murkiness**, mėr′ki·nes, n. State of being murky; darkness; gloom.

murmur, mėr′mėr, n. [Fr. *murmure*, from L. *murmur*, a reduplication of an imitative syllable *mur*, seen in G. *murren*, D. *morren*, Icel. *murra*, Dan. *murre*, to murmur.] A low sound continued or continually repeated, as that of a stream; a low indistinct sound; a hum; a complaint uttered in a low, muttering voice; a grumble or mutter.—*v i.* To utter or give out a murmur or hum; to grumble; to utter complaints; to mutter.—*v.t.* To utter indistinctly; to mutter.—**murmurer**, mėr′mėr·ėr, n. One who murmurs.—**murmuring**, mėr′-mėr·ing, p. and a. Making or consisting in a low continued noise; uttering complaints in a low voice or sullen manner.—n. A continued murmur; a low confused noise.—**murmurous**, mėr′mėr·us, a. Attended by murmurs; murmuring.—**murmurously**, mėr′mėr·us·li, adv.

murrain, mur′in, n. [O.Fr. *morine*, from L. *morior*, to die. MORTAL.] A disease that rages among cattle; a cattle plague or epizootic disease of any kind; foot-and-mouth disease. —*Murrain take you, murrain on you*, etc., plague take you, plague upon you.

murre, mėr, n. [Etymology doubtful.] A name for the common guillemot.

murrey, mur′i, n. [O.Fr. *morée*, a dark-red color, from L. *morum*, a mulberry.] A dark-red or mulberry color.

murrhine, mur′īn, a. [L. *murrhinus*, from *murrha*, a material, supposed to be fluorspar.] A name given to a delicate kind of ware anciently brought from the East, and much prized among the Romans. Called also *myrrhine*.

musaceous, mū·zā′shus, a. [From *Musa*, the typical genus.] Pertaining to the order of plants to which belong the banana and plantain.

muscadine, mus′ka·din, n. *Muscadinia rotundifolia*, a grape of the southwestern U.S.

muscatel, muscadel, mus′ka·tel, mus′ka·del, n. [Fr. *moscatelle*, from L.L. *muscatus*, smelling like musk, L. *muscus*, musk. MUSK.] The name of several sweet and strong Italian and French wines, whether white or red; the grapes which produce these wines.

muscle, mus′l, n. [Fr. *muscle*, from L. *musculus*, dim. of *mus*, a mouse.] A band or mass of contractile tissue in an animal organism by means of which bodily movement is effected, the two main kinds of muscles being the *voluntary*, which can be controlled at will, and the *involun-* *tary*, which function without regard to will, such as the muscles of the digestive tract, the heart, the blood vessels, etc.; muscular strength; power.—*v.i.* To push one's way in by force.—**muscular**, mus′kū·lėr, a. Pertaining to or consisting of muscles; performed by or dependent on muscles (*muscular* exertion); having well-developed muscles; strong; brawny.—**muscle-bound**, a. Having the muscles enlarged, overstrained, and rendered inelastic by overexercise.—**muscularity**, mus-kū·lar′i·ti, n.—**muscular dystrophy**, n. *Med.* a hereditary disease marked by a progressive deterioration of the muscles.—**musculature**, mus′kū·la·chėr, n. The muscles of all or a part of any animal.

muscovado, mus·ko·vā′dō, n. or a. [Sp. *mascabado*, from *mas*, more, and *acabado*, finished (further advanced than when in syrup).] A term applied to unrefined sugar, the raw material from which loaf and lump sugar are procured by refining.

muscovite, mus′ko·vīt, n. Ordinary mica; [*cap*.] a native of Muscovy, or Russia.—**muscovy duck**, mus′ko·vi, n. The musk duck.

muscular. See MUSCLE.

Muse, mūz, n. [Fr. *muse*, L. *musa*, from Gr. *mousa*, a muse. *Music, museum, mosaic* are derivatives.] *Greek myth.* one of the daughters of Zeus and Mnemosyne, who presided over the different kinds of poetry, and the sciences and arts, nine in number, as *Clio*, the muse of history; *Thalia*, the muse of comedy; *Melpomene*, the muse of tragedy; *Calliope*, the muse of epic poetry, etc.; [*not cap*.] hence, poetic inspiration; the inspiring goddess of song.

muse, mūz, *v.i.*—*mused, musing.* [Fr. *muser*, to muse, dawdle, loiter, from O.H.G. *muoza*, idleness, *muozon*, to be idle, G. *musze*, inactivity, leisure. From this comes *amuse* with prefix *a.*] To ponder; to think or meditate in silence; to be absent in mind.—*v.t.* To think or meditate on.—n. A fit of abstraction.—**museful**, mūz′ful, a. Musing; thoughtful.—**musing**, mū′zing. a. Meditative; absent-minded.—n. Meditation; absent-mindedness.—**musingly**, mū′zing·li, adv. In a musing way.

museum, mū·zē′um, n. [L., from Gr. *mouseion*, originally a temple of the Muses.] A place for the exhibition of objects of interest from history, the arts, or the sciences.

mush, mush, n. [G. *mus*, pap.] The meal of corn boiled in water; any mixture of watery consistency; sickening sentimentality.—**mushy**, mush′i, a.

mush, mush, *v.i.* [Fr. *marchons*, a starting order.] To journey on foot, particularly over snow, by dog team and sled.—n. Such a trip; the call of the driver to start his dogs.

mushroom, mush′röm, n. [Fr. *mousseron*, from *mousse*, L. *muscus*, moss. MOSS.] The common name of numerous fungi, especially such as are edible, having a fleshy body and a brownish color.—*v.i.* To grow or expand rapidly, as a mushroom; to spread out on the end as a mushroom.

music, mū′zik, n. [Fr. *musique*, L. *musica*, from Gr. *mousikē* (*technē*, art, understood), music, art, culture. MUSE, *n.*] A succession of sounds so modulated as to please the ear; melody or harmony; the art of producing melody or harmony; the written or printed score of a composition.—*Chamber music*, compositions suitable for performance in a private room.—**music box**, n. A small instrument, having a toothed barrel operating on vibrating tongues, which plays one or more tunes on being wound up.—**musical**, mū′zi·kal, a. Belonging to music; producing music or agreeable sounds; melodious; harmonious.—*Musical glasses*, glass vessels on which music may be played by striking them.—**musical comedy**, a theatrical production with little plot, but with much music and some dancing. —**musicale**, mū·zi·kal′, n. A social function with music as the outstanding entertainment.—**musician**, mū·zish′an, n. A person skilled in music; one that sings or performs on instruments of music.—**musicology**, mū·zi·kol′o·gi, n. The study of musical science or history.

musing. See MUSE (verb).

musk, musk, n. [Fr. *musc*, It. and Sp. *musco*, from L. *muscus*, musk, from Per. *mosk*, musk; allied to Skr. *mushka*, a testicle.] A substance obtained from a cyst or bag near the navel of the musk deer, having a strong, peculiar, and highly diffusible odor, used as a perfume; a musky smell; a popular name for one or two plants.—**musky**, mus′ki, a. Having the odor of musk.—**musk deer**, n. A deer of Central Asia, the male of which has long tusks and yields the well-known perfume musk. —**muskmelon**, n. A delicious and fragrant variety of melon.—**musk ox**, n. A kind of small hardy ox which inhabits the extreme north of North America, and smells strongly of musk.—**muskrat**, n. An American rodent allied to the beaver, which smells of musk in summer: called also *musquash*; the name is also given to two insectivorous animals smelling of musk.—**musk rose**, n. A species of rose, so called from its fragrance.

muskallonge, n. See MUSKELLUNGE.

muskellunge, mus′kel·lunj, n. [American Indian.] A large variety of pike found in the lakes and rivers of northern U. S. and Canada.

musket, mus′ket, n. [Fr. *mousquet*, O.Fr. *mousket, moschet*, originally a sparrow hawk, lit. fly-hawk, from L. *musca*, a fly (comp. *falcon, falconet, saker*, etc., as names of firearms).] A general term formerly used to mean any hand gun of smooth bore, but generally conceived of as a shoulder gun; the forerunner of the modern rifle.—**musketeer**, mus·ket·ėr′, n. A soldier armed with a musket. —**musketry**, mus′ket·ri, n. The fire of muskets; troops armed with muskets; the art or science of firing small arms.

Muslim, muz'lim, *n.* Same as *Moslem.*

muslin, muz'lin, *n.* [Fr. *mousseline,* said to be derived from *Mosul* or *Moussul,* a town in Mesopotamia where first made.] A fine thin cotton fabric, of which there are many different kinds.—*a.* Made of muslin (a *muslin* gown).—**muslin delaine,** muz'lin de•lān", *n.* [Fr. *mousseline-delaine,* muslin of wool.] A woolen, or cotton and woolen fabric of light texture, used for ladies' dresses, etc.

musquash, mus'kwosh, *n.* A muskrat.

muss, mus, *n.* [Form of *mess.*] Disorder; a dirty mess.—*v.t.* To cause to be untidy; to rumple.—**mussy,** mus'i, *a.*

mussel, mus'el, *n.* [Same as *muscle.*] The common name of various bivalve shellfish, some kinds being largely used for food.

Mussulman, mus'el•man, *n.* pl. **Mussulmans,** mus'el•manz, [Corrupted from *moslemin,* pl. of *moslem.*] A Mohammedan or believer in Mohammed; a Moslem.—**Mussulmanism,** mus'el•man•izm, *n.* Mohammedanism.

must, must, *v.i.*; without inflection and used as a present or a past tense. [A.Sax. *ic móste, wé móston,* I must, we must, a past tense; pres. *ic mót,* I may or must; similar forms in Goth., D., Sw., and G.] A defective or auxiliary verb expressing obligation or necessity, physical or moral; or often merely expressing the conviction of the speaker (you *must* be wrong).

must, must, *n.* [L. *mustum,* new wine, from *mustus,* new, fresh.] Wine or juice pressed from the grape but not fermented.

must, must, *n.* [MUSTY.] Mold or moldiness; fustiness.

mustache, mustachio, mus•täsh', mus•täsh'i•ō, *n.* [Fr. *moustache,* It. *mostaccio,* from Gr. *mystax,* the upper lip, the beard upon it.] The hair on the upper lip of men; the unshaven hair of the upper lip; often spoken of as plural.

mustang, mus'tang, *n.* [Sp. *mesteno,* belonging to the *mesta,* or body of graziers.] The wild horse of America, a descendant of horses imported.

mustard, mus'tėrd, *n.* [O.Fr. *moustarde,* It. *mostarda,* mustard, from L. *mustum,* must, because it is made with a little must mixed in it. MUST, MOIST.] An annual cruciferous plant extensively cultivated for its pungent seeds, which when ground and properly prepared form the well-known condiment of same name.—**mustard gas,** mus'tėrd, *n.* A poisonous gas with a pungent smell resembling that of mustard.

musteline, mus'te•līn, *a.* [L. *mustelinus,* from *mustela,* a weasel.] Pertaining to the weasel and kindred animals.

muster, mus'tėr, *v.t.* [O.Fr. *moustrer, mostrer, monstrer,* to exhibit, from L. *monstrare,* to show, from *monstrum,* a monster. MONSTER.] To collect, as troops for service, review, parade,

or exercise; to assemble or bring together generally; to collect for use or exhibition.—*To muster up,* to gather, collect, or summon up: generally *fig.* (to *muster up* courage).—*v.i.* To assemble or meet in one place, as soldiers.—*n.* An assembling of troops for review or for service; the act of assembling; an assemblage.—*To pass muster,* to pass without censure, as one among a number on inspection; to be allowed to pass.

musty, mus'ti, *a.* [Probably connected with *moist,* or with L. *mucidus,* moldy; comp. Sp. *mustio,* musty.] Moldy; turned sour; fusty; stale; spoiled by age; having an ill flavor; vapid.—**mustily,** mus'ti•li, *adv.* In a musty manner.—**mustiness,** mus'ti•nes, *n.* The state or quality of being musty; staleness.

mutable, mū'ta•bl, *a.* [L. *mutabilis,* from *muto,* to change; akin to *moveo,* to move.] Capable of being altered; subject to change; inconstant.—**mutably,** mū'ta•bli, *adv.*—**mutability, mutableness,** mū•ta•bil'i•ti, mū'ta•bl•nes, *n.*—**mutate,** mū'tāt, *v.t.* To change; to alter.—*v.i.* To undergo change.—**mutation,** mū•tā'shon, *n.* The act or process of changing; change; alteration; modification; *philol.* umlaut; *biol.* a sudden, marked deviation in inherited characteristics; the results of such change.—**mutant,** mū'tent, *a.*

mutchkin, much'kin, *n.* [Comp. D. *mutsje,* a little cap, a quartern; Sc. *mutch,* a kind of cap.] A liquid measure in Scotland containing four gills.

mute, mūt, *a.* [L. *mutus,* silent, dumb; akin to *mutio,* to mumble; Gr. *mu,* a sound with closed lips. MUM, MUTTER.] Silent; not speaking; incapable of utterance; not having the power of speech; dumb; *gram.* and *philol.* silent, not pronounced, or having its sound suddenly and completely checked by closure of the vocal organs; applied to certain consonants (as *t, p*).—*n.* A dumb person; one unable to use articulate speech; a hired attendant at a funeral; *gram.* and *philol.* a mute letter; *mus.* a utensil applied to a musical instrument to deaden or soften the sounds.—**mutely,** mūt'li, *adv.* In a mute manner; silently; dumbly.—**muteness, mutism,** mūt'nes, mūt'izm, *n.* The state of being mute.

mutilate, mū'ti•lāt, *v.t.*—*mutilated, mutilating.* [L. *mutilo, mutilatum,* to lop, from *mutilus,* maimed; akin Gr. *mitylos,* docked.] To cut off a limb or essential part of; to maim; to remove any material part from so as to render the thing imperfect.—**mutilation,** mū•ti•lā'shon, *n.* The act of mutilating or state of being mutilated.—**mutilator,** mū'ti•lā•tėr, *n.* One who mutilates.

mutiny, mū'ti•ni, *n.* [From Fr. *mutin,* O.Fr. *meutin,* mutinous, riotous, *meute,* a revolt, an *emeute,* from L.L. *mota,* a body of men raised for an expedition, from L. *moveo, motus,* to move. MOVE.] A resistance to or revolt against con-

stituted authority; specifically an insurrection of soldiers or seamen against the authority of their commanders; open resistance to officers or opposition to their authority.—*v.i.*—*mutinied, mutinying.* To engage in mutiny; to rise against military or naval officers; to be guilty of mutinous conduct.—**mutineer,** mū•ti•nēr', *n.* One guilty of mutiny.—**mutinous,** mū'ti•nus, *a.* Engaged in or disposed to mutiny.—**mutinously,** mū'ti•nus•li, *adv.* In a mutinous manner.—**mutinousness,** mū'ti•nus•nes, *n.* The state or quality of being rebellious or of inciting mutiny.

mutt, mut, *n.* [From *muttonhead,* a stupid person.] A mongrel dog; a stupid person.

mutter, mut'ėr, *v.i.* [An imitative word; comp. G. *muttern,* L. *muttire,* to mutter. MUMBLE.] To utter words with a low voice and compressed lips; to grumble; to murmur.—*v.t.* To utter with a low murmuring voice.—*n.* Murmur.—**mutterer,** mut'ėr•ėr, *n.*—**mutteringly,** mut'ėr•ing•li, *adv.*

mutton, mut'n, *n.* [Fr. *mouton,* It. *moltone,* a sheep; supposed to be from L. *mutilus,* mutilated, through L.L. *multo, mutilo,* a wether, a castrated ram.] The flesh of sheep, raw, or dressed for food.—**mutton-chop,** *n.* A rib-piece of mutton for broiling, having the bone cut, or *chopped* off at the small end.

mutual, mū'chu̯•al, *a.* [Fr. *mutuel,* from a L.L. *mutualis,* from L. *mutuus,* mutual, from *muto,* to change. MUTABLE.] Reciprocally given and received; pertaining alike or reciprocally to both sides; interchanged; equally relating to, affecting, proceeding from two or more together; common to two or more combined; shared alike.—**mutuality,** mū•chu̯•al'i•ti, *n.* The state or quality of being mutual.—**mutually,** mū'chu̯•al•li, *adv.* In a mutual manner; reciprocally; conjointly; in common.

mutule, mū'tūl, *n.* [L. *mutulus.*] *Arch.* a projecting block under the corona of the Doric cornice.

muzzle, muz'l, *n.* [O.Fr. *musel* (Mod. Fr. *museau*), dim. of O.Fr. *muse,* L.L. *musus,* a mouth, from L. *morsus,* a bite, from *mordeo, morsum,* to bite. MORSEL.] The projecting mouth and nose of an animal, as of a horse, dog, etc.; the open end of a gun or pistol, etc.; a fastening for the mouth which hinders an animal from biting.—*v.t.*—*muzzled, muzzling.* To put a muzzle on; to bind the mouth of, to prevent biting or eating; to put to silence.—**muzzle-loader,** *n.* A gun loaded by the muzzle; opposed to *breechloader.*

muzzy, muz'i, *a.* [Akin to *muse,* to be absent-minded.] Absent in mind; bewildered; tipsy.

my, mī, *pronom. adj.* [Contr. from *mine,* A.Sax. *min.* MINE.] Belonging to me (this is *my* book): always used before a noun or attributively, *mine* being used predicatively (this book is *mine*).—*interj*. An exclamation of surprise (Oh *my*!).

myalgia, mī·al'ji·a, *n*. [Gr. *mys*, muscle, and *algos*, pain.] Cramp.

mycelium, mī·sē'li·um, *n*. pl. **mycelia**, mī·sē'li·a. [Gr. *mykēs*, a fungus.] The cellular filamentous spawn of fungi, consisting of whitish filaments spreading like a network.—**mycelioid**, mī·sē'li·oid, *a*. *Bot*. resembling a mycelium.

mycology, mī·kol'o·ji, *n*. [Gr. *mykēs*, fungus, and *logos*.] That department of botany which investigates fungi.—**mycologist**, mī·kol'o·jist, *n*.

Mycoplasma, mī"kō·plaz'ma, *n*. [Gr. *mykēs*, and *plasma*, anything molded.] The sole genus of the family Mycoplasmataceae, which are parasitic organisms intermediate between viruses and bacteria and have complex life cycles, reportedly involving the breaking of filaments into nondivisible spherical organisms.

mycorrhiza, mī'ko·rī"za, *n*. [Gr. *mykēs*, a fungus, *rhiza*, a root.] A sheath of fungal threads surrounding a root. Probably a case of SYMBIOSIS (which see).

mydriatic, mid'ri·at"ik, *n*. [Gr. *mydriasis*, undue dilation of the pupil.] Causing dilation of the pupil; a drug for effecting this.

myelencephalous, mī'el·en·sef"al·us, *a*. [Gr. *myelos*, marrow, and *enkephalon*, the brain.] Exhibiting a nervous system concentrated in a brain and spinal cord, as the higher animals.

myelin, myeline, mī'e·lin, *n*. [Gr. *myelos*, marrow.] A white, soft, fatty material forming a thick sheath around the axis cylinder of certain nerve fibers.—**myelitis**, mī'e·lī"tis, *n*. *Med*. inflammation of the spinal cord or bone marrow.

myna, mī'na, *n*. [Ind. name.] An Indian bird of the starling family that can be taught to speak, and is often kept in cages in Europe and America.

myology, mī·ol'o·ji, *n*. [Gr. *mys*, *myos*, muscle, and *logos*, discourse.] The scientific knowledge or description of the muscles of the human body.—**myologist**, mī·ol'o·jist, *n*. One who is versed in myology.

myope, mī'ōp, *n*. [Gr. *myōps*—*myō*, to shut, and *ōps*, the eye.] A shortsighted person.—**myopia**, mī·ō'pi·a, *n*. Shortsightedness; nearsightedness; a condition in which the image is focused before reaching the retina.—**myopic**, mī·op'ik, *a*. Pertaining to or affected with myopia.

myosin, mī'o·sin, *n*. [Gr. *mys*, *myos*, a muscle.] A peculiar constituent of muscle.

myosis, mī·ō'sis, *n*. [Gr. *myō*, to close the eye.] *Pathol*. an abnormal contraction of the pupil of the eye.—**myotic**, mī·ot'ik, *a*. and *n*. Causing such contraction, or a drug that causes it.

myosotis, mī·o·sō'tis, *n*. [Gr. *mys*, *myos*, a mouse, and *ous*, *ōtos*, an ear.] The plant forget-me-not.

myriad, mir'i·ad, *n*. [Gr. *myrias*, *myriados*, from *myria*, ten thousand, innumerable.] The number of ten thousand collectively; an immense number indefinitely.—*a*. Innumerable; multitudinous but indefinite.

myriagram, mir'i·a·gram, *n*. [Gr. *myria*, ten thousand, and Fr. *gramme*, a gram.] A French weight of 10,000 grams, or 22 lbs. avoirdupois.—**myrialiter**, mir'i·a·lē·tėr, *n*. A French measure of capacity containing 10,000 liters, or 610,280 cubic inches.—**myriameter**, mir'i·a·mē·tėr, *n*. A French measure of length equal to 10 kilometers or 6.21 miles.

myriapod, mir'i·a·pod, *n*. [Gr. *myria*, ten thousand, and *pous*, *podos*, a foot.] An individual belonging to the class of animals that includes the centipedes and millipedes, having bodies of a lengthened form and in numerous segments, the segments being provided with pairs of feet.

Myrmidon, mėr'mi·don, *n*. One of an ancient Greek race in Thessaly, whom Achilles ruled, and who accompanied him to Troy; [*not cap*.] hence, a soldier of a rough character; one of a ruffianly band under a daring or unscrupulous leader; an unscrupulous follower.—*myrmidons of the law*, bailiffs, sheriffs' officers, policemen, and other law menials.

myrobalan, mī·rob'a·lan, *n*. [L. *myrobalanum*, Gr. *myrobalanos*—*myron*, unguent, and *balanus*, a nut.] A dried fruit of different species of the plum kind, brought from the East Indies, and used by dyers and tanners.

myrrh, mėr, *n*. [L. *myrrha*, Gr. *myrrha*, Ar. *murr*, bitter.] The gummy resinous exudation of a spiny shrub long in use as an aromatic in perfume, incense, and medicine.

myrtle, mėr'tl, *n*. [L. *myrtus*, Gr. *myrtos*, from *myron*, perfume.] An evergreen shrub of the south of Europe having buds and berries that yield a volatile oil, while the distilled flowers yield a perfume.—**myrtaceous**, mėr·tā'shus, *a*. Of or pertaining to the myrtles.

myself, mī·self', *pron*. pl. **ourselves**, our·selvz'. As a nominative it is used, generally after I, to express emphasis and mark distinction; I, and not another: in the objective often used reflexively and without any emphasis.

mystagogue, mis'ta·gog, *n*. [Gr. *mystagōgos*—*mystēs*, one initiated in mysteries, and *agōgos*, a leader.] One who instructs in or interprets mysteries.—**mystagogy**, mis'ta·gō·ji, *n*. The practice or doctrines of a mystagogue; the interpretation of mysteries.

mystery, mis'tėr·i, *n*. [L. *mysterium*, from Gr. *mysterion*, from *mystēs*, one initiated, from *myō*, to close, to shut.] Something hidden from human knowledge and fitted to inspire a sense of awe; something incomprehensible through being above human intelligence; something intentionally kept hidden; a secret; a species of dramatic performance in the Middle Ages; divine revelation; a mystery novel; a sacramental rite; pl. rites and ceremonies in ancient, chiefly Greek and Roman, religions, only known to, and practiced by, those who had been initiated; the

Eucharist.—**mysterious**, mis·tē'ri·us, *a*. Partaking of, or containing, mystery; occult; enigmatical.—**mysteriously**, mis·tē'ri·us·li, *adv*.—**mysteriousness**, mis·tē'ri·us·nes, *n*.—**mysterium**, mis·tē'ri·um, *n*. A space phenomenon that cannot be explained in terms of any known scientific principle.

mystic, mystical, mis'tik, mis'ti·kal, *a*. [L. *mysticus*, Gr. *mystikos*, from *mystēs*, one initiated. MYSTERY.] Hidden from or obscure to human knowledge or comprehension; involving some secret meaning or import; mysterious; occult; pertaining to the ancient mysteries; pertaining to mystics or mysticism.—**mystic**, *n*. One who is addicted to mysticism.—**mystically**, mis'ti·kal·li, *adv*. In a mystic manner.—**mysticalness**, mis'ti·kal·nes, *n*.—**mysticism**, mis'ti·sizm, *n*. Views or tendencies in religion which aspire toward a communication between man and his Maker through the inward perception of the mind, more direct than that which is afforded us through revelation; a seeking to solve the mysteries of existence by internal illumination or special revelation; a dreamy contemplation on ideas that have no foundation in human experience.

mystify, mis'ti·fī, *v.t.*—*mystified*, *mystifying*. [Coined from *mystic*, and *-fy*, Fr. *-fier*, L. *facere*, to make.] To perplex purposely; to play on the credulity of; to bewilder; to befog.—**mystification**, mis'ti·fi·kā"shon, *n*. The act of mystifying or state of being mystified.

myth, mith, *n*. [Gr. *mythos*, a word, a fable, a legend.] A fable or legend of natural upgrowth, embodying the convictions of a people as to their gods or other divine personages, their own origin and early history and the heroes connected with it, the origin of the world, etc.; in a looser sense, an invented story; something purely fabulous or having no existence in fact.—**mythical, mythic**, mith'i·kal, mith'ik, *a*. Relating to myths; described in a myth; fabulous; fabled.—**mythically**, mith'i·kal·li, *adv*. In a mythical manner.—**mythographer**, mi·thog'ra·fėr, *n*. A framer or writer of myths.—**mythological, mythologic**, mith·o·loj'i·kal, mith·o·loj'ik, *a*. Relating to mythology; proceeding from mythology; of the nature of a myth; fabulous.—**mythologically**, mith·o·loj'i·kal·li, *adv*. In a mythological manner.—**mythologist**, mi·thol'o·jist, *n*. One versed in mythology.—**mythologize**, mi·thol'o·jīz, *v.i.*—*mythologized, mythologizing*. To relate or explain myths.—**mythology**, mi·thol'o·ji, *n*. The science or doctrine of myths; the myths of a people or nation collectively.—*Comparative mythology*, the science which investigates the relationship between myths of different peoples.

myxedema, miks·i·dē'ma. [Gr. *myxa*, mucus, *oidēma*, a swelling.] A disease due to deficient secretion of the THYROID GLAND (which see).

fāte, fär, fâre, fat, fall; mē, met, hėr; pīne, pin; nōte, not, möve; tūbe, tub, bull; oil, pound.

N

N, n, en, the fourteenth letter and the eleventh consonant of the English alphabet.

nab, nab, *v.t.* [Same as Dan. *knappe,* Sw. *knappa,* to snatch; comp. D. and G. *knappen,* to snap.] To catch or seize suddenly or unexpectedly. (*Colloq.*)

nabob, nā′bob, *n.* [Corruption of Hind. *nawwâb,* from Ar. *nuwwâb,* pl. of *nâyib,* a deputy, from Ar. *nâba,* to take one's turn.] A governor of a province or commander of an army in India under the Mogul empire: a person who has acquired great wealth in the East and uses it ostentatiously.

nacelle, nä·sel′, *n.* [Fr.] An enclosed part of an aircraft which houses the engine or passengers.

nacre, nā′kér, *n.* [Fr. *nacre,* Sp. *nacar,* from Per. *nakar,* an ornament of different colors.] Mother-of-pearl.—**nacreous,** nā′krē·us, *a.* Consisting of or resembling nacre or mother-of-pearl.

nadir, nā′dér, *n.* [Fr. *nadir,* Ar. and Per. *nadir, nazir,* the nadir, from *nazara,* to correspond, to be opposite.] That point of the heavens or lower hemisphere directly opposite to the zenith; the point directly under the place where we stand; *fig.* the lowest point; the point or time of extreme depression.

nag, nag, *n.* [Same as Sc. *naig,* D. *negge,* a pony; perhaps akin to *neigh:*] A small horse, or in familiar language any horse.

nag, nag, *v.t.* and *i.* [N. and Sw. *nagga,* to gnaw, irritate, scold = G. *nagen,* E. to *gnaw.* NAIL, GNAW.] To scold pertinaciously; to find fault constantly.

nagana, na·gä′na. [Native word.] 'Fly disease' of horses in tropical Africa. Due to a microscopic parasite introduced by the bite of the tsetse fly.

naiad, nā′yad, *n.* [Gr. *naias, naiados,* a naiad, from *naō,* to flow.] A water nymph; a female deity that presides over rivers and springs.

naïf, nä·ēf, *a.* [Fr. See NAIVE.] Ingenuous; artless; having a natural luster without being cut: said of jewels.

nail, nāl, *n.* [A.Sax. *naegel,* D. and G. *nagel,* the human or a metallic nail; Icel. *nagl,* Dan. *negl,* a human nail, *nagli* and *nagle,* a metallic nail; cog. Lith. *nagas,* L. *unguis,* Skr. *nakha,* a human nail; allied to *nag* (verb).] The horny scale growing at the end of the human fingers and toes; a similar appendage in the lower animals; a claw; a small pointed piece of metal, with some sort of a head, used for driving through or into timber or other material for the purpose of holding separate pieces together, or left projecting that things may be hung on it; a stud or boss; a measure of length, being 2¼ inches, or 1-16th of a yard.—*To*

hit the nail on the head, to hit or touch the exact point, in a figurative sense.—*v.t.* To fasten with nails; to drive nails into; to stud with nails.—**nailer,** nāl′ér, *n.* One that nails; one whose occupation is to make nails.

nail file, a small file for the fingernails.

nail set, a steel rod used to drive a nailhead below the surface.

nainsook, nān′su̇k, *n.* [Hind.] A kind of muslin, plain and striped, originally made in India.

naïve, nä·ēv′, *a.* [Fr. *naïf,* fem. *naïve,* from L. *nativus,* native, latterly also rustic, simple.] Ingenuous; artless; showing candor or simplicity; unsophisticated.—**naïvely,** nä·ēv′li, *adv.* In a naïve manner.—**naïveté,** nä·ēv′te, *n.* [Fr.] Native simplicity of soul; unaffected ingenuousness.

naked, nā′ked, *a.* [A.Sax. *nacod,* naked, a participial form; D. *naakt,* Icel. *naktr, nakinn,* Dan. *nögen,* Goth. *naqviths,* G. *nackt;* same root as L. *nudus,* nude; Skr. *nagna,* naked.] Not having clothes on; bare; nude; not having a covering, especially a customary covering (a *naked* sword); *bot.* not having a calyx; not enclosed in a pod, or the like; *zool.* not having a calcareous shell; *fig.* open to view; not concealed; manifest; mere, bare, simple; unarmed; defenseless; unprovided; destitute.—*The naked eye,* the eye unassisted by any instrument, as spectacles, telescope, or microscope.—**nakedly,** nā′ked·li, *adv.* In a naked manner; without covering.—**nakedness,** nā′ked·nes, *n.* The state of being naked; nudity; bareness; plainness.

namaycush, na·mā′kush, *n.* A large North American species of fish.

namby-pamby, nam′bi-pam′bi, *a.* [Contemptuously formed from the name of *Ambrose* Phillips, a rather weak poet of Addison's time.] Affectedly pretty; weakly sentimental; insipid; vapid (*namby-pamby* sentiment, rhymes).

name, nām, *n.* [A.Sax. *nama,* a name; D. *naam,* G. *name,* Goth. *namo,* Icel. *nafn,* Dan. *navn* (for *namn*), Sw. *namn,* all cog. with L. *nomen,* for *gnomen* (whence E. *noun*), Skr. *nâman,* for *jnâman* or *gnâman,* a name; from same root as *know.*] That by which a person or thing is called or designated, in distinction from other persons or things; appellation; reputation; character (one's good or bad *name*); renown; fame; eminence; the mere word by which anything is called; sound only; not reality; authority; behalf; persons having a certain name; a family; *gram.* a noun‡.—*To call names,* to apply opprobrious names.—*Christian name,* a personal name preceding the family name, and usually bestowed at baptism: as distinguished from a surname.—*v.t.—named, naming.* To give a name or distinctive appellation to; to denominate; to mention by name; to nominate; to designate for any purpose by name; to pronounce to be; to speak of or mention as.—*To name a day,* to fix a day for

anything; *to name the day,* said of a lady's fixing her marriage day.—**namable, nameable,** nām′a·bl, *a.* Capable or worthy of being named.—**nameless,** nām′les, *a.* Without a name or appellation; not known to fame; obscure; without family or pedigree; that cannot or ought not to be named; inexpressible.—**namelessly,** nām′les·li, *adv.* In a nameless manner.—**namelessness,** nām′les·nes, *n.* The state of being nameless.—**namely,** nām′li, *adv.* To mention by name; to particularize; that is to say.—**namer,** nām′ér, *n.* One that names or calls by name.—**namesake,** nām′sāk, *n.* One that has the same name as another; one named after another.

nankeen, nankin, nan·kēn′, *n.* [*Nankin* in China.] A sort of cotton cloth, usually of a yellow color; pl. trousers or breeches made of this material.

nanny goat, a female goat.

naos, nā′os, *n.* [Gr. *naos,* a temple.] *Arch.* the body of an ancient temple.

nap, nap, *v.i.*—*napped, napping.* [A.Sax. *hnappian, hnaeppian,* to take a nap, to doze.] To have a short sleep; to drowse; to be in a careless, secure state.—*n.* A short sleep or slumber; a game at cards. (Contraction of *Napoleon.*)

nap, nap, *n.* [A.Sax. *hnoppa,* the nap of cloth = D. *nop, noppe,* Dan. *noppe,* L.G. *nobbe,* nap; allied to *knob* or *knop,* from the little tufts on coarse cloth.] The woolly substance on the surface of cloth, etc.; the pile, as of a hat; what resembles this, as the downy substance on some plants.—*v.t.—napped, napping.* To raise or put a nap on.

napalm, nā′päm, *n.* [From *naph*thenic and *palm*itic acids.] A jellied gasoline used in incendiary bombs, flamethrowers, etc.

nape, nāp, *n.* [Same as A.Sax. *cnaep,* a top; akin *nap, knob, knop.*] The back part of the neck; the prominent part of the neck behind.

napery, nā′per·i, *n.* [Fr. *napperie,* from *nappe,* a towel, from L. *mappa,* a towel, whence also *map;* akin *napkin, apron.*] A collective term for linen cloths used for domestic purposes, especially for the table.

naphtha, nap′tha or naf′tha, *n.* [Gr. Chal., Syr., and Ar. *naphtha,* Per. *naft,* naphtha.] A variety of bitumen, fluid, inflammable, emitting a strong odor, and generally of a yellow color, used as a source of light, as a solvent for caoutchouc, etc.—*Native naphtha,* petroleum or rock oil.—**naphthalene,** nap′tha·lēn, *n.* A white crystallizable solid formed during the distillation of coal for gas, or obtained by re-distilling coal tar.

napiform, nā′pi·form, *a.* [L. *napus,* a turnip, and *forma,* form.] Having the general shape of a turnip (a *napiform* root).

napkin, nap′kin, *n.* [Dim. of Fr. *nappe,* a cloth, a tablecloth, from L. *mappa,* a napkin. NAPERY.] A cloth used for wiping the hands; a towel; a handkerchief‡.

napoleon, na·pō′lē·on, *n.* [After *Na*poleon I.] Formerly, a French gold coin, worth 20 francs; a card game.

ch, *chain;* ch, Sc. lo*ch;* g, *go;* j, *job;* ng, si*ng;* TH, *then;* th, *thin;* w, *wig;* hw, *whig;* zh, a*zure.*

naprapathy, nä·prap'a·thi, n. [From Czech *naprava*, correction.] A system of treatment of disease or illness by manipulation and adjustment of joints and muscles.

narceine, när'sē·in, n. [Gr. *narkē*, torpor.] An alkaloid contained in opium.

narcissism, när·cis'sizm, n. (*Psychoanalysis*.) A morbid love and admiration of self.—**narcissist**, n.—**narcissistic**, a.

narcissus, när·sis'us, n. [L., from Gr. *narkissos*, from *narkē*, torpor; from the narcotic properties of the plants.] An extensive genus of bulbous plants, including the daffodil, the jonquil, etc.; [*cap.*] in Gr. mythology a handsome youth who died from hopeless love of his own reflection in water, and was transformed into a narcissus.

narcosis, när·kō'sis, n. [Gr. See below.] The effect of a narcotic; the state produced by narcotics.

narcotic, när·kot'ik, n. [Gr. *narkōtikos*, from *narkoō*, to render torpid, from *narkē*, torpor.] A substance which relieves pain, produces sleep, and in large doses brings on stupor, coma, and even death, as opium, hemlock, alcohol, etc.—a. Having the properties of a narcotic.—**narcotism**, när'ko·tizm, n. Narcosis.—**narcotize**, när'ko·tīz, v.t. To bring under the influence of a narcotic; to affect with stupor.

nard, närd, n. [L. *nardus*, from Gr. *nardos*, Heb. and Per. *nard*, nard.] A plant, same as *Spikenard*; an unguent prepared from the plant.

narghile, nargileh, när'gi·le, n. [Persian and Turkish name.] A kind of tobacco pipe or smoking apparatus used by the Orientals in which the smoke is passed through water. Spelled also *Nargile*.

narrate, nar·rāt', v.t.—*narrated, narrating*. [L. *narro, narratum*, to relate, for *gnarro*, from root *gna*, seen also in E. *know*; comp. *gnarus*, knowing. KNOW.] To tell or recite, as a story; to relate the particulars of in speech or writing.—**narration**, nar·rā'shon, n. The act of narrating; that which is related; a narrative; *rhet.* that part of a discourse which recites the time, manner or consequences of an action.—**narrative**, nar'a·tiv, a. Pertaining to narration.—n. That which is narrated or related; a relation or narration; a relation in words or writing of the particulars of any transaction or event.—**narratively**, nar'a·tiv·li, adv. By way of narration.—**narrator**, nar·rā'tèr, n. One who narrates or produces a narrative.

narrow, nar'ō, a. [A.Sax. *nearu, nearo*, narrow, troublesome or painful; cog. O.Sax. *naru*, Fris. *naar*;] Of little breadth; having little distance from side to side; of little extent; limited or contracted; limited as to means; straitened; contracted in mind; of confined views; bigoted; not liberal or bountiful; niggardly; near; within but a little; hence, barely sufficient to avoid evil, etc. (a *narrow* escape, majority); close; scrutinizing.—*Nar-*

row gauge, in railways, a gauge or distance between the rails of less than 4 feet 8½ inches, which is considered the standard gauge and is the most common.—n. A narrow channel of water between one sea or lake and another; a strait or sound: usually in the plural.—v.t. To make narrow or contracted, literally or figuratively.—v.i. To become narrow or narrower.—**narrowly**, nar'ō·li, adv. In a narrow manner; contractedly; sparingly; closely; rigorously; nearly; within a little.—**narrowminded**, a. Of confined views or sentiments; illiberal.—**narrowness**, nar'ō·nes, n. The quality or condition of being narrow, illiberality; want of enlarged views.

narthex, när'theks, n. [Gr.] A kind of vestibule in the afterpart of a church.

narwhal, narwal, när'hwal, när'wal, n. [Dan. *narhval*, Icel. *na-hvalr*, 'corpsewhale', Icel. *na, nár*, a corpse, from the animal's pale color.] A cetaceous mammal of northern seas, with no teeth except two canines in the upper jaw, of which one is frequently developed into a long projecting tusk; the sea unicorn.

nasal, nā'zal, a. [Fr. *nasal*, from L. *nasus*, the nose. NOSE.] Pertaining to the nose; uttered through the nose or through both the nose and mouth simultaneously (as *m* in English, *en* in French).—*Nasal fossae, anat.* the two cavities which constitute the internal part of the nose.—n. An elementary sound uttered through or partly through the nose; a medicine that operates through the nose; an errhine; the noseguard of an ancient helmet.—**nasality**, nā·zal'i·ti, n. The state or quality of being nasal. — **nasalization**, nā'zal·i·zā'shon, n. The act of nasalizing or uttering with a nasal sound.—**nasalize**, nā'zal·īz, v.t.—*nasalized, nasalizing*. To render nasal, as the sound of a letter; to insert a nasal letter in, especially *n* or *m* (L. *tundo*, is a *nasalized* form from the root *tud*, to strike).—**nasally**, nā'zal·li, adv. In a nasal manner; by or through the nose.

nascent, nas'ent, a. [L. *nascens, nascentis*, ppr. of *nascor*, to be born. NATAL.] Beginning to exist or to grow; coming into being; arising.—**nascency**, nas'en·si, n. The state of being nascent.

naseberry, nāz'ber·i, n. [Sp. *nispero*, medlar, from L. *mespilus*, medlar; modified so as to have an English form, like *barberry*.] The fruit of the sapodilla.

nasturtium, nas·tèr'shi·um, n. [L., from *nasus*, the nose, and *torqueo, tortum*, to twist, from the acridity of its smell.] A genus of herbs, including the common watercress; also a name given to the Indian cress, an American annual with pungent fruit.

nasty, nas'ti, a. [O.E. *nasky*, connected with L.G. *nask*, Sw. *naskug, nasket*, unclean, dirty.] Filthy; dirty; indecent; obscene; disgusting to taste or smell; disagreeable; troublesome;

extremely unpleasant (*nasty* weather). —**nastily**, nas'ti·li, adv. In a nasty manner; filthily; obscenely.—**nastiness**, nas'ti·nes, n. The quality of being nasty, or what is nasty; filthiness; filthy matter; obscenity.

natal, nā'tal, a. [L. *natalis*, from *nascor, natus*, to be born (whence also *nature, native, nation*); from same root as *genus, kind.* NATURE, GENUS.] Pertaining to one's birth; dating from one's birth.

natant, nā'tant, a. [L. *natans, natantis*, ppr. of *nato*, to swim, freq. of *no, natum*, to swim; same root as *navis*, a ship. NAVAL.] Floating on the surface of water; swimming, as the leaf of an aquatic plant.—**natation**, na·tā'shon, n. [L. *natatio*.] The art or act of swimming.—**natatorial**, nā·ta·tō'ri·al, a. Swimming or adapted to swimming; belonging to the Natatores.—**natatorium**, nā·ta·tō'ri·um, n. A swimming pool, particularly, one indoors.

nation, nā'shon, n. [L. *natio*, from *natus*, born, *nascor*, to be born. NATAL.] A people inhabiting a certain extent of territory, and united by common political institutions; an aggregation of persons speaking the same or a cognate language; a federation of Indian tribes; a division of students in some universities according to their place of birth; a great number; a great deal, by way of emphasis.—*Law of nations*. Same as *International Law*.—**national**, nash'on·al, a. Pertaining to a nation; common to a whole people or race; public; general.—n. A member of a particular nation, entitled to its protection.—*National air*, a popular tune peculiar to a particular nation; a tune by national consent sung or played on certain public occasions. —*National Church*, the established church of a country or nation.—*National debt*, the sum which is owing by a government to individuals who have advanced money to it for public purposes.—*National Guard*, in the U. S., organizations of militia in the several states, subject to both state and federal government.—**nationalism**, nash'on·al·izm, n. Nationality; a national idiom or trait; advocacy of making one's own nation distinct, and separate from others in social, cultural, and political matters; a socialist program for national control or ownership of industries and resources.—**nationalist**, nash'on·al·ist, n. and a.—**nationality**, nash'on·al"i·ti, n. The qualities that distinguish a nation; national character; strong attachment to one's own nation or countrymen; the people constituting a nation; a nation; a race of people; separate existence as a nation; national unity and integrity.—**nationalize**, nash'on·al·īz, v.t.—*nationalized, nationalizing*. To make national; to make the common property of the nation as a whole; to give the character of a distinct nation; to give control of properties to the government.—**nationalization**, nash·on·al·i·zā'shon, n.—**nationally**, nash'on·al·li, adv. In a national manner; as

---

fāte, fär, fâre, fat, fall; mē, met, hèr; pīne, pin; nōte, not, mōve; tūbe, tub, bull; oil, pound.

a whole nation.—**nationwide,** *a.* Extending throughout the whole of a nation.

native, nā′tiv, *a.* [L. *nativus,* born, innate, natural, native, from *nascor, natus,* to be born. NATAL.] Pertaining to the place or circumstances of one's birth; being the scene of one's origin (our *native* land); conferred by birth; belonging to one's nature or constitution; not artificial or acquired; occurring in nature pure or unmixed with other substances: said of mineral bodies (as iron or silver when found almost pure).—*n.* One born in a place or country, and not a foreigner or immigrant; an oyster raised in an artificial bed.— **natively,** nā′tiv·li, *adv.* By birth; naturally; originally.—**nativeness,** nā′tiv·nes, *n.* State of being native.— **nativity,** na·tiv′i·ti, *n.* [L. *nativitas.*] A coming into life or the world; birth; the circumstances attending birth; a picture representing the birth of Christ; *astrol.* same as *Horoscope.*—*To cast a nativity,* to draw out one's horoscope, and calculate the future influence of the predominant stars.—*The Nativity,* the birth of the Saviour.

natron, nā′tron, *n.* [Fr. and Sp. *natron,* from Ar. *natrun,* native carbonate of soda: same word as *niter.*] Native carbonate of soda, or mineral alkali, found in the ashes of several marine plants, in some lakes, and mineral springs.—**natrolite,** nā′tro·līt, *n.* [Gr. *lithos,* a stone.] A mineral substance occurring in traprocks, and containing a great quantity of soda.

natty, nat′i, *a.* [Akin to *neat.*] Neat; tidy; spruce.—**nattily,** nat′i·li, *adv.* In a natty manner; sprucely; tidily. —**nattiness,** nat′i·nes, *n.* State of being natty.

nature, nā′chėr, *n.* [Fr. *nature,* from L. *natura,* from *natus* (for *gnatus*), born, produced, from root *gna* or *gan,* seen in E. *know, kind, kin;* Skr. *jan,* to produce. GENUS.] The universe; the system of things of which ourselves are a part; the world of matter or of matter and mind; the creation, especially that part of it by which man is more immediately surrounded; often also the agent, author, or producer of things, or the powers that carry on the processes of the creation; the total of all agencies and forces in the creation; the inherent qualities of anything; the essential qualities which constitute it what it is; disposition of mind; personal character; individual constitution; quality; sort; natural affection; life or reality as distinguished from that which is artificial. —*To go the way of nature, to pay the debt of nature,* and similar phrases, to die.—*Laws of nature,* those generalizations which express the order observed in the phenomena of nature. —*In a state of nature,* naked as when born; in a state of sin; unregenerated. —**natural,** na′chėr·al, *a.* [L. *naturalis.*] Pertaining to nature; produced by nature; not artificial, acquired, or assumed (*natural* color, strength,

heat), in conformity with the laws of nature; regulated by the laws which govern events, actions, sentiments, etc. (a *natural* enemy, supposition); happening in the ordinary course of things (the *natural* consequence); connected with the existing physical system of things, or creation at large (*natural* philosophy, laws, etc.); according to life and reality; without affectation or artificiality (he was always *natural*); born out of wedlock; bastard; in a state of nature; unregenerated; *mus.* a term applied to the scale of C. —*Natural gas,* a gas issuing from fissures in the earth's crust.—*Natural history,* the study or description of nature in its widest sense, usually for the general public.—*Natural resources,* a country's wealth in terms of land, water power, minerals, etc.— *Natural science,* any of the areas of knowledge dealing with natural objects or phenomena and based on experiment, as *biology.*—*n.* One born without the usual powers of reason or understanding; an idiot; a fool; *mus.* a character marked thus ♮, the use of which is to make void a preceding sharp or flat; one who has natural talents, skills, etc. —**naturalism,** na′chėr·al·izm, *n.* Natural religion; the doctrine that there is no interference of any supernatural power in the universe; a natural mode of acting; reality in art, but usually concerned with the seamy side of life.—**naturalist,** na′chėr·al·ist, *n.* One who is versed in natural science or natural history; one who holds the doctrine of naturalism.—**naturalistic,** na′chėr·al·is″tik, *a.* Pertaining to naturalism; in accordance with nature; based on natural objects.—**naturalization,** na′chėr·al·i·zā″shon, *n.* The act of naturalizing; the act of investing an alien with the rights and privileges of a natural subject.—**naturalize,** na′chėr·al·īz, *v.t.*—*naturalized, naturalizing.* To make natural; to confer the rights and privileges of a native subject upon; to accustom to a climate; to acclimatize; to adopt as native or vernacular (to *naturalize* foreign words).—**naturally,** na′chėr·al·li, *adv.* In a natural manner; according to nature; not by art or habit; without affectation; according to the usual course of things; spontaneously; without cultivation.— **naturalness,** na′chėr·al·nes, *n.* The state of being natural; conformity to nature; absence of affectation.

naught, nat, *n.* [A.Sax. *náht, nóht, náwiht,* lit. *no whit,* not a whit (see AUGHT). *Naught* is the same and *not* is an abbreviated form.] Nought; nothing.—*To set at naught,* to slight, disregard, or despise.—*a.* Worthless; of no value or account; bad; vile.— **naughty,** na′ti, *a.* [From *naught.*] Bad: mischievous; ill-behaved; very wrong (a *naughty* child).—**naughtily,** na′ti·li, *adv.* In a naughty manner; mischievously.—**naughtiness,** na′ti·nes, *n.* The state of being naughty; misbehavior, as of children.

naumachia, naumachy, na·mā′ki·a,

na′ma·ki, *n.* [Gr. *naumachia—naus,* a ship, and *machē,* fight.] *Rom. antiq.* a show or spectacle representing a sea fight; the place where these shows were exhibited.

nauplius, na′pli·us, *n.* [Gr. *Nauplios,* a son of Neptune.] In lower Crustacea, an ovoid unsegmented larva, possessing only the three first pairs of head limbs, which are used as swimming organs.

nausea, na′shi·a, *n.* [L., from Gr. *nausia,* from *naus,* a ship. NAVAL.] Seasickness; any similar sickness of the stomach, accompanied with a propensity to vomit; loathing.— **nauseate,** na′shi·āt, *v.i.*—*nauseated, nauseating.* [L. *nauseo.*] To feel nausea; to be inclined to vomit.— *v.t.* To loathe; to reject with disgust; to affect with disgust.—**nauseous,** na′shus, *a.* Exciting or fitted to excite nausea; loathsome; disgusting. —**nauseously,** na′shus·li, *adv.* In a nauseous manner.—**nauseousness,** na′shus·nes, *n.* The quality of being nauseous; loathsomeness.

nautch girl, nach. *n.* In the East Indies, a native professional dancing girl.

nautical, na′ti·kal, *a.* [L. *nauticus* from *nauta,* a seaman, for *navita,* from *navis,* a ship. NAVAL.] Pertaining to seamanship or navigation; maritime; naval.—**nautically,** na′ti·kal·li, *adv.* In a nautical manner.

nautilus, na′ti·lus, *n.* [Gr. *nautilos,* a sailor, a nautilus, from *naus,* a ship. NAVAL.] A genus of cephalopods with many-chambered shells in the form of a flat spiral, the animal residing in the external chamber, and the others being separated by partitions; also a name for the argonaut or paper nautilus; a form of diving bell which requires no suspension, sinking and rising by means of condensed air.—*Nautilus propeller,* a hydraulic device for propelling ships.

Navaho, Navajo, na′vä·hō, *n.* [Sp. Apaches de *Navajó.*] One of a tribe of Indians living in Arizona, New Mexico and Utah.

naval, nā′val, *a.* [L. *navalis,* from *navis,* a ship (whence also *nautical, navigate, navy*); cog. Gr. *naus,* Skr. *naus;* from a root *nu* for *snu,* meaning to float or flow.] Consisting of ships, or of forces fighting in ships; pertaining to a navy or to ships of war; maritime.—*Naval officer,* one belonging to the navy of a country.— *Naval crown,* among the ancient Romans, a crown conferred for bravery at sea.—*Naval decorations,* specifically, three awards presented by the naval authorities to men in the service who perform acts of bravery beyond the call of duty: Medal of Honor, Distinguished Service Medal, and Navy Cross.

nave, nāv, *n.* [A.Sax. *nafu, nafa*=D. *nave, naaf,* Dan. *nav,* Icel. *nöf,* G. *nabe,* a nave; cog. Skr. *nâbhi,* a nave, a navel. *Navel* is a dim. from this, and *auger* is partly derived from it.] The thick piece in the center of a wheel in which the spokes and axle are inserted; the hub.

---

ch, *chain;* ch, Sc. lo*ch;* g, *go;* j, *job;* ng, si*ng;* TH, *then;* th, *thin;* w, *wig;* hw, *whig;* zh, a*zure.*

nave, nāv, *n.* [Lit. ship, from O.Fr. *nave* (Mod.Fr. *nef*), It. *nave*, from L. *navis*, a ship. NAVAL.] The middle part, lengthwise, of a church; the part between the aisles and extending from the entrance.

navel, nā´vl, *n.* [A.Sax. *nafel, nafol*= D. *navel*, Dan. *navle*, Icel. *nafle*, G. *nabel*—navel; dim. forms from words signifying nave of a wheel. NAVE.] A depression in the center of the abdomen, the point where the umbilical cord passes out of the fetus. —**navel orange**, *n.* A large, juicy orange, usually seedless, which has a navel-like indentation in its rind.

navicular, na·vik´ū·lėr, *a.* [L. *navicula*, a little ship, from *navis*, a ship. NAVAL.] Shaped like a boat (the *navicular* bone of the wrist or ankle).

navigate, nav´i·gāt, *v.i.*—navigated, navigating. [L. *navigo, navigatum*, from *navis*, a ship, *ago*, to do. NAVAL.] To pass on water in ships; to manage a ship; to sail.—*v.t.* To pass over in ships; to sail on; to steer or manage in sailing.—**navigation**, nav·i·gā´shon, *n.* [L. *navigatio.*] The act of navigating; the science or art of managing ships.—*Aerial navigation*, the art and science of operation through the air of lighter- and heavier-than-air machines; the setting of a course along a known route; the application of directional knowledge gained by the use of landmark maps, previous flying experience, and the extensive use of various instruments for dead reckoning and position finding, such as radio compass, direction finders, altimeters, artificial horizon gauges, drift indicators, barometers, and the radio telephone.—**navigator**, nav´i·gā·tėr, *n.* One that navigates; one who directs the course of a ship.— **navigable**, nav´i·ga·bl, *a.* Capable of being navigated; affording passage to ships.—**navigableness, navigability**, nav´i·ga·bl·nes, nav´i·ga·bil´i·ti, *n.* The quality or state of being navigable.

navy, nā´vi, *n.* [O.Fr. *navie*, from L. *navis*, a ship. NAVAL.] The collective name for such vessels as are built and maintained for war or for other purposes pertaining to national defense; the institutions and equipment, such as navy yards, stores, fueling stations, naval academies, etc., for the maintenance of sea defenses and vessels of war.—**navy bean**, *n.* A strain of the kidney bean. —**navy yard**, *n.* A shipyard where government vessels are built and repaired.

nawab, na·wab´, *n.* [See NABOB.] A viceroy; a deputy.

nay, nā, *adv.* [Equivalent to *ne aye* (A.Sax. *ne*, not), that is, not ever; from Icel. and Dan. *nei*, Sw. *nej*, no, nay; comp. *nor* for *ne or*, not or; *neither*, for *ne either*, not either, etc. NO.] No; a word that expresses negation or refusal; also used to intimate that something is to be added to an expression; not only so; not this alone.—*To say nay*, to deny; to refuse.—*n.* Denial; refusal.

Nazarene, naz·a·rēn´, *n.* An inhabitant of *Nazareth*; a name given to Christ and the early converts to Christianity, in contempt.

Nazarite, naz´a·rīt, *n.* [Heb. *nazir*, separated.] A Jew who by certain vows and acts devoted himself to the peculiar service of Jehovah for a certain time or for life. Num. vi. 2-21.

Nazi, nä´tsē, *a.* Of or pertaining to, or embodying the principles of, Naziism.—*n.* A member of the German National Socialist Workers' Party.—**Naziism**, nä´tsē·izm, *n.* A totalitarian form of government administered by the Nazi Party (the German National Socialist Workers' Party) which advocated the building of a highly nationalistic Aryan state, with the revival and substitution of Germanic Hero Worship for Christianity, and recognized private ownership except when the state determined otherwise.

Neanderthal, ni·an´dėr·tal, *a.* [From the Neanderthal Valley in Germany, its place of discovery.] Of or pertaining to the skeletal remains of a paleolithic man discovered in 1856. —*n.* A European paleolithic man.

neap, nēp, *a.* [A.Sax. *nep*, neap; akin to Dan. *knap*, Icel. *hneppr*, narrow, scanty, and probably to *nip*.] Low, or not rising high: applied to the lowest tides, being those that happen in the middle of the second and fourth quarters of the moon, taking place about four or five days before the new and full moons.—**neap, neap tide**, *n.* One of the lowest tides or the time of one; opposite to *spring* tide.

near, nēr, *a.* [A.Sax. *neár*, compar. of *neáh*, nigh=Icel. *nær, nærri*, Dan. *nær*, near; nearer. NEXT, NIGH.] Nigh; not far distant in place, time, or degree; closely connected by blood (*near* relations); intimate; familiar (a *near* friend); close or literal; narrow (a *near* escape); on the left of a horse (the *near* foreleg); short, or not circuitous; niggardly; approximately like the original (*nearbeer*).—*prep.* Close to.—*adv.* Almost; within a little; closely.—*v.t.* and *i.* To approach; to come near.—**nearby**, nēr·bī´, *a.* and *adv.* Close at hand.— **nearly**, nēr´li, *adv.* Almost; intimately; in a parsimonious or niggardly manner.—**nearness**, nēr´nes, *n.*— **nearsighted**, *a.* Shortsighted; seeing at a small distance only.

neat, nēt, *n.* [A.Sax. *neát* (sing, and pl.); Sc. *nowt*, Icel. *naut*. Sw. *nót*, Dan. *nód*, cattle, an ox; from verbal stem Icel. *njóta*, A.Sax. *neótan*, to use, to enjoy; Goth. *niutan*, to take.] Cattle of the bovine type, as oxen or cows: used either collectively or of one individual.— *Neat's-foot oil*, an oil obtained from the feet of *neat* cattle.

neat, nēt, *a.* [Fr. *net, nette*, from L. *nitidus*, shining, from *niteo*, to shine.] Having everything in perfect order; tidy; trim; expressed in few and well-chosen words; chaste; said of style; with all deductions made

(usually written *Net* or *Nett*).— **neatly**, nēt´li, *adv.* In a neat manner; tidily; with good taste.—**neatness**, nēt´nes, *n.* The state or quality of being neat; tidiness; simple elegance.

nebula, neb´ū·la, *n.* pl. **nebulae, nebulas**, neb´ū·lē, neb´ū·läz. [L. *nebula*, a cloud; allied to Gr. *nephēlē*, a cloud; G. *nebel*, mist.] The name for celestial objects resembling white clouds, in many cases resolved by the telescope into clusters of stars, though many nebulae consist of masses of incandescent gas; a white spot or a slight opacity of the cornea of the eye.—**nebular**, neb´ū·lėr, *a.* Pertaining to nebulae.— *Nebular hypothesis*, a hypothesis that the bodies composing the solar system once existed in the form of a nebula, from which, when condensed by refrigeration, the planets were constituted, the main body forming the sun.—**nebulosity**, neb·ū·los´i·ti, *n.* The state of being nebulous; the faint misty appearances surrounding certain stars.—**nebulous**, neb´ū·lus, *a.* [L. *nebulosus.*] Cloudy; hazy; literally or figuratively; *astron.* pertaining to or having the appearance of a nebula; nebular.—**nebulousness**, neb´ū·lus·nes, *n.*

necessary, nes´es·se·ri, *a.* [L. *necessarius*, from *necesse*, necessary, unavoidable; origin doubtful.] Such as must be; inevitable; unavoidable; indispensable; essential; that cannot be absent; acting from necessity; opposed to *free* (as regards the will).— *Necessary truths*, those truths which cannot from their very nature but be true.—*n.* Anything necessary or indispensably requisite.—**necessarily**, nes´es·se·ri·li, *adv.* In a necessary manner; by necessity; indispensably.—**necessitarian**, ne·ses´i·tâ´ri·an, *n.* One who maintains the doctrine of philosophical necessity in opposition to the freedom of the will.—**necessitarianism**, ne·ses´i·tâ´ri·an·izm, *n.* The doctrine of philosophical necessity.—**necessitate**, ne·ses´i·tāt, *v.t.*—necessitated, necessitating. To make necessary or indispensable; to render necessary; to compel; to force.—**necessitous**, ne·ses´i·tus, *a.* Exhibiting indigence; pressed with poverty; indigent; destitute.—**necessitously**, ne·ses´i·tus·li, *adv.* In a necessitous manner. —**necessitousness**, ne·ses´i·tus·nes, *n.* Extreme poverty; pressing want. —**necessity**, ne·ses´i·ti, *n.* [L. *necessitas.*] The state of being necessary; condition demanding that something must be; unavoidableness; indispensableness; need; irresistible compulsion; compulsion of circumstances; the absolute determination of the will by motives; that which is requisite; a necessary; extreme indigence; pinching poverty.

neck, nek, *n.* [A.Sax. *hnecca*, the neck=D. *nek*, Dan. *nakke*, Icel. *hnakki*, the nape; G. *nacken*, the neck; connections doubtful.] The part of an animal's body between the head and the trunk and connecting them; part of a thing corresponding to the neck of animals; a narrow tract of land connecting two larger tracts; an isthmus; the slender part of a vessel, as a bottle; that part of a violin or similar instrument which connects the scroll or head and body.—*Neck and crop.* Under CROP.—*Neck or nothing,* at every risk.—*A stiff neck,* in *Scrip.* obstinacy in sin.—*To break the neck of an affair,* to destroy the main force of it; to get over the worst part of it.—*To tread on the neck of* (*fig.*), to subdue utterly.—*Neck and neck,* close, as in a race.—*To get it in the neck,* to get the worst of it.—*On the neck of,* adhering to, or immediately following.—**neckband,** *n.* The band of a shirt round the neck, to which the collar is attached.—**neckcloth,** nek′kloth, *n.* A piece of linen or cotton cloth worn round the neck as part of a gentlemen's dress.—**neckerchief,** nek′ẽr·chif, *n.* A kerchief for the neck.—**necklace,** nek′lis, *n.* A string of beads, precious stones, or other ornamental objects worn on the neck.—**necktie,** *n.* A band of cloth worn round the neck under the collar and knotted in front; a cravat; a scarf or tie.—**necrobiosis,** nek′rō·bī·ō″sis, *n.* [Gr. *nekros,* dead, and *bios,* life.] *Med.* the degeneration or wearing away of living tissue.—**necrolatry,** nek·rol′a·tri, *n.* [Gr. *latreia,* worship.] Excessive veneration for or worship of the dead.—**necrology,** nek·rol′o·ji, *n.* A register of deaths; a collection of obituary notices.—**necrological,** nek·ro·loj′i·kal, *a.* Pertaining to a necrology.—**necrologist,** nek·rol′o·jist, *n.* One who writes obituary notices.—**necromancy,** nek′ro·man·si, *n.* [Gr. *manteia,* divination.] Divination by means of a pretended communication with the dead; the black art; the art of magic or sorcery.—**necromancer,** nek′ro·man·sẽr, *n.* One who practices necromancy; a sorcerer; a wizard.—**necromantic,** nek·ro·man′tik, *a.* Pertaining to necromancy.—**necrophagous,** nek·rof′a·gus, *a.* [Gr. *phagein,* to eat.] Feeding on the dead, or putrescent substances.—**necrophobia,** nek·ro·fō′bi·a, *n.* [Gr. *phobos,* fear.] A horror of dead bodies; exaggerated fear of death.—**necropolis,** nek·rop′o·lis, *n.* [Gr. *polis,* a city; the city of the dead.] A cemetery, especially one that is extensive and ornamentally laid out.—**necroscopy,** nek·ros′ko·pi, *n.* Examination of the dead; a postmortem examination.—**necrosis,** ne·krō′sis, *n.* [Gr. *nekrōsis,* deadness.] *Pathol.* death of the bone substance, a condition corresponding to what gangrene is to the flesh; *bot.* a disease of plants chiefly found upon the leaves and soft parts.

necrosis, ne·krō′sis, *n.* [Gr. *nekrosis,* deadness.] *Pathol.* death in a local area of the tissues.

nectar, nek′tẽr, *n.* [Gr.] *Greek myth.* the drink of the gods, ambrosia being their solid food; hence, any delicious drink; *bot.* the honey of a flower.—**nectarean,** nek·tâ′rē·an, *a.*

Resembling nectar; very delicious.—**nectareous,** nek·tâ′rē·us, *a.* Nectarean.—**nectarine,** nek′tẽr·in,—*n.* A variety of the common peach, having a smoother rind and firmer pulp.—**nectarous,** nek′tẽr·us, *a.* Sweet as nectar.—**nectary,** nek′te·ri, *n.* The part of a flower that contains or secretes the nectar.

nee, nā, *pp.* [Fr., from L. *natus,* born. NATAL.] Born; a term placed before a married woman's maiden name to indicate her parentage; as, Madame de Staël, *nee* Necker, that is, whose family name was Necker.

need, nēd, *n.* [A.Sax. *néd* = D. *nood,* Icel. *nauth,* Dan *nöd,* G. *noth,* Goth. *nauths,* need, necessity.] A state that requires supply or relief; pressing occasion for something; urgent want; necessity; want of the means of subsistence; poverty; indigence.—*v.t.* To have necessity or need for; to want, lack, require.—*v.i.* To be wanted; to be necessary.—*verb. aux.* To be under obligation, or necessity (it *needs* to be that way).—**needful,** nēd′fu̇l, *a.* Needy; necessitous; necessary; requisite.—**needfully,** nēd′fu̇l·li, *adv.*—**needfulness,** nēd′fu̇l·nes, *n.*—**neediness,** nē′di·nes, *n.*—**needless,** nēd′les, *a.* Not wanted; unnecessary; not requisite.—**needlessly,** nēd′les·li, *adv.*—**needlessness,** nēd′les·nes, *n.*—**needs,** nēdz, *adv.* Of necessity; necessarily; indispensably: generally with *must.*—**needy,** nē′di, *a.* Necessitous; indigent; very poor.

needle, nē′dl, *n.* [A.Sax. *naedl,* a needle; G. *nähen,* to sew, L. *neo,* Gr. *neō,* to spin.] A small instrument of steel pointed at one end, and having an eye or hole through which is passed a thread, used for sewing; a similar instrument used for interlacing a thread or twine in knitting, netting, embroidery, etc.; a name of sundry long and sharp-pointed surgical instruments; a magnetized bar of steel in a compass; a sharp pinnacle of rock; a needle-shaped crystal; a slender piece of steel or other material used to transmit vibrations, as from a phonograph record; *bot.* the needle-shaped leaf of a conifer.—*v.t.* To sew or pierce with a needle; to heckle; to goad into action.—*v.i.* To work with a needle; to form needle-like protuberances in crystallization.—**needlefish,** *n.* The pipefish, also the gar.—**needle point,** *n.* A kind of lace; a kind of embroidery done on canvas.—**needlewoman,** *n.* A seamstress.—**needlework,** *n.* Work executed with a needle; sewed work; embroidery; the business of a seamstress.

needless, needs, needy, etc. See NEED.

ne'er, nār. A contraction of *never.*

nefarious, ni·fâ′ri·us, *a.* [L. *nefarius,* from *nefas,* impious, unlawful, from *ne,* not, and *fas,* law, from *for, fari,* to utter. FATE.] Wicked in the extreme; impious.—**nefariously,** ni·fâ′ri·us·li, *adv.*—**nefariousness,** ni·fâ′ri·us·nes, *n.*

negation, ni·gā′shon, *n.* [L. *negatio,* a denying, from *nego,* to deny—*ne,*

not, and verbal affix, *-go, -igo.* Akin *deny, renegade.*] Denial; a declaration that something is not, has not been, or will not be; contradiction or contradictory condition: opposed to *affirmation.*—**negate,** ne·gāt′, *v.t.* To deny; to disprove or prove nonexistent.—**negative,** neg′a·tiv, *a.* Implying or containing denial or negation: opposed to *affirmative;* tending in the direction of denial without directly denying or controverting: opposed to *positive* (a *negative* result); *photog.* applied to a picture in which the lights and shades are the opposites of those in nature; *bacteriol.* not affirming the presence of an organism; *biol.* moving away from a source of stimulation.—*Negative electricity,* electricity associated with an excess of electrons.—*Negative pole,* the metal, or equivalent, placed in opposition to the *positive,* in the voltaic battery.—*Negative quantities, alg.* quantities which have the sign—(minus) prefixed to them.—*n.* A proposition by which something is denied; an opposite or contradictory term or conception; a negative proposition; a word that denies (*not, no*); that side of a question which denies or refuses; a decision or answer expressive of negation; *photog.* a photographic picture on glass or sensitized film, in which the lights and shades are the opposite of those in nature, used as a plate from which to print positive impressions; a veto or negative vote; *elec.* the negative plate of a battery.—*v.t.*—*negatived, negativing.* To disprove; to prove the contrary; to say *no* to; to reject; to refuse to enact or sanction.—**negatively,** neg′a·tiv·li, *adv.*—**negativeness, negativity,** neg′a·tiv·nes, neg·a·tiv′i·ti, *n.*—**negativism,** neg′a·tiv·izm, *n.* Atheism or agnosticism; any of the philosophies of denial; negativistic behavior.

negatron, neg′a·tron, *n.* [*Negative* and elec*tron.*] *Chem.* and *phys.* an electron.

neglect, neg·lekt′, *v.t.* [L. *negligo, neglectum,* lit. not to pick up—*neg,* not, nor, and *lego,* to pick up. LEGEND.] To treat with no regard or attention or with too little; to slight; to set at naught; to omit to do; to leave undone; to forbear; often with an infinitive as object (to *neglect* to pay a visit).—*n.* Omission; forbearance to do anything that should be done; carelessness; omission of due attention or civilities; negligence; habitual want of regard; state of being disregarded.—**neglecter,** neg·lek′tẽr, *n.* One that neglects.—**neglectful,** neg·lekt′fu̇l, *a.* Apt to neglect; treating with neglect; negligent; careless; inattentive.—**neglectfully,** neg·lekt′fu̇l·li, *adv.* In a neglectful manner.—**neglectfulness,** neg·lekt′fu̇l·nes, *n.*

negligee, neg′le·zhā′, *n.* [Fr. *negligé,* from *negliger,* to neglect.] An informal dressing gown or wrapper worn by women.

negligent, neg′li·jent, *a.* [L. *negligens, negligentis,* ppr. of *negligo,* to neglect. NEGLECT.] Characterized by neglect; apt to neglect; careless; heedless; neglectful.—**negligently**, neg'li·jent·li, adv. In a negligent manner.—**negligence**, neg'li·jens, n. [L. negligentia.] The quality of being negligent; neglect; remissness; an act of negligence.—**negligible**, neg'li·ji·bl, a. That may be neglected.

negotiate, ni·gō'shi·āt, v.i. [L. negotior, negotiatus, from negotium, want of leisure, business—neg, not, and otium, leisure.] To treat with another respecting purchase and sale; to hold intercourse in bargaining or trade; to hold diplomatic intercourse with another, as respecting a treaty, league, or other matter; to treat; to conduct communications in general.—v.t.—negotiated, negotiating. To procure or bring about by negotiation (a treaty, a loan); to pass in the way of business; to put into circulation (to negotiate a bill of exchange); to negotiate a corner, said of a motor car or other vehicle, taking an obstacle carefully in order to overcome it.—**negotiable**, ni·gō'shi·a·bl, a. Capable of being negotiated; transferable by assignment from one person to another, as a bill or promissory note.—**negotiability**, ni·gō'shi·a·bil'i·ti, n. The quality of being negotiable.—**negotiation**, ni·gō'shi·ā''shon, n. The act of negotiating; the treating with another respecting sale or purchase; the intercourse of governments by their agents, in making treaties and the like.—**negotiator, negotiant**, † ni·go'shi·ā·tėr, ni·gō'shi·ant, n. One that negotiates.

Negro, nē'grō, n. pl. **Negroes**, nē'grōz. [It. and Sp. negro, black, from L. niger, black.] A member of the African branch of the black race, formerly called the Ethiopian, which is characterized by the black or very dark color of the skin and the possession of hair of a woolly or crisp nature.—a. Relating to Negroes; black.—**Negroid**, nē'groid, a. Resembling Negroes; having Negro characteristics.—**Negrito, Negrillo**, ne·grē'tō, ne·gril'lō, n. and a. [Dim. of Negro.] A name given to the diminutive Negro-like tribes inhabiting the Philippines and the Eastern Archipelago.

negus, nē'gus, n. [From the inventor Col. Negus of Queen Anne's time.] A beverage made of wine, hot water, sugar, nutmeg, and lemon juice, or only of wine, water, and sugar; [cap.] the former ruler of Ethiopia.

neigh, nā, v.i. [A.Sax. hnaegan, Icel. hneggja, gneggja, Sw. gnägga, probably an imitative word; comp. L. hinnio.] To utter the cry of a horse; to whinny.—n. The cry of a horse; a whinnying.—**neighing**, nā'ing, n. A whinnying.

neighbor, nā'bėr, n. [A.Sax. neáh-búr, néh-búr, lit. a near-dweller, from néah, near (NIGH), and búr, gebúr, a dweller, a boor (BOOR).] One who lives near another; one who lives in a neighborhood; one in close proximity; one who lives on friendly terms with another; often used as a familiar term of address.—a. Being in the vicinity; adjoining; next.—v.t. To adjoin; to border on or be near to.—**neighborhood**, nā'bėr·hud, n. A place or district the inhabitants of which may be called neighbors; vicinity; the adjoining district or locality; neighbors collectively; a district or locality in general (a low neighborhood)—**neighboring**, nā'bėr·ing, a. Living as neighbors; being situated near.—**neighborliness**, nā'bėr·li·nes, n. State or quality of being neighborly.—**neighborly**, nā'bėr·li, a. Becoming a neighbor; acting as a good neighbor; social.

neither, nē'THėr or nī'THėr, pron. and pronominal adjective. [Used as negative of either; earlier forms nather, naither, nouther, A.Sax. náuther, náhwæther=nowhether.] Not one of two; not either; not the one or the other; used either alone or with a noun following.—conj. Not either: generally prefixed to the first of two or more co-ordinate negative propositions or clauses, the others being introduced by nor: sometimes used instead of nor in the second of two clauses, the former containing not.

nelumbo, ni·lum'bō, n. The Hindu and Chinese lotus, a beautiful water plant with rose-colored flowers.

nematocyst, nem'a·to·sist, n. [Gr. nēma, nēmatos, a thread, and kystis, a bag.] Physiol. a thread cell or stinging apparatus of coelenterate animals.

nematode, nem'ä·tōd, n. [Gr. nēma, nēmatos, a thread, from neō, to spin.] A parasitic worm of the class Nematoda, having a long cylindrical, and often filiform, body; a roundworm.

Nemean, nē'mē·an or ne·mē'an, a. Of or belonging to Nemea in Argolis. Greece.—Nemean games, ancient games or festivals celebrated at Nemea every second year.

Nemesis, nem'e·sis, n. [Gr., from nemesis, distribution of what is due.] A Greek goddess personifying retributive justice; one who takes vengeance; [often not cap.] act of retribution.

neodymium, nē'o·dim''i·um, n. [Neo, and didymium.] A metallic element of the rare-earth series. Symbol, Nd; at. no., 60; at. wt., 144.24.

Neo-Lamarckism, nē'ō·la·mark''ism, n. [Gr. neos, new, and Lamarck, an eminent French naturalist.] A theory of evolution postulating the existence of definite laws of growth.

Neolithic, nē·ō·lith'ik, a. [Gr. neos, new, and lithos, a stone.] Archeol. applied to the more recent of the two periods into which the Stone Age has been subdivided, as opposed to Paleolithic. During the Neolithic age, stone implements were polished, domesticated animals became common, cereals and fruit trees were grown, pottery made, linen woven, and boats used.

neology, ni·ol'o·ji, n. [Gr. neos, new, and logos, a word.] The introduction of a new word or of new words into a language; novel doctrines; rationalistic views in theology.—**neological**, nē·o·loj'i·kal, a. Pertaining to neology.—**neologism, neologianism**, ni·ol'o·jizm, nē·o·lō'ji·an·izm, n. A new word or phrase, or new use of a word; the use of new words or of old words in a new sense; new doctrines.—**neologist**, ni·ol'o·jist, n. One who introduces new words or phrases; an innovator in doctrines or beliefs.

neon, nē'on, n. [Gr. neon, new.] A colorless inert gaseous element occurring in the atmosphere. Symbol, Ne; at. no., 10; at. wt., 20.183.—**neon lamp**, neon contained in a vacuum tube, through which an electric current passes, producing a reddish-orange glow, valuable in electric advertising signs (neon signs), and in aeronautics for beacons.

neophyte, nē'o·fīt, n. [Gr. neos, new, and phyton, a plant, from phyō, I grow.] A new convert or proselyte; a novice; one newly admitted to the order of priest; a tyro; a beginner in learning.

neoplasm, nē'o·plasm, n. [Neo, and plasm.] Any new and abnormal body tissue, such as a tumor.

Neoplatonism, nē·o·plā'ton·izm, n. [Gr. neos, new, and E. Platonism.] A philosophical system growing up in Alexandria, and prevailing chiefly from the 3rd to the 5th century after Christ, deriving elements from the philosophy of Plato, and from Christianity, Gnosticism, and Oriental beliefs.

neoprene, nē'o·prēn, n. [Neo, and chloroprene.] A rubber-like plastic acquired through the polymerization of chloroprene.

neoteric, nē·o·ter'ik, a. [Gr. neōterikos, young, from neos, new.] New; recent in origin; modern.

Neotropical, nē·o·trop'i·kal, a. [Gr. neos, new, and E. tropical.] Applied to a region of the earth in reference to its characteristic fauna, including all America south of the isthmus of Tehuantepec.

Neozoic, nē·o·zō'ik, a. [Gr. neos, new, recent, and zōē, life.] Geol. a name given to strata from the beginning of the trias up to the most recent deposits, including the Mesozoic and Cenozoic divisions.

nepenthe, nepenthes, nē·pen'thē, nē·pen'thēz, n. [Gr. nēpenthēs—nē, not, and penthos, grief.] A kind of magic potion, supposed to make persons forget their sorrows and misfortunes; any draught or drug capable of removing pain or care.

nephew, nef'ū, n. [Fr. neveu, from L. nepos, nepotis, a nephew; cog. A.Sax. nefa, Icel. nefi, G. neffe, Skr. napat, a nephew. Akin niece.] The son of a brother or sister.

nephralgia, ne·fral'ji·a, n. [Gr. nephros, a kidney, and algos, pain.] Pain in the kidneys.—**nephrite**, nef'rīt, n. [Gr. nephritēs.] The mineral otherwise called jade.—**nephritic**, ne·frit'ik, a. Pertaining to the kidneys; relieving disorders of the kidneys.—**nephritis**, ni·frī'tis, n. [Gr. term. -itis, signifying inflammation.] Inflammation of the kidneys.—**nephrology**, ne·frol′o·ji, *n.* A description of the kidneys.—**nephrotomy**, ne·frot′o·mi, *n.* [Gr. *tomē*, a cutting.] *Surg.* the operation of cutting for stone in the kidney.

nephridium, pl. **-ia**, nef·rid′i·um, *n.* [Gr. dim. of *nephros*, a kidney.] In animals, an excretory tube placing the COELOM (which see) in communication with the interior.

nepotism, nep′o·tism, *n.* [Fr. *népotisme*, from L. *nepos*, nephew. NEPHEW.] Favoritism shown to nephews and other relations; patronage bestowed in consideration of family relationship and not of merit.—**nepotist**, nep′o·tist, *n.* One who practices nepotism.

Neptune, nep′tūn, *n.* [L. *Neptunus*.] The chief marine divinity of the Romans, identified by them with the Greek Poseidon; a planet beyond the orbit of Uranus, the third largest and second remotest from the sun.—**Neptunian**, nep·tū′ni·an, *a.* Pertaining to the ocean or sea; formed by water or aqueous solution (as rocks).—*Neptunian theory*, in *geol.* the theory of Werner, which refers the formation of all rocks and strata to the agency of water: opposed to the *Plutonic* theory.

neptunium, nep·tū′ni·um, *n.* [From *Neptune*.] A radioactive element produced artificially by neutron bombardment of uranium-238. Symbol, Np; at. no., 93; at. wt., 237.

Nereid, ni′ri·id, *n.* [Gr. *nēreis*, *nērēidos*, from *Nēreus*, a marine deity.] *Myth.* one of the daughters of Nereus, the constant attendants of Neptune; a sea nymph; a marine annelid; a sea centipede.

neroli, ner′ō·li, *n.* [The name of an Italian princess, its discoverer.] The fragrant essential oil from the flowers of the bitter orange.

nerve, nėrv, *n.* [L. *nervus*, a sinew, strength, vigor, from root *snar* (with initial *s*), seen in E. *snare*.] A sinew or tendon‡; strength; muscular power; self-command or steadiness, especially under trying circumstances; firmness of mind; courage; one of the whitish fibers which proceed from the brain and spinal cord, or from the central ganglia, of animals, and ramify through all parts of the body, and whose function is to convey sensation and originate motion; *pl.* the general tone of one's system as an indicator (*nerves* of steel); nervousness; hysteria; *bot.* one of the ribs or principal veins in a leaf.—*v.t.*—*nerved*, *nerving*. To give nerve, strength, or vigor to.—**nervation**, nėr·vā′shon, *n.* Venation.—**nerve cell**, *n. Anat.* and *physiol.* any cell containing the cellular components of nerve tissue.—**nerve-fiber**, *n.* An axon, dendrite, or process of a nerve cell.—**nerveless**, nėrv′les, *a.* Without nerve; without fear.—**nervewracking**, *a.* Very trying on the nerves; irritating; jarring.—**nervous**, nėr′vus, *a.* Pertaining to the nerves; affecting the nerves; having the nerves affected; having weak or diseased nerves; easily agitated;

strong; vigorous; sinewy; characterized by force or strength in sentiment or style.—*Nerve centers*, the organs whence the nerves originate, as the brain.—*Nervous system* the nerves and nervous centers collectively which control movement and condition behavior and consciousness, in higher animals consisting of two parts, the cerebrospinal and autonomic systems.—*Nervous temperament*, that in which the predominating characteristic is a great excitability of the nervous system, and an undue predominance of the emotional impulses.—**nervously**, nėr′vus·li, *adv.*—**nervousness**, nėr′vus·nes, *n.* The state or quality of being nervous.—**nervure**, nėr′vūr, *n. Bot.* the vein or nerve of a leaf; *entom.* one of the corneous tubes which help to expand the wing and keep it tense.—**nervy**, nėr′vi, *a.* Sinewy; vigorous; cocky, bold, nervous.

nescience, nē′shi·ens, *n.* [L. *nescientia*, from *nescio*, not to know— *ne*, not, and *scio*, to know. SCIENCE.] The state of not knowing; want of knowledge; ignorance.

ness, nes, *n.* [A.Sax. *naes*, Icel. *nes*, Dan. *naes*, a ness; probably a form of *nose*.] A promontory; a cape; a headland.

nest, nest, *n.* [A.Sax., L.G., D., and G. *nest*; allied to L. *nidus*, a nest, for *nisdus*, from root *nas*, to dwell, seen in Greek *nostos*, return.] The place or bed formed or used by a bird for incubation and rearing the young; a place where the eggs of insects, turtles, etc., are produced; a place in which the young of various small animals (as mice) are reared; a number of persons frequenting the same haunt: generally in a bad sense; a set of articles of diminishing sizes, each enveloping the one next smaller (a *nest* of boxes); a set of small drawers.—*v.i.* To build a nest; to nestle.—**nestegg**, *n.* An egg left in the nest to prevent the hen from forsaking it; something laid up as a beginning or nucleus.— **nestle**, nes′l, *v.i.*—*nestled*, *nestling*. [Freq. from *nest*.] To make or occupy a nest; to take shelter; to lie close and snug.—*v.t.* To house or shelter, as in a nest; to cherish and fondle closely.—**nestling**, nest′ling, *n.* [A dim. from *nest*.] A young bird in the nest, or just taken from the nest.

Nestor, nest′or, *n.* The type of an old and faithful counselor, from Nestor in Homer, King of Pylos in Messenia.

Nestorian, nes·tō′ri·an, *n.* An adherent of Nestorius, patriarch of Constantinople in the fifth century, who maintained that the two natures in Christ were separate.

net, net, *n.* [A.Sax. *net*, *nett*, a net = Icel., Dan., and D. *net*, Sw. *nät*, Goth. *nati*, G. *netz*, a net; cog. L. *nassa*, a basket for catching fish; from root seen in Skr. *nada*, a stream.] An instrument formed of thread, twine, or other fibrous materials, wrought or woven into meshes, used for catching fish, birds,

etc., and also for securing or containing articles of various kinds; a fabric of fine open texture.—*v.t.*—*netted*, *netting*. To make into a net or network; to take in a net; hence, to capture by wile or stratagem; to enclose in a net or network.—*v.i.* To form network.—**netted**, net′ed, *p.* and *a.* Made into a net or network; reticulated.—**netting**, net′ing, *n.* The process of making nets; a piece of network; a net of small ropes, to be stretched along the upper part of a ship's quarter to contain hammocks.—**network**, *n.* Work formed in the same manner as a net; any net-like fabric; an interlacement into a fabric or web; a complicated intermingling of lines as of a railroad system; a political undercover group, whose members are separated, but in indirect communication; in radio, a series of stations or broadcasting units called a hookup.

net, net, *n.* [M.E. Clean, clear, akin to *neat*.] A final amount remaining after all deductions.—*a.* Final; clear; remaining after all deductions have been made.—*v.t.* To make or gain as clear profit.

nether, neTH′ér, *a.* [A.Sax. *nither*, *nithor*, *neothra*, compar. of *nithe*, under, downward (whence *neothan*, *beneothan*, *beneath*); cog. L.G., D., and Dan. *neder*, Icel. *netharr*, G. *nieder*; root seen in Skr. *ni*, downward.] Lower; lying or being beneath or in the lower part; opposed to *upper*.—**nethermost**, neTH′ér·mōst, *a.* [A double superlative, like *hindmost*.] Lowest.

nettle, net′l, *n.* [A.Sax. *netele* = D. *netel*, Dan. *naelde*, *nelde*, G. *nessel*, a nettle; root doubtful.] A plant with stinging hairs, usually of the genus *Urtica*.—*v.t.*—*nettled*, *nettling*. To irritate or vex.—**nettle rash**, *n.* An eruption upon the skin much resembling the effects of the sting of a nettle; urticaria.

neural, nū′ral, *a.* [Gr. *neuron*, a nerve; akin to L. *nervus*. NERVE.] Pertaining to the nerve or nervous system.—*Neural arch*, the arch or projection posteriorly inclosing and protecting the spinal cord of the vertebra.—*Neural axis*, the central trunk of the nervous system, also called the *cerebro-spinal axis*.—**neuralgia**, nū·ral′ji·a, *n.* [Gr. *algos*, pain.] Pain in a nerve; an ailment the chief symptom of which is acute pain, apparently seated in a nerve or nerves.—**neuralgic**, nū·ral′jik, *a.* Pertaining to neuralgia.—**neurasthenia**, nū′ras·thē″ni·a, *n.* [Gr. *neuron*, nerve, *astheneia*, weakness. ASTHENIA.] *Med.* nervous debility or exhaustion; *psychol.* a form of mental disturbance characterized by excessive irritability, fatigue, and worry.—**neuration**, nū·ra′shon, *n.* The arrangement of the veins or nervures in the wings of insects; nervation.—**neuritis**, nū·rī′tis, *n. Med.* inflammation of a nerve.—**neurological**, nū·ro·loj′i·kal, *a.* Pertaining to neurology.—**neurologist**, nū·rol′o·jist, *n.* One versed in neurology.— **neurology**, nū·rol′o·ji, *n.* That branch of science which treats of the nerves.—**neuron**, nū′ron, n. The fundamental part of a nerve cell.—**neuropteran**, nū·rop′tẽr·an, n. An individual belonging to an order of insects (Neuroptera) having four membranous, transparent, naked wings, reticulated with veins, or nervures, as the dragonflies. —**neuropterous**, nu·rop′tẽr·us, a. Belonging to the Neuropters.— **neurosis**, nū·rō′sis, n. A functional disorder of the nervous system without any apparent physical counterpart.—**neurotic**, nū·rot′ik, a. Of the nerves; relating to or acting on the nerves; affected by neurosis.—n. A disease of the nerves; a medicine for nervous affections; a neurotic person.

neuter, nū′tẽr, a. [L., not either, not one nor the other—compounded of ne and uter, either of two.] Neutral‡; gram. of neither gender; neither masculine nor feminine (in Eng. gram. applied to all names of things without life); neither active nor passive; intransitive (a neuter verb); bot. having neither stamens nor pistils; zool. having no fully developed sex (neuter bees.)—n. An animal of neither sex, or incapable of propagation; one of the imperfectly developed females of certain social insects, as ants and bees; bot. a plant which has neither stamens nor pistils; gram. a noun of the neuter gender.—**neutral**, nū′tral, a. [L. neutralis.] Not taking an active part with one of certain contending parties; not interested one way or another; indifferent.—Neutral colors, those in which the hue is broken by partaking of the reflected colors of the objects which surround them.—Neutral salts, chem. salts which do not exhibit any acid or alkaline properties.—Neutral tint, a dull, grayish hue, partaking of the character of none of the brilliant colors.—n. A person or nation that takes no part in a contest between others.—**neutrality**, nū·tral′i·ti, n. The state of being neutral; the state of taking no part on either side.— **neutralization**, nū′tral·i·zā″shon, n. The act of neutralizing; chem. the process by which an acid and an alkali are so combined as to disguise each other's properties or render them inert.—**neutralize**, nū′tral·īz, v.t.—neutralized, neutralizing. To render neutral; to destroy the peculiar properties or opposite dispositions of; to render inoperative; to counteract; chem. to destroy or render inert or imperceptible the peculiar properties of, by combination with a different substance.— **neutralizer**, nū′tral·i·zẽr, n. One who or that which neutralizes.— **neutrally**, nū′tral·li, adv. In a neutral manner.

neutrino, nū·trē′nō, n. [L. neutr-, neither, and ino.] Phys. and chem. a hypothetical neutral particle of smaller mass than the neutron.— **neutron**, nū′tron, n. Phys. an uncharged particle in the nucleus of the atom, used for bombardment in atomic-energy reactions.

névé, nā′vā, n. [Fr., from L. nix, nivis, snow.] The French name for the coarsely granular snow from which glaciers are formed.

never, nev′ẽr, adv. [The neg. of ever; A.Sax. naefre, from ne, not, and aefre, ever; comp. neither, either, etc.] Not ever; at no time, whether past, present, or future; in no degree (never fear); not at all; none (never the better); not, emphatically (he answered never a word).—Never so, to any or to whatever extent or degree (never so much, little, well, etc.; now less common than ever so).—Never is much used in composition, as in never-ending, never-failing, never-dying, etc.; but in all such compounds it has its usual meaning.—**nevermore**, nev′ẽr·mōr, adv. Never again; at no future time. **nevertheless**, nev′ẽr·THE·les″, conj. [The the is the old instrumental case of the demonstrative used before comparatives; A.Sax. thý læs, the or by that less.] Not the less; notwithstanding; in spite of, or without regarding that.

nevus, nē′vus, n. [L.] A natural mark, spot, or blemish on the skin of a person; a birthmark.

new, nū, a. [A.Sax. niwe, neówe, new=D. nieuw, Goth. niujis, G. neu; cog. W. newydd, Ir. nuadh, L. novus, Gr. neos, Skr. navas, —new; connected with now.] Lately made, invented, produced, or come into being; recent in origin; novel: opposed to old, and used of things; not before known; recently discovered; recently produced by change; different from a former (to lead a new life); not habituated; not familiar; unaccustomed; fresh after any event, never used before, or recently brought into use; not secondhand (a new copy of a book); recently commenced; starting afresh (the new year, a new week).—New Testament. See TESTAMENT.—New World, a name frequently given to North and South America; the Western Hemisphere.—**newcomer**, n. One who has lately come.—**New Deal**, n. A term attached to the policies advocated by Franklin Delano Roosevelt and legislation enacted by Congress.—**newfangled**, a. New-fashioned.—**new-fashioned**, a. Made in a new fashion; lately come into fashion.—**newly**, nū′li, adv. Lately; freshly; recently; with a new form; afresh.—**new moon**, n. The moon when it is in conjunction with the sun and is totally dark.— **newness**, nū′nes, n.—**news**, nūz, n. pl. The material reported in a newspaper, magazine, or newscast; a newscast; fresh information of something that has lately taken place, or of something before unknown; tidings; a newspaper.— **newsboy**, n. A boy who sells or delivers newspapers.—**newsletter**, n. A letter-like report or analysis of a specialized nature, printed for periodic distribution to subscribers.— **newsmonger**, nūz′mung·gẽr, n. One who deals in news; a gossip; a teller

of tales.—**newspaper**, nūz′pā·pẽr, n. A periodic publication issued daily or weekly, disseminating news, opinions, and reports of immediate significance; the organization that composes, publishes, and distributes newspapers.—**newspaperman**, n. One who writes for, edits, or owns a newspaper; a gatherer of news.— **newsprint**, n. An inexpensive paper manufactured from woodpulp, machine-finished, used mostly for newspapers.—**newsreel**, nūz′rēl, n. A motion picture film depicting current news events.—**newsstand**, n. A booth or stand where newspapers and periodicals are sold.—**newsy**, nūz′i, a. Full of news.

newel, nū′l, n. [O.Fr. nouel, nouil, stone of a fruit, der. from L. nux, nucis, nut.] The post about which a winding staircase circles, hence, the main or secondary posts of a straight staircase.

Newfoundland dog, nū·found′land, or nū′fênd·land dag, n. [From the island.] A well-known and fine variety of the dog, supposed to be derived from Newfoundland, remarkable for its sagacity, good nature, and swimming powers.

newt, nūt, n. [A corruption of an ewt, ewt, evet being old forms. EFT.] One of a genus of small-tailed batrachians of lizard-like appearance, living in ponds, ditches, and moist places; an eft.

Newtonian, nū·tō′ni·an, a. Pertaining to Sir Isaac Newton, or formed or discovered by him.—Newtonian telescope, a form of reflecting telescope.

next, nekst, a. superl. of nigh. [A.Sax. néhst, néhsta, superl. of néh, neáh, nigh.] Nearest in place, time, rank, or degree. [When next stands before an object without to after it, it may be regarded as a preposition.]—Next door to, close to; allied to; not far removed from.—adv. At the time or turn nearest or immediately succeeding (who follows next?).

nexus, nek′sus, n. [L.] Tie; connection; interdependence existing.

niacin, nī′ä·sin, n. [Nicotinic acid and in.] One part of the vitamin B complex; nicotinic acid.

nib, nib, n. [Same as neb.] The bill or beak of a fowl; the point of anything, particularly of a pen; a small pen adapted to be fitted into a holder.— v.t.—nibbed, nibbing. To furnish with a nib; to mend the nib of, as a pen.

nibble, nib′l, v.t.—nibbled, nibbling. [A freq. from nib, or from nip.] To bite by little at a time; to eat in small bits; to bite, as a fish does the bait; just to catch by biting.— v.i. To bite gently; fig. to carp; to make a petty attack; with at.—n. A little bite, or the act of seizing with the mouth as if to bite.— **nibbler**, nib′lẽr, n. One that nibbles.

niblick, nib′lik, n. An iron-headed golf club with a wide face at an angle of 45 degrees or more from the vertical, that is used to lift the ball into the air from sandtraps and to approach the green.

nice, nīs, *a.* [O.Fr. *nice, nisce,* simple, from L. *nescius,* from *ne,* not, *scio,* to know. NESCIENCE.] Foolish or silly‡; unimportant‡; over-scrupulous; fastidious; punctilious; distinguishing minutely; made with scrupulous exactness; precise; pleasant to the senses; delicious; dainty; pleasing or agreeable in general: a modern sense.—**nicely,** nīs′li, *adv.* In a nice manner; fastidiously; critically; with delicate perception; accurately; exactly; becomingly; pleasantly.—**niceness,** nīs′nes, *n.* State or quality of being nice; fastidiousness; minute exactness; agreeableness; pleasantness.—**nicety,** nīs′e·ti, *n.* [O.Fr. *niceté.*] State or quality of being nice; excess of delicacy; fastidiousness; delicacy of perception; precision; delicate management; a minute difference or distinction.

Nicene, nī·sēn′, *a.* [*Nicaea,* a town of Asia Minor.] Pertaining to a summary of Christian faith, the *Nicene creed,* composed by the Council of Nice against Arianism, A.D. 325.

niche, nich, *n.* [Fr. *niche,* from It. *nicchia,* from *nicchio,* a shellfish, from L. *mytilus,* a mussel.] A recess in a wall for the reception of a statue, a vase, or some other ornament; a person's place or position.

Nick, nik, *n.* [A name among the Teutonic nations for a water-goblin; A.Sax. *nicor,* Dan. *nök,* Icel. *nykr,* N. *nykk, nök,* G. *nix, nixe.*] Originally, a goblin or spirit of the waters, but now applied only to the Evil One, generally with the addition of *Old.*

nick, nik, *n.* [Same as D. *knik,* Sw. *nick,* a nod, a wink; G *nicken;* to nod; or connected with *nick,* a notch.] The exact point of time required by necessity or convenience; the critical time.—*v.t.* To strike at the lucky time; to hit; to make a hit at by some trick (*Shak.*).

nick, nik, *n.* [Comp. G. *knick,* a flaw; also E. *notch,* O.D. *nocke,* a notch.] A notch; a notch in the shank of a type to guide the hand of the compositor in setting.—*v.t.* To make a nick or notch in; to cut in nicks or notches.

nickel, nik′el, *n.* [Sw. *nickel,* nickel; a name connected with *nick,* the evil spirit, and given to this metal because its copper-colored ore deceived the miners by giving no copper.] A hard silver-white metallic element, malleable and ductile, much used in alloys. Symbol, Ni; at. no., 28; at. wt., 58.71. The five-cent coin composed of copper and nickel. (*U.S.*)—**nickelic,** ni·kel′ik, *a.* Pertaining to or containing nickel.—**nickeliferous,** nik·el·if′er·us, *a.* Containing nickel.—**nickelplating,** *n.* The plating of metals with nickel.—**nickel silver,** *n.* An alloy composed of copper, zinc, and nickel.

nicknack, nik′nak, *n.* [KNICKKNACK.] A trinket; a gimcrack; a trifle. Spelled also *knickknack.*

nickname, nik′nām, *n.* [Probably for

ekename (Icel. *auk-nefni*), the initial *n* being that of *an,* the indef. art., like *newt* for *ewt.*] A name given to a person in contempt or derision; a familiar or contemptuous name or appellation; a familiar form of a proper name, such as "Bill," for William.

nicotine, nik′o·tin, *n.* A volatile alkaloid from tobacco, highly poisonous.

nicotinic acid, nik·o·tin′ik a′sid, *n.* [From *nicotine.*] An acid resulting from the oxidation of nicotine, $(C_5H_4 N)$ COOH, and one of the members of the vitamin B complex; niacin.

nictitate, nictate, nik′ti·tāt, nik′tāt, *v.i.*—**nictitated, nictated;** *nictitating, nictating.* [From L. *nicto, nictatum,* to wink.] To wink with the eyes.—*Nictitating membrane,* a thin movable membrane, most largely developed in birds, which covers and protects the eyes from dust or too much light.—**nictitation, nictation,** nik·ti·tā′shon, nik·tā′shon, *n.* The act of winking.

nidificate, nid′i·fi·kāt, *v.i.* [L. *nidifico,* from *nidus,* a nest, *facio,* to make. NIDULANT.] To make a nest.—**nidification,** nid′i·fi·kā″shon, *n.* The act of building a nest.

nidus, nī′dus, *n.* [L., a nest.] Any part of a living organism where a parasite finds nourishment; *med.* the bodily seat of a zymotic disease; the part of the organism where such a disease is developed.

niece, nēs, *n.* [Fr. *nièce,* O.Fr. *niepce,* from L. *neptis,* a granddaughter; allied to *nepos, nepotis,* a nephew. NEPHEW.] The daughter of a brother or sister; also, the daughter of a brother or sister in law.

nielio, ni·el′i·ō, *n.* [It., from L.L. *nigellum,* from L. *nigellus,* dim. of *niger,* black.] A method of ornamenting metal plates by cutting lines in the metal and filling them up with a black or colored composition.

nifty, nif′ti, *a.* [Slang] Very good; attractive and stylish.

niggard, nig′erd, *n.* [From Icel. *knöggr,* Sw. *njugg,* niggardly, with term. -*ard.*] A miser; a person meanly covetous; a sordid, parsimonious wretch.—**niggard, niggardly,** nig′erd·li, *a.* Miserly; meanly covetous; sordidly parsimonious.—**niggardly,** *adv.* In a niggard manner.—**niggardliness,** nig′erd·li·nes, *n.* The quality of being niggardly; sordid parsimony.

niggle, nig′l, *v.i.*—**niggled, niggling.** [N. *nigla.*] To trifle; to putter around.

nigh, nī, *a.* compar. *nigher,* superl. *next.* [A.Sax. *neáh, néh,* nigh, near; D. *na,* Icel. *ná-,* G. *nah, nahe,* near, prep. *nach,* to, Goth. *nehwa*—nigh. NEAR, NEIGHBOR.] Near; not distant or remote in place or time; closely at hand; ready to aid.—*adv.* Near; close; almost; nearly.—*prep.* Near to; at no great distance from.

night, nīt, *n.* [A.Sax. *niht, neaht*= Icel. *nátt,* Sw. *natt,* Dan. *nat,* Goth. *nahts,* D. and G. *nacht;* cog. Ir. *nochd,* W. *nos,* Armor. *noz,* Lith. *naktis,* L. *nox, noctis,* Gr. *nyx,*

nyktos, Skr. *nakti, nakta*—night; from root *nak,* to vanish, to perish.] That part of the natural day when the sun is beneath the horizon, or the time from sunset to sunrise; *fig.* a state or time of darkness, depression, misfortune, and the like; a state of ignorance or intellectual darkness; obscurity; the darkness of death or the grave; a time of sadness or sorrow.—**nightly,** nīt′li, *a.* Done by night; happening in the night; done every night.—*adv.* By night; every night.—**nightward,** nīt′wėrd, *a.* Approaching toward night. *Night* is much used as a first element in compounds, many of them self-explanatory.—**night blindness,** *n.* A disease in which the eyes can see only by day or bright light.—**nightcap,** *n.* A cap worn in bed; toddy or other potation taken before going to bed.—**night clothes,** *n.* pl. Clothes worn in bed.—**night club,** *n.* A café or restaurant, serving liquors and presenting entertainment for the enjoyment of night pleasure-seekers.—**nightcrawler,** *n.* A large angleworm which crawls about by night.—**nightfall,** nīt′fạl, *n.* The fall of night; the close of the day; evening.—**nightgown,** *n.* A loose gown worn in bed; a nightdress.—**nighthawk,** *n.* Any of the North American longwinged goatsuckers (genus *Chordeiles*) related to the whippoorwill; a person up and about during the night.—**night letter,** *n.* A telegram sent at night at a per-word rate lower than a straight telegram.—**nightlong,** *a.* Lasting a night.—**nightmare,** nīt′mār, *a.* A dream causing a state of oppression or feeling of suffocation, hence, some overpowering, oppressive, or stupefying influence.—**night rider,** *n.* A member of a band of terrorists who go about at night performing acts of violence and destruction to punish or scare.—**nightshade,** nīt′shād, *n.* [A.Sax. *nihtscada,* lit. the shade or shadow of night; so D. *nachtschade,* G. *nachtschatten,* the nightshade.] The popular name of various plants of the potato genus which possess narcotic or poisonous properties; also applied to plants of different genera.—*Deadly nightshade,* belladonna.—**nightshirt,** *n.* A pull-over sleeping garment for men and boys.—**nightwalker,** *n.* One that walks in his sleep; a somnambulist; one that roams in the night for evil purposes.—**night watch,** *n.* A watch or period of the night; a watch or guard in the night.

nightingale, nīt′in·gāl, *n.* [A.Sax. *nihtegale,* lit. the night-singer, from *niht,* night, *galan,* to sing; so D. *nachtegaal,* Dan. *nattergal,* G. *nachtigall.* The *n* medial is intrusive, as in *passenger, messenger.*] A well-known migratory bird that sings at night, often called in poetry Philomela or Philomel.

nigrescent, nī·gres′ent, *a.* [L. *nigresco,* to grow black, from *niger,* black.] Growing black; approaching to blackness.—**nigritude,** nig′ri·tūd, *n.* [L. *nigritudo.*] Blackness.

nihilism, nī′hil·izm, n. [L. nihil, nothing.] Nothingness; metaph. the denial of the basis of all knowledge; the doctrine that existence is meaningless and life has little value. —**nihilist,** nī′hil·ist, n. One who holds the doctrine or principles of nihilism; a member of a Russian secret society, the adherents of which maintained the need for an entire reconstruction of society and held revolutionary ideas generally.—**nihilistic,** nī·hil·is′tik, a.—**nihility,** nī·hil′i·ti, n. A state of being nothing; nothingness.

nil, nil, n. [L. NIHIL.] Nothing; as, his liabilities were over $5000 and his assets nil.

Nilometer, nī·lom′et·ėr, n. [Gr. Neilos, Nile, and mētron, measure.] An instrument for measuring the rise of water in the Nile during its periodical floods.—**Nilotic,** nī·lot′ik, a. Pertaining to the Nile.

nimble, nim′bl, a. [O.E. nemel, capable, A.Sax. numol, capable, catching, from niman, to take = Icel. nema, D. nemen, G. nehmen, Goth. niman, to take; akin numb, benumb.] Light and quick in motion; moving with ease and celerity; agile; prompt; swift.—**nimbleness,** nim′bl·nes, n. Agility; quickness; celerity.—**nimbly,** nim′bli, adv. In a nimble manner; with agility.

nimbus, nim′bus, n. [L., a cloud.] A cloud; a rain cloud; a kind of halo or disc surrounding the head in representations of divine or sacred personages.

nincompoop, nin′kom·pöp, n. [A corruption of L. non compos, not of sound mind.] A fool; a blockhead; a simpleton.

nine, nīn, a. [A.Sax. nigon = L.G. and D. negen, G. neun, Goth. niun, Icel. niu, Sw. niu, Dan. ni; cog. W. naw, Ir. naov, L. novem, Gr. ennea, Skr. navam—nine. NOON.] One more than eight, or one less than ten.—Nine days' wonder, a subject of astonishment and gossip for a short time.—The nine worthies, certain famous personages, often alluded to by old writers, like the seven wonders of the world, etc.—n. The number composed of eight and one.—The Nine, among English poets, the nine Muses.—**ninefold,** nīn′fōld, a. Nine times repeated.—**ninepins,** n. pl. A game with nine pins of wood set on end, at which a ball is rolled.—**nineteen,** nīn′tēn, a. and n. [A.Sax. nigontyne, i.e. nine ten.] Nine and ten.—**nineteenth,** nīn′tēnth, a. The ordinal of nineteen.—n. A nineteenth part.—**ninety,** nīn′ti, a. and n. [A.Sax. nigontig—nigon, nine, and tig, ten.] Nine times ten.—**ninetieth,** nīn′ti·eth, a. The ordinal of ninety.—n. A ninetieth part.—**ninth,** nīnth, a. The ordinal of nine; the next preceding ten.—n. A ninth part; mus. an interval containing an octave and a tone.—**ninthly,** nīnth′li, adv. In the ninth place.

ninny, nin′i, n. [A contr. for nincompoop, or from It. ninno, Sp. niño, a child.] A fool; a simpleton.

ninnyhammer, nin′i·ham·ėr, n. A simpleton.

niobium, nī·ō′bi·um, n. [From Niobe.] A gray metallic element, formerly called columbium. Symbol, Nb; at. no., 41; at. wt., 92.906.

nip, nip, v.t.—nipped or nipt, nipping. [Not found in A.Sax.; akin to Dan. nippe, to twitch, knibe, to nip, to pinch; D. knippen, to nip, nijpen, to pinch; Icel. kneif, pincers; G. kneipen, kneifen, to pinch, knippen, to fillip; akin knife, neap.] To catch and compress sharply between two surfaces or points, as of the fingers; to pinch; to cut, bite, or pinch off the end of; to blast, as by frost; to benumb; to chill.—To nip in the bud, to destroy in the first stage of growth.—n. A pinch, as with the points of the fingers, nails, etc.; a blast by frost.—**nip and tuck.** Uncertainty as to the probable success of alternate element.—**nipper,** nip′ėr, n. One who or that which nips; a foretooth of a horse.—**nippingly,** nip′ing·li, adv. In a nipping manner; sarcastically.—**nippy,** a. Brisk or tangy, as of the air or of a cheese.

nip, nip, n. [Dan. nip, a sip, nippe, D. and G. nippen, to nip; akin nipple.] A sip or small draught, especially of some strong spirituous beverage.

nipper, nip′ėr, n. In the plural, pincers; a tool.

nipple, nip′l, n. [A.Sax. nipele; probably connected with nip, a sip, L.G. nippen, Dan. nippe, to sip.] The spongy protuberance by which milk is drawn from the breasts of females; a pap; a teat; something like a nipple, as that part of a gun over which the cap is placed; a connecting piece of pipe.

nirvana, nir·vä′na, n. [Skr. nir, out, and vāna, blown; lit. blown out.] Buddhism the final beatitude attained through the extinguishing of desire and human consciousness; a state of oblivion to human reality, as pain, concern, etc.

Nisan, nī′san, n. A month of the Jewish calendar, originally called Abib.

nisei, nē′sā, n. [Jap. ni, second, and sei, generation.] An American-born child of Japanese immigrant parents.

Nissen hut, nis′n hut, n. A fairly portable wooden hut with iron roof. It was said to be warm in winter and cool in summer; actually it was the reverse.

nit, nit, n. [A.Sax. hnitu; D. neet, Icel. nitr, Dan. gnid, Sw. gnet, G. niss, a nit; cog. Gr. konis, a nit.] The egg of a louse or other small insect.

niter, nī′tėr, n. [Fr. nitre, L. nitrum, Gr. nitron, from some oriental source.] A substance called also saltpeter; potassium nitrate or sodium nitrate used for making gunpowder, in dyeing, metallurgy, medicine, etc.—**nitrate,** nī′trāt, n. A salt of nitric acid; potassium nitrate or sodium nitrate used as a fertilizer.—v.t. To join or treat with nitric acid or a nitrate; chem. to convert to a nitro

compound or a nitrate.—**nitric,** nī′trik, a. A term in the nomenclature of the oxygen compounds of nitrogen, indicating more nitrogen content, especially of higher valence than nitrous substances.—Nitric acid, an important acid, HNO_3, employed in etching, explosives, etc.—**nitrification,** nīt′rif·i·kā″shon, n. Formation of nitrates as plant food by the action of certain bacteria on organic substances.—**nitrify,** nī′tri·fī, v.t. Chem. to infuse or join with nitrogen or a nitrogen compound; to change, by oxidation, into nitrous or nitric acid or their salts.—**nitrite,** nī′trīt, n. A salt of nitrous acid.—**nitrogen,** nī′tro·jen, n. That element which is the principal ingredient of atmospheric air, of which it constitutes about four-fifths, possessing neither taste nor smell. Symbol, N; at. no., 7; at. wt., 14.0067.—Nitrogen cycle, a revolving course of natural fertilizing processes involving the passing of nitrogen through air, soil, and organisms.—**nitrogenize,** nī′tro·jen·īz, v.t. To impregnate or imbue with nitrogen.—**nitrogenous,** nī·troj′e·nus, a.—**nitroglycerin,** n. A compound produced by the action of a mixture of strong nitric and sulfuric acids on glycerin at low temperatures, a most powerful explosive.—**nitrometer,** nī·trom′et·ėr, n. An instrument for ascertaining the quality or value of niter.—**nitrous,** nī′trus, a. Chem. applied to compounds containing less oxygen than those called nitric.—Nitrous oxide gas, a combination of nitrogen and oxygen which, when inhaled, causes insensibility, and hence is used as an anaesthetic during surgical operations; diluted with air it produces an exhilarating effect, hence the name of laughing gas.

nitid, nī′tid, a. [L. nitidus.] Bright; shining; gay; spruce; bot. having a smooth polished surface.

nitwit, nit′wit, n. [G. nix, not, and E. wit.] A dull-witted or stupid person.

nix, niks, n. [G. nichts, nothing.] Nothing; no one; no.

Nizam, ni·zäm′, n. [Hind. and Ar. from Ar. nazama, to govern.] Formerly the title of the ruler of Hyderabad in India.

no, nō, adv. [A.Sax. ná, nó, no, from the negative particle, ne, no and á, ever; this negative particle = Icel. ne, Goth. ni, Bohem. and Russ. ne, Armor. and Gael. na, L. ne, Zend. na, Skr. na; akin nor, not, nay, non.] A word of denial or refusal, expressing a negative, and opposed to yes. When repeated or when used with another negative it is specially emphatic. It may be used as the correlative of whether (whether or no), though now less common than not.—n. A negative vote, or a person who votes in the negative (the noes have it).—**noway, noways, nowise,** nō′wā, nō′wāz, nō′wīz, adv. In no way, manner, or degree.—**nowhere,** nō′hwâr, adv. Not in or to any place.—**nowhither,** nō′hwiTH·ėr, *adv.* Not in any direction or to any place.

no, nō, *adv.* [A.Sax. *ná*, *nó*, no, from the negative particle, *ne*, *no* and *á*, ever; Goth. *ni*, L. *ne*, Skr. *na*; akin *nay*.] A word of denial or refusal, expressing a negative, and opposed to *yes*; a word used to emphasize or qualify a previous negative statement; not any; not at all.—*a.* Not at all; not a (I have *no* great love for him).—*n.* A negative vote; pl. persons who vote in the negative (the *noes* have it).—**noway, noways, nowise**, nō'wā, nō'wāz, nō'wīz, *adv.* In no way, manner, or degree.—**nowhere**, nō'hwâr, *adv.* Not in or to any place.

Noachian, nō·ā'ki·an, *a.* Relating to *Noah*, the patriarch, or his time.

nob, nob, *n.* [From *knob.*] The head: in humor or contempt.

nob, nob, *n.* [An abbreviation of *nobleman.*] A member of the aristocracy; a swell. (*Slang.*)—**nobby**, nob'i, *a.* Showy; stylish; smart. (*Slang.*)

nobelium, nō·bē'li·um, *n.* [From *Nobel* Institute.] A radio-active element produced artificially. Symbol, No; at. no., 102.

noble, nō'bl, *a.* [Fr. *noble*, from L. *nobilis*, high-born, noble; for *gnobilis*, from stem of *gnosco, nosco*, to know, seen also in E. *note.*] High in excellence or worth; lofty in character; magnanimous (a *noble* mind); proceeding from or characteristic of greatness of mind (*noble* sentiments); of the best kind; choice; pertaining to the nobility or peerage; magnificent; stately (a *noble* edifice).—*Noble metals*, those which have high value, superior qualities, and do not easily corrode: gold, silver, platinum, etc.—*n.* A nobleman.—**nobility**, nō·bil'i·ti, *n.* The quality of being noble; nobleness; the state of being of noble birth or rank; the peerage.—**nobly**, nō'bli, *adv.*—**nobleman**, nō'bl·man, *n.* One of the nobility.—**noblewoman**, nō'bl·wu̱·man, *n.*—**nobleness**, nō'bl·nes, *n.*—**noblesse**, nō·bles', *n.* [Fr.] The nobility.—*Noblesse oblige*, the idea that noble birth or rank necessitates honorable and beneficent behavior.

nobody, nō'bod·i, *n.* [*No* and *body.*] No person; no one; an insignificant or contemptible person; a person of no standing or position.

nock, nok, *n.* [M.E. *nocke*, prob. from Sw. *nock, nocka*, akin M.D. *nocke*, D. *nok*, L.G. *nokk*, tip or projection.] *Archery*, the notch at either end of the bow for holding the string, or the notch in the arrow for fitting it to the bow.—*v.t.* To notch the bow or arrow.

noctambulation, noctambulism, nok·tam'bū·lā'shon, nok·tam'bū·lizm, *n.* [L. *nox, noctis*, night, and *ambulo*, to walk.] Somnambulism; sleepwalking.—**noctambulist**, nok·tam'bū·list, *n.* A somnambulist.—**nocturne**, nok'tėrn, *n.* [F.] In music, a serenade concerning the night; a light, dreamy composition, variable in form; the musical piece of that name made famous by Chopin. —**nocturnal**, nok·tėr'nal, *a.* Per-

taining or belonging to the night; done or occurring at night; *zool.* active by night; *bot.* closing during the day and expanding during the night; said of flowers.—**nocturnally**, nok·tėr'nal·li, *adv.* By night; nightly.

nod, nod, *v.i.*—**nodded, nodding.** [Allied to O.H.G. *nuoton, knoton*, to shake; Dan. *noder*, gestures; or perhaps to W. and Ir. *nod*, a mark, a notice; Gael. *nodadh*, a wink or nod.] To incline the head with a quick motion; either forward or sidewise; to let the head sink from sleep; to make an inclination of the head, as in assent or in beckoning; to bend or incline the top with a quick motion (*nodding* plumes).—*v.t.* To incline, as the head or top; to signify by a nod; to beckon by a nod.—*n.* A quick downward motion of the head as a sign of assent, salutation, from drowsiness, etc.—**nodder**, nod'ėr, *n.* One who nods.

noddle, nod'l, *n.* [A dim. corresponding to D. *knod, knodde*, a knob, a knot; Dan. *knude*, a knot; akin to *knot.*] The head: used humorously.

noddy, nod'i, *n.* [Probably from *nod*, and equivalent to sleepy-head; comp. *noodle.*] A simpleton; a fool; a seafowl; so called from its being easily taken.

node, nōd, *n.* [L. *nodus* (for *gnodus*), a knot; cog. *knot, noddle.*] A knot; a knob; a protuberance; *bot.* a sort of knot on a stem where leaves arise; *mus.* a nodal point; *astron.* one of the two points in which two great circles of the celestial sphere (as the ecliptic and equator) intersect each other; one of the points in which the orbit of a satellite intersects the plane of the orbit of its primary.—*Lunar nodes*, the points at which the orbit of the moon cuts the ecliptic.—**nodal**, nō'dal, *a.* Pertaining to a node or to nodes; nodated.—*Nodal points and nodal lines*, the points or lines of a vibrating body which remain at rest during the vibration.—**nodical**, nod'i·kal, *a.* *Astron.* relating to nodes.—**nodose**, nō·dōs', *a.* [L. *nodosus.*] Knotted; jointed.—**nodosity**, nō·dos'i·ti, *n.* The state or quality of being nodose; knottiness; a knotty protuberance.—**nodular**, nod'ū·lėr, *a.* Pertaining to or in the form of a nodule.—**nodule**, nod'ūl, *n.* [L. *nodulus*, dim. from *nodus*, a knot.] A little knot or lump; *bot.* a small woody body found in bark; *geol.* a rounded irregular-shaped mineral mass.—**nodulose, nodulous**, nod'ū·lōs, nod'ū·lus, *a.* Having little knots; knotty.

noel, nō'el, *n.* [Fr. from L. *dies natalis*, birthday of Christ.] Christmas carols; [cap.] Christmas.

nog, nog, *n.* [Same as Dan. *knag, knage*, a wooden peg; D. *knog*, a yardarm; akin *knag.*] A wooden pin; a treenail or pin used in ship-building; a brick-shaped piece of wood inserted in a wall; a timber-brick; a square piece of wood used to prop up the roof of a mine.—*Eggnog*, a drink containing an egg beaten with sugar, milk, flavoring,

and usually liquors, served hot or cold.—**nogging pieces**, horizontal pieces of timber in brick work.

noggin, nog'in, *n.* [Ir. *noigin*, Gael. *noigean*, a noggin.] A small mug or wooden cup; a measure equivalent to a gill; the head.

noils, noilz, *n.* [Origin doubtful.] The knots and short wool separated out from the long wool in combing.

noise, noiz, *n.* [Fr. *noise*, strife, quarrel, noise, probably through a form *noxia*, for L. *noxa*, injury, hurt. NOXIOUS.] A sound of any kind or proceeding from any cause; more especially a din, a confused mixture of sounds; outcry; clamor; frequent talk; much public conversation or discussion.—*v.i.* noised, noising. To sound loud.—*v.t.* noised, noising. To spread by rumor or report; to report.—**noiseless**, noiz'les, *a.* Making no noise; silent.—**noiselessly**, noiz'les·li, *adv.* In a noiseless manner; silently.—**noiselessness**, noiz'les·nes, *n.* The state of being noiseless; silence.—**noisy**, noi'zi, *a.* Making a loud noise; clamorous; full of noise.—**noisily**, noi'zi·li, *adv.* In a noisy manner; with noise.—**noisiness**, noi'zi·nes, *n.* The state of being noisy.

noisome, noi'sum, *a.* [From obsol. *noye*, annoyance, to annoy, shortened from *annoy*, with term. *-some.*] Noxious to health; morally noxious or injurious; offensive to the smell or other senses; fetid.—**noisomely**, noi'sum·li, *adv.* In a noisome manner.—**noisomeness**, noi'sum·nes, *n.*

nolle prosequi, nol'i pros'e·kwī, *n.* [L. to be unwilling to prosecute.] *Law*, the refusal of a plaintiff in an action to proceed any further.

nomad, nō'mad, *n.* [Gr. *nomas, nomados*, living on pasturage, from *nemō*, to feed, to pasture.] One of those people whose chief occupation consists in feeding their flocks, and who shift their residence according to the state of the pasture.—*a.* Nomadic.—**nomadic**, nō·mad'ik, *a.* [Gr. *nomadikos.*] Pertaining to nomads; subsisting by the tending of cattle, and wandering for the sake of pasturage; pastoral.—**nomadically**, nō·mad'i·kal·li, *adv.* In a nomadic manner.—**nomadism**, nō'mad·izm, *n.* The state of being a nomad.

no man's land. The ground between hostile trenches, as belonging to neither side; unclaimed or uninhabited land.

nom de plume, nom' de plöm, *n.* Pen name.

nome, nōm, *n.* [Gr. *nomos*, a district.] A province or other political division of a country, especially of modern Greece.—**nomarch**, nom'ärk, *n.* [Gr. *archō*, to rule.] The governor or chief magistrate of a nome.—**nomarchy**, nom'är·ki, *n.* The jurisdiction of a nomarch.

nomenclator, nō'men·klā·tėr, *n.* [L., from *nomen*, name, and *calo*, to call (seen in *calendar*).] A person who gives names to things; one who settles and adjusts the names of things in any art or science.—

nomenclature, nō′men·klā·tūr, *n.* A system of names; the systematic naming of things; the vocabulary of names or technical terms which are appropriated to any branch of science. ∴ As distinguished from *terminology* it is applied to the names for individual things, while the latter is generally applied to the technical terms describing the characteristics of things.

nominal, nom′i·nal, *a.* [L. *nominalis,* from *nomen, nominis,* a name. NAME.] Pertaining to a name or term; nounal; existing in name only; not real; merely so called.—**nominalism,** nom′i·nal·izm, *n.* The principles of the nominalists.—**nominalist,** nom′i·nal·ist, *n.* One of a sect of scholastic philosophers who maintained that general notions (such as the notion of a tree) have no realities corresponding to them, and have no existence but as names (*nomina*) or words: opposed to *realist.*—**nominalistic,** nom′i·nal·is″tik, *a.* Relating to nominalism.—**nominally,** nom′i·nal·li, *adv.* In a nominal manner; in name only, not really (*nominally* king).—**nominate,** nom′i·nāt, *v.t.*—*nominated, nominating.* [L. *nomino, nominatum.*] To name; to mention by name; to designate by name for an office or place; to propose by name, or offer the name of, as a candidate for an office or place; to set down in express terms (*Shak.*).—**nomination,** nom·i·nā′shon, *n.* The act of nominating; the act of proposing by name for an office; the state of being nominated; the power of nominating or appointing to office.—**nominative,** nom′i·na·tiv, *a.* [L. *nominatus,* naming.] A term applied to that form of a noun or pronoun which is used when the noun or pronoun is the subject of a sentence.—*n.* The nominative case; a nominative word.—**nominator,** nom′i·nā·tėr, *n.* One that nominates.—**nominee,** nom·i·nē′, *n.* A person nominated; one proposed to fill a place or office.

nomography, nō·mog′ra·fi, *n.* [Gr. *nomos,* a law, and *graphō,* to write.] Exposition of the proper manner of drawing up laws.—**nomology,** nō·mol′o·ji, *n.* [Gr. *nomos,* and *logos.*] The science or knowledge of law, legislation, and government.

nonacceptance, *n.* A refusal to accept.

nonage, non′ij, *n.* [L. *non,* not, and E. *age.*] The time of life before a person becomes legally of age; minority; period of immaturity in general.

nonagenarian, non′a·je·nâ″ri·an, *n.* [L. *nonagenarius,* from *nonageni,* ninety each, *nonaginta,* ninety, *novem,* nine.] A person ninety or between ninety and a hundred years old.

nonagon, non′a·gon, *n.* [L. *nonus,* ninth, and Gr. *gonia,* an angle.] A figure having nine sides and nine angles.

nonappearance, *n.* A failure to appear; default or appearance.

nonattendance, *n.* A failure to attend; personal absence.

nonce, nons, *n.* [Same as *once,* with an initial *n* belonging to the old dative of the article, seen in the phrases *for then anes, for then ones,* for the nonce, *anes, ones,* being an adverbial genitive from A.Sax. *án,* one, used substantively; comp. *the tother,* for *that other.*] Present occasion or purpose: used only in the phrase *for the nonce.*

nonchalant, non′sha·lant or non·sha·laṅ′, *a.* [Fr., from *non,* not, *chaloir,* to care for, from L. *calere,* to be warm.] Indifferent.—**nonchalantly,** non·sha·lant′li, *adv.*—**nonchalance,** non′sha·lans or non·sha·lans′, *n.*

noncombatant, *n.* Anyone connected with a military or naval force whose duty it is not to fight; civilians in a place occupied by troops.

noncommissioned, *n.* Not having a commission.—*Noncommissioned officers,* subordinate officers below the rank of lieutenant, as sergeants and corporals in the army, and quartermasters and gunners mates in the navy.

noncommittal, *a.* Indicating a refusal to commit oneself; revealing no preference.

noncompliance, *n.* Neglect or failure of compliance.

non compos mentis, non kom′pos men′tis [L.] *Law,* not of sound mind; referring to any mental disorder.

nonconcurrence, *n.* A refusal to concur.

nonconductor, *n.* A substance which resists or conducts with difficulty such a force as heat or electricity.

nonconformist, non·kon·for′mist, *n.* One who does not conform; especially one who refuses to conform to an established church.—**nonconformity,** non·kon·for′mi·ti, *n.* Neglect or failure of conformity; the neglect or refusal to unite with an established church.

noncooperation, non·kō·op′ėr·ā″shon, *n.* Failure or refusal to cooperate or comply.

nondescript, non′di·skript, *a.* [L. *non,* not, and *descriptus,* described.] Not hitherto described or classed; not easily described; odd; indescribable.—*n.* A person or thing not easily classed.

none, nun, *n.* or *pron.* [A.Sax. *nán*—ne, not, and *án,* one.] Not one; not any; not a part; not the least portion.—*None the less,* nevertheless.—**nonesuch,** nun′such, *n.* A person or thing such as to have no parallel.

noneffective, *a.* Having no power to produce an effect; causing no effect.

nonefficient, *a.* Not efficient; specifically, *milit.* a term applied to a volunteer who has not attended a prescribed number of drills and passed a certain standard in shooting.—*n.* One who is not efficient.

nonego, *n.* [L., not I.] *Metaph.* all beyond or outside of the *ego* or conscious thinking subject; the object as opposed to the subject.

nonelastic, *a.* Not elastic; destitute of the property of elasticity.

nonelect, *n. sing.* and *pl.* One who

is or those who are not elect; those who are not chosen to salvation.—**nonelection,** *n.* Failure of election.

nonelectric, nonelectrical, *a.* Not electric; not conducting electricity.—*n.* A nonelectric substance.

nonentity, non·en′ti·ti, *n.* [L.L. *nonentitas.* ENTITY.] Nonexistence; a thing not existing; a person utterly without consequence or importance.

nones, nōnz, *n. pl.* [L. *nonae,* from *nonus,* for *novenus,* ninth, from *novem,* nine. NINE.] In the *Rom.* calendar, the fifth day of the months January, February, April, June, August, September, November, and December, and the seventh day of March, May, July, and October: so called as falling on the *ninth* day before the ides, both days included; the office for the ninth hour, one of the breviary offices of the Roman Catholic Church.

nonessential, *a.* Not essential or necessary; not absolutely necessary.—*n.* A thing that is not absolutely necessary.

nonexistence, *n.* Absence of existence; the negation of being.—**nonexistent,** *a.* Not having existence.

nonextensile, *a.* Not extensile; incapable of being stretched.

nonfeasance, *n. Law.* Omission of performance of legal duty.

nonfulfillment, *n.* Absence of fulfillment; neglect or failure to fulfill.

nonillion, nō·nil′yun, *n.* [L. *nonus,* nine, and E. *million.*] In the U.S. and France a unit with 30 ciphers annexed; in Great Britain and Germany a unit with 54 ciphers.

nonintervention, *n.* Abstention from intervening; a policy of not interfering in foreign politics excepting where a country's own interests are distinctly involved.

nonjuring, non·jür′ing, *a.* [L. *non,* not, and *juro,* to swear.] Not swearing allegiance: an epithet applied to those who would not swear allegiance to the English government after the Revolution of 1688.—**nonjuror,** non·jü′rėr, *n.* One who refused to take the oath of allegiance to the government of England at the Revolution of 1688.

nonluminous, *a.* Not luminous; not giving out light.

nonmetal, non·me′tal, *n. Chem.* an element that is not a metal, as carbon, oxygen, nitrogen, etc., none of which forms basic oxides or hydroxides.

nonobjective, non·ob·jek′tiv, *a. Art,* abstract or nonrepresentational art, involving forms that are not related to objects of the real world.

nonobservance, *n.* Neglect or failure to observe or fulfill.

nonpareil, non·pa·rel′, *n.* [Fr. *non,* not or no, and *pareil,* equal, from L. *par.* equal (whence *pair*).] A person or thing of peerless excellence; a small printing type.

nonpartisan, *n.* One not bound by party ties or obligations.

nonpayment, *n.* Neglect of payment; failure of payment.

nonperformance, *n.* A failure or neglect to perform.

---

fāte, fär, fâre, fat, fạll; mē, met, hėr; pīne, pin; nōte, not, mŏve; tūbe, tub, bụll; oil, pound.

nonplus, non′plus, *n.* [L. *non*, not, and *plus*, more, further (whence *plural*).] A state in which one is unable to proceed or decide; inability to say or do more; puzzle: usually in the phrase *at a nonplus.*—*v.t.*—*nonplussed, nonplussing.* To puzzle; to confound; to stop by embarrassment.

nonproductive, non·pro·duk′tiv, *a.* Unproductive; not directly productive.

nonprofessional, *a.* Not belonging to a profession; not done by or proceeding from professional men.

nonproficiency, *n.* Failure of proficiency.—**nonproficient,** *n.* One who has failed to improve or make progress in any study or pursuit.

nonresidence, *n.* Failure or neglect of residing where official duties require one to reside, or on one's own lands; residence by clergymen away from their cures.—**nonresident,** *a.* Not residing in a particular place, on one's own estate, or in one's proper place.—*n.* One who is nonresident.

nonresistance, *n.* The omission of resistance; submission to authority, power, or usurpation without opposition.—**nonresistant,** *a.* Making no resistance to power or oppression.—*n.* One who is nonresistant.

nonrestrictive, non·rē·strik′tiv, *a.* Not restrictive; without bounds.

nonruminant, *a.* Not ruminating or chewing the cud.

nonsectarian, non·sek·târ′ē·an, *a.* Not limited to one sect or group; open to those of all faiths.

nonsense, non′sens, *n.* Words or language conveying no just ideas; absurdity; things of no importance.—**nonsensical,** non·sen′si·kal, *a.* Having no sense; unmeaning; absurd.—**nonsensically,** non·sen′si·kal·li, *adv.* In a nonsensical manner.

nonsensitive, *a.* Not sensitive; not keenly alive to impression.

non sequitur, non sek′wi·tėr, [L., it does not follow.] *Logic,* a conclusion which does not follow the premises upon which it is based.

nonskid, *a.* Corrugated or with special tread to resist skidding.

nonsolvent, *a.* Not able to pay debts.

nonstriated, *a.* Not striated.—*Nonstriated fiber,* the fiber constituting the involuntary muscles.

nonsuit, non′sūt, *n.* A stoppage of a suit at law ordered by a judge when the plaintiff fails to make out a legal cause of action.—*v.t.* To subject to a nonsuit.

noodle, nö′dl, *n.* [G. *nudel.*] A ribbon-like flour-and-egg paste.

noodle, nö′dl, *n.* [From obsolete *noddle,* head.] (Slang) The head.

nook, nök, *n.* [Comp. Sc. *neuk,* Ir. *niuc,* a nook.] A corner; a recess; a secluded retreat.

noon, nön, *n.* [A.Sax. *nón,* L. *nona* (*hora*), the ninth hour; originally 3 p.m., the time of eating the chief meal, but afterward the term became applied to the midday hour, the chief meal being no doubt also shifted correspondingly.] The middle of the day; the time when the sun is in the

meridian; twelve o'clock; the time of greatest brilliancy or power; the prime.—**noonday,** nön′dā, *n.* Midday; twelve o'clock in the day.—*a.* Pertaining to midday; meridional.—**noontide,** nön′tīd, *n.* The time of noon; midday.

noose, nös or nöz, *n.* [Probably from O. or Prov. Fr. *nous,* a knot, from L. *nodus,* a knot. NODE.] A running knot, which binds the closer the more it is drawn.—*v.t.* (nöz)—*noosed, noosing.* To catch in a noose; to entrap; to ensnare.

nopal, nō′pal, *n.* [Mexican *nopalli.*] A name of several cactaceous plants cultivated for the cochineal insect.

nor, nor, *conj.* [*Or* with the neg. particle *ne, n-* prefixed: old forms were *nother, nouther.* OR, NO.] A word used to render negative the second or a subsequent member of a clause or sentence: correlative to *neither* or other negative; also equivalent to *and not,* and in this case not always corresponding to a foregoing negative.

Nordic, nor′dik, *a.* One of the three divisions of the Caucasian race; the blond peoples from northern Europe.—*n.* An individual with Nordic characteristics.

noria, nō′ri·a, *n.* [Sp.] A hydraulic machine used for raising water.

norm, norm, *n.* [L. *norma,* a carpenter's square, a rule, for *gnorima,* from root *gno,* to know (see NOBLE); hence *enormous.*] A rule; a pattern; a model; an authoritative standard; a type.—**normal,** nor′mal, *a.* [L. *normalis.*] According to a rule, principle, or norm; conforming with a certain type or standard; not abnormal; regular; *geom.* perpendicular.—*Normal pressure,* perpendicular; a *pressure* is said to be *normal* to a surface when it acts at right angles to it or perpendicularly thereon.—*Normal school* (from Fr. *école normale,* lit. a school that serves as a model), a school in which teachers are instructed in the principles of their profession and trained in the practice of it; a training college.—*n. Geom.* a straight line at right angles to the tangent or tangent plane at any point of a curve or curved surface.—**normalization,** nor′mal·i·zā′shon, *n.* Reduction to a standard or type.—**normalize,** nor′mal·iz, *v.t.*—*normalized, normalizing.* To make normal; to reduce to a standard or type.—**normally,** nor′mal·li, *adv.* In a normal manner or state.

Norman, nor′man, *n.* A native or inhabitant of Normandy.—*a.* Pertaining to Normandy, or the Normans.—*Norman architecture,* the round-arched style of architecture, a variety of the Romanesque.—*Norman-French,* the language of the Normans at the English Conquest, and still to a small extent made use of in several formal proceedings of state in England.

Norse, nors, *n.* The language of Norway.—*Old Norse,* the ancient language of Scandinavia, represented by the classical Icelandic and still with wonderful purity by modern

Icelandic.—*a.* Belonging to ancient Scandinavia or its language.—**Norseman,** nors′man, *n.* A native of ancient Scandinavia.

north, north, *n.* [A.Sax. *north* = Icel. *northr,* G., Sw., and Dan. *nord,* north; origin unknown.] One of the cardinal points, being that point of the horizon which is directly opposite to the sun in the meridian; the opposite of *south;* a region, tract, or country lying opposite to the south.—*a.* Northern; being in the north.—**northeast,** *n.* The point midway between the north and east.—*a.* Pertaining to, proceeding from, or directed toward that point; northeastern.—**northeaster,** *n.* A wind from the northeast.—**northeasterly,** *a.* Toward or from the northeast.—**northeastern,** *a.* Pertaining to or being in the northeast, or in a direction to the northeast.—**northeastward,** *adv.* Toward the northeast.—**northerliness,** nor′THėr·li·nes, *n.* The state of being northerly.—**northerly,** nor′THėr·li, *a.* Pertaining to or being in or toward the north; northern; proceeding from the north.—**northern,** nor′THėrn, *a.* Pertaining to or being in the north; in a direction toward the north; proceeding from the north (the *northern* wind).—*Northern diver,* a marine swimming bird. DIVER.—*Northern Hemisphere,* that half of the earth north of the equator.—*Northern lights,* the popular name of the aurora borealis.—**northern, northerner,** nor′THėr·nėr, *n.* A native or inhabitant of the north, of a northern country or part.—**northernmost,** nor′THėrn·mōst, *a.* Situated at the point farthest north.—**northing,** north′ing, *n. Navig.* and *surv.* the difference of latitude northward from the last point of reckoning: opposed to *southing.*—**Northman,** north′man, *n.* Norseman.—**North Pole,** *n.* That point of the heavens toward the north which is 90° distant from the equinoctial; the northern extremity of the earth's axis.—**North Star,** *n.* The north polar star, of the constellation Ursa Minor, toward which the earth's axis points.—**northward,** north′wėrd, *adv.* and *a.* Toward the north.—*n.* The northern part.—**northward,** north′wėrdz, *adv.* Toward the north; northward.—**northwest,** *n.* The point midway between the north and west; [cap.] that part of the United States which lies in the northwest part of the country.—*a.* Pertaining to, or being between, the north and the west; northwesterly; proceeding from the northwest (a *northwest* wind).—*adv.* Toward the northwest.—**northwester,** *n.* A wind from the northwest.—**northwesterly,** *a.* Toward the northwest; from the northwest.—**northwestern,** *a.* Pertaining to or being in the northwest; from the northwest.—**northwestward,** *adv.* Toward the northwest.

Norwegian, nor·wē′ji·an, *a.* Belonging to Norway.—*n.* A native of Norway.

nose, nöz, *n.* [A.Sax. *nosu, nasu* = Icel. *nös,* Dan. *näse;* cog., L. *nasus,* Skr.

nâsâ, nasâ—nose. *Ness* is akin.] The part of the face where the nostrils are located; the sense of smell; the olfactory organ; the forward or projecting part of anything (the *nose* of a boat).—*To thrust one's nose into*, to meddle.—*To turn up the nose*, to show contempt.—*v.t.*—*nosed, nosing*. To smell; to defeat by a narrow margin; to touch with the nose.—*v.i.* To smell; to pry officiously; to move forward slowly.—**nose bag**, *n.* A bag which may be fastened to a horse's head while he eats the provender in it.—**nose bleed**, *n.* Bleeding or hemorrhage from the nose; epistaxis. —**nose dive**, *n.* The sudden plunge of an aircraft downward; any sudden drop (the stock market took a *nose dive*).—**nosegay**, nōz′gā, *n.* A bunch of flowers; a posy.—**nosepiece**, *n.* A piece on a helmet coming down in front of the nose; a bridge on a pair of glasses.—**nosy, nosey**, nō′zē, *a.* Inquisitive; prying; meddlesome.
nosography, nō•sog′ra•fi, *n.* [Gr. *nosos*, disease, and *graphō*, to write.] The science of the description of diseases.—**nosology**, nō•sol′o•ji, *n.* [Gr. *nosos* and *logos*.] A systematic arrangement or classification of diseases; that branch of medical science which treats of the classification of diseases.—**nosological**, nos•o•loj′i•kal, *a.* Pertaining to nosology.— **nosologist**, nō•sol′o•jist, *n.* One versed in nosology.
nostalgia, nos•tal′ji•a, *n.* [Gr. *nostos*, return, and *algos*, pain.] A longing desire to revisit one's native country; homesickness.—**nostalgic**, nos•tal′-jik, *a.* Relating to nostalgia; homesick.
nostoc, nos′tok, *n.* [G. *nostok, nostoch*.] A sort of gelatinous algae often found after wet weather, especially on sandy soils.
nostril, nos′tril, *n.* [O.E. *nosethril, nosethirl*, A.Sax. *nósthyrl*, lit. nose hole, *thyrl* or *thyrel* meaning a hole, whence *thyrlian*, to bore (same word as *thrill*).] One of the two apertures of the nose which give passage to air.
nostrum, nos′trum, *n.* [L. *nostrum*, ours, that is, a medicine belonging to us alone.] A medicine, the ingredients of which are kept secret; a quack medicine; any scheme or device proposed by a quack or charlatan in any department.
not, not, *adv.* [Older *nat*, contr. from *naught*, nought, and equivalent to *ne aught*. NAUGHT.] A word that expresses negation, denial, refusal, or prohibition.
notable, nō′ta•bl, *a.* [Fr. *notable*, L. *notabilis*, from *noto*, to mark or note, from *nota*, a mark, for *gnota*, from *notus, gnotus*, known. NOTE, NOBLE.] Worthy of notice; remarkable; memorable; noted or distinguished; conspicuous; manifest; observable. —*n.* A person or thing of note or distinction; *French hist.* one of the nobles or notable men selected by the king to form a parliament, before the revolution.—**notableness**, nō′ta•bl•nes, *n.* The quality of being notable.—**notably**, nō′ta•bli, *adv.* In a notable manner; remarkably; emi-

nently; especially.—**notability**, nō•ta•bil′i•ti, *n.* The quality of being notable; a notable person or thing; a person of note.
notary, nō′te•ri, *n.* [L. *notarius*, from *nota*, a note. NOTE.] An officer authorized to attest written documents, to authenticate deeds, contracts, etc., and to administer oaths; called also *Notary Public.*—**notarial**, nō•tā′ri•al, *a.* Pertaining to a notary; done or taken by a notary.
notation, nō•tā′shon, *n.* [L. *notatio*, from *noto*, to mark. NOTE.] The act or practice of noting; the art of recording by marks or characters; a system of signs or characters used for expressing briefly facts connected with an art or science, as in arithmetic, algebra, music, etc.
notch, noch, *n.* [Softened form of old *nock*, a notch = O.D. *nock*, O.Sw. *nocka*, a notch; akin.] A hollow cut in anything; a nick; what resembles such a cutting; a gap in a mountain or hill.—*v.t.* To cut a notch or notches in; to nick; to indent; to fit to a string by the notch, as an arrow.
note, nōt, *n.* [Fr. *note*, from L. *nota*, a mark, sign, character, from *notus*, known, for *gnotus*, from *gnosco, nosco*, to know. NOBLE, KNOW.] A mark on the margin of a book‡; a mark, character, or symbol‡; a statement subsidiary to the text of a book elucidating or adding something; an explanatory or critical comment; an annotation; a memorandum or short writing intended to assist the memory or for after use or reference; a list of items; a reckoning, bill, account; a written or printed paper acknowledging a debt and promising payment (a promissory *note*; a banknote); a diplomatic or official communication in writing; a short letter; a billet; notice; heed; observation; reputation; consequence; distinction; *pl.* a newspaper reporter's or shorthand writer's report; *mus.* a character which represents a sound; a musical sound; voice; harmonious or melodious sound.—*v.t.*—*noted, noting.* To observe carefully; to heed; to attend to; to set down in writing; to make a memorandum of; to mark (a bill) as being dishonored—a proceeding done by a notary.—**notebook**, *n.* A book in which notes or memoranda are written.—**noted**, nō′ted, *a.* Being of note; much known by reputation or report; celebrated. —**notedness**, nō′ted•nes, *n.* The state or quality of being noted.—**noteless**, nōt′les, *a.* Not attracting notice; not conspicuous.—**note paper**, *n.* Paper of a small size for writing notes or letters on.—**noteworthy**, nōt′wėr•thi, *a.* Worthy of note; worthy of observation or notice.
nothing, nu′thing, *n.* [*No thing.*] Not anything; opposed to *anything* and *something*; nonexistence; nothingness; a trifle; a thing of no consideration or importance; *arith.* a cipher.— *adv.* In no degree; not at all.— **nothingness**, nu′thing•nes, *n.* Nihility; nonexistence; insignificance.
notice, nō′tis, *n.* [Fr. *notice*, from L.

notitia, notice, from *nosco, notum*, to know. NOTE.] The act of noting, observing, or remarking; heed; regard; cognizance; note; information; intelligence; direction; order; premonition; warning; intimation beforehand; a paper that communicates information; attention; respectful treatment; civility; a short statement; a brief critical review.—*v.t.* *noticed, noticing.* To take cognizance or notice of; to perceive; to become aware of; to observe; to mention or make observations on; to treat with attention and civilities.—**noticeable**, nō′tis•a•bl, *a.* Worthy of being noticed or observed; observable; likely to attract attention.—**noticeably**, nō′-tis•a•bli, *adv.* In a noticeable manner; evidently; distinctly.
notify, nō′ti•fī, *v.t.*—*notified, notifying.* [Fr. *notifier*, L. *notificare*, from *notus*, known, and *facio*, to make. NOTE.] To make known; to declare; to publish; to give notice to; to inform by words or writing.— **notification**, nō′ti•fi•kā″shon, *n.* The act of notifying or giving notice; notice given in words or writing, or by signs; intimation; the writing which communicates information; an advertisement, citation, etc.
notion, nō′shon, *n.* [L. *notio*, from *notus*, known. NOTE.] A mental conception; mental apprehension of whatever may be known or imagined; idea; an opinion; a belief or view entertained; a fancy article; an article of smallware; chiefly in the plural, needles, thread, pins, etc.; a gadget. —**notional**, nō′shon•al, *a.* Pertaining to a notion or conception; imaginary; ideal; existing in idea only; visionary; whimsical; fanciful.—*Notional words*, those words which express *notions* or objects of the understanding, as verbs and nouns, in distinction from *relational* words or words expressing relation, as prepositions.
notochord, nō′to•kord, *n.* [Gr. *nōtos*, the back, and *chordē*, a string.] A fibrocellular rod in the embryo of vertebrates, usually replaced in the adult by the vertebral column.
notorious, nō•tō′ri•us, *a.* [L.L. *notorius*, from L. *notoria, notorium*, an indictment, *notor*, a voucher, *notare*, to mark. NOTE.] Publicly or generally known and spoken of; manifest to the world; known to disadvantage; publicly known from something discreditable.—**notoriety**, nō•to•rī′-e•ti, *n.* The state or attribute of being notorious; the state of being publicly known to disadvantage; discreditable publicity.—**notoriously**, nō•tō′ri•us•li, *adv.* In a notorious manner.—**notoriousness**, nō•tō′ri-us•nes, *n.* The state of being notorious; notoriety.
notornis, nō•tor′nis, *n.* [Gr. *notos*, the south wind, the south, and *ornis*, a bird.] A genus of rare or extinct grallatorial birds of New Zealand, allied to the coots, but of larger size and with rudimentary wings.
no-trump, *n. Bridge*, and some other card games, play declared in which no suit is designated as trumps.
notwithstanding, not•with•stan′ding,

a participial compound passing into a *prep.* and a *conj.* [*Not with*, in the old sense of against, and *standing*.] In spite of; without hindrance or obstruction from; despite; nevertheless; however.

nougat, nö´gä, nö´gat, *n.* [Fr.] Candy made of egg white, sugar, corn sirup, or honey, with chopped nuts or fruits.

nought, nạt, *n.* [A.Sax. *náwiht*, i.e. no whit. NAUGHT.] Not anything; nothing; a cipher.

noumenon, nou´men·on, *n.* pl. **noumena**, nou´men·a. [Gr., the thing perceived, from *noeō*, to perceive, from *nous*, the mind.] *Metaph.* an object conceived by the understanding or thought of by the reason, as opposed to a *phenomenon*.

noun, noun, *n.* [O.Fr. *noun, non, nom*, Mod. Fr. *nom*, from L. *nomen*, name. NAME.] *Gram.* a word that denotes any object of which we speak, whether that object be animate or inanimate, material or immaterial.—**nounal**, noun´al, *a.* Pertaining to a noun; having the character of a noun.

nourish, nur´ish, *v.t.* [O.Fr. *nurrir, norrir*, Mod.Fr. *nourrir*, from L. *nutrire*, to nourish.] To feed and cause to grow; to supply with nutriment; *fig.* to supply the means of support and increase to; to encourage; to foster; to cherish; to comfort.—**nourisher**, nur´ish·ér, *n.* —**nourishing**, nur´ish·ing, *a.*—**nourishingly**, nur´ish·ing·li, *adv.*—**nourishment**, nur´ish·ment, *n.* The act of nourishing; sustenance; nutriment.

nouveau riche, nö·vō rēsh´, *n.* [Fr. —*nouveau*, new, and *riche*, rich.] A person of newly acquired riches.

nova, nō´va, *n.* [L. fem. sing. of *novus*, new.] A star which suddenly increases its brightness and energy enormously, then fades into its former obscurity.

novel, nov´el, *a.* [O.Fr. *novel*, Fr. *nouvelle*, novel, a novel, from L. *novellus*, a dim. from *novus*, new. NEW.] Of recent origin or introduction; new; unusual; strange.—*n.* A lengthy fictitious prose narrative having an almost unlimited range of subject matter and varied techniques containing one or more plots. —**novella**, nō·vel´la, *n.* A short narrative with a compact and pointed plot. —**novelette**, nov·el·et´, *n.* A short novel.—**novelist**, nov´el·ist, *n.*—**novelize**, nov´el·īz, *v.t.* To put into the form of a novel.—**novelty**, nov´el·ti, *n.* The quality of being novel; something new or strange; pl. small articles used as decoration or adornment.

November, nō·vem´bér, *n.* [L., from *novem*, nine.] The eleventh month of the year, containing 30 days.

novena, nō·vē´na, *n.* [L. *novem*, nine.] *R. Cath. Ch.* A special nine days' devotion.

novice, nov´is, *n.* [Fr., from L. *novitius*, new, fresh, from *novus*, new. NOVEL.] One who is new to the circumstances in which he or she is placed; one newly converted to the Christian faith; one that has entered a religious house, but has

not taken the vow; a probationer; one who is new in any business; a beginner.—**novitiate, noviciate**, nō-vish´i·āt, *n.* The state or time of being a novice; apprenticeship; a year or other time of probation.

novocain, nō´vo·kān´, *n.* [L. *novus*, new, and *cocaine*.] A local anesthetic.

now, nou, *adv.* [A.Sax. *nū*, a word common to all the Teutonic tongues; cog. L. *nunc*; Gr. *nun*, now; perhaps allied to *new*.] At the present time; at a particular past time (he was *now* king); at that time; after this had happened. It often implies a connection between a subsequent and a preceding proposition, or it introduces an inference or an explanation of what precedes ('*now* Barabbas was a robber').—*But now*, only a little while ago; very lately.—*Now and then*, at one time and another; indefinitely; occasionally; at intervals.—*Now .. now*, at one time—at another time; alternately. Similarly *now .. then*.—*n.* Present time or moment.—**nowadays**, nou´a·dāz, *adv.* At the present time; in these days.

noway, noways. See NO.

nowhere, nowhither, nowise, *adv.* See NO.

noxious, nok´shus, *a.* [L. *noxius*, from *noxa*, injury, from root of *noceo*, to hurt (as in *innocent, innocuous*), same as that of *night*; akin *noise, nuisance*.] Hurtful; harmful; pernicious; unwholesome; injurious, in a moral sense.—**noxiously**, nok´shus·li, *adv.* In a noxious manner; hurtfully.— **noxiousness**, nok´shus·nes, *n.*

noyade, nwä·yäd´, *n.* [Fr., from *noyer*, to drown.] A putting to death by drowning: a mode of executing victims during the reign of terror in France, practiced by Carrier at Nantes.

nozzle, noz´l, *n.* [For *nosle*, a dim. of *nose*.] The projecting spout of something; a terminal pipe or terminal part of a pipe.

nu, nū, nö, *n.* The 13th letter of the Greek alphabet.

nuance, nū´äns, *n.* [From Fr. *nuer*, to make shades of color, from L. *mutare*, to change, and Fr. *nuage*, cloud.] A delicate gradation in feeling, color, meaning, etc.

nub, nub, *n.* [From Dan. *knub*, black, L.G. *knubbe*, knot, E. *knub*, knob.] A knob; a lump; the point of a story (colloq.)—**nubbin**, nub´bin, *n.* Any small bit that projects; a small, undeveloped ear of Indian corn.— **nubby**, nub´bi, *a.*

nubile, nū´bil, *a.* [L. *nubilis*, from *nubo*, to marry. NUPTIAL.] Of an age suitable for marriage; marriageable.

nubilous, nū´bil·us, *a.* [L. *nubilus*, from *nubes*, a cloud.] Cloudy.

nucellus, nū·sel´lus. [Dim. of L. for a *kernel*.] The central part of an ovule, containing the EMBRYO SAC (which see).

nuchal, nū´kal, *a.* [L.L. *nucha*, from Ar.] Pertaining to the nape of the neck.

nuciferous, nū·sif´ér·us, *a.* [L. *nux, nucis*, a nut, and *fero*, to bear.]

Bearing or producing nuts.—**nuciform**, nū´si·form, *a.* *Bot.* resembling a nut; nut shaped.

nucleon, nū´kli·on, *n.* *Phys.* an elementary particle in the atomic nucleus; either a proton or a neutron.

nucleoprotein, nūk´li·ō·prō´tē·in. [From *nucleus* and *protein*.] A conjugated protein, combining a protein and a nucleic acid and occurring in living cells; an essential constituent of genes.

nucleus, nū´kli·us, *n.* pl. **nuclei**, nū´kli·ī. [L., a kernel, from *nux, nucis*, a nut.] A central mass about which matter is collected; *bot.* the central succulent part of an ovule in which the embryo plant is generated; *physiol.* the solid or vesicular body found in many cells; the germ of a cell; *astron.* the body of a comet, called also its head; *phys.* the central or mass part of an atom, its positive charge equal to the atomic number of the element.—**nuclear**, nū´kli·ar, *a.* Pertaining to, or having the character of, a nucleus; constituted by a nucleus; *phys.* pertaining to the atomic nucleus (*nuclear* physics).— **nucleate**, nū´kli·āt, *a.* Having a nucleus.—**nucleolus**, nū·klē´ō·lus, *n.* pl. **nucleoli**, nū·klē´ō·lī. The spherical particle found in the center of a cell nucleus.—**nucleic acid**, a complex organic compound important in the heredity and the control of the metabolism of all living cells, the groups of nucleic acids being distinguished as DNA and RNA.

nude, nūd, *a.* [L. *nudus*, naked (seen also in *denude*); same root as *naked*.] Naked; not covered with clothes or drapery.—*n.* A nude or naked figure or statue; generally the *nude*, that is, the undraped human figure.— **nudely**, nūd´li, *adv.* In a nude or naked manner; nakedly.—**nudeness**, nūd´nes, *n.* The state or quality of being nude or naked.—**nudity**, nū´di·ti, *n.* The state of being naked; nakedness.

nudge, nuj, *n.* [Allied to Prov.G. *knütschen*, Dan. *knuge*, to squeeze; E. to *knock*.] A jog with the elbow, or a poke in the ribs.—*v.t.*—**nudged, nudging**. To give a hint or signal by a private touch with the hand, elbow, or foot.

nudity. See NUDE.

nugatory, nū´ga·to·ri, *a.* [L. *nugatorius*, from *nugor, nugatus*, to trifle, from *nugae*, trifles.] Trifling; futile; worthless; of no force; inoperative.

nugget, nug´et, *n.* [Formerly *nigot, niggot*, an ingot; perhaps a corruption of *ingot* (an ingot, a ningot, a nigot).] A lump, especially, one of the larger lumps of native gold found in the diggings.

nuisance, nū´sans, *n.* [O.Fr. *nuisance, noisance*, from *nuisir, noisir* (Mod.Fr. *nuire*), L. *nocere*, to annoy. NOXIOUS.] Something that annoys or gives trouble; that which is offensive or irritating; an annoyance; a plague or pest; a bore.

null, nul, *a.* [L. *nullus*, not any, none —*ne*, not, and *ullus*, any.] Of no legal or binding force or validity; void; invalid (as in *null and void*);

having no character or expression (as the features).—**nullify,** nul´i·fī, v.t.—**nullified,** nullifying. [L. nullus, and facio, to make.] To annul; to render invalid; to deprive of legal force or efficacy.—**nullification,** nul´-i·fi·kā˝shon, n. The act of nullifying; a rendering void and of no effect.—**nullity,** nul´i·ti, n. The state or quality of being null; want of validity.

nullah, nul´la, n. In British India, a bed of a rivulet; a rivulet.

numb, num, a. [Lit. taken, being from A.Sax. numen, pp. of niman, O.E. nim, Goth. niman, to seize; hence also benumb (with prefix be); nimble. The final b is excrescent.] Torpid, benumbed, or deadened; having lost the power of sensation and motion.—v.t. To make numb or torpid.—**numbness,** num´nes, n. The state of being numb; torpidity; torpor.

number, num´bėr, n. [O.Fr. numbre, Fr. nombre, from L. numerus, number (whence also numeral, numerous, enumerate), same root as nomad, Gr. nemō, to distribute. (As to inserted b comp. humble, nimble.)] That which may be counted; an aggregate of units, or a single unit considered as part of a series; an aggregate of several individuals; not a few; many; one of a numbered series of things, as a division of a book published in parts; a part of a periodical; metrical arrangement of syllables; poetical rhythm or measure; gram. that distinction in the form which a word assumes according as it is spoken of or expresses one individual or several individuals; the form that denotes one individual being the singular number, that set apart for two the dual number, that which refers to two or more the plural number.—Number one, self.—v.t. To count; to reckon; to enumerate; to reckon, rank, or consider; to put a number or numbers on; to amount to; to reach the number of.—**numberer,** num´bėr·ėr, n. One that numbers.—**numberless,** num´bėr·les, a. That cannot be counted; innumerable.—**Numbers,** num´bėrz, n. The fourth book of the Pentateuch.

numen, nū´men, n., pl. **numina,** nū´mi·na. A divine or leading spirit, as in the Roman Catholic Church.

numerable, nū´mėr·a·bl, a. [L. numerabilis, from numerus, number. NUMBER.] Capable of being numbered or counted.—**numeral,** nū´mėr·al, a. [L. numeralis.] Pertaining to number; consisting of number; expressing number; representing number.—n. A figure or character used to express a number; gram. a word expressing a number (one, two, three, etc.).—**numerary,** nū´mėr·e·ri, a. Belonging to a certain number.—**numerate,** nū´mėr·āt, v.t. and i. [L. numero, numeratum.] To count.—**numeration,** nū·mėr·ā´shon, n. [L. numeratio.] The act or art of numbering; arith. the art of expressing in figures any number proposed in words, or of expressing in words any number proposed in figures.—

numerator, nū´mėr·ā·tėr, n. One that numbers; arith. the number in fractions which shows how many parts of a unit are taken—the number above the line.—**numerical,** nū·mer´i·kal, a. Belonging to number; denoting number; consisting in numbers.—**numerically,** nū·mer´i·kal·li, adv. In numbers; with respect to numerical quantity.—**numerology,** nū´mėr·ol˝o·ji, n. Belief in the occult influence of numbers upon the life of an individual.—**numerous,** nū´-mėr·us, a. [L. numerosus.] Consisting of many individuals.

numismatic, numismatical, nū·mis·mat´ik, nū·mis·mat´i·kal, a. [L. numisma, coin, from Gr. nomisma, coin, lit. what is sanctioned by law, from nomizō, to sanction, from nomos, law.] Pertaining to coins or medals.—**numismatics,** nū·mis·mat´iks, n. The science of coins and medals.—**numismatist,** nū·mis´mat·ist, n. One versed in numismatics.—**numismatology,** nū·mis´ma·tol˝o·ji, n. Numismatics.

numskull, num´skul, n. [Numb and skull.] A dunce; a stupid fellow.

nun, nun, n. [A.Sax. nunne, from Eccles. L. nonna, a nun, nonnus, a monk, L.Gr. nonna, nonnos, from Coptic or Egypt. nane, nanu, good, beautiful, monasteries and convents having first arisen in Egypt.] A woman devoted to a religious life who lives in a convent or nunnery, under a vow of perpetual chastity; the blue titmouse; a kind of pigeon having its head almost covered with a veil of feathers.—**nunnery,** nun´-ėr·i, n. A convent in which nuns reside.

Nunc Dimittis, nungk di·mit´tis, n. [L., now they lettest depart.] The canticle of Simeon (Luke, ii. 29-32).

nuncio, nun´shi·ō, n. [Sp. nuncio, It. nunzio, from L. nuncius, a messenger, for noventius, from novus, new; akin announce, renounce, pronounce, enunciate, etc.] An ambassador of the first rank (not a cardinal) representing the pope at the seat of a foreign government (an ambassador of the first rank who is a cardinal being styled a legate).—**nunciature,** nun´-shi·a·chėr, n.

nunnery. See NUN.

nuptial, nup´shal, a. [L. nuptialis, from nuptiæ, marriage, from nubo, nuptum, to marry; akin nubes, nimbus, a cloud (from the veiling of the bride).] Pertaining to marriage; used or done at a wedding.—**nuptials,** nup´shalz, n. pl. [L. nuptiæ (pl.), a wedding.] A wedding or marriage. ∴ Syn. under MARRIAGE.

nurl, nėrl, v.t. [Same as knurl, knarl, gnarl.] To mill or indent on the edge.

nurse, nėrs, n. [Fr. nourrice, from L. nutrix, nutricis, a nurse, from nutrio, to nourish. NOURISH.] One who tends or takes care of the young, sick, or infirm; a female who has the care of a child or children; a female attendant in a hospital; one who or that which nurtures, cherishes, or protects; hort. a shrub or tree which protects a young plant.—v.t.—nursed, nursing. To feed

and tend generally in infancy; to suckle; to rear; to nurture; to tend in sickness or infirmity; to promote growth or vigor in; to foment; to foster; to manage with care and economy, with a view to increase.—**nursemaid,** n. A maidservant employed in nursing children.—**nursery,** nėr´sėr·i, n. A place or apartment in a house set apart for children; a place where trees, shrubs, flowering plants, etc., are raised from seed or otherwise in order to be transplanted, or sold; a place where anything is fostered and the growth promoted.—**nursery rhyme,** n. A tale for children, usually written in rhyming verse.—**nurseryman,** n. One who has a nursery of plants, or is employed in one.—**nursery school,** n. A school for children usually under age 5.—**nursling,** nėrs´ling, n. One who or that which is nursed; a child; a fondling.

nurture, nėr´chėr, n. [Fr. nourriture, from nourrir, to nourish. NOURISH, NURSE.] The act of nursing or nourishing; education; that which nourishes; food; diet.—v.t.—nurtured, nurturing. To nourish; to educate; to bring or train up.

nut, nut, n. [A.Sax. hnutu=Icel. hnot, O.H.G. hnuz, Dan. nöd, G. nuss, Gael. cnudh.] The fruit of certain trees and shrubs which have the seed enclosed in a bony, woody, or leathery covering, not opening when ripe; bot. a bony pericarp containing a single seed, to which it is not closely attached; a small block of metal or wood, with an internal or female screw put upon the end of a screw bolt to keep it firmly in its place.—A nut to crack, a difficult problem to solve; a puzzle to be explained.—v.i.—nutted, nutting. To gather nuts.—**nutty,** nut´i, a. Abounding in nuts; having the flavor of nuts; enthusiastic; mentally unbalanced; crazy. (Slang)—**nutcracker,** n. An instrument for cracking hard-shelled nuts; a brown spotted bird of Europe and a related greyish-white bird of North America.—**nuthatch,** n. [Hatch is a softened form of hack.] Various small creeping birds of Europe and America, related to the titmice.—**nutshell,** n. The hard shell of a nut.—To be or lie in a nutshell, to be in small compass; to admit of a very simple explanation or statement.

nutant, nū´tant, a. [L. nutans, nutantis, ppr. of nuto, to nod, freq. of nuo, to nod. INNUENDO.] Bot. drooping or nodding.—**nutation,** nū·tā´shon, n. [L. nutatio.] A nodding; astron. a slight gyratory movement of the earth's axis tending to make the pole describe a minute ellipse, due to the attraction of the sun and moon and connected with precession.

nutmeg, nut´meg, n. [From nut, and O.Fr. muguette, nutmeg, from L. muscus, musk; lit. the scented nut.] The kernel of the fruit of a tree of the Malayan Archipelago agreeably aromatic, and much used in cookery.—

---

fāte, fär, fâre, fat, fạll; mē, met, hėr; pīne, pin; nōte, not, mõve; tūbe, tub, bụll; oil, pound.

Nutmeg butter, a solid oil extracted from the nutmeg.

nutria, nū′tri•a, *n.* [Sp. *nutria, lutria,* from L. *lutra,* an otter.] The commercial name for the skins or fur of the coypou.

nutrient, nū′tri•ent, *a.* [L. *nutrio,* to nourish. NURSE.] Nourishing; nutritious.—*n.* Any substance which nourishes.—**nutriment**, nū′tri•ment, *n.* [L. *nutrimentum.*] That which nourishes; nourishment; food; aliment.—**nutrition**, nū•trish′on, *n.* [L. *nutritio,* from *nutrio.*] The act or process by which organisms, whether vegetable or animal, absorb into their system their proper food; the process of assimilating food; that which nourishes; nutriment.—**nutritious**, nū•trish′us, *a.* Containing or serving as nutriment; promoting the growth or repairing the waste of organic bodies; nourishing.—**nutritiously**, nū•trish′us•li, *adv.* In a nutritious manner.—**nutritiousness**, nū•trish′us•nes, *n.* The quality of being nutritious.—**nutritive**, nū′tri•tiv, *a.* Having the quality of nourishing; nutritious; pertaining to nutrition.—**nutritively**, nū′tri•tiv•li, *adv.* In a nutritive manner.—**nutritiveness**, nū′tri•tiv•nes, *n.*

nuts, nuts, *interj.* (Slang) A term of anger, defiance, etc.—*a.* Insane; crazy.

nux vomica, nuks vom′i•ka, *n.* [From L. *nux,* a nut, and *vomeo,* to vomit.] The fruit of an East Indian tree, containing the virulent poison strychnine; a drug containing strychnine.

nuzzle, nuz′l, *v.t.*—*nuzzled, nuzzling.* [A form of *nozzle.*] To put a ring into the nose of; to root up with the nose.—*v.i.* To work with the nose, as a pig; to hide the head, as a child in its mother's bosom.

nyctalopia, nik•ta•lō′pi•a, *n.* [Gr. *nyktalōpia,* from *nyktalōps,* seeing by night only—*nyx, nyktos,* night, and *ōps,* the eye.] The faculty or defect of seeing in darkness or in faint light, with privation of sight in daylight; also applied to night blindness, the exactly opposite defect of vision.

nyctitropic, nik•ti•trop′ik, *a.* [Gr. *nyx, nyktos,* night, *tropos,* a turn.] *Bot.* said of certain plants, the leaves of which assume certain positions at night.

nylon, nī′lon, *n.* A synthetic material, formed when molten into fibers, sheets, or bristles of extreme toughness, strength, and elasticity, made mainly from coal, water, and air.

nymph, nimf, *n.* [L. *nympha,* Gr. *nymphē,* a nymph.] One of a numerous class of inferior divinities, imagined among the Greeks and Romans as beautiful maidens, not immortal, but always young; those who presided over rivers, brooks, and springs being called *Naiads;* over mountains *Oreads;* over woods and trees, *Dryads* and *Hamadryads;* over the sea, *Nereids;* hence, a young and attractive woman; a maiden; a damsel. Also same as *Nympha.*—**nympha**, nim′fa, *n.* The pupa or chrysalis of an insect.—

nymphal, nymphean, nim′fal, nim•fē′an, *a.* Pertaining to nymphs.

nymphomania, nim•fo•mā′ni•a, *n.* [Gr. *nymphē,* a bride, and *mania,* madness.] Morbid and uncontrollable sexual desire in females.

nystagmus, nis•tag′mus, *n.* [Gr. *nystagmos,* a nodding.] *Med.* an involuntary rolling motion of the eyes.

O

O, o, ō, the fifteenth letter and the fourth vowel in the English alphabet.

O, *interj.* An exclamation used in earnest or solemn address, appeal, or invocation, and prefixed to the noun of address; the sign of the vocative: often confounded with *Oh,* which is strictly a particle expressive of emotion prefixed to a sentence or clause. When *O* is the word, the mark of exclamation, if used, should follow the noun of address ('Hear, O Israel!'); when *oh* is the word, the mark should follow it, or the exclamatory clause of which it is a part, thus: *Oh! Oh, dear! Oh, dear me!* exclamations of surprise, uneasiness, fear, pain, etc., regarded as corruptions of Fr. *O Dieu!* It. *O Dio!* O God! It. *O Dio mio!* O my God!

oaf, ōf, *n.* [From Icel. *álfr,* an elf. ELF.] A fairy changeling; a dolt; a blockhead.—**oafish**, ōf′ish, *a.*—**oafishness**, ōf′ish•nes, *n.*

oak, ōk, *n.* [A.Sax. *ác*=Sc. *aik,* Icel. *eik,* D. *eik,* L.G. *eeke,* Dan. *eeg,* Sw. *ek,* G. *eiche;* root unknown.] A well-known and valuable timber tree, or its wood, which is hard, tough, and strong; a member of the beech family (Fagaceae).—**oak apple**, *n.* An oak gall.—**oaken**, ō′kn, *a.* Made of oak or consisting of oak.

oakum, ō′kum, *n.* [A.Sax. *ácumba,* tow, oakum, lit. matter combed out, from prefix *á,* away, out, and *camb,* a comb. COMB.] The substance of old ropes untwisted and pulled into loose fibers; used for caulking the seams of ships, stopping leaks, etc.

oar, ōr, *n.* [A.Sax. *ár;* Icel. *ár,* Dan. *aare,* Sw. *àra;* perhaps from root *ar,* seen in A.Sax. *erian,* Goth. *arjan,* L. *aro,* to plow; or allied to *rudder, row.*] A long piece of timber, flat at one end and round at the other, used to propel a boat, barge, or galley through the water.—*To feather the oars.* See FEATHER, *v.t.*—*To lie on the oars,* to suspend rowing; hence, *fig.* to cease from work; to rest.—*To muffle the oars,* to wrap some soft substance round the part that lies in the rowlock.—*To put one's oar in,* to interfere in the business or concerns of others.—*v.i.* To row.—*v.t.* To impel by rowing.—**oarlock**, *n.* A rowlock.—**oarsman**, ōrz′man, *n.* One who rows with an oar; a boatman.

oasis, ō•ā′sis, *n.* pl. **oases**, ō•ā′sēz. [L.

and Gr., from Coptic *oueh,* to dwell, and *saa,* to drink.] A fertile tract where there is water, in the midst of a desert or waste; a green spot in the midst of barrenness; often used figuratively.

oast, ōst, *n.* [D. *ast, eest, eijst,* a kiln.] A kiln to dry hops or malt.

oat, ōt, *n.* [O.E. *ote, ate, oote,* A.Sax. *áta,* the oat; Icel. *æti,* an eatable, oats; perhaps akin to *eat.*] A cereal plant valuable for the grain it produces; an oaten pipe, typical of pastoral poetry (*Mil.*); *pl.* a quantity of the plant in cultivation or of the grain (field of *oats*).—*Wild oats,* youthful excesses: generally in the phrase *to sow one's wild oats,* to indulge in youthful excesses, dissipations, or follies; *to have sown one's wild oats,* to have given up youthful follies.—**oatcake**, *n.* A cake made of the meal of oats.—**oaten**, ō′tn, *a.* Pertaining to or made of oats or oatmeal.—**oatmeal**, ōt′mēl, *n.* Meal made from oats.

oath, ōth, *n.* pl. **oaths**, ōTHZ. [A.Sax. *áth*=Sc. *aith,* Icel. *eithr,* Dan. and Sw. *ed,* Goth. *aiths,* D. *eed,* G. *eid,* oath.] A solemn affirmation or declaration, made with an appeal to God for the truth of what is affirmed; a solemn swearing; a blasphemous use of the name of the Divine Being; an imprecation.

obbligato, ob′li•gä•tō, *n.* [It. OBLIGATE.] An instrumental part or accompaniment of such importance that it cannot be dispensed with.

obcordate, ob•kor′dāt, *a.* [Prefix *ob,* and *cordate.*] *Bot.* shaped like a heart, with the apex downward.

obdurate, ob′dū•rit, *a.* [L. *obduratus,* from *obduro,* to harden—*ob,* intensive, *duro,* to harden, from *durus,* hard (seen in *indurate, endure, duration*).] Hardened in heart; persisting obstinately in sin; stubborn; inflexible; inexorable; harsh or rough†.—**obduracy**, ob′dū•re•si, *n.* The state or quality of being obdurate; invincible hardness of heart; obstinacy in wickedness.—**obdurately**, ob′dū•rit•li, *adv.* In an obdurate manner; inflexibly.—**obdurateness**, *n.* Obduracy; stubbornness.

obeah, ō′bi•a, *n.* A species of sorcery or witchcraft among the African Negroes.

obedience, ō•bē′di•ens, *n.* [Fr. *obédience,* from L. *obedientia,* obedience. OBEY.] The act or habit of obeying; compliance with a command, prohibition, or known law and rule prescribed; submission to authority.—*Passive obedience,* unqualified obedience to authority, whether the commands be reasonable or unreasonable, lawful or unlawful.—**obedient**, ō•bē′di•ent, *a.* [L. *obediens,* ppr. of *obedio.*] Submission to authority; complying with all commands; yielding compliance; dutiful.—**obediently**, ō•bē′di•ent•li, *adv.* In an obedient manner; dutifully; submissively.

obeisance, ō•bā′sans, *n.* [Fr. *obéissance,* from L. *obedientia.*—OBEDIENCE.] A bow or courtesy; an act of reverence, deference, or respect.

ch, *chain;* ch, Sc. lo*ch;* g, *go;* j, *job;* ng, si*ng;* TH, *then;* th, *thin;* w, *wig;* hw, *whig;* zh, a*zure.*

obelisk, ob′e·lisk, n. [Gr. *obeliskos*, dim. of *obelos*, a spit.] A column or monumental structure of rectangular form, diminishing toward the top, and generally finishing with a low pyramid; a mark (thus †) referring the reader to a note in the margin or at the foot of the page: called also a *dagger*.

obelus, ob′e·lus, n. [Gr. *obelos*, a spit.] A mark in ancient MSS. or old editions of the classics, indicating a suspected passage or reading.—**obelize,** ob′e·līz, v.t. To mark as spurious or suspicious.

Oberon, ōb′ẽr·on, n. [Fr. *Auberon*, *Alberon*, G. *Alberich*.] King of the fairies, married to Titania.

obese, ō·bēs′, a. [L. *obesus*, fat—*ob*, intens., and *edo*, *esum*, to eat. EAT.] Excessively corpulent; fat; fleshy.—**obesity,** ō·bes′i·ti, n. [L. *obesitas*.] The state or quality of being obese; excessive corpulency.

obey, ō·bā′, v.t. [Fr. *obéir*, from L. *obedio*, *obedire*, to obey, O.L. *obœdire*—prefix *ob*, and *audio*, to hear. AUDIBLE.] To give ear to; to comply with the commands of; to be under the government of; to be ruled by; to submit to the direction or control of.—v.i. To submit to commands or authority; to do as one is bid.—**obeyer,** ō·bā′ẽr, n. One who yields obedience.

obfuscate, ob·fus′kāt, v.t.—*obfuscated*, *obfuscating*. [L. *obfusco*, *obfuscatum*—prefix *ob*, and *fusco*, to obscure, from *fuscus*, dark.] To darken; to obscure; to bewilder; to confuse; to muddle.—**obfuscation,** ob·fus·kā′shon, n. The act of obfuscating; confusion or bewilderment of mind.

obi, ō′bē, n. [Jap.] A broad sash worn with a kimono and fastened in the back.

obit, ōb′it, n. [L. *obitus*, death, from *obeo*, *obitum*, to die—*ob*, against, and *eo*, to go. ITINERANT.] A person's decease; an obituary.—**obituary,** o·bich′ū·a·ri, n. A list of the dead; an account of a person's death.—a. Relating to, or written about, a person at his death (an *obituary* notice.)

obiter dictum [L.] A remark by the way; an off-hand aphorism or statement.

object, ob′jekt, n. [L. *objectum*, lit. something thrown before or against—*ob*, against, and *jacio*, to throw (as in *deject*, *eject*, *reject*, etc.). JET (of water).] That toward which the mind is directed in any of its states or activities; what is thought about, believed, or seen; some visible and tangible thing; a concrete reality (*objects* of interest in a museum); that to which efforts are directed; aim; end; ultimate purpose; a deformed person; *gram.* the word, clause, or member of a sentence expressing that on which the action expressed by a transitive verb is exercised, or the word or member governed by a preposition.—v.t. (ob·jekt′). [Fr. *objecter*, L. *objicio*, *objectum*.] To place before or in the way‡; to bring forward as a matter of reproach, or as an adverse ground

or reason; to state or urge in opposition; to state as an objection (I have nothing to object *against* him).—v.i. To make opposition in words or arguments; to offer adverse reasons.—**object glass,** n. In a telescope or microscope, the lens or combination of lenses directed upon the object and producing an image of it, which is viewed through the eyepiece.—**objectify,** ob·jek′ti·fī, v.t. To form into an object; to give the character of an object to.—**objection,** ob·jek′shon, n. The act of objecting; that which is or may be objected; adverse reason, argument, or charge; fault found.—**objectionable,** ob·jek′shon·a·bl, a. Such as might reasonably be objected to; justly liable to objection; calling for disapproval; reprehensible (as actions, language, etc.).—**objective,** ob·jek′tiv, a. [Fr. *objectif*.] Belonging to what is external to the mind; hence, when used of *literature* or *art*, containing no trace of the writer's or artist's own feelings or individuality: opposed to *subjective*; *gram.* belonging to the object of a transitive verb or a preposition (the *objective* case, an *objective* clause).—n. The objective case; an object glass; the aim of a military maneuver or operation.—**objectively,** ob·jek′tiv·li, adv. In an objective manner.—**objectiveness,** ob·jek′tiv·nes, n. The state or relation of being objective.—**objectivity,** ob·jek·tiv′i·ti, n. The quality or state of being objective.—**objectless,** ob′jekt·les, a.—**object lesson,** n. A lesson to the young by means of articles themselves or pictures of them.—**objector,** ob·jek′tẽr, n.

objet d'art, ob′zhe·där, n. [Fr.] Something of artistic value.

objurgate, ob′jẽr·gāt, v.t. and i.—*objurgated*, *objurgating*. [L. *objurgo*, *objurgatum*—prefix *ob*, and *jurgo*, to chide.] To chide, reprove, or reprehend.—**objurgation,** ob·jẽr·gā′shon, n. The act of objurgating; a reproof.—**objurgatory,** ob·jẽr′ga·to·ri, a.

oblate, ob′lāt, a. [L. *oblatus*, thrust forward (i.e. at the equator), also offered, devoted—*ob*, against, before, and *latus*, carried, borne.] *Geom.* flattened or depressed at the poles.—*Oblate spheroid*, a spherical body flattened at the poles, that is, having the shape of the earth.—n. *Eccles.* a secular person who offered or devoted himself and his property to some monastery, into which he was admitted as a kind of lay brother; a member of a congregation of secular priests who live in community.—**oblation,** ob·lā′shon, n. [L. *oblatio*, an offering.] Anything offered or presented in worship or sacred service.

obligate, ob′li·gāt, v.t.—*obligated*, *obligating*. [L. *obligo*, *obligatum*, to bind, to bring under an obligation—prefix *ob*, and *ligo*, to bind. LIGAMENT.] To bring or place under some obligation; to hold to some duty; a word not much used by good writers.—**obligate,** a. Of bacteria

and parasites, bound to particular conditions of life.—**obligation,** ob·li·gā′shon, n. [L. *obligatio*, from *obligo*, to bind, oblige.] That which binds or obliges to do something; binding or constraining power or effect; an external act or duty imposed by the relations of society; a claim upon one; the position in which one is bound or indebted to another for a favor received; a favor bestowed and binding to gratitude.—**obligatorily,** ob·li′ga·to·ri·li, adv. In an obligatory manner.—**obligatory,** ob·li′ga·to·ri, a. Imposing obligation or duty; binding in law or conscience; requiring performance or forbearance of some act (*obligatory on* a person).

obligato, ob·li·gä′tō. See OBBLIGATO.

oblige, o·blīj′, v.t.—*obliged*, *obliging*. [Fr. *obliger*, from L. *obligo*, to bind, to oblige—*ob*, and *ligo*, to bind. OBLIGATION.] To constrain by any force, physical, moral, or legal; to compel; to bind by any restraint; to bind by some favor done; to lay under obligation of gratitude.—**obliged,** o·blījd′, p. and a. Having received some obligement or favor; laid under obligation; indebted.—**obligee,** ob·li·jē′, n. *Law*, the person to whom another is bound.—**obliger,** o·blī′jẽr, n. One that obliges.—**obliging,** o·blī′jing, a. Having the disposition to do favors; conferring favors or kindnesses; complaisant; kind.—**obligingly,** o·blī′jing·li, adv. In an obliging manner.—**obligingness,** o·blī′jing·nes, n. The state or quality of being obliging.—**obligor,** ob·li·gor′, n. *Law*, the person who binds himself to another.

oblique, ob·lēk′ or ob·līk′, a. [Fr. *oblique*, L. *obliquus*—prefix *ob*, and *liquis*, awry.] Having a direction neither perpendicular nor parallel to some line or surface which is made the standard of reference; not direct; aslant; slanting; *fig.* indirect or by allusion; not direct in descent; collateral.—*Oblique angle*, any angle except a right angle.—*Oblique arch*, a skew arch.—*Oblique bridge*, a skewbridge.—*Oblique case*, *gram.* any case except the nominative.—*Oblique cone* or *cylinder*, one whose axis is oblique to the plane of its base.—*Oblique speech*, *oblique narration*, *rhet.* that which is quoted indirectly, or in a different person from that employed by the original speaker.—**obliquely,** ob·lēk′li or ob·līk′li, adv. In an oblique manner or direction; indirectly; by a side glance; by an allusion; not in the direct or plain meaning.—**obliqueness, obliquity,** ob·lēk′nes or ob·līk′nes, ob·lik′wi·ti, n. [L. *obliquitas*.] The state of being oblique; deviation from parallelism or a perpendicular; deviation from moral rectitude; a mental or moral twist.—*Obliquity of the ecliptic*, the angle which the plane of the ecliptic makes with that of the equator.

obliterate, ob·lit′ẽr·āt, v.t. [L. *oblitero*, to blot out, to cause to be forgotten—prefix *ob*, and *litera*, a letter. LETTER.] To efface; to erase or blot out; to make undecipherable; to cause to be forgotten.—**obliteration**, ob·lit′ĕr·ā″shon, n. The act of obliterating or effacing.

oblivion, ob·liv′i·on, n. [L. *oblivio, oblivionis,* from *obliviscor,* to forget—prefix *ob,* and *liveo,* to become black. LIVID.] The state of being blotted out from the memory; a being forgotten; forgetfulness; the act of forgetting; a forgetting of offenses, or remission of punishment.—**oblivious**, ob·liv′i·us, a. [L. *obliviosus.*] Causing forgetfulness (*Shak.*); forgetful; mentally absent. —**obliviously**, ob·liv′i·us·li, adv. In an oblivious manner.—**obliviousness**, ob·liv′i·us·nes, n. State of being oblivious.

oblong, ob′long, a. [L. *oblongus,* oblong—*ob,* against, inversely, and *longus,* long.] Rectangular, and having the length greater than the breadth; longer than broad.—n. An oblong figure.—**oblongness**, ob′long·nes, n.

obloquy, ob′lo·kwi, n. [L. *obloquium,* from *obloquor*—*ob,* against, and *loquor,* to speak. LOQUACIOUS.] Censorious speech; reproachful language; language that causes reproach and odium to rest on men or their actions; odium.

obnoxious, ob·nok′shus, a. [L. *obnoxius*—*ob,* and *noxa,* harm, hurt. NOXIOUS.] Reprehensible; censurable; odious; hateful; offensive; unpopular.—**obnoxiously**, ob·nok′shus·li, adv.—**obnoxiousness**, ob·nok′shus·nes, n.

oboe, ō′bō, n. [It. *oboe,* from Fr. *hautbois,* an oboe.] A hautboy; a wood-wind instrument made from a slender, conical tube that produces a thin, penetrating, plaintive tone by means of a double reed.—**oboist**, ō′bō·ist, n.

obolus, ob′o·lus, n. [Gr. *obolos.*] A small coin of ancient Greece.

obovate, ob·ō′vāt, a. [Prefix *ob,* implying inversion.] *Bot.* inversely ovate; having the narrow end downward.—**obovoid**, ob·ō′void, a. *Bot.* approaching the obovate form.

obscene, ob·sēn′, a. [L. *obscenus, obscaenus,* filthy, repulsive, obscene: etymol. doubtful.] Impure in language or action; indecent; offensive to chastity and delicacy; inauspicious; ill-omened.—**obscenely**, ob·sēn′li, adv. In an obscene manner.—**obsceneness, obscenity**, ob·sēn′nes, ob·sen′i·ti, n. The state or quality of being obscene; impurity; ribaldry; lewdness.

obscure, ob·skūr′, a. [Fr. *obscur,* from L. *obscurus*—prefix *ob,* and root seen in *scutum,* a shield. Skr. *sku,* to cover.] Imperfectly illuminated; gloomy; not clear or distinct to view; dim; not easily understood; not obviously intelligible; abstruse; indistinct; not much known or observed; unknown to fame; unnoticed.—v.t.—**obscured**, obscuring. To darken; to make dark or dim; to make less intelligible, legible, or visible; to hide; to prevent from being seen or known.—**obscurely**, ob·skūr′li, adv. In an obscure man-

ner; darkly; dimly; not clearly; in retirement; not conspicuously.— **obscureness**, ob·skūr′nes, n. State of being obscure; obscurity.—**obscurity**, ob·skū′ri·ti, n. [L. *obscuritas.*] The quality or state of being obscure; darkness; dimness; darkness of meaning; a state of being unknown to fame.—**obscurant, obscurantist**, ob·skū′rant, ob·skū′rant·ist, n. One who obscures; one who opposes the progress of knowledge, or labors to prevent enlightenment, inquiry, or reform.—**obscurantism**, ob·skū′rant·izm, n. The system or principles of an obscurant.—**obscuration**, ob·skū·rā′shon, n. The act of obscuring or darkening; the state of being darkened or obscured.

obsecrate, ob′si·krāt, v.t. [L. *obsecro,* to entreat—prefix *ob,* and *sacer,* sacred. SACRED.] To beseech; to entreat; to supplicate.—**obsecration**, ob·si·krā′shon, n. The act of obsecrating; entreaty; supplication.

obsequious, ob·sē′kwi·us, a. [From L. *obsequiosus,* obsequious, from *obsequium,* compliance, from *obsequor,* to follow—prefix *ob,* and *sequor,* to follow. SEQUENCE.] Promptly obedient or submissive to the will of another; compliant; officious; devoted; servilely condescending; compliant to excess; cringing; fawning.—**obsequiously**, ob·sē′kwi·us·li, adv. In an obsequious manner; servilely; cringingly.—**obsequiousness**, ob·sē′kwi·us·nes, n. The quality of being obsequious.

obsequy, ob′se·kwe, n. pl. **obsequies**, ob′se·kwēz, [O.Fr. from L. *obsequiae,* pl. funeral rites.] A funeral rite or ceremony (commonly used only in the plural).

observe, ob·zėrv′, v.t.—observed, observing. [L. *observo*—*ob,* before, in front, and *servo,* to keep or hold. SERVE.] To look on with attention; to regard attentively; to watch; to notice; to perceive; to detect; to discover; to remark in words; to mention; to keep with due ceremonies; to celebrate; to keep or adhere to in practice; to comply with; to obey. ∴ Syn. under SEE.—v.i. To be attentive; to remark; to comment.— **observer**, ob·zėr′vėr, n. One who observes.—**observingly**, ob·zėr′ving·li, adv. In an observing manner. —**observable**, ob·zėr′va·bl, a. Capable of being observed; worthy of observation.—**observably**, ob·zėr′va·bli, adv.—**observance**, ob·zėr′vans, n. The act of observing; performance; a rite or ceremony; an act of respect, worship, and the like; obedient regard or attention; respectful or servile attention; homage.—**observant**, ob·zėr′vant, a. Characterized by observation; taking notice; attentively noticing; attentive to duties or commands; obedient; adhering to in practice (*observant of* duties).—**observantly**, ob·zėr′vant·li, adv. In an observant manner.— **observation**, ob·zėr·vā′shon, n. [L. *observatio.*] The act, power, or habit of observing; a taking notice or paying attention; *science,* the act of taking notice of particular phe-

nomena as they occur in the course of nature; the observing of some phenomenon, often by the assistance of an instrument; information gained by such an act; a remark based or professing to be based on what has been observed; notice; observance†.—*Observation officer,* an artillery officer placed so as to command a view of enemy positions, and in communication by telephone with those in charge of the guns to which he is attached. He directs the laying of the guns so as to bring selected objects under fire, the objects being commonly invisible to the gunners.—*Observation post,* the position occupied by an observation officer.—**observational**, ob·zėr·vā′shon·al, a. Relating to or based on observations.— **observatory**, ob·zėr′va·to·ri, n. A place used for making observations of natural phenomena; a building constructed for astronomical observations; a place of outlook.

obsess, ob·ses′, v.t. [L. *obsideo,* to besiege—*ob,* before, *sedeo,* to sit.] To beset or besiege; to vex or harass, as an evil spirit.—**obsession**, ob·se′shon, n. Act of obsessing.

obsidian, ob·sid′i·an, n. [L. *Obsidianus,* from *Obsidius* or *Obsius,* its alleged discoverer.] Vitreous lava, or volcanic glass, a glassy mineral of several varieties.

obsolete, ob′so·lēt, a. [L. *obsoletus,* pp. of *obsolesco,* to go out of use—prefix *ob,* and *soleo,* to use, to be wont.] Gone into disuse; disused; neglected; out of fashion; *biol.* imperfectly developed or abortive. —**obsoleteness**, ob′so·lēt·nes, n. The state of being obsolete.—**obsolescence**, ob·so·les′ens, n. The state or process of becoming obsolete— **obsolescent**, ob·so·les′ent, a. [L. *obsolescens.*] Becoming obsolete; going out of use, passing into desuetude.

obstacle, ob′sta·kl, n. [Fr. *obstacle,* from L. *obstaculum,* from *obsto,* to withstand—*ob,* against, and *sto,* to stand. STATE, STAND.] Anything that stands in the way and hinders progress; a hindrance; an obstruction or impediment, either physical or moral.

obstetric, obstetrical, ob·stet′rik, ob·stet′ri·kal, a. [L. *obstetrix,* a midwife—*ob,* before, and *sto,* to stand. OBSTACLE.] Pertaining to midwifery, or care of a woman in pregnancy and labor.—**obstetrician**, ob·ste·trish′an, n. One skilled in obstetrics.—**obstetrics**, ob·stet′-riks, n. That branch of medical science which includes prenatal care, as well as childbirth and any complications arising therefrom.

obstinate, ob′sti·nit, a. [L. *obstinatus,* pp. of *obstino, obstinatum,* to resolve, from *obsto,* to stand against— *ob,* against, and *sto,* to stand. OBSTACLE.] Pertinaciously adhering to an opinion or purpose; fixed firmly in resolution; not yielding to reason, arguments, or other means; stubborn: said of persons; not yielding or not easily subdued or removed (an *obstinate* fever; an *obstinate* cough). ∴ To be *obstinate* implies the doing what we ourselves choose; to be *stubborn* denotes, rather, determination not to do what others advise or desire.— **obstinacy, obstinateness,** ob′sti•na•si, ob′sti•nit•nes, *n.* The state or quality of being obstinate.—**obstinately,** ob′sti•nit•li, *adv.* In an obstinate manner.

obstreperous, ob•strep′ér•us, *a.* [L. *obstreperus,* from *obstrepo,* to roar— *ob,* intens., and *strepo,* to make a noise.] Making a tumultuous noise; clamorous; vociferous; noisy; loud. —**obstreperously,** ob•strep′ér•us•li, *adv.* In an obstreperous manner.— **obstreperousness,** ob•strep′ér•us• nes, *n.* Clamor; noisy turbulence.

obstruct, ob•strukt′, *v.t.* [L. *obstruo, obstructum—ob,* against, and *struo,* to pile up. STRUCTURE.] To block up, stop up, or close, as a passage; to fill with obstacles or impediments that prevent passing; to hinder from passing; to impede; to stand in the way of; to retard, interrupt, render slow.—**obstructer,** ob• struk′tér, *n.* One that obstructs or hinders.—**obstruction,** ob•struk′-shon, *n.* The act of obstructing; anything that stops or closes a way, passage, or channel; obstacle; impediment; that which impedes progress; check; hindrance; the state of having the vital functions obstructed†.—**obstructionist,** ob• struk′shon•ist, *n.* One who practices obstruction; an obstructive.— **obstructive,** ob•struk′tiv, *a.* Obstructing or tending to obstruct.—*n.* One who obstructs; one who hinders the transaction of business.—**obstruent,** ob′stru•ent, *a.* [L. *obstruens,* ppr. of *obstruo.*] Blocking up; obstructing; hindering.—*n.* Anything that obstructs; something that blocks up the natural passages of the body.

obtain, ob•tān′, *v.t.* [L. *obtineo—* prefix *ob,* and *teneo,* to hold. TENANT.] To gain possession of; to gain, procure, receive, get, acquire.—*v.i.* To be received in customary or common use; to be established in practice; to hold good; to subsist (the custom still *obtains*).—**obtainable,** ob•tā′na•bl, *a.* Capable of being obtained.—**obtainer,** ob•tā′nér, *n.* One who obtains.

obtected, ob•tek′ted, *a.* [L. *obtectus—* prefix *ob,* and *tego, tectus,* to cover.] Covered; *zool.* covered with a hard shelly case.

obtest, ob•test′, *v.t.* [L. *obtestor—* prefix *ob,* and *testor,* to witness. TESTAMENT.] To call upon earnestly; to entreat, implore, conjure; to supplicate.—**obtestation,** ob•tes•tā′-shon, *n.* The act of obtesting.

obtrude, ob•tröd′, *v.t.*—*obtruded, obtruding.* [L. *obtrudo—*prefix *ob,* and *trudo,* to thrust. INTRUDE.] To thrust prominently forward; to force into any place or state unduly or without solicitation; often *refl.* (to *obtrude* one's self upon a person's notice); to offer with unreasonable importunity.—*v.i.* To obtrude one's self; to enter when not invited.— **obtruder,** ob•trö′dér, *n.* One who

obtrudes.—**obtrusion,** ob•trö′zhon, *n.* The act of obtruding.—**obtrusive,** ob•trö′siv, *a.* Disposed to obtrude; forward; intrusive.—**obtrusively,** ob•trö′siv•li, *adv.* In an obtrusive, manner.—**obtrusiveness,** ob•trö′-siv•nes, *n.*

obtuse, ob•tūs′, *a.* [L. *obtusus—* prefix *ob,* and *tundo, tudi* (Skr. *tud*), to beat. CONTUSE.] Not pointed or acute; blunt; not having acute sensibility; stupid; dull.—*Obtuse angle,* an angle greater than 90° but less than 180°.—**obtusely,** ob•tūs′li, *adv.*—**obtuseness,** ob•tūs′nes, *n.*

obverse, ob′vérs, *a.* [L. prefix *ob,* and *versus,* turned.] Pertaining to the one of two possible sides or theories; *numis.* bearing the face or head.—*n.* The one of two possible ways of looking at a thing; *numis.* that side of a coin or medal which has the face or head on it, the other being the *reverse.*—**obversely,** ob′vérs•li, *adv.* In an obverse form or manner.— **obversion,** ob•vér′shon, *n.* The act of obverting.—**obvert,** ob•vért′, *v.t.* To turn toward.—*In logic,* to infer another proposition with a contradictory predicate by changing the quality of the proposition.

obviate, ob′vi•āt, *v.t.*—*obviated, obviating.* [L. *obvio, obviatum,* to meet —*ob,* against, and *via,* a way. VOYAGE, WAY.] To meet, as difficulties or objections; to overcome; to clear out of the way.—**obviation,** ob•vi•ā′shon, *n.*

obvious, ob′vi•us, *a.* [L. *obvius,* in the way.] Easily discovered, seen, or understood; perfectly plain, manifest, or evident.—**obviously,** ob′-vi•us•li, *adv.* In an obvious manner. —**obviousness,** ob′vi•us•nes, *n.* State of being obvious.

obvolute, ob′vo•lūt, *a.* [L. *ob,* against, and *volutus,* rolled.] Rolled or turned in; *bot.* having the margins of opposite leaves alternately overlapping.

ocarina, ō•ka•rē′na, *n.* [It.] A small musical instrument of terra cotta pierced with holes, there being seven instruments in a set.

occasion, ok•kā′zhon, *n.* [L. *occasio, occasionis,* from *occido, occasum,* to fall—*ob,* and *cado,* to fall. ACCIDENT.] Time of an occurrence, incident, or event; opportunity; favorable time, season, or circumstances; incidental cause; a cause acting on the will; a motive or reason; incidental need; casual exigency; requirement (*to have occasion* or *no occasion* for a thing); peculiar position of affairs; juncture; exigency.—*v.t.* To cause incidentally; to produce; to induce.—**occasional,** ok•kā′zhon•al, *a.* Incidental; occurring at times, but not regular or systematic; made or happening as opportunity requires or admits.— **occasionally,** ok•kā′zhon•al•li, *adv.* In an occasional manner; at times; sometimes but not often.

occident, ok′si•dent, *n.* [Fr. *occident,* L. *occidens, occidentis,* ppr. of *occido,* to fall, to set, as the sun. OCCASION.] The west: the opposite of *orient;* [cap.] the Western Hemisphere and

Europe.—**occidental,** ok•si•den′tal, *a.* Western; [cap.] pertaining to the Occident or Occidentals.—*n.* [cap.] A native of the Occident.

occipital, ok•sip′i•tal, *a.* [From L. *occiput,* the back part of the head— prefix *ob,* and *caput,* the head.] Pertaining to the back part of the head. —**occiput,** ok′si•put, *n.* [L.] The hinder part of the head.

occlude, ok•klūd′, *v.t.* —*occluded, occluding.* [L. *occludo—ob,* and *claudo,* to shut.] To obstruct; to shut in or out; to cut off by closing a passage. —*v.i.* To close with the cusps fitting snugly: said of teeth.—**occlusion,** ok•klū′zhon, *n.*—**occlusive,** ok•klū′-siv, *a.*

occult, ok•kult′, *a.* [L. *occultus,* pp. of *occulo,* to cover over—prefix *ob,* and root of *celo,* to conceal, and E. *hell.*] Hidden from the eye or understanding; invisible and mysterious; unknown.—*Occult sciences,* certain so-called sciences of the Middle Ages, as alchemy, necromancy or magic, astrology.—**occultation,** ok•kul•tā′-shon, *n. Astron.* the hiding of a star or planet from our sight by passing behind some other of the heavenly bodies; the time of a planet or star being so hidden; hence, *fig.* disappearance from view; withdrawal from public notice.—**occultism,** ok′ult• izm, *n.* A system of occult or mysterious doctrines; the beliefs of the theosophists, typified in such works as Bulwer-Lytton's *Zanoni, A Strange Story; The Coming Race.*

occupy, ok′kū•pī, *v.t.*—*occupied, occupying.* [L. *occupo,* to take possession of, possess—prefix *ob,* and *capio,* to take. CAPABLE.] To take possession of; to possess; to hold and use; to take up, as room or space; to cover or fill; to employ or use (one's time); to engage; to busy: often *refl.*—*v.i.* To be an occupant; to hold possession.—**occupancy,** ok′kū•pan•si, *n.* The act of occupying; a holding in possession; term during which one is occupant.—**occupant,** ok′kū•pant, *n.* [L. *occupans, occupantis,* ppr. of *occupo,* to occupy.] An occupier.— **occupation,** ok•kū•pā′shon, *n.* [L. *occupatio.*] The act of occupying or taking possession; what engages one's time and attention; a vocation; calling; trade.—*Army of Occupation,* army provisionally occupying territory that has been overrun, until a form of government is established. —**occupational,** ok•kū•pā′shon•al, *a.* Of or pertaining to a particular occupation (an *occupational* disease). —*Occupational therapy,* mental and physical therapy by means of creative activity, such as carpentry, designed to develop confidence, muscular control, etc.

occur, ok•kér′, *v.i.*—*occurred, occurring.* [L. *occurro—ob,* against, and *curro,* to run. CURRENT.] To meet or come to the mind, imagination, or memory; to befall; to happen; to take place; to exist so as to be capable of being found or seen; to be found; to be met with.—**occurrence,** ok•kér′ens, *n.* The act of occurring or taking place; any incident or accidental event; an observed instance.

ocean, ō'shen, *n.* [L. *oceanus,* from Gr. *ōkeanos,* the ocean, the deity of the ocean.] The vast body of water which covers more than three-fifths of the surface of the globe; the sea; also, one of the great basins or areas into which it has been divided; any immense expanse (the boundless *ocean* of eternity).—*a.* Pertaining to the main or great sea (the *ocean* wave).—**oceanic,** ō·shi·an'ik, *a.* Pertaining to the ocean; occurring in or produced by the ocean, as distinguished from smaller seas; pertaining to Oceania (the islands lying between Asia and America) or its inhabitants. —*Oceanic island,* an island that has never formed part of a continent, e.g. Azores.—**oceanography,** ō·shen·og'ra·fi, *n.* The department of knowledge that deals with oceanic phenomena.

ocellus, ō·sel'lus, *n.* pl. **ocelli,** ō·sel'lī. [L. *ocellus,* dim. of *oculus,* an eye. OCULAR.] One of the minute simple eyes of insects, many spiders, crustaceans, mollusks, etc.—**ocellate, ocellated,** ō·sel'lāt, ō·sel'lā·ted, *a.* [L. *ocellatus.*] Resembling an eye; studded with the figures of little eyes.

ocelot, o'se·lot, *n.* [Nahuatl, abbrev. of *thalocelotl,* field jaguar.] A leopard-like American cat (*Felis pardalis*) about three feet long.

ocher, ochre, ō'kėr, *n.* [L. *ochra,* Gr. *ochra,* from *ochros,* pale, pale yellow.] A name applied to clays colored with the oxides of iron in various proportions, and varying in color from pale yellow to brownish red; the color of ocher.—**ocherous, ochreous,** ō'kėr·us, *a.*

ochlocracy, ok·lok're·si, *n.* [Gr. *ochlos,* the multitude, and *kratos,* power.] The rule or ascendency of the multitude or common people; a mobocracy.—**ochlocratic, ochlocratical,** ok·lō·krat'ik, ok·lō·krat'i·kal, *a.* Relating to ochlocracy.

o'clock, o·klok', *contr.* Of the clock.

ocrea, ok're·a, *n. pl.* **ocreae,** [L. *ocrea,* a greave or legging.] *Bot.* the union of two stipules around the stem in a kind of sheath.—**ocreate,** ok're·āt, *a. Bot.* furnished with ocreae.

octachord, ok'ta·kord, *n.* [Gr. *oktō,* eight, and *chorde,* a string.] A musical instrument having eight strings.

octagon, ok'ta·gon, *n.* [Gr. *oktō,* eight, and *gōnia,* angle.] *Geom.* a figure of eight sides and eight angles. —**octagonal,** ok·tag'on·al, *a.* Having eight sides and eight angles.

octahedron, ok·ta·hē'dron, *n.* [Gr. *oktō,* eight, *hedra,* a base.] *Geom.* a solid contained by eight faces, which take the form of equal and equilateral triangles.—**octahedral,** ok·ta·hē'dral, *a.* Having eight equal surfaces.

octameter, ok·tam'et·ėr, *n.* [Gr. *oktō,* eight, *metron,* a measure.] A verse of eight feet.

octane, ok·tān', *n.* [Prefix *oct-* and *-ane.*] *Chem.* any of a group of 18 isomeric hydrocarbons, C_8H_{18}, of the methane series.—**octane number, octane rating,** *n.* The numerical

statement of the anti-knock qualities of a motor fuel.

octangular, ok·tang'gū·lėr, *a.* [L. *octo,* eight; and E. *angular.*] Having eight angles.

octant, ok'tant, *n.* [L. *octans,* an eighth part, from *octo,* eight.] The eighth part of a circle; an instrument resembling a sextant or quadrant in principle, but having an arc the eighth of a circle, or 45°.

octave, ok'tiv, *n.* [L. *octavus,* eighth, from *octo,* eight.] The eighth day after a church festival, the festival itself being counted; the week immediately following a church festival; the first two stanzas in the sonnet of four verses each; a stanza of eight lines; *mus.* an eighth, or an interval of seven degrees or twelve semitones; one sound eight tones higher than another.—*a.* Consisting of eight.

octavo, ok·tā'vō, *n.* and *a.* The size of a leaf of a sheet of paper folded so as to make eight leaves: usually written *8vo*; a book of this size.

octennial, ok·ten'i·al, *a.* [L. *octo,* eight, and *annus,* a year.] Happening every eighth year; lasting eight years. —**octennially,** ok·ten'i·al·li, *adv.* Once in eight years.

octet, ok'tet, *n.* [L. *octo,* eight.] *Mus.* a musical composition for eight parts; the eight performers of such a composition; a group of eight; the first eight lines of a sonnet.

octillion, ok·til'yon, *n.* [L. *octo,* eight, and term of *million.*] The figure 1 followed by 27 zeros (*American and French*), or 1 followed by 48 zeros (*English and German*).

October, ok·tō'bėr, *n.* [L., from *octo,* eight: the eighth month of the primitive Roman year, which began in March.] The tenth month of the year; ale or cider brewed in October. —*October club,* a political club of squires in Queen Anne's day, devoted to the consumption of October ale and to the policy of enforcing strong anti-Whig measures on the Government.

octodecimo, ok·tō·des'i·mō, *n.* [L. *octodecim,* eighteen—*octo,* eight, and *decem,* ten.] The size of one leaf of a sheet of paper folded so as to make eighteen leaves; a book in which each sheet is folded into eighteen leaves: usually written *18mo.* Also used as an adjective.

octogenarian, ok'tō·je·nâ"ri·an, *n.* [L. *octogenarius,* from *octogeni,* eighty, *octo,* eight.] A person eighty years of age; any one whose age is between eighty and ninety.—*a.* Of eighty years of age; between eighty and ninety years of age.

octopus, ok'to·pus, *n.* [N.L. from Gr. *oktōpous,* eight-footed, from *okto,* eight, and *pous, podus,* foot.] Any animal of the genus (*Octopus*) that has eight arms with suckers.

octoroon, ok·to·rön', *n.* [L. *octo,* eight.] The offspring of a quadroon and a white person.

octosyllabic, ok'to·sil·lab"ik, *a.* [Gr. *oktō,* eight, and *syllabē,* a syllable.] Consisting of eight syllables.—*n.* A word of eight syllables.

octroi, ok·trwạ', *n.* [Fr., from L.

auctor, an author.] A duty levied at the gates of French cities on articles brought in.

octuple, ok'tū·pl, *a.* [L. *octuplus*—*oktō,* eight.] Eightfold.

ocular, ok'ū·lėr, *a.* [L. *ocularis,* from *oculus,* the eye, a word cognate with E. *eye.* EYE.] Pertaining to the eye; depending on the eye; received by actual sight.—*n.* The eyepiece of an optical instrument.—**oculist,** ok'ū·list, *n.* One skilled in diseases of the eyes.

od, od, *n.* The name invented by Reichenbach for a peculiar force which he fancied he had discovered associated with magnetism, and which was said to explain the phenomena of mesmerism or animal magnetism. Called also *Odic force.*— **odic,** od'ik, *a.* Pertaining to od.

odalisque, odalisk, ō'dä·lisk, *n.* [Fr. *odalisque,* from Turk., *ōdahliq,* chambermaid, from *ōdah,* chamber.] A slave in a harem, especially a Turkish sultan's harem.

odd, od, *a.* [From Icel. *oddi,* a triangle, an odd number, a tongue of land.] Not even; not exactly divisible by 2; left over; additional to a whole; not included with others: hence, unheeded; of little value or account (*odd times, odd trifles*); incidental; casual; forming one of a pair of which the other is wanting; belonging to a broken set; singular; strange; peculiar; eccentric; queer.— **Odd Fellow,** od'fel·ō, *n.* A member of an extensively ramified friendly society, originally modeled on freemasonry.—**oddity,** od'i·ti, *n.* The state or quality of being odd; singularity; something odd or singular; a singular person.—**oddly,** od'li, *adv.* In an odd manner; not evenly; strangely; whimsically; singularly.— **oddment,** od'ment, *n.* An odd article or one left over.—**oddness,** od'nes, *n.* The state of being odd; state of not being even; singularity; strangeness. —**odds,** odz, *n. sing.* or *pl.* Excess of one amount or quantity compared with another; difference in favor of one and against another; amount by which the bet of one party exceeds that of the other.—*At odds,* at variance; in controversy or quarrel. —*Odds and ends,* small miscellaneous articles.

ode, ōd, *n.* [L. *ode,* Gr. *ōdē,* song or poem, from *aoidē,* a song; seen in *parody, prosody.*] A short poem or song; a poem to be set to music or sung; a lyric poem of a lofty cast.

odeum, ō·dē'um, *n.* [Gr. *ōdeion,* from *ōdē,* a song.] A theater for musical or dramatic performances.

odic. See OD.

Odin, Woden, ō'din, wō'den, *n.* [Former from Scandinavian, latter Anglo-Saxon and German.] The chief god of Northern mythology, after whom is named Wednesday.

odious, ō'di·us, *a.* [L. *odiosus,* from *odium,* hatred, *odi,* I hate; same root as A.Sax. *atol,* hateful, horrible. ANNOY, NOISOME.] Of such a character as to be hated or greatly disliked; hateful; causing disgust or repugnance; offensive.—**odiously,**

ō'di•us•li, *adv.* In an odious manner; hatefully.—**odiousness**, ō'di•us•nes, *n.* The quality of being odious.—**odium**, ō'di•um, *n.* [L.] Hatred; dislike; the quality that provokes hatred.—*Odium theologicum*, theological hatred; the hatred of contending divines toward each other.

odometer, ō•dom'e•tẽr, *n.* [Gr. *hodometron—hodos*, way, and *metron*, measure.] A device which measures the distance traveled by a vehicle.

odontalgia, ō•don•tal'ji•a, *n.* [Gr. *odous, odontos*, tooth, *algos*, pain.] Pain in the teeth; toothache.—**odontalgic**, ō•don•tal'jik, *a.* Pertaining to the toothache.—*n.* A remedy for the toothache.—**odonto**, ō•don'tō, *n.* [Gr. *odous, odontos*.] A dentifrice; a toothwash.—**odontoglossum**, ō•don•to•glos'um, *n.* [Gr. *odous, odontos*, a tooth, and *glōssa*, a tongue.] A genus of tropical American orchids, with magnificent flowers.—**odontoid**, ō•don'toid, *a.* Tooth-like.—*Odontoid process*, the part of the first vertebra of the neck, forming a pivot for the head.—**odontological**, ō•don'to•loj'i•kal, *a.* Belonging to odontology.—**odontology**, ō•don•tol'o•ji, *n.* That branch of anatomical science which treats of the teeth.—**odontophore**, ō•don'to•fōr, *n.* [Gr. *phoros*, bearing.] The so-called tongue or lingual ribbon of certain mollusks, covered with minute teeth.

odor, ō'dẽr, *n.* [L. *odor*, a smell; allied to Gr. *ozō*, to smell; akin *olfactory*.] Any scent or smell, whether pleasant or offensive: when used alone most commonly a sweet smell; fragrance.—*In bad odor*, in bad repute; in disfavor.—*Odor of sanctity*, the reputation of being a saint.—**odoriferous**, ō•dẽr•if'ẽr•us, *a.* [L. *odoriferus*.] Giving odor or scent; diffusing fragrance; fragrant.—**odoriferously**, ō•dẽr•if'ẽr•us•li, *adv.* In an odoriferous manner.—**odoriferousness**, ō•dẽr•if'ẽr•us•nes, *n.*—**odorous**, ō'dẽr•us, *a.* Having or emitting an odor; sweet of scent; fragrant.—**odorously**, ō'dẽr•us•li, *adv.* In an odorous manner; fragrantly.—**odorousness**, ō'dẽr•us•nes, *n.* The quality of being odorous.—**odorless**, ō'dẽr•les, *a.* Having no odor.

odyssey, od'i•si, *n.* [From Homer's epic, *The Odyssey*, recounting Odysseus' years of wandering.] A long wandering or journey.

Oedipus complex, ed'i•pus kom'plex, *n.* [From Gr. *Oidipous*, son of Laius and Jocasta, who, in accordance with a prophecy, unknowingly, killed his father and married his mother.] The unconscious sexual feelings of a child (especially a male) for the parent of the opposite sex, which, if unresolved in adult life, can be a source of an emotional disorder.

oenanthic, ē•nan'thik, *a.* [Gr. *oinos*, wine, and *anthos*, a flower.] Having or imparting the characteristic odor of wine.—*Oenanthic acid*, an acid obtained from oenanthic ether.—*Oenanthic ether*, an oily liquid which gives to wine its characteristic odor.—**oenology**, ē•nol'o•ji, *n.* That

branch of knowledge which deals with wine.

o'er, ōr. A contraction (generally poetical) of *over*.

oersted, er'sted, *n.* [After *Oersted*, the physicist.] The C.G.S. unit of magnetic reluctance, equal to the reluctance of a magnetic circuit of unit length, unit area, and unit permeability.

oestrus, ēs'trŭs, *n.* [Gr. *oistros*, gadfly.] Irresistible impulse; passion; sexual impulse of animals.

of, ov, *prep.* [A.Sax. *of.*=Icel., Sw., Dan., and D. *af*, Goth. *af*, G. *ab*; cog. L. *ab*, Gr. *apo*, Skr. *apa*, from, away from. *Off* is the same word.] A word used in regard to source, cause, origin, motive, etc.; possession or ownership; attribute, quality, or condition (his state *of* mind); an aggregate or whole with a partitive reference (all, some, *of* us); the relation of object to a verbal notion (a desire *of* fame); to express concerning, relating to, about; distance or time (within a mile *of*); identity, equivalence, or apposition—appositive use of *of* (the city *of* London); on or in; with indefinite expressions of time, as a quarter *of* (an hour); so *of* late, in recent times.

off, of, *adv.* [OF.] Away; distant (a mile *off*); from or away by removal or separation (to cut *off*); not on; from, in the way of departure, abatement, remission (the fever goes *off*); so as to be less (attendance fell *off*); away from, as daily work (to take a day *off*).—*Off and on, on and off*, with interruptions and resumptions; at intervals.—*a.* Distant; as applied to horses, right hand: opposed to *near*; not on (his shoe is *off*); on the way (he is *off* to work); inaccurate (the sum is *off*); below standards; in a certain specified circumstance.—*prep.* Not on; away from; from or out of (a lane leading *off* a street); to seaward from; at the expense of (live *off* the land); relieved, or released, from (to be *off* duty); abstaining from (to be *off* liquor); below a certain level or standard.—*interj.* A command to depart: away! begone!—**offcast**, of'kast, *n.* That which is rejected as useless.—**offing**, of'ing, *n.* The portion of the sea seen from land; the near future.—**off-color**, *a.* Defective in color, as a gem; in poor taste; risque', etc.—**offhand**, *adv.* Readily; with ease.—*a.* Done without study or hesitation; unpremeditated.—**offish**, of'ish, *a.* Tending to be aloof.—**offset**, of'set, *n.* A sum set off against another as an equivalent; *print.* a printing process involving the transfer of ink from a rubber covered roller to the paper; an accidental transfer of ink.—*v.t.* of•set'. To compensate for.—**offshoot**, of'shōt, *n.* A branch from a main stem, stream, mountain range, etc.—**offspring**, of'spring, *n.* sing. or pl. Progeny; a child or children; what arises or is produced from something.

offal, of'al, *n.* [Lit. *off-fall*; so D. *afval*, Icel. *affall*, G. *abfall*, with

similar meanings.] Waste meat; a trade term for kidneys, heart, tongue, liver, and other parts of a carcass; carrion; refuse; rubbish.

offense, of•fens', *n.* [Fr. *offense*, from L. *offensa*, an offense, from *offendo*, *offensum*, to strike against — *ob*, against, and old *fendo*, to strike, seen in *defend*, also in *manifest*.] A striking against or assailing (arms of *offense*); hurt; injury; an affront, insult, or wrong; the state of being offended; displeasure; any transgression of law, divine or human; a crime or sin; a misdemeanor.—*To take offense*, to become angry or displeased at something said or done.—**offend**, of•fend', *v.t.* [L. *offendo*.] To displease; to make angry; to affront; to mortify; to shock, annoy, or pain (the taste or smell); to sin against; to disobey (Shak.).—*v.i.* To transgress the moral or divine law; to sin; to cause dislike or anger; to take offense (N.T.).—**offender**, of•fen'dẽr, *n.* One who offends; a criminal; a transgressor.—**offensive**, of•fen'siv, *a.* [Fr. *offensif*.] Causing offense; giving provocation; irritating; disgusting; disagreeable (as to the senses); pertaining to offense; used in attack: opposed to *defensive*; consisting in attack; proceeding by attack.—*Alliance offensive and defensive*, one that requires the parties to make war together, and each party to defend the other in case of being attacked.—*n.* With the definite article: the act of attacking (to act on the *offensive*).—**offensively**, of•fen'siv•li, *adv.* In an offensive manner.—**offensiveness**, of•fen'siv•nes, *n.* The quality of being offensive; unpleasantness.

offer, of'ẽr, *v.t.* [A.Sax. *offrian*, and Fr. *offrir* (*j'offre*, I offer), from L. *offerre*, to offer—*ob*, towards, and *fero*, to bring. FERTILE.] To present for acceptance or rejection; to tender; to present to notice; to proffer; to present, as an act of worship; to sacrifice (often with *up*); to attempt or do with evil intent (to *offer* violence, an insult); to bid, as a price or wages.—*v.i.* To present itself (an opportunity *offers*); to declare a willingness.—*n.* The act of offering; a proposal to be accepted or rejected; the act of bidding a price, or the sum bid.—**offerer**, of'ẽr•ẽr, *n.*—**offering**, of'ẽr•ing, *n.* That which is offered; a gift, as an oblation.—**offertory**, of'ẽr•to•ri, *n.* The oblation of the unconsecrated bread and wine to God during the Eucharist; the prayers recited and hymns sung at this time; the point at which money is offered during a religious service; the money offered.

office, of'is, *n.* [Fr. *office*, from L. *officium*, duty, office, from prefix *ob*, and *facio*, to do, or from *opem*, aid (OPULENCE), and *facio* (FACT).] Employment or business; duty or duties falling on or entrusted to a person; that which is performed or assigned to be done by a particular thing; function; act of good or ill voluntarily tendered: usually in a good sense; service; *eccles.* a formulary of devotion, or a service appointed for a particular occasion; a house or apartment in which persons transact business; a place where official acts are done; a body of persons entrusted with certain duties; persons who transact business in an office (often applied to an insurance company); *pl.* kitchens, outhouses, etc., of a mansion, dwelling house, or farm.—*Holy Office*, the Inquisition, or the authorities at Rome who direct it.—*Office hours*, the hours during which offices are open for the transaction of business.—**officer**, of′is·ẽr, *n.* A person who holds an office; a person commissioned or authorized to fill a public situation or to perform any public duty; one who holds a commission in the army or navy.—*v.t.* To furnish with officers; to appoint officers over.—**official**, of·fish′al, *a.* [L. *officialis.*] Pertaining to an office or public duty; derived from the proper office or officer, or from the proper authority (an *official* permission); communicated by virtue of authority.—*n.* One invested with an office of a public nature; *eccles.* a deputy appointed by a bishop, chapter, archdeacon, etc.—**officialism**, of·fish′al·izm, *n.* A system of official government; a system of excessive official routine; red-tapism.—**officially**, of·fish′al·li, *adv.* In an official manner; by virtue of the proper authority.—**officiate**, of·fish′i·āt, *v.i.* —*officiated, officiating.* To perform official duties.—**officiator**, of·fish′i·ā·tẽr, *n.* One who officiates.

officinal, of·fis′i·nal, *a.* [From L. *officina*, a shop; same origin as *office.*] Used in a shop, or belonging to it; *phar.* used in the preparation of recognized medical recipes (an *officinal* plant).—*n.* A drug sold in an apothecary's shop.

officious, of·fish′us, *a.* [L. *officiosus*, dutiful, obliging, from *officium*, an office. OFFICE.] Obliging‡; doing kind offices‡; excessively forward in kindness; interposing services not wanted; annoyingly eager to oblige or assist; meddling.—**officiously**, of·fish′us·li, *adv.* In an officious manner; with forward zeal; meddlesomely.—**officiousness**, of·fish′us·nes, *n.* Improper forwardness; meddlesomeness.

offing, offscouring, offset, offshoot, offspring, etc. See OFF.

oft, oft, *adv.* [A.Sax., Icel., and G. *oft*, Dan. *ofte*, Sw. *ofta*, Goth. *ufta*, oft, often; *often* is a later form; akin to *over.*] Often; frequently. (*Poet.*)—**often**, of′n, *adv.* Frequently; many times; not seldom.—*a.* Frequent.—**oftentimes**, of′n·tīmz, *adv.* Frequently; often; many times.—**ofttimes**, oft′tīmz, *adv.* Frequently; often.

ogam, og′am, *n.* See OGHAM.

ogee, ō·jē′, *n.* [Fr. *ogive, augive*; etymology doubtful.] *Arch.* a molding consisting of two members, the one concave, the other convex, the outline thus resembling the letter S (sometimes expressed by O G).

ogham, og′ham, *n.* A kind of writing practiced by the ancient Irish, the characters of which also were called *oghams.*

ogive, ō′jīv, *n.* [Fr. OGEE.] *Arch.* a French term for the Gothic or pointed arch.—**ogival**, ō·jī′val, *a. Arch.* of or pertaining to an ogive or ogee.

ogle, ō′gl, *v.t.*—*ogled, ogling.* [Same as L.G. *oegeln*, to eye, G. *äugeln*, to ogle, from *auge*, D. *oog*, the eye. EYE.] To view with side glances, as in fondness or with a design to attract notice.—*v.i.* To cast side glances.—*n.* A side glance or look.—**ogler**, ō′glẽr, *n.* One that ogles.

ogre, ō′gẽr, *n.* [Fr. *ogre*, from L. *Orcus*, the god of the infernal regions, hell.] A monster of popular legends who lived on human flesh; a person likened to an ogre.—**ogress**, ō′gres, *n.* [Fr. *ogresse.*] A female ogre.—**ogreish**, ō′gẽr·ish, *a.* Resembling or suggestive of an ogre.

oh, ō, *interj.* Expression of surprise.

ohm, ōm, *n.* [From *Ohm*, the propounder of the law known by his name.] The practical unit of electrical resistance, equal to 10^9 absolute electromagnetic units of resistance. The international ohm adopted in 1893 is the resistance of a column of mercury at $0°$ C., of 14.4521 gm. mass, of uniform cross section, and of 106.3 cm. height.—*Ohm's Law*, an important law referring to the causes that tend to impede the action of a voltaic battery.

oil, oil, *n.* [O.Fr. *oile, oille*, from L. *oleum*, oil; akin *olive.*] A substance of animal and vegetable origin, liquid at ordinary temperatures, insoluble in water, and burning with a more or less luminous flame; a substance of somewhat similar character of mineral origin (as petroleum). Oils are divided into *fixed* and *volatile* or *essential oils*, the latter being diffusible in vapor by heat.—*v.t.* To smear or rub over with oil.—*Oiled silk*, silk prepared with oil, etc., so as to be impervious to moisture and air.—*Oiled paper*, paper besmeared with oil so as to render it transparent, used for tracing designs.—**oily**, oi′li, *a.* Consisting of or containing oil; resembling oil; fat; greasy; *fig.* unctuous; sanctimonious; hypocritically pious.—**oiliness**, oi′li·ness, *n.* The quality of being oily; unctuousness.—**oil cake**, *n.* A cake or mass of compressed linseed, rape, or other seed from which oil has been extracted, linseed cake being much used as food for cattle.—**oilcloth**, *n.* Cloth treated with oil or paint, used for shelf covering, etc.—**oil color**, *n.* A pigment made by grinding a coloring substance in oil.—**oiler**, oil′ẽr, *n.* One who oils.—**oil painting**, *n.* The art of painting with oil colors, the highest branch of the painter's art; a picture painted in oil colors.—**oil palm**, *n.* A West African palm whose fruit yields palm oil.—**oilskin**, *n.* Waterproof cloth; prepared linen for making garments to keep out the rain.—**oilstone**, *n.* A fine-grained stone on which tools receive a fine edge by the aid of oil.—**oil well**, *n.* A well sunk into an oil-bearing mineral bed.

ointment, oint′ment, *n.* [From Fr. *oindre*, pp. *oint*, to anoint, from L. *ungere*. UNCTION.] Any soft unctuous substance used for smearing, particularly the body or a diseased part; an unguent.

Ojibwa, Ojibway, o·jib′wā, *n.* [Amer. Ind. *ojibway*, from *ojib, ub-way*, a kind of moccasin.] A member of a large tribe of Algonquin Indians of the Lake Superior area; the tribe itself.

OK, okay, ō·kā′, *n.* [From Democratic *O.K.* Club, supporters of van Buren, from his birthplace Old Kinderhook, N.Y.] Approval; endorsement.—*a.* and *adv.* All right; correct.—*v.t. OK'd, okayed, OK'-ing, okaying.* To approve; to authorize (to *OK* the bill).

okapi, ō·kä′pi, *n.* An African animal akin to the giraffe, but smaller and striped.

oke, ōk, *n.* An Egyptian and Turkish weight equal to about 2 ¾ lb.

okra, ō′kra, *n.* A plant of the mallow family (genus *Abelmoschus*) cultivated as a vegetable in tropical countries.

old, ōld, *a.* [A.Sax. *ald, eald*; D. *oud*, G. *alt*, Goth. *altheis*; cog. with L. *alo*, to nourish, *altus*, lofty.] Advanced far in years or life (an *old* man or tree); not new or fresh; long made or produced (*old* clothes, wine); not modern; ancient; of any duration whatever (a year *old*); former (*old* habits); long practiced; experienced (*old* offender); having the feelings of an old person; crafty or cunning (colloq.); a familiar term of affection or cordiality; worn or used.—*The old country*, an immigrant's country of origin.—*Old glory*, the flag of the United States (colloq.).—*Old Guard*, Napoleon's original bodyguard (1804).—*Old maid*, an unmarried woman no longer young; one manifesting characteristics of an old maid, primness, prudishness, etc.; a simple game of cards.—*Old school*, persons having the character, manner, or opinions of a past age (of the *old school*).—*Old Testament.* See TESTAMENT.—*Old World*, the Eastern Hemisphere, or Europe, Asia, and Africa.—*n.* An ancient or past time (days of *old*).—**olden**, ol′dn, *a.* Ancient.—**old-fashioned**, *a.* Formed according to obsolete fashion or custom; characterized by antiquated fashions or customs.—**oldness**, old′-nes, *n.*—**oldster**, *n.* An older or elderly person.—**old style**, *n. Print.* a type distinguished from modern style by having rather irregular strokes in size and thickness and slanted serifs.—**old-world**, *a.* Belonging to a far bygone age.

oleaginous, ō·li·aj′i·nus, *a.* [L. *oleaginus*, from *oleum*, oil. OIL.] Having the qualities of oil; unctuous; *fig.* (applied to persons, manners, etc.) smoothly sanctimonious; unwholesomely fawning.—**oleaginousness**, ō·li·aj′i·nus·nes, *n.* Oiliness.

oleander, ō·li·an′dẽr, *n.* [Fr. *oléandre*, from L.L. *arodandrum*, by corruption for *rhododendron.*] A beautiful evergreen flowering shrub.

oleaster, ō·li·as′tẽr, *n.* [L., from

olea, the olive tree.] The so-called wild olive, a plant resembling the olive.

olefiant, ō·lē'fi·ant, *a.* [L. *oleum,* oil, and *facio,* to make.] Forming or producing oil.—*Olefiant gas,* a gas obtained from a mixture of sulfuric acid and alcohol forming with chlorine an oily compound.—**oleic,** ō·lē'ik, *a.* Pertaining to or derived from oil.—**olein,** ōl'ē·in, *n.* [L. *oleum,* oil.] One of the chief constituents of animal fat.—**oleograph,** ō'li·o·graf, *n.* A picture produced in oils by a process analogous to that of lithographic printing.

oleomargarine, ō'li·ō·mar"ja·rēn, *n.* [L. *oleum,* and E. *margarin.*] Margarine.

oleoresin, ō'li·ō·rez"in, *n.* [Prefix *oleo,* and *resin.*] A natural combination of an essential oil and a resin, as turpentine.

olfactory, ol·fak'te·ri, *a.* [L. *olfacio, olfactum,* to smell—*oleo,* to smell, and *facio,* to make. ODOR.] Pertaining to smelling; connected with the sense of smelling.—*n.* An organ of smelling (usually pl.).—**olfaction,** ōl·fak'shon, *n.* The sense of smell; the act or process of smelling.

olibanum, o·lib'a·num, *n.* [L.L. *olibanum,* from L. *oleum,* oil, and *libanus,* frankincense.] A kind of incense; frankincense.

oligarchy, ol'i·gär·ki, *n.* [Gr. *oligarchia—oligos,* few, and *archē,* rule.] A form of government in which the supreme power is placed in the hands of a small exclusive class; those who form such a class or body.—**oligarch,** ol'i·gärk, *n.* A member of an oligarchy.—**oligarchic, oligarchical,** ol·i·gär'kik, ol·i·gär'ki·kal, *a.*

Oligocene, ol'ig·o·sēn, *a.* [Gr. *oligos,* little, and *kainos,* recent.] *Geol.* slightly recent; somewhat more recent than *eocene.*

oligoclase, ol'i·gō·klās, *n.* [Gr. *oligos,* small, and *klasis,* a fracture.] A kind of feldspar, occurring in granite, porphyry, and other metamorphic and volcanic rocks.

olio, ō'li·o, *n.* [From Sp. *olla* (pron. *olya*), a dish of meat, from L. *olla,* a pot.] A dish of stewed meat; a mixture; a medley; a miscellany.

olive, ol'iv, *n.* [Fr. *olive,* L. *oliva,* an olive, akin to Gr. *elaia,* an olive; same root as *oleum,* oil.] An evergreen tree much cultivated in Southern Europe, etc., for the valuable oil contained in its berries, formerly sacred to Minerva, furnishing wreaths used by the Greeks and Romans to crown the brows of victors, and still universally regarded as an emblem of peace; the berry or drupe of the olive; the color of the olive, a brownish-green color or one composed of violet and green mixed in nearly equal proportions.—*a.* Relating to the olive; of the color of the olive; brown, tending to a yellowish-green.—**olivaceous,** ol·i·vā'shus, *a.* Of the color of the olive; having the qualities of olives.—**olivary,** ol'i·va·ri, *a.* Resembling an olive.—**olive branch,** *n.* A branch of the olive tree: the emblem of peace; *fig.* a

child.—**olivenite,** ol'iv·en·īt, *n.* A mineral of an olive-green color, containing copper and arsenic. Called also *Olive-ore.*—**olive oil,** *n.* An oil obtained from the fruit of the olive, and much used in cookery and for medicinal and manufacturing purposes.—**olivine,** ol'iv·in, *n.* An olive-green variety of chrysolite.

olla, ol'la, *n.* [Sp. *olla,* a jar or pot, L. *olla.*] A jar or urn.—*Olla podrida,* po·drē'da. [Sp., lit. rotten or putrid pot], a favorite dish in Spain, consisting of a mixture of various kinds of meat stewed with vegetables; hence, a mixture or miscellaneous collection.

Olympiad, ō·lim'pi·ad, *n.* [Gr. *olympias, olympiados,* from *Olympia,* where the Olympic games were held.] A period of four years reckoned from one celebration of the Olympic games to another, by which the ancient Greeks computed time, from 776 B.C.—**Olympian, Olympic,** ō·lim'pi·an, ō·lim'pik, *a.* Pertaining to Olympus or to Olympia in Greece.—*Olympic games,* a great national festival of the ancient Greeks, celebrated at intervals of four years on the plain of Olympia in Peloponnesus; a modern revival (Athens, Greece, 1896) in which athletes of the world meet quadrennially in various countries.

omasum, o·mā'sum, *n.* [L.] The third stomach of ruminating animals: the manyplies.

omber, ombre, om'bėr, *n.* [Fr., from Sp. *hombre,* man, L. *homo.*] An old game at cards, usually played by three persons.

omega, o·mē'ga, o·mā'ga, ō'me·ga, *n.* [Gr. *o,* and *mega,* great, lit. the great or long *o.*] The name of the last letter of the Greek alphabet, hence in Scripture *Omega* denotes the last, the ending.

omelet, om'e·let, *n.* [Fr. *aumelette, omelette.*] Beaten eggs fried, at times with cheese, chopped meat, fruit, etc.

omen, ō'men, *n.* [L. *omen,* older *osmen,* from *os, oris,* the mouth, or connected with *auris,* the ear; hence *abominate.*] A casual event or occurrence thought to portend good or evil; a prognostic; an augury.—*v.i.* To prognosticate as an omen; to augur; to betoken.—*v.t.* To divine; to predict.—**omened,** ō'mend, *a.* Containing an omen or prognostic.—**omening,** ō'men·ing, *n.* An augury; a prognostication.—**ominous,** om'i·nus, *a.* [L. *ominosus.*] Containing an ill omen; foreboding or betokening evil; inauspicious.—**ominously,** om'i·nus·li, *adv.* In an ominous manner; with ill omen.—**ominousness,** om'i·nus·nes, *n.*

omentum, ō·men'tum, *n.* [L.] *Anat.* the caul or epiploön.—**omental,** ō·men'tal, *a.* Relating to the omentum.

omicron, ō·mī'kron, *n.* [Gr. *o mikron, lit.* little *o.*] The short *o,* the 15th letter (*O, o*) of the Greek alphabet.

omit, ō·mit', *v.t.*—**omitted, omitting.** [L. *omitto,* to neglect, disregard, say nothing of—prefix *ob,* and *mitto,* to send. MISSION.] To pass over or neglect; to let slip; to fail to do or

to use; to leave out; not to insert.—**omission,** ō·mish'on, *n.* [L. *omissio.*] The act of omitting; a neglect or failure to do something that should have been done; the act of leaving out; something omitted or left out.—**omissible,** ō·mis'i·bl, *a.* Capable of being omitted.—**omissive,** ō·mis'iv, *a.* Leaving out; neglectful.

omnibus, om'ni·bus, *n.* [L., for all.] A bus; a collection in one volume of an author's works.

omnific, om·nif'ik, *a.* [L. *omnis,* all, and *facio,* to make.] All-creating.

omnipotence, om·nip'o·tens, *n.* [L. *omnipotens,* omnipotent—*omnis,* all, and *potens,* powerful. POTENT.] Unlimited or infinite power; almighty power; an attribute of God; hence sometimes used for God (being then written with a capital).—**omnipotent,** om·nip'o·tent, *a.* Almighty; all-powerful.—*The Omnipotent,* the Almighty.—**omnipotently,** om·nip'o·tent·li, *adv.* In an omnipotent manner.

omnipresence, om·ni·prez'ens, *n.* [L. *omnis,* all, and *praesens,* present.] The faculty or power of being present in every place at the same time, an attribute peculiar to God.—**omnipresent,** om·ni·prez'ent, *a.* Present in all places at the same time; ubiquitous.

omniscience, om·nish'ens, *n.* [L. *omnis,* all, and *scientia,* knowledge. SCIENCE.] The faculty of knowing everything; knowledge unbounded or infinite; an attribute of God.—**omniscient,** om·nish'ent, *a.* Having knowledge of all things; infinitely knowing.—**omnisciently,** om·nish'ent·li, *adv.* In an omniscient manner.

omnium, om'ni·um, *n.* [L., of all (things).] A term used on the Stock Exchange to express the aggregate value of the different stocks in which a loan is funded.—**omnium-gatherum,** om'ni·um·gaTH"er·um, *n.* A miscellaneous collection of things or persons. (*Colloq.*)

omnivorous, om·niv'o·rus, *a.* [L. *omnivorus—omnis,* all, and *voro,* to eat.] All-devouring; eating food of every kind indiscriminately (*omnivorous* animals); having an insatiable appetite for anything (an *omnivorous* reader).

omphalic, om·fal'ik, *a.* [Gr. *omphalos,* the navel.] Pertaining to the navel.

on, on, *prep.* [A.Sax. *on, an,* on, in; D. *aan,* G. *an,* Goth. *ana,* Skr. *anu,* in; akin to *in* and *under.*] Above and so as to touch; not off; performing by means of (to play *on* a harp, a violin); in addition to (loss *on* loss); at or near (*on* the coast); expressing reliance, dependence, basis, etc. (a statement founded *on* error); at or in the time of (we say *on* the day, *at* the hour, *in* the week, month, year); at the time of or during (*on* public occasions); immediately after and as a result (he retired *on* the ratification of the treaty); in reference or relation to (*on* our part); toward or so as to affect (mercy *on* him); denoting a pledge, engagement, or affirmation (*on* my word, *on* his honor); *betting*, in support of the chances of; among the staff of or contributors to: with names of periodicals; pointing to a state, condition, occupation, etc. (*on* fire, *on* duty).—*On a sudden*, suddenly.—*On fire*, in a state of burning; in a passion or eager state.—*On hand*, in present possession (goods *on hand*).—*On high*, in an elevated place.—*On the way*, on the road, proceeding, journeying, or making progress.—*On the wing*, in flight; flying; *fig.* departing.—*adv.* Forward, in progression (move *on*); forward, in succession (and so *on*); without interruption or ceasing (sleep *on*, say *on*); attached to the body (his clothes are not *on*). Also used elliptically as an imperative=go on, advance.—**oncoming**, *a.* Approaching; nearing.—*n.* A coming or drawing near; approach.—**onlooker**, on'lu̇k·ėr, *n.* A looker on; a spectator.—**onrush**, on'rush, *n.* A rush or dash onward; a rapid or violent onset.—**onset**, on'set, *n.* A violent attack; an assault; an assault by an army or body of troops.—**onslaught**, on'slat, *n.* [From *on*, and A.Sax. *sleaht*, a blow, from *slagan*, *sleán*, to strike (to *slay*).] An attack or onset; an assault.

onager, on'a·jėr, *n.* [L., from Gr. *onagros—onos*, ass, and *agrios*, wild.] The wild ass of Central Asia.

once, wuns, *adv.* [O.E. *ones*, *onis*, an adverbial genit. of *one*; comp. *twice* and *thrice*. NONCE.] One time; on one occasion; at a former time.—*At once*, at the same time; immediately.—*n.* Only time; one time (at *once*, this *once*).—*conj.* As soon as; whenever.—**once-over**, *n.* A quick appraisal.

one, wun, *a.* [O.E. *oon*, A.Sax. *án*= D., L.G., and Dan. *een*, Sw. *en*, Icel. *einn*, G. *ein*, Goth. *ains*; cog. L. *unus*, W. *un*, Gael. *aon*, *an*, Armor. *unan*—one. The indefinite article *an*, *a* is the same word; *once* and *only* are derivatives, and *atone*=*at one*.] Being but a single thing or a unit; not two or more; indicating a contrast or opposition to some other thing; closely united; forming a whole; undivided; single in kind. *One* occurs in many compound words of obvious meaning, etc.—*One day*, on a certain or particular day; at an indefinite time, either past or future.—*All one*, just the same; of no consequence; no matter.—*n.* The first of the simple units; the symbol representing this (=1); a particular individual, whether thing or person (in this sense with a plural).—*At one*, in union; in concord or agreement.—*pron.* Any single person; any man, any person (*one* may speak *one's* mind).—*One another*, one or each the other.—**one-horse**, *n.* Drawn by a single horse.—**oneness**, wun'nes, *n.* The state of being one; singleness; unity.—**oneself**, wun·self', *pron.* One's self; himself or herself.—**one-sided**, *a.* Related to, or having

but one side; partial; unjust; unfair.—**onetime**, *a.* Former; past; quondam.—*adv.* Formerly.—**one-track**, *a.* Possessed of only one track, as a railroad, hence, narrow, unchanging.—**one-way**, *a.* Traffic or motion in one direction only.

oneirocritic, o·nī'ro·krit″ik, *n.* [Gr. *oneiron*, a dream, *kritikos*, discerning.] An interpreter of dreams.—**oneirocritical**, o·nī'ro·krit″i·kal, *a.* Having the power of interpreting dreams.—**oneiromancy**, o·nī'ro·man·si, *n.* [Gr. *manteia*, divination.] Divination by dreams.

onerous, on'ėr·us, *a.* [O.Fr. *onereus*, from L. *onerosus*, from *onus*, *oneris*, a load.] Burdensome; troublesome in the performance.—**onerously**, on'-ėr·us·li, *adv.* Oppressively.

onion, un'yun, *n.* [Fr. *oignon*, *ognon*, from L. *unio*, *unionis*, unity, an onion.] A biennial cultivated plant of the lily family, and particularly its bulbous root, much used as an article of food.

onlooker. See ON.

only, ōn'li, *a.* [*One*, with its old pronunciation, and term. *-ly*; A. Sax. *ánlic*.] Single; alone in its class; solitary.—*adv.* For one purpose alone; simply; merely; barely; solely; singly.—*conj.* But; excepting that.

onomatopoeia, on'o·ma·to·pē″a, *n.* [Gr. *onomatopoiia—onoma*, *onomatos*, a name, and *poieō*, to make.] The formation of words by imitation of sounds; the expressing by sound of the thing signified; thus *buzz*, *hum*, *pewit*, *whippoorwill*, etc., are produced by onomatopoeia.—**onomatopoetic**, on'o·ma·to·pō·et″ik, *a.* Pertaining to or formed by onomatopoeia.

onset, onslaught. See ON.

ontogenesis, ontogeny, on·to·jen'e·-sis, on·toj'e·ni, *n.* [Gr. *on*, *ontos*, being, and *genesis*—root *gen*, to produce.] *Biol.* the history of the individual development of an organized being.—**ontogenetic**, on'to·je·net″ik, *a.* Pertaining to ontogenesis.

ontology, on·tol'o·ji, *n.* [Gr. *on*, *ontos*, being, and *logos*, discourse.] The doctrine of being; that part of metaphysics which investigates and explains the nature of all things or existences, treating of whatever does or can exist: sometimes equivalent to *metaphysics*.—**ontological**, on·to·loj'i·kal, *a.* Pertaining to ontology, or the science of being.—**ontologist**, on·tol'o·jist, *n.* One versed in ontology.

onus, ō'nus, *n.* [L.] A burden; often used for *onus probandi*, the burden of proof; the burden of proving what has been alleged.

onward, on'wėrd, *adv.* [*On* and *ward*, denoting direction, similar to *toward*; A.Sax. *onweard*.] Toward the point before or in front; forward; on; in advance.—*a.* Advanced or advancing (an *onward* course); carried so far toward an end; forward; advanced.—**onwards**, on'wėrdz, *adv.* Same as Onward.

onyx, on'iks, *n.* [Gr. *onyx*, the nail; the color of the gem resembles

that of the nail.] A semi-pellucid gem with variously colored zones or veins; an agate with layers of chalcedony, one of which is flesh-colored: used for cameos.

oöcyte, ō'o·sīt, *n.* [Gr. *öon*, an egg, *kytos*, a cell.] *Zool.* an egg before formation of the polar bodies.

oodles, ö'dlz, *n.* pl. (colloq.) A lot; an abundance.

oögonium, ō'o·gōn″i·um, *n.* [Gr. *öon*, an egg, *gonos*, offspring.] In lower plants, the female organ, producing one or more egg cells.

oölite, ō'ol·īt, *n.* [Gr. *öon*, an egg, and *lithos*, stone, from its resemblance to the roes of fish.] *Geol.* a species of limestone composed of globules clustered together, commonly without any visible cement or base; the oölitic formation or system.—**oölitic**, ō·o·lit'ik, *a.* Pertaining to oölite; composed of oölite; resembling oölite.—*Oölitic system*, a series of strata comprehending limestones, calcareous sandstones, marls, shales, and clays which underlie the chalk formation and rest on the Trias; the Jurassic system.

oölogy, ō·ol'o·ji, *n.* [Gr. *öon*, an egg, and *logos*, a treatise.] The branch of knowledge that deals with bird's eggs.—**oölogist**, ō·ol'o·jist, *n.* One versed in oölogy.

oolong, ō'long, *n.* [Cant. pron. of Chin. (Pek.) *wu-lung*, lit. a black dragon.] A tea made from leaves partly oxidized before firing.

oöphyte, ō'o·fīt, *n.* [Gr. *öon*, an egg, *phyton*, a plant.] *Bot.* the GAMETO-PHYTE (which see).

oösperm, ō'o·sperm, *n.* [Gr. *öon*, an egg, *sperma*, seed.] A fertilized ovum; a zygote.

oöspore, ō'o·spōr, *n.* [Gr. *öon*, an egg, and E. *spore*.] *Bot.* a spore that receives impregnation before germination.

oötheca, ō·o·thē'ka, *n.* [Gr. *öon*, an egg, and *théca*, a case.] An eggcase, as that for the eggs of some insects.

ooze, öz, *v.i.*—*oozed, oozing.* [A.Sax. *wös*, juice, liquor, *wáse*, mire, mud; Icel. *vás*, wetness; same root as *water*.] To percolate, as a liquid, through the pores of a substance, or through small openings; to flow in small quantities from the pores of a body: often used figuratively (the secret *oozed* out).—*v.t.* To emit in the shape of moisture.—*n.* Soft mud or slime, as at the bottom of any sheet of water; *tanning*, a solution of tannin; the liquor of a tan-vat.

opacity. See OPAQUE.

opah, ō'pa, *n.* A large and beautiful seafish of the Eastern Seas.

opal, ō'pal, *n.* [L. *opalus*, Gr. *opallios*, an opal; comp. Skr. *upala*, a precious stone.] A precious stone of various colors and varieties, the finest characterized by its iridescent reflection of light, and formerly believed to possess magical virtues.—**opalescence**, ō·pal·es'ens, *n.* A play of colors like that of the opal; the reflection of a milky and iridescent light.—**opalescent**, ō·pal·es'ent, *a.* Resembling opal; having the iridescent tints of opal.—**opaline**, ō'-

pal·ĭn, *a.* Pertaining to or like opal.

opaque, o·pāk′, *a.* [Fr. *opaque,* from L. *opacus,* shady, dark, obscure.] Impervious to the rays of light; not transparent.—*n.* Opacity (*Young*).—**opaquely,** o·pāk′li, *adv.* In an opaque manner.—**opaqueness,** o·pāk′nes, *n.* The quality of being opaque.—**opacity,** o·pas′i·ti, *n.* [L. *opacitas.*] State or quality of being opaque; want of transparency.

ope, ōp, *v.t.* and *i.—oped, oping.* To open: used only in poetry.

open, ō′pn, *a.* [A.Sax. *open,* open=D. *open,* Icel. *opinn,* Dan. *áaben,* G. *offen,* open; akin to *up.*] Not shut; not closed; not covered; not stopped (as a bottle); unsealed (as a letter); free to be used or enjoyed; not restricted; affording free ingress; accessible; public; spread; expanded; not drawn together or contracted (an *open* hand; *open* arms); hence, free, liberal, bounteous; free from dissimulation; candid; not secret or concealed; clear; unobstructed (an *open view;* an *open* country); not frosty; free from frost and snow (an *open* winter); exposed to view; laid bare; exposed or liable to be assailed; fully prepared; attentive; not yet decided (an *open* question); not settled, balanced, or closed (an *open* account); enunciated without closing the mouth, or with a full utterance (an *open* vowel); *mus.* produced without stopping by the finger or without using a slide, key, piston, etc.—*Open verdict,* a verdict upon an inquest finding that a crime has been committed, but without specifying the criminal; or which finds that a sudden or violent death has occurred, but does not decide on the cause.—*n.* An open or clear space.—*The open,* the open country; a place or space clear of obstructions.—*v.t.* [A.Sax. *openian.*] To make open; to unclose; to remove any fastening or obstruction from, so as to afford an entrance, passage, or view of the inner parts; to spread; to expand (the fingers, the arms); to enter upon; to commence (to *open* a negotiation or correspondence); to declare open; to set in operation with some ceremony; to reveal; to disclose (to *open* one's mind).—*To open fire,* to begin to fire or discharge firearms.—*v.i.* To unclose itself; to be unclosed; to be parted; to begin to be seen from a distance; to commence; to begin; to begin to fire, as a battery.—**open and shut,** *a.* Obvious; very simple.—**open door,** *n.* An opportunity for exchange of trade and goods with equal opportunities for all; open or free admission to all.—**opener,** ō′pen·ėr, *n.*—**open-eyed,** *a.* Having the eyes open, hence, watchful; vigilant.—**open-handed,** *a.* Generous; liberal; munificent.—**open-hearted,** *a.* Candid; frank; sincere; not sly.—**openheartedly,** *adv.*—**opening,** ō′pen·ing, *n.* A break or breach in something; a hole or perforation; an aperture; beginning; commencement; a vacancy; an opportunity of

commencing a business or profession; a thinly wooded space without underbrush, as in a forest.—**open letter,** *n.* A communication of protest or appeal addressed to one person but meant for public view.—**openly,** ō′pen·li, *adv.*—**openmouthed,** *a.* Having the mouth open; gaping, as with astonishment.—**open shop,** *n.* An establishment where union and non-union workers are employed without discrimination.—**openwork,** *n.* Ornamental work, with openings through its substance.

opera, op′e·ra, *n.* [It. *opera,* work, from L. *opera,* work.] A musical drama; a dramatic composition set to music and sung and acted on the stage, accompanied with musical instruments; the score or words of a musical drama.—**opera glass,** *n.* A small binocular telescope of low magnifying power, used in theaters, etc.—**opera house,** *n.* A theater for the performance of operas.—**operatic,** op·e·rat′ik, *a.*

operate, op′e·rāt, *v.i.—operated, operating.* [L. *operor, operatum,* to work, from *opus, operis,* a work.] To exert power or strength, physical or mechanical; to work; to act; to have agency; to produce an effect; to issue in a designed result; *med.* to take appropriate effect on the human system; *surg.* to perform some manual act in a methodical manner upon a human body.—*v.t.* To effect; to accomplish; to put into operation; to work; to drive (a machine).—**operant,** op′e·rant, *a.* Having power to produce an effect; operative.—*n.* One who operates; an operator.—**operation,** op·e·rā′shon, *n.* [L. *operatio.*] The act or process of operating; a working or proceeding; process; manipulation; the carrying out of preconcerted measures by regular movements (military or naval *operations*); a surgical proceeding to which the human body is subjected for curative ends.—**operative,** op′e·ra·tiv, *a.* Operating; exerting force; active in the production of effects; efficacious; producing the effect; having to do with manual or other operations.—*n.* A skilled workman; an artisan.—**operator,** op′e·rā·tėr, *n.* One who operates; one who operates a machine (to be an IBM *operator*); one who owns, leases, or manages a mining property; (slang) one who cleverly manages people and situations to his own advantage.

operculum, ō·pėr′kū·lum, *n.* [L., from *operio,* to close or shut.] A little lid or cover; the cover or lid of the spore cases of mosses; the lid of a pitcher-form leaf; a horny or shelly plate serving to close the aperture of the shell of many mollusks when the animal is retracted within it; the bony apparatus which protects the gills of fishes.—**operculated, operculate,** ō·pėr′kū·lā·ted, ō·pėr′kū·lāt, *a.* Pertaining to or having an operculum.

operetta, op·e·ret′ta, *n.* [It. dim. of *opera.*] A short musical drama of a light character.

operose, op′e·rōs, *a.* [L. *operosus,* from *opera,* work. OPERA.] Laborious; attended with labor; tedious.—**operosely,** op′e·rōs·li, *adv.* In an operose manner.—**operoseness,** op′e·rōs·nes, *n.* Laboriousness.

ophidian, ō·fid′i·an, *a.* [Gr. *ophis,* a serpent.] Pertaining to serpents; having the characters of the serpents; serpentine.—*n.* One of an order of reptiles which comprises all the snakes or serpents.

ophiolatry, of·i·ol′a·tri, *n.* [Gr. *ophis, ophios,* a serpent, and *latreia,* worship.] Serpent worship.—**ophiological,** of·i·o·loj″i·kal, *a.* Pertaining to ophiology.—**ophiologist,** of·i·ol′o·jist, *n.* One versed in ophiology.—**ophiology,** of·i·ol′o·ji, *n.* That branch of zoology which treats of serpents; the natural history of serpents.

ophite, of′īt, *n.* [Gr. *ophis,* a serpent.] Green porphyry or serpentine, a metamorphic rock; [*cap.*] also a name for certain Gnostics of the second century, who held that the serpent by which Eve was tempted was Christ, and hence regarded the serpent as sacred.

ophthalmia, of·thal′mi·a, *n.* [Gr.. from *ophthalmos,* the eye, from root *op,* to see, as in *optic.*] Inflammation of the eye or its appendages.—**ophthalmic,** of·thal′mik, *a.* Pertaining to the eye.—**ophthalmitis,** of·thal·mī′tis, *n.* Inflammation of the eye.—**ophthalmology,** of·thal·mol′o·ji, *n.* That branch of science which deals with the eye.—**ophthalmologist,** of·thal·mol′o·jist, *n.* A person versed in ophthalmology.—**ophthalmoscope,** of·thal′mo·skōp, *n.* An instrument for viewing the interior of the eye by means of a mirror.—**ophthalmoscopy,** of·thal·mos′ko·pi, *n.* The art of using the ophthalmoscope.

opiate, ō′pi·āt, *n.* [From *opium.*] Any medicine that contains opium and has the quality of inducing sleep or repose; a narcotic; anything that dulls sensation; mental or physical.—*a.* Inducing sleep; soporific; narcotic.

opine, ō·pīn′, *v.i.* and *t.—opined, opining.* [Fr. *opiner,* from L. *opinor,* to think. OPINION.] To think; to suppose; to be of opinion.

opinion, o·pin′yun, *n.* [L. *opinio, opinionis,* from *opinor,* to think; same root as *opto,* to wish, *optimus,* best. OPTATIVE.] A judgment or belief formed without certain evidence; belief stronger than impression, less strong than positive knowledge; judgment or sentiments on persons or things as regards their character or qualities; settled judgment or persuasion; belief (religious *opinions*).—**opinionated,** o·pin′yun·ā·ted, *a.* Obstinate in opinion; opinionative; conceited.—**opinionative,** o·pin′yun·ā·tiv, *a.* Unduly attached to one's own opinions; dogmatic; obstinate in beliefs.—**opinionatively,** o·pin′yun·ā·tiv·li, *adv.* In an opinionative manner.—**opinionativeness,** o·pin′yun·ā·tiv·nes, *n.*

opium, ō′pium, *n.* [L. *opium,* Gr.

opion, from *opos*, vegetable juice.] A drug derived from dried juice of the unripe seed pod of the poppy; a narcotic or medicinal sedative.—**opium eating**, the practice of taking opium by mouth.—**opium smoking**, the habit of smoking opium.

opodeldoc, op·ō·del′dok, *n*. [Probably an arbitrary name coined by Paracelsus.] A saponaceous camphorated liniment; a solution of soap in alcohol, with the addition of camphor and essential oils.

opossum, o·pos′um, *n*. [From *opassom*, its native American name.] The name of several marsupial mammals of America.

oppidan, op′i·dan, *n*. [L. *oppidanus*, from *oppidum*, a city or town.] An inhabitant of a town‡; at Eton College a student not on the foundation, and who lives in a boarding house.

opponent, op·pō′nent, *a*. [L. *opponens, opponentis*, ppr. of *oppono*, to oppose—*ob*, against, and *pono*, to place. POSITION.] Opposing; antagonistic; opposite.—*n*. One that opposes; an adversary; an antagonist; one that supports the opposite side in controversy, disputation, or argument.

opportune, op·or·tūn′, *a*. [Fr. *opportun*, from L. *opportunis*, lit. offering a port or harbor—prefix *op*, for *ob*, and *portus*, a port, harbor, haven. PORT.] Seasonable; timely; well timed; convenient.—**opportunely**, op·or·tūn′li, *adv*. In an opportune manner.—**opportuneness**, op·or·tūn′nes, *n*. Quality of being opportune or seasonable.—**opportunism**, op·or·tūn′izm, *n*. The practice of seizing or turning opportunities to advantage; a political attitude dispensing with a fixed and moral program, but merely waiting for something to turn up to be utilized for immediate service.—**opportunity**, op·or·tū′ni·ti, *n*. [L. *opportunitas*.] Fit or convenient time or occasion; a time favorable for the purpose; a suitable time, combined with other favorable circumstances.

oppose, op·pōz′, *v.t.*—*opposed, opposing*. [Fr. *opposer*—prefix *op*, and *poser*, to place. POSE, COMPOSE.] To place in front; to set opposite; to place as an obstacle; to put with a view to hinder, defeat, destroy, or prevent effect; to act against; to resist, either by physical or other means; to act as an opponent to; to confront; to check; to withstand; to resist effectually.—*v.i.* To make objections; to act obstructively.—**opposability**, op·pō′za·bil′i·ti, *n*. The capability of being placed so as to act in opposition.—**opposable**, op·pō′za·bl, *a*. Capable of being opposed or resisted; capable of being opposed to something else.—**opposer**, op·pō′zėr, *n*. One that opposes.

opposite, op′pō·zit, *a*. [L. *oppositus*—*ob*, before, and *positus*, placed. POSITION, COMPOSE.] Standing in or situated in front; facing; adverse; opposed; hostile; different in nature or quality; mutually antagonistic; contrary; inconsistent; repugnant; *bot.* growing in pairs; each pair crosswise to that above or below it.—*n*. One who or that which opposes; one who or that which is opposite or adverse.—**oppositely**, op′pō·zit·li, *adv*. In an opposite or adverse manner.—**oppositeness**, op′pō·zit·nes, *n*. The state of being opposite or adverse.—**opposition**, op·pō·zish′on, *n*. [Partly from *oppose*, partly from *opposite*.] Situation so as to front something; a standing over against; the state of being opposed or contrasted; the state of being adverse; the act of opposing; attempt to check, restrain, or defeat resistance; that which opposes; the collective body of opposers; the party in either house of Congress or a state legislature opposed to the administration or the party in power; *astron.* the situation of two heavenly bodies when diametrically opposite to each other, or when their longitudes differ by 180°. Also used adjectively (an *opposition* scheme).

oppress, op·pres′, *v.t.* [Fr. *oppresser*, from L. *oppressus*, from *opprimo*—*ob*, and *premo, pressum*, to press. PRESS.] To load or burden with cruel, unjust, or unreasonable impositions; to treat with unjust severity, rigor, or hardship; to overburden; to overwhelm; to subdue; to sit or lie heavy on (as food in the stomach).—**oppression**, op·presh′on, *n*. The act of oppressing; excessively rigorous government; severity; hardship; calamity; depression; a sense of heaviness or weight in the mind or body.—**oppressive**, op·pres′iv, *a*. Unreasonably burdensome; unjustly severe; given to oppression; tyrannical; overpowering; overwhelming.—**oppressively**, op·pres′iv·li, *adv*. In an oppressive manner.—**oppressiveness**, op·pres′iv·nes, *n*. The quality of being oppressive.—**oppressor**, op·pres′ėr, *n*. One that oppresses or harasses.

opprobrium, op·prō′bri·um, *n*. [L., from *ob*, against, and *probrum*, a shameful or disgraceful act.] Scurrilous or abusive language; contemptuous reproaches; scurrility; disgrace; infamy.—**opprobrious**, op·prō′bri·us, *a*. Containing or expresive of opprobrium; scurrilous; abusive; infamous.—**opprobriously**, op·prō′bri·us·li, *adv*. Scurrilously.—**opprobriousness**, op·prō′bri·us·nes, *n*.

oppugn, op·pūn′, *v.t.* [L. *oppugno*—*ob*, against, and *pugno*, to fight, from *pugnus*, the fist. PUGNACIOUS.] To attack by arguments or the like, not by weapons; to oppose; to resist; to exercise hostile reasoning against.—**oppugnancy**, op·pug′nan·si, *n*. Opposition; resistance; contention.—**oppugnant**, op·pug′nant, *a*. Resisting; opposing; hostile.—**oppugner**, op·pūn′ėr, *n*. One who oppugns.

opsonic, op·son′ik, *a*. [Gr. *opson*, cooked meat.] Having the effect on bacteria of making them easier of consumption by phagocytes.—**opsonin**, op′so·nīn, *n*. The substance in a patient's blood produced by the injection of dead cultures of the bacteria of his disease.

opt, opt, *v.i.* [Fr. *opter*, from L. *optare*, to choose.] To make a choice; to choose.

optative, op′te·tiv, *a*. [L. *optativus*, from *opto*, to desire or wish (as in *adopt, option*); root same as in *opinion, opulence, optimism*.] Expressing desire or wish; *gram.* applied to that mood of the verb in which wish or desire is expressed.—*n.* Gram. the optative mood of a verb.

optic, op′tik, *a*. [Fr. *optique*, from Gr. *optikos*, from root *op*, to see—L. *oculus*, E. *eye*, being from same root.] Relating or pertaining to vision or sight; pertaining to the organ of vision; subservient to vision; relating to the science of optics.—*Optic axis*, the axis of the eye, or a line going through the middle of the pupil and the center of the eye.—*n.* An organ of sight; an eye.—**optic nerve**, the nerve of sight which connects the eye with the optic centers of the brain.—**optical**, op′ti·kal, *a*. Relating to or connected with the science of optics.—**optically**, op′ti·kal·li, *adv*.—**optician**, op·tish′an, *n*. A person skilled in the science of optics; one who makes or sells optic glasses and instruments.—**optics**, op′tiks, *n*. That branch of physical science which treats of the nature and properties of light and vision, optical instruments, etc.—**optigraph**, op′ti·graf, *n*. A telescope used in drawing landscapes.

optimates, op·ti·mā′tez, *n. pl.* [L., aristocrats, from *optimus*, best. OPTIMISM.] The Roman aristocracy; hence, an aristocracy or nobility in general.—**optime**, op′ti·mē, *n*. In the University of Cambridge, a student in the second rank of honors, next to the wranglers.

optimism, op′ti·mizm, *n*. [From L. *optimus*, best. OPTATIVE.] The doctrine that everything in nature is ordered for the best; the tendency always to take the most hopeful view of matters social or political.—**optimist**, op′ti·mist, *n*.—**optimistic**, op·ti·mis′tik, *a*.

optimum, op′ti·mum, *n*. [L. *optimus*, best.] The greatest number or degree; the most favorable of conditions, as for plant growth.

option, op′shon, *n*. [L. *optio*, option, from *opto*, to wish or desire. OPTATIVE.] The power or liberty of choosing; right of choice; the power of deciding on any course of action; choice; election; preference; *stock exchange*, a right to effect a certain transaction or not at a certain date, at the desire of the person bargaining, who pays for the right.—*Local option*, the principle by which the people of a certain locality may decide as to the sale of intoxicating liquors there.—**optional**, op′shon·al, *a*. Left to one's option or choice; depending on choice or preference.—**optionally**, op′shon·al·li, *adv*. In an optional manner; at pleasure.

optometer, op·tom′et·ėr, *n*. [From

opt- of *optic*, and Gr. *metron*, a measure. OPTIC.] An instrument for testing and measuring the visual adjustment of the eye, used to determine the focal lengths of lenses needed to correct defects of vision.

optometry, op·tom′e·tri, *n.* [From Gr. *optikos*, optic, and *metron*, measuring.] Scientific measurement of the range of vision; the fitting of lenses to effect needed adjustments. — **optometrist**, op·tom′e·trist, *n.*

opulence, opulency, op′ū·lens, op′·ū·len·si, *n.* [L. *opulentia*, from *opes*, wealth. OPTATIVE.] Wealth; riches; affluence.—**opulent**, op′ū·lent, *a.* [L. *opulentus.*] Wealthy; rich; affluent; having large means.

opuntia, ō·pun′shi·a, *n.* A kind of cactus largely cultivated in Mexico for raising the cochineal insect.

opus, ō′pus, *n.* [L. *pl.* OPERA.] A work; especially a musical composition.

opuscule, ō·pus′kūl, *n.* [L. *opusculum*, dim. from *opus*, work. OPERATE.] A small work; a little book.

or, or, *conj.* [Contr. from the older *other*, formerly used both for 'either' and 'or', the same word as *either*.] A particle that marks, or seems to mark, an alternative, frequently corresponding to a preceding *either*, and also to *whether*, with which words it is sometimes interchangeable in poetry; it often connects a series of words or propositions, presenting a choice between any two of them (he may study law *or* medicine *or* divinity, *or* he may enter into trade); beginning a sentence it expresses an alternative with the foregoing sentence.

or, or, *n.* [Fr. *or*, L. *aurum*, gold.] *Her.* gold, expressed in engraving by numerous small points or dots.

orach, orache, or′ach, *n.* [Formerly *arrach*, from Fr. *arroche*, orache; origin unknown.] A name of several plants of which a garden species is used like spinach.

oracle, or′a·kl, *n.* [L. *oraculum*, from *oro*, to speak, to pray, from *os*, *oris*, the mouth; akin *oral*, *orifice*, *orator*, *adore*, etc.] The answer of a god or the inspired priest or priestess of a god, to an inquiry made respecting some affair; the deity who gave or was supposed to give answers to inquiries; the place where the answers were given; the sanctuary (O.T.); a divine communication, revelation, or message; any person reputed uncommonly wise, and whose opinions have great weight.—**oracular**, o·rak′ū·lėr, *a.* Pertaining to an oracle or oracles; uttering oracles; resembling the utterance of an oracle; authoritative; sententious; ambiguous, like the ancient oracles.—**oracularly**, o·rak′ū·lėr·li, *adv.* In the manner of an oracle.

oral, ō′ral, *a.* [Fr., from L. *or*, *oris*, the mouth. ORACLE.] Uttered by the mouth or in words; spoken, not written; *zool.* pertaining to the mouth of animals.—**orally**, ō′ral·li, *adv.* In an oral manner; by word

of mouth; verbally.

orange, or′anj, *n.* [Fr. *orange*, It. *arancia*, *arancio*, Sp. *naranja*, from Ar. *nâranj*, an orange, the form of the word being influenced by Fr. *or*, gold.] A tree cultivated abundantly in the south of Europe, the Azores, America, etc., and also its fruit, which is imported into other countries in great quantities.—*a.* Belonging to an orange; colored as an orange.—**orangeade**, or·anj·ād′, *n.* Drink made from orange juice or flavored with orange peel.—**orange pekoe**, *n.* An Indian or Ceylon black tea.—**orangery**, or′an·jėr·i, *n.* [Fr. *orangerie*.] A place where oranges are cultivated; a house for orange trees.

Orangeman, or′anj·man, *n.* [From William III of England, Prince of *Orange*, a place now in France.] A member of a secret society instituted in Ireland in 1795, to uphold Protestant ascendency, and to oppose the Catholic religion and influence.—**Orangeism**, or′anj·izm, *n.* The tenets or principles of the Orangemen.

orangutan, orangoutang, o·rang′·ö·tan, o·rang′ö·tang, *n.* [Malay *orang-utan*, lit. man of the woods.] One of the largest of the anthropoid apes, a native of Sumatra and Borneo.

oration, o·rā′shon, *n.* [L. *oratio*, from *oro*, *oratum*, to pray. ORACLE.] A speech or discourse composed according to the rules of oratory, and spoken in public; a set speech; a formal discourse pronounced on a special occasion.—**orate**, or·āt′, *v.i.* To deliver an oration, with undercurrent idea of pomposity.—**orator**, or′a·tėr, *n.* [L.] A public speaker; one who delivers an oration; one who is skilled as a speaker; an eloquent man.—**oratorical**, or·a·tor′i·kal, *a.* Pertaining to an orator or to oratory; rhetorical.—**oratorically**, or·a·tor′i·kal·li, *adv.* In an oratorical manner.—**oratorio**, or·a·tō′ri·ō, *n.* [It.] A sacred musical composition, consisting of airs, recitatives, duets, trios, choruses, etc., the subject of which is generally taken from Scripture.—**oratory**, or′a·to·ri, *n.* [Partly from *orator*, partly from L. *oratorium*, a place of prayer.] The art of public speaking; the art of an orator; exercise of eloquence; eloquence; a place for prayer; a small apartment for private devotions.—*Priests of the Oratory*, a religious order, the members of which are not bound by any special vow.

orb, orb, *n.* [Fr. *orbe*, from L. *orbis*, a circle, a ring, a disk; seen also in *orbit*, *exorbitant*.] A spherical body; a sphere or globe; also a circular body or disk; *anc. astron.* a hollow globe or sphere forming part of the solar or sidereal system; *arch.* a plain circular boss. BOSS.—*v.i.†* To exhibit or assume the appearance of an orb.—*v.t.* To encircle; to enclose.—**orbed**, orbd, *a.* Having the form of an orb; round; circular. —**orbicular**, or·bik′ū·lėr, *a.* [L. *orbicularis.*] In the form of an orb; spherical; circular.—*Orbicular leaf*,

a circular leaf with the stalk attached to the center of it.—*Orbicular muscles*, muscles with circular fibers surrounding some natural opening of the body.—**orbicularly**, or·bik′ū·lėr·li, *adv.* Spherically; circularly.—**orbiculate, orbiculated**, or·bik′ū·lāt, or·bik′ū·lā·ted, *a.* [L. *orbiculatus.*] In the form of an orb; orbicular.

orbit, or′bit, *n.* [L. *orbita*, a wheel-track, a circuit, from *orbis*, an orb. ORB.] The path of a planet or comet through space; the curved line which a planet describes in its periodical revolution round its central body (the *orbit* of Jupiter or Mercury); *anat.* the bony cavity in which the eye is situated; *ornith.* the skin which surrounds the eye of a bird.—**orbital**, or′bi·tal, *a.* Pertaining to an orbit.—**orbitary**, or′bi·ta·ri, *a.* Connected with or surrounding the orbit (*orbitary* feathers).

orcein, or′sē·in, *n.* The chief ingredient of archil, a purple dyestuff obtained from orcinol (which see).

orchard, or′chėrd, *n.* [A.Sax. *ortgeard, wyrtgeard*, lit. a wort-yard; so Dan. *urtgaard*, Goth. *aurti-gards*, a garden. WORT, YARD.] A garden‡; an enclosure devoted to the culture of fruit growing or nut-bearing trees. —**orchardist**, or′chėrd·ist, *n.* One that cultivates orchards; a fruit grower.

orchestra, or′kes·tra, *n.* [Gr. *orchēstra*, from *orcheomai*, to dance.] The part of a theater appropriated to the musicians; in the Grecian theaters a part of the stage allotted to the chorus; the whole instrumental band performing together in public places of amusement.—**orchestral**, or·kes′tral, *a.* Pertaining to an orchestra.—**orchestration**, or·kes·trā′shon, *n.* The arrangement of music for an orchestra; instrumentation.

orchid, orchis, or′kid, or′kis, *n.* [Gr. *orchis*, a testicle, hence an orchid, from the form of the root.] The name of a family of perennial plants, with tuberous fleshy roots, and beautiful flowers of remarkable form, found almost everywhere and prized by florists; a light reddish-blue color.—**orchidaceous**, or·ki·dā′shus, *a.* Pertaining to the orchids.

orcinol, orcin, or′si·nōl, or′sin, *n.* [Fr. *orcine*, from *orchella*.] A colorless phenol obtained from lichens celebrated as dyeweeds (orchella-weed).

ordain, or·dān′, *v.t.* [O.E. *ordeyne*, *ordeine*, O.Fr. *ordener* (Fr. *ordonner*), from L. *ordino*, to order, from *ordo*, *ordinis*, order. ORDER.] To set in order or arrange‡; to decree, appoint, establish, institute; to set apart for an office; to invest with ministerial or sacerdotal functions.—**ordainer**, or·dā′nėr, *n.* One who ordains.—*Ordainers*, the Committee of Regency, composed of twenty-one members, named by Parliament in 1310, to draw up a scheme for the better management of the realm, in opposition to Edward II and Piers Gaveston.—**ordainment**, or·dān′ment, *n.* The act of ordaining; *eccles.* an appointment to a church.

fāte, fär, fâre, fat, fẹll; mē, met, hėr; pīne, pin; nōte, not, mŏve; tūbe, tub, bụll; oil, pound.

ordeal, or·de′al, *n.* [A.Sax. *ordél, ordál,* decision, ordeal, lit. *out-deal* (like D. *oordeel,* G. *urtheil,* a decision), from A.Sax. prefix *or,* Goth. *us,* out, and verb meaning to *deal.* DEAL.] An ancient form of trial to determine guilt or innocence, as by causing the accused to handle red-hot iron or put the hand into boiling water, escape from injury being considered a proof of innocence; hence, any severe trial or strict test.

order, or′dẽr, *n.* [Fr. *ordre,* from L. *ordo, ordinis,* a row, a regular series, from root *or,* seen in *orient, origin;* connected are *ordain, ordinary, ordinance, extraordinary, subordinate,* etc.] Regular disposition or methodical arrangement; established succession; a proper state or condition; the established usage or settled method; regularity; public tranquillity; absence of confusion or disturbance; a mandate, precept, or authoritative direction; a rule or regulation, oral or written; a direction, demand, or commission to supply goods; a written direction to pay money; a free pass for admission to a theater or other place of entertainment; a rank or class of men; a body of men of the same rank or profession constituting a separate class in the community; a religious fraternity; a body of men having had a common honorary distinction conferred on them; the distinction, rank, or dignity itself (the *order* of the Garter); a large division in the classification of natural objects, as plants or animals; *arch.* a column entire, with a superincumbent entablature, viewed as forming an architectural whole, there being five architectural orders, viz. Doric, Ionic, Tuscan, Corinthian, and Composite.—*Close order,* said of the ranks of soldiers when drawn up at the distance of a pace between each other.—*General orders,* the commands or notices which military headquarters issue on routine matters of general importance. *Holy orders,* the clerical or ecclesiastical character conferred on a person by ordination or consecration to the ministry in the church; often used without the word 'holy' (*to be in orders, to take orders*).—*In order,* for the purpose; with a view; to the end; as means to an end.—*Religious orders,* religious brotherhoods or communities, as monastic, military, and mendicant *orders.*—*Standing orders,* certain general rules and instructions in force until specifically changed, as in a military post or legislative body.—*Order in council,* an order issued by the British sovereign, by and with the advice of the privy-council.—*Order of battle,* the arrangement and disposition of the different parts of an army for the purpose of engaging an enemy.—*Order of the day,* a parliamentary phrase denoting the business regularly set down for consideration on the minutes or votes; *milit.* specific directions issued by a superior officer to the troops under his command.—*v.t.* To put in order; to dispose or arrange; to manage or conduct; to command; to give an order to; to give an order or commission for.—*v.i.* To give command or direction.—

orderliness, or′dẽr·li·nes, *n.* The state or quality of being orderly; regularity.—**orderly**, or′dẽr·li, *a.* In accordance with good order; well ordered; methodical; regular; *milit.* being on duty (an *orderly* officer).—*n.* A private soldier or noncommissioned officer who attends on a superior officer to carry orders or messages.—*adv.* According to due order.

ordinal, or′di·nal, *a.* [L. *ordinalis,* from *ordo, ordinis,* a row. ORDER.] Applied to a number which expresses order or succession (the *ordinal* numbers, *first, second, third,* etc.); *nat. hist.* pertaining to an order.—*n.* A number denoting order (as *first*); a book containing the ordination service.

ordinance, or′di·nans, *n.* [O.Fr. *ordenance* (Fr. *ordonnance*), from *ordener,* to ordain. ORDAIN.] A rule established by authority; a law, edict, decree, or the like; an established rite or ceremony; a law or provision enacted by a municipal government for local application.

ordinary, or′di·ne·ri, *a.* [L. *ordinarius,* from *ordo, ordinis,* order. ORDER.] Established; regular; customary; common; usual; frequent; habitual; met with at any time; hence, somewhat inferior; of little merit.—*Ordinary seaman,* a seaman capable of the common duties, but not considered fit to be rated as an able seaman.—*n.* A person who has ordinary or immediate jurisdiction in matters ecclesiastical; an ecclesiastical judge (usually a bishop); a meal prepared for all comers, as distinguished from one specially ordered; an eating house where there is a fixed price for the meal; one of the common heraldic figures formed with straight lines (as the bend, cross, saltire).—*In ordinary,* in actual and constant service; statedly attending and serving (a physician or chaplain *in ordinary*). An ambassador *in ordinary* is one constantly resident at a foreign court.—*Lord Ordinary,* one of the five judges of the Scottish Court of Session constituting the Outer House.—*A ship in ordinary* is one not in actual service, but laid up under the direction of a competent person.—**ordinarily**, or′di·ne·ri·li, *adv.* In an ordinary manner; usually; generally; in most cases.

ordinate, or′di·nāt, *a.* [L. *ordinatus,* well-ordered. ORDINARY.] Regular; methodical.—*n. Geom.* one of those lines of reference which determine the position of a point; a straight line drawn from a point in the abscissa. The abscissa and ordinate, when spoken of together, are called *coordinates.* See CO-ORDINATE.

ordination, or·di·nā′shon, *n.* [L. *ordinatio,* regulation, from *ordino,* to ordain.] The act of ordaining; the act of settling or establishing; appointment; settled order of things; the act of conferring holy orders.

ordnance, ord′nans, *n.* [Same as *ordinance,* Fr. *ordonnance,* arrangement, equipment; originally it had reference to guns of a particular size or equipment.] Cannon, mortars and howitzers collectively; artillery and small arms, ammunition and supplies, equipment for manufacture and repair of ordnance; equipment and supplies for naval warfare.—*Ordnance Department,* U.S., the department in charge of arsenals and depots and the purchase, manufacture and distribution of ordnance to the army and militia.

Ordovician, or′dō·vish″an, *n.* [L. *Ordovices,* a North Welsh tribe.] A series of strata succeeding the CAMBRIAN (which see).

ordure, or′dūr, *n.* [Fr. *ordure,* from O.Fr. *ord,* at. *ordo,* filthy, from L. *horridus,* horrid.] Dung; excrement; feces.

ore, ōr, *n.* [A.Sax. *âr,* brass, copper= Icel. *eir,* brass, O.G. *êr,* Goth. *aiz,* ore; cog. L. *aes, aeris,* ore, brass; Skr. *ayas,* iron.] A mineral consisting of a metal and some other substance, as oxygen, sulfur, or carbon, in combination, being the source from which metals are usually obtained by smelting (metals found free from such combination being called *native metals*); metal, sometimes gold *(poetical).*

oread, ō′ri·ad, *n.* [Gr. *oreias, oreiados;* from *oros,* mountain.] A mountain nymph.

organ, or′gan, *n.* [L. *organum,* from Gr. *organon,* an instrument, implement, from *ergō,* to work; same root as E. *work.*] An instrument or means; that which performs some office, duty, or function; more commonly, a part of an animal or vegetable by which some function is carried on (as the heart, the eye); a means of communication between one person or body of persons and another; a medium of conveying certain opinions; specifically, a newspaper; the largest and most harmonious of wind instruments of music, consisting of a great number of pipes and with keys similar to those of the piano.—**organic**, or·gan′ik, *a.* [L. *organicus.*] Pertaining to an organ or to organs of animals and plants; pertaining to objects that have organs, hence to the animal and vegetable worlds; exhibiting animal or vegetable life and functions (*organic* bodies, tissues, etc.); forming a whole with a systematic arrangement of parts; organized; systematized.—*Organic chemistry.* CHEMISTRY.—*Organic disease,* a disease in which the structure of an organ is morbidly altered; opposed to *functional disease.* —*Organic laws,* laws directly concerning the fundamental parts of the constitution of a state.—*Organic remains,* those organized bodies, whether animals or vegetables, found in a fossil state.—*Organic selection,* the co-operation of ACCOMMODATION and ADAPTATION (which see) in the production of new species.—**organically**, or·gan′i·kal·li, *adv.* In an organic manner; by or with organs.—

organism, or'gan·izm, *n.* Organic structure; a body exhibiting organization and organic life; member of the animal or the vegetable kingdom.—**organist,** or'gan·ist, *n.* One who plays on the organ.—**organizable,** or·gan·īz'a·bl, *a.* Capable of being organized.—**organization,** or·gan·i·zā"shon, *n.* The act or process of organizing; the act of systematizing or arranging; a whole or aggregate that is organized; organic structure; arrangement of parts or organs for the performance of vital functions.—**organize,** or'gan·īz, *v.t.*—*organized, organizing.* To give an organic structure to; to arrange the several parts of for action or work; to establish and systematize.—**organizer,** or'gan·īz·ėr, *n.* One who organizes, establishes, or systematizes.—**organogenesis,** or·gan·ō·jen"e·sis, *n.* [Gr. *organon,* an organ, and *genesis,* birth.] The development of an organ or of organs in plants or animals.—**organography,** or·gan·og'ra·fi, *n.* A description of the organs of plants or animals.—**organology,** or·gan·ol'o·ji, *n.* The physiology of the different organs of animals or plants.—**organon, organum,** or'ga·non, or'ga·num, *n.* A body of rules and canons for the direction of the scientific faculty. The *Novum Organum* of Bacon is the new, in relation to the old or Aristotelian method or instrument of logical thought.—**organotherapy,** or·gan'ō·thėr"a·pi, *n.* [Gr. *organon,* and *therapeuō,* I heal.] *Med.* the use of animal extracts for curative and other purposes.—**organdy, organdie,** or'gan·di, *n.* [Fr. *organdi.*] A fine muslin, plain or figured.

organzine, or'gan·zin, *n.* [Fr. *organsin,* It. *organzino.*] A silk thread of several threads twisted together; a fabric made of such thread.

orgasm, or'gazm, *n.* [Gr. *orgasmos,* from *orgaō,* to swell.] Extreme excitement or action, especially in coition.—**orgasmic,** or'gaz·mik, *a.*

orgeat, or'zhat, *n.* [Fr., from *orge,* barley.] A preparation extracted from barley and almonds, used to mix in certain drinks, or medicinally as a mild demulcent.

orgy, or'ji, *n.* [Gr. *orgia,* secret rites, from *orgē,* violent passion, anger.] Secret rites or ceremonies connected with the worship of some of the Greek deities, hence, a wild or frantic revel; drunken revelry.—**orgiastic,** or'jē·as"tik, *a.*

oriel, ō'ri·el, *n.* [O.Fr. *oriol,* L.L. *oriolum,* a porch, a hall; origin doubtful.] A large window projecting from a wall, and forming a bay or recess inside; a bay window.

orient, ō'ri·ent, *a.* [L. *oriens,* rising, ppr. of *orior, ortus,* to arise; whence also *origin,* (ab)*ortion;* root also in *order.*] Rising, as the sun or moon; eastern; oriental; bright; shining.—*The Orient,* the East; oriental countries.—*v.t.* [Fr. *orienter.*] *Surv.* to define the position of, in respect to the east or other points of the compass.—**oriental,** o·ri·en'tal, *a.* Eastern; situated in the east; proceeding from the east; applied to gems as a mark of excellence; precious: opposed to *occidental.*—*Oriental region,* southern Asia, together with the western part of the East Indies, the Philippines, and Formosa.—*n.* [*cap.*] A native of some eastern part of the world; an Asiatic.—**orientalism,** ō·ri·en'tal·izm, *n.* An eastern mode of thought or expression; erudition in oriental languages or literature.—**orientalist,** ō·ri·en'tal·ist, *n.* An oriental; one versed in the eastern languages and literature.—**orientalize,** ō·ri·én'tal·īz, *v.t.* To render oriental or conformed to oriental manners.—**orientate,** ō'ri·en·tāt, *v.t.* To cause to assume an easterly direction.—**orientation,** ō'ri·en·tā"shon, *n.* A turning toward the east; position east and west; as applied to churches, such a position as that the chancel shall point to the east; the determining of one's position with reference to new ideas, etc.

orifice, or'i·fis, *n.* [Fr. *orifice,* from L. *orificium—os, oris,* the mouth, and *facio,* to make. ORAL.] The mouth or aperture of a tube, pipe, or other similar object; a perforation; an opening; a vent.

oriflamme, or'i·flam, *n.* [Fr., from L. *aurum,* gold, *flamma,* flame.] The ancient royal standard of France; a piece of red silk fixed on a gilt spear with the anterior edge cut into points.

origami, o·ri·gam'ē, *n.* [Jap.] The Japanese art of folding paper into various shapes.

origin, or'i·jin, *n.* [Fr. *origine,* from L. *origo, originis,* from *orior,* to rise. ORIENT.] The first existence or beginning of anything; the commencement; fountain; source; that from which anything primarily proceeds; of a muscle, the end attached to a relatively fixed part.—**original,** o·rij'i·nal, *a.* [L. *originalis.*] Pertaining or belonging to the origin or early state of something; primitive; pristine; having the power to originate new thoughts or combinations of thought; produced by an author; not copied.—*Original sin, theol.* the first sin of Adam, namely, the eating of the forbidden fruit; hence, either the imputation of Adam's sin to his posterity, or that corruption of nature and tendency to sin inherited from him.—*n.* Origin; source; first copy; archetype; that from which anything is copied; a work not copied from another, but the work of an artist himself; the language in which any work is composed as distinguished from a translation; a person of marked individuality of character; a primary stock or type from which varieties have been developed.—**originality,** o·rij'i·nal"i·ti, *n.* The quality or state of being original; the power of originating new thoughts, or uncommon combinations of thought.—**originally,** o·rij'i·nal·li, *adv.* In an original manner; at the very beginning; from the first.—**originate,** o·rij'i·nāt, *v.t.*—*originated, originating.* To give origin or beginning to; to cause to be; to produce.—*v.i.* To take first existence; to have origin.—**origination,** o·rij'i·nā"shon, *n.* The act or mode of originating; production.—**originative,** o·rij'i·nā·tiv, *a.* Having power to originate.—**originatively,** o·rij'i·nā·tiv·li, *adv.* In an originative manner.—**originator,** o·rij'i·nā·tėr, *n.* A person who originates.

oriole, ō'ri·ōl, *n.* [O.Fr. *oriol,* from L. *aureolus,* dim. of *aureus,* golden, from *aurum,* gold.] Any of the species of the genus *Icterus,* family Icteridae, an American song bird of brilliant color, chiefly orange and black.

Orion, ō·rī'on, *n.* [A celebrated hunter of Greek mythology.] A constellation represented by the figure of a man with a sword by his side, three stars on a line forming his *belt.*

orison, or'i·zon, *n.* [O.Fr. *orison, oreison,* from L. *oratio,* a prayer, from *oro,* to pray. *Oration* is a doublet of this.] A prayer or supplication. (*Poet.*)

orle, orl, *n.* [Fr. *orle,* dim. from L. *ora,* a border.] *Her.* a figure on an escutcheon resembling a smaller escutcheon with the interior cut out; *arch.* a fillet under the ovolo of a capital (also called *orlet*).

orlon, or'lon, *n.* [From the trademark *Orlon.*] An acrylic fiber used in knitted goods; a fabric made of orlon fiber.

orlop, or'lop, *n.* [D. *overloop—over,* over, and *loopen,* to run. OVER, LEAP.] *Naut.* the lowest deck in a ship of war or merchant vessel that has three decks; sometimes a temporary deck.

ormer, or'mėr, *n.* [Fr. *ormier,* L. *auris maris,* ear of the sea.] An edible univalve shellfish.

ormolu, or'mo·lū, *n.* [Fr. *or-moulu—or,* gold, and *moulu,* pp. of *moudre,* L. *molere,* to grind.] A variety of brass containing 25 per cent zinc and 75 per cent copper, made to imitate gold.

ornament, or'na·ment, *n.* [Fr. *orne-ment,* L. *ornamentum,* from *orno, ornatum,* to adorn.] That which embellishes or adorns; something which, added to another thing, renders it more beautiful to the eye; decoration; fair outward show; that which adds beauty to the mind or character.—*v.t.* To adorn; to embellish.—**ornamental,** or·na·men'tal, *a.* Serving to ornament; pertaining to ornament.—**ornamentally,** or·na·men'tal·li, *adv.* In an ornamental manner.—**ornamentation,** or'na·men·tā"shon, *n.* The act of ornamenting; the ornaments or decorations produced.

ornate, or'nāt, *a.* [L. *ornatus,* pp. of *orno,* to adorn. ORNAMENT.] Adorned; decorated; ornamental; richly and artistically finished; much embellished.—**ornately,** or'nāt·li, *adv.* In an ornate manner.—**ornateness,** or'nāt·nes, *n.*

ornery, or'nėr·i, *a.* [Corruption of *ordinary.*] Cross in disposition or temper.—**orneriness,** or'nėr·i·nes, *n.*

ornis, or'nis, *n.* [Gr. *ornis,* a bird.] The birds of a region, or its avifauna.

ornithic, or·nith'ik, *a.* [Gr. *ornis,*

ornithos, a bird.] Of or pertaining to birds.—**ornithological,** or'ni·tho·loj'i·kal, *a*. Pertaining to ornithology.—**ornithologist,** or·ni·thol'o·jist, *n*. A person skilled in ornithology.—**ornithology,** or·ni·thol'o·ji, *n*. That branch of zoology which treats of the form, structure, classification, and habits of birds.—**ornithopter,** or·ni·thop'tẽr, *n*. [Gr. *pteron*, wing.] A form of aircraft deriving its support and propelling force from flapping surfaces.—**ornithorhynchus,** or'ni·thō·ring'kus, *n*. [Gr. *rhynchos*, a beak.] An oviparous mammal of Australia and Tasmania, one of the monotremata, with a body like that of an otter, a horny beak resembling that of a duck, and webbed feet; the duckbill, duck-mole, or water-mole.

orogeny, o·roj'e·ni, *n*. [Gr. *oros*, mountain, and root *gen*. GENUS.] The origin and formation of mountains.

orography, o·rog'ra·fi, *n*. [Gr. *oros*, a mountain, and *graphō*, to describe.] The science which describes or treats of the mountains and mountain systems of the globe; orology.—**orographic, orographical,** or·o·graf'ik, or·o·graf'i·kal, *a*. Relating to orography.

oroide, o'rō·id, *n*. [Fr. *or*, gold, and Gr. *eidos*, resemblance.] An alloy resembling gold in appearance, and used in the manufacture of cheap watchcases, trinkets, etc.—**orology,** o·rol'o·ji, *n*. [Gr. *oros*, a mountain, and *logos*, discourse.] A description of mountains; orography.—**orological,** or·o·loj'i·kal, *a*. Pertaining to orology.—**orologist,** o·rol'o·jist, *n*. A describer of mountains; one versed in orology.

orotund, or'o·tund, *a*. [L. *os, oris*, the mouth, and *rotundus*, round, rotund.] *Rhet.* characterized by fullness, richness, and clearness; rich and musical: applied to the voice or manner of utterance.

orphan, or'fan, *n*. [Gr. *orphanos*, orphaned; allied to L. *orbus*, bereaved.] A child bereft of both parents.—*a*. Being an orphan; bereaved of parents.—*v.t.* To reduce to the state of an orphan; to bereave of parents, children, or friends.—**orphanage,** or'fan·ij, *n*. The state of an orphan; a home or institution for the care of orphans.

orphean, or·fē'an, *a*. Pertaining to *Orpheus*, the legendary poet and musician of ancient Greece; hence melodious.—**orpheon,** or'fe·on, *n*. A kind of musical instrument.—**orphic,** or'fik, *a*. Orphean.

orpiment, or'pi·ment, *n*. [Fr. *orpiment*, from L. *auripigmentum*—*aurum*, gold, and *pigmentum*, a pigment.] A mineral substance, a compound of sulfur and arsenic, of a brilliant yellow color, forming the basis of the yellow paint called *king's-yellow*.—*Red orpiment*, a name of *realgar*.

orpine, or'pīn, *n*. [Fr. *orpin*.] An herb of the stonecrop species, or sedum.

orrery, or'e·ri, *n*. A machine that represents, by the movements of its parts, the motions and phases of the

planets in their orbits, named after an Earl of *Orrery*.

orris, or'is, *n*. [Fr. *or*, gold.] A sort of gold or silver lace; a pattern in which gold and silver lace is worked.

orris, or'is, *n*. [Corruption of *iris*.] A plant from which is obtained orrisroot.—**orrisroot,** *n*. The root of three species of iris which, in its dried state, is used in perfume.

ort, ort, *n*. [L.G. *ort*, O.D. *oorete*, remnants of food; from *or*, as in *ordeal*, and verb to *eat* (D. *eten*).] A scrap of food left; a fragment; a piece of refuse, commonly in the plural.

orthoclase, or'tho·klāz, *n*. [Gr. *orthos*, straight, and *klasis*, fracture.] A kind of feldspar with a straight flat fracture.

orthodontia, or·tho·don'ti·a, *n*. [Gr. *orthos*, straight, and Gr. *odontos*, teeth.] Dentistry dealing with the prevention and correction of irregularities of the teeth.—**orthodontic,** or·tho·don'tik, *a*.

orthodox, or'tho·doks, *a*. [Gr. *orthodoxos*, sound in the faith—*orthos*, right, and *doxa*, opinion (akin *dogma*).] Sound in opinion or doctrine; particularly, sound in religious opinions or doctrines: opposed to *heterodox*; in accordance with sound doctrine; sound; correct (an *orthodox* faith or proceeding).—**orthodoxly,** or'tho·doks·li, *adv*. In an orthodox way; with soundness of faith.—**orthodoxy,** or'tho·dok·si, *n*. [Gr. *orthodoxia*.] Soundness of faith; correctness of opinion or doctrine, especially in religious matters.

orthoëpy, or'thō·e·pi or or·thō'e·pi, *n*. [Gr. *orthoepeia*—*orthos*, right, *epos*, a word.] The art of uttering words with propriety; a correct pronunciation of words.—**orthoëpic,** or·thō·ep'ik, *a*. Pertaining to orthoëpy.—**orthoëpist,** or'thō·ep·ist or or·thō'ep·ist, *n*. One who is skilled in orthoëpy; one who writes on orthoëpy.

orthogamy, or·thog'a·mi, *n*. [Gr. *orthos*, straight, and *gamos*, marriage.] *Bot.* direct or immediate fertilization without the intervention of any mediate agency.

orthogenesis, or'tho·jen"e·sis, *n*. [Gr. *genesis*, origin.] The view of evolution by which all variations follow a defined direction, and are not simply accidental.

orthognathic, orthognathous, or·thŏg·nath'ik, or·thog'na·thus, *a*. [Gr. *orthos*, straight, and *gnathos*, a jaw.] Having jaws that do not protrude; having a skull in which the forehead does not recede and the jaws project. See PROGNATHIC.

orthogonal, or·thog'on·al, *a*. Right-angled.—**orthogonally,** or·thog'on·al·li, *adv*. With or at right angles.

orthography, or·thog'ra·fi, *n*. [Gr. *orthographia*—*orthos*, right, and *graphē*, writing.] The art of writing words with the proper letters; spelling; the part of grammar which treats of letters and spellings.—**orthographer,** or·thog'ra·fẽr, *n*.—**orthographic, orthographical,** or·-

tho·graf'ik, or·tho·graf'i·kal, *a*. Pertaining to orthography.—*Orthographic projection*, a projection used in drawing maps, etc., the eye being supposed to be at an infinite distance from the object.—**orthographically,** or·tho·graf'i·kal·li, *adv*. According to the rules of proper spelling; in the manner of the orthographic projection.

orthopedic, or·tho·pē'dik, *a*. [Gr. *orthos*, straight, and *pais*, a child.] Referring to the remedying of deformities; pertaining to orthopedics.—**orthopedics,** or·tho·pē'diks, *n*. A branch of surgery dealing with the correction or deformities and with the treatment of chronic diseases of the joints and spine.—**orthopedist,** *n*. A surgeon who practices orthopedics.

orthopter, orthopteran, or·thop'tẽr, or·thop'tẽr·an, *n*. [Gr. *orthos*, straight, and *pteron*, a wing.] One of an order of insects which have four wings, the anterior pair being semi-coriaceous or leathery, the posterior pair folding longitudinally like a fan, such as the cockroaches, grasshoppers, and locusts.—**orthopterous,** or·thop'tẽr·us, *a*. Pertaining to the orthopterans.

orthoscopic, or·tho·skop'ik, *a*. [Gr. *orthos*, straight, and *skopeō*, to see.] Pertaining to or giving correct vision.

orthostichy, or·thos'ti·ki, *n*. [Gr. *orthos*, straight, *stichos*, a row.] A vertical row of leaves.

orthotropous, or·thot'ro·pus, *a*. [Gr. *orthos*, straight, and *trepō*, to turn.] *Bot.* having an ovule with the foramen opposite the hilum, or an embryo with radicle next the hilum.

ortolan, or'to·lan, *n*. [It. *ortolano*, from L. *hortulanus*, from *hortus*, a garden; it frequents the hedges of gardens.] A European bird of the bunting family, much esteemed for the delicacy of its flesh; in the United States, the bobolink.

oryx, o'riks, *n*. [L. and Gr.] A name for a species of antelope, a native of the countries on both sides of the Red Sea; also the gemsbok of South Africa.

Osage orange, ō'sāj, *n*. A North American tree of the mulberry family, producing large yellow fruits resembling an orange, but not edible.

Oscan, os'kan, *n*. An ancient Italian language, of which a few fragments remain; allied to the Latin.

oscillate, os'sil·lāt, *v.i.*—oscillated, oscillating. [L. *oscillo, oscillatum*, from *oscillum*, a little face or mask hung to a tree and swaying with the wind, dim. of *os*, the mouth, the face. ORACLE.] To swing; to move backward and forward; to vibrate; to vary or fluctuate between fixed limits.—**oscillation,** os·sil·lā'shon, *n*. [L. *oscillatio*.] The act or state of oscillating or swinging backward and forward; vibration.—**oscillator,** os'sil·lā·tẽr, *n*. One who or that which oscillates.—**oscillatory,** os'sil·la·to·ri, *a*. Moving backward and forward like a pendulum.—**oscillograph,** os·sil'lo·graf, *n*. [Gr. *graphein*, to write.]

An instrument for indicating alternating-current wave forms.

oscitancy, os´si•tan•si, *n.* [L. *oscito,* to yawn, from *os,* the mouth.] The act of gaping or yawning; sleepiness; drowsiness.

osculate, os´kū•lāt, *v.t.*—*osculated, osculating.* [L. *osculor,* to kiss, from *osculum,* a kiss, dim. of *os,* the mouth. ORACLE.] To salute with a kiss; to kiss; *geom.* to touch, as one curve another.—*v.i.* To kiss one another; to kiss; *geom.* to touch at a point, as two curves coming in contact.—**osculation,** os•kū•lā´shon, *n.* The act of osculating; a kissing; specifically, *geom.* the contact between any given curve and another curve.—*Point of osculation,* the point where the osculation takes place, and where the two curves have the same curvature.—**osculatory,** os´kū•la•tō•ri, *a.* Pertaining to osculation or kissing.—**osculum,** os´kū•lum, *n.* pl. **oscula,** os´kū•la. *Lit.* a little mouth; *zool.* one of the large exhalant apertures by which a sponge is perforated; one of the suckers of the tapeworms, etc.

osier, ō´zhi•ėr, *n.* [Fr. *osier,* Fr. dial. *oisis,* Armor. *ozil, aozil,* an osier; comp. Gr. *oisos,* an osier.] The name of various species of willow, chiefly employed in basket making.—*a.* Made of osier or twigs; like osier.

Osiris, ō•sī´ris, *n.* The great Egyptian deity, the husband of Isis, and the personification of all physical and moral good.

osmium, os´mi•um, *n.* [Gr. *osmē,* odor.] A bluish-white metal, very hard, and more infusible than any other metal. Symbol, Os; at. no., 76; at. wt., 190.2.

osmose, os´mōs, *v.t.* [Gr. *ōsmos,* an impulse, a pushing, from *ōtheō,* to push.] *Chem.* to subject to diffusion through a membrane.—**osmosis,** os•mō´sis, *n.* The tendency of two solutions of different concentration, separated by a membrane with very fine pores, to pass through the membrane, mix with each other, and equalize their concentration. (The living cells of plant and animal tissues have such membranes and many of their activities depend upon osmosis.)—**osmotic,** os•mot´ik, *a.* Pertaining to osmosis.—*Osmotic pressure,* pressure exerted on a membrane through which solutions of different density are diffusing, the pressure being in the direction of the less dense solution.—**osmotically,** os•mot´i•ka•li, *adv.*

osmund, os´mund, *n.* [Fr. *osmonde.*] Any fern of the genus *Osmunda;* especially the royal fern.

osprey, os´prā, *n.* [Corrupted from *ossifrage,* L. *ossifraga,* lit. the bonebreaker—*os,* a bone, and *frango,* to break.] A well-known rapacious bird which feeds almost entirely on fish captured by suddenly darting upon them when near the surface.

ossein, os´sē•in, *n.* [From L. *osseus,* bony, from *os, ossis,* a bone; akin Gr. *osteon,* Skr. *asthi,* a bone.] Bone tissue; the soft glue-like substance of bone left after the removal of the earths.—**osseous,** os´si•us, *a.* [L. *os-*

seus.] Bony; resembling bone.—**ossicle,** os´i•kl, *n.* [L. *ossiculum,* dim. from *os,* a bone.] A small bone; some of the small bones of the human skeleton, as those of the internal ear; a small hard structure in starfishes, etc.—**ossification,** os´si•fi•kā´-shon, *n.* The act of ossifying; the change or process of changing into a bony substance.—**ossifrage,** os´si-frāj, *n.* [L. *ossifraga.* OSPREY.] A name formerly given to the osprey or its young.—**ossify,** os´si•fī, *v.t.*—*ossified, ossifying.* [L. *os, ossis,* bone, and *facio,* to form.] To form into bone; to change from a soft animal substance into bone, or a substance of the hardness of bones.—*v.i.* To become bone or bony.—**ossuary,** os´-sū•a•ri, *n.* [L. *ossuarium.*] A charnel house; a place where the bones of the dead are deposited.

osteal, os´ti•al, *a.* [Gr. *osteon,* a bone. OSSEIN.] Consisting of or pertaining to bone.

ostensible, os•ten´si•bl, *a.* [Fr. *ostensible,* from L. *ostendo, ostensum,* to show—*ob,* toward, and *tendo,* to hold out. TEND, TENT.] Put forth as having a certain character, whether worthy of it or not; hence, frequently, apparent and not real; having something of sham or pretense; pretended; professed. ∴ Syn. under COLORABLE.—**ostensibly,** os•ten´si•bli, *adv.* In an ostensible manner; professedly.—**ostensive,** os•ten´siv, *a.* [Fr. *ostensif,* from L. *ostendo,* to show.] Showing; exhibiting.—**ostensively,** os•ten´siv•li, *adv.* In an ostensive manner.—**ostentation,** os•ten•tā´shon, *n.* [L. *ostentatio,* from *ostento,* to show off, to display, intens. of *ostendo.*] Ambitious display; pretentious parade; display dictated by vanity, or to invite praise or flattery.—**ostentatious,** os•ten•tā´-shus, *a.* Characterized by ostentation; showy; intended for vain display.—**ostentatiously,** os•ten•tā´-shus•li, *adv.* In an ostentatious manner.

osteological, os•ti•o•loj´´i•kal, *a.* Pertaining to osteology.—**osteologist,** os•ti•ol´o•jist, *n.* One versed in osteology; one who describes the bones of animals.—**osteology,** os•ti•ol´o•ji, *n.* [Gr. *logos,* discourse.] That branch of anatomy which treats of bones and bone tissue.—**osteopath, osteopathist,** os´ti•o•path, os•ti•op´a•thist, *n.* One who practices osteopathy.—**osteopathy,** os•ti•op´a•thi, *n.* That system of the healing art which places the chief emphasis on the structural integrity of the body mechanism as the most important factor to maintain the organism in health.—**osteoplasty,** os´ti•o•plas•ti, *n.* [Gr. *plassō,* to form.] An operation by which the total or partial loss of a bone is remedied.—**osteotomy,** os•-ti•ot´o•mi, *n.* [Gr. *tomē,* a cutting.] The dissection of bones.

osteomyelitis, os´tē•ō•mī•e•līt´´is, *n.* [Gr. *osteo, oste,* from *osteon,* bone, and Gr. *myelitis,* from *myelos,* marrow, and Gr. suffix, *itis.*] Inflammation of the bone marrow.

ostiole, os´ti•ōl, *n.* [L. *ostiolum,* dim.

of *ostium,* door.] A small orifice or opening, as in certain sacs or cells in plants.—**ostiolar,** *a.* Of or pertaining to an ostiole.

ostler, os´lėr, *n.* [HOSTEL.] Stableman.

ostracism, os´tra•sizm, *n.* [Gr. *ostrakismos,* from *ostrakon,* a shell, a voting tablet.] A political measure among the ancient Athenians by which persons considered dangerous to the state were banished by public vote for a term of years: so called because the votes were given on shells; banishment from society; expulsion.—**ostracize,** os´tra•sīz, *v.t.*—*ostracized, ostracizing.* To exile by ostracism; to banish from society; to exclude from public or private favor.

ostrich, os´trich, *n.* [O.Fr. *ostruche, ostruce,* Fr. *autruche,* from L. *avis,* a bird, and *struthio,* Gr. *struthiōn,* an ostrich.] A large running bird inhabiting the sandy plains of Africa and Arabia, the largest of all existing birds, and whose wing and tail feathers form plumes of great beauty and value; an allied bird of S. America.

Ostrogoth, os´tro•goth, *n.* [L.L. *ostrogothus,* from *ostrus,* eastern (G. *ost,* easti, and *Gothus,* a Goth.] One of the eastern Goths, as distinguished from the Visigoths or western Goths.—**ostrogothic,** os-tro•goth´ik, *a.* Pertaining to the Ostrogoths.

otalgia, ō•tal´ji•a, *n.* [Gr. *ous, ōtos,* the ear, and *algos,* pain.] A pain in the ear; earache.

other, uTH´ėr, *a.* and *pron.* [A.Sax. *óther,*=D. and G. *ander,* Icel. *annar,* Dan. *anden,* Goth. *anthar;* cog. Lith. *antras,* L. *alter,* Skr. *anyatara* (compar. of *anya*)—other; all comparative forms.] Not the same; different; second of two; additional (get *other* knowledge as well); not this; opposite (the *other* side of the street); often used reciprocally with *each,* and applicable to any number of individuals (help *each other*). It is also used substantively, and may take the plural number and the sign of the possessive case, and frequently is opposed to *some, one, I,* or the like (*some* were right, *others* were wrong; the *one* and the *other*).—*The other day,* a day just past; quite recently.—*Every other,* every second (*every other* day, *every other* week).—**otherness,** uTH´ėr•nes, *n.*—**otherwhere,** uTH´ėr•hwâr, *n.* In some other place; elsewhere.—**otherwise,** uTH´ėr•wīz, *adv.* In a different manner; differently; not so; by other causes; in other respects.—**other world,** *n.* Pertaining to a world beyond the actual world.—**otherworldly,** uTH´´er•world´li, *a.* Concerned with a world to come.—**otherworldliness,** uTH´´er•world´´li•nes, *n.*

otic, ō´tik, *a.* [Fr. *otique,* from Gr. *ous, otos,* the ear.] Belonging or relating to the ear.

otiose, ō´shi•ōs, *a.* [L. *otiosus,* from *otium,* leisure.] Idle; unemployed; useless; futile; needless; being at leisure.—**otiosity,** ō•shi•os´i•ti, *n.* The state or quality of being otiose.

otitis, ō·tī′tis, n. [Gr. *ous, ōtos,* the ear, and term. *-itis,* signifying inflammation.] Inflammation of the tympanic cavity of the ear, accompanied with intense pain.—**otocyst,** ō′to·sist, n. [Gr. *kystis,* a bladder.] In animals, a sense organ in the form of a minute sac containing calcareous particles suspended in fluid. Probably concerned with space perception and maintenance of equilibrium.—**otolith,** ō′to·lith, n. [Gr. *lithos,* a stone.] A name of small calcareous bodies contained in the ear cavities of some of the lower animals.—**otology,** ō·tol′o·ji, n. That branch of anatomy which concerns itself with the ear.—**otorrhea,** ō·tor·rē′a, n. [Gr. *rheō,* to flow.] A purulent discharge from the ears.—**otoscope,** ō′to·skōp, n. *Surg.* an instrument for examining the interior of the ear.

ottar, ot′tär, n. See ATTAR.

ottava rima, ot·tä′va rē′ma, n. [It., eighth or octuple rhyme.] An Italian form of versification consisting of eight lines, of which the first six rhyme alternately and the last two form a couplet.

G. *otter,* Dan. *odder,* Icel. *otr*; cog. Lith. *udra,* Rus. and Pol. *wydra,* same root as *water.*] A digitigrade carnivorous mammal of amphibious habits, there being several species; they feed on fish, and their fur is much prized.

otto, ot′tō. See ATTAR.

Ottoman, ot′to·man, a. [From *Othoman* or *Osman,* the sultan who laid the foundation of the Turkish Empire in Asia.] Pertaining to or derived from the Turks.—n. A Turk; [not cap.] a kind of couch or sofa introduced from Turkey; a footstool.

oubliette, ö·bli·et′, n. [Fr., from *oublier,* L. *obliviscor,* to forget. OBLIVION.] A dungeon with an opening only at the top for the admission of air, used for persons condemned to perpetual imprisonment, or to perish secretly, and existing in some old castles or other buildings.

ouch, ouch, n. [For *nouch,* from O.Fr. *nouche, nosche,* O.H.G. *nusca,* a brooch.] The setting of a precious stone (O.T.); a jewel; a brooch.

ouch, ouch, interj. [Echoic.] An exclamation of pain.

ought, at, v. auxil. [Originally the preterite of the verb *to owe,* A.Sax. *ágan,* to possess, but now used indifferently as a present and a past; *I ought, thou oughtest, he ought, we, ye, they ought,* to do or to have done. OWE.] To be held or bound in duty or moral obligation.

ought, at, n. See AUGHT.

ought, at, n. [A corruption of *nought.*] A cipher.

Ouija, wē′ja, n. [Fr. *oui,* yes, and G. *ja,* yes.] A trademark for a board, marked with symbols and the alphabet, used with a smaller board that is moved over it with the fingertips to obtain answers and messages.

ounce, ouns, n. [From L. *uncia,* the twelfth part of anything; whence also *inch.*] A weight, the twelfth part of a pound troy, and the sixteenth of a pound avoirdupois.

ounce, ouns. [Fr. *once,* Sp. *onza,* It. *lonza,* probably from L.L. *luncea,* a lynx.] A carnivorous animal resembling a small panther inhabiting the warmer parts of Asia; a name sometimes given to the American jaguar.

our, our, a. [A.Sax. *úre,* our, contr. for *úser,* our, from *ús,* us=G. *unser,* Goth. *unsar,* our. US.] Pertaining or belonging to us (*our* country; *our* rights). Ours is a later possessive form and is used in place of *our* and a noun (the book is *ours*).—**ourself,** our′self, pron. Myself: used like *we* and *us* in the regal or formal style.—**ourselves,** our′selvz, pl. of *ourself.* We or us, not others: often when used as a nominative added to *we* by way of emphasis or opposition; when in the objective often without emphasis and simply serving as the reflexive pronoun corresponding to *us.*

ourari, ö·rä′ri, n. See CURARI.

ousel, ouzel, ö′zl, n. [A.Sax. *ósle,* an ousel, akin to O.H.G. *amisala,* G. *amsel,* an ousel.] A European blackbird.

oust, oust, v.t. [O.Fr. *ouster,* Mod. Fr. *ôter,* supposed to be from L.L. *hausto, haustare,* to remove, a freq. from L. *haurio,* to draw out (as in *exhaust*).] To eject; to turn out; to dispossess.—**ouster,** ous′tér, n. *Law,* dispossession or ejection.

out, out, adv. [A.Sax., O.Sax., O. Fris., Icel., and Goth. *út,* Sw. *ut,* Dan. *ud,* D. *uit,* G. *aus,* out; seen in *but, about, utter, utmost.*] On or toward the outside; not in or within; without: opposed to *in, into,* or *within*; not indoors; abroad; beyond usual limits (he was *out* when I called); no longer concealed or kept secret; not in a state of obscurity; public (the secret is *out*); finished; exhausted; used up; deficient; having expended (*out* of money; extinguished; no longer burning (the candle or fire is *out*); not in employment; not in office; to an end or settlement (hear me *out*); loudly; in an open and free manner (to laugh *out*); not in the hands of the owner (*out* on loan); in an error; at a loss; in a puzzle; having taken her place as a woman in society (said of a young lady); away from one's own control (parceled *out* the land); in a direction away from the inside or center; from among others (picked *out* a hat); *baseball,* so as to be retired (he struck *out*).—interj. Begone! Away!—*Out* forms a prefix in many words, especially verbs, in which it usually expresses a greater measure or degree in doing something.—n. One who is out; especially one out of office, politically; retiring of an offensive player from the game.—prep. Out through (came *out* the window); outward, along, or on (ride *out* the river road).—a. Situated at a distance; not in power (the *out* group).—v.t. To put out;

to eject.—v.i. To become public (good news will *out*).—**out of,** prep. Proceeding from as source or origin; in consequence of; taken, extracted, or quoted from; from or proceeding from a place or the interior of a place; beyond (*out of* the power of fortune); not in; excluded from (*out of* favor; *out of* use); denoting deviation from what is common, regular, or proper (*out of* order); from, by way of rescue or liberation (to be delivered *out of* afflictions); not within the limits or scope of (*out of* hearing, *out of* sight, *out of* reach); denoting loss or exhaustion (*out of* breath).—*Out-of-door,* a., out of the house; open-air (*out-of-door* exercise).—*Out-of-doors,* adv., out of the house.—*Out of hand,* immediately; without delay.—*Out of print* denotes that a book is not on sale or to be purchased, the copies printed having been all sold.—*Out of sorts,* out of order; unwell.—*Out of temper,* in bad temper; irritated.—*Out-of-the-way,* a., remote from populous districts; secluded; unfrequented; unusual; uncommon.—*Out of trim,* not in good order.—*Out of one's time,* having finished one's apprenticeship.—*Out of tune,* discordant; not harmonious.—**out-and-out,** adv. Completely; thoroughly; without reservation. (Colloq.)—a. Thorough; thoroughgoing; absolute; complete.

outbid, out·bid′, v.t. To bid more than; to go beyond in the offer of a price.—**outboard,** out′bōrd, a. *Naut.* applied to anything that is on the outside of the ship (the *outboard* works, etc.).—**outbrag,** out·brag′, v.t. To surpass in bragging, bravado, or ostentation.—**outbrave,** out·brāv′, v.t. To surpass in braving; to bear down by more daring or insolent conduct.—**outbreak,** out′brāk, n. A breaking out; a bursting forth; a sudden and violent manifestation (as of fever, anger, disease).—**outburst,** out′bérst, n. A breaking or bursting out; an outbreak (an *outburst* of wrath).

outcast, out′kast, n. One who is cast out or expelled; an exile; one driven from home or country.—a. Cast out; thrown away; rejected as useless.—**outcome,** out′kum, n. That which comes out of or results from something; the issue; the result; the consequence.—**outcrop,** out′krop, v.i. *Geol.* to crop out or appear above the surface of the ground: said of strata.—n. *Geol.* the exposure of an inclined stratum at the surface of the ground; the part so exposed; the basset.—**outcry,** out′krī, n. A vehement or loud cry; cry of distress; clamor; noisy opposition; sale at public auction.—v.t. (out·krī′). To surpass or get the better of by crying; to cry louder than.

outdare, out·dâr′, v.t. To dare or venture beyond.—**outdistance,** out·dis′tans, v.t. To excel or leave far behind in any competition or career.—**outdo,** out·dö′, v.t. To excel; to surpass; to perform beyond another.—**outdoor,** out′dōr, a. Being without the house; exterior; in the open air.—**outdoors**, out·dōrz', *adv.* Abroad; out of the house; in the open air.—**outdoor theater**, one situated in the open air without a roof.

outer, out'ér, *a.* [Compar. of *out*.] Being on the outside; farther removed from a person or fixed point. —**outer-directed**,out'ér-di·rek"ted,*a.* Directed by the rules and values of one's society.—**outermost**, out'- ér·mōst, *a.* Being on the extreme external part remotest from the midst; most distant.

outer space, out'ér spās', *n.* The region outside the earth's atmosphere.

outface, out·fās', *v.t.* To brave; to bear down with an imposing front or with effrontery; to stare down.—

outfall, out'fạl, *n.* The mouth of a river; the lower end of a watercourse; the point of discharge for, or the embouchure of a drain, culvert, or sewer.—**outfit**, out'fit, *n.* The act of fitting out for a voyage, journey, or expedition; articles for fitting out; the equipment of one going abroad.—**outfitter**, out'fit·ér, *n.* One who furnishes or makes outfits.—**outflank**, out·flangk', *v.t.* To go or extend beyond the flank or wing of; hence, to outmaneuver; to get the better of.—**outflow**, out'- flō, *n.* The act of flowing out; efflux.—*v.i.* (out·flō'). To flow out.— **outfly**, out·flī', *v.t.* To fly faster than.

outgeneral, out·jen'ér·al, *v.t.* To exceed in generalship; to gain advantage over by superior military skill.—**outgo**, out·gō', *v.t.* To advance before in going; to go faster than; to surpass; to excel.—*n.* (out'gō). That which goes out; specifically, expenditure.—**outgoing**, out'gō·ing, *p.* or *a.* Going out; removing (an *outgoing* tenant).—*n.* The act of going out; outlay; expenditure.—**outgrow**, out·grō', *v.t.* To surpass in growth; to grow too great or too old for.—**outgrowth**, out'grōth, *n.* That which grows out or proceeds from any body; an excrescence; *fig.* that which grows out of a moral cause; a result.

out-Herod, out·her'od, *v.t.* To excel in resembling Herod; to go beyond in any excess of evil or enormity.

outhouse, out'hous, *n.* An outbuilding, especially a privy.

outing, out'ing, *n.* The act of going out; an excursion; an airing.

outlandish, out·land'ish, *a.* [A.Sax. *útlændisc*, foreign, from *ut*, out, and *land*, land.] Belonging to or characteristic of a foreign country; foreign; not native; hence, strange, barbarous; uncouth; bizarre.—**outlast**, out·last', *v.i.* To last longer than; to exceed in duration; to outlive.— **outlaw**, out'lạ, *n.* [From *out* and *law*; A.Sax. *útlag*, *útlaga*.] A fugitive from justice, as a bandit, a murderer, etc.—*v.t.* To declare illegal; to taboo, as to outlaw war; to proscribe a person or a thing.—**outlawry**, out'lạ·ri, *n.* The putting of a person out of the protection of law by legal means, or the process by which a

man is deprived of that protection, being the punishment of a man who, when called into court, contemptuously refuses to appear.—**outlay**, out'lā, *n.* A laying out or expending; that which is laid out or expended; expenditure.—*v.t.* (out·lā'). To lay or spread out; to expose; to display. —**outlet**, out'let, *n.* The place or opening by which anything is let out, escapes, or is discharged; a means of egress; a place of exit; a vent.—*v.t.* To let forth; to emit.—**outlier**, out'li·ér, *n.* A part lying without, or beyond the main body; *geol.* a portion of a rock, stratum, or formation detached, and at some distance from the principal mass.— **outline**, out'līn, *n.* The line by which a figure is defined; the exterior line; contour; a drawing in which an object or scene is represented merely by lines of contour without shading; first general sketch of any scheme or design.—*v.t.* To draw in outline; to delineate.— **outlive**, out·liv', *v.t.* To live beyond; to survive.—**outlook**, out'lok, *n.* A looking out or watching; vigilant watch (to be on the *outlook* for something); the place of watch; what lies before the eye; prospect; survey.—**outlying**, out·lī'ing, *a.* Lying away from the main body or design; remote; being on the exterior or frontier.

outmaneuver, out·ma·nö'vér or out·- ma·nū'vér, *v.t.* To surpass in maneuvering.—**outmarch**, out·märch', *v.t.* To march faster than; to march so as to leave behind.—**outmost**, out'mōst, *a.* [A superlative of *out*.] Farthest outward; most remote from the middle; outermost.

outnumber, out·num'bér, *v.t.* To exceed in number.

outpatient, *n.* A patient not residing in a hospital, but who receives medical advice, etc., from the institution.—**outpost**, out'pōst, *n.* A post or station without the limits of a camp, or at a distance from the main body of an army; the troops placed at such a station.—**outpour**, out·pōr', *v.t.* To pour out; to send forth in a stream; to effuse.—*n.* (out'pōr). An outflow.—**output**, out'- pụt, *n.* The quantity of material put out or produced within a specified time, as coal from a pit or iron from a furnace, etc.

outquarters, out'kwạr·térz, *n. pl.* *Milit.* quarters away from the headquarters.

outrage, out'rāj, *n.* [Fr. *outrage*, O.Fr. *oultrage*, from L.L. *ultragium*, L. *ultra*, beyond. ULTRA.] Rude or injurious violence offered to persons or things; excessive abuse; an act of wanton mischief; an audacious transgression of law or decency.— *v.t.*—*outraged, outraging.* [Fr. *outrager*.] To treat with violence and wrong; to do violence to; to abuse; to maltreat; to commit a rape or indecent assault upon.—**outrageous**, out·rā'jus, *a.* Characterized by outrage; violent; furious; turbulent; excessive; exceeding reason or decency; enormous; atrocious.—**out-**

rageously, out·rā'jus·li, *adv.* In an outrageous manner.—**outrageousness**, out·rā'jus·nes, *n.* The quality of being outrageous.—**outride**, out·- rīd', *v.t.* To pass by riding; to ride faster than.—**outrider**, out'- rī·dér, *n.* A servant on horseback who precedes or accompanies a carriage.—**outrigger**, out'rig·ér, *n.* A structure of spars, etc., rigged out from the side of a sailing boat to steady it; an iron bracket on the outside of a boat, with the rowlock at the extremity; a light boat provided with such apparatus.— **outright**, out·rīt', *adv.* Completely; wholly; altogether (to kill him *outright*.)—**outroot**, out·rōt', *v.t.* To eradicate; to extirpate.—**outrun**, out·- run', *v.t.* To excel in running; to leave behind; to exceed or go beyond.—**outrush**, out·rush', *v.i.* To rush or issue out rapidly or forcibly. —*n.* (out'rush). A gushing or rushing out; an outflow.

outre, ö·trā', ö'trā, *a.* [Fr. pp. of *outrer*, to exaggerate.] Beyond the limits of what is considered correct; bizarre; extravagant.

outsail, out·sāl', *v.t.* To leave behind in sailing.—**outset**, out'set, *n.* A setting out; beginning; start.— **outsettlement**, out'set·l·ment, *n.* A settlement away from the main settlement.—**outsettler**, out'set·lér, *n.* One who settles at a distance from the main body.—**outshine**, out·shīn', *v.t.* To excel in luster or excellence.—*v.i.* To shine out or forth.—**outshoot**, out·shöt', *v.t.* To excel in shooting; to shoot beyond.—**outside**, out'sīd, *n.* The external outer or exposed parts or surface; superficial appearance; external aspect or features; space immediately without or beyond an enclosure; the farthest limit; the utmost; extreme estimate (with *the*). —*a.* Being on the outside; external; superficial.—*Outside broker*, a broker outside of the regular Stock Exchange.—**outsider**, out'sī·dér, *n.* One not belonging to a party, association, or set; unconnected or not admitted. —**outsit**, out·sit', *v.t.* To sit beyond the time of anything; to sit longer than.—**outskirt**, out'skért, *n.* Part near the edge or boundary of an area; border; purlieu. — **outspan**, out·span', *v.t.* and *i.*—*outspanned, outspanning.* [E. *out*, and D. *spannen*, to yoke.] To unyoke (a team of oxen) from a wagon; correlative of *inspan*. (*South Africa*.)—**outspeak**, out·spēk', *v.t.* To exceed in speaking; to say more than.—*v.i.* To speak out or aloud.—**outspoken**, out'spō·- kn, *a.* Free or bold of speech; candid; frank.—**outspokenness**, out·- spō'kn·nes, *n.* The character of being outspoken.—**outspread**, out·- spred', *v.t.* To spread out; to extend. —**outstanding**, out·stand'ing, *a.* Not collected; unpaid; prominent. —**outstare**, out·stâr', *v.t.* To stare out of countenance; to face down; to outface.—**outstay**, out·stā', *v.t.* To stay longer than; to overstay.— **outstretch**, out·strech', *v.t.* To extend; to stretch or spread out;

to expand.—**outstrip**, out·strip′, v.t. To outrun; to advance beyond; to exceed.—**outswear**, out·swâr′, v.t. To exceed in swearing.

outtalk, out·tạk′, v.t. To overpower by talking; to exceed in talking.

outvote, out·vōt′, v.t. To exceed in the number of votes given; to defeat by plurality of votes.

outwalk, out·wạk′, v.t. To walk farther, longer, or faster than; to leave behind in walking.—**outward**, out′wẽrd, a. [A.Sax. úteweard—úte, out, and weard, denoting direction.] Forming the superficial part; exterior; external; visible; appearing; tending to the exterior; derived from without; not properly belonging; adventitious.—adv. Outward; from a port or country.—**outwardly**, out′wẽrd·li, adv. Externally; on the outside; in appearance only.—**outward**, out′wẽrd, adv. Toward the outer parts.—**outwatch**, out·woch′, v.t. To surpass in watching; to watch longer than.—**outwear**, out·wâr′, v.t. To wear out; to last longer than.—**outweigh**, out·wā′, v.t. To exceed in weight or in value, influence, or importance.—**outwit**, out·wit′, v.t.—outwitted, outwitting. To defeat or frustrate by superior ingenuity; to prove too clever for; to overreach.—**outwork**, out′wẽrk, n. Part of a fortification distant from the main fortress or citadel.

ouzel, n. See OUSEL.

ova, ō′va, n. Plural of ovum.

oval, ō′val, a. [Fr. ovale, from L. ovum, an egg; cog. Gr. ōon, an egg.] Of the shape of the outline of an egg; resembling the longitudinal section of an egg; elliptical.—n. A figure in the shape of the outline of an egg; an elliptical figure.—**ovally**, ō′val·li, adv. In an oval form; so as to be oval.

ovary, ō′ve·ri, n. [Mod. L. ovarium, from L. ovum, an egg. OVAL.] The female organ in which ova, reproductive germs or eggs, are formed and developed; bot. a case enclosing ovules or young seeds, and ultimately becoming the fruit.—**ovariotomy**, ō·vã′ri·ot″o·mi, n. The operation for removing a tumor in the ovary or the ovary itself.

ovate, ō′vāt, a. [L. ovatus. OVAL.] Egg-shaped; oval.

ovation, ō·vā′shon, n. [L. ovatio, from ovare, to exult.] A kind of triumph granted to ancient Roman commanders who could not claim the distinction of a full triumph; hence, any triumphal reception of a person or marks of respect publicly shown.

oven, uv′n, n. [A.Sax. ofen=D. oven. Dan. ovn, Icel. ofn.] A closely built recess for baking, heating, or drying a substance.—**ovenbird**, uv′en·bẽrd, n. An American wood warbler (Seiurus aurocapillus) known for the oven-shaped nest it builds on the ground.

over, ō′vẽr, prep. [A.Sax. ofer, D. and Dan. over; Icel. ofr, yfir; G. über; cog. L. super, Gr. hyper, Skr. upari, above.] Above in place or position; rising to or reaching a height above; across

(implying motion); upon the surface of; through the whole extent of; above in eminence or superiority; above in authority; with oversight or watchfulness in respect to (to keep guard over); denoting motive or occasion (to rejoice over); denoting superiority as the result of a struggle or contest; upward of; more than; beyond the comprehension of (talked over their heads); by a certain means of communication (broadcast over the radio).—adv. Above; so as to turn the underside up; from side to side; in width; across; from one side to the other or to another (to roll over); on all the surface; above the top, brim, or edge; more than the quantity assigned; in excess; throughout; completely; having come to an end; past (till this heat be over); excessively; in a great degree.—**overly**, ō′vẽr·li, adv. Overmuch; too; excessively (colloq.)—Over again, once more; with repetition.—Over and above, besides; beyond what is supposed or limited.—Over against, opposite; in front of.—All over, so as to affect the whole surface; complete.—a. Upper; superior; covering; outer (overshoes).—Over forms the first element in many compounds. Of these we can only give the principal.

overact, ō′vẽr·akt′, v.t. To act or perform to excess.—v.i. To act more than is necessary.

overall, ō′vẽr·all′, a. From one end to the other (the overall length of a room); covering or including everything.

overalls, ō′vẽr·alz, n. pl. Loose trousers worn over others to protect them from being soiled.

overanxious, a. Anxious to excess.

overarch, ō·vẽr·ärch′, v.t. and i. To arch over; to cover with an arch.

overawe, ō·vẽr·ạ′, v.t. To restrain by awe, fear, or superior influence.

overbalance, ō·vẽr·bal′ans, v.t. To more than balance; to exceed in weight, value, etc.; to surpass; to destroy the balance or equilibrium of (used refl.).—n. Excess; something more than an equivalent.

overbear, ō·vẽr·bâr′, v.t. To bear down; to overpower; to overcome by argument, effrontery, or the like.—**overbearing**, ō·vẽr·bâr′ing, p. and a. Haughty and dogmatical; given to effrontery.

overblown, ō·vẽr·blōn′, a. Blown to excess; marked by larger size or proportions than is usual.

overboard, ō′vẽr·bōrd, adv. Over the side of a ship; out of a ship or from on board.—Thrown overboard (fig.), discarded; deserted; betrayed.

overbold, ō′vẽr·bōld, a. Unduly bold; forward; impudent.

overbuild, ō·vẽr·bild′, v.t. To build over; to build more than the area properly admits of, or than the population requires.—v.i. To build beyond the demand.

overburden, ō·vẽr·bẽr′dn, v.t. To load with too great weight; to overload.

overcast, ō·vẽr·kast′, v.t. To cloud;

to obscure with clouds; to cover with gloom; to sew by running the thread over a rough edge.—a. Clouded over.

overcharge, ō·vẽr·chärj′, v.t. To charge or burden to excess; to fill too numerously; to make an excessive charge against; to charge at too high a sum or price; to exaggerate.—n. ō′vẽr·chärj. An excessive charge; a charge of more than is just in an account.

overcloud, ō·vẽr·kloud′, v.t. To cover or overspread with clouds.

overcoat, ō′vẽr·kōt, n. A coat worn over all the other dress; a topcoat.

overcome, ō·vẽr·kum′, v.t. To conquer; to vanquish; to surmount; to get the better of.—v.i. To gain the superiority; to be victorious.

overconfidence, ō·vẽr·kon′fi·dens, n. Too great or excessive confidence.—**overconfident**, ō·vẽr·kon′fi·dent, a. Confident to excess.

overcrowd, ō·vẽr·kroud′, v.t. To fill or crowd to excess, especially with human beings.

overdo, ō·vẽr·dö′, v.t. To do to excess; to overact; to surpass or exceed in performance; to boil, roast, or otherwise cook too much.

overdose, ō·vẽr·dōs, n. Too great a dose.—v.t. (ō·vẽr·dōs′). To dose excessively.

overdraw, ō·vẽr·drạ′, v.t. To draw upon for a larger sum than is standing at one's credit in the books of a bank, etc.; to exaggerate either in writing, speech, or a picture.

overdress, ō·vẽr·dres′, v.t. and i. To dress to excess.

overdrive, ō′vẽr·drīv, n. Mach. an automotive transmission gear set to provide driving speed greater than the engine crankshaft speed.

overdue, ō·vẽr·dū, a. Not arrived at the proper date or assigned limit (an overdue ship); past the time of payment (an overdue bill).

overeager, ō·vẽr·ē′gẽr, a. Too eager; too vehement in desire.

overeat, ō·vẽr·ēt′, v.t. To surfeit with eating; used refl. (to overeat oneself).

overestimate, ō·vẽr·es′ti·māt, n. An estimate or calculation that is too high.—v.t. To estimate too high; to overvalue.

overexcitement, ō·vẽr·ek·sīt′ment, n. The state of being overexcited.

overexpose, ō′vẽr·ex·pōs″, v.t. Photog. to subject film too long to light.

overfatigue, ō·vẽr·fa·tēg′, n. Excessive fatigue.—v.t. To fatigue to excess.

overfeed, ō·vẽr·fēd′, v.t. and i. To feed to excess.

overflow, ō·vẽr·flō′, v.t. To run over the brim of; to deluge; to overwhelm.—v.i. To run over the brim or banks; to abound.—n. ō′vẽr·flō. An inundation; a flowing over; superabundance.

overgrow, ō·vẽr·grō′, v.t. To cover with growth or herbage; generally in pp. (a ruin overgrown with ivy).—v.i. To grow beyond the fit or natural size.—**overgrowth**, ō′vẽr·grōth, n. Exuberant or excessive growth.

overhand, ō′vėr·hand, *a.* Made with the hand brought above the shoulder (*overhand* throw); with the hand approaching over the object (*overhand* stroke).—*adv.* In an overhand manner.—*n.* Something done in an overhand manner.

overhang, ō′vėr·hang, *v.t.* To impend over; to be suspended over.—*v.i.* To project far enough to be over something.—*n.* Something that overhangs; the amount of overhang; the part of a roof extending beyond the walls of a building.

overhardy, ō·vėr·här′di, *a.* Excessively or unduly hardy or daring; foolhardy.

overhasty, ō·vėr·hās′ti, *a.* Too hasty; rash; precipitate.

overhaul, ō·vėr·hạl′, *v.t.* To turn over for examination; to examine thoroughly with a view to repairs; to re-examine (as accounts); to gain upon or overtake.—*To overhaul a ship,* to gain upon her in following; to search for contraband goods.—**overhaul, overhauling,** ō′vėr·hạl, ō′vėr·hạl·ing, *n.* Examination; inspection; repair.

overhead, ō·vėr·hed′, *adv.* Aloft; in the zenith; above one's head.—*n.* ō′vėr·hed. Expenses of a business, as rent, office expenses, taxes, depreciation, etc.—*a.* Situated above.

overhear, ō·vėr·hēr′, *v.t.* To hear though not intended or expected to hear.

overissue, ō′vėr·ish·ū, *n.* An excessive issue; an issue (as of coin or bills) in excess of the conditions which should regulate or control it.—*v.t.* To issue in excess, as bank notes or bills of exchange; to issue contrary to prudence or honesty.

overjoy, ō·vėr·joi′, *v.t.* To give great or excessive joy to; generally in *pp.*

overland, ō′vėr·land, *a.* Passing by land; made upon or across the land (an *overland* journey).

overlap, ō·vėr·lap′, *v.t.* To lap or fold over; to extend so as to lie or rest upon.—*n.* The lapping of one thing over another; *geol.* the extension of a superior stratum over an inferior so as to cover and conceal it.

overlay, ō·vėr·lā′, *v.t.*—pret. & pp. *overlaid.* To lay too much upon; to overwhelm; to cover or spread over the surface of; to coat or cover; to smother with close covering, or by lying upon; to obscure by covering.

overleap, ō·vėr·lēp′, *v.t.* To leap over; to pass by leaping; *refl.* to leap too far.

overlie, ō·vėr·lī′, *v.t.* pret. *overlay,* pp. *overlain.* To lie over or upon; to smother by lying on (to *overlie* a child; comp. OVERLAY).

overlive, ō·vėr·liv′, *v.t.* To outlive; to survive.

overload, ō·vėr·lōd′, *v.t.* To load with too heavy a burden or cargo; to overburden.

overlook, ō·vėr·luk′, *v.t.* To view from a higher place; to rise or be elevated above; to see from behind or over the shoulder of another; to inspect or superintend; to pass over indulgently; to omit to censure or punish (a fault); to slight.

overlord, ō′vėr·lord, *n.* One who is lord over another; a feudal superior.

overmaster, ō·vėr·mas′tėr, *v.t.* To overpower; to subdue; to vanquish.

overmatch, ō·vėr·mach′, *v.t.* To be too powerful for.—*n.* One superior in power; one able to overcome.

overmodest, ō·vėr·mod′est, *a.* Modest to excess; bashful.

overmuch, ō′vėr·much, *a.* Too much; exceeding what is necessary or proper.—*adv.* In too great a degree.—*n.* More than sufficient.

overnight, ō′vėr·nīt, *adv.* Through or during the night; in the course of the night or evening; in the evening before.

overpass, ō′vėr·pas, *n.* A section of a highway, etc., crossing over another road, railroad, etc.—*v.t.* (ō·vėr·pas′). To pass over; to cross.

overpay, ō·vėr·pā′, *v.t.* To pay in excess; to reward beyond the price or merit.

overpeople, ō·vėr·pē′pl, *v.t.* To overstock with inhabitants.

overplay, ō·vėr·plā′, *v.t.* To play a part on stage in an exaggerated fashion; to overemphasize; *golf,* to strike a golf ball beyond the putting green.

overplus, ō′vėr·plus, *n.* [*Over,* and L. *plus,* more.] Surplus; that which remains after a supply, or beyond a quantity proposed.

overpower, ō·vėr·pou′ėr, *v.t.* To vanquish by power or force; to subdue; to be too intense or violent for (his emotions *overpowered* him).—**overpowering,** ō·vėr·pou′ėr·ing, *p.* and *a.* Bearing down by superior power; irresistible.—**overpoweringly,** ō·vėr·pou′ėr·ing·li, *adv.* In an overpowering manner.

overprize, ō·vėr·prīz′, *v.t.* To value or prize at too high a rate.

overproduction, ō·vėr·prō·duk′shon, *n.* Production of commodities in excess of demand.

overrate, ō·vėr·rāt′, *v.t.* To rate at too much; to regard as having greater talents, abilities, or more valuable qualities than is really the case.

overreach, ō·vėr·rēch′, *v.t.* To reach beyond; to rise above; to deceive by cunning, artifice, or sagacity; to cheat; to outwit.

overrefinement, ō·vėr·rē·fīn′ment, *n.* Excessive refinement; refinement with excess of subtlety or affectation of nicety.

override, ō·vėr·rīd′, *v.t.* To ride over; hence, to trample down; to supersede; to annul—*To override one's commission,* to discharge one's office in too arbitrary a manner or with too high a hand.

overripe, ō′vėr·rīp, *a.* Ripe or matured to excess.—**overripen,** ō·vėr·rī′pn, *v.t.* To make too ripe.

overrule, ō·vėr·röl′, *v.t.* To influence or control by predominant power; to set aside (objections); *law,* to rule against or reject.

overrun, ō·vėr·run′, *v.t.* To run or spread over; to grow over; to overcome and take possession by an invasion; to outrun.—*v.i.* To run over; to defeat and occupy the conquered area.—*n.* ō′vėr·run. Act of overrunning; *print.* a run in excess of the quantity ordered.

overscrupulous, ō·vėr·skrö′pū·lus, *a.* Scrupulous to excess.

oversea, ō′vėr·sē, *a.* Foreign; from beyond sea.—**overseas,** ō′vėr·sēz, *adv.* Beyond or across the sea; abroad.

oversee, ō·vėr·sē′, *v.t.* To superintend; to overlook; to take charge of.—**overseer,** ō′vėr·sēr, *n.* One who supervises; a superintendent; an officer who has the care or superintendence of any matter.—*Overseers of the poor,* officers in England who are concerned with relief of the poor.

overset, ō·vėr·set′, *n.* An upsetting; an overturn.—*v.t.* To turn from the proper position; to turn upon the side, or to turn bottom upward (as a vehicle); to subvert; to overthrow.—*v.i.* To turn or be turned over.

overshadow, ō·vėr·shad′ō, *v.t.* To throw a shadow over; to shelter or cover with protecting influence.

overshoe, ō′vėr·shö, *n.* A shoe worn over another; an outer waterproof shoe.

overshoot, ō·vėr·shöt′, *v.t.* To shoot beyond (a mark); to venture too far.—**overshot,** ō′vėr·shot, *a.* Having the upper jaw extend beyond the lower.

oversight, ō′vėr·sīt, *n.* A mistake or inadvertence; an overlooking; omission.

oversimplify, ō′vėr·sim″pli·fī, *v.t.* To simplify to the point where meaning is distorted.—*v.i.* To engage in excessive simplification.

oversleep, ō·vėr·slēp′, *v.t.* To sleep beyond or too long.

overspread, ō·vėr·spred′, *v.t.* To spread over; to cover completely; to scatter over.—*v.i.* To be spread or scattered over.

overstate, ō·vėr·stāt′, *v.t.* To exaggerate in statement; to state in too strong terms.—**overstatement,** ō′vėr·stāt·ment, *n.* An exaggerated statement.

overstay, ō·vėr·stā′, *v.t.* To stay too long for; to stay beyond the limits or duration of.

overstep, ō·vėr·step′, *v.t.* To step over or beyond; to exceed.

overstock, ō·vėr·stok′, *v.t.* To stock to too great an extent; to fill too full; to supply with more than is wanted (the market with goods; a farm with cattle).

overstrain, ō·vėr·strān′, *v.i.* and *t.* To strain to excess; to stretch too far; to exert too much.

oversupply, ō′vėr·sup·plī, *n.* An excessive supply; a supply in excess of demand.

overt, ō′vėrt, *a.* [O.Fr. *overt,* Fr. *ouvert,* O.Fr. *ovrir,* to open, from L. *aperire,* to open.] Open to view; public; apparent; *law,* not covert or secret; manifest.—**overtly,** ō′vėrt·li, *adv.* In an overt manner; openly; publicly; in a manifest manner.

---

fāte, fär, fâre, fat, fạll; mē, met, hėr; pīne, pin; nōte, not, mōve; tūbe, tub, bụll; oil, pound.

overtake, ō·vėr·tāk´, v.t. To come up with in following; to follow and reach or catch; to come upon; to take by surprise.

overtask, ō·vėr·task´, v.t. To impose too heavy a task or duty on.

overtax, ō·vėr·taks´, v.t. To tax too heavily.

overthrow, ō·vėr·thrō´, v.t. To overset; to turn upside down; to throw down; to demolish; to defeat, conquer, vanquish; to subvert or destroy.—n. (ō´vėr·thrō). The act of overthrowing; ruin; subversion; defeat.

overtime, ō´vėr·tīm, n. Time during which one works beyond the regular hours.

overtone, ō´vėr·tōn, n. Mus. a higher, less distinct tone which, with the fundamental, makes up a complex musical tone; a secondary effect.

overtop, ō·vėr·top´, v.t. To rise above the top of; to excel; to surpass.

overtrade, ō·vėr·trād´, v.i. To trade beyond capital or too rashly.

overture, ō´vėr·chėr, n. [O.Fr. overture, Fr. ouverture, an opening, an overture. OVERT.] A proposal; something offered for consideration; a musical introduction to precede important compositions, as oratorios, operas, etc., written for a full orchestra.

overturn, ō·vėr·tėrn´, v.t. To overset or overthrow; to turn or throw from a foundation; to subvert; to ruin.—n. (ō´vėr·tėrn). State of being overturned; overthrow.

overvaluation, ō´vėr·val·ū·ā´shon, n. Too high valuation; an overestimate.

overween, ō·vėr·wēn´, v.i. To think too highly, arrogantly, or conceitedly.—**overweening**, ō·vėr·wēn´ing, p. and a. Haughty; arrogant; proud; conceited.—**overweeningly**, ō·vėr·wēn´ing·li, adv.

overweigh, ō·vėr·wā´, v.t. To exceed in weight; to outweigh.

overwhelm, ō·vėr·hwelm´, v.t. To whelm entirely; to swallow up; fig. to bear down; to crush.—**overwhelmingly**, ō·vėr·hwel´ming·li, adv.

overwind, ō·vėr·wīnd´, v.t. To wind too far (to overwind a watch).

overwise, ō´vėr·wīz, a. Wise to affectation.

overwork, ō·vėr·wėrk´, v.t. To work beyond strength; to cause to labor too much; often refl. (to overwork one's self).—n. (ō´vėr·wėrk). Excessive work or labor; work done beyond the amount required by stipulation.

overwrought, ō·vėr·rąt´, p. and a. Labored to excess; worked all over; affected or excited to excess; tasked beyond strength.

overzealous, ō´vėr·zel·us, a. Too zealous; eager to excess.

oviduct, ō´vi·dukt, n. [L. ductus, a duct.] A passage for the ovum or egg from the ovary of animals.—

oviform, ō´vi·form, a. Having the form or figure of an egg.

ovine, ō´vīn, a. [L. ovinus, from ovis, a sheep.] Pertaining to sheep; consisting of sheep.

oviparous, ō·vip´a·rus, a. [L. ovum, an egg, pario, to produce.] Producing eggs, especially eggs that are hatched after exclusion from the body (as opposed to ovoviviparous).

oviposit, ō·vi·poz´it, v.i. [L. ovum, an egg; and E. posit.] To deposit eggs: said of insects.—**oviposition**, ō´vi·po·zish″on, n. The depositing of eggs by insects.—**ovipositor**, ō·vi·poz´it·ėr, n. An organ at the extremity of the abdomen of many insects for depositing their eggs.

ovisac, ō´vi·sak, n. [L. ovum, an egg, saccus, a sack.] The cavity in the ovary which immediately contains the ovum.

ovoid, ō´void, a. [L. ovum, and Gr. eidos, form. OVAL.] Having a shape of an egg.

ovoviviparous, ō´vō·vī·vip″a·rus, a. [L. ovoviviparus—ovo, ovum, and viviparous.] Producing eggs which are hatched within the body (as is the case with vipers). OVIPAROUS.

ovulate, ō´vū·lāt, v.i. [From ovule, L. ovulum, dim. of ovum.] To produce eggs; to discharge eggs from an ovary.—**ovulation**, ō´vū·lā″shon, n.—**ovule**, ō´vūl, n. A small, immature ovum; a small pellucid body borne by the placenta of a plant, and changing into a seed.

ovum, ō´vum, n. pl. **ova**, ō´va. [L.] A small egg within the ovary of a female animal, when impregnated becoming the embryo; an egg.

owe, ō, v.t.—**owed**, **owing**. [From A.Sax. ágan, to own, to have (pret. áhte, whence ought; pp. ágen, whence own); Icel. eiga, Sw. äga, ega, O.H.G. eigan, Goth. aigan, to possess.] To possess or own‡; to be indebted in; to be bound to pay; to be obliged to ascribe; to be obliged for (he owes his safety to me); to be due or owing.—**owing**, ō´ing, ppr. [Pres. part. used in passive sense of owed, being due.] Required by obligation to be paid; remaining as a debt; ascribable, as to a cause; due; imputable, as to an agent.

owl, oul, n. [A.Sax. úle=D. uil, Icel. ugla, Dan. ugle, Sw. uggla, G. eule; names imitative of its cry; comp. L. ululo, to lament, E. howl.] One of the nocturnal birds of prey, well known for their somewhat catlike heads and their harsh and screeching note.—**owlet**, oul´et, n. [Dim. of owl.] An owl; a young owl.—**owlish**, oul´ish, a. Resembling an owl.

own, ōn, a. [A.Sax. ágen, pp. of ágan, to possess, like Dan. and Sw. egen, Icel. eiginn, D. and G. eigen, own. OWE.] Belonging to me, him, us, you, etc., distinctly and emphatically: always following a possessive pronoun, or a noun in the possessive, as my own, his own, John's own: sometimes used to impart tenderness to an expression (thine own true knight). —To hold one's own, to maintain one's own cause; not to lose ground. —v.t. [A.Sax. ágnian (from ágen=own, a.), Icel. eigna, Dan. egne, G. eignen, to own.] To have the right of property in; to hold or possess by right; to acknowledge or avow (owned him as his son); to concede; to admit to be true.—**owner**, ō´nėr, n. One who owns; the rightful proprietor.—**ownership**, ō´nėr·ship, n.

ox, oks, n. pl. **oxen**, ok´sn. [A.Sax. oxa, pl. oxan=Icel. oxi, Sw. and Dan. oxe, D. os, G. ochs, ochse, Goth. auhsa, auhsus, an ox; cog. L. vacca, a cow, Skr. ukshâ, an ox.] The general name for any animal of the cow or bovine kind; especially, a male castrated, and full grown, or nearly so.—**oxbow**, n. A curved piece of wood encircling an ox's neck when yoked; arch. an oval dormer window.—**oxlip**, oks´lip, n. A species of primrose.

oxalate, ok´sa·lāt, n. [Gr. oxalis, sorrel, from oxys, sharp, acid.] Chem. a salt or ester of oxalic acid.

oxalic acid, oks·al´ik as´id, n. A white, crystalline, poisonous solid, obtained from wood sorrel and other plants, used in dyeing, bleaching, etc.

oxeye, oks´ī, n. [Ox and eye.] Any of various plants whose flowers are formed of a disk with marginal rays (oxeye daisy).

oxford, oks´ford, n. [From the city of Oxford, England.] A low shoe laced over the instep.

Oxford clay, oks´ford, n. Geol. a bed of dark-blue clay between the lower and middle oölites, abounding in ammonites and belemnites.—**Oxford movement**, n. The Neo-Catholic movement of Newman, Keble, and Pusey, propagated by the Tracts for the Times.

oxide, ok´sīd, n. [Gr. oxys, acid, sharp.] Chem. a compound of oxygen with another element (thus rust is oxide of iron).—**oxidation**, ok·si·dā´shon, n. The operation or process of converting into an oxide.—**oxidize**, ok´si·dīz, v.t. To convert into an oxide (which see); to change an element or ion from a lower to a higher positive valence.—**oxidizer**, ok´si·dīz·ėr, n. That which oxidizes.—**oxidizable**, ok´si·dī·za·bl, a.

Oxonian, ok·sō´ni·an, n. A native or inhabitant of Oxford; a member or a graduate of the University of Oxford.

oxyacetylene, oks´i·a·set″i·len, a. [From oxy, oxygen, and acetylene.] Pertaining to a mixture of oxygen and acetylene (an oxyacetylene torch).

oxygen, ok´si·jen, n. [Gr. oxys, acid, and root gen, to generate: so named because supposed to be present in all acids.] A colorless, odorless, tasteless gas essential to respiration in most living cells, which constitutes about ⅕ of the atmosphere and supports combustion in air. Symbol, O; at. no., 8; at. wt., 15.9994.—**oxygenate**, ok´si·jen·āt, v.t. To unite or cause to combine with oxygen.—**oxygenation**, ok´si·jen·ā″shon, n.

oxyhemoglobin, oks´i·hē″mo·glō″bin, n. [From oxy, oxygen, and hemoglobin.] The bright red substance created when hemoglobin and oxygen unite loosely in the blood.

oxymoron, ok·si·mō´ron, n. [Gr. oxymóron, a smart saying which at first view appears foolish, from oxys, sharp, and móros, foolish.] Rhet. a figure in which an epithet of a quite contrary signification is added to a word: as cruel kindness; foolish wisdom.

oxytone, ok′si·tōn, *a.* [Gr. *oxys,* sharp, *tonos,* tone.] Having an acute sound; *Greek gram.* having the acute accent on the last syllable.

oyer, ō′yėr, *n.* [Norm. *oyer,* Fr. *ouir,* L. *audire,* to hear.] *Law,* a hearing or trial of causes.—*Court of oyer and terminer* (to hear and determine), a court constituted to hear and determine felonies and misdemeanors. —**oyes, oyez,** ō′yes. ['Hear ye.'] The introduction to a proclamation made by a public crier, in order to secure silence and attention, and repeated three times.

oyster, ois′tèr, *n.* [O.Fr. *oistre,* from L. *ostrea, ostreum,* from Gr. *ostreon,* an oyster, akin to *osteon,* a bone.] A well-known edible mollusk with a shell composed of two irregular valves, living in the sea and adhering to other objects.—**oyster bed,** *n.* A breeding place of oysters; a place where they are artificially or naturally reared.—**oyster catcher,** *n.* A British shore bird which feeds on small Mollusca.

ozocerite, o·zō′se·rīt, *n.* [Gr. *ozō,* to smell, and *kēros,* wax.] A mineral wax or paraffin of a brown or brownish-yellow color, made into candles.

ozone, ō′zōn, *n.* [From Gr. *ozō,* to smell.] A bluish gas (a form of oxygen, O_3) with an odor like chlorine, used as a bleaching agent.

P

P, p, pē, the sixteenth letter of the English alphabet.—*To mind one's P's and Q's,* to be very careful in behavior—a colloquial phrase of unknown origin.

pabular, pab′ū·lėr, *a.* [L. *pabulum,* food, from *pasco,* to feed. PASTOR.] Pertaining to food or pabulum.

pabulum, pab′ū·lum, *n.* [L. *pabulum,* food, from *pasco,* to feed. PASTOR.] Food; aliment; *fig.* food for the mind or intellect.

paca, pä′ka, *n.* [Pg. *paca,* from *pak,* the native name.] A large rodent animal of South America and the West Indies, much esteemed for food.

pace, pās, *n.* [Fr. *pas,* from L. *passus,* a step, from *pateo,* to lie open (whence *patent*), or from *pando, passum,* to stretch out. *Pass* has the same origin.] A step, or the space between the feet in walking (about 2½ feet); sometimes the distance from the place where either foot is taken up to that where the same foot is set down (this being the Roman pace); manner of walking; walk; gait (heavy, quick, or slow *pace*); degree of celerity; rate of progress (events followed at a great *pace*); a mode of stepping among horses.— *To keep* or *hold pace with,* to keep up with; to go or move as fast as: literally or figuratively.—*v.i.*—*paced, pacing.* To step; to walk; to step slowly or with measured tread; to stride.—*v.t.* To measure by steps; to walk over with measured paces.— **paced,** pāst, *p.* and *a.* Having a particular gait (slow-*paced*); trained in paces, as a horse; broken in. —*Thorough-paced* (*lit.* thoroughly trained), perfect in something bad; out-and-out (a *thorough-paced* scoundrel, etc.).—**pacer,** pā′sėr, *n.* One that paces; a horse well-trained in pacing.

pacha, pa·shä′, *n.* [French spelling.] PASHA.

pachymeter, pa·kim′et·ėr, *n.* [Gr. *pachys,* thick, and *metron,* a measure.] An instrument for measuring small thicknesses, as of glass or paper.— **pachyderm,** pak′i·dėrm, *n.* [Gr. *derma,* skin.] A nonruminant hoofed animal; a member of an old mammalian order including the elephant, hippopotamus, horse, hog, etc.— **pachydermatous,** pak·i·dėr′ma·tus, *a.* Belonging to the pachyderms; thickskinned; hence *fig.* not sensitive to ridicule, sarcasm, or the like.

pacify, pas′i·fī, *v.t.*—*pacified, pacifying.* [Fr. *pacifier,* L. *pacificare.*] To appease; to cause to give up anger or excited feeling; to allay the agitation or excitement of; to calm; to restore peace to; to tranquilize.— **pacifiable,** pas·i·fī′a·bl, *a.* Capable of being pacified.—**pacific,** pa·sif′ik, *a.* [L. *pacificus,* from *pacifico,* to make peace—*pax, pacis,* peace, and *facio,* to make. PEACE.] Suited to make or restore peace; conciliatory; appeasing; pacifying; calm, peaceful, tranquil; not warlike (*pacific* disposition).—*Pacific Ocean, Pacific,* the ocean situated between the west coast of America and the shores of Asia and Australia.—**pacifically,** pa·sif′i·kal·li, *adv.* In a pacific manner. —**pacification,** pa·sif′i·kā″shon, *n.* The act of pacifying; state or condition of being pacified; appeasement; reconciliation.—**pacificatory,** pa·sif′i·ka·to·ri, *a.* Tending to make peace; conciliatory.—**pacifier,** pas′i·fī·ėr, *n.* One who pacifies; a device resembling a nipple, for a baby to suck.— **pacifism,** pas′i·fizm, *n.* Opposition to war or the unrestricted use of military force; belief that all international disputes should be settled by arbitration.—**pacifist,** pas′i·fist, *n.* One who favors or supports a policy of pacifism (also used as *a.*).

pack, pak, *n.* [Either from D. *pak,* Dan. *pak, pakke,* G. *pack,* a pack or bundle; or from Armor., Ir., and Gael. *pac,* a pack.] A bundle made up to be carried; a bale; a budget; a collection; a complete set of playing cards; a number of hounds or dogs hunting or kept together; a number of persons united in a bad design or practice (a *pack* of rascals).—*v.t.* To put together for transportation or storage; to make up into a package, bundle, or bale; to stow; to fill methodically with contents (to *pack* a trunk); to assemble or bring together iniquitously and with a view to favor some particular side (to *pack* a jury; to *pack* a meeting); to dismiss without ceremony; to make begone; to make airtight by stuffing, as the piston of an engine; to stuff; to preserve in close vessels (to *pack* meat or fish).—*v.i.* To make up bundles or packs; to put up things for transportation; to depart in haste (with *off* or *away*); to gather together into flocks or bands (the grouse begin to *pack*).—**package,** pak′ij, *n.* A bundle or bale; a packet; a parcel.— *v.t.* To place in a package or packages; to make up into a package or packages (to *package* sugar).— **pack animal,** *n.* A beast of burden used on mountain and wilderness trails for transport of supplies and equipment.—**packer,** pak′ėr, *n.* One who packs; one who owns a meat-packing house; one who works in a meatpacking house.—**packet,** pak′et, *n.* [Fr. *paquet.*] A small pack or package; a little bundle or parcel; a parcel of letters; a vessel employed in carrying mails, goods, and passengers on regular days of starting; also called *packet boat, packet vessel.* —**packing,** pak′ing, *n.* Any material used for filling up empty spaces; stuffing; filling.—**packinghouse,** *n.* An establishment where meats are packed for the market.—**packman,** pak′man, *n.* One who carries a pack; a peddler.—**packsaddle,** *n.* A saddle on which burdens are laid for conveyance by pack animals.—**pack thread,** pak′thred, *n.* Strong thread or twine used in tying up parcels.

pact, pakt, *n.* [Fr. *pacte,* L. *pactum,* a bargain (as in *compact*), from *paciscor, pactus,* to fix, bargain, covenant; same root as *pax,* peace. PEACE.] A contract; an agreement or covenant.

pad, pad, *n.* [Origin uncertain; perhaps akin to *pod.*] A cushion, soft saddle, bolster, part of a garment, etc., stuffed with some soft material; a quantity of blotting paper used for blotting or writing upon (a blotting or writing *pad*).—*v.t.*—*padded, padding.* To stuff so as to make a pad; to furnish with a pad.—**padding,** pad′ing, *n.* The act of stuffing; the materials used for stuffing a saddle, bolster, etc.; literary matter inserted in a book, periodical, etc., merely to increase the bulk.

pad, pad, *n.* [A form of *path;* comp. Prov. E. *pad,* Sc. *paad,* a path.] A robber that infests the road on foot; a footpad; an easy-paced horse.

paddle, pad′l, *v.i.*—*paddled, paddling.* [A freq. and dim. from *pad,* to go = L.G. *paddeln,* to go with short steps, to paddle.] To play in the water with the hands or feet in swimming or sport; to use a paddle; to row with a paddle.—*v.t.* To propel by an oar or paddle.—*n.* A sort of short broad oar used in propelling and steering canoes and boats by a vertical motion; one of the floatboards placed on the circumference of the wheel of a steam vessel; *zool.* the swimming apparatus of the turtles and certain other animals.—**paddle box,** *n.* The wooden covering of the paddle wheel of a steamer.—**paddler,** pad′l·ėr, *n.* One that paddles.—**paddle wheel,** *n.* A wheel with boards or floats on its circumference, driven by steam and propelling a vessel over water.

---

fāte, fär, fâre, fat, fall; mē, met, hėr; pīne, pin; nōte, not, mōve; tūbe, tub, bull; oil, pound.

paddock, pad′ok, n. [A.Sax. pada, a frog or toad (with dim. suffix -ock) =Icel. and Sw. padda, Dan. padde, D. pad, padde, a frog or toad.] A toad or frog.

paddock, pad′ok, n. [For parrok, A.Sax. pearroc. PARK.] A small field enclosed for pasture; ground adjacent to racecourse stables, used for the exercising of horses.

paddy, pad′i, n. [Malay padi.] Rice in the husk whether in the field or gathered; a rice field.

padishah, pä′di·shä, n. [Per. pádishâh, from pâd, protector, master, and shâh, a king.] A title of the Turkish sultan and Persian shah.

padlock, pad′lok, n. [Either from pad, a path, lit. a lock for a gate on a path, or from pad in the local sense of a pannier.] A movable lock with a bow or semicircular link to be fastened through a staple.—v.t. To fasten or provide with a padlock or padlocks.

padre, pä′drā, n. [It. padre, L. pater, father.] A title applied in Latin countries to a minister of religion and by sailors and soldiers to a chaplain.

paduasoy, pad′ū·a·soi, n. [From Padua, in Italy, and Fr. soie, silk.] A particular kind of silk stuff.

paean, pē′an, n. [Gr.] An ancient Greek hymn in honor of Apollo, who was also called Paean; a war song before or after a battle; hence, a song of triumph generally; a loud and joyous song.

paedogenesis, pē′do·jen″e·sis, n. [Gr. pais, paidos, a child, genesis, descent.] In animals, precocious sexual reproduction by immature individuals.

paeon, pē′on, n. [Gr. paeon.] A metrical foot, consisting of four syllables, one long and three short.

pagan, pā′gan, n. [L. paganus, a peasant, from pagus, a village or country district; comp. origin of heathen. Akin peasant.] One who worships false gods; one who is neither a Christian, a Jew, nor a Mohammedan; a heathen; an idolater.—a. Pertaining to pagans or heathens; heathenish; idolatrous.—**paganish**, pā′gan·ish, a. Heathenish. —**paganism**, pā′gan·izm, n. The worship of false gods; the religious opinions and worship of pagans; heathenism.—**paganize**, pā′gan·īz, v.t.—paganized, paganizing. To render heathenish; to convert to heathenism.

page, pāj, n. [Fr. page, It. paggio, a page, from L.L. pagius, perhaps from Gr. padion, or pais, child.] A young male attendant on kings, nobles, or other persons of distinction; a lad in the service of people of rank or wealth, whose duty it is to run errands, attend to the door, etc.—v.t.—paged, paging. To attend as a page.

page, pāj, n. [Fr. page, from L. pagina, a page, from stem pag, seen in L. pango, Gr. pēgnymi, to fix; akin compact (a.), pageant.] One side of the leaf of a book; a writing or record (the page of history); printing, types set up for one side of a leaf.—v.t.

paged, paging. To mark or number the pages of.—**paginal**, paj′i·nal, a. Consisting of pages.—**paginate**, paj′i·nāt, v.t.—paginated, paginating. To number the pages of; to page.— **pagination**, paj·i·nā′shon, n. The act of paging; the marks or figures which indicate the number of pages.

pageant, paj′ent or pā′jent, n. [Old forms pagyn, pagen, originally a scaffold or stage, from L. pagina, a slab, a page (of a book). PAGE.] A spectacle or entertainment; a great display or show, as at some public rejoicing; a theatrical exhibition; anything showy, without stability or duration.—**pageantry**, paj′ent·ri, n. Pageants collectively; a showy exhibition or spectacle; splendid or ostentatious show.

paginal, pagination. See PAGE.

pagoda, pa·gō′da, n. [Fr. pagode, from Per. and Hind, but-gadah—but, an idol, and gadah, a house.] A Hindu temple in which idols are worshiped; a Buddhist temple.

Pagurus, pa·gū′rus, n. [Gr. pagouros —root pag, to fix, and oura, tail.] A genus of crabs which includes the hermit crabs, etc.—**pagurian**, pa·gū′ri·an, n. A crab of this genus or of the same family.

paid, pād, pret. and pp. of pay.

pail, pāl, n. [O.Fr. paile, paele, from L. patella, a pan, from pateo, to lie open. PATENT.] A vessel of wood, or of tin or other metal, in which milk or water is commonly carried.— **pailful**, pāl′ful, n. The quantity that a pail will hold.

paillasse, paj·yas′, n. [Fr., from paille, straw, L. palea, chaff.] An under bed of straw; an under mattress.

pain, pān, n. [Fr. peine, O.Fr. peine, paine, etc., from L. pœna, punishment, and latterly pain, torment; akin penal, penitence, pine (verb), punish, etc.] Penalty; suffering annexed to the commission of a crime (under pain of death); an uneasy sensation in animal bodies; bodily distress; suffering; the throes of travail or childbirth (generally in plural); mental distress; careful labor; close application in working; trouble (chiefly in plural).—v.t. To give pain to; to cause to endure physical or mental suffering; to afflict; to distress.—**painful**, pān′ful, a. Full of pain; giving or accompanied by pain; distressing; requiring labor or toil; difficult; executed with pains; attended with close and careful application or attention.— **painfully**, pān′ful·li, adv. In a painful manner.—**painfulness**, pān′ful·nes, n. The state or quality of being painful.—**painless**, pān′les, a. Free from pain.—**painstaking**, pānz′tā·king, a. Taking or given to taking pains; giving close application; laborious and careful.—n. The taking of pains; careful labor.

paint, pānt, v.t. [O.Fr. paindre, pp. paint (Fr. peindre), from L. pingere, pictum, to paint. PICTURE.] To lay color or colors on with a brush or otherwise; to diversify with hues; to color; to produce (a representation) in colors; to form a likeness or

representation of in colors; to represent or exhibit to the mind; to describe vividly; to delineate; to depict.—v.i. To practice painting; to lay artificial color on the face.—n. A substance used in painting; a pigment; color laid on the face; rouge.—**painter**, pān′tèr, n. One whose occupation is to paint; an artist who represents objects by means of colors or pigments.— Painter's colic, a disease to which painters and others who work with poisonous preparations of lead are liable.—**painting**, pān′ting, n. The act, art, or employment of laying on colors; the art of representing objects by means of figures and colors on a plane surface so as to produce the appearance of relief; a painted picture.

painter, pān′tèr, n. [Ir. painteir, a snare, a net.] A rope used to fasten a boat to a ship or other object.— To cut the painter, to assert one's independence by severing a connection with a person or thing.

pair, pâr, n. [Fr. paire, from L. par, equal, whence also parity, peer, compeer, disparage, etc.] Two things similar in form and suited to each other or used together (a pair of gloves or stockings); a single thing composed of two pieces suiting each other (a pair of scissors or of trousers); two of a sort; a couple; a brace; distinctively, a man and his wife; in parliament, and similar bodies, two members who would vote on opposite sides and agree not to vote for a specified time.—Pair formerly often meant a set of things; hence, we speak of a pair of stairs for a flight of stairs or steps.—v.i. To join in pairs; to couple; to mate (as birds).—To pair, to pair off, to depart from a company in pairs or couples; to form a pair in the parliamentary sense.—v.t. To unite in pairs or couples; to assort in twos.

paisley, pāz′lē, n. [For the town in Scotland.] A woolen fabric patterned in geometric designs of various colors.—a. Of a paisley pattern.

pajamas, pa·jä′mas, n. pl. [Hind.] A loose garment, usually including jacket and trousers, worn for sleeping, lounging, etc. (Seldom used in singular except attributively, as in pajama coat.)

pal, pal, n. [Of Gypsy origin.] Mate; partner; accomplice; chum. (Slang.)

palace, pal′is, n. [Fr. palais, from L. Palatium, the house of Augustus, on the hill at Rome, called by this name.] The house in which an emperor, a king, or other distinguished person resides; a splendid residence; a stately mansion.

paladin, pal′a·din, n. [Fr. paladin, from L. palatinus, attached to the palace, from palatium. PALACE.] A knight attached to a sovereign's court; a knight-errant; a heroic champion; an eminent hero.

palanquin, palankeen, pal·an·kēn′, n. [Fr. and Pg. palanquin, from Pali, pâlangki.] A covered conveyance used in India, China, etc., borne by poles on the shoulder, and carrying a single person; a covered litter.

palate, pal´at, *n.* [L. *palatum,* the palate.] The roof or upper part of the mouth; taste; relish; sometimes intellectual taste.—**palatable,** pal´at‧a‧bl, *a.* Agreeable to the taste or palate; savory.—**palatableness,** pal´at‧a‧bl‧nes, *n.* The quality of being palatable to the taste.—**palatably,** pal´at‧a‧bli, *adv.* In a palatable manner.—**palatal,** pal´at‧al, *a.* Pertaining to the palate; uttered by the aid of the palate, as certain sounds.—*n.* A sound pronounced by the aid of the palate, as that of *ch* in *church,* and that of *j.*—**palatalize,** pal´a‧tal‧īz, *v.t.* To give a palatal sound to; to convert from guttural to palatal (*church* is palatalized compared with *kirk*).

palatial, pa‧lā´shal, *a.* [From L. *palatium,* palace. PALACE.] Pertaining to a palace; becoming a palace; magnificent.—**palatine,** pal´a‧tīn, *a.* [Fr. *palatin,* L. *palatinus,* from *palatium,* palace.] Pertaining to a palace; holding office in the king's palace; possessing royal privileges.—*County palatine* is a county over which an earl, bishop, or duke had a royal jurisdiction.—*n.* One invested with royal privileges and rights; a count palatine.—**palatinate,** pa‧lat´i‧nāt, *n.* The province or seignory of a palatine.

palaver, pa‧lä´vėr, *n.* [Pg. *palavra,* Sp. *palabra,* a word, from L. *parabola,* a parable, in late times a word. PARABLE.] A talk or conference among some barbaric races; a conversation; superfluous or idle talk.—*v.t.* To flatter; to humbug by words.—*v.i.* To talk idly; to indulge in a palaver or palavers.

pale, pāl, *a.* [O.Fr. *pale* (Fr. *pâle*), from L. *pallidus,* pale. PALLID.] White or whitish; wan; not ruddy or fresh of color; not bright; of a faint luster; dim.—*v.t.*—*paled, paling.* To make pale; to diminish the brightness of.—*v.i.* To turn pale.—**paleface,** *n.* A name among the North American Indians for a white person.—**palely,** pāl´li, *adv.* In a pale manner; wanly; not ruddily.—**paleness,** pāl´nes, *n.* The quality or condition of being pale.—**palish,** pāl´ish, *a.* Somewhat pale or wan.—**paly,** pāl´i, *a.* Pale; wanting color. (*Poet.*)

pale, pāl, *n.* [A.Sax. *pal,* Fr. *pal,* from L. *palus,* a stake, from root seen in *page* (of a book), *pageant, pact.*] A pointed stake used in fencing or enclosing, fixed upright in the ground, or joined above and below to a rail; a picket; what surrounds and encloses; the space enclosed; an enclosure; an instrument for trying the quality of a cheese; in *her.* when a shield is divided into halves by a perpendicular line, it is said to be *palewise* or *per pale.*—*The Pale,* that portion of Ireland within which English rule was for some centuries confined after the conquests of Henry II.—*v.t.* To enclose with pales or stakes; to encompass.—**paling,** pāl´ing, *n.* Pales in general, or a fence formed with pales.—**paly,** pāl´i, *n.* The division of a shield into per-

pendicular bars of alternate tinctures and an even number of divisions.

palea, pā´li‧a, *n.* pl. **paleae,** pā´li‧ē. [L. *palea,* chaff.] *Bot.* one of the bracts upon the receptacle of composite plants between the florets; one of the interior bracts of the flowers of grasses.—**paleaceous,** pā‧li‧ā´shus, *a. Bot.* consisting of chaff-like scales; covered with paleae.

Palearctic, pā‧lē‧ärk´tik, *a.* [Gr. *palaios,* ancient, and E. *arctic.*] Said of a region of the earth marked by a characteristic fauna, and embracing Europe, Africa north of the Atlas, and Northern Asia.

paleobotany, pā´li‧ō‧bot″a‧ni, *n.* [Gr. *palaios,* and E. *botany.*] The study of the plants that are found in a fossil state.

paleography, pā´li‧og″ra‧fi, *n.* [Gr. *palaios,* ancient, and *graphō,* to write.] An ancient manner or form of writing; ancient writings collectively; the art of deciphering ancient documents or inscriptions.—**paleographer,** pā‧li‧og´ra‧fėr, *n.*—**paleographic,** pā‧li‧o‧graf´ik, *a.*

paleolithic, pā‧li‧o‧lith´ik, *a.* [Gr. *lithos,* stone.] Of the second period of the Stone Age, characterized by stone implements.

paleontography, pā´li‧on‧tog″ra‧fi, *n.* [Gr. *onta,* beings.] The description of fossil remains.—**paleontographical,** pā‧li‧on´to‧graf″i‧kal, *a.* Relating to paleontography.—**paleontology,** pā´li‧on‧tol″o‧ji, *n.* The science of the ancient life of the earth; that branch of biological science which treats of fossil organic remains.—**paleontological,** pā´li‧on‧to‧loj″i‧kal, *a.* Relating to paleontology.—**paleontologically,** pā´li‧on‧to‧loj″i‧kal‧li, *adv.* In a paleontological sense or point of view.—**paleozoology,** pā´li‧o‧zō‧ol″o‧ji, *n.* [Gr. *zoon,* an animal.] That branch of biology which concerns itself with the fossil remains of animals.

Paleozoic, pā‧li‧o‧zō″ik, *a.* [Gr. *zōē,* life.] A geological era that extends from the beginning of the Cambrian to the end of the Permian.

palestra, pa‧les´tra, *n.* [Gr. *palaistra,* from *palē,* wrestling.] A place appropriated to the exercise of wrestling or other athletic exercises; exercises of wrestling.

paletot, pal´e‧tō, *n.* [Fr. *paletot, paletoque,* a paletot, an overcoat, from D. *paltsrok,* a pilgrim's coat.] A loose sort of man's coat or woman's long jacket; an overcoat.

palette, pal´et, *n.* [Fr. *palette,* from L.L. *paleta,* dim. from L. *pala,* a spade or shovel.] A thin oval board or tablet, with a thumb hole at one end, on which a painter lays the pigments with which he paints his pictures; a pallet.—**palette knife,** *n.* A sort of knife used by painters for mixing colors, and by druggists to mix salves.

palfrey, pal´fri, *n.* [O.Fr. *palefrei,* from L.L. *parafredus,* L. *paraveredus,* an extra post horse, from Gr. *para,* beside, and L. *veredus,* a post horse (from *veho,* to carry, and *rheda,* a carriage).] An ordinary riding horse, or a horse used by noblemen and

others for state, distinguished from a war horse; a small horse fit for ladies.

Pali, pä´li, *n.* The sacred language of the Buddhists, a descendant of the Sanskrit, now used only in religious works.

palimpsest, pa´limp‧sest, *n.* [Gr. *palimpsestos,* rubbed again—*palin,* again, and *psaō,* to rub.] A parchment or other piece of writing material from which one writing has been erased to make room for another, often leaving the first faintly visible, a process to which many ancient manuscripts were subjected.

palindrome, pal´in‧drōm, *n.* [Gr. *palindromos,* running back—*palin,* again, and *dromos,* a running.] A word, verse, or sentence that is the same when read backward or forward.

paling. See PALE.

palingenesis, pal‧in‧jen´e‧sis, *n.* [Gr. *palin,* again, and *genesis,* birth.] A transformation from one state to another; a metamorphosis as of insects; a great geological change on the earth.

palinode, pal´i‧nōd, *n.* [Gr. *palinōdia*—*palin,* again, and *ōdē,* a song.] Originally a poetical recantation; a piece in which a poet retracts the invectives contained in a former piece; hence, a recantation in general.

palisade, pal‧i‧sād´, *n.* [Fr. *palissade,* from *palisser,* to pale, from *palis,* a pale. PALE (a stake).] A fence or fortification consisting of a row of strong stakes or posts set firmly in the ground; also applied to one of the stakes; a mass of rock, as the denuded face of a mountain.

palish. See PALE.

pall, pal, *n.* [A.Sax. *paell,* from L. *pallium,* a cloak, a pall.] An outer mantle of dignity; *eccles.* a vestment sent from Rome to patriarchs, primates, and metropolitans as an ensign of jurisdiction, and sometimes, as a mark of honor, to bishops; consisting of a band made of white lamb's wool, passing round the shoulders, and having a strip hanging down before and behind; a large black cloth thrown over a coffin at a funeral, or over a tomb; rich cloth of any kind, 'in purple and pall'.—*v.t.* To cover with a pall; to cover or invest; to shroud.—**pallbearer,** *n.* One of those who attend the coffin at a funeral.

pall, pal, *v.i.* [W. *pallu,* to fail; *pall,* loss of energy, failure; the verb *appal* was probably to some extent affected by this word.] To become vapid; to become insipid; to become devoid of agreeableness or attraction (pleasures begin to *pall*).—*v.t.* To make vapid or insipid; to cloy; to dispirit or depress‡.

Palladian, pal‧lā´di‧an, *a.* Pertaining to Andrea *Palladio,* a celebrated Italian architect (1518-80).—*Palladian architecture,* a species of Italian architecture founded upon the Roman antique.

Palladium, pal‧lā´di‧um, *n.* [From Pallas or Athene, equivalent to the Latin *Minerva.*] A sacred statue or image of *Pallas*, the Greek goddess, on the preservation of which, according to ancient legend, was said to have depended the safety of Troy.

palladium, pal·lā'di·um, *n*. [N.L., from the asteroid *Pallas*, from Gr. *Pallas*, the goddess.] *Chem.* a silver-white, malleable and ductile, metallic element of the platinum group. Symbol, Pd; at. no., 46; at. wt. 106.4.

pallet, pal'et, *n*. [Fr. *palette*, from L.L. *paletta*, dim. from L. *pala*, a spade or shovel.] A palette; a wooden instrument used by potters, etc., for forming and rounding their wares; an instrument to take up and apply goldleaf; pieces which receive the impulse from a pendulum or balance wheel.

pallet, pal'et, *n*. [From Fr. *paille*, straw; L. *palea*, chaff.] A small or rude bed; a bed or mattress of straw.

palliate, pal'i·āt, *v.t.*—*palliated*, *palliating*. [Fr. *pallier*, to cloak, palliate; from L. *pallium*, a cloak, whence also *pall* (n.).] To conceal the enormity of by excuses and apologies; to extenuate; to soften or tone down by favorable representations; to mitigate, lessen, or abate (to *palliate* a disease).—**palliation**, pal·i·ā'shon, *n*. The act of palliating; what palliates or serves to excuse; extenuation; mitigating; alleviation.—**palliative**, pal'i·ā·tiv, *a*. [Fr. *palliatif*.] Serving to palliate or extenuate; extenuating; mitigating.—*n*. That which palliates.

pallid, pal'id, *a*. [L. *pallidus*, from *palleo*, to become pale. PALE, FALLOW.] Pale; wan; deficient in color; not high colored.—**pallidly**, pal'id·li, *adv*. Palely; wanly.—**pallidness**, pal'id·nes, *n*. Paleness.

pallium, pal'li·um, *n*. [L. *pallium*, whence *pall* (n.).] An ecclesiastical or other pall; *zool*. an outgrowth of the dorsal body-wall of many mollusks, forming folds or processes which represent the foot and other parts.

pall-mall, pel-mel', *n*. [O.Fr. *pale-mail*, from It. *pallamaglio*, from *palla*, a ball (akin E. *ball*), and *maglio*, L. *malleus*, a mallet.] An ancient game in which a ball was struck with a mallet or club through a ring elevated upon a pole; the alley or walk where the game was played (hence the street in London called *Pall Mall*).

pallor, pal'or, *n*. [L. PALLID.] Paleness.

palm, päm, *n*. [L. *palma*, the palm of the hand, a palm tree (so named from the shape of its branches); cog. Gr. *palamē*, A.Sax. *folm*, O.H.G. *folma*, the palm of the hand.] The inner part of the hand; a lineal measure equal to 3 or 4 inches; a broad flat part, as of an anchor fluke; any of the plants of a well-known order of arborescent or tree-like endogens, chiefly inhabiting the tropics, of great value to man as affording food, etc.; a branch or leaf of the palm tree anciently borne as a symbol of victory or triumph; hence, superiority, vic-

tory, triumph (to carry off the *palm*); a popular name for the bloom or a branch of the willow, carried on Palm Sunday as a substitute for the Eastern palm branches.—*v.t.*—*palmed, palming*. To conceal in the palm of the hand, as jugglers or cheaters; to impose by fraud (to *palm off* trash *upon* the public).—*Palma Christi* (palm of Christ), a name for the castor-oil plant.—**palmaceous**, pal·mā'shus, *a*. Belonging to the palm tribe.—**palmar**, pal'mėr, *a*. [L. *palmaris*.] Pertaining to the palm of the hand; of the breadth of the hand.—**palmate**, **palmated**, pal'māt, pal'mā·ted, *a*. [L. *palmatus*.] Having the shape of the hand (*palmated* leaves); having the toes webbed (the *palmate* feet of aquatic birds).—**palmately**, pal'māt·li, *adv*. In a palmate manner.—**palmer**, päm'ėr, *n*. A pilgrim that returned from the Holy Land with a branch of palm; one who palms or cheats, as at cards or dice.—**palmerworm**, *n*. A name for certain hairy caterpillars.—**palmetto**, pal·met'tō, *n*. [Sp. *palmito*.] A name of several palms; the cabbage palm of the West Indies and southern United States.—**palmistry**, pä'mis·tri, *n*. The art of telling fortunes by the lines and marks in the palm of the hand; manual dexterity (humorous).—**palmitic**, pal·mit'ik, *a*. Pertaining to or obtained from palm oil (*palmitic* acid).—**palmitin**, pal'mi·tin, *n*. The principal solid ingredient of palm oil.—**palm oil**, *n*. A fatty substance resembling butter obtained from palms, chiefly from the fruit of the African oil palm, employed in the manufacture of soap and candles, for lubricating.—**Palm Sunday**, *n*. The Sunday next before Easter, commemorative of the Saviour's triumphal entry into Jerusalem, when the multitude strewed palm branches in the way.—**palmy**, pä'mi, *a*. Abounding in palms; flourishing; prosperous.—**palmyra**, **palmyra palm**, pal·mī'ra, *n*. The most common palm of India, the wood, leaves, fruit, and juice of which are all of great value and use.

palomino, pal'ō·mi"nō, *n*. [Amer. Sp. from Sp. *palomilla*.] A tan or cream-colored horse with slender legs and white mane and tail; a color like that of the horse.

palp, palpus, palp, pal'pus, *n*. (pl. **palpi**, pal'pī). [Mod. L. *palpus*, from L. *palpare*, to stroke, to feel.] A jointed sensitive organ on the head of an insect; a feeler.

palpable, pal'pa·bl, *a*. [Fr. *palpable*, from L. *palpabilis*, from *palpo*, to touch; akin *palpitate*.] Perceptible by the touch; capable of being felt; easily perceived and detected; plain; obvious; easily perceptible.—*Palpable obscure*, darkness that may be felt. (*Mil*.)—**palpability**, pal·pa·bil'i·ti, *n*. Plainness; obviousness.—**palpably**, pal'pa·bli, *adv*. Plainly; obviously.—**palpation**, pal·pā'shon, *n*. [L. *palpatio*.] The act of feeling; *pathol*. manual examination.

palpebral, pal'pe·bral, *a*. [L. *pal-*

pebra, an eyelid.] Pertaining to the eyelid or eyebrow.

palpi. See PALP.

palpitate, pal'pi·tāt, *v.i.*—*palpitated*, *palpitating*. [L. *palpito*, *palpitatum*, freq. of *palpo*, to feel. PALPABLE.] To flutter or move with slight throbs; to throb; to pulsate violently: applied particularly to an abnormal movement of the heart, as from fright or disease; hence, to tremble; to quiver.—**palpitation**, pal·pi·tā'shon, *n*. A violent and unnatural beating or pulsation of the heart, as from violent action, fright, or disease.

palsgrave, palz'grāv, *n*. [G. *pfalzgraf*, from *pfalz* (contr. from L. *palatium*, palace), and *graf*, an earl.] A count palatine; a count with the superintendence of the king's palace.—**palsgravine**, palz'gra·vin, *n*. The consort of a palsgrave.

palsy, pal'zi, *n*. [A contr. of *paralysis*, Fr. *paralysie*.] Paralysis, especially in a limb or some of the superficial muscles.—*v.t.*—*palsied*, *palsying*. To affect with palsy or as with palsy; to paralyze.—**palsied**, pal'zid, *p*. and *a*. Affected with palsy.

palter, pal'tėr, *v.i.* [Of same origin as *paltry*, and originally having reference to the haggling of dealers in old clothes.] To act insincerely; to equivocate; to haggle; to shift; to dodge; to play tricks.

paltry, pal'tri, *a*. [Same as L.G. *paltrig*, *palterig*, ragged, from *palte*, Fris. *palt*, G. *palte*, Sw. *palta* (plur. *paltor*), Dan. *pialt*, a rag; akin *palter*.] Mean; vile; worthless; despicable. ∴ Syn. under CONTEMPTIBLE.—**paltrily**, pal'tri·li, *adv*. In a paltry manner.—**paltriness**, pal'tri·nes, *n*. The state of being paltry, vile, or worthless.

paludal, pal'ū·dal, *a*. [L. *palus*, *paludis*, a marsh.] Pertaining to marshes; generated by marshes (*paludal* fever).

paludine, pal'ū·dīn, *a*. [L. *palus*, *paludis*, a pool, a marsh.] Pertaining to marshes; marshy.

paly. See PALE.

pam, pam, *n*. In five-card loo, the knave of clubs.

pampas, pam'pas, *n. pl.* [Sp.-Amer.] The grassy treeless plains of South America, resembling the prairies of North America; especially the immense plains in the southern portion of South America east of the Andes.—**pampas grass**, *n*. A variety of grass with flower stems 10 to 14 feet high growing on the pampas, introduced as an ornamental grass into Britain.—**pampean**, pam-pē'an, *a*. Pertaining to the pampas.

pamper, pam'pėr, *v.t.* [Probably akin to *pap* (with *m* inserted); comp. G. *pampen*, Bav. *pampfen*, to stuff, to cram with food.] To indulge with rich food; to feed luxuriously; to gratify to the full; to indulge to excess.—**pamperer**, pam'pėr·ėr, *n*. One who pampers.

pampero, pam·pâ'ro, *n*. [Sp.-Amer. *pampas*.] The cold wind blowing from the Andes to the Atlantic.

pamphlet, pam'flet, *n*. [Formerly

paunflet, pamfilet, pamflet: from Med. L. *Pamphilet*, name of a popular poem.] A small book consisting of a sheet of paper, or of a few sheets stitched together but not bound; a short treatise or essay published by itself.—**pamphleteer,** pam·flet·ēr´, *n.* A writer of pamphlets; a scribbler.—*v.i.* To write and issue pamphlets.

pan, pan, *n.* [A.Sax. *panne,* D. *pan,* G. *pfanne,* all from L.L. *panna,* for *patna,* L. *patina,* a pan, from *pateo,* to be wide. PATENT.] A vessel of tin, iron, or other metal, often rather shallow; a vessel of various kinds used for domestic purposes; an open vessel for boiling or evaporating or other operations (a sugar *pan,* a salt *pan,* etc.); a pond for evaporating salt water to make salt; the part of a flintlock which holds the priming; the skull or cranium (the brain*pan*).—*Pan out,* to yield a good return = 'to cut-up' well: from the phrase of miners washing out the gravel of the gold in pans; to succeed; *agri.* HARDPAN.—**pancake,** *n.* A thin cake of batter fried or baked in a pan.

Pan, pan, *n.* [Hence *panic.*] *Greek myth.* the chief god of pastures, forests, and flocks.—**Pandean,** pan·dē´an, *a.* Pertaining to Pan.—*Pandean pipes, Pan's pipes,* a musical wind instrument composed of reeds of different lengths tied together; a syrinx.

panacea, pan·a·sē´a, *n.* [L., from Gr. *panakeia,* a universal remedy—*pan,* all, and *akeomai,* to cure.] A remedy for all diseases; a universal medicine or remedy.

panada, pa·nä´da, *n.* [Fr. *panade,* from L. *panis,* bread.] A food made by boiling bread in water to the consistence of pulp.

panama, pa´na·mä, *n.* [From Panama City.] A soft straw hat made from young jipijapa leaves.

panatela, pa·na·tel´a, *n.* [Sp.] A short slender cigar.

pancake. See PAN.

panchromatic, pan·krō·mat´ik, *a.* [Prefix *pan,* and *chromatic,* color.] *Photog.* sensitive to all colors.

pancratium, pan·krā´shi·um, *n.* [Gr. *pangkration*—*pan,* all, and *kratos,* strength.] A gymnastic contest of ancient Greece consisting of boxing and wrestling.

pancreas, pan´kri·as, *n.* [Gr. *pan,* all, and *kreas,* flesh.] A large gland which secretes a digestive fluid into the intestine; the pancreas of cattle, used as food, called sweetbread.—**pancreatic,** pan·kri·at´ik, *a.*

panda, pan´da, *n.* A carnivorous quadruped of the genus *Ailurus,* found in the Himalayas and Tibet, belonging to the raccoon family, whose fur is reddish-brown on the back and sides, and black on the underside and legs.—*Giant panda,* an animal of the genus *Ailuropoda.*

pandect, pan´dekt, *n.* [Gr. *pandektēs*—*pan,* all, and *dechomai,* to contain.] A treatise which contains the whole of any science; *pl.* the digest or collection of Roman civil law,

made by order of the emperor Justinian, and consisting of fifty books.

pandemic, pan·dem´ik, *a.* [Gr. *pan,* all, and *demos,* people.] Incident to a whole people; epidemic.

pandemonium, pan·di·mō´ni·um, *n.* [Gr. *pan,* all, and *daimōn,* a demon.] The place or abode of demons or evil spirits—a name invented by Milton; hence, any lawless, disorderly place or assemblage.

pander, pan´dėr, *n.* [From *Pandarus,* who performs the part of a pimp in the story of Troilus and Cressida.] A pimp; a procurer; a male bawd; hence, one who ministers to the gratification of any of the baser passions.—*v.i.* To act as agent for the lusts of others.

Pandora, pan·dō´ra, *n.* [Gr., from *pan,* all, and *dōron,* a gift.] *Class. myth.* the name of the first woman on earth, on whom all the gods and goddesses bestowed gifts.—*Pandora's box,* a box Pandora received, containing all human ills, from which all escaped and spread over the earth, hope alone remaining.

pandour, pan´dör, *n.* [Croatian *bandur,* under a banner, later *pandur,* mounted policeman.] One of a body of Croatian foot soldiers, formerly dreaded for their savage mode of warfare.

pandurate, panduriform, pan´dū·rāt, pan·dū´ri·form, *a. Bot.* shaped like a violin; fiddle-shaped; applied to a leaf.

pane, pān, *n.* [Fr. *pan,* a panel or definite portion of a surface, from L. *pannus,* a piece of cloth, a patch (whence also *panel, pawn.*)] A distinct part of a flat surface‡; a plate of glass inserted in a window, door, etc.; a panel or division of a work; a sunken portion surrounded by a border.

panegyric, pan·e·jir´ik, *n.* [Gr. *panēgyrikos,* fit for a public assembly, from *panēgyris,* a public assembly—*pas, pan,* all, and *agyris,* an assembly.] A laudatory oration; a formal eulogy; an elaborate encomium; praise bestowed; laudation.—**panegyrical,** pan·e·jir´i·kal, *a.* Containing praise or eulogy; encomiastic;—**panegyrically,** pan·e·jir´i·kal·li, *adv.* By way of panegyric.—**panegyrist,** pan·e·jir´ist, *n.* One who bestows praise; a eulogist.—**panegyrize,** pan´e·ji·rīz, *v.t.*—*panegyrized, panegyrizing.* To write or pronounce a panegyric or eulogy on.—*v.i.* To indulge in panegyric; to bestow praises.

panel, pan´el, *n.* [O.Fr. *panel,* dim. of *pan,* a pane, a panel. PANE.] A surface or compartment of a surface more or less distinct from others; an area on a wall sunk from the general surface; a similar portion fixed in the framing of a door, shutter, etc.; a piece of wood upon which a picture is painted; *law,* a document containing the names of persons summoned to serve upon a jury; the jury; *Scots law,* the accused person in a criminal action.—*v.t.*—*paneled, paneling.* To form with panels.—**paneling,** pan´el·ing, *n.* Paneled work.

pang, pang, *n.* [Comp. W. *pang,* a pang, a convulsion.] A sudden paroxysm of extreme pain; a sudden spasm or throe.

pangenesis, pan·jen´e·sis, *n.* [Gr. *pan, genesis,* descent.] A provisional theory, now abandoned, attributing the transmission of hereditary characters to living particles migrating into the sex cells from all parts of the body.—**pangenetic,** pan·je·net´ik, *a.* Pertaining to or relating to pangenesis.

Pan-Germanism, pan·jėr´man·ism, *n.* A movement aimed at keeping Germans, resident in any part of the world, conscious of their common cultural heritage.

panhandle, pan´han·dl, *n.* A projection of land resembling a handle of a pan, as in the northwest section of Texas.—*v.t.* and *i.* To approach one on the street and beg.

Panhellenic, pan·hel·len´ik, *a.* [Gr. *pan,* all, and *Hellēnikos,* Greek, from *Hellēnes,* the Greeks.] Pertaining to all Greece.—**Panhellenism,** pan·hel´len·izm, *n.* The proposed union of all the Greeks into one political body.—**Panhellenist,** pan·hel´len·ist, *n.* One who favors Panhellenism.

panic, pan´ik, *n.* [From Gr. *panikos,* of or belonging to *Pan,* the god who was believed to inspire sudden fear, fear arising among people without visible cause.] A sudden fright, particularly without real cause; terror inspired by a trifling cause.—*a.* Extreme or causeless; applied to fright.—**panicky,** pan´ik·i, *a.* Showing or inspired by panic.—**panic-stricken, panic-struck,** *a.* Struck with a panic or sudden fear.

panic grass, pan´ik, *n.* [L. *panicum,* a kind of grass.] The name of several species of grass.

panicle, pan´i·kl, *n.* [L. *panicula,* a panicle, dim. of *panus,* thread on the bobbin in a shuttle.] A branching form of inflorescence, as in the lilac or the oat.—**Paniculate, paniculated,** pa·nik´ū·lāt, pa·nik´ū·lā·ted, *a. Bot.* furnished with or arranged in a panicle; like a panicle.

panic switch, pan´ik swich [E. panic and switch (which see).] The control on the ejector mechanism that throws a jet pilot from his plane in case of emergency.

pannier, pan´i·ėr, *n.* [Fr. *panier,* from L. *panarium,* a breadbasket, from *panis,* bread. PANTRY.] A wicker-basket, primarily a breadbasket, but now one of two baskets slung across a beast of burden, in which things are carried; a part of a lady's skirt attached to the back of the skirt; *arch.* a corbel.

pannikin, pan´i·kin, *n.* A small pan or cup.

panoply, pan´o·pli, *n.* [Gr. *panoplia*—*pan,* all, and *hopla,* arms.] Complete armor of defense; an elaborate covering.—**panoplied,** pan´o·plid, *a.* Having a panoply or full suit of armor.

panorama, pan·o·ra´ma, *n.* [Gr. *pan,* all, and *horama,* view, from *horaō,* to see.] A picture in which all the objects of nature that are visible from a single point are represented on the interior surface of a round or cylindrical wall, the point of view being in the axis of the cylinder.—**panoramic**, pan·ō·ram′ik, *a*. Pertaining to or like a panorama, or complete view.

Pan-Slavic, pan·slav′ik, *a*. [Gr. *pan*, all, and E. *Slavic*.] Pertaining to all the Slavic races.—**Pan-Slavism**, pan·slav′izm, *n*. The proposed amalgamation of all the Slavic races into one confederacy.

pansy, pan′zi, *n*. [Fr. *pensée*, thought, heart's-ease, from *penser*, to think. PENSIVE.] A name applied to the garden varieties of violet; heart's-ease.

pant, pant, *v.i*. [From or connected with O.Fr. *pantoier*, to pant, to gasp, *pantois*, a panting; Pr. *panteiar*, to be breathless.] To breathe quickly, as after exertion or from excited eagerness; to gasp; to throb or heave with unusual violence, as the heart or the breast after hard labor; to desire ardently.—*v.t*. To breathe forth; to gasp out.—*n*. A quick, short respiration; a gasp; a throb or palpitation.—**pantingly**, pan′ting·li, *adv*. In a panting manner; with gasping or rapid breathing.

pantalets, pan′ta·lets, *n. pl*. [From *pantaloon*.] Loose drawers worn by females and children.

pantaloon, pan·ta·lön′, *n*. [Fr. *pantalon*, lit. a Venetian, after their patron saint *Pantalone* or *Pantaleon*.] A character in the Italian comedy: so called from his dress; in modern pantomimes, a character usually represented as the butt of the clown; pl. a pair of trousers.

pantheism, pan′thē·izm, *n*. [Gr. *pan*, all, and *Theos*, God.] The doctrine that the universe, taken or conceived of as a whole, is God, or that all things are simply modes or manifestations of God.—**pantheist**, pan′thē·ist, *n*. One that believes in pantheism.—**pantheistic**, **pantheistical**, pan·thē·is′tik, pan·thē·is′ti·kal, *a*. Pertaining to pantheism.—**pantheistically**, pan·thē·is′ti·kal·li, *adv*. In the manner or from the point of view of a pantheist.

pantheon, pan′thē·on or pan·thē′on, *n*. [Gr. *pantheon*, *pantheion*—*pan*, all, and *theos*, a god.] A temple dedicated to all the gods, especially [*cap*.] the building so called at Rome, now converted into a church; all the divinities collectively worshiped by a people.

panther, pan′thėr, *n*. [L. *panthera*, Gr. *panthēr*; compr. Skr. *pundarika*, a leopard.] A carnivorous animal of Asia and Africa, identical with or a variety of the leopard.

pantile, pan′til, *n*. [*Pan* and *tile*.] A tile with a cross section resembling the letter S, overlapping the tile by its side as well as the one beneath.

pantofle, **pantoffle**, pan′tofl, pan·tof′l, *n*. [Fr. *pantoufle*.] A lounging slipper.

pantograph, pan′to·graf, *n*. [Gr. *pan*, *pantos*, all, and *graphō*, to write.] An instrument by means of which

drawings, maps, plans, etc., can be copied mechanically on the original scale, or on one reduced or enlarged.—**pantographic**, pan·to·graf′ik, *a*. Pertaining to a pantograph.

pantology, pan·tol′o·ji, *n*. [Gr. *pas*, *pantos*, all, and *logos*, discourse.] Universal knowledge; a systematic view of all branches of human knowledge.—**pantological**, pan·to·loj′i·kal, *a*. Relating to pantology.

pantomime, pan′to·mim, *n*. [L. *pantomimus*, Gr. *pantomimos*—*pan*, *pantos*, all, and *mimos*, a mimic.] A player who acted, not by speaking, but wholly by gesticulations; a theatrical entertainment in dumbshow; hence, dumb show generally; a popular stage entertainment usually produced about the Christmas season, the effects being heightened by gorgeous scenery and catching music.—**pantomimic**, pan·to·mim′ik, *a*. Pertaining to pantomime.—**pantomimist**, pan′to·mim·ist, *n*. One who acts in pantomime.

pantry, pan′tri, *n*. [Fr. *paneterie*, a pantry, from L. *panis* (Fr. *pain*), bread, whence also *pannier*.] A room or closet, generally entered from the kitchen, for provisions, silverware, china, and glassware.

pants, pants, *n. pl*. Shortened form of pantaloons; trousers.

panzer, pan′zėr, *a*. [G.] Armored.—*n*. A tank.

pap, pap, *n*. [D. and Dan. *pap*, G.; *pappe*, probable from an infantile cry. PAPA.] A kind of soft food for infants; the pulp of fruit.

pap, pap, *n*. [Of similar origin to *pap*, food; comp. L. *papilla*, the nipple.] A nipple of the breast; a teat; a round hill resembling a pap.

papa, pä′pa, *n*. [A reduplication of one of the earliest cries uttered by infants—Fr., G., D., and Dan. *papa*, L. *papa*, *pappa*, Gr. *pappa*; comp. *mama*, *mamma*.] Father: a word used by children.

papacy, pā′pa·si, *n*. [L.L. *papatia*, the papacy, from L. *papa*, the pope, lit. father. PAPA, POPE.] The office and dignity of the pope; papal authority and jurisdiction; the popedom; the popes collectively.

papal, pā′pal, *a*. Belonging to the pope or to popedom; proceeding from the pope.

papaw, pa′pa, *n*. A small North American tree and its pulpy fruit. (Not the same as *papaya*, which see.)

papaya, pa·pä′yä, *n*. [Sp. and Pg. *papaya*, of Malabar origin.] A tropical American tree and its edible melon-like fruit. Source of papain, a digestive ferment used in tenderizing tough meat.

paper, pā′pėr, *n*. [Fr. *papier*, It. *papiro*, from L. *papyrus*, Gr. *papyros*, the papyrus, PAPYRUS.] A well-known substance used for writing and printing on, and for various other purposes, manufactured principally of vegetable fiber reduced to a pulp; a piece, leaf, or sheet of paper; a single sheet appearing periodically; a newspaper; a journal; an essay or article on some subject; any written or printed document;

collectively, such documents as promissory notes, bills of exchange, etc.—*a*. Made of paper; appearing merely in certain documents without really existing (a *paper* army); thin; slight.—*v.t*. To cover with paper; to furnish with paper hangings; to fold or enclose in paper.—**papery**, pā′pėr·i, *a*. Like paper; having the thinness and consistency of paper.—**paper cutter**, *n*. A paper knife; a machine for cutting paper in piles, or for trimming the edges of books, etc.—**paper hanger**, *n*. One whose employment is to hang wallpaper.—**paper hangings**, *n. pl*. Paper for covering and adorning the walls of rooms; wallpaper.—**paper knife**, *n*. An instrument of bone, ivory, etc., with an edge like a blunt knife used in cutting open the leaves of books, etc., or for folding paper.—**paper money**, *n*. Banknotes or the like circulated as the representative of coin.—**paper nautilus** *n*. The paper sailor or argonaut.—**paperweight**, *n*. A small weight laid on loose papers to keep them in place.

papeterie, päp·trē′, *n*. [Fr., stationery or writing materials.] An ornamented case or box containing papers and other materials for writing.

Paphian, pā′fi·an, *a*. Pertaining to *Paphos*, a city of Cyprus sacred to Venus; hence, pertaining to Venus or her rites.

papier-mâché, päp·yā·mä·shā′, *n*. [Fr., lit masticated paper.] A material prepared by pulping different kinds of paper into a mass, which is molded into various articles, dried, and japanned.

papilionaceous, pa·pil′i·o·nā″shus, *a*. [L. *papilio*, a butterfly.] Resembling the butterfly; *bot*. having the corolla shaped like a butterfly, such as the flower of the pea.

papilla, pa·pil′la, *n. pl*. **papillae**, pa·pil′lē, [L.] A small pap or nipple; a little eminence on the surface of the skin, as on the tongue.—**papillary**, pap′il·le·ri, *a*. Pertaining to or resembling the nipple; papillose.—**papilloma**, pap′il·ō″ma, *n*. [Gr. *oma*, a tumor.] A benign tumor shaped like a papilla.—**papillose**, pap′il·lōs, *a*. Papillary.—**papillote**, pap′il·lōt, *n*. [Fr.] A curl paper.

papist, pā′pist, *n*. [Fr. *papiste*, from Fr. *pape*, L. *papa*, pope.] A Roman Catholic.—**papistic**, **papistical**, pa·pis′tik, pa·pis′ti·kal, *a*. Popish, pertaining to popery. (Usually in disparagement.)

papoose, pa·pös′, *n*. Among the native Indians of North America, a babe or young child.

pappus, pap′us, *n*. [L., from Gr. *pappos*, the down of plants.] *Bot*. the feathery appendage that crowns many single-seeded seed vessels; a form of calyx in composite plants of a downy or hairy character.—**pappose**, **pappous**, pap′ōs, pap′us, *a*. Downy; furnished with pappus.

paprika, pap·ri′ka, *n*. [Hung. *paprika*.] The ripe fruit of a pepper of the *Capsicum* genus; a spice from the fruit.

---

ch, *ch*ain; *ch*, Sc. loc*h*; g, *g*o; j, *j*ob; ng, si*ng*; TH, *th*en; th, *th*in; w, *w*ig; hw, *wh*ig; zh, a*z*ure.

papule, pap'ūl, n. [L.] A pimple.
—**papular**, pap'ū·lẽr, a.

papyrus, pa·pī'rus, n. pl. **papyri**, pa·pī'ri. [Gr. *papyros*, of Egyptian origin. Hence *paper*.] A tall sedge abundant in the valley of the Nile, the stems of which afforded the most ancient material for writing; a written scroll made of the papyrus.

par, pär, n. [L. *par*, equal, whence *pair* and *peer*.] Equality in circumstances or in value; the state of the shares of a public undertaking when they may be purchased at the original price; established value of coin or the standard value of one country expressed in the coin or standard value of another; *golf*, the number of strokes required to play a hole or a round perfectly.—*a.* Average or normal; *bus.* at or pertaining to par.—*Above par*, above the original price; at a premium.—*Below par*, below the original price, at a discount.

para- par'a. [Gr. *para-*, par, from *para*, beside.] A prefix meaning beside, with its variations; alongside, aside from, amiss, beyond, as in parallel, paragraph, etc.

para-, par'a [F. fr. Ital. imper. of *parare*, to shield or defend.] To protect from, or that which shields, as in *parasol* and *parachute*.

parable, par'a·bl, n. [Fr. *parabole*, from L. *parabola*, Gr. *parabolē*, from *paraballō*, to throw beside, to compare—*para*, beside, and *ballō*, to throw. Of same origin are *parley*, *parlor*, *parole*.] Originally, a comparison or similitude; now a fable or allegorical representation of something real in life or nature, from which a moral is drawn for instruction; *Scrip.* a proverbial or notable saying; a thing darkly or figuratively expressed.—*v.t.*—*parabled*, *parabling*. To represent by a parable.—**parabola**, pa·rab'o·la, n. [Gr. *parabolē*, so called from its axis being parallel to the side of its cone.] A geometrical figure, one of the conic sections, shown when a cone is cut by a plane parallel to one of its sides; the curve which a projectile theoretically describes.—**parabolic**, par·a·bol'ik, a. Having the form of a parabola; pertaining to a parabola, pertaining to a parable.—**parabolical**, par·a·bol'i·kal, a. Parabolic, of the nature of or having the character of a parable.—**parabolically**, par·a·bol'i·kal·li, adv. By way of parable; in the form of a parabola.—**paraboloid**, pa·rab'ol·oid, n. The solid generated by the revolution of a parabola about its axis; a parabolic conoid.

parachute, par'a·shöt, n. [Fr., from *parer*, to ward off, and *chute*, a fall.] *Avi.* an apparatus of an umbrella shape with which aircraft are provided, for the purpose of enabling safe descent by crew or troops.—*v.t.* and *i.* To descend or drop by means of a parachute.—**parachutist**, par'a·shö·tist, n.

paraclete, par'a·klēt, n. [Gr. *paraklētos*, from *parakaleō*—*para*, to, and *kaleō*, to call.] One called to aid or support; hence, [*cap.*] a term applied to the Holy Spirit.

parade, pa·rād', n. [Fr. *parade*, from Sp. *parada*, a parade, a place for the exercise of troops, from L. *paro*, *paratus*, to prepare. PARE, PREPARE.] Show; ostentation; display; a showy or pompous procession; a military display; the collection of troops for inspection or the like; the place where such display is held; a public walk or promenade.—*v.t.*—*paraded*, *parading*. To exhibit in a showy manner; to make a show of; to assemble and march in military order.—*v.i.* To assemble in military order; to go about in military procession; to walk about for show.

paradigm, par'a·dim, n. [Gr. *paradeigma*—*para*, beside, and *deigma*, example, from *deiknumi*, to show.] An example; a model; *gram.* an example of a word, as a noun, adjective, or verb, in its various inflections.—**paradigmatic**, **paradigmatical**, par'a·dig·mat″ik, par'a·dig·mat″i·kal, a. Pertaining to a paradigm; suited for being an example; exemplary.—**paradigmatically**, par'a·dig·mat″i·kal·li, adv. In the way of paradigm or example.

paradise, par'a·dīs, n. [L. *paradisus*, from Gr. *paradeisos*, a garden—properly a Persian word.] The garden of Eden, in which Adam and Eve were at first placed; hence, a place of bliss; a region of supreme felicity; the abode of sanctified souls after death.—*Bird-of-paradise*. See BIRD.—**paradisaic**, **paradisaical**, par'a·di·sā″ik, par'a·di·sā″i·kal, a. Pertaining to paradise.

paradox, par'a·doks, n. [Gr. *paradoxon*, from *para*, beyond, and *doxa*, opinion. ORTHODOX.] A tenet or proposition contrary to received opinion; a statement which seems to be at variance with common sense, or to contradict some previously ascertained truth, though when properly investigated it may be perfectly well founded,—*Hydrostatic paradox*. HYDROSTATIC.—**paradoxical**, par·a·dok'si·kal, a. Having the nature of a paradox; inclined to paradox.—**paradoxically**, par·a·dok'si·kal·li, adv. In a paradoxical manner.—**paradoxicalness**, par·a·dok'si·kal·nes, n.

paraffin, par'a·fin, n. [L. *parum*, little, and *affinis*, akin, from its resistance to chemical reagents.] A fatty substance obtained from the dry distillation of wood, bituminous coal, wax, etc., largely used in the manufacture of candles; *chem.* any member of the methane series.—*v.t.* To saturate with paraffin.

paragenesis, par·a·jen'e·sis, n. [Gr. *para*, side by side with, and *genesis*, generation.] Origin of two things side by side; that state of minerals when they are made up of an aggregate of interblended crystals or crystals which have not assumed their normal structure (as in granite, etc.).—**paragenetic**, par·a·je·net'ik, a. Characterized by or pertaining to paragenesis.

paragoge, par'a·gō·ji, n. [Gr. *para-*

gōgē—*para*, beside, and *agō*, to lead.] The addition of a letter or syllable to the end of a word.—**paragogic**, par·a·goj'ik, a. Pertaining to paragoge; lengthening a word by being affixed.

paragon, par'a·gon, n. [Fr. *parangon*, from Sp. *paragon*, *parangon*, model, from the prepositions *para*, beside, and *con*, in comparison with.] A model or pattern, especially a model or pattern of superior excellence or perfection.—*v.t.* To compare; to rival; to form a rival or equal to.

paragraph, par'a·graf, n. [Gr. *paragraphē*, a marginal note—*para*, beside, and *graphō*, to write.] Originally a marginal note; hence the character ¶ used as a reference, or to mark a division in a written composition; a distinct part of a discourse or writing, consisting of one or several sentences; a portion or section which relates to a particular point, and is generally distinguished by a break.—*v.t.* To express within a paragraph; to divide into paragraphs.—*v.i.* To work as a paragrapher.—**paragraphic**, par·a·graf'ik, a.—**paragrapher**, par'a·graf·ẽr, n.

Paraguay tea, par'a·gwā, n. See MATÉ.

parakeet, par'a·kēt, n. [Fr. *parroquet*, *perroquet*, a parakeet. PARROT.] The name given to various parrots of the Eastern Hemisphere, generally of small size and having very long tail feathers.

paraleipsis, **paralepsis**, **paralipsis**, par·a·līp'sis, par·a·lep'sis, par·a·lip'-sis, n. [Gr. *paraleipsis*, omission—*para*, beside, and *leipō*, to leave.] *Rhet.* a pretended omission; a figure by which a speaker pretends to pass by what at the same time he really mentions.

parallax, par'al·laks, n. [Gr. *parallaxis*, from *parallassō*, to vary, decline, or wander—*para*, beyond, and *allasō*, to change.] The apparent change of position of an object relatively to other objects when viewed from different places; *astron.* the difference between the position of any celestial object as viewed from the surface of the earth, and that which it would have when viewed from the center of either the earth or the sun; *optics*, the noncoincidence of the cross fibers of a telescope with the focus of the eye-glass.—**parallactic**, par·al·lak'tik, a. Pertaining to parallax.

parallel, par'al·lel, a. [Gr. *parallēlos*—*para*, side by side, and *allēlōn*, of one another.] Extended in the same direction, and in all parts equally distant; being exactly at an equal distance throughout their length or breadth (said of lines or surfaces); hence, having the same direction or tendency; running in accordance with something; equal in all essential parts, points, or features; exactly similar (a *parallel* passage or incident).—*Parallel forces*, forces which act in directions parallel to each other.—*Parallel lines*, *geom.* straight lines which are in the same plane, and being produced ever so far both ways, do not meet.—*Parallel motion*, a contrivance invented by Watt for converting a reciprocating circular motion into an alternating rectilinear motion, and applied in the steam engine.—*Parallel roads*, a phenomenon observed in some valleys of the Scottish Highlands, consisting in a series of parallel and nearly horizontal lines running along the sides of the hills, supposed to have been formed by the action of a lake. —*Parallel rod*, in locomotive engines, a rod that connects the crankpins of the driving wheels.—*Parallel ruler*, a mathematical instrument for drawing parallel lines, formed of two equal rulers, connected by two cross-bars of equal length and movable about joints.—*Parallel sailing*, sailing on a parallel of latitude.—*n*. A line which throughout its whole extent is equidistant from another line; one of the circles on a sphere parallel to its equator; a line on a map marking latitude (called also a *parallel of latitude*); resemblance or conformity in essential points; likeness; comparison (to draw a *parallel* between two historians); one who corresponds essentially to another; a counterpart; *milit.* a trench cut before a fortress, parallel to its defenses, for covering the besiegers from the guns of the place; *printing*, a mark of reference (thus ‖) used to direct attention to notes.—*v.t.*—*paralleled, paralleling* (also with *ll* in the second place); to make parallel; to form or serve as a parallel to; to match; to correspond to; to show or furnish an equal to; to compare.—**parallelepiped, parallelepipedon**, par·a·lel′e·pī″ped, par·a·lel′e·pī″ped·on, *n*. [Gr. *parallélépipedon*—*parallēlos*, parallel, and *epipedos*, plane, superficial—*epi*, upon, and *pedon*, the ground.] A solid body with six sides forming parallelograms; a solid in the shape of a brick.—**parallelism**, par′a·lel·izm, *n*. State of being parallel; resemblance in a number of important particulars; correspondence; a comparison.—*Parallelism of the earth's axis*, that feature according to which the axis is always inclined at exactly the same slope.—**parallelogram**, par·a·lel′o·gram, *n*. A four-sided figure composed of straight lines, and having its opposite sides parallel and equal; popularly, a quadrilateral figure of greater length than breadth. **paralogism**, pa·ral′o·jizm, *n*. [Gr. *paralogismos*—*para*, beyond, and *logismos*, reasoning. LOGIC.] A fallacious argument; an instance of false reasoning.—**paralogize**, pa·ral′o·jīz, *v.i.*—*paralogized, paralogizing*. To reason falsely. **paralysis**, pa·ral′i·sis, *n*. [G. *paralysis*, from *paralyō*, to loosen—*para*, beside, and *lyō*, to loose.] A loss or diminution of the power of motion in some part of the body, arising from disease of the nerves; a loss of sensation in any part of the body; palsy.—**paralyze**, par′a·līz, *v.t.*—*paralyzed, paralyzing*. To affect with *paralysis*; to destroy physical or mental energy in.—

paralytic, par·a·lit′ik, *a*. Pertaining to paralysis; affected with paralysis. —*n*. A person affected with paralysis. **paramagnetic**, par′a·mag·net″ik, *a*. A term proposed by Faraday as a substitute for *magnetic* in contradistinction to *diamagnetic*.—**paramagnetism**, par·a·mag′net·izm, *n*. Magnetism as opposed to *diamagnetism*. **paramatta**, par·a·mat′ta, *n*. A light twilled dress fabric, the weft of merino wool and the warp cotton: said to have been made originally with wool from *Paramatta* in Australia. **paramecium**, par·a·mē′shi·um *n*. [N.L. from Gr. *paramēkēs*, oblong, from *para* and *mēkos*, length.] *Zool.* a ciliate infusorian (*Paramecium*) having an elongated body with a large oral opening at the anterior end. **parameter**, pa·ram′et·ėr, *n*. [Gr. *para*, beside, and *metron*, measure.] *Geom.* a constant straight line belonging to each of the three conic sections; the constant quantity which enters into the equation of a curve. **paramo**, pä′rä·mō, *n*. In South America a mountainous district covered with stunted trees, and in which a damp cold perpetually prevails. **paramount**, par′a·mount, *a*. [O.Fr. *par* (L. *per*), through, completely, and *amont*, above. AMOUNT.] Superior in power or jurisdiction (lord *paramount*, the supreme lord of a fee or of lands, etc.); eminent; of the highest order; superior to all others.—*n*. Chief; highest in rank or order.—**paramountcy**, par′a·mount·si, *n*. The condition of being paramount. **paramour**, par′a·mör, *n*. [Fr. *par amour*, with love—*par* = L. *per*, by, *amour*, L. *amor*, love.] A lover‡; a wooer‡; one who takes the place of a husband or wife without possessing the rights. **paranoia**, par·a·noi′a, *n*. [Gr. *para*, beside, *nous*, mind.] A mental disease marked by delusions of one's importance and of being persecuted.— **paranoiac**, par·a·noi′ak, *n*. A person affected by paranoia.—*a*. Pertaining to or affected by paranoia. **paranymph**, par′a·nimf, *n*. [Gr. *paranymphos*—*para*, by and *nymphē*, a bride.] In ancient Greece, a bridesman. **parapet**, par′a·pet, *n*. [Fr. *parapet*, It. *parapetto*—*parare* (Fr. *parer*, E. *parry*), to ward off, to guard, and *petto* (L. *pectus*), the breast.] *Lit.* a wall or rampart breasthigh; *milit.* a wall or rampart to cover the soldiers from the attacks of the enemy in front; a breastwork; *arch.* a wall placed at the edges of platforms, sides of bridges, etc., to prevent people from falling over.— **parapeted**, par′a·pet·ed, *a*. Furnished with a parapet. **paraph**, par′af, *n*. [Fr. *parafe*, *paraphe*, an abbreviation of *paragraph*.] The figure formed by the flourish of a pen at the conclusion of a signature.—*v.t.* To add a paraph to; to sign.

paraphernalia, par′a·fėr·nā″li·a, *n. pl.* [L.L. *paraphernalia*, from Gr. *parapherna*, what a bride has besides her dower—*para*, beyond, and *phernē*, a dowry.] The belongings of a wife over and above her dower or portion, as apparel and ornaments; personal attire of a showy or accessory description; also, fittings, etc., of an apartment or house; appendages; ornaments; trappings. **paraphrase**, par′a·frāz, *n*. [Gr. *paraphrasis*—*para*, beside, and *phrasis*, phrase.] A restatement of a text, passage, or work, giving the sense of the original in other words; the setting forth in clearer and ampler terms of the signification of a passage or work; a sacred song or hymn based on a selected portion of Scripture.—*v.t.*—*paraphrased, paraphrasing*. To make a paraphrase of; to explain or translate with latitude. —*v.i.* To interpret or explain amply. —**paraphrast**, par′a·frast, *n*. [Gr. *paraphrastēs*.] One who paraphrases. —**paraphrastic**, par·a·fras′tik, *a*. Having the character of a paraphrase; explaining in words more clear and ample than those of the author. **parapsychology**, par′a·sī·kol″o·ji, *n*. [Prefix *para*, and *psychology*.] A branch of psychology dealing with the investigation of psychic phenomena, as clairvoyance, extrasensory perception, etc. **paraplegia**, par·a·plē′ji·a, *n*. [Gr. *paraplēgia*, paralysis—*para*, beyond, and *plēgē*, stroke.] That kind of paralysis which affects the lower part of the body. **parasang**, par′a·sang, *n*. [Gr. *parasangēs*, from Per. *farsang*, a parasang.] An ancient Persian measure of length equal to 3¾ miles. **paraselene**, par′a·se·lē″nē, *n. pl.* **paraselenae**, par′a·se·lē″nē. [Gr. *para*, about, or near, and *selēnē*, the moon.] A mock moon; a luminous ring encompassing the moon, in which sometimes are other bright spots bearing some resemblance to the moon. **parasite**, par′a·sīt, *n*. [Fr. *parasite*, from L. *parasitus*, Gr. *parasitos*, one who eats at the table of another, a parasite, a toady—*para*, beside, and *sitos*, food.] One that frequents the tables of the rich and earns his welcome by flattery; a hanger-on; a sycophant; an animal that lives upon or in, and at the expense of, other animals; a plant which grows upon another plant, and feeds upon its juices.—**parasitic, parasitical**, par·a·sit′ik, par·a·sit′i·kal, *a*. Of the nature of a parasite; meanly dependent on others for support; *bot.* and *zool.* growing or living as a parasite.—**parasitically**, par·a·sit′i·kal·li, *adv*. In the manner of a parasite.—**parasiticide**, par·a·sit′i·sīd, *n*. [E. *parasite*, and L. *caedo*, to kill.] Any agent for destroying animal or vegetable parasites.— **parasitism**, par′a·sīt·izm, *n*. The behavior or manners of a parasite; the state of being a parasite. **parasol**, par′a·sol, *n*. [Fr. *parasol*, from It. *parasole*—*parare* (L. *parare*, to prepare), to ward off, and *sole* (L. *sol*), the sun. PARRY.] A small umbrella used by ladies to defend their faces from the sun's rays.

parataxis, par·a·tak′sis, *n.* [Gr. *para*, beside, and *taxis*, arrangement.] *Gram.* the mere ranging of propositions one after another, without marking their dependence on each other by way of consequence or the like.—**paratactic,** par·a·tak′tik, *a.* Pertaining to parataxis.

parathyroid, par·a·thī′roid, *a.* [Prefix *para* and *thyroid*.] Situated beside the thyroid gland.—*Parathyroid glands*, four small glands that control the calcium content of the blood and body.

paratroop, par′a·tröp, *n. pl.* **paratroops** [Prefix *para*, and *troop*.] A military unit trained to drop by parachute from an aircraft into a specific area.—**paratrooper,** *n.*

paratyphoid, par′a·tī′foid, *n.* [Gr. *para*, beyond, *typhoid*.] A bacterial disease with symptoms resembling typhoid fever.

paravane, pa·ra·vān′, *n.* A torpedo-shaped machine fitted with an apparatus for severing the moorings of sea mines.

parboil, pär′boil, *v.t.* [Fr. *parbouillir*—*part*, part, and *bouiller*, to boil; lit. to partboil.] To boil in part; to boil in a moderate degree.

parbuckle, pär′buk·l, *n.* A purchase formed by a single rope round a heavy object for hoisting or lowering, the object itself acting as a movable pulley.—*v.t.* To hoist or lower by means of a parbuckle.

parcel, pär′sel, *n.* [Fr. *parcelle*, from a L.L. *particella*, equivalent to L. *particula*, dim. of *pars*, *partis*, a part. PART.] A portion of anything taken separately; a particle; a collection; a group; a lot; a quantity or number of things put up together; a bundle; a package: now the common meaning.—*v.t. parceled, parcelled, parceling, parcelling.* To divide or put up into parts or portions; to make up into a mass.—**parceling, parcelling,** pär′sel·ing, *n.* A dividing into small parts, as a *parceling* of land; *naut.* long narrow slips of canvas daubed with tar and bound about a rope like a bandage.—**parcel post,** *n.* The department of a post-office system by which parcels are sent.

parcener, pär′sen·ėr, *n.* [O.Fr. *parçonnier*, from *parcon*, L. *partitio*, *partitionis*, a portion. PARTITION.] A coheir or coparcener.

parch, pärch, *v.t.* [Perhaps from Fr. *percer*, Fr. dial. *percher*, to pierce, as if to pierce or penetrate with heat; or a corruption of L. *peratesco*, to grow very dry.] To burn the surface of; to scorch; to dry to extremity.—*v.i.* To become scorched or very dry.

parcheesi, parchisi, pär·chē′zē, *n.* [Hind. *pachisi*, from *pachis*, twenty-five, the highest throw in the game.] A game somewhat resembling backgammon.

parchment, pärch′ment, *n.* [Fr. *parchemin*, from L. *pergamena*, *perga-*

mina, paper of Pergamus, from *Pergamus* in Asia Minor.] The skin of a very young calf, sheep, or goat dressed or prepared and rendered fit for writing on; ordinary paper with the appearance of parchment.

pardon, pär′dn, *v.t.* [O.Fr. *pardoner*, (Fr. *pardonner*), from L.L. *perdonare*, to pardon—L. *per*, through, quite, and *dono*, to give. DONATION.] To release from liability to suffer punishment for a crime or a fault; to forgive (an offender); to remit the penalty or punishment of; to forgive (the offense).—*Pardon me, forgive me; excuse me*: a phrase often used when a person means civilly to deny or contradict what another affirms. ∴ *Pardon* means strictly to remit the punishment or retaliation we were entitled to inflict; *forgive* implies that the party who has suffered injury entirely overlooks the offense, and cherishes no ill-feeling whatever against the offender.—*n.* Forgiveness of an offender or of his offense; a passing over without, or not visiting with, punishment; remission of penalty; forgiveness; an official warrant of penalty remitted.—**pardonable,** pär′dn·a·bl, *a.* Capable of being pardoned or forgiven; excusable; venial.—**pardonably,** pär′dn·a·bli, *adv.* In a manner admitting of pardon; excusably.—**pardoner,** pär′dn·ėr, *n.* One who pardons; one licensed to sell the pope's indulgences‡.

pare, pâr, *v.t.*—*pared, paring.* [Fr. *parer*, to pare, to dress, to curry, from L. *parare*, to prepare, seen in a number of words, as *parade, parry, prepare, repair, separate,* etc.] To cut off, as the superficial substance or extremities of a thing; to shave off with a sharp instrument; to trim by shaving the surface; to diminish by little and little.—**paring,** pâr″ing, *n.* What is pared off; a piece clipped off; the rind.

paregoric, par·e·gor′ik, *a.* [Gr. *parēgorikos,* soothing, from *parēgoreō,* to exhort, console, soothe—*para,* beside, and *agoreuō,* to speak in an assembly.] *Med.* mitigating or assuaging pain.—*Paregoric elixir,* a camphorated tincture of opium, flavored by aromatics.—*n.* A medicine that mitigates pain; an anodyne.

pareira brava, pa·rā′ra brä′va, brā′va, or **pareira,** *n.* [Portuguese *pareira brava,* wild brier.] The roots of certain plants of Brazil employed in medical practice, as tonics and diuretics.

parenchyma, pa·ren′ki·ma, *n.* [Gr. *para,* beside, and *enchyma,* an infusion—*en,* in, and *cheō,* to pour.] *Anat.* the essential, functional tissue of the glands or other solid organs as distinct from the framework or supporting tissue, or stroma; *bot.* the pith or pulp of plants; the spongy and cellular tissue.—**parenchymatous,** par·en·kim′a·tus, *a.* Pertaining to or of the nature of parenchyma.

parent, pâr′ent, *n.* [L. *parens, parentis,* from *pario, parere,* to bring

forth; to beget; akin to *parere,* to appear (APPEAR), *parare,* to prepare (PARE).] A father or mother; he or she that produces young: used of animals and plants as well as of man; one who or that which produces; cause; source.—**parentage,** pâr′en·tij, *n.* Extraction; birth; origin; condition with respect to the rank or character of parents.—**parental,** pa·ren′tal, *a.* Pertaining to parents; suited to or characteristic of parents.—**parentally,** pa·ren′tal·li, *adv.* In a fatherly or parental manner.—**parenthood,** pâr′ent·hųd, *n.* The state of being a parent; the condition of a parent.

parenthesis, pa·ren′the·sis, *n. pl.* **parentheses,** pa·ren′the·sēz. [Gr. *parenthesis*—*para,* beside, *en,* in, and *thesis,* a placing, from *tithēmi,* to place.] An explanatory or qualifying sentence, or part of a sentence, inserted into the midst of another sentence, without being grammatically connected with it, generally marked off by upright curves ( ); *printing,* the parenthetical sign ( ).—**parenthetic, parenthetical,** par·en·thet′ik, par·en·thet′i·kal, *a.*—**parenthetically,** par·en·thet′i·kal·li, *adv.*

paresis, pä·rē′sis, par′e·sis, *n.* [Gr., from *pariēmi,* to relax.] *Pathol.* a slight incomplete paralysis, affecting motion but not sensation.

par excellence, pär ek′se·läns, *a.* or *adv.* [Fr.] Above all others; pre-eminent.

parfait, pär·fā′, *n.* A dessert made of beaten eggs and whipped cream, sweetened, flavored, and frozen without stirring.

parget, pär′jet, *n.* [O.E. *pariet,* O.Fr. *pariette,* from L. *paries, parietis,* a wall.] Plaster laid on roofs or walls.—*v.t.* To cover with plaster or parget; to ornament with parge work.—*v.i.* To plaster.—**pargeting,** pär′jet·ing, *n.* Plasterwork; plasterwork with patterns and ornaments raised or indented upon it, whether inside or outside a house.

parhelion, pär·hē′li·on, *n. pl.* **parhelia,** pär·hē′li·a, [Gr. *para,* near, and *hēlios,* the sun.] A mock sun, having the appearance of the sun itself, sometimes white and sometimes tinted with prismatic colors.—**parhelic,** pär·hel′ik, *a.* Relating to parhelia.

pariah, pa·rī′a, *n.* [A Tamil word.] One of a low caste of people in southern India; hence, one despised and contemned by society; an outcast.

Parian, pâ′ri·an, *a.* Pertaining to *Paros,* an isle in the Aegean Sea.—*Parian marble,* a marble of Paros, chosen by the ancients for their choicest works.—*n.* A fine variety of porcelain or porcelain clay, of which statuettes, etc., are made, resembling Parian marble.

parietal, pa·rī′et·al, *a.* [L. *parietalis,* from *paries, parietis,* a wall.] Pertaining to a wall; *anat.* pertaining to the walls of a cavity of the body, or to the bones which form the sides and upper part of the skull; *bot.* growing from the side of another organ.

pari-mutuel, par′i mū′tu·el, *n.* [Fr.] A plan of race-horse betting in which the total amount wagered on all of the horses in a race, less a small fee, is shared in proportion to amounts wagered by the betters who selected the win, place, and show horses.

paripinnate, par·i·pin′āt, *a.* [L. *par,* equal, and *pinnatus, pinnate.*] *Bot.* equally pinnate; abruptly pinnate; said of a compound pinnate leaf ending in two leaflets.

Paris green, *n.* A poisonous, green-colored arsenic compound used as an insecticide.

parish, par′ish, *n.* [Fr. *paroisse,* L.L. *paroecia,* from Gr. *paroikia,* a parish, a neighborhood, from *para,* beside, and *oikos,* a house (whence *economy*).] The district under the charge of a priest or minister; the congregation of a church; a subdivision of the state of Louisiana, equivalent to a county.—**parishioner,** pa·rish′on··ér, *n.*

parity, par′i·ti, *n.* [Fr. *parité,* L. *paritas,* from *par,* equal. PAIR.] The condition of being equal or equivalent; like state or degree; equality; *finance,* equal purchasing power at a given ratio of currency of different kinds; equal value in foreign currency.

park, pärk, *n.* [Either from Fr. *parc,* or L.L. *parcus,* a park.] A large piece of ground enclosed and set apart for beasts of chase; a piece of public ground in or near a large town, laid out and kept for the sole purpose of pleasure and recreation; a stadium for sports events, as a baseball *park; milit.* a place occupied by military equipment, supplies, etc., hence the objects themselves (a *park* of jeeps). —*v.t.* To put or keep temporarily in a place (to *park* a car); to leave in a place (he *parked* his hat); to enclose in a park.—*v.i.* To place or station a vehicle.—**parker,** pär′kér, *n.*—**parkway,** pärk′wā, *n.* A wide street or thoroughfare lined with trees, shrubs and turf.

parka, pär′ka, *n.* [Rus.] A fur outer garment or coat cut like a shirt with an attached hood.

parlance, pär′lans, *n.* [O.Fr., from *parlant,* ppr. of *parler,* to speak. PARLEY.] Conversation; talk.

parlay, pär′lā, *v.t.* and *i.* [Fr. *paroli,* from It. *paroli,* from *paro,* equal.] To place a bet on one horse, the proceeds of which are to be applied as a wager on a second horse; to so act in any similar venture.—*n.* Such a venture.

parley, pär′li, *v.i.* [Fr. *parler,* O.Fr. *paroler,* from L.L. *parabolare,* to speak, from L. *parabola,* a comparison, later, a word. PARABLE.] To confer or speak with a person on some point of mutual concern; especially to confer with an enemy.—*n.* Mutual conversation; a conference with an enemy in war.

parliament, pär′li·ment, *n.* [Fr. *parlement—parler,* to speak, and term. -*ment,* as in *complement,* etc. PARLEY.] A meeting or assembly of persons for conference or deliberation; a supreme national or general council; the legislature of the three estates of the United Kingdom of Great Britain, the lords spiritual, lords temporal, and the commons; the general council of Great Britain constituting the legislature, summoned by the sovereign's authority to consult on the affairs of the nation, and to enact and repeal laws.—*Act of parliament,* a statute or law made by the sovereign, with the advice and consent of the lords temporal and spiritual and the commons in parliament assembled.— **Parliamentarian,** pär′li·men·tā″ri·an, *n.* One of those who adhered to the parliament in the time of Charles I; [*not cap.*] one thoroughly acquainted with the rules of order for group meetings, as public assemblies, clubs, or conventions.—**parliamentary,** pär′li·men′ta·ri, *a.* Pertaining to parliament; enacted or done by parliament; according to the rules and usages of parliament, or similar legislative bodies.—*Parliamentary government,* a government whose legislature has complete power to make laws and control the administration of their enforcement.—*Parliamentary procedure,* the generally accepted rules and practices followed in conducting the business of a deliberative body.

parlor, pär′lér, *n.* [Fr. *parloir,* from *parler,* to speak. PARLEY.] A room for familiar intercourse; the room commonly used by a family; an ordinary sitting room; also applied to a certain type of business, trade or amusement place.—**parlor car,** a chair-fitted railroad car on which travelers pay extra fare.

parlous, pär′lus, *a.* [For *perilous.*] Dangerous; risky; extreme or shocking *(colloq.).*

Parmesan, pär·me·zan′, *n.* [*Parma,* in Italy.] Name of a sharp, dry type of cheese made there.

Parnassian, pär·nas′i·an, *a.* Pertaining to *Parnassus,* the celebrated mountain in Greece sacred to Apollo and the Muses.

parochial, pa·rō′ki·al, *a.* [L. *parochia,* corruption from *paroecia,* a parish. PARISH.] Belonging to a parish; restricted to a parish; hence, limited in range or scope; narrow. —*Parochial school,* an elementary school maintained by a parish, usually adding religious instruction to secular subjects.—**parochialism,** pa·rō′ki·al·izm, *n.* The state of being parochial; narrowness or contractedness of mind resulting from confining one's attention or interest to the affairs of one's parish or neighborhood.—**parochially,** pa·rō′ki·al·li, *adv.* In a parochial manner; in a parish; by parishes.

parody, par′o·di, *n.* [Fr. *parodie,* from Gr. *parōdia—para,* beside, and *ōdē,* an ode.] A literary composition in which the form and expression of serious writings are closely imitated but adapted to a ridiculous subject or a humorous method of treatment; a burlesque imitation of a serious poem.—*v.t.*—*parodied, par-*odying. To turn into a parody; to write a parody upon.

parole, pa·rōl′, *n.* [Fr. *parole,* from L.L. *parabola,* a word, a parable. PARABLE.] Word of promise; word of honor; a promise given by a prisoner of war that he will not try to escape if allowed to go about at liberty, or not to bear arms against his captors for a certain period, or the like; *milit.* a sort of countersign given out every day; *penology,* release of a convict under supervision before he has served his full sentence and on promise of good conduct; a state or condition of one on parole.—*v.t.* To free for a parole period.—*To break parole,* to conduct one's self contrary to conditions of the parole.—**parolee,** pa·rōl·ē′, *n.* A person released on parole.

paronymous, pa·ron′i·mus, *a.* [Gr. *parōnymos—para,* beside, and *onoma,* a name, a word.] Having the same or a like sound, but differing in orthography and signification, as *all, awl; ball, bawl;* having the same derivation, as *wise, wisely, wisdom.*— **paronym,** par′o·nim, *n.* A paronymous word.

paroquet, par′o·ket, *n.* See PARAKEET.

parotid, pa·rot′id, *a.* [Gr. *parōtis, parōtidos—para,* beside, and *ous, ōtos,* the ear.] *Anat.* a salivary gland on either side of the face, in front of the ear, and communicating with the mouth by a duct.—**parotitis,** par·o·tī′tis, *n.* Inflammation of the parotid gland; mumps.

paroxysm, par′ok·sizm, *n.* [Gr. *paroxysmos—para,* in excess, and *oxynō,* to sharpen, from *oxys,* sharp.] A fit or period of great intensity of a disease; a sudden and violent access of feeling (as of rage); convulsion; fit; *geol.* any sudden and violent effect of natural agency.—**paroxysmal,** par·ok·siz′mal, *a.* Pertaining to or marked by a paroxysm.

paroxytone, pa·rok′si·tōn, *a.* and *n.* [Gr.] *Gram.* said of a word having the acute accent on the penultimate syllable.

parquet, pär·kā′, *n.* [Fr. *parquet,* dim. of *parc,* a park.] First floor in a theater or music hall, frequently known as orchestra section.—*Parquet circle,* mezzanine balcony seats at rear of orchestra section.—*v.t.*—*parqueted, parqueting.* To form or ornament with parquetry.—**parquetry,** pär′ket·ri, *n.* [Fr. *parqueterie.*] Inlaid woodwork in geometric or other patterns, and generally of different colors.

parr, pär, *n.* A small fish now known to be a young salmon at a certain stage.

parrakeet, par′a·kēt, *n.* See PARAKEET.

parrel, parral, par′el, par′al, *n.* [Abbrev. from *apparel.*] *Naut.* a band of rope, or now, more generally, an iron collar which confines a yard to the mast at the center.—*v.t.* and *i.* To make fast with a parrel.

parricide, par′ri·sīd, *n.* [L. *parricida,* the criminal, *parricidium,* the crime, from *pater,* father, and *caedo,* to kill.] A person who murders his father or mother; the murder of a parent.—**parricidal**, par·ri·sĭ′dal, *a.* Pertaining to parricide; committing parricide.

parrot, par′ot, *n.* [From Fr. *Perrot*, or *Perrette*, personal names from *Pierre*, Peter (like Fr. *pierrot*, a sparrow, from *Pierre*); comp. Sp. *Perico*, a dim. for *Pedro*, Peter, also a small parrot, *periquito*, a small parrot. Comp. such names as *Magpie*, *Jackdaw*, *Robin-redbreast*, etc.] A name common to a family of scansorial or climbing birds, including the parakeets, macaws, lories, cockatoos, etc., or restricted to certain members of the family, all of which have hooked and rounded bills and fleshy tongues, some of them having the faculty of imitating the human voice in a high degree.—*v.t.* To repeat as a parrot; to repeat by rote.—**parrot fever**, *n. Med.* psittacosis.—**parrot fish**, *n.* A fish of the wrasse family, remarkable for the beak-like plates into which the teeth of either jaw are united.

parry, par′i, *v.t.*—*parried*, *parrying*. [Fr. *parer*, It. *parare*, to ward off, from L. *parare*, to prepare, keep off. PARE.] To ward off (a blow, a thrust); to stop or to put or turn aside; to prevent taking effect.—*v.i.* To put aside thrusts or strokes; to fence.

parse, pärs, *v.t.* [L. *pars orationis*, a part of a speech.] *Gram.* to analyze or describe grammatically; to show the several parts of speech composing (a sentence) and their relation to each other by government or agreement.

parsec, pär′sek, *n.* [*Parallax* and *second*.] *Astron.* an interstellar distance unit of a heliocentric parallax of one second of arc, equal to 206,265 times the distance between the earth and the sun, or 3.26 light years.

Parsee, pär·sē′, *n.* [Per. and Hind. *pârsi*, a Persian, a fire-worshiper.] One of the adherents of the Zoroastrian or ancient Persian religion in India, originally from Persia.—**Parseeism**, pär·sē′izm, *n.* The religion and customs of the Parsees.

parsimony, pär′si·mo·ni, *a.* [Fr. *parsimonie*, from L. *parsimonia*, *parcimonia*, from *parco*, *parsum*, to spare.] Closeness or sparingness in the use or expenditure of money; niggardliness; miserliness.—*Law of parsimony*, in *logic*, also called 'Occam's Razor', the principle laid down by the Nominalist leader, William of Ockham (1270-1347), the Invincible Doctor, that entities or supposed existences must not be multiplied in a theory beyond what is strictly necessary.—**parsimonious**, pär·si·mō′ni·us, *a.* Exhibiting or characterized by parsimony; niggardly; closefisted.—**parsimoniously**, pär·si·mō′ni·us·li, *adv.* In a parsimonious manner.

parsley, pärs′li, *n.* [O.E. *persely*, *persylle*, etc., Fr. *persil*, from L. *petroselinum*, Gr. *petroselinon*, rock parsley—*petra*, a rock, and *selinon*, parsley.] A well-known garden herb, the leaves of which are used for seasoning and also as a garnish.

parsnip, pärs′nip, *n.* [Corrupted from Fr. *pastinaque*, L. *pastinaca*, a parsnip, from *pastinum*, a kind of two-pronged dibble, and *nip*, *nep*, L. *napus*, a turnip.] An umbelliferous plant much cultivated for its edible roots.

parson, pär′sn, *n.* [O.Fr. *persone*, from L.L. *persona ecclesiæ*, the person of the church, L. *persona*, a person.] The priest or incumbent of a parish; one who has the parochial charge or cure of souls; a clergyman; a man that is in orders or has been licensed to preach.—**parsonage**, pär′sn·ij, *n.* The official dwelling of a parson.

part, pärt, *n.* [L. *pars*, *partis*, a part (whence also *particle*, *parcel*, *partial*, *party*, *partner*, *participate*, *apart*, etc.); same root as *parare*, to prepare, *portio*, a portion. PARE.] Any portion of a thing less than the whole; a piece or fragment separated from a whole thing; a portion or quantity not separated in fact, but considered as by itself; one of a number of equal portions or quantities that make up a whole; a constituent portion of a whole; a member of a whole; that which falls to each in division; share, portion, lot; concern or interest; side or party (to take one's *part*); allotted duty; particular office or business (to perform one's *part*); character assigned to an actor in a play or other like performance; *mus.* one of the different melodies of a concerted composition, which, heard in union, compose its harmony (the treble, tenor, or bass *part*); *pl.* qualities; powers; faculties; often excellent or superior endowments (a man of *parts*); *pl.* regions; districts; locality (well-known in these *parts*).—*For my* (*his*, *her*, etc.) *part*, so far as concerns me (him, her).—*For the most part*, commonly; oftener than otherwise.—*In part*, in some degree or extent; partly.—*In good part*, favorably; acceptably; in a friendly manner; not in displeasure.—*In ill part*, unfavorably; with displeasure.—*Part and parcel*, an essential portion; a part.—*Part of speech*, *gram.* a sort or class of words of a particular character as regards their meaning or relations to other words in a sentence.—*v.t.* [Fr. *partir*, to part, separate.] To divide; to separate or break into two or more pieces; to distribute; to share; to cause to sunder or go apart; to intervene betwixt; to interpose between; to separate, as combatants; *naut.* to break; to suffer the breaking of (the ship *parted* her cables).—*v.i.* To become separate or detached; to divide; to move apart; to go away from another or others; to quit each other; to take leave (to *part with* or *from* a person); to have a share; to share (O.T.); to break; to be torn asunder (the rope *parted*).—*To part with* a thing, to let it

leave us; to resign it.—*adv.* Partly; in some measure.—**partible**, pär′ti·bl, *a.* Capable of being parted; divisible.—**parted**, pär′ted, *p.* and *a.* Divided; separated; *bot.* cleft into divisions.—**parting**, pär′ting, *p.* and *a.* Serving to part; dividing; separating; given at separation (a *parting* kiss).—*n.* The act of dividing or separating; a division; a separation; leave-taking; *geol.* a fissure in strata.—**partly**, pärt′li, *adv.* In part; in some measure or degree; not wholly; used in stating particulars that make up a whole.—**part song**, *n.* A song adapted to be sung in two or more distinct vocal parts.—**part-time**, *a.* Involving or working less than the amount of time considered standard.

partake, pär·tāk′, *v.i.*—*partook* (pret.), *partaken* (pp.), *partaking* (ppr.). [*Part* and *take*.] To take a part, portion, or share in common with others; to have a share or part; to participate (to *partake* of a repast, *in* festivities); to have something of the character or nature of; to have features in common with: followed by *of*.—*v.t.* To have a part in; to share.—**partaker**, pär·tā′kėr, *n.* One who partakes; a sharer, a participator; usually followed by *of* or *in*.

parterre, pär·târ′, *n.* [Fr., from *par*, on, by, and *terre*, earth, ground.] *Hort.* a system of flower beds, connected together with intervening spaces of gravel or turf for walking on; the pit of a French theater.

parthenogenesis, pär′the·no·jen″e·sis, *n.* [Gr. *parthenos*, a virgin, and *genesis*, production.] Reproduction by development of an unfertilized egg, as in certain plants and insects.—**parthenogenetic**, pär′the·nō·je·net″ik, *a.*

Parthian, pär′thi·an, *a.* Pertaining to *Parthia* or its inhabitants.—*Parthian arrow*, a shaft aimed at an adversary while flying from or avoiding him; a parting shot; from the habit of the ancient Parthians in war.

partial, pär′shal, *a.* [Fr. *partial*, from L. *pars*, *partis*, a part. PART.] Affecting a part only; not general or universal; not total; inclined to favor one party in a cause, or one side of a question more than the other; not indifferent; inclined to favor without principle or reason (a fond and *partial* parent); having a predilection; inclined or favorable; with *to*; *bot.* being one of several subordinates (a *partial* umbel, a *partial* peduncle).—**partiality**, pär·shal′i·ti, *n.* The state or quality of being partial; unfair or undue bias; undue favor shown; a special liking or fondness.—**partially**, pär′shal·li, *adv.* In a partial manner; with undue bias; in part; not totally; to some extent.

partible. See PART.

participate, pär·tis′i·pāt, *v.i.*—*participated*, *participating*. [L. *participo*, *participatum*—*pars*, *partis*, a part, and *capio*, to take. PART, CAPABLE.] To partake; to take a part; to have a share in common with others; generally followed by *of* or *in*.—*v.t.*

To partake, share, receive a part of.—**participation,** pär·tis′i·pā″shon, *n.* The state of participating or sharing in common with others.—**participator,** pär·tis′i·pā·tėr, *n.* One who participates.—**participant,** pär·tis′i·pant, *a.* Sharing; having a share or part.—*n.* One participating; a partaker.

participle, pär′ti·si·pl, *n.* [L. *participium,* from *particeps,* partaking—*pars, partis,* a part, and *capio,* to take; comp. *principle,* from L. *principium.* PARTICIPATE.] *Gram.* a part of speech, so called because it partakes of the character both of a verb and an adjective, though it differs from the adjective chiefly in that it implies time, and therefore applies to a specific act, while the adjective designates a habitual quality or characteristic, without regard to time.—**participial,** pär·ti·sip′i·al, *a.* Having the nature and use of a participle; formed from a participle (a *participial* noun).—*n.* A word formed from a verb, and having the nature of a participle.—**participially,** pär·ti·sip′i·al·li, *adv.* In the sense or manner of a participle.

particle, pär′ti·kl, *n.* [Fr. *particule,* L. *particula,* dim. of *pars, partis,* part. PART.] A minute part or portion of matter, the aggregation of which parts constitutes a whole mass; any very small portion or part; an atom; a jot; *gram.* a word that is not varied or inflected, as the preposition, conjunction, etc.; *physics,* a mass of matter conceived as a point, but yet possessing inertia and other properties of matter.

particolored, pär′ti·kul·ėrd, *a.* Colored differently in different parts; of many colors.

particular, pär·tik′ū·lėr, *a.* [Fr. *particulier,* L.L. *particularis,* from L. *particula.* PARTICLE.] Pertaining to one and not to more; special; not general; individual; considered separately; peculiar; personal; private (our own *particular* wrongs); not ordinary; notable (of no *particular* importance); minute; circumstantial (a full and *particular* account); singularly nice in taste; precise; fastidious.—*n.* A single instance; a single point; a distinct, separate, or minute part; a detail.—*In particular,* specially; particularly; to particularize.—**particularity,** pär·tik′ū·lar″i·ti, *n.*—**particularization,** pär·tik′ū·lėr·i·zā″shon, *n.*—**particularize,** pär·tik′ū·lėr·īz, *v.t.* To state in detail.—*v.i.* To mention or attend to particulars; to be circumstantial.—**particularly,** pär·tik′ū·lėr·li, *adv.* In a particular or especial manner; especially; chiefly.

partisan, pär′ti·zan, *n.* [Fr., from *parti,* a party, from L. *pars, partis,* a part.] An adherent of a party or faction; one who is violently and passionately devoted to a party or interest; a guerrilla fighter.—*a.* Pertaining to a party or faction; biased in favor of a party or interest.—**partisanship,** pär′ti·zan·ship, *n.*

partisan, pär′ti·zan, *n.* [Fr. *pertuisane,* Sp. *partesana,* It. *partigiana;*

origin doubtful.] A kind of halberd or pike formerly in use; a baton; a truncheon; a quarterstaff.

partite, pär′tīt, *a.* [L. *partitus,* pp. of *partio,* to divide. PART.] *Bot.* divided to the base (as a leaf).—**partition,** pär·tish′on, *n.* [L. *partitio.*] The act of parting, dividing, or separating into portions and distributing; division; separation; that by which different parts are separated; a wall separating apartments in a building; a division between the chambers or cells of a thing; *music,* SCORE.—*v.t.* To divide by walls or partitions; to divide into shares.—**partitive,** pär′ti·tiv, *a. Gram.* denoting a part; expressing the relation of a part to a whole (a *partitive* genitive, 'the mountain's brow').—*n. Gram.* a word expressing partition.—**partitively,** pär′ti·tiv·li, *adv.* In a partitive manner.

partlet, part′let, *n.* [Fr. *Pertelote,* female proper name.] A hen.

partly. See PART.

partner, pärt′nėr, *n.* [In part directly from *part,* partly from old *parcener,* O.Fr. *parçoner,* from L. *partitio,* a sharing. PARTITION.] One who partakes or shares with another; a partaker; an associate; one who has a share with another or others in some commercial, manufacturing, or other undertaking; a member of a partnership; one who dances with another, either male or female; a husband or wife.—**partnership,** pärt′nėr·ship, *n.* The state or condition of being a partner; the association of two or more persons for the purpose of undertaking and prosecuting conjointly any business, occupation, or calling.

partridge, pär′trij, *n.* [O.E. *partryke, partriche,* from O.Fr. *pertrix,* Fr. *perdrix,* from L. and Gr. *perdix,* a partridge.] Any of a number of rasorial birds similar to the grouse, especially game birds; in America, has particular reference to the ruffed grouse and the quail.

part song. See PART.

parturient, pär·tū′ri·ent, *a.* [L. *parturiens, parturientis,* ppr. of *parturio,* from *partus,* birth, from *pario,* to bear. PARENT.] Bringing forth or about to bring forth young.—**parturition,** pär·tū·rish′on, *n.* [L. *parturitio.*] The act of bringing forth or being delivered of young.

party, pär′ti, *n.* [Fr. *partie,* a party, side, faction, a suitor or litigant, etc., from Fr. *partir,* L. *partio,* to divide, from *pars, partis,* a part. PART.] A number of persons united in opinion or design, in opposition to others in the community; persons in a state united by certain political views; a faction; persons collected for a particular purpose, often an armed force; a detached portion of a larger body or company; a detachment; a select company invited to an entertainment (a tea *party,* an evening *party*); one of two litigants; one concerned or interested in an affair (a *party* to a scheme or plot); a single person distinct from or opposed to another; a person under special consideration;

hence, a person in general; an individual (in this sense vulgar).—**party-colored,** See PARTICOLORED.—**party line,** *n.* A single telephone circuit connecting several subscribers with the exchange; a boundary line.—**party wall,** *n.* A wall between buildings to separate them from each other; a wall separating adjoining tenements.

parvenu, pär′ve·nū, *n.* [Fr. *parvenu,* lit. one who has arrived, from *parvenir,* L. *pervenire,* to arrive.] An upstart, or one newly risen into notice.

parvis, pär′vis, *n.* [Fr. *parvis,* from L.L. *parvisius, paravisus,* from L. *paradisus,* paradise.] A name formerly given to the porch of a church, now applied to the area round a church.

Pasch, pask, *n.* [L. and Gr. *pascha,* from Heb. *pascha,* passage, from *pâsach,* to pass over.] The Passover; the feast of Easter.—**paschal,** pas′kal, *a.* Pertaining to the Passover or to Easter.

pash,‡ pash, *v.t.* [Same as Sw. *paska,* Prov. G. *paschen,* to strike.] To strike violently; to dash or smash. (*Shak.*)

pasha, pa·shä′ or pash′a, *n.* [Per. *pâshâh,* contr. from *pâdishâh,* protector or great king. PADISHAH.] In Turkey, a title formerly conferred upon military commanders and governors of provinces.—**pashalic, pachalic,** pa·shä′lik, pash′a·lik, *n.* The jurisdiction of a pasha.

pasqueflower, pask, *n.* [O.Fr. *pasque,* Easter. PASCH.] A species of anemone with large handsome purple flowers, so named in consequence of its flowering about Easter.

pasquil, pasquinade, pas′kwil, pas′-kwi·nād, *n.* [From *Pasquino,* a witty and satirical tailor (or barber) of Rome, whose name after his death was bestowed upon a statue that had been dug up near his shop, and to which satirical placards were affixed at night.] A lampoon or short satirical publication.—*v.t.* and *i.*—*pasquilled, pasquilling; pasquinaded, pasquinading.* To lampoon; to satirize in writing.

pass, pas, *v.i.* pret. & pp. *passed* or sometimes *past.* [Fr. *passer,* It. *passare,* from L. *passus,* a step, a pace. PACE.] To go; to proceed (to *pass* away, from, into, over, under, etc.); to go past a certain person or place (we saw him *pass*); to alter or change condition or circumstances; to undergo transition; to vanish, disappear, be lost: hence, to depart from life; to die; to elapse; to be spent; to receive the sanction of a legislative house or body by a majority of votes (the bill has *passed*); to be current; to gain reception or be generally received (bills *pass* as a substitute for coin); to be regarded, held, or considered; to occur; to take place (what *passes* within one's own mind); to thrust; to make a push in fencing or fighting; to throw a ball, as a football or basketball; *Baseball,* four balls pitched wide of the plate entitling the batter to proceed to first base; *Cards,* to decline a privilege, as of making a bid; to go unheeded or neglected; to be transferred from an owner; to go successfully through an inspection or examination.—*To come to pass*, to happen; to occur.—*To pass away*, to move from sight; to vanish; hence, to die; to be spent (as time, life).—*To pass by*, to move near and beyond a certain person or place.—*To pass into*, to unite and blend gradually.—*To pass on*, to continue to go forward; to proceed.—*To pass over*, to go or move to another side; to cross.—*To pass through*, to undergo; to experience.—*v.t.* To move near and go beyond; to move from side to side of; to live through; to spend (to *pass* the summer); to let go by without care or notice; to take no notice of; to transcend, exceed, excel, surpass; to transfer; to make to change hands; to hand over; to send; to circulate; to undergo successfully, as an examination, ordeal, or the like; to obtain the legislative or official sanction of; to be enacted by (the bill has *passed* the house); to give legal or official sanction to; to enact or ratify; to allow as valid or just; to give forth officially; to pronounce (to *pass* a sentence of death); to void, as feces or other matter; *baseball*, to go to first base after four balls; *football*, to throw the ball to another player.—*To pass off*, to impose by fraud; to palm off.—*To pass over*, to let go by unnoticed; to disregard.—*n.* A passage; a narrow road or defile between two mountains; permission to pass, or to go or come; a ticket of free transit or admission; a thrust or push in fencing; a movement of the hand over or along anything; a manipulation of a mesmerist; state or condition of things; an embarrassing situation; the successful or satisfactory standing or going through an examination.—**passable,** pas′a‧bl, *a.* Capable of being passed, traveled, traversed, penetrated, etc.; capable of being passed from person to person; current; receivable; tolerable; allowable; admissible; mediocre.—**passably,** pas′a‧bli, *adv.* Tolerably; moderately.—**passbook,** *n.* A book in which a shopkeeper makes an entry of goods sold on credit to a customer, for the information of the customer; also, a bankbook.—**passer,** pas′ér, *n.* One who passes; a passenger.—**passer-by,** *n.* One who goes by or near.—**passing,** pas′ing, *adv.* Surpassingly; wonderfully; exceedingly (*passing* fair, *passing* strange).—*prep.* Exceeding; beyond; over.—**passing note,** *n. Music,* a note introduced between two others to form a transition, but not constituting an essential part of the harmony.—**password,** *n.* A secret parole or countersign by which a friend may be distinguished from a stranger, and allowed to pass.

passage, pas′ij, *n.* [Fr. *passage*, from *passer*, to pass. PASS.] The act of passing; transit from one place to another; a going by, through, over, or the like; transit by means of a

conveyance; a journey by a conveyance, especially a ship; liberty of passing; access; entry or exit; way by which a person or thing may pass; avenue; way of entrance or exit; a gallery or corridor leading to the various divisions of a building; a part or portion quoted or referred to in a book, poem, etc.; the act of carrying through all the steps necessary to render valid (the *passage* of a bill or of a law); an encounter (a *passage* at arms, a *passage* of love).—*Birds of passage*, birds which migrate with the season from a colder to a warmer or from a warmer to a colder climate.

passant, pas′ant, *a.* [Fr. *passant*, ppr. of *passer*, to pass. PASS.] *Her.* a term applied to an animal which appears to walk.

passé, pas‧ā′, *a.* [Fr.] Past; faded: as applied to persons, past the heyday of life.

passenger, pas′en‧jér, *n.* [O.E. *passager*, one who makes a passage; the *n* being an intrusive element, as in *messenger*.] One who passes or is on his way; a wayfarer; a traveler; one who travels, for payment, on a railroad, steamboat, coach, or other conveyance.—**passenger pigeon,** *n.* A North American wild pigeon, great flocks of which once abounded, especially in the Mississippi valley. It was widely hunted and is now extinct.

Passeres, pas′ér‧ēz, *n. pl.* [L., sparrows, so called because the bulk of them are small birds.] A name given to the extensive order of birds also called Insessores or perchers.—**passerine,** pas′ér‧in, *a.* Pertaining to the order Passeres.—*n.* A passerine bird.

passible, pas′i‧bl, *a.* [L. *passibilis*, from *patior, passus*, to suffer. PASSION.] Capable of feeling or suffering; susceptible of impressions from external agents.—**passibility,** pas‧i‧bil′i‧ti, *n.* The quality of being passible.

passion, pash′on, *n.* [L. *passio, passionis*, from *patior, passus*, to bear, to suffer; allied to Gr. *pathos*, suffering; akin *patient, passive, compatible*, etc.] The suffering of bodily pangs; [*usually cap.*] specifically, the last suffering of the Saviour. A strong feeling or emotion by which the mind is swayed, as ambition, avarice, revenge, fear, hope, joy, grief, love, hatred, etc.; a strong deep feeling; violent agitation or excitement of mind; violent anger; zeal, ardor, vehement desire (a *passion* for fame); love; ardent affection; amorous desire; a passionate display; an exhibition of deep feeling (a *passion* of tears); a pursuit to which one is devoted.—*v.i.* To bewail; to cry out in a passionate way or lament. (*Shak.*)—**passional,** pash′on‧al, *n.* A book in which are described the sufferings of saints and martyrs.—**passionate,** pash′on‧it, *a.* Characterized by passion; exhibiting or expressing passion; readily moved to anger; fiery; showing strong emotion; vehement; warm (*passionate*

affection).—**passionately,** pash′on‧‧it‧li, *adv.* In a passionate manner; ardently; vehemently; angrily.—**passionateness,** pash′on‧it‧nes, *n.* State of being passionate.—**passionflower,** *n.* A genus of plants with showy flowers, chiefly natives of tropical South America, so called because in the anthers, styles, etc., was seen a resemblance to the symbols of the Lord's passion.—**passionless,** pash′on‧les, *a.* Void of passion. —**Passion play,** *n.* A mystery or miracle play representing the different scenes in the Passion of Christ.—**Passion Sunday,** the fifth Sunday in Lent.—**Passion Week,** the week before Holy Week, beginning with Passion Sunday.

passive, pas′iv, *a.* [L. *passivus*, from *patior, passus*, to suffer. PASSION.] Not active; inert; not acting, receiving, or capable of receiving impressions from external objects; unresisting; not opposing; receiving or suffering without resistance; *gram.* expressive of suffering or being affected by some action; expressing that the nominative is the object of some action or feeling (the *passive* voice, a *passive* verb or inflection).—**passively,** pas′iv‧li, *adv.* In a passive manner; without action; unresistingly; as a passive verb; in the passive voice.—**passiveness,** pas′iv‧nes, *n.* Quality of being passive.—**passivity,** pas‧iv′i‧ti, *n.* Passiveness; the tendency of a body to continue in a given state till disturbed by another body.—**passive resistance,** *n.* Resistance to authority (especially that of government) without violence or active fighting, but rather by civil disobedience.—**passivist,** pas′iv‧ist, *n.*

Passover, pas′ō‧vėr, *n.* A feast of the Jews, instituted to commemorate the providential escape of the Hebrews in Egypt, when God, smiting the first born of the Egyptians, *passed over* the houses of the Israelites, which were marked with the blood of the paschal lamb; the sacrifice offered at the feast of the passover; the paschal lamb.

passport, pas′pōrt, *n.* [Fr. *passeport*, a safe-conduct, originally a permission to enter or leave a port. PASS, PORT.] A warrant of protection and authority to travel, granted to persons moving from place to place, by a competent authority; especially granted to persons traveling in a foreign country; something that enables one to pass with safety or certainty, or to attain any object or reach any end (the favor of the great was his *passport*); in *diplomacy*, to demand a passport is the request by an ambassador to leave a foreign country as a preliminary to war. *To receive his passports*, is to be dismissed from an enemy country at the commencement of hostilities.

past, past, *p.* and *a.* [A form of *passed*.] Gone by; belonging to a time previous to this; not present nor future; spent; ended; over; existing no more.—*n.* A past or former time or state; a bygone time;

a state of matters no longer present. —*prep.* Beyond in time; after; having lost; no longer possessing (*past* sense of feeling); beyond; out of reach of; out of the scope or influence of (*past* help), beyond in position; further than.—*adv.* By.—**past master,** *n.* One who has occupied the office or dignity of master, especially in such bodies as Freemasons, etc.; *fig.* one who has experience in his particular craft or business.—**past participle,** *n.* A participle having a past or perfect meaning.—**past perfect,** *n.* A verb form describing action or state as terminated at or before a past time referred to (she *had left* before I arrived).

paste, pāst, *n.* [O.Fr. *paste,* Fr. *pâte*; from L. *pasta,* paste, from Gr. *pastē,* a mess of barley-porridge, from *passō,* to sprinkle.] A composition in which there is just sufficient moisture to soften without liquefying the mass; a mixture of flour with milk, water, etc., used in cookery, as for pies, pastry, etc.; a kind of cement variously compounded; a composition of pounded rock crystal melted with alkaline salts, and colored with metallic oxides, used for making imitation gems; *mineral,* the mineral substance in which other minerals are embedded.—*v.t.*—*pasted, pasting.* To unite or cement with paste; to fasten with paste.—**pasteboard,** pāst'bōrd, *n.* A species of thick paper formed of several single sheets pasted one upon another, or by macerating paper and casting in molds, etc.; cardboard.—*a.* Made of pasteboard. —**pastry,** pās'tri, *n.* Viands made of paste, or of which paste constitutes the principal ingredient; the crust or cover of a pie, tart, or the like.— **pasty,** pās'ti, *a.* Like paste; of the consistence of paste.—*n.* A meat pie covered with a crust.

pastel, pas•tel', *n.* [Fr. *pastel,* a pastel, woad, from L. *pastillus,* a little roll. PASTIL.] A colored crayon; also, any of a number of pale or faint colors.

pastern, pas'tėrn, *n.* [O.Fr. *pasturon,* from *pasture,* a shackle for cattle at pasture, from L. *pasco, pastum,* to feed. PASTURE.] The part of a horse's leg between the joint next the foot and the coronet of the hoof; a shackle for horses while pasturing.

pasteurize, pas'tėr•īz, pas'tūr•īz, *v.t.* [After *Louis Pasteur,* Fr. scientist.] To sterilize liquids by heating (to *pasteurize* milk).—**pasteurization,** pas•tėr•i•zā'shon, *n.*

pastil, pastille, pas•til', pas•tēl', *n.* [Fr. *pastille,* L. *pastillus,* a little roll, from *pastus,* food, *pasco, pastum,* to feed. PASTOR.] A small roll of aromatic paste, composed of gum benzoin, sandalwood, spices, etc., for burning as a fumigator or disinfectant; a lozenge.

pastime, pas'tīm, *n.* [*Pass* and *time.*] That which amuses and serves to make time pass agreeably; sport; amusement.

pastor, pas'tor, *n.* [L. *pastor,* a shepherd, from *pasco, pastum,* to feed; same root as W. *pasg,* a feeding, Armor. *paska,* to feed, Skr. *pâ,* to

guard.] A shepherd‡; a minister of the gospel having the charge of a church and congregation.—**pastoral,** pas'tor•al, *a.* [L. *pastoralis.*] Pertaining to shepherds; rustic; rural; descriptive of the life of shepherds or of a country life (a *pastoral* poem); relating to the cure of souls, or to the pastor of a church.—*Pastoral epistles,* epistles of St. Paul to Titus and Timothy dealing with the pastoral organization of their various spheres.—*Pastoral letter,* a letter or circular addressed by a bishop to the clergy and people of his diocese.— *Pastoral theology,* that part of theology which treats of the obligations of pastors and their relations toward their flocks.—*n.* A poem describing the life and manners of shepherds; a bucolic poem; a pastoral letter or address; *mus.* a simple melody in six-eight time in a rustic style; a symphony whose simple movements are designed to suggest pastoral scenes.—**pastorale,** pas•tō•rä'le, *n.* [It.] *Mus.* a pastoral.—**pastoralism,** pas'tor•al•izm, *n.* Pastoral character. —**pastorally,** pas'tor•al•li, *adv.* In a pastoral or rural manner; in the manner of a pastor.—**pastoral staff,** *n.* The official staff of a bishop or abbot, with a curved head. See CROZIER.—**pastorate,** pas'tor•it, *n.* The office or jurisdiction of a pastor; a body of pastors.

pastry. See PASTE.

pasture, pas'chėr, *n.* [O.Fr. *pasture* (Fr. *pâture*), from L. *pastura,* from *pasco,* to feed. PASTOR.] Grass for the food of cattle or other animals; ground covered with grass for the food of animals; a grazing ground.— *v.t.*—*pastured, pasturing.* To feed on growing grass, or to supply pasture for.—*v.i.* To graze.—**pasturable,** pas'chėr•a•bl, *a.* Fit for pasture.— **pasturage,** pas'chėr•ij, *n.* [O.Fr. *pasturage.*] The business of feeding or grazing cattle; grazing ground; growing grass on which cattle feed.

pasty. See PASTE.

pat, pat, *v.t.*—*patted, patting.* [Imitative of the sound of a slight sharp blow; comp. W. *ffat,* a blow, and E. *tap. Patter* is a frequentative from this.] To strike gently with the fingers or hand; to tap.—*n.* A light quick blow with the fingers or hand; a small lump of butter molded or cut into shape.—*a.* Hitting the mark; apt; fit; convenient.—*adv.* Fitly; conveniently; just in the nick; also unmoved, as to stand *pat.*

patagium, pa•tā'ji•um, *n.* [L., the border of a dress.] The flying appendage or expansion of bats, flying squirrels, etc.

patch, pach, *n.* [Connected with Swiss *patschen,* to patch, to clap on a piece, *batsch,* a patch; also It. *pezza,* a patch, a piece.] A piece of cloth sewed on a garment to repair it; any similar piece; a small piece of silk formerly stuck on the face by way of adornment; a small piece of ground; a plot; the name of the clown in patchwork or motley; the medieval fool; any sorry or poor creature.—*v.t.* To mend with patches

or pieces; to repair clumsily; to adorn (the face) with a patch or with patches; to make up of pieces and shreds; *fig.* to make hastily or without regard to forms: usually with *up* (to *patch up* a quarrel).—**patcher,** pach'-ėr, *n.* One that patches.—**patchwork,** pach'wėrk, *n.* Work composed of various figures or colors sewed together; anything formed of ill-assorted parts.—**patchy,** pach'i, *a.* Full of patches.

patchouli, patchouly, pa•chō'li, *n.* [An Indian name.] A plant of India and China, the leaves of which furnish an odorous oil; the perfume itself.

pate, pāt, *n.* [Perhaps from Ir. *pata, pota,* Sc. *pat,* a pot, the radical meaning being the brainpan or skull.] The head of a person; the top of the head.—**pated,** pā'ted, *a.* Having a pate: in composition (shallow-*pated*).

patella, pa•tel'la, *n.* [L. dim. of *patera,* a cup, from *pateo,* to lie open. PATENT.] A small pan, vase, or dish; *anat.* the kneepan.—**patelliform,** pa•tel'li•form, *a.* Like the patella; of the form of a saucer.

paten, pat'en, *n.* [L. *patina,* a pan, from *pateo,* to lie open. PATENT.] A metallic plate or flat dish; the round metallic plate on which the bread is placed in the sacrifice of the Lord's supper.

patent, pat'ent, *a.* [From L. *patens, patentis,* ppr. of *pateo,* to lie open; same root as Gr. *petannymi,* to spread; *petalon,* a leaf; akin *pan, paten, patella.*] Open; spreading; expanded; open to the perusal of all (letters *patent*); secured by law as an exclusive privilege; patented (*patent* medicines); manifest to all; evident. —*n.* A document conferring a right; a privilege or license; a writing conveying to the individual or individuals specified therein the sole right to make, use, or dispose of some new invention or discovery for a certain limited period.—*v.t.* To make the subject of a patent; to secure by patent right.—**patentable,** pat'ent•a•bl, *a.* Capable of being patented.— **patentee,** pat'en•tē", *n.* One who holds a patent; one by whom a patent is secured.—**patent leather,** *n.* A kind of leather to which a permanent polish is given by a process of japanning.—**patent right,** *n.* An exclusive privilege in an invention, etc., granted by patent.

paterfamilias, pā'tėr•fa•mil"i•as, *n.* [L., from *pater,* father, and *familia,* a family.] The father or head of a family.

paternal, pa•tėr'nal, *a.* [Fr. *paternel,* from L. *paternus,* from *pater,* father (FATHER); akin *parricide, patriarch, patrimony, patriot, patron, pattern.*] Pertaining to a father; fatherly; derived from the father; hereditary. —**paternally,** pa•tėr'nal•li, *adv.* In a paternal manner.—**paternity,** pa•tėr'ni•ti, *n.* [Fr. *paternité.*] Fatherhood; the relation of a father to his offspring; derivation from a father (the child's *paternity*); hence, origin; authorship.

paternoster, pa'tėr•nos•tėr, *n.* [L.,

our Father, the first two words of the Lord's prayer in Latin.] [*often capped*.] The Lord's prayer; every tenth large bead in the Rosary; the Rosary itself.

path, päth, *n.* pl. **paths,** päтнz. [A. Sax. *paeth*=D. and L.G. *pad,* G. *pfad,* a path; perhaps from Gr. *patos,* a trodden way, *patein,* to walk.] A way beaten or trodden by the feet of man or beast, or made hard by wheels; a narrow or unimportant road; a footway; a way or route in general; the way or course which an animal or any object follows in the air, in water, or in space; *fig.* course of life; course of conduct or procedure.—**pathless,** päth'les, *a.* Having no beaten way; untrodden.— **pathway,** päth'wā, *n.* A path; a narrow way to be passed on foot; a way; a course of life.

Pathan, pat·hän', *n.* A person of Afghan race settled in Hindustan; an Afghan.

pathetic. See PATHOS.

pathogen, path'o·jen, *n.* [Gr. *pathos,* suffering, disease, and *gen,* born.] A disease-causing organism or virus. —**pathogenic,** path'o·jen''ik, *a.* Causing disease.

pathogeny, pa·thoj'e·ni, *n.* [Gr. *pathos,* suffering, and root *gen,* to produce.] The doctrine or science of the generation and development of disease.

pathology, pa·thol'o·ji, *n.* [Gr. *pathos,* suffering, and *logos,* discourse.] That part of medicine which explains the nature of diseases, their causes, and symptoms.—**pathologic, pathological,** path·o·loj'ik, path·o·loj'i·kal, *a.*—**pathologically,** path·o·loj'i·kal·li, *adv.*—**pathologist,** pa·thol'o·jist, *n.*

pathos, pā'thos, *n.* [Gr. *pathos,* passion, suffering, from stem of *pathein,* to suffer.] That quality, attribute, or element which awakens such tender emotions as pity, compassion, or sympathy.—**pathetic,** pa·thet'ik, *a.* Moving the feelings; exciting pity, sorrow, or other tender emotion; affecting.—**pathetical,** pa·thet'i·kal, *a.*—**pathetically,** pa·thet'i·kal·li, *adv.*

patience, pā'shens, *n.* [Fr. *patience,* from L. *patientia,* from *patiens,* patient. PASSION.] The quality of being patient; the power or capacity of physical endurance; the character or habit of mind that enables one to suffer afflictions, provocation, or other evil, with a calm unruffled temper; calmness; composure; quietness or calmness in waiting for something to happen; forbearance; long-suffering; constancy in labor or exertion; perseverance; a card game played by one person alone.— **patient,** pā'shent, *a.* [L. *patiens, patientis.*] Physically able to support or endure; proof against (*patient of* labor or pain, heat, or cold); bearing pain or trial without murmuring; sustaining afflictions with fortitude, calmness, or submission; waiting with calmness; not hasty; long-suffering; persevering; calmly diligent.—*n.* One who or that which is passively affected; a sufferer from

an ailment; a person who is under medical treatment.—**patiently,** pā'shent·li, *adv.* In a patient manner; with patience; submissively; uncomplainingly.

patina, pat'i·na, *n.* [L. *patina,* a dish, a kind of cake, from *pateo,* to be open. PATENT, PAN.] The fine green rust with which bronze and copper become covered by oxidization; a weathered surface, in general, of aesthetic value.

patio, pa'ti·ō, *n.* [Sp.] A courtyard; a paved area adjoining a dwelling and used for recreation.

patois, pat·wä', *n.* [Fr.] A dialect peculiar to the peasantry or uneducated classes; a provincial form of speech, the survival of a once literary dialect.

patriarch, pā'tri·ärk, *n.* [L. *patriarcha,* from Gr. *patriarchēs—patria,* a family, from *patēr,* father, and *archē,* rule. PATERNAL.] The father and ruler of a family; generally applied to Abraham, Isaac, Jacob, and the sons of Jacob, or to the heads of families before the flood; hence, an aged venerable man; in the *Greek Church,* a dignitary superior to an archbishop.—**patriarchal,** pā·tri·är'kal, *a.* Belonging to patriarchs; subject to a patriarch.—**patriarchate,** pā'tri·är·kāt, *n.* The office or jurisdiction of a patriarch.—**patriarchy,** pā'tri·är·ki, *n.* An ecclesiastical patriarchate.

patrician, pa·trish'an, *a.* [Fr. *patricien,* from L. *patricius,* pertaining to the *patres,* senators or patricians, from *pater,* father. PATERNAL.] Pertaining to the senatorial order in ancient Rome; hence, of noble birth; not plebeian.—*n.* A person of patrician or noble birth; a nobleman.— **patriciate,** pa·trish'i·āt, *n.* The aristocracy collectively.

patricide, pat'ri·sīd, *n.* [L. *pater, patris,* father, and *caedo,* to kill.] The murder or murderer of one's father; parricide.—**patricidal,** pat·ri·sī'dal, *a.* Relating to patricide; parricidal.

patrimony, pat'ri·mo·ni, *n.* [L. *patrimonium,* from *pater, patris,* father. PATERNAL.] A right or estate inherited from one's father or ancestors; heritage; a church estate or revenue.— **patrimonial,** pat·ri·mō'ni·al, *a.* Pertaining to a patrimony; inherited from ancestors.

patriot, pā'tri·ot, *n.* [Fr. *patriote,* from L. *patria,* one's native country, from *pater,* father. PATERNAL.] A person who loves his country, and zealously supports and defends it and its interests.—*a.* Patriotic.— **patriotic,** pā·tri·ot'ik, *a.* Having the feelings of a patriot; inspired by the love of one's country; directed by zeal for the public safety and welfare.—**patriotically,** pā·tri·ot'i·kal·li, *adv.* In a patriotic manner.—**patriotism,** pā'tri·ot·izm, *n.* Love of one's country; the passion which leads a person to serve his country with zeal.

patrist, pā'trist, *n.* [From L. *patres,* fathers.] One versed in the writings of the fathers of the Christian church. —**patristic, patristical,** pa·tris'tik, pa·tris'ti·kal, *a.* Pertaining to the

ancient fathers of the Christian church. — **patristically,** pa·tris'ti·kal·li, *adv.* In a patristic manner.

patrol, pa·trōl', *n.* [Fr. *patrouille,* from *patrouiller,* to patrol, also to paddle with the feet, from *patte,* O.Fr. *pate,* a paw=G. *pfote,* D. *poot,* a paw.] *Milit.* the marching round of a guard in the night to secure the peace and safety of a camp or other place; the persons who go the rounds; a policeman who goes round a regular beat.—*v.i.* patrolled, patrolling. To go the rounds as a guard in a camp or garrison; to go the rounds in a city, as is done by a body of police.—*Patrol flotilla,* a flotilla or fleet of vessels acting by way of patrol, that is moving about and keeping guard against the approach of hostile craft and against attempts to break a blockade.—*v.t.* To pass through or perambulate in the capacity of a patrol.

patron, pā'tron, *n.* [L. *patronus,* a protector or patron, from *pater,* a father. PATERNAL.] Among the ancient Romans, a master who had freed his slave, and still retained some rights over him; a man of distinction under whose protection another placed himself; hence, one who countenances, supports, or protects either a person or a work; a man of rank or standing who assists a person in an inferior position; a patron saint; one who has the gift and disposition of an ecclesiastical benefice.—*Patron saint,* any saint under whose special protection a church, a society, or a person is regarded as placed.—**patronage,** pat'ron·ij, *n.* The act of patronizing; protection; encouragement; guardianship, as of a saint; the right of presentation to a church or ecclesiastical benefice.—**patroness,** pā'tron·es, *n.* A female patron.— **patronize,** pat'ron·īz, *v.t.*—patronized, patronizing. To act as patron toward; to give support or countenance to; to favor; to assist; to assume the air of a patron or superior toward.—**patronizer,** pat'ron·īz·ėr, *n.* One who patronizes.—**patronizingly,** pat'ron·īz·ing·li, *adv.*

patronymic, pat·ro·nim'ik, *n.* [L. *patronymicus,* from Gr. *patēr, patros,* a father, and *onoma,* a name. PATERNAL.] A personal name derived from that of parent or ancestor (*Tydides,* the son of Tydeus; *Williamson,* the son of William).

patroon, pa·trön', *n.* [D. *patroon,* a patron.] The proprietor of land and manorial privileges granted by the old Dutch governments of New York and New Jersey.

patten, pat'en, *n.* [Fr. *patin,* a clog, patten, from *patte,* the foot. PATROL.] A wooden shoe or sole, standing on an iron ring, worn to keep the shoes from the dirt or mud; *masonry,* the base of a column or pillar; the sole for the foundation of a wall.

patter, pat'ėr, *v.i.* [Freq. from *pat,* to give a slight blow. PAT.] To strike, as falling drops of water or hail, with a quick succession of small sounds; to move with quick steps, making a succession of small sounds.—*n.* A quick succession of small sounds.

patter, pat'ẽr, *v.t.* [Perhaps from the *Paternoster,* or Lord's prayer, repeated in churches in a low tone of voice. Comp. also Icel. *pata,* to prattle, *pati,* a rumor.] To repeat in a muttering way; to mutter.—*n.* Rapid, routine talk used by magicians, comedians, etc.

pattern, pat'ẽrn, *n.* [Same word as *patron,* which has also the sense of *pattern* in French and Spanish, as has L.L. *patronus.*] An original or model proposed for imitation; that which is to be copied or imitated; a piece or part exhibited as a specimen of the whole; a design or figure corresponding in outline to an object that is to be fabricated, and serving as a guide for determining its shape and dimensions; an ornamental design on some woven fabric: the counterpart in wood of something that is to be cast in metal.

patty, pat'i, *n.* [Fr. *pâté,* pie, pasty.] A little pie; a pasty.—**pattypan,** *n.* A pan to bake patties in.

patulous, pat'ū·lus, *a.* [L. *patulus,* from *pateo,* to be open. PATENT.] Spreading slightly; expanded; opening widely; with a spreading aperture.

paucity, pa̧'si·ti, *n.* [L. *paucitas,* from *paucus,* few; cog. with E. *few.*] Fewness; smallness of number; smallness or scantness of quantity.

Pauline, pa̧l'ēn, *a.* Pertaining to St. *Paul,* or to his writings; a member of St. Paul's School in London.

paunch, pa̧nsh, *n.* [O.Fr. *panche* (Fr. *panse*), from L. *pantex, panticis,* the belly.] The belly and its contents; the abdomen; the first and largest stomach in ruminating quadrupeds, into which the food is received before rumination.—**paunchy,** pa̧n'shi, *a.* Having a prominent paunch; big-bellied.

pauper, pa̧'pẽr, *n.* [L. *pauper,* poor (whence *poverty, poor, impoverish*); akin *paucus,* few. PAUCITY.] A poor person; one in a state of indigence; particularly, one who, on account of poverty, becomes chargeable to a parish.—**pauperism,** pa̧'pẽr·izm, *n.* The state of being a pauper; a state of indigence in a community.—**pauperize,** pa̧'pẽr·īz, *v.t.*—*pauperized, pauperizing.* To reduce to pauperism.

pause, pa̧z, *n.* [Fr., from L. *pausa,* Gr. *pausis,* a stopping, from *pauō,* to stop; *pose* (seen in *compose, impose,* etc.) is of same origin.] A temporary cessation; an intermission of action, of speaking, singing, or the like; a short stop; cessation proceeding from doubt; suspense; a mark of suspension of the voice; a character marking a halt in music.—*v.i.*—*paused, pausing.* To make a pause or short stop; to intermit speaking or action; to wait; to forbear for a time; to hesitate; to hold back; to be intermitted (the music *pauses*).—**pauser,** pa̧'zẽr, *n.* One who pauses.

pave, pāv, *v.t.*—*paved,* (pp. sometimes *paven*), *paving.* [Fr. *paver,* L.L. *pavare,* from L. *pavire,* to ram, to pave.] To make a hard level surface upon by laying with stones, bricks, etc.; to floor with brick, stone, or other material.—*To pave a way* (*fig.*), to prepare a way; to remove difficulties or obstacles beforehand.—**pavement,** pāv'ment, *n.* [L. *pavimentum.*] A paved path or road; a floor or surface that is trodden on, consisting of stones, bricks, etc.; the stones or other material with which anything is paved.—**paver,** pā'vẽr, *n.* One who paves; a pavior.—**paving,** pāv'ing, *n.* Pavement; the laying of floors, streets, etc., with pavement.—*Paving stones,* large prepared stones or slabs for paving.—**pavior, paviour,** pā'vi·ẽr, *n.* One whose occupation is to pave; a slab or brick used for paving; a rammer for driving paving stones.

pavid, pav'id, *a.* [L. *pavidus,* from *paveo,* to fear.] Timid; fearful.

pavilion, pa·vil'yon, *n.* [Fr. *pavillon,* L. *papilio, papilionis,* a butterfly, also a tent, from shape of latter.] A tent; particularly, a large tent raised on posts; a canopy; *arch.* a small building or a part of a building having a tent-formed roof. —*Pavilion roof,* a roof sloping or hipped equally on all sides.—*v.t.* To furnish with tents; to shelter with a tent.

pavonine, pav'o·nīn, *a.* [L. *pavoninus,* from *pavo,* a peacock.] Belonging to a peacock; resembling a peacock; exhibiting the brilliant hues of the tail of a peacock; iridescent; applied to ores, etc.—*n.* The iridescent luster found on some ores and metallic products.

paw, pa̧, *n.* [From the Celtic: W. *pawen,* Armor. *pav, pao;* comp. D. *poot,* G. *pfote,* a paw.] The foot of quadrupeds having claws.—*v.i.* To draw the forefoot along the ground; to scrape with the forefoot (as a horse does).—*v.t.* To scrape or strike with the forefoot; to handle roughly.

pawky, pa̧'ki, *a.* Humorous, dry and satiric in tone.

pawl, pa̧l, *n.* [W. *pawl,* akin to L. *palus,* a stake. POLE.] A short bar pivoted at one end, so as to catch in a notch of a revolving body and stop its motion; a click or detent which falls into the teeth of a ratchet wheel.—*v.t.* To stop with a pawl.

pawn, pa̧n, *n.* [Fr. *pan,* a piece of a garment, formerly also a pawn or pledge, from L. *pannus,* a cloth, a rag. PANE.] Some article or chattel given or deposited as security for money borrowed; a pledge.—*In pawn, at pawn,* in the state of being pawned or pledged.—*v.t.* To give or deposit in pledge; to pledge with a pawnbroker; to pledge for the fulfillment of a promise.—**pawnbroker,** pa̧n'brō·kẽr, *n.* A person licensed to lend money at a legally fixed rate of interest on goods deposited with him.—**pawnbroking,** pa̧n'brō·king, *n.* The business of a pawnbroker.—**pawnee,** pa̧·nē', *n.*

The person to whom a pawn is delivered as security.—**pawner,** *n.* One that pawns.

pawn, pa̧n, *n.* [O.Fr. *paon, poon, peon,* properly a foot soldier. PEON.] A piece of the lowest rank at chess; an insignificant factor or person used as a tool by another.

pawpaw, pa̧'pa̧, *n.* See PAPAW.

pax, paks, *n.* [L. *pax,* peace.] In the Roman Catholic Church a small tablet engraved with sacred figures or emblems, which, having been kissed by the priest, was then kissed by others.

paxwax, paks'waks, *n.* [Also called *faxwax,* from A.Sax. *feax,* hair, and *weaxan,* to wax or grow.] A strong tendinous ligament strengthening the neck of the ox, sheep, etc.

pay, pā, *v.t.*—pret. and pp. *paid,* [O.Fr. *paier, paer* (Fr. *payer*), to pay, originally to please, being from L. *pacare,* to pacify—*pax, pacis,* peace. PEACE.] To recompense for goods received or for service rendered; to discharge one's obligation to; to compensate, remunerate, reward, requite; to discharge (as a debt) by giving or doing that which is due; to give; to render or offer; without any sense of obligation (to *pay* attention, respect, court, a visit); *naut.* to cover or coat, as the bottom of a vessel, a mast, etc.—*To pay out, naut.* to slacken or cause to run out (a rope). —*v.i.* To make payment or requital; to be worth the pains or efforts spent; to be remunerative.—*To pay for,* to make amends for; to atone for.—*To pay off,* to pay wages and discharge.—*n.* An equivalent given for money due, goods purchased, or services performed.—**payable,** pā'a·bl, *a.*—**pay dirt,** *n. Mining,* earth, ore, rock, etc., which yields a profit to the miner.—**payee,** pā·ē', *n.* The person to whom money is to be paid.—**payer,** pā'ẽr, *n.* One that pays; the person named in a bill or note who has to pay the holder.— **payload,** pā'lōd, *n.* Any useful cargo in a transport vehicle; in military rockets, the warhead.—**paymaster,** pā'mas·tẽr, *n.* One from whom wages or reward are received.—**payment,** pā'ment, *n.* The act of paying; the thing given in discharge of a debt; requital.—**payola,** pā·ō'lä, *n.* An illegal payment for commercial favors, as to a disc jockey for promoting a song.—**payroll,** pā'rōl, *n.* A list of employees and of their wages; money needed for payment of wages.

paynim, pā'nim, *n.* [O.Fr. *apienime, paienisme,* paganism, from *paien,* L. *paganus,* a pagan. PAGAN.] A pagan; a heathen.

pea, pē, *n.* [O.E. *pese, pees,* a pea, pl. *pesen, peses,* A.Sax. *pise,* from L. *pisum,* Gr. *pisos,* a pea. *Pea* is a false form, the *s* of the root being mistaken for the sign of the plural. In the plural we always write *peas* for the individual seeds, but often *pease* for an indefinite quantity (this form being the old singular): three or four *peas,* a bushel of *pease* (or *peas*).] A well-known plant with papilionaceous flowers, one of the most valuable of vegetables, cultivated in the garden and in the field; one of the seeds of the plant.—**peanut,** *n.* An American plant, whose pods grow first above and then below ground; the nutlike seed of this plant.—**peanut butter,** *n.* A paste made from crushed peanuts.

peace, pēs, *n.* [From O.Fr. *pais* (Fr. *paix*), from L. *pax, pacis,* peace—root *pac,* seen in *paciscor,* to agree (whence *pact*); of same origin as *pay, appease.*] A state of quiet or tranquility; calm, quietness, repose; especially freedom from war; a cessation of hostilities; absence of strife; tranquility of mind; quiet of conscience; harmony; concord; public tranquility.—*At peace,* in a peaceful state.—*Breach of the peace,* a violation of public tranquility by riotous or other conduct.—*To hold one's peace,* to be silent; to suppress one's thoughts; not to speak.—*To make a person's peace,* with another, to reconcile the other to him.—*Peace establishment,* the reduced number of effective men in the army during time of peace.—*Commission of the peace,* a commission appointing justices of the peace, and by virtue of which the judges sit upon circuit.—*Justices of the peace.* JUSTICE.—**peaceable,** pēs′a·bl, *a.* Tranquil; peaceful; disposed to peace; not quarrelsome. ∴ *Peaceable* usually refers to the character and disposition of men; *pacific* to designs and intentions; while *peaceful* refers to the state or condition of men or things.—**peaceableness,** pēs′a·bl·nes, *n.* The state or quality of being peaceable.—**peaceably,** pēs′a·bli, *adv.* In a peaceable manner.—**peaceful,** pēs′-ful, *a.* Full of, possessing, or enjoying peace; tranquil; quiet; removed from noise or tumult; pacific.—**peacefully,** pēs′ful·li, *adv.* In a peaceful manner; quietly; tranquilly.—**peacefulness,** pēs′ful·nes, *n.* The state or quality of being peaceful.—**peacemaker,** pēs′mā·kėr, *n.* One who reconciles parties at variance.—**peace offering,** *n.* Something offered to procure peace.—**peace pipe,** *n.* The ceremonial, long-stemmed pipe of the North American Indians, also called the *calumet,* smoked by the members to signify peace.

peach, pēch, *n.* [Fr. *pêche,* It. *pesca, persica,* from L. *persica, Persicum (malum),* the Persian apple.] A fruit tree of many varieties, grown in temperate climates; the fruit of the tree, a sweet, juicy drupe a little smaller than an apple, containing a stone; also, that which resembles a peach, as in beauty or goodness.—**peach blossom,** *n.* The delicate pink flower of the peach, which appears in early spring.

peacock, pē′kok, *n.* [*Pea*=A.Sax. *pawa,* from L. *pavo,* a peacock, the name being perhaps from the bird's cry.] A large and beautiful gallinaceous bird remarkable for the beauty

of its plumage, properly the male of the species, the female being, for distinction's sake, called a *peahen.*—**peafowl,** *n.* The peacock or peahen.

pea jacket, pē′jak·et, *n.* [*Pea* is from D. and L.G. *pije,* coarse, thick cloth, a warm jacket; akin to Goth. *paida,* a garment.] A thick loose woolen jacket worn by seamen, fishermen, etc.

peak, pēk, *n.* [Fr. *pic,* a mountain peak, a pick, *pique,* a pike, from Armor. *pic,* W. *pig.* a point, a pike, a beak; akin *beak, pike, pick, peck.*] The top of a hill or mountain, ending in a point; a projecting point; a projecting portion on a head covering (the *peak* of a cap); *naut.* the upper corner of a sail which is extended by a gaff or yard; the highest point; the point of greatest development.—*v.t.* To cause to come to a peak.—*v.i.* To reach the peak of.—**peaked,** pēkt, *a.* Pointed; having a peak.

peak, pēk, *v.i.* [Perhaps from *peak, n.,* from the sharpened features of sickly persons.] To look sickly or thin; to be or become emaciated.—**peakish,** pēk′ish, *a.* Of a thin and sickly cast or face.

peal, pēl, *n.* [A mutilated form of *appeal.*] A succession of loud sounds, as of bells, thunder, cannon, shouts of a multitude, etc.; a set of bells tuned to each other; the changes rung on such bells.—*v.i.* To utter or give out a peal.—*v.t.* To cause to ring or sound; to utter loudly and sonorously.

pean. See PAEAN.

pear, pâr, *n.* [A.Sax. *peru,* Fr. *poire,* from L. *pirum,* a pear.] A fruit tree of the genus *Pyrus,* grown in temperate climates; the fruit itself, a sweet, fleshy pome.

pearl, pėrl, *n.* [Fr. *perle,* from L.L. *perula, perla,* a pearl, either for *pirula,* from L. *pirum,* a pear, or for *pilula,* a pill, a globule.] A silvery or bluish-white, hard, smooth, lustrous body, of a roundish, oval, or pear-shaped form, produced by certain mollusks; anything very valuable; what is best.—*a.* Relating to, made of pearls.—*v.t.* To set or adorn with pearls.—**pearlash,** pėrl′-ash, *n.* Commercial carbonate of potash.—**pearl barley,** *n.* The seed of barley ground into small round grains.—**pearl nautilus,** *n.* The true nautilus as distinguished from the argonaut or paper nautilus.—**pearly,** pėr′li, *a.* Containing pearls; resembling pearls; nacreous.

peasant, pez′ant, *n.* [O.Fr. *païsant* (Fr. *paysan*), from *pais, pays,* L. *pagus,* a district of country (with *t* affixed as in *tyrant*). PAGAN, PAGE (boy).] A rustic or countryman; one occupied in rural labor.—*a.* Rustic; rural.—**peasantry,** pez′ant·-ri, *n.* Peasants collectively; the body of country people.

pease, pēz, *n.* See PEA.

peat, pēt, *n.* [For *beat, bete,* from old *bete,* to mend a fire; A.Sax. *bétan,* to make better; akin *bette, boot.*] A kind of turf used as fuel; the natural accumulation of vege-

table matter, more or less decomposed, cut and dried for fuel.—**peat moss,** pēt mos, *n.* Any moss, especially of the genus *Sphagnum,* from which peat has formed or may form.—**peaty,** pēt′i, *n.*

pebble, peb′l, *n.* [A.Sax. *papolstán,* lit. pebble-stone; etym. unknown.] A small round stone worn and rounded by the action of water; a transparent, colorless rock crystal. —*v.t.* To pelt or pave with pebbles; to grain leather, paper, etc., for a rough surface.—**pebbly,** peb′li, *a.*

pecan, pē·kan′, *n.* [Fr. *pacane,* Sp. *pacana.*] A species of hickory and its fruit.

peccable, pek′a·bl, *a.* [L.L. *peccabilis,* peccable, from L. *pecco,* to sin.] Liable to sin; subject to transgress the divine law.—**peccability,** pek·a·bil′i·ti, *n.* State of being peccable.—**peccadillo,** pek·a·dil′ō, *n.* [Sp. *pecadillo,* dim. of *pecado,* L. *peccatum,* a sin, from *pecco.*] A slight trespass or offense; a petty crime or fault.—**peccancy,** pek′an·si, *n.* State or quality of being peccant.—**peccant,** pek′ant, *a.* [L. *peccans, peccantis,* ppr. of *pecco.*] Sinning; criminal; morbid; corrupt (*peccant* humors).—**peccantly,** pek′-ant·li, *adv.*

peccary, pek′a·ri, *n.* [South American name.] A pachydermatous quadruped of America, representing the swine of the Old World, to which it is allied.

peccavi, pek·kä′vi, [L., I have sinned, from *pecco,* to sin.] A word used to express confession or acknowledgment of an offense.

peck, pek, *n.* [Perhaps a form of *pack;* but comp. Fr. *picotin,* a peck; L.L. *picotus,* a liquid measure.] The fourth part of a bushel; a dry measure of 8 quarts.

peck, pek, *v.t.* [A slightly different form of *pick.*] To strike with the beak; to pick up with the beak; to make by striking with the beak, or a pointed instrument (to *peck* a hole).—*v.i.* To make strokes with a beak, or a pointed instrument; to attack with petty criticism.—*n.* A quick, light stroke with a beak; a quick, light kiss (colloq.).—**pecker,** pek′ėr, *n.*

pecten, pek′ten, *n.* [L. *pecten,* a comb, a kind of shellfish, from *pecto, pexum,* to comb; root *pek,* also in Gr. *pekō,* to comb.] A genus of marine bivalves having a shell marked with diverging ribs and furrows.

pectic, pek′tik, *a.* [Gr. *pēktikos,* curdling, from *pēgnymi,* to fix.] Having the property of forming a jelly; said of an acid found in fruits.

pectin, pek′tin, *n.* [Gr. *pektos,* curdled, congealed.] A carbohydrate which forms the basis of vegetable jelly.

pectinal, pek′ti·nal, *a.* [L. *pecten,* a comb. PECTEN.] Pertaining to a comb; resembling a comb.—**pectinate, pectinated,** pek′ti·nāt, pek′ti·nā·ted, *a.* [L. *pectinatus.*] Having resemblance to the teeth of a comb; toothed like a comb; serrated.—**pectination,** pek·ti·nā′shon, *n.* The state of being pectinated; what is pectinated.

pectoral, pek′to·ral, *a*. [L. *pectoralis*, from *pectus*, *pectoris*, the breast.] Pertaining to the breast.—*Pectoral fins*, the two fore fins of a fish, situated near the gills.—*Pectoral theology*, heartfelt, unctuous belief.—*Pectus theologum facit* (Augustine).— *n*. A covering or protection for the breast; a breastplate; the breastplate of the Jewish high priest; a medicine for complaints of the chest; a pectoral fin.

peculate, pek′ū·lāt, *v.i.*—peculated, peculating. [L. *peculor*, *peculatus*, to steal, from *peculium*, private property, from *pecu*, cattle, in which wealth originally consisted; cog. E. *fee*. PECULIAR, PECUNIARY.] To appropriate public money, or goods entrusted to one's care; to embezzle. —**peculation**, pek·ū·lā′shon, *n*. The act of peculating; embezzlement.— **peculator**, pek′ū·lā·tėr, *n*. One who peculates.

peculiar, pi·kūl′yėr, *a*. [L. *peculiaris*, one's own, peculiar, extraordinary, from *peculium*, one's own property. PECULATE.] One's own; of private, personal, or characteristic possession and use; specially belonging (*peculiar* to that part of the country); singular; striking; unusual; eccentric.—*n*. England. A parish or church which has ecclesiastical jurisdiction within itself.—**peculiarity**, pi·kū′li·ar″i·ti, *n*. The quality of being peculiar; that which is peculiar to a person or thing; a special characteristic or feature.—**peculiarize**, pi·kū′li·ėr·īz, *v.t.*—peculiarized, peculiarizing. To make peculiar; to set apart; to appropriate.— **peculiarly**, pi·kū′li·ėr·li, *adv*. In a peculiar manner; especially; in a manner not common to others.

pecuniary, pi·kū′ni·a·ri, *a*. [Fr. *pécuniaire*, L. *pecuniarius*, from *pecunia*, money, from *pecu*, cattle. PECULATE.] Relating to or connected with money; consisting of money.

pedagogue, ped′a·gog, *n*. [Gr. *paidagōgos*—*pais*, *paidos*, a child, and *agō*, to lead.] A teacher of children; a schoolmaster; now generally by way of contempt.—**pedagogic, pedagogical**, ped·a·goj′ik, ped·a·goj′i·kal, *a*. Resembling or belonging to a pedagogue.—**pedagogics**, ped·a·goj′iks, *n*. The science or art of teaching. —**pedagogism**, ped′a·gog·izm, *n*. The business or manners of a pedagogue.—**pedagogy**, ped′a·go·ji, *n*. The art or office of a pedagogue.

pedal, ped′al, *a*. [L. *pedalis*, belonging to the foot, from *pes*, *pedis*, the foot, seen also in *pedestal*, *pedestrian*, *biped*, *quadruped*, *centipede*, *expedite*, *impede*, *dispatch*, etc. FOOT.] Pertaining to a foot (*pedal* digits); *mus.* relating to a pedal.—*n*. A lever to be pressed down by the foot; a sort of treadle; a part of a musical instrument acted on by the feet, as in the piano for strengthening or softening the sound; on the organ for opening additional sets of pipes; on the harmonium for working the bellows, etc.—*v.t.* To work the

pedal of a bicycle, to increase or decrease the speed.—*v.i.* To advance or slow down on a bicycle.

pedant, ped′ant, *n*. [Fr. *pédant*, It. Sp., and Pg. *pedante*, for *pedagogante*, from L. *paedagogans*, *paedagogantis*, ppr. of *paedagogo*, to educate. PEDAGOGUE.] A person who makes a vain display of his learning, or who prides himself on his book learning but is devoid of taste; one devoted to a system of rules.— **pedantic, pedantical**, pi·dan′tik, pi·dan′ti·kal, *a*. Pertaining to a pedant or to pedantry.—**pedantically**, pi·dan′ti·kal·li, *adv*. In a pedantic manner.—**pedantry**, ped′ant·ri, *n*. The manners or character of a pedant; ostentation or boastful display of learning; obstinate adherence to rules or established forms.

pedate, ped′āt, *a*. [L. *pedatus*, from *pes*, *pedis*, the foot. PEDAL.] Having divisions like toes; divided into distinct lobes; *bot.* applied to certain palmate leaves.—**pedatifid**, pi·dat′i·fid, *a*. [L. *findo*, *fidi*, to divide.] *Bot.* divided in a pedate manner.

peddle, ped′l, *v.i.*—peddle, peddling. [From Prov. E. *ped* or *pad*, a wicker basket, a pannier, akin to *pod*. Hence *pedlar*.] To travel about and retail small wares; to trifle.—*v.t.* To sell or retail in small quantities while traveling about.—**peddler**, ped′lėr, *n*.

pederasty, ped′ėr·as·ti, *n*. [Gr. *paiderastia*, from *pais*, *paidos*, boy, and *eraō*, to long for.] Unnatural sex relations between males.—**pederast**, ped′e·rast, *n*. One who practices pederasty.

pedestal, ped′es·tal, *n*. [Sp. *pedestal*, Fr. *piedestal*, It. *piedestallo*, from L. *pes*, *pedis*, the foot, and G. and E. *stall*.] A basement or support for a column, a statue, a vase, etc.

pedestrian, pe·des′tri·an, *a*. [L. *pedestris*, from *pes*, *pedis*, the foot. PEDAL.] Going on foot; performed on foot; walking; in literary criticism, prosaic in tone.—*n*. One that walks or journeys on foot; a remarkable walker.—**pedestrianism**, pe·des′tri·an·izm, *n*. The practice of walking; the art of a professional walker.

pediatrician, pē′di·a·trish″an, *n*. [Gr. *pais*, child, and *iatreia*, medical treatment.] A physician specializing in pediatrics.—**pediatrics**, pē·di·at′riks, *n*. The medical care of children.

pedicel, ped′i·sel, *n*. [From *pedicellus*, a form equivalent to L. *pediculus*, dim. of *pes*, *pedis*, the foot. PEDAL.] *Bot.* the stalk that supports a single flower, leaf, etc.; any short small footstalk; *zool.* a footstalk by which certain animals of the lower orders, as zoophytes, etc., are attached.— **pedicellate**, ped′i·sel·āt, *a*. Having a pedicel.—**pedicle**, ped′i·kl, *n*. See PEDICEL.

pedicular, pediculous, pe·dik′ū·lėr, pe·dik′ū·lus, *a*. [L. *pediculus*, a louse.] Lousy; being infested with lice.

pediculosis, pe·dik′ū·lō″sis, *n*. [N.L. from L. *pediculus*, louse, and Gr. suffix *osis*, signifying a condition,

state.] *Med.* infestation with lice.

pedicure, ped′i·kūr, *n*. [L. *pes*, *pedis*, foot, *cura*, *care*.] Care and grooming of the feet; one whose business is foot care; a chiropodist.

pedigree, ped′i·grē, *n*. [O.Fr. *pedegru*, Fr. *pie de grue*, crane's foot; L. *pes*, foot, *de*, of, *grus*, crane.] A line of ancestors; lineage; a genealogy; a genealogical or family tree.

pediment, ped′i·ment, *n* [From L. *pes*, *pedis*, the foot.] *Arch.* the low triangular mass resembling a gable at the end of buildings in the Greek style, surrounded with a cornice, and often ornamented with sculptures; a small gable or triangular decoration like a gable over a window, a door, etc.—**pedimental**, ped′i·men·tal, *a*. Relating to a pediment.

pedobaptism, pē·do·bap′tizm, *n*. [Gr. *pais*, *paidos*, a child.] The baptism of infants or children.

pedometer, pi·dom′et·ėr, *n*. [L. *pes*, *pedis*, the foot, and Gr. *metron*, a measure.] An instrument (often resembling a watch) by which paces are numbered as a person walks, and the distance thus ascertained.

peduncle, pi·dung′kl, *n*. [From L. *pes*, *pedis*, a foot.] *Bot.* the stalk that supports the fructification of a plant, *i.e.*, the flower and fruit; *zool.* the stem or stalk by which certain brachiopods, etc., are attached.—**peduncular**, pi·dung′kū·lėr, *a*. Pertaining to a peduncle, growing from a peduncle.—**pedunculate, pedunculated**, pi·dung′kū·lāt, pi·dung′kū·lā·ted, *a*. Having a peduncle; growing on a peduncle.

peek, pēk, *v.i.* To peep; to look or spy through half closed eyes.—*n*. A quick, secret glance.

peel, pēl, *n*. [W. *pill*, a tower, a fortress.] A name of certain strong square towers or strongholds common on the Scottish borders.

peel, pēl, *v.t.* [O.Fr. *peiler* (Fr. *peler*), to peel, from L. *pellis*, the skin (cog. with E. *fell*, a skin), whence also *pellicle*, *peltry*, *pelisse*, etc.] To strip the skin, bark, or rind from; to strip by drawing or tearing off the skin; to decorticate; to strip (bark) from the surface.—*v.i.* To lose the skin or rind; to fall off (as bark or skin).—*n*. The skin or rind of anything.—**peeler**, pēl′ėr, *n*. One that peels.

peel, pēl, *n*. [Fr. *pelle*, from L. *pala*, a spadè.] A wooden shovel used by bakers to put their bread in and take it out of the oven.

peen, pēn, *n*. [Scand.] The head of a hammer opposite the face.—*v.t.* To shape an object by striking it with the peen.

peep, pēp, *v.i.* [Imitative of sound, like D. and G. *piepen*, Dan. *pippe*, L. *pipio*, Gr. *pippizō*, to chirp; the other meaning is supposed to have been suggested from the chicken's peep or chirp closely accompanying its peeping from the shell.] To cry, as chickens; to cheep; to chirp; to begin to appear; to look through a crevice; to look narrowly, closely, or slyly.—*n*. The cry of a chicken;

a sly look, or a look through a crevice.—*Peep of day*, the dawn or daybreak.—**peeper**, pēp′ẽr, *n.* One that peeps.—**peephole**, *n.* A hole through which one may peep without being discovered.—**peep show**, *n.* A show of small pictures viewed through a hole fitted with a magnifying lens.

peer, pēr, *n.* [Lit. an equal; O.Fr. *peer*, *per*, *par* (Fr. *pair*), from L. *par*, equal. PAIR.] One of the same rank, qualities, or the like; an equal; a match; a companion; a member of one of the five degrees of British nobility (duke, marquis, earl, viscount, baron); a nobleman.—*House of Peers*. the House of Lords.—**peerage**, pēr′ij, *n.* The rank or dignity of a peer; the body of peers. —**peeress**, pēr′es, *n.* The consort of a peer; a woman ennobled by descent, by creation, or by marriage. —**peerless**, pēr′les, *a.* Unequaled; having no peer or equal.—**peerlessly**, pēr′les·li, *adv.* In a peerless manner. —**peerlessness**, pēr′les·nes, *n.*

peer, pēr, *v.i.* [O.Fr. *perer*, *pareir* from L. *pareo*, to appear; same as *-pear* in *appear*; or from L.G. *piren*, to peer.] To come just in sight; to appear (*Shak.*); to look narrowly; to pry; to peep.

peevish, pē′vish, *a.* [Comp. Dan. *piaeve*, to cry like a child; Sc. *pew*, *pyow*, a sound of complaint.] Apt to mutter and complain; easily vexed or fretted; fretful; querulous; self-willed.—**peevishly**, pē′vish·li, *adv.*—**peevishness**, pē′vish·nes, *n.*

peg, peg, *n.* [Comp. Dan. *pig*; a spike; W. *pig*, something sharp; allied probably to E. *peak*, *pick*.] A wooden pin used in fastening things, as a mark, or otherwise; one of the pins on a musical instrument for stretching the strings; a pin on which to hang anything.— *To take one down a peg*, to humiliate him.—*v.t.*—**pegged, pegging.** To put pegs into for fastening, etc.; to fasten on the sole of (a shoe) with pegs; to mark off by pegs.—*v.i.* To work diligently; generally followed by *away* or *on.* (Colloq.)—**peg top**, *n.* A child's toy, a variety of top made to spin by a string.—*a.* Tapering in shape like a top (*peg-top* pants).

Pegasus, peg′a·sus, *n.* The winged horse of Greek mythology, often regarded as the horse of the Muses, and hence connected with poets and poetry.

peignoir, pān·wär′, pān′wär, *n.* [Fr. from *peigner*, to comb, from L. *pectinare*.] A woman's loose negligee.

pejorative, pē′jor·ā·tiv, *a.* [L. *pejor*, worse.] Conveying a depreciatory meaning.—*n.* A word conveying such a meaning (*poetaster* being a *pejorative* of *poet*).

Pekingese, Pekinese, pē′king·ēz″, *n.* [From *Peking*.] A native of Peking; a small pet dog, originally from China, having a flat face and short legs.

pekoe, pē′kō, *n.* [Chinese, lit. white down.] A fine black tea.

pelage, pel′ij, *n.* [Fr. *pelage*, hair of the hide, from L. *pilus*, hair. PILE.]

Zool. the hairy covering of an animal.

Pelagian, pe·lā′ji·an, *n.* A follower of *Pelagius*, a British monk of the fourth century, who denied original sin, and asserted the doctrine of free will and the merit of good works.—**Pelagianism**, pe·lā′ji·an·izm, *n.* The doctrines of Pelagius.

pelagic, pe·laj′ik, *a.* [Gr. *pelagos*, the ocean.] Belonging to the ocean; inhabiting the open ocean.

pelargonium, pel·är·gō′ni·um, *n.* [From Gr. *pelargos*, a stork—from the shape of the capsules.] Stork's-bill, an extensive genus of highly ornamental plants, usually called *Geraniums.* See GERANIUM.

Pelasgian, Pelasgic, pe·las′ji·an, pe·las′jik, *a.* Pertaining to the Pelasgians or Pelasgi, prehistoric inhabitants of Greece, etc.

pelerine, pel′ér·in, *n.* [Fr., from *pelerin*, a pilgrim. PILGRIM.] A lady's long cape or fur tippet.

pelf, pelf, *n.* [O.Fr. *pelfre*, spoil, booty, from L. *pilare*, to rob, and *facere*, to make. PILFER.] Money; riches; filthy lucre: a contemptuous term.

pelican, pel′i·kan, *n.* [From L. *pelicanus*, Gr. *pelekanos*, a pelican, from *pelekys*, a hatchet—from shape of bill.] A web-footed bird, larger than the swan, with a very large bill, and beneath the under mandible a huge pouch for holding fish.

pelisse, pe·lēs′, *n.* [Fr. *pelisse*, from L. *pelliceus*, made of skins, from *pellis*, a skin. PEEL, *v.t.*] Originally a garment lined or trimmed with fur; now a robe of silk or other material worn by ladies.

pellagra, pe·lā′gra, *n.* [It. *pellagra*, L. *pellis*, skin, and Gr. *agra*, seizure.] A disease affecting the skin, digestive system, and nervous system caused by vitamin B deficiency.—**pellagrous**, pel·lā′grus, *a.*

pellet, pel′et, *n.* [Fr. *pelote*, from L.L. *pilota*, *pelota*, dim. of L. *pila*, a ball. PILE (heap).] A little ball; one of the globules of small shot.—*v.t.* To form into pellets.

pellicle, pel′i·kl, *n.* [L. *pellicula*, dim. of *pellis*, skin. PEEL, *v.t.*] A thin skin or film on a surface; *bot.* the outer cuticular covering of plants.— **pellicular**, pel·lik′ū·lẽr, *a.* Pertaining to a pellicle.

pellitory, pel′i·to·ri, *n.* [A corruption of L. *parietaria*, lit. the wall plant, from *paries*, *parietis*, a wall.] A name of several plants of the nettle family; also, a number of European plants which are similar to yarrow.

pellmell, pel′mel, *adv.* [Fr. *pêle-mêle*, from *pelle* (L. *pala*), a shovel, and *mêler*, to mix (MEDLEY).] With confused violence; in a disorderly body; in utter confusion; at a wild speed.—*a.* Tumultuous; disorderly; helter-skelter.—*n.* A violent disorder; an indiscriminate mingling. —*v.t.* To throw together or execute pellmell.

pellucid, pel·lū′sid, *a.* [L. *pellucidus* —*pel*, for *per*, through, and *lucidus*, bright. LUCID.] Transparent; admitting the passage of light; trans-

lucent; not opaque.—**pellucidity, pellucidness**, pel·lū·sid′i·ti, pel·lū′-sid·nes, *n.* The state or quality of being pellucid.—**pellucidly**, pel·lū′-sid·li, *adv.* In a pellucid manner.

Peloponnesian, pel′ō·pon·nē″si·an, *a.* Belonging to *Peloponnesus*, or the southern peninsula of Greece.

peloria, pi·lō′ri·a, *n.* [Gr. *pelōr*, a monster.] *Bot.* regularity of structure in the flowers of plants which normally bear irregular flowers.— **peloric**, pi·lor′ik, *a.* Characterized by peloria.

pelt, pelt, *n.* [Shortened from *peltry*, from L. *pellis*, a skin. PEEL, *v.t.*] The skin of a beast with the hair on it; a raw hide.—**peltry**, pel′tri, *n.* [Fr. *pelletrie.*] Pelts collectively; usually applied to the skins of fur-bearing animals in the raw state.

pelt, pelt, *v.t.* [O.E. *pulten*, probably from L. *pultare*, to strike or knock, from *pello*, to drive. PULSE.] To strike or assail with something thrown or driven; to drive by throwing something.—*v.i.* To throw missiles.—*n.* A blow or stroke from something thrown.—**pelter**, pel′tẽr, *n.* One who or that which pelts.

peltate, pel′tāt, *a.* [L. *pelta*, a target.] Shield-shaped; *bot.* fixed to the stalk by the center or by some point distinctly within the margin.— **peltately**, pel′tāt·li, *adv.*

pelvis, pel′vis, *n.* [L. *pelvis*, a basin.] *Anat.* the bony cavity of the body constituting a framework for the lower part of the abdomen.—**pelvic**, pel′vik, *a.* Pertaining to the pelvis.

pemmican, pem′i·kan, *n.* [North Amer. Indian.] A North American Indian preparation consisting of the lean of venison dried, pounded into a paste, and pressed into cakes so that it will keep long; beef dried and similarly preserved.

pemphigus, pem′fi·gus, *n.* [Gr. *pemphix, pemphigos*, a bubble.] A disease of the skin, consisting in an eruption of vesicles or pustules.

pen, pen, *n.* [O.Fr. *penne*, a pen, a feather, from L. *penna*, a feather, for *pesna*, from root seen in Gr. *petomai*, to fly, and in E. *feather.* FEATHER.] A quill or large feather‡; an instrument used for writing by means of a fluid ink; formerly almost always made of the quill of some large bird, but now commonly of metal; a writer; a penman; style or quality of writing; the internal bone of some cuttlefishes.— *v.t.*—**penned, penning.** To write; to compose and commit to paper.— **penknife**, pen′nīf, *n.* A small pocketknife, so called from its former use in making and mending quill pens.—**penman**, pen′man, *n.* pl. **penmen**, pen′men. A calligrapher; an author; a writer.—**penmanship**, pen′-man·ship, *n.* The use of the pen; the art of writing; manner of writing.—**pen name**, *n.* An author's pseudonym.

pen, pen, *v.t.*—**penned** or *pent*, **penning.** [Lit. to fasten with a *pin*; O.E. *pinne*, to bolt; A.Sax. *onpinnian*, to bolt in; L.G. *pinnen*, *pennen*, to shut, to bolt.] To shut in a small enclosure; to coop up; to encage. —*n.* A small enclosure, as for cows, sheep, fowls, etc.; a fold; a coop.

penal, pē′nal, *a.* [Fr. *pénal*, from L. *pœnalis*, from *pœna*, pain, punishment. PAIN.] Pertaining to punishment; enacting punishment; inflicting punishment; incurring or entailing punishment.—*Penal code*, a code of laws relating to the punishment of crimes.—*Penal law*, a law prohibiting an act and imposing a penalty for commission of it.—*Penal servitude*, a punishment consisting in imprisonment, often with hard labor at some special establishment. —**penalize**, pē′nal·īz, *v.t.* To make penal or subject to a penalty.— **penalty**, pen′al·ti, *n.* The punishment annexed to the commission of a crime, offense, or trespass; the suffering to which a person subjects himself by agreement, in case of nonfulfillment of stipulations; the sum forfeited for breaking an agreement.

penance, pen′ans, *n.* [O.Fr. *penance*, *peneance*, from L. *pœnitentia*, repentance, from *pœnitens*, penitent; it is a doublet of *penitence*. PAIN.] An ecclesiastical punishment imposed for sin; the suffering to which a person subjects himself as an expression of repentance; a sacrament of the Roman Catholic Church for remission of sin.

penates, pi·nā′tēz, *n. pl.* [L.] The household gods of the ancient Romans including the lares.

pence, pens, *n.* The plural of *penny*.

penchant, pen′shent, *n.* [Fr., from *pencher*, to incline.] Strong inclination; decided taste; liking; bias.

pencil, pen′sil, *n.* [O.Fr. *pincel*, a hair pencil, a brush; from L. *penicellus*, dim. of *penis*, a tail.] A small delicate brush used by painters for laying on their pigments; an instrument for marking, drawing, or writing, formed of graphite, colored chalk, or the like; often a lead pencil; *optics*, an aggregate of rays of light which converge to or diverge from the same point.—*v.t.*— **pencilled**, *pencilling*. To write or mark with a pencil.

pendant, pen′dant, *n.* [Fr. *pendant*, hanging, what hangs, a counterpart, from *pendre*, L. *pendere*, to hang, which with the allied *pendere*, to weigh, appears in *pensile*, *pendulum*, *depend*, *impend*, *expend*, *compensation*, *compendium*, etc.] Anything hanging down by way of ornament, but particularly from the neck; *naut.* a flag borne at the masthead of certain ships, of two kinds—the *long pendant*, and the *broad pendant*; an apparatus hanging from a roof or ceiling for giving light by gas; one of a pair of companion pictures, statues, etc.; an appendix or addition; *arch.* a hanging ornament used in the vaults and timber roofs of Gothic architecture.—**pendency**, pen′den·si, *n.* State of being pendent or suspended; the state of being continued as not yet decided.— **pendent**, pen′dent, *a.* [L. *pendens*,

pendentis, hanging, ppr. of *pendere*, to hang.] Hanging; suspended; depending; overhanging; projecting.— *n.* Something pendent or hanging.— **pendentive**, pen·den′tiv, *n.* [Fr. *pendentif*.] *Arch.* the part of a groined ceiling springing from one pillar or impost.—**pendently**, pen′dent·li, *adv.* In a pendent or projecting manner.—**pending**, pen′ding, *p.* and *a.* Depending; remaining undecided; not terminated.— *prep.* [A participle converted into a preposition, like *during*.] For the time of the continuance of; during.

pendragon, pen·drag′on, *n.* [W. *pen*, a head, and *dragon*, a leader.] A chief leader, a title among the ancient British.

pendulous, pen′dū·lus, *a.* [L. *pendulus*, from *pendeo*, to hang. PENDANT.] Hanging so as to swing freely; loosely pendent; swinging.—**pendulousness**, pen′dū·lus·nes, *n.* The state of being pendulous.—**pendulum**, pen′dū·lum, *n.* [Lit. what hangs down, from L. *pendulus*.] A body so suspended from a fixed point as to swing to and fro by the alternate action of gravity and momentum; the swinging piece in a clock serving as the regulating power, the wheelwork being attached to register the number of vibrations, and the weight or spring serving to counteract the effects of friction and resistance of the air.—*Compensation pendulum*. See COMPENSATION.

peneplain, pēn′i·plān, *n.* [L. *paene*, almost.] A denuded area approximating to a plain.

penetrate, pen′e·trāt, *v.t.*—*penetrated*, *penetrating*. [L. *penetro*, *penetratum*, to penetrate; root *pen*, denoting internality, and *tra*, to go.] To enter or pierce; to make way into the interior of; to pass into or affect the mind of; to touch; to pierce into by the intellect; to arrive at the inner meaning of; to understand.—*v.i.* To enter into or pierce anything; to pass or make way in.—**penetrating**, pen′e·trāt·ing, *p.* and *a.* Having the power of entering or piercing; sharp; acute; discerning.—**penetratingly**, pen′e·trāt·ing·li, *adv.* In a penetrating manner.—**penetration**, pen·e·trā′shon, *n.* The act of penetrating; a seeing into something obscure or difficult; discernment; mental acuteness.—**penetrative**, pen′e·trā·tiv, *a.* Sharp; subtle; acute; discerning.— **penetrable**, pen′e·tra·bl, *a.* [L. *penetrabilis*.] Capable of being penetrated, entered, or pierced by another body; susceptible of moral or intellectual impression.—**penetrability**, pen′e·tra·bil″i·ti, *n.* State of being penetrable.— **penetrably**, pen′e·tra·bli, *adv.* In a penetrable manner; so as to be penetrable.—**penetralia**, pen′e·trā″li·a, *n. pl.* [L., from *penetralis*, internal.] The inner parts of a building, as of a temple or palace; a sanctuary; hidden things.—**penetrant**, pen′e·trant, *a.* Having the power to penetrate or pierce.

penguin, pen′gwin, *n.* [Probably from W. *pen*, head, and *gwyn*, white, a

name formerly given to certain white-headed birds and transferred to penguins.] A name of swimming birds allied to the auks and guillemots, having rudimentary wings useless for flight, but effective in swimming.

penicillate, pen·i·sil′āt, *a. Bot.* consisting of a bundle of short, compact fibers or hairs; *zool.* supporting bundles of diverging hairs.

penicillin, pen′i·sil″in, *n.* An antibiotic produced from molds of the genus *Penicillium* and effective against a number of disease-producing micro-organisms.

peninsula, pe·nin′sū·la, *n.* [L., from *pene*, almost, and *insula*, an island.] A portion of land almost surrounded by water, and connected with the mainland by an isthmus.—*The Peninsula*, Spain and Portugal together. —**peninsular**, pe·nin′sū·lér, *a.* In the form of a peninsula; pertaining to a peninsula.

penis, pē′nis, *n.* [L.] The male organ of generation.

penitence, pen′i·tens, *n.* [Fr. *pénitence*, from L. *pœnitentia*, repentance. *Penance* is the same word. PENAL.] Sorrow for the commission of sin or offenses; repentance; contrition.— **penitent**, pen′i·tent, *a.* [L. *pœnitens*, repentant.] Suffering sorrow of heart on account of sins or offenses; contrite; sorry for wrongdoing and resolved on amendment.—*n.* One who is penitent; one under church censure, but admitted to penance.— **penitential**, pen·i·ten′shal, *a.* Pertaining to, proceeding from, or expressing penitence.—*Penitential psalms*, the psalms numbered vi., xxxii., xxxviii., li., cii., cxxx., cxliii. of the authorized version of the Bible.—*n.* In the *R. Cath. Ch.* a book containing the rules which relate to penance.—**penitentially**, pen·i·ten′shal·li, *adv.* In a penitential manner.—**penitentiary**, pen·i·ten′sha·ri, *a.* Relating to penance.—*n.* A penitent; an official or office of the Roman Catholic Church connected with the granting of dispensations, etc.; a house of correction in which offenders are confined for punishment and reformation, and compelled to labor.—**penitently**, pen′i·tent·li, *adv.* In a penitent manner.

penknife, **penman**, etc. See PEN.

pennant, pen′ant, *n.* [From *pennon*, but influenced by *pendant*.] A small flag; a pennon; a pendant.

pennate, pen′āt, *a.* [L. *pennatus*, winged, from *penna*, a feather.] *Bot.* same as *Pinnate*.—**penniform**, pen′i·form, *a.* Having the appearance of the barbs of a feather.—**pennigerous**, pe·nij′ér·us, *a.* Bearing feathers or quills.

pennon, pen′on, *n.* [Fr. *pennon*, from L. *penna*, a feather, a plume. PEN.] A small pointed flag or streamer formerly carried by knights attached to their spear or lance, and generally bearing a badge or device; a pennant. —**pennoncel**, **pennoncelle**, pen′on·sel, *n.* A small pennon.

penny, pen′i, *n. pl.* **pennies** or **pence**, pen′iz, pens. *Pennies* denotes the number of coins; *pence* the amount in value. [A.Sax. *penig, pening, pending*=D. *penning,* Dan. *penge,* Icel. *penningr,* O.H.G. *pfenting,* G. *pfennig;* perhaps of same origin as *pawn,* a pledge. PAWN.] A British coin, bronze, worth about one cent in U. S. money, twelve make a shilling; a cent in U. S. money, *Colloq.* Any small sum of money, as, to make an honest *penny.*—**penniless,** pen′i·les, *a.* Moneyless; destitute of money; poor.—**penny-a-liner,** *n.* A person who furnishes matter for public journals at a penny a line, or some such small price; any poor writer for hire.—**pennyroyal,** pen′i·roi·al, *n.* An aromatic plant of the mint family.—**pennyweight,** pen′i·wāt, *n.* A troy weight containing 24 grains—anciently, the weight of a silver penny.—**pennywise,** *a.* Saving small sums at the hazard of larger; niggardly on unimportant occasions: generally in the phrase 'pennywise and pound foolish'.—**pennyworth,** pen′i·wèrth, *n.* As much as is bought for a penny; a purchase; a bargain.

penology, pē·nol′o·ji, *n.* [Gr. *poinē,* punishment, and *logos,* discourse.] The science which treats of public punishments.

pensile, pen′sil, *a.* [L. *pensilis,* from *pendeo,* to hang. PENDANT.] Hanging; suspended; pendulous.

pension, pen′shon, *n.* [Fr. *pension,* from L. *pensio, pensionis,* a paying, from *pendo, pensum,* to weigh, to pay (whence *expend,* etc.). PENDANT.] A stated allowance to a person in consideration of past services; a yearly sum granted by government to retired public officers, to soldiers or sailors who have served a certain number of years or have been wounded, or others; a boardinghouse or boarding school on the Continent (in this sense pronounced pän·sē·oṅ, being French.)—*Old Age Pension.* A regular payment made by a government or institution to persons who have attained a certain age, usually 65 or over.—*v.t.* To grant a pension to.—**pensionary,** pen′shon·e·ri, *a.* Receiving a pension; consisting in a pension.—*n.* A person who receives a pension; a pensioner. —*The Grand Pensionary of Holland,* the first minister of Holland: title from 1619 to 1794.—**pensioner,** pen′shon·èr, *n.* One in receipt of a pension; a dependent on the bounty of another; in the University of Cambridge, England, one who pays for his commons out of his own income, the same as a commoner at Oxford.

pensive, pen′siv, *a.* [Fr. *pensif,* from *penser,* to think or reflect, from L. *pensare,* to weigh, to consider, a freq. from *pendo, pensum,* to weigh. PENDANT.] Thoughtful; employed in serious thought or reflection; thoughtful and somewhat melancholy; expressing thoughtfulness with sadness.—**pensively,** pen′siv·li, *adv.* In a pensive manner.—**pensiveness,** pen′siv·nes, *n.* The state or quality of being pensive.

penstock, pen′stok, *n.* [Pen, an enclosure, and *stock.*] A trough, tube, or conduit of boards for conducting water; a sluice above a water wheel.

pent, pent, pp. of *pen.* Penned or shut up; closely confined.

pentacle, pen′ta·kl, *n.* [L.L. *pentaculum,* from Gr. *pente,* five.] A figure consisting of five straight lines so joined and intersecting as to form a five-pointed star: formerly a mystic sign in astrology or necromancy.

pentad, pent′ad, *n.* [Gr. *pente,* five.] An aggregate of five; a period of five years.

pentagon, pen′ta·gon, *n.* [Gr. *pente,* five, and *gōnia,* an angle.] *Geom.* a figure of five sides and five angles; [cap.] a building in Arlington, Va., housing most of the U. S. Defense Department offices.—**pentagonal,** pen·tag′on·al,*a.*—**pentagonally,**pen·-tag′on·al·li, *adv.*

pentagram, pen′ta·gram, *n.* [Gr. *pente,* five, and *grammē,* a line.] A pentacle.

pentahedron, pen·ta·hē′dron, *n.* [Gr. *pente,* five, and *hedra,* a side or base.] A solid having five equal sides. —**pentahedral,** pen·ta·hē′dral, *a.* Having five equal sides.

pentamerous, pen·tam′er·us, *a.* [Gr. *pente,* five, and *meros,* a part.] Having or divided into five parts; *zool.* having five joints to the tarsus of each leg, a term applied to a family (Pentamera) of beetles.

pentameter, pen·tam′et·èr, *n.* [Gr. *pente,* five, and *metron,* measure.] *Pros.* a verse of five feet, belonging more especially to Greek and Latin poetry, the first two feet being either dactyls or spondees; the Greek line whose first two feet may consist of either a dactyl or a spondee, followed by a caesura, and followed in turn by two dactyls closed by a second caesura.—*a.* Having five metrical feet.

pentane, pent′ān, *n.* [Gr. *pente,* five.] Paraffin hydrocarbon occurring as a colorless fluid in petroleum and other oils.

pentarchy, pen′tär·ki, *n.* [Gr. *pente,* five, *archē,* rule.] A government in the hands of five persons.

pentastich, pen′ta·stik, *n.* [Gr. *pente,* five, and *stichos,* a verse.] A composition consisting of five verses.

Pentateuch, pen′ta·tūk, *n.* [Gr. *pente,* five, and *teuchos,* a book.] A collective term for the first five books of the Old Testament.

pentavalent, pen·ta·vā′lent, *a.* [Prefix *penta,* and *valent.*] *Chem.* having a valence of 5.

Pentecost, pen′ti·kost, *n.* [Gr. *pentēkoste (hēmera),* the fiftieth (day), from *pentēkonta,* fifty, from *pente,* five.] A solemn festival of the Jews, so called because celebrated on the fiftieth day after the Passover; Whitsuntide, which is fifty days after Easter.—**Pentecostal,** pen·ti·kos′tal, *a.* Pertaining to Pentecost.

penthouse, pent′hous, *n.* [Formerly *pentice,* from Fr. *appentis,* a penthouse.—L. *ad,* to, and *pendeo,* to hang. PENDANT.] A roof sloping up against a wall; a shed standing aslope from a building; a dwelling or apartment situated on the roof of a larger building.

penult, penultima, pē′nult, pi·nul′ti·ma, *n.* [L. *penultimus—pene,* almost, and *ultimus,* last.] The last syllable of a word except one.—**penultimate,** pi·nul′ti·māt, *a.* The last but one.—*n.* The last syllable but one of a word.

penumbra, pi·num′bra, *n.* [L. *pene,* almost, and *umbra,* shade.] The partial shadow outside of the total shadow caused by an opaque body intercepting the light from a luminous body, as in eclipses; *painting,* the boundary of shade and light, where the one blends with the other. —**penumbral,** pi·num′bral, *a.* Pertaining to a penumbra.

penury, pen′ū·ri, *n.* [Fr. *pénurie,* L. *penuria,* akin to Gr. *penia,* poverty.] Want of pecuniary means; indigence; extreme poverty.—**penurious,** pe·nū′ri·us, *a.* Pertaining to penury; niggardly; parsimonious; sordid.—**penuriously,** pe·nū′ri·us·li, *adv.* In a penurious manner.—**penuriousness,** pe·nū′ri·us·nes, *n.* The quality of being penurious.

peon, pē′on, *n.* [Sp. *peon,* a foot soldier, a day laborer, from L. *pes, pedis,* the foot. PAWN (at chess), PEDAL.] In Hindustan, a foot soldier; a native constable; in Spanish America, a day laborer; a farmer of Spanish descent; a kind of serf.—**peonage,** **peonism,** pē′on·ij, pē′on·izm, *n.* The state or condition of a peon.

peony, pē′o·ni, *n.* [L. *paeonia,* from Gr. *paiōnia,* from *Paiōn,* Apollo, who used this flower to cure the wounds of the gods.] A ranunculaceous genus of plants cultivated in gardens for their large gaudy flowers.

people, pē′pl, *n.* [O.E. *peple, puple,* etc., O.Fr. *pople, pueple,* Fr. *peuple,* from L. *populus,* people. POPULAR.] The body of persons who compose a community, race, or nation; a community; a body social (in this sense it admits the plural *peoples*); persons indefinitely; men (*people* may say what they please); with possessives, those who are closely connected with a person, as attendants, domestics, relatives, etc.—*v.t.*—*peopled, peopling.* To stock with people or inhabitants; to populate.

pep, pep, *n.* [Abbrev. of *pepper.*] (Slang) Energy; exuberance; initiative.—*v.t.* To stimulate; to give energy to (usually with *up*).

pepo, pē′pō, *n.* [L., a melon.] Any fruit of the type of the melon or gourd.

pepper, pep′èr, *n.* [A.Sax. *pipor, peppor,* from L. *piper,* Gr. *piperi, peperic* a word of Oriental origin.] A pepper plant, *Capsicum,* and its pod, which may be sweet or hot and yields a red pepper; a pepper plant, *Piper,* and its seed, which yields the table condiment black pepper.— *Cayenne pepper,* the produce of different species of capsicum.—*v.t.* To sprinkle with pepper; to pelt with shot or missiles; to cover thoroughly.—**pepperbox,** *n.* A small box with a perforated lid, for sprinkling pepper on food.—**peppercorn,** pep′èr·korn, *n.* The dried berry of the black pepper.—**peppermint,** pep′ėr·mint, *n.* A plant of the mint genus having a strong pungent taste, glowing like pepper, and followed by a sense of coolness; a liqueur; a candy flavored with peppermint.—**pepper pot,** *n.* A West Indian dish, the principal ingredient of which is cassareep, with meat or dried fish and vegetables; a pepperbox.—**peppery,** pep′ėr·i, *a.* Having the qualities of pepper; choleric; irritable.

pepsin, pep′sin, *n.* [Gr. *pepsis,* digestion, from *peptō,* to digest.] A digestive enzyme of the gastric juices; a preparation containing this enzyme.—**peptic,** pep′tik, *a.* Digestive.—**peptone,** pep′tōn, *n.* The substance into which the nitrogenous elements of the food are converted by the action of the gastric juice.

per, pėr. A Latin preposition, denoting through, by, by means of, etc.; for each.

peradventure, pėr·ad·ven′chėr, *adv.* [Prefix *per,* by, and *adventure,* Fr. *par aventure.*] Perchance; perhaps; it may be. Sometimes used as a noun=doubt; question.

perambulate, pėr·am′bū·lāt, *v.t.*— *perambulated, perambulating.* [L. *perambulo*—*per,* and *ambulo,* to walk. AMBLE.] To walk through or over; to survey the boundaries of (to *perambulate* a parish).—**perambulation,** pėr·am′bū·lā″shon, *n.* The act of perambulating; a traveling survey or inspection; a walking through or over ground for the purpose of settling boundaries.—**perambulator,** pėr·am′bū·lā·tėr, *n.* One who perambulates; a small carriage for a child, propelled from behind.

percale, pėr·kāl′, *n.* [Fr. from *par-gālah.*] A closely woven, fine cotton fabric, printed or plain.

per capita, pėr kap′i·tä, *adv.* [L.] For each individual.

perceive, pėr·sēv′, *v.t.*—*perceived, perceiving.* [Fr. *percevoir,* L. *percipio,* to perceive, to comprehend—*per,* and *capio,* to take. CAPABLE.] To have or obtain knowledge of by the senses; to apprehend or take cognizance of by the organs of sense; to apprehend by the mind; to discern, know, understand. ∴ Syn. under SEE.— **perceivable,** pėr·sē′va·bl, *a.* Capable of being perceived; perceptible.— **perceivably,** pėr·sē′va·bli, *adv.* In a perceivable manner.—**percept,** pėr′-sept, *n.* That which is perceived.— **perceptible,** pėr·sep′ti·bl, *a.* Capable of being perceived.—**perceptibly,** pėr·sep′ti·bli, *adv.* In a perceptible manner; so as to be perceived.— **perception,** pėr·sep′shon, *n.* [L. *per-ceptio, perceptionis.*] The act of perceiving; that act or process of the mind which makes known an external object; the faculty by which man holds communication with the external world or takes cognizance of objects outside the mind.—**perceptive,** pėr·sep′tiv, *a.* Relating to the act or power of perceiving; having the faculty of perceiving.

percent, pėr·sent′, *n.* [Abbrev. of L. *per centum,* by the hundred.] By the

hundred; units or parts to the hundred (used in expressing rates of interest, proportions, etc.).—**percentage,** pėr·sen′taj, *n.* Interest, a part of a whole, a proportion, etc., expressed in hundreds; a share, portion, or part.—**percentile,** pėr·-sen′til, *n.* A value of a statistical variable which divides its distribution into 100 groups having equal frequencies.

perch, pėrch, *n.* [Fr. *perche,* L. *perca,* from Gr. *perkē,* the perch, from *perkos,* dark-colored.] The popular name of certain spiny-finned fishes, one species of which is found in rivers and lakes throughout the temperate parts of the United States.

perch, pėrch, *n.* [Fr. *perche,* from L. *pertica,* a pole, a staff.] A measure of length containing 5½ yards; a pole or rod; a roost for birds; anything on which they light; hence, an elevated seat or position.—*v.i.* To sit or roost; to light or settle as a bird.—*v.t.* To place on a perch.— *Perched blocks,* blocks of stone that have been left by ancient glaciers high up on mountains.—**percher,** pėrch′ėr, *n.* One that perches; a bird belonging to the order of Insessores.

perchance, pėr·chans′, *adv.* [L. *per,* by, and E. *chance.*] Perhaps; peradventure.

perchloric, pėr·klo′rik, *a.* Applied to an acid forming a syrupy liquid very explosive.—**perchlorate,** pėr·-klō′rāt, *n.* A salt of perchloric acid.

percipient, pėr·sip′i·ent, *a.* [L. *per-cipiens,* ppr. of *percipio.* PERCEIVE.] Perceiving; having the faculty of perception.—*n.* One who perceives. —**percipience, percipiency,** pėr·-sip′i·ens, pėr·sip′i·en·si, *n.* Act or power of perceiving; perception.

percoid, pėr′koid, *a.* [Gr. *perke,* perch, and *eidos,* form.] Resembling the perch; belonging to the perch family.

percolate, pėr′ko·lāt, *v.t.*—*percolated, percolating.* [L. *percolo*—*per,* and *colo,* to strain, from *colum,* a sieve (whence *colander*).] To strain or filter.—*v.i.* To pass through small interstices or pores; to filter.—**percolator,** pėr′-ko·lā·tėr, *n.* One who or that which filters.—A kind of coffeepot in which boiling water is forced upward and filters down through the coffee.

percuss,† pėr·kus′, *v.t.* [L. *percussus,* from *percutio, percussum* — *per,* through, and *quatio,* to strike (as in *concuss*). QUASH.] To strike against; to give a shock to.—**percussion,** pėr·-kush′on, *n.* [L. *percussio.*] The act of striking one body against another with some violence; forcible collision, the shock produced by the collision of bodies; the impression or effect of sound on the ear; *med.* the method of eliciting sounds by striking the surface of the body, for the purpose of determining the condition of the organs subjacent (as the lungs or heart).—**percussion cap,** *n.* A small copper cap or cup containing fulminating powder, used in a percussion lock to explode gunpowder. —**percussion lock,** *n.* A lock for a gun, causing the ignition of the

charge by the impact of a hammer or striker.—**percussive,** pėr·kus′iv, *a.* Acting by percussion; striking against.

per diem, pėr dī′em, *adv.* [M.L.] By the day; for each day.

perdition, pėr·dish′on, *n.* [L.L. *per-ditio,* from L. *perdo, perditus,* to destroy, to ruin—*per,* thoroughly, and *do,* a verb cog. with E. *do.*] Entire ruin; utter destruction; loss of final happiness in a future state; future misery or eternal death.

perdu, perdue, pėr′dū or per·dū′, *a.* [Fr. *perdu,* lost, from *perdre,* to lose, L. *perdo.*] Hid; in concealment: generally in the phrase *to lie* or *to be perdu.*

perdurable, pėr·dū′ra·bl, *a.* [Fr., from L. *perduro*—*per,* intens., and *duro,* to last. DURABLE.] Very durable; lasting; continuing long.— **perdurably,** pėr·dū′ra·bli, *adv.* In a perdurable manner; lastingly.

peregrinate, per′e·gri·nāt, *v.i.*—*per-egrinated, peregrinating.* [L. *peregri-nor,* from *peregrinus,* a traveler or stranger—*per,* through, and *ager,* land. PILGRIM.] To travel from place to place; to wander.—**peregrination,** per′e·gri·nā″shon, *n.* A traveling, roaming, or wandering about; a journey.—**peregrinator,** per′e·gri-nā·tėr, *n.* A traveler.—**peregrine,** per′e·grin, *a.* [L. *peregrinus.*] Foreign; not native.—*Peregrine falcon,* a handsome species of European falcon.—*n.* A peregrine falcon.

peremptory, per·emp′tė·ri, *a.* [L. *peremptorius,* from *perimo, peremptus,* to destroy—*per,* thoroughly, and *emo,* to take, to buy (seen also in *exempt, example, prompt*).] Precluding debate or expostulation; decisive; authoritative; fully resolved; determined; positive in opinion or judgment; dogmatical; *law,* final; determinate. — **peremptorily,** per·emp′tė·ri·li, *adv.* In a peremptory manner.—**per-emptoriness,** per·emp′tė·ri·nes, *n.*

perennial, per·en′i·al, *a.* [L. *perennis* —*per,* through, and *annus,* a year.] Lasting or continuing without cessation through the year; continuing without stop or intermission; unceasing; never-failing; *bot.* continuing more than two years (a *perennial* plant).—*n.* A plant whose root remains alive more years than two. —**perennially,** per·en′i·al·li, *adv.*

perfect, pėr′fekt, *a.* [L. *perfectus,* pp, of *perficio,* to complete or finish—*per.* thoroughly, and *facio,* to do. FACT.] Brought to a consummation or completion; having received and possessing all its parts; finished; completed; of the best, highest, or completest type; without blemish or defect; faultless; completely skilled (*perfect* in discipline).—*Perfect gas,* a theoretical gas which satisfies several conditions, and follows exactly the law of Boyle, that the volume varies inversely as the pressure when the temperature is constant. Actual gases at best only approximate to this perfectness.— *Perfect tense, gram.* a tense which expresses an act completed.—*v.t.* To finish or complete so as to leave nothing wanting; to make perfect; to instruct fully; to make fully skillful (often *refl.*).—**perfecter**, pėr′fek·tėr, *n.* One that makes perfect.—**perfectibility**, pėr·fek′ti·bil′i·ti, *n.* The quality of being perfectible; the capacity of becoming or being made morally perfect.—**perfectible**, pėr·fek′ti·bl, *a.* Capable of becoming or being made perfect.—**perfection**, pėr·fek′shon, *n.* [L. *perfectio, perfectionis.*] The state of being perfect or complete; supreme degree of moral or other excellence; a quality of the highest worth.—**perfectionism**, pėr·fek′shon·izm, *n.* The doctrine of the Perfectionists.—**perfectionist**, pėr·fek′shon·ist, *n.* One who believes that some persons actually attain to moral perfection in the present life; [*cap.*] one of an American sect of Christians founded on socialist principles.—**perfective**, pėr·fek′tiv, *a.* Conducing to bring to perfection.—**perfectively**, pėr·fek′tiv·li, *adv.*—**perfectly**, pėr′fekt·li, *adv.*

perfecto, pėr·fek′to, *n.* [Sp. perfect.] A large cigar, tapering to both ends from a thick center.

perfervid, pėr·fėr′vid, *a.* [L. *perfervidus—per*, intens., and *fervidus*, fervid.] Very fervid; very hot or ardent.

perfidy, pėr′fi·di, *n.* [L. *perfidia*, from *perfidus*, faithless—prefix *per*, and *fidus*, faithful; *per* having the same force as in *perjure, pervert.* FAITH.] The act of violating faith or allegiance; breach of faith; treachery; faithlessness.—**perfidious**, pėr·fid′i·us, *a.* Guilty of or involving perfidy or treachery; treacherous; consisting in breach of faith; traitorous.—**perfidiously**, pėr·fid′i·us·li, *adv.* In a perfidious manner.—**perfidiousness**, pėr·fid′i·us·nes, *n.*

perfoliate, pėr·fō′li·āt, *a.* [L. *per*, through, and *folium*, a leaf.] *Bot.* applied to a leaf that has the base surrounding the stem, as if the stem ran through it.

perforate, pėr′fo·rāt, *v.t.*—*perforated, perforating.* [L. *perforo, perforatus*—prefix *per*, through, and *foro*, to bore. BORE.] To bore through; to pierce with a pointed instrument; to make a hole or holes through by boring.—**perforate, perforated**, pėr′fo·rāt, pėr′fo·rā·ted, *a.* Bored or pierced through.—**perforation**, pėr·fo·rā′shon, *n.* The act of perforating, boring, or piercing; a hole bored; a hole passing through anything.—**perforator**, pėr′fo·rā·tėr, *n.* One who or that which perforates.

perforce, pėr·fōrs′, *adv.* [Prefix *per*, through, by, and *force.*] By force or compulsion; of necessity.

perform, pėr·form′, *v.t.* [O.E. *parforme, parfourne*, from O.Fr. *parfournir*, to perform—prefix *par*, and *fournir*, to accomplish, to furnish. FURNISH.] To do; to execute; to accomplish; to fulfill, act up to, discharge (a duty); to act or represent as on the stage.—*v.i.* To act a part; to play on a musical instrument, represent a character on the stage, or the like.—**performable**, pėr·form′a·bl, *a.* Capable of being performed.

—**performance**, pėr·for′mans, *n.* The act of performing or condition of being performed; an action, deed, or thing done; a literary work; a composition; the acting or exhibition of character on the stage; an exhibition of skill and capacity; an entertainment provided at any place of amusement.—**performer**, pėr·for′mėr, *n.* One who performs; an actor, musician, etc., who exhibits his skill.

perfume, pėr′fūm or pėr·fūm′, *n.* [Fr. *parfum*, from L. *per*, through, and *fumus*, smoke; lit. smoke or vapor that disseminates itself.] A substance that emits a scent or odor which affects agreeably the organs of smelling; the scent or odor emitted from sweet-smelling substances.—*v.t.* (pėr·fūm′)—*perfumed, perfuming.* To fill or impregnate with a grateful odor; to scent.—**perfumer**, pėr·fūm′ėr, *n.* One who perfumes; one whose trade is to sell perfumes.—**perfumery**, pėr·fūm′ėr·i, *n.* Perfumes collectively; the art of preparing perfumes.

perfunctory, pėr·fungk′to·ri, *a.* [L. L. *perfunctorius*—L. *per*, and *fungor, functus*, to perform, execute. FUNCTION.] Done in a half-hearted or careless manner, and merely for the sake of getting rid of the duty; careless, slight, or not thorough; negligent. — **perfunctorily**, pėr·fungk′to·ri·li, *adv.* In a perfunctory manner. — **perfunctoriness**, pėr·fungk′to·ri·nes, *n.*

pergola, pėr′go·la, *n.* [It.] A kind of arbor or bower on which plants may grow.

perhaps, pėr·haps′, *adv.* [L. *per*, by (as in *perchance*), and E. *hap.*] Peradventure; perchance; it may be; possibly.

peri, pâ′ri, *n.* [Per. *pari*, a fairy.] *Per. myth.* a sort of spiritual being or fairy, represented as a descendant of fallen angels, excluded from paradise till the accomplishment of a task imposed as a penance.

perianth, per′i·anth, *n.* [Gr. *peri*, about, and *anthos*, a flower.] *Bot.* a term for the floral envelope when the calyx and corolla are so combined that they cannot be satisfactorily distinguished from each other.

periapt, per′i·apt, *n.* [Gr. *periapton, peri*, around, *haptō*, to fasten.] An armlet or necklet worn as a charm. (*Shak.*)

pericardium, per·i·kär′di·um, *n.* [Gr. *perikardion—peri*, around, and *kardia*, the heart.] The membranous sac that encloses the heart.—**pericardial, pericardiac**, per·i·kär′di·al, per·i·kär′di·ak, *a.* Relating to the pericardium.—**pericarditis**, per′i·kär·dī″tis, *n.* [Term. *-itis*, signifying inflammation.] Inflammation of the pericardium.

pericarp, per′i·kärp, *n.* [Gr. *peri*, about, and *karpos*, fruit.] The seed vessel of a plant, or the shell of the seed vessel; the part enclosing the seed.—**pericarpial**, per·i·kär′pi·al, *a.* Belonging to a pericarp.

perichondrium, per·i·kon′dri·um, *n.* [Gr. *peri*, around, and *chondros*, cartilage.] *Anat.* a synovial mem-

brane which covers certain cartilages.

pericranium, per·i·krā′ni·um, *n.* [Gr. *peri*, about, and *kranion*, the skull.] The membrane that invests the skull.

periderm, per′i·dėrm, *n.* [Gr. *peri*, around, and *derma*, skin.] A sort of outer layer or skin; *bot.* the outer layer of bark.

peridot, per′i·dot, *n.* A precious stone of a yellowish-green color.

perigee, per′i·jē, *n.* [Gr. *peri*, about, and *gē*, the earth.] That point of the moon's orbit which is nearest to the earth; formerly also this point in the orbit of any heavenly body. APOGEE.—**perigean**, per·i·jē′an, *a.* Pertaining to the perigee.

perigynous, pe·rij′i·nus, *a.* [Gr. *peri*, around, and *gynē*, a female.] *Bot.* having the ovary free, but the petals and stamens borne on the calyx.

perihelion, per·i·hē′li·on, *n.* [Gr. *peri*, about, and *hēlios*, the sun.] That part of the orbit of a planet or comet in which it is at its least distance from the sun: opposed to *aphelion.*

peril, per′il, *n.* [Fr. *péril*, from L. *periculum*, danger, from root seen in *perior, experior*, to try (whence *experiment*); same ultimate root as E. *fare, ferry.*] Danger; risk; hazard; jeopardy; exposure of person or property to injury, loss, or destruction.—*v.t.*—*periled, periling.* To hazard; to risk; to expose to danger.—**perilous**, per′i·lus, *a.* Full of peril; dangerous; hazardous.—**perilously**, per′i·lus·li, *adv.* In a perilous manner.—**perilousness**, per′i·lus·nes, *n.*

perimeter, pe·rim′et·ėr, *n.* [Gr. *peri*, about, and *metron*, measure.] *Geom.* the boundary of a body or figure, or the sum of all the sides.—**perimetrical**, per·i·met′ri·kal, *a.* Pertaining to the perimeter.

perimorph, per′i·morf, *n.* [Gr. *peri*, about, and *morphē*, form.] *Mineral.* a mineral or crystal enclosing other minerals or crystals. ENDOMORPH.

perineum, per·i·nē′um, *n.* [Gr. *perinaion, perineon.*] *Anat.* the inferior surface of the trunk of the body, from the anus to the external organ of generation.—**perineal**, per·i·nē′al, *a. Anat.* pertaining to the perineum.

period, pē′ri·od, *n.* [L. *periodus*, from Gr. *periodos—peri*, about, and *hodos*, way.] Originally a circuit; hence, the time taken up by the revolution of a heavenly body, or the time till it returns to the point of its orbit where it began; any round of time or series of years, days, etc., in which a revolution is completed, and the same course is to be begun; an indefinite portion of any continued state, existence, or series of events (the early *period* of life); the time in which anything is performed; termination or point of completion of any cycle or series of events; end; conclusion; limit; a complete sentence from one full stop to another; the point that marks the end of a complete sentence, or indicates an abbreviation, etc.; a full stop, thus (.).—**periodic, periodical**, pē·ri·od′ik, pē·ri·od′i·kal, *a.* Pertaining to a period or to periods; performed in a period or regular revolution; happening or returning regularly in a certain period of time; recurring; published at regular intervals, as a newspaper, magazine, etc. (in this sense *periodical* is the only form).— *Periodical diseases*, those of which the symptoms recur at stated intervals.—*Periodic law*, *chem.* the law determining the classification of elements into groups with comparable characters.—*Periodic system*, a classification of chemical elements according to their atomic weights, whereby they fall into groups having similar characters.—**periodical**, *n.* A publication which appears in successive numbers at regular intervals, as a newspaper or magazine.—**periodically**, pē·ri·od′i·kal·li, *adv.* In a periodical manner; at stated periods.—**periodicity**, pē′ri·o·dis′i·ti, *n.* The state or quality of being periodical.

periosteum, per·i·os′ti·um, *n.* [Gr. *peri*, about, and *osteon*, bone.] *Anat.* a vascular membrane immediately investing the bones of animals, and conducting the vessels by which the bone is nourished.—**periosteal**, per·i·os′ti·al, *a.* Belonging to the periosteum.—**periostitis**, per′i·os·tī″tis, *n.* Inflammation of the periosteum.

peripatetic, per′i·pa·tet″ik, *a.* [Gr. *peripatētikos*, from *peripateō*, to walk about—*peri*, about, and *pateō*, to walk. Aristotle taught his system of philosophy, and his followers disputed questions, *walking* in the Lyceum at Athens.] Walking about; itinerant; pertaining to Aristotle's system of philosophy; Aristotelian —**peripatetic**, *n.* One who walks; one who walks much; [*cap.*] a follower of Aristotle.

periphery, pe·rif′ėr·i, *n.* [Gr. *peri*, around, and *pherō*, to bear.] The outside or surface of a body; *geom.* the boundary line of a closed figure; the perimeter; in a circle, the circumference.—**peripheral**, pe·rif′ėr·al, *a.* Pertaining to or constituting a periphery.

periphrasis, pe·rif′ra·sis, *n.* pl. **periphrases**, pe·rif′ra·sēz. [Gr. *periphrasis*—*peri*, about, and *phrazō*, to speak.] A roundabout phrase or expression; circumlocution; the use of more words than are necessary to express the idea.—**periphrase**, per′i·frāz, *n.* A periphrasis.—*v.t.*—*periphrased*, *periphrasing*. To express by periphrasis or circumlocution.—*v.i.* To use circumlocution.—**periphrastic**, per·i·fras′tik, *a.* Having the character of or characterized by periphrasis —**periphrastically**, per·i·fras′ti·kal·li, *adv.* In a periphrastic manner.

peripteral, pe·rip′ter·al, *a.* [Gr. *peripteros*, from *peri*, around, and *pteron*, a wing, a row of columns.] *Greek arch.* surrounded by a single row of insulated columns.—**periptery**, pe·rip′ter·i, *n.* A surrounding row of columns.

periscope, per′i·skōp, *n.* [Gr. *peri*, round, *skopeō*, to look.] An apparatus or structure rising above the deck of a submarine vessel, giving by

means of mirrors, etc., a view of outside surroundings, though the vessel itself remains submerged, and enabling the crew to see how to direct torpedoes. A device of a similar kind is used on land in trenches or elsewhere.—**periscopic**, **periscopical**, per·i·skop′ik, per·i·skop′i·kal, *a.* Viewing on all sides: applied to spectacles having concavo-convex lenses for increasing the distinctness of objects when viewed obliquely; also to a kind of lens in microscopes.

perish, per′ish, *v.i.* [Fr. *périr*, ppr. *périssant*, to perish, from L. *perio*, to perish—*per*, through, and *eo*, to go. ITINERANT.] To lose life or vitality in any manner; to die; to be destroyed; to pass away, come to nothing, be ruined or lost.—*v.t.* To cause to perish; to destroy.—**perishable**, per′ish·a·bl, *a.* Liable to perish; subject to decay and destruction.—*Perishable goods*, goods which decay and lose their value if not consumed soon, such as fish, fruit, and the like.—**perishability**, **perishableness**, per′ish·a·bil′i·ti, per′ish·a·bl·nes, *n.* The state of being perishable.

perissodactyl, **perissodactylous**, pe·ris′o·dak″til, pe·ris′o·dak″ti·lus, *a.* [Gr. *perissos*, uneven, and *daktylos*, a finger or toe.] Having feet with toes odd in number; odd-toed: applied to a section of the ungulate or hoofed animals, including the rhinoceros, tapir, horse, etc.

peristalsis, per′i·stal″sis, *n.* [N.L. from Gr. *peristaltikos*, compressing.] *Physiol.* the wavelike constriction and release of cylindrical muscular structures in an organism (as in animal intestines) so as to push their contents forward.—**peristaltic**, per′i·stal″tik, *a.*

peristome, per′i·stōm, *n.* [Gr. *peri*, around, and *stome*, a mouth.] *Bot.* a ring or fringe of bristles or teeth that close up the orifice of the seed vessel in mosses; *zool.* a term used for the similar parts in sea urchins, etc.

peristyle, per′i·stīl, *n.* [Gr. *peri*, about, and *stylos*, a column.] *Arch.* a range of surrounding columns.

perithecium, per·i·thē′si·um, *n.* [Gr. *peri*, around, and *thēkē*, a theca or case.] *Bot.* the envelope surrounding the masses of fructification in some fungi and lichens.

peritoneum, **peritonaeum**, per′i·to·nē″um, *n.* [Gr. *peritonaion*—*peri*, about, and *teinō*, to stretch.] A thin, smooth, serous membrane investing the whole internal surface of the abdomen, and more or less all the viscera contained in it.—**peritoneal**, **peritonaeal**, per′i·to·nē″al, *a.* Pertaining to the peritoneum.—**peritonitis**, per′i·to·nī″tis, *n.* Inflammation of the peritoneum.

perivisceral, per·i·vis′ėr·al, *a.* [Gr. *peri*, about, and L. *viscera*.] *Anat.* applied to the space surrounding the viscera.

periwig, per′i·wig, *n.* [O.E. *perriwig*, *perewake*, *perwicke*, etc., corrupted from Fr. *perruque*. (PERUKE.) *Wig*

is simply the final syllable of this word.] A small wig; a peruke.—*v.t.* —*periwigged*, *periwigging*. To dress with a periwig.

periwinkle, per·i·wing′kl, *n.* [From A.Sax. *pinewincle*, from L. *pinna*, *pina*, a mussel, and A.Sax. *wincle*, a winkle or whelk.] A kind of edible sea snail abounding on the shores of the North Atlantic; the shell of this snail.

periwinkle, per·i·wing′kl, *n.* [O.E. *pervinke*, *pervenke*, Fr. *pervenche*, from L. *pervinca*, the periwinkle.] The myrtle, a trailing herb with evergreen leaves and white, blue, or purple flowers; a related species, called the *large periwinkle*.

perjure, pėr′jėr, *v.t.*—*perjured*, *perjuring*. [L. *perjuro*—*per*, and *juro*, to swear, *per* here conveying a bad sense as in *perfidia*, perfidy.] To cause to be false to oaths or vows; to swear falsely to an oath in judicial proceedings; to forswear: generally used *refl.* (the witness *perjured himself*).—**perjurer**, pėr′jėr·ėr, *n.* One that willfully takes a false oath.—**perjury**, pėr′jė·ri, *n.* The act of willfully making a false oath; knowingly making a false oath in a judicial proceeding in a matter material to the issue or cause in question; the act of violating an oath or solemn promise.

perk, pėrk, *a.* [W. *perc*, neat, trim, smart; comp. also *pert*, spruce, dapper.] Trim; smart; vain; pert.—*v.i.* To hold up the head pertly; to look narrowly or sharply.—*v.t.* To make trim or smart; to prank; to hold up (the head) pertly.—**perky**, pėr′ki, *a.* Perk; trim; saucy.

perlite, pėr′līt, *n.* A form of vitreous rock, usually occurring as a mass of enamel-like globules.

permanent, pėr′ma·nent, *a.* [L. *permanens*, permanent, from *permaneo*, to continue—*per*, through, and *maneo*, to remain. MANSION.] Continuing in the same state, or without any change that destroys the form or nature of the thing; remaining unaltered or unremoved; durable; lasting; abiding; fixed.—*Permanent way*, rail, the finished roadbed and track, including bridges, viaducts, crossings, and switches.—**permanently**, pėr′ma·nent·li, *adv.* In a permanent manner.—**permanence**, **permanency**, pėr′ma·nens, pėr′ma·nen·si, *n.* The state or quality of being permanent; continuance; fixedness.

permanganate, per·mang′ga·nāt, *n.* [L. *per*, intensive, and *manganese*.] A dark, purple, crystalline substance, containing potassium, manganese, and oxygen: used in solution as an oxidizer and disinfectant.

permeate, pėr′mi·āt, *v.t.*—*permeated*, *permeating*. [L. *permeo*, *permeatum*—*per*, through, and *meo*, to flow or pass.] To pass through the pores or interstices of; to penetrate and pass through without rupture or displacement of parts: applied particularly to fluids which pass through substances of loose texture; also used *fig.*—**permeable**, pėr′mi·a·bl, *a.* [L. *permeabilis.*] Capable of being permeated.—**permeability,** pėr'mi·-a·bil″i·ti, *n.* The quality or state of being permeable; in *magnetics,* the capacity or power of being traversed by magnetic lines of force; the unit of permeability is that of air.—**permeation,** pėr·mi·ā'shon, *n.* The act of permeating.

Permian, pėr'mi·an, *a.* [From *Perm,* in Russia, or that part of Russia which formed the ancient kingdom of *Permia,* where the series is largely developed.] *Geol.* a term applied to a system of rocks lying beneath the Triassic rocks, and immediately above the Carboniferous system, and forming the uppermost of the Paleozoic strata.

permission, etc. See PERMIT.

permit, pėr·mit', *v.t.*—*permitted, permitting.* [L. *permitto*—prefix *per,* and *mitto,* to send. MISSION.] To allow by silent consent or by not prohibiting; to suffer without giving express authority; to grant leave or liberty to by express consent; to allow expressly; to give leave to do or be done.—*v.i.* To grant leave or permission; to allow (if circumstances *permit*).—*n.* (pėr'mit). A permission; a written permission given by officers of customs or excise, or other competent authority, for conveying spirits, wine, etc., from one place to another.—**permissibility,** pėr·mis'i·bil″i·ti, *n.* The quality of being permissible.—**permissible,** pėr·mis'i·bl, *a.* Proper to being permitted or allowed; allowable.—**permissibly,** pėr·mis'i·bli, *adv.* In a permissible manner.—**permission,** pėr·mish'on, *n.* [L. *permissio.*] The act of permitting or allowing; authorization; allowance; license or liberty granted; leave.—**permissive,** pėr·mis'iv, *a.* Permitting; granting liberty; allowing.—*Permissive laws,* laws that permit certain persons to have or enjoy the use of certain things, or to do certain acts without enforcing anything.—**permissively,** pėr·mis'iv·li, *adv.* By allowance; without prohibition or hindrance.—**permitter,** pėr·mit'ėr, *n.* One who permits.

permute, pėr·mūt', *v.t.*—*permuted, permuting.* [L. *permuto*—prefix *per,* and *muto,* to change. MUTABLE.] To interchange; to change as regards order or arrangement.—**permutable,** pėr·mū'ta·bl, *a.* Capable of being permuted; exchangeable.—**permutation,** pėr·mū·tā'shon, *n.* [L. *permutatio.*] Interchange; change among various things at once; *math.* change or combination in different order of any number of quantities; any of the different ways in which a set of quantities can be arranged.

pernicious, pėr·nish'us, *a.* [L. *perniciosus,* from *pernicies,* destruction—*per,* thoroughly, and stem of *nex, necis,* death (as in *internecine*).] Having the effect of destroying; very injurious or destructive.—**perniciously,** pėr·nish'us·li, *adv.*—**pernicious anemia,** a severe form of anemia in which the red blood corpuscles become progressively

fewer and larger.

peroneal, per·o·nē'al, *a.* [Gr. *peronē,* a brooch, also a name of the fibula.] Pertaining to the fibula.

peroration, per·o·rā'shon, *n.* [L. *peroratio,* from *peroro,* to speak from beginning to end—*per,* through, and *oro,* to speak, to pray. ORATION.] The concluding part of an oration, in which the speaker recapitulates the principal points of his discourse or argument, and urges them with greater earnestness; a rhetorical passage at the conclusion of a speech.—**perorate,** per·o'·rāt, *v.i.* To make a peroration; also, to speechify; to spout.

peroxide, per·ok'sīd, *n.* [Prefix *per,* and *oxide.*] *Chem.* an oxide containing a large proportion of oxygen. —*v.t.* To bleach the hair with peroxide.

perpend, pėr·pend', *v.t.* [L. *perpendo,* to weigh carefully—*per,* intens., and *pendo,* to weigh. PENDANT.] To weigh in the mind; to consider attentively.

perpend, pėr'pend, *n.* [Fr. *parpaing, parpain,* from *par,* through, and *pan,* the side of a wall.] A long stone reaching through the thickness of a wall so as to be visible on both sides; a bonder.

perpendicular, per·pen·dik'ū·lėr, *a.* [L. *perpendicularis,* from *perpendiculum,* a plumb line—*per,* intens., and *pendeo,* to hang. PENDANT.] Perfectly upright or vertical; extending in a straight line from any point toward the center of the earth, or at right angles with the plane of the horizon; *geom.* falling directly on a line or surface at right angles; at right angles to a given line or surface or making a normal with a curved surface.—*Perpendicular style, arch.* the florid or Tudor style of Gothic; the latest style of purely English architecture.—*n.* A line at right angles to the plane of the horizon; a vertical line; *geom.* a line falling at right angles on another line or on a plane.—**perpendicularity,** pėr·pen·dik'ū·lar·i·ti, *n.* The state of being perpendicular.—**perpendicularly,** pėr·pen·dik'ū·lėr·li, *adv.* In a perpendicular manner; vertically.

perpetrate, pėr'pe·trāt, *v.t.*—*perpetrated, perpetrating.* [L. *perpetro*—*per,* through, and *patro,* to finish or perform; same root as *pater,* father. PATERNAL.] To do, execute, or perform, generally in a bad sense; to be guilty of; to commit; also used humorously for to produce something execrable or shocking (to *perpetrate* a pun).—**perpetration,** pėr·pe·trā'shon, *n.* The act of perpetrating; commission.—**perpetrator,** pėr'pe·trā·tėr, *n.* One that perpetrates.

perpetual, pėr·pet'ū·al, *a.* [Fr. *perpétuel,* L. *perpetualis,* from *perpetuus,* perpetual—*per,* through, and *peto,* to seek. PETITION.] Continuing or lasting for ever in future time; destined to be eternal; continuing or continued without intermission; uninterrupted. ∴ Syn. under CON-

TINUOUS.—*Perpetual curate,* a permanent holder of a curacy in which all the tithes are appropriated and no vicarage endowed.—*Perpetual motion,* motion that once originated, generates a power of continuing itself forever or indefinitely, by means of mechanism or some application of the force of gravity —such a motion being, however, impossible.—*Perpetual screw,* an endless screw. See ENDLESS.—**perpetually,** pėr·pet'ū·al·li, *adv.* In a perpetual manner; constantly; forever.—**perpetuate,** pėr·pet'ū·āt, *v.t.*—*perpetuated, perpetuating.* [L. *perpetuo, perpetuatum.*] To make perpetual; to cause to endure or to be continued indefinitely; to preserve from extinction or oblivion. —**perpetuation,** pėr·pet'ū·ā″shon, *n.* The act of perpetuating or making perpetual.—**perpetuity,** pėr·pe·tū'i·ti, *n.* [L. *perpetuitas.*] The state or quality of being perpetual; something of which there will be no end; duration of which there will be no end; duration to all futurity; exemption from intermission or ceasing.

perplex, pėr·pleks', *v.t.* [From L. *perplexus,* entangled, intricate, involved—*per,* intens., and *plecto, plexum,* to twist; akin to Gr. *plekō,* L. *plico,* to fold. PLY.] To involve, entangle, make complicated or intricate; to puzzle; to tease with suspense, anxiety, or ambiguity.—**perplexedly,** pėr·plek'sed·li, *adv.* In a perplexed or perplexing manner.—**perplexing,** pėr·plek'sing, *p.* and *a.* Embarrassing; difficult; intricate.—**perplexity,** pėr·plek'si·ti, *n.* The state of being perplexed, puzzled, or at a loss; the state of being intricate or involved.

perquisite, pėr'kwi·zit, *n.* [L. *perquisitum,* something sought out, from *perquiro*—*per,* intens., and *quæro,* to seek. QUERY.] Something obtained from a place or office over and above the settled wages or emoluments; something in addition to regular wages or salary.

perron, per'on, *n.* [Fr., from L.L. *petronus,* a perron, from L. and Gr. *petra,* a stone.] *Arch.* an external stair by which access is given to the entrance door of a building.

perry, per'i, *n.* [Fr. *poiré,* perry, from *poire,* L. *pirum,* a pear.] A fermented liquor made from the juice of pears and resembling cider.

per se, pėr·sā'. [L.] By or of itself; as such.

persecute, pėr'se·kūt, *v.t.*—*persecuted, persecuting.* [Fr. *persecuter,* from L. *persequor, persecutus,* to persecute —*per,* intens., and *sequor,* to follow. SEQUENCE.] To harass or afflict with repeated acts of cruelty or annoyance; to afflict persistently; specifically, to afflict or punish on account of holding particular opinions or adhering to a particular creed or mode of worship.—**persecution,** pėr·se·kū'shon, *n.* The act or practice of persecuting; the state of being persecuted.—**persecutor,** pėr'se·kū·tėr, *n.* One who persecutes.

---

fāte, fär, fâre, fat, fall; mē, met, hėr; pīne, pin; nōte, not, mŏve; tūbe, tub, bull; oil, pound.

Perseides, pėr·sē′i·dēz, *n. pl.* A name given to the August meteors because they seem to radiate from the constellation *Perseus.*

persevere, pėr·se·vėr′, *v.i.*—*persevered, persevering.* [L. *persevero,* from *perseverus,* very severe or strict—*per,* intens., and *severus,* severe, strict. SEVERE.] To continue resolutely in any business or enterprise undertaken; to pursue steadily any design or course commenced; not to give over or abandon what is undertaken. ∴ Syn. under PERSIST. —**persevering,** pėr·se·vē′ring, *p.* and *a.* Steadfast in purpose; persisting in any business or course begun.—**perseveringly,** pėr·se·vē′ring·li, *adv.* In a persevering manner.—**perseverance,** pėr·se·vē′rans, *n.* [L. *perseverantia.*] The act or habit of persevering; persistence in anything undertaken.

Persian, pėr′zhan, *a.* Pertaining to ancient Persia, the Persians or their language.—*n.* A native of Persia; the language spoken in Persia (now Iran); a silk formerly used for lining.—*Persian lamb,* the karakul lamb, the pelts of which are used in the making of outer clothing.

persiflage, pėr′si·fläzh, *n.* [Fr., from *persifler* to quiz—L. *per,* and *sibilare,* to hiss.] Idle bantering talk; a frivolous or jeering talk regarding any subject, serious or otherwise.—**persifleur,** pėr′si·flėr, *n.* One who indulges in persiflage.

persimmon, pėr·sim′on, *n.* [Virginia Indian.] An American tree of the ebony family, and also its fruit, which is about the size of a small plum and has a very sweet pulp.

persist, pėr·sist′, *v.i.* [Fr. *persister,* L. *persisto*—*per,* through, and *sisto,* to stand. STATE, STAND.] To continue steadily and firmly in the pursuit of any business or course commenced; to continue in the face of some amount of opposition; to persevere; (of things) to continue in a certain state. ∴ *Persist* is nearly synonymous with *persevere;* but *persist* frequently implies more obstinacy than *persevere,* particularly in that which is evil or injurious to others.—**persistence, persistency,** pėr·sis′tens, pėr·sis′ten·si, *n.* The state of persisting, or of being persistent; steady continuance in a course; perseverance, often in evil; *physics,* the continuance of an effect after the cause which first gave rise to it is removed, as the *persistence* of the impression of light on the retina after the luminous object is withdrawn.—**persistent,** pėr·sis′tent, *a.* Inclined to persist; persevering; tenacious of purpose; *bot.* continuing without withering or falling off.—**persistently,** pėr′sis·tent·li, *adv.* In a persistent manner.

person, pėr′son, *n.* [L. *persona,* primarily a mask used by actors, hence, a character, a person, from *personare,* to sound through—*per,* through, and *sonare,* to sound.] An individual human being; a man, woman, or child; bodily form; human frame, with its characteristic appearance (to appear in *person;* cleanly in *person*); a human being, indefinitely; one; a man (a *person* would think so); a term applied to each of the three beings of the Godhead; *gram.* one of three relations in which nouns and pronouns are regarded as standing to the act of speaking, a pronoun of the *first person* denoting the speaker, the *second person* one who is spoken to and the *third person* one who or that which is spoken of (thus including all nouns); one of the three corresponding inflections of a verb singular and plural.—*In person,* by one's self, not by representative.—**personable,** pėr′son·a·bl, *a.* Having a well-formed body or person; of good appearance.—**personage,** pėr′son·ij, *n.* A person; a man or woman of distinction (an illustrious *personage*); a being regarded as having an individuality like that of a human being (a divine or a mythological *personage*).—**personal,** pėr′son·al, *a.* [L. *personalis.*] Pertaining to a person as distinct from a thing; relating to or affecting some individual person; peculiar or proper to him or her, or to private actions or character; applying to the person, character, or conduct of an individual, generally in a disparaging manner (*personal* reflections or remarks); belonging to face and figure (*personal* charms); done in person, not by representative (a *personal* interview); *gram.* denoting or pointing to the person (a *personal* pronoun, as *I, we, thou, you, he, she, it, they*); having the modifications of the three persons.—*Personal identity, metaph.* sameness of being at every stage of life, of which consciousness is the evidence.—*Personal property, personal estate,* movables; chattels; things belonging to the person, as money, jewels, furniture, etc., as distinguished from *real* estate in land and houses.—**personality,** pėr·son·al′i·ti, *n.* The state of being personal; what constitutes an individual; a distinct person; the state of existing as a thinking intelligent being; application or applicability to a person; an application of remarks to the conduct, character, or appearance of some person; traits that characterize a nation, a group, or an individual; reference to personal traits (to indulge in *personalities*); a noted person; *law,* personal estate; personality.—**personalize,** pėr′son·al·īz, *v.t.*—*personalized, personalizing.* To make personal.—**personally,** pėr′son·al·li, *adv.* In a personal manner; in person; with respect to an individual; as regards one's personal existence or individuality.—**personalty,** pėr′son·al·ti, *n.* Law, personal property, in distinction from *realty* or real property.—**personate,** pėr′son·āt, *v.t.*—*personated, personating.* To assume the character or appearance of, whether in real life or on the stage; to represent by an assumed appearance; to act the part of; to assume or put on.—*a.* [L. *personatus,* masked.] *Bot.* a term applied to a gamopetalous corolla somewhat resembling an animal's mouth, as in the snapdragon.—**personation,** pėr·son·ā′shon, *n.* The act of counterfeiting the person or character of another.—*False personation,* the offense of personating another for the purpose of fraud.—**personator,** pėr′son·ā·tėr, *n.* One who personates; one who assumes the character of another.—**personification,** pėr·son′i·fi·kā′shon, *n.* The act of personifying; an embodiment; an impersonation; *rhet.* a species of metaphor, which consists in representing inanimate objects or abstract notions as endued with life and action, or possessing the attributes of living beings.—**personify,** pėr·son′i·fī, *v.t.*—*personified, personifying.* [L. *persona,* and *facio,* to make.] To treat or regard as a person; to treat for literary purposes as if endowed with the characters of a rational being or person; to impersonate.—**personnel,** pėr·son·el′, *n.* [Fr., from *personne,* a person.] The body of persons employed in any occupation; often opposed to *matériel.*

perspective, pėr·spek′tiv, *a.* [Fr. *perspectif,* from L. *perspicio, perspectum*—*per,* through, and *specio,* to view. SPECIES.] Producing certain optical effects when looked through; optical (a *perspective* glass); pertaining to the art of perspective.—*n.* A telescope‡; the art or science which teaches how to draw or paint objects or scenes so that they appear to have their natural dimensions, positions, and relations—*aerial* perspective dealing with light, shade, and color, *linear* perspective with form and magnitude; a representation of objects in perspective; quality of a picture as regards perspective; view; vista.—**perspectively,** pėr·spek′tiv·li, *adv.* According to the rules of perspective.

perspicacious, pėr·spi·kā′shus, *a.* [L. *perspicax, perspicācis,* from *perspicio,* to look through. PERSPECTIVE.] Quick-sighted; quickly seeing through or understanding anything; of acute discernment.—**perspicaciously,** pėr·spi·kā′shus·li, *adv.* In a perspicacious manner.—**perspicacity,** pėr·spi·kas′i·ti, *n.* The state or quality of being perspicacious; acuteness of discernment; penetration; sagacity.—**perspicuity,** pėr·spi·kū′i·ti, *n.* [L. *perspicuitas.*] The quality of being perspicuous; easiness to be understood; freedom from obscurity or ambiguity.—**perspicuous,** pėr·spik′ū·us, *a.* [L. *perspicuus.*] Clear to the understanding; not obscure or ambiguous; lucid.—**perspicuously,** pėr·spik′ū·us·li, *adv.* In a perspicuous manner.—**perspicuousness,** pėr·spik′ū·us·nes, *n.* Perspicuity; intelligibility; lucidity.

perspire, pėr·spīr′, *v.i.*—*perspired, perspiring.* [L. *perspiro*—*per,* through, and *spiro,* to breathe. SPIRIT.] To give out watery matter through the pores of the skin; to sweat; to exude. —*v.t.* To emit through the excretories of the skin; to give out through pores.—**perspiration**, pėr‧spi‧rā'shon, n. The act of perspiring; excretion of watery fluid (sweat) from the surface of the body (whether visibly or in the form of invisible vapor);—**perspiratory**, pėr‧spī'ra‧to‧ri, a. Pertaining to perspiration; causing perspiration; perspirative.

persuade, pėr‧swād', v.t.—**persuaded**, **persuading**. [L. persuadeo—per, effectively, and suadeo, to advise, urge. SUASION.] To influence by argument, advice, or expostulation; to argue or reason into a certain course of action; to advise; to try to influence; to convince by argument or reasons offered.—v.i. To use persuasion.—**persuadable**, pėr‧swā'da‧bl, a. Capable of being persuaded.—**persuader**, pėr‧swā'dėr, n. One who persuades.—**persuasible**, pėr‧swā'zi‧bl, a. [L. persuasibilis.] Capable of being persuaded.—**persuasion**, pėr‧swā'zhon, n. [L. persuasio, persuasionis.] The act of persuading; the state of being persuaded or convinced; settled opinion or conviction; a creed or belief; a sect or party adhering to a creed or system of opinions. ∴ Syn. under CONVICTION.—**persuasive**, pėr‧swā'ziv, a. Having the power of persuading; influencing to a course of action.—n. That which persuades; an incitement; an exhortation.—**persuasively**, pėr‧swā'ziv‧li, adv. In a persuasive manner.—**persuasiveness**, pėr‧swā'ziv‧nes, n. The quality of being persuasive.

pert, pėrt, a. [Partly from O.Fr. apert, appert (as in malapert), from L. apertus, open (APERIENT); partly from W. pert, perc, trim, spruce (PERK).] Lively; brisk; dapper; smart; forward; saucy; indecorously free.—**pertly**, pėrt'li, adv. In a pert manner; briskly; smartly; with indecorous boldness.—**pertness**, pėrt'nes, n. The state or quality of being pert; smartness; sauciness; forward boldness.

pertain, pėr‧tān', v.i. [L. pertineo—per, intens., and teneo, to hold, whence also tenant, contain, obtain, retain, etc. TENANT.] To belong; to be the property, right, duty of; to appertain; to have relation or bearing; always followed by to.

pertinaceous, pėr‧ti‧nā'shus, a. [L. pertinax—per, intens., and teneo, to hold; PERTAIN.] Holding or adhering to any opinion, purpose, or design with obstinacy; obstinate; perversely persistent; resolute; constant.—**pertinaciously**, pėr‧ti‧nā'shus‧li, adv. In a pertinacious manner; persistently; obstinately.—**pertinacity**, **pertinaciousness**, pėr‧ti‧nas'i‧ti, pėr‧ti‧nā'shus‧nes n. Firm or unyielding adherence to opinion or purpose; obstinacy; resolution; constancy.

pertinent, pėr'ti‧nent, a. [L. pertinens, ppr. of pertineo, to pertain. PERTAIN.] Related to the subject or matter in hand; just to the purpose; apposite; not foreign to the question.—**pertinence**, **pertinency**,

pėr'ti‧nens, pėr'ti‧nen‧si, n. The quality of being pertinent; justness of relation to the subject or matter in hand; fitness; appositeness.—**pertinently**, pėr'ti‧nent‧li, adv. In a pertinent manner; appositely; to the purpose.

perturb, pėr‧tėrb', v.t. [L. perturbo—per, intens., and turbo, to disturb, from turba, a crowd. DISTURB, TURBID.] To disturb; to agitate; to disorder; to confuse.—**perturbable**, pėr‧tėr'ba‧bl, a. Capable of being perturbed or agitated.—**perturbation**, pėr‧tėr‧bā'shon, n. [L. perturbatio.] The act of perturbing or state of being perturbed; disorder; especially, disquiet of mind; commotion of the passions; agitation; cause of disquiet.—Perturbations of the planets, their orbital irregularities or deviations from their regular elliptic orbits, arising from their attraction for one another.

pertussis, pėr‧tus'is, n. [L. per, intens., and tussis, a cough.] Med. the whooping cough.

peruke, pe‧rŭk', n. [Fr. perruque, It. perucca, It. dial. pilucca, peruke, from L. pilus, hair. Periwig is a corruption of perruque, and its final syllable has become wig.] An artificial cap of hair; a periwig; a perruque.

peruse, pe‧rūz', v.t.—**perused**, **perusing**. [From prefix per, intens., and use.] To read through; to read with attention; to observe; to examine with careful survey.—**peruser**, pe‧rū'zėr, n. One who peruses.—**perusal**, pe‧rū'zal, n. The act of perusing or reading.

Peruvian, pe‧rū'vi‧an, a. Pertaining to Peru in South America.—n. A native of Peru.—**Peruvian bark**, n. The bark of several species of Cinchona, trees of Peru, yielding quinine. See CINCHONA, QUININE.

pervade, pėr‧vād', v.t.—**pervaded**, **pervading**. [L. pervado, to go through—per, through, and vado, to go (as in invade); cog. A.Sax. wadan, E. wade.] To pass or flow through; to extend through; to spread or be diffused through the whole extent of.—**pervasion**, pėr‧vā'zhon, n. The act of pervading.—**pervasive**, pėr‧vā'siv, a. Tending or having power to pervade.

perverse, pėr‧vėrs', a. [L. perversus, from perverto, to pervert, corrupt, overthrow—per, and verto, to turn. VERSE.] Turned aside from the right; turned to evil; obstinate in the wrong; froward; stubborn; intractable; cross; petulant; untoward.—**perversely**, pėr‧vėrs'li, adv. In a perverse manner; stubbornly; obstinately in the wrong.—**perverseness**, pėr‧vėrs'nes, n. The quality of being perverse; disposition to thwart or cross.—**perversion**, pėr‧vėr'shon, n. [L. perversio.] The act of perverting; a diverting from the true intent or object; sexual aberration.—**perversity**, pėr‧vėr'si‧ti, n. [L. perversitas.] State or quality of being perverse; perverseness.—**perversive**, pėr‧vėr'siv, a. Tending or having power to pervert.—**pervert**, pėr‧vėrt', v.t. [L. per-

verto.] To turn from truth, propriety, or from its proper purpose; to distort from its true use or end; to misinterpret willfully; to turn from the right; to corrupt.—**pervert**, pėr'vėrt, n. One who has been perverted; an apostate; a degenerate; one who is sexually perverted; an invert.—**perverter**, pėr‧vėr'tėr, n. One that perverts; one that distorts, misinterprets, or misapplies.—**pervertible**, pėr‧vėr'ti‧bl, a. Capable of being perverted.

pervicacious, pėr‧vi‧kā'shus, a. [L. pervicax, headstrong.] Very obstinate; stubborn; willfully contrary or refractory.

pervious, pėr'vi‧us, a. [L. pervius—per, through, and via, a way. VOYAGE, WAY.] Capable of being penetrated by another body or substance; penetrable; allowing an entrance or a passage through; capable of being penetrated by the mental sight.—**perviousness**, pėr'vi‧us‧nes, n. The quality of being pervious.

peseta, pe‧sā'te, n. [Sp.] A Spanish gold monetary unit of 100 centimes; a silver coin of nominally equal value.

Peshito, pesh‧ē'tō, a. and n. [Syriac, single or true.] The Syrian translation of the Old and New Testaments (incomplete) made by a Christian in the second century.

pesky, pes'ki, a. [Variant of pest and risky.] Troublesome; vexatious.

peso, pā'sō, n. [Sp.] A dollar; a term used in certain of the Central and South American countries.

pessary, pes'a‧ri, n. [Med. L. pessarium, from L. pessum, Gr. pessos, a small oval stone, a medicated plug.] A device introduced into the vagina to correct uterine displacement, to prevent conception, etc.

pessimism, pes'im‧izm, n. [L. pessimus, the worst.] The belief or doctrine that man is imperfectible and that his life is essentially unhappy; the tendency to take the most unfavorable view of situations or actions: opposed to optimism.—**pessimist**, pes'im‧ist, n. One who believes in pessimism, also one who is inclined to take a despondent view of things.—**pessimistic**, pes‧si‧mis'tik, a. Pertaining to pessimism.

pest, pest, n. [Fr. peste, from L. pestis, a plague, a pest (whence pestilent, pestiferous); same root as perdo, to destroy (PERDITION).] A plague, pestilence, or deadly epidemic disease; anything very noxious, mischievous, or destructive; a mischievous or destructive person.—**pesthouse**, n. A hospital for persons infected with the plague or other pestilential disease.

Pestalozzian, pes‧ta‧lot'si‧an, a. Pertaining to the system of elementary education instituted by a Swiss philanthropist named Pestalozzi, which is substantially the system now followed.

pester, pes'tėr, v.t. [O.Fr. empestrer, originally to shackle the feet of a horse at pasture, from L.L. pasto-

rium, foot shackles, from L. *pastor*, a shepherd. PASTERN, PASTOR.] To encumber‡; to crowd or cram‡; to trouble; to disturb; to annoy with little vexations.

pestiferous, pes·tif'er·us, *a.* [L. *pestis*, plague, and *fero*, to produce. PEST.] Pestilential; noxious to health; infectious; noxious in any manner; malignant.—**pestiferously**, pes·tif'-er·us·li, *adv.* In a pestiferous manner; pestilentially.

pestilence, pes'ti·lens, *n.* [L. *pestilentia*, from *pestilens*, pestilent, from *pestis*, plague. PEST.] The disease called the plague or pest; any contagious and malignant disease that is epidemic and mortal; what is pestilential or pestiferous; something morally evil or destructive.—**pestilent**, pes'ti·lent, *a.* [L. *pestilens*.] Pestilential; mischievous; noxious to morals or society; troublesome; corrupt.—**pestilential**, pes·ti·len'-shal, *a.* Having the nature of the plague or other infectious and deadly disease; producing or tending to produce infectious disease; destructive.—**pestilently**, pes'ti·lent·li, *adv.* In a pestilent manner.

pestle, pes'l, *n.* [O.Fr. *pesteil*, from L. *pistillum*, a pestle, from *pinso*, *pistum*, to bray, to pound; akin *pistil*, *piston*.] An instrument for pounding and breaking substances in a mortar. —*v.t.*—*pestled*, *pestling*. To break or pulverize with a pestle.

pet, pet, *n.* [Possibly an abbreviated form of *petulant* or *petulance*.] A slight fit of peevishness or fretful discontent.—**pettish**, pet'ish, *a.* Proceeding from or pertaining to a pet or peevish humor.—**pettishly**, pet'-ish·li, *adv.* In a pettish manner.—**pettishness**, pet'ish·nes, *n.* Fretfulness; peevishness.

pet, pet, *n.* [From Ir. *peat*, Gael. *peata*, a pet, or perhaps from *petty*, Fr. *petit*, little.] A fondling; a darling; a favorite child; an animal fondled and indulged.—*v.t.*—*petted*, *petting*. To treat as a pet; to fondle; to indulge.—*a.* Petted; favorite (a *pet* lamb, a *pet* theory).

petal, pet'al, *n.* [From Gr. *petalon*, a leaf, from *petalos*, spread out, expanded; same root as in *patent*.] *Bot.* a flower leaf; one of the separate parts of a corolla.—**petaled**, pet'ald, *a.* Having petals.—**petaline**, pet'al·-īn, *a. Bot.* pertaining to a petal.—**petaloid**, pet'al·oid, *a.* Having the form of a petal; resembling petals.—**petalous**, pet'al·us, *a. Bot.* having petals; petaled.

petard, pe·tärd', *n.* [Fr. *pétard*, from *péter*, to break wind, to bounce, from L. *pedo*, *peditum*, with same sense.] An engine of war made of metal, to be loaded with powder and fixed on a gate, barricade, etc., in order to break it down by explosion.—*Hoist with his own petard*, (*fig.*) caught in his own trap; involved in the danger he meant for others.

petasos, **petasus**, pet'a·sos, pet'a·sus, *n.* [Gr. *petasos*.] A broad-brimmed hat; the winged cap of Mercury.

Peter, *n.*—*The Blue Peter*, the flag hoisted by a merchantman on the eve of leaving the docks.

peter out, pē·tėr·out', *v.i.* Said of a mine or vein of ore when it is exhausted and yields no return. (*Colloq.*)

Peter pence, Peter's pence, pē·tėr pens', *n. pl.* A tribute that used to be regularly offered to the popes (as the successors of St. Peter); a similar contribution still voluntarily given by some Roman Catholics.

petersham, pē'tėr·sham, *n.* [After Lord *Petersham*, who set the fashion of wearing it.] A style of overcoat formerly fashionable; the heavy, rough-napped woolen cloth of which such overcoats were made.

petiole, pet'i·ōl, *n.* [Fr., from L. *petiolus*, a dim. from *pes*, *pedis*, a foot.] *Bot.* a leafstalk; the stalk connecting the blade of the leaf with the branch or stem.—**petiolar**, pet'i·ō·lėr, *a. Bot.* pertaining to a petiole, or proceeding from it.—**petiolate**, pet'i·ō·lāt, *a.* Having a petiole.—**petiolule**, pet'i·ōl·ūl, *n.* [A dim. of *petiole*.] *Bot.* a little or partial petiole, such as belongs to the leaflets of compound leaves.

petit, pet'i or pe·tē'; **petite** (feminine form), pe·tēt', *a.* [Fr.] Little; petty; small in figure.—*Petit juror*, a person serving on a petit jury.—*Petit jury*, a group of twelve persons impaneled as a jury to decide a case tried in a law court; distinguished from *grand jury*.

petite, pe·tēt', *a.* [Fr.] Small; tiny and delicate, usually said of a woman.

petition, pe·tish'on, *n.* [L. *petitio*, *petitionis*, from *peto*, *petitum*, to seek.] An entreaty, supplication, or prayer; a formal written request; a document containing such a request, usually signed by persons supporting the request.—*v.t.* To make a petition or request to.—*v.i.* To present a petition.—**petitionary**, pe·tish'on·e·ri, *a.*—**petitioner**, pe·tish'on·ėr, *n.*

petrel, pet'rel, *n.* [Dim. of *Peter*, in allusion to St. Peter's walking on the sea, as the birds often seem to do.] The name of web-footed oceanic birds of several species, found at great distances from land, and generally in stormy weather: hence the name *stormy petrels*.

petri dish, pet'ri, *n.* [For R. J. *Petri*.] A shallow dish of thin glass with a cover, used in growing bacteriological cultures.

petrify, pet'ri·fī, *v.t.*—*petrified*, *petrifying*. [L. *petra* (from Gr. *petra*), a stone or rock (seen also in *petroleum*, *pier*), and *facio*, to make.] To convert to stone or stony substance, as by the infiltration and deposition of mineral matter; to turn into a fossil; *fig.* to make callous or obdurate; to paralyze or stupefy with fear or amazement.—*v.i.* To become stone or of a stony hardness.—**petrifaction**, pet·ri·fak'shon, *n.* The process of changing into stone; an organized body rendered hard by deposition of a stony substance in its cavities; a fossil; a state of being paralyzed as

with astonishment.—**petrifactive**, pet·ri·fak'tiv, *a.* Having power to petrify or convert into stone.

Petrine, pē'trin, *a.* Relating to St. *Peter* (the *Petrine* epistles).

petrography, pe·trog'ra·fi, *n.* [Gr. *petros*, a stone, and *graphō*, to write.] The study of rocks; a scientific description of rocks; petrology.—**petrographer**, pe·trog'ra·fėr, *n.*—**petrographic**, **petrographical**, pet·-ro·graf'ik, pet·ro·graf'i·kal, *a.*

petrol, pet'rol, *n.* [From *petroleum*.] *British*, gasoline.

petrolatum, pet·ro·lā'tum, *n.* [From *petroleum*.] A colorless, odorless, tasteless substance derived from petroleum and used in ointments and as a protective dressing.

petroleum, pe·trō'li·um, *n.* [L. *petra*, rock, and *oleum*, oil.] A natural, oily liquid consisting chiefly of hydrocarbons which, by fractional distillation, yields such products as gasoline, kerosene, lubricating oils, fuel oils, etc.

petrology, pe·trol'o·ji, *n.* [Gr. *petros*, a rock, and *logos*, a treatise.] The study of rocks; that branch of geology which determines the constitution of rocks by investigating the chemical composition of the separate mineral ingredients of which they consist. Spelled also *Petralogy*.—**petrological**, pet·ro·loj'i·kal, *a.* Of or pertaining to petrology.—**petrologist**, pe·trol'o·jist, *n.* One versed in petrology.

petronel, pet'ro·nel, *n.* [O.Fr. *petrinal*, *poictrinal*, from L. *pectus*, *pectoris*, the breast, being discharged with the stock placed against the breast.] A kind of carbine or large horseman's pistol.

petrosal, pi·trō'sal, *a.* and *n.* [L. *petrosus*.] Applied to the petrous portion of the temporal bone or to a homologous bone. See PETROUS.

petrosilex, pet·ro·si'leks, *n.* [L. *petra*, a stone, and *silex*, flint.] Rock stone; rock flint or compact feldspar.

petrous, pē'trus, *a.* [L. *petrosus*, from *petra*, a stone.] Like stone; hard; stony; *anat.* applied to that portion of the temporal bone in which the internal organs of hearing are situated, from its hardness (known as the *petrosal portion*).

petticoat, pet'i·kōt, *n.* [From *petty*, short, small, and *coat*.] A loose undergarment worn by females; hence, a woman.—*Petticoat government*, female government, either political or domestic.

pettifog, pet'i·fog, *v.i.*—*pettifogged*, *pettifogging*. [Petty and Prov.E. *fog*, to seek gain by mean practices.] To act in mean or petty cases, as a lawyer.—**pettifogger**, pet·i·fog'ėr, *n.* An inferior attorney or lawyer who is employed in mean business.—**pettifoggery**, pet·i·fog'ėr·i, *n.* The practice of a pettifogger; tricks; quibbles.

pettiness. See PETTY.

pettish. See PET.

pettitoes, pet'i·tōz, *n. pl.* [Petty and *toes*.] The toes or feet of a pig: sometimes used humorously for the human feet, as those of a child.

ch, *chain*;   ch, Sc. *loch*;   g, *go*;   j, *job*;   ng, *sing*;   TH, *then*;   th, *thin*;   w, *wig*;   hw, *whig*;   zh, *azure*.

petty, pet'i, *a*. [Fr. *petit*, little; small, akin to W. *pitw*, small, *pid*, a point.] Small; little; trifling; inconsiderable; having little power or possessions; having little importance; inferior (a *petty* prince).—*Petty averages*, the accustomed duties of anchorage, pilotage, etc., which are paid by a vessel.—*Petty cash*, money kept on hand from which change is made and small bills are paid.—*Petty-cash book*, a book in which small receipts and payments are entered.—*Petty jury*, same as PETIT JURY.—*Petty officer*, an officer in the navy whose rank corresponds with that of a noncommissioned officer in the army. —**pettily**, pet'i·li, *adv*. In a petty manner.—**pettiness**, pet'i·nes, *n*.

petulant, pet'ū·lant, *a*. [L. *petulans, petulantis*, petulant, from *peto*, to attack. PETITION.] Manifesting pique, perversity, fretfulness; saucy; pert; capricious.—**petulance, petulancy**, pet'ū·lans, pet'ū·lan·si, *n*. [L. *petulantia*.] Freakish passion; peevishness; pettishness; sauciness.— **petulantly**, pet'ū·lant·li, *adv*. In a petulant manner; with saucy pertness.

petunia, pe·tū'ni·a, *n*. [Brazil, *petun*, tobacco.] A genus of American herbaceous plants, nearly allied to the tobacco plant, and much prized by horticulturists for the beauty of their flowers.

pew, pū, *n*. [O.Fr. *pui*, a raised place, from L. *podium*, a balcony, from Gr. *podion*, from *pous, podos*, the foot.] A fixed seat in a church, enclosed and separated from those adjoining by partitions.

pewee, pē'wē, *n*. [From its call.] One of the North American flycatchers; the phoebe.

pewit, pē'wit, *n*. [From its call.] The lapwing; a small European black-headed gull.

pewter, pū'tėr, *n*. [O.Fr. *peutre, piautre*, D. *peauter*, also, *speauter*, same as *spelter*.] An alloy of tin and lead, or of tin with such proportions of lead, zinc, bismuth, antimony, or copper as experience has shown to be most conducive to the improvement of its hardness and color; a vessel, or vessels collectively, made of pewter.—*a*. Made of pewter.

pewterer, pū'tėr·ėr, *n*. One whose occupation is to make articles of pewter.

pfennig, pfen'ig, *n*. In Germany, the reichspfennig, a bronze coin worth 1/100 mark.

phaeton, fā'e·ton, *n*. [From Gr. *Phaethōn*, who obtained leave from his father Helios (the Sun) to drive the chariot of the sun, but as he was unable to restrain the horses Zeus dashed him with a thunderbolt headlong into the River Po.] An open four-wheeled carriage usually drawn by two horses.

phagedena, phagedaena, faj·e·dē'na, *n*. [Gr. *phagedaina*, from *phagein*, to eat.] A spreading obstinate ulcer.

phagocyte, fag'o·sīt, *n*. [Gr. *phagein*, to eat, *kytos*, cell.] A white blood corpuscle that absorbs and destroys disease germs.—**phagocytosis**, fag'-

o·sit·o̅"sis, *n*. The destruction of disease germs and diseased products by phagocytes.

phalange, fa·lanj', *n*. [Gr. *phalanx, phalangos*, battle array, a phalanx of soldiers, a bone of the fingers or toes.] *Anat*. one of the small bones of the fingers and toes; *bot*. a collection of several stamens joined more or less by their filaments.—**phalangal, phalangeal**, fa·lang'gal, fa·lan'ji·al, *a*. Belonging to the phalanges of the fingers and toes.—**phalanger**, fa·lan'jėr, *n*. [From two of the toes being joined as far as the last *phalanges*.] An Australian marsupial animal of several species, nocturnal in habits and living in trees.— **phalanx**, fal'angks, *n*. pl. **phalanges**, fa·lan'jēz, also, except in anatomy, **phalanxes**, fal'angk·sēz. *Greek antiq*. the heavy-armed infantry of an army, especially when formed in ranks and files close and deep; a body of troops or men in close array; *anat*. one of the small bones of the fingers or the toes.

phalanstery, fal'an·ste·ri, *n*. [Fr. *phalanstère*, from Gr. *phalanx*, a phalanx.] A socialistic community living together according to the system proposed by Fourier; the dwelling of such a community.

phalarope, fal'a·rōp, *n*. [From Gr. *phalaros*, white, and *pous, podos*, a foot.] A lobe-footed grallatorial bird resembling the sandpiper.

phallus, fal'lus, *n*. [Gr. *phallos*, the virile organ.] Image of the male organ of generation, symbolizing the power of fertility and reproductiveness in nature, as worshiped in some primitive systems of religion; in anatomy, the penis or clitoris.— **phallic**, fal'lik, *a*. Pertaining to the phallus, or to the worship of the generative principle in nature.

phanerogam, fan'ėr·o·gam, *n*. [Gr. *phaneros*, evident, and *gamos*, marriage.] *Bot*. a flowering plant or a plant with conspicuous flowers containing stamens and pistils: opposed to a *cryptogam*.—**phanerogamic, phanerogamous**, fan'ėr·o·gam"ik, fan·ėr·og'a·mus, *a*. *Bot*. belonging to the flowering plants, in contradistinction to *cryptogamic, cryptogamous*.

phantasm, fan'tazm, *n*. [Gr. *phantasma*, from *phantazein*, to show, from the stem of *phainein*, to show. PHENOMENON.] A creation of the fancy; an imaginary existence which seems to be real; an apparition; a phantom; an idea; a notion; a fancy. —**phantasmagoria**, fan·tas'ma·gō'ri·a, *n*. [Gr. *phantasma*, and *agora*, an assembly.] Any exhibition of images by means of shadows, as by the magic lantern; the apparatus used in such an exhibition; any mixed gathering of figures; illusive images. —**phantasmagorial, phantasmagoric**, fan·tas'ma·gō'ri·al, fan·tas'ma·gor"ik, *a*. Relating to a phantasmagoria.—**phantasmal**, fan'taz·mal, *a*. Pertaining to or resembling a phantasm; spectral; illusive.

phantasy, fan'ta·si, *n*. See FANTASY.

phantom, fan'tom, *n*. [Fr. *fantôme*,

from L. *phantasma*; same word as *phantasm*. PHANTASM.] An apparition or specter; a ghost; a fancied vision; a phantasm; something unreal.

Pharaoh, fâ'rō, *n*. A name given by the Hebrews to the ancient monarchs of Egypt; a game at cards. FARO.— *Pharaoh's chicken*, the Egyptian vulture.—*Pharaoh's rat*, the ichneumon. —**Pharaonic**, fâ·rā·on'ik, *a*. Pertaining to the Pharaohs, or to the old Egyptians.

Pharisee, far'i·sē, *n*. [Gr. *pharisaios*, from Heb. *pârûsh*, separated.] One of a sect among the Jews distinguished by their strict observance of rites and ceremonies and of the traditions of the elders, and who considered themselves as more righteous than other Jews; hence, a strict observer of the outward forms or ceremonies in religion without the spirit of it; a hypocrite.—**pharisaic, pharisaical**, far·i·sā'ik, far·i·sā'i·kal, *a*. Pertaining to the Pharisees; resembling the Pharisees; addicted to external forms and ceremonies; making a show of religion without the spirit of it; hypocritical.—**pharisaically**, far·i·sā'i·kal·li, *adv*. In a pharisaical manner, hypocritically. —**pharisaicalness**, far·i·sā'i·kal·nes, *n*.—**Pharisaism**, far'i·sā·izm, *n*. The doctrines and conduct of the Pharisees, as a sect; rigid observance of external rites and forms of religion without genuine piety; hypocrisy in religion.

pharmaceutic, pharmaceutical, fär·ma·sū'tik, fär·ma·sū'ti·kal, *a*. [Gr. *pharmakeutikos*, from *pharmakeuein*, to administer medicine, from *pharmakon*, a drug.] Pertaining to the knowledge or art of pharmacy or preparing medicines.—*Pharmaceutical chemistry*, chemistry applied to those substances which are employed for the cure of diseases.—**pharmaceutically**, fär·ma·sū'ti·kal·li, *adv*. In the manner of pharmacy.— **pharmaceutics**, fär·ma·sū'tiks, *n*. The science of preparing medicines; pharmacy. —**pharmaceutist**, fär·ma·sū'tist, *n*. One who prepares medicines; one who practices pharmacy; an apothecary.—**pharmacist**, fär'ma·sist, *n*. One skilled in pharmacy; a druggist.—**pharmacologist**, fär·ma·kol'o·jist, *n*. One who is skilled in pharmacology.—**pharmacology**, fär·ma·kol'o·ji, *n*. [Gr. *pharmakon* and *logos*.] The science or knowledge of drugs, or the art of preparing medicines: a branch of materia medica; a treatise on preparing medicines.—**pharmacopoeia**, fär'ma·kō·pē"a, *n*. [Gr. *pharmakon*, and *poiein*, to make.] A book of directions for the preparation, etc., of medicines, generally published by authority.—**pharmacy**, fär'ma·si, *n*. [Fr. *pharmacie*, from Gr. *pharmakeia*, from *pharmakon*.] The art of preparing and compounding medicines, and of dispensing them according to the prescriptions of medical practitioners; the occupation of an apothecary; the place where medicines are compounded or dispensed.

pharos, fâ'ros, *n*. A lighthouse or

tower which anciently stood on the isle of Pharos, at the entrance to the Port of Alexandria; hence, any lighthouse for the direction of seamen; a beacon.

pharynx, far'ingks, n. [Gr. *pharynx, pharyngos;* akin to *pharanx,* a chasm.] The muscular sac which intervenes between the cavity of the mouth and the esophagus, its contraction aiding in swallowing the food.—**pharyngeal,** fa·rin'ji·al, a. Belonging to or affecting the pharynx.—**pharyngitis,** far·in·ji'tis, n. Inflammation of the pharynx.—**pharyngotomy,** far·in··got'o·mi, n. [Gr. *pharynx,* and *tomē,* a cutting.] The operation of making an incision into the pharynx to remove anything that obstructs the passage.

phase, fāz, n. [Fr. *phase,* from Gr. *phasis,* from *phainomai,* to appear. PHENOMENON.] One of the recurring appearances or states of the moon or a planet in respect to quantity of illumination or figure of enlightened disk; the particular state, at a given instant, of a continuously varying and periodic phenomenon (the *phases* of a tide, etc.); an aspect or appearance of that which presents various aspects; one of the various aspects in which a question presents itself to the mind; a turn or chance.—*Phase rule,* an equation $(c+2-p=F)$ expressing the relation between the solid, liquid, and gaseous states (phases) of substances in solution (c=components; p=number of phases; F=degrees of freedom).

phasis, fā'sis, n. pl. **phases,** fā'sēz. *Astron.* a phase.

pheasant, fez'ant, n. [L. *phasianus,* from Gr. *phasianos,* from *Phasis,* a river of Asia, near the mouth of which these birds are said to have been numerous.] A well-known and beautiful gallinaceous bird bred as a game bird.

phenacetin, fē·nas'e·tin, n. [*Phen* (indicating a benzene derivative) and *acetin.*] A drug of coal-tar origin, used to relieve pain and fever.

phenix, fē'niks, n. See PHOENIX.

phenobarbital, fē'nō·bar''bi·tal, n. [*Pheno* and *barbital.*] A barbiturate $C_{12}H_{12}N_2O_3$ used as a sedative and hypnotic; luminal.

phenol, fē'nol, n. A name for *Carbolic Acid.*

phenology, fin·ol'o·jē, n. [Gr. *phaino,* I appear, *logos,* a discourse.] The study of times and seasons in relation to plants and animals as embodied in nature calendars.

phenolphthalein, fē'nol·thāl''ēn, n. [*Phenol* and *phthlein.*] An off-white crystalline compound $C_{20}H_{14}O_4$ used as a laxative and as an indicator for acids and bases.

phenomenon, fi·nom'e·non, n. pl. **phenomena,** fi·nom'e·na. [Gr. *phainomenon,* what appears, from *phainomai,* I appear.] An observable fact or event; a remarkable thing or person.—**phenomenal,** fi·nom'e·nal, a. Connected with, relating to, or constituted by phenomena; remarkable or extraordinary; astounding.—**phenomenalism,** fi·nom'-

e·nal·izm, n. That system of philosophy which inquires only into the causes of existing phenomena.—**phenomenally,** fi·nom'e·nal·li, adv.

phial, fī'al, n. [L. *phiala,* from Gr. *phialē,* a phial. *Vial* is another form.] A glass vessel or bottle; especially, a small glass bottle used for holding liquors, and particularly liquid medicines.—*Leyden-phial,* a vessel used in electrical experiments. LEYDEN-JAR.—*v.t.*—**phialed, phialing.** To put or keep in a phial, or as in a phial.

philander, fi·lan'dėr, v.i. [From *Philander,* a virtuous youth in Ariosto's *Orlando Furioso,* between whom and a married lady there were certain tender passages.] To make love sentimentally to a lady; to flirt; to pretend admiration.

philanthropy, fi·lan'thro·pi, n. [Gr. *philanthropia,* from *philos,* loving, and *anthrōpos,* a man.] Love toward mankind; benevolence toward the whole human family. —**philanthropic, philanthropical,** fil·an··throp'ik, fil·an·throp'i·kal, a. [Gr. *philanthrōpikos.*] Pertaining to philanthropy; possessing general benevolence; entertaining good will toward all men.—**philanthropically,** fil·an·throp'i·kal·li, adv. In a philanthropic manner.—**philanthropist,** fi·lan'throp·ist, n. One who evinces philanthropy; a person of general benevolence; one who exerts himself in doing good to his fellow men.

philately, fi·lat'e·li, n. [Fr. *philatélie,* a ridiculous compound of Gr. *philos,* loving, and *ateleia,* exemption from taxation.] The practice of collecting all sorts of postage stamps.—**philatelist,** fi·lat'e·list, n.

philharmonic, fil·här·mon'ik, a. [Gr. *philos,* loving, and *harmonia,* harmony.] Loving music, hence, referring to musical societies and their concerts. —n. A musical organization.

philhellenist, fil·hel'len·ist, n. [Fr. *philhellène,* from Gr. *philos,* loving, and *Hellen,* a Greek.] A friend of Greece; one who supports the cause and interests of the Greeks (Hellenes); one who supported them in their successful struggle with the Turks for independence.—**philhellenic,** fil·hel·len'ik, a. Loving the Greeks.—**philhellenism,** fil·hel'len··izm, n. The principles of the philhellenists.

Philippian, fi·lip'i·an, n. A native or inhabitant of Philippi, a city of ancient Macedonia ('the Epistle of Paul to the *Philippians*').

Philippic, fi·lip'ik, n. One of a series of orations delivered by Demosthenes, the Grecian orator, against *Philip,* king of Macedon; [*not cap.*] any discourse full of acrimonious invective.

Philippine, fil'i·pēn, a. [Sp. *Filipino.*] Of the Philippine Islands.

Philistine, fi·lis'tīn or fil'is·tin, n. An inhabitant of *Philistia,* now a portion of Syria; the English form of *Philister,* a term applied by German students to any one who has not been trained in a university; hence, a matter-of-fact, commonplace person deficient in liberal culture and

large intelligence, and so wanting in sentiment and taste; a person of narrow views; a prosaic, practical man.—**Philistinism,** fil'is·tin·izm, n. Manners or modes of thinking of Philistines.

philodendron, fil·o·den'dron, n. [N.L. from Gr. *philodendros,* loving trees.] A climbing plant cultivated for its showy heart-shaped leaves.

philogyny, fi·loj'i·ni, n. [Gr. *philos,* loving, and *gynē,* a woman.] Fondness for women; uxoriousness.

philology, fi·lol'o·ji, n. [Gr. *philologia,* from *phileō,* to love, and *logos,* a word.] The study of language and literature; the study of languages in connection with the whole moral and intellectual action of the peoples using them; the study of the classical languages, literature, and history; but the most common meaning now is the science of language; linguistic science; linguistics: often expressed by the qualified title of *comparative philology.*—**philologist, philologer, philologian,** fi·lol'o·jist, fi·lol'o·jėr, fil·o·lō'ji·an, n. One versed in philology, or the study of language in a scientific manner.—**philological, philologic,** fil·o·loj'i·kal, fil·o·loj'ik, a. Pertaining to philology.

philomel, fil'o·mel, n. [From *Philomela,* daughter of Pandion, king of Athens, who was changed into a nightingale.] The poetic name of the nightingale.

philoprogenitiveness, fil'o·prō·jen''-i·tiv·nes, n. [Gr. *philos,* fond, and E. *progeny.*] The love of offspring, a term used chiefly by phrenologists.

philosopher, fi·los'o·fėr, n. [Gr. *philosophos*—*philos,* loving, and *sophos,* wise.] A person versed in or devoted to philosophy; one who devotes himself to the study of moral or intellectual science; one who conforms his life to the principles of philosophy; one who lives according to reason or the rules of practical wisdom.—*Philosophers' stone,* a stone or preparation which the alchemists formerly sought, as the instrument of converting the baser metals into pure gold.—**philosophical, philosophic,** fil·o·sof'i·kal, fil·o·sof'ik, a. Pertaining, suitable, or according to philosophy; characterized or constituted by philosophy; proceeding from philosophy; characteristic of a practical philosopher; based on the rules of practical wisdom; calm; cool; temperate.—**philosophically,** fil·o·sof'i·kal·li, adv. In a philosophical manner.—**philosophism,** fi·los'of·izm, n. [Fr. *philosophisme.*] Spurious or would-be philosophy; the affectation of philosophy.—**philosophize,** fi·los'o·fīz, v.i.—*philosophized, philosophizing.* To reason like a philosopher; to form or attempt to form a philosophical system or theory.—**philosophizer,** fi·los'o·fī·zėr, n. One who philosophizes.—**philosophy,** fi·los'o·fi, n. [Gr. *philosophia,* lit. love of wisdom, from *philos,* love, and *sophia,* wisdom.] The science which aims at an explanation of all the phenomena of the universe by ultimate causes; the knowledge of phenomena as explained by, and resolved into, causes and reasons, powers and laws; a particular philosophical system or theory; the calm and unexcitable state of mind of the wise man; practical wisdom; course of studies for the degree of 'Doctor of Philosophy' in Germany or elsewhere.—*Moral philosophy*. See ETHICS.—*Mental philosophy*. See METAPHYSICS.—*Natural philosophy*. See PHYSICS.

philter, philtre, fil′tėr, *n*. [Fr. *philtre*, L. *philtrum*, from Gr. *philtron*, from *philos*, loving.] A potion supposed by the ancients, and even by the ignorant of the present day, to have the power of exciting love.—*v.t.*—*philtered, philtred; philtering, philtring*. To impregnate with a love potion; to administer a potion to.

phiz, fiz, *n*. [A contr. of *physiognomy*.] The face or visage. (*Humorous*.)

phlebitis, fle·bī′tis, *n*. [Gr. *phleps, phlebos*, a vein, and *-itis*, implying inflammation.] Inflammation of the inner membrane of a vein.—**phlebotomy,** fli·bot′o·mi, *n*. [Gr. *phlebotomia*—*phleps, phlebos*, and *tomē*, a cutting.] The act or practice of opening a vein for letting blood.—**phlebotomist,** fli·bot′o·mist, *n*. One that opens a vein for letting blood; a bloodletter. — **phlebotomize,** fli·bot′o·mīz, *v.t.*—*phlebotomized, phlebotomizing*. To let blood from; to bleed by opening a vein.

phlegm, flem, *n*. [Gr. *phlegma, phlegmatos*, a slimy humor, from *phlegō*, to burn. FLAME.] The thick viscid matter secreted in the digestive and respiratory passages, and discharged by coughing or vomiting; bronchial mucus; *fig.* coldness; sluggishness; indifference.—**phlegmatic, phlegmatical,** fleg·mat′ik, fleg·mat′i·kal, *a*. [Gr. *phlegmatikos*.] Abounding in phlegm; generating phlegm; cold or sluggish in temperament; not easily excited into action or passion; not mercurial or lively.—**phlegmatically,** fleg·mat′i·kal·li, *adv*. In a phlegmatic manner; coldly; heavily.

phloem, flō′em, *n*. [Gr. *phloios*, bark.] *Bot*. the liber or bast tissue in plants.

phlogiston, flo·jis′ton, *n*. [Gr. *phlogistos*, burnt, from *phlogizō*, to burn, from *phlegō*, to burn.] According to an obsolete theory, the supposed principle of inflammability; a hypothetical element which was thought to be pure fire fixed in combustible bodies.—**phlogistic,** flo·jis′tik, *a*. Pertaining to phlogiston; *med*. inflammatory.

phlox, floks, *n*. [Gr. *phlox*, a flame, from the appearance of the flowers.] A North American genus of plants, with red, purple, or white flowers, cultivated in gardens.

phlyctena, phlyctaena, flik·tē′na, *n*. [Gr. *phlyktaina*.] A kind of watery pustule on the skin.

phobia, fō′bi·a, *n*. [Gr. *phobos*, fear.] Any persistent, morbid fear or dread. —**phobic,** fō′bic, *a*.

phocine, fō′sīn, *a*. Pertaining to the seals.

phoebe, fē′bē, *n*. [Imitative.] Any of the small American flycatchers (genus *Sayornis*).

Phoebus, fē′bus, *n*. [Gr. *Phoibos*, lit. the brilliant one.] A name of Apollo, often used in the same sense as Sol, the sun.

Phoenician, fē·nish′i·an, *a*. Pertaining to Phoenicia.—*n*. A native of ancient Phoenicia, the region between Lebanon and the Mediterranean; the language of the Phoenicians, an extinct Semitic tongue, akin to Hebrew.

phoenix, fē′niks, *n*. [Gr. *phoinix*.] A bird of ancient legend said to be the only one of its kind and to live 500 or 600 years, at the end of which it built for itself a funeral pile, lighted it with the fanning of its wings, and rose again from its ashes; hence, an emblem of immortality; a paragon; a person of singular distinction or beauty.

phonation, fo·nā′shon, *n*. [Gr. *phonē*, voice.] The act of uttering vocal sounds.

phonautograph, fo·na′to·graf, *n*. [Gr. *phonē*, sound, *auto*, self, and *graphō*, to write.] An instrument for automatically showing sound vibrations by waved lines.

phone, fōn. Short for *Telephone*: used as noun and verb.

phoneme, fō′nēm, *n*. [Fr. *phonème*, from Gr. *phonēma*, sound.] In a language, the smallest sound unit that distinguishes one utterance from another.—**phonemic,** fō·nē′mik, *a*.—**phonemics,** fō·nē′miks, *n*. The analysis of a language by a study of its phonemes.

phonetic, phonetical, fo·net′ik, fo·net′i·kal, *a*. [Gr. *phōnetikos*, from *phōnē*, voice, sound.] Pertaining to the voice; pertaining to the representation of sounds; representing sounds.—*Phonetic spelling*, a system which aims at spelling words precisely according to their sound, and not in the loose manner in which English is spelled.—**phonetically,** fo·net′i·kal·li, *adv*. In a phonetic manner.—**phonetics,** fo·net′iks, *n*. The doctrine of sounds; the science which treats of the sounds of the human voice, and the art of representing them by writing.—**phonic,** fō′nik, *a*. Pertaining to sound.—**phonics,** fō′niks, *n*. The doctrine or science of sounds; phonetics.

phonograph, fō′no·graf, *n*. [Gr. *phonē*, sound, and *graphō*, to write.] A type or character for expressing a sound; a character used in phonography; an instrument by means of which sounds can be permanently registered, and afterward mechanically reproduced almost in the original tones from the register.—**phonogram,** fō′no·gram, *n*. A sound as reproduced by the phonograph.—**phonographer,** fo·nog′raf·ėr, *n*. One versed in phonography; one who uses or is skilled in the use of the phonograph.—**phonographic,** fo·no·graf′ik, *a*. Pertaining to or based upon phonography; pertaining to the phonograph. —**phonographically,** fo·no·graf′i·kal·li, *adv*. In a phonographic manner.—**phonography,** fo·nog′ra·fi, *n*. The description of

sounds; the representation of sounds by characters, each of which represents one sound, and always the same sound; phonetic shorthand; the art of using the phonograph.

phonolite, fō′no·līt, *n*. [Gr. *phonē*, sound, and *lithos*, stone.] Same as *Clinkstone*.

phonology, fo·nol′o·ji, *n*. [Gr. *phonē*, sound, voice, and *logos*, discourse.] The science or doctrine of the elementary sounds uttered by the human voice; phonetics.—**phonologic, phonological,** fo·no·loj′ik, fo·no·loj′i·kal, *a*. Pertaining to phonology.—**phonologist,** fo·nol′o·jist, *n*. One versed in phonology.

phonometer, fo·nom′et·ėr, *n*. [Gr. *phonē*, sound, *metron*, a measure.] An instrument for ascertaining the number of vibrations of a given sound in a given time.

phonoscope, fō′no·skōp, *n*. [Gr. *phonē*, a voice, a sound, and *skopeō*, to view.] An instrument for producing figures of light from vibrations of sound by means of an electric current.

phonotypy, fō·no·tī′pi, *n*. [Gr. *phonē*, sound, and *typos*, type.] A method of representing each of the sounds of speech by a distinct printed character or letter; phonetic printing.—**phonotype,** fō′no·tīp, *n*. A type or character used in phonetic printing. —**phonotypic,** fō·no·tip′ik, *a*.

phony, fō′nē, *a*. [Origin unknown.] Not genuine; pretentious.

phosgene, fos′jēn, *n*. [Gr. *phōs*, light, and root *gen*, to produce.] A heavy, poisonous gas with a nauseating, choking smell.

phosphorus, fos′for·us, *n*. [L. from Gr. *phosophoros*, light-bearing.] A solid, nonmetallic, glowing material. Symbol, P; at. no., 15; at. wt., 30.9738.—**phosphate,** fos′fāt, *n*. A salt of phosphoric acid; a carbonated drink.—**phosphoresce,** fos·fo·res′, *v.i.*—*phosphoresced, phosphorescing*. To emit a faint, heatless light. —**phosphorescence,** fos·fo·res′ens, *n*. The state or quality of being phosphorescent; the property which certain bodies possess of becoming luminous.—**phosphorescent,** fos·fo·res′ent, *a*. Shining by phosphorescence.—**phosphoric,** fos·for′ik, *a*. Pertaining to, obtained from, or resembling phosphorus.—**phosphoric acid,** *n*. An oxygen acid of phosphorus.—**phosphorous,** fos′for·us, *a*. Of phosphorus.—**phosphorous acid,** *n*. A crystalline acid H_3PO_3 from which phosphates are derived.

photics, fō′tiks, *n*. [Gr. *phōs, phōtos*, light.] That department of science which treats of light.

photo, fō′to, *n*. Short for *photograph* (colloq.).

photochemistry, fō·to·kem′is·tri, *n*. [Gr. *phōs, phōtos*, light, and E. *chemistry*.] That branch of chemistry which treats of the chemical action of light, especially of solar light.—**photochemical,** fō·to·kem′i·kal, *a*. Pertaining to the chemical action of light.

photochromy, fō·to·krō′mi, *n*. [Gr. *phōs, phōtos*, light, and *chrōma*, color.]

The art or operation of reproducing colors by photography.

photoelectric cell, fō′tō·i·lek″trik sel, *n.* A vacuum tube in which the action of light produces, or changes the strength of, electric current.

photoelectrotype, *n.* A process in which a photographic picture is produced in relief so as to afford, by electric deposition, a matrix for a cast, from which impressions in ink may be obtained.

photoengraving, fō′tō·en·grā″ving, *n.* [Combining form *photo* and *engraving.*] A photographic engraving process in which the printing surface is in relief; a print made by this process.

photoflash, fō′tō·flash′, *n.* [Combining form *photo* and *flash.*] An electrically operated flash lamp.

photoflood, fō′tō·flood′, *n.* [Combining form *photo* and *flood.*] A high-voltage electric lamp of intense sustained brilliance used in photography.

photogene, fō′to·jēn, *n.* [Gr. *phōs, phōtos,* light, and root *gen,* to produce.] A more or less continued impression or picture on the retina.

photogenic, fō′tō·gen′ik, *a.* [Gr. *phōs, phōtos,* light, and combining form *genic,* meaning suitable for reproduction.] Suitable for photographing; producing or generating light; *biol.* phosphorescent.

photography, fo·tog′ra·fi, *n.* [Gr. *phōs, phōtos,* light, and *graphō,* to describe.] The art of obtaining accurate representations of scenes and objects by means of the action of light on substances treated with certain chemicals.—**photograph,** fō′to·graf, *n.* A picture obtained by means of photography.—*v.t.* To take a picture with a camera.—*v.i.* To practice photography.—**photographer,** fo·tog′raf·ėr, *n.*—**photographic,** fō·to·graf′ik,—**photographically,** fō·to·graf′i·kal·li, *adv.*

photogravure, fō·to·grav·ūr′, *n.* [Gr. *phōs, phōtos,* light, Fr. *gravure,* engraving.] A process by which an engraving is produced on a metal plate by photographic methods.

photolithograph, fō′to·lith″o·graf, *n.* [Combining form *photo* and *lithograph.*] A print reproduced by any photolithography process.—**photolithography,** fō′to·li·thog′ra·fi, *n.* A mode of lithographing in which a photograph is transferred to a thin metal plate.

photometer, fō·tom′et·ėr, *n.* [Gr. *phōs, phōtos,* light, and *metron,* measure.] An instrument intended to measure the comparative intensity of different lights.—**photometric, photometrical,** fo·to·met′rik, fō·to·met′ri·kal, *a.* Pertaining to or made by a photometer.—**photometry,** fō·tom′et·ri, *n.* The measurement of the relative amounts of light emitted by different sources.

photomicrography, *n.* [Gr. *phōs, phōtos,* light, *mikros,* small, and *graphō,* to write.] The art or process of photographing minute objects when magnified by means of the microscope.

photon, fō′ton, *n.* [Combining form *photo* and Gr. suffix *on.*] *Phys.* a quantum of light energy.

photo-offset, fō′tō-of″set, *n.* [Combining form *photo* and *offset.*] A printing process in which a photographic image of design or type is used in the preparation of a plate for offset printing.

photophobia, fō·to·fō′bi·a, *n.* [Gr. *phōs, phōtos,* light, and *phobia,* dread.] An intolerance or dread of light.

photoplay, fō′to·plā, *n.* A play reproduced by motion pictures; a motion picture.

photosensitive, fō·to·sen′si·tiv, *a.* Readily affected or changed by light or other radiant energy.

photospectroscope, fō·to·spek′tro·skōp, *n.* An instrument for photographing spectra.

photosphere, fō′to·sfēr, *n.* [Gr. *phōs, phōtos,* light, and E. *sphere.*] An envelope of light; the luminous envelope, supposed to consist of incandescent matter, surrounding the sun.

photosynthesis, fō·to·sin″the·sis, *n.* [Gr. *phōs, phōtos,* light, *synthēsis,* a putting together.] In green plants, the utilization by protoplasm of the energy of light, aided by the green pigment chlorophyll, for building up organic matter from water and carbonic acid gas.

phototropism, fō·tot′rō·pizm, *n.* [Combining form *photo* and *tropism,* from Gr. *tropē,* a turning.] A tropism in which light is the stimulant.

phototype, fō′to·tīp, *n.* [Gr. *phōs, phōtos,* light, and *typos,* a type.] A plate produced from a photograph by a peculiar process, as by photolithography, and from which copies can be printed.—**phototypy,** fō·to·tī′pi, *n.* The art or process of producing phototypes.

photozincography, *n.* The process of printing from a prepared zinc plate on which a photograph has been taken.

phrase, frāz, *n.* [Gr. *phrasis,* a phrase (seen also in *periphrasis, paraphrase*), from *phrazō,* I speak.] A brief expression; two or more words forming a complete expression by themselves or being a portion of a sentence; a peculiar or characteristic expression; an idiom; the manner or style in which a person expresses himself; diction; *music,* a short part of a composition usually occupying a distinct rhythmical period of from two to four bars.—*v.t.* phrased, phrasing. To call; to style; to express.—**phraseogram,** frā′zē·o·gram, *n.* A combination of shorthand characters to represent a phrase or sentence.—**phraseological,** frā′zē·o·loj″i·kal, *a.* Pertaining to phraseology; exhibiting idiomatic phrases.—**phraseologist,** frā·zē·ol′o·jist, *n.* A stickler for a particular form of words or phraseology; a coiner of phrases.—**phraseology,** frā·zē·ol′o·ji, *n.* Manner of expression; peculiar words or phrases used in a sentence; diction; a collection of phrases in a language. ∴ Syn. under DICTION.

phrenetic, fre·net′ik, *a.* [L. *phrene-*

ticus, from Gr. *phrenetikos,* suffering from *phrenitis* or inflammation of the brain, from *phrēn,* the mind, the midriff. FRANTIC.] Having the mind disordered; frantic; frenetic.—*n.* A frantic or frenzied person; one whose mind is disordered.—**phrenetically,** fre·net′i·kal·li, *adv.* In a phrenetic manner.—**phrenic,** fren′ik, *a.* [From Gr. *phrēn,* in sense of diaphragm.] *Anat.* belonging to the diaphragm.—**phrenitis,** fre·nī′tis, *n.* [Gr., from *phrēn,* the mind, and *-itis,* term. denoting inflammation.] *Med.* an inflammation of the brain; delirium; frenzy.

phrenology, fre·nol′o·ji, *n.* [Gr. *phrēn, phrenos,* the mind, and *logos,* discourse.] A doctrine which professes to found a philosophy of the human mind upon a presumed knowledge of the functions of different portions of the brain obtained by comparing their relative forms and magnitudes in different individuals with the propensities and intellectual powers which these individuals are found respectively to possess.—**phrenologic, phrenological,** fren·o·loj′ik, fren·o·loj′i·kal, *a.* Pertaining to phrenology.—**phrenologist,** fre·nol′o·jist, *n.* One versed in phrenology.

Phrygian, frij′i·an, *a.* [From *Phrygia,* in Asia Minor.] Pertaining to Phrygia or to the Phrygians.—*Phrygian cap,* the red cap of liberty worn by the leaders during the first French Republic.—*Phrygian mode,* one of the modes in ancient music.

phthalic acid, thal′ik, fthal′ik, one of three isomeric benzene-dicarboxylic acids, the most important of which is used in making synthetic dyes, resins, etc.

phthisis, thī′sis, fthī′sis, *n.* [L. from Gr. *phthinō,* decay.] *Med.* a wasting away; pulmonary tuberculosis.

phycology, fī·kol′o·ji, *n.* [Gr. *phykos,* and *logos.*] That department of botany which treats of the algae or seaweeds.

phylactery, fi·lak′tėr·i, *n.* [Gr. *phylaktērion,* from *phylassō,* to defend or guard.] An amulet worn as a preservative from danger or disease among the Jews; a strip of parchment inscribed with certain texts from the Old Testament, enclosed within a small leather case, and fastened on the forehead or on the left arm near the region of the heart.

phyletic, fī·let′ik, *a.* [Gr. *phylē,* a tribe or race.] Pertaining to a race or tribe: applied especially in connection with the development of animal tribes.

phylloclade, fil′lō·klād, *n.* [Gr. *phyllon,* a leaf, *klados,* a branch.] A CLADODE (which see).

phyllode, fil′ōd, *n.* [Gr. *phyllon,* a leaf.] A flattened leaf stalk which performs the functions of a leaf blade.

phyllodium, fil·ō′di·um, *n.* [Gr. *phyllon,* a leaf, and *eidos,* likeness.] *Bot.* a leafstalk developed into a flattened expansion like a leaf.—**phylloid,** fil′oid, *a.* Leaf-like; shaped like a leaf.—**phyllopod,** fil′o·pod, *n.* [Gr. *phyllon,* and *pous, podos,* a foot.] One of those crustaceans that have limbs of leaf-like form for swimming.—**phyllotaxis, phyllotaxy,** fil′o·tak·sis, fil′o·tak·si, *n.* [Gr. *taxis,* order.] *Bot.* the arrangement of the leaves on the axis or stem.—**phylloxera,** fil·ok·sē′ra, *n.* [Gr. *phyllon,* a leaf, and *xēros,* parched.] An insect which infests the leaves and roots of the oak, vine, etc., one species of which has caused immense damage in some wine-producing countries.

phylogenesis, phylogeny, fī·lo·jen′e·sis, fī·loj′e·ni, *n.* [Gr. *phylē,* a tribe, and *genesis,* root *gen,* to produce.] *Biol.* the origin and history of races or types of animal forms.—**phylogenetic,** fī′lo·je·net″ik, *a.* Pertaining to phylogenesis or phylogeny, or the race history of an animal.

phylum, fī′lum, *n.* pl. **phyla.** [Gr. *phylon,* a tribe.] One of the grand subdivisions of the animal or vegetable kingdom.

physic, fiz′ik, *n.* [Gr. *physikos,* pertaining to nature, natural, from *physis,* nature, from *phyō,* to bring forth, to spring up; cog. with Skr. *bhû,* to be; E. to *be.* BE.] The science or knowledge of medicine; the art of healing; a medicine, popularly a medicine that purges; a purge; a cathartic.—*Physic garden,* an old name for a botanic garden.—*Physic nut,* the seed of one or two tropical plants (genus *Jatropha*), having strong purgative and emetic properties.—*v.t.*—*physicked, physicking.* To treat with physic; to purge with a cathartic; to remedy.—

physical, fiz′i·kal, *a.* Pertaining to nature; relating to what is material and perceived by the senses; pertaining to the material part or structure of an organized being, as opposed to what is mental or moral (*physical* force); material (the *physical* world); pertaining to physics or natural philosophy.—*Physical geography.* See GEOGRAPHY.—*Physical science.* PHYSICS.—**physically,** fiz′i·kal·li, *adv.* In a physical manner; as regards the material world; as regards the bodily constitution.—**physician,** fi·zish′an, *n.* A person skilled in the art of healing; one whose profession is to prescribe remedies for diseases.—**physicist,** fiz′i·sist, *n.* One skilled in physics; a natural philosopher.—**physics,** fiz′iks, *n.* That branch of science which treats of the laws and properties of matter; the department of science that deals with mechanics, dynamics, light, heat, sound, electricity, and magnetism; natural philosophy.

physiognomy, fiz·i·og′no·mi, *n.* [Properly *physiognomony,* from Gr. *physiognōmonia*—*physis,* nature, and *gnōmōn,* one who knows, from stem of *gignōskō,* to know.] The art of discerning the character of the mind from the features of the face; the face or countenance as an index of the mind; particular cast or expression of countenance.—**physi-ognomic, physiognomical,** fiz′i·og·nom″ik, fiz′i·og·nom″i·kal, *a.* Pertaining to physiognomy.—**physiognomist,** fiz·i·og′no·mist, *n.* One skilled in physiognomy.

physiography, fiz·i·og′ra·fi, *n.* [Gr. *physis,* nature, and *graphō,* to describe.] The science which treats of the earth's physical features, and the causes by which they have been modified, as well as of the climates, life, etc., of the globe; physical geography.—**physiographical,** fiz′i·ō·graf″i·kal, *a.* Pertaining to physiography.

physiology, fiz·i·ol′o·ji, *n.* [Fr. *physiologie,* Gr. *physiologia*—*physics,* nature, and *logos,* discourse.] That science which has for its aim the study and elucidation of the phenomena of life in animals and plants.—**physiologic, physiological,** fiz′i·o·loj″ik, fiz′i·o·loj″i·kal, *a.* Pertaining to physiology.—*Physiological selection,* partial or complete sterility of varying forms with the parent stock; a suggested cause of the isolation necessary for evolution of new species.—**physiologically,** fiz′i·o·loj″i·kal·li, *adv.* According to the principles of physiology.—**physiologist,** fiz·i·ol′o·jist, *n.* One who is versed in or who treats of physiology.

physique, fi·zēk′, *n.* [Fr.] A person's physical or bodily structure or constitution.

phytogenesis, phytogeny, fī·to·jen′e·sis, fī·toj′e·ni, *n.* [Gr. *phyton,* a plant, and *genesis.*] The doctrine of the generation of plants.

phytogeography, fī′to·jē·og″ra·fi, *n.* [Gr. *phyton,* a plant, and E. *geography.*] The geography or geographical distribution of plants.

phytography, fī·tog′ra·fi, *n.* [Gr. *phyton,* a plant, and *graphē,* description.] That branch of botany which concerns itself with the rules to be observed in describing and naming plants.

phytology, fī·tol′o·ji, *n.* [Gr. *phyton,* a plant, *logos,* discourse.] The science of plants, a name sometimes used as equivalent to botany.—**phytological,** fī′to·loj″i·kal, *a.* Relating to phytology.

phytophagous, fī·tof′a·gus, *a.* [Gr. *phyton,* a plant, *phagō,* to eat.] Eating or subsisting on plants.

pi, pī, pē, *n.* [Gr.] The 16th letter of the Greek alphabet; the symbol used to denote the ratio of the circumference of a circle to its diameter, approximate value 3.14159265.

pi, pī, *n* [Origin unknown.] *Print.* disarranged or mixed type.—*v.t.* To disarrange or mix type; to throw into confusion.

piacular, pī·ak′ū·lėr, *a.* [L. *piacularis,* from *piaculum,* expiation, from *pio,* to expiate, from *pius,* pious.] Expiatory; pertaining to expiation.

pia mater, pī′a mā′tėr, *n.* [L., lit. pious mother.] *Anat.* a vascular membrane investing the whole surface of the brain. See DURA MATER.

piano, pi·ä′nō, *a.* [It., soft, smooth, from L. *planus,* plain.] *Mus.* soft; a direction to execute a passage softly or with diminished volume of tone.—

n. (pi·an′ō). A musical metal-stringed instrument with a keyboard, by means of which the metal strings are struck by hammers.—**pianoforte,** pi·an′ō·fort, *n.* [It. *piano,* soft, smooth, and *forte* (L. *fortis*), strong.] A piano.—**pianissimo,** pi·a·nis′i·mō, [It. superl. of *piano,* soft.] *Mus.* very soft; a direction to execute a passage in the softest manner.—**pianist,** pi·an′ist, pi′an·ist, *n.* A performer on the piano.

piassava, pi·a·sä′vä, *n.* [Pg. *piaçaba.*] The fiber of a Brazilian palm tree, extensively used in making brooms and brushes for street sweeping.

piaster, piastre, pi·as′tėr, *n.* [Fr. *piastre,* It. and Sp. *piastra,* a thin plate of metal, a dollar, from L.L. *plastra,* L. *emplastrum,* Gr. *emplastron,* a plaster. PLASTER.] A denomination of money of various countries, especially Egypt and Turkey.

piazza, pi·az′za, *n.* [It. *piazza,* open place, square, market place. PLACE.] A rectangular open space surrounded by buildings or colonnades.

pibroch, pē′broch, *n.* [Gael. *piobaireachd,* from *piobair,* a piper, *piob,* a pipe.] Martial variations performed on the bagpipe, in the Highlands of Scotland.

pica, pī′ka, *n.* [L. *litera picata,* pitch-black letter.] Printing type 12 points in size; a standard printing measure, about ⅙ inch.

picador, pik′a·dor, *n.* [Sp., from *pica,* a pike or lance.] One of the horsemen armed with a lance who excites and irritates the bull in a bullfight.

picaroon, pik·a·rön′, *n.* [Sp. *picaron,* augmentative of *picaro,* a rogue.] A rogue or cheat; one that lives by his wits; an adventurer.—**picaresque,** pik·a·resk′, *a.* [Fr.] Pertaining to rogues or picaroons; describing the fortunes of rogues.

picayune, pik·a·yūn′, *n.* [Fr. *picaillon.*] A coin of small value, formerly used in Louisiana; anything of little value.

piccalilli, pik′a·lil·li, *n.* An imitation Indian pickle of various vegetables, with pungent spices.

piccolo, pik′ko·lō, *n.* [It. *piccolo,* small.] A small flute, the tones of which range an octave higher than those of the ordinary orchestral flute; an octave flute.

pice, pīs, *n. sing.* and *pl.* Small East Indian coin.

piceous, pis′i·us, *a.* [L. *piceus,* from *pix, picis,* pitch.] Of or belonging to pitch; black as pitch.

pick, pik, *v.t.* [Allied to W. *pig,* a point, a pike; Gael. *pioc, piocaid,* a pick, a pickax; *pike, peak, peck, beak;* same root also in *spike.*] To strike at with anything pointed; to peck at, as a bird, with its bill; to pierce; to clean by removing with the teeth, fingers, claws, or a small instrument, something that adheres (to *pick* a bone, the teeth); to separate from other things; to select; to choose (to *pick* the best men); to pluck; to gather, as fruit or things growing; to gather up here and there; to collect (often with *up*); to snatch thievishly (a purse); to steal the contents of (to *pick* a pocket).—*To pick off*, to separate by the fingers or a small instrument; to separate by a sharp sudden movement (to *pick off* a leaf); to aim at and kill.—*To pick out*, to draw out by anything pointed; to select from a number or quantity; to relieve with figures or lines of a different color.—*To pick up*, to take up with the fingers, or otherwise to snatch; to obtain by repeated effort or casually (to *pick up* a livelihood).—*To pick a hole in one's coat*, to find fault with one.—*To pick a lock*, to open it with some instrument other than the key.—*To pick oakum*, to make oakum by untwisting old ropes.—*To pick a quarrel*, to quarrel intentionally with a person.—*v.i.* To eat slowly or by morsels; to nibble; to pilfer.—*To pick up*, to acquire fresh strength, vigor, or the like. (*Colloq.*)—*n.* A heavy sharp-pointed iron tool, with a wooden handle, used for loosening hard earth, stones, etc., in digging, ditching, etc.; a sharp hammer used in dressing stones.—**pickax**, pik′aks, *n.* A tool with a point at one end and a blade at the other; also, simply a pick.—**picker**, pik′ér, *n.*—**pickpocket**, pik′pok·et, *n.* One who steals from others' pockets.—**pickup**, pik′up, *n.* The act of picking up; a small truck.—**pick up**, *v.t.* To lift; to gain by occasional opportunity; to take something into a vehicle; to grasp (meaning); to bring into range of reception (*pick up* a radio signal).

pickaback, pik′a·bak, *a.* or *adv.* [From the older form *pickapack*, a reduplication of *pack*.] On the back or shoulders like a pack. (*Colloq.*)

pickaninny, pik′a·nin·i, *n.* [Sp. *pequeño niño*, little infant.] A Negro or mulatto infant.

pickerel, pik′ér·el, *n.* [From *pike*.] A name applied to several small fresh-water fishes of the pike family.

picket, pik′et, *n.* [Fr. *piquet*, a dim. of *pique*, a pike. PICK.] A stake sharpened or pointed, used in fortification and encampments; a narrow pointed board; *milit.* a detachment of troops in a camp kept equipped to protect the camp from surprise; a person posted, as by a labor union, before or near a place of business where the workers are on strike; a game at cards.—*v.t.*—*picketed, picketing.* To fortify with pickets or pointed stakes; to fence with narrow pointed boards or pales; to fasten to a picket or stake; to place or post as a guard of observation.

pickle, pik′l, *n.* [D. and L.G. *pekel*, G. *pōkel, bōkel*, brine.] A solution of salt and water in which flesh, fish, or other substance is preserved; brine; vinegar, in which vegetables, fish, oysters, etc., are preserved; a thing preserved in pickle; a state of difficulty; a chemical cleaning solution.—*v.t.*—*pickled, pickling.* To preserve in brine or pickle; to treat with pickle.

picnic, pik′nik, *n.* [Fr. *piquenique*.] A pleasure party, the members of

which carry provisions along with them on an excursion to some place in the country; used also adjectively (a *picnic* party).—*v.i.*—*picnicked, picnicking.* To attend or take part in a picnic party.

picot, pē′kō, *n.* [Fr.] One of a series of ornamental loops on a border of lace, ribbon, etc.

picotee, pik·o·tē′, *n.* [Fr. *picotie*, from *Picot* de la Perousse, a French botanist.] A variety of carnation or clove pink, having the dark color only on the edge of the petals.

picric acid, pik′rik as′id, *n. Chem.* a bitter, toxic acid ($(NO_2)_3 C_6H_2OH$) used as a dye and an explosive.

Pict, pikt, *n.* [From *Picti*, the name given them by Latin writers; of uncertain origin.] One of a race of people (probably Celts) who anciently inhabited the northeast of Scotland.—**Pictish**, pik′tish, *a.* Pertaining to the Picts.

pictograph, pik′to·graf, *n.* [L. *pictura*, and *graph*.] An ancient or prehistoric drawing; a record made with pictorial symbols; a symbol in a pictographic system.

picture, pik′chér, *n.* [L. *pictura*, from *pingo, pictum*, to paint. PAINT.] A painting, drawing, or engraving exhibiting the resemblance of anything; any resemblance or representation, either to the eye or to the mind; a likeness; an image; a representation or description in words.—*Picture hat*, a large-sized hat of the Duchess of Devonshire style; the style seen in the portraits by Sir Joshua Reynolds and Gainsborough.—*Picture house*, the place of entertainment devoted to moving pictures.—*v.t.*—*pictured, picturing.* To draw or paint a resemblance of; to represent pictorially; to bring before the mind's eye; to form an ideal likeness of; to describe in a vivid manner.—**pictorial**, pik·tō′ri·al, *a.* [L. *pictor*, a painter.] Pertaining to pictures; illustrated by pictures; constituting a picture.—**pictorially**, pik·tō′ri·al·li, *adv.* In a pictorial manner; with pictures or engravings.—**picturesque**, pik·chér·esk′, *a.* Forming or fitted to form a pleasing picture; expressing that peculiar kind of beauty which is agreeable in a picture; abounding with vivid and striking imagery; graphic in style of writing.—*The picturesque*, the quality that renders a scene suitable for making into a good picture.—**picturesquely**, pik·chér·esk′li, *adv.* In a picturesque manner.—**picturesqueness**, pik·chér·esk′nes, *n.*

picul, pi′kul, *n.* In China, a weight of 133½ lbs.

piddle, pid′l, *v.i.* [A form of *peddle*.] To deal in trifles; to attend to trivial concerns.

pidgin, pij′in, *n.* [Chin. pronunciation of *business*.] A simplified speech used by persons with different languages; a jargon; originally, an English-based jargon used in Chinese commercial ports.

pie, pī, *n.* [From the Celtic; comp. Ir. *pighe*, a pie.] An article of food

consisting of dough baked with something in it or under it.

pie, pī, *n.* [Fr. *pie*, from L. *pica*, a magpie.] The magpie.

piebald, pī′bald, *a.* [From *pie*, a magpie, and *bald*, spotted with white. BALD.] Having spots or patches of white and black or other color; having patches of various colors; pied; diversified; mongrel.

piece, pēs, *n.* [Fr. *pièce*, Pr. *peza*, It. *pezza*, from L.L. *petium*, a piece, probably from the Celtic: W. *peth*, Armor. *pez*, a piece.] A fragment or part of anything separated from the whole, in any manner (to tear in *pieces*); a part of anything, though not separated or separated only in idea; a portion; a definite quantity or portion of certain things (a *piece* of muslin, a *piece* of work); an artistic or literary composition (a *piece* of poetry or sculpture); a coin (a fourpenny *piece*); a gun or single firearm (a fowling *piece*).—*To work by the piece*, to work by the measure of quantity, and not by the measure of time.—*Of a piece*, of the same sort, as if taken from the same whole; alike.—*A piece of one's mind*, a colloquial phrase for blunt and uncomplimentary statements.—*v.t.*—*pieced, piecing.* To mend by the addition of a piece; to patch; to unite; to join; to cement.—*To piece out*, to extend or enlarge by addition of a piece or pieces.—**piece goods**, *n. pl.* Goods generally sold by the piece, as cottons, shirtings, etc.—**piecemeal**, pēs′mēl, *adv.* [*Piece*, and suffix *-meal*, A.Sax. *maelum*, by parts.] In pieces; by pieces; by little and little in succession.—**piecer**, pēs′ér, *n.* One that pieces; a boy or girl employed in a spinning factory to join broken threads.—**piecework**, pēs′wérk, *n.* Work done and paid for by the measure of quantity.

pied, pīd, *a.* [From *pie*, magpie.] Particolored; variegated with spots of different colors; spotted with larger spots than if speckled.

pie plant, pī′plant, *n.* [From its use in pie.] Garden rhubarb.

pier, pēr, *n.* [O.Fr. *pere, piere*, a stone (Fr. *pierre*), from L. and Gr. *petra*, a stone.] *Arch.* the solid parts between openings in a wall, as between doors or windows; the square or other mass or post to which a gate is hung; the solid support from which an arch springs; a large pillar or shaft; one of the supports of the arches of a bridge; a mole or jetty carried out into the sea, serving to protect vessels from the open sea, to form a harbor, etc.; a projecting quay, wharf, or landing-place.—**pier glass**, *n.* A mirror or glass hanging between windows.—**pier table**, *n.* A table placed between windows.

pierce, pērs, *v.t.*—*pierced, piercing.* [Fr. *percer*, to pierce; origin uncertain.] To stab or transfix with a pointed instrument; to penetrate; to force a way into; to affect keenly; to move deeply; to penetrate into, as into a secret or purpose.—*v.i.* To

ch, *chain;* ch, Sc. *loch;* g, *go;* j, *job;* ng, *sing;* TH, *then;* th, *thin;* w, *wig;* hw, *whig;* zh, *azure.*

enter, as a pointed instrument; to penetrate.—**piercer**, pēr′sėr, *n*. An instrument that pierces; a person that pierces or perforates; that organ of an insect with which it pierces bodies; the ovipositor.—**piercingly**, pēr′sing·li, *adv*. In a piercing manner.

Pierides, pī·er′i·dēz, *n. pl.* [L.] A name of the Muses, from *Pieria*, where they were first worshiped among the Thracians.—**Pierian**, pī·ē′ri·an, *a*. Belonging to the Pierides.

Pierrot, pē′er·ō, *n*. [Fr. dim. of *Pierre*, Peter.] Itinerant minstrel or vocalist, generally at seaside places, with the dress of a clown in French pantomime.

piety, pī′e·ti, *n*. [L. *pietas*, from *pius*, pious. *Pity* is the same word.] Veneration or reverence of the Supreme Being and love of His character; the exercise of these affections in obedience to His will and devotion to His service; filial reverence; reverence toward parents or friends, with affection and devotion to them.—**pietism**, pī′et·izm, *n*. The principles or practice of the pietists.—**Pietists**, pī′et·ists, *n. pl. A* religious party in Germany who proposed to revive declining piety in the Reformed churches; hence, applied to one who makes a display of strong religious feelings.—**pietistic**, pī·et·is′tik, *a*.

piezoelectricity, pī·ē′zo·e·lek′tris″·i·ti, *n*. Electricity created by pressure as from compression along a certain axis of a crystal such as quartz.

piezometer, pī·e·zom′et·ėr, *n*. [Gr. *piezō*, to press, *metron*, measure.] An instrument for measuring compressibility.

piffle, pif′l, *n*. [Origin doubtful.] Silly spoken or written matter; trash.

pig, pig, *n*. [A.Sax. *pecga*, akin to D. *big*, *bigge*, L.G. *bigge*, a pig.] A young swine, male or female; a swine in general; an oblong mass of unforged iron, lead, or other metal. ∴ In the process of smelting, the principal channel along which the metal in a state of fusion runs, when let out of the furnace, is called the *sow*, and the lateral channels or molds are denominated *pigs*, whence the iron in this state is called *pig iron*.—*v.t.* or *i.*—*pigged*, *pigging*. To bring forth pigs; to act as pigs; to live or huddle as pigs.—**piggery**, pig′ėr·i, *n*. A place with sties and other accompaniments allotted to pigs.—**piggish**, pig′ish, *a*. Relating to or like pigs; swinish.—**pigheaded**, pig′hed·ed, *a*. Obstinate.—**pig iron**, *n*. Iron, direct from a furnace, that is to be refined.—**pigskin**, pig′skin, *n*. *Sports*, a football.—**pigsty**, *n*. A sty or pen for pigs.—**pigtail**, pig′tāl, *n*. The tail of a pig; the hair of the head tied behind in a tail; tobacco twisted into a long rope.

pigeon, pij′on, *n*. [Fr. *pigeon*, from L. *pipio*, *pipionis*, a chirping bird, from *pipio*; to peep, to chirp.] A common bird of the family Columbidae; a young woman; an easy mark

or a dupe.—**pigeonhole**, *n*. One of the holes in a dovecot where the pigeons go in and out; a little compartment or division in a case for papers.—*v.t.* To lay aside; to classify.—**pigeon-toed**, *a*. Having the toes turned inward.

piggin, pig′in, *n*. [Gael. *pigean*, Ir. *pigin*, an earthen pitcher.] A small wooden vessel with an erect handle.

pigment, pig′ment, *n*. [L. *pigmentum*, from the stem of *pingo*, to paint. PAINT.] Paint; any substance used by painters, dyers, etc., to impart colors to bodies; the coloring matter found in animal and plant bodies.—*v.t.* and *i*. To color or tint; to become colored or tinted.—**pigmentation**, pig·men·tā′shon, *n*. A deposit of pigment; coloration.

Pigmy, pig′mi, *n*. and *a*. See PYGMY.

pika, pī′ka, *n*. A species of rodent allied to the hares that has a voice like that of a quail.

pike, pīk, *n*. [Fr. *pique*, a pike; closely allied to *pick*, *peck*. PICK.] A military weapon, consisting of a long wooden shaft or staff with a flat pointed steel head; a pointed peak, hill, or mountain summit; a fresh-water fish, so named from its long shape or from the form of its snout; a turnpike, or road on which a toll is charged; also, the toll; any main highway.—**pikeman**, pīk′man, *n*. A soldier armed with a pike.—**pikestaff**, *n*. The shaft of a pike; a long staff with a sharp pike in the lower end of it.

piker, pī′ker, *n*. One who gambles, speculates, etc., in a small, cautious way.

pilaster, pi·las′tėr, *n*. [Fr. *pilastre*, It. *pilastro*, from L. *pila*, a pile.] A square pillar projecting from a pier or from a wall to a short distance.

pilau, pilaw, pi′lạ, *n*. [Per. and Turk.] An oriental dish consisting of rice cooked with fat, butter, or meat.

pilchard, pil′chėrd, *n*. [Probably a Cornish word; comp. Ir. *pilseir*, a pilchard; W. *pilcod*, a minnow.] A fish resembling the herring, but smaller.

pile, pīl, *n*. [Partly A.Sax. *pil*, a heap, a stake, partly from Fr. *pile*, a heap, a pier, a voltaic pile; both from L. *pila*, a pier or mole.] A heap; a mass or collection of things in an elevated form; a collection of combustibles arranged for burning a dead body; a large building or mass of buildings; an edifice; *elect.* a series of plates of two dissimilar metals, such as copper and zinc, laid one above the other alternately, with cloth between each pair, moistened with an acid solution, for producing a current of electricity; a galvanic or voltaic battery; a large amount of money; a fortune; an atomic reactor; a large amount; a heraldic figure resembling a wedge.—*v.t.*—*piled*, *piling*. To lay or throw into a heap; to heap up; to accumulate; to drive piles into; to furnish or support with piles.—*To pile arms*, to place three muskets

so that the butts remain firm upon the ground, and the muzzles close together.—**pile driver**, *n*. A workman whose occupation is to drive piles; a machine or contrivance worked by steam for driving in piles.

pile, pīl, *n*. [A.S. *pil*, stake.] A supporting beam; a post driven into the ground to support a structure.

pile, pīl, *n*. [O.Fr. *peil*, from L. *pilus*, hair.] A hair; a fiber of wool, cotton, etc.; the nap or fine hairy or woolly surface of cloth; also, the shag or hair on the skins of animals.—**pileous**, pī′lē·us, *a*. Pertaining to the hair; covered by or consisting of hair; pilose.

pileate, pileated, pī′lē·āt, pī′lē·ā·ted, *a*. [From L. *pileus*, a cap.] Having the form of a cap or cover for the head; *bot.* having a cap or lid like the cap of a mushroom.

pileous, pī′lē·us, *a*. See PILE (nap).

piles, pīlz, *n. pl.* [L. *pila*, a ball.] The dilatation of veins of the lower part of the rectum near the anus, the veins often forming bleeding enlargement and tumors; hemorrhoids.

pileus, pī′lē·us, *n*. [L., a cap.] *Bot.* the cap or top of a mushroom, supported by the stalk.

pilfer, pil′fėr, *v.i.* [O.Fr. *pelfrer*, to plunder, from *pelfre*, goods, spoil, booty. PELF.] To steal in small quantities; to practice petty theft.—*v.t.* To steal or gain by petty theft; to filch.—**pilferer**, pil′fėr·ėr, *n*. One who pilfers.

pilgarlic, pil·gär′lik, *n*. [*Peeled garlic*.] A poor bald-headed creature.

pilgrim, pil′grim, *n*. [Same as D. *pelgrim*, Dan. *pilegrim*, Icel. *pilagrimr*, Fr. *pelegrin*, from L. *peregrinus*, a traveler, a foreigner—*per*, through, and *ager*, land (as in *agriculture*).] A wanderer; a traveler; one that travels to a distance from his own country to visit a shrine or holy place, or to pay his devotion to the remains of dead saints; [*cap.*] one of the colonists from England who founded the colony at Plymouth, Massachusetts, in 1620, which was the first permanent New England settlement of Europeans.—**pilgrimage**, pil′gri·mij, *n*. A journey by a pilgrim; a journey to some place deemed sacred for a devotional purpose; the journey of human life.—**Pilgrim Fathers**, *n*. The Puritans who landed at Plymouth Rock, Massachusetts, in 1620, founding the first New England settlement.

pili, pī′li, *n. pl.* [L. *pilus*, a hair.] *Bot.* fine slender bodies, like hair, covering some plants.—**piliferous**, pī·lif′ėr·us, *a*. Bearing or producing hairs, as a leaf.—**piliform**, pī′li·form, *a*. Formed like or resembling down or hairs.

pill, pil, *n*. [Abbrev. of L. *pilula*, a dim. of *pila*, a ball (whence *pile*, a heap).] A little ball or small round mass of medicinal substance to be swallowed whole; something unpleasant that has to be metaphorically swallowed or accepted.—*v.t.* To dose with pills; to form into pills.

—pillbox, *n.* A box for holding pills; in military slang, a small concrete blockhouse, used in Europe as a machine gun emplacement.

pillage, pil′ij, *n.* [Fr. *pillage,* from *piller,* to rob.] Plunder; spoil; that which is taken by open force, particularly from enemies in war; the act of plundering.—*v.t.—pillaged, pillaging.* To strip of money or goods by open violence, and usually by a number of persons; to plunder; to spoil.—**pillager,** pil′-ij·ėr, *n.* One who pillages.

pillar, pil′ėr, *n.* [Fr. *pilier,* a pillar, from L.L. *pilare,* from L. *pila,* a column. PILE.] A column; a columnar mass or upright body; *fig.* a supporter; one who or that which sustains or upholds.

pillion, pil′yon, *n.* [From the Celtic; W. *pilyn,* Ir. *pillin,* Gael. *pillean,* a pillion, a packsaddle, from root of L. *pilus,* hair (whence *pile,* of cloth).] A cushion for a woman to ride on behind a person on horseback; a pad; a low saddle; the pad of a saddle that rests on the horse's back.

pillory, pil′o·ri, *n.* [Fr. *pilori,* a pillory, Pr. *espitlori,* L.L. *pilorium, spilorium,* a pillory; origin uncertain.] A frame of wood erected on a post or pole, with movable boards resembling those in the stocks, and holes through which were put the head and hands of an offender, who had to stand there by way of public punishment.—*v.t.—pilloried, pillorying.* To punish with the pillory; *fig.* to expose to ridicule, contempt, abuse, and the like.

pillow, pil′ō, *n.* [O.E. *pilwe, pulwe,* from L. *pulvinus,* a cushion.] A long cushion to support the head of a person when reposing, filled with feathers, down, or other soft material; a supporting piece for an axle or shaft; a bearing.—*v.t.* To rest or lay on for support.—**pillow-case, pillow slip,** *n.* The movable sack or case which is drawn over a pillow.—**pillow lace,** *n.* Handmade lace worked on a small pillow or cushion.

pilose, pī′lōs, *a.* [L. *pilosus,* from *pilus,* hair (whence *pile,* of cloth).] Covered with, abounding in, or full of hairs; hairy.—**pilosity,** pī·los′i·ti, *n.* Hairiness.

pilot, pī′lot, *n.* [From It. *pilota,* from Gr. *pēdon,* oar.] A helmsman; one who conducts ships into harbors, through channels, etc.; a guide; *avi.* the one who controls a spacecraft or aircraft; a test operation.—*v.t.* To act as a pilot; to guide.—**pilotage,** pī′lot·ij, *n.* The act of piloting.—**pilot fish,** *n.* A fish that often swims with sharks.—**pilot house,** *n.* A deckhouse for a ship's steering gear and pilot.—**pilot light,** *n.* A small permanent flame from which the burners of a stove are lit; a pilot lamp.

pilous, pī′lus, *a.* See PILOSE.

pilular, pil′ū·lėr, *a.* [L. *pilula,* a pill.] Pertaining to pills.—**pilule,** pil′ūl, *n.* A little pill.

pimento, pi·men′to, *n.* [Pg. *pimenta,*

It. *pimento,* from L. *pigmentum,* paint, juice of plants. PIGMENT.] Allspice, the berry of a tree of the West Indies; Jamaica pepper. See ALL.

pimp, pimp, *n.* [A nasalized form of *pipe* (Pr. *pimpa,* a pipe), a pimp being as it were one who whistles for females like a callbird.] One who provides gratifications for the lust of others; a procurer; a pander.—*v.i.* To pander; to procure lewd women for the gratification of others.

pimpernel, pim′pėr·nel, *n.* [Fr. *pimprenelle,* It. *pimpinella.*] A little red-flowered prostrate annual found in cornfields.

pimple, pim′pl, *n.* [A nasalized form of L. *papula,* a pimple; or from W. *pwmp, pwmpl,* a knob.] A small elevation of the skin, with an inflamed base, seldom containing a fluid or suppurating, and commonly terminating in scurf.—**pimpled,** pim′pld, *a.* Having pimples on the skin; full of pimples.—**pimply,** pim′pli, *a.* Full of pimples.

pin, pin, *n.* [Same as D. *pin,* Dan. *pind,* G. *pinn,* W. *pin.* a pin, a peg, etc., from L. *penna* or *pinna,* a feather, a pen. PEN.] A piece of metal, wood, or the like, used for fastening separate articles together, or as a support from which a thing may be hung; a peg; a bolt; a small piece of wire pointed at one end and with a rounded head at the other, much used as a cheap and ready means of fastening clothes, etc.; a peg in stringed musical instruments for increasing or diminishing the tension of the strings; the center of a target; a central part.—*v.t.—pinned, pinning.* To fasten with a pin or pins of any kind; to clutch; to hold fast.—*v.t.* To enclose; to confine; to pen or pound.—**pincushion,** *n.* A small cushion or pad in which pins are stuck for preservation.—**pinfeather,** pin′feTH-ėr, *n.* A small or short feather; a feather not fully grown.—**pinhole,** pin′hōl, *n.* A small hole made by the puncture of a pin; a very small aperture.—**pin money,** *n.* An allowance made by a husband to his wife for her separate use, originally *to buy pins.*—**pintail,** *n.* A variety of duck with a sharp-pointed tail.—**pinwheel,** *n.* A wheel of which the cogs are pins projecting outward.

piña cloth, pēn′ya or pī′na, *n.* [Sp. *piña,* the pineapple.] A delicate, soft, transparent cloth made from the fibers of the pineapple leaf.

pinafore, pin′a·fōr, *n.* [Because it is or was *pinned* on *before.*] A sort of apron worn by children to protect the front part of their dress; a child's apron.

pinaster, pī·nas′tėr, *n.* [L., from *pinus,* pine.] A species of pine growing in the south of Europe.

pincers, pin′sėrz, *n. pl.* [From Fr. *pincer,* to pinch (whence *pince,* pincers). PINCH.] An instrument by which anything is gripped in order to be drawn out, as a nail, or kept fast for some operation; the nippers of certain animals; prehensile claws.

pinch, pinsh, *v.t.* [Fr. *pincer,* It. *pizzare,* Sp. *pizcar, pinchar,* to pinch; of doubtful origin.] To press hard or squeeze between the ends of the fingers, the teeth, claws, or with an instrument, etc.; to nip; to distress; to afflict; to nip with frost.—*v.i.* To act with pressing force; to press painfully; to be sparing or niggardly.—*To know* or *feel where the shoe pinches,* to have practical and personal experience as to where the cause of trouble in any matter lies.—*n.* A close compression, as with the ends of the fingers; a nip; a gripe; a pang; distress inflicted or suffered; straits; difficulty; a strong iron lever; a crowbar; as much as is taken by the finger and thumb; a small quantity generally of snuff.—**pincher,** pinsh′ėr, *n.* One who or that which pinches.—**pinchers,** pinsh′ėrz, *n. pl.* See PINCERS.

pinchbeck, pinsh′bek, *n.* [From the name of the inventor, a London watchmaker of the last century.] An alloy of copper and zinc, somewhat like gold in color, and formerly much used for cheap jewelry. Hence, when used adjectively, sham; not genuine.

Pindaric, pin·dar′ik, *a.* After the style and manner of *Pindar.*—*n.* An ode in imitation of the odes of Pindar the Grecian lyric poet; an irregular ode.

pine, pīn, *n.* [From L. *pinus,* a pine-tree; same root as *pix, picis,* pitch.] The name of a valuable genus of evergreen coniferous trees, of which about seventy species are known, furnishing timber, turpentine, pitch, and resin; the pineapple, also the plant that produces it.—**pineal,** pin′-ē·al, *a.* [Fr. *pinéale,* from L. *pinea,* the cone of a pine, from *pinus,* a pine.] Resembling a pine cone in shape.—*Pineal gland,* an internal part of the brain, about the size of a pea, considered by Descartes as the seat of the soul.—**pineapple,** *n.* A tropical fruit so called from its resemblance to the cone of the pine tree; the plant itself.—*Pineapple rum,* rum flavored with sliced pineapples.—**pine cone,** *n.* The crown or strobilus of a pine tree.—**pinery,** pī′nėr·i, *n.* A hothouse in which pineapples are raised; a place where pine trees grow.—**pinetum,** pī·nē′-tum, *n.* [L., a pine plantation.] A plantation or collection of growing pine trees of different kinds, especially for ornamental or scientific purposes.

pine, pīn, *v.i.—pined, pining.* [A.Sax. *pinian,* to pain, to pine; same word as *pain.*] To languish; to lose flesh or grow weakly under any distress or anxiety of mind; to languish with desire (to *pine for* a thing).—*v.t.* To pain or torment; to grieve for.—*n.* Pain; anguish; misery.

pinfold, pin′fōld, *n.* [A.Sax. *pyndan,* to pound, to shut in, and *fold.* POUND.] A place in which cattle straying and doing damage are temporarily confined; a pound.

ping, ping, *n.* [Imitative.] The sound made by a bullet, as from a rifle, in

passing through the air.—**Ping-pong,**
n. A trademark for a kind of tennis
played on a table.

pinion, pin'yon, *n.* [Fr. *pignon,* a
pinion or small wheel; Sp. *piñon,*
a joint of a bird's wing; from L.
pinna, penna, a feather. PEN.] The
joint of a fowl's wing remotest from
the body; a wing; a small wheel
which plays in the teeth of a larger.—
v.t. To confine by binding the wings;
to disable by cutting off the first
joint of the wing; to bind the arms
of; to shackle; to fetter.

pink, pingk, *n.* [Comp. D. *pinken,* to
twinkle with the eyes, to wink—some
of them are marked with eyelike
spots.] A name of various garden
flowers, as the clove pink or carnation
and garden pink; a light red color
or pigment resembling that of the
common garden pink; anything supremely excellent (the *pink* of perfection); a fish, the minnow: so called
from the color of its abdomen in
summer.—*a.* Resembling in color
the most frequent hue of the pink.—
pinkeye, *n.* A contagious disease of
the eye; contagious conjunctivitis.

pink, pingk, *v.t.* [A nasalized form
of *pick.*] To work in eyelet-holes;
to ornament with holes, scallops, etc.;
to stab; to wound with a sword or
rapier.—**pinkroot,** *n.* The root of
the Indian pink used as a vermifuge.

pink, pingk, *n.* [D. and Dan.] A ship
with a very narrow stern, a build
now obsolete.

pinna, pin'a, *n.* pl. **pinnae,** pin'ē. [L.
pinna, penna, a feather, a wing, a fin.]
Zool. the wing or feather of a bird;
the fin of a fish; *anat.* the pavilion
of the ear, that part which projects
beyond the head; *bot.* a leaflet of
a pinnate leaf.

pinnace, pin'is, *n.* [Fr. *pinasse,* Sp.
pinaza, Pg. *pinaça,* It. *pinaccia,*
pinazza, a pinnace, from L. *pinus,*
a pine tree.] A small vessel propelled
by oars and sails, and having generally two masts rigged like those of
a schooner; a boat usually rowed
with eight oars.

pinnacle, pin'a·kl, *n.* [Fr. *pinacle,*
L.L. *pinnaculum,* from L. *pinna,* a
feather. PINION.] A rocky peak;
a sharp or pointed summit; *arch.*
any lesser structure, whatever be its
form, that rises above the roof of
a building, or that caps and terminates the higher parts of other
buildings.—*v.t.*—*pinnacled, pinna-
cling.* To put a pinnacle or pinnacles
on; to furnish with pinnacles.

pinnate, pin'āt, *a.* [L. *pinnatus,* from
pinna, a feather or fin. PEN.] *Bot.*
shaped or branching like a feather;
formed like a feather.—*Pinnate leaf,*
bot. a compound leaf wherein a
single petiole has several leaflets
attached to each side of it; *zool.*
having fins or processes resembling
fins.—**pinnately,** pin'āt·li, *adv.* In a
pinnate manner.—**pinnatifid,** pin-
nat'i·fid, *a.* [L. *pinna,* and *findo,* to
cleave.] *Bot.* said of a simple leaf
divided transversely into irregular
lobes. —**pinnatipartite,** pin·nat'i-
pär″tīt, *a.* [L. *partitus,* divided.] *Bot.*
having the lobes of the leaf separated

beyond the middle.—**pinnatiped,**
pin·nat'i·ped, *a.* [L. *pinna,* and *pes,
pedis,* a foot.] Fin-footed; having the
toes bordered by membranes, as
certain birds.—*n.* A bird which has
the toes bordered by membranes.—
pinnatisect, pin·nat'i·sekt, *a.* [L.
seco, sectum, to cut.] *Bot.* having the
lobes divided down to the midrib.

pinners, pin'ėrz, *n. pl.* A female
headdress, having long flaps hanging
down the sides of the cheeks, worn
during the early part of the eighteenth century.

pinniped, pin'i·ped, *n.* [L. *pinna,* and
pes, pedis, a foot.] A fin-footed animal.

pinnula, pin'ū·la, *n.* [L. *pinnula,* dim.
of *pinna,* a feather.] *Zool.* one of the
lateral processes of the arms of
crinoids; the barb of a feather; *bot.*
a leaflet.—**pinnulate,** pin'ū·lāt, *a.*
Bot. applied to a leaf in which each
pinna is subdivided.—**pinnule,** pin'-
ūl, *n.* A pinnula.

pinochle, pē'nuk·ėl, *n.* [Origin unknown.] A card game for two, three,
or four persons played with a special 48–card pack; in the game, the
combination of the queen of spades
and the jack of diamonds.

pint, pīnt, *n.* [D. *pint,* Fr. and G.
pinte, a pint, Sp. *pinta,* a mark, also
a pint (a quantity marked), from L.
pingo, pinctum, to paint. PICTURE.]
A measure of capacity containing
the eighth part of a gallon.

pintle, pin'tl, *n.* [Dim. of *pin.*] A pin
or bolt; *artillery,* a long iron bolt to
prevent the recoil of a cannon; *naut.*
an iron bolt by which the rudder
is hung to the sternpost; a pin
passing through an axle to hold on
a wheel.

pioneer, pī·o·nēr', *n.* [Fr. *pionnier,*
O.Fr. *peonier,* from *peon,* It. *pedone,*
a foot soldier. PEON.] One whose
business is to march with or before
an army to repair the road or clear
it of obstructions, work at intrench-
ments, etc.; anyone that goes before
to prepare the way for another
(*pioneers* of civilization).—*v.t.* To
go before and prepare a way for.—
v.i. To act as pioneer; to clear
the way.

pious, pī'us, *a.* [L. *pius,* pious, devout,
kind, whence also *piety, pity.*] Having due respect and affection for
parents or other relatives; more
commonly, duly reverencing the
Supreme Being; godly; devout; dictated by reverence to God; proceeding from piety; practiced under the
pretense of religion (*pious* frauds).—
Pious belief, a Catholic opinion not
of the importance of a dogma.—
piously, pī'us·li, *adv.* In a pious
manner.

pip, pip, *n.* [D. *pip,* L.G. *pipp,* Fr.
pipie, from L.L. *pipita,* for L. *pituita,*
phlegm, the pip.] A disease of fowls,
consisting in a secretion of thick
mucus in the mouth by which the
nostrils are stopped.

pip, pip, *n.* [Fr. *pipin,* a kernel;
derivation uncertain.] The kernel or
seed of fruit; a spot on cards.

pip, pip, *v.i.* [An imitative word,
slightly differing in form from *peep*=
Dan. *pipe,* Sw. *pipa,* G. *pipen,* to

pip. PEEP, PIPE.] To cry or chirp,
as a chicken.

pipe, pīp, *n.* [A.Sax. *pipe,* a pipe;
D. *pijp,* Icel. *pipa,* Dan. *pibe,* G.
pfeife; of imitative origin; comp. L.
pipo, pipio, to cheep, chirp.] A wind
instrument of music, consisting of
a tube of wood or metal; a long tube
or hollow body made of various materials, such as are used for the
conveyance of water, gas, steam, etc.;
a tube of clay or other material with
a bowl at one end, used in smoking
tobacco, etc.; the windpipe; the
sound of the voice; a whistle or call
of a bird; a roll in the exchequer,
so named from resembling a pipe;
a wine measure, usually containing
about 105 imperial or 126 wine
gallons; *naut.* the boatswain's whistle
used to call the men to their duties.—
v.i.—*piped, piping.* To sound or play
on a pipe; to have a shrill sound; to
whistle.—*v.t.* To play on a pipe or
other wind instrument; to utter in
a sharp or high tone; *naut.* to call
by means of the boatswain's pipe or
whistle.—**pipe clay,** *n.* The purest
kind of potter's clay, manufactured
into tobacco pipes, and used by
soldiers for cleaning belts, jackets,
trousers, etc.—*v.t.* To whiten with
pipe clay.—**pipefish,** *n.* A long and
slender fish, the thickest part of
whose body is only equal to a swan's
quill.—**piper,** pī'pėr, *n.* One who
plays on a pipe; a bagpiper; a sea
urchin common in the northern
seas.—*To pay the piper,* to be at the
expense; to suffer or make good the
loss.—**pipette,** pi·pet', *n.* [Fr., a
small pipe.] A small tube terminating
in a perforated point, used by
chemists for transferring liquids.—
piping, pī'ping, *p.* and *a.* Playing on
a pipe; having or giving out a shrill
whistling sound; accompanied by
the music of the peaceful pipe (this
piping time of peace); boiling; hissing
with heat (*piping* hot).—*n.* Pipes, as
for gas, water, etc., collectively; *hort.*
a jointed stem used for propagating
plants.

piperaceous, pī·pér·ā'shus, *a.* [L.
piper, pepper.] Belonging to the
pepper tribe of plants.—**piperin,**
piperine, pī'pėr·in, *n.* A crystalline
substance extracted from black
pepper.

pipette. See PIPE.

pipit, pip'it, *n.* [Probably imitative
of its cry.] A name of birds allied
to the lark.

pipkin, pip'kin, *n.* [Dim. of *pipe.*] A
small earthen boiler.

pippin, pip'in, *n.* [Perhaps because
grown from the *pips* or seeds.] The
name given to several kinds of
apples.

piquant, pē'kant, *a.* [Ppr. of Fr.
piquer, to prick, to be sharp, to
pique; of same origin as *pick, pike,
peak,* etc.] Making a lively, half-
pleasing, half-painful impression on
the organs of sense; sharp; racy;
lively; sparkling; interesting; sharp
or cutting to the feelings; pungent;
severe.—**piquantly,** pē'kant·li, *adv.*
In a piquant manner; tartly.—
piquancy, pē'kan·si, *n.* The state

or quality of being piquant; sharpness; pungency.

pique, pēk, *n.* [Fr. PIQUANT.] An offense taken; slight anger at persons; feeling arising from wounded pride, vanity, or self-love.—*v.t.*—*piqued, piquing.* [Fr. *piquer.*] To nettle; to irritate; to sting (less strong than *exasperate*); to stimulate; to touch with envy, jealousy, or other passion; *refl.* to pride or value one's self.—*v.i.* To cause irritation.—**piquet,** pik'et, *n.* [From Fr. *pique,* a pike, a lance, a spade at cards.] *Milit.* a picket; a game at cards played between two persons with thirty-two cards, the ace of spades being highest card.

piracy. See PIRATE.

piragua, pi·rä'gwa, *n.* A rude canoe. See PIROGUE.

piranha, pi·rän'yä, *n.* [Pg. from Tupi.] A small, voracious South American fresh-water fish of the genus *Serrasalmo.*

pirate, pī'rat, *n.* [Fr. *pirate,* L. *pirata,* from Gr. *peiratēs,* from *peiraō,* to attempt, *peira,* a trial.] A robber on the high seas; one that by open violence takes the property of another on the high seas; an armed ship or vessel engaged in piracy; a publisher or compiler who appropriates the literary labors of an author without compensation or permission.—*v.i.*—*pirated, pirating.* To play the pirate; to rob on the high seas.—*v.t.* To publish without right or permission. —**piratic, piratical,** pī·rat'ik, pī·rat'i·kal, *a.* [L. *piraticus.*] Having the character of a pirate; robbing or plundering by open violence on the high seas; pertaining to or consisting in piracy.—**piratically,** pī·rat'i·kal·li, *adv.* In a piratical manner; by piracy. —**piracy,** pī'ra·si, *n.* The act, practice, or crime of robbing on the high seas; the profession of pirate; literary theft; any infringement on the law of copyright.

pirogue, pi·rōg', *n.* [Fr. *pirogue,* Sp. *piragua;* originally a W. Indian word.] A kind of canoe made from a single trunk of a tree hollowed out.

pirouette, pi·rö·et', *n.* [Fr.; origin unknown.] A rapid whirling on the point of one foot; the short turn of a horse so as to bring his head suddenly in the opposite direction to where it was before.—*v.i.*—*pirouetted, pirouetting.* To perform a pirouette, as in dancing.

piscator, pis·kā'tor, *n.* [L., from *piscis,* a fish.] A fisherman; an angler. —**piscatorial,** pis·ka·tō'ri·al, pis'ka·tō·ri, *a.* [L. *piscatorius.*] Relating to fishermen or to fishing; pertaining to angling.—**Pisces,** pis'sēz, *n. pl.* [L. *piscis,* a fish.] *Astron.* the Fishes, the twelfth sign or constellation in the zodiac, next to Aries; the vertebrate animals of the class fishes.—**pisciculture,** pis·i·kul'chėr, *n.* [L. *piscis,* a fish, and *cultura,* culture.] The breeding, rearing, preservation, feeding, and fattening of fish by artificial means; fish culture. —**pisciform,** pis'i·form, *a.* Having the shape of a fish.—**piscina,** pis·sī'na, *n.* [L., a cistern, a fishpond.] A niche on the south side of the altar

in churches, with a small basin and water drain connected, into which the priest empties any water used.— **piscine,** pis'sin, *a.* Pertaining to fish or fishes.—**piscivorous,** pis·siv'o·rus, *a.* [L. *piscis,* and *voro,* to eat.] Feeding or subsisting on fishes.

pisiform, pī'si·form, *a.* [L. *pisum,* a pea, and *forma,* form.] Having the form of a pea; having a structure resembling peas.

pismire, pis'mīr, *n.* [E. *piss,* and *mire*=D. *mier,* Sw. *myra,* Icel. *maurr,* an ant; it discharges an irritant fluid vulgarly regarded as urine.] The ant or emmet.

pisolite, pī'sō·līt, *n.* [Gr. *pison,* a pea, and *lithos,* a stone.] A carbonate of lime slightly colored by the oxide of iron, occurring in little globular concretions of the size of a pea or larger, which usually contain each a grain of sand as a nucleus.— **pisolitic,** pī·sō·lit'ik, *a.* Composed of, containing, or resembling pisolite.

pistachio, pistachio nut, pis·tä'shi·ō, *n.* [Sp. *pistacho,* L. *pistacium,* the fruit; *pistacia,* Gr. *pistakia,* the tree, from Per. *pista,* the pistachio tree.] The nut of the pistachio tree, a member of the sumac family; a yellowish-green color.

pistil, pis'til, *n.* [L. *pistillum,* a pestle, a dim. from *pinso, pistum,* to pound, to beat in a mortar; akin *pestle, piston.*] *Bot.* the seed-bearing organ of a flower, consisting of the ovary, the stigma, and often also of a style. —**pistillate,** pis'til·lāt, *a.* Having a pistil.

pistol, pis'tol, *n.* [Fr. *pistole,* from It. *pistola,* a pistol; originally a dagger made at *Pistola* or *Pistoia,* near Florence. From diminutive poniards the name came to be given to miniature firearms.] A small firearm, the smallest used, designed to be fired with one hand only.—*v.t.*—*pistoled, pistoling.* To shoot with a pistol.

pistole, pis·tōl', *n.* [Fr. *pistole,* same as *pistol,* so named as being originally a halfcrown, a diminutive of the crown.] An old gold coin in Spain, France, etc.

piston, pis'ton, *n.* [Fr., from L. *pinso, pistum,* to beat, to pound. PISTIL.] *Mach.* a movable piece of a cylindrical form, which exactly fits a hollow cylinder, such as the barrel of a pump or the cylinder of a steam engine, and capable of being driven alternately in two directions.—**piston rod,** *n.* A rod which connects a piston to a point outside the cylinder, and either moved by the piston or moving it.

pit, pit, *n.* [A.Sax. *pyt,* pit=D. *put,* Icel. *pyttr,* a well; from L. *puteus,* a well.] A hollow or cavity more or less deep, either natural or made by digging in the earth; the shaft of a mine; a vat in tanning, bleaching, dyeing, etc.; *hort.* an excavation in the soil covered by a glazed frame, for protecting plants; a concealed hole in the ground for snaring wild beasts; any hollow, cavity, or depression in the flesh (the arm*pits*); a place or area where cocks or dogs are brought to fight, or where dogs are

trained to kill rats; part of a theater on the floor of the house, and somewhat below the level of the stage.— *The pit* (*Scrip.*), the place of the dead or the abode of evil spirits.— The *bottomless pit,* hell (N.T.).—*v.t.* —*pitted, pitting.* To lay in a pit or hole; to mark with little hollows, as by the smallpox; to set in competition; to set against one another, as in combat (*lit.* like cocks in a *pit*).— **pitfall,** pit'fal, *n.* A pit slightly covered over, forming a kind of trap. —**pitman,** pit'man, *n.* One who works in a pit.—**pit saw,** *n.* A large saw worked by two men, one of whom stands in a pit below.

pitapat, pit'a·pat, *adv.* [A reduplication of *pat,* a slight blow.] In a flutter; with palpitation or quick succession of beats.—*n.* A light quick step.

pitch, pich, *n.* [A softened form of O.E. *pik,* A.Sax. *pic,* from L. *pix, picis,* pitch, akin to *pinus,* a pine (tree).] A thick, tenacious oily substance, commonly obtained from tar, and extensively used for closing up the seams of ships, for preserving wood from the effects of water, for coating ironwork, etc.; in *acoustics,* the quality of a sound which depends upon the number of vibrations per second.—*Jew's pitch, mineral pitch,* bitumen.—*v.t.* To smear or cover over with pitch.—**pitchblende,** *n.* A mineral which constitutes one of the most important sources of the metal uranium and its compounds.— **pitch-dark,** *a.* Dark as pitch; very dark. — **pitchiness,** pich'i·nes, *n.* State or quality of being pitchy.— **pitchstone,** *n.* The glassy form of felstone; retinite.—**pitchy,** pich'i, *a.* Partaking of the qualities of pitch; like pitch; smeared with pitch; dark; dismal.

pitch, pich, *v.t.* [O.E. *picche,* to pierce, to peck, to dart or throw, a softened form of *pick, pike.* PICK.] To fix or plant, as stakes or pointed instruments; to fix by means of such; hence, to set in array; to marshal or arrange in order (to *pitch* a tent, to *pitch* a camp); to fling or throw; to cast forward; to hurl; to toss, as *pitch* a baseball; to regulate or set the keynote of; to pave or face with stones, as an embankment.—*Pitched battle,* one in which the armies are previously drawn up in form, with a regular disposition of the forces.— *v.i.* To light; to settle; to come to rest from flight; to plunge or fall headlong; to fix choice: with *on* or *upon*; to fix a tent or temporary habitation; to encamp; *naut.* to rise and fall, as the head and stern of a ship passing over waves.—*n.* A point or degree of elevation or depression; height or depth; degree; rate; loftiness; the degree of slope or inclination (the *pitch* of a hill or roof); the rise of an arch; a throw; a toss; that part of a cricket field where the wickets are put up; a cast or jerk of something from the hand; *music,* the relative height of a sound; in certain technical senses, a distance between two points (as the *pitch* of a screw, that is, the distance between its threads).—**pitcher**, pich′ėr′, *n.* One who or that which pitches.—**pitchfork**, pich′fork, *n.* A fork used in lifting or throwing hay or sheaves of grain; a tuning fork.—*v.t.* To lift or throw with a pitchfork; hence, to put suddenly or accidentally into any position.—**pitch pipe**, *n.* A small flute or free-reed pipe used in regulating the *pitch* or elevation of the key or leading note of a tune.

pitcher, pich′ėr, *n.* [O.Fr. *picher*, *pichier*, *pechier*, O.It. *pecchero*, from O.H.G. *pechar*, *behhar*, a beaker. BEAKER.] A vessel with a spout for holding liquors; an earthen or metallic vessel for holding water for domestic purposes; a water pot, jug, or jar with ears.—**pitcher plant**, *n.* A name given to several plants from their pitcher-shaped leaves.

piteous, etc. See PITY.

pitfall. See PIT.

pith, pith, *n.* [A.Sax. *pitha*, D. *pit*, marrow, pith, kernel.] A soft cellular substance occupying the center of the root, stem, and branches of exogenous plants; the spinal cord or marrow of an animal; strength, vigor, or force; closeness and vigor of thought and style; cogency; condensed substance or matter; quintessence.—**pithily**, pith′i·li, *adv.* In a pithy manner.—**pithiness**, pith′i·nes, *n.* The state or quality of being pithy. —**pithy**, pith′i, *a.* Consisting of pith; containing pith; abounding with pith; terse and striking; forcible; energetic; uttering energetic words or expressions.

pitiable, pitiful, pitiless, etc. See PITY.

pittance, pit′ans, *n.* [Fr. *pitance*, a monk's mess, from L.L. *pietantia*, *pitantia*, a monk's allowance, from L. *pietas*, piety.] An allowance of food bestowed in charity; a charity gift; a very small portion allowed or assigned.

pituitary, pi·tū′i·te·ri, *n.* [L. *pituitarius*, pertaining to phlegm.] *Anat.* the pituitary gland; *med.* an extract obtained from the pituitary gland.— **pituitary gland**, *n.* A two-lobed endocrine gland at the base of the brain; the hypophysis.

pity, pit′i, *n.* [Fr. *pitié*, O.Fr. *pité*, from L. *pietas*, piety, from *pius*, pious. (PIOUS.) *Piety* is the same word.] The suffering of one person excited by the distresses of another: commiseration; compassion; mercy; the ground or subject of pity; cause of grief; thing to be regretted; in this sense it has a plural (it is a thousand *pities* he should fail).—*To have pity upon, to take pity upon,* generally to show one's pity toward by some benevolent act.—*v.t.*—*pitied, pitying.* [O.Fr. *pitoyer*, to pity.] To feel pity or compassion toward; to feel pain or grief for; to have sympathy for; to commiserate; to compassionate.— *v.i.* To be compassionate; to exercise pity.—**pityingly**, pit′i·ing·li, *adv.* So as to show pity; compassionately.— **piteous**, pit′i·us, *a.* Fitted to excite pity; moving pity or compassion; mournful; affecting; lamentable.—

piteously, pit′i·us·li, *adv.* In a piteous manner.—**piteousness**, pit′i·us·nes, *n.* The state of being piteous. —**pitiable**, pit′i·a·bl, *a.* Deserving or exciting pity.—**pitiableness**, pit′i·a·bl·nes, *n.* State of being pitiable.— **pitiably**, pit′i·a·bli, *adv.* In a pitiable manner.—**pitiful**, pit′i·fu̱l, *a.* Full of pity; tender; compassionate; miserable; moving compassion; paltry; insignificant; contemptible. ∴ Syn. under CONTEMPTIBLE.—**pitifully**, pit′i·fu̱l·li, *adv.* In a pitiful manner.— **pitifulness**, pit′i·fu̱l·nes, *n.* The state or quality of being pitiful.—**pitiless**, pit′i·les, *a.* Destitute of pity; hardhearted; relentless; exciting no pity. —**pitilessly**, pit′i·les·li, *adv.* In a pitiless manner.—**pitilessness**, pit′i·les·ness, *n.* The state of being pitiless.

pityriasis, pit·i·rī′a·sis, *n.* [Gr. *pityron*, bran.] A cutaneous disease consisting of irregular branlike scaly patches.

pivot, piv′ot, *n.* [Fr. *pivot*, a pivot, from It. *piva*, a pipe (=Fr. and E. *pipe*).] A pin on which anything turns; a short shaft or point on which a wheel or other body revolves; *milit.* the officer or soldier upon whom the different wheelings are made in the various evolutions of the drill, etc.; that on which important results depend; a turning point.—*v.t.* To place on a pivot; to furnish with a pivot.—**pivotal**, piv′ot·al, *a.* Belonging to a pivot.

pix, piks, *n.* See PYX.

pixy, pixie, pik′si, *n.* [Perhaps for *pucksy*, from *Puck.*] A sort of fairy.

pizza, pēt′sä, *n.* [It.] A flat open pie baked with cheese, meat, spices, etc.—**pizzeria**, pēt′sä·rē′ä, *n.* A place where pizza is made or sold.

pizzicato, pit·si·kä′tō, *a.* [It., twitched.] *Mus.* to be plucked by the finger, and not played with the bow of the violin.

placable, plak′a·bl or plā′ka·bl, *a.* [L. *placabilis*, from *placo*, to soothe, pacify; akin to *placeo*, to please. PLEASE.] Capable of being appeased or pacified; appeasable.—**placability**, plak·a·bil′i·ti or plā·, *n.* The quality of being placable.—**placate**, plā′kāt, *v.t.*—*placated, placating.* To appease, pacify, or conciliate.

placard, plak′ärd or pla·kärd′, *n.* [Fr., from *plaque*, a plate, from the Teutonic; comp. D. *plak*, a flat piece of wood, a slice, *plakbriefje*, a placard; L.G. *plakke*, a piece of turf.] A written or printed paper posted in a public place; a bill posted up to draw public attention; a poster.— *v.t.* To post placards on; to make known by placard.

place, plās, *n.* [Fr. *place*, a place, post, position, an open space in a town; from L. *platea*, a street, an area, from Gr. *plateia*, from *platys*, flat, broad. PLATE.] A broad way or open space in a city; an area; a particular portion of space marked off by its use or character; a locality, spot, or site; position; a town or village; a fortified post; a passage in a book; point or degree in order of proceeding (in the first *place*); rank; order

of priority, dignity, or importance; office; employment; official station; ground or occasion; room; station in life; calling; occupation; condition; room or stead, with the sense of substitution (to act in *place* of another); the position in the heavens of a heavenly body.—*To give place,* to make room or way; to retire in favor of another; to yield.—*To have place,* to have a station, room, or seat; to have actual existence.—*To take place,* to come to pass; to happen; to occur; to take the precedence or priority.—*v.t.*—*placed, placing.* To put or set in a particular place or spot; to set or put in a certain relative position; to locate; to appoint, set, induct, or establish in an office; to put or set in any particular rank, state, or condition; to set; to fix (to *place* confidence in a friend); to invest; to lend (to *place* money in the funds).—**place kick**, *n.* In football, the act of kicking the ball after it has been placed on the ground.— **placement**, plās′ment, *n.* The act of placing or of putting in a certain spot or position.

placebo, plā·sē′bō, *n.* [L. I shall please.] *R. Cath. Ch.* vespers for the dead; a harmless medicine given to please a patient; something intended to soothe.

placenta, pla·sen′ta, *n.* [L., a cake.] The afterbirth; a temporary organ developed in mammals during pregnancy, and forming a connection between the mother and the fetus; *bot.* that part of a seed vessel on which the ovules or seeds are placed. —**placental**, pla·sen′tal, *a.* Pertaining to the placenta; possessing a placenta.—*n.* An animal that possesses a placenta.—**placentary**, pla′sen·te·ri, *n. Bot.* a placenta bearing numerous ovules.—*a.* Having reference to the placenta.—**placentation**, pla·sen·tā′shon, *n.* The disposition of the placenta, more especially in plants.

placer, plas′ėr, *n.* [Sp.] A glacial or alluvial deposit that contains particles of gold or other valuable mineral.—**placer mining**, *n.*

placid, plas′id, *a.* [L. *placidus*, from *placeo*, to please. PLEASE.] Gentle; quiet; unruffled.—**placidity, placidness**, pla·sid′i·ti, plas′id·nes, *n.*— **placidly**, plas′id·li, *adv.*

placket, plak′et, *n.* [From the Fr. *plaquer*, to lay or clap on. PLACARD.] A petticoat; the opening or slit in a petticoat or skirt.

placoid, plak′oid, *a.* [Gr. *plax, plakos,* something flat.] Applied to a certain class of fishes' scales, consisting of detached bony grains, tubercles, or plates.—*n.* A fish with such scales.

plagal, plā′gal, *a.* [Gr. *plagios*, oblique.] *Music*, applied to a cadence in which the chord of the subdominant is followed by that of the tonic.

plagiary, plā′ji·e·ri, *n.* [L. *plagiarius*, a plagiary, a kidnaper, from *plagium*, manstealing, kidnaping, from *plaga*, a snare.] One that steals or purloins the words or ideas of another and passes them off as his own; a literary thief; plagiarism.—**plagiarism**, plā´ji•a•rizm, n. The act of plagiarizing; the crime of literary theft; that which is plagiarized.—**plagiarist**, plā´ji•a•rist, n. One who plagiarizes.—**plagiarize**, plā´ji•a•rīz, v.t. and i.—plagiarized, plagiarizing. To steal or purloin the thoughts or words of another in literary composition.

plagioclase, plā´ji•o•klāz, n. [Gr. plagios, oblique, and klasis, fracture.] A name of triclinic feldspars, the two prominent cleavage directions in which are oblique to one another.—**plagioclastic**, plā´ji•o•klas˝tik, a. Of the nature of or containing plagioclase.

plague, plāg, n. [Same as D. plaag, Dan. and G. plage, Icel. plaga, Pr. plaga, O.Sp. plaga, the plague; all from L. plaga, a blow, stroke, calamity. PLAINT.] A blow or calamity; severe trouble or vexation; a pestilential disease; a malignant fever of the East eminently contagious, and attended by excessive debility, as also with carbuncles or buboes.—Plague on or upon, a kind of denunciation expressive of weariness or petty annoyance. — v.t. — plagued, plaguing. To vex; to tease; to harass; to trouble; to embarrass; to scourge with disease, calamity, or natural evil of any kind.—**plaguer**, plā´gėr, n. One who plagues or vexes.—**plaguily**, plā´gi•li, adv. Vexatiously; in a manner to vex, harass, or embarrass. (Colloq.)—**plaguy**, plā´gi, a. Vexatious; troublesome; tormenting; annoying; wearisome. (Colloq.)—adv. Vexatiously; deucedly. (Colloq.)

plaice, plās, n. [From L. platessa, a flatfish, from Gr. platys, flat.] A well-known species of the flatfish family, more flat and square than the halibut.

plaid, plād or plad, n. [Gael. plaide, from peallaid, a sheepskin, from peall, a skin or hide. PELT.] A large rectangular outer garment or wrap, frequently of tartan, worn by the Highlanders and others in Scotland.—**plaided**, plā´ded, a. Of the cloths of which plaids are made; tartan; wearing a plaid.

plain, plān, a. [Fr. plain, Pr. plan, It. piano, from L. planus, plain (same root as plango, to beat). Plan and plane are the same word.] Without elevations and depressions; level; flat; even; smooth; void of ornament; without embellishment; simple; unadorned; without beauty; homely; sometimes used as a euphemism for ugly; artless; simple; unlearned; without disguise, cunning, or affectation; without refinement; unsophisticated; honestly undisguised; open; unreserved; mere; absolute; unmistakable; without difficulties or intricacies; evident to the understanding; clear; manifest; not obscure; not highly seasoned; not rich or luxurious (a plain diet).—Plain clothes, the ordinary dress of society; nonofficial dress; opposed to uniform.—adv. In a plain manner; plainly; frankly; bluntly.—n. A piece of level land; a piece of ground with an even surface, or a surface little varied by inequalities; geog. the general term for all those parts of the dry land which cannot properly be called hilly or mountainous.—**plainly**, plān´li, adv. In a plain manner.—**plainness**, plān´nes, n. The state or quality of being plain; evenness of surface; openness; candor; intelligibility.—**plain song**, n. Music, the simple, grave, and unadorned chant in which the services of the Roman Catholic Church have been rendered from a very early age; the simple notes of an air without ornament or variation; hence, a plain unexaggerated statement.

plaint, plānt, n. [Fr. plainte, a complaint, from plaindre, to complain, from L. plango, planctum, to beat the breast, to lament, akin to plaga, a blow, Gr. plēssō, to strike. PLAGUE.] Lamentation; complaint; audible expression of sorrow; representation made of injury or wrong done.—**plaintiff**, plān´tif, n. Law, the person who commences a suit before a tribunal for the recovery of a claim; opposed to defendant.—**plaintive**, plān´tiv, a. Expressive of sorrow or melancholy; mournful; sad.—**plaintively**, plān´tiv•li, adv. In a plaintive manner.—**plaintiveness**, plān´tiv•nes, n. The quality or state of being plaintive.

plait, plāt, plat, n. [O.Fr. ploit, pleit, from L. plicatus, folded, from plicare, to twist, whence ply.] A flattened gather or fold; a doubling of cloth or any similar tissue or fabric; a braid, as of hair, straw, etc.—v.t. To fold; to double in narrow strips; to braid; to interweave the locks or strands of (to plait the hair).

plan, plan, n. [Fr. plan, from L. planus, plain, flat, level. PLAIN.] The representation of anything drawn on a plane, and forming a map or chart (the plan of a town); the representation of a horizontal section of a building, showing the extent, division, and distribution of its area into apartments, passages, etc.; a scheme devised; a project; disposition of parts according to a certain design; a method or process; a way; a mode.—v.t.—planned, planning. To invent or contrive for construction; to scheme; to devise; to form in design.—**planner**, plan´ėr, n. One who plans.

planchette, plan•shet´, n. [Fr. planchette. PLANK.] A small board, usually heartshaped, resting on two castors and the point of a pencil; when the board is touched by the fingers, the pencil is said to trace words.

plane, plān, a. [From L. planus. PLAIN.] Without elevations or depressions; even; level; flat.—n. A smooth or perfectly level surface; a part of something having a level surface; the supporting surface of an airplane; a surface such that if any two points whatever in it be joined by a straight line, the whole of the straight line will be in the surface; an ideal surface, supposed to cut and pass through solid bodies or in various directions; frequently used in astronomy (the plane of the ecliptic, the plane of a planet's orbit); a joiner's tool, consisting of a smooth-soled stock, through which passes obliquely a piece of edged steel or a chisel, used in paring or smoothing boards or wood of any kind.—v.t.—planed, planing. To make smooth, especially by the use of a plane; to travel by airplane.—Plane angle, an angle contained between two straight lines meeting in a plane.—Plane geometry, the geometry of plane figures, in contradistinction to solid geometry, or the geometry of solids.—Plane sailing, the art of determining a ship's place, on the supposition that she is moving on a plane, or that the surface of the ocean is plane instead of being spherical.—Plane trigonometry, that branch of trigonometry which treats of triangles described on a plane.

plane iron, n. The cutting iron of a plane.—**planer**, plā´nėr, n. One who planes; a wooden block used to smooth the face of a form of type before printing; a planing machine.

planet, plan´et, n. [L. planeta, a planet, from Gr. planētēs, a wanderer, from planaō, to wander.] A celestial body (such as the earth) which revolves about the sun; the nine major planets, Mercury, Venus, Earth, Mars, Jupiter, Saturn, Uranus, Neptune, and Pluto.—Primary planets, those which revolve about the sun as their center.—Secondary planets, those which revolve about other planets; satellites or moons.—**planetarium**, plan•e•tâ´ri•um, n. An astronomical machine which, by the movement of its parts, represents the motions and orbits of the planets.—**planetary**, plan´e•ta•ri, a. Pertaining to the planets; having the nature of a planet.—Planetary years, the periods of time in which the several planets make their revolutions round the sun.—**planetoid**, plan´et•oid, n. One of a numerous group of very small planets revolving round the sun between the orbits of Mars and Jupiter; an asteroid.—**planetoidal**, plan´et•oi•dal, a. Pertaining to the planetoids; relating to a planetoid.—**planet-stricken**, **planet-struck**, a. Affected by the influence of planets; blasted.—**planet wheel**, n. The exterior revolving wheel of the 'sun-and-planet' motion.

plangent,† plan´jent, a. [L. plangens, plangentis, ppr. of plango, to beat.] Beating; dashing, as a wave.—**plangency**,† plan´jen•si, n. The state or quality of being plangent.

planifolious, **planipetalous**, plā•ni•fō´li•us, plā•ni•pet´a•lus, a. [L. planus, plain, and folium, petalon, a leaf.] Applied to a flower made up of plane leaves or petals, set together in circular rows round the center.

planimeter, pla•nim´et•ėr, n. [L. planus, plain, and Gr. metron, a measure.] An instrument for measuring the area of any plane figure.—**planimetry**, pla•nim´et•ri, n. The mensuration of plane surfaces.

planish, plan'ish, v.t. [From *plane*.] To make smooth or plain, as wood; to condense, smooth, and toughen, as a metallic plate, by light blows of a hammer; to polish.

planisphere, plan'i·sfēr, n. [L. *planus*, plain, and E. *sphere*.] A sphere projected on a plane; a map exhibiting the circles of the sphere.

plank, plangk, n. [Fr. dial. *planke*, Pr. *planca*, *plancha*, Fr. *planche*, from L. *planca* (for *planica*), a board, slab, from L. *planus*, plain.] A broad piece of sawed timber, differing from a board only in being thicker; in political slang, one of the principles in the system adopted by a party. See PLATFORM.—v.t. To cover or lay with planks.

plankton, plangk'ton, n. [Gr. *plagkton*, wandering.] The mass of small organisms, plant or animal, floating or drifting in the ocean.

planner. See PLAN.

plano-concave, plā'nō, a. Plane on one side and concave on the other.— **plano-convex**, a. Plane or flat on one side and convex on the other.

planometer, plā·nom'et·ėr, n. A plane, hard surface used in machine making as a gauge for plane surfaces. —**planometry**, plā·nom'et·ri, n. The act of measuring or gauging plane surfaces; the art or act of using a planometer.

plant, plant, n. [Fr. *plante*, a plant, from L. *planta*, a plant, a twig, the sole of the foot, from root of *planus*, plain.] One of the organisms which form the vegetable kingdom; a vegetable; an organized living body deriving its sustenance from the inorganic world, generally adhering to another body, and drawing from it some of its nourishment, and having the power of propagating itself by seeds or similar reproductive bodies; popularly the word is generally applied to the smaller species of vegetables; a collective term for the fixtures, machinery, tools, apparatus, etc., necessary to carry on any trade or mechanical business; a put-up game; a swindle. (*Colloq.*)—v.t. To put in the ground and cover, as seed for growth; to set in the ground for growth; to furnish with plants; to lay out and prepare with plants; to set upright; to set firmly; to fix; to set and direct or point (to *plant* cannon against a fort); to furnish the first inhabitants of; to settle (to *plant* a colony); to introduce and establish (to *plant* Christianity).—v.i. To perform the act of planting.—**plantation**, plan·tā'shon, n. [L. *plantatio*.] The act of planting or setting in the earth for growth; the place planted; a small wood; a grove; in the Southern states, a large estate cultivated chiefly by share croppers.—**planter**, plan'tėr, n. One who plants, sets, introduces, or establishes; one who owns a plantation.—**plant louse**, n. An aphis.

plantain, plan'tin, n. [Fr. *plantain*, from L. *plantago*, from *planta*, the sole of the foot, from a vague resemblance of the leaves to the foot.] A genus of perennial or annual herbs, found in all temperate regions. They are mostly roadside weeds with elliptic ribbed leaves and spikes of small greenish flowers.

plantain, plan'tān, n. [Sp. *plantano*, *platano*, from L. *platanus*, a plane-tree.] A large herbaceous plant, with a soft succulent stem, sometimes attaining the height of 20 feet, the fruit of which is of great importance as an article of food in tropical climates.

plantar, plan'tar, a. [L. *planta*, the sole of the foot.] *Anat.* relating or belonging to the sole of the foot.

plantigrade, plan'ti·grād, a. [L. *planta*, the sole of the foot, and *gradior*, to walk.] Walking on the sole of the foot and not on the toes (digitigrade): applied to a section of carnivorous animals, including the bears.

planula, plan'ū·la, n. [L. dim. of *planus*, a wanderer.] In sponges and zoophytes, an oval ciliated larva.

plaque, plak, n. [Fr.] An ornamental plate; a brooch; the plate of a clasp; a flat plate of metal upon which enamels are painted.

plash, plash, n. [D. *plasch*, *plas*, a puddle, perhaps from sound of splashing; comp. D. *plassen*, G. *platschen*, *platschern*, to paddle in water; L.G. *plasken*, E. to *splash*.] A small collection of standing water; a puddle; a pond; a splash.—v.i. To dabble in water; to fall with a dabbling sound; to splash.—**plashy**, plash'i, a. Watery; abounding with puddles.

plash, plash, v.t. [O.Fr. *plassier*, *plessier*, from L. *plexus*, pp. of *plecto*, to weave, to twist (as in *complex*). *Pleach* is a collateral form.] To bend down and interweave the branches or twigs of (to *plash* a hedge).

plasma, plaz'ma, n. [Gr. *plasma*, something formed or molded, from *plassō*, to form, whence *plastic*.] A siliceous mineral of a color between grass green and leek green, used by the ancients for engraving upon; formless elementary matter; the liquid part of blood and lymph; specifically, *biol.* the simplest form of organized matter in the vegetable and animal body, out of which the several tissues are formed; the nearly colorless fluid in which the corpuscles of the blood are suspended.—**plasmic, plasmatic**, plaz'mik, plaz·mat'ik, a. Pertaining to plasma; having the character of a plasma.

plasmodium, plaz·mōd'i·um, n. In slime fungi (Myxomycetes), a stage in the life history consisting of a creeping mass of naked protoplasm.

plaster, plas'tėr, n. [O.Fr. *plaster* (Fr. *plâtre*), from L. *emplastrum*, Gr. *emplastron*, plaster, from *em*-*plassō*, to daub over —*en*, on, in, and *plassō*, to form, to shape (whence also *plastic*, *plasma*).] A composition of lime, water, and sand, with or without hair for binding, used for coating walls and partitions of houses; calcined gypsum, used, when mixed with water, for finishing walls, for casts, cement, etc.; *phar.* an external application of a harder consistence than an ointment, spread on linen, silk, etc.—*Plaster of Paris*, a composition of several species of gypsum, originally obtained from Montmartre near Paris, used for various purposes.—*Plaster cast*, a copy of an object obtained by pouring plaster of Paris mixed with water into a mold which forms a copy of the object in reverse.—v.t. To overlay or cover with plaster; to lay coarsely on; to bedaub.—**plasterer**, plas'tėr·ėr, n. One that overlays with plaster.—**plastery**, plas'tėr·i, a. Resembling plaster; containing plaster.

plastic, plas'tik, a. [Gr. *plastikos*, from *plassō*, to form. PLASTER.] Having the power to give form or fashion to a mass of matter; capable of being molded into various forms; capable of change or modification; capable of receiving a new bent or direction (as the mind); applied to sculpture and the kindred arts, as distinguished from painting and the graphic arts; any of a group of synthetic or natural organic materials that when soft may be molded or cast to make an infinite number of articles.—*Plastic clay*, a name given to one of the beds of the Eocene period, from its being used in the manufacture of pottery. —**plasticity**, plas·tis'i·ti, n. The state or quality of being plastic.

plastron, plas'tron, n. [Fr. *plastron*, a breastplate, same origin as *plaster*.] A piece of leather stuffed, used by fencers to defend the breast against pushes; *zool.* the lower or ventral portion of the bony case of tortoises and turtles.

plat, plat, v.t.—*platted*, *platting*. [Same as *plait*.] To interweave; to plait.—**platter**, plat'ėr, n. One who plats or forms by weaving.

plat, plat, n. [Same word as *plot*; but probably affected by Fr. *plat*, *plate*, flat. PLATE.] A small piece of ground marked out and devoted to some special purpose; a plot of ground; a map or chart.

platan, plat'an, n. [L. *platanus*.] The plane tree.

plate, plāt, n. [From Fr. *plate*, a metal plate, a piece of plate armor, and *plat*, a dish; from *plat*, *plate*, flat; perhaps (like *place*) from Gr. *platys*, broad, cog. with Skr. *prithu*, broad.] A flattened piece of metal with a uniform thickness; armor composed of broad pieces or plates; domestic vessels or utensils made of gold or silver; a small shallow vessel of metal, porcelain, or earthenware, from which food is eaten at table; a piece of timber laid horizontally in a wall to receive the ends of other timbers; a piece of metal on which anything is engraved for the purpose of being printed off on paper; a page of stereotype for printing.—v.t.—*plated*, *plating*. To cover with a plate or plates; to overlay with a thin coating of silver or other metal: used particularly of silver (*plated* vessels).—**plate**

armor, *n.* Defensive armor consisting of plates of metal.—**plate glass,** *n.* A superior kind of thick glass used for mirrors, etc.—**plater,** plā′tẽr, *n.* One who coats articles with gold or silver; horse of a poor quality competing for cups of gold or silver plate.—**plating,** plā′ting, *n.* The art of covering articles with a thin coating of metal, especially of overlaying articles made of the baser metals with a thin coating of gold or silver; a thin coating of one metal laid upon another metal.

plateau, pla·tō′, *n. pl.* **plateaus, plateaux,** pla·tōz′, *n.* [Fr., from *plat,* flat; akin to *plate.*] A broad, flat area of land in an elevated position; a tableland.

platen, plat′en, *n.* [From Fr. *plat,* flat.] *Printing,* the flat part of a press by which the impression is made; the roller of a typewriter.

platform, plat′form, *n.* [Fr. *plate-forme—plate,* flat, and *forme,* a form. PLATE.] Any flat or horizontal structure, especially if raised above some particular level; the flat roof of a building on the outside; the place where guns are mounted on a fortress or battery; the raised walk at a railroad station for landing passengers and goods; a place raised above the floor of a hall set apart for the speakers at public meetings; the aggregate of principles adopted or avowed by any body of men, such as a political party; a declared system of policy (a political *platform*).

platina, plat′i·na, *n.* [Sp. *platina,* from *plata,* silver; akin to *plate.*] The old name of platinum; twisted silver wire.

platinum, plat′i·num, *n.* [From *platina.*] A heavy, grayish-white metallic element, malleable and ductile and resistant to most chemicals; used for jewelry and scientific apparatus. Symbol, Pt; at no., 78; at. wt., 195.09.—**platinic,** pla·tin′ik, *a.* Pertaining to platinum.—**platinize,** plat′i·nīz, *v.t.* To combine or cover with platinum.—**platinoid,** plat′i·noid, *n.* [From *platinum.*] A metal of similar composition to German silver (which see), with an essential addition of 1 to 2 per cent of tungsten; any one of a series of metals allied to platinum.—**platinotype,** plat′i·nō·tīp, *n.* [*Platinum* and *type.*] A permanent photographic print produced by a process in which platinum is used.—**platinous,** plat′i·nus, *a.* Containing or consisting of platinum.

platitude, plat′i·tūd, *n.* [Fr., from *plat,* flat.] Flatness; dullness; insipidity; a trite, dull, or stupid remark; a truism.—**platitudinize,** plat·i·tū′di·nīz, *v.i.* To utter platitudes; to make stale or insipid remarks.

Platonic, Platonical, pla·ton′ik, pla·ton′i·kal, *a.* Pertaining to Plato the philosopher, or to his philosophy, his school, or his opinions.—*Platonic bodies,* the five regular geometrical solids.—*Platonic love,* a pure spiritual affection subsisting between the sexes, unmixed with carnal

desires.—*Platonic year,* a period of time determined by the revolution of the equinoxes, which is accomplished in about 26,000 years.— *n.* A follower of Plato.—**Platonically,** pla·ton′i·kal·li, *adv.* In a Platonic manner.—**Platonism,** plā′ton·izm, *n.* The doctrines, opinions, or philosophy of Plato.—**Platonist,** plā′ton·ist, *n.* One who adheres to the philosophy of Plato.—**Platonize,** plā′ton·īz, *v.i.*—*platonized, platonizing.* To adopt the opinions or philosophy of Plato.

platoon, pla·tön′, *n.* [Fr. *peloton,* a ball of thread, a platoon, from *pelote,* a ball of thread, from L.L. *pelota, pilota,* from L. *pila,* a ball.] A military unit of two or more squads or sections; a group of persons with a common characteristic.

platter, plat′ẽr, *n.* [From O.Fr. *platel,* dim. of *plat,* a plate. PLATE.] A plate; a large shallow dish for holding eatables.

platter. See PLAT.

platycephalic, platycephalous, plat′i·se·fal′ik, plat·i·sef′a·lus, *a.* [Gr. *platys,* broad, and *kephalē,* head.] Broadheaded; flatheaded.

platypus, plat′i·pus, *n.* [Gr. *platys,* broad, and *pous,* a foot.] A small aquatic mammal of Australia and Tasmania that has a fleshy bill similar to that of a duck.

plaudit, plạ′dit, *n.* [L. *plaudite,* do you applaud, imper. of *plaudo, plausum,* to applaud, seen in *plausible, applause, explode.*] Applause; praise bestowed: usually in plural.

plausible, plạ′zi·bl, *a.* [L. *plausibilis,* from *plaudo.* PLAUDIT.] Praiseworthy‡; apparently worthy of praise; apparently right; specious; using specious arguments or discourse; fair-spoken. ∴ Syn. under COLORABLE.—**plausibility, plausibleness,** plạ·zi·bil′i·ti, plạ′zi·bl·nes, *n.* The state or quality of being plausible; speciousness; superficial appearance of right.—**plausibly,** plạ′zi·bli, *adv.* In a plausible manner; speciously.

plausive, plạ′ziv, *a.* Applauding; manifesting praise.

play, plā, *v.i.* [A.Sax. *plegian,* to play, from *plega,* play, pastime; connections doubtful.] To do something not as a task or for profit, but for amusement; to act wantonly or thoughtlessly; to dally, trifle, toy; to move irregularly; to flutter; to contend in a game; to gamble; to perform on an instrument of music; to act with free motion; to work freely (the lungs *play*); to act; to behave; to act a part on the stage; to personate a character.—*To play on* or *upon,* to make sport of; to trifle with; to delude; to give a humorous or fanciful turn to (to *play upon* words).—*v.t.* To perform in sport or for sport or for a prize; to make use of in a game (to *play* a trump card); to enter into a game with; to perform music on; to perform on a musical instrument (a tune); to act on the stage; to act or represent in general; to act like; to behave in the manner of (to *play* the fool); to perform; to execute

(to *play* a trick).—*n.* Any exercise intended for pleasure, amusement, or diversion, as baseball, quoits, etc.; a game; amusement; sport; frolic; jest; not earnest; gaming; practice in any contest (sword-*play*); action; use; employment; practice; manner of acting or dealing (fair *play*); a dramatic composition; a comedy or tragedy; a dramatic performance; motion; movement, regular or irregular (the *play* of a wheel); hence, power or space for motion; liberty of action; scope; swing.—*To hold in play,* to keep occupied.—*Play of colors,* an appearance of several prismatic colors in rapid succession on turning an object, as a diamond.— *A play on words,* the giving of words a double signification; a pun.— **playbill,** plā′bil, *n.* A bill exhibited as an advertisement of a play, with the parts assigned to the actors.— **playbook,** plā′bụk, *n.* A book of dramatic compositions.—**played out,** *pp.* or *a.* Exhausted, from a game at cards which has been played to the last extremity or deal.—**player,** plā′ẽr, *n.* One who plays; an actor; a musician.—**playfellow,** plā′fel·ō, *n.* A companion in amusements or sports.—**playful,** plā′fụl, *a.* Sportive; frolicsome; frisky; indulging in gambols; full of sprightly humor; pleasantly jocular or amusing.—**playfully,** plā′fụl·li, *adv.* In a playful manner; sportively.—**playfulness,** plā′fụl·nes, *n.* The state of being playful; sportiveness.—**playgoer,** plā′gō·ẽr, *n.* One who frequents plays.—**playgoing,** plā′gō·ing, *a.* Frequenting the exhibitions of the stage.—**playground,** plā′ground, *n.* A piece of ground set apart for open-air recreation, especially connected with a school, etc., for the pupils.— **playhouse,** plā′hous, *n.* A theater.— **playmate,** plā′māt, *n.* A playfellow; a companion in diversions.—**plaything,** plā′thing, *n.* A toy; anything that serves to amuse.—**playwright,** plā′rīt, *n.* A maker of plays.

plaza, plä′zä, plaz′ä, *n.* [Sp.] A public square in a city or town.

plea, plē, *n.* [O.Fr. *plai, plaid, plait,* a suit, a plea; from L. *placitum,* an opinion, a determination, from *placeo,* to please. PLEASE.] That which is alleged by a party to a legal action in support of his demand; the answer of a defendant to the plaintiff's declaration; a suit or action; a cause in court; that which is alleged in support, justification, or defense; an excuse; a pleading.

pleach,‡ plēch, *v.t.* [Akin to *plash,* to interweave.] To plash; to interweave.

plead, plēd, *v.i.*—pret. and pp. *pleaded,* sometimes *pled.* [Fr. *plaider,* to plead, from L.L. *placitare,* from L. *placitum.* PLEA.] To argue in support of a claim, or in defense against the claim of another; to urge reasons for or against; to attempt to persuade one by argument or supplication; *law,* to present a plea; to present an answer to the declaration of a plaintiff; to deny the plaintiff's declaration and demand.—*To plead guilty* or *not guilty*, to admit or deny guilt.—*v.t.* To discuss, defend, and attempt to maintain by arguments or reasons (to *plead* one's cause); to allege or adduce in proof, support, or vindication; to offer in excuse (to *plead* poverty); to allege and offer in a legal plea or defense, or for repelling a demand in law.—**pleadable**, plē'-da·bl, *a.* Capable of being alleged in proof, defense, or vindication.—**pleader**, plē'dėr, *n.* One who pleads; a lawyer who argues in a court of justice; one that forms pleas or pleadings (a special *pleader*).—**pleading**, plē'ding, *n.* The act of advocating any cause; the act or practice of advocating client's causes in courts of law; one of the written statements containing the subject matter of a litigant's demand or claim, or of his defense or answer.

pleasant, etc. See PLEASE.

please, plēz, *v.t.*—*pleased, pleasing.* [O.Fr. *plaisir, pleisir*, etc., Mod.Fr. *plaire*, from L. *placere*, to please; of similar origin are *placid, placable, plea, plead.*] To excite agreeable sensations or emotions in; to delight; to gratify; to satisfy; to content; to seem good to: in this sense used impersonally.—*To be pleased* to do a thing, to take pleasure in doing it; to think fit or condescend to do it.—*v.i.* To give pleasure; to gain approbation; to like; to choose; to prefer; to condescend; to be pleased; to be kind enough (do it, if you *please*).—**pleasing**, plē'zing, *a.* Giving pleasure or satisfaction; agreeable; gratifying; delightful.—**pleasingly**, plē'zing·li, *adv.* In a pleasing manner; in such a way as to give pleasure.—**pleasant**, plez'ant, *a.* [Fr. *plaisant*, ppr. of *plaire*.] Pleasing; agreeable; grateful to the mind or to the senses; cheerful; gay; lively; jocular.—**pleasantly**, plez'ant·li, *adv.* In a pleasant manner; gaily; merrily; cheerfully.—**pleasantness**, plez'ant·nes, *n.* State or quality of being pleasant or agreeable; cheerfulness; gaiety.—**pleasantry**, plez'ant·ri, *n.* [Fr. *plaisanterie.*] Gaiety; merriment; a sprightly or humorous saying; a jest; raillery; lively talk; a laughable trick; a frolic.—**pleasance**, plez'ans, *n.* [Fr. *plaisance.*] Pleasure; delight; a part of a garden or pleasure-grounds secluded by trees or hedges. (*Archaic.*)—**pleasure**, plezh'ėr, *n.* [O.Fr. *plaisir, pleisir*, Mod.Fr. *plaisir*, from L. *placere*, to please; properly an infinitive but as in *leisure* the final syllable has been assimilated to that of nouns in *-ure*, L. *-ura*. PLEASE.] The gratification of the senses or of the mind; agreeable sensations or emotions; the feeling produced by enjoyment or the expectation of good; delight; opposed to *pain*; sensual or sexual gratification; vicious indulgence of the appetite; what the will dictates or prefers; choice; wish; desire; a favor; arbitrary will or choice (to go or stay at *pleasure*).—*To take pleasure in*, to have pleasure or enjoyment in.—

v.t.—*pleasured, pleasuring.* To give or afford pleasure to; to please; to gratify.—**pleasurable**, plezh'ėr·a·bl, *a.* Pleasing; giving pleasure.—**pleasurableness**, plezh'ėr·a·bl·nes, *n.*—**pleasurably**, plez'ėr·a·bli, *adv.*

pleat, plēt, *n.* [Var. of plait.] A fold of cloth or other material; a plait.—*v.t.* To fold cloth, etc.

plebe, plēb, *n.* [From *plebian*.] A freshman at a military academy.

plebeian, ple·bē'an, *a.* [L. *plebeius*, from *plebes, plebs*, the common people; same root as in PLENTY.] Pertaining to the common people; vulgar; common; belonging to the lower ranks.—*n.* One of the common people or lower ranks of men; originally applied to the common people of ancient Rome, or those free citizens who did not come under the class of the patricians.—**plebeianism**, ple·bē'an·izm, *n.* The state or quality of being plebeian; vulgarity.

plebiscite, pleb'i·sit or pleb'i·sīt, *n.* [Fr., from L. *plebiscitum—plebis*, the people, and *scitum*, a decree.] A vote of a whole people or community; a decree of a country obtained by an appeal to universal suffrage.

plectrum, plek'trum, *n.* [L. *plectrum*, from Gr. *plēktron*, from *plēssō*, to strike.] The small instrument of ivory, horn, or metal used for striking the strings of the lyre, or other stringed instrument.

pledge, plej, *n.* [Fr. *pleige*, L.L. *plegius, plegium, plivium, pluvium*, pledge; origin uncertain.] *Law*, the transfer of a chattel by a debtor to a creditor in security of a debt; the thing pawned as security for the repayment of money borrowed or for the performance of some agreement or obligation; a pawn; anything given or considered as a security for the performance of an act; a guarantee; a promise; a surety; a hostage; the drinking of another's health; a health.—*To put in pledge*, to pawn.—*To hold in pledge*, to keep in security.—*To take the pledge*, a popular method of binding one's self to observe principles of total abstinence from intoxicating drink. —*v.t.*—*pledged, pledging.* To give as a pledge or pawn; to deposit in possession of a person as a security; to gage (to *pledge* one's word or honor) to engage solemnly (to *pledge* one's self); to drink a health to; to drink to one's welfare.—

pledgee, plej·ē', *n.* The person to whom anything is pledged or pawn, promise, etc., is given.—**pledger**, plej'ėr, *n.* One who pledges or offers a pledge; one who drinks a health.

pledget, plej'et, *n.* A compress or small flat mass of lint, laid over a wound to imbibe the matter discharged and keep it clean.

Pleiad, plē'ad, *n. pl.* **Pleiades**, plē'a·dēz, [Gr. *Pleiades*, the Pleiads, from *pleo*, to sail, as the rising of the seven stars indicated the time of safe navigation.] The Pleiads are a cluster of seven stars in the neck

of the constellation Taurus; in *poetry*, a group of seven contemporaries in the reign of Ptolemy Philadelphus at Alexandria; seven poets in the reign of Henry III of France modeling their style on Latin and Greek work; seven poets in the reign of Louis XIII.

Pleiocene, plī'i·sēn. See PLIOCENE.

Pleistocene, plīs'to·sēn, *n.* [Gr. *pleistos*, most, and *kainos*, recent.] *Geol.* a division of the Quaternary period of which the fossil remains belong almost wholly to existing species.

plenary, ple'na·ri, *a.* [L.L. *plenarius*, from L. *plenus*, full. PLENTY.] Full; entire; complete.—*Plenary inspiration*, in *theol.* that kind or degree of inspiration which excludes all mixture of error.—**plenarily**, ple'na·ri·li, *adv.* In a plenary manner.

plenipotence, ple·nip'o·tens, *n.* [L. *plenus*, full, and *potentia*, power. PLENTY, POTENT.] Fullness or completeness of power.—**plenipotent**, ple·nip'o·tent, *a.* [L. *plenipotens.*] Possessing full power.—**plenipotentiary**, plen'i·pō·ten"shi·a·ri, *n.* A person invested with full power to transact any business; particularly, an ambassador or envoy to a foreign court, furnished with full power to negotiate a treaty or to transact other business.—*a.* Invested with or containing full power.

plenish, plen'ish, *v.t.* [L. *plenus*, full. REPLENISH.] To replenish.

plenitude, plen'i·tūd, *n.* [L. *plenitudo*, from *plenus*, full.] The state of being full or complete; plenty; abundance; repletion.

plenty, plen'ti, *n.* [O.Fr. *plentē*, from L.L. *plenitas*, fullness, abundance, from L. *plenus*, full, from root of *pleo*, to fill, which is seen also in Gr. *plērēs, pleos*, full, and also in E. *full, fill.*] Abundance; copiousness; a full or adequate supply; sufficiency; abundance of things necessary for man (a time of *plenty*).—*a.* Plentiful; being in abundance. (*Colloq.*)—**plenteous**, plen'tē·us, *a.* Abundant; copious; sufficient for every purpose; yielding abundance; having an abundance.—**plenteously**, plen'tē·us·li, *adv.* In a plenteous manner; plentifully.—**plenteousness**, plen'tē·us·nes, *n.* The state of being plenteous.—**plentiful**, plen'ti·ful, *a.* Existing in great plenty; copious; abundant; ample; yielding abundant crops; fruitful.—**plentifully**, plen'ti·ful·li, *adv.* In a plentiful manner.—**plentifulness**, plen'ti·ful·nes, *n.*

plenum, plē'num, *n.* [L. *plenus*, full.] That state of things in which every part of space is supposed to be full of matter; in opposition to a *vacuum*.

pleomorphism, plē'o·morf"ism, *n.* [Gr. *pleōn*, more, *morphē*, form.] In fungi, etc., the occurrence of more than one independent form in the life history.

pleonasm, plē'o·nazm, *n.* [Gr. *pleonasmos*, from *pleon, pleion*, more. PLENTY.] Redundancy of words in speaking or writing; the use of more words to express ideas than are necessary.—**pleonastic**, plē·o·nas'-

tik, *a.* Pertaining to pleonasm; redundant.—**pleonastically**, plē·o·nas'ti·kal·li, *adv.* In a pleonastic manner.

plesiosaur, plesiosaurus, plē'si·ō·sạr, plē'si·ō·sạ"rus, *n.* [Gr. *plēsios*, near, and *sauros*, a lizard.] An extinct marine saurian, chiefly remarkable for its length of neck, nearly allied to the ichthyosaurus.

plethora, pleth'e·ra, *n.* [Gr. *plēthōra*, from *plēthō*, to be full, from *pleos*, full. PLENTY.] *Med.* overfullness of blood; a redundant fullness of the blood vessels; hence, overfullness in any respect; a superabundance.—**plethoric,** ple·thor'ik, *a.* Characterized by plethora; having a full habit of body.—**plethorically,** ple·thor'i·kal·li, *adv.* In a plethoric manner.

pleura, plụ'ra, *n.* [Gr. *pleuron*, a rib, pl. *pleura*, the side.] *Anat.* a thin membrane which covers the inside of the thorax, and also invests the lungs.—**pleural,** plụ'ral, *a.* Pertaining to the pleura.—**pleurisy,** plụ'ri·si, *n.* An inflammation of the pleura. —**pleuritic,** plụ·rit'ik, *a.* Pertaining to pleurisy; diseased with pleurisy.—**pleuropneumonia,** plụ'rō·nū·mō"ni·a, *n.* [Gr. *pleura*, and *pneumōn*, the lungs.] An inflammation of the pleura and substance of the lungs; a combination of pleurisy and pneumonia.

plexiform, plek'si·form, *a.* [L. *plexus*, a fold, and *forma*, form.] In the form of network; complicated.

pleximeter, plek·sim'et·ėr, *n.* [Gr. *plēxis*, percussion, and *metron*, a measure.] *Med.* a small circular or ovoid plate, composed of ivory, india rubber, or the like, placed in contact with the body in diagnosis of disease by percussion.

plexure, plek'sūr, *n.* [L. *plexus*, an interweaving, from *plecto*, *plexum*, to interweave.] An interweaving; a texture; that which is woven together.—**plexus,** plek'sus, *n.* [L.] *Anat.* a network of vessels, nerves, or fibers.

pliable, plī'a·bl, *a.* [Fr. *pliable*, from *plier*, to bend, to fold, from L. *plico*, to fold, to bend.] Easy to be bent; flexible; pliant; flexible in disposition; easy to be persuaded.—**pliability, pliableness,** plī·a·bil'i·ti, plī'a·bl·nes, *n.* The quality of being pliable; flexibility; a yielding to force or to moral influence.—**pliably,** plī'a·bli, *adv.* In a pliable manner.—**pliant,** plī'ant, *a.* [Fr. ppr. of *plier*, to bend. PLY.] Capable of being easily bent; readily yielding to force or pressure without breaking; flexible; lithe; limber; plastic; easily yielding to moral influence; easy to be persuaded.—**pliantly,** plī'ant·li, *adv.* In a pliant manner.—**pliancy,** plī'an·si, *n.* The state or quality of being pliant; easiness to be bent; readiness to be influenced.

plica, plī'ka, *n.* [L., a fold. PLY.] *Med.* a disease of the hair, in which the hair is vascularly thickened, matted, or clotted; *bot.* a diseased state in plants in which the buds, instead of developing true branches, become short twigs, the whole

forming an entangled mass.—**plicate, plicated,** plī'kāt, plī'kā·ted, *a.* [L. *plicatus*, from *plico*, to fold, *plica*, a fold.] *Bot.* plaited; folded like a fan.—**plicately,** plī'kāt·li, *adv.* In a plicate or folded manner.—**plication,** plī·kā'shon, *n.* A folding or fold; *geol.* a bending back of strata on themselves.—**plicature,** plī·kā'chėr, *n.* [L. *plicatura*.] A plication; a folding.

pliers, plī'ėrz, *n. pl.* [Fr. *plier*, to bend. PLY.] A small pair of pincers adapted to handle small articles, and also for bending and shaping wire.

plight, plīt, *v.t.* [A.Sax. *plithan*, to pledge, to expose to danger, from *pliht*, a pledge, danger; D. *verpligten*, Dan. *forpligte*, G. *verpflichten*, to bind, oblige, or engage. See the noun.] To pledge, as one's word, hand, faith, honor; to give as a security for the performance of some act: never applied to property or goods, and therefore differing from *pledge*, which is applied to property as well as to word, honor, etc.—*n.* [A.Sax. *pliht*, a pledge, obligation, danger; D. and Dan. *pligt*, Sw. *pligt*, *plikt*, G. *pflicht*, duty.] A pledge or security‡; condition; state; predicament; generally, a risky or dangerous state; a distressed condition (to be in a wretched *plight*).—**plighter,** plī'tėr, *n.* One who plights.

Plimsoll mark, plim'sol, the line on the hull of a British merchant ship, regulating the load carried, first proposed in the Merchant Shipping Act of 1876 by Samuel Plimsoll; since 1930, ships registered in the United States have been required to carry a similar line.

plinth, plinth, *n.* [Gr. *plinthos*, a brick or tile; L. *plinthus*.] *Arch.* a flat square member, in form of a slab, which serves as the foundation of a column; the flat square table under the molding of the base and pedestal, at the bottom of the order.

Pliocene, plī'ō·sēn, *a.* and *n.* [Gr. *pleiōn*, more, and *kainos*, recent.] A geological term applied to the most modern of the divisions of the Tertiary epoch.

plod, plod, *v.i.*—*plodded, plodding.* [Akin to Prov. E. *plowd*, to wade, *plodge*, to walk through mud or water; Ir. and Gael. *plod*, *plodach*, a puddle; the primary sense being to walk laboriously, as through mire.] To travel or work slowly, or with steady laborious diligence; to study dully but with steady diligence; to toil; to trudge; to moil.— *v.t.* To go or walk over in a heavy laboring manner; to accomplish by toilsome exertion.—**plodder,** plod'ėr, *n.* A dull, heavy, laborious person.—**plodding,** plod'ing, *p.* and *a.* Given to plod or work with slow and patient diligence; patiently laborious.—**ploddingly,** plod'ing·li, *adv.* In a plodding manner.

plop, plop, *v.t.* and *i.* [Imitative.] To make a sound like that of an object striking water.—*n.* The act of plopping.

plot, plot, *n.* [A.Sax. *plot*, a spot of ground, a spot; Goth. *plats*, a patch. *Plat* is another form. *Plot* in sense of scheme is related to *plot*, piece of ground, as *plan*, a scheme, to *plan*, a design on a flat surface, only *plot* has generally the sense of ill design.] A plat or small extent of ground of a well-defined shape; *surv.* a plan or draft of a field, farm, estate, etc., on paper; a scheme, stratagem, or plan, usually a mischievous one; an intrigue; a conspiracy; the story of a play, poem, novel, or romance, comprising a complication of incidents; the intrigue.—*v.t.*—*plotted, plotting.* To make a plan of; to plan; to devise; to contrive; to trace a curve on a graph.—*v.i.* To formulate a scheme of mischief against another, or against a government or those who administer it; to conspire; to contrive a plan.—**plotter,** plot'ėr, *n.* One who plots; a conspirator.

plover, pluv'ėr, *n.* [O.Fr. *plovier*, Fr. *pluvier*, lit. the rain bird, from L. *pluvia*, rain, from *pluo*, to rain.] The common name of several species of shore birds of the family Charadriidae generally.

plow, plou, *n.* [Same as Icel. *plogr*, Dan. *ploug*, *plov*, O.Fris. *ploch*, D. *ploeg*, G. *pflug*, a plough.] An agricultural implement for breaking and turning soil preparatory to planting seed, originally operated by hand, later drawn by oxen or horses, but in modern times generally drawn by a tractor; any of a variety of implements, tools, or instruments for cutting grooves; a carpenter's or joiner's tool for grooving; *astron.* Charles's Wain, otherwise known as the Dipper or the constellation Ursa Major.—*Ice plow*, a plow for cutting grooves in ice preparatory to its removal; an ice breaker.— *Rotary snow plow*, a snow plow equipped with a large rotary fan or propeller, which plows into the snow and clears the highway by blowing the snow to one side.— *Snow plow*, a device attached to the front of a locomotive, street car, automobile, or motor truck to remove snow from sidewalks, streets, highways—*v.t.* To turn the soil; to turn the soil with a plow; to make furrows, grooves, or ridges; to *plow under*; to cut through water with a yacht, speedboat, or any other type of craft; to *plow* through water.—*v.i.* To do work with a plow; to admit of plowing, as dry snow *plows* easily.—**plowboy, plowman,** *n.* A boy or man who operates or guides a plow; a rustic person; a farmer.—**plowshare,** *n.* That part of the plow which cuts and turns the soil.

pluck, pluk, *v.t.* [A.Sax. *pluccian*, to pluck=D. and L.G. *plukken*, Dan. *plukke*, Icel. *plokka*, *plukka*, G. *pflücken*.] To gather; to pick; to cull, as berries or flowers; to pull with sudden force or effort; to twitch; by a similar action to cause the string of a musical instrument to vibrate and produce a sound;

to strip by plucking; to strip feathers from (to *pluck* a fowl); to rob (*slang*); to pull or draw, literally or figuratively.—*To pluck up courage*, to assume or resume courage.— **plucker,** pluk′er, *n.*

pluck, pluk, *n.* [Comp. Gael. and Ir. *pluc*, a lump, a knot, a bunch; as to the figurative sense compare a bold *heart*, a lily-*livered* rascal, a man of another *kidney*, *bowels* of compassion, etc.] The heart, liver, and lungs of a sheep, ox, or other animal of the butcher's market; courage or spirit (*colloq.*).—**pluckily,** pluk′i·li, *adv.* In a plucky manner; spiritedly. (*Colloq.*)—**plucky,** pluk′i, *a.* Spirited; courageous. (*Colloq.*)

plug, plug, *n.* [Same as D. *plug*, L.G. *pluck*, a block.] Any piece of wood or other material used to stop a hole; a stopper; a fitting in various electrical connections; a spark plug; a cake of tobacco, usually for chewing; that part of a cylindrical lock which is rotated by the key; a discharge pipe or hydrant for drawing water from a water main (a *water* plug); something wornout or inferior; especially a wornout horse (*slang*).—*v.t.* To insert a plug; to make tight by stopping a hole; to shoot (*slang*); to work steadily; to plod (*slang*).—**plugger,** plug′er, *n.* One who works doggedly. (*Slang*.)

plum, plum, *n.* [A.Sax. *plume,* L.G. *plumme,* G. *pflaume,* from L.L. *pruna* (Fr. *prune*), from L. *prunum,* a plum, from *prunus*＝Gr. *prounos,* the plum tree.] A well-known fleshy fruit containing a stone or kernel, and when dried being called a prune; also the tree producing it; a choice or lucrative thing.—**plum pudding,** *n.* Pudding containing raisins or currants.

plumb, plum, *n.* [Fr. *plomb,* from L. *plumbum,* lead.] A plummet.—*a.* Standing according to a plumb line; perpendicular.—*adv.* In a perpendicular direction.—*v.t.* To adjust by a plumb line; to set in a perpendicular direction; to sound with a plummet; hence to ascertain the capacity of; to test.—**plumbago,** plum·bā′gō, *n.* [L., from *plumbum,* lead.] Another name for *Graphite.*— **plumbaginous,** plum·baj′i·nus, *a.* Resembling or consisting of plumbago.—**plumbeous,** plum·bē′us, *a.* [L. *plumbum,* lead.] Consisting of lead; leaden.—**plumber,** plum′er, *n.* One who fits and repairs water and gas pipes; originally a worker in lead.—**plumbic,** plum′bik, *a.* Pertaining to lead; derived from lead.—**plumbiferous,** plum·bif′er·us, *a.* Producing lead.—**plumbing,** plum′ing, *n.* Plumber's trade or work; that which is installed by a plumber; the act of using a plumb.— **plumbism,** plum′bizm, *n.* Poisoning by lead taken into the system.— **plumb line,** *n.* A line having a metal weight attached to one end, used to determine a perpendicular; a line perpendicular to the plane of the horizon.—**plumb rule,** *n.* A narrow board with a plumb line attached,

used by masons, bricklayers, etc., for determining a perpendicular.

plume, plöm, *n.* [Fr., from L. *pluma,* the downy part of a feather, a small soft feather; cog. W. *pluf,* plumage; Skr. *plu,* to swim, to fly.] The feather of a bird, particularly a large or conspicuous feather; a feather or collection of feathers worn as an ornament; token of honor; prize of contest. *v.t.*—**plumed, pluming.** To pick and adjust the feathers of; to dress the feathers; to adorn with feathers or plumes; to pride; to boast: in this sense used reflexively. —**plumage,** plö′mij, *n.* [Fr., from *plume,* a feather.] The feathers that cover a bird.—**plumelet,** plöm′let. *n.* A small plume.—**plumose,** plö′- mōs, *a.* [L. *plumosus.*] Feathery; resembling feathers; *bot.* consisting of long hairs which are themselves hairy (*plumose* bristle).—**plumosity,** plö·mos′i·ti, *n.* The state of being plumose.

plummet, plum′et, *n.* [Fr. *plumbet,* from *plumb;* O.Fr. *plummet,* Fr. *plomet.* PLUMB.] A piece of lead or other metal attached to a line, used in sounding the depth of water.—*v.i.* To drop or plunge down.

plump, plump, *a.* [Allied to D. *plomp,* unwieldy, bulky; G., Dan., and Sw. *plump,* clumsy, massive, coarse; from a verbal root seen in E. *plim,* to swell.] Swelled with fat or flesh to the full size; fat or stout in person; fleshy; having a full skin; distended.—*v.t.* To make plump; to dilate; to fatten; to cause to fall suddenly and heavily.—*v.i.* [Perhaps an imitative word in first sense; as also in last sense above.] To plunge or fall like a heavy mass or lump of dead matter; to fall suddenly or at once; to grow plump. —*adv.* At once or with a sudden heavy fall; suddenly; heavily.— **plumper,** plump′er, *n.* One who or that which plumps; a vote given to one candidate when more than one are to be elected, which might have been divided among the number to be elected; a person who gives such a vote.—**plumply,** plump′- li, *adv.* Fully; roundly; without reserve.—**plumpness,** plump′nes, *n.* The state or quality of being plump; fullness of skin.—**plumpy,** plump′i, *a.* Plump; fat; jolly.

plumule, plö′mūl, *n.* [L. *plumula,* dim. of *pluma,* a feather. PLUME.] *Bot.* the growing point of the embryo, situated at the apex of the radicle, and at the base of the cotyledons, by which it is protected when young; the rudiment of the future stem of a plant.

plunder, plun′der, *v.t.* [G. *plündern* (from *plunder,* baggage.)＝D. *plunderen,* Sw. *plondra,* Dan. *plyndre,* to plunder. The word entered the English and other tongues about the time of the Thirty Years' War.] To take goods or valuables forcibly from; to pillage; to spoil; to rob in a hostile way; to take by pillage or open force.—*n.* The act of plundering; robbery; that which is taken

from an enemy by force; pillage; spoil; that which is taken by theft; robbery, or fraud.—**plunderer,** plun′dėr·ėr, *n.* One who plunders.

plunge, plunj, *v.t.*—**plunged, plunging.** [From Fr. *plonger,* from hypothetical Latin *plumbicare,* from *plumbum,* lead; lit. to fall like lead or to fall plumb.] To thrust into water or other fluid substance, or into any substance easily penetrable; to immerse; to thrust; to thrust or drive into any state or condition (to *plunge* a nation into war); to baptize by immersion.—*v.t.* To thrust or drive one's self into water or other fluid; to drive or to rush in; to fall or rush into distress or any state or circumstances in which the person or thing is enveloped, enclosed, or overwhelmed (to *plunge* into war); to throw the body forward and the hind legs up, as an unruly horse; to bet heavily and recklessly (*slang*).—*n.* A dive, rush, or leap into something; the act of pitching or throwing the body forward and the hind legs up, as an unruly horse; a place for diving, as a swimming tank or deep pool; a reckless speculation (*slang*).—**plunger,** plun′jėr, *n.*

plunk, plungk, *v.t.* and *i.* [Imitative.] To make a hollow metallic sound; to drop or put down suddenly.—*n.* The act or sound of plunking; a blow.—*adv.* With a plunking sound.

pluperfect, plö′pėr·fekt, *a.* and *n.* [L. *plus quam perfectum,* more than perfect.] *Gram.* applied to that tense of a verb which denotes that an action was finished at a certain period in the past; past or preterite perfect (he *had done* it).

plural, plö′ral, *a.* [L. *pluralis,* from *plus, pluris,* more.] Containing more than one; consisting of two or more, or designating two or more; *gram.* the *plural number* is that number or form of a word which designates more than one.—*n.* A form of a word expressing more than one; the plural number.—**pluralism,** plö′- ral·izm, *n.* The quality of being plural; a philosophic doctrine which maintains that there are more than one (usually more than two) fundamental substances.—**pluralist,** plö′- ral·ist, *n.*—**plurality,** plö·ral′i·ti, *n.* The state of being plural; an aggregate of two or more of the same kind; the greater number; the majority; in an election, the excess of votes of one candidate over those of any other candidate for the same office.—**pluralize,** plö′ral·- īz, *v.t.*—**pluralized, pluralizing.** To make plural by using the termination of the plural number.—**plurally,** plö′ral·li, *adv.* In a plural manner; in a sense implying more than one.

plus, plus. [L., more.] *Alg.* or *arith.* the name of a character marked thus ＋, which being placed between two numbers or quantities, signifies that they are to be added together; frequently used prepositionally, with the signification of in addition to (ability *plus* impudence.)

plush, plush, *n.* [Fr. *pluche, peluche,* It. *peluzzo,* from L. *pilus,* hair.

PILE.] A textile fabric with a sort of velvet nap or shag on one side resembling short hairs.

pluteus, plö·tē·us, *n.* [L.] A balustrade; a parapet; among the Romans a sort of wheeled shed covered with raw hides in which a besieging party made their approaches.

Pluto, plö′tō, *n.* In Greek mythology, the chief divinity of the lower regions; a planet of the solar system, the remotest known from the sun, visible only by telescope.

plutocracy, plö·tok′ra·si, *n.* [Gr. *Ploutos,* the god of wealth, and *krateia,* rule, *archē,* power.] The power or rule of wealth,—**plutocrat,** plö′to·krat, *n.* A person possessing power or influence solely or mainly owing to his riches.—**plutocratic,** plö·to·krat′ik, *a.* Pertaining to or characteristic of a plutocracy or a plutocrat.

Plutonic, Plutonian, plö·ton′ik, plö·tō′ni·an, *a.* [From *Pluto,* the king of the infernal regions among the ancient Greeks.] Of or relating to Pluto or to the regions of fire; subterranean; dark.—*Plutonic action,* the influence of volcanic heat and other subterranean causes under pressure.—*Plutonic rocks,* unstratified crystalline rocks formed at great depth beneath the earth's surface.—*Plutonic theory,* that which ascribes the changes on the earth's surface to the agency of fire. See NEPTUNIAN.

plutonium, plö·tō′ni·um, *n.* A radioactive element formed in the disintegration of neptunium. Symbol, Pu; at. no., 94.

pluvial, plö′vi·al, *a.* [L. *pluvialis,* from *pluvia,* rain, from *pluo,* to rain; same root as in *flow.*] Rainy; humid; relating to rain; *geol.* applied to results and operations which depend on or arise from the action of rain.—**pluvious,** plö′vi·us, *a.* [L. *pluviosus.*] Rainy; pluvial.

pluviometer, plö·vi·om′et·ėr, *n.* [L. *pluvia,* rain, and Gr. *metron,* measure.] A rain gauge; an instrument for measuring rainfall.—**pluviometrical,** plö′vi·o·met″ri·kal, *a.*

ply, plī, *v.t.*—**plied, plying.** [From Fr. *plier* (also *ployer*), to fold or bend, from L. *plicare,* to fold.] To fold.—*n.* A fold; a thickness; a unit of yarn, as two-ply.—**plywood,** plī′-wụd, *n.* Wood made from several thin sheets, which are glued together.

ply, plī, *v.t.* [From *apply.*] To use or wield diligently or steadily; to employ with diligence (to *ply* a needle or an oar); to keep busy; to practice or perform with diligence; to busy one's self in; to press hard, with blows or missiles; to assail briskly; to beset; to urge; to solicit, as for a favor.—*To ply with,* to present or offer to urgently and repeatedly; to press upon, especially with some ulterior object (to *ply* one *with* flattery).—*v.i.* To be steadily employed; to work steadily; to offer service; to run regularly between any two ports or places, as a vessel or vehicle; *naut.* to endeavor to make way against the wind.—*n.* A fold; a plait; a twist:

often used in composition to designate the number of twists, etc. (a three-*ply* carpet); bent; turn; direction; bias.—**plyer,** plī′ėr, *n.* One who or that which plies; *pl.* same as *Pliers.*

Plymouth Brethren, plim′uth, breTH′ren, *n. pl.* A sect of Christians who first appeared at Plymouth, England, in 1830.—**Plymouth Rock,** the spot in Plymouth harbor, Mass., where the Pilgrims landed, Dec. 21, 1620; an American breed of chicken.

pneumatic, nū·mat′ik, *a.* [Gr. *pneumatikos,* from *pneuma, pneumatos,* breath, spirit, from *pneō,* to breathe or blow.] Consisting of or resembling air; having the properties of an elastic fluid; pertaining to air, or to elastic fluids or their properties; moved or played by means of air; filled with or fitted to contain air; applied to numerous instruments, machines, apparatus, etc., for experimenting on elastic fluids, or for working by means of the compression or exhaustion of air (*pneumatic conveyors* and *pneumatic tools,* such as drills, hammers, grinders, rammers, diggers, pavement breakers, and hoists).—*Pneumatic philosophy,* a name formerly applied to the science of metaphysics.—**pneumatics,** nū·mat′iks, *n.* That branch of physics which treats of the mechanical properties of elastic fluids and particularly of atmospheric air.—**pneumatology,** nū·ma·tol′o·ji, *n.* The branch of philosophy which treats of the nature and operations of mind or spirit; psychology.—**pneumatometer,** nū·ma·tom′et·ėr, *n.* An instrument for measuring the quantity of air inhaled into the lungs at each inspiration and given out at each respiration; a spirometer.

pneumogastric, nū·mō·gas′trik, *a.* [Gr. *pneumōn,* a lung, and *gastēr,* the belly.] *Anat.* pertaining to lungs and stomach.—*Pneumogastric nerves,* a pair of nerves extending over the viscera of the chest and abdomen.

pneumonia, nū·mō′ni·a, *n.* [Gr. *pneumōn,* a lung, from *pneō,* to breathe.] *Med.* an inflammation of the lungs.—**pneumonic,** nū·mon′ik, *a.* Pertaining to the lungs; pulmonic.

poach, pōch, *v.t.* [From Fr. *pocher,* to poach eggs, from *poche* a pouch or pocket, the white of the egg forming a sort of pocket for the yolk. POUCH.] To cook (eggs) by breaking and pouring into boiling water; to cook with butter after breaking in a vessel.

poach, pōch, *v.i.* [Either from the above word, meaning originally to pouch or pocket thievishly, or a softened form of *poke,* to push, to intrude.] To intrude or encroach on the property of another to steal or plunder; to steal game or carry it away privately; to kill or destroy game contrary to law.—**poacher,** pōch′ėr, *n.* One who poaches or steals game; one who kills game unlawfully.

poach, pōch, *v.t.* [A later and softened form of *poke,* to thrust. POKE.] To stab; to pierce; to spear (to *poach* fish); to force or drive into so as to penetrate; to tread, as snow or soft ground, so as to render it broken and slushy.—*v.i.* To become soft and slushy or miry; to be swampy.

pochard, pōch′ėrd, *n.* [Lit. the *poacher,* one that poaches or pokes.] The name of a genus of oceanic ducks, natives of the Arctic Seas.

pock, pok, *n.* [A.Sax. *poc* or *pocc,* D. *pok,* G. *pok,* a vesicle or pustule; perhaps akin to *poke,* a bag. Pox= *pocks.*] A pustule raised on the surface of the body in an eruptive disease, as the small pox.—**pock-mark,** pok′märk, *n.* Mark or scar made by the small pox.

pocket, pok′et, *n.* [A dim. of *poke,* a pouch or bag.] A small bag inserted in a garment for carrying small articles; a small bag or net to receive the balls in billiards; a certain quantity, from 1½ to 2 cwt. (a *pocket* of hops); *mineral.* a small cavity in a rock, or on its surface, containing gold; a mass of rich ore.—*To be in pocket,* to have gain or profit from some transaction.—*To be out of pocket,* to expend or lose money.—*v.t.* To put or conceal in the pocket; to take clandestinely.—*To pocket an insult, affront, wrong,* or the like, to receive it without resenting it, or at least without seeking redress.—**air pocket,** *n.* A condition of the atmosphere met with by aviators in which the machine tends to drop as if into a 'pocket' empty of air, supposed to be due to a downward current at the point.—**pocketbook,** *n.* A case used for carrying papers in the pocket; a handbag or purse.—**pocket book,** *n.* A small paperbound book.—**pocket knife,** *n.* A knife that has one or more blades which fold into the handle.—**pocket money,** *n.* Money for small expenses.—**pocket veto,** *n.* An indirect veto by which an executive holds a legislative bill, without signing it, until the legislature adjourns.

pockmark, etc. See POCK.

pococurante, pō′kō·kö·ran″tā, *n.* [It. *poco,* little, and *curo,* to care.] One who cares little; an apathetic, careless, indifferent person.—**pococurantism,** pō′kō·kö·rant″izm, *n.* The character, disposition, or habits of a pococurante; extreme indifference, apathy, or carelessness.

pod, pod, *n.* [Probably connected with Dan. *pude,* Sw. *puta,* a pillow or cushion, as also with E. *pad,* a cushion.] A term applied to a number of different pericarps or seed vessels of plants, such as the legume, the loment, the siliqua, the silicle, the follicle, etc.—*v.i.*—*podded, podding.* To swell and assume the appearance of a pod; to produce pods.

podagra, pō·dag′ra, *n.* [Gr., from *pous, podos,* the foot, and *agra,* a taking or seizure.] Gout in the foot.

podesta, pō·des′ta, *n.* [It. *podesta,* a

governor, from L. *potestas*, power.]
A chief magistrate of the Italian
republics of the Middle Ages.

podgy, poj′i, *a.* Pudgy; fat and short.

podiatry, pō·dī′a·tri, *n.* [Gr. *pous,
podos*, foot, and the suffix *iatry*.]
Med. the study and treatment of
foot disorders.

podium, pō′di·um, *n.* [L. *podium*,
Gr. *pous, podos*, foot.] The low
enclosure running all round the
amphitheater; *arch.* a continuous
pedestal or low wall on which
columns rest.

podophyllin, pod·o·fil′in, *n.* [Gr.
pous, podos, a foot, and *phyllon*, a
leaf.] A resin obtained from the
root stock of the mayapple, used
in medicine as a purgative.

poem, pō′em, *n.* [Fr. *poème*, from L.
poema, from Gr. *poiēma*, lit. the
thing made, from *poieō*, to make.
POET.] A metrical composition; a
composition in which the verses
consist of certain measures, whether
in blank verse or in rhyme; a composition in which the language is
that of excited imagination.—**poesy**,
pō′e·si, *n.* [Fr. *poésie*, L. *poesis*, from
Gr. *poiēsis*, the art of writing poems.]
The art of or skill in composing
poems; poetry; metrical composition; a short conceit engraved
on a ring or other thing (*Shak.*).
POSY.—**poet**, pō′et, *n.* [Fr. *poète*,
from L. *poeta*, Gr. *poiētēs*, lit. a
maker, from *poieō*, to make. So in
England poets were formerly often
called 'makers'.] The author of a
poem; the composer of a metrical
composition; one skilled in making
poetry, or who has a particular
genius for metrical composition;
one distinguished for poetic talents.
—**poetaster**, pō′et·as·tèr, *n.* [From
poet, and the pejorative *-aster*;
comp. *criticaster*, etc.] A petty poet;
a pitiful rhymer or writer of verses.—
poetess, pō′et·es, *n.* A female poet.—
poetic, poetical, pō·et′ik, pō·et′i·kal,
a. [L. *poeticus*, Gr. *poiētikos*.] Pertaining to poetry; suitable to poetry;
expressed in poetry; having a metrical form; possessing the peculiar
beauties of poetry.—*Poetical justice*,
a distribution of rewards and punishments such as is common in
poetry and works of fiction, but
hardly in accordance with the realities of life.—*Poetic license*, a liberty
or license taken by a poet with
regard to matters of fact or language in order to produce a desired
effect.—**poetically**, pō·et′i·kal·li, *adv.*
In a poetical manner.—**poetics**, pō-
et′iks, *n.* That branch of criticism
which treats of the nature and laws
of poetry.—**poetize**, pō′et·īz, *v.i.*
[Fr. *poétiser*.] To write as a poet; to
compose verse.—**poet laureate**, *n.*
See LAUREATE.—**poetry**, pō′et·ri, *n.*
[O.Fr. *poeterie*, from *poete*, a poet.]
That one of the fine arts which
exhibits its special character and
powers by means of language; the
art which has for its object the
creation of intellectual pleasure by
means of imaginative and passionate
language, generally in verse; the
language of the imagination or

emotions rhythmically expressed, or
such language expressed in an elevated style of prose; especially that
creative writing which is divided
into lines, each containing a determined number of sounds, the sounds
being accented according to a regular
and determined rhythmical pattern;
similar creative writing, of looser
structure, in which the phrases
flow in a cadenced pattern; in a
wide sense whatever appeals to the
emotions or the sense of beauty;
verse; poems.

pogrom, pō·grom′, *n.* [Russian.] An
organized massacre or attack on a
party, e.g., Jews.

poignant, poi′nant, *a.* [Fr. *poignant*,
part. of *poindre*, from L. *pungere*,
pungo, to prick. POINT.] Stimulating
the organs of taste; piquant; pointed; keen; bitter; irritating; satirical;
severe; piercing; very painful or
acute.—**poignantly**, poi′nant·li, *adv.*
In a poignant manner.—**poignancy**,
poi′nan·si, *n.* The state or quality
of being poignant.

poilu, pwa·lü′, *a.* [Fr. 'hairy'.] A
slang term, equivalent to the English 'Tommy', and applied to a
soldier in French army; from the
custom of letting the beard grow
when on active service.

poinsettia, poin·set′i·a, *n.* [N.L. after
J. R. Poinsett (1779-1851).] A tropical plant (genus *Poinsettia*) with
lobed leaves and bright red bracts.

point, point, *n.* [Fr. *point*, a point,
a spot, a matter, moment, etc.,
pointe, something sharp or pointed,
from L. *punctum*, a puncture, from
pungo, punctum, to puncture, the
latter the fem. part of Fr. *poindre*,
to prick.] The mark made by the
end of a sharp piercing instrument;
geom. an element which has neither
length, breadth, nor thickness; a
mark of punctuation; a division of
the card of the mariner's compass,
the card of which has its circumference divided into 32 equal spaces;
north, south, east, and west, or any
intermediate direction; any place
marked in the heavens of importance
in astronomical calculations; that
which pricks, pierces, or punctures;
particularly the sharp end of a
thorn, pin, needle, knife, sword,
and the like; a tool or instrument
which pricks or pierces; a small
cape or promontory; a lace, string,
or the like, with a tag, formerly used
for fastening articles of dress; lace
worked by the needle; a lively turn
of thought or expression which
strikes with force or agreeable
surprise; the sting of an epigram;
hence, force or expression generally
(his action gave *point* to his words);
a salient trait of character; a peculiarity; a characteristic (the good or
bad *points* of a man); a certain
external peculiarity of an animal
(the *points* of a horse or a dog);
single thing or subject; matter
(right in every *point*); particular
thing desired or required; aim;
purpose (to gain one's *point*); a
single part of a complicated question,
or of a whole; an indivisible part

of time or space; the eve or verge
(at the *point* of death); a fielder
in the game of cricket who stands
a little to the off side of the batter's
wicket, or the spot where he stands;
a mark to denote the degree of
success or progress one has attained
in certain trials of skill and games,
as in rifle shooting, billiards, cards,
and the like, a single point counting
one.—*Acting point*, in *physics*, the
exact point at which any impulse
is given.—*Physical point*, the smallest or least sensible object of sight.—
Point of incidence, that point upon
the surface of a medium at which
a ray of light falls.—*Point of reflection*, the point from which a ray
is reflected.—*Point of sight*, that
point of a picture which is determined by a line from the eye of the
artist perpendicular to the perspective plane.—*Point of war*, a martial
note on a trumpet or bugle.—*Vowel
points*, in Hebrew, etc., certain
marks representing the vowels, which
precede or follow the consonant
sounds.—*To stand upon points*, to
be punctilious; to be nice or over-
scrupulous.—*v.t.* To give a point to;
to cut, forge, grind, or file to a
point; to add to the force or expression of; to direct toward an object
or place; to aim; to direct the eye
or notice to; to indicate the purpose
or point of; to punctuate; *masonry*,
to fill the joints of with mortar,
and smooth them with the point
of a trowel.—*To point out*, to show
by the finger or by other means.—
v.i. To direct the finger for designating an object and exciting attention
to it: with *at*; to indicate the presence of game by standing and
turning the nose in its direction,
as dogs do to sportsmen; to show
distinctly by any means.—**point-
blank**, *a.* [This phrase has its origin
in the directness with which an
arrow is aimed at the white mark
or blank in the center of a butt.]
In *gun.* having a horizontal direction;
fig. direct; plain; explicit; express.
As an adverb, horizontally; directly.
—**point-device,**† *a.* [From *point*,
condition, and *devise*, to imagine; lit.
in as fine a condition as could be
imagined.] Precise, nice, or finical
to excess. (*Shak.*)—**pointed**, poin′-
ted, *p.* and *a.* Having a sharp point.
aimed at or expressly referring to
some particular person (a *pointed*
remark); epigrammatical; abounding
in conceits or lively turns.—*Pointed
style*, in *arch.* a name applied to
several styles usually called *Gothic*.
—**pointedly**, poin′ted·li, *adv.* In
a pointed manner.—**pointedness**,
poin′ted·nes, *n.* The state or quality
of being pointed.—**pointer**, poin′-
tèr, *n.* One who or that which
points; a variety of dog remarkable
for its habit of pointing at game.—
Pointers, *n.* Two stars in the
Great Bear, through which a straight
line points to the polestar.—**point
lace**, *n.* A fine kind of lace wrought
with a needle.—**pointless**, point′les,
a. Having no point; blunt; obtuse;
having no smartness or keenness.—

point of view, *n.* The position from which something is observed or considered; personal standpoint; attitude.

poise, poiz, *v.t.*—*poised, poising.* [O. Fr. *poiser, peiser,* Fr. *peser,* from L. *penso,* to weigh out, from *pensus,* weighed, pp. of *pendo,* to weigh. PENDANT.] To balance in weight; to make of equal weight; to hold or place in equilibrium or equiponderance; to load with weight for balancing.—*v.i.* To be balanced or suspended; *fig.* to hang in suspense; to depend.—*n.* Weight; gravity; a thing suspended or attached as a counterweight; a counterpoise; hence, regulating power; that which balances; the weight used in weighing with steelyards, to balance the substance weighed; equipoise; balance; equilibrium.

poison, poi′zn, *n.* [Fr. *poison,* from L. *potio, potionis,* a drink, a draught, from *poto,* to drink. POTION.] Any agent capable of producing a morbid, noxious, dangerous, or deadly effect upon the animal economy, when introduced either by cutaneous absorption, respiration, or the digestive canal; that which taints or destroys moral purity or health.—*v.t.* To infect with poison; to put poison in or on; to add poison to; to attack, injure, or kill by poison; to taint; to mar, impair, vitiate, corrupt.—**poisoner,** poi′zn·ėr, *n.*—**poison gas,** *n.* A noxious gas used (as in warfare) to kill, injure, or disable.—**poison ivy,** *n.* A three-leafed, vinelike ivy having white berries, poisonous to the touch.—**poison oak,** *n.* A species of poison ivy.—**poison sumac,** *n.* A poisonous swamp shrub, related to poison ivy, having seven to thirteen leaves and greenish-white berries.—**poisonous,** poi′zn·us, *a.*—**poisonously,** poi′zn·us·li, *adv.*

poke, pōk, *n.* [O.D. a *poke,* a sack or bag; Icel. *poki,* a sack, a bag; *pouch* is a softened form of this, and *pocket* a diminutive.] A pouch; a bag; a sack.—**poke bonnet,** *n.* A long, straight, projecting bonnet formerly worn by women.

poke, pōk, *v.t.*—*poked, poking.* [D. and L.G. *poken,* to poke; Sw. *pak,* a stick; comp. Ir. *poc,* a blow; Gael. *puc,* to push.] To thrust something long or pointed against, as the hand or a stick, hence, to feel or search, as in the dark or in a hole —*To poke fun at,* to ridicule.—*v.i.* To grope; to search; to feel or push one's way, as in the dark; to busy one's self without a definite object: followed by *about.*—*n.* A gentle thrust; a jog; a sudden push.—**poker,** pō′kėr, *n.* One who pokes; a metal rod for stirring fire.

poker, pō′kėr, *n.* [Origin unknown.] A gambling game played with cards. —**poker face,** *n.* An inscrutable facial expression.

pokeweed, pōk′wēd, *n.* [Of American Indian origin.] A North American plant (genus *Phytolacca*) whose berries and roots have emetic and purgative qualities.

polar. See POLE.

polder, pōl′dėr, *n.* [D.] In the Netherlands, a tract of land below the level of the sea or nearest river, which, being originally a morass or lake, has been drained and brought under cultivation.

pole, pōl, *n.* [A.Sax. *pal,* a pole, a stake; collateral form of *pale,* L.G. and D. *paal,* from L. *palus,* a stake. PALE.] A long slender piece of wood; a tall piece of timber: frequently used in composition (a carriage-*pole,* a May-*pole*); a perch or rod, a measure of length containing 5½ yards.—*Under bare poles,* said of a ship when her sails are all furled.—*v.t.*—*poled, poling.* To furnish with poles for support; to bear or convey on poles; to impel by poles; to push forward by the use of poles; as to *pole* a skiff.

pole, pōl, *n.* [Fr. *pôle,* L. *polus,* the pole of the heavens, the heavens, from Gr. *polos,* the axis of the sphere, the firmament, from *pelō,* to turn or move.] One of the two points in which the axis of the earth is supposed to meet the sphere of the heavens; the fixed point about which the stars appear to revolve; one of the extremities of the earth's axis; a point on the surface of any sphere equally distant from every part of the circumference of a great circle of the sphere; the polestar; one of the points of a body at which its attractive or repulsive energy is concentrated, or in which a polar force is exerted; in *magnetism,* one of the two points at which the magnetic strength of a magnet is principally concentrated.—*Unit strength of pole,* or unit pole, is that pole which will attract or repel a pole of equal strength at a distance of one centimeter with unit force.—*The strength of a pole* is the force exerted between it and a unit pole at unit distance.—*Magnetic pole,* one of the points on the earth at which the dipping needle is vertical, or the magnetic intensity greatest.—*Poles of a voltaic cell* or *battery,* the connections at which the current passes from the battery to the external circuit, and *vice versa;* the current leaving the battery at the *positive* pole, and entering it at the *negative* pole.—

polestar, *n.* A star of the second magnitude, situated about 1° from the North Pole, round which it describes a small circle; *fig.* that which serves as a guide or director; a lodestar.—**polar,** pō′lėr, *a.* [L.L. *polaris,* from L. *polus,* a pole.] Pertaining to a pole or the poles of a sphere; pertaining to one of the poles of the earth or of the heavens; proceeding from the poles of the earth; pertaining to a magnetic pole or poles; pertaining to the points of a body at which its attractive or repulsive energy is concentrated.—*Polar angle,* the angle at a pole formed by two meridians.—*Polar axis,* that axis of an equatorial which is parallel to the earth's axis.—*Polar bear.* See BEAR.—**polar bodies,** *n.* Two minute cells resulting from the last stages of the cell divisions,

which end in the production of an ovum (egg cell).—*Polar circles,* the arctic and antarctic circles.—*Polar clock,* an apparatus whereby the hour of the day is found by means of the polarization of the scattered sunlight from the polar regions.—*Polar distance,* the angular distance of a heavenly body from the elevated pole of the heavens.—*Polar forces,* physical forces that are developed and act in pairs, with opposite tendencies, as in magnetism, electricity, etc.—*Polar lights,* the aurora borealis or australis.—*Polar star,* the polestar.—**polarimeter, polariscope,** pō·lar·im′et·ėr, pō·lar′i·skōp, *n.* An optical instrument, various kinds of which have been contrived, for exhibiting the polarization of light.—**polarity,** pō·lar′i·ti, *n.* That quality of a body in virtue of which peculiar properties reside in certain points called poles.—**polarization,** pō′lėr·i·zā″·shon, *n.* The act of polarizing or giving polarity to a body; the state of being polarized or of having polarity; in a voltaic cell, the setting up of a back electromotive force owing to the deposition of gases on the electrodes.—*Polarization of light,* a change produced upon light by the action of certain media, by which it exhibits the appearance of having polarity or poles possessing different properties.—**polarize,** pō′lėr·īz, *v.t.* —*polarized, polarizing.* To develop polarity in.—**polarizer,** pō·lėr·ī′zėr, *n.* That part of a polariscope by which light is polarized.

Pole, pōl, *n.* A native of Poland.

poleax, *n.* [*Pole* may here be the long stick; but perhaps it is for *poll,* the head.] A kind of ax or hatchet.

polecat, pōl′kat, *n.* [Supposed to be for *poult-cat,* that is, chicken or poultry cat, or abbrev. from *Polish cat.*] An animal of the weasel family, about 17 inches in length excluding the tail, very destructive to poultry; also, a skunk.

polemic, polemical, pō·lem′ik, pō·lem′i·kal, *a.* [Gr. *polemikos,* from *polemos,* war.] Pertaining to polemics; given to controversy; engaged in supporting an opinion or system by controversy.—**polemic,** *n.* A disputant; one who carries on a controversy; one who writes in support of an opinion or system in opposition to another.—**polemics,** pō·lem′iks, *n.* The art or practice of disputation; controversy; controversial writings.

police, po·lēs′, *n.* [Fr. *police,* from L. *politia,* from Gr. *politeia,* government, administration, from *polis,* a city.] The means instituted by a government or community to maintain public order, liberty, property, and individual security; the body of men by whom the municipal laws and regulations are enforced and public order maintained.—*Police commissioner,* one of a body of men, elected or appointed, whose duty it is to manage police affairs.—*Police court,* a court for the trial of offenders brought up on charges preferred by the police.—*Police mag-*

istrate, a judge who presides at a police court.—*Police squad*, a group of policemen operating together.—*Police squad car*, an automobile, equipped with one-way or two-way shortwave radio, in which police patrol.—*Police station*, the headquarters of the police or of a section of them.—**policeman**, po‧lēs′man, *n.* An ordinary member of the police force, (if assigned to a beat, a *patrolman*).

policy, pol′i‧si, *n.* [L. *politia*, Gr. *politeia*, polity. POLICE.] The art or manner of governing a nation; the line of conduct which the rulers of a nation adopt on particular questions, especially with regard to foreign countries; the principles on which any measure or course of action is based; prudence or wisdom of governments or individuals in the management of their affairs public or private; dexterity of management; in Scotland, the pleasure grounds around a gentleman's country residence. ∴ *Policy* is the course of conduct pursued, or the management of an affair, in certain circumstances; *polity*, the general principles on which such course of conduct is based.

policy, pol′i‧si, *n.* [Fr. *police*, from L.L. *poleticum*, a register, from L. *polyptychum*, Gr. *polyptychon*, an account book—*polys*, many, and *ptychē*, a fold.] A written contract by which a corporation or other persons engage to pay a certain sum on certain contingencies, as in the case of fire or shipwreck, in the event of death, etc., on the condition of receiving a fixed sum or percentage on the amount of the risk, or certain periodical payments.—*Insurance policy*. See INSURE.—**policyholder**, *n.* One who holds a policy or contract of insurance.

poliomyelitis, pō′li‧ō‧mī′e‧lī″tis, *n.* [N.L. from Gr. *polios*, gray and *myelitis*, inflammation of the spinal cord.] An acute virus disease marked by fever, motor paralysis, and atrophy of skeletal muscles, often permanently disabling; also called *infantile paralysis*.

Polish, pō′lish, *a.* Pertaining to Poland or to its inhabitants.—*n.* The language of the Poles.

polish, pol′ish, *v.t.* [Fr. *polir, polissant*, from L. *polio*, to smooth, whence also *polite*.] To make smooth and glossy, usually by friction; to burnish; to deprive of rudeness, rusticity, or coarseness; to make elegant and polite (to *polish* life or manners).—*v.i.* To become smooth; to take a smooth and glossy surface; to become refined.—*n.* A substance used to impart a gloss; a smooth glossy surface produced by friction; artificial gloss; refinement; elegance of manners.—**polisher**, pol′ish‧ėr, *n.* One who or that which polishes.

polite, po‧līt′, *a.* [L. *politus*, from *polio*, to polish. POLISH.] Polished or elegant in manners; refined in behavior; well bred; courteous; complaisant.—**politely**, po‧līt′li, *adv.* In a polite manner.—**politeness**, po‧-

līt′nes, *n.*

politic, pol′i‧tik, *a.* [L. *politicus*, Gr. *politikos*, from *polis*, a city. POLICE.] Consisting of citizens; constituting the state (the body *politic*); prudent and sagacious in devising and pursuing measures adapted to promote the public welfare; well devised and adapted to the public prosperity; ingenious in devising and pursuing any scheme of personal or national aggrandizement; cunning; artful; sagacious in adapting means to an end; well devised; adapted to its end, right or wrong.—**political**, po‧lit′i‧kal, *a.* Having a fixed or regular system or administration of government; relating to civil government and its administration; concerned in state affairs or national measures; pertaining to a nation or state, or to nations or states, as distinguished from *civil* or *municipal*; treating of politics or government.—*Political economy*, the science of the laws which regulate the production, distribution, and consumption of the products, necessary, useful, or agreeable to man, which it requires some portion of voluntary labor to produce, procure, or preserve.—*Political geography*. See GEOGRAPHY.—*Political science*, that science which deals with the structure, organization and government or nations and their component parts.—**politically**, po‧lit′i‧kal‧li, *adv.* In a political manner. —**politician**, pol‧i‧tish′an, *n.* One versed in the science of government and the art of governing; one skilled in politics; one who occupies himself with politics.—**politicly**, pol′i‧tik‧li, *adv.* In a politic manner.—**politics**, pol′i‧tiks, *n.* [Fr. *politique*, Gr. *politikē*.] The science of government; that part of ethics which relates to the regulation and government of a nation or state for the preservation of its safety, peace, and prosperity; political affairs, or the conduct and contests of political parties.—**polity**, pol′i‧ti, *n.* A form of political organization.

polka, pōl′ka, *n.* [Pol. *polka*, Polish woman.] A lively dance of Bohemian origin, in duple time with three steps and a hop to each bar.—*v.i.* To dance the polka.

poll, pōl, *n.* [O.D. *pol, bol*, a ball, the head; L.G. *polle*, the head, the top of a tree; allied to *ball, bowl*: *pollard* is a derivative.] The head of a person, or the back part of the head; a catalogue or register of heads, that is, of persons; the voting or registering of votes for candidates in elections (the close of the *poll*); the fish called a chub; the blunt end of a hammer, or the butt of an ax.—*v.t.* To remove the top or head of; to lop, clip, shear; to cut closely; to mow; to register or give a vote; to bring to the poll; to receive or elicit, as a number of votes or voters.—*v.i.* To vote at a poll; to record a vote, as an elector.—**polled**, pōld, *p.* and *a.* Deprived of the poll; lopped, as a tree having the top cut; having the hair cut; cropped; bald; having cast the horns, as a stag; hence, wanting

horns (*polled* cattle).—**poll tax**, *n.* A tax levied per head or person, usually on all males of mature years without regard to wealth or station.

pollack, pol′ak, *n.* [D. and G. *pollack*.] A species of marine fish belonging to the cod family.

pollard, pol′ėrd, *n.* [From *poll*, the head, and affix *-ard*.] A tree with the head cut off at some height from the ground, for the purpose of inducing it to throw out branches all round the section where amputation has taken place; a stag that has cast his horns; also, a hornless ox; a coarse product of wheat, but finer than bran.—*v.t.* To make a pollard of; to convert into a pollard by cutting off the head.

pollen, pol′en, *n.* [L. *pollen* and *pollis*, fine flour or dust.] The male element in flowering plants; the fine dust or powder which by contact with the stigma effects the fecundation of the seeds.—**polliniferous**, pol‧i‧nif′ėr‧us, *a.* Producing pollen.—**pollenize**, pol′en‧īz, *v.t.* To pollinate.—**pollinate**, pol′i‧nāt, *v.t. Bot.* to convey pollen from the anther to the stigma of.—**pollination**, pol‧i‧nā′shon, *n. Bot.* the conveyance of the pollen from the anther to the stigma.

pollex, pol′leks, *n.* [L.] The thumb in man; a corresponding digit of other animals.

pollinium, pol‧lin′i‧um, *n.*; pl. **-ia**. [L. for *dust*.] An agglutinated mass of pollen grains, as in orchids.

pollute, pol‧lūt′, *v.t.*—polluted, polluting. [L. *polluo, pollutum*, from prep. *pol, por*, used in composition, and *luō*, to wash. LAVE.] To make foul or unclean; to render impure; to defile; to soil; to taint; to corrupt or defile in a moral sense; to impair; to profane.—**pollution**, pol‧lū′shon, *n.* [L. *pollutio*.] The act of polluting; the state of being polluted.

polo, pō′lō, *n.* [Balti, ball.] A game similar to hockey, played on horseback.

polonaise, pol‧o‧nāz′, *n.* [Fr.] A robe or dress worn by ladies and adopted from the fashion of the Poles; a courtly Polish dance.

polonium, pol‧ō′ni‧um, *n.* [From *Poland*.] A radioactive element (radium F) discovered in pitchblende by M. and Mme. Curie. Symbol, Po; at. no., 84.

poltroon, pol‧trön′, *n.* [Fr. and Sp. *poltron*, from It. *poltrone*, from *poltro*, lazy, dastardly, from O.H.G. *polstar*, a pillow. BOLSTER.] An arrant coward; a dastard; a wretch; without spirit or courage.—*a.* Base; vile; contemptible.—**poltroonery**, pol‧trön′ėr‧i, *n.* Cowardice; want of spirit.

polyandrous, pol‧i‧an′drus, *a.* [Gr. *polys*, many, *anēr, andros*, a male.] *Bot.* having many stamens, that is, any number above twenty, inserted in the receptacle.

polyandry, pol‧i‧an′dri, *n.* [Gr. *polys*, many, *anēr, andros*, a man.] The practice of females having more husbands than one at the same time; plurality of husbands.

polyanthus, pol‧i‧an′thus, *n.* [Gr.

polys, many, *anthos*, a flower.] A garden variety of the oxlip primrose which has long been a favorite.

polyarchy, pol·i·är·ki, *n*. [Gr. *polys*, many, and *arche*, rule.] The government of many, whether a privileged class (aristocracy) or the people at large (democracy).

polyatomic, pol·i·a·tom″ik, *a*. [Gr. *polys*, many, E. *atomic*.] *Chem*. a term applied to elements or radicals which have an equivalency greater than one; polybasic.

polybasic, pol·i·bā′sik, *a*. [Gr. *polys* many, and E. *basic*.] *Chem*. of acids with more than one replaceable hydrogen atom.

polychromy, pol·i·krō·mi, *n*. [Gr. *polys*, many, and *chrōma*, color.] The practice of coloring statues and the exteriors and interiors of buildings; architectural ornamentation in colors. — **polychromatic**, **polychromic**, pol′i·krō·mat″ik, pol′i·krō·mik, *a*. Exhibiting a play of colors.—**polychrome**, pol′i·krōm, *a*. Having several or many colors; executed in the manner of polychromy.—*Polychrome printing*, the art of printing in one or more colors at the same time.

polycotyledon, pol′i·kot·i·lē″don, *n*. [Gr. *polys*, many, *kotylēdon*.] *Bot*. a plant that has many or more than two cotyledons or lobes to the seed.— **polycotyledonous**, pol′i·kot·i·lē″do·nus, *a*. Having more than two cotyledons.

polydactylism, pol·i·dak′til·izm, *n*. [Gr. *polys*, many, *daktylos*, a finger.] The condition of having several or many fingers or digits.—**polydactylous**, pol·i·dak′ti·lus, *a*. Having many fingers or toes.

polyester, pol·ē·es′ter, *n*. [Gr. *polys*, many, and *ester*.] An ester formed by condensation, used in clothing fibers.

polyethylene, pol′i·eth″i·lēn, *n*. [Gr. *polys*, many, and *ethylene*.] A polymer of ethylene; a plastic material.

polygamy, po·lig′a·mi, *n*. [Gr. *polys*, many, and *gamos*, marriage.] A plurality of wives or husbands at the same time, or the having of such plurality.—**polygamous**, po·lig′a·mus, *a*.—**polygamist**, po·lig′a·mist, *n*.

polygenesis, pol·i·jen′e·sis, *n*. [Gr. *polys*, many, and *genesis*.] The doctrine that beings have their origin in many cells or embryos of different kinds: opposed to *monogenesis*.— **polygenetic**, pol′i·je·net″ik, *a*. Relating to polygenesis. See MONOGENETIC.

polyglot, pol′i·glot, *n*. [Gr. *polys*, many, *glōtta*, a language.] A book containing many languages, particularly a Bible that presents the Scriptures in several languages. Also used as an adjective.

polygon, pol′i·gon, *n*. [Gr. *polys*, many, *gōnia*, an angle.] *Geom*. a plane figure of many angles and sides, or at least of more than four sides.—*Similar polygons* have their several angles equal each to each, and the sides about their equal angles proportional.—**polygonal**, po·lig′o·nal, *a*. Having the form of a polygon; having many angles. *Polygonal numbers*, the successive sums of a series of numbers in arithmetical progression.

polygraph, pol′i·graf, *n*. [Gr. *polys*, many, *graphē*, a writing.] An instrument for multiplying copies of a writing.—**polygraphic**, pol·i·graf′ik, *a*. Pertaining to polygraphy; done with a polygraph.

polygynous, po·lij′i·nus, *a*. Having many pistils or styles; polygynic.— **polygyny**, po·lij′i·ni, *n*. The practice of having more wives than one at the same time.

polyhedron, pol·i·hē′dron, *n*. [Gr. *polys*, many, *hedra*, a side.] *Geom*. a solid bounded by many faces or planes, and when all the faces are regular polygons the solid becomes a regular body; a multiplying glass with several plane surfaces; a polyscope. —**polyhedral**, pol·i·hē′dral, *a*.

polymer, pol′i·mér, *n*. [Gr. *polys*, many, and *meros*, part.] A compound of high molecular weight formed by polymerization.—**polymeric**, pol·i·mer′ik, *a*. Of or relating to a polymer.—**polymerous**, po·lim′ér·us, *a*. Containing many parts.—**polymerize**, pol′i·mér·īz, *v.t.*—**polymerized**, *polymerizing*. To subject to polymerization.—*v.i.* To undergo polymerization.—**polymerization**, pol′i·mér·i·zā″shon, *n*. The formation of large molecules from two or more smaller ones.

polymorphism, pol·i·mor′fizm, *n*. [Gr. *polys*, many, *morphe*, form.] The property of existing in different forms; the property of crystallizing in two or more fundamental forms.— **polymorphous**, **polymorphic**, pol·i·mor′fus, pol·i·mor′fik, *a*. Having many forms; assuming many forms.

Polynesian, pol·i·nē′zhi·an, *a*. [Gr. *polys*, many, *nēsos*, an island.] Pertaining to *Polynesia*, the region of many islands in the Pacific.—*n*. A native or inhabitant of Polynesia.

polynomial, pol·i·nō′mi·al, *n*. [Gr. *polys*, many and *nomen*, name.] An algebraic expression of two or more terms.—**polynomial**, *a*.

polyp, pol′ip, *n*. [L. *polypus*, a polyp, a growth or tumor, from Gr. *polypous*—*polys*, many, *pous*, a foot.] A name loosely applied to what were once known as *radiate* animals, having the mouth surrounded by more or less numerous arms or tentacles, now commonly applied to the hydra or the sea anemone; a zoophyte.— **polypary**, pol′i·pa·ri, *n*. The horny envelope or case of polyps (Hydrozoa, Polyzoa, etc.).—**polypidom**, po·lip′i·dom, *n*. [L. *polypus*, and *domus*, a house.] A stem or permanent fabric in which are the cells constituting the abodes of the polyps which fabricate it.

polypetalous, pol·i·pet′a·lus, *a*. [Gr. *polys*, many, *petalon*, a petal.] *Bot*. having or consisting of many petals (a *polypetalous* corolla).

polyphagous, po·lif′a·gus, *a*. [Gr. *polys*, many, *phagein*, to eat.] Eating or subsisting on many things or kinds of food.

polyphase, pol′i·fāz″, *a*. [Gr. *polys*, many, and *phasis*, appearance.] Of a combination of electric currents differing in their phases by constant amounts.

polyphonic, pol·i·fon′ik, *a*. [Gr. *polys*, many, *phōne*, sound.] Having or consisting of many voices or sounds; *music*, consisting of several parts progressing simultaneously according to the rules of counterpoint; contrapuntal.—**polyphony**, po·lif′o·ni, *n*. Multiplicity of sounds or voices.

polyphyllous, po·lif′i·lus, *a*. [Gr. *polys*, many, *phyllon*, a leaf.] *Bot*. many leaved.

polypody, pol′i·pō·di, *n*. [Gr. *polypodion*, from its spreading rootstock.] A name of various ferns, one of them common to Britain and North America.

polypous. See POLYPUS.

polypus, pol′i·pus, *n. pl.* **polypi**, pol′i·pī. [POLYP.] A polyp; *pathol*. a pedunculated tumor in the mucous membrane, especially that of the nostrils and uterus.—**polypous**, pol′i·pus, *a*. Pertaining to a polypus.

polysepalous, pol·i·sep′a·lus, *a*. [Gr. *polys*, many, and E. *sepal*.] *Bot*. a term applied to a calyx which has its sepals separate from each other.

polysyllable, pol′i·sil·la·bl, *n*. [Gr. *polys*, many, *syllabē*, a syllable.] A word of many syllables, that is, consisting of four or more syllables. —**polysyllabic**, **polysyllabical**, pol′i·sil·lab″ik, pol′i·sil·lab″i·kal, *a*. Consisting of many syllables or of more than three.

polysyndeton, pol·i·sin′de·ton, *n*. [Gr., from *polys*, many, *syn*, together, *deō*, I bind.] A figure of rhetoric by which the copulative conjunction is often repeated.

polytechnic, pol·i·tek′nik, *a*. [Gr. *polys*, many, and *technē*, art.] Of or designating an educational institution in which instruction is given in many technical arts and applied sciences.— *n*. A school of instruction in applied sciences; an exhibition of objects belonging to the industrial arts.

polytheism, pol·i·thē′izm, *n*. [Gr. *polys*, many, *theos*, god.] The doctrine of a plurality of gods.—**polytheist**, pol·i·thē′ist, *n*. A person who believes in a plurality of gods.— **polytheistic**, **polytheistical**, pol′i·thē·is″tik, pol′i·thē·is″ti·kal, *a*. Pertaining to polytheism; holding a plurality of gods.

Polyzoa, pol·i·zō′a, *n. pl.* [Gr. *polys*, many, *zōon*, an animal.] A class of animals, chiefly marine, forming compound groups or colonies, being the lowest members of the Mollusca, and generally known by the popular names of 'sea-mosses' and 'sea-mats'. —**polyzoarium**, pol′i·zō·ā′ri·um, *n*. A polyzoan colony or its dermal system.

polyzonal, pol·i·zō′nal, *a*. [Gr. *polys*, many, *zōnē*, a zone.] Composed of many zones or belts; a term applied to burning lenses composed of pieces united in rings.

pomace, pom′is, *n*. [From L. *pomum*, an apple.] The substance of apples or of similar fruit crushed by grinding.—**pomaceous**, po·mā′shus, *a*. Like pomace; pertaining to the apple family of trees.

pomade, po·mād′, *n*. [Fr. *pommade*,

It. *pomada*, *pomata*, from L. *pomum*, an apple. Originally it was prepared from apples.] Perfumed ointment, especially ointment for the hair; pomatum.

pomander, pō'man·dėr, *n.* [Fr. *pomme d'ambre*, apple or ball of amber.] A perfume ball, or a mixture of perfumes, formerly carried in the pocket or suspended from the neck or the girdle.

pomatum, pō·mā'tum, *n.* [From L. *pomum*, an apple. POMADE.] A perfumed unguent used in dressing the hair; pomade.

pome, pōm, *n.* [L. *pomum*, an apple.] *Bot.* a fleshy or pulpy pericarp without valves, containing a capsule or capsules, as the apple, pear, etc.

pomegranate, pom'gra·nit, *n.* [L. *pomum*, an apple, and *granatum*, grained, having many grains or seeds. GRAIN, GARNET.] A fruit as large as an orange, having a hard rind filled with a soft pulp and numerous grains or seeds; the fruit that produces pomegranates, supposed to be a native of Persia; an ornament on the robe and ephod of the Jewish high priest.

pomelo, pom'e·lō, *n.* The shaddock; the grapefruit.

Pomeranian, pom'er·ā''ni·an, *n.* A small dog from Pomerania in Prussia.

pomiferous, pō·mif'ėr·us, *a.* [L. *pomum*, an apple, and *fero*, I produce.] Apple bearing; an epithet applied to plants which bear the larger fruits (as melons, gourds, cucumbers, etc.).

pommel, pum'mel, *n.* [O.Fr. *pommel*, from L. *pomum*, an apple or similar fruit.] A knob or ball; the knob on the hilt of a sword; the protuberant part of a saddlebow; a round knob on the frame of a chair.—*v.t.*—**pommeled**, *pommeling*, To beat; to bruise. Spelled also *Pummel*.

pomology, pō·mol'o·ji, *n.* [L. *pomum*, an apple, Gr. *logos*, discourse.] The branch of knowledge that deals with fruits; the cultivation of fruit trees.—**pomological**, pō·mo·loj'i·kal, *a.* Pertaining to pomology.—**pomologist**, pō·mol'o·jist, *n.* One who is versed in pomology.

pomp, pomp, *n.* [Fr. *pompe*, L. *pompa*, from Gr. *pompē*, a procession, from *pempō*, to send.] A procession distinguished by splendor or magnificence; a pageant; magnificence; parade; splendor; display.—**pompous**, pom'pus, *a.* [Fr. *pompeux*.] Displaying pomp; splendid; showing self-importance; exhibiting an exaggerated sense of dignity; ostentatious.—**pompously**, pom'pus·li, *adv.* In a pompous manner; ostentatiously.—**pompousness, pomposity**, pom'pus·nes, pom·pos'i·ti, *n.* Pompous display; show; ostentation.

pompom, *n.* [From sound.] An automatic gun firing small shells.

pompon, pom'pon, *n.* [Fr.] An ornament of feathers, artificial flowers, etc., for a bonnet or hat; a ball on a soldier's shako.

pompous, pompously, etc. See POMP.

poncho, pon'chō, *n.* [Sp.] In Spanish America a garment like a narrow blanket with a slit in the middle for the head to pass through.

pond, pond, *n.* [A slightly different form of *pound*, A.Sax. *pund*, an enclosure.] A body of still water of less extent than a lake, either artificial or natural.—**pond lily**, *n.* The water lily.—**pondweed**, *n.* A name of several British water weeds.

ponder, pon'dėr, *v.t.* [Fr. *ponderer*, from L. *pondero*, to weigh, from *pondus*, *ponderis*, weight.] To weigh carefully in the mind; to think about; to reflect upon; to examine carefully.—*v.i.* To think; to muse; to deliberate: with *on* or *over*.—**ponderable**, pon'dėr·a·bl, *a.* [L. *ponderabilis*.] Capable of being weighed; having weight.—**ponderability**, pon'dėr·a·bil'i·ti, *n.* That property of bodies by which they possess sensible weight.—**ponderous**, pon'dėr·us, *a.* [L. *ponderosus*.] Very heavy; of great weight; massive; weighty; forcible.—**ponderously**, pon'dėr·us·li, *adv.* In a ponderous manner.—**ponderousness, ponderosity**, pon'dėr·us·nes, pon·dėr·os'i·ti, *n.* The state or quality of being ponderous; gravity; heaviness.

pongee, pon'ji, *n.* [Chinese.] Soft unbleached Chinese silk employed in the construction of balloons.

poniard, pon'yėrd, *n.* [Fr. *poignard*, from *poing*, L. *pugnus*, the fist.] A small dagger; a pointed weapon for stabbing.—*v.t.* To pierce with a poniard; to stab.

pontifex, pon'ti·feks, *n.* pl. **pontifices**, pon·tif'i·sēz. [L. *pontifex*, *pontificis*, a high priest, from *pons*, *pontis*, a bridge, and *facio*, to make.] The name by which the Romans designated the highest members of their great colleges of priests, the chief being termed *Pontifex Maximus.*—**pontiff**, pon'tif, *n.* A high priest; a designation of the pope.—**pontifical**, pon·tif'i·kal, *a.* Relating to pontiffs or priests; relating to a pope; belonging to the pope; in a lofty manner, expressive of infallibility of speaker.—*n.* A book containing rites and ceremonies ecclesiastical; *pl.* the dress and ornaments of a pope, priest, or bishop.—**pontificate**, pon·tif'i·kāt, *n.* [L. *pontificatus*.] The state or dignity of a high-priest; the office or dignity of the pope; the papacy; the reign of a pope.

pontoon, pon·tön', *n.* [Fr. *ponton*, from L. *pons*, *pontis*, a bridge.] A flat-bottomed boat, or any light framework or floating body used in the construction of a temporary military bridge over a river; a lighter, a low flat vessel resembling a barge, used in careening ships; a water-tight structure placed beneath a submerged vessel and then filled with air, to assist in refloating the vessel.—**pontonier**, pon·to·nēr', *n.* [Fr.] A soldier having charge of pontoons; one who constructs pontoon bridges.—**pontoon bridge**, *n.* A temporary military bridge supported on pontoons.

pony, pō'ni, *n.* [Gael. *ponaidh*, Ir. *poni*, a pony.] A small variety of horse; a small liqueur glass; a printed or written translation used by students to avoid work.

pood, pöd, *n.* A Russian weight, equal to 36.113 lbs.

poodle, pö'dl, *n.* [Same as G. and Dan. *pudel*, D. *poedel*, L.G. *budel*, a poodle; akin to L.G. *pudeln*, to waddle.] A small variety of dog covered with long curling hair.

pooh, pö, *interj.* Pshaw! pish! an expression of dislike, scorn, or contempt.—**pooh-pooh**, *v.t.* To turn aside with a pooh; to express scorn or contempt for; to sneer at.

pool, pöl, *n.* [A.Sax. *pól* = L.G. *pohl*, *pool*, Icel. *pollr*, D. *poll*, G. *pfuhl*, pool, fen; the word is also Celtic; W. *pwll*, a pool, a pit; perhaps akin to L. *palus*, a marsh.] A small collection of water or other liquid in a hollow place; a small piece of stagnant water; a hole in the course of a stream deeper than the ordinary bed.

pool, pöl, *n.* [Fr. *poule*, a hen.] The receptacle for the stakes at certain games of cards, billiards, etc.; the stakes themselves; games played on a table similar to a billiard table but having six pockets, usually with fifteen object balls and one cue ball; a common fund or combination of properties and interests, often arranged for speculation in grain or commodity markets.—*v.t.* to combine interests or properties.

poon, pön, *n.* [Indian name.] The name of several valuable trees of India (genus *Calophyllum*).

poop, pöp, *n.* [Fr. *poupe*, from L. *puppis*, the poop.] The highest and aftermost part of a ship's deck above the complete deck of the vessel.—*v.t.* *Naut.* to break heavily over the stern or quarter of; to drive in the stern of.

poor, pör, *a.* [O.E. *poure*, O.Fr. *poure*, *povre*, Mod.Fr. *pauvre*, from L. *pauper*, poor, from *paucus*, few, and *pario*, to produce.] Destitute of riches; not having property sufficient for a comfortable subsistence; needy; wanting good or desirable qualities; having little value or importance; trifling; insignificant; paltry; mean; destitute of fertility; barren; destitute of intellectual or artistic merit (a *poor* discourse); wanting in spirit or vigor; weak; impotent; worthy of pity; ill-fated; a word of tenderness or endearment (*poor* thing); a word of slight contempt; wretched.—*The poor*, collectively, the indigent; the needy: opposed to the rich; those unable to support themselves, and who have to depend for support on the contributions of others.—*Poor in spirit*, humble; contrite. (N.T.)—**poorhouse**, pör'hous, *n.* A residence for persons receiving public charity.—**poor law**, *n.* A law or the laws collectively established for the management of the funds for the maintenance of the poor.—**poorly**, pör'li, *adv.* In a poor manner or condition; in indigence; with little or no success; in an inferior manner; insufficiently; defectively.—*a.* Somewhat ill; indisposed; not in health. (*Colloq.*)—**poorness**, pör'nes, *n.* The state or quality of being poor; poverty.—**poor-spirited**, *a.* Of a mean spirit; cowardly.—**poor-spiritedness**, *n.*

pop, pop, *n.* [From the sound.] A small smart sound or report; a blow with a hatchet.—*v.i.*—*popped*, *popping.* To appear to the eye suddenly; to enter or issue forth with a quick, sudden motion; to dart; to start from a place suddenly.—*v.t.* To thrust forward, or offer suddenly; to thrust or push suddenly with a quick motion; to protrude (his eyes *popped*); to burst open.—*To pop corn*, to parch or roast Indian corn until it expands and 'pops' open.—*To pop the question*, in familiar language, to make an offer of marriage to a lady—*adv.* Suddenly; unexpectedly.—**popcorn**, *n.* Corn for parching; popped corn.—**popgun**, *n.* A small gun or tube used by children for shooting pellets, which makes a 'pop' when the pellet is expelled.

pope, pōp, *n.* [A.Sax. *pápa*, from L.L. *papa*, the pope, lit. father, same word as *papa*, the childish name for father. PAPA.] The Bishop of Rome, the head of the Roman Catholic Church; in the *Greek Church*, a priest or chaplain; the ruffe, a small fish closely allied to the perch.—*Pope's eye*, the gland surrounded with fat in the middle of the thigh of an ox or sheep, much prized for its delicacy.—**popedom**, pōp′dum, *n.* The place, office, dignity, or jurisdiction of the pope.—**pope joan**, *n.* A game of cards.—**popery**, pō′pėr·i, *n.* The religion of the Church of Rome, comprehending doctrines and practice: a term offensive to Catholics.—**popish**, pō′pish, *a.* Pertaining to the pope or the Roman Catholic Church: used with a shade of contempt. —**popishly**, pō′pish·li, *adv.* In a popish manner; with a tendency to popery.

popinjay, pop′in·jā, *n.* [O.E. *popingay*, Fr. *papegai*, Sp. and Pg. *papagayo*, L.Gr. *papagas*, from Ar. *babaghâ*, *babbagâ*, a parrakeet.] A parrot‡; a gay, trifling young man; a fop or coxcomb.

poplar, pop′lėr, *n.* [O.Fr. *pōplier*, Mod.Fr. *peuplier*, from L. *populus*, a poplar.] A common name of sundry well-known trees, of which there are numerous species, as the white poplar, gray poplar, trembling poplar or aspen, black poplar, etc.

poplin, pop′lin, *n.* [Fr. *Popeline*.] Corded fabric of silk or worsted, originally made in the *papal* city of Avignon, and used especially for women's clothing.

poppet, pop′et, *n.* [M.E. *popet*, doll, puppet.] A valve that rises perpendicularly from its seat; an upright support fastened at the bottom of a machine; a doll.

popple, pop′l, *v.i.* [Dim. and freq. of *pop*.] To move quickly up and down, as a cork dropped on water.

poppy, pop′i, *n.* [A.Sax. *papig*, *popig*, from L. *papaver*, a poppy.] A gay flowering plant of many species, including *Papaver californicum*, a red annual, and *P. somniferum*, the opium

poppy.

populace, pop′ū·lis, *n.* [Fr. *populace*, It. *popolazzo*, from L. *populus*, the people (whence *popular*, *people*); the root is doubtful.] The common people; the vulgar; the multitude, comprehending all persons not distinguished by rank, education, office, or profession: usually with the definite article.—**popular**, pop′ū·lėr, *a.* [L. *popularis*.] Pertaining to the common people; constituted by or depending on the people; suitable to common people; easy to be comprehended; plain; familiar; beloved by the people; pleasing to people in general.—**popularity**, pop·ū·lar′i·ti, *n.* The state or quality of being popular, or esteemed by the people at large; good will or favor proceeding from the people.—**popularization**, pop′ū·lėr·i·zā″shon, *n.* The act of making popular.—**popularize**, pop′ū·lėr·īz, *v.t.*—*popularized*, *popularizing.* To make popular; to treat in a popular manner, or so as to be generally intelligible; to spread among the people.—**popularly**, pop′ū·lėr·li, *adv.* In a popular manner; so as to please the populace; among the people at large; currently; commonly.—**populate**, pop′ū·lāt, *v.t.* —*populated*, *populating.* To furnish with inhabitants; to people.—**population**, pop·ū·lā′shon, *n.* The act or process of populating or peopling; the whole number of people in a country, town, etc.; populousness.— **Populist**, pop′ū·list, *n.* Member of a political party, formed in 1891, advocating an advanced program of national control and proprietorship of all natural means of production.— **populous**, pop′ū·lus, *a.* [L. *populosus*.] Full of inhabitants; thickly peopled.—**populously**, pop′ū·lus·li, *adv.* With many inhabitants in proportion to extent.—**populousness**, pop′ū·lus·nes, *n.* The state of being populous.

porbeagle, por′bē·gl, *n.* [Lit. hog-beagle—Fr. *porc*, a hog, and E. *beagle*, the latter term, like *dog* and *hound*, being applied to several sharks; comp. *porpoise.*] A species of shark.

porcelain, por′se·lan, *n.* [Fr. *porcelaine*, from It. *porcellana*, first a certain shell, then the nacre of the shell, and last porcelain, from L. *porcus*, a hog, from some fancied resemblance in the shell to a hog. PORK.] The finest species of pottery ware, originally manufactured in China and Japan, formed from the finest clays united with siliceous earths, which communicate a certain degree of translucency by means of their vitrification.—*a.* Belonging to or consisting of porcelain.—**porcelaneous**, por·se·lā′nē·us, *a.* Pertaining to or resembling porcelain.— *Porcelaneous shells* are those which have a compact texture, an enameled surface, and are generally beautifully variegated.

porch, pōrch, *n.* [Fr. *porche*, It. *portico*, from L. *porticus*, a porch, from *porta*, a gate, entrance. PORT.] *Arch.* an exterior appendage to a

building forming a covered approach or vestibule to a doorway; a covered walk or portico.—*The Porch*, a public portico in Athens, where Zeno, the philosopher, taught his disciples; hence, *the Porch* is equivalent to the *school of the Stoics.*

porcine, por′sīn, *a.* [L. *porcinus*, from *porcus*, a hog. PORK.] Pertaining to swine; like a swine; hoglike.

porcupine, por′kū·pīn, *n.* [O.Fr. *porcespin*, lit. spine-hog; from L. *porcus*, a pig, and *spina*, a spine or thorn. PORK, SPINE.] A rodent quadruped covered with long spines mixed with bristly hairs, which the animal can erect at pleasure, and which serve for his defense.

pore, pōr, *n.* [Fr. *pore*, from L. *porus*, Gr. *poros*, a passage, a pore. PORT (a gate).] A small opening in a solid body, especially one of the minute openings on the surface of organized bodies through which fluids and minute substances are excreted or exhaled or by which they are absorbed; one of the small interstices between the molecules of matter which compose bodies.—**porous**, pō′rus, *a.* Having many pores or minute openings or interstices; having the molecules separated by intervals or pores.—**porousness**, **porosity**, pō′rus·nes, pō·ros′i·ti, *n.* The state or quality of being porous or of having pores.

pore, pōr, *v.i.*—*pored*, *poring.* [O.E. *poure*; origin uncertain; possibly same as *pour*.] To look with steady continued attention or application; to read or examine anything with steady perseverance: generally followed by *on* (*upon*) or *over.*

porgy, por′gi, *n.* [Origin doubtful.] The name given to a number of fishes, some of them used as food.

porism, pōr′izm, *n.* [Gr. *porisma*, a corollary, from *porizō*, I gain.] *Geom.* a corollary; a proposition affirming the possibility of finding such conditions as will render a certain problem indeterminate or capable of innumerable solutions.

pork, pōrk, *n.* [Fr. *porc*, from L. *porcus*, a swine, a pig. FARROW.] The flesh of swine, fresh or salted, used for food.—**porker**, por′kėr, *n.* A hog; a pig, especially one fed for pork.—**pork barrel**, *n.* Government appropriations or projects that are designed to give patronage benefits for political advantage.

pornography, por·nog′ra·fi, *n.* [Gr. *pornē*, prostitute, *graphō*, I write.] Literature in which prostitutes figure; obscene writing.—**pornographic**, por·no·graf′ik, *a.* Pertaining to the literary treatment of such subjects.

porosity, porous, etc. See PORE.

porphyry, por′fi·ri, *n.* [Fr. *porphyre*, Pr. *porfiri*, from Gr. *porphyritēs*, lit. a purple-colored rock, from *porphyra*, purple. PURPLE.] Originally, the name given to a very hard Egyptian stone containing crystals of rose-colored feldspar, partaking of the nature of granite, susceptible of a fine polish, and consequently much used for sculpture; also applied

---

ch, *chain*;   *ch*, Sc. *loch*;   g, *go*;   j, *job*;   ng, *sing*;   TH, *then*;   th, *thin*;   w, *wig*;   hw, *whig*;   zh, *azure.*

generally to any unstratified or igneous rock in which detached crystals of feldspar or some other mineral are diffused through a compact base.—**porphyritic**, por·fi·rit'ik, *a*. Composed of, resembling, or containing porphyry.

porpoise, por'pus, *n*. [O.E. *porcpisce*, *porpesse*, etc., lit. swine fish, from L. *porcus*, a swine, and *piscis*, a fish. PORK.] A cetaceous mammal, rarely exceeding 5 feet in length, frequenting the northern seas, and frequently seen off the shores pursuing shoals of herring, mackerel, etc.

porridge, por'ij, *n*. [Perhaps from L. *porrum*, *porrus*, a leek, and meaning originally leek soup or broth; or a corruption of *pottage*.] A kind of food made by slowly stirring oatmeal, or other similar substance, into water or milk while boiling till a thickened mass is formed.—**porringer**, por'in·jėr, *n*. [From *porridge*. The *n* has intruded as in *messenger*.] A porridge dish; a small earthenware or tin vessel out of which children eat their food.

port, pōrt, *n*. [A.Sax. *port*, a port, haven, harbor, from L. *portus*, a haven; akin to *porta*, a gate; same root as *fare*. It enters into many place names, as *Portland*, *Portsmouth*, *Bridport*.] A natural or artificial harbor; a haven; any bay, cove, inlet, or recess of the sea, or of a lake, or the mouth of a river, which vessels can enter, and where they can lie safe from injury by storms.

port, pōrt, *n*. [Fr. *porte*, L. *porta*, a gate, from same root as Gr. *poros*, a passage, and E. to *fare*. See above.] A gate; an entrance; a passageway in the side of a ship; an opening in the side of a ship of war, through which cannon are discharged: called also a porthole; an aperture for the passage of steam or a fluid.—**portal**, pōr'tal, *n*. [O.Fr. *portal*, L.L. *portale*, from L. *porta*, a gate.] A door or gate: a poetical or dignified term; *arch*. the lesser gate when there are two of different dimensions at the entrance of a building; a kind of arch over a door or gate, or the framework of the gate.—*a. Anat*. belonging to a vein forming a sort of entrance (*port*) to the liver.—*Portal circulation*, a special circulation of venous blood from the intestines, etc., through the liver.—**porter**, pōr'tėr, *n*. [Fr. *portier*.] One who has charge of a door or gate; a doorkeeper; a waiter in a hall.—**porteress, portress**, pōr'tėr·es, pōr'tres, *n*. A female porter.—**porthole**, *n*. The port of a ship.

port, pōrt, *v.t*. [Fr. *porter*, from L. *porto*, to carry (seen in *export*, *import*, *report*, *transport*, *sport*, etc.); same root as *portus*, a harbor, a port.] To carry in military fashion; to carry a weapon, such as a rifle, in a slanting direction, upward toward the left, and across the body in front, as in the military command 'to *port* arms'.—*n*. [Fr. *port*, carriage, demeanor, from *porter*, L. *porto*, to carry.] Carriage; air; mien; manner of movement or walk; demeanor;

external appearance (the *port* of a gentleman).—**portability**, pōr·ta·bil'i·ti, *n*. The state of being portable.—**portable**, pōr'ta·bl, *a*. [L. *portabilis*.] Capable of being carried by the hand or about the person; capable of being carried or transported from place to place; easily carried; not bulky or heavy.—**portage**, pōr'tij, *n*. The act of carrying; the price of carriage; a break in a chain of water communication over which goods, boats, etc., have to be carried, as from one lake, river, or canal to another, or along the banks of rivers round waterfalls, rapids, etc.—**porter**, pōr'tėr, *n*. [Fr. *porteur*, from *porter*, to carry.] A carrier; a person who carries or conveys burdens, parcels, or messages for hire; a dark-colored malt liquor made wholly or partially with high-dried malt; so called from its having been originally the favorite beverage of porters.—**porterage**, pōr'tėr·ij, *n*. Money charged or paid for the carriage of burdens or parcels by a porter.

port, pōrt, *n*. [Etym. uncertain.] *Naut*. the larboard or left side of a ship.—*v.t*. and *i. Naut*. to turn or put to the left.

port, pōrt, *n*. [From *Oporto*, Portuguese city.] A rich, sweet wine, dark red in color.

portage, pōr'tij, *n*. [From Fr. *porter*, to carry.] The work of carrying; the carrying of something overland from one body of water to another.

portal. See PORT (gate).

portamento, por·ta·men'tō, *n*. [It.] *Mus*. the gliding from one note to another without a break.

portcullis, pōrt·kul'is, *n*. [Fr. *porte*, a gate, and *coulisse*, groove, from *couler*, to slip or slide.] *Fort*. a strong grating of timber or iron, resembling a harrow, made to slide in vertical grooves in the jambs of the entrance gate of a fortified place, to protect the gate in case of assault.

Porte, pōrt, *n*. [The chief office of the Ottoman Empire is styled *Babi Ali*, lit. the High Gate, from the gate (*bab*) of the palace at which justice was administered; and the French translation of this term being *Sublime Porte*, hence the use of this word.] The Ottoman court; the government of the Turkish Empire.

portend, por·tend', *v.t*. [L. *portendo*, to stretch forth, point out, portend—*por*, *pro*, forth or forward, and *tendo*, to stretch. TEND.] To foreshow ominously; to foretoken; to indicate something future by previous signs.—**portent**, por'tent or por·tent', *n*. [L. *portentum*.] That which portends or foretokens; especially, an omen of ill.—**portentous**, por·ten'tus, *a*. Of the nature of a portent; ominous; foreshowing ill; monstrous; prodigious; wonderful.—**portentously**, por·ten'tus·li, *adv*. In a portentous manner.—**portentousness**, por·ten'tus·nes, *n*.

porter. See PORT, a gate, and PORT, to carry.

portfolio, pōrt·fō'li·ō, *n*. [In imitation of Fr. *porte-feuille*, a portfolio,

the office of a minister—*porter*, to carry (L. *portare*), and *feuille*, a leaf, L. *folium*.] A portable case of the form of a large book, for holding loose drawings, prints, papers, etc.; the office and functions of a minister of state or cabinet member.

portico, pōr'ti·kō, *n*. pl. **porticoes**, pōr'ti·kōs. [It. and Sp. *portico*, from L. *porticus*. PORCH.] *Arch*. a kind of porch before the entrance of a building fronted with columns.

portion, pōr'shon, *n*. [L. *portio*, *portionis*, a portion; akin to *pars*, *partis*, a part. PART.] A part of anything separated from it; that which is divided off, as a part from a whole; a part, though not actually divided, but considered by itself; a part assigned; an allotment; fate; final state (N.T.).—*v.t*. To divide or distribute into portions or shares; to parcel out; to allot in shares; to endow with a portion or an inheritance.—**portionless**, pōr'shon·les, *a*. Having no portion.

portland cement, pōrt'land se·ment'. [Called so because of its resemblance, when set, to a stone found on the Isle of Portland, in England.] A cement of superior quality, consisting of a mixture of clay and limestone, or two similar substances, which are first ground, then heated until they form clinker, then powdered, after which they harden into stone upon the addition of water or even when immersed in water.

portly, pōrt'li, *a*. [From *port*, carriage, mien, demeanor.] Grand or dignified in mien; stately; of a noble appearance and carriage; rather tall, and inclining to stoutness.—**portliness**, pōrt'li·nes, *n*. The state or quality of being portly.

portmanteau, pōrt·man'tō, *n*. [Fr. *portemanteau*, from *porter*, to carry, and *manteau*, a cloak or mantle.] A case or trunk, usually made of leather, for carrying apparel, etc., on journeys; a leather case attached to a saddle behind the rider.

portrait, pōr'trāt, *n*. [Fr. *portrait*, pp. of *portraire*, to portray. PORTRAY.] A painted picture or representation of a person, and especially of a face drawn from the life: also used generally for engravings, photographs, crayon drawings, etc., of this character; a vivid description or delineation in words.—**portraiture**, pōr'trā·chėr, *n*. [Fr.] A portrait; the art or practice of drawing portraits, or of vividly describing in words.

portray, por·trā', *v.t*. [Fr. *portraire*, to portray, to depict, from L. *portraho*, to draw forth—L. *por*, *pro*, forward, and *trahere*, to draw, whence *traction*, *abstract*, etc.] To paint or draw the likeness of; to depict; to describe in words.—**portrayal**, por·trā'al, *n*. The act of portraying; delineation; representation.—**portrayer**, por·trā'ėr, *n*.

Portuguese, por'tū·gēz, *a*. Of or pertaining to Portugal.—*n*. The language of Portugal; the people of Portugal.

portulaca, pōr′tu·lak″ä, *n.* [L. *purslane.*] Any of the plants of the genus *Portulaca*, herbs of thick succulent leaves, sporting variously colored flowers.

pose, pōz, *v.t.*—posed, posing. [Fr. *poser*, to place, to put a question, from L. *pauso*, to halt, to stop, from *pausa*, a pause; but the meaning, as well as that of the compounds, has been influenced by *pono, positum*, to put, place, set, which gives *position*, etc. This word is seen in com*pose*, de*pose*, dis*pose*, re*pose*, etc. PAUSE.] To embarrass by a difficult question; to cause to be at a loss; to puzzle.—**poser,** pō′zér, *n.* One that poses or puzzles by asking difficult questions; something that puzzles, as a difficult question.

pose, pōz, *n.* [Fr. *pose*, an attitude, from L. *pausa*, See above.] Attitude or position taken naturally, or assumed for effect; an artistic posture or attitude.—*v.i.*—posed, posing. [Fr. *poser*.] To attitudinize; to assume characteristic airs.—*v.t.* To cause to assume a certain posture; to place so as to have a striking effect.

posit, poz′it, *v.t.* [L. *pono, positum*, to place. POSITION.] To lay down as a position or principle; to present to the consciousness as an absolute fact.

position, po·zish′on, *n.* [Fr. *position*, L. *positio*, from *pono, positum*, to place, set, which appears as -*pound* in com*pound*, etc., as -*pone* in post*pone*, and is seen also in de*posit, opposite, positive, post, posture*, etc.] State of being placed; situation; generally with reference to other objects, or to different parts of the same object; relation with regard to other persons, or to some subject; manner of standing or being placed; attitude; that on which one takes one's stand; hence, principle laid down; predication; affirmation; place or standing in society; social rank; state; condition of affairs; *arith.* a mode of solving a question by one or two suppositions.

positive, poz′i·tiv, *a.* [Fr. *positif*; L.L. *positivus*, from L. *pono, positum*. POSITION.] Definitely laid down or expressed; direct; explicit; absolute; real; existing in fact; not negative; direct (*positive* proof); confident; fully assured; dogmatic; overconfident; distinctly ascertained or ascertainable; *photog.* having the lights and shades rendered as they are in nature: opposed to *negative*; the form of an adjective which denotes simple or absolute quality; having a real force or position (a *positive* influence); *elect.* electricity produced by rubbing glass with silk; electricity arising from a deficiency of electrons in a body; *math.* greater than zero; tending to increase; indicating affirmation, lack of doubt; *pathol.* indicating the presence of a disease.—*Positive philosophy*, a philosophical system founded by Auguste Comte (1798-1857), which limits itself strictly to human experience, denies all metaphysics and all search for first or for final causes.—*Positive pole*, one of the terminals in an electric generator, battery, or circuit: opposed to *negative*.—*n. Gram.* the positive degree; *photog.* a picture in which the lights and shades are rendered as they are in nature: opposed to *negative*.—**positively,** poz′i·tiv·li, *adv.*—**positiveness,** poz′i·tiv·nes, *n.*—**positivism,** poz′i·tiv·izm, *n.* The positive philosophy.—**positivist,** poz′i·tiv·ist, *n.*

positron, poz′i·tron, *n.* [*Positive* and *electron*.] A charged particle with a mass equal to that of an electron.

posse, pos′sē. [L., to be able.] A number of people; a small body of men.—*Posse comitatus, lit.* the power of a county; *law*, the body of men which the sheriff is empowered to raise in case of riot, etc.

possess, poz·zes′, *v.t.* [L. *possideo, possessum*, to occupy, to possess—*pos* for *por*, before, near, and *sedeo*, to sit (as in *reside, preside*, etc.).] To occupy in person; to have and hold; to have as a piece of property or as a personal belonging; to be owner of; to own; to affect strongly (fear *possessed* them); to pervade; to fill or take up entirely; to have full power or mastery over; as, an evil spirit, evil influence, violent passion, etc. (*possessed* with a fury); to put in possession; to make master or owner: with *of* before the thing, and now generally in the passive or with reflexive pronouns (to be *possessed of* a large fortune; to *possess* one's *self* of another's property); to furnish or fill; to imbue or instill into: with *with* before the thing.—**possession,** poz·zesh′on, *n.* The having or holding of property; the state of owning or having in one's hands or power; the thing possessed; land, estate, or goods owned; the state of being mastered by some evil spirit or influence.—*To take possession*, to enter on the possession of property; to assume ownership.—*To give possession*, to put in another's power or occupancy.—**possessive,** poz·zes′iv, *a.* [L. *possessivus*.] Pertaining to possession; expressing possession.—*Possessive case*, the genitive case, or case of nouns and pronouns which expresses possession, ownership (*John's* book), or some relation of one thing to another (*Homer's* admirers).—*Possessive pronoun*, a pronoun denoting possession or property, as *my, thy*, etc.—*n.* A pronoun or other word denoting possession.—**possessively,** poz·zes′iv·li, *adv.* In a manner denoting possession.—**possessor,** poz·zes′ér, *n.* One who possesses.—**possessory,** poz·zes′o·ri, *a.* Pertaining to possession.

posset, pos′et, *n.* [Comp. W. *posel*, curdled milk, a posset, from *posiaw*, to gather.] A drink composed of hot milk curdled by some infusion, as wine or other liquor.—*v.t.* To curdle; to coagulate. (*Shak.*)

possible, pos′i·bl, *a.* [L. *possibilis*, from *posse*, to be able, from *potis*, able, and *esse*, to be; akin *power*.] That may be or exist; that may be now, or may happen or come to pass; that may be done; not contrary to the nature of things; capable of coming to pass, but improbable.—**possibly,** pos′i·bli, *adv.* In a possible manner; perhaps; perchance.—**possibility,** pos·i·bil′i·ti, *n.* The state or condition of being possible; a chance of happening; a thing possible; that which may take place or come into being.

post, pōst, *n.* [A.Sax. *post*, from L. *postis*, post, a doorpost, from *pono, positum*, to place, set. POSITION.] A piece of timber, metal, or other solid substance set upright, and often intended to support something else.

post, pōst, *n.* [From Fr. *poste*, (masc.), a military post or station, an office, and *poste* (fem.), a letter carrier, a post-house, a post office, etc., both from L.L. *posta*, for *posita*, from L. *positum*, placed. POST, above.] The place at which some person or thing is stationed or fixed; a station or position occupied, especially a military station; the place where a single soldier or a body of troops is stationed; a bugle call giving notice to soldiers to retire to their quarters for the night, sounded at tattoo, there being a first post and a last post, the latter sounded also at military funerals; an office or employment; an appointment; a berth; a messenger or a carrier of letters and papers; one that goes at stated times to convey the mails or dispatches; a postman; an established system for the public conveyance of letters; a post office; a size of writing and printing paper, measuring about 18¾ inches by 15¼.—*To ride post*, to be employed to carry dispatches and papers; and as such carriers rode in haste, hence the phrase signifies to ride in haste, to pass with expedition. *Post* is thus used adverbially for swiftly, expeditiously, or expressly (to travel *post*).—*v.i.* [Fr. *poster*, to post.] To travel with post horses; to travel with speed; to rise and sink on the saddle in accordance with the motion of the horse, especially when trotting.—*v.t.* To fix up in a public place, as a notice or advertisement; to expose to public reproach; to expose to opprobrium by some public action; to place; to station (to *post* troops on a hill); *bookkeeping*, to carry (accounts or items) from the journal to the ledger; to make the requisite entries in, for showing a true state of affairs; to place in the post office; to transmit by post (to *post* letters).—*To post up*, in bookkeeping, to make the requisite entries in up to date; hence, to make one master of all the details of a subject.—**postage,** pōs′tij, *n.* The charge levied on letters or other articles conveyed by post.—**postage stamp,** *n.* An adhesive stamp of various values issued by the Post Office Department for affixing to letters, packets, etc., as payment of cost of transmission.—**postal,** pōst′al, *a.* Relating to a post

office or the carrying of mails.—
post card, *n.* Any card, to which
a stamp may be affixed, transmitted
through the mail; also, officially
Postal card, a similar card, on which
a stamp has been printed, issued by
the government.—**post chaise,** *n.* A
chaise for conveying travelers from
one station to another. (*Historical.*)—
poster, pōst'ėr, *n.* One who posts;
a courier; a post horse; a large
printed bill or placard posted for advertising.—**post-free,** *a.* Franked;
paying no postage.—**posthaste,** *n.*
Haste or speed in travelling, like
that of a post or courier.—*adv.* With
speed or expedition.—**postman,**
pōst'man, *n.* A post or courier; a
letter carrier.—**postmark,** pōst'-
märk, *n.* The mark or stamp of a post
office on a letter.—**postmaster,** pōst'-
mas·tėr, *n.* The officer who has the
superintendence and direction of a
post office.—**postmaster general,** *n.*
The chief executive head of a postal
system; one of the members of the
cabinet of the President of the
United States of America, having
charge of the Post Office Department.—**post office,** *n.* An office or
house where letters are received for
transmission to various parts, and
from which letters are delivered that
have been received from places at
home and abroad; a department of
the government charged with the
conveyance of letters, etc., by post.—
General post office. See GENERAL.—
Post-office order. Money order, see
MONEY.—**postpaid,** *a.* Having the
postage prepaid.—**postroad,** *n.* A
road along which the mail is
carried.
postbellum, pōst·bel'um, *a.* [L.]
After the war, especially the American Civil War.
postdate, pōst'dāt, *v.t.*—*postdated,
postdating.* [Prefix *post,* after, and
date.] To date a check, letter, or
other document later than the current date.
postdiluvial, postdiluvian, pōst·-
di·lū'vi·al, pōst·di·lū'vi·an, *a.* [L.
post, after, and *diluvium,* the deluge.]
Being or happening posterior to the
Flood in Noah's days.—**postdiluvian,**
n. A person who lived or has lived
since the Flood.
posterior, pos·tē'ri·ėr, *a.* [L. *posterior,* compar. of *posterus,* from *post,*
after.] Later or subsequent in time;
opposed to *prior;* later in order;
coming after; situated behind; hinder (the *posterior* portion of the
skull): opposed to *anterior.*—*A posteriori.* A PRIORI.—**posteriority,** pos·-
tē'ri·or'i·ti, *n.* The state of being
later or subsequent.—**posteriorly,**
pos·tē'ri·ėr·li, *adv.* Subsequently in
time; behind.—**posteriors,** pos·tē'-
ri·ėrz, *n. pl.* The hinder part of an
animal's body.—**posterity,** pos·ter'-
i·ti, *n.* [L. *posteritas,* from *posterus,*
later.] Descendants; the race that
proceeds from a progenitor; succeeding generations.
postern, pōs'tėrn, *n.* [O.Fr. *posterne,*
from L.L. *posterna, posterula,* a
secret means of exit, from L. *posterus,*
behind, posterior, from *post,* behind.]

Primarily, a back door or gate; a
private entrance; hence, any small
door or gate; *fort.* a covered passage
leading under a rampart to the
ditch in front.
postfix, pōst'fix, *n.* [Prefix *post,* after
and *fix.*] *Gram.* an affix or suffix.—
v.t. To add or annex to the end
of a word.
postglacial, pōst·glā'shi·al, *a. Geol.*
belonging to a section of the post-
tertiary deposits. See GLACIAL.
postgraduate, pōst·grad'ū·āt, *n.* One
who engages in advanced academic
studies after receiving a degree,
usually bachelor's.—*a.* Pertaining
to such a student or to such studies.
posthumous, pos'tū·mus, *n.* [L. *pos-
tumus,* last, superl. of *posterus,*
coming after, from *post,* behind.]
Born after the death of the father;
published after the death of the
author (*posthumous* works); being
or continuing after one's decease
(*posthumous* fame).—**posthumously,**
pos'tū·mus·li, *adv.* After one's decease.
postillon, postillion, pōs·til'yon, *n.*
[Fr. *postillon,* from *poste,* a post.]
The rider of the near lead horse of
a traveling or other carriage.
postimpressionism, pōst·im·pre'-
shon·izm, *n.* [L. *post* and *impressionism.*] *Art,* a reaction from impressionism that emphasized the individual artist's reaction to objects
rather than representation of purely
visual impressions.
postliminium, postliminy, pōst·li·
min'i·um, pōst·lim'i·ni, *n.* [L., from
post, after, and *limen,* end, limit.]
That right by virtue of which persons and things taken by an enemy
in war are restored to their former
state.
postmeridian, pōst·me·rid'i·an, *a.*
[L. *postmeridianus.* MERIDIAN.] Coming after the sun has passed the
meridian; being or belonging to
the afternoon.—*n.* The afternoon.
post-mortem, pōst·mor'tem, *a.* [L.
post, after, *mors,* death.] After death.
—*Post-mortem examination,* an examination of a body made after
death.
postnatal, pōst·nā'tal, *a.* Subsequent
to birth.
postnuptial, pōst·nup'shal, *a.* Being
or happening after marriage.
post-obit, pōst·ob'it, *n.* [L. *post,
obitum,* after death.] A bond given
for the purpose of securing to a
lender a sum of money on the death
of some specified individual from
whom the borrower has expectations.
postoperative, pōst·op'ėr·ā·tiv, *a.*
[*Post* and *operative.*] Of, or pertaining to, the care of a patient
after an operation, or the results
of the operation.
postpone, pōst·pōn', *v.t.*—*postponed,
postponing.* [L. *postpono—post,* after,
and *pono,* to put. POSITION.] To
put off; to defer to a future or later
time.—**postponement,** pōst·pōn'-
ment, *n.* The act of postponing or
deferring to a future time.—
postponer, pōst·pō'nėr, *n.* One who
postpones.

postposition, pōst·pō·zish'on, *n.* The
act of placing after; the state of
being put behind; *gram.* a word or
particle placed after or at the end
of a word.—**postpositive,** pōst·poz'-
i·tiv, *a.* Placed after something else
as a word.
postprandial, pōst·pran'di·al, *a.* [L.
post, after, and *prandium,* a dinner.]
Happening after dinner.
postscript, pōst'skript, *n.* [L. *post,*
after, and *scriptum,* written.] A
paragraph added to a letter after
it is concluded and signed by the
writer; any addition made to a book
or composition after it had been
supposed to be finished; something
appended.
postulate, pos'tū·lāt, *n.* [L. *postula-
tum,* a demand, from *postulo,* to
demand, from *posco,* to ask.] A
position or supposition of which
the truth is demanded or assumed
for the purpose of future reasoning; a
necessary assumption; *geom.* something of the nature of a problem
assumed or taken for granted; the
enunciation of a self-evident problem.—*v.t.*—*postulated, postulating.*
To beg or assume without proof;
to regard as self-evident, or as too
obvious to require further proof.—
postulant, pos'tū·lant, *n.* One who
demands or requests; a candidate.—
postulation, pos·tū·lā'shon, *n.* The
act of postulating or supposing
without proof; supplication; intercession.
posture, pos'chėr, *n.* [Fr. *posture,*
from L. *positura* a placing, from
pono, positum, to place. POSITION.]
The disposition of the several parts
of the body with respect to each other,
or with respect to a particular
purpose; pose of a model or figure
used by an artist; attitude; situation;
condition; particular state with regard to something else (the *posture*
of affairs).—*v.t.*—*postured, posturing.*
To place in a particular posture.—
v.i. To dispose the body in particular postures; to contort the body
into artificial attitudes; to behave
in an artificial manner.—**posturer,**
pos'chėr·ėr, *n.* One who postures;
especially one who behaves and comports himself in a highly artificial
manner.—**postural,** pos'chėr·al, *a.*
Pertaining or relating to posture.
postwar, pōst·war', *a.* Belonging to
the period after a war, especially
one of the World Wars.
posy, pō'zi, *n.* [Corrupted from *poesy,*
being originally a piece of poetry.]
A poetical quotation or motto attached to or inscribed on something,
as on a ring; a motto or verse sent
with a nosegay; hence, a bunch of
flowers; sometimes a single flower,
as for a buttonhole.
pot, pot, *n.* [A widely spread word,
the origin of which is not clear=
Fr. *pot,* D. *pot,* Dan. *potte,* Icel.
pottr, W. *pot,* Ir. *pota,* a pot.] A
hollow vessel more deep than broad,
used for various domestic and other
purposes (an iron *pot* for boiling
meat or vegetables; an earthern *pot*
for plants, called a *flowerpot,* etc.);
a mug; a jug containing a specified

quantity of liquor; the quantity contained in a pot; definitely, a quart (a *pot* of porter); a size of paper, 12½ inches by 15 inches the sheet: said to have had originally a pot as watermark; the metal or earthenware top of a chimney.—*To go to pot*, to be destroyed or ruined; to come to an ill end; the pot being here probably that in which old metal is melted down. (*Colloq.*)—*v.t.*—*potted, potting*. To put into pots; to preserve seasoned in pots (*potted* fowl and fish); to plant or cover in pots of earth.—**potbellied**, *a*. Having a prominent belly.—**potbelly**, *n*. A protuberant belly.—**potboy**, pot′boi, *n*. A boy or man who carries pots of ale or beer for sale; a menial in a public house.—**potherb**, *n*. A herb for the pot and for cookery; a culinary plant.—**pothole**, *n*. A circular cavity in the rocky beds of rivers formed by stones being whirled round by the action of the current.—**pothook**, *n*. A hook on which pots and kettles are hung over the fire; a letter or character like a pothook, written by children in learning to write.—**pothouse**, *n*. An alehouse; a tavern.—**pothunter**, *n*. A sportsman who has more regard to winning prizes than to mere sport.—**potluck**, *n*. What may chance to be in the pot or provided for a meal.—*To take potluck*, is for an unexpected visitor to partake of the family meal, whatever it may chance to be. (*Colloq.*)—**potpourri**, pō·pö·rē′, *n*. [Fr. *pot*, pot, and *pourrir*, to putrefy, to boil very much; from L. *putere*, to rot.] A dish of different kinds of meat and vegetables cooked together; hence, a miscellaneous collection; a medley.—**potsherd**, pot′shèrd, *n*. [*Pot.* and *sherd=shard, shred*, a fragment.] A piece or fragment of an earthenware pot.—**potstone**, pot′stōn, *n*. A coarsely granular variety of steatite or soapstone, sometimes manufactured into kitchen vessels (hence the name).—**potter**, pot′ėr, *n*. [From *pot*.] One whose occupation is to make earthenware vessels or crockery of any kind; one who pots viands.—*Potter's clay*, a variety of clay of a reddish or gray color which becomes red when heated.—*Potter's wheel*, an apparatus consisting of a vertical iron axis, on which is a horizontal disk made to revolve by treadles, the clay being placed on the disk.—**pottery**, pot′ėr·i, *n*. The ware or vessels made by potters; earthenware glazed and baked; the place where earthen vessels are manufactured; the business of a potter.—**pot-valiant**, *a*. Courageous over drink; heated to valor by strong drink.—**pot-walloper**, pot·wol′lop·ėr, *n*. [*Pot*, and *wallop*, to boil; akin to *gallop*.] A parliamentary voter in some English boroughs before 1832, who was admitted to vote on proof that he had boiled a pot within the borough bounds during the six months preceding the election.

potable, pō′ta·bl, *a*. [L.L. *potabilis*, from L. *poto*, to drink, whence *potion, poison*.] Drinkable; suitable for drinking; capable of being drunk. —*n*. Something that may be drunk. —**potation**, pō·tā′shon, *n*. The act of drinking; a drinking bout; a draught; a drink.

potash, pot′ash, *n*. [*Pot*, and *ash*, from being prepared by evaporating the lixivium of wood ashes in iron pots.] Alkali in an impure state, procured from the ashes of plants by lixiviation and evaporation, largely employed in the manufacture of flint glass and soap, bleaching, making alum, etc.—*Potash water*, an aerated beverage consisting of carbonic acid water, to which is added bicarbonate of potash.

potassa, po·tas′sa, *n*. The older name for *Potash*.

potassium, po·tas′si·um, *n*. [A Latinized term from *potash*.] A soft white metallic element occurring in combination; compounds used as fertilizer, etc. Symbol, K (Latin, *kalium*); at. no., 19; at. wt., 39.102.—**potassic**, po·tas′ik, *a*.—**potassium nitrate**, *n*. A crystalline compound, KNO_3, used as a preservative and in gunpowder; saltpeter.—**potassium cyanide**. See CYANIDE.

potation. See POTABLE.

potato, po·tā′tō, *n*. pl. **potatoes**, po·tā′tōz. [Sp. *patata, batata*; said to be a Haitian word.] Originally the sweet potato; now the edible starchy tuber of a plant, *Solanum tuberosum*; the plant itself.—**potato beetle**, *n*. A leaf beetle, *Leptinotarsa decemlineata*, causing damage to potato crops.

poteen, potheen, po·tēn′, *n*. [From Ir. *poitín*, little pot.] Whisky illicitly distilled by the Irish peasantry; whisky generally. (*Irish*.)

potent, pō′tent, *a*. [L. *potens*, powerful, pres. part. of *posse*, to be able, from *potis*, able (same root as E. *father*, L. *pater*), and *esse*, to be. *Potent* is seen in *impotent, omnipotent*. POWER.] Powerful, in a physical or moral sense; efficacious; having great authority, interest, or the like. —**potency, potentness**, pō′ten·si, pō′tent·nes, *n*. The state or quality of being potent.—**potentate**, pō′ten·tāt, *n*. [Fr. *potentat*.] A person who possesses great power or sway; a prince; a sovereign; an emperor, king, or monarch.—**potential**, pō·ten′shal, *a*. [L. *potentia*, power.] Being in possibility, not in actuality; latent; that may be manifested; in *electrostatics*, at a given point, the work required to bring a unit of positive electricity from an infinite distance to that point under given conditions of electrification.—*Potential energy*, energy of position, the energy of a system which is due only to the positions of its particles; the difference between total energy and kinetic energy.—*Potential mood*, that form of the verb which is used to express the power, possibility, liberty, or necessity of an action or of being (I *may go*; he *can write*).— *n*. Anything that may be possible; a possibility.—**potentiality**, pō·ten′shi·al′i·ti, *n*. State of being potential;

possibility, but not actuality; inherent power or quality not actually exhibited.—**potentially**, pō·ten′shal·li, *adv*. In a potential manner; in possibility, not in act.—**potentiometer**, pō·ten′shi·om″et·ėr, *n*. [From *potential*, and *meter*.] An electrical instrument which can be used to measure pressure, current, or resistance.—**potently**, pō′tent·li, *adv*. In a potent manner; powerfully.

potentilla, pō·ten·til′la, *n*. [From L. *potens*, powerful, from the supposed medicinal qualities of some of the species.] An extensive genus of herbaceous perennials, of which one species is used in Lapland and the Orkney Islands to tan and dye leather.

pother, poTH′ėr, *n*. [A different form of *bother* or of *potter*.] Bustle; confusion; tumult; flutter.—*v.i.* To make a pother or bustle; to make a stir.—*v.t.* To bother; to puzzle; to tease.

potion, pō′shon, *n*. [L. *potio*, a drinking, a draught, from *poto*, to drink. *Poison* is the same word.] A draught; a liquid medicine; a dose to be drunk.

potpourri, potsherd. See POT.

pott, pot, *n*. See POT.

pottage, pot′ij *n*. [Fr. *potage*, lit. what one puts in the *pot*.] A species of food made of meat boiled to softness in water, usually with some vegetables; also, oatmeal or other porridge.

potter, pottery, etc. See POT.

potter, pot′ėr, *v.i.* [Comp. Sw. *pota*, D. *poteren, peuteren*, to poke or search with the finger or a stick; W. *pwtio*, to poke or thrust. PUT.] To busy or perplex one's self about trifles; to work with little energy or effort; to trifle.

pottle, pot′l, *n*. [Fr. *potel*, a dim. of *pot*.] Originally a liquid measure of two quarts; hence, any large tankard; a vessel or small basket for holding fruit.

pouch, pouch, *n*. [A softened form of *poke*, a bag, a pouch.] A small bag; a pocket; a bag or sac belonging to or forming an appendage of certain animals, as that of a marsupial animal.—*v.t.* To put into a pouch or pocket.—**pouched**, poucht, *a*. Having a pouch; furnished with a pouch for carrying the young, as the marsupials.

poult, pōlt, *n*. [Fr. *poulet*, a dim. of *poule*, a hen. POULTRY.] A young chicken, partridge, grouse, etc.

poultice, pōl′tis, *n*. [From L. *puls, pultis*, pottage, gruel, pap.] A soft composition of meal, bread, or the like mollifying substance, to be applied to sores, inflamed parts of the body, etc.; a cataplasm.—*v.t.* —*poulticed, poulticing*. To cover with a poultice; to apply a poultice to.

poultry, pōl′tri, *n*. [A collective from *poult*, pullet, from Fr. *poulet*, a chicken, from *poule*, a hen, L. *pullus*, a young animal, a chicken; akin to Gr. *polos*, E. *foal*.] Domestic fowls which are reared for their flesh as an article of food, for their eggs, feathers, etc., such as cocks and hens, turkeys, ducks, and geese. —**poulterer,** pōl′tėr·ėr, *n.* One who makes it his business to sell fowls for the table.

pounce, pouns, *n.* [Fr. *ponce,* It. *pomice;* from L. *pumex, pumicis,* a pumice stone.] A fine powder, such as pulverized cuttlefish bone, used to prevent ink from spreading on paper, but now almost entirely superseded by blotting paper.—*v.t.* —*pounced, pouncing.* To sprinkle or rub with pounce.

pounce, pouns, *n.* [Ultimately from L. *pungo, punctum,* to prick or pierce; comp. Fr. *poinçon,* a bodkin; Sp. *punzar,* to prick, to pierce. PUNC-TURE, PUNCH, POINT.] The claw or talon of a bird of prey.—*v.t.* *pounced, pouncing.* To seize or strike suddenly with the claws or talons: said of birds of prey.—*v.i.* To fall on and seize with the claws or talons; to dart or dash on: with *on* or *upon.*

pound, pound, *n.* [A.Sax., Dan., Sw., Icel., and Goth. *pund;* G. *pfund;* from L. *pondo,* a pound, akin to L. *pondus,* a weight. PONDEROUS, PENDANT.] A standard weight consisting of 12 ounces troy, or 16 ounces avoirdupois; the British monetary unit consisting of 20 shillings. The *pound Scots* was only equal to a twelfth of the pound sterling, that is 1*s.* 8*d.*—**poundage,** poun′dij, *n.* A sum deducted from a pound, or a certain sum or rate per pound; payment rated by the weight of a commodity.—**poundal,** poun′dal, *n.* In *physics,* the unit of force, equal to the force which in one second produces in one pound a velocity of one foot per second.—**pounder,** poun′dėr, *n.* A person or thing denominated from a certain number of pounds; often applied to pieces of ordnance along with a number to express the weight of the shell they fire (a 64-*pounder,* a cannon firing shells weighing 64 lbs.).

pound, pound, *n.* [A.Sax. *pund,* an enclosure; a different form of *pond.*] An enclosure in which cattle are confined when taken in trespassing, or going at large in violation of law; a penfold or pinfold.—*v.t.* To shut up as in a pound; to confine in a public penfold; to impound.—**pound-age,** poun′dij, *n.* Confinement of cattle in a pound; a mulct levied upon the owners of cattle impounded.

pound, pound, *v.t.* [A.Sax. *punian,* to beat, bray; the *d* has become attached, as in *sound, compound.* Hence *pun.*] To beat; to strike repeatedly with some heavy instrument; to comminute and pulverize by beating; to bruise or break into fine parts by a heavy instrument.— **pounder,** poun′dėr, *n.* One who or that which pounds.

pour, pōr, *v.t.* [Perhaps from W. *bwrw,* to cast, to shed, as in *bwrw dagrau,* to shed tears; *bwrw gwlaw,* to rain.] To cause to flow, as a liquid, either out of a vessel or into it; to send forth in a stream or continued succession; to emit; to give vent to, as under the influence of strong feeling; to throw in profusion.—*v.i.*

To flow; to issue forth in a stream; to gush; to rush in continued pro-cession.—**pourer,** pō′rėr, *n.* One who or that which pours.

poussette, pö·set′, *n.* [Comp. Fr. *poussette,* a child's game with pins, from *pousser,* to push.] A figure executed by a couple who swing together in a country-dance.—*v.i.* *poussetted, poussetting.* To swing round in couples, as in a country-dance.

pout, pout, *v.i.* [From W. *pwtiaw,* to push, or from dial. Fr. *pout, potte,* Pr. *pot,* the lip.] To thrust out the lips, as in sullenness, contempt, or displeasure; hence, to look sullen; to swell out, as the lips; to be prom-inent.—*n.* A protrusion of the lips as in sullenness; a fit of sullenness.— **pouter,** pout′ėr, *n.* One who pouts; a variety of pigeon, so called from its inflated breast.

poverty, pov′ėr·ti, *n.* [Fr. *pauvreté,* L. *paupertas,* from *pauper,* poor. POOR.] The state of being poor or indigent; indigence; a deficiency of necessary or desirable elements; bar-renness (*poverty* of soil); poorness; want of ideas or information; want or defect of words (*poverty* of lan-guage).

poverty-stricken, *a.* Reduced to a state of poverty; indigent.

powder, pou′dėr, *n.* [Fr. *poudre,* O.Fr. *pouldre,* It. *polvēre,* from L. *pulvis, pulveris,* dust, powder.] Any dry substance composed of minute particles; a substance comminuted or triturated to fine particles; gun-powder; face powder.—*v.t.* To re-duce to fine particles; to pulverize; to sprinkle with powder or as with powder; to sprinkle with salt, as meat.—*v.i.* To fall to dust; to become like powder; to pat or rub powder on the face.—**powder blue,** *n.* Powdered smalt, as generally used in laundering; pale blue blended with gray.—**powder flask,** *n.* A flask in which gunpowder is carried.— **powder horn,** *n.* A horn in which gunpowder used to be carried by sportsmen before the introduction of cartridges.—**powder mill,** *n.* A mill in which gunpowder is made.— **powder room,** *n.* The apartment in a ship where gunpowder is kept.— **powdery,** pou′dėr·i, *a.* Sprinkled or covered with powder; resembling powder; *bot.* having a surface covered with fine powder.

power, pou′ėr, *n.* [O.Fr. *pooir* (Mod. Fr. *pouvoir*), from old infinitive *podir,* from L.L. *potēre,* to be able, used for L. *posse,* to be able, from *potis,* able, and *esse,* to be; akin *possible, potent,* etc. POTENT.] Ability to act; the faculty of doing or performing something; that in virtue of which one can; capability of producing an effect; strength, force, or energy manifested in action; capacity; sus-ceptibility (great *power* of resistance); natural strength; animal strength; influence; predominance (as of the mind, imagination); faculty of the mind as manifested by a particular mode of operation (the *power* of thinking); ability; capability; the

employment of strength or influence among men; command; the right of governing or actual government; dominion; rule; authority; one who or that which exercises authority or control (the *powers* that be); a sov-ereign, or the sovereign authority of a state; a state (the great *powers* of Europe); a spirit or superhuman agent having a certain sway (celestial *powers*); legal authority; warrant; *mech.* that which produces motion or force, or that which may be applied to produce it; a mechanical agent; the moving force applied to produce the required effect; mechanical ad-vantage or effect; force or effect considered as resulting from the action of a machine; rate of doing work; the unit for practical purposes in the U. S. is HORSEPOWER (which see); *arith.* and *alg.* the product arising from the multiplication of a number or quantity into itself; *optics,* the degree to which an optical instrument magnifies the apparent dimensions of an object.—*Power of attorney,* authority given to a person to act for another. See ATTORNEY.— *European powers,* a term in modern diplomacy by which are usually meant Great Britain, France, Ger-many, Russia, and Italy.—**powerful,** pou′ėr·fṳl, *a.* Having great power; able to produce great effects; strong; potent; energetic; efficacious.—**pow-erfully,** pou′ėr·fṳl·li, *adv.* In a pow-erful manner; with great effect; forcibly.—**powerless,** pou′ėr·les, *a.* Destitute of power; weak; impotent. —**powerlessly,** pou′ėr·les·li, *adv.* In a powerless manner.—**powerless-ness,** pou′ėr·les·nes, *n.*—**power plant,** *n.* A plant, including buildings and machines, for the generation of power; a device for supplying power for a mechanical operation or proc-ess; a powerhouse.

powwow, pou′wou, *n.* [Algonquian.] A medicine-man among the North American Indians; also, a public feast, festival, or conference.—*v.i.* To confer.

pox, poks, *n.* [A peculiar spelling of *pocks,* pl. of *pock.*] A disease charac-terized by pustules, as the smallpox, chicken pox; syphilis.

pozzuolana, pozzolana, pot′zṳ·o-lä′na, pot·zo·lä′na, *n.* A volcanic product occurring near *Pozzuoli,* on the Gulf of Naples, largely employed in the manufacture of Roman or hydraulic cement.

practicable, prak′ti·ka·bl, *a.* [From L.L. *practicare,* to transact, from L. *practicus,* active; Gr. *praktikos,* active, practical, from *prassō,* to do, to work.] Capable of being effected or performed by human means, or by powers that can be applied; feasible; capable of being passed or traveled over; passable; assailable. —**practicability, practicableness,** prak′ti·ka·bil″i·ti, prak′ti·ka·bl·nes, *n.* The quality of being practicable; feasibility.—**practicably,** prak′ti·ka-bli, *adv.* In a practicable manner.— **practical,** prak′ti·kal, *a.* [L. *prac-ticus.*] Relating to practice, use, or employment: opposed to *speculative, ideal,* or *theoretical;* that may be turned to use; reducible to use in the conduct of life; given to or concerned with action or practice; capable of reducing knowledge or theories to actual use; educated by practice or experience; skilled in actual work (a *practical* gardener); derived from practice or experience. —*Practical joke*. See JOKE.—**practically,** prak'ti·kal·li, *adv.* In a practical manner; not merely theoretically; so far as actual results or effects are concerned; in effect.— **practicality,** prak·ti·kal'i·ti, *n.* The quality of being practical.—**practice,** prak'tis, *n.* [Formerly *practicke, practike,* from O.Fr. *practique,* from Gr. *praktikē,* practical knowledge.] A piece of conduct; a proceeding; a customary action; custom or habit; use or usage; state of being used; customary use; method or art of doing anything; actual performance (as opposed to *theory*); exercise of any profession (the *practice* of law); application of remedies; medical treatment of diseases; drill; exercise for instruction or discipline; skillful or artful management; stratagem; artifice: usually in a bad sense; a rule in arithmetic for expeditiously multiplying quantities expressed in different denominations.—**practice,** prak'tis, *v.t.*—*practiced, practicing.* [From the noun.] To do or perform frequently, customarily, or habitually; to use for instruction or discipline, or as a profession or art (to *practice* law or medicine); to put into practice; to perform; to do; to teach by practice; to accustom; to train.—*v.i.*—*practiced, practicing.* To perform certain acts frequently or customarily, for instruction, profit, or amusement; to form a habit of acting in any manner; to use artifices or stratagems; to exercise some profession, as that of medicine or of law. —**practiced,** prak'tist, *p.* and *a.* Skilled through practice.—**practicer,** prak'tis·er, *n.* One that practices.— **practitioner,** prak·tish'on·er, *n.* One who is engaged in the exercise of any art or profession, particularly in law or medicine.—*A general practitioner,* one who practices both medicine and surgery.

praedial, prē'di·al, *a.* See PREDIAL.

praemunire, prē·mū·nī'rē, *n.* [A corruption of L. *praemonere,* to preadmonish, from the words of the writ.] *Law,* a name given to a species of writ, to the offense for which it is granted, and also to the penalty it incurs, this penalty being forfeiture of goods and imprisonment, and being attached in former times to the offenses of asserting the jurisdiction of the pope, denying the sovereign's supremacy, etc.

praetexta, prē·teks'ta, *n.* [L., from *prae,* before, on the edge, and *textus,* woven.] Among the ancient Romans, a white robe with a narrow scarlet border worn by a youth; the white outer garment bordered with purple of the higher magistrates.

praetor, prē'tor, *n.* [L., from *prae,* before, and *eo,* I go.] In ancient Rome, a title originally of the con-

suls, in later times of two important magistrates of the city, and lastly of a number of magistrates who administered justice in the state.— **praetorial, praetorian,** prē·tō'ri·al, prē·tō'ri·an, *a.* Belonging to a praetor.—*Praetorian bands* or *guards,* bodies of troops originally formed by the emperor Augustus to protect his person and his power, and afterward long maintained by successive Roman emperors; the household troops or bodyguards of the emperors.—*n.* A soldier of the Praetorian guard.

pragmatic, pragmatical, prag·mat'ik, prag·mat'i·kal, *a.* [L. *pragmaticus,* Gr. *pragmatikos,* from *pragma,* business, from *prassō,* I do. PRACTICE.] Skilled in business‡; active or diligent‡; forward to intermeddle; impertinently busy or officious in the concerns of others.—*The pragmatic sanction,* the instrument by which the German emperor Charles VI, being without male issue, endeavored to secure the succession for his female descendants.—**pragmatically,** prag·mat'i·kal·li, *adv.* In a pragmatic manner; impertinently. — **pragmatism,** prag'ma·tizm, *n.* A nonspeculative system of philosophy, which regards the practical consequences and useful results of ideas as the test of their truthfulness, and which considers truth itself to be a process; especially the modern form of this philosophy, introduced by C. S. Pierce and William James.— **pragmatist,** prag'ma·tist, *n.*

prairie, prā'ri, *n.* [Fr., from L.L. *prataria,* from L. *pratum,* a meadow.] The extensive, mostly level tracts of land of the Middle West, including the Great Plains from the Mississippi to the Rockies, usually treeless and covered with coarse grass and flowering plants.—**prairie dog,** *n.* A small burrowing rodent allied to the marmot.—**prairie schooner,** *n.* A long, canvas-topped wagon used by settlers to cross the prairies.— **prairie wolf,** *n.* The coyote.

praise, prāz, *n.* [Formerly *preis, preys,* praise, price, value, from O.Fr. *pris, preis,* price, honor (Mod.Fr. *prix*), from L. *pretium,* price, value, reward; the same as *price* and to *prize.*] Commendation bestowed on a person; approbation; eulogy; laud; a joyful tribute of gratitude or homage paid to the Divine Being, often expressed in song; the ground or reason of praise; what makes a person worthy of praise. — *v.t.* — *praised, praising.* To commend; to applaud; to express approbation of; to extol in words or song; to laud or magnify, especially applied to the Divine Being.—**praiseless,** prāz'les, *a.* Without praise or commendation.— **praiser,** prā'zer, *n.* One who praises; a commender.—**praiseworthy,** prāz'wer·THi, *a.* Worthy or deserving of praise; commendable.—**praiseworthily,** prāz'wer·THi·li, *adv.* In a manner deserving of commendation. —**praiseworthiness,** prāz'wer·THi·nes, *n.* The quality of being praiseworthy.

Prakrit, prä'krit, *n.* [Skr. *prâkriti,* nature, hence that which is natural or vulgar.] A Hindu language or dialect based on the Sanskrit, and which has been the mother of various modern dialects.

prance, prans, *v.i.*—*pranced, prancing.* [A slightly different form of *prank.*] To spring or bound, as a horse in high mettle; to ride ostentatiously; to strut about in a showy manner or with warlike parade.— **prancer,** prans'er, *n.* A prancing horse.

prandial, pran'di·al, *a.* [L. *prandium,* dinner.] Relating to a dinner, or meal in general.

prank, prangk, *v.t.* [Allied to D. *pronk,* finery, *pronken,* to strut; Dan. *prange,* G. *prangen, prunken,* to make a show; comp. also G. *pracht,* D. and Dan. *pragt,* pomp.] To adorn in a showy manner; to dress up.—*v.i.* To have a showy or gaudy appearance.— *n.* A gambol or caper; a playful or sportive action; a merry trick; a mischievous act, generally rather for sport than injury.—**prankish,** prangk'ish, *a.* Full of pranks.

prase, prāz, *n.* [Fr., from Gr. *prason,* a leek.] A species of quartz of a leek-green color.

praseodymium, prā'zi·o·dim''i·um, *n.* [Gr. *prasios,* leek-green, and *didymium.*] A silvery-white metallic element of the rare-earth series. Symbol, Pr; at. no., 59; at. wt., 140.907.

prate, prāt, *v.i.*—*prated, prating.* [Same as L.G. *praten,* Dan. *prate;* probably of imitative origin.] To talk much and without weight; to chatter; to babble.—*v.t.* To utter foolishly.—*n.* Continued talk to little purpose; unmeaning loquacity. —**prater,** prā'ter, *n.* One that prates. —**prating,** prā'ting, *p.* and *a.* Given to prate; loquacious.—**pratingly,** prā'ting·li, *adv.* In a prating manner.

pratincole, prat'in·kōl, *n.* [From L. *pratum,* a meadow, and *incola,* an inhabitant.] A graceful bird of a genus akin to the plovers, inhabiting the temperate and warmer parts of Europe, Africa, and Asia.

pratique, pra·tēk', *n.* [Fr. *pratique,* practice, intercourse. PRACTICE.] A license to a ship to hold intercourse and trade with the inhabitants of a place, after having performed quarantine: a term used particularly in the European ports of the Mediterranean.

prattle, prat'l, *v.i.*—*prattled, prattling.* [Freq. and dim. of *prate.*] To talk much and idly; to be loquacious on trifling subjects; to talk like a child.—*n.* Puerile or trifling talk.— **prattler,** prat'ler, *n.* One who prattles.

prawn, pran, *n.* [Etym. unknown.] A small crustaceous animal of the shrimp family, highly prized for food.

praxis, prak'sis, *n.* [Gr., from *prassō,* I do. PRACTICE.] Use; practice; especially, practice or discipline for a specific purpose, as to acquire a specific art; an example or form to teach practice.

pray, prā, *v.i.* [O.Fr. *preier* (Fr. *prier*),

It. *pregare*, to pray, from L. *precari*, to pray (as in *deprecate*, *imprecate*), from *prex*, a prayer (whence also *precarious*); same root as Skr. *prach*, to demand, A.Sax. *frignan*, G. *fragen*, to inquire.] To ask something with earnestness or zeal; to supplicate; to beg (to *pray* for mercy); to make petition to the Supreme Being; to address the Supreme Being with confession of sins and supplication for benefits.—*Pray*, elliptically for *I pray you tell me*, is a common mode of introducing a question.—*v.t.* To make earnest request to; to entreat; to address with a prayer for something such as God may grant; to ask earnestly for; to beseech; to petition. —**prayer**, prā'er, *n.* One who prays.

prayer, prā'er or prâr, *n.* [Not directly from *pray*, but from O.Fr. *proiere*, Fr. *prière*, a prayer, from L.L. *precaria*, a prayer, from L. *precarius*, obtained by begging. PRAY, PRECARIOUS.] The act of asking for a favor with earnestness; a petition, supplication, entreaty; a solemn petition for benefits addressed to the Supreme Being; the words of a supplication; a formula of church service or of worship, public or private; that part of a petition to a public body which specifies the thing desired to be done or granted.— **prayer book**, *n.* A book containing prayers, used by various churches.— **prayerful**, prâr'ful or prâr'ful, *a.* Devotional; given to prayer.—**prayer meeting**, *n.* A meeting for prayer; usually a mid-week devotional service.—**prayer wheel**, *n.* Lamaism. An apparatus used mainly in Tibet; one of the commoner forms consists of a wheel to which a written prayer is attached, and each revolution of the wheel made by the devotee counts as an utterance of the prayer.

preach, prēch, *v.i.* [O.Fr. *precher* (Fr. *prêcher*), from L. *praedicare*, to declare in public—*prae*, before, and *dico*, *dicatum*, I proclaim; closely akin to *dico*, *dictum*, I say. DICTION.] To pronounce a public discourse on a religious subject, or from a text of Scripture; to deliver a sermon; to give earnest advice; to discourse in the manner of a preacher.—*v.t.* To proclaim; to publish in religious discourses; to inculcate in public discourse; to deliver (a sermon).— **preacher**, prēch'er, *n.* One who preaches.—**preachify**, prēch'i·fī, *v.i.* To give a long-winded moral advice. —**preachment**, prēch'ment, *n.* A discourse affectedly solemn: in contempt.

preamble, prē'am·bl, *n.* [Fr. *préambule*, from L. *prae*, before, and *ambulo*, I go about. AMBLE.] The introductory part of a discourse, statute, or written instrument, as the Constitution, usually beginning with *Whereas* and stating the nature and intent of the document.—*v.t.*—*preambled*, *preambling*. To preface; to introduce with previous remarks.

prebend, prē'bend, *n.* [Fr. *prébende*, from L.L. *praebenda*, things to be supplied, from L. *praebeo*, to give, grant, furnish—*prae*, and *habeo*, to

have. HABIT.] The stipend granted to a canon of a cathedral or collegiate church out of its estate.— **prebendal**, pri·ben'dal, *a.* Pertaining to a prebend.—**prebendary**, prē'-ben·de·ri, *n.* An ecclesiastic who enjoys a prebend; a canon.

Pre-Cambrian, prē·kam'bri·an, *n.* [L. *pre*, before, *Cambrian*.] The oldest known strata.

precarious, pri·kā'ri·us, *a.* [L. *precarius*, primarily, depending on request, or on the will of another, from *precor*, I pray. PRAY, PRAYER.] Depending on or held at the will or pleasure of another; hence, held by a doubtful tenure; depending on unknown or unforeseen causes or events.—**precariously**, pri·kā'ri·us·li, *adv.* In a precarious manner.— **precariousness**, pri·kā'ri·us·nes, *n.* The state of being precarious.

precative, **precatory**, prek'a·tiv, prek'a·to·ri, *a.* [From L. *precor*, I pray. PRAY.] Suppliant; beseeching.

precaution, pri·kạ'shon, *n.* [L. *praecautio*, from *praecautus*—*prae*, before, and *caveo*, *cautum*, I take care. CAUTION.] Previous caution or care; a measure taken beforehand to ward off evil or secure good.—*v.t.* To warn or advise beforehand, for preventing mischief.—**precautionary**, pri·kạ'shon·a·ri, *a.* Containing previous caution; proceeding from precaution.

precede, pri·sēd', *v.t.*—*preceded*, *preceding*. [L. *praecedo*—*prae*, before, and *cedo*, I move. CEDE.] To go before in the order of time; to be previous to; to go before in place, rank, or importance.—**precedence**, **precedency**, pri·sē'dens, pri·sē'den·si, *n.* The act or state of preceding or going before; priority in time; the state of being before in rank or dignity; the right to a more honorable place; order or adjustment of place according to rank; the foremost place in a ceremony; superior importance or influence.—**precedent**, pri·sē'dent, *a.* Going before in time; anterior; antecedent.—**precedent**, pres'e·dent, *n.* Something done or said that may serve or be adduced as an example or rule to be followed in a subsequent act of the like kind; *law*, a judicial decision, which serves as a rule for future decisions in similar or analogous cases.

precentor, pri·sen'ter, *n.* [L.L. *praecentor*—L. *prae*, before, and *cantor*, a singer, from *cano*, *cantum*, I sing. CHANT.] The leader of the choir in a cathedral, usually a minor canon; a person whose duty it is to lead the psalmody of a Presbyterian or other congregation.—**precentorship**, pri·sen'ter·ship, *n.* The office of a precentor.

precept, prē'sept, *n.* [Fr. *précepte*, L. *praeceptum*, from *praecipio*, I teach, instruct—*prae*, before, and *capio*, to take. CAPABLE.] A commandment intended as an authoritative rule of action; a command respecting moral conduct; an injunction; *law*, a mandate in writing sent by a justice of the peace, etc., for bringing a person, record, etc., before him.—**precep-**

tive, pri·sep'tiv, *a.* [L. *praeceptivus*.] Giving or containing precepts for the regulation of conduct; admonitive; instructive.—**preceptor**, pri·sep'ter, *n.* [L. *praeceptor*.] A teacher; an instructor; the head of a preceptory among the Knights Templars.— **preceptorial**, pri·sep·tō'ri·al, *a.* Pertaining to a preceptor.—**preceptory**, pri·sep'to·ri, *a.* Giving precepts.—*n.* A subordinate religious house where instruction was given; an establishment of the Knights Templars, the superior of which was called knight preceptor.—**preceptress**, pri·sep'-tres, *n.* A female teacher or preceptor.

precession, pri·sesh'on, *n.* [Fr. *précession*, from L. *praecedo*, *praecessum*, I precede. PRECEDE.] The act of going before or forward.—*Precession of the equinoxes*, an astronomical phenomenon consisting in a slow movement of the equinoctial points around the ecliptic.

precinct, prē'singt, *n.* [From L. *praecingo*, *praecinctum*, I encompass— *prae*, before, and *cingo*, to gird. CINCTURE.] The boundary line encompassing a place; a limit; a part near a border; a district within certain boundaries; a minor territorial division.

precious, presh'us, *a.* [Fr. *précieux*, from L. *pretiosus*, from *pretium*, price. PRAISE.] Of great price; costly; of great value or worth; very valuable; much esteemed; highly cherished; ironically, very great; rascally (a *precious* villain).—*Precious metals*, gold and silver.—*Precious stones*, jewels, gems.—**preciously**, presh'-us·li, *adv.* In a precious manner; at a great cost.—**preciousness**, presh'us·-nes, *n.*

precipice, pres'i·pis, *n.* [Fr. *précipice*, from L. *praecipitium*, a falling headlong, a precipice, from *praeceps*, headlong—*prae*, forward, and *caput*, head. CHIEF.] A headlong declivity; a bank or cliff extremely steep, or quite perpendicular or overhanging. —**precipitate**, pri·sip'i·tāt, *v.t.*—*precipitated*, *precipitating*. [L. *praecipito*, from *praeceps*, headlong.] To throw headlong; to cast down from a precipice or height; to urge or press with eagerness or violence; to hasten (to *precipitate* one's flight); to hurry blindly or rashly; to throw or cause to sink to the bottom of a vessel, as a substance in solution.— *v.i.* To fall to the bottom of a vessel, as sediment or any substance in solution.—*a.* Falling, flowing, or rushing with steep descent; headlong; overhasty; rashly hasty; adopted with haste or without due deliberation; hasty; hurried; headlong.—*n.* *Chem.* any matter which, having been dissolved in a fluid, falls to the bottom of the vessel on the addition of some other substance capable of producing a decomposition of the compound. ∴ Substances which fall or settle down, as earthy matter in water, are called *sediments*, the operating cause being mechanical and not chemical.—**precipitately**, pri·sip'i·tāt·li, *adv.* In a headlong or

precipitate manner; too hastily.—
precipitance, precipitancy, pri·sip´-
i·tans, pri·sip´i·tan·si, n. The quality
of being precipitate; rash haste;
haste in resolving, forming an opinion, or executing a purpose.—
precipitant, pri·sip´i·tant, a. [L.
praecipitans, praecipitantis, ppr. of
praecipito.] Falling or rushing headlong; precipitate.—n. Chem. a substance which, when added to a
solution, separates what is dissolved
and makes it fall to the bottom in a
concrete state.—**precipitantly,** pri·
sip´i·tant·li, adv. In a precipitant
manner.—**precipitation,** pri·sip´i·
tā˝shon, n. The act of precipitating,
or state of being precipitated; a
falling or rushing down with violence
and rapidity; rash, tumultuous haste;
chem. the process by which any substance is made to separate from
another or others in a solution, and
fall to the bottom.—**precipitin,** pri·
sip´it·in, n. [From *precipitate.*] A
substance formed in the blood that
precipitates disease material and
renders it harmless.—**precipitous,**
pri·sip´i·tus, a. [L. *praeceps, prae-
cipitis,* headlong.] Very steep; like
or forming a precipice; headlong in
descent.—**precipitously,** pri·sip´i·
tus·li, adv. In a precipitous manner.
—**precipitousness,** pri·sip´i·tus·nes,
n. Steepness of descent.
précis, prā·sē´, n. [Fr. *précis,* precise,
also an abstract. PRECISE.] A concise
or abridged statement; a summary;
an abstract.
precise, pri·sīs´, a. [L. *praecisus,* from
praecido, to cut off—*prae,* before, and
caedo, to cut (as in *concise, excision*).]
Sharply or exactly limited or defined
as to meaning; exact; definite; not
loose, vague, or equivocal; exact in
conduct; strict; formal; nice; punctilious.—**precisely,** pri·sīs´li, adv. In
a precise manner; exactly; accurately; with excess of formality.—
preciseness, pri·sīs´nes, n. Exactness; rigid nicety; excessive regard
to forms or rules; rigid formality.—
precisian, pri·sizh´an, n. An over-
precise person; one ceremoniously
exact in the observance of rules.—
precisianism, pri·sizh´an·izm, n.
The conduct of a precisian; excessive
exactness.—**precision,** pri·sizh´on, n.
The state of being precise as to
meaning; preciseness; exactness; accuracy.
preclude, pri·klūd´, v.t.—*precluded,
precluding.* [L. *praecludo—prae,* before, and *cludo, claudo,* to shut.
CLOSE, v.t.] To shut up; to stop; to
impede; to hinder; to hinder or
render inoperative by anticipative
action.—**preclusion,** pri·klū´zhon, n.
The act of precluding.—**preclusive,**
pri·klū´siv, a. Tending to preclude;
hindering by previous obstacles.—
preclusively, pri·klū´siv·li, abv. In
a preclusive manner.
precocious, pri·kō´shus, a. [Fr. *pré-
coce,* from L. *praecox, praecocis,* ripe
early, precocious—*prae,* before, and
coquo, to cook, to ripen. COOK.]
Ripe before the proper or natural
time‡; ripe in understanding at an
early period; developed or matured

early in life.—**precociously,** pri·
kō´shus·li, adv. In a precocious manner.—**precociousness, precocity,**
pri·kō´shus·nes, pri·kos´i·ti, n. The
state or quality of being precocious;
early development of the mental
powers.
precognition, prē·kog·nish´on, n. [L.
prae, before, and *cognitio,* knowledge.]
Previous knowledge or cognition;
Scots law, a preliminary examination
of a witness or witnesses to a criminal
act, in order to know whether there
is ground of trial.
preconceive, prē·kon·sēv´, v.t.—*preconceived, preconceiving.* To form a
conception or opinion of beforehand;
to form a previous notion or idea of.
—**preconception,** prē·kon·sep´shon,
n. The act of preconceiving; conception or opinion previously formed.
preconcert, prē·kon·sėrt´, v.t. To
concert beforehand; to settle by
previous agreement.—n. (prē·kon´-
sėrt). A previous agreement.
preconize, praeconize, prē´kon·īz,
v.t. [L. *praeco,* a public crier.] To
summon or proclaim publicly; to
bestow excessive praise.
precontract, prē·kon´trakt, n. A contract or agreement previous to another.—v.t. and i. (prē·kon·trakt´).
To contract or stipulate previously.
precursor, pri·kėr´sėr, n. [L. *prae-
cursor—prae,* before, and *cursor,* a
runner, from *curro, cursum,* I run.
CURRENT.] A forerunner; a harbinger;
one who or that which precedes an
event and indicates its approach.—
precursory, pri·kėr´so·ri, a. Preceding as the harbinger; forerunning.—
precursive, pri·kėr´siv, a. Precursory.
predaceous, pri·dā´shus, a. [From
L. *praeda,* prey, spoil, plunder, etc.
PREY.] Living by prey; given to prey
on other animals.—**predatory,** pred´-
a·to·ri, a. [L. *praedatorius.*] Plundering; pillaging; practicing rapine.
predate, prē·dāt´, v.t.—*predated, pre-
dating.* To date by anticipation; to
antedate.
predecease, prē·di·sēs´, v.t.—*prede-
ceased, predeceasing.* To die before.—
n. The decease of one before another.
predecessor, pre·di·ses´ėr, n. [L.
praedecessor—prae, before, and *deces-
sor,* one who retires, from *decedo,
decessum,* I depart—*de,* from, and
cedo, to go. CEDE.] One who precedes or goes before another in some
position; one who has preceded
another in any state, position, office,
or the like.
predestinate, prē·des´ti·nāt, v.t.—
predestinated, predestinating. [L. *prae-
destino, prdestinatum—prae,* before,
and *destino,* I determine. DESTINE.]
To predetermine or foreordain; to
appoint or ordain beforehand by an
unchangeable purpose.—a. Predestinated; foreordained.—**predestina-
rian,** pri·des´ti·nā˝ri·an, a. Belonging to predestination.—n. One who
believes in the doctrine of predestination.—**predestinarianism,** pri·des´-
ti·nā˝ri·an·izm, n. The system or
doctrines of the predestinarians.—
predestination, prē·des´ti·nā˝shon, n.
The act of decreeing or foreordaining

events; especially, *theol.* the doctrine
that God has from eternity un-
changeably appointed or determined
whatever comes to pass; particularly
that he has preordained men to
everlasting happiness or misery.—
predestine, pri·des´tin, v.t.—*predestined, predestining.* To decree beforehand; to foreordain.
predetermine, prē·di·tėr´min, v.t.—
predetermined, predetermining. To determine beforehand; to doom by
previous decree.—v.i. To make a
determination beforehand.—**predetermination,** prē·di·tėr´mi·nā˝shon.
n. Previous determination; purpose
formed beforehand.
predial, prē´di·al, a. [Fr. *prédial,*
from L. *praedium,* a farm or estate.]
Consisting of land or farms; landed;
attached to land; derived from land
(*predial* tithes).
predicable, pred´i·ka·bl, a. [L. *praedi-
cabilis,* from *praedico.* PREDICATE.]
Capable of being affirmed of something; that may be attributed to
something.—n. Anything that may
be predicated or affirmed of another;
logic, one of the five things which
can be affirmatively predicated of
several others, viz. genus, species,
difference, property, and accident.—
predicability, pred´i·ka·bil˝i·ti, n.
The quality of being predicable.—
predicament, pri·dik˝a·ment, n. [L.
L. *praedicamentum.*] *Logic,* one of
those general heads or most comprehensive terms under one or other
of which every other term may be
arranged, ten in number, according
to Aristotle, viz. substance, quantity,
quality, relation, action, passion,
time, place, situation, and habit;
hence, class or kind described by
definite marks; condition; especially,
a dangerous or trying condition or
state.—**predicant,** pred´i·kant, a.
[L. *praedicans,* ppr. of *praedico.*] One
that affirms anything; a preaching
friar; a Dominican.—a. Predicating;
preaching.
predicate, pred´i·kāt, v.t.—*predicated, predicating.* [L. *praedicare, prae-
dicatum,* to affirm, to declare—*prae,*
before, and *dicare,* to declare.
PREACH.] To affirm as an attribute
of something (to *predicate* whiteness
of snow); to declare one thing of
another.—v.i. To make an affirmation.—n. *Logic,* that which, in a
proposition, is affirmed or denied
of the subject; *gram.* the word or
words in a proposition which express
what is affirmed or denied of the
subject.—**predication,** pred·i·kā´-
shon, n. The act of predicating;
affirmation; assertion.—**predicative,**
pred´i·kā·tiv, a. Expressing affirmation or predication.—**predicatory,**
pred´i·ka·to·ri, a. Affirmative; positive.
predict pri·dikt´, v.t, [L. *praedico,
praedictum—prae,* before, and *dicere,*
to tell. DICTION.] To foretell; to
prophesy; to declare to be or happen
in the future; to prognosticate.—
prediction, pri·dik´shon, n. The
act of predicting; a foretelling; a
prophecy.—**predictive,** pri·dik´tiv,
a. Foretelling; prophetic.

predigest, prē'di·jest, _v.t._ To assimilate or digest previously.

predilection, prē·di·lek'shon, _n._ [Fr. _prédilection_—L. _prae_, before, and _dilectio_, a choice, from _diligere_, to love. DILIGENT.] A previous liking; a prepossession of mind in favor of something.

predispose, prē·dis·pōz', _v.t._—_predisposed, predisposing._ To incline beforehand; to give a previous disposition or tendency to; to fit or adapt previously.—**predisposition**, prē·dis'pi·zish"on, _n._ The state of being previously disposed toward something; previous inclination or tendency; previous fitness or adaptation to any change, impression, or purpose.

predominate, pri·dom'i·nāt, _v.i._—_predominated, predominating._ [Fr. _prédominer_—L. _prae_, before, and _dominari_, to rule, from _dominus_, lord. DOMINATE, DAME.] To have surpassing power, influence, or authority; to have controlling influence among others.—_v.t._ To rule over; to master‡.—**predominance**, **predominancy**, pri·dom'i·nans, pri·dom'i·nan·si, _n._ Prevalence over others; superiority in power, influence, or authority; ascendency.—**predominant**, pri·dom'i·nant, _a._ Prevalent over others; superior in strength, influence, or authority; ruling; controlling.—**predominantly**, pri·dom'i·nant·li, _adv._ In a predominant manner.

pre-eminence, prē·em'i·nens, _n._ The state or quality of being notably eminent among others; superior or surpassing eminence; undoubted superiority, especially superiority in excellence.—**pre-eminent**, prē·em'i·nent, _a._ Eminent above others; surpassing or highly distinguished in excellence, sometimes also in evil. —**pre-eminently**, prē·em'i·nent·li, _adv._ In a pre-eminent manner or degree.

pre-empt, prē·empt', _v.t. and i._ To acquire before others; to claim before others establish rights, as to _pre-empt_ public lands.—**pre-emption**, prē·em'shon, _n._ [L. _prae_, before, and _emptio_, a buying, from _emo_, to buy. EXEMPT.] The act or right of purchasing before others; the right of a settler to the first chance of buying land in or near which he has settled. —**pre-emptive**, prē·em'tiv, _a._

preen, prēn, _v.t._ [O.E. _proine, proigne_, to prune, to preen. PRUNE.] To trim with the beak; to clean and dress: said of birds dressing their feathers.

pre-engage, prē·en·gāj', _v.t._—_pre-engaged, pre-engaging._ To engage by previous agreement; to engage or attach by previous influence; to preoccupy.

pre-establish, prē·es·tab'lish, _v.t._ To establish or settle beforehand.

pre-exist, prē·eg·zist', _v.i._ To exist beforehand or before something else.—**pre-existence**, prē·eg·zis'tens, _n._ Existence previous to something else; existence in a previous state; existence of the soul before its union with the body.—**pre-existent**, prē·eg·zis'tent, _a._ Existing beforehand;

preceding in existence.

prefabricate, prē·fab'ri·kāt, _v.t._ To make and standardize all the parts of a structure (such as a house) at a factory so that it may be rapidly assembled.

preface, pref'is, _n._ [Fr. _préface_, from L. _praefatio_—_prae_, before, and _fari, fatum_, to speak (whence also _fate, fame_).] Something spoken as introductory to a discourse, or written as introductory to a book or other composition.—_v.t._—_prefaced, prefacing._ To introduce by preliminary remarks.—**prefatory**, pref'a·to·ri, _a._ Having the character of a preface; pertaining to a preface.—**prefatorily**, pref'a·to·ri·li, _adv._ By way of preface.

prefect, prē'fekt, _n._ [L. _praefectus_, from _praeficio_—_prae_, before, and _facio_, I make. FACT.] A governor, commander, chief magistrate, or the like; a name common to several officers, military and civil, in ancient Rome; an important functionary in France; a préfet, that is, an official who presides over and has extensive powers in a department.—**prefecture**, prē'fek·chėr, _n._ The office or jurisdiction of a prefect; _prefecture_ is also the official residence of a prefect.

prefer, pri·fėr', _v.t._—_preferred, preferring._ [L. _praefero_, to carry before, to present, to esteem more highly—_prae_, before, and _ferre_, to bear or carry. FERTILE.] To offer for one's consideration or decision; to present; said especially of petitions, prayers, etc.; to advance, as to an office or dignity; to raise; to exalt; to set above something else in estimation; to hold in greater favor or esteem; to choose rather (to _prefer_ one _to_ another).—**preferable**, pref'ėr·a·bl, _a._ Worthy to be preferred; more eligible; more desirable.—**preferableness, preferability**, pref'ėr·a·bl·nes, pref'ėr·a·bil"i·ti, _n._ The quality or state of being preferable.—**preferably**, pref'ėr·a·bli, _adv._ In or by preference.—**preference**, pref'ėr·ens, _n._ The preferring of one thing before another; choice of one thing rather than another; higher place in esteem; the object of choice; choice.—**preferred stock**, pri·fėrd', _n._ A form of capital stock given preference in payment of dividends (or other rights) over common stock.—**preferential**, pref·ėr·en'shal, _a._ In a position to which some preference is attached.—**preferment**, pri·fėr'ment, _n._ Advancement to a higher office, dignity, or station; promotion; a superior or valuable place or office, especially in the church.—**preferrer**, pri·fėr'ėr, _n._ One who prefers.

prefigure, prē·fig'yėr, _v.t._—_prefigured, prefiguring._ To exhibit by antecedent representation or by types and similitudes.—**prefiguration**, prē·fig'ū·rā"shon, _n._ The act of prefiguring; an antecedent similitude.—**prefigurative**, prē·fig'ū·rā·tiv, _a._ Showing by previous figures, types, or similitudes.

prefix, prē·fiks', _v.t._ [Fr. _préfixer_, L. _praefigo, praefixus_—_prae_, before, and

figere, to fix. FIX.] To put or fix before or at the beginning of another thing (to _prefix_ a syllable to a word, an advertisement to a book); to settle, fix, or appoint beforehand (to _prefix_ the hour of meeting).—_n._ (prē'fiks.) A letter, syllable, or word put to the beginning of a word, usually to vary its signification.—**prefixion**, prē·fik'shon, _n._ The act of prefixing.

preformation, prē·for·mā'shon, _n._ The obsolete theory that development of an organism simply consists of increase in size. Cp. EPIGENESIS.

pregnable,† preg'na·bl, _a._ [Fr. _prenable_ (with inserted _g_), from _prendre_, to take, L. _prehendo, prehensum_. PREHENSILE.] Capable of being taken or won by force; expugnable.

pregnant preg'nant, _a._ [L. _praegnans, praegnantis_—_prae_, before, and _gnans_, ppr. corresponding to _gnatus, natus_, born. NATAL, NATURE.] Being with young; great with child; gravid; full of important matter; abounding with results; full of consequence or significance (a _pregnant_ argument). —**pregnancy**, preg'nan·si, _n._ The state of being pregnant; time of going with child; the quality of being full of significance, or the like.—**pregnantly**, preg'nant·li, _adv._ In a pregnant manner.

prehensile, pri·hen'sil, _a._ [L. _prehendere, prehensus_, to lay hold of—_prae_, before, and _hendere_, to seize, as _apprehend, comprehend_, etc. PRIZE, PRISON.] Capable of or adapted to seize or grasp (a monkey's _prehensile_ tail).—**prehension**, pri·hen'shon, _n._ A taking hold of; a seizing.

prehistoric, prē·his·tor'ik, _a._ Relating to a period antecedent to that at which history begins.

preinstruct, prē·in·strukt', _v.t._ To instruct previously or beforehand.

prejudge, prē·juj', _v.t._—_prejudged, prejudging._ [Fr. _préjuger._] To judge before hearing, or before the arguments and facts are fully known; to decide by anticipation; to condemn beforehand or unheard.—**prejudgment**, prē·juj'ment, _n._ The act of prejudging; judgment without a hearing or full examination.

prejudice, prej'ū·dis, _n._ [Fr. _préjudice_, from L. _praejudicium_, from _prae_, before, and _judicium_, a judgment, from _judex, judicis_, a judge. JUDGE.] A bias or leaning, favorable or unfavorable, without reason, or for some reason other than justice; a prepossession (when used absolutely generally with the unfavorable meaning of wrong or ignorant bias or view); mischief; damage; injury (without _prejudice_ to one's interests).—_v.t._—_prejudiced, prejudicing._ To implant a prejudice in the mind of; to bias by hasty and incorrect notions; to injure by prejudices; to hurt, damage, impair; to injure in general (to _prejudice_ one's cause).—**prejudicial**, prej·ū·dish'al, _a._ Hurtful; mischievous; injurious; detrimental.—**prejudicially**, prej·ū·dish'al·li, _adv._ In a prejudicial manner.

prelate, prel'at, _n._ [Fr. _prélat_, from L.L. _praelatus_, from L. _praelatus_, pp.

of *praefero, praelatum—prae*, before and *latus*, borne.] An ecclesiastic of the higher order having authority over the lower clergy, as an archbishop, bishop, or patriarch; a dignitary of the church.—**prelacy**, prel′a·si, *n*. Episcopacy; the system of church government by prelates; prelates collectively.—**prelatic**, pre·lat′ik, *a*. Pertaining to prelates or prelacy.—**prelatist**, prel′at·ist, *n*. An advocate for prelacy.

prelect, pri·lekt′, *v.i.* and *t*. [L. *praelego, praelectus—prae*, before, and *lego*, I read. LEGEND.] To read a lecture or discourse in public.—**prelection**, pri·lek′shon, *n*. A lecture or discourse read in public or to a select company.—**prelector**, pri·lek′tor, *n*. A reader of discourses; a lecturer.

prelibation, prē·li·bā′shon, *n*. [L. *prae*, before, and *libo*, to taste. LIBATION.] Foretaste; a tasting beforehand; an effusion or libation previous to tasting.

preliminary, pri·lim′i·ne·ri, *a*. [Fr. *préliminaire*—L. *prae*, before, and *limen*, threshold. LIMIT.] Introductory; preceding the main discourse or business; prefatory.—*n*. Something introductory or preparatory; something to be examined and determined before an affair can be treated of on its own merits; a preparatory act.—**preliminarily**, pri·lim′i·ne·ri·li, *adv*. In a preliminary manner.

prelude, prē′lūd or prel′ūd, *n*. [Fr. *prélude*, from L. *prae*, before, and *ludus*, play. LUDICROUS.] Something preparatory or leading up to what follows; an introductory performance; *music*, a short introductory strain preceding the principal movement. —*v.t.* (pri·lūd′) — *preluded, preluding*. To introduce with a prelude; to serve as prelude to.—*v.i.* To serve as a prelude.—**prelusive, prelusory**, pri·lū′siv, pri·lū′so·ri, *a*. Having the character of a prelude; introductory.—**prelusively, prelusorily**, pri·lū′siv·li, pri·lū′so·ri·li, *adv*. By way of prelude.

premature, prē′ma·tūr, *a*. [L. *praematurus—prae*, before, and *maturus*, ripe.] Happening, arriving, existing, performed, or adopted before the proper time; done, said, or believed too soon; too early; untimely.—**prematurely**, prē·ma·tūr′li, *adv*. In a premature manner. — **prematureness, prematurity**, prē·ma·tūr′nes, prē·ma·tū′ri·ti, *n*. The state of being premature.

premaxillary, prē·mak′sil·la·ri, *n*. *Anat*. a bone of the upper jaw on either side anterior to the true maxillary bone.

premedical, prē·med′i·kal, *a*. [L. *prae*, before, and *medical*.] Concerning studies preceding the study of medicine.

premeditate, prē·med′i·tāt, *v.t.*— *premeditated, premeditating*. [Fr. *préméditer*, L. *praemeditor—prae*, before, and *meditor*, I meditate.] To think on and revolve in the mind beforehand.—*v.i.* To meditate beforehand.—**premeditation**, prē·med′i·tā′shon, *n*. The act of premedi-

tating; *law*, preplanning of an act showing intent to commit it.

premier, pri·mir′, *a*. [Fr. *premier*, from L. *primarius*, of the first rank, from *primus*, first. PRIME.] First; chief; principal.—*n*. The first or chief minister of state.

première, pre·myär′, *n*. [Fr.] A first showing as of a play or movie.—*v.t.* To show a play or movie for the first time.

premise, pri·mīz′, *v.t.*—*premised, premising*. [From L. *praemitto, praemissum—prae*, before, and *mitto*, I send. MISSION.] To set forth or make known beforehand; to lay down as an antecedent proposition.—*v.i.* To make an antecedent statement.—*n*. prem′is. A proposition laid down as a base of argument; *logic*, the name applied to each of the two first propositions of a syllogism, from which the inference or conclusion is drawn; *pl*. the beginning or early portion of a legal deed or document where the subject matter is stated or described in full (lit. 'the things before mentioned'); hence, lands and houses or tenements; a house and the outhouses, etc., belonging to it.

premium, prē′mi·um, *n*. [L. *praemium*, a reward—*prae*, before, and *emo*, to take. PRE-EMPTION.] A reward or prize offered for some specific thing; a bonus; an extra sum paid as an incentive; a bounty; a fee paid for the privilege of being taught a trade or profession; a sum paid periodically to an office for insurance, as against fire or loss of life or property.—*At a premium*, above par, opposed to *at a discount*: said of shares or stock; hence, in high esteem.

premolar, prē·mō′ler, *n*. *Anat*. a tooth between the canine and the molars.

premonish, pri·mon′ish, *v.t.* [Prefix *pre*, and *-monish*, as in *admonish*.] To forewarn; to admonish beforehand.—**premonition**, prē·mo·nish′on, *n*. Previous warning, notice, or information.—**premonitory**, pri·mon′i·to·ri, *a*. Giving previous warning or notice.

premorse, pri·mors′, *a*. [L. *praemorsus—prae*, before, and *mordere*, to gnaw. MORDANT.] Bitten off; applied in *bot*. to a root or leaf terminating abruptly, as if bitten off.

prenatal, prē·nā′tl, *a*. [L. *prae*, before, and *natus*, born.] Before, or prior to, birth (*prenatal* care).—**prenatally**, pre·nā′tal·li, *adv*.

prenotion, prē·nō′shon, *n*. A notion which precedes something else in time; previous notion or thought.

prentice, pren′tis. A colloquial contraction of *Apprentice*.

preoccupy, prē·ok′kū·pī, *v.t.*—*preoccupied, preoccupying*. To occupy or take possession of before another; to engage or occupy the attention of beforehand; to engross beforehand.—**preoccupancy**, prē·ok′kū·pan·si, *n*. The act or right of taking possession before another.—**preoccupation**, prē·ok′kū·pā′shon, *n*. An occupation or taking possession be-

fore another.—**preoccupied**, prē·ok′kū·pīd, *p*. and *a*. Having the attention taken up previously; absorbed.

preordain, prē·or·dān′, *v.t.* To ordain or appoint beforehand; to predetermine.—**preordination**, prē·or′di·nā′shon, *n*. The act of foreordaining.

prepare, pri·pâr′, *v.t.*—*prepared, preparing*. [Fr. *préparer*, L. *praeparo, praeparatum—prae*, before, and *parare*, to get ready. PARE.] To fit, adapt, or qualify for a particular purpose; to put into such a state as to be fit for use or application; to make ready; often, with a personal object, to make ready for something that is to happen; to give notice to (to *prepare* a person for ill news or calamity); to provide; to procure as suitable (to *prepare* arms, ammunition, etc., for troops).—*v.i.* To make ready; to put things in suitable order; to take the necessary previous measures; to make one's self ready.—**preparation**, pre·pa·rā′shon, *n*. [L. *praeparatio*.] The act of preparing; that which is prepared for a particular purpose; a substance compounded or made up for a certain use; the state of being prepared or in readiness.—**preparative**, pri·par′a·tiv, *a*. [Fr. *préparatif*.] Tending or serving to prepare or make ready; preparatory. —*n*. That which is preparative or preparatory; that which is done to prepare.—**preparatory**, pri·par′a·to·ri, *a*. Serving to prepare the way for some proceeding to follow; introductory; preparative.—**preparedly**, pri·pârd′li, *adv*. With suitable previous measures.—**preparedness**, pri·pârd′nes, *n*. The state of being prepared.—**preparer**, pri·pâ′rer, *n*. One who or that which prepares.

prepay, prē·pā′, *v.t.*—*prepaid, preparing*. To pay before obtaining possession of; to pay in advance; to pay before the payment falls due.—**prepayment**, prē·pā′ment, *n*. Act of paying beforehand; payment in advance.

prepense, pri·pens′, *a*. [L. *praepensus—prae*, before, and *pendere, pensum*, to weigh. POISE.] Deliberated or devised beforehand; premeditated; aforethought; now scarcely used except in the phrase 'malice *prepense*'.

preponderate, pri·pon′der·āt, *v.t.*— *preponderated, preponderating*. [L. *praepondero, praeponderatum—prae*, before, and *ponderare*, to weigh, from *pondus, ponderis*, a weight. PONDER.] To outweigh; to have more weight or influence than.—*v.i.* To exceed in weight, influence, or power; to have the greater weight or influence; to have sway or power superior to others.—**preponderance, preponderancy**, pri·pon′der·ans, pri·pon′der·an·si, *n*. The state or quality of preponderating or being preponderant.—**preponderant**, pri·pon′der·ant, *a*. Outweighing; superior in power, influence, or the like.—**preponderantly, preponderatingly**, pri·pon′der·ant·li, pri·pon′der·ā·ting·li, *adv*. In a preponderant manner.—**preponderation,** prē·pon'-dér·ā"shon, *n.* The state of preponderating; preponderance.

preposition, prep·o·zish'on, *n.* [L. *praepositio.* POSITION.] *Gram.* a part of speech which is used to show the relation of one noun or pronoun to another in a sentence, and is usually placed before the word which expresses the object of the relation.—**prepositional,** prep·o·zish'on·al, *a.* Pertaining to or having the nature or function of a preposition.—**prepositionally,** prep·o·zish'on·al·li, *adv.* In a prepositional manner.—**prepositive,** prē·poz'i·tiv, *a.* Put before.—*n.* A word or particle put before another word.

prepossess, prē·poz·zes', *v.t.* To take previous possession of; to preoccupy the mind or heart of; to fill or imbue beforehand with some opinion or estimate; to prejudice. ∴ *Prepossess* is more frequently used in a good sense than *prejudice.*—**prepossessing,** prē·poz·zes'ing, *a.* Creating an impression favorable to the owner; engaging: said especially of the external characteristics of a person.—**prepossession,** prē·poz·zesh'on, *n.* Prior possession; a preconceived opinion; an impression on the mind in favor or against any person or thing, especially in favor.

preposterous, pri·pos'tér·us, *a.* [L. *praeposterus*—*prae,* before, and *posterus,* coming after. POSTERIOR.] Contrary to nature, reason, or common sense; utterly and glaringly foolish; totally opposed to the fitness of things; manifestly absurd.—**preposterously,** pri·pos'tér·us·li, *adv.* In a preposterous manner.—**preposterousness,** pri·pos'tér·us·nes, *n.* The state or quality of being preposterous; utter absurdity.

prepotent, prē·pō'tent, *a.* [L. *praepotens*—*prae,* before, and *potens,* powerful. POTENT.] Very powerful; having a superiority of power or influence.—**prepotency,** prē·pō'ten·si, *n.* Superior power; predominance.

prepuce, prē'pūs, *n.* [L. *praeputium,* the foreskin.] The foreskin.—**preputial,** pri·pū'shal, *a.* Pertaining to the prepuce.

Pre-Raphaelite, prē·raf'a·el·īt, *n.* One who practices or favors the system or style of painting practiced by the early painters before Raphael, or the modern revival of their style or system, said to be a rigidly faithful representation of natural forms and effects.—**Pre-Raphaelitism,** prē·raf'a·el·it·izm, *n.* The style or practice of the pre-Raphaelites.

prerequisite, prē·rek'wi·zit, *a.* Previously requisite; necessary to something subsequent.—*n.* Something that is prerequisite.

prerogative, pri·rog'a·tiv, *n.* [L. *praerogativa,* from *praerogo,* to ask before—*prae,* before, and *rogare,* to ask (as in *interrogate, arrogate, derogate,* etc.).] An exclusive or peculiar privilege; a privilege belonging to one in virtue of his character or position; an official and hereditary

right which may be asserted without question; a special right or privilege of a sovereign or other executive of a government; the name given to the century in the Roman Comitia that by lot was empowered to record its vote first, and so was believed to be divinely commissioned to determine the vote of the rest.

presage, pres'ij or prē'sāj, *n.* [Fr. *présage,* L. *praesagium*—*prae,* before, and *sagire,* to perceive by the senses; allied to *sagacious.*] Something which portends or foreshows a future event; a foreboding.—*v.t.* pris·āj'.—*presaged, presaging.* To forebode; to foreshow; to foretell, predict, prophesy.—*v.i.* To form or utter a prediction.—**presager,** prē·sā'jér, *n.* One who predicts.

presbyopia, pres·bi·ō'pi·a, *n.* [Gr. *presbys,* old, and *ōps,* the eye.] An imperfection of vision in which near objects are seen less distinctly than those at a distance, common in old age.—**presbyopic,** pres·bi·op'ik, *a.* Pertaining to presbyopia.

presbyter, pres'bi·tér, *n.* [L. *presbyter,* from Gr. *presbyteros,* compar. of *presbys,* old. *Priest* is the same word.] An elder or a person somewhat advanced in age, who had authority in the early Christian church; a priest; a parson.—**presbyterian,** pres·bi·tē'ri·an, *a.* Pertaining to a presbyter; pertaining to ecclesiastical government by presbyteries, or to those who uphold such government.—*n.* [*cap.*] A member of that section of the Christian church who vest church government in presbyteries or associations of ministers and elders, and have no bishops.—**presbyterial,** pres·bi·tē'ri·al, *a.* Presbyterian.—**presbyterianism,** pres·bi·tē'ri·an·izm, *n.* The doctrines, principles, and discipline or government of presbyterians.—**presbytery,** pres'bi·te·ri, *n.* Presbyterianism; a judicatory consisting of Presbyterian pastors of all the churches of any particular denomination within a given district, along with one ruling elder from each church session.

preschool, prē·sköl', *a.* [L. *prae,* before, and *school.*] Referring to the period before a child enters school.

prescient, prē'shi·ent, *a.* [L. *praesciens, praescientis,* ppr. of *praescio,* to foreknow—*prae,* before, and *scio,* to know. SCIENCE.] Foreknowing; having knowledge of events before they take place.—**prescience,** prē'shi·ens, *n.* [L. *prescientia.*] Foreknowledge; knowledge of events before they take place; foresight.

prescribe, pri·skrīb', *v.t.*—*prescribed, prescribing.* [L. *praescribo*—*prae,* before, and *scribere,* to write. SCRIBE.] To lay down authoritatively for direction; to give as a rule of conduct; *med.* to direct to be used as a remedy.—*v.i.* To lay down rules or directions; to dictate; to write or give medical directions; to direct what remedies are to be used; *law,* to become extinguished or of no validity through lapse of time, as a right, debt, obligation, and the like.

—**prescriber,** pri·skrī'bér, *n.* One that prescribes.—**prescript,** prē'-skript, *a.* Directed; set down as a rule; prescribed.—*n.* Direction; precept; model prescribed.—**prescriptible,** pri·skrip'ti·bl, *a.* Suitable for being prescribed; depending or derived from prescription.—**prescription,** pri·skrip'shon, *n.* The act of prescribing; what is prescribed; a direction; prescript; *med.* a written statement of the medicines or remedies to be used by a patient; a claim, right, or title based on long use or custom; the loss of a legal right by lapse of time and neglect.—**prescriptive,** pri·skrip'tiv, *a.* Consisting in or acquired by prescription.

presence. See PRESENT.

present, prez'ent, *a.* [L. *praesens, praesentis,* from *prae,* before, and *sens, esens,* being, an old participle of *sum,* I am; comp. *absent.*] Being in a certain place; opposed to *absent;* being before the face or near; being in company; done on the spot; instant; immediate (*present* death); being now in view or under consideration; now existing, or being at this time; not past or future; ready at hand; quick in emergency. —*The present,* an elliptical expression for *the present time.*—*At present,* elliptically for *at the present time.*—*Present tense, gram.* the tense or modification of a verb which expresses action or being in the present time.—*v.t.* (pri·zent'). [Fr. *présenter,* L. *praesentare,* to present, lit. to make present.] To place or introduce into the presence or before the face of, especially of a superior; to make known; to offer for acquaintance; to exhibit or offer to view or notice (*presented* a wretched appearance); to bestow; to make a gift or donation of; generally to give formally and ceremoniously; to bestow a gift upon; to favor with a donation (to *present* a person *with* a thing); to nominate to an ecclesiastical benefice; to lay before a public body for consideration, as before a legislature, court, etc. (to *present* a memorial or the like); to point, level, aim, as a weapon, particularly some species of firearms. —*To present arms* (*milit.*), to put the arms or guns in a perpendicular position in front of the body, as in saluting a superior officer, or in token of respect.—*n.* (prez'ent). That which is presented or given; a gift; *pl.* (from the adj.), a term used in a legal deed to signify the document itself.—**presence,** prez'-ens, *n.* [L. *praesentia.*] The state of being present; the existence of a person or thing in a certain place; opposed to *absence;* the being in company with; personal attendance; the state of being within sight or call; the state of being in view of a superior; the person of a superior, as a sovereign; mien; air; personal appearance; demeanor.—*Presence of mind,* coolness and readiness of invention or resource in occasions of difficulty; quickness in devising

expedients on pressing occasions.—
presence chamber, *n.* The room in
which a great personage receives
company.—**presentable,** pri•zen′-
ta•bl, *a.* Capable of being presented;
in such trim as to be able to present
one's self without embarrassment;
suitable to be exhibited or offered.—
presentation, prez•en•tā′shon, *n.*
The act of presenting, or state of
being presented; the act or right
of presenting a clergyman or nominating a minister to a vacant
parish.—**presentative,** pri•zen′ta•-
tiv, *a.* Serving to present; presenting;
metaph. applied to what may be
apprehended directly, or to the
faculty capable of apprehending
directly.—**presentee,** prez•en•tē′, *n.*
One presented to a benefice.—
presenter, pri•zen′tėr, *n.* One who
presents; one who leads or introduces.—**presentive,** pri•zen′tiv, *a.*
Gram. applied to words which
present a definite conception of an
object to the mind; opposed to
symbolic.—*n.* A presentive word.—
presentiveness, pri•zen′tiv•nes, *n.*—
presently, prez′ent•li, *adv.* In a little
time; soon; forthwith; immediately.
—**presentment,** pri•zent′ment, *n.*
The act of presenting or state of
being presented; representation or
portrait (*Shak.*).
presentiment, pri•zen′ti•ment, *n.*
[*Pre*, before, and *sentiment*; O.Fr.
presentiment, foreboding.] Previous
conception, sentiment, or opinion;
previous apprehension of something
future; anticipation of impending
evil; foreboding.
preserve, pri•zėrv′, *v.t.*—*preserved,*
preserving. [Fr. *préserver*, L.L. *prae-
servo*—L. *prae*, before, and *servo*,
I keep. SERVE.] To keep or save from
injury or destruction; to defend from
evil; to save; to keep in the same
state; to uphold, sustain, guard;
to save from decay; to cause to
remain good and wholesome for
food by treating with salt, sugar, or
otherwise (*preserved* meats or fruits);
to prevent being hunted and killed,
except at certain seasons or by certain
persons, as game, salmon, etc.—*v.i.*
To practice the art of seasoning
fruits, etc., for preservation; to protect game for purposes of sport.—*n.*
That which is preserved; fruit, etc.,
suitably seasoned, to keep from
decay; a place set apart for the
shelter and protection of game intended for sport.—**preserver,** pri•-
zėr′vėr, *n.* A person or thing that
preserves.—**preservable,** pri•zėr′va•-
bl, *a.* Capable of being preserved.
—**preservation,** prez•ėr•vā′shon, *n.*
The act of preserving; the state of
being preserved; escape from danger;
safety.— **preservative,** pri•zėr′va•-
tiv, *a.* Having the power of keeping
safe from injury, destruction, or
decay; tending to preserve.—*n.* That
which preserves or has the power
of preserving; something that is
preventive of injury or decay.
preside, pri•zīd′, *v.i.*—*presided, presiding.* [Fr. *présider*, from L. *praesideo*
—*prae*, before, and *sedeo*, I sit. SIT.]
To be set over others; to have the

place of authority over others, as a
chairman or director: usually denoting temporary superintendence and
government, as at a public meeting;
to exercise superintendence; to watch
over as inspector. — **presidency,**
prez′i•den•si, *n.* Superintendence;
inspection and care; the office of
president; the term during which a
president holds his office; [*often
cap.*] the office of the president of the
United States.—**president,** prez′i•-
dent, *n.* One who presides; an officer
elected or appointed to preside over
and control the proceedings of a
number of persons; the chief officer
of a corporation, company, society,
etc.; the chief officer of some colleges
or universities; the highest officer of
state in a republic.—**presidential,**
prez•i•den′shal, *a.* Pertaining to a
president.—**presidentship,** prez′i•-
dent•ship, *n.* The office of president.
presidio, pri•sid′i•ō, *n.* [Sp.] A fort
or fortified station; a garrison town.
presignify, prē•sig′ni•fī, *v.t.*—*presig-
nified, presignifying.* To intimate or
signify beforehand; to show previously.
press, pres, *v.t.* [Fr. *presser*, from L.
presso, a freq. of *premere, pressum,*
to press; seen also in *compress,
depress, express, impress, repress,* etc.]
To act on with force or weight; to
squeeze; to crush; to extract the
juice of by squeezing; to squeeze for
the purpose of making smooth (to
press cloth or paper); to embrace
closely, to constrain or compel; to
urge by authority or necessity; to
impose importunately (to *press* a gift
on one); to straiten or distress (to be
pressed with want); to urge or solicit
with earnestness; to importune; to
inculcate with earnestness; to enforce; to bear hard upon; to ply
hard.—*v.i.* To exert pressure; to
act with compulsive force; to bear
heavily; to strain or strive eagerly;
to go forward with impulsive eagerness or energetic efforts; to crowd;
to throng; to force one's way; to
urge.—*To press upon,* to urge with
force; to attack closely.—*n.* [Fr.
presse, a press, a crowd, a throng.]
An instrument or machine by which
any body is squeezed, crushed, or
forced into a more compact form; a
machine for printing; a printing
press; (with *the*) printed literature
in general, often restricted to the
literature of newspapers; newspaper
reporters; a printing or publishing
establishment; also its personnel; a
crowd; a throng; multitude of individuals crowded together; a wine
vat or cistern (O.T.); an upright
cupboard in which clothes or other
articles are kept; urgency; urgent
demands of affairs.—*Freedom of the
press,* the right to publish without
political censorship.—*Press of sail*
(*naut.*), as much sail as the state of
the wind, etc., will permit.—**presser,**
pres′ėr, *n.* One who or that which
presses.—**pressing,** pres′ing, *p.* and
a. Urgent; importunate; distressing.
—**pressingly,** pres′ing•li, *adv.* In a
pressing manner.—**pressman,** pres′-
man, *n.* One who works or attends to

a printing press.—**pressroom,** *n.*
Print. the room where the printing
presses are worked, as distinguished
from a composing room; a room
where reporters assemble for a press
conference.—**pressure,** presh′ėr, *n.*
[O.Fr. *pressure*, L. *pressura.*] The
act of pressing; the state of being
squeezed or crushed; the force of
one body acting on another by weight
or the continued application of
power; a constraining force or impulse acting on the mind; severity
of grievousness, as of personal circumstances; distress, strait, or difficulty; urgency; demand on one's
time or energies (the *pressure* of
business); force exerted upon a
surface.—*v.t.* To bring pressure to
bear; to use all one's influence.—
pressurize, presh′ėr•īz, *v.t.* To cook
in a pressure cooker; to hold atmospheric pressure at average level
during a high-level flight by plane.
—**pressurization,** presh′er•ī•zā′shon,
n.—*Pressure cooker,* an apparatus
which may be sealed for cooking
or sterilizing under high-pressure
superheated steam.
press, pres, *v.t.* [Originally to *impress*
or *imprest.* See IMPRESS (in this
sense).] To force into service, especially into naval service; to impress.
Prester John, *n.* Priest John, the
mythical or legendary Christian king,
believed in the Middle Ages to be
ruling in Abyssinia.
prestidigitation, pres′ti•dij′i•tā″shon,
n. [L. *praesto*, at hand, ready, and
digitus, a finger.] Skill in legerdemain; sleight of hand; juggling.—
prestidigitator, pres•ti•dij′i•tā•tėr, *n.*
One who practices prestidigitation;
a juggler.
prestige, pres′tij or pres•tēzh′, *n.*
[Fr., from L. *praestigium*, an illusion,
a juggler's trick; hence an impression
made on spectators.] Weight or
influence derived from previous character, achievements, or associations,
especially weight or influence derived
from past success, on which a confident belief is founded of future
triumphs.
presto, pres′to, *adv.* [It. *presto*, quick,
quickly, from L. *praesto*, at hand,
ready—*prae*, before, and *sto*, to
stand.] *Music*, a direction for a quick
lively movement or performance;
also used interjectionally for quickly,
immediately, in haste.
presume, pri•zūm′, *v.t.*—*presumed,
presuming.* [Fr. *présumer*, from L.
praesumo, to presume—*prae*, before,
and *sumo*, to take, as in *assume,
consume, resume,* etc. SUMPTUOUS.]
To take for granted; to suppose on
reasonable grounds.—*v.i.* To suppose or believe without examination;
to infer; to venture without permission or beyond what is justifiable; to
take the liberty; to make bold; to act
on overconfident conclusions; to
make unwarranted advances (to *presume* upon one's good nature); to act
in a forward way; to go beyond the
boundaries laid down by reverence,
respect, or politeness.—**presumable,**
pri•zū′ma•bl, *a.* Capable of being
presumed.—**presumably,** pri•zū′-

ma·bli, *adv.* As may be presumed or reasonably supposed.—**presumer**, pri·zū'mėr, *n.* One that presumes.—**presumption**, pri·zum'shon, *n.* [L. *praesumptio.*] A supposition; a ground for presuming; a strong probability; that which is supposed to be true without direct proof; blind or headstrong confidence; unreasonable adventurousness; presumptuousness; arrogance; assurance; *law*, that which comes near to the proof of a fact, in greater or less degree.—**presumptive**, pri·zum'tiv, *a.* Based on presumption or probability; proving circumstantially, not directly (*presumptive evidence*).—*Presumptive heir*, one whose right of inheritance may be defeated by any contingency, as by the birth of a nearer relative.—**presumptively**, pri·zum'tiv·li, *adv.* In a presumptive manner.—**presumptuous**, pri·zum'chū·us, *a.* Imbued with or characterized by presumption; taking undue liberties; given to presume or act in a forward manner; arrogant; overconfident.—**presumptuously**, pri·zum'chū·us·li, *adv.* In a presumptuous manner.—**presumptuousness**, pri·zum'chū·us·nes, *n.* The quality of being presumptuous.

presuppose, prē·sup·pōz', *v.t.* To suppose or imagine as previous; to cause to be taken for granted; to imply as antecedent; to require to exist previously.—**presupposition**, prē·sup'po·zish''on, *n.* The act of presupposing; that which is presupposed.

presurmise, prē·sėr·mīz', *n.* A surmise previously formed.

pretend, pri·tend', *v.t.* [L. *praetendo*, to hold out, pretend—*prae*, before, and *tendere*, to reach or stretch. TEND.] To hold out falsely; to allege falsely; to use as a pretext; to make false appearance or representation of; to feign or affect (to *pretend* zeal); to claim or put in a claim for.—*v.i.* To feign, make believe, or sham; to put in a claim, truly or falsely: usually with *to.*—**pretender**, pri·ten'dėr, *n.* One who pretends; one who lays claim to anything; [*cap.*] *Eng. hist.* a name applied to the son and grandson of James II, the heirs to the house of Stuart, who laid claim to the British crown, from which their house had been excluded by enactment of Parliament.—**pretense**, pri·tens', *n.* [From L. *praetentum*, later *praetensum*, pp. of *praetendo.*] The act of pretending; the presenting to others, either in words or actions, of a false or hypocritical appearance; false show or statement intended to mislead; a pretext; an excuse; a claim, true or false.—*Escutcheon of pretense* (heraldry), a small shield set in the center of a husband's arms, bearing those of his wife when she is an heiress or co-heiress in blood.—**pretension**, pri·ten'shon, *n.* [Fr. *prétention.*] Claim true or false; a holding out the appearance of possessing a certain character; an alleged or assumed right.—**pretentious**, pri·ten'shus, *a.* Full of pretension; attempting to pass for more than one is worth; pretending to a superiority not

real.—**pretentiously**, pri·ten'shus·li, *adv.* In a pretentious manner.

preterit, pret'ėr·it, *a.* [L. *praeteritus*, gone by, pp. of *praetereo—praeter*, beyond, and *ire*, *itum*, to go. ITINERANT.] *Gram.* expressing past time; applied to the tense expressing action or existence perfectly past or finished; past (he *struck*); also used as equivalent to *perfect.—n. Gram.* the preterit tense.—**preterition**, prē·tėr·ish'on, *n.* [L. *praeteritio*, from *praetereo.*] *Rhet.* a figure by which, in pretending to pass over anything, we make a summary mention of it.—**preteritive**, pri·tėr'i·tiv, *a. Gram.* an epithet applied to verbs used only or chiefly in the *preterit* or past tenses.

pretermit, prē·tėr·mit', *v.t.*—pretermitted, pretermitting. [L. *praetermitto—praeter*, beyond, and *mittere*, to send.] To pass by; to omit.—**pretermission**, prē·tėr·mish'on, *n.* A passing by; omission.

preternatural, prē·tėr·nach'é·ral, *a.* [L. *praeter*, beyond, and E. *natural.*] Beyond what is natural, or different from what is natural, as distinguished from *supernatural*, above nature; and *unnatural*, contrary to nature.—**preternaturally**, prē·tėr·nach'é·ral·li, *adv.* In a preternatural manner.—**preternaturalism**, prē·tėr·nach'é·ral·izm, *n.* A state of being preternatural.

pretext, prē'tekst or pri·tekst', *n.* [Fr. *prétexte*, from L. *praetextum*, from *praetexe—prae*, before, and *texo*, to weave. TEXTURE.] An ostensible reason or motive assigned or assumed as a color or cover for the real reason or motive; a pretense.

pretor, prē'tor. See PRAETOR.

pretty, prit'i, *a.* [O.E. *pretic*, *praty*, comely, clever; A.Sax. *praetig*, crafty, from *praet*, a trick; Icel. *prettugr*, tricky, *prettr*, a trick.] Having diminutive beauty; of a pleasing and attractive form without the strong lines of beauty, or without gracefulness and dignity; pleasing; neatly arranged; affectedly nice; foppish; ironically, nice; fine; excellent: meaning the opposite.—*adv.* In some degree; moderately; expressing a degree less than *very* (*pretty* well, large, sure, etc.).—**prettily**, prit'i·li, *adv.* In a pretty manner; with prettiness; pleasingly.—**prettiness**, prit'i·nes, *n.* State or quality of being pretty; diminutive beauty; beauty without stateliness or dignity; neatness and taste exhibited on small objects; affected niceness; foppishness.—**prettyish**, prit'i·ish, *a.* Somewhat pretty.

pretzel, pret'sel, *n.* [G. *bretzel.*] A crisp, glazed, salty, knotlike cracker.

prevail, pri·vāl', *v.i.* [Fr. *prévaloir*, from L. *praevaleo—prae*, before, and *valere*, to be strong. VALID.] To overcome; to gain the victory or superiority: often with *over* or *against*; to be in force; to have extensive power or influence (a disease, a custom *prevails* in a place); to have predominant influence; to succeed; to overcome or gain over by persuasion: with *on* or *upon* (they *prevailed on* him to go).—**prevailing**,

pri·vā'ling, *p.* and *a.* Predominant; having superior influence; prevalent; most common or general.—**prevailingly**, pri·vāl'ing·li, *adv.* So as to prevail.—**prevalence**, prev'a·lens, *n.* The state or quality of being prevalent; superiority; general reception or practice; general existence or extension (the *prevalence* of vice or of a fashion).—**prevalent**, prev'a·lent, *a.* Prevailing; predominant; most generally received or current; extensively existing.—**prevalently**, prev'a·lent·li, *adv.* In a prevalent manner.

prevaricate, pri·var'i·kāt, *v.i.*—prevaricated, prevaricating. [L. *praevaricor*, *praevaricatus*, to straddle, to shuffle—*prae*, before, and *varus*, straddling.] To act or speak evasively; to evade or swerve from the truth; to shuffle; to quibble in giving answers.—**prevarication**, pri·var'i·kā''shon, *n.* The act of prevaricating; a shuffling or quibbling to evade the truth or the disclosure of truth; *law*, a collusion between an informer and a defendant, in order to a feigned prosecution; the willful concealment or misrepresentation of truth by giving evasive evidence.—**prevaricator**, pri·var'i·kā·tėr, *n.* One who prevaricates; a shuffler; a quibbler.

prevenient, prē·vē'ni·ent, *a.* [L. *praeveniens.* PREVENT.] Going before; preceding; preventing; preventive.—*Prevenient grace. Theol.* term, the grace that precedes or anticipates repentance, but which disposes the heart of man to seek God.

prevent, pri·vent', *v.t.* [L. *praevenio*, *praeventum*, to anticipate, to prevent—*prae*, before, and *venio*, to come (seen also in *advent*, *convent*, *circumvent*, *intervention*, etc.).] To anticipate‡; to forestall‡; to hinder by something done before; to stop or intercept; to impede; to thwart.—**preventable**, pri·ven'ta·bl, *a.* Capable of being prevented or hindered.—**preventer**, pri·ven'tėr, *n.* One who or that which prevents.—**prevention**, pri·ven'shon, *n.* The act of preventing.—**preventive**, pri·ven'tiv, *a.* Tending to prevent or hinder.—*Preventive medicine*, the branch of medical practice which seeks to guard against disease and its spread.—*n.* That which prevents; that which intercepts the access or approach of something; an antidote.—**preventively**, pri·ven'tiv·li, *adv.* By way of prevention.

previous, prē'vi·us, *a.* [L. *praevius—prae*, before, and *via*, a way. VOYAGE, WAY.] Going before in time; being or happening before something else; antecedent; prior.—*Previous question.* See QUESTION.—**previously**, prē'vi·us·li, *adv.* In time preceding; beforehand; antecedently. ∴ Syn. under FORMERLY.—**previousness**, prē'vi·us·nes, *n.* Priority in time.

previse, pri·vīz', *v.t.*—prevised, prevising. [L. *praevisus*, pp. of *praevideo—prae*, before, and *video*, to see. VISION.] To foresee; to forewarn.—**prevision**, pri·vizh'on, *n.* Foresight; foreknowledge; prescience.

prey, prā, *n.* [O.E. *preie*, *praie*, O.Fr.

preie, praie (Fr. *proie*), from L. *praeda*, plunder, whence *predatory, depredation.*] Spoil; booty; goods taken from an enemy in war; anything taken by violence and injustice; a victim; that which is seized by carnivorous animals to be devoured. —*Beast of prey*, a carnivorous animal, or one that feeds on the flesh of other animals.—*v.i.* To take prey or booty; to feed by violence: with *on* or *upon* before the object of rapine; to rest heavily, as on the mind; to waste gradually (grief *preyed on* him).

Priapean, prī·a·pē′an, *a.* Pertaining to the Roman deity *Priapus*, the god of procreation; grossly sensual; obscene.

price, prīs, *n.* [O.Fr. *pris, preis,* Fr. *prix,* from L. *pretium,* a price; the same word as *praise,* and *prize,* to value.] The sum of money or the value which a seller sets on his goods in market; the current value of a commodity; the equivalent for which something is bought or sold; cost; value; worth (a pearl of great *price*); estimation.—*Price of money,* in com. the price of credit; the rate of discount at which capital may be lent or borrowed.—**priced,** prīst, *a.* Set at a value; having a price: mostly in composition (high-*priced,* low-*priced*). —**priceless,** prīs′les, *a.* Invaluable; inestimable; too valuable to admit of a price being fixed.

prick, prik, *n.* [A.Sax. *prica, pricu,* a point, a dot=D. *prik,* Dan. *prik,* Sw. *prick,* dot, prick; comp. W. *pric,* a skewer, Ir. *pricadh,* a goad.] A slender pointed thing hard enough to pierce the skin; a thorn; a skewer; a puncture or wound by a prick or prickle; a sting; *fig.* a stinging or tormenting thought; remorse; a dot or small mark (*Shak.*).—*v.t.* To pierce with something sharp pointed; to puncture; to erect (said of the ears, hence, *to prick up the ears,* to listen with eager attention); to fix by a sharp point; to designate or set apart by a puncture or mark (*pricked off* for duty); to spur; to goad; to incite: often with *on*; to sting; to trace by puncturing; to render acid or pungent to the taste (the wine is *pricked*).—*v.i.* To suffer or feel penetration by a point or sharp pain; to be punctured; to become acid; to spur on; to ride rapidly.—**prick-eared,** *a.* Having pointed ears; having ears standing up prominently.— **pricker,** prik′ėr, *n.* That which pricks; a sharp-pointed instrument; one who pricks; a light horseman; one who tested whether women were witches by sticking pins into them.— **prickle,** prik′l, *n.* [Dim. of *prick.*] A little prick; a small sharp point; *bot.* a small pointed shoot or sharp process growing from the *bark,* and thus distinguished from the *thorn,* which grows from the *wood* of a plant; a sharp-pointed process or projection, as from the skin of an animal; a spine; a kind of basket.— *v.t.*—*prickled, prickling.* To prick slightly; to pierce with fine sharp points.—**prickly,** prik′li, *a.* Full of sharp points or prickles; armed

with prickles; stinging in feeling.— **prickliness,** prik′li·nes, *n.*—**prickly heat,** *n.* The popular name for a heat rash.—**prickly pear,** *n.* A variety of cactus covered with clusters of spines, and producing edible fruit.

pride, prīd, *n.* [A.Sax. *prýte,* pride, from *prút,* proud. PROUD.] The quality or state of being proud; inordinate self-esteem; an unreasonable conceit of one's own superiority over others; generous elation of heart; a noble self-esteem springing from a consciousness of worth; proud behavior; insolence; that which is or may be a cause of pride; that of which men are proud; one who or that which gives rise to pride or glorification; highest pitch; splendid show; ostentation.—*v.t.*—*prided, priding.* To indulge in pride; to value one's self: used reflexively.— **prideful,** prīd′ful, *a.* Full of pride; insolent; scornful.—**pridefully,** prīd′-ful·li, *adv.* In a prideful manner.— **pridefulness,** prīd′ful·nes, *n.* The state or quality of being prideful.

priest, prēst, *n.* [A.Sax. *preóst,* contr. from L. *presbyter.* PRESBYTER.] A clergyman of the Roman Catholic, Greek Catholic, Orthodox, or Episcopalian church; a person consecrated to the ministry of the gospel; a man who officiates in sacred offices; a minister of public worship; a minister of sacrifice or other mediatorial offices; among many non-Christian sects, the title of men selected and trained to perform sacred functions.—**priestess,** prēs′-tes, *n.* A woman who officiates in sacred rites.—**priestly,** prēst′li, *a.* Pertaining to a priest or to priests; sacerdotal; becoming a priest.— **priestliness,** prēst′li·nes, *n.* The quality of being priestly.—**priest-craft,** prēst′kraft, *n.* Priestly policy or system of management based on temporal or material interest; policy of clergy to advance their own order. —**priesthood,** prēst′hod, *n.* The office or character of a priest; the order composed of priests; priests collectively.—**priest-ridden,** *a.* Governed or entirely swayed by priests.

prig, prig, *n.* [From *prick,* in old sense of to trim or dress up.] A pert, conceited, pragmatical fellow.—**priggery, priggism,** prig′ėr·i, prig′izm, *n.* The qualities of a prig; pertness; conceit.—**priggish,** prig′ish, *a.* Conceited; affected.—**priggishly,** prig′-ish·li, *adv.* In a priggish manner; pertly.—**priggishness,** prig′ish·nes, *n.* The state or quality of being priggish.

prig, prig, *n.* [O.Fr. *briguer,* to steal, to act the highwayman; akin *brigand.*] A thief; a low or mean thief.—*v.t.*— *prigged, prigging.* To filch; to steal.

prim, prim, *a.* [O.Fr. *prim,* prime, first, also thin, slender, neat; from L. *primus,* first. PRIME.] Neat; formal; precise; affectedly nice; demure.—**primly,** prim′li, *adv.* In a prim or precise manner; with primness.—**primness,** prim′nes, *n.* Affected formality; stiffness; preciseness.

primacy. See PRIMATE.

prima donna, prē′ma don′na. [It., first lady.] The first or chief female singer in an opera.—**prima facie,** prī′ma fā′shi·ē. [L. *primus,* first, and *facies,* face.] At first view or appearance.—*Prima facie evidence, law,* evidence having such a degree of probability that it must prevail unless the contrary be proved.

primage, prī′mij, *n.* [From verb to *prime.*] A charge paid by the shipper or consigner of goods to the master and sailors for loading the same; the amount of water carried off in steam from the boiler.

primal, prī′mal, *a.* [From L. *primus,* first. PRIME.] Primary; first in time, order, or importance; original.— **primary,** prī′ma·ri, *a.* [L. *primarius.*] First in order of time; original; primitive; first; first in dignity or importance; chief; principal; elementary; preparatory, or lowest in order (*primary* schools); first in intention; radical; original; as the *primary* sense of a word.—*Primary accent,* accent (′) on the stressed syllable of a word.—*Primary cell, elect.* an ordinary voltaic cell. Comp. SECONDARY CELL, STORAGE BATTERY.— *Primary colors.* COLOR.—*Primary planets.* PLANET.—*Primary election, pol. sci.* election held to choose party candidates.—*Primary quills,* the largest feathers of the wings of a bird; primaries.—*Primary rocks, geol.* rocks of the paleozoic group; former sense, primitive igneous rocks.—*n.* That which stands highest in rank or importance, as opposed to *secondary.*—**primarily,** prī′ma·ri·li, *adv.* In a primary manner; fundamentally; essentially.

primate, prī′mit, *n.* [Fr. *primat;* L.L. *primas, primatis,* from L. *primus,* first. PRIME.] The chief ecclesiastic in certain churches, as the Anglican; an archbishop. The Archbishop of York is entitled *primate* of England; the Archbishop of Canterbury, *primate* of *all* England.— *Primates,* the order of mammals consisting of man and the apes.— **primateship, primacy,** prī′mat·ship, prī′ma·si, *n.* The office or dignity of primate or archbishop.—**primatial,** prī·mā′shi·al, *a.* Pertaining to a primate.

prime, prīm, *a.* [L. *primus,* first; superl. of *prior,* former; same root as Skr. *pra,* Gr. and L. *pro,* before; E. *fore, first,* etc. PRINCE, PRIM, PRIMITIVE, etc.] First in order of time; primitive; original (*prime* cost); first in rank, degree, or dignity (*prime* minister); first in excellence, value, or importance; first-rate; capital; early; in the first stage.— *Prime conductor, elect.* the metallic conductor opposed to the glass plate or cylinder of an electrical machine. —*Prime cost,* first or original cost; the sum or expenditure for which an article can be made or produced.— *Prime minister,* in Great Britain, the first minister of state; the premier.— *Prime mover,* the initial force which puts a machine in motion; a machine which receives and modifies force as supplied by some natural source,

as a waterwheel, a steam engine, etc.
—*Prime number, arith.* a number not divisible without remainder by any less number than itself except unity. —*Prime vertical*, in *astron.* a celestial great circle passing through the east and west points and the zenith.—*n.* The earliest stage or beginning of anything; the dawn; the morning; the spring of the year; the spring of life; youth; full health, strength, or beauty; the highest or most perfect or most flourishing condition; the best part; that which is best in quality; in *R. Cath. Ch.* the first canonical hour, succeeding to lauds. —*v.t.*—*primed, priming.* [Lit. to perform a *prime* or first operation with, to prepare.] To put into a condition for being fired: said of a gun, mine, etc.; to supply with powder for communicating fire to a charge; *painting*, to cover with a ground or first color; to instruct or prepare a person beforehand what he is to say or do; to post up (to *prime* a witness). —**primely**, prīm'li, *adv.* In a prime manner or degree; most excellently. —**primeness**, prīm'nes, *n.* The quality of being prime; supreme excellence.—**primer**, prim'ėr or prī'mėr, *n.* [Fr. *primaire*, elementary, from L. *primarius*, from *primus*, first.] A small elementary book for religious instruction or for teaching children to read; a book of elementary principles; *print.* a name given to two sizes of type, *longprimer* and *great-primer.*—**priming**, prī'ming, *n. Gun.* and *blasting*, the powder used to ignite the charge; *painting*, the first layer of paint or size laid on a surface which is to be painted; *steam engine*, the carrying over of water spray with the steam from the boiler into the cylinder—a troublesome defect.

primero, pri·mâ'ro, *n.* [Sp. *primero*, first.] An old game at cards.

primeval, prī·mē'val, *a.* [L. *primaevus*—*primus*, first, and *aevum*, age. PRIME, AGE.] Original; primitive; belonging to the first ages.—**primevally**, prī·mē'val·li, *adv.* In a primeval manner; in the earliest times.

primigenial, prī·mi·jē'ni·al, *a.* [L. *primigenius*—*primus*, first, and root *gen.* to beget.] First-born; original; primary.

primine, prī'min, *n.* [L. *primus*, first.] *Bot.* the outermost sac or covering of an ovule, the inner being termed *secundine.*

primiparous, prī·mip'a·rus, *a.* [L. *primus*, first, and *pario*, to bring forth.] Bearing young for the first time.

primitive, prim'i·tiv, *a.* [L. *primitivus*, earliest of its kind, from *primus*, first. PRIME.] Pertaining to the beginning or origin; original; first; old-fashioned; characterized by the simplicity of old times; *gram.* applied to a word in its simplest etymological form; not derived; radical; primary; *bot.* original, in opposition to forms resulting from hybridization.—*Primitive colors.* See COLOR.—*n.* A person of simple culture.—**primitively**, prim'i·tiv·li, *adv.*—**primitivism**, prim'i·tiv·izm, *n.*

A theory that cultures of primitive or early chronological date are superior to present-day culture.— **primitiveness**, prim'i·tiv·nes, *n.*

primly, primness. See PRIM.

primogeniture, prī·mo·jen'i·chėr, *n.* [Fr. *primogéniture*, from L. *primus*, first, and *genitūra*, a begetting, from *gigno, genitum*, to beget. GENDER, GENUS.] The state of being born first of the same parents; seniority by birth among children; the right or principle under which the eldest son of a family succeeds to the father's real estate, in preference to, and in absolute exclusion of the younger sons and daughters.—**primogenitor**, prī·mo·jen'i·tėr, *n.* [L. *primus*, and *genitor*, father.] The first father or forefather; an ancestor.

primordial, prī·mor'di·al, *a.* [L. *primordialis*, from *primordium*, beginning, origin—*primus*, first, and *ordior*, to commence. PRIME, ORDER.] First in order, original, existing from the beginning; *bot.* and *zool.* earliest formed.—*n.* A first principle or element.—**primordially**, prī·mor'di·al·li, *adv.* Under the first order of things; at the beginning.

primp, primp, *v.t.* [From *prim*, or perhaps a form of *prink.*] To deck one's self in a stiff and affected manner.

primrose, prim'rōz, *n.* [O.E. *primerole.* Fr. *primerole*, from L.L. *primula*, the primrose, from *primus*, first (as the first flower of spring); the last syllable was changed to *rose* to give the word an English appearance and a sort of meaning; comp. *barberry*, etc.] The common name for several beautiful herbaceous plants, both cultivated and wild, with flowers colored red, white, and yellow, and with each flower growing on a separate stem or peduncle rather than in clusters; a dye derived from coal tar, pinkish-yellow in color; when referred to as a shade, it signifies a pale greenish-yellow tint.—*a.* Resembling a primrose in color; abounding with primroses; flowery; florid; excessively ornate.— **primrose path**, *n.* The leading of a gay or merry life; indulgence in the showy and sensual pleasures of life.— **primrose yellow**, *n.* A reddish-yellow color.

prince, prins, *n.* [Fr., from L. *princeps, principis*, a prince, a chief—*primus*, first, and *capio*, to take. PRIME, CAPABLE.] A man holding the first or highest rank; a sovereign; a sovereign who has the government of a particular territory, but owes certain services to a superior; the son of a sovereign; a male member of a royal family; the chief of any body of men; a man at the head of any class, profession, etc.. (a merchant *prince*).—**princess**, prin'ses, *n.* The daughter of a sovereign; a woman of grandeur, such as a princess; the consort of a prince.—*a.* Denoting a close-fitting, one-piece dress or slip (also *princesse.*).— **princely**, prins'li, *a.* Pertaining to a prince; resembling a prince; noble; grand; august; magnificent.—**prince-**

liness, prins'li·nes, *n.*—**prince consort**, *n.* The husband of a reigning queen.

principal, prin'si·pal, *a.* [L. *principalis*, from *princeps*, first in time or order, a chief. PRINCE.] Chief; highest in rank, character, authority, or importance; first; main; essential; most considerable.—*n.* A chief or head; one who takes a leading part; the chief executive of an educational institution, particularly, of an elementary or secondary public school; *law*, the actor or absolute perpetrator of a crime, or an abettor; one who engages another person to act as his representative or agent; *com.* a capital sum lent on interest, due as a debt, or used as a fund: so called in distinction to interest; *carp.* a main timber in an assemblage of pieces.— **principality**, prin·si·pal'i·ti, *n.* [Fr. *principalité.*] Sovereignty; supreme power; a prince, or one invested with sovereignty; the territory of a prince, or the country which gives title to a prince.—**principally**, prin'si·pal·li, *adv.* In the chief place; chiefly; above all.

principle, prin'si·pl, *n.* [Fr. *principe*, from L. *principium*, a beginning, origin, element, from *princeps, principis.* PRINCE. As to the insertion of the *l* comp. *participle, syllable.*] Beginning‡; commencement‡; a source of origin; the primary source from which anything proceeds; element; primordial substance; a general truth; a law comprehending many subordinate truths; a law on which others are founded or from which others are derived; an axiom; a maxim; a tenet; a governing law of conduct; a settled rule of action; a right rule of conduct; uprightness (a man of *principle*); ground of conduct; a motive; *chem.* a component part; an element; a substance on the presence of which certain qualities common to a number of bodies depend.

prink, pringk, *v.i.* [A slightly modified form of *prank.*] To prank; to dress for show; to strut; to put on stately airs.—*v.t.* To deck; to adorn fantastically.

print, print, *v.t.* [Fr. *preinte*, from *preindre*, from L. *primo, pressum*, to press. PRESS.] To impress or imprint upon, as to mark or stamp; to impress with or convince of an idea; to apply something with pressure so as to leave a mark; to make an impression or mark with type, engraved plates, etc.; to perform all operations necessary to produce a book, periodical, etc. (to *print* a story); to stamp designs, letters, etc., on (to *print* labels); to produce or publish in print (to *print* a scandal); to form letters or words in characters similar to type, as opposed to writing them; *photog.* to transfer images from negatives or the like to a sensitized surface; to impress a design on cloth.—*v.i.* To use or practice the art of printing.—*n.* A mark made by impression; a stamp; a die, mold, or stamp; that which receives a mark or impression from a die or mold; the state or condition of being printed (it appeared in *print*); that which is produced by printing, especially an engraving; a newspaper or other periodical; printed cloth.—**printable,** print·a·ble, *a.*—**printed circuit,** *n.* A circuit for electronic devices made by depositing conductive material in continuous paths between terminals on an insulating surface.—**printer,** print′ėr, *n.*—**printing,** print′ing, *n.* The combined processes which go into the production of books, periodicals, etc., by impression from movable type, plates, etc.; all the books, etc., printed in one edition; writing in which the letters are similar in form to type; the act of a person or device that prints.—**printing press,** *n.* A press for the printing of books, etc.

prior, prī′or, *a.* [L. *prior,* a compar. to which *primus,* first, is the superl. PRIME.] Preceding, especially in the order of time; earlier; antecedent; anterior.—*adv.* Previously; antecedently (he had never been there *prior* to that time).—*n.* The superior of a priory or a monastery of lower than abbatial rank; a monk next in dignity to an abbot.—*Grand prior,* a title given to the commandants of the priories of the military orders of St. John of Jerusalem, of Malta, and of the Templars.—**priorate, priorship,** prī′or·āt, prī′or·ship, *n.* The dignity or office of a prior.—**prioress,** prī′or·es, *n.* The female head in a convent of nuns, next in rank to an abbess.—**priority,** prī·or′i·ti, *n.* The state of being prior or antecedent in time, or of preceding something else; precedence in place or rank.—**priory,** prī′e·ri, *n.* A religious house of which a prior or prioress is the superior, in dignity below an abbey.

prism, prizm, *n.* [L. and Gr. *prisma,* lit. a sawn piece, from *prizō,* to saw.] A solid whose bases or ends are any similar, equal, and parallel plane figures, and whose sides are parallelograms; a bar of glass with a triangular section, used for decomposing light, as in spectrum analysis.—**prismatic, prismatical,** priz·mat′ik, priz·mat′i·kal, *a.* Resembling or pertaining to a prism; formed or exhibited by a prism.—*Prismatic colors,* the colors into which a ray of light is decomposed in passing through a prism: red, orange, yellow, green, blue, indigo, violet.—**prismatically,** priz··mat′i·kal·li, *adv.* In the form or manner of a prism; by means of a prism.—**prismatoidal,** priz·ma·toi′dal, *a.* Having a prismlike form.—**prismoid,** priz′moid, *n.* A body that approaches to the form of a prism.—**prismoidal,** priz·moi′dal, *a.* Having the form of a prismoid.

prison, priz′on or priz′n, *n.* [Fr. *prison,* from L. *prehensio, prehensionis,* a capture, from *prehendo,* to seize (whence *prehensile,* etc.). APPREHEND.] A place of confinement or involuntary restraint; especially,

a public building for the confinement or safe custody of criminals and others committed by process of law; a jail.—*v.t.* To shut up in a prison; to confine; to imprison.—**prisoner,** priz′on·ėr, *n.* One who is confined in a prison; a person under arrest, whether in prison or not; a captive; one taken by an enemy in war; one whose liberty is restrained, as a bird in a cage.—**prisoner's base,** *n.* A game consisting chiefly of running and being pursued from goals or bases.

pristine, pris′tēn, *a.* [L. *pristinus;* same root as *prior, prime,* etc.] Belonging to a primitive or early state or period; original; primitive.

private, prī′vit, *a.* [L. *privatus,* from *privo,* to separate, from *privus,* separate, peculiar (seen also in *deprive, privilege*).] Peculiar to one's self; belonging to or concerning an individual only; personal; opposed to *public* or *national;* not known, open, or accessible to people in general; secret; not invested with public office or employment; not having a public or official character; unconnected with others; solitary; participating in knowledge; privy; *milit.* said of a common soldier.—*Private hospital,* a hospital financed from private sources, rather than public agencies.—*Private nurse,* a nurse caring for one patient.—*In private,* not publicly or openly; secretly.—*n.* A common soldier; one of the lowest rank in the army.—**privacy,** prī′va·si, *n.* A state of being private or in retirement; seclusion; secrecy; solitude; retirement.—**privately,** prī′vit·li, *adv.* In a private or secret manner; not openly or publicly; in a manner affecting an individual; personally.—**privateness,** prī′vit·nes, *n.* The state of being private.—**privateer,** prī·va·tēr′, *n.* A vessel of war owned and equipped by one or more private persons, and licensed by a government to seize or plunder the ships of an enemy in war.—*v.i.* To cruise in a privateer.—**privateersman,** prī·va·tērz′man, *n.* An officer or seaman' of a privateer.—**privation,** prī·vā′shon, *n.* [L. *privatio,* from *privo,* to bereave.] The state of being deprived; deprivation of what is necessary for comfort; destitution; want; the act of removing something possessed.—**privative,** priv′a·tiv, *a.* Causing deprivation; *gram.* changing the sense from positive to negative.—*n.* A prefix to a word which gives it a contrary sense, as *un* and *in* in *unwise, inhuman.*—**privatively,** priv′a·tiv·li, *adv.* In a private manner.

privet, priv′et, *n.* [Etym. unknown.] A shrub frequently planted to form ornamental hedges in gardens.

privilege, priv′i·lej, *n.* [L. *privilegium,* an exceptional law, from *privus,* separate, peculiar, and *lex, legis,* a law. PRIVATE, LEGAL.] A right or advantage enjoyed by a person or body of persons beyond the common advantages of other individuals; a private or personal favor

enjoyed; a peculiar advantage.—*Question of privilege,* in *parliament,* a question affecting the privileges appertaining to the members.—*v.t.* To grant some privilege, right, or exemption to; to invest with a peculiar right or immunity; to authorize; to license.

privy, priv′i, *a.* [Fr. *privé,* from L. *privatus.* PRIVATE.] Private; assigned to private uses; not public; secret; not seen openly; appropriated to retirement; sequestered (O.T.); privately knowing; admitted to the participation of knowledge with another of a secret transaction (*privy to* a thing).—*n.* A latrine or necessary house.—*Gentlemen of the privy chamber,* officers of the royal household of Britain who attend on the sovereign at court, in progresses, etc.—**privily,** priv′i·li, *adv.* In a privy manner; privately; secretly.—**privity,** priv′i·ti, *n.* Privacy‡; private knowledge; joint knowledge with another of a private concern; *pl.* secret parts; the genital organs.—**Privy Council,** *n.* The principal council of the English sovereign, the members of which are chosen at his or her pleasure.—**privy councilor,** *n.* A member of the privy council.—**privy seal,** *n.* In England, the seal appended to grants which are afterward to pass the great seal, and to documents of minor importance; the secretary of state who is entrusted with the privy seal is called *lord privy seal.*

prize, prīz, *n.* [Fr. *prise,* a taking, capture, prize, from *prendre,* to take, from L. *prehendo,* to seize. PRISON.] That which is taken from an enemy in war, particularly a ship, with the property taken in it; that which is deemed a valuable acquisition; any gain or advantage; that which is obtained or offered as the reward of exertion or contest; that which is won in a lottery, or in any similar way.—**prize court,** *n.* A court which adjudicates on captures made at sea.—**prize fight,** *n.* A pugilistic encounter or boxing match for a prize.—**prize fighter,** *n.* A professional pugilist or boxer.—**prize fighting,** *n.* Boxing in public for a reward.—**prize money,** *n.* Money distributed among the captors of a ship or place where booty has been obtained, in certain proportions according to rank, the money being realized from the sale of the prize or booty.—**prize ring,** *n.* A ring or enclosed place for prize fighting; prize fighters collectively (a member of the *prize ring*).

prize, prīz, *v.t.*—**prized, prizing.** [Fr. *priser,* to value, to set a price on, from L. *pretium,* a price. PRICE, PRECIOUS.] To set or estimate the value of; to rate; to value highly; to consider of great worth; to esteem.—*a.* Meriting award of a prize, as *prize* cattle.

pro, prō, *adv.* [L. preposition, for, in favor of.] For, opposed to *con* (against); on the affirmative side.

proa, prō′a, *n.* [Malay *prau, prahu.*]

A kind of Malay vessel with one side flat, and an outrigger adjusted sometimes to the leeward side and sometimes to both sides, remarkable for swiftness.

probable, prob′a‧bl, *a.* [Fr. *probable,* from L. *probabilis,* that may be proved, probable, from *probo,* to prove. PROVE.] Supported by or based on evidence which inclines the mind to belief, but leaves some room for doubt; likely; rendering something probable (*probable* evidence).—**probabilism,** prob′a‧bil‧izm, *n.* R. *Cath. theol.* a theory, which, when there are two contrary opinions on a point of morality, considers it lawful to adopt that which is the more in agreement with personal inclination, provided it be supported by some weighty authority.—**probabilist,** prob′a‧bil‧ist, *n.* One who maintains the theory of probabilism.—**probability,** prob‧a‧bil′i‧ti, *n.* [Fr. *probabilité,* L. *probabilitas.*] The state or quality of being probable; likelihood; appearance of truth; anything that has the appearance of reality or truth (in this sense with a plural); *math.* the ratio of the number of chances by which an event may happen, to the number by which it may both happen and fail.—**probably,** prob′a‧bli, *adv.* In a probable manner; in all likelihood; as is probable; likely.

probang, prō′bang, *n.* [Probably from *probe.*] *Surg.* a long slender elastic rod of whalebone, with a piece of sponge securely attached to one end, intended to push down anything stuck in the gullet.

probate, prō′bāt, *n.* [L. *probatus,* from *probo,* to prove.] A proceeding before proper authorities by which a person's will or testament is established as such and registered.—**probate court,** *n.* A court concerned with the probate of wills, and all matters relating thereto.

probation, prō‧bā′shon, *n.* [L. *probatio, probationis,* an approving. PROBABLE.] The act of proving; proof; any proceeding designed to ascertain character, qualifications, or the like; a preliminary or preparatory trial or examination; a period of time during which a delinquent must report at regular intervals to a probation officer.—**probationer,** prō‧bā′shon‧ėr, *n.* One who is on probation or trial; a delinquent under the supervision of a probation officer; the designation given to a student nurse during her first year of training.—**probation officer,** *n.* One to whom a probationer must report at regular intervals.—**probative,** prō′ba‧tiv, *a.* Serving for trial or proof.—**probatory,** prō′ba‧to‧ri, *a.* Serving for trial; pertaining to or serving for proof.

probe, prōb, *n.* [From L. *probo,* to test, to try, to prove. PROVE.] A surgeon's instrument for examining the depth or other circumstances of a wound, ulcer, or cavity; an investigation; a device that is launched into outer space in order to gather information.—*v.t.*—*probed, probing.*

To apply a probe to; to examine by a probe; *fig.* to search to the bottom; to examine thoroughly into.

probity, prōb′i‧ti, *n.* [L. *probitas,* from *probus,* worthy, honest, good.] Tried virtue or integrity; strict honesty; rectitude; uprightness; high principle.

problem, prob′lem, *n.* [Fr. *problème,* L. *problema,* from Gr. *problēma—pro,* before, and *ballō,* to throw.] A question proposed for solution, decision, or determination; a knotty point requiring to be cleared up; *geom.* a proposition requiring some operation to be performed, differing from a theorem in that the latter requires something to be proved.—**problematic, problematical,** prob‧le‧mat′ik, prob‧le‧mat′i‧kal, *a.* Questionable; uncertain; disputable; doubtful.—**problematically,** prob‧le‧mat′i‧kal‧li, *adv.* In a problematical manner.

proboscis, prō‧bos′sis, *n.* pl. **proboscides,** prō‧bos′si‧dēz. [L. *proboscis,* from Gr. *proboskis—pro,* before, and *boskō,* to feed.] The snout or trunk projecting from the head of an elephant and other animals; the horny tube formed by the modified jaws of insects, used for sucking blood from animals or juice from plants; the nose; used humorously or in ridicule.—**proboscidian,** prō‧bos‧sid′i‧an, *a.* Furnished with a proboscis; proboscidean.—**proboscidean,** prō‧bos‧sid′i‧an, *a.* and *n.* Pertaining to, or one of, those mammals which have the nose prolonged into a prehensile trunk, as the elephant, etc.

procaine, prō′cain, *n.* [From prefix *pro* and (co)*caine.*] A basic ester of para-amino benzoic acid used as a local anesthetic, also called novocaine.

procathedral, prō‧ka‧thē′dral, *n.* A church that serves temporarily as a cathedral.

proceed, prō‧sēd′, *v.i.* [Fr. *procéder;* L. *procedo—pro,* before, and *cedo,* to go. CEDE.] To move, pass, or go onward; to continue or renew motion or progress; to advance; to go on; to pass from one point, stage, or topic to another; to issue or come, as from an origin, source, or fountain; to set to work and go on in a certain way; to act according to some method; to begin and carry on a legal action.—**procedure,** prō‧sē′dūr, *n.* [Fr. *procédure.*] Manner of proceeding or acting; a course or mode of action; conduct; a step taken; a proceeding.—**proceeding,** prō‧sē′ding, *n.* The act of one who proceeds; a measure or step taken; a transaction; a mode of conduct; *pl.* the course of steps in the prosecution of actions at law; the record or account of the transactions of a society.—**proceeds,** prō′sēdz, *n. pl.* The amount accruing from some transaction; the value of goods sold or converted into money.

process, pros′es, *n.* [L. *processus,* from *procedo, processum,* to proceed. PROCEED.] A proceeding or moving forward; progressive course; way

in which something goes on; gradual progress; course; series of actions or experiments (a chemical *process*); series of motions or changes going on, as in growth, decay, etc., in physical bodies; course; lapse; a passing or elapsing (the *process* of time); *law,* the whole course of proceedings in a cause; a projecting portion of something; especially, in *anat.* any protuberance or projecting part of a bone or other body; printing done from photoengraved plates.—*Process printing, n.* A method of reproducing objects in natural colors, chiefly pictures, by means of three, four, or more photoengravings, each printing in a different color, and printed one over the other.—**procession,** prō‧sesh′on, *n.* [L. *processio.*] The act of proceeding or issuing forth; a train of persons walking, or riding on horseback or in vehicles, in a formal march.—**processional,** prō‧sesh′on‧al, *n.* R. *Cath. Ch.* a prayer or hymn used for religious processions.—**process server,** *n.* A bailiff or sheriff's officer.

procès-verbal, prō‧sā‧vâr′bäl, *n.* In *French law,* a detailed authentic account of an official proceeding; a statement of facts.

proclaim, prō‧klām′, *v.t.* [L. *proclamo—pro,* before, and *clamo,* to cry out. CLAIM.] To make known by public announcement; to promulgate; to announce; to publish; to outlaw by public denunciation.—**proclaimer,** prō‧klā′mėr, *n.* One who proclaims.—**proclamation,** prok‧la‧mā′shon, *n.* [L. *proclamatio.*] The act of proclaiming; an official public announcement or declaration; a published ordinance.

proclitic, prō‧klit′ik, *n.* [From Gr. *pro,* forward, and *klinō,* to lean.] *Greek gram.* a monosyllabic word so closely attached to a following word as to have no independent existence and therefore no accent.

proclivity, prō‧kliv′i‧ti, *n.* [L. *proclivitas,* from *pro,* before, and *clivus,* a slope. ACCLIVITY.] Inclination; propensity; proneness; tendency; readiness.

proconsul, prō‧kon′sul, *n.* [L., from *pro,* for, and *consul.*] In ancient Rome an officer who discharged the duties of a consul without being himself consul; generally one who had been consul.—**proconsular,** prō‧kon′sul‧ėr, *a.* Pertaining to a proconsul.—**proconsulate, proconsulship,** prō‧kon′sul‧āt, prō‧kon′sul‧ship, *n.* The office of a proconsul.

procrastinate, prō‧kras′ti‧nāt, *v.t.* —*procrastinated, procrastinating.* [L. *procrastino, procrastinatus—pro,* forward, and *crastinus,* belonging to the morrow, from *cras,* to-morrow.] To put off from day to day; to delay; to defer to a future time.—*v.i.* To delay; to be dilatory.—**procrastination,** prō‧kras‧ti‧nā″shon, *n.* The act or habit of putting off to a future time; dilatoriness.—**procrastinator,** prō‧kras′ti‧nā‧tėr, *n.* One who procrastinates.

procreate, prō′kri‧āt, *v.t.*—*procreat-*

ed, *procreating.* [L. *procreo—pro,* before, and *creo,* to create. CREATE.] To beget; to generate and produce; to engender.—**procreation,** prō·kri·ā′shon, *n.* The act of procreating or begetting.—**procreative,** prō′kri·ā·tiv, *a.* Having the power or function of procreating.—**procreator,** prō′kri·ā·tėr, *n.* One that begets; a father or sire.—**procreant,** prō′-kri·ant, *a.* [L. *procreans, procreantis,* ppr. of *procreo.*] Procreating; producing young; assisting in producing young†.—*n.* One who or that which procreates.

Procrustean, prō·krus′ti·an, *a.* Pertaining to or resembling *Procrustes,* a robber of ancient Greece, who tortured his victims by placing them on a bed, and stretching or lopping off their legs to adapt the body to its length; hence, acting similarly; producing uniformity by deforming or mutilating.

proctor, prok′tėr, *n.* [Contr. from *procurator;* comp. *proxy.*] A procurator; a person employed to manage another's cause in a court of civil or ecclesiastical law; an official in a university whose function is to see that good order is kept and that obedience is maintained.—**proctorial,** prok·tō′ri·al, *a.* Pertaining to a proctor.—**proctorship,** *n.*

procumbent, prō·kum′bent, *a.* [L. *procumbens—pro,* forward, and *cumbere,* to lie.] Lying down; prone; *bot.* trailing; prostrate; lying on the ground, but without putting forth roots (a *procumbent* stem).

procurator, prok′ū·rā·tėr, *n.* [L., one who manages, an agent, from *procuro.* PROCURE.] The manager of another's affairs; one who undertakes the care of legal proceedings for another; a governor of a province under the Roman emperors.—**procuratorial,** pro·kū′ra·tō″ri·al, *a.* Pertaining to a procurator or proctor. —**procuracy,** prok′ū·ra·si, *n.* The office or service of a procurator; the management of an affair for another.—**procuration,** pro·kū·rā′-shon, *n.* Management of another's affairs; the document by which a person is empowered to transact the affairs of another.

procure, prō·kūr′, *v.t.*—procured, *procuring.* [Fr. *procurer,* from L. *procurare,* to take care of, to attend to—*pro,* for, and *cura,* care. CURE.] To obtain, as by request, loan, effort, labor, or purchase; to get, gain, come into possession of; to bring on; to attract (modesty *procures* respect); to cause, bring about, effect, contrive.—*v.i.* To pimp. **procurable,** prō·kū′ra·bl, *a.* Capable of being procured; obtainable.— **procurement,** prō·kūr′ment, *n.* The act of procuring or obtaining.— **procurer,** prō·kū′rėr, *n.* One that procures; a pimp; a pander.— **procuress,** prō′kū·res, *n.* A female pimp; a bawd.

procurvation, prō·kėr·vā′shon, *n.* [L. *pro,* forward, and *curvatio,* a curving.] A bending forward.

prod, prod, *n.* [A form of *brod, brad.*] A pointed instrument, as a goad or an awl; a stab.—*v.t.*—prodded, *prodding.* To prick with a pointed instrument; to goad.

prodigal, prod′i·gal, *a.* [L.L. *prodigalis,* from L. *prodigus,* prodigal, from *pro,* forth, and *ago,* to drive. ACT.] Given to extravagant expenditure; expending wastefully; profuse; lavish; wasteful; lavishly bountiful.—*n.* One that expends money extravagantly; one that is profuse or lavish; a waster; a spendthrift.— **prodigality,** prod·i·gal′i·ti, *n.* Extravagance in expenditure; profusion; waste; excessive or profuse liberality. —**prodigally,** prod′i·gal·li, *adv.* In a prodigal manner; extravagantly; lavishly; wastefully; profusely.

prodigious, prō·dij′us, *a.* [Fr. *prodigieux;* L. *prodigiosus,* strange, wonderful, from *prodigium,* a prodigy.] Of the nature of a prodigy‡; extraordinary; very great; huge; enormous; excessive; intense.—**prodigiously,** prō·dij′us·li, *adv.* Enormously; astonishingly; excessively. —**prodigiousness,** prō·dij′us·nes, *n.* —**prodigy,** prod′i·ji, *n.* [L. *prodigium.*] Something extraordinary from which omens are drawn; a portent; anything very extraordinary; a wonder or miracle (he is a *prodigy* of learning); something out of the ordinary course of nature.

produce, pro·dūs′, *v.t.*—produced, *producing.* [L. *produco—pro,* before, forward, and *ducere,* to lead, bring. DUKE.] To bring forward; to bring or offer to view or notice; to exhibit; to bring forth; to give birth to; to bear, furnish, yield; to cause, effect, bring about; to make; to bring into being or form; to make accrue (money *produces* interest); *geom.* to draw out in length; to extend (to *produce* a line for a certain distance).—*v.i.* To bring forth or yield appropriate offspring, products, or consequences.

produce, prod′ūs, *n.* A total produced, brought forth, or yielded; the outcome yielded by labor and natural growth; yield or production (the *produce* of a farm or of a country).—**producer,** pro·dū′sėr, *n.* One who or that which produces; one who finances or supervises the making of motion pictures, plays, etc.—**producers' goods,** *n.* Instruments of production; tools and raw materials; economic goods that benefit the consumer only indirectly.— **producible,** pro·dū′si·bl, *a.* Capable of being produced.—**product,** prod′-ukt, *n.* [L. *productum.*] A thing which is produced by nature, as fruit, grain, or vegetables; that which is yielded by the soil; that which is produced by labor or mental application; a production; something resulting as a consequence; result; *math.* the result of, or quantity produced by, the multiplication of two numbers or quantities together.—**production,** pro·duk′-shon, *n.* [L. *productio, productionis.*] The act or process of producing; *pol. econ.* the producing of articles having an exchange value; that which is produced or made (the productions of the earth, of art, of intellect).—**productive,** pro·duk′-tiv, *a.* Having the power of producing; fertile; producing good crops; bringing into being; causing to exist (an age *productive* of great men); *pol. econ.* producing commodities of great value; adding to the wealth of the world.—**productively,** pro·duk′tiv·li, *adv.* In a productive manner.—**productiveness,** pro·duk′tiv·nes, *n.* The quality of being productive.—**productivity,** prō·duk·tiv′i·ti, *n.* Power of producing; state or quality of being productive.

proem, prō′em, *n.* [Fr. *proème,* from L. *procemium,* Gr. *prooimion—pro,* before, and *oimos,* way.] Preface; introduction; preliminary observations to a book or writing.—**proemial,** prō·ēm′i·al, *a.* Having the character of a proem.

profane, prō·fān′, *a.* [Fr. *profane,* from L. *profanus,* profane, unholy— *pro,* forth from, and *fanum,* a temple. FANE.] Not sacred or devoted to sacred purposes; not possessing any peculiar sanctity; secular; irreverent toward God or holy things; speaking or spoken, acting or acted in contempt of sacred things or implying it; blasphemous; polluted.—*Profane history,* all history other than biblical.—*v.t.*—profaned, *profaning.* To treat as if not sacred or deserving reverence; to treat with irreverence, impiety, or sacrilege; to desecrate (to *profane* the name of God, or the Sabbath); to put to a wrong use; to employ basely or unworthily.— **profanation,** prof·a·nā′shon, *n.* The act of profaning; the violating of sacred things, or the treating of them with contempt or irreverence; desecration; the act of treating with too little delicacy.—**profanely,** prō-fān′li, *adv.* In a profane manner; impiously; blasphemously. — **profaneness,** prō·fān′nes, *n.*—**profaner,** prō·fā′nėr, *n.* One who profanes.— **profanity,** prō·fan′i·ti, *n.* The quality of being profane; that which is profane; profane language or conduct.

profess, pro·fes′, *v.t.* [L. *profiteri, professus,* to declare, acknowledge, profess—*pro,* before, and *fateor,* to avow; same root as *fame, fable, fate.*] To make open declaration of; to avow, acknowledge, own; to acknowledge or own publicly to be; to lay claim openly to the character of: used *refl.* (to *profess* one's self a Christian); to make a show of; to make protestations or a pretense of; to pretend (to *profess* great friendship for a person); to declare one's self versed in (he *professes* surgery).—*v.i.* To declare openly; to make any declaration or assertion. —**professedly,** pro·fes′ed·li, *adv.* By profession; avowedly.—**profession,** pro·fesh′on, *n.* [L. *professio.*] The act of professing; a public avowal or acknowledgment of one's sentiments or belief; a declaration; a representation or protestation (*professions* of friendship or sincerity); a calling superior to a mere trade or handicraft, as that of medicine, law, architecture, etc.; a vocation; the collective body of persons engaged in such calling.—**professional,** pro·fesh'on·al, a. Pertaining to a profession; engaged in a profession. —n. A member of any profession, but more often applied, in opposition to *amateur,* to persons who make their living by arts, etc., in which nonprofessionals are accustomed to engage.—**professionally,** pro·fesh'-on·al·li, adv. In a professional manner; in the way of one's profession or calling.—**professor,** pro·fes'er, n. [L.] One who professes; one who publicly unites himself to the visible church; one who is visibly or ostensibly religious; one that publicly teaches any art, science, or branch of learning; particularly, an official in a university, college, or other seminary, whose business is to deliver lectures or instruct students.—**professorial,** pro·fes·sō'ri·al, a. Pertaining to a professor in a college, etc.—**professoriate,** pro·fes·sō'ri·āt, n. A body of professors; the teaching staff of professors.—**professorship,** pro·fes'er·ship, n. The office of a professor.

proffer, prof'er, v.t. [Fr. *proférer,* from L. *proferre,* to bring forward—*pro,* before, and *ferre,* to bring. FERTILE, BEAR.] To hold out that a person may take; to offer for acceptance.—n. An offer made; something proposed for acceptance by another.

proficient, pro·fish'ent, n. [L. *proficiens,* from *proficio,* I advance, make progress, improve—*pro,* forward, and *facio,* to make. FACT.] One who has made considerable advances in any business, art, science, or branch of learning; an adept; an expert.—a. Well versed in any business or branch of learning; well qualified; competent.—**proficiently,** pro·fish'ent·li, adv. In a proficient manner.—**proficiency,** pro·fish'en·si, n. The state of being proficient; skill and knowledge.

profile, prō'fīl, n. [Fr. *profil,* from It. *profilo;* from L. *pro,* before, and *filum,* a thread, line.] An outline or contour; especially an outline of the human face seen sideways; the side face or half face; the outline or contour of anything, such as a building, portion of country, etc., as shown by a section. Used also as adj.—v.t.—**profiled, profiling.** To draw in profile; to give a profile of.

profit, prof'it, n. [Fr. *profit,* from L. *profectus,* progress, increase, from *proficio,* to advance, to improve. PROFICIENT.] Any advantage; an accession of good from labor or exertion; especially, the advantage or gain resulting to the owner of capital from its employment in any undertaking; the difference between the original cost and selling price of anything; pecuniary gain; emolument.—*Rate of profit,* the proportion which the amount of profit bears to the capital employed.—v.t. To benefit; to advantage; to be of service to; to advance.—v.i. To

derive profit; to improve; to make progress intellectually or morally; to gain pecuniarily; to become richer; to be of use or advantage; to bring good.—**profitable,** prof'i·ta·bl, a. Yielding or bringing profit or gain; gainful; lucrative; useful; advantageous.—**profitableness,** prof'-i·ta·bl·nes, n. The quality of being profitable.—**profitably,** prof'i·ta·bli, adv. In a profitable manner; gainfully; advantageously.—**profiteer,** prof·it·ēr', n. A trader who takes advantage of abnormal conditions, such as those of wartime, to make excessive profit.—v.i. To make excess profits.—**profitless,** prof'it·les, a. Void of profit, gain, or advantage.

profligate, prof'li·git, a. [L. *profligatus,* pp. of *profligo,* to rout, to ruin—*pro,* intens., and *fligo,* to strike down; seen also in *conflict, inflict,* etc.] Ruined in morals; abandoned to vice; lost to virtue or decency; vicious; shameless in wickedness.—n. An abandoned person; one who has lost all regard to good principles, virtue, or decency.—**profligately,** prof'li·git·li, adv. In a profligate manner.—**profligacy, profligateness,** prof'li·ga·si, prof'li·git·nes, n. The quality or condition of being profligate; a profligate or very vicious course of life; abandoned conduct.

profound, pro·found', a. [Fr. *profond,* L. *profundus—pro,* forward, far, and *fundus,* bottom. FOUND, FUND.] Deep; descending or being far below the surface, or far below the adjacent places; having great depth; intellectually deep; deep in knowledge or skill (a *profound* scholar); characterized by intensity; far-reaching; deeply felt (*profound* grief); touching; bending low; humble; exhibiting or expressing humility (a *profound* bow, *profound* reverence).—n. The deep; the sea; the ocean (with *the*); an abyss; a deep immeasurable space.—**profoundly,** pro·found'li, adv. In a profound manner.—**profoundness,** pro·found'-nes, n. Profundity; depth.—**profundity,** pro·fun'di·ti, n. The quality or condition of being profound; depth of place, of knowledge, etc.

profuse, pro·fūs', a. [L. *profusus,* from *profundo—pro,* forth, and *fundere,* to pour. FUSE.] Pouring forth lavishly; extravagant; lavish; liberal to excess; prodigal; poured forth lavishly; exuberant.—**profusely,** pro·fūs'li, adv. In a profuse manner; lavishly; prodigally.—**profuseness,** pro·fūs'nes, n. The state or quality of being profuse.—**profusion,** pro·fū'zhon, n. [L. *profusio.*] Profuse or lavish expenditure; rich abundance; lavish supply; exuberant plenty.

progeny, proj'e·ni, n. [Fr. *progénie,* L. *progenies,* from *pro,* forth, and root *gen,* to bring forth; seen also in *gender, generation, genus,* etc. GENUS.] Offspring collectively; children; descendants of the human kind, or offspring of other animals.—**progenitor,** pro·jen'i·ter, n. An ancestor in the direct line; a forefather; a parent.

proglottis, prō·glot'tis, n. pl. **proglottides,** prō·glot'ti·dēz. [Gr., the tip of the tongue.] *Zool.* the generative segment or joint of a tapeworm.

prognathic, prognathous, prog·nath'ik, prog·nā'thus, a. [Gr. *pro,* before, and *gnathos,* the cheek or jawbone.] Characterized by projecting jaws; applied to human skulls when the jaw slants forward, making the lower part of the face very prominent.—**prognathism,** prog·-nā'thizm, n. The condition of being prognathic.

prognosis, prog·nō'sis, n. [Gr. *prognōsis,* a foreknowing.] Foreknowledge; a forecast, especially of the probable course of a disease.

prognostic, prog·nos'tik, a. [Gr. *prognōstikos—pro,* before, and *gignōskō,* to know. KNOW.] Foreshowing; indicating something future by signs or symptoms.—n. A sign by which a future event may be known or foretold; an omen; a token; a symptom; a foretelling; prediction.—**prognosticate,** prog·nos'ti·kāt, v.t.—*prognosticated, prognosticating.* To foretell by means of present signs; to predict; to foreshow or foretoken; to indicate as to happen in the future.—v.i. To judge or pronounce from prognostics.—**prognostication,** prog·nos'ti·kā'-shon, n. The act of prognosticating; that which foreshows; a foretoken; previous sign.—**prognosticative,** prog·nos'ti·kā·tiv, a. Having the character of a prognostic.—**prognosticator,** prog·nos'ti·kā·ter, n. One who prognosticates.

program, prō'gram, n. [Fr. *programme,* from Gr. *programma—pro,* before, and *graphō,* to write.] A plan of proceedings sketched out beforehand; an outline or detailed sketch or advertisement of the order of proceedings or subjects embraced in any entertainment, performance, or public ceremony.—v.t. To organize data on a problem so it may be solved by an electronic computer.

progress, prog'res, n. [L. *progressus,* from *progredior,* I advance—*pro,* before, and *gradior,* to go, whence also *grade, gradual,* etc. GRADE.] A moving or going forward; a proceeding onward; a moving forward in growth; increase; advance in matters of any kind; course; intellectual or moral improvement; a passage from place to place; a journey.—v.i. (pro·gres'). To move forward or onward; to advance; to proceed in any course; to advance toward something better; to make improvement.—**progression,** pro·gresh'on, n. [L. *progressio.*] The act of progressing, advancing, or moving forward; progress; advance; course; passage; *math.* regular or proportional advance in increase or decrease of numbers; continued proportion, arithmetical or geometrical (thus 2, 4, 6, 8, 10 are numbers in *arithmetical progression;* 2, 4, 8, 16, etc., in *geometrical progression.*—**progressionist,** pro·gresh'on·ist, n. One who maintains that society is in a state

of progress toward perfection.—
progressive, pro·gres′iv, *a.* Moving
forward; proceeding onward; advancing; improving; in politics, one
who advocates the passage of social
and economic reform legislation.—
progressively, pro·gres′iv·li, *adv.*—
progressiveness, pro·gres′iv·nes, *n.*
The state or quality of being progressive.

prohibit, prō·hib′it, *v.t.* [L. *prohibeo,
prohibitus*—*pro,* before, and *habeo,*
I have, I hold. HABIT.] To forbid
authoritatively; to interdict by authority (to *prohibit* a person from
doing a thing; to *prohibit* the thing
being done); to prevent; to preclude.
—**prohibition,** prō·hi·bish′on, *n.*
The act of prohibiting; a declaration
to hinder some action; interdict;
the Eighteenth Amendment of the
United States Constitution, in effect
from 1919 to 1933, which forbade
the manufacture, sale or transportation of intoxicating liquors for use
as beverages.—**prohibitionist,** *n.*—
prohibitive, prohibitory, prō·hib′i·tiv, prō·hib′i·to·ri, *a.* Serving to
prohibit; forbidding; implying prohibition.

project, pro·jekt′, *v.t.* [L. *projicio,
projectum,* to cast forth, to cause to
jut out—*pro,* forward, and *jacio,* to
throw (as in *eject, reject,* etc.). JUT.]
To throw out or forth; to cast or
shoot forward; to scheme; to contrive; to devise; to exhibit or give
a delineation of on a surface; to
delineate.—*v.i.* To shoot forward;
to extend beyond something else; to
jut; to be prominent.—*n.* (proj′ekt).
[O.Fr. *project,* Mod.Fr. *projet.*] That
which is projected or devised; a plan;
a scheme; a design.—**projectile,**
pro·jek′til, *a.* Impelling forward (a
projectile force); caused by impulse
(*projectile* motion).—*n.* A body projected or impelled through the air,
as a stone thrown from the hand or
a sling, a bullet discharged from a
cannon.—**projection,** pro·jek′shon,
n. [L. *projectio.*] The act of projecting, throwing, or shooting forward; the state of projecting or
jutting out; a part projecting or
jutting out; a prominence; the act
of projecting or scheming; the representation of something by means of
lines, etc., drawn on a surface;
especially the representation of any
object on a perspective plane; the
delineation of the earth's surface or
a portion of it by a map. See GNOMON-
IC, ORTHOGRAPHIC, STEREOGRAPHIC.—
projector, pro·jek′tẽr, *n.* One who
projects; one who forms a scheme
or design; an optical device for
throwing pictures on a screen; a sort
of magic lantern.

prolapse, prolapsus, pro·laps′, pro··
lap′sus, *n.* [L. *prolapsus*—*pro,* forward, and *labor, lapsus,* to slip, fall.
LAPSE.] *Med.* a falling down of some
internal organ from its proper position; a falling down of the womb.—
v.i.—*prolapsed, prolapsing.* To fall
down or out; to suffer a prolapse.

prolate, prō′lāt, *a.* [L. *prolatus*—*pro,*
forth, and *latus,* carried.] Extended
beyond the line of an exact sphere.—

Prolate spheroid, a spheroid produced
by the revolution of a semi-ellipse
about its larger diameter; a sphere
that projects too much at the poles.
See OBLATE.

proleg, prō′leg, *n.* [L. *pro,* for, and
E. *leg.*] One of the leglike organs of
certain larvae, used in walking, but
which disappear in the perfect insect.

prolegomenon, prō·le·gom′e·non, *n.*
pl. **prolegomena,** prō·le·gom′e·na.
[Gr., from *pro,* before, and *legō,* to
speak.] A preliminary observation:
chiefly used in plural, and applied
to an introductory discussion or
discourse prefixed to a book or
treatise.—**prolegomenous,** prō·le··
gom′e·nus, *a.* Introductory.

prolepsis, prō·lep′sis, *n.* [Gr. *pro-
lēpsis,* preconception—*pro,* before,
and *lambanō,* I take.] Something of
the nature of an anticipation; *rhet.*
a figure by which a thing is represented as already done, though in
reality it is to follow as a consequence
of the action which is described
('he washed himself *clean*'); a figure
by which objections are anticipated;
an anachronism.—**proleptic,** prō··
lep′tik, *a.* Pertaining to prolepsis;
anticipatory.

proletarian, prō·le·tâ′ri·an, *a.* [L.
proletarius, a citizen of the lowest
class, one useful to the state only
by producing children, from *proles,*
offspring, from *pro,* before, and *ol,*
root of *adolesce.* ADULT.] Pertaining
to the proletarians.—*n.* A member
of the wage-earning class; a wage
earner who does not possess capital;
formerly, one of the rabble.—
proletarianism, prō·le·tâ′ri·an·izm,
n. The condition or political influence
of the lower orders of the community.
—**proletariat,** prō·le·tâ′ri·at, *n.* Proletarians collectively; the lower
classes.

proliferation, prō·lif′ẽr·ā″shon, *n.*
[L. *proles, prolis,* offspring, and *ferre,*
to bear.] Reproduction by continued
cell division or budding; the production of proliferous growths.—
proliferous, prō·lif′ẽr·us, *a.* Bot.
bearing or producing something abnormal or adventitious (as a flower
within another flower).

prolific, prō·lif′ik, *a.* [Fr. *prolifique*;
L. *prolificus*—*proles,* offspring, and
facio, to make. PROLETARIAN.] Producing young or fruit, especially in
abundance; fruitful; productive;
serving to give rise or origin; having
the quality of generating abundantly
(a topic *prolific* of controversy).—
prolifically, prō·lif′i·kal·li, *adv.* In a
prolific manner.—**prolificness,** prō··
lif′ik·nes, *n.*

prolix, prō·liks′, *a.* [L. *prolixus,*
extended, prolix—*pro,* forth, and
root of *liqueo,* to flow. LIQUID.] Long
and wordy; extending to a great
length; diffuse; indulging in lengthy
discourse; discussing at great length;
tedious.—**prolixity, prolixness,** prō··
lik′si·ti, prō·liks′nes, *n.* The state or
quality of being prolix.—**prolixly,**
prō·liks′li, *adv.* In a prolix manner.

prolocutor, prō·lok′ū·tẽr, *n.* [L.,
from *proloquor*—*pro,* for, and *loquor,
locutus,* to speak. LOQUACIOUS.] One

who speaks for another†; the speaker
or chairman of a convocation.

prologue, prō′log, *n.* [Fr., *prologue,*
L. *prologus,* from Gr. *prologos*—*pro,*
before, and *legō,* to speak.] A preface
or introduction; the discourse or
poem spoken before a dramatic performance or play begins; the speaker
of a prologue.—*v.t.*—*prologued, pro-
loguing.* To introduce with a formal
prologue; to preface.—**prologize,**
prō′log·īz, *v.i.*—*prologized, prologiz-
ing.* To deliver a prologue.

prolong, pro·long′, *v.t.* [Fr. *prolonger*
—L. *pro,* forth, and *longus.* LONG.]
To lengthen in time; to extend the
duration of; to lengthen out; to put
off to a distant time; to extend in
space or length (to *prolong* a line).—
v.i. To put off to a distant time.—
prolongation, prō·long·gā′shon, *n.*
The act of prolonging; a part prolonged; an extension.—**prolonger,**
prō·long′ẽr, *n.* One who or that
which prolongs.

prolusion, pro·lū′zhon, *n.* [L. *pro-
lusio,* a prelude—*pro,* before, and *ludo,
lusum,* to play. LUDICROUS.] A prelude
or preliminary; a preliminary trial.

prom, prom, *n.* [From *prom*enade.]
An American school dance or ball
(colloq.)

promenade, prom·e·näd′, *n.* [Fr.,
from *promener,* from L. *pro,* forward,
and *minare,* to drive, from *mina,* a
threat. MENACE.] A walk for pleasure
and show or exercise; a place for
walking in public.—*v.i.*—*promenad-
ed, promenading.* To walk for amusement, show, or exercise.

Promethean, prō·mē′thē·an, *a.*
[From *Prometheus* of Greek mythology, lit. the forethinker, who stole
fire from heaven and imparted it to
mortals.] Pertaining to Prometheus;
pertaining to fire or heat.

promethium, pro·mē′thi·um, *n.* [PRO-
METHEAN.] A metallic element of the
rare-earth series, a fission product of
uranium. Symbol, Pm; at. no., 61.

prominence, prom′i·nens, *n.* [L.
prominentia, from *promineo*—*pro,* forward, and *minere,* to project. EMI-
NENT.] A standing out from the
surface of something; that which juts
out; protuberance; state of being
distinguished among men; conspicuousness; distinction.—**prominent,**
prom′i·nent, *a.* [L. *prominens.*]
Standing out beyond the line or
surface of something; jutting; protuberant; distinguished above others
(a *prominent* character); likely to
attract special attention from size,
position, etc.; striking; conspicuous.
—**prominently,** prom′i·nent·li, *adv.*
In a prominent manner.

promiscuous, pro·mis′kū·us, *a.* [L.
promiscuus, from *promisceo*—*pro,* and
misceo, to mix. MIX.] Consisting of
individuals united in a body or mass
without order; mingled indiscriminately; forming part of a confused
crowd or mass; random; indiscriminate; not restricted to an individual.
—**promiscuously,** pro·mis′kū·us·li,
adv. In a promiscuous manner.—
promiscuousness, promiscuity, prō··
mis′kū·us·nes, prō·mis·kū′i·ti, *n.*
The state of being promiscuous.

promise, prom'is, n. [Fr. *promesse*, from L. *promissus*, put forward—*pro*, before, and *mittere*, to send. MIS-SION.] A declaration, written or verbal, made by one person to another, which binds the person who makes it to do or forbear a certain act specified; a declaration that something will be done or given for the benefit of another; ground or basis of expectation; earnest; pledge; that which affords a ground for expectation of future distinction (a youth of great *promise*).—*v.t.*—*promised, promising*. To make a promise of; to engage to do, give, grant, or procure for some one; to afford reason to expect (the year *promises* a good harvest).—*v.i.* To make a promise; to assure one by a promise; to afford hopes or expectations.—*I promise you*, I declare to you; I assure you.—**promisee**, prom·is·ē′, n. The person to whom a promise is made.—**promiser**, prom'is·ér, n. One who promises.—**promising**, prom'-is·ing, a. Giving promise; affording reasonable ground of hope for the future; looking as if likely to turn out well.—**promisingly**, prom'is·-ing·li, adv. In a promising manner.—**promissory**, prom'is·o·ri, a. Containing a promise or binding declaration of something to be done or foreborne.—*Promissory note*, a writing which contains a promise of the payment of money to a certain person at a specified date.

promontory, prom'on·tō·ri, n. [L. *promontorium*—*pro*, forward, and *mons, montis*, a mountain. MOUNT.] A high point of land or rock projecting into the sea beyond the line of coast; a headland.

promote, pro·mōt′, v.t.—*promoted, promoting*. [L. *promotus*, pp. of *promovere*, to move forward—*pro*, forward, and *movere*, to move. MOVE.] To contribute to the growth, enlargement, increase, or power of; to forward; to advance; to help onward; to excite; to stir up (as strife); to exalt or raise to a higher post or position; to elevate.—**promoter**, pro·mō′tér, n. One who or that which promotes; an encourager; one that aids in promoting some financial undertaking; one engaged in getting up a joint-stock company.—**promotion**, pro·mō′shon, n. The act of promoting; advancement; encouragement; exaltation in rank or honor; preferment.—**promotive**, pro·mō′-tiv, a. Tending to advance or promote.

prompt, promt, a. [Fr. *prompt*, from L. *promptus*, brought out, ready, quick, from *promo, promptum*, to bring forth—*pro*, forth, and *emo*, to take. EXEMPT.] Ready and quick to act as occasion demands; acting with cheerful alacrity; ready and willing; performed without delay; quick; ready; not delayed.—*v.t.* To move or excite to action or exertion; to incite; to instigate; to assist a speaker when at a loss by pronouncing the words forgotten or next in order (to *prompt* an actor); to dictate; to suggest to the mind.—*n. Com.* an

agreement in which one party engages to sell certain goods at a given price, and the other party to take them up and pay at a specified date.—**prompter**, prom'tér, n. One that prompts; specifically, one placed behind the scenes in a theater, whose business is to assist the actors when at a loss by uttering the first words of a sentence or words forgotten.—**promptitude**, prom'ti·tūd, n. Readiness; quickness of decision and action when occasion demands; readiness of will; cheerful alacrity.—**promptly**, promt'li, adv. In a prompt manner.—**promptness**, promt'nes, n. The state or quality of being prompt; promptitude.

promulgate, prō·mul′gāt, v.t.—*promulgated, promulgating*. [L. *promulgo, promulgatus*; origin unknown.] To make known by open declaration, as laws, decrees, tidings, etc.; to publish abroad; to announce; to proclaim.—**promulgation**, prō·mul·gā′shon, n. The act of promulgating; publication; open declaration.—**promulgator**, prō′mul·gā·tér or prō·mul′-gā·tér, n. One who promulgates or publishes abroad.—**promulge**, prō·-mulj′, v.t.—*promulged, promulging*. To promulgate.

pronation, prō·nā′shon, n. [From L. *pronus*, prone, having the face downward. PRONE.] That motion of the arm whereby the palm of the hand is turned downward; position of the hand with the thumb toward the body and the palm downward.—**pronator**, prō·nā′tér, n. A muscle of the forearm which turns the palm downward.

prone, prōn, a. [L. *pronus*, hanging or leaning forwards, prone, from *pro*, before, forward; cog. Gr. *prēnēs*, Skr. *pravana*, prone.] Bending forward; lying with the face downward; rushing or falling headlong or downward; sloping downward; inclined; inclined by disposition or natural tendency; propense; disposed: usually in a bad sense (men *prone* to evil, *prone* to strife).—**pronely**, prōn′li, adv. In a prone manner or position.—**proneness**, prōn′nes, n. The state of being prone; inclination; propensity; readiness.

pronephros, prō·nef′ros, n. [L. *pro*, before, Gr. *nephros*, a kidney.] In vertebrates, the first of three successive renal organs; the 'head' kidney.

prong, prong, n. [A nasalized form of prov.E. *prog*, to prod; W. *procio*, to thrust, to poke.] A sharp-pointed instrument; the spike of a fork or of a similar instrument; a pointed projection (the *prongs* of a deer's antlers).—*v.t.* To stab, as with a fork.—**pronghorn**, n. A species of hollow-horned antelope which inhabits the western parts of North America.

pronominal, prō·nom′i·nal, a. [L. *pronomen*, a pronoun. PRONOUN.] Belonging to or of the nature of a pronoun.—**pronominally**, prō·nom′-i·nal·li, adv. With the effect of a pronoun.

pronoun, prō′noun, n. [From *pro*, for, and *noun*; L. *pronomen*, a pronoun—*pro*, for, and *nomen*, a name,

a noun.] *Gram.* one of a certain class of words or generalized terms often used instead of a noun or name, to prevent the repetition of it: classified under the heads of *personal, relative, interrogative, possessive, demonstrative, distributive*, and *indefinite* pronouns, the last four classes being commonly called *adjective pronouns* or *pronominal adjectives*.

pronounce, pro·nouns′, v.t.—*pronounced, pronouncing*. [Fr. *prononcer*, from L. *pronuntio, pronuntiatus*—*pro*, before, and *nuntio*, to declare. NUN-CIO.] To form or articulate by the organs of speech; to utter; to speak; to utter formally, officially, or solemnly (the court *pronounced* sentence of death); to declare or affirm (he *pronounced* it a forgery).—*v.i.* To speak with confidence or authority; to utter an opinion; to use a certain pronunciation.—**pronounceable**, pro·nouns′a·bl, a. Capable of being pronounced.—**pronounced**, pro·-nounst′, a. [Fr. *prononcé*, pronounced.] Strongly marked or defined; decided (a man of *pronounced* views).—**pronouncement**, pro·nouns′ment, n. The act of pronouncing; a formal announcement.—**pronouncer**, prō·-nouns′ér, n. One who pronounces.—**pronunciation**, pro·nun′si·ā″shon, n. The act of pronouncing or uttering with articulation; the mode of uttering words or letters.

pronucleus, prō·nū′kli·us, n. [L. *pro*, before, *nucleus*.] One of the two nuclei seen in the course of fertilization of an ovum, the *female pronucleus* belonging to the ovum itself, and the *male pronucleus* to the sperm.

pronunciamento, prō·nun′shi·a·-men″to, n. [Sp. *pronunciamiento*]. A manifesto or proclamation.

pronto, pron′tō, a. and adv. [Sp.] Quick; quickly; right away.

proof, pröf, n. [O.E. *profe*, Fr. *preuve*, L.L. *proba*. PROVE.] Any effort, process, or operation that ascertains truth or fact; a test; a trial; what serves as evidence; what proves or establishes; that which convinces the mind and produces belief; a test applied to certain manufactured or other articles; the act of testing the strength of alcoholic spirits: hence, also the degree of strength in spirit; *printing*, a rough impression of type, in which errors may be detected and marked for correction; *engr.* an impression taken from an engraving to prove the state of it; an early impression, or one of a limited number taken before the letters to be inserted are engraved on the plate; called a *proof-impression*, and considered the best, because taken before the plate is worn.—*a.* Impenetrable; able to resist, physically or morally (*proof against* shot, *against* temptation).—**proofreader**, n. One who reads and marks corrections on printers' proofs.—**proof sheet**, n. *Printing*, a rough impression of composed type, taken to see if any errors remain for correction.—**proof spirit**, n. Alcoholic liquor, or mixture of alcohol and water, of certain standard strength, in U. S., 50% by volume.

prop, prop, n. [Same as Ir. *propa,* Gael. *prop,* a prop.] That which sustains an incumbent weight; a fulcrum; a support; a stay.—*v.t.*—*propped, propping.* To support by placing something under or against; to support by standing under or against; to support or sustain, in a general sense.

propaedeutics, prō·pē·dū′tiks, n. [Gr. *propaideuō,* to instruct beforehand, from *pro,* before, and *paideuō,* to educate, from *pais, paidos,* a child.] The preliminary learning connected with any art or science.—**propaedeutic, propaedeutical,** prō·pē·dū′tik, prō·pē·dū′ti·kal, a. Pertaining to propaedeutics; instructing beforehand.

propaganda, prop·a·gan′da, n. [From the congregatio de *propaganda* fide, at Rome. PROPAGATE.] The dissemination and the defense of beliefs, opinions, or actions deemed salutary to the program of a particular group; the propagation of doctrines and tenets of special interests, as an effort to give credence to information partly or wholly fallacious. [*cap.*] Originally, an institution of the Roman Catholic Church, established as a proselyting agency, now, [*not cap.*] generally an intensive undertaking of political partisans.—**propagandist,** n. One who devotes himself to the spread of any system of principles or set of actions; publicity agent.—**propagandize,** v.t. To present with propaganda.

propagate, prop′a·gāt, v.t.—*propagated, propagating.* [L. *propagare, propagatus,* to peg down, to propagate—*pro,* before, and *pag,* root of *pango,* to fasten, fix, set, plant (seen in *paction, compact, impinge,* etc.).] To continue or multiply by generation or successive reproduction; to cause to reproduce itself: applied to animals and plants; to spread from person to person or from place to place; to diffuse; to generate, beget, produce, originate.—v.i. To have young or issue; to be reproduced or multiplied by generation, or by new shoots or plants.—**propagation,** prop·a·gā′shon, n. The act of propagating; the multiplication of the kind or species by generation or reproduction; the spreading or extension of anything; diffusion.—**propagator,** prop′a·gā·tėr, n. One who propagates.—**propagable,** prop′a·ga·bl, a.

propane, prō′pān, n. [*Propyl* and meth*ane.*] *Chem.* a gaseous hydrocarbon, $CH_3CH_2CH_3$, of the methane series, found in crude petroleum.

propel, pro·pel′, v.t.—*propelled, propelling.* [L. *propello*—*pro,* forward, and *pello,* to drive, as in *compel, dispel, impel,* etc. PULSATE.] To drive forward; to urge or press onward by force.—**propellant,** pro·pel′ant, n. An explosive for projectile propulsion; also rocket-engine fuel.—**propellent,** pro·pel′ent, a. Driving forward; propelling. —**propeller,** pro·pel′ėr, n. One who or that which propels; a screw for propelling a motor-driven vessel; a rotary fan for propelling an airplane.

propense, pro·pens′, a. [L. *propensus,* hanging forwards, projecting, from *propendeo*—*pro,* forward, and *pendeo,* to hang. PENDANT.] Leaning toward, in a moral sense; inclined; disposed, either to good or evil; prone.—**propension,** pro·pen′shon, n. The state of being propense; propensity.—**propensity,** pro·pen′si·ti, n. Bent of mind, natural or acquired; inclination; natural tendency or disposition, particularly to evil.

proper, prop′ėr, v. [Fr. *propre,* from L. *proprius,* one's own, peculiar, proper; allied to *prope,* near. PROPINQUITY.] Peculiar; naturally or essentially belonging to a particular individual or state; natural; particularly suited to or befitting; belonging to as one's own; *gram.* applied to a noun when it is the name of a particular person or thing (Shakespeare, Boston), as opposed to *common*; fit; suitable; adapted; appropriate; correct; just; according to right usage; hence, properly so called; real; actual (the garden *proper*); *bot.* single, or connected with something single.—*Proper motion* (*astron.*), the real motion of the sun, planets, etc., as opposed to their apparent motions.—**properly,** prop′ėr·li, adv. In a proper manner; fitly; suitably; rightly; in a strict sense; strictly.—**property,** prop′ėr·ti, n. [Fr. *propriété,* L. *proprietas,* from *proprius,* one's own.] A peculiar quality of anything; that which is inherent in a thing, or naturally essential to it; an attribute; the exclusive right of possessing, enjoying, and disposing of a thing; ownership; the subject of such a right; the thing owned; an estate, whether in lands, buildings, goods, money, etc.; in *theaters,* a stage requisite; any article necessary to be produced in some scene.—**propertied,** prop′ėr·tid, a. Possessed of property.

prophecy, prof′e·si, n. [O.Fr. *prophecie, prophetie,* L. *prophetia,* from Gr. *prophēteia,* from *prophētēs,* a prophet—*pro,* before, and *phēmi,* to tell; same root as *fame.*] A foretelling; a declaration of something to come; especially, a foretelling inspired by God; a book of prophecies; *Scrip.* interpretation of Scripture; exhortation or instruction (O.T.).—**prophesier,** prof′e·sī·ėr, n. One who predicts events.—**prophesy,** prof′e·sī, v.t.—*prophesied, prophesying.* To foretell; to predict.—v.i. To utter predictions; to make declaration of events to come; *Scrip.* to interpret or explain Scripture or religious subjects.—**prophet,** prof′et, n. [L. *propheta,* from Gr. *prophētēs.*] One who foretells future events; a predictor; a foreteller; a person inspired or instructed by God to announce future events; *Scrip.* an interpreter. —*Minor prophets,* the authors of the last twelve books of the Old Testament, as opposed to Isaiah, Jeremiah, and Ezekiel.—**prophetess,** prof′et·es, n. A female prophet.—**prophetic, prophetical,** pro·fet′ik, pro·fet′i·kal, a. Pertaining or relating to a prophet

or prophecy; having the character of prophecy; containing prophecy.—**prophetically,** pro·fet′i·kal·li, adv. In a prophetic manner; by way of prediction.

prophylactic, prō·fi·lak′tik, a. [Gr. *prophylaktikos*—*pro,* before, and *phylassō,* to guard.] *Med.* preventive; defending from or warding off disease.—n. A medicine which preserves or defends against disease; a preventive.—**prophylaxis,** prō·fi·lak′sis, n. [Gr.] Preventive or preservative treatment.

propinquity, prō·pin′kwi·ti, n. [L. *propinquitas,* from *propinquus,* near, from *prope,* near; whence also (ap)*proach.* PROXIMITY.] Nearness in place; neighborhood; nearness in time; nearness of blood; kindred.

propitiate, pro·pish′i·āt, v.t.—*propitiated, propitiating.* [L. *propitio, propitiatum,* to propitiate, from *propitius,* propitious, from *pro,* forward, and *peto,* to seek, primarily referring to a bird whose flight is of happy augury. PETITION.] To appease and render favorable; to make propitious; to conciliate.—**propitiation,** pro·pish′i·ā″shon, n. The act of propitiating; *theol.* the atonement or atoning sacrifice offered to God to assuage his wrath and render him propitious to sinners.—**propitiator,** pro·pish′i·ā·tėr, n. One who propitiates.—**propitiatory,** pro·pish′i·a·to·ri, a. Having the power to make propitious; serving to propitiate.—n. *Jewish antiq.* the mercy seat; the lid or cover of the ark of the covenant.—**propitiable,** pro·pish′i·a·bl, a. Capable of being propitiated.—**propitious,** prō·pish′us, a. Favorably disposed toward a person; disposed to be gracious or merciful; ready to forgive sins and bestow blessings; affording favorable conditions or circumstances (a *propitious* season).—**propitiously,** pro·pish′us·li, adv. In a propitious manner.—**propitiousness,** pro·pish′us·nes, n.

propolis, prop′o·lis, n. [Gr. *pro,* before, and *polis,* city.] A substance having some resemblance to wax, used by bees to stop the holes and crevices in their hives.

propone, pro·pōn′, v.t. [L. *propono*—*pro,* before, and *pono,* to place. POSITION.] To propose; to propound.

proponent, prō·pō′nent, n. [L. *proponere,* to propose.] One that makes a proposal, or lays down a proposition; *law,* one who propounds something, especially one who propounds a will for probate.

proportion, pro·pōr′shon, n. [L. *proportio*—*pro,* before, and *portio,* part or share. PORTION.] The comparative relation of one thing to another in respect to size, quantity, or degree; a quota; symmetrical arrangement; the proper relation of parts in a whole; symmetry; that which falls to one's lot when a whole is divided according to rule; just or equal share; lot; *math.* the quality or similarity of ratios; *arith.* the rule of three, that rule which enables us to find a fourth proportional to three given numbers.—*Simple proportion,* the equality of the ratio of two quantities to that of two other quantities.—*Compound proportion*, the equality of the ratio of two quantities to another ratio, the antecedent and consequent of which are respectively the products of the antecedents and consequents of two or more ratios.—*Continued proportion*, a succession of several equal ratios, as 2, 4, 8, 16, etc.—*Harmonical* or *musical proportion*. See HARMONICAL.—*Reciprocal* or *inverse proportion*. See RECIPROCAL, INVERSE.—*v.t.* To adjust in a suitable proportion; to harmoniously adjust to something else as regards dimensions or extent; to form with symmetry.—**proportionable**, pro·pōr'shon·a·bl, *a.* Capable of being proportioned; being in proportion; having a due comparative relation; corresponding; well proportioned; symmetrical.—**proportional**, pro·pōr'shon·al, *a.* Having a due proportion; being in suitable proportion or degree; *math.* having the same or a constant ratio (*proportional* quantities).—*Proportional parts*, parts of magnitude such that the corresponding ones, taken in their order, are proportional.—*n.* A quantity in proportion; *math.* one of the terms of a proportion.—*Mean proportional.* See MEAN.—**proportionality**, pro·pōr'·shon·al'i·ti, *n.* The quality or state of being in proportion.—**proportionally**, pro·pōr'shon·al·li, *adv.* In proportion; in due degree; with suitable comparative relation.—**proportionate**, pro·pōr'shon·it, *a.* Having due proportion or relation; proportional. —*v.t.*—*proportionated, proportionating.* To make proportional; to adjust in due relation.—**proportionately**, pro·pōr'shon·it·li, *adv.* With due proportion.

propose, pro·pōz', *v.t.*—*proposed, proposing.* [Fr. *proposer*, to purpose, to propose, from *pro* and *poser.* POSE, COMPOSE. *Purpose* is the same word.] To bring forward or offer for consideration or acceptance; to bring forward as something to be done, attained, or striven after: often governing an infinitive.—*v.i.* To form or declare an intention or design; to offer one's self in marriage (to *propose* to a lady).—**proposal**, pro·pō'zal, *n.* That which is proposed or offered for consideration; a scheme or design, terms or conditions proposed (*proposals* of peace, of marriage).—**proposer**, pro·pō'zėr, *n.* One that proposes.—**proposition**, prop'·o·zish'on, *n.* [Partly from *propose*, partly from L. *propositio*, from *pro*, before, and *positio*, a placing. POSITION.] That which is proposed or offered for consideration, acceptance, or adoption; a proposal; term or offer advanced; *gram.* and *logic*, a form of speech in which something is affirmed or denied of a subject; *math.* a statement of either a truth to be demonstrated, or an operation to be performed.—**propositional**, prop'o·zish'on·al, *a.* Pertaining to a proposition; considered as a proposition.

propound, pro·pound', *v.t.* [O.E.

propoune, from L. *propono*, to put forth—*pro*, before, and *pono*, to place; as to form, comp. *compound, expound.* POSITION.] To offer for consideration; to propose; to put or set, as a question.—**propounder**, pro·poun'dėr, *n.* One who propounds.

propraetor, pro·prē'tor, *n.* [L. *propraetor*—*pro*, for, and *praetor.*] A Roman magistrate who, having discharged the office of praetor at home, was sent into a province to command there.

proprietary, pro·prī'e·te·ri, *n.* [Fr. *propriétaire*, a proprietor, from *propriété*, property. PROPERTY.] A proprietor; more commonly a body of proprietors collectively.—*a.* Belonging to a proprietor or owner; belonging to ownership.—**proprietor**, pro·prī'e·tėr, *n.* An owner; the person who has the legal right or exclusive title to anything.—**proprietorship**, pro·prī'e·tėr·ship, *n.* The state or right of a proprietor.—**proprietress**, pro·prī'e·tres, *n.* A female proprietor.—**propriety**, pro·prī'e·ti, *n.* [L. *proprietas*, from *proprius*, one's own.] Property‡; possession‡; suitableness to an acknowledged or correct standard; consonance with established principles, rules, or customs; fitness; justness.— pl. *The proprieties*, conformity with established customs in social life.

propulsion, pro·pul'shon, *n.* [From L. *propello, propulsum.* PROPEL.] The act of driving forward.—**propulsive**, pro·pul'siv, *a.* Tending or having power to propel; driving or urging on.

propylaeum, prop'i·le·um, *n.* pl. **propylaea**, prop·i'le·a. [Gr. *propylaion*, from *pro*, before, and *pylē*, a gate.] The porch, vestibule, or entrance of an edifice.

pro rata, prō rā'ta. Proportionately; in accordance with some determined standard, such as a share or liability. —**prorate**, prō·rāt', *v.t.* and *i.* To distribute proportionately; to make a pro rata assessment.

prorogue, prō·rōg', *v.t.*—*prorogued, proroguing.* [Fr. *proroger*, from L. *prorogare*, to prolong, continue—*pro*, before, and *rogo*, to ask. ROGATION.] To protract or prolong, to defer or delay‡; to adjourn a parliament for an indefinite period by royal authority. *British parl. practice.*—**prorogation**, prō·rō·gā'shon, *n.* The act of proroguing.

prosaic. See PROSE.

proscenium, prō·sē'ni·um, *n.* [L. *proscenium*, from Gr. *proskēnion*— *pro*, before, and *skēnē*, a scene. SCENE.] *Arch.* the part in a theater from the curtain or drop scene to the orchestra; the curtain and the ornamental framework from which it hangs. In the ancient theater the proscenium comprised the whole stage.

proscribe, prō·skrīb', *v.t.*—*proscribed, proscribing.* [L. *proscribo*—*pro*, before, in public, and *scribo*, to write. SCRIBE.] Among the Romans, to publish the name of, as doomed to destruction and seizure of property; hence, to put out of the protection

of the law; to outlaw; to reject utterly; to interdict, exclude, prohibit.—**proscriber**, prō·skrī'bėr, *n.* One who proscribes.—**proscription**, prō·skrip'shon, *n.* [L. *proscriptio.*] The act of proscribing; outlawry; exclusion; the dooming or denouncing of citizens to death and confiscation of goods, as public enemies. —**proscriptive**, prō·skrip'tiv, *a.* Pertaining to or consisting in proscription; proscribing.—**proscriptively**, prō·skrip'tiv·li, *adv.* In a proscriptive manner.

prose, prōz, *n.* [Fr. *prose*, from L. *prosa* for *prorsa* (*oratio*, speech, understood), from *prorsus*, forward, straight on—*pro*, forward, and *versus*, turned. VERSE.] The ordinary written or spoken language of man; language unconfined to poetical measure, as opposed to *verse* or *metrical composition*; hence, dull and commonplace language or discourse. —*a.* Relating to or consisting of prose; prosaic.—*v.i.*—*prosed, prosing.* To write in prose; to write or speak tediously.—**prosaic**, prō·zā'ik, *a.* In the form of prose; dull; uninteresting; commonplace.—**prosaically**, prō·zā'i·kal·li, *adv.* In a prosaic manner.—**proser**, prō'zėr, *n.* One who proses.—**prosy**, prō'zi, *a.* Like prose; dull; tedious.—**prosily**, prō'zi·li, *adv.* In a prosy manner; tediously.—**prosiness**, prō'zi·nes *n.* State or quality of being prosy.

prosecute, pros'e·kūt, *v.t.*—*prosecuted, prosecuting.* [L. *prosequor, prosecutus*—*pro*, before, and *sequor*, to follow. SEQUENCE. *Pursue* is the same word.] To pursue with a view to attain, execute, or accomplish; to apply to with continued purpose; to carry on; to continue; *law*, to seek to obtain by legal process; to pursue for redress or punishment before a legal tribunal.—*v.i.* To carry on a legal prosecution; to act as a prosecutor.—**prosecution**, pros·e·kū'shon, *n.* The act or process of prosecuting; the proceeding with or following up any matter in hand (the *prosecution* of a design, an inquiry, etc.); the carrying on of a suit in a court of law; the process of exhibiting formal charges against an offender before a legal tribunal; the party by whom criminal proceedings are instituted. —**prosecutor**, pros'e·kū·tėr, *n.* One who prosecutes; the person who institutes and carries on proceedings in a court of justice.

proselyte, pros'e·līt, *n.* [Fr. *prosélyte*, from Gr. *prosēlytos*, one newly come —*pros*, towards, and root of *elthein*, to come.] A new convert to some religion or religious sect, or to some particular opinion, system, or party. —**proselytism**, pros'e·līt·izm, *n.* The act or system of making proselytes; conversion to a system or creed.— **proselytize**, pros'e·līt·īz, *v.t.*—*proselytized, proselytizing.* To make a proselyte or convert of.—*v.i.* To engage in making proselytes.

prosencephalon, pros·en·sef'a·lon, *n.* [Prefix *pros*, toward, and Gr. *encephalon.*] The forebrain or anterior part of the brain.

---

prosenchyma, pros·en′ki·ma, *n*. [Gr. *pros*, near, and *enchyma*, an infusion.] *Bot*. tissue of fusiform or fibriform cells, as of woody tissues.

prosody, pros′o·di, *n*. [L. *prosodia*, from Gr. *prosōdia*, a song sung to music, prosody—*pros*, to, and *odē*, a song, an ode.] That part of grammar which treats of the quantity of syllables, of accent, and of the laws of versification; the rules of rhythm or versification.—**prosodiacal**, pros··o·dī′a·kal, *a*. Pertaining to prosody. —**prosodial, prosodical**, pro·sō′di··al, pro·sod′i·kal, *a*. Pertaining to prosody; according to the rules of prosody.—**prosodist**, pros′o·dist, *n*. One skilled in prosody.

prosopopoeia, pros′o·pō·pē″ya, *n*. [Gr. *prosōpopoiia*—*prosōpon*, person, and *poieō* to make.] A figure in rhetoric by which things inanimate are spoken of as animated beings; personification.

prospect, pros′pekt, *n*. [L. *prospectus*, from *prospicio*, to look forward—*pro*, forward, and *specio*, to see. SPECIES.] View of things within the reach of the eye; sight; that which is presented to the eye; the place and the objects seen; a looking forward; anticipation; expectation or ground of expectation (little *prospect* of success).—*v.i.* and *t*. (pros·pekt′). *Mining*, to make a search; to search for metal.—**prospective**, pros·pek′tiv, *a*. Looking forward; being in prospect or expectation; looked forward to (*prospective* advantages).—**prospectively**, pros·pek′tiv·li, *adv*. In a prospective manner.—**prospector**, pros′pek·tėr, *n*. One who searches for precious stones or metals as preliminary to settled or continuous operations.—**prospectus**, pros·pek′tus, *n*. [L., prospect, sight, view.] A brief sketch issued for the purpose of making known the chief features of some commercial enterprise proposed, as the plan of a literary work, or the proposals of a new company or joint-stock association.

prosper, pros′pėr, *v.i.* [Fr. *prospérer*, L. *prosperare*, from *prosperus*, favorable, fortunate, from *pro*, before, and *spes*, hope.] To be successful; to succeed; to advance in wealth or any good: said of persons; to be in a successful state; to turn out successfully: said of affairs; to be in a healthy growing state; to thrive: said of plants and animals.—*v.t.* To make prosperous; to render successful.—**prosperity**, pros·per′i·ti, *n*. [L. *prosperitas*.] The state of being prosperous; good progress in any business or enterprise; success; attainment of the object desired; good fortune.—**prosperous**, pros′pėr·us, *a*. [L. *prosperus*.] Making good progress in the pursuit of anything desirable; thriving; successful; favorable; favoring success. ∴ Syn. under FORTUNATE.—**prosperously**, pros′pėr·us·li, *adv*. In a prosperous manner; successfully.—**prosperousness**, pros′pėr·us·nes, *n*. Prosperity.

prostate, prostatic, pros′tāt, pros··tat′ik, *a*. [Gr. *prostatēs*, standing be-

fore—*pro*, before, and stem *sta*, to stand.] Applied to a gland situated just before the neck of the bladder in males.

prosthesis, pros′the·sis, *n*. [Gr. *pros*, to, and *thesis*, a placing, from *tithēmi*, to place.] *Surg*. the addition of an artificial part to supply a defect of the body; *philol*. the adding of one or more letters to the commencement of a word (beloved).—**prosthetic**, pros·thet′ik, *a*. Pertaining to prosthesis.

prostitute, pros′ti·tūt, *v.t.*—*prostituted, prostituting*. [L. *prostituo, prostitutus*—*pro*, before, and *statuo*, to place. STATE.] To offer freely to a lewd use, or to indiscriminate lewdness for hire; to give up to any vile or infamous purpose; to sell to wickedness; to offer or expose upon vile terms or to unworthy persons.— *a*. Openly devoted to lewdness.—*n*. A female given to indiscriminate lewdness; a strumpet; a harlot; a base hireling.—**prostitution**, pros··ti·tū′shon, *n*. The act or practice of yielding the body to indiscriminate intercourse with men for hire; the act of offering to an infamous employment.—**prostitutor**, pros′ti·tū··tėr, *n*. One who prostitutes.

prostrate, pros′trāt, *a*. [L. *prostratus*, pp. of *prosterno, prostratum*, to lay flat—*pro*, before, and *sterno*, to strew. STRATUM.] Lying at length, or with the body extended on the ground; lying at mercy, as a suppliant; lying in the posture of humility or adoration; *bot*. lying flat and spreading on the ground without taking root.— *v.t.*—*prostrated, prostrating*. To lay flat or prostrate; *refl*. to throw one's self down as in humility or adoration; *fig*. to throw down; to overthrow; to ruin; to reduce to nothing (to *prostrate* one's strength).—**prostration**, pros·trā′shon, *n*. The act of prostrating or laying flat; the act of falling down, or of bowing in humility or adoration; great depression or reduction (as of strength or spirits).

prosy. See PROSE.

protactinium, prō′tak·tin″i·um, *n*. [*Proto*, first, and *actinium*.] A radioactive metallic element yielding actinium upon disintegration. Symbol, Pa; at. no., 91.

protagonist, prō·tag′o·nist, *n*. [Gr. *prōtagōnistes*—*prōtos*, first, and *agōnistēs*, an actor.] The leading character or actor in a literary work.

protasis, prō′ta·sis, *n*. [Gr. *protasis*—*pro*, before, and *teinō*, to stretch.] The first clause of a conditional sentence, being the condition on which the *apodosis* depends, as, if we run (*protasis*) we shall be in time (*apodosis*).

protean. See PROTEUS.

protect, pro·tekt′, *v.t.* [From L. *protectus*, pp. of *protego*, to protect—*pro*, before, and *tego*, to cover, from root seen also in E. *thatch*.] To cover or shield from danger or injury; to serve as a cover or shelter to; to defend; to guard.—**protectingly**, pro·tek′ting·li, *adv*. In a protecting manner.—**protection**, pro·tek′shon, *n*. The act of protecting, or state of

being protected; defense; shelter from evil; that which protects or preserves from injury; a passport or other writing which secures from molestation; exemption, as from arrest in civil suits; an artificial advantage conferred by a legislature on articles of home production, usually by duties imposed on the same articles introduced from abroad.— **protectionism**, pro·tek′shon·izm, *n*. The system of protection to commodities of home production.—**protectionist**, pro·tek′shon·ist, *n*. One who favors the protection of some branch of industry by legal enactments; one opposed to free trade; tariff booster.—**protective**, pro·tek′tiv, *a*. Affording protection; sheltering; defensive.—*Protective duties*, duties imposed on imports to prevent their obtaining an advantage in the market over commodities of home production.—*Protective substance*, an ANTITOXIN (which see).—**protector**, pro·tek′tėr, *n*. One who or that which protects; a defender; a guardian.— *Eng. hist*. one who had the care of the kingdom during the king's minority; a regent; [*cap*.] a title specifically applied to Oliver Cromwell, who assumed the title of *Lord Protector* in 1653.—**protectorate**, pro·tek′tėr··āt, *n*. Government by a protector; the period in English history during which Cromwell was protector; the protection of a weaker country by a stronger.—**protectorship**, pro·tek′tėr·ship, *n*. The office of a protector.

protégé, prō′te·zhā′, fem. **protégée**, prō′te·zhā′, *n*. [Fr., one protected.] One under the care and protection of another.

protein, prō′tē·in, *n*. [From Gr. *prōtos*, first.] One of a class of complex chemical compounds which contain carbon, hydrogen, nitrogen, oxygen, and sulfur, are essential constituents of living matter, and on decomposition yield various amino acids.—**proteide**, prō′tē·id, *n*. An older name for PROTEIN.

proteolytic, prō′ti·o·lit″ik, *a*. [*Protein* and Gr. *lysis*, a solution.] Of an enzyme, converting ordinary proteins into peptones.

proteose, prō′ti·ōs, *n*. [Gr. *prōtos*, first.] A class of products derived from proteins by hydrolysis.

protest, pro·test′, *v.i.* [L. *protestor*— *pro*, before, and *testor*, to affirm, from *testis*, a witness. TEST.] To affirm with solemnity; to asseverate; to make a solemn or formal declaration (often in writing) expressive of opposition to something.—*v.t.* To make a solemn declaration or affirmation of; to assert.—*To protest a bill of exchange*, to mark or note it, through a notary public, for non-payment or non-acceptance.—*n*. (prō′test). A solemn declaration of opinion, commonly against some act; a formal statement (usually in writing), by which a person declares that he dissents from an act to which he might otherwise be deemed to have yielded assent; *law*, a formal declaration that acceptance or payment of a bill or promissory note has been

refused.—**protestant,** prot'es·tant, *n.*
Lit. one who protests; [*cap.*] a name
given to the party who adhered to
Luther at the Reformation in 1529,
and protested against a decree of the
Emperor Charles V and the diet of
Spires; now applied to all those
Christian denominations that differ
from the Church of Rome, and that
sprang from the Reformation.—*a.*
Belonging to the religion of the
Protestants.—**Protestantism,** prot'-
es·tant·izm, *n.* The principles or
religion of Protestants.—**protestation,** prot·es·tā'shon, *n.* [L. *protes-
tatio.*] A solemn declaration; an
asseveration; a solemn declaration of
dissent; a protest.—**protester,** pro·
tes'tėr, *n.* One who protests; one who
protests a bill of exchange.

Proteus, prō'ti·us, *n.* A marine deity
of the ancient Greeks who had the
faculty of assuming different shapes;
hence, one who easily changes his
form or principles; *zool.* a small
amphibious animal with both lungs
and gills, living in certain subterranean lakes, and having rudimentary eyes.—**protean,** prō'ti·an, *a.*
Readily assuming different shapes;
exceedingly variable.

prothesis, proth'e·sis, *n.* [Gr. *prothesis*—*pro,* forth, and *thesis,* a placing.] The place in a church on which
the elements for the Eucharist are
put previous to their being placed
on the altar; a credence.

prothonotary, prō·thon'e·te·ri, *n.*
[L.L. *protonotarius*—Gr. *prōtos,* first,
and L. *notarius,* a scribe. NOTARY.
The insertion of *h* is a mistake.] A
chief notary or clerk; in the *R. Cath.
Ch.* a sort of registrar; one of twelve
constituting a college, who receive
the last wills of cardinals, etc.; in the
Eastern Church, the chief secretary
of the patriarch of Constantinople.
In some states of the U. S. a chief
clerk of a court.

prothorax, prō·thō'raks, *n.* [Gr. *pro,*
before, and *thōrax.*] *Entom.* the first
or anterior segment of the thorax
in insects.

protocol, prō'tō·kol, *n.* [Fr. *protocole,*
L.L. *protocollum,* the first leaf, the
first sheet of a legal instrument glued
to the cylinder round which the
document was rolled—Gr. *prōtos,*
first, *kolla,* glue.] The minutes or
rough draft of some diplomatic document or instrument; a document
serving as a preliminary to, or for the
opening of, any diplomatic transaction; a record or registry; rules of
etiquette and order of preference in
diplomatic ceremonies.—*v.t.*—*proto-
colled, protocolling.* To make a protocol of.

protomartyr, prō'tō·mär"tėr, *n.* [Gr.
prōtos, first, and *martyr,* martyr.] The
first martyr; a term applied to
Stephen, the first Christian martyr;
the first who suffers or is sacrificed
in any cause.

protomorphic, prō·to·mor'fik, *a.*
[Gr. *protos,* first, and *morphē,* shape.]
In the earliest form or shape.

proton, prō'ton, *n.* A positively
charged subatomic particle in the
nucleus of an atom, the number of

protons in the atomic nucleus of each
element being different.

protonema, prō·to·nē'ma, *n.* [Gr.
protos, first, *nēma,* a thread.] In
mosses, a threadlike structure resulting from germination of a spore.

protonotary, prō·ton'o·ta·ri, *n.* See
PROTHONOTARY.

protoplasm, prō'to·plazm, *n.* [Gr.
protos, first, and *plasma,* anything
formed or molded, from *plassō,* to
mold.] A transparent substance, a
complex and unstable mixture of
proteins and other compounds, and
constituting the basis of living matter
in animal and plant structures.—
protoplasmic, prō·to·plaz'mik, *a.*
Pertaining to, resembling, or consisting of protoplasm.—**protoplast,**
prō'to·plast, *n.* An original; a thing
first formed, as a copy to be imitated.
—**protoplastic,** prō·to·plas'tik, *a.*
First formed.

prototype, prō'to·tīp, *n.* [Gr. *proto-
typos*—*prōtos,* first, and *typos,* type.]
An original or model after which
anything is formed; a pattern; archetype.

protoxide, prō·tok'sīd, *n.* [Gr. *protos,*
first, and E. *oxide.*] That member of
a series of oxides having the lowest
proportion of oxygen.—**protoxidize,**
prō·tok'si·dīz, *v.t.*

Protozoa, prō·to·zō'a, *n. pl.* [Gr.
prōtos, first, and *zōon,* an animal.]
A phylum composed of the most
lowly organized members of the
animal kingdom, and which may be
defined to be animals composed of
a nearly structureless jelly-like substance without a definite body cavity
or trace of a nervous system.

protozoan, prō·to·zō'an, *n.* [Gr.
protos, first, and *zōon,* animal.] A
member of the phylum Protozoa
comprised of single-celled, microscopic animals that reproduce by
fission.—**protozoic,** prō·to·zō'ik, *a.*

protract, prō·trakt', *v.t.* [From L.
protractus, from *protraho*—*pro,* forward, and *traho,* to draw (whence
trace, traction, extract, etc.).] To
draw out or lengthen in time; to
prolong; to lengthen out in space;
to delay, defer, put off; *surv.* to draw
to a scale.—**protractile,** prō·trak'til,
a. Capable of being protracted, or
thrust forward.—**protraction,** prō·-
trak'shon, *n.* The act of protracting;
surv. the act of laying down on
paper the dimensions of a field, etc.—
protractive, prō·trak'tiv, *a.* Prolonging; continuing; delaying.—**pro-
tractor,** prō·trak'tėr, *n.* One who
protracts; *surv.* an instrument for
laying down and measuring angles
on paper; *anat.* a muscle which
draws forward a part.

protrude, prō·tröd', *v.t.*—*protruded,
protruding.* [L. *protrudo*—*pro,* forth,
forwards, and *trudo,* to thrust (seen
in *obtrude, intrude*).] To thrust forward; to shoot forth or project, or
cause to project.—*v.i.* To shoot
forward; to stand out prominently.—
protrusile, prō·trö'sīl, *a.* Capable of
being protruded and withdrawn.—
protrusion, prō·trö'zhon, *n.* The act
of protruding.—**protrusive,** prō·-
trö'ziv, *a.* Thrusting or impelling

forward.—**protrusively,** prō·trö'ziv·-
li, *adv.*

protuberate, prō·tū'bėr·āt, *v.t.*—*pro-
tuberated, protuberating.* [L.L. *pro-
tubero, protuberatus*—L. *pro,* before,
and *tuber,* a hump, a swelling, akin
to *tumeo,* to swell. TUMID.] To swell
or be prominent beyond the adjacent
surface; to bulge out.—**protuberance,** prō·tū'bėr·ans, *n.* A swelling
or tumor; a prominence; a bunch or
knob; anything swelled or pushed
beyond the surrounding or adjacent
surface.—**protuberant,** prō·tū'bėr·-
ant, *a.* Swelling; prominent beyond
the surrounding surface.—**protuber-
antly,** prō·tū'bėr·ant·li, *adv.*

protyle, prō'tīl, *n.* [Gr. *protos,* first.]
A hypothetical substance supposed
by Crookes to be the basis of all
matter.

proud, proud, *a.* [A.Sax. *prút,* proud,
whence *prýte,* pride; cog. Dan. *prud,*
stately, magnificent.] Possessing a
high and often an unreasonable opinion of one's own excellence; filled
with or showing inordinate self-
esteem; possessing a praiseworthy
self-esteem that deters from anything
mean or base; haughty; arrogant;
ready to boast; elated; priding one's
self (*proud* of one's country); arising
from pride; presumptuous; of fearless or untamable character; suggesting or exciting pride; ostentatious; grand; magnificent.—*Proud
flesh,* an excessive development of
granulations in wounds and ulcers.—
proudly, proud'li, *adv.*

prove, pröv, *v.t.*—*proved, proving.*
[O.Fr. *prover, pruver,* Fr. *prouver,*
from L. *probare,* to try, test, prove,
lit. to test the good quality of, from
probus, good (whence *probity*). *Proof*
is a derivative.] To try or ascertain
by an experiment; to test; to make
trial of (to *prove* gunpowder); to
establish the truth or reality of by
reasoning, induction, or evidence;
to demonstrate; to establish the
authenticity or validity of; to obtain
probate of (to *prove* a will); to gain
personal experience of; *arith.* to
show or ascertain the correctness of
by a further calculation.—*The exception proves the rule,* lit. the exception
tests or tries the rule.—*v.i.* To be
found or ascertained by experience
or trial; to turn out to be (the report
proved to be false); to attain certainty.—**provable,** prō'va·bl, *a.* Capable of being proved.—**proven,**
prō'vn, *pp.* [A strong form for
proved, the proper pp. Its usage in
English is rare.] Proved.—*Not prov-
en, Scots law,* a verdict given by
a jury in a criminal case when,
although there is a deficiency of
evidence to convict the prisoner,
there is sufficient to warrant grave
suspicion of his guilt.—**prover,** prō'-
vėr, *n.* One who or that which proves.
—**proving ground,** *n.* A place for
scientific testing and experiment,
hence, a practical test for something.

provenance, prov'e·nans, *n.* [Fr.—L.
pro, and *venio,* to come.] Source or
place of origin; quarter whence
something is got.

Provencal, pro·van·säl', *n.* A native

of Provence, or Southern France; the Romance language of Provence.

provender, prov'en·dėr, *n.* [From Fr. *provende* (with *r* somewhat unaccountably added), from L. *praebenda*, things to be supplied. PREBEND.] Dry food for beasts, as hay, straw, and corn; provisions; food.

proventriculus, prō'ven·trik″ū·lus, *n.* [Gr. *pro*, in front of, L. *ventriculus*, a stomach.] In birds, the first or chemical stomach.

proverb, prov'ėrb, *n.* [Fr. *proverbe*, L. *proverbium*—*pro*, before, in public, and *verbum*, a word.] A short pithy sentence expressing a truth ascertained by experience or observation; a sentence which briefly and forcibly expresses some practical truth; a wise saw; an adage; a maxim; a short dramatic composition in which some proverb or popular saying is taken as the foundation of the plot; a by-word; a reproach or object of contempt; *Scrip.* a dark saying of the wise that requires interpretation.—**proverbial,** pro·vėr'bi·al, *a.* Comprised in a proverb; used or current as a proverb; resembling a proverb.—**proverbially,** pro·vėr'bi·al·li, *adv.* In a proverbial manner or style; by way of proverb.

provide, pro·vīd', *v.t.*—*provided, providing.* [L. *provideo*, lit. to see before—*pro*, before, and *video, visum*, to see (whence *vision, visible, revise*, etc.).] To procure beforehand; to prepare (to *provide* warm clothing); to furnish; to supply (well *provided* with corn); to lay down as a previous arrangement; to make a previous condition or understanding.—*v.i.* To make provision; to take measures beforehand (we must *provide* for our wants, *against* mishaps).—**provided,** pro·vī'ded, *conj.* [A conjunction only by ellipsis = it being provided that.] On condition; on these terms; this being conceded.—**providence,** prov'i·dens, *n.* [L. *providentia.*] Foresight‡; timely care or preparation‡; prudence; the care of God over his creatures; divine superintendence; [*cap.*] God, regarded as exercising forecast, care, and direction for and over his creatures; the divine being or power; something due to an act of providential intervention; a providential circumstance.—**provident,** prov'i·dent, *a.* [L. *providens*, ppr. of *provideo*, I provide; the same word as *prudent*, as *providence* = *prudence.*] Foreseeing wants and making provision to supply them; prudent in preparing for future exigencies; frugal; economical.—**providential,** prov·i·den'shal, *a.* Effected by the providence of God; referable to divine providence.—**providentially,** prov·i·den'shal·li, *adv.* In a providential manner.—**providently,** *adv.* In a provident manner; with prudent foresight.—**provider,** pro·vī'dėr, *n.* One who provides.

province, prov'ins, *n.* [Fr., from L. *provincia*, a province—*pro*, before, and *vinco*, I conquer.] Originally, a region reduced under Roman

dominion and subjected to the command of a governor sent from Rome; hence, a territory at some distance from the metropolis (*the provinces* being often thus used in contradistinction to the metropolis); a large territorial or political division of a state; in England, a division for ecclesiastical purposes under the jurisdiction of an archbishop, there being two *provinces*, that of Canterbury and that of York; *fig.* the proper duty, office, or business of a person; sphere of action; a division in any department of knowledge or speculation; a department.—**provincial,** pro·vin'shal, *a.* Pertaining to a province; forming a province; exhibiting the manners of a province; characteristic of the inhabitants of a province; rustic; not polished; rude; pertaining to an ecclesiastical province or to the jurisdiction of an archbishop.—*n.* A person belonging to a province as distinguished from the metropolis; in some religious orders, a monastic superior in a given district.—**provincialism,** pro·vin'shal·izm, *n.* A peculiar word or manner of speaking in a district of country remote from the principal country or from the metropolis.—**provinciality,** pro·vin'shi·al″i·ti, *n.* The quality of being provincial.—**provincially,** pro·vin'shal·li, *adv.* In a provincial manner.

provision, pro·vizh'on, *n.* [L. *provisio, provisionis*, a foreseeing, foresight, purveying, from *providere, provisum*, to foresee. PROVIDE.] The act of providing or making previous preparation; a measure taken beforehand; provident care; accumulation of stores or materials beforehand; a store or stock; a stock of food provided; hence, victuals; food: usually in the plural; a stipulation or measure proposed in an enactment or the like; a proviso.—*v.t.* To provide with things necessary, especially victuals or food.—**provisional,** pro·vizh'on·al, *a.* Provided for present need or for the occasion; temporarily established; temporary.—**provisionally,** pro·vizh'on·al·li, *adv.* In a provisional manner; for the present exigency; temporarily.—**provisionary,** pro·vizh'on·e·ri, *a.* Provisional; provident.

proviso, pro·vī'zō, *n.* [L. *provisus*, pp. of *provideo*, ablative *proviso*, it being provided. PROVIDE.] An article or clause in any statute, agreement, contract, grant, or other writing, by which a condition is introduced; a conditional stipulation.—**provisory,** pro·vī'zo·ri, *a.* Temporary; provisional; conditional.

provoke, pro·vōk', *v.t.*—*provoked, provoking.* [Fr. *provoquer*, from L. *provoco*, I call forth, challenge, excite—*pro*, forth, and *voco*, to call. VOICE.] To challenge‡; to summon‡; to stimulate to action; to induce by motive; to excite or arouse (as hunger); to call forth; to instigate; to excite to anger or passion; to irritate; to enrage.—*v.i.* To produce anger.—**provoker,** pro·vō'kėr, *n.* One who or that which provokes.—

provoking, pro·vō'king, *p.* and *a.* Having the power of exciting resentment; annoying; vexatious; exasperating.—**provokingly,** pro·vō'king·li, *adv.* In a provoking manner; annoyingly.—**provocation,** prov·o·kā'shon, *n.* The act of provoking; anything that excites anger; cause of resentment; incitement; stimulus.—**provocative,** pro·vōk'a·tiv, *a.* Serving to provoke; exciting; apt to incense or enrage.—*n.* Anything that tends to excite appetite or passion; a stimulant.

provost, prov'ost, *n.* [O.Fr. *provost* (Fr. *prévôt*), from L. *praepositus*, one who is placed over others, from *praeponere*—*prae*, before, and *ponere*, to place. POSITION.] A superintendent; a university official directing educational activities; *British*, the heads of certain colleges; the chief dignitary of a cathedral or collegiate church; the chief magistrate of a Scotch burgh, corresponding to a mayor.—**provost court,** a military court for the trial of minor offenses.—**provost guard,** soldiers detailed for police duty.—**provost marshal,** *n. Milit.* an officer whose duty it is to attend to offenses committed against military discipline; *navy*, an officer who has the custody of prisoners at a court-martial.

prow, prou, *n.* [Fr. *proue*, Sp. and Pg. *proa*, from L. *prora*, from Gr. *prōra*, a prow; akin to *pro*, before.] The forepart of a ship; the bow; the beak.

prowess, prou'es, *n.* [Fr. *prouesse*, prowess, from O.Fr. *prou* (Fr. *preux*), brave; origin doubtful.] Bravery; valor; military bravery combined with skill; intrepidity and dexterity in war.

prowl, proul, *v.i.* [Origin doubtful; older forms were *proule, prolle.*] To rove or wander stealthily, as a beast in search of prey.—*v.t.* To wander stealthily over.—*n.* The act of prowling (he's on the *prowl*).—**prowler,** prou'lėr, *n.*

proximal, prok'si·mal, *a.* [L. *proximus*, nearest.] Nearest: applied to the extremity of a bone, limb, or organ of animals and plants nearest the point of attachment or insertion; opposed to *distal*.

proximate, prok'si·mit, *a.* [L. *proximatus*, pp. of *proximo*, I come near, from *proximus*, nearest, superl. of *prope*, near. PROPINQUITY.] Nearest; next.—*Proximate cause*, that which immediately precedes and produces the effect, as distinguished from the *remote, mediate*, or *predisposing cause*.—*Proximate principles*, organic compounds which are the constituents of more complex organizations, and which exist ready formed in animals and vegetables, such as albumen, gelatin, gum, starch, etc.—**proximately,** prok'si·mit·li, *adv.*—**proximity,** prok·sim'i·ti, *n.* The state of being proximate or next; immediate nearness, such as in place, time, or alliance.—**proximity fuze,** an electronic mechanism that explodes a projectile within effective range of a target.—**proxi-**

mo, prok′si·mō, *a.* In or of the next month (the 5th *proximo*).

proxy, prok′si, *n.* [Contr. from *procuracy*=L.L. *procuratia.* PRO-CURATOR.] The agency of a person who acts as a substitute for a principal; authority to act for another; the person deputed to act for another; a deputy; a writing by which one person authorizes another to vote in his place.—*v.i.*—*proxied, proxying.* To act by proxy.

prude, prōd, *n.* [Fr. *prude;* probably from L. *prudens,* prudent.] A person, particularly a woman, affecting great reserve and excessive virtue or delicacy of feeling, or who pretends to great propriety of conduct.—**prudery, prudishness,** prō′dėr·i, prō′dish·nes, *n.* The conduct of a prude; affected delicacy of feeling; coyness.—**prudish,** prō′dish, *a.* Pertaining to a prude; affecting excessive modesty or virtue; coy or reserved.—**prudishly,** prō′dish·li, *adv.* In a prudish manner.

prudent, prō′dent, *a.* [Fr. *prudent,* from L. *prudens, prudentis,* prudent, from *providens, providentis,* ppr. of *providere,* to foresee. PROVIDE.] Cautious or circumspect in determining on any action or line of conduct; careful of the consequences of enterprises, measures, or actions; dictated or directed by prudence (*prudent* behavior); frugal; economical; correct and decorous in manner.—**prudence,** prō′dens, *n.* [L. *prudentia*=*providentia.*] The state or quality of being prudent.—**prudential,** prō·den′shal, *a.* Proceeding from prudence; dictated or prescribed by prudence; exercising prudence.—**prudentially,** prō·den′shal·li, *adv.* In conformity with prudence; prudently.—**prudently,** prō′dent·li, *adv.* In a prudent manner; discreetly; cautiously; circumspectly.

pruinose, prō·in′ōs, *a.* [From L. *pruina,* hoar-frost.] Hoary; appearing as if frosted, from a covering of minute dust.

prune, prōn, *v.t.*—*pruned, pruning.* [Formerly *proine, proyne,* from Fr. *provigner,* dial. Fr. *preugner, progner,* from L. *propago, propaginis,* a slip or sucker. PROPAGATE.] To lop or cut off, as the superfluous branches of trees; to lop superfluous twigs or branches from; to trim with the knife; to clear from anything superfluous; to preen or trim, as the plumage of a bird.—**pruner,** prō′nėr, *n.* One who prunes.—**pruning hook,** *n.* An instrument for pruning trees, shrubs, etc., with a hooked blade.

prune, prōn, *n.* [Fr. *prune,* from L. *prunum,* a plum. PLUM.] A plum; specifically, a dried plum.

prunella, prō·nel′a, *n.* [Fr. *prunelle, prunella,* from its color resembling that of *prunes.* PRUNE.] A kind of woolen stuff of which clergymen's gowns were once made, afterward used for the uppers of shoes; also, a twill.

prurient, prō′ri·ent, *a.* [L. *pruriens,* from *prurire,* to itch or long for a thing, to be lecherous.] Itching after something; eagerly desirous; inclined or inclining to lascivious thoughts; having lecherous imaginations.—**pruriently,** prō′ri·ent·li, *adv.* In a prurient manner; with a longing desire.—**prurience, pruriency,** prō′ri·ens, prō′ri·en·si, *n.* The state of being prurient; lascivious suggestiveness.

prurigo, prō·rī′gō, *n.* [L., an itching, the itch.] An eruption of the skin in which the papules are diffuse and intolerably itchy. — **pruriginous,** prō·rij′i·nus, *a.* Affected by prurigo; caused by prurigo.

Prussian, prush′an, *a.* Pertaining to Prussia.—*Prussian blue,* a cyanide of iron possessed of a deep-blue color, much used as a pigment.—**prussiate,** prus′i·āt or prṳs′i·āt, *n.* A compound of cyanogen with iron and potassium; a cyanide.—**prussic acid,** prus′ik or prṳs′ik, *a.* [Originally obtained from *Prussian* blue.] The common name for *hydrocyanic acid.*

pry, prī, *v.i.*—*pried, prying.* [A modification of M.E. *prie,* to peer. PEER.] To peep narrowly; to look closely; to attempt to discover something with scrutinizing curiosity; to open with a pry.—*n.* Narrow inspection; impertinent peeping; an instrument used for prying.—**prying,** prī′ing, *p.* and *a.* Inquisitive; curious.—**pryingly,** prī′ing·li, *adv.* In a prying manner.

psalm, säm, *n.* [L. *psalmus,* a psalm, from Gr. *psalmos,* a twitching or twanging with the fingers, from *psallein,* to play a stringed instrument, to sing to the harp.] A sacred song or hymn; [*usually cap.*] especially one of the hymns composed by King David and other Jewish writers, a collection of 150 of which constitutes a book of the Old Testament; also applied to versifications of the scriptural psalms composed for the use of churches.—**psalmist,** säm′ist or säl′mist, *n.* A writer or composer of psalms.—**psalmodist,** säm′od·ist or säl′mod··ist, *n.* One who writes psalms.—**psalmody,** säm′o·di or säl′mo·di, *n.* The singing or writing of psalms; psalms collectively.

Psalter, sạl′tėr, *n.* [L. *psalterium,* Gr. *psaltērion,* a kind of harp, from *psallō.* PSALM.] The Book of Psalms, a book containing the Psalms separately printed; a version of the Psalms used in religious services.—**psalterium,** sạl·tā′ri·um, *n.* The third stomach of ruminants, called also the *Omasum* or *Manyplies.*—**psaltery,** sạl′tėr·i, *n.* An instrument of music used by the Hebrews, the form of which is not known; a form of dulcimer.

psammite, sam′mīt, *n.* [Gr. *psammos,* sand.] *Geol.* a term used for fine-grained, fissile, clayey sandstones, in contradistinction to those which are more siliceous and gritty.

pseudo-, sū′dō, [Gr. *pseudos,* falsehood.] A Greek prefix, signifying false, counterfeit, or spurious, used in many compound words, often self-explanatory, and occasionally as an independent English word.—

pseudomorph, sū′do·morf, *n.* [Gr. *morphē,* shape.] A deceptive or irregular form; a mineral having a form belonging, not to the substance of which it consists, but to some other substance which has wholly or partially disappeared.—**pseudomorphism,** sū·do·mor′fizm, *n.* The state of being a pseudomorph.—**pseudomorphous,** sū·do·mor′fus, *a.* Not having the true form; having the character of a pseudomorph.—**pseudonym,** sū′do·nim, *n.* [Gr. *onoma,* a name.] A false or feigned name; a name assumed by a writer.—**pseudonymity,** sū·do·nim′i·ti, *n.* The state of being pseudonymous; writing under an assumed name.—**pseudonymous,** sū·don′i·mus, *a.* [Gr. *pseudonymos*—*pseudos,* and *onoma,* name.] Bearing a false name or signature; applied to an author who publishes a book under a feigned name; also to the book itself.—**pseudopod,** sū′do·pod, *n.* [Gr. *pous, podos,* foot.] An animal with pseudopodia.—**pseudopodia,** sū·do·pō′di·a, *n. pl. Zool.* the organs of locomotion characteristic of the lower Protozoa, consisting of threads or processes projected from any part of the body.

psi, sī, psī, psē, *n.* [Gr.] The twenty-third letter of the Greek alphabet.

psilanthropist, sī·lan′throp·ist, *n.* [Gr. *psilos,* bare, mere, and *anthrōpos,* man.] One who believes that Christ was a mere man; a humanitarian.—**psilanthropism, psilanthropy,** sī·lan′throp·izm, sī·lan′thro·pi, *n.*

psittaceous, sit·tā′shus, *a.* [L. *psittacus,* from Gr. *psittakos,* a parrot.] Belonging to the parrot tribe.

psoas, sō′as, *n.* [From Gr. *psoa,* a muscle of the loin.] The name of two inside muscles of the loins.

psoriasis, sō·rī′a·sis, *n.* [Gr.] A cutaneous affection, consisting of patches of rough, amorphous scales, generally accompanied by chaps and fissures; also, the itch.

psych- or **psycho-,** sīk, sīk′o, *comb. form.* [Gr. *psychē,* breath, principle of life.] Soul; mental activities; brain; psychological methodology.—**psychiatrist,** sī·kī′a·trist, *n.* A physician specializing in psychiatry.—**psychiatry,** sī·kī′a·tri, *n.* That field of scientific thought and practice in medicine and psychology which aims to discover and/or correct mental derangements.—**psychic, psychical,** sī′kik, sī′ki·kal, *a.* [Gr. *psychikos.*] Belonging to the human soul, spirit, or mind; psychological; applied to that force by which spiritualists aver they produce 'spiritual' phenomena.—**psychoanalysis,** sī′kō·a·nal′i·sis, *n.* That process of revealing the subconscious thoughts of an individual by inducing him to relate without restraint the complete details of his life's experiences, in order to detect hidden mental conflicts which may produce disorders of mind and /or body.—**psychoanalyst,** sī′ko·an″a·list, *n.*—**psychoanalyze,** (-līz), *v.t.*—**psychogenesis,** sī·ko·jen′e·sis, *n.* [Gr. *psy-*

chē, and *genesis*, origin.] The origin or generation of the mind as manifested by consciousness.—**psychogenic**, sī·kō·jen'ik, *a*. Originating in the mind.—**psychological**, sī·kō·loj'i·kal, *a*.—*Psychological moment*, the apparently predestined and inevitable moment; the absolute nick of time: by confusion with the 'moment' or momentum impelling the will to act, in a psychological sense.—**psychologically**, sī·ko·loj'i·kal·li, *adv*. In a psychological manner.—**psychologist**, sī·kol'o·jist, *n*. One who studies, writes on, or is versed in psychology.—**psychology**, sī·kol'o·ji, *n*. [Gr. *psychē* and *logos*.] ō·jist, *n*.—**psychology**, sī·kol'o·ji, *n*. The science of the mind; the study of the mental and behavioral characteristics of an individual or group. —**psychoneurosis**, sī'kō·nū·ro'sis, *n*. A mental disorder less severe than psychosis but severe enough to impair social adjustment (commonly abbreviated *neurosis*).—**psychopath**, sī'kō·path, *n*. One who has a psychopathic disorder.—**psychopathic**, sī'kō·path''ik, *a*. Pertaining to psychopathy.—**psychopathy**, sī·kop'a·thē, *n*. A mental disorder characterized by an inability to restrain antisocial impulses.—**psychopharmacology**, sī'kō·fär'ma·kol''a·ji, *n*. The branch of pharmacology concerned with the effects of drugs on the mind.— **psychosis**, sī·kō'sis, *n*. Mental disorders in which social adjustment is impossible and the patient must be under medical supervision.— **psychosomatic**, sī'kō·sō·mat''ik, *a*. Of the interaction of psychic and somatic phenomena.

psyche, sī'kē, *n*. [Gr. *psyche*, the soul.] The soul; [*cap*.] a sort of mythical or allegorical personification of the human soul, as a beautiful maiden, beloved by Cupid.

psychedelic, sī'ki·del''ik, *a*. [Gr. *psyche*, the soul, and Gr. *delos*, visible.] Referring to expansion of the senses or mind, especially, to drugs, such as LSD, producing this effect.

psychotherapy, sī·kō·ther'a·pi, *n*. [Gr. *therapeuō*, I attend medically.] That branch of psychiatry which prescribes and administers, methods of treatment to eliminate maladjustments and to correct mental disorders.

psychrometer, sī·krom'et·ér, *n*. [Gr. *psychros*, cool, and *metron*, measure.] An instrument for measuring the tension of the aqueous vapor in the atmosphere; a form of hygrometer.

ptarmigan, tär'mi·gan, *n*. [Gael. *termachan*, Ir. *tarmochan*, ptarmigan.] A bird of the grouse family, of a white color in winter, frequenting northern regions.

pteridologist, ter·i·dol'o·jist, *n*. [Gr. *pteris*, *pteridos*, a fern, *logos*, discourse.] One versed in the botany of the ferns.—**pteridology**, ter·i·dol'o·ji, *n*. The science of ferns.

pteridophyte, ter'i·dō·fīt, *n*. [Gr. *pteris*, fern; *phuton*, plant.] One of the Pteridophyta, the phylum of plants which includes the ferns and their allies; formerly called a vas-

cular cryptogam.

pterodactyl, ter·o·dak'til, *n*. [Gr. *pteron*, a wing, and *daktylos*, a digit.] An extinct species of flying reptile belonging to the Mesozoic period, and exhibiting affinities to mammals, reptiles, and birds.

pteropod, ter'o·pod, *n*. [Gr. *pteron*, a wing, and *pous*, *podos*, a foot.] One of a class of mollusks which have a swimming expansion on each side of the head.

pterosaur, ter'o·sar, *n*. [Gr. *pteron*, a wing, *sauros*, a lizard.] An extinct flying reptile, such as the pterodactyl.

pterygoid, ter'i·goid, *a*. [Gr. *pteryx*, *pterygos*, a wing.] Wing-shaped; *anat*. applied to processes of the sphenoid bone which complete the osseous palate behind.

ptisan, tī'san, *n*. [L. *ptisana*, from Gr. *ptisanē*, peeled barley, barley water, from *ptissō*, to peel.] A decoction of barley with other ingredients; *med*. a drink containing little or no medicinal agent.

Ptolemaic, tol·e·mā'ik, *a*. [From *Ptolemy*, the geographer and astronomer.] Pertaining to Ptolemy.— *Ptolemaic system*, that maintained by Ptolemy, who supposed the earth to be fixed in the center of the universe, and that the sun and stars revolved around it.—**Ptolemaist**, tol·e·mā'ist, *n*. A believer in the Ptolemaic system.

ptomaine, tō'mān, *n*. [Gr. *ptōma*, a fall, a corpse, from *piptō*, to fall.] One of a class of alkaloids or organic bases which are generated in animal substances during putrefaction.— **ptomaine poisoning**, *n*. A food poisoning caused by bacteria.

ptyalin, tī'al·in, *n*. [Gr. *ptyalon*, saliva.] A ferment in saliva that converts starch into sugar.—**ptyalism**, tī'al·izm, *n*. Salivation; a morbid and copious excretion of saliva.

puberty, pū'bér·ti, *n*. [L. *pubertas*, from *puber* or *pubes*, *puberis*, of ripe age, adult, same root as *puer*, a boy, *pullus*, a chicken.] The period in both male and female marked by the functional development of the generative system; the age at which persons are capable of begetting or bearing children.—**puberulent**, pū·bér'ū·lent, *a*. *Bot*. covered with fine down.—**pubes**, pū'bēz, *n*. [L., the hair which appears on the body at puberty.] *Anat*. the middle part of the hypogastric region, so called because covered with hair at puberty; *bot*. the down or downy substance on plants; pubescence.—**pubescence**, pū·bes'ens, *n*. The state of one who has arrived at puberty; puberty; *bot*. the downy substance on plants. —**pubescent**, pū·bes'ent, *a*. Arriving at puberty; *bot*. covered with pubescence; *zool*. covered with very fine short hairs.—**pubic**, pū'bik, *a*. Pertaining to the pubes.

public, pub'lik, *a*. [Fr. *public* (masc.), *publique* (fem.), from L. *publicus*, for *populicus*, from *populus*, people. PEOPLE.] Not private; pertaining to the whole people; relating to, re-

garding, or affecting a state, nation, or community (the *public* service); proceeding from many or the many; belonging to people in general (a *public* subscription); open to the knowledge of all; general; common; notorious (*public* report): regarding not private interest; the good of the community (*public* spirit); open to common use (a *public* road). —*n*. The general body of mankind or of a nation, state, or community. —**publican**, pub'li·kan, *n*. A tax collector in ancient Rome.—**publication**, pub·li·kā'shon, *n*. The process of publishing; a published work.—**public defender**, *n*. A lawyer assigned to defend persons who cannot afford legal counsel.—**public domain**, *n*. Land owned by the government; the realm of rights that belong to the community.—**publicist**, pub'li·sist, *n*. An expert on public affairs; one who publicizes. —**publicity**, pub·li'si·tē, *n*. The dissemination of promotional material. —**publicize**, pub'li·sīz, *v.t.*—*publicized*, *publicizing*. To give publicity to.—**public relations**, *n*. The art of developing and maintaining good relations between the public and some person, organization, etc.— **public service**, *n*. The business of supplying a commodity or service to a community.—**public utility**, *n*. An organization that performs some public service.—**public works**, *n*. Works (schools and highways, e.g.) constructed for public use.—**publish**, pub'lish, *v.t.* To make generally known; to produce for publication. —*v.i.* To have a work accepted for publication.—**publishable**, pub'lish·a·bl, *a*. Capable of being published; fit for publication.—**publisher**, pub'lish·ér, *n*. One who publishes; especially, one who, as the first source of supply, issues books and other literary works, maps, engravings, etc., for sale.

puce, pūs, *a*. [Fr. *puce*, from L. *pulex*, *pulicis*, a flea.] Dark-brown; reddish-brown; of a flea color.

pucka, puk'a, *a*. [Hind. *pakka*, ripe.] Solid; substantial; permanent; genuine; an Anglo-Indian term.

pucker, puk'ér, *v.t.* [From *poke*, a bag or pocket; comp. to *purse* the lips.] To gather into small folds or wrinkles; to contract into ridges and furrows; to wrinkle.—*v.i.* To become wrinkled; to gather into folds. —*n*. A fold or wrinkle, or a collection of folds.—*To be in a pucker*, to be in a state of flutter or agitation (*colloq*.)—**puckery**, puk'ér·i, *a*. Full of puckers or wrinkles.

puckish, puk'ish, *a*. [The name *Puck* is from W. *pwca*, Ir. *puca*, a goblin.] [*also cap*.] Resembling the fairy *Puck*; elvish; freakish.

pudding, pud'ing, *n*. [From the Celtic; same as W. *poten*, Ir. *putag*, Gael. *putog*, a pudding; of the same root as *pod*.] An intestine; a gut of an animal; an intestine stuffed with meat, etc.; a sausage; a compound of flour or other farinaceous substance, with milk and eggs, sometimes enriched with raisins.—

pudding stone, *n.* A term now considered synonymous with conglomerate, but originally applied to a mass of flint pebbles cemented by a siliceous paste.

puddle, pud´l, *n.* [Akin to L.G. *pudel*, pool; D. *poedelen*, to puddle; comp. Ir. and Gael. *plod*, a pool.] A small collection of dirty water; a small muddy pool; clay or earth tempered with water and thoroughly wrought so as to be impervious to water; puddling.—*v.t.* —*puddled*, *puddling*. To make turbid or muddy; to stir up the mud or sediment in; *fig.* to befoul; to render watertight by means of puddle; to convert into wrought iron by the process of puddling.—*v.i.* To make a dirty stir. —**puddler,** pud´lêr, *n.* One who puddles; one who is employed at the process of turning cast iron into wrought iron.—**puddling,** pud´ling, *n.* The operation of working plastic clay behind piling in a cofferdam, or in other situations, to resist the penetration of water; the clay thus used; the process by which cast iron is converted into malleable iron, consisting in working it in a special furnace, hammering and rolling.— *Puddling furnace*, a kind of reverberatory furnace for puddling iron.

pudency,† pū´den·si, *n.* [L. *pudens*, *pudentis*; ppr. of *pudere*, to be ashamed (seen also in *impudent*)]. Modesty; shamefacedness.—**pudenda,** pū·den´da, *n. pl.* [L., lit. things to be ashamed of.] The parts of generation.

pudgy, puj´i, *a.* [Also *podgy*, probably akin to *pod*, *pad*.] Fat and short; thick; fleshy.

pueblo, pweb´lō, *n.* [Sp., a village.] Adobe communal apartment houses constituting the villages of U.S. southwestern Indian tribes; (cap.) any of the Indian tribes living in pueblos.

puerile, pū´êr·il, *a.* [L. *puerilis*, from *puer*, a boy; same root as *pupus*, a boy, *pullus*, a chicken. PUPIL, PULLET.] Boyish; childish; trifling.— **puerilely,** pū´êr·il·li, *adv*, In a puerile manner.—**puerility,** pū·êr·il´i·ti, *n.* [L. *puerilitas*.] The state of being puerile; boyishness; that which is puerile; a childish or silly act, thought or expression; *civil law*, the period of life from the stage of infancy to puberty.

puerperal, pū·êr´pêr·al, *a.* [L. *puerpera*, a lying-in-woman—*puer*, a boy, and *pario*, to bear.] Pertaining to childbirth.

puff, puf, *n.* [From the sound; comp. G. *puff*, a puff, a thump; Dan. *puf*, W. *pwff*, a puff.] A sudden and single emission of breath from the mouth; a sudden and short blast of wind; a fungous ball filled with dust; a puffball; a substance of loose texture, used to sprinkle powder on the hair or skin; a swelling; a kind of pastry; a loose roll of hair.— *v.i.* To blow with single and quick blasts; to blow, as an expression of scorn or contempt; to breathe with vehemence, as after violent exertion; to be dilated or inflated; to

assume importance.—*v.t.* To drive with a blast of wind or air; to inflate or dilate with air; to swell or inflate, as with pride or vanity; often with *up*; to praise with exaggeration.—**puffball,** *n.* A fungus in the form of a ball which bursts when ripe, and discharges its spores in the form of fine powder.—**puffer,** puf´êr, *n.* One that puffs.—**puffery,** puf´êr·i, *n.* Act of puffing; extravagant praise.—**puffin,** puf´in, *n.* [In allusion to its puffed-out beak.] The common name for a genus of marine diving birds of the auk family, characterized by a bill resembling that of a parrot.—**puffiness,** puf´i·nes, *n.* State or quality of being puffy.—**puff paste,** *n.* A rich dough for making the light friable covers of tarts, etc.—**puffy,** puf´i·, *a.*

pug, pug, *n.* [A form of *Puck*, the sprite or hobgoblin.] A small, sturdy dog; a small dog which bears a resemblance in miniature to the bull-dog.—**pug nose,** *n.* A snub nose.

pugaree, pug´ar·ē, pug´êr·i, **pugree,** pug´rē, *n.* [Hind. *pagri*, a turban.] A piece of muslin cloth wound round a hat or helmet to ward off the rays of the sun. (*Anglo-Indian*.)

pugilism, pū´jil·izm, *n.* [From L. *pugil*, a pugilist; same stem as *pugnus*, a fist, *pugna*, a fight. PUGNACIOUS.] The practice of boxing or fighting with the fists.—**pugilist,** pū´jil·ist, *n.* A boxer.—**pugilistic,** pū·jil·is´tik, *a.* Pertaining to boxing.

pugnacious, pug·nā´shus, *a.* [L. *pugnax*, *pugnacis*, from *pugna*, a fight, from stem of *pugnus*, a fist; akin *impugn*, *oppugn*, *repugnant*, etc.] Disposed or inclined to fighting; quarrelsome.—**pugnaciously,** pug·nā´shus·li, *adv.* In a pugnacious manner.—**pugnaciousness,** **pugnacity,** pug·nā´shus·nes, pug·nas´i·ti, *n.* Inclination to fight; quarrelsomeness.

puisne, pū´nē, *a.* [O.Fr. *puisné*, from *puis*, L. *post*, after, and *né*, L. *natus*, born. (NATAL.) *Puny* is the same word.] *Law*, younger or inferior in rank; sometimes applied to certain judges.

puissant, pū´is·ant or pū·is´ant, *a.* [Fr. *puissant*, powerful: formed as if from a participle *possens*, *possentis*, from L. *posse*, to be able. POTENT.] Powerful; strong; mighty; forcible. —**puissantly,** pū´is·ant·li, *adv.* In a puissant manner; powerfully.—**puissance,** pū´is·ans, *n.* Power; strength; might.

puke, pūk, *v.i.*—*puked*, *puking*. [Akin G. *spucken*, to spit, E. *spew*.] To vomit; to retch; to be disgusted.—*v.t.* To vomit or eject from the stomach.

pulchritude, pul´kri·tūd, *n.* [L. *pulchritudo*, from *pulcher*, beautiful.] Beauty; grace; comeliness.

pule, pūl, *v.i.*—*puled*, *puling*. [Fr. *piauler*, to make the cry represented by the syllable *piau*, to pule; an imitative word; comp. Fr. *miauler*, to mewl, to mew.] To cry like a chicken; to cry as a complaining child; to whimper.—**puler,** pū´lêr, *n.* One that pules.—**puling,** pū´ling, *p.* and *a.* Crying like a chicken; whining; infantine; childish.—*n.* A

cry as of a chicken; a whining.— **pulingly,** pū´ling·li, *adv.* In a puling or whining manner.

pull, pul, *v.t.* [A.Sax. *pullian*, to pull; L.G. *pulen*, to pick, to pluck, to pull; connections doubtful.] To draw; to draw toward one or make an effort to draw; to tug; to haul; opposed to *push*; to pluck; to gather by the hand (to *pull* fruit); to tear, rend, draw apart; in this sense followed by some qualifying word or phrase (to *pull in pieces*, to *pull asunder* or *apart*); to impress by a printing press; to move by drawing or pulling (to *pull* a bell, to *pull* a boat).—*To pull down*, to take down by pulling; to demolish (to *pull down* a house); to subvert.—*To pull off*, to separate by pulling; to pluck; also, to take off without force (to *pull off* a coat or hat).— *To pull on*, to draw on (to *pull on* boots).—*To pull out*, to draw out; to extract.—*To pull up*, to pluck up; to tear up by the roots; to apprehend or cause to be apprehended and taken before a court of justice (*colloq.*); to stop by means of the reins (to *pull up* a horse); hence, to stop in any course of conduct.—*To pull the long bow*, to exaggerate; to lie boastingly.—*To pull one through*, to help through a difficulty.—*v.i.* To give a pull; to tug; to exert strength in drawing. —*To pull through*, to get through any undertaking with difficulty.— *To pull up*, to draw the reins; to stop in riding or driving; to halt.—*n.* The act of pulling; an effort to move by drawing toward one; a pluck; a shake; a twitch; the act of rowing a boat.

pullet, pul´et, *n.* [Fr. *poulette* dim. of *poule* a hen L.L. *pulla* from L. *pullus*, a young animal. Of same origin are *poult*, *poultry*.] A young hen or chicken.

pulley, pul´i, *n. pl.* **pulleys,** pul´iz. [O.E. *poleyne*, a pulley, from Fr. *poulain*, a foal or colt, a slide for letting down casks into a cellar, a pulley rope, from L.L. *pullanus*, from L. *pullus*, the young of an animal. (PULLET.) The names of the horse, ass, goat, and other animals are given in different languages to various mechanical contrivances.] One of the simple machines or mechanical powers, used for raising weights, and consisting of a small wheel movable about an axle, and having a groove cut in its circumference over which a cord passes; used either singly or several in combination; a wheel placed upon a shaft and transmitting power to or from the different parts of machinery, or changing the direction of motion by means of a belt or band which runs over it.

Pullman car, pul´man, *n.* [After G.M. *Pullman*, U.S. inventor.] A passenger railroad car with parlor car fittings, on which additional fare is charged.

pulmonary, pulmonic, pul´mon·e·ri, pul·mon´ik, *a.* [L. *pulmonarius*, from *pulmo*, *pulmonis*, a lung; akin to Gr. *pleumōn*, *pneumōn*, a lung.] Pertaining to the lungs; affecting the lungs.—**pulmotor**, pul'mō·tẽr, n. A respirator that forces air into the lungs.

pulp, pulp, n. [Fr. *pulpe*, from L. *pulpa*, fleshy substance, pulp.] Soft undissolved animal or vegetable matter; the soft, succulent part of fruit; material for making paper reduced to a soft uniform mass; the soft vascular substance in the interior of a tooth; pl. magazines dealing with sensational matter (slang).—*v.t.* To make into pulp; to deprive of the pulp.—*v.i.* To be or become as pulp.—**pulpiness**, pul'pi·nes, n.—**pulpy,** pul'pi, a.—**pulpwood**, pulp'wụd, n. A soft wood used in making paper.

pulpit, pụl'pit, n. [L. *pulpitum*, a scaffold, stage, desk.] An elevated place or enclosed stage in a church, in which the preacher stands; frequently used adjectively, and signifying belonging, pertaining, or suitable to the pulpit (*pulpit* eloquence, *pulpit* oratory).—*The pulpit*, preachers generally; the pulpit teaching in churches (the influence of *the pulpit*).—**pulpiteer**, pụl·pi·tēr', n. A preacher, in contempt.

pulque, pụl'kā, n. [Sp.] A vinous beverage obtained by fermenting the juice of various species of the agave or American aloe.

pulsate, pul'sāt, v.i.—*pulsated, pulsating.* [L. *pulsare, pulsatum*, to beat, from *pellere, pulsum*, to drive (seen also in *expel, compel, impel, impulse, repel*, etc.).] To beat or throb.—**pulsatile**, pul'sa·tīl, a. [L. *pulsatilis.*] Played on by beating; intended to be played on by beating; *med.* beating like the pulse; throbbing.—**pulsation**, pul·sā'shon, n. The beating or throbbing of the heart or of an artery; a beat of the pulse; a throb; a beat or stroke by which some medium is affected, as in the propagation of sound.—**pulsator**, pul'sā·tẽr, n. A beater; a striker.—**pulsatory**, pul'sa·to·ri, a. Capable of pulsating or beating; throbbing, as the heart and arteries.—**pulse**, puls, n. [Fr. *pouls*, L. *pulsus*, a beating, from *pello, pulsum*.] The beating or throbbing of the heart or blood vessels, especially of the arteries; the pulsation of the radial artery at the wrist; pulsation; vibration.—*To feel one's pulse* (*fig.*), to sound one's opinion; to try or to know one's mind.—*v.i.*—*pulsed, pulsing.* To beat, as the arteries or heart.—**pulsimeter**, pul·sim'et·ẽr, n. [L. *pulsus*, and Gr. *metron*, a measure.] An instrument for measuring the strength or quickness of the pulse.—**pulsometer**, pul·som'et·ẽr, n. A sort of pump which acts by the condensation of steam sent into a reservoir, the water rushing up into the vacuum formed by the condensation.

pulse, puls, n. [From L. *puls*, pottage made of meal, pulse, etc.] Leguminous plants or their seeds; the plants whose pericarp is a legume, as beans, peas, etc.

pulverize, pul'vẽr·īz, v.t.—*pulverized, pulverizing.* [Fr. *pulvériser*, from L. *pulvis, pulveris*, powder (whence *powder*).] To reduce to fine powder, as by beating, grinding, etc.—*v.i.* To become reduced to fine powder; to fall to dust.—**pulverizable**, pul·vẽr·ī'za·bl, a. Capable of being pulverized.—**pulverizer**, pul'vẽr·ī·zẽr, n. One who or that which pulverizes.—**pulverization**, pul'vẽr·ī·zā'shon, n. The act of pulverizing.—**pulverulent**, pul·vẽr'ū·lent, a. Dusty; consisting of fine powder; powdery.

pulvilli, pul·vil'ī, n. pl. [L., little cushions, from *pulvinus*, a cushion.] A name for cushion-like masses on the feet of certain insects.—**pulvinate**, pul'vi·nāt, a. Bot. cushion-shaped.—**pulvinated**, pul'vi·nā·ted, a. Arch. a term used to express a swelling in any portion of an order.—**pulvinus**, pul'vin·us, n. The thickened base of a leaf stalk.

puma, pū'ma, n. [Peruv.] The cougar or mountain lion. See COUGAR.

pumice, pu'mis, n. [L. *pumex, pumicis*, originally *spumex*, from *spuma*, foam, from *spuo*, to spit. *Pounce* (powder) is the same word.] A sort of porous stony substance frequently ejected from volcanoes, lighter than water, used for polishing ivory, wood, marble, metals, glass, etc.—**pumiceous**, pu·mish'us, a. Pertaining to pumice; consisting of or resembling it.—**pumice stone**, n.

pummel, pum'el. See POMMEL.

pump, pump, n. [Fr. *pompe*, a pump, from D. and L.G. *pomp*, G. *pumpe*, a pump; origin unknown.] An instrument or machine employed for raising water or other liquid to a higher level, or for exhausting or compressing air or other gases.—*v.i.* To work a pump; to work something as in the motion of pumping; to raise and lower like a pump handle; to try to extract information.—*v.t.* To raise with a pump; to free from water or other fluid by a pump (to *pump* a ship); to put artful questions to for the purpose of extracting information (colloq.); to eject in spurts as by a pumping action.—**pumper**, pump'ẽr, n.

pump, pump, n. [Probably from being worn for *pomp*.] A low shoe holding to the foot only at toe and heel.

pumpernickel, pum'pẽr·nik·el, n. [G.] A species of coarse bread made from unbolted rye.

pumpkin, pump'kin, n. [From Fr. *pompon*, from L. *pepo, peponis*, a pumpkin, from Gr. *pepōn*, a melon, lit. one thoroughly ripened, from root of *peptō* (akin to L. *coquo*), to cook. COOK.] A large, round, yellow-orange, edible gourd (*Cucurbita Pepo*) borne by a vine; the plant bearing the gourd.

pun, pun, n. [Origin unknown.] A play on words that agree or resemble in sound but differ in meaning; an expression in which two different applications of a word present an odd or ludicrous idea.—*v.i.*—*punned, punning.* To play on words so as to make puns.—**punning**, pun'ing, p. and a. Given to making puns.—**punster**, pun'stẽr, n. One skilled in or given to punning.

punch, punsh, n. [Shortened from old *punchon*, a dagger, from O.Fr. *poinson*, a bodkin, from L. *punctio*, a puncturing, from *pungo, punctum*, to prick (whence *point, puncture, pungent*, etc.).] A tool employed for making apertures, as in plates of metal, in impressing dies, etc., usually made of steel, and operated by hammering; a blow, as with the fist, elbow, or knee.—*v.t.* To perforate with a punch; to give a blow or stunning knock to.—**puncher**, punsh'ẽr, n. One who or that which punches.

Punch, punsh, n. [Contr. from *punchinello* (which see).] The chief character in a popular comic exhibition of puppets, who beats to death Judy his wife, belabors a police officer, etc.

punch, punsh, n. [From Hind. *panch*, Skr. *panchan*, five.] A beverage introduced from India, and so called from its being composed of the five ingredients, arrack, tea, sugar, water, and lemon juice; in this country, a beverage made from spirits and water, and sweetened and flavored with sugar and lemon juice.—**punch bowl**, n. A bowl in which punch is made, or from which it is served to be drunk.

puncheon, punsh'on, n. [Fr. *poinçon*, a bodkin, a punch (see PUNCH, the tool); also O.Fr. *poinson*, Fr. *poinçon*, a wine vessel—perhaps one stamped with a punch as of a certain capacity.] A perforating or stamping tool; a punch; *carp.* a short upright piece of timber in framing; a measure of liquids, or a cask containing from 84 to 120 gallons.

punchinello, punsh·i·nel'lo, n. [Corrupted from It. *pulcinello*, from L. *pullus*, a chicken=my chicken.] A punch; a buffoon.

punctate, **punctated**, pungk'tāt, pungk'tā·ted, a. [From L. *punctum*, a point. POINT.] Ending in a point; pointed; *bot.* having dots scattered over the surface.

punctilio, pungk·til'i·o, n. [From Sp. *puntillo* or It. *puntiglio*, a small point, a punctilio, from L. *punctum*, a point. POINT.] A nice point in conduct, ceremony, or proceeding; particularity or exactness in forms.—**punctilious**, pungk·til'i·us, a. Attentive to punctilios; very nice or exact in the forms of behavior; sometimes, exact to excess.—**punctiliously**, pungk·til'i·us·li, adv. In a punctilious manner.—**punctiliousness**, pungk·til'i·us·nes, n.

punctual, pungk'chö·al, n. [Fr. *ponctuel*, from L. *punctum*, a point, from *pungo, punctum*, to prick. POINT, PUNCTURE, etc.] Observant of nice points‡; exact‡; exact in keeping an appointment; exact to the time agreed on; made at the exact time (*punctual* payment).—**punctuality**, pungk·chö·al'i·ti, n. The state or quality of being punctual; adherence to the exact time of attendance or appointment.—**punctually**, pungk'chö·al·li, adv. In a punctual manner; with scrupulous regard to time, appointments, promises, etc.—**punc-**

tualness, pungk′chö•al•nes, n. Punctuality.

punctuate, pungk′chö•āt, v.t.—*punctuated, punctuating.* [Fr. *ponctuer,* from L. *punctum,* a point. PUNCTUAL, PUNCTURE.] To mark with the points or stops necessary in written or printed compositions; to separate into sentences, clauses, or other divisions by points.—**punctuation,** pungk•chö•ā′shon, n. The act or art of punctuating or pointing a writing or discourse.—**punctuator,** pungk′-chö•ā•tėr, n. One who punctuates; a punctuist.

puncture, pungk′chėr, n. [L. *punctura,* from *pungo, punctum,* to prick (whence *pungent, point,* and a *punch*).] The act of perforating with a pointed instrument, or a small hole thus made; a small wound, as by a needle, prickle, or sting.—v.t.—*punctured, puncturing.* To make a puncture in; to prick.

pundit, pun′dit, n. [Skr. *pandita,* a learned man.] A learned Brahmin; one versed in the Sanskrit language, and in the science, laws, and religion of India; sometimes used ironically or contemptuously.

pungent, pun′jent, a. [L. *pungens,* ppr. of *pungo, punctum,* to prick, whence also *point, puncture, compunction, expunge,* etc.] Affecting the tongue like small sharp points; biting; acrid; sharply affecting the sense of smell; affecting the mind similarly; caustic; racy; biting.—**pungently,** pun′jent•li, adv. In a pungent manner; sharply.—**pungency,** pun′jen•si, n. The state or quality of being pungent; tartness; causticity.

Punic, pū′nik, a. [L. *punicus,* Carthaginian, from *Puni, Pœni,* the Carthaginians.] Pertaining to the Carthaginians; faithless; deceitful.—n. The language of the Carthaginians; Phoenician.

punish, pun′ish, v.t. [Fr. *punir, punissant,* from L. *punire,* to punish, from *pœna,* punishment, penalty. PAIN.] To inflict a penalty on; to visit judicially with a penalty; to castigate; to chastise; to visit with pain or suffering inflicted on the offender (to *punish* murder or theft); to inflict pain on in a loose sense (*colloq.*).—**punishable,** pun′ish•a•bl, a. Deserving punishment; liable to punishment; capable of being punished.—**punisher,** pun′ish•ėr, n. One that punishes.—**punishment,** pun′ish•ment, n. The act of punishing; pain or penalty inflicted on a person for a crime or offense; a penalty imposed in the enforcement of law.—**punitive,** pū′ni•tiv, a. Pertaining to or involving punishment; awarding or inflicting punishment.—**punitory,** pū′ni•to•ri, a. Punishing or tending to punishment.

punk, pungk, n. [Contr. from *spunk.*] Tinder made from a fungus; touchwood; spunk.

punka, punkah, pung′ka, n. A large fan slung from the ceilings of rooms in India to produce an artificial current of air.

punster. See PUN.

punt, punt, v.i. [Fr. *punter,* It. *puntare,* from L. *punctum,* a point. PUNGENT.] *Football,* to drop and kick the ball before it touches the ground; to gamble for big stakes.—**punter,** punt′ėr, n. One who punts; one who plays in games of chance against the banker or dealer.

punt, punt, n. [A punt, a pontoon, from *pons, pontis,* a bridge. PONTOON.] A square flat-bottomed vessel without masts, used as a lighter for conveying goods, etc.; a small flat-bottomed boat used in fishing and wild-fowl shooting, etc.—v.t. To propel by pushing with a pole against the bed of the water; to convey in a punt.—**punter,** punt′ėr, n. One who punts a boat; one who uses a punt.

puny, pū′ni, a. [From Fr. *puisné.* PUISNE.] Puisne; imperfectly developed in size and vigor; small and weak; petty; insignificant.—**puniness,** pū′ni•nes, n. The state or quality of being puny.

pup, pup, n. [Abbrev. of *puppy.*] A puppy; a young seal.—v.i.—*pupped, pupping.* To bring forth whelps.

pupa, pū′pa, n. pl. **pupae,** pū′pē. [L. *pupa,* a girl, a doll, fem. of *pupus,* a boy.] The chrysalis form of an insect.—**pupal,** pū′pal, a. Pertaining to a pupa.

pupil, pū′pil, n. [Fr. *pupille,* L. *pupilla,* a little girl, the apple of the eye, dim. of *pupa,* a girl; also *pupillus,* an orphan boy, dim. of *pupus,* a boy. PUPPET.] The round aperture in the middle of the iris through which the rays of light pass to reach the retina; a young person of either sex under the care of an instructor or tutor; a disciple; a ward; a young person under the care of a guardian.—**pupilage,** pū′pil•ij, n. The state of being a pupil; the state or period of being a ward under the care of a guardian.—**pupillary,** pū′pi•ler•i, a. [L. *pupillaris.*] Pertaining to a pupil or ward; pertaining to the pupil of the eye.

pupiparous, pu•pip′er•us, a. [L. *pupa,* and *pario,* to produce.] Producing pupae from the eggs before they are excluded: said of certain insects.

puppet, pup′et, n. [O.E. *popet,* O.Fr. *poupette,* dim. from L. *pupa,* a doll, a puppet. PUPA, PUPIL.] A small figure in the human form, moved by cords or wires, in a mock drama; a marionette; one actuated by the will of another; a person who is a mere tool.—**puppet show,** n. A mock drama performed by puppets.

puppy, pup′i, n. [Fr. *poupée,* a doll, a puppet, L. *pupa.* PUPA, PUPPET.] A whelp; a young dog not grown up; a conceited and insignificant fellow; a silly fop or coxcomb.

purblind, pėr′blīnd, a. [From *pure* in sense of altogether, quite, and *blind.*] Near-sighted or dim-sighted; seeing obscurely.—**purblindness,** pėr′-blīnd•nes, n. The state of being purblind; dimness of vision.

purchase, pėr′chas, v.t.—*purchased, purchasing.* [Fr. *pourchasser,* O.Fr. *purchacer,* to pursue, to get—*pour, pur,* for, and *chasser,* to chase.

CHASE.] To gain or acquire‡; to obtain by payment of money or its equivalent; to buy; to obtain by labor, danger, or other means.—n. Acquisition in general‡; the acquisition of anything by rendering an equivalent in money; buying; that which is purchased; any mechanical advantage (as is gained by a lever) used in the raising or removing of heavy bodies.—*To be worth so many years' purchase,* said of property that would bring in, in the specified time, an amount equal to the sum paid.—**purchasable,** pėr′chas•a•bl, a. Capable of being purchased.—**purchaser,** pėr′chas•ėr, n. One who purchases; a buyer.

purdah, pur′da, n. [Hind. and Per. *pardah,* veil.] A Muslim and Hindi custom of keeping women secluded by the use of screens, face veils, and voluminous clothing.

pure, pūr, a. [Fr. *pur,* from L. *purus,* pure (whence *purgo,* E. to *purge*); from root seen also in Skr. *pû,* to purify; and in *fire.*] Free from all heterogeneous or extraneous matter, especially from anything that impairs or pollutes; free from that which defiles or contaminates; innocent; spotless; chaste; stainless; genuine; ceremonially clean; unpolluted; mere; sheer; absolute (*pure* shame, hatred).—*Pure mathematics.* MATHEMATICS.—**purely,** pūr′li, adv. In a pure manner; innocently; stainlessly; chastely; merely; absolutely.—**pureness,** pūr′nes, n. The state or quality of being pure; purity.—**purify,** pū′ri•fī, v.t.—*purified, purifying.* [Fr. *purifier,* from L. *purificare—purus,* and *facio,* to make.] To make pure or clear; to free from extraneous admixture; to free from guilt or the defilement of sin.—v.i. To grow or become pure or clear.—**purification,** pū′ri•fi•kā′shon, n. [L. *purificatio.*] The act of purifying or making pure; the act of cleansing ceremonially by removing any pollution or defilement; lustration; a cleansing from guilt or the pollution of sin.—**purificatory,** pū•rif′i•ka•to•ri, a. Having power to purify; tending to cleanse.—**purifier,** pū′ri•fī•ėr, n. One who or that which purifies.—**purist,** pū′rist, n. [Fr. *puriste,* from *pur,* pure.] One who scrupulously aims at purity, particularly in the choice of language; one who is a rigorous critic of purity in literary style.—**puristic,** pū•ris′tik, a. Pertaining or relating to purism.—**purism,** pū′rizm, n. Affectation of rigid purity; excessive nicety as to the choice of words.—**purity,** pū′ri•ti, n. [L. *puritas.*] The condition of being pure; freedom from foreign matter; cleanness; innocence; chastity.

purée, pū•rā′, n. Meat, fish, or vegetables boiled into a pulp and passed through a sieve.

purfle, pėr′fl, v.t.—*purfled, purfling.* [O.Fr. *pourfiler—pour,* L. *pro,* for, before, and *fil,* L. *filum,* a thread. PROFILE.] To decorate with a wrought or flowered border; to border; to broider; to decorate richly.

purge, pėrj, v.t.—purged, purging. [L. purgare, to cleanse, from purus, clean, and agere, to do. PURE.] To cleanse or purify by carrying off whatever is impure, foreign, or superfluous; to clear from moral defilement; to clear from accusation or the charge of a crime; to remove from a position of influence, in a political party or nation, persons considered harmful or disloyal; to evacuate the bowels; to operate on by means of a cathartic. —v.i. To produce evacuations by a cathartic.—n. The act of purging; anything that purges; a cathartic medicine; the act of removing from a position of influence, in a political party or nation, persons considered harmful or disloyal.—**purgation**, pėr·gā'shon, n. [L. purgatio.] The act of purging; the act of carrying away impurities; purification; the act of cleansing from the imputation of guilt.—**purgative**, pėr'ga·tiv, a. [Fr. purgatif.] Having the power of cleansing; having the power of evacuating the intestines; cathartic.—n. A medicine that evacuates the intestines; a cathartic.—**purgatory**, pėr'ga·to·ri, a. [L. purgatorius.] Tending to cleanse; cleansing; expiatory.—n. According to R. Catholics and others, a place in which souls after death are purified from venial sins, and suffer punishment for mortal sins not atoned for; colloquially, any place or state of irritating temporary suffering.

purify. See PURE.

Purim, pu'rim, n. [Heb. purim, lots.] An annual festival among the Jews instituted to commemorate their preservation from the massacre with which they were threatened by the machinations of Haman.

purine, pūr'in, n. [Gr. pyr, burning.] A nitrogenous excretory substance.

purist. See PURE.

Puritan, pū'ri·tan, n. [From L. puritas, purity.] The name by which the dissenters from the Church of England were generally known in the reign of Elizabeth and the first two Stuarts; given (probably in derision) on account of the superior purity of doctrine or discipline which they claimed as their own.—a. Pertaining to the Puritans.—**puritanic, puritanical**, pū·ri·tan'ik, pū·ri·tan'i·kal, a. Pertaining to the Puritans or their doctrines and practice; precise in religious matters; exact; rigid. —**puritanically**, pū·ri·tan'i·kal·li, adv. In a puritanical manner.— **Puritanism**, pū'ri·tan·izm, n. The doctrines or practices of Puritans.

purity. See PURE.

purl, pėrl, n. [Contracted form of purfle.] An embroidered border; an inversion of the stitches in knitting, giving a distinctive appearance.

purl, pėrl, v.i. [Akin to Sw. porla, to purl; probably from the sound; comp. purr.] To murmur, as a shallow stream flowing among stones; to flow with a gentle murmur; to ripple.—n. A ripple; a murmuring sound, as of a shallow stream among stones; malt liquor flavored with wormwood or aromatic herbs; now

a name for beer flavored with gin, sugar, and ginger.

purlieu, pėr'lū, n. [From Norm. purlieu, puraille, O.Fr. puralée, perambulation, from pur, L. per, through, alée, a going. (ALLEY.) Both form and sense have been influenced by Fr. lieu, place.] A piece of land set apart from an ancient royal forest by perambulation of its boundaries; a part lying adjacent; the outer portion of any area; the environs.

purloin, pėr'loin, v.t. [O.Fr. porloignier, purloignier, from L. prolongare, to prolong. PROLONG.] To steal; to filch; to take by plagiarism. —v.i. To practice theft.—**purloiner**, pėr·loi'nėr, n. One who purloins; a thief; a plagiarist.

purple, pėr'pl, a. [Old form purpre, from L. purpura, purple, from Gr. porphyra, a kind of shellfish that yielded a purple dye. Akin porphyry.] Of a color composed of red and blue blended; imperial; regal—a sense derived from purple robes being formerly distinctive of great personages; bloody; dyed with blood.— n. A color compounded by the union of blue and red; a purple robe or dress; hence, from a purple robe having been the distinguishing dress of emperors, etc., used typically of imperial or regal power.—The purple, the imperial dignity; also the dignity of a cardinal.—Purple of Cassius, a pigment used in painting on glass and porcelain.—v.t.—purpled, purpling. To dye or color purple; to clothe with purple.—**purplish**, pėr'plish, a. Somewhat purple.

purport, pėr'pōrt, n. [O.Fr. purport, from pur, Fr. pour, for, and porter, to bear. PORT (demeanor).] Meaning; tenor; import.—v.t. To convey, as a certain meaning; to import; to signify.—v.i. To have a certain purport or tenor.

purpose, pėr'pus, n. [O.Fr. pourpos, Fr. propos, from L. propositum, from propono—pro, before, and ponere, positum, to place. POSITION.] That which a person sets before himself as an object to be reached or accomplished; end or aim; that which a person intends to do; design; plan; intention.—Of purpose, on purpose, with previous design; designedly; intentionally.—To the purpose, to the matter in question (to speak to the purpose).—v.t.—purposed, purposing. To intend; to resolve; to mean; to wish.—v.i. To have intention or design; to intend.—**purposeless**, pėr'pus·les, a. Having no object or purpose.—**purposely**, pėr'pus·li, adv. By purpose or design; intentionally.

purpura, pėr'pu·ra, n. [PURPLE.] A disease characterized by purple spots on the skin; the purples.

purr, pėr, v.i. [Imitative of sound.] To utter a soft murmuring sound, as a cat when pleased.—v.t. To signify by purring.—n. The sound uttered by a cat when pleased.

purse, pėrs, n. [From Fr. bourse, L.L. bursa, byrsa, a purse, from Gr. byrsa, a skin, a hide.] A small bag or case in which money is contained or

carried in the pocket; a sum of money collected as a present; a specific sum of money, namely, in Turkey 500 piasters, or about $22.00; fig. a treasury; finances.—To have a long or heavy purse, to have plenty of money; to have a short or light one, to have little.—v.t.—pursed, pursing. To put in a purse; to contract into folds or wrinkles; to pucker.—**purse-proud**, a. Proud of wealth; puffed up with the possession of riches.—**purser**, pėr'sėr, n. The ticket officer on a steamer.

pursiness, pėr'si·nes, n. See PURSY.

purslane, pėrs'lān, n. [O.Fr. porcelaine, It. porcellana, from L. porcilaca, purslane.] An annual plant with fleshy succulent leaves, used in salads, as a potherb, in pickles, etc.

pursue, pėr·sū', v.t.—pursued, pursuing. [O.Fr. poursuir, porsuir (Fr. poursuivre)—pour = L. pro, forward, and suir, suivre, to follow, L. sequor. SEQUENCE.] To follow with a view to overtake; to chase; to attend on (misfortune pursues him); to seek; to use measures to obtain; to prosecute, continue, or proceed in; to carry on; to follow up; to proceed along, with a view to some end or object; to follow (to pursue a course). —v.i. To go in pursuit; to proceed; law, to act as a prosecutor.—**pursuer**, pėr·sū'ėr, n. One who pursues; Scots law, the party who institutes an ordinary action; the plaintiff.— **pursuit**, pėr·sūt', n. [Fr. poursuite.] The act of pursuing or following with a view to overtake; a following with a view to reach or obtain; endeavor to attain; course of business or occupation; employment (mercantile pursuits).—**pursuance**, pėr·sū'ans, n. A pursuing or carrying out (of a design); prosecution.—In pursuance of, in fulfillment or execution of; in carrying out.—**pursuant**, pėr·sū'ant, a. [O.Fr. porsuiant, poursuiant.] Done in consequence of anything; agreeable; conformable; with to.—adv. Conformably; with to.—**pursuantly**, pėr·sū'ant·li, adv. Pursuant; agreeably; conformably.

pursuivant, pėr'swi·vant, n. [Fr. poursuivant, from poursuivre. PURSUE.] A state messenger; an attendant on heralds; one of the third and lowest order of heraldic officers, of whom there are four in England, named Rouge Croix, Blue Mantle, Rouge Dragon, and Portcullis.

pursy, pėr'si, a. [O.Fr. pourcif, also poulsif, from pourcer, poulser (Mod. Fr. pousser), to push, also to breathe or pant, from L. pulsare, to beat. PULSE, PUSH.] Short-winded; fat and short-winded; rank; wanton; self-indulgent. 'Pursy times' (Hamlet).— **pursiness**, pėr'si·nes, n. A state of being pursy; shortness of breath.

purtenance, pėr'te·nans, n. [Shortened from appurtenance.] Appurtenance; that which pertains or belongs to anything.

purulent, pū'ru·lent, a. [L. purulentus, from pus, puris, matter. Same root as in putrid.] Consisting of pus or matter; full of or resembling pus. —**purulently**, pū'ru·lent·li, adv. In a purulent manner.—**purulence, pu-rulency,** pū′ru·lens, pū′ru·len·si, *n.* The state of being purulent; pus.

purvey, pėr·vā′, *v.t.* [Fr. *pourvoir,* O.Fr. *proveoir, porveoir,* from L. *provideo,* to foresee, to provide. PROVIDE.] To provide, especially to provide provisions or other necessaries for a number of persons.—*v.i.* To purchase provisions, especially for a number.—**purveyance,** pėr·vā′-ans, *n.* Act of purveying; in England, the former royal prerogative of preemption of provisions and necessaries for the royal household.—**purveyor,** pėr·vā′ėr, *n.* One who supplies eatables for a number of persons; in England, an officer who formerly exacted provision for the king's household.

purview, pėr′vū, *n.* [O.Fr. *pourveu, purvieu,* Fr. *pourvu,* provided, from *pourvoir,* to provide. PURVEY.] *Law,* the body of a statute as distinguished from the *preamble;* the limit or scope of a statute; limit of sphere of authority; scope.

pus, pus, *n.* [L. *pus, puris,* matter, from same root as in *putrid, putrefy.*] The white or yellowish matter found in abscesses; matter produced in a festering sore.

Puseyism, pū′zi·izm, *n.* The name given collectively to certain doctrines promulgated by Dr. *Pusey,* in conjunction with other divines of Oxford, in a series of pamphlets entitled 'Tracts for the Times'; Tractarianism.—**Puseyite,** pū′zi·īt, *n.* An adherent of Puseyism; a Tractarian.

push, push, *v.t.* [O.E. *pusse,* from Fr. *pousser,* O.Fr. *poulser,* from L. *pulsare,* to beat, a freq. from *pello, pulsum,* to drive, whence *expel,* and other verbs in -*pel.* PULSATE.] To press against with force; to impel by pressure; to drive by steady pressure, without striking: opposed to *draw;* to press or urge forward; to advance by exertions (to *push* one's fortune); to enforce, as in argument; to press or ply hard (as an opponent in argument); to urge; to importune; to prosecute energetically (to *push* a trade).—*v.i.* To make a thrust; to make an effort; to press one's self onward; to force one's way.—*To push on,* to drive or urge one's course forward; to hasten.—*n.* The act of pushing; a short pressure or force applied; a thrust; a vigorous effort; an emergency; an extremity (to come to the *push*); persevering energy; enterprise.—**pusher,** push′-ėr, *n.* One who pushes.—**pushing,** push′ing, *a.* Pressing forward in business; enterprising; energetic.

Pushtu, push′tö, *n.* The language of the Afghans.

pusillanimous, pū·sil·lan′i·mus, *a.* [L. *pusillanimis,* from *pusillus,* very little, from *pusus,* little (same root as in *puerile*), and *animus,* the mind. PUERILE, ANIMATE.] Destitute of strength and firmness of mind; being of weak courage; faint-hearted; cowardly.—**pusillanimity,** pū′sil·la-nim″i·ti, *n.* Weakness of spirit; cowardliness; timidity.—**pusillanimous-ly,** pū·sil·lan′i·mus·li, *adv.* In a pusillanimous manner.

puss, pus, *n.* [Same as D. *poes,* L.G. *puus,* Gael. and Ir. *pus,* a cat; perhaps imitative of the spitting of a cat. The hare is so called from resembling a cat.] A name for the cat and also for the hare; a sort of pet name sometimes applied to a child or young woman.—**pussy,** pus′i, *n.* Diminutive of *puss.*

pustule, pus′chūl, *n.* [Fr. *pustule,* L. *pustula,* a form of *pusula,* a blister or pimple.] *Med.* an elevation of the cuticle, with an inflamed base, containing pus; *bot.* a pimple or little blister.—**pustular,** pus′chū·lėr, *a.* Having the character of or proceeding from a pustule or pustules.—**pustulate,** pus′chū·lāt, *v.t.*—*pustulat-ed, pustulating.* To form into pustules or blisters.—*a. Bot.* covered with glandular excrescences like pustules.

put, put, *v.t.*—pret. and pp. *put,* ppr. *putting.* [O.E. *putte,* A.Sax. *potian,* to thrust, to gore; Dan. *putte,* to put or set.] To place, set, or lay in any position or situation; to place in any state or condition (to *put* to shame, to death); to apply (to *put* one's hand, one's mind to a thing); to set before one for consideration; to propose (to *put* a case, a question).—*To put about,* to change the course of (a ship); to put to inconvenience.—*To put an end to,* to stop; to bring to a conclusion.—*To put away,* to renounce or discard; to divorce.—*To put back,* to hinder; to delay; to restore to the original place.—*To put by,* to turn away; to thrust aside; to place in safe-keeping.—*To put down,* to repress; to crush; to confute; to silence; to write down; to subscribe.—*To put forth,* to propose; to offer to notice; to stretch out; to shoot out, as leaves; to exert; to bring into action; to make known, as opinions; to publish, as in a book. —*To put in,* to introduce among others; to insert.—*To put in mind,* to remind.—*To put in practice,* to apply; to make use of.—*To put off,* to take from one's person; to lay aside; to turn aside from a purpose or demand; to delay; to postpone; to push from land.—*To put on,* to invest with as clothes or covering; to impute; to charge with (to *put* blame *on*); to assume (to *put on* a grave face); to impose; to inflict; to turn or let on; to set to work.—*To put out,* to eject; to drive out; to place (money) at interest; to extinguish; to shoot forth (to *put out* leaves); to extend; to reach out; to publish; to make public; to confuse; to disconcert; to dislocate.—*To put over,* to place in authority over; to defer; to postpone.—*To put to,* to add; to unite; to expose; to kill by; to punish by (to *put to* the sword).—*To put to it,* to press hard; to give difficulty to.—*To put the hand to,* to take hold; to begin; to undertake.—*To put this and that together,* to draw a conclusion from certain circumstances; to infer from given premises.—*To put to rights,* to arrange in an orderly condition; to set in proper order.—*To put to trial* or *on trial,* to bring before a court for

examination and decision; to bring to a test; to try.—*To put up,* to offer publicly for sale; to hoard; to pack; to hide or lay aside; to put into its ordinary place when not in use; to give entertainment to; to accommodate with lodging.—*v.i.* Used only in certain phrases.—*To put in,* to enter a harbor; to offer a claim.—*To put in for,* to put in a claim for; to stand as a candidate for.—*To put off,* to sail from land.—*To put to sea,* to set sail; to begin a voyage.—*To put up,* to take lodgings; to lodge.—*To put up with,* to suffer without showing resentment; to pocket or swallow (an affront); to accept tamely; to overlook; to endure; to tolerate.—**putter,** put′ėr, *n.* One who puts.

put, put, *v.t.*—*putted, putting.* [Akin to above.] To throw upward and forward from the shoulder.

putamen, pū·tā′men, *n.* [L., a shell.] *Bot.* the inner coat or shell of a fruit; the endocarp.

putative, pū′ta·tiv, *a.* [Fr. *putatif,* L. *putativus,* from L. *puto,* to suppose (as in *compute, impute, dispute, repute*).] Supposed; reputed (the *putative* father of a child).

putlog, put′log, *n.* [From *put* and *log.*] *Carp.* one of the short pieces of timber used in building to carry the floor of a scaffold, having one end inserted in holes in the wall.

putrefy, pū′tre·fī, *v.t.*—*putrefied, putrefying.* [Fr. *putrefier,* L. *putrefacio*—*putris,* putrid, *facio,* to make. PUTRID.] To render putrid; to cause to rot with an offensive smell; to make carious or gangrenous—*v.i.* To become putrid; to rot.—**putrefaction,** pū·tre·fak′shon, *n.* The act or process of putrefying; the decomposition of animal and vegetable substances, attended by the evolution of fetid gases; that which is putrefied.—**putrefactive,** pū·tre·fak′-tiv, *a.* Pertaining to putrefaction; tending to cause or causing putrefaction.

putrescent, pū·tres′ent, *a.* [L. *putrescens,* ppr. of *putresco,* to rot. PUTRID.] Becoming putrid; growing rotten; pertaining to the process of putrefaction.—**putrescence,** pū·tres′-ens, *n.* The state of being putrescent; a putrid state.—**putrescible,** pū-tres′i·bl, *a.* Capable of being putrefied; liable to become putrid.

putrid, pū′trid, *a.* [Fr. *putride,* L. *putridus,* from *putris,* rotten, *putreo,* to rot, from *puteo,* to stink, from a root seen also in L. *pus,* Gr. *pyon,* matter; the same root producing also E. *foul.* PUS, FOUL.] In a state of decay or putrefaction; corrupt; rotten; proceeding from putrefaction or pertaining to it.—*Putrid fever,* typhus or spotted fever.—**putridity, putridness,** pū·trid′i·ti, pū′trid·nes, *n.* The state of being putrid; corruption; rottenness.

putt, put, *n.* A stroke made on a golf green, the object being to play the ball into the cup.—*v.t.* and *i.*—*putted, putting.* To tap a golf ball while on the golf green in the direction of the cup.—**putter,** *n.* A short-shaft golf club with an almost perpendicular face, used for accurate play near the cup.—**putting green,** *n.* Smooth turf surrounding the putting holes on a golf course.

puttee, put′i, *n.* [Hind. *patti.*] Long roll of cloth wound round soldier's leg from ankle to knee as support and protection.

putty, put′i, *n.* [Fr. *potée,* calcined tin, brass, etc., putty powder, from *pot,* a pot, originally perhaps applied to a solder for pots.] A powder of calcined tin, used in polishing glass and steel; a kind of paste or cement compounded of whiting or soft carbonate of lime and linseed oil, used by glaziers for fixing in the panes or glass in window frames, etc.; a fine cement made of lime and stone dust; the mixture of ground materials in which earthenware is dipped for glazing.—*v.t.*—*puttied, puttying.* To cement with putty; to fill up with putty.

puzzle, puz′l, *v.t.*—*puzzled, puzzling.* [Freq. from *pose,* to perplex with a question; or a form of *puddle;* comp. *muddle,* to make stupid.] To perplex; to nonplus; to put to a stand; to gravel; to make intricate; to entangle; with *out,* to discover or resolve by long cogitation.—*v.i.* To be bewildered; to be awkward.—*n.* Perplexity; embarrassment; a kind of riddle; a toy or contrivance which tries the ingenuity.—**puzzlement,** puz′l·ment, *n.* The state of being puzzled; bewilderment.—**puzzler,** puz′lėr, *n.* One who or that which puzzles.—**puzzling,** puz′ling, *p.* and *a.* Such as to puzzle; perplexing; embarrassing; bewildering.

pyaemia, pī·ē′mi·a, *n.* [Gr. *pyon,* pus (PUTRID), and *haima,* blood.] Blood poisoning, a dangerous disease resulting from the introduction of decaying animal matter, pus, etc., into the system.—**pyaemic,** pī·ē′mik, *a.* Pertaining to pyaemia; characterized by or of the nature of pyaemia.

pygidium, pī·jid′i·um, *n.* [Gr. *pygē,* the posteriors.] The terminal division of the body of a trilobite, also of a flea.

Pygmy, pig′mi, *n.* [Fr. *pygmée;* L. *pygmaeus,* from Gr. *pygmaios,* from *pygmē,* the fist.] One of a Negroid people of small stature; [not cap.] a little or dwarfish person.—*a.* Pygmean; dwarfish; little.—**pygmean,** pig·mē′an, *a.*

pylon, pī′lon, *n.* [Gr. *pylōn,* from *pylē,* a gate.] A lofty massive doorway; a gateway; a large supporting post or tower, as to a bridge; a structure marking an airway.

pylorus, pī·lō′rus, *n.* [Gr. *pylōros,* from *pylē,* a gate, and *ouros,* a guard.] The outlet for the stomach, through which the food passes to the intestines.—**pyloric,** pī·lor′ik, *a.*

pyogenesis, pī·o·jen′e·sis, *n.* [Gr. *pyon,* pus, *genesis,* generation; root *gen,* to produce. PUS.] The generation or formation of pus.—**pyogenic,** pī·o·jen′ik, *a.* Having relation to formation of pus.

pyorrhea, pī′er·rē′a, *n.* [Gr. *pyon,* pus, *rrhea,* a flow.] A suppurative inflammation in and about the sockets of the teeth which results in the loosening of the teeth, abscess formation in the gums, and, unless checked, inflammation of the jawbone.

pyramid, pir′a·mid, *n.* [Fr. *pyramide;* L. *pyramis,* from Gr. *pyramis, pyramidos,* a pyramid; probably an Egyptian word.] A solid structure whose base is a rectilineal figure, and whose sides are triangular and meet at a point; one of the ancient structures of this form erected in different parts of the world, the most noted being those of Egypt, to which the name was originally applied; *geom.* strictly a solid contained by a plane triangular, square, or polygonal base, and by other planes meeting in a point; *pl.* a game at billiards played with fifteen red balls and one white, the red balls being placed together in the form of a triangle or pyramid, and the players trying who will pocket the greatest number of balls.—**pyramidal, pyramidic, pyramidical,** pi·ram′i·dal, pir·a·mid′ik, pir·a·mid′i·kal, *a.* Pertaining to a pyramid; having the form of a pyramid.

pyrargyrite, pīr·ar′ji·rīt, *n.* [Gr. *pyr,* fire, and *argyros,* silver.] An important ore of silver, chiefly sulfide of silver and antimony, with hexagonal crystallization.

pyre, pīr, *n.* [L. *pyra,* from Gr. *pyra,* a pyre, from *pyr,* fire. FIRE.] A heap of combustible materials on which a dead body was laid to be burned; a funeral pile.

pyrene, pī·rēn′, *n.* [Gr. *pyrēn.*] *Bot.* the stone found in the interior of fruits.

pyretic, pī·ret′ik, *n.* [Gr. *pyretos,* burning heat, fever, from *pyr,* fire. PYRE.] A medicine for the cure of fever.—**pyretology,** pir·e·tol′o·ji, *n.* The branch of medical science that treats of fevers.—**pyrexia,** pī·rek′si·a, *n.* [Fr. *pyrexie,* from Gr. *puressō,* to be feverish.] Fever.—**pyrexial,** pī·rek′si·al, *a.* Pertaining to fever; feverish.

pyrex, pī′reks, *n.* A heat-resistant glassware; [cap.] trademark for such glassware.

pyrheliometer, pīr·hē′li·om″et·ėr, *n.* [Gr. *pyr,* fire, *hēlios,* the sun, *metron,* a measure.] An instrument for measuring the intensity of the heat of the sun.

pyridoxin, pir·i·dok′sin, *n.* [*Pyridine* and *oxygen.*] *Biochem.* vitamin B_6 used for the prevention of pellagra.

pyriform, pīr′i·form, *a.* [L. *pyrum,* a pear, and *forma,* shape.] Having the form of a pear.

pyrites, pī·rī′tēz, *n.* [Gr. *pyritēs,* from *pyr,* fire. PYRE.] A term applied to yellow sulfide of iron, because it struck fire with steel; also applied to minerals in which sulfur exists in combination with copper, cobalt, nickel, etc.—*Arsenical pyrites.* See MISPICKEL.—*White iron pyrites.* See MARCASITE.—*Yellow* or *copper pyrites,* the sulfide of copper and iron, the most common

ore of copper.—**pyritic, pyritical,** pī·rit′ik, pī·rit′i·kal, *a.* Pertaining to pyrites; consisting of or resembling pyrites.

pyroacid, pīr·ō·as″id, *n.* A product obtained by subjecting certain organic acids to heat.

pyroelectric, pyroelectricity, pīr′ō·i·lek″trik, pīr′ō·i·lek·tris″i·ti. [Gr. *pyr, pyros,* fire, and E. *electric.*] See THERMOELECTRIC, etc.

pyrogenic, pīr·o·jen′ik, *a.* and *n.* [Gr. *pyr, pyros,* fire, and root *gen,* to produce.] Producing or that which tends to produce feverishness.—**pyrogenous,** pi·roj′e·nus, *a.* Produced by fire; igneous.

pyrognostic, pīr·og·nos′tik, *a.* [Gr. *pyr, pyros,* fire, and *gignōskō,* to know.] *Mineral,* pertaining to the phenomena exhibited on the application of the blowpipe.

pyroligneous, pyrolignic, pīr·o·lig′nē·us, pīr·o·lig′nik, *a.* [Gr. *pyr,* fire, and L. *lignum,* wood.] Generated or procured by the distillation of wood.—*Pyroligneous acid,* impure acetic acid obtained by the distillation of wood.

pyrology, pī·rol′o·ji, *n.* [Gr. *pyr,* fire, and *logos,* discourse.] The science of heat.

pyrolusite, pīr·o·lū′sīt, *n.* [Gr. *pyr,* fire, and *louō,* I wash.] A black ore of manganese, much used in chemical processes.

pyromagnetic, pīr′o·mag·net″ik, *a.* [Gr. *pyr, pyros,* fire, and E. *magnetic.*] Having the property of becoming magnetic when heated.

pyromancy, pīr′o·man·si, *n.* [Gr. *pyr, pyros,* fire, and *manteia,* divination.] Divination by fire.

pyromania, pī·rō·mā′ni·a, *n.* [N.L. *pyro,* fire, and *mania.*] *Psych.* an uncontrollable impulse for setting fires.

pyrometer, pī·rom′et·ėr, *n.* [Gr. *pyr, pyros,* fire, and *metron,* a measure.] A term applied to any instrument the object of which is to measure all gradations of temperature above those that can be indicated by the mercurial thermometer.—**pyrometric, pyrometrical,** pīr·o·met′rik, pīr·o·met′ri·kal, *a.* Pertaining to the pyrometer or its use.—**pyrometry,** pī·rom′et·ri, *n.* The use of the pyrometer; the act or art of measuring high degrees of heat.

pyrope, pīr′ōp, *n.* [Gr. *pyr, pyros,* fire, and *ōps,* the face.] Fire garnet or Bohemian garnet, a dark-red variety of garnet.

pyrophoric, pīr·o·for′ik, *a.* Light-producing.

pyrophyllite, pīr·o·fil′līt, *n.* [Gr. *pyr, pyros,* fire, and *phyllon,* a leaf.] A mineral of a foliated structure, resembling talc, and having a white, green, or yellow color and pearly luster.

pyroscope, pīr′o·skōp, *n.* [Gr. *pyr, pyros,* fire, and *skopein,* to view.] An instrument for measuring the intensity of heat radiating from a hot body.

pyrotechnic, pyrotechnical, pīr·o·tek′nik, pir·o·tek′ni·kal, *a.* [Gr. *pyr, pyros,* fire, and *technē,* art.] Pertaining to fireworks or the art of forming them.—**pyrotechnics, pyrotechny,** pĭr·o·tek'niks, pĭr·o·tek'nĭ, *n.* The art of making fireworks; the use of artificial fireworks; the management and application of fire in various operations.—**pyrotechnist,** pĭr·o·tek'nist, *n.* One skilled in pyrotechny; a manufacturer of fireworks.

pyroxene, pĭr'ok·sēn, *n.* [Gr. *pyr, pyros,* fire, and *xenos,* a stranger.] Another name for the mineral augite; any of various minerals similar to augite.—**pyroxenic,** pĭr·ok·sen'ik, *a.* Pertaining to pyroxene.

pyroxylin, pi·rok'si·lin, *n.* [Gr. *pyr,* fire, and *xylon,* wood.] A nitrocellulose compound, low in nitrogen content, soluble in an ether alcohol solution, and used in the manufacture of plastics, lacquer, etc.

pyrrhic, pĭr'ik, *n.* [Gr. *pyrrhiche,* a warlike dance.] An ancient Grecian warlike dance; a metrical foot consisting of two short syllables.—*a.* Pertaining to the Greek martial dance; *pros.* consisting of two short syllables, or of feet of two short syllables.—*Pyrrhic victory,* a victory, as of those gained by King Pyrrhus of Epirus over the Romans, costing more to the victor than to the vanquished.

Pyrrhonism, pĭr'on·izm, *n.* [From *Pyrrho,* the founder of the Skeptics.] Skepticism; universal doubt.

Pythagorean, pĭ·thag'o·rē"an, *a.* Pertaining to Pythagoras or his system of philosophy, which taught the doctrine of the transmigration of souls, and resolved all philosophy into the relations of numbers.—*Pythagorean system, astron.* the system taught by Pythagoras, afterward revived by Copernicus.—*n.* A follower of Pythagoras.—**pythagoreanism,** pi·thag'o·rē"an·izm, *n.* The doctrines or philosophy of Pythagoras.

Pythian, pith'i·an, *a.* [L. *Pythius,* Gr. *Pythios,* from *Pythō,* the older name of Delphi.] Pertaining to Delphi or to the priestess of Apollo at Delphi.—*Pythian games,* one of the four great national festivals of Greece, celebrated every fifth year in honor of Apollo near Delphi. —**Pythiad,** pith'i·ad, *n.* The period between the celebrations of the Pythian games.

pythogenic, pī·tho·jen'ik, *a.* [Gr. *pythomai,* to rot, and root *gen,* to produce.] Engendered from filth: applied to diseases, as typhus, produced by filth or by a vitiated atmosphere.

python, pī'thon, *n.* [Gr. *pythōn,* a great serpent slain by Apollo.] A genus of large nonvenomous serpents, natives of the East Indies and elsewhere.

pythoness, pī'thon·es, *n.* [Fr. *pythonisse,* from Gr. *Pythō,* old name of Delphi. PYTHIAN.] The priestess of Apollo at Delphi, who gave oracular answers; hence, any woman supposed to have a spirit of divination.—**pythonic,** pī·thon'ik, *a.* Oracular; prophetic.

pyuria, pī·ū'ri·a, *n.* [Gr. *puon,* pus, *ouron,* urine.] *Pathol.* the presence of pus in the urine.

pyx, piks, *n.* [Gr. *pyxis,* a box, especially of boxwood, from *pyxos,* the box tree.] A covered vessel used in the Roman Catholic Church for holding the consecrated host; a box or chest in which specimen coins are deposited at the British mint.— *Trial of the pyx,* the trial by weight and assay of the gold and silver coins of the United Kingdom, prior to their issue from the mint; the assay of gold and silver plate at an assay office. Written also *Pix.*—*v.t.* To test by weight and assay.

pyxidium, pik·sid'i·um, *n.* [Gr. *pyxis,* a box, and *eidos,* resemblance.] *Bot.* a capsule with a lid, as seen in the case of certain fruits; a term also applied to the theca of mosses.

Q

Q, q, kū, the seventeenth letter of the English alphabet, a consonant having the same sound as *k* or hard *c.*

qua, kwä, *adv.* [L.] In the quality or character of; as being; as.

quack, kwak, *v.i.* [Formed from the sound, like D. *kwaaken, kwakken,* G. *quaken,* Dan. *qvakke,* to croak, to quack; comp. Gr. *koax,* the croak of a frog.] To cry like the common domestic duck; to make vain and loud pretensions; to talk noisily and ostentatiously; to play the quack.—*n.* The cry of a duck; one who pretends to skill or knowledge which he does not possess; an empty pretender; a charlatan; especially, a pretender to medical skill.—*a.* Pertaining to or characterized by quackery (*quack* medicines, a *quack* doctor). —**quackery,** kwak'er·i, *n.* The boastful pretensions or mean practice of a quack, particularly in medicine; humbug; imposture.—**quackish,** kwak'ish, *a.* Like a quack or charlatan.—**quacksalver,** kwak'sal·vér, *n.* [D. *kwakzalver,* L.G. *kuaksalver,* G. *quacksalber,* lit. a *quack* that deals in *salves.*] A charlatan; a quack.

quad, kwod, *n.* [Contr. for *quadrangle.*] The quadrangle or court, as of a college or jail; hence, a jail; quod. See QUADRAT.

quadragenarian, kwod'ra·je·nâ"ri·an, *a.* [L. *quadragenarius,* from *quadrageni,* forty each, from *quadraginta,* forty.] Consisting of forty; forty years old.

Quadragesima, kwod·ra·jes'i·ma, *n.* [L. *quadragesimus,* fortieth, from *quadraginta,* forty, from *quatuor,* four.] Lent; so called because it consists of forty days.—*Quadragesima Sunday,* the first Sunday in Lent.—**quadragesimal,** kwod·ra·jes'i·mal, *a.* Connected with the number forty; [*cap.*] belonging to Lent.

quadrangle, kwod'rang·gl, *n.* [L. *quadrus*=*quatuor,* four, and *angulus,* an angle.] A quadrilateral figure; a

plain figure having four sides, and consequently four angles; a square or quadrangular court surrounded by buildings.—**quadrangular,** kwod·rang'gū·lér, *a.* Of a square shape; having four sides and four angles.

quadrant, kwod'rant, *n.* [L. *quadrans, quadrantis,* a fourth.] The quarter of a circle; the arc of a circle containing 90°; the space included between this arc and two radii drawn from the center to each extremity; an instrument for measuring angular altitudes, in principle and application the same as the sextant, by which it is superseded.— **quadrantal,** kwod·ran'tal, *a.* Pertaining to a quadrant.

quadrat, kwod'rat, *n.* [L. *quadratum,* a square, from *quadrus,* square.] *Printing,* a piece of type metal cast lower than a type, used for filling out spaces between letters, words, lines, etc., so as to leave a blank on the paper at the place.

quadrate, kwod'rāt, *a.* [L. *quadratus,* squared, pp. of *quadro, quadratum,* to make square, from *quadrus,* square.] Square in form; square, by being the product of a number multiplied into itself.—*n.* A square surface or figure.—**quadratic,** kwod·rat'ik, *a.* [Fr. *quadratique.*] Pertaining to, denoting, or containing a square, *alg.* involving the square or second power of an unknown quantity (a *quadratic* equation).—*n.* A quadratic equation; *pl.* that branch of algebra which treats of quadratic equations.—**quadrature,** kwod're·chér, *n.* [L. *quadratura.*] *Geom.* the act of squaring; the reducing of a figure to a square; thus, the finding of a square which shall contain just as much area as a certain square or triangle, is the *quadrature* of that circle or triangle; *astron.* the position of one heavenly body in respect to another when distant from it 90°.

quadrennial, kwod·ren'i·al, *a.* [From L. *quadriennium,* a space of four years—*quadrus*=*quatuor,* four, and *annus,* year.] Comprising four years; occurring once in four years.— **quadrennially,** kwod·ren'i·al·li, *adv.* Once in four years.

quadriceps, kwod'ri·seps, *n.* [L. *quadrus, quatuor,* four, *caput,* the head.] A large muscle in the front of the thigh.—**quadricipital,** kwod·ri·sip'i·tal, *a.* Four-headed; belonging to the quadriceps.

quadrifid, kwod'ri·fid, *a.* [L. *quadrus*=*quatuor,* four, and *findo, fidi,* to cleave.] Split or deeply cleft into four parts.

quadrifoliate, kwod·ri·fō'li·āt, *a.* [L. *quadrus*=*quatuor,* four, and *folium,* a leaf.] *Bot.* having four leaves attached laterally to a common stalk.

quadriga, kwod·rī'ga, *n.* pl. **quadrigae,** kwod·rī'jē. [L., contr. from *quadrijuga*—prefix *quadrus,* fourfold, and *jugum,* a yoke.] An ancient two-wheeled car or chariot drawn by four horses, harnessed all abreast.

quadrilateral, kwod·ri·lat'ér·al, *a.* [L. *quadrus*=*quatuor,* four, and *latus, lateris,* side.] Having four sides and consequently four angles.—*n.* A figure having four sides and four angles; the space enclosed between and defended by four fortresses, or the four fortresses collectively.

quadriliteral, kwod·ri·lit´ér·al, *a.* [L. *quatuor, litera,* letter.] Consisting of four letters.

quadrille, kwo·dril´, *n.* [Fr. *quadrille,* Sp. *cuadrilla,* a group of four persons, *cuadrillo,* a small square, from L. *quadra, quadrum,* a square, from *quatuor,* four.] A game played by four persons with forty cards; a dance consisting generally of five figures or movements executed by four couples each forming the side of a square; the music for such a dance.

quadrillion, kwod·ril´yon, *n.* [L. *quadrus=quatuor,* four, and E. *million.*] According to the United States and French system, a unit followed by 15 zeros; in Gt. Britain and Germany a unit followed by 24 zeros.

quadrinomial, kwod·ri·nō´mi·al, *a.* [L. *quadrus=quatuor,* four, and *nomen,* a name.] *Alg.* consisting of four denominations or terms.—*n.* *Alg.* a quantity consisting of four terms.

quadripartite, kwod·ri·pär´tīt, *a.* [L. *quadrus=quatuor,* four, and *partitus,* divided.] Divided into four parts; *bot.* divided to the base into four parts (a *quadripartite* leaf).

quadriphyllous, kwod·ri·fil´lus, *a.* [L. *quadrus=quatuor,* and Gr. *phyllon,* a leaf.] *Bot.* having four leaves; four-leaved.

quadrisyllable, kwod·ri·sil´la·bl, *n.* [L. *quadrus=quatuor,* four, and E. *syllable.*] A word consisting of four syllables.—**quadrisyllabic,** kwod´-ri·sil·lab´ik, *a.* Consisting of four syllables.

quadrivalent, kwod·riv´a·lent, *a.* [From L. *quadrus=quatuor,* four, and *valens, valentis,* ppr. of *valeo,* to be worth.] *Chem.* having a valence of four.

quadrivial, kwod·riv´i·al, *a.* [E. *quadrivium*—prefix *quadrus=quatuor,* four, and *via,* a way.] Having four roads meeting in a point.—**quadrivium,** kwod·riv´i·um, *n.* [L.L.] A collective term in the Middle Ages for the four lesser arts—arithmetic, music, geometry, and astronomy.

quadroon, kwod·rön´, *n.* [Sp. *cuarteron,* from L. *quartus,* fourth. QUARTER.] The offspring of a mulatto by a white person; a person who is one-fourth Negro.

quadruped, kwod´ru·ped, *n.* [L. *quadrupes, quadrupedis=quadrus=quatuor,* four, and *pes, pedis,* a foot.] An animal having four legs, usually restricted to four-footed mammals, though many reptiles have also four legs.—**quadrupedal,** kwod·ru´pe·dal, *a.* Belonging to a quadruped, having or walking on four feet.

quadruple, kwod´ru·pl, *a.* [L. *quadruplus—quadrus=quatuor,* four, and term. *-plus,* Gr. *ploos.* DOUBLE.] Fourfold; four times told.—*n.* Four times the sum or number.—*v.t.*—*quadrupled, quadrupling.* To make four times as much or as many; to multiply by four.—*v.i.* To become

four times as much or as many.—**quadruplet,** kwod·ru´plet, *n.* Four children born at one birth; one of these four children.

quadruplicate, kwod·ru´pli·kāt, *v.t.* [L. *quadruplico, quadruplicatum—quadrus=quatuor,* four, and *plico,* to fold.] To make fourfold; to double twice.—*a.* Fourfold; four times repeated (a *quadruplicate* ratio or proportion).—**quadruplication,** kwod·ru´pli·kā´shon, *n.* The act of making fourfold or four times as great.

quaestor, kwes´tor. See QUESTOR.

quaff, kwäf, *v.t.* [From Ir. and Gael. *cuach,* Sc. *quaich, queff,* a drinking cup.] To drink; to swallow in large draughts; to drink copiously.—*v.i.* To drink largely.—**quaffer,** kwäf´ér, *n.* One who quaffs.

quagga, kwag´a, *n.* [Hottentot; name derived from its cry.] An animal of South Africa closely allied to the zebra.

quagmire, kwag´mīr, *n.* [*Quag* for *quake,* and *mire;* lit. a mire or bog that quakes or shakes.] A piece of soft boggy land that trembles under the foot; a bog; a fen.—**quaggy,** kwag´i, *a.* Trembling under the foot, as soft wet earth; boggy; spongy.

quahog, quahaug, kwä´häg, kwa·häg´, *n.* [Algonquian origin.] An edible American clam, paricularly the hard-shelled *Venus mercenaria.*

quail, kwāl, *v.i.* [A.Sax. *cwelan,* to die=D. *quelen,* to pine away; O.H.G. *quelan,* to suffer torment. QUELL.] To have the spirits sink or give way, as before danger or difficulty; to shrink; to lose heart; to cower.

quail, kwāl, *n.* [O.Fr. *quaille,* Fr. *caille,* It. *quaglia,* a quail—names derived from its cry. Comp. D. *kwakkel,* G. *wachtel,* and Armor. *coaill,* a quail.] A common name of certain birds nearly allied to the partridges, from which they differ chiefly in being smaller.

quaint, kwänt, *a.* [O.E. *queint, coint,* from O.Fr. *coint,* neat, fine, dainty; from L. *cognitus,* known, the meaning having probably been influenced by L. *comptus,* trimmed, adorned. COGNITION, ACQUAINT.] Old and antique; singular; whimsical; curious; fanciful.—**quaintly,** kwänt´li, *adv.* In a quaint manner; oddly; fancifully; singularly; whimsically. —**quaintness,** kwänt´nes, *n.* The quality of being quaint; oddity and antiqueness.

quake, kwāk, *v.i.*—*quaked, quaking.* [A.Sax. *cwacian,* same root as *quick;* comp. Prov. G. *quacken,* to waggle, to shake. QUICK.] To shake; to tremble; to shudder (to *quake* with fear); to be shaken with more or less violent convulsions (the earth *quakes*); to shake or tremble, as the earth under the feet, through want of solidity or firmness.—*n.* A shake; a trembling; a tremulous agitation.—

quaker, kwā´kér, *n.* One that quakes; [*cap.*] one of the religious sect called the *Society of Friends* (see under FRIEND.)—**Quakeress,** kwā´-kér·es, *n.* A female Quaker.—**Qua-**

kerish, kwā´kér·ish, *a.* Relating to or resembling Quakers.—**Quakerism,** kwā´kér·izm, *n.* The peculiar manners, tenets, or worship of the Quakers.—**Quakerly,** kwā´kér·li, *a.* Resembling or characteristic of Quakers.

qualify, kwol´i·fī, *v.t.*—*qualified, qualifying.* [Fr. *qualifier,* from L.L. *qualificare,* from L. *qualis,* such, of such sort, and *facio,* to make.] To make such as is required; to fit for any place, office, or occupation; to furnish with knowledge, skill, etc., necessary for a purpose; to furnish with legal power or capacity (to *qualify* persons for the franchise); to limit or modify; to restrict; to limit by exceptions (to *qualify* a statement); to moderate, abate, soften; to modify the quality or strength of; to dilute or otherwise fit for taste (to *qualify* spirits with water).—*v.i.* To take the necessary steps for rendering one's self capable of holding any office or enjoying any privilege; to establish a right to exercise any function; followed by *for.*—**qualification,** kwol´i·fi·kā´shon, *n.* The act of qualifying, or the state of being qualified; that which qualifies or fits a person or thing for any use or purpose, as for a place, an office, an employment; legal power; ability; a qualifying or extenuating circumstance; modification; restriction; limitation; an abatement; a diminution.—**qualificative,** kwol´i·fi·kā·tiv, *a.* Serving or having the power to qualify or modify.—*n.* That which serves to qualify; a qualifying term, clause, or statement.—**qualified,** kwol´i·fīd, *p.* and *a.* Having a qualification; furnished with legal power or capacity; accompanied with some limitation or modification; modified; limited (a *qualified* statement).—**qualifiedly,** kwol´i·fīd·li, *adv.* With qualification or limitation. —**qualifier,** kwol´i·fī·ér, *n.* One who or that which qualifies.

quality, kwol´i·ti, *n.* [Fr. *qualité,* from L. *qualitas,* a quality or property, from *qualis,* such. QUALIFY.] That which makes or helps to make anything such as it is; a distinguishing property, characteristic, or attribute; a property; a trait; moral characteristic, good or bad; comparative rank; condition in relation to others; superior or high rank (ladies of *quality*).—*The quality,* persons of high rank collectively.—**qualitative,** kwol´i·tā·tiv, *a.* Pertaining to quality; estimable according to quality.— *Qualitative analysis, chem.* the process of decomposing a compound substance with a view to determine what elements it contains.—**qualitatively,** kwol´i·tā·tiv·li, *adv.* In a qualitative manner; as regards quality.

qualm, kwäm, *n.* [A.Sax. *cwealm,* pestilence, death; D. *kwalm,* Dan. *qvalm,* qualm, vapor; O.H.G. *qualm,* death; from root of *quell, quail.*] A throe or throb of pain; a sudden feeling of sickness at the stomach; a sensation of nausea; a scruple or twinge of conscience; compunction.—**qualmish**, kwäm´ish, *a*. Sick at the stomach; inclined to vomit; affected with nausea.—**qualmishly**, kwäm´ish·li, *adv*. In a qualmish manner.—**qualmishness**, kwäm´ish·nes, *n*. The state of being qualmish.

quamash, kwom´ash, *n*. An American bulbous plant with roots which were much eaten by the Indians; the Camass.

quandary, kwon·da´ri or kwon´da·ri, *n*. [Probably from Fr. *Qu'en dirai-je?* what shall I say of it?] A state of difficulty, perplexity, uncertainty, or hesitation; a pickle; a predicament.—*v.t.* quandaried, quandarying. To put into a quandary.

quantity, kwon´ti·ti, *n*. [Fr. *quantité*, L. *quantitas*, quantity, extent, from *quantus*, how great, from *quam*, to what a degree.] That property in virtue of which a thing is measurable; greatness; extent; measure; size; any amount, bulk, or aggregate (a *quantity* of earth, a *quantity* of water); often a large or considerable amount (wheat shipped in *quantities*); *math.* anything which can be multiplied, divided, or measured; anything to which mathematical processes are applicable; *gram.* the measure of a syllable or the time in which it is pronounced; the metrical value of syllables as regards length or weight in pronunciation; *logic*, the extent in which the subject of a proposition is taken.—*Quantity of electricity*, measured practically in COULOMBS (which see).—*Quantity of heat*, the unit of quantity of heat is the quantity required to raise unit mass of water through one degree of temperature; according to the unit of mass and the scales employed there are the different units known as pound-degree F., pound-degree C., gram-degree C. See CALORIE.—**quantification**, kwon´ti·fi·kā´shon, *n*. The act or process of quantifying; the act of determining the quantity or amount.—**quantify**, kwon´ti·fī, *v.t.*—*quantified, quantifying*. [L. *quantus*, how much, and *facio*, to make.] To determine the quantity of; to modify or qualify with regard to quantity; more especially a term in logic (to *quantify* the predicate, as by inserting 'all' in 'some men are (all) logicians').—**quantitative**, kwon´ti·tā·tiv, *a*. Estimable according to quantity; relating or having regard to quantity.—*Quantitative analysis, chem.* the process of decomposing a compound substance with a view to determine how much of each element it contains.—**quantitatively**, kwon´ti·tā·tiv·li, *adv*. In a quantitative manner.—**quantum**, kwan´tum, *n*. [L., how much, as much as.] A quantity; an amount; a sufficient amount.—*Quantum theory. Phys.* a theory that the emission or absorption of energy by atoms or molecules is not continuous but occurs in discrete amounts, each amount being called a quantum.

quarantine, kwor´an·tēn, *n*. [O.Fr.

quarantaine, It. *quarantana*, a space of forty days, from *quaranta*, from L. *quadraginta*, forty, from *quatuor*, four.] The period, originally of forty days, now of lesser but indeterminate length, during which a ship arriving in port is detained by health officers for investigation of the possible presence of contagious disease; a place where persons with contagious disease are detained; the place where ships are detained for inspection; the edict requiring one to be detained or the time required by health statutes for a person to be detained in his living quarters because of contagion.—*v.t.* quarantined, quarantining. To restrict the entrance to and exit from any place under observation for contagious disease.

quarrel, kwor´el, *n*. [O.Fr. *querele*, Fr. *querelle*, a quarrel, from L. *querela*, a complaint, from *queror*, to complain; akin *querulous*, also *cry*.] A brawl; an angry dispute; a wrangle; an altercation; a breach of friendship or concord; open variance between parties; the basis or ground of being at variance with another; ill-will, or reason to complain; ground of objection.—*v.i.*—*quarreled, quarreling*. To dispute violently with loud and angry words; to wrangle; to squabble; to fall out; to pick a quarrel; to get into hostilities; to find fault; to cavil.—**quarreler**, kwor´el·ėr, *n*. One who quarrels.—**quarrelsome**, kwor´el·sum, *a*. Apt to quarrel; easily irritated or provoked to contest; irascible; choleric.—**quarrelsomely**, kwor´el·sum·li, *adv*. In a quarrelsome manner.

quarrel, kwor´el, *n*. [O.Fr. *quarrel* (Fr. *carreau*), dim. of L. *quadrum*, something square, from *quatuor*, four.] A bolt to be shot from a crossbow, especially with a somewhat square-shaped head; a lozenge-shaped pane of glass in a window; a small paving stone or tile of the square or lozenge form; a glazier's diamond; a kind of graver.

quarry, kwor´i, *n*. [O.Fr. *quarriere* (Fr. *carrière*), lit. a place where stones are squared, from L. *quadro*, to square. QUADRAT, etc.] A place where stones are dug from the earth, or separated, as by blasting with gunpowder, from a large mass of rocks.—*v.t.*—*quarried, quarrying*. To dig or take from a quarry (to *quarry* marble).—**quarrier**, kwor´i·ėr, *n*. One who works in a quarry.

quarry, kwor´i, *n*. [Fr. *curée*, the portion given to the dogs, wrapped in the skin of the beast killed, from L. *corium*, a hide, leather.] A part of the entrails of a beast of chase given to the dogs; a heap of game killed; any animal pursued for prey; the game which a hawk or hound pursues; object of chase or pursuit in general.

quart, kwạrt, *n*. [Fr. *quarte*; lit. a fourth part, from L. *quartus*, fourth, from *quatuor*, four.] A unit of liquid measure ($\frac{1}{4}$ of a gallon) or dry measure ($\frac{1}{8}$ of a peck); 2 pints;

a container holding a quart.—**quartan**, kwạr´tan, *a*. [L. *quartanus*, fourth.] Intermitting so as to occur every fourth day (a *quartan* fever).

quarter, kwạr´tėr, *n*. [O.Fr. *quarter*, *quartier* (Fr. *quartier*), a quarter, from L. *quartarius*, a fourth part, from *quartus*, fourth, from *quatuor*, four.] One of four parts into which anything is divided; a fourth part or portion; the fourth part of a hundredweight, that is, 25 lbs.; the fourth of a dollar, or twenty-five cents (*U.S.*); the fourth part of the moon's period or monthly revolution; one of the four cardinal points; more widely, any region or point of the compass (from what *quarter* does the wind blow?); a particular region of a town, city, or country; a district; a locality (the Latin *quarter* of Paris; the Jews' *quarter* in Florence); the fourth part of the year; in schools, the fourth part of the teaching period of the year; the fourth part of the carcass of a quadruped, including a limb; *her.* one of the divisions of a shield when it is divided into four portions by horizontal and perpendicular lines meeting in the fess point; the piece of leather in a shoe which forms the side from the heel to the vamp; the part of a vessel's side which lies toward the stern; proper position; specific place; assigned or allotted position; the sparing of the life of a vanquished enemy; mercy shown by a conqueror (to give or show *quarter* to a person—perhaps originally to assign a lodging to, or to give a share of one's own quarters); *pl.* (in each of the following senses), temporary residence; shelter (to find *quarters* somewhere); a station or encampment occupied by troops (winter *quarters*); place of lodgment for officers and men; *naut.* the post allotted to the officers and men at the commencement of an engagement.—*On the quarter* (*naut.*), in a direction oblique to the ship's quarter.—*v.t.* To divide into four equal parts; to separate into parts; to cut to pieces; to furnish with lodgings or shelter, to find lodgings and food for (to *quarter* soldiers on the inhabitants); *her.* to add to other arms on the shield by dividing it into four or more compartments.—*v.t.* To be stationed; to lodge; to have temporary residence.—**quarterback**, *n*. In football (*U. S.*) a player who calls signals while standing behind the center from whom he may receive the ball, either carrying it or passing it to another member of the team.—*v. i.* To direct; to make plans and to give instructions for carrying out plans.—**quarter day**, *n*. One of the four days during the year on which payment of rent, interest, etc., is made.—**quarter-deck**, *n*. *Naut.* that part of the upper deck which is abaft the mainmast.—**quartering**, kwạr´tėr·ing, *n. Her.* the conjoining of coats of arms in one shield to denote the alliances of one family with the heiresses of others; one of the compartments on such a shield.—**quarterly**, kwąr'tẽr•li, *a.* Recurring at the end of each quarter of the year (*quarterly* payments of rent).—*adv.* Once in a quarter of a year.—*n.* A periodical publication issued once every three months.—**quartermaster**, *n. Milit.* an officer who has charge of the quarters, barracks, tents, etc., and supplies all foodstuffs; *naut.* a petty officer who has charge of the stowage of ballast and provisions, and attends to the steering of the ship, etc.—**quarter note**, *n.* In music, the quarter part of a whole note.—**quartersaw**, *v.t.* To saw timber into quarter sections, then into boards, so that when finished, the grain is attractive in appearance.—**quarter section**, *n.* A system of land surveying used by the governments of the U. S. and Canada, whereby farm lands are accurately divided into sections one mile square (640 acres), half sections (320 acres), and quarter sections (160 acres).—**quarterstaff**, *n.* A weapon formed of a stout pole about 6½ feet long, grasped by one hand in the middle, and by the other between the middle and the end.

quartet, kwąr•tet', *n.* [It. *quartetto*, from L. *quartus*, fourth.] A piece of music arranged for four voices or four instruments; the persons who execute a quartet; a stanza of four lines.

quartile, kwąr'tĭl, *n.* [L. *quartus*, fourth.] A point on a distribution curve indicating the division of that distribution into quarters or sections equivalent to 25% of the total number of units.

quarto, kwąr'tō, *n.* [L. *quartus*, fourth.] A book of the size of the fourth of a sheet; a size made by twice folding a sheet, which then makes four leaves; abbreviated thus, 4*to.*—*a.* Denoting the size of a book in which a sheet makes four leaves.

quartz, kwąrts, *n.* [From G. *quarz, quartz*, quartz, a word of unknown origin.] A name given to varieties of the native oxide of silicon occurring both crystallized and massive, and an important constituent of granite and the older rocks, varieties of it being known as rock crystal, flint, agate, amethyst, etc.—**quartziferous**, kwąrt•sif'ẽr•us, *a.* [*Quartz*, and L. *fero*, to bear.] Consisting of quartz, or chiefly of quartz; yielding quartz.—**quartzite**, kwąrt'sīt, *n.* A rock formed of granular quartz; quartzrock.—**quartz lamp**, *n.* A mercury lamp, used in physical therapy, which emits ultraviolet rays through a quartz lens.

quasar, kwā'sär, *n.* [*Quasi*-stellar.] One of several enormously distant, starlike sources of radio energy.

quash, kwosh, *v.t.* [O.Fr. *quasser*, Fr. *casser*, from L. *quassare*, to shake, shatter, shiver; intens. from *quatio, quassum*, to shake; seen also in *concussion, percussion, discuss.*] To sub-

due, put down, or quell; to extinguish; to put an end to (to *quash* a rebellion); *law*, to make void from insufficiency, or for other cause.

quasi, kwā'sī. [L.] As if; in a manner; sometimes forming compounds with English words, and generally implying that what it qualifies is in some degree fictitious or unreal, or only has certain features of what it professes to be (a *quasi-argument*, a *quasi-historical* account).

quassia, kwosh'a, *n.* [From *Quassy*, a Negro who first made known the medicinal virtues of one species.] A genus of South American tropical trees containing an extremely bitter principle, having marked tonic properties, and used medicinally.

quatern, kwat'ẽrn, *a.* [L. *quaterni*, four each, from *quatuor*, four.] Consisting of four; growing by fours (*quatern* leaves).—**quaternary**, kwa•tẽr'ne•ri, *a.* [L. *quaternarius*.] Consisting of four; arranged in fours; *geol.* a term applied to the strata above the tertiary; post-tertiary (which see); *chem.* applied to compounds which contain four elements.—**quaternate**, kwa•tẽr'nāt, *a.* Consisting of four.—*Quaternate leaf*, one that consists of four leaflets.

quaternion, kwa•tẽr'ni•on, *n.* [L. *quaternio*, a group of four, from *quatuor*, four.] A set or group of four; a term for a quantity employed in a method of mathematical investigation discovered by Sir W. R. Hamilton.

quatrain, kwot'rān, *n.* [Fr., from *quatre*, L. *quatuor*, four.] A stanza of four lines rhyming alternately.

quatrefoil, kä'tẽr•foil or kwą'tẽr•foil, *n.* [Fr. *quatre-feuille*—*quatre* (L. *quatuor*), four, and *feuille* (L. *folium*), a leaf.] *Arch.* an aperture or ornament somewhat resembling four leaves about a common center; an opening showing four radiating cusps.

quaver, kwā'vẽr, *v.i.* [From older *quave*, to shake, akin to *quiver*; and to L.G. *quabbeln*, to quiver; perhaps also to *quake*.] To have a tremulous motion; to vibrate; to shake in vocal utterance; to sing with tremulous modulations of voice; to produce a shake on a musical instrument.—*v.t.* To utter with a tremulous sound.—*n.* A shake or rapid vibration of the voice, or a shake on an instrument of music; a note equal to half a crotchet or the eighth of a semibreve.

quay, kē, *n.* [From Fr. *quai*, a quay, a Celtic word=Bret. *cae*, W. *cae*, an enclosure.] A built landing place along a line of coast or a river bank, or forming the side of a harbor, at which vessels are loaded and unloaded; a wharf.—*v.t.* To furnish with quays.—**quayage**, kē'ij, *n.* Quay dues; wharfage.

quean, kwēn, *n.* [A.Sax. *cwene*, a woman, a base woman. QUEEN.] A worthless woman; a slut; a strumpet.

queasy, kwē'zi, *a.* [Allied to Icel. *kveisa*, pain in the stomach; N. *kveis*, sickness after a debauch.] Sick at the stomach; affected with nausea; qualmish; apt to cause nausea.—**queasily**, kwē'zi•li, *adv.* In a queasy

manner.—**queasiness**, kwē'zi•nes, *n.* The state of being queasy; qualmishness; disgust.

quebracho, ke•brä'chō, *n.* The name of South American timber trees, the bark of one of which is used in tanning, that of another in medicine.

queen, kwēn, *n.* [A.Sax. *cwēn*, a queen, a wife (akin *quean*)=Goth. *qvens, qveins*; a woman; Icel. *kván*, a wife, *kona*, a woman; Dan. *qvinde*, a woman, *kone*, a wife; O.H.G. *quena*, a woman; Ir. and Gael. *coinne*, Gr. *gynē*, Skr. *jani*, a woman. From root *gan* Gr. and L. (*gen*), to produce. KIN, GENUS.] The consort of a king; a woman who is the sovereign of a kingdom; a female sovereign; a woman pre-eminent among others; the sovereign of a swarm of bees, or the female of the hive; a playing card on which a queen is depicted; the most powerful of all the pieces in a set of chessmen; (*slang*) an extraordinarily attractive girl or young woman.—*Queen consort*, the wife of a king. *Queen dowager*, the widow of a deceased king.—*Queen mother*, a queen dowager who is also mother of the reigning sovereign.—**queen bee**, *n.* The only fully developed and prolific female insect in a hive of bees.—**queenly**, kwēn'li, *a.* Like a queen; becoming a queen.—**queenliness**, kwēn'li•nes, *n.* The state of being queenly; queenly quality.—**queen post**, *n. Carp.* one of the two upright posts which connect two opposite rafters of a roof with the horizontal beam between them.

Queen Anne style, *n.* A period of English architecture and furniture design in the reign of Queen Anne, during the 18th century. The buildings were ornamented by modified and simplified classic designs; the characteristic furniture of the time, largely influenced by the Dutch, emphasized comfort, upholstery of simple damask, and simple, curved lines. — **Queen Anne's lace**, *n.* The wild carrot.

queer, kwēr, *a.* [From L.G. *quer, queer*, across = G. *queer, quer*, oblique, athwart, whence *querkopf*, a queer fellow.] Behaving or appearing otherwise than is usual; odd; singular; quaint.—**queerly**, kwēr'li, *adv.* In a queer manner.—**queerness**, kwēr'-nes, *n.* The state or quality of being queer; singularity.

quell, kwel, *v.t.* [A.Sax. *cwellan*, to kill=Dan. *quaele*, to stifle, torment; Icel. *kvelja*, Sw. *qvalja*, G. *quälen*, to torment; same root as to *quail*.] To subdue; to cause to cease by using force; to crush (an insurrection or the like); to quiet; to allay.—**queller**, kwel'ẽr, *n.* One that quells or crushes.

quench, kwensh, *v.t.* [A.Sax. *cwencan*, to quench, to extinguish; akin to *cwinan*, to dwindle; O.Fris. *kwinka*, to vanish.] To extinguish; to put out (fire); to allay; to slake (thirst); to suppress, stifle, check, repress.—*v.i.* To be extinguished; to go out; to lose zeal (*Shak.*).—**quenchable**, kwensh'a•bl, *a.* Capable of being quenched.—**quencher**, kwensh'ẽr, *n.*

One who or that which quenches.—**quenchless**, kwensh'les, *a.* That cannot be quenched; inextinguishable.

quercitron, kwėr'sit·ron, *n.* [L. *quercus*, an oak, and *citrus*, the citron tree.] The black or dyer's oak, a large forest tree of N. America; the bark of this tree yielding a yellow dye; the dyestuff itself.

querist. See QUERY.

quern, kwėrn, *n.* [A.Sax. *cwyrn*, *cweorn*=D. *kweern*, Icel. *kvern*, Dan. *qvaern*, Goth. *qvairnus*, a millstone, a quern; from root meaning to grind, same as in *corn*.] A stone handmill for grinding grain, still used to some extent by the Highlanders of Scotland.

querulous, kwer'ū·lus, *a.* [L. *querulus*, from *queror*, to complain. QUARREL.] Complaining or habitually complaining; apt to murmur; peevish; expressing complaint.—**querulously**, kwer'ū·lus·li, *adv.* In a querulous manner.—**querulousness**, kwer'ū·lus·nes, *n.* Disposition to complain; peevishness.

query, kwē'ri, *n.* [A modified form of L. *quaere*, imper. of *quaero*, to ask, to inquire, to seek. QUEST.] A question; an inquiry to be answered or resolved; the mark or sign of interrogation (?).—*v.i.* queried, querying. To ask a question or questions.—*v.t.* To seek by questioning; to examine by questions; to doubt of; to mark with a query.—**querist**, kwē'rist, *n.* One who puts a query; one who asks questions.

quest, kwest, *n.* [O.Fr. *queste*, Fr. *quête*, from L. *quaesitus*, pp. of *quaero*, to seek, seen also in *question*, *query*, *inquest*, *request*, *inquire*, *require*, *conquer*, etc.] The act of seeking; search; pursuit; searchers collectively (*Shak.*); inquiry; examination.—*v.i.*† To make search or inquiry.—*v.t.*† To search or seek for.

question, kwes'tyun, *n.* [Fr. *question*; L. *quaestio*, an inquiry, an investigation. QUEST.] An interrogation; something asked; an inquiry; a query; disquisition; discussion; the subject or matter of investigation or discussion; the theme of inquiry (foreign to the *question*); subject of debate; a point of doubt or difficulty; doubt; controversy (true beyond *question*); judicial trial (*Shak.*); the *question*, examination by torture.—*Question!* an exclamation used to recall a speaker to the subject under discussion; also used to express doubt as to the correctness of what a speaker is saying.—*Begging the question*, assuming something without proof; taking for granted what has to be proved.—*In question*, in debate; being at present dealt with (the point in *question*).—*To call in question*, to doubt; to challenge the truth or reality of.—*Out of question*, doubtless; undoubtedly.—*Out of the question*, not worthy of consideration; not to be thought of.—*Leading question*. See LEADING.—*Previous question*, in *parliamentary practice*, the question whether a vote shall be come to on the main issue or not, brought forward before the main or

real question is put, and for the purpose of avoiding, if the resolution is in the negative, the putting of this question. The motion is in the form, 'that the question be now put', and the mover and seconder vote against it.—*v.i.* To ask a question or questions; to debate; to doubt.—*v.t.* To inquire of by asking questions; to examine by interrogatories; to doubt of; to have no confidence in; to call in question; to challenge.—**questionable**, kwes'tyun·a·bl, *a.* Capable of being questioned or inquired of; liable to question; suspicious; doubtful; uncertain; disputable.—**questionableness**, kwes'tyun·a·bl·nes, *n.*—**questionably**, kwes'tyun·a·bli, *adv.* In a questionable manner; doubtfully.—**questionnaire**, kwes'tyun·âr″, *n.* A systematic series of questions prepared for distribution for the purpose of gathering detailed information.—**questioner**, kwes'tyun·ėr, *n.*—**question mark**, *n.* An interrogation point (?).

questor, kwes'tor, *n.* [L. *quaestor*. QUEST.] The name of certain magistrates of ancient Rome whose chief office was the management of the public treasure; a receiver of taxes, tribute, etc.—**questorship**, kwes'tor·ship, *n.* The office of questor.

quetzal, ket'zäl, *n.* [Native name.] A magnificent bird of Central America revered by Maya and Aztec.

queue, kū, *n.* [Fr., tail, from L. *cauda*, a tail. CUE.] A pigtail; a line of persons, vehicles, etc.—*v.t.* and *i.* To be or arrange in a line.

quibble, kwib'l, *n.* [A freq. of *quib*, *quip*.] A turn of language to evade the point in question; an evasion; a prevarication; a pun; a low conceit.—*v.i.*—quibbled, quibbling. To evade the point in question by artifice, play upon words, or any conceit; to prevaricate; to pun.—**quibbler**, kwib'lėr, *n.* One who quibbles; a punster.

quick, kwik, *a.* [A.Sax. *cwic*, living, lively=D. *kwik*, Icel. *kvikr*, Dan. *qvik*, Sw. *quick*, L.G. *quick*, Goth. *qvius*; same root as L. *vivus*, living, Gr. *bios*, life, Skr. *jiv*, to live.] Alive; living (the *quick* and the dead); characterized by liveliness or sprightliness; nimble; brisk; speedy; rapid; swift; perceptive in a high degree (*quick* sight); sensitive; hasty; precipitate; irritable (*quick* of temper); pregnant (*Shak.*).—*adv.* In a quick manner; quickly.—*n.* A growing plant, usually hawthorn, for hedges; with *the*, the living flesh; sensible parts; hence, *fig.* that which is susceptible of or causes keen feeling (stung to the *quick*).—**quicken**, kwik'n, *v.t.* To make alive; to revive or resuscitate; to cheer or refresh; to make quicker; to accelerate; to sharpen; to give keener perception to; to stimulate.—*v.i.* To become alive; to become quicker; to be in that state of pregnancy in which the child gives signs of life.—**quickener**, kwik'n·ėr, *n.*—**quick-freeze**, *v.t.*—pret. quick-froze, pp. quick-frozen, ppr. quick-freezing. To freeze food quickly for storage.—**quickie**,

kwik'i, *n.* Anything done or made quickly or shoddily (slang).—**quicklime**, kwik'līm, *n.* Lime burned and not yet slaked with water.—**quickly**, kwik'li, *adv.* Speedily; rapidly; nimbly; soon; without delay.—**quickness**, kwik'nes, *n.* State of being quick or alive; speed; celerity; activity; briskness; acuteness of perception; keenness; sharpness.—**quicksand**, kwik'sand, *n.* A movable sandbank in the sea, a lake, or river, dangerous to vessels or to persons who trust themselves to it; *fig.* something deceptive or treacherous.—**quickset**, kwik'set, *n.* A living plant set to grow, particularly for a hedge; hawthorn planted for a hedge.—*a.* Made of quickset.—*v.t.* To plant with living shrubs for a hedge.—**quicksilver**, kwik'sil·vėr, *n.* [Living silver, so called from its fluidity.] Mercury, metal liquid at all ordinary temperatures. See MERCURY.—**quicktempered**, *a.* Easily aroused to anger.—**quick time**, *n.* The normal rate of marching, which is 120 paces per minute in the U.S. Army.—**quick-witted**, *a.* Sharp of mind.

quid, kwid, *n.* [A form of *cud*.] A piece of tobacco chewed and rolled about in the mouth.

quiddity, kwid'i·ti, *n.* [Fr. *quiddité*, from L.L. *quidditas*, from L. *quid*, what.] An old philosophical term equivalent to essence, and comprehending both the substance and qualities; a trifling nicety; a quirk or quibble.

quidnunc, kwid'nungk, *n.* [L., what now?] One curious to know everything that passes; one who pretends to know all that goes on.

quiescent, kwī·es'ent, *a.* [L. *quiescens*, *quiescentis*, ppr. of *quiesco*, to keep quiet. QUIET.] Being in a state of repose; still; not moving; quiet; not excited; tranquil; *gram.* silent; not sounded (a *quiescent* letter).—**quiescence, quiescency**, kwī·es'ens, kwī·es'en·si, *n.* The state or quality of being quiescent; rest; repose.—**quiescently**, kwī·es'ent·li, *adv.* In a quiescent manner.

quiet, kwī'et, *a.* [Fr. *quiet*, L. *quietus*, from *quiesco*, to keep quiet, from *quies*, *quietus*, rest. *Coy*, *quit*, *quite*, have the same origin.] Not in action or motion; still; in a state of rest; free from alarm or disturbance; left at rest; tranquil; peaceable; not turbulent; free from emotion; calm; patient; retired; secluded; free from fuss or bustle; not glaring or showy (*quiet* colors).—*n.* Rest; stillness; tranquillity; repose; freedom from emotion of the mind; calmness.—*v.t.* To make or cause to be quiet; to calm; to pacify; to allay; to tranquillize; to bring to a state of rest.—*v.i.* To become quiet or still‡; to abate.—**quieter**, kwī'et·ėr, *n.* One who or that which quiets.—**quietism**, kwī'et·izm, *n.* The absorption of the feelings or faculties in religious contemplation; the practice of a class of mystics who resigned themselves to mental inactivity in order to bring the soul into direct union with the Godhead.—**quietist**, kwī'et·ist, *n.*

One who believes in or practices quietism; especially applied to one of a sect of mystics originated by Molinos, a Spanish priest, in the latter part of the seventeenth century.—**quietly**, kwī'et·li, *adv*. In a quiet state or manner; peaceably; calmly; patiently; in a manner to attract little or no observation.—**quietness**, kwī'et·nes, *n*. The state of being quiet; tranquillity; calmness.—**quietude**, kwī'e·tūd, *n*. [L. *quietudo*.] Rest; quiet; tranquillity.—**quietus**, kwī·ē'tus, *n*. [L. *quietus*, quiet. *Quietus* or *quietus est* was a formula used in discharging accounts, equivalent to quit, discharged.] A final discharge of an account; a final settlement; a quittance.

quill, kwil, *n*. [O.E. *quylle*, a cane or reed; from Fr. *quille*, a pin, a skittle, from G. *kiel*, a quill, a stalk, a pin, O.G. *kil*, a stalk.] One of the large, strong feathers of geese, swans, turkeys, crows, etc., used for pens, etc.; one of these made into an instrument of writing; the spine of a porcupine; a piece of small reed on which weavers wind the thread of the woof; a piece of quill attached to a slip of wood, by means of which certain stringed musical instruments were played; the fold of a plaited ruff or ruffle, about the size and shape of a goose quill.—*v.t.* To plait with small ridges like quills.—**quilldriver**, *n*. A contemptuous term for one who works with a quill or pen; a clerk.

quilt, kwilt, *n*. [O.Fr. *cuilte*, *coutre*, *coultre*, from L. *culcitra*, *culcita*, a mattress, a pillow, a quilt. This word by corruption or confusion gave the *counter-* of *counterpane*.] A cover or coverlet made by stitching one cloth over another, with some soft substance between; any thick or warm coverlet.—*v.t.* To stitch together, as two pieces of cloth, with some soft substance between; to stuff in the manner of a quilt.—**quilter**, kwilt'ẽr, *n*. One who quilts.—**quilting**, kwilt'-ing, *n*. The act or operation of forming a quilt; the material used for making quilts; quilted work.

quinary, kwī'na·ri, *a*. [L. *quinarius*, from *quini*, five each, from *quinque*, five.] Consisting of five or a multiple of five; arranged by fives.—**quinate**, kwī'nāt, *a*. *Bot*. applied to five similar parts arranged together, as five leaflets.

quince, kwins, *n*. [From Fr. *coignasse*, a kind of quince, from L. *cotonium*, *cydonium*, Gr. *kydōnion*, (*mēlon*), a quince, lit. Cydonian fruit, from *Cydonia*, a town in Crete.] A fruit and the tree that bears it, now widely cultivated, the fruit being golden yellow and much used in making preserves.

quincunx, kwin'kungks, *n*. [L., from *quinque*, five, and *uncia*, ounce—a five-ounce weight being marked with five spots.] An arrangement of five objects in a square, one at each corner and one in the middle; an arrangement, as of trees, in such squares continuously.—**quincuncial**, kwin·-

kun'shal, *a*. Having the form of a quincunx.

quindecagon, kwin·dek'a·gon, *n*. [L. *quinque*, five, Gr. *deka*, ten, and *gōnia*, angle.] *Geom*. a plane figure with fifteen sides and fifteen angles.

quinine, kwī'nīn, *n*. [Peruvian-Indian *kina*, *quina*, bark.] A most important vegetable alkali, obtained from the bark of several trees of the *Cinchona* genus, extensively used in medicine as a febrifuge and tonic.—**quinia**, **quinina**, kwin'i·a, kwi·nī'na, *n*. Older names for *Quinine*.—**quinidine**, kwin'i·din, *n*. A substance in some cinchona barks, with acids forming salts having febrifugal properties.

quinoline, kwin'o·lēn, *n*. [From *quinine*.] A compound from which quinine is derived.

Quinquagesima, kwin·kwa·jes'i·ma, *n*. [L.] Fiftieth.—*Quinquagesima Sunday*, so called as being about the fiftieth day before Easter; Shrove Sunday.

quinquecapsular, kwin·kwe·kap'-sū·lẽr, *a*. [L. *quinque*, five, and *capsula*, a little chest.] *Bot*. having five capsules.—**quinquefoliate**, kwin·-kwe·fō'li·āt, *a*. [L. *folium*, leaf.] Having five leaves.—**quinquelocular**, kwin·kwe·lok'ū·lẽr, *a*. [L. *loculus*, a cell.] *Bot*. five-celled.

quinquennial, kwin·kwen'i·al, *a*. [L. *quinquennium*, a period of five years—*quinque*, five, and *annus*, year.] Occurring once in five years, or lasting five years.—**quinquennium**, kwin·kwen'i·um, *n*. [L.] The space of five years. Also **quinquenniad,†** kwin·-kwen'i·ad. (*Tenn.*)

quinquepartite, kwin·kwe·pär'tīt, *a*. [L. *quinque*, five, and *partitus*, divided.] Consisting of five parts; *bot*. divided into five parts almost to the base.

quinquevalent, kwin·kwev'a·lent, *a*. [L. *quinque*, five, and *valens*, *valentis*, ppr. of *valeo*, to be worth.] *Chem*. having a valence of five.

quinsy, kwin'zi, *n*. [From Fr. *esquinancie*, *squinancie*, from L. *cynanche*, Gr. *kynanchē*, a kind of sore throat, from *kyōn*, a dog, and *anchō*, to throttle—'dog' having a pejorative effect. CYNIC.] *Med*. an inflammation of the tonsils; any inflammation of the throat or parts adjacent.

quint, kwint, *n*. [L. *quintus*, fifth.] A set or sequence of five, as in piquet.

quintain, kwin'tin, *n*. [Fr. *quintaine*, L.L. *quintana*, a quintain, from L. *quintana*, a street or broad way in a camp (from *quintus*, fifth), hence a public place, and the exercise practiced in such a place.] A figure or other object to be tilted at, often an upright post, on the top of which was a horizontal bar turning on a pivot, with a sandbag attached to one end, on the other a broad board, it being a trial of skill to tilt at the broad end with a lance, and pass on before the bag of sand could whirl round and strike the tilter.

quintal, kwin'tal, *n*. [Fr. *quintal*, from L. *centum*, a hundred, through the Sp. *quintal*, Ar. *kintâr*, a weight of 100 lb.] A weight of 100 lb.

quintan, kwin'tan, *a*. [L. *quintanus*,

from *quintus*, fifth, from *quinque*, five.] Occurring or recurring every fifth day.—*n*. An intermittent fever the paroxysms of which recur every fifth day.

quintessence, kwin·tes'ens, *n*. [L. *quinta*, *essentia*, fifth essence.] According to old notions the fifth or highest essence or most ethereal element of natural bodies; hence, an extract from anything, containing its virtues or most essential part in a small quantity; the best and purest part of a thing.—**quintessential**, kwin·tes·sen'shal, *a*. Consisting of the quintessence.

quintet, **quintette**, kwin·tet', *n*. [Fr. *quintette*, from It. *quintetto*, from *quinto*, L. *quintus*, fifth.] *Mus*. a vocal or instrumental composition in five parts; those who execute a quintet; a group of five.

quintillion, kwin·til'yon, *n*. [L. *quintus*, fifth, and term. of E. *million*.] In U.S. and France, a unit followed by 18 zeros; in Gt. Britain and Germany a unit followed by 30 zeros.

quintuple, kwin'tū·pl, *a*. [L. *quintuplus*, fivefold—*quintus*, fifth, and term. *-plus*, Gr. *pleon*. DOUBLE.] Fivefold; arranged in five or in fives; *music*, containing five notes of equal value in a bar.—*v.t.*—*quintupled*, *quintupling*. To make fivefold.

quintuplet, kwin'tū·plet, *n*. A collection or mechanism for five of a kind; any one of five offspring born at the same birth.

quip, kwip, *n*. [From L. *quippe*, indeed.] A smart sarcastic turn; a sharp or cutting jest; a jibe.—*v.t.*—*quipped*, *quipping*. To utter quips on; to sneer at.—*v.i.* To use quips; to jibe.

quire, kwīr, *n*. [O.Fr. *quayer*; Fr. *cahier*, from L.L. *quaternum*, a book of four leaves, from L. *quatuor*, four.] A collection of paper consisting of twenty-four sheets of equal size and quality; $\frac{1}{20}$ ream.

Quirinal, kwir'i·nal, *n*. The Italian court, as opposed to the Papal court of the Vatican, at Rome.

quirk, kwẽrk, *n*. [Prov.E. *quirk*, to turn sharply; comp. W. *chwired*, a sudden start, craft, deceit.] An artful turn for evasion or subterfuge; a shift; a quibble; a quip: *arch*. an acute channel or recess; also, the hollow under the abacus.

quirt, kwẽrt, *n*. [Sp. *cuarta*.] A riding whip with a short handle and braided rawhide lash.—*v.t.* To strike with a quirt.

quisling, kwis'ling, *n*. [For Vidkun *Quisling*, a Norwegian leader of the Nazi party.] A traitor, especially one who agrees to govern on behalf of the conquering nation.

quit, kwit, *a*. [From O.Fr. *quite*, Mod.Fr. *quittée*, discharged, freed, quit, from L. *quietus*, quiet. *Quiet* is thus the same word, as is also *quite*.] Discharged or released from a debt, penalty, or obligation; absolved; free; clear (with *of* before an object). It is often used in the form *quits*, as a kind of noun, to be *quits* with one, being to be on even terms, to have got even with him; hence, as an exclamation, *quits!* equivalent to, we are even.—*v.t.*—*quitted, quitting.* [O. Fr. *quiter,* Fr. *quitter,* to leave, to abandon.] To discharge, as an obligation or duty; to meet and satisfy; to repay; to set free, absolve, acquit; to relieve; to rid; to discharge from; to meet expectations entertained of; to acquit: used *refl.* (to *quit one's self* like a man); to depart from; to leave; to resign; to give up; to abandon.—*To quit cost,* to pay expenses.—*To quit scores,* to make even. —**quitclaim,** *n.* The giving up of a claim; a deed or document resigning a claim in favor of another.— **quitrent,** *n.* A small rent once paid by freeholders and copyholders of a manor in discharge of other services. —**quittance,** kwit′ans, *n.* Discharge from a debt or obligation; an acquittance; recompense; repayment. —**quitter,** kwit′ėr, *n.* One who quits; one who withdraws under adverse circumstances.—**quittor,** kwit′or, *n.* An ulcer between the hair and hoof of a horse's foot (for old *quitture,* a discharge of matter).—**quittor-bone,** *n.* A hard round swelling on a horse's coronet.

quitch, quitch grass, kwich, *n.* [A form of *quick grass*—named from its vitality and vigorous growth.] A species of worthless grass; couch grass.

quite, kwīt, *adv.* [Old form of *quit,* that is, primarily, free or clear by complete performance. QUIT.] Completely; wholly; entirely; totally; altogether; to a great extent or degree; very (*quite* warm).

quiver, kwiv′ėr, *v.i.* [Same as D. *quiveren,* to tremble, closely connected with *quaver,* and with old *quiver,* active, nimble, A.Sax. *cwifer,* perhaps also with *quick.*] To shake or tremble; to quake; to shiver; to show a slight tremulous motion; to be agitated.—*n.* The act or state of quivering; a tremulous motion; a shiver.—**quiveringly,** kwiv′er‧ing‧‧li, *adv.* In a quivering manner.

quiver, kwiv′ėr, *n.* [O.Fr. *quivre, cuivre,* from O.H.G. *kohhar, kochar,* G. *köcher,* a quiver; cog. Dan. *koger,* D. *koker,* A.Sax. *cocer*—a case, a quiver.] A case or sheath for arrows. —**quivered,** kwiv′erd, *a.* Furnished with a quiver; sheathed in a quiver.

quixotic, kwik‧sot′ik, *a.* [From Don *Quixote,* the hero of Cervantes' celebrated romance, who is painted as a half-crazy reformer and champion, and is a caricature of the ancient knights of chivalry.] Romantic to extravagance; aiming at visionary ends; ideal; high-flown.—**quixotically,** kwik‧sot′i‧kal‧li, *adv.* In a quixotic or absurdly romantic manner.—**quixotism,** kwik′sot‧izm, *n.* Romantic and absurd notions.

quiz, kwiz, *n.* [Said to have been originated simply to puzzle people, by Daly, the manager of a Dublin playhouse, who had the letters *q u i z* put on all the walls of Dublin.] Something designed to puzzle; a hoax; a jest; one who quizzes; one liable to be quizzed; a brief, informal examination, as of a class.—*v.t.*—

quizzed, quizzing. To puzzle; to banter; to make sport of by means of obscure questions; to look at through an eyeglass; to look at inquisitively; to question intensively with a view to obtaining information unwillingly revealed; curious, odd; mocking or teasing, as a *quizzical* remark.—**quizzical,** kwiz′i‧kal, *a.* Partaking of the nature of a quiz; addicted to quizzing.

quod, kwod, *n.* [A form of *quad,* a contr. of *quadrangle.*] A jail. (*Slang.*)

quoin, koin, *n.* [A slightly different spelling of *coin;* Fr. *coin,* a corner, a wedge, a quoin, a coin. COIN.] An external solid angle; the external angle of a building; a wedgelike piece of stone, wood, metal, or other material; *printing,* a wedge to wedge the types up within a chase; *gun.,* a wedge to raise a cannon to the desired elevation.

quoit, kwoit, *n.* [Origin doubtful; comp. Prov.E. and Sc. *coit; quoit,* to throw; also O.D. *koot,* a die.] A flattish ring of iron, 8 or 9 inches in diameter and of some weight, convex on the upper side and slightly concave on the under side, to be thrown at a fixed mark on the ground at play; *pl.* the game played with such rings.—*v.t.* and *i.* To throw quoits; to play at quoits.

quondam, kwon′dam, *a.* [L., formerly.] Having been formerly; former (one's *quondam* friend).

quorum, kwō′rum, *n.* [Lit. 'of whom', being the genit. pl., of L. *qui,* who—from the phraseology of commissions, etc., written in Latin certain persons being therein named generally, 'of whom' certain were specially designated as in all cases necessary and therefore constituted a quorum.] A selected group; an absolute majority unless specified to the contrary; such a number of the members of any body (a board of directors, for instance) as is competent to transact business.

quota, kwō′ta, *n.* [From L. *quotus,* which number in the series? QUOTE.] A proportional part or share; share or proportion assigned to each or which each of a number has to contribute.

quote, kwōt, *v.t.*—*quoted, quoting.* [O.Fr. *quoter,* Fr. *coter,* from L.L. *quotare,* to give chapter and verse for, from L. *quotus,* which number in the series? from *quot,* how many?] To adduce from some author or speaker; to adduce by way of authority or illustration; to cite or cite the words of (to *quote* a passage, an author); *com.* to name, as the price of an article.—*n.* A quotation; a quotation mark (colloq.).—**quotable,** kwōt′a‧bl, *a.*—**quotation,** kwō‧tā′-shon, *n.* The act of quoting; the passage quoted or cited; *com.* the current price of commodities or stocks; the statement of commodity prices.

quotidian, kwō‧tid′i‧an, *a.* [L. *quotidianus,* from *quotidie,* daily—*quot,* how many, every, and *dies,* a day.] Daily; occurring or returning daily. —*n.* Anything that returns every

day; a fever whose paroxysms return every day.

quotient, kwō′shent, *n.* [Fr., from L. *quoties,* how often? QUOTE.] *Arith.* the number resulting from the division of one number by another, and showing how often a less number is contained in a greater. —**quotum,**† kwo′tum, *n.* [Neut. of L. *quotus,* how much?] A quota; a share.

R

R, r, är, the eighteenth letter of the English alphabet.—*The three Rs,* a humorous and familiar designation for *Reading,* (*W*)*riting,* and (*A*)*rithmetic.*

rabbet, rab′et, *v.t.* [From Fr. *raboter,* to plane—prefix *re,* again, and *abouter*=E. *abut.*] To cut the edge of (as of a board) in a sloping manner, so that it may join by lapping with another piece cut in a similar manner; also, to cut a rectangular groove along the edge of to receive a corresponding projection.—*n.* The cut or groove so made. Sometimes written REBATE.— **rabbet joint,** *n.* A joint formed by rabbeting.

rabbi, rab′bī, *n. pl.* **rabbis, rabbies,** rab′bīz. [Heb. *rabî,* my master, from *rab,* master.] A title of respect given to Jewish doctors or expounders of the law.—**rabbin,** rab′bin, *n.* [A French form.] Same as *Rabbi.*—**rabbinic, rabbinical,** rab‧bin′ik, rab‧bin′i‧kal, *a.* Pertaining to the rabbins, or to their opinions, learning, and language; pertaining to the later and non-canonical Hebrew writings.— **Rabbinic,** rab‧bin′ik, *n.* The language or dialect of the rabbins; the later Hebrew.—**rabbinist,** rab′bin‧‧ist, *n.* Among the Jews, one who adhered to the Talmud and the traditions of the rabbins.

rabbit, rab′it, *n.* [O.E. *robbet,* akin to O.D. *robbe, robbeken,* a rabbit; connections doubtful.] A well-known lagomorph mammal which feeds on grass or other herbage, and burrows in the earth, characterized by long ears and soft fur.—**rabbit fever,** *n. Med.* tularemia.—**rabbit punch,** *n.* A short, sharp blow to the nape of the neck.

rabble, rab′l, *n.* [Comp. D. *rabbelen,* to gabble; G. *rabbeln, robbeln,* to chatter; perhaps imitative of noise.] A tumultuous crowd of vulgar, noisy people; a mob; with *the;* the lower class of people; the dregs of the people.—*v.t.*—*rabbled, rabbling.* To assault in a disorderly crowd; to mob.

Rabelaisian, rab′e‧lā″zi‧en, *a.* [Fr. *Rabelais.*] In the broad, indelicate style of the French author Francois Rabelais.

rabid, rab′id, *a.* [L. *rabidus,* from *rabies,* madness, from *rabo,* to rave. RAGE.] Furious; raging; mad; affected with the distemper called *rabies;* excessively or foolishly enthusiastic; rampant; intolerant (a *rabid* Tory, a *rabid* teetotaler).—**rabidity,** ra‧bid‧i′ti, *n.* The state of being rabid.—**rabidly,** rab′id‧li, *adv.* In a rabid manner; furiously.—**rabidness,** rab′id‧nes, *n.* The state of being rabid.—**rabies,** rā′bēz, *n.* [L.] Hydrophobia; an infectious disease of small animals, particularly dogs, believed to be caused by a virus transmitted to man by the bite of infected animals, and usually proving fatal unless the Pasteur treatment is instituted early in the incubation period.

raccoon, ra‧kön′, *n.* [Corruption of the American Indian, *arahkunem.*] An American plantigrade carnivorous mammal about the size of a small fox, whose skin is valuable as a fur.

race, rās, *n.* [Fr. *race,* It. *razza,* race, lineage, family.] One of the divisions of mankind; a lineage; a family, tribe, people, or nation believed or presumed to belong to the same stock; a breed or stock; a perpetuated variety of animals or plants.—**racial,** rā′shal, *a.* Of or pertaining to a race or family of man.—**racialism,** rā′shal‧izm, *n.* Racial prejudice, hatred, or discrimination.—**racism,** rās′izm, *n.* Racialism; the belief in the superiority or dominance of one race over another; the practice of this.—**racist,** rās′ist, *a.* and *n.*

race, rās, *n.* [A.Sax. *ræs,* a rush; a rapid course, a stream; same as Icel. *rās,* a race.] A rapid course; career in life; a contest of speed, especially in running, but also in riding, driving, sailing, rowing, etc., in competition; *pl.* horse races (to go to the Santa Anita *races*); a strong or rapid current of water; a powerful current or heavy sea sometimes produced by the meeting of two tides; a canal or watercourse to and from a mill or water wheel; a strong tidal rush of water, as in the Bay of Fundy; the air stream delivered by the propeller of an air machine.—*v.i.*—*raced, racing.* To run swiftly; to run or contend in running.—*v.t.* To cause to run; to cause to contend in running; to drive quickly in a trial of speed.—**race horse,** *n.* A horse bred or kept for racing; a horse that runs in competition.—**race track,** *n.* The place where races of horses, dogs, automobiles, etc., are held.—**racer,** rā′sėr, *n.* One who races; a race horse.

raceme, ra‧sēm′, *n.* [L. *racemus,* a cluster of grapes.] *Bot.* a species of inflorescence, in which a number of flowers with short and equal pedicels stand on a common slender axis, as in the currant.—**racemose,** ras′e‧mos, *a.* [L. *racemosus.*] *Bot.* resembling a raceme; in the form of a raceme; bearing flowers in racemes.

rachis, rā′kis, *n.* [Gr. *rachis,* the spine.] The vertebral column of mammals and birds; something similar to this, as the shaft of a feather, the stalk of the frond in ferns, the common stalk bearing the alternate spikelets in some grasses.—**rachitic,** ra‧kit′ik, *a.* Pertaining to rachitis; rickety.—**rachitis,** ra‧kī′tis, *n.* [Gr. *rachis,* and term. *-itis,*

signifying inflammation.] Formerly inflammation of the spine, now applied to *rickets*; a disease characterized by softening and malformation of the bones.

racily, raciness. See RACY.

rack, rak, *v.t.* [Closely allied to *reach,* Sc. *rax,* to reach; D. *rekken,* Dan. *raekke,* to stretch; G. *recken, racken,* to stretch, to torture, *reckbank,* a rack. See also noun.] To stretch unduly; to strain vehemently (as in 'to *rack* one's brains', to strain or exercise his thoughts to the utmost); to twist; to wrest; to distort; to put a false meaning on; to punish on the rack; to heighten; to exaggerate (*Shak.*); to place on or in a rack or frame (to *rack* bottles).—*n.* [Comp. D. *rak, schotel-rak,* a cupboard for dishes; G. *rack,* a rail, *recke,* a trestle, a frame, a rack for supporting things.] An appliance for straining or stretching; an instrument for the judicial torture of criminals and suspected persons, consisting of a framework on which the victim's limbs were strained by cords and levers; hence, torture; extreme pain; anguish; an open wooden framework above a manger to hold hay, grass, straw, etc., as fodder for horses and cattle; a framework on or in which articles are deposited; *mach.* a straight or very slightly curved bar, with teeth on one of its edges, adapted to work into the teeth of a wheel or pinion.

rack, rak, *n.* [A.Sax. *hracca,* O.E. and Sc. *crag,* the neck.] The neck of a carcass of veal or mutton.

rack, rak, *n.* [Icel. *rek, skȳ-rek,* drift, cloud motion; *reka,* to drive.] Thin flying broken clouds, or any portion of floating vapor in the sky.—*v.i.* To fly, as vapor or clouds.

rack, rak, *v.t.* [From Fr. *raque,* mud, dregs.] To draw off from the lees; to draw off, as pure liquor from its sediments (to *rack* cider or wine).

rack, rak, *n.* [Form of *wreck.*] Wreck; ruin; destruction; in the phrase *to go to rack and ruin.*

racket, rak′et, *n.* [Probably onomatopoetic; comp. Gael. *racaid,* noise.] A confused, clattering noise; noisy talk; clamor; din.—*v.i.* To make a racket; to frolic.—*n.* Any of a number of methods, generally unlawful, for the purpose of exorting money or gaining advantages or control of businesses by violence or threats of physical violence.—**racketeer,** rak‧e‧tēr′, *n.* One who, alone or in company with others, under threats of violence extorts money or business advantages or otherwise controls business enterprises, frequently alleging to grant protection to a victim who subscribes or consents to the racketeer's demands.—**rackety,** rak′et‧i, *a.* Making a racket or tumultuous noise.

racket, rak′et, *n.* [Fr. *raquette,* a racket; O.Fr. *rachete, rasquete,* the palm of the hand, from L.L. *racha,* the wrist, from an Arabic word.] The bat with which players at tennis or rackets strike the ball;

pl. a modern variety of the old game of tennis.—*v.t.* To strike as with a racket; to toss.

raconteur, ra‧kon‧tėr′, *n.* [Fr.] Teller of a good story; conversationalist.

racoon, ra‧kön′. See RACCOON.

racquet, rak′et. See RACKET.

racy, rā′si, *a.* [Probably from *race,* lineage, lit. partaking strongly of its race; but comp. O.H.G. *räzer,* racy, *räzer win,* racy wine; Swiss *räss,* sharp, astringent.] Strong and flavorous (*racy* wine); having a strong distinctive character of thought or language; spirited; pungent; piquant (a *racy* style, a *racy* anecdote).—**racily,** rā′si‧li, *adv.* In a racy manner.—**raciness,** rā′si‧nes, *n.* The quality of being racy.

radar, rā′där, *n.* [Short for *radio detecting* and *ranging.*] An electronic device for determining the presence and location of an object by transmitting radio signals, which are reflected by the object and picked up by a receiving system.

raddle, rad′l, *v.t.*—*raddled, raddling.* [Perhaps a corruption from *hurdle* or *riddle.*] To interweave; to twist or wind together.—*n.* A hedge formed by interweaving the shoots and branches of trees or shrubs; *weaving,* a wooden bar with a row of upright pegs to keep the warp in trim.

raddle, rad′l, *n.* [REDDLE.] A red pigment, chiefly used for marking sheep; reddle or ruddle.—*v.t.*—*raddled, raddling.* To paint, as with ruddle.

radial, rā′di‧al, *a.* [From L. *radius,* a ray, a spoke. RADIUS, RAY.] Grouped or appearing like radii or rays; shooting out as from a center; pertaining to the radius, one of the bones of the human forearm (the *radial* artery or nerve).—**radially,** rā′di‧al‧li, *adv.*—**radiance, radiancy,** rā′di‧ans, rā′di‧an‧si, *n.* [From *radiant.*] Brightness shooting in rays or beams; hence in general, brilliant or sparkling luster.—**radiant,** rā′di‧ant, *a.* Shooting or emitting rays of light or heat; shining; beaming with brightness; emitting a vivid light or splendor; *phys.* emitted by radiation.—*Radiant energy,* energy transmitted by a wave, as of light, x-rays, etc.—**radiate,** rā′di‧āt, *v.i.*—*radiated, radiating.* To issue and proceed in rays or straight lines from a point or surface, as heat or light; to beam forth; to emit rays.—*v.t.* To emit or send out in direct lines from a point or surface (a body *radiates* heat); to enlighten; to illuminate.—*a.* Having rays; having lines proceeding as from a center like radii.—**radiation,** rā‧di‧ā′shon, *n.* The act of radiating or state of being radiated; the divergence or shooting forth of anything from any point or surface.—**radiator,** rā′di‧ā‧tėr, *n.* That which radiates; an appliance for heating a room by means of hot water or steam; in automobiles, the mechanism for cooling circulating water.

radical, rad′i‧kal, *a.* [Fr. *radical,* L.

radicalis, from *radix*, *radicis*, a root (whence *radish*, *eradicate*); from root *vrad*, seen in E. *wort*; also in L. *radius*, a ray, *ramus*, a branch.] Pertaining to the root or origin; original; reaching to the principles; fundamental; thorough-going; extreme (a *radical* error, a *radical* cure or reform); implanted by nature; innate; native; *philol.* belonging to or proceeding directly from a root; (the *radical* signification of a word). —**radicalism**, rad'i·kal·izm, *n.* The doctrine or principle of the radicals or advanced liberals.—**radically**, rad'i·kal·li, *adv.* In a radical manner; in root or origin; fundamentally.— **radicate**, rad'i·kāt, *v.t.*—radicated, radicating. [L. *radicor*, *radicatus*.] To cause to take root; to plant deeply.—**radicle**, rad'i·kl, *n.* [L. *radicula*, dim. of *radix*, a root.] *Bot.* that part of the embryo or seed of a plant which, upon vegetating, becomes the root; the fibrous parts of a root; *chem.* same as RAD-ICAL.

radio, rā'di·ō, *n.* pl. radios, rā'di·ōz. [L. *radius*, a ray.] The transmission or reception of electromagnetic waves without conducting wires intervening between transmitter and receiver; the receiving set.—*a.* Of, used in, or transmitted by radio.— *v.t.* and *i.*—radioed, radioing. To transmit, or communicate with, by radio.—**radioactive**, *a.* Having the property of emitting radiation or particles from an atomic nucleus.— **radioactivity**, *n.*—**radioastronomy**, *n.* A branch of astronomy that uses radio telescopes in the study of radiation emitted by celestial bodies. —**radio beacon**, *n.* A radio station that sends out signals so that a receiver may determine his position by them.—**radiobroadcast**, *n.* The transmission of messages, music, voice, etc., by radio.—**radiocarbon**, *n.* See CARBON-14.—**radiochemistry**, *n.* A certain branch of chemistry which deals with radioactive bodies and radioactivity.—**radio-frequency**, *n.* A frequency higher than 15,000 vibrations per second.—**radiogram**, *n.* A radiotelephonic message.—**radio-isotope**, rā'di·ō·i''so·tōp, *n.* A radioactive isotope.—**radiology**, rā·di·ol'-o·ji, *n.* The science of diagnostic medicine by means of radiant energy. —**radiophone**, *n.* A radiotelephone; a device for transmission of sound by means of radiant energy.—**radiotelegraphy**, rā'di·ō·te·leg''ra·fi, *n.* Wireless telegraphy.—**radiotelegraph**, *n.* —**radiotelephony**, rā'di·ō·tel·lef''o·ni, *n.* Wireless telephony; telephoning through the air without wires. —**radiotelescope**, rā'di·ō·tel''e·skōp, *n.* A large reflector, parabolic in shape, that gathers radio signals emitted by celestial bodies.—**radiotherapy**, rā·di·ō·ther''a·pi, *n.* Treatment of diseases by radioactivity, as by the X-ray or by means of a radioactive element such as radium or thorium.—**radiothorium**, rā'di·ō·thōr''i·um, *n.* A radioactive element.—**radio tube**, *n.* An electronic valve generally consisting of an

evacuated glass or metal shell, enclosing an electron-generating device, such as a heated filament, from which electrons are propelled by electrical attraction to an anode, or plate. In the valve type of tube a mesh of fine wires is placed in the electronic stream and by suitable charging with a control current, regulates the magnitude of the electrical current flowing between the filament and plate. The tube is used in radio receivers for the amplification and rectification of electromagnetic waves.

radish, rad'ish, *n.* [Fr. *radis*, from L. *radix*, a root. RADICAL.] The name of cruciferous plants with lyre-shaped leaves, the young roots of which are eaten.—*Horse-radish.* See HORSE.

radium, rā'di·um, *n.* [RADIUS.] A radioactive metallic element discovered in pitchblende by M. and Mme. Curie in 1898. Symbol, Ra; at. no., 88; at. wt., 226.—**radium-therapy**, *n.* See RADIOTHERAPY.

radius, rā'di·us, *n.* pl. radii, radiuses, rā'di·ī, rā'di·us·ez. [L., a ray, a rod, a beam, a spoke. RADICAL, RAY.] *Geom.* a straight line extending from the center of a circle to its circumference; a circular area limited to the distance of a given radius; *anat.* the shorter, thicker bone of the two bones of the human forearm or of the forelimb of lower animals.

radix, rā'diks, *n.* [L., a root.] A root (of a plant, of a word); *math.* any number which is arbitrarily made the fundamental number or base of any system, as 10 in decimals.

radon, rā'don, *n.* [RADIUM.] A radioactive gaseous element, chemically inert, formed as a disintegration product of radium. Symbol, Rn; at. no., 86.

radula, rad'ū·la, pl. -ae, *n.* [L. for a scraper.] In mollusks, a horny tooth-studded ribbon on the floor of the ODONTOPHORE (which see).

raff, raf, *n.* [O.E. *raff*, to sweep; Fr. *raffer*, from G. *raffen*, to sweep, to snatch; akin *raffle*.] Sweepings; refuse; a person of worthless character; the scum of society; the rabble; used chiefly in the reduplicated form *riff-raff*.—**raffish**, raf'ish, *a.* Villainous; scampish; worthless.

raffia, raf'i·a, *n.* [Name in Madagascar.] A fibrous substance obtained from a palm of Madagascar, and another of South America, used for agricultural tie bands.

raffle, raf'l, *n.* [Fr. *rafle*, O.Fr. *raffle*, a kind of game at dice, from G. *raffen*, *raffeln*, to sweep or snatch. RAFF.] A lottery in which several persons deposit a part of the value of something, the winner being determined by chance (as by the drawing of a lucky number)—*v.t.*—raffled, raffling. To engage in a raffle.—*v.t.* To dispose of by means of a raffle.

Rafflesia, raf·lē'si·a, *n.* [After Sir Stamford *Raffles*, the discover of the

first known species.] A genus of parasitical plants, natives of Sumatra and Java, one of which is remarkable for its gigantic flower, about 3 feet in diameter.

raft, raft, *n.* [Properly a float made of beams or rafters; Icel. *raptr* (pron. *raftr*), Dan. *raft*, a rafter. RAFTER.] A float of logs, planks, or other pieces of timber fastened together, for the convenience of transporting them by water; a floating structure used in shipwrecks, often formed of barrels, planks, spars, etc.; a floating mass of trees, branches, etc. —*v.t.* To transport on a raft.— **raftsman**, rafts'man, *n.* A man who manages a raft.

rafter, raf'tér, *n.* [A.Sax. *raefter*= Icel-*raptr* (pron. *raftr*), Dan. *raft*, a rafter, a beam.] One of the sloping timbers of a roof, which support the outer covering.—*v.t.* To furnish with rafters.

rag, rag, *v.t.*—ragged, (ragd), ragging. [Origin doubtful.] To torment, tease, or subject to annoyance, often petty or ludicrous.

rag, rag, *n.* [Originally a tuft of rough hair; comp. Sw. and Dan. dial. *ragg*, rough hair; Icel. *rögg*, shagginess, a tuft; allied to *rug*.] Any piece of cloth torn from the rest; a tattered cloth, torn or worn; a fragment of dress; a shred; a tatter; *pl.* tattered garments or mean dress; a term for rock deposits consisting of hard irregular masses (coral-*rag*, Kentish-*rag*, etc.); ragstone.—**ragamuffin**, rag·a·muf'in, *n.* [*Ragamofin* was the name of a demon in some old mystery plays, perhaps from *rag*, and old *mof*, *muff*, a long sleeve, or from *tag*, and D. *muf*, musty.] A poorly dressed youngster.—**ragged**, rag'ed, *a.* Rent or worn into rags or tatters; tattered; having broken or rough edges; jagged; rough with sharp or irregular points; wearing tattered clothes; shabby.—*On the ragged edge*, on the verge of misfortune, failure, or collapse.—**raggedly**, rag'ed·li, *adv.* In a ragged condition. —**raggedness**, rag'ed·nes, *n.* The state of being ragged.—**ragman**, rag'man, *n.* A man who collects or deals in rags.—**ragpicker**, *n.* A collector of rags, bones, etc., from streets, ashpits, etc.; one who makes a living by scavenging.—**ragweed**, rag'wēd, *n.* A coarse, annual weed of the composite family, with some 15 species in North America, its pollen being extremely irritating to hay fever sufferers who are allergic to it.

rage, rāj, *n.* [Fr. *rage*, from L. *rabies*, rage, madness (by a change similar to that seen in *abridge*); from *rabo*, to rave, to be mad; cog. Skr. *rabh*, to desire eagerly. RABID.] Violent anger accompanied with furious words, gestures, or agitation; anger excited to fury; vehemence or violent exacerbation (the *rage* of a fever, of hunger or thirst); fury; extreme violence (the *rage* of a tempest); violent desire.—*The rage*, the object of popular and eager desire; the fashion. (*Colloq.*) ∴ Syn. under

ANGER.—*v.i.*—*raged, raging.* To be furious with anger; to be exasperated to fury; to be in a passion; to act or move furiously, or with mischievous impetuosity (the sea *rages*); to ravage; to prevail with fatal effect (the plague *rages*).

ragee, rag′ē, *n.* [Indian word.] A grain plant of India and elsewhere.

raglan, rag′lan, *n.* A type of coat or overcoat with sleeves (*raglan* sleeves) whose seams extend to the neckline, giving a slanting line to the shoulders.

ragout, ra·gö′, *n.* [Fr. *ragoût*, from L. *re*, again, *ad*, to, and *gustus*, a tasting.] A dish of stewed and highly seasoned meat.

ragtime, rag′tīm, *n.* Syncopated music with a regularly accented accompaniment, being the earliest form of jazz and probably having its origin in Negro melodies.

raid, rād, *n.* [From stem of *ride*; same as Icel. *reith*, a riding, a raid; akin to *road.*] A hostile inroad or incursion, especially one made suddenly by mounted men; a foray; an attack by violence; an unannounced entry or sudden attack by officers of the law in order to make seizures and arrests, etc.—*v.t.* To make a raid.—*v.i.* To take part in a raid.—**raider,** rād′ėr, *n.*

rail, rāl, *n.* [Same as L.G. and Sw. *regel*, G. *riegel*, a bar, a rail; akin G. *reihe*, a row.] A bar of wood or metal extending from one upright post to another, as in fences; a horizontal timber in any piece of framing or paneling; the upper pieces into which the balusters of a stair are mortised; a series of posts or balusters connected by crossbeams, bars, or rods, for enclosure; a railing; one of the parallel iron or steel bars forming a smooth track for the wheels of a locomotive and the cars which it draws, or for a streetcar, elevated, subway, etc.; a railroad (to travel or send goods by *rail*).—*v.t.* To enclose with rails; to send by rail, as goods, etc.—*v.i.* To ride or travel on a railroad.—**railer,** rā′lėr, *n.* One who makes or furnishes with rails.—**railhead,** *n.* The most advanced point of a railroad under construction; the point at which goods are transferred from a railroad to some other means of transport.—**railing,** rā′ling, *n.* A fence or barrier of wood or iron, constructed of posts and rails; rails in general, or the materials for rails. —**railroad,** rāl′rōd, *n.* A permanent roadway consisting of one or more pairs of rails laid parallel to each other and several feet apart, making a track over which locomotives, freight or passenger cars, etc., may run; in an extended sense, the road and all the land, works, buildings, machinery, franchises, and other assets required for the support and use of the road.—*Railroad train,* locomotive and cars running on railroad tracks.—*v.t.* To transport or ship by railroad; to rush through forcefully and without careful consideration, especially a bill through

a legislature (*colloq.*); to send a person to prison on a false charge (*slang*).—**railroading,** rāl′rōd·ing, *n.* Construction or operation of railroads; employment on a railroad.

rail, rāl, *n.* [O.Fr. *rasle, raale,* a rail; same origin as *rattle,* being so called from its noisy cry.] The popular name of several grallatorial birds, inhabiting sedgy places, moist herbage, etc., and comprising the land rail or corn crake and the water rail.

rail, rāl, *v.i.* [Fr. *railler,* to banter; from L.L. *radiculare,* from L. *radere,* to scrape. RASE, RASOR.] To utter reproaches; to use insolent and reproachful language; to scold.— **railer,** rā′lėr, *n.* One who rails.— **raillery,** rā′lėr·i, *n.* [Fr. *raillerie.*] Good-humored pleasantry or slight satire; satirical merriment; jesting language; banter.

raiment, rā′ment, *n.* [Contracted from obsolete *arrayment.* ARRAY.] Clothing in general; vestments; vesture; garments; now always in the *sing.*

rain, rān, *n.* [A.Sax. *regn, rén*=Icel., Dan., and Sw. *regn,* D. and G. *regen,* Goth. *rign*; same root as L. *rigare,* to wet, whence *irrigate.* As to the disappearance of *g* compare *hail* and *flail.*] The descent of water in drops from the clouds; the water thus falling; the moisture of the atmosphere condensed and deposited in drops; a shower or pouring down of anything.—*v.i.* To fall in drops from the clouds, as water: used mostly with *it* for a nominative (*it rains, it* will *rain*); to fall or drop like rain (tears *rained* from their eyes).—*v.t.* To pour or shower down, like rain from the clouds; to pour or send down abundantly.— **rainbow,** rān′bō, *n.* A bow or arc of a circle, consisting of all the prismatic colors, formed by the refraction and reflection of rays of light from drops of rain; a wide variety, as of colors.—**raincheck,** rān′chek, *n.* A ticket stub for admission to a later performance in case of a cancellation; a deferred invitation.—**raincoat,** rān′cōt, *n.* A coat of water-repellent or waterproof material.—**raindrop,** *n.* A drop of rain.—**rainfall,** rān′fal, *n.* A fall of rain; the amount of water that falls as rain.—**rainforest,** *n.* A tropical forest with an annual rainfall of more than 100 inches.—**rainy,** rā′nē, *a.*

raise, rāz, *v.t.*—*raised, raising.* [A caus. of *rise,* but coming directly from a Scandinavian source; Icel. *reisa,* to raise, caus. of *rísa,* to rise. RISE, REAR.] To cause to rise; to put, place, or remove higher; to lift upward; to elevate; to heave; to elevate in social position, rank, dignity, and the like; to increase the value or estimation of; to exalt, enhance, promote, advance; to increase the energy, strength, power, or vigor of; to excite; to heighten (to *raise* the courage, to *raise* the temperature of a room); to cause to appear from the world of spirits; to recall from death (to *raise* the dead); to cause to

assume an erect position or posture; to set upright; to awaken; to rouse to action; to incite; to stir up (to *raise* the country, to *raise* a mutiny); to set into commotion (to *raise* the sea); to cause to arise or come into being; to build up; to erect; to construct; to bring or get together; to gather, collect, to levy (to *raise* money, to *raise* an army); to cause to be produced; to breed; to rear; to grow (to *raise* wheat, to *raise* cattle, sheep, etc.); to give rise to; to originate (to *raise* a false report); to give vent or utterance to (to *raise* a cry); to strike up (to *raise* the song of victory); to cause to appear; to call up (to *raise* a smile or a blush); to heighten or elevate in pitch (a sharp *raises* a note half a tone); to increase the loudness of (to *raise* the voice); *law,* to institute or originate (to *raise* an action); to cause to swell, as dough.—*To raise steam,* to produce steam enough to drive an engine.—*To raise a blockade,* to terminate or break it up.—*To raise a siege,* to relinquish the attempt to take a place by besieging it, or to cause the attempt to be relinquished.—*To raise the wind* (*fig.*), to obtain ready money by some shift or other.—*Raised beaches.* See BEACH.

raisin, rā′zn, *n.* [Fr. *raisin,* a grape, from L. *racemus,* a cluster of grapes. RACEME.] A dried grape; a dried fruit of various species of vines.

raja, rajah, rä′jä, *n.* [Skr. and Hind. *râjâ,* a rajah; root in Skr. *râj,* to rule; cog. L. *rex* (for *regs*), a king, *rego,* to rule; Gael. and It. *righ,* a king; A.Sax. *rice,* dominion. REGAL, RICH.] In India, originally a title which belonged to princes of Hindu race who governed a territory; subsequently, a title given to Hindus of rank; a Hindu chief.

rake, rāk, *n.* [A.Sax. *raca,* a rake; cog. Icel. *reka,* a shovel or spade; Sw. *raka,* an oven rake; G. *rechen,* a rake; from root meaning to stretch. REACH.] An implement furnished with wooden or iron teeth, used for collecting hay or straw after mowing or reaping; and in gardening for smoothing the soil, covering the seed, etc.; a small implement like a hoe used for collecting the stakes on a gambling table.—*v.t.*—*raked, raking.* To apply a rake to, or something that serves the same purpose; to gather with a rake; to smooth with a rake; to gather with labor or difficulty (to *rake* together wealth); to ransack; to pass swiftly over; to scour; *milit.* to enfilade; to cannonade so that the balls range the whole length.—*To rake up* (*fig.*), to bring up or revive, as quarrels, grievances, etc.—*v.i.* To use a rake; to seek by raking; to search with minute inspection into every part.—**raker,** rā′kėr, *n.* One who or that which rakes; an implement for raking.

rake, rāk, *n.* [Shortened from M.E. *rakehell,* properly vagabond, wandering; comp. Prov. *rake,* to rove or ramble idly; Sw. *raka,* Icel.

reika, to wander; Dan. *raekel*, a lout.] A loose, disorderly vicious person; one addicted to lewdness; a libertine; a roué.—*v.i.* To play the part of a rake; to lead a dissolute debauched life; to fly wide of game; said of a hawk.—**rakish**, rā´kish, *a.* Given to the practices of a rake; dissolute; debauched.—**rakishly**, rā´kish·li, *adv.* In a rakish or dissolute manner.—**rakishness**, rā´kish·nes, *n.* Dissolute practices.

rake, rāk, *v.i.* [Same as Sw. *raka*, Dan. *rage*, to project, a Scandinavian verb=E. *reach*.] To incline; to slope; *naut.* to incline from a perpendicular direction (a mast *rakes* aft).—*n. Naut.* a slope or inclination; the projection of the stem or stern beyond the extremities of the keel; the inclination of a mast, funnel, etc., from a perpendicular direction.—**rakish**, rā´kish, *a. Naut.* having a rake or inclination of the masts forward or aft.

rallentando, ral·len·tan´dō. [It.] *Music*, a term indicating that the time of the passage over which it is written is to be gradually decreased.

ralline, ral´īn, *a.* [Mod. L. *rallus*, a rail.] *Ornith.* pertaining to the rails.

rally, ral´i, *v.t.*—*rallied, rallying.* [Fr. *rallier*, to rally—prefix *re*, and *allier*, E. *ally*, from L. *alligo*, I bind to—*ad*, to, and *ligo*, I bind. ALLY, LIGAMENT.] To collect and reduce to order, as troops dispersed or thrown into confusion; to bring together as for a fresh effort; to reunite.—*v.i.* To come back quickly to order; to reform themselves into an orderly body for a fresh effort, to resume or recover vigor or strength (the patient begins to *rally*).—*n.* A stand made by retreating troops; return of disordered troops to their ranks; the act of recovering strength; a mass meeting to arouse group enthusiasm.

rally, ral´i, *v.t.*—*rallied, rallying.* [Fr. *railler*, to banter. RAIL (to banter).] To attack with raillery; to treat with good-humor and pleasantry, or with slight contempt or satire; to tease.—*v.i.* To use pleasantry or satirical merriment.

ram, ram, *n.* [A.Sax. *ram, ramm*, D. *ram*, G. *ramm*, a ram. Root uncertain.] The male of the sheep or ovine genus; a battering-ram (under BATTER); a steam ironclad ship-of-war, armed at the prow below the waterline with a heavy iron or steel beak intended to destroy an enemy's ships by the force with which it is driven against them; the loose hammer of a pile-driving machine; the piston of a hydraulic press.—*Hydraulic ram* or *water ram*, an automatic apparatus by which a descending stream of water is made to raise by its own momentum a portion of its mass to a required height.—*The Ram*, Aries, one of the signs of the zodiac.—*v.t.*—*rammed, ramming.* [From the noun, like G. *rammen*, Dan. *ramme*, to strike, to hit.] To strike with a ram; to drive a ram or similar object against;

batter; to force in; to drive down; to fill or compact by pounding or driving; to stuff; to cram.—*v.i.* To use a battering-ram or similar object.—*a.* Strong-scented; stinking (*ram* as a fox).—**rammer**, ram´ėr, *n.* One who or that which rams or drives; a ramrod.—**rammish**, ram´ish, *a.* Ramlike; hence, lascivious; rank; strong-scented. — **ramrod**, ram´rod, *n.* A rod for ramming down the charge of a gun or other firearm; a rammer.

Ramadan, ra·ma·dän´, *n.* [Ar., the hot month, from *ramida, ramiza*, to be hot.] The ninth month of the Mohammedan year; the great annual Mohammedan fast, kept throughout the entire month from sunrise to sunset.

ramble, ram´bl, *v.i.*—*rambled, rambling.* [A dim. and freq. from *roam*; the *b* has crept in, as in *grumble, nimble, number*, etc.] To rove; to wander; to go from place to place without any determinate object in view; to think or talk in an incoherent manner; to grow without constraint.—*n.* A roving; an excursion or trip in which a person wanders from place to place; an irregular excursion.—**rambler**, ram´blėr, *n.* One who rambles; a rover; a wanderer.—**rambling**, ram´bling, *p.* and *a.* Roving; wandering; straggling; without method; confused in ideas or language.—*n.* A roving, irregular excursion.

rambunctious, ram·bungk´shus, *a.* [From *ram*, and variant of *bumptious*.] Wild and incorrigible in behavior; unruly; boisterous; impulsive.

ramekin, ramequin, ram´i·kin, *n.* [Fr.] An individual portion of a cheese preparation baked in a small dish; an individual baking dish.

rameous, rā´mē·us, *a.* [From L. *ramus*, a branch. RADIUS.] *Bot.* belonging to a branch; growing on or shooting from a branch.—**ramification**, ram´i·fi·kā″shon, *n.* The act of ramifying; the process of branching out; a small branch or offshoot from a main stock or channel; a subordinate branch; a division or subdivision in a classification, or the like.—**ramiform**, ram´i·form, *a. Bot.* resembling a branch.—**ramify**, ram´i·fī, *v.t.*—*ramified, ramifying.* [Fr. *ramifier*—L. *ramus*, a branch, and *facio*, to make.] To divide into branches or parts.—*v.i.* To shoot into branches, as the stem of a plant; to branch out; to be divided or subdivided; to branch out; as a main subject or scheme.—**ramous, ramose**, rā´mus, rā´mōs, *a.* [L. *ramosus*.] Branchy; full of branches; *bot.* branched, as a stem or root.

ramjet, ram´jet, *n.* [*Ram* and *jet*.] A jet engine that derives thrust from the addition of fuel to, and its combustion by, air compressed solely by forward speed.

rammer, rammish. See RAM.

ramose. See RAMEOUS.

ramp, ramp, *v.i.* [Fr. *ramper*, to creep, to climb=It. *rampare*, to clamber, from the German; comp. Bav. *rampfen*, to snatch; a nasalized

form corresponding to L.G. *rappen*, Sw. *rappa*, to snatch. *Romp* is the same word.] To climb, as a plant‡; to rear on the hind legs; to assume a rampant attitude; to spring or move with violence; to rage; to bound; to romp.—*n.* A sloping platform serving as a way between different levels.—**rampage**, ram´pij, *v.i.* [From *ramp*.] To romp or prance about with unrestrained spirits; to rage and storm; to prance about with fury. (*Colloq.*)—*n.* A state of passion or excitement; violent conduct. (*Colloq.*)—**rampageous**, ram·pā´jus, *a.* Boisterous; unruly. (*Colloq.*)—**rampant**, ram´pant, *a.* [Fr. *rampant*, ppr. of *ramper*, to clamber.] Springing or climbing unchecked; rank in growth; exuberant (*rampant* weeds); overleaping restraint or usual limits; excessively and obtrusively prevalent; predominant (*rampant* vice); *her.* standing upright upon his hind legs (properly on one foot) as if attacking: said of a beast of prey, as the lion.—**rampancy**, ram´pan·si, *n.* The state or quality of being rampant.—**rampantly**, ram´pant·li, *adv.* In a rampant manner.

rampart, ram´pärt, *n.* [Fr. *rempart*, a rampart, from *remparer*, to fortify a place—*re*, again, *em* for L. *in*, in, and *parer*, to defend, from L. *parare*, to prepare. PARE, PREPARE.] A bulwark; a defense; *fort.* an elevation or mound of earth round a place, capable of resisting cannon shot, and on which the parapet is raised; it also may include the parapet.—*v.t.* To fortify with ramparts.

rampion, ram´pi·on, *n.* [A nasalized form from L. *rapum*, a turnip, rape.] A perennial plant of the bellflower order, the root and leaves of which are used in salads.

ramrod. See RAM.

ramshackle, ram´shak·l, *a.* [Perhaps pp. of *ransackle, ransack*.] Ill-adjusted and threatening dissolution; carelessly constructed; rickety.

ramson, ramsons, ram´zon, ram´zonz, *n.* [A.Sax. *hramsa, hramse*, ramsons (pl. *hramsan*, so that *ramsons* is a double pl.); G. *rams, ramsel, ramsen*, Sw. *rams*, ramsons; allied to Gr. *kromyon*, an onion.] A species of garlic, having broad leaves and a bulbous root, sometimes used in salads.

ramulose, ram´ū·lōs, *a. Bot.* having many small branches.

ran, ran, *pret.* See RUN.

ranch, ranch, *n.* [Sp. *rancho*, a mess, a set of persons who eat and drink together, a messroom.] An establishment and tract of land for raising and grazing horses, cattle, sheep, etc.; the buildings of such an establishment; any farm, as for dairying or fruit growing. (*Colloq.*)—**rancher**, ran´chėr, *n.* One who owns or is employed on a ranch.—**ranchero**, ran·châ´rō, *n.* A person employed on a ranch, or who owns and manages a ranch. (*Spanish Amer.*)—**rancho**, ran´chō, *n.* Rude habitation for ranch or farm workers on a stock farm. (*Spanish Amer.*)

rancid, ran′sid, *a.* [L. *rancidus*, from *ranceo*, to be rank (whence also *rancor*).] Having a rank smell; strong-scented, from turning bad with keeping: said of oils and fats, butter, etc.; musty.—**rancidity, rancidness**, ran·sid′i·ti, ran′sid·nes, *n.* The quality of being rancid.

rancor, rang′kẻr, *n.* [L. *rancor*, an ill smell, rancor, from *ranceo*, to be rank or rancid (whence *rancid*).] The deepest malignity, enmity, or spite; deep-seated and implacable malice; inveterate enmity; malignity.—**rancorous**, rang′kẻr·us, *a.* Full of rancor; deeply malignant; intensely virulent.—**rancorously**, rang′kẻr·us·li, *adv.*

random, ran′dum, *n.* [O.Fr. *randon*, an impetuous course or efflux, vivacity, violence; *à randon*, at random; *randoner, randir*, to run rapidly; from G. *rand*, edge, brim, the word originally having reference to the violence of a stream flowing full to the brim.] A roving motion or course without direction; want of rule or method; chance; used only in the phrase, *at random*, that is, in a haphazard or fortuitous manner; *mining*, the depth below a given plane.—*a.* Done at hazard or without settled aim or purpose; left to chance; fortuitous.—*Random courses, masonry* and *paving*, courses of stones of unequal thickness.—*Random shot*, a shot not directed to a point.—**randomly**, ran′dum·li, *adv.* In a random manner; at hazard.

ranee, rän′ē, *n.* [Hind. *rani*, queen.] The wife of a rajah, or queen in her own right, in native states.

rang, rang, pret. See RING.

range, ränj, *v.t.*—*ranged, ranging.* [From Fr. *ranger*, to range, from *rang*, O.Fr. *reng*, a rank; from the German. RANK.] To set in a row or in rows; to place in regular lines or ranks; to rank; to arrange systematically; to classify; to class; to rove through or over; to pass over.—*v.i.* To be placed in order; to be ranked; to rank; to rove at large; to wander without restraint; to pass from one point to another; to fluctuate (the price *ranges* between $50 and $60); *gun.* to have range or horizontal direction.—*n.* A series of things in a line; a row; a rank (a *range* of mountains); space or room for excursion; the extent of country over which a plant or animal is naturally spread; compass or extent; discursive power; scope (a wide *range* of thought); the series of sounds belonging to a voice or a musical instrument; a kitchen grate and cooking apparatus; *gun.* the horizontal distance to which a shot or other projectile is carried; a place where gun or rifle practice is carried on.—**range finding**, *n.* The measurement of the distance in yards between a gun and the object of its aim, effected by means of instruments, the rangefinder, the mekometer, etc. The term *range-taking* is used similarly but with wider meaning.—**ranger**, rän′jẻr, *n.* One who

ranges; a member of a body of mounted, roving troops or police; a government official patrolling forest areas.—**rangership**, rän′jẻr·ship, *n.* The office of ranger.—**ranging**, rän′jing, *n.* The process of finding the elevation which should be given to a gun in order that the projectile may hit the object aimed at.

rank, rangk, *n.* [O.E. *ranc, renk*, from Fr. *rang*, O.Fr. *reng, renc*, a rank, row, range (whence also *range*), originally a circular row, from O.H.G. *hring, hrinc*, a ring, a circle. RING.] A row; a line; a tier; a range; *milit.* a line of soldiers; a line of men standing abreast or side by side: often used along with *file* (which see); hence in *pl.* the order of common soldiers (to reduce an officer to the *ranks*); an aggregate of individuals together; a social class; an order; a division; degree of dignity, eminence, or excellence; comparative station; relative place (a writer of the first *rank*); high social position; distinction; eminence (a man of *rank*).—*To fill the ranks*, to complete the whole number.—*To take rank of*, to enjoy precedence over.—*v.t.* To place abreast in a rank or line; to place in a particular class, order, or division; to class or classify; to range.—*v.i.* To be ranged, classed, or included, as in a particular class, order, or division; to have a certain rank; to occupy a certain position as compared with others; to put in a claim against the estate of a bankrupt.

rank, rangk, *a.* [A.Sax. *ranc*, fruitful, rank, proud=Icel. *rakkr*, straight, bold; Dan. *rank*, erect; D. *rank*, slender; Prov. G. *rank*, slender, upright—all nasalized forms from same root as *rack, right, reach*.] Luxuriant in growth; causing vigorous growth; fertile; strong-scented; rancid; strong to the taste; high-tasted; raised to a high degree; excessive; utter (*rank* nonsense); gross; coarse; disgusting.—**rankly**, rangk′li, *adv.* With vigorous growth; rancidly; coarsely; grossly.—**rankness**, rangk′nes, *n.* The state or quality of being rank; vigorous growth; luxuriance; strength and coarseness in smell or taste.

rankle, rang′kl, *v.i.*—*rankled, rankling.* To fester, as a sore or wound; to produce a painful sensation; *fig.* to produce bitterness or rancor in the mind; to continue to irritate.—*v.t.* To irritate; to inflame.

ransack, ran′sak, *v.t.* [A Scand. word: Icel. *rannsaka*, Sw. *ransaka*, to search, as for stolen goods—Icel. *rann* (Goth. *razns*), a house, and *saekja*, to seek. SEEK.] To search thoroughly; to enter and search every place and part of; to rummage; to plunder; to strip by plundering.

ransom, ran′sum, *n.* [Fr. *rançon*, O.Fr. *raenson, raanson*, etc., from L. *redemptio, redemptionis*, redemption, from *redimo*—*re*, back, and *emo*, I buy. (REDEEM.) The word is therefore *redemption* in another form.] Release from captivity, bond-

age, or the possession of an enemy by payment; the price paid for such release, or for goods captured by an enemy; price paid for the pardon of sins; redemption of sinners.—*v.t.* To pay a ransom for; to redeem from captivity, bondage, forfeit, or punishment; to deliver.—**ransomer**, ran′sum·ẻr, *n.* One who ransoms or redeems.

rant, rant, *v.i.* [Same as O.D. *ranten*, to be enraged, G. *ranten, ranzen*, to move noisily, Prov.G. *rant*, noisy mirth.] To rave in violent or extravagant language; to be noisy and boisterous in words or declamation.—*n.* Boisterous, empty declamation; bombast.—**ranter**, ran′tẻr, *n.* One who rants; a noisy talker; a boisterous preacher; [*cap.*] a name given by way of reproach to members of a denomination of Christians which sprang up in 1645; also vulgarly applied to the Primitive Methodists.

Ranunculus, ra·nun′kū·lus, *n.* [L. dim. of *rana*, a frog—a name first given to the aquatic ranunculùs because it floats in marshes, ditches, etc.] The crowfoot genus, a genus of flowering plants almost exclusively inhabiting the Northern Hemisphere, possessing acrid properties, and widely distributed over the Temperate Zone.—**ranunculaceous**, ra·nun′kū·lā″shus, *a.* Of the Ranunculaceae or crowfoot family.

rap, rap, *n.* [Same as Sw. *rapp*, a blow, a stroke; Dan. *rap*, a rap; imitative of sound made by a blow; comp. *pat, tap*.] A quick smart blow; a knock.—*v.i.*—*rapped, rapping.* To strike with a quick sharp blow; to knock.—*v.t.* To strike with a quick blow; to give a knock (to *rap* one's knuckles).—*To rap out*, to utter with sudden violence (to *rap out* an oath).—**rapper**, rap′ẻr, *n.* One who raps or knocks; the knocker of a door.

rap, rap, *v.t.*—*rapped, rapping.* [A Scandinavian word; Sw. *rappa*, Dan. *rappe*, to snatch; comp. Dan. *rap*, Sw. *rapp*, quick, brisk. Rape is closely allied; see also RAPT.] To affect with ecstasy or rapture; to snatch or hurry away; to seize by violence.

rap, rap, *v.t.* To criticize or censure. —**rap**, rap, *n.* (*Slang.*) A punishment (to take the *rap*).

rap, rap, *n.* [Possibly derived from the name of a coin of slight value.] Something of trifling worth, chiefly used in such phrases as, *it isn't worth a rap*. (*Colloq.*)

rapacious, ra·pā′shus, *a.* [L. *rapax, rapacis*, from *rapio*, I seize (whence also *rapine, rapture*); same root as *rapid*.] Given to plunder; accustomed to seize or take possession of property by violence; subsisting on prey or animals seized by violence; avaricious; grasping.—**rapaciously**, ra·pā′shus·li, *adv.* In a rapacious manner; by rapine.—**rapaciousness**, ra·pā′shus·nes, *n.* Disposition to plunder or to exact by oppression.—**rapacity**, ra·pas′i·ti, *n.* [L. *rapacitas*.] The quality of being rapacious;

ravenousness; the act or practice of extorting or exacting by oppressive injustice; greediness; insatiability.

rape, rāp, *n.* [From *rap*, to seize, to snatch, the meaning being influenced by L. *rapere, raptum*, to seize. RAP, to seize, RAPTURE.] The act of snatching by force; a seizing and carrying away by force or violence (the *rape* of Proserpine); *law*, the carnal knowledge of a woman forcibly and against her will; something seized and carried away.

rape, rāp, *n.* [Fr. *râpe*.] Refuse stalks and skins of raisins used by vinegar makers after the fruit has been employed in making wine.

rape, rāp, *n.* [From L. *rapa, rapum*, a turnip (whence also *rampion*).] A plant of the mustard family, cultivated for its seeds, from which oil is extracted.

raphe, rā'fē, *n.* [Gr. *raphē*, a seam or suture.] *Bot.* and *zool.* a term applied to parts which look as if they had been sewed or joined together; a suture or line of junction.—**raphides**, raf'i-dēz, *n. pl.* [Pl. of Gr. *raphis*, a needle.] *Bot.* crystals of an acicular or needle-like form occurring in plant cells.

rapid, rap'id, *a.* [Fr. *rapide*, from L. *rapidus*, rapid, from *rapio*, to seize; same root as Gr. *harpazō*, to seize. (HARPY.) *Rapine, rapacious, ravish, rapture*, etc., are from the same L. stem.] Very swift or quick; moving with celerity; advancing with speed; speed in progression (*rapid* growth); quick or swift in performance.—*n.* A swift current in a river, where the channel is descending.—**rapid-fire**, *a.* Firing or adapted to fire in quick succession, hence, proceeding or characterized by sharpness or rapidity; quick.—**rapidity**, ra·pid'i·ti, *n.*—**rapidly**, rap'id·li, *adv.*

rapier, rā'pi·ėr, *n.* [Fr. *rapière*, lit. a rasper, from Sp. *raspar*, to rasp. RASP.] A sword used only in thrusting, and usually having a four-sided blade.

rapine, rap'in, *n.* [Fr., from L. *rapina*, from *rapio*, to seize. RAPID.] The act of plundering; the seizing and carrying away of things by force.

rapparee, rap·a·rē', *n.* [Ir. *rapaire*, a noisy fellow, *rapach*, noisy, slovenly.] A wild Irish plunderer; a worthless fellow. (*Irish.*) Spelled also *Raparee*.

rappee, rap·pē', *n.* [Fr. *râpé*, ppr. of *râper*, to rasp, lit. rasped or powdered tobacco.] A strong kind of snuff made from the darker and ranker kinds of tobacco.

rapper. See RAP.

rapport, rap·pōrt', *n.* [Fr., from L. *re*, again, *ad*, to, and *portare*, to carry. PORTER.] A resemblance; a correspondence; harmony; affinity.

rapscallion, rap·skal'yun, *n.* A good-for-nothing fellow; a rascal.

rapt, rapt, *p.* and *a.* [From *rap*, to snatch, but influenced by L. *raptus*, seized, from *rapio*. RAPTURE.] Snatched away; transported; enraptured; in an ecstasy; entirely absorbed.

raptorial, rap·tō'ri·al, *a.* [L. *raptor*,

a plunderer.] Pertaining to the Raptores, or birds of prey; living by rapine or prey; adapted to the seizing of prey.

rapture, rap'chėr, *n.* [From L. *rapere, raptum*, to seize and carry away; whence also *rapine*, etc. RAPID.] A seizing by violence†; a transport of delight; ecstasy; extreme joy or pleasure; enthusiasm.—**rapturous**, rap'chėr·us, *a.* Ecstatic; transporting; ravishing.—**rapturously**, rap'chėr·us·li, *adv.* With rapture; ecstatically.

rare, râr, *a.* [Fr. *rare*, from L. *rarus*, thin, rare.] Thinly scattered; sparse; thin; porous; not dense or compact; uncommon; not frequent; possessing qualities seldom to be met with; excellent or valuable to a degree seldom found.—**rarely**, râr'li, *adv.* In a rare degree or manner; seldom. —**rareness**, râr'nes, *n.*—**rarity**, râ'ri·ti, *n.*—**rarebit**, râr'bit, *n.* Welsh rabbit.—*Rare-earth*, *chem.* any of the series of similar oxides of the rare-earth metals.—*Rare-earth metals*, *chem.* a group of trivalent rare metallic elements with the atomic numbers of 57 to 71 inclusive.

rare, râr, *v.t.* [O.E. *hrere*, boiled lightly.] Not completely cooked; underdone.

rarefy, râ're·fī, *v.t.*—*rarefied, rarefying*. [Fr. *raréfier*; L. *rarefacio*— *rarus*, rare, and *facio*, I make.] To make rare, thin, porous, or less dense; to expand by separation of constituent atoms or particles: opposed to *condense*.—*v.i.* To become rare, that is, not dense or less dense. —**rarefaction**, râ·re·fak'shon, *n.* The act of rarefying or state of being rarefied; expansion or distension by separation of constituent particles: chiefly used in speaking of the aeriform fluids, *dilatation* and *expansion* being used in speaking of solids and liquids: opposed to *condensation*.

rarely, rareness, rarity. See RARE.

rascal, ras'kal, *n.* [Lit. scrapings or refuse; O.E. *rascall, rascayle*, the rabble, also a worthless deer; from a L.L. *rasicare*, from L. *rado, rasum*, to shave or scrape. RASE.] A lean beast, especially a lean deer, not fit to hunt or kill; a mean fellow; a trickish dishonest fellow; a rogue or scoundrel.—*a.* Worthless; mean; paltry; base.—**rascality**, ras·kal'i·ti, *n.* Such qualities as make a rascal; mean trickishness or dishonesty.— **rascally**, ras'kal·li, *a.* Like a rascal; dishonest; vile; base; worthless.

rase, rāz, *v.t.*—*rased, rasing*. [Fr. *raser*, from L.L. *rasare*, freq. of L. *rado, rasum*, to scrape, seen also in *erase, razor, rascal, abrade, rally*, to *rail*.] To touch superficially in passing; to graze; to erase; to level with the ground; to overthrow; to raze (RAZE).—**rasure**, rā'zhūr, *n.* The act of scraping or erasing; an erasure.

rash, rash, *a.* [Same as L.G., Dan., and Sw. *rask*, Icel. *röskr*, D. and G. *rasch*, rash; perhaps from same root as G. *rad*, a wheel. Skr. *ratha*, a chariot.] Hasty in counsel or action; precipitate; resolving or entering on a project without due deliberation

and caution; uttered, formed, or undertaken with too little reflection. ∴ A *rash* man is one who undergoes risk from natural impulsiveness; a *foolhardy* man foolishly incurs danger in defiance of and not believing in evil consequences; a *reckless* man sees but disregards consequences.— **rashly**, rash'li, *adv.* In a rash manner; precipitately; inconsiderately.— **rashness**, rash'nes, *n.* Precipitation; inconsiderate readiness to decide or act; a rash act.

rash, rash, *n.* [O.Fr. *rasche*, rash, scurf, itch; same origin as *rascal*.] An eruption on the skin, usually in the form of red spots or patches.

rasher, rash'ėr, *n.* [Probably a piece hastily cooked, from *rash*, *a.*] *Cookery*, a slice of bacon for frying or broiling.

Rasores, ra·sō'rēz, *n. pl.* [Lit. scrapers or scratchers, from L. *rado, rasum*, to scrape. RASE.] Gallinaceous birds or scratchers, an order of birds of which the common domestic fowl may be regarded as the type.— **rasorial**, ra·sō'ri·al, *a.* Pertaining to the Rasores; scratching the ground for food.

rasp, rasp, *v.t.* [O.Fr. *rasper*, Fr. *râper*, to scrape or rasp, from O.H.G. *raspôn*, to scrape together (D. *raspen*, Dan. *raspe*, Sw. *raspa*); akin to G. *raffen*, to sweep, E. *raff, raffle, rapier*.] To rub against with some rough implement; to file with a rasp; to grate; hence, *fig.* to grate harshly upon.—*v.i.* To rub or grate.—*n.* A coarse species of file with numerous separate projections or teeth; a raspberry.—**rasper**, ras'pėr, *n.* One who or that which rasps; a scraper.— **rasping**, ras'ping, *a.* Characterized by grating or scraping.—**raspy**, ras'pi, *a.* Grating; harsh; rough.

raspberry, raz'be·ri, *n.* [*Rasp* and *berry*; so named from the roughness of the fruit. Comp. G. *kratzbeere*— *kratzen*, to scratch, and *beere*, berry.] The well-known fruit of a plant extensively used by both the cook and the confectioner, and also in the preparation of cordials; also the plant itself; a derisive sound made by vibrating the tongue and lips (*slang*).

rasure. See RASE.

rat, rat, *n.* [A.Sax. *ræt*, a rat=D. *rat*, G. *ratte* (whence Fr. *rat*), L.G. and Dan. *rotte*, Gael. *radan*, Armor. *raz*, rat; root probably in L. *rodo*, to gnaw.] Any of various long-tailed rodents resembling, and allied to, the mouse, but considerably larger, brown or gray in color, and infesting houses, barns, stables, and ships; a sneaky person; one who betrays or deserts his associates; in underworld jargon, a criminal who discloses the identity of his accomplices to the police; a section of false hair (*colloq.*).—*To smell a rat*, to be suspicious that all is not right.—*v.i.* —*ratted, ratting*. To catch or kill rats; to forsake one's associates.— **ratsbane**, rats'bān, *n.* [*Rat* and *bane*.] Poison for rats; arsenious acid.— **ratter**, rat'ėr, *n.* One who rats; one whose business it is to catch rats; a terrier which kills rats.—**rattrap,** *n.* A trap for catching rats.

ratafia, rat·a·fē′a, *n.* [Sp., from Malay *arak,* arrack, and *tafia,* a spirit distilled from molasses.] A spirituous liquor flavored with the kernels of cherries, apricots, peaches, etc.; a kind of liqueur.

ratch, rach, *n.* [A softened form of *rack.*] *Mach.* a bar having angular teeth into which a pawl drops, to prevent machines from being reversed in motion; a rack or rack-bar. —**ratchet,** rach′et, *n.* [Dim. of *ratch.*] A piece, one extremity of which abuts against the teeth of a ratchet wheel; a click, pawl, or detent.— **ratchet wheel,** *n.* A wheel with pointed and angular teeth against which a ratchet abuts, used either for converting a reciprocating into a rotatory motion or for admitting of its motion in one direction only.

rate, rāt, *n.* [O.Fr. *rate,* from L. *rata* (*pars,* part, understood), from *ratus,* reckoned, ppr. of *reor,* to reckon, to calculate; akin *ratio, reason, ratify.*] The proportion or standard by which quantity or value is adjusted; price or amount fixed on anything with relation to a standard; a settled proportion; comparative value or estimate; degree as regards speed; a tax or sum assessed on property for public use according to its income or value; *navy,* the order or class of a ship according to its magnitude or force; the daily gain or loss of a chronometer or other timepiece.— *v.t.*—*rated, rating.* To settle or fix the value, rank, or degree of; to value or estimate; to fix the relative scale, rank, or position of (to *rate* a ship).—*v.i.* To be set or considered in a class.—**rateable,** rā′ta·bl, *a.* Ratable.—**ratable,** rā′ta·bl, *a.* Capable of being rated; reckoned according to a certain rate; liable by law to taxation.—**ratability,** rā·ta·bil′i·ti, *n.* Quality of being ratable.— **ratably,** rā′ta·bli, *adv.* By rate or proportion.—*Rate of exchange,* the price per unit of money at which the currency of one country may be exchanged for the currency of another.—**rater,** rā′tėr, *n.* One who rates.—**rating,** rā′ting, *n.* The act of estimating; a fixing in rank or place; rank, as the *rating* of men and the *rating* of ships in the navy.

rate, rāt, *v.t.*—*rated, rating.* [Same word as Sw. *rata,* to blame; N. *rata,* to reject.] To chide with vehemence; to reprove; to scold; to censure violently.

ratel, rāt′el, *n.* [D. *raat,* honeycomb.] The honey-eating badger, a native of India and the Cape of Good Hope.

rather, ra′THėr, *adv.* [Compar. of *rath,* quickly, from A. Sax. *hrathor.*] Preferably; more readily or willingly; with preference or choice; with better reason; more properly; more correctly speaking; to the contrary of what has been just stated (no better but *rather* worse); somewhat (*rather* pretty).

rathskeller, rats′kel·ėr, *n.* [G. *rat,* council, and *keller,* council.] A restaurant or bar, serving wine, beer, and light food, usually located below street level.

ratify, rat′i·fī, *v.t.*—*ratified, ratifying.* [Fr. *ratifier*—*ratus,* fixed by calculation, valid, firm (RATE), and *facio,* I make.] To confirm; to settle authoritatively; to approve and sanction; to make valid, as something done by a representative, agent, or servant.—**ratifier,** rat′i·fi·ėr, *n.* One who ratifies.—**ratification,** rat′i·fi·kā″shon, *n.* The act of ratifying or confirming; confirmation; authorization.

rating, *n.* See RATE.

ratio, rā′shi·ō, *n.* [L. *ratio, rationis,* reckoning, calculation, from *reor, ratus,* to think or suppose. (RATE.) *Reason, ration* are from same word.] Relation or proportion which one thing has to another in respect of magnitude or quantity; in a narrower sense, the numerical measure which one quantity bears to another of the same kind, expressed by the number found by dividing the one by the other; thus the ratio of 3 to 4 is the same as of 6 to 8, each being equivalent to ¾; sometimes called *geometrical ratio,* in opposition to *arithmetical ratio* or the difference between two quantities.

ratiocinate, rash·i·os′i·nāt, *v.i.*—*ratiocinated, ratiocinating.* [L. *ratiocinor, ratiocinatus,* from *ratio,* reason. RATIO.] To reason; to argue.— **ratiocination,** rash·i·os′i·nā″shon, *n.* [L. *ratiocinatio.*] The act or process of reasoning, especially of reasoning deductively.—**ratiocinative,** rash·i·os′i·nā·tiv, *a.* Characterized by ratiocination; argumentative.

ration, rā′shon, ra′shon, *n.* [Fr., from L. *ratio, rationis,* proportion. RATIO.] A daily allowance of provisions to soldiers and sailors; any fixed amount or quantity dealt out; allowance.—*v.t.* To supply with rations.

rational, rash′on·al, *a.* [Fr. *rationnel,* L. *rationalis,* from *ratio, rationis,* proportion. RATIO, REASON.] Having reason or the faculty of reasoning; endowed with reason: opposed to *irrational;* agreeable to reason; not absurd, foolish, preposterous, or the like; acting in conformity to reason; judicious; *arith.* and *alg.* a term applied to an expression in finite terms, the opposite of a *surd* or *irrational* quantity.—**rationale,** rash·o·näl′, *n.* [From L. *rationalis,* from *ratio, rationis,* in sense of reason, account, plan.] A statement of reasons; an account or exposition of the principles of some process, phenomenon, etc.—**rationalism,** rash′on·al·izm, *n.* *Theol.* a system of opinions deduced from reason as distinct from inspiration or revelation, or opposed to it; the interpretation of Scripture statements upon the principles of human reason to the disregard of revelation or anything supernatural.—**rationalist,** rash′on·al·ist, *n.* An adherent of rationalism; one who rejects the supernatural element in dealing with the Old and New Testaments, and disbelieves in

revelation.—**rationalistic,** rash′on·al·is″tik, *a.* Relating to or accordant with rationalism.—**rationalistically,** rash′on·al·is″ti·kal·li, *adv.* In a rationalistic manner.—**rationality,** rash·o·nal′i·ti, *n.* The quality of being rational; power of reasoning; possession of reason; reasonableness. —**rationalize,** rash′on·al·īz, *v.t.* To explain or justify: *psych.* to devise logical or creditable motives for actions performed because of irrational, censorable, or unrecognized motives.—**rationalization,** *n.*—**rationally,** rash′on·al·li, *adv.* In a rational manner; reasonably; sensibly.

ratite, rat′īt, *a.* [From L. *ratis,* a raft.] Any of the division Ratitae with no ridge or keel on the sternum; birds such as the ostrich.

ratline, ratlin, rat′lin, *n.* [Probably from *raddling,* an E. dial. weaving term.] *Naut.* one of a series of small ropes or lines which traverse the shrouds horizontally, forming ladders for going aloft; also called *Ratling.*

ratoon, ra·tön′, *n.* [Sp. *retono,* a sprout or shoot.] A sprout from the root of the sugarcane which has been cut.

ratsbane. See RAT.

rattan, rat′an or rat·tan′, *n.* [Malay *rotan.*] The commercial name for the long trailing stems of certain species of palm from India and the Eastern Archipelago, employed for walking sticks, etc.; a cane or walking stick made of rattan.

ratteen, ra·tēn′, *n.* [Fr. *ratine,* ratteen.] A thick woolen stuff quilled or twilled.

ratten, rat′n, *v.t.* [Lit. to play a rat's trick upon, from prov. *ratten,* a rat.] To destroy or take away the tools or machinery of, a mischievous trick perpetrated upon those who work in defiance of trade unions.

ratter. See RAT.

rattle, rat′l, *v.i.*—*rattled, rattling.* [From an A.Sax. verb seen in *hraetele,* rattlewort=L.G. *ratteln,* D. *ratelen,* G. *rasseln,* Dan. *rasle,* to rattle; all from a root probably onomatopoeic.] To make a quick sharp noise rapidly repeated, as by the collision of bodies not very sonorous; to clatter; to speak eagerly and noisily; to chatter fluently.—*v.t.* To cause to make a rapid succession of sharp sounds.—*n.* A rapid succession of sharp clattering sounds; loud rapid talk; an instrument with which a clattering sound is made, formerly used by watchmen; also a child's toy constructed to produce a rattling sound; one who talks rapidly and without constraint; a jabberer; the horny organ at the extremity of the tail of the rattlesnake; the peculiar sound heard in the throat which immediately precedes and prognosticates death; the death rattle.— **rattler,** rat′lėr, *n.* One who rattles or talks away without thought; a giddy noisy person.—**rattling,** rat′ling, *p.* and *a.* Making a quick succession of sharp sounds; lively.—**rattlebrained,** *a.* Giddy; wild; rattleheaded.—

rattlehead, *n.* A giddy person.—
rattleheaded, rattlepated, *a.* Noisy;
giddy; unsteady.—**rattlesnake,** rat'-
l·snāk, *n.* A venomous American
snake having the tail terminating in
a series of articulated horny pieces,
which the animal moves in such a
manner as to make a rattling sound.
—**rattlesnake root, rattlesnake
weed,** *n.* Plants so named from being
used as a cure for the bite of the
rattlesnake.—**rattletrap,** *n.* A shaky
rickety object. (*Colloq.*)
raucous, rą'kus, *a.* [L. *raucus,* hoarse.]
Hoarse; harsh, as the voice.—**rauci-
ty,** rą'si·ti, *n.* Harshness of sound;
rough utterance; hoarseness.
ravage, rav'ij, *n.* [Fr. *ravage,* from
ravir, to carry off, to ravish (which
see).] Desolation or destruction by
violence, either by men, beasts, or
physical causes; devastation; ruin.—
v.t.—*ravaged, ravaging.* [Fr. *ravager.*]
To lay waste by force; to devastate;
to pillage.—**ravager,** rav'i·jėr, *n.*
One who ravages; a plunderer; a
spoiler.
rave, rāv, *v.i.*—*raved, raving.* [O.Fr.
raver, to be delirious, from L. *rabies,*
madness. RABID.] To wander in
mind or intellect; to be delirious,
wild, furious, or raging, as a madman; to talk with false enthusiasm;
to speak enthusiastically.—*v.t.* To
utter wildly and excitedly.—**raving,**
rā'ving, *p.* and *a.* Furious with
delirium; mad.—*n.* Furious exclamation; irrational, incoherent talk.
ravel, rav'el, *v.t.*—*ravelled, ravelling.*
[Same as O.D. *ravelen,* D. *rafelen,* to
disentangle; connections uncertain.]
To untwist; to unweave; to disentangle; to entangle; to make intricate; to involve.—*v.i.* To become
entangled; to fall into perplexity and
confusion.—**raveling,** rav'el·ing, *n.*
Anything, as a thread, detached in
the process of untwisting.
ravelin, rav'lin, *n.* [Fr. *ravelin,* from
It. *ravellino, revellino;* probably from
L. *re,* back, and *vallum,* a rampart.]
A detached triangular work in fortification, with two embankments
which form a projecting angle.
raven, rā'vn, *n.* [A.Sax. *hraefn*=Icel.
hrafn, D. *raaf,* Dan. *ravn,* O.H.G.
hraban, G. *rabe.* Like *crow,* ultimately
from its cry.] A large bird of a black
color, of the crow family, noted for
its hoarse cry and plundering habits;
found in every part of the globe.—*a.*
Resembling a raven, especially in
color; black (*raven* locks).
ravin, raven, rav'in, rav'en, *n.* [O.Fr.
ravine, from L. *rapina,* rapine. RAV-
INE.] Prey; plunder.—*v.i.* To prey
with rapacity; to show rapacity.—
v.t. To devour; to eat with voracity.
(O.T.)—**ravenous,** rav'en·us, *a.* Furiously voracious; hungry even to
rage; eager for gratification (a *ravenous* appetite).—**ravenously,** rav'en·-
us·li, *adv.* In a ravenous manner.—
ravenousness, rav'en·us·nes, *n.*
ravine, ra·vēn', *n.* [Fr. *ravine,* a
ravine, from L. *rapina,* rapine, violence, from *rapio,* to seize, or carry
away. RAPID.] A long deep hollow
worn by a stream or torrent of water;
any deep narrow gorge in a moun-

tain, etc.; a gully.
ravioli, ra·vē·ō'li, *n.* [It. pl. of
raviolo.] Small squares of dough
enclosing ground meat, etc., which
are cooked and served in a sauce.
ravish, rav'ish, *v.t.* [Fr. *ravir, ravis-
sant,* from L. *rapio, rapere,* to seize,
to snatch. RAPID.] To seize and
carry away by violence; to have
carnal knowledge of a woman by
force and against her consent; to
commit a rape upon; to deflower or
violate; to transport with joy or
delight; to enrapture; to enchant.—
ravisher, rav'ish·ėr, *n.* One that
ravishes.—**ravishing,** rav'ish·ing, *p.*
and *a.* Such as to ravish; delighting
to rapture; transporting.—**ravish-
ingly,** rav'ish·ing·li, *adv.* In a ravishing manner.—**ravishment,** rav'ish·-
ment, *n.* Ecstasy.
raw, rą, *a.* [A.Sax. *hreáw, hraew*=D.
raauw, Dan. *raa,* Icel. *hrár,* O.H.G.
rão, G. *roh,* raw; same root as L.
crudus, raw, *cruor,* blood: Gr. *kreas,*
flesh.] Not altered from its natural
state by cooking; not roasted, boiled,
or the like; not subjected to some
industrial or manufacturing process;
not manufactured (*raw* silk, *raw*
hides); not mixed or diluted (*raw*
spirits); not covered with the natural
covering; having the flesh exposed;
sore, as if galled; sensitive; immature; inexperienced; unripe in skill
(*raw* soldiers); bleak; chilly; cold
and damp (a *raw* day).—*n.* A raw,
galled, or sore place, as on a horse.—
rawboned, *a.* Having little flesh on
the bones; gaunt; lean and large-
boned.—**rawly,** rą'li, *adv.* In a raw
manner; especially, in an ignorant or
inexperienced manner.—**rawness,**
rą'nes, *n.* The state or quality of
being raw; want of cooking; state
of being inexperienced; chilliness
with dampness; bleakness.
ray, rā, *n.* [O.Fr. *ray,* a sunbeam,
from L. *radius,* a ray.] A line of light,
one of the lines that make up a
beam; *fig.* a beam of intellectual
light; a gleam; one of a number of
diverging radii; *bot.* the radiating
part of a flower; the outer part or
circumference of a compound radiate
flower; *ich.* one of the radiating bony
spines in the fins of fishes.—*Bec-
querel rays,* rays emitted by radioactive elements.—*Roentgen rays,*
rent'gen, or *X-rays,* rays of intense
penetrating power, enabling an operator to detect a body within an
organism, much used for surgical,
and to some extent for industrial,
purposes.—*Ultraviolet rays,* invisible
rays having a wave length between
the violet end of the visible spectrum
and X-rays, used in physical therapy
as a source of *Vitamin D.*—*Violet ray,*
shortest of visible wave lengths of
the spectrum.—*v.t.* To radiate; to
shoot forth or emit rays; to cause
to shine forth.—*v.i.* To shine forth
or out, as in rays.
ray, rā, *n.* [Fr. *raie,* from L. *raia,*
a ray.] One of a genus of cartilaginous
fishes, of which the skate is a well-
known example, having a flattened
body, with the pectoral fins extremely
broad and fleshy.

rayah, raia, rä'yä, *n.* In Turkey, a
person not a Mohammedan who
pays the capitation tax.
rayon, rā'on, *n.* [Arbitrarily formed
from E. *ray,* beam.] A synthetic
material formed by forcing viscose
through tiny holes and drying the
filaments.
raze, rāz, *v.t.*—*razed, razing.* [Same
word as *rase,* Fr. *raser,* to raze, to
shave, to demolish, from L. *rado,
rasum,* to scrape. RASE.] To graze;
to subvert from the foundation; to
overthrow; to demolish; to erase; to
efface; to extirpate; to destroy.
razor, rā'zor, *n.* [Fr. *rasoir,* from
raser, to shave.] A keen-edged steel
device used for shaving.—*Razorback,*
n. A species of hog having long legs
and a thin body; the rorqual whale.
See RORQUAL.
re, rē. Shortened form of Latin legal
expression *in re,* adopted in business
correspondence: with reference to,
in the matter of, a former communication or subject.
re, rā, *n. Music,* the name given to
the second of the syllables used in
solmization.
reabsorb, rē·ab·sorb', *v.t.* To absorb
or imbibe again.—**reabsorption,** rē·-
ab·sorp'shon, *n.* The act of reab-
sorbing.
reach, rēch, *v.t.* [A.Sax. *raecan,*
O.Fris. *rēka,* G. *reichen,* to reach,
to extend, to hold out; from same
root as *rich, right, rack, rake,* etc.;
L. *rego,* to govern, *rex,* a king, E.
regal.] To extend or stretch out; to
hold or put forth; to spread abroad:
often followed by *out* and *forth;* to
touch by extending the arm or
something in the hand; to extend to;
to stretch out as far, or as high as;
to give with the hand (*reach* me a
chair); to arrive at; to come to; to
get as far as (the ship *reached* her
port); to attain to by effort, labor,
or study; to gain or obtain; to
extend in action or influence to.—*v.i.*
To extend in space (to *reach* to
heaven); to extend in scope or
power; to stretch out the hand in
order to touch; to make efforts at
attainment.—*To reach after,* to make
efforts to attain to or obtain.—*n.* The
act or power of reaching; distance
to which one can reach; the sphere
to which an agency or a power is
limited; often the extent or limit of
human faculties or attainments;
scope; a stretch of water; a straight
portion of a river between any two
bendings.—**reacher,** rēch'ėr, *n.* One
who reaches.
react, ri·akt', *v.t.* To act or perform
anew.—*v.i.* To return an impulse or
impression; to resist the action of
another body by an opposite force;
to act in opposition; to act mutually
or reciprocally upon each other,
as two or more chemical agents.—
reactance, ri·ak'tans. [*Re,* back, and
act.] In an electric circuit carrying
alternating current, that part of the
impedance which is due to induction
and capacity.—**reaction,** ri·ak'shon,
n. The reciprocal action which two
bodies or two minds exert on each
other; action or tendency to revert

from a present to a previous condition; in *politics*, a tendency to revert from a more to a less advanced policy; *physics*, the resistance made by a body to anything tending to change its state; *chem.* the mutual or reciprocal action of chemical agents upon each other; *pathol.* a vital phenomenon arising from the application of an external influence; depression or exhaustion consequent on excessive excitement or stimulation, or increase of activity succeeding depression.—*Reaction wheel*, a turbine wheel.—**reactionary**, ri·ak'shon·a·ri, *a.* Pertaining to, proceeding from, or favoring reaction.—**reactionary, reactionist**, ri·ak'shon·ist, *n.* A favorer of reaction; one who attempts to check or reverse political progress.—**reactive**, ri·ak'tiv, *a.* Having power to react; tending to reaction.

reactor, ri·ak'tẽr, *n. Phys.* a device for the production and control of atomic energy.

read, rēd, *v.t.* pret. & pp. read (red). [A.Sax. *raedan*, to discern, to advise, to read; Icel. *rátha*, to advise, to read; D. *raden*, to advise, to interpret; G. *rathen*, O.H.G. *ratan*, to advise; same root as L. *reor, raius*, to suppose (RATE). Akin *riddle*. It would have been better to have retained the old spelling *red* for the pret. & pp.; comp. *lead* and *led*.] To peruse; to go over and gather the meaning of (to *read* a book, an author); to utter aloud, following something written or printed; to reproduce in sound; to see through; to understand from superficial indications (to *read* one's face); to discover by marks; to study by reading (to *read* law); to explain; to interpret (to *read* a riddle).—*To read up*, to make a special study of.—*v.i.* To perform the act of perusing; to read many books; to study for a specific object; to stand written or printed (the passage *reads* thus); to have a certain effect when read; to be coherent; to make sense: said of a sentence.—*To read between the lines*, to perceive and appreciate the real motive or meaning of a writing or work, as distinguished from what is openly professed or patent.—*n.* A reading over; perusal.—*a.* (red). Instructed or knowing by reading: hardly used except with the adverb *well* (*well read* in history).—**readable**, rē'da·bl, *a.* Capable of being read; legible; worth reading.—**readability, readableness**, rē·da·bil'i·ti, rē'da·bl·nes, *n.* The state of being readable.—**readably**, rē'da·bli, *adv.* In a readable manner.—**reader**, rē'dẽr, *n.* One who reads or peruses; one who studies; one whose office it is to read prayers, lessons, lectures, and the like to others; a reading book; one who corrects the errors in proof sheets; a corrector of the press.—**readership**, rē'dẽr·ship, *n.* The office of a reader.—**reading**, rē'ding, *n.* The act of one who reads; perusal; study of books (a man of extensive *reading*); a public recital or delivery of something written; a particular

version of a passage; a lection; view or interpretation of an author's meaning or intention; reproduction in accordance with such interpretation; rendering; *legislation*, the formal recital of a bill by the proper officer before the house which is to consider it (the bill passed the second *reading*).—*Thought reading*. See THOUGHT. —*a.* Addicted to the reading or study of books.—**reading desk**, *n.* A desk at which reading is performed.

readily, readiness. See READY.

readjust, rē·ad·just', *v.t.* To adjust or settle again; to put in order again.—**readjustment**, rē·ad·just'ment, *n.* The act of readjusting.

readmission, readmittance, rē·ad·mish'on, rē·ad·mit'ans, *n.* The act of admitting again.—**readmit**, rē·ad·mit', *v.t.* To admit again.

ready, red'i, *a.* [O.E. *redi, readi*, A.Sax. *raede*, ready=Dan. *rede*, Sw. *reda*, Icel. *reithr*, G. (be)*reit*, ready; perhaps from root of *ride*, *Array* is from this stem through the French.] Prepared at the moment; fit for immediate use; causing no delay from want of preparation; not slow, backward, dull, or hesitating (a *ready* apprehension); prompt; dexterous; not backward or reluctant; willing; inclined; offering itself at once; at hand; opportune, near, easy, convenient; on the point, eve, or brink: with *to*.—*Ready money*, means of immediate payment; cash. —*To make ready*, to make preparation; to get things in readiness.—**readily**, red'i·li, *adv.* In a ready manner; quickly; promptly; cheerfully.—**readiness**, red'i·nes, *n.* The state or quality of being ready; due preparation; aptitude; quickness; cheerfulness; alacrity.—**readymade**, *a.* Made or prepared beforehand, kept in stock ready for use or sale (*ready-made* clothes). —**ready-to-wear**, *n.* Ready-made clothes; clothes made beforehand in large quantities.—**ready-witted**, *a.* Having quick wit.

reaffirm, rē·af·fẽrm', *v.t.* To affirm again.—**reaffirmance**, rē·af·fẽr'mans, *n.* A second affirmation or confirmation.

reagent, rē·ā'jent, *n.* [REACT.] *Chem.* a substance employed to detect another by a reaction.

real, rē'al, *a.* [O.Fr. *real*, (Fr. *réel*), L.L. *realis*, from L. *res*, a thing (whence *rebus*, re- of *republic*).] Actually being or existing; not fictitious or imaginary (*real* life); genuine; not artificial, counterfeit, or fictitious; not affected; not assumed (his *real* character); *law*, pertaining to things fixed, permanent, or immovable, as to lands and tenements (*real* estate); opposed to *personal* or *movable* (property).—*Real presence*, the alleged actual presence of the body and blood of Christ in the Eucharist, or the conversion of the substance of the bread and wine into the real body and blood of Christ.—**realism**, rē'al·izm, *n.* The doctrines or principles of a realist.—**realist**, rē'al·ist, *n. Metaph.* as opposed to *idealist*, one

who holds the doctrine that there is an immediate or intuitive cognition of external objects, that external objects exist independently of our sensations or conceptions; *scholastic philos.* one who maintains that things, and not words, are the objects of dialectics: opposed to *nominalist*; *fine arts* and *literature*, one who endeavors to reproduce nature or describes real life just as it appears to him.—**realistic**, rē·al·is'tik, *a.* Pertaining to or characteristic of the realists; relating to realism.—**realistically**, rē·al·is'ti·kal·li, *adv.* In a realistic manner.—**reality**, ri·al'i·ti, *n.* [Fr. *réalité*.] The state or quality of being real; actual being or existence; actuality; truth; fact; that which is real as opposed to that which is imagination or pretense.—**realizable**, rē·al·ī·za·bl, *a.* Capable of being realized.—**realization**, rē'al·i·zā"shon, *n.* The act of realizing. —**realize**, rē'al·īz, *v.t.*—*realized, realizing*. [Fr. *réaliser*.] To make real; to bring into being or act (to *realize* a scheme or project); to feel as vividly or strongly as if real; to bring home to one's own case or experience; to acquire as the result of labor or pains; to gain (to *realize* profit from trade); to sell for or convert into money (to *realize* one's stock in a railroad).—*v.i.* To turn any kind of property into money.— **realizer**, rē'al·ī·zẽr, *n.* One who realizes.—**really**, rē'al·li, *adv.* In a real manner; in truth; actually; indeed; to tell the truth: often used familiarly as a slight corroboration of an opinion or declaration (well, *really*, I cannot say).—**realness**, rē'al·nes, *n.* The quality of being real; reality.—**realty**, rē'al·ti, *n.* [A contr. of *reality*.] *Law*, the fixed or permanent nature of that kind of property termed *real*; real property.

real, rē'al, *n.* [Sp. *real*, from royal.] A former Spanish coin.

realgar, rē·al'gar, *n.* [Fr. *réalgar*, from Sp. *rejalgar*, from Ar. *rahj*, powder, *al*, the, and *ghār*, a mine.] A mineral consisting of sulfur and arsenic in equal equivalents; red sulfide of arsenic, a brilliant red pigment. See ORPIMENT.

realm, relm, *n.* [O.Fr. *realme* (Fr. *royaume*), from L. *regalis*, from *rex, regis*, a king. REGAL.] A kingdom; a king's dominions; hence, generally, region, sphere, domain.

ream, rēm, *n.* [O.Fr. *raime*, from Sp. *resma*, a ream, from Ar. *rizmah*, a bale, a packet, a ream.] A bundle or package of paper, consisting generally of 20 quires, or 500 sheets.

ream, rēm, *v.t.* [Increase, to enlarge, from *rúm*, space. ROOM.] To bevel out, as a hole in metal; to enlarge, as the bore of a cannon; *naut.* to widen the seams between a vessel's planks for the purpose of calking them.— **reamer**, rē'mẽr, *n.* An instrument for enlarging a hole.

reanimate, rē·an'i·māt, *v.t.* To revive; to resuscitate; to restore to life or animation; to infuse new life or courage into.—**reanimation**, rē·an'i·mā"shon, *n.* The act of reanimating.

reap, rēp, *v.t.* [A.Sax. *rípan,* to reap; closely allied to Goth. *raupjan,* to pluck; D. *rapen,* to gather; L.G. *rapen,* to pluck. *Ripe* is from same stem.] To cut with a sickle, scythe, etc., as a grain crop; to cut down and gather; to gather when ripe or ready; to cut down the crop on; to clear of a grain crop (to *reap* a field); hence, to shave (*Shak.*); to receive as a reward, or as the fruit of labor or of works: in a good or bad sense.—*v.i.* To perform the act or operation of reaping; to receive the fruit of labor or works.— **reaper,** rē′pẽr, *n.* One who reaps; a machine for cutting grain; a reaping machine.—**reaping machine,** *n.* A machine for cutting down standing corn, etc., and in many cases also for forming it into sheaves, moved by horses or tractors through the field.

reappear, rē·ap·pẽr′, *v.i.* To appear again or anew.—**reappearance,** rē··ap·pē′rans, *n.* A second or new appearance.

reappoint, rē·ap·point′, *v.t.* To appoint again.—**reappointment,** rē··ap·point′ment, *n.* A renewed or second appointment.

rear, rēr, *n.* [O.F. *riere,* Pr. *reire,* from L. *retro,* behind—*re,* back, and suffix *tro,* denoting direction, from root corresponding to Skr. *tar,* to move. So *arrear,* from L. *ad,* to, and *retro.*] The part behind or at the back; the hind part; the background: generally with the definite article; specifically, the part of an army or a fleet which is behind the rest.—*a.* Pertaining to or in the rear; hindermost; last.— **rear admiral,** *n.* The third degree of the rank of admiral. ADMIRAL. —**rearmost,** rēr′mõst, *a.* Farthest in the rear; last of all.—**rearward,** rēr′ward, *n.* The rear guard; the latter part of anything.—*a.* At or toward the rear.

rear, rēr, *v.t.* [A.Sax. *raeran,* for *raeson,* to raise, caus. of *risan,* to rise. RAISE, RISE.] To lift or set up; to erect; to raise; to bring up, as young; to foster; to educate; to breed, as cattle; to build up; to construct (to *rear* an edifice).— *v.i.* To rise on the hind legs, as a horse; to assume an erect posture.

rearm, rē·ärm′, *v.t.* [Prefix, *re,* and *arm.*] To refurnish with arms.— **rearmament,** rē·är′ma·ment, *n.*

rearrange, rē′a·rānj, *v.t.* To arrange again; to put in proper order again.— **rearrangement,** rē·a·rānj′ment, *n.* A second or repeated arrangement.

reason, rē′zn, *n.* [Fr. *raison,* O.Fr. *reson,* from L. *ratio, rationis,* reason, plan, account, from *reor, ratus,* to think, to calculate. RATE, RATIFY, RATIO.] A motive, ground, or cause acting on the mind; the basis for any opinion, conclusion, or determination; a ground or a principle; what accounts for or explains a fact or phenomenon; final cause; explanation; a faculty of the mind by which it distinguishes truth from

falsehood, and which enables the possessor to deduce inferences from facts or from propositions, and to combine means for the attainment of particular ends; the act of deducing consequences from premises; ratiocination; justice; equity; fairness; that which is dictated or supported by reason; moderate demands; claims which reason and justice admit or prescribe (to bring one to *reason*).—*In reason, in all reason,* in justice; with rational ground.—*v.i.* To exercise the faculty of reason; to deduce inferences justly from premises; to argue; to ratiocinate; to discuss, in order to make something understood.— *v.t.* To examine or discuss by arguments; to debate or discuss (to *reason* the point); to persuade by reasoning or argument.—**reasonable,** rē′zn·a·bl, *a.* Having the faculty of reason; rational; governed by reason; not given to extravagant notions or expectations conformable or agreeable to reason; not extravagant, excessive, or immoderate; fair; equitable (any *reasonable* demands); being in mediocrity; moderate; tolerable.—**reasonableness,** rē′zn·a·bl·nes, *n.* The quality of being reasonable.—**reasonably,** rē′zn·a·bli, *adv.* In a reasonable manner; in consistency with reason; moderately; tolerably. — **reasoner,** rē′zn·ẽr, *n.* One who reasons or argues.—**reasoning,** rē′zn·ing, *n.* The act or process of exercising the faculty of reason; ratiocination; the arguments employed; the proofs or reasons when arranged and developed.—**reasonless,** rē′zn·les, *a.* Destitute of reason; irrational; unreasonable.

reassemble, rē·as·sem′bl, *v.t.* To collect or assemble again.—*v.i.* To assemble or meet together again.

reassume, rē·as·sūm′, *v.t.* To resume; to take again.

reassure, rē·a·shör′, *v.t.* To assure anew; to restore courage to; to free from fear or terror; also, to reinsure. —**reassurance,** rē·a·shö′rans, *n.* Assurance or confirmation repeated; also reinsurance.

reaumur, rā′o·myụr, *n.* [Inventor's name.] A thermometric scale on which the fixed points are 0° and 80°, answering respectively to 32° and 212° F.; denoted by R. See *Fahrenheit.*

rebaptize, rē·bap·tīz′, *v.t.* To baptize a second time.—**rebaptism,** rē··bap′tizm, *n.* A second baptism.

rebate, ri·bāt′, *v.t.*—*rebated, rebating.* [O.Fr. *rebatre*—*re,* back, and *batre,* L. *batuere,* to beat; akin *battle, batter, abate,* etc.] To blunt; to diminish, reduce, abate; to deduct or make a discount from.—*n.* (rē′bāt) Diminution; *com.* abatement in price; deduction.

rebate, rē·bāt′, *n.* See RABBET.

rebec, rebeck, rē′bek, *n.* [Fr. *rebec, rebebe,* from Ar. *rabāb,* a kind of musical instrument.] A stringed instrument introduced by the Moors into Spain, somewhat similar to the violin, and played with a bow.

rebel, reb′el, *n.* [Fr. *rebelle,* from L. *rebellis,* making war again—*re,* again, and *bellum,* war. DUEL.] One who revolts from the government to which he owes allegiance; one who defies and seeks to overthrow the authority to which he is rightfully subject. ∴ Syn. under INSURGENT.— *a.* Rebellious; acting in revolt.—*v.i.* (ri·bel′)—*rebelled, rebelling.* To revolt; to take up arms against the government of constituted authorities; to refuse to obey a superior; to shake off subjection; to turn with disgust or nausea; to conceive a loathing (his stomach *rebelled* at such food).—**rebellion,** ri·bel′yon, *n.* [L. *rebellio, rebellionis.*] The act of rebelling; an armed rising against a government; the taking of arms traitorously to resist the authority of lawful government; open resistence to, or refusal to obey, lawful authority. ∴ Syn. under INSURRECTION.—**rebellious,** ri·bel′yus, *a.* Engaged in, or characterized by, rebellion; mutinous.—**rebelliously,** ri·bel′yus·li, *adv.* In a rebellious manner.—**rebelliousness,** ri·bel′yus·nes, *n.*

rebirth, rē·bẽrth′, *n.* [Prefix *re,* and *birth.*] A new, or second, birth; a renaissance.

rebound, ri·bound′, *v.i.* [Prefix *re,* and *bound;* Fr. *rebondir,* to rebound.] To spring or bound back; to fly back by elastic force after impact on another body.—*v.t.* To drive back; to cause to echo; to reverberate.—*n.* (*pron.* rē′bound). The act of flying back on collision with another body; resilience.

rebuff, ri·buf′, *n.* [Prefix *re,* back, and old *buff,* a blow, from O.Fr. *buffe, bufe,* a blow. BUFFET.] A beating, forcing, or driving back; sudden check; a repulse; refusal; rejection of solicitation.—*v.t.* To beat back; to offer sudden resistance to; to repel the advances of.

rebuild, rē·bild′, *v.t.* To build again; to build after having been demolished.

rebuke, ri·būk′, *v.t.*—*rebuked, rebuking.* [Anglo-F. *rebuker,* O.Fr. *rebuchier,* to beat or strike back.] To check with reproof; to reprehend sharply and summarily; to reprimand; to reprove.—*n.* A direct and severe reprimand; reproof; reprehension; a childing.—**rebuker,** ri·bū′kẽr, *n.* One that rebukes.

rebus, rē′bus, *n.* [L., ablative plural of *res,* a thing—lit. by things, because the meaning is indicated by things.] A set of words written by figures or pictures of objects whose names resemble in sound those words or the syllables of which they are composed; thus, 'I can see you' might be expressed by figures of an eye, a can, the sea, and a ewe; hence, a kind of puzzle made up of such figures or pictures.

rebut, ri·but′, *v.t.*—*rebutted, rebutting.* [Fr. *rebuter, rebouter,* to put or thrust back—*re,* back, and *bouter,* to put, to thrust. BUTT.] To repel, as by counter evidence; to refute;

---

fāte, fär, fâre, fat, fạll; mē, met, hẽr; pīne, pin; nõte, not, mõve; tūbe, tub, bụll; oil, pound.

law, to oppose by argument, plea, or countervailing proof.—**rebuttal**, ri·but'al, *n*. The act of rebutting; refutation; confutation.—**rebutter**, ri·but'ẻr, *n. Law*, the answer of a defendant to a plaintiff's surre-joinder.

recalcitrate, ri·kal'si·trāt, *v.i.*—*recalcitrated, recalcitrating*. [L. *recalcitro*, to kick back—*re*, back, and *calcitrare*, to kick, from *calx, calcis*, the heel.] To show repugnance or resistance to something; to be refractory.—**recalcitration**, ri·kal'si·trā"shon, *n*. Act of recalcitrating; opposition; repugnance.—**recalcitrant**, ri·kal'si·trant, *a*. Exhibiting repugnance or opposition; not submissive; refractory.

recall, ri·kal', *v.t*. To call or bring back; to take back; to revoke; to annul by a subsequent act; to revive in memory; to order to come back from a place or mission (to *recall* a minister from a foreign court).—*n*. A calling back; revocation; the power of calling back or revoking; the removal of an official from office by a popular vote.

recant, ri·kant', *v.t. and i*. [L. *recantare*, to recant, to recall—*re*, back, and *canto*, freq. of *cano*, to sing. CHANT.] To retract; to unsay; to make formal contradiction of something which one had previously asserted.—**recantation**, rē·kan·tā'shon, *n*. The act of recanting; retraction; a declaration that contradicts a former one.—**recanter**, ri·kan'tẻr, *n*. One who recants.

recapitulate, rē·ka·pit'ū·lāt, *v.t.*—*recapitulated, recapitulating*. [Fr. *recapituler*, L.L. *recapitulo, recapitulatum*—prefix *re*, and *capitulum*, a head or heading. CAPITULATE.] To repeat or summarize, as the principal things mentioned in a preceding discourse; to give a summary of the principal facts, points, or arguments of.—*v.i*. To repeat in brief what has been said before.—**recapitulation**, rē·ka·pit'ū·lā"shon, *n*. The act of recapitulating; a concise statement of the principal points in a preceding discourse, argument, or essay.—*Recapitulation theory*, the theory that ancestral stages are repeated in the life history.—**recapitulatory**, rē·ka·pit'ū·la·to·ri, *a*. Containing recapitulation.

recapture, rē·kap'chẻr, *n*. The act of retaking; the retaking of goods from a captor; a prize retaken.—*v.t*. To capture back; to retake.

recast, rē·kast', *v.t*. To cast or found again; to throw again; to mold anew; to throw into a new form.

recede, ri·sēd', *v.i.*—*receded, receding*. [L. *recedo*—*re*, back, and *cedere*, to walk. CEDE.] To move back; to retreat; to withdraw; to withdraw from a claim or pretension; to relinquish what had been proposed or asserted (to *recede* from a demand, from propositions).—*v.t*. (rē·sēd'). To cede back; to grant or yield to a former possessor.

receipt, ri·sēt', *n*. [O.Fr. *recete, recepte* (Fr. *recette*), from L. *receptus*,-pp. of *recipere*, to receive. RECEIVE.]

The act of receiving (the *receipt* of a letter); that which is received; *pl*. money drawn or received; drawings (his *receipts* were $20 a day); a recipe; a prescription of ingredients for any composition, as of medicines, etc.; hence, *fig*. plan or scheme by which anything may be effected; a written acknowledgment of something received, as money, goods, etc.—*v.t*. To give a receipt for; to discharge, as an account.—**receiptor**, ri·sēt'ẻr, *n*. One who receipts; one who gives a receipt.

receive, ri·sēv', *v.t.*—*received, receiving*. [O.Fr. *recever, receveir*, Fr. *recevoir*, from L. *recipio*—*re*, again, and *capio*, to take. CAPABLE.] To get or obtain; to take, as a thing given, paid, communicated, etc.; to accept; to take into the mind; to embrace; to allow or hold, as a belief, custom, tradition, etc.; to give acceptance to; to allow to enter; to welcome; to be the object of.—*v.i*. To entertain callers; to be a recipient; to convert electrical signals so as to make them perceptible to the senses, as in telephone, radio, or television.—**receivable**, ri·sēv'a·bl, *a*. Such as may be received (accounts *receivable*).—**receiver**, ri·sē'vẻr, *n*. One who receives; a person appointed by a court to manage the affairs of an enterprise in reorganization or liquidation; a person appointed in some business for the purpose of winding up the concern; one who takes stolen goods from a thief, knowing them to be stolen; *chem*. a vessel for receiving and containing the product of distillation; a vessel to receive gases.—**receivership**, ri·sēv'ẻr·ship, *n*. The legal status of an enterprise under jurisdiction of the court for the purpose of a trust, reorganization, or liquidation.—**receiving set**, *n*. A radio instrument, or set, used in the reception of radio programs or signals.

recense,† ri·sens', *v.t.*—*recensed, recensing*. [L. *recensere*, to review or examine—*re*, again, and *censere*, to reckon. CENSOR.] To review; to revise.—**recension**, ri·sen'shon, *n*. An examination; enumeration; a revision of the text of an author by a critical editor; an edited version.

recent, rē'sent, *a*. [Fr. *récent*, from L. *recens, recentis*, recent; etym. unknown.] Of late origin, occurrence, or existence; new; not of remote date, antiquated style, and the like; modern; only made known or spoken of lately; fresh (*recent* intelligence); *geol*. applied to all accumulations and deposits whose remains belong exclusively to species still existing; occurring or formed since the glacial period.—**recently**, rē'sent·li, *adv*. Newly; lately; freshly; not long since.—**recentness**, rē'sent·nes, *n*.

receptacle, ri·sep'ta·kl or res'ep·ta·kl, *n*. [L. *receptaculum*, from *recipio, receptum*, to receive. RECEIVE.] That which receives, admits, or contains things; a place or vessel

in which anything is received and contained; a repository; *bot*. a general term given to a part which receives or bears other parts; as, that part of a flower upon which the carpels are situated; that part of the axis of a plant which forms a sort of disk bearing the flowers.

reception, ri·sep'shon, *n*. [L. *receptio*, from *recipio*, to receive. RECEIVE.] A receiving or manner of receiving; receipt; treatment at first coming; welcome; entertainment; a formal occasion or ceremony of receiving guests, official personages, etc.; admission or credence, as of an opinion or doctrine; acceptance or allowance; in *radio*, the act or process of receiving programs or signals.—**receptive**, ri·sep'tiv, *a*. Such as to receive readily (*receptive* of teaching); taking in; able to take in hold, or contain.—**receptivity**, **receptiveness**, rē'sep·tiv"i·ti, ri·sep'tiv·nes, *n*.—**receptor**, ri·sep'tẻr, *n. Physiol*. a sense organ, especially a nerve ending, which receives stimuli.

recess, ri·ses', *n*. [L. *recessus*, from *recedo, recessum*. RECEDE.] A withdrawing or retiring; a moving back (the *recess* of the tides); place of retirement or secrecy; private abode; the time or period during which public or other business is suspended (the Christmas *recess* of a school); a cavity, niche, or sunken space formed in a wall; an alcove or similar portion of a room.—*v.t*. To make a recess in; to put in a recess.—**recession**, ri·sesh'on, *n*. [L. *recessio, recessionis*, from *recedo*; in last sense directly from *re* and *cession*.] The act of receding; withdrawal; position relatively withdrawn; a cession or granting back; retrocession.—*Recession of the equinoxes*, the same as *Precession of the equinoxes*.—**recessional**, *n*. Glacial deposit remaining after the ice sheet receded; hymn or other verses sung after service, when the choir and clergy withdraw from their places.—**recessive,†** ri·ses'iv, *a*. Receding; going back.

recharter, rē·chär'tẻr, *v.t*. To charter again; to grant another charter to.

recherché, rē·shär·shā', *a*. [Fr.] Much sought after; choice; rare; exquisite.

recidivist, ri·sid'i·vist, *n*. [Fr. *récidiviste*—L. *re*, back, *cado*, to fall.] A relapsed criminal or one who returns to crime.

recipe, res'i·pē, *n*. [L. *recipe*, take, receive, imper. of *recipio*, to take or receive. RECEIVE.] The first word of a physician's prescription; hence the prescription itself; now applied to a receipt for preparing, mixing, or cooking food to produce a particular dish.

recipient, ri·sip'i·ent, *n*. [L. *recipiens, recipientis*, ppr. of *recipio*. RECEIVE.] A person or thing that receives; one to whom anything is communicated.—*a*. Receiving.—**recipience, recipiency**, ri·sip'i·ens, ri·sip'i·en·si, *n*. A receiving; act or capacity of receiving; reception.

reciprocal, ri·sip'ro·kal, *a*. [L. *reci-*

procus, Fr. *réciproque*, alternating, reciprocal, probably connected with *re*, back, and *pro*, forward.] Acting with a backward and forward motion; moving backward and forward; reciprocating; done by each to the other; mutual; mutually interchangeable; *gram.* reflexive.—*Reciprocal* or *inverse proportion.* Under INVERSE.—*Reciprocal quantities*, *math.* quantities which, multiplied together, produce unity.—*Reciprocal ratio* is the ratio between the reciprocals of two quantities; thus the *reciprocal ratio* of 4 to 9 is that of 1-4th to 1-9th.—*n.* That which is reciprocal to another thing.—*Reciprocal of a quantity*, in *math.* the quotient resulting from the division of unity by the quantity; thus, the *reciprocal* of 4 is ¼, and conversely the *reciprocal* of ¼ is 4.—**reciprocally**, ri·sip′ro·kal·li, *adv.* In a reciprocal manner; mutually; interchangeably; inversely.—**reciprocality**, ri·sip′ro·kal″i·ti, *n.* The state or quality of being reciprocal.—**reciprocate**, ri·sip′ro·kāt, *v.i.*—*reciprocated, reciprocating.* To move backward and forward; to have an alternate movement; to alternate.—*v.t.* To interchange; to give and return mutually; to give in requital (to *reciprocate* favors).—**reciprocating**, ri·sip′-ro·kāt·ing, *p.* and *a.* Alternating; moving backward and forward alternately.—*Reciprocating engine*, that form of engine in which the piston and piston rod move back and forth in a straight line, absolutely, or relatively to the cylinder.—**reciprocation**, ri·sip′ro·kā″shon, *n.* The act of reciprocating; interchange of acts; a mutual giving and returning; alternation.—**reciprocity**, res·i·pros′i·ti, *n.* The state or character of being reciprocal; reciprocal obligation or right; equal rights or benefits to be mutually yielded or enjoyed; especially equal commercial rights or privileges enjoyed mutually by two countries trading together.

recision, ri·sizh′on, *n.* [L. *recisio—re*, back, and *caedo*, to cut. EXCISION.] The act of cutting off.

recite, ri·sīt′, *v.t.*—*recited, reciting.* [Fr. *réciter*, from L. *recitare—re*, again, and *cito*, to cite. CITE.] To repeat, as something prepared, written down, or committed to memory beforehand; to rehearse, with appropriate gestures, before an audience; to tell over; to relate or narrate; to go over in particulars; to recapitulate.—*v.i.* To rehearse before an audience compositions committed to memory; to rehearse a lesson.—**reciter**, ri·sī′ter, *n.* One that recites or rehearses; a narrator.—**recital**, ri·sī′tal, *n.* The act of reciting; the repetition of the words of another; narration; a telling of the particulars of an adventure or event; that which is recited; a story; a narrative; a musical entertainment given by a single performer (an organ *recital*).—**recitation**, res·i·tā′shon, *n.* The act of reciting; the delivery aloud, with appropriate gestures, before an audience, of a composition

committed to memory, as an elocutionary exhibition; the rehearsal of a lesson by pupils before their instructor.—**recitative**, res′i·ta·tēv″, *n.* [It. *recitativo.*] *Music.* a species of vocal composition which differs from an air in having no definite rhythmical arrangement, and no strictly constructed melody; musical recitation or declamation; a piece of music to be sung recitatively.

reck, rek, *v.i.* [A.Sax. *reccan, récan*, to reck, regard; cog. O.Sax. *rókian*, Icel. *raekja*, O.H.G. *róhhian, geruochen*, to reck or care; perhaps same root as *reckon.*] *Obs.* To care; to mind; to heed; to regard; often followed by *of.*—*v.t.* To heed, regard, care for.—*It recks (impersonal)*, it concerns (*it recks* me not).—**reckless**, rek′les, *a.* Not recking; careless; heedless of consequences; mindless; with *of* before an object. ∴ Syn. under RASH.—**recklessly**, rek′les·li, *adv.* In a reckless manner.—**recklessness**, rek′les·nes, *n.* The state or quality of being reckless.

reckon, rek′n, *v.t.* [O.E. *rekken, rekenen*, A.Sax. *gerecnian, recenian*= D. *rekenen*, Dan. *regne*, Icel. *reikna*, Sw. *räkna*, G. *rechnen*, to reckon, number, esteem; perhaps from same root as *reck* or *right.*] To count; to number; to tell one by one; to calculate; to estimate by rank or quality; to esteem, account, repute, hold.—*v.i.* To make computation; to compute; to calculate; to make up or render an account; to adjust relations of desert and penalty; to think, suppose, imagine (in this sense American rather than English).—*To reckon on* or *upon*, to count or depend upon.—*To reckon with*, to call to account; to exact penalty of.—**reckoner**, rek′n·er, *n.* One who reckons; something that assists a person to reckon.—**reckoning**, rek′n·ing, *n.* The act of computing; calculation; a statement and comparison of accounts for adjustment; the charges made by a host in a hotel, tavern, etc. (to pay the *reckoning*); *naut.* the calculation of the position of a ship from the rate found by the log, and the course as determined by the compass.

reclaim, ri·klām′, *v.t.* [Re and *claim*; Fr. *réclamer*, to claim back, to reclaim a hawk, to protest; L. *reclamo—re*, back, and *clamo*, to call. CLAIM.] To claim back; to demand to have returned; to call back; to bring a hawk to the wrist by a certain call; to reduce from a wild to a tame or domestic state; to tame; to rescue from being wild, desert, or waste; to bring under cultivation; to bring back from error; to reform.—*v.i.* To cry out; to exclaim against anything; *Scots law*, to appeal to the inner house of the Court of Session.—*n.* The act of reclaiming; reformation.—**reclaimable**, ri·klā′ma·bl, *a.* Capable of being reclaimed.—**reclamation**, rek·la·mā′shon, *n.* The act of reclaiming; the act of bringing into cultivation; the bringing back of a person from evil courses; a demand;

claim made; a remonstrance or representation.

recline, ri·klīn′, *v.t.*—*reclined, reclining.* [L. *reclino*, to bend back—*re*, back, and *clino*, to bend (whence also *incline, decline*); root same as that of E. to *lean.*] To lean to one side or sidewise; to lay down to rest (to *recline* the head).—*v.i.* To rest or repose; to take a recumbent position.—**recliner**, ri·klī′ner, *n.* One who reclines.

recluse, ri·klös′, *a.* [Fr. *reclus*, fem. *recluse*, from L. *reclusus*, pp. of *recludo, reclusum*, to lay open, but in L.L. signifying to shut—*re*, again, back, and *claudere*, to shut. CLOSE.] Living shut up or apart from the world; retired; sequestered; solitary.—*n.* A person who lives in retirement or seclusion; a hermit; a religious devotee who lives in an isolated cell.—**reclusion**, ri·klö′zhon, *n.* A state of retirement from the world; seclusion.—**reclusive**, ri·klö′siv, *a.* Affording retirement from society; recluse.

recognize, rek′og·nīz, *v.t.*—*recognized, recognizing.* [From *recognisance* (which is older in English), O.Fr. *recognoissance*, from L. *recognosco—re* and *cognosco.* COGNITION, KNOW.] To recall or recover the knowledge of; to perceive the identity of, with a person or thing formerly known; to know again; to avow or admit a knowledge of; to acknowledge formally; to indicate one's notice by a bow or nod; *Parliamentary*, to give a speaker the floor in debate (by a presiding officer); to indicate appreciation of (to *recognize* services by a reward).—*v.i. Law*, to enter into recognizances.—**recognition**, rek·og·nish′on, *n.* [L. *recognitio.*] The act of recognizing or state of being recognized; a perceiving as being known; avowal; notice taken; acknowledgment.—*Recognition markings*, in birds and mammals, conspicuous markings supposed to aid mutual recognition by members of a species.—**recognitory**, ri·kog′ni·to·ri, *a.* Pertaining to recognition.—**recognizable**, rek′og·nī″za·bl, *a.* Capable of being recognized.—**recognizance**, ri·kog′ni·zans or ri·kon′i·zans, *n.* [Fr. *reconnaissance*, O.Fr. *recognoissance.*] Act of recognizing; recognition; mark or badge of recognition; token; *law*, an obligation which a man enters into before a proper tribunal, with condition to do some particular act, failure of which results in forfeiture.

recoil, ri·koil′, *v.i.* [Fr. *reculer*, from L. *re*, back, and *culus*, the posteriors; same root as in Gael. *cul*, W. *cil*, the back.] To rebound; to fall back; to take a sudden backward motion after an advance; to be forced to retreat; to return after a certain strain or impetus (the gun *recoils*); to start or draw back as from anything repulsive, alarming, or the like; to shrink.—*n.* (ré′koil). A starting or falling back; rebound; the rebound or resilience of a firearm when discharged; a shrinking back.

recoin, rē·koin′, *v.t.* To coin again.—
recoinage, rē·koi′nij, *n.* The act of coining anew.

recollect, rek′ol·lekt, *v.t.* [Lit. to collect or gather again.] To recover or recall the knowledge of; to bring back to the mind or memory; to remember; *refl.* to recover resolution or composure of mind; to collect one's self. ∴ Syn. under REMEMBER. —**recollection,** rek·ol·lek′shon, *n.* The act of recollecting or recalling to the memory; a bringing back to mind; remembrance; the power of recalling ideas to the mind, or the period over which such power extends; that which is recollected; something recalled to mind. ∴ Syn. under MEMORY.—**recollective,** rek′-ol·lek′tiv, *a.* Having the power of recollecting.

re-collect, rē·kol·lekt′, *v.t.* To collect or gather again; to collect what has been scattered.

recombine, rē·kom·bīn′, *v.t.* To combine again.

recommence, rē·kom·mens′, *v.t.* and *i.* To commence again; to begin anew.—**recommencement,** rē·kom·mens′ment, *n.* A commencement anew.

recommend, rek·om·mend′, *v.t.* [*Re* and *commend*; Fr. *recommander,* to recommend, to commend, to entrust.] To commend to another's notice; to put in a favorable light before another; to commend or give favorable representations of; to make acceptable; to attract favor to; hence, to *recommend itself,* to make itself approved; to advise, as to an action, practice, measure, remedy, etc.; to set forward as advisable.— **recommendation,** rek′om·men·dā″-shon, *n.* The act of recommending; a favorable representation; that which procures favor or a favorable reception.—**recommendatory,** rek·-om·men′da·to·ri, *a.* Serving to recommend.—**recommender,** rek·om-men′dĕr, *n.* One who recommends.

recommit, rē·kom·mit′, *v.t.* To commit again (as persons to prison); to refer again to a committee.— **recommitment, recommittal,** rē·-kom·mit′ment, rē·kom·mit′al, *n.* A second or renewed commitment; a renewed reference to a committee.

recompense, rek′om·pens, *v.t.*—*recompensed, recompensing.* [Fr. *récompenser,* L.L. *recompenso*—L. *re,* again, and *compenso, compensatum,* to compensate. COMPENSATE.] To give or render an equivalent to, as for services, loss, etc.; to reward; to requite; to compensate; to return an equivalent for; to make amends for by anything equivalent; to make compensation for.—*n.* An equivalent returned for anything given, done, or suffered, compensation, reward; amends.

reconcile, rek′on·sīl, *v.t.*—*reconciled, reconciling.* [Fr. *réconcilier,* from L. *reconcilio*—*re,* again, and *concilio,* to conciliate. CONCILIATE.] To conciliate anew; to restore to union and friendship after estrangement; to adjust or settle (differences, quarrels); to bring to acquiescence or

quiet submission (to *reconcile* one's self to afflictions); to make consistent or congruous, followed by *with* or *to*; to remove apparent discrepancies from; to harmonize.—*v.i.* To become reconciled.—**reconcilement,** rek′on·sīl′ment, *n.* Reconciliation; renewal of friendship.— **reconciliation,** rek′on·sil·i·ā″shon, *n.* [L. *reconciliate.*] The act of reconciling parties at variance; renewal of friendship after disagreement or enmity; *Scrip.* atonement; expiation; the act of harmonizing or making consistent; agreement of things seemingly opposite or inconsistent.—**reconciliatory,** rek′-on·sil′i·a·to·ri, *a.* Able or tending to reconcile.—**reconcilable,** rek·on-sī′la·bl, *a.* Capable of being again brought to friendly feelings; capable of being made to agree or be consistent; capable of being harmonized.

recondite, rek′on·dīt or re·kon′dīt, *a.* [L. *reconditus,* pp. or *recondo*—*re,* back, and *condo,* to conceal (as in *abscond*).] Hidden from the mental perception; abstruse; profound; dealing with things abstruse.

recondition, rē·kon·dish′un, *v.t.* To put something in good condition by repairing, adjusting, etc.

reconnaissance, re·kon′nā·sans, *n.* [Fr. RECONNOITER.] The act or operation of reconnoitering; preliminary examination or survey of a territory or of an enemy's position, for the purpose of directing military operations.—*Reconnaissance in force,* a demonstration by a considerable body of men for the purpose of discovering the position or strength of an enemy.

reconnoiter, reconnoitre, rek·on-noi′tĕr, *v.t.*—*reconnoitered, reconnoitering.* [O.Fr. *reconnoitre,* Fr. *reconnaître,* from L. *recognosco*—*re,* again, and *cognosco.* The elements of the word are same as in *recognize* (which see).] To make a preliminary survey of; to examine or survey, as a tract or region, for military or engineering purposes.

reconquer, rē·kong′kĕr, *v.t.* To conquer again; to recover by conquest; to recover; to regain.

reconsider, rē·kon·sid′ĕr, *v.t.* To consider again; to turn over in the mind again; to take into consideration a second time, generally with the view of rescinding.— **reconsideration,** rē′kon·sid·ĕr·ā″-shon, *n.* The act of reconsidering.

reconstruct, rē·kon·strukt′, *v.t.* To construct again; to rebuild.—**reconstruction,** rē·kon·struk′shon, *n.* Act of constructing again; something reconstructed; *U. S. History,* the governmental reorganization of the seceded states after the Civil War.

reconvene, rē·kon·vēn′, *v.t.* To convene or call together again.—*v.i.* To reassemble.

reconvert, rē·kon·vĕrt′, *v.t.* To convert again.—**reconversion,** rē·kon-vĕr′zhon, *n.* A second or renewed conversion.

reconvey, rē·kon·vā′, *v.t.* To convey back or to its former place; to transfer back to a former owner.—

reconveyance, rē·kon·vā′ans, *n.* The act of reconveying; the act of transferring back to a former proprietor.

record, ri·kord′, *v.t.* [Fr. *recorder,* to get by heart, formerly also to record, from L. *recordor,* to remember—*re,* again, and *cor, cordis,* the heart.] To preserve the memory of by written or other characters, to register; to note, to write down or enter in order to preserve evidence; to cause to be inscribed on a phonograph record, or on a wire or tape, as to *record* music; to imprint deeply on the mind or memory.—*n.* (rek′ord). Something set down in writing for the purpose of preserving the knowledge of it; a register; an authentic or official account of facts or proceedings, entered in a book for preservation; the book or document containing such; a public document; the known facts in a person's life, especially in that of a public figure; the best of recorded achievements in competitive sports as, the world's *record.*—*Court of record,* one of the higher courts in which the records of the suits are preserved. —*Phonograph record,* a cylinder or disc upon which a transcription of sound has been made.—**recorder,** ri·kor′der, *n.* One who records official transactions; in the United States, a judge with first jurisdiction in criminal cases, or a magistrate's jurisdiction; in England, the chief judicial officer of a borough or city; an old musical instrument, somewhat like a flageolet; a registering apparatus.

recount, ri·kount′, *v.t.* [Fr. *reconter* —*re,* and *conter,* to tell.] To relate in detail; to count again; to count ballots again when the result of the first count has been challenged by a defeated candidate.

recoup, ri·köp′, *n.* [From Fr. *recoupe,* cloth remaining after cutting out clothes, from *re,* back, and *couper,* to cut.] *Law,* a sum kept back; a deduction; discount.—*v.t.* *Law,* to keep back as a set-off or discount; hence, *refl.* to indemnify one's self for a loss or damage by a corresponding advantage.—**recoupment,** ri·köp′ment, *n.* The act of recouping.

recourse, ri·kōrs′, *n.* [Fr. *recours,* from L. *recursus,* a running back, a return, from *recurro,* to run back— *re,* back, and *curro,* to run. COURSE.] A going to, as for help or protection; a recurrence in difficulty, perplexity, need, or the like.

recover, ri·kuv′ĕr, *v.t.* [O.Fr. *recovrer* (Fr. *recouvrer*), from L. *recuperare,* to recover; of doubtful origin.] To regain, to get or obtain after being lost; to get back; to restore from sickness, faintness, or the like; to revive; to cure; to heal; to retrieve; to make up for; to rescue; *law,* to gain as a compensation; to obtain in return for injury or debt; to obtain title to by judgment in a court of law.—*v.i.* To regain health after sickness; to grow well again; to regain a former state or condition, as after misfortune or disturbance of mind; to succeed in a lawsuit.—**recoverable**, ri·kuv′ėr·a·bl, *a.* Capable of being regained or recovered; obtainable from a debtor or possessor. —**recoverer**, ri·kuv′ėr·ėr, *n.* One who recovers.—**recovery**, ri·kuv′ėr·i, *n.* The act or power of regaining or getting again; restoration from sickness or faintness; restoration from low condition or misfortune; *law*, the obtaining of right to something by a verdict and judgment of court from an opposing party in a suit.

recreant, rek′ri·ant, *a.* [O.Fr. *recreant*, ppr. of *recroire*, L.L. *recredere*, to give in, to confess defeat— L. *re*, again, and *credo*, to believe. See MISCREANT.] Craven; yielding to an enemy; cowardly; mean-spirited; apostate; false.—*n.* One who basely yields; one who begs for mercy; a mean-spirited, cowardly wretch.— **recreantly**, rek′ri·ant·li, *adv.* In a recreant manner; basely; falsely.— **recreancy**, rek′ri·an·si, *n.* The quality of being recreant; cowardice.

recreate, rek′ri·āt, *v.t.*—*recreated, recreating*. [L. *recreo, recreatum*—*re*, again, and *creo*, to create. CREATE.] To revive or refresh after toil or exertion; to reanimate; as languid spirits or exhausted strength; to amuse; to divert; to gratify.—*v.i.* To take recreation.—*v.t.* (rē′kri·āt′). [Directly from *re* and *create*.] To create or form anew.—**recreation**, rek·ri·ā′shon, *n.* The act of recreating or the state of being recreated; refreshment of the strength and spirits after toil; amusement; entertainment.—**recreative**, rek′ri·ā·tiv, *a.* Tending to recreate; refreshing; diverting.—**recreatively**, rek′ri·ā·tiv·li, *adv.* In a recreative manner.—**recreativeness**, rek′ri·ā·tiv·nes, *n.*

recrement, rek′ri·ment, *n.* [L. *recrementum*, from *recerno*—*re*, back, and *cerno*, to separate. SECRET.] Superfluous matter separated from that which is useful; dross; scoria; spume.—**recremental**, **recrementitious**, rek·ri·men′tal, rek′ri·men·tish″us, *a.* Drossy; consisting of superfluous matter separated from that which is valuable.

recriminate, ri·krim′i·nāt, *v.i.*—*recriminated, recriminating*. [L. *re*, again, and *criminor*, I accuse. CRIME.] To return one accusation with another; to charge an accuser with the like.—*v.t.* To accuse in return.— **recrimination**, ri·krim′i·nā″shon, *n.* The act of recriminating; the return of one accusation with another; *law*, an accusation brought by the accused against the accuser upon the same fact; a counter-accusation.—**recriminative, recriminatory**, ri·krim′i·ni·tiv, ri·krim′i·ni·to·ri, *a.* Recriminating or retorting accusation.

recross, rē·kros′, *v.t.* To cross again.

recrudescent, rē·krö·des′ent, *a.* [L. *recrudesco*—*re*, again, and *crudescere*, to become raw, from *crudus*, raw. CRUDE.] Recurring; renewing activ-

ity, as of an illness.—**recrudescence, recrudescency**, rē·krö·des′ens, rē·krö·des′en·si, *n.* The state of being recrudescent; *med.* increased severity of a disease after temporary remission.

recruit, ri·kröt′, *v.t.* [Fr. *recruter*, from *recrute*, a participial noun from O.Fr. *recroistre*, pp. *recrû*, from L. *recresco*—*re*, again, and *cresco*, to grow (seen in *crescent, increase,* etc.). CRESCENT.] To repair by fresh supplies; to restore the wasted vigor of; to renew the health, spirits, or strength of; to refresh; to supply with new men; to make up by enlistment (to *recruit* an army).— *v.i.* To gain new supplies of anything wasted; to gain flesh, health, spirits, etc.; to raise new soldiers.—*n.* A soldier newly enlisted.—**recruiter**, ri·kröt′er, *n.* One who recruits.— **recruitment**, ri·kröt′ment, *n.* The act of recruiting.

recrystallize, rē·kris′tal·īz, *v.t.* To crystallize a second time.—**recrystallization**, rē·kris′tal·i·zā′shon, *n.* The process of recrystallizing.

rectal. See RECTUM.

rectangle, rek′tang·gl, *n.* [L. *rectangulus*—*rectus*, right, and *angulus*, an angle.] A right-angled parallelogram; a quadrilateral figure having all its angles right angles.—**rectangular**, rek·tang′gū·lėr, *a.* Right angled; having an angle or angles of ninety degrees.—**rectangularly**, rek·tang′gū·lėr·li, *adv.* In a rectangular manner; with or at right angles.

rectify, rek′ti·fī, *v.t.*—*rectified, rectifying*. [Fr. *rectifier*, from L. *rectus*, right, and *facio*, to make.] To make or put right; to correct when wrong, erroneous, or false; to amend; to refine by repeated distillation or sublimation; to convert (alcohol) into gin, etc., by flavoring specially.—**rectifiable**, rek′ti·fī·a·bl, *a.* Capable of being rectified or set right.— **rectification**, rek′ti·fi·kā″shon, *n.* The act or operation of rectifying; the act of setting right that which is wrong; the process of refining or purifying by repeated distillation. —*Rectification of a globe*, the adjustment of it preparatory to the solution of a proposed problem.—**rectifier**, rek′ti·fī·ėr, *n.* One who or that which rectifies; one who refines by repeated distillations; a device for obtaining direct electric current from alternating current. See THERMIONIC VALVE.

rectilinear, rectilineal, rek·ti·lin′i·ėr, rek·ti·lin′i·al, *a.* [L. *rectus*, right, and *linea*, a line.] Bounded by straight lines; consisting of a straight line or of straight lines; straight.—**rectilinearly**, rek·ti·lin′i·ėr·li, *adv.* In a rectilinear manner; in a right line.

rectirostral, rek·ti·ros′tral, *a.* [L. *rectus*, straight, and *rostrum*, a beak.] Having a straight beak.

rectitude, rek′ti·tūd, *n.* [L. *rectitudo*, from *rectus*, pp. of *rego, rectum*, to keep or lead straight. REGENT.] Rightness of principle or practice; uprightness; integrity; honesty; probity; correctness.

recto, rek′tō, *n.* [L. *rectus*, right.] The right-hand page of an open book; the right-hand side of a sheet of paper, as opposed to *verso*, on the reverse.

rector, rek′tėr, *n.* [L. *rector*, a ruler, from *rego, rectum*, to rule, to keep right. RECTITUDE.] A clergyman of the Protestant Episcopal Church, elected by the vestrymen, who has charge of a parish, and to whom belong the parsonage and tithes; the chief elective officer of some universities, as in France and Scotland; in Scotland also the title of the headmaster of an academy or important public school.—**rectorial**, rek·tō′ri·al, *a.* Pertaining to a rector or to a rectory.—*Rectorial tithes*, great or praedial tithes.—**rectory**, rek′to·ri, *n.* A parish church or parish held by a rector; a rector's mansion or parsonage.

rectrix, rek′triks, *n.* pl. **rectrices**, rek·trī′sēz. [L. *rectrix*, a female governor. RECTOR.] One of the long quill feathers in the tail of a bird, which like a rudder direct its flight.

rectum, rek′tum, *n.* [L. *rectum*, straight, because once thought to be straight.] *Anat.* the third and last part of the large intestine opening at the anus.—**rectal**, rek′tal, *a.* Relating to the rectum.

recumbent, ri·kum′bent, *a.* [L. *recumbens, recumbentis*, ppr. of *recumbo* —*re*, back, and *cumbo*, to lie. IN-CUMBENT.] Leaning; reclining; lying down; reposing; inactive; *zool.* and *bot.* applied to a part that leans or reposes upon anything.—**recumbency**, ri·kum′ben·si, *n.* The state of being recumbent; the posture of reclining, or lying; rest; repose; idle state.—**recumbently**, ri·kum′bent·li, *adv.* In a recumbent posture.

recuperate, ri·kū′pėr·āt, *v.t.*—*recuperated, recuperating*. [L. *recupero, recuperatum*. RECOVER.] To recover; to regain.—*v.i.* To recover; to regain health.—**recuperation**, ri·kū′pėr·ā″shon, *n.* [L. *recuperatio*.] Recovery. —**recuperative, recuperatory**, ri·kū′pėr·a·tiv, ri·kū′pėr·a·to·ri, *a.* Tending to recovery; pertaining to recovery.

recur, ri·kėr′, *v.i.*—*recurred, recurring*. [L. *recurro*—*re*, and *curro*, to run. CURRENT.] To return; to return to the thought or mind; to have recourse; to turn for aid; to occur again or be repeated at a stated interval, or according to some regular rule.—**recurrence**, ri·kėr′ens, *n.* The act of recurring, or state of being recurrent; return; resort; recourse.—**recurrent**, ri·kėr′ent, *a.* Returning from time to time; turned back in its course.— **recurring**, ri·kėr′ing, *a.* Returning again.—*Recurring* or *circulating decimals*. See CIRCULATING.

recurvate, recurved, ri·kėr′vāt, ri·kėrvd′, *a.* [L. *re*, back, and *curvus*, bent.] *Bot.* bent, bowed, or curved backward or outward (a *recurvate* leaf, etc.).—**recurve**, ri·kėrv′, *v.t.* *recurved, recurving*. To bend back. **recusant**, rek′ū·zant, *a.* [Fr. *récu-*

sant, L. *recusans, recusantis,* ppr. of *recuso,* to refuse, to reject—*re,* back, and *causa,* cause.] Obstinate in refusal; refusing to acknowledge the supremacy of a sovereign, or to conform to the established rites of a church.—*n.* One obstinate in refusing; one who will not conform to general opinion or practice; specifically—*Eng. hist.* a nonconformist.—**recusancy,** rek′ū·zan·si, *n.* The state of being a recusant; the tenets of a recusant; nonconformity.

red, red, *a.* [A.Sax. *redd,* red; cog. Dan. and Sw. *röd,* Icel. *rauthr* (*raudr*), D. *rood,* G. *roth,* Goth. *rauds;* same root as in L. *rufus, ruber,* G. *erythros,* W. *rhudd,* Ir. and Gael. *ruadh,* red; Skr. *rudhira,* blood. Akin are *ruddy, russet, ruby, rubric,* etc.] Of a bright warm color resembling blood; a general term applied to many different shades or hues, as crimson, scarlet, vermillion, etc.; often used in forming compound words which are self-explanatory (*red-backed, red-breasted, red-cheeked,* etc.).—*Red admiral,* a beautiful species of butterfly.—*Red cedar,* a species of North American and West Indian juniper, of which the heartwood is in great demand for the manufacture of lead pencils. —*Red chalk.* REDDLE.—*Red deer,* the common stag, a native of the forests of Europe and Asia; still plentiful in the Highlands of Scotland.—*Red gum,* an eruptive skin disease to which infants are subject.—*Red herring,* the common herring highly salted, dried, and smoked, so as to keep for a long time; something cast in the path as a means of diverting the attention of persons, or the scent of hounds, from the real object; something to sidetrack an issue. (*Colloq.*)—*Red Indian* or *Red man,* one of the copper-colored aborigines of America.—*Red ochre,* a name common to a variety of pigments. — *Red orpiment.* REALGAR.—*Red pine,* a species of pine, the *Scotch* or *Norway Pine.*—*Red republican,* an extreme republican, so called because in the first French revolution the extreme republicans were in the habit of wearing a red cap; often contracted into *red* (he is one of the *reds*).—*n.* A red color; a color resembling that of arterial blood; one of the simple or primary colors; a red pigment; red hair; a red republican; one having radical political or social beliefs; a communist; an anarchist.—**redbreast,** red′brest, *n.* A singing bird so called from the color of its breast, also known as the *robin redbreast,* or simply as the *robin.*—**redcoat,** red′kōt, *n.* A name formerly given to a British soldier because of his uniform.—**red cross.** A rectangular red cross on a white background, as a symbol of mercy.—**Red Cross,** an international society organized to serve humanity in first aid, medical care, and relief of human suffering in times of catastrophe.—**redden,** red′n, *v.t.* To make red.—*v.i.* To

grow or become red.—**reddish,** red′-ish, *a.* Somewhat red; moderately red.—**redhand, redhanded,** *a.* With red or bloody hands; hence, in the very act, as if with red or bloody hands: said of a person caught in the perpetration of any crime.—**red-hot,** *a.* Red with heat; heated to redness. —**red lattice,** *n.* A lattice window painted red, formerly the customary badge of an inn or alehouse.— *Red-lattice phrases,* barroom talk.— **red lead,** *n.* An oxide of lead much used as a pigment, and commonly known by the name of *Minium.*— **red-letter,** *a.* Having red letters; marked by red letters.—*Red-letter day,* a fortunate or auspicious day; so called because the holidays or saints' days were marked in the old calendars with red letters.— **redness,** red′nes, *n.* The quality of being red; red color.—**redpoll,** red′pōl, *n.* [From the red color of the *poll* or head.] A name given to several species of finches.— **redskin,** *n.* A red Indian; a North American Indian.—**redstart,** red′-stärt, *n.* [*Start* is from A.Sax. *steort,* a tail.] A species of American warbler; a songbird nearly allied to the redbreast, widely diffused over Europe, Asia, and North Africa.—**red tape,** *n.* A sarcastic name for excessive regard to formality and routine without corresponding attention to essential duties: so named from the red tape used in tying up papers in government offices.—**redtapism,** *n.* Excessive official routine; strict and pedantic adherence to official formalities.—**redwing,** red′wing, *n.* An American blackbird with a red spot on the wing.—**redwood,** *n.* The name of various sorts of wood of a red color; an Indian dyewood; a coniferous tree of California, often growing 300 feet high, and its cedar-like wood.

redact, ri·dakt′, *v.t.* [L. *redigo, redactum,* to reduce to order—*re,* again, and *ago,* to bring.] To give a presentable literary form to; to act as redactor or editor of.— **redactor,** ri·dak′ter, *n.* [Fr. *redacteur.*] One who redacts; an editor.— **redaction,** ri·dak′shon, *n.* [Fr.] Preparation for publication.

redan, ri·dan′, *n.* [Fr. *redan,* O.Fr. *redent,* from *re,* back, and *dent,* L. *dens, dentis,* a tooth; from its shape.] *Field fort,* the simplest kind of work employed, consisting of two parapets of earth raised so as to form a salient angle, with the apex toward the enemy.

reddle, red′l, *n.* [From *red;* comp. G. *röthel,* from *roth,* red.] Red chalk; a species of argillaceous ironstone ore used as a pigment and to mark sheep. Spelled also *Raddle.*

redeem, ri·dēm′, *v.t.* [Fr. *redimer,* L. *redimo,* to buy back, to ransom— *red, re,* back, and *emo,* to obtain or purchase. EXAMPLE, EXEMPT.] To buy back; to release from captivity or bondage, or from any obligation or liability to suffer or be forfeited, by paying an equivalent; to pay

ransom or equivalent for; to ransom; to rescue; to perform, as a promise; to make good by performance; to make amends for; to atone for; to improve or employ to the best advantage (*redeeming* the time). —**redeemable,** ri·dē′ma·bl, *a.* Capable of being redeemed.—**redeemer,** ri·dē′mer, *n.* One who redeems or ransoms; [*cap.*] the Saviour of the world, JESUS CHRIST.—**redemption,** ri·dem′shon, *n.* [L. *redemptio:* a doublet of *ransom.*] The act of redeeming; the state of being redeemed; ransom; *theol.* the deliverance of sinners from the penalty of God's violated law by the sufferings and death of Christ.— **redemptive,** ri·dem′tiv, *a.* Redeeming; serving to redeem.—**redemptory,** ri·dem′to·ri, *a.* Paid for ransom.

redeliver, rē·di·liv′er, *v.t.* To deliver back; to return to the sender; to liberate a second time.

redemand, rē·di·mand′, *v.t.* To demand back; to demand again.

redemption. See REDEEM.

redeposit, rē·di·poz′it, *v.t.* To deposit again or anew.

redintegrate, ri·din′ti·grāt, *v.t.*— *redintegrated, redintegrating.* [L. *re,* again, and *integer,* whole. ENTIRE.] To make whole again; to restore to a perfect state.—**redintegration,** ri·din′ti·grā″shon, *n.*

rediscover, rē·dis·kuv′er, *v.t.* [L. *re,* again, and *discover.*] To discover again or afresh.

redistrict, rē·dis′trikt, *v.t.* [L. *re,* again, and *district.*] To revise the districts of, usually for legislative purposes.

redolent, red′o·lent, *a.* [L. *redolens, redolentis,* ppr. of *redolere,* to emit a scent—*red,* back, and *olere,* to smell. ODOR.] Having or diffusing a sweet scent; giving out an odor; reminiscent: often with *of.*—**redolence,** red′o·lens, *n.*

redouble, rē·dub′l, *v.i.* [Prefix *re,* and *double.*] To multiply; to repeat often; to increase by repeated or continued additions.—*v.i.* To become twice as much; to become greatly or repeatedly increased.

redoubt, ri·dout′, *n.* [Fr. *redoute, reduit,* from L.L. *reductus,* a retired spot, from L. *reductus,* retired—*re,* back, and *duco,* to lead. DUKE.] *Fort.* a general name for nearly every class of works wholly enclosed and undefended by re-entering or flanking angles; a small enclosed temporary fieldwork.

redoubtable, ri·dout′a·bl, *a.* [O.Fr. *redoutable,* from *redouter,* to fear— L. *re,* again, and *dubito,* to doubt. DOUBT.] Formidable; to be dreaded; terrible to foes; hence, valiant: often used in irony.—**redoubted,** ri·dout′ed, *p.* and *a.* Redoubtable; formidable; valiant.

redound, ri·dound′, *v.i.* [Fr. *redonder,* L. *redundo,* to overflow— *red,* back, and *undo,* to surge, from *unda,* a wave (seen also in *undulate, redundant, abound*).] To roll or flow back, as a wave; to conduce; to contribute; to result (this will *redound* to your benefit).—*n.* The coming back, as a consequence or effect; result.

redraft, rē·draft', v.t. To draw or draft anew.—n. A second draft or copy; a second draft or order drawn for money.

redraw, rē·drạ', v.t. To draw again, as a second draft or copy.—v.i. Com. to draw a new bill of exchange.

redress, ri·dres', v.t. [Fr. redresser, to straighten again, to put right. DRESS.] To remedy or put right, as a wrong; to repair, as an injury; to relieve of anything unjust or oppressive; to compensate; to make amends to.—n. Deliverance from wrong, injury, or oppression; undoing of wrong; reparation; indemnification.—**redresser**, ri·dres'ėr, n. One who gives redress.

reduce, ri·dūs', v.t.—reduced, reducing. [L. reduco—re, back, and duco, to lead. DUKE.] To bring to any state or condition, good or bad; to bring (to power, to poverty, to order, etc.); to diminish in size, quantity, or value; to make less or lower; to bring to an inferior condition; to subdue; to bring into subjection; to bring under rules or within certain limits of description; to bring from a form less fit to one more fit for operation; arith. to change from one denomination into another without altering the value; alg. to bring to the simplest form with the unknown quantity by itself on one side, and all the known quantities on the other side; metal. to separate, as a pure metal from a metallic ore; surg. to restore to its proper place or state, as a dislocated or fractured bone.—To reduce a design, to make a copy of it smaller than the original.—To reduce to the ranks, to degrade for misconduct to the position of a private soldier.—**reducer**, ri·dū'sėr, n. One that reduces.—**reducible**, ri·dū'si·bl, a. Capable of being reduced; convertible.—**reducibly**, ri·dū'si·bli, adv.—**reduction**, ri·duk'shon, n. [L. reductio.] The act of reducing; conversion into another state or form; diminution; conquest; subjugation; arith. the bringing of numbers of one denomination into another; the arithmetical rule by which this is done; alg. the process of bringing equations to their simplest forms with the unknown quantity alone on one side, and the known ones on the other; the act of making a copy of a map, design, etc., on a smaller scale, preserving the proper proportions; surg. the operation of restoring a dislocated or fractured bone to its former place; metal. the operation of obtaining pure metals from metallic ores.—**reductive**, ri·duk'tiv, a. Having the power of reducing; tending to reduce.

redundant, ri·dun'dant, a. [L. redundans, redundantis, ppr. of redundo. REDOUND.] Superfluous; exceeding what is natural or necessary; superabundant; using more words than are necessary.—**redundance**, **redundancy**, ri·dun'dans, ri·dun'-

dan·si, n. The quality of being redundant; superfluity; superabundance; that which is redundant or superfluous.—**redundantly**, ri·dun'dant·li, adv. In a redundant manner.

reduplicate, ri·dū'pli·kāt, v.t.—reduplicated, reduplicating. [L. reduplico, reduplicatum—er, and duplico, to double. DUPLICATE.] To double again; to multiply; to repeat; philol. to repeat, as the initial syllable or the root of a word, for the purpose of marking past time.—v.i. Philol. to be doubled or repeated; to undergo reduplication.—a. Redoubled; repeated; bot. applied to a form of aestivation in which the edges of the sepals or petals are turned outward.—**reduplication**, ri·dū'pli·kā"shon, n. The act of doubling or reduplicating; philol. the repetition of a root or of the initial syllable (more or less modified), as in Gr. pheugō, to flee, perfect pepheuga; did, the reduplicated past of do; the new syllable formed by reduplication.

redware, red'wâr, n. [red + ware, seaweed.] An edible brownish seaweed found off the coast of New England.

redwing. See RED.

re-echo, rē·ek'ō, v.t. and i. To echo back; to reverberate again.—n. The echo of an echo; a second or repeated echo.

reed, rēd, n. [O.E. rede, A.Sax. hreōd=O.Sax. ried, D. riet, ried, O.H.G. hriot, Mod.G. riet, ried; also Ir. readan, Gael. ribhid, a reed.] A name applied to tall broad-leaved grasses growing in marshy places, or to their hollow stems; a musical instrument made from a reed; a rustic or pastoral pipe; a little tube through which a hautboy, bassoon, or clarinet is blown; one of the thin plates of metal whose vibrations produce the notes of an accordion, harmonium, etc.; weaving, a frame of parallel flat strips of wood or metal for separating threads of the warp, and for beating the weft up to the web.—**reedbird**. RICEBIRD.—**reed grass**, n. A name given to various large grasses.—**reed pipe**, n. A musical pipe made of reed; a pipe in an organ sounding by means of a reed.—**reedy**, rēd'i, a. Abounding with reeds; resembling a reed; applied to a voice or musical instrument having a thin, harsh tone.

reef, rēf, n. [Same as D. rif, a roof; Icel. rif, Dan. rev, riv, Sw. rev, G. riff, reef; from root of rive.] A mass of rocks in the ocean lying at or near the surface of the water; among gold miners, a gold-bearing quartz vein.

reef, rēf, n. [From D. reef, a reef; L.G. reff, riff, Icel. rif, Dan. rev, reb, Sw. ref, reef; akin A.Sax. reáf, a garment. ROBE.] Naut. that part of a sail which can be drawn together by small cords, so as to contract the canvas in proportion to the increase of the wind.—v.t. Naut. to take a reef or reefs in; to reduce the extent of a sail by folding a

certain portion of it and making it fast to the yard.—**reefer**, rēf'ėr, n. One who reefs; a close-fitting jacket of strong cloth.

reek, rēk, n. [A.Sax. réc, smoke, vapor; cog. O.Fris. rék, Icel. reykr, D. and L.G. rook, Dan. rög, Sw. rök, G. rauch, Lith. rukis, smoke.] Vapor; steam; exhalation; fume; smoke.—v.i. To smoke; to steam; to exhale; to emit vapor.—**reeky**, rēk'i, a. Giving out reek or fumes. (Shak.)

reel, rēl, n. [A.Sax. hreól, reól, a reel; Icel. hraell, a weaver's rod or sley.] A machine on which yarn is wound to form it into hanks, skeins, etc.; a revolving frame on which the logline is wound; a revolving appliance attached to the butt of a fishing rod, and around which the line is wound; the photographic film of a motion picture.—v.t. To wind upon a reel.

reel, rēl, n. [Gael. righil, a reel.] A lively dance peculiar to Scotland; the music for this dance, generally written in common time of four crotchets in a bar, but sometimes in jig time of six quavers; also, the Virginia Reel.

reel, rēl, v.i. [O.E. reile, rele, to roll, to reel; perhaps from reel, the implement.] To stagger or sway in walking; to whirl; to have a whirling or giddy sensation (my brain reeled).—n. A staggering motion, as that of a drunken man.

re-elect, rē·i·lekt', v.t. To elect again.—**re-election**, rē·i·lek'shon, n. Election for a second term to an office, or a repeated election, as, for instance, the re-election of a president of the United States at the termination of his first four years in office.

re-emerge, rē·i·mėrj', v.i. To emerge after being plunged, obscured, or overwhelmed.—**re-emergence**, rē·i·mėr'jens, n. The act of emerging again.

re-enact, rē·i·nakt', v.t. To enact again.—**re-enactment**, rē·i·nakt'ment, n. The enacting or passing of a law a second time.

re-enforce, rē·in·fōrs', v.t. To enforce anew; to reinforce.

re-engage, rē·in·gāj', v.t. and i. To engage a second time.

re-enlist, rē·in·list', v.t. and i. To enlist a second time.—**re-enlistment**, rē·in·list'ment, n. The act of re-enlisting.

re-enter, rē·en'tėr, v.t. To enter again or anew; engr. to cut deeper, as the incisions of a plate which are too faint.—**re-entrance**, rē·en'trans, n. The act of entering again.—**re-entry**, rē·en'tri, n. A new or second entry; the return, through the earth's atmosphere, of a space vehicle.

re-establish, rē·es·tab'lish, v.t. To establish anew.—**re-establishment**, rē·es·tab'lish·ment, n. The act of establishing again.

reeve, rēv, n. [A.Sax. geréfa, a steward, a person in authority; origin doubtful; sheriff=shire-reeve.] In England a bailiff; a steward; a peace officer: now used only in such words as *borough-reeve*, *port-reeve*, etc.

reeve, rēv, *n.* A bird, the female of the ruff.

reeve, rēv, *v.t.* and *i.*—*reeve* or *rove*, *reeving.* [From *reef*, the nautical term.] *Naut.* to pass the end of a rope through any hole in a block, thimble, ringbolt, etc.; to run or pass through such hole.

re-examine, rē·eg·zam′in, *v.t.* To examine anew.—**re-examination,** rē·eg·zam′i·nā″shon, *n.* A renewed or repeated examination.

re-export, rē·eks·pōrt′, *v.t.* To export again; to export after having been imported.—*n.* (rē·eks′pōrt). Any commodity re-exported.—**re-exportation,** rē·eks′pōr·tā″shon, *n.* The act of re-exporting.

refashion, rē·fash′on, *v.t.* To fashion or form into shape a second time.

refasten, rē·fas′n, *v.t.* To fasten again.

refection, ri·fek′shon, *n.* [L. *refectio, refectionis*, from *reficio*, to restore, to refresh—*re*, again, and *facio*, to make.] Refreshment after hunger or fatigue; a repast.—**refectory,** ri·fek′to·ri, *n.* An eating room; an apartment in convents where meals are taken.

refer, ri·fėr′, *v.t.*—*referred, referring.* [L. *refero, referre*, to bring back, to refer, etc.—*re*, back, and *fero*, to carry. FERTILE.] To trace back; to impute; to assign; to attribute to, as the cause, motive, or ground; to hand over, as to another person or tribunal for treatment, decision, etc. (to *refer* a matter to a third party); to appeal; to assign, as to an order, genus, or class; in all senses followed by *to*.—*v.i.* To respect; to have relation; to appeal; to have recourse; to apply; to consult (to *refer* to one's notes); to allude; to make allusion; to direct the attention. ∴ Syn. under ADVERT.—**referee,** ref·ėr·ē′, *n.* One to whom a matter in dispute has been referred for settlement or decision; an arbitrator.—**reference,** ref′ėr·ens, *n.* The act of referring; the act of alluding; direct allusion; relation; respect, or regard (generally in the phrase *in* or *with reference to*); one of whom inquiries may be made in regard to a person's character, abilities, etc.; a passage or note in a work by which a person is referred to another passage.—*a.* Affording information when consulted.—*Reference Bible*, a Bible having brief explanations and references to parallel passages printed on the margin.—*Reference books*, books, such as dictionaries, etc., intended to be consulted as occasion requires. —*Reference library*, a library containing books which can be consulted on the spot.—**referendum,** ref·ėr·en′dum, *n.* [L., a thing to be referred.] The reference to public vote, for final approval or rejection, of measures proposed or passed by a representative assembly; a means of consulting public opinion by popular vote when a public body is unable to make decisions or take on itself the responsibility for a measure.

refill, rē·fil′, *v.t.* To fill again.—*n.* rē′fil, a product sold in a special container designed to be filled again when initial contents are consumed; the product made to fill again the container when original contents have been exhausted.

refine, ri·fīn′, *v.t.*—*refined, refining.* [Fr. *raffiner*, to refine—*re*, and *affiner* —*af* (for L. *ad*), to, and *fin*, fine. FINE.] To reduce to a pure state; to free from impurities; to purify; to reduce from the ore; to separate from other metals or from dross or alloy; to purify from what is coarse, inelegant, rude, and the like; to make elegant; to raise or educate, as the taste; to give culture to; to polish (to *refine* the manners, etc.).— *v.i.* To become pure or purer; to affect nicety or subtlety in thought or language.—**refined,** ri·fīnd′, *p.* and *a.* Polished or elegant in character; free from anything coarse or vulgar.—**refinement,** ri·fīn′ment, *n.* The act of refining or purifying, or state of being refined; the state of being free from what is coarse, rude, inelegant, or the like; elegance of manners, language, etc.; culture; a result of excessive elaboration, polish, or nicety; overnicety; an affected subtlety.—**refiner,** ri·fī′nėr, *n.* One that refines liquors, sugar, metals, or other things; an improver in purity and elegance; one who is overnice in discrimination, argument, reasoning, etc.—**refinery,** ri·fī′nėr·i, *n.* A place and apparatus for refining sugar, metals, or the like.

refit, rē·fit′, *v.t.*—*refitted, refitting.* To restore after damage or decay; to repair; to fit out anew.—*v.i.* To repair damages, especially to ships.— *n.* A repairing; the repair of a ship.

reflect, ri·flekt′, *v.t.* [L. *reflecto*—*re*, back, and *flecto, flexum*, to bend, seen in *flexure, deflect, inflect, inflection*, etc. FLEX.] To bend back; to turn, cast, or direct back; to throw off after striking or falling on any surface, and in accordance with certain physical laws (to *reflect* light, heat, or sound); to give back an image or likeness of; to mirror.—*v.i.* To throw back light, heat, sound, or the like; to return rays or beams; to throw or turn back the thoughts upon anything; to think or consider seriously; to revolve matters in the mind; to bring reproach; to cast censure or blame (do not *reflect* on his errors).—**reflection,** ri·flek′shon, *n.* The act of reflecting, or the state of being reflected; *physics*, the change of direction which light, heat, or sound experiences when it strikes upon a surface and is thrown back into the same medium from which it approached; that which is produced by being reflected; an image given back from a reflecting surface; attentive or continued consideration; meditation, contemplation, deliberation; a censorious remark or one attaching blame; reproach cast; *anat.* the folding of a membrane upon itself.—**reflective,** ri·flek′tiv, *a.* Throwing back rays; reflecting; exercising reflection; *gram.* reflexive.—

reflectively, ri·flek′tiv·li, *adv.* In a reflective manner.—**reflectiveness,** ri·flek′tiv·nes, *n.*—**reflector,** ri·flek′tėr, *n.* One who reflects; that which reflects; a polished surface of metal or other suitable material for reflecting light, heat, or sound in any required direction; a reflecting telescope.

reflex, rē′fleks, *a.* [L. *reflexus*, ppr. of *reflecto.* REFLECT] Turned backward; having a backward direction; reflective; introspective.—*Reflex actions*, those actions of the nervous system which are performed involuntarily, and often unconsciously, as the contraction of the pupil of the eye when exposed to strong light.—*n.* Reflection; image produced by reflection.—**reflexion,** ri·flek′shon. See REFLECTION.—**reflexive,** ri·flek′siv, *a*, Reflective; bending or turning backward; having respect to something past; *gram.* having for its direct object a pronoun which stands for the agent or subject, said of certain verbs (I *bethought myself*, the witness *forswore himself*); also applied to pronouns of this class.—**reflexively,** ri·flek′siv·li, *adv.*

refluent, ref′lu̯·ent, *a.* [L. *refluens, refluentis*—*re*, back, and *fluo*, to flow. FLUENT.] Flowing, surging, or rushing back; ebbing.—**refluence,** ref′lu̯·ens, *n.*

reflux, rē′fluks, *n.* [Prefix *re*, back, and *flux*.] A flowing back (the flux and *reflux* of the tides).

reforest, rē·for′est, *v.t.* and *i.* [L. *re*, again, and *forest*.] To replant an area with forest trees.

reform, ri·form′, *v.t.* [Fr. *réformer*, to reform or amend, from L. *reformare*—*re*, again, and *formo*, to form, from *forma*, form. FORM.] To change from worse to better; to introduce improvement in; to amend; to bring from a bad to a good state; to remove or abolish for something better.—*v.i.* To abandon evil and return to good; to amend one's behavior.—*n.* A rearrangement which either brings back a better order of things or reconstructs the present order in an entirely new form; reformation; amendment of what is defective, vicious, corrupt, or depraved.— **reformable,** ri·for′ma·bl, *a.* Capable of being reformed.—**reformation,** ref·or·mā′shon, *n.* The act of reforming or state of being reformed; correction or amendment of life, manners, or of anything objectionable or bad; the redress of grievances or abuses.—[*cap.*] The religious revolution of the sixteenth century which divided the Western Church into the two sections known as Protestant and Roman Catholic.—**reformatory,** ri·for′ma·to·ri, *a.* Tending to produce reformation.—*Reformatory*, a reform school.—*n.* An institution for the reception and reformation of juveniles who have already begun a career of criminality, and have been convicted.—**reformed,** ri·formd′, *p.* and *a.* Corrected; amended; restored to a good state; having turned from evil courses (a *reformed* profligate); [*cap.*] having accepted the principles

---

ch, *ch*ain; *ch*, Sc. lo*ch*; g, *g*o; j, *j*ob; ng, si*ng*; TH, *th*en; th, *th*in; w, *w*ig; hw, *wh*ig; zh, a*z*ure.

of the Reformation and separated from the Church of Rome; especially those churches, such as the ones constituted in various parts of Europe by Zwingli, Calvin, and others, which also separated from Luther on various doctrines.—**reformer,** ri·for′mėr, *n.* One who effects a reformation or amendment; one who promotes or urges political or social reform.

re-form, ri·form′, *v.t.* [Directly from *re* and *form.*] To form again or anew; to give the same or another disposition or arrangement to (to *re-form* troops that have been scattered).—**re-formation,** rē·for·mā′shon, *n.* The act of forming anew; a second forming in order.

refract, ri·frakt′, *v.t.* [Fr. *refracter,* from L. *refringo, refractum,* to break up—*re,* and *frango, fractum,* to break. FRACTION.] To bend back sharply or abruptly; especially, *optics,* to deflect (a ray of light) at a certain angle on passing from one medium into another of a different density.—**refracting,** ri·frak′ting, *p.* and *a.* Serving or tending to refract; turning from a direct course.—*Refracting telescope,* a telescope in which the rays are refracted by an object glass, at the focus of which they are viewed by an eyepiece.—**refraction,** ri·frak′shon, *n.* The act of refracting or state of being refracted; a deflection or change of direction impressed upon rays of light or heat passing from one transparent medium into another of different density, as from air into water or vice versa—or upon rays traversing a medium the density of which is not uniform, as the atmosphere.—*Astronomical* or *atmospheric refraction,* the apparent angular elevation of the heavenly bodies above their true places, caused by the refraction of the rays of light in their passing through the earth's atmosphere.—*Double refraction,* the separation of a ray of light into two separate parts by passing through certain transparent mediums, as Iceland spar, causing objects to appear double.—**refractive,** ri·frak′tiv, *a.* Pertaining to refraction; serving or having power to refract.—**refractiveness,** ri·frak′tiv·nes, *n.*—**refractometer,** ri·frak·tom′et·ėr, *n.* An instrument for exhibiting and measuring the refraction of light. — **refractor,** ri·frak′tėr, *n.* A refracting telescope.

refractory, ri·frak′to·ri, *a.* [Fr. *réfractaire;* from L. *refractarius,* stubborn, from *refringo, refractum.* REFRACT.] Sullen or perverse in opposition or disobedience; obstinate in noncompliance; stubborn and unmanageable (a *refractory* child); resisting ordinary treatment, as metals that are difficult of fusion.—*n.* A refractory person.—**refractorily,** ri·frak′to·ri·li, *adv.* In a refractory manner; perversely; obstinately.—**refractoriness,** ri·frak′to·ri·nes, *n.* The quality of being refractory.

refragable, ref′ra·ga·bl, *a.* [L.L. *refragabilis,* from L. *refragor,* to oppose, to resist—*re,* back, and root

of *frango,* to break. REFRACT.] Capable of being opposed or resisted; refutable.

refrain, ri·frān′, *n.* [Fr. *refrain,* from O.Fr. *refraindre,* L. *refringo*—*re,* again, and *frango,* to break. (REFRACT.) The *refrain,* therefore, is literally the break or interruption to the course of the piece.] The burden of a song; part of a poetic composition repeated at the end of every stanza; a kind of musical repetition.

refrain, ri·frān′, *v.t.* [Fr. *refréner,* to bridle in, to repress, from L. *refraeno*—*re,* back, and *fraenum,* a bit.] To hold back; to restrain; to curb; to keep from action: often *refl.*—*v.i.* To forbear; to abstain; to keep one's self from action or interference: followed by *from.*—**refrainer,** rē·frā′nėr, *n.* One who refrains.

refrangible, ri·fran′ji·bl, *a.* [L. *re,* and *frango,* to break. REFRACT.] Capable of being refracted; subject to refraction, as rays of light.—**refrangibility, refrangibleness,** ri·fran′ji·bil′′i·ti, ri·fran′ji·bl·nes, *n.* The state or quality of being refrangible; susceptibility of refraction.

refresh, ri·fresh′, *v.t.* [O.Fr. *refreschir, refraischir* (Fr. *rafraîchir*), to refresh. FRESH.] To make fresh or vigorous again; to restore vigor or energy to; to give new strength to; to reinvigorate; to recreate or revive after fatigue, want, pain, or the like; to reanimate; to freshen.—**refresher,** ri·fresh′ėr, *n.* One who or that which refreshes; among lawyers, an additional fee paid to counsel when the case is adjourned from one term or sittings to another. —**refreshing,** ri·fresh′ing, *p.* and *a.* Acting or operating so as to refresh; invigorating; reviving; reanimating. —*n.* Refreshment.—**refreshingly,** ri·fresh′ing·li, *adv.* In a refreshing manner; so as to refresh.—**refreshment,** ri·fresh′ment, *n.* The act of refreshing; that which refreshes; that which gives fresh strength or vigor, as food, drink, or rest: in the plural almost exclusively applied to food and drink.

refrigerate, ri·frij′ėr·āt, *v.t.*—*refrigerated, refrigerating.* [L. *refrigero, refrigeratum,* to refrigerate—*re,* again, and *frigus, frigoris,* cold. FRIGID.] To cool; to allay heat; to keep cool; to chill or freeze foods, etc., in order to preserve them.—**refrigerant, refrigerative,** ri·frij′ėr·ant, ri·frij′ėr·a·tiv, *a.* Cooling; allaying heat.—*n.* A cooling agency; ice, or gases used in mechanical refrigerators; a medicine which abates fever (*med.*).—**refrigeration,** ri·frij′ėr·ā′′shon, *n.* The abating of heat; the act or system of cooling or freezing foods, etc. in order to preserve them.—**refrigerator,** ri·frij′ėr·a·tėr, *n.* That which refrigerates, cools, or keeps cool; a box or room in which materials (usually foods) are kept cool, either by the action of ice or by evaporation of various liquid gases, as sulfur dioxide or ammonia; an apparatus that cools hot liquids or vapors rapidly.—**refrigeratory** ri·frij′ėr·a·to·ri, *a.* Cooling; mitigating heat.

refringent, ri·frin′jent, *a.* [L. *refringo*—*re,* back, and *frango,* to break. REFRACT.] Possessing the quality of refracting; refractive.

reft, reft, pret. & pp. of *reave.* Bereft.

refuge, ref′ūj, *n.* [Fr., from L. *refugium,* from *refugio*—*re,* again, and *fugio,* to flee (whence *fugitive*).] Shelter or protection from danger or distress; that which shelters or protects from danger, distress, or calamity; any place where one is out of the way of any evil or danger; an institution where the destitute or homeless find temporary shelter; a house of refuge; an expedient to secure protection or defense; a device, contrivance, shift.—*Cities of refuge,* among the Israelites, certain cities appointed to secure the safety of such persons as might unintentionally commit homicide.—*Harbors of refuge,* harbors which afford shelter to vessels in stress of weather.— *House of refuge,* an institution for the shelter of the homeless or destitute. —*v.t.*† To shelter; to protect.—*v.i.*† To take shelter.—**refugee,** ref·ū·jē′, *n.* [Fr. *réfugié.*] One who flees for refuge; one who in times of persecution or political commotion flees to a foreign country for safety.

refulgent, ri·ful′jent, *a.* [L. *refulgens, refulgentis,* ppr. of *refulgeo*—*re,* again, and *fulgeo,* to shine. FULGENT.] Casting a bright light; shining; splendid.—**refulgently,** ri·ful′jent·li, *adv.* In a refulgent manner.—**refulgence, refulgency,** ri·ful′jens, ri·ful′jen·si, *n.* The state or quality of being refulgent; splendor; brilliancy.

refund, ri·fund′, *v.t.* [L. *refundo,* to pour back, to restore—*re,* back, and *fundo,* to pour. FUSE.] To return in payment or compensation for what has been taken; to pay back; to restore; to reimburse.—**refunder,** ri·fun′dėr, *n.* One who refunds.

refurbish, rē·fėr′bish, *v.t.* To furbish a second time or anew.

refuse, ri·fūz′, *v.t.*—*refused, refusing.* [Fr. *réfuser,* to refuse; Pr. *refusar,* Sp. *rehusar;* supposed to owe its origin partly to L. *recusare,* to refuse; partly to *refutare,* to refute.] To deny, as a request, demand, invitation, or command; to decline to do or grant; often with an infinitive as object (he *refused* to give me the book); to decline to accept; to reject (to *refuse* an office); to deny the request of; to say no to (I could not *refuse* him).—*v.i.* To decline a request; not to comply.—*a.* (ref′ūs). Rejected; worthless; left as of no value.—*n.* That which is rejected as useless; waste matter.—**refusal,** ri·fū′zal, *n.* The act of refusing; denial of anything demanded, solicited, or offered for acceptance; option of taking or buying; preemption.—**refuser,** ri·fū′zėr, *n.* One who refuses.

refute, ri·fūt′, *v.t.*—*refuted, refuting.* [Fr. *réfuter,* L. *refutare*—*re,* back, and old *futo,* to pour, from root of *fundo,* to pour. CONFUTE, FUTILE, FUSE.] To disprove and overthrow by argument, evidence, or countervailing proof; to prove to be false or erroneous; to confute; to prove to be in error.—**refuter**, ri·fū′tėr, n. One who refutes.—**refutable**, ri··fū′ta·bl or ref′ū·ta·bl, a. Capable of being refuted.—**refutation**, ref·ū·tā′shon, n. The act of refuting or proving to be false or erroneous; overthrow by argument or countervailing proof.

regain, rē·gān′, v.t. To gain anew; to recover what has been lost; to reach again (they *regained* the shore).

regal, rē′gal, a. [L. *regalis*, from *rex, regis*, a king, from stem of *rego*, to rule, the same root being also seen in E. *right. Royal* is the same word; and *reign, regent*, etc., have the same origin, as also *-rect* in *correct, direct*, etc.] Pertaining to a king; kingly; royal. ∴ Syn. under ROYAL.—**regalia**, ri·gā′li·a, n. pl. [L. *regalia*, royal or regal things, nom. pl. neut. of *regalis*, regal.] The ensigns or symbols of royalty; the apparatus of a coronation, as the crown, scepter, etc.; the insignia or decorations of some society; showy clothes. —**regality**, ri·gal′i·ti, n. Royalty; sovereignty; kingship; sovereign right.—**regally**, rē′gal·li, adv. In a regal or royal manner; royally.

regale, ri·gāl′, v.t.—*regaled, regaling*. [Fr. *régaler*, to regale—*re*, and an old verb *galer*, to rejoice, probably from root of Goth. *gailjan*, to rejoice. GALA.] To entertain sumptuously or with something that gives great pleasure; to gratify, as the senses; to delight; to feast.—*v.i.* To feast; to fare sumptuously.—*n.* A splendid repast; a treat.—**regalement**, ri·gāl′ment, n. Entertainment; gratification.

regalia. See REGAL.

regard, ri·gärd′, v.t. [Fr. *regarder*, to regard, to observe—*re*, back, and *garder*, to guard. GUARD.] To look upon; to observe; to notice with some care; to pay attention to; to observe a certain respect toward; to respect, reverence, honor, esteem; to mind; to care for; to have or to show certain feelings toward; to view in the light of; to put on the same footing as.—*As regards* (impers.), with regard to; as respects; as concerns (as *regards* that matter I am of your opinion).—*n.* Look or gaze; aspect directed to another (*Shak.*); attention or care; heed; consideration; that feeling which springs from estimable qualities in the object; respect, esteem, reverence; relation; respect; reference; view: often in the phrases, *in regard to, with regard to; pl.* respects; good wishes; compliments (give my *regards* to the family).—**regardant**, ri·gär′dant, a. Regarding; watching; *her.* applied to an animal whose face is turned backward in an attitude of vigilance.—**regardful**, ri·gärd′ful, a. Having or paying regard.—**regardfully**, ri·gärd′ful·li, adv. In a regardful manner.—**regarding**, ri·gär′ding, prep. [Like *concerning, during*, a participle, now established as a preposition.] Respecting; concerning; in reference to (to be at a loss *regarding* something).—**regardless**,

ri·gärd′les, a. Not having regard or heed; heedless; careless.—**regardlessly**, ri·gärd′les·li, adv. In a regardless manner; heedlessly; carelessly.—**regardlessness**, ri·gärd′les·nes, n. Heedlessness; negligence.

regatta, ri·gat′a, n. [It.] Originally a gondola race in Venice; now any sailing or rowing race in which a number of yachts or boats contend for prizes.

regelation, rē·je·lā′shon, n. [L. *re*, again, and *gelatio, gelationis*, a freezing. CONGEAL.] The phenomenon presented by pieces of moist ice which when placed in contact with one another freeze together even in a warm atmosphere.

regency. See REGENT.

regenerate, ri·jen′ėr·āt, v.t.—*regenerated, regenerating*. [L. *regenero, regeneratum—re*, again, and *genero*, to generate. GENERATE.] To generate or produce anew; to reproduce; *theol.* to cause to be born again; to change, as the heart and affections, from enmity or indifference to love of God. —*a.* Reproduced; *theol.* changed from a natural to a spiritual state.—**regeneracy**, ri·jen′ėr·a·si, n. The state of being regenerated.—**regeneration**, ri·jen′ėr·ā″shon, n. The act of regenerating or producing anew; *theol.* that change by which love of God and his law is implanted in the heart.—**regenerative**, ri·jen′ėr·a·tiv, a. Producing regeneration; renewing. —**regeneratively**, ri·jen′ėr·a·tiv·li, adv.

regent, rē′jent, a. [L. *regens, regentis*, ppr. of *rego*, to rule; cog. Skr. *râj*, to rule; from same root also E. *right.* REGAL.] Ruling; governing; exercising vicarious authority.—*n.* A governor; a ruler; one who governs a kingdom in the minority, absence, or disability of the sovereign; one of a certain standing who taught in universities: the word formerly in use for a *professor*; in the English universities, one who has certain peculiar duties of instruction or government. —**regentship**, rē′jent·ship, n. The office or dignity of a regent; regency. —**regency**, rē′jen·si, n. Rule; government; the office or jurisdiction of a regent; a body of men entrusted with the power of a regent.

regicide, rej′i·sīd, n. [Fr. *régicide*, from L. *rex, regis*, a king, and *caedo*, to slay.] A king-killer; one who murders a king; the killing or murder of a king.—**regicidal**, rej·i·sī′dal, a. Pertaining to regicide.

regime, re·zhēm′, n. [Fr. *régime*, from L. *regimen*, guidance, from *rego*, to govern.] Mode or system of management; government, especially as connected with certain social features; administration; rule.—*The ancient regime*, the political system which prevailed in France before the revolution of 1789.—**regimen**, rej′i·men, n. Orderly government; the regulation of diet, exercise, etc.; *gram.* government of words.

regiment, rej′i·ment, n. [Fr. *régiment*, from L.L. *regimentum*, from L. *regimen*, rule, from *rego*, to rule. REGIME, REGENT.] An organization of

troops under the command of a colonel, consisting of several battalions, squadrons, or batteries in those branches of the army designated respectively as the infantry, cavalry, or artillery.—*v.t.* To form troops into regiments; to assign soldiers to a regiment; to organize civilians into groups to control their actions and indoctrinate their minds. —**regimentation**, rej·i·men·tā′shon, n. Strict control or uniformity imposed by external authority; the act of forming into groups.

region, rē′jun, n. [Fr. *région*, from L. *regio, regionis*, from *rego*, to rule. REGAL.] A large division of any space or surface considered as apart from others; especially, a tract of land, sea, etc., of considerable but indefinite extent; a country; a district; a part or division of the body (the *region* of the heart).—**regional**, rē′jun·al, a. Pertaining to a particular region; sectional.

register, rej′is·tėr, n. [Fr. *registre*, L.L. *registrum, regestrum*, a book of records—*re*, back, and *gero, gestum*, to carry. GESTATION.] An official written account or entry in a book regularly kept for preservation or for reference; a record; a list; the book in which records are kept; a document issued by the customs authorities as evidence of a ship's nationality; a contrivance for regulating the passage of heat or air in heating or ventilation; a device for automatically indicating the number of revolutions made or amount of work done by machinery, recording pressure, etc.; *printing*, the agreement of two printed forms to be applied to the same sheet, either on the same side, as in color printing, or on both sides as in a book or newspaper; *music*, the compass of a voice or instrument, or a portion of the compass; a stop or set of pipes in an organ.—*Lloyd's register.* See LLOYD'S.—*Lord register*, or *lord clerk register*, a Scottish officer of state who has the custody of the archives.—*v.t.* To record; to enter in a register.—*v.i. Printing*, to correspond exactly, as columns or lines of printed matter on opposite sheets.—**registered**, rej′is·tėrd, p. and a. Recorded in a register; enrolled.—*Registered company*, a joint-stock company entered in an official register, but not incorporated.— *Registered letter*, a letter the address of which is registered at a post office, for which a special fee is paid in order to secure its safe transmission. —**registrar**, rej′is·trär, n. [L.L. *registrarius*.] One whose business it is to write or keep a register; a keeper of records.—**registration**, rej·is·trā′shon, n. The act of inserting in a register.—**registry**, rej′is·tri, n. The act of entering in a register; the place where a register is kept; facts recorded; an entry.

reglet, reg′let, n. [Fr. *réglet*, from *règle*, rule, L. *regula*. REGULATE.] *Printing*, a strip of wood or metal used for separating pages in the chase, etc.; *arch.* a flat narrow molding between panels, etc.

regnal, reg'nal, *a.* [From L. *regnum*, a kingdom. REIGN.] Pertaining to the reign of a monarch.—*Regnal year*, the year of a sovereign's reign (as given in an act of the British Parliament).

regnant, reg'nant, *a.* [L. *regnans*, *regnantis*, ppr. of *regno*, to reign, from *regnum*, a kingdom.] Reigning as sovereign; predominant; prevalent.

regorge, rē·gorj', *v.t.* [Prefix *re*, and *gorge*.] To vomit up; to disgorge.

regrant, rē·grant', *v.t.* To grant back. —*n.* The act of granting back; a new or fresh grant.

regreet, rē·grēt', *v.i.* To greet or salute again.

regress, rē'gres, *n.* [L. *regressus*, from *regredior*, to go back—*re*, back, and *gradior*, to go. GRADE.] Passage back; return; power or liberty of returning or passing back.—*v.i.* (ri·gres'). To go back; to return to a former place or state.—**regression**, ri·gresh'on, *n.* [L. *regressio*.] The act of passing back or returning; retrogression.—**filial regression**. [L. *filialis*, relating to offspring.] In heredity, a tendency to return to the average.—**regressive**, ri·gres'iv, *a.* Passing back; returning.

regret, ri·gret', *n.* [Fr. *regret*, regret, *regretter*, O.Fr. *regreter*, to regret; from *re*, again, and the Teutonic verb seen in Icel. *gráta*, A.Sax. *graetan*, Sc. *greet*, to weep.] Grief or trouble caused by the want or loss of something formerly possessed; sorrowful longing; pain of mind at something done or left undone; remorse.—*v.t.*—*regretted, regretting.* To lament the loss of, or separation from; to look back at with sorrowful longing; to grieve at; to be sorry for. —**regretful**, ri·gret'ful, *a.* Full of regret.—**regretfully**, ri·gret'ful·li, *adv.* With regret.—**regrettable**, ri·gret'a·bl, *a.* Admitting of or calling for regret.

regular, reg'ū·lėr, *a.* [L. *regularis*, from *regula*, a rule, from *rego*, to rule. REGENT, REGAL.] Conformed to a rule; agreeable to a prescribed mode or customary form; normal; acting or going on by rule or rules; steady or uniform; orderly; methodical; unvarying; *geom.* applied to a figure or body whose sides and angles are equal, as a square, a cube, an equilateral triangle, an equilateral pentagon, etc.; *gram.* adhering to the common form in respect to inflectional terminations; *eccles.* belonging to a monastic order, and bound to certain rules; *bot.* symmetrical as regards figure and size and proportion of parts; colloquially, thorough, out-and-out, complete.— *Regular troops* or *regulars*; troops of a permanent army: opposed to *militia* or *volunteers*.—*Regular verb*, in English, one that forms the preterite and past participle in *d* or *ed*.—*n.* A monk who has taken the vows of some monastic order; a soldier belonging to a permanent army.— **regularity**, reg·ū·lar'i·ti, *n.* The state or quality of being regular; agreeableness to rule or established order; conformity to the customary type;

steadiness or uniformity in a course. —**regularly**, reg'ū·lėr·li, *adv.* In a regular manner; in uniform order; at fixed intervals or periods; methodically; in due order.—**regulate**, reg'ū·lāt, *v.t.*—*regulated, regulating.* [L. *regulo, regulatum,* from *regula,* a rule.] To adjust by rule or established mode; to govern by or subject to certain rules or restrictions; to direct; to put or keep in good order; to control and cause to act properly.— **regulation**, reg·ū·lā'shon, *n.* The act of regulating; a rule prescribed by a superior as to the actions of those under his control; a governing direction; a precept.—**regulative**, reg·ū·lā'tiv, *a.* Regulating; tending to regulate.—**regulator**, reg'ū·lā·tėr, *n.* One who or that which regulates; a device or contrivance of which the object is to produce uniformity of motion or action; the governor of a steam engine.

regulus, reg'ū·lus, *n.* [L., a petty king or sovereign, a dim. of *rex, regis,* a king. REGAL.] A name originally applied by the alchemists to antimony, from the facility with which it alloyed with gold (the *king* of metals), now applied to metals which still retain to a greater or less extent the impurities they contained in the state of ore; [*cap.*] a star of the first magnitude in the constellation Leo.

regurgitate, rē·gėr'ji·tāt, *v.t.*—*regurgitated, regurgitating.* [L.L. *regurgito, regurgitatum*—L. *re, back,* and *gurges, gurgitis,* a whirlpool. GORGE] To pour or cause to rush or surge back; to pour or throw back in great quantity —*v.i.* To be poured back; to rush or surge back.—**regurgitation**, rē·gėr'ji·tā'shon, *n.* The act of regurgitating; *med.* the rising of some of the contents of the stomach into the mouth.

rehabilitate, rē·ha·bil'i·tāt, *v.t.*—*rehabilitated, rehabilitating.* [Fr. *réhabiliter*—*re,* and *habiliter,* to qualify, from *habile,* qualified, able. ABLE.] To restore to a former capacity or position; to reinstate; to re-establish in the esteem of others.—**rehabilitation**, rē·ha·bil'i·tā'shon, *n.* The act of rehabilitating.

rehash, rē·hash', *v.t.* To hash anew; to work up old material in a new form.—*n.* Something made up of materials formerly used.

rehearse, ri·hėrs', *v.t.*—*rehearsed, rehearsing.* [O.E. *reherce, reherse,* from O.Fr. *rehercer, reherser,* to repeat over again—*re,* again, and *hercer, herser,* to harrow, from *herce, herse,* a harrow. HEARSE.] To repeat, as what has already been said or written; to recite; to narrate, recount, relate; to recite or repeat in private for experiment and improvement, before giving a public representation (to *rehearse* a tragedy).— *v.i.* To go through some performance in private preparatory to public representation.—**rehearsal**, ri·hėr'sal, *n.* The act of rehearsing; narration; a telling or recounting; a trial performance (as of a play) made before exhibiting to the public.—**rehearser**, ri·hėr'sėr, *n.* One who rehearses.

Reichsbank, rīchs'bänk, *n.* [G.] The state bank of Germany.

reichsmark, rīchs'märk, *n.* [G.] The German monetary unit.

reign, rān, *v.i.* [O.Fr. *reigner*, Fr. *régner*, from L. *regnare*, to rule, from *regnum*, a kingdom, from *rego*, to rule. REGAL.] To possess or exercise sovereign power or authority; to hold the supreme power; to rule; to be predominant; to prevail; to have superior or uncontrolled dominion.— *n.* [O.Fr. *reigne*, Fr. *règne*, L. *regnum*, a kingdom.] Royal authority; sovereignty; the time during which a king, queen, or emperor reigns; empire; kingdom; power; sway.

reimburse, rē·im·bėrs', *v.t.*—*reimbursed, reimbursing.* [Fr. *rembourser*— *re*, again, *en*, in, and *bourse*, a purse. PURSE.] To replace in a treasury; to pay back; to refund; to pay back to; to render an equivalent to for money or other expenditure.—**reimbursement**, rē·im·bėrs'ment, *n.* The act of reimbursing; repayment.

reimport, rē·im·pōrt', *v.t.* To import again; to carry back to the country of exportation.—*n.* (rē·im'pōrt). Something reimported.—**reimportation**, rē·im'por·tā"shon, *n.* The act of reimporting; that which is reimported.

reimpose, rē·im·pōz', *v.t.* To impose or levy anew.—**reimposition**, rē·im'pō·zish"on, *n.* Act of reimposing.

reimpression, rē·im·presh'on, *n.* A second impression; a reprint.

rein, rān, *n.* [Fr. *rêne*, O.Fr. *resne*, It. *redina*; from L. *retineo*, to retain. RETAIN.] The strap of a bridle, by which the rider or driver restrains and governs the horse, etc.; any thong or cord for the same purpose; *fig.* a means of curbing, restraining, or governing; restraint.—*To give the rein*, or *the reins*, to give license, to leave without restraint.—*To take the reins*, to take the guidance or government.—*v.t.* To govern, guide, or restrain by a bridle; to restrain.

reincarnation, rē·in·kär·na'shon, *n.* Belief that the soul returns after death to live in a new body.

reindeer, rān'dėr, *n.* [Icel. *hrein-dýri*, Sw. *rendjur*, Dan. *rensdyr*, a reindeer; said to be of Finnish or Lappish origin.] A deer of northern Europe and Asia, with broad branched antlers; used as a domestic animal among the Laplanders, to whom it furnishes food, clothing, and the means of conveyance.—**reindeer moss**, *n.* A lichen which constitutes almost the sole winter food for reindeer.

reinforce, rē·in·fōrs', *v.t.* To strengthen; to strengthen with more troops, ships, etc.—*n.* An additional thickness given to any portion of an object in order to strengthen it; the part of a cannon nearest the breech. —*Reinforced concrete*, concrete in which steel bars are embedded, so as to increase the resistance of the structure to tension. — **reinforcement**, rē·in·fōrs'ment, *n.* The act of reinforcing; additional troops or forces to augment an army or fleet.

reinsert, rē·in·sėrt', *v.t.* To insert a

second time.—**reinsertion**, rē·in·-sėr′shon, n. The act of reinsertion, or what is reinserted.

reinstall, rē·in·stạl′, v.t. To install again. —**reinstallment**, rē·in·stạl′-ment, n. The act of reinstalling.

reinstate, rē·in·stāt′, v.t. To instate again; to place again in possession or in a former state.—**reinstatement**, rē·in·stāt′ment, n. The act of rein-stating; reestablishment.

reinsurance, rē·in·shō′rans, n. A re-newed or second insurance; a con-tract by which the first insurer relieves himself from the risks he has undertaken, and devolves them upon other insurers, called *reinsurers*.

reinsure, rē·in·shōr′, v.t. To insure again.—**reinsurer**, rē·in·shō′rėr, n. One who reinsures.

reinter, rē·in·tėr′, v.t. To inter again.

reintroduce, rē·in′trō·dūs″, v.t. To introduce again.—**reintroduction**, rē·in′trō·duk″shon, n. A second in-troduction.

reinvest, rē·in·vest′, v.t. To invest anew.

reinvigorate, rē·in·vig′o·rāt, v.t. To revive vigor in; to reanimate.

reis, rīs, n. [Ar.] A head; a chief; a captain.—*Reis effendi*, one of the chief Turkish officers of state.

reissue, rē·ish′ū, v.i. To issue or go forth again.—v.t. To issue, send out, or put forth a second time (to *reissue* bank-notes).—n. A second or renewed issue.

reiterate, rē·it′ėr·āt, v.t.—*reiterated*, *reiterating*. [L. *re*, again, and *itero*, *iteratum*, to repeat, from *iterum*, again. ITERATE.] To repeat again and again; to do or say (especially to say) repeatedly.—a. Reiterated.—**reiteration**, rē·it′ėr·ā″shon, n. The act of reiterating; repetition.—**reiter-ative**, rē·it′ėr·ā·tiv, n. A word or part of a word repeated so as to form a reduplicated word; *gram.* a word signifying repeated or intense action.

reject, ri·jekt′, v.t. [L. *rejicio*, *re-jectum*, to reject—*re*, again, and *jacio*, to throw (whence also *eject*, *inject*, *project*, etc.) JET.] To throw away as useless or vile, to cast off; to discard; to refuse to receive; to decline haughtily or harshly; to refuse to grant.—n. rē′jekt, one who or that which is rejected.—**rejecter**, ri·jek′tėr, n. One who rejects or refuses.—**rejection**, ri·jek′shon, n. The act of rejecting; refusal to accept or grant.

rejoice, ri·jois′, v.i.—*rejoiced*, *rejoic-ing*. [O.E. *rejoisse*, *rejoyse*, from O.Fr. *rejoir*, *rejoissant*, Fr. *réjouir*, *réjouis-sant*; prefix *re*, and *éjouir*, older *esjoir*—L. *ex*, intens., and *gaudeo*, to rejoice. JOY.] To experience joy and gladness in a high degree; to be joyful; to exult; often with *at*, *in*, *on account of*, etc., or a sub-ordinate clause.—v.t. To make joy-ful; to gladden.—**rejoicer**, ri·jois′ėr, n. One that rejoices; one that causes to rejoice.—**rejoicing**, ri·jois′ing, n. The act of expressing joy; procedure expressive of joy; festivity.

rejoin, rē·join′, v.t. To join again;

to unite after separation; to join the company of again; to answer; to say in answer; to reply: with a clause as object.—v.i. To answer to a reply.—**rejoinder**, ri·join′dėr, n. [An infinitive form; Fr. *rejoindre*, to rejoin. *Attainder*, *remainder* are similar forms.] An answer to a reply; *law*, the fourth stage in the pleadings in an action, being the defendant's answer to the plaintiff's replication.

rejudge, rē·juj′, v.t. To judge again.

rejuvenate, rē·jū′ven·āt, v.t.—*reju-venated*, *rejuvenating*. [L. *re*, again, and *juvenis*, young. JUVENILE.] To restore to youth; to make young again.—**rejuvenation**, rē·jū′ven·ā″-shon, n. The act of rejuvenating.

rejuvenescence, rē·jū′ven·es″ens, n. [L. *re*, and *juvenesco*, to grow young.] A renewing of youth; the state of being young again.—**rejuvenescent**, rē·jū′ven·es″ent, a. Becoming or become young again.—**rejuvenize**, rē·jū′ve·nīz, v.t. To render young again.

rekindle, rē·kin′dl, v.t. To kindle again, to inflame again; to rouse anew.

relapse, ri·laps′, v.i.—*relapsed*, *re-lapsing*. [L. *relabor*, *relapsus*, to slide back—*re*, back, and *labor*, *lapsus*, to slide. LAPSE.] To slip or slide back; to return to a former bad state or practice; to backslide; to fall back or return from recovery or a convalescent state.—n. A falling back into a former bad state, either of health or of morals.

relate, ri·lāt′, v.t.—*related*, *relating*. [Fr. *relater*, to state, to mention; L. *refero*, *relatum*, to refer, to bring back—*re*, back, and *latus*, brought (as in *elate*, *oblate*, *translate*).] To tell; to recite; to recount; to narrate the particulars of; to ally by con-nection or kindred.—v.i. To have reference or respect; to regard; to stand in some relation: with *to* following.—**related**, ri·lā′ted, p. and a. Allied; connected by blood or alliance, particularly by blood, stand-ing in some relation or connection.—**relater**, ri·lā′tėr, n. One who relates. —**relation**, ri·lā′shon, n. [L. *relatio*, *relationis*.] The act of relating; that which is related or told; narrative; reference, respect, or regard; often in the phrase *in relation to*; connec-tion perceived or imagined between things; a certain position of one thing with regard to another; the condition of being such or such in respect to something else; due con-formity or harmony of parts; kin-ship; a kinsman or kinswoman; *math.* ratio; proportion; *logic*, one of the ten predicaments.—**relational**, ri·lā′shon·al, a. Indicating or spec-ifying some relation: used in con-tradistinction to *notional* (a *relational* part of speech, as the pronoun, preposition, and conjunction).—**re-lationship**, ri·lā′shon·ship, n. The state of being related by kindred, affinity, or other alliance; kinship.—**relative**, rel′a·tiv, a. [L. *relativus*.] Having relation to or bearing on something; close in connection; pertinent; relevant; not absolute or

existing by itself; depending on or incident to something else; *gram.* applied to a word which relates to another word, sentence, or part of a sentence called the antecedent, ap-plied especially to certain pronouns, as *who*, *which*, and *that*.—*Relative motion*, the change of the place of a moving body with respect to some other body also in motion.—*Relative terms*, terms which imply some relation, as *guardian* and *ward*, *master* and *servant*, etc.—n. Something con-sidered in its relation to something else; a person connected by blood or affinity, especially one allied by blood; a kinsman or kinswoman; *gram.* a word which relates to or represents another word, called its antecedent, or refers back to a statement; a relative pronoun.—**relatively**, rel′a·tiv·li, adv. In a relative manner; in relation to something else; not absolutely; com-paratively; often followed by *to* (an expenditure large *relatively to*.—**relativism**, rel′a·tiv·izm, n. A theory that knowledge is relative to the limited nature of the mind.—**rela-tivity**, rel·a·tiv′i·ti, n. The state of being relative; *phys.* a theory formulated by Albert Einstein that deals with the laws of mechanics and the velocity of light in a vacuum and considers mass and energy to be equivalent.—**relator**, ri·lā′ter, n. *law*, an individual who furnishes informa-tion of an accusatory nature, or in whose behalf, or at whose instance, an information is filed, or a writ is-sued, as in the case of a quo warranto.

relax, ri·laks′, v.t. [L. *relaxo*, to relax—*re*, back, and *laxo*, to loosen, from *laxus*, loose. LAX.] To slacken; to make less tense or rigid; to make less severe or rigorous; to remit in strictness; to remit or abate in respect to attention, effort, or labor. —v.i. To become loose, feeble, or languid; to abate in severity; to become more mild or less rigorous; to remit in close attention; to un-bend; to rest or seek recreation.—**relaxation**, ri·lak·sā′shon, n. [L. *relaxatio*.] The act of relaxing or state of being relaxed; a diminution of tension or firmness, remission of attention or application; recreation; an occupation giving mental or bodily relief after effort.

relay, rē·lā′, rē′lā, n. [Fr. *relais*, a relay of horses; originally, relief or release, from L. *re*, and *laxus*, loose.] A supply of anything stored up for affording relief from time to time, or at successive stages; a supply of horses placed on the road to be in readiness to relieve others; a squad of men to take a spell or turn of work at stated intervals; a tele-graphic apparatus which, on receiv-ing a feeble electric current, sends on a much stronger current.—v.t. To carry or pass on by stages.—**relay race**, a race between teams, in which each member of a team covers part of the total distance.

release, ri·lēs′, v.t.—*released*, *releas-ing*. [From O.Fr. *relesser*, *relaisser*, to release, to relinquish—prefix *re*, and *laisser*, to leave, from L. *laxare*, to loosen, from *laxus*, loose, lax. LAX.] To let loose again; to set free from restraint or confinement; to liberate; to free from pain, grief, or any other evil; to free from obligation or penalty; *law*, to give up or let go, as a claim.—*n.* Liberation from restraint of any kind, as from confinement or bondage; liberation from care, pain, or burden; discharge from obligation or responsibility.—**releaser**, ri‧lēs′ėr, *n.* One who releases.

re-lease, rē‧lēs′, *v.t.* [Prefix *re*, and *lease*.] To lease again or anew.

relegate, rel′e‧gāt, *v.t.*—*relegated*, *relegating*. [L. *relego*, *relegatum*, to banish—*re*, back, and *lego*, to send. LEGATE.] To send away or out of the way; to consign to some obscure or remote destination; to banish.—**relegation**, rel‧e‧gā′shon, *n.* [L. *relegatio*.] The act of relegating; banishment; in ancient Roman law, banishment to a certain place for a certain time.

relent, ri‧lent′, *v.i.* [Fr. *ralentir*, to slacken, to abate—prefix *re*, back, *a*, to, and *lent*, L. *lentus*, pliant, slow. LENIENT.] To become less harsh, cruel, or obdurate; to soften in temper; to become more mild; to yield, to comply.—**relentless**, ri‧lent′les, *a.* Incapable of relenting; insensible to the distresses of others; merciless; implacable; pitiless.—**relentlessly**, ri‧lent′les‧li, *adv.* In a relentless manner; without pity.—**relentlessness**, ri‧lent′les‧nes, *n.* The quality of being relentless.

relevant, rel′e‧vant, *a.* [Fr. *relevant*, ppr. of *relever*, to relieve, to help or aid. RELIEVE.] Lending aid or support‡; to the purpose; pertinent; applicable; bearing on the matter in hand (arguments not *relevant* to the case).—**relevantly**, rel′e‧vant‧li, *adv.* In a relevant manner.—**relevance**, **relevancy**, rel′e‧vans, rel′e‧van‧si, *n.* The quality of being relevant; pertinence.

reliable, reliance, reliant, etc. See RELY.

relic, rel′ik, *n.* [Fr. *relique*, from L. *reliquiae*, remains—*re*, back, and *linquo*, to leave (as in *delinquent*) *relinquish*; same root as *license*, Gr. *leipō*, to leave.] That which is left after the loss or decay of the rest; a remaining fragment; the body of a deceased person; usually in *pl.*; something preserved in remembrance; a memento, souvenir, or keepsake; a bone or other part of saints or martyrs, or some part of their garments, etc., preserved, and regarded as of extraordinary sanctity and often as possessing miraculous powers.

relict, rel′ikt, *n.* [O.Fr. *relicte*, a widow, L. *relicta*, fem. of *relictus*, pp. of *relinquo*, to leave. RELIC.] A widow; a woman whose husband is dead.

relief, ri‧lēf′, *n.* [Fr. *relief*, relief, a relieving, alleviation, also (like It. *rilievo*) artistic raised work, from *relever*. RELIEVE.] The removal of

anything painful or burdensome by which some ease is obtained; ease from pain; alleviation; succor; what mitigates or removes pain, grief, or other evil; help given to the poor in the form of food, money, etc.; release from duty by a substitute or substitutes; *sculp.*, *arch.*, etc., the projection or prominence of a figure above or beyond the ground or plane on which it is formed, being of three kinds; high-relief (*alto-rilievo*), low-relief (*basso-rilievo*), and middle or half relief (*mezzo-rilievo*), according to the degree of projection, hence, a piece of artistic work in one or other of these styles; *painting*, the appearance of projection and solidity in represented objects, hence, prominence or distinctness given to anything by something presenting a contrast to it; *phys. geog.* the undulations or surface elevations of a country; *fort.* the height of a parapet from the bottom of the ditch; *feudal law*, a payment by the heir of a tenant made to his lord for the privilege of taking up the estate.—**relievable**, ri‧lē′va‧bl, *a.* Capable of being relieved; fitted to receive relief.—**relieve**, ri‧lēv′, *v.t.*—*relieved*, *relieving*. [O.E. *releve*, from Fr. *relever*, to set up again, to release, to assist, from L. *relevare*, to lift up again—*re*, again, and *levare*, to raise, from *levis*, light. LEVITY.] To remove or lessen, as anything that pains or distresses; to mitigate; alleviate (pain, misery, wants); to free, wholly or partially, from pain, grief, anxiety, or anything considered to be an evil; to help, aid, or succor (the poor, the sick, etc.); to release from a post or duty by substituting another person or party (to *relieve* a sentinel); to obviate the monotony of by the introduction of some variety; to make conspicuous; to set off by contrast; to give the appearance of projection to.—**reliever**, ri‧lē′vėr, *n.* One that relieves.

relievo, ri‧lē′vō or rel‧ē‧ā′vō, *n.* A form of *Rilievo*.

relight, rē‧līt′, *v.t.* To light anew; to rekindle.

religion, ri‧lij′on, *n.* [Fr. *religion*, L. *religio*, *religionis*, perhaps from prefix *re*, and stem meaning to care for, to respect, allied to Gr. *elegō*, to heed.] The feeling of reverence which men entertain toward a Supreme Being; the recognition of God as an object of worship, love, and obedience; piety; any system of faith and worship (the *religion* of the Greeks, Jews, Hindus, Mohammedans, etc.)—*Established religion*, that form of religion in a country which is recognized and supported by the state.—*Natural religion*, the knowledge of God and of our duty which is derived from the light of nature.—*Revealed religion*, the knowledge of God and of our duty from positive revelation.—**religionism**, ri‧lij′on‧izm, *n.* The outward practice of religion; affected or false religion. —**religionist**, ri‧lij′on‧ist, *n.* A religious bigot; one who deals much

in religious discourse; a partisan of a religion.—**religious**, ri‧lij′us, *a.* [L. *religiosus*.] Pertaining or relating to religion; concerned with religion; set apart for purposes connected with religion; imbued with religion; pious; devout; devoted by vows to the practice of religion or to a monastic life (a *religious* order); bound by some solemn obligation; scrupulously faithful.—*n.* A religieux or religieuse.—**religiously**, ri‧lij′us‧li, *adv.* In a religious manner; piously; reverently; strictly; conscientiously.—**religiousness**, ri‧lij′us‧nes, *n.* The quality or state of being religious.

relinquish, ri‧ling′kwish, *v.t.* [O.Fr. *relinquir*, *relinquissant*, from L. *relinquo*, to leave. RELIC.] To give up the possession or occupancy of; to withdraw from; to leave; to abandon; to give up the pursuit or practice of; to desist from; to renounce a claim to.—**relinquisher**, ri‧ling′kwish‧ėr, *n.* One who relinquishes.—**relinquishment**, ri‧ling′kwish‧ment, *n.* The act of relinquishing; the renouncing a claim to.

reliquary, rel′i‧kwe‧ri, *n.* [Fr. *reliquaire*, from L. *reliquiae*, relics. RELIC.] A depository for relics; a casket in which relics are kept; a shrine.—**relique**, re‧lēk′ or rel′ik, *n.* A relic.

reliquiae, ri‧lik′wi‧ė, *n. pl.* [L., remnants, remains. RELIC.] Relics; remains, fossil remains.

relish, rel′ish, *v.t.* [O.Fr. *relecher*, lit. to re-lick—*re*, again, and *lécher*, from O.H.G. *lecchon*, to lick. LICK.] To like the taste or flavor of; to be pleased with or gratified by; to have a liking for; to give an agreeable taste or flavor to; to savor or smack of.—*v.i.* To have a pleasing taste; to have a flavor.—*n.* The sensation produced by anything on the palate; savor; taste, commonly a pleasing taste; inclination; liking (a *relish for* something); delight given by anything; characteristic quality; savor or flavor; smack, a small quantity just perceptible; a pickled, spiced or glazed food served with the meat or fish course.—**relishable**, rel′ish‧a‧bl, *a.* Capable of being relished.

relive, rē‧liv′, *v.i.* To live again; to revive.

reload, rē‧lōd′, *v.t.* To load again.

relucent, ri‧lū′sent, *a.* [L. *re*, back, and *luceo*, to shine. LUCID.] Throwing back light; luminous; shining; eminent.

reluctant, ri‧luk′tant, *a.* [L. *reluctans*, *reluctantis*, ppr. of *reluctor*, to struggle—*re*, back, and *luctor*, to struggle, *lucta*, a struggle.] Striving against doing something; unwilling to do what one feels called on to do; acting with repugnance; averse; loth; granted with unwillingness (*reluctant* obedience).—**reluctantly**, ri‧luk′tant‧li, *adv.* In a reluctant manner; unwillingly.—**reluctance**, **reluctancy**, ri‧luk′tans, ri‧luk′tan‧si, *n.* The state or quality of being reluctant; aversion; unwillingness; in magnetism, the resistance offered by a medium to the passage through it of lines of magnetic force; the reciprocal of permeability; also called magnetic resistance. Its unit is the OERSTED (which see).

relume, relumine, ri·lūm′, ri·lū′-min, *v.t.* [L. *re*, again, and *lumen*, light. LUMINARY.] To light anew; to illuminate again.

rely, ri·lī′, *v.t.*—*relied, relying.* [From Fr. *relier*, to bind, to attach—L. *re*, back, and *ligare*, to bind (hence *ligament*): formerly often used with reflexive pronouns (to *rely one's self upon*).] To rest with confidence, as when we are satisfied of the veracity, integrity, or ability of persons, or of the certainty of facts or of evidence; to have confidence; to trust: with *on* or *upon*.—**reliable,** ri·lī′a·bl, *a.* [This word (in use as early as 1569) was considered irregular by some 19th-century writers, but it is now considered perfectly acceptable.] Such as may be relied on; worthy of being relied on; to be depended on for support.—**reliable-ness, reliability,** ri·lī′a·bl·nes, ri·lī′a·bil″i·ti, *n.* The quality of being reliable.—**reliably,** ri·lī′a·bli, *adv.* In a reliable manner; so as to be relied on.—**reliance,** ri·lī′ans, *n.* The act of relying; dependence; confidence; trust; ground of trust.—**reliant,** ri·lī′ant, *a.* Having reliance; confident; self-reliant.—**relier,** ri·lī′ér, *n.* One who relies.

remain, ri·mān′, *v.i.* [O.Fr. *remaindre*, to remain, from L. *remaneo*—*re*, back, and *maneo, mansi*, to stay. MANSION.] To continue in a place; to abide; to continue in an unchanged form or condition; to endure; to last; to stay behind after others have gone; to be left; to be left as not included or comprised; to be still to deal with.—*n.* That which is left; remainder; relic: chiefly used in the plural; specifically, *pl.*, that which is left of a human being after life is gone, that is the dead body; *pl.* the productions, especially the literary works, of one who is dead.—**remainder,** ri·mān′-dér, *n.* [An infinitive form; comp. *rejoinder.*] That which remains; anything left after the removal of the rest; *arith.* etc., the sum or quantity that is left after subtraction or deduction; *law*, an estate limited so as to be enjoyed after the death of the present possessor or otherwise. —*a.* Remaining; left over.

remake, rē·māk′, *v.t.*—*remade, re-making.* To make anew; to make over again.

remand, ri·mand′, *v.t.* [Fr. *remander*, from L. *re*, and *mando*, to commit to one's charge. MANDATE.] To send, call, or order back; *law*, to send back to jail, as an accused party, in order to give time to collect more evidence.—*n.* The state of being remanded; the act of remanding.

remanent, rem′a·nent, *a.* [L. *remanens, remanentis*, ppr. of *remaneo.* REMAIN.] Remaining.

remark, ri·märk′, *n.* [Fr. *remarque*—*re*, and *marque.* MARK.] The act of observing or taking notice; notice or observation; a brief statement taking notice of something; an observation; a comment.—*v.t.* To observe; to note in the mind; to express, as a thought that has occurred to the speaker; to utter by way of comment or observation.—**remarkable,** ri·mär′ka·bl, *a.* Observable; worthy of notice; extraordinary; unusual; striking; noteworthy; conspicuous; distinguished.—**remarkableness,** ri·mär′ka·bl·nes, *n.*—**remarkably,** ri·mär′ka·bli, *adv.* In a remarkable manner; singularly; surprisingly.

remarry, rē·mar′i, *v.t.* To marry again or a second time.—*v.i.* To be married again or a second time.—**remarriage,** rē·mar′ij, *n.* Any marriage after the first; a repeated marriage.

remedy, rem′e·di, *n.* [L. *remedium*, from *re*, again, and *medeor*, to heal. MEDICAL.] That which cures a disease; any medicine or application which puts an end to disease and restores health (a *remedy for* the gout); that which corrects or counteracts an evil of any kind; relief; redress; legal means for recovery of a right.—*v.t.*—*remedied, remedying.* To cure; to heal; to repair or remove, as some evil; to redress; to counteract.—**remediable,** ri·mē′-di·a·bl, *a.* Capable of being remedied.—**remediably,** ri·mē′di·a·bli, *adv.*—**remedial,** ri·mē′di·al, *a.* [L. *remedialis.*] Affording a remedy; intended to remedy or cure something, or for the removal of an evil (*remedial* measures).—**remediless,** rem′e·di·les, *a.* Not admitting a remedy; incurable; irreparable.

remember, ri·mem′bér, *v.t.* [O.Fr. *remembrer, se remembrer*, from L.L. *rememorare*—L. *re*, again, and *memorare*, to bring to mind, from *memor*, mindful. MEMOIR.] To have in the mind and capable of being brought back from the past; to bear or keep in mind; to be capable of recalling; not to forget; to put in mind; to remind; to think of; to keep in mind with gratitude, favor, affection, or other emotion.—*v.i.* To have something in remembrance; to recollect. ∴ *Remember* implies that a thing exists in the memory, but not that it is actually present in the thoughts at the moment. *Recollect* means that a fact, forgotten or partially lost to memory, is after some effort recalled. See MEMORY.—**rememberer,** ri·mem′bér·ér, *n.* One that remembers.—**remembrance,** ri·mem′brans, *n.* [O.Fr. *remembrance.*] The keeping of a thing in mind; power or faculty of remembering; limit of time over which the memory extends; what is remembered; a memorial; a keepsake; state of being mindful; regard. ∴ Syn. under MEMORY.—**remembrancer,** ri·mem′bran·sér, *n.* One who reminds; [*usually cap.*] an officer in the exchequer of England whose business is to record certain papers and proceedings, make out processes, etc.; a recorder; the name of an officer who collects debts due the sovereign.

remigrate, rē·mī′grāt, *v.i.* To migrate again; to return.—**remigration,** rē·mī·grā′shon, *n.* A migration to a former place.

remind, ri·mīnd′, *v.t.* To put in mind; to cause to recollect or remember (to *remind* a person of his promise).—**reminder,** ri·mīn′dér, *n.* One who or that which reminds; a hint that serves to awaken remembrance.—**remindful,** ri·mīnd′ful, *a.* Tending or adapted to remind.

reminiscence, rem·i·nis′ens, *n.* [Fr. *réminiscence*, L. *reminiscentia*, from *reminiscor*, to recall to mind—*re*, again, and *miniscor* from root *men*, whence *mens*, the mind. MENTAL.] Recollection; that which is recollected or recalled to mind; a relation of what is recollected; a narration of past incidents within one's personal knowledge. ∴ Syn. under MEMORY.—**reminiscent,** rem·i·nis′-ent, *a.* Having remembrance; calling to mind.—*n.* One who calls to mind.

remise, ri·mīz′, *n.* [Fr., from *remettre*, L. *remitio.* REMISS.] *Law*, a granting back; a surrender; release, as of a claim.

remiss, ri·mis′, *a.* [L. *remissus*, relaxed, languid, not strict, pp. of *remitto*—*re*, back, and *mitto*, to send. MISSION.] Not energetic or diligent in performance; careless in performing duty or business; negligent; dilatory; slack; wanting earnestness or activity.—**remissibility,** ri·mis′-i·bil″i·ti, *n.* Capability of being remitted.—**remissible,** ri·mis′i·bl, *a.* Capable of being remitted or forgiven.—**remission,** ri·mish′on, *n.* The act of remitting; diminution or cessation of intensity; abatement; moderation; a giving up; the act of forgiving; forgiveness; pardon; a temporary subsidence of the force or violence of a disease or of pain.—**remissness,** ri·mis′nes, *n.* The state or quality of being remiss.—**remit,** ri·mit′, *v.t.*—*remitted, remitting.* [L. *remitto*, to send back, slacken, relax.] To relax in intensity; to make less intense or violent; to abate; to refrain from exacting; to give up in whole or in part (to *remit* punishment); to pardon; to forgive; to refrain from exacting punishment for (sins); to surrender; to resign; to send back; to put again into custody; *Scots law*, to transfer from one tribunal or judge to another; *com.* to transmit or send, as money, or other things in payment for goods received.—*v.i.* To slacken; to become less intense or rigorous; *med.* to abate in violence for a time (a fever *remits* at a certain hour every day); *com.* to transmit money, etc.— *n. Scots law*, the transferring of a cause from one tribunal or judge to another.—**remittal,** ri·mit′al, *n.* A remitting; a sending money to a distant place.—**remittance,** ri·mit′-ans, *n.* The act of transmitting money, bills, or the like, to a distant place, in return or payment for goods purchased; the sum remitted. —**remittent,** ri·mit′ent, *a.* [L. *re-mittens, remittentis*, ppr. of *remitto.*]

Temporarily ceasing; having remissions from time to time.—*Remittent fever*, any fever which suffers a decided remission of its violence during the twenty-four hours, but without entirely leaving the patient. —*n*. A remittent fever.—**remitter**, ri·mit′ẻr, *n*. One who remits.

remnant, rem′nant, *n*. [Contr. from *remanent*. REMANENT.] What remains after the removal of the rest of a thing; the remaining piece of a web of cloth after the rest is sold; that which remains after a part is done or past; a scrap, fragment, little bit.—*a*. Remaining; yet left.

remodel, rē·mod′el, *v.t.*—*remodeled*, *remodeling*. To model or fashion anew.

remold, rē·mōld′, *v.t.* To mold again or anew.

remonetize, rē·mon′e·tīz, *v.t.*—*monetized*, *remonetizing*. [L. *re*, again, and *moneta*, money. MONEY.] To restore to circulation in the shape of money; to make again the legal or standard money of account.— **remonetization**, rē·mon′et·i·zā″shon, *n*. The act of remonetizing.

remonstrate, ri·mon′strāt, *v.i.*—*remonstrated*, *remonstrating*. [O.Fr. *remonstrer* (Fr. *remontrer*); L.L. *remonstro*—L. *re*, again, and *monstro*, to show. MONSTER.] To exhibit or present strong reasons against an act, measure, or any course of proceedings; to expostulate.—**remonstrance**, ri·mon′strans, *n*. [O.Fr. *remonstrance*.] The act of remonstrating or expostulating; an expostulation; a strong statement of reasons against something; a paper containing such a statement.—**remonstrant**, **remonstrative**, ri·mon′strant, ri·mon′stra·tiv, *a*. Expostulating; remonstrating.—**remonstrant**, **remonstrator**, ri·mon′strant, ri·mon′strā·tẻr, *n*. One who remonstrates.

remora, rem′o·ra, *n*. [L., from *re*, back, and *mora*, delay.] The suckfish, a fish with flattened, adhesive disk on the top of the head, by which it attaches itself firmly to other fishes or to the bottoms of vessels; fabled by the ancients to have miraculous powers of delaying ships.

remorse, ri·mors′, *n*. [L.L. *remorsus*, a biting again, from L. *remordeo*, *remorsum*—*re*, again, and *mordeo*, to bite. MORSEL.] The keen pain or anguish excited by a sense of guilt; compunction of conscience for a crime committed; painful memory of wrongdoing.—**remorseful**, ri·mors′fụl, *a*. Full of remorse; impressed with a sense of guilt.—**remorsefully**, ri·mors′fụl·li, *adv*. In a remorseful manner.—**remorsefulness**, ri·mors′fụl·nes, *n*. The state of being remorseful.—**remorseless**, ri·mors′les, *a*. Without remorse; unpitying; cruel; insensible; pitiless.—**remorselessly**, ri·mors′les·li, *adv*. In a remorseless manner; pitilessly.—**remorselessness**, ri·mors′les·nes, *n*.

remote, ri·mōt′, *a*. [L. *remotus*, from *removeo*, to remove—*er*, and *moveo*, *motum*, to move. REMOVE.] Distant in place; far off; not near; distant in time, past or future;

not directly producing an effect; not proximate (the *remote* causes of a disease); distant in consanguinity or affinity (a *remote* kinsman); slight; inconsiderable (remote resemblance). —*Remote control*, control from a point at some distance, as by a switchboard, by a movable actuating device electrically connected to a broadcasting station.—**remotely**, ri·mōt′li, *adv*. In a remote manner; at a distance; slightly; not closely.— **remoteness**, *n*.

remount, rē·mount′, *v.t. and i*. To mount again.—*n*. A fresh horse to mount.

remove, ri·möv′, *v.t.*—*removed*, *removing*. [O.Fr. *remouvoir*, from L. *removeo*, to remove—*re*, and *moveo*, to move. MOVE.] To shift from the position occupied; to put from its place in any manner; to displace from an office, post, or position; to take away by causing to cease; to cause to leave a person or thing; to put an end to; to banish (to *remove* a disease or grievance); to make away with; to cut off (to *remove* a person by poison).—*v.i.* To change place in any manner; to move from one place to another; to change the place of residence. ∴ *Move* is a generic term, including the sense of *remove*, but the latter is never applied to a mere change of posture without a change of place or position.—*n*. The act of removing; a removal; change of place; the distance or space through which anything is removed; an interval; stage; a step in any scale of gradation; a dish removed from the table to make room for something else.—**removability**, ri·mö′va·bil′·i·ti, *n*. The capacity of being removable.—**removable**, ri·mö′va·bl, *a*. Capable of being removed.—**removal**, ri·mö′val, *n*. A moving from one place to another; change of place or site; the act of displacing from an office or post; the act of putting an end to (the *removal* of a grievance).—**removed**, ri·mövd′, *p. and a*. Changed in place; displaced from office; remote; separate from others. —**remover**, ri·mö′vẻr, *n*. One who or that which removes, as paint remover.

remunerate, ri·mū′nẻr·āt, *v.t.*—*remunerated*, *remunerating*. [L. *remunero*, *remuneratum*—*re*, back, and *munus*, *muneris*, a present, gift.] To reward; to recompense; to requite, in a good sense; to pay an equivalent to for any service, loss, or sacrifice.— **remuneration**, ri·mū′nẻr·ā″shon, *n*. The act of remunerating; what is given to remunerate.—**remunerative**, ri·mū′nẻr·a·tiv, *a*. Affording remuneration; yielding a sufficient return.

renaissance, ren′e·säns″, *n*. [Fr. regeneration or new birth—*re*, again, and *naissance*, birth, L. *nascentia*, from *nascor*, *natus*, to be born. NATAL.] The revival of anything which has long been in decay or extinct; [*cap*.] the transitional movement in Europe from the Middle Ages to the modern world; specially

applied to the time of the revival of letters and arts in the fifteenth century.—*Renaissance style*, the style of building and decoration which succeeded the Gothic, and sought to reproduce the forms of classical ornamentation.—**renascence**, ri·näs′ens, *n*. The state of being renascent; [*cap*.] also same as *Renaissance*.—**renascent**, ri·näs′ent, *a*. [L. *renascens*.] Rejuvenated.

renal, rē′nal, *a*. [L. *renalis*, from *ren*, pl. *renes*, the kidneys.] Pertaining to the kidneys.

rename, rē·nām′, *v.t.* To give a new name to.

Renard, ren′ärd, *n*. [Fr., from O.G. *Reinhard*, *Reginhart*, lit. strong in counsel, cunning—the name of a fox in a celebrated German epic poem.] A fox: a name used in fables, poetry, etc., also written *Reynard*.

rencounter, **rencontre**, ren·koun′tẻr, ren·kon′tẻr, *n*. [Fr. *rencontre*= *re-encounter*.] An abrupt or chance meeting of persons; a meeting in opposition or contest; a casual combat or action, as between individuals or small parties; a slight engagement between armies or fleets. —*v.i.*† To meet unexpectedly.—*v.i.* To meet an enemy unexpectedly; to come in collision; to fight hand to hand.

rend, rend, *v.t.*—pret. and pp. rent. [A.Sax. *rendan*, *hrendan*, to tear, to rend=O.Fris. *renda*, *randa*, N.Fris. *renne*, to cut, to rend; comp. W. *rhann*, Ir. *rann*, a part, Armor. *ranna*, to part, to separate.] To separate into parts with force or sudden violence; to tear asunder; to split; to take away with violence; to tear away.—*To rend the heart*, to affect with deep anguish or repentant sorrow.—*v.i.* To be or to become rent or torn; to split; to part asunder.—**render**, ren′dẻr, *n*. One who rends or tears by violence.

render, ren′dẻr, *v.t.* [Fr. *rendre*, from L. *reddo*, to restore, by the insertion of *n* before *d*—*re*, back, and *do*, to give.] To give in return; to give or pay back; to give, often officially, or in compliance with a request or duty; to furnish; to report (to *render* an account); to give for use or benefit (to *render* services); to make or cause to be or to convert; to invest with qualities (to *render* a fortress more secure); to translate from one language into another; to interpret or bring into full expression to others; to reproduce (to *render* a piece of music); to boil down and clarify (to *render* tallow).—*v.i. Naut.* to yield or give way to force applied; to pass freely through a block: said of a rope.—*n*. A return; a payment, especially a payment of rent.—**renderable**, ren′dẻr·a·bl, *a*. Capable of being rendered.—**renderer**, ren′dẻr·ẻr, *n*. One who renders.

rendezvous, rän′de·vö, *n*. [Fr. *rendez-vous*, lit. render yourselves, repair to a place. RENDER.] A place appointed for the assembling of troops; the port or place where ships are ordered to join company;

an appointment; a place of meeting; a place at which persons commonly meet.—*v.i.*—*rendezvoused* (rän´de‧vöd), *rendezvousing* (rän´de‧vö‧ing). To assemble at a particular place, as troops.

rendition, ren‧dish´on, *n.* [L. *redditio*. RENDER.] A rendering or giving the meaning of a word or passage; translation; the act of reproducing or exhibiting artistically; the act of rendering up or yielding possession; surrender.

renegade, renegado, ren´e‧gād, ren‧ē‧gä´dō, *n.* [Sp. *renegado*, Fr. *renégat*, L.L. *renegatus*, one who denies his religion—L. *re*, back, and *nego, negatum*, to deny. NEGATION, RUNAGATE.] An apostate from a religious faith; one who deserts to an enemy or who deserts one party and joins another: a deserter.

renege, ri‧nig´, *v.t.* and *i.* [L.L. *renego*. RENEGADE.] To deny; to renounce; to play a card of another suit when able to follow suit; to go back on a promise.

renew, ri‧nū´, *v.t.* To make new again; to restore to former freshness, completeness, or perfection; to restore to a former state, or to a good state, after decay or impairment; to make again (to *renew* a treaty); to begin again; to recommence (*renew* a fight); to grant or furnish again, as a new loan or a new note for the amount of a former one (to *renew* a bill).—*v.i.* To become new; to grow afresh; to begin again; not to desist.—**renewable,** ri‧nū´a‧bl, *a.* Capable of being renewed.—**renewal,** ri‧nū´al, *n.* The act of renewing or of forming anew.

reniform, re´ni‧form, *a.* [L. *ren*, a kidney.] Having the form or shape of the kidneys.

renitent, ri‧nī´tent, *a.* [L. *renitens, renitentis*, ppr. of *renitor*—*re*, back, and *nitor*, to struggle.] Resisting pressure; acting against impulse; persistently opposed.—**renitency,** ri‧nī´ten‧si, *n.* The state of being renitent.

rennet, ren´et, *n.* [Also written *runnet*, and formed from the verb to *run*, O.E. *renne*; A.Sax. *rinnan*, to run, *gerinnan*, to curdle or coagulate; comp. G. *rennen*, to run, to curdle, *rennse*, rennet; D. *rinnen*, to curdle.] The prepared inner membrane of the calf's stomach, which has the property of coagulating milk.

rennet, ren´et, *n.* [Fr. *reinette*, dim. of *reine*, L. *regina*, a queen.] A kind of apple said to have been introduced in the reign of Henry VIII.

rennin, ren´nin, *n.* A milk-curdling ferment contained in gastric juice.

renounce, ri‧nouns´, *v.t.*—*renounced, renouncing*. [Fr. *renoncer*, from L. *renuncio*—*re*, back, and *nuncio, nuntio*, to tell. NUNCIO.] To disown, disclaim, abjure, forswear; to refuse to own or acknowledge as belonging; to cast off or reject.—*v.i. Card playing*, not to follow suit when one has a card of the same sort; to revoke.—**renouncement,** ri‧nouns´ment, *n.* The act of disclaiming or rejecting; renunciation.—**renuncia-**

tion, ri‧nun´si‧ā˝shon, *n.* The act of renouncing; a disowning or disclaiming; rejecting.

renovate, ren´o‧vāt, *v.t.*—*renovated, renovating.* [L. *renovo, renovatum*—*re*, again, and *novo*, to make new, from *novus*, new. NOVEL.] To renew; to repair and render as good as new; to restore to freshness or to a good condition.—**renovator,** ren´o‧vā‧tėr, *n.* One who or that which renovates.—**renovation,** ren‧o‧vā´shon, *n.* The act of renovating; renewal; repair; restoration.

renown, ri‧noun´, *n.* [O.E. *renowne*, from Fr. *renom*, from L. *re*, and *nomen*, a name. NOUN.] The state of having a great or exalted name; exalted reputation derived from the widely spread praise of great achievements or accomplishments.—*v.t.* To make famous.—**renowned,** ri‧nound´, *a.* Famous; celebrated for great and heroic achievements, for distinguished qualities, or for grandeur; eminent.

rensselaerite, rens´sel‧ẚr‧it, *n.* [After Van *Rensselaer*.] A steatitic mineral with a fine compact texture, worked into inkstands and other articles.

rent, rent, pret. & pp. of *rend*.

rent, rent, *n.* [From pp. of *rend*.] An opening made by rending or tearing; a break or breach; a hole torn; schism.

rent, rent, *n.* [Fr. *rente*, It. *rendita*, that which is rendered or given up, from L.L. *rendo*, for L. *reddo*, to give up. RENDER.] A sum of money, or a certain amount of anything valuable, payable yearly for the use or occupation of lands or tenements; a compensation made to the owner by the user or occupier as a return for his occupancy.—*v.t.* To grant the possession and enjoyment of for a certain rent; to let on lease; to take and hold on the payment of rent.—*v.i.* To be leased or let for rent.—**rentable,** rent´a‧bl, *a.* Capable of being rented.—**rental,** rent´al, *n.* A schedule or account of rents; the gross amount of rents drawn from an estate.—**renter,** rent´ėr, *n.* The lessee or tenant who pays rent.

renter, rent´ėr, *v.t.* [Fr. *rentraire*—*re*, back, *en*, in, and *traire*, from L. *trahere*, to draw. TRACT.] To fine-draw; to sew together, as the edges of two pieces of cloth.

renunciation. See RENOUNCE.

reoccupy, rē‧ok´kū‧pī, *v.t.* To occupy anew.

reopen, rē‧ō´pen, *v.t.* To open again. —*v.i.* To be opened again; to open anew.

reorganize, rē‧or´gan‧īz, *v.t.* To organize anew; to reduce again to an organized condition.—**reorganization,** rē‧or´gan‧i‧zā˝shon, *n.* The act of organizing anew.

rep, repp, rep, *n.* [Perhaps from *rib*.] A dress fabric having a ribbed or corded appearance, the ribs being transverse.

repaint, rē‧pānt´, *v.t.* To paint anew.

repair, ri‧pâr´, *v.t.* [Fr. *réparer*, from L. *reparo*—*re*, again, and *paro*, to get or make ready. PARE.] To execute restoration or renovation on; to restore to a sound or good state after

decay, injury, dilapidation, or partial destruction; to make amends for, as for an injury, by an equivalent; to give indemnity for.—*n.* Restoration to a sound or good state; supply of loss; reparation; state as regards repairing (a building in good or bad *repair*).—**repairable,** ri‧pâ´ra‧bl, *a.* Capable of being repaired; reparable. —**repairer,** ri‧pâ´rėr, *n.* One who repairs.—**reparable,** rep´a‧ra‧bl, *a.* [L. *reparabilis*.] Capable of being repaired, restored to a sound state, or made good.—**reparably,** rep´a‧ra‧bli, *adv.* In a reparable manner.—**reparation,** rep‧a‧rā´shon, *n.* The act of repairing; repair; what is done to repair a wrong; indemnification for loss or damage, as demanded of Germany by the Allies after World War I for property damage done in France; satisfaction for injury; amends.—**reparative,** ri‧par´a‧tiv, *a.* Capable of effecting repair; tending to make good or amend defect.—*n.* That which restores to a good state; that which makes amends.

repair, ri‧pâr´, *v.i.* [O.Fr. *repairer*, from L.L. *repatriare*—*re*, back, and *patria*, one's native country. PATRIOT.] To go to some place; to betake one's self; to resort.—*n.* The act of betaking one's self to any place; a resorting; haunt; resort.

repand, ri‧pand´, *a.* [L. *repandus*, bent backward, turned up.] *Bot.* having an uneven, slightly sinuous margin, as a leaf.

repartee, rep‧ẚr‧tē´, *n.* [Fr. *repartie*—*re*, back, and *partir*, from L. *partire*, to share, part, from *pars, partis*, a part. PART.] A smart, ready, and witty reply.

repartition, rē‧pẚr‧tish´on, *n.* A fresh partition or division.

repass, rē‧pas´, *v.t.* To pass again; to pass or travel back over; to recross.—*v.i.* To pass or go back; to move back.

repast, ri‧past´, *n.* [O.Fr. *repast*, Fr. *repas*, from L. *re*, again, and *pasco, pastum*, to feed. PASTOR.] The act of taking food; a meal; food; victuals (*Shak.*).—*v.t.* To feed; to feast.— *v.i.* To take food; to feast.

repatriate, rē‧pā´tri‧āt, *v.t.*—*repatriated, repatriating.* [L. *repatrio, repatriatum*—*re*, again, and *patria*, one's country. PATRIOT.] To restore to one's own country.—**repatriation,** rē‧pā´tri‧ā˝shon, *n.* Return or restoration to one's own country.

repay, rē‧pā´, *v.t.* To pay back; to refund; to make return or requital for.—*v.i.* To requite either good or evil.—**repayable,** rē‧pā´a‧bl, *a.* Capable of being repaid; liable to be repaid or refunded.—**repayment,** rē‧pā´ment, *n.* The act of repaying or paying back; the money repaid.

repeal, ri‧pēl´, *v.t.* [Fr. *rappeler*—*re*, back, and *appeler*, L. *appello*, to call upon, speak to. APPEAL.] To recall, as a law or statute; to revoke; to abrogate by an authoritative act, or by the same power that made or enacted.—*n.* The act of repealing; revocation; abrogation.—**repealable,** ri‧pēl´a‧bl, *a.* Capable of being repealed.

repeat, ri·pēt', *v.t.* [Fr. *répéter*, from L. *repeto*, to seek again, to repeat—*re*, again, and *peto*, to seek. PETITION.] To do or perform again (to *repeat* an attempt); to go over, say, make, etc., again; to iterate; to recite; to rehearse; to say over (to *repeat* a lesson).—*n.* The act of repeating; repetition; *music*, a sign that a movement or part of a movement is to be twice performed.—*v.i.* To strike the hours (a *repeating* watch).—**repeatedly,** ri·pēt'ed·li, *adv.* With repetition; more than once; again and again.—**repeater,** ri·pēt'ėr, *n.* One that repeats, as illegally voting a second time in an election; a gun with extra shells in a chamber to facilitate rapid firing; one returned to prison for a further crime, having served one or more previous sentences; one that recites or rehearses; a watch that strikes the hours, etc., on the compression of a spring; *arith.* an interminate decimal in which the same figure continually recurs.—**repetend,** rep'e·tend, *n.* [L. *repetendum*, a thing to be repeated.] *Arith.* that part of a repeating decimal which recurs continually ad infinitum.—**repetition,** rep·e·tish'on, *n.* The act of doing or uttering a second time; the act of repeating or saying over; a reciting or rehearsing; what is repeated; something said or done a second time.—**repetitious,** rep·e·tish'us, *a.* Containing repetitions or statements repeated.—**repetitive,** ri·pet'i·tiv, *a.* Containing repetitions.

repel, ri·pel', *v.t.*—*repelled, repelling.* [L. *repello*—*re*, back, and *pello*, to drive, as in *expel, compel, expulsion*, etc. PULSE.] To drive back; to force to return; to check the advance of; to repulse (to *repel* an enemy); to encounter with effectual resistance; to resist or oppose successfully (to *repel* an encroachment, an argument).—*v.i.* To cause repugnance; to shock; to act with force in opposition (electricity sometimes *repels*).—**repellent,** ri·pel'ent, *a.* Having the effect of repelling; able or tending to repel; repulsive; deterring.—*n.* That which repels.—**repeller,** ri·pel'ėr, *n.* One who or that which repels.

repent, ri'pent, *a.* [L. *repens, repentis,* ppr. of *repo*, to creep.] Creeping (a *repent* root, a *repent* animal).

repent, ri·pent', *v.i.* [Fr. *repentir*—*se repentir*, to repent—L. *re*, and *poenitere*, to repent, from *poena*, pain. PENITENT, PAIN.] To feel pain, sorrow, or regret for something done or left undone by one's self; to experience such sorrow for sin as produces amendment of life; to be penitent.—*v.t.* To remember with compunction or self-reproach; to feel self-accusing pain or grief on account of (to *repent* rash words); formerly used in such phrases as I *repent me,* it *repented him* (impersonally).—**repentance,** ri·pen'tans, *n.* The act of repenting; the state of being penitent; contrition for sin; such sorrow for past conduct as produces a new life.—**repentant,** ri·-

pen'tant, *a.* Experiencing repentance; sorrowful for sin; expressing or showing sorrow for sin (*repentant* tears).—**repentantly,** ri·pen'tant·li, *adv.* In a repentant manner.—**repenter,** ri·pen'tėr, *n.* One that repents.

repeople, rē·pē'pl, *v.t.* To people anew; to furnish again with a stock of people.

repercuss, rē·pėr·kus', *v.t.* [L. *repercutio, repercussum.* PERCUSS.] To beat or drive back (as sound or air); to make rebound.—**repercussive,** rē·pėr·kus'iv, *a.* Having the power of repercussion; causing to reverberate.

repercussion, rē·per·kush'in, *n.* [L. *repercussio*, from *repercussus*, pp. of *repercutere*, to drive back.] A driving back or being driven back; reverberation; a reciprocal action or effect (the *repercussions* of the plan).

repertoire, rep'ėr·twär, *n.* [Fr. *répertoire.* REPERTORY.] A list of dramas, operas, or the like, which can be performed by a dramatic or operatic company; those parts, songs, etc., that are usually performed by an actor, vocalist, etc.

repertory, rep'ėr·to·ri, *n.* [L. *repertorium*, from *reperio*, to find again—*re*, again, and *pario*, to produce. PARENT.] A storehouse or collection of things; a repertoire.

repetition, etc. See REPEAT.

repine, ri·pīn', *v.i.*—*repined, repining* [O.E. *repoyne*, Fr. *repoindre*, to prick again—L. *re*, again, and *pungo*, to prick (PUNCTURE), influenced by verb to *pine.*] To fret one's self; to feel inward discontent which preys on the spirits; to indulge in complaint; to murmur: with *at* or *against.*

replace, ri·plās', *v.t.* To put again in the former place; to repay; to refund; to fill the place of; to be a substitute for.—**replacement,** ri·plās'ment, *n.* The act of replacing; that which replaces, as *pl.* soldiers assigned to a decimated company.

replant, rē·plant', *v.t.* To plant again; to reinstate.

repleader, rē·plē'dėr, *n. Law,* a second pleading or course of pleadings.

replenish, ri·plen'ish, *v.t.* [O.Fr. *replenir, replenissant,* from L. *re*, again, and *plenus,* full, from *pleo,* to fill. PLENARY, COMPLETE.] To fill again after having been emptied or diminished; hence, to fill completely; to stock with numbers or abundance. —**replenisher,** ri·plen'ish·ėr, *n.* One who replenishes.—**replenishment,** ri·plen'ish·ment, *n.*

replete, ri·plēt', *a.* [L. *repletus,* pp. of *repleo,* to fill again—*re,* again, and *pleo,* to fill. REPLENISH.] Completely filled; full; abounding; thoroughly imbued.—*v.t.* To fill to repletion or satiety.—**repletion,** ri·plē'shon, *n.* The state of being replete or completely filled; superabundant fullness; surfeit.

replevy, ri·plev'i, *v.t.*—*replevied, replevying.* [O.Fr. *replevir.*] *Law,* to recover possession of (as goods wrongfully seized) upon giving surety to try the right to them in court;

to take back by writ of replevin.—**repleviable, replevisable,** ri·plev'i·a·bl, ri·plev'i·za·bl, *a. Law,* capable of being replevied.—**replevin, replevy,** ri·plev'in, *n. Law,* a personal action which lies to recover possession of goods or chattels wrongfully taken or detained.

replica, rep'li·ka, *n.* [It. *replica,* a reply, a repetition—L. *re,* back, and *plica,* a fold. REPLY.] A copy of a picture or piece of sculpture made by the hand that executed the original.

replicant, rep'li·kant, *n.* [L. *replicans, replicantis,* ppr. of *replico,* reply. REPLY.] *obs.* One who makes a reply. —**replication,** rep·li·kā'shon, *n.* An answer; a reply; a repetition; a copy; a replica.

replicate, rep'li·kāt, *a.* [L. *re,* back, and *plico,* to fold. REPLY.] *Bot.* folded or bent back.

reply, ri·plī', *v.i.*—*replied, replying.* [O.Fr. *replier* (Mod.Fr. *répliquer*), to reply, from L. *replico,* to fold back, to reply—*re,* back, and *plico,* to fold. PLY, APPLY, EMPLOY.] To make answer in words or writing, as to something said or written by another; to answer; to respond; to do or give something in return for something else; to answer by deeds; to meet an attack by fitting action.—*v.t.* To return for an answer: often with a clause as object.—*n.* That which is said or written in answer to what is said or written by another; an answer; that which is done in consequence of something else; an answer by deeds; a counterattack.—**replier,** ri·plī'ėr, *n.* One who replies; an answerer, a respondent; a replicant.

report, ri·pōrt', *v.t.* [Fr. *reporter,* to carry back; *rapporter,* to carry back, relate, report; the former from L. *reporto*—*re,* and *porto,* to carry, the latter from *re, ad,* and *porto.* PORT (carriage).] To bear or bring back, as an answer; to relate, as what has been discovered by a person sent to examine or investigate; to give an account of; to relate; to tell; to circulate publicly, as a story (as in the common phrase it is *reported,* that is, it is said in public); to give an official or formal account or statement of; to give an account of for public reading; to write out or take down from the lips of the speaker (the debate was fully *reported*); to lay a charge or make a disclosure against (I will *report* you). —*To be reported of,* to be well or ill spoken of.—*To report one's self,* to make known one's whereabouts or movements to the proper quarter. —*v.i.* To make a statement of facts; to take down, in writing speeches from a speaker's lips; to discharge the office of a reporter.—*n.* An account brought back; a statement of facts given in reply to inquiry; a story circulated; hence, rumor; common fame; repute; public character (a man of good *report*); an account of a judicial decision, or of a case argued and determined in a court of law, etc.; an official statement of facts; an account of the proceedings, debates, etc., of a legislative assembly or other meeting, intended for publication; an epitome or fully written account of a speech; sound of an explosion; loud noise (the *report* of a gun).—**reportable**, ri•pōr′ta•bl, *a.* Fit to be reported.—**reporter**, ri•pōr′tér, *n.* One who reports; a member of a newspaper staff whose duty it is to give an account of the proceedings of public meetings and entertainments, collect information respecting interesting or important events, and the like.—**reportorial**, ri•pōr′tō′ri•al, *a.* Relating to a reporter or reporters.

repose, ri•pōz′, *v.t.*—*reposed, reposing.* [Fr. *reposer*, to place again, to settle, to rest—*re*, again, and *poser.* POSE.] To lay at rest; to lay for the purpose of taking rest; to refresh by rest: frequently used reflexively; to lay, place, or rest in full reliance (to *repose* trust or confidence in a person).—*v.i.* To lie at rest; to sleep; to rest in confidence; to rely: followed by *on.*—*n.* [Fr. *repos.*] The act or state of reposing; a lying at rest; sleep; rest; quiet; rest of mind; tranquillity; settled composure; absence of all show of feeling; *painting,* an avoidance of obtrusive tints or of striking action in figures.—**reposal**, ri•pō′zal, *n.* The act of reposing or resting with reliance.—**reposeful**, ri•pōz′fụl, *a.* Full of repose; affording repose or rest; trustful.

reposit, ri•poz′it, *v.t.* [L. *repono, repositum*—*re,* back, and *pono,* to place. POSITION.] To lay up; to lodge, as for safety or preservation.—**reposition**, rē•po•zish′on, *n.* Act of repositing or laying up in safety.—**repository**, ri•poz′i•to•ri, *n.* [L. *repositorium.*] A place where things are or may be deposited for safety or preservation; a depository; a storehouse; a magazine; a warehouse; a shop.

repossess, rē•poz•zes′, *v.t.* To possess again.—**repossession**, rē•poz•zesh′on, *n.* The act or state of possessing again.

reprehend, rep•ri•hend′, *v.t.* [L. *reprehendo*—*re,* back, and *prehendo,* to lay hold of; seen also in *comprehend, apprehend, prehensile,* etc.] To charge with a fault; to chide sharply; to reprove; to take exception to; to speak of as a fault; to censure.—**reprehensible**, rep•ri•hen′si•bl, *a.* Deserving to be reprehended or censured; blameworthy; censurable; deserving reproof.—**reprehensibleness**, rep•ri•hen′si•bl•nes, *n.* The quality of being reprehensible. — **reprehensibly**, rep•ri•hen′si•bli, *adv.* In a reprehensible manner; culpably. —**reprehension**, rep•ri•hen′shon, *n.* [L. *reprehensio.*] The act of reprehending; reproof; censure; blame.—**reprehensive**, rep•ri•hen′siv, *a.* Containing reprehension or reproof.—**reprehensively**, rep•ri•hen′siv•li, *adv.* With reprehension.

represent, rep•ri•zent′, *v.t.* [Fr. *représenter,* from L. *repraesento,*—*re,* again, and *praesento,* to present. PRESENT.] To exhibit the image or counterpart of; to typify; to portray by pictorial or plastic art; to act the part of; to personate; to exhibit to the mind in language; to bring before the mind; to give an account of; to describe; to supply the place of; to speak and act with authority on behalf of; to be a substitute or agent for; to serve as a sign or symbol of (words *represent* ideas or things).—**representable**, rep•ri•zen′ta•bl, *a.* Capable of being represented.—**representation**, rep′ri•zen•tā′shon, *n.* The act of representing, describing, exhibiting, portraying, etc.; that which represents; an image or likeness; a picture or statue; exhibition of a play on the stage, or of a character in a play; a dramatic performance; a statement of arguments or facts, etc.; sometimes a written expostulation; a remonstrance; the representing of a constituency in a legislative assembly (the *representation* of a county in parliament); delegates or representatives collectively.—**representative**, rep•ri•zen′ta•tive, *a.* Fitted to represent, portray, or typify; acting as a substitute for another or others; performing the functions of others (a *representative* body); conducted by the agency of delegates chosen by the people (a *representative* government); *nat. hist.* presenting the full characteristics of the type of a group (a *representative* genius).—*n.* One who or that which represents; that by which anything is represented; something standing for something else; an agent, deputy, or substitute who supplies the place of another or others, being invested with his or their authority; *law,* one that stands in the place of another as heir.—*House of Representatives,* the lower house of the supreme legislative body (Congress) in the United States.—**representatively**, rep•ri•zen′ta•tiv•li, *adv.* In a representative manner.—**representativeness**, rep•ri•zen′ta•tiv•nes, *n.*

repress, ri•pres′, *v.t.* [Prefix *re,* and *press,* L. *reprimo, repressum.* PRESS.] To press back or down effectually; to crush, quell, put down, subdue (sedition, a rising); to check; to restrain.—**represser**, ri•pres′ér, *n.* One who represses; one that crushes or subdues.—**repressible**, ri•pres′i•bl, *a.* Capable of being repressed.—**repression**, ri•presh′on, *n.* The act of repressing, restraining, or subduing; check; restraint.—**repressive**, ri•pres′iv, *a.* Having power to repress; tending to subdue or restrain.—**repressively**, ri•pres′iv•li, *adv.* In a repressive manner.

reprieve, ri•prēv′, *n.* [From O.Fr. *reprover, repruver,* to blame, condemn, from L. *reprobare,* to reject, condemn, meaning originally the rejection of a sentence already passed. REPROBATE.] The suspension of the execution of a criminal's sentence; respite; interval of ease or relief.—*v.t.*—*reprieved, reprieving.* To grant a reprieve or respite to; to suspend or delay the execution of for a time.

reprimand, rep′ri•mand, *n.* [Fr. *ré-*

primande, from L. *reprimenda,* a thing to be checked or repressed, from *reprimo, repressum,* to repress. REPRESS.] A severe reproof for a fault; a sharp rebuke; reprehension.—*v.t.* (rep•ri•mand′). To reprove severely; to reprehend; to reprove publicly and officially, in execution of a sentence.

reprint, rē•print′, *v.t.* To print again; to print a second or any new edition of; to renew the impression of.—*n.* (rē′print). A second or new impression of any printed work.

reprisal, ri•prī′zal, *n.* [Fr. *représaille,* from It. *rappresaglia,* from L.L. *reprisaliae,* from L. *reprehendo,* to take again; comp. *prize,* a capture, which is also from L. *prehendo.*] The seizure or taking of anything from an enemy by way of retaliation or indemnification; also, that which is so taken; any taking by way of retaliation; an act of severity done in retaliation.—*Letters of marque and reprisal.* See MARQUE.

reproach, ri•prōch′, *v.t.* [Fr. *reprocher,* O.Fr. *reprochier,* Pr. *repropchar,* to reproach, from L.L. *repropiare,* from L. *re,* back, and *prope,* near; lit. to bring near or set before. APPROACH, PROPINQUITY]. To charge with a fault in severe language; to censure with severity, opprobrium, or contempt, or as having suffered wrong personally; to upbraid.—*n.* A severe or cutting expression of censure or blame; blame for something considered outrageous or vile; contumely; source of blame; shame, infamy, or disgrace; object of contempt, scorn, or derision.—**reproachable**, ri•prō′cha•bl, *a.* Deserving reproach.—**reproachableness**, ri•prō′cha•bl•nes, *n.* The state of being reproachable.—**reproachably**, ri•prō′cha•bli, *adv.* In a reproachable manner.—**reproacher**, ri•prō′chér, *n.* One who reproaches.—**reproachful**, ri•prōch′fụl, *a.* Containing or expressing reproach or censure; upbraiding; scurrilous; opprobrious; worthy of reproach; shameful; infamous.—**reproachfully**, ri•prōch′fụl•li, *adv.* In a reproachful manner.—**reproachfulness**, ri•prōch′fụl•nes, *n.* Quality of being reproachful.—**reproachless**, ri•prōch′les, *a.* Without reproach.

reprobate, rep′ro•bāt, *a.* [L. *reprobatus,* disapproved, rejected, pp. of *reprobo*—*re,* denoting reverse, and *probo,* to approve. PROBABLE, REPRIEVE, REPROVE.] Abandoned in sin; morally abandoned; depraved; profligate; lost to virtue or grace.—*n.* One who is very profligate or abandoned; a person abandoned to sin; one lost to virtue; a wicked, depraved wretch.—*v.t.*—*reprobated, reprobating.* [L. *reprobo, reprobatum.*] To disapprove with detestation or marks of extreme dislike; to contemn strongly; to condemn; to reject.—**reprobation**, rep•ro•bā′shon, *n.* The act of reprobating; condemnation; censure; rejection. — **reprobative**, rep′ro•bā•tiv, *a.* Conveying reprobation.

reproduce, rē•pro•dūs′, *v.t.*—*repro-*

duced, reproducing. To produce again or anew; to renew the production of; to generate, as offspring; to portray or represent; to bring to the memory or imagination.—**reproducer**, rē‧pro‧dū′sėr, *n.* One who or that which reproduces.—**reproduction**, rē‧pro‧duk′shon, *n.* The act or process of reproducing; the process whereby new individuals are generated and the perpetuation of the species ensured; that which is produced or presented anew.—**reproductive**, rē‧pro‧duk′tiv, *a.* Pertaining to reproduction; tending to reproduce.

reproof, ri‧pröf′, *n.* [O.F. *reprueve*, reproof.] The expression of blame or censure addressed to a person; blame expressed to one's face; censure for a fault; reprehension; rebuke; reprimand.

reprove, ri‧pröv′, *v.t.*—*reproved, reproving.* [Fr. *réprouver*, to blame, to censure; O.Fr. *reprover*, from L. *reprobare.* REPROBATE.] To chide; to reprehend; to express disapproval of (to *reprove* sins); to serve to admonish.—**reprovable**, ri‧prö′va‧bl, *a.* Worthy of being reproved; deserving reproof or censure.—**reproval**, ri‧prö′val, *n.* Act of reproving; admonition; reproof.—**reprover**, ri‧prö′vėr, *n.* One that reproves.—**reprovingly**, ri‧prö′ving‧li, *adv.* In a reproving manner.

reptile, rep′til, *a.* [Fr. *reptile*, from L. *reptilis*, creeping, from *repo, reptum*, to creep; akin to *serpo*, to creep. SERPENT.] Creeping; moving on the belly, or with small, short legs; groveling; low; mean; vile.—*n.* In a general sense, an animal that moves on its belly, or by means of small, short legs; a crawling creature; specifically, *zool.* an animal belonging to the class Reptilia; a groveling, abject, or mean person.—**reptilian**, rep‧til′i‧an, *a.* Belonging to the class of reptiles.—*n.* An animal of the class Reptilia; a reptile.

republic, ri‧pub′lik, *n.* [Fr. *république*, L. *respublica—res*, an affair, interest, and *publica*, fem. of *publicus*, public. REAL, PUBLIC.] A commonwealth; a political community in which the supreme power in the state is vested either in certain privileged members of the community or in the whole community, and thus varying from the most exclusive oligarchy to a pure democracy.—*Federal republics*, of which the United States and Switzerland are examples, consist of a number of separate states bound together by treaty, so as to present the aspect of a single state with a central government, without wholly renouncing their individual powers of internal self-government.—**republican**, ri‧pub′li‧kan, *a.* Pertaining to or having the character of a republic; consonant to the principles of a republic. —*n.* One who favors or prefers a republican form of government; [*cap.*] a member of the Republican party in *U. S. politics.—Red Republican.* RED.—**republicanism**, ri‧pub′li‧kan‧izm, *n.* Republican system of government; [*cap.*] principles and

policies of the Republican party (*U.S.*); republican principles.

republication, rē‧pub′li‧kā″shon, *n.* The act of republishing; a new publication of something before published.

republish, rē‧pub′lish, *v.t.* To publish anew; to publish again, as in a new edition.

repudiate, ri‧pū′di‧āt, *v.t.*—*repudiated, repudiating.* [L. *repudio, repudiatum*, to divorce, to cast off, from *repudium*, a casting off, a divorce.] To cast away; to reject; to discard; to disavow; to divorce; to refuse to acknowledge or to pay, as debt.—**repudiation**, ri‧pū′di‧ā″shon, *n.* [L. *repudiatio.*] The act of repudiating; rejection; disavowal; divorce; refusal on the part of a government to pay debts contracted by a former government.—**repudiator**, ri‧pū′di‧ā‧tėr, *n.* One who repudiates.

repugnance, repugnancy, ri‧pug′nans, ri‧pug′nan‧si, *n.* [Fr. *répugnance*; L. *repugnantia*, from *repugno*, to resist—*re*, against, and *pugno*, to fight. PUGNACIOUS.] The state of being opposed in mind; feeling of dislike for some action; reluctance; unwillingness; opposition in nature or qualities; contrariety.—**repugnant**, ri‧pug′nant, *a.* [L. *repugnans, repugnantis*, ppr. of *repugno.*] Standing or being in opposition; contrary; at variance: usually followed by *to* (a statement *repugnant to* common sense); highly distasteful; offensive (a course *repugnant to* him).—**repugnantly**, ri‧pug′nant‧li, *adv.*

repulse, ri‧puls′, *n.* [L. *repulsa*, from *repello, repulsum—re*, back, and *pello*, to drive. REPEL.] The condition of being repelled or driven back by force; the act of driving back; a check or defeat; refusal; denial.—*v.t.* —*repulsed, repulsing.* To repel; to drive back; to refuse; to reject.—**repulser**, ri‧puls′ėr, *n.* One that repulses.—**repulsion**, ri‧pul′shon, *n.* [L. *repulsio.*] The act of repelling; *physics*, a term often applied to the action which two bodies exert upon one another when they tend to increase their mutual distance.—**repulsive**, ri‧pul′siv, *a.* Acting so as to repel; exercising repulsion; tending to deter or forbid approach or familiarity; repellent; forbidding.—**repulsively**, ri‧pul′siv‧li, *adv.* In a repulsive manner.—**repulsiveness**, ri‧pul′siv‧nes, *n.*

repurchase, rē‧pėr′ches, *v.t.* To buy back; to regain by purchase.—*n.* The act of buying again; a new purchase.

repute, ri‧pūt′, *v.t.*—*reputed, reputing.* [Fr. *réputer*, from L. *reputo*, to count over—*re*, and *puto*, to reckon; to estimate (as in *compute, impute*, etc.). PUTATIVE.] To hold in thought; to reckon, account, or consider as such or such; to deem.—*n.* Reputation; character, attributed by public report, especially good character; honorable name.—**reputed**, ri‧pū′ted, *p.* and *a.* Generally considered; commonly believed, regarded, or accounted.—**reputedly**, ri‧pū′ted‧li, *adv.* In common opinion or estimation.—**reputable**, rep′ū‧ta‧bl, *a.*

Being in good repute; held in esteem; not mean or disgraceful.—**reputably**, rep′ū‧ta‧bli, *adv.* In a reputable manner. — **reputation**, rep‧ū‧tā′shon, *n.* [L. *reputatio.*] Character by report; opinion of character generally entertained; character attributed; repute; in a good or bad sense; often favorable or honorable regard; good name.

request, ri‧kwest′, *n.* [O.Fr. *requeste* (Fr. *requête*), from L. *requisita*, a thing required, a want, from *requiro, requisitum—re*, again, and *quaero, quaesitum*, to seek. QUEST.] The expression of desire to some person for something to be granted or done; an asking; a petition, prayer, entreaty; the thing asked for or requested; a state of being esteemed and sought after, or asked for (an article in much *request*). ∴ *Request* expresses less earnestness than *entreaty* and *supplication*; and supposes a right in the person requested to deny or refuse to grant, in this differing from *demand.—v.t.* To make a request for; to solicit or express desire for; to express a request to; to ask.

Requiem, rē′kwi‧em, *n.* [Acc. case of L. *requies*, rest, respite, relaxation —*re*, again, and *quies*, rest, repose.] [*usually cap.*] A funeral dirge or service, containing the words 'Requiem aeternam', etc., sung for the rest of a person's soul; a grand musical composition performed in honor of some deceased person.

require, ri‧kwīr′, *v.t.*—*required, requiring.* [O.Fr. *requerre, requierre, requirre* (Fr. *requérir*), from L. *requiro, requirere*, to ask for. REQUEST.] To demand; to ask as of right and by authority; to insist on having; to ask as a favor; to call upon to act; to request; to have need or necessity for; to need or want (the matter *requires* great care, we *require* food); to find it necessary; to have to: with infinitives (you will *require* to go).—**requirement**, ri‧kwīr′ment, *n.* The act of requiring; demand; that which requires the doing of something; an essential condition; something required or necessary.—**requisite**, rek′wi‧zit, *a.* [L. *requisitus*, from *requiro.*] Required by the nature of things or by circumstances; necessary.—*n.* That which is necessary; something indispensable.—**requisitely**, rek′wi‧zit‧li, *adv.* In a requisite manner; necessarily.—**requisiteness**, rek′wi‧zit‧nes, *n.*—**requisition**, rek‧wi‧zish′on, *n.* [L. *requisitio.*] An application made as of a right; a demand; a demand for or a levying of necessaries by hostile troops from the people in whose country they are; a written call or invitation (a *requisition* for a public meeting); state of being required or much sought after; request.—*v.t.* To make a requisition or demand upon.

requite, ri‧kwīt′, *v.t.*—*requited, requiting.* [From *re*, back, and *quit.* QUIT.] To repay either good or evil: in a good sense, to recompense or reward: in a bad sense, to retaliate on.—**requiter**, ri‧kwī′tėr, *n.* One who requites.—**requital**, ri·kwī′tal, *n.* Return for any office, good or bad; recompense; reward.

reread, rē·rēd′, *v.t.* To read again or anew.

reredos, rēr′dos, *n.* [Fr. *arrière dos*— *arrière*, behind, and *dos*, L. *dorsum*, the back. REAR, DORSAL.] The decorated portion of the wall behind and rising above the altar in a church.

reremouse, rēr′mous, *n.* [A.Sax. *hréremus*, from *hrénan*, to raise, to move, and *mús*, a mouse.] A bat. (*Shak.*)

rerun, rē′run, *n.* An added running, as a later showing of a motion picture after its first run.—*v.t.* To run again.

resail, rē·sāl′, *v.t.* or *i.* To sail back.

resale, rē′sāl, *n.* A sale at second hand; a second sale.

rescind, ri·sind′, *v.t.* [Fr. *rescinder*, from L. *rescindo*, *rescissum*—*re*, again, and *scindo*, to cut (as in *concise*, *precise*, etc.).] To cut short‡; to abrogate; to revoke or annul by competent authority (to *rescind* a law, a judgment).—**rescission**, ri·sizh′on, *n.* [L. *rescissio*, *rescissionis*.] The act of rescinding; the act of abrogating or annulling.—**rescissory**, ri·sis′o·ri, *a.* [L. *rescissorius*.] Having power to rescind, abrogate, or annul.

rescript, rē′skript, *n.* [L. *rescriptum*, from *rescribo*, *rescriptum*, to write back—*re*, and *scribo*, to write. SCRIBE.] The answer or decision of a Roman emperor to some matter set before him; the decision by a pope of a question officially propounded; an edict or decree.

rescue, res′kū, *v.t.*—*rescued*, *rescuing*. [O.Fr. *rescoure*, *rescourre*, to rescue, from L. *re*, again, and *excutere*, to shake off.—*ex*, away, and *quiato*, *quassum*, to shake. QUASH.] To free from confinement, danger, or evil; to withdraw from a state of exposure to evil; *law*, to take by forcible or illegal means from lawful custody.— *n.* The act of rescuing; deliverance from restraint or danger; *law*, a forcible taking out of the custody of the law.—**rescuer**, res′kū·ėr, *n.* One that rescues.

research, ri·sėrch′, *n.* [Prefix *re*, and *search*; Fr. *recherche*.] Diligent inquiry or examination in seeking facts or principles; laborious or continued search after truth; investigation.—*v.t.* To search again; to examine anew.—**researcher**, ri·sėr′chėr, *n.* One engaged in research.

reseat, rē·sēt′, *v.t.* To seat or set again; to furnish with a new seat or seats.

resect, ri·sekt′, *v.t.* [L. *reseco*, *resectum*, to cut off—*re*, back, and *seco*, to cut.] To cut or pare off.— **resection**, ri·sek′shon, *n.* [L. *resectio*.] *Surg.* the removal of the articular extremity of a bone, or of the ends of the bones in a false articulation.

resell, rē·sel′, *v.t.* To sell again.

resemble, ri·zem′bl, *v.t.*—*resembled*, *resembling*. [Fr. *ressembler*—*re*, and *sembler*, to seem, from L. *similare*,

from *similis*, like. SIMILAR.] To be like; to have similarity to in form, figure, or qualities; to liken; to compare.—**resemblance**, ri·zem′blans, *n.* The state or quality of resembling; likeness; similarity either of external form or of qualities; something similar; a similitude.— *Resemblance, general*, in animals, a harmonizing with surroundings producing inconspicuousness. May be protective, aggressive (deceiving prey), or both. May be capable of adjustment, i.e. *variable*.—*Resemblance, special*, in animals, resemblance to some specific object in surroundings, causing inconspicuousness. May be protective, etc.

resend, rē·send′, *v.t.* To send again.

resent, ri·zent′, *v.t.* [Fr. *ressentir*, from L. *re*, and *sentio*, to feel. SENSE.] To consider as an injury or affront; to be in some degree angry or provoked at; to take ill; to show such feeling by words or acts.—*v.i.* To be indignant; to feel resentment. —**resentful**, ri·zent′fụl, *a.* Inclined or apt to resent; full of resentment.—**resentfully**, ri·zent′fụl·li, *adv.* In a resentful manner.—**resentment**, ri·zent′ment, *n.* The act of resenting; the feeling with which one who resents is impressed; a deep sense of injury; anger arising from a sense of wrong; strong displeasure.

reserve, ri·zėrv′, *v.t.*—*reserved*, *reserving*. [Fr. *réserver*, from L. *reservo* —*re*, back, and *servo*, to keep. SERVE.] To keep in store for future or other use; to withhold from present use for another purpose; to keep back for a time; to withdraw. *n.* The act of reserving or keeping back; that which is reserved or retained from present use or disposal; something in the mind withheld from disclosure; a reservation; the habit of keeping back or restraining the feelings; a certain closeness or coldness toward others; caution in personal behavior; banking capital retained in order to meet average liabilities; a body of troops kept for an exigency.— *Federal Reserve Bank*, any of the 12 Federal banks which comprise the Federal Reserve System, and operate by the authority, and under the supervision, of the Federal Reserve Board.—**reservation**, rez·ėr·vā′shon, *n.* The act of reserving or keeping back; concealment or withholding from disclosure; something not expressed, disclosed, or brought forward; a keeping over of part of the consecrated elements for the communion of the sick; a tract of the public land reserved for some special use, as for schools, the use of Indians, etc.; a reserve; the act of having reserved for oneself, in advance, accommodations in a public place, as a reservation in a hotel, bus, theater, ship, etc.—*Mental reservation*, an intentional reserving or holding back of some word or clause, the speaker thus intending to set his conscience at rest while being guilty of deceit, or to keep his real sentiments secret.—**reserved**,

ri·zėrvd′, *p.* and *a.* Kept for another or future use; showing reserve in behavior; distant; cold.—**reservedly**, ri·zėr′ved·li, *adv.* In a reserved manner; with reserve.—**reservist**, ri·zėr′vist, *n.* A soldier of the reserve forces of an army, navy or militia organization.

reservoir, rez′ėr·vwạr, *n.* [Fr. RESERVE.] A place where anything is kept in store; a place where water is collected and kept for use; an artificial lake or pond from which pipes convey water to a town.

reset, rē·set′, *v.t.* To set again (to *reset* a diamond); *printing*, to set over again, as a page of matter.—*n.* The act of resetting; *printing*, matter set over again.

resettle, rē·set′l, *v.t.* and *i.* To settle again.—**resettlement**, rē·set′l·ment, *n.* The act of resettling.

reshape, rē·shāp′, *v.t.* To shape again.

reship, rē·ship′, *v.t.* To ship again; to ship again what has been imported.—**reshipment**, rē·ship′ment, *n.* The act of reshipping.

reside, ri·zīd′, *v.i.*—*resided*, *residing*. [Fr. *résider*, from L. *resideo*—*re*, and *sedeo*, to sit, to settle down. SEDATE.] To dwell permanently or for a length of time; to have one's dwelling or home; to abide continuously; to abide or be inherent, as a quality; to inhere.—**residence**, rez′i·dens, *n.* The act of residing or abiding; period of abode; the place where a person resides; a dwelling; a habitation; a mansion or dwelling house.—**residency**, rez′i·den·si, *n.* The domicile of the chief executive's governmental representative to a possession or mandated territory; a territory in a protected state governed by a resident agent.—**resident**, rez′i·dent, *a.* [L. *residens*, *residentis*.] Dwelling or having an abode in a place for a continuance of time; residing.—*n.* One who resides or dwells in a place for some time; one residing; a public minister who resides at a foreign court; a kind of ambassador.—**residential**, rez·i·den′shal, *a.* Relating or pertaining to residence or to residents.— **residentiary**, rez·i·den′sher·i, *a.* Having residence.—*n.* One who is resident; an ecclesiastic who keeps a certain residence.

residue, rez′i·dū, *n.* [Fr. *résidu*, from L. *residuum*, what is left behind, from *residuus*, remaining, from *resideo*. RESIDE.] That which remains after a part is taken, separated, or dealt with in some way; that which is still over; remainder; the rest; *law*, the remainder of a testator's estate after payment of debts and legacies.—**residual**, ri·zid′ū·al, *a.* Having the character of a residue or residuum; remaining after a part is taken or dealt with.—*Residual air*, the air which remains in the chest and cannot be expelled, variously estimated at from 80 to 120 cubic inches.—**residuary**, ri·zid′ū·a·ri, *a.* Pertaining to a residue or part remaining; forming a residue or portion not dealt with.—*Residuary* *legatee*, the legatee to whom is bequeathed all that remains after deducting the debts and specific legacies.—**residuum**, re·zid′ū·um, *n*. [L.] That which is left after any process of separation or purification; a residue; the dregs or refuse; *law*, the part of an estate remaining after the payment of debts and legacies.

resign, ri·zīn′, *v.t.* [Fr. *résigner*, L. *resigno*, to resign—*re*, and *signo*, to mark, from *signum*, to sign. SIGN.] To assign or give back; to give up, as an office or post, to the person or authority that conferred it; hence, to surrender or relinquish; to give over; to withdraw, as a claim; to submit, particularly to Providence.—**resignation**, rez·ig·nā′shon, *n*. The act of resigning or giving up, as a claim, etc.; the state of being resigned or submissive; patience; quiet submission to the will of Providence; submission without discontent or repining.—**resigned**, ri·zīnd′, *p*. and *a*. Surrendered; given up; feeling resignation; submissive; patient.—**resignedly**, ri·zī′ned·li, *adv*. With resignation; submissively.

resile, ri·zīl′, *v.i.*—*resiled, resiling*. [L. *resilio*, to leap or spring back—*re*, back, and *salio*, to leap. SALIENT.] To recede or withdraw from a purpose; to recoil; to return to original position.—**resilience, resiliency**, ri·zil′i·ens, ri·zil′i·en·si, *n*. The act of resiling; the act of rebounding; rebound from being elastic; the quantity of work given out by a body, such as a spring, that is compressed and then allowed to resume its former shape.—**resilient**, ri·zil′i·ent, *a*. Inclined to resile; rebounding.

resin, rez′in, *n*. [Fr. *résine*, from L. *resina*, resin. Rosin is the same word.] A flammable substance of sundry varieties found in most plants, and often obtained by spontaneous exudation, in some cases solid and brittle at ordinary temperatures, in others viscous or semifluid (in which case they are called *balsams*), valuable as ingredients in varnishes, and several of them used in medicine. Rosin is resin from coniferous trees.—*Fossil* or *mineral resins*, amber, petroleum, asphalt, bitumen, and other mineral hydrocarbons.—**resiniferous**, rez·i·nif′ėr·us, *a*. Yielding resin.—**resinous**, rez′i·nus, *a*. Pertaining to or obtained from resin; partaking of the qualities of resin; like resin.—*Resinous electricity*, negative electricity, that kind of electricity which is excited by rubbing resinous bodies with a woolen cloth, in distinction from that excited by rubbing glass, etc., which is termed *vitreous* or *positive electricity*.

resist, ri·zist′, *v.t.* [Fr. *résister*, from L. *resisto*, to withstand—*re*, and *sisto*, to place, to stand, from *sto*, to stand. STATE, STAND.] To withstand so as not to be impressed by; to form an impediment to; to oppose passively (certain bodies *resist* acids or a cutting tool); to act in opposition to; to strive or struggle against, actively.—*v.i.* To make opposition.—*n*. A sort of paste applied to calico goods to prevent color or mordant from fixing on those parts not intended to be colored.—**resistance**, ri·zis′tans, *n*. The act of resisting, whether actively or passively; a being or acting in opposition; the quality or property in matter of not yielding to force or external impression; a force acting in opposition to another force so as to destroy it, or diminish its effect; in *elect.* the property of a body that limits the strength of an electric current in it by causing part of the electrical energy to be dissipated in the form of heat, etc.: measured practically in *ohms*.—*Unit of resistance*, the standard of measurement of electric resistance; an ohm.—**resistant**, ri·zis′tant, *n*. One who or that which resists.—*a*. Making resistance; resisting.—**resister**, ri·zis′tėr, *n*. One who resists.—**resistible**, ri·zis′ti·bl, *a*. Capable of being resisted.—**resistibility**, ri·zis′ti·bil′i·ti, *n*. The quality of being resistible.—**resistless**, ri·zist′les, *a*. Incapable of being resisted or withstood; irresistible; powerless to resist (*Keats*).—**resistlessly**, ri·zist′les·li, *adv*. In a resistless manner; irresistibly.—**resistlessness**, ri·zist′les·nes, *n*.

resoluble, rez′o·lū·bl, *a*. [Fr. *résoluble*. RESOLVE.] Capable of being melted or dissolved.

resolute, rez′o·lūt, *a*. [Fr. *résolu*, pp. of *résoudre*, L. *resolvere*, to resolve. RESOLVE.] Having a fixed purpose; determined; steadfast; bold; firm.—**resolutely**, rez′o·lūt·li, *adv*. In a resolute manner; with fixed purpose; determinedly; boldly.—**resoluteness**, rez′o·lūt·nes, *n*. The quality of being resolute; unshaken firmness.—**resolution**, rez·o·lū′shon, *n*. [Fr. *résolution*, L. *resolutio*.] The character of being resolute; a resolve taken; a fixed purpose or determination of mind; the character of acting with fixed purpose; firmness; determination; a formal decision of a legislative or other body; the operation of resolving or separating the component parts of a body; the act of unraveling a perplexing question or problem; solution; *music*, the succession of a concord immediately after a discord; *med.* a removal or disappearance, as the disappearance of a tumor.—*Resolution of an equation*, in *alg.* the bringing of the unknown quantity by itself on one side, and all the known quantities on the other.—*Resolution of forces*, in *dyn.* the dividing of any single force into two or more others, which shall produce the same effect.—**resolutioner**, rez·o·lū′shon·ėr, *n*. One who joins in a resolution or declaration.

resolve, ri·zolv′, *v.t.*—*resolved, resolving*. [L. *resolvo*, to unloose, break up, dissolve, to do away with (hence, to determine, that is, to do away with doubts or disputes)—*re*, back or again, and *solvo*, to loose. SOLVE.] To separate the component parts of; to reduce to constituent elements; to reduce to simple parts; to analyze; to disentangle of perplexities; to clear of difficulties (to *resolve* doubts); to explain; to fix in determination or purpose; to determine (usually in pp.); to melt; to dissolve; to form or constitute by resolution (the house *resolved* itself into a committee); to determine on; to express by resolution and vote; *med.* to disperse or remove, as an inflammation or a tumor; *math.* to solve.—*v.i.* To form an opinion or purpose; to determine; to determine by vote; to melt; to become fluid; to become separated into its component parts or into distinct principles.—*n*. That which has been resolved on; fixed purpose of mind; a settled determination; a resolution.—**resolved**, ri·zolvd′, *p*. and *a*. Having the mind made up; determined.—**resolvedly**, ri·zol′ved·li, *adv*. In a resolved manner; resolutely.—**resolvent**, ri·zol′vent, *a*. Having the power to resolve; causing solution.—*n*. That which has the power of causing solution; *med.* a discutient.—**resolver**, ri·zol′vėr, *n*. One who or that which resolves; one who determines.—**resolvability, resolvableness**, ri·zol′va·bil′i·ti, ri·zol′va·bl·nes, *n*. The property of being resolvable.—**resolvable**, ri·zol′va·bl, *a*. Capable of being resolved or separated into constituent parts; capable of being solved.

resonant, rez′o·nant, *a*. [L. *resonans, resonantis*, ppr. of *resono*—*re*, again, and *sono*, to sound. SOUND.] Capable of returning sound; resounding; full of sounds; echoing back.—**resonantly**, rez′o·nant·li, *adv*. In a resonant manner.—**resonance**, rez′o·nans, *n*. The state or quality of being resonant, the act of resounding.—**resonator**, rez′o·nā·tėr, *n*. An instrument for facilitating the analysis of compound sounds.

resort, ri·zort′, *v.i.* [O.Fr. *resortir*, Fr. *ressortir*, to go out again, to resort, from prefix *re*, and *sortir*, to go out, from L. *sortiri*, to obtain, to acquire by lot, from *sors, sortis*, lot. SORT.] To have recourse; to betake one's self (to *resort* to force); to go (to *resort* to a place); to repair frequently.—*n*. A betaking one's self; recourse; the act of visiting or frequenting; a place frequented; a haunt.

resound, ri·zound′, *v.t.* [O.E. *resoune*, from L. *resono*, to resound—*re*, again, and *sono*, to sound. SOUND.] To sound again; to echo; to extol.—*v.i.* To be filled with sound; to echo; to reverberate; to sound loudly; to be echoed; to be much mentioned.

resource, ri·sōrs′, *n*. [Fr. *ressource*, from O.Fr. *ressourdre*, to arise anew—*re*, again, and *sourdre*, L. *surgere*, to rise. SOURCE.] Any source of aid or support; an expedient; means yet untried; resort; *pl*. pecuniary means; funds; available means or capabilities of any kind.—**resourceful**, ri·sōrs′ful, *a*. Capable of utilizing resources.